Alfred David

PROFESSOR OF ENGLISH EMERITUS, INDIANA UNIVERSITY

E. Talbot Donaldson

LATE OF INDIANA UNIVERSITY

George M. Logan

JAMES CAPPON PROFESSOR OF ENGLISH, QUEEN'S UNIVERSITY

Hallett Smith

LATE OF THE HUNTINGTON LIBRARY

Barbara K. Lewalski

WILLIAM R. KENAN PROFESSOR OF ENGLISH AND OF HISTORY AND LITERATURE,
HARVARD UNIVERSITY

Robert M. Adams

LATE OF THE UNIVERSITY OF CALIFORNIA AT LOS ANGELES

Lawrence Lipking

PROFESSOR OF ENGLISH AND CHESTER D. TRIPP PROFESSOR OF HUMANITIES,
NORTHWESTERN UNIVERSITY

Samuel Holt Monk

LATE OF THE UNIVERSITY OF MINNESOTA

Jack Stillinger

CENTER FOR ADVANCED STUDY PROFESSOR OF ENGLISH, UNIVERSITY OF ILLINOIS

Carol T. Christ

PROFESSOR OF ENGLISH, UNIVERSITY OF CALIFORNIA AT BERKELEY

George H. Ford

LATE OF THE UNIVERSITY OF ROCHESTER

Jon Stallworthy

PROFESSOR OF ENGLISH LITERATURE, OXFORD UNIVERSITY

David Daiches

FORMERLY DIRECTOR OF THE INSTITUTE OF ADVANCED STUDIES, UNIVERSITY OF EDINBURGH

The Norton Anthology of English Literature

SEVENTH EDITION

THE MAJOR AUTHORS

VOLUME A

THE MIDDLE AGES THROUGH THE RESTORATION

AND THE EIGHTEENTH CENTURY

THE MIDDLE AGES
David / Donaldson

THE SIXTEENTH CENTURY
Logan / Greenblatt

THE EARLY SEVENTEENTH CENTURY
Lewalski / Adams

THE RESTORATION AND THE EIGHTEENTH CENTURY
Lipking / Monk

THE ROMANTIC PERIOD
Abrams / Stillinger

THE VICTORIAN AGE
Christ / Ford

THE TWENTIETH CENTURY
Stallworthy / Daiches

The Norton Anthology
of English Literature

SEVENTH EDITION

THE MAJOR AUTHORS

VOLUME A

THE MIDDLE AGES
THROUGH THE
RESTORATION AND
THE EIGHTEENTH
CENTURY

M. H. Abrams, *General Editor*

CLASS OF 1916 PROFESSOR OF ENGLISH EMERITUS,
CORNELL UNIVERSITY

Stephen Greenblatt, *Associate General Editor*

COGAN UNIVERSITY PROFESSOR,
HARVARD UNIVERSITY

W • W • NORTON & COMPANY • *New York* • *London*

The text of this book is composed in Fairfield Medium
with the display set in Bernhard Modern.
Composition by Binghamton Valley Composition.
Manufacturing by R. R. Donnelley & Sons, Inc.
Book design by Antonina Krass.

The Library of Congress has cataloged the one-volume edition as follows:

Library of Congress Cataloging-in-Publication Data

The Norton anthology of English literature. The major authors / M.H. Abrams, general
editor ; Stephen Greenblatt, associate general editor.—7th ed.
p. cm.
Includes bibliographical references and index.

ISBN 0-393-97619-X—ISBN 0-393-96150-8 (pbk.)

1. English literature. 2. Great Britain—Literary collections. I. Abrams, M. H. (Meyer
Howard), 1912–   II. Greenblatt, Stephen, 1943–

PR1109 .N6 2001
820.8—dc21   00-045229

Volume A: ISBN 0-393-96338-1 (pbk.)

W. W. Norton & Company, Inc., 500 Fifth Avenue, New York, N.Y. 10110
www.wwnorton.com

W. W. Norton & Company Ltd., 10 Coptic Street, London WC1A 1PU

1 2 3 4 5 6 7 8 9 0

Contents

MIDDLE ENGLISH LITERATURE IN THE FOURTEENTH AND FIFTEENTH CENTURIES   119

The Early Seventeenth Century (1603–1660)   577

The Restoration and the Eighteenth Century
(1660–1785)   855

Preface to the Seventh Edition

The outpouring of English literature overflows all boundaries, including the capacious boundaries of the Major Authors edition of *The Norton Anthology of English Literature*. But these pages manage to contain many of the most remarkable works written in English during centuries of restless creative effort. We have included epic poems and short lyrics; love songs and satires; plays written for performance on the commercial stage and private meditations meant to be perused in silence; prayers, popular ballads, prophecies, ecstatic visions, erotic fantasies, short stories, letters in verse and prose, critical essays, extended prose works of both fiction and nonfiction, and a great deal more. Such works generally form the core of courses that are designed to introduce students to the rich abundance of English literature, with its history not only of gradual development, continuity, and dense internal echoes, but also of radical contingency, sudden change, and startling innovation.

The meaning of the term *literature* has in the course of several centuries shifted from the whole body of writing produced in a particular language to a subset of that writing consisting of works that claim special attention because of their formal beauty and expressive power. But any individual text's claim to attention is subject to constant debate and revision; established texts are jostled both by new arrivals and by previously neglected claimants; and the boundaries between the *literary* and whatever is thought to be *nonliterary* are constantly challenged and redrawn, as are the boundaries between *major* and *minor* authors. Just as there have never been academies in English-speaking countries established to regulate the use of language, so too there have never been firm and settled guidelines for canonizing particular texts. Certain works, however, have achieved and maintained sufficient prominence to serve as widespread models for other writers and as objects of intense and enduring admiration. To present an abundant selection of these works is the purpose of the present volume.

This anthology aims to enable its readers to gauge the achievement of the principal authors it represents by providing generous samplings of their most characteristic and brilliant work. We have tried, wherever possible, not to give a brief glimpse but rather to facilitate a satisfying, sustained engagement with each writer. But we have also included some individual works whose compelling interest merits representation in these pages, even though the scope of this book does not permit a wider survey of the author's writings.

By the designation "major authors," the editors call attention to an unusual power to excite and reward close attention. Our grasp of this power—our notion of where to look for it, how to identify it, and what to do when we find it—does not stand still. There are twenty-one new writers in this Seventh Edition of the Major Authors *Norton Anthology,* eleven of whom are women. To cite a few examples: Aphra Behn's extraordinary seventeenth-century novel of slavery and revolt, *Oroonoko,* is included in its entirety; readers of Romantic poetry now encounter the remarkable Anna Letitia Barbauld, Robert Burns, and Felicia Hemans; and Thomas Carlyle, Elizabeth Gaskell, and Oscar Wilde take their places among the writers of the Victorian age. The innovations are perhaps most visible at the beginning and the end of the anthology, with a celebrated new translation by Seamus Heaney of the Anglo-Saxon epic *Beowulf* and a striking expansion of the selections of modern literature. While the Sixth Edition ended with Dylan Thomas, this edition continues with Philip Larkin, Nadine Gordimer, Derek Walcott, Seamus Heaney, J. M. Coetzee, and Salman Rushdie.

Where do we draw the boundaries? The designation *"English"* provides some obvious limits to the unstable and constantly shifting field of *literature.* But these limits are themselves in constant flux, due in part to the complexity of the territory evoked by the term (as explained in our appendix on "Geographical Nomenclature") and in part to the multinational, multicultural, and hugely expansive character of the language. As Geoffrey Nunberg's informative essay "The Persistence of English," commissioned for this Seventh Edition, makes clear, the variations in the forms of the spoken language that all go by the name of English are so great as to call into question the very notion of a single tongue, and the complex history and diffusion of the language have helped ensure that its literature is enormous. In the momentous process that transformed England into Great Britain and eventually into the center of a huge empire, more and more writers from outside England, beginning with the strong Irish and Scottish presence in the eighteenth century and gradually fanning out into the colonies, were absorbed into and at the same time transformed "English literature."

The term "English Literature" in our title designates two different things. First, it refers to the literary productions of a particular part of the world: the works we include were for the most part written by authors living in the British Isles, that is, in England, Scotland, Wales, and Ireland. Second, it refers to literary works in the English language, a language that has extended far beyond the boundaries of its point of origin. Following the lead of most college courses, we have separated off, for purposes of this anthology, English literature from American literature, but in the selections for the twentieth century we have incorporated a number of texts written in English by authors from other countries. Writers like William Butler Yeats (born in Dublin), Virginia Woolf (born in London), and Dylan Thomas (born in Swansea, Wales) are now being taught, and are here anthologized, alongside such writers as Nadine Gordimer (born in the Transvaal, South Africa), Derek Walcott (born on Saint Lucia in the West Indies), and Salman Rushdie (born in Bombay, India). English literature has ceased to be principally about the identity of a single nation; it is a global phenomenon.

The linguistic mobility and cultural interwining reflected in these texts are not new: the authors assembled in this anthology constitute a linguistic community that has never fit comfortably within any firm geographical or ethnic or national boundaries. It is fitting that among the first works in the volume is an Irish poet's translation of *Beowulf,* a powerful epic written in the Germanic language known as Old English about a singularly restless Scandinavian hero. So too, to glance at a few other authors and writings included here, in the sixteenth century William Tyndale, in exile in the Low Countries and inspired by German religious reformers, translated the New Testament from Greek and thereby changed the course of the English language; in the seventeenth century Aphra Behn deeply touched her readers with a story that moves from Africa, where its hero is born, to South America, where she herself may have briefly resided; and early in the twentieth century Joseph Conrad, born in Ukraine of Polish parents, wrote in eloquent English a celebrated novella whose vision of European empire has been powerfully challenged by such masterful writers as the African-born Nadine Gordimer and J. M. Coetzee.

One of the principal features of *The Norton Anthology of English Literature,* established by its original editors, was a commitment to provide periodic revisions in order to take advantage of newly recovered or better-edited texts, reflect scholarly discoveries and the shifting interests of readers, and keep the anthology in touch with contemporary critical and intellectual concerns. To help us honor this commitment we have, as in past years, profited from a remarkable flow of voluntary corrections and suggestions proposed by students, as well as teachers, who view the anthology with a loyal but critical eye. Moreover, we have again solicited and received detailed information on the works actually assigned, proposals for deletions and additions, and suggestions for improving the editorial matter, from dozens of reviewers from around the world, almost all of them teachers who use the book in their courses. In its evolution, then, this anthology has been the product of an ongoing collaboration among its editors, teachers, and students.

In addition to the new translation of *Beowulf* and to the augmented global approach to twentieth-century literature in English, several other important features of this Seventh Edition merit special mention. As already noted, we have greatly expanded the selection of writing by women in all of the historical periods. The extraordinary, sustained work of scholars in recent years has recovered dozens of significant authors who had been marginalized or neglected by a male-dominated literary tradition and has deepened our understanding of those women writers who had managed, against considerable odds, to claim a place in that tradition. Poets and prose writers whose names were mentioned, if at all, only in specialized literary histories—Marie de France, Mary Herbert, Aemilia Lanyer, Mary Wroth, Katherine Philips, Anne Finch, Frances Burney, Anna Letitia Barbauld, Felicia Hemans, and others—now appear in the company of their male contemporaries. There are in addition two complete long prose works by women: Aphra Behn's *Oroooko* and Virginia Woolf's *A Room of One's Own.*

The novel is, of course, a stumbling block for an anthology. The length of many great novels defies their incorporation in any volume that hopes to include a broad spectrum of literature. At the same time it is difficult to excerpt representative passages from narratives whose power often depends upon amplitude or upon the slow development of character or upon the onrushing urgency of the story. Therefore, better to represent the remarkable achievements of novelists, the publisher makes specially available, in inexpensive and well-edited Norton Anthology Editions, a range of novels, including Jane Austen's *Pride and Prejudice,* Mary Shelley's *Frankenstein,*

Charles Dickens's *Hard Times,* Charlotte Brontë's *Jane Eyre,* and Emily Brontë's *Wuthering Heights.*

Period-by-Period Revisions

The scope of the revisions we have undertaken, the most extensive in the long publishing history of the Major Authors edition of *The Norton Anthology of English Literature,* can be conveyed more fully by a list of some of the principal texts and features that have been added to the present edition.

The Middle Ages. In addition to Seamus Heaney's award-winning translation of *Beowulf,* the selection of Anglo-Saxon poems has also been augmented with *The Dream of the Rood.* We have added an entirely new section, "Legendary Histories of Britain," which provides a key bridge between the Anglo-Saxon period and the time of Chaucer, highlighting an important cluster of texts that trace the origins of Arthurian romance. This section includes legendary histories by Geoffrey of Monmouth, Wace, and Layamon, along with Marie de France's *Lanval* (a Breton lay about King Arthur's court, here in a new verse translation by Alfred David). And we have added selections from the revelations of the visionary anchoress Julian of Norwich.

The Sixteenth Century. A new section on the English Bible brings together contrasting Bible translations; also included is the beautiful marriage ceremony from the Book of Common Prayer. There are newly added letters and the celebrated "Golden Speech" by Queen Elizabeth; Sir Walter Ralegh's darkly eloquent address to Death at the end of his *History of the World;* and several additional sonnets by Sidney and Shakespeare, including "Full many a glorious morning have I seen."

The Early Seventeenth Century. John Donne's Holy Sonnet "O, to vex me, contraries meet in one" joins the already substantial selection of his works; two important parts of her *Salve Deus Rex Judaeorum,* "To the Doubtful Reader" and "Eve's Apology in Defense of Women," are added to the selection of Aemilia Lanyer; Andrew Marvell's haunting mower poems, *The Mower to the Glowworms* and *The Mower's Song,* are now included; and Katherine Philips makes her first appearance in the pages of this anthology.

The Restoration and the Eighteenth Century. Aphra Behn's novel *Oroonoko, or The Royal Slave* is included in full. Some of the issues Behn raises are echoed in a newly included work by Samuel Johnson, "A Brief to Free a Slave," and in chapters from Olaudah Equiano's ground-breaking history of his own enslavement. William Hogarth's remarkably "literary" graphic art is represented by his satiric *Marriage A-la-Mode.* The narrative gifts of Frances Burney, whose long career spans this period and the next, are newly presented by several texts, including her famous, harrowing account of her mastectomy.

The Romantic Period. Five writers have been added: the poets Anna Letitia Barbauld, Robert Burns, and Felicia Dorothea Hemans; and Mary Wollstonecraft, represented by a generous selection of her influential *Vindication,* and Dorothy Wordsworth, whose journal writings and poems are included. The presence of Barbauld, Hemans, Wollstonecraft, and Wordsworth helps to restore women writers, once marginalized in literary histories of the period, to the highly significant place they in fact occupied.

The Victorian Age. The important novelist, short story writer, and biographer Elizabeth Gaskell makes her first appearance in the Major Authors edition of the *Norton Anthology*, along with the celebrated prophet and essayist Thomas Carlyle. Newly added as well are selected works by Oscar Wilde, including his greatest play, *The Importance of Being Earnest*. We have added several poems by Elizabeth Barrett Browning, and we have moved Bernard Shaw's play *Mrs. Warren's Profession* to its chronological place in this section.

The Twentieth Century. The many changes in this section reflect a rethinking of this century's literary history. We now begin with Thomas Hardy and Joseph Conrad, both liminal figures poised between two cultural worlds. The selection from Virginia Woolf includes the whole of her feminist classic, *A Room of One's Own*. To James Joyce's works is added the poignant story *Araby*; Eliot's poems now include *The Hollow Men*; and Samuel Beckett is represented by the complete text of his masterful tragicomedy *Endgame*. Philip Larkin's subtle, ironic voice is heard for the first time in this edition in a selection of his poems. The explosion of brilliant writing in English in "postcolonial" countries around the world is represented by the addition of texts by Nadine Gordimer, Derek Walcott, J. M. Coetzee, and Salman Rushdie. Finally, the inclusion of seven poems by Seamus Heaney provides the occasion to look back again to the beginning of this volume with Heaney's new translation of *Beowulf*. This translation is a reminder that the history of literature is not a straightforward sequence, that the most recent works can double back upon the distant past, and that words set down by men and women who have crumbled into dust can speak to us with astonishing directness.

Editorial Procedures

As in past editions of the Major Authors, the editorial features—period introductions, headnotes, and annotation—are designed to give students the information needed, without imposing an interpretation. In this edition, these editorial features have been thoroughly revised in response to new scholarship. The period introductions and many headnotes have been either entirely or substantially rewritten to be more helpful to students, and all the Selected Bibliographies have been updated.

Several new features reflect the broadened scope of the selections in the anthology. The new introductory essay, "The Persistence of English" by Geoffrey Nunberg, Stanford University and Xerox Palo Alto Research Center, explores the emergence and spread of English and its apparent present-day "triumph" as a world language. It provides an informative and lively point of departure for the study of literatures in English. The endpaper maps have been reconceived and redrawn. Timelines, following each period introduction, help students place their reading in historical and cultural context. So that students can explore literature as a visual medium, the anthology newly offers graphic materials from three periods—Hogarth's *Marriage-A-la-Mode*, engravings by William Blake, and illustrations and paintings by D. G. Rossetti—supplemented with the more than one thousand images available on the Web companion to the *Norton Anthology*, described below.

An appendix, "Poems in Process," reproduces from manuscripts and printed texts the genesis and evolution of a number of poems anthologized here. The much-used section of "Poetic Forms and Literary Terminology" has been revised in this Seventh Edition, along with appendices, newly expanded, on the intricacies of English money, the baronage, and religions. An appendix, "Geographic Nomenclature," has been added to clarify the shifting place-names applied to regions of the British Isles.

Students, no less than scholars, deserve the most accurate texts available; in keeping with this policy, we continue to introduce improved versions of the selections where available. In this edition, for example, in addition to Seamus Heaney's new translation of *Beowulf*, we include Alfred David's new verse translation of Marie de France's *Lanval*. To ease a student's access, we have normalized spelling and capitalization in texts up to and including the Victorian period to follow the conventions of modern English; we leave unaltered, however, texts in which modernizing would change semantic or metrical qualities. In the Twentieth Century, we have restored the original spelling and punctuation to selections retained from the previous edition, in the belief that the authors' choices, when they pose no difficulties for student readers, should be respected.

We continue other editorial procedures that have proved useful in the past. After each work, we cite (when known) the date of composition on the left and the date of first publication on the right; in some instances, the latter is followed by the date of a revised edition for which the author was responsible. We have used square brackets to indicate titles supplied by the editors for the convenience of readers. Whenever a portion of a text has been omitted, we have indicated that omission with three asterisks. If the omitted portion is important for following the plot or argument, we have provided a brief summary within the text or in a footnote. We have extended our longstanding practice of providing marginal glossing of single words and short phrases from medieval and dialect poets (such as Robert Burns) to all the poets in the anthology. Finally, we have adopted a larger and bolder typeface and redesigned the page, so as to make the text more readable and more agreeable to the eye.

Three cardinal innovations, one print and two electronic, greatly increase the anthology's flexibility. The Seventh Edition is available in the traditional one-volume format, in clothbound and paperback versions, and in a new two-volume paperback version comprised of Volume A, covering the Middle Ages through the Restoration and the Eighteenth Century, and Volume B, covering the Romantic Period through the Twentieth Century. By maintaining the same pagination as in the original volume, the two-volume format offers a more portable option for students.

Extending beyond the printed page, the Norton Topics Online Web site (www.wwnorton.com/nael) augments the anthology's already broad representation of the sweep of English literature and greatly enlarges the representation of graphic materials that are relevant to literary studies. For students who wish to extend their exploration of the contexts of this literature, the Web site offers a huge range of related texts, prepared by the anthology editors, and by Myron Tuman, University of Alabama, and Philip Schwyzer, Oxford University. An ongoing venture, the Web site currently offers twenty-one thematic clusters—three per period—of texts and visual images, cross-referenced to the anthology, together with overviews, study explorations, and annotated links to related sites.

The Norton Topics Online Web site enables us to address effectively one of the problems that faces any anthology, however capacious and far-reaching: the need to make available at least some of the vast textual and visual resources that lie just beyond the borders of the selected literary works. The Web makes it possible as well to address another crucial problem: the need to respond to changing interests by adding new works to the printed anthology, without altogether losing the texts that considerations of space force us to drop. The solution, our second electronic innovation, is the Norton Online Archive, an ongoing project that at present includes more than 150 texts dropped from earlier editions of *The Norton Anthology of English Literature*, ranging from the Middle Ages to the early Victorian period (www.wwnorton. com/nael/noa). This archive, which will continue to grow as future editions are revised and altered, provides carefully edited Norton texts, with glosses and notes, that may be downloaded and printed. It will also constitute a valuable record of the ongoing shifts in literary and cultural interest.

Two valuable further features should be mentioned. In response to numerous requests from instructors who use the Audio Companion accompanying the anthology, we are making an expanded version available without charge to students purchasing new copies of *The Norton Anthology of English Literature*, Seventh Edition, The Major Authors. The two compact disks offer readings by the authors of the works represented in the anthology, readings of poems in Old and Middle English and in English dialects, and performances of poems written to be set to music. New to the Audio Companion, Disk 1, are a generous sampling of Seamus Heaney's reading of his translation of *Beowulf*, a selection from *The Battle of Maldon* read by R. D. Fulk, and additional Chaucer selections read by V. A. Kolve. Recordings of the poets Robert Graves, Ted Hughes, Eavan Boland, and Thom Gunn reading their work have been added to Disk 2.

The Course Guide to accompany *The Norton Anthology of English Literature*, by Alfred David (Indiana University), Kelly Hurley (University of Colorado at Boulder), and Philip Schwyzer (Oxford University), has been thoroughly revised and expanded. It contains thematic discussions of selected works in each period, sample reading lists for several kinds of survey and topical courses, study and essay questions, and cross-references to the Web materials and audio recordings that accompany the anthology. A copy of the Guide may be obtained on request from the publisher.

The editors are deeply grateful to the hundreds of teachers worldwide who have helped us to improve the Major Authors edition of *The Norton Anthology of English Literature*. A list of the advisors who prepared in-depth reviews and of the instructors who replied to a detailed questionnaire follows on a separate page, under Acknowledgments. The editors would like to express appreciation for their assistance to Tiffany Beechy (Harvard University), Mitch Cohen (Wissenschaftskolleg zu Berlin), Sandie Byrne (Oxford University), Sarah Cole (Columbia University), Dianne Ferriss (Cornell University), Robert Folkenflik (University of California, Irvine), Robert D. Fulk (Indiana University), Andrew Gurr (The University of Reading), Wendy Hyman (Harvard University), Elissa Linke (Wissenschaftskolleg zu Berlin), Joanna Lipking (Northwestern University), Linda O'Riordan (Wissenschaftskolleg zu Berlin), Ruth Perry (M.I.T.), Leah Price (Harvard University), Ramie Targoff (Yale University), and Douglas Trevor (Harvard University).

The editors give special thanks to Paul Leopold, who drafted the appendix on Geographic Nomenclature and revised the appendix on Religions in England, and to Philip Schwyzer (Oxford University), whose wide-ranging contributions include preparing texts and study materials for the Web site, assisting with the revision of numerous headnotes, and updating appendices on the British baronage and British money. We also thank the many people at Norton who contributed to the Major Authors, Seventh Edition: Julia Reidhead, who served not only as the inhouse supervisor but also as an unfailingly wise and effective collaborator in every aspect of planning and accomplishing this revision; Marian Johnson, developmental editor, who kept the project moving forward with a remarkable blend of focused energy, intelligence, and common sense; Candace Levy, Ann Tappert, Barry Katzen, Lynn Cannon Menges, David Hawkins, and Will Rigby, project and manuscript editors; Julie Tedoff, Web site editor; Diane O'Connor, production manager; Kristin Sheerin and Ann Marcy, permissions managers; Toni Krass, designer; Neil Ryder Hoos, art researcher; and Christa Grenawalt and Brian Baker, editorial assistants. All these friends provided the editors with indispensable help in meeting the challenge of representing justly the unparalleled range and variety of English literature.

M. H. Abrams
Stephen Greenblatt

Acknowledgments

Among our many critics, advisors, and friends, the following were of especial help toward the preparation of the Seventh Edition, either by offering advice or by providing critiques of particular periods of the anthology: Jonathon Allison (University of Kentucky), Rebecca Argall (University of Memphis), Christopher Baker (Armstrong Atlantic State University), Mark R. Blackwell (California State University, Chico), Mary Blockley (University of Texas at Austin), James Brown (Charleston State University), Alexander Bruce (Florida Southern College), Yvonne Bruce (The Citadel), Howard Cole (University of Illinois), Natalie B. Cole (Oakland University), Joanne Craig (Bishop's University), R. W. Crump (Louisiana State University), James E. Doan (Nova Southeastern University), Helen V. Emmitt (Virginia Military University), Laura Fasick (Moorhead State University), Suzanne Ferriss (Nova Southeastern University), Julia A. Fesmire (Middle Tennessee State University), Rosemary Fisk (Samford University), Robert Forman (St. John's University, Jamaica), Rosanne Gasse (Brandon University), Ronald W. Harris (Southeastern Louisiana University), Elizabeth Hedrick (University of Texas at Austin), Brooke Hopkins (University of Utah), Susan Jones (Palm Beach Atlantic College), Stewart Justman (University of Montana), Robert G. Laird (Carleton University), Yixiong Liang (Mohawk Valley Community College), David Lindstrom (Colorado State University), Scott Lucas (The Citadel), Paul McCarron (Texas A&M), J. McGinty (Delta College), S. Jaret McKinstry (Charleston College), K. Moore-Jumonville (Taylor University), Patricia Moran (University of California, Davis), Mary A. Papazian (Oakland University), Mary Pharr (Florida Southern College), Jim Read (Allan Hancock College), James A. W. Rembert (The Citadel), William O. Shakespeare (Brigham Young University), Isabel B. Stanley (East Tennessee State University), James W. Stick, Jr. (Des Moines Area Community College), Charlotte Templin (University of Indianapolis), Theresa Mae Thompson (Valdosta State University), Joel Westerholm (Northwestern College, Orange City), Matthew Wikander (University of Toledo), Thomas Willard (University of Arizona), Lloyd Worley (University of North Colorado).

The Persistence of English

Geoffrey Nunberg

Stanford University and Xerox Palo Alto Research Center

THE TRIUMPH OF ENGLISH?

If you measure the success of a language in purely quantitative terms, English is entering the twenty-first century at the moment of its greatest triumph. It has between 400 and 450 million native speakers, perhaps 300 million more who speak it as a second language—well enough, that is, to use it in their daily lives—and somewhere between 500 and 750 million who speak it as a foreign language with various degrees of fluency. The resulting total of between 1.2 billion and 1.5 billion speakers, or roughly a quarter of the world's population, gives English more speakers than any other language (though Chinese has more native speakers). Then, too, English is spoken over a much wider geographical area than any other language and is the predominant lingua franca of most fields of international activity, such as diplomacy, business, travel, science, and technology.

But figures like these can obscure a basic question: what exactly do we mean when we talk about the "English language" in the first place? There is, after all, an enormous range of variation in the forms of speech that go by the name of English in the various parts of the world—or often, even within the speech of a single nation—and it is not obvious why we should think of all of these as belonging to a single language. Indeed, there are some linguists who prefer to talk about "world Englishes," in the plural, with the implication that these varieties may not have much more to unite them than a single name and a common historical origin.

To the general public, these reservations may be hard to understand; people usually assume that languages are natural kinds like botanical species, whose boundaries are matters of scientific fact. But as linguists observe, there is nothing in the forms of English themselves that tells us that it is a single language. It may be that the varieties called "English" have a great deal of vocabulary and structure in common and that English-speakers can usually manage to make themselves understood to one another, more or less (though films produced in one part of the English-speaking world often have to be dubbed or subtitled to make them intelligible to audiences in another). But there are many cases where we find linguistic varieties that are mutually intelligible and grammatically similar, but where speakers nonetheless identify separate languages—for example, Danish and Norwegian, Czech and Slovak, or Dutch and Afrikaans. And on the other hand, there are cases where speakers identify varieties as belonging to a single language even though they are linguistically quite distant from one another: the various "dialects" of Chinese are more different from one another than the Latin offshoots that we identify now as French, Italian, Spanish, and so forth.

Philosophers sometimes compare languages to games, and the analogy is apt here, as well. Trying to determine whether American English and British English or Dutch and Afrikaans are "the same language" is like trying to determine whether baseball and softball are "the same game"—it is not something you can find out just by looking at their rules. It is not surprising, then, that linguists should throw up their hands when someone asks them to determine on linguistic grounds alone whether two varieties belong to a single language. That, they answer, is a political or social determination, not a linguistic one, and they usually go on to cite a well-known quip: "a language is just a dialect with an army and a navy."

There is something to this remark. Since the eighteenth century, it has been widely believed that every nation deserved to have its own language, and declarations of political independence have often been followed by declarations of linguistic independence. Until recently, for example, the collection of similar language varieties that were spoken in most of central Yugoslavia was regarded as a single language, Serbo-Croatian, but once the various regions became independent, their inhabitants began to speak of Croatian, Serbian, and Bosnian as separate languages, even though they are mutually comprehensible and grammatically almost identical.

The English language has avoided this fate (though on occasion it has come closer to breaking up than most people realize). But the unity of a language is never a foregone conclusion. In any speech-community, there are forces always at work to create new differences and varieties: the geographic and social separation of speech-communities, their distinct cultural and practical interests, their contact with other cultures and other languages, and, no less important, a universal fondness for novelty for its own sake, and a desire to speak differently from one's parents or the people in the next town. Left to function on their own, these centrifugal pressures can rapidly lead to the linguistic fragmentation of the speech-community. That is what happened, for example, to the vulgar (that is, "popular") Latin of the late Roman Empire, which devolved into hundreds or thousands of separate dialects (the emergence of the eight or ten standard varieties that we now think of as the Romance languages was a much later development).

Maintaining the unity of a language over an extended time and space, then, requires a more or less conscious determination by its speakers that they have certain communicative interests in common that make it worthwhile to try to curb or modulate the natural tendency to fragmentation and isolation. This determination can be realized in a number of ways. The speakers of a language may decide to use a common spelling system even when dialects become phonetically distinct, to defer to a common set of literary models, to adopt a common format for their dictionaries and grammars, or to make instruction in the standard language a part of the general school curriculum, all of which the English-speaking world has done to some degree. Or in some other places, the nations of the linguistic community may establish academies or other state institutions charged with regulating the use of the language, and even go so far as to publish lists of words that are unacceptable for use in the press or in official publications, as the French have done in recent years. Most important, the continuity of the language rests on speakers' willingness to absorb the linguistic and cultural influences of other parts of the linguistic community.

THE EMERGENCE OF THE ENGLISH LANGUAGE

To recount the history of a language, then, is not simply to trace the development of its various sounds, words, and constructions. Seen from that exclusively linguistic point of view, there would be nothing to distinguish the evolution of Anglo-Saxon into the varieties of modern English from the evolution of Latin into modern French, Italian, and so forth—we would not be able to tell, that is, why English continued to be considered a single language while the Romance languages did not. We also have to follow the play of centrifugal and centripetal forces that kept the language always more or less a unity—the continual process of creation of new dialects and varieties, the countervailing rise of new standards and of mechanisms aimed at maintaining the linguistic center of gravity.

Histories of the English language usually put its origin in the middle of the fifth century, when several Germanic peoples first landed in the place we now call England and began to displace the local inhabitants, the Celts. There is no inherent linguistic reason why we should locate the beginning of the language at this time, rather than with the Norman Conquest of 1066 or in the fourteenth century, say, and in fact the determination that English began with the Anglo-Saxon period was not generally accepted until the nineteenth century. But this point of view has been to a certain extent self-fulfilling, if only because it has led to the addition of Anglo-Saxon works to the canon of English literature, where they remain. Languages are constructions over time as well as over space.

Wherever we place the beginnings of English, though, there was never a time when the language was not diverse. The Germanic peoples who began to arrive in England in the fifth century belonged to a number of distinct tribes, each with its own dialect, and tended to settle in different parts of the country—the Saxons in the southwest, the Angles in the east and north, the Jutes (and perhaps some Franks) in Kent. These differences were the first source of the distinct dialects of the language we now refer to as Anglo-Saxon or Old English. As time went by, the linguistic divisions were reinforced by geography and by the political fragmentation of the country, and later, through contact with the Vikings who had settled the eastern and northern parts of England in the eighth through eleventh centuries.

Throughout this period, though, there were also forces operating to consolidate the language of England. Over the centuries, cultural and political dominance passed from Northumbria in the north to Mercia in the center and then to Wessex in the southwest, where a literary standard emerged in the ninth century, owing in part to the unification of the kingdom and in part to the singular efforts of Alfred the Great (849–899), who encouraged literary production in English and himself translated Latin works into the language. The influence of these standards and the frequent communication between the regions worked to level many of the dialect differences. There is a striking example of the process in the hundreds of everyday words derived from the language of the Scandinavian settlers, which include *dirt, lift, sky, skin, die, birth, weak, seat,* and *want.* All of these spread to general usage from the northern and eastern dialects in which they were first introduced, an indication of how frequent and ordinary were the contacts among the Anglo-Saxons of various parts of the country—and initially, between the Anglo-Saxons and the Scandinavians themselves. (By contrast, the Celtic peoples that the Anglo-Saxons had displaced made relatively few contributions to the language, apart from place-names like *Thames, Avon,* and *Dover.*)

The Anglo-Saxon period came to an abrupt end with the Norman Conquest of 1066. With the introduction of a French-speaking ruling class, the written use of English was greatly reduced for a hundred and fifty years. English did not reappear extensively in written records until the beginning of the thirteenth century, and even then it was only one of the languages of a multilingual community: French was widely used for another two hundred years or so (Parliament was conducted in French until 1362), and Latin was the predominant language of scholarship until the Renaissance. The English language that re-emerged in this period was considerably changed from the language of Alfred's period. Its grammar was simplified, continuing a process already under way before the Conquest, and its vocabulary was enriched by thousands of French loan words. Not surprisingly, given the preeminent role of French among the elite, these included the language of government (*majesty, state, rebel*); of religion (*pastor, ordain, temptation*); of fashion and social life (*button, adorn, dinner*); and of art, literature, and medicine (*painting, chapter, paper, physician*). But the breadth of French influence was not limited to those domains; it also provided simple words like *move, aim, join, solid, chief, clear, air,* and *very.* All of this left the language sufficiently different from Old English to warrant describing it with the name of Middle English, though we should bear in mind that language change is always gradual and that the division of English into neat periods is chiefly a matter of scholarly convenience.

Middle English was as varied a language as Old English was: Chaucer wrote in *Troilus and Criseyde* that "ther is so gret diversite in Englissh" that he was fearful that the text would be misread in other parts of the country. It was only in the fifteenth century or so that anything like a standard language began to emerge, based in the speech of the East Midlands and in particular of London, which reflected the increased centralization of political and economic power in that region. Even then, though, dialect differences remained strong; John Palsgrave complained in 1540 that the speech of university students was tainted by "the rude language used in their native countries [i.e., counties]," which left them unable to express themselves in their "vulgar tongue."

The language itself continued to change as it moved into what scholars describe as the Early Modern English period, which for convenience sake we can date from the year 1500. Around this time, it began to undergo the Great Vowel Shift, as the long vowels engaged in an intricate dance that left them with new phonetic values. (In Chaucer's time, the word *bite* had been pronounced roughly as "beet," *beet* as "bate," *name* as "nahm," and so forth.) The grammar was changing as well; for example, the pronoun *thee* began to disappear, as did the verbal suffix-*eth*, and the modern form of questions began to emerge: in place of "See you that house?" people began to say "Do you see that house?" Most significantly, at least so far as contemporary observers were concerned, the Elizabethans and their successors coined thousands of new words based on Latin and Greek in an effort to make English an adequate replacement for Latin in the writing of philosophy, science, and literature. Many of these words now seem quite ordinary to us—for example, *accommodation*, *frugal*, *obscene*, *premeditated*, and *submerge*, all of which are recorded for the first time in Shakespeare's works. A large proportion of these linguistic experiments, though, never gained a foothold in the language—for example, *illecebrous* for "delicate," *deruncinate* for "to weed," *obtestate* for "call on," or Shakespeare's *disquantity* to mean "diminish." Indeed, some contemporaries ridiculed the pretension and obscurity of these "inkhorn words" in terms that sound very like modern criticisms of bureaucratic and corporate jargon—the rhetorician Thomas Wilson wrote in 1540 of the writers who affected "outlandish English" such that "if some of their mothers were alive, they were not able to tell what they say." But this effect was inevitable: the additions to the standard language that made it a suitable vehicle for art and scholarship could only increase the linguistic distance between the written language used by the educated classes and the spoken language used by other groups.

DICTIONARIES AND RULES

These were essentially growing pains for the standard language, which continued to gain ground in the sixteenth and seventeenth centuries, abetted by a number of developments: the ever-increasing dominance of London and the Southeast, the growth in social and geographic mobility, and in particular the introduction and spread of print, which led both to higher levels of literacy and schooling and to the gradual standardization of English spelling. But even as this process was going on, other developments were both creating new distinctions and investing existing ones with a new importance. For one thing, people were starting to pay more attention to accents based on social class, rather than region, an understandable preoccupation as social mobility increased and speech became a more important indicator of social background. Not surprisingly, the often imperfect efforts of the emerging middle class to speak and dress like their social superiors occasioned some ridicule; Thomas Gainsford wrote in 1616 of the "foppish mockery" of commoners who tried to imitate gentlemen by altering "habit, manner of life, conversation, and even their phrase of speech." Yet even the upper classes were paying more attention to speech as a social indicator than they had in previous ages; as one writer put it, "it is a pitty when a Noble man is better distinguished from a Clowne by his golden laces, than by his good language." (Shakespeare plays on this theme in *I Henry IV* [3.1.250, 257–58] when he has Hotspur tease his wife for swearing too daintily, which makes her sound like "a comfit-maker's wife," rather than "like a lady as thou art," with "a good mouth-filling oath.")

Over the course of the seventeenth and eighteenth centuries, print began to exercise a paradoxical effect on the perception of the language: even as it was serving to codify the standard, it was also making people more aware of variation and more anxious about its consequences. This was largely the result of the growing importance of print, as periodicals, novels, and other new forms became increasingly influential in shaping public opinion, together with the perception that the contributors to the print discourse were drawn from a wider range of backgrounds than in previous periods. As Samuel Johnson wrote: "The present age . . . may be styled, with great propriety, the Age of Authors; for, perhaps, there was never a time when men of all degrees of ability, of every kind of education, of every profession and employment were posting with ardor so general to the press. . . ."

This anxiety about the language was behind the frequent eighteenth-century lamentations that English was "unruled," "barbarous," or, as Johnson put it, "copious without order, and energetick without rule." Some writers looked for a remedy in public institutions modeled on the French Academy. This idea was advocated by John Dryden, Daniel Defoe, Joseph Addison, and most notably by Jonathan Swift, in a 1712 pamphlet called A *Proposal for Correcting, Improving, and Ascertaining* [i.e., "fixing"] *the English Tongue*, which did receive some official attention from the Tory government. But the idea was dropped as a Tory scheme when the Whigs came to power two years later, and by the middle of the eighteenth century, there was wide agreement among all parties that an academy would be an unwarranted intervention in the free conduct of public discourse. Samuel Johnson wrote in the Preface to his *Dictionary* of 1775 that he hoped that "the spirit of English liberty will hinder or destroy" any attempt to set up an academy; and the scientist and radical Joseph Priestly called such an institution "unsuitable to the genius of a *free nation*."

The rejection of the idea of an academy was to be important in the subsequent development of the language. From that time forward, it was clear that the state was not to play a major role in regulating and reforming the language, whether in England or in the other nations of the language community—a characteristic that makes English different from many other languages. (In languages like French and German, for example, spelling reforms can be introduced by official commissions charged with drawing up rules which are then adopted in all textbooks and official publications, a procedure that would be unthinkable in any of the nations of the English-speaking world.) Instead, the task of determining standards was left to private citizens, whose authority rested on their ability to gain general public acceptance.

The eighteenth century saw an enormous growth in the number of grammars and handbooks, which formulated most of the principles of correct English that, for better or worse, are still with us today—the rules for using *who* and *whom*, for example, the injunction against constructions like "very unique," and the curious prejudice against the split infinitive. Even more important was the development of the modern English dictionary. Before 1700, English speakers had to make do with alphabetical lists of "hard-words," a bit like the vocabulary improvement books that are still frequent today; it was only in the early 1700s that scholars began to produce anything like a comprehensive dictionary in the modern sense, a process that culminated in the publication of Samuel Johnson's magisterial *Dictionary* of 1755. It would be hard to argue that these dictionaries did much in fact to reduce variation or to arrest the process of linguistic change (among the words that Johnson objected to, for example, were *belabor*, *budge*, *cajole*, *coax*, *doff*, *gambler*, and *job*, all of which have since become part of the standard language). But they did serve to ease the sense of linguistic crisis, by providing a structure for describing the language and points of reference for resolving disputes about grammar and meaning. And while both the understanding of language and the craft of lexicography have made a great deal of progress since Johnson's time, the form of the English-language dictionary is still pretty much as he laid it down. (In this regard, Johnson's *Dictionary* is likely to present a much more familiar appearance to a modern reader than his poetry or periodical essays.)

THE DIFFUSION OF ENGLISH

The Modern English period saw the rise of another sort of variation, as well, as English began to spread over an increasingly larger area. By Shakespeare's time, English was displacing the Celtic languages in Wales, Cornwall, and Scotland, and then in Ireland, where the use of Irish was brutally repressed on the assumption—in retrospect a remarkably obtuse one—that people who were forced to become English in tongue would soon become English in loyalty as well. People in these new parts of the English-speaking world—a term we can begin to use in this period, for English was no longer the language of a single country—naturally used the language in accordance with their own idiom and habits of thought and mixed it with words drawn from the Celtic languages, a number of which eventually entered the speech of the larger linguistic community, for example, *baffle, bun, clan, crag, drab, galore, hubbub, pet, slob, slogan,* and *trousers.*

The development of the language in the New World followed the same process of differentiation. English settlers in North America rapidly developed their own characteristic forms of speech. They retained a number of words that had fallen into disuse in England (*din, clod, trash,* and *fall* for *autumn*) and gave old words new senses (like *corn,* which in England meant simply "grain," or *creek,* originally "an arm of the sea"). They borrowed freely from the other languages they came in contact with. By the time of the American Revolution, the colonists had already taken *chowder, cache, prairie,* and *bureau* from French; *noodle* and *pretzel* from German; *cookie, boss,* and *scow* and *yankee* from the Dutch; and *moose, skunk, chipmunk, succotash, toboggan,* and *tomahawk* from various Indian languages. And they coined new words with abandon. Some of these answered to their specific needs and interests—for example, *squatter, clearing, foothill, watershed, congressional, sidewalk*—but there were thousands of others that had no close connection to the American experience as such, many of which were ultimately adopted by the other varieties of English. *Belittle, influential, reliable, comeback, lengthy, turn down, make good*—all of these were originally American creations; they and other words like them indicate how independently the language was developing in the New World.

This process was repeated wherever English took root—in India, Africa, the Far East, the Caribbean, and Australia and New Zealand; by the late nineteenth century, English bore thousands of souvenirs of its extensive travels. From Africa (sometimes via Dutch) came words like *banana, boorish, palaver, gorilla,* and *guinea;* from the aboriginal languages of Australia came *wombat* and *kangaroo;* from the Caribbean languages came *cannibal, hammock, potato,* and *canoe;* and from the languages of India came *bangle, bun-*

galow, chintz, cot, dinghy, jungle, loot, pariah, pundit, and *thug.* And even lists like these are misleading, since they include only words that worked their way into the general English vocabulary and don't give a sense of the thousands of borrowings and coinages that were used only locally. Nor do they touch on the variation in grammar from one variety to the next. This kind of variation occurs everywhere, but it is particularly marked in regions like the Caribbean and Africa, where the local varieties of English are heavily influenced by English-based creoles—that is, language varieties that use English-based vocabulary with grammars largely derived from African languages. This is the source, for example, of a number of the distinctive syntactic features of the variety used by many inner-city African Americans, like the "invariant *be*" of sentences like *We be living in Chicago,* which signals a state of affairs that holds for an extended period. (Some linguists have suggested that Middle English, in fact, could be thought of as a kind of creolized French.)

The growing importance of these new forms of English, particularly in America, presented a new challenge to the unity of the language. Until the eighteenth century, English was still thought of as essentially a national language. It might be spoken in various other nations and colonies under English control, but it was nonetheless rooted in the speech of England and subject to a single standard. Not surprisingly, Americans came to find this picture uncongenial, and when the United States first declared its independence from Britain, there was a strong sentiment for declaring that "American," too, should be recognized as a separate language. This was the view held by John Adams, Thomas Jefferson, and above all by America's first and greatest lexicographer, Noah Webster, who argued that American culture would naturally come to take a distinct form in the soil of the New World, free from what he described as "the old feudal and hierarchical establishments of England." And if a language was naturally the product and reflection of a national culture, then Americans could scarcely continue to speak "English." As Webster wrote in 1789: "Culture, habits, and language, as well as government should be national. America should have her own distinct from the rest of the world. . . ." It was in the interest of symbolically distinguishing American from English that Webster introduced a variety of spelling changes, such as *honor* and *favor* for *honour* and *favour, theater* for *theatre, traveled* for *travelled,* and so forth—a procedure that new nations often adopt when they want to make their variety of a language look different from its parent tongue.

In fact Webster's was by no means an outlandish suggestion. Even at the time of American independence, the linguistic differences between America and Britain were as great as those that separate many languages today, and the differences would have become much more salient if Americans had systematically adopted all of the spelling reforms that Webster at one time proposed, such as *wurd, reezon, tung, iz,* and so forth, which would ultimately have left English and American looking superficially no more similar than German and Dutch. Left to develop on their own, English and American might soon have gone their separate ways, perhaps paving the way for the separation of the varieties of English used in other parts of the world.

In the end, of course, the Americans and British decided that neither their linguistic nor their cultural and political differences warranted recognizing distinct languages. Webster himself conceded the point in 1828, when he entitled his magnum opus *An American Dictionary of the English Language*. And by 1862 the English novelist Anthony Trollope could write:

> An American will perhaps consider himself to be as little like an Englishman as he is like a Frenchman. But he reads Shakespeare through the medium of his own vernacular, and has to undergo the penance of a foreign tongue before he can understand Molière. He separates himself from England in politics and perhaps in affection; but he cannot separate himself from England in mental culture.

ENGLISH AND ENGLISHNESS

This was a crucial point of transition, which set the English language on a very different course from most of the European languages, where the association of language and national culture was being made more strongly than ever before. But the detachment of English from Englishness did not take place overnight. For Trollope and his Victorian contemporaries, the "mental culture" of the English-speaking world was still a creation of England, the embodiment of English social and political values. "The English language," said G. C. Swayne in 1862, "is like the English constitution . . . and perhaps also the English Church, full of inconsistencies and anomalies, yet flourishing in defiance of theory." The monumental *Oxford English Dictionary* that the Victorians undertook was conceived in this patriotic spirit. In the words of Archbishop Richard Chevenix Trench, one of the guiding spirits of the OED project:

> We could scarcely have a lesson on the growth of our English tongue, we could scarcely follow upon one of its significant words, without having unawares a lesson in English history as well, without not merely falling upon some curious fact illustrative of our national life, but learning also how the great heart which is beating at the centre of that life, was being gradually shaped and moulded.

It was this conception of the significance of the language that led, too, to the insistence that the origin of the English language should properly be located in Anglo-Saxon, rather than in the thirteenth or fourteenth centuries, as scholars argued that contemporary English laws and institutions could be traced to a primordial "Anglo-Saxon spirit" in an almost racial line of descent, and that the Anglo-Saxon language was "immediately connected with the original introduction and establishment of their present language and their laws, their liberty, and their religion."

This view of English as the repository of "Anglo-Saxon" political ideals had its appeal in America, as well, particularly in the first decades of the twentieth century, when the crusade to "Americanize" recent immigrants led a number of states to impose severe restrictions on the use of other languages in schools, newspapers, and public meetings, a course that was often justified on the grounds that only speakers of English were in a position to fully appreciate the nuances of democratic thought. As a delegate to a New York State constitutional convention in 1916 put the point: "You have got to learn our language because that is the vehicle of the thought that has been handed down from the men in whose breasts first burned the fire of freedom at the signing of the Magna Carta."

But this view of the language is untenable on both linguistic and historical grounds. It is true that the nations of the English-speaking world have a common political heritage that makes itself known in similar legal systems and an (occasionally shaky) predilection for democratic forms of government. But while there is no doubt that the possession of a common language has helped to reinforce some of these connections, it is not responsible for them. Languages do work to create a common worldview, but not at such a specific level. Words like *democracy* move easily from one language to the next, along with the concepts they name—a good thing for the English-speaking world, since a great many of those ideals of "English democracy," as the writer calls it, owe no small debt to thinkers in Greece, Italy, France, Germany, and a number of other places, and those ideals have been established in many nations that speak languages other than English. (Thirteenth-century England was one of them. We should bear in mind that the Magna Carta that people sometimes like to mention in this context was a Latin document issued by a French-speaking king to French-speaking barons.) For that matter, there are English-speaking nations where democratic institutions have not taken root—nor should we take their continuing health for granted even in the core nations of the English-speaking world.

In the end, the view of English as the repository of Englishness has the effect of marginalizing or disenfranchising large parts of the English-speaking world, particularly those who do not count the political and cultural imposition of Englishness as an unmixed blessing. In most of the places where English has been planted, after all, it has had the British flag flying above it. And for many nations, it has been hard to slough off the sense of English as a colonial language. There is a famous passage in James Joyce's *Portrait of the Artist as a Young Man*, for example, where Stephen Daedelus says of the speech of an English-born dean, "The language in which we are speaking is his not mine," and there are still many people in Ireland and other parts of the English-speaking world who have mixed feelings about the English language: they may use and even love English, but they resent it, too.

Today the view of English as an essentially English creation is impossible to sustain even on purely linguistic grounds; the influences of the rest of the English-speaking world have simply been too great. Already in Trollope's time there were vociferous complaints in England about the growing use of Americanisms, a sign that the linguistic balance of payments between the two communities was tipping westward, and a present-day English writer would have a hard time producing a single paragraph that contained no words that originated in other parts of the linguistic community. Nor, what is more important, could you find a modern British or North American writer whose work was not heavily influenced, directly or indirectly, by the literature of the rest of the linguistic community, particularly after the extraordinary twentieth-century efflorescence of the English-language literatures of other parts of the world. Trying to imagine modern English literature without the contributions of writers like Yeats, Shaw, Joyce, Beckett, Heaney, Walcott, Lessing, Gordimer, Rushdie, Achebe, and Naipaul (to take only some of the writers who are included in this collection) is like trying to imagine an "English" cuisine that made no use of potatoes, tomatoes, corn, noodles, eggplant, olive oil, almonds, bay leaf, curry, or pepper.

THE FEATURES OF "STANDARD ENGLISH"

Where should we look, then, for the common "mental culture" that English-speakers share? This is always a difficult question to answer, partly because the understanding of the language changes from one place and time to the next, and partly because it is hard to say just what sorts of things languages are in the abstract. For all that we may want to think of the English-speaking world as a single community united by a common worldview, it is not a social group comparable to a tribe or people or nation—the sorts of groups that can easily evoke the first-person plural pronoun *we*. (Americans and Australians travel around saying "We gave the world Shakespeare," even though one might think that as paid-up members of the English-speaking community they would be entirely within their rights to do so.)

But we can get some sense of the ties that connect the members of the English-speaking community by starting with the language itself—not just in its forms and rules, but in the centripetal forces spoken of earlier. Forces like these are operating in every language community, it's true, but what gives each language its unique character is the way they are realized, the particular institutions and cultural commonalties which work to smooth differences and create a basis for continued communication—which ensure, in short, that English will continue as a single language, rather than devolve into a collection of dialects that are free to wander wherever they will.

People often refer to this basis for communication as "Standard English," but that term is misleading. There are many linguistic communities that do have a genuine standard variety, a fixed and invariant form of the language that is used for certain kinds of communication. But that notion of the standard would be unsuitable to a language like English, which recognizes no single cultural center and has to allow for a great deal of variation even in the language of published texts. (It is rare to find a single page of an English-language novel or newspaper that does not reveal what nation it was written in.) What English does have, rather, is a collection of standard features—of spelling, of grammar, and of word use—which taken together ensure that certain kinds of communication will be more or less comprehensible in any part of the language community.

The standard features of English are as notable for what they don't contain as for what they do. One characteristic of English, for example, is that it has no standard pronunciation. People pronounce the language according to whatever their regional practice happens to be, and while certain pronunciations may be counted as "good" or "bad" according to local standards, there are no general rules about this, the way there are in French or Italian. (Some New Yorkers may be stigmatized for pronouncing words like *car* and *bard* as 'kah' and 'bahd', but roughly the same *r*-less pronunciation is standard in parts of the American South and in England, South Africa, Australia, and New Zealand.) In this sense, "standard English" exists only as a written language. Of course there is some variation in the rules of written English, as well, such as the American spellings that Webster introduced, but these are relatively minor and tend to date from earlier periods. A particular speech-community can pronounce the words *half* or *car* however it likes, but it can't unilaterally change the way the words are spelled. Indeed, this is one of the unappreciated advantages of the notoriously irregular English spelling system—it is so plainly *un*phonetic that there's no temptation to take it as codifying any particular spoken variety. When you want to define a written standard in a linguistic community that embraces no one standard accent, it's useful to have a spelling system that doesn't tip its hand.

The primacy of the written language is evident in the standard English vocabulary, too, if only indirectly. The fact is that English as such does not give us a complete vocabulary for talking about the world, but only for certain kinds of topics. If you want to talk about vegetables in English, for example, you have to choose among the usages common in one or another region: depending on where you do your shopping, you will talk about *rutabagas*, *scallions*, and *string beans* or *Swedes*, *spring onions*, and *French beans*. That is, you can only talk about vegetables in your capacity as an American, an Englishman, or whatever, not in your capacity as an English-speaker in general. And similarly for fashion (*sweater* vs. *jumper*, *bobby pin* vs. *hair grip*, *vest* vs. *waistcoat*), for car parts (*hood* vs. *bonnet*, *trunk* vs. *boot*), and for food, sport, transport, and furniture, among many other things.

The English-language vocabulary is much more standardized, though, in other areas of the lexicon. We have a large common vocabulary for talking about aspects of our social and moral life—*blatant*, *vanity*, *smug*, *indifferent*, and the like. We have a common repertory of grammatical constructions and "signpost" expressions—for example, adverbs like *arguably*, *literally*, and *of course*—which we use to organize our discourse and tell readers how to interpret it. And there is a large number of common words for talking about the language itself—for example, *slang*, *usage*, *jargon*, *succinct*, and *literate*. (It is striking how many of these words are particular to English. No other language has an exact synonym for *slang*, for example, or a single word that covers the territory that *literate* covers in English, from "able to read and write" to "knowledgeable or educated.")

The common "core vocabulary" of English is not limited to these notions, of course—for example, it includes as well the thousands of technical and scientific terms that are in use throughout the English-speaking world, like *global warming* and *penicillin*, which for obvious reasons are not particularly susceptible to cultural variation. Nor would it be accurate to say that the core vocabulary includes all the words we use to refer to our language or to our social and moral life, many of which have a purely local character. But the existence of a core vocabulary of common English words, as fuzzy as it may prove to be, is an indication of the source of our cultural commonalities. What is notable about words like *blatant*, *arguably*, and *succinct* is that their meanings are defined by reference to our common literature, and in particular to the usage of what the eighteenth-century philosopher George Campbell described as "authors of reputation"—writers whose authority is determined by "the esteem of the public." We would not take the usage of Ezra Pound or Bernard Shaw as authoritative in deciding what words like *sweater* or *rutabaga* mean—they could easily have been wrong about either—but their precedents carry a lot of weight when we come to talking about the meaning of *blatant* and *succinct*. In fact the body of English-language "authors of reputation" *couldn't* be wrong about the meanings of words like these, since it is their usage by these authors that collectively determines what these words mean. And for purposes of defining these words it does not matter where a writer is from. The *American Heritage Dictionary*, for example, uses citations from the Irish writer Samuel Beckett to illustrate the meanings of *exasperate* and *impulsion*, from the African-born Doris Lessing to illustrate the meaning of *efface*, and from the Englishman E. M. Forster to illustrate the meaning of *solitude;* and dictionaries from other communities feel equally free to draw on the whole of English literature to illustrate the meanings of the words of the common vocabulary.

It is this strong connection between our common language and our common literature that gives both the language and the linguistic community their essential unity. Late in the eighteenth century, Samuel Johnson said that Britain had become "a nation of readers," by which he meant not just that people were reading more than ever before, but that participation in the written discourse of English had become in some sense constitutive of the national identity. And while the English-speaking world and its ongoing conversation can no longer be identified with a single nation, that world is still very much a community of readers in this sense. Historically, at least, we use the language in the same way because we read and talk about the same books—not *all* the same books, of course, but a loose and shifting group of works that figure as points of reference for our use of language.

This sense of the core vocabulary based on a common literature is intimately connected to the linguistic culture that English-speakers share—the standards, beliefs, and institutions that keep the various written dialects of the language from flying apart. The English dictionary is a good example. It is true that each part of the linguistic community requires its own dictionaries, given the variation in vocabulary and occasionally in spelling and the rest, but they are all formed on more or less the same model, which is very different from that of the French or the Germans. They all organize their entries in the same way, use the same form of definitions, include the same kind of information, and so on, to the point where we often speak of "*the* dictionary," as if the book were a single, invariant text like "the periodic table." By the same token, the schools in every English-speaking nation generally teach the same principles of good usage, a large number of which date from the grammarians of the eighteenth century. There are a few notable exceptions to this generality (Americans and most other communities outside England abandoned some time ago the effort to keep *shall* and *will* straight and seem to be none the worse off for it), but even in these cases grammarians justify their prescriptions using the same terminology and forms of argument.

THE CONTINUITY OF ENGLISH

To be sure, our collective agreement on standards of language and literature is never more than approximate and is always undergoing redefinition and change. Things could hardly be otherwise, given the varied constitution of the English-speaking community, the changing social background, and the insistence of English-speakers that they must be left to decide these matters on their own, without the intervention of official commissions or academies. It is not surprising that the reference points that we depend on to maintain the continuity of the language should often be controversial, even within a single community, and even less so that different national communities should have different ideas as to who counts as authority or what kinds of texts should be relevant to defining the common core of English words. The most we can ask of our common linguistic heritage is that it give us a general format for adapting the language to new needs and for reinterpreting its significance from one time and place to another.

This is the challenge posed by the triumph of English. Granted, there is no threat to the hegemony of English as a worldwide medium for practical communication. It is a certainty that the nations of the English-speaking community will continue to use the various forms of English to communicate with each other, as well as with the hundreds of millions of people who speak English as a second language (and who in fact outnumber the native speakers of the language by a factor of two or three to one). And with the growth of travel and trade and of media like the Internet, the number of English-speakers is sure to continue to increase.

But none of this guarantees the unity of English as a means of cultural expression. What is striking about the accelerating spread of English over the past two centuries is not so much the number of speakers that the language has acquired, but the remarkable variety of the cultures and communities who use it. The heterogeneity of the linguistic community is evident not just in the emergence of the rich new literatures of Africa, Asia, and the Caribbean, but also in the literatures of what linguists sometimes call the "inner circle" of the English-speaking world—nations like Britain, the United States, Australia, and Canada—where the language is being asked to describe a much wider range of experience than ever before, particularly on behalf of groups who until recently have been largely excluded or marginalized from the collective conversation of the English-speaking world.

Not surprisingly, the speakers of the "new Englishes" use the language with different voices and different rhythms and bring to it different linguistic and cultural backgrounds. The language of a writer like Chinua Achebe reflects the influence not just of Shakespeare and Wordsworth but of proverbs and other forms of discourse drawn from West African oral traditions. Indian writers like R. K. Narayan and Salman Rushdie ground their works not just in the traditional English-language canon but in Sanskrit classics like the epic *Rāmāyana*. The continuing sense that all English-speakers are engaged in a common discourse depends on the linguistic community's being able to accommodate and absorb these new linguistic and literary influences, as it has been able to do in the past.

In all parts of the linguistic community, moreover, there are questions posed by the new media of discourse. Over the past hundred years, the primacy of print has been challenged first by the growth of film, recordings, and the broadcast media, and more recently by the remarkable growth of the Internet, each of which has had its effects on the language. With film and the rest, we have begun to see the emergence of spoken standards that coexist with the written standard of print, not in the form of a standardized English pronunciation—if anything, pronunciation differences among the communities of the English-speaking world have become more marked over the course of the century—but rather in the use of words, expressions, and rhythms that are particular to speech (there is no better example of this than the universal adoption of the particle *okay*). And the Internet has had the effect of projecting what were previously private forms of written communication, like the personal letter, into something more like models of public discourse, but with a language that is much more informal than the traditional discourse of the novel or newspaper.

It is a mistake to think that any of these new forms of discourse will wholly replace the discourse of print (the Internet, in particular, has shown itself to be an important vehicle for marketing and diffusing print works with much greater efficiency than has ever been possible before). It seems reasonable to assume that a hundred years from now the English-speaking world will still be at heart a community of readers—and of readers of books, among other things. And it is likely, too, that the English language will still be at heart a means of written expression, not just for setting down air schedules and trade statistics, but for doing the kind of cultural work that we have looked for literature to do for us in the past; a medium, that is, for poetry, criticism, history, and fiction. But only time will tell if English will remain a single language—if in the midst of all the diversity, cultural and communicative, people will still be able to discern a single "English literature" and a characteristic English-language frame of mind.

Geographic Nomenclature: England, Great Britain, The United Kingdom

The **British Isles** refers to the prominent group of islands off the northwest coast of Europe, especially to the two largest, **Great Britain** and **Ireland**. At present these comprise two sovereign states: **The Republic of Ireland**, or **Eire**, and **The United Kingdom of Great Britain and Northern Ireland**—known for short as **The United Kingdom** or **The U.K.** Most of the smaller islands are part of **The U.K.** but a few, like the **Isle of Man** and the tiny **Channel Islands,** are very largely independent. **The U.K.** is often loosely referred to as "**Britain**" or "**Great Britain**" and is sometimes simply called "**England.**" The latter usage, though technically inaccurate and occasionally confusing, is common among Englishmen as well as foreigners, though, for obvious reasons, it is rarely heard among the inhabitants of the other countries of **The U.K.**—**Scotland, Wales,** and **Northern Ireland** (sometimes called **Ulster**). England is by far the most populous part of the kingdom, as well as the seat of its capital, London.

From the first to the fifth century C.E. most of what is now **England** and **Wales** was a province of the Roman Empire called **Britain** (in Latin, **Britannia**). After the fall of Rome, much of the island was invaded and settled by peoples from northern Germany and Denmark speaking what we now call Old English. They are collectively known as the Anglo-Saxons, and the word **England** is related to the first element of their name. By the time of the Norman Conquest (1066) most of the kingdoms founded by the Anglo-Saxons and subsequent Viking invaders had coalesced into the kingdom of **England**, which, in the latter Middle Ages, conquered and largely absorbed the neighboring Celtic kingdom of **Wales**. In 1603 James VI of **Scotland** inherited the island's other throne as James I of **England,** and for the next hundred years—except for the brief period of Puritan rule—**Scotland** and **England** (with **Wales**) were two kingdoms under a single king. In 1707 the Act of Union welded them together as **The United Kingdom of Great Britain,** which, upon the incorporation of **Ireland** in 1801, became **The United Kingdom of Great Britain and Ireland**. With the division of Ireland and the establishment of **The Irish Free State** after World War I, this name was modified to its present form. In 1949 **The Irish Free State** became **The Republic of Ireland**; and in 1997 **Scotland** voted to restore the separate parliament it had relinquished in 1707, without, however, ceasing to be part of **The United Kingdom.**

The **British Isles** are further divided into counties, which in **Great Britain** are also known as shires. This word, with its vowel shortened in pronunciation, forms the suffix in the names of many counties, such as **Yorkshire, Wiltshire, Somersetshire.**

The Latin names **Britannia (Britain), Caledonia (Scotland),** and **Hibernia (Ireland)** are sometimes used in poetic diction; so too is **Britain**'s ancient Celtic name, **Albion.** Because of its accidental resemblance to *albus* (Latin for "white"), **Albion** is especially associated with the chalk cliffs which seem to gird much of the English coast like defensive walls.

The **British Empire** took its name from **The British Isles** because it was created not only by the **English** but by the **Irish, Scots,** and **Welsh,** as well as by civilians and servicemen from other constituent countries of the Empire.

British Money

Since 1971, British money has been calculated on the decimal system, with 100 pence to the pound; the pound has fluctuated from a bit more than 2 American dollars to virtual parity—whatever dollars may be worth. Before 1971, the pound consisted of 20 shillings, each containing 12 pence, making 240 pence to the pound. In paper money the change has not been great; 5- and 10-pound notes constitute the mass of bills under both the old and the new systems; nowadays, in addition, 20- and 50-pound notes have been added. But in the smaller coinage the change has been considerable and the simplification remarkable. Most notable is the abolition of the shilling, which goes into retirement now with the mark (worth in its day two-thirds of a pound or 13 shillings 4 pence) and the angel (once 10 shillings but replaced by the 10-shilling note, now in its turn abolished). The guinea, an oddity of the old currency, amounted to a pound and a shilling; though it has not been minted since 1813, a very few quality items or prestige awards (like horse races) may still be quoted in guineas. Colloquially, a pound was (and is) called a quid; a shilling a bob; sixpence a tanner; a penny, half-penny, or farthing, a copper. The common signs were £ for pound, s. for shilling, d. for a penny (from Latin *denarius*). A sum would normally be written £2.19.3, i.e., 2 pounds, 19 shillings, 3 pence. In Joyce's *Ulysses*, that is Leopold Bloom's budget for June 16, 1904. In new currency, it would be about £2.96.

Old	New
1 pound note	1 pound coin (or note in Scotland)
10 shilling (half-pound note)	50 pence
5 shilling (crown)	
	20 pence
2½ shilling (half crown)	
2 shilling (florin)	10 pence
1 shilling	5 pence
6 pence	
2½ pence	1 penny
2 pence	
1 penny	
½ penny	
¼ penny (farthing)	

What the pound was worth at any point in history is ever easy to state. In the first part of the twentieth century, 1 pound equaled about 5 American dollars; but those dollars bought three or four times what they would today. Historians sometimes attempt to calculate the value of the pound in terms of the goods and services it would purchase, but these too vary radically with special circumstances such as wars and poor harvests. Nevertheless, it is clear that money used to be worth much more than it is now. In the early sixteenth century, according to Hugh Latimer, people would say, "Oh, he's a rich man, he's worth £500." Four centuries later, Virginia Woolf argued that £500 a year (along with a room of one's own) was the bare minimum necessary for a woman to be able to write. Whatever Latimer meant by "rich," or Woolf by "necessary," it is clear that the value of the pound had declined drastically over this period, as it has continued to do in the course of the twentieth century. In Britain today, a worker on minimum wage earns more than £500 a month, an income associated with severe poverty.

In the Anglo-Saxon period, the silver penny was the biggest coin in general circulation; 4 of them would buy a sheep. Peasants and craftsmen before the Black Death of the fourteenth century made at most 2 or 3 pence a day—an annual income of £3 or £4; after the onset of the plague, wages nearly doubled, due to the shortage of laborers. Throughout the medieval period, kings and commoners worried less about inflation than about the debasement of the silver currency. In 1124, dozens of mintmasters had their right hands chopped off on Christmas Day for issuing inferior coinage. In the early sixteenth century, under Henry VIII and his son Edward VI, the silver content of coins fell as low as 25 percent. Elizabeth I considered the revaluation of the silver coinage to be one of her greatest achievements as queen. Nevertheless, her reign was marked by sustained inflation of prices, caused in part by the influx of gold and silver from the New World, and in part by the rising population.

In the Elizabethan era, admission to the public theaters cost a penny for those who stood throughout the performance. Playwrights were paid about £6 for each play, so to make a living a writer had to be prolific (or, like Shakespeare, own shares in the theater company). In the same period, 40 pounds a year in independent income (generally rent from lands) was the minimum requirement for a justice of the peace; it marked the threshold of gentry status and was also the sum fixed by King James I at which a man could be forced to accept knighthood (paying a fee to the crown). In 1661, following further inflation, Samuel Pepys calculated his worth at a modest £650 just after he had begun working for the navy; five years later, that good bourgeois was worth more than £6000, and his annual income was about £3000. Of course, he was working for most of this income. Pepys was a rising official and would become a very important one; but he never achieved a title or even knighthood because the smell of commerce had never been washed from his money by possession of land.

Various writers provide examples of the incomes of rich and poor in the eighteenth and nineteenth centuries. Joseph Andrews (in Fielding's novel, published 1742) worked as a footman in the house of Lady Booby for £8 a year; in addition, he got his room, board, and livery, plus the occasional tip. Among the comfortable classes, Mr. Bennet of Jane Austen's *Price and Prejudice* (1813) enjoyed an income of £2000 a year (with a family of five nonearning females to support), while Mr. Darcy had close to £10,000, nearing the level of the aristocracy. In his deepest degradation David Copperfield (of Dickens's 1850 novel) worked in the warehouse of Murdstone & Grinby for 6 or 7 shillings a week (£15 to £18 a year). Mr. Murdstone paid extra for his lodging and laundry, but even so the boy was bitterly impoverished, though he had only himself to feed. When his father died, his mother was thought to be pretty well taken care of with £105 a year, less than £9 per month. Even in 1888, Annie Besant reports workers in Bryant and May's match factory made 4 to 9 shillings a week and paid for their own lodging—this, in the words of Ada Nield Chew, was not a living wage, but "a lingering, dying wage." Far removed from this world is Jack Worthing in Wilde's comedy *The Importance of Being Earnest* (1895), who receives £7000 or £8000 a year from investments and has a country house with about fifteen hundred acres attached to it, though it yields no income worth talking about.

While incomes have risen enormously over the centuries, and the value of the pound declined accordingly, the gap between rich and poor has remained. So too has the gap between the country and the city: London has always been very expensive, and elsewhere a small income goes further. To a large extent, one's position in terms of class and geography determines not only what money can buy but what it means.

We have only to contrast Jack Worthing's vague estimate of his income with the factory workers' exact sense of the value of a shilling. As Woolf acknowledged, having a purse with the power "to breed ten-shilling notes automatically," changes one's view of money and of the world. Perhaps it is because British currency has been so important in shaping people's views of themselves and their society that many Britons are reluctant to let it go. The question of whether the United Kingdom should relinquish the pound and the penny to join the single European currency (the Euro) is a matter of fierce and prolonged debate. For some, the pound, far more than the flag, is an enduring symbol of the nation. Whether or not one holds this view, it can at least be said that over the centuries the pound has undergone as many crises and transformations as the nation itself.

The British Baronage

The English monarchy is in principle hereditary, though at times during the Middle Ages the rules were subject to dispute. In general, authority passes from father to eldest surviving son, from daughters in order of seniority if there is no son, to a brother if there are no children, and in default of direct descendants to collateral lines (cousins, nephews, nieces) in order of closeness. There have been breaks in the order of succession (1066, 1399, 1688), but so far as possible the usurpers have always sought to paper over the break with a legitimate, i.e., a hereditary claim. When a queen succeeds to the throne and takes a husband, he does not become king unless he is in the line of blood succession; rather, he is named prince consort, as Albert was to Victoria. He may father kings, but is not one himself.

The original Saxon nobles were the king's thanes, ealdormen, or earls, who provided the king with military service and counsel in return for booty, gifts, or landed estates. William the Conqueror, arriving from France, where feudalism was fully developed, considerably expanded this group. In addition, as the king distributed the lands of his new kingdom, he also distributed dignities to men who became known collectively as "the baronage." "Baron" in its root meaning signifies simply "man," and barons were the king's men. As the title was common, a distinction was early made between greater and lesser barons, the former gradually assuming loftier and more impressive titles. The first English "duke" was created in 1337; the title of "marquess," or "marquis" (pronounced "markwis"), followed in 1385, and "viscount" ("vyekount") in 1440. Though "earl" is the oldest title of all, it now comes between a marquess and a viscount in order of dignity and precedence, and the old term "baron" now designates a rank just below viscount. "Baronets" were created in 1611 as a means of raising revenue for the crown (the title could be purchased for about £1000); they are marginal nobility and do not sit in the House of Lords.

Kings and queens are addressed as "Your Majesty," princes and princesses as "Your Highness," the other hereditary nobility as "My Lord" or "Your Lordship." Peers receive their titles either by inheritance (like Lord Byron, the sixth baron of that line) or from the monarch (like Alfred Lord Tennyson, created first Baron Tennyson by Victoria). The children, even of a duke, are commoners unless they are specifically granted some other title or inherit their father's title from him. A peerage can be forfeited by act of attainder, as for example when a lord is convicted of treason; and, when forfeited, or lapsed for lack of a successor, can be bestowed on another family. Thus Robert Cecil was made in 1605 first earl of Salisbury in the third creation, the first creation dating from 1149, the second from 1337, the title having been in abeyance since 1539. Titles descend by right of succession and do not depend on tenure of land; thus, a title does not always indicate where a lord dwells or holds power. Indeed, noble titles do not always refer to a real place at all. At Prince Edward's marriage in 1999, the queen created him earl of Wessex, although the old kingdom of Wessex has had no political existence since the Anglo-Saxon period, and the name was all but forgotten until it was resurrected by Thomas Hardy as the setting of his novels. (This is perhaps but one of many ways in which the world of the aristocracy increasingly resembles the realm of literature.)

The king and queen	(These are all of the royal line.)
Prince and princess	
Duke and duchess	(These may or may not be of the royal line, but are
Marquess and marchioness	ordinarily remote from the succession.)
Earl and countess	
Viscount and viscountess	
Baron and baroness	
Baronet and lady	

Scottish peers sat in the parliament of Scotland, as English peers did in the parliament of England, till at the Act of Union (1707) Scots peers were granted sixteen seats in the English House of Lords, to be filled by election. Similarly, Irish peers, when the Irish parliament was abolished in 1801, were granted the right to elect twenty-eight of their number to the House of Lords in Westminster. (Now that the Republic of Ireland is a separate nation, of course, this no longer applies.) The House of Lords still retains some power to influence or delay legislation. But this upper house is now being reformed. All or most of the hereditary peers are to be expelled, while recipients of nonhereditary Life Peerages will remain and vote as before.

Below the peerage the chief title of honor is "knight." Knighthood, which is not hereditary, is generally a reward for services rendered. A knight (Sir John Black) is addressed, using his first name, as "Sir John"; his wife, using the last name, is "Lady Black"—unless she is the daughter of an earl or nobleman of higher rank, in which case she will be "Lady Arabella." The female equivalent of a knight bears the title of "Dame."

Though the word itself comes from the Anglo-Saxon *cniht*, there seems to be some doubt as to whether knighthood amounted to much before the arrival of the Normans. The feudal system required military service as a condition of land tenure, and a man who came to serve his king at the head of an army of tenants required a title of authority and badges of identity—hence the title of knighthood and the coat of arms. During the Crusades, when men were far removed from their land (or had even sold it in order to go on crusade), more elaborate forms of fealty sprang up that soon expanded into orders of knighthood. The Templars, Hospitallers, Knights of the Teutonic Order, Knights of Malta, and Knights of the Golden Fleece were but a few of these companionships; not all of them were available at all times in England.

Gradually, with the rise of centralized government and the decline of feudal tenures, military knighthood became obsolete, and the rank largely honorific; sometimes, as under James I, it degenerated into a scheme of the royal government for making money. For hundreds of years after its establishment in the fourteenth century, the Order of the Garter was the only English order of knighthood, an exclusive courtly companionship. Then, during the late seventeenth, the eighteenth, and the nineteenth centuries, a number of additional orders were created, with names such as the Thistle, Saint Patrick, the Bath, Saint Michael and Saint George, plus a number of special Victorian and Indian orders. They retain the terminology, ceremony, and dignity of knighthood, but the military implications are vestigial.

Although the British Empire now belongs to history, appointments to the Order of the British Empire continue to be conferred for services to that empire at home or abroad. Such honors (commonly referred to as "gongs") are granted by the monarch in her New Year's and Birthday lists, but the decisions are now made by the government in power. In recent years there have been efforts to popularize and democratize the dispensation of honors, with recipients including rock stars and actors. But this does not prevent large sectors of British society from regarding both knighthood and the peerage as largely irrelevant to modern life.

The Royal Lines of England and Great Britain

England

SAXONS AND DANES

Egbert, king of Wessex	802–839
Ethelwulf, son of Egbert	839–858
Ethelbald, son of Ethelwulf	858–860
Ethelbert, second son of Ethelwulf	860–866
Ethelred I, third son of Ethelwulf	866–871
Alfred the Great, fourth son of Ethelwulf	871–899
Edward the Elder, son of Alfred	899–924
Athelstan the Glorious, son of Edward	924–940
Edmund I, third son of Edward	940–946
Edred, fourth son of Edward	946–955
Edwy the Fair, son of Edmund	955–959
Edgar the Peaceful, second son of Edmund	959–975
Edward the Martyr, son of Edgar	975–978 (murdered)
Ethelred II, the Unready, second son of Edgar	978–1016
Edmund II, Ironside, son of Ethelred II	1016–1016
Canute the Dane	1016–1035
Harold I, Harefoot, natural son of Canute	1035–1040
Hardecanute, son of Canute	1040–1042
Edward the Confessor, son of Ethelred II	1042–1066
Harold II, brother-in-law of Edward	1066–1066 (died in battle)

HOUSE OF NORMANDY

William I the Conqueror	1066–1087
William II, Rufus, third son of William I	1087–1100 (shot from ambush)
Henry I, Beauclerc, youngest son of William I	1100–1135

HOUSE OF BLOIS

Stephen, son of Adela, daughter of William I	1135–1154

HOUSE OF PLANTAGENET

Henry II, son of Geoffrey Plantagenet by Matilda, daughter of Henry I	1154–1189
Richard I, Coeur de Lion, son of Henry II	1189–1199
John Lackland, son of Henry II	1199–1216
Henry III, son of John	1216–1272
Edward I, Longshanks, son of Henry III	1272–1307
Edward II, son of Edward I	1307–1327
Edward III of Windsor, son of Edward II	1327–1377
Richard II, grandson of Edward III	1377–1400

HOUSE OF LANCASTER

Henry IV, son of John of Gaunt, son of Edward III	1399–1413
Henry V, Prince Hal, son of Henry IV	1413–1422
Henry VI, son of Henry V	1422–1471 (deposed)

HOUSE OF YORK

Edward IV, great-great-grandson of Edward III	1461–1483
Edward V, son of Edward IV	1483–1483 (murdered)
Richard III, Crookback	1483–1485 (died in battle)

HOUSE OF TUDOR

Henry VII, married daughter of Edward IV	1485–1509
Henry VIII, son of Henry VII	1509–1547
Edward VI, son of Henry VIII	1547–1553
Mary I, "Bloody," daughter of Henry VIII	1553–1558
Elizabeth I, daughter of Henry VIII	1558–1603

HOUSE OF STUART

James I (James VI of Scotland)	1603–1625
Charles I, son of James I	1625–1649 (executed)

COMMONWEALTH & PROTECTORATE

Council of State	1649–1653
Oliver Cromwell, Lord Protector	1653–1658
Richard Cromwell, son of Oliver	1658–1660 (resigned)

HOUSE OF STUART (RESTORED)

Charles II, son of Charles I	1660–1685
James II, second son of Charles I	1685–1688

(INTERREGNUM, 11 DECEMBER 1688 TO 13 FEBRUARY 1689)

William III of Orange, by Mary, daughter of Charles I	1685–1701
and Mary II, daughter of James II	–1694
Anne, second daughter of James II	1702–1714

Great Britain

HOUSE OF HANOVER

George I, son of Elector of Hanover and Sophia, granddaughter of James I	1714–1727
George II, son of George I	1727–1760
George III, grandson of George II	1760–1820
George IV, son of George III	1820–1830
William IV, third son of George III	1830–1837
Victoria, daughter of Edward, fourth son of George III	1837–1901

HOUSE OF SAXE-COBURG AND GOTHA

Edward VII, son of Victoria   1901–1910

HOUSE OF WINDSOR (NAME ADOPTED 17 JULY 1917)

George V, second son of Edward VII   1910–1936
Edward VIII, eldest son of George V   1936–1936 (abdicated)
George VI, second son of George V   1936–1952
Elizabeth II, daughter of George VI   1952–

Religions in England

Religious distinctions and denominations are important in British social history, hence deeply woven into the nation's literature. The numerous (over three hundred) British churches and sects divide along a scale from high to low, depending on the amount of authority they give to the church or the amount of liberty they concede to the individual conscience. At one end of the scale is the Roman Catholic Church, asserting papal infallibility, universal jurisdiction, and the supreme importance of hierarchy as guide and intercessor. For political and social reasons, Catholicism struck deep roots in Ireland but in England was the object of prolonged, bitter hatred on the part of Protestants from the Reformation through the nineteenth century. The Established English (Anglican) Episcopal church has been the official national church since the sixteenth century; it enjoys the support (once direct and exclusive, now indirect and peripheral) of the national government. Its creed is defined by Thirty-Nine Articles, but these are intentionally vague, so there are numerous ways of adhering to the Church of England. Roughly and intermittently, the chief classes of Anglicans have been known as High Church (with its highest portion calling itself Anglo-Catholic); Broad Church, or Latitudinarian (when they get so broad that they admit anyone believing in God, they may be known as Deists, or some may leave the church altogether and be known as Unitarians); and Low Church, whose adherents may stay in the English church and yet come close to shaking hands with Presbyterians or Methodists. These various groups may be arranged, from the High down to the Low Church, in direct relation to the amount of ritual each prefers and in the degree of authority conceded to the upper clergy—and in inverse relation to the importance ascribed to a saving faith directly infused by God into an individual conscience.

All English Protestants who decline to subscribe to the English established church are classed as Dissenters or Nonconformists; for a time in the sixteenth and seventeenth centuries, they were also known as Puritans. (Nowadays, though Puritanism has less distinct theological meaning, it marks a distinct character type; because of his passionate emphasis on individual conscience and moral economy, Bernard Shaw was a prototypical Puritan.) The Presbyterians model their church government on that established by John Calvin in the Swiss city of Geneva. It has no bishops, and therefore is more democratic for the clergy; but it gains energy by associating lay elders with clergymen in matters of social discipline and tends to be strict with the ungodly. From its first reformation the Scottish Kirk was fixed on the Presbyterian model. During the civil wars of the seventeenth century, a great many sects sprang up on the left wing of the Presbyterians, most of them touched by Calvinism but some rebelling against it; a few of these still survive. The Independents became our modern Congregationalists; the Quakers are still Quakers, as Baptists are still Baptists, though multiply divided. But many of the sects flourished and perished within the space of a few years. Among these now vanished groups were the Shakers (though a few groups still exist in America), the Seekers, the Ranters, the Anabaptists, the Muggletonians, the Fifth Monarchy Men, the Family of Love, the Sweet Singers of Israel, and many others, forgotten by all except scholars. During the eighteenth and nineteenth centuries, new sects arose, supplanting old ones; the Methodists, under John and Charles Wesley, became numerous and important, taking root particularly in Wales. (The three "subject" nationalities, Ireland, Scotland, and Wales, thus turned three different ways to avoid the Anglican church.) With the passage of time a small number of Swedenborgians sprang up, followers of the Swedish mystic Emanuel Swedenborg—to be followed by the Plymouth Brethren, Christian Scientists, Jehovah's Witnesses, and countless other nineteenth-century groups. All these sects constantly grow, shrink, split, and occasionally disappear as they succeed or fail in attracting new converts.

Within the various churches and sects, independent of them all but amazingly persistent, there has always survived a stream of esoteric or hermetic thought—a belief in occult powers, and sometimes in magic also, exemplified by the pseudo-sciences of astrology and alchemy but taking many other forms as well. From the mythical Egyptian seer Hermes Trismegistus through Paracelsus, Cornelius Agrippa, Giordano Bruno, Jakob Boehme, the society of Rosicrucians, and a hundred other shadowy figures, the line can be traced to William Blake and William Butler Yeats, who both in their different ways brought hermetic Protestantism close to its ultimate goal, a mystic church of a single consciousness, poised within its mind-elaborated cosmos.

Christianity is not, of course, the only religion present on the British Isles. The few Jews in medieval England were regarded as resident aliens, as were those in other European countries. In 1290 all English Jews who refused baptism were expelled from the kingdom, and officially, there were no Jews living in England between that time and the mid-1650s, when Cromwell encouraged Jewish merchants to settle in London. A considerable number of east European Jews emigrated to England in the first half of the twentieth century (many as refugees), but the country's Jewish population as a whole remains quite small (less than half a million). Hardly any Muslims or Hindus lived in the U.K. before the dissolution of the Empire shortly after World War II. Today both religions have a large and growing representation among ex-colonial immigrants and their children.

The Norton Anthology
of English Literature

SEVENTH EDITION

THE MAJOR AUTHORS

VOLUME A

THE MIDDLE AGES THROUGH
THE RESTORATION AND THE
EIGHTEENTH CENTURY

The Middle Ages
to ca. 1485

43–ca. 420:	Roman invasion and occupation of Britain
ca. 450:	Anglo-Saxon Conquest
597:	St. Augustine arrives in Kent; beginning of Anglo-Saxon conversion to Christianity
871–899:	Reign of King Alfred
1066:	Norman Conquest
1154–1189:	Reign of Henry II
ca. 1200:	Beginnings of Middle English literature
1360–1400:	Geoffrey Chaucer; *Piers Plowman; Sir Gawain and the Green Knight*
1485:	William Caxton's printing of Sir Thomas Malory's *Morte Darthur*, one of the first books printed in England

The Middle Ages designates the time span roughly from the collapse of the Roman Empire to the Renaissance. The adjective "medieval," coined from Latin *medium* (middle) and *aevum* (age), refers to whatever was made, written, or thought during the Middle Ages. The Renaissance was so named by nineteenth-century historians and critics because they associated it with an outburst of creativity attributed to a "rebirth" or revival of Latin and, especially, of Greek learning and literature. The Renaissance was seen as spreading from Italy in the fourteenth and fifteenth centuries to the rest of Europe. The very idea of a "rebirth," however, implies something dormant or lacking in the preceding era. More recently, there has been a tendency to emphasize the continuities between the Middle Ages and the later time now often called the Early Modern period. Medieval authors, of course, did not think of themselves as living in the "middle"; they sometimes expressed the idea that the world was growing old and that theirs was a declining age, close to the end of time. Yet art, literature, and science flourished during the Middle Ages, rooted in the Christian culture that preserved, transmitted, and transformed classical tradition.

Although the Roman Catholic Church provided continuity, the period was one of enormous historical, social, and linguistic change. To emphasize these changes and the events underlying them, we have divided the period into three primary sections: Anglo-Saxon England, Anglo-Norman England, and Middle English Literature in the Fourteenth and Fifteenth Centuries. The Anglo-Saxon invaders, who began their conquest of the southeastern part of Britain around 450, spoke an early form of the language we now call Old English. Old English displays its kinship with other Germanic languages (German or Dutch, for example) much more clearly than does contemporary British and American English, of which Old English is the remote ancestor.

As late as the tenth century, part of an Old Saxon poem written on the Continent was transcribed and transliterated into the West Saxon dialect of Old English without presenting problems to its English readers. In form and content Old English literature also has much in common with other Germanic literatures with which it shared a body of heroic as well as Christian stories. The major characters in *Beowulf* are pagan Danes and Geats, and the only connection to England is an obscure allusion to the ancestor of one of the kings of the Angles.

The changes already in progress in the language and culture of Anglo-Saxon England were greatly accelerated by the Norman Conquest of 1066. The ascendancy of a French-speaking ruling class had the effect of adding a vast number of French loan words to the English vocabulary. The conquest resulted in new forms of political organization and administration, architecture, and literary expression. In the twelfth century, through the interest of the Anglo-Normans in British history before the Anglo-Saxon Conquest, not only England but all of Western Europe became fascinated with a legendary hero named Arthur who makes his earliest appearances in Celtic literature. King Arthur and his knights became a staple subject of medieval French, English, and German literature.

Literature in English was performed orally and written throughout the Middle Ages, but the awareness of and pride in a uniquely *English* literature does not actually exist before the late fourteenth century. In 1336 Edward III began a war to enforce his claims to the throne of France; the war continued intermittently for one hundred years until finally the English were driven from all their French territories except for the port of Calais. One result of the war and these losses was a keener sense on the part of England's nobility of their English heritage and identity. Toward the close of the fourteenth century English finally began to displace French as the language for conducting business in Parliament and in the courts of law. Although the high nobility continued to speak French by preference, they were certainly bilingual, whereas some of the earlier Norman kings had known no English at all. It was becoming possible to obtain patronage for literary achievement in English. Chaucer's decision to emulate French and Italian poetry in his own vernacular is an indication of the change taking place in the status of English, and Chaucer's works were greatly to enhance the prestige of English as a vehicle for important literature. He was acclaimed by fifteenth-century poets as the embellisher of the English tongue; later writers called him the English Homer and the father of English poetry. His friend John Gower (1325?–1408) wrote long poems in French and Latin before producing his last major work, the *Confessio Amantis* (The Lover's Confession), which in spite of its Latin title is composed in English. The third and longest of the three primary sections, Middle English Literature in the Fourteenth and Fifteenth Centuries, is thus not only a chronological and linguistic division but implies a new sense of English as a literary medium that could compete with French and Latin in elegance and seriousness.

Texts in Old English and *Sir Gawain and the Green Knight*, which is in a difficult regional dialect of Middle English, are given in translation. Chaucer and other Middle English works may be read in the original, even by the beginner, with the help of marginal glosses and notes. These texts have been spelled in a way that is intended to aid the reader. Analyses of the sounds and grammar of Middle English and of Old and Middle English prosody are discussed on pages 12–18.

ANGLO-SAXON ENGLAND

From the first to the fifth century, England was a province of the Roman Empire and was named Britannia after its Celtic-speaking inhabitants, the Britons. The Britons adapted themselves to Roman civilization, of which the ruins survived to impress the poet of *The Wanderer*, who refers to them as "the old works of giants." The withdrawal of the Roman legions during the fifth century, in a vain attempt to protect Rome itself from the threat of Germanic conquest, left the island vulnerable to seafaring Germanic invaders. These belonged primarily to three related tribes, the Angles, the Saxons, and the Jutes. The name *English* derives from the Angles, and the names of the counties Essex, Sussex, and Wessex refer to the territories occupied by the East, South, and West Saxons.

The Anglo-Saxon occupation was no sudden conquest but extended over decades of fighting against the native Britons. The latter were finally confined to the mountainous region of Wales, where the modern form of their language is spoken alongside English to this day. The Britons had become Christians in the fourth century after the conversion of Emperor Constantine along with most of the rest of the Roman Empire, but for about 150 years after the beginning of the invasion, Christianity was maintained only in the remoter regions where the as yet pagan Anglo-Saxons failed to penetrate. In the year 597, however, a Benedictine monk (afterward St. Augustine of Canterbury) was sent by Pope Gregory as a missionary to King Ethelbert of Kent, the most southerly of the kingdoms into which England was then divided, and about the same time missionaries from Ireland began to preach Christianity in the north. Within 75 years the island was once more predominantly Christian. Before Christianity there had been no books. The impact of Christianity on literacy is evident from the fact that the first extended written specimen of the Old English (Anglo-Saxon) language is a code of laws promulgated by Ethelbert, the first English Christian king.

In the centuries that followed the conversion, England produced many distinguished churchmen. One of the earliest of these was Bede, whose Latin *Ecclesiastical History of the English People*, which tells the story of the conversion and of the English church, was completed in 731; this remains one of our most important sources of knowledge about the period. In the next generation Alcuin (735–804), a man of wide culture, became the friend and adviser of the Frankish emperor Charlemagne, whom he assisted in making the Frankish court a great center of learning; thus by the year 800 English culture had developed so richly that it overflowed its insular boundaries.

In the ninth century the Christian Anglo-Saxons were themselves subjected to new Germanic invasions by the Danes who in their longboats repeatedly ravaged the coast, sacking Bede's monastery among others. The Danes also occupied the northern part of the island, threatening to overrun the rest. They were stopped by Alfred, king of the West Saxons from 871 to 899, who for a time united all the kingdoms of southern England. This most active king was also an enthusiastic patron of literature. He himself translated various works from Latin, the most important of which was Boethius's *Consolation of Philosophy*, a sixth-century Roman work also translated in the fourteenth century by Chaucer. Practically all of Old English poetry is preserved in copies made in the West Saxon dialect after the reign of Alfred.

Old English Poetry

The Anglo-Saxon invaders brought with them a tradition of oral poetry. Because nothing was written down before the conversion to Christianity, we have only circumstantial evidence of what that poetry must have been like. Aside from a few short inscriptions on small artifacts, the earliest records in the English language are in manuscripts produced at monasteries and other religious establishments, beginning in the seventh century. Literacy was mainly restricted to servants of the church, and so it is natural that the bulk of Old English literature deals with religious subjects and is mostly drawn from Latin sources. Manuscripts were costly and time-consuming to produce, because they required the copying of texts word by word onto parchment, a durable material made from the prepared skins of domestic animals (paper would not be used in Europe before the twelfth century). Under these difficult circumstances, few texts were written down that did not pertain directly to the work of the church. Most of Old English poetry is contained in just four manuscripts.

These poems show that the aristocratic heroic and kinship values of Germanic society continued to inspire both clergy and laity in the Christian era. As represented in the relatively small body of Anglo-Saxon heroic poetry that survives, this world shares many characteristics with the heroic world described by Homer. Nations are reckoned as groups of people related by kinship rather than by geographical areas, and kinship is the basis of the heroic code. The tribe is ruled by a chieftain who is called *king*, a word that has "kin" for its root. The *lord* (a word derived from Old English *hlaf*, "loaf," plus *weard*, "protector") surrounds himself with a band of retainers (many of them his blood kindred) who are members of his household. He leads his men in battle and rewards them with the spoils; royal generosity was one of the most important aspects of heroic behavior. In return, the retainers are obligated to fight for their lord to the death, and if he is slain, to avenge him or die in the attempt. Blood vengeance is regarded as a sacred duty, and in poetry, everlasting shame awaits those who fail to observe it.

Even though the heroic world of poetry could be invoked to rally resistance to the Viking invasions, it was already remote from the Christian world of Anglo-Saxon England. Nevertheless, Christian writers like the *Beowulf* poet were fascinated by the distant culture of their pagan ancestors and by the inherent conflict between the heroic code and a religion that teaches that we should "forgive those who trespass against us" and that "all they that take the sword shall perish with the sword." The *Beowulf* poet looks back on that ancient world with admiration for the courage of which it was capable and at the same time with elegiac sympathy for its inevitable doom.

For Anglo-Saxon poetry, it is difficult and probably futile to draw a line between "heroic" and "Christian," for the best poetry crosses that boundary. Much of the Christian poetry is also cast in the heroic mode: although the Anglo-Saxons adapted themselves readily to the ideals of Christianity, they did not do so without adapting Christianity to their own heroic ideal. Thus

Moses and St. Andrew, Christ and God the Father are represented in the style of heroic verse. In the *Dream of the Rood*, the Cross speaks of Christ as "the young hero, . . . strong and stouthearted."

The world of Old English poetry is predominantly harsh. Men are said to be cheerful in the mead hall, but even there they think of struggle in war, of possible triumph but more possible failure. Romantic love—one of the principal topics of later literature—appears hardly at all. Even so, at some of the bleakest moments, the poets powerfully recall the return of spring. The blade of the magic sword with which Beowulf has killed Grendel's mother in her sinister underwater lair begins to melt, "as ice melts / when the Father eases the fetters off the frost / and unravels the water ropes, He who wields power."

Poetic language is created out of a special vocabulary that contains a multiplicity of terms for *lord, warrior, spear, shield*, and so on. Synecdoche and metonymy are common figures of speech as when *keel* is used for "ship" or *iron*, for "sword." A particularly striking effect is achieved by the kenning, a compound of two words in place of another as when *sea* becomes "whale-road" or *body* is called "life-house." The figurative use of language finds playful expression in poetic riddles, of which about one hundred survive. Common (and sometimes uncommon) creatures, objects, or phenomena are described in an enigmatic passage of alliterative verse, and the reader must guess their identity. Sometimes they are personified and ask, "What is my name?"

The overall effect of the language is to formalize and elevate speech. Instead of being straightforward, it moves at a slow and stately pace with steady indirection. A favorite mode of this indirection is irony. A grim irony pervades heroic poetry even at the level of diction where *fighting* is called "battle-play." A favorite device, known by the rhetorical term *litotes*, is ironic understatement. After the monster Grendel has slaughtered the Danes in the great hall Heorot, it stands deserted. The poet observes, "It was easy then to meet with a man / shifting himself to a safer distance."

More than a figure of speech, irony is also a mode of perception in Old English poetry. *Beowulf* is full of ironic balances and contrasts—between the aged Danish king and the youthful Beowulf, and between Beowulf, the high-spirited young warrior at the beginning, and Beowulf, the gray-haired king at the end, facing the dragon and death.

The formal and dignified speech of Old English poetry was always distant from the everyday language of the Anglo-Saxons, and this poetic idiom remained remarkably uniform for the roughly three hundred years before the Norman Conquest. This clinging to old forms—grammatical and orthographic as well as literary—by the Anglo-Saxon church and aristocracy conceals from us the enormous changes that were taking place in the English language and the diversity of its dialects. The dramatic changes between Old and Middle English did not happen overnight or over the course of a single century. The Normans displaced the English ruling class with their own barons and clerics, whose native language was a dialect of Old French that we call Anglo-Norman. Without a ruling literate class to preserve English traditions, the custom of transcribing vernacular texts in an earlier form of the West-Saxon dialect was abandoned, and both language and literature were allowed to develop unchecked in new directions.

ANGLO-NORMAN ENGLAND

The Normans, who took possession of England after the decisive Battle of Hastings (1066), were, like the Anglo-Saxons, descendants of Germanic adventurers who at the beginning of the tenth century had seized a wide part of northern France. Their name is actually a contraction of "Norsemen." A highly adaptable people, they had adopted the French language of the land they had settled in and its Christian religion. Both in Normandy and in Britain they were great builders of castles, with which they enforced their political dominance, and magnificent churches. Norman bishops, who held land and castles like the barons, wielded both political and spiritual authority. The earlier Norman kings of England, however, were often absentee rulers, as much concerned with defending their Continental possessions as with ruling over their English holdings. The English Crown's French territories were enormously increased in 1154 when Henry II, the first of England's Plantagenet kings, ascended the throne. Through his marriage with Eleanor of Aquitaine, the divorced wife of Louis VII of France, Henry had acquired vast provinces in the south of France.

The presence of a French-speaking ruling class in England created exceptional opportunities for linguistic and cultural exchange. Four languages coexisted in the realm of Anglo-Norman England: Latin, as it had been for Bede, remained the international language of learning, used for theology, science, and history. It was not by any means a written language only but a lingua franca by which different nationalities communicated in the church and the newly founded universities. The Norman aristocracy for the most part spoke French, but intermarriage with the native English nobility and the business of daily life between masters and servants encouraged bilingualism. Different branches of the Celtic language group were spoken in Ireland, Wales, Cornwall, and Brittany.

Inevitably there was also literary intercourse among the different languages. The Latin Bible and Latin saints' lives provided subjects for a great deal of Old English as well as Old French poetry and prose. The first medieval drama in the vernacular, *The Play of Adam*, with elaborate stage directions in Latin and realistic dialogue in the Anglo-Norman dialect of French, was probably produced in England during the twelfth century.

The Anglo-Norman aristocracy was especially attracted to Celtic legends and tales that had been circulating orally for centuries. The twelfth-century poets Marie de France and Chrétien de Troyes both claim to have obtained their narratives from Breton storytellers, who were probably bilingual performers of native tales for French audiences. "Breton" may indicate that they came from Brittany, or it may have been a generic term for a Celtic bard. Marie speaks respectfully of the storytellers; Chrétien accuses them of marring their material, which, he boasts, he has retold with an elegant fusion of form and meaning. Marie wrote a series of short romances, which she refers to as "lays" originally told by Bretons. Her versions are the most original and sophisticated examples of the genre that came to be known as the Breton lay, represented here by Marie's *Lanval*. It is very likely that Henry II is the "noble king" to whom she dedicated her lays and that they were written for his court. Chrétien is the principal creator of the romance of chivalry in which knightly adventures are a means of exploring psychological and ethical dilemmas that the knights must solve, in addition to displaying martial prowess in saving ladies from monsters, giants, and wicked knights. Chrétien, like Marie, is thought to have spent time in England at the court of Henry II. Both Marie de France and Chrétien de Troyes were innovators of the genre that has become known as "romance." The word *roman* was initially applied in French to a work written in the French vernacular. Thus the thirteenth-century *Roman de Troie* is a long poem about the Trojan War in French. While this work deals mainly with the siege of Troy, it also includes stories about the love of Troilus for Cressida and of Achilles for the Trojan princess Polyxena. Eventually "romance" acquired the generic associations it has for us as a story about love and adventure. In the late twelfth century, Andreas Capellanus (Andrew the Chaplain) wrote a Latin treatise, the title of which may be translated *The Art of Loving Correctly* [*honeste*]. In one part, Eleanor of Aquitaine, her daughter, the countess Marie de Champagne, and other noble women are cited as a supreme court rendering decisions on difficult questions of love—for example, whether there is greater passion between lovers or between married couples. Whether such "courts of love" were purely imaginary or whether they represent some actual court entertainment, they imply that the literary taste and judgment of women had a significant role in determining the rise of romance in France and Anglo-Norman England.

In Marie's *Lanval* and in Chrétien's romances, the court of King Arthur had already acquired for French audiences a reputation as the most famous center of chivalry. That eminence is owing in large measure to a remarkable book in Latin, *The History of the Kings of Britain*, completed by Geoffrey of Monmouth, ca. 1136–38. Geoffrey claimed to have based his "history" on a book in the British tongue (i.e., Welsh), but no one has ever found such a book. He drew on a few earlier Latin chronicles, but the bulk of his history was probably fabricated from Celtic oral tradition, his familiarity with Roman history and literature, and his own fertile imagination. The climax of the book is the reign of King Arthur, who defeats the Roman armies but is forced to turn back to Britain to counter the treachery of his nephew Mordred. Geoffrey's Latin was rendered into French rhyme by an Anglo-Norman poet called Wace, and Wace's poem was turned by Layamon, an English priest, into a much longer poem that combines English alliterative verse with sporadic rhyme.

Layamon's work is one of many instances where English receives new material directly through French sources, which may be drawn from Celtic or Latin sources. There are two Middle English versions of Marie's *Lanval*, and the English romance called *Yvain and Gawain* is a cruder version of Chrétien's *Le Chevalier au Lion* (The Knight of the Lion). There is a marvelous English lay, *Sir Orfeo*, a version of the Orpheus story in which Orpheus succeeds in rescuing his wife from the other world, for which a French original, if there was one, has never been found. Romance, stripped of its courtly, psychological, and ethical subtleties, had an immense popular appeal for English readers and listeners. Many of these romances are simplified adaptations of more aristocratic French poems and recount in a rollicking and rambling style the adventures of heroes like Guy of Warwick, a poor steward who must prove his knightly worth to win the love of Fair

Phyllis. The ethos of many romances, aristocratic and popular alike, involves a knight proving his worthiness through nobility of character and brave deeds rather than through high birth. In this respect romances reflect the aspirations of a lower order of the nobility to rise in the world, as historically some of these nobles did. William the Marshall, for example, the fourth son of a baron of middle rank, used his talents in war and in tournaments to become tutor to the oldest son of Henry II and Eleanor of Aquitaine. He married a great heiress and became one of the most powerful nobles in England and the subject of a verse biography in French, which often reads like a romance.

MIDDLE ENGLISH LITERATURE IN THE FOURTEENTH AND FIFTEENTH CENTURIES

Throughout the thirteenth and early fourteenth centuries, there are many kinds of evidence that, although French continued to be the principal language of Parliament, law, business, and high culture, English was gaining ground. Several authors of religious and didactic works in English state that they are writing for the benefit of those who do not understand Latin or French. Anthologies are made of miscellaneous works adapted from French for English readers and original pieces in English. Most of the nobility are by now bilingual, and the author of an English romance written early in the fourteenth century declares that he has seen many nobles who cannot speak French. Children of the nobility and the merchant class are now learning French as a second language. By the 1360s the linguistic, political, and cultural climate had been prepared for the flowering of Middle English literature in the writings of Chaucer, Langland, and the *Gawain* poet.

The Fourteenth Century

War and disease were prevalent throughout the Middle Ages but never more devastatingly than during the fourteenth century. In the wars against France, the gains of two spectacular English victories, at Crécy in 1346 and Poitiers in 1356, were gradually frittered away in futile campaigns that ravaged the French countryside without obtaining any clear advantage for the English. In 1348 the first and most virulent epidemic of the bubonic plague—the Black Death—swept Europe, wiping out a quarter to a third of the population. The toll was higher in crowded urban centers. Giovanni Boccaccio's description of the plague in Florence, with which he introduces the *Decameron*, vividly portrays its ravages: "So many corpses would arrive in front of a church every day and at every hour that the amount of holy ground for burials was certainly insufficient for the ancient custom of giving each body its individual place; when all the graves were full, huge trenches were dug in all of the cemeteries of the churches and into them the new arrivals were dumped by the hundreds; and they were packed in there with dirt, one on top of another, like a ship's cargo, until the trench was filled." The resulting scarcity of labor and a sudden expansion of the possibilities for social mobility fostered popular discontent. In 1381 attempts to enforce wage controls and to collect oppressive new taxes provoked a rural uprising in Essex and Kent that dealt a profound shock to the English ruling class. The participants were for the most part tenant farmers, day laborers, apprentices, and rural workers not attached to the big manors. A few of the lower clergy sided with the rebels against their wealthy church superiors; the priest John Ball was among the leaders. The movement was quickly suppressed, but not before sympathizers in London had admitted the rebels through two city gates, which had been barred against them. The insurgents burned down the palace of the hated duke of Lancaster, and they summarily beheaded the archbishop of Canterbury and the treasurer of England, who had taken refuge in the Tower of London. The church had become the target of popular resentment because it was among the greatest of the oppressive landowners and because of the wealth, worldliness, and venality of many of the higher clergy.

These calamities and upheavals nevertheless did not stem the growth of international trade and the influence of the merchant class. In the portrait of Geoffrey Chaucer's merchant, we see the budding of capitalism based on credit and interest. Cities like London ran their own affairs under politically powerful mayors and aldermen. Edward III, chronically in need of money to finance his wars, was obliged to negotiate for revenues with the Commons in the English Parliament, an institution that became a major political force during this period. A large part of the king's revenues depended on taxing the profitable export of English wool to the Continent. The Crown thus became involved in the country's economic affairs, and this involvement led to a need for capable administrators. These were no longer drawn mainly from the church, as in the past, but from a newly educated laity that occupied a rank somewhere between that of the lesser nobility and the upper bourgeoisie. The career of Chaucer, who served Edward III and his successor Richard II in a number of civil posts, is typical of this class—with the exception that Chaucer was also a great poet.

In the fourteenth century, a few poets and intellectuals achieved the status and respect formerly accorded only to the ancients. Marie de France and Chrétien de Troyes had dedicated their works to noble patrons and, in their role as narrators, address themselves as entertainers and sometimes as instructors to court audiences. Dante (1265–1321) made himself the protagonist of *The Divine Comedy*, the sacred poem, as he called it, in which he revealed the secrets of the afterlife. After his death, manuscripts of the work were provided with lengthy commentaries as though it were Scripture, and public readings and lectures were devoted to it. Francesco Petrarch (1304–1374) won an international reputation as a man of letters. He wrote primarily in Latin and contrived to have himself crowned "poet laureate" in emulation of the Roman poets whose works he imitated, but his most famous work is the sonnet sequence he wrote in Italian. Giovanni Boccaccio (1313–1375) was among Petrarch's most ardent admirers and carried on a literary correspondence with him.

Chaucer read these authors along with the ancient Roman poets and drew on them in his own works. Chaucer's *Clerk's Tale* is based on a Latin version Petrarch made from the last tale in Boccaccio's *Decameron*; in his prologue, the Clerk refers to Petrarch as "lauriat poete" whose sweet rhetoric illuminated all Italy with his poetry. Yet in his own time, the English poet Chaucer never attained the kind of laurels that he and others accorded to Petrarch. In his earlier works, Chaucer portrayed himself comically as a diligent reader of old books, as an aspiring apprentice writer, and as an eager spectator on the fringe of a fashionable world of courtiers and poets. In *The House of*

Fame, he relates a dream of being snatched up by a huge golden eagle (the eagle and many other things in this work were inspired by Dante), who transports him to the palace of the goddess of Fame. There he gets to see phantoms, like the shades in Dante's poem, of all the famous authors of antiquity. At the end of his romance *Troilus and Criseyde*, Chaucer asks his "litel book" to kiss the footsteps where the great ancient poets had passed before. Like Dante and Petrarch, Chaucer had an ideal of great poetry and, in his *Troilus* at least, strove to emulate it. But in *The House of Fame* and in his final work, *The Canterbury Tales*, he also views that ideal ironically and distances himself from it. The many surviving documents that record Geoffrey Chaucer's career as a civil servant do not contain a single word to show that he was also a poet. Only in the following centuries would he be canonized as the father of English poetry.

Native traditions held out longest in the west and north, away from London, where Chaucer and his audience were more open to literary fashions from the Continent. Those areas saw a final flowering in the late fourteenth century of the verse form that goes all the way back to Anglo-Saxon England, known as the "Alliterative Revival." An important poem in that tradition is William Langland's dream vision allegory *Piers Plowman*, which assailed corruption in church and state. Admiration for Chaucer's poetry and the controversial nature of Langland's writing assured the survival of their work in many manuscripts. The work of a third major fourteenth-century English poet, who remains anonymous, is known only through a single manuscript, which contains four poems all thought to be by a single author: *Cleanness* and *Patience*, two biblical narratives in alliterative verse; *Pearl*, a moving dream vision in which a grief-stricken father is visited and consoled by his dead child, who has been transformed into a queen in the kingdom of heaven; and *Sir Gawain and the Green Knight*, the finest of all English romances. The plot of *Gawain* involves a folklore motif of a challenge by a supernatural visitor, first found in an Old Irish tale. The poet has made this motif a challenge to King Arthur's court and has framed the tale with allusions at the beginning and end to the legends that link Arthur's reign with the Trojan War and the founding of Rome and of Britain. The poet has a sophisticated awareness of romance as a literary genre and plays a game with both the hero's and the readers' expectations of what is supposed to happen in a romance. One could say that the broader subject of *Sir Gawain and the Green Knight* is "romance" itself, and in this respect the poem resembles Chaucer's *Canterbury Tales* in its author's interest in literary form.

The Fifteenth Century

In 1399 Henry Bolingbroke, the duke of Lancaster, deposed his cousin Richard II, who was murdered in prison. As Henry IV, he successfully defended his crown against several insurrections and passed it on to Henry V, who briefly united the country once more and achieved one last apparently decisive victory over the French at the Battle of Agincourt (1415). The premature death of Henry V, however, left England exposed to the civil wars known as the Wars of the Roses, the red rose being the emblem of the house of Lancaster; the white, of York. These wars did not end until 1485, when Henry Tudor defeated Richard III at Bosworth Field and acceded to the throne as Henry VII.

Social, economic, and literary life continued as they had throughout all of the previous wars. The prosperity of the towns was shown by performances of the mystery plays—a sequence or "cycle" of plays based on the Bible and produced by the city guilds, the organizations representing the various trades and crafts. The cycles of several towns are lost, but those of York, Wakefield, and Chester have been preserved. The play of *Noah's Flood* continued to be performed at Chester until late in the sixteenth century.

While religious works of all kinds continued to be produced, the fourteenth and fifteenth centuries are notable (both in England and on the Continent) for mystical writings in which the authors, many of whom were women, tell of their direct personal experience of God. The anchoress Julian of Norwich spent her life meditating and writing about a series of visions, which she called "showings," that she had received in 1373, when she was thirty years old. Early in the fifteenth century she was still in her cell, attached to a church in Norwich, when she was consulted by Margery Kempe, whom a series of visions had directed to lead a spiritual life. Kempe, a controversial figure, made a pilgrimage to the Holy Land and during the 1430s dictated the first autobiography in English. Both Julian of Norwich and Margery Kempe, in highly individual ways, allow us to see the medieval church and its doctrines from female points of view.

The works of Sir Thomas Malory gave the definitive form in English to the saga of King Arthur and his knights. Malory spent years in prison Englishing a series of Arthurian romances that he translated and abridged chiefly from several enormously long thirteenth-century French prose romances. Malory was a passionate devotee of chivalry, which he personified in his hero Sir Lancelot. In the jealousies and rivalries that finally break up the round table and destroy Arthur's kingdom, Malory saw a distant image of the civil wars of his own time. A manuscript of Malory's works fell into the hands of William Caxton (1422?–1491), who had introduced the new art of printing by movable type to England in 1476. Caxton divided Malory's tales into the chapters and books of a single long work, as though it were a chronicle history, and gave it the title *Morte Darthur*, which has stuck to it ever since. Caxton also printed *The Canterbury Tales*, some of Chaucer's earlier works, and Gower's *Confessio Amantis*. Caxton himself translated many of the works he printed for English readers: a history of Troy, a book on chivalry, Aesop's fables, and *The Game and Playe of Chesse*. The new technology extended literacy and made books more easily accessible to new classes of readers. Printing made the production of literature a business and made possible the bitter political and doctrinal disputes that, in the sixteenth century, were waged in print as well as on the field of battle.

MEDIEVAL ENGLISH

The medieval works in this book were composed in different states of our language. Old English, the language that took shape among the Germanic settlers of England, preserved its integrity until the Norman Conquest radically altered English civilization. Middle English, the earliest records of which date from the early twelfth century, was continually changing. Shortly after the introduction of printing at the end of the fifteenth century, it attained the form designated as Early Modern English. Old English is a very heavily inflected language. (That is, the words change form to indicate changes in usage, such as person, number, tense, case, mood, and so on. Most languages have some inflection—for example, the personal pronouns in Modern English have different forms when used as objects—but a "heavily inflected" language is one in which almost all classes of words undergo elaborate patterns of change.) The vocabulary of Old English is almost entirely Germanic. In Middle English, the inflectional system was weakened, and a large number of words were introduced into it from French, so that many of the older native words disappeared. Because of the difficulty of Old English, all selections from it in this book have been given in translation. The present discussion, then, is concerned primarily with the relatively late form of Middle English used by Chaucer and the East Midland dialect in which he wrote.

The chief difficulty with Middle English for the modern reader is caused not by its inflections so much as by its spelling, which may be described as a rough-and-ready phonetic system, and by the fact that it is not a single standardized language, but consists of a number of regional dialects, each with its own peculiarities of sound and its own systems for representing sounds in writing. The Midland dialect—the dialect of London and of Chaucer, which is the ancestor of our own standard speech—differs greatly from the dialect spoken in the west of England (the original dialect of *Piers Plowman*), from that of the northwest (*Sir Gawain and the Green Knight*), and from that of the north (*The Second Shepherds' Play*). In this book, the long texts composed in the more difficult dialects have been translated or modernized, and those that—like Chaucer, *Everyman*, the lyrics, and the ballads—appear in the original, have been re-spelled in a way that is designed to aid the reader. The remarks that follow apply chiefly to Chaucer's Midland English, although certain non-Midland dialectal variations are noted if they occur in some of the other selections.

I. The Sounds of Middle English: General Rules

The following general analysis of the sounds of Middle English will enable the reader who has not time for detailed study to read Middle English aloud so as to preserve some of its most essential characteristics, without, however, giving heed to many important details. The next section, "Detailed Analysis," is designed for the reader who wishes to go more deeply into the pronunciation of Middle English.

Middle English differs from Modern English in three principal respects: (1) the pronunciation of the long vowels *a, e, i* (or *y*), *o,* and *u* (spelled *ou, ow*); (2) the fact that Middle English final *e* is often sounded; and (3) the fact that all Middle English consonants are sounded.

1. LONG VOWELS

Middle English vowels are long when they are doubled (*aa, ee, oo*) or when they are terminal (*he, to, holy*); *a, e,* and *o* are long when followed by a single consonant plus a vowel (*name, mete, note*). Middle English vowels are short when they are followed by two consonants.

Long *a* is sounded like the *a* in Modern English "father": *maken, madd*.

Long *e* may be sounded like the *a* in Modern English "name" (ignoring the distinction between the close and open vowel): *be, sweete.*

Long *i* (or *y*) is sounded like the *i* in Modern English "machine": *lif, whit; myn, holy.*

Long *o* may be sounded like the *o* in Modern English "note" (again ignoring the distinction between the close and open vowel): *do, soone.*

Long *u* (spelled *ou, ow*) is sounded like the *oo* in Modern English "goose": *hous, flowr.*

Note that in general Middle English long vowels are pronounced like long vowels in modern European languages other than English. Short vowels and diphthongs, however, may be pronounced as in Modern English.

2. FINAL E

In Middle English syllabic verse, final *e* is sounded like the *a* in "sofa" to provide a needed unstressed syllable: *Another Nonnë with hire haddë she.* But (cf. *hire* in the example) final *e* is suppressed when not needed for the meter. It is commonly silent before words beginning with a vowel or *h.*

3. CONSONANTS

Middle English consonants are pronounced separately in all combinations—*gnat: g-nat; knave: k-nave; write: w-rite; folk: fol-k.* In a simplified system of pronunciation the combination *gh* as in *night* or *thought* may be treated as if it were silent.

II. The Sounds of Middle English: Detailed Analysis

1. SIMPLE VOWELS

Sound	Pronunciation	Example
long *a* (spelled *a, aa*)	*a* in "father"	*maken, maad*
short *a*	*o* in "hot"	*cappe*
long *e* close (spelled *e, ee*)	*a* in "name"	*be, sweete*
long *e* open (spelled *e, ee*)	*e* in "there"	*mete, heeth*
short *e*	*e* in "set"	*setten*
final *e*	*a* in "sofa"	*large*
long *i* (spelled *i, y*)	*i* in "machine"	*lif, mym*
short *i*	*i* in "wit"	*wit*
long *o* close (spelled *o, oo*)	*o* in "note"	*do, soone*
long *o* open (spelled *o, oo*)	*oa* in "broad"	*go, goon*
short *o*	*o* in "oft"	*pot*
long *u* when spelled *ou, ow*	*oo* in "goose"	*hous, flowr*
long *u* when spelled *u*	*u* in "pure"	*vertu*
short *u* (spelled *u, o*)	*u* in "full"	*ful, love*

Doubled vowels and terminal vowels are always long, whereas single vowels before two consonants other than *th, ch* are always short. The vowels *a*, *e*, and *o* are long before a single consonant followed by a vowel: *nāmë, sēkë* (sick), *hōly.* In general, words that have descended into Modern English reflect their original Middle English quantity: *līven* (to live), but *līf* (life).

The close and open sounds of long *e* and long *o* may often be identified by the Modern English spellings of the words in which they appear. Original long close *e* is generally represented in Modern English by *ee*: "sweet," "knee," "teeth," "see" have close *e* in Middle English, but so does "be"; original long open *e* is generally represented in Modern English by *ea*: "meat," "heath," "sea," "great," "breath" have open *e* in Middle English. Similarly, original long close *o* is now generally represented by *oo*: "soon," "food," "good," but also "do," "to"; original long open *o* is represented either by *oa* or by *o*: "coat," "boat," "moan," but also "go," "bone," "foe," "home." Notice that original close *o* is now almost always pronounced like the *oo* in "goose," but that original open *o* is almost never so pronounced; thus it is often possible to identify the Middle English vowels through Modern English sounds.

The nonphonetic Middle English spelling of *o* for short *u* has been preserved in a number of Modern English words ("love," "son," "come"), but in others *u* has been restored: "sun" (*sonne*), "run" (*ronne*).

For the treatment of final *e*, see "General Rules," "Final *e*."

2. DIPHTHONGS

Sound	Pronunciation	Example
ai, ay, ei, ay	between *ai* in "aisle" and *ay* in "day"	*saide, day, veine, preye*
au, aw	*ou* in "out"	*chaunge, bawdy*
eu, ew	*ew* in "few"	*newe*
oi, oy	*oy* in "joy"	*joye, point*
ou, ow	*ou* in "thought"	*thought, lowe*

Note that in words with *ou, ow* that in Modern English are sounded with the *ou* of "about," the combination indicates not the diphthong but the simple vowel long *u* (see "Simple Vowels").

3. CONSONANTS

In general, all consonants except *h* were always sounded in Middle English, including consonants that have become silent in Modern English, such as the *g* in *gnaw*, the *k* in *knight*, the *l* in *folk*, and the *w* in *write*. In noninitial *gn*, however, the *g* was silent as in Modern English "sign." Initial *h* was silent in short common English words and in words borrowed from French and may have been almost silent in all words. The combination *gh* as in *night* or *thought* was sounded like the *ch* of German *ich* or *nach*. Note that Middle English *gg* represents both the hard sound of "dagger" and the soft sound of "bridge."

III. Parts of Speech and Grammar

1. NOUNS

The plural and possessive *s* of nouns end in *es*, formed by adding *s* or *es* to the singular: *knight, knightes; roote, rootes*; a final consonant is frequently doubled before *es: bed, beddes*. A common irregular plural is *yën*, from *yë*, eye.

2. PRONOUNS

The chief differences from Modern English are as follows:

Modern English	Middle English
I	I, *ich* (*ik* is a northern form)
you (singular)	*thou* (subjective); *thee* (objective)
her	*hir(e)*, *her(e)*
its	*his*
you (plural)	*ye* (subjective); *you* (objective)
their	*hir*
them	*hem*

In formal speech, the second person plural is often used for the singular. The possessive adjectives *my*, *thy* take *n* before a word beginning with a vowel or *h*: *thyn yë*, *myn host*.

3. ADJECTIVES

Adjectives ending in a consonant add final *e* when they stand before the noun they modify and after another modifying word such as *the*, *this*, *that*, or nouns or pronouns in the possessive: *a good hors*, but *the* (*this*, *my*, *the kinges*) *goode hors*. They also generally add *e* when standing before and modifying a plural noun, a noun in the vocative, or any proper noun: *goode men*, *oh goode man*, *faire Venus*.

Adjectives are compared by adding *er(e)* for the comparative, *est(e)* for the superlative. Sometimes the stem vowel is shortened or altered in the process: *sweete, swettere, swettest; long, lenger, lengest*.

4. ADVERBS

Adverbs are formed from adjectives by adding *e*, *ly*, or *liche*; the adjective *fair* thus yields *faire, fairly, fairliche*.

5. VERBS

Middle English verbs, like Modern English verbs, are either "weak" or "strong." Weak verbs form their preterites and past participles with a *t* or *d* suffix and preserve the same stem vowel throughout their systems, although it is sometimes shortened in the preterite and past participle: *love, loved; bend, bent; hear, heard; meet, met*. Strong verbs do not use the *t* or *d* suffix, but vary their stem vowel in the preterite and past participle: *take, took, taken; begin, began, begun; find, found, found*.

The inflectional endings are the same for Middle English strong verbs and weak verbs except in the preterite singular and the imperative singular. In the following paradigms, the weak verbs *loven* (to love) and *heeren* (to hear), and the strong verbs *taken* (to take) and *ginnen* (to begin) serve as models.

	Present Indicative	Preterite Indicative
I	*love, heere*	*loved(e), herde*
	take, ginne	*took, gan*
thou	*lovest, heerest*	*lovedest, herdest*
	takest, ginnest	*tooke, gonne*
he, she, it	*loveth, heereth*	*loved(e), herde*
	taketh, ginneth	*took, gan*
we, ye, they	*love(n) (th), heere(n) (th)*	*loved(e) (en), herde(n)*
	take(n) (th), ginne(n) (th)	*tooke(n), gonne(n)*

The present plural ending *eth* is southern, whereas the *e(n)* ending is Midland and characteristic of Chaucer. In the north, *s* may appear as the ending of all persons of the present. In the weak preterite, when the ending *e* gave a verb three or more syllables, it was frequently dropped. Note that in certain strong verbs like *ginnen* there are two distinct stem vowels in the preterite; even in Chaucer's time, however, one of these had begun to replace the other, and Chaucer occasionally writes *gan* for all persons of the preterite.

	Present Subjunctive	Preterite Subjunctive
Singular	*love, heere*	*lovede, herde*
	take, ginne	*tooke, gonne*
Plural	*love(n), heere(n)*	*lovede(n), herde(n)*
	take(n), ginne(n)	*tooke(n), gonne(n)*

In verbs like *ginnen*, which have two stem vowels in the indicative preterite, it is the vowel of the plural and of the second person singular that is used for the preterite subjunctive.

The imperative singular of most weak verbs is *e: (thou) love*, but of some weak verbs and all strong verbs, the imperative singular is without termination: *(thou) heer, taak, gin*. The imperative plural of all verbs is either *e* or *eth: (ye) love(th), heere(th), take(th), ginne(th)*.

The infinitive of verbs is *e* or *en: love(n), heere(n), take(n), ginne(n)*.

The past participle of weak verbs is the same as the preterite without inflectional ending: *loved, herd*. In strong verbs the ending is either *e* or *en: take(n), gonne(n)*. The prefix *y* often appears on past participles: *yloved, yherd, ytake(n)*.

OLD AND MIDDLE ENGLISH PROSODY

All the poetry of Old English is in the same verse form. The verse unit is the single line, because rhyme was not used to link one line to another, except very occasionally in late Old English. The organizing device of the line is alliteration, the beginning of several words with the same sound ("Foemen fled"). The Old English alliterative line contains, on the average, four principal stresses and is divided into two half-lines of two stresses each by a strong medial caesura, or pause. These two half-lines are linked to each other by the alliteration; at least one of the two stressed words in the first half-line, and often both of them, begin with the same sound as the first stressed

word of the second half-line (the second stressed word is generally nonal-
literative). The fourth line of *Beowulf* is an example (*sc* has the value of
modern *sh*; þ is a runic symbol with the value of modern *th*):

> Oft Scyld Scefing   sceaþena þreatum.

It will be noticed that any vowel alliterates with any vowel. In addition
to the alliteration, the length of the unstressed syllables and their number
and pattern is governed by a highly complex set of rules. When sung or
intoned—as it was—to the rhythmic strumming of a harp, Old English poetry
must have been wonderfully impressive in the dignified, highly formalized
way that aptly fits both its subject matter and tone.

The majority of Middle English verse is either in alternately stressed rhyming verse, adapted from French after the conquest, or in alliterative verse
that is descended from Old English. The latter preserves the caesura of Old
English and in its purest form the same alliterative system, the two stressed
words of the first half-line (or at least one of them) alliterating with the first
stressed word in the second half-line. But most of the alliterative poets
allowed themselves a number of deviations from the norm. All four stressed
words may alliterate, as in the first line of *Piers Plowman:*

> In a summer season   when soft was the sun.

Or the line may contain five, six, or even more stressed words, of which all
or only the basic minimum may alliterate:

> A *fair field full* of   *folk found* I therebetween.

There is no rule determining the number of unstressed syllables, and at times
some poets seem to ignore alliteration entirely. As in Old English, any vowel
may alliterate with any other vowel; furthermore, since initial *h* was silent or
lightly pronounced in Middle English, words beginning with *h* are treated as
though they began with the following vowel.

There are two general types of stressed verse with rhyme. In the more
common, stressed and unstressed syllables alternate regularly as x X x X x X
or, with two unstressed syllables intervening as x x X x x X x x X or a combination of the two as x x X x X x x X (of the reverse patterns, only X x X x X x
is common in English). There is also a line that can only be defined as
containing a predetermined number of stressed syllables but an irregular
number and pattern of unstressed syllables. Much Middle English verse has
to be read without expectation of regularity; some of this was evidently composed in the irregular meter, but some was probably originally composed
according to a strict metrical system that has been obliterated by scribes
careless of fine points. One receives the impression that many of the lyrics—
as well as the *Second Shepherds' Play*—were at least composed with regular
syllabic alternation. In the play *Everyman*, only the number of stresses is
generally predetermined but not the number or placement of unstressed
syllables.

In pre-Chaucerian verse the number of stresses, whether regularly or irregularly alternated, was most often four, although sometimes the number was three and rose in some poems to seven. Rhyme in Middle English (as in Modern English) may be either between adjacent or alternate lines, or may occur in more complex patterns. Most of the *Canterbury Tales* are in rhymed couplets, the line containing five stresses with regular alternation—technically known as iambic pentameter, the standard English poetic line, perhaps introduced into English by Chaucer. In reading Chaucer and much pre-Chaucerian verse one must remember that the final *e*, which is silent in Modern English, could be pronounced at any time to provide a needed unstressed syllable. Evidence seems to indicate that it was also pronounced at the end of the line, even though it thus produced a line with eleven syllables. Although he was a very regular metricist, Chaucer used various conventional devices that are apt to make the reader stumble until he or she understands them. Final *e* is often not pronounced before a word beginning with a vowel or *h*, and may be suppressed whenever metrically convenient. The same medial and terminal syllables that are slurred in Modern English are apt to be suppressed in Chaucer's English: *Canterb'ry* for *Canterbury*; *ev'r* (perhaps *e'er*) for *evere*. The plural in *es* may either be syllabic or reduced to *s* as in Modern English. Despite these seeming irregularities, Chaucer's verse is not difficult to read if one constantly bears in mind the basic pattern of the iambic pentameter line.

THE MIDDLE AGES

TEXTS	CONTEXTS
	43–ca. 420 Romans conquer Britons; Brittania a province of the Roman Empire
	307–37 Reign of Constantine the Great leads to adoption of Christianity as official religion of the Roman Empire
ca. 405 St. Jerome completes *Vulgate,* Latin translation of the Bible that becomes standard for the Roman Catholic Church	
	432 St. Patrick begins mission to convert Ireland
	ca. 450 Withdrawal of Roman legions; Anglo-Saxon conquest of Britons begins
523 Boethius, *Consolation of Philosophy* (Latin)	
	597 St. Augustine of Canterbury's mission to Kent begins conversion of Anglo-Saxons to Christianity
ca. 658–80 *Cædmon's Hymn,* earliest poem recorded in English	
731 Bede completes *Ecclesiastical History of the English People*	
? ca. 750 *Beowulf* composed	
	ca. 787 First Viking raids on England
	871–99 Reign of King Alfred
ca. 1000 Unique *Beowulf* manuscript written	
	1066 Norman Conquest by William I establishes French-speaking ruling class in England
	1095–1221 Crusades
ca. 1135–38 Geoffrey of Monmouth's Latin *History of the Kings of Britain* gives pseudohistorical status to Arthurian and other legends	
	1152 Future Henry II marries Eleanor of Aquitaine, bringing vast French territories to the English crown
1154 End of *Peterborough Chronicle,* last branch of the *Anglo-Saxon Chronicle*	
? ca. 1165–80 Marie de France, *Lais* in Anglo-Norman French from Breton sources	
ca. 1170–91 Chrétien de Troyes, chivalric romances about knights of the Round Table	**1170** Archbishop Thomas Becket murdered in Canterbury Cathedral
	1182 Birth of St. Francis of Assisi
? ca. 1200 Layamon's *Brut*	
? ca. 1215–25 *Ancrene Riwle*	
	1215 Fourth Lateran Council requires annual confession. English barons force King John to seal Magna Carta (the Great Charter) guaranteeing baronial rights

TEXTS	CONTEXTS
ca. 1304–21 Dante Alighieri writing *Divine Comedy*	
	ca. 1337–1453 Hundred Years' War
	1348 Black Death ravages Europe
	1362 English first used in law courts and Parliament
1368 Chaucer, *Book of the Duchess*	**1372** Chaucer's first journey to Italy
ca. 1375–1400 *Sir Gawain and the Green Knight*	
	1376 Earliest record of performance of drama at York
1377–79 William Langland, *Piers Plowman* (B-Text)	
ca. 1380 John Wycliffe and his followers begin first complete translation of the Bible into English	
	1381 People's uprising briefly takes control of London before being suppressed
ca. 1385–87 Chaucer, *Troilus and Criseyde*	
ca. 1387–89 Chaucer working on *The Canterbury Tales*	
ca. 1390–92 John Gower, *Confessio Amantis*	
	1399 Richard II deposed by his cousin, who succeeds him as Henry IV
	1400 Richard II murdered
	1401 Execution of William Sawtre, first Lollard burned at the stake under new law against heresy
	1415 Henry V defeats French at Agincourt
	1431 English burn Joan of Arc at Rouen
ca. 1432–38 Margery Kempe, *The Book of Margery Kempe*	
ca. 1450–75 Wakefield mystery cycle, *Second Shepherds' Play*	
	1455–85 Wars of the Roses
ca. 1470 Sir Thomas Malory in prison working on *Morte Darthur*	
	1476 William Caxton sets up first printing press in England
1485 Caxton publishes *Morte Darthur,* one of the first books in English to be printed	**1485** The earl of Richmond defeats the Yorkist king, Richard III, at Bosworth Field and succeeds him as Henry VII, founder of the Tudor dynasty
ca. 1510 *Everyman*	**1575** Last performance of mystery plays at Chester

Anglo-Saxon England

THE DREAM OF THE ROOD

The *Dream of the Rood* (i.e., of the Cross) is the finest of a rather large number of religious poems in Old English. Neither its author nor its date of composition is known. It appears in a late tenth-century manuscript located in Vercelli in northern Italy, a manuscript made up of Old English religious poems and sermons. The poem may antedate its manuscript, because some passages from the Rood's speech were carved, with some variations, in runes on a stone cross at some time after its construction early in the eighth century; this is the famous Ruthwell Cross, which is preserved near Dumfries in southern Scotland. The precise relation of the poem to this cross is, however, uncertain.

The experience of the Rood—its humiliation at the hands of those who changed it from tree to instrument of punishment for criminals, its humility when the young hero Christ mounts it, and its pride as the restored "tree of glory"—has a suggestive relevance to the condition of the sad, lonely, sin-stained Dreamer. His isolation and melancholy is typical of exile figures in Old English poetry. For the Rood, however, glory has replaced torment, and at the end, the Dreamer's description of Christ's triumphant entry into heaven with the souls He has liberated from hell reflects the Dreamer's response to the hope that has been brought to him.

The Dream of the Rood[1]

Listen, I will speak of the best of dreams, of what I dreamed at midnight when men and their voices were at rest. It seemed to me that I saw a most rare tree reach high aloft, wound in light, brightest of beams. All that beacon[2] was covered with gold; gems stood fair where it met the ground, five were above about the crosspiece. Many hosts of angels gazed on it, fair in the form created for them. This was surely no felon's gallows, but holy spirits beheld it there, men upon earth, and all this glorious creation. Wonderful was the triumph-tree, and I stained with sins, wounded with wrongdoings. I saw the tree of glory shine splendidly, adorned with garments, decked with gold: jewels had worthily covered the Lord's tree. Yet through that gold I might perceive ancient agony of wretches, for now it began to bleed on the right side.[3] I was all afflicted with sorrows, I was afraid for that fair sight. I saw that bright beacon change in clothing and color: now it was wet with moisture, drenched with flowing of blood, now adorned with treasure. Yet I, lying

1. This prose translation, by E. T. Donaldson, has been based in general on the edition of the poem by John C. Pope, *Seven Old English Poems* (1966).
2. The Old English word *beacen* also means token or sign and battle standard.
3. The wound Christ received on the Cross was supposed to have been on the right side.

there a long while troubled, beheld the Saviour's tree until I heard it give voice: the best of trees began to speak words.

"It was long ago—I remember it still—that I was hewn down at the wood's edge, taken from my stump. Strong foes seized me there, hewed me to the shape they wished to see, commanded me to lift their criminals. Men carried me on their shoulders, then set me on a hill; foes enough fastened me there. Then I saw the Lord of mankind hasten with stout heart, for he would climb upon me. I dared not bow or break against God's word when I saw earth's surface tremble. I might have felled all foes, but I stood fast. Then the young Hero stripped himself—that was God Almighty—strong and stouthearted. He climbed on the high gallows, bold in the sight of many, when he would free mankind. I trembled when the Warrior embraced me, yet I dared not bow to earth, fall to the ground's surface; but I must stand fast. I was raised up, a cross; I lifted up the Mighty King, Lord of the Heavens: I dared not bend. They pierced me with dark nails: the wounds are seen on me, open gashes of hatred. Nor did I dare harm any of them. They mocked us both together. I was all wet with blood, drenched from the side of that Man after he had sent forth his spirit. I had endured many bitter happenings on that hill. I saw the God of Hosts cruelly racked. The shades of night had covered the Ruler's body with their mists, the bright splendor. Shadow came forth, dark beneath the clouds. All creation wept, bewailed the King's fall; Christ was on Cross.

"Yet from afar some came hastening to the Lord.[4] All that I beheld. I was sore afflicted with griefs, yet I bowed to the men's hands, meekly, eagerly. Then they took Almighty God, lifted him up from his heavy torment. The warriors left me standing, covered with blood. I was all wounded with arrows. They laid him down weary of limb, stood at the body's head, looked there upon Heaven's Lord; and he rested there a while, tired after the great struggle. Then warriors began to build him an earth-house in the sight of his slayer,[5] carved it out of bright stone; they set there the Wielder of Triumphs. Then they began to sing him a song of sorrow, desolate in the evening. Then they wished to turn back, weary, from the great Prince; he remained with small company.[6] Yet we[7] stood in our places a good while, weeping. The voice of the warriors departed. The body grew cold, fair house of the spirit. Then some began to fell us to earth—that was a fearful fate! Some buried us in a deep pit. Yet thanes[8] of the Lord, friends, learned of me there. . . . decked me in gold and silver.[9]

"Now you might understand, my beloved man, that I had endured the work of evildoers, grievous sorrows. Now the time has come that men far and wide upon earth honor me—and all this glorious creation—and pray to this beacon. On me God's Son suffered awhile; therefore I tower now glorious under the heavens, and I may heal every one of those who hold me in awe. Of old I became the hardest of torments, most loathed by men, before I opened the right road of life to those who have voices. Behold, the Lord of Glory honored

4. According to John 19.38–39, it was Joseph of Arimathea and Nicodemus who received Christ's body from the Cross.
5. I.e., the Cross.
6. I.e., alone (an understatement).
7. I.e., Christ's Cross and those on which the two thieves were crucified.

8. Members of the king's body of warriors.
9. A number of lines describing the finding of the Cross have apparently been lost here. According to the legend, St. Helen, the mother of Constantine the Great, the first Christian emperor, led a Roman expedition that discovered the true Cross in the 4th century.

me over all the trees of the wood, the Ruler of Heaven, just as also he honored his mother Mary, Almighty God for all men's sake, over all woman's kind.

"Now I command you, my beloved man, that you tell men of this vision. Disclose with your words that it is of the tree of glory on which Almighty God suffered for mankind's many sins and the deeds Adam did of old. He tasted death there; yet the Lord arose again to help mankind in his great might. Then he climbed to the heavens. He will come again hither on this earth to seek mankind on Doomsday, the Lord himself, Almighty God, and his angels with him, for then he will judge, he who has power to judge, each one just as in this brief life he has deserved. Nor may any one be unafraid of the word the Ruler will speak. Before his host he will ask where the man is who in the name of the Lord would taste bitter death as he did on the Cross. But then they will be afraid, and will think of little to begin to say to Christ. There need none be afraid who bears on his breast the best of tokens, but through the Cross shall the kingdom be sought by each soul on this earthly journey that thinks to dwell with the Lord."

Then I prayed to the tree, blithe-hearted, confident, there where I was alone with small company. My heart's thoughts were urged on the way hence. I endured many times of longing. Now is there hope of life for me, that I am permitted to seek the tree of triumph, more often than other men honor it well, alone. For it my heart's desire is great, and my hope of protection is directed to the Cross. I do not possess many powerful friends on earth, but they have gone hence from the delights of the world, sought for themselves the King of Glory. They live now in the heavens with the High Father, dwell in glory. And every day I look forward to when the Lord's Cross that I beheld here on earth will fetch me from this short life and bring me then where joy is great, delight in the heavens, where the Lord's folk are seated at the feast, where bliss is eternal. And then may it place me where thenceforth I may dwell in glory, fully enjoy bliss with the saints. May the Lord be my friend, who once here on earth suffered on the gallows-tree for man's sins: he freed us and granted us life, a heavenly home. Hope was renewed, with joys and with bliss, to those who endured fire.[1] The Son was victorious in that foray, mighty and successful. Then he came with his multitude, a host of spirits, into God's kingdom, the Almighty Ruler; and the angels and all the saints who dwelt then in glory rejoiced when their Ruler, Almighty God, came where his home was.

---

1. This and the following sentences refer to the Harrowing (i.e., pillaging) of Hell; after His death on the Cross, Christ descended into Hell, from which He released the souls of certain of the patriarchs and prophets, conducting them triumphantly to Heaven.

BEOWULF

Beowulf, the oldest of the great long poems written in English, may have been composed more than twelve hundred years ago, in the first half of the eighth century, although some scholars would place it as late as the tenth century. As is the case with most Old English poems, the title has been assigned by modern editors, for the manuscripts do not normally give any indication of title or authorship. Linguistic evidence shows that the poem was originally composed in the dialect of what was then Mercia, the Midlands of England today. But in the unique late-tenth-century manuscript preserving the poem, it has been converted into the West-Saxon dialect of the south-west in which most of Old English literature survives. In 1731, before any modern transcript of the text had been made, the manuscript was seriously damaged in a fire that destroyed the building in London that housed the extraordinary collection of medieval English manuscripts made by Sir Robert Bruce Cotton (1571–1631). As a result of the fire and subsequent deterioration, a number of lines and words have been lost from the poem.

It is possible that *Beowulf* may be the lone survivor of a genre of Old English long epics, but it must have been a remarkable and difficult work even in its own day. The poet was reviving the heroic language, style, and pagan world of ancient Germanic oral poetry, a world that was already remote for his contemporaries and that is stranger to the modern reader, in many respects, than the epic world of Homer and Virgil. With the help of *Beowulf* itself, a few shorter heroic poems in Old English, and later poetry and prose in Old Saxon, Old Icelandic, and Middle High German, we can only conjecture what Germanic oral epic must have been like when performed by the Germanic *scop*, or bard. The *Beowulf* poet himself imagines such oral performances by having King Hrothgar's court poet recite a heroic lay at a feast celebrating Beowulf's defeat of Grendel. Many of the words and formulaic expressions in *Beowulf* can be found in other Old English poems, but there are also an extraordinary number of what linguists call *hapax legomena*—that is, words recorded only once in a language. The poet may have found them elsewhere, but the high incidence of such words suggests that he was an original wordsmith in his own right.

Although the poem itself is English in language and origin, it deals not with native Englishmen but with their Germanic forebears, especially with two south Scandinavian tribes, the Danes and the Geats, who lived on the Danish island of Zealand and in southern Sweden. Thus the historical period the poem concerns—insofar as it may be said to refer to history at all—is some centuries before it was written—that is, a time after the initial invasion of England by Germanic tribes in the middle of the fifth century but before the Anglo-Saxon migration was completed. The one datable fact of history mentioned in the poem is a raid on the Franks in which Hygelac, the king of the Geats and Beowulf's lord, was killed, and this raid occurred in the year 520. Yet the poet's elliptical references to quasihistorical and legendary material show that his audience was still familiar with many old stories, the outlines of which we can only infer, sometimes with the help of later analogous tales in other Germanic languages. This knowledge was probably kept alive by other heroic poetry, of which little has been preserved in English, although much may once have existed.

It is now widely believed that *Beowulf* is the work of a single poet who was a Christian and that his poem reflects well-established Christian tradition. The conversion of the Germanic settlers in England had been largely completed during the seventh century. The Danish king Hrothgar's poet sings a song about the Creation (lines 87–98) reminiscent of Cædmon's *Hymn*. The monster Grendel is said to be a descendant of Cain. There are allusions to God's judgment and to fate (*wyrd*) but none to pagan deities. References to the New Testament are notably absent, but Hrothgar and Beowulf often speak of God as though their religion is monotheistic. With sadness the poet relates that, made desperate by Grendel's attacks, the Danes pray for help at heathen shrines—apparently backsliding as the children of Israel and the earliest Anglo-Saxon Christians had sometimes done.

Although Hrothgar and Beowulf are portrayed as morally upright and enlightened pagans, they fully espouse and frequently affirm the values of Germanic heroic poetry. In the poetry depicting this warrior society, the most important of human relationships was that which existed between the warrior—the thane—and his lord, a relationship based less on subordination of one man's will to another's than on mutual trust and respect. When a warrior vowed loyalty to his lord, he became not so much his servant as his voluntary companion, one who would take pride in defending him and fighting in his wars. In return, the lord was expected to take care of his thanes and to reward them richly for their valor; a good king, one like Hrothgar or Beowulf, is referred to by such poetic epithets as "ring-giver" and as the "helmet" and "shield" of his people.

The relationship between kinsmen was also of deep significance to this society. If one of his kinsmen had been slain, a man had a moral obligation either to kill the slayer or to exact the payment of *wergild* (man-price) in compensation. Each rank of society was evaluated at a definite price, which had to be paid to the dead man's kin by the killer if he wished to avoid their vengeance—even if the killing had been an accident. In the absence of any legal code other than custom or any body of law enforcement, it was the duty of the family (often with the lord's support) to execute justice. The payment itself had less significance as wealth than as proof that the kinsmen had done what was right. The failure to take revenge or to exact compensation was considered shameful. Hrothgar's anguish over the murders committed by Grendel is not only for the loss of his men but also for the shame of his inability either to kill Grendel or to exact a "death-price" from the killer. "It is always better / to avenge dear ones than to indulge in mourning" (lines 1384–85), Beowulf says to Hrothgar, who has been thrown back into despair by the revenge-slaying of his old friend Aeschere by Grendel's mother.

Yet the young Beowulf's attempt to comfort the bereaved old king by invoking the code of vengeance may be one of several instances of the poet's ironic treatment of the tragic futility of the never-ending blood feuds. The most graphic example in the poem of that irony is the Finnsburg episode, the lay sung by Hrothgar's hall-poet. The Danish princess Hildeburh, married to the Frisian king Finn—probably to put an end to a feud between those peoples—loses both her brother and her son when a bloody fight breaks out in the hall between a visiting party of Danes and her husband's men. The bodies are cremated together on a huge funeral pyre: "The glutton element flamed and consumed / the dead of both sides. Their great days were gone" (lines 1124–25).

Such feuds, the staple subject of Germanic epic and saga, have only a peripheral place in the poem. Instead, the poem turns on Beowulf's three great fights against preternatural evil, which inhabits the dangerous and demonic space surrounding human society. He undertakes the fight against Grendel to save the Danes from the monster and to exact vengeance for the men Grendel has slain. Another motive is to demonstrate his strength and courage and thereby to enhance his personal glory. Hrothgar's magnificent gifts become the material emblems of that glory. Revenge and glory also motivate Beowulf's slaying of Grendel's mother. He undertakes his last battle against the dragon, however, only because there is no other way to save his own people.

A somber and dignified elegiac mood pervades *Beowulf*. The poem opens and closes with the description of a funeral and is filled with laments for the dead. Our first view of Beowulf is of an ambitious young hero. At the end, he has become an old king, facing the dragon and death. His people mourn him and praise him, as does the poet, for his nobility, generosity, courage, and, what is less common in Germanic heroes, kindness to his people. The poet's elegiac tone may be informed by something more than the duty to "praise a prince whom he holds dear / and cherish his memory when that moment comes / when he has to be convoyed from his bodily home" (lines 3175–77). The entire poem could be viewed as the poet's lament for heroes like Beowulf who went into the darkness without the light of his own Christian faith.

The present verse translation is by the Irish poet Seamus Heaney, who received the Nobel Prize for literature in 1995. Selections from Heaney's own poems appear in this anthology. His *Beowulf* is both a translation of one of the oldest English poems and a personal response to a work that speaks to a modern poet about the violence of our own century and the courage with which some men and women have faced up to it.

TRIBES AND GENEALOGIES

1. The Danes (Bright-, Half-, Ring-, Spear-, North-, East-, South-, West-Danes; Shieldings, Honor-, Victor-, War-Shieldings; Ing's friends)

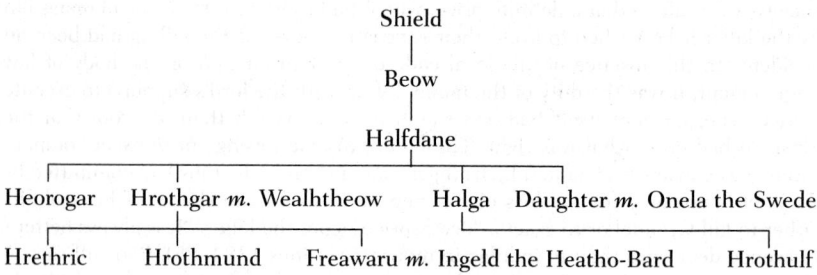

2. The Geats (Sea-, War-, Weather-Geats)

3. The Swedes

4. Miscellaneous

A. The Half-Danes (also called Shieldings) involved in the fight at Finnsburg may represent a different tribe from the Danes described above. Their king Hoc had a son, Hnaef, who succeeded him, and a daughter Hildeburh, who married Finn, king of the Jutes.

B. The Jutes or Frisians are represented as enemies of the Danes in the fight at Finnsburg and as allies of the Franks or Hugas at the time Hygelac the Geat made the attack in which he lost his life and from which Beowulf swam home. Also allied with the Franks at this time were the Hetware.

C. The Heatho-Bards (i.e., "Battle-Bards") are represented as inveterate enemies of the Danes. Their king Froda had been killed in an attack on the Danes, and Hrothgar's attempt to make peace with them by marrying his daughter Freawaru to Froda's son Ingeld failed when the latter attacked Heorot. The attack was repulsed, although Heorot was burned.

---

* The daughter of Hygelac who was given to Eofor may have been born to him by a former wife, older than Hygd.

A NOTE ON NAMES

Old English, like Modern German, contained many compound words, most of which have been lost in Modern English. Most of the names in *Beowulf* are compounds. Hrothgar is a combination of words meaning "glory" and "spear"; the name of his older brother, Heorogar, comes from "army" and "spear"; Hrothgar's sons Hrethric and Hrothmund contain the first elements of their father's name combined, respectively, with *ric* (kingdom, empire; Modern German *Reich*) and *mund* (hand, protection). As in the case of the Danish dynasty, family names often alliterate. Masculine names of the warrior class have military associations. The importance of family and the demands of alliteration frequently lead to the designation of characters by formulas identifying them in terms of relationships. Thus Beowulf is referred to as "son of Ecgtheow" or "kinsman of Hygelac" (his uncle and lord).

The Old English spellings of names are mostly preserved in the translation. A few rules of pronunciation are worth keeping in mind. Initial *H* before *r* was sounded, and so Hrothgar's name alliterates with that of his brother Heorogar. The combination *cg* has the value of *dg* in words like "edge." The first element in the name of Beowulf's father "Ecgtheow" is the same word as "edge," and, by the figure of speech called synecdoche (a part of something stands for the whole), *ecg* stands for *sword* and Ecgtheow means "sword-servant."

Beowulf

[PROLOGUE: THE RISE OF THE DANISH NATION]

So. The Spear-Danes[1] in days gone by
and the kings who ruled them had courage and greatness.
We have heard of those princes' heroic campaigns.
There was Shield Sheafson,[2] scourge of many tribes,
5   a wrecker of mead-benches, rampaging among foes.
This terror of the hall-troops had come far.
A foundling to start with, he would flourish later on
as his powers waxed and his worth was proved.
In the end each clan on the outlying coasts
10   beyond the whale-road had to yield to him
and begin to pay tribute. That was one good king.
   Afterward a boy-child was born to Shield,
a cub in the yard, a comfort sent
by God to that nation. He knew what they had tholed,[3]
15   the long times and troubles they'd come through
without a leader; so the Lord of Life,
the glorious Almighty, made this man renowned.
Shield had fathered a famous son:
Beow's name was known through the north.

1. There are different compound names for tribes, often determined by alliteration in Old English poetry. Line 1 reads, *"Hwæt, we Gar-dena in geardagum,"* where alliteration falls on *Gar* (spear) and *gear* (year). Old English hard and soft *g* (spelled *y* in Modern English) alliterate. The compound *geardagum* derives from "year," used in the special sense of "long ago," and "days" and survives in the archaic expression "days of yore."

2. Shield is the name of the founder of the Danish royal line. Sheafson translates *Scefing*, i.e., *sheaf* + the patronymic suffix *-ing*. Because Sheaf was a "foundling" (line 7: *feasceaft funden*, i.e., found destitute) who arrived by sea (lines 45–46), it is likely that as a child Shield brought with him only a sheaf, a symbol of fruitfulness.

3. Suffered, endured.

20   And a young prince must be prudent like that,
       giving freely while his father lives
       so that afterward in age when fighting starts
       steadfast companions will stand by him
       and hold the line. Behavior that's admired
25   is the path to power among people everywhere.
          Shield was still thriving when his time came
       and he crossed over into the Lord's keeping.
       His warrior band did what he bade them
       when he laid down the law among the Danes:
30   they shouldered him out to the sea's flood,
       the chief they revered who had long ruled them.
       A ring-whorled prow rode in the harbor,
       ice-clad, outbound, a craft for a prince.
       They stretched their beloved lord in his boat,
35   laid out by the mast, amidships,
       the great ring-giver. Far-fetched treasures
       were piled upon him, and precious gear.
       I never heard before of a ship so well furbished
       with battle-tackle, bladed weapons
40   and coats of mail. The massed treasure
       was loaded on top of him: it would travel far
       on out into the ocean's sway.
       They decked his body no less bountifully
       with offerings than those first ones did
45   who cast him away when he was a child
       and launched him alone out over the waves.[4]
       And they set a gold standard up
       high above his head and let him drift
       to wind and tide, bewailing him
50   and mourning their loss. No man can tell,
       no wise man in hall or weathered veteran
       knows for certain who salvaged that load.
          Then it fell to Beow to keep the forts.
       He was well regarded and ruled the Danes
55   for a long time after his father took leave
       of his life on earth. And then his heir,
       the great Halfdane,[5] held sway
       for as long as he lived, their elder and warlord.
       He was four times a father, this fighter prince:
60   one by one they entered the world,
       Heorogar, Hrothgar, the good Halga,
       and a daughter, I have heard, who was Onela's queen,
       a balm in bed to the battle-scarred Swede.
          The fortunes of war favored Hrothgar.
65   Friends and kinsmen flocked to his ranks,
       young followers, a force that grew
       to be a mighty army. So his mind turned

---

4. See n. 2, above. Since Shield was found destitute, "no less bountifully" is litotes or understatement; the ironic reminder that he came with
nothing (line 43) emphasizes the reversal of his
fortunes.

5. Probably named so because, according to one
source, his mother was a Swedish princess.

to hall-building: he handed down orders
for men to work on a great mead-hall
70   meant to be a wonder of the world forever;
it would be his throne-room and there he would dispense
his God-given goods to young and old—
but not the common land or people's lives.[6]
Far and wide through the world, I have heard,
75   orders for work to adorn that wallstead
were sent to many peoples. And soon it stood there
finished and ready, in full view,
the hall of halls. Heorot was the name[7]
he had settled on it, whose utterance was law.
80   Nor did he renege, but doled out rings
and torques at the table. The hall towered,
its gables wide and high and awaiting
a barbarous burning.[8] That doom abided,
but in time it would come: the killer instinct
85   unleashed among in-laws, the blood-lust rampant.[9]

[HEOROT IS ATTACKED]

Then a powerful demon,[1] a prowler through the dark,
nursed a hard grievance. It harrowed him
to hear the din of the loud banquet
every day in the hall, the harp being struck
90   and the clear song of a skilled poet
telling with mastery of man's beginnings,
how the Almighty had made the earth
a gleaming plain girdled with waters;
in His splendor He set the sun and the moon
95   to be earth's lamplight, lanterns for men,
and filled the broad lap of the world
with branches and leaves; and quickened life
in every other thing that moved.
So times were pleasant for the people there
100   until finally one, a fiend out of hell,
began to work his evil in the world.
Grendel was the name of this grim demon
haunting the marches, marauding round the heath
and the desolate fens; he had dwelt for a time
105   in misery among the banished monsters,
Cain's clan, whom the Creator had outlawed
and condemned as outcasts.[2] For the killing of Abel
the Eternal Lord had exacted a price:
Cain got no good from committing that murder
110   because the Almighty made him anathema

6. The king could not dispose of land used by all, such as a common pasture, or of slaves.
7. I.e., "Hart," from antlers fastened to the gables or because the crossed gable-ends resembled a stag's antlers; the hart was also an icon of royalty.
8. An allusion to the future destruction of Heorot by fire, probably in a raid by the Heatho-Bards.
9. As told later (lines 2020–69), Hrothgar plans to marry a daughter to Ingeld, chief of the Heatho-Bards, in hopes of resolving a long-standing feud. See previous note.
1. The poet withholds the name for several lines. He does the same with the name of the hero as well as others.
2. See Genesis 4.9–12.

and out of the curse of his exile there sprang
ogres and elves and evil phantoms
and the giants too who strove with God
time and again until He gave them their reward.
115   So, after nightfall, Grendel set out
for the lofty house, to see how the Ring-Danes
were settling into it after their drink,
and there he came upon them, a company of the best
asleep from their feasting, insensible to pain
120   and human sorrow. Suddenly then
the God-cursed brute was creating havoc:
greedy and grim, he grabbed thirty men
from their resting places and rushed to his lair,
flushed up and inflamed from the raid,
125   blundering back with the butchered corpses.
        Then as dawn brightened and the day broke,
Grendel's powers of destruction were plain:
their wassail was over, they wept to heaven
and mourned under morning. Their mighty prince,
130   the storied leader, sat stricken and helpless,
humiliated by the loss of his guard,
bewildered and stunned, staring aghast
at the demon's trail, in deep distress.
He was numb with grief, but got no respite
135   for one night later merciless Grendel
struck again with more gruesome murders.
Malignant by nature, he never showed remorse.
It was easy then to meet with a man
shifting himself to a safer distance
140   to bed in the bothies,[3] for who could be blind
to the evidence of his eyes, the obviousness
of the hall-watcher's hate? Whoever escaped
kept a weather-eye open and moved away.
        So Grendel ruled in defiance of right,
145   one against all, until the greatest house
in the world stood empty, a deserted wallstead.
For twelve winters, seasons of woe,
the lord of the Shieldings[4] suffered under
his load of sorrow; and so, before long,
150   the news was known over the whole world.
Sad lays were sung about the beset king,
the vicious raids and ravages of Grendel,
his long and unrelenting feud,
nothing but war; how he would never
155   parley or make peace with any Dane
nor stop his death-dealing nor pay the death-price.[5]
No counselor could ever expect
fair reparation from those rabid hands.

---

3. Huts, outlying buildings. Evidently Grendel wants only to dominate the hall.
4. The descendants of Shield, another name for the Danes.

5. I.e., *wergild* (man-price); monetary compensation for the life of the slain man is the only way, according to Germanic law, to settle a feud peacefully.

All were endangered; young and old
160 were hunted down by that dark death-shadow
who lurked and swooped in the long nights
on the misty moors; nobody knows
where these reavers from hell roam on their errands.
    So Grendel waged his lonely war,
165 inflicting constant cruelties on the people,
atrocious hurt. He took over Heorot,
haunted the glittering hall after dark,
but the throne itself, the treasure-seat,
he was kept from approaching; he was the Lord's outcast.
170   These were hard times, heartbreaking
for the prince of the Shieldings; powerful counselors,
the highest in the land, would lend advice,
plotting how best the bold defenders
might resist and beat off sudden attacks.
175 Sometimes at pagan shrines they vowed
offerings to idols, swore oaths
that the killer of souls⁶ might come to their aid
and save the people. That was their way,
their heathenish hope; deep in their hearts
180 they remembered hell. The Almighty Judge
of good deeds and bad, the Lord God,
Head of the Heavens and High King of the World,
was unknown to them. Oh, cursed is he
who in time of trouble has to thrust his soul
185 in the fire's embrace, forfeiting help;
he has nowhere to turn. But blessed is he
who after death can approach the Lord
and find friendship in the Father's embrace.

[THE HERO COMES TO HEOROT]

    So that troubled time continued, woe
190 that never stopped, steady affliction
for Halfdane's son, too hard an ordeal.
There was panic after dark, people endured
raids in the night, riven by the terror.
    When he heard about Grendel, Hygelac's thane
195 was on home ground, over in Geatland.
There was no one else like him alive.
In his day, he was the mightiest man on earth,
highborn and powerful. He ordered a boat
that would ply the waves. He announced his plan:
200 to sail the swan's road and seek out that king,
the famous prince who needed defenders.
Nobody tried to keep him from going,
no elder denied him, dear as he was to them.
Instead, they inspected omens and spurred
205 his ambition to go, whilst he moved about
like the leader he was, enlisting men,

6. I.e., the devil. Heathen gods were thought to be devils.

the best he could find; with fourteen others
the warrior boarded the boat as captain,
a canny pilot along coast and currents.
210   Time went by, the boat was on water,
in close under the cliffs.
Men climbed eagerly up the gangplank,
sand churned in surf, warriors loaded
a cargo of weapons, shining war-gear
215   in the vessel's hold, then heaved out,
away with a will in their wood-wreathed ship.
Over the waves, with the wind behind her
and foam at her neck, she flew like a bird
until her curved prow had covered the distance,
220   and on the following day, at the due hour,
those seafarers sighted land,
sunlit cliffs, sheer crags
and looming headlands, the landfall they sought.
It was the end of their voyage and the Geats vaulted
225   over the side, out on to the sand,
and moored their ship. There was a clash of mail
and a thresh of gear. They thanked God
for that easy crossing on a calm sea.
    When the watchman on the wall, the Shieldings' lookout
230   whose job it was to guard the sea-cliffs,
saw shields glittering on the gangplank
and battle-equipment being unloaded
he had to find out who and what
the arrivals were. So he rode to the shore,
235   this horseman of Hrothgar's, and challenged them
in formal terms, flourishing his spear:
"What kind of men are you who arrive
rigged out for combat in your coats of mail,
sailing here over the sea-lanes
240   in your steep-hulled boat? I have been stationed
as lookout on this coast for a long time.
My job is to watch the waves for raiders,
any danger to the Danish shore.
Never before has a force under arms
245   disembarked so openly—not bothering to ask
if the sentries allowed them safe passage
or the clan had consented. Nor have I seen
a mightier man-at-arms on this earth
than the one standing here: unless I am mistaken,
250   he is truly noble. This is no mere
hanger-on in a hero's armor.
So now, before you fare inland
as interlopers, I have to be informed
about who you are and where you hail from.
255   Outsiders from across the water,
I say it again: the sooner you tell
where you come from and why, the better."
    The leader of the troop unlocked his word-hoard;

the distinguished one delivered this answer:
260 "We belong by birth to the Geat people
and owe allegiance to Lord Hygelac.
In his day, my father was a famous man,
a noble warrior-lord named Ecgtheow.
He outlasted many a long winter
265 and went on his way. All over the world
men wise in counsel continue to remember him.
We come in good faith to find your lord
and nation's shield, the son of Halfdane.
Give us the right advice and direction.
270 We have arrived here on a great errand
to the lord of the Danes, and I believe therefore
there should be nothing hidden or withheld between us.
So tell us if what we have heard is true
about this threat, whatever it is,
275 this danger abroad in the dark nights,
this corpse-maker mongering death
in the Shieldings' country. I come to proffer
my wholehearted help and counsel.
I can show the wise Hrothgar a way
280 to defeat his enemy and find respite—
if any respite is to reach him, ever.
I can calm the turmoil and terror in his mind.
Otherwise, he must endure woes
and live with grief for as long as his hall
285 stands at the horizon on its high ground."
     Undaunted, sitting astride his horse,
the coast-guard answered: "Anyone with gumption
and a sharp mind will take the measure
of two things: what's said and what's done.
290 I believe what you have told me, that you are a troop
loyal to our king. So come ahead
with your arms and your gear, and I will guide you.
What's more, I'll order my own comrades
on their word of honor to watch your boat
295 down there on the strand—keep her safe
in her fresh tar, until the time comes
for her curved prow to preen on the waves
and bear this hero back to Geatland.
May one so valiant and venturesome
300 come unharmed through the clash of battle."
     So they went on their way. The ship rode the water,
broad-beamed, bound by its hawser
and anchored fast. Boar-shapes[7] flashed
above their cheek-guards, the brightly forged
305 work of goldsmiths, watching over
those stern-faced men. They marched in step,
hurrying on till the timbered hall
rose before them, radiant with gold.

---

7. Carved images of boars were placed on helmets, probably as good luck charms to protect the warriors.

Nobody on earth knew of another
310 building like it. Majesty lodged there,
its light shone over many lands.
So their gallant escort guided them
to that dazzling stronghold and indicated
the shortest way to it; then the noble warrior
315 wheeled on his horse and spoke these words:
"It is time for me to go. May the Almighty
Father keep you and in His kindness
watch over your exploits. I'm away to the sea,
back on alert against enemy raiders."
320   It was a paved track, a path that kept them
in marching order. Their mail-shirts glinted,
hard and hand-linked; the high-gloss iron
of their armor rang. So they duly arrived
in their grim war-graith[8] and gear at the hall,
325 and, weary from the sea, stacked wide shields
of the toughest hardwood against the wall,
then collapsed on the benches; battle-dress
and weapons clashed. They collected their spears
in a seafarers' stook, a stand of grayish
330 tapering ash. And the troops themselves
were as good as their weapons.
                     Then a proud warrior
questioned the men concerning their origins:
"Where do you come from, carrying these
decorated shields and shirts of mail,
335 these cheek-hinged helmets and javelins?
I am Hrothgar's herald and officer.
I have never seen so impressive or large
an assembly of strangers. Stoutness of heart,
bravery not banishment, must have brought you to Hrothgar."
340   The man whose name was known for courage,
the Geat leader, resolute in his helmet,
answered in return: "We are retainers
from Hygelac's band. Beowulf is my name.
If your lord and master, the most renowned
345 son of Halfdane, will hear me out
and graciously allow me to greet him in person,
I am ready and willing to report my errand."
    Wulfgar replied, a Wendel chief
renowned as a warrior, well known for his wisdom
350 and the temper of his mind: "I will take this message,
in accordance with your wish, to our noble king,
our dear lord, friend of the Danes,
the giver of rings. I will go and ask him
about your coming here, then hurry back
355 with whatever reply it pleases him to give."
    With that he turned to where Hrothgar sat,
an old man among retainers;

8. "Graith": archaic for apparel.

the valiant follower stood foursquare
in front of his king: he knew the courtesies.
360 Wulfgar addressed his dear lord:
"People from Geatland have put ashore.
They have sailed far over the wide sea.
They call the chief in charge of their band
by the name of Beowulf. They beg, my lord,
365 an audience with you, exchange of words
and formal greeting. Most gracious Hrothgar,
do not refuse them, but grant them a reply.
From their arms and appointment, they appear well born
and worthy of respect, especially the one
370 who has led them this far: he is formidable indeed."
     Hrothgar, protector of Shieldings, replied:
"I used to know him when he was a young boy.
His father before him was called Ecgtheow.
Hrethel the Geat⁹ gave Ecgtheow
375 his daughter in marriage. This man is their son,
here to follow up an old friendship.
A crew of seamen who sailed for me once
with a gift-cargo across to Geatland
returned with marvelous tales about him:
380 a thane, they declared, with the strength of thirty
in the grip of each hand. Now Holy God
has, in His goodness, guided him here
to the West-Danes, to defend us from Grendel.
This is my hope; and for his heroism
385 I will recompense him with a rich treasure.
Go immediately, bid him and the Geats
he has in attendance to assemble and enter.
Say, moreover, when you speak to them,
they are welcome to Denmark."
                              At the door of the hall,
390 Wulfgar duly delivered the message:
"My lord, the conquering king of the Danes,
bids me announce that he knows your ancestry;
also that he welcomes you here to Heorot
and salutes your arrival from across the sea.
395 You are free now to move forward
to meet Hrothgar in helmets and armor,
but shields must stay here and spears be stacked
until the outcome of the audience is clear."
     The hero arose, surrounded closely
400 by his powerful thanes. A party remained
under orders to keep watch on the arms;
the rest proceeded, led by their prince
under Heorot's roof. And standing on the hearth
in webbed links that the smith had woven,
405 the fine-forged mesh of his gleaming mail-shirt,
resolute in his helmet, Beowulf spoke:

9. Hygelac's father and Beowulf's grandfather.

"Greetings to Hrothgar. I am Hygelac's kinsman,
one of his hall-troop. When I was younger,
I had great triumphs. Then news of Grendel,
410   hard to ignore, reached me at home:
sailors brought stories of the plight you suffer
in this legendary hall, how it lies deserted,
empty and useless once the evening light
hides itself under heaven's dome.
415   So every elder and experienced councilman
among my people supported my resolve
to come here to you, King Hrothgar,
because all knew of my awesome strength.
They had seen me boltered[1] in the blood of enemies
420   when I battled and bound five beasts,
raided a troll-nest and in the night-sea
slaughtered sea-brutes. I have suffered extremes
and avenged the Geats (their enemies brought it
upon themselves; I devastated them).
425   Now I mean to be a match for Grendel,
settle the outcome in single combat.
And so, my request, O king of Bright-Danes,
dear prince of the Shieldings, friend of the people
and their ring of defense, my one request
430   is that you won't refuse me, who have come this far,
the privilege of purifying Heorot,
with my own men to help me, and nobody else.
I have heard moreover that the monster scorns
in his reckless way to use weapons;
435   therefore, to heighten Hygelac's fame
and gladden his heart, I hereby renounce
sword and the shelter of the broad shield,
the heavy war-board: hand-to-hand
is how it will be, a life-and-death
440   fight with the fiend. Whichever one death fells
must deem it a just judgment by God.
If Grendel wins, it will be a gruesome day;
he will glut himself on the Geats in the war-hall,
swoop without fear on that flower of manhood
445   as on others before. Then my face won't be there
to be covered in death: he will carry me away
as he goes to ground, gorged and bloodied;
he will run gloating with my raw corpse
and feed on it alone, in a cruel frenzy
450   fouling his moor-nest. No need then
to lament for long or lay out my body:[2]
if the battle takes me, send back
this breast-webbing that Weland[3] fashioned
and Hrethel gave me, to Lord Hygelac.
455   Fate goes ever as fate must."

1. Clotted, sticky.
2. I.e., for burial. Hrothgar will not need to give

Beowulf an expensive funeral.
3. Famed blacksmith in Germanic legend.

Hrothgar, the helmet of Shieldings, spoke:
"Beowulf, my friend, you have traveled here
to favor us with help and to fight for us.
There was a feud one time, begun by your father.
460 With his own hands he had killed Heatholaf
who was a Wulfing; so war was looming
and his people, in fear of it, forced him to leave.
He came away then over rolling waves
to the South-Danes here, the sons of honor.
465 I was then in the first flush of kingship,
establishing my sway over the rich strongholds
of this heroic land. Heorogar,
my older brother and the better man,
also a son of Halfdane's, had died.
470 Finally I healed the feud by paying:
I shipped a treasure-trove to the Wulfings,
and Ecgtheow acknowledged me with oaths of allegiance.
  "It bothers me to have to burden anyone
with all the grief that Grendel has caused
475 and the havoc he has wreaked upon us in Heorot,
our humiliations. My household-guard
are on the wane, fate sweeps them away
into Grendel's clutches—but God can easily
halt these raids and harrowing attacks!
480   "Time and again, when the goblets passed
and seasoned fighters got flushed with beer
they would pledge themselves to protect Heorot
and wait for Grendel with their whetted swords.
But when dawn broke and day crept in
485 over each empty, blood-spattered bench,
the floor of the mead-hall where they had feasted
would be slick with slaughter. And so they died,
faithful retainers, and my following dwindled.
Now take your place at the table, relish
490 the triumph of heroes to your heart's content."

[FEAST AT HEOROT]

Then a bench was cleared in that banquet hall
so the Geats could have room to be together
and the party sat, proud in their bearing,
strong and stalwart. An attendant stood by
495 with a decorated pitcher, pouring bright
helpings of mead. And the minstrel sang,
filling Heorot with his head-clearing voice,
gladdening that great rally of Geats and Danes.
  From where he crouched at the king's feet,
500 Unferth, a son of Ecglaf's, spoke
contrary words. Beowulf's coming,
his sea-braving, made him sick with envy:
he could not brook or abide the fact
that anyone else alive under heaven
505 might enjoy greater regard than he did:

"Are you the Beowulf who took on Breca
in a swimming match on the open sea,
risking the water just to prove that you could win?
It was sheer vanity made you venture out
510   on the main deep. And no matter who tried,
friend or foe, to deflect the pair of you,
neither would back down: the sea-test obsessed you.
You waded in, embracing water,
taking its measure, mastering currents,
515   riding on the swell. The ocean swayed,
winter went wild in the waves, but you vied
for seven nights; and then he outswam you,
came ashore the stronger contender.
He was cast up safe and sound one morning
520   among the Heatho-Reams, then made his way
to where he belonged in Bronding country,
home again, sure of his ground
in strongroom and bawn.⁴ So Breca made good
his boast upon you and was proved right.
525   No matter, therefore, how you may have fared
in every bout and battle until now,
this time you'll be worsted; no one has ever
outlasted an entire night against Grendel."
    Beowulf, Ecgtheow's son, replied:
530   "Well, friend Unferth, you have had your say
about Breca and me. But it was mostly beer
that was doing the talking. The truth is this:
when the going was heavy in those high waves,
I was the strongest swimmer of all.
535   We'd been children together and we grew up
daring ourselves to outdo each other,
boasting and urging each other to risk
our lives on the sea. And so it turned out.
Each of us swam holding a sword,
540   a naked, hard-proofed blade for protection
against the whale-beasts. But Breca could never
move out farther or faster from me
than I could manage to move from him.
Shoulder to shoulder, we struggled on
545   for five nights, until the long flow
and pitch of the waves, the perishing cold,
night falling and winds from the north
drove us apart. The deep boiled up
and its wallowing sent the sea-brutes wild.
550   My armor helped me to hold out;
my hard-ringed chain-mail, hand-forged and linked,
a fine, close-fitting filigree of gold,
kept me safe when some ocean creature
pulled me to the bottom. Pinioned fast

---

4. Fortified outwork of a court or castle. The word was used by English planters in Ulster to describe
fortified dwellings they erected on lands confiscated from the Irish [Translator's note].

555 and swathed in its grip, I was granted one
final chance: my sword plunged
and the ordeal was over. Through my own hands,
the fury of battle had finished off the sea-beast.
      "Time and again, foul things attacked me,
560 lurking and stalking, but I lashed out,
gave as good as I got with my sword.
My flesh was not for feasting on,
there would be no monsters gnawing and gloating
over their banquet at the bottom of the sea.
565 Instead, in the morning, mangled and sleeping
the sleep of the sword, they slopped and floated
like the ocean's leavings. From now on
sailors would be safe, the deep-sea raids
were over for good. Light came from the east,
570 bright guarantee of God, and the waves
went quiet; I could see headlands
and buffeted cliffs. Often, for undaunted courage,
fate spares the man it has not already marked.
However it occurred, my sword had killed
575 nine sea-monsters. Such night dangers
and hard ordeals I have never heard of
nor of a man more desolate in surging waves.
But worn out as I was, I survived,
came through with my life. The ocean lifted
580 and laid me ashore, I landed safe
on the coast of Finland.
                              Now I cannot recall
any fight you entered, Unferth,
that bears comparison. I don't boast when I say
that neither you nor Breca were ever much
585 celebrated for swordsmanship
or for facing danger on the field of battle.
You killed your own kith and kin,
so for all your cleverness and quick tongue,
you will suffer damnation in the depths of hell.
590 The fact is, Unferth, if you were truly
as keen or courageous as you claim to be
Grendel would never have got away with
such unchecked atrocity, attacks on your king,
havoc in Heorot and horrors everywhere.
595 But he knows he need never be in dread
of your blade making a mizzle of his blood
or of vengeance arriving ever from this quarter—
from the Victory-Shieldings, the shoulderers of the spear.
He knows he can trample down you Danes
600 to his heart's content, humiliate and murder
without fear of reprisal. But he will find me different.
I will show him how Geats shape to kill
in the heat of battle. Then whoever wants to
may go bravely to mead, when the morning light,
605 scarfed in sun-dazzle, shines forth from the south

and brings another daybreak to the world."
    Then the gray-haired treasure-giver was glad;
far-famed in battle, the prince of Bright-Danes
and keeper of his people counted on Beowulf,
610 on the warrior's steadfastness and his word.
So the laughter started, the din got louder
and the crowd was happy. Wealhtheow came in,
Hrothgar's queen, observing the courtesies.
Adorned in her gold, she graciously saluted
615 the men in the hall, then handed the cup
first to Hrothgar, their homeland's guardian,
urging him to drink deep and enjoy it
because he was dear to them. And he drank it down
like the warlord he was, with festive cheer.
620 So the Helming woman went on her rounds,
queenly and dignified, decked out in rings,
offering the goblet to all ranks,
treating the household and the assembled troop,
until it was Beowulf's turn to take it from her hand.
625 With measured words she welcomed the Geat
and thanked God for granting her wish
that a deliverer she could believe in would arrive
to ease their afflictions. He accepted the cup,
a daunting man, dangerous in action
630 and eager for it always. He addressed Wealhtheow;
Beowulf, son of Ecgtheow, said:
"I had a fixed purpose when I put to sea.
As I sat in the boat with my band of men,
I meant to perform to the uttermost
635 what your people wanted or perish in the attempt,
in the fiend's clutches. And I shall fulfill that purpose,
prove myself with a proud deed
or meet my death here in the mead-hall."
This formal boast by Beowulf the Geat
640 pleased the lady well and she went to sit
by Hrothgar, regal and arrayed with gold.
    Then it was like old times in the echoing hall,
proud talk and the people happy,
loud and excited; until soon enough
645 Halfdane's heir had to be away
to his night's rest. He realized
that the demon was going to descend on the hall,
that he had plotted all day, from dawn-light
until darkness gathered again over the world
650 and stealthy night-shapes came stealing forth
under the cloud-murk. The company stood
as the two leaders took leave of each other:
Hrothgar wished Beowulf health and good luck,
named him hall-warden and announced as follows:
655 "Never, since my hand could hold a shield
have I entrusted or given control
of the Danes' hall to anyone but you.

Ward and guard it, for it is the greatest of houses.
Be on your mettle now, keep in mind your fame,
660   beware of the enemy. There's nothing you wish for
that won't be yours if you win through alive."

[THE FIGHT WITH GRENDEL]

Hrothgar departed then with his house-guard.
The lord of the Shieldings, their shelter in war,
left the mead-hall to lie with Wealhtheow,
665   his queen and bedmate. The King of Glory
(as people learned) had posted a lookout
who was a match for Grendel, a guard against monsters,
special protection to the Danish prince.
And the Geat placed complete trust
670   in his strength of limb and the Lord's favor.
He began to remove his iron breast-mail,
took off the helmet and handed his attendant
the patterned sword, a smith's masterpiece,
ordering him to keep the equipment guarded.
675   And before he bedded down, Beowulf,
that prince of goodness, proudly asserted:
"When it comes to fighting, I count myself
as dangerous any day as Grendel.
So it won't be a cutting edge I'll wield
680   to mow him down, easily as I might.
He has no idea of the arts of war,
of shield or sword-play, although he does possess
a wild strength. No weapons, therefore,
for either this night: unarmed he shall face me
685   if face me he dares. And may the Divine Lord
in His wisdom grant the glory of victory
to whichever side He sees fit."
    Then down the brave man lay with his bolster
under his head and his whole company
690   of sea-rovers at rest beside him.
None of them expected he would ever see
his homeland again or get back
to his native place and the people who reared him.
They knew too well the way it was before,
695   how often the Danes had fallen prey
to death in the mead-hall. But the Lord was weaving
a victory on His war-loom for the Weather-Geats.
Through the strength of one they all prevailed;
they would crush their enemy and come through
700   in triumph and gladness. The truth is clear:
Almighty God rules over mankind
and always has.
              Then out of the night
came the shadow-stalker, stealthy and swift.
The hall-guards were slack, asleep at their posts,
705   all except one; it was widely understood
that as long as God disallowed it,

the fiend could not bear them to his shadow-bourne.
One man, however, was in fighting mood,
awake and on edge, spoiling for action.
710　　　In off the moors, down through the mist-bands
God-cursed Grendel came greedily loping.
The bane of the race of men roamed forth,
hunting for a prey in the high hall.
Under the cloud-murk he moved toward it
715　until it shone above him, a sheer keep
of fortified gold. Nor was that the first time
he had scouted the grounds of Hrothgar's dwelling—
although never in his life, before or since,
did he find harder fortune or hall-defenders.
720　Spurned and joyless, he journeyed on ahead
and arrived at the bawn.[5] The iron-braced door
turned on its hinge when his hands touched it.
Then his rage boiled over, he ripped open
the mouth of the building, maddening for blood,
725　pacing the length of the patterned floor
with his loathsome tread, while a baleful light,
flame more than light, flared from his eyes.
He saw many men in the mansion, sleeping,
a ranked company of kinsmen and warriors
730　quartered together. And his glee was demonic,
picturing the mayhem: before morning
he would rip life from limb and devour them,
feed on their flesh; but his fate that night
was due to change, his days of ravening
had come to an end.
735　　　　　　　　　　　　Mighty and canny,
Hygelac's kinsman was keenly watching
for the first move the monster would make.
Nor did the creature keep him waiting
but struck suddenly and started in;
740　he grabbed and mauled a man on his bench,
bit into his bone-lappings, bolted down his blood
and gorged on him in lumps, leaving the body
utterly lifeless, eaten up
hand and foot. Venturing closer,
745　his talon was raised to attack Beowulf
where he lay on the bed, he was bearing in
with open claw when the alert hero's
comeback and armlock forestalled him utterly.
The captain of evil discovered himself
750　in a handgrip harder than anything
he had ever encountered in any man
on the face of the earth. Every bone in his body
quailed and recoiled, but he could not escape.
He was desperate to flee to his den and hide
755　with the devil's litter, for in all his days

5. See p. 38, n. 4.

he had never been clamped or cornered like this.
Then Hygelac's trusty retainer recalled
his bedtime speech, sprang to his feet
and got a firm hold. Fingers were bursting,
760　the monster back-tracking, the man overpowering.
The dread of the land was desperate to escape,
to take a roundabout road and flee
to his lair in the fens. The latching power
in his fingers weakened; it was the worst trip
765　the terror-monger had taken to Heorot.
And now the timbers trembled and sang,
a hall-session[6] that harrowed every Dane
inside the stockade: stumbling in fury,
the two contenders crashed through the building.
770　The hall clattered and hammered, but somehow
survived the onslaught and kept standing:
it was handsomely structured, a sturdy frame
braced with the best of blacksmith's work
inside and out. The story goes
775　that as the pair struggled, mead-benches were smashed
and sprung off the floor, gold fittings and all.
Before then, no Shielding elder would believe
there was any power or person upon earth
capable of wrecking their horn-rigged hall
780　unless the burning embrace of a fire
engulf it in flame. Then an extraordinary
wail arose, and bewildering fear
came over the Danes. Everyone felt it
who heard that cry as it echoed off the wall,
785　a God-cursed scream and strain of catastrophe,
the howl of the loser, the lament of the hell-serf
keening his wound. He was overwhelmed,
manacled tight by the man who of all men
was foremost and strongest in the days of this life.
790　　But the earl-troop's leader was not inclined
to allow his caller to depart alive:
he did not consider that life of much account
to anyone anywhere. Time and again,
Beowulf's warriors worked to defend
795　their lord's life, laying about them
as best they could, with their ancestral blades.
Stalwart in action, they kept striking out
on every side, seeking to cut
straight to the soul. When they joined the struggle
800　there was something they could not have known at the time,
that no blade on earth, no blacksmith's art
could ever damage their demon opponent.
He had conjured the harm from the cutting edge
of every weapon.[7] But his going away

---

6. In Hiberno-English the word "session" (*seissiún*
in Irish) can mean a gathering where musicians
and singers perform for their own enjoyment

[Translator's note].
7. Grendel is protected by a charm against metals.

805 out of this world and the days of his life
  would be agony to him, and his alien spirit
  would travel far into fiends' keeping.
   Then he who had harrowed the hearts of men
  with pain and affliction in former times
810 and had given offense also to God
  found that his bodily powers failed him.
  Hygelac's kinsman kept him helplessly
  locked in a handgrip. As long as either lived,
  he was hateful to the other. The monster's whole
815 body was in pain; a tremendous wound
  appeared on his shoulder. Sinews split
  and the bone-lappings burst. Beowulf was granted
  the glory of winning; Grendel was driven
  under the fen-banks, fatally hurt,
820 to his desolate lair. His days were numbered,
  the end of his life was coming over him,
  he knew it for certain; and one bloody clash
  had fulfilled the dearest wishes of the Danes.
  The man who had lately landed among them,
825 proud and sure, had purged the hall,
  kept it from harm; he was happy with his nightwork
  and the courage he had shown. The Geat captain
  had boldly fulfilled his boast to the Danes:
  he had healed and relieved a huge distress,
830 unremitting humiliations,
  the hard fate they'd been forced to undergo,
  no small affliction. Clear proof of this
  could be seen in the hand the hero displayed
  high up near the roof: the whole of Grendel's
835 shoulder and arm, his awesome grasp.

[CELEBRATION AT HEOROT]

   Then morning came and many a warrior
  gathered, as I've heard, around the gift-hall,
  clan-chiefs flocking from far and near
  down wide-ranging roads, wondering greatly
840 at the monster's footprints. His fatal departure
  was regretted by no one who witnessed his trail,
  the ignominious marks of his flight
  where he'd skulked away, exhausted in spirit
  and beaten in battle, bloodying the path,
845 hauling his doom to the demons' mere.[8]
  The bloodshot water wallowed and surged,
  there were loathsome upthrows and overturnings
  of waves and gore and wound-slurry.
  With his death upon him, he had dived deep
850 into his marsh-den, drowned out his life
  and his heathen soul: hell claimed him there.
   Then away they rode, the old retainers

---

8. A lake or pool, although we learn later that it has an outlet to the sea. Grendel's habitat.

with many a young man following after,
a troop on horseback, in high spirits
855   on their bay steeds. Beowulf's doings
were praised over and over again.
Nowhere, they said, north or south
between the two seas or under the tall sky
on the broad earth was there anyone better
860   to raise a shield or to rule a kingdom.
Yet there was no laying of blame on their lord,
the noble Hrothgar; he was a good king.
    At times the war-band broke into a gallop,
letting their chestnut horses race
865   wherever they found the going good
on those well-known tracks. Meanwhile, a thane
of the king's household, a carrier of tales,
a traditional singer deeply schooled
in the lore of the past, linked a new theme
870   to a strict meter.[9] The man started
to recite with skill, rehearsing Beowulf's
triumphs and feats in well-fashioned lines,
entwining his words.
                He told what he'd heard
repeated in songs about Sigemund's exploits,[1]
875   all of those many feats and marvels,
the struggles and wanderings of Waels's son,[2]
things unknown to anyone
except to Fitela, feuds and foul doings
confided by uncle to nephew when he felt
880   the urge to speak of them: always they had been
partners in the fight, friends in need.
They killed giants, their conquering swords
had brought them down.
                After his death
Sigemund's glory   grew and grew
885   *because of his courage   when he killed the dragon,*
the guardian of the hoard.   Under gray stone
he had dared to enter   all by himself
to face the worst   without Fitela.
But it came to pass   that his sword plunged
890   *right through   those radiant scales*
and drove into the wall.   The dragon died of it.
His daring had given him   total possession
of the treasure-hoard,   his to dispose of
however he liked.   He loaded a boat:
895   *Waels's son   weighted her hold*
with dazzling spoils.   The hot dragon melted.
Sigemund's name   was known everywhere.

9. I.e., an extemporaneous heroic poem in alliterative verse about Beowulf's deeds.
1. Tales about Sigemund, his nephew Sinfjotli
(Fitela), and his son Sigurth are found in a 13th-
century Old Icelandic collection of legends known
as the *Volsung Saga.* Analogous stories must have
been known to the poet and his audience, though
details differ.
2. Waels is the father of Sigemund.

He was utterly valiant   and venturesome,
a fence round his fighters   and flourished therefore
900 *after King Heremod's[3]   prowess declined*
and his campaigns slowed down.   The king was betrayed,
ambushed in Jutland,   overpowered
and done away with.   The waves of his grief
had beaten him down,   made him a burden,
905 *a source of anxiety   to his own nobles:*
that expedition   was often condemned
in those earlier times   by experienced men,
men who relied   on his lordship for redress,
who presumed that the part   of a prince was to thrive
910 *on his father's throne   and defend the nation,*
the Shielding land   where they lived and belonged,
its holdings and strongholds.   Such was Beowulf
in the affection of his friends   and of everyone alive.
But evil entered   into Heremod.

915   Meanwhile, the Danes kept racing their mounts
down sandy lanes. The light of day
broke and kept brightening. Bands of retainers
galloped in excitement to the gabled hall
to see the marvel; and the king himself,
920 guardian of the ring-hoard, goodness in person,
walked in majesty from the women's quarters
with a numerous train, attended by his queen
and her crowd of maidens, across to the mead-hall.
    When Hrothgar arrived at the hall, he spoke,
925 standing on the steps, under the steep eaves,
gazing toward the roofwork and Grendel's talon:
"First and foremost, let the Almighty Father
be thanked for this sight. I suffered a long
harrowing by Grendel. But the Heavenly Shepherd
930 can work His wonders always and everywhere.
Not long since, it seemed I would never
be granted the slightest solace or relief
from any of my burdens: the best of houses
glittered and reeked and ran with blood.
935 This one worry outweighed all others—
a constant distress to counselors entrusted
with defending the people's forts from assault
by monsters and demons. But now a man,
with the Lord's assistance, has accomplished something
940 none of us could manage before now
for all our efforts. Whoever she was
who brought forth this flower of manhood,
if she is still alive, that woman can say
that in her labor the Lord of Ages
945 bestowed a grace on her. So now, Beowulf,
I adopt you in my heart as a dear son.

---

3. Heremod was a bad king, held up by the bard as the opposite of Beowulf, as Sigemund is held up as a
heroic prototype of Beowulf.

Nourish and maintain this new connection,
you noblest of men; there'll be nothing you'll want for,
no worldly goods that won't be yours.
950   I have often honored smaller achievements,
recognized warriors not nearly as worthy,
lavished rewards on the less deserving.
But you have made yourself immortal
by your glorious action. May the God of Ages
955   continue to keep and requite you well."
      Beowulf, son of Ecgtheow, spoke:
"We have gone through with a glorious endeavor
and been much favored in this fight we dared
against the unknown. Nevertheless,
960   if you could have seen the monster himself
where he lay beaten, I would have been better pleased.
My plan was to pounce, pin him down
in a tight grip and grapple him to death—
have him panting for life, powerless and clasped
965   in my bare hands, his body in thrall.
But I couldn't stop him from slipping my hold.
The Lord allowed it, my lock on him
wasn't strong enough; he struggled fiercely
and broke and ran. Yet he bought his freedom
970   at a high price, for he left his hand
and arm and shoulder to show he had been here,
a cold comfort for having come among us.
And now he won't be long for this world.
He has done his worst but the wound will end him.
975   He is hasped and hooped and hirpling with pain,
limping and looped in it. Like a man outlawed
for wickedness, he must await
the mighty judgment of God in majesty."
      There was less tampering and big talk then
980   from Unferth the boaster, less of his blather
as the hall-thanes eyed the awful proof
of the hero's prowess, the splayed hand
up under the eaves. Every nail,
claw-scale and spur, every spike
985   and welt on the hand of that heathen brute
was like barbed steel. Everybody said
there was no honed iron hard enough
to pierce him through, no time-proofed blade
that could cut his brutal, blood-caked claw.
990   Then the order was given for all hands
to help to refurbish Heorot immediately:
men and women thronging the wine-hall,
getting it ready. Gold thread shone
in the wall-hangings, woven scenes
995   that attracted and held the eye's attention.
But iron-braced as the inside of it had been,
that bright room lay in ruins now.
The very doors had been dragged from their hinges.

Only the roof remained unscathed
1000 by the time the guilt-fouled fiend turned tail
in despair of his life. But death is not easily
escaped from by anyone:
all of us with souls, earth-dwellers
and children of men, must make our way
1005 to a destination already ordained
where the body, after the banqueting,
sleeps on its deathbed.
                          Then the due time arrived
for Halfdane's son to proceed to the hall.
The king himself would sit down to feast.
1010 No group ever gathered in greater numbers
or better order around their ring-giver.
The benches filled with famous men
who fell to with relish; round upon round
of mead was passed; those powerful kinsmen,
1015 Hrothgar and Hrothulf, were in high spirits
in the raftered hall. Inside Heorot
there was nothing but friendship. The Shielding nation
was not yet familiar with feud and betrayal.[4]
    Then Halfdane's son presented Beowulf
1020 with a gold standard as a victory gift,
an embroidered banner; also breast-mail
and a helmet; and a sword carried high,
that was both precious object and token of honor.
So Beowulf drank his drink, at ease;
1025 it was hardly a shame to be showered with such gifts
in front of the hall-troops. There haven't been many
moments, I am sure, when men exchanged
four such treasures at so friendly a sitting.
An embossed ridge, a band lapped with wire
1030 arched over the helmet: head-protection
to keep the keen-ground cutting edge
from damaging it when danger threatened
and the man was battling behind his shield.
Next the king ordered eight horses
1035 with gold bridles to be brought through the yard
into the hall. The harness of one
included a saddle of sumptuous design,
the battle-seat where the son of Halfdane
rode when he wished to join the sword-play:
1040 wherever the killing and carnage were the worst,
he would be to the fore, fighting hard.
Then the Danish prince, descendant of Ing,
handed over both the arms and the horses,
urging Beowulf to use them well.
1045 And so their leader, the lord and guard
of coffer and strongroom, with customary grace

---

4. Probably an ironic allusion to the future usurpation of the throne from Hrothgar's sons by Hrothulf, although no such treachery is recorded of
Hrothulf, who is the hero of other Germanic stories.

bestowed upon Beowulf both sets of gifts.
A fair witness can see how well each one behaved.
   The chieftain went on to reward the others:
1050 each man on the bench who had sailed with Beowulf
and risked the voyage received a bounty,
some treasured possession. And compensation,
a price in gold, was settled for the Geat
Grendel had cruelly killed earlier—
1055 as he would have killed more, had not mindful God
and one man's daring prevented that doom.
Past and present, God's will prevails.
Hence, understanding is always best
and a prudent mind. Whoever remains
1060 for long here in this earthly life
will enjoy and endure more than enough.
   They sang then and played to please the hero,
words and music for their warrior prince,
harp tunes and tales of adventure:
1065 there were high times on the hall benches,
and the king's poet performed his part
with the saga of Finn and his sons, unfolding
the tale of the fierce attack in Friesland
where Hnaef, king of the Danes, met death.[5]

1070 *Hildeburh*
                  had little cause
to credit the Jutes:
                son and brother,
she lost them both
                on the battlefield.
She, bereft
                and blameless, they
foredoomed, cut down
                and spear-gored. She,
1075 *the woman in shock,*
                waylaid by grief,
Hoc's daughter—
                how could she not
lament her fate
                when morning came
and the light broke
                on her murdered dears?
And so farewell
                delight on earth,
1080 *war carried away*

5. The bard's lay is known as the Finnsburg Episode. Its allusive style makes the tale obscure in
many details, although some can be filled in from
a fragmentary Old English lay, which modern editors have entitled *The Fight at Finnsburg*. Hildeburh, the daughter of the former Danish king Hoc,
was married to Finn, king of Friesland, presumably
to help end a feud between their peoples. As the
episode opens, the feud has already broken out
again when a visiting party of Danes, led by Hildeburh's brother Hnaef, who has succeeded their
father, is attacked by a tribe called the Jutes. The
Jutes are subject to Finn but may be a clan distinct
from the Frisians, and Finn does not seem to have
instigated the attack. In the ensuing battle, both
Hnaef and the son of Hildeburh and Finn are
killed, and both sides suffer heavy losses.

Finn's troop of thanes
all but a few.
     How then could Finn
hold the line
     or fight on
to the end with Hengest,
      how save
the rump of his force
      from that enemy chief?

1085 *So a truce was offered*
      as follows:[6] *first*
separate quarters
      to be cleared for the Danes,
hall and throne
      to be shared with the Frisians.
Then, second:
      every day
at the dole-out of gifts
      Finn, son of Folcwald,
1090 *should honor the Danes,*
      bestow with an even
hand to Hengest
      and Hengest's men
the wrought-gold rings,
      bounty to match
the measure he gave
      his own Frisians—
to keep morale
      in the beer-hall high.
1095 *Both sides then*
      sealed their agreement.
With oaths to Hengest
      Finn swore
openly, solemnly,
      that the battle survivors
would be guaranteed
      honor and status.
No infringement
      by word or deed,
1100 *no provocation*
      would be permitted.
Their own ring-giver
      after all
was dead and gone,
      they were leaderless,
in forced allegiance
      to his murderer.
So if any Frisian
      stirred up bad blood
1105 *with insinuations*

---

6. The truce was offered by Finn to Hengest, who succeeded Hnaef as leader of the Danes.

             or taunts about this,
the blade of the sword
             would arbitrate it.
A funeral pyre
             was then prepared,
effulgent gold
             brought out from the hoard.
The pride and prince
             of the Shieldings lay
1110   *awaiting the flame.*
             Everywhere
there were blood-plastered
             coats of mail.
The pyre was heaped
             with boar-shaped helmets
forged in gold,
             with the gashed corpses
of wellborn Danes—
             many had fallen.
1115   *Then Hildeburh*
             ordered her own
son's body
             be burnt with Hnaef's
the flesh on his bones
             to sputter and blaze
beside his uncle's.
             The woman wailed
and sang keens,
             the warrior went up.[7]
1120   *Carcass flame*
             swirled and fumed,
they stood round the burial
             mound and howled
as heads melted,
             crusted gashes
spattered and ran
             bloody matter.
The glutton element
             flamed and consumed
1125   *the dead of both sides.*
             Their great days were gone.
Warriors scattered
             to homes and forts
all over Friesland,
             fewer now, feeling
loss of friends.
             Hengest stayed,
lived out that whole
             resentful, blood-sullen

---

7. The meaning may be, the warrior was placed up on the pyre, or went up in smoke. "Keens": lamentations or dirges for the dead.

1130 *winter with Finn,*
        homesick and helpless.
    No ring-whorled prow
            could up then
    and away on the sea.
            Wind and water
    raged with storms,
            wave and shingle
    were shackled in ice
            until another year
1135 *appeared in the yard*
            as it does to this day,
    the seasons constant,
            the wonder of light
    coming over us.
            Then winter was gone,
    earth's lap grew lovely,
            longing woke
    in the cooped-up exile
            for a voyage home—
1140 *but more for vengeance,*
            some way of bringing
    things to a head:
            his sword arm hankered
    to greet the Jutes.
            So he did not balk
    once Hunlafing
            placed on his lap
    Dazzle-the-Duel,
            the best sword of all,[8]
1145 *whose edges Jutes*
            knew only too well.
    Thus blood was spilled,
            the gallant Finn
    slain in his home
            after Guthlaf and Oslaf[9]
    back from their voyage
            made old accusation:
    the brutal ambush,
            the fate they had suffered,
1150 *all blamed on Finn.*
            The wildness in them
    had to brim over.
            The hall ran red
    with blood of enemies.
            Finn was cut down,
    the queen brought away
            and everything

---

8. Hunlafing may be the son of a Danish warrior called Hunlaf. The placing of the sword in Hengest's lap is a symbolic call for revenge. 9. It is not clear whether the Danes have traveled home and then returned to Friesland with reinforcements, or whether the Danish survivors attack once the weather allows them to take ship.

the Shieldings could find
                    inside Finn's walls—
1155 the Frisian king's
                    gold collars and gemstones—
swept off to the ship.
                    Over sea-lanes then
back to Daneland
                    the warrior troop
bore that lady home.

                    The poem was over,
the poet had performed, a pleasant murmur
1160 started on the benches, stewards did the rounds
with wine in splendid jugs, and Wealhtheow came to sit
in her gold crown between two good men,
uncle and nephew, each one of whom
still trusted the other;[1] and the forthright Unferth,
1165 admired by all for his mind and courage
although under a cloud for killing his brothers,
reclined near the king.
                    The queen spoke:
"Enjoy this drink, my most generous lord;
raise up your goblet, entertain the Geats
1170 duly and gently, discourse with them,
be open-handed, happy and fond.
Relish their company, but recollect as well
all of the boons that have been bestowed on you.
The bright court of Heorot has been cleansed
1175 and now the word is that you want to adopt
this warrior as a son. So, while you may,
bask in your fortune, and then bequeath
kingdom and nation to your kith and kin,
before your decease. I am certain of Hrothulf.
1180 He is noble and will use the young ones well.
He will not let you down. Should you die before him,
he will treat our children truly and fairly.
He will honor, I am sure, our two sons,
repay them in kind, when he recollects
1185 all the good things we gave him once,
the favor and respect he found in his childhood."
She turned then to the bench where her boys sat,
Hrethric and Hrothmund, with other nobles' sons,
all the youth together; and that good man,
1190 Beowulf the Geat, sat between the brothers.
    The cup was carried to him, kind words
spoken in welcome and a wealth of wrought gold
graciously bestowed: two arm bangles,
a mail-shirt and rings, and the most resplendent
1195 torque of gold I ever heard tell of
anywhere on earth or under heaven.

1. See n. 4, p. 48.

There was no hoard like it since Hama snatched
the Brosings' neck-chain and bore it away
with its gems and settings to his shining fort,
1200 away from Eormenric's wiles and hatred,[2]
and thereby ensured his eternal reward.
Hygelac the Geat, grandson of Swerting,
wore this neck-ring on his last raid;[3]
at bay under his banner, he defended the booty,
1205 treasure he had won. Fate swept him away
because of his proud need to provoke
a feud with the Frisians. He fell beneath his shield,
in the same gem-crusted, kingly gear
he had worn when he crossed the frothing wave-vat.
1210 So the dead king fell into Frankish hands.
They took his breast-mail, also his neck-torque,
and punier warriors plundered the slain
when the carnage ended; Geat corpses
covered the field.
                    Applause filled the hall.
1215 Then Wealhtheow pronounced in the presence of the company:
"Take delight in this torque, dear Beowulf,
wear it for luck and wear also this mail
from our people's armory: may you prosper in them!
Be acclaimed for strength, for kindly guidance
1220 to these two boys, and your bounty will be sure.
You have won renown: you are to all men
far and near, now and forever.
Your sway is wide as the wind's home,
as the sea around cliffs. And so, my prince,
1225 I wish you a lifetime's luck and blessings
to enjoy this treasure. Treat my sons
with tender care, be strong and kind.
Here each comrade is true to the other,
loyal to lord, loving in spirit.
1230 The thanes have one purpose, the people are ready:
having drunk and pledged, the ranks do as I bid."
     She moved then to her place. Men were drinking wine
at that rare feast; how could they know fate,
the grim shape of things to come,
1235 the threat looming over many thanes
as night approached and King Hrothgar prepared
to retire to his quarters? Retainers in great numbers
were posted on guard as so often in the past.
Benches were pushed back, bedding gear and bolsters
1240 spread across the floor, and one man
lay down to his rest, already marked for death.

2. The necklace presented to Beowulf is compared
to one worn by the goddess Freya in Germanic
mythology. In another story it was stolen by Hama
from the Gothic king Eormenric, who is treated as
a tyrant in Germanic legend, but how Eormenric
came to possess it is not known.
3. Later we learn that Beowulf gave the necklace
to Hygd, the queen of his lord Hygelac. Hygelac is
here said to have been wearing it on his last expedition. This is the first of several allusions to Hygelac's death on a raid up the Rhine, the one incident
in the poem that can be connected to a historical
event documented elsewhere.

At their heads they placed their polished timber
battle-shields; and on the bench above them,
each man's kit was kept to hand:
1245   a towering war-helmet, webbed mail-shirt
and great-shafted spear. It was their habit
always and everywhere to be ready for action,
at home or in the camp, in whatever case
and at whatever time the need arose
1250   to rally round their lord. They were a right people.

[ANOTHER ATTACK]

They went to sleep. And one paid dearly
for his night's ease, as had happened to them often,
ever since Grendel occupied the gold-hall,
committing evil until the end came,
1255   death after his crimes. Then it became clear,
obvious to everyone once the fight was over,
that an avenger lurked and was still alive,
grimly biding time. Grendel's mother,
monstrous hell-bride, brooded on her wrongs.
1260   She had been forced down into fearful waters,
the cold depths, after Cain had killed
his father's son, felled his own
brother with a sword. Branded an outlaw,
marked by having murdered, he moved into the wilds,
1265   shunned company and joy. And from Cain there sprang
misbegotten spirits, among them Grendel,
the banished and accursed, due to come to grips
with that watcher in Heorot waiting to do battle.
The monster wrenched and wrestled with him,
1270   but Beowulf was mindful of his mighty strength,
the wondrous gifts God had showered on him:
he relied for help on the Lord of All,
on His care and favor. So he overcame the foe,
brought down the hell-brute. Broken and bowed,
1275   outcast from all sweetness, the enemy of mankind
made for his death-den. But now his mother
had sallied forth on a savage journey,
grief-racked and ravenous, desperate for revenge.
She came to Heorot. There, inside the hall,
1280   Danes lay asleep, earls who would soon endure
a great reversal, once Grendel's mother
attacked and entered. Her onslaught was less
only by as much as an amazon warrior's
strength is less than an armed man's
1285   when the hefted sword, its hammered edge
and gleaming blade slathered in blood,
razes the sturdy boar-ridge off a helmet.
Then in the hall, hard-honed swords
were grabbed from the bench, many a broad shield
1290   lifted and braced; there was little thought of helmets
or woven mail when they woke in terror.

The hell-dam was in panic, desperate to get out,
in mortal terror the moment she was found.
She had pounced and taken one of the retainers
1295   in a tight hold, then headed for the fen.
To Hrothgar, this man was the most beloved
of the friends he trusted between the two seas.
She had done away with a great warrior,
ambushed him at rest.
              Beowulf was elsewhere.
1300   Earlier, after the award of the treasure,
the Geat had been given another lodging.
    There was uproar in Heorot. She had snatched their trophy,
Grendel's bloodied hand. It was a fresh blow
to the afflicted bawn. The bargain was hard,
1305   both parties having to pay
with the lives of friends. And the old lord,
the gray-haired warrior, was heartsore and weary
when he heard the news: his highest-placed adviser,
his dearest companion, was dead and gone.
1310   Beowulf was quickly brought to the chamber:
the winner of fights, the arch-warrior,
came first-footing in with his fellow troops
to where the king in his wisdom waited,
still wondering whether Almighty God
1315   would ever turn the tide of his misfortunes.
So Beowulf entered with his band in attendance
and the wooden floorboards banged and rang
as he advanced, hurrying to address
the prince of the Ingwins, asking if he'd rested
1320   since the urgent summons had come as a surprise.
    Then Hrothgar, the Shieldings' helmet, spoke:
"Rest? What is rest? Sorrow has returned.
Alas for the Danes! Aeschere is dead.
He was Yrmenlaf's elder brother
1325   and a soul-mate to me, a true mentor,
my right-hand man when the ranks clashed
and our boar-crests had to take a battering
in the line of action. Aeschere was everything
the world admires in a wise man and a friend.
1330   Then this roaming killer came in a fury
and slaughtered him in Heorot. Where she is hiding,
glutting on the corpse and glorying in her escape,
I cannot tell; she has taken up the feud
because of last night, when you killed Grendel,
1335   wrestled and racked him in ruinous combat
since for too long he had terrorized us
with his depredations. He died in battle,
paid with his life; and now this powerful
other one arrives, this force for evil
1340   driven to avenge her kinsman's death.
Or so it seems to thanes in their grief,
in the anguish every thane endures

at the loss of a ring-giver, now that the hand
that bestowed so richly has been stilled in death.
1345   "I have heard it said by my people in hall,
counselors who live in the upland country,
that they have seen two such creatures
prowling the moors, huge marauders
from some other world. One of these things,
1350   as far as anyone ever can discern,
looks like a woman; the other, warped
in the shape of a man, moves beyond the pale
bigger than any man, an unnatural birth
called Grendel by the country people
1355   in former days. They are fatherless creatures,
and their whole ancestry is hidden in a past
of demons and ghosts. They dwell apart
among wolves on the hills, on windswept crags
and treacherous keshes, where cold streams
1360   pour down the mountain and disappear
under mist and moorland.
                        A few miles from here
a frost-stiffened wood waits and keeps watch
above a mere; the overhanging bank
is a maze of tree-roots mirrored in its surface.
1365   At night there, something uncanny happens:
the water burns. And the mere bottom
has never been sounded by the sons of men.
On its bank, the heather-stepper halts:
the hart in flight from pursuing hounds
1370   will turn to face them with firm-set horns
and die in the wood rather than dive
beneath its surface. That is no good place.
When wind blows up and stormy weather
makes clouds scud and the skies weep,
1375   out of its depths a dirty surge
is pitched toward the heavens. Now help depends
again on you and on you alone.
The gap of danger where the demon waits
is still unknown to you. Seek it if you dare.
1380   I will compensate you for settling the feud
as I did the last time with lavish wealth,
coffers of coiled gold, if you come back."

[BEOWULF FIGHTS GRENDEL'S MOTHER]

Beowulf, son of Ecgtheow, spoke:
"Wise sir, do not grieve. It is always better
1385   to avenge dear ones than to indulge in mourning.
For every one of us, living in this world
means waiting for our end. Let whoever can
win glory before death. When a warrior is gone,
that will be his best and only bulwark.
1390   So arise, my lord, and let us immediately
set forth on the trail of this troll-dam.

I guarantee you: she will not get away,
not to dens under ground nor upland groves
nor the ocean floor. She'll have nowhere to flee to.
1395 Endure your troubles today. Bear up
and be the man I expect you to be."
     With that the old lord sprang to his feet
and praised God for Beowulf's pledge.
Then a bit and halter were brought for his horse
1400 with the plaited mane. The wise king mounted
the royal saddle and rode out in style
with a force of shield-bearers. The forest paths
were marked all over with the monster's tracks,
her trail on the ground wherever she had gone
1405 across the dark moors, dragging away
the body of that thane, Hrothgar's best
counselor and overseer of the country.
So the noble prince proceeded undismayed
up fells and screes, along narrow footpaths
1410 and ways where they were forced into single file,
ledges on cliffs above lairs of water-monsters.
He went in front with a few men,
good judges of the lie of the land,
and suddenly discovered the dismal wood,
1415 mountain trees growing out at an angle
above gray stones: the bloodshot water
surged underneath. It was a sore blow
to all of the Danes, friends of the Shieldings,
a hurt to each and every one
1420 of that noble company when they came upon
Aeschere's head at the foot of the cliff.
     Everybody gazed as the hot gore
kept wallowing up and an urgent war-horn
repeated its notes: the whole party
1425 sat down to watch. The water was infested
with all kinds of reptiles. There were writhing sea-dragons
and monsters slouching on slopes by the cliff,
serpents and wild things such as those that often
surface at dawn to roam the sail-road
1430 and doom the voyage. Down they plunged,
lashing in anger at the loud call
of the battle-bugle. An arrow from the bow
of the Geat chief got one of them
as he surged to the surface: the seasoned shaft
1435 stuck deep in his flank and his freedom in the water
got less and less. It was his last swim.
He was swiftly overwhelmed in the shallows,
prodded by barbed boar-spears,
cornered, beaten, pulled up on the bank,
1440 a strange lake-birth, a loathsome catch
men gazed at in awe.
                    Beowulf got ready,
donned his war-gear, indifferent to death;

his mighty, hand-forged, fine-webbed mail
would soon meet with the menace underwater.
1445   It would keep the bone-cage of his body safe:
no enemy's clasp could crush him in it,
no vicious armlock choke his life out.
To guard his head he had a glittering helmet
that was due to be muddied on the mere bottom
1450   and blurred in the upswirl. It was of beaten gold,
princely headgear hooped and hasped
by a weapon-smith who had worked wonders
in days gone by and adorned it with boar-shapes;
since then it had resisted every sword.
1455   And another item lent by Unferth
at that moment of need was of no small importance:
the brehon[4] handed him a hilted weapon,
a rare and ancient sword named Hrunting.
The iron blade with its ill-boding patterns
1460   had been tempered in blood. It had never failed
the hand of anyone who hefted it in battle,
anyone who had fought and faced the worst
in the gap of danger. This was not the first time
it had been called to perform heroic feats.
1465   When he lent that blade to the better swordsman,
Unferth, the strong-built son of Ecglaf,
could hardly have remembered the ranting speech
he had made in his cups. He was not man enough
to face the turmoil of a fight under water
1470   and the risk to his life. So there he lost
fame and repute. It was different for the other
rigged out in his gear, ready to do battle.
        Beowulf, son of Ecgtheow, spoke:
"Wisest of kings, now that I have come
1475   to the point of action, I ask you to recall
what we said earlier: that you, son of Halfdane
and gold-friend to retainers, that you, if I should fall
and suffer death while serving your cause,
would act like a father to me afterward.
1480   If this combat kills me, take care
of my young company, my comrades in arms.
And be sure also, my beloved Hrothgar,
to send Hygelac the treasures I received.
Let the lord of the Geats gaze on that gold,
1485   let Hrethel's son take note of it and see
that I found a ring-giver of rare magnificence
and enjoyed the good of his generosity.
And Unferth is to have what I inherited:
to that far-famed man I bequeath my own
1490   sharp-honed, wave-sheened wonder-blade.
With Hrunting I shall gain glory or die."

---

4. One of an ancient class of lawyers in Ireland [Translator's note]. The Old English word for Unferth's office, *thyle*, has been interpreted as "orator" and "spokesman."

After these words, the prince of the Weather-Geats
was impatient to be away and plunged suddenly:
without more ado, he dived into the heaving
1495 depths of the lake. It was the best part of a day
before he could see the solid bottom.
Quickly the one who haunted those waters,
who had scavenged and gone her gluttonous rounds
for a hundred seasons, sensed a human
1500 observing her outlandish lair from above.
So she lunged and clutched and managed to catch him
in her brutal grip; but his body, for all that,
remained unscathed: the mesh of the chain-mail
saved him on the outside. Her savage talons
1505 failed to rip the web of his war-shirt.
Then once she touched bottom, that wolfish swimmer
carried the ring-mailed prince to her court
so that for all his courage he could never use
the weapons he carried; and a bewildering horde
1510 came at him from the depths, droves of sea-beasts
who attacked with tusks and tore at his chain-mail
in a ghastly onslaught. The gallant man
could see he had entered some hellish turn-hole
and yet the water there did not work against him
1515 because the hall-roofing held off
the force of the current; then he saw firelight,
a gleam and flare-up, a glimmer of brightness.
The hero observed that swamp-thing from hell,
the tarn-hag in all her terrible strength,
1520 then heaved his war-sword and swung his arm:
the decorated blade came down ringing
and singing on her head. But he soon found
his battle-torch extinguished; the shining blade
refused to bite. It spared her and failed
1525 the man in his need. It had gone through many
hand-to-hand fight, had hewed the armor
and helmets of the doomed, but here at last
the fabulous powers of that heirloom failed.
Hygelac's kinsman kept thinking about
1530 his name and fame: he never lost heart.
Then, in a fury, he flung his sword away.
The keen, inlaid, worm-loop-patterned steel
was hurled to the ground: he would have to rely
on the might of his arm. So must a man do
1535 who intends to gain enduring glory
in a combat. Life doesn't cost him a thought.
Then the prince of War-Geats, warming to this fight
with Grendel's mother, gripped her shoulder
and laid about him in a battle frenzy:
1540 he pitched his killer opponent to the floor
but she rose quickly and retaliated,
grappled him tightly in her grim embrace.
The sure-footed fighter felt daunted,

the strongest of warriors stumbled and fell.
1545 So she pounced upon him and pulled out
a broad, whetted knife: now she would avenge
her only child. But the mesh of chain-mail
on Beowulf's shoulder shielded his life,
turned the edge and tip of the blade.
1550 The son of Ecgtheow would have surely perished
and the Geats lost their warrior under the wide earth
had the strong links and locks of his war-gear
not helped to save him: holy God
decided the victory. It was easy for the Lord,
1555 the Ruler of Heaven, to redress the balance
once Beowulf got back up on his feet.
    Then he saw a blade that boded well,
a sword in her armory, an ancient heirloom
from the days of the giants, an ideal weapon,
1560 one that any warrior would envy,
but so huge and heavy of itself
only Beowulf could wield it in a battle.
So the Shieldings' hero hard-pressed and enraged,
took a firm hold of the hilt and swung
1565 the blade in an arc, a resolute blow
that bit deep into her neck-bone
and severed it entirely, toppling the doomed
house of her flesh; she fell to the floor.
The sword dripped blood, the swordsman was elated.
1570   A light appeared and the place brightened
the way the sky does when heaven's candle
is shining clearly. He inspected the vault:
with sword held high, its hilt raised
to guard and threaten, Hygelac's thane
1575 scouted by the wall in Grendel's wake.
Now the weapon was to prove its worth.
The warrior determined to take revenge
for every gross act Grendel had committed—
and not only for that one occasion
1580 when he'd come to slaughter the sleeping troops,
fifteen of Hrothgar's house-guards
surprised on their benches and ruthlessly devoured,
and as many again carried away,
a brutal plunder. Beowulf in his fury
1585 now settled that score: he saw the monster
in his resting place, war-weary and wrecked,
a lifeless corpse, a casualty
of the battle in Heorot. The body gaped
at the stroke dealt to it after death:
1590 Beowulf cut the corpse's head off.
    Immediately the counselors keeping a lookout
with Hrothgar, watching the lake water,
saw a heave-up and surge of waves
and blood in the backwash. They bowed gray heads,
1595 spoke in their sage, experienced way

about the good warrior, how they never again
expected to see that prince returning
in triumph to their king. It was clear to many
that the wolf of the deep had destroyed him forever.
1600   The ninth hour of the day arrived.
The brave Shieldings abandoned the cliff-top
and the king went home; but sick at heart,
staring at the mere, the strangers held on.
They wished, without hope, to behold their lord,
Beowulf himself.
1605   Meanwhile, the sword
began to wilt into gory icicles
to slather and thaw. It was a wonderful thing,
the way it all melted as ice melts
when the Father eases the fetters off the frost
1610   and unravels the water-ropes, He who wields power
over time and tide: He is the true Lord.
      The Geat captain saw treasure in abundance
but carried no spoils from those quarters
except for the head and the inlaid hilt
1615   embossed with jewels; its blade had melted
and the scrollwork on it burned, so scalding was the blood
of the poisonous fiend who had perished there.
Then away he swam, the one who had survived
the fall of his enemies, flailing to the surface.
1620   The wide water, the waves and pools,
were no longer infested once the wandering fiend
let go of her life and this unreliable world.
      The seafarers' leader made for land,
resolutely swimming, delighted with his prize,
1625   the mighty load he was lugging to the surface.
His thanes advanced in a troop to meet him,
thanking God and taking great delight
in seeing their prince back safe and sound.
Quickly the hero's helmet and mail-shirt
1630   were loosed and unlaced. The lake settled,
clouds darkened above the bloodshot depths.
      With high hearts they headed away
along footpaths and trails through the fields,
roads that they knew, each of them wrestling
1635   with the head they were carrying from the lakeside cliff,
men kingly in their courage and capable
of difficult work. It was a task for four
to hoist Grendel's head on a spear
and bear it under strain to the bright hall.
1640   But soon enough they neared the place,
fourteen Geats in fine fettle,
striding across the outlying ground
in a delighted throng around their leader.
      In he came then, the thanes' commander,
1645   the arch-warrior, to address Hrothgar:
his courage was proven, his glory was secure.

Grendel's head was hauled by the hair,
dragged across the floor where the people were drinking,
a horror for both queen and company to behold.
1650   They stared in awe. It was an astonishing sight.

[ANOTHER CELEBRATION AT HEOROT]

    Beowulf, son of Ecgtheow, spoke:
"So, son of Halfdane, prince of the Shieldings,
we are glad to bring this booty from the lake.
It is a token of triumph and we tender it to you.
1655   I barely survived the battle under water.
It was hard-fought, a desperate affair
that could have gone badly; if God had not helped me,
the outcome would have been quick and fatal.
Although Hrunting is hard-edged,
1660   I could never bring it to bear in battle.
But the Lord of Men allowed me to behold—
for He often helps the unbefriended—
an ancient sword shining on the wall,
a weapon made for giants, there for the wielding.
1665   Then my moment came in the combat and I struck
the dwellers in that den. Next thing the damascened
sword blade melted; it bloated and it burned
in their rushing blood. I have wrested the hilt
from the enemies' hand, avenged the evil
1670   done to the Danes; it is what was due.
And this I pledge, O prince of the Shieldings:
you can sleep secure with your company of troops
in Heorot Hall. Never need you fear
for a single thane of your sept or nation,
1675   young warriors or old, that laying waste of life
that you and your people endured of yore."
    Then the gold hilt was handed over
to the old lord, a relic from long ago
for the venerable ruler. That rare smithwork
1680   was passed on to the prince of the Danes
when those devils perished; once death removed
that murdering, guilt-steeped, God-cursed fiend,
eliminating his unholy life
and his mother's as well, it was willed to that king
1685   who of all the lavish gift-lords of the north
was the best regarded between the two seas.
    Hrothgar spoke; he examined the hilt,
that relic of old times. It was engraved all over
and showed how war first came into the world
1690   and the flood destroyed the tribe of giants.
They suffered a terrible severance from the Lord;
the Almighty made the waters rise,
drowned them in the deluge for retribution.
In pure gold inlay on the sword-guards
1695   there were rune-markings correctly incised,
stating and recording for whom the sword

had been first made and ornamented
with its scrollworked hilt. Then everyone hushed
as the son of Halfdane spoke this wisdom:
1700 "A protector of his people, pledged to uphold
truth and justice and to respect tradition,
is entitled to affirm that this man
was born to distinction. Beowulf, my friend,
your fame has gone far and wide,
1705 you are known everywhere. In all things you are even-tempered,
prudent and resolute. So I stand firm by the promise of friendship
we exchanged before. Forever you will be
your people's mainstay and your own warriors'
helping hand.
          Heremod was different,
1710 the way he behaved to Ecgwela's sons.
His rise in the world brought little joy
to the Danish people, only death and destruction.
He vented his rage on men he caroused with,
killed his own comrades, a pariah king
1715 who cut himself off from his own kind,
even though Almighty God had made him
eminent and powerful and marked him from the start
for a happy life. But a change happened,
he grew bloodthirsty, gave no more rings
1720 to honor the Danes. He suffered in the end
for having plagued his people for so long:
his life lost happiness.
                    So learn from this
and understand true values. I who tell you
have wintered into wisdom.
                    It is a great wonder
1725 how Almighty God in His magnificence
favors our race with rank and scope
and the gift of wisdom; His sway is wide.
Sometimes He allows the mind of a man
of distinguished birth to follow its bent,
1730 grants him fulfillment and felicity on earth
and forts to command in his own country.
He permits him to lord it in many lands
until the man in his unthinkingness
forgets that it will ever end for him.
1735 He indulges his desires; illness and old age
mean nothing to him; his mind is untroubled
by envy or malice or the thought of enemies
with their hate-honed swords. The whole world
conforms to his will, he is kept from the worst
1740 until an element of overweening
enters him and takes hold
while the soul's guard, its sentry, drowses,
grown too distracted. A killer stalks him,
an archer who draws a deadly bow.
1745 And then the man is hit in the heart,

the arrow flies beneath his defenses,
the devious promptings of the demon start.
His old possessions seem paltry to him now.
He covets and resents; dishonors custom
1750   and bestows no gold; and because of good things
that the Heavenly Powers gave him in the past
he ignores the shape of things to come.
Then finally the end arrives
when the body he was lent collapses and falls
1755   prey to its death; ancestral possessions
and the goods he hoarded are inherited by another
who lets them go with a liberal hand.
    "O flower of warriors, beware of that trap.
Choose, dear Beowulf, the better part,
1760   eternal rewards. Do not give way to pride.
For a brief while your strength is in bloom
but it fades quickly; and soon there will follow
illness or the sword to lay you low,
or a sudden fire or surge of water
1765   or jabbing blade or javelin from the air
or repellent age. Your piercing eye
will dim and darken; and death will arrive,
dear warrior, to sweep you away.
    "Just so I ruled the Ring-Danes' country
1770   for fifty years, defended them in wartime
with spear and sword against constant assaults
by many tribes: I came to believe
my enemies had faded from the face of the earth.
Still, what happened was a hard reversal
1775   from bliss to grief. Grendel struck
after lying in wait. He laid waste to the land
and from that moment my mind was in dread
of his depredations. So I praise God
in His heavenly glory that I lived to behold
1780   this head dripping blood and that after such harrowing
I can look upon it in triumph at last.
Take your place, then, with pride and pleasure,
and move to the feast. Tomorrow morning
our treasure will be shared and showered upon you."
1785   The Geat was elated and gladly obeyed
the old man's bidding; he sat on the bench.
And soon all was restored, the same as before.
Happiness came back, the hall was thronged,
and a banquet set forth; black night fell
and covered them in darkness.
1790   Then the company rose
for the old campaigner: the gray-haired prince
was ready for bed. And a need for rest
came over the brave shield-bearing Geat.
He was a weary seafarer, far from home,
1795   so immediately a house-guard guided him out,
one whose office entailed looking after

whatever a thane on the road in those days
might need or require. It was noble courtesy.

[BEOWULF RETURNS HOME]

That great heart rested. The hall towered,
1800 gold-shingled and gabled, and the guest slept in it
until the black raven with raucous glee
announced heaven's joy, and a hurry of brightness
overran the shadows. Warriors rose quickly,
impatient to be off: their own country
1805 was beckoning the nobles; and the bold voyager
longed to be aboard his distant boat.
Then that stalwart fighter ordered Hrunting
to be brought to Unferth, and bade Unferth
take the sword and thanked him for lending it.
1810 He said he had found it a friend in battle
and a powerful help; he put no blame
on the blade's cutting edge. He was a considerate man.
    And there the warriors stood in their war-gear,
eager to go, while their honored lord
1815 approached the platform where the other sat.
The undaunted hero addressed Hrothgar.
Beowulf, son of Ecghteow, spoke:
"Now we who crossed the wide sea
have to inform you that we feel a desire
1820 to return to Hygelac. Here we have been welcomed
and thoroughly entertained. You have treated us well.
If there is any favor on earth I can perform
beyond deeds of arms I have done already,
anything that would merit your affections more,
1825 I shall act, my lord, with alacrity.
If ever I hear from across the ocean
that people on your borders are threatening battle
as attackers have done from time to time,
I shall land with a thousand thanes at my back
1830 to help your cause. Hygelac may be young
to rule a nation, but this much I know
about the king of the Geats: he will come to my aid
and want to support me by word and action
in your hour of need, when honor dictates
1835 that I raise a hedge of spears around you.
Then if Hrethric should think about traveling
as a king's son to the court of the Geats,
he will find many friends. Foreign places
yield more to one who is himself worth meeting."
1840   Hrothgar spoke and answered him:
"The Lord in his wisdom sent you those words
and they came from the heart. I have never heard
so young a man make truer observations.
You are strong in body and mature in mind,
1845 impressive in speech. If it should come to pass
that Hrethel's descendant dies beneath a spear,

if deadly battle or the sword blade or disease
fells the prince who guards your people
and you are still alive, then I firmly believe
1850 the seafaring Geats won't find a man
worthier of acclaim as their king and defender
than you, if only you would undertake
the lordship of your homeland. My liking for you
deepens with time, dear Beowulf.
1855 What you have done is to draw two peoples,
the Geat nation and us neighboring Danes,
into shared peace and a pact of friendship
in spite of hatreds we have harbored in the past.
For as long as I rule this far-flung land
1860 treasures will change hands and each side will treat
the other with gifts; across the gannet's bath,
over the broad sea, whorled prows will bring
presents and tokens. I know your people
are beyond reproach in every respect,
1865 steadfast in the old way with friend or foe."
  Then the earls' defender furnished the hero
with twelve treasures and told him to set out,
sail with those gifts safely home
to the people he loved, but to return promptly.
1870 And so the good and gray-haired Dane,
that highborn king, kissed Beowulf
and embraced his neck, then broke down
in sudden tears. Two forebodings
disturbed him in his wisdom, but one was stronger:
1875 nevermore would they meet each other
face to face. And such was his affection
that he could not help being overcome:
his fondness for the man was so deep-founded,
it warmed his heart and wound the heartstrings
tight in his breast.
1880   The embrace ended
and Beowulf, glorious in his gold regalia,
stepped the green earth. Straining at anchor
and ready for boarding, his boat awaited him.
So they went on their journey, and Hrothgar's generosity
1885 was praised repeatedly. He was a peerless king
until old age sapped his strength and did him
mortal harm, as it has done so many.
  Down to the waves then, dressed in the web
of their chain-mail and war-shirts the young men marched
1890 in high spirits. The coast-guard spied them,
thanes setting forth, the same as before.
His salute this time from the top of the cliff
was far from unmannerly; he galloped to meet them
and as they took ship in their shining gear,
1895 he said how welcome they would be in Geatland.
Then the broad hull was beached on the sand
to be cargoed with treasure, horses and war-gear.

The curved prow motioned; the mast stood high
above Hrothgar's riches in the loaded hold.
1900   The guard who had watched the boat was given
a sword with gold fittings, and in future days
that present would make him a respected man
at his place on the mead-bench.
                              Then the keel plunged
and shook in the sea; and they sailed from Denmark.
1905   Right away the mast was rigged with its sea-shawl;
sail-ropes were tightened, timbers drummed
and stiff winds kept the wave-crosser
skimming ahead; as she heaved forward,
her foamy neck was fleet and buoyant,
1910   a lapped prow loping over currents,
until finally the Geats caught sight of coastline
and familiar cliffs. The keel reared up,
wind lifted it home, it hit on the land.
        The harbor guard came hurrying out
1915   to the rolling water: he had watched the offing
long and hard, on the lookout for those friends.
With the anchor cables, he moored their craft
right where it had beached, in case a backwash
might catch the hull and carry it away.
1920   Then he ordered the prince's treasure-trove
to be carried ashore. It was a short step
from there to where Hrethel's son and heir,
Hygelac the gold-giver, makes his home
on a secure cliff, in the company of retainers.
1925   The building was magnificent, the king majestic,
ensconced in his hall; and although Hygd, his queen,
was young, a few short years at court,
her mind was thoughtful and her manners sure.
Haereth's daughter behaved generously
1930   and stinted nothing when she distributed
bounty to the Geats.
                    Great Queen Modthryth
perpetrated terrible wrongs.[5]
If any retainer ever made bold
to look her in the face, if an eye not her lord's[6]
1935   stared at her directly during daylight,
the outcome was sealed: he was kept bound,
in hand-tightened shackles, racked, tortured
until doom was pronounced—death by the sword,
slash of blade, blood-gush, and death-qualms
1940   in an evil display. Even a queen
outstanding in beauty must not overstep like that.

5. The story of Queen Modthryth's vices is
abruptly introduced as a foil to Queen Hygd's virtues. A transitional passage may have been lost, but
the poet's device is similar to that of using the earlier reference to the wickedness of King Heremod
to contrast with the good qualities of Sigemund
and Beowulf.

6. This could refer to her husband or her father
before her marriage. The story resembles folktales
about a proud princess whose unsuccessful suitors
are all put to death, although the unfortunate victims in this case seem to be guilty only of looking
at her.

A queen should weave peace, not punish the innocent
with loss of life for imagined insults.
But Hemming's kinsman[7] put a halt to her ways
1945 and drinkers round the table had another tale:
she was less of a bane to people's lives,
less cruel-minded, after she was married
to the brave Offa, a bride arrayed
in her gold finery, given away
1950 by a caring father, ferried to her young prince
over dim seas. In days to come
she would grace the throne and grow famous
for her good deeds and conduct of life,
her high devotion to the hero king
1955 who was the best king, it has been said,
between the two seas or anywhere else
on the face of the earth. Offa was honored
far and wide for his generous ways,
his fighting spirit and his farseeing
1960 defense of his homeland; from him there sprang Eomer,
Garmund's grandson, kinsman of Hemming,[8]
his warriors' mainstay and master of the field.

　　Heroic Beowulf and his band of men
crossed the wide strand, striding along
1965 the sandy foreshore; the sun shone,
the world's candle warmed them from the south
as they hastened to where, as they had heard,
the young king, Ongentheow's killer
and his people's protector,[9] was dispensing rings
1970 inside his bawn. Beowulf's return
was reported to Hygelac as soon as possible,
news that the captain was now in the enclosure,
his battle-brother back from the fray
alive and well, walking to the hall.
1975 Room was quickly made, on the king's orders,
and the troops filed across the cleared floor.

　　After Hygelac had offered greetings
to his loyal thane in a lofty speech,
he and his kinsman, that hale survivor,
1980 sat face to face. Haereth's daughter
moved about with the mead-jug in her hand,
taking care of the company, filling the cups
that warriors held out. Then Hygelac began
to put courteous questions to his old comrade
1985 in the high hall. He hankered to know
every tale the Sea-Geats had to tell:

---

7. I.e., Offa I, a legendary king of the Angles. We know nothing about Hemming other than that Offa was related to him. Offa II (757–96) was king of Mercia, and although the story is about the second Offa's ancestor on the Continent, this is the only English connection in the poem and has been taken as evidence to date its origins to 8th-century Mercia.

8. I.e., Eomer, Offa's son. See previous note. Garmund was presumably the name of Offa's father.

9. I.e., Hygelac. Ongentheow was king of the Swedish people called the Shylfings. This is the first of the references to wars between the Geats and the Swedes. One of Hygelac's war party named Eofer was the actual slayer of Ongentheow.

"How did you fare on your foreign voyage,
dear Beowulf, when you abruptly decided
to sail away across the salt water
1990 and fight at Heorot? Did you help Hrothgar
much in the end? Could you ease the prince
of his well-known troubles? Your undertaking
cast my spirits down, I dreaded the outcome
of your expedition and pleaded with you
1995 long and hard to leave the killer be,
let the South-Danes settle their own
blood-feud with Grendel. So God be thanked
I am granted this sight of you, safe and sound."
    Beowulf, son of Ecgtheow, spoke:
2000 "What happened, Lord Hygelac, is hardly a secret
any more among men in this world—
myself and Grendel coming to grips
on the very spot where he visited destruction
on the Victory-Shieldings and violated
2005 life and limb, losses I avenged
so no earthly offspring of Grendel's
need ever boast of that bout before dawn,
no matter how long the last of his evil
family survives.
          When I first landed
2010 I hastened to the ring-hall and saluted Hrothgar.
Once he discovered why I had come,
the son of Halfdane sent me immediately
to sit with his own sons on the bench.
It was a happy gathering. In my whole life
2015 I have never seen mead enjoyed more
in any hall on earth. Sometimes the queen
herself appeared, peace-pledge between nations,
to hearten the young ones and hand out
a torque to a warrior, then take her place.
2020 Sometimes Hrothgar's daughter distributed
ale to older ranks, in order on the benches:
I heard the company call her Freawaru
as she made her rounds, presenting men
with the gem-studded bowl, young bride-to-be
2025 to the gracious Ingeld,[1] in her gold-trimmed attire.
The friend of the Shieldings favors her betrothal:
the guardian of the kingdom sees good in it
and hopes this woman will heal old wounds
and grievous feuds.
          But generally the spear
2030 is prompt to retaliate when a prince is killed,
no matter how admirable the bride may be.
    "Think how the Heatho-Bards are bound to feel,
their lord, Ingeld, and his loyal thanes,
when he walks in with that woman to the feast:
2035 Danes are at the table, being entertained,

---

1. King of the Heatho-Bards; his father, Froda, was killed by the Danes.

honored guests in glittering regalia,
burnished ring-mail that was their hosts' birthright,
looted when the Heatho-Bards could no longer wield
their weapons in the shield-clash, when they went down
2040 with their beloved comrades and forfeited their lives.
Then an old spearman will speak while they are drinking,
having glimpsed some heirloom that brings alive
memories of the massacre; his mood will darken
and heart-stricken, in the stress of his emotion,
2045 he will begin to test a young man's temper
and stir up trouble, starting like this:
'Now, my friend, don't you recognize
your father's sword, his favorite weapon,
the one he wore when he went out in his war-mask
2050 to face the Danes on that final day?
After Withergeld[2] died and his men were doomed,
the Shieldings quickly claimed the field;
and now here's a son of one or other
of those same killers coming through our hall
2055 overbearing us, mouthing boasts,
and rigged in armor that by right is yours.'
And so he keeps on, recalling and accusing,
working things up with bitter words
until one of the lady's retainers lies
2060 spattered in blood, split open
on his father's account.[3] The killer knows
the lie of the land and escapes with his life.
Then on both sides the oath-bound lords
will break the peace, a passionate hate
2065 will build up in Ingeld, and love for his bride
will falter in him as the feud rankles.
I therefore suspect the good faith of the Heatho-Bards,
the truth of their friendship and the trustworthiness
of their alliance with the Danes.
                        But now, my lord,
2070 I shall carry on with my account of Grendel,
the whole story of everything that happened
in the hand-to-hand fight.
                    After heaven's gem
had gone mildly to earth, that maddened spirit,
the terror of those twilights, came to attack us
2075 where we stood guard, still safe inside the hall.
There deadly violence came down on Hondscio
and he fell as fate ordained, the first to perish,
rigged out for the combat. A comrade from our ranks
had come to grief in Grendel's maw:
2080 he ate up the entire body.
There was blood on his teeth, he was bloated and dangerous,
all roused up, yet still unready

---

2. One of the Heatho-Bard leaders.
3. I.e., the young Danish attendant is killed
because his father killed the father of the young

Heatho-Bard who has been egged on by the old
veteran of that campaign.

to leave the hall empty-handed;
renowned for his might, he matched himself against me,
2085   wildly reaching. He had this roomy pouch,
a strange accoutrement, intricately strung
and hung at the ready, a rare patchwork
of devilishly fitted dragon-skins.
I had done him no wrong, yet the raging demon
2090   wanted to cram me and many another
into this bag—but it was not to be
once I got to my feet in a blind fury.
It would take too long to tell how I repaid
the terror of the land for every life he took
2095   and so won credit for you, my king,
and for all your people. And although he got away
to enjoy life's sweetness for a while longer,
his right hand stayed behind him in Heorot,
evidence of his miserable overthrow
2100   as he dived into murk on the mere bottom.
    "I got lavish rewards from the lord of the Danes
for my part in the battle, beaten gold
and much else, once morning came
and we took our places at the banquet table.
2105   There was singing and excitement: an old reciter,
a carrier of stories, recalled the early days.
At times some hero made the timbered harp
tremble with sweetness, or related true
and tragic happenings; at times the king
2110   gave the proper turn to some fantastic tale,
or a battle-scarred veteran, bowed with age,
would begin to remember the martial deeds
of his youth and prime and be overcome
as the past welled up in his wintry heart.
2115   "We were happy there the whole day long
and enjoyed our time until another night
descended upon us. Then suddenly
the vehement mother avenged her son
and wreaked destruction. Death had robbed her,
2120   Geats had slain Grendel, so his ghastly dam
struck back and with bare-faced defiance
laid a man low. Thus life departed
from the sage Aeschere, an elder wise in counsel.
But afterward, on the morning following,
2125   the Danes could not burn the dead body
nor lay the remains of the man they loved
on his funeral pyre. She had fled with the corpse
and taken refuge beneath torrents on the mountain.
It was a hard blow for Hrothgar to bear,
2130   harder than any he had undergone before.
And so the heartsore king beseeched me
in your royal name to take my chances
underwater, to win glory

and prove my worth. He promised me rewards.
2135   Hence, as is well known, I went to my encounter
with the terror-monger at the bottom of the tarn.
For a while it was hand-to-hand between us,
then blood went curling along the currents
and I beheaded Grendel's mother in the hall
2140   with a mighty sword. I barely managed
to escape with my life; my time had not yet come.
But Halfdane's heir, the shelter of those earls,
again endowed me with gifts in abundance.
         "Thus the king acted with due custom.
2145   I was paid and recompensed completely,
given full measure and the freedom to choose
from Hothgar's treasures by Hrothgar himself.
These, King Hygelac, I am happy to present
to you as gifts. It is still upon your grace
2150   that all favor depends. I have few kinsmen
who are close, my king, except for your kind self."
Then he ordered the boar-framed standard to be brought,
the battle-topping helmet, the mail-shirt gray as hoar-frost,
and the precious war-sword; and proceeded with his speech:
2155   "When Hrothgar presented this war-gear to me
he instructed me, my lord, to give you some account
of why it signifies his special favor.
He said it had belonged to his older brother,
King Heorogar, who had long kept it,
2160   but that Heorogar had never bequeathed it
to his son Heoroward, that worthy scion,
loyal as he was. Enjoy it well."
         I heard four horses were handed over next.
Beowulf bestowed four bay steeds
2165   to go with the armor, swift gallopers,
all alike. So ought a kinsman act,
instead of plotting and planning in secret
to bring people to grief, or conspiring to arrange
the death of comrades. The warrior king
2170   was uncle to Beowulf and honored by his nephew:
each was concerned for the other's good.
         I heard he presented Hygd with a gorget,
the priceless torque that the prince's daughter,
Wealhtheow, had given him; and three horses,
2175   supple creatures brilliantly saddled.
The bright necklace would be luminous on Hygd's breast.
         Thus Beowulf bore himself with valor;
he was formidable in battle yet behaved with honor
and took no advantage; never cut down
2180   a comrade who was drunk, kept his temper
and, warrior that he was, watched and controlled
his God-sent strength and his outstanding
natural powers. He had been poorly regarded
for a long time, was taken by the Geats

2185 for less than he was worth:[4] and their lord too
had never much esteemed him in the mead-hall.
They firmly believed that he lacked force,
that the prince was a weakling; but presently
every affront to his deserving was reversed.

2190 The battle-famed king, bulwark of his earls,
ordered a gold-chased heirloom of Hrethel's[5]
to be brought in; it was the best example
of a gem-studded sword in the Geat treasury.
This he laid on Beowulf's lap

2195 and then rewarded him with land as well,
seven thousand hides; and a hall and a throne.
Both owned land by birth in that country,
ancestral grounds; but the greater right
and sway were inherited by the higher born.

[THE DRAGON WAKES]

2200 A lot was to happen in later days
in the fury of battle. Hygelac fell
and the shelter of Heardred's shield proved useless
against the fierce aggression of the Shylfings:[6]
ruthless swordsmen, seasoned campaigners,

2205 they came against him and his conquering nation,
and with cruel force cut him down
so that afterwards
        the wide kingdom
reverted to Beowulf. He ruled it well
for fifty winters, grew old and wise

2210 as warden of the land
        until one began
to dominate the dark, a dragon on the prowl
from the steep vaults of a stone-roofed barrow
where he guarded a hoard; there was a hidden passage,
unknown to men, but someone[7] managed

2215 to enter by it and interfere
with the heathen trove. He had handled and removed

---

4. There is no other mention of Beowulf's unpromising youth. This motif of the "Cinderella hero" and others, such as Grendel's magic pouch, are examples of folklore material, probably circulating orally, that made its way into the poem.
5. Hygelac's father and Beowulf's grandfather.
6. There are several references, some of them lengthy, to the wars between the Geats and the Swedes. Because these are highly allusive and not in chronological order, they are difficult to follow and keep straight. This outline, along with the Genealogies (p. 26), may serve as a guide. *Phase 1:* After the death of the Geat patriarch, King Hrethel (lines 2462–70), Ohthere and Onela, the sons of the Swedish king Ongentheow, invade Geat territory and inflict heavy casualties in a battle at Hreosnahill (lines 2472–78). *Phase 2:* The Geats invade Sweden under Haethcyn, King Hrethel's son who has succeeded him. At the battle of Ravenswood, the Geats capture Ongentheow's queen, but Ongentheow counterattacks, rescues the queen, and kills Haethcyn. Hygelac, Haethcyn's younger brother, arrives with reinforcements; Ongentheow is killed in savage combat with two of Hygelac's men; and the Swedes are routed (lines 2479–89 and 2922–90). *Phase 3:* Eanmund and Eadgils, the sons of Ohthere (presumably dead), are driven into exile by their uncle Onela, who is now king of the Swedes. They are given refuge by Hygelac's son Heardred, who has succeeded his father. Onela invades Geatland and kills Heardred; his retainer Weohstan kills Eanmund; and after the Swedes withdraw, Beowulf becomes king (lines 2204–8, which follow, and 2379–90). *Phase 4:* Eadgils, supported by Beowulf, invades Sweden and kills Onela (lines 2391–96).
7. The following section was damaged by fire. In lines 2215–31 entire words and phrases are missing or indicated by only a few letters. Editorial attempts to reconstruct the text are conjectural and often disagree.

a gem-studded goblet; it gained him nothing,
though with a thief's wiles he had outwitted
the sleeping dragon. That drove him into rage,
2220 as the people of that country would soon discover.
     The intruder who broached the dragon's treasure
and moved him to wrath had never meant to.
It was desperation on the part of a slave
fleeing the heavy hand of some master,
2225 guilt-ridden and on the run,
going to ground. But he soon began
to shake with terror;[8] . . . . in shock
the wretch . . . .
. . . . panicked and ran
2230 away with the precious . . . . . .
metalwork. There were many other
heirlooms heaped inside the earth-house,
because long ago, with deliberate care,
somebody now forgotten
2235 had buried the riches of a highborn race
in this ancient cache. Death had come
and taken them all in times gone by
and the only one left to tell their tale,
the last of their line, could look forward to nothing
2240 but the same fate for himself: he foresaw that his joy
in the treasure would be brief.
                              A newly constructed
barrow stood waiting, on a wide headland
close to the waves, its entryway secured.
Into it the keeper of the hoard had carried
2245 all the goods and golden ware
worth preserving. His words were few:
"Now, earth, hold what earls once held
and heroes can no more; it was mined from you first
by honorable men. My own people
2250 have been ruined in war; one by one
they went down to death, looked their last
on sweet life in the hall. I am left with nobody
to bear a sword or to burnish plated goblets,
put a sheen on the cup. The companies have departed.
2255 The hard helmet, hasped with gold,
will be stripped of its hoops; and the helmet-shiner
who should polish the metal of the war-mask sleeps;
the coat of mail that came through all fights,
through shield-collapse and cut of sword,
2260 decays with the warrior. Nor may webbed mail
range far and wide on the warlord's back
beside his mustered troops. No trembling harp,
no tuned timber, no tumbling hawk
swerving through the hall, no swift horse
2265 pawing the courtyard. Pillage and slaughter

---

8. Lines 2227–30 are so damaged that they defy guesswork to reconstruct them.

have emptied the earth of entire peoples."
And so he mourned as he moved about the world,
deserted and alone, lamenting his unhappiness
day and night, until death's flood
brimmed up in his heart.
2270   Then an old harrower of the dark
happened to find the hoard open,
the burning one who hunts out barrows,
the slick-skinned dragon, threatening the night sky
with streamers of fire. People on the farms
2275 are in dread of him. He is driven to hunt out
hoards under ground, to guard heathen gold
through age-long vigils, though to little avail.
For three centuries, this scourge of the people
had stood guard on that stoutly protected
2280 underground treasury, until the intruder
unleashed its fury; he hurried to his lord
with the gold-plated cup and made his plea
to be reinstated. Then the vault was rifled,
the ring-hoard robbed, and the wretched man
2285 had his request granted. His master gazed
on that find from the past for the first time.
    When the dragon awoke, trouble flared again.
He rippled down the rock, writhing with anger
when he saw the footprints of the prowler who had stolen
2290 too close to his dreaming head.
So may a man not marked by fate
easily escape exile and woe
by the grace of God.
                    The hoard-guardian
scorched the ground as he scoured and hunted
2295 for the trespasser who had troubled his sleep.
Hot and savage, he kept circling and circling
the outside of the mound. No man appeared
in that desert waste, but he worked himself up
by imagining battle; then back in he'd go
2300 in search of the cup, only to discover
signs that someone had stumbled upon
the golden treasures. So the guardian of the mound,
the hoard-watcher, waited for the gloaming
with fierce impatience; his pent-up fury
2305 at the loss of the vessel made him long to hit back
and lash out in flames. Then, to his delight,
the day waned and he could wait no longer
behind the wall, but hurtled forth
in a fiery blaze. The first to suffer
2310 were the people on the land, but before long
it was their treasure-giver who would come to grief.
    The dragon began to belch out flames
and burn bright homesteads; there was a hot glow
that scared everyone, for the vile sky-winger
2315 would leave nothing alive in his wake.

Everywhere the havoc he wrought was in evidence.
Far and near, the Geat nation
bore the brunt of his brutal assaults
and virulent hate. Then back to the hoard
2320   he would dart before daybreak, to hide in his den.
He had swinged the land, swathed it in flame,
in fire and burning, and now he felt secure
in the vaults of his barrow; but his trust was unavailing.
    Then Beowulf was given bad news,
2325   the hard truth: his own home,
the best of buildings, had been burned to a cinder,
the throne-room of the Geats. It threw the hero
into deep anguish and darkened his mood:
the wise man thought he must have thwarted
2330   ancient ordinance of the eternal Lord,
broken His commandment. His mind was in turmoil,
unaccustomed anxiety and gloom
confused his brain; the fire-dragon
had razed the coastal region and reduced
2335   forts and earthworks to dust and ashes,
so the war-king planned and plotted his revenge.
The warriors' protector, prince of the hall-troop,
ordered a marvelous all-iron shield
from his smithy works. He well knew
2340   that linden boards would let him down
and timber burn. After many trials,
he was destined to face the end of his days,
in this mortal world, as was the dragon,
for all his long leasehold on the treasure.
2345   Yet the prince of the rings was too proud
to line up with a large army
against the sky-plague. He had scant regard
for the dragon as a threat, no dread at all
of its courage or strength, for he had kept going
2350   often in the past, through perils and ordeals
of every sort, after he had purged
Hrothgar's hall, triumphed in Heorot
and beaten Grendel. He outgrappled the monster
and his evil kin.
               One of his cruelest
2355   hand-to-hand encounters had happened
when Hygelac, king of the Geats, was killed
in Friesland: the people's friend and lord,
Hrethel's son, slaked a sword blade's
thirst for blood. But Beowulf's prodigious
2360   gifts as a swimmer guaranteed his safety:
he arrived at the shore, shouldering thirty
battle-dresses, the booty he had won.
There was little for the Hetware[9] to be happy about
as they shielded their faces and fighting on the ground

9. A tribe of the Franks allied with the Frisians.

2365 began in earnest. With Beowulf against them,
few could hope to return home.
        Across the wide sea, desolate and alone,
the son of Ecgtheow swam back to his people.
There Hygd offered him throne and authority
2370 as lord of the ring-hoard: with Hygelac dead,
she had no belief in her son's ability
to defend their homeland against foreign invaders.
Yet there was no way the weakened nation
could get Beowulf to give in and agree
2375 to be elevated over Heardred as his lord
or to undertake the office of kingship.
But he did provide support for the prince,
honored and minded him until he matured
as the ruler of Geatland.
                        Then over sea-roads
2380 exiles arrived, sons of Ohthere.[1]
They had rebelled against the best of all
the sea-kings in Sweden, the one who held sway
in the Shylfing nation, their renowned prince,
lord of the mead-hall. That marked the end
2385 for Hygelac's son: his hospitality
was mortally rewarded with wounds from a sword.
Heardred lay slaughtered and Onela returned
to the land of Sweden, leaving Beowulf
to ascend the throne, to sit in majesty
2390 and rule over the Geats. He was a good king.
        In days to come, he contrived to avenge
the fall of his prince; he befriended Eadgils
when Eadgils was friendless, aiding his cause
with weapons and warriors over the wide sea,
2395 sending him men. The feud was settled
on a comfortless campaign when he killed Onela.
        And so the son of Ecgtheow had survived
every extreme, excelling himself
in daring and in danger, until the day arrived
2400 when he had to come face to face with the dragon.
The lord of the Geats took eleven comrades
and went in a rage to reconnoiter.
By then he had discovered the cause of the affliction
being visited on the people. The precious cup
2405 had come to him from the hand of the finder,
the one who had started all this strife
and was now added as a thirteenth to their number.
They press-ganged and compelled this poor creature
to be their guide. Against his will
2410 he led them to the earth-vault he alone knew,
an underground barrow near the sea-billows
and heaving waves, heaped inside
with exquisite metalwork. The one who stood guard

1. See p. 74, n. 6, Phases 3 and 4.

was dangerous and watchful, warden of the trove
2415 buried under earth: no easy bargain
would be made in that place by any man.
    The veteran king sat down on the cliff-top.
He wished good luck to the Geats who had shared
his hearth and his gold. He was sad at heart,
2420 unsettled yet ready, sensing his death.
His fate hovered near, unknowable but certain:
it would soon claim his coffered soul,
part life from limb. Before long
the prince's spirit would spin free from his body.
2425   Beowulf, son of Ecgtheow, spoke:
"Many a skirmish I survived when I was young
and many times of war: I remember them well.
At seven, I was fostered out by my father,
left in the charge of my people's lord.
2430 King Hrethel kept me and took care of me,
was openhanded, behaved like a kinsman.
While I was his ward, he treated me no worse
as a wean[2] about the place than one of his own boys,
Herebeald and Haethcyn, or my own Hygelac.
2435 For the eldest, Herebeald, an unexpected
deathbed was laid out, through a brother's doing,
when Haethcyn bent his horn-tipped bow
and loosed the arrow that destroyed his life.
He shot wide and buried a shaft
2440 in the flesh and blood of his own brother.
That offense was beyond redress, a wrongfooting
of the heart's affections; for who could avenge
the prince's life or pay his death-price?
It was like the misery felt by an old man
2445 who has lived to see his son's body
swing on the gallows. He begins to keen
and weep for his boy, watching the raven
gloat where he hangs: he can be of no help.
The wisdom of age is worthless to him.
2450 Morning after morning, he wakes to remember
that his child is gone; he has no interest
in living on until another heir
is born in the hall, now that his first-born
has entered death's dominion forever.
2455 . He gazes sorrowfully at his son's dwelling,
the banquet hall bereft of all delight,
the windswept hearthstone; the horsemen are sleeping,
the warriors under ground; what was is no more.
No tunes from the harp, no cheer raised in the yard.
2460 Alone with his longing, he lies down on his bed
and sings a lament; everything seems too large,
the steadings and the fields.
                        Such was the feeling

---

2. A young child [Northern Ireland; Translator's note].

of loss endured by the lord of the Geats
after Herebeald's death. He was helplessly placed
2465   to set to rights the wrong committed,
could not punish the killer in accordance with the law
of the blood-feud, although he felt no love for him.
Heartsore, wearied, he turned away
from life's joys, chose God's light
2470   and departed, leaving buildings and lands
to his sons, as a man of substance will.
     "Then over the wide sea Swedes and Geats
battled and feuded and fought without quarter.
Hostilities broke out when Hrethel died.[3]
2475   Ongentheow's sons were unrelenting,
refusing to make peace, campaigning violently
from coast to coast, constantly setting up
terrible ambushes around Hreosnahill.
My own kith and kin avenged
2480   these evil events, as everybody knows,
but the price was high: one of them paid
with his life. Haethcyn, lord of the Geats,
met his fate there and fell in the battle.
Then, as I have heard, Hygelac's sword
2485   was raised in the morning against Ongentheow,
his brother's killer. When Eofor cleft
the old Swede's helmet, halved it open,
he fell, death-pale: his feud-calloused hand
could not stave off the fatal stroke.
2490   "The treasures that Hygelac lavished on me
I paid for when I fought, as fortune allowed me,
with my glittering sword. He gave me land
and the security land brings, so he had no call
to go looking for some lesser champion,
2495   some mercenary from among the Gifthas
or the Spear-Danes or the men of Sweden.
I marched ahead of him, always there
at the front of the line; and I shall fight like that
for as long as I live, as long as this sword
2500   shall last, which has stood me in good stead
late and soon, ever since I killed
Dayraven the Frank in front of the two armies.
He brought back no looted breastplate
to the Frisian king but fell in battle,
2505   their standard-bearer, highborn and brave.
No sword blade sent him to his death:
my bare hands stilled his heartbeats
and wrecked the bone-house. Now blade and hand,
sword and sword-stroke, will assay the hoard."

---

3. See p. 74, n. 6, Phases 1 and 2.

[BEOWULF ATTACKS THE DRAGON]

2510   Beowulf spoke, made a formal boast
for the last time: "I risked my life
often when I was young. Now I am old,
but as king of the people I shall pursue this fight
for the glory of winning, if the evil one will only
2515 abandon his earth-fort and face me in the open."
    Then he addressed each dear companion
one final time, those fighters in their helmets,
resolute and highborn: "I would rather not
use a weapon if I knew another way
2520 to grapple with the dragon and make good my boast
as I did against Grendel in days gone by.
But I shall be meeting molten venom
in the fire he breathes, so I go forth
in mail-shirt and shield. I won't shift a foot
2525 when I meet the cave-guard: what occurs on the wall
between the two of us will turn out as fate,
overseer of men, decides. I am resolved.
I scorn further words against this sky-borne foe.
    "Men-at-arms, remain here on the barrow,
2530 safe in your armor, to see which one of us
is better in the end at bearing wounds
in a deadly fray. This fight is not yours,
nor is it up to any man except me
to measure his strength against the monster
2535 or to prove his worth. I shall win the gold
by my courage, or else mortal combat,
doom of battle, will bear your lord away."
    Then he drew himself up beside his shield.
The fabled warrior in his war-shirt and helmet
2540 trusted in his own strength entirely
and went under the crag. No coward path.
    Hard by the rock-face that hale veteran,
a good man who had gone repeatedly
into combat and danger and come through,
2545 saw a stone arch and a gushing stream
that burst from the barrow, blazing and wafting
a deadly heat. It would be hard to survive
unscathed near the hoard, to hold firm
against the dragon in those flaming depths.
2550 Then he gave a shout. The lord of the Geats
unburdened his breast and broke out
in a storm of anger. Under gray stone
his voice challenged and resounded clearly.
Hate was ignited. The hoard-guard recognized
2555 a human voice, the time was over
for peace and parleying. Pouring forth
in a hot battle-fume, the breath of the monster
burst from the rock. There was a rumble under ground.
Down there in the barrow, Beowulf the warrior

2560 lifted his shield: the outlandish thing
writhed and convulsed and viciously
turned on the king, whose keen-edged sword,
an heirloom inherited by ancient right,
was already in his hand. Roused to a fury,
2565 each antagonist struck terror in the other.
Unyielding, the lord of his people loomed
by his tall shield, sure of his ground,
while the serpent looped and unleashed itself.
Swaddled in flames, it came gliding and flexing
2570 and racing toward its fate. Yet his shield defended
the renowned leader's life and limb
for a shorter time than he meant it to:
that final day was the first time
when Beowulf fought and fate denied him
2575 glory in battle. So the king of the Geats
raised his hand and struck hard
at the enameled scales, but scarcely cut through:
the blade flashed and slashed yet the blow
was far less powerful than the hard-pressed king
2580 had need of at that moment. The mound-keeper
went into a spasm and spouted deadly flames:
when he felt the stroke, battle-fire
billowed and spewed. Beowulf was foiled
of a glorious victory. The glittering sword,
2585 infallible before that day,
failed when he unsheathed it, as it never should have.
For the son of Ecgtheow, it was no easy thing
to have to give ground like that and go
unwillingly to inhabit another home
2590 in a place beyond; so every man must yield
the leasehold of his days.
                              Before long
the fierce contenders clashed again.
The hoard-guard took heart, inhaled and swelled up
and got a new wind; he who had once ruled
2595 was furled in fire and had to face the worst.
No help or backing was to be had then
from his highborn comrades; that hand-picked troop
broke ranks and ran for their lives
to the safety of the wood. But within one heart
2600 sorrow welled up: in a man of worth
the claims of kinship cannot be denied.
    His name was Wiglaf, a son of Weohstan's,
a well-regarded Shylfing warrior
related to Aelfhere.[4] When he saw his lord
2605 tormented by the heat of his scalding helmet,
he remembered the bountiful gifts bestowed on him,

---

4. Although Wiglaf is here said to be a Shylfing (i.e., a Swede), in line 2607 we are told his family are Waegmundings, a clan of the Geats, which is also Beowulf's family. It was possible for a family to owe allegiance to more than one nation and to shift sides as a result of feuds. Nothing is known of Aelfhere.

how well he lived among the Waegmundings,
the freehold he inherited from his father[5] before him.
He could not hold back: one hand brandished
2610 the yellow-timbered shield, the other drew his sword—
an ancient blade that was said to have belonged
to Eanmund, the son of Ohthere, the one
Weohstan had slain when he was an exile without friends.
He carried the arms to the victim's kinfolk,
2615 the burnished helmet, the webbed chain-mail
and that relic of the giants. But Onela returned
the weapons to him, rewarded Weohstan
with Eanmund's war-gear. He ignored the blood-feud,
the fact that Eanmund was his brother's son.[6]
2620 Weohstan kept that war-gear for a lifetime,
the sword and the mail-shirt, until it was the son's turn
to follow his father and perform his part.
Then, in old age, at the end of his days
among the Weather-Geats, he bequeathed to Wiglaf
innumerable weapons.
2625   And now the youth
was to enter the line of battle with his lord,
his first time to be tested as a fighter.
His spirit did not break and the ancestral blade
would keep its edge, as the dragon discovered
2630 as soon as they came together in the combat.
    Sad at heart, addressing his companions,
Wiglaf spoke wise and fluent words:
"I remember that time when mead was flowing,
how we pledged loyalty to our lord in the hall,
2635 promised our ring-giver we would be worth our price,
make good the gift of the war-gear,
those swords and helmets, as and when
his need required it. He picked us out
from the army deliberately, honored us and judged us
2640 fit for this action, made me these lavish gifts—
and all because he considered us the best
of his arms-bearing thanes. And now, although
he wanted this challenge to be one he'd face
by himself alone—the shepherd of our land,
2645 a man unequaled in the quest for glory
and a name for daring—now the day has come
when this lord we serve needs sound men
to give him their support. Let us go to him,
help our leader through the hot flame
2650 and dread of the fire. As God is my witness,
I would rather my body were robed in the same
burning blaze as my gold-giver's body

---

5. I.e., Weohstan, who, as explained below, was the slayer of Onela's nephew Eanmund. Possibly, Weohstan joined the Geats under Beowulf after Eanmund's brother, with Beowulf's help, avenged Eanmund's death on Onela and became king of the Shylfings. See p. 74, n. 6, Phase 2.

6. An ironic comment: since Onela wanted to kill Eanmund, he rewarded Weohstan for killing his nephew instead of exacting compensation or revenge.

than go back home bearing arms.
That is unthinkable, unless we have first
2655   slain the foe and defended the life
of the prince of the Weather-Geats. I well know
the things he has done for us deserve better.
Should he alone be left exposed
to fall in battle? We must bond together,
2660   shield and helmet, mail-shirt and sword."
Then he waded the dangerous reek and went
under arms to his lord, saying only:
"Go on, dear Beowulf, do everything
you said you would when you were still young
2665   and vowed you would never let your name and fame
be dimmed while you lived. Your deeds are famous,
so stay resolute, my lord, defend your life now
with the whole of your strength. I shall stand by you."
    After those words, a wildness rose
2670   in the dragon again and drove it to attack,
heaving up fire, hunting for enemies,
the humans it loathed. Flames lapped the shield,
charred it to the boss, and the body armor
on the young warrior was useless to him.
2675   But Wiglaf did well under the wide rim
Beowulf shared with him once his own had shattered
in sparks and ashes.
                    Inspired again
by the thought of glory, the war-king threw
his whole strength behind a sword stroke
2680   and connected with the skull. And Naegling snapped.
Beowulf's ancient iron-gray sword
let him down in the fight. It was never his fortune
to be helped in combat by the cutting edge
of weapons made of iron. When he wielded a sword,
2685   no matter how blooded and hard-edged the blade,
his hand was too strong, the stroke he dealt
(I have heard) would ruin it. He could reap no advantage.
    Then the bane of that people, the fire-breathing dragon,
was mad to attack for a third time.
2690   When a chance came, he caught the hero
in a rush of flame and clamped sharp fangs
into his neck. Beowulf's body
ran wet with his life-blood: it came welling out.
    Next thing, they say, the noble son of Weohstan
2695   saw the king in danger at his side
and displayed his inborn bravery and strength.
He left the head alone,[7] but his fighting hand
was burned when he came to his kinsman's aid.
He lunged at the enemy lower down
2700   so that his decorated sword sank into its belly
and the flames grew weaker.

---

7. I.e., he avoided the dragon's flame-breathing head.

Once again the king
gathered his strength and drew a stabbing knife
he carried on his belt, sharpened for battle.
He stuck it deep in the dragon's flank.
2705 Beowulf dealt it a deadly wound.
They had killed the enemy, courage quelled his life;
that pair of kinsmen, partners in nobility,
had destroyed the foe. So every man should act,
be at hand when needed; but now, for the king,
2710 this would be the last of his many labors
and triumphs in the world.
Then the wound
dealt by the ground-burner earlier began
to scald and swell; Beowulf discovered
deadly poison suppurating inside him,
2715 surges of nausea, and so, in his wisdom,
the prince realized his state and struggled
toward a seat on the rampart. He steadied his gaze
on those gigantic stones, saw how the earthwork
was braced with arches built over columns.
2720 And now that thane unequaled for goodness
with his own hands washed his lord's wounds,
swabbed the weary prince with water,
bathed him clean, unbuckled his helmet.
Beowulf spoke: in spite of his wounds,
2725 mortal wounds, he still spoke
for he well knew his days in the world
had been lived out to the end—his allotted time
was drawing to a close, death was very near.
"Now is the time when I would have wanted
2730 to bestow this armor on my own son,
had it been my fortune to have fathered an heir
and live on in his flesh. For fifty years
I ruled this nation. No king
of any neighboring clan would dare
2735 face me with troops, none had the power
to intimidate me. I took what came,
cared for and stood by things in my keeping,
never fomented quarrels, never
swore to a lie. All this consoles me,
2740 doomed as I am and sickening for death;
because of my right ways, the Ruler of mankind
need never blame me when the breath leaves my body
for murder of kinsmen. Go now quickly,
dearest Wiglaf, under the gray stone
2745 where the dragon is laid out, lost to his treasure;
hurry to feast your eyes on the hoard.
Away you go: I want to examine
that ancient gold, gaze my fill
on those garnered jewels; my going will be easier
2750 for having seen the treasure, a less troubled letting-go
of the life and lordship I have long maintained."

And so, I have heard, the son of Weohstan
quickly obeyed the command of his languishing
war-weary lord; he went in his chain-mail
2755   under the rock-piled roof of the barrow,
exulting in his triumph, and saw beyond the seat
a treasure-trove of astonishing richness,
wall-hangings that were a wonder to behold,
glittering gold spread across the ground,
2760   the old dawn-scorching serpent's den
packed with goblets and vessels from the past,
tarnished and corroding. Rusty helmets
all eaten away. Armbands everywhere,
artfully wrought. How easily treasure
2765   buried in the ground, gold hidden
however skillfully, can escape from any man!
    And he saw too a standard, entirely of gold,
hanging high over the hoard,
a masterpiece of filigree; it glowed with light
2770   so he could make out the ground at his feet
and inspect the valuables. Of the dragon there was no
remaining sign: the sword had dispatched him.
Then, the story goes, a certain man
plundered the hoard in that immemorial howe,
2775   filled his arms with flagons and plates,
anything he wanted; and took the standard also,
most brilliant of banners.
                    Already the blade
of the old king's sharp killing-sword
had done its worst: the one who had for long
2780   minded the hoard, hovering over gold,
unleashing fire, surging forth
midnight after midnight, had been mown down.
    Wiglaf went quickly, keen to get back,
excited by the treasure. Anxiety weighed
2785   on his brave heart—he was hoping he would find
the leader of the Geats alive where he had left him
helpless, earlier, on the open ground.
    So he came to the place, carrying the treasure
and found his lord bleeding profusely,
2790   his life at an end; again he began
to swab his body. The beginnings of an utterance
broke out from the king's breast-cage.
The old lord gazed sadly at the gold.
    "To the everlasting Lord of all,
2795   to the King of Glory, I give thanks
that I behold this treasure here in front of me,
that I have been allowed to leave my people
so well endowed on the day I die.
Now that I have bartered my last breath
2800   to own this fortune, it is up to you
to look after their needs. I can hold out no longer.
Order my troop to construct a barrow

on a headland on the coast, after my pyre has cooled.
It will loom on the horizon at Hronesness[8]
2805 and be a reminder among my people—
so that in coming times crews under sail
will call it Beowulf's Barrow, as they steer
ships across the wide and shrouded waters."
    Then the king in his great-heartedness unclasped
2810 the collar of gold from his neck and gave it
to the young thane, telling him to use
it and the war-shirt and gilded helmet well.
"You are the last of us, the only one left
of the Waegmundings. Fate swept us away,
2815 sent my whole brave highborn clan
to their final doom. Now I must follow them."
    That was the warrior's last word.
He had no more to confide. The furious heat
of the pyre would assail him. His soul fled from his breast
2820 to its destined place among the steadfast ones.

[BEOWULF'S FUNERAL]

    It was hard then on the young hero,
having to watch the one he held so dear
there on the ground, going through
his death agony. The dragon from underearth,
2825 his nightmarish destroyer, lay destroyed as well,
utterly without life. No longer would his snakefolds
ply themselves to safeguard hidden gold.
Hard-edged blades, hammered out
and keenly filed, had finished him
2830 so that the sky-roamer lay there rigid,
brought low beside the treasure-lodge.
    Never again would he glitter and glide
and show himself off in midnight air,
exulting in his riches: he fell to earth
2835 through the battle-strength in Beowulf's arm.
There were few, indeed, as far as I have heard,
big and brave as they may have been,
few who would have held out if they had had to face
the outpourings of that poison-breather
2840 or gone foraging on the ring-hall floor
and found the deep barrow-dweller
on guard and awake.
                    The treasure had been won,
bought and paid for by Beowulf's death.
Both had reached the end of the road
through the life they had been lent.
2845   Before long
the battle-dodgers abandoned the wood,
the ones who had let down their lord earlier,
the tail-turners, ten of them together.

8. A headland by the sea. The name means "Whalesness."

When he needed them most, they had made off.
2850 Now they were ashamed and came behind shields,
in their battle-outfits, to where the old man lay.
They watched Wiglaf, sitting worn out,
a comrade shoulder to shoulder with his lord,
trying in vain to bring him round with water.
2855 Much as he wanted to, there was no way
he could preserve his lord's life on earth
or alter in the least the Almighty's will.
What God judged right would rule what happened
to every man, as it does to this day.
2860   Then a stern rebuke was bound to come
from the young warrior to the ones who had been cowards.
Wiglaf, son of Weohstan, spoke
disdainfully and in disappointment:
"Anyone ready to admit the truth
2865 will surely realize that the lord of men
who showered you with gifts and gave you the armor
you are standing in—when he would distribute
helmets and mail-shirts to men on the mead-benches,
a prince treating his thanes in hall
2870 to the best he could find, far or near—
was throwing weapons uselessly away.
It would be a sad waste when the war broke out.
Beowulf had little cause to brag
about his armed guard; yet God who ordains
2875 who wins or loses allowed him to strike
with his own blade when bravery was needed.
There was little I could do to protect his life
in the heat of the fray, but I found new strength
welling up when I went to help him.
2880 Then my sword connected and the deadly assaults
of our foe grew weaker, the fire coursed
less strongly from his head. But when the worst happened
too few rallied around the prince.
    "So it is good-bye now to all you know and love
2885 on your home ground, the open-handedness,
the giving of war-swords. Every one of you
with freeholds of land, our whole nation,
will be dispossessed, once princes from beyond
get tidings of how you turned and fled
2890 and disgraced yourselves. A warrior will sooner
die than live a life of shame."
    Then he ordered the outcome of the fight to be reported
to those camped on the ridge, that crowd of retainers
who had sat all morning, sad at heart,
2895 shield-bearers wondering about
the man they loved: would this day be his last
or would he return? He told the truth
and did not balk, the rider who bore
news to the cliff-top. He addressed them all:
2900 "Now the people's pride and love,

the lord of the Geats, is laid on his deathbed,
brought down by the dragon's attack.
Beside him lies the bane of his life,
dead from knife-wounds. There was no way
2905 Beowulf could manage to get the better
of the monster with his sword. Wiglaf sits
at Beowulf's side, the son of Weohstan,
the living warrior watching by the dead,
keeping weary vigil, holding a wake
for the loved and the loathed.
2910   Now war is looming
over our nation, soon it will be known
to Franks and Frisians, far and wide,
that the king is gone. Hostility has been great
among the Franks since Hygelac sailed forth
2915 at the head of a war-fleet into Friesland:
there the Hetware harried and attacked
and overwhelmed him with great odds.
The leader in his war-gear was laid low,
fell among followers: that lord did not favor
2920 his company with spoils. The Merovingian king
has been an enemy to us ever since.
     "Nor do I expect peace or pact-keeping
of any sort from the Swedes. Remember:
at Ravenswood,⁹ Ongentheow
2925 slaughtered Haethcyn, Hrethel's son,
when the Geat people in their arrogance
first attacked the fierce Shylfings.
The return blow was quickly struck
by Ohthere's father.¹ Old and terrible,
2930 he felled the sea-king and saved his own
aged wife, the mother of Onela
and of Ohthere, bereft of her gold rings.
Then he kept hard on the heels of the foe
and drove them, leaderless, lucky to get away
2935 in a desperate rout into Ravenswood.
His army surrounded the weary remnant
where they nursed their wounds; all through the night
he howled threats at those huddled survivors,
promised to axe their bodies open
2940 when dawn broke, dangle them from gallows
to feed the birds. But at first light
when their spirits were lowest, relief arrived.
They heard the sound of Hygelac's horn,
his trumpet calling as he came to find them,
2945 the hero in pursuit, at hand with troops.
     "The bloody swathe that Swedes and Geats
cut through each other was everywhere.
No one could miss their murderous feuding.

---

9. The messenger describes in greater detail the
Battle of Ravenswood. See the outline of the Swedish wars on p. 74, n. 6.
1. I.e., Ongentheow.

Then the old man made his move,
2950 pulled back, barred his people in:
Ongentheow withdrew to higher ground.
Hygelac's pride and prowess as a fighter
were known to the earl; he had no confidence
that he could hold out against that horde of seamen,
2955 defend his wife and the ones he loved
from the shock of the attack. He retreated for shelter
behind the earthwall. Then Hygelac swooped
on the Swedes at bay, his banners swarmed
into their refuge, his Geat forces
2960 drove forward to destroy the camp.
There in his gray hairs, Ongentheow
was cornered, ringed around with swords.
And it came to pass that the king's fate
was in Eofor's hands,[2] and in his alone.
2965 Wulf, son of Wonred, went for him in anger,
split him open so that blood came spurting
from under his hair. The old hero
still did not flinch, but parried fast,
hit back with a harder stroke:
2970 the king turned and took him on.
Then Wonred's son, the brave Wulf,
could land no blow against the aged lord.
Ongentheow divided his helmet
so that he buckled and bowed his bloodied head
2975 and dropped to the ground. But his doom held off.
Though he was cut deep, he recovered again.
    "With his brother down, the undaunted Eofor,
Hygelac's thane, hefted his sword
and smashed murderously at the massive helmet
2980 past the lifted shield. And the king collapsed,
the shepherd of people was sheared of life.
Many then hurried to help Wulf,
bandaged and lifted him, now that they were left
masters of the blood-soaked battle-ground.
2985 One warrior stripped the other,
looted Ongenteow's iron mail-coat,
his hard sword-hilt, his helmet too,
and carried the graith[3] to King Hygelac;
he accepted the prize, promised fairly
2990 that reward would come, and kept his word.
For their bravery in action, when they arrived home,
Eofor and Wulf were overloaded
by Hrethel's son, Hygelac the Geat,
with gifts of land and linked rings
2995 that were worth a fortune. They had won glory,
so there was no gainsaying his generosity.

2. I.e., he was at Eofor's mercy. Eofor's slaying of Ongetheow was described in lines 2486–89, where no mention is made of his brother Wulf's part in the battle. They are the sons of Wonred. *Eofor* means boar, and *Wulf* is the Old English spelling of wolf.
3. Possessions, apparel.

And he gave Eofor his only daughter
to bide at home with him, an honor and a bond.
"So this bad blood between us and the Swedes,
3000 this vicious feud, I am convinced,
is bound to revive; they will cross our borders
and attack in force when they find out
that Beowulf is dead. In days gone by
when our warriors fell and we were undefended,
3005 he kept our coffers and our kingdom safe.
He worked for the people, but as well as that
he behaved like a hero.
                                    We must hurry now
to take a last look at the king
and launch him, lord and lavisher of rings,
3010 on the funeral road. His royal pyre
will melt no small amount of gold:
heaped there in a hoard, it was bought at heavy cost,
and that pile of rings he paid for at the end
with his own life will go up with the flame,
3015 be furled in fire: treasure no follower
will wear in his memory, nor lovely woman
link and attach as a torque around her neck—
but often, repeatedly, in the path of exile
they shall walk bereft, bowed under woe,
3020 now that their leader's laugh is silenced,
high spirits quenched. Many a spear
dawn-cold to the touch will be taken down
and waved on high; the swept harp
won't waken warriors, but the raven winging
3025 darkly over the doomed will have news,
tidings for the eagle of how he hoked and ate,
how the wolf and he made short work of the dead."[4]
      Such was the drift of the dire report
that gallant man delivered. He got little wrong
in what he told and predicted.
3030   The whole troop
rose in tears, then took their way
to the uncanny scene under Earnaness.[5]
There, on the sand, where his soul had left him,
they found him at rest, their ring-giver
3035 from days gone by. The great man
had breathed his last. Beowulf the king
had indeed met with a marvelous death.
      But what they saw first was far stranger:
the serpent on the ground, gruesome and vile,
3040 lying facing him. The fire-dragon
was scaresomely burned, scorched all colors.
From head to tail, his entire length

4. The raven, eagle, and wolf—the scavengers
who will feed on the slain—are "the beasts of battle," a common motif in Germanic war poetry.
"Hoked": rooted about [Northern Ireland,
Translator's note].
5. The site of Beowulf's fight with the dragon. The
name means "Eaglesness."

was fifty feet. He had shimmered forth
on the night air once, then winged back
3045 down to his den; but death owned him now,
he would never enter his earth-gallery again.
Beside him stood pitchers and piled-up dishes,
silent flagons, precious swords
eaten through with rust, ranged as they had been
3050 while they waited their thousand winters under ground.
That huge cache, gold inherited
from an ancient race, was under a spell—
which meant no one was ever permitted
to enter the ring-hall unless God Himself,
3055 mankind's Keeper, True King of Triumphs,
allowed some person pleasing to Him—
and in His eyes worthy—to open the hoard.
    What came about brought to nothing
the hopes of the one who had wrongly hidden
3060 riches under the rock-face. First the dragon slew
that man among men, who in turn made fierce amends
and settled the feud. Famous for his deeds
a warrior may be, but it remains a mystery
where his life will end, when he may no longer
3065 dwell in the mead-hall among his own.
So it was with Beowulf, when he faced the cruelty
and cunning of the mound-guard. He himself was ignorant
of how his departure from the world would happen.
The highborn chiefs who had buried the treasure
3070 declared it until doomsday so accursed
that whoever robbed it would be guilty of wrong
and grimly punished for their transgression,
hasped in hell-bonds in heathen shrines.
Yet Beowulf's gaze at the gold treasure
3075 when he first saw it had not been selfish.
    Wiglaf, son of Weohstan, spoke:
"Often when one man follows his own will
many are hurt. This happened to us.
Nothing we advised could ever convince
3080 the prince we loved, our land's guardian,
not to vex the custodian of the gold,
let him lie where he was long accustomed,
lurk there under earth until the end of the world.
He held to his high destiny. The hoard is laid bare,
3085 but at a grave cost; it was too cruel a fate
that forced the king to that encounter.
I have been inside and seen everything
amassed in the vault. I managed to enter
although no great welcome awaited me
3090 under the earthwall. I quickly gathered up
a huge pile of the priceless treasures
handpicked from the hoard and carried them here
where the king could see them. He was still himself,
alive, aware, and in spite of his weakness

3095   he had many requests. He wanted me to greet you
and order the building of a barrow that would crown
the site of his pyre, serve as his memorial,
in a commanding position, since of all men
to have lived and thrived and lorded it on earth
3100   his worth and due as a warrior were the greatest.
Now let us again go quickly
and feast our eyes on that amazing fortune
heaped under the wall. I will show the way
and take you close to those coffers packed with rings
3105   and bars of gold. Let a bier be made
and got ready quickly when we come out
and then let us bring the body of our lord,
the man we loved, to where he will lodge
for a long time in the care of the Almighty."
3110   Then Weohstan's son, stalwart to the end,
had orders given to owners of dwellings,
many people of importance in the land,
to fetch wood from far and wide
for the good man's pyre:
                    "Now shall flame consume
3115   our leader in battle, the blaze darken
round him who stood his ground in the steel-hail,
when the arrow-storm shot from bowstrings
pelted the shield-wall. The shaft hit home.
Feather-fledged, it finned the barb in flight."
3120   Next the wise son of Weohstan
called from among the king's thanes
a group of seven: he selected the best
and entered with them, the eighth of their number,
under the God-cursed roof; one raised
3125   a lighted torch and led the way.
No lots were cast for who should loot the hoard
for it was obvious to them that every bit of it
lay unprotected within the vault,
there for the taking. It was no trouble
3130   to hurry to work and haul out
the priceless store. They pitched the dragon
over the cliff-top, let tide's flow
and backwash take the treasure-minder.
Then coiled gold was loaded on a cart
3135   in great abundance, and the gray-haired leader,
the prince on his bier, borne to Hronesness.
       The Geat people built a pyre for Beowulf,
stacked and decked it until it stood foursquare,
hung with helmets, heavy war-shields
3140   and shining armor, just as he had ordered.
Then his warriors laid him in the middle of it,
mourning a lord far-famed and beloved.
On a height they kindled the hugest of all
funeral fires; fumes of woodsmoke
3145   billowed darkly up, the blaze roared

and drowned out their weeping, wind died down
and flames wrought havoc in the hot bone-house,
burning it to the core. They were disconsolate
and wailed aloud for their lord's decease.
3150 A Geat woman too sang out in grief;
with hair bound up, she unburdened herself
of her worst fears, a wild litany
of nightmare and lament: her nation invaded,
enemies on the rampage, bodies in piles,
3155 slavery and abasement. Heaven swallowed the smoke.
  Then the Geat people began to construct
a mound on a headland, high and imposing,
a marker that sailors could see from far away,
and in ten days they had done the work.
3160 It was their hero's memorial; what remained from the fire
they housed inside it, behind a wall
as worthy of him as their workmanship could make it.
And they buried torques in the barrow, and jewels
and a trove of such things as trespassing men
3165 had once dared to drag from the hoard.
They let the ground keep that ancestral treasure,
gold under gravel, gone to earth,
as useless to men now as it ever was.
Then twelve warriors rode around the tomb,
3170 chieftains' sons, champions in battle,
all of them distraught, chanting in dirges,
mourning his loss as a man and a king.
They extolled his heroic nature and exploits
and gave thanks for his greatness; which was the proper thing,
3175 for a man should praise a prince whom he holds dear
and cherish his memory when that moment comes
when he has to be convoyed from his bodily home.
So the Geat people, his hearth-companions,
sorrowed for the lord who had been laid low.
3180 They said that of all the kings upon earth
he was the man most gracious and fair-minded,
kindest to his people and keenest to win fame.

Anglo-Norman England

LEGENDARY HISTORIES OF BRITAIN

During the twelfth century, three authors, who wrote in Latin, Anglo-Norman French, and Middle English, respectively, created a mostly legendary history of Britain for their Norman overlords (see pp. 6–7). This "history" was set in the remote past, beginning with a foundation myth—a heroic account of national origins—modeled on Virgil's *Aeneid* and ending with the Anglo-Saxon conquest of the native island-ers, the Britons, in the fifth and sixth centuries. The chief architect of the history is Geoffrey of Monmouth, who was writing his *History of the Kings of Britain* in Latin prose ca. 1136–38. His work was freely translated into French verse by Wace in 1155, and Wace in turn was translated into English alliterative poetry by Layamon.

Geoffrey of Monmouth and Wace wrote their histories of Britain primarily for an audience of noblemen and prelates who were descendants of the Norman conquerors of the Anglo-Saxons. Geoffrey wrote several dedications of his *History*, first to sup-porters of Matilda, the heiress presumptive of Henry I, and, when the Crown went instead to Stephen of Blois, to the new king's allies and to Stephen himself. Layamon tells us that Wace wrote his French version for Eleanor of Aquitaine, queen of Ste-phen's successor, Henry II. The prestige and power of ancient Rome still dominated the historical and political imagination of the feudal aristocracy, and the legendary history of the ancient kings of the Britons, especially of King Arthur, who had defeated Rome itself, served to flatter the self-image and ambitions of the Anglo-Norman bar-ons. Perhaps the destruction of Arthur's kingdom also provided a timely object lesson of the disastrous consequences of civil wars such as those over the English succession in which these lords were engaged.

The selections from Geoffrey of Monmouth and Wace are translated by Alfred David. The Layamon selections are translated by Rosamund Allen.

GEOFFREY OF MONMOUTH

The author of the *History of the Kings of Britain* was a churchman, probably of Welsh or Breton ancestry, who spent much of his life at Oxford. One of his motives in writing the work was undoubtedly to obtain advancement in the church. In the dedications of the *History*, Geoffrey claims that it is merely a translation into Latin of "a very old book in the British language [i.e., Welsh]," which had been loaned to him by his friend Walter, archdeacon of Oxford, but scholars have discounted this story as another one of Geoffrey's many fictions.

Geoffrey began his history with a British foundation myth modeled upon Virgil's *Aeneid*. Out of legends that Rome had been founded by refugees from the fall of Troy, the poet Virgil had created his epic poem the *Aeneid* for Augustus Caesar. Aeneas, carrying his father upon his back, had escaped from the ruins of Troy and, fulfilling prophecies, became the founding father of a new Troy in Italy. The Brit-ons had developed an analogous foundation myth in which a great-grandson of Aeneas called Brutus had led another band of Trojan exiles to establish another Troy, which was named Britain after him. Geoffrey drew upon earlier Latin chron-icles and Welsh oral tradition, but he himself provided his history with a chronol-ogy, a genealogy, a large cast of both historical and legendary characters (among many other stories, he is the first to tell of King Lear and his daughters), and a cyclical sense of the rise and fall of empires. The longest and most original part of the work (over one-fifth of the *History*) is devoted to the birth and reign of King Arthur. In the first part of Arthur's reign, he defeats and drives out the pagan Anglo-Saxon invaders. At the end of his reign the Saxons return at the invitation of the traitor Mordred and, though defeated again by Arthur in his last battle, they ultimately triumph over his successors.

The historicity of Geoffrey's book, although questioned by some of Geoffrey's con-temporary historians, was widely accepted and not fully discredited until the seven-teenth century. In the course of time Arthur was adopted as a national and cultural hero by the English against whose ancestors he had fought, and his court became the international ideal of a splendid chivalric order in the past of which contemporary knighthood was only a faint imitation. Geoffrey of Monmouth himself already declares that in Arthur's time, "Womenfolk became chaste and more virtuous and for their love the knights were ever more daring."

In the following selections, Geoffrey relates the British foundation myth, which he historicizes, amplifies, and fleshes out with details that he regards as classical.

From The History of the Kings of Britain

[THE STORY OF BRUTUS AND DIANA'S PROPHECY]

After the Trojan War, Aeneas with his son Ascanius fled from the destruction of the city and sailed to Italy. Although King Latinus would have received him there with honor, Turnus, the king of the Rutuli, was envious and made war on him. In their rivalry Aeneas prevailed and, having slain Turnus, obtained the kingdom of Italy and Latinus's daughter, Lavinia.

At the end of Aeneas's days, Ascanius was elevated to royal power and founded the city of Alba on the banks of the Tiber. He fathered a son whose name was Silvius. The latter had a secret love affair with a niece of Lavinia's whom he married and got with child. When his father Ascanius learned about this he ordered his wise men to find out the sex of the child that the girl had conceived. When the wise men had made sure of the truth, they said that she would bear a son who would be the death of his father and mother. After travelling through many lands as an exile, he would nevertheless attain to the highest honor. Their prophecies did not turn out to be mistaken. For when her time had come, the woman bore a boy and died in childbirth. The boy was handed over to the midwife and named Brutus. At last, after fifteen years had gone by, the boy went hunting with his father and killed him with a misdirected bowshot. For as the servants were driving some stags into their path, Brutus, believing that he was aiming at them, hit his father below the breast. On account of this death, his relatives, outraged that he should have done such a deed, drove him from Italy.* * *

[The exiled Brutus travels to Greece, where he discovers descendants of Trojan prisoners of war living in slavery. He organizes a successful rebellion against their Greek masters and, like Aeneas before him, leads them on a quest for a new homeland.]

Driven by favorable winds, the Trojans sailed for two days and one night until they made land on an island called Leogetia, which was uninhabited because long ago it had been devastated by pirate raids. So Brutus sent three hundred armed men to explore the island and see whether anything was living on it. They found no one but they killed several kinds of wild animals that they came across in the woods and thickets.

They came to a deserted city where they found a temple of Diana in which a statue of the goddess rendered oracles if someone should consult it. At last they returned to their ships, loaded down with game, and told their comrades about the land and the city. They suggested to their chief that he go to the temple and, after making propitiatory sacrifices, inquire of the goddess what land might afford them a permanent home. When everyone agreed, Brutus with the soothsayer Gero and twelve elders set out for the temple, taking along everything necessary for the sacrifice. When they got there, they bound their brows with headbands and, in preparation of the most ancient rite, they erected three hearths to three gods, namely to Jupiter, Mercury, and Diana. They poured out libations to each one in turn. Before the altar of the goddess, Brutus himself, holding a sacrificial vessel filled with wine and the blood of a white doe in his right hand, raised his face to her statue and broke the silence with these words:[1]

> Mighty goddess of woodlands, terror of the wild boar,
> Thou who art free to traverse the ethereal heavens
> And the mansions of hell, disclose my rights on this earth
> And say what lands it is your wish for us to inhabit,
> What dwelling-place where I shall worship you all my life,
> Where I shall dedicate temples to you with virgin choirs.

After he had spoken this prayer nine times, he walked four times around the altar and poured out the wine he was holding upon the hearth. Then he spread out the hide of the doe before the altar and lay down on it. He tried to doze off and finally fell asleep. It was now the third hour of the night when sweetest slumber overcomes mortals. Then it seemed to him that the goddess was standing before him and speaking to him like this:

> Brutus, where the sun sets beyond the kingdoms of Gaul
> Is an isle in the ocean, closed all around by the sea.
> Once on a time giants lived on that isle in the ocean,
> But now it stands empty and fit to receive your people.
> Seek it out, for it shall be your homeland forever;
> It shall be a second Troy for your descendants.
> There kings shall be born of your seed and to them
> All nations of the round earth shall be subject.

When the vision vanished, Brutus remained in doubt whether what he had seen was only a phantom or whether the actual voice of the goddess had foretold the homeland to which he was to travel. Finally he called his comrades and told them point by point what had happened to him while he slept. Waves of great joy swept over them, and they urged that they return to the ships and, while the wind blew behind them, head with swiftest sail toward the ocean to seek out what the goddess had promised. Without delay they rejoined their comrades and set out on the high seas.

---

1. Brutus's prayer and Diana's prophecy are written as Latin poetry and employ a more formal diction than the prose narrative. The entire episode is meant to show off Geoffrey's classical learning and familiarity with pagan ritual.

WACE

Wace (ca. 1110–ca. 1180) was a Norman cleric, born on the island of Jersey in the English Channel, which was then part of the dukedom of Normandy. Although educated for the church, he seems to have served the laity, perhaps in a secretarial function. All of his extant works, which include saints' lives, *Le Roman de Brut*, and *Le Roman de Rou*, were written in French verse for a lay audience that would have included women like Eleanor of Aquitaine, to whom he dedicated the *Brut*, and Marie de France, who drew on that work in her lays. *Roman* in these titles refers to the fact that they are, respectively, chronicles in French verse about the dynasties of Brutus (first of the kings of Britain) and Rollo (first of the dukes of Normandy).

The *Roman de Brut* is a very free translation in eight-syllable couplets of Geoffrey of Monmouth's Latin prose *History of the Kings of Britain*. Wace has cut some details and added a good deal, including the first mention of the Round Table. He is far more interested than Geoffrey in creating an atmosphere of courtliness—in the way his characters dress, think, speak, and behave. The following selection covers a challenge delivered to Arthur by the Roman emperor Lucius and Arthur's response. This climactic sequence follows an elaborate coronation scene attended by a large gathering of kings and dukes from Britain and overseas who owe allegiance to Arthur and whose lands comprise what might be called the Arthurian Empire. At the feast following his coronation, Arthur's authority is challenged by ambassadors who present an insulting letter from Lucius. Arthur's reply is a masterpiece of feudal rhetoric that would have been admired by Wace's audience.

From Le Roman de Brut

[THE ROMAN CHALLENGE]

Arthur was seated on a dais surrounded by counts and kings when a dozen white-haired, very well-dressed men came into the hall in pairs, one holding the other's hand. Each held an olive branch. They crossed the hall very slowly in an orderly and solemn procession, approached the king and hailed him. They said they had come from Rome as messengers. They unfolded a letter, which one of them gave to Arthur on behalf of the Roman emperor. Listen to what it said:

"Lucius who holds Rome in his domain and is sovereign lord of the Romans, proclaims to King Arthur, his enemy, what he has deserved. I am disdainful in amazement and am amazed with disdain at the inordinate and insane pride with which you have set your sights on Rome. With disdain and amazement I ask myself at whose prompting and from what quarters you have undertaken to pick a quarrel with Rome as long as a single Roman remains alive. You have acted with great recklessness in attacking us who have the right to rule the world and hold supremacy over it. You still don't know, but we shall teach you; you are blind, but we shall make you see what a great thing it is to anger Rome, which has the power to rule over everything. You have presumed beyond your place and crossed the bounds of your authority! Have you any idea who you are and where you come from—you who are taking and holding back the tribute that belongs to us? You are taking our tribute and our lands: why do you hold them, why don't you turn them over, why do you keep them, what right do you have to them? If you keep them any longer, you will be acting most recklessly. And if you are capable of holding them without our forcing you to give them up, you might as well say—an unprecedented miracle!—that the lion flees from the lamb, the wolf from the goat, the greyhound from the hare. But that could never happen, for Nature would not suffer it. Julius Caesar, our ancestor—but maybe you have little respect for him—conquered Britain and imposed a tribute that our people have collected since that time. And we have also been receiving tribute for a long time from the other islands surrounding you. And you have foolishly presumed to take tribute from both of them. Already you were guilty of senseless behavior, but you have committed an even greater insult that touches us still more closely than the losses we have sustained: you killed our vassal Frollo[1] and illegally occupied France. Therefore, since you are not afraid of Rome nor its great power, the Senate summons and orders you—for the summons is an order—to come before it in mid-August, ready, at whatever cost, to make full restitution of what you have taken from them. And thus you will give satisfaction for the wrongs of which we accuse you. But if you delay in any fashion to do what I command you, I will cross the Alps with an army and will deprive you of Britain and France. But I can't imagine that you will await my coming or will defend France against me. I don't think you will dare to face me on this side of the Channel. And even if you stay over there, you will never await my coming. You won't know a place to hide where I won't flush you out. I'll lead you to Rome in chains and hand you over to the Senate."

At these words there was a great uproar, and all were greatly enraged. You could have heard the Britons shouting loudly, calling God as witness and swearing by his name that they were going to punish the messengers. They would have showered them with abuse and insults, but the king rose to his feet and called out to them, "Silence! Silence! Don't lay a hand on these men. They are messengers; they have a master, they are bringing his message; they can say whatever they like. No one shall do them the slightest harm."

When the noise quieted down and the retainers recovered their composure, the king ordered his dukes and counts and his personal advisers to accompany him to a stone tower called the Giant Tower. There he wanted to seek advice on what to reply to the messengers. Side by side the barons and counts were already mounting the stairs, when Cador, the duke of Cornwall, with a smile spoke to the king, who was in front of him, as follows: "I've been afraid," he said, "and have often thought that leisure and peace might spoil the Britons, for leisure is conducive to bad habits and causes many a man to become lazy. Leisure diminishes prowess, leisure promotes lechery, leisure kindles clandestine love affairs. Through prolonged repose and leisure youth gets preoccupied with entertainment and pleasure and backgammon and other games of diversion. By staying put and resting for a long time, we could lose our reputation. Well, we've been asleep, but God has given us a little wake-up call—let us thank him for encouraging the Romans to challenge our country and the others we have conquered. Should the Romans find it in themselves to carry out what they say in that letter, the Britons will still retain their reputation for valor and strength. I never like peace for long, nor shall I love a peace that lasts a long time."

"My lord," said Gawain, "in faith, you're getting upset over nothing. Peace after war is a good thing. The land is better and more beautiful on account of it. It's very good to amuse oneself and to make love. It's for love and for their ladies that knights perform chivalrous deeds."

While bantering in this way, they entered the tower and took their seats. When Arthur saw them sitting down and waiting in silence with full attention, he paused for a moment in thought, then raised his head and spoke:

"Barons," he said, "you who are here, my companions and friends, you have stood by me in good times and bad; you have supported me when I had

---

1. Roman governor of France.

to go to war; you have taken my part whether I won or lost; you have been partners in my loss, and in my gain when I conquered. Thanks to you and your help, I have won many a victory. I have led you through many dangers by land and by sea, in places near and far. I have found you loyal in action and in counsel. I have tested your mettle many times and always found it good. Thanks to you the neighboring countries are subject to me. You have heard the Romans' order, the tenor of the letter, and the overbearingness and arrogance of their demands. They have provoked and threatened us enough, but if God protects us, we shall do away with the Romans. They are rich and have great power, and now we must carefully consider what we can properly and reasonably say and do. Trouble is dealt with better when a strategy has been worked out in advance. If someone sees the arrow in flight, he must get out of the way or shield himself. That is how we must proceed. The Romans want to shoot at us, and we must get ready so that they cannot wound us. They demand tribute from Britain and must have it, so they tell us; they demand the same from the other islands and from France.

"But first I shall reply how matters stand with regard to Britain. They claim that Caesar conquered it; Caesar was a powerful man and carried out his will by force. The Britons could not defend themselves against him, and he exacted tribute from them by force. But might is not right; it is force and superior power. A man does not possess by right what he has taken by force. Therefore, we are allowed to keep by right what they formerly took by force. They have held up to us the damages, losses, humiliations, the sufferings and fears that they inflicted on our ancestors. They boasted that they conquered them and extorted tribute and rents from them. We have all the more right to make them suffer; they have all the more restitution to make to us. We ought to hate those who hated our ancestors and to injure those who injured them. They remind us that they made them suffer, got tribute from them, and demand tribute from us. They want us to suffer the same shame and extortion as our ancestors. They once got tribute from Britain, and so they want to get it from us. By the same reason and with equal cause we can challenge the Romans and dispute our rights. Belinus, who was king of the Britons, and Brennus,[2] duke of the Burgundians, two brothers born in Britain, valiant and wise knights, marched on Rome, laid siege to the city, and took it by assault. They hanged twenty-four hostages in plain sight of their families. When Belinus returned from Rome, he entrusted the city to his brother.

"I won't dwell on Belinus and Brennus but will speak of Constantine. He was British by birth, the son of Helen; he held Rome in his own right. Maximian, king of Britain, conquered France and Germany, crossed the Alps and Lombardy and reigned over Rome. These were my ancestors by direct descent, and each one held Rome in his possession. Now you may hear and understand that we have just as much right to possess Rome as they do to possess Britain. The Romans had our tribute, and my ancestors had theirs.

---

2. Brennus was not a Briton but a Gaulish chieftain who sacked Rome in the 4th century. Belinus is fictional. Constantine I, who adopted Christianity as the official religion of the Roman Empire, was believed to be British. Maximian (Maximus) was a 5th-century Roman general serving in Britain who abandoned the island when his army proclaimed him emperor and usurped the imperium in civil wars that weakened Rome and left Britain at the mercy of attacks by the Picts, Scots, and Germanic tribes. Geoffrey of Monmouth's earlier accounts of these personages had conflated a tiny amount of fact with a great deal of fiction.

They claim Britain, and I claim Rome. This is the gist of my counsel: that they may have the land and tribute who can take it away from another. As for France and the other lands we have taken from them, they have no right to dispute them since they would not or could not defend them, or perhaps had no right to them because they held them in bondage through force and greed. So let him who can hold all. There is no need to look for any other kind of right. The emperor threatens us. God forbid that he should do us any harm. He says that he will take away our lands and lead me to Rome as a prisoner. He has small regard or fear of me. But, God willing, if he comes to this land, before he leaves again he'll have no stomach to make threats. He defies me, and I defy him: may he possess the lands who is able to take them!"

When King Arthur had spoken what he wanted to his barons, the others spoke in turn while the rest listened. Hoël, king of Brittany, spoke next: "Sire," he said, "in faith, you have spoken many just words; none could have said it better. Send after and mobilize your forces along with us who are here at court. Without delay pass over the sea, pass through Burgundy and France, pass the Alps, conquer Lombardy! Throw the emperor who is defying you into confusion and panic so that he will not have the chance to cause you harm. The Romans have begun a suit that will ruin them. God wants to exalt you: don't hold back and lose any time! Make yourself master of the empire, which is ready to surrender to you of its own will. Remember what is written in the Sibyl's prophecies.[3] Three Britons will be born in Britain who shall conquer Rome by might. Two have already lived and been sovereigns over Rome. The first was Belinus and the second, Constantine. You shall be the third to possess Rome and conquer it by force; in you the Sibyl's prophecy will be fulfilled. Why delay to seize that which God wants to bestow on you? Increase your glory and ours to which we aspire. We may say truly that we are not afraid of blows or wounds or death or hardship or prison so long as we strive for honor. As long as you are in danger, I will lead ten thousand armed knights in your host, and if that should not be enough, I shall mortgage all my lands and give you the gold and silver. I won't keep back a farthing so long as you have need of it!"

3. Reference to the Sibylline books containing prophecies of the Roman Sibyl of Cumae, but these no longer existed and could have been known only by reputation. This prophecy was probably invented by Geoffrey of Monmouth.

LAYAMON

Layamon, an English priest, adapted Wace's *Roman de Brut* into Middle English alliterative verse. His *Brut* (ca. 1190) runs to 16,095 lines, expanding on Wace and adding much new material.

After winning the continental campaign against Lucius, Arthur is forced to return to Britain upon learning that his nephew, Mordred, whom he had left behind as regent, has usurped Arthur's throne and queen. The following selection, a passage added by Layamon, presents Arthur's dream of Mordred's treachery.

Layamon employs a long alliterative line that harks back to Old English poetry, but the two halves of his line are often linked by rhyme as well as by alliteration. Layamon reveals his ties with Germanic literary tradition in other ways. In Arthur's nightmare, the king and Gawain are sitting astride the roof beam of a building like the mead hall Heorot in *Beowulf*—a symbol of the control a king wields over his house and kingdom. On the ground below, Mordred is chopping away at the foundations like the gigantic rodent in Norse mythology that is gnawing away at the roots of Yggdrasil, the great tree, which holds together earth, heaven, and hell.

From Brut

[ARTHUR'S DREAM]

Then came to pass what Merlin spoke of long before,
13965   That the walls of Rome would fall down before Arthur;
This had already happened there in relation to the emperor
Who had fallen in the fighting with fifty thousand men:
That's when Rome with her power was pushed to the ground.
   And so Arthur really expected to possess all of Rome,
13970   And the most mighty of kings remained there in Burgundy.
   Now there arrived at this time a bold man on horseback;
News he was bringing for Arthur the king
From Modred, his sister's son: to Arthur he was welcome,
For he thought that he was bringing very pleasant tidings.
13975   Arthur lay there all that long night, talking with the young knight,
Who simply did not like to tell him the truth of what had happened.
The next day, as dawn broke, the household started moving,
And then Arthur got up, and, stretching his arms,
He stood up, and sat down again, as if he felt very sick.
Then a good knight questioned him: "My Lord, how did you get on
13980   last night?"
Arthur responded (his heart was very heavy):
"Tonight as I was sleeping, where I was lying in my chamber,
There came to me a dream which has made me most depressed:
I dreamed someone had lifted me right on top of some hall
13985   And I was sitting on the hall, astride, as if I was going riding;
All the lands which I possess, all of them I was surveying,
And Gawain sat in front of me, holding in his hands my sword.
Then Modred came marching there with a countless host of men,
Carrying in his hand a massive battle-axe.
13990   He started to hew, with horrible force,
And hacked down all the posts which were holding up the hall.
I saw Guinevere there as well, the woman I love best of all:
The whole roof of that enormous hall with her hands she was
      pulling down;
The hall started tottering, and I tumbled to the ground,
13995   And broke my right arm, at which Modred said 'Take that!'
Down then fell the hall and Gawain fell as well,
Falling on the ground where both his arms were broken,
So with my left hand I clutched my beloved sword
And struck off Modred's head and it went rolling over the ground,
14000   And I sliced the queen in pieces with my beloved sword,

And after that I dropped her into a dingy pit.
And all my fine subjects set off in flight,
And what in Christendom became of them I had no idea,
Except that I was standing by myself in a vast plain,
14005 And then I started roaming all around across the moors;
There I could see griffins and really gruesome birds.
   "Then a golden lioness came gliding over the downs,
As really lovely a beast as any Our Lord has made.
The lioness ran up to me and put her jaws around my waist,
14010 And off she set, moving away towards the sea,
And I could see the waves, tossing in the sea,
And taking me with her, the lioness plunged into the water.
When we two were in the sea, the waves swept her away from me;
Then a fish came swimming by and ferried me ashore.
14015 Then I was all wet and weary, and I was sick with sorrow.
And upon waking, I started quaking,
And then I started to shudder as if burning up with fire,
And so all night I've been preoccupied with my disturbing dream,
For I know of a certainty this is the end of my felicity,
14020 And all the rest of my life I must suffer grief.
O alas that I do not have here my queen with me, my Guinevere!"
   Then the knight responded: "My Lord, you are mistaken;
Dreams should never be interpreted as harbingers of sorrow!
You are the most mighty prince who has rule in any land,
14025 And the most intelligent of all inhabitants on the earth.
If it should have happened—as may Our Lord not allow it—
That your sister's son, Lord Modred, your own queen might have
    wedded,
And all your royal domains might have annexed in his own name,
Those which you entrusted to him when you intended going to
    Rome,
14030 And if he should have done all this by his treacherous deeds,
Even then you might avenge yourself honorably with arms,
And once again possess your lands and rule over your people,
And destroy your enemies who wish you so much evil,
And slay them, every one alive, so that there is none who survives!"
14035   Then Arthur answered him, most excellent of all kings:
"For as long as is for ever, I have no fear whatever,
That Modred who is my relative, the man I love best,
Would betray all my trust, not for all of my realm,
Nor would Guinevere, my queen, weaken in her allegiance,
14040 She will not begin to, for any man in the world!"
Immediately after these words, the knight gave his answer:
"I am telling you the truth, dear king, for I am merely your
    underling:
Modred has done these things: he has adopted your queen,
And has placed in his own hands your lovely land;
14045 He is king and she is queen; they don't expect your return,
For they don't believe it will be the case that you'll ever come back
    from Rome.
I am your loyal liegeman, and I did see this treason,
And so I have come to you in person to tell you the truth.

Let my head be as pledge of what I have told you,
14050　The truth and no lie, about your beloved queen,
And about Modred, your sister's son, and how he has snatched
　　Britain from you."
Then everything went still in King Arthur's hall;
There was great unhappiness for the excellent king,
And because of it the British men were utterly depressed;
14055　Then after a while came the sound of a voice;
All over could be heard the reactions of the British
As they started to discuss in many kinds of expression
How they wished to condemn Modred and the queen
And destroy all the population who had supported Modred.
14060　Most courteous of all Britons, Arthur then called out aloud,
"Sit down quietly, my knights in this assembly,
And then I shall tell you some very strange tales.
Now tomorrow when daylight is sent by our Lord to us,
I wish to be on my way toward entering Britain,
14065　And there I shall kill Modred and burn the queen to death,
And I shall destroy all of them who gave assent to the treason."

MARIE DE FRANCE

Much of twelfth-century French literature was composed in England in the Anglo-Norman dialect (see pp. 6–7). Prominent among the earliest poets writing in the French vernacular, who shaped the genres, themes, and styles of later medieval European poetry, is the author who, in an epilogue to her *Fables*, calls herself Marie de France. That signature tells us only that her given name was Marie and that she was born in France, but circumstantial evidence from her writings shows that she spent much of her life in England. A reference to her in a French poem written in England around 1180 speaks of "dame Marie" who wrote "lais" much loved and praised, read, and heard by counts, barons, and knights and indicates that her poems also appealed to ladies who listened to them gladly and joyfully.

Three works can be safely attributed to Marie, probably written in the following order: the *Lais* [English "lay" refers to a short narrative poem in verse], the *Fables*, and *St. Patrick's Purgatory*. Marie's twelve lays are short romances (they range from 118 to 1,184 lines), each of which deals with a single event or crisis in the affairs of noble lovers. In her prologue, Marie tells us that she had heard these *performed*, and in several of the lays she refers to the Breton language and Breton storytellers—that is, professional minstrels from the French province of Brittany or the Celtic parts of Great Britain. Because no sources of Marie's stories have survived, it is not possible to determine the exact nature of the materials she worked from, but they were probably oral and were presented with the accompaniment of a stringed instrument. Marie's lays provide the basis of the genre that came to be known as the "Breton lay." In the prologue Marie dedicates the work to a "noble king," who is most likely to have been Henry II of England, who reigned from 1154 to 1189.

The portrait of the author that emerges from the combination of these works is of a highly educated noblewoman, proficient in Latin and English as well as her native French, with ideas of her own and a strong commitment to writing. Scholars have proposed several Maries of the period who fit this description to identify the author. A likely candidate is Marie, abbess of Shaftesbury, an illegitimate daughter of Geoffrey of Anjou and thus half-sister of Henry II. Correct or not, such an identification points to the milieu in which Marie moved and to the kind of audience she was addressing.

Many of Marie's lays contain elements of magic and mystery. Medieval readers would recognize that *Lanval* is about a mortal lover and a fairy bride, although the word "fairy" is not used in the tale. In the Middle Ages fairies were not thought of as the small creatures they became in Elizabethan and later literature. Fairies are supernatural, sometimes dangerous, beings who possess magical powers and inhabit another world. Their realm in some respects resembles the human (fairies have kings and queens), and fairies generally keep to themselves and disappear when humans notice them. But the tales are often about crossovers between the human and fairy worlds. Chaucer's *Wife of Bath's Tale* is such a story. In *Lanval* the female fairy world eclipses King Arthur's chivalric court (which Marie had read about in Wace's *Roman de Brut*) in splendor, riches, and generosity.

With Chrétien de Troyes, Marie is among the twelfth-century writers who made love the means of analyzing the individual's relation to his or her society. The only woman writer known to be among the creators of this literature, Marie explores both female and male desire. Her lays portray different kinds of love relationships, both favorably and unfavorably, with both happy and tragic resolutions. They resist reduction to a pattern.

Two Middle English versions of Marie's *Lanval* exist, but we prefer to offer a modern verse translation of the original. Marie wrote in eight-syllable couplets, which was the standard form of French narrative verse, employed also by Wace and Chrétien de Troyes. Here is what the beginning of Marie's prologue to the *Lais* says about her view of a writer's duty and, implicitly, of her own talent:

Ki Deu ad duné escïence	He to whom God has given knowledge
E de parler bon' eloquence	And the gift of speaking eloquently,
Ne s'en deit taisir ne celer,	Must not keep silent nor conceal the gift,
Ainz se deit volunters mustrer.	But he must willingly display it.

Lanval[1]

> Another lay to you I'll tell,
> Of the adventure that befell
> A noble vassal whom they call
> In the Breton tongue Lanval.
> 5   Arthur, the brave and courtly king,
> At Carlisle was sojourning
> Because the Scots and Picts allied
> Were ravaging the countryside;
> Of Logres° they had crossed the border   *Arthur's kingdom*
> 10 Where often they caused great disorder.
>   He had come there with his host
> That spring to hold the Pentecost.

1. The translation is by Alfred David and is based on *Marie de France: Lais*, edited by Alfred Ewert (1947).

He lavished ample patronage
On all his noble baronage—
15 That is the knights of the Round Table
(In all the world none are so able).
Lands and wives he gave outright
To all his servants save one knight:
That was Lanval; him he forgot.
20 His men disliked him, too; the lot
Were envious of his handsomeness,
His strength, his courage, his largesse.
There were a few who friendship feigned,
But would by no means have complained
25 Had Lanval met some evil fate.
He was a prince of great estate,
But all his personal property
He gave away for amity,
And he got nothing from the king,
30 Nor would he ask for anything.
Now Lanval is much preoccupied,
Gloomy, seeing the darker side.
My lords, please do not think it rare:
A foreigner is filled with care
35 And sadness in a distant land,
Finding no help at any hand.
The knight of whom I'm telling you,
In the king's service tried and true,
Mounting upon his steed one day,
40 For pleasure's sake set on his way.
Outside the town he went to ride
Alone into the countryside.
He got off by a running brook,
But there his horse trembled and shook.
45 He unlaced the saddle, set it free,
And let it ramble on the lee.
He folded up his riding gown
To make a pillow and lay down.
Much troubled by his luck's declining,
50 He can't see any silver lining.
There as he lay without a clue,
Two damoiselles hove into view,
The fairest he had ever eyed,
Riding along the riverside.
55 Their clothes were in expensive taste,
Close-fitting tunics, tightly laced,
Made of deep-dyed purple wool.
Their faces were most beautiful.
The elder bore a well-made pair
60 Of basins; of purest gold they were.
My lords, I swear that I'm not lying!
The other held a towel for drying.
The two of them went straightaway
Right to the spot where the knight lay.

65 Lanval, the soul of courtesy,
  Rose to his feet immediately.
  They greeted him first by his name
  And told the reason why they came.
  "Sir Lanval, our damoiselle,
70 Who is so worthy, wise, and *belle*,[2]
  Dispatched us to come after you,
  For she has come here with us, too.
  We shall bring you safely to her:
  See, her pavillion's over there."
75 The knight followed without regard
  For the horse left grazing on the sward.
  The tent to which they bring the knight
  Was fairly pitched, a beauteous sight.
  Not Queen Semiramis of yore,
80 Had she been owner of even more
  Wealth, power, and *savoir*,°   *wisdom, know-how*
  Nor Octavian, the emperor,
  Could have afforded to pay for
  The right-hand flap of the front door.
85 On top was set an eagle of gold,
  The cost of which cannot be told,
  Nor of the cords and poles which brace
  That structure and hold it in place.
  No earthly king could own this tent
90 For any treasure that he spent.
  Inside the tent the maiden was:
  Not rose nor lily could surpass
  Her beauty when they bloom in May.
  The sumptuous bed on which she lay
95 Was beautiful. The drapes and tassel,
  Sheets and pillows were worth a castle.
  The single gown she wore was sheer
  And made her shapely form appear.
  She'd thrown, in order to keep warm,
100 An ermine stole over her arm,
  White fur with the lining dyed
  Alexandrian purple. But her side,
  Her face, her neck, her bosom
  Showed whiter than the hawthorn blossom.
105 The knight moved toward the bed's head.
  She asked him to sit down and said,
  "Lanval, fair friend, for you I've come,
  For you I've traveled far from home.
  If you are brave and courteous,
110 You'll be more glad and prosperous
  Than ever was emperor or king,
  For I love you over everything."
  Her loveliness transfixed his gaze.

2. Beautiful. Several words and phrases are in French, partly for the sake of rhyme but also as an indication of the great influence that the French language exercised on English. Most of these words can be found in a modern English dictionary.

Love pierced his eyes with its bright rays,
115 Set fire to and scorched his heart.
He gave fair answer on his part.
"Lady," he said, "if this should be
Your wish (and such joy meant for me),
To have me for your paramour,
120 There's no command, you may be sure,
Wise or foolish, what you will,
Which I don't promise to fulfill.
I'll follow only your behest.
For you I'll give up all the rest."
125 When the lady heard him say
That he would love her in this way,
She bestowed on him her heart
And her body, every part.
Now Lanval is on easy street!
130 Whatever his needs are she will meet:
As a gift to him she granted
He should get whatever he wanted—
Money, as fast as he can spend it,
No matter how much, she will send it.
135 The more largesse he gives, the more
Gold and silver in his store.
Now Sir Lanval is harbored well.
To him then spoke the damoiselle:
"Ami,"[3] she said, "please understand,
140 I warn and pray you and command:
You must never tell anyone
About the love that you have won.
The consequence I shall declare:
Should people learn of this affair,
145 You shall never again see me,
Nor have my body in your fee."
He promised her that he would do
Whatever thing she told him to.
He lay beside her on the bed:
150 Now is Lanval well bestead.
He stayed with her all afternoon
Until it would be evening soon
And gladly would have stayed all night
Had she consented that he might.
155 But she told him, "Rise up, Ami.
You may no longer stay with me.
Get on your way; I shall remain.
But one thing I will tell you plain:
When you would like to talk to me
160 At any rendezvous that's free
Of blame or of unseemliness,
Where one his true love may possess,
I shall attend you at your will

---

3. Literally "friend," but used as a term of endearment for a lover. The feminine form is *amie*.

All your wishes to fulfill."
165 These words gave him great happiness.
He kissed her, then got up to dress.
The damsels who had brought him there
Gave him expensive clothes to wear.
This world has no such comely squire
170 As Lanval in his new attire.
He was no simpleton or knave.
Water to wash his hands they gave,
Also the towel with which he dried,
And next he was with food supplied.
175 His love ate supper with Lanval,
A thing he did not mind at all.
They served him with great courtesy,
Which he accepted with much glee.
There were many special dishes
180 That the knight found most delicious.
And many times the gallant knight
Kissed his love and held her tight.
After they had cleared the table,
They fetched his horse out of the stable,
185 Harnessed just as it should be.
He had been served luxuriously.
He took his leave, mounted the horse,
And toward town he held his course,
Oftentimes looking to his rear.
190 Lanval was very much in fear
As he went thinking about the maiden,
And his heart with doubts was laden.
What to believe he's all astir;
He thinks he's seen the last of her.
195 Arrived back home, Sir Lanval sees
His men dressed in new liveries.
That night the lavish host he plays,
But no one knows from whence he pays.
In town there is no *chevalier*[4]
200 Who badly needs a place to stay
Whom Lanval doesn't make his guest
And serves him richly of the best.
Lanval gives expensive presents;
Lanval remits the captive's sentence;
205 Lanval puts minstrels in new dress;
Lanval does honors in excess.
There's no stranger nor private friend
On whom Lanval does not spend.
He lives in joy and in delight,
210 Whether it be by day or night.
He sees his lady often, and
Has all the world at his command.
    That same summer, I would say,

---

4. Knight. Rhymes with -*ay* in French pronunciation.

After the feast of St. John's Day,
215 Thirty knights made an excursion,
For the sake of their diversion,
To a garden beneath the tower
In which the queen had her bower.
Among that party was Gawain
220 And his cousin, the good Yvain.
Sir Gawain spoke, brave and sincere,
Whom everybody held so dear,
"By God, my lords, we've not done right
By our companion, that good knight—
225 Lanval, so free, courtly, and loyal,
Son of a king who's rich and royal—
To leave that nobleman behind."
And straightway they turn back and find
Sir Lanval at his residence
230 And beg that they might take him thence.
    From a window with fine molding
The queen herself leaned out beholding
(Waited on by damsels three)
King Arthur's festive company.
235 She gazed at Lanval and knew him well.
She called out to one damoiselle
And sent her for her maids-in-waiting,
The fairest and most captivating.
With her into the garden then
240 They went to relax with the men.
Thirty she took along and more,
Down the stairs and out the door.
Rejoiced to have the ladies meet them,
The *chevaliers* advance to greet them.
245 Each girl by a knight's hand is led:
Such pleasant talk is not ill-bred.
Lanval goes off alone and turns
Aside from all the rest. He yearns
To hold his love within his arms,
250 To kiss, embrace, and feel her charms.
The joy of others is less pleasant
To him, his own not being present.
When she perceives him stand alone,
The queen straightway to him has gone
255 To sit beside him and reveals
All the passion that she feels:
"Lanval, I've honored you sincerely,
Have cherished you and loved you dearly.
All my love is at your disposal.
260 What do you say to my proposal?
Your mistress I consent to be;
You should receive much joy from me."
"Lady," he said, "hold me excused
Because your love must be refused.
265 I've served the king for many a day;

My faith to him I won't betray.
Never for love, and not for you,
Would I be to my lord untrue."
Made angry by these words, the queen
270 Insultingly expressed her spleen.
"Lanval," she said, "It's evident
That to such pleasures you have no bent.
Often I have heard men aver
That women are not what you prefer.
275 But you have many pretty boys
With whom you like to take your joys.
Faithless coward of low degree,
My lord was badly served when he
Suffered your person to come near.
280 For that he could lose God, I fear."
   Hearing this, Lanval was dismayed;
His answer was not long delayed.
With spite, as he was much upset,
He spoke what soon he would regret.
285 "My lady queen," was his retort,
"I know nothing about that sport.
But I love one, and she loves me;
From every woman I know of, she
Deserves to bear the prize away.
290 And one more thing I wish to say,
So that you may know it plain:
Each serving-maid in her domain,
The poorest girl of the whole crew,
My lady, is worth more than you
295 In beauty of both figure and face,
In good breeding and bounteous grace."
In tears the queen at once repairs
Back to her chamber up the stairs.
Dolorous she is and mortified
300 To be by him thus villified.
She goes to bed where sick she lies,
Vowing never again to rise,
Unless the king grants her redress
For that which caused her such distress.
305   The king had come back from the wood
Cheerful because the day was good.
To the queen's bedroom he attained;
As soon as she saw him, she complained.
Fallen at his feet, she cried, "*Merci!*[5]
310 Lanval has done me infamy."
To be her lover he had affected.
When his advances were rejected,
He had reviled her shamefully
And boasted he had an *amie*
315 So chic, noble, and proud, he said,

---

5. Exclamation appealing for compassion and favor.

That even her lowliest chambermaid,
The poorest one that might be seen,
Was worthier than she—the queen.
The king grew marvelously wroth,
320 And solemnly he swore an oath:
Unless the knight proved what he'd boasted,
The king would have him hanged or roasted.
Leaving the chamber, the king then
Summoned three of his noblemen.
325 After Lanval they were to go,
Who, feeling enough of grief and woe,
Had returned to his habitation,
Well aware of his situation.
Since he had told of their *amour*,
330 He had lost his love for sure.
In his room alone he languished,
Melancholy and sorely anguished.
He calls his love time and again,
But all his pleadings are in vain.
335 Sighs he utters and complaints,
And from time to time he faints.
A hundred times he cries *merci*
And begs her speak to her *ami*.
He curses both his heart and tongue;
340 A wonder 'tis he lives so long
Without committing suicide.
However much he roared and cried,
Fought with himself and scratched his face,
She would not show him any grace—
345 Even to see her once again.
Alas, how can he bear the pain?
   The king's men have arrived to say
He must to court without delay.
The king had summoned him for this reason:
350 The queen had charged the knight with treason.
Lanval went with them very sadly.
Should he be killed, he'd bear it gladly.
The knight was brought before the king,
Grief-stricken, not saying anything,
355 Like someone in great misery.
The king spoke out indignantly:
"Vassal, you've done lèse-majesté.[6]
You have begun a churlish play,
Me to dishonor and demean
360 And to speak slander of the queen.
It was a foolish boast to call
Your love the noblest one of all,
And her servant—to declare her
Worthier than the queen and fairer.
365   Lanval protested, word for word,

6. Treason against the highest authority.

Any dishonor done to his lord
Respecting the queen's accusation
Of a guilty solicitation.
But of his speech—to give her due—
370 He confessed that it was true.
The mistress he had boasted of
He mourned, for he had lost her love.
Regarding that, he said he'd do
Whatever the court told him to.
375 This put the king in a great fury.
He summoned his knights to act as jury
To tell how to proceed by law
So none might catch him in a flaw.[7]
They obeyed him—the entire lot,
380 Whether they wanted to or not.
They met together to consult
And deemed and judged with this result:
A court day set, Lanval goes free
But must find pledges to guarantee
385 His lord that judgment he'll abide,
Return to court and there be tried
By Arthur's entire baronage,
Not just the palace entourage.[8]
Back to the king the barons bring
390 The judgment of their parleying.
The king demands his sureties,
Thus putting Lanval ill at ease.
A foreigner, he felt chagrin
Since he had neither friend nor kin.
395 Gawain stepped forth and pledged that he
Would stand as Lanval's surety.
And his companions in succession
Each one made the same profession.
The king replied, "He's in your hands
400 At risk to forfeit all your lands
And fiefs, whatever they may be,
Which each of you obtained from me."
The pledges made, the court adjourned,
And Lanval to his place returned.
405 The knights escort him on his way.
They blame and warn him, and they say
To shun excessive melancholy;
And they lay curses on love's folly.
Worried about his mental state,
410 Each day they go investigate
Whether he's taking nourishment
Or to himself is violent.

7. The trial of Lanval shows precise knowledge of 12th-century legal procedure concerning the respective rights of the king and his barons. So as not to violate baronial rights, Arthur asks the knights of his household to determine the proper ways to proceed against one of their own.
8. The case is important enough to require judgment by all of Arthur's vassals, not just the immediate household. Hence the delay of the trial.

On the day that had been set,
All King Arthur's barons met.
415 Attending were the king and queen;
Pledges brought Lanval on the scene.
They were all sad on his account—
A hundred of them I could count
Who would have done their best to see
420 Him without trial go scot-free,
For he'd been wrongfully arraigned.
On the charge, the king maintained,
And his response, he must be tried:
And now the barons must decide.
425 To the judgment they go next
Greatly worried and perplexed,
Since the noble foreign guest
In their midst is so hard-pressed.
Some were willing to condemn
430 To oblige their sovereign.
The Duke of Cornwall counselled thus:
"No fault shall be ascribed to us:
Though some may weep and some may play,
Justice must take its lawful way.
435 A vassal by the king denounced,
Whose name—"Lanval"—I heard pronounced,
Has been accused of felony
And charged that mischievously he
To a mistress had pretended
440 And Madame the Queen offended.
By the faith I owe you duly,
In this case, should one speak truly,
The king being the sole adversary,
No defense were necessary,
445 Save for the sake of his lord's name
A man must never speak him shame.
Sir Lanval by his oath must stand,
And the king quitclaim our land,
If the knight can guarantee
450 The coming here of his *amie*.
Should it prove true what he has claimed,
By which the queen felt so defamed,
Of that he'll be judged innocent,
Since he spoke without base intent.
455 But if he cannot prove it so,
In that case we must let him know,
All the king's service he must lose
And banished say his last adieus.
The knight was sent the court's decree
460 And informed by them that he
Must summon his *amie* and send her
To be his witness and defender.
The knight responded that he could not:
To his rescue come she would not.

465 To the judges they made report
That he looked for no support.
The king pressed them to make an ending
And not to keep the queen attending.
    When they came to lay down the law,
470 Two maidens from afar they saw
On two fine steeds, riding apace,
Who were extremely fair of face.
Of purple taffeta a sheath
They wore with nothing underneath.
475 The men took pleasure in the view.
Sir Gawain and three of his crew
Went to Sir Lanval to report
And show the girls coming to court.
Happy, he asked him earnestly
480 If one of them were his *amie*.
He told them that he knew not who
They were, where from, or going to.
The damoiselles rode on withal
Upon their mounts into the hall,
485 And they got off before the dais
There where the king sat at his place.
Their features were of beauty rare;
Their form of speech was debonair:
"King, clear your chambers, if you please,
490 And hang them with silk draperies,
Where my lady may make arrest,
For she wishes to be your guest.
The king gladly gave his consent.
Two of his courtiers he sent
495 To show them to their rooms upstairs.
No more was said of these affairs.
    The king ordered his retinue
To render up their judgment due.
The long procrastination had,
500 He said, made him extremely mad.
"My lord," they answered, "we have acted.
But our attention was distracted
By those ladies we have seen.
But now the court shall reconvene."
505 They reassembled much perturbed,
By too much noise and strife disturbed.
    While they engaged in this debate,
Two damoiselles of high estate—
In silks produced in Phrygia,
510 On mules from Andalusia—
Came riding up the street just then.
This gave great joy to Arthur's men,
Who told each other this must be
The worthy Lanval's remedy.
515 To him there hastened Sir Gawain
With his companions in his train.

"Sir knight," he said, "be of good cheer.
For God's sake speak to us! See here,
Two maidens are approaching us,
520   Most beautiful and decorous;
Surely one must be your *amie.*"
Lanval made answer hastily.
He said that he recognized neither.
He didn't know or love them either.
525   Meanwhile the damoiselles had gone
And dismounted before the throne
Where the king was sitting on the dais.
From many there they won great praise
For figure, visage, and complexion.
530   They came much nearer to perfection
Than did the queen, so people said.
The elder was courteous and well-bred.
She spoke her message with much flair:
"King, tell your household to prepare
535   A suite to lodge my lady, who
Is coming here to speak with you."
The king had them conducted where
His men had lodged the previous pair.
As soon as they were from him gone,
540   He told his barons to have done
And give their verdict right away.
There had been far too much delay;
The queen had found it most frustrating
That they so long had kept her waiting.
545   When they were just about to bring
Judgment, a girl was entering
The town, whose beauty, it was clear,
In all the world could have no peer.
She rode upon a milkwhite horse,
550   Which bore her gently down the course.
Its neck and head were shapeliest;
Of all creatures, it was the best.
Splendidly furnished was this mount:
Beneath the heavens, no king or count
555   Could have afforded gear so grand
Unless he sold or pawned his land.
And this is how she was arrayed:
A white linen shift displayed—
There where it was with laces tied—
560   Her slender flanks on either side.
Slim-hipped, her form was *comme il faut;*[9]
Her neck, whiter than branch in snow;
Her eyes were gray; her face was bright;
Her mouth, lovely; nose, set just right;
565   Eyebrows black, forehead fair;
Blonde and curly was her hair.

9. As required, perfectly correct.

Golden wire sheds no such ray
As did her locks against the day.
A mantle was around her drawn,
570 A cloak of deep-dyed purple lawn.
A falcon on her wrist sat still;
A greyhound followed her at will.
In town was neither high nor low,
Old man or child, who did not go
575 And line the streets along the way
To watch as she made her entrée.
And as they stood gazing at her,
Her beauty was no laughing matter.
She rode up to the castle slowly.
580 The judges, seeing her, were wholly
Astonished at that spectacle
And held it for a miracle.
The heart of every single knight
Among them warmed with sheer delight.
585 Those who loved Sir Lanval well
Quickly went to him to tell
About the maiden who perchance,
Please God, brought him deliverance.
"Comrade," they said, "here comes one,
590 Who is neither swart nor dun.
Of all women by land and sea,
She is the fairest that may be.
Lanval heard and raised his eye;
He knew her well and gave a sigh.
595 The blood shot up into his cheeks,
And somewhat hastily he speaks:
"In faith," he said, "that's my *amie*!
Now I don't care if they kill me
If but her mercy is assured,
600 For when I see her, I am cured."
The maid rode through the palace door,
So fair came never there before.
In front of Arthur she got down
With the whole company looking on.
605 Softly she let her mantle fall,
The better to be seen by all.
King Arthur, who was most discreet,
To greet her got up on his feet.
In turn, to honor her the rest
610 Offered their service to the guest.
When they had satisfied their gaze
And greatly sung her beauty's praise,
She made her speech in such a way
As she did not intend to stay:
615 "King, I have loved one of your band—
It's Lanval, there you see him stand.
I would not have the man ill-used—
In your court he has been accused

Of lies he spoke. Take it from me,
620 The queen committed perjury;
He never asked her for her love.
As for the things he boasted of,
If I may be his warranty,
Your barons ought to speak him free."
625 The king agreed he would abide
By what they lawfully decide.
Among them there was no dissent;
Lanval was pronounced innocent.
The damoiselle set off again,
630 Though the king asked her to remain.
Outside there stood a marble rock
With steps to make a mounting block,
From which armed men would get astride
When they from court set out to ride.
635 Lanval climbed up on it before
The damoiselle rode out the door.
Swiftly he sprang the horse to straddle
And sat behind her on the saddle.
To Avalon they came away,
640 Which Breton storytellers say
An island is, most ravishing,
There Lanval has gone, vanishing.
No man has heard more of his fate;
I've nothing further to relate.
                              FINIS

Middle English Literature in the Fourteenth and Fifteenth Centuries

SIR GAWAIN AND THE GREEN KNIGHT
ca. 1375–1400

The finest Arthurian romance in English survives in only one manuscript, which also contains three religious poems—*Pearl, Patience,* and *Purity*—generally believed to be by the same poet. Nothing is known about the author except what can be inferred from the works. The dialect of the poems locates them in a remote corner of the northwest midlands between Cheshire and Staffordshire, and details of Sir Gawain's journey north show that the author was familiar with the geography of that region. But if author and audience were provincials, *Sir Gawain* and the other poems in the manuscript reveal them to have been highly sophisticated and well acquainted both with the international culture of the high Middle Ages and with ancient native traditions.

Sir Gawain belongs to the so-called Alliterative Revival. After the Norman Conquest, alliterative verse doubtless continued to be recited by oral poets. At the beginning, the *Gawain* poet pretends that this romance is an oral poem and asks the audience to "listen" to a story, which he has "heard." Alliterative verse also continued to appear in Early Middle English texts. Layamon's *Brut* (see pp. 102–04) is the outstanding example. During the late fourteenth century there was a renewed flowering of alliterative poetry, especially in the north and west of Britain, which includes *Piers Plowman* and a splendid poem known as *The Alliterative Morte Darthur*.

The *Gawain* poet's audience evidently valued the kind of alliterative verse that Chaucer's Parson caricatures as "Rum-Ram-Ruf by lettre" (see p. 275, line 43). They would also have understood archaic poetic diction surviving from Old English poetry such as *athel* (noble) and words of Scandinavian origin such as *skete* (quickly) and *skifted* (alternated). They were well acquainted with French Arthurian romances and the latest fashions in clothing, armor, and castle building. In making Sir Gawain, Arthur's sister's son, the preeminent knight of the Round Table, the poet was faithful to an older tradition. The thirteenth-century French romances, which in the next century became the main sources of Sir Thomas Malory, had made Sir Lancelot the best of Arthur's knights and Lancelot's adultery with Queen Guinevere the central event on which the fate of Arthur's kingdom turns. In *Sir Gawain* Lancelot is only one name in a list of Arthur's knights. Arthur is still a youth, and the court is in its springtime. Sir Gawain epitomizes this first blooming of Arthurian chivalry, and the reputation of the court rests upon his shoulders.

Ostensibly, Gawain's head is what is at stake. The main plot belongs to a type folklorists classify as the "Beheading Game," in which a supernatural challenger offers to let his head be cut off in exchange for a return blow. The earliest written occurrence of this motif is in the Middle Irish tale of *Bricriu's Feast*. The *Gawain* poet could have encountered it in several French romances as well as in oral tradition. But the outcome of the game here does not turn only on the champion's courage as it does in

Bricriu's Feast. The *Gawain* poet has devised another series of tests for the hero that link the beheading with his truth, the emblem of which is the pentangle—a five-pointed star—displayed on Gawain's coat of arms and shield. The word *truth* in Middle English means not only what it still means now—a fact, belief, or idea held to be "true"—but what is conveyed by the old-fashioned variant from the same root: *troth*— that is, faith pledged by one's word and owed to a lord, a spouse, or anyone who puts someone else under an obligation. In this respect, Sir Gawain is being measured against a moral and Christian ideal of chivalry. Whether or not he succeeds in that contest is a question carefully left unresolved—perhaps as a challenge for the reader.

The poet has framed Gawain's adventure with references in the first and last stanzas to what are called the "Brutus books," the foundation stories that trace the origins of Rome and Britain back to the destruction of Troy. See, for example, the selection from Geoffrey of Monmouth's *History of the Kings of Britain* (p. 96). A cyclical sense of history as well as of the cycles of the seasons of the year, the generations of humankind, and of individual lives runs through *Sir Gawain and the Green Knight*.

The poem is written in stanzas that contain a group of alliterative lines (the number of lines in a stanza varies). The line is longer and does not contain a fixed number or pattern of stresses like the classical alliterative measure of Old English poetry. Each stanza closes with five short lines rhyming *a b a b a*. The first of these rhyming lines contains just two (rarely three) syllables and is called the "bob"; the four three-stress lines that follow are called the "wheel." For details on alliterative verse, see "Old and Middle English Prosody" (pp. 16–18). The opening stanza is printed below in Middle English with an interlinear translation. The alliterating sounds, which should be stressed, have been italicized.

Sithen the *sege* and the *assaut* was *sesed* at Troye,
After the siege and the assault was ceased at Troy,

The *borgh* *brittened* and *brent* to *brondes* and askes,
The city crumbled and burned to brands and ashes,

The *tulk* that the *trammes* of *tresoun* ther *wroght*
The man who the plots of treason there wrought

Was *tried* for his *tricherie*, the *trewest* on erthe.
Was tried for his treachery, the truest on earth.

Hit was *Ennias* the *athel* and his highe kynde,
It was Aeneas the noble and his high race,

That sithen *depreced* *provinces*, and *patrounes* bicome
Who after subjugated provinces, and lords became

Welneghe of al the *wele* in the *west* iles.
Wellnigh of all the wealth in the west isles.

Fro *riche* *Romulus* to *Rome* *ricchis* hym swythe,
Then noble Romulus to Rome proceeds quickly,

With gret *bobbaunce* that *burghe* he *biges* upon fyrst
With great pride that city he builds at first

And *nevenes* hit his aune *nome*, as hit *now* hat;
And names it his own name, as it now is called;

Ticius to Tuskan and *t*eldes bigynnes,
Ticius (goes) to Tuscany and houses begins,

*L*angaberde in *L*umbardie *l*yftes up homes,
Longbeard in Lombardy raises up homes,

And *f*er over the French *f*lod, Felix Brutus
And far over the English Channel, Felix Brutus

On mony *b*onkkes ful *b*rode *B*retayn he settes
On many banks very broad Brittain he sets

Wyth wynne,
With joy,

Where *w*erre and *w*rake and *w*onder
Where war and revenge and wondrous happenings

Bi sythes has wont therinne,
On occasions have dwelled therein

And oft *b*othe *b*lysse and *b*lunder
And often both joy and strife

Ful skete has skyfted synne.
Very swiftly have alternated since.

Sir Gawain and the Green Knight[1]

Part 1

Since the siege and the assault was ceased at Troy,
The walls breached and burnt down to brands and ashes,
The knight that had knotted the nets of deceit
Was impeached for his perfidy, proven most true,[2]
5 It was high-born Aeneas and his haughty race
That since prevailed over provinces, and proudly reigned
Over well-nigh all the wealth of the West Isles.[3]
Great Romulus[4] to Rome repairs in haste;
With boast and with bravery builds he that city
10 And names it with his own name, that it now bears.
Ticius to Tuscany, and towers raises,
Langobard[5] in Lombardy lays out homes,
And far over the French Sea, Felix Brutus[6]
On many broad hills and high Britain he sets,
15   most fair.

---

1. The Modern English translation is by Marie Borroff (1967), who has reproduced the alliterative meter of the original as well as the "bob" and "wheel," the five-line rhyming group that concludes each of the long irregular stanzas.
2. The treacherous knight is Aeneas, who was a traitor to his city, Troy, according to medieval tradition, but Aeneas was actually tried ("impeached") by the Greeks for his refusal to hand over to them his sister Polyxena.
3. Perhaps Western Europe.
4. The legendary founder of Rome is here given Trojan ancestry, like Aeneas.
5. The reputed founder of Lombardy. "Ticius": not otherwise known.
6. Great-grandson of Aeneas and legendary founder of Britain; not elsewhere given the name Felix (Latin "happy").

Where war and wrack and wonder
By shifts have sojourned there,
And bliss by turns with blunder
In that land's lot had share.

20 And since this Britain was built by this baron great,
Bold boys bred there, in broils delighting,
That did in their day many a deed most dire.
More marvels have happened in this merry land
Than in any other I know, since that olden time,
25 But of those that here built, of British kings,
King Arthur was counted most courteous of all,
Wherefore an adventure I aim to unfold,
That a marvel of might some men think it,
And one unmatched among Arthur's wonders.
30 If you will listen to my lay but a little while,
As I heard it in hall, I shall hasten to tell
anew.
As it was fashioned featly
In tale of derring-do,
35 And linked in measures meetly
By letters tried and true.

This king lay at Camelot[7] at Christmastide;
Many good knights and gay his guests were there,
Arrayed of the Round Table[8] rightful brothers,
40 With feasting and fellowship and carefree mirth.
There true men contended in tournaments many,
Joined there in jousting these gentle knights,
Then came to the court for carol-dancing,
For the feast was in force full fifteen days,
45 With all the meat and the mirth that men could devise,
Such gaiety and glee, glorious to hear,
Brave din by day, dancing by night.
High were their hearts in halls and chambers,
These lords and these ladies, for life was sweet.
50 In peerless pleasures passed they their days,
The most noble knights known under Christ,
And the loveliest ladies that lived on earth ever,
And he the comeliest king, that that court holds,
For all this fair folk in their first age
55 were still.
Happiest of mortal kind,
King noblest famed of will;
You would now go far to find
So hardy a host on hill.

60 While the New Year was new, but yesternight come,
This fair folk at feast two-fold was served,

7. Capital of Arthur's kingdom, presumably located in southwest England or southern Wales.
8. According to legend, Merlin made the Round Table after a dispute broke out among Arthur's knights about precedence: it seated one hundred knights. The table described in the poem is not round.

When the king and his company were come in together,
The chanting in chapel achieved and ended.
Clerics and all the court acclaimed the glad season,
65 Cried Noel anew, good news to men;
Then gallants gather gaily, hand-gifts to make,
Called them out clearly, claimed them by hand,
Bickered long and busily about those gifts.
Ladies laughed aloud, though losers they were,
70 And he that won was not angered, as well you will know.[9]
All this mirth they made until meat was served;
When they had washed them worthily, they went to their seats,
The best seated above, as best it beseemed,
Guenevere the goodly queen gay in the midst
75 On a dais well-decked and duly arrayed
With costly silk curtains, a canopy over,
Of Toulouse and Turkestan tapestries rich,
All broidered and bordered with the best gems
Ever brought into Britain, with bright pennies
80   to pay.
                    Fair queen, without a flaw,
                    She glanced with eyes of grey.
                    A seemlier that once he saw,
                    In truth, no man could say.

85 But Arthur would not eat till all were served;
So light was his lordly heart, and a little boyish;
His life he liked lively—the less he cared
To be lying for long, or long to sit,
So busy his young blood, his brain so wild.
90 And also a point of pride pricked him in heart,
For he nobly had willed, he would never eat
On so high a holiday, till he had heard first
Of some fair feat or fray some far-borne tale,
Of some marvel of might, that he might trust,
95 By champions of chivalry achieved in arms,
Or some suppliant came seeking some single knight
To join with him in jousting, in jeopardy each
To lay life for life, and leave it to fortune
To afford him on field fair hap or other.
100 Such is the king's custom, when his court he holds
At each far-famed feast amid his fair host
                              so dear.
                    The stout king stands in state
                    Till a wonder shall appear;
105   He leads, with heart elate,
                    High mirth in the New Year.

So he stands there in state, the stout young king,
Talking before the high table of trifles fair.
There Gawain the good knight by Guenevere sits,
110 With Agravain à la dure main on her other side,

9. The dispensing of New Year's gifts seems to have involved kissing.

Both knights of renown, and nephews of the king.
Bishop Baldwin above begins the table,
And Yvain, son of Urien, ate with him there.
These few with the fair queen were fittingly served;
115   At the side-tables[1] sat many stalwart knights.
Then the first course comes, with clamor of trumpets
That were bravely bedecked with bannerets bright,
With noise of new drums and the noble pipes.
Wild were the warbles that wakened that day
120   In strains that stirred many strong men's hearts.
There dainties were dealt out, dishes rare,
Choice fare to choose, on chargers so many
That scarce was there space to set before the people
The service of silver, with sundry meats,
125   on cloth.
            Each fair guest freely there
            Partakes, and nothing loth;
            Twelve dishes before each pair;
            Good beer and bright wine both.

130   Of the service itself I need say no more,
For well you will know no tittle was wanting.
Another noise and a new was well-nigh at hand,
That the lord might have leave his life to nourish;
For scarce were the sweet strains still in the hall,
135   And the first course come to that company fair,
There hurtles in at the hall-door an unknown rider,
One the greatest on ground in growth of his frame:
From broad neck to buttocks so bulky and thick,
And his loins and his legs so long and so great,
140   Half a giant on earth I hold him to be,
But believe him no less than the largest of men,
And that the seemliest in his stature to see, as he rides,
For in back and in breast though his body was grim,
His waist in its width was worthily small,
145   And formed with every feature in fair accord
                   was he.
            Great wonder grew in hall
            At his hue most strange to see,
            For man and gear and all
150   Were green as green could be.

And in guise all of green, the gear and the man:
A coat cut close, that clung to his sides,
And a mantle to match, made with a lining
Of furs cut and fitted—the fabric was noble,
155   Embellished all with ermine, and his hood beside,
That was loosed from his locks, and laid on his shoulders.
With trim hose and tight, the same tint of green,

---

1. The side tables are on the main floor and run along the walls at a right angle with the high table, which is on a dais.

His great calves were girt, and gold spurs under
He bore on silk bands that embellished his heels,
160 And footgear well-fashioned, for riding most fit.
And all his vesture verily was verdant green;
Both the bosses on his belt and other bright gems
That were richly ranged on his raiment noble
About himself and his saddle, set upon silk,
165 That to tell half the trifles would tax my wits,
The butterflies and birds embroidered thereon
In green of the gayest, with many a gold thread.
The pendants of the breast-band, the princely crupper,
And the bars of the bit were brightly enameled;
170 The stout stirrups were green, that steadied his feet,
And the bows of the saddle and the side-panels both,
That gleamed all and glinted with green gems about.
The steed he bestrides of that same green
                    so bright.
175   A green horse great and thick;
                A headstrong steed of might;
                In broidered bridle quick,
                Mount matched man aright.

Gay was this goodly man in guise all of green,
180 And the hair of his head to his horse suited;
Fair flowing tresses enfold his shoulders;
A beard big as a bush on his breast hangs,
That with his heavy hair, that from his head falls,
Was evened all about above both his elbows,
185 That half his arms thereunder were hid in the fashion
Of a king's cap-à-dos,[2] that covers his throat.
The mane of that mighty horse much to it like,
Well curled and becombed, and cunningly knotted
With filaments of fine gold amid the fair green,
190 Here a strand of the hair, here one of gold;
His tail and his foretop twin in their hue,
And bound both with a band of a bright green
That was decked adown the dock with dazzling stones
And tied tight at the top with a triple knot
195 Where many bells well burnished rang bright and clear.
Such a mount in his might, nor man on him riding,
None had seen, I dare swear, with sight in that hall
                    so grand.
                As lightning quick and light
200   He looked to all at hand;
                It seemed that no man might
                His deadly dints withstand.

Yet had he no helm, nor hauberk neither,
Nor plate, nor appurtenance appending to arms,

---

2. The word *capados* occurs in this form in Middle English only in *Gawain*, here and in line 572. The translator has interpreted it, as the poet apparently did also, as *cap-à-dos*, i.e., a garment covering its wearer "from head to back," on the model of *cap-à-pie*, "from head to foot," referring to armor.

205   Nor shaft pointed sharp, nor shield for defense,
But in his one hand he had a holly bob
That is goodliest in green when groves are bare,
And an ax in his other, a huge and immense,
A wicked piece of work in words to expound:
210   The head on its haft was an ell long;
The spike of green steel, resplendent with gold;
The blade burnished bright, with a broad edge,
As well shaped to shear as a sharp razor;
Stout was the stave in the strong man's gripe,
215   That was wound all with iron to the weapon's end,
With engravings in green of goodliest work.
A lace lightly about, that led to a knot,
Was looped in by lengths along the fair haft,
And tassels thereto attached in a row,
220   With buttons of bright green, brave to behold.
This horseman hurtles in, and the hall enters;
Riding to the high dais, recked he no danger;
Not a greeting he gave as the guests he o'erlooked,
Nor wasted his words, but "Where is," he said,
225   "The captain of this crowd? Keenly I wish
To see that sire with sight, and to himself say

my say."
He swaggered all about
To scan the host so gay;
230   He halted, as if in doubt
Who in that hall held sway.

There were stares on all sides as the stranger spoke,
For much did they marvel what it might mean
That a horseman and a horse should have such a hue,
235   Grow green as the grass, and greener, it seemed,
Than green fused on gold more glorious by far.
All the onlookers eyed him, and edged nearer,
And awaited in wonder what he would do,
For many sights had they seen, but such a one never,
240   So that phantom and faerie the folk there deemed it,
Therefore chary of answer was many a champion bold,
And stunned at his strong words stone-still they sat
In a swooning silence in the stately hall.
As all were slipped into sleep, so slackened their speech

245   apace.
Not all, I think, for dread,
But some of courteous grace
Let him who was their head
Be spokesman in that place.

250   Then Arthur before the high dais that entrance beholds,
And hailed him, as behooved, for he had no fear,
And said "Fellow, in faith you have found fair welcome;
The head of this hostelry Arthur am I;
Leap lightly down, and linger, I pray,

255 And the tale of your intent you shall tell us after."
"Nay, so help me," said the other, "He that on high sits,
To tarry here any time, 'twas not mine errand;
But as the praise of you, prince, is puffed up so high,
And your court and your company are counted the best,
260 Stoutest under steel-gear on steeds to ride,
Worthiest of their works the wide world over,
And peerless to prove in passages of arms,
And courtesy here is carried to its height,
And so at this season I have sought you out.
265 You may be certain by the branch that I bear in hand
That I pass here in peace, and would part friends,
For had I come to this court on combat bent,
I have a hauberk at home, and a helm beside,
A shield and a sharp spear, shining bright,
270 And other weapons to wield, I ween well, to boot,
But as I willed no war, I wore no metal.
But if you be so bold as all men believe,
You will graciously grant the game that I ask
by right."
275 Arthur answer gave
And said, "Sir courteous knight,
If contest bare you crave,
You shall not fail to fight."

"Nay, to fight, in good faith, is far from my thought;
280 There are about on these benches but beardless children,
Were I here in full arms on a haughty steed,
For measured against mine, their might is puny.
And so I call in this court for a Christmas game,
For 'tis Yule and New Year, and many young bloods about;
285 If any in this house such hardihood claims,
Be so bold in his blood, his brain so wild,
As stoutly to strike one stroke for another,
I shall give him as my gift this gisarme noble,
This ax, that is heavy enough, to handle as he likes,
290 And I shall bide the first blow, as bare as I sit.
If there be one so wilful my words to assay,
Let him leap hither lightly, lay hold of this weapon;
I quitclaim it forever, keep it as his own,
And I shall stand him a stroke, steady on this floor,
295 So you grant me the guerdon to give him another,
sans blame.
In a twelvemonth and a day
He shall have of me the same;
Now be it seen straightway
300 Who dares take up the game."

If he astonished them at first, stiller were then
All that household in hall, the high and the low;
The stranger on his green steed stirred in the saddle,
And roisterously his red eyes he rolled all about,

305   Bent his bristling brows, that were bright green,
      Wagged his beard as he watched who would arise.
      When the court kept its counsel he coughed aloud,
      And cleared his throat coolly, the clearer to speak:
      "What, is this Arthur's house," said that horseman then,
310   "Whose fame is so fair in far realms and wide?
      Where is now your arrogance and your awesome deeds,
      Your valor and your victories and your vaunting words?
      Now are the revel and renown of the Round Table
      Overwhelmed with a word of one man's speech,
315   For all cower and quake, and no cut felt!"
      With this he laughs so loud that the lord grieved;
      The blood for sheer shame shot to his face,
                  and pride.
             With rage his face flushed red,
320   And so did all beside.
             Then the king as bold man bred
             Toward the stranger took a stride.

      And said "Sir, now we see you will say but folly,
      Which whoso has sought, it suits that he find.
325   No guest here is aghast of your great words.
      Give to me your gisarme, in God's own name,
      And the boon you have begged shall straight be granted."
      He leaps to him lightly, lays hold of his weapon;
      The green fellow on foot fiercely alights.
330   Now has Arthur his ax, and the haft grips,
      And sternly stirs it about, on striking bent.
      The stranger before him stood there erect,
      Higher than any in the house by a head and more;
      With stern look as he stood, he stroked his beard,
335   And with undaunted countenance drew down his coat,
      No more moved nor dismayed for his mighty dints
      Than any bold man on bench had brought him a drink
                  of wine.
             Gawain by Guenevere
340   Toward the king doth now incline:
             "I beseech, before all here,
             That this melee may be mine."

      "Would you grant me the grace," said Gawain to the king,
      "To be gone from this bench and stand by you there,
345   If I without discourtesy might quit this board,
      And if my liege lady misliked it not,
      I would come to your counsel before your court noble.
      For I find it not fit, as in faith it is known,
      When such a boon is begged before all these knights,
350   Though you be tempted thereto, to take it on yourself
      While so bold men about upon benches sit,
      That no host under heaven is hardier of will,
      Nor better brothers-in-arms where battle is joined;
      I am the weakest, well I know, and of wit feeblest;

355 And the loss of my life would be least of any;
That I have you for uncle is my only praise;
My body, but for your blood, is barren of worth;
And for that this folly befits not a king,
And 'tis I that have asked it, it ought to be mine,
360 And if my claim be not comely let all this court judge,
                    in sight."
           The court assays the claim,
           And in counsel all unite
           To give Gawain the game
365   And release the king outright.

Then the king called the knight to come to his side,
And he rose up readily, and reached him with speed,
Bows low to his lord, lays hold of the weapon,
And he releases it lightly, and lifts up his hand,
370 And gives him God's blessing, and graciously prays
That his heart and his hand may be hardy both.
"Keep, cousin," said the king, "what you cut with this day,
And if you rule it aright, then readily, I know,
You shall stand the stroke it will strike after."
375 Gawain goes to the guest with gisarme in hand,
And boldly he bides there, abashed not a whit.
Then hails he Sir Gawain, the horseman in green:
"Recount we our contract, ere you come further.
First I ask and adjure you, how you are called
380 That you tell me true, so that trust it I may."
"In good faith," said the good knight, "Gawain am I
Whose buffet befalls you, what'er betide after,
And at this time twelvemonth take from you another
With what weapon you will, and with no man else
385   alive."
           The other nods assent:
           "Sir Gawain, as I may thrive,
           I am wondrous well content
           That you this dint shall drive."

390 "Sir Gawain," said the Green Knight, "By God, I rejoice
That your fist shall fetch this favor I seek,
And you have readily rehearsed, and in right terms,
Each clause of my covenant with the king your lord,
Save that you shall assure me, sir, upon oath,
395 That you shall seek me yourself, wheresoever you deem
My lodgings may lie, and look for such wages
As you have offered me here before all this host."
"What is the way there?" said Gawain. "Where do you dwell?
I heard never of your house, by him that made me,
400 Nor I know you not, knight, your name nor your court.
But tell me truly thereof, and teach me your name,
And I shall fare forth to find you, so far as I may,
And this I say in good certain, and swear upon oath."
"That is enough in New Year, you need say no more,"

405 Said the knight in the green to Gawain the noble,
"If I tell you true, when I have taken your knock,
And if you handily have hit, you shall hear straightway
Of my house and my home and my own name;
Then follow in my footsteps by faithful accord.
410 And if I spend no speech, you shall speed the better:
You can feast with your friends, nor further trace
           my tracks.
        Now hold your grim tool steady
        And show us how it hacks."
415   "Gladly, sir; all ready,"
        Says Gawain; he strokes the ax.

The Green Knight upon ground girds him with care:
Bows a bit with his head, and bares his flesh:
His long lovely locks he laid over his crown,
420 Let the naked nape for the need be shown.
Gawain grips to his ax and gathers it aloft—
The left foot on the floor before him he set—
Brought it down deftly upon the bare neck,
That the shock of the sharp blow shivered the bones
425 And cut the flesh cleanly and clove it in twain,
That the blade of bright steel bit into the ground.
The head was hewn off and fell to the floor;
Many found it at their feet, as forth it rolled;
The blood gushed from the body, bright on the green,
430 Yet fell not the fellow, nor faltered a whit,
But stoutly he starts forth upon stiff shanks,
And as all stood staring he stretched forth his hand,
Laid hold of his head and heaved it aloft,
Then goes to the green steed, grasps the bridle,
435 Steps into the stirrup, bestrides his mount,
And his head by the hair in his hand holds,
And as steady he sits in the stately saddle
As he had met with no mishap, nor missing were
           his head.
440   His bulk about he haled,
        That fearsome body that bled;
        There were many in the court that quailed
        Before all his say was said.

For the head in his hand he holds right up;
445 Toward the first on the dais directs he the face,
And it lifted up its lids, and looked with wide eyes,
And said as much with its mouth as now you may hear:
"Sir Gawain, forget not to go as agreed,
And cease not to seek till me, sir, you find,
450 As you promised in the presence of these proud knights.
To the Green Chapel come, I charge you, to take
Such a dint as you have dealt—you have well deserved
That your neck should have a knock on New Year's morn.
The Knight of the Green Chapel I am well-known to many,

455 Wherefore you cannot fail to find me at last;
Therefore come, or be counted a recreant knight."
With a roisterous rush he flings round the reins,
Hurtles out at the hall-door, his head in his hand,
That the flint-fire flew from the flashing hooves.
460 Which way he went, not one of them knew
Nor whence he was come in the wide world
                        so fair.
            The king and Gawain gay
            Make game of the Green Knight there,
465   Yet all who saw it say
            'Twas a wonder past compare.

Though high-born Arthur at heart had wonder,
He let no sign be seen, but said aloud
To the comely queen, with courteous speech,
470 "Dear dame, on this day dismay you no whit;
Such crafts are becoming at Christmastide,
Laughing at interludes, light songs and mirth,
Amid dancing of damsels with doughty knights.
Nevertheless of my meat now let me partake,
475 For I have met with a marvel, I may not deny."
He glanced at Sir Gawain, and gaily he said,
"Now, sir, hang up your ax,³ that has hewn enough,"
And over the high dais it was hung on the wall
That men in amazement might on it look,
480 And tell in true terms the tale of the wonder.
Then they turned toward the table, these two together,
The good king and Gawain, and made great feast,
With all dainties double, dishes rare,
With all manner of meat and minstrelsy both,
485 Such happiness wholly had they that day
                        in hold.
            Now take care, Sir Gawain,
            That your courage wax not cold
            When you must turn again
490   To your enterprise foretold.

Part 2

This adventure had Arthur of handsels⁴ first
When young was the year, for he yearned to hear tales;
Though they wanted for words when they went to sup,
Now are fierce deeds to follow, their fists stuffed full.
495 Gawain was glad to begin those games in hall,
But if the end be harsher, hold it no wonder,
For though men are merry in mind after much drink,
A year passes apace, and proves ever new;
First things and final conform but seldom.

3. A colloquial expression equivalent to "bury the
hatchet," but here with an appropriate literal sense

also.
4. New Year's presents.

500 And so this Yule to the young year yielded place,
And each season ensued at its set time;
After Christmas there came the cold cheer of Lent,
When with fish and plainer fare our flesh we reprove;
But then the world's weather with winter contends:
505 The keen cold lessens, the low clouds lift;
Fresh falls the rain in fostering showers
On the face of the fields; flowers appear.
The ground and the groves wear gowns of green;
Birds build their nests, and blithely sing
510 That solace of all sorrow with summer comes
                          ere long.
                    And blossoms day by day
                    Bloom rich and rife in throng;
                    Then every grove so gay
515   Of the greenwood rings with song.

And then the season of summer with the soft winds,
When Zephyr sighs low over seeds and shoots;
Glad is the green plant growing abroad,
When the dew at dawn drops from the leaves,
520 To get a gracious glance from the golden sun.
But harvest with harsher winds follows hard after,
Warns him to ripen well ere winter comes;
Drives forth the dust in the droughty season,
From the face of the fields to fly high in air.
525 Wroth winds in the welkin wrestle with the sun,
The leaves launch from the linden and light on the ground,
And the grass turns to gray, that once grew green.
Then all ripens and rots that rose up at first,
And so the year moves on in yesterdays many,
530 And winter once more, by the world's law,
                          draws nigh.
                    At Michaelmas° the moon   *September 29*
                    Hangs wintry pale in sky;
                    Sir Gawain girds him soon
535   For travails yet to try.

Till All-Hallows' Day⁵ with Arthur he dwells,
And he held a high feast to honor that knight
With great revels and rich, of the Round Table.
Then ladies lovely and lords debonair
540 With sorrow for Sir Gawain were sore at heart;
Yet they covered their care with countenance glad:
Many a mournful man made mirth for his sake.
So after supper soberly he speaks to his uncle
Of the hard hour at hand, and openly says,
545 "Now, liege lord of my life, my leave I take;
The terms of this task too well you know—
To count the cost over concerns me nothing.

---

5. All Saints' Day, November 1.

But I am bound forth betimes to bear a stroke
From the grim man in green, as God may direct."
550 Then the first and foremost came forth in throng:
Yvain and Eric and others of note,
Sir Dodinal le Sauvage, the Duke of Clarence,
Lionel and Lancelot and Lucan the good,
Sir Bors and Sir Bedivere, big men both,
555 And many manly knights more, with Mador de la Porte.
All this courtly company comes to the king
To counsel their comrade, with care in their hearts;
There was much secret sorrow suffered that day
That one so good as Gawain must go in such wise
560 To bear a bitter blow, and his bright sword
          lay by.
      He said, "Why should I tarry?"
      And smiled with tranquil eye;
      "In destinies sad or merry,
565   True men can but try."

He dwelt there all that day, and dressed in the morning;
Asked early for his arms, and all were brought.
First a carpet of rare cost was cast on the floor
Where much goodly gear gleamed golden bright;
570 He takes his place promptly and picks up the steel,
Attired in a tight coat of Turkestan silk
And a kingly cap-à-dos, closed at the throat,
That was lavishly lined with a lustrous fur.
Then they set the steel shoes on his sturdy feet
575 And clad his calves about with comely greaves,
And plate well-polished protected his knees,
Affixed with fastenings of the finest gold.
Fair cuisses enclosed, that were cunningly wrought,
His thick-thewed thighs, with thongs bound fast,
580 And massy chain-mail of many a steel ring
He bore on his body, above the best cloth,
With brace burnished bright upon both his arms,
Good couters and gay, and gloves of plate,
And all the goodly gear to grace him well
585   that tide.
      His surcoat blazoned bold;
      Sharp spurs to prick with pride;
      And a brave silk band to hold
      The broadsword at his side.

590 When he had on his arms, his harness was rich,
The least latchet or loop laden with gold;
So armored as he was, he heard a mass,
Honored God humbly at the high altar.
Then he comes to the king and his comrades-in-arms,
595 Takes his leave at last of lords and ladies,
And they clasped and kissed him, commending him to Christ.
By then Gringolet was girt with a great saddle

That was gaily agleam with fine gilt fringe,
New-furbished for the need with nail-heads bright;
600 The bridle and the bars bedecked all with gold;
The breast-plate, the saddlebow, the side-panels both,
The caparison and the crupper accorded in hue,
And all ranged on the red the resplendent studs
That glittered and glowed like the glorious sun.
605 His helm now he holds up and hastily kisses,
Well-closed with iron clinches, and cushioned within;
It was high on his head, with a hasp behind,
And a covering of cloth to encase the visor,
All bound and embroidered with the best gems
610 On broad bands of silk, and bordered with birds,
Parrots and popinjays preening their wings,
Lovebirds and love-knots as lavishly wrought
As many women had worked seven winters thereon,
                              entire.
615   The diadem costlier yet
                That crowned that comely sire,
                With diamonds richly set,
                That flashed as if on fire.

Then they showed forth the shield, that shone all red,
620 With the pentangle[6] portrayed in purest gold.
About his broad neck by the baldric he casts it,
That was meet for the man, and matched him well.
And why the pentangle is proper to that peerless prince
I intend now to tell, though detain me it must.
625 It is a sign by Solomon sagely devised
To be a token of truth, by its title of old,
For it is a figure formed of five points,
And each line is linked and locked with the next
For ever and ever, and hence it is called
630 In all England, as I hear, the endless knot.
And well may he wear it on his worthy arms,
For ever faithful five-fold in five-fold fashion
Was Gawain in good works, as gold unalloyed,
Devoid of all villainy, with virtues adorned
635   in sight.
                On shield and coat in view
                He bore that emblem bright,

6. A five-pointed star, formed by five lines that are drawn without lifting the pencil from the paper, supposed to have mystical significance; as Solomon's sign (line 625) it was enclosed in a circle.

As to his word most true
And in speech most courteous knight.
640 And first, he was faultless in his five senses,
Nor found ever to fail in his five fingers,
And all his fealty was fixed upon the five wounds
That Christ got on the cross, as the creed tells;
And wherever this man in melee took part,
645 His one thought was of this, past all things else,
That all his force was founded on the five joys[7]
That the high Queen of heaven had in her child.
And therefore, as I find, he fittingly had
On the inner part of his shield her image portrayed,
650 That when his look on it lighted, he never lost heart.
The fifth of the five fives followed by this knight
Were beneficence boundless and brotherly love
And pure mind and manners, that none might impeach,
And compassion most precious—these peerless five
655 Were forged and made fast in him, foremost of men.
Now all these five fives were confirmed in this knight,
And each linked in other, that end there was none,
And fixed to five points, whose force never failed,
Nor assembled all on a side, nor asunder either,
660 Nor anywhere at an end, but whole and entire
However the pattern proceeded or played out its course.
And so on his shining shield shaped was the knot
Royally in red gold against red gules,
That is the peerless pentangle, prized of old
665   in lore.
          Now armed is Gawain gay,
          And bears his lance before,
          And soberly said good day,
          He thought forevermore.

670 He struck his steed with the spurs and sped on his way
So fast that the flint-fire flashed from the stones.
When they saw him set forth they were sore aggrieved,
And all sighed softly, and said to each other,
Fearing for their fellow, "Ill fortune it is
675 That you, man, must be marred, that most are worthy!
His equal on this earth can hardly be found;
To have dealt more discreetly had done less harm,
And have dubbed him a duke, with all due honor.
A great leader of lords he was like to become,
680 And better so to have been than battered to bits,
Beheaded by an elf-man,° for empty pride!   supernatural being
Who would credit that a king could be counseled so,
And caught in a cavil in a Christmas game?"
Many were the warm tears they wept from their eyes
685 When goodly Sir Gawain was gone from the court
                    that day.

---

7. Most commonly in Middle English literature, the Annunciation, Nativity, Resurrection, Ascension, and Assumption, although the list varies. These overlap but are not identical with the Five Joyful Mysteries of the Rosary, which were not formally established until the 16th century.

No longer he abode,
But speedily went his way
Over many a wandering road,
690   As I heard my author say.

Now he rides in his array through the realm of Logres,[8]
Sir Gawain, God knows, though it gave him small joy!
All alone must he lodge through many a long night
Where the food that he fancied was far from his plate;
695 He had no mate but his mount, over mountain and plain,
Nor man to say his mind to but almighty God,
Till he had wandered well-nigh into North Wales.
All the islands of Anglesey he holds on his left,
And follows, as he fares, the fords by the coast,
700 Comes over at Holy Head, and enters next
The Wilderness of Wirral[9]—few were within
That had great good will toward God or man.
And earnestly he asked of each mortal he met
If he had ever heard aught of a knight all green,
705 Or of a Green Chapel, on ground thereabouts,
And all said the same, and solemnly swore
They saw no such knight all solely green
                    in hue.
            Over country wild and strange
710   The knight sets off anew;
            Often his course must change
            Ere the Chapel comes in view.

Many a cliff must he climb in country wild;
Far off from all his friends, forlorn must he ride;
715 At each strand or stream where the stalwart passed
'Twere a marvel if he met not some monstrous foe,
And that so fierce and forbidding that fight he must.
So many were the wonders he wandered among
That to tell but the tenth part would tax my wits.
720 Now with serpents he wars, now with savage wolves,
Now with wild men of the woods, that watched from the rocks,
Both with bulls and with bears, and with boars besides,
And giants that came gibbering from the jagged steeps.
Had he not borne himself bravely, and been on God's side,
725 He had met with many mishaps and mortal harms.
And if the wars were unwelcome, the winter was worse,
When the cold clear rains rushed from the clouds
And froze before they could fall to the frosty earth.
Near slain by the sleet he sleeps in his irons
730 More nights than enough, among naked rocks,
Where clattering from the crest the cold stream ran
And hung in hard icicles high overhead.
Thus in peril and pain and predicaments dire

8. One of the names for Arthur's kingdom.
9. Gawain went from Camelot north to the northern coast of Wales, opposite the islands of Anglesey; there he turned east across the Dee to the
forest of Wirral in Cheshire.

He rides across country till Christmas Eve,
735   our knight.
     And at that holy tide
     He prays with all his might
     That Mary may be his guide
     Till a dwelling comes in sight.

740   By a mountain next morning he makes his way
   Into a forest fastness, fearsome and wild;
   High hills on either hand, with hoar woods below,
   Oaks old and huge by the hundred together.
   The hazel and the hawthorn were all intertwined
745   With rough raveled moss, that raggedly hung,
   With many birds unblithe upon bare twigs
   That peeped most piteously for pain of the cold.
   The good knight on Gringolet glides thereunder
   Through many a marsh and mire, a man all alone;
750   He feared for his default, should he fail to see
   The service of that Sire that on that same night
   Was born of a bright maid, to bring us his peace.
   And therefore sighing he said, "I beseech of Thee, Lord,
   And Mary, thou mildest mother so dear,
755   Some harborage where haply I might hear mass
   And Thy matins tomorrow—meekly I ask it,
   And thereto proffer and pray my pater and ave
         and creed."
     He said his prayer with sighs,
760   Lamenting his misdeed;
     He crosses himself, and cries
     On Christ in his great need.

   No sooner had Sir Gawain signed himself thrice
   Than he was ware, in the wood, of a wondrous dwelling,
765   Within a moat, on a mound, bright amid boughs
   Of many a tree great of girth that grew by the water—
   A castle as comely as a knight could own,
   On grounds fair and green, in a goodly park
   With a palisade of palings planted about
770   For two miles and more, round many a fair tree.
   The stout knight stared at that stronghold great
   As it shimmered and shone amid shining leaves,
   Then with helmet in hand he offers his thanks
   To Jesus and Saint Julian,[1] that are gentle both,
775   That in courteous accord had inclined to his prayer;
   "Now fair harbor," said he, "I humbly beseech!"
   Then he pricks his proud steed with the plated spurs,
   And by chance he has chosen the chief path
   That brought the bold knight to the bridge's end
780   in haste.
     The bridge hung high in air;

1. Patron saint of hospitality.

> The gates were bolted fast;
> The walls well-framed to bear
> The fury of the blast.

785 The man on his mount remained on the bank
Of the deep double moat that defended the place.
The wall went in the water wondrous deep,
And a long way aloft it loomed overhead.
It was built of stone blocks to the battlements' height,
790 With corbels under cornices in comeliest style;
Watch-towers trusty protected the gate,
With many a lean loophole, to look from within:
A better-made barbican the knight beheld never.
And behind it there hoved a great hall and fair:
795 Turrets rising in tiers, with tines° at their tops,   *spikes*
Spires set beside them, splendidly long,
With finials° well-fashioned, as filigree fine.   *gable ornaments*
Chalk-white chimneys over chambers high
Gleamed in gay array upon gables and roofs;
800 The pinnacles in panoply, pointing in air,
So vied there for his view that verily it seemed
A castle cut of paper for a king's feast.[2]
The good knight on Gringolet thought it great luck
If he could but contrive to come there within
805 To keep the Christmas feast in that castle fair
> and bright.
> There answered to his call
> A porter most polite;
> From his station on the wall
810 > He greets the errant knight.

"Good sir," said Gawain, "Wouldst go to inquire
If your lord would allow me to lodge here a space?"
"Peter!" said the porter, "For my part, I think
So noble a knight will not want for a welcome!"
815 Then he bustles off briskly, and comes back straight,
And many servants beside, to receive him the better.
They let down the drawbridge and duly went forth
And kneeled down on their knees on the naked earth
To welcome this warrior as best they were able.
820 They proffered him passage—the portals stood wide—
And he beckoned them to rise, and rode over the bridge.
Men steadied his saddle as he stepped to the ground,
And there stabled his steed many stalwart folk.
Now come the knights and the noble squires
825 To bring him with bliss into the bright hall.
When his high helm was off, there hied forth a throng
Of attendants to take it, and see to its care;
They bore away his brand° and his blazoned shield;   *sword*
Then graciously he greeted those gallants each one,

2. A common table decoration at feasts.

830   And many a noble drew near, to do the knight honor.
        All in his armor into hall he was led,
        Where fire on a fair hearth fiercely blazed.
        And soon the lord himself descends from his chamber
        To meet with good manners the man on his floor.
835   He said, "To this house you are heartily welcome:
        What is here is wholly yours, to have in your power
                    and sway."
           "Many thanks," said Sir Gawain;
           "May Christ your pains repay!"
840   The two embrace amain
           As men well met that day.

        Gawain gazed on the host that greeted him there,
        And a lusty fellow he looked, the lord of that place:
        A man of massive mold, and of middle age;
845   Broad, bright was his beard, of a beaver's hue,
        Strong, steady his stance, upon stalwart shanks,
        His face fierce as fire, fair-spoken withal,
        And well-suited he seemed in Sir Gawain's sight
        To be a master of men in a mighty keep.
850   They pass into a parlor, where promptly the host
        Has a servant assigned him to see to his needs,
        And there came upon his call many courteous folk
        That brought him to a bower where bedding was noble,
        With heavy silk hangings hemmed all in gold,
855   Coverlets and counterpanes curiously wrought,
        A canopy over the couch, clad all with fur,
        Curtains running on cords, caught to gold rings,
        Woven rugs on the walls of eastern work,
        And the floor, under foot, well-furnished with the same.
860   Amid light talk and laughter they loosed from him then
        His war-dress of weight and his worthy clothes.
        Robes richly wrought they brought him right soon,
        To change there in chamber and choose what he would.
        When he had found one he fancied, and flung it about,
865   Well-fashioned for his frame, with flowing skirts,
        His face fair and fresh as the flowers of spring,
        All the good folk agreed, that gazed on him then,
        His limbs arrayed royally in radiant hues,
        That so comely a mortal never Christ made
870   as he.
           Whatever his place of birth,
           It seemed he well might be
           Without a peer on earth
           In martial rivalry.

875   A couch before the fire, where fresh coals burned,
        They spread for Sir Gawain splendidly now
        With quilts quaintly stitched, and cushions beside,
        And then a costly cloak they cast on his shoulders
        Of bright silk, embroidered on borders and hems,

880 With furs of the finest well-furnished within,
And bound about with ermine, both mantle and hood;
And he sat at that fireside in sumptuous estate
And warmed himself well, and soon he waxed merry.
Then attendants set a table upon trestles broad,
885 And lustrous white linen they laid thereupon,
A saltcellar of silver, spoons of the same.
He washed himself well and went to his place,
Men set his fare before him in fashion most fit.
There were soups of all sorts, seasoned with skill,
890 Double-sized servings, and sundry fish,
Some baked, some breaded, some broiled on the coals,
Some simmered, some in stews, steaming with spice,
And with sauces to sup that suited his taste.
He confesses it a feast with free words and fair;
895 They requite him as kindly with courteous jests,
well-sped.
"Tonight you fast[3] and pray;
Tomorrow we'll see you fed."
The knight grows wondrous gay
900 As the wine goes to his head.

Then at times and by turns, as at table he sat,
They questioned him quietly, with queries discreet,
And he courteously confessed that he comes from the court,
And owns him of the brotherhood of high-famed Arthur,
905 The right royal ruler of the Round Table,
And the guest by their fireside is Gawain himself,
Who has happened on their house at that holy feast.
When the name of the knight was made known to the lord,
Then loudly he laughed, so elated he was,
910 And the men in that household made haste with joy
To appear in his presence promptly that day,
That of courage ever-constant, and customs pure,
Is pattern and paragon, and praised without end:
Of all knights on earth most honored is he.
915 Each said solemnly aside to his brother,
"Now displays of deportment shall dazzle our eyes
And the polished pearls of impeccable speech;
The high art of eloquence is ours to pursue
Since the father of fine manners is found in our midst.
920 Great is God's grace, and goodly indeed,
That a guest such as Gawain he guides to us here
When men sit and sing of their Savior's birth
in view.
With command of manners pure
925 He shall each heart imbue;
Who shares his converse, sure,
Shall learn love's language true."

3. Gawain is said to be "fasting" because the meal, although elaborate, consisted only of fish dishes,
appropriate to a fasting day.

When the knight had done dining and duly arose,
The dark was drawing on; the day nigh ended.
930　Chaplains in chapels and churches about
Rang the bells aright, reminding all men
Of the holy evensong of the high feast.
The lord attends alone: his fair lady sits
In a comely closet, secluded from sight.
935　Gawain in gay attire goes thither soon;
The lord catches his coat, and calls him by name,
And has him sit beside him, and says in good faith
No guest on God's earth would he gladlier greet.
For that Gawain thanked him; the two then embraced
940　And sat together soberly the service through.
Then the lady, that longed to look on the knight,
Came forth from her closet with her comely maids.
The fair hues of her flesh, her face and her hair
And her body and her bearing were beyond praise,
945　And excelled the queen herself, as Sir Gawain thought.
He goes forth to greet her with gracious intent;
Another lady led her by the left hand
That was older than she—an ancient, it seemed,
And held in high honor by all men about.
950　But unlike to look upon, those ladies were,
For if the one was fresh, the other was faded:
Bedecked in bright red was the body of one;
Flesh hung in folds on the face of the other;
On one a high headdress, hung all with pearls;
955　Her bright throat and bosom fair to behold,
Fresh as the first snow fallen upon hills;
A wimple the other one wore round her throat;
Her swart chin well swaddled, swathed all in white;
Her forehead enfolded in flounces of silk
960　That framed a fair fillet, of fashion ornate,
And nothing bare beneath save the black brows,
The two eyes and the nose, the naked lips,
And they unsightly to see, and sorrily bleared.
A beldame, by God, she may well be deemed,
　　　　　　　　　　　　of pride!
965
　　　　　She was short and thick of waist,
　　　　　Her buttocks round and wide;
　　　　　More toothsome, to his taste,
　　　　　Was the beauty by her side.

970　When Gawain had gazed on that gay lady,
With leave of her lord, he politely approached;
To the elder in homage he humbly bows;
The lovelier he salutes with a light embrace.
He claims a comely kiss, and courteously he speaks;
975　They welcome him warmly, and straightway he asks
To be received as their servant, if they so desire.
They take him between them; with talking they bring him
Beside a bright fire; bade then that spices

Be freely fetched forth, to refresh them the better,
980 And the good wine therewith, to warm their hearts.
The lord leaps about in light-hearted mood;
Contrives entertainments and timely sports;
Takes his hood from his head and hangs it on a spear,
And offers him openly the honor thereof
985 Who should promote the most mirth at that Christmas feast;
"And I shall try for it, trust me—contend with the best,
Ere I go without my headgear by grace of my friends!"
Thus with light talk and laughter the lord makes merry
To gladden the guest he had greeted in hall
990   that day.
                    At the last he called for light
                    The company to convey;
                    Gawain says goodnight
                    And retires to bed straightway.

995 On the morn when each man is mindful in heart
That God's son was sent down to suffer our death,
No household but is blithe for his blessed sake;
So was it there on that day, with many delights.
Both at larger meals and less they were lavishly served
1000 By doughty lads on dais, with delicate fare;
The old ancient lady, highest she sits;
The lord at her left hand leaned, as I hear;
Sir Gawain in the center, beside the gay lady,
Where the food was brought first to that festive board,
1005 And thence throughout the hall, as they held most fit,
To each man was offered in order of rank.
There was meat, there was mirth, there was much joy,
That to tell all the tale would tax my wits,
Though I pained me, perchance, to paint it with care;
1010 But yet I know that our knight and the noble lady
Were accorded so closely in company there,
With the seemly solace of their secret words,
With speeches well-sped, spotless and pure,
That each prince's pastime their pleasures far
1015   outshone.
                    Sweet pipes beguile their cares,
                    And the trumpet of martial tone;
                    Each tends his affairs
                    And those two tend their own.

1020 That day and all the next, their disport was noble,
And the third day, I think, pleased them no less;
The joys of St. John's Day° were justly praised,   *December 27*
And were the last of their like for those lords and ladies;
Then guests were to go in the gray morning,
1025 Wherefore they whiled the night away with wine and with mirth,
Moved to the measures of many a blithe carol;
At last, when it was late, took leave of each other,
Each one of those worthies, to wend his way.
Gawain bids goodbye to his goodly host

1030 Who brings him to his chamber, the chimney beside,
And detains him in talk, and tenders his thanks
And holds it an honor to him and his people
That he has harbored in his house at that holy time
And embellished his abode with his inborn grace.
1035 "As long as I may live, my luck is the better
That Gawain was my guest at God's own feast!"
"Noble sir," said the knight, "I cannot but think
All the honor is your own—may heaven requite it!
And your man to command I account myself here
1040 As I am bound and beholden, and shall be, come
what may."
The lord with all his might
Entreats his guest to stay;
Brief answer makes the knight:
1045 Next morning he must away.

Then the lord of that land politely inquired
What dire affair had forced him, at that festive time,
So far from the king's court to fare forth alone
Ere the holidays wholly had ended in hall.
1050 "In good faith," said Gawain, "you have guessed the truth:
On a high errand and urgent I hastened away,
For I am summoned by myself to seek for a place—
I would I knew whither, or where it might be!
Far rather would I find it before the New Year
1055 Than own the land of Logres, so help me our Lord!
Wherefore, sir, in friendship this favor I ask,
That you say in sober earnest, if something you know
Of the Green Chapel, on ground far or near,
Or the lone knight that lives there, of like hue of green.
1060 A certain day was set by assent of us both
To meet at that landmark, if I might last,
And from now to the New Year is nothing too long,
And I would greet the Green Knight there, would God but allow,
More gladly, by God's Son, than gain the world's wealth!
1065 And I must set forth to search, as soon as I may;
To be about the business I have but three days
And would as soon sink down dead as desist from my errand."
Then smiling said the lord, "Your search, sir, is done,
For we shall see you to that site by the set time.
1070 Let Gawain grieve no more over the Green Chapel;
You shall be in your own bed, in blissful ease,
All the forenoon, and fare forth the first of the year,
And make the goal by midmorn, to mind your affairs,
no fear!
1075 Tarry till the fourth day
And ride on the first of the year.
We shall set you on your way;
It is not two miles from here."

Then Gawain was glad, and gleefully he laughed:
1080 "Now I thank you for this, past all things else!

Now my goal is here at hand! With a glad heart I shall
Both tarry, and undertake any task you devise."
Then the host seized his arm and seated him there;
Let the ladies be brought, to delight them the better,
1085 And in fellowship fair by the fireside they sit;
So gay waxed the good host, so giddy his words,
All waited in wonder what next he would say.
Then he stares on the stout knight, and sternly he speaks:
"You have bound yourself boldly my bidding to do—
1090 Will you stand by that boast, and obey me this once?"
"I shall do so indeed," said the doughty knight;
"While I lie in your lodging, your laws will I follow."
"As you have had," said the host, "many hardships abroad
And little sleep of late, you are lacking, I judge,
1095 Both in nourishment needful and nightly rest;
You shall lie abed late in your lofty chamber
Tomorrow until mass, and meet then to dine
When you will, with my wife, who will sit by your side
And talk with you at table, the better to cheer
1100   our guest.
           A-hunting I will go
           While you lie late and rest."
           The knight, inclining low,
           Assents to each behest.

1105 "And Gawain," said the good host, "agree now to this:
Whatever I win in the woods I will give you at eve,
And all you have earned you must offer to me;
Swear now, sweet friend, to swap as I say,
Whether hands, in the end, be empty or better."
1110 "By God," said Sir Gawain, "I grant it forthwith!
If you find the game good, I shall gladly take part."
"Let the bright wine be brought, and our bargain is done,"
Said the lord of that land—the two laughed together.
Then they drank and they dallied and doffed all constraint,
1115 These lords and these ladies, as late as they chose,
And then with gaiety and gallantries and graceful adieux
They talked in low tones, and tarried at parting.
With compliments comely they kiss at the last;
There were brisk lads about with blazing torches
1120 To see them safe to bed, for soft repose
            long due.
           Their covenants, yet awhile,
           They repeat, and pledge anew;
           That lord could well beguile
1125   Men's hearts, with mirth in view.

Part 3

Long before daylight they left their beds;
Guests that wished to go gave word to their grooms,
And they set about briskly to bind on saddles,
Tend to their tackle, tie up trunks.

1130 The proud lords appear, appareled to ride,
Leap lightly astride, lay hold of their bridles,
Each one on his way to his worthy house.
The liege lord of the land was not the last
Arrayed there to ride, with retainers many;
1135 He had a bite to eat when he had heard mass;
With horn to the hills he hastens amain.
By the dawn of that day over the dim earth,
Master and men were mounted and ready.
Then they harnessed in couples the keen-scented hounds,
1140 Cast wide the kennel-door and called them forth,
Blew upon their bugles bold blasts three;
The dogs began to bay with a deafening din,
And they quieted them quickly and called them to heel,
A hundred brave huntsmen, as I have heard tell,
1145   together.
        Men at stations meet;
        From the hounds they slip the tether;
        The echoing horns repeat,
        Clear in the merry weather.

1150 At the clamor of the quest, the quarry trembled;
Deer dashed through the dale, dazed with dread;
Hastened to the high ground, only to be
Turned back by the beaters, who boldly shouted.
They harmed not the harts, with their high heads,
1155 Let the bucks go by, with their broad antlers,
For it was counted a crime, in the close season,
If a man of that demesne should molest the male deer.
The hinds were headed up, with "Hey!" and "Ware!"
The does with great din were driven to the valleys.
1160 Then you were ware, as they went, of the whistling of arrows;
At each bend under boughs the bright shafts flew
That tore the tawny hide with their tapered heads.
Ah! they bray and they bleed, on banks they die,
And ever the pack pell-mell comes panting behind;
1165 Hunters with shrill horns hot on their heels—
Like the cracking of cliffs their cries resounded.
What game got away from the gallant archers
Was promptly picked off at the posts below
When they were harried on the heights and herded to the streams:
1170 The watchers were so wary at the waiting-stations,
And the greyhounds so huge, that eagerly snatched,
And finished them off as fast as folk could see
           with sight.
        The lord, now here, now there,
1175   Spurs forth in sheer delight.
        And drives, with pleasures rare,
        The day to the dark night.

So the lord in the linden-wood leads the hunt
And Gawain the good knight in gay bed lies,
1180 Lingered late alone, till daylight gleamed,

Under coverlet costly, curtained about.
And as he slips into slumber, slyly there comes
A little din at his door, and the latch lifted,
And he holds up his heavy head out of the clothes;
1185 A corner of the curtain he caught back a little
And waited there warily, to see what befell.
Lo! it was the lady, loveliest to behold,
That drew the door behind her deftly and still
And was bound for his bed—abashed was the knight,
1190 And laid his head low again in likeness of sleep;
And she stepped stealthily, and stole to his bed,
Cast aside the curtain and came within,
And set herself softly on the bedside there,
And lingered at her leisure, to look on his waking.
1195 The fair knight lay feigning for a long while,
Conning in his conscience what his case might
Mean or amount to—a marvel he thought it.
But yet he said within himself, "More seemly it were
To try her intent by talking a little."
1200 So he started and stretched, as startled from sleep,
Lifts wide his lids in likeness of wonder,
And signs himself swiftly, as safer to be,
                              with art.
                    Sweetly does she speak
1205   And kindling glances dart,
                    Blent white and red on cheek
                    And laughing lips apart.

"Good morning, Sir Gawain," said that gay lady,
"A slack sleeper you are, to let one slip in!
1210 Now you are taken in a trice—a truce we must make,
Or I shall bind you in your bed, of that be assured."
Thus laughing lightly that lady jested.
"Good morning, good lady," said Gawain the blithe,
"Be it with me as you will; I am well content!
1215 For I surrender myself, and sue for your grace,
And that is best, I believe, and behooves me now."
Thus jested in answer that gentle knight.
"But if, lovely lady, you misliked it not,
And were pleased to permit your prisoner to rise,
1220 I should quit this couch and accoutre me better,
And be clad in more comfort for converse here."
"Nay, not so, sweet sir," said the smiling lady;
"You shall not rise from your bed; I direct you better:
I shall hem and hold you on either hand,
1225 And keep company awhile with my captive knight.
For as certain as I sit here, Sir Gawain you are,
Whom all the world worships, whereso you ride;
Your honor, your courtesy are highest acclaimed
By lords and by ladies, by all living men;
1230 And lo! we are alone here, and left to ourselves:
My lord and his liegemen are long departed,

The household asleep, my handmaids too,
The door drawn, and held by a well-driven bolt,
And since I have in this house him whom all love,
1235 I shall while the time away with mirthful speech
                              at will.
                    My body is here at hand,
                    Your each wish to fulfill;
                    Your servant to command
1240   I am, and shall be still."

"In good faith," said Gawain, "my gain is the greater,
Though I am not he of whom you have heard;
To arrive at such reverence as you recount here
I am one all unworthy, and well do I know it.
1245 By heaven, I would hold me the happiest of men
If by word or by work I once might aspire
To the prize of your praise—'twere a pure joy!"
"In good faith, Sir Gawain," said that gay lady,
"The well-proven prowess that pleases all others,
1250 Did I scant or scout it, 'twere scarce becoming.
But there are ladies, believe me, that had liefer far
Have thee here in their hold, as I have today,
To pass an hour in pastime with pleasant words,
Assuage all their sorrows and solace their hearts,
1255 Than much of the goodly gems and gold they possess.
But laud be to the Lord of the lofty skies,
For here in my hands all hearts' desire
                              doth lie."
                    Great welcome got he there
1260   From the lady who sat him by;
                    With fitting speech and fair
                    The good knight makes reply.

"Madame," said the merry man, "Mary reward you!
For in good faith, I find your beneficence noble.
1265 And the fame of fair deeds runs far and wide,
But the praise you report pertains not to me,
But comes of your courtesy and kindness of heart."
"By the high Queen of heaven" (said she) "I count it not so,
For were I worth all the women in this world alive,
1270 And all wealth and all worship were in my hands,
And I should hunt high and low, a husband to take,
For the nurture I have noted in thee, knight, here,
The comeliness and courtesies and courtly mirth—
And so I had ever heard, and now hold it true—
1275 No other on this earth should have me for wife."
"You are bound to a better man," the bold knight said,
"Yet I prize the praise you have proffered me here,
And soberly your servant, my sovereign I hold you,
And acknowledge me your knight, in the name of Christ."
1280 So they talked of this and that until 'twas nigh noon,
And ever the lady languishing in likeness of love.

With feat words and fair he framed his defense,
For were she never so winsome, the warrior had
The less will to woo, for the wound that his bane
1285   must be.
          He must bear the blinding blow,
          For such is fate's decree:
          The lady asks leave to go;
          He grants it full and free.

1290 Then she gaily said goodbye, and glanced at him, laughing,
And as she stood, she astonished him with a stern speech:
"Now may the Giver of all good words these glad hours repay!
But our guest is not Gawain—forgot is that thought."
"How so?" said the other, and asks in some haste,
1295 For he feared he had been at fault in the forms of his speech.
But she held up her hand, and made answer thus:
"So good a knight as Gawain is given out to be,
And the model of fair demeanor and manners pure,
Had he lain so long at a lady's side,
1300 Would have claimed a kiss, by his courtesy,
Through some touch or trick of phrase at some tale's end."
Said Gawain, "Good lady, I grant it at once!
I shall kiss at your command, as becomes a knight,
And more, lest you mislike, so let be, I pray."
1305 With that she turns toward him, takes him in her arms,
Leans down her lovely head, and lo! he is kissed.
They commend each other to Christ with comely words,
He sees her forth safely, in silence they part,
And then he lies no later in his lofty bed,
1310 But calls to his chamberlain, chooses his clothes,
Goes in those garments gladly to mass,
Then takes his way to table, where attendants wait,
And made merry all day, till the moon rose
                  in view
1315   Was never knight beset
          'Twixt worthier ladies two:
          The crone and the coquette;
          Fair pastimes they pursue.

And the lord of the land rides late and long,
1320 Hunting the barren hind over the broad heath.
He had slain such a sum, when the sun sank low,
Of does and other deer, as would dizzy one's wits.
Then they trooped in together in triumph at last,
And the count of the quarry quickly they take.
1325 The lords lent a hand with their liegemen many,
Picked out the plumpest and put them together
And duly dressed the deer, as the deed requires.
Some were assigned the assay of the fat:
Two fingers' width fully they found on the leanest.
1330 Then they slit the slot open and searched out the paunch,
Trimmed it with trencher-knives and tied it up tight.

They flayed the fair hide from the legs and trunk,
Then broke open the belly and laid bare the bowels,
Deftly detaching and drawing them forth.
1335 And next at the neck they neatly parted
The weasand° from the windpipe, and cast away the guts.　　　*esophagus*
At the shoulders with sharp blades they showed their skill,
Boning them from beneath, lest the sides be marred;
They breached the broad breast and broke it in twain,
1340 And again at the gullet they begin with their knives,
Cleave down the carcass clear to the breach;
Two tender morsels they take from the throat,
Then round the inner ribs they rid off a layer
And carve out the kidney-fat, close to the spine,
1345 Hewing down to the haunch, that all hung together,
And held it up whole, and hacked it free,
And this they named the numbles,[4] that knew such terms
　　　　　　　of art.
　　　　　They divide the crotch in two,
1350 　　　　And straightway then they start
　　　　　To cut the backbone through
　　　　　And cleave the trunk apart.

With hard strokes they hewed off the head and the neck,
Then swiftly from the sides they severed the chine,
1355 And the corbie's bone[5] they cast on a branch.
Then they pierced the plump sides, impaled either one
With the hock of the hind foot, and hung it aloft,
To each person his portion most proper and fit.
On a hide of a hind the hounds they fed
1360 With the liver and the lights,° the leathery paunches,　　　*lungs*
And bread soaked in blood well blended therewith.
High horns and shrill set hounds a-baying,
Then merrily with their meat they make their way home,
Blowing on their bugles many a brave blast.
1365 Ere dark had descended, that doughty band
Was come within the walls where Gawain waits
　　　　　　　at leisure.
　　　　　Bliss and hearth-fire bright
　　　　　Await the master's pleasure;
1370 　　　　When the two men met that night,
　　　　　Joy surpassed all measure.

Then the host in the hall his household assembles,
With the dames of high degree and their damsels fair.
In the presence of the people, a party he sends
1375 To convey him his venison in view of the knight.
And in high good-humor he hails him then,
Counts over the kill, the cuts on the tallies,
Holds high the hewn ribs, heavy with fat.
"What think you, sir, of this? Have I thriven well?

---

4. The other internal organs.　　　　　5. A bit of gristle assigned to the ravens ("corbies").

1380 Have I won with my woodcraft a worthy prize?"
"In good earnest," said Gawain, "this game is the finest
I have seen in seven years in the season of winter."
"And I give it to you, Gawain," said the goodly host,
"For according to our convenant, you claim it as your own."
1385 "That is so," said Sir Gawain, "the same say I:
What I worthily have won within these fair walls,
Herewith I as willingly award it to you."
He embraces his broad neck with both his arms,
And confers on him a kiss in the comeliest style.
1390 "Have here my profit, it proved no better;
Ungrudging do I grant it, were it greater far."
"Such a gift," said the good host, "I gladly accept—
Yet it might be all the better, would you but say
Where you won this same award, by your wits alone."
1395 "That was no part of the pact; press me no further,
For you have had what behooves; all other claims
     forbear."
    With jest and compliment
    They conversed, and cast off care;
1400   To the table soon they went;
    Fresh dainties wait them there.

And then by the chimney-side they chat at their ease;
The best wine was brought them, and bounteously served;
And after in their jesting they jointly accord
1405 To do on the second day the deeds of the first:
That the two men should trade, betide as it may,
What each had taken in, at eve when they met.
They seal the pact solemnly in sight of the court;
Their cups were filled afresh to confirm the jest;
1410 Then at last they took their leave, for late was the hour,
Each to his own bed hastening away.
Before the barnyard cock had crowed but thrice
The lord had leapt from his rest, his liegemen as well.
Both of mass and their meal they made short work:
1415 By the dim light of dawn they were deep in the woods
     away.
    With huntsmen and with horns
    Over plains they pass that day;
    They release, amid the thorns,
1420   Swift hounds that run and bay.

Soon some were on a scent by the side of a marsh;
When the hounds opened cry, the head of the hunt
Rallied them with rough words, raised a great noise.
The hounds that had heard it came hurrying straight
1425 And followed along with their fellows, forty together.
Then such a clamor and cry of coursing hounds
Arose, that the rocks resounded again.
Hunters exhorted them with horn and with voice;
Then all in a body bore off together

1430 Between a mere in the marsh and a menacing crag,
To a rise where the rock stood rugged and steep,
And boulders lay about, that blocked their approach.
Then the company in consort closed on their prey:
They surrounded the rise and the rocks both,
1435 For well they were aware that it waited within,
The beast that the bloodhounds boldly proclaimed.
Then they beat on the bushes and bade him appear,
And he made a murderous rush in the midst of them all;
The best of all boars broke from his cover,
1440 That had ranged long unrivaled, a renegade old,
For of tough-brawned boars he was biggest far,
Most grim when he grunted—then grieved were many,
For three at the first thrust he threw to the earth,
And dashed away at once without more damage.
1445 With "Hi!" "Hi!" and "Hey!" "Hey!" the others followed,
Had horns at their lips, blew high and clear.
Merry was the music of men and of hounds
That were bound after this boar, his bloodthirsty heart
                                   to quell.
1450   Often he stands at bay,
                         Then scatters the pack pell-mell;
                         He hurts the hounds, and they
                         Most dolefully yowl and yell.

Men then with mighty bows moved in to shoot,
1455 Aimed at him with their arrows and often hit,
But the points had no power to pierce through his hide,
And the barbs were brushed aside by his bristly brow;
Though the shank of the shaft shivered in pieces,
The head hopped away, wheresoever it struck.
1460 But when their stubborn strokes had stung him at last,
Then, foaming in his frenzy, fiercely he charges,
Hies at them headlong that hindered his flight,
And many feared for their lives, and fell back a little.
But the lord on a lively horse leads the chase;
1465 As a high-mettled huntsman his horn he blows;
He sounds the assembly and sweeps through the brush,
Pursuing this wild swine till the sunlight slanted.
All day with this deed they drive forth the time
While our lone knight so lovesome lies in his bed,
1470 Sir Gawain safe at home, in silken bower
                                   so gay.
                         The lady, with guile in heart,
                         Came early where he lay;
                         She was at him with all her art
1475   To turn his mind her way.

She comes to the curtain and coyly peeps in;
Gawain thought it good to greet her at once,
And she richly repays him with her ready words,
Settles softly at his side, and suddenly she laughs,

1480 And with a gracious glance, she begins on him thus:
"Sir, if you be Gawain, it seems a great wonder—
A man so well-meaning, and mannerly disposed,
And cannot act in company as courtesy bids,
And if one takes the trouble to teach him, 'tis all in vain.
1485 That lesson learned lately is lightly forgot,
Though I painted it as plain as my poor wit allowed."
"What lesson, dear lady?" he asked all alarmed;
"I have been much to blame, if your story be true."
"Yet my counsel was of kissing," came her answer then,
1490 "Where favor has been found, freely to claim
As accords with the conduct of courteous knights."
"My dear," said the doughty man, "dismiss that thought;
Such freedom, I fear, might offend you much;
It were rude to request if the right were denied."
1495 "But none can deny you," said the noble dame,
"You are stout enough to constrain with strength, if you choose,
Were any so ungracious as to grudge you aught."
"By heaven," said he, "you have answered well,
But threats never throve among those of my land,
1500 Nor any gift not freely given, good though it be.
I am yours to command, to kiss when you please;
You may lay on as you like, and leave off at will."
                    With this,
              The lady lightly bends
1505   And graciously gives him a kiss;
              The two converse as friends
              Of true love's trials and bliss.

"I should like, by your leave," said the lovely lady,
"If it did not annoy you, to know for what cause
1510 So brisk and so bold a young blood as you,
And acclaimed for all courtesies becoming a knight—
And name what knight you will, they are noblest esteemed
For loyal faith in love, in life as in story;
For to tell the tribulations of these true hearts,
1515 Why, 'tis the very title and text of their deeds,
How bold knights for beauty have braved many a foe,
Suffered heavy sorrows out of secret love,
And then valorously avenged them on villainous churls
And made happy ever after the hearts of their ladies.
1520 And you are the noblest knight known in your time;
No household under heaven but has heard of your fame,
And here by your side I have sat for two days
Yet never has a fair phrase fallen from your lips
Of the language of love, not one little word!
1525 And you, that with sweet vows sway women's hearts,
Should show your winsome ways, and woo a young thing,
And teach by some tokens the craft of true love.
How! are you artless, whom all men praise?
Or do you deem me so dull, or deaf to such words?

1530   Fie! Fie!
          In hope of pastimes new
          I have come where none can spy;
          Instruct me a little, do,
          While my husband is not nearby."

1535 "God love you, gracious lady!" said Gawain then;
     "It is a pleasure surpassing, and a peerless joy,
     That one so worthy as you would willingly come
     And take the time and trouble to talk with your knight
     And content you with his company—it comforts my heart.
1540 But to take to myself the task of telling of love,
     And touch upon its texts, and treat of its themes
     To one that, I know well, wields more power
     In that art, by a half, than a hundred such
     As I am where I live, or am like to become,
1545 It were folly, fair dame, in the first degree!
     In all that I am able, my aim is to please,
     As in honor behooves me, and am evermore
     Your servant heart and soul, so save me our Lord!"
     Thus she tested his temper and tried many a time,
1550 Whatever her true intent, to entice him to sin,
     But so fair was his defense that no fault appeared,
     Nor evil on either hand, but only bliss
                they knew.
          They linger and laugh awhile;
1555   She kisses the knight so true,
          Takes leave in comeliest style
          And departs without more ado.

     Then he rose from his rest and made ready for mass,
     And then a meal was set and served, in sumptuous style;
1560 He dallied at home all day with the dear ladies,
     But the lord lingered late at his lusty sport;
     Pursued his sorry swine, that swerved as he fled,
     And bit asunder the backs of the best of his hounds
     When they brought him to bay, till the bowmen appeared
1565 And soon forced him forth, though he fought for dear life,
     So sharp were the shafts they shot at him there.
     But yet the boldest drew back from his battering head,
     Till at last he was so tired he could travel no more,
     But in as much haste as he might, he makes his retreat
1570 To a rise on rocky ground, by a rushing stream.
     With the bank at his back he scrapes the bare earth,
     The froth foams at his jaws, frightful to see.
     He whets his white tusks—then weary were all
     Those hunters so hardy that hoved round about
1575 Of aiming from afar, but ever they mistrust
              his mood.
         He had hurt so many by then
         That none had hardihood

To be torn by his tusks again,
1580   That was brainsick, and out for blood.

Till the lord came at last on his lofty steed,
Beheld him there at bay before all his folk;
Lightly he leaps down, leaves his courser,
Bares his bright sword, and boldly advances;
1585 Straight into the stream he strides towards his foe.
The wild thing was wary of weapon and man;
His hackles rose high; so hotly he snorts
That many watched with alarm, lest the worst befall.
The boar makes for the man with a mighty bound
1590 So that he and his hunter came headlong together
Where the water ran wildest—the worse for the beast,
For the man, when they first met, marked him with care,
Sights well the slot, slips in the blade,
Shoves it home to the hilt, and the heart shattered,
1595 And he falls in his fury and floats down the water,
     ill-sped.
     Hounds hasten by the score
     To maul him, hide and head;
     Men drag him in to shore
1600   And dogs pronounce him dead.

With many a brave blast they boast of their prize,
All hallooed in high glee, that had their wind;
The hounds bayed their best, as the bold men bade
That were charged with chief rank in that chase of renown.
1605 Then one wise in woodcraft, and worthily skilled,
Began to dress the boar in becoming style:
He severs the savage head and sets it aloft,
Then rends the body roughly right down the spine;
Takes the bowels from the belly, broils them on coals,
1610 Blends them well with bread to bestow on the hounds.
Then he breaks out the brawn in fair broad flitches,
And the innards to be eaten in order he takes.
The two sides, attached to each other all whole,
He suspended from a spar that was springy and tough;
1615 And so with this swine they set out for home;
The boar's head was borne before the same man
That had stabbed him in the stream with his strong arm,
     right through.
     He thought it long indeed
1620   Till he had the knight in view;
     At his call, he comes with speed
     To claim his payment due.

The lord laughed aloud, with many a light word,
When he greeted Sir Gawain—with good cheer he speaks.
1625 They fetch the fair dames and the folk of the house;
He brings forth the brawn, and begins the tale
Of the great length and girth, the grim rage as well,

Of the battle of the boar they beset in the wood.
The other man meetly commended his deeds
1630 And praised well the prize of his princely sport,
For the brawn of that boar, the bold knight said,
And the sides of that swine surpassed all others.
Then they handled the huge head; he owns it a wonder,
And eyes it with abhorrence, to heighten his praise.
1635 "Now, Gawain," said the good man, "this game becomes yours
By those fair terms we fixed, as you know full well."
"That is true," returned the knight, "and trust me, fair friend,
All my gains, as agreed, I shall give you forthwith."
He clasps him and kisses him in courteous style,
1640 Then serves him with the same fare a second time.
"Now we are even," said he, "at this evening feast,
And clear is every claim incurred here to date,
                    and debt."
               "By Saint Giles!" the host replies,
1645   "You're the best I ever met!
               If your profits are all this size,
               We'll see you wealthy yet!"

Then attendants set tables on trestles about,
And laid them with linen; light shone forth,
1650 Wakened along the walls in waxen torches.
The service was set and the supper brought;
Royal were the revels that rose then in hall
At that feast by the fire, with many fair sports:
Amid the meal and after, melody sweet,
1655 Carol-dances comely and Christmas songs,
With all the mannerly mirth my tongue may describe.
And ever our gallant knight beside the gay lady;
So uncommonly kind and complaisant was she,
With sweet stolen glances, that stirred his stout heart,
1660 That he was at his wits' end, and wondrous vexed;
But he could not rebuff her, for courtesy forbade,
Yet took pains to please her, though the plan might
                    go wrong.
               When they to heart's delight
1665   Had reveled there in throng,
               To his chamber he calls the knight,
               And thither they go along.

And there they dallied and drank, and deemed it good sport
To enact their play anew on New Year's Eve,
1670 But Gawain asked again to go on the morrow,
For the time until his tryst was not two days.
The host hindered that, and urged him to stay,
And said, "On my honor, my oath here I take
That you shall get to the Green Chapel to begin your chores
1675 By dawn on New Year's Day, if you so desire.
Wherefore lie at your leisure in your lofty bed,
And I shall hunt hereabouts, and hold to our terms,

And we shall trade winnings when once more we meet,
For I have tested you twice, and true have I found you;
1680 Now think this tomorrow: the third pays for all;
Be we merry while we may, and mindful of joy,
For heaviness of heart can be had for the asking."
This is gravely agreed on and Gawain will stay.
They drink a last draught and with torches depart
1685   to rest.
                    To bed Sir Gawain went:
                    His sleep was of the best;
                    The lord, on his craft intent,
                    Was early up and dressed.

1690 After mass, with his men, a morsel he takes;
Clear and crisp the morning; he calls for his mount;
The folk that were to follow him afield that day
Were high astride their horses before the hall gates.
Wondrous fair were the fields, for the frost was light;
1695 The sun rises red amid radiant clouds,
Sails into the sky, and sends forth his beams.
They let loose the hounds by a leafy wood;
The rocks all around re-echo to their horns;
Soon some have set off in pursuit of the fox,
1700 Cast about with craft for a clearer scent;
A young dog yaps, and is yelled at in turn;
His fellows fall to sniffing, and follow his lead,
Running in a rabble on the right track,
And he scampers all before; they discover him soon,
1705 And when they see him with sight they pursue him the faster,
Railing at him rudely with a wrathful din.
Often he reverses over rough terrain,
Or loops back to listen in the lee of a hedge;
At last, by a little ditch, he leaps over the brush,
1710 Comes into a clearing at a cautious pace,
Then he thought through his wiles to have thrown off the hounds
Till he was ware, as he went, of a waiting-station
Where three athwart his path threatened him at once,
                                        all gray.
1715   Quick as a flash he wheels
                    And darts off in dismay;
                    With hard luck at his heels
                    He is off to the wood away.

Then it was heaven on earth to hark to the hounds
1720 When they had come on their quarry, coursing together!
Such harsh cries and howls they hurled at his head
As all the cliffs with a crash had come down at once.
Here he was hailed, when huntsmen met him;
Yonder they yelled at him, yapping and snarling;
1725 There they cried "Thief!" and threatened his life,
And ever the harriers at his heels, that he had no rest.
Often he was menaced when he made for the open,

And often rushed in again, for Reynard was wily;
And so he leads them a merry chase, the lord and his men,
1730 In this manner on the mountains, till midday or near,
While our hero lies at home in wholesome sleep
Within the comely curtains on the cold morning.
But the lady, as love would allow her no rest,
And pursuing ever the purpose that pricked her heart,
1735 Was awake with the dawn, and went to his chamber
In a fair flowing mantle that fell to the earth,
All edged and embellished with ermines fine;
No hood on her head, but heavy with gems
Were her fillet and the fret° that confined her tresses;   ornamental net
1740 Her face and her fair throat freely displayed;
Her bosom all but bare, and her back as well.
She comes in at the chamber-door, and closes it with care,
Throws wide a window—then waits no longer,
But hails him thus airily with her artful words,
1745   with cheer:
    "Ah, man, how can you sleep?
    The morning is so clear!"
    Though dreams have drowned him deep,
    He cannot choose but hear.

1750 Deep in his dreams he darkly mutters
As a man may that mourns, with many grim thoughts
Of that day when destiny shall deal him his doom
When he greets his grim host at the Green Chapel
And must bow to his buffet, bating all strife.
1755 But when he sees her at his side he summons his wits,
Breaks from the black dreams, and blithely answers.
That lovely lady comes laughing sweet,
Sinks down at his side, and salutes him with a kiss.
He accords her fair welcome in courtliest style;
1760 He sees her so glorious, so gaily attired,
So faultless her features, so fair and so bright,
His heart swelled swiftly with surging joys.
They melt into mirth with many a fond smile,
Nor was fair language lacking, to further that hour's
1765   delight.
    Good were their words of greeting;
    Each joyed in other's sight;
    Great peril attends that meeting
    Should Mary forget her knight.

1770 For that high-born beauty so hemmed him about,
Made so plain her meaning, the man must needs
Either take her tendered love or distastefully refuse.
His courtesy concerned him, lest crass he appear,
But more his soul's mischief, should he commit sin
1775 And belie his loyal oath to the lord of that house.
"God forbid!" said the bold knight. "That shall not befall!"
With a little fond laughter he lightly let pass

All the words of special weight that were sped his way;
"I find you much at fault," the fair one said,
1780 "Who can be cold toward a creature so close by your side,
Of all women in this world most wounded in heart,
Unless you have a sweetheart, one you hold dearer,
And allegiance to that lady so loyally knit
That you will never love another, as now I believe.
1785 And, sir, if it be so, then say it, I beg you;
By all your heart holds dear, hide it no longer
                         with guile."
                    "Lady, by Saint John,"
                    He answers with a smile,
1790   "Lover have I none,
                    Nor will have, yet awhile."

"Those words," said the woman, "are the worst of all,
But I have had my answer, and hard do I find it!
Kiss me now kindly: I can but go hence
1795 To lament my life long like a maid lovelorn."
She inclines her head quickly and kisses the knight,
Then straightens with a sigh, and says as she stands,
"Now, dear, ere I depart, do me this pleasure:
Give me some little gift, your glove or the like,
1800 That I may think on you, man, and mourn the less."
"Now by heavens," said he, "I wish I had here
My most precious possession, to put it in your hands,
For your deeds, beyond doubt, have often deserved
A repayment far passing my power to bestow.
1805 But a love-token, lady, were of little avail;
It is not to your honor to have at this time
A glove as a guerdon from Gawain's hand,
And I am here on an errand in unknown realms
And have no bearers with baggage with becoming gifts,
1810 Which distresses me, madame, for your dear sake.
A man must keep within his compass: account it neither grief
                         nor slight."
                    "Nay, noblest knight alive,"
                    Said that beauty of body white,
1815   "Though you be loath to give,
                    Yet you shall take, by right."

She reached out a rich ring, wrought all of gold,
With a splendid stone displayed on the band
That flashed before his eyes like a fiery sun;
1820 It was worth a king's wealth, you may well believe.
But he waved it away with these ready words:
"Before God, good lady, I forgo all gifts;
None have I to offer, nor any will I take."
And she urged it on him eagerly, and ever he refused,
1825 And vowed in very earnest, prevail she would not.
And she sad to find it so, and said to him then,
"If my ring is refused for its rich cost—

You would not be my debtor for so dear a thing—
I shall give you my girdle; you gain less thereby."
1830 She released a knot lightly, and loosened a belt
That was caught about her kirtle, the bright cloak beneath,
Of a gay green silk, with gold overwrought,
And the borders all bound with embroidery fine,
And this she presses upon him, and pleads with a smile,
1835 Unworthy though it were, that it would not be scorned.
But the man still maintains that he means to accept
Neither gold nor any gift, till by God's grace
The fate that lay before him was fully achieved.
"And be not offended, fair lady, I beg,
1840 And give over your offer, for ever I must
     decline.
    I am grateful for favor shown
    Past all deserts of mine,
    And ever shall be your own
1845   True servant, rain or shine."

"Now does my present displease you," she promptly inquired,
"Because it seems in your sight so simple a thing?
And belike, as it is little, it is less to praise,
But if the virtue that invests it were verily known,
1850 It would be held, I hope, in higher esteem.
For the man that possesses this piece of silk,
If he bore it on his body, belted about,
There is no hand under heaven that could hew him down,
For he could not be killed by any craft on earth."
1855 Then the man began to muse, and mainly he thought
It was a pearl for his plight, the peril to come
When he gains the Green Chapel to get his reward:
Could he escape unscathed, the scheme were noble!
Then he bore with her words and withstood them no more,
1860 And she repeated her petition and pleaded anew,
And he granted it, and gladly she gave him the belt,
And besought him for her sake to conceal it well,
Lest the noble lord should know—and, the knight agrees
That not a soul save themselves shall see it thenceforth
1865   with sight.
    He thanked her with fervent heart,
    As often as ever he might;
    Three times, before they part,
    She has kissed the stalwart knight.

1870 Then the lady took her leave, and left him there,
For more mirth with that man she might not have.
When she was gone, Sir Gawain got from his bed,
Arose and arrayed him in his rich attire;
Tucked away the token the temptress had left,
1875 Laid it reliably where he looked for it after.
And then with good cheer to the chapel he goes,
Approached a priest in private, and prayed to be taught

To lead a better life and lift up his mind,
Lest he be among the lost when he must leave this world.
1880　And shamefaced at shrift he showed his misdeeds
From the largest to the least, and asked the Lord's mercy,
And called on his confessor to cleanse his soul,
And he absolved him of his sins as safe and as clean
As if the dread Day of Doom were to dawn on the morrow.
1885　And then he made merry amid the fine ladies
With deft-footed dances and dalliance light,
As never until now, while the afternoon wore
　　　　　　　　　away.
　　　　　　He delighted all around him,
1890　　　　And all agreed, that day,
　　　　　　They never before had found him
　　　　　　So gracious and so gay.

Now peaceful be his pasture, and love play him fair!
The host is on horseback, hunting afield;
1895　He has finished off this fox that he followed so long:
As he leapt a low hedge to look for the villain
Where he heard all the hounds in hot pursuit,
Reynard comes racing out of a rough thicket,
And all the rabble in a rush, right at his heels.
1900　The man beholds the beast, and bides his time,
And bares his bright sword, and brings it down hard,
And he blenches from the blade, and backward he starts;
A hound hurries up and hinders that move,
And before the horse's feet they fell on him at once
1905　And ripped the rascal's throat with a wrathful din.
The lord soon alighted and lifted him free,
Swiftly snatched him up from the snapping jaws,
Holds him over his head, halloos with a will,
And the dogs bayed the dirge, that had done him to death.
1910　Hunters hastened thither with horns at their lips,
Sounding the assembly till they saw him at last.
When that comely company was come in together,
All that bore bugles blew them at once,
And the others all hallooed, that had no horns.
1915　It was the merriest medley that ever a man heard,
The racket that they raised for Sir Reynard's soul
　　　　　　　　　that died.
　　　　　　Their hounds they praised and fed,
　　　　　　Fondling their heads with pride,
1920　　　　And they took Reynard the Red
　　　　　　And stripped away his hide.

And then they headed homeward, for evening had come,
Blowing many a blast on their bugles bright.
The lord at long last alights at his house,
1925　Finds fire on the hearth where the fair knight waits,
Sir Gawain the good, that was glad in heart.

With the ladies, that loved him, he lingered at ease;
He wore a rich robe of blue, that reached to the earth
And a surcoat lined softly with sumptuous furs;
1930 A hood of the same hue hung on his shoulders;
With bands of bright ermine embellished were both.
He comes to meet the man amid all the folk,
And greets him good-humoredly, and gaily he says,
"I shall follow forthwith the form of our pledge
1935 That we framed to good effect amid fresh-filled cups."
He clasps him accordingly and kisses him thrice,
As amiably and as earnestly as ever he could.
"By heaven," said the host, "you have had some luck
Since you took up this trade, if the terms were good."
1940 "Never trouble about the terms," he returned at once,
"Since all that I owe here is openly paid."
"Marry!" said the other man, "mine is much less,
For I have hunted all day, and nought have I got
But this foul fox pelt, the fiend take the goods!
1945 Which but poorly repays such precious things
That you have cordially conferred, such kisses three
                    so good."
                "Enough!" said Sir Gawain;
                "I thank you, by the rood!"
1950   And how the fox was slain
                He told him, as they stood.

With minstrelsy and mirth, with all manner of meats,
They made as much merriment as any men might
(Amid laughing of ladies and light hearted girls;
1955 So gay grew Sir Gawain and the goodly host)
Unless they had been besotted, or brainless fools.
The knight joined in jesting with that joyous folk,
Until at last it was late; ere long they must part,
And be off to their beds, as behooved them each one.
1960 Then politely his leave of the lord of the house
Our noble knight takes, and renews his thanks:
"The courtesies countless accorded me here,
Your kindness at this Christmas, may heaven's King repay!
Henceforth, if you will have me, I hold you my liege,
1965 And so, as I have said, I must set forth tomorrow,
If I may take some trusty man to teach, as you promised,
The way to the Green Chapel, that as God allows
I shall see my fate fulfilled on the first of the year."
"In good faith," said the good man, "with a good will
1970 Every promise on my part shall be fully performed."
He assigns him a servant to set him on the path,
To see him safe and sound over the snowy hills,
To follow the fastest way through forest green
                    and grove.
1975   Gawain thanks him again,
                So kind his favors prove,

> And of the ladies then
> He takes his leave, with love.

Courteously he kissed them, with care in his heart,
1980 And often wished them well, with warmest thanks,
Which they for their part were prompt to repay.
They commend him to Christ with disconsolate sighs;
And then in that hall with the household he parts—
Each man that he met, he remembered to thank
1985 For his deeds of devotion and diligent pains,
And the trouble he had taken to tend to his needs;
And each one as woeful, that watched him depart,
As he had lived with him loyally all his life long.
By lads bearing lights he was led to his chamber
1990 And blithely brought to his bed, to be at his rest.
How soundly he slept, I presume not to say,
For there were matters of moment his thoughts might well
> pursue.
> Let him lie and wait;
1995 > He has little more to do,
> Then listen, while I relate
> How they kept their rendezvous.

Part 4

Now the New Year draws near, and the night passes,
The day dispels the dark, by the Lord's decree;
2000 But wild weather awoke in the world without:
The clouds in the cold sky cast down their snow
With great gusts from the north, grievous to bear.
Sleet showered aslant upon shivering beasts;
The wind warbled wild as it whipped from aloft,
2005 And drove the drifts deep in the dales below.
Long and well he listens, that lies in his bed;
Though he lifts not his eyelids, little he sleeps;
Each crow of the cock he counts without fail.
Readily from his rest he rose before dawn,
2010 For a lamp had been left him, that lighted his chamber.
He called to his chamberlain, who quickly appeared,
And bade him get him his gear, and gird his good steed,
And he sets about briskly to bring in his arms,
And makes ready his master in manner most fit.
2015 First he clad him in his clothes, to keep out the cold,
And then his other harness, made handsome anew,
His plate-armor of proof, polished with pains,
The rings of his rich mail rid of their rust,
And all was fresh as at first, and for this he gave thanks
2020 > indeed.
> With pride he wears each piece,
> New-furbished for his need:
> No gayer from here to Greece;
> He bids them bring his steed.

2025 In his richest raiment he robed himself then:
His crested coat-armor, close-stitched with craft,
With stones of strange virtue on silk velvet set;
All bound with embroidery on borders and seams
And lined warmly and well with furs of the best.
2030 Yet he left not his love-gift, the lady's girdle;
Gawain, for his own good, forgot not that:
When the bright sword was belted and bound on his haunches,
Then twice with that token he twined him about.
Sweetly did he swathe him in that swatch of silk,
2035 That girdle of green so goodly to see,
That against the gay red showed gorgeous bright.
Yet he wore not for its wealth that wondrous girdle,
Nor pride in its pendants, though polished they were,
Though glittering gold gleamed at the tips,
2040 But to keep himself safe when consent he must
To endure a deadly dint, and all defense
                              denied.
               And now the bold knight came
               Into the courtyard wide;
2045   That folk of worthy fame
               He thanks on every side.

Then was Gringolet girt, that was great and huge,
And had sojourned safe and sound, and savored his fare;
He pawed the earth in his pride, that princely steed.
2050 The good knight draws near him and notes well his look,
And says sagely to himself, and soberly swears,
"Here is a household in hall that upholds the right!
The man that maintains it, may happiness be his!
Likewise the dear lady, may love betide her!
2055 If thus they in charity cherish a guest
That are honored here on earth, may they have his reward
That reigns high in heaven—and also you all;
And might I live in this land but a little while,
I should willingly reward you, and well, if I might."
2060 Then he steps into the stirrup and bestrides his mount;
His shield is shown forth; on his shoulder he casts it;
Strikes the side of his steed with his steel spurs,
And he starts across the stones, nor stands any longer
                              to prance.
               On horseback was the swain
2065   That bore his spear and lance;
               "May Christ this house maintain
               And guard it from mischance!"

The bridge was brought down, and the road gates
2070 Unbarred and carried back upon both sides;
He commended him to Christ, and crossed over the planks;
Praised the noble porter, who prayed on his knees
That God save Sir Gawain, and bade him good day,
And went on his way alone with the man

2075   That was to lead him ere long to that luckless place
Where the dolorous dint must be dealt him at last.
Under bare boughs they ride, where steep banks rise,
Over high cliffs they climb, where cold snow clings;
The heavens held aloof, but heavy thereunder
2080   Mist mantled the moors, moved on the slopes.
Each hill had a hat, a huge cape of cloud;
Brooks bubbled and broke over broken rocks,
Flashing in freshets that waterfalls fed.
Roundabout was the road that ran through the wood
2085   Till the sun at that season was soon to rise,
              that day.
         They were on a hilltop high;
         The white snow round them lay;
         The man that rode nearby
2090   Now bade his master stay.

"For I have seen you here safe at the set time,
And now you are not far from that notable place
That you have sought for so long with such special pains.
But this I say for certain, since I know you, sir knight,
2095   And have your good at heart, and hold you dear—
Would you heed well my words, it were worth your while—
You are rushing into risks that you reck not of:
There is a villain in yon valley, the veriest on earth,
For he is rugged and rude, and ready with his fists,
2100   And most immense in his mold of mortals alive,
And his body bigger than the best four
That are in Arthur's house, Hector[6] or any.
He gets his grim way at the Green Chapel;
None passes by that place so proud in his arms
2105   That he does not dash him down with his deadly blows,
For he is heartless wholly, and heedless of right,
For be it chaplain or churl that by the Chapel rides,
Monk or mass-priest or any man else,
He would as soon strike him dead as stand on two feet.
2110   Wherefore I say, just as certain as you sit there astride,
You cannot but be killed, if his counsel holds,
For he would trounce you in a trice, had you twenty lives
              for sale.
         He has lived long in this land
2115   And dealt out deadly bale;
         Against his heavy hand
         Your power cannot prevail.

"And so, good Sir Gawain, let the grim man be;
Go off by some other road, in God's own name!
2120   Leave by some other land, for the love of Christ,
And I shall get me home again, and give you my word
That I shall swear by God's self and the saints above,
By heaven and by my halidom[7] and other oaths more,

---

6. Either the Trojan hero or one of Arthur's knights.   7. Holiness or, more likely, patron saints.

To conceal this day's deed, nor say to a soul
2125 That ever you fled for fear from any that I knew."
"Many thanks!" said the other man—and demurring he speaks—
"Fair fortune befall you for your friendly words!
And conceal this day's deed I doubt not you would,
But though you never told the tale, if I turned back now,
2130 Forsook this place for fear, and fled, as you say,
I were a caitiff coward; I could not be excused.
But I must to the Chapel to chance my luck
And say to that same man such words as I please,
Befall what may befall through Fortune's will
2135   or whim.
            Though he be a quarrelsome knave
            With a cudgel great and grim,
            The Lord is strong to save:
            His servants trust in him."

2140 "Marry," said the man, "since you tell me so much,
And I see you are set to seek your own harm,
If you crave a quick death, let me keep you no longer!
Put your helm on your head, your hand on your lance,
And ride the narrow road down yon rocky slope
2145 Till it brings you to the bottom of the broad valley.
Then look a little ahead, on your left hand,
And you will soon see before you that self-same Chapel,
And the man of great might that is master there.
Now goodbye in God's name, Gawain the noble!
2150 For all the world's wealth I would not stay here,
Or go with you in this wood one footstep further!"
He tarried no more to talk, but turned his bridle,
Hit his horse with his heels as hard as he might,
Leaves the knight alone, and off like the wind
2155   goes leaping.
            "By God," said Gawain then,
            "I shall not give way to weeping;
            God's will be done, amen!
            I commend me to his keeping."

2160 He puts his heels to his horse, and picks up the path;
Goes in beside a grove where the ground is steep,
Rides down the rough slope right to the valley;
And then he looked a little about him—the landscape was wild,
And not a soul to be seen, nor sign of a dwelling,
2165 But high banks on either hand hemmed it about,
With many a ragged rock and rough-hewn crag;
The skies seemed scored by the scowling peaks.
Then he halted his horse, and hoved there a space,
And sought on every side for a sight of the Chapel,
2170 But no such place appeared, which puzzled him sore,
Yet he saw some way off what seemed like a mound,
A hillock high and broad, hard by the water,
Where the stream fell in foam down the face of the steep
And bubbled as if it boiled on its bed below.

2175 The knight urges his horse, and heads for the knoll;
Leaps lightly to earth; loops well the rein
Of his steed to a stout branch, and stations him there.
He strides straight to the mound, and strolls all about,
Much wondering what it was, but no whit the wiser;
2180 It had a hole at one end, and on either side,
And was covered with coarse grass in clumps all without,
And hollow all within, like some old cave,
Or a crevice of an old crag—he could not discern
aright.
2185   "Can this be the Chapel Green?
     Alack!" said the man, "here might
     The devil himself be seen
     Saying matins at black midnight!"

"Now by heaven," said he, "it is bleak hereabouts;
2190 This prayer-house is hideous, half-covered with grass!
Well may the grim man mantled in green
Hold here his orisons, in hell's own style!
Now I feel it is the Fiend, in my five wits,
That has tempted me to this tryst, to take my life;
2195 This is a Chapel of mischance, may the mischief take it!
As accursed a country church as I came upon ever!"
With his helm on his head, his lance in his hand,
He stalks toward the steep wall of that strange house.
Then he heard, on the hill, behind a hard rock,
2200 Beyond the brook, from the bank, a most barbarous din:
Lord! it clattered in the cliff fit to cleave it in two,
As one upon a grindstone ground a great scythe!
Lord! it whirred like a mill-wheel whirling about!
Lord! it echoed loud and long, lamentable to hear!
Then "By heaven," said the bold knight, "that business
2205   up there
Is arranged for my arrival, or else I am much
     misled.
     Let God work! Ah me!
     All hope of help has fled!
2210   Forfeit my life may be
     But noise I do not dread."

Then he listened no longer, but loudly he called,
"Who has power in this place, high parley to hold?
For none greets Sir Gawain, or gives him good day;
2215 If any would a word with him, let him walk forth
And speak now or never, to speed his affairs."
"Abide," said one on the bank above over his head,
"And what I promised you once shall straightway be given."
Yet he stayed not his grindstone, nor stinted its noise,
2220 But worked awhile at his whetting before he would rest,
And then he comes around a crag, from a cave in the rocks,
Hurtling out of hiding with a hateful weapon,
A Danish° ax devised for that day's deed,   *i.e., long-bladed*

With a broad blade and bright, bent in a curve,
2225 Filed to a fine edge—four feet it measured
By the length of the lace that was looped round the haft.
And in form as at first, the fellow all green,
His lordly face and his legs, his locks and his beard,
Save that firm upon two feet forward he strides,
2230 Sets a hand on the ax-head, the haft to the earth;
When he came to the cold stream, and cared not to wade,
He vaults over on his ax, and advances amain
On a broad bank of snow, overbearing and brisk
                    of mood.
2235   Little did the knight incline
              When face to face they stood;
              Said the other man, "Friend mine,
              It seems your word holds good!"

"God love you, Sir Gawain!" said the Green Knight then,
2240 "And well met this morning, man, at my place!
And you have followed me faithfully and found me betimes,
And on the business between us we both are agreed:
Twelve months ago today you took what was yours,
And you at this New Year must yield me the same.
2245 And we have met in these mountains, remote from all eyes:
There is none here to halt us or hinder our sport;
Unhasp your high helm, and have here your wages;
Make no more demur than I did myself
When you hacked off my head with one hard blow."
2250 "No, by God," said Sir Gawain, "that granted me life,
I shall grudge not the guerdon, grim though it prove;
Bestow but one stroke, and I shall stand still,
And you may lay on as you like till the last of my part
                    be paid."
2255   He proffered, with good grace,
              His bare neck to the blade,
              And feigned a cheerful face:
              He scorned to seem afraid.

Then the grim man in green gathers his strength,
2260 Heaves high the heavy ax to hit him the blow.
With all the force in his frame he fetches it aloft,
With a grimace as grim as he would grind him to bits;
Had the blow he bestowed been as big as he threatened,
A good knight and gallant had gone to his grave.
2265 But Gawain at the great ax glanced up aside.
As down it descended with death-dealing force,
And his shoulders shrank a little from the sharp iron.
Abruptly the brawny man breaks off the stroke,
And then reproved with proud words that prince among knights.
2270 "You are not Gawain the glorious," the green man said,
"That never fell back on field in the face of the foe,
And now you flee for fear, and have felt no harm:
Such news of that knight I never heard yet!

I moved not a muscle when you made to strike,
2275   Nor caviled at the cut in King Arthur's house;
My head fell to my feet, yet steadfast I stood,
And you, all unharmed, are wholly dismayed—
Wherefore the better man I, by all odds,
               must be."
2280   Said Gawain, "Strike once more;
             I shall neither flinch nor flee;
             But if my head falls to the floor
             There is no mending me!"

"But go on, man, in God's name, and get to the point!
2285   Deliver me my destiny, and do it out of hand,
For I shall stand to the stroke and stir not an inch
Till your ax has hit home—on my honor I swear it!"
"Have at thee then!" said the other, and heaves it aloft,
And glares down as grimly as he had gone mad.
2290   He made a mighty feint, but marred not his hide;
Withdrew the ax adroitly before it did damage.
Gawain gave no ground, nor glanced up aside,
But stood still as a stone, or else a stout stump
That is held in hard earth by a hundred roots.
2295   Then merrily does he mock him, the man all in green:
"So now you have your nerve again, I needs must strike;
Uphold the high knighthood that Arthur bestowed,
And keep your neck-bone clear, if this cut allows!"
Then was Gawain gripped with rage, and grimly he said,
2300   "Why, thrash away, tyrant, I tire of your threats;
You make such a scene, you must frighten yourself."
Said the green fellow, "In faith, so fiercely you speak
That I shall finish this affair, nor further grace
               allow."
2305   He stands prepared to strike
             And scowls with both lip and brow;
             No marvel if the man mislike
             Who can hope no rescue now.

He gathered up the grim ax and guided it well:
2310   Let the barb at the blade's end brush the bare throat;
He hammered down hard, yet harmed him no whit
Save a scratch on one side, that severed the skin;
The end of the hooked edge entered the flesh,
And a little blood lightly leapt to the earth.
2315   And when the man beheld his own blood bright on the snow,
He sprang a spear's length with feet spread wide,
Seized his high helm, and set it on his head,
Shoved before his shoulders the shield at his back,
Bares his trusty blade, and boldly he speaks—
2320   Not since he was a babe born of his mother
Was he once in this world one-half so blithe—
"Have done with your hacking—harry me no more!
I have borne, as behooved, one blow in this place;

If you make another move I shall meet it midway
2325 And promptly, I promise you, pay back each blow
      with brand.
    One stroke acquits me here;
    So did our covenant stand
    In Arthur's court last year—
2330   Wherefore, sir, hold your hand!"

He lowers the long ax and leans on it there,
Sets his arms on the head, the haft on the earth,
And beholds the bold knight that bides there afoot,
How he faces him fearless, fierce in full arms,
2335 And plies him with proud words—it pleases him well.
Then once again gaily to Gawain he calls,
And in a loud voice and lusty, delivers these words:
"Bold fellow, on this field your anger forbear!
No man has made demands here in manner uncouth,
2340 Nor done, save as duly determined at court.
I owed you a hit and you have it; be happy therewith!
The rest of my rights here I freely resign.
Had I been a bit busier, a buffet, perhaps,
I could have dealt more directly, and done you some harm.
2345 First I flourished with a feint, in frolicsome mood,
And left your hide unhurt—and here I did well
By the fair terms we fixed on the first night;
And fully and faithfully you followed accord:
Gave over all your gains as a good man should.
2350 A second feint, sir, I assigned for the morning
You kissed my comely wife—each kiss you restored.
For both of these there behooved two feigned blows
      by right.
    True men pay what they owe;
2355   No danger then in sight.
    You failed at the third throw,
    So take my tap, sir knight.

"For that is my belt about you, that same braided girdle,
My wife it was that wore it; I know well the tale,
2360 And the count of your kisses and your conduct too,
And the wooing of my wife—it was all my scheme!
She made trial of a man most faultless by far
Of all that ever walked over the wide earth;
As pearls to white peas, more precious and prized,
2365 So is Gawain, in good faith, to other gay knights.
Yet you lacked, sir, a little in loyalty there,
But the cause was not cunning, nor courtship either,
But that you loved your own life; the less, then, to blame."
The other stout knight in a study stood a long while,
2370 So gripped with grim rage that his great heart shook.
All the blood of his body burned in his face
As he shrank back in shame from the man's sharp speech.
The first words that fell from the fair knight's lips:

"Accursed be a cowardly and covetous heart!
2375 In you is villainy and vice, and virtue laid low!"
Then he grasps the green girdle and lets go the knot,
Hands it over in haste, and hotly he says:
"Behold there my falsehood, ill hap betide it!
Your cut taught me cowardice, care for my life,
2380 And coveting came after, contrary both
To largesse and loyalty belonging to knights.
Now am I faulty and false, that fearful was ever
Of disloyalty and lies, bad luck to them both!
      and greed.
2385   I confess, knight, in this place,
      Most dire is my misdeed;
      Let me gain back your good grace,
      And thereafter I shall take heed."

Then the other laughed aloud, and lightly he said,
2390 "Such harm as I have had, I hold it quite healed.
You are so fully confessed, your failings made known,
And bear the plain penance of the point of my blade,
I hold you polished as a pearl, as pure and as bright
As you had lived free of fault since first you were born.
2395 And I give you, sir, this girdle that is gold-hemmed
And green as my garments, that, Gawain, you may
Be mindful of this meeting when you mingle in throng
With nobles of renown—and known by this token
How it chanced at the Green Chapel, to chivalrous knights.
2400 And you shall in this New Year come yet again
And we shall finish out our feast in my fair hall,
      with cheer."
      He urged the knight to stay,
      And said, "With my wife so dear
2405   We shall see you friends this day,
      Whose enmity touched you near."

"Indeed," said the doughty knight, and doffed his high helm,
And held it in his hands as he offered his thanks,
"I have lingered long enough—may good luck be yours,
2410 And he reward you well that all worship bestows!
And commend me to that comely one, your courteous wife,
Both herself and that other, my honoured ladies,
That have trapped their true knight in their trammels so quaint.
But if a dullard should dote, deem it no wonder,
2415 And through the wiles of a woman be wooed into sorrow,
For so was Adam by one, when the world began,
And Solomon by many more, and Samson the mighty—
Delilah was his doom, and David thereafter
Was beguiled by Bathsheba, and bore much distress;
2420 Now these were vexed by their devices—'twere a very joy
Could one but learn to love, and believe them not.
For these were proud princes, most prosperous of old,
Past all lovers lucky, that languished under heaven,

bemused.

2425
And one and all fell prey
To women that they had used;
If I be led astray,
Methinks I may be excused.

"But your girdle, God love you! I gladly shall take
2430 And be pleased to possess, not for the pure gold,
Nor the bright belt itself, nor the beauteous pendants,
Nor for wealth, nor worldly state, nor workmanship fine,
But a sign of excess it shall seem oftentimes
When I ride in renown, and remember with shame
2435 The faults and the frailty of the flesh perverse,
How its tenderness entices the foul taint of sin;
And so when praise and high prowess have pleased my heart,
A look at this love-lace will lower my pride.
But one thing would I learn, if you were not loath,
2440 Since you are lord of yonder land where I have long sojourned
With honor in your house—may you have His reward
That upholds all the heavens, highest on throne!
How runs your right name?—and let the rest go."
"That shall I give you gladly," said the Green Knight then;
2445 "Bercilak de Hautdesert this barony I hold,
Through the might of Morgan le Faye,[8] that lodges at my house,
By subtleties of science and sorcerers' arts,
The mistress of Merlin,[9] she has caught many a man,
For sweet love in secret she shared sometime
2450 With that wizard, that knows well each one of your knights
and you.
Morgan the Goddess, she,
So styled by title true;
None holds so high degree
2455
That her arts cannot subdue.

"She guided me in this guise to your glorious hall,
To assay, if such it were, the surfeit of pride
That is rumored of the retinue of the Round Table.
She put this shape upon me to puzzle your wits,
2460 To afflict the fair queen, and frighten her to death
With awe of that elvish man that eerily spoke
With his head in his hand before the high table.
She was with my wife at home, that old withered lady,
Your own aunt[1] is she, Arthur's half-sister,
2465 The Duchess' daughter of Tintagel, that dear King Uther
Got Arthur on after, that honored is now.
And therefore, good friend, come feast with your aunt;
Make merry in my house; my men hold you dear,

---

8. Arthur's half-sister, an enchantress who sometimes abetted him, sometimes made trouble for
him.
9. The wise magician who had helped Arthur
become king.

1. Morgan was the daughter of Igraine, duchess
of Tintagel, and her husband the duke; Igraine
conceived Arthur when his father, Uther, lay with
her through one of Merlin's trickeries.

And I wish you as well, sir, with all my heart,
2470 As any man God ever made, for your great good faith."
But the knight said him nay, that he might by no means.
They clasped then and kissed, and commended each other
To the Prince of Paradise, and parted with one
                              assent.
2475   Gawain sets out anew;
               Toward the court his course is bent;
               And the knight all green in hue,
               Wheresoever he wished, he went.

Wild ways in the world our worthy knight rides
2480 On Gringolet, that by grace had been granted his life.
He harbored often in houses, and often abroad,
And with many valiant adventures verily he met
That I shall not take time to tell in this story.
The hurt was whole that he had had in his neck,
2485 And the bright green belt on his body he bore,
Oblique, like a baldric, bound at his side,
Below his left shoulder, laced in a knot,
In betokening of the blame he had borne for his fault;
And so to court in due course he comes safe and sound.
2490 Bliss abounded in hall when the high-born heard
That good Gawain was come; glad tidings they thought it.
The king kisses the knight, and the queen as well,
And many a comrade came to clasp him in arms,
And eagerly they asked, and awesomely he told,
2495 Confessed all his cares and discomfitures many,
How it chanced at the Chapel, what cheer made the knight,
The love of the lady, the green lace at last.
The nick on his neck he naked displayed
That he got in his disgrace at the Green Knight's hands,
2500   alone.
               With rage in heart he speaks,
               And grieves with many a groan;
               The blood burns in his cheeks
               For shame at what must be shown.

2505 "Behold, sir," said he, and handles the belt,
"This is the blazon of the blemish that I bear on my neck;
This is the sign of sore loss that I have suffered there
For the cowardice and coveting that I came to there;
This is the badge of false faith that I was found in there,
2510 And I must bear it on my body till I breathe my last.
For one may keep a deed dark, but undo it no whit,
For where a fault is made fast, it is fixed evermore."
The king comforts the knight, and the court all together
Agree with gay laughter and gracious intent
2515 That the lords and the ladies belonging to the Table,
Each brother of that band, a baldric should have,
A belt borne oblique, of a bright green,
To be worn with one accord for that worthy's sake.

So that was taken as a token by the Table Round,
2520　And he honored that had it, evermore after,
As the best book of knighthood bids it be known.
In the old days of Arthur this happening befell;
The books of Brutus' deeds bear witness thereto
Since Brutus, the bold knight, embarked for this land
2525　After the siege ceased at Troy and the city fared
amiss.
Many such, ere we were born,
Have befallen here, ere this.
May He that was crowned with thorn
2530　Bring all men to His bliss! Amen.

Hony Soyt Qui Mal Pense[2]

2. "Shame be to the man who has evil in his mind." This is the motto of the Order of the Garter, founded ca. 1350: apparently a copyist of the poem associated this order with the one founded to honor Gawain.

GEOFFREY CHAUCER
ca. 1343–1400

Medieval social theory held that society was made up of three "estates": the nobility, composed of a small hereditary aristocracy, whose mission on earth was to rule over and defend the body politic; the church, whose duty was to look after the spiritual welfare of that body; and everyone else, the large mass of commoners who were supposed to do the work that provided for its physical needs. By the late fourteenth century, however, these basic categories were layered into complex, interrelated, and unstable social strata among which birth, wealth, profession, and personal ability all played a part in determining one's status in a world that was rapidly changing economically, politically, and socially. Chaucer's life and his works, especially *The Canterbury Tales,* were profoundly influenced by these forces. A growing and prosperous middle class was beginning to play increasingly important roles in church and state, blurring the traditional class boundaries, and it was into this middle class that Chaucer was born.

Chaucer was the son of a prosperous wine merchant and probably spent his boyhood in the mercantile atmosphere of London's Vintry, where ships docked with wines from France and Spain. Here he would have mixed daily with people of all sorts, heard several languages spoken, become fluent in French, and received schooling in Latin. Instead of apprenticing Chaucer to the family business, however, his father was apparently able to place him, in his early teens, as a page in one of the great aristocratic households of England, that of the countess of Ulster who was married to Prince Lionel, the second son of Edward III. There Chaucer would have acquired the manners and skills required for a career in the service of the ruling class, not only in the role of personal attendant in royal households but in a series of administrative posts.

We can trace Chaucer's official and personal life in a considerable number of surviving historical documents, beginning with a reference, in Elizabeth of Ulster's household accounts, to an outfit he received as a page (1357). He was captured by the French and ransomed in one of Edward III's campaigns during the Hundred Years

War (1359). He was a member of King Edward's personal household (1367) and took part in several diplomatic missions to Spain (1366), France (1368), and Italy (1372). As controller of customs on wool, sheepskins, and leather for the port of London (1374–85), Chaucer audited and kept books on the export taxes, which were one of the Crown's main sources of revenue. During this period he was living in a rent-free apartment over one of the gates in the city wall, probably as a perquisite of the customs job. He served as a justice of the peace and knight of the shire (the title given to members of Parliament) for the county of Kent (1385–86) where he moved after giving up the controllership. As clerk of the king's works (1389–91), Chaucer was responsible for the maintenance of numerous royal residences, parks, and other hold-ings; his duties included supervision of the construction of the nave of Westminster Abbey and of stands and lists for a celebrated tournament staged by Richard II. While the records show Chaucer receiving many grants and annuities in addition to his salary for these services, they also show that at times he was being pressed by creditors and obliged to borrow money.

These activities brought Chaucer into association with the ruling nobility of the kingdom, with Prince Lionel and his younger brother John of Gaunt, duke of Lan-caster, England's most powerful baron during much of Chaucer's lifetime; with their father, King Edward; and with Edward's grandson, who succeeded to the throne as Richard II. Near the end of his life Chaucer addressed a comic *Complaint to His Purse* to Henry IV—John of Gaunt's son, who had usurped the crown from his cousin Richard—as a reminder that the treasury owed Chaucer his annuity. Chaucer's wife, Philippa, served in the households of Edward's queen and of John of Gaunt's second wife, Constance, daughter of the king of Castile. A Thomas Chaucer, who was prob-ably Chaucer's son, was an eminent man in the next generation, and Thomas's daugh-ter Alice was married successively to the earl of Salisbury and the duke of Suffolk. The gap between the commoners and the aristocracy would thus have been bridged by Chaucer's family in the course of three generations.

None of these documents contains any hint that this hardworking civil servant wrote poetry, although poetry would certainly have been among the diversions cul-tivated at English courts in Chaucer's youth. That poetry, however, would have been in French, which still remained the fashionable language and literature of the English aristocracy, whose culture in many ways had more in common with that of the French nobles with whom they warred than with that of their English subjects. Chaucer's earliest models, works by Guillaume de Machaut (1300?–1377) and Jean Froissart (1333?–1400?), the leading French poets of the day, were lyrics and narratives about courtly love, often cast in the form of a dream in which the poet acted as a protagonist or participant in some aristocratic love affair. The poetry of Machaut and Froissart derives from the thirteenth-century *Romance of the Rose*, a long dream allegory in which the dreamer suffers many agonies and trials for the love of a symbolic rosebud. Chaucer's apprentice work may well have been a partial translation of the twenty-one-thousand-line *Romance*. His first important original poem is *The Book of the Duchess*, an elegy in the form of a dream vision commemorating John of Gaunt's first wife, the young duchess of Lancaster, who died in 1368.

The diplomatic mission that sent Chaucer to Italy in 1372 was in all likelihood a milestone in his literary development. Although he may have acquired some knowl-edge of the language and literature from Italian merchants and bankers posted in London, this visit and a subsequent one to Florence (1378) brought him into direct contact with the Italian Renaissance. Probably he acquired manuscripts of works by Dante, Petrarch, and Boccaccio—the last two still alive at the time of Chaucer's visit, although he probably did not meet them. These writers provided him with models of new verse forms, new subject matter, and new modes of representation. *The House of Fame*, still a dream vision, takes the poet on a journey in the talons of a gigantic eagle to the celestial palace of the goddess Fame, a trip that at many points affec-tionately parodies Dante's journey in the *Divine Comedy*. In his dream vision *The*

Parliament of Fowls, all the birds meet on St. Valentine's Day to choose their mates; their "parliament" humorously depicts the ways in which different classes in human society think and talk about love. Boccaccio provided sources for two of Chaucer's finest poems—although Chaucer never mentions his name. *The Knight's Tale,* the first of *The Canterbury Tales,* is based on Boccaccio's romance *Il Teseida* (The Story of Theseus). His longest completed poem, *Troilus and Criseyde* (ca. 1385), which tells the story of how Trojan Prince Troilus loved and finally lost Criseyde to the Greek warrior Diomede, is an adaptation of Boccaccio's *Il Filostrato* (The Love-Stricken). Chaucer reworked the latter into one of the greatest love poems in any language. Even if he had never written *The Canterbury Tales,* *Troilus* would have secured Chaucer a place among the major English poets.

A final dream vision provides the frame for Chaucer's first experiment with a series of tales, the unfinished *Legend of Good Women.* In the dream, Chaucer is accused of heresy and antifeminism by Cupid, the god of love himself, and ordered to do penance by writing a series of "legends," i.e., saints' lives, of Cupid's martyrs, women who were betrayed by false men and died for love. Perhaps a noble patron, possibly Queen Anne, asked the poet to write something to make up for telling about Criseyde's betrayal of Troilus.

Throughout his life Chaucer also wrote moral and religious works, chiefly translations. Besides French, which was a second language for him, and Italian, Chaucer also read Latin. He made a prose translation of the Latin *Consolation of Philosophy,* written by the sixth-century Roman statesman Boethius while in prison awaiting execution for crimes for which he had been unjustly condemned. The *Consolation* became a favorite book for the Middle Ages, providing inspiration and comfort through its lesson that worldly fortune is deceitful and ephemeral and through the platonic doctrine that the body itself is only a prison house for the soul that aspires to eternal things. The influence of Boethius is deeply ingrained in *The Knight's Tale* and *Troilus.* The ballade *Truth* compresses the Boethian and Christian teaching into three stanzas of homely moral advice.

Thus long before Chaucer conceived of *The Canterbury Tales,* his writings were many faceted: they embrace prose and poetry; human and divine love; French, Italian, and Latin sources; secular and religious influences; comedy and philosophy. Moreover, different elements are likely to mix in the same work, often making it difficult to extract from Chaucer simple, direct, and certain meanings.

This Chaucerian complexity owes much to the wide range of Chaucer's learning and his exposure to new literary currents on the Continent but perhaps also to the special social position he occupied as a member of a new class of civil servants. Born into the urban middle class, Chaucer, through his association with the court and service of the Crown, had attained the rank of "esquire," roughly equivalent to what would later be termed a "gentleman." His career brought him into contact with overlapping bourgeois and aristocratic social worlds, without his being securely anchored in either. Although he was born a commoner and continued to associate with commoners in his official life, he did not live as a commoner; and although his training and service at court, his wife's connections, and probably his poetry brought him into contact with the nobility, he must always have been conscious of the fact that he did not really belong to that society of which birth alone could make one a true member. Situated at the intersection of these social worlds, Chaucer had the gift of being able to view with both sympathy and humor the behaviors, beliefs, and pretensions of the diverse people who comprised the levels of society. Chaucer's art of being at once involved in and detached from a given situation is peculiarly his own, but that art would have been appreciated by a small group of friends close to Chaucer's social position—men like Sir Philip de la Vache, to whom Chaucer addressed the humorous envoy to *Truth.* Chaucer belongs to an age when poetry was read aloud. A beautiful frontispiece to a manuscript of *Troilus* pictures the poet's public performance before a magnificently dressed royal audience, and he may well have been invited at times to read his poems at court. But besides addressing a listening audience, to whose allegedly superior taste and sensibility the poet often ironically defers (for example, *The General Prologue*, lines 745–48), Chaucer has in mind discriminating readers whom he might expect to share his sense of humor and his complex attitudes toward the company of "sondry folk" who make the pilgrimage to Canterbury.

The text given here is from E. T. Donaldson's *Chaucer's Poetry: An Anthology for the Modern Reader* (1958, 1975) with some modifications. For *The Canterbury Tales* the Hengwrt Manuscript has provided the textual basis. The spelling has been altered to improve consistency and has been modernized in so far as is possible without distorting the phonological values of the Middle English. A discussion of Middle English pronunciation, grammar, and prosody is included in the introduction to "The Middle Ages" (pp. 11–18).

The Canterbury Tales   Chaucer's original plan for *The Canterbury Tales*—if we assume it to be the same as that which the fictional Host proposes at the end of *The General Prologue*—projected about one hundred twenty stories, two for each pilgrim to tell on the way to Canterbury and two more on the way back. Chaucer actually completed only twenty-two and the beginnings of two others. He did write an ending, for the Host says to the Parson, who tells the last tale, that everyone except him has told "his tale." Indeed, the pilgrims never even get to Canterbury. The work was probably first conceived in 1386, when Chaucer was living in Greenwich, some miles east of London. From his house he might have been able to see the pilgrim road that led toward the shrine of the famous English saint, Thomas à Becket, the archbishop of Canterbury who was murdered in his cathedral in 1170. Medieval pilgrims were notorious tale tellers, and the sight and sound of the bands riding toward Canterbury may well have suggested to Chaucer the idea of using a fictitious pilgrimage as a framing device for a number of stories. Collections of stories linked by such a device were common in the later Middle Ages. Chaucer's contemporary John Gower had used one in his *Confessio Amantis*. The most famous medieval framing tale besides Chaucer's is Boccaccio's *Decameron*, in which ten different narrators each tell a tale a day for ten days. Chaucer could have known the *Decameron*, which contains tales with plots analogous to plots found also in *The Canterbury Tales*, but these stories were widespread, and there is no proof that Chaucer got them from Boccaccio.

Chaucer's artistic exploitation of the device is, in any case, altogether his own. Whereas in Gower a single speaker relates all the stories, and in Boccaccio the ten speakers—three young gentlemen and seven young ladies—all belong to the same sophisticated social elite, Chaucer's pilgrim narrators represent a wide spectrum of ranks and occupations. This device, however, should not be mistaken for "realism." It is highly unlikely that a group like Chaucer's pilgrims would ever have joined together and communicated on such seemingly equal terms. That is part of the fiction, as is the tacit assumption that a group so large could have ridden along listening to one another tell tales in verse. The variety of tellers is matched by the diversity of their tales: tales are assigned to appropriate narrators and juxtaposed to bring out contrasts in genre, style, tone, and values. Thus the Knight's courtly romance about the rivalry of two noble lovers for a lady is followed by the Miller's fabliau of the seduction of an old carpenter's young wife by a student. In several of *The Canterbury Tales* there is a fascinating accord between the narrators and their stories, so that the story takes on rich overtones from what we have learned of its teller in *The General Prologue* and elsewhere, and the character itself grows and is revealed by the story. Chaucer conducts two fictions simultaneously—that of the individual tale and that of the pilgrim to whom he has assigned it. He develops the second fiction not only through *The General Prologue* but also through the "links," the interchanges among pilgrims connecting the stories. These interchanges sometimes lead to quarrels. Thus *The Miller's Tale* offends the Reeve, who takes the figure of the Miller's foolish, cuckolded carpenter as directed personally at himself, and he retaliates with a story satirizing an arrogant miller very much like the pilgrim Miller. The antagonism of the two tellers provides comedy in the links and enhances the comedy of their tales. The links also offer interesting literary commentary on the tales by members of the pilgrim audience, especially the Host, whom the pilgrims have declared "governour" and "juge" of the storytelling. Further dramatic interest is created by the fact that several tales respond to topics taken up by previous tellers. The Wife of Bath's thesis that women should have sovereignty over men in marriage gets a reply from the Clerk, which in turn elicits responses from the Merchant and the Franklin. The tales have their own logic and interest quite apart from the framing fiction; no other medieval framing fiction, however, has such varied and lively interaction between the frame and the individual stories.

The composition of none of the tales can be accurately dated; most of them were written during the last fourteen years of Chaucer's life, although a few were probably written earlier and inserted into *The Canterbury Tales*. The popularity of the poem in late medieval England is attested by the number of surviving manuscripts: more than eighty, none from Chaucer's lifetime. It was also twice printed by William Caxton, who introduced printing to England in 1476, and often reprinted by Caxton's early successors. The manuscripts reflect the unfinished state of the poem—the fact that when he died Chaucer had not made up his mind about a number of details and hence left many inconsistencies. The poem appears in the manuscripts as nine or ten "fragments" or blocks of tales; the order of the poems within each fragment is generally the same, but the order of the fragments themselves varies widely. The fragment containing *The General Prologue*; the Knight's, Miller's, and Reeve's tales; and the Cook's unfinished tale, always comes first, and the fragment consisting of *The Parson's Tale* and *The Retraction* always comes last. But the others, such as that containing the Wife of Bath, the Friar, and the Summoner or that consisting of the Physician and Pardoner or the longest fragment, consisting of six tales concluding with the Nun's Priest's, are by no means stable in relation to one another. The order followed here, that of the Ellesmere manuscript, has been adopted as the most nearly satisfactory.

The General Prologue

Chaucer did not need to make a pilgrimage himself to meet the types of people that his fictitious pilgrimage includes, because most of them had long inhabited literature as well as life: the ideal Knight, who had taken part in all the major expeditions and battles of the crusades during the last half-century; his fashionably dressed son, the Squire, a typical young lover; the lady Prioress, the hunting Monk, and the flattering Friar, who practice the little vanities and larger vices for which such ecclesiastics were conventionally attacked; the prosperous Franklin; the fraudulent Doctor; the lusty and domineering Wife of Bath; the austere Parson; and so on down through the lower orders to that spellbinding preacher and mercenary, the Pardoner, peddling his paper indulgences and phony relics. One meets all these types throughout medieval literature, but particularly in a genre called estates satire, which sets out to expose and pillory typical examples of corruption at all levels of society. A remarkable number of details in *The General Prologue* could have been taken straight out of books as well as drawn from life. Although it has been argued that some of the pilgrims are portraits of actual people, the impression that they are drawn from life is more likely to be a function of Chaucer's art, which is able to endow types with a reality we generally associate only with people we know. The salient features of each pilgrim leap out randomly at the reader, as they might to an observer concerned only with what meets the eye. This imitation of the way our minds actually perceive reality may make us fail to notice the care with which Chaucer has selected his details to give an integrated sketch of the person being described. Most of these details give something more than mere verisimilitude to the description. The pilgrims' facial features, the clothes they wear, the foods they like to eat, the things they say, the work they do are all clues not only to their social rank but to their moral and spiritual condition and, through the accumulation of detail, to the condition of late-medieval society, of which, collectively, they are representative. What uniquely distinguishes Chaucer's prologue from more conventional estates satire, such as the *Prologue* to *Piers Plowman*, is the suppression in all but a few flagrant instances of overt moral judgment. The narrator, in fact, seems to be expressing chiefly admiration and praise at the superlative skills and accomplishments of this particular group, even such dubious ones as the Friar's begging techniques or the Manciple's success in cheating the learned lawyers who employ him. The reader is left free to draw out the ironic implications of details presented with such seeming artlessness, even while falling in with the easygoing mood of "felaweship" that pervades Chaucer's prologue to the pilgrimage.

FROM THE CANTERBURY TALES

The General Prologue

Whan that April with his° showres soote°	*its/fresh*
The droughte of March hath perced to the roote,	
And bathed every veine[1] in swich° licour,°	*such/liquid*
Of which vertu[2] engendred is the flowr;	
5 Whan Zephyrus eek° with his sweete breeth	*also*
Inspired[3] hath in every holt° and heeth°	*grove/field*
The tendre croppes,° and the yonge sonne[4]	*shoots*
Hath in the Ram his halve cours yronne,	
And smale fowles° maken melodye	*birds*
10 That sleepen al the night with open yë°—	*eye*
So priketh hem° Nature in hir corages[5]—	*them*
Thanne longen folk to goon° on pilgrimages,	*go*
And palmeres for to seeken straunge strondes	
To ferne halwes,[6] couthe° in sondry° londes;	*known/various*
15 And specially from every shires ende	
Of Engelond to Canterbury they wende,	
The holy blisful martyr[7] for to seeke	
That hem hath holpen° whan that they were seke.°	*helped/sick*
Bifel° that in that seson on a day,	*It happened*
20 In Southwerk[8] at the Tabard as I lay,	
Redy to wenden on my pilgrimage	
To Canterbury with ful° devout corage,	*very*
At night was come into that hostelrye	

1. I.e., in plants.
2. By the power of which.
3. Breathed into. "Zephyrus": the west wind.
4. The sun is young because it has run only half-way through its course in Aries, the Ram—the first sign of the zodiac in the solar year.
5. Their hearts.
6. Far-off shrines. "Palmeres": palmers, wide-ranging pilgrims—especially those who sought out the "straunge strondes" (foreign shores) of the Holy Land.
7. St. Thomas à Becket, murdered in Canterbury Cathedral in 1170.
8. Southwark, site of the Tabard Inn, was then a suburb of London, south of the Thames River.

Wel nine and twenty in a compaignye
25 Of sondry folk, by aventure° yfalle   *chance*
In felaweshipe, and pilgrimes were they alle
That toward Canterbury wolden° ride.   *would*
The chambres and the stables weren wide,
And wel we weren esed° at the beste.⁹   *accommodated*
30 And shortly,° whan the sonne was to reste,¹   *in brief*
So hadde I spoken with hem everichoon°   *every one*
That I was of hir felaweshipe anoon,°   *at once*
And made forward² erly for to rise,
To take oure way ther as³ I you devise.°   *describe*
35   But nathelees,° whil I have time and space,⁴   *nevertheless*
Er° that I ferther in this tale pace,°   *before / proceed*
Me thinketh it accordant to resoun⁵
To telle you al the condicioun
Of eech of hem, so as it seemed me,
40 And whiche they were, and of what degree,°   *social rank*
And eek° in what array that they were inne: *also*
And at a knight thanne° wol I first biginne.   *then*
    A Knight ther was, and that a worthy man,
That fro the time that he first bigan
45 To riden out, he loved chivalrye,
Trouthe and honour, freedom and curteisye.⁶
Ful worthy was he in his lordes werre,°   *war*
And therto hadde he riden, no man ferre,°   *farther*
As wel in Cristendom as hethenesse,°   *heathen lands*
50 And⁷ evere honoured for his worthinesse.
    At Alisandre⁸ he was whan it was wonne;
Ful ofte time he hadde the boord bigonne⁹
Aboven alle nacions in Pruce;
In Lettou had he reised,° and in Ruce,   *campaigned*
55 No Cristen man so ofte of his degree;
In Gernade° at the sege eek hadde he be   *Granada*
Of Algezir, and riden in Belmarye;
At Lyeis was he, and at Satalye,
Whan they were wonne; and in the Grete See¹
60 At many a noble arivee° hadde he be.   *military landing*
    At mortal batailes² hadde he been fifteene,
And foughten for oure faith at Tramissene
In listes³ thries,° and ay° slain his fo.   *thrice / always*
    This ilke° worthy Knight hadde been also   *same*
65 Sometime with the lord of Palatye⁴

9. In the best possible way.
1. Had set.
2. I.e., (we) made an agreement.
3. Where.
4. I.e., opportunity.
5. It seems to me according to reason.
6. Courtesy. "Trouthe": integrity. "Freedom": generosity of spirit.
7. I.e., and he was.
8. The Knight has taken part in campaigns fought against three groups who threatened Christian Europe during the 14th century: the Muslims in the Near East, from whom Alexandria was seized after a famous siege; the northern barbarians in Prussia, Lithuania, and Russia; and the Moors in North Africa. The place names in the following lines refer to battlegrounds in these continuing wars.
9. Sat in the seat of honor at military feasts.
1. The Mediterranean.
2. Tournaments fought to the death.
3. Lists, tournament grounds.
4. A Muslim: alliances of convenience were often made during the Crusades between Christians and Muslims.

Again° another hethen in Turkye;   *against*
And everemore he hadde a soverein pris.°   *reputation*
And though that he were worthy, he was wis,[5]
And of his port° as meeke as is a maide.   *demeanor*
70 He nevere yit no vilainye° ne saide   *rudeness*
In al his lif unto no manere wight:[6]
He was a verray,° parfit,° gentil° knight.   *true/perfect/noble*
But for to tellen you of his array,
His hors° were goode, but he was nat gay.[7]   *horses*
75 Of fustian° he wered° a gipoun[8]   *thick cloth/wore*
Al bismotered with his haubergeoun,[9]
For he was late° come from his viage,°   *lately/expedition*
And wente for to doon his pilgrimage.
    With him ther was his sone, a yong Squier,[1]
80 A lovere and a lusty bacheler,
With lokkes crulle° as° they were laid in presse.   *curly/as if*
Of twenty yeer of age he was, I gesse.
Of his stature he was of evene° lengthe,   *moderate*
And wonderly delivere,° and of greet° strengthe.   *agile/great*
85 And he hadde been som time in chivachye[2]
In Flandres, in Artois, and Picardye,
And born him wel as of so litel space,[3]
In hope to stonden in his lady° grace.   *lady's*
    Embrouded° was he as it were a mede,[4]   *embroidered*
90 Al ful of fresshe flowres, white and rede;°   *red*
Singing he was, or floiting,° al the day: *whistling*
He was as fressh as is the month of May.
Short was his gowne, with sleeves longe and wide.
Wel coude he sitte on hors, and faire ride;
95 He coude songes make, and wel endite,°   *compose verse*
Juste[5] and eek° daunce, and wel portraye° and write.   *also/sketch*
So hote° he loved that by nightertale[6]   *hotly*
He slepte namore than dooth a nightingale.
Curteis he was, lowely,° and servisable,   *humble*
100 And carf biforn his fader at the table.[7]
    A Yeman hadde he[8] and servants namo°   *no more*
At that time, for him liste[9] ride so;
And he[1] was clad in cote and hood of greene.
A sheef of pecok arwes,° bright and keene,   *arrows*
105 Under his belt he bar° ful thriftily;°   *bore/properly*
Wel coude he dresse° his takel° yemanly:[2]   *tend to/gear*
His arwes drouped nought with fetheres lowe.

---

5. I.e., he was wise as well as bold.
6. Any sort of person. In Middle English, negatives are multiplied for emphasis, as in these two lines: "nevere," "no," "ne," "no."
7. I.e., gaily dressed.
8. Tunic worn underneath the coat of mail.
9. All rust-stained from his hauberk (coat of mail).
1. The vague term "Squier" (Squire) here seems to be the equivalent of "bacheler" (line 80), a young knight still in the service of an older one.
2. On cavalry expeditions. The places in the next line are sites of skirmishes in the constant warfare between the English and the French.

3. I.e., considering the little time he had been in service.
4. Mead, meadow.
5. Joust, fight in a tournament.
6. At night.
7. It was a squire's duty to carve his lord's meat.
8. I.e., the Knight. The "Yeman" (Yeoman) is an independent commoner who acts as the Knight's military servant.
9. It pleased him to.
1. I.e., the Yeoman.
2. In a workmanlike way.

And in his hand he bar a mighty bowe.

A not-heed° hadde he with a brown visage.   *close-cut head*

110 Of wodecraft wel coude° he al the usage.   *knew*

Upon his arm he bar a gay bracer,[3]

And by his side a swerd° and a bokeler,[4]   *sword*

And on that other side a gay daggere,

Harneised° wel and sharp as point of spere;   *mounted*

115 A Cristophre[5] on his brest of silver sheene;°   *bright*

An horn he bar, the baudrik[6] was of greene.

A forster° was he soothly,° as I gesse.   *forester / truly*

    Ther was also a Nonne, a Prioresse,

That of hir smiling was ful simple and coy.[7]

120 Hir gretteste ooth was but by sainte Loy!°   *Eloi*

And she was cleped° Madame Eglantine.   *named*

Ful wel she soong° the service divine,   *sang*

Entuned° in hir nose ful semely;[8]   *chanted*

And Frenssh she spak ful faire and fetisly,°   *elegantly*

125 After the scole° of Stratford at the Bowe[9]—   *school*

For Frenssh of Paris was to hire unknowe.

At mete° wel ytaught was she withalle:°   *meals / besides*

She leet° no morsel from hir lippes falle,   *let*

Ne wette hir fingres in hir sauce deepe;

130 Wel coude she carye a morsel, and wel keepe°   *take care*

That no drope ne fille° upon hir brest.   *should fall*

In curteisye was set ful muchel hir lest.[1]

Hir over-lippe° wiped she so clene   *upper lip*

That in hir coppe° ther was no ferthing° seene   *cup / bit*

135 Of grece,° whan she dronken hadde hir draughte;   *grease*

Ful semely after hir mete she raughte.°   *reached*

And sikerly° she was of greet disport,[2]   *certainly*

And ful plesant, and amiable of port,°   *mien*

And pained hire to countrefete cheere[3]

140 Of court, and to been statlich° of manere,   *dignified*

And to been holden digne[4] of reverence.

But, for to speken of hir conscience,

She was so charitable and so pitous°   *merciful*

She wolde weepe if that she saw a mous

145 Caught in a trappe, if it were deed° or bledde.   *dead*

Of[5] smale houndes hadde she that she fedde

With rosted flessh, or milk and wastelbreed;°   *fine white bread*

But sore wepte she if oon of hem were deed,

Or if men smoot it with a yerde smerte;[6]

150 And al was conscience and tendre herte.

Ful semely hir wimpel° pinched° was,   *headdress / pleated*

Hir nose tretis,° hir yën° greye as glas,   *well-formed / eyes*

---

3. Wrist guard for archers.
4. Buckler (a small shield).
5. St. Christopher medal.
6. Baldric (a supporting strap).
7. Sincere and shy. The Prioress is the mother superior of her nunnery.
8. In a seemly, proper manner.
9. The French learned in a convent school in

Stratford-at-the-Bow, a suburb of London, was evidently not up to the Parisian standard.
1. I.e., her chief delight lay in good manners.
2. Of great good cheer.
3. And took pains to imitate the behavior.
4. And to be considered worthy.
5. I.e., some.
6. If someone struck it with a rod sharply.

Hir mouth ful smal, and therto° softe and reed,°   *moreover/red*
But sikerly° she hadde a fair forheed: *certainly*
155 It was almost a spanne brood,[7] I trowe,°   *believe*
For hardily,° she was nat undergrowe.   *assuredly*
Ful fetis° was hir cloke, as I was war;°   *becoming/aware*
Of smal° coral aboute hir arm she bar   *dainty*
A paire of bedes, gauded all with greene,[8]
160 And theron heeng° a brooch of gold ful sheene,°   *hung/bright*
On which ther was first writen a crowned A,[9]
And after, *Amor vincit omnia.*[1]
   Another Nonne with hire hadde she
That was hir chapelaine,° and preestes three.[2]   *secretary*
165   A Monk ther was, a fair for the maistrye,[3]
An outridere[4] that loved venerye,°   *hunting*
A manly man, to been an abbot able.°   *worthy*
Ful many a daintee° hors hadde he in stable,   *fine*
And whan he rood,° men mighte his bridel heere   *rode*
170 Ginglen° in a whistling wind as clere   *jingle*
And eek° as loude as dooth the chapel belle   *also*
Ther as this lord was kepere of the celle.[5]
The rule of Saint Maure or of Saint Beneit,
By cause that it was old and somdeel strait[6]—
175 This ilke° Monk leet olde thinges pace,°   *same/pass away*
And heeld° after the newe world the space.°   *held/course*
He yaf° nought of that text a pulled hen[7]   *gave*
That saith that hunteres been° nought holy men,   *are*
Ne that a monk, whan he is recchelees,[8]
180 Is likned til° a fissh that is waterlees—   *to*
This is to sayn, a monk out of his cloistre;
But thilke° text heeld he nat worth an oystre.   *that same*
And I saide his opinion was good:
What° sholde he studye and make himselven wood°   *why/crazy*
185 Upon a book in cloistre alway to poure,°   *pore*
Or swinke° with his handes and laboure,   *work*
As Austin bit?[9] How shal the world be served?
Lat Austin have his swink to him reserved!
Therefore he was a prikasour° aright.   *hard rider*
190 Grehoundes he hadde as swift as fowl in flight.
Of priking° and of hunting for the hare   *riding*
Was al his lust,° for no cost wolde he spare.   *pleasure*
I sawgh his sleeves purfiled° at the hand   *fur lined*
With gris,° and that the fineste of a land;   *gray fur*
195 And for to festne his hood under his chin
He hadde of gold wrought a ful curious[1] pin:

---

7. A handsbreadth wide.
8. Provided with green beads to mark certain prayers. "A paire": string (i.e., a rosary).
9. An *A* with an ornamental crown on it.
1. "Love conquers all."
2. The three get reduced to just one nun's priest.
3. I.e., a superlatively fine one.
4. A monk charged with supervising property distant from the monastery. Monasteries obtained income from large landholdings.

5. Prior of an outlying cell (branch) of the monastery.
6. Somewhat strict. St. Maurus and St. Benedict were authors of monastic rules.
7. He didn't give a plucked hen for that text.
8. Reckless, careless of rule.
9. I.e., as St. Augustine bids. St. Augustine had written that monks should perform manual labor.
1. Of careful workmanship.

A love-knotte in the grettere° ende ther was.   *greater*
His heed was balled,° that shoon as any glas,   *bald*
And eek his face, as he hadde been anoint:
200 He was a lord ful fat and in good point;²
His yën steepe,° and rolling in his heed,   *protruding*
That stemed as a furnais of a leed,³
His bootes souple,° his hors in greet estat°   *supple/condition*
Now certainly he was a fair prelat.⁴
205 He was nat pale as a forpined° gost: *wasted away*
A fat swan loved he best of any rost.
His palfrey° was as brown as is a berye.   *saddle horse*
     A Frere ther was, a wantoune° and a merye,   *jovial*
A limitour,⁵ a ful solempne° man.   *ceremonious*
210 In alle the ordres foure is noon that can°   *knows*
So muche of daliaunce° and fair langage: *sociability*
He hadde maad ful many a mariage
Of yonge wommen at his owene cost;
Unto his ordre he was a noble post.⁶
215 Ful wel biloved and familier was he
With frankelains over al⁷ in his contree,
And with worthy wommen of the town—
For he hadde power of confessioun,
As saide himself, more than a curat,°   *parish priest*
220 For of° his ordre he was licenciat.⁸   *by*
Ful swetely herde he confessioun,
And plesant was his absolucioun.
He was an esy man to yive penaunce
Ther as he wiste to have⁹ a good pitaunce;°   *donation*
225 For unto a poore ordre for to yive
Is signe that a man is wel yshrive,¹
For if he yaf, he dorste make avaunt°   *boast*
He wiste° that a man was repentaunt;   *knew*
For many a man so hard is of his herte
230 He may nat weepe though him sore smerte:²
Therfore, in stede of weeping and prayeres,
Men mote° yive silver to the poore freres.³   *may*
     His tipet° was ay farsed° ful of knives   *hood/stuffed*
And pinnes, for to yiven faire wives;
235 And certainly he hadde a merye note;
Wel coude he singe and playen on a rote;°   *fiddle*
Of yeddinges he bar outrely the pris.⁴
His nekke whit was as the flowr-de-lis;°   *lily*
Therto he strong was as a champioun.

2. In good shape, plump.
3. That glowed like a furnace with a pot in it.
4. Prelate (an important churchman).
5. The "Frere" (Friar) is a member of one of the four religious orders whose members live by begging; as a "limitour" he has been granted by his order exclusive begging rights within a certain limited area.
6. I.e., pillar, a staunch supporter.
7. I.e., with franklins everywhere. Franklins were well-to-do country men.

8. I.e., licensed to hear confessions.
9. Where he knew he would have.
1. Shriven, absolved.
2. Although he is sorely grieved.
3. Before granting absolution, the confessor must be sure the sinner is contrite; moreover, the absolution is contingent on the sinner's performance of an act of satisfaction. In the case of Chaucer's Friar, a liberal contribution served both as proof of contrition and as satisfaction.
4. He absolutely took the prize for ballads.

240 He knew the tavernes wel in every town,
And every hostiler° and tappestere,°   *innkeeper/barmaid*
Bet° than a lazar or a beggestere.[5]   *better*
For unto swich a worthy man as he
Accorded nat, as by his facultee,[6]
245 To have with sike° lazars aquaintaunce: *sick*
It is nat honeste,° it may nought avaunce,°   *dignified/profit*
For to delen with no swich poraile,[7]
But al with riche, and selleres of vitaile;°   *foodstuffs*
And over al ther as[8] profit sholde arise,
250 Curteis he was, and lowely of servise.
Ther was no man nowher so vertuous:°   *effective*
He was the beste beggere in his hous.°   *friary*
And yaf a certain ferme for the graunt:[9]
Noon of his bretheren cam ther in his haunt.[1]
255 For though a widwe° hadde nought a sho,°   *widow/shoe*
So plesant was his *In principio*[2]
Yit wolde he have a ferthing° er he wente;   *small coin*
His purchas was wel bettre than his rente.[3]
And rage he coude as it were right a whelpe;[4]
260 In love-dayes[5] ther coude he muchel° helpe,   *much*
For ther he was nat lik a cloisterer,
With a thredbare cope, as is a poore scoler,
But he was lik a maister[6] or a pope.
Of double worstede was his semicope,°   *short robe*
265 And rounded as a belle out of the presse.°   *bell mold*
Somwhat he lipsed° for his wantounesse°   *lisped/affectation*
To make his Englissh sweete upon his tonge;
And in his harping, whan he hadde songe,°   *sung*
His yën twinkled in his heed aright
270 As doon the sterres° in the frosty night.   *stars*
This worthy limitour was cleped Huberd.
      A Marchant was ther with a forked beerd,
In motelee,[7] and hye on hors he sat,
Upon his heed a Flandrissh° bevere hat,   *Flemish*
275 His bootes clasped faire and fetisly.°   *elegantly*
His resons° he spak ful solempnely,   *opinions*
Souning° alway th' encrees of his winning.°   *implying/profit*
He wolde the see were kept for any thing[8]
Bitwixen Middelburgh and Orewelle.
280 Wel coude he in eschaunge sheeldes[9] selle.

5. "Beggestere": female beggar. "Lazar:" leper.
6. It was not suitable because of his position.
7. I.e., poor trash. The oldest order of friars had been founded by St. Francis to administer to the spiritual needs of precisely those classes the Friar avoids.
8. Everywhere.
9. And he paid a certain rent for the privilege of begging.
1. Assigned territory.
2. A friar's usual salutation: "In the beginning [was the Word]" (John 1.1).
3. I.e., the money he got through such activity was more than his proper income.

4. And he could flirt wantonly, as if he were a puppy.
5. Days appointed for the settlement of lawsuits out of court.
6. A man of recognized learning.
7. Motley, a cloth of mixed color.
8. I.e., he wished the sea to be guarded at all costs. The sea route between Middelburgh (in the Netherlands) and Orwell (in Suffolk) was vital to the Merchant's export and import of wool—the basis of England's chief trade at the time.
9. Shields were units of transfer in international credit, which he exchanged at a profit.

This worthy man ful wel his wit bisette:° employed
Ther wiste° no wight° that he was in dette, knew/person
So statly° was he of his governaunce,[1] dignified
With his bargaines,° and with his chevissaunce.° bargainings/borrowing
285 Forsoothe° he was a worthy man withalle; in truth
But, sooth to sayn, I noot° how men him calle. don't know
A Clerk[2] ther was of Oxenforde also
That unto logik hadde longe ygo.[3]
As lene was his hors as is a rake,
290 And he was nought right fat, I undertake,
But looked holwe,° and therto sobrely. hollow
Ful thredbare was his overeste courtepy,
For he hadde geten him yit no benefice,[4]
Ne was so worldly for to have office.° secular employment
295 For him was levere[5] have at his beddes heed
Twenty bookes, clad in blak or reed,
Of Aristotle and his philosophye,
Than robes riche, or fithele,° or gay sautrye.[6] fiddle
But al be that he was a philosophre[7]
300 Yit hadde he but litel gold in cofre;° coffer
But al that he mighte of his freendes hente,° take
On bookes and on lerning he it spente,
And bisily gan for the soules praye
Of hem that yaf him wherwith to scoleye.° study
305 Of studye took he most cure° and most heede. care
Nought oo° word spak he more than was neede, one
And that was said in forme[8] and reverence,
And short and quik,° and ful of heigh sentence:[9] lively
Souning° in moral vertu was his speeche, resounding
310 And gladly wolde he lerne, and gladly teche.
    A Sergeant of the Lawe, war and wis,[1]
That often hadde been at the Parvis[2]
Ther was also, ful riche of excellence.
Discreet he was, and of greet reverence—
315 He seemed swich, his wordes weren so wise.
Justice he was ful often in assise° circuit courts
By patente[3] and by plein° commissioun. full
For his science° and for his heigh renown knowledge
Of fees and robes hadde he many oon.
320 So greet a purchasour° was nowher noon; speculator in land
Al was fee simple[4] to him in effect—
His purchasing mighte nat been infect.[5]

---

1. The management of his affairs.
2. The Clerk is a student at Oxford; to become a student, he would have had to signify his intention of becoming a cleric, but he was not bound to proceed to a position of responsibility in the church.
3. Who had long since matriculated in philosophy.
4. Ecclesiastical living, such as the income a parish priest receives. "Courtepy": outer cloak.
5. He would rather.
6. Psaltery (a kind of harp).
7. The word may also mean alchemist, someone who tries to turn base metals into gold. The Clerk's

"philosophy" does not pay either way.
8. With decorum.
9. Elevated thought.
1. Wary and wise. The Sergeant is not only a practicing lawyer but one of the high justices of the nation.
2. The Paradise, the porch of St. Paul's Cathedral, a meeting place for lawyers and their clients.
3. Royal warrant.
4. Owned outright without legal impediments.
5. Invalidated on a legal technicality.

Nowher so bisy a man as he ther nas;°   *was not*
And yit he seemed bisier than he was.
325 In termes hadde he caas and doomes[6] alle
That from the time of King William[7] were falle.
Therto he coude endite and make a thing,[8]
Ther coude no wight pinchen° at his writing;   *cavil*
And every statut coude° he plein° by rote.[9]   *knew/entire*
330 He rood but hoomly° in a medlee cote,[1]   *unpretentiously*
Girt with a ceint° of silk, with barres[2] smale.   *belt*
Of his array telle I no lenger tale.
    A Frankelain[3] was in his compaignye:
Whit was his beerd as is the dayesye;°   *daisy*
335 Of his complexion he was sanguin.[4]
Wel loved he by the morwe a sop in win.[5]
To liven in delit° was evere his wone,°   *sensual delight/wont*
For he was Epicurus[6] owene sone,
That heeld opinion that plein° delit   *full*
340 Was verray° felicitee parfit.°   *true/perfect*
An housholdere and that a greet was he:
Saint Julian[7] he was in his contree.
His breed, his ale, was always after oon;[8]
A bettre envined° man was nevere noon.   *wine-stocked*
345 Withouten bake mete was nevere his hous,
Of fissh and flessh, and that so plentevous°   *plenteous*
It snewed° in his hous of mete° and drinke,   *snowed/food*
Of alle daintees that men coude thinke.
After° the sondry sesons of the yeer   *according to*
350 So chaunged he his mete° and his soper.°   *dinner/supper*
Ful many a fat partrich hadde he in mewe,°   *cage*
And many a breem,° and many a luce° in stewe.[9] *carp/pike*
Wo was his cook but if his sauce were
Poinant° and sharp, and redy all his gere.   *spicy*
355 His table dormant in his halle alway
Stood redy covered all the longe day.[1]
At sessions ther was he lord and sire.
Ful ofte time he was Knight of the Shire.[2]
An anlaas° and a gipser° al of silk   *dagger/purse*
360 Heeng at his girdel,[3] whit as morne° milk.   *morning*
A shirreve° hadde he been, and countour.[4]   *sheriff*
Was nowhere swich a worthy vavasour.[5]

---

6. Law cases and decisions. "By termes": i.e., by heart.
7. I.e., the Conqueror (reigned 1066–87).
8. Compose and draw up a deed.
9. By heart.
1. A coat of mixed color.
2. Transverse stripes.
3. The "Frankelain" (Franklin) is a prosperous country man, whose lower-class ancestry is no impediment to the importance he has attained in his county.
4. A reference to the fact that the Franklin's temperament, "humor," is dominated by blood as well as to his red face (see p. 188, n. 8).
5. I.e., in the morning he was very fond of a piece of bread soaked in wine.

6. The Greek philosopher whose teaching is popularly believed to make pleasure the chief goal of life.
7. The patron saint of hospitality.
8. Always of the same high quality.
9. Fishpond.
1. Tables were usually dismounted when not in use, but the Franklin kept his mounted and set ("covered"), hence "dormant."
2. County representative in Parliament. "Sessions": i.e., sessions of the justices of the peace.
3. Hung at his belt.
4. Auditor of county finances.
5. Feudal landholder of lowest rank; a provincial gentleman.

An Haberdasshere and a Carpenter,
A Webbe,° a Dyere, and a Tapicer°— *weaver/tapestry maker*
365 And they were clothed alle in oo liveree⁶
Of a solempne and greet fraternitee.
Ful fresshe and newe hir gere apiked° was; *trimmed*
Hir knives were chaped° nought with bras, *mounted*
But al with silver; wrought ful clene and weel
370 Hir girdles and hir pouches everydeel.° *altogether*
Wel seemed eech of hem a fair burgeis° *burgher*
To sitten in a yeldehalle° on a dais. *guildhall*
Everich, for the wisdom that he can,⁷
Was shaply° for to been an alderman. *suitable*
375 For catel° hadde they ynough and rente,° *property/income*
And eek hir wives wolde it wel assente—
And elles certain were they to blame:
It is ful fair to been ycleped° "Madame," *called*
And goon to vigilies all bifore,⁸
380 And have a mantel royalliche ybore.⁹
A Cook they hadde with hem for the nones,¹
To boile the chiknes with the marybones,° *marrowbones*
And powdre-marchant tart and galingale.²
Wel coude he knowe° a draughte of London ale. *recognize*
385 He coude roste, and seethe,° and broile, and frye, *boil*
Maken mortreux,° and wel bake a pie. *stews*
But greet harm was it, as it thoughte° me, *seemed to*
That on his shine a mormal° hadde he, *ulcer*
For blankmanger,³ that made he with the beste.
390 A Shipman was ther, woning° fer by weste—° *dwelling/in the west*
For ought I woot,° he was of Dertemouthe.⁴ *know*
He rood upon a rouncy° as he couthe,⁵ *large nag*
In a gowne of falding° to the knee. *heavy wool*
A daggere hanging on a laas° hadde he *strap*
395 Aboute his nekke, under his arm adown.
The hote somer hadde maad his hewe° al brown; *color*
And certainly he was a good felawe.
Ful many a draughte of win hadde he drawe⁶
Fro Burdeuxward, whil that the chapman sleep:⁷
400 Of nice° conscience took he no keep;° *fastidious/heed*
If that he faught and hadde the hyer° hand, *upper*
By water he sente hem hoom to every land.⁸
But of his craft, to rekene wel his tides,
His stremes° and his daungers° him bisides,⁹ *currents/hazards*
405 His herberwe° and his moone, his lodemenage,¹ *anchorage*

6. In one livery, i.e., the uniform of their "frater-nitee" or guild, a partly religious, partly social organization.
7. Was capable of.
8. I.e., at the head of the procession. "Vigiles": feasts held on the eve of saints' days.
9. Royally carried.
1. For the occasion.
2. "Powdre-marchant" and "galingale" are flavoring materials.

3. A white stew or mousse.
4. Dartmouth, a port in the southwest of England.
5. As best he could.
6. Drawn, i.e., stolen.
7. Merchant slept. "Fro Burdeuxward": from Bordeaux; i.e., while carrying wine from Bordeaux (the wine center of France).
8. He drowned his prisoners.
9. Around him.
1. Pilotage, art of navigation.

There was noon swich from Hulle to Cartage.[2]
Hardy he was and wis to undertake;[3]
With many a tempest hadde his beerd been shake;
He knew alle the havenes° as they were   *harbors*
410 Fro Gotlond to the Cape of Finistere,[4]
And every crike° in Britaine° and in Spaine.   *inlet/Brittany*
His barge ycleped was the Maudelaine.°   *Magdalene*
      With us ther was a Doctour of Physik:°   *medicine*
In al this world ne was ther noon him lik
415 To speken of physik and of surgerye.
For° he was grounded in astronomye,°   *because/astrology*
He kepte° his pacient a ful greet deel[5]   *tended to*
In houres by his magik naturel.[6]
Wel coude he fortunen the ascendent
420 Of his images[7] for his pacient.
He knew the cause of every maladye,
Were it of hoot or cold or moiste or drye,
And where engendred and of what humour:[8]
He was a verray parfit praktisour.[9]
425 The cause yknowe,° and of his° harm the roote,   *known/its*
Anoon he yaf the sike man his boote.°   *remedy*
      Ful redy hadde he his apothecaries
To senden him drogges° and his letuaries,°   *drugs/medicines*
For eech of hem made other for to winne:
430 Hir frendshipe was nought newe to biginne.
Wel knew he the olde Esculapius,[1]
And Deiscorides and eek Rufus,
Olde Ipocras, Hali, and Galien,
Serapion, Razis, and Avicen,
435 Averrois, Damascien, and Constantin,
Bernard, and Gatesden, and Gilbertin.
Of his diete mesurable° was he,   *moderate*
For it was of no superfluitee,
But of greet norissing° and digestible.   *nourishment*
440 His studye was but litel on the Bible.
In sanguin° and in pers° he clad was al,   *blood red/blue*
Lined with taffata and with sendal;°   *silk*
And yit he was but esy of dispence;°   *expenditure*

2. From Hull (in northern England) to Cartagena
(in Spain).
3. Shrewd in his undertakings.
4. From Gotland (an island in the Baltic) to Fin-
isterre (the westernmost point in Spain).
5. Closely.
6. Natural—as opposed to black—magic. "In
houres": i.e., the astrologically important hours
(when conjunctions of the planets might help his
recovery).
7. Assign the propitious time, according to the
position of stars, for using talismanic images. Such
images, representing either the patient himself or
points in the zodiac, were thought to be influential
on the course of the disease.
8. Diseases were thought to be caused by a disturbance of one or another of the four bodily
"humors," each of which, like the four elements,
was a compound of two of the elementary qualities

mentioned in line 422: the melancholy humor,
seated in the black bile, was cold and dry (like
earth); the sanguine, seated in the blood, hot and
moist (like air); the choleric, seated in the yellow
bile, hot and dry (like fire); the phlegmatic, seated
in the phlegm, cold and moist (like water).
9. True perfect practitioner.
1. The Doctor is familiar with the treatises that
the Middle Ages attributed to the "great names" of
medical history, whom Chaucer names: the purely
legendary Greek demigod Aesculapius; the Greeks
Dioscorides, Rufus, Hippocrates, Galen, and Serapion; the Persians Hali and Rhazes; the Arabians
Avicenna and Averroës; the early Christians John
(?) of Damascus and Constantine Afer; the Scotsman Bernard Gordon; the Englishmen John of
Gatesden and Gilbert, the former an early contemporary of Chaucer.

He kepte that he wan in pestilence.[2]
445 For° gold in physik is a cordial,[3]   *because*
Therfore he loved gold in special.
    A good Wif was ther of biside Bathe,
But she was somdeel deef,° and that was scathe.°   *a bit deaf/a pity*
Of cloth-making she hadde swich an haunt,°   *skill*
450 She passed° hem of Ypres and of Gaunt.[4]   *surpassed*
In al the parissh wif ne was ther noon
That to the offring[5] bifore hire sholde goon,
And if ther dide, certain so wroth° was she   *angry*
That she was out of alle charitee.
455 Hir coverchiefs° ful fine were of ground°—   *headcovers/texture*
I dorste° swere they weyeden° ten pound   *dare/weighed*
That on a Sonday weren° upon hir heed.   *were*
Hir hosen° weren of fin scarlet reed,°   *leggings/red*
Ful straite yteyd,[6] and shoes ful moiste° and newe.   *supple*
460 Bold was hir face and fair and reed of hewe.
She was a worthy womman al hir live:
Housbondes at chirche dore[7] she hadde five,
Withouten° other compaignye in youthe—   *not counting*
But therof needeth nought to speke as nouthe.°   *now*
465 And thries hadde she been at Jerusalem;
She hadde passed many a straunge° streem;   *foreign*
At Rome she hadde been, and at Boloigne,
In Galice at Saint Jame, and at Coloigne:[8]
She coude° muchel of wandring by the waye: *knew*
470 Gat-toothed[9] was she, soothly for to saye.
Upon an amblere[1] esily she sat,
Ywimpled° wel, and on hir heed an hat   *veiled*
As brood as is a bokeler or a targe,[2]
A foot-mantel° aboute hir hipes large,   *riding skirt*
475 And on hir feet a paire of spores° sharpe.   *spurs*
In felaweshipe wel coude she laughe and carpe:°   *talk*
Of remedies of love she knew parchaunce,°   *as it happened*
For she coude of that art the olde daunce.[3]
    A good man was ther of religioun,
480 And was a poore Person° of a town,   *parson*
But riche he was of holy thought and werk.
He was also a lerned man, a clerk,
That Cristes gospel trewely° wolde preche;   *faithfully*
His parisshens° devoutly wolde he teche.   *parishioners*
485 Benigne he was, and wonder° diligent,   *wonderfully*
And in adversitee ful pacient,

---

2. He saved the money he made during the plague time.
3. A stimulant. Gold was thought to have some medicinal properties.
4. Ypres and Ghent ("Gaunt") were Flemish cloth-making centers.
5. The offering in church, when the congregation brought its gifts forward.
6. Tightly laced.
7. In medieval times, weddings were performed at the church door.
8. Rome, Boulogne (in France), St. James (of Compostella) in Galicia (Spain), and Cologne (in Germany) were all sites of shrines much visited by pilgrims.
9. Gap-toothed, thought to be a sign of amorousness.
1. Horse with an easy gait.
2. "Bokeler" and "targe": small shields.
3. I.e., she knew all the tricks of that trade.

And swich he was preved° ofte sithes.°   *proved/times*
Ful loth were him to cursen for his tithes,[4]
But rather wolde he yiven, out of doute,[5]
490   Unto his poore parisshens aboute
Of his offring[6] and eek of his substaunce:°   *property*
He coude in litel thing have suffisaunce.°   *sufficiency*
Wid was his parissh, and houses fer asonder,
But he ne lafte° nought for rain ne thonder,   *neglected*
495   In siknesse nor in meschief,° to visite   *misfortune*
The ferreste° in his parissh, muche and lite,[7]   *farthest*
Upon his feet, and in his hand a staf.
This noble ensample° to his sheep he yaf   *example*
That first he wroughte,[8] and afterward he taughte.
500   Out of the Gospel he tho° wordes caughte,°   *those/took*
And this figure° he added eek therto: *metaphor*
That if gold ruste, what shal iren do?
For if a preest be foul, on whom we truste,
No wonder is a lewed° man to ruste.   *uneducated*
505   And shame it is, if a preest take keep,°   *heed*
A shiten° shepherde and a clene sheep.   *befouled*
Wel oughte a preest ensample for to yive
By his clennesse how that his sheep sholde live.
He sette nought his benefice[9] to hire
510   And leet° his sheep encombred in the mire   *left*
And ran to London, unto Sainte Poules,[1]
To seeken him a chaunterye[2] for soules,
Or with a bretherhede to been withholde,[3]
But dwelte at hoom and kepte wel his folde,
515   So that the wolf ne made it nought miscarye:
He was a shepherde and nought a mercenarye.
And though he holy were and vertuous,
He was to sinful men nought despitous,°   *scornful*
Ne of his speeche daungerous° ne digne,°   *disdainful/haughty*
520   But in his teching discreet and benigne,
To drawen folk to hevene by fairnesse
By good ensample—this was his bisinesse.
But it° were any persone obstinat,   *if there*
What so he were, of heigh or lowe estat,
525   Him wolde he snibben° sharply for the nones:[4]   *scold*
A bettre preest I trowe° ther nowher noon is.   *believe*
He waited after[5] no pompe and reverence,
Ne maked him a spiced conscience,[6]
But Cristes lore° and his Apostles twelve   *teaching*

---

4. He would be most reluctant to invoke excommunication in order to collect his tithes.
5. Without doubt.
6. The offering made by the congregation of his church was at the Parson's disposal.
7. Great and small.
8. I.e., he practiced what he preached.
9. I.e., his parish. A priest might rent his parish to another and take a more profitable position.
1. St. Paul's Cathedral.
2. Chantry, i.e., a foundation that employed priests for the sole duty of saying masses for the souls of wealthy persons. St. Paul's had many of them.
3. Or to be employed by a brotherhood; i.e., to take a lucrative and fairly easy position as chaplain with a parish guild (see p. 187, 1st n. 6).
4. On the spot, promptly.
5. I.e., expected.
6. Nor did he assume an overfastidious conscience, a holier-than-thou attitude.

530 He taughte, but first he folwed it himselve.
         With him ther was a Plowman, was his brother,
     That hadde ylad° of dong° ful many a fother.[7]   carried / dung
     A trewe swinkere° and a good was he,   worker
     Living in pees° and parfit charitee.   peace
535 God loved he best with al his hoole° herte   whole
     At alle times, though him gamed or smerte,[8]
     And thanne his neighebor right as himselve.
     He wolde thresshe, and therto dike° and delve,°   work hard / dig
     For Cristes sake, for every poore wight,
540 Withouten hire, if it laye in his might.
     His tithes payed he ful faire and wel,
     Bothe of his propre swink[9] and his catel.°   property
     In a tabard° he rood upon a mere.°   workman's smock / mare
         Ther was also a Reeve° and a Millere,   estate manager
545 A Somnour, and a Pardoner[1] also,
     A Manciple,° and myself—ther were namo.   steward
         The Millere was a stout carl° for the nones.   fellow
     Ful big he was of brawn° and eek of bones—   muscle
     That preved[2] wel, for overal ther he cam
550 At wrastling he wolde have alway the ram.[3]
     He was short-shuldred, brood,° a thikke knarre.[4]   broad
     Ther was no dore that he nolde heve of harre,[5]
     Or breke it at a renning° with his heed.°   running / head
     His beerd as any sowe or fox was reed,°   red
555 And therto brood, as though it were a spade;
     Upon the cop right[6] of his nose he hade
     A werte,° and theron stood a tuft of heres,   wart
     Rede as the bristles of a sowes eres;°   ears
     His nosethirles° blake were and wide.   nostrils
560 A swerd and a bokeler° bar° he by his side.   shield / bore
     His mouth as greet was as a greet furnais.°   furnace
     He was a janglere° and a Goliardais,[7]   chatterer
     And that was most of sinne and harlotries.°   obscenities
     Wel coude he stelen corn and tollen thries[8]—
565 And yit he hadde a thombe[9] of gold, pardee.°   by heaven
     A whit cote and a blew hood wered° he.   wore
     A baggepipe wel coude he blowe and soune,°   sound
     And therwithal° he broughte us out of towne.   therewith
         A gentil Manciple[1] was ther of a temple,
570 Of which achatours° mighte take exemple   buyers of food
     For to been wise in bying of vitaile;°   victuals
     For wheither that he paide or took by taile,[2]

7. Load.
8. Whether he was pleased or grieved.
9. His own work.
1. "Somnour" (Summoner): server of summonses to the ecclesiastical court. "Pardoner": dispenser of papal pardons (see p. 193, 1st n. 8, and p. 194, n. 5).
2. Proved, i.e., was evident.
3. A ram was frequently offered as the prize in wrestling, a village sport.
4. Sturdy fellow.

5. He would not heave off (its) hinge.
6. Right on the tip.
7. Goliard, teller of ribald stories.
8. Take toll thrice—i.e., deduct from the grain far more than the lawful percentage.
9. Thumb. Ironic allusion to a proverb: "An honest miller has a golden thumb."
1. The Manciple is the business agent of a community of lawyers in London (a "temple").
2. By talley, i.e., on credit.

Algate he waited so in his achat[3]
That he was ay biforn and in good stat.[4]
575   Now is nat that of God a ful fair grace
That swich a lewed° mannes wit shal pace°   *uneducated/surpass*
The wisdom of an heep of lerned men?
Of maistres° hadde he mo than thries ten   *masters*
That weren of lawe expert and curious,°   *cunning*
580 Of whiche ther were a dozeine in that hous
Worthy to been stiwardes of rente° and lond   *income*
Of any lord that is in Engelond,
To make him live by his propre good[5]
In honour dettelees but if he were wood,[6]
585 Or live as scarsly° as him list° desire,   *economically/it pleases*
And able for to helpen al a shire
In any caas° that mighte falle° or happe,   *event/befall*
And yit this Manciple sette hir aller cappe![7]
The Reeve was a sclendre° colerik[8] man;   *slender*
590 His beerd was shave as neigh° as evere he can;   *close*
His heer was by his eres ful round yshorn;
His top was dokked[9] lik a preest biforn;°   *in front*
Ful longe were his legges and ful lene,
Ylik a staf, ther was no calf yseene.°   *visible*
595 Wel coude he keepe° a gerner° and a binne—   *guard/granary*
Ther was noon auditour coude on him winne.[1]
Wel wiste° he by the droughte and by the rain   *knew*
The yeelding of his seed and of his grain.
His lordes sheep, his neet,° his dayerye,°   *cattle/dairy herd*
600 His swin, his hors, his stoor,° and his pultrye   *stock*
Was hoolly° in this Reeves governinge,   *wholly*
And by his covenant yaf[2] the rekeninge,
Sin° that his lord was twenty-yeer of age.   *since*
There coude no man bringe him in arrerage.[3]
605 Ther nas baillif, hierde, nor other hine,
That he ne knew his sleighte and his covine[4]—
They were adrad° of him as of the deeth.°   *afraid/plague*
His woning° was ful faire upon an heeth;°   *dwelling/meadow*
With greene trees shadwed was his place.
610 He coude bettre than his lord purchace.°   *acquire goods*
Ful riche he was astored° prively.°   *stocked/secretly*
His lord wel coude he plesen subtilly,
To yive and lene° him of his owene good,°   *lend/property*
And have a thank, and yit a cote and hood.
615 In youthe he hadde lerned a good mister:°   *occupation*
He was a wel good wrighte, a carpenter.
This Reeve sat upon a ful good stot°   *stallion*

3. Always he was on the watch in his purchasing.
4. Financial condition. "Ay biforn": i.e., ahead of the game.
5. His own money.
6. Out of debt unless he were crazy.
7. This Manciple made fools of them all.
8. Choleric describes a person whose dominant humor is yellow bile (choler)—i.e., a hot-tempered person. The Reeve is the superintendent of a large farming estate.
9. Cut short; the clergy wore the head partially shaved.
1. I.e., find him in default.
2. And according to his contract he gave.
3. Convict him of being in arrears financially.
4. There was no bailiff (i.e., foreman), shepherd, or other farm laborer whose craftiness and plots he didn't know.

That was a pomely° grey and highte° Scot.   *dapple / was named*
A long surcote° of pers° upon he hade,⁵   *overcoat / blue*
620 And by his side he bar° a rusty blade.   *bore*
Of Northfolk was this Reeve of which I telle,
Biside a town men clepen Baldeswelle.°   *Bawdswell*
Tukked⁶ he was as is a frere aboute,
And evere he rood the hindreste of oure route.⁷
625   A Somnour⁸ was ther with us in that place
That hadde a fir-reed° cherubinnes⁹ face,   *fire-red*
For saucefleem° he was, with yën narwe,   *pimply*
And hoot° he was, and lecherous as a sparwe,°   *hot / sparrow*
With scaled° browes blake and piled¹ beerd: *scabby*
630 Of his visage children were aferd.°   *afraid*
Ther nas quiksilver, litarge, ne brimstoon,
Boras, ceruce, ne oile of tartre noon,²
Ne oinement that wolde clense and bite,
That him mighte helpen of his whelkes° white,   *pimples*
635 Nor of the knobbes° sitting on his cheekes.   *lumps*
Wel loved he garlek, oinons, and eek leekes,
And for to drinke strong win reed as blood.
Thanne wolde he speke and crye as he were wood;°   *mad*
And whan that he wel dronken hadde the win,
640 Thanne wolde he speke no word but Latin:
A fewe termes hadde he, two or three,
That he hadde lerned out of som decree;
No wonder is—he herde it al the day,
And eek ye knowe wel how that a jay°   *parrot*
645 Can clepen "Watte"³ as wel as can the Pope—
But whoso coude in other thing him grope,°   *examine*
Thanne hadde he spent all his philosophye;⁴
Ay *Questio quid juris*⁵ wolde he crye.
He was a gentil harlot° and a kinde;   *rascal*
650 A bettre felawe sholde men nought finde:
He wolde suffre,° for a quart of win,   *permit*
A good felawe to have his concubin
A twelfmonth, and excusen him at the fulle;⁶
Ful prively° a finch eek coude he pulle.⁷   *secretly*
655 And if he foond° owher° a good felawe   *found / anywhere*
He wolde techen him to have noon awe
In swich caas of the Ercedekenes curs,⁸
But if⁹ a mannes soule were in his purs,

---

5. He had on.
6. With clothing tucked up like a friar.
7. Hindmost of our group.
8. The "Somnour" (Summoner) is an employee of the ecclesiastical court, whose duty is to bring to court persons whom the archdeacon—the justice of the court—suspects of offenses against canon law. By this time, however, summoners had generally transformed themselves into corrupt detectives who spied out offenders and blackmailed them by threats of summonses.
9. Cherubs, often depicted in art with red faces.
1. Uneven, partly hairless.
2. These are all ointments for diseases affecting

the skin, probably diseases of venereal origin.
3. Call out: "Walter"—like modern parrots' "Polly."
4. I.e., learning.
5. "What point of law does this investigation involve?" A phrase frequently used in ecclesiastical courts.
6. Fully. Ecclesiastical courts had jurisdiction over many offenses that today would come under civil law, including sexual offenses.
7. "To pull a finch" (pluck a bird) is to have sexual relations with a woman.
8. Archdeacon's sentence of excommunication.
9. Unless.

For in his purs he sholde ypunisshed be.
660 "Purs is the Ercedekenes helle," saide he.
But wel I woot he lied right in deede:
Of cursing° oughte eech gilty man him drede,   excommunication
For curs wol slee° right as assoiling° savith—   slay/absolution
And also war him of a *significavit*.[1]
665 In daunger[2] hadde he at his owene gise°   disposal
The yonge girles of the diocise,
And knew hir conseil,° and was al hir reed.[3]   secrets
A gerland hadde he set upon his heed
As greet as it were for an ale-stake,[4]
670 A bokeler hadde he maad him of a cake.
With him ther rood a gentil Pardoner[5]
Of Rouncival, his freend and his compeer,°   comrade
That straight was comen fro the Court of Rome.[6]
Ful loude he soong,° "Com hider, love, to me."   sang
675 This Somnour bar to him a stif burdoun:[7]
Was nevere trompe° of half so greet a soun.   trumpet
This Pardoner hadde heer as yelow as wex,
But smoothe it heeng° as dooth a strike° of flex;°   hung/hank/flax
By ounces[8] heenge his lokkes that he hadde,
680 And therwith he his shuldres overspradde,°   overspread
But thinne it lay, by colpons,° oon by oon;   strands
But hood for jolitee° wered° he noon,   nonchalance/wore
For it was trussed up in his walet:°   pack
Him thoughte he rood al of the newe jet.°   fashion
685 Dischevelee° save his cappe he rood al bare.   with hair down
Swiche glaring yën hadde he as an hare.
A vernicle[9] hadde he sowed upon his cappe,
His walet biforn him in his lappe,
Bretful° of pardon, come from Rome al hoot.°   brimful/hot
690 A vois he hadde as smal° as hath a goot;°   high-pitched/goat
No beerd hadde he, ne nevere sholde have;
As smoothe it was as it were late yshave:
I trowe° he were a gelding[1] or a mare.   believe
But of his craft, fro Berwik into Ware,[2]
695 Ne was ther swich another pardoner;
For in his male° he hadde a pilwe-beer°   bag/pillowcase
Which that he saide was Oure Lady veil;
He saide he hadde a gobet° of the sail   piece
That Sainte Peter hadde whan that he wente
700 Upon the see, til Jesu Crist him hente.°   seized

---

1. And also one should be careful of a *significavit* (the writ that transferred the guilty offender from the ecclesiastical to the civil arm for punishment).
2. Under his domination.
3. Was their chief source of advice.
4. A tavern was signalized by a pole ("ale-stake"), rather like a modern flagpole, projecting from its front wall; on this hung a garland, or "bush."
5. A Pardoner dispensed papal pardon for sins to those who contributed to the charitable institution that he was licensed to represent; this Pardoner purported to be collecting for the hospital of

Roncesvalles ("Rouncival") in Spain, which had a London branch.
6. The papal court.
7. I.e., provided him with a strong bass accompaniment.
8. I.e., thin strands.
9. Portrait of Christ's face as it was said to have been impressed on St. Veronica's handkerchief, i.e., a souvenir reproduction of a famous relic in Rome.
1. A neutered stallion, i.e., a eunuch.
2. I.e., from one end of England to the other.

He hadde a crois° of laton,° ful of stones,   *cross / brassy metal*
And in a glas he hadde pigges bones,
But with thise relikes[3] whan that he foond°   *found*
A poore person° dwelling upon lond,[4]   *parson*
705 Upon° a day he gat° him more moneye   *in / got*
Than that the person gat in monthes twaye;
And thus with feined° flaterye and japes°   *false / tricks*
He made the person and the peple his apes.°   *dupes*
But trewely to tellen at the laste,
710 He was in chirche a noble ecclesiaste;
Wel coude he rede a lesson and a storye,°   *liturgical narrative*
But alderbest° he soong an offertorye,[5]   *best of all*
For wel he wiste° whan that song was songe,   *knew*
He moste° preche and wel affile° his tonge   *must / sharpen*
715 To winne silver, as he ful wel coude—
Therefore he soong the merierly° and loude.   *more merrily*
Now have I told you soothly in a clause[6]
Th'estaat, th'array, the nombre, and eek the cause
Why that assembled was this compaignye
720 In Southwerk at this gentil hostelrye
That highte the Tabard, faste° by the Belle;[7]   *close*
But now is time to you for to telle
How that we baren us[8] that ilke° night   *same*
Whan we were in that hostelrye alight;
725 And after wol I telle of oure viage,°   *trip*
And al the remenant of oure pilgrimage.
But first I praye you of youre curteisye
That ye n'arette it nought my vilainye[9]
Though that I plainly speke in this matere
730 To telle you hir wordes and hir cheere,°   *behavior*
Ne though I speke hir wordes proprely;°   *accurately*
For this ye knowen also wel as I:
Who so shal telle a tale after a man
He moot° reherce,° as neigh as evere he can,   *must / repeat*
735 Everich a word, if it be in his charge,°   *responsibility*
Al speke he[1] nevere so rudeliche and large,°   *broadly*
Or elles he moot telle his tale untrewe,
Or feine° thing, or finde° wordes newe;   *make up / devise*
He may nought spare[2] although he were his brother:
740 He moot as wel saye oo word as another.
Crist spak himself ful brode° in Holy Writ,   *broadly*
And wel ye woot no vilainye° is it;   *rudeness*
Eek Plato saith, who so can him rede,
The wordes mote be cosin to the deede.
745   Also I praye you to foryive it me
Al° have I nat set folk in hir degree   *although*
Here in this tale as that they sholde stonde:

---

3. Relics, i.e., the pigs' bones that the Pardoner represented as saints' bones.
4. Upcountry.
5. Part of the mass sung before the offering of alms.
6. I.e., in a short space.

7. Another tavern in Southwark.
8. Bore ourselves.
9. That you do not attribute it to my boorishness.
1. Although he speak.
2. I.e., spare anyone.

My wit is short, ye may wel understonde.
  Greet cheere made oure Host[3] us everichoon,
750 And to the soper sette he us anoon.°   *at once*
He served us with vitaile° at the beste.   *food*
Strong was the win, and wel to drinke us leste.°   *it pleased*
A semely man oure Hoste was withalle
For to been a marchal[4] in an halle;
755 A large man he was, with yën steepe,°   *prominent*
A fairer burgeis° was ther noon in Chepe[5]—   *burgher*
Bold of his speeche, and wis, and wel ytaught,
And of manhood him lakkede right naught.
Eek therto he was right a merye man,
760 And after soper playen he bigan,
And spak of mirthe amonges othere thinges—
Whan that we hadde maad oure rekeninges[6]—
And saide thus, "Now, lordinges, trewely,
Ye been to me right welcome, hertely.°   *heartily*
765 For by my trouthe, if that I shal nat lie,
I sawgh nat this yeer so merye a compaignye
At ones in this herberwe° as is now.   *inn*
Fain° wolde I doon you mirthe, wiste I[7] how.   *gladly*
And of a mirthe I am right now bithought,
770 To doon you ese, and it shal coste nought.
  "Ye goon to Canterbury—God you speede;
The blisful martyr quite you youre meede.[8]
And wel I woot as ye goon by the waye
Ye shapen you[9] to talen° and to playe,   *converse*
775 For trewely, confort ne mirthe is noon
To ride by the waye domb as stoon;°   *stone*
And therefore wol I maken you disport
As I saide erst,° and doon you som confort;   *before*
And if you liketh alle, by oon assent,
780 For to stonden at[1] my juggement,
And for to werken as I shall you saye,
Tomorwe whan ye riden by the waye—
Now by my fader° soule that is deed,   *father's*
But° ye be merye I wol yive you myn heed!° *unless / head*
785 Holde up youre handes withouten more speeche."
  Oure counseil was nat longe for to seeche;°   *seek*
Us thought it was not worth to make it wis,[2]
And graunted him withouten more avis,°   *deliberation*
And bade him saye his voirdit° as him leste.[3]   *verdict*
790   "Lordinges," quod he, "now herkneth for the beste;
But taketh it nought, I praye you, in desdain.
This is the point, to speken short and plain,
That eech of you, to shorte° with oure waye   *shorten*
In this viage, shal tellen tales twaye°—   *two*

---

3. The landlord of the Tabard Inn.
4. Marshal, one who was in charge of feasts.
5. Cheapside, business center of London.
6. Had paid our bills.
7. If I knew.
8. Pay you your reward.

9. Intend.
1. Abide by.
2. We didn't think it worthwhile to make an issue of it.
3. It pleased.

795   To Canterburyward, I mene it so,
      And hoomward he shal tellen othere two,
      Of aventures that whilom° have bifalle;   *once upon a time*
      And which of you that bereth him best of alle—
      That is to sayn, that telleth in this cas
800   Tales of best sentence° and most solas°—   *meaning/delight*
      Shal have a soper at oure aller cost,[4]
      Here in this place, sitting by this post,
      Whan that we come again fro Canterbury.
      And for to make you the more mury°   *merry*
805   I wol myself goodly° with you ride—   *kindly*
      Right at myn owene cost—and be youre gide.
      And who so wol my juggement withsaye°   *contradict*
      Shal paye al that we spende by the waye.
      And if ye vouche sauf that it be so,
810   Telle me anoon, withouten wordes mo,°   *more*
      And I wol erly shape me[5] therefore."
          This thing was graunted and oure othes swore
      With ful glad herte, and prayden[6] him also
      That he wolde vouche sauf for to do so,
815   And that he wolde been oure governour,
      And of oure tales juge and reportour,°   *accountant*
      And sette a soper at a certain pris,°   *price*
      And we wol ruled been at his devis,°   *disposal*
      In heigh and lowe; and thus by oon assent
820   We been accorded to his juggement.
      And therupon the win was fet° anoon;   *fetched*
      We dronken and to reste wente eechoon°   *each one*
      Withouten any lenger° taryinge.   *longer*
         Amorwe° whan that day bigan to springe   *in the morning*
825   Up roos oure Host and was oure aller cok,[7]
      And gadred us togidres in a flok,
      And forth we riden, a litel more than pas,°   *walking pace*
      Unto the watering of Saint Thomas;[8]
      And ther oure Host bigan his hors arreste,°   *halt*
830   And saide, "Lordes, herkneth if you leste:°   *it please*
         Ye woot youre forward° and it you recorde:[9]   *agreement*
      If evensong and morwesong° accorde,°   *morning song/agree*
      Lat see now who shal telle the firste tale.
      As evere mote° I drinken win or ale,   *may*
835   Who so be rebel to my juggement
      Shal paye for al that by the way is spent.
      Now draweth cut er that we ferrer twinne:[1]
      He which that hath the shorteste shal biginne.
         "Sire Knight," quod he, "my maister and my lord,
840   Now draweth cut, for that is myn accord.°   *will*
      Cometh neer," quod he, "my lady Prioresse,
      And ye, sire Clerk, lat be youre shamefastnesse°—   *modesty*

---

4. At the cost of us all.
5. Prepare myself.
6. I.e., we prayed.
7. Was rooster for us all.

8. A watering place near Southwark.
9. You recall it.
1. Go farther. "Draweth cut": i.e., draw straws.

Ne studieth nought. Lay hand to, every man!"
    Anoon to drawen every wight bigan,
845 And shortly for to tellen as it was
    Were it by aventure, or sort, or cas,[2]
    The soothe° is this, the cut fil° to the Knight;   *truth/fell*
    Of which ful blithe and glad was every wight,
    And telle he moste° his tale, as was resoun,   *must*
850 By forward and by composicioun,[3]
    As ye han herd. What needeth wordes mo?
    And whan this goode man sawgh that it was so,
    As he that wis was and obedient
    To keepe his forward by his free assent,
855 He saide, "Sin° I shal biginne the game,   *since*
    What, welcome be the cut, in Goddes name!
    Now lat us ride, and herkneth what I saye."
    And with that word we riden forth oure waye,
    And he bigan with right a merye cheere°   *countenance*
860 His tale anoon, and saide as ye may heere.

2. Whether it was luck, fate, or chance.   3. By agreement and compact.

[*The Knight's Tale* is a romance of 2,350 lines, which Chaucer had written before beginning *The Canterbury Tales*—one of several works assumed to be earlier that he inserted into the collection. It is probably the same story, with only minor revisions, that Chaucer referred to in *The Legend of Good Women* as "al the love of Palamon and Arcite." These are the names of the two heroes of *The Knight's Tale*, kinsmen and best friends who are taken prisoner at the siege and destruction of ancient Thebes by Theseus, the ruler of Athens. Gazing out from their prison cell in a tower, they fall in love at first sight and almost at the same moment with Theseus's sister-in-law, Emily, who is taking an early-morning walk in a garden below their window. After a bitter rivalry, they are at last reconciled through a tournament in which Emily is the prize. Arcite wins the tournament but, as he lies dying after being thrown by his horse, he makes a noble speech encouraging Palamon and Emily to marry. The tale is an ambitious combination of classical setting and mythology, romance plot, and themes of fortune and destiny.]

The Miller's Prologue and Tale

The Miller's Tale belongs to a genre known as the "fabliau": a short story in verse that deals satirically, often grossly and fantastically as well as hilariously, with intrigues and deceptions about sex or money (and often both these elements in the same story). These are the tales Chaucer is anticipating in *The General Prologue* when he warns his presumably genteel audience that they must expect some rude speaking (see lines 727–44). An even more pointed apology follows at the end of *The Miller's Prologue*. Fabliau tales exist everywhere in oral literature; as a literary form they flourished in France, especially in the thirteenth century. By having Robin the Miller tell a fabliau to "quit" (to requite or pay back) the Knight's aristocratic romance, Chaucer sets up a dialectic between classes, genres, and styles that he exploits throughout *The Canterbury Tales*.

The Prologue

Whan that the Knight hadde thus his tale ytold,
In al the route° nas° ther yong ne old   *group / was not*
That he ne saide it was a noble storye,
And worthy for to drawen° to memorye,   *recall*
5 And namely° the gentils everichoon.   *especially*
    Oure Hoste lough° and swoor, "So mote I goon,¹   *laughed*
This gooth aright: unbokeled is the male.°   *pouch*
Lat see now who shal telle another tale.
For trewely the game is wel bigonne.
10 Now telleth ye, sire Monk, if that ye conne,°   *can*
Somwhat to quite° with the Knightes tale."   *repay*
    The Millere, that for dronken² was al pale,
So that unnethe° upon his hors he sat,   *with difficulty*
He nolde° avalen° neither hood ne hat,   *would not / take off*
15 Ne abiden no man for his curteisye,
But in Pilates vois³ he gan to crye,
And swoor, "By armes⁴ and by blood and bones,
I can° a noble tale for the nones,   *know*
With which I wol now quite the Knightes tale."
20 Oure Hoste sawgh that he was dronke of ale,
And saide, "Abide, Robin, leve° brother,   *dear*
Som bettre man shal telle us first another.
Abide, and lat us werken thriftily."°   *with propriety*
    "By Goddes soule," quod he, "that wol nat I,
25 For I wol speke or elles go my way."
    Oure Host answerde, "Tel on, a devele way!⁵
Thou art a fool; thy wit is overcome."
    "Now herkneth," quod the Millere, "alle and some.⁶
But first I make a protestacioun°   *public affirmation*
30 That I am dronke: I knowe it by my soun.°   *tone of voice*
And therfore if that I misspeke° or saye,   *speak or say wrongly*
Wite it⁷ the ale of Southwerk, I you praye;
For I wol telle a legende° and a lif   *saint's life*
Bothe of a carpenter and of his wif,
35 How that a clerk hath set the wrightes cappe."⁸
    The Reeve answerde and saide, "Stint thy clappe!⁹
Lat be thy lewed° dronken harlotrye.°   *ignorant / obscenity*
It is a sinne and eek° a greet folye   *also*
To apairen° any man or him defame,   *injure*
40 And eek to bringen wives in swich fame.°   *reputation*
Thou maist ynough of othere thinges sayn."
    This dronken Millere spak ful soone again,
And saide, "Leve° brother Osewold,   *dear*
Who hath no wif, he is no cokewold.°   *cuckold*
45 But I saye nat therfore that thou art oon.

---

1. So might I walk—an oath.
2. I.e., drunkenness.
3. The harsh voice usually associated with the character of Pontius Pilate in the mystery plays.
4. I.e., by God's arms, a blasphemous oath.

5. I.e., in the devil's name.
6. Each and every one.
7. Blame it on.
8 I.e., how a clerk made a fool of a carpenter.
9. Stop your chatter.

Ther ben ful goode wives many oon,°   *a one*
And evere a thousand goode ayains oon badde.
That knowestou wel thyself but if thou madde.°   *rave*
Why artou angry with my tale now?
50 I have a wif, pardee,° as wel as thou,   *by God*
Yit nolde° I, for the oxen in my plough,   *would not*
Take upon me more than ynough°   *enough*
As deemen of myself that I were oon:[1]
I wol bileve wel that I am noon.
55 An housbonde shal nought been inquisitif
Of Goddes privetee,° nor of his wif.   *secrets*
So[2] he may finde Goddes foison° there,   *plenty*
Of the remenant° needeth nought enquere."°   *rest / inquire*
   What sholde I more sayn but this Millere
60 He nolde his wordes for no man forbere,
But tolde his cherles tale in his manere.
M'athinketh° that I shal reherce° it here,   *I regret / repeat*
And therefore every gentil wight I praye,
Deemeth nought, for Goddes love, that I saye
65 Of yvel entente, but for° I moot reherse   *because*
Hir tales alle, be they bet° or werse,   *better*
Or elles falsen° som of my matere.   *falsify*
And therfore, whoso list it nought yheere°   *hear*
Turne over the leef,° and chese° another tale,   *page / choose*
70 For he shal finde ynowe,° grete and smale,   *enough*
Of storial[3] thing that toucheth gentilesse,°   *gentility*
And eek moralitee and holinesse:
Blameth nought me if that ye chese amis.
The Millere is a cherl, ye knowe wel this,
75 So was the Reeve eek, and othere mo,
And harlotrye° they tolden bothe two.   *ribaldry*
Aviseth you,[4] and putte me out of blame:
And eek men shal nought maken ernest of game.

The Tale

   Whilom° ther was dwelling at Oxenforde   *once upon a time*
80 A riche gnof° that gestes heeld to boorde,[5]   *churl*
And of his craft he was a carpenter.
With him ther was dwelling a poore scoler,
Hadde lerned art,[6] but al his fantasye°   *desire*
Was turned for to lere° astrologye,   *learn*
85 And coude a certain of conclusiouns,
To deemen by interrogaciouns,[7]
If that men axed° him in certain houres   *asked*
Whan that men sholde have droughte or elles showres,
Or if men axed him what shal bifalle

---

1. To think that I were one (a cuckold).
2. Provided that.
3. Historical, i.e., true.
4. Take heed.
5. I.e., took in boarders.

6. Who had completed the first stage of university education (the trivium).
7. I.e., and he knew a number of propositions on which to base astrological analyses (which would reveal the matters in the next three lines).

90 Of every thing—I may nat rekene hem alle.
   This clerk was cleped° hende[8] Nicholas.　　　　　　*called*
   Of derne love he coude, and of solas,[9]
   And therto he was sly and ful privee,°　　　　　　　*secretive*
   And lik a maide meeke for to see.
95 A chambre hadde he in that hostelrye
   Allone, withouten any compaignye,
   Ful fetisly ydight[1] with herbes swoote,°　　　　　　*sweet*
   And he himself as sweete as is the roote
   Of licoris or any setewale.[2]
100 His *Almageste*[3] and bookes grete and smale,
   His astrelabye, longing for[4] his art,
   His augrim stones,[5] layen faire apart
   On shelves couched° at his beddes heed;　　　　　　　*set*
   His presse° ycovered with a falding reed;[6]　　　*storage chest*
105 And al above ther lay a gay sautrye,°　　　　　*psaltery (harp)*
   On which he made a-nightes melodye
   So swetely that al the chambre roong,°　　　　　　　*rang*
   And *Angelus ad Virginem*[7] he soong,
   And after that he soong the *Kinges Note:*[8]
110 Ful often blessed was his merye throte.
   And thus this sweete clerk his time spente
   After his freendes finding and his rente.[9]
   This carpenter hadde wedded newe° a wif　　　　　　*lately*
   Which that he loved more than his lif.
115 Of eighteteene yeer she was of age;
   Jalous he was, and heeld hire narwe in cage,
   For she was wilde and yong, and he was old,
   And deemed himself been lik a cokewold.[1]
   He knew nat Caton,[2] for his wit was rude,
120 That bad men sholde wedde his similitude:[3]
   Men sholde wedden after hir estat,[4]
   For youthe and elde° is often at debat.　　　　　　　*age*
   But sith that he was fallen in the snare,
   He moste endure, as other folk, his care.
125　　Fair was this yonge wif, and therwithal
   As any wesele° hir body gent and smal.[5]　　　　　*weasel*
   A ceint she wered, barred[6] al of silk;
   A barmcloth° as whit as morne° milk　　　　　*apron / morning*
   Upon hir lendes,° ful of many a gore;°　　　　　*loins / flounce*
130 Whit was hir smok,° and broiden° al bifore　　*undergarment / embroidered*
   And eek bihinde, on hir coler° aboute,　　　　　　　*collar*

8. Courteous, handy, attractive.
9. I.e., he knew about secret love and pleasurable practices.
1. Elegantly furnished.
2. Setwall, a spice.
3. The 2nd-century treatise by Ptolemy, still the standard astronomy textbook.
4. Belonging to. "Astrelabye": astrolabe, an astronomical instrument.
5. Counters used in arithmetic.
6. Red coarse woolen cloth.
7. "The Angel to the Virgin," an Annunciation

hymn.
8. Probably a popular song of the time.
9. In accordance with his friends' provision and his own income.
1. I.e., suspected of himself that he was like a cuckold.
2. Dionysius Cato, the supposed author of a book of maxims used in elementary education.
3. Commanded that one should wed his equal.
4. Men should marry according to their condition.
5. Slender and delicate.
6. A belt she wore, with transverse stripes.

Of° col-blak silk, withinne and eek withoute;   *with*
The tapes° of hir white voluper°   *ribbons/cap*
Were of the same suite of⁷ hir coler;
135 Hir filet° brood° of silk and set ful hye;   *headband/broad*
And sikerly° she hadde a likerous° yë;   *certainly/wanton*
Ful smale ypulled⁸ were hir browes two,
And tho were bent,° and blake as any slo.°   *arching/sloeberry*
She was ful more blisful on to see
140 Than is the newe perejonette° tree,   *pear*
And softer than the wolle° is of a wether;°   *wool/ram*
And by hir girdel° heeng° a purs of lether,   *belt/hung*
Tasseled with silk and perled with latoun.⁹
In al this world, to seeken up and down,
145 Ther nis no man so wis that coude thenche°   *imagine*
So gay a popelote° or swich° a wenche.   *doll/such*
Ful brighter was the shining of hir hewe
Than in the Towr¹ the noble° yforged newe.   *gold coin*
But of hir song, it was as loud and yerne°   *lively*
150 As any swalwe° sitting on a berne.°   *swallow/barn*
Therto she coude skippe and make game°   *play*
As any kide or calf folwing his dame.°   *mother*
Hir mouth was sweete as bragot or the meeth,²
Or hoord of apples laid in hay or heeth.°   *heather*
155 Winsing° she was as is a joly° colt,   *skittish/high-spirited*
Long as a mast, and upright° as a bolt.°   *straight/arrow*
A brooch she bar upon hir lowe coler
As brood as is the boos° of a bokeler;°   *boss/shield*
Hir shoes were laced on hir legges hye.
160 She was a primerole,° a piggesnye,³   *primrose*
For any lord to leggen° in his bedde,   *lay*
Or yit for any good yeman to wedde.

    Now sire, and eft° sire, so bifel the cas   *again*
That on a day this hende Nicholas
165 Fil° with this yonge wif to rage° and playe,   *happened/flirt*
Whil that hir housbonde was at Oseneye⁴
(As clerkes been ful subtil and ful quainte),°   *clever*
And prively he caughte hire by the queinte,⁵
And saide, "Ywis,° but° if ich° have my wille,   *truly/unless/I*
170 For derne° love of thee, lemman, I spille,"°   *secret/die*
And heeld hire harde by the haunche-bones,°   *thighs*
And saide, "Lemman,° love me al atones,⁶   *sweetheart*
Or I wol dien, also° God me save."   *so*
And she sproong° as a colt dooth in a trave,⁷   *sprang*
175 And with hir heed she wried° faste away;   *twisted*
She saide, "I wol nat kisse thee, by my fay.°   *faith*
Why, lat be," quod she, "lat be, Nicholas!
Or I wol crye 'Out, harrow,° and allas!'   *help*
Do way youre handes, for your curteisye!"

---

7. The same kind as, i.e., black.
8. Delicately plucked.
9. I.e., with brassy spangles on it.
1. The Tower of London, the Mint.
2. "Bragot" and "meeth" are honey drinks.
3. A pig's eye, a name for a common flower.

4. A town near Oxford.
5. Elegant (thing); a euphemism for the female genitals.
6. Right now.
7. Frame for holding a horse to be shod.

180 This Nicholas gan mercy for to crye,
And spak so faire, and profred him so faste,[8]
That she hir love him graunted atte laste,
And swoor hir ooth by Saint Thomas of Kent[9]
That she wolde been at his comandement,
185 Whan that she may hir leiser[1] wel espye.
"Myn housbonde is so ful of jalousye
That but ye waite° wel and been privee   be on guard
I woot right wel I nam but deed,"[2] quod she.
"Ye moste been ful derne° as in this cas."   secret
190 "Nay, therof care thee nought," quod Nicholas.
"A clerk hadde litherly biset his while,[3]
But if he coude a carpenter bigile."
And thus they been accorded and ysworn
To waite° a time, as I have told biforn.   watch for
195 Whan Nicholas hadde doon this everydeel,°   every bit
And thakked° hire upon the lendes° weel,   patted / loins
He kiste hire sweete, and taketh his sautrye,
And playeth faste, and maketh melodye.
Thanne fil° it thus, that to the parissh chirche,   befell
200 Cristes owene werkes for to wirche,°   perform
This goode wif wente on an haliday:°   holy day
Hir forheed shoon as bright as any day,
So was it wasshen whan she leet° hir werk.   left
Now was ther of that chirche a parissh clerk,[4]
205 The which that was ycleped° Absolon: called
Crul° was his heer, and as the gold it shoon,   curly
And strouted° as a fanne[5] large and brode;   spread out
Ful straight and evene lay his joly shode.[6]
His rode° was reed, his yën greye as goos.°   complexion / goose
210 With Poules window corven[7] on his shoos,
In hoses° rede he wente fetisly.°   stockings / elegantly
Yclad he was ful smale° and proprely,   finely
Al in a kirtel° of a light waget°—   tunic / blue
Ful faire and thikke been the pointes[8] set—
215 And therupon he hadde a gay surplis,°   surplice
As whit as is the blosme upon the ris.°   bough
A merye child° he was, so God me save.   young man
Wel coude he laten blood, and clippe,[9] and shave,
And maken a chartre of land, or acquitaunce;[1]
220 In twenty manere° coude he trippe and daunce   ways
After the scole of Oxenforde tho,°   then
And with his legges casten° to and fro,   prance
And playen songes on a smal rubible;°   fiddle
Therto he soong somtime a loud quinible,[2]
225 And as wel coude he playe on a giterne:°   guitar

8. I.e., made such vigorous advances.
9. Thomas à Becket.
1. I.e., opportunity.
2. I am no more than dead, I am done for.
3. Poorly employed his time.
4. Assistant to the parish priest, not a cleric or student.
5. Wide-mouthed basket for separating grain from chaff.
6. Parting of the hair.
7. Carved with intricate designs, like the tracery in the windows of St. Paul's.
8. Laces for fastening the tunic and holding up the hose.
9. Let blood and give haircuts. Bleeding was a medical treatment performed by barbers.
1. Legal release. "Chartre": deed.
2. Part requiring a very high voice.

In al the town nas brewhous ne taverne
That he ne visited with his solas,°   *entertainment*
Ther any gailard tappestere³ was.
But sooth to sayn, he was somdeel squaimous°   *a bit squeamish*
230   Of° farting, and of speeche daungerous.⁴   *about*
     This Absolon, that joly° was and gay,   *pretty, amorous*
Gooth with a cencer° on the haliday,   *incense burner*
Cencing the wives of the parissh faste,
And many a lovely look on hem he caste,
235   And namely° on this carpenteres wif: *especially*
To looke on hire him thoughte a merye lif.
She was so propre° and sweete and likerous,⁵   *neat*
I dar wel sayn, if she hadde been a mous,
And he a cat, he wolde hire hente° anoon.   *pounce on*
240   This parissh clerk, this joly Absolon,
Hath in his herte swich a love-longinge°   *lovesickness*
That of no wif ne took he noon offringe—
For curteisye he saide he wolde noon.
The moone, whan it was night, ful brighte shoon,°   *shone*
245   And Absolon his giterne° hath ytake—   *guitar*
For paramours° he thoughte for to wake—   *love*
And forth he gooth, jolif° and amorous,   *pretty*
Til he cam to the carpenteres hous,
A litel after cokkes hadde ycrowe,
250   And dressed him up by a shot-windowe⁶
That was upon the carpenteres wal.
He singeth in his vois gentil and smal,°   *dainty*
"Now dere lady, if thy wille be,
I praye you that ye wol rewe° on me,"   *have pity*
255   Ful wel accordant to his giterninge.⁷
This carpenter awook and herde him singe,
And spak unto his wif, and saide anoon,
"What, Alison, heerestou nought Absolon
That chaunteth thus under oure bowres° wal?"   *bedroom's*
260   And she answerde hir housbonde therwithal,
"Yis, God woot, John, I heere it everydeel."°   *every bit*
     This passeth forth. What wol ye bet than weel?⁸
Fro day to day this joly Absolon
So woweth° hire that him is wo-bigoon: *woos*
265   He waketh° al the night and al the day;   *stays awake*
He kembed° his lokkes brode⁹ and made him gay;   *combed*
He woweth hire by menes and brocage,¹
And swoor he wolde been hir owene page°   *personal servant*
He singeth, brokking° as a nightingale;   *trilling*
270   He sente hire piment,° meeth,° and spiced ale,   *spiced wine / mead*
And wafres° piping hoot out of the gleede;°   *pastries / coals*
And for she was of towne,² he profred meede°—   *money*

---

3. Gay barmaid.
4. Prudish about (vulgar) talk.
5. Wanton, appetizing.
6. Took his position by a hinged window.
7. In harmony with his guitar playing.

8. Better than well.
9. I.e., wide-spreading.
1. By go-betweens and agents.
2. Because she was a town woman.

      For som folk wol be wonnen for richesse,
      And som for strokes,° and som for gentilesse.   *blows (force)*
275   Somtime to shewe his lightnesse and maistrye,³
      He playeth Herodes⁴ upon a scaffold° hye.   *platform, stage*
      But what availeth him as in this cas?
      She loveth so this hende Nicholas
      That Absolon may blowe the bukkes horn;⁵
280   He ne hadde for his labour but a scorn.
      And thus she maketh Absolon hir ape,⁶
      And al his ernest turneth til° a jape.°   *to/joke*
      Ful sooth is this proverbe, it is no lie;
      Men saith right thus: "Alway the nye slye
285   Maketh the ferre leve to be loth."⁷
      For though that Absolon be wood° or wroth,   *furious*
      By cause that he fer was from hir sighte,
      This nye° Nicholas stood in his lighte.   *nearby*
       Now beer° thee wel, thou hende Nicholas,   *bear*
290   For Absolon may waile and singe allas.
       And so bifel it on a Saterday
      This carpenter was goon til Oseney,
      And hende Nicholas and Alisoun
      Accorded been to this conclusioun,
295   That Nicholas shal shapen° hem a wile°   *arrange/trick*
      This sely⁸ jalous housbonde to bigile,
      And if so be this game wente aright,
      She sholden sleepen in his arm al night—
      For this was his desir and hire° also.   *hers*
300   And right anoon, withouten wordes mo,
      This Nicholas no lenger wolde tarye,
      But dooth ful softe unto his chambre carye
      Bothe mete and drinke for a day or twaye,
      And to hir housbonde bad hire for to saye,
305   If that he axed after Nicholas,
      She sholde saye she niste° wher he was—   *didn't know*
      Of al that day she sawgh him nought with yë:
      She trowed° that he was in maladye,   *believed*
      For for no cry hir maide coude him calle,
310   He nolde answere for no thing that mighte falle.°   *happen*
       This passeth forth al thilke° Saterday   *this*
      That Nicholas stille in his chambre lay,
      And eet,° and sleep,° or dide what him leste,⁹   *ate/slept*
      Til Sonday that the sonne gooth to reste.
315   This sely carpenter hath greet mervaile
      Of Nicholas, or what thing mighte him aile,
      And saide, "I am adrad,° by Saint Thomas,   *afraid*
      It stondeth nat aright with Nicholas.
      God shilde° that he deide sodeinly!   *forbid*

---

3. Facility and virtuosity.
4. Herod, a role traditionally played as a bully in the mystery plays.
5. Blow the buck's horn, i.e., go whistle, waste his time.
6. I.e., thus she makes a monkey out of Absolon.
7. Always the sly man at hand makes the distant dear one hated.
8. Poor innocent.
9. He wanted.

320 This world is now ful tikel,° sikerly: *precarious*
 I sawgh today a corps yborn to chirche
 That now a° Monday last I sawgh him wirche.° *on/work*
 Go up," quod he unto his knave° anoon,   *manservant*
 "Clepe° at his dore or knokke with a stoon.° *call/stone*
325 Looke how it is and tel me boldely."
  This knave gooth him up ful sturdily,
 And at the chambre dore whil that he stood
 He cride and knokked as that he were wood,° *mad*
 "What? How? What do ye, maister Nicholay?
330 How may ye sleepen al the longe day?"
 But al for nought: he herde nat a word.
 An hole he foond ful lowe upon a boord,
 Ther as the cat was wont in for to creepe,
 And at that hole he looked in ful deepe,
335 And atte laste he hadde of him a sighte.
  This Nicholas sat evere caping° uprighte *gaping*
 As he hadde kiked° on the newe moone.   *gazed*
 Adown he gooth and tolde his maister soone
 In what array° he saw this ilke° man. *condition/same*
340 This carpenter to blessen him[1] bigan,
 And saide, "Help us, Sainte Frideswide!
 A man woot litel what him shal bitide.
 This man is falle, with his astromye,°   *astronomy*
 In som woodnesse° or in som agonye.   *madness*
345 I thoughte ay° wel how that it sholde be: *always*
 Men sholde nought knowe of Goddes privetee.
 Ye, blessed be alway a lewed° man   *ignorant*
 That nought but only his bileve° can.° *creed/knows*
 So ferde° another clerk with astromye: *fared*
350 He walked in the feeldes for to prye°   *gaze*
 Upon the sterres,° what ther sholde bifalle, *stars*
 Til he was in a marle-pit[2] yfalle—
 He saw nat that. But yit, by Saint Thomas,
 Me reweth sore[3] for hende Nicholas.
355 He shal be rated of[4] his studying,
 If that I may, by Jesus, hevene king!
 Get me a staf that I may underspore,°   *pry up*
 Whil that thou, Robin, hevest° up the dore. *heave*
 He shal[5] out of his studying, as I gesse."
360 And to the chambre dore he gan him dresse.[6]
 His knave was a strong carl° for the nones,° *fellow/purpose*
 And by the haspe he haaf° it up atones: *heaved*
 Into° the floor the dore fil° anoon.   *on/fell*
 This Nicholas sat ay as stille as stoon,
365 And evere caped up into the air.
 This carpenter wende° he were in despair, *thought*
 And hente° him by the shuldres mightily, *seized*
 And shook him harde, and cride spitously,° *vehemently*

---

1. Cross himself.   4. Scolded for.
2. Pit from which a fertilizing clay is dug. 5. I.e., shall come.
3. I sorely pity.   6. Took his stand.

"What, Nicholay, what, how! What! Looke adown!
370 Awaak and thenk on Cristes passioun![7]
I crouche[8] thee from elves and fro wightes."°   *wicked creatures*
Therwith the nightspel saide he anoonrightes[9]
On foure halves° of the hous aboute,   *sides*
And on the thresshfold° on the dore withoute: *threshold*
375 "Jesu Crist and Sainte Benedight,°   *Benedict*
Blesse this hous from every wikked wight!
For nightes nerye the White Pater Noster.[1]
Where wentestou,° thou Sainte Petres soster?°   *did you go / sister*
And at the laste this hende Nicholas
380 Gan for to sike° sore, and saide, "Allas,   *sigh*
Shal al the world be lost eftsoones° now?"   *again*
     This carpenter answerde, "What saistou?
What, thenk on God as we doon, men that swinke."°   *work*
     This Nicholas answerde, "Fecche me drinke,
385 And after wol I speke in privetee
Of certain thing that toucheth me and thee.
I wol telle it noon other man, certain."
     This carpenter gooth down and comth again,
And broughte of mighty° ale a large quart,   *strong*
390 And when that eech of hem hadde dronke his part,
This Nicholas his dore faste shette,°   *shut*
And down the carpenter by him he sette,
And saide, "John, myn hoste lief° and dere,   *beloved*
Thou shalt upon thy trouthe° swere me here   *word of honor*
395 That to no wight thou shalt this conseil° wraye;°   *secret / disclose*
For it is Cristes conseil that I saye,
And if thou telle it man,[2] thou art forlore,°   *lost*
For this vengeance thou shalt have therfore,
That if thou wraye me, thou shalt be wood."[3]
400   "Nay, Crist forbede it, for his holy blood,"
Quod tho this sely° man. "I nam no labbe,°   *innocent / tell-tale*
And though I saye, I nam nat lief to gabbe.[4]
Say what thou wilt, I shal it nevere telle
To child ne wif, by him that harwed helle."[5]
405   "Now John," quod Nicholas, "I wol nought lie.
I have yfounde in myn astrologye,
As I have looked in the moone bright,
That now a Monday next, at quarter night,[6]
Shal falle a rain, and that so wilde and wood,°   *furious*
410 That half so greet was nevere Noees° flood.   *Noah's*
This world," he saide, "in lasse° than an hour   *less*
Shal al be dreint,° so hidous is the showr.   *drowned*
Thus shal mankinde drenche° and lese° hir lif."   *drown / lose*

---

7. I.e., the Crucifixion.
8. Make the sign of the cross on.
9. The night-charm he said right away (to ward off evil spirits).
1. Pater Noster is Latin for "Our Father," the beginning of the Lord's Prayer. The line is obscure, but a conjectural reading would be, "May the White 'Our Father' (or 'Our White Father') [either a prayer or the personification of a protecting

power] defend [*nerye*] (us) against nights." The "nightspel" is a jumble of Christian references and pagan superstition.
2. To anyone.
3. Go mad.
4. And though I say it myself, I don't like to gossip.
5. By Him that despoiled hell—i.e., Christ.
6. I.e., shortly before dawn.

This carpenter answerde, "Allas, my wif!
415 And shal she drenche? Allas, myn Alisoun!"
For sorwe of this he fil almost[7] adown,
And saide, "Is there no remedye in this cas?"
"Why yis, for[8] Gode," quod hende Nicholas,
"If thou wolt werken after lore and reed[9]—
420 Thou maist nought werken after thyn owene heed;°   head
For thus saith Salomon that was ful trewe,
'Werk al by conseil and thou shalt nought rewe.'°   be sorry
And if thou werken wolt by good conseil,
I undertake, withouten mast or sail,
425 Yit shal I save hire and thee and me.
Hastou nat herd how saved was Noee
Whan that oure Lord hadde warned him biforn
That al the world with water sholde be lorn?"°   lost
"Yis," quod this carpenter, "ful yore° ago."   long
430 "Hastou nat herd," quod Nicholas, "also
The sorwe of Noee with his felaweshipe?
Er° that he mighte gete his wif to shipe,   before
Him hadde levere,[1] I dar wel undertake,
At thilke time than alle his wetheres[2] blake
435 That she hadde had a ship hirself allone.[3]
And therfore woostou° what is best to doone?   do you know
This axeth° haste, and of an hastif° thing   requires / urgent
Men may nought preche or maken tarying.
Anoon go gete us faste into this in°   lodging
440 A kneeding trough or elles a kimelin°   brewing tub
For eech of us, but looke that they be large,°   wide
In whiche we mowen swimme as in a barge,[4]
And han therinne vitaile suffisaunt[5]
But for a day—fy° on the remenaunt!   fie
445 The water shal aslake° and goon away   diminish
Aboute prime[6] upon the nexte day.
But Robin may nat wite° of this, thy knave,   know
Ne eek thy maide Gille I may nat save.
Axe nought why, for though thou axe me,
450 I wol nought tellen Goddes privetee.°   secrets
Suffiseth thee, but if thy wittes madde,°   go mad
To han° as greet a grace as Noee hadde.   have
Thy wif shal I wel saven, out of doute.
Go now thy way, and speed thee heraboute.
455 But whan thou hast for hire° and thee and me   her
Ygeten us thise kneeding-tubbes three,
Thanne shaltou hangen hem in the roof ful hye,
That no man of oure purveyance° espye.   preparations
And whan thou thus hast doon as I have said,
460 And hast oure vitaile faire in hem ylaid,

7. Almost fell.
8. I.e., by.
9. Act according to learning and advice.
1. He had rather.
2. Rams. I.e., he'd have given all the black rams
he had.

3. The reluctance of Noah's wife to board the ark
is a traditional comic theme in the mystery plays.
4. In which we can float as in a vessel.
5. Sufficient food.
6. 9 A.M.

And eek an ax to smite the corde atwo,
Whan that the water comth that we may go,
And broke an hole an heigh[7] upon the gable
Unto the gardinward,[8] over the stable,
465 That we may freely passen forth oure way,
Whan that the grete showr is goon away,
Thanne shaltou swimme as merye, I undertake,
As dooth the white doke° after hir drake.   duck
Thanne wol I clepe,° 'How, Alison? How, John?   call
470 Be merye, for the flood wol passe anoon.'
And thou wolt sayn, 'Hail, maister Nicholay!
Good morwe, I see thee wel, for it is day!'
And thanne shal we be lordes al oure lif
Of al the world, as Noee and his wif.
475 But of oo thing I warne thee ful right:
Be wel avised° on that ilke night   warned
That we been entred into shippes boord
That noon of us ne speke nought a word,
Ne clepe, ne crye, but been in his prayere,
480 For it is Goddes owene heeste dere.[9]
Thy wif and thou mote hange fer atwinne,[1]
For that bitwixe you shal be no sinne—
Namore in looking than ther shal in deede.
This ordinance is said: go, God thee speede.
485 Tomorwe at night whan men been alle asleepe,
Into oure kneeding-tubbes wol we creepe,
And sitten there, abiding Goddes grace.
Go now thy way, I have no lenger space°   time
To make of this no lenger sermoning.
490 Men sayn thus: 'Send the wise and say no thing.'
Thou art so wis it needeth thee nat teche:
Go save oure lif, and that I thee biseeche."
   This sely carpenter gooth forth his way:
Ful ofte he saide allas and wailaway,
495 And to his wif he tolde his privetee,
And she was war,° and knew it bet° than he,   aware / better
What al this quainte cast was for to saye.[2]
But nathelees she ferde° as she wolde deye,   acted
And saide, "Allas, go forth thy way anoon.
500 Help us to scape,° or we been dede eechoon.   escape
I am thy trewe verray wedded wif:
Go, dere spouse, and help to save oure lif."
   Lo, which a greet thing is affeccioun!°   emotion
Men may dien of imaginacioun,
505 So deepe° may impression be take.   deeply
This sely carpenter biginneth quake;
Him thinketh verrailiche° that he may see   truly
Noees flood come walwing° as the see   rolling

7. On high.   1. Far apart.
8. Toward the garden.   2. What all this clever plan meant.
9. Precious commandment.

To drenchen° Alison, his hony dere.   drown
510 He weepeth, waileth, maketh sory cheere;
He siketh° with ful many a sory swough,°   sighs / groan
And gooth and geteth him a kneeding-trough,
And after a tubbe and a kimelin,
And prively he sente hem to his in,°   dwelling
515 And heeng° hem in the roof in privetee;   hung
His° owene hand he made laddres three,   with his
To climben by the ronges° and the stalkes°   rungs / uprights
Unto the tubbes hanging in the balkes,°   rafters
And hem vitailed,° bothe trough and tubbe,   victualed
520 With breed and cheese and good ale in a jubbe,°   jug
Suffising right ynough as for a day.
But er° that he hadde maad al this array,   before
He sente his knave, and eek his wenche also,
Upon his neede[3] to London for to go.
525 And on the Monday whan it drow to[4] nighte,
He shette° his dore withouten candel-lighte,   shut
And dressed° alle thing as it sholde be,   arranged
And shortly up they clomben° alle three.   climbed
They seten° stille wel a furlong way.[5]   sat
530 "Now, Pater Noster, clum,"[6] saide Nicholay,
And "Clum" quod John, and "Clum" saide Alisoun.
This carpenter saide his devocioun,
And stille he sit° and biddeth° his prayere,   sits / prays
Awaiting on the rain, if he it heere.°   might hear
535   The dede sleep, for wery bisinesse,
Fil° on this carpenter right as I gesse   fell
Aboute corfew time,[7] or litel more.
For travailing of his gost[8] he groneth sore,
And eft° he routeth,° for his heed mislay.[9]   then / snores
540   Down of the laddre stalketh Nicholay,
And Alison ful softe adown she spedde:
Withouten wordes mo they goon to bedde
Ther as the carpenter is wont to lie.
Ther was the revel and the melodye,
545 And thus lith° Alison and Nicholas   lies
In bisinesse of mirthe and of solas,°   pleasure
Til that the belle of Laudes[1] gan to ringe,
And freres° in the chauncel° gonne singe.   friars / chancel
This parissh clerk, this amorous Absolon,
550 That is for love alway so wo-bigoon,
Upon the Monday was at Oseneye,
With compaignye him to disporte and playe,
And axed upon caas a cloisterer[2]
Ful prively after John the carpenter;

---

3. On an errand for him.
4. Drew toward.
5. The time it takes to go a furlong (i.e., a few minutes).
6. Hush (?). "Pater Noster": Our Father.
7. Probably about 8 P.M.

8. Affliction of his spirit.
9. Lay in the wrong position.
1. The first church service of the day, before daybreak.
2. Here a member of the religious order of Osney Abbey. "Upon caas": by chance.

555 And he drow him apart out of the chirche,
And saide, "I noot:[3] I sawgh him here nought wirche°   work
Sith Saterday. I trowe that he be went
For timber ther oure abbot hath him sent.
For he is wont for timber for to go,
560 And dwellen atte grange[4] a day or two.
Or elles he is at his hous, certain.
Where that he be I can nought soothly sayn."
    This Absolon ful jolif was and light,[5]
And thoughte, "Now is time to wake al night,
565 For sikerly,° I sawgh him nought stiringe   certainly
Aboute his dore sin day bigan to springe.
So mote° I thrive, I shal at cokkes crowe   may
Ful prively knokken at his windowe
That stant° ful lowe upon his bowres° wal.   stands / bedroom's
570 To Alison now wol I tellen al
My love-longing,° for yet I shal nat misse   lovesickness
That at the leeste way[6] I shal hire kisse.
Som manere confort shal I have, parfay.°   in faith
My mouth hath icched al this longe day:
575 That is a signe of kissing at the leeste.
Al night me mette[7] eek I was at a feeste.
Therfore I wol go sleepe an hour or twaye,
And al the night thanne wol I wake and playe."
    Whan that the firste cok hath crowe, anoon
580 Up rist° this joly lovere Absolon,   rises
And him arrayeth gay at point devis.[8]
But first he cheweth grain[9] and licoris,
To smellen sweete, er he hadde kembd° his heer.   combed
Under his tonge a trewe-love[1] he beer,°   bore
585 For therby wende° he to be gracious.°   supposed / pleasing
He rometh° to the carpenteres hous,   strolls
And stille he stant° under the shot-windowe—   stands
Unto his brest it raughte,° it was so lowe—   reached
And ofte he cougheth with a semisoun.°   small sound
590 "What do ye, hony-comb, sweete Alisoun,
My faire brid,[2] my sweete cinamome?°   cinnamon
Awaketh, lemman° myn, and speketh to me.   sweetheart
Wel litel thinken ye upon my wo
That for your love I swete° ther I go.   sweat
595 No wonder is though that I swelte° and swete: melt
I moorne as doth a lamb after the tete.°   teat
Ywis, lemman, I have swich love-longinge,
That lik a turtle° trewe is my moorninge: dove
I may nat ete namore than a maide."
600   "Go fro the windowe, Jakke fool," she saide.
"As help me God, it wol nat be com-pa-me.°   come-kiss-me

3. Don't know.
4. The outlying farm belonging to the abbey.
5. Was very amorous and cheerful.
6. I.e., at least.
7. I dreamed.

8. To perfection.
9. Grain of paradise; a spice.
1. Sprig of a cloverlike plant.
2. Bird or bride.

I love another, and elles I were to blame,
Wel bet° than thee, by Jesu, Absolon.   *better*
Go forth thy way or I wol caste a stoon,
605 And lat me sleepe, a twenty devele way."[3]
    "Allas," quod Absolon, "and wailaway,
That trewe love was evere so yvele biset.[4]
Thanne kis me, sin that it may be no bet,
For Jesus love and for the love of me."
610   "Woltou thanne go thy way therwith?" quod she.
    "Ye, certes, lemman," quod this Absolon.
    "Thanne maak thee redy," quod she. "I come anoon."
And unto Nicholas she saide stille,°   *quietly*
    "Now hust,° and thou shalt laughen al thy fille."   *hush*
615   This Absolon down sette him on his knees,
And said, "I am a lord at alle degrees,[5]
For after this I hope ther cometh more.
Lemman, thy grace, and sweete brid, thyn ore!"°   *mercy*
The windowe she undooth, and that in haste.
620 "Have do," quod she, "come of and speed thee faste,
Lest that oure neighebores thee espye."
    This Absolon gan wipe his mouth ful drye:
Derk was the night as pich or as the cole,
And at the windowe out she putte hir hole,
625 And Absolon, him fil no bet ne wers,[6]
But with his mouth he kiste hir naked ers,
Ful savourly,° er he were war of this.   *with relish*
Abak he sterte,° and thoughte it was amis,   *started*
For wel he wiste a womman hath no beerd.°   *beard*
630 He felte a thing al rough and longe yherd,°   *haired*
And saide, "Fy, allas, what have I do?"
    "Teehee," quod she, and clapte the windowe to.
And Absolon gooth forth a sory pas.[7]
    "A beerd, a beerd!"[8] quod hende Nicholas,
635 "By Goddes corpus,° this gooth faire and weel."   *body*
    This sely Absolon herde everydeel,°   *every bit*
And on his lippe he gan for anger bite,
And to himself he saide, "I shal thee quite."°   *repay*
    Who rubbeth now, who froteth° now his lippes   *wipes*
640 With dust, with sond,° with straw, with cloth, with chippes, *sand*
But Absolon, that saith ful ofte allas?
    "My soule bitake° I unto Satanas,°   *commit / Satan*
But me were levere[9] than all this town," quod he,
    "Of this despit° awroken° for to be.   *insult / avenged*
645 Allas," quod he, "allas I ne hadde ybleint!"°   *turned aside*
His hote love was cold and al yqueint,°   *quenched*
For fro that time that he hadde kist hir ers
Of paramours he sette nought a kers,[1]
For he was heled° of his maladye.   *cured*

---

3. In the name of twenty devils.
4. Ill-used.
5. In every way.
6. It befell him neither better nor worse.

7. I.e., walking sadly.
8. A trick (slang), but with a play on line 629.
9. I had rather.
1. He didn't care a piece of cress for woman's love.

650 Ful ofte paramours he gan defye,°   *renounce*
And weep° as dooth a child that is ybete.   *wept*
A softe paas² he wente over the streete
Until° a smith men clepen daun Gervais,³   *to*
That in his forge smithed plough harneis:°   *equipment*
655 He sharpeth shaar and cultour⁴ bisily.
This Absolon knokketh al esily,°   *quietly*
And saide, "Undo, Gervais, and that anoon."°   *at once*
    "What, who artou?" "It am I, Absolon."
"What, Absolon? What, Cristes sweete tree!°   *cross*
660 Why rise ye so rathe?° Ey, benedicite,°   *early/bless me*
What aileth you? Som gay girl, God it woot,
Hath brought you thus upon the viritoot.⁵
By Sainte Note, ye woot wel what I mene."
    This Absolon ne roughte nat a bene⁶
665 Of al his play. No word again he yaf:
He hadde more tow on his distaf⁷
Than Gervais knew, and saide, "Freend so dere,
This hote cultour in the chimenee° here,   *fireplace*
As lene⁸ it me: I have therwith to doone.
670 I wol bringe it thee again ful soone."
    Gervais answerde, "Certes, were it gold,
Or in a poke nobles alle untold,⁹
Thou sholdest have, as I am trewe smith.
Ey, Cristes fo,¹ what wol ye do therwith?"
675   "Therof," quod Absolon, "be as be may.
I shal wel telle it thee another day."
And caughte the cultour by the colde stele.°   *handle*
Ful softe out at the dore he gan to stele,
And wente unto the carpenteres wal:
680 He cougheth first and knokketh therwithal
Upon the windowe, right as he dide er.°   *before*
    This Alison answerde, "Who is ther
That knokketh so? I warante² it a thief."
    "Why, nay," quod he, "God woot, my sweete lief,°   *dear*
685 I am thyn Absolon, my dereling.°   *darling*
Of gold," quod he, "I have thee brought a ring—
My moder yaf it me, so God me save;
Ful fin it is and therto wel ygrave:°   *engraved*
This wol I yiven thee if thou me kisse."
690   This Nicholas was risen for to pisse,
And thoughte he wolde amenden³ al the jape:°   *joke*
He sholde kisse his ers er that he scape.
And up the windowe dide he hastily,
And out his ers he putteth prively,
695 Over the buttok to the haunche-boon.
    And therwith spak this clerk, this Absolon,

---

2. I.e., quiet walk.
3. Master Gervais.
4. He sharpens plowshare and coulter (the turf
cutter on a plow).
5. I.e., on the prowl.
6. Didn't care a bean.

7. I.e., more on his mind.
8. I.e., please lend.
9. Or gold coins all uncounted in a bag.
1. Foe, i.e., Satan.
2. I.e., wager.
3. Improve on.

"Speek, sweete brid, I noot nought wher thou art."
This Nicholas anoon leet flee[4] a fart
As greet as it hadde been a thonder-dent°   thunderbolt
700   That with the strook he was almost yblent,°   blinded
And he was redy with his iren hoot,°   hot
And Nicholas amidde the ers he smoot:°   smote
Of° gooth the skin an hande-brede° aboute;   off/handsbreadth
The hote cultour brende so his toute°   buttocks
705   That for the smert° he wende for to[5] die;   pain
As he were wood° for wo he gan to crye,   crazy
"Help! Water! Water! Help, for Goddes herte!"
This carpenter out of his slomber sterte,
And herde oon cryen "Water!" as he were wood,
710   And thoughte, "Allas, now cometh Noweles[6] flood!"
He sette him up[7] withoute wordes mo,
And with his ax he smoot the corde atwo,
And down gooth al: he foond neither to selle
Ne breed ne ale til he cam to the celle,[8]
715   Upon the floor, and ther aswoune° he lay.   in a faint
Up sterte hire[9] Alison and Nicholay,
And criden "Out" and "Harrow" in the streete.
The neighebores, bothe smale and grete,
In ronnen for to gauren° on this man   gape
720   That aswoune lay bothe pale and wan,
For with the fal he brosten° hadde his arm;   broken
But stonde he moste° unto his owene harm,   must
For whan he spak he was anoon bore down[1]
With° hende Nicholas and Alisoun: by
725   They tolden every man that he was wood—
He was agast so of Noweles flood,
Thurgh fantasye, that of his vanitee°   folly
He hadde ybought him kneeding-tubbes three,
And hadde hem hanged in the roof above,
730   And that he prayed hem, for Goddes love,
To sitten in the roof, par compaignye.[2]
The folk gan laughen at his fantasye.
Into the roof they kiken° and they cape,°   peer/gape
And turned al his harm unto a jape,°   joke
735   For what so that this carpenter answerde,
It was for nought: no man his reson° herde;   argument
With othes grete he was so sworn adown,
That he was holden° wood in al the town,   considered
For every clerk anoonright heeld with other:
740   They saide, "The man was wood, my leve brother,"
And every wight gan laughen at this strif.°   fuss
Thus swived[3] was the carpenteres wif
For al his keeping° and his jalousye,   guarding

4. Let fly.
5. Thought he would.
6. The carpenter is confusing Noah and Noel
(Christmas).
7. Got up.
8. He found time to sell neither bread nor ale until

he arrived at the foundation, i.e., he did not take
time out.
9. Started.
1. Refuted.
2. For company's sake.
3. The vulgar verb for having sexual intercourse.

And Absolon hath kist hir nether° yë,   *lower*
745   And Nicholas is scalded in the toute:
This tale is doon, and God save al the route!°   *company*

The Man of Law's Epilogue

The Reeve has taken *The Miller's Tale* personally and retaliates with a fabliau about a miller whose wife and daughter are seduced by two clerks. Next the Cook begins yet another fabliau, which breaks off after fifty-five lines, thereby closing Fragment I of *The Canterbury Tales*. Chaucer may never have settled on a final order for the tales he completed, but all modern editors, following many manuscripts, agree in putting *The Man of Law's Tale* next. The Man of Law tells a long moralistic tale about the many trials of a heroine called Constance for the virtue she personifies. This tale is finished, but Fragment II shows that *The Canterbury Tales* reaches us as a work in progress, which Chaucer kept revising, creating many problems for its scribes and editors. In the link that introduces him, the Man of Law says he will tell a tale in prose, but the story of Constance turns out to be in a seven-line stanza called rhyme royal. That inconsistency has led to speculation that at one time the Man of Law was assigned a long prose allegory, which Chaucer later reassigned to his own pilgrim persona. In thirty-five manuscripts *The Man of Law's Tale* is followed by an *Epilogue* omitted in twenty-two of the manuscripts that contain more or less complete versions of *The Canterbury Tales*. The often-missing link begins with the Host praising the *Man of Law's Tale* and calling upon the Parson to tell another uplifting tale. The Parson, however, rebukes the Host for swearing. The Host angrily accuses the Parson of being a "Lollard," a derogatory term for followers of the reformist preacher John Wycliffe. This is Chaucer's only overt reference to an important religious and political controversy that anticipates the sixteenth-century English Reformation.

A third speaker, about whose identity the manuscripts disagree (six read "Summoner"; twenty-eight, "Squire"; one, "Shipman"), interrupts with the promise to tell a merry tale. Several modern editions, including the standard one used by scholars, print *The Man of Law's Epilogue* at the end of Fragment II, and begin Fragment III with *The Wife of Bath's Prologue*. Because the third speaker in the former *sounds* like the Wife, an argument has been made that she is the pilgrim who refers to "My joly body" (line 23), who at one time told a fabliau tale in which the narrator speaks of married women in the first person plural ("we," "us," "our"). Chaucer, so the argument goes, later gave that story to the Shipman. If in fact the Wife of Bath did once tell what is now *The Shipman's Tale*, that would be an indication of the exciting new possibilities he discovered in the literary form he had invented.

Oure Host upon his stiropes stood anoon
And saide, "Goode men, herkneth everichoon,
This was a thrifty° tale for the nones,°   *proper / occasion*
Sire parissh Preest," quod he, "for Goddes bones,
5   Tel us a tale as was thy forward° yore.°   *agreement / earlier*
I see wel that ye lerned men in lore°   *teaching*
Can° muche good, by Goddes dignitee."   *know*
The Person him answerde, "Benedicite,°   *bless me*
What aileth the man so sinfully to swere?"
10   Oure Host answerede, "O Jankin, be ye there?[1]
I smelle a lollere[2] in the wind," quod he.

1. Is that where you're coming from? "Jankin": Johnny; derogatory name for a priest.

2. Contemptuous term for a religious reformer considered radical; a heretic.

"Now, goode men," quod oure Hoste, "herkneth me:
Abideth, for Goddes digne° passioun,   *worthy*
For we shal have a predicacioun.°   *sermon*
15 This lollere here wol prechen us somwhat."
"Nay, by my fader soule, that shal he nat,"
Saide the [Wif of Bathe],³ "here shal he nat preche:
He shal no gospel glosen⁴ here ne teche.
We leven° alle in the grete God," quod [she].   *believe*
20 He wolde sowen som difficultee
Or sprengen cokkel in oure clene corn.⁵
And therfore, Host, I warne thee biforn,
My joly body shal a tale telle
And I shal clinken you so merye a belle
25 That I shal waken al this compaignye.
But it shal nat been of philosophye,
Ne physlias,⁶ ne termes quainte of lawe:
There is but litel Latin in my mawe."°   *stomach*

The Wife of Bath's Prologue and Tale

In creating the Wife of Bath, Chaucer drew upon a centuries-old tradition of anti-feminist writings that was particularly nurtured by the medieval church. In their conviction that the rational, intellectual, spiritual, and, therefore, higher side of human nature predominated in men, whereas the irrational, material, earthly, and, therefore, lower side of human nature predominated in women, St. Paul and the early Church fathers exalted celibacy and virginity above marriage, although they were also obliged to concede the necessity and sanctity of matrimony. In the fourth century, a monk called Jovinian wrote a tract in which he apparently presented marriage as a positive good rather than as a necessary evil. That tract is known only through St. Jerome's extreme attack upon it. Jerome's diatribe and other antifeminist and anti-matrimonial literature provided Chaucer with a rich body of bookish male "auctoritee" (authority) against which the Wife of Bath asserts her female "experience" and defends her rights and justifies her life as a five-time married woman. In her polemical wars with medieval clerks and her matrimonial wars with her five husbands, the last of whom was once a clerk of Oxenford, the Wife of Bath seems ironically to confirm the accusations of the clerks, but at the same time she succeeds in satirizing the shallowness of the stereotypes of women and marriage in antifeminist writings and in demonstrating how much the largeness and complexity of her own character rise above that stereotype.

The Prologue

Experience, though noon auctoritee
Were in this world, is right ynough for me
To speke of wo that is in mariage:
For lordinges,° sith I twelf yeer was of age—   *gentlemen*
5 Thanked be God that is eterne on live—
Housbondes at chirche dore¹ I have had five

---

3. On the speaker here, see discussion in headnote.
4. Gloss, with the sense of distorting the meaning of scripture.
5. Sow tares (impure doctrine) in our pure wheat.

6. No such word exists. The speaker is coining a professional-sounding term in philosophy, law, or medicine.
1. The actual wedding ceremony was celebrated at the church door, not in the chancel.

(If I so ofte mighte han wedded be),
And alle were worthy men in hir degree.
But me was told, certain, nat longe agoon is,
10 That sith that Crist ne wente nevere but ones°   *once*
To wedding in the Cane[2] of Galilee,
That by the same ensample° taughte he me   *example*
That I ne sholde wedded be but ones.
Herke eek,° lo, which° a sharp word for the nones,[3]   *also/what*
15 Biside a welle, Jesus, God and man,
Spak in repreve° of the Samaritan: *reproof*
"Thou hast yhad five housbondes," quod he,
"And that ilke° man that now hath thee   *same*
Is nat thyn housbonde." Thus saide he certain.
20 What that he mente therby I can nat sayn,
But that I axe° why the fifthe man   *ask*
Was noon housbonde to the Samaritan?[4]
How manye mighte she han in mariage?
Yit herde I nevere tellen in myn age
25 Upon this nombre diffinicioun.°   *definition*
Men may divine° and glosen° up and down,   *guess/interpret*
But wel I woot,° expres,° withouten lie,   *know/expressly*
God bad us for to wexe[5] and multiplye:
That gentil text can I wel understonde.
30   Eek wel I woot° he saide that myn housbonde   *know*
Sholde lete° fader and moder and take to me,[6]   *leave*
But of no nombre mencion made he—
Of bigamye or of octogamye:[7]
Why sholde men thanne speke of it vilainye?
35   Lo, here the wise king daun° Salomon: *master*
I trowe° he hadde wives many oon,[8]   *believe*
As wolde God it leveful° were to me   *permissible*
To be refresshed half so ofte as he.
Which yifte[9] of God hadde he for alle his wives!
40 No man hath swich° that in this world alive is.   *such*
God woot this noble king, as to my wit,°   *knowledge*
The firste night hadde many a merye fit°   *bout*
With eech of hem, so wel was him on live.[1]
Blessed be God that I have wedded five,
45 Of whiche I have piked out the beste,[2]
Bothe of hir nether purs[3] and of hir cheste.°   *money box*
Diverse scoles maken parfit° clerkes,   *perfect*
And diverse practikes[4] in sondry werkes
Maken the werkman parfit sikerly:°   *certainly*
50 Of five housbondes scoleying° am I.   *schooling*

---

2. Cana (see John 2.1).
3. To the purpose.
4. Christ was actually referring to a sixth man who was not married to the Samaritan woman (cf. John 4.6 ff.).
5. I.e., increase (see Genesis 1.28).
6. See Matthew 19.5.
7. I.e., of two or even eight marriages. The Wife of Bath is referring to successive, rather than simultaneous, marriages.
8. Solomon had seven hundred wives and three hundred concubines (1 Kings 11.3).
9. What a gift.
1. I.e., so pleasant a life he had.
2. Whom I have cleaned out of everything worthwhile.
3. Lower purse, i.e., testicles.
4. Practical experiences.

Welcome the sixte whan that evere he shal![5]
For sith I wol nat kepe me chast in al,
Whan my housbonde is fro the world agoon,
Som Cristen man shal wedde me anoon.°   right away
55 For thanne th'Apostle[6] saith that I am free
To wedde, a Goddes half, where it liketh me.[7]
He saide that to be wedded is no sinne:
Bet is to be wedded than to brinne.[8]
What rekketh me[9] though folk saye vilainye
60 Of shrewed° Lamech[1] and his bigamye?   cursed
I woot wel Abraham was an holy man,
And Jacob eek, as fer as evere I can,°   know
And eech of hem hadde wives mo than two,
And many another holy man also.
65   Where can ye saye in any manere age
That hye God defended° mariage   prohibited
By expres word? I praye you, telleth me.
Or where comanded he virginitee?
I woot as wel as ye, it is no drede,°   doubt
70 Th'Apostle, whan he speketh of maidenhede,°   virginity
He saide that precept therof hadde he noon:
Men may conseile a womman to be oon,°   single
But conseiling nis° no comandement.   is not
He putte it in oure owene juggement.
75 For hadde God comanded maidenhede,
Thanne hadde he dampned° wedding with the deede;[2]   condemned
And certes, if there were no seed ysowe,
Virginitee, thanne wherof sholde it growe?
Paul dorste nat comanden at the leeste
80 A thing of which his maister yaf° no heeste.°   gave/command
The dart[3] is set up for virginitee:
Cacche whoso may, who renneth° best lat see.   runs
But this word is nought take of[4] every wight,°   person
But ther as[5] God list° yive it of his might.   it pleases
85 I woot wel that th'Apostle was a maide,°   virgin
But nathelees, though that he wroot and saide
He wolde that every wight were swich° as he,   such
Al nis but conseil to virginitee;
And for to been a wif he yaf me leve
90 Of indulgence; so nis it no repreve°   disgrace
To wedde me[6] if that my make° die,   mate
Withouten excepcion of bigamye[7]—
Al° were it good no womman for to touche[8]   although
(He mente as in his bed or in his couche,

5. I.e., shall come along.
6. St. Paul.
7. I please. "A Goddes half": on God's behalf.
8. "It is better to marry than to burn" (1 Corinthians 7.9). Many of the Wife's citations of St. Paul are from this chapter, often secondhand from St. Jerome's tract *Against Jovinian*.
9. What do I care.
1. The first man whom the Bible mentions as having two wives (Genesis 4.19–24); he is cursed, however, not for his marriages but for murder.
2. I.e., at the same time.
3. I.e., prize in a race.
4. Understood for, i.e., applicable to.
5. Where.
6. For me to marry.
7. I.e., without there being any legal objection on the score of remarriage.
8. "It is good for a man not to touch a woman" (1 Corinthians 7.1).

95 For peril is bothe fir° and tow° t'assemble—   *fire/flax*
    Ye knowe what this ensample may resemble).⁹
    This al and som,¹ he heeld virginitee
    More parfit than wedding in freletee.°   *frailty*
    (Freletee clepe I but if² that he and she
100 Wolde leden al hir lif in chastitee.)
    I graunte it wel, I have noon envye
    Though maidenhede preferre° bigamye:°   *excel/remarriage*
    It liketh hem to be clene in body and gost.°   *spirit*
    Of myn estaat ne wol I make no boost;
105 For wel ye knowe, a lord in his houshold
    Ne hath nat every vessel al of gold:
    Some been of tree,° and doon hir lord servise.   *wood*
    God clepeth° folk to him in sondry wise,   *calls*
    And everich hath of God a propre³ yifte,
110 Som this, som that, as him liketh shifte.°   *ordain*
    Virginitee is greet perfeccioun,
    And continence eek with devocioun,
    But Crist, that of perfeccion is welle,°   *source*
    Bad nat every wight he sholde go selle
115 Al that he hadde and yive it to the poore,
    And in swich wise folwe him and his fore:°⁴   *footsteps*
    He spak to hem that wolde live parfitly°—   *perfectly*
    And lordinges, by youre leve, that am nat I.
    I wol bistowe the flour of al myn age
120 In th'actes and in fruit of mariage.
       Telle me also, to what conclusioun°   *end*
    Were membres maad of generacioun
    And of so parfit wis a wrighte ywrought?⁵
       Trusteth right wel, they were nat maad for nought.
125 Glose° whoso wol, and saye bothe up and down   *interpret*
    That they were maked for purgacioun
    Of urine, and oure bothe thinges smale
    Was eek° to knowe a femele from a male,   *also*
    And for noon other cause—saye ye no?
130 Th'experience woot it is nought so.
    So that the clerkes be nat with me wrothe,
    I saye this, that they been maad for bothe—
    That is to sayn, for office° and for ese°   *use/pleasure*
    Of engendrure,° ther we nat God displese.   *procreation*
135 Why sholde men elles in hir bookes sette
    That man shal yeelde⁶ to his wif hir dette?°   *(marital) debt*
    Now wherwith sholde he make his payement
    If he ne used his sely° instrument?   *innocent*
    Thanne were they maad upon a creature
140 To purge urine, and eek for engendrure.
       But I saye nought that every wight is holde,°   *bound*
    That hath swich harneis° as I to you tolde,   *equipment*

---

9. I.e., what this metaphor may apply to.   4. Matthew 19.21.
1. This is all there is to it.   5. And wrought by so perfectly wise a maker.
2. Frailty I call it unless.   6. I.e., pay.
3. I.e., his own.

To goon and usen hem in engendrure:
Thanne sholde men take of chastitee no cure.°   *heed*
145 Crist was a maide° and shapen as a man,   *virgin*
And many a saint sith that the world bigan,
Yit lived they evere in parfit chastitee.
I nil° envye no virginitee: *will not*
Lat hem be breed° of pured° whete seed,   *bread/refined*
150 And lat us wives hote° barly breed—   *be called*
And yit with barly breed, Mark telle can,
Oure Lord Jesu refresshed many a man.[7]
In swich estaat as God hath cleped us
I wol persevere: I nam nat precious.°   *fastidious*
155 In wifhood wol I use myn instrument
As freely° as my Makere hath it sent.   *generously*
If I be daungerous[8], God yive me sorwe:
Myn housbonde shal it han both eve and morwe,°   *morning*
Whan that him list[9] come forth and paye his dette.
160 An housbonde wol I have, I wol nat lette,[1]
Which shal be bothe my dettour° and my thral,°   *debtor/slave*
And have his tribulacion withal°   *as well*
Upon his flessh whil that I am his wif.
I have the power during al my lif
165 Upon his propre° body, and nat he: *own*
Right thus th'Apostle tolde it unto me,
And bad oure housbondes for to love us weel.
Al this sentence° me liketh everydeel.°   *sense/entirely*

[AN INTERLUDE]

Up sterte° the Pardoner and that anoon: *started*
170 "Now dame," quod he, "by God and by Saint John,
Ye been a noble prechour in this cas.
I was aboute to wedde a wif: allas,
What° sholde I bye° it on my flessh so dere?   *why/purchase*
Yit hadde I levere° wedde no wif toyere."°   *rather/this year*
175 "Abid," quod she, "my tale is nat bigonne.
Nay, thou shalt drinken of another tonne,°   *tun, barrel*
Er° that I go, shal savoure wors than ale.   *before*
And whan that I have told thee forth my tale
Of tribulacion in mariage,
180 Of which I am expert in al myn age—
This is to saye, myself hath been the whippe—
Thanne maistou chese° wheither thou wolt sippe   *choose*
Of thilke° tonne that I shal abroche;°   *this same/open*
Be war of it, er thou too neigh approche,
185 For I shal telle ensamples mo than ten.
'Whoso that nil° be war by othere men,   *will not*
By him shal othere men corrected be.'

7. In the descriptions of the miracle of the loaves and fishes, it is actually John, not Mark, who mentions barley bread (6.9).
8. In romance *dangerous* is a term for disdainfulness with which a woman rejects a lover. The Wife means she will not withhold sexual favors, in emulation of God's generosity (line 156).
9. When he wishes to.
1. I will not leave off, desist.

Thise same wordes writeth Ptolomee:
Rede in his *Almageste* and take it there."[2]
190   "Dame, I wolde praye you if youre wil it were,"
Saide this Pardoner, "as ye bigan,
Telle forth youre tale; spareth for no man,
And teche us yonge men of youre practike."°   *mode of operation*
    "Gladly," quod she, "sith it may you like;°   *please*
195   But that I praye to al this compaignye,
If that I speke after my fantasye,[3]
As taketh nat agrief° of that I saye,   *amiss*
For myn entente nis but for to playe."

[THE WIFE CONTINUES]

    Now sire, thanne wol I telle you forth my tale.
200 As evere mote I drinke win or ale,
I shal saye sooth: tho° housbondes that I hadde,   *those*
As three of hem were goode, and two were badde.
The three men were goode, and riche, and olde;
Unnethe° mighte they the statut holde   *scarcely*
205 In which they were bounden unto me—
Ye woot wel what I mene of this, pardee.
As help me God, I laughe whan I thinke
How pitously anight I made hem swinke;°   *work*
And by my fay,° I tolde of it no stoor:[4]   *faith*
210 They hadde me yiven hir land and hir tresor;
Me needed nat do lenger diligence
To winne hir love or doon hem reverence.
They loved me so wel, by God above,
That I ne tolde no daintee of[5] hir love.
215 A wis womman wol bisye hire evere in oon[6]
To gete hire love, ye, ther as she hath noon.
But sith I hadde hem hoolly in myn hand,
And sith that they hadde yiven me al hir land,
What° sholde I take keep° hem for to plese,   *why/care*
220 But it were for my profit and myn ese?
I sette hem so awerke,° by my fay,   *awork*
That many a night they songen° wailaway.   *sang*
The bacon was nat fet° for hem, I trowe,   *brought back*
That some men han in Essexe at Dunmowe.[7]
225 I governed hem so wel after° my lawe   *according to*
That eech of hem ful blisful was and fawe°   *glad*
To bringe me gaye thinges fro the faire;
They were ful glade whan I spak hem faire,
For God it woot, I chidde° hem spitously.°   *chided/cruelly*
230   Now herkneth how I bar me[8] proprely:

---

2. "He who will not be warned by the example of others shall become an example to others." The *Almagest*, an astronomical work by the Greek astronomer and mathematician Ptolemy (2nd century C.E.), contains no such aphorism.
3. If I speak according to my fancy.
4. I set no store by it.

5. Set no value on.
6. Busy herself constantly.
7. At Dunmow, a side of bacon was awarded to the couple who after a year of marriage could claim no quarrels, no regrets, and the desire, if freed, to remarry one another.
8. Bore myself, behaved.

Ye wise wives, that conne understonde,
Thus sholde ye speke and bere him wrong on honde⁹—
For half so boldely can ther no man
Swere and lie as a woman can.

235 I saye nat this by wives that been wise,
But if it be whan they hem misavise.¹
A wis wif, if that she can hir good,²
Shal bere him on hande the cow is wood,³
And take witnesse of hir owene maide

240 Of hir assent.⁴ But herkneth how I saide:
"Sire olde cainard,° is this thyn array?⁵   *sluggard*
Why is my neighebores wif so gay?
She is honoured overal° ther she gooth: *wherever*
I sitte at hoom; I have no thrifty° cloth.   *decent*

245 What doostou at my neighebores hous?
Is she so fair? Artou so amorous?
What roune° ye with oure maide, benedicite?⁶   *whisper*
Sire olde lechour, lat thy japes° be.   *tricks, intrigues*
And if I have a gossib° or a freend   *confidant*

250 Withouten gilt, ye chiden as a feend,
If that I walke or playe unto his hous.
Thou comest hoom as dronken as a mous,
And prechest on thy bench, with yvel preef.⁷
Thou saist to me, it is a greet meschief°   *misfortune*

255 To wedde a poore womman for costage.⁸
And if that she be riche, of heigh parage,°   *descent*
Thanne saistou that it is a tormentrye
To suffre hir pride and hir malencolye.°   *bad humor*
And if that she be fair, thou verray knave,

260 Thou saist that every holour° wol hire have: *lecher*
She may no while in chastitee abide
That is assailed upon eech a side.
"Thou saist som folk desiren us for richesse,
Som⁹ for oure shap, and som for oure fairnesse,

265 And som for she can outher° singe or daunce,   *either*
And som for gentilesse and daliaunce,°   *flirtatiousness*
Som for hir handes and hir armes smale°—   *slender*
Thus gooth al to the devel by thy tale!¹
Thou saist men may nat keepe² a castel wal,

270 It may so longe assailed been overal.°   *everywhere*
And if that she be foul,° thou saist that she   *ugly*
Coveiteth° every man that she may see;   *desires*
For as a spaniel she wol on him lepe,
Til that she finde som man hire to chepe.°   *bargain for*

275 Ne noon so grey goos gooth ther in the lake,

---

9. Accuse him falsely.
1. Unless it happens that they make a mistake.
2. If she knows what's good for her.
3. Shall persuade him the chough has gone crazy.
The chough, a talking bird, was popularly supposed
to tell husbands of their wives' infidelity.
4. And call as a witness her maid, who is on her
side.

5. I.e., is this how you behave?
6. Bless me.
7. I.e., (may you have) bad luck.
8. Because of the expense.
9. "Som," in this and the following lines, means
"one."
1. I.e., according to your story.
2. I.e., keep safe.

As, saistou, wol be withoute make;°   *mate*
And saist it is an hard thing for to weelde°   *possess*
A thing that no man wol, his thankes, heelde.³
Thus saistou, lorel,° whan thou goost to bedde,   *wretch*
280 And that no wis man needeth for to wedde,
Ne no man that entendeth° unto hevene—   *aims*
With wilde thonder-dint° and firy levene°   *thunderbolt/lightning*
Mote thy welked nekke be tobroke!⁴
Thou saist that dropping° houses and eek smoke   *leaking*
285 And chiding wives maken men to flee
Out of hir owene hous: a, benedicite,
What aileth swich an old man for to chide?
Thou saist we wives wil oure vices hide
Til we be fast,⁵ and thanne we wol hem shewe—
290 Wel may that be a proverbe of a shrewe!°   *rascal*
Thou saist that oxen, asses, hors,° and houndes,   *horses*
They been assayed° at diverse stoundes;°   *tried out/times*
Bacins, lavours,° er that men hem bye,°   *washbowls/buy*
Spoones, stooles, and al swich housbondrye,°   *household goods*
295 And so be° pottes, clothes, and array°—   *are/clothing*
But folk of wives maken noon assay
Til they be wedded—olde dotard shrewe!
And thanne, saistou, we wil oure vices shewe.
Thou saist also that it displeseth me
300 But if ° that thou wolt praise my beautee,   *unless*
And but thou poure° alway upon my face,   *gaze*
And clepe me 'Faire Dame' in every place,
And but thou make a feeste on thilke day
That I was born, and make me fressh and gay,
305 And but thou do to my norice° honour,   *nurse*
And to my chamberere within my bowr,⁶
And to my fadres folk, and his allies⁷—
Thus saistou, olde barel-ful of lies.
And yit of our apprentice Janekin,
310 For his crispe° heer, shining as gold so fin,   *curly*
And for° he squiereth me bothe up and down,   *because*
Yit hastou caught a fals suspecioun;
I wil° him nat though thou were deed° tomorwe.   *want/dead*
"But tel me this, why hidestou with sorwe⁸
315 The keyes of thy cheste° away fro me?   *money box*
It is my good° as wel as thyn, pardee.   *property*
What, weenestou° make an idiot of oure dame?⁹   *do you think to*
Now by that lord that called is Saint Jame,
Thou shalt nought bothe, though thou were wood,°   *furious*
320 Be maister of my body and of my good:
That oon thou shalt forgo, maugree thine yën.¹
"What helpeth it of me enquere° and spyen?   *inquire*

I trowe thou woldest loke° me in thy cheste.   *lock*
Thou sholdest saye, 'Wif, go wher thee leste.°   *it may please*
325 Taak youre disport.² I nil leve° no tales: *believe*
I knowe you for a trewe wif, dame Alis.'
We love no man that taketh keep or charge³
Wher that we goon: we wol been at oure large.⁴
Of alle men yblessed mote he be
330 The wise astrologen° daun Ptolomee,   *astronomer*
That saith this proverbe in his *Almageste*:
'Of alle men his wisdom is the hyeste
That rekketh° nat who hath the world in honde.'⁵   *cares*
By this proverbe thou shalt understonde,
335 Have thou⁶ ynough, what thar° thee rekke or care   *need*
How merily that othere folkes fare?
For certes, olde dotard, by youre leve,
Ye shal han queinte⁷ right ynough at eve:
He is too greet a nigard that wil werne°   *refuse*
340 A man to lighte a candle at his lanterne;
He shal han nevere the lasse° lighte, pardee.   *less*
Have thou ynough, thee thar nat plaine thee.⁸
    "Thou saist also that if we make us gay
With clothing and with precious array,
345 That it is peril of oure chastitee,
And yit, with sorwe, thou moste enforce thee,⁹
And saye thise wordes in th' Apostles¹ name:
'In habit° maad with chastitee and shame   *clothing*
Ye wommen shal apparaile you,' quod he,
350 'And nat in tressed heer² and gay perree,°   *jewelry*
As perles, ne with gold ne clothes riche.'³
After thy text, ne after thy rubriche,⁴
I wol nat werke as muchel as a gnat.
Thou saidest this, that I was lik a cat:
355 For whoso wolde senge° a cattes skin,   *singe*
Thanne wolde the cat wel dwellen in his in;°   *lodging*
And if the cattes skin be slik° and gay,   *sleek*
She wol nat dwelle in house half a day,
But forth she wol, er any day be dawed,⁵
360 To shewe her skin and goon a-caterwawed.°   *caterwauling*
This is to saye, if I be gay, sire shrewe,
I wol renne° out, my borel° for to shewe.   *run / clothing*
Sir olde fool, what helpeth⁶ thee t'espyen?
Though thou praye Argus with his hundred yën⁷
365 To be my wardecors,° as he can best,   *bodyguard*
In faith, he shal nat keepe° me but me lest:⁸   *guard*

2. Enjoy yourself.
3. Notice or interest.
4. I.e., liberty.
5. Who rules the world.
6. If you have.
7. Elegant, pleasing thing; a euphemism for sexual enjoyment.
8. I.e., you need not complain.
9. Strengthen your position.
1. I.e., St. Paul's.

2. I.e., elaborate hairdo.
3. See 1 Timothy 2.9.
4. Rubric, i.e., direction.
5. Has dawned.
6. What does it help.
7. Argus was a monster whom Juno set to watch over one of Jupiter's mistresses. Mercury put all one hundred of his eyes to sleep and slew him.
8. Unless I please.

Yit coude I make his beerd,⁹ so mote I thee.°   *prosper*
  "Thou saidest eek that ther been thinges three,
The whiche thinges troublen al this erthe,
370 And that no wight may endure the ferthe.°   *fourth*
O leve° sire shrewe, Jesu shorte° thy lif!   *dear / shorten*
Yit prechestou and saist an hateful wif
Yrekened° is for oon of thise meschaunces.¹   *is counted*
Been ther nat none othere resemblaunces
375 That ye may likne youre parables to,²
But if° a sely° wif be oon of tho?   *unless / innocent*
  "Thou liknest eek wommanes love to helle,
To bareine° land ther water may nat dwelle;   *barren*
Thou liknest it also to wilde fir—
380 The more it brenneth,° the more it hath desir   *burns*
To consumen every thing that brent° wol be;   *burned*
Thou saist right° as wormes shende° a tree,   *just / destroy*
Right so a wif destroyeth hir housbonde—
This knowen they that been to wives bonde."°   *bound*
385   Lordinges, right thus, as ye han understonde,
Bar I stifly mine olde housbondes on honde³
That thus they saiden in hir dronkenesse—
And al was fals, but that I took witnesse
On Janekin and on my nece also.
390 O Lord, the paine I dide hem and the wo,
Ful giltelees, by Goddes sweete pine!°   *suffering*
For as an hors I coude bite and whine;°   *whinny*
I coude plaine° and° I was in the gilt,   *complain / if*
Or elles often time I hadde been spilt.°   *ruined*
395 Whoso that first to mille comth first grint.°   *grinds*
I plained first: so was oure werre stint.⁴
They were ful glade to excusen hem ful blive°   *quickly*
Of thing of which they nevere agilte hir live.⁵
Of wenches wolde I beren hem on honde,⁶
400 Whan that for sik⁷ they mighte unnethe° stonde,   *scarcely*
Yit tikled I his herte for that he
Wende° I hadde had of him so greet cheertee.°   *thought / affection*
I swoor that al my walking out by nighte
Was for to espye wenches that he dighte.⁸
405 Under that colour⁹ hadde I many a mirthe.
For al swich wit is yiven us in oure birthe:
Deceite, weeping, spinning God hath yive
To wommen kindely° whil they may live.   *naturally*
And thus of oo thing I avaunte me:¹
410 At ende I hadde the bet° in eech degree,   *better*
By sleighte or force, or by som manere thing,
As by continuel murmur° or grucching;°   *complaint / grumbling*

---

9. I.e., deceive him.
1. For the other three misfortunes see Proverbs 30.21–23.
2. Are there no other (appropriate) similitudes to which you might draw analogies?
3. I rigorously accused my old husbands.
4. Our war brought to an end.

5. Of which they were never guilty in their lives.
6. Falsely accuse them.
7. I.e., sickness.
8. Had intercourse with.
9. I.e., pretense.
1. Boast.

Namely° abedde hadden they meschaunce: *especially*
Ther wolde I chide and do hem no plesaunce;[2]
415   I wolde no lenger in the bed abide
If that I felte his arm over my side,
Til he hadde maad his raunson° unto me;   *ransom*
Thanne wolde I suffre him do his nicetee.°   *foolishness (sex)*
And therfore every man this tale I telle:
420   Winne whoso may, for al is for to selle;
With empty hand men may no hawkes lure.
For winning° wolde I al his lust endure,   *profit*
And make me a feined° appetit—   *pretended*
And yit in bacon[3] hadde I nevere delit.
425   That made me that evere I wolde hem chide;
For though the Pope hadde seten° hem biside,   *sat*
I wolde nought spare hem at hir owene boord.°   *table*
For by my trouthe, I quitte° hem word for word.   *repaid*
As help me verray God omnipotent,
430   Though I right now sholde make my testament,
I ne owe hem nat a word that it nis quit.
I broughte it so aboute by my wit
That they moste yive it up as for the beste,
Or elles hadde we nevere been in reste;
435   For though he looked as a wood° leoun,   *furious*
Yit sholde he faile of his conclusioun.°   *object*
    Thanne wolde I saye, "Goodelief, taak keep,[4]
How mekely looketh Wilekin,[5] oure sheep!
Com neer my spouse, lat me ba° thy cheeke—   *kiss*
440   Ye sholden be al pacient and meeke,
And han a sweete-spiced° conscience,   *mild*
Sith ye so preche of Jobes pacience;
Suffreth alway, sin ye so wel can preche;
And but ye do, certain, we shal you teche
445   That it is fair to han a wif in pees.
Oon of us two moste bowen, doutelees,
And sith a man is more resonable
Than womman is, ye mosten been suffrable.°   *patient*
What aileth you to grucche° thus and grone?   *grumble*
450   Is it for ye wolde have my queinte° allone?   *sexual organ*
Why, taak it al—lo, have it everydeel.°   *all of it*
Peter,[6] I shrewe° you but ye° love it weel.   *curse / if you don't*
For if I wolde selle my bele chose,[7]
I coude walke as fressh as is a rose;
455   But I wol keepe it for youre owene tooth.°   *taste*
Ye be to blame. By God, I saye you sooth!"°   *the truth*
Swiche manere° wordes hadde we on honde.   *kind of*
Now wol I speke of my ferthe° housbonde.   *fourth*
    My ferthe housbonde was a revelour°   *reveler*
460   This is to sayn, he hadde a paramour°   *mistress*

---

2. Give them no pleasure.
3. I.e., old meat.
4. Good friend, take notice.
5. I.e., Willie.

6. By St. Peter.
7. French for "beautiful thing"; a euphemism for sexual organs.

And I was yong and ful of ragerye,°   *passion*
Stibourne° and strong and joly as a pie:°   *untamable/magpie*
How coude I daunce to an harpe smale,°   *gracefully*
And singe, ywis,° as any nightingale,   *indeed*
465 Whan I hadde dronke a draughte of sweete win.
Metellius, the foule cherl, the swin,
That with a staf birafte° his wif hir lif   *deprived*
For° she drank win, though I hadde been his wif,   *because*
Ne sholde nat han daunted° me fro drinke;   *frightened*
470 And after win on Venus moste° I thinke,   *must*
For also siker° as cold engendreth hail,   *sure*
A likerous° mouth moste han a likerous° tail: *greedy/lecherous*
In womman vinolent° is no defence—   *who drinks*
This knowen lechours by experience.
475   But Lord Crist, whan that it remembreth me[8]
Upon my youthe and on my jolitee,
It tikleth me aboute myn herte roote—
Unto this day it dooth myn herte boote°   *good*
That I have had my world as in my time.
480 But age, allas, that al wol envenime,°   *poison*
Hath me biraft[9] my beautee and my pith°—   *vigor*
Lat go, farewel, the devel go therwith!
The flour is goon, ther is namore to telle:
The bren° as I best can now moste I selle;   *bran*
485 But yit to be right merye wol I fonde.°   *strive*
Now wol I tellen of my ferthe housbonde.
     I saye I hadde in herte greet despit
That he of any other hadde delit,
But he was quit,° by God and by Saint Joce: *paid back*
490 I made him of the same wode a croce[1]—
Nat of my body in no foul manere—
But, certainly, I made folk swich cheere[2]
That in his owene grece I made him frye,
For angre and for verray jalousye.
495 By God, in erthe I was his purgatorye,
For which I hope his soule be in glorye.
For God it woot, he sat ful ofte and soong°   *sang*
Whan that his sho ful bitterly him wroong.°   *pinched*
Ther was no wight save God and he that wiste° *knew*
500 In many wise how sore I him twiste.
He deide whan I cam fro Jerusalem,
And lith ygrave under the roode-beem,[3]
Al° is his tombe nought so curious[4]   *although*
As was the sepulcre of him Darius,
505 Which that Apelles wroughte subtilly:[5]
It nis but wast to burye him preciously.°   *expensively*
Lat him fare wel, God yive his soule reste;

---

8. When I look back.
9. Has taken away from me.
1. I made him a cross of the same wood. The proverb has much the same sense as the one quoted in line 493.
2. Pretended to be in love with others.

3. And lies buried under the rood beam (the crucifix beam running between nave and chancel).
4. Carefully wrought.
5. Accordingly to medieval legend, the artist Apelles decorated the tomb of Darius, king of the Persians.

He is now in his grave and in his cheste.°   *coffin*
     Now of my fifthe housbonde wol I telle—
510   God lete his soule nevere come in helle—
And yit he was to me the moste shrewe:[6]
That feele I on my ribbes al by rewe,[7]
And evere shal unto myn ending day.
But in oure bed he was so fressh and gay,
515   And therwithal so wel coulde he me glose°   *flatter, coax*
Whan that he wolde han my bele chose,
That though he hadde me bet° on every boon,°   *beaten / bone*
He coude winne again my love anoon.°   *immediately*
I trowe I loved him best for that he
520   Was of his love daungerous[8] to me.
We wommen han, if that I shal nat lie,
In this matere a quainte fantasye:[9]
Waite what[1] thing we may nat lightly° have,   *easily*
Therafter wol we crye al day and crave;
525   Forbede us thing, and that desiren we;
Preesse on us faste, and thanne wol we flee.
With daunger oute we al oure chaffare:[2]
Greet prees° at market maketh dere° ware,   *crowd / expensive*
And too greet chepe is holden at litel pris.[3]
530   This knoweth every womman that is wis.
     My fifthe housbonde—God his soule blesse!—
Which that I took for love and no richesse,
He somtime was a clerk at Oxenforde,
And hadde laft° scole and wente at hoom to boorde   *left*
535   With my gossib,° dwelling in oure town   *confidante*
God have hir soule!—hir name was Alisoun;
She knew myn herte and eek my privetee°   *secrets*
Bet° than oure parissh preest, as mote I thee.°   *better / prosper*
To hire biwrayed° I my conseil° al,   *disclosed / secrets*
540   For hadde myn housbonde pissed on a wal,
Or doon a thing that sholde han cost his lif,
To hire,° and to another worthy wif,   *her*
And to my nece which I loved weel,
I wolde han told his conseil everydeel;°   *entirely*
545   And so I dide ful often, God it woot,
That made his face often reed° and hoot°   *red / hot*
For verray shame, and blamed himself for he
Hadde told to me so greet a privetee.
     And so bifel that ones° in a Lente—   *once*
550   So often times I to my gossib wente,
For evere yit I loved to be gay,
And for to walke in March, Averil, and May,
From hous to hous, to heere sondry tales—
That Janekin clerk and my gossib dame Alis
555   And I myself into the feeldes wente.
     Myn housbonde was at London al that Lente:

---

6. Worst rascal.
7. In a row.
8. I.e., he played hard to get.
9. Strange fancy.

1. Whatever.
2. (Meeting) with reserve, we spread out our merchandise.
3. Too good a bargain is held at little value.

I hadde the better leiser for to playe,
And for to see, and eek for to be seye°   seen
Of lusty folk—what wiste I wher my grace°   luck
560 Was shapen° for to be, or in what place?   destined
Therfore I made my visitaciouns
To vigilies[4] and to processiouns,
To preching eek, and to thise pilgrimages,
To playes of miracles and to mariages,
565 And wered upon[5] my gaye scarlet gites°—   gowns
Thise wormes ne thise motthes ne thise mites,
Upon my peril,[6] frete° hem neveradeel: ate
And woostou why? For they were used weel.
     Now wol I tellen forth what happed me.
570 I saye that in the feeldes walked we,
Til trewely we hadde swich daliaunce,°   flirtation
This clerk and I, that of my purveyaunce°   foresight
I spak to him and saide him how that he,
If I were widwe, sholde wedde me.
575 For certainly, I saye for no bobaunce,°   boast
Yit was I nevere withouten purveyaunce
Of mariage n'of othere thinges eek:
I holde a mouses herte nought worth a leek
That hath but oon hole for to sterte° to,   run
580 And if that faile thanne is al ydo.[7]
I bar him on hand[8] he hadde enchaunted me
(My dame° taughte me that subtiltee);   mother
And eek I saide I mette° of him al night: dreamed
He wolde han slain me as I lay upright,°   on my back
585 And al my bed was ful of verray blood—
"But yit I hope that ye shul do me good;
For blood bitokeneth° gold, as me was taught."   signifies
And al was fals, I dremed of it right naught,
But as I folwed ay my dames° lore°   mother's / teaching
590 As wel of that as othere thinges more.
But now sire—lat me see, what shal I sayn?
Aha, by God, I have my tale again.
     Whan that my ferthe housbonde was on beere,°   funeral bier
I weep,° algate,° and made sory cheere,   wept / anyhow
595 As wives moten,° for it is usage,°   must / custom
And with my coverchief covered my visage;
But for I was purveyed° of a make.°   provided / mate
I wepte but smale, and that I undertake.°   guarantee
     To chirche was myn housbonde born amorwe;[9]
600 With neighebores that for him maden sorwe,
And Janekin oure clerk was oon of tho.
As help me God, whan that I saw him go
After the beere, me thoughte he hadde a paire
Of legges and of feet so clene[1] and faire,
605 That al myn herte I yaf unto his hold.°   possession

4. Evening service before a religious holiday.   8. I pretended to him.
5. Wore.   9. In the morning.
6. On peril (to my soul), an oath.   1. I.e., neat.
7. I.e., the game is up.

He was, I trowe,° twenty winter old,   *believe*
And I was fourty, if I shal saye sooth—
But yit I hadde alway a coltes tooth:[2]
Gat-toothed[3] was I, and that bicam me weel;
610 I hadde the prente[4] of Sainte Venus seel.°   *seal*
As help me God, I was a lusty oon,
And fair and riche and yong and wel-bigoon,°   *well-situated*
And trewely, as mine housbondes tolde me,
I hadde the beste quoniam[5] mighte be.
615 For certes I am al Venerien
In feeling, and myn herte is Marcien:[6]
Venus me yaf my lust, my likerousnesse,°   *amorousness*
And Mars yaf me my sturdy hardinesse.
Myn ascendent was Taur[7] and Mars therinne—
620 Allas, allas, that evere love was sinne!
I folwed ay° my inclinacioun   *ever*
By vertu of my constellacioun;[8]
That made me I coude nought withdrawe
My chambre of Venus from a good felawe.
625 Yit have I Martes° merk upon my face,   *Mars's*
And also in another privee place.
For God so wis° be my savacioun,°   *surely / salvation*
I loved nevere by no discrecioun,°   *moderation*
But evere folwede myn appetit,
630 Al were he short or long or blak or whit;
I took no keep,° so that he liked° me,   *heed / pleased*
How poore he was, ne eek of what degree.
       What sholde I saye but at the monthes ende
This joly clerk Janekin that was so hende°   *courteous, nice*
635 Hath wedded me with greet solempnitee,°   *splendor*
And to him yaf I al the land and fee°   *property*
That evere was me yiven therbifore—
But afterward repented me ful sore:
He nolde suffre no thing of my list.°   *wish*
640 By God, he smoot° me ones on the list°   *struck / ear*
For that I rente° out of his book a leef,   *tore*
That of the strook° myn ere weex° al deef.   *blow / grew*
Stibourne° I was as is a leonesse,   *stubborn*
And of my tonge a verray jangleresse,°   *chatterbox*
645 And walke I wolde, as I hadde doon biforn,
From hous to hous, although he hadde it[9] sworn;
For which he often times wolde preche,
And me of olde Romain geestes° teche,   *stories*
How he Simplicius Gallus lafte° his wif,   *left*
650 And hire forsook for terme of al his lif,
Nought but for open-heveded he hire sey[1]

---

2. I.e., youthful appetites.
3. Gap-toothed women were considered to be amorous.
4. Print, i.e., a birthmark.
5. Latin for "because"; another euphemism for a sexual organ.
6. Influenced by Mars. "Venerien": astrologically

influenced by Venus.
7. My birth sign was the constellation Taurus, a sign in which Venus is dominant.
8. I.e., horoscope.
9. I.e., the contrary.
1. Just because he saw her bareheaded.

Looking out at his dore upon a day.
   Another Romain tolde he me by name
That, for his wif was at a someres° game   *summer's*
655 Withouten his witing,° he forsook hire eke;   *knowledge*
And thanne wolde he upon his Bible seeke
That ilke proverbe of Ecclesiaste[2]
Where he comandeth and forbedeth faste°   *strictly*
Man shal nat suffre his wif go roule° aboute;   *roam*
660 Thanne wolde he saye right thus withouten doute:
"Whoso that buildeth his hous al of salwes,°   *willow sticks*
And priketh° his blinde hors over the falwes,[3]   *rides*
And suffreth° his wif to go seeken halwes,°   *allows/shrines*
Is worthy to be hanged on the galwes."°   *gallows*
665 But al for nought—I sette nought an hawe[4]
Of his proverbes n'of his olde sawe;
N' I wolde nat of him corrected be:
I hate him that my vices telleth me,
And so doon mo, God woot, of us than I.
670 This made him with me wood al outrely:°   *entirely*
I nolde nought forbere° him in no cas.   *submit to*
   Now wol I saye you sooth, by Saint Thomas,
Why that I rente° out of his book a leef,   *tore*
For which he smoot me so that I was deef.
675 He hadde a book that gladly night and day
For his disport° he wolde rede alway.   *entertainment*
He cleped it *Valerie*[5] *and Theofraste,*
At which book he lough° alway ful faste;   *laughed*
And eek ther was somtime a clerk at Rome,
680 A cardinal, that highte Saint Jerome,
That made a book[6] again° Jovinian;   *against*
In which book eek ther was Tertulan,
Crysippus, Trotula, and Helouis,[7]
That was abbesse nat fer fro Paris;
685 And eek the Parables of Salomon,
Ovides *Art,*[8] and bookes many oon—
And alle thise were bounden in oo volume.
And every night and day was his custume,
Whan he hadde leiser and vacacioun°   *free time*
690 From other worldly occupacioun,
To reden in this book of wikked wives.
He knew of hem mo legendes and lives
Than been of goode wives in the Bible.
For trusteth wel, it is an impossible°   *impossibility*
695 That any clerk wol speke good of wives,
But if it be of holy saintes lives,

2. Ecclesiasticus (25.25).
3. Plowed land.
4. I did not rate at the value of a hawthorn berry.
5. "Valerie": i.e., the *Letter of Valerius Concerning Not Marrying*, by Walter Map; "*Theofraste*": Theophrastus's *Book Concerning Marriage.* Medieval manuscripts often contained a number of different works, sometimes, as here, dealing with the same subject.

6. St. Jerome's antifeminist *Against Jovinian.*
7. "Tertulan": i.e., Tertullian, author of treatises on sexual modesty. "Crysippus": mentioned by Jerome as an antifeminist. "Trotula": a female doctor whose presence here is unexplained. "Helouis": i.e., Eloise, whose love affair with the great scholar Abelard was a medieval scandal.
8. Ovid's *Art of Love.* "Parables of Salomon": the biblical Book of Proverbs.

N'of noon other womman nevere the mo—
Who painted the leon, tel me who?[9]
By God, if wommen hadden writen stories,
700   As clerkes han within hir oratories,°   *chapels*
They wolde han writen of men more wikkednesse
Than al the merk[1] of Adam may redresse.
The children of Mercurye and Venus[2]
Been in hir werking° ful contrarious:°   *operation / opposed*
705   Mercurye loveth wisdom and science,
And Venus loveth riot° and dispence;°   *revelry / spending*
And for hir diverse disposicioun
Each falleth in otheres exaltacioun,[3]
And thus, God woot, Mercurye is desolat
710   In Pisces wher Venus is exaltat,[4]
And Venus falleth ther Mercurye is raised:
Therfore no womman of no clerk is praised.
The clerk, whan he is old and may nought do
Of Venus werkes worth his olde sho,°   *shoe*
715   Thanne sit° he down and writ° in his dotage   *sits / writes*
That wommen can nat keepe hir mariage.
        But now to purpose why I tolde thee
That I was beten for a book, pardee:
Upon a night Janekin, that was our sire,[5]
720   Redde on his book as he sat by the fire
Of Eva first, that for hir wikkednesse
Was al mankinde brought to wrecchednesse,
For which that Jesu Crist himself was slain
That boughte° us with his herte blood again—   *redeemed*
725   Lo, heer expres of wommen may ye finde
That womman was the los° of al mankinde.[6]   *ruin*
        Tho° redde he me how Sampson loste his heres: *then*
Sleeping his lemman° kitte° it with hir sheres,   *lover / cut*
Thurgh which treson loste he both his yën.
730   Tho redde he me, if that I shal nat lien,
Of Ercules and of his Dianire,[7]
That caused him to sette himself afire.
        No thing forgat he the sorwe and wo
That Socrates hadde with his wives two—
735   How Xantippa caste pisse upon his heed:
This sely° man sat stille as he were deed;   *poor, hapless*
He wiped his heed, namore dorste° he sayn   *dared*
But "Er that thonder stinte,° comth a rain."   *stops*
        Of Pasipha[8] that was the queene of Crete—
740   For shrewednesse° him thoughte the tale sweete—   *malice*

9. In one of Aesop's fables, the lion, shown a picture of a man killing a lion, asked who painted the
picture. Had a lion been the artist, of course, the
roles would have been reversed.
1. Mark, sex.
2. I.e., clerks and women, astrologically ruled by
Mercury and Venus, respectively.
3. Because of their contrary positions (as planets),
each one descends (in the belt of the zodiac) as the
other rises, hence one loses its power as the other

becomes dominant.
4. I.e., Mercury is deprived of power in Pisces (the
sign of the Fish), where Venus is most powerful.
5. My husband.
6. The stories of wicked women Chaucer drew
mainly from St. Jerome and Walter Map.
7. Dejanira unwittingly gave Hercules a poisoned
shirt, which hurt him so much that he committed
suicide by fire.
8. Pasiphaë, who had intercourse with a bull.

Fy, speek namore, it is a grisly thing
Of hir horrible lust and hir liking.°   *pleasure*
    Of Clytermistra⁹ for hir lecherye
That falsly made hir housbonde for to die,
745   He redde it with ful good devocioun.
    He tolde me eek for what occasioun
Amphiorax¹ at Thebes loste his lif:
Myn housbonde hadde a legende of his wif
Eriphylem, that for an ouche° of gold   *trinket*
750   Hath prively unto the Greekes told
Wher that hir housbonde hidde him in a place,
For which he hadde at Thebes sory grace.
    Of Livia tolde he me and of Lucie:²
They bothe made hir housbondes for to die,
755   That oon for love, that other was for hate;
Livia hir housbonde on an even late
Empoisoned hath for that she was his fo;
Lucia likerous° loved hir housbonde so   *lecherous*
That for° he sholde alway upon hire thinke,   *in order that*
760   She yaf him swich a manere love-drinke
That he was deed er it were by the morwe.³
And thus algates° housbondes han sorwe.   *in every way*
    Thanne tolde he me how oon Latumius
Complained unto his felawe Arrius
765   That in his garden growed swich a tree,
On which he saide how that his wives three
Hanged hemself for herte despitous.⁴
    "O leve° brother," quod this Arrius,   *dear*
"Yif me a plante of thilke blessed tree,
770   And in my gardin planted shal it be."
    Of latter date of wives hath he red
That some han slain hir housbondes in hir bed
And lete hir lechour dighte⁵ hire al the night,
Whan that the cors° lay in the floor upright;°   *corpse / on his back*
775   And some han driven nailes in hir brain
Whil that they sleepe, and thus they han hem slain;
Some han hem yiven poison in hir drinke.
He spak more harm than herte may bithinke,°   *imagine*
And therwithal he knew of mo proverbes
780   Than in this world ther growen gras or herbes:
"Bet° is," quod he, "thyn habitacioun   *better*
Be with a leon or a foul dragoun
Than with a womman using° for to chide."   *accustomed*
"Bet is," quod he, "hye in the roof abide
785   Than with an angry wif down in the hous:
They been so wikked° and contrarious,   *perverse*
They haten that hir housbondes loveth ay."

9. Clytemnestra, who, with her lover, Aegisthus, slew her husband, Agamemnon.
1. Amphiaraus, betrayed by his wife, Eriphyle, and forced to go to the war against Thebes.
2. Livia murdered her husband in behalf of her lover, Sejanus. "Lucie": i.e., Lucilla, who was said to have poisoned her husband, the poet Lucretius, with a potion designed to keep him faithful.
3. He was dead before it was near morning.
4. For malice of heart.
5. Have intercourse with.

He saide, "A womman cast° hir shame away   *casts*
When she cast of° hir smok,"⁶ and ferthermo,   *off*
790 "A fair womman, but she be chast also,
Is like a gold ring in a sowes nose."
Who wolde weene,° or who wolde suppose   *think*
The wo that in myn herte was and pine?°   *suffering*
 And whan I sawgh he wolde nevere fine°   *end*
795 To reden on this cursed book al night,
Al sodeinly three leves have I plight°   *snatched*
Out of his book right as he redde, and eke
I with my fist so took⁷ him on the cheeke
That in oure fir he fil° bakward adown.   *fell*
800 And up he sterte as dooth a wood° leoun,   *raging*
And with his fist he smoot me on the heed°   *head*
That in the floor I lay as I were deed.°   *dead*
And whan he sawgh how stille that I lay,
He was agast, and wolde have fled his way,
805 Til atte laste out of my swough° I braide:° *swoon / started*
"O hastou slain me, false thief?" I saide,
"And for my land thus hastou mordred° me?   *murdered*
Er I be deed yit wol I kisse thee."
And neer he cam and kneeled faire adown,
810 And saide, "Dere suster Alisoun,
As help me God, I shal thee nevere smite.
That I have doon, it is thyself to wite.°   *blame*
Foryif it me, and that I thee biseeke."°   *beseech*
And yit eftsoones° I hitte him on the cheeke, *another time*
815 And saide, "Thief, thus muchel am I wreke.°   *avenged*
Now wol I die: I may no lenger speke."
 But at the laste with muchel care and wo
We fille⁸ accorded by us selven two.
He yaf me al the bridel° in myn hand,   *bridle*
820 To han the governance of hous and land,
And of his tonge and his hand also;
And made⁹ him brenne° his book anoonright tho. *burn*
And whan that I hadde geten unto me
By maistrye° al the sovereinetee,°   *skill / dominion*
825 And that he saide, "Myn owene trewe wif,
Do as thee lust° the terme of al thy lif;   *it pleases*
Keep thyn honour, and keep eek myn estat,"
After that day we hadde nevere debat.
God help me so, I was to him as kinde
830 As any wif from Denmark unto Inde,°   *India*
And also trewe, and so was he to me.
I praye to God that sit° in majestee,   *sits*
So blesse his soule for his mercy dere.
Now wol I saye my tale if ye wol heere.

---

6. Undergarment.   8. I.e., became.
7. I.e., hit.   9. I.e., I made.

[ANOTHER INTERRUPTION]

835   The Frere lough° whan he hadde herd all this: *laughed*
        "Now dame," quod he, "so have I joye or blis,
        This is a long preamble of a tale."
        And whan the Somnour herde the Frere gale,°   *exclaim*
        "Lo," quod the Somnour, "Goddes armes two,
840   A frere wol entremette him¹ everemo!
        Lo, goode men, a flye and eek a frere
        Wol falle in every dissh and eek matere.
        What spekestou of preambulacioun?
        What, amble or trotte or pisse or go sitte down!
845   Thou lettest° oure disport in this manere."   *hinder*
            "Ye, woltou so, sire Somnour?" quod the Frere.
        "Now by my faith, I shal er that I go
        Telle of a somnour swich a tale or two
        That al the folk shal laughen in this place."
850   "Now elles, Frere, I wol bishrewe° thy face,"   *curse*
        Quod this Somnour, "and I bishrewe me,
        But if I telle tales two or three
        Of freres, er I come to Sidingborne,²
        That I shal make thyn herte for to moorne°—   *mourn*
855   For wel I woot thy pacience is goon."
            Oure Hoste cride, "Pees, and that anoon!"
        And saide, "Lat the womman telle hir tale:
        Ye fare as folk that dronken been of ale.
        Do, dame, tel forth youre tale, and that is best."
860   "Al redy, sire," quod she, "right as you lest°—   *it pleases*
        If I have licence of this worthy Frere."
        "Yis, dame," quod he, "tel forth and I wol heere."

The Tale

As was suggested in the headnote to *The Man of Law's Epilogue*, Chaucer may have
originally written the fabliau that became *The Shipman's Tale* for the Wife of Bath.
If so, then he replaced it with a tale that is not simply appropriate to her character
but that develops it even beyond the complexity already revealed in her *Prologue*. The
story survives in two other versions in which the hero is Sir Gawain, whose courtesy
contrasts sharply with the behavior of the knight in the Wife's tale. As Chaucer has
the Wife tell it, the tale expresses her views about the relations of the sexes, her wit
and humor, and her fantasies. Like Marie de France's lay *Lanval* (see pp. 105–18),
the Wife's tale is about a fairy bride who seeks out and tests a mortal lover.

        In th'olde dayes of the King Arthour,
        Of which that Britouns speken greet honour,
865   Al was this land fulfild of faïrye:³
        The elf-queene° with hir joly compaignye   *queen of the fairies*
        Daunced ful ofte in many a greene mede°—   *meadow*
        This was the olde opinion as I rede;

---

1. Intrude himself.   don).
2. Sittingbourne (a town forty miles from Lon-   3. I.e., filled full of supernatural creatures.

I speke of many hundred yeres ago.
870 But now can no man see none elves mo,
For now the grete charitee and prayeres
Of limitours,[4] and othere holy freres,
That serchen every land and every streem,
As thikke as motes° in the sonne-beem,   *dust particles*
875 Blessing halles, chambres, kichenes, bowres,
Citees, burghes,° castels, hye towres,   *townships*
Thropes, bernes, shipnes,[5] dayeries—
This maketh that ther been no faïries.
For ther as wont to walken was an elf
880 Ther walketh now the limitour himself,
In undermeles° and in morweninges,°   *afternoons / mornings*
And saith his Matins and his holy thinges,
As he gooth in his limitacioun.[6]
Wommen may go saufly° up and down: *safely*
885 In every bussh or under every tree
Ther is noon other incubus[7] but he,
And he ne wol doon hem but[8] dishonour.
    And so bifel it that this King Arthour
Hadde in his hous a lusty bacheler,°   *young knight*
890 That on a day cam riding fro river,[9]
And happed° that, allone as he was born,   *it happened*
He sawgh a maide walking him biforn;
Of which maide anoon, maugree hir heed,[1]
By verray force he rafte° hir maidenheed;   *deprived her of*
895 For which oppression° was swich clamour,   *rape*
And swich pursuite° unto the King Arthour,   *petitioning*
That dampned was this knight for to be deed[2]
By cours of lawe, and sholde han lost his heed—
Paraventure° swich was the statut tho—   *perchance*
900 But that the queene and othere ladies mo
So longe prayeden the king of grace,
Til he his lif him graunted in the place,
And yaf him to the queene, al at hir wille,
To chese° wheither she wolde him save or spille.[3]   *choose*
905 The queene thanked the king with al hir might,
And after this thus spak she to the knight,
Whan that she saw hir time upon a day:
"Thou standest yit," quod she, "in swich array°   *condition*
That of thy lif yit hastou no suretee.°   *guarantee*
910 I graunte thee lif if thou canst tellen me
What thing it is that wommen most desiren:
Be war and keep thy nekke boon° from iren.   *bone*
And if thou canst nat tellen me anoon,°   *right away*
Yit wol I yive thee leve for to goon
915 A twelfmonth and a day to seeche° and lere°   *search / learn*

4. Friars licensed to beg in a certain territory.
5. Thorps (villages), barns, stables.
6. I.e., the friar's assigned area. His "holy thinges" are prayers.
7. An evil spirit that seduces mortal women.
8. "Ne . . . but": only.
9. Hawking, usually carried out on the banks of a stream.
1. Despite her head, i.e., despite anything she could do.
2. This knight was condemned to death.
3. Put to death.

An answere suffisant° in this matere,   *satisfactory*
And suretee wol I han er that thou pace,°   *pass*
Thy body for to yeelden in this place."
    Wo was this knight, and sorwefully he siketh.°   *sighs*
920 But what, he may nat doon al as him liketh,
And atte laste he chees° him for to wende,   *chose*
And come again right at the yeres ende,
With swich answere as God wolde him purveye,°   *provide*
And taketh his leve and wendeth forth his waye.
925 He seeketh every hous and every place
Wher as he hopeth for to finde grace,
To lerne what thing wommen love most.
But he ne coude arriven in no coost⁴
Wher as he mighte finde in this matere
930 Two creatures according in fere.⁵
    Some saiden wommen loven best richesse;
Some saide honour, some saide jolinesse;°   *pleasure*
Some riche array, some saiden lust abedde,
And ofte time to be widwe and wedde.
935 Some saide that oure herte is most esed
Whan that we been yflatered and yplesed—
He gooth ful neigh the soothe, I wol nat lie:
A man shal winne us best with flaterye,
And with attendance° and with bisinesse°   *attention / solicitude*
940 Been we ylimed,° bothe more and lesse.   *ensnared*
    And some sayen that we loven best
For to be free, and do right as us lest,°   *it pleases*
And that no man repreve° us of oure vice,   *reprove*
But saye that we be wise and no thing nice.°   *foolish*
945 For trewely, ther is noon of us alle,
If any wight wol clawe° us on the galle,°   *rub / sore spot*
That we nil kike° for° he saith us sooth: *kick / because*
Assaye° and he shal finde it that so dooth.   *try*
For be we nevere so vicious withinne,
950 We wol be holden° wise and clene of sinne.   *considered*
    And some sayn that greet delit han we
For to be holden stable and eek secree,⁶
And in oo° purpos stedefastly to dwelle,   *one*
And nat biwraye° thing that men us telle—   *disclose*
955 But that tale is nat worth a rake-stele.°   *rake handle*
Pardee,° we wommen conne no thing hele:°   *by God / conceal*
Witnesse on Mida.° Wol ye heere the tale?   *Midas*
    Ovide, amonges othere thinges smale,
Saide Mida hadde under his longe heres,
960 Growing upon his heed, two asses eres,
The whiche vice° he hidde as he best mighte   *defect*
Ful subtilly from every mannes sighte,
That save his wif ther wiste° of it namo.   *knew*
He loved hire most and trusted hire also.

---

4. I.e., country.   6. Reliable and also closemouthed.
5. Agreeing together.

965 He prayed hire that to no creature
 She sholde tellen of his disfigure.°   *deformity*
   She swoor him nay, for al this world to winne,
 She nolde do that vilainye or sinne
 To make hir housbonde han so foul a name:
970 She nolde nat telle it for hir owene shame.
 But nathelees, hir thoughte that she dyde°   *would die*
 That she so longe sholde a conseil° hide;   *secret*
 Hire thoughte it swal° so sore about hir herte   *swelled*
 That nedely som word hire moste asterte,[7]
975 And sith she dorste nat telle it to no man,
 Down to a mareis° faste° by she ran—   *marsh/close*
 Til she cam there hir herte was afire—
 And as a bitore bombleth[8] in the mire,
 She laide hir mouth unto the water down:
980 "Biwray° me nat, thou water, with thy soun,"°   *betray/sound*
 Quod she. "To thee I telle it and namo:°   *to no one else*
 Myn housbonde hath longe asses eres two.
 Now is myn herte al hool,[9] now is it oute.
 I mighte no lenger keep it, out of doute."
985 Here may ye see, though we a time abide,
 Yit oute it moot:° we can no conseil hide.   *must*
 The remenant of the tale if ye wol heere,
 Redeth Ovide, and ther ye may it lere.[1]
   This knight of which my tale is specially,
990 Whan that he sawgh he mighte nat come thereby—
 This is to saye what wommen loven most—
 Within his brest ful sorweful was his gost,°   *spirit*
 But hoom he gooth, he mighte nat sojourne:°   *delay*
 The day was come that hoomward moste° he turne. *must*
995 And in his way it happed him to ride
 In al this care under° a forest side,   *by*
 Wher as he sawgh upon a daunce go
 Of ladies foure and twenty and yit mo;
 Toward the whiche daunce he drow ful yerne,[2]
1000 In hope that som wisdom sholde he lerne.
 But certainly, er he cam fully there,
 Vanisshed was this daunce, he niste° where.   *knew not*
 No creature sawgh he that bar° lif,   *bore*
 Save on the greene he sawgh sitting a wif°—   *woman*
1005 A fouler wight ther may no man devise.°   *imagine*
 Again[3] the knight this olde wif gan rise,
 And saide, "Sire knight, heer forth lith° no way.° *lies/road*
 Telle me what ye seeken, by youre fay.°   *faith*
 Paraventure it may the better be:
1010 Thise olde folk conne° muchel thing," quod she. *know*
   "My leve moder,"° quod this knight, "certain,   *mother*
 I nam but deed but if that I can sayn

---

7. Of necessity some word must escape her.
8. Makes a booming noise. "Bittore": bittern, a heron.
9. I.e., sound.

1. Learn. The reeds disclosed the secret by whispering *"aures aselli"* (ass's ears).
2. Drew very quickly.
3. I.e., to meet.

What thing it is that wommen most desire.
Coude ye me wisse,° I wolde wel quite youre hire."⁴   *teach*
1015   "Plight° me thy trouthe here in myn hand," quod she,   *pledge*
"The nexte thing that I requere° thee,   *require of*
Thou shalt it do, if it lie in thy might,
And I wol telle it you er it be night."
     "Have heer my trouthe," quod the knight. "I graunte."
1020   "Thanne," quod she, "I dar me wel avaunte°   *boast*
Thy lif is sauf,° for I wol stande therby.   *safe*
Upon my lif the queene wol saye as I.
Lat see which is the pruddeste° of hem alle   *proudest*
That wereth on⁵ a coverchief or a calle°   *headdress*
1025   That dar saye nay of that I shal thee teche.
Lat us go forth withouten lenger speeche."
Tho rouned° she a pistel° in his ere,   *whispered / message*
And bad him to be glad and have no fere.
     Whan they be comen to the court, this knight
1030   Saide he hadde holde his day as he hadde hight,°   *promised*
And redy was his answere, as he saide.
Ful many a noble wif, and many a maide,
And many a widwe—for that they been wise—
The queene hirself sitting as justise,
1035   Assembled been this answere for to heere,
And afterward this knight was bode° appere.   *bidden to*
To every wight comanded was silence,
And that the knight sholde telle in audience°   *open hearing*
What thing that worldly wommen loven best.
1040   This knight ne stood nat stille as dooth a best,°   *beast*
But to his question anoon answerde
With manly vois that al the court it herde.
     "My lige° lady, generally," quod he,   *liege*
"Wommen desire to have sovereinetee°   *dominion*
1045   As wel over hir housbonde as hir love,
And for to been in maistrye him above.
This is youre moste desir though ye me kille.
Dooth as you list:° I am here at youre wille."   *please*
     In al the court ne was ther wif ne maide
1050   Ne widwe that contraried° that he saide,   *contradicted*
But saiden he was worthy han° his lif.   *to have*
     And with that word up sterte° that olde wif,   *started*
Which that the knight sawgh sitting on the greene;
"Mercy," quod she, "my soverein lady queene,
1055   Er that youre court departe, do me right.
I taughte this answere unto the knight,
For which he plighte me his trouthe there
The firste thing I wolde him requere°   *require*
He wolde it do, if it laye in his might.
1060   Bifore the court thanne praye I thee, sire knight,"
Quod she, "that thou me take unto thy wif,
For wel thou woost that I have kept° thy lif.   *saved*

---

4. Repay your trouble.   5. That wears.

If I saye fals, say nay, upon thy fay."
   This knight answerde, "Allas and wailaway,
1065 I woot right wel that swich was my biheeste.°   *promise*
For Goddes love, as chees° a newe requeste: *choose*
Taak al my good and lat my body go."
   "Nay thanne," quod she, "I shrewe° us bothe two.   *curse*
For though that I be foul and old and poore,
1070 I nolde for al the metal ne for ore
That under erthe is grave° or lith° above,   *buried/lies*
But if thy wif I were and eek thy love."
   "My love," quod he. "Nay, my dampnacioun!°   *damnation*
Allas, that any of my nacioun[6]
1075 Sholde evere so foule disparaged° be."   *degraded*
But al for nought, th'ende is this, that he
Constrained was: he needes moste hire wedde,
And taketh his olde wif and gooth to bedde.
   Now wolden some men saye, paraventure,
1080 That for my necligence I do no cure[7]
To tellen you the joye and al th'array
That at the feeste was that ilke day.
To which thing shortly answere I shal:
I saye ther nas no joye ne feeste at al;
1085 Ther nas but hevinesse and muche sorwe.
For prively he wedded hire on morwe,[8]
And al day after hidde him as an owle,
So wo was him, his wif looked so foule.
   Greet was the wo the knight hadde in his thought:
1090 Whan he was with his wif abedde brought,
He walweth° and he turneth to and fro.   *tosses*
His olde wif lay smiling everemo,
And saide, "O dere housbonde, benedicite,°   *bless me*
Fareth° every knight thus with his wif as ye?   *behaves*
1095 Is this the lawe of King Arthures hous?
Is every knight of his thus daungerous?°   *standoffish*
I am youre owene love and youre wif;
I am she which that saved hath youre lif;
And certes yit ne dide I you nevere unright.
1100 Why fare ye thus with me this firste night?
Ye faren like a man hadde lost his wit.
What is my gilt? For Goddes love, telle it,
And it shal been amended if I may."
   "Amended!" quod this knight. "Allas, nay, nay,
1105 It wol nat been amended neveremo.
Thou art so lothly° and so old also,   *hideous*
And therto comen of so lowe a kinde,°   *lineage*
That litel wonder is though I walwe and winde.°   *turn*
So wolde God myn herte wolde breste!"°   *break*
1110   "Is this," quod she, "the cause of youre unreste?"
   "Ye, certainly," quod he. "No wonder is."

---

6. I.e., family.
7. I do not take the trouble.

8. In the morning.

"Now sire," quod she, "I coude amende al this,
If that me liste, er it were dayes three,
So° wel ye mighte bere you⁹ unto me.   *provided that*
1115 "But for ye speken of swich gentilesse°   *nobility*
As is descended out of old richesse—
That therfore sholden ye be gentilmen—
Swich arrogance is nat worth an hen.
Looke who that is most vertuous alway,
1120 Privee and apert,¹ and most entendeth° ay° *tries/always*
To do the gentil deedes that he can,
Taak him for the gretteste° gentilman.   *greatest*
Crist wol° we claime of him oure gentilesse, *desires that*
Nat of oure eldres for hir 'old richesse.'
1125 For though they yive us al hir heritage,
For which we claime to been of heigh parage,° *descent*
Yit may they nat biquethe for no thing
To noon of us hir vertuous living,
That made hem gentilmen ycalled be,
1130 And bad² us folwen hem in swich degree.
 "Wel can the wise poete of Florence,
That highte Dant,³ speken in this sentence;° *topic*
Lo, in swich manere rym is Dantes tale:
'Ful selde° up riseth by his braunches⁴ smale *seldom*
1135 Prowesse° of man, for God of his prowesse *excellence*
Wol that of him we claime oure gentilesse.'
For of oure eldres may we no thing claime
But temporel thing that man may hurte and maime.
Eek every wight woot this as wel as I,
1140 If gentilesse were planted natureelly
Unto a certain linage down the line,
Privee and apert, thanne wolde they nevere fine° *cease*
To doon of gentilesse the faire office°— *function*
They mighte do no vilainye or vice.
1145 "Taak fir and beer° it in the derkeste hous *bear*
Bitwixe this and the Mount of Caucasus,
And lat men shette° the dores and go thenne,° *shut/thence*
Yit wol the fir as faire lye° and brenne° *blaze/burn*
As twenty thousand men mighte it biholde:
1150 His° office natureel ay wol it holde,   *its*
Up° peril of my lif, til that it die.   *upon*
Heer may ye see wel how that genterye° *gentility*
Is nat annexed° to possessioun,⁵   *related*
Sith folk ne doon hir operacioun
1155 Alway, as dooth the fir, lo, in his kinde.° *nature*
For God it woot, men may wel often finde
A lordes sone do shame and vilainye;
And he that wol han pris of his gentrye,⁶
For he was boren° of a gentil° hous, *born/noble*

---

9. Behave.
1. Privately and publicly.
2. I.e., they bade.
3. Dante (see his *Convivio*).

4. I.e., by the branches of a man's family tree.
5. I.e., inheritable property.
6. Have credit for his noble birth.

1160 And hadde his eldres noble and vertuous,
And nil himselven do no gentil deedes,
Ne folwen his gentil auncestre that deed° is,   *dead*
He nis nat gentil, be he duc or erl—
For vilaines sinful deedes maken a cherl.
1165 Thy gentilesse[7] nis but renomee°   *renown*
Of thine auncestres for hir heigh bountee,°   *magnanimity*
Which is a straunge° thing for thy persone. *external*
For gentilesse[8] cometh fro God allone.
Thanne comth oure verray gentilesse of grace:
1170 It was no thing biquethe us with oure place.
Thenketh how noble, as saith Valerius,[9]
Was thilke Tullius Hostilius
That out of poverte° roos to heigh noblesse. *poverty*
Redeth Senek° and redeth eek Boece:° *Seneca/Boethius*
1175 Ther shul ye seen expres that no drede° is *doubt*
That he is gentil that dooth gentil deedes.
And therfore, leve housbonde, I thus conclude:
Al° were it that mine auncestres weren rude,[1] *although*
Yit may the hye God—and so hope I—
1180 Graunte me grace to liven vertuously.
Thanne am I gentil whan that I biginne
To liven vertuously and waive° sinne.   *avoid*
  "And ther as ye of poverte me repreve,° *reprove*
The hye God, on whom that we bileve,
1185 In wilful° poverte chees° to live his lif; *voluntary/chose*
And certes every man, maiden, or wif
May understonde that Jesus, hevene king,
Ne wolde nat chese° a vicious living.   *choose*
Glad poverte is an honeste° thing, certain; *honorable*
1190 This wol Senek and othere clerkes sayn.
Whoso that halt him paid of[2] his poverte,
I holde him riche al hadde he nat a sherte.° *shirt*
He that coveiteth[3] is a poore wight,
For he wolde han that is nat in his might;
1195 But he that nought hath, ne coveiteth° have, *desires to*
Is riche, although we holde him but a knave.
Verray° poverte it singeth proprely.° *true/appropriately*
Juvenal saith of poverte, 'Merily
The poore man, whan he gooth by the waye,
1200 Biforn the theves he may singe and playe.'
Poverte is hateful good, and as I gesse,
A ful greet bringere out of bisinesse;[4]
A greet amendere eek of sapience°   *wisdom*
To him that taketh it in pacience;
1205 Poverte is thing, although it seeme elenge,° *wretched*
Possession that no wight wol chalenge;[5]

---

7. I.e., the gentility you claim.   2. Considers himself satisfied with.
8. I.e., true gentility.   3. I.e., suffers desires.
9. A Roman historian.   4. I.e., remover of cares.
1. I.e., low born.   5. Claim as his property.

Poverte ful often, whan a man is lowe,
Maketh[6] his God and eek himself to knowe;
Poverte a spectacle° is, as thinketh me,   *pair of spectacles*
1210 Thurgh which he may his verray° freendes see.   *true*
And therfore, sire, sin that I nought you greve,
Of my poverte namore ye me repreve.°   *reproach*
 "Now sire, of elde° ye repreve me: *old age*
And certes sire, though noon auctoritee
1215 Were in no book, ye gentils of honour
Sayn that men sholde an old wight doon favour,
And clepe him fader for youre gentilesse—
And auctours[7] shal I finde, as I gesse.
 "Now ther ye saye that I am foul and old:
1220 Thanne drede you nought to been a cokewold,°   *cuckold*
For filthe and elde, also mote I thee,[8]
Been grete wardeins° upon chastitee.   *guardians*
But nathelees, sin I knowe your delit,
I shal fulfille youre worldly appetit.
1225 "Chees° now," quod she, "oon of thise thinges twaye: *choose*
To han me foul and old til that I deye
And be to you a trewe humble wif,
And nevere you displese in al my lif,
Or elles ye wol han me yong and fair,
1230 And take youre aventure° of the repair[9]   *chance*
That shal be to youre hous by cause of me—
Or in some other place, wel may be.
Now chees youreselven wheither° that you liketh."   *whichever*
 This knight aviseth him[1] and sore siketh;°   *sighs*
1235 But atte laste he saide in this manere:
"My lady and my love, and wif so dere,
I putte me in youre wise governaunce:
Cheseth° yourself which may be most plesaunce°   *choose/pleasure*
And most honour to you and me also.
1240 I do no fors the wheither[2] of the two,
For as you liketh it suffiseth° me."   *satisfies*
 "Thanne have I gete° of you maistrye," quod she,   *got*
"Sin I may chese and governe as me lest?"°   *it pleases*
 "Ye, certes, wif," quod he. "I holde it best."
1245 "Kisse me," quod she. "We be no lenger wrothe.
For by my trouthe, I wol be to you bothe—
This is to sayn, ye, bothe fair and good.
I praye to God that I mote sterven wood,[3]
But° I to you be al so good and trewe   *unless*
1250 As evere was wif sin that the world was newe.
And but I be tomorn° as fair to seene   *tomorrow morning*
As any lady, emperisse, or queene,
That is bitwixe the eest and eek the west,

---

6. I.e., makes him.   1. Considers.
7. I.e., authorities.   2. I do not care whichever.
8. So may I prosper.   3. Die mad.
9. I.e., visits.

Do with my lif and deeth right as you lest:
1255 Caste up the curtin,[4] looke how that it is."
And whan the knight sawgh verraily al this,
That she so fair was and so yong therto,
For joye he hente° hire in his armes two;   *took*
His herte bathed in a bath of blisse;
1260 A thousand time arewe° he gan hire kisse,   *in a row*
And she obeyed him in every thing
That mighte do him plesance or liking.°   *pleasure*
And thus they live unto hir lives ende
In parfit° joye. And Jesu Crist us sende   *perfect*
1265 Housbondes meeke, yonge, and fresshe abedde—
And grace t'overbide° hem that we wedde.   *outlive*
And eek I praye Jesu shorte° hir lives   *shorten*
That nought wol be governed by hir wives,
And olde and angry nigardes of dispence°—   *spending*
1270 God sende hem soone a verray° pestilence!   *veritable*

The Pardoner's Prologue and Tale

As with *The Wife of Bath's Prologue* and *Tale*, *The Pardoner's Prologue* and *Tale* develop in profound and surprising ways the portrait sketched in *The General Prologue*. In his *Prologue* the Pardoner boasts to his fellow pilgrims about his own depravity and the ingenuity with which he abuses his office and extracts money from poor and ignorant people.

The medieval pardoner's job was to collect money for the charitable enterprises, such as hospitals, supported by the church. In return for donations he was licensed by the pope to award token remission of sins that the donor should have repented and confessed. By canon law pardoners were permitted to work only in a prescribed area; within that area they might visit churches during Sunday service, briefly explain their mission, receive contributions, and in the pope's name issue indulgence, which was not considered to be a sale but a gift from the infinite treasury of Christ's mercy made in return for a gift of money. In practice, pardoners ignored the restrictions on their office, made their way into churches at will, preached emotional sermons, and claimed extraordinary power for their pardons.

The Pardoner's Tale is a bombastic sermon against gluttony, gambling, and swearing, which he preaches to the pilgrims to show off his professional skills. The sermon is framed by a narrative that is supposed to function as an *exemplum* (that is, an illustration) of the scriptural text, the one on which the Pardoner, as he tells the pilgrims, always preaches: "*Radix malorum est cupiditas*" (Avarice is the root of evil).

The Introduction

Oure Hoste gan to swere as he were wood°   *insane*
"Harrow,"° quod he, "by nailes and by blood,[1]   *help*
This was a fals cherl and a fals justise.[2]

---

4. The curtain around the bed.
1. I.e., God's nails and blood.
2. The Host has been affected by the Physicians's sad tale of the Roman maiden Virginia, whose great beauty caused a judge to attempt to obtain her person by means of a trumped-up lawsuit in which he connived with a "churl" who claimed her as his slave; in order to preserve her chastity, her father killed her.

As shameful deeth as herte may devise
5 Come to thise juges and hir advocats.
Algate° this sely° maide is slain, allas!   *at any rate/innocent*
Allas, too dere boughte she beautee!
Wherfore I saye alday° that men may see   *always*
The yiftes of Fortune and of Nature
10 Been cause of deeth to many a creature.
As bothe yiftes that I speke of now,
Men han ful ofte more for harm than prow.°   *benefit*
 "But trewely, myn owene maister dere,
This is a pitous tale for to heere.
15 But nathelees, passe over, is no fors:³
I praye to God to save thy gentil cors,°   *body*
And eek thine urinals and thy jurdones,⁴
Thyn ipocras and eek thy galiones,⁵
And every boiste° ful of thy letuarye°—   *box/medicine*
20 God blesse hem, and oure lady Sainte Marye.
So mote I theen,⁶ thou art a propre man,
And lik a prelat, by Saint Ronian!⁷
Saide I nat wel? I can nat speke in terme.⁸
But wel I woot, thou doost° myn herte to erme° *make/grieve*
25 That I almost have caught a cardinacle.⁹
By corpus bones,¹ but if° I have triacle,°   *unless/medicine*
Or elles a draughte of moiste° and corny° ale, *fresh/malty*
Or but I here anoon° a merye tale,   *at once*
Myn herte is lost for pitee of this maide.
30 "Thou bel ami,² thou Pardoner," he saide,
"Tel us som mirthe or japes° right anoon."   *jokes*
 "It shal be doon," quod he, "by Saint Ronion.
But first," quod he, "here at this ale-stake³
I wol bothe drinke and eten of a cake."° *flat loaf of bread*
35 And right anoon thise gentils gan to crye,
"Nay, lat him telle us of no ribaudye.°   *ribaldry*
Tel us som moral thing that we may lere,°   *learn*
Som wit,⁴ and thanne wol we gladly heere."
 "I graunte, ywis,"° quod he, "but I moot thinke *certainly*
40 Upon som honeste° thing whil that I drinke." *decent*

The Prologue

Lordinges—quod he—in chirches whan I preche,
I paine me⁵ to han° an hautein° speeche,   *have/loud*
And ringe it out as round as gooth a belle,
For I can al by rote⁶ that I telle.

---

3. I.e., never mind.
4. Jordans (chamber pots): the Host is somewhat confused in his endeavor to use technical medical terms. "Urinals": vessels for examining urine.
5. A medicine, probably invented on the spot by the Host, named after Galen. "Ipocras": a medicinal drink named after Hippocrates.
6. So might I prosper.
7. St. Ronan or St. Ninian, with a possible play on "runnion" (sexual organ).

8. Speak in technical idiom.
9. Apparently a cardiac condition, confused in the Host's mind with a cardinal.
1. An illiterate oath, mixing "God's bones" with *corpus dei* ("God's body").
2. Fair friend.
3. Sign of a tavern.
4. Take, something with significance.
5. Take pains.
6. I know all by heart.

45 My theme is alway oon,[7] and evere was:
    Radix malorum est cupiditas.[8]
    First I pronounce whennes° that I come,   *whence*
    And thanne my bulles shewe I alle and some:[9]
    Oure lige lordes seel on my patente,[1]
50 That shewe I first, my body to warente,°   *keep safe*
    That no man be so bold, ne preest ne clerk,
    Me to destourbe of Cristes holy werk.
    And after that thanne telle I forth my tales[2]—
    Bulles of popes and of cardinales,
55 Of patriarkes and bisshopes I shewe,
    And in Latin I speke a wordes fewe,
    To saffron with[3] my predicacioun,°   *preaching*
    And for to stire hem to devocioun.
      Thanne shewe I forth my longe crystal stones,°   *jars*
60 Ycrammed ful of cloutes° and of bones   *rags*
    Relikes been they, as weenen° they eechoon.   *suppose*
    Thanne have I in laton° a shulder-boon   *brass*
    Which that was of an holy Jewes sheep.
    "Goode men," I saye, "take of my wordes keep:°   *notice*
65 If that this boon be wasshe in any welle,
    If cow, or calf, or sheep, or oxe swelle,
    That any worm hath ete or worm ystonge,[4]
    Take water of that welle and wassh his tonge,
    And it is hool[5] anoon. And ferthermoor,
70 Of pokkes° and of scabbe and every soor°   *pox, pustules/sore*
    Shal every sheep be hool that of this welle
    Drinketh a draughte. Take keep eek° that I telle: *also*
    If that the goode man that the beestes oweth°   *owns*
    Wol every wike,° er° that the cok him croweth,   *week/before*
75 Fasting drinken of this welle a draughte—
    As thilke° holy Jew oure eldres taughte—   *that same*
    His beestes and his stoor° shal multiplye.   *stock*
    "And sire, also it heleth jalousye:
    For though a man be falle in jalous rage,
80 Lat maken with this water his potage,°   *soup*
    And nevere shal he more his wif mistriste,°   *mistrust*
    Though he the soothe of hir defaute wiste,[6]
    Al hadde she[7] taken preestes two or three.
    "Here is a mitein° eek that ye may see: *mitten*
85 He that his hand wol putte in this mitein
    He shal have multiplying of his grain,
    Whan he hath sowen, be it whete or otes—
    So that he offre pens or elles grotes.[8]
    "Goode men and wommen, oo thing warne I you:

---

7. I.e., the same. "Theme": biblical text on which the sermon is based.
8. Avarice is the root of evil (1 Timothy 6.10).
9. Each and every one. "Bulles": papal bulls, official documents.
1. I.e., the pope's or bishop's seal on my papal license.
2. I go on with my yarn.

3. To add spice to.
4. That has eaten any worm or been bitten by any snake.
5. I.e., sound.
6. Knew the truth of her infidelity.
7. Even if she had.
8. Pennies, groats, coins.

90 If any wight be in this chirche now
   That hath doon sinne horrible, that he
   Dar nat for shame of it yshriven° be,   *confessed*
   Or any womman, be she yong or old,
   That hath ymaked hir housbonde cokewold,°   *cuckold*
95 Swich° folk shal have no power ne no grace   *such*
   To offren to⁹ my relikes in this place;
   And whoso findeth him out of swich blame,
   He wol come up and offre in Goddes name,
   And I assoile° him by the auctoritee   *absolve*
100 Which that by bulle ygraunted was to me."
      By this gaude° have I wonne, yeer by yeer,   *trick*
   An hundred mark¹ sith° I was pardoner.   *since*
   I stonde lik a clerk in my pulpet,
   And whan the lewed° peple is down yset,   *ignorant*
105 I preche so as ye han herd bifore,
   And telle an hundred false japes° more.   *tricks*
   Thanne paine I me² to strecche forth the nekke,
   And eest and west upon the peple I bekke°   *nod*
   As dooth a douve,° sitting on a berne;°   *dove/barn*
110 Mine handes and my tonge goon so yerne°   *fast*
   That it is joye to see my bisinesse.
   Of avarice and of swich cursednesse°   *sin*
   Is al my preching, for to make hem free°   *generous*
   To yiven hir pens, and namely° unto me,   *especially*
115 For myn entente is nat but for to winne,³
   And no thing for correccion of sinne:
   I rekke° nevere whan that they been beried°   *care/buried*
   Though that hir soules goon a-blakeberied.⁴
   For certes, many a predicacioun°   *sermon*
120 Comth ofte time of yvel entencioun:
   Som for plesance of folk and flaterye,
   To been avaunced° by ypocrisye,   *promoted*
   And som for vaine glorye, and som for hate;
   For whan I dar noon otherways debate,°   *fight*
125 Thanne wol I stinge him⁵ with my tonge smerte°   *sharply*
   In preching, so that he shal nat asterte°   *escape*
   To been defamed falsly, if that he
   Hath trespassed to my bretheren⁶ or to me.
   For though I telle nought his propre name,
130 Men shal wel knowe that it is the same
   By signes and by othere circumstaunces.
   Thus quite° I folk that doon us displesaunces;⁷   *pay back*
   Thus spete° I out my venim under hewe°   *spit/false colors*
   Of holinesse, to seeme holy and trewe.
135 But shortly myn entente I wol devise:°   *explain*
   I preche of no thing but for coveitise;°   *covetousness*
   Therfore my theme is yit and evere was

---

9. To make gifts in reverence of.
1. Marks (pecuniary units).
2. I take pains.
3. My intent is only to make money.

4. Go blackberrying, i.e., go to hell.
5. An adversary critical of pardoners.
6. Injured my fellow pardoners.
7. Make trouble for us.

Radix malorum est cupiditas.

Thus can I preche again that same vice
140 Which that I use, and that is avarice.
But though myself be gilty in that sinne,
Yit can I make other folk to twinne°   *separate*
From avarice, and sore to repente—
But that is nat my principal entente:
145 I preche no thing but for coveitise.
Of this matere it oughte ynough suffise.
Thanne telle I hem ensamples[8] many oon
Of olde stories longe time agoon,
For lewed° peple loven tales olde—   *ignorant*
150 Swiche° thinges can they wel reporte and holde.[9]   *such*
What, trowe° ye that whiles I may preche,   *believe*
And winne gold and silver for° I teche,   *because*
That I wol live in poverte wilfully?°   *voluntarily*
Nay, nay, I thoughte° it nevere, trewely,   *intended*
155 For I wol preche and begge in sondry landes;
I wol nat do no labour with mine handes,
Ne make baskettes and live therby,
By cause I wol nat beggen idelly.[1]
I wol none of the Apostles countrefete:°   *imitate*
160 I wol have moneye, wolle,° cheese, and whete,   *wool*
Al were it[2] yiven of the pooreste page,
Or of the pooreste widwe in a village—
Al sholde hir children sterve[3] for famine.
Nay, I wol drinke licour of the vine
165 And have a joly wenche in every town.
But herkneth, lordinges, in conclusioun,
Youre liking° is that I shal telle a tale: *pleasure*
Now have I dronke a draughte of corny ale,
By God, I hope I shal you telle a thing
170 That shal by reson been at youre liking;
For though myself be a ful vicious man,
A moral tale yit I you telle can,
Which I am wont to preche for to winne.
Now holde youre pees, my tale I wol biginne.

The Tale

175   In Flandres whilom° was a compaignye   *once*
Of yonge folk that haunteden° folye—   *practiced*
As riot, hasard, stewes,[4] and tavernes,
Wher as with harpes, lutes, and giternes°   *guitars*
They daunce and playen at dees° bothe day and night, *dice*
180 And ete also and drinke over hir might,[5]
Thurgh which they doon the devel sacrifise

---

8. Exempla (stories illustrating moral principles).
9. Repeat and remember.
1. I.e., without profit.
2. Even though it were.

3. Even though her children should die.
4. Wild parties, gambling, brothels.
5. Beyond their capacity.

Within that develes temple in cursed wise
By superfluitee° abhominable.   *overindulgence*
Hir othes been so grete and so dampnable
185   That it is grisly for to heere hem swere:
Oure blessed Lordes body they totere⁶—
Hem thoughte that Jewes rente° him nought ynough.   *tore*
And eech of hem at otheres sinne lough.°   *laughed*
And right anoon thanne comen tombesteres,°   *dancing girls*
190   Fetis° and smale,° and yonge frutesteres,⁷   *shapely/slender*
Singeres with harpes, bawdes,° wafereres⁸—   *pimps*
Whiche been the verray develes officeres,
To kindle and blowe the fir of lecherye
That is annexed unto glotonye:⁹
195   The Holy Writ take I to my witnesse
That luxure° is in win and dronkenesse.   *lechery*
Lo, how that dronken Lot¹ unkindely°   *unnaturally*
Lay by his doughtres two unwitingly:
So dronke he was he niste° what he wroughte.°   *didn't know/did*
200   Herodes, who so wel the stories soughte,²
Whan he of win was repleet° at his feeste,   *filled*
Right at his owene table he yaf his heeste°   *command*
To sleen° the Baptist John, ful giltelees.   *slay*
    Senek³ saith a good word doutelees:
205   He saith he can no difference finde
Bitwixe a man that is out of his minde
And a man which that is dronkelewe,°   *drunken*
But that woodnesse, yfallen in a shrewe,⁴
Persevereth lenger than dooth dronkenesse.
210   O glotonye, ful of cursednesse!°   *wickedness*
O cause first of oure confusioun!°   *downfall*
O original of oure dampnacioun,°   *damnation*
Til Crist hadde bought° us with his blood again!   *redeemed*
Lo, how dere, shortly for to sayn,
215   Abought° was thilke° cursed vilainye;   *paid for/that same*
Corrupt was al this world for glotonye:
Adam oure fader and his wif also
Fro Paradis to labour and to wo
Were driven for that vice, it is no drede.°   *doubt*
220   For whil that Adam fasted, as I rede,
He was in Paradis; and whan that he
Eet° of the fruit defended° on a tree,   *ate/forbidden*
Anoon he was out cast to wo and paine.
O glotonye, on thee wel oughte us plaine!°   *complain*
225   O, wiste a man⁵ how manye maladies
Folwen of excesse and of glotonies,

6. Tear apart (a reference to oaths sworn by parts of His body, such as "God's bones!" or "God's teeth!").
7. Fruit-selling girls.
8. Girl cake vendors.
9. I.e., closely related to gluttony.
1. See Genesis 19.30–36.

2. For the story of Herod and St. John the Baptist, see Mark 6.17–29. "Who so . . . soughte": i.e., whoever looked it up in the Gospel would find.
3. Seneca, the Roman Stoic philosopher.
4. But that madness, occurring in a wicked man.
5. If a man knew.

He wolde been the more mesurable°   *moderate*
Of his diete, sitting at his table.
Allas, the shorte throte, the tendre mouth,
230   Maketh that eest and west and north and south,
In erthe, in air, in water, men to swinke,°   *work*
To gete a gloton daintee mete° and drinke.   *food*
Of this matere, O Paul, wel canstou trete:
"Mete unto wombe,° and wombe eek unto mete,   *belly*
235   Shal God destroyen bothe," as Paulus saith.[6]
Allas, a foul thing is it, by my faith,
To saye this word, and fouler is the deede
Whan man so drinketh of the white and rede[7]
That of his throte he maketh his privee°   *toilet*
240   Thurgh thilke cursed superfluitee.°   *overindulgence*
    The Apostle[8] weeping saith ful pitously,
"Ther walken manye of which you told have I—
I saye it now weeping with pitous vois—
They been enemies of Cristes crois,°   *cross*
245   Of whiche the ende is deeth—wombe is hir god!"[9]
O wombe, O bely, O stinking cod,°   *bag*
Fulfilled° of dong° and of corrupcioun!   *filled full / dung*
At either ende of thee foul is the soun.°   *sound*
How greet labour and cost is thee to finde!°   *provide for*
250   Thise cookes, how they stampe° and straine and grinde,   *pound*
And turnen substance into accident[1]
To fulfillen al thy likerous° talent!°   *greedy / appetite*
Out of the harde bones knokke they
The mary,° for they caste nought away   *marrow*
255   That may go thurgh the golet[2] softe and soote.°   *sweetly*
Of spicerye° of leef and bark and roote   *spices*
Shal been his sauce ymaked by delit,
To make him yit a newer appetit.
But certes, he that haunteth swiche delices°   *pleasures*
260   Is deed° whil that he liveth in tho° vices.   *dead / those*
    A lecherous thing is win, and dronkenesse
Is ful of striving° and of wrecchednesse.   *quarreling*
O dronke man, disfigured is thy face!
Sour is thy breeth, foul artou to embrace!
265   And thurgh thy dronke nose seemeth the soun
As though thou saidest ay,° "Sampsoun, Sampsoun."   *always*
And yit, God woot,° Sampson drank nevere win.[3]   *knows*
Thou fallest as it were a stiked swin;°   *stuck pig*
Thy tonge is lost, and al thyn honeste cure,[4]
270   For dronkenesse is verray sepulture°   *burial*
Of mannes wit° and his discrecioun.   *intelligence*
In whom that drinke hath dominacioun

6. See 1 Corinthians 6.13.
7. I.e., white and red wines.
8. I.e., St. Paul.
9. See Philippians 3.18.
1. A philosophic joke, depending on the distinction between inner reality (substance) and outward
appearance (accident).
2. Through the gullet.
3. Before Samson's birth an angel told his mother
that he would be a Nazarite throughout his life;
members of this sect took no strong drink.
4. Care for self-respect.

He can no conseil° keepe, it is no drede.°   *secrets/doubt*
Now keepe you fro the white and fro the rede—
275 And namely° fro the white win of Lepe[5]   *particularly*
That is to selle in Fisshstreete or in Chepe:[6]
The win of Spaine creepeth subtilly
In othere wines growing faste° by,   *close*
Of which ther riseth swich fumositee°   *heady fumes*
280 That whan a man hath dronken draughtes three
And weeneth° that he be at hoom in Chepe,   *supposes*
He is in Spaine, right at the town of Lepe,
Nat at The Rochele ne at Burdeux town;[7]
And thanne wol he sayn, "Sampsoun, Sampsoun."
285   But herkneth, lordinges, oo° word I you praye, *one*
That alle the soverein actes,[8] dar I saye,
Of victories in the Olde Testament,
Thurgh verray God that is omnipotent,
Were doon in abstinence and in prayere:
290 Looketh° the Bible and ther ye may it lere.° *behold/learn*
   Looke Attila, the grete conquerour,[9]
Deide° in his sleep with shame and dishonour,   *died*
Bleeding at his nose in dronkenesse:
A capitain sholde live in sobrenesse.
295   And overal this, aviseth you[1] right wel
What was comanded unto Lamuel[2]—
Nat Samuel, but Lamuel, saye I—
Redeth the Bible and finde it expresly,
Of win-yiving° to hem that han[3] justise: *wine-serving*
300 Namore of this, for it may wel suffise.
   And now that I have spoken of glotonye,
Now wol I you defende° hasardrye:° *prohibit/gambling*
Hasard is verray moder° of lesinges,°   *mother/lies*
And of deceite and cursed forsweringes,°   *perjuries*
305 Blaspheme of Crist, manslaughtre, and wast° also *waste*
Of catel° and of time; and ferthermo,   *property*
It is repreve° and contrarye of honour   *disgrace*
For to been holden a commune hasardour,°   *gambler*
And evere the hyer he is of estat
310 The more is he holden desolat.[4]
If that a prince useth hasardrye,
In alle governance and policye
He is, as by commune opinioun,
Yholde the lasse° in reputacioun.   *less*
315   Stilbon, that was a wis embassadour,
Was sent to Corinthe in ful greet honour
Fro Lacedomye° to make hir alliaunce,   *Sparta*

5. A town in Spain.
6. Fishstreet and Cheapside in the London market district.
7. The Pardoner is joking about the illegal custom of adulterating fine wines of Bordeaux and La Rochelle with strong Spanish wine.
8. Distinguished deeds.
9. Attila was the leader of the Huns who almost captured Rome in the 5th century.
1. Consider.
2. Lemuel's mother told him that kings should not drink (Proverbs 31.4–5).
3. I.e., administer.
4. I.e. dissolute.

And whan he cam him happede° parchaunce   *it happened*
That alle the gretteste° that were of that lond   *greatest*
320 Playing at the hasard he hem foond,°   *found*
For which as soone as it mighte be
He stal him[5] hoom again to his contree,
And saide, "Ther wol I nat lese° my name,   *lose*
N'I wol nat take on me so greet defame°   *dishonor*
325 You to allye unto none hasardours:
Sendeth othere wise embassadours,
For by my trouthe, me were levere[6] die
Than I you sholde to hasardours allye.
For ye that been so glorious in honours
330 Shal nat allye you with hasardours
As by my wil, ne as by my tretee."°   *treaty*
This wise philosophre, thus saide he.
    Looke eek that to the king Demetrius
The King of Parthes,° as the book[7] saith us,   *Parthians*
335 Sente him a paire of dees° of gold in scorn,   *dice*
For he hadde used hasard therbiforn,
For which he heeld his glorye or his renown
At no value or reputacioun.
Lordes may finden other manere play
340 Honeste° ynough to drive the day away.   *honorable*
    Now wol I speke of othes false and grete
A word or two, as olde bookes trete:
    Greet swering is a thing abhominable,
And fals swering is yit more reprevable.°   *reprehensible*
345 The hye God forbad swering at al—
Witnesse on Mathew.[8] But in special
Of swering saith the holy Jeremie,[9]
"Thou shalt swere sooth thine othes and nat lie,
And swere in doom° and eek in rightwisnesse,°   *equity/righteousness*
350 But idel swering is a cursednesse."°   *wickedness*
    Biholde and see that in the firste Table[1]
Of hye Goddes heestes° honorable   *commandments*
How that the seconde heeste of him is this:
"Take nat my name in idel or amis."
355 Lo, rather° he forbedeth swich swering   *sooner*
Than homicide, or many a cursed thing.
I saye that as by ordre thus it stondeth—
This knoweth that[2] his heestes understondeth
How that the seconde heeste of God is that.
360 And fertherover,° I wol thee telle al plat°   *moreover/plain*
That vengeance shal nat parten° from his hous   *depart*
That of his othes is too outrageous.
"By Goddes precious herte!" and "By his nailes!"°   *fingernails*
And "By the blood of Crist that is in Hailes,[3]

---

5. He stole away.
6. I had rather.
7. The book that relates this and the previous incident is the *Policraticus* of the 12th-century Latin writer John of Salisbury.
8. "But I say unto you, Swear not at all" (Matthew

5.34).
9. Jeremiah 4.2.
1. I.e., the first three of the Ten Commandments.
2. I.e., he that.
3. An abbey in Gloucestershire supposed to possess some of Christ's blood.

365	Sevene is my chaunce,° and thyn is cink and traye!"[4]	*winning number*
	"By Goddes armes, if thou falsly playe	
	This daggere shal thurghout thyn herte go!"	
	This fruit cometh of the bicche bones[5] two—	
	Forswering, ire, falsnesse, homicide.	
370	Now for the love of Crist that for us dyde,°	*died*
	Lete° youre othes bothe grete and smale.	*leave*
	But sires, now wol I telle forth my tale.	
	Thise riotoures° three of whiche I telle,	*revelers*
	Longe erst er prime[6] ronge of any belle,	
375	Were set hem in a taverne to drinke,	
	And as they sat they herde a belle clinke	
	Biforn a cors° was caried to his grave.	*corpse*
	That oon of hem gan callen to his knave:°	*servant*
	Go bet,"[7] quod he, "and axe° redily°	*ask/promptly*
380	What cors is this that passeth heer forby,	
	And looke° that thou reporte his name weel."°	*be sure/well*
	"Sire," quod this boy, "it needeth neveradeel:[8]	
	It was me told er ye cam heer two houres.	
	He was, pardee,° an old felawe of youres,	*by God*
385	And sodeinly he was yslain tonight,°	*last night*
	Fordronke° as he sat on his bench upright;	*very drunk*
	Ther cam a privee° thief men clepeth° Deeth,	*stealthy/call*
	That in this contree al the peple sleeth,°	*slays*
	And with his spere he smoot his herte atwo,	
390	And wente his way withouten wordes mo.	
	He hath a thousand slain this° pestilence.	*during this*
	And maister, er ye come in his presence,	
	Me thinketh that it were necessarye	
	For to be war of swich an adversarye;	
395	Beeth redy for to meete him everemore:	
	Thus taughte me my dame.° I saye namore."	*mother*
	"By Sainte Marye," saide this taverner,	
	"The child saith sooth, for he hath slain this yeer,	
	Henne° over a mile, within a greet village,	*hence*
400	Bothe man and womman, child and hine[9] and page.	
	I trowe° his habitacion be there.	*believe*
	To been avised° greet wisdom it were	*wary*
	Er that he dide a man a dishonour."	
	"Ye, Goddes armes," quod this riotour,	
405	"Is it swich peril with him for to meete?	
	I shal him seeke by way and eek by streete,[1]	
	I make avow to Goddes digne° bones.	*worthy*
	Herkneth, felawes, we three been alle ones:°	*of one mind*
	Lat eech of us holde up his hand to other	
410	And eech of us bicome otheres brother,	
	And we wol sleen this false traitour Deeth.	
	He shal be slain, he that so manye sleeth,	

---

4. Five and three.
5. I.e., damned dice.
6. Long before 9 A.M.
7. Better, i.e., quick.

8. It isn't a bit necessary.
9. Farm laborer.
1. By highway and byway.

By Goddes dignitee, er it be night."
    Togidres han thise three hir trouthes plight[2]
415 To live and dien eech of hem with other,
As though he were his owene ybore° brother.   *born*
And up they sterte,° al dronken in this rage,   *started*
And forth they goon towardes that village
Of which the taverner hadde spoke biforn,
420 And many a grisly ooth thanne han they sworn,
And Cristes blessed body they torente:°   *tore apart*
Deeth shal be deed° if that they may him hente.°   *dead / catch*
    Whan they han goon nat fully half a mile,
Right as they wolde han treden° over a stile,   *stepped*
425 An old man and a poore with hem mette;
This olde man ful mekely hem grette,°   *greeted*
And saide thus, "Now lordes, God you see."[3]
    The pruddeste° of thise riotoures three   *proudest*
Answerde again, "What, carl° with sory grace,   *fellow*
430 Why artou al forwrapped° save thy face?   *muffled up*
Why livestou so longe in so greet age?"
    This olde man gan looke in his visage,
And saide thus, "For° I ne can nat finde   *because*
A man, though that I walked into Inde,°   *India*
435 Neither in citee ne in no village,
That wolde chaunge his youthe for myn age;
And therefore moot° I han myn age stille,   *must*
As longe time as it is Goddes wille.
    "Ne Deeth, allas, ne wol nat have my lif.
440 Thus walke I lik a restelees caitif,°   *wretch*
And on the ground which is my modres° gate   *mother's*
I knokke with my staf bothe erly and late,
And saye, 'Leve° moder, leet me in: *dear*
Lo, how I vanisshe, flessh and blood and skin.
445 Allas, whan shal my bones been at reste?
Moder, with you wolde I chaunge° my cheste[4]   *exchange*
That in my chambre longe time hath be,
Ye, for an haire-clout[5] to wrappe me.'
But yit to me she wol nat do that grace,
450 For which ful pale and welked° is my face.   *withered*
But sires, to you it is no curteisye
To speken to an old man vilainye,°   *rudeness*
But° he trespasse° in word or elles in deede.   *unless / offend*
In Holy Writ ye may yourself wel rede,
455 'Agains[6] an old man, hoor° upon his heed,   *hoar*
Ye shall arise.'[7] Wherfore I yive you reed,°   *advice*
Ne dooth unto an old man noon harm now,
Namore than that ye wolde men dide to you
In age, if that ye so longe abide.[8]
460 And God be with you wher ye go° or ride: *walk*

2. Pledged their words of honor.
3. May God protect you.
4. Chest for one's belongings, used here as the symbol for life—or perhaps a coffin.
5. Haircloth, for a winding sheet.
6. In the presence of.
7. Cf. Leviticus 19.32.
8. I.e., if you live so long.

I moot go thider as I have to go."
   "Nay, olde cherl, by God thou shalt nat so,"
Saide this other hasardour anoon.
"Thou partest nat so lightly,° by Saint John!   *easily*
465 Thou speke° right now of thilke traitour Deeth,   *spoke*
That in this contree alle oure freendes sleeth:
Have here my trouthe, as thou art his espye,°   *spy*
Tel wher he is, or thou shalt it abye,°   *pay for*
By God and by the holy sacrament!
470 For soothly thou art oon of his assent[9]
To sleen us yonge folk, thou false thief."
   "Now sires," quod he, "if that ye be so lief°   *anxious*
To finde Deeth, turne up this crooked way,
For in that grove I lafte° him, by my fay,°   *left/faith*
475 Under a tree, and ther he wol abide:
Nat for youre boost° he wol him no thing hide.   *boast*
See ye that ook?° Right ther ye shal him finde.   *oak*
God save you, that boughte again[1] mankinde,
And you amende." Thus saide this olde man.
480   And everich of thise riotoures ran
Til he cam to that tree, and ther they founde
Of florins° fine of gold ycoined rounde   *coins*
Wel neigh an eighte busshels as hem thoughte—
Ne lenger thanne after Deeth they soughte,
485 But eech of hem so glad was of the sighte,
For that the florins been so faire and brighte,
That down they sette hem by this precious hoord.
The worste of hem he spak the firste word:
   "Bretheren," quod he, "take keep° what that I saye: *heed*
490 My wit is greet though that I bourde° and playe.   *joke*
This tresor hath Fortune unto us yiven
In mirthe and jolitee oure lif to liven,
And lightly° as it cometh so wol we spende.   *easily*
Ey, Goddes precious dignitee, who wende[2]
495 Today that we sholde han so fair a grace?
But mighte this gold be caried fro this place
Hoom to myn hous—or elles unto youres—
For wel ye woot that al this gold is oures—
Thanne were we in heigh felicitee.
500 But trewely, by daye it mighte nat be:
Men wolde sayn that we were theves stronge,°   *flagrant*
And for oure owene tresor doon us honge.[3]
This tresor moste ycaried be by nighte,
As wisely and as slyly as it mighte.
505 Therefore I rede° that cut° amonges us alle   *advise/straws*
Be drawe, and lat see wher the cut wol falle;
And he that hath the cut with herte blithe
Shal renne° to the town, and that ful swithe,°   *run/quickly*
And bringe us breed and win ful prively;

---

9. I.e., one of his party.   2. Who would have supposed.
1. Redeemed.   3. Have us hanged.

510 And two of us shal keepen° subtilly   *guard*
This tresor wel, and if he wol nat tarye,
Whan it is night we wol this tresor carye
By oon assent wher as us thinketh best."
That oon of hem the cut broughte in his fest°   *fist*
515 And bad hem drawe and looke wher it wol falle;
And it fil° on the yongeste of hem alle,   *fell*
And forth toward the town he wente anoon.
And also° soone as that he was agoon,° *as/gone away*
That oon of hem spak thus unto that other:
520 "Thou knowest wel thou art my sworen brother;
Thy profit wol I telle thee anoon:
Thou woost wel that oure felawe is agoon,
And here is gold, and that ful greet plentee,
That shall departed° been among us three.   *divided*
525 But nathelees, if I can shape° it so   *arrange*
That it departed were among us two,
Hadde I nat doon a freendes turn to thee?"
  That other answerde, "I noot⁴ how that may be:
He woot that the gold is with us twaye.
530 What shal we doon? What shal we to him saye?"
  "Shal it be conseil?"⁵ saide the firste shrewe.° *villain*
"And I shal telle in a wordes fewe
What we shul doon, and bringe it wel aboute."
  "I graunte," quod that other, "out of doute,
535 That by my trouthe I wol thee nat biwraye."°   *expose*
  "Now," quod the firste, "thou woost wel we be twaye,
And two of us shal strenger° be than oon: *stronger*
Looke whan that he is set that right anoon
Aris as though thou woldest with him playe,
540 And I shal rive° him thurgh the sides twaye,   *pierce*
Whil that thou strugelest with him as in game,
And with thy daggere looke thou do the same;
And thanne shal al this gold departed be,
My dere freend, bitwixe thee and me.
545 Thanne we may bothe oure lustes° al fulfille,   *desires*
And playe at dees° right at oure owene wille."   *dice*
And thus accorded been thise shrewes twaye
To sleen the thridde, as ye han herd me saye.
  This yongeste, which that wente to the town,
550 Ful ofte in herte he rolleth up and down
The beautee of thise florins newe and brighte.
"O Lord," quod he, "if so were that I mighte
Have al this tresor to myself allone,
Ther is no man that liveth under the trone°   *throne*
555 Of God that sholde live so merye as I."
And at the laste the feend oure enemy
Putte in his thought that he sholde poison beye,°   *buy*
With which he mighte sleen his felawes twaye—

---

4. Don't know.   5. A secret.

	Forwhy° the feend° foond him in swich livinge	because / devil
560	That he hadde leve° him to sorwe bringe:[6]	permission
	For this was outrely° his fulle entente,	plainly
	To sleen hem bothe, and nevere to repente.	
	And forth he gooth—no lenger wolde he tarye—	
	Into the town unto a pothecarye,°	apothecary
565	And prayed him that he him wolde selle	
	Som poison that he mighte his rattes quelle,°	kill
	And eek ther was a polcat[7] in his hawe°	yard
	That, as he saide, his capons hadde yslawe,°	slain
	And fain he wolde wreke him[8] if he mighte	
570	On vermin that destroyed him[9] by nighte.	
	The pothecarye answerde, "And thou shalt have	
	A thing that, also° God my soule save,	as
	In al this world there is no creature	
	That ete or dronke hath of this confiture°	mixture
575	Nat but the mountance° of a corn° of whete—	amount / grain
	That he ne shal his lif anoon forlete.°	lose
	Ye, sterve° he shal, and that in lasse° while	die / less
	Than thou wolt goon a paas[1] nat but a mile,	
	The poison is so strong and violent."	
580	This cursed man hath in his hand yhent°	taken
	This poison in a box and sith° he ran	then
	Into the nexte streete unto a man	
	And borwed of him large botels three,	
	And in the two his poison poured he—	
585	The thridde he kepte clene for his drinke,	
	For al the night he shoop him[2] for to swinke°	work
	In carying of the gold out of that place.	
	And whan this riotour with sory grace	
	Hadde filled with win his grete botels three,	
590	To his felawes again repaireth he.	
	What needeth it to sermone of it more?	
	For right as they had cast° his deeth bifore,	plotted
	Right so they han him slain, and that anoon.	
	And whan that this was doon, thus spak that oon:	
595	"Now lat us sitte and drinke and make us merye,	
	And afterward we wol his body berye."°	bury
	And with that word it happed him par cas[3]	
	To take the botel ther the poison was,	
	And drank, and yaf his felawe drinke also,	
600	For which anoon they storven° bothe two.	died
	But certes I suppose that Avicen	
	Wroot nevere in no canon ne in no fen[4]	
	Mo wonder signes[5] of empoisoning	
	Than hadde thise wrecches two er hir ending:	

6. Christian doctrine teaches that the devil may not tempt people except with God's permission.
7. A weasellike animal.
8. He would gladly avenge himself.
9. I.e., were ruining his farming.
1. Take a walk.
2. He was preparing.
3. By chance.
4. The *Canon of Medicine*, by Avicenna, an 11th-century Arabic philosopher, was divided into sections called "fens."
5. More wonderful symptoms.

605 Thus ended been thise homicides two,
And eek the false empoisonere also.
O cursed sinne of alle cursednesse!
O traitours homicide, O wikkednesse!
O glotonye, luxure,° and hasardrye!   *lechery*
610 Thou blasphemour of Crist with vilainye
And othes grete of usage° and of pride!   *habit*
Allas, mankinde, how may it bitide
That to thy Creatour which that thee wroughte,
And with his precious herte blood thee boughte,°   *redeemed*
615 Thou art so fals and so unkinde,° allas?   *unnatural*
Now goode men, God foryive you youre trespas,
And ware° you fro the sinne of avarice: *guard*
Myn holy pardon may you alle warice°—   *save*
So that ye offre nobles or sterlinges,⁶
620 Or elles silver brooches, spoones, ringes.
Boweth your heed under this holy bulle!
Cometh up, ye wives, offreth of youre wolle!°   *wool*
Youre name I entre here in my rolle: anoon
Into the blisse of hevene shul ye goon.
625 I you assoile° by myn heigh power—   *absolve*
Ye that wol offre—as clene and eek as cleer
As ye were born.—And lo, sires, thus I preche.
And Jesu Crist that is oure soules leeche°   *physician*
So graunte you his pardon to receive,
630 For that is best—I wol you nat deceive.

The Epilogue

"But sires, oo word forgat I in my tale:
I have relikes and pardon in my male°   *bag*
As faire as any man in Engelond,
Whiche were me yiven by the Popes hond.
635 If any of you wol of devocioun
Offren and han myn absolucioun,
Come forth anoon, and kneeleth here adown,
And mekely receiveth my pardoun,
Or elles taketh pardon as ye wende,°   *ride along*
640 Al newe and fressh at every miles ende—
So that ye offre alway newe and newe⁷
Nobles or pens whiche that be goode and trewe.
It is an honour to everich° that is heer   *everyone*
That ye have a suffisant° pardoner   *competent*
645 T'assoile you in contrees as ye ride,
For aventures° whiche that may bitide: *accidents*
Paraventure ther may falle oon or two
Down of his hors and breke his nekke atwo;
Looke which a suretee° is it to you alle   *safeguard*
650 That I am in youre felaweshipe yfalle
That may assoile you, bothe more and lasse,⁸

6. "Nobles" and "sterlinges" were valuable coins.   8. Both high and low (i.e., everybody).
7. Over and over.

Whan that the soule shal fro the body passe.
I rede° that oure Hoste shal biginne,   advise
For he is most envoluped° in sinne.   involved
655   Com forth, sire Host, and offre first anoon,
And thou shalt kisse the relikes everichoon,°   each one
Ye, for a grote: unbokele° anoon thy purs."   unbuckle
"Nay, nay," quod he, "thanne have I Cristes curs!
Lat be," quod he, "it shal nat be, so theech!°   may I prosper
660   Thou woldest make me kisse thyn olde breech°   breeches
And swere it were a relik of a saint,
Though it were with thy fundament° depeint.°   anus / stained
But, by the crois which that Sainte Elaine foond,⁹
I wolde I hadde thy coilons° in myn hond,   testicles
665   In stede of relikes or of saintuarye.°   relic-box
Lat cutte hem of: I wol thee helpe hem carye.
They shal be shrined in an hogges tord."°   turd
This Pardoner answerde nat a word:
So wroth he was no word ne wolde he saye.
670   "Now," quod oure Host, "I wol no lenger playe
With thee, ne with noon other angry man."
But right anoon the worthy Knight bigan,
Whan that he sawgh that al the peple lough,°   laughed
"Namore of this, for it is right ynough.
675   Sire Pardoner, be glad and merye of cheere,
And ye, sire Host that been to me so dere,
I praye you that ye kisse the Pardoner,
And Pardoner, I praye thee, draw thee neer,
And as we diden lat us laughe and playe."
680   Anoon they kiste and riden forth hir waye.

The Nun's Priest's Tale

In the framing story, *The Nun's Priest's Tale* is linked to a dramatic exchange that follows *The Monk's Tale*. The latter consists of brief tragedies, the common theme of which is the fall of famous men and one woman, most of whom are rulers, through the reversals of Fortune. Like *The Knight's Tale*, this was probably an earlier work of Chaucer's, one that he never finished. As the Monk's tragedies promise to go on and on monotonously, the Knight interrupts and politely tells the Monk that his tragedies are too painful. The Host chimes in to say that the tragedies are "nat worth a botterflye" and asks the Monk to try another subject, but the Monk is offended and refuses. The Host then turns to the Nun's Priest, that is, the priest who is accompanying the Prioress. The three priests said in *The General Prologue* to have been traveling with her have apparently been reduced to one.

The Nun's Priest's Tale is an example of the literary genre known as the "beast fable," familiar from the fables of Aesop in which animals, behaving like human beings, point a moral. In the Middle Ages fables often functioned as elementary texts to teach boys Latin. Marie de France's fables in French are the earliest known vernacular translations. This particular fable derives from an episode in the French

9. I.e., by the cross that St. Helena found. Helena, mother of Constantine the Great, was reputed to have found the True Cross.

Roman de Renard, a "beast epic," which satirically represents a feudal animal society ruled over by Noble the Lion. Reynard the Fox is a wily trickster hero who is constantly preying upon and outwitting the other animals, although sometimes Reynard himself is outwitted by one of his victims.

In *The Nun's Priest's Tale*, morals proliferate: both the priest-narrator and his hero, Chauntecleer the rooster, spout examples, learned allusions, proverbs, and sententious generalizations, often in highly inflated rhetoric. The simple beast fable is thus inflated into a delightful satire of learning and moralizing and of the pretentious rhetoric by which medieval writers sometimes sought to elevate their works. Among them, we we may include Chaucer himself who in this tale seems to be making affectionate fun of some of his own works like the tragedies which became *The Monk's Tale*.

	A poore widwe somdeel stape° in age	*advanced*
	Was whilom° dwelling in a narwe[1] cotage,	*once upon a time*
	Biside a grove, stonding in a dale:	
	This widwe of which I telle you my tale,	
5	Sin thilke° day that she was last a wif,	*that same*
	In pacience ladde° a ful simple lif.	*led*
	For litel was hir catel° and hir rente,°	*property / income*
	By housbondrye° of swich as God hire sente	*economy*
	She foond° hirself and eek hir doughtren two.	*provided for*
10	Three large sowes hadde she and namo,	
	Three kin,° and eek a sheep that highte° Malle.	*cows / was called*
	Ful sooty was hir bowr° and eek hir halle.	*bedroom*
	In which she eet ful many a sclendre° meel;	*scanty*
	Of poinant° sauce hire needed neveradeel:°	*pungent / not a bit*
15	No daintee morsel passed thurgh hir throte—	
	Hir diete was accordant to hir cote.°	*cottage*
	Repleccioun° ne made hire nevere sik:	*overeating*
	Attempre° diete was al hir physik,°	*moderate / medicine*
	And exercise and hertes suffisaunce.°	*contentment*
20	The goute lette hire nothing for to daunce,[2]	
	N'apoplexye shente° nat hir heed.°	*hurt / head*
	No win ne drank she, neither whit ne reed:°	*red*
	Hir boord° was served most with whit and blak,[3]	*table*
	Milk and brown breed, in which she foond no lak;[4]	
25	Seind bacon, and somtime an ey° or twaye,	*egg*
	For she was as it were a manere daye.[5]	
	A yeerd° she hadde, enclosed al withoute	*yard*
	With stikkes, and a drye dich aboute,	
	In which she hadde a cok heet° Chauntecleer:	*named*
30	In al the land of crowing nas° his peer.	*was not*
	His vois was merier than the merye orgon	
	On massedayes that in the chirche goon;[6]	
	Wel sikerer[7] was his crowing in his logge°	*dwelling*
	Than is a clok or an abbeye orlogge;°	*timepiece*
35	By nature he knew eech ascensioun	

---

1. I.e., small.
2. The gout didn't hinder her at all from dancing.
3. I.e., milk and bread.
4. Found no fault.

5. I.e., a kind of dairywoman. "Seind": scorched (i.e., broiled).
6. I.e., is played.
7. More reliable.

Of th'equinoxial[8] in thilke town:
For whan degrees fifteene were ascended,
Thanne crew° he that it mighte nat been amended.°   *crowed/improved*
His comb was redder than the fin coral,
40 And batailed° as it were a castel wal;   *battlemented*
His bile° was blak, and as the jeet° it shoon;   *bill/jet*
Like asure[9] were his legges and his toon;°   *toes*
His nailes whitter° than the lilye flowr,   *whiter*
And lik the burned° gold was his colour.   *burnished*
45 This gentil° cok hadde in his governaunce   *noble*
Sevene hennes for to doon al his plesaunce,°   *pleasure*
Whiche were his sustres and his paramours,[1]
And wonder like to him as of colours;
Of whiche the faireste hewed° on hir throte   *colored*
50 Was cleped° faire damoisele Pertelote: *called*
Curteis she was, discreet, and debonaire,°   *meek*
And compaignable,° and bar° hirself so faire,   *companionable/bore*
Sin thilke day that she was seven night old,
That trewely she hath the herte in hold
55 Of Chauntecleer, loken° in every lith.°   *locked/limb*
He loved hire so that wel was him therwith.[2]
But swich a joye was it to heere hem singe,
Whan that the brighte sonne gan to springe,
In sweete accord *My Lief is Faren in Londe*[3]—
60 For thilke time, as I have understonde,
Beestes and briddes couden speke and singe.
    And so bifel that in a daweninge,
As Chauntecleer among his wives alle
Sat on his perche that was in the halle,
65 And next him sat this faire Pertelote,
This Chauntecleer gan gronen in his throte,
As man that in his dreem is drecched° sore.   *troubled*
    And whan that Pertelote thus herde him rore,°   *roar*
She was agast, and saide, "Herte dere,
70 What aileth you to grone in this manere?
Ye been a verray slepere,[4] fy, for shame!"
    And he answerde and saide thus, "Madame,
I praye you that ye take it nat agrief.°   *amiss*
By God, me mette I was in swich meschief[5]
75 Right now, that yit myn herte is sore afright.
Now God," quod he, "my swevene recche aright,[6]
And keepe my body out of foul prisoun!
Me mette° how that I romed up and down   *dreamed*
Within oure yeerd, wher as I sawgh a beest,
80 Was lik an hound and wolde han maad arrest[7]

8. I.e., he knew by instinct each step in the progression of the celestial equator. The celestial
equator was thought to make a 360° rotation
around the earth every twenty-four hours;
therefore, a progression of 15° would be equal to
the passage of an hour (line 37).
9. Blue (lapis lazuli).
1. His sisters and his mistresses.

2. That he was well contented.
3. "My Love Has Gone Away," a popular song of
the time.
4. Sound sleeper.
5. I dreamed that I was in such misfortune.
6. Interpret my dream correctly (i.e., in an auspicious manner).
7. Would have laid hold.

Upon my body, and han had me deed.[8]
His colour was bitwixe yelow and reed,
And tipped was his tail and bothe his eres
With blak, unlik the remenant° of his heres;°   *rest/hairs*
85   His snoute smal, with glowing yën twaye.
Yit of his look for fere almost I deye:°   *die*
This caused me my groning, doutelees."
     "Avoi,"° quod she, "fy on you, hertelees!°   *fie/coward*
Allas," quod she, "for by that God above,
90   Now han ye lost myn herte and al my love!
I can nat love a coward, by my faith.
For certes, what so any womman saith,
We alle desiren, if it mighte be,
To han housbondes hardy, wise, and free,°   *generous*
95   And secree,° and no nigard, ne no fool,   *discreet*
Ne him that is agast of every tool,°   *weapon*
Ne noon avauntour.° By that God above,   *boaster*
How dorste° ye sayn for shame unto youre love   *dare*
That any thing mighte make you aferd?
100 Have ye no mannes herte and han a beerd?°   *beard*
Allas, and conne° ye been agast of swevenes?°   *can/dreams*
No thing, God woot, but vanitee[9] in swevene is!
Swevenes engendren of replexiouns,[1]
And ofte of fume° and of complexiouns,°   *gas/bodily humors*
105 Whan humours been too habundant in a wight.[2]
Certes, this dreem which ye han met° tonight   *dreamed*
Comth of the grete superfluitee
Of youre rede colera,[3] pardee,
Which causeth folk to dreden° in hir dremes   *fear*
110 Of arwes,° and of fir with rede lemes,°   *arrows/flames*
Of rede beestes, that they wol hem bite,
Of contek,° and of whelpes grete and lite[4]—   *strife*
Right° as the humour of malencolye[5]   *just*
Causeth ful many a man in sleep to crye
115 For fere of blake beres° or boles° blake,   *bears/bulls*
Or elles blake develes wol hem take.
Of othere humours coude I tell also
That werken many a man in sleep ful wo,
But I wol passe as lightly° as I can.   *quickly*
120 Lo, Caton,[6] which that was so wis a man,
Saide he nat thus? 'Ne do no fors of[7] dremes.'
Now, sire," quod she, "whan we flee fro the bemes,[8]
For Goddes love, as take som laxatif.
Up° peril of my soule and of my lif,   *upon*
125 I conseile you the beste, I wol nat lie,

8. I.e., killed me.
9. I.e., empty illusion.
1. Dreams have their origin in overeating.
2. I.e., when humors (bodily fluids) are too abundant in a person. Pertelote's diagnosis is based on the familiar concept that an excess of one of the bodily humors in a person affected his or her temperament (see p. 188, n. 8).
3. Red bile.
4. And of big and little dogs.
5. I.e., black bile.
6. Dionysius Cato, supposed author of a book of maxims used in elementary education.
7. Pay no attention to.
8. Fly down from the rafters.

That bothe of colere and of malencolye
Ye purge you; and for° ye shal nat tarye,   *in order that*
Though in this town is noon apothecarye,
I shal myself to herbes techen you,
130 That shal been for youre hele° and for youre prow,°   *health/benefit*
And in oure yeerd tho° herbes shal I finde,   *those*
The whiche han of hir propretee by kinde°   *nature*
To purge you binethe and eek above.
Foryet° nat this, for Goddes owene love.   *forget*
135 Ye been ful colerik° of complexioun;   *bilious*
Ware° the sonne in his ascencioun   *beware that*
Ne finde you nat repleet° of humours hote;°   *filled/hot*
And if it do, I dar wel laye° a grote   *bet*
That ye shul have a fevere terciane,[9]
140 Or an agu° that may be youre bane.°   *ague/death*
A day or two ye shul han digestives
Of wormes, er° ye take youre laxatives   *before*
Of lauriol, centaure, and fumetere,[1]
Or elles of ellebor° that groweth there,   *hellebore*
145 Of catapuce, or of gaitres beries,[2]
Of herb-ive° growing in oure yeerd ther merye is[3]—   *herb ivy*
Pekke hem right up as they growe and ete hem in.
Be merye, housbonde, for youre fader° kin!   *father's*
Dredeth no dreem: I can saye you namore."
150   "Madame," quod he, "graunt mercy of youre lore,[4]
But nathelees, as touching daun° Catoun,   *master*
That hath of wisdom swich a greet renown,
Though that he bad no dremes for to drede,
By God, men may in olde bookes rede
155 Of many a man more of auctoritee°   *authority*
Than evere Caton was, so mote I thee,°   *prosper*
That al the revers sayn of his sentence,°   *opinion*
And han wel founden by experience
That dremes been significaciouns
160 As wel of joye as tribulaciouns
That folk enduren in this lif present.
Ther needeth make of this noon argument:
The verray preve[5] sheweth it in deede.
    "Oon of the gretteste auctour[6] that men rede
165 Saith thus, that whilom two felawes wente
On pilgrimage in a ful good entente,
And happed so they comen in a town,
Wher as ther was swich congregacioun
Of peple, and eek so strait of herbergage,[7]
170 That they ne founde as muche as oo cotage
In which they bothe mighte ylogged° be;   *lodged*
Wherfore they mosten° of necessitee   *must*

9. Tertian (recurring every other day).
1. Of laureole, centaury, and fumitory. These, and
the herbs mentioned in the next lines, were all
common medieval medicines used as cathartics.
2. Of caper berry or of gaiter berry.
3. Where it is pleasant.

4. Many thanks for your instruction.
5. Actual experience.
6. I.e., one of the greatest authors (perhaps Cicero
or Valerius Maximus).
7. And also such a shortage of lodging.

As for that night departe° compaignye.　　　　　*part*
And eech of hem gooth to his hostelrye,
175　And took his logging as it wolde falle.°　　　*befall*
That oon of hem was logged in a stalle,
Fer° in a yeerd, with oxen of the plough;　　　*far away*
That other man was logged wel ynough,
As was his aventure° or his fortune,　　　　*lot*
180　That us governeth alle as in commune.
And so bifel that longe er it were day,
This man mette° in his bed, ther as he lay,　　*dreamed*
How that his felawe gan upon him calle,
And saide, 'Allas, for in an oxes stalle
185　This night I shal be mordred° ther I lie!　　*murdered*
Now help me, dere brother, or I die!
In alle haste com to me,' he saide.
　　"This man out of his sleep for fere abraide,°　*started up*
But whan that he was wakened of his sleep,
190　He turned him and took of this no keep:°　*heed*
Him thoughte his dreem nas but a vanitee.°　*illusion*
Thus twies in his sleeping dremed he,
And atte thridde time yit his felawe
Cam, as him thoughte, and saide, 'I am now slawe:°　*slain*
195　Bihold my bloody woundes deepe and wide.
Aris up erly in the morwe tide,[8]
And atte west gate of the town,' quod he,
'A carte ful of dong° ther shaltou see,　　*dung*
In which my body is hid ful prively:
200　Do thilke carte arresten boldely.[9]
My gold caused my mordre, sooth to sayn'
—And tolde him every point how he was slain,
With a ful pitous face, pale of hewe.
And truste wel, his dreem he foond° ful trewe,　*found*
205　For on the morwe° as soone as it was day,　*morning*
To his felawes in° he took the way,　　*lodging*
And whan that he cam to this oxes stalle,
After his felawe he bigan to calle.
　　"The hostiler° answerde him anoon,　　*innkeeper*
210　And saide, 'Sire, youre felawe is agoon:°　*gone away*
As soone as day he wente out of the town.'
　　"This man gan fallen in suspecioun,
Remembring on his dremes that he mette;°　*dreamed*
And forth he gooth, no lenger wolde he lette,°　*tarry*
215　Unto the west gate of the town, and foond
A dong carte, wente as it were to donge° lond,　*put manure on*
That was arrayed in that same wise
As ye han herd the dede° man devise;　　*dead*
And with an hardy herte he gan to crye,
220　'Vengeance and justice of this felonye!
My felawe mordred is this same night,
And in this carte he lith° gaping upright!°　*lies/on his back*
I crye out on the ministres,' quod he,

---

8. In the morning.　　　　　9. Boldly have this same cart seized.

'That sholde keepe and rulen this citee.
225 Harrow,° allas, here lith my felawe slain!'   *help*
What sholde I more unto this tale sayn?
The peple up sterte° and caste the carte to grounde,   *started*
And in the middel of the dong they founde
The dede man that mordred was al newe.[1]
230   "O blisful God that art so just and trewe,
Lo, how that thou biwrayest° mordre alway!   *disclose*
Mordre wol out, that see we day by day:
Mordre is so wlatsom° and abhominable   *loathsome*
To God that is so just and resonable,
235 That he ne wol nat suffre it heled° be,   *concealed*
Though it abide a yeer or two or three.
Mordre wol out: this my conclusioun.
And right anoon ministres of that town
Han hent° the cartere and so sore him pined,[2]   *seized*
240 And eek the hostiler so sore engined,°   *racked*
That they biknewe° hir wikkednesse anoon,   *confessed*
And were anhanged° by the nekke boon.   *hanged*
Here may men seen that dremes been to drede.[3]
      "And certes, in the same book I rede—
245 Right in the nexte chapitre after this—
I gabbe° nat, so have I joye or blis—   *lie*
Two men that wolde han passed over see
For certain cause into a fer contree,
If that the wind ne hadde been contrarye
250 That made hem in a citee for to tarye,
That stood ful merye upon an haven° side—   *harbor's*
But on a day again° the even-tide   *toward*
The wind gan chaunge, and blewe right as hem leste:[4]
Jolif° and glad they wenten unto reste,   *merry*
255 And casten° hem ful erly for to saile.   *determined*
      "But to that oo man fil° a greet mervaile;   *befell*
That oon of hem, in sleeping as he lay,
Him mette[5] a wonder dreem again the day:
Him thoughte a man stood by his beddes side,
260 And him comanded that he sholde abide,
And saide him thus, 'If thou tomorwe wende,
Thou shalt be dreint:° my tale is at an ende.'   *drowned*
      "He wook and tolde his felawe what he mette,
And prayed him his viage° to lette;°   *voyage/delay*
265 As for that day he prayed him to bide.
      "His felawe that lay by his beddes side
Gan for to laughe, and scorned him ful faste.°   *hard*
'No dreem,' quod he, 'may so myn herte agaste°   *terrify*
That I wol lette for to do my thinges.°   *business*
270 I sette nat a straw by thy dreminges,[6]
For swevenes been but vanitees and japes:[7]
Men dreme alday° of owles or of apes,[8]   *constantly*

---

1. Recently.   5. He dreamed.
2. Tortured.   6. I don't care a straw for your dreamings.
3. Worthy of being feared.   7. Dreams are but illusions and frauds.
4. Just as they wished.   8. I.e., of absurdities.

And of many a maze° therwithal—— *delusion*
Men dreme of thing that nevere was ne shal.[9]
275 But sith I see that thou wolt here abide,
And thus forsleuthen° wilfully thy tide,° *waste/time*
God woot, it reweth me;[1] and have good day.'
And thus he took his leve and wente his way.
But er that he hadde half his cours ysailed——
280 Noot I nat why ne what meschaunce it ailed——
But casuelly the shippes botme rente,[2]
And ship and man under the water wente,
In sighte of othere shippes it biside,
That with hem sailed at the same tide.
285 And therfore, faire Pertelote so dere,
By swiche ensamples olde maistou lere° *learn*
That no man sholde been too recchelees° *careless*
Of dremes, for I saye thee doutelees
That many a dreem ful sore is for to drede.
290   "Lo, in the lif of Saint Kenelm[3] I rede——
That was Kenulphus sone, the noble king
Of Mercenrike°——how Kenelm mette a thing *Mercia*
A lite° er he was mordred on a day. *little*
His mordre in his avision° he sey.° *dream/saw*
295 His norice° him expounded everydeel° *nurse/every bit*
His swevene, and bad him for to keepe him[4] weel
For traison, but he nas but seven yeer old,
And therfore litel tale hath he told
Of any dreem,[5] so holy was his herte.
300 By God, I hadde levere than my sherte[6]
That ye hadde rad° his legende as have I. *read*
  "Dame Pertelote, I saye you trewely,
Macrobeus,[7] that writ the *Avisioun*
In Affrike of the worthy Scipioun,
305 Affermeth° dremes, and saith that they been *confirms*
Warning of thinges that men after seen.
  "And ferthermore, I praye you looketh wel
In the Olde Testament of Daniel,
If he heeld° dremes any vanitee.[8] *considered*
310   "Rede eek of Joseph[9] and ther shul ye see
Wher° dremes be somtime—I saye nat alle— *whether*
Warning of thinges that shul after falle.
  "Looke of Egypte the king daun Pharao,
His bakere and his botelere° also, *butler*
315 Wher they ne felte noon effect in dremes.[1]
Whoso wol seeke actes of sondry remes° *realms*
May rede of dremes many a wonder thing.

---

9. I.e., shall be.
1. I'm sorry.
2. I don't know why nor what was the trouble with it—but accidentally the ship's bottom split.
3. Kenelm succeeded his father as king of Mercia at the age of seven, but was slain by his aunt (in 821).
4. Guard himself.
5. Therefore he has set little store by any dream.

6. I.e., I'd give my shirt.
7. Macrobius wrote a famous commentary on Cicero's account in *De Republica* of the dream of Scipio Africanus Minor; the commentary came to be regarded as a standard authority on dream lore.
8. See Daniel 7.
9. See Genesis 37.
1. See Genesis 39–41.

   "Lo Cresus, which that was of Lyde° king,   *Lydia*
   Mette° he nat that he sat upon a tree,   *dreamed*
320 Which signified he sholde anhanged° be?   *hanged*
   "Lo here Andromacha, Ectores° wif,   *Hector's*
   That day that Ector sholde lese° his lif,   *lose*
   She dremed on the same night biforn
   How that the lif of Ector sholde be lorn,°   *lost*
325 If thilke° day he wente into bataile;   *that same*
   She warned him, but it mighte nat availe:°   *do any good*
   He wente for to fighte nathelees,
   But he was slain anoon° of Achilles.   *right away*
   But thilke tale is al too long to telle,
330 And eek it is neigh day, I may nat dwelle.
   Shortly I saye, as for conclusioun,
   That I shal han of this avisioun[2]
   Adversitee, and I saye ferthermoor
   That I ne telle of[3] laxatives no stoor,
335 For they been venimes,° I woot it weel: *poisons*
   I hem defye, I love hem neveradeel.°   *not a bit*
   "Now lat us speke of mirthe and stinte° al this.   *stop*
   Madame Pertelote, so have I blis,
   Of oo thing God hath sente me large grace:
340 For whan I see the beautee of youre face—
   Ye been so scarlet reed° aboute youre yën—   *red*
   It maketh al my drede for to dien.
   For also siker° as *In principio*,[4]   *certain*
   Mulier est hominis confusio.[5]
345 Madame, the sentence° of this Latin is,   *meaning*
   'Womman is mannes joye and al his blis.'
   For whan I feele anight youre softe side—
   Al be it that I may nat on you ride,
   For that oure perche is maad so narwe, allas—
350 I am so ful of joye and of solas°   *delight*
   That I defye bothe swevene and dreem."
   And with that word he fleigh° down fro the beem,   *flew*
   For it was day, and eek his hennes alle,
   And with a "chuk" he gan hem for to calle,
355 For he hadde founde a corn lay in the yeerd.
   Real° he was, he was namore aferd:°   *regal / afraid*
   He fethered[6] Pertelote twenty time,
   And trad hire as ofte er it was prime.[7]
   He looketh as it were a grim leoun,
360 And on his toes he rometh up and down:
   Him deined[8] nat to sette his foot to grounde.
   He chukketh whan he hath a corn yfounde,
   And to him rennen° thanne his wives alle.   *run*
   Thus royal, as a prince is in his halle,

2. Divinely inspired dream (as opposed to the more ordinary "swevene" or "dreem").
3. Set by.
4. Beginning of the Gospel of St. John that gives the essential premises of Christianity: "In the beginning was the Word."
5. Woman is man's ruination.
6. I.e., embraced.
7. 9 A.M. "Trad": trod, copulated with.
8. He deigned.

365 Leve I this Chauntecleer in his pasture,
And after wol I telle his aventure.
     Whan that the month in which the world bigan,
That highte° March, whan God first maked man,   *is called*
Was compleet, and passed were also,
370 Sin March biran,° thritty days and two,[9]   *passed by*
Bifel that Chauntecleer in al his pride,
His sevene wives walking him biside,
Caste up his yën to the brighte sonne,
That in the signe of Taurus hadde yronne
375 Twenty degrees and oon and somwhat more,
And knew by kinde,° and by noon other lore,   *nature*
That it was prime, and crew with blisful stevene.°   *voice*
"The sonne," he saide, "is clomben[1] up on hevene
Fourty degrees and oon and more, ywis.°   *indeed*
380 Madame Pertelote, my worldes blis,
Herkneth thise blisful briddes° how they singe,   *birds*
And see the fresshe flowers how they springe:
Ful is myn herte of revel and solas."
But sodeinly him fil° a sorweful cas,°   *befell / chance*
385 For evere the latter ende of joye is wo—
God woot that worldly joye is soone ago,
And if a rethor° coude faire endite,   *rhetorician*
He in a cronicle saufly° mighte it write,   *safely*
As for a soverein notabilitee.[2]
390 Now every wis man lat him herkne me:
This storye is also° trewe, I undertake,   *as*
As is the book of *Launcelot de Lake*,[3]
That wommen holde in ful greet reverence.
Now wol I turne again to my sentence.°   *main point*
395   A colfox[4] ful of sly iniquitee,
That in the grove hadde woned° yeres three,   *dwelled*
By heigh imaginacion forncast,[5]
The same night thurghout the hegges° brast°   *hedges / burst*
Into the yeerd ther Chauntecleer the faire
400 Was wont, and eek his wives, to repaire;
And in a bed of wortes° stille he lay   *cabbages*
Til it was passed undren° of the day,   *midmorning*
Waiting his time on Chauntecleer to falle,
As gladly doon thise homicides alle,
405 That in await liggen to mordre[6] men.
O false mordrour, lurking in thy den!
O newe Scariot! Newe Geniloun![7]
False dissimilour!° O Greek Sinoun,[8]   *dissembler*
That broughtest Troye al outrely° to sorwe!   *utterly*

---

9. The rhetorical time telling yields the date May 3.
1. Has climbed.
2. Indisputable fact.
3. Romances of the courteous knight Lancelot of the Lake were very popular.
4. Fox with black markings.
5. Predestined by divine planning.

6. That lie in ambush to murder.
7. I.e., Ganelon, who betrayed Roland to the Saracens (in the medieval French epic *The Song of Roland*). "Scariot": Judas Iscariot.
8. Sinon, who persuaded the Trojans to take the Greeks' wooden horse into their city—with, of course, the result that the city was destroyed.

410 O Chauntecleer, accursed be that morwe°　　　　　　　*morning*
　　That thou into the yeerd flaugh° fro the bemes!　　　　*flew*
　　Thou were ful wel ywarned by thy dremes
　　That thilke day was perilous to thee;
　　But what that God forwoot° moot° needes be,　　　　*foreknows / must*
415 After° the opinion of certain clerkes:　　　　　　　*according to*
　　Witnesse on him that any parfit° clerk is　　　　　*perfect*
　　That in scole is greet altercacioun
　　In this matere, and greet disputisoun,°　　　　　　*disputation*
　　And hath been of an hundred thousand men.
420 But I ne can nat bulte it to the bren,⁹
　　As can the holy doctour Augustin,
　　Or Boece, or the bisshop Bradwardin¹—
　　Wheither that Goddes worthy forwiting°　　　　　*foreknowledge*
　　Straineth me nedely² for to doon a thing
425 ("Nedely" clepe I simple necessitee),
　　Or elles if free chois be graunted me
　　To do that same thing or do it naught,
　　Though God forwoot° it er that I was wrought;　　　*foreknew*
　　Or if his witing° straineth neveradeel,　　　　　*knowledge*
430 But by necessitee condicionel³—
　　I wol nat han to do of swich matere:
　　My tale is of a cok, as ye may heere,
　　That took his conseil of his wif with sorwe,
　　To walken in the yeerd upon that morwe
435 That he hadde met° the dreem that I you tolde.　　　*dreamed*
　　Wommenes conseils been ful ofte colde,⁴
　　Wommanes conseil broughte us first to wo,
　　And made Adam fro Paradis to go,
　　Ther as he was ful merye and wel at ese.
440 But for I noot° to whom it mighte displese　　　　*don't know*
　　If I conseil of wommen wolde blame,
　　Passe over, for I saide it in my game°—　　　　　*sport*
　　Rede auctours where they trete of swich matere,
　　And what they sayn of wommen ye may heere—
445 Thise been the cokkes wordes and nat mine:
　　I can noon harm of no womman divine.°　　　　　*guess*
　　　　Faire in the sond° to bathe hire merily　　　　*sand*
　　Lith° Pertelote, and alle hir sustres by,　　　　*lies*
　　Again° the sonne, and Chauntecleer so free°　　*in / noble*
450 Soong° merier than the mermaide in the see—　　*sang*
　　For Physiologus⁵ saith sikerly
　　How that they singen wel and merily.
　　　　And so bifel that as he caste his yë
　　Among the wortes on a boterflye,°　　　　　　*butterfly*

455 He was war of this fox that lay ful lowe.
No thing ne liste him[6] thanne for to crowe,
But cride anoon "Cok cok!" and up he sterte,°   *started*
As man that[7] was affrayed in his herte—
For naturelly a beest desireth flee
460 Fro his contrarye[8] if he may it see,
Though he nevere erst° hadde seen it with his yë.   *before*
This Chauntecleer, whan he gan him espye,
He wolde han fled, but that the fox anoon
Saide, "Gentil sire, allas, wher wol ye goon?
465 Be ye afraid of me that am youre freend?
Now certes, I were worse than a feend
If I to you wolde° harm or vilainye.   *meant*
I am nat come youre conseil° for t'espye,   *secrets*
But trewely the cause of my cominge
470 Was only for to herkne how ye singe:
For trewely, ye han as merye a stevene°   *voice*
As any angel hath that is in hevene.
Therwith ye han in musik more feelinge
Than hadde Boece,[9] or any that can singe.
475 My lord your fader—God his soule blesse!—
And eek youre moder, of hir gentilesse,°   *gentility*
Han in myn hous ybeen, to my grete ese.
And certes sire, ful fain° wolde I you plese.   *gladly*
"But for men speke of singing, I wol saye,
480 So mote I brouke[1] wel mine yën twaye,
Save ye, I herde nevere man to singe
As dide youre fader in the morweninge.
Certes, it was of herte° al that he soong.°   *heartfelt / sang*
And for to make his vois the more strong,
485 He wolde so paine him[2] that with bothe his yën
He moste winke,[3] so loude wolde he cryen;
And stonden on his tiptoon therwithal,
And strecche forth his nekke long and smal;
And eek he was of swich discrecioun
490 That ther nas no man in no regioun
That him in song or wisdom mighte passe.
I have wel rad° in *Daun Burnel the Asse*[4]   *read*
Among his vers how that ther was a cok,
For a preestes sone yaf him a knok[5]
495 Upon his leg whil he was yong and nice,°   *foolish*
He made him for to lese° his benefice.[6]   *lose*
But certain, ther nis no comparisoun
Bitwixe the wisdom and discrecioun
Of youre fader and of his subtiltee.[7]

6. He wished.
7. Like one who.
8. I.e., his natural enemy.
9. Boethius also wrote a treatise on music.
1. So might I enjoy the use of.
2. Take pains.
3. He had to shut his eyes.
4. Master Brunellus, a discontented donkey, was
the hero of a 12th-century satirical poem by Nigel
Wireker.
5. Because a priest's son gave him a knock.
6. The offended cock neglected to crow so that his
master, now grown to manhood, overslept, missing
his ordination and losing his benefice.
7. His (the cock in the story) cleverness.

500	Now singeth, sire, for sainte° charitee!	*holy*
	Lat see, conne° ye youre fader countrefete?"°	*can/imitate*
	This Chauntecleer his winges gan to bete,	
	As man that coude his traison nat espye,	
	So was he ravisshed with his flaterye.	
505	Allas, ye lordes, many a fals flatour°	*flatterer*
	Is in youre court, and many a losengeour°	*deceiver*
	That plesen you wel more, by my faith,	
	Than he that soothfastnesse° unto you saith!	*truth*
	Redeth Ecclesiaste[8] of flaterye.	
510	Beeth war, ye lordes, of hir trecherye.	
	This Chauntecleer stood hye upon his toos,	
	Strecching his nekke, and heeld his yën cloos,	
	And gan to crowe loude for the nones;°	*occasion*
	And daun Russel the fox sterte° up atones,	*jumped*
515	And by the gargat° hente° Chauntecleer,	*throat/seized*
	And on his bak toward the wode him beer,°	*bore*
	For yit ne was ther no man that him sued.°	*followed*
	O destinee that maist nat been eschued!°	*eschewed*
	Allas that Chauntecleer fleigh° fro the bemes!	*flew*
520	Allas his wif ne roughte nat of[9] dremes!	
	And on a Friday fil° al this meschaunce!	*befell*
	O Venus that art goddesse of plesaunce,	
	Sin that thy servant was this Chauntecleer,	
	And in thy service dide al his power—	
525	More for delit than world[1] to multiplye—	
	Why woldestou suffre him on thy day[2] to die?	
	O Gaufred,[3] dere maister soverein,	
	That, whan thy worthy king Richard was slain	
	With shot,[4] complainedest his deeth so sore,	
530	Why ne hadde I now thy sentence and thy lore,[5]	
	The Friday for to chide as diden ye?	
	For on a Friday soothly slain was he.	
	Thanne wolde I shewe you how that I coude plaine°	*lament*
	For Chauntecleres drede and for his paine.	
535	Certes, swich cry ne lamentacioun	
	Was nevere of ladies maad when Ilioun°	*Ilium, Troy*
	Was wonne, and Pyrrus[6] with his straite° swerd,	*drawn*
	Whan he hadde hent° King Priam by the beerd	*seized*
	And slain him, as saith us *Eneidos*,[7]	
540	As maden alle the hennes in the cloos,°	*yard*
	Whan they hadde seen of Chauntecleer the sighte.	
	But sovereinly° Dame Pertelote shrighte°	*supremely/shrieked*
	Ful louder than dide Hasdrubales[8] wif	
	Whan that hir housbonde hadde lost his lif,	

---

8. The Book of Ecclesiasticus, in the Apocrypha.
9. Didn't care for.
1. I.e., population.
2. Friday is Venus's day.
3. Geoffrey of Vinsauf, a famous medieval rhetorician, who wrote a lament on the death of Richard I in which he scolded Friday, the day on which the king died.

4. I.e., a missile.
5. Thy wisdom and thy learning.
6. Pyrrhus was the Greek who slew Priam, king of Troy.
7. As the *Aeneid* tells us.
8. Hasdrubal was king of Carthage when it was destroyed by the Romans.

545 And that the Romains hadden brend° Cartage: *burned*
    She was so ful of torment and of rage°   *madness*
    That wilfully unto the fir she sterte,°   *jumped*
    And brende hirselven with a stedefast herte.
      O woful hennes, right so criden ye
550 As, whan that Nero brende the citee
    Of Rome, criden senatoures wives
    For that hir housbondes losten alle hir lives:[9]
    Withouten gilt this Nero hath hem slain.
    Now wol I turne to my tale again.
555   The sely° widwe and eek hir doughtres two   *innocent*
    Herden thise hennes crye and maken wo,
    And out at dores sterten° they anoon,   *leapt*
    And sien° the fox toward the grove goon,   *saw*
    And bar upon his bak the cok away,
560 And criden, "Out, harrow,° and wailaway,   *help*
    Ha, ha, the fox," and after him they ran,
    And eek with staves many another man;
    Ran Colle oure dogge, and Talbot and Gerland,[1]
    And Malkin with a distaf in hir hand,
565 Ran cow and calf, and eek the verray hogges,
    Sore aferd° for berking of the dogges   *frightened*
    And shouting of the men and wommen eke.
    They ronne° so hem thoughte hir herte breke;[2]   *ran*
    They yelleden as feendes doon in helle;
570 The dokes° criden as men wolde hem quelle;°   *ducks/kill*
    The gees for fere flowen° over the trees;   *flew*
    Out of the hive cam the swarm of bees;
    So hidous was the noise, a, benedicite,°   *bless me*
    Certes, he Jakke Straw[3] and his meinee°   *company*
575 Ne made nevere shoutes half so shrille
    Whan that they wolden any Fleming kille,
    As thilke day was maad upon the fox:
    Of bras they broughten bemes° and of box,°   *trumpets/boxwood*
    Of horn, of boon,° in whiche they blewe and pouped,°   *bone/tooted*
580 And therwithal they skriked° and they houped°—   *shrieked/whooped*
    It seemed as that hevene sholde falle.
      Now goode men, I praye you herkneth alle:
    Lo, how Fortune turneth° sodeinly   *reverses, overturns*
    The hope and pride eek of hir enemy.
585 This cok that lay upon the foxes bak,
    In al his drede unto the fox he spak,
    And saide, "Sire, if that I were as ye,
    Yit sholde I sayn, as wis° God helpe me,   *surely*
    'Turneth ayain, ye proude cherles alle!
590 A verray pestilence upon you falle!
    Now am I come unto this wodes side,
    Maugree your heed,[4] the cok shal here abide.

---

9. According to the legend, Nero not only set fire to Rome (in 64 C.E.) but also put many senators to death.
1. Two other dogs.
2. Would break.

3. One of the leaders of the Uprising of 1381, which was partially directed against the Flemings living in London.
4. Despite your head—i.e., despite anything you can do.

I wol him ete, in faith, and that anoon.' "
  The fox answerde, "In faith, it shal be doon."
595 And as he spak that word, al sodeinly
  The cok brak from his mouth deliverly,°   *nimbly*
  And hye upon a tree he fleigh° anoon.   *flew*
    And whan the fox sawgh that he was agoon,
  "Allas," quod he, "O Chauntecleer, allas!
600 I have to you," quod he, "ydoon trespas,
  In as muche as I maked you aferd
  Whan I you hente° and broughte out of the yeerd.   *seized*
  But sire, I dide it in no wikke° entente: *wicked*
  Come down, and I shal telle you what I mente.
605 I shal saye sooth to you, God help me so."
    "Nay thanne," quod he, "I shrewe° us bothe two: *curse*
  But first I shrewe myself, bothe blood and bones,
  If thou bigile me ofter than ones;
  Thou shalt namore thurgh thy flaterye
610 Do° me to singe and winken with myn yëe.   *cause*
  For he that winketh whan he sholde see,
  Al wilfully, God lat him nevere thee."°   *prosper*
    "Nay," quod the fox, "but God yive him meschaunce
  That is so undiscreet of governaunce°   *self-control*
615 That jangleth° whan he sholde holde his pees."   *chatters*
    Lo, swich it is for to be reccheless°   *careless*
  And necligent and truste on flaterye.
  But ye that holden this tale a folye
  As of a fox, or of a cok and hen,
620 Taketh the moralitee, goode men.
  For Saint Paul saith that al that writen is
  To oure doctrine it is ywrit, ywis:[5]
  Taketh the fruit, and lat the chaf be stille.[6]
  Now goode God, if that it be thy wille,
625 As saith my lord, so make us alle goode men,
  And bringe us to his hye blisse. Amen.

Close of *Canterbury Tales*

At the end of *The Canterbury Tales*, Chaucer invokes a common allegorical theme, that life on earth is a pilgrimage. As Chaucer puts it in his moral ballade *Truth*, "Here in noon home . . . / Forth, pilgrim, forth!" In the final fragment, he makes explicit a metaphor that has been implicit all along in the journey to Canterbury. The pilgrims never arrive at the shrine of St. Thomas, but in *The Parson's Tale*, and in its short introduction and in the "Retraction" that follows it, Chaucer seems to be making an end for two pilgrimages that had become one, that of his fiction and that of his life.

In the introduction to the tale we find the twenty-nine pilgrims moving through a nameless little village as the sun sinks to within twenty-nine degrees of the horizon. The atmosphere contains something of both the chill and the urgency of a late autumn afternoon, and we are surprised to find that the pilgrimage is almost over,

---

5. See Romans 15.4.
6. The "fruit" refers to the kernel of moral or doctrinal meaning; the "chaf," or husk, is the narrative containing that meaning. The metaphor was commonly applied to scriptural interpretation.

that there is need for haste to make that "good end" that every medieval Christian hoped for. This delicately suggestive passage, rich with allegorical overtones, introduces an extremely long penitential treatise, translated by Chaucer from Latin or French sources. Although often assumed to be an earlier work, it may well have been written by Chaucer to provide the ending for *The Canterbury Tales*.

In the "Retraction" that follows *The Parson's Tale*, Chaucer acknowledges, lists, revokes, and asks forgiveness for his "giltes" (that is, his sins), which consist of having written most of the works on which his reputation as a great poet depends. He thanks Christ and Mary for his religious and moral works. One need not take this as evidence of a spiritual crisis or conversion at the end of his life. The "Retraction" seems to have been written to appear at the end of *The Canterbury Tales*, without censoring any of the tales deemed to be sinful. At the same time, one need not question Chaucer's sincerity. A readiness to deny his own reality before the reality of his God is implicit in many of Chaucer's works, and the placement of the "Retraction" within or just outside the border of the fictional pilgrimage suggests that although Chaucer finally rejected his fictions, he recognized that he and they were inseparable.

From The Parson's Tale

The Introduction

By that[1] the Manciple hadde his tale al ended,
The sonne fro the south line[2] was descended
So lowe, that he has nat to my sighte
Degrees nine and twenty as in highte.
5   Four of the clokke it was, so as I gesse,
For elevene foot, or litel more or lesse,
My shadwe was at thilke time as there,
Of swich feet as° my lengthe parted° were   *as if / divided*
In sixe feet equal of proporcioun.[3]
10 Therwith the moones exaltacioun[4]—
I mene Libra—always gan ascende,
As we were entring at a thropes° ende.   *village's*
For which oure Host, as he was wont to gie°   *lead*
As in this caas oure joly compaignye,
15 Saide in this wise, "Lordinges everichoon,
Now lakketh us no tales mo than oon:
Fulfild is my sentence° and my decree;   *purpose*
I trowe° that we han herd of ech degree;   *believe*
Almost fulfild is al myn ordinaunce.
20 I praye to God, so yive him right good chaunce
That telleth this tale to us lustily.
Sire preest," quod he, "artou a vicary,°   *vicar*
Or arte a Person? Say sooth, by thy fay.°   *faith*
Be what thou be, ne breek° thou nat oure play,   *break*
25 For every man save thou hath told his tale.
Unbokele and shew us what is in thy male!°   *bag*
For trewely, me thinketh by thy cheere°   *expression*
Thou sholdest knitte up wel a greet matere.
Tel us a fable anoon, for cokkes bones!"[5]

1. By the time that.
2. I.e., the line that runs some 28° to the south of the celestial equator and parallel to it.
3. This detailed analysis merely says that the shad-
ows are lengthening.
4. I.e., the astrological sign in which the moon's influence was dominant.
5. Cock's bones, a euphemism for God's bones.

30   This Person answerde al atones,°   *immediately*
    "Thou getest fable noon ytold for me,
    For Paul, that writeth unto Timothee,
    Repreveth° hem that waiven soothfastnesse,[6]   *reproves*
    And tellen fables and swich wrecchednesse.
35   Why sholde I sowen draf° out of my fest,°   *chaff/fist*
    Whan I may sowen whete if that me lest?[7]
    For which I saye that if you list to heere
    Moralitee and vertuous matere,
    And thanne that ye wol yive me audience,
40   I wol ful fain,° at Cristes reverence,   *gladly*
    Do you plesance leveful° as I can.   *lawful*
    But trusteth wel, I am a southren man:
    I can nat geeste Rum-Ram-Ruf by lettre[8]—
    Ne, God woot, rym holde° I but litel bettre.   *consider*
45   And therfore, if you list—I wol nat glose[9]—
    I wol you telle a merye tale in prose
    To knitte up al this feeste and make an ende.
    And Jesu for his grace wit me sende
    To shewe you the way in this viage°   *journey*
50   Of thilke parfit glorious pilgrimage
    That highte° Jerusalem celestial.   *is called*
    And if ye vouche sauf, anoon I shal
    Biginne upon my tale, for which I praye
    Telle youre avis:° I can no bettre saye.   *opinion*
55   But nathelees, this meditacioun
    I putte it ay under correccioun
    Of clerkes, for I am nat textuel:[1]
    I take but the sentence,° trusteth wel.   *meaning*
    Therefore I make protestacioun°   *public acknowledgment*
60   That I wol stonde to correccioun."
      Upon this word we han assented soone,
    For, as it seemed, it was for to doone[2]
    To enden in som vertuous sentence,°   *doctrine*
    And for to yive him space° and audience;   *time*
65   And bede[3] oure Host he sholde to him saye
    That alle we to telle his tale him praye.
      Oure Hoste hadde the wordes for us alle:
    "Sire preest," quod he, "now faire you bifalle:
    Telleth," quod he, "youre meditacioun.
70   But hasteth you; the sonne wol adown.
    Beeth fructuous,° and that in litel space,°   *fruitful/time*
    And to do wel God sende you his grace.
    Saye what you list, and we wol gladly heere."
    And with that word he saide in this manere.

---

6. Depart from truth (see 1 Timothy 1.4).
7. It pleases me.
8. I.e., I cannot tell stories in the alliterative measure (without rhyme): this form of poetry was not common in southeastern England.
9. I.e., speak in order to please.
1. Literal, faithful to the letter.
2. Necessary to be done.
3. I.e., we bade.

Chaucer's Retraction

Here taketh the makere of this book his leve[4]

Now praye I to hem alle that herkne this litel tretis[5] or rede, that if ther be any thing in it that liketh[6] hem, that therof they thanken oure Lord Jesu Crist, of whom proceedeth al wit[7] and al goodnesse. And if ther be any thing that displese hem, I praye hem also that they arrette it to the defaute of myn unconning,[8] and nat to my wil, that wolde ful fain have said bettre if I hadde had conning. For oure book saith, "Al that is writen is writen for oure doctrine,"[9] and that is myn entente. Wherfore I biseeke[1] you mekely, for the mercy of God, that ye praye for me that Crist have mercy on me and foryive me my giltes, and namely of my translacions and enditinges[2] of worldly vanitees, the whiche I revoke in my retraccions: as is the *Book of Troilus;* the Book also of *Fame;* the *Book of the Five and Twenty Ladies;*[3] the *Book of the Duchesse;* the *Book of Saint Valentines Day of the Parlement of Briddes;* the *Tales of Canterbury,* thilke that sounen into[4] sinne; the *Book of the Leon;*[5] and many another book, if they were in my remembrance, and many a song and many a leccherous lay: that Crist for his grete mercy foryive me the sinne. But of the translacion of Boece[6] *De Consolatione,* and othere bookes of legendes of saintes, and omelies,[7] and moralitee, and devocion, that thanke I oure Lord Jesu Crist and his blisful Moder and alle the saintes of hevene, biseeking hem that they from hennes[8] forth unto my lives ende sende me grace to biwaile my giltes and to studye to the salvacion of my soule, and graunte me grace of verray penitence, confession, and satisfaccion to doon in this present lif, thurgh the benigne grace of him that is king of kinges and preest over alle preestes, that boughte[9] us with the precious blood of his herte, so that I may been oon of hem at the day of doom that shulle be saved. *Qui cum patre et Spiritu Sancto vivis et regnas Deus per omnia saecula.*[1] Amen.

1386–1400

4. "Chaucer's Retraction" is the title given to this passage by modern editors. The heading, "*Here . . . leve,*" which does appear in all manuscripts, may be by Chaucer himself or by a scribe.
5. Hear this little treatise, i.e., *The Parson's Tale.*
6. Pleases.
7. Understanding.
8. Ascribe it to the defect of my lack of skill.
9. Romans 15.4.
1. Beseech.

2. Compositions. "Namely": especially.
3. I.e., the *Legend of Good Women.*
4. Those that tend toward.
5. The *Book of the Lion* has not been preserved.
6. Boethius.
7. Homilies.
8. Hence.
9. Redeemed.
1. Who with the Father and the Holy Spirit livest and reignest God forever.

JULIAN OF NORWICH
1342–ca.1416

The "Showings," or "Revelations" as they are also called, were sixteen mystical visions received by the woman known as Julian of Norwich. The name may be one that she adopted when she became an anchoress in a cell attached to the church of St. Julian that still stands in that town on the northeast coast of England. An anchorite (m.) or anchoress (f.) is a religious recluse confined to an enclosure, which he or she has vowed never to leave. At the time of such an enclosing the burial service was performed, signifying that the enclosed person was dead to the world and that the enclosure corresponded to a grave. The point of this confinement was, of course, to pursue more actively the contemplative or spiritual life.

Julian may well have belonged to a religious order at the time that her visions led her to choose the life of an anchoress. We know very little about her except what she tells us in her writings. She is, however, very precise about the date of her visions. They occurred, she tells us, at the age of thirty and a half on May 13, 1373. Four extant wills bequeath sums for Julian's maintenance in her anchorage. The most important document witnessing her life is *The Book of Margery Kempe*. Kempe sought out Julian's advice whether there might be any deception in Kempe's own visions, "for the anchoress," she says, "was expert in such things." Kempe's description of Julian's conversation accords well with the doctrines and personality that emerge from Julian's own book.

A *Book of Showings* survives in a short and a long version. The longer text, from which the following excerpts are taken, was the product of fifteen and more years of meditation on the meaning of the visions in which much had been obscure to Julian. Apparently the mystical experiences were never repeated, but through constant study and contemplation the showings acquired a greater clarity, richness, and profundity as they continued to be turned over in a mind both gifted with spiritual insight and learned in theology. Her editors document her extensive use of the Bible and her familiarity with medieval religious writings in both English and Latin.

Julian's showings are, in her words, both "ghostly" (that is, spiritual) and "bodily." They embrace powerful visual phenomena such as blood drops running from the crown of thorns and revelations that take place in pure mind. The years of meditation on these showings led her ultimately to a personal, profound, and difficult understanding of the Trinity—the one God in the three persons of the father, the son, and the Holy Spirit—and humanity's participation in that oneness. For Julian, God the father generates the human soul (conceived of as immortal "substance," co-eternal with God); God the son is the mother who bears, nourishes, and redeems (through his own incarnation) sensual human nature; God the Holy Spirit binds deity and humanity in eternal love and grace. Julian expresses such sophisticated theological concepts in language that can be intricate in its logic yet at other times transparently simple. She herself is amazed that God, who is so great and awe inspiring, can be so "homely" (so direct, intimate, and familial) with "a sinful creature." The blood of Christ reminds her of water dripping from the eaves of a house and of the scales of herring. Her concept of Jesus as mother has antecedents in both the Old and New Testaments, in medieval theology, and in the writings of medieval mystics (both men and women).

Julian is an accomplished prose stylist, inheriting a tradition of English religious prose that goes back to the Old English period. Her book is one of many distinguished devotional and mystical works, both English and Continental, composed during the late Middle Ages, such as the *Dialogue* of Catherine of Siena (translated into Middle English as *The Orchard of Syon*) or the anonymous *Cloud of Unknowing*. Julian wrote and rewrote *A Book of Showings* to come to terms with her visions, but, like other visionaries, she felt the visions were not only a personal gift but an obligation. "We are all one," she says, "and I am sure I saw it for the profit of many other."

From A Book of Showings to the Anchoress Julian of Norwich[1]

[THE FIRST REVELATION]

And when I was thirty year old and a half, God sent me a bodily sickness in the which I lay three days and three nights; and on the fourth night I took all my rites of holy church, and went[2] not to have liven till day. And after this I lay two days and two nights; and on the third night I weened[3] oftentimes to have passed, and so weened they that were with me. And yet in this I felt a great loathsomeness[4] to die, but for nothing that was on earth that me liketh to live for, ne[5] for no pain that I was afraid of, for I trusted in God of his mercy. But it was for I would have lived to have loved God better and longer time, that I might by the grace of that living have the more knowing and loving of God in the bliss of heaven. For me thought[6] all that time that I had lived here so little and so short in regard of[7] that endless bliss, I thought: Good Lord, may my living no longer be to thy worship?[8] And I understood by my reason and by the feeling of my pains that I should die; and I assented fully with all the will of my heart to be at God's will.

Thus I endured till day, and by then was my body dead from the middes downward, as to my feeling.[9] Then was I holpen[1] to be set upright, underset[2] with help, for to have the more freedom of my heart to be at God's will, and thinking on God while my life lasted. My curate was sent for to be at my ending, and before he came I had set up my eyen[3] and might not speak. He set the cross before my face and said: "I have brought the image of thy savior; look thereupon and comfort thee therewith." Me thought I was well, for my eyen was set upright into heaven, where I trusted to come by the mercy of God; but nevertheless I assented to set my eyen in the face of the crucifix, if I might, and so I did, for me thought I might longer dure to look even forth than right up.[4] After this my sight began to fail. It waxed as dark about me in the chamber as if it had been night, save in the image of the cross, wherein held a common light; and I wist[5] not how. All that was beside the cross was ugly and fearful to me as[6] it had been much occupied with fiends.

After this the over[7] part of my body began to die so farforth that unneth[8] I had any feeling. My most pain was shortness of breath and failing of life. Then went[9] I verily to have passed. And in this suddenly all my pain was taken from me, and I was as whole, and namely in the over part of my body, as ever I was before. I marvelled of this sudden change, for me thought that it was a privy working of God, and not of kind;[1] and yet by feeling of this ease I trusted never more to have lived, ne the feeling of this ease was no full ease to me, for me thought I had liever[2] have been delivered of this world, for my heart was willfully set thereto.

---

1. The text is based on that given by Edmund Colledge, O.S.A., and James Walsh, S. J., for the Pontifical Institute of Mediaeval Studies, Toronto (1978), but it has been freely edited and modern spelling has been used where possible.
2. Thought.
3. Supposed.
4. Reluctance.
5. Nor.
6. I thought, [it] thought me.
7. In comparison with.
8. Glory.

9. As it felt to me.
1. Helped.
2. Supported.
3. Eyes.
4. Endure to look straight ahead than straight up.
5. Knew.
6. As if.
7. Upper.
8. To the extent that scarcely.
9. Thought.
1. Nature.
2. Rather.

Then came suddenly to my mind that I should desire the second wound of our Lord's gift and of his grace, that my body might be fulfilled with mind and feeling of his blessed passion, as I had before prayed,[3] for I would that his pains were my pains, with compassion and afterward longing to God. Thus thought me that I might with his grace have the wounds that I had before desired; but in this I desired never no bodily sight ne no manner showing of God, but compassion as me thought that a kind soul might have with our Lord Jesu, that for love would become a deadly[4] man. With him I desired to suffer, living in my deadly body, as God would give me grace.

And in this suddenly I saw the red blood running down from under the garland, hot and freshly, plenteously and lively, right as it was in the time that the garland of thorns was pressed on his blessed head. Right so, both God and man, the same that suffered for me, I conceived truly and mightily that it was himself that shewed it me without any mean.[5]

And in the same showing suddenly the Trinity fulfilled my heart most of joy, and so I understood it shall be in heaven without end to all that shall come there. For the Trinity is God, God is the Trinity. The Trinity is our maker, the Trinity is our keeper, the Trinity is our everlasting lover, the Trinity is endless joy and our bliss, by our Lord Jesu Christ, and in our Lord Jesu Christ. And this was showed in the first sight and in all, for where Jesu appeareth, the blessed Trinity is understand, as to my sight.[6] And I said, "Benedicite dominus."[7] This I said for reverence in my meaning,[8] with a mighty voice, and full greatly was I astoned[9] for wonder and marvel that I had, that he that is so reverend and so dreadful[1] will be so homely[2] with a sinful creature living in this wretched flesh.

* * *

In this same time that I saw this sight of the head bleeding, our good Lord showed a ghostly sight of his homely loving. I saw that he is to us all thing that is good and comfortable to our help. He is our clothing that for love wrappeth us and windeth us, halseth us[3] and all becloses us, hangeth about us for tender love that[4] he may never leave us. And so in this sight I saw that he is all thing that is good, as to my understanding.

And in this he showed a little thing, the quantity of an hazelnut, lying in the palm of my hand, as me seemed, and it was as round as a ball. I looked thereon with the eye of my understanding, and thought: What may this be? And it was answered generally thus: It is all that is made. I marvelled how it might last, for me thought it might suddenly have fallen to nought for[5] littleness. And I was answered in my understanding: It lasteth and ever shall, for God loveth it; and so hath all thing being by the love of God.

* * *

And in all that time that he showed this that I have now said in ghostly sight, I saw the bodily sight lasting of the plenteous bleeding of the head.

---

3. Julian had prayed for three gifts: direct experience of Christ's passion, mortal sickness, and the wounds of true contrition, loving compassion, and a willed desire for God.
4. Mortal.
5. Intermediary.
6. Is understood, as I see it.
7. Blessed be the Lord.
8. Intention.
9. Astonished.
1. Awe-inspiring.
2. Familiar, intimate (the quality of being "at home").
3. Envelops us and embraces us.
4. So that.
5. Because of.

The great drops of blood fell down fro under the garland like pellets, seeming as it had come out of the veins. And in the coming out they were brown red, for the blood was full thick; and in the spreading abroad they were bright red. And when it came at the brows, there they vanished; and not withstanding the bleeding continued till many things were seen and understanded. Nevertheless the fairhead and livelihead continued in the same beauty and liveliness.

The plenteoushead is like to the drops of water that fall of the evesing[6] of an house after a great shower of rain, that fall so thick that no man may number them with no bodily wit.[7] And for the roundness they were like to the scale of herring in the spreading of the forehead.

[JESUS AS MOTHER]

And thus is Jesu our very[8] mother in kind of our first making, and he is our very mother in grace by taking of our kind made. All the fair working and all the sweet kindly offices of dearworthy motherhood is impropered to[9] the second person, for in him we have this goodly will, whole and safe without end, both in kind and in grace, of his own proper goodness.

I understood three manner of beholdings of motherhood in God. The first is ground of our kind making, the second is taking of our kind, and there beginneth the motherhood of grace, the third is motherhood in working.[1] And therein is a forthspreading[2] by the same grace of length and breadth, of high and of deepness without end. And all is one love.

But now me behooveth to say a little more of this forthspreading, as I understood, in the meaning of our Lord: how that we be brought again by the motherhood of mercy and grace into our kindly stead, where that we were in,[3] made by the motherhood of kind love, which kind love never leaveth us.

Our kind mother, our gracious mother (for he would[4] all wholly become our mother in all thing) he took the ground of his work full low[5] and full mildly in the maiden's womb. And that showed he first, where he brought that meek maiden before the eye of my understanding, in the simple stature as she was when she conceived;[6] that is to say our high god, the sovereign wisdom of all, in this low place he arrayed him and dight him[7] all ready in our poor flesh, himself to do the service, he and the office of motherhood in all thing. The mother's service is nearest, readiest, and surest: nearest for it is most of kind, readiest for it is most of love, and sikerest[8] for it is most of truth. This office ne might nor could never none doon to the full but he alone. We wit[9] that all our mothers bear us to pain and to dying. Ah, what is that? But our very Mother Jesu, he alone beareth us to joy and to endless living, blessed moot[1] he be. Thus he sustaineth us within him in love and travail, into the full time that he would suffer the sharpest thorns and griev-

6. Eaves.
7. Intelligence.
8. True.
9. Appropriated to.
1. At work.
2. (Infinite) spreading out, expansion.
3. The natural condition, i.e., the state of grace, that we were in originally.
4. Because he wanted to.

5. I.e., he laid the groundwork for his mission in a very humble place.
6. The appearance of the Virgin in Julian's first vision.
7. Arrayed and dressed himself.
8. Surest.
9. Know.
1. May.

ous pains that ever were or ever shall be, and died at the last. And when he had done, and so borne us to bliss, yet might not all this make aseeth[2] to his marvelous love. And that showed he in these high overpassing words of love: "If I might suffer more I would suffer more."[3] He might no more die, but he would not stint[4] working.

Wherefore him behooveth to find[5] us, for the dearworthy love of mother-hood hath made him debtor to us.[6] The mother may give her child sucken her milk, but our precious mother Jesu, he may feed us with himself, and doth full courteously and full tenderly with the blessed sacrament, that is precious food of very life; and with all the sweet sacraments he sustaineth us full mercifully and graciously, and so meant he in these blessed words, where he said: "I it am that holy church preacheth thee and teacheth thee." That is to say: All the health and the life of sacraments, all the virtue and the grace of my word, all the goodness that is ordained in holy church to thee, I it am.

The mother may lay her child tenderly to her breast, but our tender mother Jesu, he may homely lead us into his blessed breast by his sweet open side,[7] and show us therein in party of[8] the godhead and the joys of heaven with ghostly sureness of endless bliss. And that showed he in the tenth revelation, giving the same understanding in this sweet word where he sayeth: "Lo, how I love thee."

*　*　*

The mother may suffer the child to fall sometime and be diseased[9] in diverse manner of peril come to her child for love. And though our earthly mother may suffer her child to perish, our heavenly mother Jesu may never suffer us that be his children to perish, for he is all mighty, all wisdom, and all love, and so is none but he, blessed mote he be.

But oft times when our falling and our wretchedness is showed to us, we be so sore adread and so greatly ashamed of ourself that unnethes[1] we wit where that we may hold us. But then will not our courteous mother that we flee away, for him were nothing loather;[2] for then he will that we use[3] the condition of a child. For when it is diseased and afeared, it runneth hastily to the mother; and if it may do no more, it crieth on the mother for help with all the might. So will he that we do as the meek child, saying thus: "My kind mother, my gracious mother, my dearworthy mother, have mercy on me. I have made myself foul and unlike to thee, and I may not nor can amend it but with thine help and grace."

And if we feel us not then eased, as soon be we sure that he useth[4] the condition of a wise mother. For if he see that it be for profit to us to mourn and to weep, he suffereth with ruth[5] and pity, into the best time,[6] for love. And he will then that we use the property of a child that ever more kindly trusteth to the love of the mother in weal and in woe. And he will that we

<hr />

2. Bring satisfaction.
3. These and other quotations refer back to Jul-ian's earlier revelations.
4. Stop.
5. Nourish, feed.
6. As any mother is obligated to look after her child.
7. The wound inflicted by a soldier in John 19.34.

8. A part of.
9. Unhappy.
1. Scarcely.
2. Nothing would be more hateful to him.
3. He wants us to experience.
4. Right away we are sure he is practicing.
5. Compassion.
6. Until the right time.

take us mightily to the faith of holy church and find there our dearworthy mother in solace and true understanding with all the blessed common.[7] For one singular person may oftentimes be broken, as it seemeth to the self, but the whole body of holy church was never broken, nor never shall be without end. And therefore a sure thing it is, a good and a gracious, to willen meekly and mightily been fastened and oned to our mother holy church, that is Christ Jesu. For the flood of his mercy that is his dearworthy blood and precious water is plenteous to make us fair and clean. The blessed wounds of our savior be open and enjoy[8] to heal us. The sweet gracious hands of our mother be ready and diligent about us; for he in all this working useth the very office of a kind nurse that hath not else to do but to entend[9] the salvation of her child.

It is his office to save us, it is his worship to do it, and it is his will we know it; for he will we love him sweetly and trust in him meekly and mightily. And this showed he in these gracious words: "I keep thee full surely."

[CONCLUSION]

This book is begun by God's gift and his grace, but it is not yet performed,[1] as to my sight. For charity, pray we all together with God's working, thanking, trusting, enjoying, for thus will our good Lord be prayed, but the understanding that I took in all his own meaning, and in the sweet words where he sayeth full merrily: "I am ground of thy beseeching." For truly I saw and understood in our Lord's meaning that he showed it for he will have it known more than it is. In which knowing he will give us grace to love him and cleave to him, for he beheld his heavenly treasure with so great love on earth that he will give us more light, and solace in heavenly joy, in drawing of our hearts fro sorrow and darkness which we are in.

And fro the time that it was showed, I desired oftentimes to wit[2] in what was our Lord's meaning. And fifteen year after and more, I was answered in ghostly understanding, saying thus: "What, wouldst thou wit thy Lord's meaning in this thing? Wit it well, love was his meaning. Who showeth it thee? Love. What showed he thee? Love. Wherefore showeth he it thee? For love. Hold thee therein, thou shalt wit more in the same. But thou shalt never wit therein other withouten end."

Thus was I learned,[3] that love is our Lord's meaning. And I saw full surely in this and in all, that ere God made us he loved us, which love was never slaked[4] ne never shall. And in this love he hath done all his works, and in this love he hath made all things profitable to us, and in this love our life is everlasting. In our making we had beginning, but the love wherein he made us was in him fro without beginning. In which love we have our beginning, and all this shall we see in God withouten end.

Deo gracias. Explicit liber revelacionum Julyane anacorite Norwyche, cuius anime propicietur deus.[5]

ca. 1390

---

7. Community.
8. Rejoice.
9. Be busy about.
1. Completed.
2. Know.

3. Taught.
4. Abated.
5. Thanks be to God. Here ends the book of revelations of Julian, anchorite of Norwich, on whose soul may God have mercy.

MYSTERY PLAYS

The word *mystery*, as applied to medieval drama, refers to the spiritual mystery of Christ's redemption of humankind, and mystery plays are dramatizations of the Old Testament, which foretells that redemption, and of the New, which recounts it. In England the mysteries were generally composed in cycles containing as many as forty-eight individual plays: a typical cycle would begin with the Creation, continue with the Fall of Man, and proceed through the most significant events of the Old Testament, such as the Flood, to the New Testament, which provided plays on the Nativity, the chief events of Christ's life, the Crucifixion, the Harrowing of Hell (based on sources now deemed apocryphal), and the Last Judgment.

The church had its own drama in Latin, dating back to the tenth century, which developed through the dramatization and elaboration of the liturgy—the regular service—for certain holidays, the Easter morning service in particular. The vernacular drama was once thought to have evolved from the liturgical, passing by stages from the church into the streets of the town. However, even though the vernacular plays at times echo their Latin counterparts and although their authors may have been clerics, the mysteries represent an old and largely independent tradition of vernacular religious drama. As early as the twelfth century a *Play of Adam* in Anglo-Norman French was performed in England, a dramatization of the Fall with highly sophisticated dialogue, characterization, and stagecraft.

During the late fourteenth and the fifteenth centuries the great English mystery cycles, four of which have survived complete, were formed in the towns that, in spite of war and plague, became increasingly prosperous and independent. Most of our knowledge of the plays, apart from the texts themselves, comes through municipal and guild records. Every trade in urban society had its guild, an organization combining the functions of a modern trade union, club, religious society, and political action group. The guilds, which played a major role in the governance of the towns, produced the plays; each guild was responsible for putting on a traditional play during the holidays when the cycles were presented.

The town and guild documents tell us a great deal about the evolution, staging, and all aspects of the production of the cycles. In some of the towns each company had a wagon that served as a stage. The wagon would proceed from one strategic point in the city to another, and the play would be performed a number of times on the same day. The spectators gathered at any one place would never be without a play before them and might see the whole cycle without moving. In other towns, plays were probably acted out in sequence on a platform erected at a single location such as the main city square.

The cycles were performed every year at the time of one of two great early summer festivals—Whitsuntide, the week following the seventh Sunday after Easter, or Corpus Christi, a week later. They served as both religious instruction and entertainment for wide audiences, including unlearned folk like the carpenter in *The Miller's Tale* (lines 405–74), who recalls from them the trouble Noah had getting his wife aboard the ark, but also educated laypeople and clerics, who besides enjoying the sometimes boisterous comedy would find the plays acting out traditional interpretations of Scripture such as the ark as a type, or prefiguration, of the church.

Thus the cycles were public spectacles watched by every layer of society, and they paved the way for the professional theater in the age of Elizabeth I. The rainbow in *Noah's Flood* with its messages of mercy and hope, unites actors and audience in a common faith.

The Chester Play of Noah's Flood   The most durable of the four surviving English mystery cycles was that of Chester, which was still occasionally performed when Shakespeare was a boy and was produced for the last time in 1575. The plays, however, remained of great interest to antiquarians and were a source of municipal pride. The five surviving manuscripts are all later than the final performance. Because the cycle had been extensively revised during the sixteenth century, we cannot know what it was like during the medieval period. The text we have is certainly very late. God's lengthy instructions to Noah concerning "clean" and "unclean" beasts reflect a new, probably Protestant, interest in Jewish law, also seen in other plays of the Chester cycle. But the revisers were also concerned to preserve what they felt to be traditional medieval features and, in the case of *Noah's Flood*, to introduce such a feature when it was missing. Thus the entertaining scene in which Noah and his wife quarrel and she gives him a box on the ear is an interpolation based on an old comic tradition that is well attested in the other cycle plays and in Chaucer's *The Miller's Tale*. The Chester play is a typical example of the composite authorship so characteristic of many medieval works, by which a text, passing through many hands and generations, carries with it traces of its past that blend in a rich, although not always smooth mixture. An interesting feature of the play is its stage directions, which show how such business as the animals on the ark was managed. A few additional stage directions are provided in braces.

Noah's Flood[1]

The Waterleaders and Drawers of Dee[2]

CAST OF CHARACTERS

GOD	NOAH'S WIFE
NOAH	SHEM'S WIFE
SHEM	HAM'S WIFE
HAM	JAPHET'S WIFE
JAPHETH	GOSSIPS

And first in some high place—or in the clouds, if it may be—God speaketh to Noah, standing without the ark[3] with all his family.

GOD   I, God, that[4] all this world hath wrought,
　　　Heaven and earth, and all of nought,
・　　I see my people in deed and thought
　　　Are set foully° in sin.　　　　　　　　　　　　　　　　　　*are mired*
5　　My ghost shall not leng in mon,
　　　That through flesh-liking is my fon,
　　　But till six score years be comen and gone,
　　　To look if they will blin.[5]

---

1. The text is based on that of R. M. Lumiansky and David Mills in *The Chester Mystery Cycle* (1974), but has been freely edited. Spelling has been normalized except in some cases for the sake of rhyme and meter. Stage directions are original except for a few added in braces.
2. The guild responsible for the production of the play, the Waterleaders and Drawers, carted and sold water, a trade appropriate for the producers of Noah's flood.
3. Outside the ark. Evidently the ark is already on stage, although Noah and his family will simulate its building.
4. Who. *That* is used throughout as the relative pronoun.
5. My spirit shall remain with mankind, who through fleshly lust are my foes, only till six score [120] years be come and gone, to see if they will stop [sinning]. I.e., God allows the human race a probationary period to reform (cf. lines 149–50),

Man that I made will I destroy,
10 Beast, worm, and fowl to fly;[6]
For on earth they do me noy,°   harm
     The folk that are thereon.
It harmes me so hurtfully,°   grievously
The malice that doth now multiply,
15 That sore it grieves me inwardly
     That ever I made mon.

Therefore Noah, my servant free,°   noble
That righteous man art as I see,
A ship soon thou shalt make thee
20   Of trees dry and light.
Little chambers therein thou make
And binding slitch also thou take;
Within and without thou ne slake
To annoint it through all thy might.[7]

25 Three hundred cubits it shall be long
And fifty broad to make it strong;
Of height sixty. The meet thou fong;[8]
     Thus measure thou it about.
One window work through thy wit;
30 A cubit of length and breadth make it.
Upon the side a door shall shut,
     For to come in and out.

Eating-places thou make also,
Three roofed chambers on a row,[9]
35 For with water I think to flow°   drown
     Man that I can° make.   did
Destroyed all the world shall be—
Save thou, thy wife, thy sonnes three,
And their wives also with thee—
40   Shall saved be for thy sake.

NOAH   A, Lord, I thank thee loud and still[1]
That to me art in such will
And spares me and my household to spill.[2]
     As now I soothly° find.   truly
45 Thy bidding, Lord, I shall fulfill
Nor never more Thee grieve ne grill,°   offend
That such grace has sent me till°   to me
     Amonges all mankind.

---

probably a misunderstanding of Genesis 6.3,
where God limits the human life span to 120 years.
"Mon": man. In the West-Midland dialect, *a* is
rounded before a nasal and rhymes with the vowel
of *gone* and *on*. Both spellings *mon* and *man* occur
in the manuscripts.
6. Animal, reptile, and bird flying.
7. Do not slacken to smear it [to make it water-

tight], inside and out, with all your might. "Slitch":
mud (for caulking).
8. Take thou the measurement.
9. May refer to three decks, but the text is
obscure.
1. Aloud and silent, i.e., at all times.
2. Who are so minded toward me and refrain from
destroying me and my household.

Have done, you men and women all,
50 Hie° you, lest this water fall,   *haste*
To work this ship, chamber and hall,
     As God hath bidden us do.
     SHEM   Father, I am already boun:°   *prepared*
     An ax I have, by my crown,[3]
55 As sharp as any in all this town,
     For to go thereto.

     HAM   I have a hatchet wonder keen
     To bite well, as may be seen;
     A better ground,° as I ween,°   *sharpened / think*
60   Is not in all this town.
     JAPHETH   And I can well make a pin°   *peg*
     And with this hammer knock it in.
     Go we work but° more din,°   *without / fuss*
     And I am ready boun.

65 NOAH'S WIFE   And we shall bring timber to,°   *thereto*
     For we mun° nothing else do—   *may*
     Woman been weak to underfo°   *undertake*
     Any great travail.°   *labor*
     SHEM'S WIFE   Here is a good hackestock;°   *chopping block*
70   On this you may hewe and knock,
     Shall none be idle in this flock,
     Ne now may no man fail.

     HAM'S WIFE   And I will go gather slitch,°   *pitch*
     The ship for to cleam° and pitch.   *caulk*
75   Annoint° it must be every stitch—   *smeared*
     Board, tree,° and pin.   *mast*
     JAPHETH'S WIFE   And I will gather chippes here
     To make a fire for you in fere,°   *together*
     And for to dighte° your dinner   *prepare*
80   Against° you come in.   *before*

[*Then they make signs as if they were working with different tools.*]

     NOAH   Now in the name of God I begin
     To make the ship that we shall in,°   *go in*
     That we may be ready for to swim°   *float*
     At the coming of the flood.
85   These boards I pin here together
     To bear us safe from the weather
     That we may row both hither and thither
     And safe be from this flood.

     Of this tree will I make a mast
90   Tied with cables that will last,

_____
3. By my head (an oath).

With a sail-yard° for each blast,   *spar*
   And each thing in their kind.
With topcastle[4] and bowsprit,
Both cords and ropes I have all meet°   *suitable*
95 To sail forth at the nexte wet;°   *rain*
   This ship is at an end.

⟨Wife, in this vessel we shall be kept;
My children and thou, I would in ye leapt.[5]
NOAH'S WIFE   In faith, Noah, I had as lief thou slept.
100   For all thy frankish fare,
   I will not do after thy rede.[6]
NOAH   Good wife, do now as I thee bid.
NOAH'S WIFE   By Christ, not ere I see more need,
   Though thou stand all day and stare.

105 NOAH   Lord, that° women been crabbed ay,°   *how / always*
And none are meek, I dare well say.
That is well seen by me today
   In witness of you each one.[7]
Good wife, let be all this bear°   *behavior*
110 That thou makest in this place here,
For all they ween° that thou art master—   *think*
   And so thou art, by Saint John.⟩

GOD   Noah, take thou thy meinie,°   *household*
And in the ship hie° that ye be;   *hasten*
115 For none so righteous man to me
   Is now on earth living.
Of clean beasts with thee thou take
Seven and seven ere then thou slake;[8]
He and she, make to make,°   *mate with mate*
120   Belive in that thou bring.[9]

Of beasts unclean two and two,
Male and female, but mo;°   *no more*
Of clean fowls seven also
   The he and she together;
125 Of fowls unclean, twain and no more,
   As I of beasts said before,

4. An armed platform at the masthead. "And each thing in their kind": and each kind of thing (required).
5. I would like you to jump aboard. The behavior of Noah's Wife in the next two stanzas and in lines 193–252, both enclosed in angle brackets, is inconsistent with her cooperation and meek words in lines 65–68 and elsewhere. Nor does it make sense that Noah orders her to board the ark before God tells him to take his family inside. Stylistic evidence strongly suggests that these comic exchanges were added, probably in the early 16th century, to bring the Chester play in line with the tradition of the shrewish and recalcitrant Wife of the other mystery cycles.
6. I'd just as soon have you go to bed. In spite of your polite ("Frenchified") manner, I won't follow your direction.
7. As each one of you (i.e., in the audience) witnesses.
8. I.e., seven by seven before you leave off. See Genesis 7.2–4, where God's instructions follow Jewish dietary laws. According to Genesis 6.19–21, Noah is to take only one pair of each.
9. [See] that you bring in quickly.

That shall be saved through my lore,°   *teaching*
    Against° I send this weather.   *before*

Of meats° that may be eaten,   *foods*
130   Into the ship look they be gotten,
For that may be no way forgotten.
    And do this al bedene.°   *at once*
To sustain man and beasts therein.
Ay till the water cease and blin.°   *stop*
135   This world is filled full of sin,
    And that is now well seen.

Seven days been yet coming;°   *are yet to come*
You shall have space° them in to bring.   *time*
After that it is my liking
140   Mankind to annoy.°   *afflict*
Forty days and forty nights
Rain shall fall for their unrights,°   *sins*
And that I have made through mights[1]
    Now think I to destroy.

145   NOAH   Lord, at Your bidding I am bain.°   *ready*
Sithen° no other grace will gain,°   *since/avail*
It will I fulfill fain,°   *gladly*
    For gracious I Thee find.
An hundred winters and twenty
150   This ship-making tarried° have I,   *delayed*
If through amendment Thy mercy
    Would fall to mankind.[2]

Have done, ye men and women all;
Hie you lest this water fall,
155   That each beast were in his stall
    And into the ship brought.
Of clean beastes seven shall be,
Of unclean two; thus God bade me.
The flood is nigh, you may well see;
160   Therefore tarry you nought.

[*Then* NOAH *shall go into the ark with all his family, his wife except, and the ark must be boarded[3] round about. And on the boards all the beasts and fowls hereafter rehearsed must be painted, that their words may agree with the pictures.*]

SHEM   Sir, here are lions, leopards in;
Horses, mares, oxen, and swine,
Goats, calves, sheep, and kine

---

1. That [which] I have made through [my] power.
2. If through reform mankind would obtain Thy
   mercy (cf. lines 7–8).
3. Supplied with boards.

Here sitten thou may see.
165 HAM   Camels, asses, man may find,
Buck and doe, hart and hind.
All beasts of all manner kind
Here been, as thinketh me.

JAPHETH   Take here cattes, dogges too,
170 Otters and foxes, fulmarts° also;   polecats
Hares hopping gaily can go
Here have cole° for to eat.   cabbage
NOAH'S WIFE   And here are bears, wolves set,
Apes, owls, marmoset,
175 Weasels, squirrels, and ferret;
Here they eat their meat.°   food

SHEM'S WIFE   Here are beasts in this house;
Here cats maken it crouse;[4]
Here a raton,° here a mouse   rat
180 That standen near together.
HAM'S WIFE   And here are fowles less and more—
Herons, cranes, and bittor,°   bittern
Swanes, peacocks—and them before,
Meat for this weather.

185 JAPHETH'S WIFE   Here are cockes, kites, crowes,
Rookes, ravens, many rowes,
Duckes, curlews, whoever knowes,
Each one in this kind.
And here are doves, digges,° drakes,   ducks
190 Redshanks running through the lakes;
And each fowl that leden° makes   song
In this ship man may find.

⟨NOAH   Wife, come in. Why stands thou there?
Thou art ever froward;[5] that dare I swear.
195 Come, in God's name! Time it were,
For fear lest that we drown!
NOAH'S WIFE   Yea, sir, set up your sail
And row forth with evil hail;°   ill luck
For withouten any fail°   doubt
200 I will not out of this town.

But° I have my gossips° every one,   unless/friends
One foot further I will not gone.°   go
They shall not drown, by Saint John,
And° I may save their life.   if
205 They loved me full well, by Christ.
But thou wilt let them into thy chist,°   ark (chest)

---

4. Have a merry time.   5. Bold, presumptuous.

Else row forth, Noah, when thee list°   *you please*
And get thee a new wife.

NOAH   Shem, son, lo thy mother is wrow;°   *angry*
210   By God, such another I do not know.
SHEM   Father, I shall fetch her in, I trow,°   *trust*
Withouten any fail.
Mother, my father after thee send
And bids thee into yonder ship wend.°   *go*
215   Look up and see the wind,
For we been ready to sail.

NOAH'S WIFE   Son, go again to him and say
I will not come therein today.
NOAH   Come in, Wife, in twenty devils way,[6]
220   Or else stand there without.°   *outside*
HAM   Shall we all fetch her in?
NOAH   Yea, son, in Christ's blessing and mine,
I would ye hied you betime,
For of this flood I stand in doubt.[7]

Song

225   THE GOOD GOSSIPS   The flood comes fleeting in full fast,[8]
On every side that spreadeth full far.
For fear of drowning I am aghast;
Good gossip, let us draw near.

And let us drink ere we depart,
230   For oftentimes we have done so.
For at one draught thou drink a quart,
And so will I do ere I go.

NOAH'S WIFE   Here is a pottle of Malmsey[9] good and strong;
It will rejoice both heart and tongue.
235   Though Noah think us never so long,
Yet we will drink atyte.°   *at once*

JAPHETH   Mother, we pray you all together—
For we are here, your own childer°—   *children*
Come into the ship for fear of the weather,
240   For his love that you bought![1]
NOAH'S WIFE   That will I not for all your call
But° I have my gossips all.   *unless*
SHEM   I° faith, mother, yet thou shall,   *in*
Whether thou will or nought.   *{Drags her aboard.}*

---

6. In the name of twenty devils.
7. I want you to hurry before it's too late because I'm afraid of the flood.
8. The flood comes flowing in very fast.

9. A sweet wine. "Pottle": two-quart measure.
1. For the love of him who redeemed you (i.e., Christ).

245 NOAH Welcome, wife, into this boat.
    NOAH'S WIFE {*slaps him*} Have thou that for thy note!°   *trouble*
    NOAH Aha, Mary,[2] this is hot!
      It is good for to be still.
      Ah, children, methinks my boat removes.°   *moves off*
250   Our tarrying here me highly grieves.
      Over the land the water spreads;
        God do as He will.⟩

[*Then they sing and* NOAH *shall speak again.*[3]]

    NOAH Ah, great God that art so good,
      That° workes not thy will is wood.°   *whoever/crazy*
255   Now all this world is on a flood.
        As we see well in sight.
      The windows I will shut anon,
      And into my chamber I will gone.
      Till this water, so great one,
260   Is slaked° through Thy might.   *diminished*

[*Then shall* NOAH *shut the window of the ark, and for a little space within the boards he shall be silent; and afterward opening the window and looking round about saying:*]

      Now forty days are fully gone.
      Send a raven I will anon,
      If aughtwhere° earth, tree, or stone   *anywhere*
        Be dry in any place.
265   And if this fowl come not again,
      It is a sign, sooth to sayn,°   *truth to say*
      That dry it is on hill or plain,
        And God hath done some grace.

[*Then he shall send forth a raven, and taking a dove in his hands, let him say:*]

      Ah, Lord, wherever this raven be,
270   Somewhere is dry, well I see;
      But yet a dove, by my lewty,°   *faith*
        After I will send.
      Thou wilt turn again to me,
      For of all fowls that may fle°   *fly*
275   Thou art most meek and hend.°   *gentle*

[*Then he shall send forth the dove; and there shall be another dove in the ship, bearing an olive branch in its mouth, which someone shall let*]

---

2. [By] Mary (an oath).
3. The manuscripts do not indicate what song

Noah and his family sing. A song might originally
have followed after line 192.

down from the mast into NOAH's *hands with a rope; and then let* NOAH
say:]

Ah, Lord, blessed be thou ay,
That me hast comfort° thus today.   *comforted*
By this sight I may well say
   This flood begins to cease.
280   My sweet dove to me brought has
A branch of olive from some place,
This betokeneth God has done us some grace,
   And is a sign of peace.

Ah, Lord, honored must Thou be;
285   All earth dries now I see.
But yet till thou command me,
   Hence I will not hie.
All this water is away;
Therefore, as soon as I may,
290   Sacrifice I shall do in fay°   *faith*
   To Thee devoutly.

GOD   Noah, take thy wife anon,
And thy children every one;
Out of the ship thou shalt gone,
295   And they all with thee.
Beasts and all that can fly,
Out anon they shall hie.
On earth to grow and multiply.
   I will that it so be.

300 NOAH   Lord, I thank Thee through Thy might;
Thy bidding shall be done in hight,°   *haste*
And, as fast as I may dight,°   *get ready*
   I will do Thee honor.
And to Thee offer sacrifice
305   Therefore comes in all wise,[4]
For of these beasts that been His,
   Offer I will this store.°   *great number*

[*Then, going out of the ark with his whole family he shall take his animals
and birds and offer and sacrifice them.*]

Lord God in majesty,
That such grace has granted me,
310   Where all was lorn,° safe to be,   *lost*
   Therefore now am I boun,°   *ready*
My wife, my children, and my meinie,°   *household*
With sacrifice to honor Thee

---

4. Is, therefore, becoming in every way.

Of beasts, fowls, as Thou mayst see,
315   And full devotioun.

GOD   Noah, to me thou art full able°   *very worthy*
And thy sacrifice acceptable,
For I have found thee true and stable,
      On thee now must I min.[5]
320   Wary° earth I will no more   *curse*
For man's sins that grieve me sore;
For of youth man full yore
      Has been inclined to sin.[6]

Ye shall now grow and multiply
325   And earth again to edify.°   *replenish*
Each beast, and fowl that may fly,
      Shall be feared° of you;   *afraid*
And fish in sea, all that may flete,°   *swim*
Shall sustain you, I thee beheet;°   *promise*
330   To eat of them ye ne let
      That clean been you may know.[7]

Thereas° ye have eaten before   *whereas*
Trees and roots since ye were bore,°   *born*
Of clean beasts now, less and more,
335   I give you leave to eat—
Save blood and flesh both in fere.[8]
Of wrong dead carrion that is here,
Eat ye not of that in no manner,
      For that ay ye shall let.[9]

340   Manslaughter also ay ye shall flee,
For that is not pleasant unto me.
They that shed blood, he or she,
      Aughtwhere° amongst mankin,°   *anywhere / mankind*
That blood foully shed shall be
345   And vengeance have, that men shall see.
Therefore beware now all ye,
      Ye fall not into that sin.

A forward,° Noah, with thee I make   *covenant*
And all thy seed for thy sake,
350   Of such vengeance for to slake,[1]
      For now I have my will.
Here I beheet thee an hest[2]

5. I must now be mindful of you.
6. Because for a very long time man, from his youth, has been inclined to sin.
7. Do not abstain from eating those you know to be clean (Genesis 9.1–3). The eating of meat will henceforth be permissible so long as the dietary laws are observed. "Ye": God speaks not just to Noah but to all the human race.
8. Except for blood and flesh both together (Genesis 9.4).
9. Of wrongly dead carrion (i.e., meat not killed according to dietary law), which is here, of that do not eat at all, for you must always leave that alone.
1. To give over such vengeance (as the flood).
2. Here I make you a promise.

That man, woman, fowl, ne beast,
With water while this world shall last
355   I will no more spill.°   *destroy*

My bow° between you and me   *rainbow*
In the firmament shall be
By very° tokening that you may see   *true*
That such vengeance shall cease.
360   That man ne woman shall never more
Be wasted by water as hath before;[3]
But for sin that grieveth me sore,
Therefore this vengeance was.

Where cloudes in the welkin° been,   *sky*
365   That ilke° bow shall be seen,   *same*
In tokening that my wrath and teen°   *anger*
Shall never thus wroken° be.   *avenged*
The string is turned towards you,
And towards me is bent the bow,[4]
370   That such weather shall never show;[5]
And this beheet° I thee.   *promise*

My blessing now I give thee here,
To thee, Noah, my servant dear,
For vengeance shall no more appear;
375   And now farewell, my darling dear.

3. Be destroyed by water as has happened.   from the earth at the sky.
4. The rainbow is visualized as a bow aimed away   5. [A sign] that such a flood shall never appear.

SIR THOMAS MALORY
ca. 1405–1471

Morte Darthur (Death of Arthur) is the title that William Caxton, the first English printer, gave to Malory's volume, which Caxton described more accurately in his Preface as "the noble histories of * * * King Arthur and of certain of his knights." The volume begins with the mythical story of Arthur's birth. King Uther Pendragon falls in love with the wife of one of his barons. Merlin's magic transforms Uther into the likeness of her husband, and Arthur is born of this union. The volume ends with the destruction of the Round Table and the deaths of Arthur, Queen Guinevere, and Sir Lancelot, who is Arthur's best knight and the queen's lover. The bulk of the work is taken up with the separate adventures of the knights of the Round Table.

On the evolution of the Arthurian saga, see the headnote to *Legendary Histories of Britain*, p. 94. During the thirteenth century the stories about Arthur and his knights had been turned into a series of enormously long prose romances in French, and it was these, as Caxton informed his readers, "Sir Thomas Malory did take out of certain books of French and reduced into English."

Little was known about the author until the early twentieth century when scholars began to unearth the criminal record of a Sir Thomas Malory of Newbold Revell in Warwickshire. In 1451 he was arrested for the first time to prevent his doing injury—presumably further injury—to a priory in Lincolnshire, and shortly thereafter he was accused of a number of criminal acts. These included escaping from prison after his first arrest, twice breaking into and plundering the Abbey of Coombe, extorting money from various persons, and committing rape. Malory pleaded innocent of all charges. The Wars of the Roses—in which Malory, like the formidable earl of Warwick (the "kingmaker"), whom he seems to have followed, switched sides from Lancaster to York and back again—may account for some of his troubles with the law. After a failed Lancastrian revolt, the Yorkist king, Edward IV, specifically excluded Malory from four amnesties he granted to the Lancastrians.

The identification of this Sir Thomas Malory (there is another candidate with the same name) as the author of the *Morte* was strengthened by the discovery in 1934 of a manuscript that differed from Caxton's text, the only version previously known. The manuscript contained eight separate romances. Caxton, in order to give the impression of a continuous narrative, had welded these together into twenty-one books, subdivided into short chapters with summary chapter headings. Caxton suppressed all but the last of the personal remarks the author had appended to individual tales in the manuscript. At the very end of the book Malory asks "all gentlemen and gentlewomen that readeth this book * * * pray for me while I am alive that God send me good deliverance." The discovery of the manuscript revealed that at the close of the first tale he had written: "this was drawyn by a knight presoner Sir Thomas Malleoré, that God sende him good recover." There is strong circumstantial evidence, therefore, that the book from which the Arthurian legends were passed on to future generations to be adapted in literature, art, and film was written in prison by a man whose violent career might seem at odds with the chivalric ideals he professes.

Such a contradiction—if it really is one—should not be surprising. Nostalgia for an ideal past that never truly existed is typical of much historical romance. Like the slave-owning plantation society of Margaret Mitchell's *Gone with the Wind*, whose southern gentlemen cultivate chivalrous manners and respect for gentlewomen, Malory's Arthurian world is a fiction. In our terms, it cannot even be labeled "historical," although the distinction between romance and history is not one that Malory would have made. Only rarely does he voice skepticism about the historicity of his tale; one such example is his questioning of the myth of Arthur's return. Much of the tragic power of his romance lies in his sense of the irretrievability of past glory in comparison with the sordidness of his own age.

The success of Malory's retelling owes much to his development of a terse and direct prose style, especially the naturalistic dialogue that keeps his narrative close to earth. And both he and many of his characters are masters of understatement who express themselves, in moments of great emotional tension, with a bare minimum of words.

In spite of its professed dedication to service of women, Malory's chivalry is primarily devoted to the fellowship and competitions of aristocratic men. Fighting consists mainly of single combats in tournaments, chance encounters, and battles, which Malory never tires of describing in professional detail. Commoners rarely come into view; when they do, the effect can be chilling—as when pillagers by moonlight plunder the corpses of the knights left on the field of Arthur's last battle. Above all, Malory cherishes an aristocratic male code of honor for which his favorite word is "worship." Men win or lose "worship" through their actions in war and love.

The most "worshipful" of Arthur's knights is Sir Lancelot, the "head of all Christian knights," as he is called in a moving eulogy by his brother, Sir Ector. But Lancelot is compromised by his fatal liaison with Arthur's queen and torn between the incompatible loyalties that bind him as an honorable knight, on the one hand, to his lord Arthur and, on the other, to his lady Guinevere. Malory loves his character Lancelot even to the point of indulging in the fleeting speculation, after Lancelot has been admitted to the queen's chamber, that their activities might have been innocent, "for love that time was not as love is nowadays." But when the jealousy and malice of two wicked knights forces the affair into the open, nothing can avert the breaking up of the fellowship of the Round Table and the death of Arthur himself, which Malory relates with somber magnificence as the passing of a great era.

From Morte Darthur[1]

[THE CONSPIRACY AGAINST LANCELOT AND GUINEVERE]

In May, when every lusty[2] heart flourisheth and burgeoneth, for as the season is lusty to behold and comfortable,[3] so man and woman rejoiceth and gladdeth of summer coming with his fresh flowers, for winter with his rough winds and blasts causeth lusty men and women to cower and to sit fast by the fire—so this season it befell in the month of May a great anger and unhap that stinted not[4] till the flower of chivalry of all the world was destroyed and slain. And all was long upon two unhappy[5] knights which were named Sir Agravain and Sir Mordred that were brethren unto Sir Gawain.[6] For this Sir Agravain and Sir Mordred had ever a privy[7] hate unto the Queen, Dame Guinevere, and to Sir Lancelot, and daily and nightly they ever watched upon Sir Lancelot.

So it misfortuned Sir Gawain and all his brethren were in King Arthur's chamber, and then Sir Agravain said thus openly, and not in no counsel,[8] that many knights might hear: "I marvel that we all be not ashamed both to see and to know how Sir Lancelot lieth daily and nightly by the Queen. And all we know well that it is so, and it is shamefully suffered of us all[9] that we should suffer so noble a king as King Arthur is to be shamed."

Then spoke Sir Gawain and said, "Brother, Sir Agravain, I pray you and charge you, move no such matters no more afore[1] me, for wit you well, I will not be of your counsel."[2]

"So God me help," said Sir Gaheris and Sir Gareth,[3] "we will not be known of your deeds."[4]

"Then will I!" said Sir Mordred.

"I lieve[5] you well," said Sir Gawain, "for ever unto all unhappiness, sir, ye will grant.[6] And I would that ye left all this and make you not so busy, for I know," said Sir Gawain, "what will fall of it."[7]

"Fall whatsoever fall may," said Sir Agravain, "I will disclose it to the King."

"Not by my counsel," said Sir Gawain, "for and[8] there arise war and wrack betwixt[9] Sir Lancelot and us, wit you well, brother, there will many kings and

---

1. The selections given here are from the section that Caxton called book 20, chaps. 1–4, 8–10, and book 21, chaps. 3–7, 10–12, with omissions. In the Winchester manuscript this section is titled "The Most Piteous Tale of the Morte Arthur Saunz Guerdon" (i.e., the death of Arthur without reward or compensation). The text has been based on Winchester, with some readings introduced from the Caxton edition; spelling has been modernized and modern punctuation added.
2. Merry.
3. Pleasant.
4. Misfortune that ceased not.
5. On account of two ill-fated.
6. Gawain and Agravain are sons of King Lot of Orkney and his wife, Arthur's half-sister Morgause.

Mordred is the illegitimate son of Arthur and Morgause.
7. Secret.
8. Secret manner.
9. Put up with by all of us.
1. Before. "Move": propose.
2. On your side. "Wit you well": know well, i.e., give you to understand.
3. Sons of King Lot and Gawain's brothers.
4. A party to your doings.
5. Believe.
6. You will consent to all mischief.
7. Come of it.
8. If.
9. Strife between.

great lords hold with Sir Lancelot. Also, brother, Sir Agravain," said Sir Gawain, "ye must remember how often times Sir Lancelot hath rescued the King and the Queen. And the best of us all had been full cold at the heart-root[1] had not Sir Lancelot been better than we, and that has he proved himself full oft. And as for my part," said Sir Gawain, "I will never be against Sir Lancelot for[2] one day's deed, when he rescued me from King Carados of the Dolorous Tower and slew him and saved my life. Also, brother, Sir Agravain and Sir Mordred, in like wise Sir Lancelot rescued you both and three score and two[3] from Sir Tarquin. And therefore, brother, methinks such noble deeds and kindness should be remembered."

"Do as ye list,"[4] said Sir Agravain, "for I will layne[5] it no longer."

So with these words came in Sir Arthur.

"Now, brother," said Sir Gawain, "stint your noise."[6]

"That will I not," said Sir Agravain and Sir Mordred.

"Well, will ye so?" said Sir Gawain. "Then God speed you, for I will not hear of your tales, neither be of your counsel."

"No more will I," said Sir Gaheris.

"Neither I," said Sir Gareth, "for I shall never say evil by[7] that man that made me knight." And therewithal they three departed making great dole.[8]

"Alas!" said Sir Gawain and Sir Gareth, "now is this realm wholly destroyed and mischieved,[9] and the noble fellowship of the Round Table shall be disparbeled."[1]

So they departed, and then King Arthur asked them what noise they made. "My lord," said Sir Agravain, "I shall tell you, for I may keep[2] it no longer. Here is I and my brother Sir Mordred broke[3] unto my brother Sir Gawain, Sir Gaheris, and to Sir Gareth—for this is all, to make it short—how that we know all that Sir Lancelot holdeth your queen, and hath done long; and we be your sister[4] sons, we may suffer it no longer. And all we woot[5] that ye should be above Sir Lancelot, and ye are the king that made him knight, and therefore we will prove it that he is a traitor to your person."

"If it be so," said the King, "wit[6] you well, he is none other. But I would be loath to begin such a thing but[7] I might have proofs of it, for Sir Lancelot is an hardy knight, and all ye know that he is the best knight among us all. And but if he be taken with the deed,[8] he will fight with him that bringeth up the noise, and I know no knight that is able to match him. Therefore, and[9] it be sooth as ye say, I would that he were taken with the deed."

For, as the French book saith, the King was full loath that such a noise should be upon Sir Lancelot and his queen. For the King had a deeming[1] of it, but he would not hear of it, for Sir Lancelot had done so much for him and for the Queen so many times that, wit you well, the King loved him passingly[2] well.

---

1. Would have been dead.
2. On account of.
3. I.e., sixty-two.
4. You please.
5. Conceal.
6. Stop making scandal.
7. About.
8. Lamentation.
9. Put to shame.
1. Dispersed.

2. Conceal.
3. Revealed.
4. Sister's.
5. Know.
6. Know.
7. Unless.
8. Unless he is caught in the act.
9. If.
1. Suspicion.
2. Exceedingly.

"My lord," said Sir Agravain, "ye shall ride tomorn[3] on hunting, and doubt ye not, Sir Lancelot will not go with you. And so when it draweth toward night, ye may send the Queen word that ye will lie out all that night, and so may ye send for your cooks. And then, upon pain of death, that night we shall take him with the Queen, and we shall bring him unto you, quick[4] or dead."

"I will well,"[5] said the King. "Then I counsel you to take with you sure fellowship."

"Sir," said Sir Agravain, "my brother, Sir Mordred, and I will take with us twelve knights of the Round Table."

"Beware," said King Arthur, "for I warn you, ye shall find him wight."[6]

"Let us deal!"[7] said Sir Agravain and Sir Mordred.

So on the morn King Arthur rode on hunting and sent word to the Queen that he would be out all that night. Then Sir Agravain and Sir Mordred got to them[8] twelve knights and hid themself in a chamber in the castle of Carlisle. And these were their names: Sir Colgrevance, Sir Mador de la Porte, Sir Guingalen, Sir Meliot de Logres, Sir Petipace of Winchelsea, Sir Galeron of Galway, Sir Melion de la Mountain, Sir Ascamore, Sir Gromore Somyr Jour, Sir Curselayne, Sir Florence, and Sir Lovell. So these twelve knights were with Sir Mordred and Sir Agravain, and all they were of Scotland, or else of Sir Gawain's kin, or well-willers[9] to his brother.

So when the night came, Sir Lancelot told Sir Bors[1] how he would go that night and speak with the Queen.

"Sir," said Sir Bors, "ye shall not go this night by my counsel."

"Why?" said Sir Lancelot.

"Sir," said Sir Bors, "I dread me[2] ever of Sir Agravain that waiteth upon[3] you daily to do you shame and us all. And never gave my heart against no going that ever ye went[4] to the queen so much as now, for I mistrust[5] that the King is out this night from the Queen because peradventure he hath lain[6] some watch for you and the Queen. Therefore, I dread me sore of some treason."

"Have ye no dread," said Sir Lancelot, "for I shall go and come again and make no tarrying."

"Sir," said Sir Bors, "that me repents,[7] for I dread me sore that your going this night shall wrath[8] us all."

"Fair nephew," said Sir Lancelot, "I marvel me much why ye say thus, sithen[9] the Queen hath sent for me. And wit you well, I will not be so much a coward, but she shall understand I will[1] see her good grace."

"God speed you well," said Sir Bors, "and send you sound and safe again!"

So Sir Lancelot departed and took his sword under his arm, and so he walked in his mantel,[2] that noble knight, and put himself in great jeopardy.

---

3. Tomorrow.
4. Alive.
5. Readily agree.
6. Strong.
7. Leave it to us.
8. Gathered to themselves.
9. Partisans.
1. Nephew and confidant of Sir Lancelot.
2. I am afraid.
3. Lies in wait.

4. Never misgave my heart against any visit you made.
5. Suspect.
6. Perhaps he has set.
7. I regret.
8. Cause injury to.
9. Since.
1. Wish to.
2. Cloak. Lancelot goes without armor.

And so he passed on till he came to the Queen's chamber, and so lightly he was had[3] into the chamber. And then, as the French book saith, the Queen and Sir Lancelot were together. And whether they were abed or at other manner of disports, me list[4] not thereof make no mention, for love that time[5] was not as love is nowadays.

But thus as they were together there came Sir Agravain and Sir Mordred with twelve knights with them of the Round Table, and they said with great crying and scaring[6] voice: "Thou traitor, Sir Lancelot, now are thou taken!" And thus they cried with a loud voice that all the court might hear it. And these fourteen knights all were armed at all points, as[7] they should fight in a battle.

"Alas!" said Queen Guinevere, "now are we mischieved[8] both!"

"Madam," said Sir Lancelot, "is there here any armor within your chamber that I might cover my body withal? And if there be any, give it me, and I shall soon stint[9] their malice, by the grace of God!"

"Now, truly," said the Queen, "I have none armor neither helm, shield, sword, neither spear, wherefore I dread me sore our long love is come to a mischievous end. For I hear by their noise there be many noble knights, and well I woot they be surely[1] armed, and against them ye may make no resistance. Wherefore ye are likely to be slain, and then shall I be burned! For and[2] ye might escape them," said the Queen, "I would not doubt but that ye would rescue me in what danger that ever I stood in."

"Alas!" said Sir Lancelot, "in all my life thus was I never bestead[3] that I should be thus shamefully slain for lack of mine armor."

But ever in one[4] Sir Agravain and Sir Mordred cried: "Traitor knight, come out of the Queen's chamber! For wit thou well thou art beset so that thou shalt not escape."

"Ah, Jesu mercy!" said Sir Lancelot, "this shameful cry and noise I may not suffer, for better were death at once than thus to endure this pain." Then he took the Queen in his arms and kissed her and said, "Most noblest Christian queen, I beseech you, as ye have been ever my special good lady, and I at all times your poor knight and true unto[5] my power, and as I never failed you in right nor in wrong sithen the first day King Arthur made me knight, that ye will pray for my soul if that I be slain. For well I am assured that Sir Bors, my nephew, and all the remnant of my kin, with Sir Lavain and Sir Urry,[6] that they will not fail you to rescue you from the fire. And therefore, mine own lady, recomfort yourself,[7] whatsoever come of me, that ye go with Sir Bors, my nephew, and Sir Urry and they all will do you all the pleasure that they may, and ye shall live like a queen upon my lands."

"Nay, Sir Lancelot, nay!" said the Queen. "Wit thou well that I will not live long after thy days. But and[8] ye be slain I will take my death as meekly as ever did martyr take his death for Jesu Christ's sake."

"Well, Madam," said Sir Lancelot, "sith it is so that the day is come that

---

3. Quickly he was received.
4. I care. "Disports": pastimes.
5. At that time.
6. Terrifying.
7. Completely, as if.
8. Come to grief.
9. Stop.
1. Securely.
2. If.

3. Beset.
4. In unison.
5. To the utmost of.
6. The brother of Elaine, the Fair Maid of Astolat, and a knight miraculously healed of his wound by Sir Lancelot. "Remnant": rest.
7. Take heart again.
8. If.

our love must depart,[9] wit you well I shall sell my life as dear as I may. And a thousandfold," said Sir Lancelot, "I am more heavier[1] for you than for myself! And now I had liefer[2] than to be lord of all Christendom that I had sure armor upon me, that men might speak of my deeds ere ever I were slain."

"Truly," said the Queen, "and[3] it might please God, I would that they would take me and slay me and suffer[4] you to escape."

"That shall never be," said Sir Lancelot. "God defend me from such a shame! But, Jesu Christ, be Thou my shield and mine armor!" And therewith Sir Lancelot wrapped his mantel about his arm well and surely; and by then they had gotten a great form[5] out of the hall, and therewith they all rushed at the door. "Now, fair lords," said Sir Lancelot, "leave[6] your noise and your rushing, and I shall set open this door, and then may ye do with me what it liketh you."[7]

"Come off,[8] then," said they all, "and do it, for it availeth thee not to strive against us all. And therefore let us into this chamber, and we shall save thy life until thou come to King Arthur."

Then Sir Lancelot unbarred the door, and with his left hand he held it open a little, that but one man might come in at once. And so there came striding a good knight, a much[9] man and a large, and his name was called Sir Colgrevance of Gore. And he with a sword struck at Sir Lancelot mightily. And he put aside[1] the stroke and gave him such a buffet[2] upon the helmet that he fell groveling dead within the chamber door. Then Sir Lancelot with great might drew the knight within[3] the chamber door. And then Sir Lancelot, with help of the Queen and her ladies, he was lightly[4] armed in Colgrevance's armor. And ever stood Sir Agravain and Sir Mordred, crying, "Traitor knight! Come forth out of the Queen's chamber!"

"Sirs, leave[5] your noise," said Sir Lancelot, "for wit you well, Sir Agravain, ye shall not prison me this night. And therefore, and[6] ye do by my counsel, go ye all from this chamber door and make you no such crying and such manner of slander as ye do. For I promise you by my knighthood, and ye will depart and make no more noise, I shall as tomorn appear afore you all and before the King, and then let it be seen which of you all, other else ye all,[7] that will deprove[8] me of treason. And there shall I answer you, as a knight should, that hither I came to the Queen for no manner of mal engine,[9] and that will I prove and make it good upon you with my hands."

"Fie upon thee, traitor," said Sir Agravain and Sir Mordred, "for we will have thee malgré thine head[1] and slay thee, and we list. For we let thee wit we have the choice of[2] King Arthur to save thee other slay thee."

"Ah, sirs," said Sir Lancelot, "is there none other grace with you? Then keep[3] yourself!" And then Sir Lancelot set all open the chamber door and

---

9. Come to an end.
1. More grieved.
2. Rather.
3. If.
4. Allow.
5. Bench.
6. Stop.
7. Pleases you.
8. Go ahead.
9. Big.
1. Fended off.

2. Blow.
3. Inside.
4. Quickly.
5. Stop.
6. If.
7. Or else all of you.
8. Accuse.
9. Evil design.
1. In spite of you.
2. From.
3. Defend.

mightily and knightly he strode in among them. And anon[4] at the first stroke he slew Sir Agravain, and after twelve of his fellows. Within a little while he had laid them down cold to the earth, for there was none of the twelve knights might stand Sir Lancelot one buffet.[5] And also he wounded Sir Mordred, and therewithal he fled with all his might.

And then Sir Lancelot returned again unto the Queen and said, "Madam, now wit you well, all our true love is brought to an end, for now will King Arthur ever be my foe. And therefore, Madam, and it like you[6] that I may have you with me, I shall save you from all manner adventurous[7] dangers."

"Sir, that is not best," said the Queen, "me seemeth, for[8] now ye have done so much harm, it will be best that ye hold you still with this. And if ye see that as tomorn they will put me unto death, then may ye rescue me as ye think best."

"I will well,"[9] said Sir Lancelot, "for have ye no doubt, while I am a man living I shall rescue you." And then he kissed her, and either of them gave other a ring, and so there he left the Queen and went until[1] his lodging.

[WAR BREAKS OUT BETWEEN ARTHUR AND LANCELOT][2]

Then said King Arthur unto Sir Gawain, "Dear nephew, I pray you make ready in your best armor with your brethren, Sir Gaheris and Sir Gareth, to bring my Queen to the fire, there to have her judgment and receive the death."

"Nay, my most noble king," said Sir Gawain, "that will I never do, for wit you well I will never be in that place where so noble a queen as is my lady Dame Guinevere shall take such a shameful end. For wit you well," said Sir Gawain, "my heart will not serve me for to see her die, and it shall never be said that ever I was of your counsel for her death."

"Then," said the King unto Sir Gawain, "suffer[3] your brethren Sir Gaheris and Sir Gareth to be there."

"My lord," said Sir Gawain, "wit you well they will be loath to be there present because of many adventures[4] that is like to fall, but they are young and full unable to say you nay."

Then spake Sir Gaheris and the good knight Sir Gareth unto King Arthur: "Sir, ye may well command us to be there, but wit you well it shall be sore against our will. But and[5] we be there by your straight commandment, ye shall plainly[6] hold us there excused—we will be there in peaceable wise and bear none harness of war upon us."

"In the name of God," said the King, "then make you ready, for she shall have soon[7] her judgment."

"Alas," said Sir Gawain, "that ever I should endure[8] to see this woeful day."

---

4. Right away.
5. Withstand Sir Lancelot one blow.
6. If it please you.
7. Perilous.
8. Because.
9. Agree.
1. To.
2. Lancelot and Sir Bors mobilize their friends for the rescue of Guinevere. In the morning Mordred reports the events of the night to Arthur who, against Gawain's strong opposition, condemns the queen to be burned, for "the law was such in those days that whatsoever they were, of what estate or degree, if they were found guilty of treason there should be none other remedy but death."
3. Allow.
4. Chance occurrences.
5. If.
6. Openly. "Straight": strict.
7. Right away.
8. Live.

So Sir Gawain turned him and wept heartily, and so he went into his chamber.

And then the Queen was led forth without[9] Carlisle, and anon she was dispoiled into[1] her smock. And then her ghostly father[2] was brought to her to be shriven of her misdeeds.[3] Then was there weeping and wailing and wringing of hands of many lords and ladies, but there were but few in comparison that would bear any armor for to strengthen[4] the death of the Queen.

Then was there one that Sir Lancelot had sent unto that place, which went to espy what time the Queen should go unto her death. And anon as[5] he saw the Queen dispoiled into her smock and shriven, then he gave Sir Lancelot warning. Then was there but spurring and plucking up[6] of horses, and right so they came unto the fire. And who[7] that stood against them, there were they slain—there might none withstand Sir Lancelot. So all that bore arms and withstood them, there were they slain, full many a noble knight. * * * And so in this rushing and hurling, as Sir Lancelot thrang[8] here and there, it misfortuned him[9] to slay Sir Gaheris and Sir Gareth, the noble knight, for they were unarmed and unwares.[1] As the French book saith, Sir Lancelot smote Sir Gaheris and Sir Gareth upon the brain-pans, wherethrough[2] that they were slain in the field, howbeit[3] Sir Lancelot saw them not. And so were they found dead among the thickest of the press.

Then when Sir Lancelot had thus done, and slain and put to flight all that would withstand him, then he rode straight unto Queen Guinevere and made a kirtle[4] and a gown to be cast upon her, and then he made her to be set behind him and prayed her to be of good cheer. Now wit you well the Queen was glad that she was escaped from death, and then she thanked God and Sir Lancelot.

And so he rode his way with the Queen, as the French book saith, unto Joyous Garde,[5] and there he kept her as a noble knight should. And many great lords and many good knights were sent him, and many full noble knights drew unto him. When they heard that King Arthur and Sir Lancelot were at debate,[6] many knights were glad, and many were sorry of their debate.

Now turn we again unto King Arthur, that when it was told him how and in what manner the Queen was taken away from the fire, and when he heard of the death of his noble knights, and in especial Sir Gaheris and Sir Gareth, then he swooned for very pure[7] sorrow. And when he awoke of his swoon, then he said: "Alas, that ever I bore crown upon my head! For now have I lost the fairest fellowship of noble knights that ever held Christian king[8] together. Alas, my good knights be slain and gone away from me. Now within these two days I have lost nigh forty knights and also the noble fellowship of Sir Lancelot and his blood,[9] for now I may nevermore hold them together with my worship.[1] Alas, that ever this war began!"

"Now, fair fellows," said the King, "I charge you that no man tell Sir

---

9. Outside.
1. Undressed down to.
2. Spiritual father, i.e., her priest.
3. For her to be confessed of her sins.
4. Secure.
5. As soon as.
6. Urging forward.
7. Whoever.
8. Pressed. "Hurling": turmoil.
9. He had the misfortune.

1. Unaware.
2. Through which.
3. Although.
4. Petticoat.
5. Lancelot's castle in England.
6. Strife.
7. Sheer.
8. That Christian king ever held.
9. Kin.
1. Glory.

Gawain of the death of his two brethren, for I am sure," said the King, "when he heareth tell that Sir Gareth is dead, he will go nigh out of his mind. Mercy Jesu," said the King, "why slew he Sir Gaheris and Sir Gareth? For I dare say, as for Sir Gareth, he loved Sir Lancelot above all men earthly."[2]

"That is truth," said some knights, "but they were slain in the hurling,[3] as Sir Lancelot thrang in the thickest of the press. And as they were unarmed, he smote them and wist[4] not whom that he smote, and so unhappily[5] they were slain."

"Well," said Arthur, "the death of them will cause the greatest mortal war that ever was, for I am sure that when Sir Gawain knoweth hereof that Sir Gareth is slain, I shall never have rest of him[6] till I have destroyed Sir Lancelot's kin and himself both, other else he to destroy me. And therefore," said the King, "wit you well, my heart was never so heavy as it is now. And much more I am sorrier for my good knights' loss[7] than for the loss of my fair queen; for queens I might have enough, but such a fellowship of good knights shall never be together in no company. And now I dare say," said King Arthur, "there was never Christian king that ever held such a fellowship together. And alas, that ever Sir Lancelot and I should be at debate. Ah, Agravain, Agravain!" said the King, "Jesu forgive it thy soul, for thine evil will that thou and thy brother Sir Mordred haddest unto Sir Lancelot hath caused all this sorrow." And ever among these complaints the King wept and swooned.

Then came there one to Sir Gawain and told him how the Queen was led away with[8] Sir Lancelot, and nigh a four-and-twenty knights slain. "Ah, Jesu, save me my two brethren!" said Sir Gawain. "For full well wist I," said Sir Gawain, "that Sir Lancelot would rescue her, other else he would die in that field. And to say the truth he were not of worship but if he had[9] rescued the Queen, insomuch as she should have been burned for his sake. And as in that," said Sir Gawain, "he hath done but knightly, and as I would have done myself and I had stood in like case. But where are my brethren?" said Sir Gawain. "I marvel that I hear not of them."

Then said that man, "Truly, Sir Gaheris and Sir Gareth be slain."

"Jesu defend!"[1] said Sir Gawain. "For all this world I would not that they were slain, and in especial my good brother Sir Gareth."

"Sir," said the man, "he is slain, and that is great pity."

"Who slew him?" said Sir Gawain.

"Sir Lancelot," said the man, "slew them both."

"That may I not believe," said Sir Gawain, "that ever he slew my good brother Sir Gareth, for I dare say my brother loved him better than me and all his brethren and the King both. Also I dare say, an[2] Sir Lancelot had desired my brother Sir Gareth with him, he would have been with him against the King and us all. And therefore I may never believe that Sir Lancelot slew my brethren."

"Verily, sir," said the man, "it is noised[3] that he slew him."

"Alas," said Sir Gawain, "now is my joy gone." And then he fell down and

---

2. Earthly men.
3. Turmoil.
4. Knew.
5. Unluckily.
6. He will never give me any peace.
7. The loss of my good knights.

8. By.
9. Of honor if he had not.
1. Forbid.
2. If.
3. Reported.

swooned, and long he lay there as he had been dead. And when he arose out of his swoon, he cried out sorrowfully and said, "Alas!" And forthwith he ran unto the King, crying and weeping, and said, "Ah, mine uncle King Arthur! My good brother Sir Gareth is slain, and so is my brother Sir Gaheris, which were two noble knights."

Then the King wept and he both, and so they fell on swooning. And when they were revived, then spake Sir Gawain and said, "Sir, I will go and see my brother Sir Gareth."

"Sir, ye may not see him," said the King, "for I caused him to be interred and Sir Gaheris both, for I well understood that ye would make overmuch sorrow, and the sight of Sir Gareth should have caused your double sorrow."

"Alas, my lord," said Sir Gawain, "how slew he my brother Sir Gareth? Mine own good lord, I pray you tell me."

"Truly," said the King, "I shall tell you as it hath been told me—Sir Lancelot slew him and Sir Gaheris both."

"Alas," said Sir Gawain, "they bore none arms against him, neither of them both."

"I woot not how it was," said the King, "but as it is said, Sir Lancelot slew them in the thickest of the press and knew them not. And therefore let us shape a remedy for to revenge their deaths."

"My king, my lord, and mine uncle," said Sir Gawain, "wit you well, now I shall make you a promise which I shall hold by my knighthood, that from this day forward I shall never fail[4] Sir Lancelot until that one of us have slain the other. And therefore I require you, my lord and king, dress[5] you unto the wars, for wit you well, I will be revenged upon Sir Lancelot; and therefore, as ye will have my service and my love, now haste you thereto and assay[6] your friends. For I promise unto God," said Sir Gawain, "for the death of my brother Sir Gareth I shall seek Sir Lancelot throughout seven kings' realms, but I shall slay him, other else he shall slay me."

"Sir, ye shall not need to seek him so far," said the King, "for as I hear say, Sir Lancelot will abide me and us all within the castle of Joyous Garde. And much people draweth unto him, as I hear say."

"That may I right well believe," said Sir Gawain, "but my lord," he said, "assay your friends and I will assay mine."

"It shall be done," said the King, "and as I suppose I shall be big[7] enough to drive him out of the biggest tower of his castle."

So then the King sent letters and writs throughout all England, both the length and the breadth, for to summon all his knights. And so unto King Arthur drew many knights, dukes, and earls, that he had a great host, and when they were assembled the King informed them how Sir Lancelot had bereft him his Queen. Then the King and all his host made them ready to lay siege about Sir Lancelot where he lay within Joyous Garde.

---

4. Give up the pursuit of.
5. Prepare.
6. Appeal to.
7. Strong.

[THE DEATH OF ARTHUR][8]

So upon Trinity Sunday at night King Arthur dreamed a wonderful dream, and in his dream him seemed that he saw upon a chafflet[9] a chair, and the chair was fast to a wheel, and thereupon sat King Arthur in the richest cloth of gold that might be made. And the King thought there was under him, far from him, an hideous deep black water, and therein was all manner of serpents, and worms, and wild beasts, foul and horrible. And suddenly the King thought that the wheel turned upside down, and he fell among the serpents, and every beast took him by a limb. And then the King cried as he lay in his bed, "Help, help!"

And then knights, squires, and yeomen awaked the King, and then he was so amazed that he wist[1] not where he was. And then so he awaked[2] until it was nigh day, and then he fell on slumbering again, not sleeping nor thoroughly waking. So the King seemed[3] verily that there came Sir Gawain unto him with a number of fair ladies with him. So when King Arthur saw him, he said, "Welcome, my sister's son. I weened ye had been dead. And now I see thee on-live, much am I beholden unto Almighty Jesu. Ah, fair nephew and my sister's son, what been these ladies that hither be come with you?"

"Sir," said Sir Gawain, "all these be ladies for whom I have foughten for when I was man living. And all these are tho[4] that I did battle for in righteous quarrels, and God hath given them that grace, at their great prayer, because I did battle for them for their right, that they should bring me hither unto you. Thus much hath given me leave God, for to warn you of your death. For and ye fight as tomorn[5] with Sir Mordred, as ye both have assigned,[6] doubt ye not ye must be slain, and the most party of your people on both parties. And for the great grace and goodness that Almighty Jesu hath unto you, and for pity of you and many mo other good men there[7] shall be slain, God hath sent me to you of his special grace to give you warning that in no wise ye do battle as tomorn, but that ye take a treatise for a month-day.[8] And proffer you largely,[9] so that tomorn ye put in a delay. For within a month shall come Sir Lancelot with all his noble knights and rescue you worshipfully and slay Sir Mordred and all that ever will hold with him."

Then Sir Gawain and all the ladies vanished. And anon the King called upon his knights, squires, and yeomen, and charged them wightly[1] to fetch his noble lords and wise bishops unto him. And when they were come the King told them of his avision,[2] that Sir Gawain had told him and warned him that, and he fought on the morn, he should be slain. Then the King commanded Sir Lucan the Butler[3] and his brother Sir Bedivere the Bold, with

---

8. The pope arranges a truce, Guinevere is returned to Arthur, and Lancelot and his kin leave England to become rulers of France. At Gawain's instigation Arthur invades France to resume the war against Lancelot. Word comes to the king that Mordred has seized the kingdom, and Arthur leads his forces back to England. Mordred attacks them upon their landing, and Gawain is mortally wounded and dies, although not before he has repented for having insisted that Arthur fight Lancelot and has written Lancelot to come to the aid of his former lord.
9. Scaffold. "Him seemed": it seemed to him.
1. Knew.
2. Lay awake.

3. It seemed to the king.
4. Those.
5. If you fight tomorrow.
6. Decided.
7. I.e., who there. "Mo": more.
8. For a month from today. "Treatise": treaty, truce.
9. Make generous offers.
1. Quickly.
2. Dream.
3. "Butler" here is probably only a title of high rank, although it was originally used to designate the officer who had charge of wine for the king's table.

two bishops with them, and charged them in any wise to take a treatise for a month-day with Sir Mordred. "And spare not: proffer him lands and goods as much as ye think reasonable."

So then they departed and came to Sir Mordred where he had a grim host of an hundred thousand, and there they entreated[4] Sir Mordred long time. And at the last Sir Mordred was agreed for to have Cornwall and Kent by King Arthur's days,[5] and after that, all England, after the days of King Arthur.

Then were they condescended[6] that King Arthur and Sir Mordred should meet betwixt both their hosts, and everich[7] of them should bring fourteen persons. And so they came with this word unto Arthur. Then said he, "I am glad that this is done," and so he went into the field.

And when King Arthur should depart, he warned all his host that, and they see any sword drawn, "Look ye come on fiercely and slay that traitor Sir Mordred, for I in no wise trust him." In like wise Sir Mordred warned his host that "And ye see any manner of sword drawn, look that ye come on fiercely, and so slay all that ever before you standeth, for in no wise I will not trust for this treatise." And in the same wise said Sir Mordred unto his host, "For I know well my father will be avenged upon me."

And so they met as their pointment[8] was and were agreed and accorded thoroughly. And wine was fetched and they drank together. Right so came an adder out of a little heath-bush, and it stung a knight in the foot. And so when the knight felt him so stung, he looked down and saw the adder. And anon he drew his sword to slay the adder, and thought[9] none other harm. And when the host on both parties saw that sword drawn, then they blew beams,[1] trumpets, and horns, and shouted grimly. And so both hosts dressed them[2] together. And King Arthur took his horse and said, "Alas, this unhappy day!" and so rode to his party, and Sir Mordred in like wise.

And never since was there never seen a more dolefuller battle in no Christian land, for there was but rushing and riding, foining[3] and striking; and many a grim word was there spoken of either to other, and many a deadly stroke. But ever King Arthur rode throughout the battle[4] of Sir Mordred many times and did full nobly, as a noble king should do, and at all times he fainted never. And Sir Mordred did his devoir[5] that day and put himself in great peril.

And thus they fought all the long day, and never stinted[6] till the noble knights were laid to the cold earth. And ever they fought still till it was near night, and by then was there an hundred thousand laid dead upon the down. Then was King Arthur wood-wroth[7] out of measure when he saw his people so slain from him. And so he looked about him and could see no mo[8] of all his host, and good knights left no mo on-live, but two knights: the t'one[9] was Sir Lucan the Butler and [the other] his brother Sir Bedivere. And yet they were full sore wounded.

"Jesu, mercy," said the King, "where are all my noble knights become?[1]

4. Dealt with.
5. During King Arthur's lifetime.
6. Agreed.
7. Each.
8. Arrangement.
9. Meant.
1. A kind of trumpet.
2. Prepared to come.

3. Lunging.
4. Battalion.
5. Knightly duty.
6. Stopped.
7. Mad with rage.
8. Others.
9. That one, i.e., the first.
1. What has become of all my noble knights?

Alas that ever I should see this doleful day! For now," said King Arthur, "I am come to mine end. But would to God," said he, "that I wist[2] now where were that traitor Sir Mordred that has caused all this mischief."

Then King Arthur looked about and was ware where stood Sir Mordred leaning upon his sword among a great heap of dead men.

"Now give me my spear," said King Arthur unto Sir Lucan, "for yonder I have espied the traitor that all this woe hath wrought."

"Sir, let him be," said Sir Lucan, "for he is unhappy.[3] And if ye pass this unhappy day ye shall be right well revenged upon him. And, good lord, remember ye of your night's dream, and what the spirit of Sir Gawain told you tonight, and yet God of his great goodness hath preserved you hitherto. And for God's sake, my lord, leave off by this,[4] for, blessed be God, ye have won the field: for yet we been here three on-live, and with Sir Mordred is not one on-live. And therefore if ye leave off now, this wicked day of destiny is past."

"Now, tide[5] me death, tide me life," said the King, "now I see him yonder alone, he shall never escape mine hands. For at a better avail[6] shall I never have him."

"God speed you well!" said Sir Bedivere.

Then the King got his spear in both his hands and ran toward Sir Mordred, crying and saying, "Traitor, now is thy deathday come!"

And when Sir Mordred saw King Arthur he ran until him with his sword drawn in his hand, and there King Arthur smote Sir Mordred under the shield, with a foin[7] of his spear, throughout the body more than a fathom.[8] And when Sir Mordred felt that he had his death's wound, he thrust himself with the might that he had up to the burr[9] of King Arthur's spear, and right so he smote his father King Arthur with his sword holden in both his hands, upon the side of the head, that the sword pierced the helmet and the tay[1] of the brain. And therewith Sir Mordred dashed down stark dead to the earth.

And noble King Arthur fell in a swough[2] to the earth, and there he swooned oftentimes, and Sir Lucan and Sir Bedivere ofttimes heaved him up. And so, weakly betwixt them, they led him to a little chapel not far from the seaside, and when the King was there, him thought him reasonably eased. Then heard they people cry in the field. "Now go thou, Sir Lucan," said the King, "and do me to wit[3] what betokens that noise in the field."

So Sir Lucan departed, for he was grievously wounded in many places. And so as he yede[4] he saw and harkened by the moonlight how that pillers[5] and robbers were come into the field to pill and to rob many a full noble knight of brooches and bees[6] and of many a good ring and many a rich jewel. And who that were not dead all out there they slew them for their harness[7] and their riches. When Sir Lucan understood this work, he came to the King as soon as he might and told him all what he had heard and seen. "Therefore by my read,"[8] said Sir Lucan, "it is best that we bring you to some town."

---

2. Knew.
3. I.e., unlucky for you.
4. I.e., with this much accomplished.
5. Betide.
6. Advantage.
7. Thrust.
8. I.e., six feet.
9. Hand guard.

1. Edge.
2. Swoon.
3. Let me know.
4. Walked.
5. Plunderers.
6. Bracelets.
7. Armor. "All out": entirely.
8. Advice.

"I would it were so," said the King, "but I may not stand, my head works[9] so. Ah, Sir Lancelot," said King Arthur, "this day have I sore missed thee. And alas that ever I was against thee, for now have I my death, whereof Sir Gawain me warned in my dream."

Then Sir Lucan took up the King the t'one party[1] and Sir Bedivere the other party; and in the lifting up the King swooned and in the lifting Sir Lucan fell in a swoon that part of his guts fell out of his body, and therewith the noble knight's heart burst. And when the King awoke he beheld Sir Lucan how he lay foaming at the mouth and part of his guts lay at his feet.

"Alas," said the King, "this is to me a full heavy[2] sight to see this noble duke so die for my sake, for he would have holpen[3] me that had more need of help than I. Alas that he would not complain him for[4] his heart was so set to help me. Now Jesu have mercy upon his soul."

Then Sir Bedivere wept for the death of his brother.

"Now leave this mourning and weeping, gentle knight," said the King, "for all this will not avail me. For wit thou well, and[5] I might live myself, the death of Sir Lucan would grieve me evermore. But my time passeth on fast," said the King. "Therefore," said King Arthur unto Sir Bedivere, "take thou here Excalibur[6] my good sword and go with it to yonder water's side; and when thou comest there I charge thee throw my sword in that water and come again and tell me what thou sawest there."

"My lord," said Sir Bedivere, "your commandment shall be done, and [I shall] lightly[7] bring you word again."

So Sir Bedivere departed. And by the way he beheld that noble sword, that the pommel and the haft[8] was all precious stones. And then he said to himself, "If I throw this rich sword in the water, thereof shall never come good, but harm and loss." And then Sir Bedivere hid Excalibur under a tree. And so, as soon as he might, he came again unto the King and said he had been at the water and had thrown the sword into the water.

"What saw thou there?" said the King.

"Sir," he said, "I saw nothing but waves and winds."

"That is untruly said of thee," said the King. "And therefore go thou lightly again and do my commandment; as thou art to me lief[9] and dear, spare not, but throw it in."

Then Sir Bedivere returned again and took the sword in his hand. And yet him thought[1] sin and shame to throw away that noble sword. And so eft[2] he hid the sword and returned again and told the King that he had been at the water and done his commandment.

"What sawest thou there?" said the King.

"Sir," he said, "I saw nothing but waters wap and waves wan."[3]

"Ah, traitor unto me and untrue," said King Arthur, "now hast thou betrayed me twice. Who would have weened that thou that has been to me so lief and dear, and thou art named a noble knight, and would betray me for the riches of this sword. But now go again lightly, for thy long tarrying

---

9. Aches.
1. On one side.
2. Sorrowful.
3. Helped.
4. Because.
5. If.
6. The sword that Arthur had received as a young man from the Lady of the Lake; it is presumably she who catches it when Bedivere finally throws it

into the water.
7. Quickly.
8. Handle. "Pommel": rounded knob on the hilt.
9. Beloved.
1. It seemed to him.
2. Again.
3. The phrase seems to mean "waters wash the shore and waves grow dark."

putteth me in great jeopardy of my life, for I have taken cold. And but if thou do now as I bid thee, if ever I may see thee I shall slay thee mine[4] own hands, for thou wouldest for my rich sword see me dead."

Then Sir Bedivere departed and went to the sword and lightly took it up, and so he went to the water's side; and there he bound the girdle[5] about the hilts, and threw the sword as far into the water as he might. And there came an arm and an hand above the water and took it and clutched it, and shook it thrice and brandished; and then vanished away the hand with the sword into the water. So Sir Bedivere came again to the King and told him what he saw.

"Alas," said the King, "help me hence, for I dread me I have tarried over-long."

Then Sir Bedivere took the King upon his back and so went with him to that water's side. And when they were at the water's side, even fast[6] by the bank hoved[7] a little barge with many fair ladies in it; and among them all was a queen; and all they had black hoods, and all they wept and shrieked when they saw King Arthur.

"Now put me into that barge," said the King; and so he did softly. And there received him three ladies with great mourning, and so they set them[8] down. And in one of their laps King Arthur laid his head, and then the queen said, "Ah, my dear brother, why have ye tarried so long from me? Alas, this wound on your head hath caught overmuch cold." And anon they rowed fromward the land, and Sir Bedivere beheld all tho ladies go froward him.

Then Sir Bedivere cried and said, "Ah, my lord Arthur, what shall become of me, now ye go from me and leave me here alone among mine enemies?"

"Comfort thyself," said the King, "and do as well as thou mayest, for in me is no trust for to trust in. For I must into the vale of Avilion[9] to heal me of my grievous wound. And if thou hear nevermore of me, pray for my soul."

But ever the queen and ladies wept and shrieked that it was pity to hear. And as soon as Sir Bedivere had lost the sight of the barge he wept and wailed and so took the forest, and went[1] all that night. And in the morning he was ware betwixt two holts hoar[2] of a chapel and an hermitage.[3]

* * *

Thus of Arthur I find no more written in books that been authorized,[4] neither more of the very certainty of his death heard I never read,[5] but thus was he led away in a ship wherein were three queens: that one was King Arthur's sister, Queen Morgan la Fée, the t'other[6] was the Queen of North Wales, and the third was the Queen of the Waste Lands. * * *

Now more of the death of King Arthur could I never find but that these ladies brought him to his burials,[7] and such one was buried there that the hermit bore witness that sometime was Bishop of Canterbury.[8] But yet the

4. I.e., with mine.
5. Sword belt.
6. Close.
7. Waited.
8. I.e., they sat.
9. A legendary island, sometimes identified with the earthly paradise.
1. Walked. "Took": took to.
2. Ancient copses.
3. In the passage here omitted, Sir Bedivere meets the former bishop of Canterbury, now a hermit, who describes how on the previous night a com-

pany of ladies had brought to the chapel a dead body, asking that it be buried. Sir Bedivere exclaims that the dead man must have been King Arthur and vows to spend the rest of his life there in the chapel as a hermit.
4. That have authority.
5. Tell.
6. The second.
7. Grave.
8. Of whom the hermit, who was formerly bishop of Canterbury, bore witness.

hermit knew not in certain that he was verily the body of King Arthur, for this tale Sir Bedivere, a Knight of the Table Round, made it to be written. Yet some men say in many parts of England that King Arthur is not dead, but had by the will of our Lord Jesu into another place. And men say that he shall come again and he shall win the Holy Cross. Yet I will not say that it shall be so, but rather I will say, Here in this world he changed his life. And many men say that there is written upon his tomb this verse: *Hic iacet Arthurus, rex quondam, rexque futurus.*[9]

[THE DEATHS OF LANCELOT AND GUINEVERE][1]

And thus upon a night there came a vision to Sir Lancelot and charged him, in remission[2] of his sins, to haste him unto Amesbury: "And by then[3] thou come there, thou shalt find Queen Guinevere dead. And therefore take thy fellows with thee, and purvey them of an horse-bier,[4] and fetch thou the corse[5] of her, and bury her by her husband, the noble King Arthur. So this avision[6] came to Lancelot thrice in one night. Then Sir Lancelot rose up ere day and told the hermit.

"It were well done," said the hermit, "that ye made you ready and that ye disobey not the avision."

Then Sir Lancelot took his eight fellows with him, and on foot they yede[7] from Glastonbury to Amesbury, the which is little more than thirty mile, and thither they came within two days, for they were weak and feeble to go. And when Sir Lancelot was come to Amesbury within the nunnery, Queen Guinevere died but half an hour afore. And the ladies told Sir Lancelot that Queen Guinevere told them all ere she passed that Sir Lancelot had been priest near a twelve-month:[8] "and hither he cometh as fast as he may to fetch my corse, and beside my lord King Arthur he shall bury me." Wherefore the Queen said in hearing of them all, "I beseech Almighty God that I may never have power to see Sir Lancelot with my worldly eyes."

"And thus," said all the ladies, "was ever her prayer these two days till she was dead."

Then Sir Lancelot saw her visage, but he wept not greatly, but sighed. And so he did all the observance of the service himself, both the *dirige*[9] and on the morn he sang mass. And there was ordained[1] an horse-bier, and so with an hundred torches ever burning about the corse of the Queen, and ever Sir Lancelot with his eight fellows went about[2] the horse-bier, singing and reading many an holy orison,[3] and frankincense upon the corse incensed.[4]

Thus Sir Lancelot and his eight fellows went on foot from Amesbury unto Glastonbury, and when they were come to the chapel and the hermitage, there she had a *dirige* with great devotion.[5] And on the morn the hermit that

9. "Here lies Arthur, who was once king and king will be again."
1. Guinevere enters a convent at Amesbury where Lancelot, returned with his companions to England, visits her, but she commands him never to see her again. Emulating her example, Lancelot joins the bishop of Canterbury and Bedivere in their hermitage where he takes holy orders and is joined in turn by seven of his fellow knights.
2. For the remission.
3. By the time.

4. Provide them with a horse-drawn hearse.
5. Body.
6. Dream.
7. Went.
8. Nearly twelve months.
9. Funeral service.
1. Prepared.
2. Around.
3. Reciting many a prayer.
4. Burned frankincense over the body.
5. Solemnity.

sometime[6] was Bishop of Canterbury sang the mass of requiem with great devotion, and Sir Lancelot was the first that offered, and then als[7] his eight fellows. And then she was wrapped in cered cloth of Rennes, from the top[8] to the toe, in thirtyfold, and after she was put in a web[9] of lead, and then in a coffin of marble.

And when she was put in the earth Sir Lancelot swooned and lay long still, while[1] the hermit came and awaked him, and said, "Ye be to blame, for ye displease God with such manner of sorrow-making."

"Truly," said Sir Lancelot, "I trust I do not displease God, for He knoweth mine intent—for my sorrow was not, nor is not, for any rejoicing of sin, but my sorrow may never have end. For when I remember of her beaulté and of her noblesse[2] that was both with her king and with her,[3] so when I saw his corse and her corse so lie together, truly mine heart would not serve to sustain my careful[4] body. Also when I remember me how by my defaute and mine orgule[5] and my pride that they were both laid full low, that were peerless that ever was living of Christian people, wit you well," said Sir Lancelot, "this remembered, of their kindness and mine unkindness, sank so to mine heart that I might not sustain myself." So the French book maketh mention.

Then Sir Lancelot never after ate but little meat,[6] nor drank, till he was dead, for then he sickened more and more and dried and dwined[7] away. For the Bishop nor none of his fellows might not make him to eat, and little he drank, that he was waxen by a kibbet[8] shorter than he was, that the people could not know him. For evermore, day and night, he prayed, but sometime he slumbered a broken sleep. Ever he was lying groveling on the tomb of King Arthur and Queen Guinevere, and there was no comfort that the Bishop nor Sir Bors, nor none of his fellows could make him—it availed not.

So within six weeks after, Sir Lancelot fell sick and lay in his bed. And then he sent for the Bishop that there was hermit, and all his true fellows. Then Sir Lancelot said with dreary steven,[9] "Sir Bishop, I pray you give to me all my rights that longeth[1] to a Christian man."

"It shall not need you,"[2] said the hermit and all his fellows. "It is but heaviness of your blood. Ye shall be well mended by the grace of God tomorn."

"My fair lords," said Sir Lancelot, "wit you well my careful body will into the earth; I have warning more than now I will say. Therefore give me my rights."

So when he was houseled and annealed[3] and had all that a Christian man ought to have, he prayed the Bishop that his fellows might bear his body to Joyous Garde. (Some men say it was Alnwick, and some men say it was Bamborough.) "Howbeit," said Sir Lancelot, "me repenteth[4] sore, but I made mine avow sometime that in Joyous Garde I would be buried. And because

6. Once.
7. Also. "Offered": made his donation.
8. Head. "Cloth of Rennes": A shroud made of fine linen smeared with wax, produced at Rennes.
9. Afterward she was put in a sheet.
1. Until.
2. Her beauty and nobility.
3. That she and her king both had.
4. Sorrowful.

5. My fault and my haughtiness.
6. Food.
7. Wasted.
8. Grown by a cubit.
9. Sad voice.
1. Pertains. "Rights": last sacrament.
2. You shall not need it.
3. Given communion and extreme unction.
4. I am sorry.

of breaking[5] of mine avow, I pray you all, lead me thither." Then there was weeping and wringing of hands among his fellows.

So at a season of the night they all went to their beds, for they all lay in one chamber. And so after midnight, against[6] day, the Bishop that was hermit, as he lay in his bed asleep, he fell upon a great laughter. And therewith all the fellowship awoke and came to the Bishop and asked him what he ailed.[7]

"Ah, Jesu mercy," said the Bishop, "why did ye awake me? I was never in all my life so merry and so well at ease."

"Wherefore?" said Sir Bors.

"Truly," said the Bishop, "here was Sir Lancelot with me, with mo[8] angels than ever I saw men in one day. And I saw the angels heave[9] up Sir Lancelot unto heaven, and the gates of heaven opened against him."

"It is but dretching of swevens,"[1] said Sir Bors, "for I doubt not Sir Lancelot aileth nothing but good."[2]

"It may well be," said the Bishop. "Go ye to his bed and then shall ye prove the sooth."

So when Sir Bors and his fellows came to his bed, they found him stark dead. And he lay as he had smiled, and the sweetest savor[3] about him that ever they felt. Then was there weeping and wringing of hands, and the greatest dole they made that ever made men. And on the morn the Bishop did his mass of Requiem, and after the Bishop and all the nine knights put Sir Lancelot in the same horse-bier that Queen Guinevere was laid in tofore that she was buried. And so the Bishop and they all together went with the body of Sir Lancelot daily, till they came to Joyous Garde. And ever they had an hundred torches burning about him.

And so within fifteen days they came to Joyous Garde. And there they laid his corse in the body of the choir,[4] and sang and read many psalters[5] and prayers over him and about him. And ever his visage was laid open and naked, that all folks might behold him; for such was the custom in tho[6] days that all men of worship should so lie with open visage till that they were buried.

And right thus as they were at their service, there came Sir Ector de Maris that had seven year sought all England, Scotland, and Wales, seeking his brother, Sir Lancelot. And when Sir Ector heard such noise and light in the choir of Joyous Garde, he alight and put his horse from him and came into the choir. And there he saw men sing and weep, and all they knew Sir Ector, but he knew not them. Then went Sir Bors unto Sir Ector and told him how there lay his brother, Sir Lancelot, dead. And then Sir Ector threw his shield, sword, and helm from him, and when he beheld Sir Lancelot's visage, he fell down in a swoon. And when he waked, it were hard any tongue to tell the doleful complaints that he made for his brother.

"Ah, Lancelot!" he said, "thou were head of all Christian knights. And now I dare say," said Sir Ector, "thou Sir Lancelot, there thou liest, that thou were never matched of earthly knight's hand. And thou were the courteoust[7]

---

5. In order not to break.
6. Toward.
7. Ailed him.
8. More.
9. Lift.
1. Illusion of dreams.
2. Has nothing wrong with him.

3. Odor. A sweet scent is a conventional sign in saints' lives of a sanctified death.
4. The center of the chancel, the place of honor.
5. Psalms.
6. Those.
7. Most courteous.

knight that ever bore shield. And thou were the truest friend to thy lover that ever bestrode horse, and thou were the truest lover, of a sinful man,[8] that ever loved woman, and thou were the kindest man that ever struck with sword. And thou were the goodliest person that ever came among press of knights, and thou was the meekest man and the gentlest that ever ate in hall among ladies, and thou were the sternest knight to thy mortal foe that ever put spear in the rest."[9]

Then there was weeping and dolor out of measure.

Thus they kept Sir Lancelot's corse aloft fifteen days, and then they buried it with great devotion. And then at leisure they went all with the Bishop of Canterbury to his hermitage, and there they were together more than a month.

Then Sir Constantine that was Sir Cador's son of Cornwall was chosen king of England, and he was a full noble knight, and worshipfully he ruled this realm. And then this King Constantine sent for the Bishop of Canterbury, for he heard say where he was. And so he was restored unto his bishopric and left that hermitage, and Sir Bedivere was there ever still hermit to his life's end.

Then Sir Bors de Ganis, Sir Ector de Maris, Sir Gahalantine, Sir Galihud, Sir Galihodin, Sir Blamour, Sir Bleoberis, Sir Villiars le Valiant, Sir Clarrus of Clermount, all these knights drew them to their countries. Howbeit[1] King Constantine would have had them with him, but they would not abide in this realm. And there they all lived in their countries as holy men.

And some English books make mention that they went never out of England after the death of Sir Lancelot—but that was but favor of makers.[2] For the French book maketh mention—and is authorized—that Sir Bors, Sir Ector, Sir Blamour, and Sir Bleoberis went into the Holy Land, thereas Jesu Christ was quick[3] and dead, and anon as they had stablished their lands;[4] for the book saith so Sir Lancelot commanded them for to do ere ever he passed out of this world. There these four knights did many battles upon the miscreaunts,[5] or Turks, and there they died upon a Good Friday for God's sake.

Here is the end of the whole book of King Arthur and of his noble knights of the Round Table, that when they were whole together there was ever an hundred and forty. And here is the end of *The Death of Arthur*.[6]

I pray you all gentlemen and gentlewomen that readeth this book of Arthur and his knights from the beginning to the ending, pray for me while I am alive that God send me good deliverance. And when I am dead, I pray you all pray for my soul.

For this book was ended the ninth year of the reign of King Edward the Fourth, by Sir Thomas Malory, knight, as Jesu help him for His great might, as he is the servant of Jesu both day and night.

1469–70   1485

---

8. Of any man born in original sin.
9. Support for the butt of the lance.
1. However.
2. The authors' bias.
3. Living. "Thereas": where.
4. As soon as they had put their lands in order.

5. Infidels.
6. By the "whole book" Malory refers to the entire work; the *Death of Arthur*, which Caxton made the title of the entire work, refers to the last part of Malory's book.

The Sixteenth Century
1485–1603

At the beginning of the sixteenth century, the English language had almost no prestige abroad, and there were those at home who doubted that it could serve as a suitable medium for serious, elevated, or elegant discourse. Yet by the century's end there were signs of a great increase in what we might call linguistic self-confidence, signs that at least some contemporary observers were aware that something extraordinary had happened to their language. Though in 1600 England still remained somewhat peripheral to the Continent, English had been fashioned into an immensely powerful expressive medium, one whose cadences in the works of Marlowe, Shakespeare, or the translators of the Bible continue after more than four centuries to thrill readers.

How did it come about that by the century's end so many remarkable poems, plays, and prose works were written in English? The answer lies in part in the spectacular creativity of a succession of brilliant writers, the best of whom are represented in these pages. Still, a vital literary culture is the product of a complex process, involving thousands of more modest, half-hidden creative acts sparked by a wide range of motives, some of which we will briefly explore.

THE COURT AND THE CITY

The development of the English language in the sixteenth century is linked at least indirectly to the consolidation and strengthening of the English state. Preoccupied by violent clashes between the thuggish feudal retainers of rival barons, England through most of the fifteenth century had rather limited time and inclination to cultivate rhetorical skills. The social and economic health of the nation had been severely damaged by the so-called Wars of the Roses, a vicious, decades-long struggle for royal power between the noble houses of York and Lancaster. The struggle was resolved with the establishment by Henry VII of the Tudor dynasty that ruled England from 1485 to 1603. The wily Henry was able to counter the multiple and competing power structures characteristic of feudal society and to impose a much stronger central authority and order on the nation. Initiated by the first Tudor sovereign, this consolidation progressed throughout the sixteenth century; by the reign of the last Tudor—Henry's granddaughter, Elizabeth I—though the ruler still needed the consent of Parliament on crucial matters (including the all-important one of raising taxes), the royal court had concentrated in itself much of the nation's power.

The court was a center of culture as well as power: court entertainments such as theater and masque (a sumptuous, elaborately costumed performance of dance, song, and poetry); court fashions in dress and speech; court tastes in painting, music, and poetry—all shaped the taste and the imagination of the country as a whole. Culture and power were not, in any case, easily separable in Tudor England. In a society with no freedom of speech as we understand it and with relatively limited means of mass communication, important public issues were often aired indirectly, through what we might now regard as entertainment, while lyrics that to us seem slight and nonchalant could serve as carefully crafted manifestations of rhetorical agility by aspiring courtiers.

Court culture simultaneously spawned an art of intrigue and one of ostentation. Ambitious men and women sought to call attention to themselves. They did so by the gorgeous, immensely costly clothes they wore—Elizabethan high fashion was among the most extravagantly ornamented in European history—and by the display of their artistic and social skills. The goal was close proximity to the monarch's body (one of the coveted positions in the court of Henry VIII was Groom of the Stool, "close stool" being the Tudor term for toilet). But if proximity held out the promise of wealth and power, it also harbored danger. Festive evenings with the likes of the ruthless Henry VIII were not occasions for relaxation. The court fostered paranoia and an attendant obsession with secrecy, spying, duplicity, and betrayal. Courtiers were highly gifted at crafting and deciphering graceful words with double or triple meanings. Sixteenth-century poets had much to learn from courtiers, the Elizabethan critic George Puttenham observed; indeed many of the best poets in the period, Sir Thomas Wyatt, Sir Philip Sidney, Sir Walter Ralegh, and others, were courtiers.

If court culture fostered performances for a small coterie audience, other forces in Tudor England pulled toward a more public sphere. Markets expanded significantly, international trade flourished, and cities throughout the realm experienced a rapid surge in size and importance. London's population in particular soared, from 60,000 in 1520 to 120,000 in 1550 to 375,000 a century later, making it the largest and fastest-growing city not only in England but in all of Europe. Every year in the first half of the seventeenth century about 10,000 people migrated to London from other parts of England—wages in London tended to be around 50 percent higher than in the rest of the country—and it is estimated that one in eight English people lived in London at some point in their lives.

About a decade before Henry VII won his throne, the art of printing from movable metal type, a German invention, had been introduced into England by William Caxton (ca. 1422–1491), who had learned and practiced it in the Low Countries. Though reliable statistics are impossible to come by, literacy seems to have increased during the fifteenth century and still more during the sixteenth, when Protestantism encouraged a direct encounter with the Bible. Printing made books cheaper and more plentiful, providing more opportunity to read and more incentive to learn. The greater availability of books may also have reinforced the trend toward silent reading, a trend that gradually transformed what had been a communal experience into a more intimate encounter with a text.

Yet it would be a mistake to imagine these changes as sudden and dramatic. Manuscripts retained considerable prestige among the elite; throughout the sixteenth and well into the seventeenth centuries court poets in particular were wary of the "stigma of print" that might mark their verse as less exclusive.

RENAISSANCE HUMANISM

During the fifteenth century a few English clerics and government officials had journeyed to Italy and had seen something of the extraordinary cultural and intellectual movement flourishing in the city-states there. That movement, generally known as the Renaissance, involved a rebirth of letters and arts stimulated by the recovery of texts and artifacts from classical antiquity, the development of techniques such as linear perspective, and the creation of powerful new aesthetic norms based on classical models. It also unleashed new ideas and new social, political, and economic forces that gradually displaced the otherworldly and communal values of the Middle Ages. In the brilliant, intensely competitive, and vital world of Leonardo da Vinci and Michelangelo, the submission of the human spirit to penitential discipline gave way to unleashed curiosity, individual self-assertion, and a powerful conviction that man was the measure of all things. "We have made thee neither of heaven nor of earth, neither mortal nor immortal," God tells Adam, in the Florentine Pico della Mirandola's *Oration on the Dignity of Man* (1486), "so that with freedom of choice and with honor, as though the maker and molder of thyself, thou mayest fashion thyself in whatever shape thou shalt prefer." "As though the maker and molder of thyself": this vision of self-fashioning may be glimpsed in the poetry of Petrarch, the sculpture of Donatello, and the statecraft of Lorenzo de' Medici. But in England it was not until Henry VII's reign brought some measure of political stability that the Renaissance could take root, and it was not until the accession of Henry VIII that it began to flower.

This flowering, when it occurred, came not, as in Italy, in the visual arts and architecture. It came rather in the spiritual and intellectual orientation known as humanism. In England and elsewhere, humanism was bound up with struggles over the purposes of education and curriculum reform. Education—predominantly male and conducted by tutors in wealthy families or in grammar schools—was ordered according to the subjects of the medieval *trivium* (grammar, logic, and rhetoric) and *quadrivium* (arithmetic, geometry, astronomy, and music), but humanists helped to shift its focus from training for the church to the general acquisition of "literature," in the sense both of literacy and of cultural knowledge. For some of the more intellectually ambitious humanists, that knowledge extended to ancient Greek, whose enthusiastic adherents began to challenge the entrenched prestige of Latin.

Still, at the core of the curriculum remained the study of Latin, the mastery of which was in effect a prolonged male puberty rite involving pain as well as pleasure. Though some educators counseled mildness, punishment was an established part of the pedagogy of the age, and even gifted students could scarcely have escaped recurrent flogging. The purpose was to train the sons of the nobility and gentry to speak and write good Latin, the language of diplomacy, of the professions, and of all higher learning. Their sisters were always educated at home or in other noble houses. They chiefly learned modern languages, religion, music, and needlework, but they very seldom received the firm grounding in ancient languages and classical literature so central to Renaissance culture.

Humanists committed to classical learning were faced with the question of whether to write their own works in Latin or in English. To many learned men, influenced both by the humanist exaltation of the classical languages and by the characteristic Renaissance desire for eternal fame, the national languages seemed relatively unstable and ephemeral. Intellectuals had long shared a pan-European world of scientific inquiry, so that works by such English scientists as William Gilbert, William Harvey, and Francis Bacon easily joined those by Nicolaus Copernicus, Johannes Kepler, and Andreas Vesalius on the common linguistic ground of Latin. But throughout Europe nationalism and the expansion of the reading public were steadily strengthening the power and allure of the vernacular. The famous schoolmaster Richard Mulcaster (ca. 1530–1611), teacher of the poet Edmund Spenser, captured this emergent sense of national identity in singing the praises of his native tongue: "I love Rome, but London better; I favor Italy, but England more; I honor the Latin, but I worship the English."

THE REFORMATION

There had long been serious ideological and institutional tensions in the religious life of England, but officially at least England in the early sixteenth century had a single religion, Catholicism, whose acknowledged head was the pope in Rome. For its faithful adherents the Catholic church was the central institution in their lives, a universal infallible guide to human existence from cradle to grave and on into the life to come. They were instructed by its teachings, corrected by its discipline, sustained by its sacraments, and comforted by its promises. At Mass, its most sacred ritual, the congregation could witness a miracle, as the priest held aloft the Host and uttered the words that transformed the bread and wine into the body and blood of God incarnate. A vast system of confession, pardons, penance, absolution, indulgences, sacred relics, and ceremonies gave the unmarried male clerical hierarchy great power, at once spiritual and material, over their largely illiterate flock. The Bible, the liturgy, and most of the theological discussions were in Latin, which few lay people could understand; however, religious doctrine and spirituality were mediated to them by the priests, by beautiful church art and music, and by the liturgical ceremonies of daily life—festivals, holy days, baptisms, marriages, exorcisms, and funerals.

Several of the key doctrines and practices of the Catholic church had been challenged in fourteenth-century England by the teachings of John Wycliffe and his followers, known as the Lollards. But the heretical challenge had been ruthlessly suppressed, and the embers of dissent lay largely dormant until they were ignited once again in Germany by Martin Luther, an Augustinian monk and professor of theology at the University of Wittenberg. What began in November 1517 as an academic disputation grew with amazing speed into a bitter, far-reaching, and bloody revolt that forever ruptured the unity of Western Christendom.

When Luther rose up against the ancient church, he did so in the name of private conscience enlightened by a personal reading of the Scriptures. A person of formidable intellectual energy, eloquence, and rhetorical violence, Luther charged that the pope and his hierarchy were the servants of Satan and that the church had degenerated into a corrupt, worldly conspiracy designed to bilk the credulous and subvert secular authority. Salvation depended upon destroying this conspiracy and enabling all of the people to regain direct access to the word of God by means of vernacular translations of the Bible. The common watchwords of the Reformation, as the movement Luther sparked came to be known, were *sola scriptura* and *sola fide*: only the Scriptures (not the church or tradition or the clerical hierarchy) have authority in matters of religion and should determine what an individual must believe and practice; only the faith of the individual (not good works or the scrupulous observance of religious rituals) can effect a Christian's salvation.

These tenets, heretical in the eyes of the Catholic Church, spread and gathered force, especially in Northern Europe, where major leaders like the Swiss pastor Ulrich Zwingli in Zurich and the French theologian John Calvin in Geneva, elaborating various and sometimes conflicting doctrinal principles, organized the populace to overturn the existing church and established new institutional structures. In England, however, the Reformation began less with popular discontent and theological disputation than with dynastic politics and royal greed. Henry VIII, who had received from Pope Leo X the title Defender of the Faith for writing a book against Luther, craved a legitimate son to succeed to the throne, and his queen, Catherine of Aragon, failed to give him one. (Catherine had borne six children, but only a daughter, Mary, survived infancy.) After lengthy negotiations, the pope, under pressure from Catherine's powerful Spanish family, refused to grant the king the divorce he sought in order to marry Anne Boleyn. A series of momentous events followed, as England lurched away from the Church of Rome. In 1531 Henry charged the entire clergy of England with having usurped royal authority in the administration of canon law (the law that governed such matters as divorce). Under extreme pressure, including the threat of mass confiscations and imprisonment, the Convocation of the Clergy begged for pardon and made a donation to the royal coffers of over one hundred thousand pounds.

In 1533 Henry's marriage to Catherine was officially declared null and void and Anne Boleyn was crowned queen. The king was promptly excommunicated by the pope, Clement VII. In the following year, a parliamentary

Act of Succession required an oath from all adult male subjects confirming the new dynastic settlement. Thomas More, the distinguished humanist and former chancellor, and John Fisher, the bishop of Rochester, were among the small number who refused. The Act of Supremacy, passed later in the year, formally declared the king to be "Supreme Head of the Church in England" and again required an oath to this effect. In 1535 and 1536 further acts made it treasonous to refuse the oath of royal supremacy or, as More had tried to do, to remain silent. The first victims were three Carthusian monks who rejected the oath—"How could the king, a layman," said one of them, "be Head of the Church of England?"—and in May 1535 were duly hanged, drawn, and quartered. A few weeks later Fisher and More were convicted and beheaded. Between 1536 and 1539, under the direction of Henry's powerful secretary of state, Thomas Cromwell, England's monasteries were suppressed and their vast wealth seized by the crown.

Royal defiance of the authority of Rome was a key element in the Reformation but did not by itself constitute the establishment of Protestantism in England. On the contrary, in the same year that Fisher and More were martyred for their adherence to Roman Catholicism, twenty-five Protestants, members of a sect known as Anabaptists, were burned for heresy on a single day. Through most of his reign, Henry remained an equal-opportunity persecutor, pitiless to Catholics loyal to Rome and hostile to many of those who espoused Reformation ideas, though these ideas gradually established themselves on English soil.

Even when Henry (in his brief stint as Defender of the Faith) was eager to do so, it proved impossible to eradicate Protestantism, as it would later prove impossible for Protestant monarchs to eradicate Catholicism. In part this persistence in the face of ferocious persecution arose from the willingness of a small core of ardent believers to die for their faith; in part it arose from the ability of even a small number of clandestine printing presses to flood the country with texts that the authorities were unable to suppress. Hence in his role as Defender of the Faith, Henry had driven the great English translator of the Bible, William Tyndale, into exile on the Continent, where he was eventually seized and garroted by Catholic authorities. But Tyndale's eloquent—and distinctly Protestant—translation of the New Testament circulated widely in England, despite repeated attempts by officials to burn every copy. After Henry's break with Rome, Tyndale's version served as the core of the so-called Great Bible, the authorized translation that made the Scriptures available in English to anyone who could read.

Upon Henry's death in 1547, his son, Edward (by his third wife, Jane Seymour), came to the throne, with his maternal uncle, Edward Seymour, the duke of Somerset, as Lord Protector. Both the ten-year-old Edward and his uncle were staunch Protestants, and reformers hastened to transform the English church accordingly. During Edward's brief reign, Thomas Cranmer, the archbishop of Canterbury, formulated the forty-two articles of religion which became the core of Anglican orthodoxy and wrote the first *Book of Common Prayer*, which was officially adopted in 1549 as the basis of English worship services.

The sickly Edward died in 1553, only six years after his accession to the throne, and was succeeded by his half-sister Mary (Henry VIII's daughter by his first wife, Catherine), who immediately took steps to return her kingdom to Roman Catholicism. Though she was unable to get Parliament to agree to return church lands seized under Henry VIII, she restored the Catholic Mass, once again affirmed the authority of the pope, and put down a rebellion that sought to depose her. Seconded by her ardently Catholic husband, Philip II, king of Spain, she initiated a series of religious persecutions that earned her (from her enemies) the name Bloody Mary. Hundreds of Protestants took refuge abroad in cities like Calvin's Geneva; almost three hundred less fortunate Protestants were condemned as heretics and burned at the stake.

Mary died childless in 1558, and her younger half-sister, Elizabeth, became queen. Elizabeth's succession had been by no means assured. For if Protestants regarded Henry VIII's marriage to Catherine as invalid and hence deemed Mary illegitimate, so Catholics regarded his marriage to Anne Boleyn as invalid and hence deemed her daughter, Elizabeth, illegitimate. Henry VIII himself seemed to support both views, since only three years after divorcing Catherine, he beheaded Anne on charges of treason and adultery and urged Parliament to invalidate the marriage. Moreover, though during her sister's reign Elizabeth outwardly complied with the official Catholic religious observance, Mary and her advisers suspected her of Protestant leanings, and the young princess's life was in grave danger. Poised and circumspect, Elizabeth warily evaded the traps that were set for her. When she ascended the throne, her actions were scrutinized for some indication of the country's future course. During her coronation procession, when a girl in an allegorical pageant presented her with a Bible in English translation—banned under Mary's reign—Elizabeth kissed the book, held it up reverently, and laid it to her breast. England had returned to the Reformation.

Many English men and women, of all classes, remained loyal to the old Catholic faith, but English authorities under Elizabeth moved steadily, if cautiously, toward ensuring at least an outward conformity to the official Protestant settlement. Recusants, those who refused to attend regular Sunday services in their parish churches, were heavily fined. Anyone who wished to receive a university degree, to be ordained as a priest in the Church of England, or to be named as an officer of the state had to swear an oath to the royal supremacy. Commissioners were sent throughout the land to confirm that religious services were following the officially approved liturgy and to investigate any reported backsliding into Catholic practice or, alternatively, any attempts to introduce reforms more radical than the queen and her bishops had chosen to embrace, for the Protestant exiles who streamed back were eager not only to undo the damage Mary had done but also to carry the Reformation much further than it had gone. They sought to dismantle the church hierarchy, to purge the calendar of folk customs deemed pagan and the church service of ritual practices deemed superstitious, to dress the clergy in simple garb, and, at the extreme edge, to smash "idolatrous" statues, crucifixes, and altarpieces. Throughout her long reign, however, Elizabeth herself remained cautiously conservative and determined to hold religious zealotry in check.

In the space of a single lifetime, England had gone officially from Roman Catholicism, to Catholicism under the supreme headship of the English king, to a guarded Protestantism, to a more radical Protestantism, to a renewed and aggressive Roman Catholicism, and finally to Protestantism again. Each of these shifts was accompanied by danger, persecution, and death. It was enough to make people wary. Or skeptical. Or extremely agile.

THE ENGLISH AND OTHERNESS

Elizabethan London had a large population of resident aliens, mainly artisans and merchants and their families, from Portugal, Italy, Spain, Germany, and, above all, France and the Netherlands. Many of these people were Protestant refugees, and they were accorded some legal and economic protection by the government. But they were not always welcome to the local populace. Throughout the sixteenth century London was the site of repeated demonstrations and, on occasion, bloody riots against the communities of foreign artisans, who were accused of taking jobs away from Englishmen. There was widespread hostility as well toward the Welsh, the Scots, and above all the Irish, whom the English had for centuries been struggling unsuccessfully to subdue. The kings of England claimed to be rulers of Ireland, but in reality they effectively controlled only a small area known as the Pale, extending north from Dublin. The great majority of the population remained stubbornly Catholic and, despite endlessly reiterated English repression, burning of villages, destruction of crops, seizure of land, and massacres, incorrigibly independent.

Medieval England's Jewish population, the recurrent object of persecution, extortion, and massacre, had been officially expelled by King Edward I in 1290, but Elizabethan England harbored a tiny number of Jews or Jewish converts to Christianity. They were the objects of suspicion and hostility. Elizabethans appear to have been fascinated by Jews and Judaism but quite uncertain whether the terms referred to a people, a foreign nation, a set of strange practices, a living faith, a defunct religion, a villainous conspiracy, or a messianic inheritance. Protestant Reformers brooded deeply on the Hebraic origins of Christianity; government officials ordered the arrest of those "suspected to be Jews"; villagers paid pennies to itinerant fortunetellers who claimed to be descended from Abraham or masters of kabbalistic mysteries; and London playgoers enjoyed the spectacle of the downfall of the wicked Barabas in Christopher Marlowe's *The Jew of Malta* and the forced conversion of Shylock in Shakespeare's *The Merchant of Venice*. Jews were not officially permitted to resettle in England until the middle of the seventeenth century, and even then their legal status was ambiguous.

Sixteenth-century England also had a small African population whose skin color was the subject of pseudoscientific speculation and theological debate. Some Elizabethans believed that Africans' blackness resulted from the climate of the regions where they lived, where, as one traveler put it, they were "so scorched and vexed with the heat of the sun, that in many places they curse it when it riseth." Others held that blackness was a curse inherited from their forefather Cush, the son of Ham (who had, according to Genesis, wickedly exposed the nakedness of his drunken father, Noah). George Best, a proponent of this theory of inherited skin color, reported that "I myself have seen an Ethiopian as black as coal brought into England, who taking a fair English woman to wife, begat a son in all respects as black as the father was, although England were his native country, and an English woman his mother: whereby it seemeth this blackness proceedeth rather of some natural infection of that man."

As the word "infection" suggests, Elizabethans frequently regarded blackness as a physical defect, though the black people who lived in England and Scotland throughout the sixteenth century were also treated as exotic curiosities. At his marriage to Anne of Denmark, James VI of Scotland (the son of Mary, Queen of Scots; as James I of England, he succeeded Elizabeth in 1603) entertained his bride and her family by commanding four naked black youths to dance before him in the snow. (The youths died of exposure shortly afterward.) In 1594, in the festivities celebrating the baptism of James's son, a "Black-Moor" entered pulling an elaborately decorated chariot that was, in the original plan, supposed to be pulled by a lion. In England there was a black trumpeter in the courts of Henry VII and Henry VIII, while Elizabeth had at least two black servants, one an entertainer, the other a page. Africans became increasingly popular as servants in aristocratic and gentle households in the last decades of the sixteenth century.

Some of these Africans were almost certainly slaves, though the legal status of slavery in England was ambiguous. In Cartwright's Case (1569), the court ruled "that England was too Pure an Air for Slaves to breathe in," but there is evidence that black slaves were owned in Elizabethan and Jacobean England. Moreover, by the mid-sixteenth century the English had become involved in the profitable trade that carried African slaves to the New World. In 1562 John Hawkins embarked on his first slaving voyage, transporting some three hundred Africans from the Guinea coast to Hispaniola, where they were sold for ten thousand pounds. Elizabeth is reported to have said of this venture that it was "detestable, and would call down the Vengeance of Heaven upon the Undertakers." Nevertheless, she invested in Hawkins's subsequent voyages and loaned him ships.

Elizabeth also invested in other enterprises that combined aggressive nationalism and the pursuit of profit. In 1493 the pope had divided the New World between the Spanish and the Portuguese by drawing a line from pole to pole (hence Brazil speaks Portuguese today and the rest of Latin America speaks Spanish): the English were not in the picture. But by the end of Edward VI's reign the Company of Merchant Adventurers was founded, and Englishmen began to explore Asia and North America. Some of these adventurers turned to piracy, preying on Spanish ships that were returning laden with wealth extracted from their New World possessions. (The pope had ruled that the Indians were human beings—and hence could be converted to Christianity—but the ruling did nothing to prevent their enslavement and brutal exploitation.) English acts of piracy soon became a private undeclared war, with the queen and her courtiers covertly investing in the raids but accepting no responsibility for them. The greatest of many astounding exploits was the voyage of Francis Drake (1577–80): he sailed through the Strait of Magellan, pillaged Spanish towns on the Pacific, reached as far north as San Francisco, crossed to the Philippines, and returned around the Cape of Good Hope; he came back with a million pounds in treasure, and his investors earned a dividend of 5,000 percent. Queen Elizabeth knighted him on the deck of his ship, *The Golden Hind*.

A FEMALE MONARCH IN A MALE WORLD

In the last year of Mary's reign, the Scottish Calvinist minister John Knox thundered against what he called "the monstrous regiment of women." After the Protestant Elizabeth came to the throne the following year, Knox and his religious brethren were less inclined to denounce all female rulers, but in England, as elsewhere in Europe, there remained a widespread conviction that women were unsuited to wield power over men. Many men seem to have regarded the capacity for rational thought as exclusively male; women, they assumed, were led only by their passions. While gentlemen mastered the arts of rhetoric and warfare, gentlewomen were expected to display the virtues of silence and good housekeeping. Among upper-class males, the will to dominate others was acceptable and indeed admired; the same will in women was condemned as a grotesque and dangerous aberration.

Apologists for the queen countered these prejudices by appealing to historical precedent and legal theory. History offered inspiring examples of just female rulers, notably Deborah, the biblical prophetess who had judged Israel. In the legal sphere, crown lawyers advanced the theory of "the king's two bodies." As England's crowned head, Elizabeth's person was mystically divided between her mortal "body natural" and the immortal "body politic." While the queen's natural body was inevitably subject to the failings of human flesh, the body politic was timeless and perfect. In political terms, therefore, Elizabeth's sex was a matter of no consequence, a thing indifferent.

Elizabeth, who had received a fine humanist education and an extended, dangerous lesson in the art of survival, made it immediately clear that she intended to rule in more than name only. Like many Renaissance monarchs, Elizabeth was drawn to the idea of royal absolutism, the theory that ultimate power was quite properly concentrated in her person and indeed that God had appointed her to be His deputy in the kingdom. In reality, Elizabeth's power was not absolute. The government had a network of spies, informers and *agents provocateurs*, but it lacked a standing army, a national police force, an efficient system of communication, and an extensive bureaucracy. Above all, the queen had limited financial resources and needed to turn periodically to an independent and often recalcitrant Parliament, which by long tradition had the sole right to levy taxes and to grant subsidies. Members of the House of Commons were elected from their boroughs, not appointed by the monarch, and though the queen had considerable influence over their decisions, she could by no means dictate policy. Under these constraints, Elizabeth ruled through a combination of adroit political maneuvering and imperious command, all the while enhancing her authority in the eyes of both court and country by means of an extraordinary cult of love.

"We all loved her," Elizabeth's godson Sir John Harington wrote, with just a touch of irony, a few years after the queen's death, "for she said she loved us." Ambassadors, courtiers, and parliamentarians all submitted to Elizabeth's cult of love, in which the queen's gender was transformed from a potential liability into a significant asset. Those who approached her generally did so on their knees and were expected to address her with the most extravagant compliments; she in turn spoke, when it suited her to do so, in a comparable language of love. The court moved in an atmosphere of romance, with music, dancing, plays, and the elaborate, fancy-dress entertainments called masques. The queen adorned herself in dazzling clothes and rich jewels. When she went on one of her summer "progresses," ceremonial journeys through her land, she looked like an exotic, sacred image in a religious cult of love, and her noble hosts virtually bankrupted themselves to lavish upon her the costliest pleasures. England's leading artists, such as the poet Spenser and the painter Nicholas Hilliard, enlisted themselves in the celebration of Elizabeth's mystery, likening her to the goddesses of mythology and the heroines of the Bible: Diana, Astraea, Cynthia, Deborah.

There was a sober, even grim aspect to these poetical fantasies: Elizabeth was brilliant at playing one dangerous faction off against another, now turning her gracious smiles on one favorite, now honoring his hated rival, now suddenly looking elsewhere and raising an obscure upstart to royal favor. And when she was disobeyed or when she felt that her prerogatives had been challenged, she was capable of an anger that, as Harington put it, "left no doubtings whose daughter she was." Thus when Sir Walter Ralegh, one of the queen's glittering favorites, married without her knowledge or consent, he found himself promptly imprisoned in the Tower of London. Or when the Protestant polemicist John Stubbs ventured to publish a pamphlet stridently denouncing the queen's proposed marriage to the French Catholic duke of Anjou, Stubbs and his publisher were arrested and had their right hands chopped off. (After receiving the blow, the now prudent Stubbs lifted his hat with his remaining hand and cried, "God save the Queen!")

The queen's marriage negotiations were a particularly fraught issue. When she came to the throne at twenty-five, speculation about a suitable match, already widespread, intensified and remained for decades at a fever pitch, for the stakes were high. If Elizabeth died childless, the Tudor line would come to an end. The nearest heir was her cousin Mary, Queen of Scots, a Catholic whose claim was supported by France and by the papacy and whose penchant for sexual and political intrigue confirmed the worst fears of English Protestants. The obvious way to avert the nightmare was for Elizabeth to marry and produce an heir, and the pressure upon her to do so was intense.

More than the royal succession hinged on the question of the queen's marriage; Elizabeth's perceived eligibility was a vital factor in the complex machinations of international diplomacy. A dynastic marriage between the queen of England and a foreign ruler would forge an alliance sufficient to alter the balance of power in Europe. The English court hosted a steady stream of ambassadors from kings and princelings eager to win the hand of the royal maiden, and Elizabeth, who prided herself on speaking fluent French and Italian (and on reading Latin and Greek), played her romantic part with exemplary skill, sighing and spinning the negotiations out for months and even years. Most probably, she never meant to marry any of her numerous foreign (and domestic) suitors. Such a decisive act would have meant the end of her independence, as well as the end of the marriage game by which she played one power off against another. One day she would seem to be on the verge of accepting a proposal; the next, she would vow never to forsake her virginity. "She is a princess," the French ambassador remarked, "who can act any part she pleases."

THE KINGDOM IN DANGER

Beset by Catholic and Protestant extremists, Elizabeth contrived to forge a moderate compromise that enabled her realm to avert the massacres and civil wars that poisoned France and other countries on the Continent. But menace was never far off, and there were continual fears of conspiracy, rebellion, and assassination. Many of the fears swirled around Mary, Queen of Scots, who had been driven from her own kingdom in 1567 and had taken refuge in England. Her presence, under a kind of house arrest, was the source of intense anxiety and helped generate continual rumors of plots, some of them real enough, others imaginary, still others fabricated by the secret agents of the government's intelligence service under the direction of Sir Francis Walsingham.

The queen's life seemed to be in great danger after Pope Gregory XIII's proclamation in 1580 that the assassination of the great heretic Elizabeth (who had been excommunicated a decade before) would not constitute a mortal sin. The immediate effect of the proclamation was to make life more difficult for English Catholics, most of whom were loyal to the queen but who fell under grave suspicion. Suspicion was intensified by the clandestine presence of English Jesuits, trained at seminaries abroad and smuggled back into England to serve the Roman Catholic cause. When, after several botched conspiracies had been disclosed, Elizabeth's spymaster Walsingham unearthed another assassination plot in the correspondence between the Queen of Scots and the Catholic Anthony Babington, the wretched Mary's fate was sealed. After vacillating, a very reluctant Elizabeth signed the death warrant, and her cousin was beheaded.

The long-anticipated military confrontation with Catholic Spain was now unavoidable. Elizabeth learned that Philip II, her former brother-in-law and one-time suitor, was preparing to send an enormous fleet against her island realm. The Armada was to sail to the Netherlands, where a Spanish army would be waiting to embark and invade England. Barring its way was England's small fleet of well-armed and highly maneuverable fighting vessels, backed up by ships from the merchant navy. The Invincible Armada reached English waters in July 1588, only to be routed in one of the most famous and decisive naval battles in European history. Then, in what many viewed as an Act of God on behalf of Protestant England, the Spanish fleet was dispersed and all but destroyed by violent storms.

As England braced itself to withstand the invasion that never came, Elizabeth appeared in person to review a detachment of soldiers assembled at Tilbury. Dressed in a white gown and a silver breastplate, she declared that though some among her councillors had urged her not to appear before a large crowd of armed men, she would never fail to trust the loyalty of her faithful and loving subjects. Nor did she fear the Spanish armies. "I know I have the body but of a weak and feeble woman," Elizabeth declared, "but I have the heart and stomach [i.e., valor] of a king, and of a king of England too." In this celebrated speech, Elizabeth displayed many of her most memorable qualities: her self-consciously theatrical command of grand public occasion, her subtle blending of magniloquent rhetoric and the language of love, her strategic appropriation of traditionally masculine qualities, and her great personal courage. "We princes," she once remarked, "are set on stages in the sight and view of all the world."

WRITERS, PRINTERS, AND PATRONS

The career of professional writer in sixteenth-century England was almost impossible: there was no such thing as author's copyright, no royalties paid to an author according to the sales of his book, and virtually no notion that anyone could make a decent living through the creation of works of literature. Writers sold their manuscripts to the printer or bookseller outright, for what now seem like ridiculously low prices. Freedom of the press did not exist. Writers and printers were supposed to abide by stringent government regulations. The political, judicial, and ecclesiastical authorities that enforced these regulations could mete out severe punishments for breaches of censorship and other infractions: fines, interrogation, imprisonment; even branding, mutilation, and execution. Not surprisingly, therefore, literary texts sometimes bear traces of self-censorship and often deploy strategies of indirection designed to evade official scrutiny. It was potentially dangerous to put pen to paper and so unprofitable that it is a wonder that any serious original writing was published at all.

Fortunately, the system of state censorship was inefficient, and many men and women of the sixteenth century had a passionate determination to make themselves heard. The *Short-Title Catalogue* of the Bibliographical Society, which lists works published in English between 1475 and 1640, includes more than 26,000 items, and that is an incomplete list. To these we must add the many manuscripts in which poems and other literary texts were circulated, especially those by authors of higher rank, and the commonplace books in which people jotted down poems and prose passages they considered worth keeping.

Elizabethan writers of exalted social standing, like the earl of Surrey or Sir Philip Sidney, thought of themselves as courtiers, statesmen, and landowners; poetry was for them an indispensable social grace and a deeply pleasurable, exalted form of play. Writers of lower rank sought careers as civil servants, secretaries, tutors, and clerics; they might take up more or less permanent residence in a noble household, or, more casually, offer their literary work to actual or prospective patrons, in the hope of protection, career advancement, or financial reward. Remuneration for writing prose or poetry came mostly in the form of gifts from wealthy patrons, who sought to enhance their status and gratify their vanity through the achievements and lavish praises of their clients. Some Elizabethan patrons, though, were well-educated humanists motivated by aesthetic interests, and with them, patronage extended beyond financial support to the creation of lively literary and intellectual circles.

In addition to the court and the great families as dispensers of patronage, the city of London and the two universities also had a substantial impact on the period's literature. London was the center of the book trade, the nursery of a fledgling middle-class reading public, and, most important, the home of the public theaters. Before Elizabeth's time, the universities were mainly devoted to educating the clergy, and that remained an important part of their function. But in the second half of the century, the sons of the gentry and the aristocracy were going in increasing numbers to the universities and the Inns of Court (law schools), not in order to take religious orders or to practice law but to prepare for public service or the management of their estates. Other, less affluent students, such as Marlowe and Spenser, attended Oxford and Cambridge on scholarship. A group of graduates, including Thomas Nashe, enlivened the literary scene in London in the 1590s, but the precarious lives of these so-called "university wits" testify to the difficulties they encountered in their quixotic attempt to survive by their writing skill. The diary of Philip Henslowe, a leading theatrical manager, has entry after entry showing university graduates in prison or in debt or at best eking out a miserable existence patching plays.

Women had no access to grammar schools, the universities, or the Inns of Court and, when not altogether illiterate, received for the most part only a rudimentary education. While Protestantism, with its emphasis on reading Scripture, certainly helped to improve female literacy in the sixteenth century, girls were rarely encouraged to pursue their studies. Indeed, while girls were increasingly taught to read, they were not necessarily taught to write, for the latter skill in women was considered to be at the very least useless, at the worst dangerous. When the prominent humanist Sir Thomas Smith thinks of how he should describe his country's social order, he declares that "we do reject women, as those whom nature hath made to keep home and to nourish their family and children, and not to meddle with matters abroad, nor to bear office in a city or commonwealth." Then, with a kind of nervous glance over his shoulder, he makes an exception of those few in whom "the blood is respected, not the age nor the sex": for example, the queen. Every piece of writing by a woman from this period is a triumph over nearly impossible odds.

TUDOR STYLE: ORNAMENT, PLAINNESS, AND WONDER

Renaissance literature is the product of a rhetorical culture, a culture steeped in the arts of persuasion and trained to process complex verbal signals. (The contemporary equivalent would be the ease with which we deal with complex visual signals, effortlessly processing such devices as fade-out, montage, crosscutting, and morphing.) In 1512, Erasmus published a work called *De copia* that taught its readers how to cultivate "copiousness," verbal richness, in discourse. The work obligingly provides, as a sample, a list of 144 different ways of saying "Thank you for your letter."

In Renaissance England, certain syntactic forms of patterns of words known as "figures" (also called "schemes") were shaped and repeated in order to confer beauty or heighten expressive power. Figures were usually known by their Greek and Latin names, though in an Elizabethan rhetorical manual, *The Arte of English Poesie*, George Puttenham made a valiant if short-lived attempt to give them English equivalents, such as "Hyperbole, or the Overreacher," "Ironia, or the Dry Mock," and "Ploce, or the Doubler." Those who received a grammar-school education throughout Europe at almost any point between the Roman Empire and the eighteenth century probably knew by heart the names of up to one hundred such figures, just as they knew by heart their multiplication tables. According to one scholar's count, William Shakespeare knew and made use of about two hundred.

As certain grotesquely inflated Renaissance texts attest, lessons from *De copia* and similar rhetorical guides could encourage prolixity and verbal self-display. Elizabethans had a taste for elaborate ornament in language as in clothing, jewelry, and furniture, and, if we are to appreciate their accomplishments, it helps to set aside the modern preference, particularly in prose, for unadorned simplicity and directness. When, in one of the age's most fashionable works of prose fiction, John Lyly wishes to explain that the vices of his young hero, Euphues, are tarnishing his virtues, he offers a small flood of synonymous images: "The freshest colors soonest fade, the teenest [i.e., keenest] razor soonest turneth his edge, the finest cloth is soonest eaten with moths." The euphistic multiplication of figures was soon ridiculed by Shakespeare and others, but its pleasure is deeply rooted in rhetorical culture, and most of the greatest Renaissance writers used to it extraordinary effect. Consider, for example, the succession of images in Shakespeare's sonnet 73:

> That time of year thou mayst in me behold
> When yellow leaves, or none, or few, do hang
> Upon those boughs which shake against the cold,
> Bare ruined choirs, where late the sweet birds sang.
> In me thou seest the twilight of such day
> As after sunset fadeth in the west;
> Which by and by black night doth take away,
> Death's second self that seals up all in rest.
> In me thou seest the glowing of such fire
> That on the ashes of his youth doth lie,
> As the deathbed whereon it must expire,
> Consumed with that which it was nourished by.
> This thou perceiv'st, which makes thy love more strong,
> To love that well, which thou must leave ere long.

What seems merely repetitious in Lyly here becomes a subtle, poignant amplification of the perception of decay, through the succession of images from winter (or late fall) to twilight to the last glow of a dying fire. Each of these images is in turn sensitively explored, so that, for example, the season is figured by bare boughs that shiver, as if they were human, and then these anthropomorphized tree branches in turn are figured as the ruined choirs of a church where services were once sung. No sooner is the image of singers in a church choir evoked than these singers are instantaneously transmuted back into the songbirds who, in an earlier season, had sat upon the boughs, while these sweet birds in turn conjure up the poet's own vanished youth. And this nostalgic gaze extends, at least glancingly, to the chancels of the Catholic abbeys reduced to ruins by Protestant iconoclasm and the dissolution of the monasteries. All of this within the first four lines: here and elsewhere Shakespeare, along with other poets of his time, contrives to freight the small compass and tight formal constraints of the sonnet—fourteen lines of iambic pentameter in three principal rhyming patterns—with remarkable emotional intensity, psychological nuance, and imagistic complexity. The effect is what Christopher Marlowe called "infinite riches in a little room."

Elizabethans were certainly capable of admiring plainness of speech, and such poets as Thomas Nashe and, in the early seventeenth century, Ben Jonson wrote restrained, aphoristic, moralizing lyrics in a plain style whose power depends precisely on the avoidance of richly figurative verbal pyrotechnics. This power is readily apparent in the wintry spareness of Nashe's *A Litany in Time of Plague*, with its grim refrain:

> Wit with his wantonness
> Tasteth death's bitterness;
> Hell's executioner
> Hath no ears for to hear
> What vain art can reply.
> I am sick, I must die.
> Lord, have mercy on us!

Here the linguistic playfulness beloved by Elizabethan culture is scorned as an ineffectual "vain art" to which the executioner, death, is utterly indifferent.

But here and in other plain-style poetry, the somber, lapidary effect depends on a tacit recognition of the allure of the suppleness, grace, and sweet harmony that the dominant literary artists of the period so assiduously cultivated. Many sixteenth-century poems were written to be set to music, but even those that were not often aspire in their metrical and syllabic virtuosity to the complex pleasures of madrigals or to the sweet fluency of airs. In poetry and music, as in gardens, architecture and dance, Elizabethans had a taste for elaborate, intricate, but perfectly regular designs. They admired form, valued the artist's manifest control of the medium, and took pleasure in the highly patterned surfaces of things. Suspicion of surfaces, impatience with order, the desire to rip away the mask in order to discover a hidden core of experiential truth: these responses to art, highly characteristic of later periods, are far less in evidence in Renaissance aesthetics than is a delight in pattern.

Such an emphasis on conspicuous pattern might seem to encourage an art as stiff as the starched ruffs that ladies and gentlemen wore around their necks, but the period's fascination with order was conjoined with a profound interest in persuasively conveying the movements of the mind and heart. Syntax in the sixteenth century was looser, more flexible than our own and punctuation less systematic. If the effect is sometimes confusing, it also enabled writers confidently to follow the twists and turns of thought or perception. Such confidence emanates from Sir Walter Ralegh's deeply melancholy, deeply ironic apostrophe to Death at the close of *The History of the World*, written when he was a prisoner in the Tower:

> O eloquent, just, and mighty Death! Whom none could advise, thou hast persuaded; what none hath dared, thou hast done; and whom all the world hath flattered, thou only hast cast out of the world and despised; thou hast drawn together all the far-stretched greatness, all the pride, cruelty, and ambition of man, and covered it all over with these two narrow words: *Hic jacet!* [Here lies]

Death is triumphant here, but so is Ralegh's eloquent, just, and mighty language.

The power of *wonder* that animates much Elizabethan prose—as if the world were being seen clearly and distinctly for the first time—characterizes much of the period's poetry as well. In his *Defense of Poesy*, the most important work of literary criticism in sixteenth-century England, Sidney claims that this power is also a moral power. All other arts, he argues, are subjected to fallen, imperfect nature, but the poet alone is free to range "within the zodiac of his own wit" and create a second nature, superior to the one we are condemned to inhabit: "Her world is brazen, the poets only deliver a golden." The poet's golden world in this account is not an escapist fantasy; it is a model to be emulated in actual life, an ideal to be brought into reality as completely as possible. It is difficult to say, of course, how seriously this project of realization was taken—though the circumstances of Sidney's own death suggest that he may have been attempting to enact on the battlefield an ideal image of Protestant chivalry. A didactic role for poetry is, in any case, urged not by Sidney alone but by most Elizabethan poets. Human sinfulness has corrupted life, robbing it of the sweet wholesomeness that it had once possessed in Eden, but poetry can mark the way back to a more virtuous and fulfilled existence. And not only mark the way: poetry, Sidney and others argue, has a unique persuasive force that shatters inertia and impels readers toward the good they glimpse in its ravishing lines.

This force, attributed to the energy and vividness of figurative language, made poetry a fitting instrument not only for such high-minded enterprises as moral exhortation, prayer, and praise, and for such uplifting narratives as the legends of religious and national heroes, but also for such verbal actions as cursing, lamenting, flattering, and seducing. The almost inexhaustible range of motives was given some order by literary conventions that functioned as shared cultural codes, enabling poets to elicit particular responses from readers and to relate their words to other times, other languages, and other cultures. We can glimpse a few of the ways in which these literary codes worked by looking briefly at the two that are, for modern readers, the least familiar: pastoral and heroic.

The conventions of the pastoral mode present a world inhabited by shepherds and shepherdesses who are chiefly concerned to tend their flocks, fall in love, and engage in friendly singing contests. The mode celebrated leisure, humility, and contentment, exalting the simple country life over the city and its business, the military camp and its violence, the court and its burdens of rule. Pastoral motifs could be deployed in different genres. Pastoral songs commonly expressed the joys of the shepherd's life or disappointment in love. Pastoral dialogues between shepherds might conceal serious, satiric comment on abuses in the great world under the guise of homely, local concerns. There were pastoral funeral elegies, pastoral dramas, pastoral romances (prose fiction), and even pastoral episodes within epics. Probably the most famous pastoral poem of the period is Marlowe's *The Passionate Shepherd to His Love*, an erotic invitation whose promise of gold buckles, coral clasps, and amber studs serves to remind us that, however much it sings of naïve innocence, the mode is ineradicably sophisticated and urban.

With its rustic characters, simple concerns, and modest scope, the pastoral mode was regarded as situated at the opposite extreme from heroic, with its values of honor, martial courage, loyalty, leadership, and endurance and its glorification of a nation or people. The chief genre here was the epic, typically a long, exalted poem in the high style, based on a heroic story from the nation's distant past and imitating Homer and Virgil in structure and motifs. Renaissance poets throughout Europe undertook to honor their nations and their vernacular languages by writing this most prestigious kind of poetry. In sixteenth-century England the major success in heroic poetry is Spenser's *Faerie Queene*, properly speaking, a romantic epic in that it draws more heavily on the romance conventions employed by the great Italian poets Ariosto and Tasso—tangled, episodic plots, exotic adventures and marvels, and a fundamental concern with love as well as war—than on the classical epics. To these basic elements Spenser also conjoins medieval allegory, pastoral, satire, mythological narrative, comedy, philosophical meditation, and many other literary conventions in a strange, wonderful blend. The spectacular mixing of genres in Spenser's poem is only an extreme instance of a general Elizabethan indifference to the generic purity admired by writers, principally on the Continent, who adhered to Aristotle's *Poetics*. Where such neoclassicists attempted to observe rigid stylistic boundaries, English poets tended to approach the different genres in the spirit of Sidney's inclusivism: "if severed they be good, the conjunction cannot be hurtful."

THE ELIZABETHAN THEATER

If Sidney welcomed the experimental intertwining of genres in both poetry and prose—and his own *Arcadia*, a prose romance incorporating both pastoral and heroic elements, confirms that he did—there was one place where he found it absurd: the theater. He condemned the conjunction of high and low characters in "mongrel" tragicomedies that mingled "kings and clowns." Moreover, in the spirit of neoclassical advocacy of the "dramatic unities," Sidney disliked the ease with which the action on the bare stage ("where you shall have Asia of the one side, and Afric of the other") violated the laws of time and space. "Now you shall have three ladies walk to gather flowers," he writes in *The Defense of Poesy*, "and then we must believe the stage to be a garden. By and by we hear news of shipwreck in the same place: and then we are to blame if we accept it not for a rock." The irony is that this mocking account, written probably in 1579, anticipates by a few years the stupendous achievements of Marlowe and Shakespeare, whose plays joyously break every rule that Sidney thought it essential to observe.

A permanent, freestanding public theater in England dates only from Shakespeare's own lifetime. A London playhouse, the Red Lion, is first mentioned in 1567, and James Burbage's playhouse, The Theater, was built in 1576. But it is quite misleading to identify English drama exclusively with the new, specially constructed playhouses, for in fact there was a rich and vital theatrical tradition in England stretching back for centuries. Several towns in late medieval England were the sites of annual festivals that mounted elaborate cycles of plays depicting the great biblical stories, from the creation of the world to Christ's Passion and its miraculous aftermath.

But early English theater was not restricted to these civic and religious festivals. Performers acted in town halls and the halls of guilds and aristocratic mansions, on scaffolds erected in town squares and marketplaces, on pageant wagons in the streets, and in innyards. By the fifteenth century, and probably earlier, there were organized companies of players traveling under noble patronage. Such companies earned a precarious living providing amusement, while enhancing the prestige of the patron whose livery they wore and whose protection they enjoyed. (Otherwise, by statutes enjoining productive labor, actors without another, ordinary trade could have been classified as vagabonds and whipped or branded.) This practice explains why the professional acting companies of Shakespeare's time, including Shakespeare's own, attached themselves to a nobleman and were technically his servants (the Lord Chamberlain's Men, the Lord Admiral's Men, etc.), even though virtually all their time was devoted to entertaining the public from whom most of their income derived.

Before the construction of the public theaters, the playing companies often performed short plays called "interludes" that were, in effect, staged dialogues on religious, moral, and political themes. The structure of such plays reflects the training in argumentation that students received in Tudor schools and, in particular, the sustained practice in examining both sides of a difficult question. Some of Shakespeare's amazing ability to look at critical issues from multiple perspectives may be traced back to this practice and the dramatic interludes it helped to inspire.

Another major form of theater that flourished in England in the fifteenth century and continued on into the sixteenth was the morality play. Like the mysteries, moralities addressed questions of the ultimate fate of the soul. They did so, however, not by rehearsing scriptural stories but by dramatizing allegories of spiritual struggle. Typically, a person named Human or Mankind or Youth is faced with a choice between a pious life in the company of such associates as Mercy, Discretion, and Good Deeds and a dissolute life among riotous companions like Lust or Mischief.

If such plays sound more than a bit like sermons, it is because they were. The church was a profoundly different institution from the theater, but its professionals shared some of the same rhetorical skills. It would be grossly misleading to regard churchgoing and playgoing as comparable entertainments, but clerical attacks on the theater sometimes make it sound as if ministers thought themselves to be in direct competition with professional players. The players, for their part, were generally too discreet to present themselves in a similar light, yet they almost certainly understood their craft as relating to sermons with an uneasy blend of emulation and rivalry.

Play-acting, whether of tragedies, comedies, or any of the other Elizabethan forms, took its place alongside other forms of public expression and entertainment as well. Perhaps the most important, from the perspective of the theater, were music and dance, since these were directly and repeatedly incorporated into plays. Moreover, virtually all plays in the period, including Shakespeare's, apparently ended with a dance. Brushing off the theatrical gore and changing their expressions from woe to pleasure, the actors in plays like *Doctor Faustus* and *King Lear* would presumably have received the audience's applause and then bid for a second round by performing a stately pavane or a lively jig.

Plays, music, and dancing were by no means the only shows in town. There were jousts, tournaments, royal entries, religious processions, pageants in honor of newly installed civic officials or ambassadors arriving from abroad;

wedding masques, court masques, and costumed entertainments known as Disguisings or Mummings; juggling acts, fortune tellers, exhibitions of swordsmanship, mountebanks, folk healers, storytellers, magic shows; bear-baiting, bullbaiting, cockfighting, and other blood sports; folk festivals such as Maying, the Feast of Fools, Carnival, and Whitsun Ales. For several years, Elizabethan Londoners were delighted by a trained animal—Banks's Horse—that could, it was thought, do arithmetic and answer questions. And there was always the grim but compelling spectacle of public shaming, mutilation, and execution.

Most English towns had stocks and whipping posts. Drunks, fraudulent merchants, adulterers, and quarrelers could be placed in carts or mounted backward on asses and paraded through the streets for crowds to jeer and throw refuse at. Women accused of being scolds could be publicly muzzled by an iron device called a brank or tied to a "cucking stool" and dunked in the river. Convicted criminals could have their ears cut off, their noses slit, their foreheads branded. Public beheadings and hangings were common. In the worst cases, felons were sentenced to be "hanged by the neck, and being alive cut down, and your privy members to be cut off, and your bowels to be taken out of your belly and there burned, you being alive." In the dismem-berment with which Marlowe's *Doctor Faustus* ends, the audience was wit-nessing the theatrical equivalent of the execution of criminals and traitors that they could have also watched in the flesh, as it were, nearby.

Doctor Faustus was performed by the Lord Admiral's Men at the Rose Theater, one of four major public playhouses that by the mid-1590s were feverishly competing for crowds of spectators. These playhouses (including Shakespeare's famous Globe Theater, which opened in 1599) each accom-modated some two thousand spectators and generally followed the same design: they were oval in shape, with an unroofed yard in the center where stood the groundlings (apprentices, servants, and others of the lower classes) and three rising tiers around the yard for men and women able to pay a higher price for places to sit and a roof over their heads. A large platform stage jutted out into the yard, surrounded on three sides by spectators (see the conjectural drawing of an Elizabethan playhouse, in the appendices to this volume). These financially risky ventures relied on admission charges—it was an innovation of this period to have money advanced in the expectation of pleasure rather than offered to servants as a reward—and counted on habitual playgoing fueled by a steady supply of new plays. The public play-houses were all located outside the limits of the city of London and, accord-ingly, beyond the jurisdiction of city authorities generally hostile to dramatic spectacles. Eventually, indoor theaters, artificially lighted and patronized by a more select audience, were also built, secured under conditions that would allow them some protection from those who wished to shut them down.

Why should what we now regard as one of the undisputed glories of the age have aroused so much hostility? One answer, curiously enough, is traffic: plays drew large audiences, and residents objected to the crowds, the noise, and the crush of carriages. Other, more serious concerns were public health and crime. It was thought that many diseases, including the dreaded bubonic plague, were spread by noxious odors, and the packed playhouses were obvi-ous breeding grounds for infection. (Patrons often tried to protect themselves by sniffing nosegays or stuffing cloves in their nostrils.) The large crowds drew pickpockets, cutpurses, and other scoundrels. On one memorable afternoon a pickpocket was caught in the act and tied for the duration of the play to one of the posts that held up the canopy above the stage. The theater was, moreover, a well-known haunt of prostitutes, and, it was alleged, a place where innocent maids were seduced and respectable matrons corrupted. It was darkly rumored that "chambers and secret places" adjoined the theater galleries, and, in any case, taverns, disreputable inns, and whorehouses were close at hand.

There were other charges as well. Plays were performed in the afternoon and therefore drew people, especially the young, away from their work. They were schools of idleness, luring apprentices from their trades, law students from their studies, housewives from their kitchens, and potentially pious souls from the sober meditations to which they might otherwise devote themselves. Moralists warned that the theaters were nests of sedition, and religious polemicists, especially Puritans, obsessively focusing on the use of boy actors to play the female parts, charged that theatrical transvestism excited illicit sexual desires, both heterosexual and homosexual.

But the playing companies had powerful allies, including Queen Elizabeth herself, and continuing popular support. One theater historian has estimated that between the late 1560s and 1642, when the playhouses were shut down by the English Civil War, well over fifty million visits were paid to the London theater, an astonishing figure for a city that had, by our standards, a very modest population. Plays were performed without the scene breaks and intermissions to which we are accustomed; there was no scenery and few props, but costumes were usually costly and elaborate. The players formed what would now be called repertory companies—that is, they filled the roles of each play from members of their own group, not employing outsiders. They performed a number of different plays on consecutive days, and the principal actors were shareholders in the profits of the company. Boys were apprenticed to actors just as they had been apprenticed to master craftsmen in the guilds; they took the women's parts in plays until their voices changed. The plays might be bought for the company from hack writers, or, as in Shakespeare's company, the group might include an actor-playwright who could supply it with some (though by no means all) of its plays. The script remained the property of the company, but a popular play was eagerly sought by the printers, and the companies, which generally tried to keep their plays from appearing in print, sometimes had trouble guarding their rights. The editors of the first collected edition of Shakespeare, the First Folio (1623), complain about the prior publication of "divers stolen and surreptitious copies" of his plays, "maimed and deformed by the frauds and stealths of injurious imposters."

SURPRISED BY TIME

All of the ways we cut up time into units are inevitably distortions. The dividing line between centuries was not, as far as we can tell, a highly significant one for people in the Renaissance, and many of the most important literary careers cross into the seventeenth century without a self-conscious moment of reflection. But virtually everyone must have been aware that the long reign of England's Queen Elizabeth was nearing its end, and this impending closure occasioned considerable anxiety. Childless, the last of her line, Elizabeth had steadfastly refused to name a successor. She continued to make brilliant speeches, to receive the extravagant compliments of her flatterers, and to exercise her authority—in 1601, she had her favorite, the headstrong earl of Essex, executed for attempting to raise an insurrection. But, as her seventieth birthday approached, she was clearly, as Ralegh put it, "a lady surprised by time." She suffered from bouts of ill health and melancholy; her godson, Sir John Harington, was dismayed to see her pacing through the rooms of her palace, striking at the tapestries with a sword. Her more astute advisers—among them Lord Burghley's son, Sir Robert Cecil, who had succeeded his father as her principal counselor—secretly entered into correspondence with the likeliest claimant to the throne, James VI of Scotland. Though the English queen had executed his Catholic mother, Mary, Queen of Scots, the Protestant James had continued to exchange polite letters with Elizabeth. It was at least plausible, as officially claimed, that in her dying breath, on March 24, 1603, Elizabeth designated James as her successor. A jittery nation that had feared a possible civil war lit bonfires to welcome its new king. But in a very few years, the English began to express nostalgia for the rule of "Good Queen Bess" and to look back on her reign as a magnificent high point in the history and culture of their nation.

THE SIXTEENTH CENTURY

TEXTS	CONTEXTS
	1485 Accession of Henry VII inaugurates Tudor dynasty
	1499 Desiderius Erasmus first visits England; meets Thomas More
ca. 1504 Amerigo Vespucci, *New World* and *Four Voyages*	**ca. 1504** Leonardo paints Mona Lisa
	1508–12 Michelangelo paints Sistine Chapel ceiling
	1509 Death of Henry VII; accession of Henry VIII
1511 Erasmus, *Praise of Folly*	
	1513 James IV of Scotland killed at Battle of Flodden; succeeded by James V
1516 More, *Utopia*. Ludovico Ariosto, *Orlando furioso*	
ca. 1517 John Skelton, *The Tunning of Elinour Rumming*	**1517** Martin Luther's Ninety-Five Theses; beginning of the Reformation in Germany
	1519 Cortés invades Mexico. Magellen begins his voyage around the world
1520s–30s Thomas Wyatt's poems circulating in manuscript	**1521** Pope Leo X names Henry VIII "Defender of the Faith"
1525 William Tyndale's English translation of the New Testament	
1528 Baldessare Castiglione, *The Courtier*	
	1529–32 More is Lord Chancellor
1532 Nicolò Machiavelli, *The Prince* (written 1513)	**1532–34** Henry VIII divorces Catherine of Aragon to marry Anne Boleyn; Elizabeth I born; Henry declares himself head of the English church
	1535 More beheaded
1537 John Calvin, *The Institution of Christian Religion*	**1537** Establishment of Calvin's theocracy at Geneva
	1542 Roman Inquisition. James IV of Scotland dies; succeeded by daughter Mary
1543 Copernicus, *On the Revolution of the Spheres*	
1547 *Book of Homilies*	**1547** Death of Henry VIII; accession of Protestant Edward VI
1549 *Book of Common Prayer*	**1553** Death of Edward VI; accession of Catholic Queen Mary, daughter of Catherine of Aragon
	1555–56 Archbishop Cranmer and former bishops Latimer and Ridley burned at the stake
1557 Tottel's *Songs and Sonnets* (printed poems by Wyatt, Surrey, and others)	
	1558 Mary dies; succeeded by Protestant Elizabeth I

TEXTS	CONTEXTS
1563 John Foxe, *Acts and Monuments*	
1565 Thomas Norton and Thomas Sackville, *Gorboduc*, first English blank-verse tragedy (acted in 1561)	
1567 Arthur Golding, translation of Ovid's *Metamorphoses*	1567 Mary, Queen of Scots, abdicates; succeeded by her son James VI; Mary imprisoned in England
	1570 Elizabeth I excommunicated by Pope Pius V
	1576 James Burbage's playhouse, The Theater, built in London
	1576–77 Frobisher's voyage to North America
	1577–80 Drake's circumnavigation
1578 John Lyly, *Euphues*	
1579 Edmund Spenser, *Shepheardes Calender*	
1580 Montaigne, *Essays*	
	1583 Irish rebellion crushed
	1584–87 Sir Walter Ralegh's earliest attempts to colonize Virginia
	1586–87 Mary, Queen of Scots, tried for treason and executed
ca. 1587–90 Marlowe's *Tamburlaine* acted. Shakespeare begins career as actor and playwright	
1588 Thomas Hariot, *A Brief and True Report of Virginia*	1588 Failed invasion of the Spanish Armada
1589 Richard Hakluyt, *The Principal Navigations . . . of the English Nation*	
1590 Sir Philip Sidney, *Arcadia* (posthumously published); Spenser, *The Faerie Queene*, Books 1–3	
1591 Sidney, *Astrophil and Stella*	
ca. 1592 John Donne's earliest poems circulating in manuscript	
1595 Sidney, *The Defense of Poesy*	1595 Ralegh's voyage to Guiana
1596 Spenser, *The Faerie Queene*, Books 4–6 (with Books 1–3)	
1598 Ben Jonson, *Every Man in His Humor*	1599 Globe Theater opens
	1603 Elizabeth I dies; succeeded by James VI of Scotland (as James I), inaugurating the Stuart dynasty

SIR THOMAS WYATT THE ELDER
1503–1542

Thomas Wyatt made his career in the shifting, dangerous currents of Renaissance courts, and court culture, with its power struggles, sexual intrigues, and sophisticated tastes, shaped his remarkable achievements as a poet. The son of a gentleman who early linked his fortunes to the Tudor dynasty, Wyatt was educated at St. John's College, Cambridge, and then entered the service of Henry VIII, becoming clerk of the king's jewels, a member of diplomatic missions to France and the Low Countries, and, in 1537–39, ambassador to the court of the Emperor Charles V in Spain. The years he spent abroad as a diplomat had a significant impact upon his writing, most obvious in his translations. Diplomacy, with its veiled threats, subtle indirection, and cynical role-playing, may have had a more indirect impact as well, reinforcing the lessons in self-display and self-concealment that Wyatt would have received at the English court.

Life in the orbit of the ruthless, unpredictable Henry VIII was competitive and risky. When, in the late 1530s, Wyatt wrote to his son of the "thousand dangers and hazards, enmities, hatreds, prisonments, despites, and indignations" he had faced, he was not exaggerating. He probably came closest to the executioner's axe when in 1536 he was imprisoned in the Tower of London along with several others accused of having adulterous affairs with the queen, Anne Boleyn. As his poem *Who list his wealth and ease retain* implies, Wyatt may have watched from his cell the execution of the queen and her alleged lovers, but he himself was spared, as he was spared a few years later, when he was again imprisoned in the Tower on charges of high treason brought by his enemies at court. His death, at the age of thirty-nine, came from a fever.

It is not surprising, given his career, that many of Wyatt's poems express an intense longing for "steadfastness" and an escape from the corruption, anxiety, and duplicity of the court. But of course the eloquent celebration of simplicity and truthfulness can itself be a cunning strategy. Wyatt was a master of the game of poetic self-display. Again and again he represents himself as a plain-speaking and steadfast man, betrayed by the "doubleness" of a fickle mistress or the instability of fortune. At this distance it is impossible to know how much this account corresponds to reality, but we can admire, as Wyatt's contemporaries did, the rhetorical deftness of the performance.

In a move with momentous consequences for English poetry, Wyatt introduced into English the sonnet, a fourteen-line poem in pentameter with a complex, inter-twining rhyme scheme. For the most part, he took his subject matter from Petrarch's sonnets, but his rhyme schemes came from other Italian models. The most common rhyme scheme in Wyatt's sonnets is *abba abba cddc ee*; the more typical Italian struc-ture—an octave (the first eight lines) followed, after a turn in the sense, by a sestet (the last six lines)—was already beginning to change into the characteristic "English" structure for the sonnet, three quatrains and a couplet.

In his translations of Petrarchan sonnets, such as *Whoso list to hunt*, Wyatt tends to turn the idealizing of the woman into disillusionment and complaint. For the lover in Petrarch's poems, love is a transcendent experience; for the lover in Wyatt's poems, it is obsessive and embittering. The tone of bitterness carries over to many poems less closely linked to Italian and French models, poems with short stanzas and refrains in the manner of the native English "ballet" (pronounced to rhyme with *mallet*) or dance-song. Some of the ballets, to be sure, strike a note of jaunty independence, often tinged with misogyny, but melancholy complaint is rarely very distant. Perhaps the poem that most brilliantly captures Wyatt's blend of passion, anger, cynicism, longing, and pain is *They flee from me*.

Wyatt never published a collection of his own poems, and very little of his verse appeared in print during his lifetime. In 1557 (fifteen years after his death), the printer Richard Tottel included 97 poems attributed to Wyatt among the 271 poems in his miscellany, *Songs and Sonnets*. Wyatt was not primarily concerned with regularity of accent and smoothness of rhythm. By the time Tottel's collection was published, Wyatt's deliberately rough, vigorous, and expressive metrical practice was felt to be crude, and Tottel (or someone in his printing house) smoothed out the versification. We print Wyatt's poems in the versions found in the Egerton Manuscript (E. MS.), a manuscript that contains poems in Wyatt's own hand and corrections in his hand of scribal copies of his poems, and in the Arundel Manuscript (A. MS.).

The long love that in my thought doth harbor[1]

The long love that in my thought doth harbor,
And in mine heart doth keep his residence,
Into my face presseth with bold pretense
And therein campeth, spreading his banner.[2]
5 She that me learneth to love and suffer
And will that my trust and lust's negligence[3]
Be reined by reason, shame,° and reverence,   modesty
With his hardiness taketh displeasure.
Wherewithal unto the heart's forest he fleeth,
10 Leaving his enterprise with pain and cry,
And there him hideth, and not appeareth.
What may I do, when my master feareth,
But in the field with him to live and die?
For good is the life ending faithfully.

E. MS.

Whoso list to hunt[1]

Whoso list° to hunt, I know where is an hind,°   cares / female deer
But as for me, alas, I may no more.
The vain travail hath wearied me so sore,
I am of them that farthest cometh behind.
5 Yet may I, by no means, my wearied mind
Draw from the deer, but as she fleeth afore,
Fainting I follow. I leave off, therefore,
Since in a net I seek to hold the wind.
Who list her hunt, I put him out of doubt,

1. Wyatt's version of poem 140 of Petrarch's *Rime sparse* (Scattered Rhymes); his younger friend, the earl of Surrey, also translated it (p. 344).
2. I.e., the speaker's blush. The first four lines of this sonnet introduce the "conceit" (or elaborately sustained metaphor) of Love as a warrior who, "with bold pretense" (i.e., making bold claim), flaunts his presence by means of the "banner." Elaborate metaphors of this kind are common in Petrarchan (and Elizabethan) love poetry, and often, as in this instance, an entire sonnet will turn on a single conceit.
3. I.e., my open and careless revelation of my love. "Learneth": teaches.
1. An adaptation of Petrarch's *Rima* 190, perhaps influenced by commentators on Petrarch, who said that *Noli me tangere quia Caesaris sum* ("Touch me not, for I am Caesar's") was inscribed on the collars of Caesar's hinds, which were then set free and were presumably safe from hunters. Wyatt's sonnet is usually supposed to refer to Anne Boleyn, in whom Henry VIII became interested in 1526.

10 As well as I, may spend his time in vain.
And graven with diamonds in letters plain
There is written, her fair neck round about,
"*Noli me tangere,* for Caesar's I am,
And wild for to hold, though I seem tame."

E. MS.

They flee from me

They flee from me, that sometime did me seek
With naked foot stalking° in my chamber.   *walking softly*
I have seen them gentle, tame, and meek
That now are wild and do not remember
5   That sometime they put themself in danger
To take bread at my hand; and now they range,
Busily seeking with a continual change.

Thanked be fortune it hath been otherwise
Twenty times better; but once in special,
10 In thin array, after a pleasant guise,
When her loose gown from her shoulders did fall,
And she me caught in her arms long and small,°   *slender*
Therewithal sweetly did me kiss
And softly said, "Dear heart, how like you this?"

15 It was no dream, I lay broad waking.
But all is turned, thorough my gentleness,
Into a strange fashion of forsaking;
And I have leave to go, of her goodness,
And she also to use newfangleness.°   *fickleness*
20 But since that I so kindely[1] am served,
I fain would know what she hath deserved.

E. MS.

My lute, awake!

My lute, awake! Perform the last
Labor that thou and I shall waste,
And end that I have now begun;
For when this song is sung and past,
5   My lute, be still, for I have done.

As to be heard where ear is none,
As lead to grave in marble stone,[1]

---

1. Naturally, but with an ironic suggestion of the modern meaning of "kindly." In Wyatt's spelling, the word should presumably be pronounced as three syllables.

1. I.e., when sound may be heard with no ear to hear it or when soft lead is able to carve ("grave") hard marble.

My song may pierce her heart as soon.
Should we then sigh or sing or moan?
10 No, no, my lute, for I have done.

The rocks do not so cruelly
Repulse the waves continually
As she my suit and affectiön.
So that I am past remedy,
15 Whereby my lute and I have done.

Proud of the spoil that thou hast got
Of simple hearts, thorough love's shot,
By whom, unkind, thou hast them won,
Think not he hath his bow forgot,
20 Although my lute and I have done.

Vengeance shall fall on thy disdain
That makest but game on earnest pain.
Think not alone under the sun
Unquit° to cause thy lovers plain,°   *unrevenged / to complain*
25 Although my lute and I have done.

Perchance thee lie withered and old
The winter nights that are so cold,
Plaining in vain unto the moon.
Thy wishes then dare not be told.
30 Care then who list,° for I have done.   *likes*

And then may chance thee to repent
The time that thou hast lost and spent
To cause thy lovers sigh and swoon.
Then shalt thou know beauty but lent,
35 And wish and want as I have done.

Now cease, my lute. This is the last
Labor that thou and I shall waste,
And ended is that we begun.
Now is this song both sung and past;
40 My lute, be still, for I have done.

                                        E. MS.

Stand whoso list[1]

Stand whoso list° upon the slipper° top   *cares to / slippery*
Of court's estates,° and let me here rejoice   *high positions*
And use me quiet without let or stop,[2]
Unknown in court, that hath such brackish joys.
5 In hidden place so let my days forth pass
That when my years be done withouten noise,

---

1. A translation of Seneca, *Thyestes*, lines 391–403.

2. Comport myself quietly without hindrance or impediment from others.

I may die aged after the common trace.°   *way*
For him death grippeth right hard by the crop°   *throat*
That is much known of other, and of himself, alas,
10   Doth die unknown, dazed, with dreadful° face.   *fearful*

A. MS.

HENRY HOWARD, EARL OF SURREY
1517–1547

The axe that beheaded Surrey at the age of thirty had been hanging over his head for much of his life. In the court of Henry VIII, it was dangerous to be a potential claimant to the throne, and Surrey was descended from kings on both sides of his family. He was brought up at Windsor Castle as the close companion of Henry VIII's illegitimate son, the duke of Richmond, who married Surrey's sister. As the eldest son of the duke of Norfolk, the chief bulwark of the old Catholic aristocracy against the rising tide of "new men" and the reformed religion, Surrey was the heir not only to the Howard family's great wealth but also to their immense pride, their sense at once of noble privilege and of obligation. Like his father and grandfather, he was a brave and able soldier, serving in Henry VIII's French wars as "Lieutenant General of the King on Sea and Land." He was also repeatedly imprisoned for rash behavior, on one occasion for striking a courtier, on another for wandering through the streets of London breaking the windows of sleeping townspeople. In 1541 Surrey used his family connections—his first cousin, Catherine Howard, was queen—to secure the release from the Tower of his close friend, the poet Thomas Wyatt, who had been accused of treason. But a year later, Catherine Howard was executed for adultery. Power returned to the rival family of the former queen Jane Seymour, who had died in childbirth giving a son and heir to the aging Henry VIII. Surrey's situation was already precarious, and his vocal opposition to the Seymours, with their strong Protestant leanings, sealed his fate. Convicted of treason, he had the grim distinction of being Henry's last victim.

Poets and critics of the later sixteenth century, fascinated by Surrey's noble rank and his tragic fate, routinely praised him as one of the very greatest English poets. The full title of Tottel's influential miscellany, published in 1557 (ten years after Surrey's death), is *Songs and Sonnets written by the Right Honorable Lord Henry Howard Late Earl of Surrey and Other*. The principal "other" here is his older friend Wyatt, with whose poetry Surrey's is closely linked. Poets who circulated their verse in manuscript in a courtly milieu, both shared a passion for French and Italian poetry, especially for Petrarch's sonnets. Surrey established a form for these that was used by Shakespeare and that has become known as the English sonnet: three quatrains and a couplet, all in iambic pentameter and rhyming *abab cdcd efef gg*. Even more significant, he was the first English poet to publish in blank verse—unrhymed iambic pentameter—a verse form so popular in the succeeding centuries that it has come to seem almost indigenous to the language. The work in which he used his "strange meter," as the publisher called it, was a translation of part of Virgil's *Aeneid*. (Book 4 was published in 1554 and Book 2 in 1557.) Whether in blank verse or in rhyming forms, Surrey managed with exceptional skill the rhythmic fluency of the five-stress line, initiating the ease and grace that distinguish so many Elizabethan lyrics.

Love, that doth reign and live within my thought[1]

Love, that doth reign and live within my thought,
And built his seat within my captive breast,
Clad in the arms wherein with me he fought,
Oft in my face he doth his banner rest.
5 But she that taught me love and suffer pain,
My doubtful hope and eke° my hot desire   *also*
With shamefast° look to shadow and refrain,   *modest*
Her smiling grace converteth straight to ire.
And coward Love, then, to the heart apace
10 Taketh his flight, where he doth lurk and plain,°   *complain*
His purpose lost, and dare not show his face.
For my lord's guilt thus faultless bide I pain,
Yet from my lord shall not my foot remove:
Sweet is the death that taketh end by love.

1557

1. Cf. Surrey's version of Petrarch's *Rima* 140 with Wyatt's adaptation of the same original (p. 340).

THE ENGLISH BIBLE

Protestantism required direct lay access to the Bible, which meant in practice the widespread availability of vernacular translations. The Roman Catholic Church had not always and everywhere opposed such translations, but it generally preferred that the populace encounter the Scriptures through the interpretations of the priests, trained to read the Latin translation known as the Vulgate. In times of great conflict this preference for clerical mediation hardened into outright prohibition of vernacular translation and into persecution and book burning.

Zealous Protestants set out, in the teeth of fierce opposition, to put the Bible into the hands of the laity. A remarkable translation of the New Testament, by an English Lutheran named William Tyndale, was printed on the Continent and smuggled into England in 1525; Tyndale's translation of the Pentateuch, the first five books of the Hebrew Bible, followed in 1530. Many copies of these translations were seized and destroyed, as was the translator himself, but the printing press made it extremely difficult for authorities to eradicate books for which there was a passionate demand. The English Bible was a force that could not be suppressed, and it became, in its various forms, the single most important book of the sixteenth century.

Tyndale's translation was completed by an associate, Miles Coverdale, whose rendering of the Psalms proved to be particularly influential. Their joint labor was the basis for the Great Bible (1539), the first authorized version of the Bible in English, a copy of which was ordered to be placed in every church in the kingdom. With the accession of Edward VI, many editions of the Bible followed, but the process was sharply reversed when Mary came to the throne in 1553. Along with people condemned as heretics, English Bibles were burned in great bonfires.

Marian persecution was indirectly responsible for what would become the most scholarly Protestant English Bible, the translation known as the Geneva Bible, prepared, with extensive, learned, and often fiercely polemical marginal notes, by English exiles in Calvin's Geneva and widely diffused in England after Elizabeth came to the throne. In addition, Elizabethan church authorities ordered a careful revision of the Great Bible, and this version, known as the Bishops' Bible, was the one read in the churches. The success of the Geneva Bible in particular prompted those Elizabethan Catholics who now in turn found themselves in exile to bring out a vernacular translation of their own, the Douay-Rheims version, in order to counter the Protestant readings and glosses.

After Elizabeth's death in 1603, King James I and his bishops ordered that a revised translation of the entire Bible be undertaken by a group of forty-seven scholars. The result was the Authorized Version, more popularly known as the King James Bible.

In the passage selected here, 1 Corinthians 13, Tyndale's use of the word "love," echoed by the Geneva Bible, is set against the Catholic "charity." The latter term would gesture toward the religious doctrine of "works," against the Protestant insistence on salvation by faith alone. It is a sign of the conservative, moderate Protestantism of the King James version that it too opts for "charity."

From Tyndale's Translation

Though I spake with the tongues of men and angels, and yet had no love, I were even as sounding brass: or as a tinkling cymbal. And though I could prophesy, and understood all secrets, and all knowledge: yea, if I had all faith, so that I could move mountains out of their places, and yet had no love, I were nothing. And though I bestowed all my goods to feed the poor, and though I gave my body even that I burned, and yet had no love, it profiteth me nothing.

Love suffereth long, and is courteous. Love envieth not. Love doth not frowardly,[1] swelleth not, dealeth not dishonestly, seeketh not her own, is not provoked to anger, thinketh not evil, rejoiceth not in iniquity: but rejoiceth in the truth, suffereth all things, believeth all things, hopeth all things, endureth in all things. Though that prophesying fail, other[2] tongues shall cease, or knowledge vanish away, yet love falleth never away.

For our knowledge is unperfect and our prophesying is unperfect. But when that which is perfect is come, then that which is unperfect shall be done away. When I was a child, I spake as a child, I understood as a child, I imagined as a child. But as soon as I was a man, I put away childishness. Now we see in a glass,[3] even in a dark speaking: but then shall we see face to face. Now I know unperfectly: but then shall I know even as I am known. Now abideth faith, hope, and love, even these three: but the chief of these is love.

1525, 1535

From The Geneva Bible[1]

Though I speak with the tongues of men and Angels, and have not love, I am as sounding brass, or a tinkling cymbal. [2]And though I had the gift of

---

1. Perversely, evilly.
2. Or.
3. Mirror. "Dark": obscure, unclear. This metaphor of indirect and imperfect sight seems to

derive from Plato's Allegory of the Cave (*Republic* 7).
1. The Geneva Bible is the earliest English version printed with verse divisions.

prophecy, and knew all secrets and all knowledge, yea, if I had all faith, so that I could remove mountains, and had not love, I were nothing. [3]And though I feed the poor with all my goods, and though I give my body, that I be burned, and have not love, it profiteth me nothing. [4]Love suffereth long: it is bountiful: love envieth not: love doth not boast itself: it is not puffed up: [5]It disdaineth not: it seeketh not her own things: it is not provoked to anger: it thinketh not evil: [6]It rejoiceth not in iniquity, but rejoiceth in the truth: [7]It suffereth all things: it believeth all things: it hopeth all things: it endureth all things. [8]Love doth never fall away, though that prophesyings be abolished, or the tongues cease, or knowledge vanish away. [9]For we know in part, and we prophesy in part. [10]But when that which is perfect is come, then that which is in part shall be abolished. [11]When I was a child, I spake as a child, I understood as a child, I thought as a child: but when I became a man, I put away childish things. [12]For now we see through a glass darkly:[2] but then shall we see face to face. Now I know in part: but then shall I know even as I am known. [13]And now abideth faith, hope, and love, even these three: but the chiefest of these is love.

1560, 1602

From The Douay-Rheims Version

If I speak with the tongues of men and of Angels, and have not charity, I am become as sounding brass, or a tinkling cymbal. [2]And if I should have prophecy, and knew all mysteries, and all knowledge, and if I should have all faith so that I could remove mountains, and have not charity, I am nothing. [3]And if I should distribute all my goods to be meat[1] for the poor, and if I should deliver my body so that I burn, and have not charity, it doth profit me nothing.

[4]Charity is patient, is benign: charity envieth not, dealeth not perversely: is not puffed up, [5]is not ambitious, seeketh not her own, is not provoked to anger, thinketh not evil: [6]rejoiceth not upon iniquity, but rejoiceth with the truth: [7]suffereth all things, believeth all things, hopeth all things, beareth all things. [8]Charity never falleth away: whether prophecies shall be made void, or tongues shall cease, or knowledge shall be destroyed. [9]For in part we know, and in part we prophesy. [10]But when that shall come that is perfect, that shall be made void that is in part. [11]When I was a little one, I spake as a little one, I understood as a little one, I thought as a little one. But when I was made a man, I did away the things that belonged to a little one. [12]We see now by a glass in a dark sort: but then face to face. Now I know in part: but then I shall know as also I am known. [13]And now there remain faith, hope, charity, these three, but the greater of these is charity.

1582

---

2. By means of a mirror, obscurely.   1. Food (in general).

From The Authorized (King James) Version

Though I speak with the tongues of men and of angels, and have not charity, I am become as sounding brass, or a tinkling cymbal. ²And though I have the gift of prophecy, and understand all mysteries, and all knowledge; and though I have all faith, so that I could remove mountains, and have no charity, I am nothing. ³And though I bestow all my goods to feed the poor, and though I give my body to be burned, and have not charity, it profiteth me nothing. ⁴Charity suffereth long, and is kind; charity envieth not; charity vaunteth not itself, is not puffed up, ⁵doth not behave itself unseemly, seeketh not her own, is not easily provoked, thinketh no evil; ⁶rejoiceth not in iniquity, but rejoiceth in the truth; ⁷beareth all things, believeth all things, hopeth all things, endureth all things. ⁸Charity never faileth: but whether there be prophecies, they shall fail; whether there be tongues, they shall cease; whether there be knowledge, it shall vanish away. ⁹For we know in part, and we prophesy in part. ¹⁰But when that which is perfect is come, then that which is in part shall be done away. ¹¹When I was a child, I spake as a child, I understood as a child, I thought as a child: but when I became a man, I put away childish things. ¹²For now we see through a glass, darkly; but then face to face: now I know in part; but then shall I know even as also I am known. And now abideth faith, hope, charity, these three; but the greatest of these is charity.

1611

BOOK OF COMMON PRAYER

The Protestant attack on Catholic rituals and the demand for worship in the vernacular led during the reign of Edward VI to the preparation of an English liturgical book, authorized to be the official and only text for public worship in England. Initiated by the Act of Uniformity in 1549, the work's principal architect was Thomas Cranmer (1489–1556). Cranmer, the archbishop of Canterbury, was at first careful to translate and shape the old Latin liturgy into a moderate, occasionally ambiguous compromise between Catholic and Protestant positions. His thorough revision in 1552 put the *Book of Common Prayer* much more decisively into the Protestant camp. Banned by the Catholic Mary Tudor, during whose reign Cranmer was executed, the *Book of Common Prayer* was restored, with small revisions, by Elizabeth, and has remained the basis of Anglican worship ever since. Cranmer was, among his other accomplishments, a brilliant prose stylist, and the cadences of the *Book of Common Prayer* have had a profound influence on the English language. The selection, part of the marriage service, is from the version used during the reign of Elizabeth.

From The Book of Common Prayer and Administration of the Sacraments and Other Rites and Ceremonies in the Church of England

From The Form of Solemnization of Matrimony

* * * At the day appointed for solemnization of matrimony, the persons to be married shall come into the body of the church with their friends and neighbors. And there the priest shall thus say:

Dearly beloved friends, we are gathered together here in the sight of God, and in the face of his congregation, to join together this man and this woman in holy matrimony, which is an honorable estate,[1] instituted of God in paradise, in the time of man's innocency, signifying unto us the mystical union that is betwixt Christ and his church: which holy estate Christ adorned and beautified with his presence and first miracle that he wrought in Cana of Galilee,[2] and is commended of Saint Paul to be honorable among all men,[3] and therefore is not to be enterprised[4] nor taken in hand unadvisedly, lightly, or wantonly, to satisfy men's carnal lusts and appetites, like brute beasts that have no understanding; but reverently, discreetly, advisedly, soberly, and in the fear of God, duly considering the causes for the which matrimony was ordained. One was, the procreation of children, to be brought up in the fear and nurture of the Lord, and praise of God. Secondly, it was ordained for a remedy against sin, and to avoid fornication, that such persons as have not the gift of continency might marry, and keep themselves undefiled members of Christ's body.[5] Thirdly, for the mutual society, help, and comfort that the one ought to have of the other, both in prosperity and adversity: into the which holy estate these two persons present come now to be joined. Therefore if any man can show any just cause why they may not lawfully be joined together, let him now speak, or else hereafter forever hold his peace.

And also speaking to the persons that shall be married, he shall say:

I require and charge you (as you will answer at the dreadful day of judgment, when the secrets of all hearts shall be disclosed) that if either of you do know any impediment why ye may not be lawfully joined together in matrimony, that ye confess it. For be ye well assured, that so many as be coupled together otherwise than God's word doth allow are not joined together by God, neither is their matrimony lawful.

At which day of marriage, if any man do allege and declare any impediment why they may not be coupled together in matrimony by God's law or the laws of this realm; and will be bound, and sufficient sureties with him, to the parties, or else put in a caution,[6] to the full value of such charges as the persons to be married doth sustain, to prove his allegation: then the solemnization must be deferred unto such time as the truth be tried. If no impediment be alleged, then shall the curate[7] say unto the man,

1. State, condition.
2. He changed water into wine (John 2.1–11).
3. "Marriage is honorable in all, and the bed undefiled: but whoremongers and adulterers God will judge" (Hebrews 13.4).

4. Undertaken.
5. The church.
6. Surety.
7. A clergyman who has charge of a parish.

N.[8] Wilt thou have this woman to thy wedded wife, to live together after God's ordinance in the holy estate of matrimony? Wilt thou love her, comfort her, honor and keep her, in sickness and in health? And forsaking all other, keep thee only to her, so long as you both shall live?

The man shall answer,
I will.
Then shall the priest say to the woman,

N. Wilt thou have this man to thy wedded husband, to live together after God's ordinance in the holy estate of matrimony? Wilt thou obey him and serve him, love, honor, and keep him, in sickness and in health, and forsaking all other, keep thee only unto him, so long as you both shall live?

The woman shall answer,
I will.
Then shall the minister say,

Who giveth this woman to be married unto this man?

And the minister receiving the woman at her father or friend's hands, shall cause the man to take the woman by the right hand, and so either to give their troth[9] to other. The man first saying:

I N. take thee N. to my wedded wife, to have and to hold from this day forward, for better, for worse, for richer, for poorer, in sickness and in health, to love and to cherish, till death us depart,[1] according to God's holy ordinance: and thereto I plight thee my troth.

Then shall they loose their hands, and the woman taking again the man by the right hand shall say:

I N. take thee N. to my wedded husband, to have and to hold from this day forward, for better, for worse, for richer, for poorer, in sickness and in health, to love, cherish, and to obey, till death us depart, according to God's holy ordinance: and thereto I give thee my troth.

Then shall they again loose their hands, and the man shall give unto the woman a ring, laying the same upon the book with the accustomed duty[2] to the priest and clerk. And the priest taking the ring, shall deliver it unto the man, to put it upon the fourth finger of the woman's left hand. And the man taught by the priest shall say:

With this ring I thee wed: with my body I thee worship: and with all my worldly goods I thee endow. In the name of the Father, and of the Son, and of the Holy Ghost. Amen.

Then the man leaving the ring upon the fourth finger of the woman's left hand, the minister shall say:

O eternal God, creator and preserver of all mankind, giver of all spiritual grace, the author of everlasting life: send thy blessing upon these thy servants, this man and this woman, whom we bless in thy name; that as Isaac

8. Name—i.e., the minister inserts the man's given name here.
9. Truth—i.e., pledge.

1. Part.
2. Payment. "Book": Bible.

and Rebecca lived faithfully together,[3] so these persons may surely perform and keep the vow and covenant betwixt them made, whereof this ring given and received is a token and pledge, and may ever remain in perfect love and peace together, and live according unto thy laws: through Jesus Christ our Lord. Amen.

Then shall the priest join their right hands together, and say:

Those whom God hath joined together, let no man put asunder.

Then shall the minister speak unto the people:

Forasmuch as N. and N. have consented together in holy wedlock, and have witnessed the same before God and this company, and thereto have given and pledged their troth, either to other, and have declared the same by giving and receiving of a ring, and by joining of hands: I pronounce that they be man and wife together. In the name of the Father, and of the Son, and of the Holy Ghost. Amen.

And the minister shall add this blessing:

God the Father, God the Son, God the Holy Ghost, bless, preserve, and keep you: the Lord mercifully with his favor look upon you, and so fill you with all spiritual benediction and grace that you may so live together in this life that in the world to come you may have life everlasting. Amen.

1559

3. In Genesis 24–27.

QUEEN ELIZABETH
1533–1603

Elizabeth I, queen of England from 1558 to 1603, set her mark indelibly on the age that has come to bear her name. Endowed with intelligence, courage, cunning, and a talent for self-display, she managed to survive and flourish in a world that would have easily crushed a weaker person. Her birth was a disappointment to her father, Henry VIII, who had hoped for a male heir to the throne, and her prospects were further dimmed when her mother, Anne Boleyn, was executed three years later on charges of adultery and treason. At six years old, observers noted, Elizabeth had as much gravity as if she had been forty.

Under distinguished tutors, including the Protestant humanist Roger Ascham, the young princess received a rigorous education, with training in classical and modern languages, history, rhetoric, theology, and moral philosophy. Her religious orientation was Protestant, which put her in great danger during the reign of her Catholic older half-sister, Mary. Imprisoned in the Tower, interrogated and constantly spied upon, Elizabeth steadfastly professed innocence, loyalty, and a pious abhorrence of heresy. Upon Mary's death, she ascended the throne and quickly made clear that the official religion of the land would be Protestantism.

Elizabeth also made it clear that she would not be a figurehead. She gathered around her an able group of advisers, but she held firmly to the reins of power, playing one faction against another, conducting diplomatic affairs in her fluent French and Latin, and negotiating with an often contentious Parliament. Under great pressure to marry, she entered into protracted courtships with princely suitors, including the French duke of Anjou, but she ultimately refused all offers and declared repeatedly that she was wedded to her country.

In the face of deep skepticism about the ability of any woman to rule, Elizabeth strategically blended imperiousness with an elaborate cult of love. Her courtiers and advisers, on their knees, approached the queen, glittering in jewels and gorgeous gowns, and addressed her in extravagant terms that conjoined romantic passion and religious veneration. Artists and poets celebrated her in mythological dress—as Diana, the chaste goddess of the moon; Astraea, the goddess of justice; Gloriana, the queen of the fairies. Though she could suddenly veer whenever she chose toward bluntness and anger, Elizabeth herself often contrived to transform the language of politics into the language of love. "We all loved her," her godson John Harington wrote with a touch of irony, "for she said she loved us."

Throughout her life Elizabeth took pride in her command of languages and her felicity of expression. Her own writing includes carefully crafted letters and speeches on several state occasions; verse translations of selections from the Psalms, Petrarch, Seneca, and Horace; prose translations from Boethius, Plutarch, and the French Protestant Queen Margaret of Navarre; and a few original poems. The original poems known to be hers deal with actual events in her life. They are chiefly in octosyllabics or poulter's measure (rhyming couplets in which the first line has twelve and the second line fourteen syllables) and are rough-hewn, vigorous, and moralistic.

The doubt of future foes[1]

The doubt° of future foes exiles my present joy,	*fear*
And wit° me warns to shun such snares as threaten mine	*intelligence*
annoy.[2]	
For falsehood now doth flow, and subjects' faith doth ebb,[3]	
Which would not be, if reason ruled or wisdom weaved the web.	
5 But clouds of toys untried do cloak aspiring minds,	
Which turn to rain of late repent, by course of changèd winds.[4]	
The top of hope supposed, the root of ruth° will be,	*sorrow*
And fruitless all their graffèd guiles, as shortly ye shall see.[5]	
The dazzled eyes with pride, which great ambition blinds,	
10 Shall be unsealed by worthy wights° whose foresight falsehood	*men*
finds.	
The daughter of debate,[6] that eke° discord doth sow	*also*
Shall reap no gain where former rule[7] hath taught still° peace to	*stable*
grow.	
No foreign banished wight shall anchor in this port;	

---

1. The poem concerns Elizabeth's Roman Catholic cousin Mary Stuart, queen of Scotland, who in 1567 sought refuge in England from her rebellious subjects. Mary was the focus of several Catholic conspiracies to place her on the English throne in place of Elizabeth.
2. I.e., threaten to harm ("annoy") me.
3. I.e., the tide of faith (loyalty) is ebbing, yielding to the rising tide of falsehood.
4. Clouds of tricks ("toys") not yet tested and detected ("untried") hide the "aspiring minds" of

ambitious foes, but those clouds will turn at last into rains of repentance.
5. The deceptions ("guiles") grafted ("graffèd") into them will not bear fruit.
6. Mary Stuart also was sometimes called "Mother of Debate," because she was constantly the focus of conspiracies and plots.
7. "Former rule": either the reign of Henry VIII or that of Edward VI, which established the Reformation in England.

Our realm it brooks no stranger's force, let them elsewhere resort.
15   Our rusty sword with rest,[8] shall first his edge employ
To poll their tops[9] that seek such change and gape for future joy.

ca. 1568   1589

On Monsieur's Departure[1]

I grieve and dare not show my discontent,
I love and yet am forced to seem to hate,
I do, yet dare not say I ever meant,
I seem stark mute but inwardly do prate.°   chatter
5   I am and not, I freeze and yet am burned,
Since from myself another self I turned.

My care is like my shadow in the sun,
Follows me flying, flies when I pursue it,
Stands and lies by me, doth what I have done.[2]
10   His too familiar care[3] doth make me rue° it.   regret
No means I find to rid him from my breast,
Till by the end of things it be suppressed.

Some gentler passion slide into my mind,
For I am soft and made of melting snow;
15   Or be more cruel, love, and so be kind.
Let me or° float or sink, be high or low.   either
Or let me live with some more sweet content,
Or die and so forget what love ere meant.

ca. 1582   1823

Letters

To Sir Amyas Paulet[1]

[ca. September 1586]

Amyas, my most faithful and careful servant, God reward thee treblefold
in the double for thy most troublesome charge[2] so well discharged. If you
knew, my Amyas, how kindly, besides most dutifully, my grateful heart
accepts and prizes your spotless endeavors and faultless actions, your wise
orders and safe regard, performed in so dangerous and crafty a charge, it
would ease your travails and rejoice your heart, in which I charge you place

---

8. Sword rusty from disuse.
9. Strike off their heads.
1. The heading, present in two manuscripts, identifies the occasion of this poem as the breaking off
of marriage negotiations between Queen Elizabeth
and the French duke of Anjou in 1582. A third
manuscript implies instead an association with
Elizabeth's favorite, the earl of Essex, who led an
abortive rebellion and was executed for treason in
1601.
2. Does everything I do.

3. I.e., my own care (i.e., sorrow) that he caused.
1. Paulet was the keeper of Mary, Queen of Scots,
who had been imprisoned in England since 1567.
In 1586 a number of her supporters, led by
Anthony Babington, plotted to murder Elizabeth
and place Mary on the throne. The plot was discovered, and the plotters were executed in September. Mary, who had been complicit with them, was
placed under stricter confinement.
2. Duty, responsibility.

this most just thought, that I cannot balance in any weight of my judgment the value that I prize you at, and suppose no treasures to countervail such a faith. If I reward not such deserts, let me lack when I have most need of you, if I acknowledge not such merit, *non omnibus dictum*.[3]

Let your wicked murderess know how, with hearty sorrow, her vile deserts compel these orders; and bid her from me, ask God forgiveness for her treacherous dealings towards the savior of her life many a year, to the intolerable peril of my own, and yet, not contented with so many forgivenesses, must fault again so horribly, far passing woman's thought, much less a princess; instead of excusing whereof, not one can sorrow, it being so plainly confessed by the authors[4] of my guiltless death. Let repentance take place, and let not the fiend possess her, so as her better part may not be lost, for which I pray with hands lifted up to Him that may both save and spill.[5]

With my most loving adieu and prayer for thy long life, your most assured and loving sovereign, as thereby by good deserts induced.

1854

To Henry III, king of France[1]

January 1587

Sir, my Good Brother,

The old ground, on which I have often based my letters, appears to me so changed at present, that I am compelled to alter the style, and instead of returning thanks, to use complaints. My God! How could you be so unreasonable as to reproach the injured party, and to compass the death of an innocent one by allowing her to become the prey of a murderess? But, without reference to my rank, which is nowise inferior to your own, nor to my friendship to you, most sincere, for I have wellnigh forfeited all reputation among the princes of my own religion,[2] by neglecting them in order to prevent disturbances in your dominions; exposed to dangers such as scarcely any prince ever was before; expecting, at least, some ostensible reasons and offers for security against the daily danger, for the epilogue of this whole negotiation: you are, in spite of all this, so blinded by the words of those who I pray may not ruin you, that instead of a thousand thanks, which I had merited for such singular services, Monsieur de Bellievre has addressed language to my ears, which, in truth, I know not well how to interpret. For that you should be angry at my saving my own life seems to me the threat of an enemy, which, I assure you, will never put me in fear, but is the shortest way to make me dispatch the cause of so much mischief. Let me, I pray you, understand in what sense I am to take these words; for I will not live an hour to endure that any prince whatsoever should boast that he had humbled me

---

3. In context, the phrase (which means "not said to [or by] all") is obscure. Perhaps Elizabeth's meaning is "if indeed I do not proclaim such merit to all."
4. I.e., the conspirators.
5. Destroy.
1. Translated from the original French by Agnes Strickland. In the aftermath of the conspiracy to set her on the throne, Mary was tried, convicted, and sentenced to death. On January 6, 1587, Mon-

sieur de Bellievre, a special ambassador from the king of France, Henry III (to whose predecessor, Henry II, Mary had briefly enjoyed a dynastic marriage, ended by the young king's death in 1560), pleaded Mary's cause before Elizabeth. The threats included in his remarks prompted her to write this strong letter to his master. On February 8 Mary was beheaded.
2. I.e., other Protestant monarchs.

into drinking such a cup as that. Monsieur de Bellievre has, indeed, somewhat softened his language, by adding that you in nowise wish any danger to accrue to me, and still less to cause me any. I therefore write you these few words, and if it please you to act accordingly, you shall never find a truer friend; but if otherwise, I neither am in so low a place, nor govern realms so inconsiderable, that I should in right and honor yield to any living prince who would injure me; and I doubt not, by the grace of God, to make my cause good for my own security.

I beseech you to think rather of the means of maintaining than of diminishing my friendship. Your realm, my good brother, cannot abide many enemies. Give not the rein, in God's name, to wild horses, lest they should shake you from your saddle. I say this to you out of a true and upright heart, and implore the Creator to grant you long and happy life.

Elizabeth

1854

Speech to the Troops at Tilbury[1]

My loving people: We have been persuaded by some that are careful of[2] our safety, to take heed how we commit ourselves to armed multitudes, for fear of treachery. But I assure you I do not desire to live to distrust my faithful and loving people. Let tyrants fear! I have always so behaved myself that, under God, I have placed my chief strength and safeguard in the loyal hearts and goodwill of my subjects; and therefore I am come amongst you, as you see, at this time, not for my recreation and disport, but being resolved, in the midst of the heat of the battle, to live or die amongst you all; to lay down for my God, and for my kingdom, and for my people, my honor and my blood, even in the dust. I know I have the body but of a weak and feeble woman; but I have the heart and stomach of a king, and of a king of England too,[3] and think foul scorn that Parma[4] or Spain, or any prince of Europe, should dare to invade the borders of my realm; to which, rather than any dishonor should grow by me, I myself will take up arms, I myself will be your general, judge, and rewarder of every one of your virtues in the field. I know already, for your forwardness you have deserved rewards and crowns;[5] and we do assure you on the word of a prince, they shall be duly paid you. In the meantime, my lieutenant-general[6] shall be in my stead, than whom never prince commanded a more noble or worthy subject; not doubting but by your obedience to my general, by your concord in the camp, and your valor in the

---

1. Delivered by Elizabeth to the land forces assembled at Tilbury (Essex) to repel the anticipated invasion of the Spanish Armada, a fleet of warships sent by Philip II. The Armada was defeated at sea and never reached England, a miraculous deliverance and sign of God's special favor to Elizabeth and to England, in the general view.
2. Anxious about.
3. An allusion to the concept of the king's (or queen's) two bodies, the one natural and mortal,

the other an ideal and enduring political construct. "Stomach": valor.
4. Alexander Farnese, duke of Parma, allied with (the king of) Spain and expected to join with him in the invasion of England.
5. An English monetary unit.
6. Robert Dudley, earl of Leicester, led her armies; he was the queen's favorite courtier and at one time rumored to be her lover and a prospective husband.

field, we shall shortly have a famous victory over those enemies of my God, of my kingdoms, and of my people.

1588   1752

The "Golden Speech"[1]

Mr. Speaker: We have heard your declaration and perceive your care of our state,[2] by falling into the consideration of a grateful acknowledgment of such benefits as you have received; and that your coming is to present thanks unto us, which I accept with no less joy than your loves can have desire to offer such a present.

I do assure you that there is no prince that loveth his subjects better, or whose love can countervail our love. There is no jewel, be it of never so rich a price, which I prefer before this jewel, I mean your love, for I do more esteem it than any treasure or riches: for that we know how to prize, but love and thanks I count inestimable. And though God has raised me high, yet this I count the glory of my crown, that I have reigned with your loves. This makes me that I do not so much rejoice that God hath made me to be a queen as to be a queen over so thankful a people. Therefore I have cause to wish nothing more than to content the subject, and that is a duty which I owe. Neither do I desire to live longer days than that I may see your prosperity, and that is my only desire. And as I am that person that still, yet under God, hath delivered you, so I trust, by the almighty power of God, that I still shall be His instrument to preserve you from envy, peril, dishonor, shame, tyranny, and oppression, partly by means of your intended helps, which we take very acceptably, because it manifests the largeness of your loves and loyalties unto your sovereign.

Of myself I must say this: I never was any greedy, scraping grasper, nor a strait fast-holding prince, nor yet a waster; my heart was never set on worldly goods, but only for my subjects' good. What you do bestow on me I will not hoard up, but receive it to bestow on you again. Yea, mine own properties I count yours, to be expended for your good. Therefore render unto them, I beseech you, Mr. Speaker, such thanks as you imagine my heart yieldeth, but my tongue cannot express.

1. Elizabeth's speech to her last Parliament, 1601. The designation "Golden Speech" stems from the headnote to a version of it printed near the end of the Puritan interregnum (1659?): "This speech ought to be set in letters of gold, that as well the majesty, prudence, and virtue of this royal queen might in general most exquisitely appear, as also that her religious love and tender respect which she particularly and constantly did bear to her Parliament in unfeigned sincerity might (to the shame and perpetual disgrace and infamy of some of her successors) be nobly and truly vindicated."

The royal prerogatives included the right to grant or sell "letters patent," which gave the recipient monopoly control of some branch of commerce. (Sir Walter Ralegh, for example, was given the exclusive right, for a period of thirty years, to license all taverns.) Discontent with the monopolies—which had resulted in higher prices for a wide range of commodities, including such basic ones as salt and starch—came to a head in the Parliament of 1601. Under parliamentary pressure (and in return for a subsidy granted to her treasury), Elizabeth agreed to revoke some of the most obnoxious patents and to allow the courts to rule freely on charges brought against the holders of others. She invited members of Parliament who wished to offer thanks for this largess to come to her in a body, and on November 30 received about 150 of them at Whitehall palace. After effusive remarks by the speaker of the House of Commons (John Croke), the queen responded more or less as recorded here. (Elizabeth revised the speech for publication; and none of the surviving versions of it—which differ considerably—was printed earlier than about 1628.)

2. Rank, position.

Mr. Speaker, I would wish you and the rest to stand up, for I shall yet trouble you with longer speech.[3]

Mr. Speaker, you give me thanks, but I doubt me I have more cause to thank you all than you me: and I charge you to thank them of the House of Commons from me, for had I not received a knowledge from you, I might have fallen into the lap of an error only for lack of true information.

Since I was queen, yet never did I put my pen to any grant but that upon pretext and semblance made unto me that it was both good and beneficial to the subjects in general, though a private profit to some of my ancient servants who had deserved well. But the contrary being found by experience, I am exceedingly beholding to such subjects as would move the same at first. And I am not so simple to suppose but that there be some of the Lower House[4] whom these grievances never touched, and for them I think they speak out of zeal to their countries[5] and not out of spleen or malevolent affection, as being parties grieved. And I take it exceeding grateful from them, because it gives us to know that no respects or interests had moved them other than the minds[6] they bear to suffer no diminution of our honor and our subjects' love unto us. The zeal of which affection, tending to ease my people and knit their hearts unto me, I embrace with a princely care.

Far above all earthly treasure I esteem my people's love, more than which I desire not to merit. That my grants should be grievous to my people and oppressions to be privileged under color of our patents, our kingly dignity shall not suffer[7] it. Yea, when I heard it, I could give no rest to my thoughts until I had reformed it.[8] Shall they think to escape unpunished that have thus oppressed you and have been respectless of their duty and regardless of our honor? No, Mr. Speaker, I assure you, were it more for conscience' sake than for any glory or increase of love that I desire these errors, troubles, vexations, and oppressions done by these varlets and lewd[9] persons, not worthy the name of subjects, should not escape without condign punishment. But I perceive they dealt with me like physicians who, ministering a drug, make it more acceptable by giving it a good aromatical savor, or, when they give pills, do gild them all over.

I have ever used to set the last judgment day before mine eyes and so to rule as I shall be judged to answer before a higher Judge. To Whose judgment seat I do appeal that never thought was cherished in my heart that tended not to my people's good. And if my kingly bounty have been abused and my grants turned to the hurt of my people, contrary to my will and meaning, or if any in authority under me have neglected or perverted what I have committed to them, I hope God will not lay their culps[1] and offenses to my charge. And though there were danger in repealing our grants, yet what danger would not I rather incur for your own good, than I would suffer them still to continue?

I know the title of a king is a glorious title, but assure yourself that the shining glory of princely authority hath not so dazzled the eyes of our understanding but that we well know and remember that we also are to yield an account of our actions before the Great Judge. To be a king and wear a crown

---

3. Up to this point, the assemblage had evidently been kneeling.
4. The House of Commons.
5. Their constituents.
6. Intentions.
7. Allow. "Color": pretext.

8. In fact, Elizabeth was extremely slow to respond to the grievances, which had, for example, previously been raised in the Parliament of 1597.
9. Base.
1. Sins.

is more glorious to them that see it than it is pleasure to them that bear it. For myself, I was never so much enticed with the glorious name of a king or royal authority of a queen as delighted that God hath made me this instrument to maintain His truth and glory, and to defend this kingdom, as I said, from peril, dishonor, tyranny, and oppression.

There will never queen sit in my seat with more zeal to my country or care to my subjects, and that will sooner with willingness yield and venture her life for your good and safety than myself. And though you have had and may have many princes more mighty and wise sitting in this seat, yet you never had or shall have any that will be more careful and loving.

Should I ascribe anything to myself and my sexly weakness, I were not worthy to live then, and of all most unworthy of the mercies I have had from God, Who hath ever yet given me a heart which never yet feared foreign or home enemies. I speak it to give God the praise as a testimony before you, and not to attribute anything unto myself. For I, O Lord, what am I, whom practices and perils past should not fear?[2] O what can I do? That I should speak for any glory, God forbid!

This, Mr. Speaker, I pray you deliver unto the House, to whom heartily recommend me. And so I commit you all to your best fortunes and further counsels. And I pray you, Mr. Comptroller, Mr. Secretary,[3] and you of my council, that before these gentlemen depart into their countries,[4] you bring them all to kiss my hand.

1601   ca. 1628

2. Frighten. "Practices": treacherous schemes.   Cecil, earl of Salisbury.
3. William Knollys, earl of Banbury, and Robert   4. Districts.

EDMUND SPENSER
1552–1599

Edmund Spenser set out, consciously and deliberately, to become the great English poet of his age. In a culture in which most accomplished poetry was written by those who were, or at least professed to be, principally interested in something else— advancement at court, diplomacy, statecraft, or the church—Spenser's ambition was altogether remarkable, and it is still more remarkable that he succeeded in reaching his goal. Unlike such poets as Wyatt, Surrey, and Sidney, born to privilege and social distinction, Spenser was born to parents of modest means and station, in London, probably in 1552. He nonetheless received an impressive education, first at the Merchant Taylors' School, under its demanding humanist headmaster, Richard Mulcaster, then at Pembroke College, Cambridge, where he was enrolled as a "sizar" or poor (meaning impoverished) scholar. In the Puritan environment of Cambridge, where the popular preacher Thomas Cartwright was beginning to make the authorities uneasy, Spenser started as a poet by translating some poems for a volume of anti-Catholic propaganda. He also began his friendship with Gabriel Harvey, an eccentric Cambridge don, humanist, and pamphleteer. Their correspondence shows that both men were passionately interested in theories of poetry and in experiments in quantitative versification in English.

After receiving the B.A. degree in 1573 and the M.A. in 1576, Spenser served as personal secretary and aide to several prominent men, including Dr. John Young, bishop of Rochester; and the earl of Leicester, the queen's principal favorite. During his employment in Leicester's household he came to know Sir Philip Sidney and his friend Sir Edward Dyer, courtiers who sought to promote a new English poetry. Spenser's contribution to the movement was *The Shepheardes Calender*, published in 1579 and dedicated to Sidney.

In *The Shepheardes Calender* Spenser used a deliberately archaic language, partly in homage to Chaucer, whose work he praised as a "well of English undefiled," and partly to achieve a rustic effect, in keeping with the feigned simplicity of pastoral poetry's shepherd singers. Sidney did not approve; in his *Defense of Poesy* he wrote, "*The Shepheardes Calender* hath much poetry in his eclogues, indeed worthy the reading, if I be not deceived. (That same framing of his style to an old rustic language I dare not allow, since neither Theocritus in Greek, Virgil in Latin, nor Sannazzaro in Italian did affect it.)" Another classical purist, Ben Jonson, growled that Spenser "writ no language," and, in the eighteenth century, Samuel Johnson described the language of *The Shepheardes Calender* as "studied barbarity." Johnson's characterization is, in a way, quite accurate, for Spenser was attempting to conjure up a native English style to which he could wed the classical mode of the pastoral. Moreover, since pastoral was traditionally viewed as the prelude in a great national poet's career to more ambitious undertakings, Spenser was also in effect announcing his extravagant ambition.

There are thirteen different meters in *The Shepheardes Calender*. Some of these Spenser invented, some he adapted, but most of them were novel; only three or four were at all common in 1579. Spenser was a prolific experimenter who went on to make further innovations in his later poems: the special rhyme scheme of the Spenserian sonnet; the remarkably beautiful adaptation of the Italian *canzone* forms for the *Epithalamion* and *Prothalamion*; and the nine-line stanza of *The Faerie Queene*, with its hexameter (six-stress) line at the end, are the best known. Spenser is sometimes called the "poet's poet" because so many later English poets learned the art of versification from him. In the nineteenth century alone his influence may be seen in Shelley's *Revolt of Islam*, Byron's *Childe Harold's Pilgrimage*, Keats's *Eve of St. Agnes*, and Tennyson's *The Lotus-Eaters*.

The year after the publication of *The Shepheardes Calender*, Spenser went to Ireland as secretary and aide to Lord Grey of Wilton, lord deputy of Ireland. Although he tried continually to obtain appointments in England and to secure the patronage of the queen, he spent the rest of his career in Ireland, holding various minor government posts and hence participating actively in the English struggle against those who resisted their colonial authority. The grim realities of that struggle—massacre, the burning of miserable hovels and of crops with the deliberate intention of starving the inhabitants, the forced relocation of whole communities, the manipulation of treason charges so as to facilitate the seizure of lands, the endless repetition of acts of military "justice" calculated to intimidate and break the spirit—may be glimpsed in distorted and on occasion direct form throughout Spenser's writings, along with dreamlike depictions of the beauty of the Irish landscape. Those writings probably include *A View of the Present State of Ireland*, an anonymously published apology for the repressive English regime.

Spenser was rewarded for his efforts in Ireland with a castle and 3,028 acres of expropriated land at Kilcolman in the province of Munster. There he was visited by another colonist and poet, the powerful and well-connected Sir Walter Ralegh, to whom Spenser showed the great chivalric epic on which he was at work. With Ralegh's influential backing, Spenser traveled to England and published, in 1590, the first three books of *The Faerie Queene*, which made a strong bid for the queen's favor and patronage. He was rewarded with a handsome pension of fifty pounds a year for life, though the queen's principal councilor, Lord Burghley, is said to have complained that it was a lot for a song. Soon after, Spenser published a volume of poems called *Complaints;* a pastoral called *Colin Clouts Come Home Againe* (1595), commenting on the courtiers and ladies at the center of English court life at the time of his 1590 visit; his sonnet cycle, *Amoretti;* and two wedding poems, *Epithalamion* and *Protha-lamion.* The six-book *Faerie Queene* was published in 1596, with some revisions in the first part and a changed ending to Book 3 to provide a bridge to the added books; the two so-called Mutability cantos and two stanzas of a third—perhaps part of an intended seventh book—appeared posthumously in the edition of 1609.

In 1598 there was an uprising in Munster, and rebels burned down the house in which Spenser lived. The poet fled with his wife; their newborn baby is said to have died in the flames. Spenser was sent to England with messages from the besieged English garrison. He died in Westminster on January 13, 1599, and was buried near his beloved Chaucer in what is now called the Poets' Corner of Westminster Abbey.

Spenser cannot be put into neatly labeled categories. His work is steeped in Renais-sance Neoplatonism but is also earthy and practical. He is a lover and celebrator of physical beauty yet also a profound analyst of good and evil in all their perplexing shapes and complexities. In his early days he was strongly influenced by Puritanism, remained a thoroughgoing Protestant all his life, and portrayed the Roman Catholic church as a demonic villain in *The Faerie Queene;* yet his understanding of faith and of sin owes much to Catholic thinkers. He is a poet of sensuous images yet also something of an iconoclast, deeply suspicious of the power of images (material and verbal) to turn into idols. He is an idealist, drawn to courtesy, gentleness, and exqui-site moral refinement, yet also a celebrant of English nationalism, empire, and martial power. He is in some ways a backward-looking poet who paid homage to Chaucer, used archaic language, and compared his own age unfavorably with the feudal past. Yet as a British epic poet and poet-prophet, he points forward to the poetry of the Romantics and especially Milton—who himself paid homage to the "sage and serious" Spenser as "a better teacher than Scotus or Aquinas."

Because it was a deliberate choice on Spenser's part that his language should seem antique, his poetry is always printed in the original spelling and punctuation; a few of the most confusing punctuation marks have, however, been altered in the present text. Spenser also spells words variably in such a way as to suggest rhymes to the eye or to suggest etymologies (often incorrect ones). This inconsistency in his spelling is typical of his time; in the sixteenth century people varied even the spelling of their own names.

The Faerie Queene   In a letter to Sir Walter Ralegh, appended to the first, 1590, edition of *The Faerie Queene,* Spenser describes his exuberant, multifaceted poem as an allegory—an extended metaphor or "dark conceit"—and invites us to interpret the characters and adventures in the several books in terms of the particular virtues and vices they enact or come to embody. Thus the Redcrosse Knight in Book 1 is the knight of Holiness (and also St. George, the patron saint of England); Sir Guyon in Book 2 is the knight of Temperance; the female knight Britomart in Book 3 is the knight of Chastity (chastity here meaning chaste love leading to marriage). The heroes of Books 4, 5, and 6 represent Friendship, Justice, and Courtesy. The poem's general end, Spenser writes, is "to fashion a gentleman or noble person in vertuous and gentle discipline," and the individual moral qualities, taken together, constitute the ideal human being.

However, Spenser's allegory is not as simple as the letter to Ralegh might suggest, and the fashioning of identity proves to be anything but straightforward. Far from being the static embodiments of abstract moral precepts, the knights have a surprisingly complex, altogether human relation to their allegorical identities, identities into which they grow only through painful trial and error in the course of their adventures. These adventures repeatedly take the form of mortal combat with sworn enemies—hence the Redcrosse Knight of Holiness smites the "Saracen" (that is, Muslim) Sansfoy (literally, "without faith")—but the enemies are revealed more often than not to be weirdly dissociated aspects of the knights themselves: when he encounters Sansfoy, Redcrosse has just been faithless to his lady Una, and his most dangerous enemy ultimately proves to be his own despair. Accordingly, the meaning of the various characters, episodes, and places is richly complex, revealed to us (and to the characters themselves) only by degrees.

The complexity is heightened by the inclusion, in addition to the moral allegory, of an historical allegory to which Spenser calls attention, in the letter to Ralegh, by observing that both the Faerie Queene and Britomart are personifications of Queen Elizabeth. Throughout the poem there is a dense network of allusions to events, issues, and particular persons in England and Ireland—for example, the queen, her rival Mary, Queen of Scots, the Spanish Armada, the English Reformation, the controversies over religious images, and the bitter colonial struggles against Irish rebellion. Some of Spenser's characters are identified by conventional symbols and attributes that would have been obvious to every reader of his time. For example, such a reader would know immediately that a woman who wears a miter and scarlet clothes and who dwells near the river Tiber represents (in one sense at least) the Roman Catholic Church, which had often been identified by Protestant preachers with the Whore of Babylon in the Book of Revelation. Marginal notes jotted in early copies of *The Faerie Queene* suggest, however, that there was no consensus among Spenser's contemporaries about the precise historical referents of others of the poem's myriad figures. (Sir Walter Ralegh's wife Bess, for example, seems to have identified many of the virtuous female characters as allegorical representations of herself.) Spenser's poem may be enjoyed as a fascinating story with multiple meanings, a story that works on several levels at once and continually eludes the full and definitive allegorical explanation it constantly promises to deliver.

The poem is also an epic. The organization of each book into twelve cantos imitates the twelve books of Virgil's great Latin epic, the *Aeneid*, and, like Virgil, Spenser is deeply concerned with the dangerous struggles and painful renunciations required to achieve the highest values of human civilization. The heroic deeds of Spenser's brave knights are the achievements of individual aristocratic men and women, not the triumphs of armies or communities united in serving a common purpose, not even the triumph of the virtually invisible royal court of Gloriana, the Faerie Queene. Yet, taken together, the disjointed adventures of these solitary warriors constitute in Spenser's fervent vision the glory of Britain, the collective memory of its heroic past and the promise of a still more glorious future. And if the Faerie Queene herself is consigned to the margins of the poem that bears her name, she nonetheless is the symbolic embodiment of a shared national destiny, a destiny that reaches beyond mere political success to participate in the ultimate, millennial triumph of good over evil.

If *The Faerie Queene* is thus an epic celebration of Queen Elizabeth, the Protestant faith, and the English nation, it is also a chivalric romance, full of jousting knights and damsels in distress, dragons, witches, enchanted trees, wicked magicians, giants, dark caves, shining castles, and "paynims" (with French names). A clear, pleasant stream may be dangerous to drink from because to do so produces loss of strength. A pious hermit may prove to be a cunningly disguised villain. Houses, castles, and gardens are often places of education and challenge or of especially dense allegorical significance, as if they possess special, half-hidden keys to the meaning of the books in which they appear. As a romance, Spenser's poem is designed to produce wonder, to enthrall its readers with sprawling plots, marvelous adventures, heroic characters, ravishing descriptions, and esoteric mysteries.

The Faerie Queene constantly intertwines diverse literary and pictorial traditions. Entire episodes are adapted from two great Italian romantic epics, Orlando furioso (Orlando Mad, 1516), by Ariosto, and Gerusalemme liberata (Jerusalem Delivered, 1575), by Tasso. Ariosto and Tasso in turn were closely following Homer, Virgil, and Ovid, as well as other ancient poets. (For a Renaissance poet, borrowing from and reworking older materials was thought praiseworthy.) Places such as Lucifera's castle, individual attributes such as Una's lamb, and certain stock characters, with their names, physiognomies, and costumes, came to Spenser from the classics and the Bible, from theologians, from folk tales and medieval pageants, from tapestries, paintings, and collections of emblems.

The whole of The Faerie Queene is written in a remarkable nine-line stanza of closely interlocking rhymes (ababbcbcc), the first eight lines with five stresses each (iambic pentameter) and the final line with six stresses (iambic hexameter or alexandrine). The stanza gives the work a certain formal regularity, but the various books are composed on quite different structural principles. Book 1 is almost entirely self-contained; it has been called a miniature epic in itself, centering on the adventures of one principal hero, Redcrosse, who at length achieves the quest he undertakes at Una's behest: killing the dragon who has imprisoned her parents and thereby winning her as his bride. The spiritual allegory is similarly self-contained; it presents the Christian struggling heroically against many evils and temptations—doctrinal error, hypocrisy, the Seven Deadly Sins, and despair—to some of which he succumbs before finally emerging triumphant. It shows him separated from the one true faith and, aided by many interventions of divine grace, at length reunited with it once more. Then it treats his purgation from sin, his education in the House of Holiness, and his final salvation.

To some degree a lack of closure characterizes all of The Faerie Queene, including the more self-contained of the six finished books, and it is fitting that there survives the fragment of another book, the cantos of Mutability, in which Spenser broods on the tension in nature between systematic order and ceaseless change. The poem as a whole is built around principles that pull tautly against one another: a commitment to a life of constant struggle and a profound longing for rest; a celebration of human heroism and a perception of ineradicable human sinfulness; a vision of evil as a terrifyingly potent force and a vision of evil as mere emptiness and filth; a faith in the supreme value of visionary art and a recurrent suspicion that art is dangerously allied to graven images and deception. That Spenser's knights never quite reach the havens they seek may reflect irresolvable tensions to which we owe much of the power and beauty of this great, unfinished work.

From THE FAERIE QUEENE

From The First Booke of The Faerie Queene

Contayning
The Legende of the
Knight of the Red Crosse,
or
Of Holinesse

Canto 1

The Patron of true Holinesse,
Foule Errour doth defeate:
Hypocrisie him to entrappe,
Doth to his home entreate.

1

A Gentle Knight was pricking° on the plaine,   *spurring*
Ycladd in mightie armes and silver shielde,
Wherein old dints of deepe wounds did remaine,
The cruell markes of many a bloudy fielde;
5   Yet armes till that time did he never wield:[1]
His angry steede did chide his foming bitt,
As much disdayning to the curbe to yield:
Full jolly° knight he seemd, and faire did sitt,   *gallant*
As one for knightly giusts° and fierce encounters fitt.   *tourneys, jousts*

2

10   But on his brest a bloudie Crosse he bore,
The deare remembrance of his dying Lord,
For whose sweete sake that glorious badge he wore,
And dead as living ever him adored:
Upon his shield the like was also scored,
15   For soveraine[2] hope, which in his helpe he had:
Right faithfull true[3] he was in deede and word,
But of his cheere[4] did seeme too solemne sad;°   *grave*
Yet nothing did he dread, but ever was ydrad.°   *dreaded, feared*

3

Upon a great adventure he was bond,
20   That greatest Gloriana to him gave,
That greatest Glorious Queene of Faerie Lond,
To winne him worship,° and her grace to have,   *honor*
Which of all earthly things he most did crave;

---

1. Redcrosse wears the armor of the Christian
man, as Spenser explained in the letter to Ralegh.
It bears the dents of every Christian's fight against
evil.
2. Having greatest power (often applied to medical

remedies).
3. An echo of Revelation 19.11: "And I saw heaven
opened; and behold a white horse; and he that sat
upon him was called Faithful and True."
4. Facial expression, mood.

And ever as he rode, his hart did earne°   *yearn*
25   To prove his puissance in battell brave
        Upon his foe, and his new force to learne;
    Upon his foe, a Dragon horrible and stearne.

4

    A lovely Ladie rode him faire beside,
        Upon a lowly Asse more white then snow,
30   Yet she much whiter, but the same did hide
        Under a vele, that wimpled° was full low,   *lying in folds*
        And over all a blacke stole she did throw,
        As one that inly mournd: so was she sad,
        And heavie sat upon her palfrey slow:
35   Seemèd in heart some hidden care she had,
    And by her in a line a milke white lambe she lad.

5

    So pure an innocent, as that same lambe,
        She was in life and every vertuous lore,
        And by descent from Royall lynage came
40   Of ancient Kings and Queenes, that had of yore
        Their scepters stretcht from East to Westerne shore,
        And all the world in their subjection held;
        Till that infernall feend with foule uprore
        Forwasted° all their land, and them expeld: *laid waste*
45   Whom to avenge, she had this Knight from far compeld.°   *summoned*

6

    Behind her farre away a Dwarfe did lag,
        That lasie seemd in being ever last,
        Or wearied with bearing of her bag
        Of needments at his backe. Thus as they past,
50   The day with cloudes was suddeine overcast,
        And angry Jove an hideous storme of raine
        Did poure into his Lemans⁵ lap so fast,
        That every wight° to shrowd° it did constrain,   *creature / cover*
    And this faire couple eke° to shroud themselves were fain.°   *also / eager*

7

55   Enforst to seeke some covert nigh at hand,
        A shadie grove not far away they spide,
        That promist ayde the tempest to withstand:
        Whose loftie trees yclad with sommers pride,
        Did spred so broad, that heavens light did hide,
60   Not perceable° with power of any starre: *penetrable*
        And all within were pathes and alleies wide,
        With footing worne, and leading inward farre:
    Faire harbour that them seemes; so in they entred arre.

---

5. His lover's, i.e., the earth's.

8

And foorth they passe, with pleasure forward led,
65   Joying to heare the birdes sweete harmony,
Which therein shrouded from the tempest dred,°   *fearful*
Seemd in their song to scorne the cruell sky.
Much can° they prayse the trees, so straight and hy,   *did*
The sayling Pine, the Cedar proud and tall,
70   The vine-prop Elme, the Poplar never dry,
The builder Oake, sole king of forrests all,
The Aspine good for staves, the Cypresse funerall.

9

The Laurell, meed° of mightie Conquerours   *reward*
And Poets sage, the Firre that weepeth still,[6]
75   The Willow worne of forlorne Paramours,
The Eugh° obedient to the benders will,   *yew*
The Birch for shaftes, the Sallow° for the mill,   *willow*
The Mirrhe sweete bleeding in the bitter wound,
The warlike Beech, the Ash for nothing ill,
80   The fruitfull Olive, and the Platane° round,   *plane-tree*
The carver Holme,[7] the Maple seeldom inward sound.

10

Led with delight, they thus beguile the way,
Untill the blustring storme is overblowne;
When weening° to returne, whence they did stray,   *thinking*
85   They cannot finde that path, which first was showne,
But wander too and fro in wayes unknowne,
Furthest from end then, when they neerest weene,
That makes them doubt, their wits be not their owne:
So many pathes, so many turnings seene,
90   That which of them to take, in diverse doubt they been.

11

At last resolving forward still to fare,
Till that some end they finde or° in or out,   *either*
That path they take, that beaten seemed most bare,
And like to lead the labyrinth about°   *out of*
95   Which when by tract they hunted had throughout,
At length it brought them to a hollow cave,
Amid the thickest woods. The Champion stout
Eftsoones° dismounted from his courser brave,   *forthwith*
And to the Dwarfe a while his needlesse spere[8] he gave.

12

100   "Be well aware,"° quoth then that Ladie milde,   *watchful*
"Least suddaine mischiefe° ye too rash provoke: *misfortune*

---

6. I.e., exudes resin continuously. Spenser in these stanzas imitates Chaucer's catalog of trees in the *Parliament of Fowls*; the convention goes back to Ovid.

7. Holly or holm-oak, both suitable for carving.
8. "Needlesse" because the spear is used only on horseback. "By tract" (line 95): by following the track.

The danger hid, the place unknowne and wilde,
Breedes dreadfull doubts: Oft fire is without smoke,
And perill without show: therefore your stroke
105   Sir knight with-hold, till further triall made."
"Ah Ladie," said he, "shame were to revoke°   *draw back*
The forward footing for° an hidden shade: *because of*
Vertue gives her selfe light, through darkenesse for to wade."

13

"Yea but," quoth she, "the perill of this place
110   I better wot then° you, though now too late   *know than*
To wish you backe returne with foule disgrace,
Yet wisedome warnes, whilest foot is in the gate,
To stay the stepe, ere forcèd to retrate.
This is the wandring wood, this Errours den,
115   A monster vile, whom God and man does hate:
Therefore I read° beware." "Fly fly," quoth then   *advise*
The fearefull Dwarfe: "this is no place for living men."

14

But full of fire and greedy hardiment,°   *boldness*
The youthfull knight could not for ought° be staide,   *anything*
120   But forth unto the darksome hole he went,
And lookèd in: his glistring° armor made   *shining*
A litle glooming light, much like a shade,
By which he saw the ugly monster plaine,
Halfe like a serpent horribly displaide,[9]
125   But th' other halfe did womans shape retaine,
Most lothsom, filthie, foule, and full of vile disdaine.°   *loathsomeness*

15

And as she lay upon the durtie ground,
Her huge long taile her den all overspred,
Yet was in knots and many boughtes° upwound,   *coils*
130   Pointed with mortall sting. Of her there bred
A thousand yong ones, which she dayly fed,
Sucking upon her poisonous dugs, eachone
Of sundry shapes, yet all ill favorèd:
Soone as that uncouth° light upon them shone,   *unfamiliar*
135 Into her mouth they crept, and suddain all were gone.

16

Their dam upstart, out of her den effraide,°   *alarmed*
And rushèd forth, hurling her hideous taile
About her cursèd head, whose folds displaid°   *extended*
Were stretcht now forth at length without entraile.°   *coiling*
140   She lookt about, and seeing one in mayle
Armèd to point,° sought backe to turne againe;   *i.e., completely*
For light she hated as the deadly bale,°   *injury*

---

9. That Errour is half serpent reminds us of the primal error in Eden, which the serpent instigated. The description echoes both classical and biblical monsters (cf. Revelation 9.7–10).

Ay wont° in desert darknesse to remain,   *ever accustomed*
Where plaine none might her see, nor she see any plaine.

17

145 Which when the valiant Elfe[1] perceived, he lept
    As Lyon fierce upon the flying pray,
    And with his trenchand° blade her boldly kept   *cutting*
    From turning backe, and forcèd her to stay:
    Therewith enraged she loudly gan to bray,
150   And turning fierce, her speckled taile advaunst,
    Threatning her angry sting, him to dismay:°   *defeat*
    Who nought aghast, his mightie hand enhaunst:°   *lifted up*
  The stroke down from her head unto her shoulder glaunst.

18

  Much daunted with that dint,° her sence was dazd,   *blow*
155   Yet kindling rage, her selfe she gathered round,
    And all attonce her beastly body raizd
    With doubled forces high above the ground:
    Tho° wrapping up her wrethèd sterne arownd,   *then*
    Lept fierce upon his shield, and her huge traine°   *tail*
160   All suddenly about his body wound,
    That hand or foot to stirre he strove in vaine:
  God helpe the man so wrapt in Errours endlesse traine.

19

  His Lady sad to see his sore constraint,°   *fettered state*
    Cride out, "Now now Sir knight, shew what ye bee,
165   Add faith unto your force, and be not faint:
    Strangle her, else she sure will strangle thee."
    That when he heard, in great perplexitie,[2]
    His gall did grate for griefe° and high disdaine,   *wrath*
    And knitting all his force got one hand free,
170   Wherewith he grypt her gorge° with so great paine,   *throat*
  That soone to loose her wicked bands did her constraine.

20

  Therewith she spewd out of her filthy maw
    A floud of poyson horrible and blacke,
    Full of great lumpes of flesh and gobbets raw,
175   Which stunck so vildly, that it forst him slacke
    His grasping hold, and from her turne him backe:
    Her vomit full of bookes and papers was,[3]
    With loathly frogs and toades, which eyes did lacke,
    And creeping sought way in the weedy gras:
180 Her filthy parbreake° all the place defilèd has.[4]   *vomit*

---

1. I.e., knight of Faerie Land.
2. In both the usual sense and the sense of "entangled condition."
3. Alluding (at one level) to books and pamphlets of Catholic propaganda, notably attacks on Queen Elizabeth.
4. Revelation 16.13: "And I saw three unclean spirits like frogs come out of the mouth of the dragon, and out of the mouth of the beast, and out of the mouth of the false prophet."

21

As when old father Nilus gins to swell
   With timely° pride above the Aegyptian vale,   *in season*
   His fattie° waves do fertile slime outwell,   *rich*
   And overflow each plaine and lowly dale:
185   But when his later spring gins to avale,°   *subside*
   Huge heapes of mudd he leaves, wherein there breed
   Ten thousand kindes of creatures, partly male
   And partly female of his fruitfull seed;
Such ugly monstrous shapes elswhere may no man reed.°   *see*

22

190 The same so sore annoyèd has the knight,
   That welnigh chokèd with the deadly stinke,
   His forces faile, ne can no longer fight.
   Whose corage when the feend perceived to shrinke,
   She pourèd forth out of her hellish sinke
195 Her fruitfull cursèd spawne of serpents small,
   Deformèd monsters, fowle, and blacke as inke,
   Which swarming all about his legs did crall,
And him encombred sore, but could not hurt at all.

23

As gentle Shepheard in sweete even-tide,
200 When ruddy Phoebus gins to welke° in west,   *sink*
   High on an hill, his flocke to vewen wide,
   Markes° which do byte their hasty supper best;   *observes*
   A cloud of combrous° gnattes do him molest,   *encumbering*
   All striving to infixe their feeble stings,
205 That from their noyance he no where can rest,
   But with his clownish° hands their tender wings   *rustic*
He brusheth oft, and oft doth mar their murmurings.

24

Thus ill bestedd,° and fearful more of shame,   *situated*
   Then of the certaine perill he stood in,
210 Halfe furious unto his foe he came,
   Resolved in minde all suddenly to win,
   Or soone to lose, before he once would lin;°   *cease*
   And strooke at her with more then manly force,
   That from her body full of filthie sin
215 He raft° her hatefull head without remorse;   *cut away*
A streame of cole black bloud forth gushèd from her corse.

25

Her scattred brood, soone as their Parent deare
   They saw so rudely° falling to the ground,   *with great force*
   Groning full deadly, all with troublous feare,
220 Gathred themselves about her body round,
   Weening° their wonted entrance to have found   *thinking*
   At her wide mouth: but being there withstood

They flockèd all about her bleeding wound,
And suckèd up their dying mothers blood,
225 Making her death their life, and eke° her hurt their good.   *also*

26

That detestable sight him much amazde,°   *stunned*
To see th' unkindly Impes° of heaven accurst,   *unnatural offspring*
Devoure their dam; on whom while so he gazd,
Having all satisfide their bloudy thurst,
230 Their bellies swolne he saw with fulnesse burst,
And bowels gushing forth: well worthy end
Of such as drunke her life, the which them nurst;
Now needeth him no lenger labour spend,
His foes have slaine themselves, with whom he should contend.

27

235 His Ladie seeing all, that chaunst, from farre
Approcht in hast to greet° his victorie,   *congratulate*
And said, "Faire knight, borne under happy starre,
Who see your vanquisht foes before you lye;
Well worthy be you of that Armorie,°   *armor*
240 Wherein ye have great glory wonne this day,
And prooved your strength on a strong enimie,
Your first adventure: many such I pray,
And henceforth ever wish, that like succeed it may."

28

Then mounted he upon his Steede againe,
245 And with the Lady backward sought to wend;°   *go*
That path he kept, which beaten was most plaine,
Ne ever would to any by-way bend,
But still did follow one unto the end,
The which at last out of the wood them brought.
250 So forward on his way (with God to frend)°   *with God as friend*
He passèd forth, and new adventure sought;
Long way he travelèd, before he heard of ought.

29

At length they chaunst to meet upon the way
An aged Sire, in long blacke weedes yclad,[5]
255 His feete all bare, his beard all hoarie gray,
And by his belt his booke he hanging had;
Sober he seemde, and very sagely sad,°   *grave*
And to the ground his eyes were lowly bent,
Simple in shew, and voyde of malice bad,
260 And all the way he prayèd, as he went,
And often knockt his brest, as one that did repent.

30

He faire the knight saluted, louting° low,   *bowing*
Who faire him quited,° as that courteous was: *answered*

---

5. Dressed in long black garments.

And after askèd him, if he did know
265   Of straunge adventures, which abroad did pas.
"Ah my deare Sonne," quoth he, "how should, alas,
Silly° old man, that lives in hidden cell,   *simple*
Bidding his beades° all day for his trespas,   *saying his prayers*
Tydings of warre and worldly trouble tell?
270   With holy father sits not with such things to mell.[6]

31

"But if of daunger which hereby doth dwell,
And homebred evill ye desire to heare,
Of a straunge man I can you tidings tell,
That wasteth all this countrey farre and neare."
275   "Of such," said he, "I chiefly do inquere,
And shall you well reward to shew the place,
In which that wicked wight his dayes doth weare.°   *spend*
For to all knighthood it is foule disgrace,
That such a cursed creature lives so long a space."

32

280   "Far hence," quoth he, "in wastfull° wildernesse   *desolate*
His dwelling is, by which no living wight
May ever passe, but thorough great distresse."
"Now," sayd the Lady, "draweth toward night,
And well I wote, that of your later° fight   *recent*
285   Ye all forwearied be: for what so strong,
But wanting rest will also want of might?
The Sunne that measures heaven all day long,
At night doth baite° his steedes the Ocean waves emong.   *feed, refresh*

33

"Then with the Sunne take Sir, your timely rest,
290   And with new day new worke at once begin:
Untroubled night they say gives counsell best."
"Right well Sir knight ye have advisèd bin,"
Quoth then that agèd man; "the way to win
Is wisely to advise:° now day is spent;   *take thought*
295   Therefore with me ye may take up your In°   *lodging*
For this same night." The knight was well content.
So with that godly father to his home they went.

34

A little lowly Hermitage it was,
Downe in a dale, hard by a forests side,
300   Far from resort of people, that did pas
In travell to and froe: a little wyde°   *apart*
There was an holy Chappell edifyde,°   *built*
Wherein the Hermite dewly wont° to say   *was accustomed*
His holy things° each morne and eventyde: *prayers*
305   Thereby a Christall streame did gently play,
Which from a sacred fountaine wellèd forth alway.

---

6. I.e., it is not fitting for a holy hermit to meddle ("mell") with such things.

35

Arrivèd there, the little house they fill,
      Ne looke for entertainement, where none was:
      Rest is their feast, and all things at their will;
310   The noblest mind the best contentment has.
      With faire discourse the evening so they pas:
      For that old man of pleasing wordes had store,
      And well could file° his tongue as smooth as glas;   *polish*
      He told of Saintes and Popes, and evermore
315 He strowd an *Ave-Mary*[7] after and before.

36

The drouping Night thus creepeth on them fast,
      And the sad humour;° loading their eye liddes,   *heavy moisture*
      As messenger of Morpheus° on them cast   *god of dreams*
      Sweet slombring deaw, the which to sleepe them biddes.
320   Unto their lodgings then his guestes he riddes:°   *leads*
      Where when all drownd in deadly sleepe;° he findes,   *sleep like death*
      He to his study goes, and there amiddes
      His Magick bookes and artes of sundry kindes,
      He seekes out mighty charmes, to trouble sleepy mindes.

37

325 Then choosing out few wordes most horrible
      (Let none them read), thereof did verses frame,
      With which and other spelles like terrible,
      He bade awake blacke Plutoes griesly Dame,[8]
      And cursèd heaven, and spake reprochfull shame
330   Of highest God, the Lord of life and light;
      A bold bad man, that dared to call by name
      Great Gorgon,[9] Prince of darknesse and dead night,
      At which Cocytus quakes, and Styx is put to flight.

38

And forth he cald out of deepe darknesse dred
335   Legions of Sprights, the which like little flyes;[1]
      Fluttring about his ever damnèd hed,
      A-waite whereto their service he applyes,
      To aide his friends, or fray° his enimies: *frighten*
      Of those he chose out two, the falsest twoo,
340   And fittest for to forge true-seeming lyes;
      The one of them he gave a message too,
      The other by him selfe staide other worke to doo.

39

He making speedy way through spersèd° ayre,   *dispersed*
      And through the world of waters wide and deepe,
345 To Morpheus house doth hastily repaire.

---

7. "Hail Mary"—that is, a Catholic prayer.
8. Proserpine, as patron of witchcraft.
9. Demogorgon, in some myths the progenitor of all the gods, so powerful that the mention of his

name causes hell's rivers (Styx and Cocytus) to tremble.
1. The simile associates him with Beelzebub (Lord of Flies).

Amid the bowels of the earth full steepe,
And low, where dawning day doth never peepe,
His dwelling is; there Tethys° his wet bed   *the wife of Ocean*
Doth ever wash, and Cynthia[2] still° doth steepe   *continually*
350   In silver deaw his ever-drouping hed,
Whiles sad° Night over him her mantle black doth spred.   *sober*

40

Whose double gates he findeth lockèd fast,
The one faire framed of burnisht Yvory,
The other all with silver overcast;
355   And wakefull dogges before them farre do lye,
Watching to banish Care their enimy,
Who oft is wont° to trouble gentle Sleepe.   *accustomed to*
By them the Sprite doth passe in quietly,
And unto Morpheus comes, whom drownèd deepe
360   In drowsie fit he findes: of nothing he takes keepe.°   *notice*

41

And more, to lulle him in his slumber soft,
A trickling streame from high rocke tumbling downe
And ever-drizling raine upon the loft,
Mixt with a murmuring winde, much like the sowne°   *sound*
365   Of swarming Bees, did cast him in a swowne:°   *swoon*
No other noyse, nor peoples troublous cryes,
As still° are wont t'annoy the wallèd towne,   *always*
Might there be heard: but carelesse° Quiet lyes,   *free from care*
Wrapt in eternall silence farre from enemyes.[3]

42

370   The messenger approching to him spake,
But his wast° wordes returnd to him in vaine: *wasted*
So sound he slept, that nought mought° him awake.   *might*
Then rudely he him thrust, and pusht with paine,°   *effort*
Whereat he gan to stretch: but he againe
375   Shooke him so hard, that forcèd him to speake.
As one then in a dreame, whose dryer braine[4]
Is tost with troubled sights and fancies° weake,   *fantasies*
He mumbled soft, but would not all his silence breake.

43

The Sprite then gan more boldly him to wake,
380   And threatned unto him the dreaded name
Of Hecate:° whereat he gan to quake,   *queen of Hades*
And lifting up his lumpish head, with blame
Halfe angry askèd him, for what° he came.   *why*
"Hither," quoth he, "me Archimago[5] sent,
385   He that the stubborne Sprites can wisely tame,

2. Diana, the goddess of the moon.
3. Spenser is imitating descriptions of the house of Morpheus in Chaucer and Ovid.
4. According to the old physiology, elderly people and other light sleepers had too little moisture in the brain.
5. The name can be construed as meaning both "archmagician" and "architect of images."

He bids thee to him send for his intent
A fit false dreame, that can delude the sleepers sent."°   *senses*

44

The God obayde, and calling forth straight way
A diverse° dreame out of his prison darke,   *distracting*
390 Delivered it to him, and downe did lay
His heavie head, devoide of carefull carke,°   *anxious concerns*
Whose sences all were straight benumbd and starke.
He backe returning by the Yvorie dore,[6]
Remounted up as light as chearefull Larke,
395 And on his litle winges the dreame he bore
In hast unto his Lord, where he him left afore.

45

Who all this while with charmes and hidden artes,
Had made a Lady of that other Spright,
And framed of liquid ayre her tender partes
400 So lively,° and so like in all mens sight,   *lifelike*
That weaker° sence it could have ravisht quight: *too weak*
The maker selfe for all his wondrous witt,
Was nigh beguilèd with so goodly sight:
Her all in white he clad, and over it
405 Cast a blacke stole, most like to seeme for Una[7] fit.°   *fitting*

46

Now when that ydle dreame was to him brought
Unto that Elfin knight he bad him fly,
Where he slept soundly void of evill thought
And with false shewes abuse his fantasy,°   *imagination*
410 In sort as° he him schoolèd privily: *in the way that*
And that new creature borne without her dew°   *unnaturally*
Full of the makers guile, with usage sly
He taught to imitate that Lady trew,
Whose semblance she did carrie under feignèd hew.°   *form*

47

415 Thus well instructed, to their worke they hast
And comming where the knight in slomber lay
The one upon his hardy head him plast,°   *placed*
And made him dreame of loves and lustfull play
That nigh his manly hart did melt away,
420 Bathèd in wanton blis and wicked joy:
Then seemèd him his Lady by him lay,
And to him playnd,° how that false wingèd boy;°   *complained / Cupid*
Her chast hart had subdewd, to learne Dame pleasures toy.°   *lustful play*

---

6. According to Homer (*Odyssey* 19.562–67) and Virgil (*Aeneid* 6.893–96), false dreams come through Sleep's ivory gate, true dreams through his gate of horn.

7. Her name means "one, unity." Elizabethan readers would know the Latin phrase *Una Vera Fides* ("one true faith") and also the proverb "Truth is one."

48

And she her selfe of beautie soveraigne Queene
425 Faire Venus seemde unto his bed to bring
Her, whom he waking evermore did weene°   *think*
To be the chastest flowre, that ay° did spring   *ever*
On earthly braunch, the daughter of a king,
Now a loose Leman° to vile service bound: *paramour*
430 And eke° the Graces seemèd all to sing,   *also*
Hymen iô Hymen, dauncing all around,
Whilst freshest Flora her with Yvie girlond crownd.[8]

49

In this great passion of unwonted° lust,   *unaccustomed*
Or wonted feare of doing ought amis,
435 He started up, as seeming to mistrust°   *suspect*
Some secret ill, or hidden foe of his:
Lo there before his face his Lady is,
Under blake stole hyding her bayted hooke,
And as halfe blushing offred him to kis,
440 With gentle blandishment and lovely° looke,   *loving*
Most like that virgin true, which for her knight him took.

50

All cleane dismayd to see so uncouth° sight,   *unseemly*
And halfe enragèd at her shamelesse guise,
He thought have slaine her in his fierce despight:°   *indignation*
445 But hasty heat tempring with sufferance wise,
He stayde his hand, and gan himselfe advise
To prove his sense, and tempt° her faignèd truth.   *test*
Wringing her hands in wemens pitteous wise,
Tho can° she weepe, to stirre up gentle ruth,°   *then did / pity*
450 Both for her noble bloud, and for her tender youth.

51

And said, "Ah Sir, my liege Lord and my love,
Shall I accuse the hidden cruell fate,
And mightie causes wrought in heaven above,
Or the blind God, that doth me thus amate,°   *dismay*
455 For° hopèd love to winne me certaine hate?   *instead of*
Yet thus perforce° he bids me do, or die.   *forcibly*
Die is my dew:[9] yet rew° my wretched state   *pity*
You, whom my hard avenging destinie
Hath made judge of my life or death indifferently.

52

460 "Your owne deare sake forst me at first to leave
My Fathers kingdome," There she stopt with teares;

8. The three graces of classical mythology were personifications of grace and beauty; here they sing a call to the pleasures of the marriage bed (Hymen was god of marriage). In the March eclogue of The *Shepheardes Calender*, E. K. glossed Flora as "the Goddesse of flowres, but indede (as saith Tacitus) a famous harlot."
9. I.e., I deserve to die.

Her swollen hart her speach seemd to bereave,
And then againe begun, "My weaker yeares
Captived to fortune and frayle worldly feares,
465 Fly to your faith for succour and sure ayde:
Let me not dye in languor° and long teares.   sorrow
"Why Dame," quoth he, "what hath ye thus dismayd?
What frayes° ye, that were wont to comfort me affrayd?"   frightens

53
"Love of your selfe," she said, "and deare° constraint   dire
470 Lets me not sleepe, but wast the wearie night
In secret anguish and unpittied plaint,
Whiles you in carelesse sleepe are drownèd quight."
Her doubtfull words made that redoubted[1] knight
Suspect her truth: yet since no untruth he knew,
475 Her fawning love with foule disdainefull spight
He would not shend,° but said, "Deare dame I rew,   reject
That for my sake unknowne such griefe unto you grew.

54
"Assure your selfe, it fell not all to ground;
For all so deare as life is to my hart,
480 I deeme your love, and hold me to you bound;
Ne let vaine feares procure your needlesse smart,°   pain
Where cause is none, but to your rest depart."
Not all content, yet seemd she to appease°   cease
Her mournefull plaintes, beguilèd° of her art,   foiled
485 And fed with words, that could not chuse but please,
So slyding softly forth, she turnd° as to her ease.   returned

55
Long after lay he musing at her mood,
Much grieved to thinke that gentle Dame so light,°   frivolous
For whose defence he was to shed his blood.
490 At last dull wearinesse of former fight
Having yrockt a sleepe his irkesome spright,°   weary mind
That troublous dreame gan freshly tosse his braine,
With bowres and beds, and Ladies deare delight:
But when he saw his labour all was vaine,
495 With that misformèd spright[2] he backe returnd againe.

1. Dreaded, also doubting again. "Doubtfull":   2. I.e., with the spirit impersonating Una.
fearful, also questionable.

From *Canto 2*

[REDCROSSE WINS "FIDESSA"]

The guilefull great Enchaunter parts
The Redcrosse Knight from Truth:
Into whose stead faire falshood steps,
And workes him wofull ruth.

I

By this the Northerne wagoner had set
　　His seven fold teame behind the stedfast starre,[3]
　　That was in Ocean waves yet never wet,
　　But firme is fixt, and sendeth light from farre
5　　To all, that in the wide deepe wandring arre:
　　And chearefull Chaunticlere with his note shrill
　　Had warnèd once, that Phoebus fiery carre[4]
　　In hast was climbing up the Easterne hill,
Full envious that night so long his roome did fill.

2

10　When those accursèd messengers of hell,
　　That feigning dreame, and that faire-forgèd Spright
　　Came to their wicked maister, and gan tell
　　Their bootelesse° paines, and ill succeeding night:　　　　useless
　　Who all in rage to see his skilfull might
15　Deluded so, gan threaten hellish paine
　　And sad Proserpines wrath, them to affright.
　　But when he saw his threatning was but vaine,
He cast about, and searcht his balefull° bookes againe.　　deadly

3

Eftsoones° he tooke that miscreated faire,　　　　　　　forthwith
20　And that false other Spright, on whom he spred
　　A seeming body of the subtile° aire,　　　　　　　　　rarefied
　　Like a young Squire, in loves and lusty-hed
　　His wanton dayes that ever loosely led,
　　Without regard of armes and dreaded fight:
25　Those two he tooke, and in a secret bed,
　　Covered with darknesse and misdeeming° night,　　　misleading
Them both together laid, to joy in vaine delight.

4

Forthwith he runnes with feignèd faithfull hast
　　Unto his guest, who after troublous sights
30　And dreames, gan now to take more sound repast,°　　　rest
　　Whom suddenly he wakes with fearefull frights,
　　As one aghast with feends or damnèd sprights,
　　And to him cals, "Rise rise unhappy Swaine,

3. I.e., by this time the Big Dipper had set behind　4. The chariot of the sun. "Chaunticlere": Chan-
the North Star.　　　　　　　　　　　　　　　　ticleer is the generic name for a rooster.

That here wex° old in sleepe, whiles wicked wights   *grow*
35   Have knit themselves in Venus shamefull chaine;
Come see, where your false Lady doth her honour staine."

5

All in amaze he suddenly up start
With sword in hand, and with the old man went;
Who soone him brought into a secret part,
40   Where that false couple were full closely ment°   *mingled*
In wanton lust and lewd embracèment:
Which when he saw, he burnt with gealous fire,
The eye of reason was with rage yblent,°   *blinded*
And would have slaine them in his furious ire,
45   But hardly° was restreinèd of° that aged sire.   *with difficulty / by*

6

Returning to his bed in torment great,
And bitter anguish of his guiltie sight,
He could not rest, but did his stout heart eat,
And wast his inward gall with deepe despight,°   *malice*
50   Yrkesome° of life, and too long lingring night.   *tired*
At last faire Hesperus[5] in highest skie
Had spent his lampe, and brought forth dawning light,
Then up he rose, and clad him hastily;
The Dwarfe him brought his steed: so both away do fly.

7

55   Now when the rosy-fingred Morning faire,
Weary of aged Tithones[6] saffron bed,
Had spred her purple robe through deawy aire,
And the high hils Titan° discoverèd,°   *the sun / revealed*
The royall virgin shooke off drowsy-hed,
60   And rising forth out of her baser° bowre,   *too lowly*
Lookt for her knight, who far away was fled,
And for her Dwarfe, that wont to wait each houre:
Then gan she waile and weepe, to see that woefull stowre.°   *affliction*

8

And after him she rode with so much speede
65   As her slow beast could make; but all in vaine:
For him so far had borne his light-foot steede,
Prickèd with wrath and fiery fierce disdaine,°   *indignation*
That him to follow was but fruitlesse paine;
Yet she her weary limbes would never rest,
70   But every hill and dale, each wood and plaine
Did search, sore grievèd in her gentle brest,
He so ungently left her, whom she lovèd best.

5. The morning star.
6. Tithonus is the husband of Aurora, goddess of the dawn.

9

But subtill° Archimago, when his guests   *cunning*
    He saw divided into double parts,
75   And Una wandring in woods and forrests,
    Th' end of his drift,° he praisd his divelish arts   *plot*
    That had such might over true meaning harts;
    Yet rests not so, but other meanes doth make,
    How he may worke unto her further smarts:
80   For her he hated as the hissing snake,
And in her many troubles did most pleasure take.

10

He then devisde himselfe how to disguise;
    For by his mightie science° he could take   *knowledge*
    As many formes and shapes in seeming wise,°   *in appearance*
85   As ever Proteus[7] to himselfe could make:
    Sometime a fowle, sometime a fish in lake,
    Now like a foxe, now like a dragon fell,°   *fierce*
    That of himselfe he oft for feare would quake,
    And oft would flie away. O who can tell
90   The hidden power of herbes, and might of Magicke spell?

11

But now seemde best, the person to put on
    Of that good knight, his late beguilèd guest:
    In mighty armes he was yclad anon,
    And silver shield: upon his coward brest
95   A bloudy crosse, and on his craven crest
    A bounch of haires discolourd diversly:°   *variously colored*
    Full jolly° knight he seemde, and well addrest,°   *gallant / armed*
    And when he sate upon his courser free,
Saint George himself ye would have deemèd him to be.

12

100   But he the knight, whose semblaunt° he did beare,   *likeness*
    The true Saint George was wandred far away,
    Still flying from° his thoughts and gealous feare;   *because of*
    Will was his guide,[8] and griefe led him astray.
    At last him chaunst to meete upon the way
105   A faithlesse Sarazin° all armed to point,   *Saracen*
    In whose great shield was writ with letters gay
    Sans foy:[9] full large of limbe and every joint
He was, and carèd not for God or man a point.°   *at all*

13

He had a faire companion of his way,
110   A goodly Lady clad in scarlot red,

7. A sea god who could change his shape at will (*Odyssey* 4.398–424).
8. Will should itself be under the guidance of rea-
son or truth.
9. Literally, without faith, faithless.

Purfled° with gold and pearle of rich assay,[1]   *decorated*
And like a Persian mitre on her hed
She wore, with crownes and owches° garnishèd,   *brooches*
The which her lavish lovers to her gave;[2]
115   Her wanton° palfrey all was overspred   *unruly*
With tinsell trappings, woven like a wave,
Whose bridle rung with golden bels and bosses brave.°   *handsome studs*

14

With faire disport° and courting dalliaunce   *diversion*
        She intertainde her lover all the way:
120   But when she saw the knight his speare advaunce,
        She soone left off her mirth and wanton play,
        And bad her knight addresse him to the fray:
        His foe was nigh at hand. He prickt with pride
        And hope to winne his Ladies heart that day,
125   Forth spurrèd fast: adowne his coursers side
The red bloud trickling staind the way, as he did ride.

15

The knight of the Redcrosse when him he spide,
        Spurring so hote with rage dispiteous,°   *cruel*
        Gan fairely couch° his speare, and towards ride: *lower*
130   Soone meete they both, both fell and furious,
        That daunted with their forces hideous,
        Their steeds do stagger, and amazèd stand,
        And eke° themselves too rudely rigorous,°   *also / violent*
        Astonied° with the stroke of their owne hand,   *stunned*
135 Do backe rebut,° and each to other yeeldeth land.   *recoil*

16

As when two rams stird with ambitious pride,
        Fight for the rule of the rich fleecèd flocke,
        Their hornèd fronts so fierce on either side
        Do meete, that with the terrour of the shocke
140   Astonied both, stand sencelesse as a blocke,
        Forgetfull of the hanging° victory: *in the balance*
        So stood these twaine, unmovèd as a rocke,
        Both staring fierce, and holding idely
The broken reliques of their former cruelty.

17

145 The Sarazin sore daunted with the buffe
        Snatcheth his sword, and fiercely to him flies;
        Who well it wards, and quyteth° cuff with cuff: *requites*
        Each others equall puissaunce envies,

---

1. Proven valuable by analysis.
2. The lady's garb associates her with the Whore of Babylon (Revelation 17.3–4): "And I saw a woman sit upon a scarlet colored beast, full of names of blasphemy, having seven heads and ten horns. And the woman was arrayed in purple and scarlet color, and decked with gold and precious stones and pearls, having a golden cup in her hand full of abominations and filthiness of her fornication."

And through their iron sides with cruell spies° *looks*
150 Does seeke to perce: repining courage yields
No foote to foe. The flashing fier flies
As from a forge out of their burning shields,
And streames of purple bloud new dies the verdant fields.

18

"Curse on that Crosse," quoth then the Sarazin,
155 "That keepes thy body from the bitter fit;° *death pangs*
Dead long ygoe I wote° thou haddest bin, *thought*
Had not that charme from thee forwarnèd° it: *prevented*
But yet I warne thee now assurèd° sitt, *securely*
And hide thy head." Therewith upon his crest
160 With rigour° so outrageous he smitt, *violence*
That a large share it hewd out of the rest,
And glauncing downe his shield, from blame him fairely blest.³

19

Who thereat wondrous wroth, the sleeping spark
Of native vertue° gan eftsoones revive, *strength*
165 And at his haughtie helmet making mark,
So hugely° stroke, that it the steele did rive, *mightily*
And cleft his head. He tumbling downe alive,
With bloudy mouth his mother earth did kis
Greeting his grave: his grudging° ghost did strive *complaining*
170 With the fraile flesh; at last it flitted is,
Whither the soules do fly of men, that live amis.

20

The Lady when she saw her champion fall,
Like the old ruines of a broken towre,
Staid not to waile his woefull funerall,° *death*
175 But from him fled away with all her powre;
Who after her as hastily gan scowre,° *scurry*
Bidding the Dwarfe with him to bring away
The Sarazins shield, signe of the conqueroure.
Her soone he overtooke, and bad to stay,
180 For present cause was none of dread her to dismay.

21

She turning backe with ruefull countenaunce,
Cride, "Mercy mercy Sir vouchsafe to show
On silly° Dame, subject to hard mischaunce, *helpless*
And to your mighty will." Her humblesse low
185 In so ritch weedes° and seeming glorious show, *clothes*
Did much emmove his stout heroicke heart,
And said, "Deare dame, your suddein overthrow
Much rueth° me; but now put feare apart, *grieves*
And tell, both who ye be, and who that tooke your part."

---

3. Preserved him from harm.

22

190 Melting in teares, then gan she thus lament;
"The wretched woman, whom unhappy howre
Hath now made thrall° to your commandèment,   *slave*
Before that angry heavens list to lowre,°   *frown*
And fortune false betraide me to your powre
195 Was (O what now availeth that I was!)
Borne the sole daughter of an Emperour,
He that the wide West under his rule has,
And high hath set his throne, where Tiberis doth pas.⁴

23

"He in the first flowre of my freshest age,
200 Betrothèd me unto the onely haire°   *heir*
Of a most mighty king, most rich and sage;
Was never Prince so faithfull and so faire,
Was never Prince so meeke and debonaire;°   *gracious*
But ere my hopèd day of spousall shone,
205 My dearest Lord fell from high honours staire,
Into the hands of his accursèd fone,°   *foes*
And cruelly was slaine, that shall I ever mone.⁵

24

"His blessed body spoild of lively breath,
Was afterward, I know not how, convaid°   *carried away*
210 And fro me hid: of whose most innocent death
When tidings came to me unhappy maid,
O how great sorrow my sad soule assaid.°   *afflicted*
Then forth I went his woefull corse to find,
And many yeares throughout the world I straid,
215 A virgin widow, whose deepe wounded mind
With love, long time did languish as the striken hind.° *deer*

25

"At last it chauncèd this proud Sarazin
To meete me wandring, who perforce° me led   *by violence*
With him away, but yet could never win
220 The fort, that Ladies hold in soveraigne dread.
There lies he now with foule dishonour dead,
Who whiles he livde, was callèd proud Sans foy,
The eldest of three brethren, all three bred
Of one bad sire, whose youngest is Sans joy,
225 And twixt them both was borne the bloudy bold Sans loy.⁶

26

"In this sad plight, friendlesse, unfortunate,
Now miserable I Fidessa° dwell,   *Faith*

4. The Tiber River runs through Rome. The lady is hence associated with the Catholic church. Her father, she says, is ruler of the west—but Una's father had the rule of both east *and* west (1.1.41); historically, the true church once embraced east and west.
5. The lady claims to have been betrothed to Christ, bridegroom of the church.
6. Literally, without law. *Sans joy* means "without joy, darkness of spirit."

      Craving of you in pitty of my state,
      To do none° ill, if please ye not do well."   *no*
230   He in great passion all this while did dwell,°   *continue*
      More busying his quicke eyes, her face to view,
      Then his dull eares, to heare what she did tell;
      And said, "Faire Lady hart of flint would rew
      The undeservèd woes and sorrowes, which ye shew.

27

235   "Henceforth in safe assuraunce may ye rest,
      Having both found a new friend you to aid,
      And lost an old foe, that did you molest:
      Better new friend than an old foe is° said."   *it is*
      With chaunge of cheare the seeming simple maid
240   Let fall her eyen, as shamefast° to the earth,   *as if modestly*
      And yeelding soft, in that she nought gain-said,
      So forth they rode, he feining° seemely merth,   *simulating*
      And she coy lookes: so dainty they say maketh derth.[7]

Summary   In the second half of the canto, Redcrosse and his new companion seek relief from the blazing sun in the shade of two trees. Plucking a bough from one of them to make a garland for the lady, he is astonished to hear a groaning voice from within the tree. The voice is that of a knight named Fradubio (Brother Doubt), who explains that he and his beloved have been metamorphosed into trees by a wicked witch named Duessa. Unbeknownst to him, Redcrosse is in the company of this witch.

Canto 3 Summary   In search of the knight who has abandoned her, Una encounters a lion who licks her hands and accompanies her in her wanderings. They take refuge for the night in the cottage of a superstitious old woman and her daughter. During the night the daughter's lover, a robber of churches, returns to the cottage with booty for her and is torn to pieces by the lion. Seeking revenge, the old woman encounters Archimago and tells him where to find Una. The magician presents himself to Una disguised as Redcrosse, but his plan backfires when he is attacked by the Saracen Sans loy (brother of the slain Sans foy). Sans loy then kills the faithful lion and abducts Una, leaving Archimago lying wounded.

From *Canto 4*

[THE HOUSE OF PRIDE]

To sinfull house of Pride, Duessa
   guides the faithfull knight,
Where brothers death to wreak° Sansjoy   *avenge*
   doth chalenge him to fight.

1

   Young knight, what ever that dost armes professe,
     And through long labours huntest after fame,
     Beware of fraud, beware of ficklenesse,
     In choice, and change of thy deare lovèd Dame,

---

7. Proverbial: what's dear is rare; here, coyness creates unsatisfied desire.

5 Least thou of her beleeve too lightly blame,
 And rash misweening° doe thy hart remove: *misjudgment*
 For unto knight there is no greater shame,
 Then lightnesse and inconstancie in love;
That doth this Redcrosse knights ensample° plainly prove. *example*

2

10 Who after that he had faire Una lorne,°   *forsaken*
 Through light misdeeming° of her loialtie,   *misjudging*
 And false Duessa in her sted had borne,° *taken as companion*
 Called Fidess', and so supposd to bee;
 Long with her traveild, till at last they see
15 A goodly building, bravely garnishèd,°   *adorned*
 The house of mightie Prince it seemd to bee:
 And towards it a broad high way[8] that led,
All bare through peoples feet, which thither traveilèd.

3

 Great troupes of people traveild thitherward
20 Both day and night, of each degree and place,°   *rank*
 But few returnèd, having scapèd hard,°   *with difficulty*
 With balefull° beggerie, or foule disgrace,   *wretched*
 Which ever after in most wretched case,
 Like loathsome lazars,° by the hedges lay.   *lepers*
25 Thither Duessa bad him bend his pace:° *direct his steps*
 For she is wearie of the toilesome way,
 And also nigh consumèd is the lingring day.

4

 A stately Pallace built of squarèd bricke,
 Which cunningly was without morter laid,
30 Whose wals were high, but nothing strong, nor thick,
 And golden foile° all over them displaid, *thin layer of gold*
 That purest skye with brightnesse they dismaid:° *outdid*
 High lifted up were many loftie towres,
 And goodly galleries farre over laid,°   *placed above*
35 Full of faire windowes, and delightfull bowres;
And on the top a Diall told the timely howres.[9]

5

 It was a goodly heape° for to behould,   *building*
 And spake the praises of the workmans wit;°   *skill*
 But full great pittie, that so faire a mould°   *structure*
40 Did on so weake foundation ever sit:
 For on a sandie hill,[1] that still did flit,°   *shift*
 And fall away, it mounted was full hie,
 That every breath of heaven shakèd it:

---

8. "Broad is the way that leadeth to destruction" (Matthew 7.13).
9. A sundial measured the hours of the day.
1. Matthew 7.26–27: "A foolish man . . . built his house upon the sand: And the rain descended, and the floods came, and the winds blew, and beat upon that house; and it fell; and great was the fall of it."

And all the hinder parts, that few could spie,
45   Were ruinous and old, but painted cunningly.

6

Arrivèd there they passèd in forth right;
  For still to all the gates stood open wide,
  Yet charge of them was to a Porter hight°   committed
  Cald Malvenù,[2] who entrance none denide:
50   Thence to the hall, which was on every side
  With rich array and costly arras dight:[3]
  Infinite sorts of people did abide
  There waiting long, to win the wishèd sight
Of her, that was the Lady of that Pallace bright.

7

55   By them they passe, all gazing on them round,
  And to the Presence[4] mount; whose glorious vew
  Their frayle amazèd senses did confound:
  In living Princes court none ever knew
  Such endlesse richesse, and so sumptuous shew;
60   Ne Persia selfe, the nourse of pompous pride
  Like ever saw. And there a noble crew
  Of Lordes and Ladies stood on every side,
Which with their presence faire, the place much beautifide.

8

High above all a cloth of State° was spred,   canopy
65   And a rich throne, as bright as sunny day,
  On which there sate most brave embellishèd°   handsomely clad
  With royall robes and gorgeous array,
  A mayden Queene, that shone as Titans° ray,   the sun's
  In glistring gold, and peerelesse pretious stone:
70   Yet her bright blazing beautie did assay°   attempt
  To dim the brightnesse of her glorious throne,
As envying her selfe, that too exceeding shone.

9

Exceeding shone, like Phoebus fairest childe,
  That did presume his fathers firie wayne,°   chariot
75   And flaming mouthes of steedes unwonted° wilde   unusually
  Through highest heaven with weaker° hand to rayne;   too weak
  Proud of such glory and advancement vaine,
  While flashing beames do daze his feeble eyen,
  He leaves the welkin° way most beaten plaine,   heavenly
80   And rapt° with whirling wheeles, inflames the skyen, carried away
With fire not made to burne, but fairely for to shyne.[5]

---

2. The name means unwelcome. In courtly love allegories, the porter is often called Bienvenu or Bel-accueil ("welcome").
3. Decorated with costly wall hangings.

4. Presence chamber, where a sovereign receives guests.
5. Phaëthon tried to drive the chariot of Phoebus, his father, but set the skies on fire and fell.

10

So proud she shynèd in her Princely state,
   Looking to heaven; for earth she did disdayne,
   And sitting high; for lowly° she did hate: *lowliness*
85   Lo underneath her scornefull feete, was layne
   A dreadfull Dragon with an hideous trayne,°   *tail*
   And in her hand she held a mirrhour bright,[6]
   Wherein her face she often vewèd fayne,°   *with pleasure*
   And in her selfe-loved semblance tooke delight;
90   For she was wondrous faire, as any living wight.

11

Of griesly° Pluto she the daughter was,   *horrid*
   And sad Proserpina the Queene of hell;
   Yet did she thinke her pearelesse worth to pas°   *surpass*
   That parentage, with pride so did she swell,
95   And thundring Jove, that high in heaven doth dwell,
   And wield° the world, she claymèd for her syre,   *govern*
   Or if that any else did Jove excell:
   For to the highest she did still aspyre,
Or if ought° higher were then that, did it desyre.   *anything*

12

100 And proud Lucifera men did her call,
   That made her selfe a Queene, and crownd to be,
   Yet rightfull kingdome she had none at all,
   Ne heritage of native soveraintie,
   But did usurpe with wrong and tyrannie
105 Upon the scepter, which she now did hold:
   Ne ruld her Realmes with lawes, but pollicie,°   *political cunning*
   And strong advizement of six wisards old,
That with their counsels bad her kingdome did uphold.

13

Soone as the Elfin knight in presence came,
110 And false Duessa seeming Lady faire,
   A gentle Husher,° Vanitie by name   *usher*
   Made rowme, and passage for them did prepaire:
   So goodly° brought them to the lowest staire   *graciously*
   Of her high throne, where they on humble knee
115 Making obeyssance,° did the cause declare,   *submission*
   Why they were come, her royall state to see,
To prove° the wide report of her great Majestee.   *verify*

14

With loftie eyes, halfe loth to looke so low,
   She thankèd them in her disdainefull wise,°   *manner*
120 Ne other grace vouchsafèd them to show

6. Pride and figures associated with her in Renaissance literature and art often hold a mirror, emblematic of self-love.

Of Princesse worthy, scarse them bad arise.
Her Lordes and Ladies all this while devise°   *make ready*
Themselves to setten forth to straungers sight:
Some frounce° their curlèd haire in courtly guise,   *frizzle*
125 Some prancke° their ruffes, and others trimly dight°   *pleat / arrange*
Their gay attire: each others greater pride does spight.[7]

15

Goodly they all that knight do entertaine,
Right glad with him to have increast their crew:
But to Duess' each one himselfe did paine
130 All kindnesse and faire courtesie to shew;
For in that court whylome° her well they knew: *formerly*
Yet the stout Faerie mongst the middest° crowd   *thickest*
Thought all their glorie vaine in knightly vew,
And that great Princesse too exceeding prowd,
135 That to strange° knight no better countenance° allowd.   *stranger / favor*

16

Suddein upriseth from her stately place
The royall Dame, and for her coche doth call:
All hurtlen° forth and she with Princely pace,   *rush*
As faire Aurora in her purple pall,[8]
140 Out of the East the dawning day doth call:
So forth she comes: her brightnesse brode° doth blaze;   *abroad*
The heapes of people thronging in the hall,
Do ride° each other, upon her to gaze: *climb up*
Her glorious glitterand° light doth all mens eyes amaze.   *glittering*

17

145 So forth she comes, and to her coche does clyme,
Adornèd all with gold, and girlonds gay,
That seemd as fresh as Flora in her prime,
And strove to match, in royall rich array,
Great Junos golden chaire,° the which they say   *chariot*
150 The Gods stand gazing on, when she does ride
To Joves high house through heavens bras-pavèd way
Drawne of faire Pecocks, that excell in pride,
And full of Argus eyes their tailes dispredden wide.[9]

18

But this was drawne of six unequall beasts,
155 On which her six sage Counsellours did ryde,
Taught to obey their bestiall beheasts,
With like conditions to their kinds applyde:[1]

7. Each begrudges the others' greater pride.
8. Goddess of dawn, in her crimson robe ("purple pall").
9. Peacocks, with their tails outspread ("dispredden wide"), are a symbol of pride. The hundred-eyed monster Argus was set by Juno to watch Io, Jupiter's love. When Mercury killed Argus, his eyes were put in the peacock's tail feathers.
1. Because riders and their mounts are alike bestial, the same conditions pertain (are "applyde") to both natures ("kinds"). This procession of the Seven Deadly Sins—of which Pride is queen—had a long tradition in medieval art and literature (see also Marlowe, *Dr. Faustus* 5.280–330, pp. 475–76).

Of which the first, that all the rest did guyde,
Was sluggish Idlenesse the nourse of sin;
160   Upon a slouthfull Asse he chose to ryde,
Arayd in habit blacke, and amis thin,[2]
Like to an holy Monck, the service to begin.

19

And in his hand his Portesse° still he bare,   *breviary*
That much was worne, but therein little red,
165   For of devotion he had little care,
Still drownd in sleepe, and most of his dayes ded;
Scarse could he once uphold his heavie hed,
To looken, whether it were night or day:
May seeme the wayne° was very evill led,   *chariot*
170   When such an one had guiding of the way,
That knew not, whether right he went, or else astray.

20

From worldly cares himselfe he did esloyne,°   *withdraw*
And greatly shunnèd manly exercise,
From every worke he chalengèd essoyne,°   *claimed exemption*
175   For contemplation sake: yet otherwise,
His life he led in lawlesse riotise;°   *riotous conduct*
By which he grew to grievous malady;
For in his lustlesse° limbs through evill guise°   *feeble / living*
A shaking fever raignd continually:
180   Such one was Idlenesse, first of this company.

21

And by his side rode loathsome Gluttony,
Deformèd creature, on a filthie swyne,
His belly was up-blowne with luxury.°   *indulgence*
And eke with fatnesse swollen were his eyne,
185   And like a Crane his necke was long and fyne,[3]
With which he swallowd up excessive feast,
For want whereof poore people oft did pyne;°   *starve*
And all the way, most like a brutish beast,
He spuèd up his gorge,[4] that° all did him deteast.   *so that*

22

190   In greene vine leaves he was right fitly clad;
For other clothes he could not weare for heat,
And on his head an yvie girland had,[5]
From under which fast trickled downe the sweat:
Still as he rode, he somewhat° still did eat,   *something*

2. Idleness wears the gown ("habit") and hood or amice ("amis") of a monk. Traditionally, Idleness led the procession of the deadly sins.
3. The crane is a common symbol of gluttony because its long and thin ("fyne") neck allows extended pleasure in swallowing.
4. Vomited up what he had swallowed.
5. He resembles the drunken satyr Silenus, foster father of Bacchus, god of wine; ivy is sacred to Bacchus.

195 And in his hand did beare a bouzing° can,   *drinking*
Of which he supt so oft, that on his seat
His dronken corse° he scarse upholden can,   *body*
In shape and life more like a monster, then° a man.   *than*

23

Unfit he was for any worldly thing,
200 And eke unhable once° to stirre or go,°   *at all / walk*
Not meet° to be of counsell to a king,   *fit*
Whose mind in meat and drinke was drownèd so,
That from his friend he seldome knew his fo:
Full of diseases was his carcas blew,
205 And a dry dropsie through his flesh did flow:
Which by misdiet daily greater grew:
Such one was Gluttony, the second of that crew.

24

And next° to him rode lustfull Lechery,   *just after*
Upon a bearded Goat,[6] whose rugged haire,
210 And whally° eyes (the signe of gelosy,°)   *glaring / jealousy*
Was like the person selfe, whom he did beare:
Who rough, and blacke, and filthy did appeare,
Unseemely man to please faire Ladies eye;
Yet he of Ladies oft was lovèd deare,
215 When fairer faces were bid standen by:°   *away*
O who does know the bent of womens fantasy?

25

In a greene gowne he clothèd was full faire,
Which underneath did hide his filthinesse,
And in his hand a burning hart he bare,
220 Full of vaine follies, and new fangleness:°   *fickleness*
For he was false, and fraught with ficklenesse,
And learnèd had to love with secret lookes,
And well could daunce, and sing with ruefulnesse,°   *pathos*
And fortunes tell, and read in loving bookes,[7]
225 And thousand other wayes, to bait his fleshly hookes.

26

Inconstant man, that lovèd all he saw,
And lusted after all, that he did love,
Ne would his looser life be tide to law,
But joyd weake wemens hearts to tempt and prove°   *try*
230 If from their loyall loves he might them move;
Which lewdnesse fild him with reprochfull paine
Of that fowle evill, which all men reprove,
That rots the marrow, and consumes the braine:°   *i.e., syphilis*
Such one was Lecherie, the third of all this traine.

---

6. Traditional symbol of Lust.
7. Either manuals on the art of love (e.g., Ovid's *Ars Amatoria*) or erotic books.

27

235 And greedy Avarice by him did ride,
   Upon a Camell loaden all with gold;[8]
   Two iron coffers hong on either side,
   With precious mettall full, as they might hold,
   And in his lap an heape of coine he told;°   *counted*
240 For of his wicked pelfe° his God he made,   *money*
   And unto hell him selfe for money sold;
   Accursèd usurie was all his trade,
   And right and wrong ylike in equall ballaunce waide.[9]

28

   His life was nigh unto deaths doore yplast,
245 And thread-bare cote, and cobled shoes he ware,
   Ne scarse good morsell all his life did tast,
   But both from backe and belly still did spare,
   To fill his bags, and richesse to compare;°   *acquire*
   Yet chylde ne kinsman living had he none
250 To leave them to; but thorough daily care
   To get, and nightly feare to lose his owne,
   He led a wretched life unto him selfe unknowne.

29

   Most wretched wight, whom nothing might suffise,
   Whose greedy lust did lacke in greatest store,°   *plenty*
255 Whose need had end, but no end covetise,
   Whose wealth was want, whose plenty made him pore,
   Who had enough, yet wishèd ever more;
   A vile disease, and eke in foote and hand
   A grievous gout tormented him full sore,
260 That well he could not touch, not go,° nor stand: *walk*
   Such one was Avarice, the fourth of this faire band.

30

   And next to him malicious Envie rode,
   Upon a ravenous wolfe, and still° did chaw   *continually*
   Betweene his cankred° teeth a venemous tode,   *infected*
265 That all the poison ran about his chaw;°   *jaw*
   But inwardly he chawèd his owne maw°   *entrails*
   At neighbours wealth, that made him ever sad;
   For death it was, when any good he saw,
   And wept, that cause of weeping none he had,
270 But when he heard of harme, he wexèd wondrous glad.

31

   All in a kirtle of discolourd say[1]
   He clothèd was, ypainted full of eyes;

---

8. The camel as a symbol of avarice is based on Matthew 19.24: "It is easier for a camel to go through the eye of a needle, than for a rich man to enter into the kingdom of God."

9. I.e., he made no distinction between right and wrong.

1. Jacket of many-colored wool.

And in his bosome secretly there lay
An hatefull Snake,[2] the which his taile uptyes

275 In many folds, and mortall sting implyes.°   *enfolds*
Still as he rode, he gnasht his teeth, to see
Those heapes of gold with griple Covetyse,°   *grasping Avarice*
And grudgèd at the great felicitie
Of proud Lucifera, and his owne companie.

32

280 He hated all good workes and vertuous deeds,
And him no lesse, that any like did use,°   *perform*
And who with gracious bread the hungry feeds,
His almes for want of faith he doth accuse;[3]
So every good to bad he doth abuse:°   *twist*

285 And eke° the verse of famous Poets witt   *also*
He does backebite, and spightfull poison spues
From leprous mouth on all, that ever writt:
Such one vile Envie was, that fifte in row did sitt.

33

And him beside rides fierce revenging Wrath,

290 Upon a Lion, loth for to be led;
And in his hand a burning brond° he hath,   *sword*
The which he brandisheth about his hed;
His eyes did hurle forth sparkles fiery red,
And starèd sterne on all, that him beheld,

295 As ashes pale of hew and seeming ded;
And on his dagger still his hand he held,
Trembling through hasty rage, when choler° in him sweld.   *anger*

34

His ruffin° raiment all was staind with blood,   *disorderly*
Which he had spilt, and all to rags yrent,°   *torn*

300 Through unadvisèd rashnesse woxen wood,[4]
For of his hands he had no governement,°   *control*
Ne cared for bloud in his avengement:
But when the furious fit was overpast,
His cruell facts° he often would repent;   *actions*

305 Yet wilfull man he never would forecast,
How many mischieves should ensue his heedlesse hast.[5]

35

Full many mischiefes follow cruell Wrath;
Abhorrèd bloudshed, and tumultuous strife,
Unmanly murder, and unthrifty scath,[6]

310 Bitter despight,° with rancours rusty knife,   *malice*
And fretting griefe the enemy of life;

2. Traditional attribute of Envy.
3. Envy perversely discounts others' good works by attributing them to a selfish motive: the desire to compensate (in God's eyes) for lack of faith.
4. Grown insane.
5. I.e., he never would foresee ("forecast") the calamities his "heedless haste" caused.
6. I.e., inhuman murder and destructive harm.

All these, and many evils moe° haunt ire,°   *more / anger*
The swelling Splene,[7] and Frenzy raging rife,
The shaking Palsey, and Saint Fraunces fire:[8]
315   Such one was Wrath, the last of this ungoldly tire.°   *train*

36

And after all, upon the wagon beame
Rode Sathan, with a smarting whip in hand,
With which he forward lasht the laesie teme,
So oft as Slowth° still in the mire did stand.   *Idleness*
320   Huge routs° of people did about them band,   *crowds*
Showting for joy, and still before their way
A foggy mist had covered all the land;
And underneath their feet, all scattered lay
Dead sculs and bones of men, whose life had gone astray.

Summary   In the remainder of the canto, the third Saracen brother, Sans joy, arrives at the House of Pride and demands to do battle with Redcrosse. Lucifera intervenes and orders them to meet in a formal combat on the following day. Duessa visits Sans joy in the night, warning him of the power of Redcrosse's invulnerable armor, and promising him her secret aid.

Canto 5 *Summary*   Just as Redcrosse is about to slay Sans joy in combat, the Saracen vanishes in a magical cloud created by Duessa. To heal the wounded Sans joy, the witch enlists the help of Night, the queen of darkness who is grandmother of the three Saracen brothers. Together they take Sans joy down to Hades, the classical underworld. There he will be healed by the legendary physician Aesculapius, who has the power to raise the dead and is himself immortal, but doomed to live forever in Hades. Meanwhile, Redcrosse's companion the dwarf discovers Lucifera's dungeon, where the bodies of the proud are cast in heaps. With the dwarf, Redcrosse flees in the night, stumbling over piled-up corpses as he makes his escape, and Duessa returns to find him gone.

Canto 6 *Summary*   Sans loy intends to rape Una, but is frightened away by a band of fauns and satyrs (mythological creatures who are men above the waist and goats below). They take Una and proceed to worship her as a goddess, in spite of her attempts to teach them true religion. She is discovered among them by Satyrane, a wild but virtuous knight born of a human mother and a satyr father. Together they escape her idolators. They then meet with a pilgrim who informs them that Redcrosse has been slain by Sans loy. Satyrane seeks out the Saracen and they do battle. Una flees in terror and is pursued by the pilgrim, who is revealed as Archimago in disguise.

Cantos 7 and 8 *Summary*   Still disguised as Fidessa, Duessa pursues and finds Redcrosse. He drinks from a fountain which robs him of strength. The enfeebled knight is discovered lying with Duessa by the giant Orgoglio (Pride), who easily conquers Redcrosse and casts him into his dungeon. The giant pampers Duessa, attiring her as the Whore of Babylon in Revelation (a figure associated by Protestants with the papacy), and mounting her on a seven-headed beast. Meanwhile, the dwarf finds Una and reveals to her what has happened. Una sets out in search of Redcrosse and meets with Prince Arthur—the future king of Britain whose story runs through all the books of *The Faerie Queene*. She tells Arthur her story, explaining that Redcrosse

---

7. Organ associated with anger in Renaissance physiology.

8. St. Anthony's fire, erysipelas, or the flaming itch; appropriate to Wrath.

has been assigned by the Faerie Queene to rescue her parents, the king and queen of Eden, from a dragon. Arthur promises to rescue Redcrosse. In an epic fight, he defeats and kills Orgoglio, after stunning the giant and the beast with the divine brightness of his shield. Arthur seizes the keys to Orgoglio's dungeon from the giant's ancient foster-father, Ignaro (Ignorance), and liberates the starving Redcrosse. They strip Duessa, who is revealed as a filthy, bestial hag. She hides herself in the wilderness.

From *Canto 9*

His loves and lignage° Arthur tells: *lineage*
  The knights knit friendly bands:°   *bonds*
Sir Trevisan flies from Despayre,
  Whom Redcrosse knight withstands.

Summary   In the first part of the canto, Arthur tells Redcrosse and Una of his past life. Taken from his mother at birth, Arthur is ignorant of his lineage, but has been told by the magician Merlin that he is heir to a king. After being visited by the Faerie Queene in a dream, in which she lay beside him on the grass, he has fallen in love with her. The knights then exchange vows of friendship and gifts. Arthur gives Redcrosse a precious liquid which heals wounds, while Redcrosse gives him the New Testament. Arthur then rides off in search of the Faerie Queene. Una looks with concern at Redcrosse, who remains weak and weary from his recent ordeal.

[REDCROSSE MEETS DESPAIRE]

21

So as they traveild, lo they gan espy
  An armèd knight towards them gallop fast,
  That seemèd from some fearèd foe to fly,
  Or other griesly thing, that him agast.°   *terrified*
185 Still as he fled, his eye was backward cast,
  As if his feare still followed him behind;
  Als flew his steed, as he his bands had brast,°   *broken*
  And with his wingèd heeles did tread the wind,
As he had beene a fole of Pegasus his kind.[9]

22

190 Nigh as he drew, they might perceive his head
  To be unarmd, and curld uncombèd heares
  Upstaring° stiffe, dismayd with uncouth° dread; *bristling/unknown*
  Nor drop of bloud in all his face appeares
  Nor life in limbe: and to increase his feares,
195 In fowle reproch° of knighthoods faire degree,° *disgrace/condition*
  About his neck an hempen rope he weares,
  That with his glistring armes does ill agree;
But he of rope or armes has now no memoree.

23

The Redcrosse knight toward him crossèd fast,
200 To weet, what mister° wight was so dismayd: *kind of*

---

9. I.e., as if he had been a foal of a horse like Pegasus (a flying horse).

There him he finds all sencelesse and aghast,
That of him selfe he seemd to be afrayd;
Whom hardly he from flying forward stayd,
Till he these wordes to him deliver might;
205   "Sir knight, aread° who hath ye thus arayd,   *declare*
And eke from whom make ye this hasty flight:
For never knight I saw in such misseeming° plight."   *unseemly*

24

He answerd nought at all, but adding new
Feare to his first amazment, staring wide
210   With stony eyes, and hartlesse hollow hew,[1]
Astonisht stood, as one that had aspide
Infernall furies, with their chaines untide.
Him yet againe, and yet againe bespake
The gentle knight; who nought to him replide,
215   But trembling every joynt did inly quake,
And foltring tongue at last these words seemd forth to shake.

25

"For Gods deare love, Sir knight, do me not stay;
For loe he comes, he comes fast after mee."
Eft° looking backe would faine have runne away;   *again*
220   But he him forst to stay, and tellen free
The secret cause of his perplexitie:°   *distress*
Yet nathemore° by his bold hartie speach,   *not at all*
Could his bloud-frosen hart emboldned bee,
But through his boldnesse rather feare did reach,
225   Yet forst, at last he made through silence suddein breach.

26

"And am I now in safetie sure," quoth he,
"From him, that would have forcèd me to dye?
And is the point of death now turnd fro mee,
That I may tell this haplesse history?"
230   "Feare nought:" quoth he, "no daunger now is nye."
"Then shall I you recount a ruefull cace,"°   *event*
Said he, "the which with this unlucky eye
I late beheld, and had not greater grace
Me reft° from it, had bene partaker of the place.[2]   *carried*

27

235   "I lately chaunst (Would I had never chaunst)
With a faire knight to keepen companee,
Sir Terwin[3] hight,° that well himselfe advaunst   *named*
In all affaires, and was both bold and free,
But not so happie as mote happie bee:
240   He loved, as was his lot, a Ladie gent,°   *gentle*

---

1. I.e., with blanched, bloodless countenance.   3. His name may connote weariness or fatigue
2. I.e., shared the same fate.   ("terwyn").

That him againe° loved in the least degree: *in return*
For she was proud, and of too high intent,°   *mind*
And joyd to see her lover languish and lament.

28

"From whom returning sad and comfortlesse,°   *desolate*
245 As on the way together we did fare,
We met that villen (God from him me blesse°)   *defend*
That cursèd wight, from whom I scapt whyleare,°   *a while before*
A man of hell, that cals himselfe Despaire;[4]
Who first us greets, and after faire areedes°   *tells*
250 Of tydings strange, and of adventures rare:
So creeping close, as Snake in hidden weedes,
Inquireth of our states, and of our knightly deedes.

29

"Which when he knew, and felt our feeble harts
Embost° with bale,° and bitter byting griefe,   *exhausted / sorrow*
255 Which love had launchèd° with his deadly darts,   *pierced*
With wounding words and termes of foule repriefe°   *insult*
He pluckt from us all hope of due reliefe,
That earst us held in love of lingring life;
Then hopelesse hartlesse, gan the cunning thiefe
260 Perswade us die, to stint° all further strife: *end*
To me he lent this rope, to him a rustie knife.

30

"With which sad instrument of hastie death,
That wofull lover, loathing lenger° light,   *longer*
A wide way made to let forth living breath.
265 But I more fearefull, or more luckie wight,
Dismayd with that deformèd dismall sight,
Fled fast away, halfe dead with dying feare:°   *fear of death*
Ne yet assur'd of life by you, Sir knight,
Whose like infirmitie like chaunce may beare:
270 But God you never let his charmèd speeches heare."[5]

31

"How may a man," said he, "with idle speach
Be wonne, to spoyle° the Castle of his health?"   *destroy*
"I wote," quoth he, "whom triall° late did teach,   *experience*
That like would not[6] for all this worldes wealth:
275 His subtill tongue, like dropping honny, mealt'th°   *melts*
Into the hart, and searcheth every vaine,
That ere one be aware, by secret stealth
His powre is reft, and weaknesse doth remaine.
O never Sir desire to try° his guilefull traine."°   *test / treachery*

4. Despair is the ultimate Christian sin, denying   izing ("charmed") speeches.
the possibility of Divine mercy and grace.   6. I.e., would not do the like again.
5. I.e., may God never let you hear his mesmer-

32

280 "Certes,"° said he, "hence shall I never rest,   *surely*
    Till I that treachours art have heard and tride;
    And you Sir knight, whose name mote° I request,   *might*
    Of grace° do me unto his cabin° guide."   *favor/cave*
    "I that hight° Trevisan," quoth he, "will ride   *am called*
285 Against my liking backe, to doe you grace:°   *a favor*
    But nor for gold nor glee⁷ will I abide
    By you, when ye arrive in that same place;
    For lever° had I die, then° see his deadly face."   *rather/than*

33

    Ere long they come, where that same wicked wight
290 His dwelling has, low in an hollow cave,
    Farre underneath a craggie clift ypight,°   *placed*
    Darke, dolefull, drearie, like a greedie grave,
    That still for carrion carcases doth crave:
    On top whereof aye dwelt the ghastly Owle,⁸
295 Shrieking his balefull note, which ever drave
    Farre from that haunt all other chearefull fowle;
And all about it wandring ghostes did waile and howle.

34

And all about old stockes° and stubs of trees,   *stumps*
    Whereon nor fruit, nor leafe was ever seene,
300 Did hang upon the ragged rocky knees;°   *crags*
    On which had many wretches hangèd beene,
    Whose carcases were scattered on the greene,
    And throwne about the cliffs. Arrivèd there,
    That bare-head knight for dread and dolefull teene,° *grief*
305 Would faine° have fled, ne durst approachen neare,   *gladly*
But th' other forst him stay, and comforted in feare.

35

That darkesome cave they enter, where they find
    That cursèd man, low sitting on the ground,
    Musing full sadly in his sullein° mind;   *morose*
310 His griesie° lockes, long growen, and unbound,   *gray*
    Disordred hong about his shoulders round,
    And hid his face; through which his hollow eyne
    Lookt deadly dull, and starèd as astound;
    His raw-bone cheekes through penurie and pine,°   *starvation*
315 Were shronke into his jawes, as° he did never dine.   *as if*

36

His garment nought but many ragged clouts,°   *rags*
    With thornes together pind and patchèd was,
    The which his naked sides he wrapt abouts;
    And him beside there lay upon the gras

---

7. Song; i.e., anything you can say to me.   8. Traditionally a messenger of death.

320   A drearie° corse, whose life away did pas,   *bloody*
      All wallowd in his owne yet luke-warme blood,
      That from his wound yet wellèd fresh alas;
      In which a rustie° knife fast fixèd stood,   *bloodstained*
      And made an open passage for the gushing flood.

37

325   Which piteous spectacle, approving° trew   *confirming*
      The wofull tale that Trevisan had told,
      When as the gentle Redcrosse knight did vew,
      With firie zeale he burnt in courage bold,
      Him to avenge, before his bloud were cold,
330   And to the villein said, "Thou agèd damnèd wight,
      The author of this fact,° we here behold,   *deed*
      What justice can but judge against thee right,
  With thine owne bloud to price° his bloud, here shed in sight?" *pay for*

38

      "What franticke fit," quoth he,° "hath thus distraught   *i.e., Despaire*
335   Thee, foolish man, so rash a doome° to give?   *judgment*
      What justice ever other judgement taught,
      But he should die, who merites not to live?
      None else to death this man despayring drive,°   *drove*
      But his owne guiltie mind deserving death.
340   Is then unjust to each his due to give?
      Or let him die, that loatheth living breath?
      Or let him die at ease, that liveth here uneath?°   *in unease*

39

      "Who travels by the wearie wandring way,
      To come unto his wishèd home in haste,
345   And meetes a flood, that doth his passage stay,
      Is not great grace to helpe him over past,
      Or free his feet, that in the myre sticke fast?
      Most envious man, that grieves at neighbours good,
      And fond,° that joyest in the woe thou hast,   *foolish*
350   Why wilt not let him passe, that long hath stood
  Upon the banke, yet wilt thy selfe not passe the flood?

40

      "He there does now enjoy eternall rest
      And happie ease, which thou doest want and crave,
      And further from it daily wanderest:
355   What if some litle paine the passage have,
      That makes fraile flesh to feare the bitter wave?
      Is not short paine well borne, that brings long ease,
      And layes the soule to sleepe in quiet grave?
      Sleepe after toyle, port after stormie seas,
360   Ease after warre, death after life does greatly please."⁹

9. Despaire's arguments on behalf of suicide as against a painful life are derived, like those of Hamlet in his third soliloquy (*Hamlet* 3.1.58–90), principally from Seneca, Marcus Aurelius, other ancient Stoics, and Old Testament statements on divine justice.

41

The knight much wondred at his suddeine wit,° *quick intelligence*
And said, "The terme of life is limited,
Ne may a man prolong, nor shorten it;
The souldier may not move from watchfull sted,[1]
365 Nor leave his stand, untill his Captaine bed."° *commands*
"Who life did limit by almightie doome,"
Quoth he,° "knowes best the termes establishèd; *Despaire*
And he, that points the Centonell his roome,° *station*
Doth license him depart at sound of morning droome.[2]

42

370 "Is not his deed, what ever thing is donne,
In heaven and earth? did not he all create
To die againe? all ends that was begonne.
Their times in his eternall booke of fate
Are written sure, and have their certaine° date. *fixed*
375 Who then can strive with strong necessitie,
That holds the world in his still chaunging state,
Or shunne the death ordaynd by destinie?
When houre of death is come, let none aske whence, nor why.

43

"The lenger° life, I wote° the greater sin, *longer/know*
380 The greater sin, the greater punishment:
All those great battels, which thou boasts to win,
Through strife, and bloud-shed, and avengement,
Now praysd, hereafter deare° thou shalt repent: *bitterly*
For life must life, and bloud must bloud repay.[3]
385 Is not enough thy evill life forespent?
For he, that once hath missèd the right way,
The further he doth goe, the further he doth stray.

44

"Then do no further goe, no further stray,
But here lie downe, and to thy rest betake,
390 Th' ill to prevent, that life ensewen may.[4]
For what hath life, that may it lovèd make,
And gives not rather cause it to forsake?
Feare, sicknesse, age, losse, labour, sorrow, strife,
Paine, hunger, cold, that makes the hart to quake;
395 And ever fickle fortune rageth rife,
All which, and thousands mo° do make a loathsome life. *more*

45

"Thou wretched man, of death hast greatest need,
If in true ballance thou wilt weigh thy state:

---

1. The sentry post assigned him.
2. Drum, with a pun on *doom.*
3. An echo of Genesis 9.6: "Whoso sheddeth man's blood, by man shall his blood be shed."
4. I.e., to prevent the evil that will ensue in the rest of your life.

For never knight, that darèd warlike deede,
400 More lucklesse disaventures° did amate:°   *mishaps/daunt*
Witnesse the dongeon deepe, wherein of late
Thy life shut up, for death so oft did call;
And though good lucke prolongèd hath thy date,°   *span of life*
Yet death then, would the like mishaps forestall,
405 Into the which hereafter thou maiest happen fall.°   *happen to fall*

46

"Why then doest thou, O man of sin, desire
To draw thy dayes forth to their last degree?
Is not the measure of thy sinfull hire°   *service to sin*
High heapèd up with huge iniquitie,
410 Against the day of wrath,° to burden thee?   *Judgment Day*
Is not enough that to this Ladie milde
Thou falsèd° hast thy faith with perjurie,   *betrayed*
And sold thy selfe to serve Duessa vilde,°   *vile*
With whom in all abuse thou hast thy selfe defilde?

47

415 "Is not he just, that all this doth behold
From highest heaven, and beares an equall° eye?   *impartial*
Shall he thy sins up in his knowledge fold,
And guiltie be of thine impietie?
Is not his law, Let every sinner die:⁵
420 Die shall all flesh? what then must needs be donne,
Is it not better to doe willinglie,
Then linger, till the glasse° be all out ronne?   *hourglass*
Death is the end of woes: die soone, O faeries sonne."

48

The knight was much enmovèd with his speach,
425 That as a swords point through his hart did perse,
And in his conscience made a secret breach,
Well knowing true all, that he did reherse°   *recount*
And to his fresh remembrance did reverse°   *bring back*
The ugly vew of his deformèd crimes,
430 That all his manly powres it did disperse,
As he were charmèd with inchaunted rimes,
That oftentimes he quakt, and fainted oftentimes.

49

In which amazement, when the Miscreant°   *misbeliever*
Perceivèd him to waver weake and fraile,
435 Whiles trembling horror did his conscience dant,°   *daunt*
And hellish anguish° did his soule assaile,   *i.e., fear of hell*
To drive him to despaire, and quite to quaile,°   *be dismayed*
He shewed him painted in a table° plaine,   *picture*

---

5. Despaire cites only half of the Scripture verse: "The wages of sin is death; but the gift of God is eternal life through Jesus Christ our Lord" (Romans 6.23).

The damnèd ghosts, that doe in torments waile,
440   And thousand feends that doe them endlesse paine
With fire and brimstone, which for ever shall remaine.

50

The sight whereof so throughly him dismaid,
    That nought but death before his eyes he saw,
    And ever burning wrath before him laid,
445   By righteous sentence of th' Almighties law:
    Then gan the villein him to overcraw,°   *exult over*
    And brought unto him swords, ropes, poison, fire,
    And all that might him to perdition draw;
    And bad him choose, what death he would desire:
450 For death was due to him, that had provokt Gods ire.

51

But when as none of them he saw him take,
    He to him raught° a dagger sharpe and keene,   *reached*
    And gave it him in hand: his hand did quake,
    And tremble like a leafe of Aspin greene,
455   And troubled bloud through his pale face was seene
    To come, and goe with tydings from the hart,
    As it a running messenger had beene.
    At last resolved to worke his finall smart,
He lifted up his hand, that backe againe did start.

52

460 Which when as Una saw, through every vaine
    The crudled° cold ran to her well of life,°   *congealing/heart*
    As in a swowne: but soone relived° againe,   *revived*
    Out of his hand she snatcht the cursèd knife,
    And threw it to the ground, enragèd rife,°   *deeply*
465   And to him said, "Fie, fie, faint harted knight,
    What meanest thou by this reprochfull° strife? *deserving reproach*
    Is this the battell, which thou vauntst to fight
With the fire-mouthèd Dragon, horrible and bright?

53

"Come, come away, fraile, feeble, fleshly wight,
470   Ne let vaine words bewitch thy manly hart,
    Ne divelish thoughts dismay thy constant spright.
    In heavenly mercies hast thou not a part?
    Why shouldst thou then despeire, that chosen[6] art?
    Where justice growes, there grows eke° greater grace, *also*
475   The which doth quench the brond of hellish smart,
    And that accurst hand-writing[7] doth deface.°   *blot out*
Arise, Sir knight arise, and leave this cursèd place."

6. Cf. 2 Thessalonians 2.13: "God hath from the beginning chosen you to salvation through sanctification of the Spirit and belief of the truth."
7. An echo of Colossians 2.14: "Blotting out the handwriting of ordinances [i.e., the Old Testament Law] that was against us, which was contrary to us, and took it out of the way, nailing it to his cross."

54

So up he rose, and thence amounted° streight.	*mounted his horse*
Which when the carle° beheld, and saw his guest	*churl*
Would safe depart, for° all his subtill sleight,	*in spite of*
He chose an halter from among the rest,	
And with it hung himselfe, unbid° unblest.	*unprayed for*
But death he could not worke himselfe thereby;	
For thousand times he so himselfe had drest,°	*made ready*
Yet nathelesse it could not doe° him die,	*make*
Till he should die his last, that is eternally.	

480 ... 485

From *Canto 10*

Her faithfull knight faire Una brings
to house of Holinesse,
Where he is taught repentance, and
the way to heavenly blesse.°   *bliss*

Summary   In the first part of the canto, Una brings Redcrosse to the House of Holinesse to be healed in body and spirit. The house is kept by Dame Caelia (Heavenly) with her three daughters Fidelia (Faith), Speranza (Hope), and Charissa (Charity, or Love). Redcrosse is welcomed and given counsel by Fidelia and Speranza, but remains wracked by guilt and suicidal impulses. He is entrusted to the doctor Patience and undergoes a painful cure with Penance, Remorse, and Repentance. He next comes to Charissa, who instructs him in love and good deeds and places him in the hands of a godly matron, Mercie. She leads him along a narrow and thorny path to a holy Hospitall (hostel), kept by seven Bead-men (men of prayer), where Redcrosse learns to frame his life in righteousness. Redcrosse and Mercie then continue on their way.

46

Thence forward by that painfull way they pas,	
Forth to an hill, that was both steepe and hy;	
On top whereof a sacred chappell was,	
And eke a litle Hermitage thereby,	
Wherein an agèd holy man did lye,°	*live*
That day and night said his devotion,	
Ne other worldly busines did apply;⁸	
His name was heavenly Contemplation;	
Of God and goodnesse was his meditation.	

410

47

Great grace that old man to him given had;	
For God he often saw from heavens hight,	
All° were his earthly eyen both blunt° and bad,	*although / dim*
And through great age had lost their kindly° sight,	*natural*
Yet wondrous quick and persant° was his spright,°	*piercing / spirit*
As Eagles eye, that can behold the Sunne:	
That hill they scale with all their powre and might,	
That his frayle thighes nigh wearie and fordonne°	*exhausted*
Gan faile, but by her helpe the top at last he wonne.	

415 ... 420

8. I.e., he did not attend to any worldly activities.

48

There they do finde that godly agèd Sire,
425   With snowy lockes adowne his shoulders shed,
    As hoarie frost with spangles doth attire
    The mossy braunches of an Oke halfe ded.
    Each bone might through his body well be red,°   *seen*
    And every sinew seene through° his long fast: *because of*
430   For nought he cared his carcas long unfed;
    His mind was full of spirituall repast,
And pynèd° his flesh, to keepe his body low° and chast.   *starved / thin*

49

Who when these two approching he aspide,
    At their first presence grew agrievèd sore,[9]
435   That forst him lay his heavenly thoughts aside;
    And had he not that Dame respected more,°   *greatly*
    Whom highly he did reverence and adore,
    He would not once have movèd for the knight.
    They him saluted standing far afore;°   *away*
440   Who well them greeting, humbly did requight,°   *respond*
And askèd, to what end they clomb° that tedious height.   *had climbed*

50

"What end," quoth she, "should cause us take such paine,
    But that same end, which every living wight
    Should make his marke,° high heaven to attaine?   *goal*
445   Is not from hence the way, that leadeth right
    To that most glorious house, that glistreth bright
    With burning starres, and everliving fire,
    Whereof the keyes are to thy hand behight°   *entrusted*
    By wise Fidelia? she doth thee require,
450 To shew it to this knight, according° his desire."   *granting*

51

"Thrise happy man," said then the father grave,
    "Whose staggering steps thy° steady hand doth lead,   *i.e., Mercy's*
    And shewes the way, his sinfull soule to save.
    Who better can the way to heaven aread°   *direct*
455   Then thou thy selfe, that was both borne and bred
    In heavenly throne, where thousand Angels shine?
    Thou doest the prayers of the righteous sead°   *seed*
    Present before the majestie divine,
And his avenging wrath to clemencie incline.

52

460 "Yet since thou bidst, thy pleasure shalbe donne.
    Then come thou man of earth,[1] and see the way,
    That never yet was seene of Faeries sonne,
    That never leads the traveiler astray,

9. I.e., he was at first sorely grieved at their arrival.
1. An allusion to humankind's formation from the dust of the earth (Genesis 2.7) and also to the knight's name (see below, stanza 66 and note 2).

But after labours long, and sad delay,
465   Brings them to joyous rest and endlesse blis.
   But first thou must a season fast and pray,
   Till from her bands the spright assoilèd° is,   *spirit released*
   And have her strength recured° from fraile infirmitis."   *recovered*

53

That done, he leads him to the highest Mount;
470   Such one, as that same mighty man of God,
   That bloud-red billowes like a wallèd front
   On either side disparted° with his rod,   *parted asunder*
   Till that his army dry-foot through them yod,°   *went*
   Dwelt fortie dayes upon; where writ in stone
475   With bloudy letters by the hand of God,
   The bitter doome of death and balefull mone[2]
He did receive, whiles flashing fire about him shone.

54

Or like that sacred hill, whose head full hie,
   Adornd with fruitfull Olives all arownd,
480   Is, as it were for endlesse memory
   Of that deare Lord, who oft thereon was fownd,
   For ever with a flowring girlond crownd:
   Or like that pleasaunt Mount, that is for ay
   Through famous Poets verse each where° renownd,   *everywhere*
485   On which the thrise three learned Ladies play
Their heavenly notes, and make full many a lovely lay.[3]

55

From thence, far off he unto him did shew
   A litle path, that was both steepe and long,
   Which to a goodly Citie led his vew;
490   Whose wals and towres were builded high and strong
   Of perle and precious stone, that earthly tong
   Cannot describe, nor wit of man can tell;
   Too high a ditty° for my simple song;   *subject*
   The Citie of the great king hight it well,
495 Wherein eternall peace and happinesse doth dwell.

56

As he thereon stood gazing, he might see
   The blessed Angels to and fro descend
   From highest heaven, in gladsome companee,
   And with great joy into that Citie wend,
500   As commonly° as friend does with his frend.[4]   *familiarly*
   Whereat he wondred much, and gan enquere,

2. I.e., the Ten Commandments ("bloudy letters") carried with them the judgment ("doome") of death and pain (causing sorrowful moans—"balefull mone").
3. Song. The mountain is successively compared with Mount Sinai, where Moses, after parting the "bloud-red billowes" of the Red Sea, received the tablets of the Ten Commandments; to the Mount of Olives, associated with Christ; and to Mount Parnassus, where the Nine Muses of art and poetry dwelt.
4. Cf. Jacob's ladder, which "reached to heaven; and behold the angels of God ascending and descending on it" (Genesis 28.12).

What stately building durst so high extend
Her loftie towres unto the starry sphere,
And what unknowen nation there empeopled were.

57

505 "Faire knight," quoth he, "Hierusalem that is,
The new Hierusalem, that God has built
For those to dwell in, that are chosen his,
His chosen people purged from sinfull guilt,
With pretious bloud, which cruelly was spilt
510 On cursèd tree, of that unspotted lam,[5]
That for the sinnes of all the world was kilt:
Now are they Saints all in that Citie sam,°   together
More deare unto their God, then younglings to their dam."[6]

58

"Till now," said then the knight, "I weenèd well,
515 That great Cleopolis,[7] where I have beene,
In which that fairest Faerie Queene doth dwell,
The fairest Citie was, that might be seene;
And that bright towre all built of christall cleene,°   clear
Panthea,[8] seemd the brightest thing, that was:
520 But now by proofe all otherwise I weene;
For this great Citie that[9] does far surpas,
And this bright Angels towre quite dims that towre of glas."

59

"Most trew," then said the holy agèd man;
"Yet is Cleopolis for earthly frame,°   structure
525 The fairest peece,° that eye beholden can: masterpiece
And well beseemes° all knights of noble name,   becomes
That covet in th' immortall booke of fame
To be eternizèd, that same to haunt,°   frequent
And doen their service to that soveraigne Dame,
530 That glorie does to them for guerdon° graunt: reward
For she is heavenly borne, and heaven may justly vaunt.° claim

60

"And thou faire ymp,° sprong out from English race,   youth
How ever now accompted° Elfins sonne,   accounted
Well worthy doest thy service for her grace,°   favor
535 To aide a virgin desolate foredonne.°   undone
But when thou famous victorie hast wonne,
And high emongst all knights hast hong thy shield,
Thenceforth the suit° of earthly conquest shonne,   pursuit

---

5. Lamb; a reference to Christ (the lamb of God),
whose death on the cross ("cursèd tree") purged
the guilt of sin from those "chosen his."
6. The New Jerusalem is described in Revelation
21–22; "the nations of them which are saved shall
walk in the light of it" (21.24).
7. London, Camelot—the earthly counterpart of
the Heavenly Kingdom.
8. Reminiscent of the temple of glass in Chaucer's
House of Fame; perhaps intended to allude to Richmond Palace or Westminster Abbey.
9. I.e., The New Jerusalem far surpasses Cleopolis
("that").

And wash thy hands from guilt of bloudy field:
540   For bloud can nought but sin, and wars but sorrowes yield.

61

"Then seeke this path, that I to thee presage,°   *show prophetically*
Which after all to heaven shall thee send;
Then peaceably thy painefull° pilgrimage   *laborious*
To yonder same Hierusalem do bend,
545   Where is for thee ordaind a blessèd end:
For thou emongst those Saints, whom thou doest see,
Shalt be a Saint, and thine owne nations frend
And Patrone: thou Saint George shalt callèd bee,
Saint George of mery England, the signe of victoree."[1]

62

550   "Unworthy wretch," quoth he, "of so great grace,
How dare I thinke such glory to attaine?"
"These that have it attaind, were in like cace,"
Quoth he, "as wretched, and lived in like paine."
"But deeds of armes must I at last be faine,°   *content (to leave)*
555   And Ladies love to leave so dearely bought?"
"What need of armes, where peace doth ay remaine,"
Said he, "and battailes none are to be fought?
As for loose loves are° vaine, and vanish into nought."   *i.e., they are*

63

"O let me not," quoth he, "then turne againe
560   Backe to the world, whose joyes so fruitlesse are;
But let me here for aye in peace remaine,
Or streight way on that last long voyage fare,
That nothing may my present hope empare."°   *impair*
"That may not be," said he, "ne maist thou yit
565   Forgo that royall maides bequeathèd care,°   *charge*
Who did her cause into thy hand commit,
Till from her cursèd foe thou have her freely quit."°   *released*

64

"Then shall I soone," quoth he, "so God me grace,
Abet° that virgins cause disconsolate,   *maintain*
570   And shortly backe returne unto this place
To walke this way in Pilgrims poore estate.
But now aread,° old father, why of late   *declare*
Didst thou behight° me borne of English blood,   *call*
Whom all a Faeries sonne doen nominate?"°   *name*
575   "That word shall I," said he, "avouchen° good,   *prove*
Sith° to thee is unknowne the cradle of thy brood.   *since*

---

1. Spenser's conception of St. George, patron saint of England, draws on the *Legenda Aurea* (*The Golden Legend*—a medieval manual of ecclesiastical lore, translated into English by William Caxton in 1487) and on pictures, tapestries, pageants, and folklore.

65

"For well I wote,° thou springst from ancient race   *know*
    Of Saxon kings, that have with mightie hand
    And many bloudie battailes fought in place°   *there*
580   High reard their royall throne in Britane land,
    And vanquisht them, unable to withstand:
    From thence a Faerie thee unweeting reft,°   *secretly stole*
    There as thou slepst in tender swadling band,
    And her base Elfin brood there for thee left.
585 Such men do Chaungelings call, so chaungd by Faeries theft.

66

"Thence she thee brought into this Faerie lond,
    And in an heapèd furrow did thee hyde,
    Where thee a Ploughman all unweeting° fond,   *unknowing*
    As he his toylesome teme° that way did guyde,   *team of oxen*
590   And brought thee up in ploughmans state to byde,
    Whereof Georgos he thee gave to name;[2]
    Till prickt° with courage, and thy forces pryde,   *spurred*
    To Faery court thou cam'st to seeke for fame,
    And prove thy puissaunt armes, as seemes thee best
        became."°   *as best suited you*

67

595 "O holy Sire," quoth he, "how shall I quight°   *repay*
    The many favours I with thee have found,
    That hast my name and nation red aright,
    And taught the way that does to heaven bound?"°   *go*
    This said, adowne he lookèd to the ground,
600   To have returnd, but dazèd° were his eyne,   *dazzled*
    Through passing° brightnesse, which did quite confound   *surpassing*
    His feeble sence, and too exceeding shyne.
    So darke are earthly things compard to things divine.

68

At last whenas himselfe he gan to find,°   *recover*
605   To Una back he cast him to retire;
    Who him awaited still with pensive° mind.   *anxious*
    Great thankes and goodly meed° to that good syre,   *gift*
    He thence departing gave for his paines hyre.°   *reward*
    So came to Una, who him joyd to see,
610   And after litle rest, gan him desire,
    Of her adventure mindfull for to bee.
    So leave they take of Caelia, and her daughters three.

---

2. I.e., as a name. *Georgos* is Greek for "farmer" (cf. Virgil's *Georgics*, on farming).

Canto 11

The knight with that old Dragon fights
two dayes incessantly:
The third him overthrowes, and gayns
most glorious victory.

1

High time now gan it wex° for Una faire,   *grow*
   To thinke of those her captive Parents deare,
   And their forwasted kingdome to repaire:[3]
   Whereto whenas they now approachèd neare,
5   With hartie° words her knight she gan to cheare,   *bold*
   And in her modest manner thus bespake;
   "Deare knight, as deare, as ever knight was deare,
   That all these sorrowes suffer for my sake,
High heaven behold the tedious toyle, ye for me take.

2

10 "Now are we come unto my native soyle,
   And to the place, where all our perils dwell;
   Here haunts that feend, and does his dayly spoyle,
   Therefore henceforth be at your keeping well,° *be well on your guard*
   And ever ready for your foeman fell.
15 The sparke of noble courage now awake,
   And strive your excellent selfe to excell;
   That shall ye evermore renowmèd make,
Above all knights on earth, that batteill undertake."

3

And pointing forth, "lo yonder is," said she,
20 "The brasen towre in which my parents deare
   For dread of that huge feend emprisond be,
   Whom I from far see on the walles appeare,
   Whose sight my feeble soule doth greatly cheare:
   And on the top of all I do espye
25 The watchman wayting tydings glad to heare,
   That O my parents might I happily
Unto you bring, to ease you of your misery."

4

With that they heard a roaring hideous sound,
   That all the ayre with terrour fillèd wide,
30 And seemd uneath° to shake the stedfast ground.   *almost*
   Eftsoones that dreadfull Dragon they espide,
   Where stretcht he lay upon the sunny side
   Of a great hill, himselfe like a great hill.
   But all so soone, as he from far descride

---

3. I.e., to restore their kingdom, laid waste (by the dragon).

35   Those glistring armes, that heaven with light did fill,
    He rousd himselfe full blith,° and hastned them untill.° *joyfully/toward*

5

   Then bad the knight his Lady yede° aloofe,   *go*
    And to an hill her selfe withdraw aside,
    From whence she might behold that battailles proof° *outcome*
40   And eke° be safe from daunger far descryde: *also*
    She him obayd, and turnd a little wyde.°   *aside*
    Now O thou sacred Muse, most learnèd Dame,
    Faire ympe° of Phoebus, and his aged bride,[4] *child*
    The Nourse of time, and everlasting fame,
45   That warlike hands ennoblest with immortall name;

6

   O gently come into my feeble brest,
    Come gently, but not with that mighty rage,
    Wherewith the martiall troupes thou doest infest,° *arouse*
    And harts of great Heroës doest enrage,
50   That nought their kindled courage may aswage,
    Soone as thy dreadfull trompe° begins to sownd; *trumpet*
    The God of warre with his fiers equipage
    Thou doest awake, sleepe never he so sownd,° *sound*
    And scarèd nations doest with horrour sterne astown.° *appall*

7

55   Faire Goddesse lay that furious fit° aside,   *strain*
    Till I of warres and bloudy Mars do sing[5]
    And Briton fields with Sarazin bloud bedyde,
    Twixt that great faery Queene and Paynim king,
    That with their horrour heaven and earth did ring,
60   A worke of labour long, and endlesse prayse:
    But now a while let downe that haughtie string,
    And to my tunes thy second tenor rayse,[6]
    That I this man of God his godly armes may blaze.° *proclaim*

8

   By this the dreadfull Beast drew nigh to hand,
65   Halfe flying, and halfe footing° in his hast, *walking*
    That with his largenesse measurèd much land,
    And made wide shadow under his huge wast;° *girth*
    As mountaine doth the valley overcast.
    Approching nigh, he rearèd high afore
70   His body monstrous, horrible, and vast,
    Which to increase his wondrous greatnesse more,
   Was swolne with wrath, and poyson, and with bloudy gore.

---

4. I.e., Mnemosyne (memory), mother of the Muses.
5. Perhaps a reference to a projected but unwritten book of *The Faerie Queene.*

6. The "haughtie" (high-pitched) mode would be appropriate to a large-scale epic war; the "second tenor" (lower in pitch) to this present battle.

9

And over, all with brasen scales was armd,
 Like plated coate of steele, so couchèd neare,°   *placed so closely*
75 That nought mote perce,[7] ne might his corse° be harmd   *body*
 With dint of sword, nor push of pointed speare;
 Which as an Eagle, seeing pray appeare,
 His aery Plumes doth rouze,° full rudely dight,° *shake / ruggedly arrayed*
 So shakèd he, that horrour was to heare,
80 For as the clashing of an Armour bright,
Such noyse his rouzèd scales did send unto the knight.

10

His flaggy° wings when forth he did display,   *drooping*
 Were like two sayles, in which the hollow wynd
 Is gathered full, and worketh speedy way:
85 And eke the pennes,° that did his pineons bynd,   *quills*
 Were like mayne-yards, with flying canvas lynd,
 With which whenas him list the ayre to beat,
 And there by force unwonted° passage find,   *unaccustomed*
 The cloudes before him fled for terrour great,
90 And all the heavens stood still amazèd with his threat.

11

His huge long tayle wound up in hundred foldes,
 Does overspred his long bras-scaly backe,
 Whose wreathèd boughts° when ever he unfoldes,   *coils*
 And thicke entangled knots adown does slacke,
95 Bespotted as with shields° of red and blacke,   *scales*
 It sweepeth all the land behind him farre,
 And of three furlongs does but litle lacke;
 And at the point two stings in-fixèd arre,
Both deadly sharpe, that sharpest steele exceeden farre.

12

100 But stings and sharpest steele did far exceed° *i.e., were far exceeded by*
 The sharpnesse of his cruell rending clawes;
 Dead was it sure, as sure as death in deed,°   *in its effect*
 What ever thing does touch his ravenous pawes,
 Or what within his reach he ever drawes.
105 But his most hideous head my toung to tell
 Does tremble: for his deepe devouring jawes
 Wide gapèd, like the griesly° mouth of hell,   *horrid*
Through which into his darke abisse all ravin° fell. *prey, booty*

13

And that° more wondrous was, in either jaw   *what*
110 Three ranckes of yron teeth enraungèd were,
 In which yet trickling bloud and gobbets raw° *chunks of undigested food*

---

7. Nothing might pierce.

Of late° devourèd bodies did appeare,   *recently*
That sight thereof bred cold congealèd feare:
Which to increase, and all at once to kill,
115   A cloud of smoothering smoke and sulphur seare°   *burning*
Out of his stinking gorge° forth steemèd still,   *maw*
That all the ayre about with smoke and stench did fill.

14

His blazing eyes, like two bright shining shields,
Did burne with wrath, and sparkled living fyre;
120   As two broad Beacons, set in open fields,
Send forth their flames farre off to every shyre,°   *shire*
And warning give, that enemies conspyre,
With fire and sword the region to invade;
So flamed his eyne° with rage and rancorous yre:°   *eyes/ire*
125   But farre within, as in a hollow glade,
Those glaring lampes were set, that made a dreadfull shade.

15

So dreadfully he towards him did pas,
Forelifting up aloft his speckled brest,
And often bounding on the brusèd gras,
130   As for great joyance of his newcome guest.
Eftsoones he gan advance his haughtie crest,
As chauffèd° Bore his bristles doth upreare,   *angry*
And shoke his scales to battell readie drest;°   *prepared*
That made the Redcrosse knight nigh quake for feare,
135 As bidding bold defiance to his foeman neare.

16

The knight gan fairely couch° his steadie speare,   *rest, aim*
And fiercely ran at him with rigorous° might: *violent*
The pointed steele arriving rudely° theare,   *roughly*
His harder hide would neither perce, nor bight,
140   But glauncing by forth passèd forward right;
Yet sore amovèd with so puissant push,
The wrathfull beast about him turnèd light,°   *quickly*
And him so rudely passing by, did brush
With his long tayle, that horse and man to ground did rush.

17

145 Both horse and man up lightly rose againe,
And fresh encounter towards him addrest:
But th' idle stroke yet backe recoyld in vaine,
And found no place his° deadly point to rest.   *its*
Exceeding rage enflamed the furious beast,
150   To be avengèd of so great despight;°   *outrage*
For never felt his imperceable brest
So wondrous force, from hand of living wight;
Yet had he provèd° the powre of many a puissant knight.   *tested*

18

Then with his waving wings displayèd wyde,
155   Himselfe up high he lifted from the ground,
  And with strong flight did forcibly divide
  The yielding aire, which nigh too feeble found
  Her flitting° partes, and element unsound,°   *moving / weak*
  To beare so great a weight: he cutting way
160   With his broad sayles, about him soarèd round:
  At last low stouping with unweldie sway,°   *ponderous force*
Snatcht up both horse and man, to beare them quite away.

19

Long he them bore above the subject plaine,°   *i.e., the ground below*
  So farre as Ewghen° bow a shaft may send,   *yewen, of yew*
165   Till struggling strong did him at last constraine,
  To let them downe before his flightès end:
  As hagard° hauke presuming to contend   *untamed*
  With hardie fowle, above his hable might,°   *able power*
  His wearie pounces° all in vaine doth spend,   *claws*
170   To trusse° the pray too heavie for his flight;   *seize*
Which comming downe to ground, does free it selfe by fight.

20

He so disseizèd of his gryping grosse,[8]
  The knight his thrilant° speare againe assayd   *piercing*
  In his bras-plated body to embosse,°   *plunge*
175   And three mens strength unto the stroke he layd;
  Wherewith the stiffe beame quakèd, as affrayd,
  And glauncing from his scaly necke, did glyde
  Close under his left wing, then broad displayd.
  The percing steele there wrought a wound full wyde,
180 That with the uncouth° smart the Monster lowdly cryde.   *unfamiliar*

21

He cryde, as raging seas are wont to rore,
  When wintry storme his wrathfull wreck does threat,
  The rolling billowes beat the ragged shore,
  As they the earth would shoulder from her seat,
185   And greedie gulfe° does gape, as he would eat   *i.e., the sea*
  His neighbour element° in his revenge: *earth*
  Then gin the blustring brethren° boldly threat,   *the winds*
  To move the world from off his stedfast henge,°   *axis*
And boystrous battell make, each other to avenge.

22

190 The steely head stucke fast still in his flesh,
  Till with his cruell clawes he snatcht the wood,
  And quite a sunder broke. Forth flowèd fresh

8. Freed from his formidable grip.

A gushing river of blacke goarie° blood,   *clotted*
That drownèd all the land, whereon he stood;
195   The stream thereof would drive a water-mill.
Trebly augmented was his furious mood
With bitter sense of his deepe rooted ill,°   *injury*
That flames of fire he threw forth from his large nosethrill.

23

His hideous tayle then hurlèd he about,
200   And therewith all enwrapt the nimble thyes°   *thighs*
Of his froth-fomy steed, whose courage stout
Striving to loose the knot, that fast him tyes,
Himselfe in streighter° bandes too rash implyes,⁹   *tighter*
That to the ground he is perforce constraynd
205   To throw his rider: who can° quickly ryse   *did*
From off the earth, with durty bloud distaynd,°   *defiled*
For that reprochfull fall right fowly he disdaynd.

24

And fiercely tooke his trenchand° blade in hand,   *sharp*
With which he stroke so furious and so fell,
210   That nothing seemd the puissance could withstand:
Upon his crest the hardned yron fell,
But his more hardned crest was armd so well,
That deeper dint therein it would not make;¹
Yet so extremely did the buffe° him quell,°   *blow/dismay*
215   That from thenceforth he shund the like to take,
But when he saw them come, he did them still forsake.° *avoid*

25

The knight was wrath to see his stroke beguyld,°   *foiled*
And smote againe with more outrageous might;
But backe againe the sparckling steele recoyld,
220   And left not any marke, where it did light;
As if in Adamant rocke it had bene pight.°   *struck against*
The beast impatient of his smarting wound,
And of so fierce and forcible despight,°   *powerful injury*
Thought with his wings to stye° above the ground; *mount*
225   But his late wounded wing unserviceable found.

26

Then full of griefe and anguish vehement,
He lowdly brayd, that like was never heard,
And from his wide devouring oven sent
A flake° of fire, that flashing in his beard,   *flash*
230   Him all amazd, and almost made affeard;
The scorching flame sore swingèd° all his face,   *singed*
And through his armour all his bodie seard,

---

9. I.e., too quickly entangles.   1. I.e., it could not make a deep gash there.

That he could not endure so cruell cace,°   *plight*
But thought his armes to leave, and helmet to unlace.

27

235   Not that great Champion of the antique world,
      Whom famous Poetes verse so much doth vaunt,
      And hath for twelve huge labours high extold,
      So many furies and sharpe fits did haunt,
      When him the poysoned garment did enchaunt
240   With Centaures bloud, and bloudie verses charmed,
      As did this knight twelve thousand dolours° daunt,   *pains*
      Whom fyrie steele now burnt, that earst° him armed,   *formerly*
That erst him goodly armed, now most of all him harmed.[2]

28

      Faint, wearie, sore, emboylèd, grievèd, brent°   *burned*
245   With heat, toyle, wounds, armes, smart, and inward fire
      That never man such mischiefes° did torment;   *misfortunes*
      Death better were, death did he oft desire,
      But death will never come, when needes require.
      Whom so dismayd when that his foe beheld,
250   He cast to suffer him no more respire,°   *live*
      But gan his sturdie sterne° about to weld,°   *tail/lash*
And him so strongly stroke, that to the ground him feld.

29

      It fortunèd (as faire it then befell)
      Behind his backe unweeting,° where he stood,   *unnoticed*
255   Of auncient time there was a springing well,
      From which fast trickled forth a silver flood,
      Full of great vertues, and for med'cine good.
      Whylome,° before that cursèd Dragon got   *formerly*
      That happie land, and all with innocent blood
260   Defyld those sacred waves, it rightly hot°   *was called*
The Well of Life,[3] ne yet his vertues° had forgot.   *powers*

30

      For unto life the dead it could restore,
      And guilt of sinfull crimes cleane wash away,
      Those that with sicknesse were infected sore,
265   It could recure, and agèd long decay
      Renew, as one were borne that very day.
      Both Silo this, and Jordan did excell,
      And th' English Bath, and eke the german Spau,

2. Redcrosse's fire baptism is compared with the burning shirt of Nessus, which killed Hercules, "that great Champion of the antique world" (line 235). His "twelve huge labours" are paralleled to the knight's "twelve thousand dolours."
3. An allusion to Revelation 22.1–2: "And he showed me a pure river of water of life, clear as crystal, proceeding out of the throne of God, and of the Lamb. In the midst of the street of it, and on either side of the river, was the tree of life which bare twelve manner of fruits and yielded her fruit every month: and the leaves of the tree were for the healing of the nations."

Ne can Cephise, nor Hebrus match this well:
270 Into the same the knight backe overthrowen, fell.[4]

31

Now gan the golden Phoebus for to steepe
His fierie face in billowes of the west,
And his faint steedes watred in Ocean deepe,
Whiles from their journall° labours they did rest,   *daily*
275 When that infernall Monster, having kest°   *cast*
His wearie foe into that living well,
Can° high advaunce his broad discoloured brest,   *did*
Above his wonted pitch,° with countenance fell,°   *height / sinister*
And clapt his yron wings, as victor he did dwell.°   *remain*

32

280 Which when his pensive Ladie saw from farre,
Great woe and sorrow did her soule assay,°   *assail*
As weening that the sad end of the warre,
And gan to highest God entirely° pray,   *earnestly*
That fearèd chaunce° from her to turne away;   *fate*
285 With folded hands and knees full lowly bent
All night she watcht, ne once adowne would lay
Her daintie limbs in her sad dreriment,°   *dismal condition*
But praying still did wake, and waking did lament.

33

The morrow next gan early to appeare,
290 That° Titan° rose to runne his daily race;   *when / the sun god*
But early ere the morrow next gan reare
Out of the sea faire Titans deawy face,
Up rose the gentle virgin from her place,
And lookèd all about, if she might spy
295 Her lovèd knight to move his manly pace:
For she had great doubt of his safety,
Since late she saw him fall before his enemy.

34

At last she saw, where he upstarted brave
Out of the well, wherein he drenchèd lay;
300 As Eagle fresh out of the Ocean wave,
Where he hath left his plumes all hoary gray,
And deckt himselfe with feathers youthly gay,
Like Eyas° hauke up mounts unto the skies,   *young*
His newly budded pineons to assay,
305 And marveiles at himselfe, still as he flies:
So new this new-borne knight to battell new did rise.[5]

4. The Well of Life, with its powers of renewal, is successively compared with waters of the Bible, of England and Europe, and of classical antiquity. In Siloam ("Silo") a blind man was cured by Christ (John 9.7); the crossing of the river Jordan saved the Jews (Deuteronomy 27.2–9), and Christ was baptized therein (Matthew 3.16). "Bath" and "Spau" (Spa) were famed for their medicinal waters. "Cephise" and "Hebrus" in Greece were noted for purifying and healing powers.
5. Legend had it that the eagle could renew its youth by bathing in a spring.

35

Whom when the damnèd feend so fresh did spy,
  No wonder if he wondred at the sight,
  And doubted, whether his late enemy
310 It were, or other new supplièd knight.
  He, now to prove his late renewèd might,
  High brandishing his bright deaw-burning blade,
  Upon his crested scalpe so sore did smite,
  That to the scull a yawning wound it made:
315 The deadly dint° his dullèd senses all dismaid.   *blow*

36

I wote° not, whether the revenging steele   *know*
  Were hardnèd with that holy water dew,
  Wherein he fell, or sharper edge did feele,
  Or his baptizèd hands now greater° grew;   *stronger*
320 Or other secret vertue° did ensew;   *power*
  Else never could the force of fleshly arme,
  Ne molten mettall in his bloud embrew:°   *plunge*
  For till that stownd° could never wight him harme,   *moment*
By subtilty, nor slight,° nor might, nor mighty charme. *trickery*

37

325 The cruell wound enragèd him so sore,
  That loud he yellèd for exceeding paine;
  As hundred ramping Lyons seemed to rore,
  Whom ravenous hunger did thereto constraine:
  Then gan he tosse aloft his stretchèd traine,°   *tail*
330 And therewith scourge the buxome° aire so sore, *yielding*
  That to his force to yeelden it was faine;°   *obliged*
  Ne ought his sturdie strokes might stand afore,[6]
That high trees overthrew, and rocks in peeces tore.

38

The same advancing high above his head,
335 With sharpe intended° sting so rude° him smot, *extended/roughly*
  That to the earth him drove, as stricken dead,
  Ne living wight would have him life behot:[7]
  The mortall sting his angry needle shot
  Quite through his shield, and in his shoulder seasd,
340 Where fast it stucke, ne would there out be got:
  The griefe° thereof him wondrous sore diseasd,° *pain/afflicted*
Ne might his ranckling paine with patience be appeasd.

39

But yet more mindfull of his honour deare,
  Then of the grievous smart, which him did wring,° *torment*
345 From loathèd soile he can° him lightly reare,   *did*

---

6. I.e., neither could anything ("ought") stand
before his violent ("sturdie") strokes.

7. Promised. I.e., no one would have thought he
could survive the blow.

And strove to loose the farre infixèd sting:
Which when in vaine he tryde with struggeling,
Inflamed with wrath, his raging blade he heft,°   *heaved*
And strooke so strongly, that the knotty string
350 Of his huge taile he quite a sunder cleft,
Five joynts thereof he hewd, and but the stump him left.

40

Hart cannot thinke, what outrage,° and what cryes,   *violent clamor*
With foule enfouldred[8] smoake and flashing fire,
The hell-bred beast threw forth unto the skyes,
355 That all was coverèd with darknesse dire:
Then fraught° with rancour, and engorgèd° ire,   *filled/swollen*
He cast at once him to avenge for all,
And gathering up himselfe out of the mire,
With his uneven wings did fiercely fall
360 Upon his sunne-bright shield, and gript it fast withall.

41

Much was the man encombred with his hold,
In feare to lose his weapon in his paw,
Ne wist yet, how his talents° to unfold;   *talons*
Nor harder was from Cerberus[9] greedie jaw
365 To plucke a bone, then° from his cruell claw   *than*
To reave° by strength the gripèd gage° away: *seize/prize*
Thrise he assayd it from his foot to draw,
And thrise in vaine to draw it did assay,
It booted nought to thinke, to robbe him of his pray.

42

370 Tho° when he saw no power might prevaile,   *then*
His trustie sword he cald to his last aid,
Wherewith he fiercely did his foe assaile,
And double blowes about him stoutly laid,
That glauncing fire out of the yron plaid;
375 As sparckles from the Andvile° use to fly,   *anvil*
When heavie hammers on the wedge are swaid;°   *struck*
Therewith at last he forst him to unty°   *loosen*
One of his grasping feete, him to defend thereby.

43

The other foot, fast fixèd on his shield,
380 Whenas no strength, nor stroks mote° him constraine   *might*
To loose, ne yet the warlike pledge to yield,
He smot thereat with all his might and maine,
That nought so wondrous puissance might sustaine;
Upon the joynt the lucky steele did light,
385 And made such way, that hewd it quite in twaine;
The paw yet missèd not his minisht° might,   *lessened*
But hong still on the shield, as it at first was pight.°   *placed*

---

8. Black as a thundercloud.   9. The dog that guards the mouth of hell.

44

For griefe thereof, and divelish despight,
  From his infernall fournace forth he threw
390   Huge flames, that dimmèd all the heavens light,
  Enrold in duskish smoke and brimstone blew;
  As burning Aetna from his boyling stew°   *cauldron*
  Doth belch out flames, and rockes in peeces broke,
  And ragged ribs of mountaines molten new
395   Enwrapt in coleblacke clouds and filthy smoke,
That all the land with stench, and heaven with horror choke.

45

The heate whereof, and harmefull pestilence
  So sore him noyd,° that forst him to retire   *troubled*
  A little backward for his best defence,
400   To save his bodie from the scorching fire,
  Which he from hellish entrailes did expire.°   *breathe out*
  It chaunst (eternall God that chaunce did guide)
  As he recoylèd backward, in the mire
  His nigh forwearied feeble feet did slide,
405   And downe he fell, with dread of shame sore terrifide.

46

There grew a goodly tree him faire beside,
  Loaden with fruit and apples rosie red,
  As they in pure vermilion had beene dide,
  Whereof great vertues over all were red:°   *everywhere were told*
410   For happie life to all, which thereon fed,
  And life eke everlasting did befall:
  Great God it planted in that blessed sted°   *place*
  With his almightie hand, and did it call
The Tree of Life, the crime of our first fathers fall.[1]

47

415   In all the world like was not to be found,
  Save in that soile, where all good things did grow,
  And freely sprong out of the fruitfull ground,
  As incorrupted Nature did them sow,
  Till that dread Dragon all did overthrow.
420   Another like faire tree eke grew thereby,
  Whereof who so did eat, eftsoones did know
  Both good and ill: O mornefull memory:
That tree through one mans fault hath doen us all to dy.°   *i.e., killed us*

48

From that first tree forth flowd, as from a well,
425   A trickling streame of Balme, most soveraine°   *powerful for cures*

1. Genesis 2.9 describes the Tree of Life and also the Tree of Knowledge of Good and Evil, both of which God planted in the Garden of Eden. The "crime of our first fathers fall" is that Adam, in eating of the second and being banished from Eden, separated himself—and (according to Christian doctrine) us—from the first. The Tree of Life appears again in the New Jerusalem (Revelation 22.2).

    And daintie deare,° which on the ground still fell,   *precious*
    And overflowèd all the fertill plaine,
    As it had deawèd bene with timely° raine: *seasonable*
    Life and long health that gratious° ointment gave,   *full of grace*
430   And deadly woundes could heale, and reare° againe   *raise*
    The senselesse corse appointed° for the grave.   *made ready*
Into that same he fell: which did from death him save.[2]

49

For nigh thereto the ever damnèd beast
    Durst not approch, for he was deadly made,°   *i.e., a child of death*
435   And all that life preservèd, did detest:
    Yet he it oft adventured° to invade.   *attempted*
    By this the drouping day-light gan to fade,
    And yeeld his roome to sad succeeding night,
    Who with her sable mantle gan to shade
440   The face of earth, and wayes of living wight,
And high her burning torch set up in heaven bright.

50

When gentle Una saw the second fall
    Of her deare knight, who wearie of long fight,
    And faint through losse of bloud, moved not at all,
445   But lay as in a dreame of deepe delight,
    Besmeard with pretious Balme, whose vertuous might
    Did heale his wounds, and scorching heat alay,[3]
    Againe she stricken was with sore affright,
    And for his safetie gan devoutly pray;
450 And watch the noyous° night, and wait for joyous day.   *noxious*

51

The joyous day gan early to appeare,
    And faire Aurora from the deawy bed
    Of aged Tithone gan her selfe to reare,[4]
    With rosie cheekes, for shame as blushing red;
455   Her golden lockes for haste were loosely shed
    About her eares, when Una her did marke
    Clymbe to her charet, all with flowers spred,
    From heaven high to chase the chearelesse darke;
With merry note her loud salutes the mounting larke.

52

460 Then freshly up arose the doughtie knight,
    All healèd of his hurts and woundès wide,
    And did himselfe to battell readie dight;°   *prepare*
    Whose early foe awaiting him beside

---

2. The healing balm flowing from the Tree of Life is understood to be Christ's blood, shed to redeem humankind from eternal damnation.
3. Cf. Revelation 2.7, 11: "To him that overcometh will I give to eat of the tree of life" and "He that overcometh shall not be hurt of the second death."
4. Aurora is goddess of the dawn, Tithonus her husband ("aged" because he was granted everlasting life without everlasting youth).

To have devourd, so soone as day he spyde,
465 When now he saw himselfe so freshly reare,
As if late fight had nought him damnifyde,°   *injured*
He woxe° dismayd, and gan his fate to feare;   *grew*
Nathlesse° with wonted rage he him advauncèd neare.   *nevertheless*

53

And in his first encounter, gaping wide,
470 He thought attonce him to have swallowed quight,
And rusht upon him with outragious pride;
Who him r'encountring fierce, as hauke in flight,
Perforce rebutted° backe. The weapon bright   *drove*
Taking advantage of his open jaw,
475 Ran through his mouth with so importune° might,   *violent*
That deepe emperst his darksome hollow maw,
And back retyrd,⁵ his life bloud forth with all did draw.

54

So downe he fell, and forth his life did breath,
That vanisht into smoke and cloudès swift;
480 So downe he fell, that th' earth him underneath
Did grone, as feeble so great load to lift;
So downe he fell, as an huge rockie clift,
Whose false° foundation waves have washt away,   *insecure*
With dreadfull poyse° is from the mayneland rift,°   *falling weight/split*
485 And rolling downe, great Neptune doth dismay;
So downe he fell, and like an heapèd mountaine lay.

55

The knight himselfe even trembled at his fall,
So huge and horrible a masse it seemed;
And his deare Ladie, that beheld it all,
490 Durst not approch for dread, which she misdeemed,°   *misjudged*
But yet at last, when as the direfull feend
She saw not stirre, off-shaking vaine affright,
She nigher drew, and saw that joyous end:
Then God she praysd, and thankt her faithfull knight,
495 That had atchiev'd so great a conquest by his might.

Canto 12 *Summary*   The king and queen of Eden emerge from the castle with all their followers and gaze in wonder at the dead dragon. A great banquet is held in the castle, and Redcrosse and Una are betrothed, though Redcrosse must still fulfill his pledge to serve the Faerie Queene in war for six more years. A messenger arrives bearing a letter from Fidessa (Duessa), in which she charges Redcrosse with breach of promise and seeks to prevent his marriage to Una. Redcrosse explains to the king how he was led astray by Duessa's wicked arts. The messenger is revealed by Una as Archimago and thrown into a dungeon. The king then performs the wedding ceremony. They live in happiness for some time, until Redcrosse must return to the Faerie Queene, leaving Una to mourn.

---

5. I.e., on being drawn back.

From The Second Booke of The Faerie Queene

Contayning
The Legend of Sir Guyon,
or
Of Temperaunce

Summary Book 2 deals with Temperance, a virtue encompassing moderation, balance, and self-discipline. Sir Guyon, the Knight of Temperance, is accompanied for most of his journey by the faithful Palmer, who represents reason. His quest is to capture the lustful enchantress Acrasia, who seduces men and turns them into beasts. On his journey, Guyon must face and overcome a series of challenges involving different kinds of passion and desire: wrath, lust, mirth, ambition, and greed. In the seventh canto he enters the underworld realm of Mammon, god of wealth, and survives three days there without succumbing to any of a host of temptations. This experience leaves him exhausted spiritually and physically. After a sojourn with Prince Arthur in the House of Alma, an allegorical representation of the properly disciplined human body ruled by the rational soul, Guyon and the Palmer resume their quest. Together they travel by boat to Acrasia's Bower of Bliss, passing by a host of dangers and temptations on the way.

From *Canto 12*

[THE BOWER OF BLISS][1]

42

370 Thence passing forth, they shortly do arrive,
 Whereas the Bowre of Blisse was situate;
 A place pickt out by choice of best alive,°   *the best living artisans*
 That natures worke by art can imitate:
 In which what ever in this worldly state
375 Is sweet, and pleasing unto living sense,
 Or that may dayntiest fantasie aggrate,°   *please, satisfy*
 Was pourèd forth with plentifull dispence,°   *liberality*
 And made there to abound with lavish affluence.

43

 Goodly it was enclosèd round about,
380 Aswell their entred guests to keepe within,
 As those unruly beasts to hold without;
 Yet was the fence thereof but weake and thin;
 Nought feard their force, that fortilage° to win,   *fortress*
 But wisedomes powre, and temperaunces might,
385 By which the mightiest things efforcèd bin:°   *are compelled*
 And eke° the gate was wrought of substaunce light, *also*
 Rather for pleasure, then° for battery or fight.   *than*

44

 Yt framèd was of precious yvory,
 That seemd a worke of admirable wit;°   *marvelous skill*

1. The Bower of Bliss, perhaps the most famous of Spenser's symbolic places, has been variously interpreted. Some critics emphasize its aspects of sterility and artifice; others, its seductive and threatening eroticism and idolatry akin to that associated with the New World and Ireland.

390   And therein all the famous history
       Of Jason and Medaea was ywrit;
       Her mighty charmes, her furious loving fit,
       His goodly conquest of the golden fleece,
       His falsèd° faith, and love too lightly flit,°   *violated / altering*
395   The wondred° Argo, which in venturous peece[2]   *admired*
       First through the Euxine seas bore all the flowr of Greece.[3]

45

    Ye might have seene the frothy billowes fry°   *foam*
       Under the ship, as thorough them she went,
       That seemd the waves were into yvory,
400   Or yvory into the waves were sent;
       And other where the snowy substaunce sprent°   *sprinkled*
       With vermell,° like the boyes bloud[4] therein shed,   *vermilion*
       A piteous spectacle did represent,
       And otherwhiles° with gold besprinkelèd;   *elsewhere*
405 Yt seemd th' enchaunted flame, which did Creüsa wed.[5]

46

    All this, and more might in that goodly gate
       Be red; that ever open stood to all,
       Which thither came: but in the Porch there sate
       A comely personage of stature tall,
410   And semblaunce° pleasing, more then naturall,   *appearance*
       That travellers to him seemd to entize;
       His looser° garment to the ground did fall,   *too loose*
       And flew about his heeles in wanton wize,
       Not fit for speedy pace, or manly exercize.

47

415 They in that place him Genius° did call: *presiding spirit*
       Not that celestiall powre,[6] to whom the care
       Of life, and generatiön of all
       That lives, pertaines in charge particulare,
       Who wondrous things concerning our welfare,
420   And strange phantomes doth let us oft forsee,
       And oft of secret ill bids us beware:
       That is our Selfe, whom though we do not see,
       Yet each doth in him selfe it well perceive to bee.

48

    Therefore a God him sage Antiquity
425   Did wisely make, and good Agdistes call:
       But this same was to that quite contrary,

---

2. I.e., adventurous vessel.
3. Jason, in his ship the *Argo*, sought the Golden Fleece of the king of Colchis; the witch Medea, the king's daughter, fell in love with him and used "her mighty charmes" to help him obtain it.
4. Refers to Absyrtus, Medea's younger brother, whose body she cut into pieces and scattered to delay her father's pursuit.

5. Jason later deserted Medea for Creüsa. In revenge, Medea gave the girl a dress that burst into flame when she put it on; the flame consumed and thus "wed" her.
6. I.e., not Agdistes (see next stanza), the god of generation. The true Agdistes appears in the Garden of Adonis canto (3.6, stanzas 31–33).

The foe of life, that good envyes° to all,   *grudges*
That secretly doth us procure° to fall,   *cause*
Through guilefull semblaunts,° which he makes us see.   *illusions*
He of this Gardin had the governall,°   *management*
And Pleasures porter was devizd° to bee,   *appointed*
Holding a staffe in hand for more formalitee.

49

With diverse flowres he daintily was deckt,
And strowèd round about, and by his side
A mighty Mazer bowle[7] of wine was set,
As if it had to him bene sacrifide;°   *consecrated*
Wherewith all new-come guests he gratifide:
So did he eke Sir Guyon passing by:
But he his idle curtesie defide,
And overthrew his bowle disdainfully;
And broke his staffe, with which he charmèd semblants sly.[8]

50

Thus being entred, they behold around
A large and spacious plaine, on every side
Strowed with pleasauns,° whose faire grassy ground   *gardens*
Mantled with greene, and goodly beautifide
With all the ornaments of Floraes° pride,   *goddess of flowers*
Wherewith her mother Art, as halfe in scorne
Of niggard Nature, like a pompous bride
Did decke her, and too lavishly adorne,
When forth from virgin bowre she comes in th' early morne.

51

Thereto the Heavens alwayes Joviall,[9]
Lookt on them lovely,° still in stedfast state,   *lovingly*
Ne° suffred storme nor frost on them to fall,   *nor*
Their tender buds or leaves to violate,
Nor scorching heat, nor cold intemperate
T' afflict the creatures, which therein did dwell,
But the milde aire with season moderate
Gently attempred, and disposd so well,
That still it breathèd forth sweet spirit° and holesome smell.   *breath*

52

More sweet and holesome, then the pleasaunt hill
Of Rhodope, on which the Nimphe, that bore
A gyaunt babe, her selfe for griefe did kill;
Or the Thessalian Tempe, where of yore
Faire Daphne Phoebus hart with love did gore;
Or Ida, where the Gods lov'd to repaire,°   *resort*

---

7. A drinking cup of maple.
8. Raised deceitful apparitions. The rod and bowl are traditional emblems of enchantment (cf.

Duessa's cup, 1.8, stanza 14).
9. Serene and beneficent, as influenced by the planet Jupiter.

When ever they their heavenly bowres forlore;°   *deserted*
Or sweet Parnasse, the haunt of Muses faire;[1]
Or Eden selfe, if ought with Eden mote compaire.

53

Much wondred Guyon at the faire aspect
470   Of that sweet place, yet suffred no delight
To sincke into his sence, nor mind affect,
But passèd forth, and lookt still forward right,°   *straight ahead*
Bridling his will, and maistering his might:
Till that he came unto another gate;
475   No gate, but like one, being goodly dight°   *arrayed*
With boughes and braunches, which did broad dilate°   *spread out*
Their clasping armes, in wanton wreathings intricate.

54

So fashionèd a Porch with rare device,°   *design*
Archt over head with an embracing vine,
480   Whose bounches hanging downe, seemed to entice
All passers by, to tast their lushious wine,
And did themselves into their hands incline,
As freely offering to be gatherèd:
Some deepe empurpled as the Hyacint,[2]
485   Some as the Rubine,° laughing sweetly red,   *ruby*
Some like faire Emeraudes, not yet well ripenèd.

55

And them amongst, some were of burnisht gold,
So made by art, to beautifie the rest,
Which did themselves amongst the leaves enfold,
490   As lurking from the vew of covetous guest,
That the weake bowes,° with so rich load opprest,   *boughs*
Did bowe adowne, as over-burdenèd.
Under that Porch a comely dame did rest,
Clad in faire weedes,° but fowle disorderèd,   *garments*
495   And garments loose, that seemd unmeet for womanhed.°   *womanhood*

56

In her left hand a Cup of gold she held,
And with her right the riper° fruit did reach,   *overripe*
Whose sappy liquor, that with fulnesse sweld,
Into her cup she scruzd,° with daintie breach°   *squeezed/crushing*
500   Of her fine fingers, without fowle empeach,°   *injury*
That so faire wine-presse made the wine more sweet:
Thereof she usd to give to drinke to each,

---

1. The nymph Rhodope, who had a "gyaunt babe," Athos, by Neptune, was turned into a mountain. Daphne, another nymph, charmed Apollo so that he pursued her until she prayed for aid and was turned into a laurel tree. Mount Ida was the scene of the rape of Ganymede by Jupiter, the judgment of Paris, and the gods' vantage point for viewing the Trojan War. Mount Parnassus is the home of the Muses.
2. The hyacinth or jacinth, a sapphire-colored stone.

Whom passing by she happenèd to meet:
It was her guise,° all Straungers goodly so to greet.   *custom*

57

505 So she to Guyon offred it to tast;
    Who taking it out of her tender hond,
    The cup to ground did violently cast,
    That all in peeces it was broken fond,°   *found*
    And with the liquor stainèd all the lond:°   *land*
510   Whereat Excesse exceedingly was wroth,
    Yet no'te° the same amend, ne yet withstond,   *knew not how to*
    But suffered him to passe, all° were she loth;   *although*
Who nought regarding her displeasure forward goth.

58

There the most daintie Paradise on ground,
515   It selfe doth offer to his sober eye,
    In which all pleasures plenteously abound,
    And none does others happinesse envye:
    The painted° flowres, the trees upshooting hye,   *brightly colored*
    The dales for shade, the hilles for breathing space,
520   The trembling groves, the Christall° running by;   *clear stream*
    And that, which all faire workes doth most aggrace,°   *add grace to*
The art, which all that wrought, appearèd in no place.

59

One would have thought (so cunningly, the rude,
    And scornèd parts were mingled with the fine)
525   That nature had for wantonesse ensude°   *imitated*
    Art, and that Art at nature did repine;°   *complain*
    So striving each th' other to undermine,
    Each did the others worke more beautifie;
    So diff'ring both in willes, agreed in fine:°   *in the end*
530   So all agreed through sweete diversitie,
This Gardin to adorne with all varietie.

60

And in the midst of all, a fountaine stood,
    Of richest substaunce, that on earth might bee,
    So pure and shiny, that the silver flood
535   Through every channell running one might see;
    Most goodly it with curious imageree
    Was over-wrought, and shapes of naked boyes,
    Of which some seemd with lively jollitee,
    To fly about, playing their wanton toyes,°   *sports*
540 Whilest others did them selves embay° in liquid joyes.   *bathe*

61

And over all, of purest gold was spred,
    A trayle of yvie in his native hew:
    For the rich mettall was so colourèd,

That wight, who did not well avis'd° it vew,   *carefully*
545   Would surely deeme it to be yvie trew:
      Low his lascivious armes adown did creepe,
      That themselves dipping in the silver dew,
      Their fleecy flowres they tenderly did steepe,
Which° drops of Christall seemd for wantones°   *on which/wantonness*
      to weepe.

62

550 Infinit streames continually did well
      Out of this fountaine, sweet and faire to see,
      The which into an ample laver° fell,   *basin*
      And shortly grew to so great quantitie,
      That like a little lake it seemd to bee;
555   Whose depth exceeded not three cubits[3] hight,
      That through the waves one might the bottom see,
      All pav'd beneath with Jaspar shining bright,
That seemd the fountaine in that sea did sayle upright.

63

And all the margent° round about was set,   *border*
560   With shady Laurell trees, thence to defend°   *ward off*
      The sunny beames, which on the billowes bet,°   *beat*
      And those which therein bathèd, mote offend.°   *harm*
      As Guyon hapned by the same to wend,
      Two naked Damzelles he therein espyde,
565   Which therein bathing, seemèd to contend,
      And wrestle wantonly, ne car'd to hyde,
Their dainty parts from vew of any, which them eyde.

64

Sometimes the one would lift the other quight
      Above the waters, and then downe againe
570   Her plong,° as over maisterèd by might,   *plunge*
      Where both awhile would coverèd remaine,
      And each the other from to rise° restraine;   *rising*
      The whiles their snowy limbes, as through a vele,
      So through the Christall waves appearèd plaine:
575   Then suddeinly both would themselves unhele,°   *uncover*
And th' amarous sweet spoiles to greedy eyes revele.

65

As that faire Starre, the messenger of morne,[4]
      His deawy face out of the sea doth reare:
      Or as the Cyprian goddess,[5] newly borne
580   Of th' Oceans fruitfull froth,° did first appeare: *foam*
      Such seemèd they, and so their yellow heare

---

3. A cubit is about twenty inches (thus the depth is less than five feet).
4. "His" in the next line implies that the reference is not to Venus but to Phosphorus (or Heophorus),
the minor male divinity sometimes identified with the morning star.
5. Venus, one of whose principal shrines was on the island of Cyprus.

Christalline humour° droppèd downe apace.   *clear water*
Whom such when Guyon saw, he drew him neare,
And somewhat gan relent his earnest pace,
585   His stubborne brest gan secret pleasaunce to embrace.

66

The wanton Maidens him espying, stood
    Gazing a while at his unwonted guise;°   *manner*
    Then th' one her selfe low duckèd in the flood,
    Abasht, that her a straunger did avise:°   *see*
590   But th' other rather higher did arise,
    And her two lilly paps aloft displayd,
    And all, that might his melting hart entise
    To her delights, she unto him bewrayed:°   *revealed*
The rest hid underneath, him more desirous made.

67

595   With that, the other likewise up arose,
    And her faire lockes, which formerly were bownd
    Up in one knot, she low adowne did lose:°   *loosen*
    Which flowing long and thick, her cloth'd arownd,
    And th' yvorie in golden mantle gownd:
600   So that faire spectacle from him was reft,°   *taken*
    Yet that, which reft it, no lesse faire was fownd:
    So hid in lockes and waves from lookers theft,
Nought but her lovely face she for his looking left.

68

Withall she laughèd, and she blusht withall,
605   That blushing to her laughter gave more grace,
    And laughter to her blushing, as did fall:
    Now when they spide the knight to slacke his pace,
    Them to behold, and in his sparkling face
    The secret signes of kindled lust appeare,
610   Their wanton meriments they did encreace,
    And to him beckned, to approch more neare,
And shewd him many sights, that courage cold could reare.[6]

69

On which when gazing him the Palmer saw,
    He much rebukt those wandring eyes of his,
615   And counseld well, him forward thence did draw.
    Now are they come nigh to the Bowre of blis
    Of her fond favorites so named amis:
    When thus the Palmer; "Now Sir, well avise;°   *take care*
    For here the end of all our travell is:
620   Here wonnes° Acrasia, whom we must surprise,   *dwells*
Else she will slip away, and all our drift° despise."   *plan, effort*

---

6. That could arouse sexual desire ("courage") when cold.

70

Eftsoones they heard a most melodious sound,
　Of all that mote delight a daintie eare,
　Such as attonce might not on living ground,
625　Save in this Paradise, be heard elswhere:
　Right hard it was, for wight, which did it heare,
　To read,° what manner musicke that mote bee:　　　　　*discern*
　For all that pleasing is to living eare,
　Was there consorted in one harmonee,
630　Birdes, voyces, instruments, windes, waters, all agree.

71

The joyous birdes shrouded in chearefull shade,
　Their notes unto the voyce attempred° sweet;　　　　　*attuned*
　Th' Angelicall soft trembling voyces made
　To th' instruments divine respondence meet:°　　　　　*fitting*
635　The silver sounding instruments did meet°　　　　　*join*
　With the base murmure of the waters fall:
　The waters fall with difference discreet,°　　　*distinct variations*
　Now soft, now loud, unto the wind did call:
　The gentle warbling wind low answerèd to all.

72

640　There, whence that Musick seemèd heard to bee,
　Was the faire Witch her selfe[7] now solacing,
　With a new Lover, whom through sorceree
　And witchcraft, she from farre did thither bring:
　There she had him now layd a slombering,
645　In secret shade, after long wanton joyes:
　Whilst round about them pleasauntly did sing
　Many faire Ladies, and lascivious boyes,
　That ever mixt their song with light licentious toyes.°　　*amorous play*

73

And all that while, right over him she hong,
650　With her false° eyes fast fixèd in his sight,　　　　　*deceitful*
　As seeking medicine, whence she was stong,
　Or greedily depasturing° delight:　　　　　*feeding on*
　And oft inclining downe with kisses light,
　For feare of waking him, his lips bedewd,
655　And through his humid eyes did sucke his spright,
　Quite molten into lust and pleasure lewd;
　Wherewith she sighèd soft, as if his case she rewd.°　　*pitied*

74

The whiles some one did chaunt this lovely lay:[8]
　"Ah see, who so faire thing doest faine° to see,　　　　*delight*

7. Acrasia—whose name means both "excess" and "impotence"—bears many resemblances to Circe (in *Odyssey* 10 as well as the more witchlike and seductive figure in Ovid's *Metamorphoses* 14) and also to the enchantresses of Italian romance who derive from Circe: Acratia in Trissino's *L'Italia liberata* and Armida in Tasso's *Gerusalemme liberata*.

Much of the description in this scene is imitated from Armida's garden.
8. The song ("lay") of stanzas 74 and 75 imitates that in *Gerusalemme liberata* 16.14–15; this is a classic statement of the *carpe florem* theme—pick the flower of youth before it fades.

660 In springing flowre the image of thy day;
    Ah see the Virgin Rose, how sweetly shee
    Doth first peepe forth with bashfull modestee,
    That fairer seemes, the lesse ye see her may;
    Lo see soone after, how more bold and free
665 Her barèd bosome she doth broad display;
    Loe see soone after, how she fades, and falles away.

75

    "So passeth, in the passing of a day,
        Of mortall life the leafe, the bud, the flowre,
        Ne more doth flourish after first decay,
670   That earst° was sought to decke both bed and bowre,   *formerly*
        Of many a Ladie, and many a Paramowre:°   *lover*
        Gather therefore the Rose, whilest yet is prime,°   *(its) springtime*
        For soone comes age, that will her pride deflowre:
        Gather the Rose of love, whilest yet is time,
675   Whilest loving thou mayst lovèd be with equal crime."

76

    He ceast, and then gan all the quire of birdes
        Their diverse notes t' attune unto his lay,
        As in approvance of his pleasing words.
        The constant paire[9] heard all, that he did say,
680   Yet swarvèd not, but kept their forward way,
        Through many covert groves, and thickets close,
        In which they creeping did at last display°   *discover*
        That wanton Ladie, with her lover lose,°   *loose, wanton*
    Whose sleepie head she in her lap did soft dispose.

77

685 Upon a bed of Roses she was layd,
        As faint through heat, or dight to° pleasant sin,   *ready for*
        And was arayd, or rather disarayd,
        All in a vele of silke and silver thin,
        That hid no whit her alablaster skin,
690   But rather shewd more white, if more might bee:
        More subtile web Arachne° cannot spin,   *the spider*
        Nor the fine nets, which oft we woven see
    Of scorchèd deaw, do not in th' aire more lightly flee.° *float*

78

    Her snowy brest was bare to readie spoyle
695   Of hungry eies, which n'ote° therewith be fild,   *could not*
        And yet through languor of her late sweet toyle,
        Few drops, more cleare then Nectar, forth distild,
        That like pure Orient perles[1] adowne it trild,°   *trickled*
        And her faire eyes sweet smyling in delight,
700   Moystened their fierie beames, with which she thrild° *pierced*

---

9. I.e., Guyon and the Palmer.   1. Lustrous pearls of the East.

Fraile harts, yet quenchèd° not; like starry light   *killed*
Which sparckling on the silent waves, does seeme more bright.

79

The young man sleeping by her, seemd to bee
  Some goodly swayne of honorable place,°   *rank*
705   That certès it great pittie was to see
  Him his nobilitie so foule deface;°   *disgrace*
  A sweet regard,° and amiable grace,   *demeanor*
  Mixèd with manly sternnesse did appeare
  Yet sleeping, in his well proportioned face,
710   And on his tender lips the downy heare
Did now but freshly spring, and silken blossomes beare.

80

His warlike armes, the idle instruments
  Of sleeping praise,° were hong upon a tree,   *worthiness*
  And his brave shield, full of old moniments,°   *marks of honor*
715   Was fowly ra'st,° that none the signes might see;   *erased*
  Ne for them, ne for honour carèd hee,
  Ne ought, that did to his advauncement tend,
  But in lewd loves, and wastfull luxuree,°   *licentiousness*
  His dayes, his goods, his bodie he did spend:
720 O horrible enchantment, that him so did blend.°   *blind*

81

The noble Elfe,[2] and carefull Palmer drew
  So nigh them, minding nought, but lustfull game,
  That suddein forth they on them rusht, and threw
  A subtile net, which onely for the same
725   The skilfull Palmer formally° did frame.   *expressly*
  So held them under fast, the whiles the rest
  Fled all away from feare of fowler shame.
  The faire Enchauntresse, so unwares opprest,°   *surprised*
Tryde all her arts, and all her sleights, thence out to wrest.

82

730 And eke° her lover strove: but all in vaine;   *also*
  For that same net so cunningly was wound,
  That neither guile, nor force might it distraine.°   *tear*
  They tooke them both, and both them strongly bound
  In captive bandes,° which there they readie found: *bonds*
735   But her in chaines of adamant[3] he tyde;
  For nothing else might keepe her safe and sound;
  But Verdant[4] (so he hight°) he soone untyde,   *was called*
And counsell sage in steed° thereof to him applyde.   *instead*

---

2. Knight of Faerie Land, here, Guyon.
3. Steel or some other extremely hard substance.

4. His name, meaning "green," points to aspects of his nature.

83

But all those pleasant bowres and Pallace brave,°   *splendid*
740 Guyon broke downe, with rigour pittilesse;
Ne ought their goodly workmanship might save
Them from the tempest of his wrathfulnesse,
But that their blisse he turn'd to balefulnesse:°   *distress*
Their groves he feld, their gardins did deface,
745 Their arbers spoyle, their Cabinets° suppresse,   *bowers*
Their banket° houses burne, their buildings race,°   *banquet / raze*
And of the fairest late, now made the fowlest place.

84

Then led they her away, and eke that knight
They with them led, both sorrowfull and sad:
750 The way they came, the same retourn'd they right,
Till they arrivèd, where they lately had
Charm'd those wild-beasts, that rag'd with furie mad.
Which now awaking, fierce at them gan fly,
As in their mistresse reskew, whom they lad;°   *led*
755 But them the Palmer soone did pacify.
Then Guyon askt, what meant those beastes, which there did ly.

85

Said he, "These seeming beasts are men indeed,
Whom this Enchauntresse hath transformèd thus,
Whylome° her lovers, which her lusts did feed,   *formerly*
760 Now turnèd into figures hideous,
According to their mindes like monstruous."⁵
"Sad end," quoth he, "of life intemperate,
And mournefull meed° of joyes delicious: *reward*
But Palmer, if it mote thee so aggrate,°   *please*
765 Let them returnèd be unto their former state."

86

Streight way he with his vertuous° staffe them strooke,   *powerful*
And streight of beasts they comely men became;
Yet being men they did unmanly looke,
And starèd ghastly, some for inward shame,
770 And some for wrath, to see their captive Dame:
But one above the rest in speciall,
That had an hog beene late, hight° Grille⁶ by name,   *called*
Repinèd greatly, and did him miscall,°   *revile*
That had from hoggish forme him brought to naturall.

87

775 Said Guyon, "See the mind of beastly man,
That hath so soone forgot the excellence
Of his creation, when he life began,

---

5. Even as their own minds were similarly monstrous. Circe changed Odysseus's companions into animals, but Odysseus had a charm to release them.

6. According to one of Plutarch's dialogues, a man named Gryllus ("fierce," "cruel"), having been changed into a hog by Circe, refused to be restored to human form by Odysseus.

That now he chooseth, with vile difference,°   *preference*
To be a beast, and lacke intelligence."
780   To whom the Palmer thus, "The donghill kind
Delights in filth and foule incontinence:
Let Grill be Grill, and have his hoggish mind,
But let us hence depart, whilest wether serves and wind."

1590, 1596

Amoretti and Epithalamion

In the early 1590s the widowed Spenser wooed and won Elizabeth Boyle, who became his wife in 1594. The next year he published a small volume that included the sonnet sequence *Amoretti* ("little loves" or "little cupids") and the *Epithalamion*. Several of the sonnets explicitly address an "Elizabeth," and the volume's subtitle, "Written not long since," suggest that these poems, taken together, are a portrait of Spenser's recent courtship and marriage. It was unusual to write sonnets about a happy and successful love; traditionally, the sonneteer's love was for someone painfully inaccessible. Spenser rehearses some of the conventional motifs of frustration and longing, but his cycle of polished, eloquent poems leads toward joyous possession. Thus, for example, in sonnet 67 ("Lyke as a huntman after weary chace"), he transforms a Petrarchan lament into a vision of unexpected fulfillment.

Spenser's great celebration of this fulfillment is the *Epithalamion*. A learned poet, he was acutely conscious that he was writing within a tradition: an epithalamion is a wedding song whose Greek name conveys that it was sung on the threshold of the bridal chamber. The genre, which goes back at least as far as Sappho (ca. 612 B.C.E.), was widely practiced by the Latin poets, particularly Catullus, and imitated in the Renaissance. Its elements typically include an invocation of the Muses, followed by a celebratory description of the procession of the bride, the religious rites, the singing and dancing at the wedding party, the preparations for the wedding night, and the sexual consummation of the marriage.

In long, flowing stanzas, Spenser follows these conventions closely, adapting them with exquisite delicacy to his small-town Irish setting and native folklore. But his first stanza announces a major innovation: "So I unto myselfe alone will sing." Traditionally, the poet of an epithalamion was an admiring observer, a kind of master of ceremonies; by combining the roles of poet and bridegroom, Spenser transforms a genial social performance into a passionate lyric utterance. Equally remarkable innovations are the complex stanza form, for which no direct model has been discovered, and the still more complex overall structure. That structure is a triumph of symbolic patterning; the more scholars have studied it, the more elaborate the order they have uncovered. For example, the poem has exactly 365 long lines (composed of five or more metrical feet) matching the number of days in the year. There are twenty-four stanzas, counting the closing "envoy," matching the hours of one full day. Of these stanzas, the first sixteen describe the course of the day, in which the woods echo the various sounds; the last eight describe the night, a time of silence in which the woods no longer echo. (At the summer solstice [cf. line 266 and note 2] in the latitude of Ireland, night falls after sixteen hours of daylight.)

This subtle and rich poetic structure conjures up not only a single day of celebration but also, beyond this particular event, an orderly, harmonious universe, with a hidden pattern of coherence and regularity. If the *Epithalamion* goes to remarkable lengths to affirm this pattern, it is perhaps because it also registers so insistently all that threatens the enduring happiness of wedded love and indeed of human life itself. The greatest threat is the force over which the poem exercises its greatest power: time.

From Amoretti

Sonnet 1

Happy ye leaves[1] when as those lilly hands,
   Which hold my life in their dead doing° might,   *killing*
   Shall handle you and hold in loves soft bands,°   *bonds*
   Lyke captives trembling at the victors sight.
5 And happy lines, on which with starry light,
   Those lamping° eyes will deigne sometimes to look   *flashing*
   And reade the sorrowes of my dying spright,°   *spirit*
   Written with teares in harts close° bleeding book.   *secret*
   And happy rymes bath'd in the sacred brooke
10   Of Helicon[2] whence she derivèd is,
   When ye behold that Angels blessèd looke,
   My soules long lackèd foode, my heavens blis.
   Leaves, lines, and rymes, seeke her to please alone,
   Whom if ye please, I care for other none.

Sonnet 34[3]

Lyke as a ship that through the Ocean wyde,
   By conduct of some star doth make her way,
   Whenas a storme hath dimd her trusty guyde,
   Out of her course doth wander far astray:
5 So I whose star, that wont° with her bright ray   *was accustomed*
   Me to direct, with cloudes is overcast,
   Doe wander now in darknesse and dismay,
   Through hidden perils round about me plast.°   *placed*
   Yet hope I well, that when this storme is past
10   My Helice[4] the lodestar of my lyfe
   Will shine again, and looke on me at last,
   With lovely light to cleare my cloudy grief.
   Till then I wander carefull° comfortlesse,   *full of cares*
   In secret sorow and sad pensivenesse.

Sonnet 54

Of this worlds Theatre in which we stay,
   My love like the Spectator ydly sits
   Beholding me that all the pageants° play,   *roles*
   Disguysing diversly my troubled wits.
5 Sometimes I joy when glad occasion fits,
   And mask in myrth lyke to a Comedy:
   Soone after when my joy to sorrow flits,
   I waile and make my woes a Tragedy.
   Yet she beholding me with constant eye,

---

1. I.e., of the book: pages.
2. The "sacred brooke" is Hippocrene, which flows from Mount Helicon, the mountain sacred to the Muses.
3. An adaptation of Petrarch's *Rima* 189.
4. The Big Dipper or North Star.

10   Delights not in my merth nor rues my smart:°   *pities my hurt*
      But when I laugh she mocks, and when I cry
      She laughes and hardens evermore her hart.
What then can move her? if nor merth nor mone,°   *moan*
      She is no woman, but a sencelesse stone.

Sonnet 64[5]

Comming to kisse her lyps (such grace I found)
      Me seemd I smelt a gardin of sweet flowres
      That dainty odours from them threw around,
      For damzels fit to decke their lovers bowres.
5   Her lips did smell lyke unto Gillyflowers,°   *carnations*
      Her ruddy cheeks lyke unto Roses red;
      Her snowy browes lyke budded Bellamoures,[6]
      Her lovely eyes like Pincks but newly spred,
Her goodly bosome lyke a Strawberry bed,
10   Her neck lyke to a bounch of Cullambynes;
      Her brest lyke lillyes, ere theyr leaves be shed,
      Her nipples lyke yong blossomd Jessemynes.°   *jasmines*
Such fragrant flowres doe give most odorous smell,
      But her sweet odour did them all excell.

Sonnet 67[7]

Lyke as a huntsman after weary chace,
      Seeing the game from him escapt away,
      Sits downe to rest him in some shady place,
      With panting hounds beguilèd of their pray:
5   So after long pursuit and vaine assay,°   *attempt*
      When I all weary had the chace forsooke,
      The gentle deare returnd the selfe-same way,
      Thinking to quench her thirst at the next° brooke.   *nearby*
There she beholding me with mylder looke,
10   Sought not to fly, but fearelesse still did bide:
      Till I in hand her yet halfe trembling tooke,
      And with her owne goodwill hir fyrmely tyde.
Strange thing me seemd to see a beast so wyld,
      So goodly wonne with her owne will beguyld.°   *entangled*

Sonnet 75

One day I wrote her name upon the strand,°   *beach*
      But came the waves and washèd it away:

5. Much of the imagery of this sonnet is imitated from the Song of Solomon 4.10–16.
6. Unidentified flower, evidently white.

7. An imitation of Petrarch's *Rima* 190 but with a very different ending. Cf. Wyatt's *Whoso list to hunt*, p. 340.

Agayne I wrote it with a second hand,
But came the tyde, and made my paynes his pray.°   *prey*
5   "Vayne man," sayd she, "that doest in vaine assay,°   *attempt*
A mortall thing so to immortalize,
For I my selve shall lyke to this decay,
And eek° my name bee wypèd out lykewize."   *also*
"Not so," quod° I, "let baser things devize°   *quoth/contrive*
10   To dy in dust, but you shall live by fame:
My verse your vertues rare shall eternize,
And in the heavens wryte your glorious name.
Where whenas death shall all the world subdew,
Our love shall live, and later life renew."

Sonnet 79

Men call you fayre, and you doe credit° it,   *believe*
For that your selfe ye dayly such doe see:
But the trew fayre,° that is the gentle wit,   *beauty*
And vertuous mind, is much more praysd of me.
5   For all the rest, how ever fayre it be,
Shall turne to nought and loose that glorious hew:°   *form*
But onely that is permanent and free
From frayle corruption, that doth flesh ensew.°   *outlast*
That is true beautie: that doth argue you
10   To be divine and borne of heavenly seed:
Deriv'd from that fayre Spirit,° from whom al true   *i.e., God*
And perfect beauty did at first proceed.
He onely fayre, and what he fayre hath made:
All other fayre, lyke flowres, untymely fade.

1595

Epithalamion

Ye learnèd sisters which have oftentimes
Beene to me ayding, others to adorne:[1]
Whom ye thought worthy of your gracefull rymes,
That even the greatest did not greatly scorne
5   To heare theyr names sung in your simple layes,
But joyèd in theyr prayse.
And when ye list° your owne mishaps to mourne,   *chose*
Which death, or love, or fortunes wreck did rayse,
Your string could soone to sadder tenor° turne,   *mood*
10   And teach the woods and waters to lament
Your dolefull dreriment.°   *sorrow*
Now lay those sorrowfull complaints aside,
And having all your heads with girland crownd,
Helpe me mine owne loves prayses to resound,
15   Ne let the same of° any be envide: *by*

---

1. To write poems in praise of others. The "learned sisters" are the Muses.

So Orpheus did for his owne bride,[2]
So I unto my selfe alone will sing,
The woods shall to me answer and my Eccho ring.

Early before the worlds light giving lampe,
His golden beame upon the hils doth spred,   20
Having disperst the nights unchearefull dampe,
Doe ye awake, and with fresh lustyhed°   *vigor*
Go to the bowre° of my belovèd love,   *bedchamber*
My truest turtle dove,
Bid her awake; for Hymen[3] is awake,   25
And long since ready forth his maske to move,
With his bright Tead[4] that flames with many a flake,°   *spark*
And many a bachelor to waite on him,
In theyr fresh garments trim.
Bid her awake therefore and soone her dight,°   *dress*   30
For lo the wishèd day is come at last,
That shall for al the paynes and sorrowes past,
Pay to her usury° of long delight: *interest*
And whylest she doth her dight,
Doe ye to her of joy and solace sing,   35
That all the woods may answer and your Eccho ring.

Bring with you all the Nymphes that you can
    heare°   *that can hear you*
Both of the rivers and the forrests greene:
And of the sea that neighbours to her neare,
Al with gay girlands goodly wel beseene.°   *beautified*   40
And let them also with them bring in hand,
Another gay girland
For my fayre love of lillyes and of roses,
Bound truelove wize° with a blew silke riband.   *i.e., in a love knot*
And let them make great store of bridale poses,°   *posies*   45
And let them eeke° bring store of other flowers   *also*
To deck the bridale bowers.
And let the ground whereas her foot shall tread,
For feare the stones her tender foot should wrong
Be strewed with fragrant flowers all along,   50
And diapred lyke the discolored mead.[5]
Which done, doe at her chamber dore awayt,
For she will waken strayt,°   *straightway*
The whiles doe ye this song unto her sing,
The woods shall to you answer and your Eccho ring.   55

Ye Nymphes of Mulla[6] which with careful heed,
The silver scaly trouts doe tend full well,
And greedy pikes which use therein to feed,

---

2. Orpheus, archetype of the poet in classical antiquity, was famous for his love for his wife, Eurydice.
3. The god of marriage, who leads a "maske" or procession at weddings.

4. A ceremonial torch, associated with marriages since classical times.
5. Ornamented like the many-colored meadow.
6. The vale of Mulla, near Spenser's home in Ireland.

(Those trouts and pikes all others doo excell)
60   And ye likewise, which keepe the rushy lake,
    Where none doo fishes take,
    Bynd up the locks the which hang scatterd light,
    And in his waters which your mirror make,
    Behold your faces as the christall bright,
65   That when you come whereas° my love doth lie,   *where*
    No blemish she may spie.
    And eke° ye lightfoot mayds which keepe the deere,   *also*
    That on the hoary mountayne use to towre,[7]
    And the wylde wolves which seeke them to devoure,
70   With your steele darts doo chace from comming neer
    Be also present heere,
    To helpe to decke her and to help to sing,
    That all the woods may answer and your Eccho ring.

    Wake, now my love, awake; for it is time,
75   The Rosy Morne long since left Tithones bed,[8]
    All ready to her silver coche° to clyme,   *coach*
    And Phoebus gins to shew his glorious hed.
    Hark how the cheerefull birds do chaunt theyr laies°   *songs*
    And carroll of loves praise.
80   The merry Larke hir mattins° sings aloft,   *morning prayers*
    The thrush replyes, the Mavis descant playes,
    The Ouzell shrills, the Ruddock warbles soft,[9]
    So goodly all agree with sweet consent,
    To this dayes merriment.
85   Ah my deere love why doe ye sleepe thus long,
    When meeter° were that ye should now awake,   *more fitting*
    T' awayt the comming of your joyous make,°   *mate*
    And hearken to the birds lovelearnèd song,
    The deawy leaves among.
90   For they of joy and pleasance to you sing,
    That all the woods them answer and theyr Eccho ring.

    My love is now awake out of her dreame,
    And her fayre eyes like stars that dimmèd were
    With darksome cloud, now shew theyr goodly beams
95   More bright then Hesperus° his head doth rere.   *evening star*
    Come now ye damzels, daughters of delight,
    Helpe quickly her to dight,°   *adorn*
    But first come ye fayre houres which were begot
    In Joves sweet paradice, of Day and Night,
100   Which doe the seasons of the yeare allot,

7. A falconry term meaning to occupy heights. "The deere": all wild animals, kept by the forest nymphs.
8. See Song of Solomon 2.10–13: "Rise up, my love, my fair one, and come away. For, lo, the winter is past, the rain is over and gone; the flowers appear on the earth; the time of the singing of birds is come." In classical myth, Tithonus is the aged husband of Aurora, the dawn.
9. "Descant": a melody or counterpoint written above a musical theme—a soprano obbligato. The "Mavis" is the song thrush; the "Ouzell," the blackbird (which sings in England); and the "Ruddock," the European robin. The birds' concert is a convention of medieval love poetry.

And al that ever in this world is fayre
Doe make and still° repayre.   *continuously*
And ye three handmayds of the Cyprian Queene,[1]
The which doe still adorne her beauties pride,
105   Helpe to addorne my beautifullest bride:
And as ye her array, still throw betweene°   *at intervals*
Some graces to be seene,
And as ye use° to Venus, to her sing,   *are accustomed*
The whiles the woods shal answer and your Eccho ring.

110   Now is my love all ready forth to come,
Let all the virgins therefore well awayt,
And ye fresh boyes that tend upon her groome
Prepare your selves; for he is comming strayt.°   *straightway*
Set all your things in seemly good aray°   *order*
115   Fit for so joyfull day,
The joyfulst day that ever sunne did see.
Faire Sun, shew forth thy favourable ray,
And let thy lifull° heat not fervent be   *life-giving*
For feare of burning her sunshyny face,
120   Her beauty to disgrace.
O fayrest Phoebus, father of the Muse,[2]
If ever I did honour thee aright,
Or sing the thing, that mote° thy mind delight,   *might*
Doe not thy servants simple boone° refuse,   *request*
125   But let this day let this one day be myne,
Let all the rest be thine.
Then I thy soverayne prayses loud wil sing,
That all the woods shal answer and theyr Eccho ring.

Harke how the Minstrels gin° to shrill aloud   *begin*
130   Their merry Musick that resounds from far,
The pipe, the tabor,° and the trembling Croud,[3]   *small drum*
That well agree withouten breach or jar.°   *discord*
But most of all the Damzels doe delite,
When they their tymbrels° smyte,   *tambourines*
135   And thereunto doe daunce and carrol sweet,
That all the sences they doe ravish quite,
The whyles the boyes run up and downe the street,
Crying aloud with strong confusèd noyce,
As if it were one voyce.
140   *Hymen iô Hymen, Hymen*[4] they do shout,
That even to the heavens theyr shouting shrill
Doth reach, and all the firmament doth fill,
To which the people standing all about,
As in approvance doe thereto applaud

1. The Graces attending on Venus ("Cyprian Queene"), representing brightness, joy, and bloom.
2. Phoebus (Apollo), god of the sun, was also god of music and poetry, but he was not normally regarded as the father of the Nine Muses (Zeus was).

3. Primitive fiddle. Spenser here designates Irish, not classical, instruments and music for the classical masque or ballet.
4. The name of the god of marriage, used as a conventional exclamation at weddings.

145 And loud advaunce her laud,°   *praise*
      And evermore they *Hymen Hymen* sing,
      That all the woods them answer and theyr Eccho ring.

      Loe where she comes along with portly° pace   *stately*
      Lyke Phoebe from her chamber of the East,
150 Arysing forth to run her mighty race,[5]
      Clad all in white, that seemes° a virgin best.   *beseems, suits*
      So well it her beseemes that ye would weene°   *think*
      Some angell she had beene.
      Her long loose yellow locks lyke golden wyre,
155 Sprinckled with perle, and perling° flowres a tweene,   *winding*
      Doe lyke a golden mantle her attyre,
      And being crownèd with a girland greene,
      Seeme lyke some mayden Queene.
      Her modest eyes abashèd to behold
160 So many gazers, as on her do stare,
      Upon the lowly ground affixèd are.
      Ne dare lift up her countenance too bold,
      But blush to heare her prayses sung so loud,
      So farre from being proud.
165 Nathlesse doe ye still loud her prayses sing.
      That all the woods may answer and your Eccho ring.

      Tell me ye merchants daughters did ye see
      So fayre a creature in your towne before,
      So sweet, so lovely, and so mild as she,
170 Adornd with beautyes grace and vertues store,
      Her goodly eyes lyke Saphyres shining bright,
      Her forehead yvory white,
      Her cheekes lyke apples which the sun hath rudded,°   *made red*
      Her lips lyke cherryes charming men to byte,
175 Her brest like to a bowle of creame uncrudded,°   *uncurdled*
      Her paps lyke lyllies budded,
      Her snowie necke lyke to a marble towre,
      And all her body like a pallace fayre,
      Ascending uppe with many a stately stayre,
180 To honors seat and chastities sweet bowre.[6]
      Why stand ye still ye virgins in amaze,
      Upon her so to gaze,
      Whiles ye forget your former lay to sing,
      To which the woods did answer and your Eccho ring.

185 But if ye saw that which no eyes can see,
      The inward beauty of her lively spright,°   *living spirit, soul*
      Garnisht with heavenly guifts of high degree,
      Much more then would ye wonder at that sight,

5. Phoebe is the moon, a virgin like the bride; the reference to her anticipates the night.
6. The head, where the higher faculties are. The catalog of qualities is a convention in love poetry (cf. Song of Solomon 4–8).

And stand astonisht lyke to those which red°   *saw*
190 Medusaes mazeful hed.[7]
There dwels sweet love and constant chastity,
Unspotted fayth and comely womanhood,
Regard of honour and mild modesty,
195 There vertue raynes as Queene in royal throne,
And giveth lawes alone.
The which the base° affections doe obay,   *lower*
And yeeld theyr services unto her will,
Ne thought of thing uncomely ever may
Thereto approch to tempt her mind to ill.
200 Had ye once seene these her celestial threasures,
And unrevealèd pleasures,
Then would ye wonder and her prayses sing,
That all the woods should answer and your Eccho ring.

Open the temple gates unto my love,
205 Open them wide that she may enter in,[8]
And all the postes adorne as doth behove,[9]
And all the pillours deck with girlands trim,
For to recyve this Saynt with honour dew,
That commeth in to you.
210 With trembling steps and humble reverence,
She commeth in, before th' almighties vew,
Of her ye virgins learne obedience,
When so ye come into those holy places,
To humble your proud faces:
215 Bring her up to th' high altar, that she may
The sacred ceremonies there partake,
The which do endless matrimony make,
And let the roring Organs loudly play
The praises of the Lord in lively notes,
220 The whiles with hollow throates
The Choristers the joyous Antheme sing,
That all the woods may answere and theyr Eccho ring.

Behold whiles she before the altar stands
Hearing the holy priest that to her speakes
225 And blesseth her with his two happy hands,
How the red roses flush up in her cheekes,
And the pure snow with goodly vermill° stayne,   *vermilion*
Like crimsin dyde in grayne,°   *fast color*
That even th' Angels which continually,
230 About the sacred Altare doe remaine,
Forget their service and about her fly,
Ofte peeping in her face that seemes more fayre,
The more they on it stare.

7. Medusa, one of the Gorgons, had serpents instead of hair (hence a "mazeful hed"): the effect on beholders was to turn them to stone.
8. Cf. Psalm 24.7: "Lift up your heads, O ye gates; and be ye lift up, ye everlasting doors; and the King of glory shall come in."
9. As is proper. The doorposts were trimmed for weddings in classical times, and the custom was often referred to in classical and later love poetry.

But her sad° eyes still fastened on the ground,   *serious*
235 Are governèd with goodly modesty,
That suffers not one looke to glaunce awry,
Which may let in a little thought unsownd.
Why blush ye love to give to me your hand,
The pledge of all our band?°   *bond, tie*
240 Sing ye sweet Angels, Alleluya sing,
That all the woods may answere and your Eccho ring.

Now al is done; bring home the bride againe,
Bring home the triumph of our victory,
Bring home with you the glory of her gaine,[1]
245 With joyance bring her and with jollity.
Never had man more joyfull day then this,
Whom heaven would heape with blis.
Make feast therefore now all this live long day,
This day for ever to me holy is,
250 Poure out the wine without restraint or stay,
Poure not by cups, but by the belly full,
Poure out to all that wull,°   *want it*
And sprinkle all the postes and wals with wine,
That they may sweat, and drunken be withall.
255 Crowne ye God Bacchus° with a coronall,° *god of wine/garland*
And Hymen also crowne with wreathes of vine,
And let the Graces daunce unto the rest;
For they can doo it best:
The whiles the maydens doe theyr carroll sing,
260 To which the woods shall answer and theyr Eccho ring.

Ring ye the bels, ye young men of the towne,
And leave your wonted° labors for this day: *usual*
This day is holy; doe ye write it downe,
That ye for ever it remember may.
265 This day the sunne is in his chiefest hight,
With Barnaby the bright,[2]
From whence declining daily by degrees,
He somewhat loseth of his heat and light,
When once the Crab[3] behind his back he sees.
270 But for this time it ill ordainèd was,
To chose the longest day in all the yeare,
And shortest night, when longest fitter weare:
Yet never day so long, but late° would passe.   *at last*
Ring ye the bels, to make it weare away,
275 And bonefiers° make all day,   *bonfires*
And daunce about them, and about them sing:
That all the woods may answer, and your Eccho ring.

Ah when will this long weary day have end,
And lende me leave to come unto my love?

1. I.e., the glory of gaining her.
2. St. Barnabas's Day, at the time of the summer solstice.
3. The constellation Cancer between Gemini and Leo. The sun, passing through the zodiac, leaves the Crab behind toward the end of July.

280 How slowly do the houres theyr numbers spend?
How slowly does sad Time his feathers move?
Hast thee O fayrest Planet to thy home
Within the Westerne fome:
Thy tyred steedes long since have need of rest.[4]
285 Long though it be, at last I see it gloome,
And the bright evening star° with golden creast°   *Hesperus/crest*
Appeare out of the East.
Fayre childe of beauty, glorious lampe of love
That all the host of heaven in rankes doost lead,
290 And guydest lovers through the nightès dread,
How chearefully thou lookest from above,
And seemst to laugh atweene thy twinkling light
As joying in the sight
Of these glad many which for joy doe sing,
295 That all the woods them answer and theyr Eccho ring.

Now ceasse ye damsels your delights forepast;
Enough is it, that all the day was youres:
Now day is doen, and night is nighing fast:
Now bring the Bryde into the brydall boures.
300 Now night is come, now soone her disaray,
And in her bed her lay;
Lay her in lillies and in violets,
And silken courteins over her display,°   *spread*
And odourd° sheetes, and Arras° coverlets.   *perfumed/tapestry*
305 Behold how goodly my faire love does ly
In proud humility;
Like unto Maia,[5] when as Jove her tooke,
In Tempe,[6] lying on the flowry gras,
Twixt sleepe and wake, after she weary was,
310 With bathing in the Acidalian brooke.[7]
Now it is night, ye damsels may be gon,
And leave my love alone,
And leave likewise your former lay to sing:
The woods no more shall answere, nor your Eccho ring.

315 Now welcome night, thou night so long expected,
That long daies labour doest at last defray,°   *pay for*
And all my cares, which cruell love collected,
Hast sumd in one, and cancellèd for aye:
Spread thy broad wing over my love and me,
320 That no man may us see,
And in thy sable mantle us enwrap,
From feare of perrill and foule horror free.
Let no false treason seeke us to entrap,
Nor any dread disquiet once annoy

---

4. The sun's chariot completes its daily course in the western sea.
5. The eldest and most beautiful of the seven daughters of Atlas. (They were stellified as the Pleiades.) Jove fathered Mercury on her.

6. The Vale of Tempe in Thessaly (not, however, traditionally the site of Jove's encounter with Maia).
7. The Acidalian brook is associated with Venus.

325 The safety of our joy:
But let the night be calme and quietsome,
Without tempestuous storms or sad afray:°   *fear*
Lyke as when Jove with fayre Alcmena[8] lay,
When he begot the great Tirynthian groome:
330 Or lyke as when he with thy selfe[9] did lie,
And begot Majesty.
And let the mayds and yongmen cease to sing:
Ne let the woods them answer, nor theyr Eccho ring.

Let no lamenting cryes, nor dolefull teares,
335 Be heard all night within nor yet without:
Ne let false whispers, breeding hidden feares,
Breake gentle sleepe with misconceivèd dout.°   *fear*
Let no deluding dreames, nor dreadful sights
Make sudden sad affrights;
340 Ne let housefyres, nor lightnings helpelesse harmes,
Ne let the Pouke,[1] nor other evill sprights,
Ne let mischivous witches with theyr charmes,
Ne let hob Goblins, names whose sence we see not,
Fray° us with things that be not.   *terrify*
345 Let not the shriech Oule, nor the Storke be heard:
Nor the night Raven that still° deadly yels,[2]   *continuously*
Nor damnèd ghosts cald up with mighty spels,
Nor griesly° vultures make us once affeard: *horrid*
Ne let th' unpleasant Quyre of Frogs still croking
350 Make us to wish theyr choking.
Let none of these theyr drery accents sing;
Ne let the woods them answer, nor theyr Eccho ring.

But let stil Silence trew night watches keepe,
That sacred peace may in assurance rayne,
355 And tymely Sleep, when it is tyme to sleepe,
May poure his limbs forth on your pleasant playne,
The whiles an hundred little wingèd loves,°   *cupids (or amoretti)*
Like divers fethered doves,
Shall fly and flutter round about your bed,
360 And in the secret darke, that none reproves,
Their prety stealthes shal worke, and snares shal spread
To filch away sweet snatches of delight,
Conceald through covert night.
Ye sonnes of Venus, play your sports at will,
365 For greedy pleasure, carelesse of your toyes,°   *amorous dallying*
Thinks more upon her paradise of joyes,
Then° what ye do, albe it good or ill.   *than*
All night therefore attend your merry play,
For it will soone be day:

8. The mother of Hercules ("the great Tirynthian groome"). Jove made that first night last as long as three.
9. Night. This is Spenser's own myth.
1. Puke, Robin Goodfellow—here more powerful

and evil than Shakespeare made him.
2. The owl and the night raven were birds of ill omen; the stork, in Chaucer's *Parliament of Fowls*, is called an avenger of adultery.

370 Now none doth hinder you, that say or sing,
Ne will the woods now answer, nor your Eccho ring.

Who is the same, which at my window peepes?
Or whose is that faire face, that shines so bright,
Is it not Cinthia,[3] she that never sleepes,
375 But walkes about high heaven al the night?
O fayrest goddesse, do thou not envy
My love with me to spy:
For thou likewise didst love, though now unthought,°   *not thought of*
And for a fleece of woll,° which privily,   *wool*
380 The Latmian shephard[4] once unto thee brought,
His pleasures with thee wrought,
Therefore to us be favorable now;
And sith° of wemens labours thou hast charge,[5]   *since*
And generation goodly dost enlarge,
385 Encline thy will t' effect our wishfull vow,
And the chast wombe informe° with timely seed,   *give life to*
That may our comfort breed:
Till which we cease our hopefull hap° to sing,   *fortune we hope for*
Ne let the woods us answer, nor our Eccho ring.

390 And thou great Juno, which with awful might
The lawes of wedlock still dost patronize,
And the religion° of the faith first plight   *sanctity*
With sacred rites hast taught to solemnize:
And eeke° for comfort often callèd art   *also*
395 Of women in their smart,°   *labor*
Eternally bind thou this lovely band,°   *bond*
And all thy blessings unto us impart.
And thou glad Genius,[6] in whose gentle hand,
The bridale bowre and geniall bed remaine,
400 Without blemish or staine,
And the sweet pleasures of theyr loves delight
With secret ayde doest succour and supply,
Till they bring forth the fruitfull progeny,
Send us the timely fruit of this same night.
405 And thou fayre Hebe,[7] and thou Hymen free,
Grant that it may so be.
Til which we cease your further prayse to sing,
Ne any woods shall answer, nor your Eccho ring.

And ye high heavens, the temple of the gods,
410 In which a thousand torches flaming bright
Doe burne, that to us wretched earthly clods,
In dreadful darknesse lend desirèd light;
And all ye powers which in the same remayne,
More than we men can fayne,°   *imagine*

---

3. Cynthia (or Diana) is goddess of the moon.
4. Endymion, beloved by the moon. The "fleece of woll," however, comes from another story—that of Pan's enticement of the moon.

5. Diana is, as Lucina, patroness of births. The "labours" are, of course, those of childbirth.
6. Patron of sex, pregnancy, and reproduction.
7. Patron of youth and freedom.

415 Poure out your blessing on us plentiously,
     And happy influence upon us raine,
     That we may raise a large posterity,
     Which from the earth, which they may long possesse,
     With lasting happinesse,
420 Up to your haughty pallaces may mount,
     And for the guerdon° of theyr glorious merit   *reward*
     May heavenly tabernacles there inherit,
     Of blessèd Saints for to increase the count.
     So let us rest, sweet love, in hope of this,
425 And cease till then our tymely joyes to sing,
     The woods no more us answer, nor our Eccho ring.

     Song made in lieu of many ornaments,
     With which my love should duly have bene dect,°   *adorned*
     Which cutting off through hasty accidents,
430 Ye would not stay your dew time to expect,°   *await*
     But promist both to recompens,
     Be unto her a goodly ornament,
     And for short time an endlesse moniment.[8]

                                                                      1595

8. The envoy is traditionally apologetic in tone: the poem is offered as a substitute for wedding presents ("ornaments") that did not arrive in time for the wedding. But this elaborate poem is itself a "goodly ornament," for it stands as a timeless monument of art to the passing day that it celebrates.

SIR WALTER RALEGH
1552–1618

The brilliant and versatile Sir Walter Ralegh was a soldier, courtier, philosopher, explorer and colonist, student of science, historian, and poet. Born to West Country gentry of modest means, Ralegh amassed great wealth thanks to his position at court, leading him to be denounced by some as an upstart and hated by others as a rapacious monopolist. He fought ruthlessly in Ireland and Cádiz, directed the colonization of Virginia, introduced the potato to Ireland and tobacco to Europe, brought Spenser from Ireland to the English court, conducted scientific experiments, led expeditions to Guiana in an unsuccessful effort to find gold, and wrote several reports urging England to challenge Spanish dominance in the New World. He was known for his violent temper, his dramatic sense of life, his extravagant dress, his skepticism in religious matters, his bitter hatred of Spain, and his great favor with Queen Elizabeth, interrupted in 1592 when he seduced, and then married, one of her ladies-in-waiting. His long poem to the queen, *The Ocean to Cynthia,* remains in fragments of manuscript, one of more than five hundred lines. His best-known shorter poems include the reply to Marlowe's *Passionate Shepherd* and *The Lie,* an attack on social classes and institutions which itself provoked many replies. His active resistance to printing his poems—in one case he forced a printer to recall a volume and paste a slip of paper over his initials—makes it very difficult to put the copies that circulated in manuscript in any reliable chronological order.

King James suspected Ralegh of opposing his succession and threw him into the Tower of London in 1603 on trumped-up charges of treason; there he remained for the rest of his life save for an ill-fated last voyage to Guiana in 1617, which again failed to discover gold. In prison he wrote his long, unfinished *History of the World*, which begins with the Creation, emphasizes the providential punishment of evil princes, and projects a treatment of English history—although not of recent events because, he declared, he who follows truth too closely at the heels might get kicked in the teeth. The work was to have been dedicated to Henry, prince of Wales, Ralegh's most powerful friend and supporter, who declared, "Only my father would keep such a bird in a cage." But Henry died in 1612, and Ralegh broke off his narrative at 168 B.C.E. Six years later James, bowing to Spanish pressure, had Ralegh executed on the old treason charge.

The Nymph's Reply to the Shepherd

If all the world and love were young,
And truth in every shepherd's tongue,
These pretty pleasures might me move
To live with thee and be thy love.

5   Time drives the flocks from field to fold
When rivers rage and rocks grow cold,
And Philomel° becometh dumb;   *the nightingale*
The rest complains of cares to come.

The flowers do fade, and wanton fields
10 To wayward winter reckoning yields;
A honey tongue, a heart of gall,
Is fancy's spring, but sorrow's fall.

Thy gowns, thy shoes, thy beds of roses,
Thy cap, thy kirtle,° and thy posies   *skirt, outer petticoat*
15 Soon break, soon wither, soon forgotten—
In folly ripe, in reason rotten.

Thy belt of straw and ivy buds,
Thy coral clasps and amber studs,
All these in me no means can move
20 To come to thee and be thy love.

But could youth last and love still breed,
Had joys no date° nor age no need,   *ending*
Then these delights my mind might move
To live with thee and be thy love.

1600

From The History of the World

[CONCLUSION: ON DEATH]

It is * * * Death alone that can suddenly make man to know himself. He tells the proud and insolent that they are but abjects,[1] and humbles them at the instant; makes them cry, complain, and repent, yea, even to hate their forepassed happiness. He takes the account of the rich, and proves him a beggar, a naked beggar, which hath interest in nothing but in the gravel that fills his mouth. He holds a glass before the eyes of the most beautiful, and makes them see therein their deformity and rottenness, and they acknowledge it.

O eloquent, just, and mighty Death! Whom none could advise, thou hast persuaded; what none hath dared, thou hast done; and whom all the world hath flattered, thou only hast cast out of the world and despised; thou hast drawn together all the far-stretched greatness, all the pride, cruelty, and ambition of man, and covered it all over with these two narrow words: *Hic jacet!*[2] * * *

1614

1. Castoffs.
2. Latin for "Here lies," often carved on tombstones.

SIR PHILIP SIDNEY
1554–1586

Knight, soldier, poet, friend, and patron, Sidney seemed to the Elizabethans to embody all the traits of character and personality they admired. When he was killed in battle in the Low Countries at the age of thirty-two, fighting for the Protestant cause against the hated Spanish, all England mourned. Stories, possibly apocryphal, began immediately to circulate about his gallantry on the battlefield—grievously wounded, he gave his water to a dying footsoldier with the words "Thy necessity is yet greater than mine"—and about his astonishing self-composure as he himself lay dying: suffering from his putrifying, gangrenous wound, Sidney composed a song and had it sung by his deathbed. When his corpse was brought back to England for burial, the spectacular funeral procession, one of the most elaborate ever staged, almost bankrupted his father-in-law, Francis Walsingham, the wealthy head of Queen Elizabeth's secret service.

Philip Sidney's father was Sir Henry Sidney, thrice lord deputy (governor) of Ireland, and his mother was a sister of Robert Dudley, earl of Leicester, the most spectacular and powerful of all the queen's favorites. He attended Oxford but left without taking a degree and completed his education by extended travels on the Continent. There he met many of the most important people of the time, from kings and queens to philosophers, theologians, and poets. In France he witnessed the Massacre of St. Bartholomew's Day, which began in Paris on August 24, 1572, and raged through France for more than a month, as Catholic mobs incited by Queen Catherine de Medici slaughtered perhaps 50,000 Huguenots (French Protestants). This experience undoubtedly strengthened Sidney's ardent Protestantism, which had been inculcated by his family background and education. In an intense correspondence with his mentor, the Burgundian humanist Hubert Languet, he brooded on how he could help to save Europe from what he viewed as the Roman Catholic menace.

When he returned to England Sidney found the direct path to heroic action blocked by the caution and hard-nosed realism of Queen Elizabeth and her principal advisers. Though she sent him on some diplomatic missions, the queen clearly regarded the zealous young man with considerable skepticism. As a prominent, well-connected courtier with literary interests, Sidney actively encouraged authors such as Edward Dyer, Fulke Greville, and, most important, the young Edmund Spenser. But he clearly longed to be something more than an influential patron of letters. In 1580 his Protestant convictions led him publicly to oppose Queen Elizabeth's projected marriage to the Catholic duke of Anjou. The queen, who hated interference with her diplomatic maneuvers, angrily dismissed Sidney from the court.

He retired to Wilton, the estate of his beloved and learned sister, Mary Herbert, countess of Pembroke, and there he wrote a long, elaborate epic romance in prose called *Arcadia*. Two other influential works by Sidney have had still more lasting importance. One of these was a major piece of critical prose that was published after his death under two titles, *The Defense of Poesy* and *An Apology for Poetry*. In this long essay Sidney eloquently defends poetry (his term for all imaginative literature) against its attackers and, in the process, greatly exalts the role of the poet, the freedom of the imagination, and the moral value of fiction.

Perhaps Sidney's finest literary achievement is *Astrophil and Stella* ("Starlover and Star"), the first of the major Elizabethan sonnet cycles. The 108 sonnets and eleven songs rely heavily, as do virtually all sonnets in the period, on the conventions established by the great fourteenth-century Italian poet Petrarch and his many Italian, French, and Spanish imitators. These conventions bequeathed a loose framework of plot, marking the stages of a love relationship from its starting point in the lover's attraction to the lady's beauty, through various trials, sufferings, conflicts, and occasional encouragements, to a conclusion in which nothing is resolved. The poet undertook to produce an anatomy of love, displaying its shifting and often contradictory states: hope and despair, tenderness and bitterness, exultation and modesty, bodily desire and spiritual transcendence. Petrarch had deployed a series of ingenious metaphors to describe these states, but by Sidney's time the metaphors—love as a freezing fire, the beloved's glance as an arrow striking the lover's heart, and so forth—had through endless repetition become familiar and predictable.

In an elaborate game of literary masks, psychological risk-taking, and open secrets, Sidney manages to infuse these conventions with an extraordinary vigor and freshness. The sequence of poems, with its dazzling display of technical virtuosity, provides tantalizing glimpses of identifiable characters and, still more, a sustained and remarkably intimate portrait of the poet's inner life. Sidney was hardly indifferent to his privacy: "I assure you before God," he had written once in an angry letter to his father's private secretary, "that if ever I know you do so much as read any letter I write to my father, without his commandment or my consent, I will thrust my dagger into you. And trust to it, for I speak it in earnest." Yet in *Astrophil and Stella* he seems to hold up a mirror to every nuance of his emotional being. The sense of the poet's daring self-exposure, his hinting at intimate psychological and social secrets, has provoked much biographical speculation centered on Sidney's ambiguous relationship with Penelope Devereux, the original of Stella. A marriage between the two had been proposed in 1576 and was talked about for some years, but in 1581 she married Lord Robert Rich, and two years later Sidney also married. (At their high social rank, marriages were negotiated in the interests of the powerful families involved, not of the individuals.) Some of the sonnets contain sly puns on the name *Rich*, and it seems likely that there are autobiographical elements in the shadowy narrative sketched by the work. But the principal focus of the sonnets is not a narrative of events or an unfolding relationship. Rather, *Astrophil and Stella* explores the lover's state of mind and soul, the contradictory impulses, intense desires, and frustrations that haunt him.

In 1585 Sidney tried to join Sir Francis Drake's West Indian expedition but was prevented by the queen; instead, she appointed him governor of Flushing in the Netherlands, where as a volunteer and knight-errant he engaged in several vicious skirmishes in the war against Spain. At Zutphen on September 13, 1586, leading a charge against great odds, Sidney was wounded in the thigh, shortly after he had thrown away his thigh armor in an ill-fated chivalric gesture. He died after lingering for twenty-six days.

Sidney called poetry his "unelected vocation," and, in keeping with the norms of his class, he did not publish any of his major literary works himself. His ambition, continually thwarted, was to be a man of action whose deeds would affect his country's destiny. Yet he was the author of the most ambitious work of prose fiction, the most important piece of literary criticism, and the most influential sonnet cycle of the Elizabethan age.

From Astrophil and Stella

1[1]

Loving in truth, and fain° in verse my love to show,		*desirous*
That the dear She might take some pleasure of my pain,		
Pleasure might cause her read, reading might make her know,		
Knowledge might pity win, and pity grace obtain,		
5 I sought fit words to paint the blackest face of woe,		
Studying inventions fine, her wits to entertain,		
Oft turning others' leaves, to see if thence would flow		
Some fresh and fruitful showers upon my sunburned brain.		
But words came halting forth, wanting Invention's stay;°		*prop*
10 Invention, Nature's child, fled step-dame Study's blows,		
And others' feet still seemed but strangers in my way.		
Thus great with child to speak, and helpless in my throes,		
Biting my trewand° pen, beating myself for spite,		*truant*
"Fool," said my Muse to me, "look in thy heart and write."		

2

Not at first sight, nor with a dribbèd[2] shot		
Love gave the wound, which while I breathe will bleed,		
But known worth did in mine[3] of time proceed,		
Till by degrees it had full conquest got.		
5 I saw and liked, I liked but lovèd not,		
I loved, but straight did not what *Love* decreed;		
At length to Love's decrees, I, forced, agreed,		
Yet with repining at so partial° lot.		*unfair*
Now even that footstep of lost liberty		
10 Is gone, and now like slave-borne Muscovite,[4]		

1. One of six sonnets in the sequence written in hexameters.
2. Ineffectual or at random.
3. Tunnel dug to undermine a besieged fortress.

4. Inhabitant of Muscovy, an important Russian principality ruled from Moscow; 16th-century travel books describe Muscovites as contented slaves.

I call it praise to suffer tyranny;
And now employ the remnant of my wit,°   *intelligence*
  To make myself believe that all is well,
  While with a feeling skill I paint my hell.

6

Some lovers speak, when they their muses entertain,
Of hopes begot by fear, of wot° not what desires,   *know*
Of force of heavenly beams infusing hellish pain,
Of living deaths, dear wounds, fair storms, and freezing fires;⁵
5   Some one his song in Jove, and Jove's strange tales attires,
Broidered with bulls and swans, powdered with golden rain;⁶
Another humbler wit to shepherd's pipe retires,
Yet hiding royal blood full oft in rural vein.⁷
    To some a sweetest plaint a sweetest style affords,⁸
10   While tears pour out his ink, and sighs breathe out his words,
His paper pale despair, and pain his pen doth move.
  I can speak what I feel, and feel as much as they,
  But think that all the map of my state I display,
When trembling voice brings forth that I do Stella love.

20

Fly, fly, my friends, I have my death-wound, fly;
See there that boy, that murth'ring° boy, I say,   *murdering*
Who, like a thief, hid in dark bush doth lie
Till bloody bullet get him wrongful prey.
5   So tyran° he no fitter place could spy,   *tyrant*
Nor so fair level° in so secret stay,°   *aim/stopping place*
As that sweet black° which veils the heav'nly eye;   *pupil*
There himself with his shot he close° doth lay.   *secretly*
  Poor passenger,° pass now thereby I did,   *passerby*
10 And stay'd, pleas'd with the prospect of the place,
While that black hue from me the bad guest hid;
  But straight I saw motions of lightning grace,
    And then descried the glist'ring° of his dart;   *glittering*
    But ere I could fly thence, it pierc'd my heart.

28

You that with allegory's curious frame
  Of others' children changelings use to make,
  With me those pains, for God's sake, do not take;
I list not° dig so deep for brazen fame.   *I don't care to*
5 When I say Stella, I do mean the same
  Princess of beauty for whose only sake

---

5. Conventional Petrarchan oxymorons.
6. I.e., embroidered with mythological figures. Jove courted Europa in the shape of a bull; Leda, as a swan; and Danaë, as a golden shower.
7. Pastoral allegory. By convention, a pastoral

poet pipes his songs on an oaten or reed pipe.
8. Overuse of the word *sweet* in love complaints, with allusion to the very musical *dolce stil nuovo* (sweet new style) associated with Dante and his Italian contemporaries.

The reins of love I love, though never slake,°   slack
And joy therein, though nations count it shame.
I beg no subject to use eloquence,⁹
10   Nor in hid ways do guide philosophy;
Look at my hands for no such quintessence,¹
But know that I in pure simplicity
    Breathe out the flames which burn within my heart,
    Love only reading unto me this art.

31

With how sad steps, O Moon, thou climb'st the skies,
    How silently, and with how wan a face!
    What, may it be that even in heavenly place
That busy archer° his sharp arrows tries?   Cupid
5   Sure, if that long-with-love-acquainted eyes
    Can judge of love, thou feel'st a lover's case;
    I read it in thy looks: thy languished grace,
To me that feel the like, thy state descries.
    Then even of fellowship, O Moon, tell me,
10   Is constant love deemed there but want of wit?
Are beauties there as proud as here they be?
    Do they above love to be loved, and yet
    Those lovers scorn whom that love doth possess?
    Do they call virtue there ungratefulness?²

52

A strife is grown between Virtue and Love,
    While each pretends° that Stella must be his: claims
    Her eyes, her lips, her all, saith Love, do this,
Since they do wear his badge,³ most firmly prove.
5   But Virtue thus that title doth disprove:
    That Stella (O dear name) that Stella is
    That virtuous soul, sure heir of heavenly bliss;
Not this fair outside, which our hearts doth move.
    And therefore, though her beauty and her grace
10   Be Love's indeed, in Stella's self he may
By no pretence claim any manner° place.   kind of
Well, Love, since this demur° our suit⁴ doth stay,°   objection/stop
    Let Virtue have that Stella's self; yet thus,
    That Virtue but° that body grant to us.   only

71

Who will in fairest book of Nature know
    How Virtue may best lodged in beauty be,

---

9. I.e., I don't ask for a topic simply as an excuse to display my rhetorical skills.
1. The mysterious "fifth element" of matter (supplementary to earth, air, fire, and water), which alchemists labored to extract.
2. I.e., is the lady's ingratitude considered virtue in heaven (as here)? Also, is the lover's virtue (fidelity) considered distasteful in heaven (as here)?
3. Device or livery worn to identify someone's (here, Cupid's) servants.
4. "Courtship," in addition to the legal meaning.

Let him but learn of Love to read in thee,
Stella, those fair lines, which true goodness show.
5 There shall he find all vices' overthrow,
     Not by rude force, but sweetest sovereignty
     Of reason, from whose light those night-birds[5] fly;
That inward sun in thine eyes shineth so.
     And not content to be Perfection's heir
10 Thyself, dost strive all minds that way to move,
Who mark° in thee what is in thee most fair.[6]   *perceive*
So while thy beauty draws the heart to love,
     As fast° thy Virtue bends that love to good;   *at the same rate*
     "But, ah," Desire still cries, "give me some food."

72

Desire, though thou my old companion art,
     And oft so clings to my pure Love that I
     One from the other scarcely can descry,°   *distinguish*
While each doth blow the fire of my heart,
5 Now from thy fellowship I needs must part:
     Venus is taught with Dian's wings to fly;[7]
     I must no more in thy sweet passions lie;
Virtue's gold now must head my Cupid's dart.
     Service and honor, wonder with delight,
10 Fear to offend, will worthy to appear,[8]
Care shining in mine eyes, faith in my sprite:°   *spirit*
These things are left me by my only dear;
     But thou, Desire, because thou wouldst have all,
     Now banished art. But yet alas how shall?

74

I never drank of Aganippe well,
     Nor ever did in shade of Tempe[9] sit;
And Muses scorn with vulgar brains to dwell;
Poor layman I, for sacred rites unfit.
5   Some do I hear of Poets' fury° tell,   *inspiration*
     But God wot,° wot not what they mean by it;   *knows*
And this I swear by blackest brook of hell,[1]
I am no pick-purse of another's wit.
     How falls it then that with so smooth an ease
10 My thoughts I speak, and what I speak doth flow
In verse, and that my verse best wits doth please?
Guess we the cause. "What, is it thus?" Fie no.
     "Or so?" Much less. "How then?" Sure thus it is:
     My lips are sweet, inspired with Stella's kiss.[2]

5. The owl, for example, was an emblem of various
vices.
6. I.e., her virtue, which is fairer even than her
beauty.
7. Diana, goddess of the moon and patron of chastity; Venus, goddess of beauty and love, mother of
Cupid.
8. The phrase can mean either "the wish to appear
worthy" or "desire that is worthy to appear [i.e., not

shameful]."
9. Valley beside Mount Olympus, sacred to
Apollo, the god of song. "Aganippe": fountain at
the foot of Mount Helicon in Greece, sacred to the
Muses.
1. The most binding of all oaths were those sworn
by the river Styx.
2. A kiss he stole from Stella when he caught her
napping (Song 2).

108[3]

When Sorrow (using mine own fire's might)
   Melts down his lead into my boiling breast,
   Through that dark furnace to my heart oppressed
There shines a joy from thee, my only light;
5 But soon as thought of thee breeds my delight,
   And my young soul flutters to thee, his nest,
   Most rude Despair, my daily unbidden guest,
Clips straight° my wings, straight wraps me in his night,   *immediately*
   And makes me then bow down my head and say,
10 "Ah, what doth Phoebus'° gold that wretch avail,   *god of the sun*
Whom iron doors do keep from use of day?"
So strangely (alas) thy works in me prevail,
   That in my woes for thee thou art my joy,
   And in my joys for thee my only annoy.

1582?   1591, 1598

Leave me, O Love[1]

Leave me, O Love which reachest but to dust,
And thou my mind aspire to higher things;
Grow rich in that which never taketh rust:
Whatever fades but fading pleasure brings.

5 Draw in thy beams, and humble all thy might
To that sweet yoke where lasting freedoms be;
Which breaks the clouds and opens forth the light,
That doth both shine and give us sight to see.

O take fast hold; let that light be thy guide
10 In this small course which birth draws out to death,
And think how evil becometh him to slide,
Who seeketh heav'n, and comes of heav'nly breath.[2]
   Then farewell world, thy uttermost I see;
   Eternal Love, maintain thy life in me.

ca. 1581   1598

---

3. In many sonnet sequences, as here, the final sonnet brings no resolution.
1. This poem is from *Certain Sonnets*, a miscellany of thirty-two poems (not all of them sonnets in the modern sense) apparently written before *Astrophil and Stella*.
2. I.e., it ill becomes one who has a soul and seeks heaven to "slide" to earthly things.

MARY (SIDNEY) HERBERT, COUNTESS OF PEMBROKE
1562–1621

When her brother, the celebrated courtier and author Philip Sidney, died in 1586, Mary Sidney, the countess of Pembroke, became the custodian not only of his writings but also of his last name. Though her marriage in 1577 to Henry Herbert, the second earl of Pembroke, represented a great social advance for her family—her offspring would no longer be members of the gentry but rather would be among the nation's tiny number of landed aristocrats—yet throughout her life the countess of Pembroke held onto her identity as a Sidney.

She had good reason to do so. The Sidneys were celebrated for their generous support of poets, clergy, alchemists, naturalists, scientists, and musicians. The Pembroke country estate, Wilton, quickly became a gathering place for thinkers who enjoyed the countess's patronage and shared her staunch Protestant convictions and her literary interests. Books, pamphlets, and scores of poems were dedicated in the 1590s and thereafter to her, as well as to her brother Robert (his country house, Penshurst, is praised in a well-known poem by Ben Jonson). Nicholas Breton and Samuel Daniel in particular benefited from her support, as did her niece, goddaughter, and frequent companion, Mary Wroth.

In one of the dedicatory poems to *Salve Deus Rex Judaeorum*, Aemilia Lanyer praises Mary Sidney not only for her generosity toward poets but also for those "works that are more deep and more profound." These include her translation of Robert Garnier's neoclassical French tragedy *Antonius* and a prose translation of the religious tract *A Discourse of Life and Death* by the French Protestant Philippe de Mornay. Her translation of Petrarch's *Triumph of Death* was the first in English to maintain the original *terza rima* (a particularly challenging rhyme scheme for an English versifier). Although translation was considered an especially appropriate genre for women to work in, it is a mistake to assume that Mary Sidney's efforts as a poet are merely derivative: Elizabethans understood that translation offered the opportunity not only for the display of linguistic and technical skills but also for the indirect expression of personal and political concerns. Mary Sidney also expressed these concerns directly: among her original poems was a powerful elegy for her brother Philip and a short pastoral entertainment for Queen Elizabeth.

Mary Sidney was best known for having prepared a composite edition of Philip Sidney's *Arcadia* and for contributing the larger number (107) of the series of 150 poetic translations of the psalms begun by her brother. Her very free renderings recreate the psalms as English poems, using an amazing variety of stanzaic and metrical patterns and some strikingly effective images. This widely circulated and influential volume was an important bridge between the many metrical paraphrases of psalms in this period and the works of the great religious lyric poets of the seventeenth century, especially George Herbert. Donne's poem *Upon the Translation of the Psalms by Sir Philip Sidney and the Countess of Pembroke His Sister* testifies to that importance: "They tell us *why*, and teach us *how* to sing."

To the Angel Spirit of the Most Excellent Sir Philip Sidney[1]

> To thee, pure sprite,° to thee alone's addressed   *spirit*
> This coupled work, by double int'rest thine:

---

1. This is the dedicatory poem to the translation of the Psalms begun by Philip Sidney and completed, after his death, by Mary.

First raised by thy blessed hand, and what is mine
Inspired by thee, thy secret power impressed.°   *i.e., investing her*
5   So dared my Muse with thine itself combine,
As mortal stuff with that which is divine.
Thy light'ning beams give luster to the rest,

That heaven's king may deign his own transformed
In substance no, but superficial tire°   *attire*
10   By thee put on; to praise, not to aspire
To those high tones, so in themselves adorned,
Which angels sing in their celestial choir,
And all of tongues with soul and voice admire
These sacred hymns thy kingly prophet[2] formed.

15   Oh, had that soul which honor brought to rest
Too soon not left, and reft° the world of all   *deprived*
What man could show, which we perfection call,
This half-maimed piece had sorted° with the best.   *consorted, equaled*
Deep wounds enlarged, long festered in their gall,
20   Fresh bleeding smart;° not eye- but heart-tears fall.   *pain, grief*
Ah memory, what needs this new arrest?°   *delay*

Yet here behold (oh, wert thou to behold!)
This° finished now, thy matchless Muse begun,   *the translation*
The rest but pieced, as left by thee undone.
25   Pardon (oh, blessed soul) presumption too too bold,
If love and zeal such error ill become,[3]
'Tis zealous love, love which hath never done,
Nor can enough in world of words unfold.

And sith° it hath no further scope to go,   *since*
30   Nor other purpose but to honor thee,
Thee in thy works, where all the Graces[4] be,
As little streams with all their all do flow
To their great sea, due tribute's grateful fee;
So press my thoughts, my burdened thoughts, in me,
35   To pay the debt of infinites I owe

To thy great worth. Exceeding Nature's store,°   *abundance*
Wonder of men, sole° born perfection's kind,   *alone*
Phoenix[5] thou wert. So rare thy fairest mind,
Heav'nly adorned, Earth justly might adore,
40   Where truthful praise in highest glory shined,
For there alone° was praise to truth confined;   *i.e., in heaven*
And where but there to live forevermore?

---

2. The Old Testament King David, supposed author of the Psalms. Herbert says that in translating the Psalms her brother intended not to rival the originals—which angels sing and which all those learned in ancient languages ("all of tongues") admire—but simply to praise God.
3. I.e., if it's unbecoming for (her) love and zeal to

have presumed to complete the translation.
4. The three Graces of classical mythology, goddesses who presided over all social pleasures and polite accomplishments.
5. The phoenix was a mythical Arabian bird, only one of which existed at any one time. Often associated with Christ, it symbolizes unique perfection.

Oh! When to this accompt,° this cast-up° sum,　　　　　*account / totaled*
　　This reckoning made, this audit of my woe,
45　I call my thoughts, whence so strange passions flow,
　　How works my heart, my senses stricken dumb?
　　　　That would thee[6] more than ever heart could show,
　　　　And all too short:° who knew thee best doth know　　　*inadequate*
　　There lives no wit° that may thy praise become.°　　　*mind / express*

50　Truth I invoke (who scorn elsewhere to move,
　　　Or here in aught my blood should partialize),[7]
　　Truth, sacred Truth, thee sole to solemnize.
　　Those precious rights well known best minds approve;
　　　And who but doth, hath wisdom's open eyes,
55　　Not owly blind the fairest light still flies,
　　Confirm no less?[8] At least 'tis sealed above,°　　　*acknowledged in heaven*

Where thou art fixed among thy fellow lights:
　　My day put out, my life in darkness cast,
　　Thy angel's soul with highest angels placed
60　There blessèd sings enjoying heav'n-delights,
　　Thy maker's praise, as far from earthly taste
　　As here thy works so worthily embraced
By all of worth, where never envy bites.

As goodly buildings to some glorious end
65　Cut off by Fate, before the Graces had
　　Each wond'rous part in all their beauties clad,
　　Yet so much done, as art could not amend;[9]
　　So thy rare works to which no wit can add,
　　In all men's eyes, which are not blindly mad,
70　Beyond compare, above all praise extend.

Immortal monuments of thy fair fame,
　　Though not complete, nor in the reach of thought,
　　How on that passing peacetime would have wrought,
　　Had Heav'n so spared the life of life to frame
75　The rest?[1] But ah, such loss! Hath this world aught
　　Can equal it? Or which like grievance brought?
Yet there will live thy ever-praisèd name.

To which these dearest off'rings of my heart,
　　Dissolved to ink, while pen's impressions move
80　The bleeding veins of never-dying love,
　　I render here: these wounding lines of smart,
　　Sad characters indeed of simple love,
　　Not art nor skill, which abler wits do prove,°　　　*experience*
Of my full soul receive the meanest part.[2]

6. I.e., my thoughts would (if they could) praise
you.
7. I scorn demonstrating partiality to my kinsman.
8. I.e., those who have the open eyes of wisdom—
are not blind like an owl always fleeing the fairest
light—will confirm what I've said about Sidney's
worth.
9. I.e., the part that was completed could not be

improved upon; the same is true of Sidney's unfinished literary works.
1. If heaven had spared your life so that you could
have completed your representation of human life.
2. The least part—all that she, with her limitations
as a writer, is able to express. Professions of a
writer's inadequacy are conventional.

⁸⁵ Receive these hymns,° these obsequies° receive: *the psalms / funeral rites*
    If any mark of thy sweet sprite appear,
    Well are they born; no title else shall bear.
I can no more. Dear soul, I take my leave;
    Sorrow still strives, would mount thy highest sphere,
⁹⁰   Presuming so just cause might meet thee there.³
Oh happy change, could so I take my leave!

ca. 1595   1623

Psalm 52

Tyrant, why swell'st thou thus,
    Of mischief vaunting?
Since help from God to us
    Is never wanting.

⁵ Lewd lies thy tongue contrives,
    Loud lies it soundeth;
Sharper than sharpest knives
    With lies it woundeth.

Falsehood thy wit° approves,   *mind*
¹⁰   All truth rejected:
Thy will all vices loves,
    Virtue neglected.

Not words from cursèd thee,
    But gulfs° are pourèd;   *abysses, yawning chasms*
¹⁵ Gulfs wherein daily be
    Good men devourèd.

Think'st thou to bear it° so?   *bear it off, triumph*
    God shall displace thee;
God shall thee overthrow,
²⁰   Crush thee, deface thee.

The just shall fearing see
    These fearful chances,
And laughing shoot at thee
    With scornful glances.

²⁵ Lo, lo, the wretched wight,
    Who, God disdaining,
His mischief made his might,
    His guard his gaining.°   *riches*

I as an olive tree
³⁰   Still green shall flourish:

---

3. My sorrow would mount to heaven to meet you, presuming that the justness of my cause would allow me (however personally unworthy) entrance there.

God's house the soil shall be
    My roots to nourish.

My trust on his true love
    Truly attending,
35 Shall never thence remove,
    Never see ending.

Thee will I honor still,
    Lord, for this justice;
There fix my hopes I will
40 Where thy saints' trust is.

Thy saints trust in thy name,
    Therein they joy them:
Protected by the same,
    Nought° can annoy° them.   *nothing / harm*

ca. 1595   1823

MICHAEL DRAYTON
1563–1631

Michael Drayton was born about a year before Shakespeare and in the same county, Warwickshire. He had a long career as poet, extending from the early 1590s until well into the seventeenth century. He collaborated on plays, wrote scriptural paraphrases, pastorals, odes, poetic epistles, verse legends, and a historical epic called *The Barons' Wars*. His self-styled masterpiece is *Poly-Olbion,* a thirty-thousand-line historical-geographical poem celebrating all the counties of England and Wales. He made a significant contribution as well to the period's vogue for sonnets, publishing a sequence called *Idea's Mirror* (1594) that, following substantial revision, he republished as *Idea*. It was in fact Drayton's standard practice to revise and add to his poems in each new edition, so that one can trace his response to shifting fashions, his rethinking of his antiquarian fascinations, and his development from an Elizabethan to a seventeenth-century poet.

From Idea

61

Since there's no help, come, let us kiss and part;
Nay, I have done, you get no more of me,
And I am glad, yea glad with all my heart
That thus so cleanly I myself can free.
5 Shake hands forever, cancel all our vows,
And when we meet at any time again,
Be it not seen in either of our brows

That we one jot of former love retain.
Now at the last gasp of love's latest breath,
10   When, his pulse failing, passion speechless lies,
When faith is kneeling by his bed of death,
And innocence is closing up his eyes;
Now if thou wouldst, when all have given him over,
From death to life thou mightst him yet recover.

1619

CHRISTOPHER MARLOWE
1564–1593

The son of a Canterbury shoemaker, Christopher Marlowe was born two months before William Shakespeare. In 1580 he went to Corpus Christi College, Cambridge, on a scholarship that was ordinarily awarded to students preparing for the ministry. He held the scholarship for the maximum time, six years, but did not take holy orders. Instead, he began to write plays. When he applied for his Master of Arts degree in 1587, the university was about to deny it to him on the ground that he intended to go abroad to Rheims, the center of Catholic intrigue and propaganda against Elizabeth, and remain there. But the Privy Council intervened and requested that because Marlowe had done the queen "good service"—evidently as some kind of secret agent—he be granted his degree at the next commencement. "It is not Her Majesty's pleasure," the government officials added, "that anyone employed as he had been in matters touching the benefit of his country should be defamed by those that are ignorant in the affairs he went about." Although much sensational information about Marlowe has been discovered in modern times, we are still largely "ignorant in the affairs he went about." The likeliest possibility is that he served as a spy or *agent provocateur* against English Catholics who were conspiring to overthrow the Protestant regime.

Before he left Cambridge, Marlowe had certainly written his tremendously successful play *Tamburlaine* and perhaps also, in collaboration with his younger Cambridge contemporary, Thomas Nashe, the tragedy of *Dido, Queen of Carthage*. *Tamburlaine* dramatizes the exploits of a fourteenth-century Mongol warrior who rose from humble origins to conquer a huge territory that extended from the Black Sea to Delhi. In some sixteenth-century chronicles, Tamburlaine is represented as God's scourge, the instrument of divine wrath. In Marlowe's play there are few if any glimpses of a transcendent design. His hero is the vehicle for the expression of boundless energy and ambition, the impulse to strive ceaselessly for absolute power. When one of his victims accuses him of bloody cruelty, Tamburlaine answers that strife, restlessness, and unfettered ambition are embedded in the laws of nature and in basic human psychology:

> Nature that framed us of four elements
> Warring within our breasts for regiment,
> Doth teach us all to have aspiring minds;
> Our souls, whose faculties can comprehend
> The wondrous architecture of the world

And measure every wandering planet's course,
Still climbing after knowledge infinite,
And always moving as the restless spheres,
Wills us to wear ourselves and never rest
Until we reach the ripest fruit of all,
That perfect bliss and sole felicity,
The sweet fruition of an earthly crown.

The English theater audience had never before heard such resonant, immensely energetic blank verse. The great period of Elizabethan drama was launched by what Marlowe called his "high astounding terms."

From the time of his first theatrical success, when he was twenty-three, Marlowe had only six years to live. They were not calm years. In 1589 he was involved in a brawl with one William Bradley, in which the poet Thomas Watson intervened and killed Bradley. Both poets were jailed, but Watson got off on a plea of self-defense, and Marlowe was released. In 1591 Marlowe was living in London with the playwright Thomas Kyd, who later, under torture, gave information to the Privy Council accusing him of atheism and treason. On May 30, 1593, at an inn in the London suburb of Deptford, Marlowe was killed by a dagger thrust, purportedly in an argument over the bill. Modern scholars have discovered that the murderer and the others present in the room at the inn had connections to the world of spies, double agents, and swindlers to which Marlowe himself was in some way linked. Those who were arrested in connection with the murder were briefly held and then quietly released.

In the turbulent years before his death at the age of twenty-nine, Marlowe composed five more plays: a sequel to *Tamburlaine*; *The Massacre at Paris*; two major tragedies, *The Jew of Malta* and *Doctor Faustus*; and a chronicle history play about the tragic fate of a homosexual king, *Edward II*.

The Passionate Shepherd to His Love[1]

Come live with me and be my love,
And we will all the pleasures prove°   test, experience
That valleys, groves, hills, and fields,
Woods, or steepy mountain yields.

5   And we will sit upon the rocks,
Seeing the shepherds feed their flocks,
By shallow rivers to whose falls
Melodious birds sing madrigals.

And I will make thee beds of roses
10 And a thousand fragrant posies,
A cap of flowers, and a kirtle°   skirt
Embroidered all with leaves of myrtle;

A gown made of the finest wool
Which from our pretty lambs we pull;
15 Fair linèd slippers for the cold,
With buckles of the purest gold;

1. This pastoral lyric of invitation is one of the most famous of Elizabethan songs, and a few lines from it are sung in Shakespeare's *Merry Wives of* *Windsor*. Many poets have written replies to it, the best known of which is by Sir Walter Ralegh (p. 443).

A belt of straw and ivy buds,
With coral clasps and amber studs:
And if these pleasures may thee move,
20 Come live with me, and be my love.

The shepherd swains shall dance and sing
For thy delight each May morning:
If these delights thy mind may move,
Then live with me and be my love.

1599, 1600

Doctor Faustus

Marlowe's major dramas, *Tamburlaine, The Jew of Malta*, and *Doctor Faustus*, all portray heroes who passionately seek power—the power of rule, the power of money, and the power of knowledge, respectively. Each of the heroes is an overreacher, striving to get beyond the conventional boundaries established to contain the human will.

Unlike Tamburlaine, whose aim and goal is "the sweet fruition of an earthly crown," and Barabas, the Jew of Malta, who lusts for "infinite riches in a little room," Faustus seeks the power and voluptuous pleasure that come from forbidden knowledge. To get this power Faustus must make—or chooses to make—a bargain with Lucifer. This is an old folklore motif, but it would have been taken seriously in a time when belief in the reality of devils was almost universal. The story's power over its original audience is vividly suggested by the numerous accounts of uncanny events at performances of the play: strange noises in the theater or extra devils who suddenly appeared among the actors on stage, causing panic.

In the opening soliloquy, Marlowe's Faustus bids farewell to each of his studies—logic, medicine, law, and divinity—as something he has used up. He turns instead to black magic, but the devil exacts a fearful price in exchange: the eternal damnation of Faustus's soul. This fate would also have been taken literally by an Elizabethan audience. Faustus aspires to be more than a man: "A sound magician is a mighty god," he declares. His fall is caused by the same pride and ambition that caused the fall of the angels in heaven and of humankind in the Garden of Eden. But it is characteristic of Marlowe that he makes those aspirations nonetheless magnificent.

The immediate source of the play is a German narrative called, in its English translation, *The History of the Damnable Life and Deserved Death of Doctor John Faustus*. That source supplies Marlowe's drama with the scenes of horseplay and low practical joking that contrast so markedly with the passages of huge ambition. It is quite possible that these comic scenes are the work of a collaborator; but no other Elizabethan could have written the first scene (with its brilliant representation of the insatiable aspiring mind of the hero), the ecstatic address to Helen of Troy, or the searing scene of Faustus's last hour. And though compared with these celebrated passages, the comic scenes often seem crude, they too contribute to the overarching vision of Faustus's fate: the half-trivial, half-daring exploits, the alternating states of bliss and despair, the questions that are not answered and the answers that bring no real satisfaction, the heroic wanderings that lead nowhere.

Marlowe's play exists in two very different forms: the A text (1604) and the much longer B text (1616), which, according to theatrical records, contains yet more scenes by other hands and which has also been revised to conform to the severe censorship statutes of 1606. We use Roma Gill's edition, based on the A text.

The Tragical History
of Doctor Faustus

DRAMATIS PERSONAE[1]

CHORUS
DR. JOHN FAUSTUS
WAGNER, *his servant, a student*
VALDES
CORNELIUS } *his friends, magicians*
THREE SCHOLARS
GOOD ANGEL
EVIL ANGEL
MEPHASTOPHILIS
LUCIFER
BELZEBUB
OLD MAN
CLOWN
ROBIN
RAFE } *ostlers at an inn*
VINTNER
HORSE-COURSER
THE POPE
THE CARDINAL OF LORRAINE
CHARLES V, EMPEROR OF GERMANY
A KNIGHT *at the* EMPEROR'*s court*
DUKE OF VANHOLT
DUCHESS OF VANHOLT

Spirits presenting
THE SEVEN DEADLY SINS
  PRIDE
  COVETOUSNESS
  WRATH
  ENVY
  GLUTTONY
  SLOTH
  LECHERY
ALEXANDER THE GREAT *and his* PARAMOUR
HELEN OF TROY

ATTENDANTS, FRIARS, *and* DEVILS

Prologue

[*Enter* CHORUS.][2]
CHORUS Not marching now in fields of Thrasimene,
  Where Mars[3] did mate° the Carthaginians,   *join with*
  Nor sporting in the dalliance of love,

1. There is no list of characters in the A text. The one here is an editorial construction.
2. A single actor who recited a prologue to an act or a whole play, and occasionally delivered an epi-logue.
3. God of war. The battle of Lake Trasimene (217 B.C.E.) was one of the Carthaginian leader Hannibal's great victories.

In courts of kings where state° is overturned,   *political power*
5   Nor in the pomp of proud audacious deeds,
     Intends our Muse to vaunt his heavenly verse:
     Only this (Gentlemen) we must perform,
     The form of Faustus' fortunes good or bad.
     To patient judgments we appeal our plaud,°   *applause*
10   And speak for Faustus in his infancy:
     Now is he born, his parents base of stock,
     In Germany, within a town called Rhodes;
     Of riper years to Wittenberg[4] he went,
     Whereas° his kinsmen chiefly brought him up.   *where*
15   So soon he profits in divinity,
     The fruitfull plot of scholarism graced,
     That shortly he was graced with doctor's name,[5]
     Excelling all, whose sweet delight disputes[6]
     In heavenly matters of theology.
20   Till, swollen with cunning,° of a self-conceit,   *knowledge*
     His waxen wings did mount above his reach,
     And melting heavens conspired his overthrow.[7]
     For falling to a devilish exercise,
     And glutted more with learning's golden gifts,
25   He surfeits upon cursed necromancy:°   *black magic*
     Nothing so sweet as magic is to him,
     Which he prefers before his chiefest bliss.[8]
     And this the man[9] that in his study sits.   [*Exit.*]

SCENE 1

[*Enter* FAUSTUS *in his study.*]
FAUSTUS   Settle thy studies, Faustus, and begin
     To sound the depth of that thou wilt profess:
     Having commenced, be a divine in show,[1]
     Yet level° at the end of every art,   *aim*
5   And live and die in Aristotle's works.
     Sweet *Analytics,* 'tis thou hast ravished me:
     Bene disserere est finis logices.[2]
     Is, to dispute well, logic's chiefest end?
     Affords this art no greater miracle?
10   Then read no more, thou hast attained the end;
     A greater subject fitteth Faustus' wit.°   *intellect*
     Bid *on kai me on* farewell; Galen[3] come:
     Seeing, *ubi desinit philosophus, ibi incipit medicus.*[4]
     Be a physician, Faustus, heap up gold,

4. The famous university where Martin Luther studied, as did Shakespeare's Hamlet and Horatio. "Rhodes": Roda, or Stadtroda, in Germany.
5. The lines play on two senses of *graced*: he so (1) adorned the place ("plot") of scholarship—i.e., the university—that shortly he was (2) honored with a doctor's degree.
6. Referring to formal disputations, academic exercises that took the place of examinations.
7. In Greek myth, Icarus flew too near the sun on wings of feathers and wax made by his father, Daedalus; the wax melted, and he fell into the sea and drowned.
8. The salvation of his soul.

9. Apparently a cue for the Chorus to draw aside the curtain to the enclosed space at the rear of the stage.
1. In external appearance. "Commenced": graduated, i.e., received the doctor's degree.
2. To carry on a disputation well is the end or purpose of logic. "*Analytics*": the title of two treatises on logic by Aristotle.
3. The ancient authority on medicine (2nd century C.E.). The Greek means, "Being and not being," i.e., philosophy.
4. Where the philosopher leaves off the physician begins.

15   And be eternized for some wondrous cure.
      Summum bonum medicinae sanitas:[5]
      The end of physic° is our body's health.   *medicine*
      Why Faustus, hast thou not attained that end?
      Is not thy common talk found aphorisms?[6]
20   Are not thy bills° hung up as monuments,   *prescriptions*
      Whereby whole cities have escaped the plague,
      And thousand desperate maladies been eased?
      Yet art thou still but Faustus, and a man.
      Couldst thou make men to live eternally,
25   Or, being dead, raise them to life again,
      Then this profession were to be esteemed.
      Physic farewell! Where is Justinian?[7]
      Si una eademque res legatur duobus,
      Alter rem alter valorem rei, etc.[8]
30   A pretty case of paltry legacies:
      Exhereditare filium non potest pater nisi . . . [9]
      Such is the subject of the Institute,
      And universal body of the law:
      This study fits a mercenary drudge
35   Who aims at nothing but external trash!
      Too servile and illiberal for me.
      When all is done, divinity is best:
      Jerome's Bible,[1] Faustus, view it well:
      Stipendium peccati mors est: ha! *Stipendium, etc.*[2]
40   The reward of sin is death? That's hard.
      Si pecasse negamus, fallimur, et nulla est in nobis veritas.[3]
      If we say that we have no sin,
      We deceive ourselves, and there's no truth in us.
      Why then belike we must sin,
45   And so consequently die.
      Ay, we must die an everlasting death.
      What doctrine call you this? *Che sarà, sarà:*[4]
      What will be, shall be! Divinity, adieu!
      These metaphysics° of magicians,   *basic principles*
50   And necromantic books are heavenly!
      Lines, circles, schemes, letters, and characters!
      Ay, these are those that Faustus most desires.
      O what a world of profit and delight,
      Of power, of honor, of omnipotence
55   Is promised to the studious artisan![5]
      All things that move between the quiet° poles   *unmoving*
      Shall be at my command: emperors and kings
      Are but obeyed in their several provinces,
      Nor can they raise the wind, or rend the clouds;
60   But his dominion that exceeds in this
      Stretcheth as far as doth the mind of man:

---

5. The Latin is translated in the line below.
6. I.e., generally accepted wisdom.
7. Roman emperor and authority on law (483–565 C.E.), author of the *Institutes.*
8. If something is bequeathed to two persons, one shall have the thing itself, the other something of equal value.
9. A father cannot disinherit his son unless . . .

1. The Latin translation, or "Vulgate," of St. Jerome (ca. 340–420 C.E.).
2. Romans 6.23, translated in the line below.
3. 1 John 1.8, translated in the next two lines.
4. Translated in the first half of the next line.
5. A master of the occult arts, such as necromancy.

A sound magician is a mighty god.
Here Faustus, try thy brains to gain a deity.
                    [*Enter* WAGNER.]
Wagner, commend me to my dearest friends,
65   The German Valdes, and Cornelius,
Request them earnestly to visit me.
WAGNER   I will sir.   [*Exit.*]
FAUSTUS   Their conference will be a greater help to me
Than all my labors, plod I ne'er so fast.
                    [*Enter the* GOOD ANGEL *and the* EVIL ANGEL.]
70   GOOD ANGEL   O Faustus, lay that damnèd book aside,
And gaze not on it, lest it tempt thy soul,
And heap God's heavy wrath upon thy head:
Read, read the Scriptures; that is blasphemy.
EVIL ANGEL   Go forward, Faustus, in that famous art,
75   Wherein all nature's treasury is contained:
Be thou on earth as Jove[6] is in the sky,
Lord and commander of these elements.   [*Exeunt.*]
FAUSTUS   How am I glutted with conceit° of this!   *filled with the idea*
Shall I make spirits fetch me what I please,
80   Resolve me of all ambiguities,
Perform what desperate enterprise I will?
I'll have them fly to India[7] for gold,
Ransack the ocean for orient pearl,
And search all corners of the new-found world
85   For pleasant fruits and princely delicates.
I'll have them read me strange philosophy,
And tell the secrets of all foreign kings;
I'll have them wall all Germany with brass,
And make swift Rhine circle fair Wittenberg;[8]
90   I'll have them fill the public schools[9] with silk,
Wherewith the students shall be bravely° clad.   *splendidly*
I'll levy soldiers with the coin they bring,
And chase the Prince of Parma[1] from our land,
And reign sole king of all our provinces.
95   Yea, stranger engines for the brunt of war
Than was the fiery keel at Antwerp's bridge,[2]
I'll make my servile spirits to invent.
Come German Valdes and Cornelius,
And make me blest with your sage conference.
                    [*Enter* VALDES *and* CORNELIUS.]
100   Valdes, sweet Valdes, and Cornelius,
Know that your words have won me at the last
To practise magic and concealed arts;
Yet not your words only, but mine own fantasy,
That will receive no object[3] for my head,

---

6. God, a common substitution in Elizabethan drama.
7. "India" could refer to the West Indies, America, or Ophir (in the east).
8. Wittenberg is in fact on the Elbe River.
9. The university lecture rooms.
1. The duke of Parma was the Spanish governor-

general of the Low Countries, 1579–92.
2. A reference to the burning ship sent by the Netherlanders in 1585 against the barrier on the river Scheldt that Parma had built as a part of the blockade of Antwerp.
3. That will pay no attention to physical reality.

105 But ruminates on necromantic skill.
Philosophy is odious and obscure,
Both law and physic are for petty wits;
Divinity is basest of the three,
Unpleasant, harsh, contemptible, and vile.
110 'Tis magic, magic that hath ravished me.
Then, gentle friends, aid me in this attempt,
And I, that have with concise syllogisms
Graveled° the pastors of the German church,   *confounded*
And made the flowering pride of Wittenberg
115 Swarm to my problems,[4] as the infernal spirits
On sweet Musaeus when he came to hell,
Will be as cunning as Agrippa was,
Whose shadows made all Europe honor him.[5]
  VALDES   Faustus, these books, thy wit, and our experience
120 Shall make all nations to canonize us.
As Indian Moors[6] obey their Spanish lords,
So shall the spirits of every element
Be always serviceable to us three.
Like lions shall they guard us when we please,
125 Like Almaine rutters° with their horsemen's staves,   *German horsemen*
Or Lapland giants trotting by our sides;
Sometimes like women, or unwedded maids,
Shadowing° more beauty in their airy brows   *harboring*
Than in the white breasts of the Queen of Love.
130 From Venice shall they drag huge argosies,
And from America the golden fleece
That yearly stuffs old Philip's° treasury,   *Philip II, king of Spain*
If learnèd Faustus will be resolute.
  FAUSTUS   Valdes, as resolute am I in this
135 As thou to live, therefore object it not.[7]
  CORNELIUS   The miracles that magic will perform
Will make thee vow to study nothing else.
He that is grounded in astrology,
Enriched with tongues,° well seen° in minerals,   *languages/expert*
140 Hath all the principles magic doth require:
Then doubt not, Faustus, but to be renowned
And more frequented for this mystery°   *craft*
Than heretofore the Delphian oracle.[8]
The spirits tell me they can dry the sea,
145 And fetch the treasure of all foreign wrecks,
Ay, all the wealth that our forefathers hid
Within the massy° entrails of the earth.   *massive*
Then tell me, Faustus, what shall we three want?
  FAUSTUS   Nothing, Cornelius. O this cheers my soul!
150 Come, show me some demonstrations magical,
That I may conjure in some lusty° grove,   *flourishing, beautiful*

4. Lectures in logic and mathematics.
5. Musaeus was a mythical singer, son of Orpheus; it was, however, Orpheus who charmed the denizens of hell with his music. Cornelius Agrippa, German author of *The Vanity and Uncertainty of Arts and Sciences* (1530), was popularly supposed to have had the power of calling up the "shadows" or shades of the dead.
6. Dark-skinned native Americans.
7. Do not make it a condition.
8. The oracle of Apollo at Delphi in Greece.

And have these joys in full possessiön.
VALDES   Then haste thee to some solitary grove,
And bear wise Bacon's and Abanus'[9] works,
155   The Hebrew Psalter, and New Testament;
And whatsoever else is requisite
We will inform thee ere our conference cease.
CORNELIUS   Valdes, first let him know the words of art,
And then, all other ceremonies learned,
160   Faustus may try his cunning by himself.
VALDES   First, I'll instruct thee in the rudiments,
And then wilt thou be perfecter than I.
FAUSTUS   Then come and dine with me, and after meat
We'll canvass every quiddity° thereof: essential feature
165   For ere I sleep, I'll try what I can do.
This night I'll conjure,° though I die therefore.   call up spirits
[Exeunt.]

SCENE 2

[Enter two SCHOLARS.]
1 SCHOLAR   I wonder what's become of Faustus, that was wont to
make our schools ring with sic probo.[1]
2 SCHOLAR   That shall we know; for see, here comes his boy.[2]
[Enter WAGNER.]
SCHOLAR   How now sirra, where's thy master?
5   WAGNER   God in heaven knows.
2 SCHOLAR   Why, dost not thou know?
WAGNER   Yes I know, but that follows not.
1 SCHOLAR   Go to sirra, leave your jesting, and tell us where he is.
WAGNER   That follows not necessary by force of argument, that you,
10   being licentiates,[3] should stand upon't; therefore acknowledge your
error, and be attentive.
2 SCHOLAR   Why, didst thou not say thou knew'st?
WAGNER   Have you any witness on't?
1 SCHOLAR   Yes sirra, I heard you.
15   WAGNER   Ask my fellow if I be a thief.
2 SCHOLAR   Well, you will not tell us.
WAGNER   Yes sir, I will tell you; yet if you were not dunces you would
never ask me such a question. For is not he corpus naturale? And
is not that mobile?[4] Then wherefore should you ask me such a ques-
20   tion? But that I am by nature phlegmatic,[5] slow to wrath, and prone
to lechery—to love I would say—it were not for you to come within
forty foot of the place of execution,[6] although I do not doubt to see
you both hanged the next sessions. Thus having triumphed over
you, I will set my countenance like a precisian,[7] and begin to speak
25   thus: Truly my dear brethren, my master is within at dinner with
Valdes and Cornelius, as this wine, if it could speak, it would inform

9. Roger Bacon, the medieval friar and scientist
popularly thought to be a magician, and Pietro
d'Abano, 13th-century alchemist.
1. Thus I prove; a phrase in scholastic disputation.
2. Poor student acting as servant to earn his living.
3. Graduate students.
4. Corpus naturale et mobile ("matter natural and
movable") was a scholastic definition of the subject

matter of physics. Wagner is here parodying the
language of learning at the university.
5. Dominated by the phlegm, one of the four
humors of medieval medicine and psychology.
6. The dining room.
7. Puritan. The rest of his speech is in the style of
the Puritans.

your worships. And so the Lord bless you, preserve you, and keep
you, my dear brethren, my dear brethren.   [*Exit.*]
1 SCHOLAR   Nay then, I fear he is fallen into that damned art, for
30   which they two are infamous through the world.
2 SCHOLAR   Were he a stranger, and not allied to me, yet should I
grieve for him. But come, let us go and inform the Rector,[8] and see
if he by his grave counsel can reclaim him.
1 SCHOLAR   Ay, but I fear me nothing can reclaim him.
35   2 SCHOLAR   Yet let us try what we can do.   [*Exeunt.*]

SCENE 3

[*Enter* FAUSTUS *to conjure.*]
FAUSTUS   Now that the gloomy shadow of the earth,
Longing to view Orion's drizzling look,[9]
Leaps from th'antarctic world unto the sky,
And dims the welkin° with her pitchy breath,   sky
5   Faustus, begin thine incantations,
And try if devils will obey thy hest,
Seeing thou hast prayed and sacrificed to them.
Within this circle[1] is Jehovah's name,
Forward and backward anagrammatized;
10   Th'abbreviated names of holy saints,
Figures of every adjunct to the heavens,
And characters of signs and erring stars,[2]
By which the spirits are enforced to rise.
Then fear not Faustus, but be resolute,
15   And try the uttermost magic can perform.
Sint mihi dei Acherontis propitii! Valeat numen triplex Jehovae!
Ignei, aerii, aquatici, terreni spiritus salvete! Orientis princeps, Bel-
zebub inferni ardentis monarcha, et Demogorgon, propitiamus vos ut
appareat et surgat Mephastophilis. Quid tu moraris? Per Jehovam,
20   *Gehennam, et consecratam aquam quam nunc spargo, signumque*
crucis quod nunc facio, et per vota nostra, ipse nunc surgat nobis
dicatus Mephastophilis.[3]
[*Enter a* DEVIL.]
I charge thee to return and change thy shape,
Thou art too ugly to attend on me;
25   Go and return an old Franciscan friar,
That holy shape becomes a devil best.   [*Exit* DEVIL.]
I see there's virtue° in my heavenly words!   power
Who would not be proficient in this art?
How pliant is this Mephastophilis,
30   Full of obedience and humility,
Such is the force of magic and my spells.

8. The head of a German university.
9. The constellation Orion appears at the beginning of winter. The phrase is a reminiscence of
Virgil.
1. The magic circle drawn on the ground, within
which the magician would be safe from the spirits
he conjured.
2. The moving planets. "Adjunct": heavenly body,
thought to be joined to the solid firmament of the
sky. "Characters of signs": signs of the zodiac and
the planets.

3. May the gods of the lower regions favor me!
Farewell to the Trinity! Hail, spirits of fire, air,
water, and earth! Prince of the East, Belzebub,
monarch of burning hell, and Demogorgon, we
pray to you that Mephastophilis may appear and
rise. What are you waiting for? By Jehovah,
Gehenna, and the holy water that I now sprinkle,
and the sign of the cross that I now make, and by
our vows, may Mephastophilis himself now rise to
serve us.

Now Faustus, thou art conjurer laureate
That canst command great Mephastophilis.
Quin redis, Mephastophilis, fratris imagine![4]
[*Enter* MEPHASTOPHILIS.]
35 MEPHASTOPHILIS Now Faustus, what would'st thou have me do?
FAUSTUS I charge thee wait upon me whilst I live,
To do whatever Faustus shall command,
Be it to make the moon drop from her sphere,
Or the ocean to overwhelm the world.
40 MEPHASTOPHILIS I am a servant to great Lucifer,
And may not follow thee without his leave;
No more than he commands must we perform.
FAUSTUS Did not he charge thee to appear to me?
MEPHASTOPHILIS No, I came now hither of mine own accord.
45 FAUSTUS Did not my conjuring speeches raise thee? Speak!
MEPHASTOPHILIS That was the cause, but yet *per accidens*,[5]
For when we hear one rack[6] the name of God,
Abjure the Scriptures, and his savior Christ,
We fly in hope to get his glorious soul;
50 Nor will we come unless he use such means
Whereby he is in danger to be damned:
Therefore the shortest cut for conjuring
Is stoutly to abjure the Trinity,
And pray devoutly to the prince of hell.
55 FAUSTUS So Faustus hath already done, and holds this principle:
There is no chief but only Belzebub,
To whom Faustus doth dedicate himself.
This word damnation terrifies not him,
For he confounds hell in Elysium:
60 His ghost be with the old philosophers.[7]
But leaving these vain trifles of men's souls,
Tell me, what is that Lucifer thy lord?
MEPHASTOPHILIS Arch-regent and commander of all spirits.
FAUSTUS Was not that Lucifer an angel once?
65 MEPHASTOPHILIS Yes Faustus, and most dearly loved of God.
FAUSTUS How comes it then that he is prince of devils?
MEPHASTOPHILIS O, by aspiring pride and insolence,
For which God threw him from the face of heaven.
FAUSTUS And what are you that live with Lucifer?
70 MEPHASTOPHILIS Unhappy spirits that fell with Lucifer,
Conspired against our God with Lucifer,
And are forever damned with Lucifer.
FAUSTUS Where are you damned?
MEPHASTOPHILIS In hell.
75 FAUSTUS How comes it then that thou art out of hell?
MEPHASTOPHILIS Why this is hell, nor am I out of it.
Think'st thou that I, who saw the face of God,
And tasted the eternal joys of heaven,
Am not tormented with ten thousand hells

---

4. Return, Mephastophilis, in the shape of a friar.
5. The immediate, not ultimate, cause.
6. Torture (by anagrammatizing).

7. Faustus considers hell to be the Elysium of the classical philosophers, not the Christian hell of torment.

80   In being deprived of everlasting bliss?[8]
       O Faustus, leave these frivolous demands,
       Which strike a terror to my fainting soul.
    FAUSTUS What, is great Mephastophilis so passionate
       For being deprivèd of the joys of heaven?
85   Learn thou of Faustus manly fortitude,
       And scorn those joys thou never shalt possess.
       Go bear these tidings to great Lucifer,
       Seeing Faustus hath incurred eternal death
       By desperate thoughts against Jove's deity:
90   Say, he surrenders up to him his soul
       So he will spare him four and twenty years,
       Letting him live in all voluptuousness,
       Having thee ever to attend on me,
       To give me whatsoever I shall ask,
95   To tell me whatsoever I demand,
       To slay mine enemies, and aid my friends,
       And always be obedient to my will.
       Go, and return to mighty Lucifer,
       And meet me in my study at midnight
100   And then resolve me of thy master's mind.[9]
    MEPHASTOPHILIS I will, Faustus.   *[Exit.]*
    FAUSTUS Had I as many souls as there be stars,
       I'd give them all for Mephastophilis.
       By him I'll be great emperor of the world,
105   And make a bridge through the moving air
       To pass the ocean with a band of men;
       I'll join the hills that bind the Afric shore,
       And make that land continent to Spain,
       And both contributory to my crown.
110   The emperor[1] shall not live but by my leave,
       Nor any potentate of Germany.
       Now that I have obtained what I desire,
       I'll live in speculation° of this art   *contemplation*
       Till Mephastophilis return again.   *[Exit.]*

SCENE 4

    [*Enter* WAGNER *and the* CLOWN.[2]]
    WAGNER Sirra boy, come hither.
    CLOWN How, boy? Zounds, boy! I hope you have seen many boys
    with such pickadevants as I have. Boy, quotha![3]
    WAGNER Tell me sirra, hast thou any comings in?[4]
5 CLOWN Ay, and goings out too; you may see else.[5]
    WAGNER Alas poor slave, see how poverty jesteth in his nakedness!
    The villain is bare, and out of service,[6] and so hungry that I know

---

8. This is the punishment of loss of God's presence, which is supposed to be the greatest torment of hell.
9. I.e., give me his decision.
1. The Holy Roman Emperor.
2. Not a court jester (as in some of Shakespeare's plays) but an older stock character, a rustic buffoon.

3. Says he. The point of the clown's retort is that he is a man and wears a beard. "Zounds": an oath, meaning "God's wounds." "Pickadevants": small, pointed beards.
4. Income, but the clown then puns on the literal meaning.
5. I.e., if you don't believe me.
6. Out of a job.

he would give his soul to the devil for a shoulder of mutton, though
it were blood raw.

10 CLOWN   How, my soul to the devil for a shoulder of mutton though
'twere blood raw? Not so good friend; by'rlady,[7] I had need have it
well roasted, and good sauce to it, if I pay so dear.

WAGNER   Well, wilt thou serve me, and I'll make thee go like *qui
mihi discipulus?*[8]

15 CLOWN   How, in verse?

WAGNER   No sirra; in beaten silk and stavesacre.[9]

CLOWN   How, how, knavesacre?[1] Ay I thought that was all the land
his father left him! Do ye hear, I would be sorry to rob you of your
living.

20 WAGNER   Sirra, I say in stavesacre.

CLOWN   Oho, oho, stavesacre! Why then belike, if I were your man,
I should be full of vermin.

WAGNER   So thou shalt, whether thou be'st with me or no. But sirra,
leave your jesting, and bind your self presently unto me for seven

25 years, or I'll turn all the lice about thee into familiars,[2] and they
shall tear thee in pieces.

CLOWN   Do you hear, sir? You may save that labor: they are too familiar with me already—zounds, they are as bold with my flesh as if
they had paid for my meat and drink.

30 WAGNER   Well, do you hear, sirra? Hold, take these guilders.[3]

CLOWN   Gridirons; what be they?

WAGNER   Why, French crowns.[4]

CLOWN   'Mass, but for the name of French crowns a man were as
good have as many English counters![5] And what should I do with

35 these?

WAGNER   Why, now, sirra, thou art at an hour's warning whensoever
or wheresoever the devil shall fetch thee.

CLOWN   No, no, here take your gridirons again.

WAGNER   Truly I'll none of them.

40 CLOWN   Truly but you shall.

WAGNER   Bear witness I gave them him.

CLOWN   Bear witness I give them you again.

WAGNER   Well, I will cause two devils presently to fetch thee away.
Baliol[6] and Belcher!

45 CLOWN   Let your Baliol and your Belcher come here, and I'll knock[7]
them, they were never so knocked since they were devils! Say I
should kill one of them, what would folks say? Do ye see yonder tall
fellow in the round slop?[8] He has killed the devil! So I should be
called "Killdevil" all the parish over.

[*Enter two* DEVILS, *and the* CLOWN *runs up and down crying.*]

50 WAGNER   Baliol and Belcher, spirits, away!   [*Exeunt* DEVILS.]

CLOWN   What, are they gone? A vengeance on them! They have vile
long nails. There was a he devil and a she devil. I'll tell you how

7. An oath: "by Our Lady."
8. You who are my pupil (the opening phrase of a
poem on how students should behave, from Lily's
Latin Grammar, ca. 1509). Wagner means "like a
proper servant of a learned man."
9. A kind of delphinium used for killing vermin.
1. Wordplay, here and below.
2. Familiar spirits, demons.

3. Coins.
4. French crowns, legal tender in England at this
period, were easily counterfeited.
5. Worthless tokens.
6. Probably a corruption of Belial.
7. Beat.
8. Baggy pants. "Tall": fine.

you shall know them: all he devils has horns, and all she devils has clefts and cloven feet.

55 WAGNER Well sirra, follow me.

CLOWN But do you hear? If I should serve you, would you teach me to raise up Banios and Belcheos?

WAGNER I will teach thee to turn thyself to anything, to a dog, or a cat, or a mouse, or a rat, or anything.

60 CLOWN How! A Christian fellow to a dog, or a cat, a mouse, or a rat? No, no sir, if you turn me into anything, let it be in the likeness of a little pretty frisking flea, that I may be here, and there, and everywhere. O I'll tickle the pretty wenches' plackets! I'll be amongst them, i'faith.⁹

65 WAGNER Well sirra, come.

CLOWN But, do you hear, Wagner . . . ?

WAGNER How? Baliol and Belcher!

CLOWN O Lord I pray, sir, let Banio and Belcher go sleep.

WAGNER Villain, call me Master Wagner; and let thy left eye be dia-
70 metarily fixed upon my right heel, with *quasi vestigias nostras insistere*.¹ [Exit.]

CLOWN God forgive me, he speaks Dutch fustian!² Well, I'll follow him, I'll serve him; that's flat. [Exit.]

SCENE 5

[Enter FAUSTUS *in his study*.]

FAUSTUS Now Faustus, must thou needs be damned,
And canst thou not be saved.
What boots° it then to think of God or heaven?   avails
Away with such vain fancies, and despair,
5   Despair in God, and trust in Belzebub.
Now go not backward: no, Faustus, be resolute;
Why waverest thou? O, something soundeth in mine ears:
"Abjure this magic, turn to God again."
Ay, and Faustus will turn to God again.
10   To God? He loves thee not:
The god thou servest is thine own appetite
Wherein is fixed the love of Belzebub.
To him I'll build an altar and a church,
And offer lukewarm blood of newborn babes.
                     [Enter GOOD ANGEL *and* EVIL.]
15 GOOD ANGEL Sweet Faustus, leave that execrable art.

FAUSTUS Contrition, prayer, repentance: what of them?

GOOD ANGEL O they are means to bring thee unto heaven.

EVIL ANGEL Rather illusions, fruits of lunacy,
That makes men foolish that do trust them most.
20 GOOD ANGEL Sweet Faustus, think of heaven, and heavenly things.

EVIL ANGEL No Faustus, think of honor and of wealth.
                     [Exeunt.]
FAUSTUS Of wealth!
Why, the signory of Emden³ shall be mine,

9. In faith. "Plackets": slits in garments—but with an obvious sexual allusion.
1. A pedantic way of saying "Follow my footsteps."

"Diametarily": diametrically.
2. Gibberish.
3. A wealthy German trade center.

When Mephastophilis shall stand by me.
25 What god can hurt thee, Faustus? Thou art safe,
Cast no more doubts. Come, Mephastophilis,
And bring glad tidings from great Lucifer.
Is't not midnight? Come, Mephastophilis:
Veni, veni, Mephastophile![4]
    [*Enter* MEPHASTOPHILIS.]
30 Now tell, what says Lucifer thy lord?
MEPHASTOPHILIS   That I shall wait on Faustus whilst he lives,
So he will buy my service with his soul.
FAUSTUS   Already Faustus hath hazarded that for thee.
MEPHASTOPHILIS   But Faustus, thou must bequeath it solemnly,
35 And write a deed of gift with thine own blood,
For that security craves great Lucifer.
If thou deny it, I will back to hell.
FAUSTUS   Stay, Mephastophilis, and tell me,
What good will my soul do thy lord?
40 MEPHASTOPHILIS   Enlarge his kingdom.
FAUSTUS   Is that the reason he tempts us thus?
MEPHASTOPHILIS   *Solamen miseris socios habuisse doloris.*[5]
FAUSTUS   Have you any pain that tortures others?
MEPHASTOPHILIS   As great as have the human souls of men.
45 But tell me Faustus, shall I have thy soul?
And I will be thy slave and wait on thee,
And give thee more than thou hast wit to ask.
FAUSTUS   Ay Mephastophilis, I give it thee.
MEPHASTOPHILIS   Then stab thine arm courageously,
50 And bind thy soul, that at some certain day
Great Lucifer may claim it as his own,
And then be thou as great as Lucifer.
FAUSTUS   Lo Mephastophilis, for love of thee,
I cut my arm, and with my proper° blood   *own*
55 Assure my soul to be great Lucifer's,
Chief lord and regent of perpetual night.
View here the blood that trickles from mine arm,
And let it be propitious for my wish.
MEPHASTOPHILIS   But Faustus, thou must write it
60 In manner of a deed of gift.
FAUSTUS   Ay, so I will; but, Mephastophilis,
My blood congeals and I can write no more.
MEPHASTOPHILIS   I'll fetch thee fire to dissolve it straight.   [*Exit.*]
FAUSTUS   What might the staying of my blood portend?
65 Is it unwilling I should write this bill?°   *contract*
Why streams it not, that I may write afresh:
"Faustus gives to thee his soul"? Ah, there it stayed!
Why should'st thou not? Is not thy soul thine own?
Then write again: "Faustus gives to thee his soul."
    [*Enter* MEPHASTOPHILIS *with a chafer° of coals.*]   *a portable grate*
70 MEPHASTOPHILIS   Here's fire, come Faustus, set it on.
FAUSTUS   So, now the blood begins to clear again.

4. Come, come, Mephastophilis!   5. Misery loves company.

Now will I make an end immediately.

MEPHASTOPHILIS   Oh what will not I do to obtain his soul!

FAUSTUS   *Consummatum est,*[6] this bill is ended,

75   And Faustus hath bequeathed his soul to Lucifer.
But what is this inscription on mine arm?
Homo fuge.° Whither should I fly?   O *man, fly*
If unto God, he'll throw me down to hell;
My senses are deceived, here's nothing writ;

80   I see it plain, here in this place is writ,
Homo fuge! Yet shall not Faustus fly.

MEPHASTOPHILIS   I'll fetch him somewhat to delight his mind.   [*Exit.*]
[*Enter with* DEVILS, *giving crowns and rich apparel to* FAUS-
TUS, *and dance, and then depart.*]

FAUSTUS   Speak, Mephastophilis, what means this show?

MEPHASTOPHILIS   Nothing, Faustus, but to delight thy mind withal,

85   And to show thee what magic can perform.

FAUSTUS   But may I raise up spirits when I please?

MEPHASTOPHILIS   Ay, Faustus, and do greater things than these.

FAUSTUS   Then there's enough for a thousand souls!
Here, Mephastophilis, receive this scroll,

90   A deed of gift of body and of soul:
But yet conditionally, that thou perform
All articles prescribed between us both.

MEPHASTOPHILIS   Faustus, I swear by hell and Lucifer
To effect all promises between us made.

95   FAUSTUS   Then hear me read them. On these conditions following:
First, that Faustus may be a spirit[7] *in form and substance.*
Secondly, that Mephastophilis shall be his servant, and at his com-
mand.
Thirdly, that Mephastophilis shall do for him, and bring him whatso-

100   *ever.*
Fourthly, that he shall be in his chamber or house invisible.
Lastly, that he shall appear to the said John Faustus at all times, in
what form or shape soever he please.
I, John Faustus of Wittenberg, doctor, by these presents,[8] *do give both*

105   *body and soul to Lucifer, Prince of the East, and his minister Mephas-*
tophilis; and furthermore grant unto them that, four and twenty years
being expired, the articles above-written inviolate, full power to fetch
or carry the said John Faustus, body and soul, flesh, blood, or goods,
into their habitation wheresoever.

110   *By me John Faustus.*

MEPHASTOPHILIS   Speak, Faustus: do you deliver this as your deed?

FAUSTUS   Ay, take it; and the devil give thee good on't.

MEPHASTOPHILIS   Now, Faustus, ask what thou wilt.

FAUSTUS   First will I question with thee about hell:

115   Tell me, where is the place that men call hell?

MEPHASTOPHILIS   Under the heavens.

FAUSTUS   Ay, but whereabouts?

MEPHASTOPHILIS   Within the bowels of these elements,
Where we are tortured and remain for ever.

---

6. It is finished; a blasphemy, because these are   7. I.e., have the supernatural powers of a spirit.
the words of Christ on the Cross (John 19.30).   8. Legal articles.

120 Hell hath no limits, nor is circumscribed
In one self place; for where we are is hell,
And where hell is, there must we ever be.
And to conclude, when all the world dissolves,
And every creature shall be purified,
125 All places shall be hell that is not heaven.
FAUSTUS Come, I think hell's a fable.
MEPHASTOPHILIS Ay, think so still, till experience change thy
mind.
FAUSTUS Why? think'st thou then that Faustus shall be damned?
130 MEPHASTOPHILIS Ay, of necessity, for here's the scroll
Wherein thou hast given thy soul to Lucifer.
FAUSTUS Ay, and body too; but what of that?
Think'st thou that Faustus is so fond° to imagine   *foolish*
That after this life there is any pain?
135 Tush, these are trifles and mere old wives' tales.
MEPHASTOPHILIS But Faustus, I am an instance to prove the con-
trary;
For I am damned, and am now in hell.
FAUSTUS How, now in hell? Nay, and this be hell, I'll willingly be
damned here! What? walking, disputing, etc. . . . . But leaving off
140 this, let me have a wife, the fairest maid in Germany, for I am
wanton and lascivious, and cannot live without a wife.
MEPHASTOPHILIS How, a wife? I prithee Faustus, talk not of a wife.⁹
FAUSTUS Nay sweet Mephastophilis, fetch me one, for I will have
one.
145 MEPHASTOPHILIS Well, thou wilt have one; sit there till I come.
I'll fetch thee a wife in the devil's name.   [*Exit.*]
[*Enter with a* DEVIL *dressed like a woman, with fireworks.*]
MEPHASTOPHILIS Tell, Faustus, how dost thou like thy wife?
FAUSTUS A plague on her for a hot whore!
MEPHASTOPHILIS Tut, Faustus, marriage is but a ceremonial toy;
150 If thou lovest me, think no more of it.
I'll cull thee out the fairest courtesans
And bring them every morning to thy bed:
She whom thine eye shall like, thy heart shall have,
Be she as chaste as was Penelope,
155 As wise as Saba,¹ or as beautiful
As was bright Lucifer before his fall.
Hold, take this book, peruse it thoroughly:
The iterating° of these lines brings gold;   *repeating*
The framing° of this circle on the ground   *drawing*
160 Brings whirlwinds, tempests, thunder and lightning.
Pronounce this thrice devoutly to thyself,
And men in armor shall appear to thee,
Ready to execute what thou desirest.
FAUSTUS Thanks, Mephastophilis, yet fain would I have a book
165 wherein I might behold all spells and incantations, that I might raise
up spirits when I please.
MEPHASTOPHILIS Here they are in this book. [*There turn to them.*]

9. Mephastophilis cannot produce a wife for Faustus because marriage is a sacrament.

1. The queen of Sheba. "Penelope": the wife of Ulysses, famed for chastity and fidelity.

FAUSTUS Now would I have a book where I might see all characters
and planets of the heavens, that I might know their motions and
170   dispositions.
MEPHASTOPHILIS Here they are too.   [*Turn to them.*]
FAUSTUS Nay, let me have one book more, and then I have done,
wherein I might see all plants, herbs, and trees that grow upon the
earth.
175   MEPHASTOPHILIS Here they be.
FAUSTUS O thou art deceived!
MEPHASTOPHILIS Tut, I warrant thee.   [*Turn to them.*]
FAUSTUS When I behold the heavens, then I repent,
And curse thee, wicked Mephastophilis,
180   Because thou hast deprived me of those joys.
MEPHASTOPHILIS Why Faustus,
Think'st thou that heaven is such a glorious thing?
I tell thee 'tis not half so fair as thou,
Or any man that breathes on earth.
185   FAUSTUS How prov'st thou that?
MEPHASTOPHILIS It was made for man, therefore is man more excel-
lent.
FAUSTUS If it were made for man, 'twas made for me:
I will renounce this magic, and repent.
[*Enter* GOOD ANGEL *and* EVIL ANGEL.]
190   GOOD ANGEL Faustus, repent, yet° God will pity thee.   *still*
EVIL ANGEL Thou art a spirit,° God cannot pity thee.   *evil spirit, devil*
FAUSTUS Who buzzeth in mine ears I am a spirit?
Be I a devil, yet God may pity me.
Ay, God will pity me if I repent.
195   EVIL ANGEL Ay, but Faustus never shall repent.   [*Exeunt.*]
FAUSTUS My heart's so hardened[2] I cannot repent!
Scarce can I name salvation, faith, or heaven,
But fearful echoes thunders in mine ears,
"Faustus, thou are damned"; then swords and knives,
200   Poison, guns, halters,° and envenomed steel   *ropes for hanging*
Are laid before me to dispatch myself:
And long ere this I should have slain myself,
Had not sweet pleasure conquered deep despair.
Have I not made blind Homer sing to me
205   Of Alexander's[3] love, and Oenon's death?
And hath not he that built the walls of Thebes
With ravishing sound of his melodious harp,[4]
Made music with my Mephastophilis?
Why should I die then, or basely despair?
210   I am resolved! Faustus shall ne'er repent.
Come, Mephastophilis, let us dispute again,
And argue of divine astrology.
Tell me, are there many heavens above the moon?

2. Hardness of heart is the desperate spiritual
state of the reprobate who will suffer eternal damnation.
3. Alexander is another name for Paris, the lover
of Oenone; later he deserted her and abducted
Helen, causing the Trojan War. Oenone refused to
heal the wounds Paris received in battle, and when
he died of them, she killed herself in remorse.
4. The legendary musician Amphion, whose harp
caused stones, of themselves, to form the walls of
Thebes.

Are all celestial bodies but one globe,
215 As is the substance of this centric earth?[5]
MEPHASTOPHILIS As are the elements, such are the spheres,
Mutually folded in each other's orb.
And, Faustus, all jointly move upon one axletree
Whose termine° is termed the world's wide pole,   *end*
220 Nor are the names of Saturn, Mars, or Jupiter
Feigned, but are erring stars.[6]
FAUSTUS But tell me, have they all one motion, both *situ et tempore?*[7]
MEPHASTOPHILIS All jointly move from east to west in four-and-
twenty hours upon the poles of the world, but differ in their motion
225 upon the poles of the zodiac.[8]
FAUSTUS Tush, these slender trifles Wagner can decide!
Hath Mephastophilis no greater skill?
Who knows not the double motion of the planets?
The first is finished in a natural day, the second thus: as Saturn in
230 thirty years; Jupiter in twelve; Mars in four; the Sun, Venus, and
Mercury in a year; the Moon in twenty-eight days. Tush, these are
freshmen's suppositions. But tell me, hath every sphere a dominion
or *intelligentia?*[9]
MEPHASTOPHILIS Ay.
235 FAUSTUS How many heavens or spheres are there?
MEPHASTOPHILIS Nine: the seven planets, the firmament, and the
empyreal heaven.[1]
FAUSTUS Well, resolve me then in this question: why have we not
conjunctions, oppositions,[2] aspects, eclipses, all at one time, but in
240 some years we have more, in some less?
MEPHASTOPHILIS *Per inaequalem motum respectu totius.*[3]
FAUSTUS Well, I am answered. Tell me who made the world?
MEPHASTOPHILIS I will not.
FAUSTUS Sweet Mephastophilis, tell me.
245 MEPHASTOPHILIS Move° me not, for I will not tell thee.   *anger*
FAUSTUS Villain, have I not bound thee to tell me anything?
MEPHASTOPHILIS Ay, that is not against our kingdom; but this is.
Think thou on hell, Faustus, for thou art damned.
FAUSTUS Think, Faustus, upon God, that made the world.
250 MEPHASTOPHILIS Remember this.   [*Exit.*]
FAUSTUS Ay, go accursèd spirit, to ugly hell,
'Tis thou hast damned distressèd Faustus' soul:
Is't not too late?
[*Enter* GOOD ANGEL *and* EVIL.]
EVIL ANGEL Too late.
255 GOOD ANGEL Never too late, if Faustus will repent.
EVIL ANGEL If thou repent, devils shall tear thee in pieces.

---

5. Faustus asks whether all the apparently different heavenly bodies form really "one globe" like the
earth. Mephastophilis answers that like the elements, which are separate but combined, the heavenly bodies are separate but their spheres are
enfolded and they move on one axletree.
6. It is appropriate to give individual names to Saturn, Mars, Jupiter, and the other planets—which
are called wandering, or "erring" stars. The fixed
stars were in the eighth sphere (the firmament, or
crystalline sphere).
7. In position and time.

8. The common axletree on which all the spheres
revolve.
9. An angel, or intelligence, thought to be the
source of motion in each sphere.
1. The ninth sphere was the immovable empyrean.
2. "Conjunctions": the apparent joinings of two
planets. "Oppositions": when two planets are most
remote.
3. Because of their unequal velocities within the
system.

GOOD ANGEL   Repent, and they shall never raze° thy skin.   *tear*
        [*Exeunt.*]
FAUSTUS   Ah Christ my Savior! seek to save
   Distressèd Faustus' soul!
        [*Enter* LUCIFER, BELZEBUB, *and* MEPHASTOPHILIS.]
260 LUCIFER   Christ cannot save thy soul, for he is just.
   There's none but I have interest in the same.
FAUSTUS   O who art thou that look'st so terrible?
LUCIFER   I am Lucifer, and this is my companion prince in hell.
FAUSTUS   O Faustus, they are come to fetch away thy soul!
265 LUCIFER   We come to tell thee thou dost injure us.
   Thou talk'st of Christ, contrary to thy promise.
   Thou should'st not think of God; think of the devil,
   And his dam⁴ too.
FAUSTUS   Nor will I henceforth: pardon me in this,
270   And Faustus vows never to look to heaven,
   Never to name God, or to pray to him,
   To burn his Scriptures, slay his ministers,
   And make my spirits pull his churches down.
LUCIFER   Do so, and we will highly gratify thee. Faustus, we are
275   come from hell to show thee some pastime; sit down, and thou shalt
   see all the Seven Deadly Sins⁵ appear in their proper shapes.
FAUSTUS   That sight will be as pleasing unto me as Paradise was to
   Adam, the first day of his creation.
LUCIFER   Talk not of Paradise, nor creation, but mark this show; talk
280   of the devil and nothing else. Come away.
        [*Enter the* SEVEN DEADLY SINS.]
   Now Faustus, examine them of their several names and dispositions.
FAUSTUS   What art thou, the first?
PRIDE   I am Pride: I disdain to have any parents. I am like to Ovid's
285   flea,⁶ I can creep into every corner of a wench: sometimes like a
   periwig, I sit upon her brow; or like a fan of feathers, I kiss her lips.
   Indeed I do—what do I not! But fie, what a scent is here? I'll not
   speak another word, except the ground were perfumed and covered
   with cloth of arras.⁷
290 FAUSTUS   What art thou, the second?
COVETOUSNESS   I am Covetousness, begotten of an old churl in an
   old leathern bag; and might I have my wish, I would desire that this
   house, and all the people in it, were turned to gold, that I might
   lock you up in my good chest. O my sweet gold!
295 FAUSTUS   What art thou, the third?
WRATH   I am Wrath. I had neither father nor mother: I leaped out
   of a lion's mouth when I was scarce half an hour old, and ever since
   I have run up and down the world, with this case of rapiers, wounding myself when I had nobody to fight withal. I was born in hell—
300   and look to it, for some of you shall be my father.
FAUSTUS   What art thou, the fourth?

4. Mother. "The devil and his dam" was a common colloquial expression.
5. Pride, avarice, lust, anger, gluttony, envy, and sloth, called deadly because they lead to spiritual death. All other sins are said to grow out of them (cf. the procession of the Seven Deadly Sins in

Spenser's *The Faerie Queene* 1.4, stanzas 16–36, pp. 385–90).
6. A salacious medieval poem *Carmen de Pulice* (Song of the Flea) was attributed to Ovid.
7. Arras in Flanders exported fine cloth used for tapestry hangings. "Except": unless.

ENVY   I am Envy, begotten of a chimney-sweeper and an oyster-wife. I cannot read, and therefore wish all books were burnt; I am lean with seeing others eat—O that there would come a famine through all the world, that all might die, and I live alone; then thou should'st see how fat I would be! But must thou sit and I stand? Come down, with a vengeance!

FAUSTUS   Away, envious rascal! What art thou, the fifth?

305

GLUTTONY   Who, I sir? I am Gluttony. My parents are all dead, and the devil a penny they have left me but a bare pension, and that is thirty meals a day and ten bevers[8]—a small trifle to suffice nature. O, I come of a royal parentage: my grandfather was a gammon[9] of bacon, my grandmother a hogshead of claret wine; my godfathers were these: Peter Pickled-Herring, and Martin Martlemas-Beef.[1] O, but my godmother! She was a jolly gentlewoman, and well-beloved in every good town and city; her name was Mistress Margery March-Beer.[2] Now, Faustus, thou hast heard all my progeny;[3] wilt thou bid me to supper?

310

315

FAUSTUS   No, I'll see thee hanged; thou wilt eat up all my victuals.

GLUTTONY   Then the devil choke thee!

320

FAUSTUS   Choke thyself, Glutton. What art thou, the sixth?

SLOTH   I am Sloth; I was begotten on a sunny bank, where I have lain ever since—and you have done me great injury to bring me from thence. Let me be carried thither again by Gluttony and Lechery. I'll not speak another word for a king's ransom.

325

FAUSTUS   What are you, Mistress Minx, the seventh and last?

LECHERY   Who, I sir? I am one that loves an inch of raw mutton better than an ell of fried stockfish;[4] and the first letter of my name begins with Lechery.

LUCIFER   Away! To hell, to hell!   [Exeunt the SINS.]

330

Now Faustus, how dost thou like this?

FAUSTUS   O this feeds my soul!

LUCIFER   Tut, Faustus, in hell is all manner of delight.

FAUSTUS   O might I see hell, and return again, how happy were I then!

335

LUCIFER   Thou shalt; I will send for thee at midnight. In meantime, take this book, peruse it thoroughly, and thou shalt turn thyself into what shape thou wilt.

FAUSTUS   Great thanks, mighty Lucifer; this will I keep as chary[5] as my life.

340

LUCIFER   Farewell, Faustus; and think on the devil.

FAUSTUS   Farewell, great Lucifer; come, Mephastophilis.

[Exeunt OMNES.]

SCENE 6

[Enter ROBIN the ostler[6] with a book in his hand.]

ROBIN   O this is admirable! here I ha' stolen one of Doctor Faustus' conjuring books, and i'faith I mean to search some circles[7] for my

---

8. Snacks.
9. The lower side of pork, including the leg.
1. Meat, salted to preserve it during the winter, was prepared around Martinmas (November 11).
2. A rich ale, made in March.
3. Ancestry, lineage.

4. Dried cod. "Mutton": frequently a bawdy term in Elizabethan English; here, the penis. "Ell": forty-five inches.
5. Carefully.
6. Hostler, stablehand.
7. Magicians' circles, but with a sexual innuendo.

own use: now will I make all the maidens in our parish dance at my pleasure stark naked before me, and so by that means I shall see
5 more than ere I felt or saw yet.

[*Enter* RAFE *calling* ROBIN.]

RAFE   Robin, prithee come away, there's a gentleman tarries to have his horse, and he would have his things rubbed and made clean. He keeps such a chafing[8] with my mistress about it, and she has sent me to look thee out. Prithee, come away.
10 ROBIN   Keep out, keep out; or else you are blown up, you are dismembered, Rafe. Keep out, for I am about a roaring[9] piece of work.

RAFE   Come, what dost thou with that same book? Thou canst not read!

ROBIN   Yes, my master and mistress shall find that I can read—he
15 for his forehead,[1] she for her private study. She's born to bear with me,[2] or else my art fails.

RAFE   Why Robin, what book is that?

ROBIN   What book? Why the most intolerable[3] book for conjuring that ere was invented by any brimstone devil.
20 RAFE   Canst thou conjure with it?

ROBIN   I can do all these things easily with it: first, I can make thee drunk with 'ipocrase[4] at any tavern in Europe for nothing, that's one of my conjuring works.

RAFE   Our master parson says that's nothing.
25 ROBIN   True, Rafe! And more, Rafe, if thou hast any mind to Nan Spit, our kitchen maid, then turn her and wind her to thy own use, as often as thou wilt, and at midnight.

RAFE   O brave Robin! Shall I have Nan Spit, and to mine own use? On that condition I'll feed thy devil with horsebread as long as he
30 lives, of free cost.[5]

ROBIN   No more, sweet Rafe; let's go and make clean our boots which lie foul upon our hands, and then to our conjuring in the devil's name.   [*Exeunt.*]

CHORUS 2

[*Enter* WAGNER *solus.*]

WAGNER   Learned Faustus,
        To know the secrets of astronomy
        Graven in the book of Jove's high firmament,
        Did mount himself to scale Olympus'[6] top.
5   Being seated in a chariot burning bright,
        Drawn by the strength of yokèd dragons' necks.
        He now is gone to prove cosmography,[7]
        And, as I guess, will first arrive at Rome
        To see the pope, and manner of his court,
10   And take some part of holy Peter's feast,[8]
        That to this day is highly solemnized.   [*Exit* WAGNER.]

---

8. Scolding.
9. Dangerous.
1. That is, Robin intends to give his master horns—cuckold him.
2. I.e., bear his weight, or bear him a child.
3. Irresistible.

4. Robin's pronunciation of *hippocras*, a spiced wine.
5. Free of charge. "Horsebread": fodder.
6. The home of the gods in Greek mythology.
7. To test the accuracy of maps.
8. St. Peter's feast is June 29.

SCENE 7

[*Enter* FAUSTUS *and* MEPHASTOPHILIS.]

FAUSTUS   Having now, my good Mephastophilis,
Passed with delight the stately town of Trier,[9]
Environed round with airy mountain tops,
With walls of flint, and deep entrenchèd lakes,°   *moats*
5   Not to be won by any conquering prince;
From Paris next, coasting° the realm of France,   *traversing*
We saw the river Main fall into Rhine,
Whose banks are set with groves of fruitful vines;
Then up to Naples, rich Campania,
10   With buildings fair and gorgeous to the eye,
The streets straight forth, and paved with finest brick,
Quarters the town in four equivalents;
There saw we learned Maro's[1] golden tomb,
The way° he cut, an English mile in length,   *tunnel*
15   Thorough a rock of stone in one night's space.
From thence to Venice, Padua, and the rest,
In midst of which a sumptuous temple° stands   *St. Mark's in Venice*
That threats the stars with her aspiring top.
Thus hitherto hath Faustus spent his time.
20   But tell me now, what resting place is this?
Hast thou, as erst° I did command,   *earlier*
Conducted me within the walls of Rome?
MEPHASTOPHILIS   Faustus, I have; and because we will not be unpro-
vided, I have taken up his holiness' privy chamber for our use.
25   FAUSTUS   I hope his holiness will bid us welcome.
MEPHASTOPHILIS   Tut, 'tis no matter, man, we'll be bold with his
good cheer.
And now, my Faustus, that thou may'st perceive
What Rome containeth to delight thee with,
30   Know that this city stands upon seven hills
That underprop the groundwork of the same;
Just through the midst runs flowing Tiber's stream,
With winding banks, that cut it in two parts;
Over the which four stately bridges lean,
35   That makes safe passage to each part of Rome.
Upon the bridge called Ponte Angelo
Erected is a castle passing strong,[2]
Within whose walls such store of ordinance are
And double cannons, framed of carvèd brass,
40   As match the days within one complete year—
Besides the gates and high pyramides°   *obelisks*
Which Julius Caesar brought from Africa.
FAUSTUS   Now by the kingdoms of infernal rule,
Of Styx, Acheron, and the fiery lake
45   Of ever-burning Phlegethon,[3] I swear
That I do long to see the monuments
And situation of bright-splendent Rome.

9. Treves (in Prussia).
1. Virgil's. In medieval legend the Roman poet Virgil was considered a magician whose powers produced a tunnel on the promontory of Posilippo at Naples, near his tomb.
2. Actually the castle is on the bank, not the bridge. "Passing": surpassingly.
3. Classical names for rivers of the underworld.

Come therefore, let's away.

MEPHASTOPHILIS   Nay, Faustus, stay. I know you'd fain see the pope,
50   And take some part of holy Peter's feast,
Where thou shalt see a troup of bald-pate friars,
Whose *summum bonum*[4] is in belly-cheer.

FAUSTUS   Well, I am content to compass[5] then some sport,
And by their folly make us merriment.
55   Then charm me that I may be invisible, to do what I please unseen
of any whilst I stay in Rome.

MEPHASTOPHILIS [*casts a spell on him*].   So Faustus, now do what
thou wilt, thou shalt not be discerned.

> [*Sound a sennet;*[6] *enter the* POPE *and the* CARDINAL OF LOR-
> RAINE *to the banquet, with* FRIARS *attending.*]

POPE   My lord of Lorraine, will't please you draw near.
60   FAUSTUS   Fall to; and the devil choke you and[7] you spare.

POPE   How now, who's that which spake? Friars, look about.

1 FRIAR   Here's nobody, if it like[8] your holiness.

POPE   My lord, here is a dainty dish was sent to me from the bishop
of Milan.
65   FAUSTUS   I thank you, sir.   [*Snatch it.*]

POPE   How now, who's that which snatched the meat from me? Will
no man look? My lord, this dish was sent me from the cardinal of
Florence.

FAUSTUS   You say true? I'll have't.   [*Snatch it.*]
70   POPE   What, again! My lord, I'll drink to your grace.

FAUSTUS   I'll pledge your grace.   [*Snatch the cup.*]

LORRAINE   My lord, it may be some ghost newly crept out of purgatory come to beg a pardon of your holiness.

POPE   It may be so; friars; prepare a dirge[9] to lay the fury of this ghost.
75   Once again my lord, fall to.   [*The* POPE *crosseth himself.*]

FAUSTUS   What, are you crossing of your self? Well, use that trick no
more, I would advise you.

> [*Cross again.*]

FAUSTUS   Well, there's the second time; aware the third! I give you
fair warning.

> [*Cross again, and* FAUSTUS *hits him a box of the ear, and they
> all run away.*]

80   FAUSTUS   Come on, Mephastophilis, what shall we do?

MEPHASTOPHILIS   Nay, I know not; we shall be cursed with bell,
book, and candle.[1]

FAUSTUS   How! Bell, book, and candle; candle, book, and bell,
Forward and backward, to curse Faustus to hell.
85   Anon you shall hear a hog grunt, a calf bleat, and an ass bray,
Because it is St. Peter's holy day.

> [*Enter all the* FRIARS *to sing the Dirge.*]

1 FRIAR   Come brethren, let's about our business with good devotion.

> [*Sing this.*]

---

4. The greatest good; often refers to God.
5. Take part in.
6. A set of notes on the trumpet or cornet.
7. If. "Fall to": get on with it.
8. Please.

9. A requiem mass. But what actually follows is a litany of curses. "Pledge": toast.
1. The traditional paraphernalia for cursing and excommunication.

Cursed be he that stole away his holiness' meat from the table.
90   Maledicat Dominus.[2]
Cursed be he that struck his holiness a blow on the face.
    Maledicat Dominus.
Cursed be he that took Friar Sandelo a blow on the pate.
    Maledicat Dominus.
95   Cursed be he that disturbeth our holy dirge.
    Maledicat Dominus.
Cursed be he that took away his holiness' wine.
    Maledicat dominus.
        Et omnes sancti.[3] Amen.
    [*Beat the* FRIARS, *and fling fireworks among them, and so Exeunt.*]

SCENE 8

[*Enter* ROBIN *and* RAFE *with a silver goblet.*]
ROBIN   Come, Rafe, did not I tell thee we were forever made by this
Doctor Faustus' book? *Ecce signum!*[4] Here's a simple purchase for
horsekeepers: our horses shall eat no hay as long as this lasts.
    [*Enter the* VINTNER.]
RAFE   But Robin, here comes the vintner.
5 ROBIN   Hush, I'll gull him supernaturally! Drawer,[5] I hope all is paid;
God be with you. Come, Rafe.
VINTNER   Soft, sir, a word with you. I must yet have a goblet paid
from you ere you go.
ROBIN   I, a goblet, Rafe? I, a goblet? I scorn you: and you are but a
10   &c.[6] . . . I, a goblet? Search me.
VINTNER   I mean so, sir, with your favor.   [*Searches* ROBIN.]
ROBIN   How say you now?
VINTNER   I must say somewhat to your fellow; you, sir!
RAFE   Me, sir? Me, sir? Search your fill. Now sir, you may be ashamed
15   to burden honest men with a matter of truth.
VINTNER [*searches* RAFE]   Well, t'one of you hath this goblet about
you.
ROBIN   You lie, drawer; 'tis afore me. Sirra you, I'll teach ye to
impeach honest men: [*to* RAFE] stand by. [*to the* VINTNER] I'll scour
20   you for a goblet—stand aside, you were best—I charge you in the
name of Belzebub—look to the goblet, Rafe!
VINTNER   What mean you, sirra?
ROBIN   I'll tell you what I mean: [*he reads*] *Sanctobulorum Periphras-
ticon*—nay, I'll tickle you, vintner—look to the goblet, Rafe—*Poly-*
25   *pragmos Belseborams framanto pacostiphos tostis Mephastophilis,*
&c. . . . [7]
        [*Enter* MEPHASTOPHILIS: *sets squibs*[8] *at their backs: they run*
        about.]
VINTNER   O *nomine Domine!*[9] What mean'st thou, Robin? Thou hast
no goblet.
RAFE   *Peccatum peccatorum!*[1] Here's thy goblet, good vintner.

---

2. May the Lord curse him.
3. And all the saints (also curse him).
4. Behold the proof.
5. Wine-drawer. "Gull": trick.
6. The actor might ad lib abuse at this point.
7. Dog-Latin, as Robin attempts to conjure from Faustus's book.

8. Firecrackers. Evidently Mephastophilis is on stage only long enough to set off the firecrackers and is not seen by Robin, Rafe, or the Vintner. He then reenters at line 32.
9. In the name of the Lord; the Latin invocations are used in swearing.
1. Sin of sins!

30 ROBIN *Misericordia pro nobis!*[2] What shall I do? Good devil, forgive
me now, and I'll never rob thy library more.
[*Enter to them* MEPHASTOPHILIS.]
MEPHASTOPHILIS Vanish, villains, th'one like an ape, another like a
bear, the third an ass, for doing this enterprise. [*Exit* VINTNER.]
Monarch of hell, under whose black survey
35 Great potentates do kneel with awful fear;
Upon whose altars thousand souls do lie;
How am I vexèd with these villains' charms!
From Constantinople am I hither come,
Only for pleasure of these damnèd slaves.
40 ROBIN How, from Constantinople? You have had a great journey!
Will you take sixpence in your purse to pay for your supper, and be
gone?
MEPHASTOPHILIS Well, villains, for your presumption, I transform
thee into an ape, and thee into a dog; and so begone! [*Exit.*]
45 ROBIN How, into an ape? That's brave: I'll have fine sport with the
boys; I'll get nuts and apples enow.[3]
RAFE And I must be a dog.
ROBIN I'faith, thy head will never be out of the potage[4] pot.
[*Exeunt.*]

CHORUS 3

[*Enter* CHORUS.[5]]
CHORUS When Faustus had with pleasure ta'en the view
Of rarest things, and royal courts of kings,
He stayed his course, and so returnèd home;
Where such as bare his absence but with grief—
5 I mean his friends and nearest companions—
Did gratulate his safety with kind words.
And in their conference of what befell,
Touching his journey through the world and air,
They put forth questions of astrology,
10 Which Faustus answered with such learnèd skill,
As they admired and wondered at his wit.
Now is his fame spread forth in every land:
Amongst the rest the emperor is one,
Carolus the Fifth,[6] at whose palace now
15 Faustus is feasted 'mongst his noblemen.
What there he did in trial of his art
I leave untold: your eyes shall see performed. [*Exit.*]

SCENE 9

[*Enter* EMPEROR, FAUSTUS, *and a* KNIGHT, *with Attendants.*]
EMPEROR Master Doctor Faustus, I have heard strange report of thy
knowledge in the black art, how that none in my empire, nor in the
whole world, can compare with thee for the rare effects of magic.
They say thou hast a familiar spirit, by whom thou canst accomplish
5 what thou list! This therefore is my request: that thou let me see

2. Have mercy on us!
3. Enough. "Brave": splendid.
4. Porridge.

5. I.e., Wagner.
6. The Holy Roman Emperor Charles V (reigned
1519–1556).

some proof of thy skill, that mine eyes may be witnesses to confirm
what mine ears have heard reported. And here I swear to thee, by
the honor of mine imperial crown, that whatever thou dost, thou
shalt be in no ways prejudiced or endamaged.

10 KNIGHT [aside]   I'faith, he looks much like a conjuror.

FAUSTUS   My gracious sovereign, though I must confess myself far
inferior to the report men have published, and nothing answerable
to the honor of your imperial majesty, yet for that love and duty
binds me thereunto, I am content to do whatsoever your majesty

15 shall command me.

EMPEROR   Then Doctor Faustus, mark what I shall say. As I was
sometime solitary set within my closet,[7] sundry thoughts arose
about the honor of mine ancestors—how they had won by prowess
such exploits, got such riches, subdued so many kingdoms, as we

20 that do succeed, or they that shall hereafter possess our throne,
shall (I fear me) never attain to that degree of high renown and
great authority. Amongst which kings is Alexander the Great,[8] chief
spectacle of the world's pre-eminence:
The bright shining of whose glorious acts

25 Lightens the world with his reflecting beams;
As when I hear but motion° made of him,   *mention*
It grieves my soul I never saw the man.
If therefore thou, by cunning of thine art,
Canst raise this man from hollow vaults below,

30 Where lies entombed this famous conqueror,
And bring with him his beauteous paramour,[9]
Both in their right shapes, gesture, and attire
They used to wear during their time of life,
Thou shalt both satisfy my just desire,

35 And give me cause to praise thee whilst I live.

FAUSTUS   My gracious lord, I am ready to accomplish your request,
so far forth as by art and power of my spirit I am able to perform.

KNIGHT [aside]   I'faith, that's just nothing at all.

FAUSTUS   But, if it like your grace, it is not in my ability to present

40 before your eyes the true substantial bodies of those two deceased
princes, which long since are consumed to dust.

KNIGHT [aside]   Ay, marry,[1] master doctor, now there's a sign of grace
in you, when you will confess the truth.

FAUSTUS   But such spirits as can lively resemble Alexander and his

45 paramour shall appear before your grace, in that manner that they
best lived in, in their most flourishing estate: which I doubt not
shall sufficiently content your imperial majesty.

EMPEROR   Go to, master doctor, let me see them presently.[2]

KNIGHT   Do you hear, master doctor? You bring Alexander and his

50 paramour before the emperor!

FAUSTUS   How then, sir?

KNIGHT   I'faith, that's as true as Diana turned me to a stag.

FAUSTUS   No sir; but when Actaeon died, he left the horns[3] for you!
Mephastophilis, begone!   [Exit MEPHASTOPHILIS.]

---

7. Private chamber.
8. The emperor traces his ancestry to the great
world conqueror (356–323 B.C.E.).
9. Probably Roxana, Alexander's wife.
1. To be sure.
2. Immediately.

3. Horns were traditionally a sign of the cuckolded
husband (cf. Scene 6, lines 14–15). "Actaeon": the
hunter of classical legend who happened to see the
goddess Diana bathing. For punishment he was
changed into a stag; he was then chased and killed
by his own hounds.

55 KNIGHT   Nay, and[4] you go to conjuring I'll be gone.   [*Exit* KNIGHT.]
  FAUSTUS   I'll meet with you anon for interrupting me so. Here they
  are, my gracious lord.
      [*Enter* MEPHASTOPHILIS *with* ALEXANDER *and his* PARAMOUR.]
  EMPEROR   Master doctor, I heard this lady, while she lived, had a
  wart or mole in her neck; how shall I know whether it be so or no?
60 FAUSTUS   Your highness may boldly go and see.
      [*The* EMPEROR *examines the lady's neck.*]
  EMPEROR   Sure, these are no spirits, but the true substantial bodies
  of those two deceased princes.
      [*Exit* ALEXANDER (*and his* PARAMOUR).]
  FAUSTUS   Will't please your highness now to send for the knight that
  was so pleasant with me here of late?
65 EMPEROR   One of you call him forth.
      [*Enter the* KNIGHT *with a pair of horns on his head.*]
  EMPEROR   How now, sir knight? Why, I had thought thou hadst
  been a bachelor, but now I see thou hast a wife that not only gives
  thee horns but makes thee wear them! Feel on thy head.
  KNIGHT   Thou damnèd wretch and execrable dog,
70 Bred in the concave of some monstrous rock,
  How dar'st thou thus abuse a gentleman?
  Villain, I say, undo what thou hast done.
  FAUSTUS   O not so fast, sir, there's no haste but good. Are you
  remembered[5] how you crossed me in my conference with the
75 emperor? I think I have met with[6] you for it.
  EMPEROR   Good master doctor, at my entreaty release him; he hath
  done penance sufficient.
  FAUSTUS   My gracious lord, not so much for the injury he offered me
  here in your presence as to delight you with some mirth, hath Faus-
80 tus worthily requited this injurious knight; which being all I desire,
  I am content to release him of his horns. And, sir knight, hereafter
  speak well of scholars: Mephastophilis, transform him straight.[7]
  Now, my good lord, having done my duty, I humbly take my leave.
  EMPEROR   Farewell, master doctor; yet ere you go, expect from me a
85 bounteous reward.
      [*Exit* EMPEROR (*and his* ATTENDANTS).]
  FAUSTUS   Now, Mephastophilis, the restless course
  That time doth run with calm and silent foot,
  Shortening my days and thread of vital life,
  Calls for the payment of my latest years;
90 Therefore, sweet Mephastophilis, let us make haste to Wittenberg.
  MEPHASTOPHILIS   What, will you go on horseback or on foot?
  FAUSTUS   Nay, till I am past this fair and pleasant green, I'll walk on
  foot.

SCENE 10

[*Enter a* HORSE-COURSER.[8]]
  HORSE-COURSER   I have been all this day seeking one Master Fustian: 'mass,[9] see where he is! God save you, master doctor.

4. If.
5. Have you forgotten. "No haste but good": a
proverb: no point hurrying, unless it's to good
effect.
6. Been revenged upon.

7. Immediately.
8. Horse trader, traditionally a sharp bargainer or
cheat.
9. By the Mass. "Fustian": the horse-courser's
mispronunciation of Faustus's name.

FAUSTUS   What, horse-courser: you are well met.

HORSE-COURSER   Do you hear, sir; I have brought you forty dollars[1]
5   for your horse.

FAUSTUS   I cannot sell him so: if thou lik'st him for fifty, take him.

HORSE-COURSER   Alas sir, I have no more. I pray you speak for me.

MEPHASTOPHILIS   I pray you let him have him; he is an honest fellow,
and he has a great charge[2]—neither wife nor child.

10   FAUSTUS   Well, come, give me your money; my boy will deliver him
to you. But I must tell you one thing before you have him: ride him
not into the water at any hand.

HORSE-COURSER   Why sir, will he not drink of all waters?

FAUSTUS   O yes, he will drink of all waters, but ride him not into the
15   water. Ride him over hedge or ditch, or where thou wilt, but not
into the water.

HORSE-COURSER   Well sir. Now am I made man forever: I'll not leave
my horse for forty! If he had but the quality of hey ding ding, hey
ding ding,[3] I'd make a brave living on him! He has a buttock as slick
20   as an eel. Well, God b'y,[4] sir; your boy will deliver him me. But hark
ye sir, if my horse be sick, or ill at ease, if I bring his water[5] to you,
you'll tell me what it is?
   [*Exit* HORSE-COURSER.]

FAUSTUS   Away, you villain! What, dost think I am a horse-doctor?
What art thou, Faustus, but a man condemned to die?
25   Thy fatal time doth draw to final end.
Despair doth drive distrust unto my thoughts:
Confound these passions with a quiet sleep.
Tush, Christ did call the thief upon the cross;[6]
Then rest thee, Faustus, quiet in conceit.°   *in mind*
   [*Sleep in his chair.*]
   [*Enter* HORSE-COURSER *all wet, crying.*]

30   HORSE-COURSER   Alas, alas, Doctor Fustian, quoth 'a: 'mass, Doctor
Lopus[7] was never such a doctor! H'as given me a purgation, h'as
purged me of forty dollars! I shall never see them more. But yet,
like an ass as I was, I would not be ruled by him; for he bade me I
should ride him into no water. Now I, thinking my horse had had
35   some rare quality that he would not have had me known of, I, like
a vent'rous youth, rid him into the deep pond at the town's end. I
was no sooner in the middle of the pond, but my horse vanished
away, and I sat upon a bottle[8] of hay, never so near drowning in my
life! But I'll seek out my doctor, and have my forty dollars again, or
40   I'll make it the dearest[9] horse. O, yonder is his snipper-snapper! Do
you hear, you hey-pass,[1] where's your master?

MEPHASTOPHILIS   Why, sir, what would you? You cannot speak with
him.

HORSE-COURSER   But I will speak with him.

45   MEPHASTOPHILIS   Why, he's fast asleep; come some other time.

1. Common German coins.
2. Burden.
3. I.e., he wishes his horse were a stallion, not a
gelding, so he could put him to stud.
4. Good-bye (contracted from "God be with you").
5. Urine.
6. In Luke 23.39–43 one of the two thieves crucified with Jesus is promised paradise.

7. In February 1594 Roderigo Lopez, the queen's
personal physician, was executed for plotting to
poison her. Obviously Marlowe, who died in 1593,
did not write the line.
8. Bundle.
9. Most expensive.
1. A conjurer's phrase. "Snipper-snapper": insignificant youth, whipper-snapper.

HORSE-COURSER I'll speak with him now, or I'll break his glass-windows[2] about his ears.

MEPHASTOPHILIS I tell thee, he has not slept this eight nights.

HORSE-COURSER And he have not slept this eight weeks I'll speak
50 with him.

MEPHASTOPHILIS See where he is, fast asleep.

HORSE-COURSER Ay, this is he; God save ye master doctor, master doctor, master Doctor Fustian, forty dollars, forty dollars for a bottle of hay.

55 MEPHASTOPHILIS Why, thou seest he hears thee not.

HORSE-COURSER So ho ho; so ho ho.[3] [halloo in his ear] No, will you not wake? I'll make you wake ere I go. [pull him by the leg, and pull it away] Alas, I am undone! What shall I do?

FAUSTUS O my leg, my leg! Help, Mephastophilis! Call the officers!
60 My leg, my leg!

MEPHASTOPHILIS Come villain, to the constable.

HORSE-COURSER O Lord, sir! Let me go, and I'll give you forty dollars more.

MEPHASTOPHILIS Where be they?

65 HORSE-COURSER I have none about me: come to my ostry[4] and I'll give them you.

MEPHASTOPHILIS Begone quickly!
    [HORSE-COURSER runs away.]

FAUSTUS What, is he gone? Farewell he: Faustus has his leg again, and the horse-courser—I take it—a bottle of hay for his labor! Well,
70 this trick shall cost him forty dollars more.
    [Enter WAGNER.]
How now, Wagner, what's the news with thee?

WAGNER Sir, the Duke of Vanholt doth earnestly entreat your company.

FAUSTUS The Duke of Vanholt! An honorable gentleman, to whom
75 I must be no niggard of my cunning. Come, Mephastophilis, let's away to him.   [Exeunt.]

SCENE 11

    [FAUSTUS and MEPHASTOPHILIS return to the stage. Enter to
    them the DUKE and the DUCHESS; the DUKE speaks.]

DUKE Believe me, master doctor, this merriment hath much pleased me.

FAUSTUS My gracious Lord, I am glad it contents you so well: but it may be, madam, you take no delight in this; I have heard that great-
5 bellied women do long for some dainties or other—what is it, madam? Tell me, and you shall have it.

DUCHESS Thanks, good master doctor; and for I see your courteous intent to pleasure me, I will not hide from you the thing my heart desires. And were it now summer, as it is January and the dead of
10 winter, I would desire no better meat than a dish of ripe grapes.

FAUSTUS Alas madam, that's nothing! Mephastophilis, begone! [Exit MEPHASTOPHILIS.] Were it a greater thing than this, so it would

2. Spectacles.   4. Hostelry, inn.
3. The huntsman's cry, when he sights the quarry.

content you, you should have it. [*Enter* MEPHASTOPHILIS *with the grapes.*] Here they be, madam; will't please you taste on them?

15 DUKE Believe me, master doctor, this makes me wonder above the rest: that being in the dead time of winter, and in the month of January, how you should come by these grapes?

FAUSTUS If it like your grace, the year is divided into two circles over the whole world, that when it is here winter with us, in the contrary
20 circle it is summer with them, as in India, Saba,[5] and farther countries in the east; and by means of a swift spirit that I have, I had them brought hither, as ye see. How do you like them, madam; be they good?

DUCHESS Believe me, master doctor, they be the best grapes that ere
25 I tasted in my life before.

FAUSTUS I am glad they content you so, madam.

DUKE Come madam, let us in, where you must well reward this learned man for the great kindness he hath showed to you.

DUCHESS And so I will, my lord; and whilst I live, rest beholding for
30 this courtesy.

FAUSTUS I humbly thank your grace.

DUKE Come, master doctor, follow us, and receive your reward.

[*Exeunt.*]

CHORUS 4

[*Enter* WAGNER *solus.*]

WAGNER I think my master means to die shortly,
For he hath given to me all his goods!
And yet methinks, if that death were near,
He would not banquet, and carouse, and swill
5 Amongst the students, as even now he doth,
Who are at supper with such belly-cheer
As Wagner ne'er beheld in all his life.
See where they come: belike the feast is ended.

[*Exit.*]

SCENE 12

[*Enter* FAUSTUS (*and* MEPHASTOPHILIS), *with two or three*
SCHOLARS.]

1 SCHOLAR Master Doctor Faustus, since our conference about fair ladies, which was the beautifulest in all the world, we have determined with ourselves that Helen of Greece was the admirablest lady that ever lived. Therefore, master doctor, if you will do us that favor
5 as to let us see that peerless dame of Greece, whom all the world admires for majesty, we should think ourselves much beholding unto you.

FAUSTUS Gentlemen, for that I know your friendship is unfeigned,
And Faustus' custom is not to deny
10 The just requests of those that wish him well,
You shall behold that peerless dame of Greece,
No otherways for pomp and majesty
Than when Sir Paris crossed the seas with her

5. Sheba, Yemen.

And brought the spoils to rich Dardania.°   *Troy*
15   Be silent then, for danger is in words.
     [*Music sounds, and* HELEN *passeth over the stage.*]
   2 SCHOLAR   Too simple is my wit to tell her praise,
     Whom all the world admires for majesty.
   3 SCHOLAR   No marvel though the angry Greeks pursued
     With ten years' war the rape of such a queen,
20   Whose heavenly beauty passeth all compare.
   1 SCHOLAR   Since we have seen the pride of Nature's works
     And only paragon of excellence,
     Let us depart; and for this glorious deed
     Happy and blest be Faustus evermore.
25   FAUSTUS   Gentlemen farewell; the same I wish to you.
                             [*Exeunt* SCHOLARS.]
     [*Enter an* OLD MAN.]
   OLD MAN   Ah Doctor Faustus, that I might prevail
     To guide thy steps unto the way of life,
     By which sweet path thou may'st attain the goal
     That shall conduct thee to celestial rest.
30   Break heart, drop blood, and mingle it with tears,
     Tears falling from repentant heaviness
     Of thy most vile and loathsome filthiness,
     The stench whereof corrupts the inward soul
     With such flagitious° crimes of heinous sins,   *villainous*
35   As no commiseration may expel
     But mercy, Faustus, of thy savior sweet,
     Whose blood alone must wash away thy guilt.
   FAUSTUS   Where art thou, Faustus? Wretch, what hast thou done!
     Damned art thou, Faustus, damned; despair and die!
40   Hell calls for right, and with a roaring voice
     Says, "Faustus, come: thine hour is come!"
     [MEPHASTOPHILIS *gives him a dagger.*]
     And Faustus will come to do thee right.
   OLD MAN   Ah stay, good Faustus, stay thy desperate steps!
     I see an angel hovers o'er thy head
45   And with a vial full of precious grace
     Offers to pour the same into thy soul!
     Then call for mercy, and avoid despair.
   FAUSTUS   Ah my sweet friend, I feel thy words
     To comfort my distressed soul;
50   Leave me awhile to ponder on my sins.
   OLD MAN   I go, sweet Faustus; but with heavy cheer,°   *i.e., heavy heart*
     Fearing the ruin of thy hopeless soul.   [*Exit.*]
   FAUSTUS   Accursèd Faustus, where is mercy now?
     I do repent, and yet I do despair:
55   Hell strives with grace for conquest in my breast!
     What shall I do to shun the snares of death?
   MEPHASTOPHILIS   Thou traitor, Faustus: I arrest thy soul
     For disobedience to my sovereign lord.
     Revolt,[6] or I'll in piecemeal tear thy flesh.
60   FAUSTUS   Sweet Mephastophilis, entreat thy lord
     To pardon my unjust presumptiön;

6. Turn back (to your allegiance to Lucifer).

And with my blood again I will confirm
My former vow I made to Lucifer.
MEPHASTOPHILIS   Do it then quickly, with unfeignèd heart,
65   Lest greater danger do attend thy drift.°   *intent*
FAUSTUS   Torment, sweet friend, that base and crooked age
That durst dissuade me from thy Lucifer,
With greatest torments that our hell affords.
MEPHASTOPHILIS   His faith is great, I cannot touch his soul,
70   But what I may afflict his body with
I will attempt—which is but little worth.
FAUSTUS   One thing, good servant, let me crave of thee,
To glut the longing of my heart's desire:
That I might have unto my paramour
75   That heavenly Helen which I saw of late,
Whose sweet embracings may extinguish clean
These thoughts that do dissuade me from my vow:
And keep mine oath I made to Lucifer.
MEPHASTOPHILIS   Faustus, this, or what else thou shalt desire,
80   Shall be performed in twinkling of an eye.
[*Enter* HELEN.]
FAUSTUS   Was this the face that launched a thousand ships,
And burnt the topless[7] towers of Ilium?°   *Troy*
Sweet Helen, make me immortal with a kiss:
Her lips sucks forth my soul, see where it flies!
85   Come Helen, come, give me my soul again.
Here will I dwell, for heaven be in these lips,
And all is dross that is not Helena!
[*Enter* OLD MAN.]
I will be Paris, and for love of thee,
Instead of Troy shall Wittenberg be sacked;
90   And I will combat with weak Menelaus,°   *Helen's husband*
And wear thy colors on my plumèd crest:
Yea, I will wound Achilles in the heel,[8]
And then return to Helen for a kiss.
O thou art fairer than the evening air,
95   Clad in the beauty of a thousand stars,
Brighter art thou than flaming Jupiter
When he appeared to hapless Semele;[9]
More lovely than the monarch of the sky
In wanton Arethusa's azured arms;[1]
100   And none but thou shalt be my paramour.
[*Exeunt* (FAUSTUS *and* HELEN).]
OLD MAN   Accursèd Faustus, miserable man,
That from thy soul exclud'st the grace of heaven
And fliest the throne of His tribunal seat!
[*Enter the* DEVILS.]
Satan begins to sift me with his pride,[2]

---

7. So high they seemed to have no tops.
8. Achilles could only be wounded in his heel—
where he was shot by Paris.
9. A Theban girl, loved by Jupiter and destroyed
by the fire of his lightning when he appeared to her
in his full splendor.

1. Arethusa was the nymph of a fountain, as well
as the fountain itself; she excited the passion of
the river god Alpheus, who was by some accounts
related to the sun.
2. To test me with his strength.

105 As in this furnace God shall try my faith.
My faith, vile hell, shall triumph over thee!
Ambitious fiends, see how the heavens smiles
At your repulse, and laughs your state° to scorn.   *royal power*
Hence hell, for hence I fly unto my God.   [*Exeunt.*]

SCENE 13

[*Enter* FAUSTUS *with the* SCHOLARS.]

FAUSTUS Ah, gentlemen!

1 SCHOLAR What ails Faustus?

FAUSTUS Ah, my sweet chamber-fellow, had I lived with thee, then had I lived still; but now I die eternally. Look, comes he not, comes
5 he not?

2 SCHOLAR What means Faustus?

3 SCHOLAR Belike he is grown into some sickness by being over-solitary.

1 SCHOLAR If it be so, we'll have physicians to cure him; 'tis but a
10 surfeit:[3] never fear, man.

FAUSTUS A surfeit of deadly sin, that hath damned both body and soul.

2 SCHOLAR Yet Faustus, look up to heaven; remember God's mercies are infinite.

15 FAUSTUS But Faustus' offense can ne'er be pardoned! The serpent that tempted Eve may be saved, but not Faustus. Ah gentlemen, hear me with patience, and tremble not at my speeches, though my heart pants and quivers to remember that I have been a student here these thirty years—O would I had never seen Wittenberg,
20 never read book—and what wonders I have done, all Wittenberg can witness—yea, all the world; for which Faustus hath lost both Germany and the world—yea, heaven itself—heaven, the seat of God, the throne of the blessed, the kingdom of joy; and must remain in hell forever—hell, ah, hell forever! Sweet friends, what shall
25 become of Faustus, being in hell forever?

3 SCHOLAR Yet Faustus, call on God.

FAUSTUS On God, whom Faustus hath abjured? On God, whom Faustus hath blasphemed? Ah my God—I would weep, but the devil draws in my tears! gush forth blood, instead of tears—yea, life and
30 soul! O, he stays my tongue! I would lift up my hands, but see, they hold them, they hold them!

ALL Who, Faustus?

FAUSTUS Lucifer and Mephastophilis! Ah gentlemen, I gave them my soul for my cunning.

35 ALL God forbid!

FAUSTUS God forbade it indeed, but Faustus hath done it: for the vain pleasure of four-and-twenty years hath Faustus lost eternal joy and felicity. I writ them a bill with mine own blood, the date is expired, the time will come, and he will fetch me.

40 1 SCHOLAR Why did not Faustus tell us of this before, that divines might have prayed for thee?

FAUSTUS Oft have I thought to have done so, but the devil threatened to tear me in pieces if I named God, to fetch both body and

---

3. Indigestion caused by overeating.

soul, if I once gave ear to divinity; and now 'tis too late. Gentlemen
45   away, lest you perish with me!
2 SCHOLAR   O what shall we do to save Faustus?
3 SCHOLAR   God will strengthen me. I will stay with Faustus.
1 SCHOLAR   Tempt not God, sweet friend, but let us into the next
room, and there pray for him.
50 FAUSTUS   Ay, pray for me, pray for me; and what noise soever ye hear,
come not unto me, for nothing can rescue me.
2 SCHOLAR   Pray thou, and we will pray, that God may have mercy
upon thee.
FAUSTUS   Gentlemen, farewell. If I live till morning, I'll visit you; if
55   not, Faustus is gone to hell.
ALL   Faustus, farewell.   [*Exeunt* SCHOLARS.]
       [*The clock strikes eleven.*]
FAUSTUS   Ah Faustus,
Now hast thou but one bare hour to live,
And then thou must be damned perpetually.
60   Stand still, you ever-moving spheres of heaven,
That time may cease, and midnight never come.
Fair Nature's eye, rise, rise again, and make
Perpetual day, or let this hour be but
A year, a month, a week, a natural day,
65   That Faustus may repent and save his soul.
O lente, lente currite noctis equi![4]
The stars move still, time runs, the clock will strike,
The devil will come, and Faustus must be damned.
O I'll leap up to my God! Who pulls me down?
70   See, see where Christ's blood streams in the firmament!
One drop would save my soul, half a drop: ah my Christ—
Ah, rend not my heart for naming of my Christ;
Yet will I call on him—O spare me, Lucifer!
Where is it now? 'Tis gone: and see where God
75   Stretcheth out his arm, and bends his ireful brows!
Mountains and hills, come, come and fall on me,
And hide me from the heavy wrath of God.
No, no?
Then will I headlong run into the earth:
80   Earth, gape! O no, it will not harbor me.
You stars that reigned at my nativity,
Whose influence hath allotted death and hell,
Now draw up Faustus like a foggy mist
Into the entrails of yon laboring cloud,
85   That when you vomit forth into the air
My limbs may issue from your smoky mouths,
So that my soul may but ascend to heaven.[5]
       [*The watch strikes.*]
Ah, half the hour is past: 'twill all be past anon.
O God, if thou wilt not have mercy on my soul,
90   Yet for Christ's sake, whose blood hath ransomed me,
Impose some end to my incessant pain:

---

4. Slowly, slowly run, O horses of the night;
adapted from a line in Ovid's *Amores.*
5. Faustus wants to be drawn up into a cloud,
which would compact his body into a thunderstone
so that his soul, thus purified, might ascend to
heaven.

Let Faustus live in hell a thousand years,
A hundred thousand, and at last be saved.
O no end is limited to damnèd souls!
95 Why wert thou not a creature wanting soul?
Or why is this immortal that thou hast?
Ah, Pythagoras' *metempsychosis*⁶—were that true,
This soul should fly from me, and I be changed
Unto some brutish beast:
100 All beasts are happy, for when they die,
Their souls are soon dissolved in elements;
But mine must live still° to be plagued in hell.   *always*
Cursed be the parents that engendered me:
No, Faustus, curse thy self, curse Lucifer,
105 That hath deprived thee of the joys of heaven.
    [*The clock striketh twelve.*]
O it strikes, it strikes! Now body, turn to air,
Or Lucifer will bear thee quick° to hell.   *alive*
    [*Thunder and lightning.*]
O soul, be changed into little water drops,
And fall into the ocean, ne'er be found.
110 My God, my God, look not so fierce on me!
    [*Enter* DEVILS.]
Adders and serpents, let me breathe awhile!
Ugly hell gape not! Come not, Lucifer!
I'll burn my books—ah, Mephastophilis!
    [*Exeunt with him.*]

Epilogue

    [*Enter* CHORUS.]
Cut is the branch that might have grown full straight,
And burnèd is Apollo's laurel bough,⁷
That sometime grew within this learnèd man.
Faustus is gone! Regard his hellish fall,
5 Whose fiendful fortune° may exhort the wise   *devilish fate*
Only to wonder at⁸ unlawful things:
Whose deepness doth entice such forward wits
To practice more than heavenly power permits.   [*Exit.*]

*Terminat hora diem, terminat author opus.*⁹

1604, 1616

---

6. Pythagoras's doctrine of the transmigration of souls.
7. The laurel crown of Apollo symbolizes (among other things) learning and wisdom.
8. Be content simply to observe with awe.
9. The hour ends the day, the author ends his work; this motto was probably added by the printer.

WILLIAM SHAKESPEARE
1564–1616

William Shakespeare was born in the small market town of Stratford-on-Avon in April (probably April 23) 1564. His father, a successful glovemaker, landowner, money-lender, and dealer in agricultural commodities, was elected to several important posts in local government but later suffered financial and social reverses, possibly as a result of adherence to the Catholic faith. Shakespeare almost certainly attended the free Stratford grammar school, where he could have acquired a reasonably impressive education, including a respectable knowledge of Latin, but he did not proceed to Oxford or Cambridge. There are legends about Shakespeare's youth but no docu-mented facts. The first record we have of his life after his christening is that of his marriage in 1582, at age eighteen, to Anne Hathaway, eight years his senior. A daugh-ter, Susanna, was born six months later, in 1583, and twins, Hamnet and Judith, in 1585. We possess no information about his activities for the next seven years, but by 1592 he was in London as an actor and apparently already well known as a playwright, for a rival dramatist, Robert Greene, refers to him resentfully in A *Groatsworth of Wit* as "an upstart crow, beautified with our feathers."

At this time, there were several companies of professional actors in London and in the provinces. What connection Shakespeare had with one or more of them before 1592 is conjectural, but we do know of his long and fruitful connection with the most successful troupe, the Lord Chamberlain's Men, who later, when James I came to the throne, became the King's Men. Shakespeare not only acted with this company but eventually became a leading shareholder and the principal playwright. Then as now, making a living in the professional theater was not easy: competition among the repertoire companies was stiff, civic officials and religious moralists regarded play-acting as a sinful, time-wasting nuisance and tried to ban it altogether, government officials exercised censorship over the contents of the plays, and periodic outbreaks of bubonic plague led to temporary closing of the London theaters. But Shakespeare's company, which included some of the most famous actors of the day, nonetheless thrived and in 1599 began to perform in the Globe, a fine, open-air theater that the company built for itself on the south bank of the Thames. The company also per-formed frequently at court and, after 1608, at Blackfriars, an indoor London theater. Already by 1597 Shakespeare had so prospered that he was able to purchase New Place, a handsome house in Stratford; he could now call himself a gentleman, as his father had (probably with the financial assistance of his successful playwright son) been granted a coat of arms the previous year.

Shakespeare himself evidently had no interest in preserving for posterity the sum of his writings, let alone in clarifying the chronology of his works or in specifying which plays he wrote alone and which with collaborators. He wrote plays for perfor-mance by his company, and his scripts existed in his own handwritten manuscripts or in scribal copies, in playhouse prompt books, and probably in pirated texts based on shorthand reports of a performance or on reconstructions from memory by an actor or spectator. None of these manuscript versions has survived. Eighteen of his plays were published during his lifetime in the small-format, inexpensive books called quartos; to these were added eighteen other plays, never before printed, in the large, expensive folio volume of Mr. *William Shakespeares Comedies, Histories, & Tragedies* (1623), published seven years after his death. This First Folio, edited by two of his friends and fellow actors, John Heminges and Henry Condell, is organized by genre and makes no attempt to establish a chronology. We do not know how long a time would normally have elapsed between the writing of a play and its first per-formance, nor, with a very few exceptions, do we know with any certainty the month or even the year of the first performance of Shakespeare's plays. But scholars have gradually assembled a considerable archive of evidence, both external and internal, for dating the composition of the plays.

Shakespeare began his career, probably in the early 1590s, by writing both comedies and history plays. The earliest of these histories, generally based on the accounts of English kings written by Raphael Holinshed and other sixteenth-century chroniclers, seem theatrically vital but crude, as does an early attempt at tragedy, *Titus Andronicus*. But Shakespeare very quickly moved on to create, in *Richard III* (ca. 1592), a brilliantly conceived central character and to display a dazzling command of histrionic rhetoric and an overarching moral vision of English history. In the later 1590s he wrote a sequence of profoundly searching and ambitious history plays— *Richard II*, the first and second parts of *Henry IV*, and *Henry V*—which together explore the death throes of feudal England and the birth of the modern nation-state ruled by a charismatic monarch.

Shakespeare's first comedies show even fewer signs of an apprenticeship. *The Comedy of Errors*, one of his early efforts in this genre, already displays a rare command of the resources of comedy—mistaken identity, madcap confusion, and the threat of disaster, giving way in the end to reconciliation, recovery, and love. Successful as are these early histories and comedies, and indicative of an extraordinary theatrical talent, Shakespeare's achievement only a few years later would still have been all but impossible to foresee. Starting with *A Midsummer Night's Dream* (ca. 1595), he wrote an unprecedented succession of romantic comedies—*The Merchant of Venice*, *The Merry Wives of Windsor*, *Much Ado About Nothing*, *As You Like It*, and *Twelfth Night* (ca. 1601)—whose poetic richness and emotional complexity remain unmatched.

In the same year that Shakespeare wrote *Twelfth Night*, often regarded as the greatest of his comedies, he also probably wrote *Hamlet*, initiating an outpouring of great tragic dramas: *Othello*, *King Lear*, *Macbeth*, *Antony and Cleopatra*, and *Coriolanus*. These plays, written from 1601 to 1607, seem to mark a major shift in sensibility, an existential and metaphysical darkening that many readers think must have originated in a deep personal anguish, perhaps caused by the death of his father, John, in 1601.

Whatever the truth of these speculations—and we have no direct testimony either to support or to undermine them—there appears to have occurred in the same period a shift as well in Shakespeare's comic sensibility. The comedies written between 1601 and 1604, *Troilus and Cressida*, *All's Well That Ends Well*, and *Measure for Measure*, are sufficiently different from the earlier comedies—more biting in tone, more uneasy with comic conventions, more ruthlessly questioning of the values of the characters and the resolutions of the plots—to have led some modern scholars to classify them as "problem plays" or "dark comedies." Another group of plays, among the last that Shakespeare wrote, similarly constitutes a distinct category not recognized by the editors of the First Folio. *Pericles*, *Cymbeline*, *The Winter's Tale*, and *The Tempest*, written between 1608 and 1611, when Shakespeare had developed a remarkably fluid, dreamlike sense of plot and a poetic style that could veer, apparently effortlessly, from the tortured to the ineffably sweet, are now commonly known as the "romances." These plays share an interest in the moral and emotional life less of the adolescents who dominate the earlier comedies than of their parents. The "romances" are deeply concerned with patterns of loss and recovery, suffering and redemption, despair and renewal. They have seemed to many critics to constitute a self-conscious conclusion to a career that opened with histories and comedies and passed through the dark and tormented tragedies. Shakespeare evidently wrote the last of his plays in Stratford, where he retired about 1610. He died in 1616, shortly after the marriage festivities for his daughter Judith. His best epitaph is a famous line from a poem that his friend and rival Ben Jonson wrote in the First Folio: "He was not of an age, but for all time!"

Sonnets   In Elizabethan England aristocratic patronage, with the money, protection and prestige it alone could provide, was probably a professional writer's most important asset. This patronage, or at least Shakespeare's quest for it, is most visible in his dedication in 1593 and 1594 of his narrative poems, *Venus and Adonis* and *The Rape of Lucrece*, to the young nobleman Henry Wriothesley, earl of Southampton. What return the poet got for his exquisite offerings is unknown. We do know that among wits and gallants the narrative poems won Shakespeare a fine reputation as an immensely stylish and accomplished poet. This reputation was enhanced as well by manuscript circulation of his sonnets, which were mentioned admiringly in print more than ten years before they were published in 1609 (apparently without his personal supervision and perhaps without his consent).

Shakespeare's sonnets are quite unlike the other sonnet sequences of his day, notably in his almost unprecedented choice of a beautiful young man (rather than a lady) as the principal object of praise, love, and idealizing devotion and in his portrait of a dark, sensuous, and sexually promiscuous mistress (rather than the usual chaste and aloof blond beauty). Nor are the moods confined to what the Renaissance thought were those of the despairing Petrarchan lover: they include delight, pride, melancholy, shame, disgust, and fear. Shakespeare's sequence suggests a story, although the details are vague, and there is even doubt whether the sonnets as published are in an order established by the poet himself. Certain motifs are evident: an introductory series (1 to 17) celebrates the beauty of a young man and urges him to marry and beget children who will bear his image. The subsequent long sequence (18 to 126), passionately focused on the same beloved young man, develops as a dominant motif the transience and destructive power of time, countered only by the force of love and the permanence of poetry. The remaining sonnets focus chiefly on the so-called Dark Lady as an alluring but degrading object of desire. Some sonnets (like 144) intimate a love triangle involving the speaker, the male friend, and the woman; others take note of a rival poet (sometimes identified as George Chapman or Christopher Marlowe). The biographical background of the sonnets has inspired a mountain of speculation, but very little of it has any factual support.

Though there are many variations, Shakespeare's most frequent rhyme scheme in the sonnets is *abab cdcd efef gg*. This so-called Shakespearean pattern often (though not always) calls attention to three distinct quatrains (each of which may develop a separate metaphor), followed by a closing couplet that may either confirm or pull sharply against what has gone before. Startling shifts in direction may occur in lines other than the closing ones; consider, for example, the twists and turns in the opening lines of sonnet 138: "When my love swears that she is made of truth, / I do believe her, though I know she lies." Shakespeare's sonnets as a whole are strikingly intense, conveying a sense of high psychological and moral stakes. They are also remarkably dense, written with a daunting energy, concentration, and compression. Often the main idea of the poem may be grasped quickly, but the precise movement of thought and feeling, the links among the shifting images, the syntax, tone, and rhetorical structure prove immensely challenging. These are poems that famously reward rereading.

SONNETS

To the Only Begetter of
These Ensuing Sonnets
Mr. W. H. All Happiness
and That Eternity
Promised
By
Our Ever-Living Poet
Wisheth
the Well-Wishing
Adventurer in
Setting Forth
T. T.[1]

3

Look in thy glass° and tell the face thou viewest   *mirror*
Now is the time that face should form another,
Whose fresh repair if now thou not renewest,
Thou dost beguile the world, unbless some mother.
5   For where is she so fair whose uneared° womb   *unplowed*
Disdains the tillage of thy husbandry?
Or who is he so fond° will be the tomb   *foolish*
Of his self-love, to stop posterity?
Thou art thy mother's glass, and she in thee
10   Calls back the lovely April of her prime;
So thou through windows of thine age shalt see,
Despite of wrinkles, this thy golden time.
    But if thou live rememb'red not to be,
    Die single, and thine image dies with thee.

12

When I do count the clock that tells the time
And see the brave° day sunk in hideous night,   *splendid*
When I behold the violet past prime
And sable curls all silvered o'er with white,
5   When lofty trees I see barren of leaves,
Which erst° from heat did canopy the herd   *formerly*
And summer's green all girded up in sheaves
Borne on the bier with white and bristly beard:

1. This odd dedication bears the initials of the publisher, Thomas Thorpe. The W. H. addressed here may or may not be the male friend addressed in sonnets 1 to 126. Leading candidates for that role are Henry Wriothesley, earl of Southampton, the dedicatee of *Venus and Adonis* (1593) and *The Rape of Lucrece* (1594), and William Herbert, earl of Pembroke, a dedicatee of the First Folio. But there is no hard evidence to support these or other suggested identifications of the male friend or of the so-called Dark Lady; these sonnet personages may or may not have had real-life counterparts.
    Since all the sonnets save two were first published in 1609, we do not repeat the date after each one. Numbers 138 and 144 were first published in 1599, in a verse miscellany called *The Passionate Pilgrim*.

Then of thy beauty do I question make°   *speculate*
10 That thou among the wastes of time must go,
Since sweets and beauties do themselves forsake,
And die as fast as they see others grow,
  And nothing 'gainst Time's scythe can make defense
  Save breed, to brave[2] him when he takes thee hence.

15

When I consider every thing that grows
Holds° in perfection but a little moment;   *remains*
That this huge stage presenteth naught but shows
Whereon the stars in secret influence comment;[3]
5 When I perceive that men as plants increase,
Cheerèd and checked[4] even by the selfsame sky,
Vaunt[5] in their youthful sap, at height decrease,
And wear their brave state out of memory;[6]
Then the conceit° of this inconstant stay   *conception*
10 Sets you most rich in youth before my sight,
Where wasteful Time debateth[7] with Decay
To change your day of youth to sullied° night,   *soiled, blackened*
  And all in war with Time for love of you,
  As he takes from you, I ingraft[8] you new.

18

Shall I compare thee to a summer's day?
Thou art more lovely and more temperate:
Rough winds do shake the darling buds of May,
And summer's lease hath all too short a date;
5 Sometime too hot the eye of heaven shines,
And often is his gold complexion dimmed;
And every fair from fair sometime declines,
By chance or nature's changing course untrimmed.[9]
But thy eternal summer shall not fade,
10 Nor lose possession of that fair thou ow'st;°   *ownest*
Nor shall death brag thou wander'st in his shade,
When in eternal lines to time thou grow'st:°   *are grafted*
  So long as men can breathe or eyes can see,
  So long lives this, and this gives life to thee.[1]

2. Defy. "Breed": offspring.
3. The stars secretly affect human actions. "Shows": (1) appearances, (2) performances.
4. Encouraged and reproached or stopped.
5. Exult, display themselves.
6. Wear their showy splendor out and are forgotten.
7. (1)Fights, (2) joins forces.
8. Renew by grafting, implant beauty again (by my verse).
9. Stripped of gay apparel.
1. The boast of immortality for one's verse was a convention going back to the classics. It may be thought to imply not egotism on the part of the poet but faith in the permanence of poetry.

19

Devouring Time, blunt thou the lion's paws,
And make the earth devour her own sweet brood;
Pluck the keen teeth from the fierce tiger's jaws,
And burn the long-lived phoenix in her blood;[2]
5 Make glad and sorry seasons as thou fleet'st,
And do whate'er thou wilt, swift-footed Time,
To the wide world and all her fading sweets,
But I forbid thee one most heinous crime:
O carve not with thy hours my love's fair brow,
10 Nor draw no lines there with thine antique[3] pen;
Him in thy course untainted[4] do allow,
For beauty's pattern to succeeding men.
    Yet do thy worst, old Time: despite thy wrong,
    My love shall in my verse ever live young.

20

A woman's face with Nature's own hand painted[5]
Hast thou, the master mistress of my passion;[6]
A woman's gentle heart but not acquainted
With shifting change as is false women's fashion;
5 An eye more bright than theirs, less false in rolling,°   *roving*
Gilding the object whereupon it gazeth;
A man in hue all hues[7] in his controlling,
Which steals men's eyes and women's souls amazeth.
And for a woman wert thou first created,
10 Till Nature as she wrought thee fell a-doting,[8]
And by addition me of thee defeated,
By adding one thing to my purpose nothing.
    But since she pricked[9] thee out for women's pleasure,
    Mine be thy love, and thy love's use their treasure.[1]

29

When, in disgrace° with Fortune and men's eyes,   *disfavor*
I all alone beweep my outcast state,
And trouble deaf heaven with my bootless° cries,   *futile*
And look upon myself and curse my fate,
5 Wishing me like to one more rich in hope,
Featured like him, like him with friends possessed,[2]
Desiring this man's art° and that man's scope,°   *skill / ability*

---

2. In full vigor of life (a hunting term). The phoenix was a mythical bird that lived five hundred years, then died in flames to rise again from its ashes.
3. (1) Old, (2) fantastic.
4. (1) Undefiled, (2) untouched by a weapon (a term from jousting).
5. I.e., not made up with cosmetics.
6. (1) Strong feeling, (2) poem.
7. "Hue" probably means appearance or form. In

the first edition, "hues" is spelled "*Hews*," which some have taken as indicating a pun on a proper name. It has also been suggested that "man in" is a copyist's or compositor's misreading of "maiden."
8. (1) Crazy, (2) infatuated.
9. Marked, with obvious sexual pun.
1. (1) Sexual enjoyment, (2) interest (as in usury).
2. I.e., I wish I had one man's looks, another man's friends.

With what I most enjoy contented least;
Yet in these thoughts myself almost despising,
10 Haply I think on thee, and then my state³
(Like to the lark at break of day arising
From sullen earth) sings hymns at heaven's gate;
    For thy sweet love remembered such wealth brings
    That then I scorn to change my state with kings.

30

When to the sessions⁴ of sweet silent thought
I summon up remembrance of things past,
I sigh the lack of many a thing I sought,
And with old woes new wail° my dear time's waste: *bewail anew*
5 Then can I drown an eye (unused to flow)
For precious friends hid in death's dateless° night,   *endless*
And weep afresh love's long since canceled woe,
And moan th' expense° of many a vanished sight: *loss*
Then can I grieve at grievances foregone,°   *former*
10 And heavily from woe to woe tell° o'er   *count*
The sad account of fore-bemoanèd moan,
Which I new pay as if not paid before.
    But if the while I think on thee, dear friend,
    All losses are restored and sorrows end.

33

Full many a glorious morning have I seen
Flatter the mountain tops with sovereign eye,°   *sunlight*
Kissing with golden face the meadows green,
Gilding pale streams with heavenly alchemy;
5 Anon° permit the basest° clouds to ride   *(but) soon / darkest*
With ugly rack° on his celestial face,   *cloudy mask*
And from the forlorn world his visage hide,
Stealing unseen to west with this disgrace.
Even so my sun one early morn did shine
10 With all triumphant splendor on my brow;
But out, alack,° he was but one hour mine;   *alas*
The region° cloud hath masked him from me now.   *high*
    Yet him for this my love no whit disdaineth:
    Suns of the world may stain° when heaven's sun staineth.   *darken*

35

No more be grieved at that which thou hast done:
Roses have thorns, and silver fountains mud.

---

3. Condition, state of mind; but in line 14 there is a pun on *state* meaning chair of state, throne.

4. Sittings of court. "Summon up" (next line) continues the metaphor.

Clouds and eclipses stain° both moon and sun,   *dim*
And loathsome canker° lives in sweetest bud.   *rose worm*
5 All men make faults, and even I in this,
Authorizing thy trespass with compare,
Myself corrupting, salving thy amiss,°   *palliating your offense*
Excusing thy sins more than thy sins are;
For to thy sensual fault I bring in sense°—   *reason*
10 Thy adverse party is thy advocate—
And 'gainst myself a lawful plea commence.
Such civil war is in my love and hate,
   That I an accessary needs must be
   To that sweet thief which sourly robs from me.

55

Not marble, nor the gilded monuments
Of princes, shall outlive this powerful rhyme;
But you shall shine more bright in these contents
Than unswept stone, besmeared with sluttish time.[5]
5 When wasteful war shall statues overturn,
And broils root out the work of masonry,
Nor Mars his° sword nor war's quick fire shall burn   *neither Mars's*
The living record of your memory.
'Gainst death and all-oblivious enmity[6]
10 Shall you pace forth; your praise shall still find room
Even in the eyes of all posterity
That wear this world out to the ending doom.°   *Judgment Day*
   So, till the judgment that yourself arise,[7]
   You live in this, and dwell in lovers' eyes.

60

Like as the waves make towards the pebbled shore,
So do our minutes hasten to their end;
Each changing place with that which goes before,
In sequent toil all forwards do contend.[8]
5 Nativity, once in the main° of light,   *broad expanse*
Crawls to maturity, wherewith being crowned,
Crooked eclipses 'gainst his glory fight,
And Time that gave doth now his gift confound.
Time doth transfix the flourish set on youth
10 And delves the parallels[9] in beauty's brow,
Feeds on the rarities of nature's truth,
And nothing stands but for his scythe to mow.

---

5. I.e., than in a stone tomb or effigy that time
wears away and covers with dust.
6. The enmity of oblivion, of being forgotten.
7. Until you rise from the dead on Judgment Day.
8. Toiling and following each other, the waves
struggle to press forward.
9. Digs the parallel furrows (wrinkles). "Transfix
the flourish": remove the embellishment. To
"flourish" is also to blossom.

And yet to times in hope° my verse shall stand,   *future times*
Praising thy worth, despite his cruel hand.

65

Since[1] brass, nor stone, nor earth, nor boundless sea,
But sad mortality o'ersways their power,
How with this rage° shall beauty hold a plea,   *destructive power*
Whose action is no stronger than a flower?
5   O how shall summer's honey breath hold out
Against the wrackful° siege of batt'ring days,   *destructive*
When rocks impregnable are not so stout,
Nor gates of steel so strong, but Time decays?
O fearful meditation! where, alack,
10 Shall Time's best jewel from Time's chest[2] lie hid?
Or what strong hand can hold his swift foot back?
Or who his spoil° of beauty can forbid?   *ravaging*
   O none, unless this miracle have might,
   That in black ink my love may still shine bright.

71

No longer mourn for me when I am dead
Than you shall hear the surly sullen bell[3]
Give warning to the world that I am fled
From this vile world, with vilest worms to dwell:
5   Nay, if you read this line, remember not
The hand that writ it; for I love you so,
That I in your sweet thoughts would be forgot,
If thinking on me then should make you woe.
Oh, if, I say, you look upon this verse
10 When I perhaps compounded am with clay,
Do not so much as my poor name rehearse,
But let your love even with my life decay;
   Lest the wise world should look into your moan,
   And mock you with me after I am gone.

73

That time of year thou mayst in me behold
When yellow leaves, or none, or few, do hang
Upon those boughs which shake against the cold,
Bare ruined choirs,[4] where late the sweet birds sang.
5   In me thou seest the twilight of such day

---

1. I.e., because there is neither.
2. I.e., from being coffered up by Time.
3. The bell was tolled to announce the death of a member of the parish—one stroke for each year of

his or her life.
4. The part of a church where divine service was sung.

As after sunset fadeth in the west;
Which by and by black night doth take away,
Death's second self that seals up all in rest.
In me thou seest the glowing of such fire

10 That on the ashes of his youth doth lie,
As the deathbed whereon it must expire,
Consumed with that which it was nourished by.[5]
    This thou perceiv'st, which makes thy love more strong,
    To love that well, which thou must leave ere long.

74

But be contented; when that fell[6] arrest
Without all bail shall carry me away,
My life hath in this line some interest,[7]
Which for memorial still° with thee shall stay.   *always*

5 When thou reviewest this, thou dost review
The very part was° consecrate to thee.   *i.e., which was*
The earth can have but earth, which is his due;
My spirit is thine, the better part of me.
So then thou hast but lost the dregs of life,

10 The prey of worms, my body being dead,
The coward conquest of a wretch's knife,[8]
Too base of thee to be rememberèd.
    The worth of that is that which it contains,[9]
    And that is this, and this with thee remains.

87

Farewell: thou art too dear[1] for my possessing,
And like enough thou know'st thy estimate.°   *value*
The charter° of thy worth gives thee releasing;   *deed, contract for property*
My bonds in thee are all determinate.°   *expired*

5 For how do I hold thee but by thy granting,
And for that riches where is my deserving?
The cause of this fair gift in me is wanting,
And so my patent° back again is swerving.   *title*
Thy self thou gav'st, thy own worth then not knowing,

10 Or me, to whom thou gav'st it, else mistaking;
So thy great gift, upon misprision° growing,   *mistake, oversight*
Comes home again, on better judgment making.
    Thus have I had thee as a dream doth flatter,
    In sleep a king, but waking no such matter.

---

5. Choked by the ashes of that which once nourished its flame.
6. Cruel. Hamlet says, "this fell sergeant / Death
is strict in his arrest" (5.2.278–79).
7. Share, participation. "In this line": i.e., poetry.

8. Death's weapon (like Time's scythe).
9. I.e., the only value of the body is that it contains
the spirit.
1. (1) Expensive, (2) beloved.

94

They that have power to hurt and will do none,
That do not do the thing they most do show,°   *seem to do*
Who, moving others, are themselves as stone,
Unmovèd, cold, and to temptation slow;
5 They rightly do inherit heaven's graces
And husband nature's riches from expense;[2]
They are the lords and owners of their faces,
Others but stewards of their excellence.
The summer's flower is to the summer sweet,
10 Though to itself it only live and die,
But if that flower with base infection meet,
The basest weed outbraves° his dignity: *surpasses*
    For sweetest things turn sourest by their deeds;
    Lilies that fester smell far worse than weeds.[3]

97

How like a winter hath my absence been
From thee, the pleasure of the fleeting year!
What freezings have I felt, what dark days seen!
What old December's bareness everywhere!
5 And yet this time removed[4] was summer's time,
The teeming autumn, big with rich increase,
Bearing the wanton burthen of the prime,[5]
Like widowed wombs after their lords' decease;
Yet this abundant issue seemed to me
10 But hope of orphans and unfathered fruit;
For summer and his pleasures wait on thee,
And, thou away, the very birds are mute;
    Or, if they sing, 'tis with so dull a cheer°   *disposition*
    That leaves look pale, dreading the winter's near.

106

When in the chronicle of wasted° time   *past*
I see descriptions of the fairest wights,°   *persons*
And beauty making beautiful old rhyme
In praise of ladies dead and lovely knights,
5 Then, in the blazon[6] of sweet beauty's best,
Of hand, of foot, of lip, of eye, of brow,
I see their antique pen would have expressed

---

2. I.e., they do not squander nature's gifts.
3. This line also appears in *Edward III* (2.1.451), an apocryphal Shakespearean play licensed December 1, 1595.
4. I.e., when I was absent.

5. Spring, which has engendered the lavish crop ("wanton burthen") that autumn is now left to bear.
6. Catalog of excellencies.

Even such a beauty as you master now.
So all their praises are but prophecies
10 Of this our time, all you prefiguring;
And, for they looked but with divining eyes,[7]
They had not skill enough your worth to sing:
 For we, which now behold these present days,
 Have eyes to wonder, but lack tongues to praise.

107

Not mine own fears, nor the prophetic soul
Of the wide world dreaming on things to come,[8]
Can yet the lease of my true love control,
Supposed as forfeit to a confinèd doom.[9]
5 The mortal moon hath her eclipse endured,
And the sad augurs mock their own presage;[1]
Incertainties now crown themselves assured,
And peace[2] proclaims olives of endless age.
Now with the drops of this most balmy time
10 My love looks fresh, and death to me subscribes,°   *submits*
Since, spite of him, I'll live in this poor rhyme,
While he insults o'er dull and speechless tribes:
 And thou in this shalt find thy monument,
 When tyrants' crests and tombs of brass are spent.°   *wasted away*

116

Let me not to the marriage of true minds
Admit impediments;[3] love is not love
Which alters when it alteration finds,
Or bends with the remover to remove:
5 O, no, it is an ever-fixèd mark,[4]
That looks on tempests and is never shaken;
It is the star to every wand'ring bark,
Whose worth's unknown, although his highth[5] be taken.
Love's not Time's fool,° though rosy lips and cheeks *plaything, victim*
10 Within his[6] bending sickle's compass come;
Love alters not with his brief hours and weeks,
But bears it out even to the edge of doom.°   *brink of Judgment Day*

7. Because ("for") they were able only ("but") to foresee prophetically.
8. This sonnet refers to contemporary events and the prophecies, common in Elizabethan almanacs, of disaster.
9. I.e., can yet put an end to my love, which I thought doomed to early forfeiture.
1. The "mortal moon" is Queen Elizabeth; her "eclipse" is probably her climacteric year, her sixty-third (thought meaningful because the product of two "significant" numbers, 7 and 9), which ended in September 1596. The sober astrologers ("sad augurs") now ridicule their own predictions ("pres-age") of catastrophe, because they turned out to be false.
2. Probably the agreement between Henry IV of France and Elizabeth.
3. From the marriage service: "If any of you know cause or just impediment why these persons should not be joined together . . ."
4. Seamark (cf. *landmark*).
5. The star's value is incalculable, although its "highth" (altitude) may be known and used for practical purposes.
6. Time's (as also in line 11).

If this be error and upon me proved,
I never writ, nor no man ever loved.

129

Th' expense of spirit in a waste of shame
Is lust in action;[7] and till action, lust
Is perjured, murd'rous, bloody, full of blame,
Savage, extreme, rude,° cruel, not to trust;   brutal
5   Enjoyed no sooner but despisèd straight:
Past reason hunted; and no sooner had,
Past reason hated, as a swallowed bait,
On purpose laid to make the taker mad:
Mad in pursuit, and in possession so;
10 Had, having, and in quest to have, extreme;
A bliss in proof[8] and proved, a very° woe;   true
Before, a joy proposed; behind, a dream.
    All this the world well knows; yet none knows well
    To shun the heaven that leads men to this hell.

130

My mistress' eyes are nothing like the sun;[9]
Coral is far more red than her lips' red;
If snow be white, why then her breasts are dun;
If hairs be wires, black wires grow on her head.
5   I have seen roses damasked,° red and white,   variegated
But no such roses see I in her cheeks;
And in some perfumes is there more delight
Than in the breath that from my mistress reeks.[1]
I love to hear her speak, yet well I know
10 That music hath a far more pleasing sound;
I grant I never saw a goddess go;°   walk
My mistress, when she walks, treads on the ground.
    And yet, by heaven, I think my love as rare°   admirable, extraordinary
    As any she belied° with false compare.   misrepresented

135

Whoever hath her wish, thou hast thy *Will*,[2]
And *Will* to boot, and *Will* in overplus;

7. The word order here is inverted and slightly
obscures the meaning. Lust, when put into action,
expends "spirit" (life, vitality; also semen) in a
"waste" (desert; also with a pun on *waist*) of shame.
8. A bliss during the experience.
9. An anti-Petrarchan sonnet. All of the details
commonly attributed by other Elizabethan sonneteers to their ladies are here denied to the poet's
mistress.
1. Not with our pejorative sense, but simply "emanates."
2. (1) Wishes, (2) carnal desire, (3) the male and
female sexual organs, (4) a lover—Shakespeare?—
named Will. This is one of three, possibly four,
sonnets punning on the word.

More than enough am I that vex thee still,°   *always*
To thy sweet will making addition thus.
5 Wilt thou, whose will is large and spacious,
   Not once vouchsafe° to hide my will in thine?   *consent*
   Shall will in others seem right gracious,
   And in° my will no fair acceptance shine?   *in the case of*
   The sea, all water, yet receives rain still,
10 And in abundance addeth to his store,°   *plenty*
   So thou being rich in *Will* add to thy *Will*
   One will of mine to make thy large *Will* more.
       Let no unkind, no fair beseechers kill;[3]
       Think all but one, and me in that one *Will*.

138

When my love swears that she is made of truth,
I do believe her, though I know she lies,[4]
That she might think me some untutored youth,
Unlearnèd in the world's false subtleties.
5 Thus vainly thinking that she thinks me young,
   Although she knows my days are past the best,[5]
   Simply° I credit her false-speaking tongue: *like a simpleton*
   On both sides thus is simple truth suppressed.
   But wherefore says she not she is unjust?°   *unfaithful*
10 And wherefore say not I that I am old?
   Oh, love's best habit[6] is in seeming trust,
   And age in love loves not to have years told.°   *counted*
       Therefore I lie with her and she with me,
       And in our faults by lies we flattered be.

144

Two loves I have of comfort and despair,[7]
Which like two spirits do suggest me still:°   *tempt me constantly*
The better angel is a man right fair,
The worser spirit a woman colored ill.°   *dark*
5 To win me soon to hell, my female evil
   Tempteth my better angel from my side,
   And would corrupt my saint to be a devil,
   Wooing his purity with her foul pride.[8]
   And whether that my angel be turned fiend
10 Suspect I may, yet not directly tell;
   But being both from me, both to each[9] friend,
   I guess one angel in another's hell.[1]

3. I.e., do not kill with unkindness any of your
wooers.
4. With the obvious sexual pun (as also in lines
13–14). "Made of truth": (1) is utterly honest, (2)
is faithful.
5. Shakespeare was thirty-five or younger when he
wrote this sonnet (it first appeared in *The Passion-*

ate Pilgrim, 1599).
6. Appearance, deportment.
7. I have two beloveds, one bringing me comfort
and the other despair.
8. (1) Vanity, (2) sexuality.
9. Each other. "From": away from.
1. A double entendre.

Yet this shall I ne'er know, but live in doubt,
Till my bad angel fire my good one out.[2]

146

Poor soul, the center of my sinful earth,
Lord of[3] these rebel powers that thee array,[4]
Why dost thou pine within and suffer dearth,
Painting thy outward walls so costly gay?
5 Why so large cost, having so short a lease,
Dost thou upon thy fading mansion spend?
Shall worms, inheritors of this excess,
Eat up thy charge?[5] Is this thy body's end?
Then, soul, live thou upon thy servant's loss,
10 And let that pine to aggravate thy store;[6]
Buy terms divine in selling hours of dross;[7]
Within be fed, without be rich no more.
  So shalt thou feed on death, that feeds on men,
  And death once dead, there's no more dying then.

147

My love is as a fever, longing still°   continually
For that which longer nurseth[8] the disease,
Feeding on that which doth preserve the ill,°   maintain the illness
Th' uncertain sickly appetite[9] to please.
5 My reason, the physician to my love,
Angry that his prescriptions are not kept,
Hath left me, and I desperate now approve
Desire is death, which physic did except.[1]
Past cure I am, now reason is past care,[2]
10 And frantic mad with evermore unrest;
My thoughts and my discourse as madmen's are,
At random from the truth, vainly expressed;[3]
  For I have sworn thee fair, and thought thee bright,
  Who art as black as hell, as dark as night.

1 Henry IV   With a succession of plays written in the 1590s, Shakespeare helped to invent and perfect a theatrical genre known as the history play, a staging of momentous events and crucial figures from England's past. Depicting on the public

---

2. I.e., until she infects him with venereal disease.
3. An emendation. The 1609 edition repeats the last three words of line 1. Other suggestions are "Thrall to," "Starved by," "Pressed by," and leaving the repetition but dropping "that thee" in line 2.
4. Dress out, often used in a military sense.
5. What you have spent so much on.
6. Let "that" (i.e., the body) deteriorate to increase ("aggravate") the soul's riches ("thy store").

7. Refuse, rubbish. "Terms": long periods.
8. (1) Nourishes, (2) takes care of.
9. (1) Desire for food, (2) lust.
1. I.e., I learn by experience that desire, which rejected reason's medicine, is death.
2. I.e., medical care (of me). The line is a version of the proverb "past cure, past care."
3. Wide of the mark and senselessly uttered.

stage contemporary figures such as Queen Elizabeth or her glittering courtiers would not have been at all prudent: both the Elizabethan theater and the printing press were censored, and it was dangerous to represent or to reflect in public on those in power. As Sir Walter Ralegh remarked, explaining why he was writing a history of the ancient past, he who follows truth too close on the heels is likely to have his teeth kicked out. But Shakespeare contrived to reflect with remarkable candor on his own society and on the underlying forces that shaped the nation's destiny. He did so by powerfully chronicling a series of violent struggles in the fourteenth and fifteenth centuries that, as he depicts them, constituted the birth pangs of the modern world.

Henry IV, Part One is part of what is often termed Shakespeare's Second Tetralogy (that is, the sequence of four plays comprising *Richard II,* the two parts of *Henry IV,* and *Henry V*). But each of these was clearly intended to be enjoyed independently of the others. First printed in 1598, *1 Henry IV* had been performed on the stage and at court before publication, and from that time to this it has remained one of Shakespeare's most popular plays.

In *Richard II,* the tough, efficient Bullingbrook overthrows his weak, irresponsible young cousin, King Richard II. Vain, surrounded by flatterers, and deluded by poetic dreams of his own grandeur, Richard had precipitated the events that led to his downfall by unjustly exiling Bullingbrook and then seizing his inheritance. At the close of the play, Bullingbrook, now on the throne as King Henry IV, has the imprisoned Richard II murdered. By this act—ridding himself, as he puts it, of his "buried fear"—he hopes to stabilize and secure his rule and the rule after him of his son and heir Prince Hal.

But the buried fear proves to be a persistent nightmare. Deposing a legitimate king, one who had been duly anointed by the church and thereby invested with enormous symbolic significance, is an act whose long-term consequences are difficult to control. Several characters express the anxious sense that there is a curse now hanging over the land, a curse that will bring what the bishop of Carlisle grimly predicts: "Disorder, horror, fear, and mutiny" (*Richard II* 4.1.137). And, even without metaphysical dread, there are ample grounds for concern, since a variety of political and social forces are threatening to tear the kingdom apart. The usurper Bullingbrook's struggle to maintain his power in the face of a succession of civil wars and rebellions lies at the heart of the two parts of *Henry IV.* Bound up with this struggle is the transformation of his son, Prince Hal, from a dissolute wastrel to a staunch prop of the regime and a worthy successor to monarchical authority. In *Henry V,* Hal, having succeeded to his father's throne, secures this transformation, becoming in the process an English national hero. Leading his brave, heavily outnumbered troops, he conquers France at the Battle of Agincourt.

Shakespeare drew his historical material from prose chronicle histories, specifically Raphael Holinshed's *Chronicle of England, Scotland, and Ireland,* as well as from Samuel Daniel's historical poem, *The Civil Wars,* and an earlier anonymously authored play about Henry V, *The Famous Victories of Henry V.* These sources gave him the main outlines of his plot: the beleaguered Henry IV is threatened by a rebellion among his nobles, especially the powerful Percy family that had earlier helped him topple Richard II. This family, whose stronghold lay in Northumberland, in the north of England, is joined by other dangerous forces situated on the Celtic-speaking peripheries of the kingdom: the Scots, led by the redoubtable Earl of Douglas, and the Welsh, led by the charismatic, volatile magician Owen Glendower. These menacing powers had been kept at bay by Henry IV's allies, but the erstwhile allies have now become the king's most dangerous enemies: the gallant, impetuous Henry Percy or Hotspur, who has naturally followed his father, the earl of Northumberland, and his uncle, the earl of Worcester, into rebellion, and Edmund Mortimer, who had a strong claim to succeed Richard II to the throne and who has now married Glendower's daughter.

From his sources Shakespeare also derived a portrait of Prince Hal as a prodigal son, a wild youth cavorting with a disorderly crew of drunks, thieves, and whores. The chief among these dissipated friends was a fat knight whom Shakespeare originally called Sir John Oldcastle. The choice of name turned out to be an unfortunate one. The historical Oldcastle had at one time fought for Henry IV but was charged with rebellion and executed; Protestants in the sixteenth century said that he was a martyr who had actually been killed for his religious beliefs, many of which anticipated the tenets of the Reformation. Oldcastle's powerful descendants vehemently objected to the identification of their illustrious ancestor with the corrupt, wheezing, hilarious scoundrel on stage, and Shakespeare was forced to come up with another name. Under the altered name—Sir John Falstaff—the character has come to be widely regarded as Shakespeare's greatest comic creation.

Shakespeare, who never felt tied to a strict observance of historical accuracy, made many changes in his source materials, most notably, perhaps, reconceiving the character of Hotspur. In the *Chronicle,* he is older than Hal's father, but Shakespeare makes him Hal's foil, coeval, and rival—a charismatic and brave warrior, as Hal finally proves to be, but also (unlike Hal) fiery and impatient, scornful of the soft, civilized arts of music and poetry, and single-mindedly driven by ambition for honor and fame. In reworking his sources Shakespeare highlights psychological conflicts: Hal's need to define himself in relation to two very different fathers—the tense, care-worn Henry IV and his witty, disreputable surrogate father, Falstaff—and against his glittering, siblinglike rival, Hotspur.

1 Henry IV is centrally concerned with political power: its sources, uses, theatrical manifestations, ambiguities, psychological costs, and subversions. Recent criticism has focused attention on several key questions: how far does this play (and the tetralogy) serve to reinforce the "Tudor myth" of providential kingship? And to what extent does it undermine that myth of divinely-sanctioned legitimacy by exposing the basis of kingship as Machiavellian force and fraud? How far does Prince Hal's transformation make him the embodiment of an ideal monarch who fulfills his filial and regal responsibilities? And to what extent is that idealization undercut by Hal's self-proclaimed hypocrisy and play-acting (and in *2 Henry IV* by his cold-hearted repudiation of Falstaff)? The scheme of Hal's moral redemption is carefully laid out in his soliloquy at the close of the first tavern scene: "By how much better than my word I am," he declares, "By so much shall I falsify men's hopes" (1.2.165–66). To falsify men's hopes is to exceed their expectations, but it is also to disappoint their expectations, to deceive men, to turn hopes into fictions, to betray.

At issue are not only the contradictory desires and expectations centered on Hal—the competing hopes of his royal father and his tavern cronies—but also the fantasies continually aroused by the play of innate grace, limitless playfulness, absolute friendship, generosity, and trust. Those fantasies are symbolized by certain echoing, talismanic phrases ("when thou art king?"), and they are bound up with the overall vividness, intensity, and richness of the theatrical practice itself: the play's multiplicity of brilliant characters, its intensely differentiated settings, its dazzling verbal wit, its mingling of high comedy, farce, epic heroism, and tragedy. *1 Henry IV* awakens a dream of superabundance, which is given its irresistible embodiment in Falstaff.

In structure, the play moves back and forth between court (whether that of the king or of the rebels) and tavern, and it sets the affairs of state in counterpoint to the affairs of bawds, thieves, and drunkards. The fulcrum in this precarious balance is Falstaff, for generations of readers and critics the play's most fascinating figure. A number of literary antecedents lie behind Shakespeare's character: the braggart soldier of Roman comedy, the stock character called the Vice in medieval morality plays, the carnival Lord of Misrule, the figure of Gluttony from the pageant of the Seven Deadly Sins, the picaresque rogue or highwayman, and the sanctimonious hypocrite from popular satires on Elizabethan puritanism. What is most striking about Falstaff perhaps is his sheer comic excess: he is liar, glutton, knave, coward, thief, lecher, drunkard, wit, philosopher, skilled rhetorician, cynic, master parodist, confidence man, parasite, and friend. Shakespeare continued to mine his inexhaustible exuberance in 2 *Henry IV* and also (reportedly by Queen Elizabeth's express command) in a comedy of middle-class life, *The Merry Wives of Windsor*.

The First Part of King Henry the Fourth

DRAMATIS PERSONAE

KING HENRY THE FOURTH
HENRY, *Prince of Wales*
PRINCE JOHN OF LANCASTER } *Sons to the* KING
EARL OF WESTMORELAND
SIR WALTER BLUNT
THOMAS PERCY, *Earl of Worcester*
HENRY PERCY, *Earl of Northumberland*
HENRY PERCY, *surnamed* HOTSPUR, *his son*
EDMUND MORTIMER, *Earl of March*
RICHARD SCROOP, *Archbishop of York*
ARCHIBALD, *Earl of Douglas*
OWEN GLENDOWER
SIR RICHARD VERNON
SIR MICHAEL, *a friend to the* ARCHBISHOP OF YORK
SIR JOHN FALSTAFF
POINS
GADSHILL
PETO } *Companions of* FALSTAFF
BARDOLPH
LADY PERCY, *wife to* HOTSPUR, *and sister to* MORTIMER
LADY MORTIMER, *daughter to* GLENDOWER, *and wife to* MORTIMER
MISTRESS QUICKLY, *hostess of a tavern in Eastcheap*
LORDS, OFFICERS, SHERIFF, VINTNER, CHAMBERLAIN, DRAWERS, *two* CARRIERS, TRAVELERS, *and* ATTENDANTS

England and Wales

Act 1

SCENE 1

[*Enter the* KING, PRINCE JOHN OF LANCASTER, THE EARL OF WEST-
MORELAND, SIR WALTER BLUNT, *with others.*]

KING   So shaken as we are, so wan with care,
Find we a time for frighted peace to pant,[1]
And breathe short-winded accents of new broils[2]
To be commenced in stronds° afar remote.   strands, regions
5   No more the thirsty entrance[3] of this soil
Shall daub her lips with her own children's blood;
No more shall trenching war channel her fields,

1. I.e., let us allow peace to catch her breath.   3. Parched mouth.
2. I.e., news of new wars.

Nor bruise her flow'rets with the armèd hoofs
Of hostile paces.⁴ Those opposèd eyes,
10   Which, like the meteors of a troubled heaven,
All of one nature, of one substance bred,
Did lately meet in the intestine shock⁵
And furious close° of civil butchery,   *encounter*
Shall now, in mutual well-beseeming ranks,
15   March all one way and be no more opposed
Against acquaintance, kindred, and allies.
The edge of war, like an ill-sheathèd knife,
No more shall cut his master. Therefore, friends,
As far as to the sepulchre of Christ,—
20   Whose soldier now, under whose blessed cross
We are impressèd° and engaged to fight,   *enlisted*
Forthwith a power⁶ of English shall we levy,
Whose arms were molded in their mother's womb
To chase these pagans in those holy fields
25   Over whose acres walked those blessed feet
Which fourteen hundred years ago were nailed
For our advantage on the bitter cross.
But this our purpose now is twelve month old,
And bootless° 'tis to tell you we will go.   *useless*
30   Therefore we meet not now.⁷ Then let me hear
Of you, my gentle cousin° Westmoreland,   *kinsman*
What yesternight our Council did decree
In forwarding this dear expedience.⁸
WESTMORELAND   My liege, this haste was hot in questiòn,
35   And many limits of the charge⁹ set down
But yesternight, when all athwart¹ there came
A post° from Wales loaden with heavy news,   *messenger*
Whose worst was that the noble Mortimer,
Leading the men of Herefordshire to fight
40   Against the irregular° and wild Glendower,   *guerrilla*
Was by the rude hands of that Welshman taken,
A thousand of his people butcherèd,
Upon whose dead corpse° there was such misuse,   *corpses*
Such beastly shameless transformatiòn,
45   By those Welshwomen done as may not be
Without much shame retold or spoken of.
KING   It seems then that the tidings of this broil
Brake off our business for the Holy Land.
WESTMORELAND   This matched with other did, my gracious lord,
50   For more uneven and unwelcome news
Came from the north, and thus it did import:
On Holyrood Day² the gallant Hotspur there,

---

4. The tread of war horses.
5. Internal violence, civil war.
6. Army. He is planning a crusade, in expiation of his guilt for the death of Richard II.
7. I.e., that is not the reason for our present meeting.

8. Important, urgent matter.
9. Assignment of military responsibilities. "Hot in question": actively discussed.
1. Interrupting, crossing our purpose.
2. Holy Cross Day (September 14).

Young Harry Percy, and brave Archibald,
That ever-valiant and approvèd Scot,
55 At Holmedon met,
Where they did spend a sad and bloody hour,
As by discharge of their artillery,
And shape of likelihood,[3] the news was told;
For he that brought them[4] in the very heat
60 And pride° of their contention did take horse,   *height*
Uncertain of the issue any way.
KING   Here is a dear, a true industrious friend,
Sir Walter Blunt, new lighted from his horse,
Stained with the variation of each soil
65 Betwixt that Holmedon and this seat of ours;
And he hath brought us smooth and welcome news.
The Earl of Douglas is discomfited;
Ten thousand bold Scots, two and twenty knights
Balked° in their own blood did Sir Walter see   *heaped*
70 On Holmedon's plains. Of prisoners Hotspur took
Mordake Earl of Fife, and eldest son
To beaten Douglas, and the Earl of Athol,
Of Murray, Angus, and Menteith;
And is not this an honorable spoil,
75 A gallant prize? Ha, cousin, is it not?
WESTMORELAND   In faith,
It is a conquest for a prince to boast of.
KING   Yea, there thou mak'st me sad and mak'st me sin
In envy that my Lord Northumberland
80 Should be the father to so blest a son,
A son who is the theme of honor's tongue,
Amongst a grove the very straightest plant,
Who is sweet Fortune's minion° and her pride;   *favorite*
Whilst I, by looking on the praise of him,
85 See riot and dishonor stain the brow
Of my young Harry. O that it could be proved
That some night-tripping fairy had exchanged
In cradle-clothes our children where they lay,
And called mine Percy, his Plantagenet![5]
90 Then would I have his Harry, and he mine.
But let him from my thoughts. What think you, coz,
Of this young Percy's pride? The prisoners
Which he in this adventure hath surprised
To his own use he keeps, and sends me word
95 I shall have none but Mordake Earl of Fife.
WESTMORELAND   This is his uncle's teaching, this is Worcester,
Malevolent to you in all aspects,[6]
Which makes him prune himself,[7] and bristle up

---

3. Probable inference.
4. I.e., the news (usually a plural in Shakespeare).
5. The family name of the English royal family.
6. Hostile in every way. The figure is from astrology.
7. Plume himself. "Bristle up" and "crest" continue the image, which is that of a fighting cock.

The crest of youth against your dignity.
100 KING   But I have sent for him to answer this;
And for this cause awhile we must neglect
Our holy purpose to Jerusalem.
Cousin, on Wednesday next our council we
Will hold at Windsor, so inform the lords;
105 But come yourself with speed to us again,
For more is to be said and to be done
Than out of anger can be utterèd.
WESTMORELAND   I will, my liege.   [*Exeunt.*]

SCENE 2

[*Enter* HENRY, PRINCE OF WALES, *and* SIR JOHN FALSTAFF.]
FALSTAFF   Now Hal, what time of day is it, lad?
PRINCE   Thou art so fat-witted with drinking of old sack,[8] and unbuttoning
thee after supper, and sleeping upon benches after noon, that thou hast
forgotten to demand that truly which thou wouldst truly know. What a
5   devil hast thou to do with the time of the day? Unless hours were cups
of sack, and minutes capons, and clocks the tongues of bawds, and dials
the signs of leaping-houses,[9] and the blessed sun himself a fair hot wench
in flame-colored taffeta, I see no reason why thou shouldst be so superfluous to demand the time of the day.
10 FALSTAFF   Indeed you come near me now, Hal, for we that take purses go
by the moon and the seven stars, and not by Phoebus,[1] he, "that wandering knight so fair." And I prithee, sweet wag, when thou art king, as,
God save thy grace—majesty I should say, for grace[2] thou wilt have
none—
15 PRINCE   What, none?
FALSTAFF   No, by my troth, not so much as will serve to be prologue to an
egg and butter.
PRINCE   Well, how then? come, roundly, roundly.[3]
FALSTAFF   Marry then, sweet wag, when thou art king, let not us that are
20   squires of the night's body be called thieves of the day's beauty;[4] let us
be Diana's foresters, gentlemen of the shade, minions of the moon; and
let men say we be men of good government, being governed as the sea
is, by our noble and chaste mistress the moon, under whose countenance
we steal.
25 PRINCE   Thou sayest well, and it holds well too, for the fortune of us that
are the moon's men doth ebb and flow like the sea, being governed as
the sea is by the moon. As for proof now: a purse of gold most resolutely
snatched on Monday night and most dissolutely spent on Tuesday morning, got with swearing "Lay by" and spent with crying "Bring in," now in

---

8. Dry Spanish wine.
9. Whorehouses.
1. The sun. Falstaff then quotes from a popular ballad.
2. A triple pun: (1) "your Grace," the correct manner of addressing a prince or duke; (2) the divine influence that produces sanctity; and (3) a short

prayer before a meal—hence Falstaff's allusion to "egg and butter," a common hasty breakfast.
3. Plainly.
4. Two puns: (1) a "squire of the body" was an attendant on a knight and (2) "body" would be pronounced *bawdy.* "Beauty" also puns with *booty,* which thieves take. Diana is the moon goddess.

30   as low an ebb as the foot of the ladder and by and by in as high a flow
as the ridge of the gallows.[5]

FALSTAFF   By the Lord thou sayest true, lad. And is not my hostess of the
tavern a most sweet wench?

PRINCE   As the honey of Hybla, my old lad of the castle.[6] And is not a buff
35   jerkin a most sweet robe of durance?[7]

FALSTAFF   How now, how now, mad wag! what, in thy quips and thy quid-
dities?[8] what a plague have I to do with a buff jerkin?

PRINCE   Why, what a pox[9] have I to do with my hostess of the tavern?

FALSTAFF   Well, thou hast called her to a reckoning[1] many a time and oft.

40 PRINCE   Did I ever call for thee to pay thy part?

FALSTAFF   No, I'll give thee thy due, thou hast paid all there.

PRINCE   Yea, and elsewhere, so far as my coin would stretch, and where
it would not I have used my credit.

FALSTAFF   Yea, and so used it that were it not here apparent that thou art
45   heir apparent[2]—but I prithee, sweet wag, shall there be gallows standing
in England when thou art king? and resolution thus fobbed as it is with
the rusty curb of old father antic[3] the law? Do not thou, when thou art
king, hang a thief.

PRINCE   No, thou shalt.

50 FALSTAFF   Shall I? O rare! By the Lord, I'll be a brave judge.

PRINCE   Thou judgest false already; I mean thou shalt have the hanging
of the thieves and so become a rare hangman.

FALSTAFF   Well, Hal, well; and in some sort it jumps with my humor[4] as
well as waiting in the court, I can tell you.

55 PRINCE   For obtaining of suits?[5]

FALSTAFF   Yea, for obtaining of suits, whereof the hangman hath no lean
wardrobe. 'Sblood, I am as melancholy as a gib cat or a lugged[6] bear.

PRINCE   Or an old lion, or a lover's lute.

FALSTAFF   Yea, or the drone of a Lincolnshire bagpipe.

60 PRINCE   What sayest thou to a hare, or the melancholy of Moorditch?[7]

FALSTAFF   Thou hast the most unsavory similes and art indeed the most
comparative,[8] rascalliest, sweet young prince. But Hal, I prithee, trouble
me no more with vanity. I would to God thou and I knew where a commodity of good names were to be bought. An old lord of the council rated[9]
65   me the other day in the street about you, sir, but I marked him not; and
yet he talked very wisely, but I regarded him not; and yet he talked wisely,
and in the street too.

---

5. The "foot of the ladder" is at the bottom of the
gallows (robbery was a hanging offense); the
"ridge" is the crosspiece at the top. "Lay by": hand
over (a robber's command to the victim). "Bring
in": a customer's command for more drink at a tavern.
6. A reference to Falstaff's original name, Oldcastle. Hybla is a town in Sicily, famous for honey.
7. A pun: (1) lasting quality, (2) imprisonment.
"Buff jerkin": the leather jacket worn by a sheriff's
sergeant.
8. Quibbles.
9. Common oath, alluding to venereal disease.
1. The bill; also (here) sexual intercourse.
2. "Here" and "heir" would pun in Elizabethan

pronunciation.
3. A clown. "Resolution": bravery. "Fobbed":
cheated.
4. I.e., agrees with my disposition.
5. Special favors, but "clothing" in the next line.
The hangman was given the clothes of his victims.
6. Baited (in the bearbaiting pits a bear was
attacked by dogs as a public amusement).
" 'Sblood": God's blood, a common oath. "Gib cat":
tomcat.
7. A foul-smelling ditch on the outskirts of London. The "hare" was traditionally associated with
melancholy.
8. Given to (insulting) comparisons.
9. Scolded, berated.

PRINCE   Thou didst well, for wisdom cries out in the streets and no man regards it.[1]

70   FALSTAFF   O, thou hast damnable iteration[2] and art indeed able to corrupt a saint. Thou hast done much harm upon me, Hal, God forgive thee for it! Before I knew thee, Hal, I knew nothing, and now am I, if a man should speak truly, little better than one of the wicked. I must give over this life, and I will give it over; by the Lord, an[3] I do not, I am a villain;

75   I'll be damned for never a king's son in Christendom.

PRINCE   Where shall we take a purse tomorrow, Jack?

FALSTAFF   Zounds, where thou wilt, lad; I'll make one; an I do not, call me villain and baffle[4] me.

PRINCE   I see a good amendment of life in thee—from praying to purse-

80   taking.

FALSTAFF   Why, Hal, 'tis my vocation,[5] Hal; 'tis no sin for a man to labor in his vocation.

[Enter POINS.]

Poins! Now shall we know if Gadshill[6] have set a match. O, if men were to be saved by merit, what hole in hell were hot enough for him? This is

85   the most omnipotent villain that ever cried "stand" to a true man.

PRINCE   Good morrow, Ned.

POINS   Good morrow, sweet Hal. What says Monsieur Remorse? what says Sir John Sack and Sugar? Jack! how agrees the devil and thee about thy soul, that thou soldest him on Good Friday last for a cup of Madeira and

90   a cold capon's leg?

PRINCE   Sir John stands to his word; the devil shall have his bargain, for he was never yet a breaker of proverbs; he will give the devil his due.

POINS   Then art thou damned for keeping thy word with the devil.

PRINCE   Else he had been damned for cozening[7] the devil.

95   POINS   But my lads, my lads, tomorrow morning by four o'clock, early at Gadshill, there are pilgrims going to Canterbury with rich offerings, and traders riding to London with fat purses. I have vizards for you all, you have horses for yourselves; Gads hill lies[8] tonight in Rochester; I have bespoke supper tomorrow night in Eastcheap;[9] we may do it as secure

100   as sleep. If you will go, I will stuff your purses full of crowns; if you will not, tarry at home and be hanged.

FALSTAFF   Hear ye, Yedward[1] if I tarry at home and go not, I'll hang you for going.

POINS   You will, chops?[2]

105   FALSTAFF   Hal, wilt thou make one?

PRINCE   Who, I rob? I a thief? not I, by my faith.

---

1. Prince Hal is quoting Proverbs 1.20 and 24.
2. Repetition, especially of sacred texts.
3. If.
4. A knight in the days of chivalry was "baffled" or disgraced by having his shield hung upside down, signaling his loss of rank. "Zounds": a common oath, a contraction of "by God's wounds" (i.e., Jesus' wounds on the Cross).
5. Falstaff is here making fun of the Puritan doctrine of "calling" or vocation, based on the parable of the talents (Matthew 25.25ff.).
6. Both a man and a place: the place is a hill

twenty-seven miles from London on the road to Rochester; it was notorious for robberies. The man, so called from the place, is the thieves' "setter," who arranges when and where the robbery will occur.
7. Cheating.
8. Lodges. "Vizards": masks.
9. A thoroughfare in London, site of Mistress Quickly's tavern.
1. Dialect for Edward.
2. Fat face.

FALSTAFF   There's neither honesty, manhood, nor good fellowship in thee, nor thou camest not of the blood royal, if thou darest not stand for[3] ten shillings.

110   PRINCE   Well then, once in my days I'll be a madcap.

FALSTAFF   Why, that's well said.

PRINCE   Well, come what will, I'll tarry at home.

FALSTAFF   By the Lord, I'll be a traitor then, when thou art king.

PRINCE   I care not.

115   POINS   Sir John, I prithee leave the prince and me alone; I will lay him down such reasons for this adventure that he shall go.

FALSTAFF   Well, God give thee the spirit of persuasion and him the ears of profiting, that what thou speakest may move and what he hears may be believed, that the true prince may (for recreation sake) prove a false
120   thief; for the poor abuses of the time want countenance.[4] Farewell; you shall find me in Eastcheap.

PRINCE   Farewell, thou latter spring, farewell, Allhallown summer![5]
         [⟨*Exit* FALSTAFF.⟩][6]

POINS   Now, my good sweet honey lord, ride with us tomorrow; I have a jest to execute that I cannot manage alone. Falstaff, Bardolph, Peto, and
125   Gadshill shall rob those men that we have already waylaid;[7] yourself and I will not be there, and when they have the booty, if you and I do not rob them, cut this head off from my shoulders.

PRINCE   How shall we part with them in setting forth?

POINS   Why, we will set forth before or after them, and appoint them a
130   place of meeting, wherein it is at our pleasure to fail, and then will they adventure upon the exploit themselves, which they shall have no sooner achieved but we'll set upon them.

PRINCE   Yea, but 'tis like that they will know us by our horses, by our habits,[8] and by every other appointment to be ourselves.

135   POINS   Tut, our horses they shall not see—I'll tie them in the wood; our vizards we will change after we leave them: and, sirrah, I have cases of buckram for the nonce,[9] to immask our noted outward garments.

PRINCE   Yea, but I doubt they will be too hard[1] for us.

POINS   Well, for two of them, I know them to be as true-bred cowards as
140   ever turned back; and for the third, if he fight longer than he sees reason, I'll forswear arms. The virtue of this jest will be the incomprehensible lies that this same fat rogue will tell us when we meet at supper: how thirty at least he fought with; what wards,[2] what blows, what extremities he endured; and in the reproof[3] of this lies the jest.

---

3. A pun: "stand for" means both "represent" and "fight for." "Royal" is also a pun: the coin called *royal* was worth ten shillings.
4. A satirical reference to the common complaint that the nobility did not properly give "countenance" to (i.e., encourage) good causes and to the Puritan habit of attacking the "abuses of the time." This entire speech parodies the language of the Puritans.
5. I.e., Indian summer; All Hallows' Day (All Saints' Day) is November 1. The two epithets are intended to suggest how unseasonable it is for Falstaff, an old man, to be engaged in youthful, hood-

lum exploits.
6. This stage direction, like some others in the play, does not appear in the earliest editions; it was added by a later editor. All such interpolated directions are indicated in our text by the special double brackets used here.
7. Set an ambush for.
8. Clothes.
9. I.e., outer clothes (of a coarse, stiff cloth) for the occasion.
1. I.e., too many. "Doubt": suspect.
2. Defensive postures.
3. Disproof.

145 PRINCE   Well, I'll go with thee. Provide us all things necessary and meet
        me tomorrow night[4] in Eastcheap; there I'll sup. Farewell.
     POINS   Farewell, my lord.   [*Exit* POINS.]
     PRINCE   I know you all, and will awhile uphold
          The unyoked humor° of your idleness;   *undisciplined whim*
150   Yet herein will I imitate the sun,
          Who doth permit the base contagious° clouds   *pestilence-breeding*
          To smother up his beauty from the world,
          That, when he please again to be himself,
          Being wanted, he may be more wondered at
155   By breaking through the foul and ugly mists
          Of vapors that did seem to strangle him.
          If all the year were playing holidays,
          To sport would be as tedious as to work;
          But when they seldom come, they wished-for come,
160   And nothing pleaseth but rare accidents.
          So, when this loose behavior I throw off
          And pay the debt I never promisèd,
          By how much better than my word I am,
          By so much shall I falsify men's hopes,
165   And like bright metal on a sullen ground,°   *dull background*
          My reformation, glitt'ring o'er my fault,
          Shall show more goodly and attract more eyes
          Than that which hath no foil° to set it off.   *contrast*
          I'll so offend to make offense a skill,
170   Redeeming time[5] when men think least I will.   [*Exit.*]

SCENE 3

[*Enter the* KING, NORTHUMBERLAND, WORCESTER, HOTSPUR,
   SIR WALTER BLUNT, *with others.*]

     KING   My blood hath been too cold and temperate,
          Unapt to stir at these indignities,
          And you have found me,[6] for accordingly
          You tread upon my patience; but be sure
5   I will from henceforth rather be myself,
          Mighty and to be feared, than my condition,°   *disposition*
          Which hath been smooth as oil, soft as young down,
          And therefore lost that title of respect
          Which the proud soul ne'er pays but to the proud.
10   WORCESTER   Our house, my sovereign liege, little deserves
          The scourge of greatness to be used on it,
          And that same greatness too which our own hands
          Have holp° to make so portly.°   *helped/stately*
     NORTHUMBERLAND   My lord—

---

4. Either the text should read "tonight" (before the
robbery) or else Shakespeare intends to show
Prince Hal's mind intent, not on the robbery, but
on its aftermath. The soliloquy of the Prince that
follows has provoked much critical discussion.

5. Making good use of time, following the advice
given to Christians in a non-Christian world (see
Ephesians 5.16). "Skill": piece of good policy.
6. Discovered this to be true.

15 KING   Worcester, get thee gone, for I do see
          Danger and disobedience in thine eye;
          O, sir, your presence is too bold and peremptory,
          And majesty might never yet endure
          The moody frontier of a servant brow.[7]
20   You have good leave to leave us; when we need
          Your use and counsel we shall send for you.   [*Exit* WORCESTER.]
          You were about to speak.   [⟨*to* NORTHUMBERLAND⟩]
     NORTHUMBERLAND.   Yea, my good lord.
          Those prisoners in your highness' name demanded,
          Which Harry Percy here at Holmedon took,
25   Were, as he says, not with such strength denied
          As is delivered to your majesty.
          Either envy° therefore or misprisiòn°   *malice / mistake*
          Is guilty of this fault, and not my son.
     HOTSPUR   My liege, I did deny no prisoners.
30   But I remember, when the fight was done,
          When I was dry with rage and extreme toil,
          Breathless and faint, leaning upon my sword,
          Came there a certain lord, neat and trimly dressed,
          Fresh as a bridegroom, and his chin new reaped
35   Showed like a stubble-land at harvest-home.
          He was perfumèd like a milliner,[8]
          And 'twixt his finger and his thumb he held
          A pouncet box,° which ever and anon   *perfume box*
          He gave his nose and took 't away again;
40   Who therewith angry, when it next came there,
          Took it in snuff;[9] and still he smiled and talked,
          And as the soldiers bore dead bodies by,
          He called them untaught knaves, unmannerly,
          To bring a slovenly° unhandsome corse°   *disgusting / corpse*
45   Betwixt the wind and his nobility.
          With many holiday and lady terms[1]
          He questioned me; amongst the rest, demanded
          My prisoners in your majesty's behalf.
          I then, all smarting with my wounds being cold,
50   To be so pestered with a popinjay,°   *parrot*
          Out of my grief and my impatience
          Answered neglectingly I know not what,
          He should, or he should not—for he made me mad
          To see him shine so brisk and smell so sweet
55   And talk so like a waiting-gentlewoman
          Of guns and drums and wounds, God save the mark!
          And telling me the sovereign'st° thing on earth   *most curative*
          Was parmaceti[2] for an inward bruise,

---

7. I.e., a servant's brow showing defiance, like a
fortification ("frontier").
8. Not a maker of hats, but a dealer in perfumes,
women's gloves, etc.

9. I.e., was annoyed at it, with a pun on *snuffing
it up.*
1. Affected and effeminate language.
2. Spermaceti, whale oil used as an ointment.

And that it was great pity, so it was,
60 This villanous saltpeter³ should be digged
Out of the bowels of the harmless earth,
Which many a good tall° fellow had destroyed   *brave*
So cowardly, and but for these vile guns
He would himself have been a soldier.
65 This bald° unjointed chat of his, my lord,   *trivial*
I answered indirectly as I said,
And I beseech you, let not his report
Come current⁴ for an accusation
Betwixt my love and your high majesty.
70 BLUNT   The circumstance considered, good my lord,
Whate'er Lord Harry Percy then had said
To such a person and in such a place,
At such a time, with all the rest retold,
May reasonably die and never rise
75 To do him wrong or any way impeach
What then he said, so he unsay it now.
KING   Why, yet° he doth deny his prisoners,   *still*
But° with proviso and exceptiòn,   *except*
That we at our own charge shall ransom straight°   *immediately*
80 His brother-in-law, the foolish Mortimer,
Who, on my soul, hath willfully betrayed
The lives of those that he did lead to fight
Against that great magician, damned Glendower,
Whose daughter, as we hear, the Earl of March
85 Hath lately married. Shall our coffers then
Be emptied to redeem a traitor home?
Shall we buy treason? and indent with fears,⁵
When they have lost and forfeited themselves?
No, on the barren mountains let him starve;
90 For I shall never hold that man my friend
Whose tongue shall ask me for one penny cost
To ransom home revolted Mortimer.
HOTSPUR   Revolted Mortimer!
He never did fall off, my sovereign liege,
95 But by the chance of war. To prove that true
Needs no more but one tongue for all those wounds,
Those mouthèd wounds which valiantly he took
When on the gentle Severn's⁶ sedgy bank
In single opposition, hand to hand,
100 He did confound° the best part of an hour   *spend*
In changing hardiment⁷ with great Glendower;
Three times they breathed° and three times   *paused for breath*
    did they drink

---

3. Used in gunpowder.
4. Be considered valid.
5. Enter into a contract with cowards.
6. A river on the England-Wales border. Wounds are often likened to mouths in Shakespeare. The image may derive from their appearance and from the idea that they could speak as witnesses to what caused them (cf. *Julius Caesar* 3.2.229–231 and *Richard III* 1.2.55–56).
7. Testing prowess and exchanging blows.

Upon agreement of swift Severn's flood,
Who then, affrighted with their bloody looks,
05 Ran fearfully among the trembling reeds,
And hid his crisp[8] head in the hollow bank
Bloodstainèd with these valiant combatants.
Never did bare and rotten policy°   *craftiness, conspiracy*
Color° her working with such deadly wounds,   *disguise*
10 Nor never could the noble Mortimer
Receive so many, and all willingly;
Then let not him be slandered with revolt.
KING   Thou dost belie him, Percy, thou dost belie him;
He never did encounter with Glendower.
15 I tell thee,
He durst as well have met the devil alone
As Owen Glendower for an enemy.
Art thou not ashamed? But, sirrah,[9] henceforth
Let me not hear you speak of° Mortimer;   *mention*
20 Send me your prisoners with the speediest means,
Or you shall hear in such a kind from me
As will displease you. My Lord Northumberland,
We license your departure with your son.
Send us your prisoners, or you will hear of it.
      [*Exeunt* KING, ⟨BLUNT, *and train*⟩.]
25 HOTSPUR   An if the devil come and roar for them
I will not send them; I will after straight
And tell him so, for I will ease my heart
Albeit I make a hazard of my head.
NORTHUMBERLAND   What, drunk with choler?° stay and   *anger*
      pause awhile.
Here comes your uncle.
      [*Enter* WORCESTER.]
30 HOTSPUR   Speak of Mortimer!
Zounds, I will speak of him, and let my soul
Want mercy if I do not join with him;
Yea, on his part° I'll empty all these veins,   *behalf*
And shed my dear blood drop by drop in the dust,
35 But I will lift the downtrod Mortimer
As high in the air as this unthankful king,
As this ingrate° and cankered° Bullingbrook.   *ungrateful/malignant*
NORTHUMBERLAND   Brother, the king hath made your nephew mad.
WORCESTER   Who struck this heat up after I was gone?
40 HOTSPUR   He will, forsooth, have all my prisoners;
And when I urged the ransom once again
Of my wife's brother, then his cheek looked pale,
And on my face he turned an eye of death,
Trembling even at the name of Mortimer.
45 WORCESTER   I cannot blame him; was not he proclaimed

---

8. I.e., curly (because of the waves).
9. A form of "sir," but used familiarly, and sometimes, as here, with a tone of contempt.

By Richard, that dead is, the next of blood?
NORTHUMBERLAND   He was—I heard the proclamatiòn;
    And then it was when the unhappy king
    (Whose wrongs in us God pardon!¹) did set forth
150   Upon his Irish expeditiòn;
    From whence he intercepted did return
    To be deposed and shortly murderèd.
WORCESTER   And for whose death we in the world's wide mouth
    Live scandalized and foully spoken of.
155 HOTSPUR   But soft, I pray you; did King Richard then
    Proclaim my brother² Edmund Mortimer
    Heir to the crown?
NORTHUMBERLAND   He did; myself did hear it.
HOTSPUR   Nay, then I cannot blame his cousin king
    That wished him on the barren mountains starve.
160   But shall it be that you, that set the crown
    Upon the head of this forgetful man
    And for his sake wear the detested blot
    Of murderous subornation³—shall it be
    That you a world of curses undergo,
165   Being the agents, or base second means,°   *tools, helpers*
    The cords, the ladder, or the hangman rather?
    O pardon me that I descend so low
    To show the line and the predicament
    Wherein you range⁴ under this subtle king!
170   Shall it for shame be spoken in these days,
    Or fill up chronicles in time to come,
    That men of your nobility and power
    Did gage° them both in an unjust behalf,°   *pledge/cause*
    As both of you—God pardon it!—have done,
175   To put down Richard, that sweet lovely rose,
    And plant this thorn, this canker,⁵ Bullingbrook?
    And shall it in more shame be further spoken,
    That you are fooled, discarded, and shook off
    By him for whom these shames ye underwent?
180   No; yet time serves wherein you may redeem
    Your banished honors and restore yourselves
    Into the good thoughts of the world again,
    Revenge the jeering and disdained° contempt   *disdainful*
    Of this proud king, who studies day and night
185   To answer all the debt he owes to you
    Even with the bloody payment of your deaths:
    Therefore, I say—
WORCESTER   Peace, cousin, say no more;
    And now I will unclasp a secret book,
    And to your quick-conceiving discontents
190   I'll read you matter deep and dangerous,
    As full of peril and adventurous spirit

1. I.e., God pardon in us the wrongs we did to him.
2. Brother-in-law.
3. I.e., the stain of aiding and abetting murder.
4. I.e., to show the position and the category (or class) in which you are placed.
5. A wild rose, also a diseased spot in a nose.

As to o'er-walk a current roaring loud
On the unsteadfast footing of a spear.⁶
HOTSPUR   If he fall in, good night, or sink or swim.
195 Send danger from the east unto the west,
So° honor cross it from the north to south,   *provided that*
And let them grapple. O, the blood more stirs
To rouse a lion than to start⁷ a hare!
NORTHUMBERLAND   Imagination of some great exploit
200 Drives him beyond the bounds of patience.
HOTSPUR   By heaven, methinks it were an easy leap
To pluck bright honor from the pale-faced moon,
Or dive into the bottom of the deep,
Where fathom line could never touch the ground,
205 And pluck up drownèd honor by the locks,
So he that doth redeem her thence might wear
Without corrival° all her dignities;   *rival*
But out upon this half-faced fellowship!⁸
WORCESTER   He apprehends a world of figures⁹ here,
210 But not the form of what he should attend.
Good cousin, give me audience for a while.
HOTSPUR   I cry you mercy.¹
WORCESTER   Those same noble Scots
That are your prisoners—
HOTSPUR   I'll keep them all;
By God, he shall not have a Scot of them;
215 No, if a Scot would save his soul he shall not.
I'll keep them, by his hand.
WORCESTER   You start away
And lend no ear unto my purposes.
Those prisoners you shall keep.
HOTSPUR   Nay, I will; that's flat.
He said he would not ransom Mortimer,
220 Forbade my tongue to speak of Mortimer,
But I will find him when he lies asleep,
And in his ear I'll holla "Mortimer!"
Nay,
I'll have a starling shall be taught to speak²
225 Nothing but "Mortimer," and give it him
To keep his anger still in motion.
WORCESTER   Hear you, cousin, a word.
HOTSPUR   All studies here I solemnly defy,
Save how to gall° and pinch this Bullingbrook,   *irritate*
230 And that same sword-and-buckler³ Prince of Wales,
But that I think his father loves him not
And would be glad he met with some mischance,
I would have him poisoned with a pot of ale.⁴

---

6. A spear laid down as a footbridge.
7. Arouse, in hunting.
8. Miserable sharing (of honor) with someone else.
9. Rhetorical figures of speech.
1. Beg your pardon.

2. Starlings used to be taught to speak, as parrots are now.
3. Weapons used by the lowest class of soldiers and servants. Gentlemen used rapiers.
4. The drink of the lower classes.

WORCESTER   Farewell, kinsman; I'll talk to you
235   When you are better tempered to attend.
NORTHUMBERLAND   Why, what a wasp-stung and impatient fool
   Art thou to break into this woman's mood,
   Tying thine ear to no tongue but thine own!
HOTSPUR   Why, look you, I am whipped and scourged with rods,
240   Nettled and stung with pismires,° when I hear   *ants*
   Of this vile politician Bullingbrook.
   In Richard's time—what do you call the place?—
   A plague upon it, it is in Gloucestershire—
   'Twas where the madcap duke his uncle kept,°   *lived*
245   His uncle York, where I first bow'd my knee
   Unto this king of smiles, this Bullingbrook
   'Sblood!—
   When you and he came back from Ravenspurgh.
NORTHUMBERLAND   At Berkeley castle.
250   HOTSPUR   You say true.
   Why, what a candy deal of courtesy
   This fawning greyhound⁵ then did proffer me!
   "Look when his infant fortune came to age,"
   And "gentle Harry Percy," and "kind cousin";
255   O, the devil take such cozeners!⁶ God forgive me!
   Good uncle, tell your tale; I have done.
WORCESTER   Nay, if you have not, to it again;
   We will stay your leisure.
HOTSPUR   I have done, i' faith.
WORCESTER   Then once more to your Scottish prisoners.
260   Deliver them up without their ransom straight,
   And make the Douglas' son your only mean
   For powers in Scotland, which, for divers reasons
   Which I shall send you written, be assured
   Will easily be granted. You, my lord, [⟨*to* NORTHUMBERLAND⟩]
265   Your son in Scotland being thus employed,
   Shall secretly into the bosom creep
   Of that same noble prelate well beloved,
   The archbishop.
HOTSPUR   Of York, is it not?
270   WORCESTER   True; who bears hard
   His brother's death at Bristol, the Lord Scroop.
   I speak not this in estimation,°   *by conjecture*
   As what I think might be, but what I know
   Is ruminated, plotted, and set down,
275   And only stays but to behold the face
   Of that occasion that shall bring it on.
HOTSPUR   I smell it; upon my life, it will do well.
NORTHUMBERLAND   Before the game is afoot, thou still let'st slip.⁷

5. A complex image that occurs in Shakespeare several times (cf. *Hamlet* 3.2.50–52 and *Antony and Cleopatra* 4.12.20–23). The idea of fawning or flattery called up to Shakespeare's mind the image of a dog begging for sweetmeats ("candy").

6. Cheaters, with, of course, a pun on *cousin*.
7. An image from hunting. The meaning is "You always ('still') release the dogs before we are ready to pursue the game."

HOTSPUR   Why, it cannot choose but be a noble plot;
280   And then the power of Scotland and of York
      To join with Mortimer, ha?
WORCESTER   And so they shall.
HOTSPUR   In faith, it is exceedingly well aimed.
WORCESTER   And 'tis no little reason bids us speed,
      To save our heads by raising of a head;[8]
285   For, bear ourselves as even as we can,
      The king will always think him in our debt,
      And think we think ourselves unsatisfied,
      Till he hath found a time to pay us home;
      And see already how he doth begin
290   To make us strangers to his looks of love.
HOTSPUR   He does, he does; we'll be revenged on him.
WORCESTER   Cousin, farewell. No further go in this
      Than I by letters shall direct your course.
      When time is ripe, which will be suddenly,
295   I'll steal to Glendower and Lord Mortimer,
      Where you and Douglas and our powers at once,
      As I will fashion it, shall happily meet,
      To bear our fortunes in our own strong arms,
      Which now we hold at much uncertainty.
300 NORTHUMBERLAND   Farewell, good brother; we shall thrive, I trust.
HOTSPUR   Uncle, adieu; O, let the hours be short
      Till fields and blows and groans applaud our sport!   *[Exeunt.]*

Act 2

SCENE 1

[Enter a CARRIER *with a lantern in his hand.]*
FIRST CARRIER   Heigh-ho! an it be not four by the day, I'll be hanged;
    Charles' wain[9] is over the new chimney, and yet our horse not packed.
    What, ostler!
OSTLER *[within]*   Anon, anon.
5 FIRST CARRIER   I prithee, Tom, beat Cut's saddle,[1] put a few flocks in the
    point;[2] poor jade, is wrung in the withers out of all cess.[3]
        [Enter another CARRIER.]
SECOND CARRIER   Peas and beans are as dank here as a dog, and that is
    the next way to give poor jades the bots;[4] this house is turned upside
    down since Robin Ostler died.
10 FIRST CARRIER   Poor fellow, never joyed since the price of oats rose; it was
    the death of him.
SECOND CARRIER   I think this be the most villainous house in all London
    road for fleas; I am stung like a tench.[5]
FIRST CARRIER   Like a tench! by the mass, there is ne'er a king christen[6]
15   could be better bit than I have been since the first cock.

---

8. Raising an army.
9. The constellation of the Great Bear, or Big Dipper.
1. A saddle was beaten to make it soft. "Cut" is a name for a horse with a docked tail.
2. Pieces of wool under the point of the saddle.

3. I.e., is sore excessively in the shoulders.
4. I.e., that is the easiest way to give poor nags worms in the stomach.
5. A fish covered with red spots, like fleabites.
6. Christian king.

SECOND CARRIER   Why, they will allow us ne'er a jordan, and then we leak
in your chimney, and your chamber-lye breeds fleas like a loach.[7]

FIRST CARRIER   What, ostler! come away and be hanged, come away!

SECOND CARRIER   I have a gammon of bacon and two razes[8] of ginger, to
be delivered as far as Charing Cross.

FIRST CARRIER   God's body! the turkeys in my pannier[9] are quite starved.
What, ostler! A plague on thee, hast thou never an eye in thy head? canst
not hear? An 'twere not as good deed as drink to break the pate on thee,
I am a very villain. Come and be hanged! hast no faith in thee?

[*Enter* GADSHILL.]

GADSHILL   Good morrow, carriers. What's o'clock?

FIRST CARRIER   I think it be two o'clock.

GADSHILL   I prithee lend me thy lantern to see my gelding in the stable.

FIRST CARRIER   Nay, by God, soft; I know a trick worth two of that, i' faith.

GADSHILL   I pray thee lend me thine.

SECOND CARRIER   Aye, when? canst tell?[1] Lend me thy lantern, quoth he?
marry, I'll see thee hanged first.

GADSHILL   Sirrah carrier, what time do you mean to come to London?

SECOND CARRIER   Time enough to go to bed with a candle, I warrant thee.
Come, neighbor Mugs, we'll call up the gentlemen; they will along with
company, for they have great charge.[2]

[*Exeunt* ⟨CARRIERS⟩.]

GADSHILL   What ho! chamberlain!

[*Enter* CHAMBERLAIN.]

CHAMBERLAIN   At hand, quoth pickpurse.

GADSHILL   That's even as fair as At hand, quoth the chamberlain, for thou
variest no more from picking of purses than giving direction doth from
laboring; thou layest the plot how.[3]

CHAMBERLAIN   Good morrow, Master Gadshill. It holds current[4] that I
told you yesternight; there's a franklin in the weald of Kent[5] hath brought
three hundred marks with him in gold—I heard him tell it to one of his
company last night at supper—a kind of auditor, one that hath abundance of charge[6] too, God knows what. They are up already and call for
eggs and butter; they will away presently.[7]

GADSHILL   Sirrah, if they meet not with Saint Nicholas' clerks,[8] I'll give
thee this neck.

CHAMBERLAIN   No, I'll none of it; I pray thee, keep that for the hangman,
for I know thou worshipest Saint Nicholas as truly as a man of falsehood
may.

GADSHILL   What talkest thou to me of the hangman? if I hang, I'll make
a fat pair of gallows; for if I hang, old Sir John hangs with me, and thou
knowest he is no starveling. Tut! there are other Trojans[9] that thou

---

7. A fish that breeds prolifically. "Jordan": chamber pot. "Chamber-lye": urine.
8. Roots. "Gammon": haunch.
9. Basket.
1. A colloquial expression of contemptuous
refusal.
2. Valuable cargo.
3. A pun: "giving direction" means supervising, as
contrasted with "laboring," but it was also the
name for informing thieves about the journeys of

prospective victims (laying "the plot how").
4. Remains true.
5. A section of that county, formerly wooded.
"Franklin": a freeholder, just below a gentleman in
rank.
6. Considerable property. "Auditor": revenue officer.
7. At once.
8. Highwaymen.
9. Roisterers, good fellows.

55 dream'st not of, the which for sport sake are content to do the profession some grace, that would, if matters should be looked into, for their own credit sake make all whole. I am joined with no foot land-rakers, no long-staff sixpenny strikers,[1] none of these mad mustachio purple-hued malt-worms, but with nobility and tranquility, burgomasters and great oneyers,

60 such as can hold in,[2] such as will strike sooner than speak, and speak sooner than drink, and drink sooner than pray; and yet, zounds, I lie, for they pray continually to their saint, the commonwealth, or rather, not pray to her but prey on her, for they ride up and down on her and make her their boots.[3]

65 CHAMBERLAIN What, the commonwealth their boots? will she hold out water in foul way?[4]

GADSHILL She will, she will; justice hath liquored her.[5] We steal as in a castle, cocksure; we have the receipt of fern seed,[6] we walk invisible.

CHAMBERLAIN Nay, by my faith, I think you are more beholding to the
70 night than to fern seed for your walking invisible.

GADSHILL Give me thy hand; thou shalt have a share in our purchase,[7] as I am a true man.

CHAMBERLAIN Nay, rather let me have it, as you are a false thief.

GADSHILL Go to; *homo* is a common name to all men. Bid the ostler bring
75 my gelding out of the stable. Farewell, you muddy[8] knave.[*Exeunt.*]

SCENE 2

[*Enter* PRINCE *and* POINS.]

POINS Come shelter, shelter; I have removed Falstaff's horse, and he frets like a gummed velvet.

PRINCE Stand close.[9]

[*Enter* FALSTAFF.]

FALSTAFF Poins! Poins, and be hanged! Poins!

5 PRINCE Peace, ye fat-kidneyed rascal! what a brawling dost thou keep!

FALSTAFF Where's Poins, Hal?

PRINCE He is walked up to the top of the hill; I'll go seek him.

[⟨*He pretends to go, but hides onstage with* POINS.⟩]

FALSTAFF I am accursed to rob in that thief's company; the rascal hath removed my horse, and tied him I know not where. If I travel but four
10 foot by the squier[1] further afoot, I shall break my wind. Well, I doubt not but to die a fair death for all this, if I 'scape hanging for killing that rogue. I have forsworn his company hourly any time this two and twenty years, and yet I am bewitched with the rogue's company. If the rascal have not given me medicines to make me love him, I'll be hanged; it
15 could not be else; I have drunk medicines. Poins! Hal! a plague upon you both! Bardolph! Peto! I'll starve ere I'll rob a foot further. An 'twere

1. Small-time thieves. "Land-rakers": footpads.
2. Keep secret. "Purple-hued maltworms": flushed, swaggering barflies. "Oneyers": dignitaries.
3. Booty.
4. Keep one dry in muddy roads, i.e., give protection.
5. I.e., those who control the laws have greased (or bribed) her.

6. I.e., we have the recipe for fern seed (supposed to make one invisible).
7. Takings.
8. Muddleheaded.
9. Hide. "Gummed velvet": cheap velvet was treated with gum to make the pile stiff; as a result it soon fretted or wore away.
1. Ruler, yardstick.

not as good a deed as drink to turn true man and to leave these rogues, I am the veriest varlet that ever chewed with a tooth. Eight yards of uneven ground is threescore and ten miles afoot with me, and the stony-hearted villains know it well enough; a plague upon it when thieves cannot be true one to another! [*They whistle.*] Whew! A plague upon you all! Give me my horse, you rogues; give me my horse, and be hanged!

PRINCE   Peace, ye fat-guts! lie down; lay thine ear close to the ground and list if thou canst hear the tread of travelers.

FALSTAFF   Have you any levers to lift me up again, being down? 'Sblood, I'll not bear my own flesh so far afoot again for all the coin in thy father's exchequer. What a plague mean ye to colt me thus?

PRINCE   Thou liest; thou art not colted, thou art uncolted.[2]

FALSTAFF   I prithee, good Prince, Hal, help me to my horse, good king's son.

PRINCE   Out, ye rogue! shall I be your ostler?

FALSTAFF   Go hang thyself in thine own heir-apparent garters![3] If I be ta'en, I'll peach for this. An I have not ballads made on you all and sung to filthy tunes, let a cup of sack be my poison; when a jest is so forward, and afoot too! I hate it.

[*Enter* GADSHILL.]

GADSHILL   Stand.

FALSTAFF   So I do, against my will.

POINS [*coming forward with* BARDOLPH *and* PETO]   O, 'tis our setter; I know his voice. Bardolph, what news?

BARDOLPH   Case[4] ye, case ye, on with your vizards; there's money of the king's coming down the hill; 'tis going to the king's exchequer.

FALSTAFF   You lie, you rogue; 'tis going to the king's tavern.

GADSHILL   There's enough to make us all.

FALSTAFF   To be hanged.

PRINCE   Sirs, you four shall front them in the narrow lane; Ned Poins and I will walk lower; if they 'scape from your encounter, then they light on us.

PETO   How many be there of them?

GADSHILL   Some eight or ten.

FALSTAFF   Zounds, will they not rob us?

PRINCE   What, a coward, Sir John Paunch?

FALSTAFF   Indeed, I am not John of Gaunt, your grandfather, but yet no coward, Hal.

PRINCE   Well, we leave that to the proof.

POINS   Sirrah Jack, thy horse stands behind the hedge; when thou need'st him, there thou shalt find him. Farewell, and stand fast.

FALSTAFF   Now cannot I strike him, if I should be hanged.

PRINCE [⟨*aside to* POINS⟩]   Ned, where are our disguises?

POINS [⟨*aside*⟩]   Here, hard by; stand close.

[⟨*Exeunt* PRINCE *and* POINS.⟩]

---

2. You have had your horse stolen. "To colt": trick.
3. As heir apparent to the throne, Hal would be a

knight of the Order of the Garter.
4. Mask.

FALSTAFF   Now, my masters, happy man be his dole,[5] say I; every man to his business.

[*Enter the* TRAVELERS.]

FIRST TRAVELER   Come, neighbor, the boy shall lead our horses down the hill; we'll walk afoot awhile, and ease our legs.

THIEVES   Stand!

TRAVELERS   Jesus bless us!

FALSTAFF   Strike; down with them; cut the villains' throats. Ah, whoreson caterpillars,[6] bacon-fed knaves, they hate us youth! Down with them, fleece them.

TRAVELERS   O, we are undone, both we and ours forever!

FALSTAFF   Hang ye, gorbellied knaves, are ye undone? No, ye fat chuffs,[7] I would your store were here! On, bacons, on! What, ye knaves, young men must live! You are grand jurors, are ye? we'll jure ye, faith.

[*Here they rob them and bind them. Exeunt.*]

[*Enter the* PRINCE *and* POINS *in buckram.*]

PRINCE   The thieves have bound the true men. Now could thou and I rob the thieves and go merrily to London; it would be argument[8] for a week, laughter for a month, and a good jest forever.

POINS   Stand close; I hear them coming.

[*Enter the* THIEVES *again.*]

FALSTAFF   Come, my masters, let us share, and then to horse before day. An the Prince and Poins be not two arrant cowards, there's no equity stirring;[9] there's no more valor in that Poins than in a wild duck.

PRINCE   Your money!

POINS   Villains!

[*As they are sharing, the* PRINCE *and* POINS *set upon them; they all run away; and* FALSTAFF, *after a blow or two, runs away too, leaving the booty behind them.*]

PRINCE   Got with much ease. Now merrily to horse;
The thieves are all scattered and possessed with fear
So strongly that they dare not meet each other;
Each takes his fellow for an officer.
Away, good Ned. Falstaff sweats to death,
And lards the lean earth as he walks along;
Were't not for laughing, I should pity him.

POINS   How the fat rogue roared!   [*Exeunt.*]

SCENE 3

[*Enter* HOTSPUR, *alone, reading a letter.*]

HOTSPUR   "But for mine own part, my lord, I could be well contented to be there, in respect of the love I bear your house." He could be contented; why is he not, then? In respect of the love he bears our house, he shows in this, he loves his own barn better than he loves our house. Let me see some more. "The purpose you undertake is dangerous." Why, that's cer-

---

5. I.e., good luck!
6. "Caterpillars of the commonwealth" was a common phrase, referring to rogues. Falstaff here applies ridiculously inappropriate terms to the

travelers and to himself (e.g., "youth").
7. Misers. "Gorbellied": fat.
8. Subject of stories.
9. There's no justice.

tain. 'Tis dangerous to take a cold, to sleep, to drink; but I tell you, my lord fool, out of this nettle, danger, we pluck this flower, safety.[1] "The purpose you undertake is dangerous, the friends you have named uncertain, the time itself unsorted,[2] and your whole plot too light for the counterpoise of so great an opposition." Say you so, say you so? I say unto you again, you are a shallow cowardly hind,[3] and you lie. What a lackbrain is this! By the Lord, our plot is a good plot as ever was laid, our friends true and constant; a good plot, good friends, and full of expectation; an excellent plot, very good friends. What a frosty-spirited rogue is this! Why, my lord of York[4] commends the plot and the general course of the action. Zounds, an I were now by this rascal I could brain him with his lady's fan. Is there not my father, my uncle, and myself? Lord Edmund Mortimer, my lord of York, and Owen Glendower? is there not besides the Douglas? have I not all their letters to meet me in arms by the ninth of the next month, and are they not some of them set forward already? What a pagan rascal is this, an infidel! Ha! you shall see now in very sincerity of fear and cold heart, will he to the king and lay open all our proceedings. O, I could divide myself and go to buffets,[5] for moving[6] such a dish of skim milk with so honorable an action! Hang him! let him tell the king. We are prepared; I will set forward tonight.

    [*Enter his* LADY.]

How now, Kate! I must leave you within these two hours.

LADY   O, my good lord, why are you thus alone?
For what offense have I this fortnight been
A banished woman from my Harry's bed?
Tell me, sweet lord, what is 't that takes from thee
Thy stomach,° pleasure, and thy golden sleep?   *appetite*
Why dost thou bend thine eyes upon the earth,
And start so often when thou sit'st alone?
Why hast thou lost the fresh blood in thy cheeks,
And given my treasures and my rights of thee
To thick-eyed musing and cursed melancholy?
In thy faint slumbers I by thee have watched
And heard thee murmur tales of iron wars,
Speak terms of manage° to thy bounding steed,   *horsemanship*
Cry "Courage! to the field!" And thou hast talked
Of sallies and retires, of trenches, tents,
Of palisadoes, frontiers, parapets,
Of basilisks, of cannon, culverin,[7]
Of prisoners' ransom and of soldiers slain,
And all the currents of a heady fight.
Thy spirit within thee hath been so at war
And thus hath so bestirred thee in thy sleep
That beads of sweat have stood upon thy brow
Like bubbles in a late-disturbèd stream,

1. The nettle if touched tenderly will sting; if grasped firmly, will not.
2. Unsuitable.
3. Peasant.
4. The archbishop of York.

5. Split myself in two and let the parts fight each other.
6. Urging.
7. Three kinds of artillery (named here in decreasing order of weight).

50 And in thy face strange motions have appeared
Such as we see when men restrain their breath
On some great sudden hest.° O, what portents are these?   *command*
Some heavy business hath my lord in hand
And I must know it, else he loves me not.
HOTSPUR What, ho!
          [⟨*Enter* SERVANT.⟩]
55   Is Gilliams with the packet gone?
SERVANT He is, my lord, an hour ago.
HOTSPUR Hath Butler brought those horses from the sheriff?
SERVANT One horse, my lord, he brought even now.
HOTSPUR What horse? a roan, a crop-ear, is it not?
SERVANT It is, my lord.
60 HOTSPUR   That roan shall be my throne.
Well, I will back° him straight; O Esperance!⁸   *mount*
Bid Butler lead him forth into the park.   [⟨*Exit* SERVANT.⟩]
LADY But hear you, my lord.
HOTSPUR What say'st thou, my lady?
65 LADY What is it carries you away?
HOTSPUR Why, my horse, my love, my horse.
LADY Out, you mad-headed ape!
A weasel hath not such a deal of spleen⁹
As you are tossed with. In faith
70 I'll know your business, Harry, that I will.
I fear my brother Mortimer doth stir
About his title, and hath sent for you
To line° his enterprise; but if you go¹—   *support*
HOTSPUR So far afoot, I shall be weary, love.
75 LADY Come, come, you paraquito,° answer me   *parrot*
Directly unto this question that I ask.
In faith, I'll break thy little finger, Harry,
An if thou wilt not tell me all things true.
HOTSPUR Away,
80 Away, you trifler! Love! I love thee not,
I care not for thee, Kate; this is no world
To play with mammets° and to tilt with lips;   *dolls*
We must have bloody noses and cracked crowns,²
And pass them current too. God's me, my horse!
85 What say'st thou, Kate? what wouldst thou have with me?
LADY Do you not love me? do you not, indeed?
Well, do not then, for since you love me not
I will not love myself. Do you not love me?
Nay, tell me if you speak in jest or no.
90 HOTSPUR Come, wilt thou see me ride?
And when I am o' horseback, I will swear

---

8. The battle cry of the Percies: "Hope!"
9. The spleen was supposed to be the source of sudden and violent emotions. The weasel was considered a very impetuous animal.
1. Besides its ordinary sense, which Lady Percy uses, "go" also meant "walk," the sense in which Hotspur takes it.
2. Broken heads, with a pun on *crowns* as coins and with allusion to the overthrow of kings.

I love thee infinitely. But hark you, Kate,
I must not have you henceforth question me
Whither I go, nor reason whereabout;
95 Whither I must, I must; and, to conclude,
This evening must I leave you, gentle Kate.
I know you wise, but yet no farther wise
Than Harry Percy's wife; constant you are,
But yet a woman, and for secrecy
100 No lady closer; for I well believe
Thou wilt not utter what thou dost not know,
And so far will I trust thee, gentle Kate.
LADY How! so far?
HOTSPUR Not an inch further. But hark you, Kate,
105 Whither I go, thither shall you go too;
Today will I set forth, tomorrow you.
Will this content you, Kate?
LADY   It must of force.[3]   [*Exeunt.*]

SCENE 4

[*Enter the* PRINCE *and* POINS.]
PRINCE Ned, prithee come out of that fat[4] room, and lend me thy hand
to laugh a little.
POINS Where hast been, Hal?
PRINCE With three or four loggerheads[5] amongst three or four-score hogs-
5 heads. I have sounded the very bass string of humility. Sirrah, I am sworn
brother to a leash of drawers,[6] and can call them all by their christen
names, as Tom, Dick, and Francis. They take it already upon their salvation, that though I be but Prince of Wales, yet I am the king of courtesy, and tell me flatly I am no proud Jack, like Falstaff, but a Corinthian,[7]
10 a lad of mettle, a good boy—by the Lord, so they call me—and when I
am king of England I shall command all the good lads in Eastcheap.
They call drinking deep, dyeing scarlet, and when you breathe in your
watering[8] they cry "hem!" and bid you play it off. To conclude, I am so
good a proficient in one quarter of an hour that I can drink with any
15 tinker in his own language during my life. I tell thee, Ned, thou hast lost
much honor, that thou wert not with me in this action. But, sweet Ned—
to sweeten which name of Ned, I give thee this penny worth of sugar,
clapped even now into my hand by an underskinker,[9] one that never
spake other English in his life than "Eight shillings and sixpence," and
20 "You are welcome," with this shrill addition, "Anon, anon, sir! Score a
pint of bastard in the Half-Moon,"[1] or so. But, Ned, to drive away the
time till Falstaff come, I prithee do thou stand in some by-room, while
I question my puny drawer to what end he gave me the sugar, and do

---

3. Of necessity.
4. Vat. This establishes that the scene is a tavern.
5. Blockheads.
6. Group of tapsters, waiters.
7. Good fellow.
8. Drink.

9. Assistant waiter.
1. I.e., charge a pint of "bastard" (a sweet Spanish wine) to a customer in the room called "Half-Moon." "Anon": immediately (the reply of a servant when called, equivalent to "Coming!").

thou never leave calling "Francis," that his tale to me may be nothing
25 but "Anon." Step aside, and I'll show thee a precedent.[2]
POINS   Francis!
PRINCE   Thou art perfect.
POINS   Francis!   [⟨*Exit* POINS.⟩]
        [*Enter* DRAWER.]
FRANCIS   Anon, anon, sir. Look down into the Pomgarnet,[3] Ralph.
30 PRINCE   Come hither, Francis.
FRANCIS   My lord?
PRINCE   How long hast thou to serve,[4] Francis?
FRANCIS   Forsooth, five years, and as much as to—
POINS [*within*]   Francis!
35 FRANCIS   Anon, anon, sir.
PRINCE   Five year! by 'r Lady, a long lease for the clinking of pewter. But,
        Francis, darest thou be so valiant as to play the coward with thy indenture
        and show it a fair pair of heels and run from it?
FRANCIS   O Lord, sir, I'll be sworn upon all the books[5] in England, I could
40 find in my heart—
POINS [*within*]   Francis!
FRANCIS   Anon, sir.
PRINCE   How old art thou, Francis?
FRANCIS   Let me see—about Michaelmas[6] next I shall be—
45 POINS [*within*]   Francis!
FRANCIS   Anon, sir. Pray stay a little, my lord.
PRINCE   Nay, but hark you, Francis: for the sugar thou gavest me, 'twas a
        pennyworth, was't not?
FRANCIS   O Lord, I would it had been two!
50 PRINCE   I will give thee for it a thousand pound; ask me when thou wilt,
        and thou shalt have it.
POINS [*within*]   Francis!
FRANCIS   Anon, anon.
PRINCE   Anon, Francis? No, Francis, but tomorrow, Francis; or Francis,
55 o' Thursday, or indeed, Francis, when thou wilt. But, Francis!
FRANCIS   My lord?
PRINCE   Wilt thou rob this leathern-jerkin, crystal-button, not-pated,
        agate-ring, puke-stocking, caddis-garter,[7] smooth-tongue, Spanish-
        pouch—
60 FRANCIS   O Lord, sir, who do you mean?
PRINCE   Why, then, your brown bastard is your only drink, for
        look you, Francis, your white canvas doublet will sully. In Barbary, sir,
        it cannot come to so much.[8]
FRANCIS   What, sir?
65 POINS [*within*]   Francis!
PRINCE   Away, you rogue, dost thou not hear them call?

---

2. Example.
3. Pomegranate (another room in the tavern).
4. I.e., to finish out his apprenticeship, usually a
seven-year period under an "indenture" or agreement.
5. I.e., Bibles.
6. September 29.

7. Worsted   tape   garter.   "Leathern-jerken":
leather-jacketed. "Not-pated": with short hair.
"Puke": dark gray.
8. Deliberate nonsense to confuse Francis and
one of the first instances of double-talk in English
literature.

[Here they both call him; the drawer stands amazed, not knowing which way to go.]
[Enter VINTNER.*]*

VINTNER   What, stand'st thou still, and hear'st such a calling? Look to the guests within. *[Exit* FRANCIS.*]* My lord, old Sir John with half-a-dozen more are at the door; shall I let them in?

70   PRINCE   Let them alone awhile, and then open the door. *[Exit* VINTNER.*]* Poins!
[Enter POINS.*]*

POINS   Anon, anon, sir.

PRINCE   Sirrah, Falstaff and the rest of the thieves are at the door; shall we be merry?

75   POINS   As merry as crickets, my lad. But hark ye, what cunning match have you made with this jest of the drawer? come, what's the issue?

PRINCE   I am now of all humors[9] that have showed themselves humors since the old days of goodman Adam to the pupil[1] age of this present twelve o'clock at midnight.
[⟨Enter FRANCIS.⟩*]*

80   What's o'clock, Francis?

FRANCIS   Anon, anon, sir.   *[⟨Exit.⟩]*

PRINCE   That ever this fellow should have fewer words than a parrot, and yet the son of a woman! His industry is upstairs and downstairs, his eloquence the parcel[2] of a reckoning. I am not yet of Percy's mind, the
85   Hotspur of the north, he that kills me some six or seven dozen of Scots at a breakfast, washes his hands, and says to his wife "Fie upon this quiet life! I want work." "O my sweet Harry," says she, "how many hast thou killed today?" "Give my roan horse a drench," says he, and answers "Some fourteen," an hour after, "a trifle, a trifle." I prithee, call in Falstaff; I'll
90   play Percy, and that damned brawn shall play Dame Mortimer his wife. "Rivo!"[3] says the drunkard. Call in ribs, call in tallow.
[Enter FALSTAFF, ⟨GADSHILL, BARDOLPH, *and* PETO, FRANCIS *following with wine*⟩.*]*

POINS   Welcome, Jack; where hast thou been?

FALSTAFF   A plague of all cowards, I say, and a vengeance too, marry and amen! Give me a cup of sack, boy. Ere I lead this life long, I'll sew nether
95   stocks[4] and mend them and foot them too. A plague of all cowards! Give me a cup of sack, rogue. Is there no virtue extant?   *[He drinks.]*

PRINCE   Didst thou ever see Titan[5] kiss a dish of butter, pitiful-hearted butter that melted at the sweet tale of the sun's? If thou didst, then behold that compound.

100   FALSTAFF   You rogue, here's lime in this sack too;[6] there is nothing but roguery to be found in villainous man, yet a coward is worse than a cup of sack with lime in it. A villainous coward! Go thy ways, old Jack, die when thou wilt; if manhood, good manhood, be not forgot upon the face of the earth, then am I a shotten herring.[7] There lives not three good
105   men unhanged in England, and one of them is fat and grows old. God

---

9. Temperaments, dispositions, i.e., as a result of teasing the servant, I am now in the mood for anything.
1. Youthful.
2. Item.

3. Drink up!
4. Stockings.
5. The sun.
6. Lime was used to make wine sparkle.
7. A herring that has cast its spawn and is lean.

help the while; a bad world, I say. I would I were a weaver; I could sing
psalms[8] or anything. A plague of all cowards, I say still.

PRINCE How now, woolsack, what mutter you?

FALSTAFF A king's son! If I do not beat thee out of thy kingdom with a
110 dagger of lath,[9] and drive all thy subjects afore thee like a flock of wild
geese, I'll never wear hair on my face more. You Prince of Wales!

PRINCE Why, you whoreson round man, what's the matter?

FALSTAFF Are not you a coward? answer me to that; and Poins there?

POINS Zounds, ye fat paunch, an ye call me coward, by the Lord I'll stab
115 thee.

FALSTAFF I call thee coward! I'll see thee damned ere I call thee coward;
but I would give a thousand pound I could run as fast as thou canst. You
are straight enough in the shoulders, you care not who sees your back;
call you that backing of your friends? A plague upon such backing! give
120 me them that will face me. Give me a cup of sack; I am a rogue if I drunk
today.

PRINCE O villain! thy lips are scarce wiped since thou drunk'st last.

FALSTAFF All's one for that. [*He drinks.*] A plague of all cowards, still
say I.

125 PRINCE What's the matter?

FALSTAFF What's the matter! there be four of us here have ta'en a thousand pound this day morning.

PRINCE Where is it, Jack? where is it?

FALSTAFF Where is it? taken from us it is—a hundred upon poor four
130 of us.

PRINCE What, a hundred, man?

FALSTAFF I am a rogue if I were not at half-sword[1] with a dozen of them
two hours together. I have 'scaped by miracle. I am eight times thrust
through the doublet, four through the hose,[2] my buckler cut through and
135 through, my sword hacked like a handsaw—*ecce signum!*[3] I never dealt
better since I was a man; all would not do. A plague of all cowards! Let
them speak; if they speak more or less than truth, they are villains and
the sons of darkness.

PRINCE Speak, sirs; how was it?

140 GADSHILL We four set upon some dozen—

FALSTAFF Sixteen at least, my lord.

GADSHILL And bound them.

PETO No, no, they were not bound.

FALSTAFF You rogue, they were bound, every man of them, or I am a Jew
145 else, an Ebrew Jew.

GADSHILL As we were sharing, some six or seven fresh men set upon us—

FALSTAFF And unbound the rest, and then come in the other.

PRINCE What, fought you with them all?

FALSTAFF All! I know not what you call all, but if I fought not with fifty
150 of them, I am a bunch of radish; if there were not two or three and fifty
upon poor old Jack, then am I no two-legged creature.

PRINCE Pray God you have not murdered some of them.

---

8. Protestant weavers from Flanders were notorious for singing psalms.
9. A stick used by Vice in the old morality plays.

1. At half a sword's length.
2. Breeches.
3. Here's the proof!

FALSTAFF Nay, that's past praying for; I have peppered two of them. Two
I am sure I have paid, two rogues in buckram suits. I tell thee what, Hal,
if I tell thee a lie, spit in my face, call me horse. Thou knowest my old
ward; here I lay,[4] and thus I bore my point. Four rogues in buckram let
drive at me—

PRINCE What, four? thou saidst but two even now.

FALSTAFF Four, Hal; I told thee four.

POINS Aye, aye, he said four.

FALSTAFF These four came all a-front, and mainly[5] thrust at me. I made
me no more ado but took all their seven points in my target,[6] thus.

PRINCE Seven? why, there were but four even now.

FALSTAFF In buckram?

POINS Aye, four, in buckram suits.

FALSTAFF Seven, by these hilts, or I am a villain else.

PRINCE Prithee, let him alone; we shall have more anon.

FALSTAFF Dost thou hear me, Hal?

PRINCE Aye, and mark thee too, Jack.

FALSTAFF Do so, for it is worth the listening to. These nine in buckram
that I told thee of—

PRINCE So, two more already.

FALSTAFF Their points being broken—

POINS Down fell their hose.[7]

FALSTAFF Began to give me ground; but I followed me close, came in foot
and hand, and with a thought[8] seven of the eleven I paid.

PRINCE O monstrous! eleven buckram men grown out of two!

FALSTAFF But, as the devil would have it, three misbegotten knaves in
Kendal green[9] came at my back and let drive at me, for it was so dark,
Hal, that thou couldst not see thy hand.

PRINCE These lies are like their father that begets them—gross as a mountain, open, palpable. Why, thou clay-brained guts, thou knotty-pated
fool, thou whoreson, obscene, greasy tallow-catch[1]—

FALSTAFF What, art thou mad? art thou mad? is not the truth the truth?

PRINCE Why, how couldst thou know these men in Kendal green, when
it was so dark thou couldst not see thy hand? come, tell us your reason.
What sayest thou to this?

POINS Come, your reason, Jack, your reason.

FALSTAFF What, upon compulsion? Zounds, an I were at the strappado,
or all the racks[2] in the world, I would not tell you on compulsion. Give
you a reason on compulsion! if reasons[3] were as plentiful as blackberries,
I would give no man a reason upon compulsion, I.

PRINCE I'll be no longer guilty of this sin; this sanguine coward, this bed-
presser, this horseback-breaker, this huge hill of flesh—

FALSTAFF 'Sblood, you starveling, you eelskin, you dried neat's tongue,
you bull's pizzle, you stockfish![4] O for breath to utter what is like thee!

4. This was my stance. "Ward": defense.
5. Strongly.
6. Shield.
7. Poins puns on the other meaning of *points*: the laces used to tie a man's hose to his doublet.
8. As quick as thought.
9. A coarse cloth.

1. Piece of tallow from which chandlers made candles
2. "Strappado" and "racks" are methods of torture.
3. A pun on the word *raisin*, which was spelled and pronounced like *reason* in Elizabethan England.
4. I.e., you ox tongue, you bull's penis, you dried cod!

you tailor's yard, you sheath, you bow case, you vile standing-tuck[5]—

PRINCE   Well, breathe awhile, and then to it again; and when thou hast
tired thyself in base comparisons, hear me speak but this.

200   POINS   Mark, Jack.

PRINCE   We two saw you four set on four and bound them, and were
masters of their wealth. Mark now, how a plain tale shall put you down.
Then did we two set on you four; and, with a word, outfaced you from
your prize, and have it, yea, and can show it you here in the house; and,

205   Falstaff, you carried your guts away as nimbly, with as quick dexterity,
and roared for mercy and still run and roared, as ever I heard bullcalf.
What a slave art thou, to hack thy sword as thou hast done, and then say
it was in fight! What trick, what device, what starting-hole,[6] canst thou
now find out to hide thee from this open and apparent shame?

210   POINS   Come, let's hear, Jack; what trick hast thou now?

FALSTAFF   By the Lord, I knew ye as well as he that made ye. Why, hear
you, my masters: was it for me to kill the heir apparent? should I turn
upon the true prince? why, thou knowest I am as valiant as Hercules;
but beware instinct; the lion will not touch the true prince.[7] Instinct is

215   a great matter; I was now a coward on instinct. I shall think the better
of myself and thee during my life; I for a valiant lion, and thou for a true
prince. But, by the Lord, lads, I am glad you have the money. Hostess,
clap to the doors; watch[8] tonight, pray tomorrow. Gallants, lads, boys,
hearts of gold, all the titles of good fellowship come to you! What, shall

220   we be merry? shall we have a play extempore?

PRINCE   Content; and the argument[9] shall be thy running away.

FALSTAFF   Ah, no more of that, Hal, an thou lovest me!

[Enter HOSTESS.]

HOSTESS   O Jesu, my lord the prince!

PRINCE   How now, my lady the hostess! what sayest thou to me?

225   HOSTESS   Marry, my lord, there is a nobleman of the court at door would
speak with you; he says he comes from your father.

PRINCE   Give him as much as will make him a royal[1] man, and send him
back again to my mother.

FALSTAFF   What manner of man is he?

230   HOSTESS   An old man.

FALSTAFF   What doth gravity out of his bed at midnight? Shall I give him
his answer?

PRINCE   Prithee, do, Jack.

FALSTAFF   Faith, and I'll send him packing.   [Exit.]

235   PRINCE   Now, sirs. By 'r Lady, you fought fair; so did you, Peto; so did
you, Bardolph; you are lions too, you ran away upon instinct, you will
not touch the true prince; no, fie!

BARDOLPH   Faith, I ran when I saw others run.

PRINCE   Faith, tell me now in earnest, how came Falstaff's sword so

240   hacked?

---

5. Stiff rapier.
6. Evasion.
7. In many medieval romances the lion, as king of
beasts, shows respect for royalty.

8. Stay up.
9. Plot or story.
1. A "royal" was half of a pound sterling, a "noble"
was a third.

PETO Why, he hacked it with his dagger, and said he would swear truth out of England but he would make you believe it was done in fight, and persuaded us to do the like.

BARDOLPH Yea, and to tickle our noses with speargrass to make them bleed, and then to beslubber our garments with it and swear it was the blood of true men. I did that I did not this seven year before, I blushed to hear his monstrous devices.

PRINCE O villain, thou stolest a cup of sack eighteen years ago, and wert taken with the manner,[2] and ever since thou hast blushed extempore. Thou hadst fire and sword on thy side, and yet thou ran'st away; what instinct hadst thou for it?

BARDOLPH My lord, do you see these meteors? do you behold these exhalations?[3]

PRINCE I do.

BARDOLPH What think you they portend?

PRINCE Hot livers and cold purses.[4]

BARDOLPH Choler, my lord, if rightly taken.

PRINCE No, if rightly taken, halter.[5]

[*Enter* FALSTAFF.]

Here comes lean Jack, here comes bare-bone. How now, my sweet creature of bombast,[6] how long is 't ago, Jack, since thou sawest thine own knee?

FALSTAFF My own knee! when I was about thy years, Hal, I was not an eagle's talon in the waist; I could have crept into any alderman's thumb ring. A plague of sighing and grief—it blows a man up like a bladder. There's villainous news abroad; here was Sir John Bracy from your father; you must to the court in the morning. That same mad fellow of the north, Percy, and he of Wales, that gave Amamon the bastinado[7] and made Lucifer cuckold and swore the devil his true liegeman upon the cross of a Welsh hook[8]—what a plague call you him?

POINS O, Glendower.

FALSTAFF Owen, Owen, the same; and his son-in-law Mortimer, and old Northumberland, and that sprightly Scot of Scots, Douglas, that runs o' horseback up a hill perpendicular—

PRINCE He that rides at high speed and with his pistol kills a sparrow flying.

FALSTAFF You have hit it.

PRINCE So did he never the sparrow.

FALSTAFF Well, that rascal hath good mettle in him; he will not run.

PRINCE Why, what a rascal art thou then, to praise him so for running!

FALSTAFF O' horseback, ye cuckoo; but afoot he will not budge a foot.

PRINCE Yes, Jack, upon instinct.

FALSTAFF I grant ye, upon instinct. Well, he is there too, and one Mordake, and a thousand blue-caps[9] more. Worcester is stolen away tonight; thy father's beard is turned white with the news; you may buy land now

---

2. In the act.
3. "Fire" and the allusions to "meteors" and "exhalations" (shooting stars) refer to Bardolph's red nose.
4. I.e., drunkenness and poverty.
5. Hangman's noose, with a pun on *collar*.

"Choler": fiery complexion, indicating a choleric (angry) temperament.
6. Padding, stuffing.
7. A beating, cudgeling. "Amamon": a devil.
8. A long spear with a hook on it.
9. Scots.

85   as cheap as stinking mackerel.

PRINCE   Why then, it is like, if there come a hot June, and this civil buf-
feting hold, we shall buy maidenheads as they buy hobnails, by the hundreds.

FALSTAFF   By the mass, lad, thou sayest true; it is like we shall have good
90   trading that way. But tell me, Hal, art not thou horrible afeard? thou
being heir apparent, could the world pick thee out three such enemies
again as that fiend Douglas, that spirit Percy, and that devil Glendower?
Art thou not horribly afraid? doth not thy blood thrill at it?

PRINCE   Not a whit, i' faith; I lack some of thy instinct.

295 FALSTAFF   Well, thou wilt be horribly chid tomorrow when thou comest
to thy father; if thou love me, practice an answer.

PRINCE   Do thou stand for[1] my father and examine me upon the particulars of my life.

FALSTAFF   Shall I? Content. This chair shall be my state,[2] this dagger my
300   scepter, and this cushion my crown.

PRINCE   Thy state is taken for a joint-stool,[3] thy golden scepter for a leaden
dagger, and thy precious rich crown for a pitiful bald crown!

FALSTAFF   Well, an the fire of grace be not quite out of thee, now shalt
thou be moved. Give me a cup of sack to make my eyes look red, that it
305   may be thought I have wept, for I must speak in passion, and I will do it
in King Cambyses'[4] vein.

PRINCE   Well, here is my leg.[5]

FALSTAFF   And here is my speech. Stand aside, nobility.

HOSTESS   O Jesu, this is excellent sport, i' faith!

310 FALSTAFF   Weep not, sweet queen, for trickling tears are vain.

HOSTESS   O, the father, how he holds his countenance!

FALSTAFF   For God's sake, lords, convey my tristful queen,
For tears do stop the floodgates of her eyes.[6]

HOSTESS   O Jesu, he doth it as like one of these harlotry players as ever I
315   see!

FALSTAFF   Peace, good pint pot, peace, good ticklebrain. Harry, I do not
only marvel where thou spendest thy time, but also how thou art accompanied, for though the camomile,[7] the more it is trodden on the faster it
grows, so youth, the more it is wasted the sooner it wears. That thou art
320   my son, I have partly thy mother's word, partly my own opinion, but
chiefly a villainous trick of thine eye and a foolish hanging of thy nether
lip that doth warrant[8] me. If then thou be son to me, here lies the point;
why, being son to me, art thou so pointed at? Shall the blessed sun of
heaven prove a micher[9] and eat blackberries? a question not to be asked.
325   Shall the son of England prove a thief and take purses? a question to be
asked. There is a thing, Harry, which thou hast often heard of and it is
known to many in our land by the name of pitch. This pitch, as ancient
writers do report, doth defile; so doth the company thou keepest: for,

---

1. Represent.
2. Throne.
3. An ordinary stool, made by a joiner (cabinet-maker).
4. Like the bombastic hero of the old play *Cambyses*.
5. I.e., he bows, makes an obeisance.

6. Falstaff's blank verse lines parody the old-fashioned tragedies of the 1570s and 1580s.
7. An aromatic herb. The style in this speech is a parody of Euphuism, the ornate, elaborate, bal-anced style made popular by Lyly's *Euphues*.
8. Assure.
9. Truant.

Harry, now I do not speak to thee in drink but in tears, not in pleasure
330   but in passion, not in words only, but in woes also: and yet there is a
virtuous man whom I have often noted in thy company, but I know not
his name.

PRINCE   What manner of man, an it like[1] your majesty?

FALSTAFF   A goodly portly man, i' faith, and a corpulent; of a cheerful look,
335   a pleasing eye and a most noble carriage, and, as I think, his age some
fifty, or, by 'r Lady, inclining to threescore; and now I remember me, his
name is Falstaff. If that man should be lewdly given, he deceiveth me,
for, Harry, I see virtue in his looks. If then the tree may be known by the
fruit, as the fruit by the tree, then, peremptorily I speak it, there is virtue
340   in that Falstaff; him keep with, the rest banish. And tell me now, thou
naughty varlet, tell me, where hast thou been this month?

PRINCE   Dost thou speak like a king? Do thou stand for me, and I'll play
my father.

FALSTAFF   Depose me? if thou dost it half so gravely, so majestically, both
345   in word and matter, hang me up by the heels for a rabbit-sucker[2] or a
poulter's hare.

PRINCE   Well, here I am set.[3]

FALSTAFF   And here I stand; judge, my masters.

PRINCE   Now, Harry, whence come you?

350 FALSTAFF   My noble lord, from Eastcheap.

PRINCE   The complaints I hear of thee are grievous.

FALSTAFF   'Sblood, my lord, they are false: nay, I'll tickle ye for a young
prince, i' faith.

PRINCE   Swearest thou, ungracious boy? Henceforth ne'er look on me.
355   Thou art violently carried away from grace; there is a devil haunts thee
in the likeness of an old fat man; a tun[4] of man is thy companion. Why
dost thou converse with that trunk of humors, that bolting-hutch of
beastliness, that swollen parcel of dropsies, that huge bombard[5] of sack,
that stuffed cloak-bag of guts, that roasted Manningtree ox with the pud-
360   ding in his belly, that reverend vice,[6] that gray iniquity, that father ruffian, that vanity in years? Wherein is he good, but to taste sack and drink
it? wherein neat and cleanly, but to carve a capon and eat it? wherein
cunning, but in craft? wherein crafty, but in villainy? wherein villainous,
but in all things? wherein worthy, but in nothing?

365 FALSTAFF   I would your grace would take me with you; whom means your
grace?

PRINCE   That villainous abominable misleader of youth, Falstaff, that old
white-bearded Satan.

FALSTAFF   My lord, the man I know.

370 PRINCE   I know thou dost.

FALSTAFF   But to say I know more harm in him than in myself were to say
more than I know. That he is old the more the pity, his white hairs do
witness it; but that he is, saving your reverence, a whoremaster, that I

---

1. If it please.
2. Suckling rabbit.
3. Seated.
4. Large barrel.
5. Leather wine vessel. "Bolting-hutch": trough.

6. The Vice was a comic character in the old
morality plays. Falstaff is in some respects a
descendant of this type character. "Manningtree":
a town in Essex, noted for barbecues. "Pudding":
sausage.

utterly deny. If sack and sugar be a fault, God help the wicked! if to be
375 old and merry be a sin, then many an old host that I know is damned; if
to be fat be to be hated, then Pharaoh's lean kine[7] are to be loved. No,
my good lord, banish Peto, banish Bardolph, banish Poins, but for sweet
Jack Falstaff, kind Jack Falstaff, true Jack Falstaff, valiant Jack Falstaff,
and therefore more valiant, being as he is old Jack Falstaff, banish not
380 him thy Harry's company, banish not him thy Harry's company; banish
plump Jack, and banish all the world.

PRINCE   I do, I will.   [⟨*A knocking heard.*⟩]
                                             [⟨*Exeunt* HOSTESS *and* BARDOLPH.⟩]
           [*Enter* BARDOLPH, *running.*]
BARDOLPH   O, my lord, my lord, the sheriff with a most monstrous watch
is at the door.
385 FALSTAFF   Out, ye rogue! Play out the play; I have much to say in the
behalf of that Falstaff.
           [*Enter the* HOSTESS.]
HOSTESS   O Jesu, my lord, my lord!
FALSTAFF   Heigh, heigh! the devil rides upon a fiddlestick;[8] what's the matter?
390 HOSTESS   The sheriff and all the watch are at the door; they are come to
search the house. Shall I let them in?
FALSTAFF   Dost thou hear, Hal? never call a true piece of gold a counterfeit; thou art essentially mad, without seeming so.[9]
PRINCE   And thou a natural coward, without instinct.
395 FALSTAFF   I deny your major;[1] if you will deny the sheriff, so; if not, let
him enter. If I become not a cart as well as another man, a plague on
my bringing up! I hope I shall as soon be strangled with a halter as
another.[2]
PRINCE   Go hide thee behind the arras; the rest walk up above.[3] Now my
400 masters, for a true face and good conscience.
FALSTAFF   Both which I have had; but their date is out,[4] and therefore I'll
hide me.
PRINCE   Call in the sheriff.
                                     [*Exeunt* ⟨*all except the* PRINCE *and* POINS⟩.]
           [*Enter* SHERIFF *and the* CARRIER.]
Now, master sheriff, what is your will with me?
405 SHERIFF   First pardon me, my lord. A hue and cry
Hath followed certain men unto this house.
PRINCE   What men?
SHERIFF   One of them is well known, my gracious lord,
A gross fat man.
CARRIER   As fat as butter.
410 PRINCE   The man, I do assure you, is not here,

---

7. In the dream Joseph interpreted (Genesis
41.19–21).
8. I.e., there's a commotion.
9. I.e., don't give a true man (me, Falstaff) away
as a thief. He goes on to accuse the prince, in his
reversal of values in the play scene, of being out of
his mind, though he appears rational.
1. Your major premise (that I, Falstaff, am a cow-

ard).
2. I.e., I hope my fat neck will not make the process of strangling on the gallows longer for me than
for the rest of you. The "cart" is the wagon on
which criminals were taken to be hanged.
3. On the balcony. "Arras": the hangings or draperies that covered the walls.
4. Lease has expired.

For I myself at this time have employed him,
And, sheriff, I will engage my word to thee
That I will by tomorrow dinnertime
Send him to answer thee or any man
415 For anything he shall be charged withal;
And so let me entreat you leave the house.
SHERIFF   I will, my lord. There are two gentlemen
Have in this robbery lost three hundred marks.
PRINCE   It may be so; if he have robbed these men
420 He shall be answerable; and so farewell.
SHERIFF   Good night, my noble lord.
PRINCE   I think it is good morrow, is it not?
SHERIFF   Indeed, my lord, I think it be two o'clock.
          [*Exeunt* ⟨SHERIFF *and* CARRIER.⟩]
PRINCE   This oily rascal is known as well as Paul's.[5] Go call him forth.
425 POINS   Falstaff!—Fast asleep behind the arras, and snorting like a horse.
PRINCE   Hark, how hard he fetches breath. Search his pockets. [*He
          searcheth his pockets, and findeth certain papers.*] What hast thou found?
POINS   Nothing but papers, my lord.
PRINCE   Let's see what they be: read them.
430 POINS [*reads*] "Item, a capon. .   .   .   .   2s. 2d.
                     Item, sauce. .   .   .   .   .   4d.
                     Item, sack, two gallons. .   .   5s. 8d.
                     Item, anchovies and sack   2s. 6d.
                         after supper. .   .   .   .
                     Item, bread. .   .   .   .   .   ob."[6]
435 PRINCE   O monstrous! but one halfpennyworth of bread to this intolerable
          deal of sack! What there is else, keep close; we'll read it at more advan-
          tage; there let him sleep till day. I'll to the court in the morning. We
          must all to the wars, and thy place shall be honorable. I'll procure this
          fat rogue a charge of foot,[7] and I know his death will be a march of
440 twelvescore. The money shall be paid back again with advantage. Be with
          me betimes[8] in the morning, and so good morrow, Poins.
POINS   Good morrow, good my lord.   [*Exeunt.*]

Act 3

SCENE 1

[*Enter* HOTSPUR, WORCESTER, LORD MORTIMER, *and* OWEN GLEN-
DOWER.]
MORTIMER   These promises are fair, the parties sure,
And our induction° full of prosperous hope.   initial step
HOTSPUR   Lord Mortimer, and cousin Glendower,
Will you sit down?
5 And uncle Worcester; a plague upon it,
I have forgot the map.
GLENDOWER   No, here it is.

---

5. St. Paul's Cathedral.   7. Company of infantry.
6. Oble, a halfpenny.   8. Early. "Twelvescore": i.e., 240 yards.

Sit, cousin Percy, sit, good cousin Hotspur,
For by that name as oft as Lancaster[9]
Doth speak of you, his cheek looks pale and with
10   A rising sigh he wisheth you in heaven.
HOTSPUR   And you in hell as often as he hears Owen Glendower spoke of.
GLENDOWER   I cannot blame him; at my nativity
The front° of heaven was full of fiery shapes,   *forehead*
Of burning cressets,° and at my birth   *lamps*
15   The frame and huge foundation of the earth
Shaked like a coward.
HOTSPUR   Why, so it would have done at the same season if your mother's
cat had but kittened, though yourself had never been born.
GLENDOWER   I say the earth did shake when I was born.
20   HOTSPUR   And I say the earth was not of my mind,
If you suppose as fearing you it shook.
GLENDOWER   The heavens were all on fire, the earth did tremble.
HOTSPUR   O then the earth shook to see the heavens on fire,
And not in fear of your nativity.
25   Diseasèd nature oftentimes breaks forth
In strange eruptions; oft the teeming earth
Is with a kind of colic pinched and vexed
By the imprisoning of unruly wind
Within her womb, which for enlargement striving
30   Shakes the old beldam° earth and topples down   *old woman*
Steeples and moss-grown towers. At your birth
Our grandam earth, having this distemperature,°   *ailment*
In passion shook.
GLENDOWER   Cousin, of many men
I do not bear these crossings. Give me leave
35   To tell you once again that at my birth
The front of heaven was full of fiery shapes,
The goats ran from the mountains, and the herds
Were strangely clamorous to the frighted fields.
These signs have marked me extraordinary,
40   And all the courses of my life do show
I am not in the roll of common men.
Where is he living, clipped in with[1] the sea
That chides the banks of England, Scotland, Wales,
Which calls me pil or hath read to me?
45   And bring him out that is but woman's son
Can trace me in the tedious ways of art[2]
And hold me pace in deep experiments.
HOTSPUR   I think there's no man speaks better Welsh. I'll to dinner.
MORTIMER   Peace, cousin Percy; you will make him mad.
50   GLENDOWER   I can call spirits from the vasty deep.
HOTSPUR   Why, so can I, or so can any man;
But will they come when you do call for them?

---

9. I.e., King Henry IV. To call him by his lesser
title is insulting.

1. Within the limits of.
2. Follow me in practicing difficult magic.

GLENDOWER   Why, I can teach you, cousin, to command
 The devil.
55 HOTSPUR   And I can teach thee, coz, to shame the devil
 By telling truth; tell truth and shame the devil.[3]
 If thou have power to raise him, bring him hither,
 And I'll be sworn I have power to shame him hence.
 O, while you live, tell truth and shame the devil!
60 MORTIMER   Come, come, no more of this unprofitable chat.
 GLENDOWER   Three times hath Henry Bullingbrook made head
 Against my power, thrice from the banks of Wye
 And sandy-bottomed Severn have I sent him
 Bootless[4] home and weather-beaten back.
65 HOTSPUR   Home without boots, and in foul weather too!
 How 'scapes he agues,° in the devil's name?   *fevers and chills*
 GLENDOWER   Come, here is the map; shall we divide our right
 According to our threefold order ta'en?[5]
 MORTIMER   The archdeacon hath divided it
70 Into three limits very equally:
 England, from Trent and Severn hitherto,
 By south and east is to my part assigned;
 All westward, Wales beyond the Severn shore,
 And all the fertile land within that bound,
75 To Owen Glendower; and, dear coz, to you
 The remnant northward lying off from Trent.
 And our indentures tripartite are drawn,
 Which being sealèd interchangeably,
 A business that this night may execute,
80 Tomorrow, cousin Percy, you and I
 And my good Lord of Worcester will set forth
 To meet your father and the Scottish power,
 As is appointed us, at Shrewsbury.
 My father[6] Glendower is not ready yet,
85 Nor shall we need his help these fourteen days.
 Within that space you may have drawn together
 Your tenants, friends, and neighboring gentlemen.
 GLENDOWER   A shorter time shall send me to you, lords,
 And in my conduct shall your ladies come,
90 From whom you ow must steal and take no leave,
 For there will be a world of water shed
 Upon the parting of your wives and you.
 HOTSPUR   Methinks my moiety,° north from Burton here,   *share*
 In quantity equals not one of yours;
95 See how this river comes me cranking° in,   *curving*
 And cuts me from the best of all my land
 A huge half-moon, a monstrous cantle° out.   *corner*
 I'll have the current in this place dammed up;
 And here the smug° and silver Trent shall run   *smooth*

---

3. A proverb.
4. Unsuccessful; but Hotspur takes it in the other
sense.

5. Divide our property according to the arrangement for division into three parts.
6. Father-in-law.

100   In a new channel, fair and evenly;
      It shall not wind with such a deep indent
      To rob me of so rich a bottom° here.   *valley*
    GLENDOWER   Not wind? it shall, it must; you see it doth.
    MORTIMER   Yea, but
105   Mark how he bears his course, and runs me up
      With like advantage on the other side;
      Gelding the opposèd continent⁷ as much
      As on the other side it takes from you.
    WORCESTER   Yea, but a little charge will trench him here
110   And on this north side win this cape of land,
      And then he runs straight and even.
    HOTSPUR   I'll have it so; a little charge will do it.
    GLENDOWER   I'll not have it altered.
    HOTSPUR   Will not you?
    GLENDOWER   No, nor you shall not.
    HOTSPUR   Who shall say me nay?
115   GLENDOWER   Why, that will I.
    HOTSPUR   Let me not understand you then; speak it in Welsh.
    GLENDOWER   I can speak English, lord, as well as you,
      For I was trained up in the English court,
      Where, being but young, I framèd to the harp
120   Many an English ditty lovely well
      And gave the tongue a helpful ornament,
      A virtue that was never seen in you.
    HOTSPUR   Marry,
      And I am glad of it with all my heart;
125   I had rather be a kitten and cry mew
      Than one of these same meter ballad-mongers;
      I had rather hear a brazen canstick turned,⁸
      Or a dry wheel grate on the axletree,
      And that would set my teeth nothing on edge,
130   Nothing so much as mincing° poetry;   *affected*
      'Tis like the forced gait of a shuffling° nag.   *hobbled*
    GLENDOWER   Come, you shall have Trent turned.
    HOTSPUR   I do not care; I'll give thrice so much land
      To any well-deserving friend;
135   But in the way of bargain, mark ye me,
      I'll cavil° on the ninth part of a hair.   *quibble*
      Are the indentures drawn? shall we be gone?
    GLENDOWER   The moon shines fair; you may be away by night.
      I'll haste the writer, and withal
140   Break with° your wives of your departure hence.   *inform*
      I am afraid my daughter will run mad,
      So much she doteth on her Mortimer.   [*Exit.*]
    MORTIMER   Fie, cousin Percy, how you cross my father!
    HOTSPUR   I cannot choose; sometime he angers me

---

7. I.e., cutting off from the opposite side.   8. A brass candlestick turned on a lathe.

145 With telling me of the moldwarp[9] and the ant,
Of the dreamer Merlin and his prophecies,
And of a dragon and a finless fish,
A clip-winged griffin and a molten raven,
A couching lion and a ramping[1] cat,
150 And such a deal of skimble-skamble stuff
As puts me from my faith. I tell you what;
He held me last night at least nine hours
In reckoning up the several devils' names
That were his lackeys. I cried "hum" and "well, go to,"
155 But marked him not a word. O, he is as tedious
As a tired horse, a railing° wife,   *nagging*
Worse than a smoky house. I had rather live
With cheese and garlic in a windmill,[2] far,
Than feed on cates° and have him talk to me   *delicacies*
160 In any summer house in Christendom.
MORTIMER   In faith, he is a worthy gentleman,
Exceedingly well read, and profited
In strange concealments,[3] valiant as a lion
And wondrous affable and as bountiful
165 As mines of India. Shall I tell you, cousin?
He holds your temper° in a high respect   *character*
And curbs himself even of his natural scope
When you come 'cross his humor; faith, he does.
I warrant you that man is not alive
170 Might so have tempted him as you have done
Without the taste of danger and reproof;
But do not use it oft, let me entreat you.
WORCESTER   In faith, my lord, you are too willful-blame,
And since your coming hither have done enough
175 To put him quite beside his patience.
You must needs learn, lord, to amend this fault.
Though sometimes it show greatness, courage, blood°—   *breeding*
And that's the dearest grace it renders you—
Yet oftentimes it doth present harsh rage,
180 Defect of manners, want of government,°   *self-control*
Pride, haughtiness, opinion,° and disdain;   *arrogance*
The least of which haunting a nobleman
Loseth men's hearts and leaves behind a stain
Upon the beauty of all parts besides,
185 Beguiling them of commendation.
HOTSPUR   Well, I am schooled; good manners be your speed!
Here come our wives, and let us take our leave.
[*Enter* GLENDOWER *with the ladies.*]

---

9. Mole. According to the chronicler Holinshed there were prophecies in which Henry IV was referred to as "a moldwarp, cursed of God." Merlin was the famous prophet of King Arthur's court; many later prophecies were attributed to him.
1. "Couching" and "ramping" are Hotspur's ver-

sions of the heraldic terms "couchant" (lying down) and "rampant" (erect, on hind feet).
2. Cheese and garlic would be smelly, and the living quarters in a mill would be noisy.
3. Experienced in secret mysteries.

MORTIMER   This is the deadly spite that angers me;
My wife can speak no English, I no Welsh.
90   GLENDOWER   My daughter weeps; she will not part with you,
She'll be a soldier too, she'll to the wars.
MORTIMER   Good father, tell her that she and my aunt Percy
Shall follow in your conduct speedily.
      [GLENDOWER *speaks to her in Welsh, and she answers him in the same.*]
GLENDOWER   She is desperate here; a peevish self-willed harlotry,[4] one
95   that no persuasion can do good upon.
      [*The lady speaks in Welsh.*]
MORTIMER   I understand thy looks; that pretty Welsh
Which thou pour'st down from these swelling heavens[5]
I am too perfect in; and, but for shame,
In such a parley should I answer thee.[6]
      [*The lady speaks again in Welsh.*]
200   I understand thy kisses and thou mine,
And that's a feeling disputation,
But I will never be a truant, love,
Till I have learned thy language, for thy tongue
Makes Welsh as sweet as ditties highly penned,
205   Sung by a fair queen in a summer's bower,
With ravishing division,° to her lute.   *musical variation*
GLENDOWER   Nay, if you melt, then will she run mad.
      [*The lady speaks again in Welsh.*]
MORTIMER   O, I am ignorance itself in this!
GLENDOWER   She bids you on the wanton rushes[7] lay you down
210   And rest your gentle head upon her lap,
And she will sing the song that pleaseth you
And on your eyelids crown the god of sleep,
Charming your blood with pleasing heaviness,°   *drowsiness*
Making such difference 'twixt wake and sleep
215   As is the difference betwixt day and night
The hour before the heavenly-harnessed team[8]
Begins his golden progress in the east.
MORTIMER   With all my heart I'll sit and hear her sing;
By that time will our book,[9] think, be drawn.
220   GLENDOWER   Do so:
And those musicians that shall play to you
Hang in the air a thousand leagues from hence,
And straight they shall be here; sit, and attend.
HOTSPUR   Come, Kate, thou art perfect in lying down; come, quick,
225   quick, that I may lay my head in thy lap.
LADY PERCY   Go, ye giddy goose.
      [*The music plays.*]
HOTSPUR   Now I perceive the devil understands Welsh,
And 'tis no marvel, he is so humorous.[1]

4. Wench; used affectionately, not seriously.
5. I.e., tears from her eyes.
6. Cry likewise.
7. The dry reeds used as a floor covering in Eliz-

abethan England.
8. The horses of the sun.
9. The indenture.
1. Capricious, governed by humors.

By 'r Lady, he is a good musician.

230 LADY PERCY   Then should you be nothing but musical, for you are altogether governed by humors. Lie still, ye thief, and hear the lady sing
in Welsh.

HOTSPUR   I had rather hear Lady, my brach,[2] howl in Irish.

LADY PERCY   Wouldst thou have thy head broken?

235 HOTSPUR   No.

LADY PERCY   Then be still.

HOTSPUR   Neither; 'tis a woman's fault.[3]

LADY PERCY   Now God help thee.

HOTSPUR   To the Welsh lady's bed.

240 LADY PERCY   What's that?

HOTSPUR   Peace! she sings.

[Here the lady sings a Welsh song.]

HOTSPUR   Come, Kate, I'll have your song too.

LADY PERCY   Not mine, in good sooth.°   truth

HOTSPUR   Not yours, in good sooth! Heart! you swear like a comfitmaker's[4]

245 wife. "Not you, in good sooth," and "as true as I live," and "as God shall
mend me," and "as sure as day,"
And givest such sarcenet° surety for thy oaths   thin silk
As if thou never walk'st further than Finsbury.[5]
Swear me, Kate, like a lady as thou art,

250 A good mouth-filling oath, and leave "in sooth,"
And such protest of pepper-gingerbread,
To velvet-guards and Sunday citizens.[6]
Come, sing.

LADY PERCY   I will not sing.

255 HOTSPUR   'Tis the next way to turn tailor, or be redbreast teacher.[7] An the
indentures be drawn, I'll away within these two hours; and so, come in
when ye will.   [Exit.]

GLENDOWER   Come, come, Lord Mortimer, you are as slow
As hot Lord Percy is on fire to go.

260 By this our book is drawn; we will but seal,
And then to horse immediately.

MORTIMER   With all my heart.   [Exeunt.]

SCENE 2

[Enter the KING, PRINCE OF WALES, and others.]

KING   Lords, give us leave; the Prince of Wales and I
Must have some private conference; but be near at hand,
For we shall presently have need of you.   [Exeunt LORDS.]
I know not whether God will have it so

2. My bitch hound, Lady.
3. Hotspur sarcastically reverses the usual saying
about women and talkativeness.
4. Confectioner's.
5. A recreation ground outside London, frequented by citizens and their wives on Sundays,
but not by ladies of Lady Percy's class.
6. City folk out for a stroll on Sunday. "Pepper-

gingerbread": i.e., such tame oaths, as crumbly and
unsubstantial as gingerbread. "Velvet-guards":
respectable people of the middle class, who wore
velvet stripes on their clothes.
7. I.e., it is the easiest way to become a tailor (supposedly tailors sang at their work) or a person who
teaches birds to sing. Hotspur is equally scornful
of music and of people who work for a living.

5   For some displeasing service I have done,
    That, in his secret doom, out of my blood[8]
    He'll breed revengement and a scourge for me;
    But thou dost in thy passages° of life   *actions*
    Make me believe that thou art only marked
10   For the hot vengeance and the rod of heaven
    To punish my mistreadings.° Tell me else,   *misdeeds*
    Could such inordinate and low desires,
    Such poor, such bare, such lewd,° such mean attempts,   *low*
    Such barren pleasures, rude society
15   As thou art matched withal and grafted to
    Accompany the greatness of thy blood
    And hold their level with thy princely heart?
    PRINCE   So please your majesty, I would I could
    Quit[9] all offenses with as clear excuse
20   As well as I am doubtless° I can purge   *sure*
    Myself of many I am charged withal;
    Yet such extenuation let me beg,
    As, in reproof of many tales devised
    (Which oft the ear of greatness needs must hear)
25   By smiling pickthanks° and base newsmongers,°   *flatterers / tattletales*
    I may, for some things true, wherein my youth
    Hath faulty wandered and irregular,
    Find pardon on my true submissiòn.
    KING   God pardon thee; yet let me wonder, Harry,
30   At thy affections, which doth hold a wing
    Quite from the flight of all thy ancestors.
    Thy place in council thou hast rudely lost,
    Which by thy younger brother is supplied,
    And art almost an alien to the hearts
35   Of all the court and princes of my blood.
    The hope and expectation of thy time[1]
    Is ruined, and the soul of every man
    Prophetically do forethink thy fall.
    Had I so lavish of my presence been,
40   So common-hackneyed[2] in the eyes of men,
    So stale and cheap to vulgar company,
    Opinion,[3] that did help me to the crown,
    Had still kept loyal to possessiòn
    And left me in reputeless banishment,
45   A fellow of no mark nor likelihood.
    By being seldom seen, I could not stir
    But like a comet I was wondered at,
    That men would tell their children "This is he";
    Others would say "Where, which is Bullingbrook?"
50   And then I stole all courtesy from heaven,

8. Unknown judgment, through my son.   2. Cheapened, vulgarized.
9. Acquit myself of.   3. Popularity, public opinion.
1. Lifetime.

And dressed myself in such humility.
That I did pluck allegiance from men's hearts,
Loud shouts and salutations from their mouths,
Even in the presence of the crownèd king.
55   Thus did I keep my person fresh and new,
My presence like a robe pontifical,
Ne'er seen but wondered at; and so my state,[4]
Seldom but sumptuous, showed like a feast
And wan° by rareness such solemnity.[5]   *won*
60   The skipping king, he ambled up and down
With shallow jesters and rash° bavin[6] wits,   *quick*
Soon kindled and soon burnt, carded his state,[7]
Mingled his royalty with cap'ring fools,
Had his great name profanèd with their scorns
65   And gave his countenance° against his name[8]   *authority*
To laugh at gibing boys and stand the push
Of every beardless vain comparative,[9]
Grew a companion to the common streets,
Enfeoffed himself to popularity,[1]
70   That, being daily swallowed by men's eyes,
They surfeited with honey and began
To loathe the taste of sweetness, whereof a little
More than a little is by much too much.
So when he had occasion to be seen
75   He was but as the cuckoo is in June,[2]
Heard, not regarded, seen, but with such eyes
As, sick and blunted with community,°   *commonness*
Afford no extraordinary gaze
Such as is bent on sunlike majesty
80   When it shines seldom in admiring eyes,
But rather drowsed and hung their eyelids down,
Slept in his face[3] and rendered such aspèct°   *looks*
As cloudy° men use to their adversaries,   *sullen*
Being with his presence glutted, gorged, and full.
85   And in that very line, Harry, standest thou,
For thou hast lost thy princely privilege
With vile participation.[4] Not an eye
But is a-weary of thy common sight,
Save mine, which hath desired to see thee more,
90   Which now doth that I would not have it do,
Make blind itself with foolish tenderness.
PRINCE   I shall hereafter, my thrice gracious lord,

---

4. Public ceremonial appearances.
5. "Such solemnity": i.e., the greatest possible majestic effect.
6. Brushwood; the image is explained in the next line.
7. Degraded his royal dignity; "card" also means "to adulterate wine."
8. Reputation.

9. Tolerate the impertinent witticisms of every beardless youth.
1. Made himself the common property of the public.
2. The cuckoo is noticed in April, when its song is first heard; by June it is commonplace.
3. I.e., yawned in his face.
4. Association with vile companions.

Be more myself.

KING   For all the world
As thou art to this hour was Richard then
95   When I from France set foot at Ravenspurgh,
And even as I was then is Percy now.
Now, by my scepter and my soul to boot,
He hath more worthy interest to the state
Than thou the shadow of successiòn;[5]
100 For of no right, nor color[6] like to right,
He doth fill fields with harness° in the realm,   *armor*
Turns head against the lion's armèd jaws,[7]
And, being no more in debt to years than thou,
Leads ancient lords and reverend bishops on
105 To bloody battles and to bruising arms.
What never-dying honor hath he got
Against renownèd Douglas! whose high deeds,
Whose hot incursions° and great name in arms   *raids*
Holds from all soldiers chief majority°   *superiority*
110 And military title capital[8]
Through all the kingdoms that acknowledge Christ.
Thrice hath this Hotspur, Mars in swaddling clothes,
This infant warrior, in his enterprises
Discomfited great Douglas, ta'en him once,
115 Enlargèd° him and made a friend of him,   *freed*
To fill the mouth of deep defiance up[9]
And shake the peace and safety of our throne.
And what say you to this? Percy, Northumberland,
The Archbishop's grace of York, Douglas, Mortimer,
120 Capitulate[1] against us and are up.
But wherefore do I tell these news to thee?
Why, Harry, do I tell thee of my foes,
Which art my nearest and dearest enemy?
Thou that art like enough through vassal fear,
125 Base inclinatiòn and the start of spleen,[2]
To fight against me under Percy's pay,
To dog his heels and curtsy at his frowns,
To show how much thou art degenerate.

PRINCE   Do not think so; you shall not find it so;
130 And God forgive them that so much have swayed
Your majesty's good thoughts away from me.
I will redeem all this on Percy's head
And in the closing of some glorious day
Be bold to tell you that I am your son,
135 When I will wear a garment all of blood

---

5. I.e., Hotspur's claim to the throne is more solid, because of his achievements, than is Hal's, which rests only on shadowy rights of succession by birth.
6. False pretense.
7. I.e., takes military action against the king's

army.
8. Has the greatest reputation among soldiers.
9. I.e., to swell the chorus of defiance.
1. Raise a head, revolt.
2. Unreasoning impulse.

And stain my favors° in a bloody mask,   *features*
Which, washed away, shall scour my shame with it;
And that shall be the day, whene'er it lights,
That this same child of honor and renown,
140   This gallant Hotspur, this all-praisèd knight,
And your unthought-of Harry chance to meet.
For every honor sitting on his helm—
Would they were multitudes, and on my head
My shames redoubled!—for the time will come
145   That I shall make this northern youth exchange
His glorious deeds for my indignities.
Percy is but my factor,° good my lord,   *agent*
To engross up° glorious deeds on my behalf,   *collect, aquire*
And I will call him to so strict account,
150   That he shall render every glory up,
Yea, even the slightest worship° of his time,   *honor*
Or I will tear the reckoning from his heart.
This in the name of God I promise here,
The which if He be pleased I shall perform,
155   I do beseech your majesty, may salve
The long-grown wounds of my intemperance;
If not, the end of life cancels all bands,°   *bonds, debts*
And I will die a hundred thousand deaths
Ere break the smallest parcel of this vow.
160   KING   A hundred thousand rebels die in this;
Thou shalt have charge and sovereign trust herein.
      [*Enter* BLUNT.]
How now, good Blunt? thy looks are full of speed.
BLUNT   So hath the business that I come to speak of.
Lord Mortimer of Scotland hath sent word
165   That Douglas and the English rebels met
The eleventh of this month at Shrewsbury;
A mighty and a fearful head° they are,   *power*
If promises be kept on every hand,
As ever offered foul play in a state.
170   KING   The Earl of Westmoreland set forth today,
With him my son, Lord John of Lancaster,
For this advertisement° is five days old.   *news*
On Wednesday next, Harry, you shall set forward;
On Thursday we ourselves will march. Our meeting
175   Is Bridgenorth and, Harry, you shall march
Through Gloucestershire, by which account,°   *method*
Our business valued,³ some twelve days hence
Our general forces at Bridgenorth shall meet.
Our hands are full of business: let's away;
180   Advantage feeds him fat while men delay.⁴   [*Exeunt.*]

---

3. According to estimates.
4. I.e., the rebels' "advantage" (opportunity) grows as the king's men delay.

SCENE 3

[*Enter* FALSTAFF *and* BARDOLPH.]

FALSTAFF   Bardolph, am I not fall'n away vilely[5] since this last action? do I not bate? do I not dwindle? Why, my skin hangs about me like an old lady's loose gown; I am withered like an old applejohn. Well, I'll repent, and that suddenly, while I am in some liking;[6] I shall be out of heart
5   shortly, and then I shall have no strength to repent. An I have not forgotten what the inside of a church is made of, I am a peppercorn, a brewer's horse. The inside of a church! Company, villainous company, hath been the spoil of me.

BARDOLPH   Sir John, you are so fretful you cannot live long.
10   FALSTAFF   Why, there is it; come sing me a bawdy song, make me merry. I was as virtuously given as a gentleman need to be: virtuous enough: swore little; diced not above seven times a week; went to a bawdyhouse not above once in a quarter—of an hour; paid money that I borrowed three or four times; lived well and in good compass; and now I live out
15   of all order, out of all compass.

BARDOLPH   Why, you are so fat, Sir John, that you must needs be out of all compass, out of all reasonable compass, Sir John.

FALSTAFF   Do thou amend thy face, and I'll amend my life; thou art our admiral,[7] thou bearest the lantern in the poop, but 'tis in the nose of
20   thee; thou art the Knight of the Burning Lamp.

BARDOLPH   Why, Sir John, my face does you no harm.

FALSTAFF   No, I'll be sworn; I make as good use of it as many a man doth of a death's-head or a *memento mori.*[8] I never see thy face but I think upon hell-fire and Dives[9] that lived in purple, for there he is in his robes,
25   burning, burning. If thou wert any way given to virtue, I would swear by thy face; my oath should be "By this fire, that's God's angel"; but thou art altogether given over, and wert indeed, but for the light in thy face, the son of utter darkness. When thou ran'st up Gadshill in the night to catch my horse, if I did not think thou hadst been an *ignis fatuus* or a
30   ball of wildfire,[1] there's no purchase in money. O, thou art a perpetual triumph, an everlasting bonfire light![2] Thou hast saved me a thousand marks in links[3] and torches, walking with thee in the night betwixt tavern and tavern, but the sack that thou hast drunk me would have bought me lights as good cheap at the dearest chandler's in Europe. I have main-
35   tained that salamander[4] of yours with fire any time this two and thirty years, God reward me for it.

BARDOLPH   'Sblood, I would my face were in your belly!

FALSTAFF   God-a-mercy! so should I be sure to be heartburnt.

[*Enter* HOSTESS.]

---

5. Lose weight. "Last action": i.e., the Gadshill robbery.
6. In good condition, in the mood. "Applejohn": an apple with a wrinkled skin.
7. Flagship.
8. I.e., a skull or some other reminder of death.
9. The rich man who would not give food to Lazarus and was punished in hell for it (Luke 16.19–

31).
1. A firework used for military purposes. "*Ignis fatuus*": will-o'-the-wisp.
2. Illumination at a public festival.
3. Small torches carried at night.
4. Lizards that supposedly lived in fire and ate it. "Chandler's": candlemaker's.

How now, Dame Partlet[5] the hen! have you inquired yet who picked my
40   pocket?

HOSTESS   Why, Sir John, what do you think, Sir John? do you think I keep
thieves in my house? I have searched, I have inquired, so has my husband, man by man, boy by boy, servant by servant; the tithe[6] of a hair
was never lost in my house before.

45 FALSTAFF   Ye lie, hostess; Bardolph was shaved and lost many a hair, and
I'll be sworn my pocket was picked. Go to, you are a woman, go.

HOSTESS   Who, I? no, I defy thee; God's light, I was never called so in
mine own house before.

FALSTAFF   Go to, I know you well enough.

50 HOSTESS   No, Sir John; you do not know me, Sir John. I know you, Sir
John; you owe me money, Sir John, and now you pick a quarrel to beguile
me of it; I bought you a dozen of shirts to your back.

FALSTAFF   Dowlas, filthy dowlas; I have given them away to bakers' wives,
and they have made bolters[7] of them.

55 HOSTESS   Now, as I am a true woman, holland of eight shillings an ell.[8]
You owe money here besides, Sir John, for your diet and by-drinkings,[9]
and money lent you, four and twenty pound.

FALSTAFF   He had his part of it; let him pay.

HOSTESS   He? alas, he is poor; he hath nothing.

60 FALSTAFF   How! poor? look upon his face; what call you rich? let them
coin his nose, let them coin his cheeks; I'll not pay a denier. What, will
you make a younker[1] of me? shall I not take mine ease in mine inn but
I shall have my pocket picked? I have lost a seal ring of my grandfather's
worth forty mark.[2]

65 HOSTESS   O Jesu, I have heard the prince tell him I know not how oft that
that ring was copper.

FALSTAFF   How! the prince is a Jack, a sneak-up;[3] 'sblood, an he were here,
I would cudgel him like a dog if he would say so.

       [Enter the PRINCE *⟨and* POINS⟩, *marching, and* FALSTAFF *meets them*
       playing upon his truncheon like a fife.]

How now, lad, is the wind in that door, i' faith? must we all march?

70 BARDOLPH   Yea, two and two, Newgate fashion.[4]

HOSTESS   My lord, I pray you hear me.

PRINCE   What say'st thou, Mistress Quickly? How doth thy husband? I
love him well; he is an honest man.

HOSTESS   Good my lord, hear me.

75 FALSTAFF   Prithee let her alone, and list to me.

PRINCE   What say'st thou, Jack?

FALSTAFF   The other night I fell asleep here behind the arras and had my
pocket picked; this house is turned bawdyhouse, they pick pockets.

PRINCE   What didst thou lose, Jack?

80 FALSTAFF   Wilt thou believe me, Hal? three or four bonds of forty pound
apiece, and a seal ring of my grandfather's.

---

5. A nickname from the hen in Chaucer's *The
Nun's Priest's Tale*; in Shakespeare's time a conventional name for a scolding woman.
6. Tenth part.
7. Sieves for flour. "Dowlas": a coarse cloth.
8. Forty-five inches. "Holland": fine linen.

9. Drinks between meals.
1. Youngster, novice. "Denier": French penny,
worth a tenth of an English penny.
2. A mark was worth two-thirds of a pound.
3. A sneak. "Jack": rascal.
4. Chained together, like prisoners at Newgate.

PRINCE A trifle, some eightpenny matter.

HOSTESS So I told him, my lord, and I said I heard your grace say so; and,
my lord, he speaks most vilely of you, like a foul-mouthed man as he is,
and said he would cudgel you.

PRINCE What, he did not?

HOSTESS There's neither faith, truth, nor womanhood in me else.

FALSTAFF There's no more faith in thee than in a stewed prune, nor no
more truth in thee than in a drawn[5] fox, and for womanhood Maid Marian may be the deputy's wife of the ward[6] to thee. Go, you thing, go.

HOSTESS Say, what thing, what thing?

FALSTAFF What thing! why, a thing to thank God on.

HOSTESS I am no thing to thank God on, I would thou shouldst know it;
I am an honest man's wife, and, setting thy knighthood aside,[7] thou art
a knave to call me so.

FALSTAFF Setting thy womanhood aside, thou art a beast to say otherwise.

HOSTESS Say, what beast, thou knave, thou?

FALSTAFF What beast? why, an otter.

PRINCE An otter, Sir John, why an otter?

FALSTAFF Why, she's neither fish nor flesh, a man knows not where to
have her.[8]

HOSTESS Thou art an unjust man in saying so; thou or any man knows
where to have me, thou knave, thou!

PRINCE Thou sayest true, hostess, and he slanders thee most grossly.

HOSTESS So he doth you, my lord, and said this other day you ought[9] him
a thousand pound.

PRINCE Sirrah, do I owe you a thousand pound?

FALSTAFF A thousand pound, Hal! A million. Thy love is worth a million;
thou owest me thy love.

HOSTESS Nay, my lord, he called you Jack, and said he would
cudgel you.

FALSTAFF Did I, Bardolph?

BARDOLPH Indeed, Sir John, you said so.

FALSTAFF Yea, if he said my ring was copper.

PRINCE I say 'tis copper; darest thou be as good as thy word now?

FALSTAFF Why, Hal, thou knowest, as thou art but man, I dare; but as
thou art prince, I fear thee as I fear the roaring of the lion's whelp.

PRINCE And why not as the lion?

FALSTAFF The king himself is to be feared as the lion; dost thou think I'll
fear thee as I fear thy father? Nay, an I do, I pray God my girdle[1] break.

PRINCE O, if it should, how would thy guts fall about thy knees! But,
sirrah, there's no room for faith, truth, nor honesty in this bosom of thine;
it is all filled up with guts and midriff. Charge an honest woman with
picking thy pocket! Why, thou whoreson, impudent, embossed rascal[2] if

---

5. Hunted. Stewed prunes were commonly served
in bawdyhouses, as a supposed protection against
venereal disease.
6. "Maid Marian" was a female character of low
morals in the popular Robin Hood plays; a "deputy's wife of the ward" would be a respectable
woman.
7. I.e., ignoring, or intending no disrespect to, the

rank of knighthood. Falstaff intentionally misun-
derstands the phrase.
8. I.e., how to understand her. But the Hostess's
retort is, unconsciously, equivalent to saying that
she is completely promiscuous.
9. Owed.
1. Belt.
2. Swollen rascal.

125 there were anything in thy pocket but tavern-reckonings, memorandums
of bawdyhouses, and one poor pennyworth of sugar candy to make thee
long-winded, if thy pocket were enriched with any other injuries[3] but
these, I am a villain. And yet you will stand to it, you will not pocket up
wrong; art thou not ashamed?

130 FALSTAFF   Dost thou hear, Hal? thou knowest in the state of innocency
Adam fell, and what should poor Jack Falstaff do in the days of villainy?
Thou seest I have more flesh than another man, and therefore more
frailty.[4] You confess then, you picked my pocket?

PRINCE   It appears so by the story.

135 FALSTAFF   Hostess, I forgive thee; go make ready breakfast, love thy husband, look to thy servants, cherish thy guests; thou shalt find me tractable to any honest reason; thou seest I am pacified still.[5] Nay, prithee
begone. [*Exit* HOSTESS.] Now, Hal, to the news at court; for the robbery,
lad, how is that answered?

140 PRINCE   O, my sweet beef, I must still be good angel to thee; the money
is paid back again.

FALSTAFF   O, I do not like that paying back; 'tis a double labor.

PRINCE   I am good friends with my father and may do anything.

FALSTAFF   Rob me the exchequer the first thing thou doest, and do it with
145 unwashed hands[6] too.

BARDOLPH   Do, my lord.

PRINCE   I have procured thee, Jack, a charge of foot.

FALSTAFF   I would it had been of horse.[7] Where shall I find one that can
steal well? O for a fine thief, of the age of two and twenty or thereabouts!
150 I am heinously unprovided. Well, God be thanked for these rebels, they
offend none but the virtuous; I laud them, I praise them.

PRINCE   Bardolph!

BARDOLPH   My lord?

PRINCE   Go bear this letter to Lord John of Lancaster, to my brother John;
155 this to my Lord of Westmoreland. [*Exit* BARDOLPH.] Go, Poins, to horse,
to horse; for thou and I have thirty miles to ride yet ere dinnertime. [*Exit*
POINS.] Jack, meet me tomorrow in the Temple Hall at two o'clock in
the afternoon.
There shalt thou know thy charge, and there receive
160 Money and order for their furniture.[8]
The land is burning, Percy stands on high,
And either we or they must lower lie.   [⟨*Exit.*⟩]

FALSTAFF   Rare words, brave world! Hostess, my breakfast, come.
O, I could wish this tavern were my drum![9]   [*Exit.*]

Act 4

SCENE 1

[*Enter* HOTSPUR, WORCESTER, *and* DOUGLAS.]

HOTSPUR   Well said, my noble Scot. If speaking truth
In this fine age were not thought flattery,

---

3. Things, the loss of which you claim as injuries.
4. "The flesh is frail is proverbial" (cf. Matthew 26.41), meaning the flesh is weak.
5. Always easily pacified.
6. I.e., hastily.

7. Cavalry. "A charge of foot": command of a company of foot soldiers.
8. Furnishings, equipment.
9. Headquarters.

Such attribution° should the Douglas have   *praise*
As not a soldier of this season's stamp
5   Should go so general current[1] through the world.
By God, I cannot flatter; I do defy
The tongues of soothers,° but a braver[2] place   *flatterers*
In my heart's love hath no man than yourself;
Nay, task me to my word,[3] approve° me, lord.   *prove, test*
10 DOUGLAS   Thou art the king of honor;
No man so potent breathes upon the ground
But I will beard him.[4]
HOTSPUR   Do so, and 'tis well.
      [*Enter a* MESSENGER *with letters.*]
What letters hast thou there?—I can but thank you.
MESSENGER   These letters come from your father.
15 HOTSPUR   Letters from him! why comes he not himself?
MESSENGER   He cannot come, my lord; he is grievous sick.
HOTSPUR   Zounds! how has he the leisure to be sick
In such a justling° time? Who leads his power?   *turbulent*
Under whose government come they along?
20 MESSENGER   His letters bears his mind, not I, my lord.
WORCESTER   I prithee tell me, doth he keep his bed?
MESSENGER   He did, my lord, four days ere I set forth,
And at the time of my departure thence
He was much feared by his physicíans.
25 WORCESTER   I would the state of time[5] had first been whole
Ere he by sickness had been visited;
His health was never better worth than now.
HOTSPUR   Sick now! droop now! this sickness doth infect
The very lifeblood of our enterprise;
30 'Tis catching hither, even to our camp.
He writes me here that inward sickness—
And that his friends by deputation could not
So soon be drawn,[6] nor did he think it meet
To lay so dangerous and dear a trust
35 On any soul removed[7] but on his own.
Yet doth he give us bold advertisement
That with our small conjunction[8] we should on
To see how fortune is disposed to us;
For, as he writes, there is no quailing now,
40 Because the king is certainly possessed°   *informed*
Of all our purposes. What say you to it?
WORCESTER   Your father's sickness is a maim to us.
HOTSPUR   A perilous gash, a very limb lopped off;
And yet in faith it is not; his present want[9]
45 Seems more than we shall find it. Were it good
To set the exact wealth of all our states

---

1. I.e., that not a soldier of this age's coinage should achieve such currency.
2. More distinguished.
3. Compare my actions with my speech.
4. I.e., I will take on anybody, however powerful.

5. Public affairs. "Feared by": feared for by.
6. Could not quickly be organized under a deputy.
7. Other person.
8. Unified forces.
9. Our present awareness of his absence.

All at one cast, to set so rich a main
On the nice hazard[1] of one doubtful hour?
It were not good, for therein should we read
50   The very bottom and the soul of hope,[2]
The very list,° the very utmost bound   limit
Of all our fortunes.
DOUGLAS   Faith, and so we should,
Where now remains a sweet reversiòn.[3]
We may boldly spend upon the hope of what
55   Is to come in;
A comfort of retirement[4] lives in this.
HOTSPUR   A rendezvous, a home to fly unto,
If that the devil and mischance look big
Upon the maidenhead of our affairs.[5]
60   WORCESTER   But yet I would your father had been here.
The quality and hair° of our attempt   character
Brooks° no division; it will be thought   allows
By some that know not why he is away
That wisdom, loyalty, and mere dislike
65   Of our proceedings kept the earl from hence.
And think how such an apprehensiòn
May turn the tide of fearful factiòn°   conspiracy
And breed a kind of question in our cause,
For well you know we of the off'ring° side   challenging
70   Must keep aloof from strict arbitrement,°   investigation
And stop all sight-holes, every loop° from whence   loophole
The eye of reason may pry in upon us.
This absence of your father's draws a curtain,
That shows the ignorant a kind of fear
Before not dreamt of.
75   HOTSPUR   You strain too far.
I rather of his absence make this use:
It lends a luster and more great opinion,
A larger dare to our great enterprise,
Than if the earl were here, for men must think,
80   If we without his help can make a head
To push against a kingdom, with his help
We shall o'erturn it topsy-turvy down.
Yet all goes well, yet all our joints are whole.
DOUGLAS   As heart can think; there is not such a word
85   Spoke of in Scotland as this term of fear.
[Enter SIR RICHARD VERNON.]
HOTSPUR   My cousin Vernon, welcome, by my soul!
VERNON   Pray God my news be worth a welcome, lord.
The Earl of Westmoreland, seven thousand strong,
Is marching hitherwards; with him Prince John.
HOTSPUR   No harm; what more?

1. Risky chance. "Main": stake, in betting.   4. Sustaining place to fall back on.
2. Foundation and essence of our expectations.   5. I.e., threaten the beginning of our affairs.
3. A fund to be inherited in the future.

90 VERNON   And further I have learned
    The king himself in person is set forth,
    Or hitherwards intended speedily,
    With strong and mighty preparatiòn.
HOTSPUR   He shall be welcome too. Where is his son,
95   The nimble-footed madcap Prince of Wales,
    And his comrades that daft° the world aside   *push*
    And bid it pass?
VERNON   All furnished, all in arms,
    All plumed like estridges° that with the wind   *ostriches*
    Bated, like eagles having lately bathed,[6]
100   Glittering in golden coats like images,
    As full of spirit as the month of May,
    And gorgeous as the sun at midsummer,
    Wanton as youthful goats, wild as young bulls.
    I saw young Harry, with his beaver° on,   *helmet*
105   His cushes[7] on his thighs, gallantly armed,
    Rise from the ground like feathered Mercury,
    And vaulted with such ease into his seat,
    As if an angel dropped down from the clouds,
    To turn and wind° a fiery Pegasus[8]   *direct*
110   And witch the world with noble horsemanship.
HOTSPUR   No more, no more. Worse than the sun in March
    This praise doth nourish agues.[9] Let them come;
    They come like sacrifices in their trim,
    And to the fire-eyed maid of smoky war[1]
115   All hot and bleeding will we offer them;
    The mailèd Mars shall on his altar sit
    Up to the ears in blood. I am on fire
    To hear this rich reprisal° is so nigh   *prize*
    And yet not ours. Come, let me taste my horse,
120   Who is to bear me like a thunderbolt
    Against the bosom of the Prince of Wales;
    Harry to Harry shall, hot horse to horse,
    Meet and ne'er part till one drop down a corse.
    O that Glendower were come!
VERNON   There is more news;
125   I learned in Worcester, as I rode along,
    He cannot draw his power[2] this fourteen days.
DOUGLAS   That's the worst tidings that I hear of yet.
WORCESTER   Aye, by my faith, that bears a frosty sound.
HOTSPUR   What may the king's whole battle° reach unto?   *army*
VERNON   To thirty thousand.
130 HOTSPUR   Forty let it be;
    My father and Glendower being both away,

---

6. Eagles were supposed to renew their youth by bathing in the ocean. "Bated": fluttering their wings.
7. Cuisses, armor for the thighs.
8. A winged horse.

9. Fevers. Malaria was thought to be caused by vapors from the marshes, drawn up by the sun in spring.
1. Bellona, goddess of war.
2. Assemble his forces.

The powers of us may serve so great a day.
Come, let us take a muster speedily;
Doomsday is near; die all, die merrily.
135 DOUGLAS Talk not of dying; I am out of fear
Of death or death's hand for this one-half year.   [*Exeunt.*]

SCENE 2

[*Enter* FALSTAFF *and* BARDOLPH.]

FALSTAFF Bardolph, get thee before to Coventry; fill me a bottle of sack,
our soldiers shall march through. We'll to Sutton Co'fil'³ tonight.
BARDOLPH Will you give me money, captain?
FALSTAFF Lay out, lay out.
5   BARDOLPH This bottle makes an angel.⁴
FALSTAFF An if it do, take it for thy labor; and if it make twenty, take them
all; I'll answer the coinage. Bid my lieutenant Peto meet me at town's
end.
BARDOLPH I will, captain; farewell.   [*Exit.*]
10 FALSTAFF If I be not ashamed of my soldiers, I am a soused gurnet. I have
misused the king's press⁵ damnably. I have got in exchange of a hundred
and fifty soldiers three hundred and odd pounds. I press me none but
good householders, yeomen's sons, inquire me out contracted bachelors,
such as had been asked twice on the banns,⁶ such a commodity of warm
15 slaves as had as lieve hear the devil as a drum, such as fear the report of
a caliver⁷ worse than a struck fowl or a hurt wild duck. I pressed me
none but such toasts-and-butter⁸ with hearts in their bellies no bigger
than pins' heads, and they have bought out their services, and now my
whole charge consists of ancients,⁹ corporals, lieutenants, gentlemen of
20 companies, slaves as ragged as Lazarus in the painted cloth where the
glutton's dogs licked his sores, and such as indeed were never soldiers,
but discarded unjust serving-men, younger sons to younger brothers,
revolted tapsters and ostlers trade-fall'n,¹ the cankers² of a calm world
and a long peace, ten times more dishonorable ragged than an old-fac'd
25 ancient,³ and such have I to fill up the rooms of them that have bought
out their services, that you would think that I had a hundred and fifty
tattered prodigals lately come from swine-keeping, from eating draff⁴ and
husks. A mad fellow met me on the way and told me I had unloaded all
the gibbets and pressed the dead bodies. No eye hath seen such scare-
30 crows. I'll not march through Coventry with them, that's flat; nay, and
the villains march wide betwixt the legs, as if they had gyves⁵ on, for
indeed I had the most of them out of prison. There's but a shirt and a
half in all my company, and the half shirt is two napkins tacked together

---

3. Sutton Coldfield, about twenty-five miles from
Coventry.
4. Ten shillings' worth.
5. The draft or impressment of soldiers into service. "Soused gurnet": pickled anchovy.
6. Notice of approaching marriage, announced
three times publicly in church before the marriage
could take place.
7. Musket. "Commodity": collection. "Warm":

well-to-do.
8. Sissies.
9. Ensigns.
1. Hostlers out of work.
2. Canker worms.
3. Frayed flag.
4. Garbage. The prodigal son, in the Bible, fed on
husks before returning to the paternal board.
5. Leg-irons.

35 and thrown over the shoulders like a herald's coat without sleeves, and the shirt, to say the truth, stolen from my host at Saint Alban's, or the red-nose innkeeper of Daventry. But that's all one; they'll find linen enough on every hedge.[6]

[*Enter the* PRINCE *and the* LORD OF WESTMORELAND.]

PRINCE How now, blown Jack! how now, quilt![7]

FALSTAFF What, Hal, how now, mad wag! what a devil dost thou in War-
40 wickshire? My good Lord of Westmoreland, I cry you mercy; I thought your honor had already been at Shrewsbury.

WESTMORELAND Faith, Sir John, 'tis more than time that I were there, and you too; but my powers are there already. The king, I can tell you, looks for us all; we must away all night.

45 FALSTAFF Tut, never fear me; I am as vigilant as a cat to steal cream.

PRINCE I think, to steal cream indeed, for thy theft hath already made thee butter. But tell me, Jack, whose fellows are these that come after?

FALSTAFF Mine, Hal, mine.

PRINCE I did never see such pitiful rascals.

50 FALSTAFF Tut, tut, good enough to toss,[8] food for powder, food for powder; they'll fill a pit as well as better; tush, man, mortal men, mortal men.

WESTMORELAND Aye, but, Sir John, methinks they are exceeding poor and bare, too beggarly.

FALSTAFF Faith, for their poverty I know not where they had that, and for
55 their bareness I am sure they never learned that of me.

PRINCE No, I'll be sworn, unless you call three fingers[9] on the ribs bare. But, sirrah, make haste; Percy is already in the field.

FALSTAFF What, is the king encamped?

WESTMORELAND He is, Sir John; I fear we shall stay too long.

60 FALSTAFF Well,
To the latter end of a fray and the beginning of a feast
Fits a dull fighter and a keen guest.   [*Exeunt.*]

SCENE 3

[*Enter* HOTSPUR, WORCESTER, DOUGLAS, *and* VERNON.]

HOTSPUR We'll fight with him tonight.

WORCESTER   It may not be.

DOUGLAS You give him then advantage.

VERNON   Not a whit.

HOTSPUR Why say you so? looks he not for supply?

VERNON So do we.

HOTSPUR   His is certain, ours is doubtful.

5 WORCESTER Good cousin, be advised; stir not tonight.

VERNON Do not, my lord.

DOUGLAS   You do not counsel well;
You speak it out of fear and cold heart.

VERNON Do me no slander, Douglas; by my life,

---

6. Laundry was customarily hung on hedges to dry.
7. Padded material, a substitute for armor.

8. I.e., on a pike, or long spear.
9. Layers of fat. A finger was three-quarters of an inch.

And I dare well maintain it with my life,
10 If well-respected honor[1] bid me on,
I hold as little counsel with weak fear
As you, my lord, or any Scot that this day lives.
Let it be seen tomorrow in the battle
Which of us fears.
DOUGLAS   Yea, or tonight.
VERNON   Content.
15 HOTSPUR   Tonight, say I.
VERNON   Come, come, it may not be. I wonder much,
Being men of such great leading as you are,
That you foresee not what impediments
Drag back our expedition;[2] certain horse
20 Of my cousin Vernon's are not yet come up,
Your uncle Worcester's horse came but today,
And now their pride and mettle is asleep,
Their courage with hard labor tame and dull,
That not a horse is half the half of himself.
25 HOTSPUR   So are the horses of the enemy
In general, journey-bated[3] and brought low;
The better part of ours are full of rest.
WORCESTER   The number of the king exceedeth ours;
For God's sake, cousin, stay till all come in.
[*The trumpet sounds a parley. Enter* SIR WALTER BLUNT.]
30 BLUNT   I come with gracious offers from the king,
If you vouchsafe me hearing and respect.
HOTSPUR   Welcome, Sir Walter Blunt; and would to God
You were of our determinàtion!
Some of us love you well, and even those some
35 Envy your great deservings and good name
Because you are not of our quality,[4]
But stand against us like an enemy.
BLUNT   And God defend° but still° I should stand so,   *forbid/always*
So long as out of limit and true rule
40 You stand against anointed majesty.
But to my charge. The king hath sent to know
The nature of your griefs, and whereupon
You conjure from the breast of civil peace
Such bold hostility, teaching his duteous land
45 Audacious cruelty. If that the king
Have any way your good deserts forgot,
Which he confesseth to be manifold,
He bids you name your griefs, and with all speed
You shall have your desires with interest
50 And pardon absolute for yourself and these
Herein misled by your suggestiòn.°   *temptation*
HOTSPUR   The king is kind, and well we know the king

---

1. Well-considered (not rash, like Hotspur's).   3. Tired from travel.
2. Retard our speed.   4. Fellowship, party.

Knows at what time to promise, when to pay.
My father and my uncle and myself
55 Did give him that same royalty he wears;
And when he was not six and twenty strong,
Sick in the world's regard, wretched and low,
A poor unminded outlaw sneaking home,
My father gave him welcome to the shore;
60 And when he heard him swear and vow to God
He came but to be Duke of Lancaster,
To sue his livery⁵ and beg his peace,
With tears of innocency and terms of zeal,
My father, in kind heart and pity moved,
65 Swore him assistance and performed it too.
Now when the lords and barons of the realm
Perceived Northumberland did lean to him,
The more and less came in with cap and knee,⁶
Met him in boroughs, cities, villages,
70 Attended him on bridges, stood in lanes,
Laid gifts before him, proffered him their oaths,
Gave him their heirs as pages, followed him
Even at the heels in golden multitudes.
He presently, as greatness knows itself,
75 Steps me a little higher than his vow,
Made to my father while his blood was poor
Upon the naked shore at Ravenspurgh,
And now, forsooth, takes on him to reform
Some certain edicts and some strait° decrees   *strict*
80 That lie too heavy on the commonwealth,
Cries out upon abuses, seems to weep
Over his country's wrongs, and by this face,°   *pretense*
This seeming brow of justice, did he win
The hearts of all that he did angle for;
85 Proceeded further, cut me off the heads
Of all the favorites that the absent king
In deputation left behind him here,
When he was personal⁷ in the Irish war.
BLUNT   Tut, I came not to hear this.
HOTSPUR   Then to the point.
90 In short time after he deposed the king,
Soon after that deprived him of his life,
And in the neck of that tasked⁸ the whole state;
To make that worse, suffered his kinsman March
(Who is, if every owner were well placed,
95 Indeed his king) to be engaged⁹ in Wales,
There without ransom to lie forfeited;
Disgraced¹ me in my happy victories,

---

5. I.e., claim title to his late father's lands (held by
King Richard II).
6. Cap in hand and on bended knee; i.e., offering
homage.
7. Actively participating in person.
8. I.e., immediately after that, (he) taxed.
9. Pawned as a hostage.
1. I.e., did not favor.

Sought to entrap me by intelligence,°   *spying*
Rated² mine uncle from the council board,
In rage dismissed my father from the court,
Broke oath on oath, committed wrong on wrong,
And in conclusion drove us to seek out
This head of safety,³ and withal to pry
Into his title, the which we find
Too indirect for long continuance.
BLUNT   Shall I return this answer to the king?
HOTSPUR   Not so, Sir Walter; we'll withdraw awhile.
Go to the king, and let there be impawned°   *pledged*
Some surety° for a safe return again,   *guarantee*
And in the morning early shall mine uncle
Bring him our purposes; and so farewell.
BLUNT   I would you would accept of grace and love.
HOTSPUR   And may be so we shall.
BLUNT   Pray God you do.   [*Exeunt.*]

SCENE 4

[*Enter the* ARCHBISHOP OF YORK *and* SIR MICHAEL.]
ARCHBISHOP   Hie, good Sir Michael; bear this sealèd brief°   *letter*
With wingèd haste to the lord marshal,
This to my cousin Scroop, and all the rest
To whom they are directed. If you knew
How much they do import you would make haste.
SIR MICHAEL   My good lord,
I guess their tenor.
ARCHBISHOP   Like enough you do.
Tomorrow, good Sir Michael, is a day
Wherein the fortune of ten thousand men
Must bide the touch;⁴ for, sir, at Shrewsbury,
As I am truly given to understand,
The king with mighty and quick-raisèd power
Meets with Lord Harry; and I fear, Sir Michael,
What with the sickness of Northumberland,
Whose power was in the first proportiòn,⁵
And what with Owen Glendower's absence thence,
Who with them was a rated⁶ sinew too
And comes not in, o'er-ruled by prophecies—
I fear the power of Percy is too weak
To wage an instant trial with the king.
SIR MICHAEL   Why, my good lord, you need not fear;
There is Douglas and Lord Mortimer.
ARCHBISHOP   No, Mortimer is not there.
SIR MICHAEL   But there is Mordake, Vernon, Lord Harry Percy,
And there is my Lord of Worcester and a head

2. Angrily dismissed.
3. Army for our safety.
4. Stand the test.

5. The largest part.
6. Highly regarded.

Of gallant warriors, noble gentlemen.
ARCHBISHOP   And so there is; but yet the king hath drawn
The special head[7] of all the land together:
The Prince of Wales, Lord John of Lancaster,
30 The noble Westmoreland, and warlike Blunt,
And many more corrivals° and dear° men   *associates/noble*
O estimation and command in arms.
SIR MICHAEL   Doubt not, my lord, they shall be well opposed.
ARCHBISHOP   I hope no less, yet needful 'tis to fear,
35 And to prevent° the worst, Sir Michael, speed;   *forestall*
For if Lord Percy thrive not, ere the king
Dismiss his power, he means to visit° us,   *attack*
For he hath heard of our confederacy,
And 'tis but wisdom to make strong against him;
40 Therefore make haste. I must go write again
To other friends; and so farewell, Sir Michael.   [*Exeunt.*]

Act 5

SCENE 1

[*Enter the* KING, PRINCE OF WALES, PRINCE JOHN OF LANCASTER, SIR
WALTER BLUNT, *and* FALSTAFF.]
KING   How bloodily the sun begins to peer
Above yon busky° hill! The day looks pale   *wooded*
At his distemp'rature.[8]
PRINCE   The southern wind
Doth play the trumpet to his purposes,[9]
5 And by his hollow whistling in the leaves
Foretells a tempest and a blustering day.
KING   Then with the losers let it sympathize,
For nothing can seem foul to those that win.
[*The trumpet sounds. Enter* WORCESTER ⟨*and* VERNON⟩.]
How now, my lord of Worcester! 'Tis not well
10 That you and I should meet upon such terms
As now we meet. You have deceived our trust
And made us doff our easy robes of peace,
To crush° our old limbs in ungentle steel;   *enfold, cramp*
This is not well, my lord, this is not well.
15 What say you to it? will you again unknit
This churlish knot of all-abhorrèd war
And move in that obedient orb[1] again
Where you did give a fair and natural light,
And be no more an exhaled meteor,[2]
20 A prodigy of fear and a portent
Of broachèd mischief to the unborn times?[3]

---

7. Principal army.
8. I.e., the sun's illness or malevolence.
9. I.e., the sun's intentions; the southern wind
supports them.
1. Regular orbit, as of a planet.
2. Meteors were thought to be made of gas

exhaled by a planet and were commonly associated
with civil commotion.
3. I.e., of harm or disaster opened up ("broached")
to plague the future. "Mischief" conveyed a tron-
ger meaning to Shakespeare than it does to us.

WORCESTER   Hear me, my liege:
　　For mine own part I could be well content
　　To entertain the lag end of my life
25　With quiet hours, for I do protest
　　I have not sought the day of this dislike.
KING   You have not sought it! how comes it then?
FALSTAFF   Rebellion lay in his way, and he found it.
PRINCE   Peace, chewet,[4] peace!
30　WORCESTER   It pleased your majesty to turn your looks
　　Of favor from myself and all our house,
　　And yet I must remember° you, my lord,　　　　　　　　*remind*
　　We were the first and dearest of your friends.
　　For you my staff of office did I break
35　In Richard's time, and posted day and night
　　To meet you on the way and kiss your hand
　　When yet you were in place and in account
　　Nothing so strong and fortunate as I.
　　It was myself, my brother, and his son
40　That brought you home and boldly did outdare
　　The dangers of the time. You swore to us,
　　And you did swear that oath at Doncaster,
　　That you did nothing purpose 'gainst the state
　　Nor claim no further than your new-fall'n[5] right,
45　The seat of Gaunt, dukedom of Lancaster.
　　To this we swore our aid. But in short space
　　It rained down fortune showering on your head
　　And such a flood of greatness fell on you,
　　What with our help, what with the absent king,
50　What with the injuries of a wanton time,
　　The seeming sufferances° that you had borne,　　　　　*sufferings*
　　And the contrarious winds that held the king
　　So long in his unlucky Irish wars
　　That all in England did repute him dead;
55　And from this swarm of fair advantages
　　You took occasion to be quickly wooed
　　To gripe the general sway[6] into your hand,
　　Forgot your oath to us at Doncaster,
　　And being fed by us you used us so
60　As that ungentle gull[7] the cuckoo's bird
　　Useth the sparrow, did oppress our nest,
　　Grew by our feeding to so great a bulk
　　That even our love durst not come near your sight
　　For fear of swallowing;[8] but with nimble wing
65　We were enforced for safety sake to fly
　　Out of your sight and raise this present head,
　　Whereby we stand opposèd by such means

---

4. Chattering bird.
5. Recently inherited.
6. Seize power over the whole state.

7. Rude nestling; the cuckoo hatches its young in
other birds' nests.
8. Being swallowed.

As you yourself have forged against yourself
By unkind usage, dangerous countenance,[9]
70 And violation of all faith and troth
Sworn to us in your younger enterprise.
KING These things indeed you have articulate,[1]
Proclaimed at market crosses, read in churches,
To face° the garment of rebellìon   decorate
75 With some fine color that may please the eye
Of fickle changelings and poor discontents,
Which gape and rub the elbow at the news
Of hurlyburly innovatìon;
And never yet did insurrection want
80 Such water colors to impaint his cause,
Nor moody beggars starving for a time
Of pellmell havoc and confusìon.
PRINCE In both our armies there is many a soul
Shall pay full dearly for this encounter,
85 If once they join in trial. Tell your nephew
The Prince of Wales doth join with all the world
In praise of Henry Percy; by my hopes,
This present enterprise set off his head,[2]
I do not think a braver gentleman,
90 More active-valiant or more valiant-young,
More daring or more bold, is now alive
To grace this latter age with noble deeds.
For my part, I may speak it to my shame,
I have a truant been to chivalry—
95 And so I hear he doth account me too—
Yet this before my father's majesty:
I am content that he shall take the odds
Of his great name and estimatìon,
And will, to save the blood on either side,
100 Try fortune with him in a single fight.
KING And, Prince of Wales, so dare we venture thee,
Albeit considerations infinite
Do make° against it. No, good Worcester, no,   weigh
We love our people well; even those we love
105 That are misled upon your cousin's part;
And, will they take the offer of our grace,
Both he and they and you, yea, every man
Shall be my friend again and I'll be his.
So tell your cousin, and bring me word
110 What he will do; but if he will not yield,
Rebuke and dread correction wait on° us   accompany
And they shall do their office. So, be gone;
We will not now be troubled with reply.

9. Threatening looks.   2. Deducted from his account.
1. Drawn up in detail.

We offer fair; take it advisedly.
[*Exit* WORCESTER ⟨*and* VERNON.⟩]

115   PRINCE   It will not be accepted, on my life;
The Douglas and the Hotspur both together
Are confident against the world in arms.

KING   Hence, therefore, every leader to his charge,
For on their answer will we set on them,

120   And God befriend us, as our cause is just!
[*Exeunt all but the* PRINCE *and* FALSTAFF.]

FALSTAFF   Hal, if thou see me down in the battle and bestride me, so; 'tis a point of friendship.

PRINCE   Nothing but a colossus can do thee that friendship. Say thy prayers, and farewell.

125   FALSTAFF   I would 'twere bedtime, Hal, and all well.

PRINCE   Why, thou owest God a death.   [⟨*Exit.*⟩]

FALSTAFF   'Tis not due yet; I would be loath to pay him before his day. What need I be so forward with him that calls not on me? Well, 'tis no matter; honor pricks me on. Yea, but how if honor prick me off when I

130   come on? How then? can honor set to a leg? No. Or an arm? No. Or take away the grief³ of a wound? No. Honor hath no skill in surgery, then? No. What is honor? A word. What is in that word honor? what is that honor? Air. A trim reckoning!⁴ Who hath it? He that died o'Wednesday. Doth he feel it? No. Doth he hear it? No. 'Tis insensible,⁵ then? Yea,

135   to the dead. But will it not live with the living? No. Why? Detraction will not suffer it. Therefore I'll none of it; Honor is a mere scutcheon.⁶ And so ends my catechism.   [*Exit.*]

SCENE 2

[*Enter* WORCESTER *and* SIR RICHARD VERNON.]

WORCESTER   O no, my nephew must not know, Sir Richard,
The liberal and kind offer of the king.

VERNON   'Twere best he did.

WORCESTER   Then are we all undone.
It is not possible, it cannot be,

5   The king should keep his word in loving us;
He will suspect us still and find a time
To punish this offense in other faults.
Suspicion all our lives shall be stuck full of eyes,
For treason is but trusted like the fox

10   Who, ne'er so tame, so cherished and locked up,
Will have a wild trick of his ancestors;
Look how we can, or sad or merrily,
Interpretation will misquote° our looks,   *misinterpret*
And we shall feed like oxen at a stall,

15   The better cherished, still the nearer death.
My nephew's trespass may be well forgot;

---

3. Pain.
4. A fine totaling of the bill.

5. Not capable of being felt.
6. A coat of arms, often put on a tombstone.

It hath the excuse of youth and heat of blood
And an adopted name of privilege,[7]
A harebrained Hotspur, governed by a spleen.[8]
20 All his offenses live upon my head
And on his father's; we did train° him on,   *entice*
And, his corruption being ta'en from us,[9]
We, as the spring of all, shall pay for all.
Therefore, good cousin, let not Harry know
25 In any case the offer of the king.
VERNON   Deliver what you will; I'll say 'tis so.
Here comes your cousin.
      [*Enter* HOTSPUR ⟨*and* DOUGLAS⟩.]
HOTSPUR   My uncle is returned;
Deliver up my Lord of Westmoreland.
30 Uncle, what news?
WORCESTER   The king will bid you battle presently.°   *immediately*
DOUGLAS   Defy him by the Lord of Westmoreland.
HOTSPUR   Lord Douglas, go you and tell him so.
DOUGLAS   Marry, and shall, and very willingly.   [*Exit.*]
35 WORCESTER   There is no seeming mercy in the king.
HOTSPUR   Did you beg any? God forbid!
WORCESTER   I told him gently of our grievances,
Of his oath-breaking, which he mended thus,
By now forswearing[1] that he is forsworn;
40 He calls us rebels, traitors, and will scourge
With haughty arms this hateful name in us.
      [*Enter* DOUGLAS.]
DOUGLAS   Arm, gentlemen, to arms! for I have thrown
A brave defiance in King Henry's teeth,
And Westmoreland, that was engaged,[2] did hear it,
45 Which cannot choose but bring him quickly on.
WORCESTER   The Prince of Wales stepped forth before the king,
And, nephew, challenged you to single fight.
HOTSPUR   O, would the quarrel lay upon our heads,
And that no man might draw short breath today
50 But I and Harry Monmouth! Tell me, tell me,
How showed his tasking?° seemed it in contempt?   *challenge*
VERNON   No, by my soul; I never in my life
Did hear a challenge urged more modestly,
Unless a brother should a brother dare
55 To gentle exercise and proof of arms.
He gave you all the duties[3] of a man,
Trimmed up your praises with a princely tongue,
Spoke your deservings like a chronicle,
Making you ever better than his praise
60 By still dispraising praise valued° with you;   *compared*

7. A nickname that gives him privileges.
8. Impetuous temperament.
9. Being attributed to.

1. Swearing falsely.
2. Held as a hostage.
3. Good qualities.

And, which became him like a prince indeed,
He made a blushing cital[4] of himself,
And chid his truant youth with such a grace
As if he mastered there a double spirit
65   Of teaching and of learning instantly.
There did he pause; but let me tell the world,
If he outlive the envy° of this day,   *malice*
England did never owe° so sweet a hope,   *own*
So much miscònstrued in his wantonness.°   *frivolity*
70   HOTSPUR   Cousin, I think thou art enamoured
On his follies; never did I hear
Of any prince so wild a liberty.[5]
But be he as he will, yet once ere night
I will embrace him with a soldier's arm,
75   That he shall shrink under my courtesy.
Arm, arm with speed; and, fellows, soldiers, friends,
Better consider what you have to do
Than I, that have not well the gift of tongue,
Can lift your blood up with persuasiòn.
     [*Enter a* MESSENGER.]
80   MESSENGER   My lord, here are letters for you.
HOTSPUR   I cannot read them now.
O gentlemen, the time of life is short!
To spend that shortness basely were too long,
If life did ride upon a dial's point,
85   Still° ending at the arrival of an hour;[6]   *always*
And if we live, we live to tread on kings,
If die, brave death when princes die with us!
Now, for our consciences, the arms are fair,
When the intent of bearing them is just.
     [*Enter another* MESSENGER.]
90   MESSENGER   My lord, prepare; the king comes on apace.
HOTSPUR   I thank him that he cuts me from my tale,
For I profess not talking; only this—
Let each man do his best; and here draw I
A sword whose temper I intend to stain
95   With the best blood that I can meet withal
In the adventure of this perilous day.
Now, *Esperance! Percy!*[7] and set on.
Sound all the lofty instruments of war,
And by that music let us all embrace;
100   For, heaven to earth,[8] some of us never shall
A second time do such a courtesy.
     [*The trumpets sound. They embrace and exeunt.*]

---

4. Mention, recital.
5. Reckless dissipation.
6. Hotspur's meaning is that a base life would be too long even if it lasted only one hour. "Dial's

point": hands of a clock.
7. Hope, Percy! (the family motto).
8. I.e., the odds are heaven to earth that.

SCENE 3

[*The* KING *enters with his power. Alarum*[9] *to the battle.*
Then enter DOUGLAS *and* SIR WALTER BLUNT.]

BLUNT   What is thy name, that in the battle thus
  Thou crossest me? what honor dost thou seek
  Upon my head?
DOUGLAS   Know then, my name is Douglas,
  And I do haunt thee in the battle thus
5   Because some tell me that thou art a king.[1]
BLUNT   They tell thee true.
DOUGLAS   The Lord of Stafford dear° today hath bought   expensively
  Thy likeness, for instead of thee, King Harry,
  This sword hath ended him; so shall it thee,
10   Unless thou yield thee as my prisoner.
BLUNT   I was not born a yielder, thou proud Scot,
  And thou shalt find a king that will revenge
  Lord Stafford's death.   [*They fight.* DOUGLAS *kills* BLUNT.]
          [*Enter* HOTSPUR.]
HOTSPUR   O Douglas, hadst thou fought at Holmedon thus,
15   I never had triumphed upon a Scot.
DOUGLAS   All's done, all's won; here breathless lies the king.
HOTSPUR   Where?
DOUGLAS   Here.
HOTSPUR   This, Douglas? No, I know this face full well;
20   A gallant knight he was, his name was Blunt;
  Semblably furnished like the king himself.
DOUGLAS   Ah fool, go with thy soul whither it goes!
  A borrowed title hast thou bought too dear;
  Why didst thou tell me that thou wert a king?
25 HOTSPUR   The king hath many marching in his coats.
DOUGLAS   Now, by my sword, I will kill all his coats;
  I'll murder all his wardrobe, piece by piece,
  Until I meet the king.
HOTSPUR   Up and away!
  Our soldiers stand full fairly for the day.   [*Exeunt.*]
          [*Alarum. Enter* FALSTAFF *alone.*]
30 FALSTAFF   Though I could 'scape shot-free[2] at London, I fear the shot here;
  here's no scoring but upon the pate. Soft, who are you? Sir Walter Blunt;
  there's honor for you, here's no vanity! I am as hot as molten lead, and
  as heavy too; God keep lead out of me! I need no more weight than mine
  own bowels. I have led my ragamuffins where they are peppered; there's
35   not three of my hundred and fifty left alive, and they are for the town's
  end, to beg during life. But who comes here?
          [*Enter the* PRINCE.]
PRINCE   What, stand'st thou idle here? lend me thy sword;
  Many a nobleman lies stark and stiff

9. Trumpet signal.
1. Blunt and others are dressed to look like the king.

2. Scot-free, without paying the bill at a tavern. "Scoring" continues the pun; it means (1) marking up a charge, (2) cutting with a sword.

Under the hoofs of vaunting enemies,
40   Whose deaths are yet unrevenged; I prithee, lend me thy sword.
FALSTAFF   O Hal, I prithee give me leave to breathe awhile. Turk Gregory[3]
        never did such deeds in arms as I have done this day. I have paid Percy,
        I have made him sure.
PRINCE   He is indeed, and living to kill thee. I prithee, lend me thy sword.
45   FALSTAFF   Nay, before God, Hal, if Percy be alive, thou get'st not my
        sword; but take my pistol if thou wilt.
PRINCE   Give it me; what, is it in the case?
FALSTAFF   Aye, Hal; 'tis hot, 'tis hot; there's that will sack a city.
        [*The* PRINCE *draws it out, and finds it to be a bottle of sack.*]
PRINCE   What, is it a time to jest and dally now?
        [*He throws the bottle at him. Exit.*]
50   FALSTAFF   Well, if Percy be alive, I'll pierce him. If he do come in my way,
        so; if he do not, if I come in his willingly, let him make a carbonado[4] of
        me. I like not such grinning honor as Sir Walter hath; give me life, which
        if I can save, so; if not, honor comes unlooked for, and there's an end.
                                                              [*Exit.*]

SCENE 4

[*Alarum. Excursions.*[5] *Enter the* KING, *the* PRINCE, PRINCE JOHN OF
LANCASTER, *and* EARL OF WESTMORELAND.]
KING   I prithee,
        Harry, withdraw thyself; thou bleed'st too much.
        Lord John of Lancaster, go you with him.
LANCASTER   Not I, my lord, unless I did bleed too.
5   PRINCE   I beseech your majesty, make up,°   advance
        Lest your retirement do amaze° your friends.   dismay
KING   I will do so.
        My Lord of Westmoreland, lead him to his tent.
WESTMORELAND   Come, my lord, I'll lead you to your tent.
10   PRINCE   Lead me, my lord? I do not need your help,
        And God forbid a shallow scratch should drive
        The Prince of Wales from such a field as this,
        Where stained nobility lies trodden on,
        And rebels' arms triumph in massacres!
15   LANCASTER   We breathe too long; come, cousin Westmoreland,
        Our duty this way lies; for God's sake, come.
        [⟨*Exeunt* PRINCE JOHN *and* WESTMORELAND.⟩]
PRINCE   By God, thou hast deceived me, Lancaster;
        I did not think thee lord of such a spirit.
        Before, I loved thee as a brother, John,
20   But now I do respect thee as my soul.
KING   I saw him hold Lord Percy at the point
        With lustier maintenance than I did look for
        Of such an ungrown warrior.
PRINCE   O, this boy

---

3. Falstaff combines Pope Gregory VII, of whom   4. A cubed steak.
fantastic stories were told, with "Turk" (the Turks   5. Brief appearances and exits of soldiers fighting.
were noted for ferocity).

Lends mettle to us all! [*Exit.*]
    [*Enter* DOUGLAS.]
25 DOUGLAS   Another king! they grow like Hydra's heads.[6]
    I am the Douglas, fatal to all those
    That wear those colors on them; what art thou,
    That counterfeit'st the person of a king?
    KING   The king himself, who, Douglas, grieves at heart
30   So many of his shadows° thou hast met   *likenesses*
    And not the very king. I have two boys
    Seek Percy and thyself about the field,
    But seeing thou fall'st on me so luckily
    I will assay thee; so defend thyself.
35 DOUGLAS   I fear thou art another counterfeit,
    And yet, in faith, thou bearest thee like a king;
    But mine I am sure thou art, whoe'er thou be.
    And thus I win thee.
        [*They fight; the* KING *being in danger, enter* PRINCE OF WALES.]
    PRINCE   Hold up thy head, vile Scot, or thou art like
40   Never to hold it up again! the spirits
    Of valiant Shirley, Stafford, Blunt, are in my arms;
    It is the Prince of Wales that threatens thee,
    Who never promiseth but he means to pay.
        [*They fight;* DOUGLAS *flieth.*]
    Cheerly, my lord; how fares your grace?
45   Sir Nicholas Gawsey hath for succor sent,
    And so hath Clifton; I'll to Clifton straight.
    KING   Stay, and breathe awhile.
    Thou hast redeemed thy lost opiniòn,°   *reputation*
    And showed thou makest some tender of[7] my life
50   His fair rescue thou hast brought to me.
    PRINCE   O God, they did me too much injury
    That ever said I hearkened for your death.
    If it were so, I might have let alone
    The insulting hand of Douglas over you,
55   Which would have been as speedy in your end
    As all the poisonous potions in the world
    And saved the treacherous labor of your son.
    KING   Make up to Clifton; I'll to Sir Nicholas Gawsey.   [*Exit.*]
    [*Enter* HOTSPUR.]
    HOTSPUR   If I mistake not, thou art Harry Monmouth.
60   PRINCE   Thou speak'st as if I would deny my name.
    HOTSPUR   My name is Harry Percy.
    PRINCE   Why then I see
    A very valiant rebel of the name.
    I am the Prince of Wales, and think not, Percy,
    To share with me in glory any more:
65   Two stars keep not their motion in one sphere,°   *orbit*

6. The heads of this fabulous monster grew back   7. I.e., you have some concern for.
as fast as they could be cut off.

Nor can one England brook° a double reign   *endure*
Of Harry Percy and the Prince of Wales.
HOTSPUR Nor shall it, Harry, for the hour is come
To end the one of us; and would to God
70 Thy name in arms were now as great as mine!
PRINCE I'll make it greater ere I part from thee,
And all the budding honors on thy crest
I'll crop to make a garland for my head.
HOTSPUR I can no longer brook thy vanities.   *[They fight.]*
  [Enter FALSTAFF.]
75 FALSTAFF Well said, Hal, to it, Hal! Nay, you shall find no boy's play here,
I can tell you.
  [Enter DOUGLAS; *he fighteth with* FALSTAFF, *who falls down as if he were dead. ⟨Exit* DOUGLAS.⟩ *The* PRINCE *killeth* PERCY.]
HOTSPUR O Harry, thou hast robbed me of my youth!
I better brook the loss of brittle life
Than those proud titles thou hast won of me;
80 They wound my thoughts worse than thy sword my flesh;
But thought's the slave of life, and life time's fool,
And time, that takes survey of all the world,
Must have a stop. O, I could prophesy,
But that the earthy and cold hand of death
85 Lies on my tongue; no, Percy, thou art dust,
And food for—   *[⟨Dies.⟩]*
PRINCE For worms, brave Percy; fare thee well, great heart!
Ill-weaved ambition, how much art thou shrunk!
When that this body did contain a spirit
90 A kingdom for it was too small a bound,
But now two paces of the vilest earth
Is room enough; this earth that bears thee dead
Bears not alive so stout° a gentleman.   *valiant*
If thou wert sensible of courtesy,
95 I should not make so dear° a show of zeal;   *open*
But let my favors hide thy mangled face[8]
And, even in thy behalf, I'll thank myself
For doing these fair rites of tenderness.
Adieu, and take thy praise with thee to heaven;
100 Thy ignominy sleep with thee in the grave,
But not remembered in thy epitaph!
  [He spieth FALSTAFF *on the ground.]*
What, old acquaintance, could not all this flesh
Keep in a little life? Poor Jack, farewell;
I could have better spared a better man.
105 O, I should have a heavy miss of thee,
If I were much in love with vanity!°   *frivolity*
Death hath not struck so fat a deer today,
Though many dearer,° in this bloody fray.   *nobler*
Emboweled° will I see thee by and by;   *embalmed*
110 Till then in blood by noble Percy lie.   *[Exit.]*

8. Prince Hal here covers Hotspur's face with a scarf.

FALSTAFF [*rising up*]   Emboweled! if thou embowel me today, I'll give you
leave to powder[9] me and eat me tomorrow. 'Sblood, 'twas time to counterfeit, or that hot termagant Scot had paid me scot and lot[1] too. Counterfeit? I lie, I am no counterfeit; to die is to be a counterfeit, for he is but
115   the counterfeit of a man who hath not the life of a man; but to counterfeit
dying when a man thereby liveth is to be no counterfeit, but the true and
perfect image of life indeed. The better part[2] of valor is discretion, in the
which better part I have saved my life. Zounds, I am afraid of this gunpowder Percy, though he be dead; how if he should counterfeit too and
120   rise? By my faith, I am afraid he would prove the better counterfeit.
Therefore I'll make him sure; yea, and I'll swear I killed him. Why may
not he rise as well as I? Nothing confutes me but eyes, and nobody sees
me. Therefore, sirrah [*stabbing him*], with a new wound in your thigh,
come you along with me.
                                             [*He takes up* HOTSPUR *on his back.*]
          [*Enter the* PRINCE *and* JOHN OF LANCASTER.]
125   PRINCE   Come, brother John, full bravely hast thou fleshed°   initiated
Thy maiden sword.
LANCASTER   But soft, whom have we here?
Did you not tell me this fat man was dead?
PRINCE   I did; I saw him dead,
Breathless and bleeding on the ground. Art thou alive?
130   Or is it fantasy° that plays upon our eyesight?   illusion
I prithee speak; we will not trust our eyes
Without our ears; thou art not what thou seem'st.
FALSTAFF   No, that's certain, I am not a double man; but if I be not Jack
Falstaff, then am I a Jack.[3] There is Percy [*throwing the body down*]; if
135   your father will do me any honor, so; if not, let him kill the next Percy
himself. I look to be either earl or duke, I can assure you.
PRINCE   Why, Percy I killed myself and saw thee dead.
FALSTAFF   Didst thou? Lord, Lord, how this world is given to lying! I grant
you I was down and out of breath, and so was he; but we rose both at
140   an instant and fought a long hour by Shrewsbury clock. If I may be
believed, so; if not, let them that should reward valor bear the sin upon
their own heads. I'll take it upon my death, I gave him this wound in the
thigh; if the man were alive and would deny it, zounds, I would make
him eat a piece of my sword.
145   LANCASTER   This is the strangest tale that ever I heard.
PRINCE   This is the strangest fellow, brother John.
Come, bring your luggage nobly on your back;
For my part, if a lie may do thee grace,
I'll gild it with the happiest terms I have.
          [*A retreat is sounded.*]
150   The trumpet sounds retreat;[4] the day is ours.
Come, brother, let us to the highest[5] of the field,
To see what friends are living, who are dead.

9. Pickle.
1. Completely. "Termagant": violent.
2. Quality, not "portion."
3. I.e., a worthless fellow.

4. The signal to stop pursuit of the defeated
enemy.
5. Highest part.

[*Exeunt* ⟨PRINCE OF WALES *and* LANCASTER⟩.]

FALSTAFF   I'll follow, as they say, for reward. He that rewards me, God
reward him! If I do grow great, I'll grow less, for I'll purge[6] and leave
155   sack, and live cleanly as a nobleman should do.   [*Exit.*]

SCENE 5

[*The trumpets sound. Enter the* KING, PRINCE OF WALES, PRINCE JOHN
OF LANCASTER, EARL OF WESTMORELAND, *with* WORCESTER *and* VER-
NON *prisoners.*]

KING   Thus ever did rebellion find rebuke.
   Ill-spirited Worcester, did not we send grace,
   Pardon, and terms of love to all of you?
   And wouldst thou turn our offers contrary,
5   Misuse the tenor of thy kinsman's trust?
   Three knights upon our party slain today,
   A noble earl and many a creature else
   Had been alive this hour,
   If like a Christian thou hadst truly borne
10   Betwixt our armies true intelligence.
WORCESTER   What I have done my safety urged me to,
   And I embrace this fortune patiently,
   Since not to be avoided it falls on me.
KING   Bear Worcester to the death and Vernon too;
15   Other offenders we will pause upon.
      [*Exeunt* WORCESTER *and* VERNON ⟨*guarded*⟩.]
   How goes the field?
PRINCE   The noble Scot, Lord Douglas, when he saw
   The fortune of the day quite turned from him,
   The noble Percy slain, and all his men
20   Upon the foot of fear,[7] fled with the rest,
   And falling from a hill he was so bruised
   That the pursuers took him. At my tent
   The Douglas is, and I beseech your grace
   I may dispose of him.
KING   With all my heart.
25   PRINCE   Then, brother John of Lancaster, to you
   This honorable bounty shall belong;
   Go to the Douglas and deliver him
   Up to his pleasure, ransomless and free;
   His valor shown upon our crests today
30   Hath taught us how to cherish such high deeds
   Even in the bosom of our adversaries.
LANCASTER   I thank your grace for this high courtesy,
   Which I shall give away immediately.
KING   Then this remains, that we divide our power.
35   You, son John and my cousin Westmoreland,
   Towards York shall bend you with your dearest° speed   *greatest*

---

6. Take laxatives, also repent. "Grow great": i.e.,   7. Fleeing in panic.
become either earl or duke.

To meet Northumberland and the prelate Scroop,
Who, as we hear, are busily in arms;
Myself and you, son Harry, will towards Wales
40   To fight with Glendower and the Earl of March.
Rebellion in this land shall lose his sway,
Meeting the check[8] of such another day;
And since this business so fair is done,
Let us not leave till all our own be won.   [*Exeunt.*]

1598

8. (1) Hindrance, (2) rebuke.

THOMAS NASHE
1567–1601

Thomas Nashe, a Cambridge graduate, was a versatile writer of controversial pamphlets, satires, plays, a novel, and lyric verse. He was one of the so-called University Wits who in the late 1580s came to London and wrote for the stage and the press. They lived short and precarious lives: Nashe was about thirty-three when he died; his friend Christopher Marlowe died at twenty-nine; George Peele, at thirty; and Robert Greene, at thirty-two. Nashe's polemical enemy was an older man, Gabriel Harvey, Spenser's friend; Nashe exchanged a series of vituperative and slanderous pamphlets with Harvey in which Nashe's talent for invective and mockery was exploited to the fullest. In June 1599 the ecclesiastical authorities ordered that "all Nashe's books and Doctor Harvey's books be taken wheresoever they may be found and that none of their books be ever printed hereafter."

Nashe wrote a festive comedy, *Summer's Last Will and Testament*; an attack on women called *The Anatomy of Absurdity*; an attack on social abuses of every kind titled *Pierce Penniless, His Supplication to the Devil*; and a strident comparison between the sins of the Jews that led to the destruction of Jerusalem and the current morals and manners of London, called *Christ's Tears Over Jerusalem*. His picaresque narrative, *The Unfortunate Traveler or the Life of Jack Wilton*, recounts the adventures of the young hero all over Europe, including fictive encounters with Erasmus and the poet Surrey, the massacre of the Protestant radicals in Germany, and harrowing, melodramatic exploits in seductive, corrupt, and plague-ridden Italy. Nashe's outlook, like that of many satirists, was conservative; he attacked innovation and praised the purported stability and order of the past. But there is something wild and extreme in his vision of the world, and his prose style, which sometimes sounds like modern experimental fiction, is headlong, impatient, colloquial, and vivid.

A Litany in Time of Plague[1]

Adieu, farewell, earth's bliss,
This world uncertain is;

1. This lyric is from *A Pleasant Comedy Called Summer's Last Will and Testament*, acted before the archbishop of Canterbury in his palace at Croydon in 1592 and published in 1600.

Fond° are life's lustful joys,　　　　　*foolish*
Death proves them all but toys,°　　　　*trifles*
5　None from his darts can fly;
I am sick, I must die.
　Lord, have mercy on us!

Rich men, trust not in wealth,
Gold cannot buy you health;
10　Physic himself must fade,
All things to end are made.
The plague full swift goes by;
I am sick, I must die.
　Lord, have mercy on us!

15　Beauty is but a flower
Which wrinkles will devour;
Brightness falls from the air,
Queens have died young and fair,
Dust hath closèd Helen's eye.
20　I am sick, I must die.
　Lord, have mercy on us!

Strength stoops unto the grave,
Worms feed on Hector brave;
Swords may not fight with fate,
25　Earth still holds ope her gate.
"Come, come!" the bells do cry.
I am sick, I must die.
　Lord, have mercy on us!

Wit with his wantonness
30　Tasteth death's bitterness;
Hell's executioner
Hath no ears for to hear
What vain art can reply.
I am sick, I must die.
35　　Lord, have mercy on us!

Haste, therefore, each degree,
To welcome destiny;
Heaven is our heritage,
Earth but a player's stage;
40　Mount we unto the sky.
I am sick, I must die.
　Lord, have mercy on us!

1592　　　　　　　　　　　　　　　　　1600

The Early Seventeenth Century 1603–1660

1603: Death of Elizabeth I; accession of James I, first Stuart king of England
1605: The Gunpowder Plot, a failed effort by Catholic extremists to blow up Parliament and the king
1620: Arrival of the Pilgrims in the New World aboard the *Mayflower*
1625: Death of James I; accession of Charles I
1642: Outbreak of civil war: theaters closed
1649: Execution of Charles I; beginning of Commonwealth and Protectorate, known inclusively as the Interregnum (1649–60)
1660: End of the Protectorate; Restoration of Charles II

When Queen Elizabeth died on March 24, 1603, after more than four decades on the throne, her kinsman James VI of Scotland succeeded her as James I of England without the disruptions or attempted *coups* that had been feared. The nation breathed a sigh of relief and expected a new beginning. The change from an aged queen without progeny to a thirty-six-year-old king, with an attractive queen, Anne of Denmark, and children who could assure the succession, was cause for celebration. But there was also cause for unease, as the nation saw itself exchanging an English Deborah, whom God had favored with a miraculous victory over the Spanish Armada and who had declared herself married to her people, for an aloof Scotsman with a foreign entourage that might displace English place-seekers. The atmosphere and anxieties at the change of regimes are suggested by an entry in the diary of Lady Anne Clifford, then thirteen years old:

> About 10 o'clock King *James* was proclaimed in *Cheapside* by all the Council with great joy and triumph. I went to see and hear. This peaceable coming-in of the King was unexpected of all sorts of people. . . . At this time we used to go very much to *Whitehall*, and walked much in the garden which was frequented by lords and ladies, my Mother [Margaret Clifford, countess of Cumberland] being all full of hopes, every man expecting mountains and finding molehills. . . . We all went to *Tibbalds* [Theobalds] to see the King who used my Mother and aunt very graciously, but we all saw a great change between the fashion of the Court as it is now and of that in the Queen's time, for we were all lousy by sitting in the chamber of Sir *Thomas Erskine*. . . . About this time my Aunt *Warwick* went to meet the Queen [enroute from Scotland]. . . . Then my Mother and I went on our journey to overtake her, and killed three horses that day with extremity of heat. . . .

Upon the 25th of July the King and Queen were crowned at *West-minster*, my Father and Mother both attended in their robes, my Aunt of *Bath* and my Uncle *Russell*, which solemn sight my Mother would not let me see because the plague was hot in *London*.

Because of the plague, public celebrations of the coronation were postponed until the following year, when the king made an elaborate progress through the City of London. He passed through ceremonial arches and viewed pageants that represented him in terms suited to his patriarchal and absolutist royal style: a Roman Augustus, a wise Solomon, a Sun King, and the ruler of a newly constituted Britain with England and Scotland linked. The progress was designed to testify to an ideal relationship between a ruler and his people, but it revealed tensions and misunderstandings on both sides. Unlike Elizabeth, James thoroughly disliked exposing himself at such close quarters to the tumultuous crowds. His plans for a full union between his two kingdoms found little favor with the English people. The relationships between the monarch and his people and between England and Scotland would be sources of deep and recurrent conflict throughout his reign, and long afterward.

Traditional literary and historical periods are arbitrary, and their association with monarchs' reigns even more so. Broad political and cultural movements—the Reformation, exploration and colonization, the rising bourgeois class in the cities, the printing press and the expansion of literacy, conflicts over gender roles, changes in perceptions of the self and of authorship—have a much longer time-frame. They span the centuries (roughly 1500–1700) that scholars refer to as the Renaissance when they mean to emphasize breaks with medieval culture and the Early Modern Period when they mean to emphasize seeds of the modern world. Nor do authors' lives and careers neatly conform to the conventional periods. Shakespeare wrote his great tragedies and romances in James I's reign; Donne wrote his elegies, satires, and some love poems in the last decade of Queen Elizabeth's. Milton completed *Paradise Lost* and wrote two other major poems in the 1660s. Yet recognizing the years 1603–60 as a period brings into focus important political, intellectual, cultural, and stylistic currents that bear directly upon literary production. It also permits attention to changes in worldview that helped shape the cultural and literary scene: Galileo's astronomy, Bacon's empiricism, justifications for revolution, and the seismic shift in consciousness that, in 1649, allowed for the formal trial, conviction, and execution of an anointed king.

STATE AND CHURCH, 1603–40

Soon after James I's ascension, the Elizabethan settlement in church and state began to unravel. By great astuteness, by appointing brilliant ministers, and by playing complex roles as female monarch and Petrarchan lady, eliciting both obedience and love, Elizabeth had managed to maintain control over her Parliaments, retain the loyalty and devotion of most of her subjects, and win respect abroad. The Stuart kings, James I and his son Charles I, were unable to do this, engaging in constant confrontations with their Parliaments and subjects over taxes, religion, unpopular ministers, and parliamentary rights. Elizabeth did not try to define precisely how power is divided in what was usually described as a "mixed" government of Monarch, Lords, and Commons. James, while yet in Scotland, published two arguments for royal absolutism, *The True Law of Free Monarchies* (1597) and *Basilikon Doran* (1598). These works, both reissued in 1603, proclaim the divine right of kings as God's deputies and as fathers of their people and explain that monarchs are "free" in that they are accountable only to God. A series of analogies is seen to structure a patriarchal social order: as God is absolute ruler of the universe, so is the king of his people and the father of his family. James also claimed a role as shaper of culture in other published works, among them original poems, a translation of the psalms, a treatise on witchcraft, and a vigorous polemic against tobacco.

By contrast with Elizabeth's, James's court was disorderly and indecorous, marked by hard drinking and late-night feasting, a craze for hunting, and great extravagance. While Elizabeth had created eight new peers, James created sixty, selling peerages and noble titles as a means of raising funds. The court was in a constant state of financial crisis. As early as 1605, the king lamented that "it is a horror to me to think of the height of my place, the greatness of my debts, and the smallness of my means." Unlike Elizabeth, James had to maintain separate households for his queen and for the heir apparent, Prince Henry. The three courts had markedly different styles. The queen's household had places for female as well as male courtiers and separate channels for patronage, the most important being the queen's favorite, Lucy Russell, countess of Bedford, who was a major patron of Donne and Jonson. Prince Henry also patronized authors and scholars (among them Sir Walter Ralegh, who was writing, in prison, his *History of the World*, and George Chapman, who was translating Homer). His household became a focus for militant Protestants who were seeking more reform at home and more vigorous support of Protestantism abroad.

James himself relied increasingly on favorites who became channels for patronage in all spheres: first Robert Car, earl of Somerset, then George Villiers, duke of Buckingham. The attachment James formed for these favorites was highly romantic. "God so love me," the king wrote to Buckingham, "as I only desire to live in the world for your sake, and that I would rather live banished in any part of the earth with you than live a sorrowful widow's life without you." Such sentiments, not surprisingly, gave rise to widespread rumors of homosexual activities at court. The rumors are certainly plausible, though the surviving evidence of same-sex relationships in Early Modern England is extremely difficult to interpret. Sodomy was a crime punishable by death, but prosecutions were extremely rare. English law simply declined to recognize the possibility of lesbian acts. From Shakespeare's sonnets to James's letters, we find avowals of love and desire between men which may sometimes be formal expressions of affection based on classical models, or, alternatively, expressions of passionate physical and spiritual love. The interpretive difficulty is compounded by the absence in the period of any clear reference to homosexual "identity," though there are many references to same-sex acts and feelings. What is clear is that male friendships at the court of James and elsewhere were suffused with an eroticism, at once delightful and threatening, that subsequent periods policed more anxiously.

Religious tensions mounted during James's reign. The divisive energies of the Reformation had been tamed under Elizabeth by the establishment of a national church that accommodated, more or less comfortably, the great majority of her subjects, whether mostly Catholic or mostly Protestant in their religious views. During the first decade of James's reign, this accommodation held. The discovery and thwarting of the "Gunpowder Plot" in 1605, in which Guy Fawkes and a band of Roman Catholic conspirators plotted to blow up the Houses of Parliament and seize control of the government, unified English Protestants in a wave of anti-Catholic sentiment and support for the monarch. James, it seemed, had been preserved by a divine miracle even as Elizabeth had been by the defeat of the Armada. Also, the king's sponsorship of the so-called King James Bible (the Authorized Version, 1611) was a powerful force for Protestant unity.

Religion was such a vital cement for maintaining social and political order that, for almost everybody, genuine separation of church and state was unthinkable. Yet Christians thought it absolutely vital for their salvation or damnation to make right decisions about controversial theological issues: what to believe about predestination? how to conduct public worship? how to read, understand, and explicate scripture? what private devotions and meditations to use? what church was established by Christ? how to know if one is saved? So it is not surprising that Roman Catholics and various kinds of Puritans resisted the Established Church and that the Established Church tried to repress that opposition.

There were still many open or covert Roman Catholics who paid stiff fines for recusancy (failing to take the sacrament in the Established Church). They were also barred from taking degrees in the universities or holding public office or practicing at the bar, since to do so required an oath recognizing the monarch's supremacy over the church. Catholic priests, if captured, might be executed as traitors in the usual grisly fashion of hanging, drawing, disemboweling, and quartering. Yet there were Catholics in high places. Some ancient noble houses held to the old religion. And when Queen Anne refused to take the sacrament at her coronation there was intense speculation that she was a covert Catholic, speculation that continued (without being actually proved) throughout the reign.

From the other side, Puritans, as they were disparagingly called, pressed for more reformation in doctrine, ritual, and especially in church government, so as to bring the English church into closer conformity with the Presbyterian Church organization in Geneva, as established by the Protestants reformer John Calvin. Theology as such was not the issue, since much of the clergy accepted some version of Calvinism, as did King James. However, within that consensus Puritans tended to hold more extreme views about predestination (God's consignment of individuals to salvation or damnation—election and reprobation—without reference to their own acts or merit) and about the total depravity of humankind after the Fall. Many Puritans sought to remain within the Established Church but wanted to eliminate what they saw as the "popish" elements in the liturgy of *The Book of Common Prayer* and the "idolatrous" religious images in churches, e.g., religious statues, stained-glass windows, and an ornate high altar. They emphasized preaching and reading the Bible, not sacraments, as the core of religious practice; they sought moral and social reform through laws governing recreation, sabbath-keeping, drunkenness, and public order; and they emphasized the individual's direct responsibility for his or her own faith and for fulfilling his or her vocation or calling in the world, counting success as a possible indicator of election to salvation. The largest Puritan denomination, the Presbyterians, held that the Bible mandated church government by Presbyters (ministers), Lay Elders, and Synods (regional and national convocations) and agitated to substitute that organization for the Established Church hierarchy of archbishops, bishops, and priests. Some separatist Puritans (Congregationalists, Brownists, Anabaptists) wanted no national church, only individual gathered churches of the elect; some of them went to Holland or New England to escape repression.

Prince Henry's sudden death in 1612 dashed the hopes of Puritans and other reformist Protestants, prompting an outpouring of funeral elegies and laments reminiscent of the response to Sir Philip Sidney's early death in 1586. Prince Charles became heir apparent, and Henry's role as a potential leader of international Protestantism was partly filled by Frederick, Elector Palatine, who married James's daughter Elizabeth in 1613. Reformist Protestants urged James to take an active military role in the Thirty-Years' War (1618–48), which erupted over Frederick's claims to Bohemia and raged all over Europe, pitting Protestant against Roman Catholic nations. But James sought, unsuccessfully, to play peacemaker in that conflict. In 1623 he set plans in motion to marry Prince Charles to the Catholic Infanta of Spain, but when those plans collapsed over religious issues the nation was overjoyed. When Charles married the French princess Henrietta Maria instead there was little objection: though Catholic, she was at least not Spanish. The English antipathy to Catholic Spain reached back to Mary Tudor's reign (with her Spanish husband, Phillip II) and it intensified to white heat with the threat of invasion by the Spanish Armada (1588).

The ascent of Charles I to the throne in 1625 brought a palpable change in monarchical style. Unlike his father, Charles was not a theorist of royal absolutism and the divine right of kings, but he acted on those principles with consistency and inflexibility. By temperament James was given to compromise, whereas Charles held out for his royal prerogatives. He dissolved Parliament three times and in 1629 began nearly a decade of "personal rule" without Parliament, raising money through special taxes that were widely denounced as illegal and governing through a much-hated cabinet council: Buckingham, the earl of Strafford, and Archbishop Laud. Religious conflicts also intensified. Queen Henrietta Maria brought with her from France to England an entourage of Roman Catholic priests and followers and promoted the conversion to Catholicism of several English noblewomen in her court. The appointment in 1633 of William Laud as archbishop of Canterbury, the ecclesiastical head of the English Church, proved to be a watershed event. Throughout the 1630s Laud promoted the rapid growth of a high Anglican faction within the church, conforming its ceremony, ritual, and doctrine more closely to Roman Catholicism. The altar rather than the pulpit again dominated the church, making the eucharist the primary element in worship, rather than preaching. Ministers of Puritan tendency were dispossessed of their livings, and the full liturgy of The Book of Common Prayer was required in every parish. In theology Laud threw down the gauntlet to much of the nation by imposing an Arminian rather than a Calvinist interpretation on the

Thirty-Nine Articles of the Church of England—a doctrine of Free Will, that is, rather than Predestination.

Through both reigns, but especially that of Charles, resistance to Stuart absolutism came from several quarters. The Commons in Parliament insisted on their own rights and powers and demanded reforms in return for voting subsidies. As the peerage grew more impoverished, due in part to changes in agriculture but also to the expense of maintaining their status in the lavish courts, many peers of ancient lineage grew increasingly disaffected. Some Puritans and reform-minded clergy found ways to urge their causes in the pulpit and the press. Also, the wealthy bourgeois in the cities gained considerable power as sources of needed funds: they often supplied loans to the Crown and also funded exploration and colonization in the New World and elsewhere through such corporations as the East and West India Companies.

As the 1630s drew to a close, Archbishop Laud and Charles attempted to impose *The Book of Common Prayer* and episcopal organization upon Presbyterian Scotland. When the Scots resisted, Charles took this as a direct challenge to his authority, being persuaded that to dismantle ecclesiastical hierarchy threatened hierarchy everywhere and ultimately the Crown: "No Bishop, No King." Charles's military action against Scotland (The First and Second Bishops' Wars in 1639–40) was funded by extra-legal taxes, but met with abject failure. Exacerbating the situation, Laud laid down new canons for the English church, requiring full conformity in liturgy and preaching and an oath from all clergy opposing any change in the church government then in place. Riots in the London streets and Scots occupation of several northern English cities forced Charles to call the so-called "Long Parliament," which would soon be managing a revolution.

LITERATURE AND CULTURE, 1603–40

The earlier seventeenth century brought old and new ideas about the nature of things into sharp opposition. An inherited body of concepts and images was still available to be used by Donne, Burton, and others, even as they were being questioned or displaced: the Ptolemaic universe with its nine concentric spheres whose movements produce music, its circling sun and fixed earth, and its assumption of perfection above the moon and corruption beneath; the four elements—fire, air, water, earth—that comprise the matter of all things; and the four humors of the body—choler, blood, phlegm, and melancholy—that determine temperament and in great imbalance make for disease, mental and physical. Jacobeans thought of themselves as especially prone to melancholy: Shakespeare's Hamlet and Jacques in *As You Like It* are melancholics, and Robert Burton wrote a massive and thoroughly delightful treatise on the malady, which he thought universal, *The Anatomy of Melancholy* (1621). Milton's title figure in *Il Penseroso* is a benign exemplar of that temperament, which was commonly associated with scholars. Key concepts of this inherited system were order and analogy, often rendered in striking literary images. Donne was especially fond of the macrocosm/microcosm parallel according to which the human being is seen as "a little world" or recapitulation of the world itself; and almost everyone believed in some version of the "chain" of being that links and orders all species hierarchically.

But this system, with its *a priori* assumptions and reliance upon ancient authority, was challenged by Francis Bacon's new emphasis on scientific method, as well as by actual experiments such as Gabriel Harvey's discovery of the circulation of the blood and Galileo's telescope, which supplied evidence confirming the Copernican astronomy. Galileo dislodged the earth from its former fixed and stable position at the center of the cosmos and, in defiance of all ordinary observation, sent it whirling about the sun; he also found evidence of change and corruption in the heavens and advanced mind-boggling speculations about life on other planets and infinite universes. Donne, like other writers of his age, responded to the new ideas, giving voice to the anxieties they produced in his *Anatomy of the World*:

> And new philosophy calls all in doubt,
> The element of fire is quite put out;
> The sun is lost, and the earth, and no man's wit
> Can well direct him where to look for it.

Milton, however, embraced the new science, referring with pride to a visit during his European tour to "the famous Galileo, grown old, a prisoner to the Inquisition for thinking in astronomy otherwise than the Franciscan and Dominican licensers thought." In *Paradise Lost* he made complex poetic use of the astronomical controversy.

In both reigns, the court was an important site of literary activity. Births, marriages, and funerals in the royal family prompted celebratory or elegiac verse, as did other royal occasions. Queen Anne played a major role in giving distinctive form and prominence to the court masque, traditionally presented at Christmastide and most often on Twelfth Night (January 6). The spectacular and extravagant masques devised by Inigo Jones, written by Ben Jonson, and danced by royal and noble personages portray King James as source of all power and splendor in the kingdom. Masques customarily end with the masquers unmasking and dancing with other courtiers, symbolizing the fusion of the ideal world and the Stuart court. But masques produced and danced by Queen Anne and her ladies also served to assert their own interests and power and to enact some resistance to the king's control.

Beyond the court, some noblemen retained their status as powerful local patrons with many clients, including poets and playwrights. Especially prominent were the interrelated families of the Sidneys at Penshurst and the Herberts at Wilton. Ben Jonson's country-house poem *To Penshurst* celebrates the Sidney estate as an alternative ideal to the court, hospitable alike to poets and kings; his collection of poems *The Forest* also includes several other poems associated with the Sidney family. Aemilia Lanyer's country-house poem of about the same date, *The Description of Cooke-Ham*, celebrates the estate occupied by Margaret Clifford, countess of Cumberland, and her daughter Anne (author of the *Diary* quoted above), crediting her residence there with nurturing her poetry. Jonson's book of *Epigrams* and Lanyer's dedicatory poems construct imagined communities of worthy personages and patrons honored by and honoring the poet. Coteries of friends also promoted and circulated literary works. Donne addressed several verse letters and some of his *Songs and Sonnets* to male friends in the law courts and at court; later he became part of a coterie formed around his patron, Lucy Russell, countess of Bedford, with whom he sometimes exchanged poems.

The church also promoted writing of several kinds: treatises of devotion, meditation, and instruction; controversial tracts (like Donne's *Pseudo-Martyr* against the Roman Catholics); cases of conscience that work out difficult moral issues in complex situations; and especially sermons. This is an age in which everyone heard sermons at least once and often twice on Sunday, as well as on all days of special religious or national celebration. Sermons were at least an hour long and often much longer. Congregants, especially children, were urged to outline them, repeat them later, and meditate on them. The essence of a sermon, Protestants agreed, is the careful exposition of Scripture, and its purpose is to instruct and move. Gifted Church of England preachers like Donne called on all the resources of artful rhetoric and elegant style to enthrall their congregations. They probed the words and phrases of a Scripture text by wordplay, allusions, conceits, and quotations from the learned languages. By contrast, many Puritans sought a logical, undecorated style that would display God's word in its own splendor, unadorned by human wit.

The City of London was also an important site for literary creation. City officials commissioned Lord Mayors' pageants and other civic entertainments. Also, the numerous booksellers contracted for and published books of domestic advice, devotional treatises, "how-to-do-it" manuals, and tracts of political and religious controversy. The theaters continued to flourish in the Liberties just outside the City, and therefore not under London's jurisdiction; this was the only sphere in which authors could support themselves by writing. Shakespeare was at the height of his powers: *King Lear, Othello, Macbeth, Twelfth Night, The Tempest*, and several others were staged during the early years of James's reign. So were Ben Jonson's major comedies—*Volpone, The Alchemist*, and *Epicoene*—as well as *Bartholomew Fair*, Jonson's contribution to City Comedy. That new kind, practiced by Thomas Middleton, Thomas Heywood, and others, drew satirical and comic matter from the life of London. The most important new playwright was John Webster, whose dark tragedies *The Duchess of Malfi* and *The White Devil* combined gothic horror with poetry of stunning beauty.

This era saw important changes in poetic fashion. Several prominent Elizabethan genres were no longer much in evidence: long allegorical or mythological narratives, sonnet sequences, and pastoral poems. Nor were such stylistic features as nature imagery, florid ornament, and sonorous lyricism. The norm was coming to be short, very concentrated poems in a colloquial and often witty "plain style." The major poets of these years, Donne, Jonson, and George Herbert, led this shift, as well as the rise to prominence of other genres: love elegy and satire after the classical models of Ovid and Horace, epigram, verse epistle, dramatic monologue, meditative religious lyric, and country-house poem. These three poets represent three distinct modes of authorship, but have in common a pronounced anxiety about the nature of literary production and the relation of the author to society. All three exercised an important influence on poets of the next generation.

John Donne, whose imprudent marriage cost him a much-desired career in the court bureaucracy but who later became a famous preacher and dean of St. Paul's Cathedral, cast himself in the older mold of gentleman amateur, circulating his poems in manuscript to friends and coterie circles, and largely avoiding print publication (his poems were published posthumously in

1633). In both their style and their content, Donne's poems were designed to be read by a select few rather than the public at large. His best poems explore the private worlds of love and religion, often developing passionate dialectical arguments that set them in anxious opposition to the public world. His style is characterized by learned terms and images, speechlike and often unmelodic verses, and strikingly dramatic language that often evokes a scene in progress. It is also characterized by witty play with paradoxes, ironies and the conjunction of opposites, as in the so-called "metaphysical conceit"—a surprising metaphor that (as Samuel Johnson later observed) links together images from very different ranges of experience. Donne took particular delight in challenging his sophisticated readers by interchanging the vocabularies of sexual and religious love both in his love poems and in his religious poems. Donne has sometimes been regarded as the founder of a "metaphysical school" of poetry, but that classification is not very useful. We find some echoes of Donne's style in some later poets such as Thomas Carew, who praised Donne as "Monarch of wit," John Cleveland, Abraham Cowley, and Andrew Marvell. But neither they nor the other poets sometimes linked with Donne (Herbert, Vaughan, Crashaw, Traherne) can be usefully classified as members of a "school," since none of them is very like Donne, nor are they like one another.

Ben Jonson staked his claim as a new kind of professional author when he published his court masques, his plays for the public theater, and two collections of poems in an elegant folio titled *Works* in the same year (1616) that King James published his treatises and poems under the same title. Jonson's finest poems celebrate the social world of friendship and community and embody the classical values of simplicity, restraint, economy, decorum, good workmanship, and art. Important principles of his poetics can be gleaned from his comments on poets and poetry to his friend, William Drummond of Hawthornden, and from his volume of extracts from classical sources: that nature first and then art makes the poet; that the poet's formation demands wit, judgment, and the proper imitation of models; and that the ideal poetic style is strong and plain (not abstruse like Donne's): "Pure and neat language I love, yet plain and customary." A ruling principle for Jonson is decorum—the proper fit of style to subject. Another is that the best art conceals art. In contrast to Donne, Jonson cast himself as the father of a brood of poetic sons—known as the Tribe or Sons of Ben—and met regularly with some of them in the Apollo Room of the Devil Tavern in London. Robert Herrick and many of the poets known as Cavaliers for their attachment to the court—Carew, Lovelace, Suckling—either acknowledged the relationship or gave some evidence of it.

George Herbert, pastor to a small country parish, was a very different kind of author from Donne, who wrote to please his friends and patrons, or Jonson, who wrote to instruct the court and country. Herbert destroyed his secular verse in English and turned his volume of religious verse over to a friend on his deathbed, desiring him to print it if he thought it would be useful "to some dejected poor soul" and otherwise to burn it. The 177 lyrics contained in that volume, *The Temple* (1633), display a complex religious sensibility and great artistic subtlety in an amazing variety of kinds, stanzaic forms, and rhythmic patterns. In several of these poems, Herbert agonized about the paradoxical necessity, and at the same time impossibility, of a

Christian poet giving fit and sincere praise to God. He also questioned whether literary art is appropriate to divine praises and if so, what kind of art? Several poems renounce old poetic styles and ornaments for a new, plain, devotional, and biblical mode, exploring the question posed in *Jordan I*, "Is there in truth no beauty?" Herbert was the major influence on the next generation of religious lyric poets and was explicitly recognized as such by Henry Vaughan and Richard Crashaw.

The Jacobean era (so-called from King James I) also saw the emergence of what would become a major new prose genre, the familiar essay. Francis Bacon brought it to England in a form very different from the intimate, tentative, conversational essay developed some decades earlier in France by Montaigne. Bacon's fifty-eight short sketches have, by contrast, a pithy, sententious style and a tone of cool objectivity, as if presenting society's accumulated practical wisdom on such topics as *Marriage and the Single Life, Truth, Simulation and Dissimulation, Ambition, Followers and Friends*, and *Suitors*. Bacon's other works are analyses of the state of knowledge in England and proposals for placing it on a scientific basis of induction and experimentation. His fictional utopia *The New Atlantis* imagines a society based on the Baconian dream of scientific learning and research.

These years mark the entry of Englishwomen, in some numbers, into authorship and publication. Their works rewrite discourses that repress or diminish women—patriarchy, gender hierarchy, the apostle Paul's teachings on marriage—and shape several genres to women's concerns. Most of these women were from the nobility or gentry and all were educated above the norm for women in the period. Some wrote private diaries and autobiographies that remained in manuscript, published mothers' manuals, or polemics defending women's worthiness against attacks. Aemilia Lanyer is the first Englishwoman to publish a substantial volume of original poems (1611), containing poetic dedications, a long poem on Christ's passion, and a country-house poem, all defending women's interests and worth. Elizabeth Cary, Lady Falkland, is the first Englishwoman to publish a tragedy, *Mariam* (1613), a Senecan closet drama that probes the situation of a queen-wife subjected to domestic and political tyranny. Lady Mary Wroth, niece of Sir Philip Sidney and the countess of Pembroke, wrote three works that are firsts for an Englishwoman. Her Petrarchan sonnet sequence *Pamphilia to Amphilanthus* (1621) gives voice and subjectivity to the woman lover-poet. It was published with her long prose romance *Urania* (1621), which presents a range of women's responses to life and love as well as many spheres for women's exercise of agency and power—as rulers, counselors, scholars, storytellers, poets, and seers. Her unpublished pastoral tragicomedy *Love's Victory* depicts a nonhierarchical pastoral world whose ideality depends on female friendships and female control.

When Charles and Henrietta Maria came to the throne in 1625, the changed court style in this Caroline era directly affected the arts and literature. As the Puritan Lucy Hutchinson recalled, "The fools and bawds, mimics and catamites of the former court grew out of fashion," to be replaced by a new sophistication and refinement and a courtly code idealizing female beauty, heterosexual love, and harmony. Charles and his queen were art collectors on a large scale and patrons of such painters as Rubens and Van Dyke; the latter portrayed Charles in magnificent, heroic poses, mounted on a splendid white stallion. A fashionable artistic and literary cult of platonic love mythologized the two monarchs as the ideal Platonic hermaphrodite, their union joining together heroic virtue and divine beauty or love. In this milieu several courtier-poets—Carew, Suckling, Waller—wrote playful, sophisticated, sometimes delicate and sometimes licentious love lyrics on *carpe diem* themes: seize the day, time passes swiftly, make love now.

During the 1630s, the culture wars intensified between the Caroline court and the Laudian church on the one hand and the reformist Protestant and Puritan opposition on the other. In 1633 Charles reissued James I's *Book of Sports*, prescribing the continuation of traditional holiday festivities and Sunday sports in every parish in an effort to extend the cultural control of the court throughout the country. Puritans denounced both court festivities and country sports on religious grounds: they regarded masques, maypoles, and morris dances as palpable occasions of sin and the Sunday sports as profanations of the Sabbath. Also, many saw connections between the sophisticated pastoralism, Neoplatonism, and representations of ritual in the court masques and the Queen's Roman Catholicism. William Prynne had staked out the most extreme Puritan position, publishing in November 1632 a passionate tirade of over one thousand pages against stage-plays, masques, masque dancing, maypoles, and rural festivals, country sports on the Sabbath, Laudian ritual, stained-glass windows, and much more. He associated the court arts—"effeminate mixed dancing, lascivious pictures, wanton fashions, face painting . . . amorous pastorals, lascivious effeminate music"— with licentiousness, effeminacy, and seduction to popery. Worse, his reference to "Women actors, notorious whores" was thought to refer to the queen and her ladies, then rehearsing a pastoral play at court. For this cultural critique Prynne was stripped of his academic degrees, ejected from the legal profession, set in the pillory at Westminster and Cheapside, had his books burned and his ears cut off, and was sentenced to life imprisonment. The severity of the punishment indicates the perceived danger of his book, which one judge claimed would "effect disobedience to the state, and a general dislike unto all governments."

Milton's early poems display astonishing artistic virtuosity rooted in literary and generic traditions, but they also respond to the tensions of these years. Milton repudiated courtly and Laudian aesthetics and also Prynne's wholesale prohibitions, developing reformed versions of pastoral, masque, and hymn. His lovely hymn *On the Morning of Christ's Nativity* (1629) contains a long section on the casting out of idols at Christ's birth which resonates with contemporary Puritan resistance to Laudian "idolatry." And his magnificent pastoral funeral elegy *Lycidas* contains a vehement denunciation of the establishment clergy as "Blind Mouths"—both ignorant and greedy— who deprive their flocks of spiritual nourishment.

THE REVOLUTIONARY ERA, 1640–60

Now almost four hundred years after the execution of Charles I, the English Revolution is still not quite over. Its aftershocks can be felt in the politically heated debate over its causes, which continues to this day. On the one hand, many historians see the revolution as the consequence, at least in part, of long-term changes in the English society and economy. They point to the conflict between new (capitalist) and old (feudal) modes of production in agriculture, industry, and trade and to the rising power and ambition of the gentry, the urban bourgeoisie, and those known as the "middling sort" of people in town and country. The frustrated demands of these classes for a greater measure of economic, political, and religious freedom led to rising social tensions and eventually civil war and revolution. This view, championed by Marxists among others, has been opposed by a revisionist school which emphasizes short-term and avoidable causes of the war. These historians point to a number of unlucky chance events, personal psychological factors, and poor decisions made by a small group of individuals. The political overtones of this clash of historians are unmistakeable. The debate over whether this was Europe's first bourgeois revolution or merely the consequence (as one scholar has argued) of Charles I's attempts to compensate for a sense of masculine inadequacy is ultimately a debate about the nature of history. As such it is not only about the events of the past, but about the shape of the future.

Whatever causes contributed to the outbreak of hostilities, there is no doubt that the twenty-year revolutionary period left the English economy far more open to the development of capitalist production. It also saw the development of concepts central to bourgeois liberal thought and soon to influence John Locke and the theorists of the American and French revolutions: religious toleration, separation of church and state, social contract, popular sovereignty, representative government, and republicanism. These concepts developed out of years of prolonged and bitter dispute centering around three fundamental questions: What kind of church government is laid down in Scripture and should therefore be settled in England? What should be the relation between church and state? What is the ultimate source of political power? The theories that evolved in response to these questions contain the seeds of much that is familiar in modern thought, mixed with much that seems forbiddingly alien. It is vital to bear in mind that the participants in these debates were not working their way (vaguely and haphazardly) toward modern liberalism, but responding (clearly and powerfully) to the most fundamental problems of their day. The debate was especially bitter and the need to find the right answers particularly intense for the many Millenarians among them, who believed that their day was very near to being the last day of all.

When the so-called "Long Parliament" convened in 1640, it had no intention of mounting a revolution and executing a king, but it was intent on securing and expanding its rights in the face of the king's perceived absolutist tendencies. Parliament set about to abolish extra-legal taxes and courts; to bring to trial and at length execute the king's hated ministers, Strafford and Laud; to rein in the bishops' power; to provide for triennial parliaments; and to remain in session until they themselves agreed to disband. As Parliament debated such matters, legitimate and underground presses poured forth a flood of treatises denouncing or supporting the bishops, *The Book of Common Prayer*, and the competing ecclesiastical models, creating a lively public forum for political discussion. That forum was also shaped by the little weekly newsbooks—the ancestors of our newpapers—which reported events at home and abroad from different political perspectives: royalist, parliamentarian, republican, army. Some of these so-called "Mercuries" were official government publications; some were licensed and quasi-official; some were fly-by-night affairs that lasted a few weeks, disappeared when the censors came after them, and then reappeared under different names.

Puritans were united in passionate opposition to the bishops, associating them with popery, tyranny over conscience, evil counsel to the king, and pompous excesses in lifestyle. Many, including Milton, demanded that they be cast out of the church, "root and branch." Puritan pamphlets sounded watchwords that were to be constantly repeated over the next two decades. One such was the call for "Godly Preachers." Another was "Holy Community," which some found embodied in the nation as a whole, some in a national church, and some in gathered churches of elect "saints." Another was "Covenant," registering the Puritan sense of being in a covenantal relation with God, whether as individuals, families, church members, or nation. Still another was the reference to England as a "New Israel," a new chosen people called to reform church and state, perhaps in preparation for Christ's Millennial Kingdom—the thousand-year reign of Christ with the saints which was to follow the Last Judgment.

In late 1641 events began to move quickly, though not inevitably, toward war. As the rift widened between Parliament and the king, and mobs of London apprentices kept up the pressure, horrific news came of an uprising in Ireland, with perhaps thirty thousand English and Scottish Protestants massacred by the enraged Catholic populace which they had dispossessed, persecuted for religion, and reduced to poverty. Parliament refused to fund the king for an invasion of Ireland, fearing he would instead invade England with an Irish army. When Charles sought to arrest five members of Parliament for treason, Londoners rose in arms against him. Negotiations for compromise broke down over the issues that would derail them at every future stage: control of the army and episcopacy. On July 12, 1642, Parliament voted to raise an army, and on August 22 the king stood before a force of some two thousand horse and foot at Nottingham, unfurled his royal standard, and summoned his liegemen to his aid. Civil war had officially begun with its agonizing divisions, not only between but within regions of the country, cities, towns, rural communities, social classes, Parliament, the army, and even families.

Parliament and the Presbyterian clergy who managed the First Civil War (1642–46) had limited aims: to secure the rights of Parliament, to limit the king's control over the army and the church, and to settle some version of Presbyterianism as the national established church. They had no desire to depose the king, and indeed both Scots and English swore in their *Solemn League and Covenant* to uphold the king's person and authority even as they also swore to advance reformation, the rights of Parliament, and the peoples' liberties. They justified taking arms against the king by the Calvinist theory of contract, according to which political power was transferred by the people to "Magistrates" generally, so that "subordinate magistrates" (Parliament) could mount resistance to a king when, like Charles, he endangered religion and his subjects' liberties. The king set up court and an alternative parliament in Oxford, to which many in the House of Lords and some in the Commons resorted. As the Puritan armies moved through the country, fighting at Edgehill, Marston Moor, Naseby, and elsewhere, they also undertook an iconoclastic crusade to stamp out idolatry, often destroying religious images and stained-glass windows and lopping the heads off of statues, as an earlier generation of radical Protestants had done at the time of the English Reformation. The effects of these ravages can still be seen in English cathedrals and churches.

The Toleration Controversy that erupted in 1643 exposed deep divisions among Puritans. Presbyterians insisted that it was the Christian magistrates' duty to settle a national Presbyterian Church and enforce conformity to it, repressing all dissent. But some secular-minded Parliamentarians thought that broad toleration was the key to civic harmony, while Congegationalists, Independents, and Baptists in the gathered churches and in the army vehemently opposed any national church and pressed for toleration. Most, however, stopped well short of the argument in *The Bloody Tenant* (1644) by the Baptist Roger Williams, recently returned from New England, that Christ has mandated complete separation of church and state and toleration of all religions, even Roman Catholics, Jews, and Muslims. As the revolution wore on, other sects sprang up, also seeking toleration: Seekers, Finders, Antinomians, the Family of Love, Fifth Monarchists, Quakers, Muggletonians, Ranters, and more. The orthodox were aghast, attempting unsuccessfully to stem the tide with laws against blasphemy and for censorship and with treatises like Thomas Edward's massive catalogue of dangerous sects and heresies, *Gangreana* (1646). Milton joined the toleration controversy with *Areopagitica* (1644), arguing vigorously against press censorship and for a very broad though not complete religious toleration.

The defeat of the royalist army in 1646 led to difficult, protracted negotiations and a brief Second Civil War in 1648, in which the king was again beaten, and at length brought to trial. That dramatic spectacle began on January 20 in the crowded Great Hall at Westminster, where Charles heard himself accused of "High Treason and other High Crimes," specifically that he had broken his coronation oath, sought "unlimited and tyrannical power," attempted to overthrow the peoples' liberties and their foundation in successive Parliaments, and "traitorously and maliciously" made war against the Parliament and people. Every day Charles wore his hat in defiance of the court's authority and refused to answer the charges, insisting that a divinely anointed king could not be judged by any earthly power. On January 27 he was sentenced to be beheaded as a "Tyrant, Traitor, Murderer, and public Enemy," with fifty-nine commissioners signing the death warrant. On January 30, on a black-draped scaffold stage erected, ironically enough, outside the Banquetting Room at Whitehall where Charles had danced so many masque roles, he now acted his last role with dignity and courage. Andrew Marvell described the execution scene memorably in *An Horatian Ode*.

The Rump Parliament, the part of the House of Commons that was allowed to remain after the army expelled royalist and Presbyterian members (Pride's Purge), immediately established a new government "in way of a republic, without King or House of Lords" and with a Council of State as executive. Some classically educated supporters of the revolution saw themselves as reviving the forms of Athenian democracy and the Roman republic. As Hobbes later remarked, these men had absorbed the works of Demosthenes, Cicero, Livy, and others in which "popular government was extolled by the glorious name of liberty, and monarchy disgraced by the name of tyranny," and so "fell in love with their forms of government." But whatever their ideals, those in power in the infant republic (1649–54) found they could not afford to be doctrinaire or hold new elections while the state was threatened on all sides. The Scots and Irish immediately proclaimed the exiled prince—in France with his mother, Henrietta Maria—as Charles II and gathered armies to invade England; invasion was also threatened from Europe. Royalist newsletters and Presbyterian pulpits exploded in fury, pronouncing it sacrilege to execute a king anointed by God. The government party, including Milton, had to argue somewhat uncomfortably that popular sovereignty for the present could only extend to the "well affected" and that the good men raised up by God to serve the cause of liberty—the Rump and the army—could act for the whole people.

But the new establishment was not threatened by royalists alone. The Rump and the army were at odds with one another, divided within themselves, and attacked by a chorus of voices demanding far more radical religious and political reform. Millenarians and Fifth Monarchists called for political power to be given to regenerate "Saints," in preparation for the last days and the thousand-year reign of Christ. Quakers were seen to defy state and church authority by refusing to take oaths or remove their hats and by denouncing ministers in their own pulpits—practices that often landed them in prison. The rank and file of the army contained many so-called Levellers, who held that "all power is originally and essentially in the whole body of the people" and insisted that voting rights should not be limited to men of property. Still more threatening in principle if not in fact were the "True Levellers" or Diggers, a few poor men who set out on April 1, 1649, to cultivate waste lands in Surrey as a symbolic claim to rights in the common lands and, in theory, to all property; their leader, Gerrard Winstanley, wrote eloquent manifestos urging their Christian communist program. Most alarming of all, out of all proportion to their scant numbers, were the Ranters, who believed that because God dwelt in them none of their acts could be sinful; some acted on that belief by running naked in the streets, or by open sexual license, or by blaspheming and swearing (hence their name).

The threat of invasion was dispelled by Oliver Cromwell's victories in Ireland and Scotland. The war in Ireland was especially bloody as Cromwell's army slaughtered the native Irish without quarter in a frenzy of religious hatred. The republic gained international prestige by winning notable sea victories in the Anglo-Dutch War (1652–54), which erupted over trade rivalries and supremacy in the English Channel. But, given continued popular disaffection, the republic's leaders still could not find a way to call new elections, and relations between the Rump and army grew worse. In 1653 Cromwell expelled the Rump and convened a new legislature dominated by radical sectaries and Millenarians. This so-called "Barebones" Parliament, nicknamed for a prominent member, Praisegod Barebone, self-destructed in less than six months, and at the end of the year Cromwell was sworn in as Protector for life under England's first written constitution. The transition was comparatively smooth, save for outraged republicans opposed to any "single person," Fifth Monarchists who thought Cromwell had usurped the place of "King Jesus" soon to appear, and royalists who continued to act in the interests of Charles II. Many property owners adhered to Cromwell as the only hope for stability and settlement, while others, including Milton, did so because religious liberty was more secure with him than with the Rump or the other parliaments. Quakers and Ranters continued to receive harsh treatment, though Cromwell intervened sometimes to rescue Quakers from prison. He also began a program to readmit Jews to England, partly in the interests of trade but also to open the way for their conversion, supposedly a precursor of the last days as prophesied in the New Testament Book of Revelation.

Cromwell succumbed to a virulent influenza epidemic and died on September 3, 1658. Had he lived longer he might have restored monarchy to England by having himself crowned; his last constitution contained several monarchical features. In early 1660, in conditions of mounting chaos, General George Monk marched from Scotland to London proclaiming his firm support for the republic, but he soon called elections for a new "full and free" parliament that everyone knew would restore the king. As Monk played out his hand and negotiated secretly with Charles, royalist and Presbyterian preachers ridiculed and denounced the republic in pulpit and press. A few republicans and radicals made last-ditch efforts to stave off the inevitable: the last polemic plea for the Good Old Cause was probably Milton's *Ready and Easy Way to Establish a Free Commonwealth*, published in late April 1660. On May 8, 1660, Charles II was officially proclaimed king; he landed at Dover on May 25 and made a triumphal entry into London four days later.

Over the next few years some regicides were executed and others were imprisoned, the court and the Anglican church were restored to full glory, and Puritan dissenters were harshly repressed. But royal absolutism was not restored. Parliament was now a force to be reckoned with; and the merchant classes, filled with dissenters, had powerful economic leverage. Less than three decades after Charles II returned, his brother, the Roman Catholic King James II, who had succeeded because Charles had no legitimate progeny, was frightened into fleeing the country in the so-called "Glorious Revolution" of 1688. The throne was transferred to the Dutch Protestant William of Orange and his wife, Mary, a daughter of James II. The English revolution was apparently dismantled in 1660, but its long-term effects profoundly changed English institutions and English society.

LITERATURE AND CULTURE, 1640–60

One of Parliament's first acts after hostilities began in 1642 was to abolish public sports and stage plays as unsuited to the calamitous times, "being spectacles of pleasure, too commonly expressing lascivious mirth and levity." The last play produced was Richard Brome's *A Jovial Crew: Or, The Merry Beggars*. During the next fifteen years, London theaters were dismantled and destroyed: the Globe, Blackfriars, the Phoenix, the Fortune, and the beargardens. Dramatic literature continued to be published—some Caroline plays in the 1640s and Brome's play in 1652. Also, both royalists and antiroyalists wrote play-pamphlets about real-life dramas, such as *The Famous Tragedie of King Charles I. Basely Butchered* (1649). Despite the prohibitions, some plays were put on stage in England. Beaumont and Fletcher's *Wit without Money* was performed in February 1648 at the Red Bull Theater. Under the Protectorate, some erstwhile royalist playwrights used the new fashion for opera to develop "reformed" dramas. William Davenant's *First Day's Entertainment at Rutland House* (1656) and James Shirley's *Cupid and Death* were presented in quasi-private circumstances, but Davenant's *Cruelty of the Spaniards in Peru* (1658) was performed in the more public venue of the Cockpit Theater. This and other Davenant plays of the late 1650s dramatize crusades against the Turks and the Spaniards, emphasizing colonial and imperial myths.

During the revolutionary era many royalist authors found support in hard times from circles of friends. Also, with the disruption of their usual patronage networks, many decided to publish their verse. During the 1640s the bookseller Herbert Moseley collected and published volumes of poems by the Cavalier poets Thomas Carew, Sir John Denham, Edmund Waller, Sir John Suckling, James Shirley, Richard Lovelace, and Robert Herrick. Some of these poets fought for their king; others were imprisoned or fled abroad with the queen or went into "internal exile" at home. Their poems, some dating from the 1630s, celebrate royalist culture and the courtly ideal of the good life: wine, good food, good friends, good verses, hospitality, and loyalty to the king. One characteristic genre for them is the elegant love lyric, often with a *carpe diem* theme; other common themes are friendship and retirement. Stylistically, their verses are characterized by urbanity, smoothness, and (especially with Herrick) diligent attention to classical models. Several poems in Herrick's delightful collection of short lyrics, *Hesperides* (1648), celebrate those rural, quasi-pagan harvest festivals and May-day rituals so much criticized by Puritans. Others underscore the volume's dominant theme: "time's trans-shifting," the transience of all life, beauty, and poetry. Waller and Denham helped set the fashion for melodic rhymed stanzas and iambic pentameter couplets, which were to become normative verse patterns after the Restoration. The poems of Suckling and Lovelace construct a quintessential Cavalier persona with the qualities usually associated with those supporters of the king and queen. He talks amusingly, bawdily, charmingly, and sometimes sadly about the joys and tribulations of love, the conflicts of love and honor, loyalty to friends, and the trials of the times. He presents himself as an amateur, writing verse in the midst of a life devoted to more important matters: war, love, the king's service, and the endurance of loss.

During the 1650s, royalists wrote lyric poems in places removed from the hostile centers of parliamentary power. Henry Vaughan in Wales wrote religious verse expressing his intense longing for past biblical eras of innocence and for the perfection of heaven or the millennium, and representing himself in the present as a solitary wanderer seeking out the vestiges of God in nature. Also in Wales, Katherine Philips wrote and circulated in manuscript poems that celebrate female friends in the Platonic terms normally reserved for male friendships. Their publication after the Restoration brought Philips some celebrity as "The Matchless Orinda." Richard Crashaw, an exile in Paris and Rome and a convert to Roman Catholicism, is England's only major baroque poet. His poems treat typical baroque topics—weeping Magdalens, infant Saviors, rosy cherubs, tender Virgins, tormented martyrs, ecstatic saints—in the lush, sensuous language that, according to Counter-Reformation aesthetics, could reveal the spiritual by stimulating the senses. Margaret Cavendish, duchess of Newcastle, also in exile with the queen in Paris, published two collections of lyrics when she returned to England in

1653; a number of these poems are about her own role as poet. After the Restoration she published several dramas and her remarkable utopian romance, *The Blazing World* (1668), which imagines a world governed by an empress with absolute power to rule as she will and learn what she wishes. Cavendish claims for herself as author a comparable absolutism in creating fictional worlds.

The most important English philosopher and political theorist of the earlier seventeenth century, Thomas Hobbes, was also an exile in Paris, as longtime tutor and secretary in the Cavendish family. While there he developed his materialist philosophy and psychology, his critique of language, and, in *Leviathan* (1651), his unflinching analysis and defense of absolute and indivisible sovereignty based on social contract. As his argument validates whatever government is in power and can preserve peace and security—whether Stuart kings, the republic, or Cromwell—he was distrusted by royalists and republicans alike. Claims of royal legitimacy and assertions of the rights and liberties of the people are alike irrelevant in Hobbes's political theory.

Several prose works by royalists have become classics of their respective prose genres. They seem to have little or nothing to do with the contemporary scene but in fact they carry a political charge. In his *Life of Donne*, Izaak Walton went some distance toward producing a scholarly biography: he drew on his personal knowledge of Donne in his later years, collected facts and sometimes dubious anecdotes from those who knew him, and read his letters and personal papers. But Walton's overall design presents Donne as a latter-day St. Augustine—rakish in youth, saintly in his later life as dean of St. Paul's. Published as a preface to a collection of Donne's sermons in 1640, when religious tensions were growing and war loomed on the horizon, Walton's work makes Donne a modern "saint" of Anglicanism. Later, Walton wrote an enormously popular treatise on fishing, *The Complete Angler* (1653), presenting it as a dialogue between Walton's warm-hearted persona, Piscator the angler, and a hunter, Venator, a figure for busy, warlike Puritans. Sir Thomas Browne published *Religio Medici* (A Doctor's Religion) in 1642/43, offering it as a portrait of his mind. Browne presents himself as a genial, speculative doctor who contains in himself many paradoxes and idiosyncratic views but willingly submits his judgment to the Church of England, who loves ritual and ceremony, who finds nothing human foreign to him, and who can sympathize with and worship with all Christians, even Roman Catholics. The subtext presents him as a model of Anglican inclusiveness and charity, a sharp contrast to reforming Puritans bent on ridding the church of its errors. Browne's other works published in this period display his Baconian, antiquarian, and mystical sides. The omnipresent prose genre of the revolutionary era was the polemic tract. Tracts large and small addressed all aspects of all the religious, social, and political controversies. Many voices are memorable for their rhetorical and literary power amid that hubbub: the Leveller John Lilburne, the Digger Gerrard Winstanley, the tolerationist Roger Williams, the prophet Anna Trapnall, and Milton.

It is no surprise that the revolutionary era gave new impetus to women's writing. The overturning of boundaries and the circumstances of war that placed women in novel and sometimes dangerous situations gave them unusual events to chronicle and prompted self-discovery. Autobiographies of three royalist women, Lady Anne Halkett, Lady Anne Fanshaw, and Margaret Cavendish, duchess of Newcastle, all published after the Restoration, report their emotions, their love relationships, and their sometimes daring activities during those trying days. On the revolutionary side, Lucy Hutchinson's *Memoir* of her husband, Colonel John Hutchinson, treats his life with her and his significant role in the war and in government within a narrative that is also a republican history of those times; it was first published in 1806, along with an autobiographical fragment dealing with her early life. She left in manuscript several poems on personal and political themes. Leveller women joined the polemic fray, offering petitions and manifestos in support of their imprisoned husbands and their cause. Quaker women came into their own as preachers and sometimes writers of tracts, authorized by Quaker belief that all persons should testify to what the Inner Light of the Spirit communicates to them. Among the Quaker Margaret Fell's several treatises is one justifying women speaking in church. Female prophets came forth in some numbers during the revolution, their claims to divine inspiration gaining currency from the widespread belief that the Spirit was moving in unexpected ways. The published prophecies of Lady Eleanor Davies, Mary Cary, and Anna Trapnell often carried a strong political critique of Charles or Cromwell. Trapnell dictated her ecstatic visions to scribes, but she also wrote a lively autobiographical report of her adventures and persecution during a missionary journey in the west of England.

If the royalist side claimed most of the poets and the writers of literary prose during this period, the revolution could claim the best of them: Marvell and Milton. During several regimes, Andrew Marvell maintained his independent vision and his firm commitment to religious toleration. He wrote most of his supremely artful lyrics and political poems while at Nunappleton in 1650–52, tutoring the daughter of the retired parliamentary general Sir Thomas Fairfax; in 1657 he joined his friend Milton in the office of Cromwell's Latin Secretariat. All of his poems play wittily with genre and literary convention. His love poems span the spectrum from *carpe diem* invitations to love to neoplatonic affirmations of the absolute split between soul and body, to near-postmodern perceptions that what attracts love is only an unstable set of shifting images. His pastorals, spoken as dramatic monologues by such unusual figures as Damon the Mower, disrupt pastoral norms of contentment and harmony between humans and nature. Several of his political poems are praises of Cromwell, but the finest of them, *An Horatian Ode upon Cromwell's Return from Ireland,* also invites sympathy for the executed king. It recognizes Cromwell as a providential force and celebrates his Irish victory, but also indicates the potential danger in his military successes and meteoric rise to power as a kind of Caesar. Marvell's very long poem celebrating his patron's estate, *Upon Appleton House,* attains something like epic scope, as it locates the static, mythic features traditionally celebrated in country-house poems within the course of providential history in Israel and England, a history that includes the chaotic events of the English revolution.

Milton's commitment to the revolution was unwavering, early to late, despite his disillusion when it failed to realize his fundamental ideals: religious toleration for all Protestants and the free circulation of ideas without prior censorship. He argued for those ideals in the most impressive and enduring polemic of the age, his eloquent, brilliantly imagistic *Areopagitica*

(1644). First as self-appointed advisor to the state, then as its official defender, he addressed the other great issues under debate and argued for his own positions: removal of the bishops "root and branch"; the necessity of divorce for incompatibility so as to relieve widespread human unhappiness; justifications for tyrannicide and republican government based on natural law and popular sovereignty; the right of those who love liberty to act, if necessary, for the whole people; denial to magistrates of any power over religion; church disestablishment; the manifest evils of kingship; and the divine preference for republican government. He was a Puritan, but both his theological heterodoxies and his poetic vision mark him as a distinctly unusual one.

During the twenty years in which he wrote polemics in support of these causes, Milton also wrote several sonnets, revising that small kind to accommodate large public and private topics: a threatened attack by the royalist army on London; praise of and advice to Cromwell about the church; agonizing questions posed by his blindness; and the massacre of the proto-Protestant Waldensians by Roman Catholic forces in the Piedmont. In 1645 he published his collected poems in a double volume, English and Latin, offering it as a counterstatement to the royalist volumes of the 1640s. He wrote some part of *Paradise Lost* in the 1650s and completed it after the Restoration, encompassing in it all he had thought, read, and experienced of tyranny, political rhetoric, evil, deception, love, the need for human companionship, the woes and the good of human life. This stunning, cosmic, blank-verse epic assimilates and critiques the epic tradition and Milton's entire intellectual and literary heritage, classical and Christian. Yet it has at its center not martial heroes but a domestic pair, whose challenge is to discover how to live the good human life day by day, in Eden and later in the fallen world, amid intense emotional pressures and the seductions of evil.

Seventeenth-century poetry and prose retains its hold on readers because so much of it is so very good, fusing (as T. S. Eliot recognized) intellectual strength, emotional passion, and linguistic artfulness. We have in Donne and Marvell love poetry at once cerebral, witty, and passionate; in Donne and Herbert religious poetry at once deeply felt and highly artful; in Jonson tough-minded analyses of what is worthy of praise and blame in the social order; in Herrick some of the most exquisite short lyrics in the English language; in Crashaw the most extravagantly baroque as well as, arguably, the most musical poet in our literature. We watch English prose become a highly flexible instrument, suited to informal essays, scientific or political treatises, religious meditation, biography and autobiography, and vigorous polemic. We observe a number of literary forms evolve for the analysis or dramatization or representation of the self: dramatic monologues portraying the self or several imagined selves in various love situations; religious meditations on the state of the soul; meditations on personal experiences like illness; intellectual or spiritual autobiographies; sermons in which the preacher takes himself as example. Finally, we have in Milton an epic poet who assumed the role of inspired prophet, envisioning a world produced by God but shaped by human choice and imagination.

THE EARLY SEVENTEENTH CENTURY

TEXTS	CONTEXTS
1603　James I, *Basilikon Doran* reissued	1603　Death of Elizabeth I; accession of James I. Plague
1604　William Shakespeare, *Othello*	
1605　Shakespeare, *King Lear*. Ben Jonson, *The Masque of Blackness*. Francis Bacon, *The Advancement of Learning*	1605　Gunpowder Plot, failed effort by Roman Catholic extremists to blow up Parliament
1606　Jonson, *Volpone*. Shakespeare, *MacBeth*	
	1607　Founding of Jamestown colony in Virginia
1609　Shakespeare, *Sonnets*	1609　Galileo's telescope
1611　"King James" Bible (Authorized Version). Shakespeare, *The Tempest*. John Donne, *The First Anniversary*. Aemilia Lanyer, *Salve Deus Rex Judaeorum*	
1612　Donne, *The Second Anniversary*	1612　Death of Prince Henry
1613　Elizabeth Cary, *The Tragedy of Mariam*	
1614　John Webster, *The Duchess of Malfi*	
1616　Jonson, *Works*. James I, *Works*	1616　Death of Shakespeare
	1618　Beginning of the Thirty Years War
	1619　First African slaves in North America exchanged by Dutch frigate for food and supplies at Jamestown
1620　Bacon, *Novum Organum*	1620　Pilgrims land at Plymouth
1621　Mary Wroth, *The Countess of Montgomery's Urania*. Robert Burton, *Anatomy of Melancholy*	1621　Donne appointed dean of St. Paul's Cathedral
1623　Shakespeare, First Folio	
	1625　Death of James I; accession of Charles I; Charles I marries Henrietta Maria
	1629　Charles I dissolves Parliament
1633　Donne, *Poems*. George Herbert, *The Temple*	1633　Galileo forced by the Inquisition to recant the Copernican theory
1637　John Milton, *Lycidas*	
1640　Thomas Carew, *Poems*	1640　Long Parliament called (1640–53). Archbishop Laud impeached
1642　Thomas Browne, *Religio Medici*. Milton, *Reason of Church Government*	1642　First Civil War begins (1642–46). Parliament closes the theaters
1643　Milton, *Doctrine and Discipline of Divorce*	1643　Accession of Louis XIV of France
1644　Milton, *Areopagitica*	
1645　Milton, *Poems*. Edmund Waller, *Poems*	1645　Archbishop Laud executed. Royalists defeated at Naseby

TEXTS	CONTEXTS
1648 Robert Herrick, *Hesperides*	**1648** Second Civil War. Pride's Purge of Parliament
1649 Milton, *Eikonoklastes*	**1649** Trial and execution of Charles I. Republic declared. Milton becomes Latin Secretary (1649–59)
1650 Henry Vaughan, *Silex Scintillans* (Part II, 1655)	
1651 Thomas Hobbes, *Leviathan.* Andrew Marvell, *Upon Appleton House* (unpublished)	
	1652 Dutch War (1652–53)
	1653 Cromwell made Lord Protector
	1658 Death of Cromwell; his son Richard made Protector
1660 Milton, *Ready and Easy Way to Establish a Free Commonwealth*	**1660** Restoration of Charles II to throne. Royal Society founded
	1662 Charles II marries Catherine of Braganza
	1665 The Great Plague
1666 Margaret Cavendish, *The Blazing World*	**1666** The Great Fire
1667 Milton, *Paradise Lost* (in ten books). Katherine Philips, *Collected Poems.* John Dryden, *Annus Mirabilis*	
1671 Milton, *Paradise Regained* and *Samson Agonistes*	
1674 Milton, *Paradise Lost* (in twelve books)	**1674** Death of Milton
1681 Marvell, *Poems,* published posthumously	

JOHN DONNE
1572–1631

Lovers' eyeballs threaded on a string. A god who assaults the human heart with a battering ram. A teardrop that encompasses and drowns the world. John Donne's poems abound with startling images, some of them exalting and others grotesque. With his strange and playful intelligence, expressed in puns, paradoxes, and the elaborately sustained metaphors known as "conceits," Donne has enthralled and sometimes enraged readers from his day to our own. The tired clichés of love poetry—cheeks like roses, hearts pierced by the arrows of love—emerge reinvigorated and radically transformed by his hand, demanding from the reader an unprecedented level of mental alertness and engagement. Donne prided himself on his wit and displayed it not only in his conceits but in his grasp of learned and obscure discourses ranging from theology to alchemy, from cosmology to law. Yet for all their ostentatious intellectuality, Donne's poems never give the impression of being academic exercises put into verse. Rather, they are intense dramatic monologues in which the speaker's ideas and feelings seem to shift and evolve from one line to the next. Donne's prosody is equally dramatic, mirroring in its variable and jagged rhythms the effect of speech (and eliciting from his classically minded contemporary Ben Jonson the gruff observation that "Donne, for not keeping of accent deserved hanging").

Donne began life as an outsider, and in some respects remained one until death. He was born in London in 1572 into a devout Roman Catholic household. The family was prosperous, but, as the poet later remarked, none had suffered more heavily for its loyalty to the Catholic Church: "I have been ever kept awake in a meditation of martyrdom." Donne was distantly related to the great Catholic humanist and martyr Sir Thomas More. Closer to home, a Jesuit uncle was executed by the brutal method of hanging, drawing, quartering, and disemboweling, and his own brother Henry, arrested for harboring a priest, died in prison of the plague. As a Catholic in Protestant England, growing up in decades when anti-Roman feeling reached new heights, Donne could not expect any kind of public career, nor even to receive a university degree (he left Oxford without one and studied law for a time at the Inns of Court). What he could reasonably expect instead was prejudice, official harrassment, and crippling financial penalties. He chose not to live under such conditions. At some point in the 1590s, having returned to London after travels abroad, and having devoted some years to studying theological issues, Donne converted to the English Church.

The poems that belong with certainty to this period of his life—the five Satires and most of the Elegies—reveal a man both fascinated by and keenly critical of English society. Four of the satires treat commonplace Elizabethan topics—foppish and obsequious courtiers, bad poets, corrupt lawyers and a corrupt court—but are unique both in their visceral revulsion and in their intellectual excitement. Donne uses striking images of pestilence, itchy lust, vomit, excrement, and pox to create a unique satiric world, busy, vibrant, and corrupt, in which his dramatic speakers have only to step outside the door to be innundated by all the fools and knaves in Christendom. By contrast, the third satire treats the quest for true religion—the question that preoccupied him above all others in these years—in terms that are serious, passionately witty, and deeply felt. Donne argues that honest doubting search is better than the facile acceptance of any religious tradition, epitomizing that point brilliantly in the image of Truth on a high and craggy hill, very difficult to climb. What is certain is that society's values are of no help whatsoever to the individual seeker—none will escape the final judgment by pleading that "A Harry, or a Martin taught [them] this." In the love Elegies Donne seems intent on making up for his social powerlessness through witty representations of mastery in the bedroom and of adventurous travel.

In *Elegy 16* he imagines his speaker embarking on a journey "O'er the white Alps" and with mingled tenderness and condescension argues down a naive mistress's proposal to accompany him. And in *Elegy 19*, his fondling of a naked lover becomes in a famous conceit the equivalent of exploration in America. Donne's interest in satire and elegy—classical Roman genres which he helped introduce to English verse—is itself significant. He wrote in English, but he reached out to other traditions.

If Donne's conversion to the Church of England promised him security, social acceptance, and the possibility of a public career, that promise was soon to be cruelly withdrawn. In 1596–97 he participated in the earl of Essex's military expeditions against Catholic Spain in Cádiz and the Azores (the experience prompted two remarkable descriptive poems of life at sea, *The Storm* and *The Calm*) and upon his return became secretary to Sir Thomas Egerton, Lord Keeper of the Great Seal. This should have been the beginning of a successful public career. But his secret marriage in 1601 to Egerton's seventeen-year-old niece Ann More enraged Donne's employer and the bride's wealthy father; Donne was briefly imprisoned and dismissed from service. The poet was reduced to a retired country life beset by financial insecurity and a rapidly increasing family; Ann bore twelve children (not counting miscarriages) by the time she died at age thirty-three. At one point, Donne wrote despairingly that while the death of a child would mean one less mouth to feed, he could not afford the burial expenses. In this bleak period, he wrote but dared not publish a paradoxical defense of suicide (*Biathanatos*).

As his family grew, Donne made every effort to reinstate himself in the favor of the great. To win the approval of James I, he penned *Pseudo-Martyr* (1610), defending the king's insistence that Catholics take the Oath of Allegiance. This set an irrevocable public stamp on his renunciation of Catholicism, and Donne followed up with a witty satire on the Jesuits, *Ignatius his Conclave* (1611). In the same period he was producing a steady stream of occasional poems for friends and patrons such as Somerset (the king's favorite), the countess of Bedford, and Magdalen Herbert, and for small coteries of courtiers and ladies. Like most gentlemen of his era, Donne saw poetry as a polite accomplishment rather than as a trade or vocation, and in consequence he circulated his poems in manuscript but left most of them uncollected and unpublished. In 1611 and 1612, however, he published the first and second *Anniversaries* on the death of the daughter of his patron, Sir Robert Drury.

For some years King James had urged an ecclesiastical career on Donne, denying him any other means of advancement. In 1615 Donne finally consented, overcoming his sense of unworthiness and the pull of other ambitions. He was ordained in the Church of England and entered upon a distinguished career as court preacher, reader in divinity at Lincoln's Inn, and dean of St. Paul's. Donne's metaphorical style, bold erudition, and dramatic wit established him as a great preacher in an age that appreciated learned sermons powerfully delivered. Some 160 of his sermons survive, preached to monarchs and courtiers, lawyers and London magistrates, city merchants and trading companies. As a distinguished clergyman in the Church of England, Donne had traveled an immense distance from the religion of his childhood and the adventurous life of his twenties. Yet in his sermons and late poems we find the same brilliant and idiosyncratic mind at work, refashioning his profane conceits to serve a new and higher purpose. In *Expostulation 19* he praises God as the greatest of literary stylists: "a figurative, a metaphorical God," imagining God as a conceit-maker like himself. In poems, meditations, and sermons, Donne came increasingly to be engaged in anxious contemplation of his own mortality. In *A Hymn to God my God in my Sickness*, Donne imagines himself spread out on his deathbed like a map showing the route to the next world. Only a few days before his death he preached *Death's Duel*, a terrifying analysis of all life as a decline toward death and dissolution which contemporaries termed his own funeral sermon. On his deathbed, according to his contemporary biographer Izaak Walton, Donne had a portrait made of himself in his shroud and meditated on it daily. Meditations upon skulls as emblems of mortality were common in the period, but nothing is more characteristic of Donne than to find a way to meditate on his own skull.

Given the shape of Donne's career, it is no surprise that his poems and prose works display an astonishing variety of attitudes, viewpoints, and feelings on the great subjects of love and religion. Yet this variety cannot be fully explained in biographical terms. The poet's own attempt to distinguish between Jack Donne, the young rake, and Dr. Donne, the grave and religious dean of St. Paul's, is (perhaps intentionally) misleading. We do not know the time and circumstances for most of Donne's verses, but it is clear that many of his finest religious poems predate his ordination, and it is possible that he continued to add to the love poems known as his *Songs and Sonnets* after he entered the Church. Theological language abounds in his love poetry, and daringly erotic images occur in his religious verse.

Although they were not widely known in his lifetime, Donne's *Songs and Sonnets* have been the cornerstone of his reputation almost since their publication in 1633. The title associates them with the popular miscellanies of love poems and sonnet sequences in the Petrarchan tradition, but they directly challenge the popular Petrarchan sonnet sequences of the 1590s. The collection contains only one formal sonnet, the "Songs" are not notably lyrical, and Donne draws upon and transforms a whole range of literary traditions concerned with love. Like Petrarch, Donne can present himself as the despairing lover of an unattainable lady (*The Funeral*); like Ovid he can be lighthearted, witty, cynical, and frankly lustful (*The Flea, The Indifferent*); like the Neoplatonists, he espouses a theory of transcendant love, but he breaks from them with his insistence in many poems on the union of physical and spiritual love. What binds these poems together and grants them enduring power is their compelling immediacy. The speaker is always in the throes of intense emotion, and that emotion is not static but constantly shifting and evolving with the turns of the poet's thought. Donne seems supremely present in these poems, standing behind their various speakers. Where Petrarchan poets exhaustively catalogue their beloved's physical features (though in highly conventional terms), Donne's speakers tell us little or nothing about the loved woman, or about the male friends imagined as audience for many poems. Donne's repeated insistence that the private world of lovers is superior to the wider public world, or that it somehow contains all of that world, or obliterates it, is understandable in light of the many disappointments of his career. Yet this was also a poet who threw himself headlong into life, love, and sexuality, and later into the very visible public role of court and city preacher.

Donne was long grouped with Herbert, Vaughan, Crashaw, Marvell, Traherne, and Cowley under the heading of "Metaphysical Poets." The expression was first employed by critics like Samuel Johnson and William Hazlitt, who found the intricate conceits and self-conscious learning of these poets incompatible with poetic beauty and sincerity. Early in the twentieth century, T. S. Eliot sought to restore their reputation, attributing to them a unity of thought and feeling which had since their time been lost. Today the term "Metaphysicals" seems more an obstacle than an aid to understanding these very different poets. There was certainly no formal "school" of metaphysical poetry, and the characteristics ascribed to it by later critics pertain chiefly to Donne. Like Ben Jonson, John Donne had a large influence on the succeeding generation, but he remains a singularity.

FROM SONGS AND SONNETS[1]

The Flea[2]

Mark but this flea, and mark in this,
How little that which thou deniest me is;
Me it sucked first, and now sucks thee,
And in this flea our two bloods mingled be;
5 Thou know'st that this cannot be said
A sin, or shame, or loss of maidenhead,
    Yet this enjoys before it woo,
    And pampered swells with one blood made of two,[3]
    And this, alas, is more than we would do.

10 Oh stay, three lives in one flea spare,
Where we almost, nay more than married are.
This flea is you and I, and this
Our marriage bed and marriage temple is;
Though parents grudge, and you, we are met,
15 And cloistered[4] in these living walls of jet.°   *black*
    Though use° make you apt to kill[5] me,   *habit*
    Let not to that, self-murder added be,
    And sacrilege, three sins in killing three.

  Cruel and sudden, hast thou since
20 Purpled thy nail in blood of innocence?
Wherein could this flea guilty be,
Except in that drop which it sucked from thee?
Yet thou triumph'st, and say'st that thou
Find'st not thy self nor me the weaker now;
25   'Tis true; then learn how false fears be:
    Just so much honor, when thou yield'st to me,
    Will waste, as this flea's death took life from thee.

1633

The Good-Morrow

I wonder, by my troth, what thou and I
Did, till we loved? Were we not weaned till then,
But sucked on country pleasures, childishly?

1. Donne's love poems were written over nearly two decades, beginning around 1595; they were not published in Donne's lifetime but circulated widely in manuscript. The title *Songs and Sonnets* was supplied in the second edition (1635), which grouped the poems by kind, but neither this arrangement nor the more haphazard organization of the first edition (1633) is Donne's own. In Donne's time the term *sonnet* often meant simply "love lyric," and in fact there is only one formal sonnet in this collection. For the poems we present we follow the 1635 edition, beginning with the extremely popular poem *The Flea*.
2. This insect afforded a popular erotic theme for poets all over Europe, deriving from a pseudo-Ovidian medieval poem in which a lover envies the flea for the liberties it takes with his mistress's body.
3. The swelling suggests pregnancy.
4. As in a convent or monastery.
5. "Kill" carries an allusion to sexual intercourse.

Or snorted° in the seven sleepers' den?[1]   *snored*
5   'Twas so; but° this, all pleasures fancies be.   *except for*
     If ever any beauty I did see,
     Which I desired, and got, 'twas but a dream of thee.

     And now good morrow to our waking souls,
     Which watch not one another out of fear;
10 For love all love of other sights controls,
     And makes one little room an everywhere.
     Let sea-discoverers to new worlds have gone,
     Let maps to others, worlds on worlds have shown:
     Let us possess one world;[2] each hath one, and is one.

15 My face in thine eye, thine in mine appears,
     And true plain hearts do in the faces rest;
     Where can we find two better hemispheres,
     Without sharp North, without declining West?
     Whatever dies was not mixed equally;[3]
20 If our two loves be one, or thou and I
     Love so alike that none do slacken, none can die.

1633

Song

     Go and catch a falling star,
       Get with child a mandrake root,[1]
     Tell me where all past years are,
       Or who cleft the Devil's foot,
5   Teach me to hear mermaids° singing,   *sirens*
     Or to keep off envy's stinging,
        And find
        What wind
     Serves to advance an honest mind.

10 If thou beest born to strange sights,
       Things invisible to see,
     Ride ten thousand days and nights,
       Till age snow white hairs on thee,
     Thou, when thou return'st, wilt tell me
15 All strange wonders that befell thee,
       And swear
       No where
     Lives a woman true, and fair.

1. Cave in Ephesus where, according to legend, seven Christian youths hid from pagan persecutors and slept for 187 years.
2. "Our world" in many manuscripts.
3. Scholastic philosophy taught that when the elements were imperfectly ("not equally") mixed, matter was mutable and mortal; conversely, when the elements were perfectly mixed, matter was immutable and hence immortal.
1. The mandrake root, or mandragora, is forked like the lower part of the human body. It was thought to shriek when pulled from the ground and to kill all humans who heard it; it was also (paradoxically) thought to help women conceive.

If thou find'st one, let me know,
20   Such a pilgrimage were sweet;
Yet do not, I would not go,
      Though at next door we might meet;
Though she were true when you met her,
And last till you write your letter,
25   Yet she
        Will be
False, ere I come, to two, or three.

1633

The Undertaking

I have done one braver thing
      Than all the Worthies[1] did,
And yet a braver thence doth spring,
      Which is, to keep that hid.

5   It were but madness now t' impart
      The skill of specular stone,[2]
When he which can have learned the art
      To cut it, can find none.

So, if I now should utter this,
10   Others (because no more
Such stuff to work upon, there is)
      Would love but as before.

But he who loveliness within
      Hath found, all outward loathes,
15   For he who color loves, and skin,
      Loves but their oldest clothes.

If, as I have, you also do
      Virtue attired in woman see,
And dare love that, and say so too,
20   And forget the He and She;

And if this love, though placèd so,
      From profane men you hide,
Which will no faith on this bestow,
      Or, if they do, deride;

25   Then you have done a braver thing
      Than all the Worthies did;

1. According to medieval legend, the Nine Worthies, or supreme heroes of history, included three Jews (Joshua, David, Judas Maccabeus), three pagans (Hector, Alexander, Julius Caesar), and three Christians (Arthur, Charlemagne, Godfrey of Bouillon).
2. A transparent or translucent material, reputed to have been used in antiquity for windows, but no longer known. Great skill was needed to cut it.

And a braver thence will spring,
Which is, to keep that hid.

1633

The Sun Rising[1]

Busy old fool, unruly sun,
Why dost thou thus
Through windows and through curtains call on us?
Must to thy motions lovers' seasons run?
5   Saucy pedantic wretch, go chide
Late schoolboys and sour prentices,
Go tell court huntsmen that the King will ride,[2]
Call country ants to harvest offices;[3]
Love, all alike, no season knows nor clime,
10   Nor hours, days, months, which are the rags of time.

Thy beams, so reverend and strong
Why shouldst thou think?
I could eclipse and cloud them with a wink,
But that I would not lose her sight so long;
15   If her eyes have not blinded thine,
Look, and tomorrow late, tell me,
Whether both th' Indias of spice and mine[4]
Be where thou leftst them, or lie here with me.
Ask for those kings whom thou saw'st yesterday,
20   And thou shalt hear, All here in one bed lay.

She is all states,° and all princes I,   *nations*
Nothing else is.
Princes do but play us; compared to this,
All honor's mimic, all wealth alchemy.
25   Thou, sun, art half as happy as we,
In that the world's contracted thus;
Thine age asks ease, and since thy duties be
To warm the world, that's done in warming us.
Shine here to us, and thou art everywhere;
30   This bed thy center is,[5] these walls thy sphere.

1633

The Indifferent[1]

I can love both fair and brown,[2]
Her whom abundance melts, and her whom want betrays,

---

1. Some lines of this poem recall Ovid, *Amores*
1.13.
2. King James was very fond of hunting.
3. Autumn chores. "Country ants": farm drudges.
4. The India of "spice" is East India; that of "mine"
(gold) is the West Indies.

5. According to the old Ptolemaic astronomy, the
earth was the center of the sun's orbit, and the
sun's motion was contained within its sphere.
1. Some lines of this poem recall Ovid, *Amores*
2.4.
2. Both blond and brunet.

Her who loves loneness best, and her who masks and plays,
Her whom the country formed, and whom the town,
5 Her who believes, and her who tries,°   *tests*
Her who still weeps with spongy eyes,
And her who is dry cork, and never cries;
I can love her, and her, and you, and you,
I can love any, so she be not true.

10 Will no other vice content you?
Will it not serve your turn to do as did your mothers?
Or have you all old vices spent, and now would find out others?
Or doth a fear that men are true torment you?
O we are not, be not you so;
15 Let me, and do you, twenty know.
Rob me, but bind me not, and let me go.
Must I, who came to travail thorough³ you,
Grow your fixed subject, because you are true?

Venus heard me sigh this song,
20 And by love's sweetest part, variety, she swore,
She heard not this till now; and that it should be so no more.
She went, examined, and returned ere long,
And said, Alas, some two or three
Poor heretics in love there be,
25 Which think to 'stablish dangerous constancy.
But I have told them, Since you will be true,
You shall be true to them who are false to you.

                 1633

The Canonization¹

For God's sake hold your tongue, and let me love,
 Or chide my palsy, or my gout,
My five gray hairs, or ruined fortune, flout,
  With wealth your state, your mind with arts improve,
5   Take you a course, get you a place,²
   Observe His Honor, or His Grace,³
Or the King's real, or his stampèd face⁴
  Contemplate; what you will, approve,°   *try, test*
  So you will let me love.

10 Alas, alas, who's injured by my love?
  What merchant's ships have my sighs drowned?
 Who says my tears have overflowed his ground?
  When did my colds a forward° spring remove?⁵   *early*
   When did the heats which my veins fill

3. Through. "Travail": grief, but also journey, travel.
1. The poem plays off against the Roman Catholic process of determining that certain persons are saints, proper objects of veneration and prayer.
2. An appointment, at court or elsewhere. "Take you a course": follow some career.
3. Pay court to some lord or bishop.
4. On coins; "real" (royal) refers also to a particular Spanish coin.
5. Petrarchan lovers traditionally sigh, weep, and are frozen by their mistresses' neglect.

15   Add one man to the plaguy bill?[6]
        Soldiers find wars, and lawyers find out still
            Litigious men, which quarrels move,
            Though she and I do love.

        Call us what you will, we are made such by love;
20   Call her one, me another fly,
        We're tapers too, and at our own cost die,[7]
            And we in us find the eagle and the dove.[8]
                The phoenix riddle hath more wit
                By us: we two being one, are it.
25   So, to one neutral thing both sexes fit.
            We die and rise the same, and prove
            Mysterious by this love.

        We can die by it, if not live by love,
            And if unfit for tombs and hearse
30   Our legend be, it will be fit for verse;
            And if no piece of chronicle we prove,
                We'll build in sonnets pretty rooms;[9]
                As well a well-wrought urn becomes°   *befits*
            The greatest ashes, as half-acre tombs,
35   And by these hymns,[1] all shall approve°   *confirm*
            Us canonized for love:

        And thus invoke us: You whom reverend love
            Made one another's hermitage;
        You, to whom love was peace, that now is rage;
40   Who did the whole world's soul contract,[2] and drove
            Into the glasses of your eyes
            (So made such mirrors, and such spies,°   *spyglasses, telescopes*
        That they did all to you epitomize)
            Countries, towns, courts:[3] Beg from above
45   A pattern of your love!

                                                            1633

---

6. Deaths from the plague, which raged in summer, were recorded by parish in weekly bills.
7. Flies were emblems of transience and lustfulness; tapers (candles) attract flies to their death and also consume themselves. "Die" in the punning terminology of the period means to experience orgasm, and there was a superstition that intercourse shortens life.
8. The eagle signifies strength and vision; the dove, meekness and mercy. The phoenix was a mythic Arabian bird, only one of which existed at any one time. After living five hundred years, it was consumed by fire, then rose triumphantly from its ashes a new bird. Thus it was a symbol of immor-

tality and sometimes associated with Christ. "Eagle" and "dove" are also alchemical terms for processes leading to the rise of "phoenix," a stage in the transmutation of metals to gold.
9. "Rooms" (punning on the Italian meaning of "stanza") will contain their exploits, as prose chronicle histories contain great deeds done in the world.
1. The lover's own poems.
2. An alternative meaning is "extract."
3. "Countries, towns, courts" are objects of the verb "drove." The notion is that eyes both see and reflect the outside world, and so can contain all of it.

Air and Angels

Twice or thrice had I loved thee,
Before I knew thy face or name;
So in a voice, so in a shapeless flame,
Angels affect us oft, and worshipped be;
5   Still° when, to where thou wert, I came,   *always*
Some lovely glorious nothing[1] I did see.
But since my soul, whose child love is,
Takes limbs of flesh, and else could nothing do,[2]
More subtle° than the parent is   *rarified*
10   Love must not be, but take a body too;
And therefore what thou wert, and who,
I bid love ask, and now
That it assume thy body I allow,
And fix itself in thy lip, eye, and brow.
15   Whilst thus to ballast love I thought,
And so more steadily to have gone,
With wares which would sink° admiration,   *overwhelm*
I saw I had love's pinnace° overfraught;°   *small boat/overballasted*
Every thy hair for love to work upon
20   Is much too much, some fitter must be sought;
For, nor in nothing, nor in things
Extreme and scatt'ring° bright, can love inhere.   *diffused, dazzling*
Then as an angel, face and wings
Of air, not pure as it, yet pure doth wear,
25   So thy love may be my love's sphere;[3]
Just such disparity
As is 'twixt air and angels' purity,
'Twixt women's love and men's will ever be.[4]

1633

Break of Day[1]

'Tis true, 'tis day; what though it be?
O wilt thou therefore rise from me?
Why should we rise because 'tis light?
Did we lie down because 'twas night?
5   Love, which in spite of darkness brought us hither,
Should in despite of light keep us together.
Light hath no tongue, but is all eye;
If it could speak as well as spy,
This were the worst that it could say,

---

1. Spiritual beauty, the true object of love in Neo-platonic philosophy.
2. My soul could not function unless it were in a body.
3. Each sphere was thought to be governed by an angel (an intelligence).
4. It was commonly believed that angels, when they appeared to humans, assumed a body of air

which, though pure, was less so than the angel's spiritual essence.
1. An aubade, or song of the lovers' parting at dawn, this poem is unusual for Donne in having a female speaker. The poem was given a musical setting and published in 1622, in William Corkine's *Second Book of Ayers*.

10   That being well, I fain would stay,
      And that I loved my heart and honor so
      That I would not from him, that had them, go.

      Must business thee from hence remove?
      O, that's the worst disease of love.
15   The poor, the foul, the false, love can
      Admit, but not the busied man.
      He which hath business, and makes love, doth do
      Such wrong, as when a married man doth woo.

1622, 1633

A Valediction:[1] Of Weeping

      Let me pour forth
My tears before thy face whilst I stay here,
For thy face coins them, and thy stamp° they bear,   *image*
And by this mintage they are something worth,
5   For thus they be
      Pregnant of thee;
Fruits of much grief they are, emblems° of more—   *symbols*
When a tear falls, that Thou falls which it bore,
So thou and I are nothing then, when on a diverse° shore.   *different*

10   On a round ball
A workman that hath copies by can lay
An Europe, Afric, and an Asia,
And quickly make that, which was nothing, all;[2]
      So doth each tear
15   Which thee doth wear,[3]
A globe, yea world, by that impression grow,
Till thy tears mixed with mine do overflow
This world; by waters sent from thee, my heaven dissolvèd so.

      O more than moon,
20 Draw not up seas to drown me in thy sphere;[4]
Weep me not dead in thine arms, but forbear
To teach the sea what it may do too soon.
      Let not the wind
      Example find
25 To do me more harm than it purposeth;
Since thou and I sigh one another's breath,
Whoe'er sighs most is cruelest, and hastes the other's death.

1633

1. A farewell poem, one of four so titled in the *Songs and Sonnets*. Another is *A Valediction: Forbidding Mourning*, p. 611.
2. I.e., on a blank globe one can place maps of the continents and so convert a cypher ("nothing") into the whole world ("all").
3. Bears your image.
4. A star or planet with more power of attraction than the moon might not only affect tides but draw the very seas unto itself.

Love's Alchemy

Some that have deeper digged love's mine than I,
Say where his centric° happiness doth lie: *central*
   I have loved, and got, and told,
   But should I love, get, tell, till I were old,
5   I should not find that hidden mystery;
      O, 'tis imposture all:
And as no chemic° yet the elixir[1] got,   *alchemist*
   But glorifies his pregnant pot[2]
   If by the way to him befall
10   Some odoriferous thing, or medicinal;
    So lovers dream a rich and long delight,
    But get a winter-seeming summer's night.[3]

Our ease, our thrift, our honor, and our day,
Shall we for this vain bubble's shadow pay?
15   Ends love in this, that my man°   *servant*
Can be as happy as I can, if he can
Endure the short scorn of a bridegroom's play?
    That loving wretch that swears
   'Tis not the bodies marry, but the minds,
20   Which he in her angelic finds,
    Would swear as justly that he hears,
In that day's rude hoarse minstrelsy, the spheres.[4]
    Hope not for mind in women; at their best
    Sweetness and wit, they are but mummy, possessed.[5]

1633

The Apparition

When by thy scorn, O murderess, I am dead,
   And that thou thinkst thee free
   From all solicitation from me,
Then shall my ghost come to thy bed,
5   And thee, feigned vestal,[1] in worse arms shall see;
Then thy sick taper will begin to wink,°   *flicker*
And he whose thou art then, being tired before,
Will, if thou stir, or pinch to wake him, think
   Thou call'st for more,

---

1. A magic medicine sought by alchemists and reputed to heal all ills.
2. A fertile (and womb-shaped) retort, calling up the common analogy between producing the elixir of life and human generation.
3. A night cold as in winter and short as in summer.
4. The perfect harmony of the planets, moving in concentric crystalline spheres, is contrasted with the boistrous serenade of pots, pans, and trumpets,

performed on the wedding night.
5. The syntax of the last two lines is unclear, and they are punctuated differently in various copies. The 1633 edition reads: "at their best, / Sweetnesse, and wit they'are, but, *mummy*, possesst." Many modern editors punctuate as we do here. "Mummy" suggests a corpselike body, without mind or spirit.
1. Virgins consecrated to the Roman goddess Vesta.

¹⁰ And in false sleep will from thee shrink,
And then, poor aspen wretch,² neglected thou
Bathed in a cold quicksilver sweat³ wilt lie
    A verier° ghost than I;   *truer*
What I will say, I will not tell thee now,
¹⁵ Lest that preserve thee; and since my love is spent,
I had rather thou shouldst painfully repent,
Than by my threatenings rest still innocent.

                                                                      1633

A Valediction: Forbidding Mourning¹

As virtuous men pass mildly away,
    And whisper to their souls to go,
Whilst some of their sad friends do say
    The breath goes now, and some say, No;

⁵ So let us melt, and make no noise,
    No tear-floods, nor sigh-tempests move;
'Twere profanation° of our joys   *desecration*
    To tell the laity our love.

Moving of th' earth brings harms and fears,
¹⁰   Men reckon what it did and meant;
But trepidation of the spheres,
    Though greater far, is innocent.²

Dull sublunary³ lovers' love
    (Whose soul is sense) cannot admit
¹⁵ Absence, because it doth remove
    Those things which elemented° it.   *composed*

But we, by a love so much refined
    That our selves know not what it is,
Inter-assurèd of the mind,
²⁰   Care less, eyes, lips, and hands to miss.

Our two souls therefore, which are one,
    Though I must go, endure not yet
A breach, but an expansion,
    Like gold to airy thinness beat.

2. Aspen leaves flutter in the slightest breeze.
3. Sweating in terror; quicksilver (mercury) was a stock prescription for venereal disease, and sweating was part of the cure.
1. For "valediction" see p. 609, n. 1. Izaak Walton speculated that this poem was addressed to Donne's wife on the occasion of his trip to the Continent in 1611, but there is no proof of that. Donne was, however, apprehensive about that trip; Walton also heard that, while abroad, Donne had a startling vision of his wife holding a dead baby at about the time she gave birth to a stillborn child.
2. Earthquakes cause damage and were thought to be portentous. Trepidation (in the Ptolemaic cosmology, an oscillation of the ninth or crystalline sphere imparted to all the inner spheres), though a much more violent motion than an earthquake, is neither destructive nor sinister.
3. Beneath the moon, therefore earthly, sensual, and subject to change.

25   If they be two, they are two so
      As stiff twin compasses⁴ are two;
    Thy soul, the fixed foot, makes no show
    To move, but doth, if th' other do.

    And though it in the center sit,
30   Yet when the other far doth roam,
    It leans and hearkens after it,
    And grows erect, as that comes home.

    Such wilt thou be to me, who must,
      Like th' other foot, obliquely run;
35   Thy firmness makes my circle just,
    And makes me end where I begun.

1633

The Ecstasy¹

    Where, like a pillow on a bed,
      A pregnant bank swelled up to rest
    The violet's reclining head,
      Sat we two, one another's best.

5   Our hands were firmly cemented
      With a fast balm° which thence did spring,   *perspiration*
    Our eye-beams² twisted, and did thread
      Our eyes upon one double string;

    So to intergraft our hands, as yet
10   Was all our means to make us one,
    And pictures in our eyes to get°   *beget*
      Was all our propagation.³

    As 'twixt two equal armies Fate
      Suspends uncertain victory,
15   Our souls (which to advance their state
      Were gone out) hung 'twixt her and me;

    And whilst our souls negotiate there,
      We like sepulchral statues lay;
    All day the same our postures were,
20   And we said nothing all the day.

    If any, so by love refined
      That he soul's language understood,

---

4. The two legs of a geometer's or draughtsman's compass. This simile is the most famous example of the "metaphysical conceit" (see "Figurative language," in the "Literary Terminology" appendix to this volume).
1. From *ekstasis* (Greek), a movement of the soul outside of the body.
2. Invisible shafts of light, thought of as going out of the eyes and thereby enabling one to see things.
3. Reflections of each in the other's eyes, often called "making babies."

And by good love were grown all mind,
   Within convenient distance stood,

25 He (though he know not which soul spake,
   Because both meant, both spake the same)
   Might thence a new concoction[4] take,
   And part far purer than he came.

This ecstasy doth unperplex,
30   We said, and tell us what we love;
We see by this it was not sex;
   We see we saw not what did move;°   *motivate us*

But as all several° souls contain   *separate*
   Mixture of things, they know not what,
35 Love these mixed souls doth mix again,
   And makes both one, each this and that.

A single violet transplant,
   The strength, the color, and the size
(All which before was poor and scant)
40   Redoubles still, and multiplies.

When love with one another so
   Interinanimates two souls,
That abler soul, which thence doth flow,
   Defects of loneliness controls.

45 We then, who are this new soul, know
   Of what we are composed and made,
For th' atomies° of which we grow   *components*
   Are souls, whom no change can invade.

But O alas, so long, so far
50   Our bodies why do we forbear?
They are ours, though they are not we; we are
   The intelligences, they the sphere.[5]

We owe them thanks because they thus
   Did us to us at first convey,
55 Yielded their forces, sense, to us,
   Nor are dross to us, but allay.[6]

On man heaven's influence works not so
   But that it first imprints the air:[7]
So soul into the soul may flow,
60   Though it to body first repair.°   *go*

4. In the alchemical sense of sublimation or purification.
5. In Ptolemaic astronomy, each planet, set in a
transparent "sphere" that revolved and so carried
it around the earth, was inhabited by a controlling

angelic "intelligence."
6. "Dross" is an impurity that weakens metal;
"allay" (alloy) strengthens it.
7. Astrological influences were thought to work on
people through the medium of the surrounding air.

As our blood labors to beget
    Spirits[8] as like souls as it can,
Because such fingers need° to knit   *are needed*
    That subtle knot which makes us man,

65 So must pure lovers' souls descend
    T' affections, and to faculties
Which sense may reach and apprehend;
    Else a great prince in prison lies.

To our bodies turn we then, that so
70   Weak men on love revealed may look;
Love's mysteries[9] in souls do grow,
    But yet the body is his book.

And if some lover, such as we,
    Have heard this dialogue of one,[1]
75 Let him still mark° us; he shall see   *observe*
    Small change when we are to bodies gone.

1633

The Funeral

Whoever comes to shroud me, do not harm
    Nor question much
That subtle wreath of hair which crowns my arm;
The mystery, the sign you must not touch,
5   For 'tis my outward soul,
Viceroy to that, which then to heaven being gone,
    Will leave this to control,
And keep these limbs, her[1] provinces, from dissolution.

For if the sinewy thread[2] my brain lets fall
10   Through every part
Can tie those parts and make me one of all,
These hairs which upward grew, and strength and art
    Have from a better brain,
Can better do it; except° she meant that I   *unless*
15   By this should know my pain,
As prisoners then are manacled, when they're condemned to die.

Whate'er she meant by it, bury it with me,
    For since I am
Love's martyr, it might breed idolatry,

8. Subtle substances thought to be produced by the blood to serve as intermediaries between body and soul.
9. The implied comparison is with God's mysteries, which are revealed and may be read in the book of Nature and the book of Scripture.

1. "Dialogue of one" because "both meant, both spake the same" (line 26).
1. The soul's, but also the mistress's (cf. "she," line 14).
2. The nervous system.

20 If into others' hands these relics[3] came:
        As 'twas humility
    To afford to it all that a soul can do,
        So 'tis some bravery,
    That since you would save[4] none of me, I bury some of you.

                                                    1633

The Relic

        When my grave is broke up again
        Some second guest to entertain
        (For graves have learned that woman-head°   *female trait*
        To be to more than one a bed),[1]
5   And he that digs it spies
        A bracelet of bright hair about the bone,
            Will he not let us alone,
        And think that there a loving couple lies,
        Who thought that this device might be some way
10   To make their souls, at the last busy day,°   *Judgment Day*
        Meet at this grave, and make a little stay?

        If this fall in a time, or land,
        Where mis-devotion[2] doth command,
        Then he that digs us up will bring
15   Us to the Bishop and the King,
            To make us relics; then
        Thou shalt be a Mary Magdalen, and I
            A something else thereby;
        All women shall adore us, and some men;
20   And since at such times, miracles are sought,
        I would have that age by this paper taught
        What miracles we harmless lovers wrought.

        First, we loved well and faithfully,
        Yet knew not what we loved, nor why,
25   Difference of sex no more we knew,
            Than our guardian angels do;
            Coming and going, we
        Perchance might kiss, but not between those meals;[3]
            Our hands ne'er touched the seals°   *sexual organs*
30   Which nature, injured by late law, sets free:[4]
        These miracles we did: but now, alas,

3. Body parts or other objects belonging to a saint, venerated by Roman Catholics.
4. All the early printed texts read "have" (which carries sexual connotations), while many manuscripts read "save."
1. Graves were often used to inter successive corpses, the bones of previous occupants being deposited in charnel houses.
2. False devotion, superstition, i.e., Roman Catholicism.
3. The kiss of salutation and parting.
4. Human law forbids the free love permitted by nature. "Late": recent (comparatively speaking).

All measure and all language I should pass,
Should I tell what a miracle she was.

1633

Elegy[1] 16. On His Mistress

By our first strange and fatal interview,
By all desires which thereof did ensue,
By our long starving hopes, by that remorse°   *pity*
Which my words' masculine persuasive force
5 Begot in thee, and by the memory
Of hurts which spies and rivals threatened me,
I calmly beg; but by thy father's wrath,
By all pains which want and divorcement hath,
I conjure thee; and all the oaths which I
10 And thou have sworn to seal joint constancy
Here I unswear and overswear them thus:
Thou shalt not love by ways so dangerous.
Temper, oh fair love, love's impetuous rage;
Be my true mistress still, not my feigned page.[2]
15 I'll go, and, by thy kind leave, leave behind
Thee, only worthy to nurse in my mind
Thirst to come back. Oh, if thou die before,
My soul from other lands to thee shall soar.
Thy (else almighty) beauty cannot move
20 Rage from the seas, nor thy love teach them love,
Nor tame wild Boreas' harshness.[3] Thou hast read
How roughly he in pieces shiverèd
Fair Orithea, whom he swore he loved.
Fall ill or good, 'tis madness to have proved°   *sought out*
25 Dangers unurged; feed on this flattery,
That absent lovers one in th' other be.
Dissemble nothing, not a boy, nor change
Thy body's habit,° nor mind's; be not strange   *clothing*
To thyself only; all will spy in thy face
30 A blushing womanly discovering grace.
Richly clothed apes are called apes, and as soon
Eclipsed as bright we call the moon the moon.
Men of France, changeable chameleons,
Spitals° of diseases, shops of fashions,   *hospitals*
35 Love's fuellers[4] and the rightest company

---

1. In Latin poetry, an elegy is not necessarily a funeral lament but simply a discursive or reflective poem written in "elegiacs" (unrhymed couplets of alternating dactylic hexameters and pentameters). The subject matter primarily associated with this meter was sex, the most famous collection of elegies being Ovid's *Amores*. Several of Donne's elegies—almost all written in the 1590s—take Ovid as their principal model and resemble him in ingenious wit and in frank and unapologetic erot-icism. *Elegy 16* is highly dramatic.
2. The speaker's mistress wanted to accompany him abroad, disguised as a page boy. Such escapades occasionally took place in real life; in 1605, Elizabeth Southwell, disguised as a page, went abroad with Sir Robert Dudley.
3. God of the north wind; Ovid in *Metamorphoses* 6 describes the wild force with which Boreas abducted Orithea.
4. Providers of aphrodisiacs.

Of players which upon the world's stage be,
Will quickly know thee, and know⁵ thee; and alas!
Th' indifferent° Italian, as we pass   *bisexual*
His warm land, well content to think thee page,
40 Will hunt thee with such lust and hideous rage
As Lot's fair guests were vexed.⁶ But none of these
Nor spongy, hydroptic⁷ Dutch shall thee displease
If thou stay here. O stay here, for, for thee,
England is only a worthy gallery
45 To walk in expectation, till from thence
Our greatest king call thee to his presence.⁸
When I am gone, dream me some happiness,
Nor let thy looks our long-hid love confess;
Nor praise nor dispraise me, bless nor curse
50 Openly love's force, nor in bed fright thy nurse
With midnight's startings, crying out "Oh, oh!
Nurse, oh my love is slain, I saw him go
O'er the white Alps alone; I saw him, I,
Assailed, fight, taken, stabbed, bleed, fall, and die."
55 Augur me better chance, except dread Jove
Think it enough for me t' have had thy love.

1635

Elegy 19. To His Mistress Going to Bed¹

Come, Madam, come, all rest my powers defy,
Until I labor, I in labor lie.²
The foe oft-times, having the foe in sight,
Is tired with standing though he never fight.
5 Off with that girdle,° like heaven's zone° glistering,   *belt/zodiac*
But a far fairer world encompassing.
Unpin that spangled breastplate³ which you wear
That th' eyes of busy fools may be stopped there.
Unlace yourself, for that harmonious chime
10 Tells me from you that now it is bed-time.
Off with that happy busk,° which I envy,   *bodice*
That still can be and still can stand so nigh.
Your gown going off, such beauteous state reveals
As when from flowery meads th' hill's shadow steals.
15 Off with that wiry coronet and show
The hairy diadem which on you doth grow;
Now off with those shoes, and then safely tread

5. "Know" in the sexual sense. "Alas" may pun on "a lass."
6. The inhabitants of Sodom brought destruction on themselves when they tried to rape two angels who visited Lot in the guise of young men (Genesis 19.1–11).
7. Dropsical, thus insatiably thirsty.
8. Throne rooms commonly had antechambers (galleries) where visitors waited until the monarch

was ready to see them.
1. This poem reworks the central situation of Ovid's *Amores* 1.5 in much more dramatic terms.
2. Labor in the dual sense of "get to work (sexually)" and "distress."
3. The stomacher, an ornamental, often jeweled, covering for the chest, worn under the lacing of the bodice.

In this love's hallowed temple, this soft bed.
In such white robes, heaven's angels used to be
20 Received by men; thou, angel, bring'st with thee
A heaven like Mahomet's paradise;[4] and though
Ill spirits walk in white, we easily know
By this these angels from an evil sprite,
Those set our hairs, but these our flesh upright.
25   License my roving hands, and let them go
Before, behind, between, above, below.
O my America! my new-found-land,
My kingdom, safeliest when with one man manned,
My mine of precious stones, my empery,°   empire
30 How blest am I in this discovering thee!
To enter in these bonds is to be free;
There where my hand is set, my seal shall be.[5]
    Full nakedness! All joys are due to thee.
As souls unbodied, bodies unclothed must be,
35 To taste whole joys. Gems which you women use
Are like Atalanta's balls,[6] cast in men's views,
That when a fool's eye lighteth on a gem,
His earthly soul may covet theirs, not them.
Like pictures, or like books' gay coverings, made
40 For laymen, are all women thus arrayed;
Themselves are mystic books, which only we
(Whom their imputed grace will dignify)
Must see revealed.[7] Then since that I may know,
As liberally as to a midwife show
45 Thyself: cast all, yea, this white linen hence,
Here is no penance, much less innocence.[8]
    To teach thee, I am naked first; why then
What need'st thou have more covering than a man?

1669

Satire 3

In satire the author holds a subject up to ridicule or to scorn. Like his elegies, Donne's five verse satires were written in his twenties and are in the forefront of an effort in the 1590s (by Donne, Ben Jonson, Joseph Hall, and John Marston) to naturalize those classical forms in England. While elements of satire figure in many different kinds of literature, the great models for formal verse satire were the Roman poets Horace and Juvenal, the former for an ubanely witty style, the latter for an indignant or angry manner. While Donne's other satires call on these models, his

4. A place of sensual pleasure, thought to be populated by seductive houris for the delectation of the faithful.
5. The jokes mingle law with sex: where he has signed a document (placed his hand) he will now place his seal; and in the bonds of her arms he will find freedom.
6. Atalanta, running a race against her suitor Hippomenes, was beaten when he dropped golden balls (apples) for her to pick up. Donne reverses the story.

7. By granting favors to their lovers, women impute to them grace that they don't deserve, as God (in Calvinist doctrine) imputes grace to undeserving sinners. Laymen can only look at the covers of mystic books (women) but "we" elect can read them.
8. Some manuscripts read: "There is no penance due to innocence." White garments would be appropriate either for the innocent virgin or for the sinner doing formal penance.

third satire more nearly resembles a third Roman satirist, Persius, known for an abstruse style and moralizing manner. This work is a strenuous discussion of an acute theological problem, for the age and for Donne himself: How may one discover the true Christian church among so many claimants to that role? At the time Donne wrote this, he was in the process of leaving the Roman Catholic Church of his heritage for the Church of England.

Satire 3

Kind pity chokes my spleen;[1] brave scorn forbids
Those tears to issue which swell my eyelids;
I must not laugh, nor weep° sins, and be wise: *lament*
Can railing then cure these worn maladies?
5   Is not our mistress, fair Religion,
As worthy of all our souls' devotion
As virtue was to the first blinded age?[2]
Are not heaven's joys as valiant to assuage
Lusts, as earth's honor was to them?° Alas,   *pagans*
10   As we do them in means, shall they surpass
Us in the end, and shall thy father's spirit
Meet blind philosophers in heaven, whose merit
Of strict life may be imputed faith,[3] and hear
Thee, whom he taught so easy ways and near
15   To follow, damned? O, if thou dar'st, fear this;
This fear great courage and high valor is.
Dar'st thou aid mutinous Dutch,[4] and dar'st thou lay
Thee in ships, wooden sepulchers, a prey
To leaders' rage, to storms, to shot, to dearth?°   *famine*
20   Dar'st thou dive seas and dungeons° of the earth?   *mines, caves*
Hast thou courageous fire to thaw the ice
Of frozen North discoveries?[5] and thrice
Colder than salamanders, like divine
Children in the oven,[6] fires of Spain, and the line,
25   Whose countries limbecks to our bodies be,
Canst thou for gain bear?[7] And must every he
Which cries not "Goddess!" to thy mistress, draw,°   *fight a duel*
Or eat thy poisonous words? Courage of straw!
O desperate coward, wilt thou seem bold, and
30   To thy foes and his° (who made thee to stand   *God's*
Sentinel in his world's garrison) thus yield,
And for forbidden wars leave th' appointed field?[8]

1. The seat of bile, hence scorn and ridicule.
2. The age of paganism, blind to Christianity but capable of natural morality ("virtue").
3. Donne's formulation wittily turns on its head the key concept of reformed Protestant theology—that salvation is to be achieved only by imputing Christ's merits to Christians through faith—by suggesting that virtuous pagans might be saved by imputing faith to them on the basis of their moral life.
4. English volunteers took frequent part with the Dutch in their wars against Spain. Donne himself had sailed in two raiding expeditions against the Spanish.
5. Many explorers tried to find a northwest passage to the Pacific.
6. In the biblical story (Daniel 3), Shadrach, Meshack, and Abednego were rescued from a fiery furnace. The salamander (a lizardlike creature) was thought to be so cold-blooded that it could live in fire.
7. The object of "bear" is "fires of Spain, and the line"—inquisitorial and equatorial heats, which roast people as chemists heat materials in "limbecks" (alembics, or vessels for distilling).
8. Of moral struggle.

Know thy foes: The foul Devil (whom thou
Strivest to please) for hate, not love, would allow
35 Thee fain his whole realm to be quit;° and as   to satisfy you
The world's all parts wither away and pass,⁹
So the world's self, thy other loved foe, is
In her decrepit wane, and thou, loving this,
Dost love a withered and worn strumpet; last,
40 Flesh (itself's death) and joys which flesh can taste
Thou lovest; and thy fair goodly soul, which doth
Give this flesh power to taste joy, thou dost loathe.
Seek true religion. O, where? Mirreus,¹
Thinking her unhoused here, and fled from us,
45 Seeks her at Rome; there, because he doth know
That she was there a thousand years ago.
He loves her rags so, as we here obey
The statecloth² where the Prince sat yesterday.
Crantz to such brave loves will not be enthralled,
50 But loves her only, who at Geneva is called
Religion—plain, simple, sullen, young,
Contemptuous, yet unhandsome; as among
Lecherous humors,° there is one that judges   temperaments
No wenches wholesome but coarse country drudges.
55 Graius stays still at home here, and because
Some preachers, vile ambitious bawds, and laws
Still new, like fashions, bid him think that she
Which dwells with us is only perfect, he
Embraceth her whom his godfathers will
60 Tender to him, being tender, as wards still
Take such wives as their guardians offer, or
Pay values.³ Careless Phrygius doth abhor
All, because all cannot be good, as one
Knowing some women whores, dares marry none.
65 Graccus loves all as one, and thinks that so
As women do in divers countries go
In divers habits, yet are still one kind,
So doth, so is religion; and this blind-
ness too much light breeds;⁴ but unmoved thou
70 Of force° must one, and forced but one allow;   necessity
And the right; ask thy father which is she,
Let him ask his; though truth and falsehood be
Near twins, yet truth a little elder is;
Be busy to seek her, believe me this,
75 He's not of none, nor worst, that seeks the best.⁵
To adore, or scorn an image, or protest,
May all be bad; doubt wisely; in strange way

9. The common belief that the world was growing
old and becoming decrepit.
1. The satiric types in this passage represent different creeds: "Mirreus" is a Roman Catholic;
"Crantz" an austere Calvinist Presbyterian of
Geneva; "Graius" a Church of England Erastian
who believes in any religion sponsored by the state;
"Phrygius" a skeptic; and "Graccus" a complete rel-
ativist.

2. The royal canopy, a symbol of kingly power.
3. If minors in care of a guardian (in wardship)
rejected the wives offered ("tendered") to them
they had to pay fines ("values").
4. I.e., being blind to the differences between
religions, Graccus has too much light to see where
truth might lie.
5. The person who seeks the best church is neither an unbeliever nor the worst sort of believer.

To stand inquiring right, is not to stray;
To sleep, or run wrong, is. On a huge hill,
80 Cragged and steep, Truth stands, and he that will
Reach her, about must, and about must go,
And what the hill's suddenness resists, win so;
Yet strive so, that before age, death's twilight,
Thy soul rest, for none can work in that night.[6]
85 To will° implies delay, therefore now do.   *intend a future act*
Hard deeds, the body's pains; hard knowledge too
The mind's endeavors reach,° and mysteries   *achieve*
Are like the sun, dazzling, yet plain to all eyes.
Keep the truth which thou hast found; men do not stand
90 In so ill case here, that God hath with his hand
Signed kings' blank charters to kill whom they hate,
Nor are they vicars, but hangmen to fate.[7]
Fool and wretch, wilt thou let thy soul be tied
To man's laws, by which she shall not be tried
95 At the last day? O, will it then boot° thee   *profit*
To say a Philip, or a Gregory,
A Harry, or a Martin taught thee this?[8]
Is not this excuse for mere° contraries   *complete*
Equally strong? Cannot both sides say so?
100 That thou mayest rightly obey power, her bounds know;
Those passed, her nature and name is changed; to be
Then humble to her is idolatry.
As streams are, power is; those blest flowers that dwell
At the rough stream's calm head, thrive and prove well,
105 But having left their roots, and themselves given
To the stream's tyrannous rage, alas, are driven
Through mills, and rocks, and woods, and at last, almost
Consumed in going, in the sea are lost:
So perish souls, which more choose men's unjust
110 Power from God claimed, than God himself to trust.

1633

From Holy Sonnets[1]

1

Thou hast made me, and shall thy work decay?
Repair me now, for now mine end doth haste;
I run to death, and death meets me as fast,
And all my pleasures are like yesterday.

6. Echoes John 9.4, "the night cometh, when no man can work."
7. Kings are not God's vicars on earth, with license ("blank charters") to persecute or kill whomever they wish on grounds of religion.
8. "Philip" is Philip II of Spain, "Gregory" is Pope Gregory XIII or XIV, "Harry" is England's Henry VIII, and "Martin" is Martin Luther.
1. Donne wrote a variety of religious poems (called "Divine Poems"), including a group of nine-teen *Holy Sonnets* that reflect his interest in Jesuit and especially Protestant meditative procedures. He probably began writing them about 1609, a decade or so after leaving the Catholic church. Our selections follow the traditional numbering established in Sir Herbert Grierson's influential edition, since for most of these sonnets we cannot tell when they were written or in what order they were intended to appear.

5   I dare not move my dim eyes any way,
     Despair behind, and death before doth cast
     Such terror, and my feeble flesh doth waste
     By sin in it, which it towards hell doth weigh.°   *incline, weigh down*
     Only thou art above, and when towards thee
10   By thy leave I can look, I rise again;
     But our old subtle foe so tempteth me
     That not one hour myself I can sustain.
     Thy grace may wing° me to prevent° his art,   *give wings to / forestall*
     And thou like adamant° draw mine iron heart.   *magnetic lodestone*

1635

5

     I am a little world[2] made cunningly
     Of elements, and an angelic sprite;°   *spirit, soul*
     But black sin hath betrayed to endless night
     My world's both parts, and O, both parts must die.
5   You which beyond that heaven which was most high
     Have found new spheres, and of new lands can write,[3]
     Pour new seas in mine eyes, that so I might
     Drown my world with my weeping earnestly,
     Or wash it if it must be drowned no more.[4]
10   But O, it must be burnt! Alas, the fire
     Of lust and envy have burnt it heretofore,
     And made it fouler; let their flames retire,
     And burn me, O Lord, with a fiery zeal
     Of thee and thy house, which doth in eating heal.[5]

1635

7

     At the round earth's imagined corners,[6] blow
     Your trumpets, angels; and arise, arise
     From death, you numberless infinities
     Of souls, and to your scattered bodies go:
5   All whom the flood did, and fire[7] shall, o'erthrow,
     All whom war, dearth,° age, agues,° tyrannies,   *famine / fevers*
     Despair, law, chance hath slain, and you whose eyes
     Shall behold God, and never taste death's woe.[8]
     But let them sleep, Lord, and me mourn a space;
10   For, if above all these, my sins abound,
     'Tis late to ask abundance of thy grace
     When we are there. Here on this lowly ground,

2. The traditional idea of the human being as microcosm (a "little world"), containing in miniature all the features of the macrocosm or great world.
3. Astronomers, especially Galileo.
4. God promised Noah (Genesis 9.11) never to flood the earth again.
5. See Psalm 69.9: "For the zeal of thine house hath eaten me up." These lines refer to three kinds of flame—those of the Last Judgment, those of lust and envy, and those of zeal, which alone save.
6. Cf. Revelations 7.1: "I saw four angels standing on the four corners of the earth."
7. Noah's flood, and the universal conflagration at the end of the world (Revelation 6.11).
8. Those who will be alive at the Second Coming (cf. Luke 9.27).

Teach me how to repent; for that's as good
As if thou hadst sealed my pardon with thy blood.

1633

9

If poisonous minerals, and if that tree[9]
Whose fruit threw death on else-immortal us,
If lecherous goats, if serpents envious[1]
Cannot be damned, alas! why should I be?
5   Why should intent or reason, born in me,
Make sins, else equal, in me more heinous?
And, mercy being easy and glorious
To God, in his stern wrath why threatens he?
But who am I that dare dispute with thee
10   O God? Oh, of thine only worthy blood
And my tears, make a heavenly Lethean[2] flood,
And drown in it my sin's black memory.
That thou remember them some claim as debt;
I think it mercy if thou wilt forget.[3]

1633

10

Death, be not proud, though some have callèd thee
Mighty and dreadful, for thou art not so;
For those whom thou think'st thou dost overthrow
Die not, poor Death, nor yet canst thou kill me.
5   From rest and sleep, which but thy pictures be,
Much pleasure; then from thee much more must flow,
And soonest our best men with thee do go,
Rest of their bones, and soul's delivery.[4]
Thou art slave to fate, chance, kings, and desperate men,
10   And dost with poison, war, and sickness dwell,
And poppy° or charms can make us sleep as well   opium
And better than thy stroke; why swell'st° thou then?   puff with pride
One short sleep past, we wake eternally
And death shall be no more; Death, thou shalt die.[5]

1633

13

What if this present were the world's last night?
Mark in my heart, O soul, where thou dost dwell,

9. The Tree of Knowledge of Good and Evil, whose fruit was forbidden to Adam and Eve in Eden.
1. Traits commonly associated with these creatures.
2. In classical mythology, the waters of the river Lethe in the underworld caused total forgetful-ness.
3. Cf. Jeremiah 31.34: "I will forgive their iniquity, and I will remember their sins no more."
4. I.e., to find rest for their bones and freedom ("delivery") for their souls.
5. Cf. 1 Corinthians 15.26: "The last enemy that shall be destroyed is death."

The picture of Christ crucified, and tell
Whether that countenance can thee affright.
5 Tears in his eyes quench the amazing light,
Blood fills his frowns, which from his pierced head fell;
And can that tongue adjudge thee unto hell
Which prayed forgiveness for his foes' fierce spite?
No, no; but as in my idolatry
10 I said to all my profane° mistresses,   *earthly*
Beauty of pity, foulness only is
A sign of rigor:⁶ so I say to thee,
To wicked spirits are horrid shapes assigned,
This beauteous form assures a piteous mind.

1633

14

Batter my heart, three-personed God; for you
As yet but knock, breathe, shine, and seek to mend;
That I may rise and stand, o'erthrow me, and bend
Your force to break, blow, burn, and make me new.
5 I, like an usurped town, to another due,
Labor to admit you, but O, to no end;
Reason, your viceroy⁷ in me, me should defend,
But is captived, and proves weak or untrue.
Yet dearly I love you, and would be loved fain,°   *gladly*
10 But am betrothed⁸ unto your enemy.
Divorce me, untie or break that knot again;
Take me to you, imprison me, for I,
Except° you enthrall me, never shall be free,   *unless*
Nor ever chaste, except you ravish⁹ me.

1633

18

Show me, dear Christ, thy spouse¹ so bright and clear.
What! is it she which on the other shore
Goes richly painted? or which, robbed and tore,
Laments and mourns in Germany and here?²
5 Sleeps she a thousand, then peeps up one year?
Is she self-truth, and errs? now new, now outwore?
Doth she, and did she, and shall she evermore
On one, on seven, or on no hill appear?³

6. In Neoplatonic theory, beautiful features are the sign of a compassionate mind, while ugliness signifies the contrary.
7. The governor in your stead.
8. Humanity's relationship with God has been described in terms of marriage and adultery from the time of the Hebrew prophets.
9. Rape, also overwhelm with wonder. "Enthrall": enslave, also enchant.
1. The church is commonly called the bride of Christ. Cf. Revelation 19.7–8: "The marriage of

the Lamb is come, and his wife hath made herself ready. / And to her was granted that she should be arrayed in fine linen, clean and white."
2. I.e., neither the painted woman (the Church of Rome) nor the ravished virgin (the Lutheran and Calvinist churches in Germany and England) seem very like a bride.
3. The church on one hill is probably Solomon's temple on Mount Moriah; that on seven hills is the Church of Rome; that on no hill is the Presbyterian church of Geneva.

Dwells she with us, or like adventuring knights
10 First travel we to seek, and then make love?
Betray, kind husband, thy spouse to our sights,
And let mine amorous soul court thy mild dove,
Who is most true and pleasing to thee then
When she is embraced and open to most men.[4]

1899

19

Oh, to vex me, contraries meet in one:
Inconstancy unnaturally hath begot
A constant habit; that when I would not
I change in vows, and in devotion.
5 As humorous is my contrition
As my profane love, and as soon forgot:
As riddlingly distempered, cold and hot,[5]
As praying, as mute, as infinite, as none.
I durst not view heaven yesterday; and today
10 In prayers, and flattering speeches I court God:
Tomorrow I quake with true fear of his rod.
So my devout fits come and go away
Like a fantastic ague:[6] save that here
Those are my best days, when I shake with fear.

1899

Hymn to God My God, in My Sickness[1]

Since I am coming to that holy room
    Where, with thy choir of saints for evermore,
I shall be made thy music; as I come
    I tune the instrument here at the door,
5   And what I must do then, think[2] now before.

Whilst my physicians by their love are grown
    Cosmographers, and I their map, who lie
Flat on this bed, that by them may be shown
    That this is my southwest discovery[3]
10   *Per fretum febris*,[4] by these straits to die,

4. The final lines wittily rework, with startling sexual associations, Song of Solomon 5.2: "Open to me, my sister, my love, my dove, my undefiled." That biblical book was often interpreted as the song of love between Christ and the church.
5. Arising from the unbalanced humors, changeable.
6. A fever, attended with paroxysms of hot and cold and trembling fits. "Fantastic": capricious, extravagant.
1. Though Izaak Walton, Donne's pious biographer, assigns this poem to the last days of his life, it was probably written in December 1623.
2. This and the previous poem are less hymns (songs of praise) than meditations preparing (tuning the instrument) for such hymns.
3. South is the region of heat, west the region of sunset and death.
4. Through the straits of fever, with a pun on straits as sufferings, rigors, and a geographical reference to the Strait of Magellan.

I joy, that in these straits, I see my West;
  For, though their currents yield return to none,
What shall my West hurt me? As West and East
  In all flat maps (and I am one) are one,[5]
15   So death doth touch the resurrection.

Is the Pacific Sea my home? Or are
  The Eastern riches?° Is Jerusalem?   *Cathay, China*
Anyan,[6] and Magellan, and Gibraltar,
  All straits, and none but straits, are ways to them,
20   Whether where Japhet dwelt, or Cham, or Shem.[7]

We think that Paradise and Calvary,
  Christ's cross and Adam's tree, stood in one place;
Look, Lord and find both Adams[8] met in me;
  As the first Adam's sweat surrounds my face,
25   May the last Adam's blood my soul embrace.

So, in his purple wrapped,[9] receive me, Lord;
  By these his thorns give me his other crown;
And, as to others' souls I preached thy word,
  Be this my text, my sermon to mine own:
30   Therefore that he may raise the Lord throws down.

1635

A Hymn to God the Father[1]

Wilt thou forgive that sin where I begun,
  Which is my sin, though it were done before?[2]
Wilt thou forgive that sin through which I run,
  And do run still, though still I do deplore?
5   When thou hast done,[3] thou hast not done,
      For I have more.

Wilt thou forgive that sin by which I have won
  Others to sin? and made my sin their door?
Wilt thou forgive that sin which I did shun
10   A year or two, but wallowed in a score?
      When thou hast done, thou hast not done,
        For I have more.

5. If a flat map is pasted on a round globe, west and east meet.
6. Anian, a strait on the west coast of America, shown on early maps as separating America from Asia.
7. The three sons of Noah by whom the world was repopulated after the Flood (Genesis 10). The descendants of Japhet were thought to inhabit Europe; those of Cham (Ham), Africa; and those of Shem, Asia.
8. Adam and Christ. Legend had it that Christ's cross was erected on the spot, or at least in the region, where the tree forbidden to Adam in Eden had stood.
9. In his blood, also in his kingly robes.
1. This hymn was used as a congregational hymn. Walton tells us that Donne wrote it during his illness of 1623, had it set to music, and was delighted to hear it performed (as it frequently was) by the choir of St. Paul's Cathedral.
2. I.e., he inherits the original sin of Adam and Eve.
3. In the refrains, Donne puns on his own name and may pun on his wife's maiden name, Ann More.

I have a sin of fear, that when I have spun
　My last thread, I shall perish on the shore;
15　Swear by thy self, that at my death thy Son
　Shall shine as he shines now and heretofore;
　And, having done that, thou hast done,
　I fear[4] no more.

1633

From Devotions upon Emergent Occasions[1]

Meditation 17

Nunc lento sonitu dicunt, morieris.
Now this bell tolling softly for another, says to me, Thou must die.

Perchance he for whom this bell[2] tolls may be so ill as that he knows not it tolls for him; and perchance I may think myself so much better than I am, as that they who are about me and see my state may have caused it to toll for me, and I know not that. The church is catholic, universal, so are all her actions; all that she does belongs to all. When she baptizes a child, that action concerns me; for that child is thereby connected to that head which is my head too, and ingrafted into that body[3] whereof I am a member. And when she buries a man, that action concerns me: all mankind is of one author and is one volume; when one man dies, one chapter is not torn out of the book, but translated[4] into a better language; and every chapter must be so translated. God employs several translators; some pieces are translated by age, some by sickness, some by war, some by justice; but God's hand is in every translation, and his hand shall bind up all our scattered leaves again for that library where every book shall lie open to one another. As therefore the bell that rings to a sermon calls not upon the preacher only, but upon the congregation to come, so this bell calls us all; but how much more me, who am brought so near the door by this sickness. There was a contention as far as a suit[5] (in which piety and dignity, religion and estimation,[6] were mingled) which of the religious orders should ring to prayers first in the morning; and it was determined that they should ring first that rose earliest. If we understand aright the dignity of this bell that tolls for our evening prayer, we would be glad to make it ours by rising early, in that application, that it might be ours as well as his whose indeed it is. The bell doth toll for him that thinks it doth; and though it intermit again, yet from that minute that that occasion wrought upon him, he is united to God. Who casts not up his eye to the sun when it rises? but who takes off his eye from a comet when that breaks out?

4. Some manuscripts read "have."
1. Donne's *Devotions* were composed in the aftermath of his serious illness in the winter of 1623, though Donne characteristically writes as if the events of the illness were happening as he describes them. The *Devotions* recount in twenty-three sections the stages ("emergent occasions") of the illness and recovery: the term associates the exercise with a popular kind of Protestant meditation on the occasions that daily life presents to us. Each section contains a "meditation upon our

human condition," an "expostulation and debatement with God," and a prayer to God. The book was published almost immediately, offering its meditation on an intensely personal experience as exemplary for others.
2. The "passing bell" for the dying.
3. The church.
4. Punning on the literal sense, "carried across."
5. Controversy that went as far as a lawsuit.
6. Self-esteem.

Who bends not his ear to any bell which upon any occasion rings? but who can remove it from that bell which is passing a piece of himself out of this world? No man is an island, entire of itself; every man is a piece of the continent, a part of the main.[7] If a clod be washed away by the sea, Europe is the less, as well as if a promontory were, as well as if a manor of thy friend's or of thine own were. Any man's death diminishes me, because I am involved in mankind; and therefore never send to know for whom the bell tolls; it tolls for thee.[8] Neither can we call this a begging of misery or a borrowing of misery, as though we were not miserable enough of ourselves but must fetch in more from the next house, in taking upon us the misery of our neighbors. Truly it were an excusable covetousness if we did; for affliction is a treasure, and scarce any man hath enough of it. No man hath affliction enough that is not matured and ripened by it, and made fit for God by that affliction. If a man carry treasure in bullion, or in a wedge of gold, and have none coined into current moneys, his treasure will not defray[9] him as he travels. Tribulation is treasure in the nature of it, but it is not current money in the use of it, except we get nearer and nearer our home, heaven, by it. Another man may be sick too, and sick to death, and this affliction may lie in his bowels as gold in a mine and be of no use to him; but this bell that tells me of his affliction digs out and applies that gold to me, if by this consideration of another's danger I take mine own into contemplation and so secure myself by making my recourse to my God, who is our only security.

1623   1624

7. Mainland.
8. This phrase gave Hemingway the title for his

novel *For Whom the Bell Tolls.*
9. Meet his expenses.

AEMILIA LANYER
1569–1645

Aemilia Lanyer was the first Englishwoman to publish a substantial volume of original poems and the first to make an overt bid for patronage, as previously only a male poet of the era might. She was daughter to an Italian-Jewish family of court musicians (the Bassanos), and for some years the mistress of Queen Elizabeth's Lord Chamberlain, Henry Cary, Lord Hunsdon, forty-five years her senior and a notable patron of the arts, including Shakespeare's company. Apparently to cover a pregnancy by him that resulted in a son named Henry, she married into another family of gentlemen musicians attached to the courts of Elizabeth I and James I. Educated in the aristocratic household of the countess of Kent and supported in style by Hunsdon, her fortunes declined after her marriage to Alfonso Lanyer, and her efforts to find some niche at the Jacobean court came to nothing. The gossipy notebooks of the astrologer Simon Forman record some of these facts from information Lanyer provided when consulting him about her fortunes. She evidently resided for some time in the bookish and cultivated household of Margaret Clifford, countess of Cumberland, and Margaret's young daughter Anne Clifford, receiving there some encouragement in learning, piety, and poetry, as well as, perhaps, some support in the unusual venture of offering her poems for publication.

Lanyer's single volume of poems, *Salve Deus Rex Judaeorum* (1611), has a decided feminist thrust. A series of dedicatory poems to former and would-be patronesses praises them as a community of contemporary good women. The title poem, a baroque meditation on Christ's Passion which at times invites some comparison with Donne and Crashaw, contrasts the good women who are part of the Passion story with the weak and evil men portrayed there and also incorporates a defense of Eve and all women. That defense and Lanyer's prose epistle "To the Virtuous Reader" are spirited contributions to the so-called *querelle des femmes*, a massive body of writings both serious and satiric that extends over several centuries and argues the issue of women's worthiness or faultiness in several genres and languages: some examples include Chaucer's *Wife of Bath's Prologue and Tale*, John Knox's denunciation of Mary Queen of Scots, and Shakespeare's *Taming of the Shrew*. The final poem in Lanyer's volume, *The Description of Cooke-ham*, celebrates in elegiac mode the crown estate occasionally occupied by the countess of Cumberland, portraying it as an Edenic paradise of women, now lost. This poem may or may not have been written before Ben Jonson's *To Penshurst*—commonly thought to have inaugurated the "country-house" genre in English literature—but Lanyer's poem can claim priority in publication. These two poems offer an instructive comparison, constructing male and female conceptions of an idealized social order that respond in very different ways to contemporary gender ideology.

From Salve Deus Rex Judaeorum[1]

To the Doubtful Reader[2]

Gentle Reader, if thou desire to be resolved, why I give this title, *Salve Deus Rex Judaeorum*, know for certain, that it was delivered unto me in sleep many years before I had any intent to write in this manner, and was quite out of my memory, until I had written the Passion of Christ, when immediately it came into my remembrance, what I had dreamed long before. And thinking it a significant token[3] that I was appointed to perform this work, I gave the very same words I received in sleep as the fittest title I could devise for this book.

Eve's Apology in Defense of Women[4]

Now Pontius Pilate is to judge the cause°   *case*
Of faultless Jesus, who before him stands,
Who neither hath offended prince, nor laws,
Although he now be brought in woeful bands.
5 O noble governor, make thou yet a pause,
Do not in innocent blood inbrue° thy hands;   *stain*
   But hear the words of thy most worthy wife,[5]
   Who sends to thee, to beg her Savior's life.

1. "Hail God, King of the Jews," a variant of the inscription affixed to Christ's cross.
2. Lanyer placed this explanation at the end of her volume, not the beginning, as a further authorizing gesture. Invoking the familiar genre of the dream vision, she lays claim to some kind of poetic, and even divine, inspiration. "Doubtful": doubting.
3. Sign.
4. Lanyer supplies the title for this subsection of the *Salve Deus* on her title page. Eve is not, however, the speaker; rather, the narrator presents

Eve's "Apology" (defense of her actions), which is also a defense of all women. She does so by means of an apostrophe (impassioned address) to Pilate, the Roman official who authorized the crucifixion of Jesus. Lanyer makes Pilate and Adam representatives of the male gender, whereas Eve and Pilate's wife represent womankind.
5. Pilate's wife wrote her husband a letter urging Pilate to spare Jesus, about whom she had a warning dream (Matthew 27.19).

Let barb'rous cruelty far depart from thee,
10 And in true justice take affliction's part;
Open thine eyes, that thou the truth may'st see.
Do not the thing that goes against thy heart,
Condemn not him that must thy Savior be;
But view his holy life, his good desert.
15   Let not us women glory in men's fall.[6]
Who had power given to overrule us all.

Till now your indiscretion sets us free.
And makes our former fault much less appear;
Our mother Eve, who tasted of the tree,
20 Giving to Adam what she held most dear,
Was simply good, and had no power to see;[7]
The after-coming harm did not appear:
    The subtle serpent that our sex betrayed
    Before our fall so sure a plot had laid.

25 That undiscerning ignorance perceived
No guile or craft that was by him intended;
For had she known of what we were bereaved,[8]
To his request she had not condescended.
But she, poor soul, by cunning was deceived;
30 No hurt therein her harmless heart intended:
    For she alleged° God's word, which he° denies,   *asserted / serpent*
    That they should die, but even as gods be wise.

But surely Adam cannot be excused;
Her fault though great, yet he was most to blame;
35 What weakness offered, strength might have refused,
Being lord of all, the greater was his shame.
Although the serpent's craft had her abused,
God's holy word ought all his actions frame,°   *determine*
    For he was lord and king of all the earth,
40   Before poor Eve had either life or breath,

Who being framed° by God's eternal hand   *fashioned*
The perfectest man that ever breathed on earth;
And from God's mouth received that strait° command,   *strict*
The breach whereof he knew was present death;
45 Yea, having power to rule both sea and land,
Yet with one apple won to lose that breath[9]
    Which God had breathed in his beauteous face,
    Bringing us all in danger and disgrace.

6. The fall of Adam, and the prospective fall of Pilate.
7. In Eden, Eve ate the forbidden fruit first, at the serpent's bidding. Genesis commentary usually emphasized Eve's full knowledge that God had forbidden them on pain of death and banishment from Eden to eat the fruit of the Tree of Knowledge of Good and Evil; her action was usually ascribed to intemperance, pride, and ambition.

8. Deprived, specifically of eternal life. In Genesis 3, Eve was enticed by the serpent to eat the forbidden fruit; she in turn enticed her husband. God expelled them from Eden, condemning Adam to hard labor, Eve to pain in childbirth and subjection to her husband, and both to suffering and death.
9. The breath of life, which would have been eternal.

And then to lay the fault on Patience' back,
50 That we (poor women) must endure it all.
We know right well he did discretion lack,
Being not persuaded thereunto at all.
If Eve did err, it was for knowledge sake;
The fruit being fair persuaded him to fall:
55   No subtle serpent's falsehood did betray him;
If he would eat it, who had power to stay° him?   *prevent*

Not Eve, whose fault was only too much love,
Which made her give this present to her dear,
That what she tasted he likewise might prove,°   *experience*
60 Whereby his knowledge might become more clear;
He never sought her weakness to reprove
With those sharp words which he of God did hear;
Yet men will boast of knowledge, which he took
From Eve's fair hand, as from a learned book.

65 If any evil did in her remain,
Being made of him,[1] he was the ground of all.
If one of many worlds[2] could lay a stain
Upon our sex, and work so great a fall
To wretched man by Satan's subtle train,[3]
70 What will so foul a fault amongst you all?
Her weakness did the serpent's words obey,
But you in malice God's dear Son betray,

Whom, if unjustly you condemn to die,
Her sin was small to what you do commit;
75 All mortal sins[4] that do for vengeance cry
Are not to be compared unto it.
If many worlds would altogether try
By all their sins the wrath of God to get,
This sin of yours surmounts them all as far
80   As doth the sun another little star.[5]

Then let us have our liberty again,
And challenge° to yourselves no sovereignty.   *claim*
You came not in the world without our pain,
Make that a bar against your cruelty;
85 Your fault being greater, why should you disdain
Our being your equals, free from tyranny?
If one weak woman simply did offend,
This sin of yours hath no excuse nor end,

To which, poor souls, we never gave consent.
90 Witness, thy wife, O Pilate, speaks for all,

---

1. Genesis 2.21–22 reports God's creation of Eve from Adam's rib.
2. May allude to the commonplace that man is a little world, applying it here to woman.
3. Tradition identifies Satan with the serpent, although that identification is not made in Genesis.
4. Sins punishable by damnation.
5. In the Ptolemaic system, the sun was larger than the other planets and the fixed stars.

Who did but dream, and yet a message sent
That thou shouldest have nothing to do at all
With that just man[6] which, if thy heart relent,
Why wilt thou be a reprobate° with Saul[7]   *damned*
95   To seek the death of him that is so good,
For thy soul's health to shed his dearest blood?

1611

The Description of Cooke-ham[1]

Farewell (sweet *Cooke-ham*) where I first obtained
Grace[2] from that grace where perfect grace remained;
And where the muses gave their full consent,
I should have power the virtuous to content;
5   Where princely palace[3] willed me to indite,
The sacred story of the soul's delight.
Farewell (sweet place) where virtue then did rest,
And all delights did harbor in her breast;
Never shall my sad eyes again behold
10   Those pleasures which my thoughts did then unfold.
Yet you (great Lady) Mistress of that place,
From whose desires did spring this work of grace;
Vouchsafe to think upon those pleasures past,
As fleeting worldly joys that could not last,
15   Or, as dim shadows of celestial pleasures,
Which are desired above all earthly treasures.
Oh how (methought) against° you thither came,   *in preparation for*
Each part did seem some new delight to frame!
The house received all ornaments to grace it,
20   And would endure no foulness to deface it.
And walks put on their summer liveries,[4]
And all things else did hold like similes:[5]
The trees with leaves, with fruits, with flowers clad,
Embraced each other, seeming to be glad,
25   Turning themselves to beauteous Canopies,
To shade the bright sun from your brighter eyes;
The crystal streams with silver spangles graced,
While by the glorious sun they were embraced;

---

6. Christ.
7. King of Israel who sought the death of God's annointed prophet-king, David. The parallel is with Pilate, who sought Christ's death.
1. The poem was written in honor of Margaret Clifford, countess of Cumberland, and celebrates a royal estate leased to her brother, at which the countess occasionally resided. The poem should be compared with Jonson's *To Penshurst*. Lanyer's poem is based on a familiar classical topic, the "Farewell to a Place," which had its most famous development in Virgil's *Eclogue* 1. Lanyer makes extensive use of the common pastoral motif of nature's active sympathy with and response to human emotion—which later came to be called

the "pathetic fallacy."
2. Here, both God's grace and the favor of Her Grace, the Countess of Cumberland. Lanyer attributes both her religious conversion and her vocation as poet to a period of residence at Cookeham in the countess's household. We do not know how long or under what circumstances Lanyer resided there.
3. Apparently a reference to the countess as her patron, commissioning her Passion poem.
4. Distinctive garments worn by persons in the service of great families, to indicate whose servants they were.
5. Behaved in similar fashion.

The little birds in chirping notes did sing,
30 To entertain both you and that sweet spring.
And *Philomela*[6] with her sundry lays,
Both you and that delightful place did praise.
Oh how me thought each plant, each flower, each tree
Set forth their beauties then to welcome thee!
35 The very hills right humbly did descend,
When you to tread on them did intend.
And as you set your feet, they still did rise,
Glad that they could receive so rich a prize.
The gentle winds did take delight to be
40 Among those woods that were so graced by thee,
And in sad murmur uttered pleasing sound,
That pleasure in that place might more abound.
The swelling banks delivered all their pride
When such a *Phoenix*[7] once they had espied.
45 Each arbor, bank, each seat, each stately tree,
Thought themselves honored in supporting thee.
The pretty birds would oft come to attend thee,
Yet fly away for fear they should offend thee;
The little creatures in the burrough by
50 Would come abroad to sport them in your eye,
Yet fearful of the bow in your fair hand,
Would run away when you did make a stand.
Now let me come unto that stately tree,
Wherein such goodly prospects you did see;
55 That oak that did in height his fellows pass,
As much as lofty trees, low growing grass,
Much like a comely cedar straight and tall,
Whose beauteous stature far exceeded all.
How often did you visit this fair tree,
60 Which seeming joyful in receiving thee,
Would like a palm tree spread his arms abroad,
Desirous that you there should make abode;
Whose fair green leaves much like a comely veil,
Defended° *Phoebus* when he would assail;   *defended against, resisted*
65 Whose pleasing boughs did yield a cool fresh air,
Joying° his happiness when you were there.   *enjoying*
Where being seated, you might plainly see
Hills, vales, and woods, as if on bended knee
They had appeared, your honor to salute,
70 Or to prefer some strange unlooked-for suit;[8]
All interlaced with brooks and crystal springs,
A prospect fit to please the eyes of kings.
And thirteen shires appeared all in your sight,

6. In myth, Philomela was raped by her brother-in-law Tereus, who also tore out her tongue; the gods transformed her into a nightingale. Here the bird's song is joyous but later mournful (line 189), associating her own woes with those of Cookeham at the women's departure.
7. Mythical bird that lived alone of its kind for five hundred years, then was consumed in flame and reborn from its own ashes; metaphorically, a person of rare excellence. "All their pride": fish (cf. *To Penshurst*, lines 31–36).
8. To urge some unexpected petition, as to a monarch.

Europe could not afford much more delight.
75 What was there then but gave you all content,
While you the time in meditation spent
Of their Creator's power, which there you saw,
In all his creatures held a perfect law;
And in their beauties did you plain descry°   perceive
80 His beauty, wisdom, grace, love, majesty.
In these sweet woods how often did you walk,
With Christ and his Apostles there to talk;
Placing his holy Writ in some fair tree
To meditate what you therein did see.
85 With *Moses* you did mount his holy hill
To know his pleasure, and perform his will.[9]
With lowly *David* you did often sing
His holy hymns to Heaven's eternal King.[1]
And in sweet music did your soul delight
90 To sound his praises, morning, noon, and night.
With blessed *Joseph* you did often feed
Your pined brethren, when they stood in need.[2]
And that sweet Lady sprung from *Clifford's* race,
Of noble *Bedford's* blood, fair stem of grace,[3]
95 To honorable *Dorset* now espoused,[4]
In whose fair breast true virtue then was housed,
Oh what delight did my weak spirits find
In those pure parts of her well framéd mind.
And yet it grieves me that I cannot be
100 Near unto her, whose virtues did agree
With those fair ornaments of outward beauty,
Which did enforce from all both love and duty.
Unconstant Fortune, thou art most to blame,
Who casts us down into so low a frame
105 Where our great friends we cannot daily see,
So great a difference is there in degree.[5]
Many are placed in those orbs of state,
Parters[6] in honor, so ordained by Fate,
Nearer in show, yet farther off in love,
110 In which, the lowest always are above.[7]
But whither am I carried in conceit,
My wit too weak to conster° of the great.   construe
Why not? although we are but born of earth,
We may behold the heavens, despising death;
115 And loving heaven that is so far above,

9. You sought out and followed God's law, like Moses, who received the Ten Commandments on Mount Sinai.
1. You often sang David's psalms.
2. Like Joseph, who fed the starving Israelites in Egypt, you fed the hungry.
3. Main line of the family tree. Anne Clifford, only surviving child of the seaman-adventurer George Clifford, third earl of Cumberland, and the countess, a Russell (of "Bedford's blood"). She was tutored by Samuel Daniel and her *Diary* offers interesting insights into this period.
4. Anne Clifford was married to Richard Sackville, third earl of Dorset, on February 25, 1609; the reference helps date Lanyer's poem.
5. These lines and lines 117–25 probably exaggerate Lanyer's former familiarity with Anne Clifford.
6. Separators, i.e., the various honorific ranks "orbs of state" act to separate person from person.
7. An egalitarian sentiment playing on the Christian notion that in spiritual things—love and charity—the poor and lowly surpass the great ones.

May in the end vouchsafe us entire love.[8]
Therefore sweet memory do thou retain
Those pleasures past, which will not turn again:
Remember beauteous *Dorset's* former sports,[9]
120 So far from being touched by ill reports,
Wherein myself did always bear a part,
While reverend love presented my true heart.
Those recreations let me bear in mind,
Which her sweet youth and noble thoughts did find,
125 Whereof deprived, I evermore must grieve,
Hating blind Fortune, careless to relieve.
And you sweet Cooke-ham, whom these ladies leave,
I now must tell the grief you did conceive
At their departure, when they went away,
130 How everything retained a sad dismay.
Nay long before, when once an inkling came,
Methought each thing did unto sorrow frame:
The trees that were so glorious in our view,
Forsook both flowers and fruit, when once they knew
135 Of your depart, their very leaves did wither,
Changing their colors as they grew together.
But when they saw this had no power to stay you,
They often wept, though, speechless, could not pray you,
Letting their tears in your fair bosoms fall,
140 As if they said, Why will ye leave us all?
This being vain, they cast their leaves away
Hoping that pity would have made you stay:
Their frozen tops, like age's hoary hairs,
Shows their disasters, languishing in fears.
145 A swarthy riveled rind° all over spread,   bark
Their dying bodies half alive, half dead.
But your occasions[1] called you so away
That nothing there had power to make you stay.
Yet did I see a noble grateful mind
150 Requiting each according to their kind,
Forgetting not to turn and take your leave
Of these sad creatures, powerless to receive
Your favor, when with grief you did depart,
Placing their former pleasures in your heart,
155 Giving great charge to noble memory
There to preserve their love continually.
But specially the love of that fair tree,
That first and last you did vouchsafe to see,
In which it pleased you oft to take the air
160 With noble *Dorset*, then a virgin fair,
Where many a learned book was read and scanned,
To this fair tree, taking me by the hand,
You did repeat the pleasures which had passed,

---

8. I.e., we (lowly) may also love God and enjoy God's love, and hence are equal to anyone.
9. As was common, Anne Clifford is here referred to by her husband's title.

1. After her husband's death (1605) Margaret Clifford chiefly resided in her dower properties in the north; Anne Clifford was married in 1609.

Seeming to grieve they could no longer last.
165 And with a chaste, yet loving kiss took leave,
Of which sweet kiss I did it soon bereave,°   *take from it*
Scorning a senseless creature should possess
So rare a favor, so great happiness.
No other kiss it could receive from me,
170 For fear to give back what it took of thee,
So I ungrateful creature did deceive it
Of that which you in love vouchsafed to leave it.
And though it oft had given me much content,
Yet this great wrong I never could repent;
175 But of the happiest made it most forlorn,
To show that nothing's free from Fortune's scorne,
While all the rest with this most beauteous tree
Made their sad comfort sorrow's harmony.
The flowers that on the banks and walks did grow,
180 Crept in the ground, the grass did weep for woe.
The winds and waters seemed to chide together
Because you went away they knew not whither;
And those sweet brooks that ran so fair and clear,
With grief and trouble wrinkled did appear.
185 Those pretty birds that wonted were to sing,
Now neither sing, nor chirp, nor use their wing,
But with their tender feet on some bare spray,
Warble forth sorrow, and their own dismay.
Fair *Philomela* leaves her mournful ditty,
190 Drowned in deep sleep, yet can procure no pity.
Each arbor, bank, each seat, each stately tree
Looks bare and desolate now for want of thee,
Turning green tresses into frosty gray,
While in cold grief they wither all away.
195 The sun grew weak, his beams no comfort gave,
While all green things did make the earth their grave.
Each brier, each bramble, when you went away
Caught fast your clothes, thinking to make you stay;
Delightful Echo wonted° to reply   *was accustomed*
200 To our last words, did now for sorrow die;
The house cast off each garment that might grace it,
Putting on dust and cobwebs to deface it.
All desolation then there did appear,
When you were going whom they held so dear.
205 This last farewell to *Cooke-ham* here I give,
When I am dead thy name in this may live,
Wherein I have performed her noble hest°   *commission*
Whose virtues lodge in my unworthy breast,
And ever shall, so long as life remains,
210 Tying my life to her by those rich chains.[2]

1611

2. Her virtues.

BEN JONSON
1572–1637

In 1616 Ben Jonson published his *Works*, earning howls of derision and incredulity from many who were astounded to see mere plays and poems collected under the same title the king gave to his political treatises. Many of Jonson's contemporaries shied away from publication, either because, like Donne, they wrote for small coterie audiences, or because, like Shakespeare, they wrote for theater companies which preferred not to let go of the scripts. Jonson knew and admired both Donne and Shakespeare, and more than any Jacobean belonged to both of their very different worlds, but in publishing his *Works* he broke with them and laid claim to an altogether higher literary status. He had risen from very humble beginnings to become England's unofficial poet laureate, with a pension from the king and honorary degrees from both universities. If he was not the first professional author in England, he was the first to invest that role with dignity and respectability. His published *Works*, over which he labored with painstaking and pedantic care, are designed to testify to an extraordinary feat of self-transformation.

Jonson's early life was tough and turbulent. The posthumous son of a London clergyman, he was educated at Westminster school under the great antiquarian scholar William Camden. There he developed his love of classical learning, but lacking the resources to continue his education, Jonson was forced to turn to his stepfather's trade of bricklaying, a life he "could not endure." He escaped by joining the English forces in Flanders, where, as he later boasted, he killed a man in single combat before the eyes of two armies. Back in London, his attempt to make a living as an actor and playwright almost ended in early disaster. He was imprisoned in 1597 for collaborating with Thomas Nashe on the scandalous play *The Isle of Dogs* (now lost), and shortly after his release he killed one of his fellow actors in a duel. Jonson escaped the gallows by pleading benefit of clergy (a medieval privilege allowing felons who could read Latin to be tried by a more lenient ecclesiastical court). His learning had saved his life, but he emerged from captivity branded on the thumb, and with another mark against him as well. Under the influence of a priest imprisoned with him, he had converted to Catholicism (around the time that John Donne was abandoning that faith). Jonson was now more than ever a marginal figure, distrusted by the society that he satirized brilliantly in his early plays.

Jonson's fortunes improved with the accession of James I, though not at once. In 1603 he was called before the Privy Council to answer charges of "popery and treason" found in his play *Sejanus*. Little more than a year later he was in jail again for his part in the play *Eastward Ho*, which openly mocked the king's Scots accent and propensity for selling knighthoods. But Jonson was now on the way to establishing himself at the new court. In 1605 he received the commission to organize the Twelfth Night entertainment; *The Masque of Blackness* was the first of twenty-four masques he would produce for the court, most of them in collaboration with the architect and scene designer Inigo Jones. In the same years that he was writing the masques he produced his greatest works for the public theater. His first successful play, *Every Man in His Humor* (1598), had inaugurated the so-called "comedy of humors," in which the ruling eccentricities or passions of the characters (thought to be caused by physiological imbalance) are exposed to ridicule. He capitalized on this success with the comedies *Volpone* (1606), *The Alchemist* (1610), and *Bartholomew Fair* (1614). Jonson preserved the detached, satiric perspective of an outsider, but he was rising in society and making accommodations where necessary. In 1605, when suspicion fell upon him as a Catholic following the exposure of the Gunpowder Plot, he showed his loyalty by agreeing to serve as a spy for the Privy Council. Five years later he would return to the Church of England.

Although he rose to a position of eminent respectability, Jonson seems to have been possessed all his life by an uncontrollably quarrelsome spirit. Indeed, much of his best work emerged out of fierce tensions with his collaborators and contemporaries. At the turn of the century he became embroiled in the so-called "War of the Theaters," in which he satirized and was satirized by his fellow playwrights John Marston and Thomas Dekker. Later, his long collaborative partnership with Inigo Jones was marked by ever more bitter rivalry over the relative importance of words and scenery in the making of masques. Jonson also poured scorn and invective on the public theater audiences who failed, in his view, to appreciate the classical unities he brought to his plots. The failure of his play *The New Inn* elicited his *Ode to Himself* (1629), a disgusted farewell to the "loathed stage." Yet even after a stroke in 1629 left him partially paralyzed and confined to his home, Jonson continued to write for the stage, and was at work on a new play when he died in 1637.

In spite of his antagonistic nature, Jonson had a great capacity for friendship. His friends included Shakespeare, Donne, Francis Bacon, and John Selden, and in later years he gathered about himself a group of admiring younger men known as the "Sons of Ben," whose numbers included Herrick, Carew, and Suckling. He was a fascinating and inexhaustible conversationalist, as recorded by his friend William Drummond of Hawthornden, who carefully noted down Jonson's off-the-cuff opinions on a wide variety of subjects, ranging from his fellow poets to his sexual predilections. Jonson also moved easily among the great of the land, though in poems like *Celebration of Charis* he shows himself cutting a ridiculous figure in the fashionable world. His patrons included Lady Mary Wroth and Sir Walter Ralegh and members of the Sidney and Herbert families. In *To Penshurst,* a celebration of Robert Sidney's country estate, Jonson offers an ideal image of a social order in which a virtuous patriarchal governor offers ready hospitality to guests of all stations, from poets to kings.

To Penshurst, together with Aemilia Lanyer's *Description of Cooke-ham,* inaugurated the small genre of the "country-house poem" in England. Jonson tried his hand, usually with success, at a wide range of poetic genres, including epitaph and epigram, love and funeral elegy, verse satire and verse letter, song and ode. More often than not he looked back to classical precedents. From the Roman poets Horace and Martial he derived not only generic models but an ideal vision of the artist and society against which he measured himself and the court he served. In many poems he adopted the persona of "bluff Ben," a witty, keenly perceptive, and scrupulously honest judge of men and women. The classical values Jonson most admired are enumerated in his longest epigram, *Inviting a Friend to Supper,* which describes a dinner party characterized by moderation, civility, graciousness, and pleasure that delights without enslaving—all contrasting sharply with the excess and licentiousness that marked the banquets and entertainments of imperial Rome and Stuart England. Yet the poet who produced this image of perfect moderation was notorious in his life as a drinker and a glutton with, as he puts it in *My Picture Left in Scotland,* a "mountain belly." Jonson was a man of immense appetites, which found expression in his art as well as in his life. His best works seethe with an almost uncontrollable imaginative energy and lust for abundance. Even his profound classical learning manifests this impulse. The notes and references to learned authorities which spill across the margins of his *Works* can be seen as the literary equivalent of food and drink piled high on the poet's table. Years of hardship had taught Jonson to seek his feasts in his imagination, and he could make the most mundane object the basis for flights of high fancy. As he told Drummond, he once "consumed a whole night in lying looking to his great toe, about which he had seen Tartars and Turks, Romans and Carthaginians fight in his imagination." In Drummond's view, Jonson was "oppressed with fantasy." Perhaps it was so—but Jonson's capacity for fantasy also produced a wide variety of plays, masques, and poems, in styles ranging from witty comedy to delicate lyricism.

FROM EPIGRAMS[1]

To My Book

It will be looked for, book, when some but see
   Thy title, *Epigrams*, and named of me,
Thou should'st be bold, licentious, full of gall,
   Wormwood° and sulphur, sharp and toothed[2] withal,   *bitter-tasting plant*
5 Become a petulant thing, hurl ink and wit
   As madmen stones, not caring whom they hit.
Deceive their malice who could wish it so,
   And by thy wiser temper let men know
Thou art not covetous of least self-fame
10   Made from the hazard of another's shame[3]—
Much less with lewd, profane, and beastly phrase
   To catch the world's loose laughter or vain gaze.
He that departs° with his own honesty   *parts*
   For vulgar praise, doth it too dearly buy.

1616

On My First Daughter[1]

Here lies, to each her parents' ruth,°   *grief*
   Mary, the daughter of their youth;
Yet all heaven's gifts being heaven's due,
   It makes the father less to rue.
5 At six months' end she parted hence
   With safety of her innocence;
Whose soul heaven's queen, whose name she bears,
   In comfort of her mother's tears,
Hath placed amongst her virgin-train:
10   Where, while that severed doth remain,
This grave partakes the fleshly birth;°   *the body*
   Which cover lightly, gentle earth![2]

1616

1. Epigrams are commonly thought of as brief, witty, incisive poems of personal invective, often with a surprise turn at the end. But when Jonson included in his collected *Works* of 1616 a separate section headed "Epigrams (Book 1)," he was using the word in a more liberal sense. His "epigrams" included (besides some sharp and satiric verses) several poems of compliment and courtesy, some memorial epitaphs, and a verse letter, *Inviting a Friend to Supper*. *To My Book* and the next several poems come from this section. The "Book 1" of Jonson's title implied a "Book 2"; there are a num-

ber of epigramlike verses scattered through his later poetry, but Jonson never assembled them under any such title.
2. The distinction between toothed (biting) and toothless (general) satires—originally made by Joseph Hall (1574–1656), who claimed to be the first English satirist—was a commonplace.
3. Here, as often elsewhere, Jonson echoes the greatest Roman epigrammatist, Martial.
1. Probably written in the late 1590s, in Jonson's Roman Catholic period (ca. 1598–1610).
2. A common sentiment in Latin epitaphs.

To John Donne

Donne, the delight of Phoebus° and each Muse,   *god of poetry*
Who, to thy one, all other brains refuse;[1]
Whose every work, of thy most early wit,
Came forth example and remains so yet;
5 Longer a-knowing than most wits do live,
And which no affection praise enough can give.
To it[2] thy language, letters, arts, best life,
Which might with half mankind maintain a strife.
All which I meant to praise, and yet I would,
10 But leave, because I cannot as I should.

1616

On Giles and Joan

Who says that Giles and Joan at discord be?
Th' observing neighbors no such mood can see.
Indeed, poor Giles repents he married ever,
But that his Joan doth too. And Giles would never
5 By his free will be in Joan's company;
No more would Joan he should. Giles riseth early,
And having got him out of doors is glad;
The like is Joan. But turning home is sad,
And so is Joan. Ofttimes, when Giles doth find
10 Harsh sights at home, Giles wisheth he were blind:
All this doth Joan. Or that his long-yearned[1] life
Were quite outspun. The like wish hath his wife.
The children that he keeps Giles swears are none
Of his begetting; and so swears his Joan.
15 In all affections she concurreth still.
If now, with man and wife, to will and nill°   *not will*
The self-same things a note of concord be,
I know no couple better can agree.

1616

On My First Son

Farewell, thou child of my right hand,[1] and joy;
My sin was too much hope of thee, loved boy:
Seven years thou wert lent to me, and I thee pay,
Exacted by thy fate, on the just day.
5 O could I lose all father now! For why
Will man lament the state he should envy,

---

1. I.e., the muses shower their favors exclusively
on you.
2. In addition to your wit.
1. Spun from long skeins of yarn.

1. A literal translation of the Hebrew name "Benjamin," which implies the meaning "dexterous" or "fortunate." The boy was born in 1596 and died on his birthday in 1603.

To have so soon 'scaped world's and flesh's rage,
   And, if no other misery, yet age?
Rest in soft peace, and asked, say, "Here doth lie
10   Ben Jonson his best piece of poetry."[2]
For whose sake henceforth all his vows be such
   As what he loves may never like too much.[3]

1616

To Lucy, Countess of Bedford, with Mr. Donne's Satires[1]

Lucy, you brightness[2] of our sphere, who are
   Life of the Muses' day, their morning star!
If works, not th' authors, their own grace should look,°   *have regard to*
   Whose poems would not wish to be your book?
5   But these, desired by you, the maker's ends
   Crown with their own. Rare poems ask rare friends.
Yet satires, since the most of mankind be
   Their unavoided° subject, fewest see: *inevitable*
For none e'er took that pleasure in sin's sense,
10   But, when they heard it taxed, took more offense.
They then that, living where the matter is bred,[3]
   Dare for these poems yet both ask and read
And like them too, must needfully, though few,
   Be of the best: and 'mongst those, best are you;
15 Lucy, you brightness of our sphere, who are
   The Muses' evening, as their morning star.[4]

1616

Inviting a Friend to Supper

Tonight, grave sir, both my poor house and I
   Do equally desire your company:
Not that we think us worthy such a guest,
   But that your worth will dignify our feast
5 With those that come; whose grace may make that seem
   Something, which else could hope for no esteem.
It is the fair acceptance, Sir, creates
   The entertainment perfect: not the cates.°   *food*
Yet shall you have, to rectify your palate,
10   An olive, capers, or some better salad
Ushering the mutton; with a short-legged hen,

2. Poet and father are both makers, Jonson's favorite term for the poet.
3. The obscure grammar of the last lines allows for various readings; "like" may carry the sense of "please."
1. With this poem, Jonson offered a manuscript collection of Donne's satires (see p. 618), such as commonly passed from hand to hand in court cir-

cles.
2. Lucy's name derives from the Latin *lux*, meaning light.
3. I.e., at court.
4. The planet Venus is called Lucifer (light-bearing) when it appears before sunrise, Hesperus when it appears after sunset.

If we can get her, full of eggs, and then
Lemons and wine for sauce; to these, a coney°   *rabbit*
Is not to be despaired of for our money;

15   And though fowl now be scarce, yet there are clerks,°   *scholars*
The sky not falling, think we may have larks.
I'll tell you of more, and lie, so you will come:
Of partridge, pheasant, woodcock, of which some
May yet be there; and godwit if we can,

20   Knot, rail, and ruff, too.[1] Howsoe'er, my man°   *servant*
Shall read a piece of Virgil, Tacitus,
Livy, or of some better book to us,
Of which we'll speak our minds amidst our meat;
And I'll profess° no verses to repeat: *promise*

25   To this,° if aught appear which I not know of,   *add to this*
That will the pastry, not my paper, show of.[2]
Digestive cheese and fruit there sure will be;
But that which most doth take my muse and me
Is a pure cup of rich Canary wine,

30   Which is the Mermaid's now, but shall be mine;
Of which, had Horace or Anacreon[3] tasted,
Their lives, as do their lines, till now had lasted.
Tobacco, Nectar, or the Thespian spring[4]
Are all but Luther's beer to this I sing.

35   Of this we will sup free but moderately,
And we will have no Pooly or Parrot[5] by;
Nor shall our cups make any guilty men,
But at our parting we will be as when
We innocently met. No simple word

40   That shall be uttered at our mirthful board
Shall make us sad next morning, or affright
The liberty that we'll enjoy tonight.

                                                        1616

Epitaph on S. P., a Child of Queen Elizabeth's Chapel[1]

Weep with me, all you that read
     This little story;
And know for whom a tear you shed,
     Death's self is sorry.
5   'Twas a child that so did thrive
     In grace and feature,
As Heaven and Nature seemed to strive
     Which owned the creature.
Years he numbered scarce thirteen

1. All these are edible birds.
2. I.e., papers may appear, but they will be under pies (to keep them from sticking to the pan), not for declamation.
3. Horace and Anacreon (one in Latin, the other in Greek) wrote many poems in praise of wine. The Mermaid tavern was a favorite haunt of the poets; sweet wine from the Canary Islands was popular in England.
4. One of two springs on Mount Helicon, both reputed to be sources of poetic inspiration. Com-pared to Canary, all these other intoxicants are no better than inferior German beer.
5. Pooly and Parrot were government spies, though their conjunction also suggests a talkative bird, Poll Parrot. While a Roman Catholic and even after, Jonson had reason to be wary of under-cover agents.
1. Salomon Pavy, a boy actor in the troupe known as the Children of Queen Elizabeth's Chapel, who had appeared in several of Jonson's plays; he died in 1602.

10 When Fates turned cruel,
Yet three filled zodiacs had he been
 The stage's jewel;[2]
And did act (what now we moan)
 Old men so duly,°   *aptly*
15 As, sooth, the Parcae° thought him one,   *Fates*
He played so truly.
So, by error, to his fate
 They all consented;
But, viewing him since (alas, too late),
20 They have repented,
And have sought (to give new birth)
 In baths[3] to steep him;
But, being so much too good for earth,
 Heaven vows to keep him.

                   1616

From The Forest[1]

To Penshurst[2]

Thou art not, Penshurst, built to envious show,
 Of touch[3] or marble; nor canst boast a row
Of polished pillars, or a roof of gold;
 Thou hast no lantern° whereof tales are told, *cupola*
5 Or stair, or courts; but stand'st an ancient pile,
 And, these grudged at,[4] art reverenced the while.
Thou joy'st in better marks, of soil, of air,
 Of wood, of water; therein thou art fair.
Thou hast thy walks for health, as well as sport;
10 Thy mount, to which the dryads° do resort, *wood nymphs*
Where Pan and Bacchus their high feasts have made,
 Beneath the broad beech and the chestnut shade;
That taller tree, which of a nut was set
 At his great birth where all the Muses met.[5]
15 There in the writhèd bark are cut the names
 Of many a sylvan,° taken with his flames; *countryman*
And thence the ruddy satyrs[6] oft provoke
 The lighter fauns to reach thy Lady's Oak.[7]
Thy copse° too, named of Gamage,[8] thou hast there, *little woods*

---

2. He had been on the stage for three seasons.
3. Perhaps such magic baths as that of Medea, which restored Jason's father to his first youth (Ovid, *Metamorphoses* 7).
1. In the 1616 *Works*, Jonson grouped some of his nonepigrammatic poems under the heading *The Forest*, a translation of the term *Sylvae*, meaning a poetic miscellany. *To Penshurst* and the two following poems are from that group.
2. Penshurst, in Kent, was the estate of Robert Sidney, Viscount Lisle (later, earl of Leicester), a younger brother of the poet Sir Philip Sidney (see p. 444). Along with Lanyer's *The Description of Cooke-ham* (p. 632), this poem inaugurated the small genre of English "country-house" poems.
3. Touchstone, a fine black (and expensive) variety of basalt.
4. More pretentious houses attract envy.
5. Sir Philip Sidney was born at Penshurst.
6. Satyrs and fauns were woodland spirits. Satyrs, with the body of a man and the legs (and horns) of a goat, were symbols of lechery. "Provokes": challenges to a race.
7. Named after a lady of the house who went into labor under its branches.
8. Lady Barbara (Gamage) Sidney, wife of Sir Robert.

20   That never fails to serve thee seasoned deer
    When thou wouldst feast or exercise thy friends.
      The lower land, that to the river bends,
    Thy sheep, thy bullocks, kine,° and calves do feed;   *cattle*
      The middle grounds thy mares and horses breed.
25   Each bank doth yield thee conies;° and the tops,°   *rabbits / high ground*
    Fertile of wood, Ashore and Sidney's copse,
      To crown thy open table, doth provide
      The purpled pheasant with the speckled side;
    The painted partridge lies in every field,
30   And for thy mess is willing to be killed.
    And if the high-swollen Medway⁹ fail thy dish,
      Thou hast thy ponds, that pay thee tribute fish:
    Fat agèd carps that run into thy net,
      And pikes, now weary their own kind to eat,
35   As loath the second draught or cast to stay,
      Officiously° at first themselves betray;   *dutifully*
    Bright eels that emulate them, and leap on land
      Before the fisher, or into his hand.
    Then hath thy orchard fruit, thy garden flowers,
40   Fresh as the air, and new as are the hours.
    The early cherry, with the later plum,
      Fig, grape, and quince, each in his time doth come;
    The blushing apricot and woolly peach
      Hang on thy walls, that every child may reach.
45   And though thy walls be of the country stone,
      They're reared with no man's ruin, no man's groan;
    There's none that dwell about them wish them down;
      But all come in, the farmer and the clown,°   *peasant*
    And no one empty-handed, to salute
50   Thy lord and lady, though they have no suit.°   *request to make*
    Some bring a capon, some a rural cake,
      Some nuts, some apples; some that think they make
    The better cheeses bring them, or else send
      By their ripe daughters, whom they would commend
55   This way to husbands, and whose baskets bear
      An emblem of themselves in plum or pear.
    But what can this (more than express their love)
      Add to thy free provisions, far above
    The need of such? whose liberal board doth flow
60   With all that hospitality doth know;
    Where comes no guest but is allowed to eat,
      Without his fear, and of thy lord's own meat;
    Where the same beer and bread, and selfsame wine,
      That is his lordship's shall be also mine,
65   And I not fain to sit (as some this day
      At great men's tables), and yet dine away.¹
    Here no man tells° my cups; nor, standing by,   *counts*
      A waiter doth my gluttony envy,

---

9. The local river.
1. Different courses might be served to different guests, depending on their social status. The lord would have the best food.

But gives me what I call, and lets me eat;
70   He knows below° he shall find plenty of meat.   *in the servants' quarters*
Thy tables hoard not up for the next day;
    Nor, when I take my lodging, need I pray
For fire, or lights, or livery; all is there,
    As if thou then wert mine, or I reigned here:
75   There's nothing I can wish, for which I stay.°   *wait*
That found King James when, hunting late this way
With his brave son, the Prince,² they saw thy fires
    Shine bright on every hearth, as the desires
Of thy Penates° had been set on flame   *Roman household gods*
80   To entertain them; or the country came
With all their zeal to warm their welcome here.
    What (great I will not say, but) sudden cheer
Didst thou then make 'em! and what praise was heaped
    On thy good lady then, who therein reaped
85   The just reward of her high housewifery;
    To have her linen, plate, and all things nigh,
When she was far; and not a room but dressed
    As if it had expected such a guest!
These, Penshurst, are thy praise, and yet not all.
90   Thy lady's noble, fruitful, chaste withal.
His children thy great lord may call his own,
    A fortune in this age but rarely known.
They are, and have been, taught religion; thence
    Their gentler spirits have sucked innocence.
95   Each morn and even they are taught to pray,
    With the whole household, and may, every day,
Read in their virtuous parents' noble parts
    The mysteries of manners, arms, and arts.
Now, Penshurst, they that will proportion° thee   *compare*
100   With other edifices, when they see
Those proud, ambitious heaps, and nothing else,
    May say, their lords have built, but thy lord dwells.

1616

Song: To Celia¹

Drink to me only with thine eyes,
    And I will pledge with mine;
Or leave a kiss but in the cup,
    And I'll not look for wine.
5   The thirst that from the soul doth rise
    Doth ask a drink divine:
But might I of Jove's nectar sup,
    I would not change for thine.

2. Prince Henry, the heir apparent, who died in November 1612.
1. These famous lines are a patchwork of five separate prose passages by Philostratus, a Greek sophist (3rd century C.E.). The music that has made it a barroom favorite is by an anonymous 18th-century composer.

I sent thee late a rosy wreath,
10   Not so much honoring thee,
As giving it a hope that there
    It could not withered be.
But thou thereon didst only breathe,
    And sent'st it back to me;
15 Since when it grows and smells, I swear,
    Not of itself, but thee.

1616

To Heaven

Good and great God, can I not think of thee
    But it must straight my melancholy be?
Is it interpreted in me disease
    That, laden with my sins, I seek for ease?
5 Oh, be thou witness, that the reins[1] dost know
    And hearts of all, if I be sad for show,
And judge me after, if I dare pretend
    To aught but grace, or aim at other end.
As thou art all, so be thou all to me,
10   First, midst, and last, converted° one and three,   *interchanging*
My faith, my hope, my love; and in this state,
    My judge, my witness, and my advocate.
Where have I been this while exiled from thee,
    And whither rapt,° now thou but stoop'st to me?   *carried off*
15 Dwell, dwell here still: Oh, being everywhere,
    How can I doubt to find thee ever here?
I know my state, both full of shame and scorn,
    Conceived in sin and unto labor born,
Standing with fear, and must with horror fall,
20   And destined unto judgment after all.
I feel my griefs too, and there scarce is ground
    Upon my flesh to inflict another wound.
Yet dare I not complain or wish for death
    With holy Paul,[2] lest it be thought the breath
25 Of discontent; or that these prayers be
    For weariness of life, not love of thee.

1616

My Picture Left in Scotland[1]

I now think Love is rather deaf than blind,
    For else it could not be

---

1. Literally, kidneys, but also the seat of the affections, with a glance at Psalm 7.9: "the righteous God trieth the hearts and reins."
2. "Who shall deliver me from the body of this death?" (Roman 7.24).

1. After his walking tour of Scotland in 1618–19, Jonson sent a manuscript version of this poem to William Drummond, with whom he had stayed. The woman of the poem may or may not be a real person.

That she
Whom I adore so much should so slight me
5   And cast my love behind;
I'm sure my language to her was as sweet,
    And every close° did meet   *cadence*
    In sentence° of as subtle feet,   *wise sayings*
    As hath the youngest he
10   That sits in shadow of Apollo's tree.[2]

O, but my conscious fears
    That fly my thoughts between,
    Tell me that she hath seen
    My hundreds of gray hairs,
15   Told seven and forty years,
Read so much waist[3] as she cannot embrace
My mountain belly and my rocky face;
And all these through her eyes have stopped her ears.

1619   1640–41

Queen and Huntress[1]

Queen and huntress, chaste and fair,
Now the sun is laid to sleep,
Seated in thy silver chair,
State in wonted manner keep;
5   Hesperus entreats thy light,
Goddess excellently bright.

Earth, let not thy envious shade
Dare itself to interpose;[2]
Cynthia's shining orb was made
10   Heaven to clear, when day did close.
Bless us then with wishèd sight,
Goddess excellently bright.

Lay thy bow of pearl apart,
And thy crystal-shining quiver;
15   Give unto the flying hart
Space to breathe, how short soever.
Thou that mak'st a day of night,
Goddess excellently bright.

1600

---

2. The god of poetry.
3. With a pun on waste.
1. Also from *Cynthia's Revels* (4.3), this song is sung by Hesperus, the evening star, to Cynthia or

Diana, goddess of chastity and the moon—with whom Queen Elizabeth was constantly compared.
2. Eclipses were thought to portend evil.

Though I Am Young[1]

Though I am young and cannot tell
Either what Death or Love is well,
Yet I have heard they both bear darts,
And both do aim at human hearts.
5   And then again, I have been told
Love wounds with heat, as Death with cold;
So that I fear they do but bring
Extremes to touch, and mean one thing.

As in a ruin we it call
10   One thing to be blown up or fall;
Or to our end like way may have
By a flash of lightning or a wave;
So Love's inflamèd shaft or brand
May kill as soon as Death's cold hand;
15   Except[2] Love's fires the virtue have
To fright the frost out of the grave.

1640–41

Still to Be Neat[1]

Still to be neat, still to be dressed
As° you were going to a feast,   *as though*
Still to be powdered, still perfumed;
Lady, it is to be presumed,
5   Though art's hid causes are not found,
All is not sweet, all is not sound.

Give me a look, give me a face
That makes simplicity a grace;
Robes loosely flowing, hair as free—
10   Such sweet neglect more taketh me
Than all the adulteries of art.
They strike mine eyes, but not my heart.

1609

To the Memory of My Beloved, The Author, Mr. William Shakespeare, and What He Hath Left Us[1]

To draw no envy, Shakespeare, on thy name,
Am I thus ample° to thy book and fame,   *copious*

---

1. This song is sung in *The Sad Shepherd*, by Karolin; the pastoral simplicity of his character is caught in the naive monosyllables of the poem.
2. Unless.

1. Sung in the play *Epicoene*, this song concerns the art of makeup, but also art more generally.
1. This poem was prefixed to the first Folio of Shakespeare's plays (1623).

While I confess thy writings to be such
    As neither man nor muse can praise too much.
5 'Tis true, and all men's suffrage.° But these ways   *consent*
    Were not the paths I meant unto thy praise;
For silliest° ignorance on these may light,   *simplest*
    Which, when it sounds at best, but echoes right;
Or blind affection, which doth ne'er advance
10   The truth, but gropes, and urgeth all by chance;
Or crafty malice might pretend this praise,
    And think to ruin where it seemed to raise.
These are as° some infamous bawd or whore   *as though*
    Should praise a matron. What could hurt her more?
15 But thou art proof against them, and, indeed,
    Above th' ill fortune of them, or the need.
I therefore will begin. Soul of the age!
    The applause! delight! the wonder of our stage!
My Shakespeare, rise; I will not lodge thee by
20   Chaucer or Spenser, or bid Beaumont lie
A little further to make thee a room:[2]
    Thou art a monument without a tomb,
And art alive still while thy book doth live,
    And we have wits to read and praise to give.
25 That I not mix thee so, my brain excuses,
    I mean with great, but disproportioned° Muses;   *not comparable*
For, if I thought my judgment were of years,
    I should commit thee surely with thy peers,
And tell how far thou didst our Lyly outshine,
30   Or sporting Kyd, or Marlowe's mighty line.[3]
And though thou hadst small Latin and less Greek,[4]
    From thence to honor thee I would not seek°   *lack*
For names, but call forth thund'ring Aeschylus,
    Euripides, and Sophocles to us,
35 Pacuvius, Accius, him of Cordova dead,[5]
    To life again, to hear thy buskin° tread   *symbol of tragedy*
And shake a stage; or, when thy socks° were on,   *symbol of comedy*
    Leave thee alone for the comparison
Of all that insolent Greece or haughty Rome
40   Sent forth, or since did from their ashes come.
Triumph, my Britain; thou hast one to show
    To whom all scenes° of Europe homage owe.   *stages*
He was not of an age, but for all time!
    And all the Muses still were in their prime
45 When like Apollo he came forth to warm
    Our ears, or like a Mercury to charm.
Nature herself was proud of his designs,

2. Chaucer, Spenser, and Francis Beaumont were buried in Westminster Abbey; Shakespeare, in Stratford.
3. John Lily, Thomas Kyd, and Christopher Marlowe were Elizabethan dramatists contemporary or nearly contemporary with Shakespeare.
4. Shakespeare's Latin was pretty good, but Jon-son is judging by the standard of his own remarkable scholarship.
5. Marcus Pacuvius, Lucius Accius (2nd century B.C.E.) and "him of Cordova," Seneca the Younger (Ist century C.E.), were Latin tragedians. Seneca's tragedies had a large influence on Elizabethan revenge tragedy.

And joyed to wear the dressing of his lines,
Which were so richly spun, and woven so fit,
50   As, since, she will vouchsafe no other wit:
The merry Greek, tart Aristophanes,
Neat Terence, witty Plautus[6] now not please,
But antiquated and deserted lie,
As they were not of Nature's family.
55   Yet must I not give Nature all; thy Art,
My gentle Shakespeare, must enjoy a part.
For though the poet's matter° Nature be,   subject matter
His Art doth give the fashion;° and that he   form, style
Who casts° to write a living line must sweat   undertakes
60   (Such as thine are) and strike the second heat
Upon the Muses' anvil; turn the same,
And himself with it, that he thinks to frame,
Or for the laurel he may gain a scorn;
For a good poet's made as well as born.
65   And such wert thou! Look how the father's face
Lives in his issue; even so the race
Of Shakespeare's mind and manners brightly shines
In his well-turnèd and true-filèd lines,
In each of which he seems to shake a lance,[7]
70   As brandished at the eyes of ignorance.
Sweet swan of Avon, what a sight it were
To see thee in our waters yet appear,
And make those flights upon the banks of Thames
That so did take Eliza and our James![8]
75   But stay; I see thee in the hemisphere
Advanced and made a constellation there![9]
Shine forth, thou star of poets, and with rage
Or influence[1] chide or cheer the drooping stage,
Which, since thy flight from hence, hath mourned like night,
80   And despairs day, but for thy volume's light.

1623

6. Aristophanes, an ancient Greek satirist and writer of comedy; Terence and Plautus (2nd and 3rd centuries B.C.E.), Roman writers of comedy.
7. Pun on Shake-speare.
8. Queen Elizabeth and King James.

9. Heroes and demigods were typically exalted after death to a place among the stars.
1. "Rage" and "influence" describe the supposed effects of the planets on earthly affairs. "Rage" also implies poetic inspiration.

MARY WROTH
1587–1651?

Lady Mary Wroth was the most prolific, self-conscious, and impressive female author
of the Jacobean era. Her published work (1621) include two firsts for an Englishwoman: a 558-page romance, *The Countess of Montgomery's Urania*, which includes
more than fifty poems; and appended to it a Petrarchan lyric sequence that had

circulated some years in manuscript, 103 sonnets and elegant songs titled *Pamphilia to Amphilanthus*. Wroth left unpublished a very long but unfinished continuation of the *Urania* and a pastoral drama, *Love's Victory*, also a first for an Englishwoman. Her achievement was fostered by her strong sense of identity as a Sidney, heir to the literary talent and cultural role of her famous uncle Sir Philip Sidney, her famous aunt Mary Sidney Herbert, countess of Pembroke, who may have served as mentor to her, and her father Robert Sidney, Viscount Lisle, author of a recently discovered sonnet sequence. But she used that heritage transgressively to replace heroes with heroines in genres employed by the male Sidney authors—notably Philip Sidney's *Astrophil and Stella* and *The Countess of Pembroke's Arcadia*—transforming their gender politics and exploring the poetics and situation of women writers.

As Robert Sidney's eldest daughter, she lived and was educated at Penshurst, the Sidney country house celebrated by Ben Jonson, and was often at her aunt's "little college" at Wilton. She danced at court in *The Masque of Blackness* and perhaps in other masques; she was married (incompatibly) at age seventeen to Sir Robert Wroth of Durrance and Loughton Manor, whose office it was to facilitate the king's hunting; and she was patron to several poets, including Jonson. He celebrated her in two epigrams and in a verse letter honoring her husband, dedicated his great comedy *The Alchemist* to her, and claimed in his only sonnet (p. 1408) that the artistry and erotic power of her sonnets had made him "a better lover, and much better poet." After her husband's death she carried on a long-standing love affair with her married first cousin, William Herbert, earl of Pembroke, himself a poet, a powerful courtier, and a patron of the theater and of literature. That relationship produced two children and occasioned some scandal.

The significant names in the title of Wroth's Petrarchan sequence, *Pamphilia* ("all-loving") *to Amphilanthus* ("lover of two"), are from characters in her romance who at times shadow Wroth and her lover Pembroke. Though it was passé by Wroth's time, the Petrarchan lyric sequence had long served as the major genre for analyzing a male lover's desire, passions, frustrations, and fantasies (and sometimes his career anxieties), so it was the obvious beginning point for a woman poet undertaking the construction of subjectivity in a female lover-speaker. Wroth does not, however, simply reverse roles: Pamphilia addresses very few sonnets to Amphilanthus and seldom assumes the Petrarchan lover's position of abject servitude to a cruel beloved; instead, she proclaims subjection to Cupid, usually identified with the force of her own desire. This radical revision identifies female desire as the source and center of the love relationship and celebrates the woman lover-poet's movement from the bondage of chaotic passion to the freedom of self-chosen constancy.

Wroth's romance, *Urania*, breaks the romance convention of a plot centered on courtship, portraying instead married heroines and their love relationships, both inside and outside of marriage. It is in part an idealizing fantasy in which all the principal characters are queens, kings, and emperors, with the power and comparative freedom such positions allow. However the landscape is not Arcadia or Fairyland but war-torn Europe and Asia, and the romance fantasy, with Spenserian symbolic places and knights fighting evil tyrants and monsters, only partially overlays a rigidly patriarchal Jacobean world rife with rape, incest, arranged or forced marriages, jealous husbands, tortured women, and endangered children. Those conditions, affecting all women from shepherdesses to queens, are rendered in large part through the numerous stories interpolated in romance fashion within the principal plots. The male heroes are courageous fighters and attractive lovers, but all are flawed by inconstancy. The higher heroism involves attainment or preservation of personal integrity and agency in love amid intense social and psychological pressures and constraints, and it belongs to a few women, chief among them Pamphilia, the good queen and heroine of constancy; Urania, the wise counselor who wins through to self-knowledge and makes wise choices in love; and Veralinda, who marries her true lover after great trials. A major means of self-definition and agency for almost all Wroth's female characters is storytelling and making poems. Women compose twice as many of the poems as men do, and Pamphilia (Wroth's surrogate) is singled out as a poet by vocation by the number and recognized excellence of her poems.

The *Urania* was widely assumed by contemporaries to be a *roman á clef*, alluding not only to Sidney-Pembroke-Wroth affairs but also at times to notable scandals and personages of the Jacobean court. A public outcry from one such target, Lord Edward Denny, elicited from Wroth a spirited and satiric response; she also made an offer to the king's minister Buckingham to withdraw the work from circulation. There is, however, no evidence that she actually did so, though the uproar may have discouraged her from publishing part II of the romance and her pastoral drama.

From The Countess of Montgomery's Urania[1]

From *The First Book*

When the spring began to appear like the welcome messenger of summer, one sweet (and in that more sweet) morning, after Aurora[2] had called all careful eyes to attend the day, forth came the fair shepherdess Urania[3] (fair indeed; yet that far too mean a title for her, who for beauty deserved the highest style[4] could be given by best-knowing judgments). Into the mead[5] she came, where usually she drove her flocks to feed, whose leaping and wantonness showed they were proud of such a guide: but she, whose sad thoughts led her to another manner of spending her time, made her soon leave them, and follow her late-begun custom; which was (while they delighted themselves) to sit under some shade, bewailing her misfortune; while they fed, to feed upon her own sorrow and tears, which at this time she began again to summon, sitting down under the shade of a well-spread beech; the ground (then blest) and the tree, with full and fine-leaved branches, growing proud to bear and shadow such perfections. But she regarding nothing, in comparison of her woe, thus proceeded in her grief: "Alas Urania," said she (the true servant to misfortune), "of any misery that can befall woman, is not this the most and greatest which thou art fallen into? Can there be any near the unhappiness of being ignorant, and that in the highest kind, not being certain of mine own estate or birth? Why was I not still continued in the belief I was, as I appear, a shepherdess, and daughter to a shepherd? My ambition then went no higher than this estate, now flies it to a knowledge; then was I contented, now perplexed. O ignorance, can thy dullness yet procure so sharp a pain? and that such a thought as makes me now aspire unto knowledge? How did I joy in this poor life, being quiet? blest in the love of those I took for parents, but now by them I know the contrary, and by that knowledge, now to know myself. Miserable Urania,

1. Wroth's title echoes *The Countess of Pembroke's Arcadia*, the romance written by her uncle, Sir Philip Sidney. The countess of Montgomery was Susan (Vere) Herbert, Wroth's close friend and the sister-in-law of her lover, William Herbert. The opening of *Urania* is meant to be compared to (and contrasted with) the opening of the *Arcadia*, in which two shepherds lament the absence of their beloved, the mysterious shepherdess Urania.
2. The Greek goddess of the dawn.
3. The name has multiple associations: the Muse of Astronomy, the Muse of Christian Poetry, a sur-

name for Aphrodite (Venus) designating Heavenly Beauty. It was also an honorific commonly bestowed on Wroth's aunt, Mary Sidney, countess of Pembroke. In Wroth's romance, Urania is a foundling adopted by shepherds but actually the daughter of the king of Naples: after losing one lover and gaining another, she marries, becomes a matriarch, and is throughout (as in this episode) a counselor of others.
4. Title.
5. Meadow.

worse art thou now than these thy lambs; for they know their dams, while thou dost live unknown of any." By this were others come into that mead with their flocks: but she, esteeming her sorrowing thoughts her best and choicest company, left that place, taking a little path which brought her to the further side of the plain, to the foot of the rocks, speaking as she went these lines, her eyes fixed upon the ground, her very soul turned into mourning.

> Unseen, unknown, I here alone complain
> To rocks, to hills, to meadows, and to springs,
> Which can no help return to ease my pain,
> But back my sorrows the sad Echo[6] brings.
> 5 Thus still increasing are my woes to me,
> Doubly resounded by that moanful voice,
> Which seems to second me in misery,
> And answer gives like friend of mine own choice.
> Thus only she doth my companion prove,
> 10 The others silently do offer ease.
> But those that grieve, a grieving note do love;
> Pleasures to dying eyes bring but disease:
> And such am I, who daily ending live,
> Wailing a state which can no comfort give.

In this passion she went on, till she came to the foot of a great rock, she thinking of nothing less than ease, sought how she might ascend it; hoping there to pass away her time more peaceably with loneliness, though not to find least respite from her sorrow, which so dearly she did value, as by no means she would impart it to any. The way was hard, though by some windings making the ascent pleasing. Having attained the top, she saw under some hollow trees the entry into the rock: she fearing nothing but the continuance of her ignorance, went in; where she found a pretty room, as if that stony place had yet in pity, given leave for such perfections to come into the heart as chiefest, and most beloved place, because most loving. The place was not unlike the ancient (or the descriptions of ancient) Hermitages, instead of hangings, covered and lined with ivy, disdaining aught else should come there, that being in such perfection. This richness in Nature's plenty made her stay to behold it, and almost grudge the pleasant fulness of content that place might have, if sensible, while she must know to taste of torments. As she was thus in passion mixed with pain, throwing her eyes as wildly as timorous lovers do for fear of discovery, she perceived a little light, and such a one, as a chink doth oft discover to our sights. She curious to see what this was, with her delicate hands put the natural ornament aside, discerning a little door, which she putting from her, passed through it into another room, like the first in all proportion; but in the midst there was a square stone, like to a pretty table, and on it a wax-candle burning; and by that a paper,[7] which had suffered itself patiently to receive the discovering of

---

6. In classical mythology Echo was a wood nymph who pined away in unrequited love for the handsome Narcissus until only her voice remained (Ovid, *Metamorphoses* 3).
7. The episode alludes to an episode in Sidney's *Old Arcadia* (181) in which one of the heroines, Cleophila, enters a darkened cave illuminated by a single candle and finds a poem on top of a stone table.

so much of it, as presented this sonnet (as it seemed newly written) to her sight.

> Here all alone in silence might I mourn:
> But how can silence be where sorrows flow?
> Sighs with complaints have poorer pains out-worne;
> But broken hearts can only true grief show.
> 5 Drops of my dearest blood shall let Love know
> Such tears for her I shed, yet still do burn,
> As no spring can quench least part of my woe,
> Till this live earth, again to earth doe turne.
> Hateful all thought of comfort is to me,
> 10 Despised day, let me still night possess;
> Let me all torments feel in their excesse,
> And but this light allow my state to see.
> Which still doth waste, and wasting as this light,
> Are my sad days unto eternal night.

"Alas Urania!" sighed she. "How well do these words, this place, and all agree with thy fortune? Sure poor soul thou wert here appointed to spend they days, and these rooms ordained to keep thy tortures in; none being assuredly so matchlessly unfortunate."

Turning from the table, she discerned in the room a bed of boughs, and on it a man lying, deprived of outward sense, as she thought, and of life, as she at first did fear, which struck her into a great amazement: yet having a brave spirit, though shadowed under a mean habit,[8] she stepped unto him, whom she found not dead, but laid upon his back, his head a little to her wards, his arms folded on his breast, hair long, and beard disordered, manifesting all care;[9] but care itself had left him: curiousness thus far afforded him, as to be perfectly discerned the most exact piece of misery; apparel he had suitable to the habitation, which was a long gray[1] robe. This grieveful spectacle did much amaze the sweet and tender-hearted Shepherdess; especially, when she perceived (as she might by the help of the candle) the tears which distilled from his eyes; who seeming the image of death, yet had this sign of worldly sorrow, the drops falling in that abundance, as if there were a kind strife among them, to rid their Master first of that burdenous[2] carriage; or else meaning to make a flood, and so drown their woeful patient in his own sorrow, who yet lay still, but then fetching a deep groan from the profoundest part of his soul, he said:

"Miserable Perissus,[3] canst thou thus live, knowing she that gave thee life is gone? Gone, O me! and with her all my joy departed. Wilt thou (unblessed creature) lie here complaining for her death, and know she died for thee? Let truth and shame make thee do something worthy of such a love, ending thy days like thyself, and one fit to be her servant. But that I must not do: then thus remain and foster storms, still to torment thy wretched soul withall, since all are little, and too too little for such a loss. O dear Limena,[4] loving Limena, worthy Limena, and more rare, constant Limena: perfections deli-

8. Garment.
9. Trouble.
1. Gray is typically associated with mourning and despair.

2. Burdensome.
3. Perissus: Lost one.
4. Limena: Woman of home or threshold.

cately feigned to be in women were verified in thee, was such worthiness framed only to be wondered at by the best, but given as a prey to base and unworthy jealousy? When were all worthy parts joined in one, but in thee (my best Limena)? Yet all these grown subject to a creature ignorant of all but ill; like unto a Fool, who in a dark Cave, that hath but one way to get out, having a candle, but not the understanding what good it doth him, puts it out: this ignorant wretch not being able to comprehend thy virtues, did so by thee in thy murder, putting out the world's light, and men's admiration: Limena, Limena, O my Limena."

With that he fell from complaining into such a passion, as weeping and crying were never in so woeful a perfection, as now in him; which brought as deserved a compassion from the excellent Shepherdess, who already had her heart so tempered with grief, as that it was apt to take any impression that it would come to seal withall. Yet taking a brave courage to her, she stepped unto him, kneeling down by his side, and gently pulling him by the arm, she thus spoke.

"Sir," said she, "having heard some part of your sorrows, they have not only made me truly pity you, but wonder at you; since if you have lost so great a treasure, you should not lie thus leaving her and your love unrevenged, suffering her murderers to live, while you lie here complaining; and if such perfections be dead in her, why make you not the Phoenix[5] of your deeds live again, as to new life raised out of the revenge you should take on them? Then were her end satisfied, and you deservedly accounted worthy of her favor, if she were so worthy as you say."

"If she were, O God," cried out Perissus, "what devilish spirit art thou, that thus dost come to torture me? But now I see you are a woman; and therefore not much to be marked, and less resisted: but if you know charity, I pray now practice it, and leave me who am afflicted sufficiently without your company; or if you will stay, discourse not to me."

"Neither of these will I do," said she.

"If you be then," said he, "some fury of purpose sent to vex me, use your force to the uttermost in martyring me; for never was there a fitter subject, then the heart of poor Perissus is."

"I am no fury," replied the divine Urania, "nor hither come to trouble you, but by accident lighted on this place; my cruel hap being such, as only the like can give me content, while the solitariness of this like cave might give me quiet, though not ease. Seeking for such a one, I happened hither; and this is the true cause of my being here, though now I would use it to a better end if I might: Wherefore favor me with the knowledge of your grief; which heard, it may be I shall give you some counsel, and comfort in your sorrow."

"Cursed may I be," cried he, "if ever I take comfort, having such cause of mourning: but because you are, or seem to be afflicted, I will not refuse to satisfy your demand, but tell you the saddest story that ever was rehearsed by dying man to living woman, and such a one, as I fear will fasten too much sadness in you; yet should I deny it, I were to blame, being so well known to these senseless places; as were they sensible of sorrow, they would condole,

---

5. Mythical bird which could rise with new life after being consumed in flame.

or else amazed at such cruelty stand dumb as they do, to find that man should be so inhuman."

*   *   *

SONG[6]

Love what art thou? A vain thought
In our minds by fant'sy wrought.
Idle smiles did thee beget,
While fond wishes made the net
5   Which so many fools have caught.

Love what art thou? Light and fair,
Fresh as morning, clear as th' air.
But too soon thy evening change
Makes thy worth with coldness range;
10   Still thy joy is mixt with care.

Love what art thou? A sweet flower
Once full blown,° dead in an hour.   *in full bloom*
Dust in wind as staid remains
As thy pleasure or our gains,
15   If thy humor° change, to lour.   *whim*

Love what art thou? Childish, vain,
Firm as bubbles made by rain,
Wantonness thy greatest pride.
These foul faults thy virtues hide—
20   But babes can no staidness gain.

Love what art thou? Causeless cursed,
Yet alas these not the worst:
Much more of thee may be said.
But thy law I once obeyed,
25   Therefore say no more at first.

1621

From Pamphilia to Amphilanthus[1]

1

When night's black mantle could most darkness prove,
And sleep, death's image, did my senses hire

6. This song, one of a group of eclogues that marks the conclusion of book 1 of the *Urania*, is sung to a shepherdess by a shepherd, "being, as it seemed, fallen out with Love."
1. Pamphilia ("All-loving") is the protagonist of *Urania*. Her unfaithful beloved's name means "Lover of Two." These characters are first cousins, like Mary Wroth and William Herbert; their names adumbrate the main theme of both the romance and the appended sonnet sequence, constancy in

the face of unfaithfulness.
    Pamphilia to Amphilanthus is broken into several separately numbered series (the first of which includes forty-eight sonnets, with songs inserted after every sixth sonnet except the last). In Josephine A. Roberts's edition of Wroth's poetry, the poems are numbered consecutively throughout the work; we have adopted this convenient renumbering.

From knowledge of myself, then thoughts did move
Swifter than those most swiftness need require.
5 In sleep, a chariot drawn by winged desire
I saw, where sat bright Venus, Queen of Love,
And at her feet, her son,[2] still adding fire
To burning hearts, which she did hold above.
But one heart flaming more than all the rest
10 The goddess held, and put it to my breast.
"Dear son, now shut,"[3] said she: "thus must we win."
He her obeyed, and martyred my poor heart.
I, waking, hoped as dreams it would depart:
Yet since, O me, a lover I have been.

16

Am I thus conquered? Have I lost the powers
That to withstand, which joys to ruin me?[4]
Must I be still while it my strength devours,
And captive leads me prisoner, bound, unfree?
5 Love first shall leave men's fant'sies to them free,[5]
Desire shall quench Love's flames, spring hate sweet showers,
Love shall loose all his darts, have sight, and see
His shame, and wishings hinder happy hours.
Why should we not Love's purblind° charms resist?   *completely blind*
10 Must we be servile, doing what he list?°   *what pleases him*
No, seek some host to harbor thee: I fly
Thy babish tricks, and freedom do profess.
But O my hurt makes my lost heart confess
I love, and must: So farewell liberty.

40

False hope which feeds but to destroy, and spill[6]
What it first breeds; unnatural to the birth
Of thine own womb; conceiving but to kill,
And plenty gives to make the greater dearth,[7]
5 So tyrants do who falsely ruling earth
Outwardly grace them,[8] and with profits fill,
Advance those who appointed are to death,
To make their greater fall to please their will.
Thus shadow° they their wicked vile intent,   *conceal*
10 Coloring evil with a show of good
While in fair shows their malice so is spent;[9]
Hope kills the heart, and tyrants shed the blood.
For hope deluding brings us to the pride
Of our desires the farther down to slide.

2. Cupid.
3. I.e., shut the burning heart into Pamphilia's breast.
4. I.e., have I lost the power to withstand love ("That"), which takes pleasure in ruining me?
5. I.e., this and the other impossibilities that follow will occur before I surrender to love.

6. Kill. The image is of miscarriage or infanticide.
7. I.e., gives abundance only to make scarcity more painful afterward.
8. I.e., those whom they mean to destroy (see the next line).
9. Expended, employed. "Shows": appearances.

68

My pain, still smothered in my grievèd breast,
  Seeks for some ease, yet cannot passage find
To be discharged of this unwelcome guest:
  When most I strive, most fast his burdens bind,
5 Like to a ship on Goodwin's[1] cast by wind,
  The more she strives, more deep in sand is pressed,
Till she be lost; so am I, in this kind,°   *manner*
  Sunk, and devoured, and swallowed by unrest,
Lost, shipwrecked, spoiled, debarred of smallest hope,
10 Nothing of pleasure left; save thoughts have scope,
  Which wander may. Go then, my thoughts, and cry
Hope's perished, Love tempest-beaten, Joy lost:
  Killing Despair hath all these blessings crossed.
  Yet Faith still cries, Love will not falsify.

74

SONG

Love a child is ever crying,
  Please him, and he straight is flying;
  Give him, he the more is craving,
  Never satisfied with having.

5 His desires have no measure,
  Endless folly is his treasure;
  What he promiseth he breaketh:
  Trust not one word that he speaketh.

He vows nothing but false matter,
10 And to cozen you he'll flatter.
  Let him gain the hand,° he'll leave you,   *the upper hand*
  And still glory to deceive you.

He will triumph in your wailing,
  And yet cause be of your failing:
15 These his virtues are, and slighter
  Are his gifts, his favors lighter.

Feathers are as firm in staying,
  Wolves no fiercer in their preying.
  As a child then leave him crying,
20 Nor seek him, so given to flying.

1. Goodwin Sands, a line of shoals at the entrance to the Strait of Dover.

From *A Crown of Sonnets Dedicated to Love*[2]

77

In this strange labyrinth how shall I turn?
Ways° are on all sides, while the way I miss: *paths*
If to the right hand, there in love I burn;
Let me go forward, therein danger is;
5   If to the left, suspicion hinders bliss,
Let me° turn back, Shame cries I ought return,   *if I*
Nor faint though crosses[3] with my fortunes kiss;
Stand still is harder, although sure to mourn.[4]
Then let me take the right- or left-hand way;
10   Go forward, or stand still, or back retire;
I must these doubts endure without allay°   *abatement*
Or help, but travail find for my best hire.[5]
Yet that which most my troubled sense doth move
Is to leave all, and take the thread of love.[6]

1621

2. The "crown" is a difficult poetic form (originally Italian and usually known by its Italian name, *corona*) in which the last line of each poem serves as the first line of the next, until a circle is completed by the last line of the final poem, which is the same as the first line of the first one. The number of poems varies from seven to (as in Wroth's *corona*) fourteen.
   In contrast to the errant-child Cupid of the preceding part of the sequence, Love in this series is a mature and just monarch, whose true service ennobles lovers. The crown is in part a recantation of the harsh judgment of love earlier in the sequence. But Pamphilia relapses into melancholy afterward.
3. Troubles, adversity. "Faint": lose heart.
4. I.e., certain to make me mourn.
5. I.e., I find travail (with a pun on "travel," the spelling in the 1621 edition) is my only reward.
6. Ariadne gave Theseus a thread to follow so as to find his way out of the Labyrinth, after killing the Minotaur at its center.

GEORGE HERBERT
1593–1633

Unlike the learned and witty style of the work of his friend John Donne, Herbert's style in his single volume of religious poetry, *The Temple*, is deceptively simple, marked by ease and grace. But it is also marked by self-irony, a remarkable intellectual and emotional range, and a highly conscious artistry that is evident in the poems' tight construction, exact diction, perfect control of tone, and great variety of stanzaic forms and rhythmic patterns. As well, these poems reflect Herbert's struggle to define his relationship to God through biblical metaphors that are also invested with the tensions and anxieties those relationships held in his own society: king and subject, lord and courtier, master and servant, father and child, bridegroom and bride, friend to friend of inferior status. None of Herbert's secular English poems survives, so his reputation rests on this single volume, published posthumously. *The Temple* contains a long prefatory poem, *The Church-Porch*, and a long concluding poem, *Church Militant,* which together enclose a collection of 177 short lyrics entitled *The Church*, among which are sonnets, songs, hymns, laments, meditative poems, dialogue poems, acrostic poems, emblematic poems, and more. Herbert's own description of the collection is apt: "a picture of the many spiritual conflicts that have passed between God and my soul." Izaak Walton reports that Herbert gave the manuscript to his friend

Nicholas Farrar, head of a quasi-monastic community at Little Gidding, with instructions to publish it if he thought it would "turn to the advantage of any dejected poor soul" and otherwise to burn it. Fortunately, Farrar chose to publish, and *The Temple* became the major influence on the religious lyric poets of the Caroline age: Henry Vaughan, Richard Crashaw, Thomas Traherne, and even Edward Taylor, the American colonial poet.

The fifth son of an eminent Welsh family, Herbert's upbringing and that of his nine siblings was carefully monitored by his mother, Magdalen Herbert, patron and friend of Donne and several other scholars and poets. Herbert was educated at Westminster School and at Trinity College, Cambridge, where he subsequently held a fellowship and wrote Latin poetry: elegies on the death of Prince Henry (1612), witty epigrams, poems on Christ's passion and death, and poems defending the rites of the English Church. In 1620 he was appointed "public orator," the official spokesman and correspondent for the university; this was a step toward a career at court or in public service, as was his election as Member of Parliament from Montgomery in 1624. But that route was closed off by the death of influential patrons and the change of monarchs. Like Donne, Herbert hesitated for some years before being ordained, but in 1630 he took up pastoral duties in the small country parish at Bemerton in Wiltshire. Whereas Donne preached to monarchs and statesmen, Herbert ministered to a few cottagers and none of his sermons survive. His small book on the duties of his new life, *A Priest to the Temple; or, The Country Parson*, testifies to the earnestness and joy (but also to the aristocratic uneasiness) with which he embraced that role. In chronic bad health he lived only three more years—performing pastoral duties assiduously, writing and revising his poems, playing music, and listening to organ and choir at nearby Salisbury cathedral.

Herbert locates himself in the church through many poems that treat church liturgy, architecture, and art—e.g., *Church Monuments* and *The Windows*—but his primary emphasis is always on the soul's inner architecture. Unlike Donne's poems, Herbert's poems do not voice anxious fears about his salvation or about his desperate sins and helplessness; his anxieties center rather on his relationship with Christ, most often represented as that of friend with friend. Many poems register the speaker's distress over the vacillations and regressions in this relationship, over his lack of "fruition" in God's service, and over the instability in his own nature, purposes, and temperament. In several dialogic poems the speaker's difficulties and anxieties are alleviated or resolved by the voice of a divine friend heard within or recalled through a scripture text (as in *The Collar*). In poem after poem he resists but has to come to terms with the fact that his relationship with Christ is always radically unequal, that Christ must both initiate it and make possible his own response. He struggles constantly with the paradox that, as the works of a Christian poet, his poems ought to give fit and sincere praise to God but that they cannot possibly do so—an issue explored in *The Altar,* the two *Jordan* poems, *Easter, The Forerunners*, and many more.

His recourse is to develop a biblical poetics that renounces conventional poetic styles—"fiction and false hair"—so as to depend on God's "art" wrought in his own soul and displayed in the language, metaphors, and symbolism of the Bible. He makes scant use of Donnean learned imagery drawn from such areas as cosmology or medicine or Scholastic philosophy, but his allusions carry profound significances. A biblical metaphor provides the unifying motif for the volume: the New Testament temple in the human heart (1 Corinthians 3.16). Another recurring biblical metaphor represents the Christian as plant or tree or flower in God's garden, needing pruning, rain, and nurture. Many poems are related to religious emblems: shaped poems like *The Altar* that present image and picture at once, or others like *Life* that might stand as commentaries on an emblem, here, a posy. Other poems allude to typological symbolism, which reads persons and events in the Old Testament as types or foreshadowings of Christ, the fulfillment or antitype; often, as in *The Bunch of Grapes,* Herbert locates both type and antitype in the speaker's soul.

FROM *THE TEMPLE*[1]

The Altar[2]

A broken A L T A R , Lord, thy servant rears,
Made of a heart, and cemented with tears:
Whose parts are as thy hand did frame;
No workman's tool hath touched the same.[3]
5   A H E A R T alone
Is such a stone,
As nothing but
Thy power doth cut.
Wherefore each part
10   Of my hard heart
Meets in this frame,
To praise thy Name:
That, if I chance to hold my peace,
These stones to praise thee may not cease.[4]
15 Oh let thy blessed S A C R I F I C E be mine,
And   sanctify   this   A L T A R   to   be   thine.

Redemption[1]

Having been tenant long to a rich lord,
Not thriving, I resolvèd to be bold,
And make a suit unto him, to afford
A new small-rented lease, and cancel th' old.[2]

5   In heaven at his manor I him sought:
They told me there that he was lately gone
About some land which he had dearly bought
Long since on earth, to take possession.

I straight returned, and knowing his great birth,
10   Sought him accordingly in great resorts—
In cities, theaters, gardens, parks, and courts:
At length I heard a ragged noise and mirth

1. The title of Herbert's volume sets his poems in
relation to David's Psalms for the Temple at Jerusalem; his are new covenant "psalms" for the New
Testament temple in the heart. All of the following
poems come from this volume, published in 1633.
2. A variety of emblem poem. Emblems customarily have three parts: a picture, a motto, and a
poem. This kind collapses picture and poem into
one, presenting the emblem image by its very
shape. Shaped poems have been used by the occasional author from Hellenistic times to Dylan Thomas.
3. A reference to Exodus 20.25, in which the Lord
enjoins Moses to build an altar of uncut stones,

not touched by any tool, and also to Psalm 51.7:
"A broken and the contrite heart, O God, thou wilt
not despise."
4. A reference to Luke 19.40: "I tell you that, if
these should hold their peace, the stones would
immediately cry out." Herbert's poems obtain
much of their resonance from the biblical echoes
they incorporate.
1. Literally, "buying back." In this beautifully concise sonnet Herbert figures God as a landlord, himself a discontented tenant.
2. I.e., to ask him for a new lease, with a smaller
rent; the figure points to the New Testament supplanting the Old.

Of thieves and murderers; there I him espied,
Who straight, "Your suit is granted," said, and died.

Easter Wings[1]

Lord, who createdst man in wealth and store,°   *abundance*
Though foolishly he lost the same,
Decaying more and more
Till he became
5   Most poor:
With thee
O let me rise
As larks, harmoniously,
And sing this day thy victories:
10   Then shall the fall further the flight in me.[2]

My tender age in sorrow did begin:
And still with sicknesses and shame
Thou didst so punish sin,
That I became
15   Most thin.
With thee
Let me combine,
And feel this day thy victory;
For, if I imp[3] my wing on thine,
20   Affliction shall advance the flight in me.

Jordan (1)[1]

Who says that fictions only and false hair
Become a verse? Is there in truth no beauty?
Is all good structure in a winding stair?
May no lines pass, except they do their duty°   *pay reverence to*
5   Not to a true, but painted chair?[2]

Is it no verse, except enchanted groves
And sudden arbors shadow coarse-spun lines?[3]
Must purling° streams refresh a lover's loves?   *rippling*
Must all be veiled,[4] while he that reads, divines,
10   Catching the sense at two removes?

1. Another emblem poem whose shape presents the emblem picture; the lines, increasing and decreasing, imitate flight, and also the spiritual experience of falling and rising. Early editions printed the poem with the lines running vertically, making the wing shape more apparent.
2. The idea of the "Fortunate Fall," which brought humankind so great a redeemer.
3. In falconry, to insert feathers in a bird's wing.
1. The river Jordan, which the Israelites crossed to enter the promised land, was also taken as a symbol for baptism.
2. It was the custom for men to bow before a throne, whether it was occupied or not (see Donne, *Satire* 3, lines 47–48, p. 618), but to require bowing before a throne in a painting would be ridiculous.
3. "Sudden," i.e., that appear unexpectedly (an artificial effect much sought after in landscape gardening). "Shadow": shade.
4. As in allegory.

Shepherds[5] are honest people: let them sing;
Riddle who list,° for me, and pull for prime:[6]   *wishes*
I envy no man's nightingale or spring;
Nor let them punish me with loss of rhyme,
15   Who plainly say, *My God, My King*.[7]

The Collar[1]

I struck the board[2] and cried, "No more;
        I will abroad!
What? shall I ever sigh and pine?
My lines and life are free, free as the road,
5   Loose as the wind, as large as store.
        Shall I be still in suit?[3]
Have I no harvest but a thorn
To let me blood, and not restore
What I have lost with cordial° fruit?   *restorative to the heart*
10   Sure there was wine
Before my sighs did dry it; there was corn
        Before my tears did drown it.
Is the year only lost to me?
        Have I no bays[4] to crown it,
15 No flowers, no garlands gay? all blasted?
                All wasted?
Not so, my heart; but there is fruit,
        And thou hast hands.
Recover all thy sigh-blown age
20 On double pleasures: leave thy cold dispute
Of what is fit and not. Forsake thy cage,
                Thy rope of sands,
Which petty thoughts have made, and made to thee
Good cable,[5] to enforce and draw,
25   And be thy law,
While thou didst wink and wouldst not see.
        Away! take heed;
        I will abroad.
Call in thy death's-head[6] there; tie up thy fears.
30   He that forbears
        To suit and serve his need,
        Deserves his load."
But as I raved and grew more fierce and wild
        At every word,

5. Conventional pastoral poets.
6. To draw a lucky card in the game of primero.
"For me": as far as I am concerned.
7. Echoes Psalm 145.1: "my God, O king."
1. The emblematic title at first suggests a clerical
collar that has become a slave's collar; also, punningly, it comes to suggest the speaker's choler
(anger) and, perhaps, the caller that he at last
hears.
2. Table, with perhaps an allusion to the communion table.
3. In attendance, waiting on someone for a favor.
4. The poet's laurel wreath, symbol of recognized
accomplishment.
5. Christian restrictions on behavior, which the
"petty thoughts" of the docile believer have made
into strong bonds.
6. Skull, emblem of human mortality, and often
used as an object for meditation.

35   Methoughts I heard one calling, *Child!*[7]
      And I replied, *My Lord.*

The Pulley[1]

When God at first made man,
Having a glass of blessings standing by,
"Let us," said he, "pour on him all we can:
Let the world's riches, which dispersèd lie,
5   Contract into a span."

So strength first made a way;
Then beauty flowed, then wisdom, honor, pleasure.
When almost all was out, God made a stay,
Perceiving that, alone of all his treasure,
10   Rest in the bottom lay.[2]

"For if I should," said he,
"Bestow this jewel also on my creature,
He would adore my gifts instead of me,
And rest in Nature, not the God of Nature;
15   So both should losers be.

"Yet let him keep the rest,
But keep them with repining restlessness:
Let him be rich and weary, that at least,
If goodness lead him not, yet weariness
20   May toss him to my breast."

The Flower

How fresh, O Lord, how sweet and clean
Are thy returns! even as the flowers in spring,
    To which, besides their own demesne,°   *domain, demeanor*
The late-past frosts tributes of pleasure bring.
5   Grief melts away
        Like snow in May,
    As if there were no such cold thing.

Who would have thought my shriveled heart
Could have recovered greenness? It was gone
10   Quite underground; as flowers depart
    To see their mother-root, when they have blown,°   *bloomed*
        Where they together

7. The call "Child" reminds the speaker of Paul's words (Romans 8.14–17) that Christians are not in "bondage again to fear" but are children of God, "and if children, then heirs."
1. The poem inverts the legend of Pandora's box, which released all manner of evils when opened, but left Hope trapped inside.
2. "Rest" has two senses: "remainder" and "repose."

All the hard weather,
Dead to the world, keep house unknown.

15 These are thy wonders, Lord of power,
Killing and quickening, bringing down to hell
And up to heaven in an hour,
Making a chiming of a passing-bell.[1]
We say amiss
20 This or that is:
Thy word is all, if we could spell.

O that I once past changing were,
Fast in thy Paradise, where no flower can wither!
Many a spring I shoot up fair,
25 Offering° at heaven, growing and groaning thither;   *aiming*
Nor doth my flower
Want a spring shower,[2]
My sins and I joining together.

But while I grow in a straight line,
30 Still upwards bent, as if heaven were mine own,
Thy anger comes, and I decline:
What frost to that? what pole is not the zone
Where all things burn,
When thou dost turn,
35 And the least frown of thine is shown?[3]

And now in age I bud again,
After so many deaths I live and write;
I once more smell the dew and rain,
And relish versing. O my only light,
40 It cannot be
That I am he
On whom thy tempests fell all night.

These are thy wonders, Lord of love,
To make us see we are but flowers that glide;°   *slip silently away*
45 Which when we once can find and prove,[4]
Thou hast a garden for us where to bide;
Who would be more,
Swelling through store,
Forfeit their Paradise by their pride.

Love (3)

Love bade me welcome: yet my soul drew back,
Guilty of dust and sin.

1. The "passing-bell," intended to mark the death of a parishioner, is tolled in a monotone; a chiming bell offers pleasant variety.
2. Tears of contrition.
3. I.e., compared with God's wrath, what polar chill would not seem like the heat of the equator?
4. Experience.

But quick-eyed Love, observing me grow slack°   *hesitant*
    From my first entrance in,
5 Drew nearer to me, sweetly questioning
    If I lacked anything.[1]

"A guest," I answered, "worthy to be here":
    Love said, "You shall be he."
"I, the unkind, ungrateful? Ah, my dear,
10   I cannot look on thee."
Love took my hand, and smiling did reply,
    "Who made the eyes but I?"

"Truth, Lord; but I have marred them; let my shame
    Go where it doth deserve."
15 "And know you not," says Love, "who bore the blame?"
    "My dear, then I will serve."
"You must sit down," says Love, "and taste my meat."
    So I did sit and eat.[2]

1. The first question of shopkeepers and tavern waiters to an entering customer would be "What d'ye lack?" (i.e., want).
2. In addition to the sacrament of Communion, the reference is especially to the final communion in heaven, when the Lord "shall gird himself, and make them to sit down to meat, and will come forth and serve them" (Luke 12.37).

ROBERT HERRICK
1591–1674

Robert Herrick is the most devoted of the Sons of Ben, though his epigrams and lyrics (like Jonson's) also show the direct influence of classical poets: Horace, Anacreon, Catullus, Tibullus, Ovid, and Martial. Born in London the son of a goldsmith and apprenticed for some years in that craft, Herrick took B.A. and M.A. degrees at Cambridge and consorted in the early 1620s with Jonson and his "tribe," meeting regularly at the Apollo Room. After his ordination in 1623, he apparently served as chaplain to various noblemen and in that role joined Buckingham's failed military expedition to rescue French Protestants at Rhé in 1627. In 1630 he was installed as vicar of Dean Prior in Devonshire but found much to dislike about rural life in the West Country. Expelled as a royalist in 1647, he apparently lived in and about London until the Restoration, when he was reinstated at Dean Prior and lived there until his death.

His single volume of poems, *Hesperides* (1648), with its appended book of religious poems, *Noble Numbers*, contains over four hundred short poems which, at first glance, seem mostly playful and charming, remarkable for their exquisite and unerring artistry and perfect decorum. Many are love poems on the *Carpe Diem* theme—seize the day, time is fleeting, make love now; a famous example is the elegant song *To the Virgins, to Make Much of Time*. But Herrick's range is much wider than is sometimes recognized: he moves from the pastoral to the cynical, from an almost rococo elegance to coarse, even vulgar, epigrams, and from the didactic to the dramatic. Also, he derives mythic energy and power from certain recurring motifs. One is metamorphosis, "times trans-shifting," the transience of all natural things. Another is celebration—festivals and feasts—evoking the social, ritualistic, and even anthropological signficances and energies contained in rural harvest festivals (*The Hock-Cart*) or the May Day rituals described in what is perhaps his finest poem, *Corinna's Going A-Maying*. Yet another is the classical but also perennial ideal of the "good life," defined in his terms as "cleanly wantonness." For Herrick this involves love devoid of high passion (the several mistresses he addresses seem interchangeable and not very real); the pleasures of food, drink, and song; delight in the beauty of surfaces (as in *Upon Julia's Clothes*); and finally, the creation of poetry as some ballast against the ravages of time.

These poems, published just months before the execution of Charles I, seem almost oblivious to the catastrophes of the war and the political turmoil. But they are not. Poems celebrating rural feasts and festivals, ceremonial social occasions, and the rituals of good fellowship reinforce the old conservative values of social stability, tradition, and order threatened by the Puritan revolution. Several poems that draw upon the Celtic mythology of fairy folk make their feasts, temples, worship, and ceremonies stand in for the forbidden ceremonies of the Laudian church and a life governed by ritual. Still other poems, like *The Hock-Cart* and *Corinna's Going A-Maying*, celebrate the kind of rural festivals that were at the center of the culture wars between royalists and Puritans. Both James I and Charles I urged such activities in their *Book of Sports* as a means of reinforcing hierarchical relations and traditional institutions in the countryside and deflecting discontent, while Puritans vigorously opposed these activities on those accounts and as occasions for drunkenness and licentiousness.

The Vine

I dreamed this mortal part of mine
Was metamorphosed to a vine,
Which, crawling one and every way,
Enthralled my dainty Lucia.[1]
5   Methought, her long small legs and thighs
I with my tendrils did surprise;
Her belly, buttocks, and her waist
By my soft nervelets were embraced.
About her head I writhing hung,
10   And with rich clusters (hid among
The leaves) her temples I behung,
So that my Lucia seemed to me
Young Bacchus ravished by his tree.°   *the grapevine*
My curls about her neck did crawl,
15   And arms and hands they did enthrall,
So that she could not freely stir
(All parts there made one prisoner).
But when I crept with leaves to hide
Those parts which maids keep unespied,
20   Such fleeting pleasures there I took
That with the fancy I awoke,

1. For the sake of both rhyme and meter, the name of this lady is given three syllables here; in line 12 it has only two.

And found (ah me!) this flesh of mine
More like a stock than like a vine.

Delight in Disorder[1]

    A sweet disorder in the dress
Kindles in clothes a wantonness.
A lawn° about the shoulders thrown   *fine linen scarf*
Into a fine distraction;
5 An erring° lace, which here and there   *wandering*
Enthralls the crimson stomacher;[2]
A cuff neglectful, and thereby
Ribbons to flow confusedly;
A winning wave, deserving note,
10 In the tempestuous petticoat;
A careless shoestring, in whose tie
I see a wild civility:
Do more bewitch me than when art
Is too precise[3] in every part.

Corinna's Going A-Maying

Get up! get up for shame! the blooming morn
Upon her wings presents the god unshorn.[1]
    See how Aurora throws her fair
    Fresh-quilted colors through the air:[2]
5 Get up, sweet slug-a-bed, and see
    The dew bespangling herb and tree.
Each flower has wept and bowed toward the east
Above an hour since, yet you not dressed;
    Nay, not so much as out of bed?
10 When all the birds have matins° said,   *morning prayer*
    And sung their thankful hymns, 'tis sin,
    Nay, profanation° to keep in,   *impiety*
Whenas a thousand virgins on this day
Spring, sooner than the lark, to fetch in May.[3]

15 Rise, and put on your foliage, and be seen
To come forth, like the springtime, fresh and green,
    And sweet as Flora.[4] Take no care
    For jewels for your gown or hair;
    Fear not; the leaves will strew

1. One of several poems in this period in which women's dress is a means by which to explore the relation of nature and art. See Jonson's *Still to Be Neat*, p. 648.
2. An ornamental covering of the chest, worn under the laces of the bodice.
3. "Precise" and "precision" were terms used satirically about Puritans. Herrick, in praising feminine disarray, is at one level praising the "sprezzatura"

or careless grace of Cavalier art.
1. Apollo, the sun god; sunbeams are seen as his flowing locks.
2. Aurora is goddess of the dawn.
3. On May Day morning, it was the custom to gather whitethorn blossoms and trim the house with them.
4. Flora, Italian goddess of flowers, had her festival in the spring.

20   Gems in abundance upon you;
        Besides, the childhood of the day has kept,
        Against° you come, some orient pearls⁵ unwept;   *until*
            Come and receive them while the light
            Hangs on the dew-locks of the night,
25   And Titan° on the eastern hill   *the sun*
        Retires himself, or else stands still
        Till you come forth. Wash, dress, be brief in praying:
        Few beads⁶ are best when once we go a-Maying.

        Come, my Corinna, come; and, coming, mark
30   How each field turns° a street, each street a park   *turns into*
            Made green and trimmed with trees; see how
            Devotion gives each house a bough
        Or branch: each porch, each door ere this,
            An ark, a tabernacle is,⁷
35   Made up of whitethorn neatly interwove,
        As if here were those cooler shades of love.
            Can such delights be in the street
            And open fields, and we not see 't?
            Come, we'll abroad; and let's obey
40   The proclamation⁸ made for May,
        And sin no more, as we have done, by staying;
        But, my Corinna, come, let's go a-Maying.

        There's not a budding boy or girl this day
        But is got up and gone to bring in May;
45   A deal of youth, ere this, is come
            Back, and with whitethorn laden, home.
        Some have dispatched their cakes and cream
            Before that we have left to dream;
        And some have wept, and wooed, and plighted troth,
50   And chose their priest, ere we can cast off sloth.
            Many a green-gown⁹ has been given,
            Many a kiss, both odd and even;¹
            Many a glance, too, has been sent
            From out the eye, love's firmament;
55   Many a jest told of the keys betraying
        This night, and locks picked; yet we're not a-Maying.

        Come, let us go while we are in our prime,
        And take the harmless folly of the time.
            We shall grow old apace, and die
60   Before we know our liberty.
            Our life is short, and our days run
            As fast away as does the sun;

5. Pearls from the orient were especially lustrous, like drops of dew.
6. Rosary beads of the "old" Catholic religion, but more generally, a casual term for prayers.
7. The doorways, ornamented with whitethorn, are like the Hebrew Ark of the Covenant, or the sanctuary that housed it (Leviticus 23.40–42: "Ye shall take you on the first day the boughs of goodly trees . . . ").
8. Probably a reference to Charles I's "Declaration to his subjects concerning lawful sports."
9. Got by rolling in the grass.
1. Kisses are odd and even in kissing games.

And, as a vapor or a drop of rain,
Once lost, can ne'er be found again,
65 So when or you or I are made
A fable, song, or fleeting shade,
All love, all liking, all delight
Lies drowned with us in endless night.[2]
Then while time serves, and we are but decaying,
70 Come, my Corinna, come, let's go a-Maying.

To the Virgins, to Make Much of Time

Gather ye rosebuds while ye may,
Old time is still a-flying;[1]
And this same flower that smiles today,
Tomorrow will be dying.

5 The glorious lamp of heaven, the sun,
The higher he's a-getting,
The sooner will his race be run,[2]
And nearer he's to setting.

That age is best which is the first,
10 When youth and blood are warmer;
But being spent, the worse, and worst
Times still succeed the former.

Then be not coy, but use your time,
And while ye may, go marry;
15 For having lost but once your prime,
You may forever tarry.

Upon Julia's Clothes

Whenas in silks my Julia goes,
Then, then, methinks, how sweetly flows
That liquefaction of her clothes.

Next, when I cast mine eyes and see
5 That brave[1] vibration each way free,
Oh, how that glittering taketh me!

---

2. Some echoes of the apocryphal book Wisdom of Solomon 2.1–8: "For the ungodly said . . . the breath of our nostrils is as smoke, and a little spark . . . and our life shall pass away as the trace of a cloud. . . . Come on therefore . . . Let us crown ourselves with rose buds before they be withered." This *carpe diem* sentiment is a frequent theme in classical love poetry.

1. Translates the Latin *tempus fugit*.
2. In classical myth, the sun was taken to be the chariot of Phoebus Apollo, which he drove across the heavens daily.
1. Splendid, glorious.

RICHARD LOVELACE
1618–1657

Usually linked with Suckling as a quintessential Cavalier, Richard Lovelace was described by a contemporary as "the most amiable and beautiful person that ever eye beheld." Born into a wealthy Kentish family, he was educated at Oxford, and, like Suckling, fought for his king in Scotland (in both expeditions, 1639 and 1640). But he was not a libertine and his poems, in contrast with Suckling's, often exalt women, love, and honor. Also, he shared with his king a serious interest in art, especially the paintings of Rubens, Van Dyke, and Lely. He was imprisoned for a few months in 1642 for supporting the "Kentish Petition" that urged restoration of the king to his ancient rights; in *To Althea, from Prison*, he finds freedom from external bondage in the Cavalier ideals of women, wine, and royalism. During 1643–46 he fought in Holland and France and in the king's armies in England, and was wounded abroad. In a general roundup of known royalists in 1648 he was imprisoned for ten months, and while there prepared his poems for publication under the title *Lucasta* (1649). Besides witty and charming love songs, that volume includes the plaintive ballad about the conflict between love and honor, *To Lucasta, Going to the Wars*, and also a poem that presents the Cavalier ideal at its most attractive: *The Grasshopper*. That emblematic summer creature is taken to symbolize the loss of the king and the carefree Cavalier life in the Puritan "winter," but Lovelace finds in the fellowship of Cavalier friends a nobler version of the good life and a truer kingship. After 1649 he endured a decade of penury, largely dependent on the largess of his friend and fellow royalist, Charles Cotton. His remaining poems appeared in 1659 as *Lucasta: Postume Poems*.

FROM LUCASTA

To Lucasta, Going to the Wars

Tell me not, sweet, I am unkind,
    That from the nunnery
Of thy chaste breast and quiet mind
    To war and arms I fly.

5   True, a new mistress now I chase,
    The first foe in the field;
And with a stronger faith embrace
    A sword, a horse, a shield.

Yet this inconstancy is such
10   As you too shall adore;
I could not love thee, dear, so much,
    Loved I not honor more.

1649

To Althea, from Prison

When Love with unconfinèd wings
    Hovers within my gates,

And my divine Althea brings
   To whisper at the grates;
5 When I lie tangled in her hair
   And fettered to her eye,
The gods[1] that wanton° in the air   *play*
   Know no such liberty.

When flowing cups run swiftly round,
10   With no allaying Thames,[2]
Our careless heads with roses bound,
   Our hearts with loyal flames;
When thirsty grief in wine we steep,
   When healths and draughts go free,
15 Fishes that tipple in the deep
   Know no such liberty.

When, like committed linnets,[3] I
   With shriller throat shall sing
The sweetness, mercy, majesty,
20   And glories of my king;
When I shall voice aloud how good
   He is, how great should be,
Enlargèd winds, that curl the flood,
   Know no such liberty.

25 Stone walls do not a prison make,
   Nor iron bars a cage;
Minds innocent and quiet take
   That for an hermitage.
If I have freedom in my love,
30   And in my soul am free,
Angels alone, that soar above,
   Enjoy such liberty.

1649

1. Some versions read "birds" instead of "gods."   in the wine.
2. No mixture of water (as from the River Thames)   3. Caged finches.

KATHERINE PHILIPS
1632–1664

The best-known woman poet of her own and the next generation, Katherine Philips
was honored as "The Matchless Orinda," the classical name she chose for herself in
her poetic addresses to a coterie of chiefly female friends, especially Mary Aubrey
(M. A.) and Anne Owen (Lucasia). Sometimes reminiscent of Donne's love lyrics and
sometimes of the ancient Greek Sappho's erotic lyrics to women, these poems develop

an exalted ideal of female friendship as a Platonic union of souls. Born to a well-to-do Presbyterian family and educated at Mrs. Salmon's Presbyterian school, Philips was taken to Wales when her mother remarried. In 1648 at age seventeen she was married to James Philips, thirty-eight years her senior and a prominent Presbyterian magistrate and Member of Parliament. They lived together twelve years, chiefly in the small Welsh town of Cardigan, and had two children: Hector, whose death a few days after birth prompted one of her most moving poems, and Katherine, who lived to adulthood. A royalist despite her Puritan family connections, Philips forged connections with other displaced royalists. Her poems circulated in manuscript and elicited high praise from Vaughan in *Olor Iscanus*. They include elegies, epitaphs, poems at parting, and friendship poems to women and men, but also poetry on political themes: a denunciation of the regicide, *Upon the Double Murder of King Charles*, and panegyrics on the restored Stuarts. At the Restoration, James Philips barely escaped execution as a regicide, had his estates confiscated, and lost his seat in parliament, but Katherine became a favorite at Court, promoted by her friend Sir Charles Cotterell ("Poliarchus"), who was master of ceremonies. In Ireland attempting (unsuccessfully) to redeem an investment, she translated Corneille's *Pompey* and her friend the earl of Orrery produced and printed it in Dublin in 1663. The first edition of her poems, apparently pirated, appeared in 1664, the same year she died of smallpox. Her friend Cotterell brought out an authorized edition in 1667.

A Married State[1]

A married state affords but little ease
The best of husbands are so hard to please.
This in wives' careful° faces you may spell   *full of cares*
Though they dissemble their misfortunes well.
5   A virgin state is crowned with much content;[2]
It's always happy as it's innocent.
No blustering husbands to create your fears;
No pangs of childbirth to extort your tears;
No children's cries for to offend your ears;
10 Few worldly crosses to distract your prayers:
Thus are you freed from all the cares that do
Attend on matrimony and a husband too.
Therefore Madam, be advised by me
Turn, turn apostate to love's levity,
15 Suppress wild nature if she dare rebel.
There's no such thing as leading apes in hell.[3]

ca. 1646   Ms; 1988

1. In a manuscript (Orielton MSS Box 24 at the National Library of Wales) this poem appears with another by Philips, addressed to Anne Barlow (whom she probably met in 1646); this one is probably also for Barlow. Both are signed by her maiden name, C. Fowler, so were evidently written before her marriage in 1648.
2. Praise of the single life is a common topic in women's poetry.
3. Proverbially, the fate of spinsters.

Upon the Double Murder of King Charles

In Answer to a Libelous Rhyme made by V. P.[1]

I think not on the state, nor am concerned
Which way soever that great helm[2] is turned,
But as that son whose father's danger nigh
Did force his native dumbness, and untie
His fettered organs: so here is a cause
That will excuse the breach of nature's laws.[3]
Silence were now a sin: nay passion now
Wise men themselves for merit would allow.[4]
What noble eye could see (and careless pass)
The dying lion kicked by every ass?
Hath Charles so broke God's laws, he must not have
A quiet crown, nor yet a quiet grave?
Tombs have been sanctuaries; thieves lie here
Secure from all their penalty and fear.
Great Charles his double misery was this,
Unfaithful friends, ignoble enemies;
Had any heathen been this prince's foe,
He would have wept to see him injured so.
His title was his crime, they'd reason good
To quarrel at the right they had withstood.
He broke God's laws, and therefore he must die,
And what shall then become of thee and I?
Slander must follow treason; but yet stay,
Take not our reason with our king away.
Though you have seized upon all our defense,
Yet do not sequester° our common sense.   *confiscate*
But I admire not at this new supply:
No bounds will hold those who at scepters fly.
Christ will be King, but I ne'er understood,
His subjects built his kingdom up with blood
(Except their own) or that he would dispense
With his commands, though for his own defense.
Oh! to what height of horror are they come
Who dare pull down a crown, tear up a tomb![5]

1649?   1664

1. The itinerant Welsh preacher Vavasour Powell was a Fifth Monarchist and an ardent republican who justified the regicide on the ground that Christ's second coming was imminent, when he would rule with his saints, putting down all earthly kings. His poem, which Philips is answering, has not survived, but the likelihood is that both were written shortly after Charles I's execution (January 30, 1649).

2. Steering wheel for the "ships" of state.
3. Breaking the supposed law of nature that excludes women from speaking about public affairs.
4. Wise men, especially Stoic philosophers, normally counsel the firm control or elimination of passions.
5. Their slanders tear up Charles's tomb after his death.

Friendship's Mystery, To My Dearest *Lucasia*[1]

1

Come, my *Lucasia*, since we see
That Miracles Men's faith do move,
By wonder and by prodigy
To the dull angry world let's prove
5   There's a Religion in our Love.

2

For though we were designed t' agree,
That Fate no liberty destroys,
But our Election is as free
As Angels, who with greedy choice
10   Are yet determined to their joys[2]

3

Our hearts are doubled by the loss,
Here Mixture is Addition grown;
We both diffuse,° and both engross:°   *spread out / collect*
And we whose minds are so much one,
15   Never, yet ever are alone.

4

We court our own Captivity
Than Thrones more great and innocent:
'Twere banishment to be set free,
Since we wear fetters whose intent
20   Not bondage is, but Ornament.

5

Divided joys are tedious found,
And griefs united easier grow:
We are selves but by rebound,
And all our Titles shuffled so,
25   Both Princes, and both Subjects too.[3]

6

Our Hearts are mutual Victims laid,
While they (such power in Friendship lies)
Are Altars, Priests, and Off'rings made:
And each Heart which thus kindly° dies,   *benevolently, naturally*
30   Grows deathless by the Sacrifice.

1655, 1664

---

1. This poem was first printed, with a musical setting by the royalist musician and composer Henry Lawes, as "Mutual Affection betweene *Orinda* and *Lucasia*" in Lawes's *The Second Book of Ayres* (1655); our text is from *Poems by the most deservedly admired Mrs. Katherine Philips, the matchless Orinda* (1667). Lucasia is Philips's name for her friend Anne Owen.
2. Angels, though created with free will, were thought to have become fixed in goodness when they turned toward God in the first moments after their creation.
3. Compare Donne, *The Sun Rising*, lines 21–22: "She is all states, and all princes, I" (p. 605).

To Mrs. M. A.[1] at Parting

I have examined and do find,
  Of all that favor me
There's none I grieve to leave behind
  But only only thee.
5 To part with thee I needs must die,
Could parting separate thee and I.

But neither chance nor compliment
  Did element our love:
'Twas sacred sympathy was lent
10 Us from the choir above.
(That friendship fortune did create,
Still fears a wound from time or fate.)

Our changed and mingled souls are grown
  To such acquaintance now,
15 That if each would resume their own,
  Alas! we know not how.
We have each other so engrossed
That each is in the union lost.[2]

And thus we can no absence know,
20 Nor shall we be confined;
Our active souls will daily go
  To learn each other's mind.
Nay, should we never meet to sense,
Our souls would hold intelligence.°   *would still commune*

25 Inspirèd with a flame divine,
  I scorn to court a stay;[3]
For from that noble soul of thine
  I ne'er can be away.
But I shall weep when thou dost grieve;
30 Nor can I die whilst thou dost live.

By my own temper I shall guess
  At thy felicity,
And only like my happiness
  Because it pleaseth thee.
35 Our hearts at any time will tell
If thou or I be sick or well.

1. M. A. was Mary Aubrey, the first and, until she married, the dearest member of Philips's "Society of Friendship." Orinda's valedictory poem to her—which Keats admired enough to copy it out in full in an early letter—recalls some of Donne's lyrics, especially *A Valediction: Forbidding Mourning* (p. 611).
2. These lines play upon the Neoplatonic idea of friendship and spiritual love—two souls become one.
3. Postponement (of their parting).

All honor, sure, I must pretend,°   *aspire to*
   All that is good or great:
She that would be Rosania's⁴ friend
40   Must be at least complete.
   If I have any bravery,
   'Tis cause I have so much of thee.

Thy leiger° soul in me shall lie,   *ambassadorial*
   And all thy thoughts reveal;
45 Then back again with mine shall fly,
   And thence to me shall steal.
   Thus still to one another tend:
   Such is the sacred name of friend.

Thus our twin souls in one shall grow,
50   And teach the world new love,
   Redeem the age and sex, and show
      A flame fate dares not move:
   And courting death to be our friend,
   Our lives, together too, shall end.

55 A dew shall dwell upon our tomb
      Of such a quality
   That fighting armies, thither come,
      Shall reconcilèd be.
   We'll ask no epitaph, but say:
60 ORINDA and ROSANIA.

                                                                  1664

On the Death of My First and Dearest Child, Hector Philips[1]

Twice forty months in wedlock[2] I did stay,
   Then had my vows crowned with a lovely boy.
And yet in forty days[3] he dropped away;
   O swift vicissitude of human joy!

5 I did but see him, and he disappeared,
   I did but touch the rosebud, and it fell;
A sorrow unforeseen and scarcely feared,
   So ill can mortals their afflictions spell.°   *discern*

And now, sweet babe, what can my trembling heart
10   Suggest to right my doleful fate or thee?

4. The poetic name Philips gave to Mary Aubrey.
1. In a manuscript the subtitle reads, "born the
23d of April, and died the 2d of May 1655. Set by
Mr. Lawes." There is however no extant musical
setting.
2. Philips was married in August 1648.
3. The subtitle indicates that he lived barely ten
days; the change here is clearly for the parallelism.

Tears are my muse, and sorrow all my art,
So piercing groans must be thy elegy.

Thus whilst no eye is witness of my moan,
I grieve thy loss (Ah, boy too dear to live!),
15   And let the unconcernèd world alone,
Who neither will, nor can, refreshment give.

An off'ring too for thy sad tomb I have,
Too just a tribute to thy early hearse.
Receive these gasping numbers to thy grave,
20   The last of thy unhappy mother's verse.[4]

1655   1667

4. This was not in fact Philips's last poem, but the sentiment is both true to human feeling and common in elegy. She had one other child, a year later—a daughter, Katherine, who survived her.

ANDREW MARVELL
1621–1678

Andrew Marvell's finest poems are second to none in this or any other period. He wrote less than Donne, Jonson, and Herbert did, but his range is in some ways greater, as he claimed both the private worlds of love and religion and the public worlds of political and satirical poetry and prose. His overriding concern with art, his elegant, well-crafted, limpid style, and the cool balance and reserve of some poems align him with Ben Jonson, but his paradoxes and complexities of tone, his use of dramatic monologue, and his witty, dialectical arguments associate him with Donne. Above all, he is a supremely original poet, so complex and elusive that it is often hard to know what he really thought about the subjects he treats. Many of his poems were published posthumously in 1681, some thirty years after they were written, by a woman who claimed to be his widow but was probably his housekeeper. So their date and order of composition is often in doubt, as is his authorship of some anonymous works.

The son of a Church of England clergyman, Marvell grew up in Yorkshire, attended Trinity College, Cambridge (perhaps deriving the persistant strain of Neoplatonism in his poetry from the academics known as the Cambridge Platonists), ran off to London, and converted to Roman Catholicism until his father put an end to both ventures. He returned to Cambridge, took his degree in 1639, and stayed on as a scholar until his father's death in 1641. During the years of the Civil Wars (1642–47), he traveled in France, Italy, Holland and Spain; much later he said of the Puritan "Good Old Cause" that it was "too good to have been fought for." While his earliest poems associate him with royalists, those after 1649 celebrate the Commonwealth and Cromwell, sometimes with ambivalence but recognizing divine providence in the political changes. From 1650 to 1652 he lived at Nunappleton as tutor to the twelve-year-old daughter of Thomas Fairfax, who had given over his command of the Parliamentary army to Cromwell because he was unwilling to invade Scotland. In these years of retirement and ease, Marvell probably wrote most of his love lyrics and pastorals as well as *Upon Appleton House*. Subsequently he was tutor to Cromwell's ward, William Dutton, and traveled with him on the Continent; in 1657 he joined the blind

Milton, at Milton's request, in the post of Latin secretary to Cromwell's Council of State. Marvell accepted the Restoration but maintained his own independent vision and his abiding belief in religious toleration, a mixed state, and constitutional government. He helped his friend Milton avoid execution for his revolutionary polemics and helped negotiate Milton's release from a brief imprisonment. Elected a Member of Parliament in 1659 from his hometown, Hull in Yorkshire, he held that post until 1678, focusing his attention on the needs of his district; on two occasions he went on diplomatic missions—to Holland and Russia. His (necessarily anonymous) antiroyalist polemics of these years include his best-known prose work, *The Rehearsal Transprosed* (1672–73), which defends Puritan dissenters and denounces censorship with verve and wit, and several verse satires that ridicule Charles II and his ministers. He also wrote a brilliant poem of criticism and interpretation on Milton's *Paradise Lost* that was prefixed to the second edition (1674).

Many of Marvell's poems explore the human condition in terms of fundamental dichotomies that resist resolution. In religious or philosophical poems like *The Coronet* or *The Dialogue Between the Soul and Body*, the conflict is between nature and grace, or body and soul, or poetic creation and sacrifice. In love poems such as *The Definition of Love* or *To His Coy Mistress* it is often between flesh and spirit, or physical sex and platonic love, or idealizing courtship and the ravages of time. In pastorals like the Mower poems and *The Garden* the opposition is between nature and art, or the fallen and Edenic state, or violent passion and contentment. Marvell's most subtle and complex political poem, *An Horatian Ode upon Cromwell's Return from Ireland*, sets stable traditional order and ancient right against providential revolutionary change, and the goods and costs of retirement and peace against those of action and war. *Upon Appleton House* also opposes the attractions of various kinds of retirement to the duties of action and reformation.

Marvell's stylistic experiments and transformations of genres produce striking aesthetic effects. Many of his dramatic monologues are voiced by named, naive personas— the Mower, the Nymph complaining—who stand at some remove from the author. One of his most striking figures—the phrase "Like a green thought in a green shade" from *The Garden*—derives its power from the unanalyzable suggestiveness the entire poem invests in the term "green." *To His Coy Mistress*, perhaps the best known of the century's *carpe diem* poems, is voiced by a witty and urbane speaker in balanced and artful couplets, but its rapid shifts from the world of fantasy to the charnal house of reality raise questions as to whether this is a clever seduction poem or a probing of existential angst, and whether Marvell intends to endorse or critique this speaker's view of passion and sex.

To His Coy Mistress[1]

Had we but world enough, and time,
This coyness, lady, were no crime.
We would sit down, and think which way
To walk, and pass our long love's day.
5   Thou by the Indian Ganges' side

---

1. One of the most famous *carpe diem* (seize the day) poems of the period, it develops the motifs of time and space, introduced in line 1.

Shouldst rubies find; I by the tide
Of Humber would complain.[2] I would
Love you ten years before the Flood,
And you should, if you please, refuse
10   Till the conversion of the Jews.[3]
My vegetable love should grow
Vaster than empires, and more slow;
An hundred years should go to praise
Thine eyes, and on thy forehead gaze;
15   Two hundred to adore each breast,
But thirty thousand to the rest:
An age at least to every part,
And the last age should show your heart.
For, lady, you deserve this state,°   *dignity*
20   Nor would I love at lower rate.
      But at my back I always hear
Time's wingèd chariot hurrying near;
And yonder all before us lie
Deserts of vast eternity.
25   Thy beauty shall no more be found,
Nor, in thy marble vault, shall sound
My echoing song; then worms shall try
That long-preserved virginity,
And your quaint[4] honor turn to dust,
30   And into ashes all my lust:
The grave's a fine and private place,
But none, I think, do there embrace.
      Now therefore, while the youthful hue
Sits on thy skin like morning dew,[5]
35   And while thy willing soul transpires
At every pore with instant fires,[6]
Now let us sport us while we may,
And now, like amorous birds of prey,
Rather at once our time devour
40   Than languish in his slow-chapped[7] power.
Let us roll all our strength and all
Our sweetness up into one ball,
And tear our pleasures with rough strife
Thorough° the iron gates of life:[8]   *through*
45   Thus, though we cannot make our sun
Stand still, yet we will make him run.[9]

---

2. The exotic river Ganges is on one side of the world, the Humber river flows past Marvell's city, Hull, on the opposite side. Complaints are poems of plaintive, unavailing love.
3. Popular belief had it that the Jews were to be converted just before the Last Judgment. The exaggerated offers in this stanza play off against conventional hyperbolic declarations of love in Petrarchan poetry.
4. "Quaint" puns on "out of date" and *queynte*, a term for the female genitals.

5. The text reads "glew," which could be correct, but "dew" is a common emendation.
6. Urgent, sudden enthusiasm. "Transpires": breathes forth.
7. Slowly devouring jaws.
8. One manuscript reads "grates," a somewhat different figure for the sexual act proposed.
9. The sun stood still for Joshua (Joshua 10.12) in his war against Gibeon; see the very different resolution in Donne's *The Sun Rising* (p. 605).

The Definition of Love

My Love is of a birth as rare
As 'tis, for object, strange and high;
It was begotten by Despair
Upon Impossibility.

5   Magnanimous Despair alone
Could show me so divine a thing,
Where feeble Hope could ne'er have flown
But vainly flapped its tinsel wing.

And yet I quickly might arrive
10   Where my extended soul is fixed;[1]
But Fate does iron wedges drive,
And always crowds itself betwixt.

For Fate with jealous eye does see
Two perfect loves, nor lets them close;°   *unite*
15   Their union would her ruin be,
And her tyrannic power depose.[2]

And therefore her decrees of steel
Us as the distant poles have placed
(Though Love's whole world on us doth wheel),[3]
20   Not by themselves to be embraced,

Unless the giddy heaven fall,
And earth some new convulsion tear,
And, us to join, the world should all
Be cramped into a planisphere.[4]

25   As lines, so loves oblique may well
Themselves in every angle greet;[5]
But ours, so truly parallel,
Though infinite, can never meet.

Therefore the love which us doth bind,
30   But Fate so enviously debars,
Is the conjunction of the mind,
And opposition of the stars.[6]

1. The soul has extended itself from the speaker's body and fixed itself to his lover.
2. Two perfections, united, would not be subject to change and thereby to Fate.
3. Rotates as on its axis.
4. A two-dimensional map of the world; Marvell images a round globe collapsed into a flat pancake shape, top to bottom, which would bring the two poles together.
5. Oblique lines can touch in angles, as might "oblique" lovers that (in one meaning of the term) "deviate from right conduct or thought."
6. Conjunction is the coming together of two heavenly bodies in the same sign of the zodiac; "opposition" places them at diametrical opposites.

The Mower to the Glowworms

Ye living lamps, by whose dear light
The nightingale does sit so late,
And studying all the summer night
Her matchless songs does meditate,

5   Ye country comets, that portend
No war nor prince's funeral,
Shining unto no higher end
Than to presage the grass's fall;

Ye glowworms, whose officious° flame   *zealous, attentive*
10 To wand'ring mowers shows the way,
That in the night have lost their aim,
And after foolish fires° do stray;   *will-o-the-wisps*

Your courteous fires in vain you waste,
Since Juliana here is come,
15 For she my mind hath so displaced
That I shall never find my home.

The Mower's Song

My mind was once the true survey
Of all these meadows fresh and gay,
And in the greenness of the grass
Did see its hopes[1] as in a glass;°   *mirror*
5 When Juliana came, and she,
What I do to the grass, does to my thoughts and me.[2]

But these, while I with sorrow pine,
Grew more luxuriant still and fine,
That not one blade of grass you spied
10 But had a flower on either side;
When Juliana came, and she,
What I do to the grass, does to my thoughts and me.

Unthankful meadows, could you so
A fellowship so true forego,
15 And in your gaudy May-games[3] meet,
While I lay trodden under feet?
When Juliana came, and she,
What I do to the grass, does to my thoughts and me.

But what you in compassion ought
20 Shall now by my revenge be wrought,
And flowers, and grass, and I, and all,

---

1. Green is the color of hope.
2. The alexandrine (12-syllable line) used here is the only example of a refrain in Marvell.
3. Festivals and merrymaking marked the first of May.

Will in one common ruin fall;
For Juliana comes, and she,
What I do to the grass, does to my thoughts and me.

25 And thus ye meadows, which have been
Companions of my thoughts more green,
Shall now the heraldry become
With which I shall adorn my tomb;
For Juliana comes, and she,
30 What I do to the grass, does to my thoughts and me.

The Garden

How vainly men themselves amaze°   *bewilder*
To win the palm, the oak, or bays,[1]
And their uncessant labors see
Crowned from some single herb or tree,
5 Whose short and narrow-vergèd° shade   *edged*
Does prudently their toils upbraid;
While all flowers and all trees do close°   *unite, agree*
To weave the garlands of repose!

Fair Quiet, have I found thee here,
10 And Innocence, thy sister dear?
Mistaken long, I sought you then
In busy companies of men.
Your sacred plants, if here below,°   *on earth*
Only among the plants will grow;
15 Society is all but rude,
To° this delicious solitude.   *compared to*

No white nor red[2] was ever seen
So amorous as this lovely green.
Fond lovers, cruel as their flame,
20 Cut in these trees their mistress' name:
Little, alas, they know or heed
How far these beauties hers exceed!
Fair trees, wheresoe'er your barks I wound,
No name shall but your own be found.[3]

25 When we have run our passion's heat,
Love hither makes his best retreat.
The gods, that mortal beauty chase,
Still in a tree did end their race:
Apollo hunted Daphne so,
30 Only that she might laurel grow;
And Pan did after Syrinx speed,
Not as a nymph, but for a reed.[4]

1. Honors, respectively, for military, civic, and poetic achievement.
2. Colors traditionally associated with female beauty.
3. Marvell proposes to carve in the bark of trees, not *Sylvia* or *Laura,* but *Beech* and *Oak.*

4. Apollo, the god of poetry, chased Daphne until she turned into a laurel (the emblematic reward of poets); Pan pursued Syrinx until she became a reed, out of which he made panpipes. The gods' motives were, of course, sexual, not horticultural.

What wondrous life in this I lead!
Ripe apples drop about my head;
35 The luscious clusters of the vine
Upon my mouth do crush their wine;
The nectarine and curious° peach   *exquisite*
Into my hands themselves do reach;
Stumbling on melons[5] as I pass,
40 Insnared with flowers, I fall on grass.

Meanwhile the mind, from pleasure less,[6]
Withdraws into its happiness;
The mind, that ocean where each kind
Does straight° its own resemblance find;[7]   *immediately*
45 Yet it creates, transcending these,
Far other worlds and other seas,
Annihilating all that's made
To a green thought in a green shade.

Here at the fountain's sliding foot,
50 Or at some fruit tree's mossy root,
Casting the body's vest° aside,   *garment*
My soul into the boughs does glide:
There like a bird it sits and sings,
Then whets° and combs its silver wings,   *preen*
55 And, till prepared for longer flight,
Waves in its plumes the various light.[8]

Such was that happy garden-state,
While man there walked without a mate:
After a place so pure and sweet,
60 What other help could yet be meet![9]
But 'twas beyond a mortal's share
To wander solitary there:
Two paradises 'twere in one
To live in paradise alone.

65 How well the skillful gardener drew
Of flowers and herbs this dial new,[1]
Where from above the milder sun
Does through a fragrant zodiac run;

---

5. "Melons," with etymological roots in the Greek word for *apple*, may recall the apple over which all humankind stumbled.
6. "Less" may modify either "pleasure" or "mind."
7. As the ocean supposedly contained a counterpart of every creature on land, so the ocean of the mind holds the innate ideas of all things (in Neo-platonic philosophy).
8. The multicolored light of this world, contrasted with the white radiance of eternity.
9. Genesis 2.18 recounts the Lord's decision to make a "help meet" for Adam, Eve.
1. The garden itself is laid out as a sundial.

And as it works, th' industrious bee
70 Computes its time[2] as well as we!
How could such sweet and wholesome hours
Be reckoned but with herbs and flowers?

2. With a pun on thyme.

MARGARET CAVENDISH
1623–1673

Margaret (Lucas) Cavendish, duchess of Newcastle, wrote and published numerous works during the Interregnum and Restoration era, in a great variety of genres: poetry (*Poems and Fancies*, 1653), essays (*Philosophical Fancies*, 1653, *The World's Olio*, 1655), short fiction (*Nature's Pictures*, 1656), autobiography (*A True Relation of My Birth, Breeding, and Life*, 1656), utopian romance (*The Blazing World*, 1666), scientific essays chiefly critical of the new science, letters, a biography of her husband (*The Life of . . . William Cavendish*, 1667), and some eighteen plays, of which one, *The Forced Marriage*, was produced in 1670. Most were published in lavish editions, at the Newcastles' own expense, and at the time they elicited more derision than praise: for a woman, especially an aristocratic woman, to publish works dealing so intimately with her desires, opinions, personal circumstances, and aspirations to fame and authorship was seen by many as disgraceful. Samuel Pepys concluded, after reading her life of her husband the duke, that she was "a mad, conceited, ridiculous woman, and he an ass to suffer [her] to write what she writes to him and of him." Her fantastic dress and sometimes idiosyncratic social behavior abetted that characterization: she took pride in "singularity" and even insisted on paying a visit to the all-male Royal Society. But the philosopher Thomas Hobbes thought well of her, and her rediscoverers in recent decades have been impressed by her works and her self-construction as a female author.

Her autobiography analyzes her responses to the circumstances of her life: born into a wealthy royalist family that encouraged her disposition to read and write; accepted as maid of honor by Queen Henrietta Maria, whom she followed into exile in Paris; married there (1645) to the widowed William Cavendish, thirty years her senior, who was one of Charles I's generals and later duke of Newcastle; exiled with him for fifteen years on the Continent, where (his estates having been sequestered) they ran up exorbitant debts; and restored to status and fortune after the Restoration. The duke, who was himself something of a poet, playwright, and philosopher, encouraged, supported, and promoted Margaret's literary endeavors—for which she was profoundly grateful. In polemical prefaces to her several works, she develops a fragmentary poetics, trenchantly defends her right to publish and to participate in contemporary intellectual exchange, defends women's rational powers, and decries their educational disadvantages and exclusion from the public domain.

The Blazing World Part romance, part utopia, and part science fiction, *The Blazing World* is also an idealized version of Cavendish's own ideas and fantasies in that it portrays the effortless rise of a woman to absolute power. It begins in the vein of romance: a young woman is abducted and miraculously saved as a tempest carries the abductors' boat to the North Pole and on to another universe, the Blazing World, whose emperor promptly marries her and turns over the entire government of the realm to her. It takes on a utopian character, as the new Empress learns from the fantastically diverse inhabitants about their numerous scientific experiments and about the royalist politics and religious uniformity of the place. She then brings Margaret Cavendish to be her scribe and returns with Margaret (in the state of disembodied spirits and platonic friends) to visit and learn about Margaret's world and Margaret's husband, the duke; she also puts down a rebellion at home and subjects other nations to her beneficent rule. Cavendish's preface makes a bold claim for authorial self-sufficiency, equating her creation and rule over her textual world with the conquering and ruling of empires by Caesar and Alexander. She undertakes to emphasize the satisfactions of authorship, but in doing so she also underscores the social and political restrictions on women that have confined her sphere of action to an imagined world.

The Description of a New World, Called The Blazing World[1]

To the Reader

* * * This is the reason, why I added this piece of fancy to my philosophical observations, and joined them as two worlds at the ends of their poles; both for my own sake, to divert my studious thoughts, which I employed in the contemplation thereof, and to delight the reader with variety, which is always pleasing. But lest my fancy should stray too much, I chose such a fiction as would be agreeable to the subject treated of in the former parts; it is a description of a *new world*, not such as *Lucian's* or the *French*-man's world in the moon;[2] but a world of my own creating, which I call the *Blazing World*: the first part whereof is *romancical*, the second philosophical, and the third is merely *fancy*, or (as I may call it) *fantastical*, which if it add any satisfaction to you, I shall account my self a happy *creatoress*; if not, I must be content to live a melancholy life in my own world; I cannot call it a poor world, if poverty be only want of gold, silver, and jewels; for there is more gold in it than all the chemists ever did, and (as I verily believe) will ever be able to make. As for the rocks of diamonds, I wish with all my soul they might be shared amongst my noble female friends, and upon that condition, I would willingly quit my part; and of the gold I should only desire so much as might suffice to repair my noble lord and husband's losses:[3] for I am not covetous, but as ambitious as ever any of my sex was, is, or can be; which makes, that though I cannot be *Henry* the Fifth, or *Charles* the Second, yet I endeavor to be *Margaret* the *First*; and although I have neither power, time nor occasion to conquer the world as *Alexander* and *Caesar* did; yet rather than not to be mistress of one, since Fortune and the Fates would give me none, I

---

1. *The Blazing World* was published in 1666 and 1668, together with Newcastle's *Observations upon Experimental Philosophy*, a critique of the new science emphasizing the limitations of experiment founded on human perception, and such machines as the microscope and telescope.
2. Cyrano de Bergerac (1620–1655), author of *Histoire comique conenant les états et empires de la lune* (1657). The Greek satirist Lucian of Samo-

sata (125–200? C.E.) wrote dialogues about an imaginary voyage, translated in 1634.
3. Cavendish's husband, William, was formally banished from England and his estates confiscated in 1649; they were all restored after the Restoration. During his banishment Margaret estimated that he suffered financial losses of around £940,000.

have made a world of my own: for which no body, I hope, will blame me, since it is in every one's power to do the like.

———————

* * * No sooner was the Lady brought before the Emperor, but he conceived her to be some goddess, and offered to worship her; which she refused, telling him, (for by that time she had pretty well learned their language) that although she came out of another world, yet was she but a mortal; at which the Emperor rejoicing, made her his wife, and gave her an absolute power to rule and govern all that world as she pleased. But her subjects, who could hardly be persuaded to believe her mortal, tendered her all the veneration and worship due to a deity . . .

Their priests and governors were princes of the imperial blood, and made eunuchs for that purpose; and as for the ordinary sort of men in that part of the world where the Emperor resided, they were of several complexions; not white, black, tawny, olive or ash-coloured; but some appeared of an azure, some of a deep purple, some of a grass-green, some of a scarlet, some of an orange color, etc. Which colors and complexions, whether they were made by the bare reflection of light, without the assistance of small particles, or by the help of well-ranged and ordered atoms; or by a continual agitation of little globules; or by some pressing and reacting motion, I am not able to determine. The rest of the inhabitants of that world, were men of several different sorts, shapes, figures, dispositions, and humors, as I have already made mention heretofore; some were bear-men, some worm-men, some fish- or mear-men,[4] otherwise called sirens; some bird-men, some fly-men, some ant-men, some geese-men, some spider-men, some lice-men, some fox-men, some ape-men, some jackdaw-men, some magpie-men, some parrot-men, some satyrs, some giants, and many more, which I cannot all remember; and of these several sorts of men, each followed such a profession as was most proper for the nature of their species, which the Empress encouraged them in, especially those that had applied themselves to the study of several arts and sciences; for they were as ingenious and witty in the invention of profitable and useful arts, as we are in our world, nay, more; and to that end she erected schools, and founded several societies. The bear-men were to be her experimental philosophers, the bird-men her astronomers, the fly-, worm- and fish-men her natural philosophers, the ape-men her chemists, the satyrs her Galenic physicians, the fox-men her politicians, the spider- and lice-men her mathematicians, the jackdaw-, magpie- and parrot-men her orators and logicians, the giants her architects, etc. But before all things, she having got a sovereign power from the Emperor over all the world, desired to be informed both of the manner of their religion and government, and to that end she called the priests and statesmen, to give her an account of either. Of the statesmen she enquired, first, why they had so few laws? To which they answered, that many laws made many divisions, which most commonly did breed factions, and at last break out into open wars. Next, she asked, why they preferred the monarchical form of government before any other? They answered, that as it was natural for one body to have but one head, so it was also natural for a politic body to have but one governor; and that a

———

4. Mermen, the male counterparts of mermaids.

commonwealth, which had many governors was like a monster with many heads: besides, said they, a monarchy is a divine form of government, and agrees most with our religion; for as there is but one God, whom we all unanimously worship and adore with one faith, so we are resolved to have but one Emperor, to whom we all submit with one obedience.

Then the Empress seeing that the several sorts of her subjects had each their churches apart, asked the priests whether they were of several religions? They answered her Majesty, that there was no more but one religion in all that world, nor no diversity of opinions in that same religion; for though there were several sorts of men, yet had they all but one opinion concerning the worship and adoration of God. The Empress asked them, whether they were Jews, Turks, or Christians? We do not know, said they, what religions those are; but we do all unanimously acknowledge, worship and adore the only, omnipotent, and eternal God, with all reverence, submission, and duty. Again, the Empress enquired, whether they had several forms of worship? They answered, no: for our devotion and worship consists only in prayers, which we frame according to our several necessities, in petitions, humiliations, thanksgiving, etc. Truly, replied the Empress, I thought you had been either Jews, or Turks, because I never perceived any women in your congregations; but what is the reason, you bar them from your religious assemblies? It is not fit, said they, that men and women should be promiscuously together in time of religious worship; for their company hinders devotion, and makes many, instead of praying to God, direct their devotion to their mistresses. But, asked the Empress, have they no congregation of their own, to perform the duties of divine worship, as well as men? No, answered they: but they stay at home, and say their prayers by themselves in their closets.[5] Then the Empress desired to know the reason why the priests and governors of their world were made eunuchs? They answered, to keep them from marriage: for women and children most commonly make disturbance both in church and state. But, said she, women and children have no employment in church or state. 'Tis true, answered they; but although they are not admitted to public employments, yet are they so prevalent[6] with their husbands and parents, that many times by their importunate persuasions, they cause as much, nay, more mischief secretly, than if they had the management of public affairs.

✳ ✳ ✳

[THE EMPRESS BRINGS THE DUCHESS OF NEWCASTLE TO THE BLAZING WORLD]

After some time, when the spirits had refreshed themselves in their own vehicles, they sent one of their nimblest spirits, to ask the Empress, whether she would have a scribe. ✳ ✳ ✳ Then the spirit asked her, whether she would have the soul of a living or a dead man? Why, said the Empress, can the soul quit a living body, and wander or travel abroad? Yes, answered he, for according to Plato's doctrine, there is a conversation of souls, and the souls of lovers live in the bodies of their beloved. Then I will have, answered she, the soul of some ancient famous writer, either of Aristotle, Pythagoras, Plato, Epicurus,[7] or the like. The spirit said, that those famous men were very learned,

<hr />

5. Private chambers.
6. I.e., they prevail so much.
7. Classical philosophers and founders, respec-

tively, of schools of philosophy: the Peripatetics, the Pythagoreans, the Academics, the Epicureans.

subtle, and ingenious writers, but they were so wedded to their own opinions, that they would never have the patience to be scribes. Then, said she, I'll have the soul of one of the most famous modern writers, as either of Galileo, Gassendus, Descartes, Helmont, Hobbes, H. More, etc.[8] The spirit answered, that they were fine ingenious writers, but yet so self-conceited, that they would scorn to be scribes to a woman. But, said he, there's a lady, the Duchess of Newcastle, which although she is not one of the most learned, eloquent, witty and ingenious, yet is she a plain and rational writer, for the principle of her writings, is sense and reason, and she will without question, be ready to do you all the service she can. This lady then, said the Empress, will I choose for my scribe, neither will the Emperor have reason to be jealous, she being one of my own sex. In truth, said the spirit, husbands have reason to be jealous of platonic lovers, for they are very dangerous, as being not only very intimate and close, but subtle and insinuating. You say well, replied the Empress; wherefore I pray send me the Duchess of Newcastle's soul; which the spirit did; and after she came to wait on the Empress, at her first arrival the Empress embraced and saluted her with a spiritual kiss.

* * *

[THE DUCHESS WANTS A WORLD TO RULE]

Well, said the Duchess, setting aside this dispute, my ambition is, that I would fain be as you are, that is, an Empress of a world, and I shall never be at quiet until I be one. I love you so well, replied the Empress, that I wish with all my soul, you had the fruition of your ambitious desire, and I shall not fail to give you my best advice how to accomplish it; the best informers are the immaterial spirits, and they'll soon tell you, whether it be possible to obtain your wish. But, said the Duchess, I have little acquaintance with them, for I never knew any before the time you sent for me. They know you, replied the Empress; for they told me of you, and were the means and instrument of your coming hither: wherefore I'll confer with them, and enquire whether there be not another world, whereof you may be Empress as well as I am of this? No sooner had the Empress said this, but some immaterial spirits came to visit her, of whom she enquired, whether there were but there worlds in all, to wit, the Blazing World where she was in, the world which she came from, and the world where the Duchess lived? The spirits answered, that there were more numerous worlds than the stars which appeared in these three mentioned worlds. Then the Empress asked, whether it was not possible, that her dearest friend the Duchess of Newcastle, might be Empress of one of them?[9] Although there be numerous, nay, infinite worlds, answered the spirits, yet none is without government. But is none of these worlds so weak, said she, that it may be surprised or conquered? The spirits answered, that Lucian's world of lights, had been for some time in a snuff, but of late years one Helmont had got it, who since he was Emperor

8. Galileo Galilei (1564–1642), Italian astronomer and defender of the Copernican system; Pierre Gassendi (1592–1655), proponent of a mechanistic theory of matter; René Descartes (1596–1650), French mathematician and philosopher who had a major influence on the new science; Jan Baptista Van Helmont (1577–1644), Flemish chemist; Thomas Hobbes, English mechanistic philosopher and political scientist, author of *Leviathan*; Henry More (1614–1687), one of the antimaterialist Cambridge Platonists.

9. Speculation about multiple inhabited worlds was an occasional topic in texts on the new astronomy. Milton's Raphael introduces the idea to Adam (*Paradise Lost* 8.148–52).

of it, had so strengthened the immortal parts thereof with mortal out-works, as it was for the present impregnable. Said the Empress, if there be such an infinite number of worlds, I am sure, not only my friend, the Duchess, but any other might obtain one. Yes, answered the spirits, if those worlds were uninhabited; but they are as populous as this, your Majesty governs. Why, said the Empress, it is not impossible to conquer a world. No, answered the spirits, but, for the most part, conquerors seldom enjoy their conquest, for they being more feared than loved, most commonly come to an untimely end. If you will but direct me, said the Duchess to the spirits, which world is easiest to be conquered, her Majesty will assist me with means, and I will trust to fate and fortune; for I had rather die in the adventure of noble achievements, than live in obscure and sluggish security; since by the one, I may live in a glorious fame, and by the other I am buried in oblivion. The spirits answered, that the lives of fame were like other lives; for some lasted long, and some died soon. 'Tis true, said the Duchess; but yet the shortest-lived fame lasts longer than the longest life of man. But, replied the spirits, if occasion does not serve you, you must content yourself to live without such achievements that may gain you a fame: but we wonder, proceeded the spirits, that you desire to be Empress of a terrestrial world, whenas you can create yourself a celestial world if you please. What, said the Empress, can any mortal be a creator? Yes, answered the spirits; for every human creature can create an immaterial world fully inhabited by immaterial creatures, and populous of immaterial subjects, such as we are, and all this within the compass of the head or skull; nay, not only so, but he may create a world of what fashion and government he will, and give the creatures thereof such motions, figures, forms, colors, perceptions, etc. as he pleases, and make whirlpools, lights, pressures and reactions, etc. as he thinks best; nay, he may make a world full of veins, muscles, and nerves, and all these to move by one jolt or stroke: also he may alter that world as often as he pleases, or change it from a natural world, to an artificial; he may make a world of ideas, a world of atoms, a world of lights, or whatsoever his fancy leads him to. And since it is in your power to create such a world, what need you to venture life, reputation and tranquility, to conquer a gross material world? . . . You have converted me, said the Duchess to the spirits, from my ambitious desire; wherefore I'll take your advice, reject and despise all the worlds without me, and create a world of my own.

* * *

The Epilogue to the Reader

By this poetical description, you may perceive, that my ambition is not only to be Empress, but Authoress of a whole world; and that the worlds I have made, both the Blazing and the other Philosophical World, mentioned in the first part of this description, are framed and composed of the most pure, that is, the rational parts of matter, which are the parts of my mind; which creation was more easily and suddenly effected, than the conquests of the two famous monarchs of the world, Alexander and Caesar:[1] neither have I made such disturbances, and caused so many dissolutions of particulars, otherwise named deaths, as they did; for I have destroyed but some

1. Alexander the Great and Julius Caesar were both famed as conquerors of much of the world known to them.

few men in a little boat, which died through the extremity of cold, and that by the hand of Justice, which was necessitated to punish their crime of stealing away a young and beauteous lady.[2] And in the formation of those worlds, I take more delight and glory, than ever Alexander or Caesar did in conquering this terrestrial world; and though I have made my Blazing World, a peaceable world, allowing it but one religion, one language, and one government; yet could I make another world, as full of factions, divisions, and wars, as this is of peace and tranquility; and the rational figures of my mind might express as much courage to fight, as Hector and Achilles[3] had; and be as wise as Nestor, as eloquent as Ulysses, and as beautiful as Helen. But I esteeming peace before war, wit before policy, honesty before beauty; instead of the figures of Alexander, Caesar, Hector, Achilles, Nestor, Ulysses, Helen, etc. chose rather the figure of honest Margaret Newcastle, which now I would not change for all this terrestrial world; and if any should like the world I have made, and be willing to be my subjects, they may imagine themselves such, and they are such, I mean, in their minds, fancies or imaginations; but if they cannot endure to be subjects, they may create worlds of their own, and govern themselves as they please: but yet let them have a care, not to prove unjust usurpers, and to rob me of mine; for concerning the Philosophical World, I am Empress of it myself; and as for the Blazing World, it having an Empress already, who rules it with great wisdom and conduct, which Empress is my dear Platonic friend; I shall never prove so unjust, treacherous and unworthy to her, as to disturb her government, much less to depose her from her imperial throne, for the sake of any other; but rather choose to create another world for another friend.

1666, 1668

2. A reference to the romancelike incident with which *The Blazing World* begins, the abduction of a young woman by a party of adventurers, whose boat was blown in a tempest to the North Pole, where they perished (except for the woman, who entered into the Blazing World).

3. The principal heroes of Homer's *Iliad*, Hector the Trojan and Achilles the Greek. "Nestor": wise advisor to the Greeks. "Ulysses": hero of Homer's *Odyssey*. "Helen": her beauty caused the Trojan War, as it prompted the Trojan Paris to steal her away from her Greek husband, Menelaus.

JOHN MILTON
1608–1674

When he was thirty, John Milton proclaimed himself the future author of a great English epic. He promised a poem devoted to the glory of the nation, centering around the deeds of King Arthur or some other ancient hero. When Milton finally published his epic thirty years later, readers found instead a poem set in Heaven, Hell, and the garden of Eden, in which traditional heroism is denigrated and England not once mentioned. What lay between the youthful promise and the eventual fulfillment was a career marked by private tragedy and public controversy. Milton tells us much about both these experiences in his works, which combine an intense self-scrutiny and concern with authorship with urgent intervention in the great questions of his time. It is scarcely possible to treat Milton's career separately from the history of England in his lifetime, not only because he was an active participant in public affairs but also because he himself refused to distinguish between his private life and affairs of church and state. When he signed himself, as he often did, "John Milton, Englishman," he did not simply mean *an* Englishman. As England's self-appointed prophetic bard, Milton saw himself as spokesman for the nation as a whole, even when he found himself in a minority of one. Milton was a man who devoted his life to public causes, but whose understanding of those causes often arose out of the most personal concerns.

The young Milton self-consciously set out to follow the steps of the ideal poetic career—beginning with pastoral and ending with epic—modeled on that of the Roman poet Virgil. In this approach to his vocation, he stood at the opposite end of the spectrum from such Cavalier contemporaries as Suckling and Lovelace, who turned to verse with an air of studied carelessness. Milton began by writing occasional poems in Latin and several English poems in the pastoral mode: lyrics, the masque *Comus* (1634), and the pastoral elegy *Lycidas* (1683). These are extraordinary works in their own right, which crown and transform their respective genres, but Milton also undertook them as preparation for the greater genres of tragedy and epic. He was embarking on a road previously traveled by Edmund Spenser, whom he called "a better teacher than Scotus or Aquinas." Milton resembles Spenser in certain ways, above all in his constant use of myth and archetype, alluding to and juxtaposing biblical and classical stories. But Milton's learning was greater than Spenser's. As part of his preparation for a poetic career, he undertook a six-year program of self-directed reading in ancient and modern theology, philosophy, history, science, politics, and literature. His command of languages included Latin, Greek, Hebrew and its dialects, Italian, French, Spanish, and Dutch. The sum of the western literary and intellectual heritage impinged on his writing as immediately and directly as the circumstances of his own life, but he continually reconceived the ideas, literary forms, and values of this heritage to make them relevant to himself and his age.

For Milton to devote six years of his adult life to an obscure course of private study required extraordinary confidence in the service he hoped to perform for God and country. It also, of course, required money, which was provided by his father, who was a successful scrivener—a combination of solicitor, investment advisor, and money lender. Although Milton enjoyed the company of some aristocrats and was profoundly grateful that his father spared him from the grubby business of making money, he belonged to the London bourgeoisie. His father's business dealings and loans at interest paid for private tutors in his youth, for his education at St. Paul's, one of the finest schools in the land, for his seven years at Cambridge and the six years of reading that followed, and for his "grand tour" of France, Italy, and Switzerland at the age of thirty. Yet Milton's connection with the class that stood to benefit most directly from Europe's first bourgeois revolution does not account for his passionate political views. His brother, Christopher, fought on the royalist side. For the Milton brothers, as for most of their contemporaries, the civil wars did not appear as a confrontation of class interests, but as a conflict between radically differing theories of government and, above all, religion.

From the outbreak of the conflict until his death, Milton was allied with the Puritan cause. Yet his religious opinions developed throughout his life, from relative orthodoxy in his youth to ever more heretical positions in his later years. Milton went up to Cambridge in 1625 with every intention of taking orders in the Church of England. In the hindsight of 1642, he blamed the lack of reformation and the corruption in the English Church under Archbishop Laud for forcing him to abandon that goal, proclaiming himself "church-outed by the Prelates." Milton's change of direction must also have been linked to the fastidious contempt he expressed for the ignorant and clownish clergymen-in-making who were his fellow students at Cambridge: "They thought themselves gallant men, and I thought them fools." Those fellow students dubbed Milton "The Lady of Christ's College." Above all, Milton came to believe that he was destined to serve his language, his country, and his God as a poet. In his first major English poem, the hymn *On the Morning of Christ's Nativity* (written at the age of twenty-one), Milton had already begun to construct himself as a prophetic bard. His sense of poetic mission grew over the next decade, accompanied by growing disillusion with the Church of England. Both are present in *Lycidas* (1638), written to lament the untimely death of his Cambridge contemporary Edward King. The figure of King recedes in the poem next to Milton's anxious contemplation of poetry as a vocation and his furious diatribe against the corrupt Anglican clergy who leave their charges prey to the "grim wolf" of Catholicism. Yet while he was in Italy on the Grand Tour (1638–39), Milton delighted in exchanging verses and learned compliments with various Catholic intellectuals and men of letters, some of whom became friends. Milton could always maintain friendships and family relationships across ideological divides.

Upon his return to England, Milton opened a school and was soon involved in Presbyterian efforts to depose the bishops and reform Church liturgy, writing five "Antiprelatical" tracts denouncing and satirizing bishops. These were the first in a remarkable series of political interventions which occupied Milton for the next twenty years, until the disaster (for him) of the Restoration. He wrote successively on church government, divorce, education, freedom of the press, regicide, and republicanism. He also served as Latin Secretary to the Commonwealth Government (1649–53) and to Oliver Cromwell's Protectorate (1654–58), writing the official letters—mostly in Latin—to foreign governments and heads of state. Yet Milton was the very opposite of a faceless spokesman for a party line. From the beginning to the end of his polemical career, his publications show an extraordinary courage and independence of thought. In his tracts advocating divorce on the grounds of incompatibility and with the right to remarry, he adopted and vigorously defended a position almost unheard of at the time, one which required a boldly antiliteral reading of the gospels. In *Areopagitica*, he put forward an impassioned defense of a free press against a Parliament determined to restore effective censorship. And just as he was among the first to attack the power of the bishops, so he was virtually the last defender of the "Good Old Cause" of the Revolution; the second edition of his *Ready and Easy Way to Establish a Free Commonwealth* appeared in late April 1660, scarcely two weeks before the Restoration.

Several of these treatises were also prompted by personal concerns or crises. In his polemical tract *The Reason of Church Government Urged Against Prelaty*, Milton devoted several pages to a discussion of his poetic vocation and the great works he might produce in the future. His writings on divorce, which can hardly have seemed the most pressing of issues in the strife-torn years 1643–45, were motivated by his personal experience of a disastrous marriage. Aged thirty-three, inexperienced with women, and idealistic about marriage as in essence a union of minds and spirits, he had wedded a young woman of seventeen, Mary Powell, who returned to her royalist family just a few months after the marriage. Milton responded by turning his private grief into a matter of public controversy. The fact that his tracts on divorce could not be licensed and were roundly denounced in Parliament, from pulpits, and in print prompted him in turn to write *Areopagitica*, his famous defense of a free press and the free commerce in ideas. Yet he saw all these personal issues—a reformed poetry, the domestic liberty to be achieved through needful divorce, and a free press—as vital to the creation of a reformed English culture.

In the years that followed, Milton suffered a series of agonizing tragedies. Mary Powell returned to him in 1645, but died in childbirth in 1652, leaving four children; the only son, John, died a few months later. In the same year, Milton became totally blind. Whatever the medical causes, Milton himself attributed his blindness to late nights of reading in his youth and his exertions in writing defenses of the execution of Charles I and the new republic. Milton married again in 1656, apparently happily, but his new wife, Katherine Woodcock, was dead two years later, along with their infant daughter. Katherine is probably the subject of his sonnet *Methought I Saw My Late Espousèd Saint*, a moving dream-vision poignant with the sense of loss—both of sight and of love. Milton had little time for poetry in these years, but his few sonnets revolutionized the genre, overlaying the Petrarchan metrical structure with an urgent rhetorical voice and using the small sonnet form, hitherto confined mainly to matters of love, for new and grand subjects: praise of Cromwell mixed with admonition and political advice; a prophetic denunciation calling down God's vengeance for Protestants massacred in Piedmont; an emotion-filled account of his continuing struggle to come to terms with his blindness as part of God's providence.

Milton's courageous defense of the Revolution down to the last possible moment could have spelled disaster for him upon the return of Charles II. For several months after that event, he was in hiding, his life in danger, but friends, especially the poet Andrew Marvell, managed his pardon and later his release from a brief imprisonment. He lived out his last years in reduced circumstances, plagued by ever more serious attacks of gout but grateful for the domestic comforts provided by his third wife, Elizabeth Minshull, whom he married in 1663 and who survived him. In such conditions, dismayed by the defeat of his political and religious cause, totally blind and often ill, threatened by the horrific plague of 1665 and the great fire of 1666, and entirely dependent on amanuenses and friends to transcribe his dictation, he completed the great epic poem that undertakes to "justify the ways of God to men." *Paradise Lost* radically reconceives the epic genre and epic heroism, choosing as protagonists a domestic couple rather than martial heroes, and degrading the military glory celebrated in epic tradition in favor of the "better fortitude / Of patience and heroic martyrdom." Michael's prophecy to Adam makes clear that the course of human history is tragic, that the world will remain "to good malignant, to bad men benign" until the Second Coming of Christ. Yet it also makes clear that throughout history God will raise up prophets and heroes to resist wicked tyrants and corrupt societies.

In his final years, Milton continued to pursue subjects that had interested him from his youth, publishing works on grammar and logic chiefly written during his days as schoolmaster, a *History of Britain* (1670) from earliest times to the Norman Conquest, and a treatise urging toleration for Puritan dissenters (1673). He also continued work on his *Christian Doctrine*, a Latin treatise which reveals how far Milton had moved from the orthodoxies of his day. The work denies the Trinity (making Christ and the Holy Spirit much inferior to God the Father), insists upon free will (against Calvinist predestination), and privileges the inspiration of the Spirit over the Scriptures and the Ten Commandments. Such radical and heterodox positions could not be made public in his lifetime, certainly not in the repressive conditions of the Restoration, and Milton's *Christian Doctrine* was lost to view for over 150 years.

In 1671 Milton published two poems which resonate with echoes of the harsh repression and the moral and political challenges Puritan dissenters faced after the Restoration. *Paradise Regained*, a brief epic in four books, treats Jesus' Temptation in the Wilderness as a hard intellectual struggle through which the hero comes to understand himself and his mission and defeats Satan by renouncing the whole panoply of false or faulty versions of the good life and of his kingdom. *Samson Agonistes*, a classical tragedy, is the more harrowing for the resemblances between its tragic hero and its author. The deeply flawed, pain-wracked, blind, and defeated Samson struggles, in dialogues with his visitors, to gain self-knowledge, discovering at last a desperate way to triumph over his captors and offer his people a chance to regain their freedom. In these last poems, Milton sought to educate his readers in moral and political wisdom and virtue. Only through such inner transformation, Milton now firmly believed, would men and women come to value—and so perhaps reclaim—the intellectual, religious, and political freedom he so vigorously promoted in his prose and poetry.

On Shakespeare[1]

What needs my Shakespeare for his honored bones
The labor of an age in pilèd stones,
Or that his hallowed relics should be hid
Under a star-ypointing[2] pyramid?
5 Dear son of memory,[3] great heir of fame,
What° need'st thou such weak witness of thy name?   *why*
Thou in our wonder and astonishment
Hast built thyself a livelong° monument.   *enduring*
For whilst to th' shame of slow-endeavoring art
10 Thy easy numbers flow, and that each heart
Hath from the leaves of thy unvalued° book   *invaluable*
Those Delphic[4] lines with deep impression took,
Then thou, our fancy of itself bereaving,
Dost make us marble with too much conceiving;[5]
15 And so sepùlchered in such pomp dost lie,
That kings for such a tomb would wish to die.

1630   1632

L'Allegro[1]

Hence loathèd Melancholy,[2]
Of Cerberus[3] and blackest midnight born,
In Stygian[4] cave forlorn
'Mongst horrid shapes, and shrieks, and sights unholy,
5 Find out some uncouth° cell,   *desolate*
Where brooding Darkness spreads his jealous wings,
And the night-raven sings;
There under ebon shades and low-browed rocks,
As ragged as thy locks,
10   In dark Cimmerian[5] desert ever dwell.
But come thou goddess fair and free,
In heaven yclept Euphrosyne,[6]

1. This tribute, Milton's first published poem, appeared in the Second Folio of Shakespeare's plays (1632).
2. A Spenserian archaism.
3. As "son of memory" Shakespeare is a brother of the Muses, who are the daughters of Mnemosyne (Memory).
4. Apollo, god of poetry, had his oracle at Delphi.
5. Shakespeare's mesmerized readers are themselves his (marble) monument.
1. The companion poems *L'Allegro* and *Il Penseroso* are both written in tetrameter couplets, but Milton's virtuosity produces entirely different tempos and sound qualities in the two poems. The Italian titles name, respectively, the cheerful, mirthful man and the melancholy, contemplative man. The poems are carefully balanced and their different values celebrated, though *Penseroso*'s greater length and final coda may intimate that life's superiority. Mirth, the presiding deity of *Allegro*, is described in terms that evoke Botticelli's presen-

tation of the Grace Euphrosone (youthful mirth) and her sisters in his *Primavera*.
2. The black Melancholy recognized and here exorcized by Mirth's man is a disease leading to madness; *Il Penseroso* celebrates melancholy as the temperament of the scholarly, contemplative man, represented in Durer's famous engraving *Melancholy*. Robert Burton's *Anatomy of Melancholy* treats the entire range of possibilities.
3. The three-headed hellhound of classical mythology.
4. Near the river Styx, in the underworld.
5. Homer's Cimmereans (*Odyssey* 11.13–19) live on the outer edge of the world, in perpetual darkness.
6. The three Graces—Euphrosyne (four syllables) figuring Youthful Mirth, Aglaia, Brilliance, and Thalia, Bloom—were commonly taken to be offspring of Venus (Love and Beauty) and Bacchus (god of wine). Milton proceeds, however, to devise another, more innocent parentage for Euphrosyne

And by men, heart-easing Mirth,
Whom lovely Venus at a birth
15   With two sister Graces more
To ivy-crownèd Bacchus bore;
Or whether (as some sager sing)
The frolic wind that breathes the spring,
Zephyr with Aurora playing,
20   As he met her once a-Maying,
There on beds of violets blue,
And fresh-blown° roses washed in dew,   *newly opened*
Filled her with thee a daughter fair,
So buxom,° blithe, and debonair.   *lively*
25   Haste thee nymph, and bring with thee
Jest and youthful Jollity,
Quips° and Cranks,° and wanton Wiles,   *witty sayings/jokes*
Nods, and Becks,° and wreathèd Smiles,   *beckonings*
Such as hang on Hebe's⁷ cheek,
30   And love to live in dimple sleek;
Sport that wrinkled Care derides,
And Laughter holding both his sides.
Come, and trip it° as ye go   *dance*
On the light fantastic toe,
35   And in thy right hand lead with thee
The mountain nymph, sweet Liberty;
And if I give thee honor due,
Mirth, admit me of thy crew
To live with her and live with thee,
40   In unreprovèd° pleasures free;   *irreproachable*
To hear the lark begin his flight,
And, singing, startle the dull night,
From his watch-tower in the skies,
Till the dappled dawn doth rise;
45   Then to come in spite of° sorrow,   *in defiance of*
And at my window bid good morrow,
Through the sweetbriar or the vine,
Or the twisted eglantine.
While the cock with lively din
50   Scatters the rear of darkness thin,
And to the stack or the barn door,
Stoutly struts his dames before;
Oft listening how the hounds and horn
Cheerly rouse the slumbering morn,
55   From the side of some hoar hill,
Through the high wood echoing shrill.
Sometime walking not unseen
By hedgerow elms, on hillocks green,
Right against the eastern gate,
60   Where the great sun begins his state,⁸
Robed in flames and amber light,

(ascribing it to "some sager," lines 17–24): Zephyr,
the West Wind, and Aurora, goddess of the Dawn.

7. Goddess of youth and cupbearer to the gods.
8. Stately procession, as by a monarch.

The clouds in thousand liveries dight;°   *dressed*
While the plowman near at hand
Whistles o'er the furrowed land,
65   And the milkmaid singeth blithe,
And the mower whets his scythe,
And every shepherd tells his tale
Under the hawthorn in the dale.
Straight mine eye hath caught new pleasures
70   Whilst the landscape round it measures,
Russet lawns and fallows° gray,   *plowed land*
Where the nibbling flocks do stray,
Mountains on whose barren breast
The laboring clouds do often rest;
75   Meadows trim with daisies pied,°   *multicolored*
Shallow brooks, and rivers wide.
Towers and battlements it sees
Bosomed high in tufted trees,
Where perhaps some beauty lies,
80   The cynosure[9] of neighboring eyes.
Hard by, a cottage chimney smokes
From betwixt two agèd oaks,
Where Corydon and Thyrsis met
Are at their savory dinner set
85   Of herbs and other country messes,
Which the neat-handed° Phyllis dresses;   *dexterous*
And then in haste her bower she leaves,
With Thestylis[1] to bind the sheaves;
Or if the earlier season lead
90   To the tanned° haycock in the mead.   *sun-dried*
Sometimes with secure° delight   *careless*
The upland hamlets will invite,
When the merry bells ring round
And the jocund rebecks[2] sound
95   To many a youth and many a maid,
Dancing in the checkered shade;
And young and old come forth to play
On a sunshine holiday,
Till the livelong daylight fail;
100   Then to the spicy nut-brown ale,
With stories told of many a feat,
How fairy Mab the junkets[3] eat;
She was pinched and pulled, she said,
And he, by friar's lantern led,
105   Tells how the drudging goblin[4] sweat
To earn his cream-bowl duly set,
When in one night, ere glimpse of morn,

---

9. Literally, the bright polestar, by which mariners steer; here, a splendid object, much gazed at.
1. Milton uses traditional names from classical pastoral—"Corydon," "Thyrsis," "Phyllis," "Thestylis"—for his rustic English shepherds.
2. A small three-stringed fiddle. "Jocund": merry, sprightly.

3. Sweetmeats, especially with cream. Queen Mab is the fairy queen, consort of Oberon. "She" and "he" in the next two lines are country folk telling of their experiences with fairies.
4. Robin Goodfellow, alias Puck, Pook, or Hobgoblin. "Friar's lantern": will-o-the-wisp.

His shadowy flail hath threshed the corn
That ten day-laborers could not end;
110 Then lies him down the lubber fiend,[5]
And stretched out all the chimney's° length,   *fireplace's*
Basks at the fire his hairy strength;
And crop-full out of doors he flings
Ere the first cock his matin rings.
115 Thus done the tales, to bed they creep,
By whispering winds soon lulled asleep.
Towered cities please us then,
And the busy hum of men,
Where throngs of knights and barons bold
120 In weeds of peace high triumphs[6] hold,
With store of ladies, whose bright eyes
Rain influence,[7] and judge the prize
Of wit or arms, while both contend
To win her grace, whom all commend.
125 There let Hymen[8] oft appear
In saffron robe, with taper clear,
And pomp and feast and revelry,
With masque and antique° pageantry;   *ancient, also antic*
Such sights as youthful poets dream
130 On summer eves by haunted stream.
Then to the well-trod stage anon,
If Jonson's learned sock be on,
Or sweetest Shakespeare, fancy's child,
Warble his native wood-notes wild.[9]
135 And ever against eating cares;[1]
Lap me in soft Lydian airs,[2]
Married to immortal verse
Such as the meeting soul may pierce
In notes with many a winding bout°   *circuit*
140 Of linkèd sweetness long drawn out,
With wanton heed and giddy cunning,
The melting voice through mazes running,
Untwisting all the chains that tie
The hidden soul of harmony;
145 That Orpheus' self may heave his head
From golden slumber on a bed
Of heaped Elysian flowers, and hear
Such strains as would have won the ear
Of Pluto, to have quite set free
150 His half-regained Eurydice.[3]

5. Robin traditionally did all manner of drudging work for people, to be rewarded with a bowl of cream.
6. Pageants. "Weeds of peace": courtly raiment.
7. The ladies' eyes are stars and so have astrological influence over the men.
8. Roman god of marriage. An orange-yellow (saffron) robe and a torch are his attributes.
9. It was conventional to contrast Jonson as a "learned" poet and Shakespeare as a "natural" one, but L'Allegro's views and choices of literature also

suits with his nature. "Sock": the comedian's low-heeled slipper, contrasted with the tragedian's buskin, a high-heeled boot.
1. "Eating cares" (Horace, *Odes* 2.11.18) is one of many classical echoes in the poem.
2. Plato considered "Lydian airs" to be enervating, soft, and sensual; he preferred the solemn Doric mode. Some others thought Lydian airs relaxing and delightful.
3. Orpheus's music so moved Pluto that he agreed to release his dead wife Eurydice (four syllables,

These delights if thou canst give,
Mirth, with thee I mean to live.[4]

ca. 1631   1645

Il Penseroso[1]

Hence vain deluding Joys,[2]
    The brood of Folly without father bred,
How little you bestead,°   *avail*
    Or fill the fixèd mind with all your toys°   *trifles*
5 Dwell in some idle brain,
    And fancies fond° with gaudy shapes possess,   *foolish*
As thick and numberless
    As the gay motes that people the sunbeams,
Or likest hovering dreams,
10   The fickle pensioners of Morpheus'[3] train.
But hail thou Goddess sage and holy,
    Hail, divinest Melancholy,
Whose saintly visage is too bright
    To hit° the sense of human sight,   *suit*
15 And therefore to our weaker view
O'erlaid with black, staid Wisdom's hue;[4]
    Black, but such as in esteem,
Prince Memnon's sister[5] might beseem,
    Or that starred Ethiope queen[6] that strove
20 To set her beauty's praise above
    The sea nymphs, and their powers offended.
Yet thou art higher far descended;
    Thee bright-haired Vesta long of yore
To solitary Saturn bore;[7]
25 His daughter she (in Saturn's reign
    Such mixture was not held a stain).
Oft in glimmering bowers and glades
    He met her, and in secret shades
Of woody Ida's inmost grove,
30   While yet there was no fear of Jove.
    Come pensive nun, devout and pure,

accent on the second) from the underworld, but
he violated the condition set—that he not look
back at her—and so lost her again. Milton often
uses Orpheus as a figure for the poet.
4. The final lines echo Marlowe's *The Passionate
Shepherd to His Love* (p. 457): "If these delights
thy mind may move, / Then live with me, and be
my love."
1. Melancholy's man celebrates a melancholy that
does not produce madness but the scholarly temperament, ruled by Saturn. See note 2 to *L 'Allegro*.
2. For Melancholy's man, Mirth is not the innocent joys of *L'Allegro*, but "vain deluding Joys."
3. Morpheus is the god of sleep. "Pensioners": followers.
4. The melancholy humor, caused by black bile,
was thought to make the face dark or saturnine—

from the ancient god, Saturn, allegorized in Neoplatonic philosophy as "the collective angelic
mind."
5. Memnon, in *Odyssey* 11, was a handsome Ethiopian prince; his sister Himera's beauty was mentioned by later commentators. Cf. Song of
Solomon 1.5, "I am black but comely."
6. Cassiopeia was turned into a constellation
("starred") for bragging that she was more beautiful than the sea nymphs.
7. Vesta, daughter of Saturn, was goddess of the
household and a virgin, as were her priestesses.
Milton invented the story of her sexual congress
with Saturn on Mount Ida, resulting in Melancholy's birth. Saturn ruled the gods and the world
during the Golden Age, which ended when he was
murdered by his son Jove.

Sober, steadfast, and demure,
All in a robe of darkest grain,°   *color*
Flowing with majestic train,
35 And sable stole[8] of cypress lawn
Over thy decent° shoulders drawn.   *comely, modestly covered*
Come, but keep thy wonted state,
With even step and musing gait,
And looks commercing with the skies,
40 Thy rapt soul sitting in thine eyes:
There held in holy passion still,
Forget thyself to marble,[9] till
With a sad° leaden downward cast°   *grave, dignified / glance*
Thou fix them on the earth as fast.
45 And join with thee calm Peace and Quiet,
Spare Fast, that oft with gods doth diet,
And hears the Muses in a ring
Aye° round about Jove's altar sing.   *continually*
And add to these retired Leisure,
50 That in trim gardens takes his pleasure;
But first, and chiefest, with thee bring
Him that yon soars on golden wing,
Guiding the fiery-wheelèd throne,
The cherub Contemplation;[1]
55 And the mute Silence hist° along,   *summon*
'Less Philomel[2] will deign a song,
In her sweetest, saddest plight,
Smoothing the rugged brow of night,
While Cynthia[3] checks her dragon yoke
60 Gently o'er th' accustomed oak;
Sweet bird that shunn'st the noise of folly,
Most musical, most melancholy!
Thee chantress oft the woods among
I woo to hear thy evensong;[4]
65 And missing thee, I walk unseen
On the dry smooth-shaven green,
To behold the wandering moon,
Riding near her highest noon,
Like one that had been led astray
70 Through the heaven's wide pathless way;
And oft as if her head she bowed,
Stooping through a fleecy cloud.
Oft on a plat° of rising ground,   *plot, open field*
I hear the far-off curfew sound
75 Over some wide-watered shore,
Swinging slow with sullen° roar;   *deep, mournful*

---

8. A delicate black cloth.
9. Still as a statue.
1. The special function of cherubim is contemplation of God; Milton alludes also (line 53) to their identification with the wheels of the mystical chariot/throne of God described by Ezekiel (Ezekiel 10).
2. The nightingale (the bird into which Philomela was transformed after her rape by her brother-in-

law Tereus) traditionally sings a mournful song.
3. Goddess of the moon, also associated with Hecate, goddess of the underworld, who drives a pair of sleepless dragons.
4. The evening liturgy traditionally sung by cloistered monks and nuns ("chantress" evokes such a singer); *L'Allegro*'s cock, by contrast, calls hearers to the morning liturgy, matins (line 114).

Or if the air will not permit,
Some still removèd place will fit,
Where glowing embers through the room
80 Teach light to counterfeit a gloom,
Far from all resort of mirth,
Save the cricket on the hearth,
Or the bellman's;[5] drowsy charm,
To bless the doors from nightly harm;
85 Or let my lamp at midnight hour
Be seen in some high lonely tower,
Where I may oft outwatch the Bear,[6]
With thrice-great Hermes,[7] or unsphere
The spirit of Plato to unfold
90 What words or what vast regions hold
The immortal mind that hath forsook
Her mansion in this fleshly nook;
And of those demons[8] that are found
In fire, air, flood, or under ground,
95 Whose power hath a true consent°   *agreement*
With planet, or with element.
Sometime let gorgeous Tragedy
In sceptered pall[9] come sweeping by,
Presenting Thebes, or Pelops' line,
100 Or the tale of Troy divine,[1]
Or what (though rare) of later age
Ennobled hath the buskined[2] stage.
But, O sad virgin, that thy power
Might raise Musaeus[3] from his bower,
105 Or bid the soul of Orpheus[4] sing
Such notes as, warbled to the string,
Drew iron tears down Pluto's cheek,
And made Hell grant what Love did seek.
Or call up him[5] that left half told
110 The story of Cambuscan bold,
Of Camball and of Algarsife,
And who had Canacee to wife,
That owned the virtuous° ring and glass,   *having magical powers*
And of the wondrous horse of brass,
115 On which the Tartar king did ride;
And if aught else great bards beside
In sage and solemn tunes have sung,

5. Night watchman who rang a bell to mark the hours.
6. The Great Bear constellation never sets in northern skies.
7. Various esoteric books (actually written in the 3rd and 4th centuries) were attributed to an ancient Egyptian, Hermes Trismegistus ("thrice great"). Neoplatonists made him the father of all knowledge; later he became a patron of magicians and alchemists. To "unsphere" Plato is to bring him magically back to earth from whatever sphere he now inhabits—in practical terms, by reading his books.
8. Demons, halfway between gods and men, pre-side over the four elements.
9. Royal robe, worn by tragic actors.
1. Tragedies about Thebes include Sophocles' *Oedipus* cycle, those about the line of Pelops, Aeschylus's *Oresteia*, and those about Troy, Euripedes' *Trojan Women*.
2. The buskin (high boot) of tragedy, constrasted with the sock of comedy (*L'Allegro*, line 132).
3. Mythical poet-priest of the pre-Homeric age, supposedly a son or pupil of Orpheus.
4. For the story of Orpheus, see *L'Allegro*, line 145, and note.
5. Chaucer, whose *Squire's Tale* is unfinished.

Of tourneys and of trophies hung,
Of forests and enchantments drear,
120 Where more is meant than meets the ear.[6]
Thus, Night, oft see me in thy pale career,
Till civil-suited Morn[7] appear,
Not tricked and frounced as she was wont
With the Attic boy to hunt,
125 But kerchiefed in a comely cloud,
While rocking winds are piping loud,
Or ushered with a shower still,°   gentle
When the gust hath blown his fill,
Ending on the rustling leaves,
130 With minute drops from off the eaves.
And when the sun begins to fling
His flaring beams, me, Goddess, bring
To archèd walks of twilight groves,
And shadows brown that Sylvan[8] loves
135 Of pine or monumental oak,
Where the rude ax with heavèd stroke
Was never heard the nymphs to daunt,
Or fright them from their hallowed haunt.
There in close covert° by some brook,   hidden place
140 Where no profaner eye may look,
Hide me from day's garish eye,
While the bee with honeyed thigh,
That at her flowery work doth sing,
And the waters murmuring
145 With such consort° as they keep,   musical harmony
Entice the dewy-feathered sleep;
And let some strange mysterious dream
Wave at his wings in airy stream
Of lively portraiture displayed
150 Softly on my eyelids laid.
And as I wake, sweet music breathe
Above, about, or underneath,
Sent by some spirit to mortals good,
Or th' unseen genius° of the wood.   guardian deity
155 But let my due feet never fail
To walk the studious cloister's pale,°   enclosure
And love the high embowèd roof,
With antic pillars massy proof,[9]
And storied windows richly dight,[1]
160 Casting a dim religious light.
There let the pealing organ blow
To the full-voiced choir below,
In service high and anthems clear,
As may with sweetness, through mine ear,

---

6. A capsule definition of allegory.
7. The now soberly dressed Aurora, goddess of the dawn, once fell in love with Cephalus ("the Attic boy") and hunted with him. "Tricked and frounced": adorned and with frizzled hair.
8. Roman god of woodlands.
9. Massive and strong. "Antic": covered with quaint or grotesque carvings, also antique.
1. Dressed. "Storied windows": stained-glass windows depicting biblical stories.

165   Dissolve me into ecstasies,
      And bring all heaven before mine eyes.
      And may at last my weary age
      Find out the peaceful hermitage,
      The hairy gown and mossy cell,
170   Where I may sit and rightly spell°   *study*
      Of every star that heaven doth shew,
      And every herb that sips the dew,
      Till old experience do attain
      To something like prophetic strain.
175   These pleasures, Melancholy, give,[2]
      And I with thee will choose to live.

ca. 1631   1645

Lycidas   Milton wrote this pastoral elegy for a volume of Latin, Greek, and English poems, *Justa Eduourdo King Naufrago* (1638), commemorating the death by shipwreck of his college classmate Edward King, three years younger than himself. King was not a close friend, but Milton's deepest emotions, anxieties, and fears are engaged here because, as poet and minister, King could serve him as a kind of alter ego. Still engaged in preparing himself, at the age of twenty-nine, for his projected poetic career, Milton was forced to recognize the uncertainty of all human endeavors. King's death posed the problem of mortality in its most agonizing form: the death of the young, the unfulfilled, the good, seems to deny all meaning to life, to demonstrate the uselessness of exceptional talent, lofty ambition, and noble ideals of service to God.

While the poem expresses Milton's anxieties, it also serves as an announcement of his grand ambitions. Like Edmund Spenser, Milton saw mastery of pastoral mode as the first step in a great poetic career. In *Lycidas* that mastery is complete. In the tradition which Milton received from classical and Renaissance predecessors, including Theocritus, Virgil, Petrarch, and Spenser, the pastoral landscape was invested with profound significances that had little indeed to do with the hard life of agricultural labor. The carefree shepherds who engage in singing contests, watch contentedly over their grazing sheep, fall in love, and write poetry offer an image or human life in harmony with nature and the seasonal processes of fruition and mellowing before the winter of death. The classical image of the shepherd as poet is mingled with the Christian understanding of the shepherd as pastor (Christ is the Good Shepherd), and sometimes as the prophet called to his mission from the fields, like David or Isaiah. Milton calls on all these associations, along with other motifs specific to pastoral funeral elegy: the recollection of past friendship, a questioning of destiny for cutting short this life, a procession of mourners (often mythological figures), and a "flower passage" in which nature pays tribute to the dead shepherd.

Lycidas uses but continually tests and challenges the assumptions and conventions of pastoral elegy, making for profound tensions and clashes of tone. The pastoral "oaten flute" is interrupted by divine pronouncements and bitter invective; nature seems rife with examples of meaningless waste and early death; the "blind Fury" often cuts off the poet's "thin-spun life" before he can win fame; good pastors die young while corrupt "Blind Mouths" remain; and Nature cannot even pay her tribute of

---

2. Compare this version of the echo from Marlowe's *Passionate Shepherd* with that with which *L'Allegro* ends.

flowers to Lycidas's funeral bier since he welters in the deep, his bones hurled to the "bottom of the monstrous world." In response to these fierce challenges come pronouncements by Apollo and St. Peter, and images of protection and resurrection in nature and myth, culminating in a new vision of pastoral: in heaven Lycidas enjoys a perfected pastoral existence, and in the coda, the consoled shepherd arises and carries his song to "pastures new." Milton's questioning thus leads to a final reassertion of confidence in his calling as national poet. Moreover, in the headnote added in the 1645 volume of his *Poems*, he lays claim to prophetic authority, for the Anglican clergy he denounced as corrupt in 1638 had mostly been expelled from their livings by Puritan reformers in 1645.

Lycidas

IN THIS MONODY[1] THE AUTHOR BEWAILS A LEARNED FRIEND,
UNFORTUNATELY DROWNED IN HIS PASSAGE FROM CHESTER ON THE
IRISH SEAS, 1637. AND BY OCCASION FORETELLS THE RUIN OF OUR
CORRUPTED CLERGY, THEN IN THEIR HEIGHT.

    Yet once more, O ye laurels, and once more
Ye myrtles brown, with ivy never sere,[2]
I come to pluck your berries harsh and crude,°   *unripe*
And with forced fingers rude,°   *unskilled*
5 Shatter your leaves before the mellowing year.
Bitter constraint, and sad occasion dear,°   *heartfelt, also dire*
Compels me to disturb your season due;
For Lycidas is dead, dead ere his prime,[3]
Young Lycidas, and hath not left his peer.
10 Who would not sing for Lycidas? He knew
Himself to sing, and build the lofty rhyme.[4]
He must not float upon his watery bier
Unwept, and welter° to the parching wind,   *be tossed about*
Without the meed° of some melodious tear.°   *reward / elegy*
15   Begin then, sisters of the sacred well[5]
That from beneath the seat of Jove doth spring,
Begin, and somewhat loudly sweep the string.
Hence with denial vain, and coy excuse;
So may some gentle Muse[6]
20 With lucky words favor my destined urn,
And as he passes turn,
And bid fair peace be to my sable shroud.
For we were nursed upon the selfsame hill,
Fed the same flock, by fountain, shade, and rill.
25   Together both, ere the high lawns° appeared   *upland pastures*
Under the opening eyelids of the morn,

1. A dirge sung by a single voice, though this one incorporates several other voices. This Miltonic headnote was added in the edition of 1645; it identifies Milton as a prophet in the passage denouncing the clergy in this 1638 poem (lines 112–31) and invites the reader to remember Milton's 1641–42 polemics against the English bishops and church government (now dismantled).
2. "Laurels," associated with Apollo and poetry; "myrtle," associated with Venus and love; "ivy,"

associated with Bacchus and frenzy (also learning). All three are evergreens ("never sere") linked to poetic inspiration.
3. King was twenty-five.
4. King had written several poems of compliment in the patronage mode, chiefly on members of the royal family.
5. The nine (sister) Muses called (probably) from the fountain Aganippe, near Mount Helicon.
6. Here, some kindly poet.

We drove afield, and both together heard
What time the grayfly winds her sultry horn,[7]
Battening our flocks with the fresh dews of night,
30 Oft till the star that rose at evening bright
Toward heaven's descent had sloped his westering wheel.[8]
Meanwhile the rural ditties were not mute,
Tempered to th' oaten flute,[9]
Rough satyrs danced, and fauns with cloven heel
35 From the glad sound would not be absent long,
And old Damoetas[1] loved to hear our song.
    But O the heavy change, now thou art gone,
Now thou art gone, and never must return!
Thee, shepherd, thee the woods and desert caves,
40 With wild thyme and the gadding° vine o'ergrown,   *wandering*
And all their echoes mourn.
The willows and the hazel copses green
Shall now no more be seen,
Fanning their joyous leaves to thy soft lays.
45 As killing as the canker° to the rose,   *cankerworm*
Or taint-worm[2] to the weanling herds that graze,
Or frost to flowers that their gay wardrobe wear
When first the white-thorn blows;[3]
Such, Lycidas, thy loss to shepherd's ear.
50   Where were ye, nymphs,[4] when the remorseless deep
Closed o'er the head of your loved Lycidas?
For neither were ye playing on the steep
Where your old bards, the famous Druids,[5] lie,
Nor on the shaggy top of Mona high,
55 Nor yet where Deva spreads her wizard stream:[6]
Ay me! I fondly dream—
Had ye been there—for what could that have done?
What could the Muse[7] herself that Orpheus bore,
The Muse herself, for her enchanting[8] son
60 Whom universal Nature did lament,
When by the rout[9] that made the hideous roar
His gory visage down the stream was sent,
Down the swift Hebrus to the Lesbian shore?
    Alas! What boots° it with incessant care   *profits*
65 To tend the homely slighted shepherd's trade,
And strictly meditate the thankless Muse?[1]

---

7. I.e., heard the grayfly when she buzzes. "Battening" (next line): feeding.
8. Hesperus, the evening star.
9. Panpipes, played traditionally by shepherds in pastoral.
1. A type name from pastoral poetry, possibly referring to some particular tutor at Cambridge. "Satyrs": goat-legged woodland creatures, Pan's boisterous attendants.
2. Internal parasite fatal to newly weaned lambs.
3. Hawthorne in bloom.
4. Nature deities.
5. Priestly poet-kings of Celtic Britain, who worshiped the forces of nature. They are buried on the mountain ("steep") Kerig-y-Druidion in Wales.
6. Deva, the river Dee in Cheshire, was magic

("wizard") because its shifting stream foretold prosperity or dearth for the land. "Mona" is the island of Anglesey. All these places are in the West Country, near where King drowned.
7. Calliope, Muse of epic poetry, was the mother of Orpheus.
8. Implies both song and magic; the root word survives in "incantation."
9. Orpheus's song was drowned out by the screams of a mob ("rout") of Thracian women, the Bacchantes, who then were able to tear him to pieces and throw his gory head into the river Hebrus, which carried it—still singing—to the island of Lesbos, bringing that island the gift of poetry.
1. I.e., study to write poetry (a Virgilian phrase).

Were it not better done as others use,
To sport with Amaryllis in the shade,
Or with the tangles of Neaera's hair?[2]
70 Fame is the spur that the clear spirit doth raise
(That last infirmity of noble mind)
To scorn delights, and live laborious days;
But the fair guerdon° when we hope to find,   reward
And think to burst out into sudden blaze,
75 Comes the blind Fury[3] with th' abhorrèd shears,
And slits the thin-spun life. "But not the praise,"
Phoebus replied, and touched my trembling ears;[4]
"Fame is no plant that grows on mortal soil,
Nor in the glistering foil[5]
80 Set off to th' world, nor in broad rumor lies,
But lives and spreads aloft by those pure eyes,
And perfect witness of all-judging Jove;
As he pronounces lastly on each deed,
Of so much fame in heaven expect thy meed."°   reward
85   O fountain Arethuse, and thou honored flood,
Smooth-sliding Mincius, crowned with vocal reeds,
That strain I heard was of a higher mood.[6]
But now my oat° proceeds,   pastoral flute
And listens to the herald of the sea[7]
90 That came in Neptune's plea.
He asked the waves, and asked the felon° winds,   savage
"What hard mishap hath doomed this gentle swain?"
And questioned every gust of rugged° wings   stormy
That blows from off each beakèd promontory;
95 They knew not of his story,
And sage Hippotades[8] their answer brings,
That not a blast was from his dungeon strayed;
The air was calm, and on the level brine,
Sleek Panope[9] with all her sisters played.
100 It was that fatal and perfidious bark,
Built in th' eclipse,[1] and rigged with curses dark,
That sunk so low that sacred head of thine.
    Next Camus,[2] reverend sire, went footing slow,
His mantle hairy, and his bonnet sedge,°   formed of reeds
105 Inwrought with figures dim, and on the edge
Like to that sanguine flower inscribed with woe.[3]
"Ah! who hath reft," quoth he, "my dearest pledge?"

2. "Amaryllis" and "Neaera" (*Nee-eye-ra*), conventional names for pretty shepherdesses wooed in song by pastoral shepherds.
3. Atropos, one of the three Fates, whose scissors cuts the thread of human life after her sisters spin and measure it. Milton makes her a savage, and blind, Fury.
4. Phoebus Apollo, god of poetic inspiration. In *Eclogue* 6.3–4 he plucked Virgil's ears, warning him against impatient ambition.
5. Flashy, glittering metal foil, set under a gem to enhance its brilliance.
6. Arethusa was a fountain in Sicily associated with Greek pastoral poetry (Theocritus), Mincius

a river in Lombardy associated with Latin pastoral (Virgil); Milton invokes them as a return to the pastoral after the "higher mood" of Apollo's speech.
7. Triton, who comes gathering evidence about the accident for Neptune's court.
8. Aeolus, god of winds.
9. The chief Nereid or sea nymph.
1. Eclipses were taken as evil omens.
2. God of the river Cam, representing Cambridge University.
3. Like the AI AI cry of grief supposedly found on the hyacinth, a "sanguine flower" sprung from the blood of the youth Hyacinthus, beloved of Apollo and accidentally killed by him.

Last came and last did go
The pilot of the Galilean lake;[4]
110   Two massy keys he bore of metals twain
(The golden opes, the iron shuts amain).°   *forever*
He shook his mitered locks, and stern bespake:
"How well could I have spared for° thee, young swain,   *in place of*
Enow° of such as for their bellies' sake   *enough (plural)*
115   Creep and intrude and climb into the fold![5]
Of other care they little reckoning make,
Than how to scramble at the shearers' feast,[6]
And shove away the worthy bidden guest.
Blind mouths![7] that scarce themselves know how to hold
120   A sheep-hook, or have learned aught else the least
That to the faithful herdsman's art belongs!
What recks it them? What need they? They are sped;[8]
And when they list,° their lean° and flashy songs   *choose / meager*
Grate on their scrannel° pipes of wretched straw.   *harsh, thin*
125   The hungry sheep look up, and are not fed,
But swoln with wind, and the rank mist they draw,°   *inhale*
Rot inwardly,[9] and foul contagion spread,
Besides what the grim wolf with privy paw[1]
Daily devours apace, and nothing said.
130   But that two-handed engine at the door[2]
Stands ready to smite once, and smite no more."
      Return, Alpheus,[3] the dread voice is past,
That shrunk thy streams; return, Sicilian muse,
And call the vales, and bid them hither cast
135   Their bells and flowerets of a thousand hues.[4]
Ye valleys low where the mild whispers use,°   *frequent*
Of shades and wanton winds, and gushing brooks,
On whose fresh lap the swart star sparely looks,[5]
Throw hither all your quaint enameled eyes,[6]
140   That on the green turf suck the honeyed showers,
And purple all the ground with vernal flowers.

---

4. St. Peter, originally a fisherman on the sea of Galilee, was Christ's chief apostle; his keys open and shut the gates of heaven. He wears a bishop's miter (line 112): Milton in his antiprelatical tracts allows for a special role for apostles but denies any distinction in office between bishops and ministers in the later church.
5. Cf. John 10.1: "He that entereth not by the door into the sheepfold, but climbeth up some other way, the same is a thief and a robber."
6. Festive suppers for the sheepshearers (hence, the material rewards of their ministry). "Worthy bidden guest": cf. Matthew 22.8, the parable of the marriage feast, "they which were bidden were not worthy."
7. This audacious metaphor collapses them into these reprehensible qualities, blindness, as opposed to the oversight the term *episcopus* (bishop) signifies; gluttony, as opposed to the feeding of flocks proper to pastors. "Sheep-hook" (line 120): the bishop's staff is in the form of a shepherd's crook.
8. Provided for. "What recks it them?": what do they care?

9. Sheep-rot is used as an allegory of church corruption by both Petrarch and Dante.
1. I.e., Roman Catholicism, whose agents operated in secret ("privy"). Conversions in the court of the Roman Catholic queen Henrietta Maria were notorious.
2. A celebrated crux, variously explained as the two houses of Parliament, St. Peter's keys, the two-edged sword of the gospel, a sword wielded by two hands, and by other guesses; what is clear is the denunciation of impending, apocalyptic vengeance. In Matthew 24.33 the Last Judgment is said to be "even at the doors."
3. A river in Arcadia, fabled to pass unmixed through the sea before mixing its waters with the "fountain Arethuse" in Sicily, again reviving the pastoral mode after the fierce denunciation of Peter (see lines 85–87).
4. A catalogue of flowers was a common pastoral topic. "Bells": bell-shaped flowers.
5. The Dog Star, Sirius, associated with the heats of late summer.
6. Flowers curiously patterned and adorned with many colors.

Bring the rathe° primrose that forsaken dies,   early
The tufted crow-toe, and pale jessamine,[7]
The white pink, and the pansy freaked° with jet,   flecked
145   The glowing violet,
The musk-rose, and the well-attired woodbine,
With cowslips wan° that hang the pensive head,   pale
And every flower that sad embroidery wears:
Bid amaranthus[8] all his beauty shed,
150   And daffadillies fill their cups with tears,
To strew the laureate hearse° where Lycid lies.   laurel-decked bier
For so to interpose a little ease,
Let our frail thoughts dally with false surmise.[9]
Ay me! whilst thee the shores and sounding seas
155   Wash far away, where'er thy bones are hurled,
Whether beyond the stormy Hebrides,[1]
Where thou perhaps under the whelming° tide   roaring, overwhelming
Visit'st the bottom of the monstrous world;
Or whether thou, to our moist vows denied,
160   Sleep'st by the fable of Bellerus old,[2]
Where the great vision of the guarded mount
Looks toward Namancos and Bayona's hold;[3]
Look homeward angel now, and melt with ruth:°   pity
And, O ye dolphins,[4] waft the hapless youth.
165   Weep no more, woeful shepherds, weep no more,
For Lycidas your sorrow is not dead,
Sunk though he be beneath the wat'ry floor;
So sinks the day-star° in the ocean bed,   the sun
And yet anon repairs his drooping head,
170   And tricks° his beams, and with new-spangled ore   adorns, trims
Flames in the forehead of the morning sky:
So Lycidas sunk low, but mounted high,
Through the dear might of him[5] that walked the waves,
Where, other groves and other streams along,[6]
175   With nectar pure his oozy° locks he laves,   moist
And hears the unexpressive nuptial song,[7]
In the blest kingdoms meek of joy and love.
There entertain him all the saints above,
In solemn troops and sweet societies
180   That sing, and singing in their glory move,
And wipe the tears forever from his eyes.

---

7. White jasmine. "Tufted crow-toe": hyacinth or buttercup, growing in clusters. "Woodbine" (line 146): honeysuckle.
8. In Greek, "unfading," a legendary flower of immortality, one that never fades.
9. False, because Lycidas's body is not here to receive floral and poetic tributes.
1. Islands off the coast of Scotland, the northern terminus of the Irish Sea.
2. A fabulous giant invented by Milton as the origin of the Latin name for Land's End in Cornwall, *Bellerium*. "Monstrous world" (line 158): filled with monsters, also, immense.
3. St. Michael's Mount in Cornwall, where the archangel was said to have appeared to fishermen

in 495, and from which he is envisioned as looking over the Atlantic toward a region and fortress (Bayona's hold) in northern Spain, thereby guarding Protestant England against the continuing Roman Catholic threat.
4. Dolphins brought the Greek poet Arion safely ashore, for love of his verse, and also performed other sea rescues.
5. Christ, who rescued Peter when he tried and failed to do so (Matthew 14.25–31).
6. See Revelation 22.1–2, on the "pure river of water of life," and the "tree of life, which bare twelve manner of fruits."
7. Inexpressible hymn of joy sung "at the marriage supper of the Lamb" (Revelation 19).

Now, Lycidas, the shepherds weep no more;
Henceforth thou art the genius[8] of the shore,
In thy large recompense, and shalt be good
185   To all that wander in that perilous flood.
    Thus sang the uncouth swain[9] to th' oaks and rills,
While the still morn went out with sandals gray;
He touched the tender stops of various quills,[1]
With eager thought warbling his Doric[2] lay:
190   And now the sun had stretched out all the hills,
And now was dropped into the western bay;
At last he rose, and twitched his mantle blue:[3]
Tomorrow to fresh woods, and pastures new.

November 1637   1638

Areopagitica   In this most literary of his tracts, Milton sets forth a trenchant defense of intellectual liberty that has had a powerful influence on the evolving liberal conception of the freedom of speech, press, and thought. His target is the Press Ordinance of June 14, 1643, Parliament's attempt to crack down on the flood of pamphlets (including Milton's own controversial treatises on divorce) that poured forth both from legal and from underground presses as the Civil War raged. Like Tudor and Stuart censorship laws, Parliament's ordinance demanded that works be registered with the Stationers and licensed by the censors before publication, and that both author and publisher be identified, on pain of fines and imprisonment for both. Milton vigorously protests the prepublication licensing of books, arguing that such measures have only been used by, and are only fit for, degenerate cultures. In the regenerate English nation, now "rousing herself like a strong man after sleep," men and women must be allowed to develop in virtue by participating in the clash and conflict of ideas. Truth will always overcome falsehood in reasoned debate. Thus, in opposition to the Presbyterians then in power, Milton defends widespread religious toleration, though with restrictions on Roman Catholicism, which, like most of his Protestant contemporaries, he viewed as a political threat and a tyranny binding individual conscience to the Pope.

    The title associates the tract with the speech of the Greek orator Isocrates to the Areopagus, the Council of the Wise in Athens. Learned readers would have recognized the irony of this; while Isocrates instructed the council to reform Athens by careful supervision of the private lives of citizens, Milton argues that only liberty and removal of censorship can advance reformation. This association explains the oratorical tone of the tract, which was, in fact, subtitled "A Speech." Milton's style is elevated, eloquent, dense with poetic figures, and ranges in tone from satire and ridicule to urgent pleading and florid praise. His arguments and principles are often couched in striking images and phrases. One example is his passionate testimony to the potency and inestimable value of books: "As good almost kill a man as kill a good book . . ." Most memorable is his ringing credo that echoes down the centuries to protest every new tyranny: "Give me the liberty to know, to utter, and to argue freely according to conscience, above all liberties."

8. Local guardian spirit.
9. Another voice now seems to take over from the previously heard voice of the "uncouth swain" (unknown, unskilled shepherd).
1. The oaten stalks of panpipes.

2. Rustic, the dialect of Theocritus and other famous Greek pastoral poets.
3. The color of hope. "Twitched": pulled up around his shoulders.

From Areopagitica

I deny not, but that it is of greatest concernment in the Church and Commonwealth, to have a vigilant eye how Books demean[1] themselves as well as men; and thereafter to confine, imprison, and do sharpest justice on them as malefactors:[2] For Books are not absolutely dead things, but do contain a potency of life in them to be as active as that soul was whose progeny they are; nay they do preserve as in a vial the purest efficacy and extraction of that living intellect that bred them. I know they are as lively, and as vigorously productive, as those fabulous Dragon's teeth; and being sown up and down, may chance to spring up armed men.[3] And yet on the other hand unless wariness be used, as good almost kill a Man as kill a good Book; who kills a Man kills a reasonable creature, God's Image; but he who destroys a good Book, kills reason it self, kills the Image of God, as it were in the eye. Many a man lives a burden to the Earth; but a good Book is the precious life-blood of a master spirit, embalmed and treasured up on purpose to a life beyond life. 'Tis true, no age can restore a life, whereof perhaps there is no great loss; and revolutions of ages do not oft recover the loss of a rejected truth, for the want of which whole Nations fare the worse. We should be wary therefore what persecution we raise against the living labors of public men, how we spill that seasoned life of man preserved and stored up in Books; since we see a kind of massacre, whereof the execution ends not in the slaying of an elemental life, but strikes at that ethereal and fifth essence,[4] the breath of reason it self, slays an immortality rather then a life. But lest I should be condemned of introducing licence, while I oppose Licensing, I refuse not the pains to be so much Historical, as will serve to show what hath been done by ancient and famous Commonwealths, against this disorder, till the very time that this project of licensing crept out of the *Inquisition*,[5] was catched up by our Prelates, and hath caught some of our Presbyters.[6]* * *

* * *Good and evil we know in the field of this world grow up together almost inseparably; and the knowledge of good is so involved and interwoven with the knowledge of evil, and in so many cunning resemblances hardly to be discerned, that those confused seeds which were imposed on Psyche as an incessant labor to cull out and sort asunder[7] were not more intermixed. It was from out the rind of one apple tasted, that the knowledge of good and evil, as two twins cleaving together, leaped forth into the world. And perhaps this is that doom which Adam fell into of knowing good and evil, that is to say of knowing good by evil.

1. Behave.
2. Milton allows that books may be called to account after publication, if they are proved to contain libels or other manifest crimes (he leaves this quite vague).
3. After Cadmus killed a dragon on his way to founding Thebes, on a god's advice he sowed the dragon's teeth, which sprang up as an army, the belligerent forefathers of Sparta.
4. Quintessence, a pure, mystical substance above the four elements (fire, air, water, earth).
5. The Roman Catholic institution for suppressing heresy, especially strong in Spain.

6. The Presbyterians, powerful in the Parliament, were striving to establish theirs as the national church and suppress others; Milton, who began by supporting them in *The Reason of Church Government* and his other antiprelatical tracts (1641–42), now rejects them, in large part because they seek to supplant one repressive church with another.
7. Angry at her son Cupid's love for Psyche, Venus set the girl many trials, among them to sort out a vast mound of mixed seeds, but the ants took pity on her and did the work.

As therefore the state of man now is, what wisdom can there be to choose, what continence to forbear, without the knowledge of evil? He that can apprehend and consider vice with all her baits and seeming pleasures, and yet abstain, and yet distinguish, and yet prefer that which is truly better, he is the true wayfaring[8] Christian. I cannot praise a fugitive and cloistered virtue, unexercised and unbreathed,[9] that never sallies out and sees her adversary, but slinks out of the race where that immortal garland is to be run for, not without dust and heat. Assuredly we bring not innocence into the world, we bring impurity much rather; that which purifies us is trial, and trial is by what is contrary. That virtue therefore which is but a youngling in the contemplation of evil, and knows not the utmost that vice promises to her followers, and rejects it, is but a blank virtue, not a pure; her whiteness is but an excremental[1] whiteness; which was the reason why our sage and serious poet Spenser (whom I dare be known to think a better teacher than Scotus or Aquinas[2]), describing true temperance under the person of Guyon, brings him in with his palmer through the cave of Mammon and the bower of earthly bliss, that he might see and know, and yet abstain.

Since therefore the knowledge and survey of vice is in this world so necessary to the constituting of human virtue, and the scanning of error to the confirmation of truth, how can we more safely, and with less danger, scout into the regions of sin and falsity than by reading all manner of tractates and hearing all manner of reason? And this is the benefit which may be had of books promiscuously read.

But of the harm that may result hence, three kinds are usually reckoned. First is feared the infection that may spread; but then all human learning and controversy in religious points must remove out of the world, yea, the Bible itself; for that ofttimes relates blasphemy not nicely,[3] it describes the carnal sense of wicked men not unelegantly, it brings in holiest men passionately murmuring against providence through all the arguments of Epicurus;[4] in other great disputes it answers dubiously and darkly to the common reader.[5]

* * *

To sequester out of the world into Atlantic and Utopian politics,[6] which never can be drawn into use, will not mend our condition, but to ordain wisely as in this world of evil, in the midst whereof God hath placed us unavoidably. . . . Impunity and remissness, for certain, are the bane of a

8. The printed text reads "wayfaring," calling up the image of the Christian pilgrim; several presentation copies correct it (by hand) to "warfaring," calling up the image of the Christian warrior. Both suit the passage.
9. Not forced by exertion to breathe hard. "Immortal garland" (next line): the prize for the winner of a race, as figure for the "crown of life" promised to those who endure temptation (James 1.12).
1. Exterior only.
2. Duns Scotus and Thomas Aquinas, major Scholastic theologians. Guyon, the hero of Book II of the *Faerie Queene*, passes through the Cave of Mammon (symbolic of all worldly goods and honors) without his Palmer-guide, but that figure does accompany him through the Bower of

Bliss.
3. Daintily.
4. Greek philosopher (342–270 B.C.E.) who taught that happiness is the greatest good, and that virtue should be practiced because it brings happiness; some of his followers equated happiness with sensual enjoyment. Milton may be thinking of the biblical book of Ecclesiastes.
5. Milton goes on to argue that a fool can find material for folly in the best books, and a wise person cannot remove evil by censoring books without also censoring ballads, fiddlers, clothing, conversation, and all social life.
6. Milton alludes to Thomas More's *Utopia* and Francis Bacon's *New Atlantis*.

commonwealth; but here the great art lies, to discern in what the law is to bid restraint and punishment, and in what things persuasion only is to work. If every action which is good or evil in man at ripe years were to be under pittance[7] and prescription and compulsion, what were virtue but a name, what praise could be then due to well-doing, what gramercy[8] to be sober, just, or continent?

Many there be that complain of divine providence for suffering Adam to transgress; foolish tongues! when God gave him reason, he gave him freedom to choose, for reason is but choosing; he had been else a mere artificial Adam, such an Adam as he is in the motions.[9] We ourselves esteem not of that obedience, or love, or gift, which is of force: God therefore left him free, set before him a provoking object, ever almost in his eyes; herein consisted his merit, herein the right of his reward, the praise of his abstinence.[1] Wherefore did he create passions within us, pleasures round about us, but that these rightly tempered are the very ingredients of virtue? They are not skillful considerers of human things, who imagine to remove sin by removing the matter of sin; for, besides that it is a huge heap increasing under the very act of diminishing, though some part of it may for a time be withdrawn from some persons, it cannot from all, in such a universal thing as books are; and when this is done, yet the sin remains entire. Though ye take from a covetous man all his treasure, he has yet one jewel left: ye cannot bereave him of his covetousness. Banish all objects of lust, shut up all youth into the severest discipline that can be exercised in any hermitage, ye cannot make them chaste that came not thither so: such great care and wisdom is required to the right managing of this point.

Suppose we could expel sin by this means; look how much we thus expel of sin, so much we expel of virtue: for the matter of them both is the same; remove that, and ye remove them both alike. This justifies the high providence of God, who, though he commands us temperance, justice, continence, yet pours out before us, even to a profuseness, all desirable things, and gives us minds that can wander beyond all limit and satiety. Why should we then affect a rigor contrary to the manner of God and of nature, by abridging or scanting those means, which books freely permitted are, both to the trial of virtue and the exercise of truth? It would be better done to learn that the law must needs be frivolous which goes to restrain things uncertainly and yet equally working to good and to evil. And were I the chooser, a dram of well-doing should be preferred before many times as much the forcible hindrance of evil-doing. For God sure esteems the growth and completing of one virtuous person more than the restraint of ten vicious.

*   *   *

What advantage is it to be a man over it is to be a boy at school, if we have only scaped the ferula[2] to come under the fescue of an Imprimatur; if serious and elaborate writings, as if they were no more than the theme of a grammar-

---

7. Rationing.
8. Reward, thanks.
9. Puppet shows.
1. Compare Milton's representation of Adam and Eve in Eden in *Paradise Lost*.

2. "Ferula": a schoolmaster's rod; "fescue": a pointer. Milton's keen sense of the affront to scholars and scholarship, and to himself, is evident in this passage.

lad under his pedagogue, must not be uttered without the cursory eyes of a temporizing and extemporizing licenser?[3] He who is not trusted with his own actions, his drift not being known to be evil, and standing to the hazard of law and penalty, has no great argument to think himself reputed, in the commonwealth wherein he was born, for other than a fool or a foreigner.

When a man writes to the world, he summons up all his reason and deliberation to assist him; he searches, meditates, is industrious, and likely consults and confers with his judicious friends, after all which done he takes himself to be informed in what he writes, as well as any that writ before him. If in this the most consummate act of his fidelity and ripeness, no years, no industry, no former proof of his abilities can bring him to that state of maturity as not to be still mistrusted and suspected (unless he carry all his considerate diligence, all his midnight watchings, and expense of Palladian[4] oil, to the hasty view of an unleisured licenser, perhaps much his younger, perhaps far his inferior in judgment, perhaps one who never knew the labor of bookwriting), and if he be not repulsed, or slighted, must appear in print like a puny[5] with his guardian, and his censor's hand on the back of his title to be his bail and surety that he is no idiot, or seducer; it cannot be but a dishonor and derogation to the author, to the book, to the privilege and dignity of learning. * * *

And how can a man teach with authority, which is the life of teaching, how can he be a doctor in his book as he ought to be, or else had better be silent, whenas all he teaches, all he delivers, is but under the tuition, under the correction of his patriarchal[6] licenser to blot or alter what precisely accords not with the hide-bound humor which he calls his judgment? When every acute reader upon the first sight of a pedantic license, will be ready with these like words to ding the book a quoit's[7] distance from him: "I hate a pupil teacher, I endure not an instructor that comes to me under the wardship of an overseeing fist. I know nothing of the licenser, but that I have his own hand here for his arrogance; who shall warrant me his judgment?"

"The State, sir," replies the stationer, but has a quick return: "The State shall be my governors, but not my critics; they may be mistaken in the choice of a licenser, as easily as this licenser may be mistaken in an author."

* * *

Well knows he who uses to consider, that our faith and knowledge thrives by exercise, as well as our limbs and complexion.[8] Truth is compared in Scripture to a streaming fountain;[9] if her waters flow not in a perpetual progression, they sicken into a muddy pool of conformity and tradition. A man may be a heretic in the truth; and if he believe things only because his pastor says so, or the Assembly[1] so determines, without knowing other reason, though his belief be true, yet the very truth he holds becomes his heresy.

* * *

3. He temporizes in following the times, and acts by whim (extemporizes).
4. Pertaining to Pallas Athena, goddess of wisdom.
5. A minor, hence, young, unseasoned.
6. Taking on the role of a father; also, standing in for ecclesiastical patriarchs or prelates (like Archbishop Laud).
7. A flat disc of stone or metal, thrown as an exercise of strength or skill.
8. Constitution, the proper mingling of qualities in the body.
9. In Psalm 85.11.
1. The Westminster Assembly, convened by Parliament in 1643 to reorganize the English church along Presbyterian lines.

Truth indeed came once into the world with her Divine Master, and was a perfect shape most glorious to look on: but when he ascended, and his apostles after him were laid asleep, then straight arose a wicked race of deceivers, who, as that story goes of the Egyptian Typhon with his conspirators, how they dealt with the good Osiris,[2] took the virgin Truth, hewed her lovely form into a thousand pieces, and scattered them to the four winds. From that time ever since, the sad friends of Truth, such as durst appear, imitating the careful search that Isis made for the mangled body of Osiris, went up and down gathering up limb by limb, still as they could find them. We have not yet found them all, Lords and Commons, nor ever shall do, till her Master's second coming; he shall bring together every joint and member, and shall mold them into an immortal feature of loveliness and perfection. Suffer not these licensing prohibitions to stand at every place of opportunity, forbidding and disturbing them that continue seeking, that continue to do our obsequies[3] to the torn body of our martyred saint.

We boast our light; but if we look not wisely on the sun itself, it smites us into darkness. Who can discern those planets that are oft combust,[4] and those stars of brightest magnitude that rise and set with the sun, until the opposite motion of their orbs bring them to such a place in the firmament where they may be seen evening or morning? The light which we have gained was given us, not to be ever staring on, but by it to discover onward things more remote from our knowledge. It is not the unfrocking of a priest, the unmitering of a bishop, and the removing him from off the Presbyterian shoulders, that will make us a happy nation. No, if other things as great in the church, and in the rule of life both economical and political, be not looked into and reformed, we have looked so long upon the blaze that Zwinglius and Calvin[5] hath beaconed up to us, that we are stark blind.

There be who perpetually complain of schisms and sects, and make it such a calamity that any man dissents from their maxims. 'Tis their own pride and ignorance which causes the disturbing, who neither will hear with meekness, nor can convince; yet all must be suppressed which is not found in their syntagma.[6] They are the troublers, they are the dividers of unity, who neglect and permit not others to unite those dissevered pieces which are yet wanting to the body of Truth. To be still searching what we know not by what we know, still closing up truth to truth as we find it (for all her body is homogeneal and proportional), this is the golden rule in theology as well as in arithmetic, and makes up the best harmony in a church; not the forced and outward union of cold and neutral and inwardly divided minds.

Lords and Commons of England, consider what nation it is whereof ye are, and whereof ye are the governors: a nation not slow and dull, but of a quick, ingenious, and piercing spirit, acute to invent, subtle and sinewy to discourse, not beneath the reach of any point the highest that human capacity can soar to. Therefore the studies of learning in her deepest sciences have been so ancient and so eminent among us, that writers of good antiquity and

---

2. Plutarch tells, in *Isis and Osiris*, of Typhon's scattering the fragments of his brother Osiris and of Isis's efforts to recover them.
3. Funeral or commemorative rites.
4. Burned up; in astrology, so close to the sun as

not to be visible.
5. Zwingli and Calvin, famous Protestant reformers, were mainstays of the Presbyterian cause. "Economical": domestic.
6. Compilations of beliefs, creeds.

ablest judgment have been persuaded that even the school of Pythagoras and the Persian wisdom took beginning from the old philosophy of this island.[7] And that wise and civil Roman, Julius Agricola, who governed once here for Caesar, preferred the natural wits of Britain before the labored studies of the French. Nor is it for nothing that the grave and frugal Transylvanian sends out yearly from as far as the mountainous borders of Russia, and beyond the Hercynian wilderness, not their youth, but their staid men, to learn our language and our theologic arts.[8]

Yet that which is above all this, the favor and the love of heaven we have great argument to think in a peculiar manner propitious and propending[9] towards us. Why else was this nation chosen before any other, that out of her, as out of Zion,[1] should be proclaimed and sounded forth the first tidings and trumpet of Reformation to all Europe? And had it not been the obstinate perverseness of our prelates against the divine and admirable spirit of Wycliffe to suppress him as a schismatic and innovator, perhaps neither the Bohemian Huss and Jerome,[2] no, nor the name of Luther or of Calvin, had been ever known: the glory of reforming all our neighbors had been completely ours. But now, as our obdurate clergy have with violence demeaned the matter, we are become hitherto the latest and the backwardest scholars of whom[3] God offered to have made us the teachers.

Now once again by all concurrence of signs, and by the general instinct of holy and devout men, as they daily and solemnly express their thoughts, God is decreeing to begin some new and great period in his church, even to the reforming of Reformation itself; what does he then but reveal himself to his servants, and as his manner is, first to his Englishmen? I say, as his manner is, first to us, though we mark not the method of his counsels, and are unworthy. Behold now this vast city: a city of refuge,[4] the mansion house of liberty, encompassed and surrounded with his protection; the shop of war hath not there more anvils and hammers waking, to fashion out the plates[5] and instruments of armed justice in defense of beleaguered truth, than there be pens and heads there, sitting by their studious lamps, musing, searching, revolving new notions and ideas wherewith to present, as with their homage and their fealty, the approaching Reformation: others as fast reading, trying all things, assenting to the force of reason and convincement.

What could a man require more from a nation so pliant and so prone to seek after knowledge? What wants there to such a towardly[6] and pregnant soil, but wise and faithful laborers, to make a knowing people, a nation of prophets,[7] of sages, and of worthies? We reckon more than five months yet

---

7. Some speculation existed as to whether the Pythagorean notion of the transmigration of souls might trace back to the Druids, but the notion was mostly denied.
8. The "civil" (cultured, civilized) Agricola's opinion of the British intellect (referred to next) is found in Tacitus's *Life of Agricola*. Transylvania (now Romania) was an independent Protestant country whose citizens sometimes came to England to study. "Hercynian wilderness": Roman name for a forested and mountainous region of Germany.
9. Inclining, favorable. "Argument": reason.
1. Mount Zion, in Jerusalem, the site of the Temple.

2. John Wycliffe was a 14th-century English reformer and translator of the Bible, whose books were forbidden by Pope Alexander V in 1409. John Huss spread Wycliffe's doctrines on the Continent; he was burned at the stake in 1415, as was (the next year) his follower Jerome of Prague.
3. Of those whom. "Demeaned": conducted, degraded.
4. Numbers 35 instructs the Jews to establish "cities of refuge" where those accused of crimes are protected from "revengers of blood."
5. Plate mail, for armor.
6. Favorable.
7. In Numbers 11.29 Moses reproaches Joshua, who complained of the presence of other prophets:

to harvest; there need not be five weeks; had we but eyes to lift up, the fields are white already.[8] Where there is much desire to learn, there of necessity will be much arguing, much writing, many opinions; for opinion in good men is but knowledge in the making. Under these fantastic terrors of sect and schism we wrong the earnest and zealous thirst after knowledge and understanding which God hath stirred up in this city.

What some lament of, we rather should rejoice at, should rather praise this pious forwardness among men, to reassume the ill-deputed care of their religion into their own hands again. A little generous prudence, a little forbearance of one another, and some grain of charity might win all these diligences to join, and unite into one general and brotherly search after truth; could we but forego this prelatical tradition of crowding free consciences and Christian liberties into canons and precepts of men. I doubt not, if some great and worthy stranger should come among us, wise to discern the mold and temper of a people, and how to govern it, observing the high hopes and aims, the diligent alacrity of our extended thoughts and reasonings in the pursuance of truth and freedom, but that he would cry out as Pyrrhus did, admiring the Roman docility and courage: "If such were my Epirots, I would not despair the greatest design that could be attempted, to make a church or kingdom happy."[9] Yet these are the men cried out against for schismatics and sectaries;[1] as if, while the temple of the Lord was building, some cutting, some squaring the marble, others hewing the cedars, there should be a sort of irrational men, who could not consider there must be many schisms and many dissections[2] made in the quarry and in the timber, ere the house of God can be built. And when every stone is laid artfully together, it cannot be united into a continuity, it can but be contiguous in this world; neither can every piece of the building be of one form; nay rather the perfection consists in this, that out of many moderate varieties and brotherly dissimilitudes that are not vastly disproportional, arises the goodly and the graceful symmetry that commends the whole pile and structure. Let us therefore be more considerate builders, more wise in spiritual architecture, when great reformation is expected. For now the time seems come, wherein Moses the great prophet may sit in heaven rejoicing to see that memorable and glorious wish of his fulfilled, when not only our seventy elders, but all the Lord's people, are become prophets.[3]

* * *

Methinks I see in my mind a noble and puissant nation rousing herself like a strong man after sleep, and shaking her invincible locks:[4] methinks I see her as an eagle mewing[5] her mighty youth, and kindling her undazzled

---

"Enviest thou for my sake? Would God that all the Lord's people were prophets."

8. Milton is paraphrasing Christ's words to his disciples (John 4.35): "Lift up your eyes, and look on the fields: for they are white already to harvest."

9. Though King Pyrrhus of Epirus beat the Roman armies at Heraclea in 280 B.C.E., he was much impressed by their discipline.

1. "Schismatics": those who cut up or divide the church; "sectaries": members of Protestant communions outside the national church.

2. Milton is playing on the literal meaning of

"schism," cutting up or dividing.

3. Again alluding to Numbers 11.29, Milton equates the English assembly of clergy to set doctrine and church order (the Westminster Assembly) with the Jewish Sanhedrin of seventy elders.

4. The allusion is to Samson, whose uncut hair made him invincible, when he frustrated the first three attempts of Delilah and the Philistines to subdue him in sleep (Judges 16.6–14).

5. Molting, when the eagle sheds it feathers and thereby renews its coat; eagles were thought to be able to look directly at the sun.

eyes at the full midday beam; purging and unscaling her long-abused sight at the fountain itself of heavenly radiance; while the whole noise of timorous and flocking birds, with those also that love the twilight, flutter about, amazed at what she means, and in their envious gabble would prognosticate[6] a year of sects and schisms.

What should ye do then, should ye suppress all this flowery crop of knowledge and new light sprung up and yet springing daily in this city? Should ye set an oligarchy of twenty engrossers[7] over it, to bring a famine upon our minds again, when we shall know nothing but what is measured to us by their bushel? Believe it, Lords and Commons, they who counsel ye to such a suppressing do as good as bid ye suppress yourselves; and I will soon show how.[8]

* * *

And now the time in special is by privilege to write and speak what may help to the further discussing of matters in agitation. The temple of Janus with his two controversial faces might now not unsignificantly be set open.[9] And though all the winds of doctrine were let loose to play upon the earth, so Truth be in the field, we do injuriously by licensing and prohibiting to misdoubt her strength. Let her and Falsehood grapple; who ever knew Truth put to the worse in a free and open encounter? Her[1] confuting is the best and surest suppressing. He who hears what praying there is for light and clearer knowledge to be sent down among us would think of other matters to be constituted beyond the discipline of Geneva framed and fabricked already to our hands.[2]

Yet when the new light which we beg for shines in upon us, there be who envy and oppose if it come not first in at their casements. What a collusion is this, whenas we are exhorted by the wise man to use diligence, to seek for wisdom as for hidden treasures early and late,[3] that another order shall enjoin us to know nothing but by statute. When a man hath been laboring the hardest labor in the deep mines of knowledge, hath furnished out his findings in all their equipage, drawn forth his reasons as it were a battle[4] ranged, scattered and defeated all objections in his way, calls out his adversary into the plain, offers him the advantage of wind and sun if he please, only that he may try the matter by dint of argument; for his opponents then to skulk, to lay ambushments, to keep a narrow bridge of licensing where the challenger should pass, though it be valor enough in soldiership, is but weakness and cowardice in the wars of Truth.

For who knows not that Truth is strong, next to the Almighty? She needs no policies nor stratagems nor licensings to make her victorious—those are

---

6. Predict.
7. Engrossers, much hated in the English countryside, bought up great quantities of grain and held it for times of famine, selling it at high prices; Milton equates them with the twenty authorized printers, the stationers.
8. Milton argues that Parliament, by its own liberalizing reforms to date, has created the vigorous and inquiring minds it now seeks to suppress.
9. Janus, as god of beginnings and endings, had two faces looking in opposite directions; a door

dedicated to him in Rome was kept open in time of war, closed in time of peace.
1. I.e., Falsehood's.
2. Milton was already disenchanted with Genevan "Discipline" (Presbyterian church government) and within a year or so would be writing, "New Presbyter is but Old Priest, writ large." "Fabricked": fabricated.
3. Solomon's advice in Proverbs 8.11.
4. Line of battle. Wind and sun (below) were significant advantages in a fight with swords.

the shifts and the defenses that error uses against her power. Give her but room, and do not bind her when she sleeps, for then she speaks not true, as the old Proteus[5] did, who spake oracles only when he was caught and bound, but then rather she turns herself into all shapes except her own, and perhaps tunes her voice according to the time, as Micaiah did before Ahab,[6] until she be adjured into her own likeness.

Yet it is not impossible that she may have more shapes than one. What else is all that rank of things indifferent, wherein Truth may be on this side or on the other without being unlike herself? What but a vain shadow else is the abolition of those ordinances, that handwriting nailed to the cross?[7] what great purchase is this Christian liberty which Paul so often boasts of? His doctrine is that he who eats or eats not, regards a day or regards it not, may do either to the Lord.[8] How many other things might be tolerated in peace and left to conscience, had we but charity, and were it not the chief stronghold of our hypocrisy to be ever judging one another? I fear yet this iron yoke of outward conformity hath left a slavish print upon our necks; the ghost of a linen decency[9] yet haunts us. We stumble and are impatient at the least dividing of one visible congregation from another, though it be not in fundamentals; and through our forwardness to suppress and our backwardness to recover any enthralled piece of truth out of the grip of custom, we care not[1] to keep truth separated from truth, which is the fiercest rent and disunion of all. We do not see that while we still affect by all means a rigid and external formality, we may as soon fall again into a gross conforming stupidity, a stark and dead congealment of "wood and hay and stubble," forced and frozen together, which is more to the sudden degenerating of a church than many sub-dichotomies of petty schisms.

Not that I can think well of every light separation, or that all in a church is to be expected "gold and silver and precious stones."[2] It is not possible for man to sever the wheat from the tares, the good fish from the other fry; that must be the angels' ministry at the end of mortal things.[3] Yet if all cannot be of one mind—as who looks they should be?— this doubtless is more wholesome, more prudent, and more Christian, that many be tolerated rather than all compelled. I mean not tolerated popery and open superstition, which, as it extirpates all religions and civil supremacies, so itself should be extirpate, provided first that all charitable and compassionate means be used to win and regain the weak and the misled; that also which is impious or evil absolutely, either against faith or manners,[4] no law can possibly permit that intends not to unlaw itself; but those neighboring differences or rather indifferences are what I speak of, whether in some point of doctrine or of discipline, which though they

---

5. The sea god who could change shape at will, to avoid capture (*Odyssey* 4).
6. Micaiah, a prophet of God, tried for a time to disguise an unpleasant prophecy from King Ahab but then spoke truth when adjured to do so (1 Kings 22.10–28).
7. The locution, from Colossians 2.14, implies that the crucifixion canceled all the rules and penalties of the Mosaic law. Paul's doctrine of Christian liberty is expressed in Galatians 5 and elsewhere.
8. In the Lord's service.

9. The scraps of white linen around the necks and wrists of gentlemen (and white bands around the necks of clergymen) are made emblems of formal piety.
1. Scruple not.
2. The contrast between "wood, hay, stubble" and "gold, silver, precious stones" is from 1 Corinthians 3.12.
3. In Matthew 13.24–30, 36–43, Christ in a parable tells his disciples to let the wheat and tares (weeds) grow up together till harvest time.
4. Morals.

may be many yet need not interrupt "the unity of spirit," if we could but find among us the "bond of peace."[5]

In the meanwhile, if anyone would write and bring his helpful hand to the slow-moving reformation which we labor under, if truth have spoken to him before others, or but seemed at least to speak, who hath so beje-suited[6] us that we should trouble that man with asking license to do so worthy a deed? And not consider this, that if it come to prohibiting, there is not aught more likely to be prohibited than truth itself; whose first appearance to our eyes bleared and dimmed with prejudice and custom is more unsightly and unplausible than many errors, even as the person is of many a great man slight and contemptible to see to. And what do they tell us vainly of new opinions, when this very opinion of theirs, that none must be heard but whom they like, is the worst and newest opinion of all others, and is the chief cause why sects and schisms do so much abound, and true knowledge is kept at distance from us; besides yet a greater danger which is in it. For when God shakes a kingdom[7] with strong and healthful commotions to a general reforming, it is not untrue that many sectaries and false teachers are then busiest in seducing; but yet more true it is that God then raises to his own work men of rare abilities and more than common industry, not only to look back and revise what hath been taught heretofore, but to gain further and go on some new enlightened steps in the discovery of truth.

✳ ✳ ✳

1644

Sonnets

Between 1630 and 1658 Milton wrote twenty-four sonnets. Five in Italian constitute a mini-Petrarchan sequence on a perhaps imaginary Italian lady. The rest, in English, are individual poems on a wide variety of topics and occasions though not on the usual sonnet topics (love, as in the sequences of Sidney, Spenser, and Shakespeare, or religious devotion, as in that of Donne). Milton writes sometimes about personal crises (his blindness, the death of his wife), sometimes about political issues or personages (Cromwell, the persecuting Parliament), sometimes about friends and friendship (Cyriack Skinner, Lady Margaret Ley), sometimes about historical events (a threatened royalist attack on London, the massacre of Protestants in Piedmont); and his tone ranges from Jonsonian urbanity to prophetic denunciation. The form of the sonnets is Petrarchan (see "Poetic Forms and Literary Terminology," in the appendices to this volume), but in the later sonnets especially (e.g., the Blindness and Piedmont sonnets) the sense runs on from line to line, overriding the expected end-stopped lines and the octave/sestet shift. There is some precedent for this in the Italian sonneteer Giovanni Della Casa, but not for the powerful tension Milton creates as meaning and emotion strive within and against the metrical form of the Petrarchan sonnet. Milton's new ways with the sonnet had a profound and acknowledged influence on the Romantic poets, especially Wordsworth and Shelley.

---

5. The quoted phrases are from Ephesians 4.3.
6. Imposed on us Jesuit ideas (of censorship).
7. Milton alludes to Haggai 2.7: "I will shake all nations, and the desire of all nations shall come, and I will fill this house with glory, saith the Lord of hosts."

Sonnets

How Soon Hath Time

How soon hath Time, the subtle thief of youth,
Stol'n on his wing my three and twentieth year!
My hasting days fly on with full career,
But my late spring no bud or blossom shew'th.
5   Perhaps my semblance might deceive[1] the truth,
That I to manhood am arrived so near,
And inward ripeness doth much less appear,
That some more timely-happy spirits endu'th.°   *endows*
Yet be it less or more, or soon or slow,
10   It shall be still in strictest measure even[2]
To that same lot, however mean or high,
Toward which Time leads me, and the will of Heaven;
All is, if I have grace to use it so,
As ever in my great Taskmaster's eye.[3]

1632?   1645

When I Consider How My Light Is Spent[1]

When I consider how my light is spent,°   *extinguished*
Ere half my days,[2] in this dark world and wide,
And that one talent which is death to hide[3]
Lodged with me useless, though my soul more bent
5   To serve therewith my Maker, and present
My true account, lest he returning chide;
"Doth God exact day-labor, light denied?"[4]
I fondly° ask; but Patience to prevent°   *foolishly / forestall*
That murmur, soon replies, "God doth not need
10   Either man's work or his own gifts; who best
Bear his mild yoke, they serve him best. His state°   *splendor*
Is kingly.[5] Thousands at his bidding speed
And post o'er land and ocean without rest:
They also serve who only stand and wait."

1652?   1673

1. Misrepresent. "Semblance": appearance.
2. Equal, adequate. "It": Milton's inner growth. "Even / To that same lot": conformed to the appointed destiny.
3. The final lines allow for various readings. "Taskmaster" identifies God with the parable (Matthew 20.1–16) in which a vineyard keeper takes on workers throughout the day, paying the same wages to those hired at the first and at the eleventh hour.
1. Apparently written soon after Milton lost his sight entirely in 1652.
2. Milton was forty-three in 1652; he is obviously not thinking of the biblical lifespan of seventy, but perhaps of that of his father, who died at eighty-four.
3. In the parable of the talents (Matthew 25.14–

30), a crucial text for Puritans, the servants who put their master's money ("talents") to earn interest for him were praised while the servant who buried the single talent he was given was deprived of it and cast into outer darkness. Milton puns on "literary talent." "Useless" (line 4) carries a pun on usury, the return expected by the Master.
4. Milton also alludes here to the parable of the vineyard keeper (see *How Soon Hath Time*, n. 3). Also to John 9.4, spoken by Jesus before curing a blind man: "I must work the works of him that sent me, while it is day: the night cometh, when no man can work."
5. The changed metaphor for God—from master who needs to profit from his workers to King—allows the inference that those who "stand and wait" may be placed nearest the throne.

On the Late Massacre in Piedmont[1]

Avenge,[2] O Lord, thy slaughtered saints, whose bones
Lie scattered on the Alpine mountains cold;
Even them who kept thy truth so pure of old
When all our fathers worshiped stocks and stones,[3]
5 Forget not: in thy book[4] record their groans
Who were thy sheep and in their ancient fold
Slain by the bloody Piemontese that rolled
Mother with infant down the rocks. Their moans
The vales redoubled to the hills, and they
10 To heaven. Their martyred blood and ashes sow
O'er all th' Italian fields, where still doth sway
The triple tyrant:[5] that from these may grow
A hundredfold, who having learnt thy way
Early may fly the Babylonian woe.[6]

1655   1673

Methought I Saw My Late Espousèd Saint[1]

Methought I saw my late espousèd saint
Brought to me like Alcestis[2] from the grave,
Whom Jove's great son to her glad husband gave,
Rescued from death by force though pale and faint.
5 Mine, as whom[3] washed from spot of childbed taint,
Purification in the old law did save,[4]
And such, as yet once more I trust to have
Full sight of her in heaven without restraint,
Came vested all in white, pure as her mind.
10 Her face was veiled, yet to my fancied sight[5]

1. The Waldensians (or Vaudois) were a proto-Protestant sect dating to the 12th century, who lived in the valleys of northern Italy (the Piedmont) and southern France; Protestants considered them a remnant retaining Apostolic purity, free of Catholic superstitions and graven images ("stocks and stones"). The treaty that had allowed them freedom of worship was bypassed in 1655 when the armies of the Catholic duke of Savoy conducted a massacre, razing villages, committing unspeakable atrocities, and hurling women and children from the mountaintops. Protestant Europe was outraged, and in his capacity as Cromwell's Latin secretary Milton translated and wrote several letters about the episode. The sonnet incorporates details from such letters and the contemporary newsbooks. Here Milton transforms the sonnet into a prophetic denunciation.
2. Cf. Revelation 6.9–10: "The souls of them that were slain for the word of God . . . cried with a loud voice, saying 'How long, O Lord, holy and true, dost thou not judge and avenge our blood?' "
3. Pagan gods of wood and stone, but with allusion to Roman Catholic "idols."
4. Cf. Revelation 20.12: "The dead were judged out of those things which were written in the books, according to their works." "Sheep": echoes Romans 8.36: "We are accounted as sheep for the slaughter."

5. The pope, wearing his tiara with three crowns. The passage alludes to Tertullian's maxim that "the blood of the martyrs is the seed of the church"; also to the parable of the sower (Matthew 13.3), some of whose seed brought forth fruit "an hundredfold"; and also to Cadmus, who sowed dragon's teeth that sprang forth armed men.
6. Protestants often identified the Roman Church with the whore of Babylon (Revelation 17–18).
1. There is some critical debate as to whether this poem refers to Milton's first wife, Mary Powell, who died in May 1652 three days after giving birth to her third daughter, or his second wife, Katherine Woodcock, who died in February 1658, after giving birth (in October 1657) to a daughter. The text can support either, but the latter seems more likely. The sonnet is couched as a dream vision.
2. In Euripedes' Alcestis, Alcestis, wife of Admetus, is rescued from the underworld by Hercules ("Jove's great son") and restored, veiled, to Admetus; he is overjoyed when he lifts the veil, but she must remain silent until she is ritually cleansed.
3. As one whom.
4. The Mosaic Law (Leviticus 12.4–8) prescribed periods for the purification of women after childbirth (eighty days for a daughter).
5. She is veiled like Alcestes and Milton's sight of her is only "fancied"; he never saw the face of his second wife, Katherine.

Love, sweetness, goodness, in her person shined
So clear, as in no face with more delight.
But O, as to embrace me she inclined,
I waked, she fled, and day brought back my night.

1658   1673

Paradise Lost

Paradise Lost   The setting of Milton's great epic encompasses Heaven, Hell, primordial Chaos, and the planet Earth. It features battles among immortal spirits, voyages through space, and lakes of fire. Yet its protagonists are a married couple living in a garden, and its climax consists in the eating of a piece of fruit. *Paradise Lost* is ultimately about the human condition, the Fall that caused "all our woe," and the promise and means of restoration. It is also about knowing and choosing, about free will. In the opening passages of Books 1, 3, 7, and 9, Milton highlights the choices and difficulties he faced in creating his poem. His central characters—Satan, Beelzebub, Abdiel, Adam, and Eve—are confronted with hard choices under the pressure of powerful desires and sometimes devious temptations. Milton's readers, too, are continually challenged to choose and to reconsider their most basic assumptions about freedom, heroism, work, pleasure, language, nature, and love. The great themes of *Paradise Lost* are intimately linked to the political questions at stake in the English Revolution and Restoration, but the connection is by no means simple or straightforward. This is a poem in which Satan leads a revolution against an absolute monarch and in which questions of tyranny, servitude, and liberty are debated in a Parliament in Hell. Milton's readers are hereby challenged to rethink these topics and, like Abdiel debating with Satan in Books 5 and 6, to make crucial distinctions.

In Milton's time, the conventions of epic poetry comprised a familiar recipe. The action should begin *in medias res* (in the middle of things), following the poet's statement of his theme and invocation of his Muse. The reader could expect grand battles and love affairs, supernatural intervention, a descent into the underworld, catalogs of warriors, and epic similes. Milton had absorbed the epic tradition in its entirety, and his poem abounds with echoes of Homer and Virgil, the fifteenth-century Italians Tasso and Ariosto, and the English Spenser. But in *Paradise Lost* he at once heightens epic conventions and utterly transforms them. This is the epic to end all epics. Milton gives us the first and greatest of all wars (between God and Satan) and the first and greatest of love affairs (between Adam and Eve). His theme is the destiny of the entire human race, caught up in the temptation and Fall of our first "grand parents."

Milton challenges his readers in *Paradise Lost*, at once fulfilling and defying all of our expectations. Nothing in the epic tradition or in biblical interpretation can prepare us for the Satan who hurtles into view in Book 1, with his awesome energy and defiance, incredible fortitude, and, above all, magnificent rhetoric. For some readers, including Blake and Shelley, Satan has been the true hero of the poem. But Milton is engaged in a radical re-evaluation of epic values, and Satan's version of heroism must be contrasted with those of the loyal Abdiel and the Son of God. Moreover, the poem's truly epic action takes place not on the battlefield but in the moral and domestic arena. Milton's Adam and Eve are not conventional epic heroes, but neither are they the conventional Adam and Eve. Their state of innocence is not childlike, tranquil, and free of sexual desire. Instead, the first couple enjoy sex, experience tension and passion, make mistakes of judgment, and grow in knowledge. Their task is to prune what is unruly in their own natures as they prune the vegetation in their garden, for both have the capacity to grow wild. Their relationship exhibits gender hierarchy, but Milton's early readers may have been surprised by the fullness and complexity of Eve's character and the centrality of her role, not only in the Fall but in the promised restoration.

We expect in epics a grand style, and Milton's style engulfs us from the outset with its energy and power, as those rushing, enjambed, blank-verse lines propel us along with only a few pauses for line endings or grammar (there is only one full-stop in the first twenty-six lines). The elevated diction and complex syntax, the sonorities and patternings, make a magnificent music. But that music is an entire orchestra of tones, including the high political rhetoric of Satan in Books 1 and 2, the evocative sensuousness of the descriptions of Eden, the delicacy of Eve's love lyric to Adam in Book 4, the relatively plain speech of God in Book 3, and the speech rhythms of Adam and Eve's marital quarrel in Book 9. This majestic achievement depends on the poet's rejection of heroic couplets, the norm for epic and tragedy in the Restoration, vigorously defended by Dryden, but denounced by Milton in his note on "The Verse." The choice of verse form was, like so many other things in Milton's life, in part a question of politics. Milton's terms associate the "troublesome and modern bondage of rhyming" with Restoration monarchy and repression of dissidents and present his use of unrhymed blank verse as a recovery of "ancient liberty."

FROM PARADISE LOST

SECOND EDITION (1674)[1]

The Verse

The measure is English heroic verse without rhyme, as that of Homer in Greek and of Virgil in Latin; rhyme being no necessary adjunct or true ornament of poem or good verse, in longer works especially, but the invention of a barbarous age, to set off wretched matter[2] and lame meter; graced indeed since by the use of some famous modern poets,[3] carried away by custom, but much to their own vexation, hindrance, and constraint to express many things otherwise, and for the most part worse than else they would have expressed them. Not without cause therefore some both Italian[4] and Spanish poets of prime note have rejected rhyme both in longer and shorter works, as have also long since our best English tragedies, as a thing of itself, to all judicious ears, trivial and of no true musical delight; which consists only in apt numbers,[5] fit quantity of syllables, and the sense variously drawn out from one verse into another, not in the jingling sound of like endings, a fault avoided by the learned ancients both in poetry and all good oratory. This neglect then of rhyme so little is to be taken for a defect, though it may seem so perhaps to vulgar readers, that it rather is to be esteemed an example set,

---

1. The first edition (1667) presented *Paradise Lost* in ten books; the second (1674) recast it into twelve books after the Virgilian model, splitting the original Books 7 and 10.
2. Perhaps the bawdy content of the Latin songs composed by Goliardic poets of the Middle Ages;

they learned rhyme from medieval hymns.
3. Notably, Dryden. See his *Essay of Dramatic Poesy*, p. 913.
4. Trissino and Tasso.
5. Appropriate rhythm.

the first in English, of ancient liberty recovered to heroic poem from the troublesome and modern bondage of rhyming.

Book 1

The Argument[1]

 This first book proposes, first in brief, the whole subject, man's disobedience, and the loss thereupon of Paradise wherein he was placed: then touches the prime cause of his fall, the Serpent, or rather Satan in the Serpent; who revolting from God, and drawing to his side many legions of angels, was by the command of God driven out of Heaven with all his crew into the great deep. Which action passed over, the poem hastes into the midst of things,[2] presenting Satan with his angels now fallen into Hell, described here, not in the center[3] (for Heaven and Earth may be supposed as yet not made, certainly not yet accursed) but in a place of utter darkness, fitliest called Chaos: here Satan with his angels lying on the burning lake, thunderstruck and astonished, after a certain space recovers, as from confusion, calls up him who next in order and dignity lay by him; they confer of their miserable fall. Satan awakens all his legions, who lay till then in the same manner confounded; they rise, their numbers, array of battle, their chief leaders named, according to the idols known afterwards in Canaan and the countries adjoining. To these Satan directs his speech, comforts them with hope yet of regaining Heaven, but tells them lastly of a new world and new kind of creature to be created, according to an ancient prophecy or report in Heaven; for that angels were long before this visible creation, was the opinion of many ancient Fathers.[4] To find out the truth of this prophecy, and what to determine[5] thereon he refers to a full council. What his associates thence attempt. Pandemonium the palace of Satan rises, suddenly built out of the deep: the infernal peers there sit in council.

 Of man's first disobedience, and the fruit[1]
 Of that forbidden tree, whose mortal° taste   *deadly*
 Brought death into the world, and all our woe,
 With loss of Eden, till one greater Man[2]
5 Restore us, and regain the blissful seat,
 Sing Heav'nly Muse,[3] that on the secret top
 Of Oreb, or of Sinai, didst inspire
 That shepherd, who first taught the chosen seed,
 In the beginning how the heav'ns and earth
10 Rose out of Chaos: or if Sion hill[4]

1. *Paradise Lost* appeared originally without any sort of prose aid to the reader, but the printer asked Milton for some "Arguments," or summary explanations of the action in the various books, and these were prefixed to later issues of the poem. We reprint the "Argument" for the first book.
2. According to Horace, the epic poet should begin, "*in medias res.*"
3. I.e., of the earth.
4. Church Fathers, the Christian writers of the first centuries.
5. I.e., what action to take.
1. Eve's apple, and all the consequences of eating

it. This first Proem (lines 1–26) combines the epic statement of theme and invocation.
2. Christ, the second Adam.
3. In Greek mythology, Urania, Muse of astronomy; here, however, by the references to Oreb and Sinai, identified with the Muse who inspired Moses ("that shepherd") to write Genesis and the other four books of the Pentateuch for the instruction of the Jews ("the chosen seed").
4. Mount Zion: the site of Solomon's Temple. "Siloa's Brook": a spring near the Temple where Christ cured a blind man.

Delight thee more, and Siloa's brook that flowed
Fast by the oracle of God; I thence
Invoke thy aid to my advent'rous song,
That with no middle flight intends to soar
15 Above th' Aonian mount,[5] while it pursues
Things unattempted yet in prose or rhyme.[6]
And chiefly thou O Spirit,[7] that dost prefer
Before all temples th' upright heart and pure,
Instruct me, for thou know'st; thou from the first
20 Wast present, and with mighty wings outspread
Dove-like sat'st brooding[8] on the vast abyss
And mad'st it pregnant: what in me is dark
Illumine, what is low raise and support;
That to the height of this great argument°   *subject, theme*
25 I may assert Eternal Providence,
And justify° the ways of God to men.   *show the justice of*
    Say first, for Heav'n hides nothing from thy view
Nor the deep tract of Hell, say first what cause[9]
Moved our grand parents in that happy state,
30 Favored of Heav'n so highly, to fall off
From their Creator, and transgress his will
For° one restraint, lords of the world besides?°   *because of / otherwise*
Who first seduced them to that foul revolt?
Th' infernal Serpent; he it was, whose guile
35 Stirred up with envy and revenge, deceived
The mother of mankind, what time° his pride   *when*
Had cast him out from Heav'n, with all his host
Of rebel angels, by whose aid aspiring
To set himself in glory above his peers,°   *equals*
40 He trusted to have equaled the Most High,
If he opposed; and with ambitious aim
Against the throne and monarchy of God
Raised impious war in Heav'n and battle proud
With vain attempt. Him the Almighty Power
45 Hurled headlong flaming from th' ethereal sky
With hideous ruin and combustion down
To bottomless perdition, there to dwell
In adamantine[1] chains and penal fire,
Who durst defy th' Omnipotent to arms.
50 Nine times the space[2] that measures day and night
To mortal men, he with his horrid crew
Lay vanquished, rolling in the fiery gulf
Confounded though immortal: but his doom
Reserved him to more wrath; for now the thought
55 Both of lost happiness and lasting pain

5. Helicon, home of the classical Muses. Milton will attempt to surpass Homer and Virgil.
6. Paradoxically, Milton vaunts his originality in a translated line from Ariosto's *Orlando Furioso* 1.2. The allusion also challenges the romantic epic in Ariosto's tradition.
7. An impulse or voice or power of God.
8. A composite of phrases and ideas from Genesis 1.2 ("And the earth was without form, and void, and darkness was upon the face of the deep. And

the Spirit of God moved upon the face of the waters"). Only a small number of Milton's many allusions to the Bible (in many versions) can be indicated in the notes. Milton's brooding dove image comes from the Latin (Tremellius) Bible version, "incubabat."
9. An opening question like this is an epic convention.
1. A mythical substance of great hardness.
2. Extent of time, linear distances.

Torments him; round he throws his baleful° eyes   *malignant*
That witnessed huge affliction and dismay
Mixed with obdúrate pride and steadfast hate:
At once as far as angels ken° he views   *range of sight*
60 The dismal situation waste and wild,
A dungeon horrible, on all sides round
As one great furnace flamed, yet from those flames
No light,[3] but rather darkness visible
Served only to discover sights of woe,
65 Regions of sorrow, doleful shades, where peace
And rest can never dwell, hope never comes
That comes to all;[4] but torture without end
Still urges,° and a fiery deluge, fed   *always provokes*
With ever-burning sulphur unconsumed:
70 Such place Eternal Justice had prepared
For those rebellious, here their prison ordained
In utter darkness, and their portion set
As far removed from God and light of Heav'n
As from the center thrice to th' utmost pole.[5]
75 O how unlike the place from whence they fell!
There the companions of his fall, o'erwhelmed
With floods and whirlwinds of tempestuous fire,
He soon discerns, and welt'ring° by his side   *rolling in the waves*
One next himself in power, and next in crime,
80 Long after known in Palestine, and named
Beëlzebub.[6] To whom th' Arch-Enemy,
And thence in Heav'n called Satan,[7] with bold words
Breaking the horrid silence thus began.
  "If thou beest he; but O how fall'n![8] how changed
85 From him, who in the happy realms of light
Clothed with transcendent brightness didst outshine
Myriads though bright: if he whom mutual league,
United thoughts and counsels, equal hope
And hazard in the glorious enterprise,
90 Joined with me once, now misery hath joined
In equal ruin: into what pit thou seest
From what height fall'n, so much the stronger proved
He with his thunder:° and till then who knew   *thunderbolt*
The force of those dire arms? Yet not for those,
95 Nor what the potent victor in his rage
Can else inflict, do I repent or change,
Though changed in outward luster, that fixed mind

3. Omitting the verb conveys abruptly the paradox, fire without light.
4. The phrase alludes to Dante ("All hope abandon, ye who enter here").
5. Milton makes use of various images of the cosmos in *Paradise Lost*: (1) The earth is the center of the (Ptolemaic) cosmos of ten concentric spheres; (2) The earth and the whole cosmos are an appendage hanging from Heaven by a golden chain; (3) The cosmos seems Copernican from the angels' perspective (see Book 8). Here, the fall from Heaven to Hell is described as thrice as far as the distance from the center (earth) to the outermost sphere.

6. A Phoenician deity, or Baal (the name means "Lord of Flies"). He is called the prince of devils in Matthew 12.24. As with the other fallen angels, his angelic name has been obliterated, and he is now called by the name he will bear as a pagan deity. That literary strategy evokes all the evil associations attaching to those names in human history.
7. In Hebrew the name means "adversary."
8. Alludes to Isaiah 14.12: "How art thou fallen from heaven, O Lucifer, Son of the morning."

And high disdain, from sense of injured merit,
That with the mightiest raised me to contend,
100 And to the fierce contention brought along
Innumerable force of Spirits armed
That durst dislike his reign, and me preferring,
His utmost power with adverse power opposed
In dubious° battle on the plains of Heav'n,   *of uncertain outcome*
105 And shook his throne. What though the field be lost?
All is not lost; the unconquerable will,
And study° of revenge, immortal hate,   *intense consideration*
And courage never to submit or yield:
And what is else not to be overcome?[9]
110 That glory never shall his wrath or might
Extort from me. To bow and sue for grace
With suppliant knee, and deify his power
Who from the terror of this arm so late
Doubted° his empire, that were low indeed,   *feared for*
115 That were an ignominy and shame beneath
This downfall; since by fate the strength of gods[1]
And this empyreal substance cannot fail,°   *cease to exist*
Since through experience of this great event
In arms not worse, in foresight much advanced,
120 We may with more successful hope resolve
To wage by force or guile eternal war
Irreconcilable, to our grand foe,
Who now triúmphs, and in th' excess of joy
Sole reigning holds the tyranny of Heav'n."
125   So spake th' apostate angel, though in pain,
Vaunting aloud, but racked with deep despair:
And him thus answered soon his bold compeer.°   *comrade, equal*
    "O Prince, O Chief of many thronéd Powers,
That led th' embattled Seraphim[2] to war
130 Under thy conduct, and in dreadful deeds
Fearless, endangered Heav'ns perpetual King;
And put to proof his high supremacy,
Whether upheld by strength, or chance, or fate;
Too well I see and rue the dire event,°   *outcome*
135 That with sad overthrow and foul defeat
Hath lost us Heav'n, and all this mighty host
In horrible destruction laid thus low,
As far as gods and heav'nly essences
Can perish: for the mind and spirit remains
140 Invincible, and vigor soon returns,
Though all our glory extinct, and happy state
Here swallowed up in endless misery.
But what if he our conqueror (whom I now
Of force° believe almighty, since no less   *necessarily*

9. I.e., what else does it mean not to be overcome?
1. A term commonly used in the poem for angels. But to Satan and his followers it means more, as Satan claims the position of a god, subject to fate but nothing else. Their substance is "empyreal" (of the empyrean).

2. According to tradition, there were nine orders of angels, arranged hierarchically—seraphim, cherubim, thrones, dominions, virtues, powers, principalities, archangels, and angels. The poem makes use of some of these titles, but does not keep this hierarchy.

145 Than such could have o'erpow'red such force as ours)
Have left us this our spirit and strength entire
Strongly to suffer and support our pains,
That we may so suffice° his vengeful ire,   *satisfy*
Or do him mightier service as his thralls
150 By right of war, whate'er his business be
Here in the heart of Hell to work in fire,
Or do his errands in the gloomy deep;
What can it then avail though yet we feel
Strength undiminished, or eternal being
155 To undergo eternal punishment?"
Whereto with speedy words th' Arch-Fiend replied.
   "Fall'n Cherub, to be weak is miserable
Doing or suffering: but of this be sure,
To do aught good never will be our task,
160 But ever to do ill our sole delight,
As being the contrary to his high will
Whom we resist. If then his providence
Out of our evil seek to bring forth good,
Our labor must be to pervert that end,
165 And out of good still to find means of evil;
Which ofttimes may succeed, so as perhaps
Shall grieve him, if I fail° not, and disturb   *err*
His inmost counsels from their destined aim.
But see the angry victor hath recalled
170 His ministers of vengeance and pursuit
Back to the gates of Heav'n: the sulphurous hail
Shot after us in storm, o'erblown hath laid°   *calmed*
The fiery surge, that from the precipice
Of Heav'n received us falling, and the thunder,
175 Winged with red lightning and impetuous rage,
Perhaps hath spent his shafts, and ceases now
To bellow through the vast and boundless deep.
Let us not slip° th' occasion, whether scorn,   *let slip*
Or satiate fury yield it from our foe.
180 Seest thou yon dreary plain, forlorn and wild,
The seat of desolation, void of light,
Save what the glimmering of these livid° flames   *bluish*
Casts pale and dreadful? Thither let us tend
From off the tossing of these fiery waves,
185 There rest, if any rest can harbor there,
And reassembling our afflicted powers,°   *armies*
Consult how we may henceforth most offend°   *harm, vex*
Our enemy, our own loss how repair,
How overcome this dire calamity,
190 What reinforcement we may gain from hope,
If not what resolution from despair."[3]
   Thus Satan talking to his nearest mate
With head uplift above the wave, and eyes
That sparkling blazed, his other parts besides

---

3. Five of the last nine lines of Satan's speech rhyme.

195 Prone on the flood, extended long and large
    Lay floating many a rood,[4] in bulk as huge
    As whom° the fables name of monstrous size,   *as those whom*
    Titanian, or Earth-born, that warred on Jove,
    Briareos or Typhon,[5] whom the den
200 By ancient Tarsus held, or that sea-beast
    Leviathan,[6] which God of all his works
    Created hugest that swim th' ocean stream:
    Him haply slumb'ring on the Norway foam
    The pilot of some small night-foundered° skiff,   *overcome by night*
205 Deeming some island, oft, as seamen tell,[7]
    With fixèd anchor in his scaly rind
    Moors by his side under the lee,° while night   *out of the wind*
    Invests° the sea, and wishèd morn delays: *covers*
    So stretched out huge in length the Arch-Fiend lay
210 Chained on the burning lake, nor ever thence
    Had ris'n or heaved his head, but that the will
    And high permission of all-ruling Heaven
    Left him at large to his own dark designs,
    That with reiterated crimes he might
215 Heap on himself damnation, while he sought
    Evil to others, and enraged might see
    How all his malice served but to bring forth
    Infinite goodness, grace and mercy shown
    On man by him seduced, but on himself
220 Treble confusion, wrath and vengeance poured.
    Forthwith upright he rears from off the pool
    His mighty stature; on each hand the flames
    Driv'n backward slope their pointing spires,° and rolled   *points of flames*
    In billows, leave i' th' midst a horrid° vale.   *dreadful, bristling*
225 Then with expanded wings he steers his flight
    Aloft, incumbent on° the dusky air   *resting on*
    That felt unusual weight, till on dry land
    He lights,° if it were land that ever burned   *alights*
    With solid, as the lake with liquid fire,
230 And such appeared in hue; as when the force
    Of subterranean wind transports a hill
    Torn from Pelorus, or the shattered side
    Of thund'ring Etna,[8] whose combustible
    And fueled entrails thence conceiving fire,
235 Sublimed° with mineral fury, aid the winds,   *vaporized*
    And leave a singèd bottom all involved°   *enveloped*
    With stench and smoke: such resting found the sole
    Of unblest feet. Him followed his next mate,

4. An old unit of measure, between six and eight yards.
5. Both the Titans, led by Briareos (said to have had a hundred hands), and the earth-born Giants, represented by Typhon (who lived in Cilicea near Tarsus and was said to have had a hundred heads), fought with Jove. They were punished by being thrown into the underworld. Christian mythographers found in these stories an analogy to Satan's revolt and punishment.

6. The whale, often identified with the great sea-monster and enemy of the Lord in Isaiah 17.1 and the crocodilelike dragon of Job 41. Both were also identified with Satan.
7. The story of the deceived sailor and the illusory island was a commonplace, but the reference to Norway suggests a 16th-century version by Olaus Magnus, a Swedish historian.
8. Pelorus and Etna are volcanic mountains in Sicily.

Both glorying to have scaped the Stygian° flood   *Styxlike, hellish*
240 As gods, and by their own recovered strength,
Not by the sufferance° of supernal power.   *permission*
    "Is this the region, this the soil, the clime,"
Said then the lost Archangel, "this the seat°   *estate*
That we must change for Heav'n, this mournful gloom
245 For that celestial light? Be it so, since he
Who now is sovran can dispose and bid
What shall be right: farthest from him is best
Whom reason hath equaled, force hath made supreme
Above his equals. Farewell happy fields
250 Where joy for ever dwells: Hail horrors, hail
Infernal world, and thou profoundest Hell
Receive thy new possessor: one who brings
A mind not to be changed by place or time.
The mind is its own place, and in itself
255 Can make a Heav'n of Hell, a Hell of Heav'n.⁹
What matter where, if I be still the same,
And what I should be, all but less than° he   *barely less than*
Whom thunder hath made greater? Here at least
We shall be free; th' Almighty hath not built
260 Here for his envy,¹ will not drive us hence:
Here we may reign secure, and in my choice
To reign is worth ambition though in Hell:
Better to reign in Hell, than serve in Heav'n.²
But wherefore let we then our faithful friends,
265 Th' associates and copartners of our loss
Lie thus astonished° on th' oblivious pool,³   *stunned*
And call them not to share with us their part
In this unhappy mansion, or once more
With rallied arms to try what may be yet
270 Regained in Heav'n, or what more lost in Hell?"
    So Satan spake, and him Beëlzebub
Thus answered. "Leader of those armies bright,
Which but th' Omnipotent none could have foiled,
If once they hear that voice, their liveliest pledge
275 Of hope in fears and dangers, heard so oft
In worst extremes, and on the perilous edge°   *front lines*
Of battle when it raged, in all assaults
Their surest signal, they will soon resume
New courage and revive, though now they lie
280 Groveling and prostrate on yon lake of fire,
As we erewhile, astounded and amazed,
No wonder, fall'n such a pernicious highth."
    He scarce had ceased when the superior Fiend
Was moving toward the shore; his ponderous shield
285 Ethereal temper,⁴ massy, large and round,

9. Compare Satan's soliloquy, 4.33–113.
1. I.e., because he desires this place.
2. An ironic echo of *Odyssey* 11.489–91, where the shade of Achilles tells Odysseus that it is better to be a farmhand on earth than king among the dead.
3. The epithet "oblivious" is transferred from the fallen angels to the pool in which they have fallen.
4. I.e., tempered in celestial fire.

Behind him cast; the broad circumference
Hung on his shoulders like the moon, whose orb
Through optic glass the Tuscan artists views[5]
At evening from the top of Fesole,
290 Or in Valdarno, to descry new lands,
Rivers or mountains in her spotty globe.
His spear, to equal which the tallest pine
Hewn on Norwegian hills, to be the mast
Of some great ammiral,° were but a wand,   *admiral's ship*
295 He walked with to support uneasy steps
Over the burning marl,° not like those steps   *soil*
On heaven's azure; and the torrid clime
Smote on him sore besides, vaulted with fire;
Nathless° he so endured, till on the beach   *nevertheless*
300 Of that inflamed° sea, he stood and called   *flaming*
His legions, angel forms, who lay entranced
Thick as autumnal leaves that strow the brooks
In Vallombrosa,[6] where th' Etrurian shades
High overarched embow'r;° or scattered sedge°   *form bowers / seaweed*
305 Afloat, when with fierce winds Orion[7] armed
Hath vexed the Red Sea coast, whose waves o'erthrew
Busiris[8] and his Memphian chivalry,
While with perfidious hatred they pursued
The sojourners of Goshen, who beheld
310 From the safe shore their floating carcasses
And broken chariot wheels; so thick bestrown
Abject and lost lay these, covering the flood,
Under amazement of their hideous change.
He called so loud, that all the hollow deep
315 Of Hell resounded. "Princes, Potentates,
Warriors, the flow'r of heav'n, once yours, now lost,
If such astonishment as this can seize
Eternal Spirits: or have ye chos'n this place
After the toil of battle to repose
320 Your wearied virtue,° for the ease you find   *strength, valor*
To slumber here, as in the vales of Heav'n?
Or in this abject posture have ye sworn
To adore the conqueror? who now beholds
Cherub and Seraph rolling in the flood
325 With scattered arms and ensigns,° till anon   *battle flags*
His swift pursuers from Heav'n gates discern
Th' advantage, and descending tread us down
Thus drooping, or with linkèd thunderbolts
Transfix us to the bottom of this gulf.
330 Awake, arise, or be for ever fall'n."

---

5. Galileo, who looked through a telescope ("optic glass") from the hill town of Fiesole outside Florence, in the valley of the Arno river ("Valdarno," val d'Arno). In 1610 he published a book describing the mountains on the moon.
6. The name means "shady valley," a region high in the Apennines, about twenty miles from Florence, in Tuscany ("Etruria"). Similes comparing the numberless dead to falling leaves are frequent

in epic (e.g., *Aeneid* 6.309–10).
7. Orion is a constellation whose rising near sunset in late summer and autumn was associated with storms in the Red Sea.
8. Mythical Egyptian pharaoh, whom Milton associates with the pharaoh of Exodus 14 who pursued the Israelites ("sojourners of Goshen") into the Red Sea, which God parted for them. His "chivalry" are horsemen from Memphis.

They heard, and were abashed, and up they sprung
Upon the wing, as when men wont to watch
On duty, sleeping found by whom they dread,
Rouse and bestir themselves ere well awake.
335 Nor did they not perceive⁹ the evil plight
In which they were, or the fierce pains not feel;
Yet to their general's voice they soon obeyed
Innumerable. As when the potent rod
Of Amram's son¹ in Egypt's evil day
340 Waved round the coast, up called a pitchy cloud
Of locusts, warping° on the eastern wind,   *floating*
That o'er the realm of impious Pharaoh hung
Like night, and darkened all the land of Nile:
So numberless were those bad angels seen
345 Hovering on wing under the cope° of Hell   *roof*
'Twixt upper, nether, and surrounding fires;
Till, as a signal giv'n, th' uplifted spear
Of their great Sultan² waving to direct
Their course, in even balance down they light
350 On the firm brimstone, and fill all the plain;
A multitude, like which the populous North
Poured never from her frozen loins, to pass
Rhene or the Danaw, when her barbarous sons
Came like a deluge on the South, and spread
355 Beneath Gibraltar to the Libyan sands.³
Forthwith from every squadron and each band
The heads and leaders thither haste where stood
Their great commander; godlike shapes and forms
Excelling human, princely dignities,
360 And powers that erst in Heaven sat on thrones;
Though of their names in heav'nly records now
Be no memorial, blotted out and razed°   *erased*
By their rebellion, from the Books of Life.
Nor had they yet among the sons of Eve
365 Got them new names, till wand'ring o'er the earth,
Through God's high sufferance for the trial of man,
By falsities and lies the greatest part
Of mankind they corrupted to forsake
God their Creator, and th' invisible
370 Glory of him that made them, to transform
Oft to the image of a brute, adorned
With gay religions° full of pomp and gold,   *showy rites*
And devils to adore for deities:
Then were they known to men by various names,
375 And various idols through the heathen world.
   Say, Muse, their names then known, who first, who last,⁴
Roused from the slumber on that fiery couch,

---

9. The double negatives make a positive: they did perceive both plight and pain.
1. Moses, who drew down a plague of locusts on Egypt (Exodus 10.12–15).
2. A first use of this description of Satan as an Oriental despot.

3. The barbarian invasions of Rome began with crossings of the Rhine ("Rhene") and Danube ("Danaw") rivers and spread across Spain, via Gibraltar, to North Africa.
4. The catalog of gods here is an epic convention; Homer catalogs ships; Virgil, warriors.

At their great emperor's call, as next in worth
Came singly° where he stood on the bare strand,   *one at a time*
380 While the promiscuous° crowd stood yet aloof.   *mixed*
    The chief were those who from the pit of Hell
Roaming to seek their prey on earth, durst fix
Their seats long after next the seat of God,[5]
Their altars by his altar, gods adored
385 Among the nations round, and durst abide
Jehovah thund'ring out of Zion, throned
Between the Cherubim;[6] yea, often placed
Within his sanctuary itself their shrines,
Abomination; and with cursèd things
390 His holy rites, and solemn feasts profaned,
And with their darkness durst affront his light.
First Moloch,[7] horrid king besmeared with blood
Of human sacrifice, and parents' tears,
Though for the noise of drums and timbrels° loud   *tambourines*
395 Their children's cries unheard, that passed through fire
To his grim idol. Him the Ammonite[8]
Worshiped in Rabba and her wat'ry plain,
In Argob and in Basan, to the stream
Of Utmost Arnon. Nor content with such
400 Audacious neighborhood, the wisest heart
Of Solomon he led by fraud to build
His temple right against the temple of God
On that opprobrious hill, and made his grove
The pleasant valley of Hinnom, Tophet thence
405 And black Gehenna called, the type of Hell.[9]
Next Chemos,[1] th' obscene dread of Moab's sons,
From Aroer to Nebo, and the wild
Of southmost Abarim; in Hesebon
And Horanaim, Seon's realm, beyond
410 The flow'ry dale of Sibma clad with vines,
And Elealè to th' Asphaltic Pool.[2]
Peor[3] his other name, when he enticed
Israel in Sittim on their march from Nile
To do him wanton rites, which cost them woe.
415 Yet thence his lustful orgies he enlarged
Even to that hill of scandal,[4] by the grove
Of Moloch homicide, lust hard by hate;

5. The first group of devils come from the Middle East, close neighbors of Jehovah "throned" in his sanctuary in Jerusalem.
6. Golden cherubim adorned opposite ends of the gold cover on the Ark of the Covenant.
7. Moloch was a sun god, sometimes represented as a roaring bull or with a calf's head, within whose brazen image living children were supposedly burned as sacrifices.
8. The Ammonites lived east of the Jordan. "Rabba" is modern Amman, in Jordan; "Argob," "Basan," "utmost Arnon" are lands east of the Dead Sea.
9. The rites of Moloch on "that opprobrious hill" (the Mount of Olives), just opposite the Jewish temple, and in the valley of Hinnom so polluted

those places that they were turned into the refuse dump of Jerusalem. Under the name "Tophet" and "Gehenna," Hinnom became a type of Hell.
1. Chemos or Chemosh, associated with Moloch in 1 Kings 11.7, was the god of the Moabites, whose lands (many drawn from Isaiah 15–16) are mentioned in the following lines.
2. The Dead Sea.
3. The story of Peor seducing the Israelites in Sittim is told in Numbers 15.
4. The Mount of Olives where Solomon built temples for Chemos and Moloch (1 Kings 11.7); epithets were commonly attached to the names of gods, as here, Moloch "homicide." Josiah (next line) destroyed pagan idols in Jerusalem and other cities (2 Chronicles 34).

Till good Josiah drove them thence to Hell.
With these came they, who from the bord'ring flood
420   Of old Euphrates to the brook that parts
Egypt from Syrian ground,[5] had general names
Of Baalim and Ashtaroth, those male,
These feminine.[6] For Spirits when they please
Can either sex assume, or both; so soft
425   And uncompounded is their essence pure,
Not tied or manacled with joint or limb,
Nor founded on the brittle strength of bones,
Like cumbrous flesh; but in what shape they choose
Dilated or condensed, bright or obscure,
430   Can execute their airy purposes,
And works of love or enmity fulfill.
For those the race of Israel oft forsook
Their Living Strength, and unfrequented left
His righteous altar, bowing lowly down
435   To bestial gods; for which their heads as low
Bowed down in battle, sunk before the spear
Of despicable foes. With these in troop
Came Astoreth, whom the Phoenicians called
Astartè, queen of Heav'n, with crescent horns;
440   To whose bright image nightly by the moon
Sidonian virgins[7] paid their vows and songs,
In Sion also not unsung, where stood
Her temple on th' offensive mountain,[8] built
By that uxorious king, whose heart though large,
445   Beguiled by fair idolatresses, fell
To idols foul. Thammuz[9] came next behind,
Whose annual wound in Lebanon allured
The Syrian damsels to lament his fate
In amorous ditties all a summer's day,
450   While smooth Adonis[1] from his native work
Ran purple to the sea, supposed with blood
Of Thammuz yearly wounded: the love-tale
Infected Sion's daughters with like heat,
Whose wanton passions in the sacred porch
455   Ezekiel[2] saw, when by the vision led
His eye surveyed the dark idolatries
Of alienated Judah. Next came one
Who mourned in earnest, when the captive ark
Maimed his brute image, head and hands lopped off
460   In his own temple, on the grunsel edge,[3]

---

5. Palestine lies between the Euphrates and "the brook of Besor" (1 Samuel 30.10).
6. Plural forms, masculine and feminine, respectively, denoting aspects of the sun god Baal and the moon goddess Astarte.
7. Sidon and Tyre were the chief cities of Phoenicia.
8. The Mount of Olives again. "That uxorious king" (next line) is Solomon, who "loved many strange women" (2 Kings 11.1–8).
9. A Syrian god, supposedly killed by a boar in Lebanon; his Greek form was Adonis, beloved of Aphrodite and god of the solar year. Annual festivals mourned his death and celebrated his revival as signifying the death and rebirth of vegetation.
1. Here, the Lebanese river named for the deity because every spring it turned blood-red from sedimentary mud.
2. The prophet complained that Jewish women were worshipping Thammuz (Ezekiel 8.14).
3. When the Philistines stole the ark of God, they placed it in the temple of their sea god, Dagon, but

Where he fell flat, and shamed his worshipers:
Dagon his name, sea monster, upward man
And downward fish: yet had his temple high
Reared in Azotus, dreaded through the coast
465 Of Palestine, in Gath and Ascalon⁴
And Accaron and Gaza's frontier bounds.
Him followed Rimmon,⁵ whose delightful seat
Was fair Damascus, on the fertile banks
Of Abbana and Pharphar, lucid streams.
470 He also against the house of God was bold:
A leper once he lost and gained a king,⁶
Ahaz his sottish conqueror, whom he drew
God's altar to disparage and displace
For one of Syrian mode, whereon to burn
475 His odious off'rings, and adore the gods
Whom he had vanquished. After these appeared
A crew who under names of old renown,
Osiris, Isis, Orus⁷ and their train
With monstrous shapes and sorceries abused
480 Fanatic Egypt and her priests, to seek
Their wand'ring gods disguised in brutish forms
Rather than human. Nor did Israel scape
Th' infection when their borrowed gold composed
The calf in Oreb:⁸ and the rebel king
485 Doubled that sin in Bethel and in Dan,
Lik'ning his Maker to the grazèd ox,⁹
Jehovah, who in one night when he passed
From Egypt marching, equaled° with one stroke   *levelled*
Both her first-born and all her bleating gods.¹
490 Belial came last,² than whom a spirit more lewd
Fell not from Heaven, or more gross to love
Vice for itself: to him no temple stood
Or altar smoked; yet who more oft than he
In temples and at altars, when the priest
495 Turns atheist, as did Eli's sons,³ who filled
With lust and violence the house of God.
In courts and palaces he also reigns
And in luxurious cities, where the noise
Of riot ascends above their loftiest tow'rs,

---

in the morning the mutilated statue of Dagon was found on the threshhold ("grunsel edge") (1 Samuel 5.1–5).
4. The five chief cities of the Philistines, sites of Dagon's worship.
5. A Phoenician god whose temple was in Damascus.
6. A Syrian general, Naaman, was cured of leprosy and converted from worship of Rimmon by the waters of the Jordan (2 Kings 5), while King Ahaz, an Israelite monarch who conquered Damascus, was converted there to Rimmon's worship.
7. The second group of devils include the Egyptian gods driven from Heaven by the revolt of the giants (Ovid, *Metamorphoses* 5) and forced to wander in "monstrous" (next line) animal disguises.
8. In the wilderness of Egypt, while Moses was

receiving the Law, Aaron made a golden calf, thought to be an idol of the Egyptian god Apis and made of ornaments brought out of Egypt (Exodus 32).
9. Jereboam, "the rebel king" who led the ten tribes of Israel in revolt against Solomon's son, Reheboam; he doubled Aaron's sin by making two golden calves (1 Kings 12–30).
1. Jehovah smote the firstborn of all Egyptian families as well as their gods (Exodus 12.12).
2. Belial was never worshiped as a god; his name means "wickedness," but its use in phrases like "sons of Belial" encouraged personification.
3. Priests who were termed "sons of Belial" because they seized for themselves offerings made to God and lay with prostitutes (1 Samuel 2.12–22).

500 And injury and outrage: and when night
Darkens the streets, then wander forth the sons
Of Belial, flown° with insolence and wine.⁴   *flushed*
Witness the streets of Sodom, and that night
In Gibeah,⁵ when the hospitable door
505 Exposed a matron to avoid worse rape.
    These were the prime in order and in might;
The rest were long to tell, though far renowned,
Th' Ionian gods, of Javan's issue held
Gods, yet confessed later than Heav'n and Earth
510 Their boasted parents;⁶ Titan Heav'n's first-born
With his enormous brood, and birthright seized
By younger Saturn, he from mightier Jove,
His own and Rhea's son, like measure found;
So Jove usurping reigned:⁷ these first in Crete
515 And Ida known, thence on the snowy top
Of cold Olympus ruled the middle air
Their highest heav'n; or on the Delphian cliff,
Or in Dodona, and through all the bounds
Of Doric land;⁸ or who with Saturn old
520 Fled over Adria to th' Hesperian fields,
And o'er the Celtic roamed the utmost isles.⁹
    All these and more came flocking; but with looks
Downcast and damp,° yet such wherein appeared   *depressed, dazed*
Obscure some glimpse of joy, to have found their chief
525 Not in despair, to have found themselves not lost
In loss itself; which on his count'nance cast
Like doubtful hue:¹ but he his wonted pride
Soon recollecting, with high words, that bore
Semblance of worth, not substance, gently raised
530 Their fainting courage, and dispelled their fears.
Then straight commands that at the warlike sound
Of trumpets loud and clarions be upreared
His mighty standard; that proud honor claimed
Azazel² as his right, a Cherub tall:
535 Who forthwith from the glittering staff unfurled
Th' imperial ensign, which full high advanced
Shone like a meteor streaming to the wind
With gems and golden luster rich emblazed,
Seraphic arms and trophies:³ all the while

4. This passage, with its present-tense verbs, invites application to current examples—like Cavaliers at court and Restoration London.
5. Lot begged the Sodomites to rape his daughter rather than his (male) angel guests (Genesis 19); in Gibeah a Levite avoided worse (homosexual) rape by surrendering his concubine to riotous "sons of Belial" (Judges 19.21–30).
6. The Ionian Greeks ("Javan's issue," i.e., of the line of Javan, grandson of Noah) regarded the Titans as gods; their supposed parents were Heaven (Uranus) and Earth (Gaea).
7. The Titan Chronos, or Saturn, deposed his elder brother, married his sister Rhea, and ruled until he was deposed by his son, Zeus (Jove), who

had been reared in secret on Mount Ida in Crete.
8. Zeus and the other Olympian gods had their seat on Mount Olympus, in "middle air"; they were worshiped in Delphi, Dodona, and throughout Greece ("Doric lands").
9. Saturn, after his downfall, fled over "Adria" (the Adriatic Sea) to "the Hesperian fields" (Italy), crossed the "Celtic" fields of France, and thence to Britain, the "utmost isles."
1. Satan's face reflected the same mixed emotions.
2. Traditionally, one of the four standard-bearers in Satan's army. "Clarions" (line 532): small, shrill trumpets.
3. Their flags bear the heraldic arms of the various orders of angels and memorials of their battles.

540 Sonorous metal° blowing martial sounds: *trumpets*
At which the universal host upsent
A shout that tore Hell's concave,° and beyond *vault*
Frighted the reign of Chaos and old Night.[4]
All in a moment through the gloom were seen
545 Ten thousand banners rise into the air
With orient° colors waving: with them rose *lustrous*
A forest huge of spears: and thronging helms
Appeared, and serried° shields in thick array *pushed close together*
Of depth immeasurable: anon they move
550 In perfect phalanx to the Dorian[5] mood
Of flutes and soft recorders; such as raised
To highth of noblest temper heroes old
Arming to battle, and instead of rage
Deliberate valor breathed, firm and unmoved
555 With dread of death to flight or foul retreat,
Nor wanting power to mitigate and swage° *assuage*
With solemn touches, troubled thoughts, and chase
Anguish and doubt and fear and sorrow and pain
From mortal or immortal minds. Thus they
560 Breathing united force with fixèd thought
Moved on in silence to soft pipes that charmed
Their painful steps o'er the burnt soil; and now
Advanced in view they stand, a horrid° front *bristling with spears*
Of dreadful length and dazzling arms, in guise
565 Of warriors old with ordered spear and shield,
Awaiting what command their mighty chief
Had to impose. He through the armèd files
Darts his experienced eye, and soon traverse° *across*
The whole battalion views, their order due,
570 Their visages and stature as of gods,
Their number last he sums. And now his heart
Distends with pride, and hard'ning in his strength
Glories: for never since created man[6]
Met such embodied force, as named° with these *composed*
575 Could merit more than that small infantry[7]
Warred on by cranes: though all the giant brood
Of Phlegra with th' heroic race were joined
That fought at Thebes and Ilium,[8] on each side
Mixed with auxiliar° gods; and what resounds *allied*
580 In fable or romance of Uther's son
Begirt with British and Armoric knights;
And all who since, baptized or infidel
Jousted in Aspramont or Montalban,
Damasco, or Marocco, or Trebisond,

4. In *Paradise Lost* 2.894–909, 959–70 Chaos and Night rule the region of unformed matter between Heaven and earth.
5. Severe, martial music used by the Spartans marching to battle. "Phalanx": battle formation.
6. I.e., since the creation of man.
7. Pygmies (little people, with a pun on *infants*) had periodic fights with the cranes, in Pliny's account. Compared with Satan's forces, all other armies are puny.
8. In Greek mythology, the Giants fought the gods at Phlegra in Macedonia; in Roman myth, it was at Phlegra in Italy. Satan's forces surpass them, even if joined with the Seven who fought against Thebes and the whole Greek host that besieged Troy ("Illium").

585   Or whom Biserta sent from Afric shore
       When Charlemain with all his peerage fell
       By Fontarabbia.⁹ Thus far these beyond
       Compare of mortal prowess, yet observed°   *obeyed*
       Their dread commander: he above the rest
590   In shape and gesture proudly eminent
       Stood like a tow'r; his form had yet not lost
       All her¹ original brightness, nor appeared
       Less than Archangel ruined, and th' excess
       Of glory obscured: as when the sun new-ris'n
595   Looks through the horizontal° misty air   *on the horizon*
       Shorn of his beams, or from behind the moon
       In dim eclipse° disastrous twilight sheds   *ill-starred*
       On half the nations, and with fear of change
       Perplexes monarchs. Darkened so, yet shone
600   Above them all th' Archangel: but his face
       Deep scars of thunder had intrenched,° and care   *furrowed*
       Sat on his faded cheek, but under brows
       Of dauntless courage, and considerate° pride   *conscious, deliberate*
       Waiting revenge: cruel his eye, but cast
605   Signs of remorse and passion° to behold   *compassion, pain*
       The fellows of his crime, the followers rather
       (Far other once beheld in bliss) condemned
       For ever now to have their lot in pain,
       Millions of Spirits for his fault amerced°   *deprived*
610   Of Heav'n, and from eternal splendors flung
       For his revolt, yet faithful how they stood,
       Their glory withered: as when Heaven's fire
       Hath scathed the forest oaks, or mountain pines,
       With singèd top their stately growth though bare
615   Stands on the blasted heath. He now prepared
       To speak; whereat their doubled ranks they bend
       From wing to wing, and half enclose him round
       With all his peers: attention held them mute.
       Thrice he essayed, and thrice, in spite of scorn,
620   Tears such as angels weep burst forth: at last
       Words interwove with sighs found out their way.
       "O myriads of immortal Spirits, O Powers
       Matchless, but with th' Almighty, and that strife
       Was not inglorious, though th' event° was dire,   *outcome*
625   As this place testifies, and this dire change
       Hateful to utter: but what power of mind
       Foreseeing or presaging, from the depth
       Of knowledge past or present, could have feared,
       How such united force of gods, how such
630   As stood like these, could ever know repulse?
       For who can yet believe, though after loss,

---

9. Satan's forces also surpass the "British or Armoric" (from Brittany) knights who fought with King Arthur ("Uther's son"), and all the romance knights who fought at the famous named sites in the following lines. Roncevalles, near Fontarabba, was the place where Charlemagne's "peerage," including his best knight, Roland, were defeated in battle (though not Charlemagne himself).

1. "Forma" in Latin is feminine.

That all these puissant° legions, whose exile   *potent, powerful*
Hath emptied Heav'n, shall fail to reascend
Self-raised, and repossess their native seat?
635 For me, be witness all the host of Heav'n,
If counsels different,° or danger shunned   *contradictory*
By me, have lost our hopes. But he who reigns
Monarch in Heav'n, till then as one secure
Sat on his throne, upheld by old repute,
640 Consent or custom, and his regal state
Put forth at full, but still his strength concealed,
Which tempted our attempt,² and wrought our fall.
Henceforth his might we know, and know our own
So as not either to provoke, or dread
645 New war, provoked; our better part remains
To work in close design, by fraud or guile
What force effected not: that he no less
At length from us may find, who overcomes
By force, hath overcome but half his foe.
650 Space may produce new worlds; whereof so rife°   *common*
There went a fame° in Heav'n that he ere long   *rumor*
Intended to create, and therein plant
A generation, whom his choice regard
Should favor equal to the sons of Heaven:
655 Thither, if but to pry, shall be perhaps
Our first eruption,° thither or elsewhere: *breaking out*
For this infernal pit shall never hold
Celestial Spirits in bondage, not th' abyss
Long under darkness cover. But these thoughts
660 Full counsel must mature: peace is despaired,
For who can think submission? War then, war
Open or understood° must be resolved."   *covert*
    He spake: and to confirm his words, out flew
Millions of flaming swords, drawn from the thighs
665 Of mighty Cherubim; the sudden blaze
Far round illumined Hell: highly they raged
Against the Highest, and fierce with graspèd arms
Clashed on their sounding shields the din of war,³
Hurling defiance toward the vault of Heav'n.
670   There stood a hill not far whose grisly top
Belched fire and rolling smoke; the rest entire
Shone with a glossy scurf,° undoubted sign   *crust*
That in his womb was hid metallic ore,
The work of sulphur.⁴ Thither winged with speed
675 A numerous brígade hastened. As when bands
Of pioneers° with spade and pickax armed   *military engineers*
Forerun the royal camp, to trench a field,
Or cast a rampart. Mammon⁵ led them on,

---

2. Satan is an inveterate punster.
3. Like Roman legionaires, the fallen angels applaud by beating swords on shields.
4. Sulfur and mercury were considered the basic substances of all metals.

5. Mammon, an abstract word for riches, came to be personified and associated with the god of wealth, Plutus, and so with Pluto, god of the underworld. Cf. Matthew 6.24: "Ye cannot serve God and Mammon."

Mammon, the least erected Spirit that fell
680 From Heav'n, for ev'n in Heav'n his looks and thoughts
Were always downward bent, admiring more
The riches of Heav'n's pavement, trodden gold,
Than aught divine or holy else enjoyed
In vision beatific: by him first
685 Men also, and by his suggestion taught,
Ransacked the center, and with impious hands
Rifled the bowels of their mother earth
For treasures better hid. Soon had his crew
Opened into the hill a spacious wound
690 And digged out ribs of gold. Let none admire°   *wonder*
That riches grow in Hell; that soil may best
Deserve the precious bane.° And here let those   *poison*
Who boast in mortal things, and wond'ring tell
Of Babel, and the works of Memphian kings,[6]
695 Learn how their greatest monuments of fame,
And strength and art are easily outdone
By Spirits reprobate, and in an hour
What in an age they with incessant toil
And hands innumerable scarce perform.
700 Nigh on the plain in many cells prepared,
That underneath had veins of liquid fire
Sluiced from the lake, a second multitude
With wondrous art founded° the massy ore,   *melted*
Severing° each kind, and scummed the bullion dross:° *separating/boiling dregs*
705 A third as soon had formed within the ground
A various mold, and from the boiling cells
By strange conveyance filled each hollow nook,
As in an organ from one blast of wind
To many a row of pipes the soundboard breathes.
710 Anon out of the earth a fabric huge
Rose like an exhalation, with the sound
Of dulcet symphonies and voices sweet,[7]
Built like a temple, where pilasters° round   *columns set in a wall*
Were set, and Doric pillars[8] overlaid
715 With golden architrave; nor did there want
Cornice or frieze, with bossy° sculptures grav'n;   *embossed*
The roof was fretted° gold. Not Babylon,   *richly ornamented*
Nor great Alcairo such magnificence
Equaled in all their glories, to enshrine
720 Belus or Serapis[9] their gods, or seat
Their kings, when Egypt with Assyria strove
In wealth and luxury. Th' ascending pile
Stood fixed° her stately height, and straight° the doors *complete/at once*
Opening their brazen folds discover wide
725 Within, her ample spaces, o'er the smooth
And level pavement: from the archèd roof

---

6. The Tower of Babel and the pyramids of Egypt.
7. After melting the gold with fire from the lake and pouring it into molds, the devils cause their building to rise as by magic, to the sounds of marvelous music.
8. Doric pillars are severe and plain. The devils'

palace combines classical architectural features with elaborate ornamentation, suggesting, perhaps, St. Peter's in Rome.
9. At Babylon in Assyria there were temples to "Belus" or Baal; at Alcairo (modern Cairo, ancient Memphis) in Egypt they were to Osiris ("Serapis").

Pendent by subtle magic many a row
Of starry lamps and blazing cressets[1] fed
With naphtha and asphaltus yielded light
730 As from a sky. The hasty multitude
Admiring entered, and the work some praise
And some the architect: his hand was known
In Heav'n by many a towered structure high,
Where sceptered angels held their residence,
735 And sat as princes, whom the Súpreme King
Exalted to such power, and gave to rule,
Each in his hierarchy, the orders bright.
Nor was his name unheard or unadored
In ancient Greece and in Ausonian land
740 Men called him Mulciber[2] and how he fell
From Heav'n, they fabled, thrown by angry Jove
Sheer o'er the crystal battlements: from morn
To noon he fell, from noon to dewy eve,
A summer's day; and with the setting sun
745 Dropped from the zenith like a falling star,
On Lemnos th' Aégean isle: thus they relate,
Erring; for he with this rebellious rout
Fell long before; nor aught availed him now
To have built in Heav'n high tow'rs; nor did he scape
750 By all his engines, but was headlong sent
With his industrious crew to build in Hell.
    Meanwhile the wingèd heralds by command
Of sovran power, with awful ceremony
And trumpet's sound throughout the host proclaim
755 A solemn council forthwith to be held
At Pandemonium,[3] the high capitol
Of Satan and his peers:° their summons called   *nobles*
From every band and squarèd regiment
By place° or choice° the worthiest; they anon   *rank/election*
760 With hundreds and with thousands trooping came
Attended: all access was thronged, the gates
And porches wide, but chief the spacious hall
(Though like a covered field, where champions bold
Wont ride in armed, and at the Soldan's° chair   *sultan's*
765 Defied the best of paynim° chivalry   *pagan*
To mortal combat or career with lance)
Thick swarmed, both on the ground and in the air,
Brushed with the hiss of rustling wings. As bees
In springtime, when the sun with Taurus[4] rides,
770 Pour forth their populous youth about the hive
In clusters; they among fresh dews and flowers
Fly to and fro, or on the smoothèd plank,
The suburb of their straw-built citadel,
New rubbed with balm, expatiate and confer[5]

1. Basketlike lamps, hung from the ceiling.
2. Hephaestus, or Vulcan, was sometimes known in "Ausonian land" (Italy) as "Mulciber." The story of Jove's tossing him out of heaven is told in book 1 of the *Iliad*.
3. "Pandemonium" (a Miltonic coinage) means

literally "All-Demons," an inversion of Pantheon, "All Gods."
4. The sun is in the zodiacal sign of Taurus from about April 19 to May 20.
5. Spread out and discuss. Bee similes were common in epic from Homer on; also, the bees' (roy-

775 Their state affairs. So thick the aery crowd
Swarmed and were straitened; till the signal giv'n,
Behold a wonder! They but now who seemed
In bigness to surpass Earth's giant sons
Now less than smallest dwarfs, in narrow room
780 Throng numberless, like that Pygmean race
Beyond the Indian mount,[6] or fairy elves,
Whose midnight revels, by a forest side
Or fountain some belated peasant sees,
Or dreams he sees, while overhead the moon
785 Sits arbitress,° and nearer to the earth   *witness*
Wheels her pale course: they on their mirth and dance
Intent, with jocund° music charm his ear;[7]   *merry*
At once with joy and fear his heart rebounds.
Thus incorporeal Spirits to smallest forms
790 Reduced their shapes immense, and were at large,
Though without number still amidst the hall
Of that infernal court. But far within
And in their own dimensions like themselves
The great Seraphic Lords and Cherubim
795 In close recess and secret conclave sat,
A thousand demi-gods on golden seats,
Frequent and full.[8] After short silence then
And summons read, the great consult[9] began.

Book 2

High on a throne of royal state, which far
Outshone the wealth of Ormus and of Ind,[1]
Or where the gorgeous East with richest hand
Show'rs on her kings barbaric pearl and gold,
5 Satan exalted sat, by merit raised
To that bad eminence; and from despair
Thus high uplifted beyond hope, aspires
Beyond thus high, insatiate to pursue
Vain war with Heav'n, and by success° untaught   *the outcome*
10 His proud imaginations° thus displayed.   *schemes*
     "Powers and Dominions,[2] deities of Heaven,
For since no deep within her gulf can hold
Immortal vigor, though oppressed and fall'n,
I give not Heav'n for lost. From this descent
15 Celestial Virtues rising, will appear
More glorious and more dread than from no fall,
And trust themselves to fear no second fate.
Me though just right, and the fixed laws of Heav'n
Did first create your leader, next, free choice,

---

alist) society was often cited in political argument.
The simile prepares for the sudden contraction of
the devils, who can shrink or dilate at will.
6. The pygmies were supposed to live beyond the
Himalayas.
7. The belated peasant's.

8. Crowded together, and in full complement.
9. Consultation, often secret and seditious.
1. India. "Ormus": an island in the Persian Gulf,
modern Hormuz, famous for pearls.
2. Angelic orders.

20 With what besides, in counsel or in fight,
  Hath been achieved of merit, yet this loss
  Thus far at least recovered, hath much more
  Established in a safe unenvied throne
  Yielded with full consent. The happier state
25 In Heaven, which follows dignity, might draw
  Envy from each inferior; but who here
  Will envy whom the highest place exposes
  Foremost to stand against the Thunderer's aim
  Your bulwark, and condemns to greatest share
30 Of endless pain? Where there is then no good
  For which to strive, no strife can grow up there
  From faction; for none sure will claim in Hell
  Precédence, none, whose portion is so small
  Of present pain, that with ambitious mind
35 Will covet more. With this advantage then
  To union, and firm faith, and firm accord,
  More than can be in Heav'n, we now return
  To claim our just inheritance of old,
  Surer to prosper than prosperity
40 Could have assured us;[3] and by what best way,
  Whether of open war or covert guile,[4]
  We now debate; who can advise, may speak."
   He ceas'd, and next him Moloch, sceptered king
  Stood up, the strongest and the fiercest Spirit
45 That fought in Heav'n; now fiercer by despair:
  His trust was with th' Eternal to be deemed
  Equal in strength, and rather than be less
  Cared not to be at all; with that care lost
  Went all his fear: of God, or Hell, or worse
50 He recked° not, and these words thereafter spake.   *cared*
   "My sentence° is for open war: of wiles,   *judgment*
  More unexpert,° I boast not: them let those *less experienced*
  Contrive who need, or when they need, not now.
  For while they sit contriving, shall the rest,
55 Millions that stand in arms, and longing wait
  The signal to ascend, sit lingering here
  Heav'n's fugitives, and for their dwelling-place
  Accept this dark opprobrious den of shame,
  The prison of his tyranny who reigns
60 By our delay? No, let us rather choose
  Armed with Hell flames and fury all at once
  O'er Heav'n's high tow'rs to force resistless way,
  Turning our tortures into horrid° arms   *bristling, horrifying*
  Against the Torturer; when to meet the noise
65 Of his almighty engine° he shall hear   *the thunderbolt*
  Infernal thunder, and for lightning see
  Black fire and horror shot with equal rage
  Among his angels; and his throne itself

---

3. Note the play on "sure—prosper—prosperity— assure," a favorite device of Milton's.
4. A typical epic convention (in Homer, Virgil, Tasso, and elsewhere) involved councils debating war or peace, with spokesmen on each side. Satan offers only the option of war, open or covert.

Mixed with Tartarean⁵ sulfur, and strange fire,
His own invented torments. But perhaps
The way seems difficult and steep to scale
With upright wing against a higher foe.
Let such bethink them, if the sleepy drench°   *large draught*
Of that forgetful° lake benumb not still,   *causing oblivion*
That in our proper° motion we ascend   *natural*
Up to our native seat: descent and fall
To us is adverse. Who but felt of late
When the fierce foe hung on our broken rear
Insulting,⁶ and pursued us through the deep,
With what compulsion and laborious flight
We sunk thus low? Th' ascent is easy then;
Th' event° is feared; should we again provoke   *outcome*
Our stronger, some worse way his wrath may find
To our destruction: if there be in Hell
Fear to be worse destroyed: what can be worse
Than to dwell here, driven out from bliss, condemned
In this abhorrèd deep to utter woe;
Where pain of unextinguishable fire
Must exercise° us without hope of end   *vex, afflict*
The vassals⁷ of his anger, when the scourge
Inexorably, and the torturing hour
Calls us to penance? More destroyed than thus
We should be quite abolished and expire.
What fear we then? What° doubt we to incense   *why*
His utmost ire? which to the high enraged,
Will either quite consume us, and reduce
To nothing this essential,° happier far   *essence*
Than miserable to have eternal being:
Or if our substance be indeed divine,
And cannot cease to be, we are at worst
On this side nothing;⁸ and by proof we feel
Our power sufficient to disturb his Heav'n,
And with perpetual inroads to alarm,
Though inaccessible, his fatal⁹ throne:
Which if not victory is yet revenge."
    He ended frowning, and his look, denounced°   *portended*
Desperate revenge, and battle dangerous
To less than gods. On th' other side up rose
Belial, in act more graceful and humane;°   *civil, polite*
A fairer person lost not Heav'n; he seemed
For dignity composed and high exploit:
But all was false and hollow; though his tongue
Dropped manna, and could make the worse appear
The better reason,¹ to perplex and dash°   *confuse*

---

5. Tartarus is a classical name for hell.
6. With the Latin sense of stamping on; also, triumphantly scorning.
7. Servants, but perhaps also, vessels.
8. I.e., we cannot be worse off than we are now, and still live.
9. Established by Fate; also, deadly.

1. The Sophists, mercenary teachers of rhetoric in ancient Greece, were denounced by Plato for making "the worse appear / The better reason." "His tongue / Dropped manna": his honeyed words seemed like the manna supplied to the Israelites in the desert.

15   Maturest counsels: for his thoughts were low;
To vice industrious, but to nobler deeds
Timorous and slothful: yet he pleased the ear,
And with persuasive accent thus began.
      "I should be much for open war, O Peers,
20   As not behind in hate; if what was urged
Main reason to persuade immediate war,
Did not dissuade me most, and seem to cast
Ominous conjecture on the whole success:
When he who most excells in fact° of arms,   *feat*
25   In what he counsels and in what excels
Mistrustful, grounds his courage on despair
And utter dissolution, as the scope
Of all his aim, after some dire revenge.
First, what revenge? The tow'rs of Heav'n are filled
30   With armèd watch, that render all access
Impregnable; oft on the bordering deep
Encamp their legions, or with óbscure wing
Scout far and wide into the realm of Night,
Scorning surprise. Or could we break our way
35   By force, and at our heels all Hell should rise
With blackest insurrection, to confound
Heav'n's purest light, yet our great enemy
All incorruptible would on his throne
Sit unpolluted, and th' ethereal mold²
40   Incapable of stain would soon expel
Her mischief, and purge off the baser fire
Victorious. Thus repulsed, our final hope
Is flat despair: we must exasperate
Th' almighty victor to spend all his rage,
45   And that must end us, that must be our cure,
To be no more; sad cure; for who would lose,
Though full of pain, this intellectual being,
Those thoughts that wander through eternity,
To perish rather, swallowed up and lost
50   In the wide womb of uncreated night,
Devoid of sense and motion? And who knows,
Let this be good, whether our angry foe
Can give it, or will ever? How he can
Is doubtful; that he never will is sure.
55   Will he, so wise, let loose at once his ire,
Belike° through impotence, or unaware,   *perhaps*
To give his enemies their wish, and end
Them in his anger, whom his anger saves
To punish endless? 'Wherefore cease we then?'
60   Say they who counsel war, 'We are decreed,
Reserved and destined to eternal woe;
Whatever doing, what can we suffer more,
What can we suffer worse?' Is this then worst,
Thus sitting, thus consulting, thus in arms?

2. Heavenly substance, derived from "ether," the fifth and purest element, thought to be incorruptible.

165   What when we fled amain,° pursued and strook°   *headlong/struck*
With Heav'n's afflicting thunder, and besought
The deep to shelter us? This Hell then seemed
A refuge from those wounds. Or when we lay
Chained on the burning lake? That sure was worse.
170   What if the breath that kindled those grim fires
Awaked should blow them into sevenfold rage
And plunge us in the flames? Or from above
Should intermitted° vengeance arm again   *suspended*
His red right hand to plague us? What if all
175   Her° stores were opened, and this firmament   *Hell's*
Of Hell should spout her cataracts° of fire,   *cascades*
Impendent[3] horrors, threat'ning hideous fall
One day upon our heads; while we perhaps
Designing or exhorting glorious war,
180   Caught in a fiery tempest shall be hurled
Each on his rock transfixed, the sport and prey
Of racking whirlwinds, or for ever sunk
Under yon boiling ocean, wrapped in chains;
There to converse with everlasting groans,
185   Unrespited, unpitied, unreprieved,
Ages of hopeless end; this would be worse.
War therefore, open or concealed, alike
My voice dissuades; for what can force or guile[4]
With him, or who deceive his mind, whose eye
190   Views all things at one view? He from Heav'n's high
All these our motions° vain, sees and derides;   *proposals*
Not more almighty to resist our might
Than wise to frustrate all our plots and wiles.
Shall we then live thus vile, the race of Heav'n
195   Thus trampled, thus expelled to suffer here
Chains and these torments? Better these than worse
By my advice; since fate inevitable
Subdues us, and omnipotent decree,
The victor's will. To suffer, as to do,
200   Our strength is equal, nor the law unjust
That so ordains: this was at first resolved,
If we were wise, against so great a foe
Contending, and so doubtful what might fall.
I laugh, when those who at the spear are bold
205   And vent'rous, if that fail them, shrink and fear
What yet they know must follow, to endure
Exile, or ignominy, or bonds, or pain,
The sentence of their conqueror: This is now
Our doom; which if we can sustain and bear,
210   Our Súpreme Foe in time may much remit
His anger, and perhaps thus far removed
Not mind us not offending, satisfied
With what is punished; whence these raging fires

3. In the Latin sense, hanging down, threatening.
4. The verb "accomplish" or "achieve" is understood.

Will slacken, if his breath stir not their flames.
215 Our purer essence then will overcome
Their noxious vapor, or inured° not feel,   accustomed
Or changed at length, and to the place conformed
In temper and in nature, will receive
Familiar the fierce heat, and void of pain;
220 This horror will grow mild, this darkness light,
Besides what hope the never-ending flight
Of future days may bring, what chance, what change
Worth waiting, since our present lot appears
For happy though but ill, for ill not worst,[5]
225 If we procure not to ourselves more woe."
        Thus Belial, with words clothed in reason's garb,
Counseled ignoble ease and peaceful sloth,
Not peace: and after him thus Mammon spake.
        "Either to disenthrone the King of Heav'n
230 We war, if war be best, or to regain
Our own right lost: him to unthrone we then
May hope when everlasting fate shall yield
To fickle chance, and Chaos judge the strife:
The former vain to hope argues° as vain   proves
235 The latter: for what place can be for us
Within Heav'n's bound, unless Heav'n's Lord supreme
We overpower? Suppose he should relent
And publish grace to all, on promise made
Of new subjection; with what eyes could we
240 Stand in his presence humble, and receive
Strict laws imposed, to celebrate his throne
With warbled hymns, and to his Godhead sing
Forced hallelujahs; while he lordly sits
Our envied Sovran, and his altar breathes
245 Ambrosial° odors and ambrosial flowers,   fragrant, immortal
Our servile offerings. This must be our task
In Heav'n, this our delight; how wearisome
Eternity so spent in worship paid
To whom we hate. Let us not then pursue
250 By force impossible, by leave obtained
Unácceptable, though in Heav'n, our state
Of splendid vassalage,° but rather seek   servitude
Our own good from ourselves, and from our own
Live to ourselves, though in this vast recess,
255 Free, and to none accountable, preferring
Hard liberty before the easy yoke
Of servile pomp. Our greatness will appear
Then most conspicuous, when great things of small,
Useful of hurtful, prosperous of adverse
260 We can create, and in what place soe'er
Thrive under evil, and work ease out of pain
Through labor and endurance. This deep world

---

5. I.e., from the point of view of happiness, the devils are in ill state; from the point of view of evil, they
could be worse.

Of darkness do we dread? How oft amidst
Thick clouds and dark doth Heav'n's all-ruling Sire
265 Choose to reside, his glory unobscured,
And with the majesty of darkness round
Covers his throne; from whence deep thunders roar
Must'ring their rage, and Heav'n resembles Hell?
As he our darkness, cannot we his light
270 Imitate when we please? This desert soil
Wants° not her hidden luster, gems and gold;   lacks
Nor want we skill or art, from whence to raise
Magnificence; and what can Heav'n show more?
Our torments also may in length of time
275 Become our elements, these piercing fires
As soft as now severe, our temper° changed   constitution
Into their temper; which must needs remove
The sensible of pain.⁶ All things invite
To peaceful counsels, and the settled state
280 Of order, how in safety best we may
Compose° our present evils, with regard   come to terms with
Of what we are and where, dismissing quite
All thoughts of war: ye have what I advise."
       He scarce had finished, when such murmur filled
285 Th' assembly, as when hollow rocks retain
The sound of blust'ring winds, which all night long
Had roused the sea, now with hoarse cadence lull
Seafaring men o'erwatched,° whose bark by chance   worn out from watching
Or pinnace° anchors in a craggy bay   boat
290 After the tempest: such applause was heard
As Mammon ended, and his sentence pleased,
Advising peace: for such another field°   battlefield
They dreaded worse than Hell: so much the fear
Of thunder and the sword of Michaël⁷
295 Wrought still within them; and no less desire
To found this nether empire, which might rise
By policy,° and long process of time,   statecraft
In emulation opposite to Heav'n.
Which then Beëlzebub perceived, than whom,
300 Satan except, none higher sat, with grave
Aspect he rose, and in his rising seemed
A pillar of state; deep on his front° engraven   brow
Deliberation sat and public care;
And princely counsel in his face yet shone,
305 Majestic though in ruin: sage he stood
With Atlantean⁸ shoulders fit to bear
The weight of mightiest monarchies; his look
Drew audience and attention still as night
Or summer's noontide air, while thus he spake.
310   "Thrones and imperial Powers, offspring of Heav'n
Ethereal Virtues; or these titles⁹ now
Must we renounce, and changing style be called

---

6. Pain felt by the senses.
7. The warrior angel, chief of the angelic armies.
8. Worthy of Atlas, the Titan who as a punishment

for rebellion was condemned to hold up the heavens on his shoulders.
9. The official titles of angelic orders.

Princes of Hell? for so the popular vote
Inclines, here to continue, and build up here
15 A growing empire. Doubtless! while we dream,
And know not that the King of Heav'n hath doomed
This place our dungeon, not our safe retreat
Beyond his potent arm, to live exempt
From Heav'n's high jurisdiction, in new league
20 Banded against his throne, but to remain
In strictest bondage, though thus far removed,
Under th' inevitable curb, reserved
His captive multitude: for he, be sure,
In height or depth, still first and last will reign
25 Sole King, and of his kingdom lose no part
By our revolt, but over Hell extend
His empire, and with iron scepter rule
Us here, as with his golden those in Heav'n.
What° sit we then projecting peace and war?   *why*
30 War hath determined us,[1] and foiled with loss
Irreparable; terms of peace yet none
Vouchsafed or sought; for what peace will be giv'n
To us enslaved, but custody severe,
And stripes, and arbitrary punishment
35 Inflicted? And what peace can we return,
But, to our power,[2] hostility and hate,
Untamed reluctance,° and revenge though slow,   *resistance*
Yet ever plotting how the conqueror least
May reap his conquest, and may least rejoice
40 In doing what we most in suffering feel?
Nor will occasion want,° nor shall we need   *be lacking*
With dangerous expedition to invade
Heav'n, whose high walls fear no assault or siege,
Or ambush from the deep. What if we find
45 Some easier enterprise? There is a place
(If ancient and prophetic fame° in Heav'n   *rumor*
Err not) another world, the happy seat
Of some new race called Man, about this time
To be created like to us, though less
50 In power and excellence, but favored more
Of him who rules above; so was his will
Pronounced among the gods, and by an oath,
That shook Heav'n's whole circumference, confirmed.
Thither let us bend all our thoughts, to learn
55 What creatures there inhabit, of what mold,
Or substance, how endued,° and what their power,   *endowed*
And where their weakness, how attempted° best,   *attacked, tempted*
By force or subtlety. Though Heav'n be shut,
And Heav'n's high arbitrator sit secure
60 In his own strength, this place may lie exposed,
The utmost border of his kingdom, left
To their defense who hold it:[3] here perhaps

---

1. I.e., war has decided the question for us, but also limited us.
2. I.e., to the best of our power.
3. To be defended by the occupants.

Some advantageous act may be achieved
By sudden onset, either with Hell fire
365 To waste° his whole creation, or possess   *lay waste*
All as our own, and drive as we were driven,
The puny habitants, or if not drive,
Seduce them to our party, that their God
May prove their foe, and with repenting hand
370 Abolish his own works.⁴ This would surpass
Common revenge, and interrupt his joy
In our confusion, and our joy upraise
In his disturbance; when his darling sons
Hurled headlong to partake with us, shall curse
375 Their frail original,° and faded bliss,   *originator, parent*
Faded so soon. Advise° if this be worth   *consider*
Attempting, or to sit in darkness here
Hatching vain empires." Thus Beëlzebub
Pleaded his devilish counsel, first devised
380 By Satan, and in part proposed: for whence,
But from the author of all ill could spring
So deep a malice, to confound° the race   *ruin*
Of mankind in one root,⁵ and earth with Hell
To mingle and involve, done all to spite
385 The great Creator? But their spite still serves
His glory to augment. The bold design
Pleased highly those infernal States,° and joy   *nobles*
Sparkled in all their eyes; with full assent
They vote: whereat his speech he thus renews.
390   "Well have ye judged, well ended long debate,
Synod of gods, and like to what ye are,
Great things resolved, which from the lowest deep
Will once more lift us up, in spite of fate,
Nearer our ancient seat; perhaps in view
395 Of those bright confines, whence with neighboring arms
And opportune excursion we may chance
Re-enter Heav'n; or else in some mild zone
Dwell not unvisited of Heav'n's fair light
Secure, and at the bright'ning orient beam
400 Purge off this gloom; the soft delicious air,
To heal the scar of these corrosive fires
Shall breathe her balm. But first whom shall we send
In search of this new world, whom shall we find
Sufficient? Who shall tempt° with wand'ring feet   *attempt, venture*
405 The dark unbottomed infinite abyss
And through the palpable obscure⁶ find out
His uncouth° way, or spread his aery flight   *unknown*
Upborne with indefatigable wings
Over the vast abrupt,⁷ ere he arrive

---

4. Cf. Genesis 6.7: "And the Lord said, I will destroy man [and all other creatures]; for it repenteth me that I have made them."
5. Adam, the first man, is the "root" of the human race.

6. Darkness so thick it can be felt (cf. Exodus 10.21).
7. Chaos, a striking example of sound imitating sense.

410 The happy isle? what strength, what art can then
Suffice, or what evasion bear him safe
Through the strict senteries° and stations thick   *sentries*
Of angels watching round? Here he had need
All circumspection, and we now no less
415 Choice° in our suffrage; for on whom we send,   *discrimination*
The weight of all and our last hope relies."
    This said, he sat; and expectation held
His look suspense,[8] awaiting who appeared
To second, or oppose, or undertake
420 The perilous attempt: but all sat mute,
Pondering the danger with deep thoughts; and each
In other's count'nance read his own dismay
Astonished. None among the choice and prime
Of those Heav'n-warring champions could be found
425 So hardy as to proffer or accept
Alone the dreadful voyage; till at last
Satan, whom now transcendent glory raised
Above his fellows, with monarchal pride
Conscious of highest worth, unmoved thus spake.
430   "O progeny of Heav'n, empyreal Thrones,
With reason hath deep silence and demur°   *hesitation*
Seized us, though undismayed: long is the way
And hard, that out of Hell leads up to light;
Our prison strong, this huge convex of fire,
435 Outrageous to devour, immures us round
Ninefold,[9] and gates of burning adamant
Barred over us prohibit all egress.
These passed, if any pass, the void profound
Of unessential Night receives him next
440 Wide gaping, and with utter loss of being
Threatens him, plunged in that abortive gulf.[1]
If thence he scape into whatever world,
Or unknown region, what remains him less°   *awaits him except*
Than unknown dangers and as hard escape?
445 But I should ill become this throne, O Peers,
And this imperial sovranty, adorned
With splendor, armed with power, if aught proposed
And judged of public moment,° in the shape   *importance*
Of difficulty or danger could deter
450 Me from attempting. Wherefore do I assume
These royalties, and not refuse to reign,
Refusing° to accept as great a share   *if I refuse*
Of hazard as of honor, due alike
To him who reigns, and so much to him due
455 Of hazard more, as he above the rest
High honored sits? Go therefore mighty Powers,
Terror of Heav'n, though fall'n; intend° at home,   *consider*
While here shall be our home, what best may ease

---

8. I.e., everyone sat waiting in suspense.
9. Hell's fiery walls and gate have nine thicknesses
(see lines 645ff.).

1. Chaos is a womb in which all potential forms
fragment (see lines 900ff.) "Unessential" (line
439): i.e., having no real essence.

The present misery, and render Hell
460 More tolerable; if there be cure or charm
To respite or deceive, or slack the pain
Of this ill mansion: intermit no watch
Against a wakeful foe, while I abroad
Through all the coasts of dark destruction seek
465 Deliverance for us all: this enterprise
None shall partake with me." Thus saying rose
The monarch, and prevented° all reply,   *forestalled*
Prudent, lest from his resolution raised°   *roused*
Others among the chief might offer now
470 (Certain to be refused) what erst they feared;
And so refused might in opinion stand
His rivals, winning cheap the high repute
Which he through hazard huge must earn. But they
Dreaded not more th' adventure than his voice
475 Forbidding; and at once with him they rose;
Their rising all at once was as the sound
Of thunder heard remote. Towards him they bend
With awful° reverence prone; and as a god   *full of awe*
Extol him equal to the Highest in Heav'n:
480 Nor failed they to express how much they praised,
That for the general safety he despised
His own: for neither do the Spirits damned
Lose all their virtue; lest bad men should boast
Their specious° deeds on earth, which glory excites,   *pretending to worth*
485 Or close° ambition varnished o'er with zeal.   *secret*
    Thus they their doubtful consultations dark
Ended rejoicing in their matchless chief:
As when from mountain tops the dusky clouds
Ascending, while the north wind sleeps, o'erspread
490 Heav'n's cheerful face, the louring element°   *threatening sky*
Scowls o'er the darkened landscape snow, or show'r;
If chance the radiant sun with farewell sweet
Extend his evening beam, the fields revive,
The birds their notes renew, and bleating herds
495 Attest their joy, that hill and valley rings.
O shame to men! Devil with devil damned
Firm concord holds, men only disagree
Of creatures rational, though under hope
Of heavenly grace: and God proclaiming peace,
500 Yet live in hatred, enmity, and strife
Among themselves, and levy cruel wars,
Wasting the earth, each other to destroy:
As if (which might induce us to accord)
Man had not hellish foes enow° besides,   *enough*
505 That day and night for his destruction wait.
    The Stygian council thus dissolved; and forth
In order came the grand infernal peers:
Midst came their mighty paramount,° and seemed   *supreme ruler*
Alone th' antagonist of Heav'n, nor less
510 Than Hell's dread emperor with pomp supreme,

And god-like imitated state; him round
A globe° of fiery Seraphim enclosed   *band, circle*
With bright emblazonry and horrent² arms.
Then of their session ended they bid cry
515 With trumpet's regal sound the great result:
Toward the four winds four speedy Cherubim
Put to their mouths the sounding alchemy³
By herald's voice explained; the hollow abyss
Heard far and wide, and all the host of hell
520 With deaf'ning shout, returned them loud acclaim.
Thence more at ease their minds and somewhat raised
By false presumptuous hope, the rangèd° powers   *arrayed in ranks*
Disband, and wand'ring, each his several way
Pursues, as inclination or sad choice
525 Leads him perplexed, where he may likeliest find
Truce to his restless thoughts, and entertain°   *while away*
The irksome hours, till his great chief return.
Part on the plain, or in the air sublime°   *aloft*
Upon the wing, or in swift race contend,
530 As at th' Olympian games or Pythian fields;⁴
Part curb their fiery steeds, or shun the goal⁵
With rapid wheels, or fronted° brígades form.   *confronting*
As when to warn proud cities war appears
Waged in the troubled sky, and armies rush
535 To battle in the clouds,⁶ before each van°   *vanguard*
Prick° forth the aery knights, and couch their spears   *spur*
Till thickest legions close; with feats of arms
From either end of Heav'n the welkin° burns.   *sky*
Others with vast Typhoean⁷ rage more fell
540 Rend up both rocks and hills, and ride the air
In Whirlwind; Hell scarce holds the wild uproar.
As when Alcides from Oechalia crowned
With conquest, felt th' envenomed robe, and tore
Through pain up by the roots Thessalian pines,
545 And Lichas from the top of Oeta threw
Into th' Euboic sea.⁸ Others more mild,
Retreated in a silent valley, sing
With notes angelical to many a harp
Their own heroic deeds and hapless fall
550 By doom of battle; and complain that fate
Free virtue should enthrall to force or chance.
Their song was partial,° but the harmony   *prejudiced*
(What could it less when Spirits immortal sing?)
Suspended° Hell, and took with ravishment   *held in suspense*
555 The thronging audience. In discourse more sweet

2. Bristling. "Emblazonry": decorated shields.
3. Trumpets (made of the goldlike alloy, brass).
4. The Olympic games were held at Olympia, the Pythian games at Delphi. Games celebrating a (usually dead) hero are an epic convention.
5. To drive a chariot as close as possible around a column without hitting it.
6. The appearance of warfare in the skies, reported before several notable battles, portends trouble on earth.
7. Like that of Typhon, the hundred-headed Titan (see 1.199).
8. Wearing a poisoned robe given him in a deception, Hercules in his dying agonies threw his beloved companion Lichas, along with a good part of Mount Oeta, into the sea of Euboea, near Thermopylae.

(For eloquence the soul, song charms the sense)
Others apart sat on a hill retired,
In thoughts more elevate, and reasoned high
Of providence, foreknowledge, will, and fate,
560 Fixed fate, free will, foreknowledge absolute,
And found no end, in wand'ring mazes lost.
Of good and evil much they argued then,
Of happiness and final misery,
Passion and apathy,[9] and glory and shame,
565 Vain wisdom all, and false philosophy:
Yet with a pleasing sorcery could charm
Pain for a while or anguish, and excite
Fallacious hope, or arm th' obdurèd° breast   *hardened*
With stubborn patience as with triple steel.
570 Another part in squadrons and gross° bands,   *solid, dense*
On bold adventure to discover wide
That dismal world, if any clime perhaps
Might yield them easier habitation, bend
Four ways their flying march, along the banks
575 Of four infernal rivers that disgorge
Into the burning lake their baleful streams:[1]
Abhorrèd Styx the flood of deadly hate,
Sad Acheron of sorrow, black and deep;
Cocytus, named of lamentation loud
580 Heard on the rueful stream; fierce Phlegethon
Whose waves of torrent fire inflame with rage.
Far off from these a slow and silent stream,
Lethe the river of oblivion rolls
Her wat'ry labyrinth, whereof who drinks,
585 Forthwith his former state and being forgets,
Forgets both joy and grief, pleasure and pain.
Beyond this flood a frozen continent
Lies dark and wild, beat with perpetual storms
Of whirlwind and dire hail, which on firm land
590 Thaws not, but gathers heap,[2] and ruin seems
Of ancient pile; all else deep snow and ice,
A gulf profound as that Serbonian bog[3]
Betwixt Damiata and Mount Casius old,
Where armies whole have sunk: the parching air
595 Burns frore,° and cold performs th' effect of fire.   *frozen*
Thither by harpy-footed[4] Furies haled,
At certain revolutions° all the damned   *recurring times*
Are brought: and feel by turns the bitter change
Of fierce extremes, extremes by change more fierce,
600 From beds of raging fire to starve° in ice   *make numb*

9. The Stoic goal of freedom from passion.
1. These four rivers are traditional in hellish geography. Milton distinguishes them by the original meanings of their Greek names: Styx means "hateful," Acheron "woeful," etc. Lethe is "far off" and quite different from the others, oblivion being a desired state in Hell.

2. In a heap, resembling the ruin of an old building ("ancient pile").
3. Lake Serbonis, once famous for its quicksands, lies near the city of Damiata, just east of the Nile.
4. Taloned. In Greek mythology the harpies (monsters with women's faces) carried off individuals to the Furies, who avenged crimes.

Their soft ethereal warmth, and there to pine
Immovable, infixed, and frozen round,
Periods of time; thence hurried back to fire.
They ferry over this Lethean sound
05 Both to and fro, their sorrow to augment,
And wish and struggle, as they pass, to reach
The tempting stream, with one small drop to lose
In sweet forgetfulness all pain and woe,
All in one moment, and so near the brink;
10 But fate withstands, and to oppose th' attempt
Medusa[5] with Gorgonian terror guards
The ford, and of itself the water flies
All taste of living wight, as once it fled
The lip of Tantalus.[6] Thus roving on
15 In cónfused march forlorn, th' advent'rous bands
With shudd'ring horror pale, and eyes aghast
Viewed first their lamentable lot, and found
No rest: through many a dark and dreary vale
They passed, and many a region dolorous,
20 O'er many a frozen, many a fiery alp,°   *volcano*
Rocks, caves, lakes, fens, bogs, dens, and shades of death,
A universe of death, which God by curse
Created evil, for evil only good,
Where all life dies, death lives, and nature breeds,
25 Perverse, all monstrous, all prodigious things,
Abominable, inutterable, and worse
Than fables yet have feigned, or fear conceived,
Gorgons and Hydras, and Chimeras[7] dire.
   Meanwhile the Adversary of God and man,
30 Satan, with thoughts inflamed of highest design,
Puts on swift wings,° and towards the gates of hell   *flies swiftly*
Explores his solitary flight; sometimes
He scours the right-hand coast, sometimes the left,
Now shaves with level wing the deep, then soars
35 Up to the fiery concave° tow'ring high.   *vault*
As when far off at sea a fleet descried
Hangs on the clouds, by equinoctial winds°   *from the equator*
Close sailing from Bengala,° or the isles   *Bengal*
Of Ternate and Tidore,[8] whence merchants bring
40 Their spicy drugs: they on the trading flood
Through the wide Ethiopian to the Cape
Ply stemming nightly toward the pole:[9] so seemed
Far off the flying Fiend. At last appear
Hell bounds high reaching to the horrid roof,
45 And thrice threefold the gates; three folds were brass,

---

5. One of the three Gorgons, women with snaky hair, scaly bodies, and boar's tusks, the sight of whose faces changed men to stone.
6. Tantalus, afflicted with a raging thirst, stood in the middle of a lake, the water of which always receded when he tried to drink (hence, "tantalize").
7. The Hydra was a serpent whose multiple heads grew back when severed; the Chimera was a fire-breathing creature, part lion, part dragon, part goat.
8. Two of the Molucca or "Spice" Islands, modern Indonesia.
9. The South Pole. "Ethiopian": the Indian Ocean. "The Cape" is the Cape of Good Hope.

Three iron, three of adamantine rock,
Impenetrable, impaled with circling fire,
Yet unconsumed. Before the gates there sat
On either side a formidable shape;[1]
650 The one seemed woman to the waist, and fair,
But ended foul in many a scaly fold
Voluminous and vast, a serpent armed
With mortal sting: about her middle round
A cry° of hell-hounds never ceasing barked   *pack*
655 With wide Cerberean[2] mouths full loud, and rung
A hideous peal: yet, when they list, would creep,
If aught disturbed their noise, into her womb,
And kennel there, yet there still barked and howled,
Within unseen. Far less abhorred than these
660 Vexed Scylla[3] bathing in the sea that parts
Calabria from the hoarse Trinacrian shore:
Nor uglier follow the night-hag,[4] when called
In secret, riding through the air she comes
Lured with the smell of infant blood, to dance
665 With Lapland witches, while the laboring° moon   *troubled*
Eclipses at their charms.° The other shape,   *magic*
If shape it might be called that shape had none
Distinguishable in member, joint, or limb,
Or substance might be called that shadow seemed,
670 For each seemed either; black it stood as night,
Fierce as ten Furies, terrible as hell,
And shook a dreadful dart; what seemed his head
The likeness of a kingly crown had on.
Satan was now at hand, and from his seat
675 The monster moving onward came as fast
With horrid strides. Hell trembled as he strode.
Th' undaunted Fiend what this might be admired,°   *wondered*
Admired, not feared; God and his Son except,
Created thing naught valued he nor shunned;
680 And with disdainful look thus first began.
    "Whence and what art thou, execrable shape,
That dar'st, though grim and terrible, advance
Thy miscreated front° athwart my way   *misshapen face*
To yonder gates? Through them I mean to pass,
685 That be assured, without leave asked of thee:
Retire, or taste° thy folly, and learn by proof,   *experience*
Hell-born, not to contend with Spirits of Heav'n."
    To whom the goblin full of wrath replied:
"Art thou that traitor angel, art thou he,
690 Who first broke peace in Heav'n and faith, till then

---

1. The allegorical figures of Sin and Death are founded on James 1.15: "Then when lust hath conceived, it bringeth forth sin: and sin, when it is finished, bringeth forth death." But the incestuous relations of Sin and Death are Milton's own invention. Physically, Sin is modeled on Virgil's or Ovid's Scylla, with some touches adopted from Spenser's Error. Death is a traditional figure, vague and vast.
2. Like Cerberus, the multiheaded hound of Hell.

3. Circe, out of jealousy, threw poison into the water where Scylla bathed, in the straits between Calabria and Sicily ("Trinacria"); the poison caused Scylla to develop a ring of barking, snapping dogs around her waist.
4. Hecate (three syllables), goddess of sorcery. She attends orgies of witches in Lapland (famous for witchcraft), drawn by the blood of babies sacrificed for the occasion.

Unbroken, and in proud rebellious arms
Drew after him the third part of Heav'n's sons
Conjured° against the Highest, for which both thou   *sworn together*
And they outcast from God, are here condemned
595 To waste eternal days in woe and pain?
And reckon'st thou thyself with Spirits of Heav'n,
Hell-doomed, and breath'st defiance here and scorn,
Where I reign king, and to enrage thee more,
Thy king and lord? Back to thy punishment,
600 False fugitive, and to thy speed add wings,
Lest with a whip of scorpions I pursue
Thy ling'ring, or with one stroke of this dart
Strange horror seize thee, and pangs unfelt before."
       So spake the grisly terror, and in shape,
605 So speaking and so threat'ning, grew tenfold
More dreadful and deform: on th' other side
Incensed with indignation Satan stood
Unterrified, and like a comet burned
That fires the length of Ophiuchus⁵ huge
610 In th' arctic sky, and from his horrid° hair   *bristling*
Shakes pestilence and war. Each at the head
Leveled his deadly aim; their fatal hands
No second stroke intend, and such a frown
Each cast at th' other, as when, two black clouds
615 With Heav'n's artillery fraught,⁶ come rattling on
Over the Caspian,⁷ then stand front to front
Hov'ring a space, till winds the signal blow
To join their dark encounter in mid-air:
So frowned the mighty combatants, that Hell
620 Grew darker at their frown, so matched they stood;
For never but once more was either like
To meet so great a foe.⁸ And now great deeds
Had been achieved, whereof all Hell had rung,
Had not the snaky sorceress that sat
625 Fast by Hell gate, and kept the fatal key,
Ris'n, and with hideous outcry rushed between.
       "O father, what intends thy hand," she cried,
"Against thy only son?⁹ What fury O son,
Possesses thee to bend that mortal dart
630 Against thy father's head? And know'st for whom;
For him who sits above and laughs the while
At thee ordained his drudge, to execute
Whate'er his wrath, which he calls justice, bids,
His wrath which one day will destroy ye both."
635   She spake, and at her words the hellish pest
Forbore, then these to her Satan returned.
       "So strange thy outcry, and thy words so strange
Thou interposest, that my sudden hand

5. A vast northern constellation, "The Serpent Bearer."
6. Loaded with thunderbolts.
7. The Caspian is a particularly stormy area.

8. I.e., the Son of God.
9. Sin, Death, and Satan, in their various interrelations, parody obscenely the relations between God and the Son, Adam and Eve.

Prevented° spares to tell thee yet by deeds　　　　　　*forestalled*
740　What it intends; till first I know of thee,
What thing thou art, thus double-formed, and why
In this infernal vale first met thou call'st
Me father, and that phantasm call'st my son?
I know thee not, nor ever saw till now
745　Sight more detestable than him and thee."
　　　T' whom thus the portress of Hell gate replied:
"Hast thou forgot me then, and do I seem
Now in thine eye so foul, once deemed so fair
In Heav'n, when at th' assembly, and in sight
750　Of all the Seraphim with thee combined
In bold conspiracy against Heav'n's King,
All on a sudden miserable pain
Surprised thee, dim thine eyes, and dizzy swum
In darkness, while thy head flames thick and fast
755　Threw forth, till on the left side op'ning wide,
Likest to thee in shape and count'nance bright,
Then shining heav'nly fair, a goddess armed
Out of thy head I sprung:[1] amazement seized
All th' host of Heav'n; back they recoiled afraid
760　At first, and called me Sin, and for a sign
Portentous held me; but familiar grown,
I pleased, and with attractive graces won
The most averse, thee chiefly, who full oft
Thyself in me thy perfect image viewing
765　Becam'st enamored, and such joy thou took'st
With me in secret, that my womb conceived
A growing burden. Meanwhile war arose,
And fields were fought in Heav'n; wherein remained
(For what could else) to our almighty foe
770　Clear victory, to our part loss and rout
Through all the empyrean: down they fell
Driv'n headlong from the pitch° of Heaven, down　　　*summit*
Into this deep, and in the general fall
I also; at which time this powerful key
775　Into my hand was giv'n, with charge to keep
These gates for ever shut, which none can pass
Without my op'ning. Pensive here I sat
Alone, but long I sat not, till my womb
Pregnant by thee, and now excessive grown
780　Prodigious motion felt and rueful throes.
At last this odious offspring whom thou seest
Thine own begotten, breaking violent way
Tore through my entrails, that with fear and pain
Distorted, all my nether shape thus grew
785　Transformed: but he my inbred enemy
Forth issued, brandishing his fatal dart
Made to destroy: I fled, and cried out 'Death';
Hell trembled at the hideous name, and sighed

---

1. As Athena sprang full-grown from the head of Zeus.

From all her caves, and back resounded 'Death.'
790 I fled, but he pursued (though more, it seems,
Inflamed with lust than rage) and swifter far,
Me overtook his mother all dismayed,
And in embraces forcible and foul
Engend'ring with me, of that rape begot
795 These yelling monsters that with ceaseless cry
Surround me, as thou saw'st, hourly conceived
And hourly born, with sorrow infinite
To me, for when they list,° into the womb   *wish*
That bred them they return, and howl and gnaw
800 My bowels, their repast; then bursting forth
Afresh with conscious terrors vex me round,
That rest or intermission none I find.
Before mine eyes in opposition sits
Grim Death my son and foe, who sets them on,
805 And me his parent would full soon devour
For want of other prey, but that he knows
His end with mine involved; and knows that I
Should prove a bitter morsel, and his bane,
Whenever that shall be; so fate pronounced.
810 But thou O father, I forewarn thee, shun
His deadly arrow; neither vainly hope
To be invulnerable in those bright arms,
Though tempered heav'nly, for that mortal dint,°   *blow*
Save he who reigns above, none can resist."
815 She finished, and the subtle Fiend his lore°   *lesson*
Soon learned, now milder, and thus answered smooth.
"Dear daughter, since thou claim'st me for thy sire,
And my fair son here show'st me, the dear pledge
Of dalliance had with thee in Heav'n, and joys
820 Then sweet, now sad to mention, through dire change
Befall'n us unforeseen, unthought of, know
I come no enemy, but to set free
From out this dark and dismal house of pain,
Both him and thee, and all the heav'nly host
825 Of Spirits that in our just pretenses° armed   *claims*
Fell with us from on high: from them I go
This uncouth errand sole,[2] and one for all
Myself expose, with lonely steps to tread
Th' unfounded° deep, and through the void immense *bottomless*
830 To search with wand'ring quest a place foretold
Should be, and, by concurring signs, ere now
Created vast and round, a place of bliss
In the purlieus° of Heav'n, and therein placed   *outskirts*
A race of upstart creatures, to supply
835 Perhaps our vacant room, though more removed,
Lest Heav'n surcharged° with potent multitude *overcrowded*
Might hap to move new broils:° be this or aught *controversies*
Than this more secret now designed, I haste

---

2. Unknown journey—a parody of Christ's errand on earth (3.236–65).

To know, and this once known, shall soon return,
840 And bring ye to the place where thou and Death
Shall dwell at ease, and up and down unseen
Wing silently the buxom° air, embalmed°   *yielding/made fragrant*
With odors; there ye shall be fed and filled
Immeasurably, all things shall be your prey."
845 He ceased, for both seemed highly pleased, and Death
Grinned horrible a ghastly smile, to hear
His famine° should be filled, and blessed his maw   *ravenous hunger*
Destined to that good hour: no less rejoiced
His mother bad, and thus bespake her sire.
850   "The key of this infernal pit by due,
And by command of Heav'n's all-powerful King
I keep, by him forbidden to unlock
These adamantine gates; against all force
Death ready stands to interpose his dart,
855 Fearless to be o'ermatched by living might.
But what owe I to his commands above
Who hates me, and hath hither thrust me down
Into this gloom of Tartarus profound,
To sit in hateful office here confined,
860 Inhabitant of Heav'n, and heav'nly-born,
Here in perpetual agony and pain,
With terrors and with clamors compassed round
Of mine own brood, that on my bowels feed?
Thou art my father, thou my author, thou
865 My being gav'st me; whom should I obey
But thee, whom follow? Thou wilt bring me soon
To that new world of light and bliss, among
The gods who live at ease, where I shall reign
At thy right hand voluptuous,[3] as beseems
870 Thy daughter and thy darling, without end."
    Thus saying, from her side the fatal key,
Sad instrument of all our woe, she took;
And towards the gate rolling her bestial train,[4]
Forthwith the huge portcullis high up drew,
875 Which but herself not all the Stygian powers°   *armies of Hell*
Could once have moved; then in the key-hole turns
Th' intrícate wards, and every bolt and bar
Of massy iron or solid rock with ease
Unfastens: on a sudden open fly
880 With impetuous recoil and jarring sound
Th' infernal doors, and on their hinges grate
Harsh thunder, that the lowest bottom shook
Of Erebus.° She opened, but to shut   *Hell*
Excelled° her power; the gates wide open stood,   *exceeded*
885 That with extended wings a bannered host
Under spread ensigns° marching might pass through   *flags, standards*
With horse and chariots ranked in loose array;

---

3. As the Son sits at God's right hand, Sin will at   *Paradise Lost* 3.250–80.
Satan's, a blasphemous parody of the Creed and of   4. I.e. accompanied by her yelping offspring.

So wide they stood, and like a furnace mouth
Cast forth redounding° smoke and ruddy flame.   *billowing*
90 Before their eyes in sudden view appear
The secrets of the hoary deep, a dark
Illimitable° ocean without bound,   *without limit*
Without dimension, where length, breadth, and height,
And time and place are lost; where eldest Night
95 And Chaos, ancestors of Nature, hold
Eternal anarchy, amidst the noise
Of endless wars, and by confusion stand.
For Hot, Cold, Moist, and Dry, four champions fierce
Strive here for mastery, and to battle bring
100 Their embryon atoms;[5] they around the flag
Of each his faction, in their several clans,
Light-armed or heavy, sharp, smooth, swift or slow,
Swarm populous, unnumbered as the sands
Of Barca or Cyrene's torrid soil,[6]
105 Levied to side with warring winds, and poise[7]
Their lighter wings. To whom these most adhere,
He rules a moment; Chaos[8] umpire sits,
And by decision more embroils the fray
By which he reigns: next him high arbiter
110 Chance governs all. Into this wild abyss,
The womb of Nature and perhaps her grave,
Of neither sea, nor shore, nor air, nor fire,
But all these in their pregnant causes° mixed   *seeds*
Confus'dly, and which thus must ever fight,
115 Unless th' Almighty Maker them ordain
His dark materials to create more worlds,
Into this wild abyss the wary Fiend
Stood on the brink of Hell and looked a while,
Pondering his voyage; for no narrow frith°   *channel, firth*
120 He had to cross. Nor was his ear less pealed°   *dinned*
With noises loud and ruinous (to compare
Great things with small) than when Bellona[9] storms,
With all her battering engines bent to raze
Some capital city; or less than if this frame°   *structure*
125 Of Heav'n were falling, and these elements
In mutiny had from her axle torn
The steadfast earth. At last his sail-broad vans°   *wings*
He spreads for flight, and in the surging smoke
Uplifted spurns the ground, thence many a league
130 As in a cloudy chair ascending rides
Audacious, but that seat soon failing, meets
A vast vacuity: all unawares
Flutt'ring his pennons[1] vain plumb down he drops

---

5. These subatomic qualities combine together in nature to form the four elements, fire, earth, water, and air, but they struggle endlessly in Chaos, where the atoms of these elements remain undeveloped (in "embryon").
6. Cities built on the shifting sands of North Africa.
7. Give weight to. "Levied": both enlisted and raised up.
8. Chaos is both the place where confusion reigns and personified confusion itself.
9. Goddess of war.
1. Useless wings ("pinions").

Ten thousand fathom deep, and to this hour
935 Down had been falling, had not by ill chance
The strong rebuff° of some tumultuous cloud   *counterblast*
Instinct° with fire and niter° hurried him   *filled/saltpeter*
As many miles aloft: that fury stayed,
Quenched in a boggy Syrtis,[2] neither sea,
940 Nor good dry land: night foundered on he fares,
Treading the crude consistence, half on foot,
Half flying; behoves° him now both oar and sail.   *befits*
As when a gryphon through the wilderness
With wingèd course o'er hill or moory° dale,   *marshy*
945 Pursues the Arimaspian, who by stealth
Had from his wakeful custody purloined
The guarded gold:[3] so eagerly the Fiend
O'er bog or steep, through strait, rough, dense, or rare,
With head, hands, wings, or feet pursues his way,
950 And swims or sinks, or wades, or creeps, or flies:
At length a universal hubbub wild
Of stunning sounds and voices all confused
Borne through the hollow dark assaults his ear
With loudest vehemence: thither he plies,
955 Undaunted to meet there whatever Power
Or Spirit of the nethermost abyss
Might in that noise reside, of whom to ask
Which way the nearest coast of darkness lies
Bordering on light; when straight behold the throne
960 Of Chaos, and his dark pavilion spread
Wide on the wasteful deep; with him enthroned
Sat sable-vested Night, eldest of things,
The consort of his reign; and by them stood
Orcus and Ades,[4] and the dreaded name
965 Of Demogorgon,[5] Rumor next and Chance,
And Tumult and Confusion all embroiled,
And Discord with a thousand various mouths.
    T' whom Satan turning boldly, thus. "Ye Powers
And Spirits of this nethermost abyss,
970 Chaos and ancient Night, I come no spy,
With purpose to explore or to disturb
The secrets of your realm, but by constraint
Wand'ring this darksome desert, as my way
Lies through your spacious empire up to light,
975 Alone, and without guide, half lost, I seek
What readiest path leads where your gloomy bounds
Confine with° Heav'n; or if some other place   *border on*
From your dominion won, th' Ethereal King
Possesses lately, thither to arrive
980 I travel this profound;° direct my course;   *deep pit*
Directed, no mean recompense it brings

2. Quicksand in North African gulfs, famous for their shifting sandbars.
3. Gryphons, fabulous creatures, half-eagle, half-lion, hoarded gold which was stolen from them by the one-eyed Arimaspians.
4. Latin and Greek names of Pluto, god of Hell.
5. A mysterious deity associated with Fate; Milton elsewhere identifies him with Chaos.

To your behoof,° if I that region lost,   *on your behalf*
All usurpation thence expelled, reduce
To her original darkness and your sway
85 (Which is my present journey)[6] and once more
Erect the standard there of ancient Night;
Yours be th' advantage all, mine the revenge."
    Thus Satan; and him thus the anarch[7] old
With falt'ring speech and visage incomposed°   *disordered*
90 Answered. "I know thee, stranger, who thou art,
That mighty leading angel, who of late
Made head against Heav'n's King, though overthrown.
I saw and heard, for such a numerous host
Fled not in silence through the frighted deep
95 With ruin upon ruin, rout on rout,
Confusion worse confounded; and Heav'n gates
Poured out by millions her victorious bands
Pursuing. I upon my frontiers here
Keep residence; if all I can will serve,
100 That little which is left so to defend,
Encroached on still° through our intestine broils°   *constantly/civil wars*
Weak'ning the scepter of old Night: first Hell
Your dungeon stretching far and wide beneath;
Now lately heaven and earth,[8] another world
105 Hung o'er my realm, linked in a golden chain
To that side Heav'n from whence your legions fell:
If that way be your walk, you have not far;
So much the nearer danger; go and speed;
Havoc and spoil and ruin are my gain."
110   He ceased; and Satan stayed not to reply,
But glad that now his sea should find a shore,
With fresh alacrity and force renewed
Springs upward like a pyramid of fire
Into the wild expanse, and through the shock
115 Of fighting elements, on all sides round
Environed wins his way; harder beset
And more endangered, than when Argo passed
Through Bosporus betwixt the justling rocks:[9]
Or when Ulysses on the larboard shunned
120 Charybdis, and by th' other whirlpool steered.[1]
So he with difficulty and labor hard
Moved on, with difficulty and labor he;
But he once passed, soon after when man fell,
Strange alteration! Sin and Death amain°   *at full speed*
125 Following his track, such was the will of Heav'n,
Paved after him a broad and beaten way
Over the dark abyss, whose boiling gulf

6. The purpose of my present journey.
7. Chaos is not monarch of his realm but, appropriately, "anarch," nonruler.
8. The cosmos, with its own "heaven" (not the empyrean, the Heaven of God and the angels).
9. Jason and his fifty Argonauts, sailing through the Bosporus to the Black Sea in pursuit of the Golden Fleece, had to pass through the Symplegades, or clashing rocks.
1. Homer's Ulysses, sailing where Italy almost touches Sicily, had to pass between Charybdis, a whirlpool, and Scylla, a monster who devoured six of his men (not another whirlpool, as used here).

Tamely endured a bridge of wondrous length
From Hell continued reaching th' utmost orb[2]
1030 Of this frail world; by which the Spirits perverse
With easy intercourse pass to and fro
To tempt or punish mortals, except whom
God and good angels guard by special grace.
But now at last the sacred influence
1035 Of light appears, and from the walls of Heav'n
Shoots far into the bosom of dim Night
A glimmering dawn; here Nature first begins
Her farthest verge,° and Chaos to retire   threshold
As from her outmost works a broken foe
1040 With tumult less and with less hostile din,
That° Satan with less toil, and now with ease   so that
Wafts on the calmer wave by dubious light
And like a weather-beaten vessel holds°   makes for
Gladly the port, though shrouds and tackle torn;
1045 Or in the emptier waste, resembling air
Weighs° his spread wings, at leisure to behold   balances
Far off th' empyreal Heav'n, extended wide
In circuit, undetermined square or round,
With opal tow'rs and battlements adorned
1050 Of living sapphire, once his native seat;
And fast by hanging in a golden chain
This pendent world,° in bigness as a star   universe
Of smallest magnitude close by the moon.
Thither full fraught with mischievous revenge,
1055 Accursed, and in a curséd hour, he hies.

From Book 3

[THE INVOCATION, THE COUNCIL IN HEAVEN, AND THE CONCLUSION OF SATAN'S JOURNEY]

Hail holy Light, offspring of Heav'n first-born,
Or of th' Eternal coeternal beam
May I express thee unblamed?[1] Since God is light,
And never but in unapproachèd light
5 Dwelt from eternity, dwelt then in thee,
Bright effluence of bright essence increate.°   uncreated, eternal
Or hear'st thou rather[2] pure ethereal stream,
Whose fountain who shall tell? Before the sun,
Before the heavens thou wert, and at the voice
10 Of God, as with a mantle didst invest°   cover
The rising world of waters dark and deep,
Won from the void and formless infinite.
Thee I revisit now with bolder wing,

2. The bridge ends on the outermost sphere of the ten concentric spheres making up the universe.
1. This second Proem or invocation (3.1–55) is a hymn to Light, addressed either as the first crea-

ture of God or as coeternal with God, with allusion to 1 John 1.5, "God is Light, and in him is no darkness at all."
2. I.e., would you rather be called (a Latinism).

Escaped the Stygian pool, though long detained
15 In that obscure sojourn, while in my flight
Through utter and through middle darkness³ borne
With other notes than to th' Orphéan lyre⁴
I sung of Chaos and eternal Night,
Taught by the Heav'nly Muse⁵ to venture down
20 The dark descent, and up to reascend,
Though hard and rare: thee I revisit safe,
And feel thy sovran vital lamp; but thou
Revisit'st not these eyes, that roll in vain
To find thy piercing ray, and find no dawn;
25 So thick a drop serene hath quenched their orbs,
Or dim suffusion⁶ veiled. Yet not the more
Cease I to wander where the Muses haunt
Clear spring, or shady grove, or sunny hill,
Smit with the love of sacred song; but chief
30 Thee Sion⁷ and the flow'ry brooks beneath
That wash thy hallowed feet, and warbling flow,
Nightly I visit: nor sometimes forget°   *always remember*
Those other two equaled with me in fate,⁸
So were I equaled with them in renown,
35 Blind Thamyris and blind Maeonides,
And Tiresias and Phineus prophets old,⁹
Then feed on thoughts, that voluntary move
Harmonious numbers;° as the wakeful bird°   *verses / nightingale*
Sings darkling,° and in shadiest covert hid   *in the dark*
40 Tunes her nocturnal note. Thus with the year
Seasons return, but not to me returns
Day, or the sweet approach of ev'n or morn,
Or sight of vernal bloom, or summer's rose,
Or flocks, or herds, or human face divine;
45 But cloud instead, and ever-during dark
Surrounds me, from the cheerful ways of men
Cut off, and for the book of knowledge° fair   *Book of Nature*
Presented with a universal blank
Of nature's works to me expunged and razed,°   *erased*
50 And wisdom at one entrance quite shut out.
So much the rather thou celestial Light
Shine inward, and the mind through all her powers
Irradiate, there plant eyes, all mist from thence
Purge and disperse, that I may see and tell
55 Of things invisible to mortal sight.
    Now had the Almighty Father from above,
From the pure empyrean where he sits
High throned above all height, bent down his eye,

3. Hell is "utter" (i.e., outer) darkness; Chaos is
middle darkness.
4. One of the so-called Orphic Hymns is *To Night*,
and Orpheus himself visited the underworld. But
Milton's song, Christian and epic, is of a different
kind.
5. Urania (though not named until 7.1).
6. Cataract—*suffusio nigra*. "Drop serene": *gutta
serena*, the medical term for Milton's kind of blindness.
7. The mountain of scriptural inspiration, with its
brooks Siloa and Kidron.
8. I.e., blind like me.
9. Thamyris was a blind Thracian poet, who lived
before Homer; "Maeonides" is an epithet of
Homer; Tiresias was the blind prophet of Thebes;
Phineus was a blind king and seer (*Aeneid* 3).

His own works and their works at once to view:
Above him all the sanctities° of Heaven   *angels*
Stood thick as stars, and from his sight received
Beatitude past utterance; on his right
The radiant image of his glory sat,
His only Son; on earth he first beheld
Our two first parents, yet the only two
Of mankind, in the happy garden placed,
Reaping immortal fruits of joy and love,
Uninterrupted joy, unrivaled love
In blissful solitude; he then surveyed
Hell and the gulf between, and Satan there
Coasting the wall of Heav'n on this side Night
In the dun° air sublime,° and ready now   *dusky / above*
To stoop with wearied wings, and willing feet
On the bare outside of this world,° that seemed   *universe*
Firm land embosomed without firmament,°   *atmosphere*
Uncertain which, in ocean or in air.
Him God beholding from his prospect high,
Wherein past, present, future he beholds,
Thus to his only Son foreseeing spake.
      "Only begotten Son, seest thou what rage
Transports our Adversary, whom no bounds
Prescribed, no bars of Hell, nor all the chains
Heaped on him there, nor yet the main° abyss   *vast*
Wide interrupt¹ can hold; so bent he seems
On desperate revenge, that shall redound
Upon his own rebellious head. And now
Through all restraint broke loose he wings his way
Not far off Heav'n, in the precincts of light,
Directly towards the new-created world,
And man there placed, with purpose to essay
If him by force he can destroy, or worse,
By some false guile pervert; and shall pervert;
For man will hearken to his glozing° lies,   *flattering*
And easily transgress the sole command,
Sole pledge of his obedience: so will fall
He and his faithless progeny: whose fault?
Whose but his own? Ingrate, he had of me
All he could have; I made him just and right,
Sufficient to have stood, though free to fall.
Such I created all th' ethereal Powers
And Spirits, both them who stood and them who failed;
Freely they stood who stood, and fell who fell.
Not free, what proof could they have giv'n sincere
Of true allegiance, constant faith or love,
Where only what they needs must do, appeared,
Not what they would? What praise could they receive?
What pleasure I from such obedience paid,

---

1. Forming a wide breach between Heaven and Hell.

When will and reason (reason also is choice)
Useless and vain, of freedom both despoiled,
10 Made passive both, had served necessity,
Not me. They therefore as to right belonged,
So were created, nor can justly accuse
Their Maker, or their making, or their fate,
As if predestination overruled
15 Their will, disposed by absolute decree
Or high foreknowledge; they themselves decreed
Their own revolt, not I: if I foreknew,
Foreknowledge had no influence on their fault,
Which had no less proved certain unforeknown.[2]
20 So without least impulse or shadow of fate,
Or aught by me immutably foreseen,
They trespass, authors to themselves in all
Both what they judge and what they choose; for so
I formed them free, and free they must remain,
25 Till they enthrall themselves: I else must change
Their nature, and revoke the high decree
Unchangeable, eternal, which ordained
Their freedom, they themselves ordained their fall.
The first sort[3] by their own suggestion fell,
30 Self-tempted, self-depraved: man falls deceived
By the other first: man therefore shall find grace,
The other none: in mercy and justice both,
Through Heav'n and earth, so shall my glory excel,
But mercy first and last shall brightest shine."
35   Thus while God spake, ambrosial fragrance filled
All Heav'n, and in the blessèd Spirits elect°   *unfallen*
Sense of new joy ineffable diffused:
Beyond compare the Son of God was seen
Most glorious, in him all his Father shone
40 Substantially expressed, and in his face
Divine compassion visibly appeared,
Love without end, and without measure grace,
Which uttering thus he to his Father spake.
    "O Father, gracious was that word which closed
45 Thy sovran sentence, that man should find grace;
For which both Heav'n and earth shall high extol
Thy praises, with th' innumerable sound
Of hymns and sacred songs, wherewith thy throne
Encompassed shall resound thee ever blessed.
50 For should man finally be lost, should man
Thy creature late so loved, thy youngest son
Fall circumvented thus by fraud, though joined
With his own folly? That be from thee far,
That far be from thee, Father, who art judge
55 Of all things made, and judgest only right.[4]

2. I.e., if I had not foreknown it.
3. Satan and his crew.
4. The Son echoes (or rather foreshadows) Abra-

ham pleading with the Lord to spare Sodom: "That
be far from thee to do after this manner, to slay
the righteous with the wicked . . . that be far from

Or shall the Adversary[5] thus obtain
His end, and frustrate thine, shall he fulfill
His malice, and thy goodness bring to naught,
Or proud return though to his heavier doom,
160 Yet with revenge accomplished, and to Hell
Draw after him the whole race of mankind,
By him corrupted? Or wilt thou thyself
Abolish thy creation, and unmake,
For him, what for thy glory thou hast made?
165 So should thy goodness and thy greatness both
Be questioned and blasphemed° without defense."   °reviled
  To whom the great Creator thus replied.
"O Son, in whom my soul hath chief delight,
Son of my bosom, Son who art alone
170 My Word, my wisdom, and effectual might,[6]
All hast thou spoken as my thoughts are, all
As my eternal purpose hath decreed:
Man shall not quite be lost, but saved who will,
Yet not of will in him, but grace in me
175 Freely vouchsafed; once more I will renew
His lapsèd powers, though forfeit and enthralled
By sin to foul exorbitant desires;
Upheld by me, yet once more he shall stand
On even ground against his mortal foe,
180 By me upheld, that he may know how frail
His fall'n condition is, and to me owe
All his deliv'rance, and to none but me.
Some I have chosen of peculiar grace
Elect above the rest;[7] so is my will:
185 The rest shall hear me call, and oft be warned°   °warned about
Their sinful state, and to appease betimes
Th' incensèd Deity, while offered grace
Invites; for I will clear their senses dark,
What may suffice, and soften stony hearts
190 To pray, repent, and bring obedience due.
To prayer, repentance, and obedience due,
Though but endeavored with sincere intent,
Mine ear shall not be slow, mine eye not shut.
And I will place within them as a guide
195 My umpire conscience, whom if they will hear,
Light after light well used they shall attain,[8]
And to the end persisting, safe arrive.
This my long sufferance and my day of grace
They who neglect and scorn, shall never taste;
200 But hard be hardened, blind be blinded more,

---

thee. Shall not the Judge of all the earth do right?"
(Genesis 18.25).
5. *Satan* in Hebrew means "adversary."
6. God's speech is rhythmic and sometimes
rhymed.
7. In this speech, Milton's God rejects the Calvinist doctrine that he had from the beginning predestined the damnation or salvation of each

individual soul; he claims rather that grace sufficient for salvation is offered to all, enabling everyone, if they choose to do so, to believe and
persevere. He does, however, assert his right to give
special grace to some.
8. By using the light of conscience well they will
gain more light.

That they may stumble on, and deeper fall;
And none but such from mercy I exclude.
But yet all is not done; man disobeying,
Disloyal breaks his fealty, and sins
205 Against the high supremacy of Heav'n,
Affecting° Godhead, and so losing all,   *aspiring to*
To expiate his treason hath naught left,
But to destruction sacred and devote,°   *consecrated*
He with his whole posterity must die,
210 Die he or justice must; unless for him
Some other able, and as willing, pay
The rigid satisfaction, death for death.
Say heav'nly Powers, where shall we find such love,
Which of ye will be mortal to redeem
215 Man's mortal crime,[9] and just th' unjust to save,
Dwells in all heaven charity so dear?"
    He asked, but all the heav'nly choir stood mute,[1]
And silence was in Heav'n; on man's behalf
Patron or intercessor none appeared,
220 Much less that durst upon his own head draw
The deadly forfeiture, and ransom set.
And now without redemption all mankind
Must have been lost, adjudged to death and Hell
By doom severe, had not the Son of God,
225 In whom the fullness dwells of love divine,
His dearest mediation° thus renewed.   *intercession*
    "Father, thy word is passed, man shall find grace;
And shall grace not find means, that finds her way,
The speediest of thy wingèd messengers,
230 To visit all thy creatures, and to all
Comes unprevented,° unimplored, unsought,   *unanticipated*
Happy for man, so coming; he her aid
Can never seek, once dead in sins and lost;
Atonement for himself or offering meet,
235 Indebted and undone, hath none to bring:
Behold me then, me for him, life for life
I offer, on me let thine anger fall;
Account me man; I for his sake will leave
Thy bosom, and this glory next to thee
240 Freely put off, and for him lastly die
Well pleased, on me let Death wreck all his rage;
Under his gloomy power I shall not long
Lie vanquished; thou hast giv'n me to possess
Life in myself forever, by thee I live,
245 Though now to Death I yield, and am his due
All that of me can die, yet that debt paid,
Thou wilt not leave me in the loathsome grave
His prey, nor suffer my unspotted soul
Forever with corruption there to dwell;

9. "Mortal" means "human" in line 214, but "deadly" in line 215.

1. Compare the devils in the Great Consult, 2.420–26.

250 But I shall rise victorious, and subdue
My vanquisher, spoiled of his vaunted spoil;
Death his death's wound shall then receive, and stoop
Inglorious, of his mortal sting disarmed.
I through the ample air in triumph high
255 Shall lead Hell captive maugre° Hell, and show   *in spite of*
The powers of darkness bound.[2] Thou at the sight
Pleased, out of Heaven shalt look down and smile,
While by thee raised I ruin[3] all my foes,
Death last, and with his carcass glut the grave:
260 Then with the multitude of my redeemed
Shall enter Heaven long absent, and return,
Father, to see thy face, wherein no cloud
Of anger shall remain, but peace assured,
And reconcilement; wrath shall be no more
265 Thenceforth, but in thy presence joy entire."
     His words here ended, but his meek aspéct
Silent yet spake, and breathed immortal love
To mortal men, above which only shone
Filial obedience: as a sacrifice
270 Glad to be offered, he attends the will
Of his great Father. Admiration° seized   *wonder*
All Heav'n, what this might mean, and wither tend
Wond'ring; but soon th' Almighty thus replied:
"O thou in Heav'n and earth the only peace
275 Found out for mankind under wrath, O thou
My sole complacence!° well thou know'st how dear   *pleasure, delight*
To me are all my works, nor man the least
Though last created, that for him I spare
Thee from my bosom and right hand, to save,
280 By losing thee a while, the whole race lost.
Thou therefore whom[4] thou only canst redeem,
Their nature also to thy nature join;
And be thy self man among men on earth,
Made flesh, when time shall be, of virgin seed,
285 By wondrous birth: be thou in Adam's room
The head of all mankind, though Adam's son.[5]
As in him perish all men, so in thee
As from a second root shall be restored,
As many as are restored, without thee none.
290 His crime makes guilty all his sons; thy merit
Imputed shall absolve them who renounce
Their own both righteous and unrighteous deeds,[6]
And live in thee transplanted, and from thee
Receive new life. So man, as is most just,

2. The Son's triumph is represented in a series of paradoxes—a vanquisher vanquished, a spoiler spoiled, Death dead, Hell captured in all Hell's despite.
3. In the Latin sense, throw down.
4. The antecedent of "whom" is, loosely construed, the "their nature" that follows it.
5. The Son of God, who long antedates the creation of Adam and who is actually the first created

being (3.383), is later incarnated in Jesus Christ; he is called Second Adam and "Son of Man" by reason of his descent from the first man, Adam. Cf. 1 Corinthians 15.22: "For as in Adam all die, even so in Christ shall all be made alive."
6. The merit of Christ attributed vicariously ("imputed") to human beings frees from original sin those who renounce their own deeds, good and bad, and hope to be saved by faith.

95 Shall satisfy for man, be judged and die,
    And dying rise, and rising with him raise
    His brethren, ransomed with his own dear life.
    So heav'nly love shall outdo hellish hate,
    Giving to death, and dying to redeem,
00 So dearly to redeem what hellish hate
    So easily destroyed, and still destroys
    In those who, when they may, accept not grace.
    Nor shalt thou by descending to assume
    Man's nature, lessen or degrade thine own.
05 Because thou hast, though throned in highest bliss
    Equal to God, and equally enjoying
    God-like fruition,° quitted all to save   state
    A world from utter loss, and hast been found
    By merit more than birthright Son of God,⁷
10 Found worthiest to be so by being good,
    Far more than great or high; because in thee
    Love hath abounded more than glory abounds.
    Therefore thy humiliation shall exalt
    With thee thy manhood also to this throne;
15 Here shalt thou sit incarnate, here shalt reign
    Both God and man, Son both of God and man,
    Anointed⁸ universal King; all power
    I give thee, reign forever, and assume
    Thy merits; under thee as Head Supreme
20 Thrones, Princedoms, Powers, Dominions⁹ I reduce:
    All knees to thee shall bow, of them that bide
    In Heaven, or earth, or under earth in Hell;
    When thou attended gloriously from Heav'n
    Shalt in the sky appear, and from thee send
25 The summoning Archangels to proclaim
    Thy dread tribunal: forthwith from all winds°   directions
    The living, and forthwith the cited° dead   summoned
    Of all past ages to the general doom
    Shall hasten, such a peal shall rouse their sleep.
30 Then all thy saints assembled, thou shalt judge
    Bad men and angels, they arraigned° shall sink   accursed
    Beneath thy sentence; Hell, her numbers full,
    Thenceforth shall be forever shut. Meanwhile
    The world shall burn, and from her ashes spring
35 New Heav'n and earth, wherein the just shall dwell,¹
    And after all their tribulations long
    See golden days, fruitful of golden deeds,
    With joy and love triumphing, and fair truth.
    Then thou thy regal scepter shalt lay by,
40 For regal scepter then no more shall need,°   be needed
    God shall be all in all. But all ye gods,°   angels

7. A heterodox doctrine, that Christ was Son of God by merit. Compare with Satan (2.5).
8. "The Anointed" in Hebrew means messiah.
9. Orders of angels.
1. Milton's description of the Last Judgment
draws on several biblical texts, including Matthew 24.30–31, and 25.31–32; the account of the burning and re-creation of Heaven and earth is from 2 Peter 3.12–13.

Adore him, who to compass all this dies,
Adore the Son, and honor him as me."
    No sooner had th' Almighty ceased, but all
345 The multitude of angels with a shout
Loud as from numbers without number, sweet
As from blest voices, uttering joy, Heav'n rung[2]
With jubilee, and loud hosannas filled
Th' eternal regions: lowly reverent
350 Towards either throne[3] they bow, and to the ground
With solemn adoration down they cast
Their crowns inwove with amarant[4] and gold,
Immortal amarant, a flow'r which once
In Paradise, fast by the Tree of Life
355 Began to bloom, but soon for man's offense
To Heav'n removed where first it grew, there grows,
And flow'rs aloft shading the Fount of Life,
And where the river of bliss through midst of Heav'n
Rolls o'er Elysian[5] flow'rs her amber° stream;   pure
360 With these that never fade the Spirits elect
Bind their resplendent locks inwreathed with beams,
Now in loose garlands thick thrown off, the bright
Pavement that like a sea of jasper shone
Impurpled with celestial roses smiled.
365 Then crowned again their golden harps they took,
Harps ever tuned, that glittering by their side
Like quivers hung, and with preamble sweet
Of charming symphony they introduce
Their sacred song, and waken raptures high;
370 No voice exempt,° no voice but well could join   excluded
Melodious part, such concord is in Heav'n.
    Thee Father first they sung omnipotent,
Immutable, immortal, infinite,
Eternal King; thee Author of all being,
375 Fountain of light, thyself invisible
Amidst the glorious brightness where thou sitt'st
Throned inaccessible, but when thou shad'st
The full blaze of thy beams, and through a cloud
Drawn round about thee like a radiant shrine,[6]
380 Dark with excessive bright thy skirts appear,
Yet dazzle Heav'n, that brightest Seraphim
Approach not, but with both wings veil their eyes.
Thee next they sang of all creation first,[7]
Begotten Son, Divine Similitude,
385 In whose conspicuous count'nance, without cloud
Made visible, th' Almighty Father shines,
Whom else no creature can behold;[8] on thee

2. "Multitude" (line 345) is the subject of the sentence, "rung" the verb, and "Heav'n" the object.
3. Thrones of God and the Son.
4. In Greek, "unfading," a legendary immortal flower.
5. Milton draws freely, for his Christian Heaven, on descriptions of the classical paradisal place, the Elysian Fields.

6. Note the turn from theological debate to images that evoke a more mystical aspect of God.
7. The Son is not eternal, as in Trinitarian doctrine, but rather, God's first creation.
8. If it were not for the Son who is God's image, no creature could see God.

Impressed th' effulgence of his glory abides,
Transfused on thee his ample spirit rests.
390 He Heav'n of heavens and all the Powers therein
By thee created, and by thee threw down
Th' aspiring Dominations.[9] Thou that day
Thy Father's dreadful thunder didst not spare,
Nor stop thy flaming chariot wheels, that shook
395 Heav'n's everlasting frame, while o'er the necks
Thou drov'st of warring angels disarrayed.
Back from pursuit thy Powers° with loud acclaim   *angels*
Thee only extolled, Son of thy Father's might,
To execute fierce vengeance on his foes,
400 Not so on man; him through their malice fall'n,
Father of mercy and grace, thou didst not doom
So strictly, but much more to pity incline:
No sooner did thy dear and only Son
Perceive thee purposed not to doom° frail man   *judge*
405 So strictly, but much more to pity inclined,
He to appease thy wrath, and end the strife
Of mercy and justice in thy face discerned,
Regardless of the bliss wherein he sat
Second to thee, offered himself to die
410 For man's offense. O unexampled love,
Love nowhere to be found to be found less than divine!
Hail Son of God, Saviour of men, thy name
Shall be the copious matter of my[1] song
Henceforth, and never shall my harp thy praise
415 Forget, nor from thy Father's praise disjoin.
  Thus they in Heav'n, above the starry sphere,
Their happy hours in joy and hymning spent.
Meanwhile upon the firm opacous° globe   *opaque*
Of this round world, whose first convex divides
420 The luminous inferior orbs, enclosed
From Chaos and th' inroad of Darkness old,
Satan alighted walks:[2] a globe far off
It seemed, now seems a boundless continent
Dark, waste, and wild, under the frown of Night
425 Starless exposed, and ever-threatening storms
Of Chaos blust'ring round, inclement sky;
Save on that side which from the wall of Heav'n
Though distant far some small reflection gains
Of glimmering air less vexed with tempest loud:
430 Here walked the Fiend at large in spacious field.
As when a vulture on Imaus bred,
Whose snowy ridge the roving Tartar bounds,[3]
Dislodging from a region scarce of prey
To gorge the flesh of lambs or yeanling° kids   *newborn*

9. The rebel angels.
1. Either Milton here quotes the angels singing as a single chorus, or he associates himself with their song, or both.
2. Satan is on the outermost of the ten concentric spheres that make up the cosmos.
3. Imaus, a ridge of mountains beyond the modern Himalayas, runs north through Asia from modern Afghanistan to the Arctic Circle.

435 On hills where flocks are fed, flies toward the springs
Of Ganges or Hydaspes, Indian streams;[4]
But in his way lights on the barren plains
Of Sericana, where Chineses drive
With sails and wind their cany wagons light:
440 So on this windy sea of land, the Fiend
Walked up and down alone bent on his prey,
Alone, for other creature in this place
Living or lifeless to be found was none,
None yet, but store hereafter from the earth
445 Up hither like aërial vapors flew
Of all things transitory and vain, when sin
With vanity had filled the works of men:
Both all things vain, and all who in vain things
Built their fond hopes of glory or lasting fame,
450 Or happiness in this or th' other life;
All who have their reward on earth, the fruits
Of painful superstition and blind zeal,
Naught seeking but the praise of men, here find
Fit retribution, empty as their deeds;
455 All th' unaccomplished° works of nature's hand,   *imperfect*
Abortive, monstrous, or unkindly° mixed,   *unnatural*
Dissolved on earth, fleet° hither, and in vain,   *float*
Till final dissolution, wander here,
Not in the neighboring moon, as some[5] have dreamed;
460 Those argent° fields more likely habitants,   *silver*
Translated saints,[6] or middle Spirits hold
Betwixt th' angelical and human kind:
Hither of ill-joined sons and daughters born
First from the ancient world those giants came
465 With many a vain exploit, though then renowned:[7]
The builders next of Babel on the plain
Of Sennaär,[8] and still with vain design
New Babels, had they wherewithal, would build:
Others came single; he who to be deemed
470 A god, leaped fondly° into Etna flames,   *foolishly*
Empedocles, and he who to enjoy
Plato's Elysium, leaped into the sea,
Cleombrotus, and many more too long,[9]
Embryos and idiots, eremites° and friars   *hermits*
475 White, black, and gray, with all their trumpery.[1]
Here pilgrims roam, that strayed so far to seek
In Golgotha[2] him dead, who lives in Heav'n;

---

4. Both the Ganges and Hydaspes (a tributary of the Indus) rise from the mountains of northern India. Sericana (line 438) is a region in Northwest China.
5. Milton's Paradise of Fools (named in line 496) was inspired by Ariosto's Limbo of Vanity in *Orlando Furioso* (book 34, lines 73ff.); Milton's region is reserved for deluded victims of misplaced devotion, chiefly Roman Catholics.
6. Holy men like Enoch and Elijah, transported to Heaven while yet alive.
7. Giants, born of unnatural marriages between

the "sons of God" and the daughters of men (Genesis 6.4), are creatures unkindly mixed.
8. Shinar, the plain of Babel (Genesis 11.2–9); the Tower of Babel is an emblem of human pride and folly.
9. I.e., it would take too long to name them. Both Empedocles and Cleombrotus foolishly carried piety to the point of suicide.
1. The white friars are Carmelites; the black, Dominicans; and the gray, Franciscans. "Trumpery": religious paraphernalia.
2. Place where Christ was crucified.

And they who to be sure of paradise
Dying put on the weeds° of Dominic,   garments
80 Or in Franciscan think to pass disguised;³
They pass the planets seven, and pass the fixed,
And that crystálline sphere whose balance weighs
The trepidation talked, and that first moved;⁴
And now Saint Peter at Heav'n's wicket seems
85 To wait them with his keys, and now at foot
Of Heav'n's ascent they lift their feet, when lo
A violent crosswind from either coast
Blows them transverse ten thousand leagues awry
Into the devious° air. Then might ye see   erratic
90 Cowls, hoods and habits⁵ with their wearers tossed
And fluttered into rags; then relics, beads,
Indulgences, dispenses, pardons, bulls,
The sport of winds: all these upwhirled aloft
Fly o'er the backside° of the world far off   rump
95 Into a limbo large and broad, since called
The Paradise of Fools, to few unknown
Long after, now unpeopled, and untrod;
All this dark globe the Fiend found as he passed,
And long he wandered, till at last a gleam
100 Of dawning light turned thitherward in haste
His traveled° steps; far distant he descries   travel-weary
Ascending by degrees° magnificent   steps
Up to the wall of heaven a structure high,
At top whereof, but far more rich appeared
105 The work as of a kingly palace gate
With frontispiece° of diamond and gold   pediment
Embellished; thick with sparkling orient° gems   lustrous
The portal shone, inimitable on earth,
By model, or by shading pencil drawn.
110 The stairs were such as whereon Jacob saw
Angels ascending and descending, bands
Of guardians bright, when he from Esau fled
To Padan-Aram in the field of Luz,
Dreaming by night under the open sky,
115 And waking cried, "This is the gate of Heav'n."⁶
Each stair mysteriously was meant, nor stood
There always, but drawn up to Heav'n sometimes
Viewless,° and underneath a bright sea flowed   invisible
Of jasper, or of liquid pearl, whereon
120 Who after came from earth, sailing arrived,
Wafted by angels, or flew o'er the lake
Rapt in a chariot drawn by fiery steeds.⁷
The stairs were then let down, whether to dare

3. Some try to trick God into granting them salvation by wearing on their deathbeds the garb of
various religious orders.
4. Milton follows their souls through the spheres
of the moon and sun, the five then-known planets,
the fixed stars, and the sphere responsible for the
"trepidation" (a periodic corrective shudder of the
cosmos), up to the *primum mobile* or prime mover.
The next step seems to be the empyreal Heaven.

5. The dress of religious orders, together with
(next lines) rosary beads, saints' relics, various
kinds of pardon for sins, and papal decrees
("bulls").
6. The story of Jacob's vision is summarized from
Genesis 28.1–19; the stairs of the ladder allegori-
cally ("mysteriously") represent stages of spiritual
growth.
7. Elijah was wafted to heaven in a chariot.

The Fiend by easy ascent, or aggravate
525 His sad exclusion from the doors of bliss.
Direct against which opened from beneath,
Just o'er the blissful seat of Paradise,
A passage down to th' earth, a passage wide,[8]
Wider by far than that of aftertimes
530 Over Mount Zion, and, though that were large,
Over the Promised Land to God so dear,
By which, to visit oft those happy tribes,
On high behests his angels to and fro
Passed frequent, and his eye with choice° regard   *discriminating*
535 From Paneas the fount of Jordan's flood
To Beërsaba, where the Holy Land
Borders on Egypt and the Arabian shore;[9]
So wide the op'ning seemed, where bounds were set
To darkness, such as bound the ocean wave.
540 Satan from hence now on the lower stair
That scaled by steps of gold to Heaven gate
Looks down with wonder at the sudden view
Of all this world at once. As when a scout
Through dark and desert ways with peril gone
545 All night; at last by break of cheerful dawn
Obtains° the brow of some high-climbing hill,   *gains*
Which to his eye discovers unaware
The goodly prospect of some foreign land
First seen, or some renowned metropolis
550 With glistering spires and pinnacles adorned,
Which now the rising sun gilds with his beams.
Such wonder seized, though after Heaven seen,
The Spirit malign, but much more envy seized
At sight of all this world beheld so fair.
555 Round he surveys, and well might, where he stood
So high above the circling canopy
Of night's extended shade; from eastern point
Of Libra to the fleecy star that bears
Andromeda far off Atlantic seas[1]
560 Beyond th' horizon; then from pole to pole
He views in breadth, and without longer pause
Down right into the world's first region throws
His flight precipitant, and winds with ease
Through the pure marble° air his oblique way   *sparkling*
565 Amongst innumerable stars, that shone
Stars distant, but nigh hand seemed other worlds,
Or other worlds they seemed, or happy isles,
Like those Hesperian gardens famed of old,
Fortunate fields, and groves and flow'ry vales,[2]
570 Thrice happy isles, but who dwelt happy there

8. A passage through the crystalline spheres, otherwise impenetrable.
9. From Paneas (or Dan) in northern Palestine to Beersaba, or Beersheba, near the Egyptian border—the entire land of Israel.
1. In the zodiac, Libra is diametrically opposite Aries, or the Ram ("the fleecy star"), which seems to carry the constellation Andromeda on its back.
2. The gardens of the Hesperides and the "fortunate isles" of Greek mythology, classical versions of paradise, lay far out in the Atlantic.

He stayed not to inquire: above them all
The golden sun in splendor likest Heaven
Allured his eye: thither his course he bends
Through the calm firmament; but up or down
By center, or eccentric, hard to tell,
Or longitude,[3] where the great luminary
Aloof the vulgar constellations thick,
That from his lordly eye keep distance due,
Dispenses light from far; they as they move
Their starry dance in numbers that compute
Days, months, and years, towards his all-cheering lamp
Turn swift their various motions, or are turned
By his magnetic beam, that gently warms
The universe, and to each inward part
With gentle penetration, though unseen,
Shoots invisible virtue° even to the deep: *influence, strength*
So wondrously was set his station bright.

Summary   Landing on the bright orb of the sun, Satan disguises himself as a youthful cherub and approaches the solar guardian, the archangel Uriel. Pretending interest in the new great works of God, he gets directions to Earth and Adam's bower, then spirals down and on Mount Niphates (in modern Iran), overlooking the site of Paradise.

From Book 4

[SATAN'S ENTRY INTO PARADISE; ADAM AND EVE IN THEIR BOWER]

O for that warning voice, which he who saw
Th' Apocalypse, heard cry in heaven aloud,
Then when the Dragon, put to second rout,
Came furious down to be revenged on men,
"Woe to the inhabitants on earth!"[1] that now,
While time was, our first parents had been warned
The coming of their secret foe, and scaped
Haply° so scaped his mortal° snare; for now   *happily / deadly*
Satan, now first inflamed with rage, came down,
The tempter ere° th' accuser of mankind,   *before being*
To wreck° on innocent frail man his loss   *avenge, wreak*
Of that first battle, and his flight to Hell:
Yet not rejoicing in his speed, though bold,
Far off and fearless, nor with cause to boast,
Begins his dire attempt, which nigh the birth
Now rolling, boils in his tumultuous breast,
And like a devilish engine back recoils

---

3. Milton leaves open whether the sun or the earth is at the center of the cosmos.
1. John of Patmos, in Revelation 12.3–12, hears such a cry during a second war in Heaven, between the Dragon and the angels.

Upon himself; horror and doubt distract
His troubled thoughts, and from the bottom stir
20 The Hell within him, for within him Hell
He brings, and round about him, nor from Hell
One step no more than from himself can fly
By change of place: now conscience wakes despair
That slumbered, wakes the bitter memory
25 Of what he was, what is, and what must be
Worse; of worse deeds worse sufferings must ensue.
Sometimes towards Eden which now in his view
Lay pleasant, his grieved look he fixes sad,
Sometimes towards Heav'n and the full-blazing sun,
30 Which now sat high in his meridian tow'r:[2]
Then much revolving,° thus in sighs began.   *pondering*
    "O thou that with surpassing glory crowned,[3]
Look'st from thy sole dominion like the god
Of this new world: at whose sight all the stars
35 Hide their diminished heads; to thee I call,
But with no friendly voice, and add thy name
O sun, to tell thee how I hate thy beams
That bring to my remembrance from what state
I fell, how glorious once above thy sphere;
40 Till pride and worse ambition threw me down
Warring in Heav'n against Heav'n's matchless King:
Ah wherefore! he deserved no such return
From me, whom he created what I was
In that bright eminence, and with his good
45 Upbraided none,[4] nor was his service hard.
What could be less than to afford him praise,
The easiest recompense, and pay him thanks,
How due! yet all his good proved ill in me,
And wrought but malice; lifted up so high
50 I 'sdained° subjection, and thought one step higher   *disdained*
Would set me highest, and in a moment quit°   *pay*
The debt immense of endless gratitude,
So burthensome still° paying, still to owe;   *always*
Forgetful what from him I still received,
55 And understood not that a grateful mind
By owing owes not, but still pays, at once
Indebted and discharged; what burden then?
O had his powerful destiny ordained
Me some inferior angel, I had stood
60 Then happy; no unbounded hope had raised
Ambition. Yet why not? some other Power°   *angel*
As great might have aspired, and me though mean
Drawn to his part; but other Powers as great
Fell not, but stand unshaken, from within

---

2. Midday, the height of noon.
3. Milton's nephew, Edward Phillips, said that this soliloquy was written "several years before the poem was begun," and was intended to begin a

drama on the topic, *Adam Unparadised*.
4. Demanded no return for his benefits (James 1.5).

₆₅ Or from without, to all temptations armed.
Hadst thou[5] the same free will and power to stand?
Thou hadst: whom hast thou then or what to accuse,
But Heav'n's free love dealt equally to all?
Be then his love accursed, since love or hate,
₇₀ To me alike, it deals eternal woe.
Nay cursed be thou; since against his thy will
Chose freely what it now so justly rues.
Me miserable![6] which way shall I fly
Infinite wrath, and infinite despair?
₇₅ Which way I fly is Hell; myself am Hell;[7]
And in the lowest deep a lower deep
Still threat'ning to devour me opens wide,
To which the Hell I suffer seems a Heav'n.
O then at last relent! is there no place
₈₀ Left for repentance, none for pardon left?
None left but by submission; and that word
Disdain forbids me, and my dread of shame
Among the Spirits beneath, whom I seduced
With other promises and other vaunts
₈₅ Than to submit, boasting I could subdue
Th' Omnipotent. Ay me, they little know
How dearly I abide° that boast so vain,   *pay the penalty for*
Under what torments inwardly I groan:
While they adore me on the throne of hell,
₉₀ With diadem and scepter high advanced
The lower still I fall, only supreme
In misery; such joy ambition finds.
But say I could repent and could obtain
By act of grace[8] my former state; how soon
₉₅ Would hight recall high thoughts, how soon unsay
What feigned submission swore: ease would recant
Vows made in pain, as violent° and void.   *forced*
For never can true reconcilement grow
Where wounds of deadly hate have pierced so deep:
₀₀ Which would but lead me to a worse relapse,
And heavier fall: so should I purchase dear
Short intermission bought with double smart.
This knows my punisher; therefore as far
From granting he, as I from begging peace:
₀₅ All hope excluded thus, behold instead
Of us outcast, exiled, his new delight,
Mankind created, and for him this world.
So farewell hope, and with hope farewell fear,
Farewell remorse: all good to me is lost;
₁₀ Evil be thou my good; by thee at least
Divided empire with Heav'n's King I hold

---

5. Compare Satan's address to himself here with Adam's soliloquy in parallel circumstances (10.758ff.).
6. A Latinism, *me miserum!*

7. Compare Satan's earlier claim that "the mind is its own place" (1.254).
8. The technical term for a formal pardon.

By thee, and more than half perhaps will reign;
As man ere long, and this new world shall know."
    Thus while he spake, each passion dimmed his face
115 Thrice changed with pale,° ire, envy and despair,   *pallor*
Which marred his borowed visage, and betrayed
Him counterfeit, if any eye beheld.
For heav'nly minds from such distempers foul
Are ever clear. Whereof he soon aware,
120 Each perturbation smoothed with outward calm,
Artificer of fraud; and was the first
That practiced falsehood under saintly show,
Deep malice to conceal, couched° with revenge: *hidden*
Yet not enough had practiced to deceive
125 Uriel once warned; whose eye pursued him down
The way he went, and on th' Assyrian mount°   *Niphates*
Saw him disfigured, more than could befall
Spirit of happy sort: his gestures fierce
He marked and mad demeanor, then alone,
130 As he supposed, all unobserved, unseen.
    So on he fares, and to the border comes
Of Eden, where delicious Paradise,[9]
Now nearer, crowns with her enclosure green,
As with a rural mound the champaign head°   *open summit*
135 Of a steep wilderness, whose hairy sides
With thicket overgrown, grotesque[1] and wild,
Access denied; and overhead up grew
Insuperable highth of loftiest shade,
Cedar, and pine, and fir, and branching palm,
140 A sylvan scene, and as the ranks ascend
Shade above shade, a woody theater[2]
Of stateliest view. Yet higher than their tops
The verdurous wall of Paradise up sprung:
Which to our general sire gave prospect large
145 Into his nether empire neighboring round.
And higher than that wall a circling row
Of goodliest trees loaden with fairest fruit,
Blossoms and fruits at once of golden hue
Appeared, with gay enameled° colors mixed: *bright*
150 On which the sun more glad impressed his beams
Than in fair evening cloud, or humid bow,°   *rainbow*
When God hath show'red the earth; so lovely seemed
That landscape: and of pure now purer air[3]
Meets his approach, and to the heart inspires°   *infuses*
155 Vernal delight and joy, able to drive°   *drive out*
All sadness but despair: now gentle gales
Fanning their odoriferous° wings dispense   *fragrance-bearing*
Native perfumes, and whisper whence they stole
Those balmy spoils. As when to them who sail

---

9. Paradise is a delightful ("delicious") garden on top of a steep hill situated in the east of the land of Eden.
1. Characterized by interwoven, tangled vines and branches.
2. As if in a Greek amphitheater, the trees are set row on row.
3. The air becomes still purer.

60 Beyond the Cape of Hope,° and now are past   *Cape of Good Hope*
    Mozambic, off at sea northeast winds blow
    Sabean odors from the spicy shore
    Of Araby the Blest,[4] with such delay
    Well pleased they slack their course, and many a league
65 Cheered with the grateful° smell old Ocean smiles.   *pleasing*
    So entertained those odorous sweets the Fiend
    Who came their bane, though with them better pleased
    Than Asmodeus with the fishy fume,
    That drove him, though enamored, from the spouse
70 Of Tobit's son,[5] and with a vengeance sent
    From Media post to Egypt, there fast bound.
       Now to th'ascent of that steep savage° hill   *wooded, wild*
    Satan had journeyed on, pensive and slow;
    But further way found none, so thick entwined,
75 As one continued brake,° the undergrowth   *thicket*
    Of shrubs and tangling bushes had perplexed
    All path of man or beast that passed that way:
    One gate there only was, and that looked east
    On th' other side: which when th' arch-felon saw
80 Due entrance he disdained, and in contempt,
    At one slight bound high overleaped all bound
    Of hill or highest wall, and sheer within
    Lights on his feet. As when a prowling wolf,
    Whom hunger drives to seek new haunt for prey,
85 Watching where shepherds pen their flocks at eve
    In hurdled cotes° amid the field secure,   *pens of woven reeds*
    Leaps o'er the fence with ease into the fold:
    Or as a thief bent to unhoard the cash
    Of some rich burgher, whose substantial doors,
90 Cross-barred and bolted fast, fear no assault,
    In at the window climbs, or o'er the tiles;
    So clomb° this first grand thief into God's fold: *climbed*
    So since into his church lewd hirelings[6] climb.
    Thence up he flew, and on the Tree of Life,
95 The middle tree and highest there that grew,
    Sat like a cormorant;[7] yet not true life
    Thereby regained, but sat devising death
    To them who lived; nor on the virtue° thought   *power*
    Of that life-giving plant, but only used
100 For prospect,° what well used had been the pledge   *as a lookout*
    Of immortality. So little knows
    Any, but God alone, to value right
    The good before him, but perverts best things
    To worst abuse, or to their meanest use.
105   Beneath him with new wonder now he views

---

4. *Arabia Felix* (modern Yemen). "Sabean": the biblical Sheba.

5. The Apocryphal book of Tobit tells of Tobias, Tobit's son, who married Sara and avoided the fate of her previous seven husbands (killed on their wedding night by the demon Asmodeus) by following the instructions of the angel Raphael and mak-ing a fishy smell to drive him off; Asmodeus then fled to Egypt where Raphael bound him.

6. Base men interested only in money; Milton would have clergymen not paid by the state, to ensure their purity of motive.

7. A sea bird, noted for gluttony.

To all delight of human sense exposed
In narrow room nature's whole wealth, yea more,
A heav'n on earth: for blissful Paradise
Of God the garden was, by him in the east
210 Of Eden planted; Eden stretched her line
From Auran eastward to the royal tow'rs
Of great Seleucia, built by Grecian kings,
Or where the sons of Eden long before
Dwelt in Telassar:[8] in this pleasant soil
215 His far more pleasant garden God ordained;
Out of the fertile ground he caused to grow
All trees of noblest kind for sight, smell, taste;
And all amid them stood the Tree of Life,
High eminent, blooming ambrosial° fruit   *divinely fragrant*
220 Of vegetable gold; and next to life
Our death the Tree of Knowledge grew fast by,
Knowledge of good bought dear by knowing ill.
Southward through Eden[9] went a river large,
Nor changed his course, but through the shaggy hill
225 Passed underneath engulfed, for God had thrown
That mountain as his garden mold° high raised   *rich earth*
Upon the rapid current, which through veins
Of porous earth with kindly° thirst up drawn,   *natural*
Rose a fresh fountain, and with many a rill
230 Watered the garden; thence united fell
Down the steep glade, and met the nether flood,
Which from his darksome passage now appears,
And now divided into four main streams,
Runs diverse, wand'ring many a famous realm
235 And country whereof here needs no account,
But rather to tell how, if art could tell,
How from that sapphire fount the crispèd° brooks,   *wavy, rippling*
Rolling on orient pearl and sands of gold,
With mazy error[1] under pendent shades
240 Ran nectar, visiting each plant, and fed
Flow'rs worthy of Paradise which not nice° art   *fastidious*
In beds and curious knots, but nature boon°   *bounteous*
Poured forth profuse on hill and dale and plain,
Both where the morning sun first warmly smote
245 The open field, and where the unpierced shade
Embrowned° the noontide bow'rs. Thus was this place,   *darkened*
A happy rural seat of various view,[2]
Groves whose rich trees wept odorous gums and balm,
Others whose fruit burnished with golden rind
250 Hung amiable,° Hesperian fables true,[3]   *lovely*

---

8. "Auran" is the province of Hauran on the eastern border of Israel. "Selucia," a powerful city on the Tigris, near modern Baghdad, was founded by one of Alexander's generals ("built by Grecian kings"). "Telassar" is another Near Eastern kingdom.
9. The Tigris (identified at 9.71) flowed under the hill.

1. From Latin *errare*, wandering.
2. Like a country estate, with a variety of prospects.
3. These were real golden apples, by contrast to those feigned golden apples of the Hesperides, fabled paradisal islands in the Western Ocean.

If true, here only, and of delicious taste:
Betwixt them lawns, or level downs, and flocks
Grazing the tender herb, were interposed,
Or palmy hillock, or the flow'ry lap
55 Of some irriguous° valley spread her store,   *well-watered*
Flow'rs of all hue, and without thorn the rose:
Another side, umbrageous° grots and caves   *shady*
Of cool recess, o'er which the mantling° vine   *enveloping*
Lays forth her purple grape, and gently creeps
60 Luxuriant; meanwhile murmuring waters fall
Down the slope hills, dispersed, or in a lake,
That to the fringèd bank with myrtle crowned,
Her crystal mirror holds, unite their streams.
The birds their choir apply; airs,[4] vernal airs,
65 Breathing the smell of field and grove, attune
The trembling leaves, while universal Pan[5]
Knit° with the Graces and the Hours in dance   *clasping hands*
Led on th' eternal spring. Not that fair field
Of Enna, where Proserpine gathering flow'rs
70 Herself a fairer flow'r by gloomy Dis
Was gathered, which cost Ceres all that pain
To seek her through the world; nor that sweet grove
Of Daphne by Orontes, and th' inspired
Castalian spring,[6] might with this Paradise
75 Of Eden strive; nor that Nyseian isle
Girt with the river Triton, where old Cham,
Whom Gentiles Ammon call and Libyan Jove,
Hid Amalthea and her florid° son   *wine-flushed*
Young Bacchus from his stepdame Rhea's eye;[7]
80 Nor where Abassin kings their issue guard,
Mount Amara,[8] though this by some supposed
True Paradise under the Ethiop line°   *equator*
By Nilus'° head, enclosed with shining rock,   *Nile's*
A whole day's journey high, but wide remote
85 From this Assyrian garden,° where the Fiend   *Eden*
Saw undelighted all delight, all kind
Of living creatures new to sight and strange:
    Two of far nobler shape erect and tall,
God-like erect, with native honor clad
90 In naked majesty seemed lords of all,
And worthy seemed, for in their looks divine
The image of their glorious Maker shone,
Truth, wisdom, sanctitude severe and pure,

---

4. Both breezes and melodies. "Their choir apply": practice their songs.
5. The god of all nature—"pan" in Greek means "all."
6. Milton compares Paradise with famous beauty spots of antiquity. Enna in Sicily was a lovely meadow from which "Proserpine" was kidnapped by "gloomy Dis" (i.e., Pluto); her mother Ceres sought her throughout the world. The grove of Daphne, near Antioch and the Orontes River in the Near East, had a spring called "Castalia" after the Muses' fountain near Parnassus.
7. The isle of Nysa in the river Triton in Tunisia was where Ammon (an Egyptian god, identified with Cham or Ham, the son of Noah) hid Bacchus, his child by Amalthea (who later became the god of wine), away from the eyes of his wife Rhea.
8. Atop Mount Amara, the "Abassin" (Abyssinian) king had a splendid palace in a paradisal garden.

Severe but in true filial freedom placed;
295 Whence true authority in men;[9] though both
Not equal, as their sex not equal seemed;
For contemplation he and valor formed,
For softness she and sweet attractive grace,
He for God only, she for God in him:[1]
300 His fair large front° and eye sublime declared   *forehead*
Absolute rule; and hyacinthine[2] locks
Round from his parted forelock manly hung
Clust'ring, but not beneath his shoulders broad:
She as a veil down to the slender waist
305 Her unadorned golden tresses wore
Disheveled, but in wanton ringlets waved
As the vine curls her tendrils,[3] which implied
Subjection, but required with gentle sway,°   *persuasion*
And by her yielded, by him best received,
310 Yielded with coy° submission, modest pride,   *shyly reserved*
And sweet reluctant amorous delay.
Nor those mysterious parts were then concealed,
Then was not guilty shame, dishonest° shame   *unchaste*
Of nature's works, honor dishonorable,
315 Sin-bred, how have ye troubled all mankind
With shows instead, mere shows of seeming pure,
And banished from man's life his happiest life,
Simplicity and spotless innocence.
So passed they naked on, nor shunned the sight
320 Of God or angel, for they thought no ill:
So hand in hand they passed, the loveliest pair
That ever since in love's embraces met,
Adam the goodliest man of men since born
His sons, the fairest of her daughters Eve.
325 Under a tuft of shade that on a green
Stood whispering soft, by a fresh fountain side
They sat them down, and after no more toil
Of their sweet gard'ning labor than sufficed
To recommend cool Zephyr,[4] and made ease
330 More easy, wholesome thirst and appetite
More grateful, to their supper fruits they fell,
Nectarine° fruits which the compliant boughs   *sweet as nectar*
Yielded them, sidelong as they sat recline
On the soft downy bank damasked with flow'rs:
335 The savory pulp they chew, and in the rind
Still as they thirsted scoop the brimming stream;
Nor gentle purpose,° nor endearing smiles   *conversation*
Wanted,° nor youthful dalliance as beseems   *lacked*
Fair couple, linked in happy nuptial league,
340 Alone as they. About them frisking played

9. This phrase underscores Milton's idea that true freedom involves obedience to natural superiors (i.e., God).
1. The phrase has as its context 1 Corinthians 11.3: "The head of every man is Christ; and the head of the woman is the man."

2. A classical metaphor for hair curled in the form of hyacinth petals, and perhaps also implying dark or flowing.
3. Eve's hair is curly, abundant, not subjected to rigid control, like the vegetation in Paradise.
4. I.e., to make a cool breeze welcome.

All beasts of th' earth, since wild, and of all chase° *a game preserve*
In wood or wilderness, forest or den;
Sporting the lion ramped,° and in his paw *stood on hind legs*
Dandled the kid; bears, tigers, ounces,° pards° *lynxes / leopards*
45 Gamboled before them; th' unwieldy elephant
To make them mirth used all his might, and wreathed
His lithe proboscis;° close the serpent sly *trunk*
Insinuating,° wove with Gordian twine *writhing, twisting*
His braided train,[5] and of his fatal guile
50 Gave proof unheeded; others on the grass
Couched, and now filled with pasture gazing sat,
Or bedward ruminating:° for the sun *chewing the cud*
Declined was hasting now with prone° career *sinking*
To th' Ocean Isles,° and in th' ascending scale *the Azores*
55 Of Heav'n the stars that usher evening rose:
When Satan still in gaze, as first he stood,
Scarce thus at length failed speech recovered sad.
 "O Hell! what do mine eyes with grief behold,
Into our room of bliss thus high advanced
360 Creatures of other mold, earth-born perhaps,
Not Spirits, yet to heav'nly Spirits bright
Little inferior; whom my thoughts pursue
With wonder, and could love, so lively shines
In them divine resemblance, and such grace
365 The hand that formed them on their shape hath poured.
Ah gentle pair, ye little think how nigh
Your change approaches, when all these delights
Will vanish and deliver ye to woe,
More woe, the more your taste is now of joy;
370 Happy, but for so happy° ill secured *such happiness*
Long to continue, and this high seat your heav'n
Ill fenced for heav'n to keep out such a foe
As now is entered; yet no purposed foe
To you whom I could pity thus forlorn
375 Though I unpitied: league with you I seek,
And mutual amity so strait,° so close, *intimate*
That I with you must dwell, or you with me
Henceforth; my dwelling haply may not please
Like this fair Paradise, your sense, yet such
380 Accept your Maker's work; he gave it me,
Which I as freely give; Hell shall unfold,
To entertain you two, her widest gates,
And send forth all her kings; there will be room,
Not like these narrow limits, to receive
385 Your numerous offspring; if no better place,
Thank him who puts me loath to this revenge
On you who wrong me not for° him who wronged. *in place of*
And should I at your harmless innocence
Melt, as I do, yet public reason just,

---

5. Checkered body. "Gordian twine": cords as convoluted as the Gordian knot which Alexander the Great had to cut with his sword.

390 Honor and empire with revenge enlarged
By conquering this new world, compels me now
To do what else though damned I should abhor."⁶
    So spake the Fiend, and with necessity,
The tyrant's plea, excused his devilish deeds.
395 Then from his lofty stand on that high tree
Down he alights among the sportful herd
Of those four-footed kinds, himself now one,
Now other, as their shape served best his end
Nearer to view his prey, and unespied
400 To mark what of their state he more might learn
By word or action marked: about them round
A lion now he stalks with fiery glare,
Then as a tiger, who by chance hath spied
In some purlieu° two gentle fawns at play,   *outskirts of a forest*
405 Straight couches close, then rising changes oft
His couchant watch, as one who chose his ground
Whence rushing he might surest seize them both
Gripped in each paw: when Adam first of men
To first of women Eve thus moving speech
410 Turned him all ear to hear new utterance flow:
    "Sole partner and sole° part of all these joys,   *chief*
Dearer thyself than all; needs must the Power
That made us, and for us this ample world
Be infinitely good, and of his good
415 As liberal and free as infinite,
That raised us from the dust and placed us here
In all this happiness, who at his hand
Have nothing merited, nor can perform
Aught whereof he hath need, he who requires
420 From us no other service than to keep
This one, this easy charge, of all the trees
In Paradise that bear delicious fruit
So various, not to taste that only Tree
Of Knowledge, planted by the Tree of Life,
425 So near grows death to life, whate'er death is,
Some dreadful thing no doubt; for well thou know'st
God hath pronounced it death to taste that Tree,
The only sign of our obedience left
Among so many signs of power and rule
430 Conferred upon us, and dominion giv'n
Over all other creatures that possess
Earth, air, and sea. Then let us not think hard
One easy prohibition, who enjoy
Free leave so large to all things else, and choice
435 Unlimited of manifold delights:
But let us ever praise him, and extol
His bounty, following our delightful task
To prune these growing plants, and tend these flow'rs,
Which were it toilsome, yet with thee were sweet."

---

6. Satan's excuse—reason of state, public interest, empire, etc.—is called "the tyrant's plea" in line 394.

₄₀   To whom thus Eve replied. "O thou for whom
And from whom I was formed flesh of thy flesh,
And without whom am to no end, my guide
And head, what thou hast said is just and right.
For we to him indeed all praises owe,
₄₅ And daily thanks, I chiefly who enjoy
So far the happier lot, enjoying thee
Preeminent by so much odds,° while thou   *advantage*
Like consort to thyself canst nowhere find.
That day I oft remember, when from sleep
₅₀ I first awaked, and found myself reposed°   *resting*
Under a shade on flowers, much wond'ring where
And what I was, whence thither brought, and how.
Not distant far from thence a murmuring sound
Of waters issued from a cave and spread
₅₅ Into a liquid plain, then stood unmoved
Pure as th' expanse of Heav'n; I thither went
With unexperienced thought, and laid me down
On the green bank, to look into the clear
Smooth lake, that to me seemed another sky.
₆₀ As I bent down to look, just opposite,
A shape within the wat'ry gleam appeared
Bending to look on me, I started back,
It started back, but pleased I soon returned,
Pleased it returned as soon with answering looks
₆₅ Of sympathy and love; there I had fixed
Mine eyes till now, and pined with vain° desire,[7]   *futile*
Had not a voice thus warned me, 'What thou seest,
What there thou seest fair creature is thyself,
With thee it came and goes: but follow me,
₇₀ And I will bring thee where no shadow stays°   *hinders*
Thy coming, and thy soft embraces, he
Whose image thou art, him thou shalt enjoy
Inseparably thine, to him shalt bear
Multitudes like thyself, and thence be called
₇₅ Mother of human race': what could I do,
But follow straight° invisibly thus led?   *at once*
Till I espied thee, fair indeed and tall,
Under a platan,° yet methought less fair,   *plane tree*
Less winning soft, less amiably mild,
₈₀ Than that smooth wat'ry image; back I turned,
Thou following cried'st aloud, 'Return fair Eve,
Whom fli'st thou? Whom thou fli'st, of him thou art,
His flesh, his bone; to give thee being I lent
Out of my side to thee, nearest my heart
₈₅ Substantial life, to have thee by my side
Henceforth an individual° solace dear;   *inseparable, distinct*
Part of my soul I seek thee, and thee claim
My other half': with that thy gentle hand

---

7. Eve's experience reprises (but with significant differences) the story of Narcissus, who fell in love with
his own reflection and was transformed into a flower.

Seized mine, I yielded, and from that time see
490 How beauty is excelled by manly grace
And wisdom, which alone is truly fair."
    So spake our general mother, and with eyes
Of conjugal attraction unreproved,
And meek surrender, half embracing leaned
495 On our first father, half her swelling breast
Naked met his under the flowing gold
Of her loose tresses hid: he in delight
Both of her beauty and submissive charms
Smiled with superior love, as Jupiter
500 On Juno smiles, when he impregns° the clouds   *impregnates*
That shed May flowers; and pressed her matron lip
With kisses pure: aside the Devil turned
For envy, yet with jealous leer malign
Eyed them askance, and to himself thus plained.°   *complained*
505   "Sight hateful, sight tormenting! thus these two
Imparadised in one another's arms
The happier Eden, shall enjoy their fill
Of bliss on bliss, while I to Hell am thrust,
Where neither joy nor love, but fierce desire,
510 Among our other torments not the least,
Still° unfulfilled with pain of longing pines;   *always*
Yet let me not forget what I have gained
From their own mouths; all is not theirs it seems:
One fatal tree there stands of Knowledge called,
515 Forbidden them to taste: Knowledge forbidden?
Suspicious, reasonless. Why should their Lord
Envy° them that? Can it be sin to know,   *begrudge*
Can it be death? And do they only stand
By ignorance, is that their happy state,
520 The proof of their obedience and their faith?
O fair foundation laid whereon to build
Their ruin! Hence I will excite their minds
With more desire to know, and to reject
Envious commands, invented with design
525 To keep them low whom knowledge might exalt
Equal with gods; aspiring to be such,
They taste and die: what likelier can ensue?
But first with narrow search I must walk round
This garden, and no corner leave unspied;
530 A chance, but chance[8] may lead where I may meet
Some wand'ring Spirit of Heav'n, by fountain side,
Or in thick shade retired, from him to draw
What further would be learnt. Live while ye may,
Yet happy pair; enjoy, till I return,
535 Short pleasures, for long woes are to succeed."
    So saying, his proud step he scornful turned,
But with sly circumspection, and began
Through wood, through waste, o'er hill, o'er dale his roam.°   *act of wandering*

---

8. An opportunity, even if only by luck.

Meanwhile in utmost longitude, where Heav'n
540 With earth and ocean meets, the setting sun
Slowly descended, and with right aspéct
Against the eastern gate of Paradise
Leveled his evening rays.⁹ it was a rock
Of alabaster,¹ piled up to the clouds,
545 Conspicuous far, winding with one ascent
Accessible from earth, one entrance high;
The rest was craggy cliff, that overhung
Still as it rose, impossible to climb.
Betwixt these rocky pillars Gabriel² sat
550 Chief of th' angelic guards, awaiting night;
About him exercised heroic games
Th' unarmèd youth of Heav'n, but nigh at hand
Celestial armory, shields, helms, and spears
Hung high with diamond flaming, and with gold.
555 Thither came Uriel, gliding through the even
On a sunbeam, swift as a shooting star
In autumn thwarts° the night, when vapors fired   *passes across*
Impress the air, and shows the mariner
From what point of his compass to beware
560 Impetuous winds:³ he thus began in haste.
      "Gabriel, to thee thy course by lot hath giv'n
Charge and strict watch that to this happy place
No evil thing approach or enter in;
This day at hight of noon came to my sphere
565 A Spirit, zealous, as he seemed, to know
More of th' Almighty's works, and chiefly man
God's latest image: I described° his way   *descried, observed*
Bent all on speed, and marked his airy gait;°   *path*
But in the mount that lies from Eden north,
570 Where he first lighted, soon discerned his looks
Alien from Heav'n, with passions foul obscured:
Mine eye pursued him still, but under shade°   *trees*
Lost sight of him; one of the banished crew
I fear, hath ventured from the deep, to raise
575 New troubles; him thy care must be to find."
      To whom the wingèd warrior thus returned:
"Uriel, no wonder if thy perfect sight,
Amid the sun's bright circle where thou sitt'st,
See far and wide. In at this gate none pass
580 The vigilance here placed, but such as come
Well known from Heav'n; and since meridian hour°   *noon*
No creature thence: if Spirit of other sort,
So minded, have o'erleaped these earthy bounds
On purpose, hard thou know'st it to exclude
585 Spiritual substance with corporeal bar.
But if within the circuit of these walks,

---

9. Setting in the west, the sun struck the eastern
gate from the inside, at a 90-degree angle.
1. White, translucent marble veined with colors.
2. In Hebrew, "Strength of God." A tradition (cf.

Enoch 20.7) gave Gabriel charge of Paradise.
3. Shooting stars were thought to indicate by the
direction of their fall the source of oncoming
storms. "Vapors fired": heat lightning.

In whatsoever shape he lurk, of whom
Thou tell'st, by morrow dawning I shall know."
    So promised he, and Uriel to his charge
590 Returned on that bright beam, whose point now raised
Bore him slope downward to the sun now fall'n
Beneath th' Azorès; whether the prime orb,
Incredible how swift, had thither rolled
Diurnal,° or this less volúble° earth   *daily/swift-turning*
595 By shorter flight to th' east,⁴ had left him there
Arraying with reflected purple and gold
The clouds that on his western throne attend.
Now came still evening on, and twilight gray
Had in her sober livery all things clad;
600 Silence accompanied, for beast and bird,
They to their grassy couch, these to their nests
Were slunk, all but the wakeful nightingale;
She all night long her amorous descant° sung;   *melody*
Silence was pleased: now glowed the firmament
605 With living sapphires: Hesperus⁵ that led
The starry host, rode brightest, till the moon
Rising in clouded majesty, at length
Apparent° queen unveiled her peerless light,   *clearly seen*
And o'er the dark her silver mantle threw.
610   When Adam thus to Eve: "Fair consort, th' hour
Of night, and all things now retired to rest
Mind us of like repose, since God hath set
Labor and rest, as day and night to men
Successive, and the timely dew of sleep
615 Now falling with soft slumbrous weight inclines
Our eyelids; other creatures all day long
Rove idle unemployed, and less need rest;
Man hath his daily work of body or mind
Appointed, which declares his dignity,
620 And the regard of Heav'n on all his ways;
While other animals unactive range,
And of their doings God takes no account.
Tomorrow ere fresh morning streak the east
With first approach of light, we must be ris'n,
625 And at our pleasant labor, to reform
Yon flow'ry arbors, yonder alleys green,
Our walk at noon, with branches overgrown,
That mock our scant manuring,° and require   *cultivating*
More hands than ours to lop their wanton growth:
630 Those blossoms also, and those dropping gums,
That lie bestrown unsightly and unsmooth,
Ask riddance,° if we mean to tread with ease;   *need to be cleared*
Meanwhile, as nature wills, night bids us rest."
    To whom thus Eve with perfect beauty adorned.
635 "My author and disposer, what thou bidd'st

---

4. Here and elsewhere Milton leaves open the
question of whether the sun moves around the
earth, or vice versa.
5. The evening star, Venus.

Unargued I obey; so God ordains,
God is thy law, thou mine: to know no more
Is woman's happiest knowledge and her praise.
With thee conversing I forget all time.
540 All seasons° and their change, all please alike.   *times of day*
Sweet[6] is the breath of morn, her rising sweet,
With charm[7] of earliest birds; pleasant the sun
When first on this delightful land he spreads
His orient beams, on herb, tree, fruit, and flow'r,
545 Glist'ring with dew; fragrant the fertile earth
After soft showers; and sweet the coming on
Of grateful evening mild, then silent night
With this her solemn bird° and this fair moon,   *the nightingale*
And these the gems of heav'n, her starry train:
550 But neither breath of morn when she ascends
With charm of earliest birds, nor rising sun
On this delightful land, nor herb, fruit, flow'r,
Glist'ring with dew, nor fragrance after showers,
Nor grateful evening mild, nor silent night
555 With this her solemn bird, nor walk by moon,
Or glittering starlight without thee is sweet.
But wherefore all night long shine these, for whom
This glorious sight, when sleep hath shut all eyes?"
    To whom our general ancestor replied.
560 "Daughter of God and man, accomplished Eve,[8]
Those have their course to finish, round the earth,
By morrow evening, and from land to land
In order, though to nations yet unborn,
Minist'ring light prepared, they set and rise;
565 Lest total darkness should by night regain
Her old possession, and extinguish life
In nature and all things, which these soft° fires   *agreeable*
Not only enlighten, but with kindly° heat   *natural, benevolent*
Of various influence foment and warm,
570 Temper or nourish, or in part shed down
Their stellar virtue on all kinds that grow
On earth, made hereby apter to receive
Perfection from the sun's more potent ray.[9]
These then, though unbeheld in deep of night,
575 Shine not in vain, nor think, though men were none,
That Heav'n would want spectators, God want praise;
Millions of spiritual creatures walk the earth
Unseen, both when we wake, and when we sleep:
All these with ceaseless praise his works behold
580 Both day and night: how often from the steep
Of echoing hill or thicket have we heard
Celestial voices to the midnight air,

---

6. With this embedded lyric, Eve displays her literary talents as author of an elegant love song, sonnetlike and replete with striking rhetorical figures of circularity and repetition.
7. Blended singing of many birds.

8. Having many talents and achievements; perfect, complete.
9. The stars were thought to have their own occult influence, and also to moderate that of the sun.

Sole, or responsive each to other's note
Singing their great Creator: oft in bands
685 While they keep watch, or nightly rounding walk,
With heav'nly touch of instrumental sounds
In full harmonic number joined, their songs
Divide[1] the night, and lift our thoughts to Heaven."
    Thus talking hand in hand alone they passed
690 On to their blissful bower; it was a place
Chos'n by the sovran Planter, when he framed°   *fashioned*
All things to man's delightful use; the roof
Of thickest covert was inwoven shade
Laurel and myrtle, and what higher grew
695 Of firm and fragrant leaf; on either side
Acanthus, and each odorous bushy shrub
Fenced up the verdant wall; each beauteous flow'r,
Iris all hues, roses, and jessamine°   *jasmine*
Reared high their flourished° heads between, and wrought   *flowering*
700 Mosaic; underfoot the violet,
Crocus, and hyacinth with rich inlay
Broidered the ground, more colored than with stone
Of costliest emblem:° other creature here   *inlaid work*
Beast, bird, insect, or worm durst enter none,
705 Such was their awe of man. In shadier bower
More sacred and sequestered,° though but feigned,   *secluded*
Pan or Silvanus never slept, nor nymph,
Nor Faunus[2] haunted. Here in close recess
With flowers, garlands, and sweet-smelling herbs
710 Espousèd Eve decked first her nuptial bed,
And heav'nly choirs the hymenean° sung,   *wedding song*
What day the genial[3] angel to our sire
Brought her in naked beauty more adorned,
More lovely than Pandora, whom the gods
715 Endowed with all their gifts, and O too like
In sad event,° when to the unwiser son   *outcome*
Of Japhet brought by Hermes, she ensnared
Mankind with her fair looks, to be avenged
On him who had stole Jove's authentic fire.[4]
720   Thus at their shady lodge arrived, both stood,
Both turned, and under open sky adored
The God that made both sky, air, earth and Heav'n
Which they beheld, the moon's resplendent globe
And starry pole:° "Thou also mad'st the night,   *sky*
725 Maker Omnipotent, and thou the day,
Which we in our appointed work employed
Have finished happy in our mutual help

---

1. Mark the watches of the night; also, perform musical "divisions," elaborate melodic passages.
2. Forest and field divinities of classical mythology.
3. Presiding over marriage and generation.
4. Pandora (the name means "all gifts") was an artificial woman, molded of clay, bestowed by the gods on Epimetheus, brother of Prometheus (who angered Jove by stealing fire from heaven). She brought a box that foolish Epimetheus opened, releasing all the ills of the human race, leaving only hope inside. The brothers were sons of Iapetos, whom Milton identifies with Japhet, Noah's third son. The Eve-Pandora parallel was often noted.

And mutual love, the crown of all our bliss
Ordained by thee, and this delicious place
30 For us too large, where thy abundance wants
Partakers, and uncropped falls to the ground.
But thou hast promised from us two a race
To fill the earth, who shall with us extol
Thy goodness infinite, both when we wake,
35 And when we seek, as now, thy gift of sleep."
    This said unanimous, and other rites
Observing none, but adoration pure
Which God likes best,[5] into their inmost bow'r
Handed° they went; and eased° the putting off   *hand in hand / spared*
40 These troublesome disguises which we wear,
Straight side by side were laid, nor turned I ween°   *surmise*
Adam from his fair spouse, nor Eve the rites
Mysterious[6] of connubial love refused:
Whatever hypocrites austerely talk
45 Of purity and place and innocence,
Defaming as impure what God declares
Pure, and commands to some, leaves free to all.
Our Maker bids increase,[7] who bids abstain
But our destroyer, foe to God and man?
50 Hail wedded Love, mysterious law, true source
Of human offspring, sole propriety°   *private property*
In Paradise of all things common else.
By thee adulterous lust was driv'n from men
Among the bestial herds to range, by thee
55 Founded in reason, loyal, just, and pure,
Relations dear, and all the charities°   *loves*
Of father, son, and brother first were known.
Far be it, that I should write thee sin or blame,
Or think thee unbefitting holiest place,
60 Perpetual fountain of domestic sweets,
Whose bed is undefiled and chaste pronounced,
Present, or past, as saints and patriarchs used.[8]
Here Love his golden shafts employs, here lights
His constant lamp, and waves his purple wings,
65 Reigns here and revels;[9] not in the bought smile
Of harlots, loveless, joyless, unendeared,
Casual fruition, nor in court amours,
Mixed dance, or wanton masque, or midnight ball,
Or serenade, which the starved° lover sings   *perished with cold*
70 To his proud fair, best quitted with disdain.
These lulled by nightingales embracing slept,
And on their naked limbs the flow'ry roof

5. Like many Puritans, Milton objected to set forms of prayer, so Adam and Eve pray spontaneously (therefore sincerely), but also, paradoxically, together. Their prayer develops variations on Psalm 104.20–24.
6. Awe-inspiring. St. Paul (Ephesians 5.32) calls the union of man and woman a "mystery" parallel-ing that of Christ and the Church.
7. Genesis 1.28.
8. Throughout history ("present or past"), Old and New Testament worthies have "used" matrimony as a noble estate.
9. The "golden shafts" (arrows) of Cupid produce true love, his lead-tipped arrows, hate.

Show'red roses, which the morn repaired.° Sleep on,   *replaced*
Blest pair; and O yet happiest if ye seek
775   No happier state, and know to know no more.[1]

Summary   Fulfilling his promise to Uriel, Gabriel divides his night watch into search parties, assigning Ithuriel and Zephon to guard closely the bower of Adam and Eve. They find Satan in the bower, whispering in the ear of the sleeping Eve, and bring him before Gabriel. A battle impends, but is averted by a heavenly signal, and Satan flees out of Paradise.

From Book 5

[EVE'S DREAM: TROUBLE IN PARADISE]

Now Morn her rosy steps in th' eastern clime
Advancing, sowed the earth with orient pearl,°   *sparkling dew*
When Adam waked, so customed, for his sleep
Was aery light, from pure digestion bred,
5   And temperate vapors bland,° which th' only sound   *gentle, balmy*
Of leaves and fuming rills, Aurora's fan,[1]
Lightly dispersed, and the shrill matin° song   *morning*
Of birds on every bough; so much the more
His wonder was to find unawakened Eve
10   With tresses discomposed, and glowing cheek,
As through unquiet rest: he on his side
Leaning half-raised, with looks of cordial° love   *heartfelt*
Hung over her enamored, and beheld
Beauty, which whether waking or asleep,
15   Shot forth peculiar° graces; then with voice   *its own*
Mild, as when Zephyrus on Flora[2] breathes,
Her hand soft touching, whispered thus: "Awake
My fairest, my espoused, my lastest found,
Heav'n's last best gift, my ever new delight,
20   Awake, the morning shines, and the fresh field
Calls us, we lose the prime, to mark how spring
Our tended plants, how blows° the citron grove,   *blooms*
What drops the myrrh, and what the balmy reed,°   *balsam*
How nature paints her colors, how the bee
25   Sits on the bloom extracting liquid sweet."[3]
    Such whispering waked her, but with startled eye
On Adam, whom embracing, thus she spake:
    "O sole in whom my thoughts find all repose,

---

1. Know enough to be content with what you know.
1. Rustling leaves stirred by Aurora, goddess of the dawn.
2. Zephyrus is god of the gentle west wind, Flora goddess of flowers.
3. Adam sings a morning love song (*aubade*) to Eve, which works variations on Song of Solomon 2.10–12: "Rise up, my love, my fair one, and come away. . . . The flowers appear on the earth; the time of the singing of birds is come." Compare Satan's serenade (5.38–47), a parody of Adam's *aubade* and the Song of Solomon. "Prime" (line 21): first hour of the day.

My glory, my perfection, glad I see
30 Thy face, and morn returned, for I this night,
Such night till this I never passed, have dreamed,
If dreamed, not as I oft am wont, of thee,
Works of day past, or morrow's next design,
But of offense and trouble, which my mind
35 Knew never till this irksome night. Methought
Close at mine ear one called me forth to walk
With gentle voice, I thought it thine; it said,
'Why sleep'st thou Eve? now is the pleasant time,
The cool, the silent, save where silence yields
40 To the night-warbling bird, that now awake
Tunes sweetest his love-labored song; now reigns
Full-orbed the moon, and with more pleasing light
Shadowy sets off the face of things, in vain,
If none regard; heav'n wakes with all his eyes,°   stars
45 Whom to behold but thee, nature's desire,
In whose sight all things joy, with ravishment
Attracted by thy beauty still° to gaze.'   continually
I rose as at thy call, but found thee not;
To find thee I directed then my walk;
50 And on, me thought, alone I passed through ways
That brought me on a sudden to the tree
Of interdicted knowledge: fair it seemed,
Much fairer to my fancy than by day:
And as I wond'ring looked, beside it stood
55 One shaped and winged like one of those from Heav'n
By us oft seen; his dewy locks distilled
Ambrosia;° on that tree he also gazed;   heavenly fragrance
And 'O fair plant,' said he, 'with fruit surcharged,
Deigns none to ease thy load and taste thy sweet,
60 Nor god,° nor man; is knowledge so despised?   angel
Or envy, or what reserve forbids to taste?[4]
Forbid who will, none shall from me withhold
Longer thy offered good, why else set here?'
This said he paused not, but with vent'rous arm
65 He plucked, he tasted; me damp horror chilled
At such bold words vouched with° a deed so bold: backed by
But he thus overjoyed, 'O fruit divine,
Sweet of thyself, but much more sweet thus cropped,
Forbidden here, it seems, as only fit
70 For gods, yet able to make gods of men:
And why not gods of men, since good, the more
Communicated, more abundant grows,
The author not impaired,° but honored more?   injured, diminished
Here, happy creature, fair angelic Eve,
75 Partake thou also; happy though thou art,
Happier thou may'st be, worthier canst not be:
Taste this, and be henceforth among the gods
Thyself a goddess, not to earth confined,

4. I.e., does envy or some other barrier ("reserve") forbid your being tasted?

But sometimes in the air, as we, sometimes
80 Ascend to Heav'n, by merit thine, and see
What life the gods live there, and such live thou.'
So saying, he drew nigh, and to me held,
Even to my mouth of that same fruit held part
Which he had plucked; the pleasant savory smell
85 So quickened appetite, that I, me thought,
Could not but taste. Forthwith up to the clouds
With him I flew, and underneath beheld
The earth outstretched immense, a prospect wide
And various: wond'ring at my flight and change
90 To this high exaltation: suddenly
My guide was gone, and I, methought, sunk down,
And fell asleep; but O how glad I waked
To find this but a dream!" Thus Eve her night
Related, and thus Adam answered sad.°   gravely, soberly
95   "Best image of myself and dearer half,
The trouble of thy thoughts this night in sleep
Affects me equally; nor can I like
This uncouth° dream, of evil sprung I fear;   strange, unpleasant
Yet evil whence? in thee can harbor none,
100 Created pure. But know that in the soul
Are many lesser faculties[5] that serve
Reason as chief; among these fancy next
Her office holds; of all external things,
Which the five watchful senses represent,
105 She forms imaginations,° aery shapes,   images
Which reason joining or disjoining, frames
All what we affirm or what deny, and call
Our knowledge or opinion; then retires
Into her private cell when nature rests.
110 Oft in her absence mimic fancy wakes
To imitate her; but misjoining shapes,
Wild work produces oft, and most in dreams,
Ill matching words and deeds long past or late.
Some such resemblances methinks I find
115 Of our last evening's talk in this thy dream,[6]
But with addition strange; yet be not sad.
Evil into the mind of god[7] or man
May come and go, so unapproved,[8] and leave
No spot or blame behind: which gives me hope
120 That what in sleep thou didst abhor to dream,
Waking thou never wilt consent to do.
Be not disheartened then, nor cloud those looks
That wont to be more cheerful and serene
Than when fair morning first smiles on the world,
125 And let us to our fresh employments rise

5. Adam's explanation of the dream (lines 100–
113) summarizes the orthodox faculty psychology
and dream theory of Milton's time—one among
many kinds of knowledge with which unfallen man
was endowed.
6. Adam recalls his own words in 4.411–39.

7. Probably "angel" as elsewhere, but perhaps
God, whose omniscience must encompass knowledge of evil as well as good.
8. If not approved of, or not acted on (put to the
proof).

Among the groves, the fountains, and the flow'rs
That open now their choicest bosomed smells
Reserved from night, and kept for thee in store."
   So cheered he his fair spouse, and she was cheered,
30 But silently a gentle tear let fall
From either eye, and wiped them with her hair;
Two other precious drops that ready stood,
Each in their crystal sluice, he ere they fell
Kissed as the gracious signs of sweet remorse
35 And pious° awe, that feared to have offended.   *dutiful*

Summary   Before going to work at their rural tasks, Adam and Eve recite their spontaneous morning prayers. God, seeing and pitying their unprotected innocence, dispatches Raphael to warn them of approaching dangers. The affable archangel enters the bower just about noontime and is promptly invited to join the midday meal, an invitation that he gladly accepts.

[A VISIT WITH THE ANGEL. THE SCALE OF NATURE]

    * * * So to the sylvan lodge
They came, that like Pomona's[9] arbor smiled
With flow'rets decked° and fragrant smells; but Eve   *covered*
80 Undecked, save with herself more lovely fair
Than wood-nymph, or the fairest goddess feigned
Of three that in Mount Ida naked strove,[1]
Stood to entertain her guest from Heav'n; no veil   ,
She needed, virtue-proof,° no thought infirm   *armored in virtue*
85 Altered her cheek. On whom the Angel "Hail"
Bestowed, the holy salutation used
Long after to blest Mary, second Eve.[2]
   "Hail mother of mankind, whose fruitful womb
Shall fill the world more numerous with thy sons
90 Than with these various fruits the trees of God
Have heaped this table." Raised of grassy turf
Their table was, and mossy seats had round,
And on her ample square from side to side
All autumn piled, though spring and autumn here
,95 Danced hand in hand. A while discourse they hold;
No fear lest dinner cool; when thus began
Our author:° "Heav'nly stranger, please to taste   *forefather*
These bounties which our Nourisher, from whom
All perfect good unmeasured out, descends,
,00 To us for food and for delight hath caused

---

9. The Roman goddess of fruit trees.
1. On Mount Ida, Venus, Juno, and Minerva "strove" naked for the title of the most beautiful; Paris awarded the prize (the apple of discord) to Venus, which led to the rape of Helen and the Tro-

jan War.
2. Cf. the angel's words to Mary announcing that she would bear a son, Jesus (Luke 1.28): "Hail, thou that art highly favored, the Lord is with thee: blessed art thou among women."

The earth to yield; unsavory food perhaps
To spiritual natures; only this I know,
That one Celestial Father gives to all."
   To whom the angel: "Therefore what he gives
405 (Whose praise be ever sung) to man in part
Spiritual, may of° purest Spirits be found   *by*
No ingrateful food: and food alike those pure
Intelligential substances require³
As doth your rational; and both contain
410 Within them every lower faculty
Of sense, whereby they hear, see, smell, touch, taste,
Tasting concoct, digest, assimilate,⁴
And corporeal to incorporeal turn.
For know, whatever was created, needs
415 To be sustained and fed; of elements
The grosser feeds the purer, earth the sea,
Earth and the sea feed air, the air those fires
Ethereal, and as lowest first the moon;
Whence in her visage round those spots, unpurged
420 Vapors not yet into her substance turned.⁵
Nor doth the moon no nourishment exhale
From her moist continent to higher orbs.⁶
The sun that light imparts to all, receives
From all his alimental° recompense   *nourishing*
425 In humid exhalations, and at even
Sups with the ocean:⁷ though in Heav'n the trees
Of life ambrosial fruitage bear, and vines
Yield nectar,⁸ though from off the boughs each morn
We brush mellifluous° dews, and find the ground   *honey-flowing*
430 Covered with pearly grain; yet God hath here
Varied his bounty so with new delights,
As may compare with Heaven; and to taste
Think not I shall be nice."° So down they sat,   *fastidious, finicky*
And to their viands fell, nor seemingly°   *in show*
435 The angel, nor in mist, the common gloss°   *explanation*
Of theologians, but with keen dispatch
Of real hunger, and concoctive° heat   *digestive*
To transubstantiate;⁹ what redounds, transpires
Through Spirits with ease; nor wonder, if by fire
440 Of sooty coal the empiric° alchemist   *experimental*

3. Milton's angels ("intelligential substances") require real food, even as "rational" men do (see below, lines 430–38). As a monist (believer that all creation is of one matter), Milton denied the more common (dualistic) idea that angels are pure spirit, holding instead that they are of a very highly refined material substance.

4. Three stages in digestion.

5. Here Raphael describes lunar spots as still-undigested vapors (in keeping with his exposition of the universal need of nourishment); in 1.287–91 he referred to moonspots in Galileo's terms, as landscape features.

6. A double negative: the moon does exhale such nourishment to other planets.

7. Milton explains evaporation as the sun dining off moisture exhaled from the oceans.

8. Ambrosia is the food and nectar the drink of the classical gods; Milton adds "pearly grain" (line 430), like the manna showered on the Israelites in the desert (Exodus 16.14).

9. In common theological use, transubstantiation is the Roman Catholic doctrine that the bread and wine of the eucharist become the body and blood of Christ. Milton vigorously denied that doctrine, but he describes the angels' transforming of earthly food into their more highly refined spiritual substance as a true transubstantiation. The excess ("what redounds") is exhaled ("transpires") through angelic pores.

Can turn, or holds it possible to turn
Metals of drossiest ore to perfect gold
As from the mine. Meanwhile at table Eve
Ministered naked, and their flowing cups
With pleasant liquors crowned.° O innocence   *filled to the brim*
Deserving Paradise! if ever, then,
Then had the Sons of God excuse t' have been
Enamored at that sight,[1] but in those hearts
Love unlibidinous° reigned, nor jealousy   *without lust*
Was understood, the injured lover's hell.
    Thus when with meats and drinks they had sufficed,
Not burdened nature, sudden mind arose
In Adam, not to let th' occasion pass
Given him by this great conference to know
Of things above his world, and of their being
Who dwell in Heav'n, whose excellence he saw
Transcend his own so far, whose radiant forms
Divine effulgence,° whose high power so far   *shining forth*
Exceeded human, and his wary speech
Thus to th' empyreal minister he framed:
    "Inhabitant with God, now know I well
Thy favor, in this honor done to man,
Under whose lowly roof thou hast vouchsafed
To enter and these earthly fruits to taste,
Food not of angels, yet accepted so,
As that more willingly thou couldst not seem
At Heav'n's high feasts t' have fed: yet what compare?"
    To whom the wingèd Hierarch replied:
"O Adam, one Almighty is, from whom
All things proceed, and up to him return,
If not depraved from good, created all
Such to perfection, one first matter all,[2]
Endued with various forms, various degrees
Of substance, and in things that live, of life;
But more refined, more spiritous, and pure,
As nearer to him placed or nearer tending
Each in their several active spheres assigned,
Till body up to spirit work, in bounds
Proportioned to each kind.[3] So from the root
Springs lighter the green stalk, from thence the leaves
More airy, last the bright consummate flow'r
Spirits odórous breathes:[4] flow'rs and their fruit

1. Genesis 6.2 tells of the marriage of the daughters of men with the sons of God, usually identified as sons of Seth, but a patristic tradition (alluded to here) identifies them as angels.
2. Milton held that the universe was created out of Chaos, not out of nothing: the primal matter of Chaos had its origin in God, who subsequently created all things from that matter (see 7.168–73, 210–42). This materialist "monism" denies sharp distinctions between angels and men, spirit and matter: all beings are of one substance, of varying degrees of refinement and life.
3. Milton's version of the chain of being qualifies

natural hierarchy by allowing for movement up or down; beings may become increasingly "spiritual" or increasingly gross (as the rebel angels do), depending on their moral choices—"nearer tending."
4. The plant figure—root, stalk, leaves, flowers, and fruit—provides an illustration of the dynamism of being in the universe and further explains why Raphael can eat the fruit. Such food is then transformed (next lines) into various orders of "spirits"—"vital," "animal," and "intellectual" (fluids in the blood that sustain life, sensation, motion, and finally intellect and its functions, "fancy,"

Man's nourishment, by gradual scale sublimed°   *purified*
To vital spirits aspire, to animal,
485   To intellectual, give both life and sense,
Fancy° and understanding, whence the soul   *imagination*
Reason receives, and reason is her being,
Discursive, or intuitive;⁵ discourse
Is oftest yours, the latter most is ours,
490   Differing but in degree, of kind the same.
Wonder not then, what God for you saw good
If I refuse not, but convert, as you,
To proper° substance; time may come when men   *our own*
With angels may participate, and find
495   No inconvenient diet, nor too light fare:
And from these corporal nutriments perhaps
Your bodies may at last turn all to spirit,
Improved by tract° of time, and winged ascend   *passage*
Ethereal as we, or may at choice
500   Here or in heav'nly paradises dwell;
If ye be found obedient, and retain
Unalterably firm his love entire
Whose progeny you are. Meanwhile enjoy
Your fill what happiness this happy state
505   Can comprehend, incapable° of more."   *unable to contain*
     To whom the patriarch of mankind replied:
"O favorable Spirit, propitious guest,
Well hast thou taught the way that might direct
Our knowledge, and the scale of nature set
510   From center to circumference, whereon
In contemplation of created things
By steps we may ascend to God. * * *

Summary   After this mingled explanation and warning, Raphael, by way of emphasizing the danger that threatens Adam and Eve, enters upon the story of Satan's revolt and fall. Satan, pretending that God's exaltation of the Son was an offense to angelic dignity, persuaded the angels under his command—a third of the heavenly host—to go off and set up a camp in the north of Heaven. When he revealed his rebellious purpose, however, one of these angels refused to embrace it. The seraph Abdiel, though scorned by Satan and all his legions, denounced the rebellion and returned, heroically alone, to the ranks of God's followers.

Book 6 Summary   Continuing the story of the war in Heaven, Raphael describes the assembling of the armies and a first skirmish in which Satan is both

---

"understanding," and "reason"), indicating that the soul is also material.
5. Traditionally, on the dualist assumption that angels are pure spirit and humans a combination of matter and spirit, angelic intuition (immediate apprehension of truth) was absolutely distinguished from human "discourse" of reason (arguing from premises to conclusions). Milton, denying that assumption, makes the distinction only relative, a matter of "degree" (line 490).

insulted and wounded by Abdiel. After the first day's battle, the evil angels retire discomfited; but overnight Satan invents cannon, with which, on the second day, the good angels are put to some disorder. In the fury of the fight, however, they pull up mountains by the roots and bury the cannon beneath them; thus the issue remains inconclusive. On the third day, God withdraws all His armies and sends the Son alone into battle; the Son drives His enemies irresistibly over the wall of Heaven, and after falling nine days through Chaos they are swallowed up in Hell.

From Book 7

[THE INVOCATION]

Descend from Heav'n Urania,[1] by that name
If rightly thou art called, whose voice divine
Following, above th' Olympian hill I soar,
Above the flight of Pegasean wing.[2]
5   The meaning, not the name I call: for thou
Nor of the muses nine, nor on the top
Of old Olympus dwell'st, but heav'nly born
Before the hills appeared, or fountain flowed,
Thou with eternal Wisdom[3] didst converse,°   *associate*
10 Wisdom thy sister, and with her didst play
In presence of th' Almighty Father, pleased
With thy celestial song. Up led by thee
Into the Heav'n of Heav'ns I have presumed,
An earthly guest, and drawn empyreal air,
15 Thy temp'ring;° with like safety guided down   *made suitable by thee*
Return me to my native element:
Lest from this flying steed unreined (as once
Bellerophon,[4] though from a lower clime)°   *region*
Dismounted, on th' Aleian field I fall
20 Erroneous° there to wander and forlorn.   *straying*
Half yet remains unsung, but narrower bound
Within the visible diurnal sphere;[5]
Standing on earth, not rapt° above the pole,   *transported, enraptured*
More safe I sing with mortal voice, unchanged
25 To hoarse or mute, though fall'n on evil days,
On evil days though fall'n on evil tongues;
In darkness, and with dangers compassed round,[6]

1. Urania, the Greek Muse of Astronomy, had been made into the Muse of Christian Poetry by DuBartas and other religious poets. Milton, however, constructs another derivation for her (line 5ff.). Milton begins Book 7 with a third Proem (lines 1–39).
2. Pegasus, the flying horse of inspired poetry, suggests (in connection with Bellerophon, line 18) Milton's sense of perilous audacity in writing this poem.
3. In Proverbs 8.24–31 Wisdom tells of her activities before the Creation: "Then I was by him [God], as one brought up with him; and I was daily his delight, rejoicing always before him." Milton describes "eternal Wisdom" as a "daughter" of God (personification of his wisdom), and devises a myth in which the Muse of Divine Poetry ("celestial song," line 12) is Wisdom's "sister"—also, thereby, originating from God.
4. Bellerophon incurred the gods' anger when he tried to fly to heaven upon Pegasus; Zeus sent an insect to sting the horse, and Bellerophon fell down to the "Aleian field" (plain of error), where he wandered alone and blind until his death.
5. The universe, which appears to rotate daily.
6. After the Restoration of Charles II (May 1660) and until the passage of the Act of Oblivion (August 1660), Milton was in danger of death and dismemberment (like Orpheus, lines 34–35); several of his republican colleagues were hanged, drawn, and quartered for their part in the revolution and regicide.

And solitude; yet not alone, while thou
Visit'st my slumbers nightly, or when morn
30 Purples the east: still govern thou my song,
Urania, and fit audience find, though few.
But drive far off the barbarous dissonance
Of Bacchus and his revelers,[7] the race
Of that wild rout that tore the Thracian bard
35 In Rhodope, where woods and rocks had ears
To rapture, till the savage clamor drowned
Both harp and voice; nor could the Muse[8] defend
Her son. So fail not thou, who thee implores:
For thou art heav'nly, she an empty dream.

Summary   At Adam's request, Raphael continues his narration and describes how God, to replace the fallen angels, created the world, its creatures, and finally man, in the course of six days; the story of the creation concludes, on the seventh day, with a chorus of thanksgiving by the angels.

From Book 8

Summary   Adam, to prolong his visit with Raphael, asks why so many and such splendid stars seem to be at the service of the earth, which appears smaller and less noble than they. At this point Eve discreetly takes her leave. Replying to Adam's question, Raphael proposes various astronomical possibilities, but gives no conclusive answer, advising Adam to concern himself with matters closer to home. The angel, on the other hand, is much interested to hear the story, which Adam proposes to tell, of his own creation.

[ADAM DESCRIBES HIS OWN CREATION AND THAT OF EVE; HAVING
REPEATED HIS WARNING, THE ANGEL DEPARTS]

So spake the godlike Power, and thus our sire:
250 "For man to tell how human life began
Is hard; for who himself beginning knew?[1]
Desire with thee still longer to converse
Induced me. As new-waked from soundest sleep
Soft on the flow'ry herb I found me laid
255 In balmy sweat, which with his beams the sun
Soon dried, and on the reeking° moisture fed.   *steaming*
Straight toward heav'n my wond'ring eyes I turned,
And gazed a while the ample sky, till raised
By quick instinctive motion up I sprung

---

7. The music of the "Thracian Bard" Orpheus, type of the poet, charmed even "woods and rocks," but his song was drowned out by the Bacchantes, a "wild rout" of screaming women who murdered and dismembered him and threw his body parts into the Hebrus River, which rises in the "Rhodope" mountains. Milton fears that a similar "bar-

barous dissonance" unleashed by the Restoration will drown out his voice and threaten his life.
8. Orpheus's mother is Calliope, Muse of Epic Poetry.
1. Compare Satan's inability to remember his origins (5.859–63) from which he infers self-creation, whereas Adam infers a Maker (278).

60 As thitherward endeavoring, and upright
    Stood on my feet; about me round I saw
    Hill, dale, and shady woods, and sunny plains,
    And liquid lapse° of murmuring streams; by these,   *flow*
    Creatures that lived, and moved, and walked, or flew,
65 Birds on the branches warbling; all things smiled,
    With fragrance and with joy my heart o'erflowed.
    Myself I then perused, and limb by limb
    Surveyed, and sometimes went,° and sometimes ran   *walked*
    With supple joints, as lively vigor led:
70 But who I was, or where, or from what cause,
    Knew not; to speak I tried, and forthwith spake,
    My tongue obeyed and readily could name
    Whate'er I saw.² 'Thou sun,' said I, 'fair light,
    And thou enlightened earth, so fresh and gay,
75 Ye hills and dales, ye rivers, woods, and plains,
    And ye that live and move, fair creatures, tell,
    Tell, if ye saw, how came I thus, how here?
    Not of myself; by some great Maker then,
    In goodness and in power preeminent;
80 Tell me, how may I know him, how adore,
    From whom I have that thus I move and live,
    And feel that I am happier than I know.'
    While thus I called, and strayed I knew not whither,
    From where I first drew air, and first beheld
85 This happy light, when answer none returned,
    On a green shady bank profuse of flow'rs
    Pensive I sat me down; there gentle sleep
    First found me, and with soft oppression seized
    My drowsèd sense, untroubled, though I thought
90 I then was passing to my former state
    Insensible, and forthwith to dissolve:
    When suddenly stood at my head a dream,
    Whose inward apparition gently moved
    My fancy to believe I yet had being,
95 And lived: one came, methought, of shape divine,
    And said, 'Thy mansion° wants° thee, Adam, rise,   *habitation / lacks*
    First man, of men innumerable ordained
    First father, called by thee I come thy guide
    To the garden of bliss, thy seat° prepared.'   *residence*
00 So saying, by the hand he took me raised,
    And over fields and waters, as in air
    Smooth sliding without step, last led me up
    A woody mountain whose high top was plain,
    A circuit wide, enclosed, with goodliest trees
05 Planted, with walks, and bowers, that what I saw
    Of earth before scarce pleasant seemed. Each tree
    Load'n with fairest fruit, that hung to the eye
    Tempting, stirred in me sudden appetite
    To pluck and eat; whereat I waked, and found

---

2. Adam's ability to name the creatures was said to signify his intuitive understanding of their natures.

310 Before mine eyes all real, as the dream
Had lively° shadowed: here had new begun   *vividly*
My wand'ring, had not he who was my guide
Up hither, from among the trees appeared,
Presence Divine. Rejoicing, but with awe
315 In adoration at his feet I fell
Submiss:° he reared me, and 'Whom thou sought'st I am,'   *submissive*
Said mildly, 'Author of all this thou seest
Above, or round about thee or beneath.
This paradise I give thee, count it thine
320 To till and keep,° and of the fruit to eat: *care for*
Of every tree that in the garden grows
Eat freely with glad heart; fear here no dearth:
But of the tree whose operation° brings   *action*
Knowledge of good and ill, which I have set
325 The pledge of thy obedience and thy faith,
Amid the garden by the Tree of Life,
Remember what I warn thee, shun to taste,
And shun the bitter consequence: for know,
The day thou eat'st thereof, my sole command
330 Transgressed, inevitably thou shalt die;
From that day mortal, and this happy state
Shalt lose, expelled from hence into a world
Of woe and sorrow.'³ Sternly he pronounced
The rigid interdiction,° which resounds   *prohibition*
335 Yet dreadful in mine ear, though in my choice
Not to incur; but soon his clear aspéct
Returned and gracious purpose° thus renewed: *speech*
'Not only these fair bounds, but all the earth
To thee and to thy race I give; as lords
340 Possess it, and all things that therein live,
Or live in sea, or air, beast, fish, and fowl.
In sign whereof each bird and beast behold
After their kinds; I bring them to receive
From thee their names, and pay thee fealty
345 With low subjection; understand the same
Of fish within their wat'ry residence,
Not hither summoned, since they cannot change
Their element to draw the thinner air.'
As thus he spake, each bird and beast behold
350 Approaching two and two, these° cow'ring low   *the beasts*
With blandishment,° each bird stooped on his wing.   *flattering gesture*
I named them, as they passed, and understood
Their nature, with such knowledge God endued
My sudden apprehension:⁴ but in these
355 I found not what methought I wanted still;
And to the heav'nly Vision thus presumed:
    " 'O by what name, for thou above all these,

---

3. Compare God's commands to Adam (Genesis 1.28–39, 2.16–17) with Milton's elaboration here.
4. Adam had already begun naming the sun and features of the earth (lines 72–73), but here he names (and thereby shows he understands) all living creatures.

Above mankind, or aught than mankind higher,
Surpassest far my naming,[5] how may I
360 Adore thee, Author of this universe,
And all this good to man, for whose well-being
So amply, and with hands so liberal
Thou hast provided all things: but with me
I see not who partakes. In solitude
365 What happiness, who can enjoy alone,
Or all enjoying, what contentment find?'
Thus I presumptuous; and the Vision bright,
As with a smile more brightened, thus replied:
    " 'What call'st thou solitude? Is not the earth
370 With various living creatures, and the air
Replenished,° and all these at thy command   *fully stocked*
To come and play before thee? Know'st thou not
Their language and their ways? They also know,°   *have understanding*
And reason not contemptibly; with these
375 Find pastime, and bear rule; thy realm is large.'
So spake the Universal Lord, and seemed
So ordering. I with leave of speech implored,
And humble deprecation thus replied:
    " 'Let not my words offend thee, Heav'nly Power,
380 My Maker, be propitious while I speak.
Hast thou not made me here thy substitute,
And these inferior far beneath me set?
Among unequals what society
Can sort,° what harmony or true delight?   *agree*
385 Which must be mutual, in proportion due
Giv'n and received; but in disparity
The one intense, the other still remiss[6]
Cannot well suit with either, but soon prove
Tedious alike. Of fellowship I speak
390 Such as I seek, fit to participate°   *partake of*
All rational delight, wherein the brute
Cannot be human consort; they rejoice
Each with their kind, lion with lioness;
So fitly them in pairs thou hast combined;
395 Much less can bird with beast, or fish with fowl
So well converse,° nor with the ox the ape;   *associate*
Worse then can man with beast, and least of all.'
    "Whereto th' Almighty answered, not displeased:
'A nice° and subtle happiness I see   *fastidious*
400 Thou to thyself proposest, in the choice
Of thy associates, Adam, and wilt taste
No pleasure, though in pleasure, solitary.
What think'st thou then of me, and this my state?
Seem I to thee sufficiently possessed

---

5. Adam reasons, as the Scholastics did, from the creatures to the fact of a Creator, but he cannot name (and so indicates that he cannot understand) God, except as God reveals himself.

6. As with poorly matched musical instruments, Adam's string is too taut ("intense") and the animals' is too slack ("remiss") to be in harmony ("suit").

405 Of happiness, or not? who am alone
     From all eternity, for none I know
     Second to me or like, equal much less.
     How have I then with whom to hold converse
     Save with the creatures which I made, and those
410 To me inferior, infinite descents
     Beneath what other creatures are to thee?'
        "He ceased, I lowly answered: 'To attain
     The height and depth of thy eternal ways
     All human thoughts come short, Supreme of things;
415 Thou in thyself art perfect, and in thee
     Is no deficience found; not so is man,
     But in degree, the cause of his desire
     By conversation with his like to help,
     Or solace his defects.[7] No need that thou
420 Shouldst propagate, already infinite;
     And through all numbers absolute, though One;[8]
     But man by number is to manifest
     His single imperfection, and beget
     Like of his like, his image multiplied,
425 In unity defective, which requires
     Collateral° love, and dearest amity.   *mutual*
     Thou in thy secrecy° although alone,   *seclusion*
     Best with thyself accompanied, seek'st not
     Social communication, yet so pleased,
430 Canst raise thy creature to what height thou wilt
     Of union or communion, deified;
     I by conversing cannot these erect
     From prone, nor in their ways complacence° find.'   *satisfaction*
     Thus I emboldened spake, and freedom used
435 Permissive,° and acceptance found, which gained   *permitted*
     This answer from the gracious Voice Divine:
        " 'Thus far to try thee, Adam, I was pleased,
     And find thee knowing not of beasts alone,
     Which thou hast rightly named, but of thyself,
440 Expressing well the spirit within thee free,
     My image, not imparted to the brute,
     Whose fellowship therefore unmeet for thee
     Good reason was thou freely shouldst dislike,
     And be so minded still. I, ere thou spak'st,
445 Knew it not good for man to be alone,
     And no such company as then thou saw'st
     Intended thee, for trial only brought,
     To see how thou couldst judge of fit and meet:
     What next I bring shall please thee, be assured,
450 Thy likeness, thy fit help, thy other self,
     Thy wish, exactly to thy heart's desire.'[9]

---

7. God is absolutely perfect, man only relatively so
("in degree"), and thereby needs companionship
with a fit mate to assuage ("solace") the "defects"
arising from solitariness.
8. God, though One, contains all numbers, but
man has to remedy the "imperfection" of being sin-

gle (line 423) by procreating and thereby multiplying his single and thereby "defective" image (line
425).
9. Compare the account in Genesis 2.18 with Milton's elaboration.

"He ended, or I heard no more, for now
My earthly by his heav'nly overpowered,
Which it had long stood under,° strained to the height   *been exposed to*
55 In that celestial colloquy sublime,
As with an object that excels° the sense,   *exceeds*
Dazzled and spent, sunk down, and sought repair
Of sleep, which instantly fell on me, called
By nature as in aid, and closed mine eyes.
60 Mine eyes he closed, but open left the cell
Of fancy° my internal sight, by which   *imagination*
Abstract° as in a trance methought I saw.   *withdrawn*
Though sleeping, where I lay, and saw the shape
Still glorious before whom awake I stood;
65 Who stooping opened my left side, and took
From thence a rib, with cordial° spirits warm,   *from the heart*
And life-blood streaming fresh; wide was the wound,
But suddenly with flesh filled up and healed:
The rib he formed and fashioned with his hands;
70 Under his forming hands a creature grew,[1]
Manlike, but different sex, so lovely fair
That what seemed fair in all the world seemed now
Mean, or in her summed up, in her contained
And in her looks, which from that time infused
75 Sweetness into my heart, unfelt before,
And into all things from her air° inspired   *mien, look*
The spirit of love and amorous delight.
She disappeared, and left me dark, I waked
To find her, or for ever to deplore
80 Her loss, and other pleasures all abjure:
When out of hope, behold her, not far off,
Such as I saw her in my dream, adorned
With what all earth or heaven could bestow
To make her amiable:° on she came,   *lovely*
85 Led by her heav'nly Maker, though unseen,[2]
And guided by his voice, nor uninformed
Of nuptial sanctity and marriage rites:
Grace was in all her steps, Heav'n in her eye,
In every gesture dignity and love.
90 I overjoyed could not forbear aloud:
    " 'This turn hath made amends; thou hast fulfilled
Thy words, Creator bounteous and benign,
Giver of all things fair, but fairest this
Of all thy gifts, nor enviest.° I now see   *give reluctantly*
95 Bone of my bone, flesh of my flesh, my self
Before me; woman is her name, of man
Extracted; for this cause he shall forgo
Father and mother, and to his wife adhere;
And they shall be one flesh, one heart, one soul.'[3]
100   "She heard me thus, and though divinely brought,

---

1. Compare the *Creation of Eve* by the Italian painter Paolo Veronese (1528–1588).
2. Compare Eve's version of these events (4.440–

91).
3. Compare the account in Genesis 2.23–24.

Yet innocence and virgin modesty,
Her virtue and the conscience°   *consciousness*
That would be wooed, and not unsought be won,
Not obvious,° not obtrusive,° but retired,   *bold / forward*
505 The more desirable, or to say all,
Nature herself, though pure of sinful thought,
Wrought in her so that, seeing me, she turned;
I followed her, she what was honor knew,
And with obsequious° majesty approved   *compliant*
510 My pleaded reason. To the nuptial bow'r
I led her blushing like the morn: all heav'n,
And happy constellations on that hour
Shed their selectest influence; the earth
Gave sign of gratulation,° and each hill;   *rejoicing, congratulation*
515 Joyous the birds; fresh gales and gentle airs⁴
Whispered it to the woods, and from their wings
Flung rose, flung odors from the spicy shrub,
Disporting,° till the amorous bird of night°   *frolicking / nightingale*
Sung spousal, and bid haste the evening star°   *Venus*
520 On his hill top, to light the bridal lamp.
     Thus I have told thee all my state, and brought
My story to the sum of earthly bliss
Which I enjoy, and must confess to find
In all things else delight indeed, but such
525 As used or not, works in the mind no change,
Nor vehement desire, these delicacies
I mean of taste, sight, smell, herbs, fruits, and flow'rs,
Walks, and the melody of birds; but here
Far otherwise, transported° I behold,   *enraptured*
530 Transported touch; here passion first I felt,
Commotion° strange, in all enjoyments else   *mental agitation*
Superior and unmoved, here only weak
Against the charm of beauty's powerful glance.
Or° nature failed in me, and left some part   *either*
535 Not proof enough such object to sustain,°   *withstand*
Or from my side subducting,° took perhaps   *subtracting*
More than enough; at least on her bestowed
Too much of ornament, in outward show
Elaborate, of inward less exact.
540 For well I understand in the prime end
Of nature her th' inferior, in the mind
And inward faculties, which most excel,
In outward also her resembling less
His image who made both, and less expressing
545 The character of that dominion giv'n
O'er other creatures; yet when I approach
Her loveliness, so absolute° she seems   *perfect, independent*
And in herself complete, so well to know
Her own, that what she wills to do or say,
550 Seems wisest, virtuousest, discreetest, best;
All higher knowledge in her presence falls

---

4. Both breezes and melodies. "Gales": winds.

Degraded, wisdom in discourse with her
Loses discount'nanced,° and like folly shows;   *disconcerted, abashed*
Authority and reason on her wait,
55 As one intended first, not after made
Occasionally;° and to consúmmate all,   *incidentally*
Greatness of mind and nobleness their seat
Build in her loveliest, and create an awe
About her, as a guard angelic placed."
60 To whom the angel with contracted brow:
    "Accuse not nature, she hath done her part;
Do thou but thine, and be not diffident°   *mistrustful*
Of wisdom, she deserts thee not, if thou
Dismiss not her, when most thou need'st her nigh,
65 By áttributing overmuch to things
Less excellent, as thou thyself perceiv'st.
For what admir'st thou, what transports thee so,
An outside? Fair no doubt, and worthy well
Thy cherishing, thy honoring, and thy love,
70 Not thy subjection: weigh with her thyself;
Then value: ofttimes nothing profits more
Than self-esteem, grounded on just and right
Well managed; of that skill the more thou know'st,
The more she will acknowledge thee her head,[5]
75 And to realities yield all her shows:
Made so adorn for thy delight the more,
So awful,° that with honor thou may'st love   *awe-inspiring*
Thy mate, who sees when thou art seen least wise.
But if the sense of touch whereby mankind
80 Is propagated seem such dear delight
Beyond all other, think the same vouchsafed
To cattle and each beast; which would not be
To them made common and divulged,° if aught   *imparted generally*
Therein enjoyed were worthy to subdue
85 The soul of man, or passion in him move.
What higher in her society thou find'st
Attractive, human, rational, love still;
In loving thou dost well, in passion not,
Wherein true love consists not; love refines
90 The thoughts, and heart enlarges, hath his seat
In reason, and is judicious, is the scale[6]
By which to heav'nly love thou may'st ascend,
Not sunk in carnal pleasure, for which cause
Among the beasts no mate for thee was found."
95   To whom thus half abashed Adam replied.
"Neither her outside formed so fair, nor aught
In procreation common to all kinds
(Though higher of the genial[7] bed by far,
And with mysterious reverence I deem)

---

5. See 1 Corinthians 11.31: "The head of every man is Christ; and the head of the woman is the man; and the head of Christ is God."
6. The ladder of love, a Neoplatonic concept for the movement from sensual love to higher forms, and ultimately to love of God.

7. Both nuptial and generative. Adam takes respectful issue with the apparent denigration of human sex in Raphael's account of the Neoplatonic ladder, which prompts his question about angelic sex (lines 615–17).

600 So much delights me, as those graceful acts,
Those thousand decencies° that daily flow   *fitting acts*
From all her words and actions, mixed with love
And sweet compliance, which declare unfeigned
Union of mind, or in us both one soul;
605 Harmony to behold in wedded pair
More grateful than harmonious sound to the ear.
Yet these subject not; I to thee disclose
What inward thence I feel, not therefore foiled,°   *overcome*
Who meet with various objects, from the sense
610 Variously representing;[8] yet still free
Approve the best, and follow what I approve.
To love thou blam'st me not, for love thou say'st
Leads up to Heav'n, is both the way and guide;
Bear with me then, if lawful what I ask;
615 Love not the heav'nly Spirits, and how their love
Express they, by looks only, or do they mix
Irradiance, virtual or immediate° touch?"   *actual*
  To whom the angel with a smile that glowed
Celestial rosy red, love's proper hue,[9]
620 Answered. "Let it suffice thee that thou know'st
Us happy, and without love no happiness.
Whatever pure thou in the body enjoy'st
(And pure thou wert created) we enjoy
In eminence,° and obstacle find none   *surprisingly*
625 Of membrane, joint, or limb, exclusive bars:
Easier than air with air, if Spirits embrace,
Total they mix, union of pure with pure
Desiring; nor restrained conveyance need
As flesh to mix with flesh, or soul with soul.
630 But I can now no more; the parting sun
Beyond the earth's green cape[1] and verdant isles
Hesperian sets, my signal to depart.
Be strong, live happy, and love, but first of all
Him whom to love is to obey, and keep
635 His great command; take heed lest passion sway
Thy judgment to do aught, which else free will
Would not admit;° thine and of all thy sons   *permit*
The weal or woe in thee is placed; beware.
I in thy persevering shall rejoice,
640 And all the blest: stand fast; to stand or fall
Free in thine own arbitrament° it lies.   *determination*
Perfect within, no outward aid require;°   *depend on*
And all temptation to transgress repel."
  So saying, he arose; whom Adam thus
645 Followed with benediction. "Since to part,
Go heavenly guest, ethereal messenger,

---

8. I.e., various objects, variously represented to me by my senses.
9. This is not likely to be an embarrassed blush: red is the color traditionally associated with Seraphim who burn with ardor. Raphael's smile also

glows with friendship for Adam and appreciation of his perceptive inference about angelic love.
1. Cape Verde near Dakar and the islands off that coast are the westernmost ("Hesperian") points of Africa.

Sent from whose sovran goodness I adore.
Gentle to me and affable hath been
Thy condescension, and shall be honored ever
50 With grateful memory: thou to mankind
Be good and friendly still, and oft return."
  So parted they, the angel up to Heav'n
From the thick shade, and Adam to his bow'r.

Book 9

No more of talk where God or angel guest
With man, as with his friend, familiar used
To sit indulgent, and with him partake
Rural repast, permitting him the while
5 Venial° discourse unblamed: I now must change   *pardonable*
Those notes to tragic; foul distrust, and breach
Disloyal on the part of man, revolt,
And disobedience: on the part of Heav'n
Now alienated, distance and distaste,°   *aversion*
10 Anger and just rebuke, and judgment giv'n,
That brought into this world a world of woe,
Sin and her shadow Death, and misery
Death's harbinger: sad task, yet argument
Not less but more heroic than the wrath
15 Of stern Achilles on his foe pursued
Thrice fugitive about Troy wall; or rage
Of Turnus for Lavinia disespoused,
Or Neptune's ire or Juno's, that so long
Perplexed the Greek and Cytherea's son;[1]
20 If answerable° style I can obtain   *fitting*
Of my celestial patroness, who deigns
Her nightly visitation unimplored,[2]
And dictates to me slumb'ring, or inspires
Easy my unpremeditated verse:
25 Since first this subject for heroic song
Pleased me long choosing, and beginning late;
Not sedulous° by nature to indite   *eager*
Wars, hitherto the only argument°   *subject*
Heroic deemed, chief mastery to dissect
30 With long and tedious havoc fabled knights
In battles feigned; the better fortitude
Of patience and heroic martyrdom
Unsung; or to describe races and games,
Or tilting furniture,[3] emblazoned shields,

---

1. In this fourth proem (lines 1–47), after signaling his change from pastoral to tragic mode (lines 1–6), Milton emphasizes tragic elements in several classical epics: Achilles pursuing Hector three times around Troy wall before killing him (*Iliad* 22); Turnus fighting Aeneas over the loss of his betrothed Lavinia and killed by him; Odysseus ("the Greek") and Aeneas ("Cytherea's son," i.e., Venus's son) tormented ("perplexed") by Neptune (Poseidon) and Juno, respectively.
2. Milton does not here invoke the Muse but testifies to her customary nightly visits. Milton's nephew reports that he often awoke in the morning with lines of poetry fully formed in his head, ready to dictate them to an amanuensis.
3. Equipment for jousting; "impresses quaint": cunningly designed heraldic devices on shields; "caparisons": ornamental trappings or armor for

35   Impresses quaint, caparisons and steeds;
Bases and tinsel trappings, gorgeous knights
At joust and tournament; then marshaled feast
Served up in hall with sewers,° and seneschals;°   *waiters/stewards*
The skill of artifice° or office mean,   *mechanic art*
40   Not that which justly gives heroic name
To person or to poem. Me of these
Nor skilled nor studious, higher argument
Remains,⁴ sufficient of itself to raise
That name, unless an age too late, or cold
45   Climate, or years damp my intended wing
Depressed, and much they may, if all be mine,
Not hers who brings it nightly to my ear.
    The sun was sunk, and after him the star
Of Hesperus,⁵ whose office is to bring
50   Twilight upon the earth, short arbiter
'Twixt day and night, and now from end to end
Night's hemisphere had veiled the horizon round:
When Satan who late fled⁶ before the threats
Of Gabriel out of Eden, now improved°   *increased*
55   In meditated fraud and malice, bent
On man's destruction, maugre what might hap
Of heavier on himself,⁷ fearless returned.
By night he fled, and at midnight returned
From compassing the earth, cautious of day,
60   Since Uriel regent of the sun descried
His entrance, and forewarned the Cherubim
That kept their watch; thence full of anguish driv'n,
The space of seven continued nights he rode
With darkness, thrice the equinoctial line°   *equator*
65   He circled, four times crossed the car of Night
From pole to pole, traversing each colure;⁸
On the eighth returned, and on the coast averse°   *turned away*
From entrance on Cherubic watch, by stealth
Found unsuspected way. There was a place,
70   Now not, though sin, not time, first wrought the change,
Where Tigris at the foot of Paradise
Into a gulf shot under ground, till part
Rose up a fountain by the Tree of Life;
In with the river sunk, and with it rose
75   Satan involved in rising mist, then sought
Where to lie hid. Sea he had searched and land
From Eden over Pontus,⁹ and the pool

---

horses; "bases": cloth coverings for horses. After rejecting the classical epic subjects, Milton here rejects the familiar topics of romance.

4. For a heroic poem. He proceeds to recap worries he has voiced before: that the times might not be receptive to such poems ("age too late"), that the "cold/Climate" of England or his own advanced age might "damp" (benumb, dampen) his "intended wing/Depressed" (poetic flights held down, kept from soaring).

5. Venus, the Evening Star.

6. At the end of Book 4.

7. I.e., despite ("maugre") what might result in

heavier punishments for himself.

8. The colures are two great circles that intersect at right angles at the poles. By circling the globe from east to west at the equator and then over the north and south poles, Satan can remain in darkness, keeping the earth between himself and the sun. "Car of Night" (line 65): the earth's shadow, imagined as the chariot of the goddess Night.

9. The Black Sea. Satan's journey (lines 77–82) takes him from there to the Sea of Azov in Russia ("Maeotis"), beyond the river "Ob" in Siberia, which flows into the Arctic Ocean, then south to Antarctica; thence west from "Orontes" (a river in

Maeotis, up beyond the river Ob;
Downward as far Antarctic; and in length
80 West from Orontes to the ocean barred
At Darien, thence to the land where flows
Ganges and Indus: thus the orb he roamed
With narrow search; and with inspection deep
Considered every creature, which of all
85 Most opportune might serve his wiles, and found
The serpent subtlest beast of all the field.[1]
Him after long debate, irresolute°   undecided
Of° thoughts revolved, his final sentence° chose   among / decision
Fit vessel, fittest imp° of fraud, in whom   offshoot
90 To enter, and his dark suggestions hide
From sharpest sight: for in the wily snake,
Whatever sleights° none would suspicious mark,   artifices
As from his wit and native subtlety
Proceeding, which in other beasts observed
95 Doubt° might beget of diabolic pow'r   suspicion
Active within beyond the sense of brute.
Thus he resolved, but first from inward grief
His bursting passion into plaints thus poured:
    "O earth, how like to Heav'n, if not preferred
00 More justly, seat worthier of gods, as built
With second thoughts, reforming what was old!
For what God after better worse would build?
Terrestrial heav'n, danced round by other heav'ns
That shine, yet bear their bright officious° lamps,   dutiful
05 Light above light, for thee alone, as seems,[2]
In thee concent'ring all their precious beams
Of sacred influence: as God in Heav'n
Is center, yet extends to all, so thou
Centring receiv'st from all those orbs; in thee,
10 Not in themselves, all their known virtue appears
Productive in herb, plant, and nobler birth
Of creatures animate with gradual life
Of growth, sense, reason,[3] all summed up in man.
With what delight could I have walked thee round,
15 If I could joy in aught, sweet interchange
Of hill and valley, rivers, woods and plains,
Now land, now sea, and shores with forest crowned,
Rocks, dens, and caves; but I in none of these
Find place or refuge; and the more I see
20 Pleasures about me, so much more I feel
Torment within me, as from the hateful siege°   conflict
Of contraries; all good to me becomes
Bane,° and in Heav'n much worse would be my state.   poison
But neither here seek I, no nor in Heav'n
25 To dwell, unless by mastering Heav'n's Supreme;

Syria) across the Atlantic to "Darien" (the Isthmus
of Panama), then across the Pacific and Asia to
India where the "Ganges" and "Indus" rivers flow.
1. The serpent is so described in Genesis 3.1.
2. Like Adam (8.15ff.) and Eve (4.657) but not

Raphael (8.114–78), Satan assumes a Ptolemaic
universe centered on the earth and humankind.
3. Graduated in steps ("gradual," line 113) from
vegetable to animal to rational forms (souls); cf.
5.469–90.

Nor hope to be myself less miserable
By what I seek, but others to make such
As I, though thereby worse to me redound:
For only in destroying I find ease
130 To my relentless thoughts; and him[4] destroyed,
Or won to what may work his utter loss,
For whom all this was made, all this will soon
Follow, as to him linked in weal or woe:
In woe then; that destruction wide may range:
135 To me shall be the glory sole among
The infernal Powers, in one day to have marred
What he Almighty styled, six nights and days
Continued making, and who knows how long
Before had been contriving, though perhaps
140 Not longer than since I in one night freed
From servitude inglorious well-nigh half
Th' angelic name, and thinner left the throng
Of his adorers. He to be avenged,
And to repair his numbers thus impaired,
145 Whether such virtue° spent of old now failed   *power*
More angels to create, if they at least
Are his created, or to spite us more,
Determined to advance into our room
A creature formed of earth, and him endow,
150 Exalted from so base original,°   *origin*
With heav'nly spoils, our spoils: what he decreed
He effected; man he made, and for him built
Magnificent this world, and earth his seat,
Him lord pronounced, and, O indignity!
155 Subjected to his service angel wings,
And flaming ministers to watch and tend
Their earthy charge: of these the vigilance
I dread, and to elude, thus wrapped in mist
Of midnight vapor glide obscure, and pry
160 In every bush and brake, where hap° may find   *luck*
The serpent sleeping, in whose mazy folds
To hide me, and the dark intent I bring.
O foul descent![5] that I who erst contended
With gods to sit the highest, am now constrained
165 Into a beast, and mixed with bestial slime,
This essence to incarnate and imbrute,
That to the height of deity aspired;
But what will not ambition and revenge
Descend to? Who aspires must down as low
170 As high he soared, obnoxious° first or last   *exposed*
To basest things. Revenge, at first though sweet,
Bitter ere long back on itself recoils;
Let it; I reck° not, so it light well aimed,   *care*
Since higher I fall short, on him who next

---

4. Adam. "This" (line 132): the universe.
5. Satan "imbruting" himself in a snake parodies,
grotesquely, the Son's incarnation in human form,
as Christ.

75   Provokes my envy, this new favorite
Of Heav'n, this man of clay, son of despite,
Whom us the more to spite his Maker raised
From dust: spite then with spite is best repaid."
   So saying, through each thicket dank or dry,
180 Like a black mist low creeping, he held on
His midnight search, where soonest he might find
The serpent: him fast sleeping soon he found
In labyrinth of many a round self-rolled,
His head the midst, well stored with subtle wiles:
185 Not yet in horrid shade or dismal den,
Nor nocent° yet, but on the grassy herb   *harmful, guilty*
Fearless unfeared he slept: in at his mouth
The Devil entered, and his brutal° sense,   *animal*
In heart or head, possessing soon inspired
190 With act intelligential: but his sleep
Disturbed not, waiting close° th' approach of morn.   *hidden*
Now whenas sacred light began to dawn
In Eden on the humid flow'rs, that breathed
Their morning incense, when all things that breathe,
195 From th' earth's great altar send up silent praise
To the Creator, and his nostrils fill
With grateful° smell, forth came the human pair   *pleasing*
And joined their vocal worship to the choir
Of creatures wanting° voice; that done, partake   *lacking*
200 The season, prime° for sweetest scents and airs: *best*
Then cómmune how that day they best may ply
Their growing work; for much their work outgrew
The hands' dispatch of two gard'ning so wide.
And Eve first to her husband thus began:
205   "Adam, well may we labor still° to dress   *continually*
This garden, still to tend plant, herb and flow'r,
Our pleasant task enjoined, but till more hands
Aid us, the work under our labor grows,
Luxurious° by restraint; what we by day   *luxuriant*
210 Lop overgrown, or prune, or prop, or bind,
One night or two with wanton growth derides,
Tending to wild. Thou therefore now advise
Or hear what to my mind first thoughts present,
Let us divide our labors, thou where choice
215 Leads thee, or where most needs, whether to wind
The woodbine round this arbor, or direct
The clasping ivy where to climb, while I
In yonder spring° of roses intermixed   *growth*
With myrtle, find what to redress° till noon: *set upright*
220 For while so near each other thus all day
Our task we choose, what wonder if so near
Looks intervene and smiles, or object new
Casual discourse draw on, which intermits
Our day's work brought to little, though begun
225 Early, and th' hour of supper comes unearned."
   To whom mild answer Adam thus returned:

"Sole Eve, associate sole,[6] to me beyond
Compare above all living creatures dear,
Well hast thou motioned,° well thy thoughts employed   *proposed*
230 How we might best fulfill the work which here
God hath assigned us, nor of me shalt pass
Unpraised: for nothing lovelier can be found
In woman, than to study household good,
And good works in her husband to promote.[7]
235 Yet not so strictly hath our Lord imposed
Labor, as to debar us when we need
Refreshment, whether food, or talk between,
Food of the mind, or this sweet intercourse
Of looks and smiles, for smiles from reason flow,
240 To brute denied, and are of love the food,
Love not the lowest end of human life.
For not to irksome toil, but to delight
He made us, and delight to reason joined.
These paths and bowers doubt not but our joint hands
245 Will keep from wilderness with ease, as wide
As we need walk, till younger hands ere long
Assist us: but if much convérse perhaps
Thee satiate, to short absence I could yield.
For solitude sometimes is best society,
250 And short retirement urges sweet return.
But other doubt possesses me, lest harm
Befall thee severed from me; for thou know'st
What hath been warned us, what malicious foe
Envying our happiness, and of his own
255 Despairing, seeks to work us woe and shame
By sly assault; and somewhere nigh at hand
Watches, no doubt, with greedy hope to find
His wish and best advantage, us asunder,
Hopeless to circumvent us joined, where each
260 To other speedy aid might lend at need;
Whether his first design be to withdraw
Our fealty from God, or to disturb
Conjugal love, than which perhaps no bliss
Enjoyed by us excites his envy more;
265 Or° this, or worse, leave not the faithful side   *whether*
That gave thee being, still shades thee and protects.
The wife, where danger or dishonor lurks,
Safest and seemliest by her husband stays,
Who guards her, or with her the worst endures."
270   To whom the virgin[8] majesty of Eve,
As one who loves, and some unkindness meets,
With sweet austere composure thus replied.
   "Offspring of Heav'n and earth, and all earth's lord,
That such an enemy we have, who seeks

---

6. Adam puns on "sole" as "unrivaled" and "only" (cf. 4.411).
7. Adam's compliments owe something to the praises of a good wife in Proverbs 31.

8. The term here means unspotted or peerless; Milton has insisted at the end of Books 4 and 8 that Adam and Eve have sex.

75   Our ruin, both by thee informed I learn,
    And from the parting angel overheard
    As in a shady nook I stood behind,
    Just then returned at shut of evening flow'rs.[9]
80   But that thou shouldst my firmness therefore doubt
    To God or thee, because we have a foe
    May tempt it, I expected not to hear.
    His violence thou fear'st not, being such,
    As we, not capable of death or pain,
    Can either not receive, or can repel.
85   His fraud is then thy fear, which plain infers
    Thy equal fear that my firm faith and love
    Can by his fraud be shaken or seduced;
    Thoughts, which how found they harbor in thy breast,
    Adam, misthought of° her to thee so dear?"   *misapplied to*
90   To whom with healing words Adam replied.
    "Daughter of God and man, immortal Eve,
    For such thou art, from sin and blame entire:°   *untouched*
    Not diffident° of thee do I dissuade   *distrustful*
    Thy absence from my sight, but to avoid
95   Th' attempt itself, intended by our foe.
    For he who tempts, though in vain, at least asperses°   *bespatters*
    The tempted with dishonor foul, supposed
    Not incorruptible of faith, not proof
    Against temptation: thou thyself with scorn
100   And anger wouldst resent the offered wrong,
    Though ineffectual found; misdeem not then,
    If such affront I labor to avert
    From thee alone, which on us both at once
    The enemy, though bold, will hardly dare,
105   Or daring, first on me th' assault shall light.
    Nor thou his malice and false guile contemn;
    Subtle he needs must be, who could seduce
    Angels, nor think superfluous others' aid.
    I from the influence of thy looks receive
110   Access° in every virtue, in thy sight   *increase*
    More wise, more watchful, stronger, if need were
    Of outward strength; while shame, thou looking on,
    Shame to be overcome or overreached°   *outwitted*
    Would utmost vigor raise, and raised unite.
115   Why shouldst not thou like sense within thee feel
    When I am present, and thy trial choose
    With me, best witness of thy virtue tried."
       So spake domestic Adam in his care
    And matrimonial love; but Eve, who thought
120   Less° attribúted to her faith sincere,   *too little*
    Thus her reply with accent sweet renewed.
       "If this be our condition, thus to dwell

9. Somewhat confusing, since Eve heard the full story of the war in Heaven and Raphael's earlier warnings; Raphael's parting words (8.630–43), overheard by Eve, do not mention Satan but warn Adam to resist his passion for Eve. He does, however, reiterate the charge to obey the "great command" and repel temptation.

In narrow circuit straitened° by a foe,   *confined*
Subtle or violent, we not endued
325 Single with like defense, wherever met,
How are we happy, still° in fear of harm?   *always*
But harm precedes not sin: only our foe
Tempting affronts us with his foul esteem
Of our integrity: his foul esteem
330 Sticks no dishonor on our front,° but turns   *forehead*
Foul on himself; then wherefore shunned or feared
By us? who rather double honor gain
From his surmise proved false, find peace within,
Favor from Heav'n, our witness from th' event.°   *outcome*
335 And what is faith, love, virtue unassayed
Alone, without exterior help sustained?[1]
Let us not then suspect our happy state
Left so imperfect by the Maker wise,
As not secure to single° or combined.   *one alone*
340 Frail is our happiness, if this be so,
And Eden were no Eden thus exposed."
    To whom thus Adam fervently replied.
"O woman, best are all things as the will
Of God ordained them, his creating hand
345 Nothing imperfect or deficient left
Of all that he created, much less man,
Or aught that might his happy state secure,
Secure from outward force; within himself
The danger lies, yet lies within his power:
350 Against his will he can receive no harm.
But God left free the will, for what obeys
Reason, is free, and reason he made right,[2]
But bid her well beware, and still erect,°   *alert*
Lest by some fair appearing good surprised
355 She dictate false, and misinform the will
To do what God expressly hath forbid.
Not then mistrust, but tender love enjoins,
That I should mind° thee oft, and mind thou me. *remind, pay heed to*
Firm we subsist,° yet possible to swerve,   *stand, exist*
360 Since reason not impossibly may meet
Some specious° object by the foe suborned,   *deceptively attractive*
And fall into deception unaware,
Not keeping strictest watch, as she was warned.
Seek not temptation then, which to avoid
365 Were better, and most likely if from me
Thou sever not: trial will come unsought.
Wouldst thou approve° thy constancy, approve   *prove*
First thy obedience; th' other who can know,
Not seeing thee attempted, who attest?
370 But if thou think, trial unsought may find
Us both securer° than thus warned thou seem'st, *overconfident*

---

1. Compare and contrast *Areopagitica*, p. 710.
2. Right reason, a classical concept accommodated to Christian thought, is the God-given power
to apprehend truth and moral law.

Go; for thy stay, not free, absents thee more;
Go in thy native innocence, rely
On what thou hast of virtue, summon all,
5 For God towards thee hath done his part, do thine."
    So spake the patriarch of mankind, but Eve
Persisted, yet submiss, though last, replied:
    "With thy permission then, and thus forewarned
Chiefly by what thy own last reasoning words
380 Touched only, that our trial, when least sought,
May find us both perhaps far less prepared,
The willinger I go, nor much expect
A foe so proud will first the weaker seek;
So bent, the more shall shame him his repulse."
385 Thus saying, from her husband's hand her hand
Soft she withdrew, and like a wood-nymph light[3]
Oread or Dryad, or of Delia's train,
Betook her to the groves, but Delia's self
In gait surpassed and goddess-like deport,°   *bearing*
390 Though not as she with bow and quiver armed,
But with such gardening tools as art yet rude,
Guiltless of fire[4] had formed, or angels brought.
To Pales, or Pomona, thus adorned,
Likest she seemed[5] Pomona when she fled
395 Vertumnus, or to Ceres in her prime,
Yet virgin of Proserpina from Jove.
Her long with ardent look his eye pursued
Delighted, but desiring more her stay.
Oft he to her his charge of quick return
400 Repeated, she to him as oft engaged
To be returned by noon amid the bow'r,
And all things in best order to invite
Noontide repast, or afternoon's repose.
O much deceived, much failing,° hapless° Eve,   *erring / unlucky*
405 Of thy presumed return! event perverse!
Thou never from that hour in Paradise
Found'st either sweet repast, or sound repose;
Such ambush hid among sweet flow'rs and shades
Waited with hellish rancor imminent
410 To intercept thy way, or send thee back
Despoiled of innocence, of faith, of bliss.
For now, and since first break of dawn the Fiend,
Mere serpent in appearance, forth was come,
And on his quest, where likeliest he might find
415 The only two of mankind, but in them
The whole included race, his purposed prey.

3. Light-footed, with overtones of "fickle" or "frivolous." "Oread": a mountain nymph. "Dryad": a
wood nymph. "Delia": Diana, born on the isle of
Delos, hunted with a "train" of nymphs.
4. Having no experience of fire, not needed in Paradise. Milton may be alluding to the guilt of Prometheus, who stole fire from heaven.
5. These goddesses, like Eve, are associated with
agriculture (lines 393–96)—Pales, with flocks and
pastures; Pomona, with fruit trees, Ceres with harvests—and the latter two foreshadow Eve's situation. Pomona was chased by the wood god
"Vertumnus" in many guises before surrendering
to him; Ceres was impregnated by Jove with Proserpina—later carried off to Hades by Pluto.

In bow'r and field he sought, where any tuft
Of grove or garden-plot more pleasant lay,
Their tendance or plantation⁶ for delight,
420 By fountain or by shady rivulet
He sought them both, but wished his hap° might find   *luck*
Eve separate; he wished, but not with hope
Of what so seldom chanced, when to his wish,
Beyond his hope, Eve separate he spies,
425 Veiled in a cloud of fragrance, where she stood,
Half spied, so thick the roses bushing round
About her glowed, oft stooping to support
Each flow'r of slender stalk, whose head though gay
Carnation, purple, azure, or specked with gold,
430 Hung drooping unsustained, them she upstays
Gently with myrtle band, mindless° the while,   *heedless*
Herself, though fairest unsupported flow'r
From her best prop so far, and storm so nigh.⁷
Nearer he drew, and many a walk traversed
435 Of stateliest covert, cedar, pine, or palm,
Then voluble° and bold, now hid, now seen   *undulating*
Among thick-woven arborets° and flow'rs   *small trees*
Embordered on each bank, the hand° of Eve: *handiwork*
Spot more delicious than those gardens feigned
440 Or of revived Adonis, or renowned
Alcinous, host of old Laertes' son,
Or that, not mystic, where the sapient king
Held dalliance with his fair Egyptian spouse.⁸
Much he the place admired, the person more.
445 As one who long in populous city pent,
Where houses thick and sewers annoy° the air,   *make noisome, befoul*
Forth issuing on a summer's morn to breathe
Among the pleasant villages and farms
Adjoined, from each thing met conceives delight,
450 The smell of grain, or tedded grass, or kine,⁹
Or dairy, each rural sight, each rural sound;
If chance with nymph-like step fair virgin pass,
What pleasing seemed, for° her now pleases more,   *because of*
She most, and in her look sums all delight.
455 Such pleasure took the Serpent to behold
This flow'ry plat,° the sweet recess° of Eve   *plot / retreat*
Thus early, thus alone; her heav'nly form
Angelic, but more soft, and feminine,
Her graceful innocence, her every air°   *manner*
460 Of gesture or least action overawed
His malice, and with rapine sweet¹ bereaved
His fierceness of the fierce intent it brought:

---

6. I.e., which they had cultivated or planted for their pleasure.
7. The conceit of the flower-gatherer who is herself gathered evokes the story of Proserpina, to whom it was applied in 4.269–71.
8. The gardens of Adonis were beauty spots named for the lovely youth loved by Venus, killed by a boar, and subsequently revived; Odysseus ("Laertes' son") was entertained by "Alcinous" in

his beautiful gardens; Solomon ("the sapient king") entertained his "fair Egyptian spouse," the Queen of Sheba, in a real garden (not "mystic," or "feigned," as the others were).
9. Cattle. "Tedded": spread out to dry, like hay.
1. From Latin "rapere," to seize, the root of both "rape" and "rapture," underscoring the paradox of the ravisher (temporarily) ravished.

That space the Evil One abstracted° stood   *withdrawn*
From his own evil, and for the time remained
65   Stupidly good,° of enmity disarmed,   *good because stupefied*
Of guile, of hate, of envy, of revenge;
But the hot hell that always in him burns,
Though in mid-heav'n, soon ended his delight,
And tortures him now more, the more he sees
70   Of pleasure not for him ordained: then soon
Fierce hate he recollects, and all his thoughts
Of mischief gratulating,° thus excites: *greeting*
    "Thoughts, whither have ye led me, with what sweet
Compulsion thus transported to forget
75   What hither brought us, hate, not love, nor hope
Of Paradise for Hell, hope here to taste
Of pleasure, but all pleasure to destroy,
Save what is in destroying, other joy
To me is lost. Then let me not let pass
80   Occasion which now smiles, behold alone
The woman, opportune° to all attempts,   *open*
Her husband, for I view far round, not nigh,
Whose higher intellectual more I shun,
And strength, of courage haughty,° and of limb   *exalted*
85   Heroic built, though of terrestrial° mold,   *earthly*
Foe not informidable, exempt from wound,
I not; so much hath Hell debased, and pain
Enfeebled me, to what I was in Heav'n.
She fair, divinely fair, fit love for gods,
90   Not terrible,° though terror be in love   *terrifying*
And beauty, not° approached by stronger hate,   *unless*
Hate stronger, under show of love well feigned,
The way which to her ruin now I tend."
    So spake the Enemy of mankind, enclosed
95   In serpent, inmate bad, and toward Eve
Addressed his way, not with indented° wave,   *zigzag*
Prone on the ground, as since, but on his rear,
Circular base of rising folds, that tow'red
Fold above fold a surging maze, his head
00   Crested aloft, and carbuncle° his eyes;   *deep red*
With burnished neck of verdant gold, erect
Amidst his circling spires,° that on the grass   *coils*
Floated redundant:° pleasing was his shape,   *in swelling waves*
And lovely, never since of serpent kind
05   Lovelier, not those that in Illyria changed
Hermione and Cadmus, or the god
In Epidaurus;[2] nor to which transformed
Ammonian Jove, or Capitoline was seen,
He with Olympias, this with her who bore
10   Scipio, the height of Rome.[3] With tract° oblique   *course*

2. The legendary founder of Thebes, "Cadmus," and his wife Harmonia (Milton's "Hermione") were changed to serpents when they went to "Illyria" in old age; Aesculapius, god of healing, sometimes came forth as a serpent fron his temple in "Epidaurus."

3. Jupiter Ammon ("Ammonian Jove") made love to "Olympias" in the form of a snake, and sired Alexander the Great; the Jupiter worshipped in Rome ("Capitoline") also in serpent form, sired Scipio Africanus, the savior and great leader ("height") of Rome.

At first, as one who sought accéss, but feared
To interrupt, sidelong he works his way.
As when a ship by skilful steersman wrought
Nigh river's mouth or foreland, where the wind
515 Veers oft, as oft so steers, and shifts her sail;
So varied he, and of his tortuous train
Curled many a wanton° wreath in sight of Eve,   luxuriant, sportive
To lure her eye; she busied heard the sound
Of rustling leaves, but minded not, as used
520 To such disport before her through the field,
From every beast, more duteous at her call,
Than at Circean⁴ call the herd disguised.
He bolder now, uncalled before her stood;
But as in gaze admiring: oft he bowed
525 His turret crest, and sleek enameled° neck,   multicolored
Fawning, and licked the ground whereon she trod.
His gentle dumb expression turned at length
The eye of Eve to mark his play; he glad
Of her attention gained, with serpent tongue
530 Organic, or impulse of vocal air,⁵
His fraudulent temptation thus began.
    "Wonder not, sovran mistress, if perhaps
Thou canst, who art sole wonder, much less arm
Thy looks, the heav'n of mildness, with disdain,
535 Displeased that I approach thee thus, and gaze
Insatiate, I thus single, nor have feared
Thy awful brow, more awful thus retired.
Fairest resemblance of thy Maker fair,
Thee all things living gaze on, all things thine
540 By gift, and thy celestial beauty adore
With ravishment beheld, there best beheld
Where universally admired; but here
In this enclosure wild, these beasts among,
Beholders rude, and shallow to discern
545 Half what in thee is fair, one man except,
Who sees thee? (and what is one?) who shouldst be seen
A goddess among gods, adored and served
By angels numberless, thy daily train."⁶
    So glozed° the Tempter, and his proem° tuned;   flattered / prelude
550 Into the heart of Eve his words made way,
Though at the voice much marveling; at length
Not unamazed she thus in answer spake.
"What may this mean? Language of man pronounced
By tongue of brute, and human sense expressed?
555 The first at least of these I thought denied
To beasts, whom God on their creation-day
Created mute to all articulate sound;
The latter I demur,° for in their looks   hesitate about
Much reason, and in their actions oft appears.

4. Circe, in the *Odyssey*, transformed men to beasts and was attended by an obedient herd.
5. Satan either used the actual tongue of the serpent or impressed the air with his own voice.
6. Satan's entire speech is couched in the extravagant praises of the Petrarchan love convention.

60   Thee, serpent, subtlest beast of all the field
    I knew, but not with human voice endued;°   *endowed*
    Redouble then this miracle, and say,
    How cam'st thou speakable° of mute, and how   *able to speak*
    To me so friendly grown above the rest
65   Of brutal kind, that daily are in sight?
    Say, for such wonder claims attention due."
      To whom the guileful Tempter thus replied:
    "Empress of this fair world, resplendent Eve,
    Easy to me it is to tell thee all
70   What thou command'st, and right thou shouldst be obeyed:
    I was at first as other beasts that graze
    The trodden herb, of abject thoughts and low,
    As was my food, nor aught but food discerned
    Or sex, and apprehended nothing high:
75   Till on a day roving the field, I chanced
    A goodly tree far distant to behold
    Loaden with fruit of fairest colors mixed,
    Ruddy and gold: I nearer drew to gaze;
    When from the boughs a savory odor blown,
80   Grateful to appetite, more pleased my sense
    Than smell of sweetest fennel, or the teats
    Of ewe or goat dropping with milk at ev'n,[7]
    Unsucked of lamb or kid, that tend their play.
    To satisfy the sharp desire I had
85   Of tasting those fair apples, I resolved
    Not to defer;° hunger and thirst at once,   *delay*
    Powerful persuaders, quickened at the scent
    Of that alluring fruit, urged me so keen.
    About the mossy trunk I wound me soon,
90   For high from ground the branches would require
    Thy utmost reach or Adam's: round the tree
    All other beasts that saw, with like desire
    Longing and envying stood, but could not reach.
    Amid the tree now got, where plenty hung
95   Tempting so nigh, to pluck and eat my fill
    I spared° not, for such pleasure till that hour   *refrained*
    At feed or fountain never had I found.
    Sated at length, ere long I might perceive
    Strange alteration in me, to degree
00   Of reason in my inward powers,[8] and speech
    Wanted° not long, though to this shape retained.   *lacked*
    Thenceforth to speculations high or deep
    I turned my thoughts, and with capacious mind
    Considered all things visible in Heav'n,
05   Or earth, or middle,° all things fair and good;   *regions between*

---

7. According to Pliny, serpents ate fennel to aid in shedding their skins and to sharpen their eyesight; folklore had it that they drank the milk of sheep and goats.

8. There is no precedent in Genesis or the inter-pretative tradition for Satan's powerfully persuasive argument by analogy based on the snake's supposed experience of attaining to reason and speech by eating the forbidden fruit.

But all that fair and good in thy divine
Semblance, and in thy beauty's heav'nly ray
United I beheld; no fair° to thine   *beauty*
Equivalent or second, which compelled
610 Me thus, though importune° perhaps, to come   *inopportunely*
And gaze, and worship thee of right declared
Sovran of creatures, universal dame."⁹
    So talked the spirited¹ sly snake; and Eve
Yet more amazed unwary thus replied:
615   "Serpent, thy overpraising leaves in doubt
The virtue° of that fruit, in thee first proved: *power*
But say, where grows the tree, from hence how far?
For many are the trees of God that grow
In Paradise, and various, yet unknown
620 To us, in such abundance lies our choice,
As leaves a greater store of fruit untouched,
Still hanging incorruptible, till men
Grow up to their provision,² and more hands
Help to disburden nature of her birth."
625   To whom the wily adder, blithe and glad:
"Empress, the way is ready, and not long,
Beyond a row of myrtles, on a flat,
Fast by a fountain, one small thicket past
Of blowing myrrh and balm;³ if thou accept
630 My conduct,° I can bring thee thither soon."   *guidance*
    "Lead then," said Eve. He leading swiftly rolled
In tangles, and made intricate seem straight,
To mischief swift. Hope elevates, and joy
Brightens his crest, as when a wand'ring fire,°   *will-o'-the-wisp*
635 Compact° of unctuous° vapor, which the night   *composed/oily*
Condenses, and the cold environs round,
Kindled through agitation to a flame,
Which oft, they say, some evil spirit attends,
Hovering and blazing with delusive light,
640 Misleads th' amazed° night-wanderer from his way   *bewildered*
To bogs and mires, and oft through pond or pool,
There swallowed up and lost, from succor far.
So glistered the dire snake, and into fraud
Led Eve our credulous mother, to the tree
645 Of prohibition, root of all our woe;
Which when she saw, thus to her guide she spake:
    "Serpent, we might have spared our coming hither,
Fruitless to me, though fruit be here to excess,
The credit of whose virtue° rest with thee,   *power*
650 Wondrous indeed, if cause of such effects.
But of this tree we may not taste nor touch;
God so commanded, and left that command

---

9. Satan continues his Petrarchan language of
courtship.
1. Both inspired by and possessed by an evil spirit,
Satan.

2. I.e., until the numbers of the human race are
such as to consume the food God has provided.
3. Blooming trees that exude the aromatic gums,
myrrh and balm (balsam).

Sole daughter of his voice;[4] the rest, we live
Law to ourselves, our reason is our law."
55 To whom the Tempter guilefully replied:
"Indeed? hath God then said that of the fruit
Of all these garden trees ye shall not eat,
Yet lords declared of all in earth or air?"
 To whom thus Eve yet sinless: "Of the fruit
60 Of each tree in the garden we may eat,
But of the fruit of this fair tree amidst
The garden, God hath said, 'Ye shall not eat
Thereof, nor shall ye touch it, lest ye die.'"[5]
 She scarce had said, though brief, when now more bold
65 The Tempter, but with show of zeal and love
To man, and indignation at his wrong,
New part puts on, and as to passion moved,
Fluctuates disturbed, yet comely, and in act
Raised,[6] as of some great matter to begin.
70 As when of old some orator renowned
In Athens or free Rome, where eloquence
Flourished, since mute, to some great cause addressed,
Stood in himself collected, while each part,
Motion, each act won audience ere the tongue,°   *before speaking*
75 Sometimes in high began, as no delay
Of preface brooking[7] through his zeal of right.
So standing, moving, or to high upgrown
The Tempter all impassioned thus began:
 "O sacred, wise, and wisdom-giving plant,
80 Mother of science,° now I feel thy power   *knowledge*
Within me clear, not only to discern
Things in their causes, but to trace the ways
Of highest agents, deemed however wise.
Queen of this universe, do not believe
85 Those rigid threats of death; ye shall not die:
How should ye? By the fruit? It gives you life
To knowledge.[8] By the Threat'ner? Look on me,
Me who have touched and tasted, yet both live,
And life more perfect have attained than fate
90 Meant me, by vent'ring higher than my lot.
Shall that be shut to man, which to the beast
Is open? Or will God incense his ire
For such a petty trespass, and not praise
Rather your dauntless virtue,° whom the pain   *courage*
95 Of death denounced,° whatever thing death be,   *threatened*
Deterred not from achieving what might lead
To happier life, knowledge of good and evil;

<hr>

4. God's only direct commandment (in Hebrew, *Bath Kol*, "daughter of a voice" from heaven). Otherwise, they follow the moral law of nature, known to them perfectly by their unfallen reason, "our reason is our law."
5. Eve's formulation indicates her "sufficient" understanding of the prohibition and the conditions of life in Eden.
6. Drawn up to full dignity. Satan as the snake

takes on the role of a Greek or Roman orator defending liberty (lines 671–72), a Demosthenes or a Cicero.
7. Bursting into the middle of his speech without a preface, and "upgrown" to the impassioned high style ("high") at once (lines 675–78).
8. I.e., life as well as knowledge, and a better life enhanced by knowledge, which Satan in the snake presents as a "magical" property of the tree.

Of good, how just?[9] Of evil, if what is evil
Be real, why not known, since easier shunned?
700 God therefore cannot hurt ye, and be just;
Not just, not God;[1] not feared then, nor obeyed:
Your fear itself of death removes the fear.
Why then was this forbid? Why but to awe,
Why but to keep ye low and ignorant,
705 His worshipers; he knows that in the day
Ye eat thereof, your eyes that seem so clear,
Yet are but dim, shall perfectly be then
Opened and cleared, and ye shall be as gods,
Knowing both good and evil as they know.
710 That ye should be as gods, since I as man,
Internal man, is but proportion meet,
I of brute human, ye of human gods.[2]
So ye shall die perhaps, by putting off
Human, to put on gods, death to be wished,
715 Though threatened, which no worse than this can bring.
And what are gods that man may not become
As they, participating° godlike food?   *partaking of*
The gods[3] are first, and that advantage use
On our belief, that all from them proceeds;
720 I question it, for this fair earth I see,
Warmed by the sun, producing every kind,
Them nothing: if they all° things, who enclosed   *produce all*
Knowledge of good and evil in this tree,
That whoso eats thereof, forthwith attains
725 Wisdom without their leave? And wherein lies
Th' offense, that man should thus attain to know?
What can your knowledge hurt him, or this tree
Impart against his will if all be his?
Or is it envy, and can envy dwell
730 In heav'nly breasts? These, these and many more
Causes import° your need of this fair fruit.   *prove*
Goddess humane,[4] reach then, and freely taste."
    He ended, and his words replete with guile
Into her heart too easy entrance won:
735 Fixed on the fruit she gazed, which to behold
Might tempt alone, and in her ears the sound
Yet rung of his persuasive words, impregned°   *impregnated*
With reason, to her seeming, and with truth;
Meanwhile the hour of noon drew on, and waked
740 An eager appetite, raised by the smell
So savory of that fruit, which with desire,
Inclinable now grown to touch or taste,
Solicited her longing eye;[5] yet first
Pausing a while, thus to herself she mused:

9. I.e., how can it be just to forbid the knowledge of good?
1. Satan's sophism invites atheism: if God forbids knowledge of good and evil he is not just, therefore not God, therefore his threat of death need not be feared.

2. Satan invites the aspiration to divinity, based on analogy to the supposed experience of the snake.
3. Hereafter, Satan speaks of "gods," not God.
4. Both "human" and "gracious" or "kindly."
5. All Eve's senses—sight, hearing, smell, taste, and touch—are solicited by the fruit.

45   "Great are thy virtues,° doubtless, best of fruits,   *powers*
Though kept from man, and worthy to be admired,
Whose taste, too long forborne, at first assay°   *try*
Gave elocution to the mute, and taught
The tongue not made for speech to speak thy praise:
50   Thy praise he also who forbids thy use,
Conceals not from us, naming thee the Tree
Of Knowledge, knowledge both of good and evil;
Forbids us then to taste, but his forbidding
Commends thee more, while it infers° the good   *implies*
55   By thee communicated, and our want:°   *lack*
For good unknown, sure is not had, or had
And yet unknown, is as not had at all.
In plain° then, what forbids he but to know,   *in plain words*
Forbids us good, forbids us to be wise?
60   Such prohibitions bind not. But if death
Bind us with after-bands,° what profits then   *later bonds*
Our inward freedom? In the day we eat
Of this fair fruit, our doom is, we shall die.
How dies the serpent? He hath eat'n and lives,
65   And knows, and speaks, and reasons, and discerns,
Irrational till then. For us alone
Was death invented? Or to us denied
This intellectual food, for beasts reserved?
For beasts it seems: yet that one beast which first
70   Hath tasted, envies° not, but brings with joy   *begrudges*
The good befall'n him, author unsuspect,[6]
Friendly to man, far from deceit or guile.
What fear I then, rather what know to fear
Under this ignorance of good and evil,
75   Of God or death, of law or penalty?
Here grows the cure of all, this fruit divine,
Fair to the eye, inviting to the taste,
Of virtue° to make wise: what hinders then   *power*
To reach, and feed at once both body and mind?"
80   So saying, her rash hand in evil hour
Forth reaching to the fruit, she plucked, she eat.[7]
Earth felt the wound, and nature from her seat
Sighing through all her works gave signs of woe,
That all was lost. Back to the thicket slunk
85   The guilty serpent, and well might, for Eve
Intent now wholly on her taste, naught else
Regarded, such delight till then, as seemed,
In fruit she never tasted, whether true
Or fancied so, through expectation high
90   Of knowledge, nor was Godhead from her thought.
Greedily she engorged without restraint,
And knew not eating death:[8] satiate at length,
And heightened as with wine, jocund° and boon,°   *merry/jolly*

---

6. An authority or informant beyond suspicion.
7. Ate: an accepted past tense, pronounced *et*.
8. I.e., she is eating death and doesn't know it, or

experience it yet, but also, punning, death is eating her too.

Thus to herself she pleasingly began:

795   "O sovran, virtuous, precious of all trees
In Paradise, of operation blest
To sapience, hitherto obscured, infamed,[9]
And thy fair fruit let hang, as to no end
Created; but henceforth my early care,

800 Not without song, each morning, and due praise
Shall tend thee, and the fertile burden ease
Of thy full branches offered free to all;
Till dieted by thee I grow mature
In knowledge, as the gods who all things know;

805 Though others envy what they cannot give;
For had the gift been theirs,[1] it had not here
Thus grown. Experience, next to thee I owe,
Best guide; not following thee, I had remained
In ignorance, thou open'st wisdom's way,

810 And giv'st accéss, though secret° she retire.   *hidden*
And I perhaps am secret° Heav'n is high,   *unseen*
High and remote to see from thence distinct
Each thing on earth; and other care perhaps
May have diverted from continual watch

815 Our great Forbidder, safe with all his spies
About him. But to Adam in what sort°   *guise*
Shall I appear? shall I to him make known
As yet my change, and give him to partake
Full happiness with me, or rather not,

820 But keep the odds° of knowledge in my power   *advantage*
Without copartner? so to add what wants°   *lacks*
In female sex, the more to draw his love,
And render me more equal, and perhaps,
A thing not undesirable, sometime

825 Superior; for inferior who is free?[2]
This may be well: but what if God have seen,
And death ensue? Then I shall be no more,
And Adam wedded to another Eve,
Shall live with her enjoying, I extinct;

830 A death to think. Confirmed then I resolve,
Adam shall share with me in bliss or woe:
So dear I love him, that with him all deaths
I could endure, without him live no life."

    So saying, from the tree her step she turned,
835 But first low reverence done, as to the power
That dwelt within,[3] whose presence had infused
Into the plant sciential° sap, derived   *knowledge-producing*
From nectar, drink of gods. Adam the while
Waiting desirous her return, had wove

840 Of choicest flow'rs a garland to adorn
Her tresses, and her rural labors crown,
As reapers oft are wont their harvest queen.

---

9. Slandered. "Sapience": both knowledge and tasting (Latin, *sapere*).
1. Like Satan, Eve now conflates gods and God,

ascribing envy but also lack of power to "them."
2. Cf. Satan, 1.248–63, 5.790–97.
3. Eve ends with idolatry, worship of the tree.

Great joy he promised to his thoughts, and new
Solace in her return, so long delayed;
45　Yet oft his heart, divine of° something ill,　　　　　　　　　　　*foreboding*
Misgave him; he the falt'ring measure° felt;　　　　　　　　　　　*heartbeat*
And forth to meet her went, the way she took
That morn when first they parted; by the Tree
Of Knowledge he must pass; there he her met,
50　Scarce from the tree returning; in her hand
A bough of fairest fruit that downy smiled,
New gathered, and ambrosial smell diffused.
To him she hasted, in her face excuse
Came prologue,⁴ and apology to prompt,
55　Which with bland° words at will she thus addressed.　　　　　　*mild, coaxing*
　　"Hast thou not wondered, Adam, at my stay?
Thee I have missed, and thought it long, deprived
Thy presence, agony of love till now
Not felt, nor shall be twice, for never more
60　Mean I to try, what rash untried I sought,
The pain of absence from thy sight. But strange
Hath been the cause, and wonderful to hear:
This tree is not as we are told, a tree
Of danger tasted,° nor to evil unknown　　　　　　　　　　　　　*if tasted*
65　Op'ning the way, but of divine effect
To open eyes, and make them gods who taste;
And hath been tasted such: the serpent wise,
Or° not restrained as we, or not obeying,　　　　　　　　　　　　*either*
Hath eaten of the fruit, and is become,
70　Not dead, as we are threatened, but thenceforth
Endued with human voice and human sense,
Reasoning to admiration,° and with me　　　　　　　　　　　　　*cause wonder*
Persuasively° hath so prevailed, that I　　　　　　　　　　　　　*by persuasion*
Have also tasted, and have also found
75　Th' effects to correspond, opener mine eyes,
Dim erst,° dilated spirits, ampler heart,　　　　　　　　　　　　*before*
And growing up to godhead; which for thee
Chiefly I sought, without thee can despise.
For bliss, as thou hast part, to me is bliss,
80　Tedious, unshared with thee, and odious soon.
Thou therefore also taste, that equal lot
May join us, equal joy, as equal love;
Lest thou not tasting, different degree°　　　　　　　　　　　　　*rank*
Disjoin us, and I then too late renounce
85　Deity for thee, when fate will not permit."⁵
　　Thus Eve with count'nance blithe her story told;
But in her cheek distemper⁶ flushing glowed.
On th' other side, Adam, soon as he heard
The fatal trespass done by Eve, amazed,°　　　　　　　　　　　　*stunned*
90　Astonied° stood and blank, while horror chill　　　　　　　　　　*petrified*
Ran through his veins, and all his joints relaxed;

4. I.e., excuse came like the prologue in a play, and apology (justification, self-defense) served as prompter.

5. Compare Eve in soliloquy, lines 817–31.
6. I.e., disorder arising from disturbance of the balance of humors in the body, intoxication.

From his slack hand the garland wreathed for Eve
Down dropped, and all the faded roses shed:
Speechless he stood and pale, till thus at length
895 First to himself he inward silence broke:
    "O fairest of creation, last and best
Of all God's works, creature in whom excelled
Whatever can to sight or thought be formed,
Holy, divine, good, amiable, or sweet!
900 How art thou lost, how on a sudden lost,
Defaced, deflow'red, and now to death devote?°   doomed
Rather how hast thou yielded to transgress
The strict forbiddance, how to violate
The sacred° fruit forbidd'n! some cursèd fraud   consecrated
905 Of enemy hath beguiled thee, yet unknown,
And me with thee hath ruined, for with thee
Certain my resolution is to die;
How can I live without thee, how forgo
Thy sweet converse and love so dearly joined,
910 To live again in these wild woods forlorn?
Should God create another Eve, and I
Another rib afford, yet loss of thee
Would never from my heart; no no, I feel
The link of nature draw me: flesh of flesh,
915 Bone of my bone thou art,[7] and from thy state
Mine never shall be parted, bliss or woe."
    So having said, as one from sad dismay
Recomforted, and after thoughts disturbed
Submitting to what seemed remédiless,
920 Thus in calm mood his words to Eve he turned:
    "Bold deed thou hast presumed, advent'rous Eve,
And peril great provoked, who thus hast dared
Had it been only coveting to eye
That sacred fruit, sacred° to abstinence,   set apart
925 Much more to taste it under ban to touch.
But past who can recall, or done undo?
Not God omnipotent, nor fate; yet so
Perhaps thou shalt not die, perhaps the fact°   deed
Is not so heinous now, foretasted fruit,
930 Profaned first by the serpent, by him first
Made common and unhallowed ere our taste;
Nor yet on him found deadly, he yet lives,
Lives, as thou saidst, and gains to live as man
Higher degree of life, inducement strong
935 To us, as likely tasting to attain
Proportional ascent, which cannot be
But to be gods, or angels demi-gods.
Nor can I think that God, Creator wise,
Though threat'ning, will in earnest so destroy
940 Us his prime creatures, dignified so high,
Set over all his works, which in our fall,

7. Adam echoes Genesis 2.23–24.

For us created, needs with us must fail,
Dependent made; so God shall uncreate,
Be frustrate, do, undo, and labor lose,
945 Not well conceived of God, who though his power
Creation could repeat, yet would be loath
Us to abolish, lest the Adversary°   Satan
Triumph and say; 'Fickle their state whom God
Most favors, who can please him long? Me first
950 He ruined, now mankind; whom will he next?'
Matter of scorn, not to be given the Foe.
However I with thee have fixed my lot,
Certain° to undergo like doom; if death   resolved
Consort° with thee, death is to me as life;   associate
955 So forcible within my heart I feel
The bond of nature draw me to my own,
My own in thee, for what thou art is mine;
Our state cannot be severed, we are one,
One flesh; to lose thee were to lose myself."
960   So Adam, and thus Eve to him replied:
"O glorious trial of exceeding⁸ love,
Illustrious evidence, example high!
Engaging me to emulate, but short
Of thy perfection, how shall I attain,
965 Adam, from whose dear side I boast me sprung,
And gladly of our union hear thee speak,
One heart, one soul in both; whereof good proof
This day affords, declaring thee resolved,
Rather than death or aught° than death more dread   anything other
970 Shall separate us, linked in love so dear,
To undergo with me one guilt, one crime,
If any be, of tasting this fair fruit,
Whose virtue,° for of good still good proceeds,   power
Direct, or by occasion° hath presented   indirectly
975 This happy trial of thy love, which else
So eminently never had been known.
Were it° I thought death menaced would ensue°   if/result from
This my attempt, I would sustain alone
The worst, and not persuade thee, rather die
980 Deserted, than oblige° thee with a fact°   bind/deed
Pernicious to thy peace, chiefly assured
Remarkably so late of thy so true,
So faithful love unequaled;⁹ but I feel
Far otherwise th' event,° not death, but life   result
985 Augmented, opened eyes, new hopes, new joys,
Taste so divine, that what of sweet before
Hath touched my sense, flat seems to this, and harsh.
On my experience, Adam, freely taste,
And fear of death deliver to the winds."
990   So saying, she embraced him, and for joy

---

8. The word, which Eve intends as praise, carries   9. I.e., since I have so recently been assured of
the implication of "excessive."   your unparalleled love.

Tenderly wept, much won that he his love
Had so ennobled, as of choice to incur
Divine displeasure for her sake, or death.
In recompense (for such compliance bad
995 Such recompense best merits) from the bough
She gave him of that fair enticing fruit
With liberal hand: he scrupled not to eat
Against his better knowledge, not deceived,[1]
But fondly° overcome with female charm.   foolishly
1000 Earth trembled from her entrails, as again
In pangs, and nature gave a second groan;
Sky loured, and muttering thunder, some sad drops
Wept at completing of the mortal sin
Original;[2] while Adam took no thought,
1005 Eating his fill, nor Eve to iterate°   repeat
Her former trespass feared, the more to soothe
Him with her loved society, that now
As with new wine intoxicated both
They swim in mirth, and fancy that they feel
1010 Divinity within them breeding wings
Wherewith to scorn the earth: but that false fruit
Far other operation first displayed,
Carnal desire inflaming, he on Eve
Began to cast lascivious eyes, she him
1015 As wantonly repaid; in lust they burn:
Till Adam thus 'gan Eve to dalliance move:
    "Eve, now I see thou art exact of taste,
And elegant, of sapience[3] no small part,
Since to each meaning savor we apply,
1020 And palate call judicious; I the praise
Yield thee, so well this day thou hast purveyed.°   provided
Much pleasure we have lost, while we abstained
From this delightful fruit, nor known till now
True relish, tasting; if such pleasure be
1025 In things to us forbidden, it might be wished,
For this one tree had been forbidden ten.
But come, so well refreshed, now let us play,
As meet° is, after such delicious fare;   appropriate
For never did thy beauty since the day
1030 I saw thee first and wedded thee, adorned
With all perfections, so inflame my sense
With ardor to enjoy thee, fairer now
Than ever, bounty of this virtuous tree."
    So said he, and forbore not glance or toy°   caress
1035 Of amorous intent, well understood
Of° Eve, whose eye darted contagious fire.   by
Her hand he seized, and to a shady bank,

1. Cf. 1 Timothy 2.14: "And Adam was not deceived, but the woman being deceived was in the transgression."
2. The theological doctrine that all Adam's descendants are stained by Adam's sin, and are thereby subject to physical death and (unless saved by grace) to damnation.
3. Adam commends Eve for her fine ("exact") and discriminating ("elegant") taste, as a part of "sapience," which means both "taste" and "wisdom."

Thick overhead with verdant roof embow'red
He led her nothing loath; flow'rs were the couch,
940 Pansies, and violets, and asphodel,
And hyacinth, earth's freshest softest lap.
There they their fill of love and love's disport
Took largely, of their mutual guilt the seal,
The solace of their sin, till dewy sleep
945 Oppressed them, wearied with their amorous play.
Soon as the force of that fallacious fruit,
That with exhilarating vapor bland°   *pleasing*
About their spirits had played, and inmost powers
Made err, was now exhaled, and grosser sleep
950 Bred of unkindly° fumes,° with conscious dreams   *unnatural / vapors*
Encumbered,° now had left them, up they rose   *oppressed*
As from unrest, and each the other viewing,
Soon found their eyes how opened, and their minds
How darkened; innocence, that as a veil
955 Had shadowed them from knowing ill, was gone,
Just confidence, and native righteousness,
And honor from about them, naked left
To guilty shame: he° covered, but his robe   *shame*
Uncovered more. So rose the Danite strong
960 Hercúlean Samson from the harlot-lap
Of Philistéan Dálilah, and waked
Shorn of his strength,[4] they destitute and bare
Of all their virtue: silent, and in face
Confounded long they sat, as strucken mute,
965 Till Adam, though not less than Eve abashed,
At length gave utterance to these words constrained:°   *forced*
    "O Eve, in evil[5] hour thou didst give ear
To that false worm, of whomsoever taught
To counterfeit man's voice, true in our fall,
970 False in our promised rising; since our eyes
Opened we find indeed, and find we know
Both good and evil, good lost and evil got,[6]
Bad fruit of knowledge, if this be to know,
Which leaves us naked thus, of honor void,
975 Of innocence, of faith, of purity,
Our wonted° ornaments now soiled and stained,   *former*
And in our faces evident the signs
Of foul concupiscence;[7] whence evil store;
Even shame, the last of evils; of the first
980 Be sure then. How shall I behold the face
Henceforth of God or angel, erst with joy
And rapture so oft beheld? Those heav'nly shapes

---

4. Samson, of the tribe of Dan, told the "harlot" Philistine Delilah that the secret of his strength (like that of Hercules) lay in his hair; she sheared it off while he slept, and when he awoke he was easily captured and blinded by his enemies.
5. Adam's bitter pun—Eve, evil—repudiates the actual etymology of Eve, "life," which Adam will later reaffirm (11.159–61).

6. Milton, like most commentators, derives the tree's name from the event (4.222, 11.84–89).
7. The theological term for the unruly human passions and desires seen as one effect of the Fall, a sign of abundance ("store") of evils. If "shame" is the "last" evil, the "first" is probably the guiltiness that produces it, according to Milton's *Christian Doctrine* (1.12).

Will dazzle now this earthly, with their blaze
Insufferably bright. O might I here
1085 In solitude live savage, in some glade
Obscured, where highest woods impenetrable
To star or sunlight, spread their umbrage° broad,   *shadow, foliage*
And brown as evening: cover me ye pines,
Ye cedars, with innumerable boughs
1090 Hide me, where I may never see them more.
But let us now, as in bad plight, devise
What best may for the present serve to hide
The parts of each from other, that seem most
To shame obnoxious,° and unseemliest seen,   *exposed*
1095 Some tree whose broad smooth leaves together sewed,
And girded on our loins, may cover round
Those middle parts, that this newcomer, shame,
There sit not, and reproach us as unclean."
        So counseled he, and both together went
1100 Into the thickest wood, there soon they chose
The fig tree,[8] not that kind for fruit renowned,
But such as at this day to Indians known
In Malabar or Deccan spreads her arms
Branching so broad and long, that in the ground
1105 The bended twigs take root, and daughters grow
About the mother tree, a pillared shade
High overarched, and echoing walks between;
There oft the Indian herdsman shunning heat
Shelters in cool, and tends his pasturing herds
1110 At loopholes cut through thickest shade: those leaves
They gathered, broad as Amazonian targe,°   *shields*
And with what skill they had, together sewed,
To gird their waist, vain covering if to hide
Their guilt and dreaded shame. O how unlike
1115 To that first naked glory. Such of late
Columbus found th' American so girt
With feathered cincture,° naked else and wild,   *belt*
Among the trees on isles and woody shores.
Thus fenced, and as they thought, their shame in part
1120 Covered, but not at rest or ease of mind,
They sat them down to weep, nor only tears
Rained at their eyes, but high winds worse within
Began to rise, high passions, anger, hate,
Mistrust, suspicion, discord, and shook sore
1125 Their inward state of mind, calm region once
And full of peace, now tossed and turbulent:
For understanding ruled not, and the will
Heard not her lore, both in subjection now
To sensual appetite, who from beneath
1130 Usurping over sovran reason claimed

---

8. The banyan, or Indian fig, has small leaves, but the account Milton draws on from Gerard's *Herbal* (1597) contains the details of lines 1104–11; "Malabar" and "Deccan" are in southern India.

Superior sway: from thus distempered breast,[9]
Adam, estranged° in look and altered style,   *unlike himself*
Speech intermitted thus to Eve renewed:
 "Would thou hadst hearkened to my words, and stayed
435 With me, as I besought thee, when that strange
Desire of wand'ring this unhappy morn,
I know not whence possessed thee; we had then
Remained still happy, not as now, despoiled
Of all our good, shamed, naked, miserable.
440 Let none henceforth seek needless cause to approve°   *prove*
The faith they owe; when earnestly they seek
Such proof, conclude, they then begin to fail."
 To whom soon moved with touch of blame thus Eve:
"What words have passed thy lips, Adam severe,
445 Imput'st thou that to my default, or will
Of wand'ring, as thou call'st it, which who knows
But might as ill have happened thou being by,
Or to thyself perhaps: hadst thou been there,
Or here th' attempt, thou couldst not have discerned
450 Fraud in the serpent, speaking as he spake;
No ground of enmity between us known,
Why he should mean me ill, or seek to harm.
Was I to have never parted from thy side?
As good have grown there still a lifeless rib.
455 Being as I am, why didst not thou the head
Command me absolutely not to go,
Going into such danger as thou saidst?
Too facile° then thou didst not much gainsay,   *easy, mild*
Nay didst permit, approve, and fair dismiss.
460 Hadst thou been firm and fixed in thy dissent,
Neither had I transgressed, nor thou with me."
 To whom then first incensed Adam replied.
"Is this the love, is this the recompense
Of mine to thee, ingrateful Eve, expressed°   *demonstrated*
465 Immutable when thou wert lost, not I,
Who might have lived and joyed immortal bliss,
Yet willingly chose rather death with thee:
And am I now upbraided, as the cause
Of thy transgressing? not enough severe,
470 It seems, in thy restraint: what could I more?
I warned thee, I admonished thee, foretold
The danger, and the lurking enemy
That lay in wait; beyond this had been force,
And force upon free will hath here no place.
475 But confidence then bore thee on, secure°   *self-assured*
Either to meet no danger, or to find
Matter of glorious trial; and perhaps
I also erred in overmuch admiring
What seemed in thee so perfect, that I thought

---

9. The immediate psychological effects of the Fall are evident in the subjection of reason to the lower faculties of sensual appetite.

1180 No evil durst attempt thee, but I rue
That error now, which is become my crime,
And thou th' accuser. Thus it shall befall
Him who to worth in women overtrusting
Lets her will rule; restraint she will not brook,°   accept
1185 And left to herself, if evil thence ensue,
She first his weak indulgence will accuse."
　　　Thus they in mutual accusation spent
The fruitless hours, but neither self-condemning,
And of their vain contést appeared no end.

From Book 10

Summary　When it is known in Heaven that man has fallen, God sends his Son to pass judgment on the sinners. Having found them in the garden, he hears their confession and passes instant sentence, cursing the serpent, condemning Eve to the pains of childbirth and Adam to those of daily toil; but in mercy, he clothes the human couple both outwardly with skins of beasts and inwardly with his righteousness. Meanwhile Sin and Death, sitting by Hell-gate, feel new strength, and pass across Chaos, leaving a great bridge behind them. On their way they meet with their parent, Satan, learn of his success on Earth, and press eagerly forward in hopes of destroying humankind altogether. Satan, on the other hand, continues his flight back toward Hell, where he is to report to his constituents.

[CONSEQUENCES OF THE FALL]

　　　* * *　　Th' other way Satan went down
415 The causey° to Hell gate; on either side   causeway
Disparted Chaos over-built exclaimed,
And with rebounding surge the bars assailed,
That scorned his indignation.[1] Through the gate,
Wide open and unguarded, Satan passed,
420 And all about found desolate; for those[2]
Appointed to sit there, had left their charge,
Flown to the upper world; the rest were all
Far to the inland retired, about the walls
Of Pandemonium, city and proud seat
425 Of Lucifer, so by allusion° called,   metaphor
Of that bright star[3] to Satan paragoned.
There kept their watch the legions, while the grand[4]
In council sat, solicitous° what chance   anxious
Might intercept their emperor sent, so he
430 Departing gave command, and they observed.
As when the Tartar[5] from his Russian foe

1. Chaos is the instinctive enemy of all order, so hostile to the bridge built over it.
2. Sin and Death.
3. Satan before his fall was Lucifer, the Light-bringer, and the Morning Star is named Lucifer because it is compared ("paragoned") to him.
4. The "grand infernal peers" who govern (cf. 2.507).
5. The simile compares the fallen angels, withdrawn from other regions of Hell to guard their metropolis, to Tartars retiring before attacking Russians and Persians before the attacking Turks (lines 431–39). "Astracan": a region west of the Caspian Sea inhabited by Russia and defended against Turks and Tartars; "Aladule": the region of Armenia, from which the last Persian ruler, called "Anadule," a "Bactrian Sophi" (Persian Shah), was forced to retreat from the Turks, to Tabriz ("Tauris") and Kazvin ("Casbeen").

By Astracan over the snowy plains
Retires, or Bactrian Sophi from the horns
Of Turkish crescent, leaves all waste beyond
35 The realm of Aladule, in his retreat
To Tauris or Casbeen: so these the late
Heav'n-banished host, left desert utmost Hell
Many a dark league, reduced° in careful watch   *drawn together*
Round their metropolis, and now expecting
40 Each hour their great adventurer from the search
Of foreign worlds: he through the midst unmarked,°   *unnoticed*
In show plebeian angel militant
Of lowest order,° passed; and from the door   *private*
Of that Plutonian[6] hall, invisible
45 Ascended his high throne, which under state°   *canopy*
Of richest texture spread, at th' upper end
Was placed in regal luster. Down a while
He sat, and round about him saw unseen:
At last as from a cloud his fulgent head
50 And shape star-bright appeared, or brighter, clad
With what permissive° glory since his fall   *permitted*
Was left him, or false glitter: all amazed
At that so sudden blaze the Stygian[7] throng
Bent their aspéct, and whom they wished beheld,
55 Their mighty chief returned: loud was th' acclaim:
Forth rushed in haste the great consulting peers,
Raised from their dark divan,[8] and with like joy
Congratulant approached him, who with hand
Silence, and with these words attention won:
60   "Thrones, Dominations, Princedoms, Virtues, Powers,
For in possession such, not only of right,
I call ye[9] and declare ye now, returned
Successful beyond hope, to lead ye forth
Triumphant out of this infernal pit
65 Abominable, accurst, the house of woe,
And dungeon of our tyrant: now possess,
As lords, a spacious world, to our native heaven
Little inferior, by my adventure hard
With peril great achieved. Long were to tell
70 What I have done, what suffered, with what pain
Voyaged th' unreal,° vast, unbounded deep   *unformed*
Of horrible confusion, over which
By Sin and Death a broad way now is paved
To expedite your glorious march; but I
75 Toiled out my uncouth° passage, forced to ride   *strange*
Th' untractable abyss, plunged in the womb
Of unoriginal[1] Night and Chaos wild,
That jealous of their secrets fiercely opposed

6. Pertaining to Pluto, ruler of the classical underworld.
7. Of the river Styx in Hades, the river of hate.
8. The Turkish Council of State (continuing the

comparisons with oriental despotism).
9. I.e., you now have these titles not only by right
but by possession (from the conquest on earth).
1. Having no origin, uncreated.

My journey strange, with clamorous uproar
480   Protesting[2] Fate supreme; thence how I found
The new-created world, which fame in Heav'n
Long had foretold, a fabric wonderful
Of absolute perfection, therein man
Placed in a paradise, by our exile
485   Made happy: him by fraud I have seduced
From his Creator, and the more to increase
Your wonder, with an apple. He thereat
Offended, worth your laughter, hath giv'n up
Both his beloved man and all his world,
490   To Sin and Death a prey, and so to us,
Without our hazard, labor, or alarm,
To range in, and to dwell, and over man
To rule, as over all he should have ruled.
True is, me also he hath judged, or rather
495   Me not, but the brute serpent in whose shape
Man I deceived; that which to me belongs,
Is enmity, which he will put between
Me and mankind; I am to bruise his heel;
His seed, when is not set, shall bruise my head:
500   A world who would not purchase with a bruise,
Or much more grievous pain? Ye have th' account
Of my performance: what remains, ye gods,
But up and enter now into full bliss."[3]
       So having said, a while he stood, expecting
505   Their universal shout and high applause.
To fill his ear, when contrary he hears
On all sides, from innumerable tongues
A dismal universal hiss, the sound
Of public scorn; he wondered, but not long
510   Had leisure, wond'ring at himself now more;
His visage drawn he felt to sharp and spare,
His arms clung to his ribs, his legs entwining
Each other, till supplanted° down he fell   *tripped up*
A monstrous serpent on his belly prone,
515   Reluctant,° but in vain, a greater power   *struggling*
Now ruled him, punished in the shape he sinned,
According to his doom: he would have spoke,
But hiss for hiss returned with forkèd tongue
To forkèd tongue, for now were all transformed
520   Alike, to serpents[4] all as accessories
To his bold riot:° dreadful was the din   *revolt*
Of hissing through the hall, thick swarming now
With complicated° monsters, head and tail,   *tangled*
Scorpion[5] and asp, and amphisbaena dire,

---

2. Protesting both to, and against, Fate.
3. Ironically, the final word of Satan's proud, triumphal speech rhymes with and so prepares for the "hiss" that will soon greet him, as his would-be triumph is turned by God to abject humiliation.
4. The scene recalls Dante's vivid description of the thieves metamorphosed to snakes in *Inferno* 24–25.

5. The "Scorpion" has a venomous sting at the tip of the tail; "asp" is a small Egyptian viper; "amphisbaena" supposedly had a head at each end; "Cerastes" is an asp with horny projections over each eye; "hydrus" and "ellops" were mythical water snakes; "dipsas" was a mythical snake whose bite caused raging thirst.

25 Cerastes horned, hydrus, and ellops drear,
And dipsas (not so thick swarmed once the soil
Bedropped with blood of Gorgon,⁶ or the isle
Ophiusa) but still greatest he the midst,
Now dragon grown, larger than whom the sun
30 Engendered in the Pythian vale on slime,
Huge Python,⁷ and his power no less he seemed
Above the rest still to retain; they all
Him followed issuing forth to th' open field,
Where all yet left of that revolted rout
35 Heav'n-fall'n, in station stood or just array,⁸   *raised up*
Sublime° with expectation when to see
In triumph issuing forth their glorious chief;
They saw, but other sight instead, a crowd
Of ugly serpents; horror on them fell,
40 And horrid sympathy; for what they saw,
They felt themselves now changing; down their arms,
Down fell both spear and shield, down they as fast,
And the dire hiss renewed, and the dire form
Catched by contagion, like in punishment,
45 As in their crime. Thus was th' applause they meant,
Turned to exploding hiss, triumph to shame
Cast on themselves from their own mouths. There stood
A grove hard by, sprung up with this their change,
His will who reigns above, to aggravate
50 Their penance,° laden with fair fruit, like that   *punishment*
Which grew in Paradise, the bait of Eve
Used by the Tempter: on that prospect strange
Their earnest eyes they fixed, imagining
For one forbidden tree a multitude
55 Now ris'n, to work them further woe or shame;
Yet parched with scalding thirst and hunger fierce,
Though to delude them sent, could not abstain,
But on they rolled in heaps, and up the trees
Climbing, sat thicker than the snaky locks
60 That curled Megaera:⁹ greedily they plucked
The fruitage fair to sight, like that which grew
Near that bituminous lake where Sodom flamed;¹
This more delusive, not the touch, but taste
Deceived; they fondly° thinking to allay   *foolishly*
65 Their appetite with gust,° instead of fruit   *relish*
Chewed bitter ashes, which th' offended taste
With spattering noise rejected: oft they assayed,°   *attempted*
Hunger and thirst constraining, drugged as oft,
With hatefulest disrelish writhed their jaws
70 With soot and cinders filled; so oft they fell

6. Drops of blood from the Gorgon Medusa's severed head turned into snakes; "Ophiusa" in Greek
means "isle of snakes."
7. A gigantic serpent engendered from the slime
left by Deucalion's flood; Apollo slew him and
appropriated the "Pythian" vale and shrine at Delphi.

8. I.e., at their posts or on parade.
9. One of three Furies with snaky hair.
1. Sodom apples reputedly grew on the spot where
the accursed city once stood, now the Dead Sea
("that bituminous lake"); the apples look good, but
dissolve into ashes when eaten.

Into the same illusion, not as man
Whom they triumphed once lapsed.[2] Thus were they plagued
And worn with famine, long and ceaseless hiss,
Till their lost shape, permitted, they resumed,[3]
575　Yearly enjoined, some say, to undergo
This annual humbling certain numbered days,
To dash their pride, and joy for man seduced.
However some tradition they dispersed
Among the heathen of their purchase° got,　　　　　　　　　　　*plunder*
580　And fabled how the serpent, whom they called
Ophion with Eurynome,[4] the wide-
Encroaching Eve perhaps, had first the rule
Of high Olympus, thence by Saturn driv'n
And Ops, ere yet Dictaean Jove was born.

Summary　Sin and Death proceed without further interruption to Earth, and
enter into possession of it. God sees their arrival and declines to interfere, but proph-
esies that their triumph will be only temporary; in due course they will be forced back
to Hell again, and forever. Meanwhile, the angels are ordered to twist the Earth on
its axis, disorder the planets so their influence will in future be bad as well as good,
and rearrange the cosmos generally. In consequence, the temperate climate of Paradise at once gives way to extremes of heat and cold, and furious winds begin to blow
across the ruined planet.

[ADAM, EVE, AND THE FIRST STEPS TO REDEMPTION]

*　*　* Thus began
Outrage from lifeless things; but Discord first
Daughter of Sin, among th' irrational,
Death introduced through fierce antipathy:[5]
710　Beast now with beast gan war, and fowl with fowl,
And fish with fish; to graze the herb° all leaving,　　　　　　　　*grass*
Devour'd each other; nor stood much in awe
Of man, but fled him, or with count'nance grim
Glared on him passing: these were from without
715　The growing miseries, which Adam saw
Already in part, though hid in gloomiest shade,
To sorrow abandoned, but worse felt within,
And in a troubled sea of passion tossed,
Thus to disburden sought with sad complaint:
720　"O miserable of happy![6] Is this the end

2. Unlike man who fell once, they try to eat the
dissolving apples over and over again.
3. God permitted them to regain their "lost form"
as fallen angels; but they are undergoing a slower,
natural metamorphosis into grosser substance by
their continuing commitment to and choice of evil.
4. The Titan "Ophion" (whose name means
"snake") and his wife "Eurynome" ("the wide-
reacher") ruled Olympus until driven away by "Saturn" and his wife "Ops," who were in turn

overthrown by "Jove," who lived on the mountain
"Dicte." Milton suggests that these may represent
versions of the story transmitted by the fallen
angels to the pagans (lines 578–84).
5. "Discord" (personified as daughter of Sin)
introduced Death among the animals ("the irrational") by stirring up "antipathy" among them.
6. Adam's complaint begins with the classical formula for a tragic fall or *peripeteia*, the change from
happiness to misery.

Of this new glorious world, and me so late
The glory of that glory, who now become
Accurst of blessèd, hide me from the face
Of God, whom to behold was then my height
725 Of happiness: yet well, if here would end
The misery, I deserved it, and would bear
My own deservings; but this will not serve;
All that I eat or drink, or shall beget,
Is propagated⁷ curse. O voice once heard
730 Delightfully, 'Increase and multiply,'
Now death to hear! For what can I increase
Or multiply, but curses on my head?
Who of all ages to succeed, but feeling
The evil on him brought by me, will curse
735 My head: 'Ill fare our ancestor impure,
For this we may thank Adam'; but his thanks
Shall be the execration; so besides
Mine own that bide upon⁸ me, all from me
Shall with a fierce reflux on me redound,
740 On me as on their natural center light
Heavy, though in their place. O fleeting joys
Of Paradise, dear bought with lasting woes!
Did I request thee, Maker, from my clay
To mold me man, did I solicit thee
745 From darkness to promote me, or here place
In this delicious garden? As my will
Concurred not to my being, it were but right
And equal° to reduce me to my dust,   *just*
Desirous to resign, and render back
750 All I received, unable to perform
Thy terms too hard, by which I was to hold
The good I sought not. To the loss of that,
Sufficient penalty, why hast thou added
The sense of endless woes? Inexplicable
755 Thy justice seems; yet to say truth, too late
I thus contest; then should have been refused
Those terms whatever, when they were proposed:
Thou⁹ didst accept them; wilt thou enjoy the good,
Then cavil the conditions? And though God
760 Made thee without thy leave, what if thy son
Prove disobedient, and reproved, retort,
'Wherefore didst thou beget me? I sought it not:'
Wouldst thou admit for his contempt of thee
That proud excuse? Yet him not thy election,°   *choice*
765 But natural necessity begot.

---

7. Handed down from one generation to the next.
8. I.e., Adam's "own" curse will remain ("bide") with him, and the curse ("execration") of "all" who descend from him will "redound" on him as to their natural "center"; objects so placed ("in their place,"

line 741) were thought to be weightless ("light")
but these curses will be "heavy."
9. Adam turns from addressing God to address himself.

God made thee of choice his own, and of his own
To serve him, thy reward was of his grace,
Thy punishment then justly is at his will.
Be it so, for I submit, his doom is fair,
770 That dust I am, and shall to dust return:
O welcome hour whenever! Why delays
His hand to execute what his decree
Fixed on this day? Why do I overlive,
Why am I mocked with death, and lengthened out
775 To deathless pain? How gladly would I meet
Mortality my sentence, and be earth
Insensible, how glad would lay me down
As in my mother's lap! There I should rest
And sleep secure; his dreadful voice no more
780 Would thunder in my ears, no fear of worse
To me and to my offspring would torment me
With cruel expectation. Yet one doubt
Pursues me still, lest all I° cannot die,   *all of me*
Lest that pure breath of life, the spirit of man
785 Which God inspired, cannot together perish
With this corporeal clod; then in the grave,
Or in some other dismal place, who knows
But I shall die a living death? O thought
Horrid, if true! Yet why? It was but breath
790 Of life that sinned; what dies but what had life
And sin? The body properly hath neither.
All of me then shall die:[1] let this appease
The doubt, since human reach no further knows.
For though the Lord of all be infinite,
795 Is his wrath also? Be it, man is not so,
But mortal doomed. How can he exercise
Wrath without end on man whom death must end?
Can he make deathless death? That were to make
Strange contradiction, which to God himself
800 Impossible is held, as argument
Of weakness, not of power. Will he draw out,
For anger's sake, finite to infinite
In punished man, to satisfy his rigor
Satisfied never; that were to extend
805 His sentence beyond dust and nature's law,
By which all causes else according still
To the reception of their matter act,
Not to th' extent of their own sphere.[2] But say
That death be not one stroke, as I supposed,
810 Bereaving° sense, but endless misery   *taking away*

---

1. After debating the matter, Adam concludes that the soul dies with the body; Milton in his *Christian Doctrine* worked out this "mortalist" doctrine, with its corollary, that both soul and body rise at the Last Judgment.

2. Adam convinces himself that "finite" matter (line 802) cannot suffer "infinite" punishment by an axiom of traditional philosophy, that by "nature's law" (line 805) the actions of agents are limited by the nature of the object they act upon.

From this day onward, which I feel begun
Both in me, and without° me, and so last   outside of
To perpetuity; ay me, that fear
Comes thund'ring back with dreadful revolution°   recurrence
15 On my defenseless head; both Death and I
Am found eternal, and incorporate° both,   made one body
Nor I on my part single, in me all
Posterity stands cursed: fair patrimony
That I must leave ye, sons; O were I able
20 To waste it all myself, and leave ye none!
So disinherited how would ye bless
Me now your curse! Ah, why should all mankind
For one man's fault thus guiltless be condemned,
If guiltless? But from me what can proceed,
25 But all corrupt, both mind and will depraved,
Not to do° only, but to will the same   act
With me? How can they then acquitted stand
In sight of God? Him after all disputes
Forced I absolve: all my evasions vain
30 And reasonings, though through mazes, lead me still
But to my own conviction: first and last
On me, me only, as the source and spring
Of all corruption, all the blame lights due;
So might the wrath.³ Fond° wish! Couldst thou support   foolish
35 That burden heavier than the earth to bear,
Than all the world much heavier, though divided
With that bad woman? Thus what thou desir'st,
And what thou fear'st, alike destroys all hope
Of refuge, and concludes thee miserable
40 Beyond all past example and future,
To Satan only like both crime and doom.
O conscience, into what abyss of fears
And horrors hast thou driv'n me; out of which
I find no way, from deep to deeper plunged!"
45   Thus Adam to himself lamented loud
Through the still night, not now, as ere man fell,
Wholesome and cool, and mild, but with black air
Accompanied, with damps° and dreadful gloom,   noxious vapors
Which to his evil conscience represented
50 All things with double terror: on the ground
Outstretched he lay, on the cold ground, and oft
Cursed his creation, Death as oft accused
Of tardy execution, since denounced°   pronounced
The day of his offense: "Why comes not Death,"
55 Said he, "with one thrice-ácceptáble stroke
To end me? Shall Truth fail to keep her word,
Justice divine not hasten to be just?
But Death comes not at call, Justice divine

3. Cf. the Son's offer to accept all humankind's guilt (3.236), and Eve's similar offer (10.935–36).

Mends not her slowest pace for prayers or cries.
860 O woods, O fountains, hillocks, dales and bow'rs,
With other echo late I taught your shades
To answer, and resound far other song."[4]
Whom thus afflicted when sad Eve beheld,
Desolate where she sat, approaching nigh,
865 Soft words to his fierce passion she assayed;
But her with stern regard he thus repelled:
    "Out of my sight, thou serpent,[5] that name best
Befits thee with him leagued, thyself as false
And hateful; nothing wants,° but that thy shape,   is lacking
870 Like his, and color serpentine may show
Thy inward fraud, to warn all creatures from thee
Henceforth; lest that too heav'nly form, pretended[6]
To hellish falsehood, snare them. But° for thee   except
I had persisted happy, had not thy pride
875 And wand'ring vanity, when least was safe,
Rejected my forewarning, and disdained
Not to be trusted, longing to be seen
Though by the Devil himself, him overweening°   overconfident
To overreach, but with the serpent meeting
880 Fooled and beguiled, by him thou, I by thee,
To trust thee from my side, imagined wise,
Constant, mature, proof against all assaults,
And understood not all was but a show
Rather than solid virtue, all but a rib
885 Crooked by nature, bent, as now appears,
More to the part siníster° from me drawn,   the left side
Well if thrown out, as supernumerary[7]
To my just number found. O why did God,
Creator wise, that peopled highest heav'n
890 With Spirits masculine,[8] create at last
This novelty on earth, this fair defect
Of nature,[9] and not fill the world at once
With men as angels without feminine,
Or find some other way to generate
895 Mankind? This mischief had not then befall'n,
And more that shall befall, innumerable
Disturbances on earth through female snares,
And strait conjunction[1] with this sex: for either
He never shall find out fit mate, but such
900 As some misfortune brings him, or mistake,
Or whom he wishes most shall seldom gain

4. Cf. their morning hymn (5.153–208).
5. Adam's bitter, misogynistic outcry begins with reference to the patristic notion that the name Eve, aspirated, means "serpent."
6. Held in front of, as a cover or mask.
7. It was supposed that Adam had thirteen ribs on the left side, so he could spare one for the creation of Eve and still retain the proper ("just") number,
twelve.
8. The Miltonic Bard indicated that angels can assume at will "either sex . . . or both" (1.424).
9. Aristotle had claimed that the female is a defective male.
1. Close, hard-pressing, binding union: Adam goes on to project the problems of future marriages.

Through her perverseness, but shall see her gained
By a far worse, or if she love, withheld
By parents, or his happiest choice too late
905   Shall meet, already linked and wedlock-bound
To a fell° adversary, his hate or shame: *bitter*
Which infinite calamity shall cause
To human life, and household peace confound."
    He added not, and from her turned, but Eve
910   Not so repulsed, with tears that ceased not flowing,
And tresses all disordered, at his feet
Fell humble, and embracing them, besought
His peace, and thus proceeded in her plaint:
    "Forsake me not thus, Adam, witness Heav'n
915   What love sincere, and reverence in my heart
I bear thee, and unweeting° have offended,   *unintentionally*
Unhappily deceived; thy suppliant
I beg, and clasp thy knees;[2] bereave me not,
Whereon I live, thy gentle looks, thy aid,
920   Thy counsel in this uttermost distress,
My only strength and stay: forlorn of thee,
Whither shall I betake me, where subsist?
While yet we live, scarce one short hour perhaps,
Between us two let there be peace, both joining,
925   As joined in injuries, one enmity
Against a foe by doom express° assigned us,   *explicit judgment*
That cruel serpent: on me exercise not
Thy hatred for this misery befall'n,
On me already lost, me than thyself
930   More miserable; both have sinned, but thou
Against God only, I against God and thee,
And to the place of judgment will return,
There with my cries importune Heaven, that all
The sentence from thy head removed may light
935   On me, sole cause to thee of all this woe,
Me me only just object of his ire."[3]
    She ended weeping, and her lowly plight,°   *posture*
Immovable till peace obtained from fault
Acknowledged and deplored, in Adam wrought
940   Commiseration; soon his heart relented
Towards her, his life so late and sole delight,
Now at his feet submissive in distress,
Creature so fair his reconcilement seeking,
His counsel whom she had displeased, his aid;
945   As one disarmed, his anger all he lost,
And thus with peaceful words upraised her soon:
    "Unwary, and too desirous, as before,
So now of what thou know'st not, who desir'st

---

2. Eve assumes the posture of the classical suppliant, clasping the knees of the one she begs from.

3. Eve also echoes the Son's offer (3.236). Cf.
Adam's cry (10.832).

The punishment all on thyself; alas!
950 Bear thine own first, ill able to sustain
His full wrath whose thou feel'st as yet least part,[4]
And my displeasure bear'st so ill. If prayers
Could alter high decrees, I to that place
Would speed before thee, and be louder heard,
955 That on my head all might be visited,
Thy frailty and infirmer sex forgiv'n,
To me committed and by me exposed.
But rise, let us no more contend, nor blame
Each other, blamed enough elsewhere, but strive
960 In offices of love, how we may light'n
Each other's burden in our share of woe;
Since this day's death denounced, if aught I see,
Will prove no sudden, but a slow-paced evil,
A long day's dying to augment our pain,
965 And to our seed (O hapless seed!) derived."°   *passed on*
    To whom thus Eve, recovering heart, replied:
"Adam, by sad experiment I know
How little weight my words with thee can find,
Found so erroneous, thence by just event°   *consequence*
970 Found so unfortunate; nevertheless,
Restored by thee, vile as I am, to place
Of new acceptance, hopeful to regain
Thy love, the sole contentment of my heart
Living or dying, from thee I will not hide
975 What thoughts in my unquiet breast are ris'n,
Tending to some relief of our extremes,
Or end, though sharp and sad, yet tolerable,
As in our evils, and of easier choice.
If care of our descent perplex us most,[5]
980 Which must be born to certain woe, devoured
By Death at last, and miserable it is
To be to others cause of misery,
Our own begotten, and of our loins to bring
Into this cursèd world a woeful race,
985 That after wretched life must be at last
Food for so foul a monster, in thy power
It lies, yet ere conception to prevent
The race unblest, to being yet unbegot.
Childless thou art, childless remain; so Death
990 Shall be deceived° his glut, and with us two   *cheated of*
Be forced to satisfy his rav'nous maw.
But if thou judge it hard and difficult,
Conversing, looking, loving, to abstain
From love's due rites, nuptial embraces sweet,

---

4. I.e., you could hardly bear God's "full wrath" since you are so distraught when you feel only the smallest part of it, and you can "ill" bear my displeasure (line 952).
5. I.e., if concern for our descendants most torment ("perplex") us.

95   And with desire to languish without hope,
     Before the present object[6] languishing
     With like desire, which would be misery
     And torment less than none of what we dread,
     Then both ourselves and seed at once to free
100 From what we fear for both, let us make short,°   *lose no time*
     Let us seek Death, or he not found, supply
     With our own hands his office on ourselves;
     Why stand we longer shivering under fears,
     That show no end but death, and have the power,
105 Of many ways to die the shortest choosing,
     Destruction with destruction to destroy."
         She ended here, or vehement despair
     Broke off the rest; so much of death her thoughts
     Had entertained, as dyed her cheeks with pale.
110 But Adam with such counsel nothing swayed,
     To better hopes his more attentive mind
     Laboring had raised, and thus to Eve replied.
         "Eve thy contempt of life and pleasure seems
     To argue in thee something more sublime
115 And excellent than what thy mind contemns;°   *despises*
     But self-destruction therefore sought, refutes
     That excellence thought in thee, and implies,
     Not thy contempt, but anguish and regret
     For loss of life and pleasure overloved.
120 Or if thou covet death, as utmost end
     Of misery, so thinking to evade
     The penalty pronounced, doubt not but God
     Hath wiselier armed his vengeful ire than so
     To be forestalled; much more I fear lest death
125 So snatched will not exempt us from the pain
     We are by doom to pay: rather such acts
     Of contumácy° will provoke the Highest   *contempt*
     To make death in us live. Then let us seek
     Some safer resolution, which methinks
130 I have in view, calling to mind with heed
     Part of our sentence, that thy seed shall bruise
     The serpent's head; piteous amends, unless
     Be meant, whom I conjecture, our grand foe
     Satan, who in the serpent hath contrived
135 Against us this deceit: to crush his head
     Would be revenge indeed; which will be lost
     By death brought on ourselves, or childless days
     Resolved, as thou proposest; so our foe
     Shall scape his punishment ordained, and we
140 Instead shall double ours upon our heads.
     No more be mentioned then of violence

---

6. I.e., Eve herself, who then projects her own frustrated desire if they were to forgo sex.

Against ourselves, and wilful barrenness,
That cuts us off from hope, and savors only
Rancor and pride, impatience and despite,
1045 Reluctance° against God and his just yoke   *resistance*
Laid on our necks. Remember with what mild
And gracious temper he both heard and judged
Without wrath or reviling; we expected
Immediate dissolution, which we thought
1050 Was meant by death that day, when lo, to thee
Pains only in child-bearing were foretold,
And bringing forth, soon recompensed with joy,
Fruit of thy womb:⁷ on me the curse aslope
Glanced on the ground,⁸ with labor I must earn
1055 My bread; what harm? Idleness had been worse;
My labor will sustain me; and lest cold
Or heat should injure us, his timely care
Hath unbesought provided, and his hands
Clothed us unworthy, pitying while he judged;
1060 How much more, if we pray him, will his ear
Be open, and his heart to pity incline,
And teach us further by what means to shun
Th' inclement seasons, rain, ice, hail and snow,
Which now the sky with various face begins
1065 To show us in this mountain, while the winds
Blow moist and keen, shattering° the graceful locks   *scattering*
Of these fair spreading trees; which bids us seek
Some better shroud,° some better warmth to cherish   *shelter*
Our limbs benumbed, ere this diurnal star°   *the sun*
1070 Leave cold the night, how we his gathered beams
Reflected, may with matter sere foment,
Or by collision of two bodies grind
The air attrite to fire,⁹ as late the clouds
Justling or pushed with winds rude in their shock
1075 Tine° the slant lightning, whose thwart° flame driv'n down   *ignite / slanting*
Kindles the gummy bark of fir or pine,
And sends a comfortable heat from far,
Which might supply° the sun: such fire to use,   *take the place of*
And what may else be remedy or cure
1080 To evils which our own misdeeds have wrought,
He will instruct us praying, and of grace
Beseeching him, so as we need not fear
To pass commodiously this life, sustained
By him with many comforts, till we end
1085 In dust, our final rest and native home.
What better can we do, than to the place

7. Adam's unconscious echo of Elizabeth's address to Mary, mother of Jesus (Luke 1.41–42), "Blessed is the fruit of thy womb," lays the ground for their fuller understanding of the promise about the "seed" of the woman.
8. I.e., the curse, like a spear that almost missed its target, glanced aside and hit the ground.
9. Adam projects the invention of fire: they might, by striking two bodies together, rub ("attrite") the air into fire by fiction; or else (line 1070) focus reflected sunbeams (through some equivalent of glass) on dry ("sere") matter.

Repairing where he judged us, prostrate fall
Before him reverent, and there confess
Humbly our faults, and pardon beg, with tears
990 Watering the ground, and with our sighs the air
Frequenting,° sent from hearts contrite, in sign   *filling*
Of sorrow unfeigned, and humiliation meek.
Undoubtedly he will relent and turn
From his displeasure; in whose look serene,
995 When angry most he seemed and most severe,
What else but favor, grace, and mercy shone?"
    So spake our father penitent, nor Eve
Felt less remorse: they forthwith to the place
Repairing where he judged them prostrate fell
1100 Before him reverent, and both confessed
Humbly their faults, and pardon begged, with tears
Watering the ground, and with their sighs the air
Frequenting, sent from hearts contrite, in sign
Of sorrow unfeigned, and humiliation meek.[1]

Book 11 *Summary*   The prayers of Adam and Eve prove acceptable to God.
But while humankind may now hope for ultimate redemption, humans may no longer
dwell in Paradise; and Michael, the warrior archangel, is dispatched to explain the
sentence, offer some hope for the future, and dismiss Adam and Eve from the happy
garden. Adam is at first overcome with grief; but the angel encourages him, and while
Eve is put in a trance, Adam is raised to the peak of a high hill and shown in a vision
the future of the human race as far as the flood of Noah.

From Book 12

Summary   Continuing his instruction of Adam, Michael relates the history of
the world from the time of Noah through the coming of Christ, whose ascent into
Heaven and triumph over Death after the Crucifixion he describes.

[THE DEPARTURE FROM EDEN]

    So spake th' Archangel Michaël, then paused,
As at the world's great period;° and our sire   *consummation*
Replete with joy and wonder thus replied:
    "O goodness infinite, goodness immense!
470 That all this good of evil shall produce,
And evil turn to good; more wonderful
Than that which by creation first brought forth
Light out of darkness! Full of doubt I stand,
Whether I should repent me now of sin
475 By me done and occasioned, or rejoice
Much more, that much more good thereof shall spring,
To God more glory, more good will to men

---

1. The final six lines repeat, almost word for word, lines 1086–92, with only six lines separating them; this provides strong closure, as the poet describes Adam's proposed gesture of repentance carried out in every detail.

From God, and over wrath grace shall abound.[1]
But say, if our Deliverer up to Heav'n
480   Must reascend, what will betide the few
His faithful, left among th' unfaithful herd,
The enemies of truth; who then shall guide
His people, who defend? Will they not deal
Worse with his followers than with him they dealt?"
485   "Be sure they will," said th' angel; "but from Heav'n
He to his own a Comforter will send,[2]
The promise of the Father, who shall dwell
His Spirit within them, and the law of faith
Working through love, upon their hearts shall write,
490   To guide them in all truth, and also arm
With spiritual armor, able to resist
Satan's assaults, and quench his fiery darts,[3]
What° man can do against them, not afraid,   *as much as*
Though to the death, against such cruelties
495   With inward consolations recompensed,
And oft supported so as shall amaze
Their proudest persecutors: for the Spirit
Poured first on his apostles, whom he sends
To evangelize the nations, then on all
500   Baptized, shall them with wondrous gifts endue°   *endow*
To speak all tongues, and do all miracles,
As did their Lord before them. Thus they win
Great numbers of each nation to receive
With joy the tidings brought from Heav'n: at length
505   Their ministry performed, and race well run,
Their doctrine and their story written left,[4]
They die; but in their room, as they forewarn,
Wolves shall succeed for teachers, grievous wolves,
Who all the sacred mysteries of Heav'n
510   To their own vile advantages shall turn
Of lucre and ambition, and the truth
With superstitions and traditions taint,[5]
Left only in those written records pure,
Though not but by the Spirit understood.
515   Then shall they seek to avail themselves of names,°   *honors*
Places° and titles, and with these to join   *offices*
Secular power, though feigning still to act

---

1. These lines do not formulate the medieval idea of the *felix culpa*—that the Fall was fortunate in bringing humans greater happiness than they would otherwise have enjoyed—only that the Fall has provided God an occasion to bring still greater good out of evil. The poem makes clear that Adam and Eve would have grown in perfection and advanced to Heaven had they not sinned.
2. The Holy Spirit, who for Milton is much subordinate to both Father and Son.
3. Cf. Ephesians 6.11–16: "Put on the whole armor of God, that ye may be able to stand against the wiles of the devil. . . . Above all, taking the shield of faith, wherewith ye shall be able to

quench all the fiery darts of the wicked." The subsequent history (lines 493–505) is that of the early Christian church in apostolic times.
4. I.e., in the Gospels and Epistles.
5. The history summarized in lines 510–40 is of the corruption of the Christian church by superstitions, traditions, and persecutions of conscience in patristic times under the popes and the Christian emperors, but also extending to the Last Day. The terms point especially to what Milton saw as the revival of "popish" superstitions in the English Church of the Restoration, and to the fierce persecution of Dissenters.

By spiritual, to themselves appropriating
The Spirit of God, promised alike and giv'n
20 To all believers;[6] and from that pretense,
Spiritual laws by carnal° power shall force   *fleshly, worldly*
On every conscience; laws which none shall find
Left them enrolled, or what the Spirit within
Shall on the heart engrave.[7] What will they then
25 But force the Spirit of Grace itself, and bind
His consort Liberty; what, but unbuild
His living temples,[8] built by faith to stand,
Their own faith not another's: for on earth
Who against faith and conscience can be heard
30 Infallible?[9] Yet many will presume:
Whence heavy persecution shall arise
On all who in the worship persevere
Of Spirit and Truth; the rest, far greater part,
Will deem in outward rites and specious forms
35 Religion satisfied; Truth shall retire
Bestuck with sland'rous darts, and works of faith
Rarely be found: so shall the world go on,
To good malignant, to bad men benign,
Under her own weight groaning, till the day
40 Appear of respiration° to the just,   *respite*
And vengeance to the wicked, at return
Of him so lately promised to thy aid,
The Woman's Seed,[1] obscurely then foretold,
Now ampler known thy Saviour and thy Lord,
45 Last in the clouds from Heav'n to be revealed
In glory of the Father, to dissolve
Satan with his perverted world, then raise
From the conflagrant mass,° purged and refined,   *the burning world*
New heav'ns, new earth, ages of endless date
50 Founded in righteousness and peace of love,
To bring forth fruits joy and eternal bliss."
    He ended; and thus Adam last replied:
"How soon hath thy prediction, seer blest,
Measured this transient world, the race of time,
55 Till time stand fixed: beyond is all abyss,
Eternity, whose end no eye can reach.
Greatly instructed I shall hence depart,
Greatly in peace of thought, and have my fill
Of knowledge, what° this vessel can contain;   *as much as*

6. These lines affirm the Protestant principle of every Christian's right to interpret Scripture according to the "inner light" of the Spirit, and denounce (as Milton consistently did in his tracts) the use of civil ("carnal") power to enforce orthodoxy.
7. I.e., there is nothing in Scripture or in the Spirit's inner teaching that sanctions persecution for conscience.
8. Cf. 1 Corinthians 3.16: "Know ye not that ye are the temple of God?" "His consort Liberty": Mil-

ton typically insists that Christ's gospel and the Spirit of God teach liberty, religious and civil, alluding as here to 2 Corinthians 3.17: "Where the Spirit of the Lord is, there is Liberty."
9. An attack on papal claims to infallibility, asserted though not yet proclaimed as doctrine.
1. Michael's story ends with the full explication of the promised "Woman's Seed" as Christ, and with the renewal of all things after the Last Judgment (lines 545–51).

560 Beyond which was my folly to aspire.
Henceforth I learn, that to obey is best,
And love with fear the only God, to walk
As in his presence, ever to observe
His providence, and on him sole depend,
565 Merciful over all his works, with good
Still overcoming evil, and by small
Accomplishing great things, by things deemed weak
Subverting worldly strong, and worldly wise
By simply meek; that suffering for truth's sake
570 Is fortitude to highest victory,
And to the faithful death the gate of life;
Taught this by his example whom I now
Acknowledge my Redeemer ever blest."
　　To whom thus also th' angel last replied:
575 "This having learnt, thou hast attained the sum
Of wisdom; hope no higher, though all the stars
Thou knew'st by name,[2] and all th' ethereal powers,
All secrets of the deep, all nature's works,
Or works of God in heav'n, air, earth, or sea,
580 And all the riches of this world enjoy'dst,
And all the rule, one empire; only add
Deeds to thy knowledge answerable,° add faith,　　　　　*corresponding*
Add virtue, patience, temperance, add love,
By name to come called charity, the soul
585 Of all the rest: then wilt thou not be loath
To leave this Paradise, but shalt possess
A paradise within thee, happier far.
Let us descend now therefore from this top
Of speculation;° for the hour precise　　　　　*hill of speculation*
590 Exacts° our parting hence; and see the guards,　　　　　*requires*
By me encamped on yonder hill, expect
Their motion,° at whose front a flaming sword,　　　　　*await their orders*
In signal of remove, waves fiercely round;
We may no longer stay: go, waken Eve;
595 Her also I with gentle dreams have calmed
Portending good, and all her spirits composed
To meek submission: thou at season fit
Let her with thee partake what thou hast heard,
Chiefly what may concern her faith to know,
600 The great deliverance by her seed to come
(For by the Woman's Seed) on all mankind.
That ye may live, which will be many days,
Both in one faith unanimous though sad,
With cause for evils past, yet much more cheered
605 With meditation on the happy end."
　　He ended, and they both descend the hill;
Descended, Adam to the bow'r where Eve

2. Michael glances back at Raphael's warning in Book 8 that Adam should concern himself first with matters pertaining to his own life and world, rather than speculating overmuch about the cosmos.

Lay sleeping ran before, but found her waked;
And thus with words not sad she him received:
10   "Whence thou return'st, and whither went'st, I know;
For God is also in sleep, and dreams advise,[3]
Which he hath sent propitious, some great good
Presaging, since with sorrow and heart's distress
Wearied I fell asleep: but now lead on;
15   In me is no delay; with thee to go,
Is to stay here; without thee here to stay,
Is to go hence unwilling; thou to me
Art all things under heav'n,[4] all places thou,
Who for my wilful crime art banished hence.
20   This further consolation yet secure
I carry hence; though all by me is lost,
Such favor I unworthy am vouchsafed,
By me the Promised Seed shall all restore."
     So spake our mother Eve, and Adam heard
25   Well pleased, but answered not; for now too nigh
Th' Archangel stood, and from the other hill
To their fixed station, all in bright array
The Cherubim descended; on the ground
Gliding metéorous,° as evening mist   like a meteor
30   Ris'n from a river o'er the marish° glides,   marsh
And gathers ground fast at the laborer's heel
Homeward returning. High in front advanced,
The brandished sword of God before them blazed
Fierce as a comet; which with torrid heat,
35   And vapor° as the Libyan air adust,°   smoke/parched
Began to parch that temperate clime; whereat
In either hand the hast'ning angel caught
Our ling'ring parents, and to th' eastern gate
Led them direct, and down the cliff as fast
40   To the subjected° plain; then disappeared.   low-lying
They looking back, all th' eastern side beheld
Of Paradise, so late their happy seat,°   estate
Waved over by that flaming brand,° the gate   sword
With dreadful faces thronged and fiery arms:
45   Some natural tears they dropped, but wiped them soon;
The world was all before them, where to choose
Their place of rest, and Providence their guide:
They hand in hand with wand'ring steps and slow,
Through Eden took their solitary way.[5]

1674

---

3. The lines suggest that Eve's dream has provided her a parallel (if lesser) prophecy to Adam's visions and instruction. Cf. Numbers 12.6: "If there be a prophet among you, I the Lord will make myself known unto him in a vision, and will speak to him in a dream."
4. Eve has the last word in the poem, a love-song recalling her lovely prelapsarian lyric (4.641ff.).

Her language also recalls Ruth's promise to accompany her mother-in-law, Naomi (Ruth 1.16). In her last lines (621–23) she rather surprisingly characterizes herself as the central epic protagonist of Milton's poem.
5. The paradox, "hand in hand" / "solitary," is especially resonant.

The Restoration and the Eighteenth Century 1660–1785

1660:   Charles II restored to the English throne
1688–89: The Glorious Revolution: deposition of James II and accession
              of William of Orange
1700:   Death of John Dryden
1707:   Act of Union unites Scotland and England, which thus become
              "Great Britain"
1714:   Rule by House of Hanover begins with accession of George I
1744–45: Deaths of Alexander Pope and Jonathan Swift
1784:   Death of Samuel Johnson

The Restoration and the eighteenth century were times of enormous growth and change in England—or Great Britain, as the nation came to be called after 1707, when the Act of Union joined Scotland to England and Wales. Britain became a world power, an empire on which the sun never set. But it also changed internally. England had always been an agricultural nation; most people were farmers who spent their lives in the neighborhoods where they were born. Gradually their horizons expanded. As the population doubled, to more than ten million, the balance of power shifted toward cities, while trades and industries multiplied and standards of living rose. Moreover, Great Britain became a literate nation, a nation of readers. Almost everyone read the new periodicals and novels that reflected the lives of ordinary women and men, and writers learned to cater to the public. Common interests linked the British Isles; among famous authors, Jonathan Swift, Edmund Burke, Richard Sheridan, and Oliver Goldsmith came from Ireland, and James Thomson, David Hume, and James Boswell came from Scotland. Britons also ventured abroad. In a series of wars against France from 1689 to 1763, colonies were annexed around the world, from Canada in the west to India in the east, and an aggressive market economy—including a lucrative slave trade—brought in unprecedented wealth. At the same time, such developments strained the old ways of life. The gulf widened between rich and poor; individual interests and rights took the place of hierarchical values; and new class conflicts turned people against one another. Regret for what had been lost—the communities and beliefs that gave each person a place to belong to—competed with an eagerness for what had been gained—new ideas and pleasures, new chances to rise. The struggle between these opposing visions affects every phase of eighteenth-century life.

RELIGION AND POLITICS

The Restoration of 1660—the return of Charles Stuart to England—brought hope to a nation divided against itself, exhausted by twenty years of civil wars. Almost all of Charles's subjects welcomed him home, for after the abdication of Richard Cromwell in 1659 the country had seemed at the brink of chaos, and Britons were eager to believe that their king would bring order and law and a spirit of mildness back into the national life. But no political settlement could be stable until religious issues had been resolved. The restoration of the monarchy meant that the established church would also be restored, and though Charles was willing to pardon or ignore many former enemies (such as Milton), the bishops and Anglican clergy were less tolerant of dissent. When Parliament reimposed the Book of Common Prayer in 1662, and then in 1664 barred Nonconformists from religious meetings outside the established church, thousands of clergyman resigned their livings, and the jails were filled with preachers like John Bunyan who refused to be silenced. In 1673 the Test Act required all holders of civil and military offices to take the sacrament in an Anglican Church and to deny belief in transubstantiation. Thus Protestant Dissenters and Roman Catholics were largely excluded from public life; for instance, Alexander Pope, a Catholic, could not attend a university, own land, or vote. The scorn of Anglicans for Nonconformist zeal or "enthusiasm" (a belief in private revelation) bursts out in Samuel Butler's popular *Hudibras* (1663), a caricature of Presbyterians and Independents. And English Catholics were widely regarded as potential traitors who had probably set the great fire that destroyed much of London in 1666.

Yet the triumph of the established church did not resolve the constitutional issues that had divided Charles I and Parliament. Charles II had promised to govern through Parliament, but slyly tried to consolidate royal power. Steering away from crises, he hid his Catholic sympathies and avoided a test of strength with Parliament—except on one occasion. In 1678 the report of the Popish Plot, in which Catholics would rise and murder their Protestant foes, terrified London; and though the charge turned out to be a fraud, the House of Commons exploited the fear by trying to force Charles to exclude his Catholic brother, James, duke of York, from succession to the throne. The turmoil of this period is captured brilliantly by Dryden's *Absalom and Achitophel* (1681). Finally, Charles defeated the Exclusion Bill by dissolving Parliament. But the crisis resulted in a basic division of the country between two new political parties. The party that supported the king came to be called Tories; the king's opponents, Whigs. By the end of the century the two parties had developed opposing attitudes on most important issues. The Tories, who drew their strength from the landed gentry and country clergy, represented conservative values; they strongly supported the Crown and the Anglican Church as the pillars of social and political stability. Convinced that only those with local ties and deep roots in the land could rule responsibly, they were hostile to the rising influence of the new moneyed interests. The Whigs were more progressive and diverse: many powerful nobles, jealous of the powers of the Crown; the merchants and financiers of London; a number of bishops and low-church clergymen; and the Dissenters. What held them together were policies of toleration and support of commerce.

Neither party could live with James II. After he came to the throne in 1685, he claimed the right to make his own laws, suspended the Test Act, and began to fill the army and government with fellow Catholics. Matters came to a head in 1688, when the birth of a son confronted the nation with the prospect of a Catholic dynasty. Secret negotiations paved the way for the Dutchman William of Orange, a champion of Protestantism and the husband of James's Protestant daughter Mary. William landed with a small army in southwestern England and marched toward London. As he advanced, the king's allies faded away, and James fled to a permanent exile in France. The house of Stuart would be heard from again. For more than half a century some loyal Jacobites (from the Latin *Jacobus,* "James"), especially in Scotland, supported James, his son ("the Old Pretender"), and his grandson ("the Young Pretender" or "Bonnie Prince Charlie") as the legitimate rulers of Britain. Moreover, a good many writers, from Aphra Behn and Dryden (and arguably Pope and Johnson) to Robert Burns, privately sympathized with Jacobitism. But after the failure of one last rising in 1745, the cause would dwindle gradually into a wistful sentiment. In retrospect, the coming of William and Mary in 1688—the Glorious, or Bloodless, Revolution—had calmed the fierce divisions within the nation and prepared the way for a unified Great Britain.

A lasting settlement followed. In 1689 a Bill of Rights revoked James's actions; it limited the powers of the Crown, reaffirmed the supremacy of Parliament, and guaranteed some individual rights. The same year the Toleration Act relaxed the strain of religious conflict by granting a limited freedom of worship to Dissenters (although not to Catholics or Jews) so long as they swore allegiance to the Crown. This proved to be a workable compromise; and with the passage of the Act of Settlement in 1701, putting Sophia, electress of Hanover, and her descendants in line for the throne (as the granddaughter of James I, she was the closest Protestant relative of Princess Anne, James II's younger daughter, whose sole surviving child died in that year), the difficult problems that had so long divided England seemed resolved. The principles established in 1689 endured unaltered in essentials until the Reform Bill of 1832.

During Anne's reign (1702–14), new political tensions embittered the nation. England and its allies defeated France and Spain in the War of the Spanish Succession (1702–13)—a Whig war, supported by Whig lords and London merchants, who grew rich on war profits and gained by weakening the power of France and Spain. The spoils included new colonies and the *asiento,* a contract to supply slaves to the Spanish Empire. The hero of the war, Captain-General John Churchill, duke of Marlborough, won the famous victory of Blenheim; was showered with honors and wealth; and with his duchess, dominated the queen until 1710. But the Whigs and Marlborough pushed their luck too hard. When the Whigs tried to reward the Dissenters for their loyalty by removing the Test, Anne fought back to defend the established church. She dismissed her Whig ministers and the Marlboroughs and called in Robert Harley and the brilliant young Henry St. John to form a Tory ministry. These ministers were popular with writers; they employed

Defoe and Swift and commissioned Matthew Prior to negotiate the Peace of Utrecht (1713). But to Swift's despair—he later burlesqued events at court in *Gulliver's Travels*—a bitter rivalry broke out between Harley (then earl of Oxford) and St. John (then Viscount Bolingbroke). Though Bolingbroke succeeded in ousting Oxford, the death of Anne in 1714 reversed his fortunes. George I (Sophia's son) became the first Hanoverian king, and the vindictive Whigs returned to power. Harley was imprisoned in the Tower of London until 1717; and Bolingbroke, charged with being a Jacobite traitor, fled to France. Pardoned in 1723, he came back to England and directed the opposition to Robert Walpole, while playing the gentleman-philosopher-farmer and helping Pope to plan *An Essay on Man*. Government was now securely in the hands of the Whigs.

The three Georges who occupied the throne during the rest of the century presided over a nation that grew increasingly prosperous through war, trade, colonization, consumer capitalism, and the beginnings of industrialism. George I (reigned 1714–27) and George II (reigned 1727–60) were German at heart; they spoke broken English and took little interest in England's affairs. Hence ministers became more important and more independent of the Crown than they had ever been before. Through royal indifference and the ambition and skill of Walpole, the first "prime minister," the modern system of ministerial government began to develop. Walpole rose to power as a result of the "South Sea bubble" (1720), a stock market crash; and his ability to restore confidence and keep the country running smoothly—as well as to juggle money—would mark his long ascendancy (1721–42). He was a master of the patronage system, installing his dependents in government offices and controlling the House of Commons by buying off its members. But he did not buy off the wits, and they were offended. Gay's *Beggar's Opera* (1728) and Fielding's *Jonathan Wild* (1743) draw interesting parallels between great criminals and great politicians, and Pope's *Dunciad* uses Walpole as an emblem of the corruption and commercialization of the whole social fabric. Yet Pope himself had made a fortune by marketing his poems as cleverly as he wrote them. Increasingly, authors, like politicians, rose in the world by giving the public what it wanted. Walpole was unwilling to go to war (and fell because he managed it badly); but the next major English statesman, William Pitt the Elder, appealed to the patriotism of common people and called for the expansion of British power and commerce overseas. The defeat of the French in the Seven Years' War (1756–63), especially in North America, was largely his doing.

The long reign of George III (1760–1820) was dominated by two great concerns: the emergence of Britain as a colonial power and the cry for a new social order based on liberty and radical reform. In 1763 the Peace of Paris consolidated British rule over Canada and India, and not even the later loss of the American colonies could stem the rise of the empire. Great Britain was no longer an isolated island but a nation with interests and responsibilities around the world. At home, however, there was discontent. The wealth brought to England by industrialism and foreign trade had not spread to the working classes. It seemed to many that the bonds of custom that once held people together had broken, and now money alone was respected. Protestants turned against Catholics; in 1780 the Gordon Riots put London temporarily under mob rule. The king was popular with his subjects and tried to take government into his own hands, rising above all parties, but his efforts often backfired—as when the American colonists mistook him for a tyrant. From 1788 to the end of his life, moreover, an inherited disease (porphyria) periodically unhinged his mind, as in a memorable scene described by Frances Burney. Meanwhile, reformers such as John Wilkes and Richard Price called for a new political democracy. Fear of their radicalism would contribute to the British reaction against the French Revolution. In the last decades of the century, British authors would be torn between two opposing attitudes: loyalty to the old traditions of subordination, mutual obligations, and local self-sufficiency; and yearning for a new dispensation founded on principles of liberty, the rule of reason, and human rights.

THE CONTEXT OF IDEAS

The political turbulence of the seventeenth century subsided only gradually during the period after the Restoration (1660–1700), and literature also registered a conflict of values. John Milton's major poems, a culmination of Renaissance art, appeared at the same time that John Dryden was leading the way to a new age of elegance. Bunyan's *Pilgrim's Progress* expressed the Nonconformist conscience at the same time that the earl of Rochester expressed the creed of a libertine and rake. In the theater, witty, bawdy comedies—written and acted by women as well as men—reflected the style of a fun-loving, dissolute court. Charles set a mixed example for the nation. A lover of pleasure and women, he was always ready to sacrifice principles to live in comfort. But he also took a genuine interest in new ideas and supported the arts and sciences. French and Italian musicians, as well as painters from the Low Countries, migrated to England; and playhouses—closed by the Puritans since 1642—sprang back to life. In 1660 Charles authorized two new companies of actors: the King's Players and the Duke's. Two years later he chartered the Royal Society of London for the Improving of Natural Knowledge, thus giving official approval to the scientific revolution that was reshaping views of the world. Early in the century, Francis Bacon had called for an advancement of learning based on direct observations of nature; and two wonderful inventions, the microscope and telescope, had begun to reveal that nature is more extravagant—teeming with tiny creatures and boundless galaxies—than anyone had ever imagined. Now experiments came into vogue, in thought and morals as well as science and art. The sense that new worlds were being discovered could be unnerving, but it was also exciting.

Skepticism and freethinking flourished during the late seventeenth century. The civil wars had turned the world upside down; if a king could be executed, what authority was safe? Even after the Restoration, the question remained. One answer had been offered by Thomas Hobbes, whose *Leviathan* (1651) had argued that only an absolute government could check the "perpetual and restless desire of power" in all human beings, a competition that would lead to the "war of every man against every man" unless the final power were vested in some sovereign. Hobbes's emphasis on the predatory passions that drive both human nature and society was detested by the church and attacked on all sides. Yet his ideas influenced many young people, especially the libertines who devoted their lives to a quest for pleasure and power. His pessimistic view of human nature also provoked, by way of reaction, an optimistic insistence on the natural goodness of humanity, which would become an article of faith for many in the eighteenth century. Another influential point of view was philosophic skepticism. Originating in ancient Greece, skepticism revived in the all-questioning essays of the Frenchman Michel de Montaigne (1533–1592). The skeptic argued that all knowledge derives from our senses but that, because our senses do not report the world accurately, reliable knowledge is impossible to achieve. The safest course is to remember that most beliefs rest on opinion and not to hunger for some ultimate, inaccessible truth. Butler, Dryden, and Rochester were among those who followed this doctrine. But though skeptics might doubt the results of human reasoning, they were not precluded from religious beliefs. As Dryden asserted after converting to Catholicism, to accept the mysteries of Christianity one needs faith alone.

The new science also encouraged a challenge to traditional wisdom and learning. The ancients (and the fathers of the church) had not known about the solar system, the circulation of the blood, the existence of microscopic organisms, or the law of gravity. In this respect the moderns were much wiser. But the school curriculum still began with years of Latin and Greek. Humanistic education had long relied on standard ancient texts, which were supposed to teach the student everything necessary for understanding life. Hence a battle of books broke out in the late seventeenth century between the champions of ancient and of modern learning; Swift, Pope, and other British writers fought for the ancients. Nevertheless, modern habits of thought began to dominate intellectual life as scientists discovered new worlds in outer space or under the microscope, other thinkers began to speculate that our world is plural (or multicultural) and that its most basic institutions—systems of government, marriage, the church, the distribution of wealth—could always be organized in some different way. Schemes for reforming society preoccupied many writers. Both Mary Astell and Daniel Defoe, for instance, proposed model schools for the education of women.

As views of nature changed, so did philosophy and religion. What we call "science" today was then grouped under "natural history" (the collection and description of facts of nature), "natural philosophy" (the study of the causes of what happens in nature), and "natural religion" (the study of nature as a book written by God). And the discovery of laws of nature, such as Boyle's law (the pressure and volume of a gas are inversely proportional) or Newton's laws of optics and celestial mechanics, seemed evidence of a universal order in creation. Theologically, the elegant simplicity of that order supported the idea of a divine intelligence whose presence might be deduced from his works, as a watch implies a watchmaker. For Deists like Bolingbroke, religion did not depend on mystery or superstition, but only on reason, which taught the goodness and wisdom of natural law and its creator. Many orthodox Christians shuddered at the vision of a vast, impersonal machine of nature. Instead they rested their faith on the revelation of Scripture, the scheme of salvation in which Christ died to redeem our sins. Newton himself spent much of his life exploring mysteries of Scripture. Yet many others, like Pope in *An Essay on Man*, insisted that they saw no contradiction between the books of nature and Relevation.

Philosophers also claimed to be following nature. The main line of British philosophy—which runs from Bacon and Hobbes through John Locke, George Berkeley, and David Hume—can be characterized broadly as empiricism, the doctrine that regards all knowledge as derived from experience. However much they disagree with one another, eighteenth-century philosophers typically shun metaphysics—the search for essential or ultimate principles of reality, transcending the physical—in favor of more practical concerns: how do we know what we know, and how can we best put that knowledge to use? Reasoning from what they know most immediately, their own minds and perceptions, they draw conclusions about the natural basis of the ways that human beings behave, especially in morals and politics. British philosophers like to appeal to common sense. Accepting the limits of human intelligence and power, they settle for the possible. Thus Locke, the philosopher who most influenced others, expresses the temper of his times in the *Essay Concerning Human Understanding* (1690):

> If by this inquiry into the nature of the understanding, I can discover the powers thereof; how far they reach; to what things they are in any degree proportionate; and where they fail us, I suppose it may be of use, to prevail with the busy mind of man to be more cautious in meddling with things exceeding its comprehension; to stop when it is at the utmost extent of its tether; and to sit down in a quiet ignorance of those things which, upon examination, are found to be beyond the reach of our capacities. . . . Our business here is not to know all things, but those which concern our conduct.

These words might be taken as the creed of eighteenth-century England. Such a position is Swift's, when he inveighs against metaphysics, abstract logical deductions, and theoretical science. It is similar to Pope's warning against human presumption in *An Essay on Man*. It prompts Johnson to talk of "the business of living" and to restrain the flights of unbridled imagination. And it helps account for the Anglican clergy's dislike of emotion and "enthusiasm" in religion, and for their emphasis on good works, rather than faith, as the way to salvation. Locke's empiricism pervaded eighteenth-century British thought on politics, education, and morals as well as philosophy; Johnson's great *Dictionary* (1755) uses more than fifteen hundred illustrations from his writings.

During the early eighteenth century, the most heated challenges to authority tended to cool. The Act of Settlement and the Act of Union, reducing some tensions within the nation, seemed paralleled by a growing consensus in manners and ideas. Addison and Steele are the masters of that consensus. Attracting a national audience, the *Tatler* (1709–11) and the *Spectator* (1711–12; 1714) both produced and reflected an urbane social ideal, an intellectual life in which all sorts of people could mingle, as in the streets and parks of a thriving city like London. Here a large middle-class public learned to think and behave politely. Through most of the century, as prosperity grew, the rifts in the nation seemed patched. In the provinces as well as in London, in Scotland as well as in England, a standard of good manners came to be shared.

An optimistic view of the ties that bind people together extended to human nature. Rejecting Hobbes, and minimizing original sin, some eighteenth-century thinkers asserted that human beings are naturally good and find their highest happiness by being good to others. In midcentury a new word, *sen-*

timental, suddenly came into fashion. Those who trusted humanity looked for virtue in instinctive and social impulses rather than in a code of conduct sanctioned by divine law. The cult of sensibility fostered a philanthropy that led to social reforms seldom envisioned in earlier times—to the improvement of jails, the relief of imprisoned debtors, the establishment of foundling hospitals and homes for penitent prostitutes, and ultimately the abolition of the slave trade. And it also loosed a ready flow of feeling and tears, sympathetic responses to the joys and sorrows of fellow human beings. The doctrine of natural goodness, popularized by Rousseau, suggested that civilization corrupts us and that if we lived in a state of nature, like "noble savages," we might retain a childlike innocence and virtue. Such notions encouraged an interest in primitive societies and in poets who were reputed to draw their inspiration directly from nature, like the thresher Stephen Duck, the milkmaid Ann Yearsley, and the plowman Robert Burns. William Wordsworth's fascination with children and simple, rural people grows out of the eighteenth-century wish to believe in natural goodness and genius.

As the wave of sentimentalism mounted, it was balanced by a rise of religious feeling. The evangelical revival known as Methodism began in the 1730s, led by three Oxford graduates: John Wesley (1703–1791), his brother Charles (1707–1788), and George Whitefield (1714–1770). The Methodists took their gospel to the common people, warning that all were sinners and damned, unless they accepted "amazing grace," salvation through faith. Nor did the insistence of Methodists on faith over works as the way to salvation prevent them or their Anglican allies from fighting for social reforms. The campaign to abolish slavery and the slave trade was driven largely by a passion to save souls.

Both sentimentalism and evangelicalism placed a new importance on individuals—their private encounters with one another or with a personal god. The older hierarchical system had tended to subordinate individuals to their social rank or station. In the eighteenth century that fixed system began to break down, and people's sense of themselves began to change. The difference between the self as it appears to us in introspection and the identity that others fasten on us—for instance, between the person a woman feels herself to be and the generic "woman" whose role she is supposed to fill— becomes a major interest of eighteenth-century writing. Anne Finch, Lady Mary Wortley Montagu, and Burney all grapple, in their own ways, with the problem of how to stay true to their own core of feelings in spite of social expectations. Similarly, a new kind of fiction, the novel, devotes unprecedented attention to what particular characters are thinking and feeling. In such a world, an institution like marriage begins to be defined as a means to self-fulfillment and personal happiness rather than as a family alliance. By the end of the century many issues of politics and the law revolve around rights, not traditions. The modern individual had been invented; no product of the age is more enduring.

LITERARY PRINCIPLES

The literature of the period between 1660 and 1785 divides conveniently into three lesser periods of about forty years each. The first, extending to the death of Dryden in 1700, is characterized by an effort to bring a new refinement to English literature according to sound critical principles of what is fitting and right; the second, ending with the deaths of Pope in 1744 and Swift in 1745, extends that effort to a wider circle of readers, with special satirical attention to what is unfitting and wrong; the third, concluding with the death of Johnson in 1784 and the publication of Cowper's *The Task* in 1785, confronts the old principles with revolutionary ideas that would come to the fore in the Romantic movement of the late eighteenth and early nineteenth centuries.

Apparently, a sudden change of taste took place about 1660. The change had been long prepared, however, by a trend in European culture, especially in seventeenth-century France: the desire for an elegant simplicity. Reacting against the difficulty and occasional extravagance of late Renaissance literature, writers and critics called for a new restraint, clarity, regularity, and good sense. Donne's "metaphysics" and Milton's bold storming of heaven, for instance, seemed overdone to some Restoration readers. Hence Dryden and Andrew Marvell both were tempted to revise *Paradise Lost,* smoothing away its sublime but arduous idiosyncrasies. The "easy, natural" wit that such writers prefer, surprising but seldom shocking, may well reflect a yearning for peace and order after the violent extremism of the civil wars. Postwar writing aims to be disarming, to counsel a middle way among opposing parties.

This movement produced in France an impressive body of classical literature that distinguished the age of Louis XIV. In England it produced a literature often termed "Augustan," after the writers—Virgil, Horace, and Ovid—who flourished during the reign of Augustus Caesar, the first Roman emperor. In 1660 there was hope that Charles would be a better Augustus, bringing England the civilized virtues of an Augustan age. The King and his followers brought back from exile an admiration of French literature, as well as French fashions, and the theoretical "correctness" of such writers as Pierre Corneille, René Rapin, and Nicolas Boileau came into vogue. The effort to formulate rules of good writing appealed to Dryden and later to Pope. Even Shakespeare had sometimes been careless; and although writers could not expect to surpass his genius, they might hope to avoid his faults. But "neoclassical" English literature aimed to be not only classical but *new.* When Dryden and Pope make use of Greek or Latin or French poets, they convert them to English traditions of variety, freewheeling fancy, and humor. Chaucer, Spenser, Shakespeare, Jonson, and Milton (as well as Homer, Virgil, Horace, Longinus, and Corneille) helped form the literary consciousness of the new age.

If Charles had never lived abroad, English literature would probably still have turned toward an ideal of elegant simplicity. Jonson's poems and criticism had brought the classicizing tendencies of the English Renaissance to a focus. His closed heroic couplets set an example for Edmund Waller and Sir John Denham, whom Dryden considered the principal "refiners" of English metrics. By 1625 one "son of Ben," Sir John Beaumont, anticipated the critical standards of Dryden and Pope, in couplets very much like theirs:

> Pure phrase, fit epithets, a sober care
> Of metaphors, descriptions clear, yet rare,

> Similitudes contracted, smooth and round,
> Not vexed by learning, but with Nature crowned:
> Strong figures drawn from deep inventions, springs,
> Consisting less in words, and more in things:
> A language not affecting ancient times,
> Nor Latin shreds, by which the pedant climbs.
> (*To His Late Majesty, Concerning the True Form of
> English Poetry*)

Such standards, alien to the verse of Donne, Richard Crashaw, or Milton, suggest that a native classicism, serene and graceful, existed side by side with metaphysical poetry. The emphasis on the correct ("pure"), the appropriate ("fit"), restraint and discipline ("sober care"), clarity, the fresh and surprising ("rare"), nature, strength, freedom from pedantry indicates exactly the direction English poets were to follow after the Restoration.

Above all, the new simplicity of style aimed to give pleasure to readers— to write about passions that everyone could recognize in language that everyone could understand. According to Dryden, Donne's amorous verse mistakenly "perplexes the minds of the fair sex with nice speculations of philosophy, when he should engage their hearts, and entertain them with the softnesses of love." Dryden's poems would not make that mistake; like subsequent English critics, he values poetry according to its power to move an audience. Readers, in turn, were supposed to cooperate with authors through the exercise of their own imaginations, creating pictures in the mind.

What poets most tried to see and represent was *Nature*—a word of many meanings. The Augustans focused especially on one meaning: Nature as the universal and permanent elements in human experience. External nature— the landscape—attracted attention throughout the eighteenth century as a source of pleasure and an object of inquiry. But as Finch muses on the landscape, in *A Nocturnal Reverie*, it is her own soul she discovers. Pope's injunction to the critic, "First follow Nature," has primarily *human* nature in view. Nature consists of the enduring, general truths that have been, are, and will be true for everyone in all times, everywhere. Hence the business of the poet, according to Johnson's *Rasselas*, is not "to number the streaks of the tulip" but "to examine, not the individual, but the species; to remark general properties and large appearances . . . to exhibit in his portraits of nature such prominent and striking features as recall the original to every mind." The general need not exclude the particular. In *The Vanity of Human Wishes*, Johnson describes the sorrows of an old woman: "Now kindred Merit fills the sable Bier, / Now lacerated Friendship claims a tear." Here "kindred Merit" refers particularly to a worthy relative who has died, and "lacerated Friendship" refers to a friend who has been wasted by violence or disease. Yet Merit and Friendship are also personifications, and the lines imply that the woman may be mourning the passing of goodness like her own or a broken friendship; values and sympathies can die as well as people. This play on words is not a pun. Rather, it indicates a state of mind in which life assumes the form of a perpetual allegory and some abiding truth shines through each circumstance and moment as it passes. The particular is already the general, in good eighteenth-century verse.

To study Nature was also to study the ancients. Nature and Homer, according to Pope, were the same; and both Pope and his readers applied

Horace's satires on Rome to their own world, because Horace had expressed the perennial forms of life. Moreover, modern writers could learn from the ancients how to practice their craft. If a poem is an object to be made, the *poet* (a word derived from the Greek for "maker") must make the object to proper specifications. Thus poets were taught to plan their works in one of the classical "kinds" or genres—epic, tragedy, comedy, pastoral, satire, or ode—to choose a language appropriate to that genre, and to select the right style and tone and rhetorical figures. The rules of art, as Pope had said, "are Nature methodized." At the same time, however, writers needed *wit:* quickness of mind, inventiveness, a knack for conceiving images and metaphors and for perceiving resemblances between things apparently unlike. Shakespeare had surpassed the ancients themselves in wit, and no one could deny that Pope was witty. Hence a major project of the age was to combine good method with wit, or judgment with fancy. Nature intended them to be one, and the role of judgment was not to suppress passion, energy, and originality but to make them more effective through discipline: "The wingèd courser, like a generous horse, / Shows most true mettle when you check his course."

The test of a poet's true mettle is language. When Wordsworth, in the preface to *Lyrical Ballads* (1800), declared that he wrote "in a selection of the language really used by men," he went on to attack eighteenth-century poets for their use of an artificial and stock "poetic diction." Many poets did employ a special language. When used mechanically it could become a mannerism. But Thomas Gray contrives subtle, expressive effects from artificial diction and syntax, as in the ironic inflation of *Ode on the Death of a Favorite Cat* or a famous stanza from *Elegy Written in a Country Churchyard*:

> The boast of heraldry, the pomp of power,
> And all that beauty, all that wealth e'er gave,
> Awaits alike the inevitable hour.
> The paths of glory lead but to the grave.

It is easy to misread the first sentence. What is the subject of *awaits*? The answer must be *hour* (the only available singular noun), which lurks at the end of the sentence, ready to spring a trap not only on the reader but on all those aristocratic, powerful, beautiful, wealthy people who forget that their hour will come. Moreover, the intricacy of that sentence sets off the simplicity of the next, which says the same thing with deadly directness. The artful mix in the *Elegy* of a special poetic language—a language that nobody speaks—with sentiments that everybody feels helps account for the poem's enduring popularity.

Versification also tests a poet's skill. The heroic couplet was brought to such perfection by Pope, Johnson thought, that "to attempt any further improvement of versification will be dangerous." Pope's couplets, in rhymed iambic pentameter, typically present a complete statement, closed by a punctuation mark. Within the binary system of these two lines, as in a digital computer, a world of distinctions can be compressed. The second line of the couplet might closely parallel the first in structure and meaning, for instance, or the two lines might antithetically play against each other. Similarly, because normally the length of a pentameter line requires a slight pause called a "caesura" ("Know then thyself, presume not God to scan"), one part of the line can be made parallel with or antithetical to the other or even to one part of the following line. Sir John Denham's *Cooper's Hill* (1642) includes a passage, quoted and parodied for many years, that illustrates these effects. The poem addresses the Thames and builds up a witty comparison between the flow of a river and the flow of verse (italics are added to highlight the terms compared):

	O could I flow like thee,	and make thy stream
Parallelism:	*My great example,*	as it is *my theme!*
Double balance:	Though *deep,* yet *clear,*	though *gentle,* yet not *dull,*
Double balance:	*Strong* without *rage,*	without *o'erflowing, full.*

Once Dryden and Pope had bound such passages more tightly together with alliteration and assonance, the typical metrical-rhetorical wit of the new age had been perfected. For most of the eighteenth century its only metrical rival was blank verse: iambic pentameter that does not rhyme and is not closed in couplets. Milton's blank verse in *Paradise Lost* provided one model, and the dramatic blank verse of Shakespeare and Dryden provided another. This more expansive form appealed to poets who cared less for wit than for stories and thoughts with plenty of room to develop.

Yet not all poets chose to compete with Pope's wit or Milton's heroic striving. Ordinary people also wrote and read verse, and many of them neither knew nor regarded the classics. Only a minority of men, and very few women, had the chance to study Latin and Greek, but that did not keep a good many from playing with verse as a pastime or writing about their own lives. Hence the eighteenth century is the first age to reflect the modern tension between "high" and "low" art. While the heroic couplet was being perfected, doggerel also thrived, and Milton's blank verse was sometimes reduced to describing a drunk or an oyster. Burlesque and broad humor characterize the common run of eighteenth-century verse. As the audience for poetry became more diversified, so did the subject matter. No readership was too small to address; Isaac Watts, and later Anna Laetitia Barbauld and William Blake, wrote songs for children. The rise of unconventional forms and topics of verse subverted an older poetic ideal: the Olympian art that only a handful of the elect could possibly master. The eighteenth century brought poetry down to earth. In the future, art that claimed to be high would have to find ways to distinguish itself from the low.

RESTORATION LITERATURE, 1660–1700

Dryden brought England a *modern* literature between 1660 and 1700. He combined a cosmopolitan outlook on the latest European trends with some of the richness and variety he admired in Chaucer and Shakespeare. In most of the important contemporary forms—occasional verse, comedy, tragedy, heroic play, ode, satire, translation, and critical essay—both his example and his precepts influenced others. As a critic, he spread the word that English literature, particularly his own, could vie with the best of the past. As a translator, he made such classics as Ovid and Virgil available to a wide public; for the first time, a large number of women and men without a formal education could feel included in the literary world.

The effort to reach a new audience is clearly marked by Restoration prose.

The styles of Donne's sermons, of Milton's pamphlets, or of Browne's treatises now seemed too elaborate and rhetorical for simple communication. In polite literature, exemplified by Cowley, Dryden, and Sir William Temple, the ideal of good prose came to be a style with the ease and poise of well-bred urbane conversation. This is a social prose for a sociable age. Later, it became the mainstay of essayists like Addison and Steele, of eighteenth-century novelists, and of the host of brilliant eighteenth-century letter writers, including Montagu, Horace Walpole, Gray, Cowper, and Burney, who still give readers the sense of being their intimate friends.

Yet despite its broad appeal to the public, Restoration literature kept its ties to an aristocratic heroic ideal. The "fierce wars and faithful loves" of epic poems were expected to offer patterns of virtue for noble emulation. These ideals lived on in popular French prose romances, in Behn's *Oroonoko*, and in heroic plays like those written by Dryden, which push to extremes the conflict between love and honor in the hearts of impossibly valiant heroes and impossibly high-minded and attractive heroines.

But comedy was the real distinction of Restoration drama. The best plays of Sir George Etherege (*The Man of Mode*, 1676), William Wycherley (*The Country Wife*, 1675), Aphra Behn (*The Rover*, 1677), William Congreve (*Love for Love*, 1695; *The Way of the World*, 1700), and later George Farquhar (*The Beaux' Stratagem*, 1707) can still hold the stage today. These "comedies of manners" pick social behavior apart, exposing the nasty struggles for power among the upper classes, who use wit, manners and sex as weapons.

During the 1690s "Societies for the Reformation of Manners" began to attack the blasphemy and obscenity they detected on stage, and they sometimes brought offenders to trial. The clergyman Jeremy Collier spoke for the moral outrage of the pious middle classes. The wits retreated. The temper of comedy softened; at the end of the century, the heroes and heroines were often good-natured and decent. Ladies could safely attend the theater, where several of the leading playwrights were women, such as Mary Pix, Susanna Centlivre, and Catharine Trotter. When Dryden died in 1700, a more respectable society was coming into being. One of the tasks that, early in the next century, Steele and Addison undertook in the *Tatler* and *Spectator* and Pope in *An Essay on Criticism* was to rehabilitate "wit" by making it the servant of social and moral decorum.

Decorum was also enforced by the clubs where literary people gathered. The coffeehouses of London served as informal meeting places; first founded in 1652, they numbered in the hundreds by the turn of the century. Collectively they functioned as a new kind of national forum, a public sphere. There men could smoke, drink chocolate or coffee, read newspapers, write and receive letters, gossip, do business, argue, and observe the oddities of character for which the English were famous. Eventually clubs like Addison's imaginary Spectator Club came to preside over literary life. Their members helped determine the tone of literature, the reputations of writers, the success or failure of plays, and the character of the *Spectator* itself. At first women were excluded. Around 1750, however, some intellectual women (known as bluestockings because they wore homely worsted hose instead of black silk) established clubs of their own under the leadership of Elizabeth Montagu, and gradually men joined them for literary conversation.

EIGHTEENTH-CENTURY LITERATURE, 1700–45

Early in the century a new and brilliant group of writers took the stage: Swift, with *A Tale of a Tub* (1704–10); Addison, with *The Campaign* (1705), a poetic celebration of the battle of Blenheim; Prior, with *Poems on Several Occasions* (1707); Steele, with the *Tatler* (1709); and the youthful Pope, in the same year, with his *Pastorals*. These writers consolidate and popularize the social graces of the previous age. Determined to preserve good sense and civilized values, they turn their wit against fanaticism and innovation. Hence this is a great age of satire. Deeply conservative but also playful, the finest works often cast a strange light on modern times by viewing them through the screen of classical myths and classical forms. Thus Pope exposes the frivolity of fashionable London, in *The Rape of the Lock,* through the incongruity of verse that casts the idle rich as epic heroes. Such incongruities are not entirely negative. They also provide a fresh perspective on things that had once seemed too low for poetry to notice them—for instance, in *The Rape of the Lock,* a girl putting on her makeup. In this way a parallel with classical literature can show not only how far the modern world has fallen but also how much has stayed the same in the lives of ordinary, unheroic people.

At the same time, a new sort of reading matter began to appeal to an audience eager to be entertained. The reading public expanded dramatically during the eighteenth century, and its recruits included upper-class women and the prosperous men and women of the growing middle class. The popular press churned out a succession of newspapers; periodical essays in the manner of the *Tatler;* miscellaneous collections of verse and prose; and finally, in 1731, the first magazine, the *Gentleman's Magazine*, followed not only by imitations but also by successful literary journals like the *Monthly Review* (1749) and the *Critical Review* (1756). Each audience attracted some periodical tailored to it, as with the *Female Tatler* (1709) and Eliza Haywood's *Female Spectator* (1744–46). The new journalism satisfied a hunger for information about politics, science, philosophy, and literature as well as for scandal and gossip. As the number of readers grew, so did the demand for writers. Grub Street, where many poor London writers lived, became a synonym for hacks and scandal mongers. To Pope and Swift, these drudges represented a serious threat to the dignity of authorship and humanistic learning. But it was the public, not a few wealthy patrons, that eighteenth-century writers had to please. Johnson began his career as an employee of the *Gentleman's Magazine,* then took the job of putting together a dictionary, and only gradually emerged as a major author. Nor could the novel have come into being without the new customers for print, who wanted to read about people whose lives were like their own.

As the readership changed, so did kinds of literature. Lyric poetry, one of the glories of the late sixteenth and early seventeenth centuries, became in the Restoration a minor, graceful mode, often used to flatter a patron or mistress. Between 1700 and 1740, however, the forms of poetry shifted. The sonnet now seemed an archaic, courtly form; lyrics went out of fashion, replaced by descriptive and didactic verse, along with such popular genres as the ballad, the hymn, the burlesque. A similar shift in taste occurred in the drama. The moral reform of the 1690s, together with an increasingly optimistic view of human nature, made Restoration rakes seem libels on humanity. The old comedy of manners was replaced by a new kind, later called "sentimental" not only because goodness triumphs over vice but also because it deals in high moral sentiments rather than witty dialogue and because the embarrassments of its heroines and heroes move the audience not to laughter but to tears. Some plays resisted the tide. Gay's cynical *Beggar's Opera* (1728) was a tremendous success, and later in the century the comedies of Goldsmith and Sheridan proved that sentiment is not necessarily an enemy to wit and laughter. Yet larger and larger audiences responded more to spectacles and special effects than to sophisticated writing. Although the *stage* prospered during the eighteenth century, and the star system produced idolized actors and actresses (such as David Garrick and Sarah Siddons), the authors of *drama* tended to fade to the background.

The rising tide of popular taste also provoked a reaction. Pope and Swift and other satirists turned their weapons against what they perceived as the coarsening and corruption of public life and the arts. Early in his career, Pope (like Dryden before him) had set out to make the texts and principles of classical literature available to everyone who could read English. His translations of Homer brought the epic tradition home to Britain, earning him enormous profits. But eventually he came to fear that the barbarians were winning. Politics contributed to this despair; both Pope and Swift were Tory satirists in an age of Whig domination. Tories stood fast against the social and economic changes that were transforming Britain from an island kingdom into a world power and from an agrarian into a mercantile society. A new nexus of cash and credit seemed to be driving out the civic humanism that put the nation ahead of private interests. Moral revulsion—especially against the wheeling and dealing perfected by Walpole—fueled the satirists' rage. In his last great work, *The Dunciad*, Pope imagines the tragic victory of Chaos and Night over Order and Art. Swift emphasizes that the world is going mad. The abandonment of practical reality to crackbrained theories of science, religious fanaticism, and romantic illusions leaves no recourse—except a saving remnant of laughter.

A wholly different sort of poetry accompanied the age of satire. Since the seventeenth century, no poems had been more popular than those about the pleasures of retirement, which invited the reader to dream about a safe retreat in the country or to meditate, like Finch, on scenery and the soul. But after 1726, when Thomson published *Winter*, the first of his cycle on the seasons, the poetry of natural description came into its own. Tourists as well as poets roamed the countryside, frequently quoting verse as they gazed at some evocative scene. Wordsworth's love of external nature draws on eighteenth-century sources; *Tintern Abbey* is very much a poem of the century in which it was written. During the course of the century, Britons learned to enjoy not only the tamed and gentrified nature of landscape gardens and fields but also a thrilling pleasure or fear in the presence of "the sublime" in nature: rushing waters, wild prospects, and mountains shrouded in mist. Whether enthusiasts went to the landscape in search of God or merely of heightened sensations, they came back feeling that they had been touched by something beyond the life they knew, by something that could hardly be expressed. Pope had written of "a grace beyond the reach of art, / Which, without passing through the judgment, gains / The heart, and all its end at once attains"; but many of his successors identified that appeal to feeling—and avoidance of judgment—with poetry itself. The presence of the sublime in nature, as well as in the emotions of writers and readers, would be a staple of literature for decades to come.

THE EMERGENCE OF NEW LITERARY THEMES AND MODES, 1740–85

When Matthew Arnold called the eighteenth century an "age of prose," he meant to belittle its poetry, but he also stated a significant fact: great prose does dominate the age. Until the 1740s, poetry tended to set the standards of literature. But the growth of new kinds of prose took the initiative away from verse. Novelists became better known than poets; no writers of mid-century were more admired or popular than Samuel Richardson and Henry Fielding. And intellectual prose also flourished, with the achievements of Johnson in the essay and literary criticism; of Boswell in biography; of Hume in philosophy; of Burke in politics; of Edward Gibbon in history; of Sir Joshua Reynolds in aesthetics; of Gilbert White in natural history; and of Adam Smith in economics. Each of these authors is a master stylist, whose effort to express himself clearly and fully demands an art as carefully wrought as poetry. An unprecedented effort to formulate the first principles of philosophy, history, psychology, and art required a new style of persuasion.

Johnson helped codify that language, not only with his writings but with the first great English *Dictionary* (1755). This work established him as a national man of letters; eventually the period would be known as "the Age of Johnson." But his dominance was based on an ideal of service to others. The *Dictionary* illustrates its definitions with more than 114,000 quotations from the best English writers, thus building a bridge from past to present usage; and Johnson's essays, poems, and criticism also reflect his desire to preserve the lessons of the past. Yet he looks to the future as well, trying both to reach and to mold a nation of readers. If Johnson speaks for his age, one reason is his faith in common sense and the common reader. "By the common sense of readers uncorrupted with literary prejudices," he wrote in the last of his *Lives of the Poets* (1781), "must be finally decided all claim to poetical honors." A similar respect for the good judgment of ordinary people, and for standards of taste and behavior that anyone can share, marks many writers of the age. Both Burke, the great conservative statesman and author, and Thomas Paine, his radical adversary, proclaim themselves apostles of common sense. Moreover, the poets whom everyone read relied on verse that could do justice to the feelings of simple people. Gray's *Elegy*, Goldsmith's *The Deserted Village*, Crabbe's *The Village*, and the lyrics of Burns all strive to make poetry from and for the lives of common men and women.

Nevertheless, an age of great prose can burden its poets. The generation of talented young poets who emerged about the time of Pope's death, a group that includes Gray, William Collins, Mark Akenside, and the brothers Joseph and Thomas Warton, seems afraid that the spirit of poetry might be dying, driven out by the spirit of prose, by uninspiring truth, by the end of superstitions that had once peopled the land with poetic fairies and demons. In an age barren of magic, they ask, where has poetry gone? That question haunts many poems, suffusing them with melancholy. The prototype of the mid-eighteenth-century poet was Milton's *Il Penseroso*, a night-loving solitary who broods on the "far-off curfew" or the plangent organ in the twilight of a Gothic church. Such a figure has little in common with poets like Dryden and Pope, social beings who live in a crowded world and seldom confess their private feelings in public. The melancholy poet withdraws into himself and yearns to be living in some other time and place.

Poets who muse in silence are never far from thoughts of death, and a morbid fascination with suicide and the grave preoccupies many midcentury poets. Pope's *Essay on Man* had taken a sunny view of providence; Edward Young's *The Complaint: or Night Thoughts on Life, Death, and Immortality* (1742–46), an immensely long poem in blank verse, is darkened by Christian fear of the life to come. But the "graveyard school" pays less attention to religion than to images of decay. Surrounded by medieval ruins and tombs, the spirits of graveyard poets tremble and sink. The revival of Gothic architectural styles, most famously in Horace Walpole's tiny pseudo-Gothic castle, Strawberry Hill, influenced literary styles as well. Walpole's *Castle of Otranto* (1765), a dreamlike tale of terror set in a simulacrum of Strawberry Hill, created a mode of fiction that retains its popularity to the present day. In a typical Gothic romance, amid the glooms and secret passages of some remote castle, the laws of nightmare replace the laws of probability. Forbidden themes—incest, murder, necrophilia, atheism, and the torments of sexual desire—are allowed free play; repressed anxieties and terrors rise to the surface of the narrative. In serious novels of social purpose, like William Godwin's *Caleb Williams* (1794) and Mary Wollstonecraft's *Maria, or The Wrongs of Woman* (1798); and Mary Shelley, the daughter of Wollstonecraft and Godwin, eventually composed a romantic nightmare, *Frankenstein* (1818), that continues to haunt our dreams.

When poets looked for a renewal of poetry, however, they sought it not so much in the Gothic as in their own imaginations and feelings. In his *Ode to Fancy* (1746), Joseph Warton associated "fancy" with visions in the wilderness and spontaneous passions; the true poet was no longer defined as a craftsman or maker but as a seer or nature's priest. "The public has seen all that art can do," William Shenstone wrote in 1761, welcoming James Macpherson's *Ossian*, "and they want the more striking efforts of wild, original, enthusiastic genius." Macpherson filled the bill. His primitive, sentimental epics, supposedly translated from an ancient Gaelic warrior-bard, won the hearts of readers around the world; Napoleon and Thomas Jefferson, for instance, both thought that Ossian was greater than Homer. At the same time, many of the best poets of the period identified with the recluse or the outcast. Collins, Smart, and Cowper all were isolated from society by fits of madness, and only a handful of readers noticed the extraodinary work of Smart or later of William Blake.

Meanwhile, a different sort of poetry flourished: humorous, personal, and down to earth. As the reading public expanded, so did the number of people who tried their hand at verse; and they wrote about whatever interested them. Women and men described the details of their lives in homely images and graphic language. Such poets were not afraid to deal with beggars and barbers and chimney sweeps, or to sing the joys of village sports or the bustle of washing day. For much of the public, poetry offered the pleasures of self-expression and companionship. Cowper, the most popular poet of the later part of the century, won his readers with a modest, intimate kind of verse, seldom departing far from the accents of friendly conversation. Women especially prized his poems, and poets like Anna Seward and Charlotte Smith helped revive the lyric. Amid revolutions in society and thought, poets were asked to teach their readers how to respond—above all, how to feel. The next generation would try to answer that call.

THE BEGINNING OF THE NOVEL

The modern novel came into its own in the 1740s. Prose fiction had existed, to be sure, since ancient times; the Greeks and Romans wrote stories about the tribulations of love, and narrative traditions lie behind the Bible and most other sacred writings. Other early types of prose fiction include Sir Philip Sidney's courtly *Arcadia* and Lady Mary Wroth's *Urania*; the earthy tales of Thomas Nashe and Thomas Deloney; the long French romances of the seventeenth century, blending chivalric adventure and courtly love; and in a world apart, Bunyan's vivid allegories of the spiritual quests and battles of wayfaring Christians. Nor were clear distinctions drawn between history and fiction; Behn's *Oroonoko* is both. In the early eighteenth century, writers often mixed facts with their fiction, as when they whipped up scandalous versions of current events or reported some famous criminal's "true story." The master of this genre was Daniel Defoe. A middle-class writer, he did not seek upper-class readers (though *Robinson Crusoe*, 1719, appealed to all classes). Instead he aimed at shopkeepers, apprentices, and servants, a readership avid for racy stories, usually laced with moral indignation. Defoe shows his readers a world that they know, where unheroic people try to cope with practical problems, like finding a trustworthy spouse or simply staying alive. Nor was he alone in writing about and for women. For the first time in British history, a critical mass of female readers and writers carried weight with publishers. Jane Barker and Mary Davys, along with many others, brought women's work and daily lives as well as love affairs to fiction. Such stories were not only amusing but also served as models of conduct; they influenced the stories that real people told about themselves.

Samuel Richardson conceived the idea of *Pamela, or Virtue Rewarded* (1740) while compiling a little book of model letters. The letters grew into a story about a captivating young servant who resists her master's base designs on her virtue until he gives up and marries her. The combination of a high moral tone with sexual titillation and a minute analysis of the heroine's emotions and state of mind proved irresistible to readers. Richardson caught the attention of all literate Europe and once and for all established the novel as we know it: a serious form that can also be a popular success. He topped that success with *Clarissa* (1747–48). In the conflict between the libertine Lovelace, an attractive and diabolical aristocrat, and the angelic Clarissa, a middle-class paragon who struggles to stay pure, Richardson caught the ideals and tensions of a society whose values were in flux. No earlier author had involved readers so much in the feelings and motives of characters, examined minute by minute—this is the longest novel in English—until they seem more real than people we meet every day.

Like Richardson, Henry Fielding had a gift for writing dramatic scenes; in the 1730s he had been the best comic playwright in England. But Fielding looked down on Richardson's pious middle-class values. *Joseph Andrews* (1742) begins by turning *Pamela* farcically upside-down, as Joseph (Pamela's brother) defends his chastity from the lewd advances of Lady Booby. Fielding's true model, however, is Cervantes' great *Don Quixote* (1605–15), from which he took an ironic, antiromantic style, a plot of wandering around the countryside, and an idealistic central character (Parson Adams) who keeps mistaking appearances for reality. The ambition of writing what Fielding called "a comic epic-poem in prose" went still further in *The History of Tom Jones, A Foundling* (1749). Crowded with incidents and comments on the state of England, the novel contrasts a good-natured, generous, wayward hero (who needs to learn prudence) with cold-hearted people who use moral codes and the law for their own selfish interests. This emphasis on instinctive virtue and vice, instead of Richardson's devotion to good principles, put off respectable readers like Johnson and Burney. But Coleridge thought that *Tom Jones* (along with *Oedipus Rex* and Jonson's *Alchemist*) was one of "the three most perfect plots ever planned."

Remarkable experiments in fiction run through the later part of the century, anticipating many of the forms that novelists still use today. Tobias Smollett's picaresque *Roderick Random* (1748) and *Humphry Clinker* (1771) delight in coarse practical jokes, the freaks and strong odors of life. But the most *novel* novelist of the age was Laurence Sterne, a humorous, sentimental clergyman who loves to play tricks on his readers. *The Life and Opinions of Tristram Shandy* (1760–67) abandons clock time for psychological time, whimsically follows chance associations, interrupts its own stories, violates the conventions of print by putting chapters 18 and 19 after chapter 25, sneaks in double entendres, and seems ready to go on forever. And yet these games get us inside the characters' minds, as if the world were as capricious as our thoughts. Sterne's self-conscious art implies that people's private obsessions shape their lives—or help create reality itself. Present-day novelists still play the games he invented.

At the same time, the focus on eccentric or individual points of view, along with the popularity of fiction—Gothic or sentimental—that indulged in extreme states of feeling, freed many writers to question the norms of behavior. Identifying with characters in novels, readers might find themselves. That seems to have been especially true for women. By the end of the century most of the leading British novelists were women—Burney, Ann Radcliffe, and later Maria Edgeworth—and the novel was often considered a feminine preserve. For that reason, perhaps, it lost some prestige. When two young women spend their time reading novels together, in *Northanger Abbey*, the young Jane Austen defends them against some critic (presumably male) who might accuse them of frivolity: " 'It is only a novel!' . . . only some work in which the greatest powers of the mind are displayed, in which the most thorough knowledge of human nature, the happiest delineation of its varieties, the liveliest effusions of wit and humour, are conveyed to the world in the best chosen language." Novels, she argues, not only give pleasure to women but foster their education. Yet men were already beginning to take back the novel. Although today no English novelist of manners seems greater than Austen, early in the nineteenth century it was Walter Scott whose novels everyone read; and the historical novel, filled with scenes of men at work and war, largely superseded more intimate forms. That broader canvas would mark out the future of fiction.

CONTINUITY AND REVOLUTION

The history of eighteenth-century literature was first composed by the Romantics, who wrote it to serve their own interests. Prizing originality, they naturally preferred to stress how different they were from writers of the previous age. Later historians have tended to follow their lead, competing to prove that everything changed in 1776, or 1789, or 1798. This revolutionary view of history accounts for what happened to the word *revolution*. The older meaning referred to a movement around a point, a recurrence or cycle, as in the revolutions of the planets; the newer meaning signified a violent break with the past, an overthrow of the existing order, as in the Big Bang or the French Revolution. Romantic rhetoric made heavy use of such dramatic upheavals. Yet every history devoted to truth must take account of both sorts of revolution, of continuities as well as changes. The ideals that many Romantics made their own—the passion for liberty and equality, the founding of justice on individual rights, the distrust of institutions, the love of nature, the reverence for imagination, and even the embrace of change—were grown from seeds that had been planted long before. Nor did Augustan literature abruptly vanish on that day in 1798 when Wordsworth and Coleridge anonymously published a small and unsuccessful volume of poems called *Lyrical Ballads*. Even when they rebel against the work of Pope and Johnson and Gray, Romantic writers incorporate much of their language and values.

What Restoration and eighteenth-century literature passed on to the future, in fact, was chiefly a set of unresolved problems. The age of Enlightenment was also, in England, an age that insisted on holding fast to older beliefs and customs; the age of population explosion was also an age of individualism; the age that developed the slave trade was also the age that gave rise to the abolitionist movement; the age that codified rigid standards of conduct for women was also an age when many women took the chance to read and write and think for themselves; the age of reason was also the age when sensibility flourished; the last classical age was also the first modern age. These contradictions are far from abstract; writers were forced to choose their own directions. When young James Boswell looked for a mentor whose biography he might write, he considered not only Samuel Johnson but also David Hume, whose skeptical views of morality, truth, and religion were everything Johnson abhorred. The two writers seem to inhabit different worlds, yet Boswell traveled freely between them. That was exciting and also instructive. "Without Contraries is no progression," according to one citizen of Johnson's London, William Blake, who also thought that "Opposition is true Friendship." Good conversation was a lively eighteenth-century art, and sharp disagreements did not keep people from talking. The conversations the period started have not ended yet.

THE RESTORATION AND THE EIGHTEENTH CENTURY

TEXTS	CONTEXTS
1660 Samuel Pepys begins his diary.	1660 Charles II restored to the throne. Reopening of the theaters
1662 Samuel Butler, *Hudibras*, part 1	1662 Act of Uniformity requires all clergy to obey the Church of England. Chartering of the Royal Society
	1666 Fire destroys the City of London
1667 John Milton, *Paradise Lost*	
1668 John Dryden, *Essay of Dramatic Poesy*	1668 Dryden becomes Poet Laureate
	1673 Test Act requires all officeholders to swear allegiance to Anglicanism
1678 John Bunyan, *Pilgrim's Progress*, part 1	1678 The "Popish Plot" inflames anti-Catholic feeling
1681 Dryden, *Absalom and Achitophel*	1681 Charles II dissolves Parliament
	1685 Death of Charles II. James II, his Catholic brother, takes the throne
1687 Sir Isaac Newton, *Principia Mathematica*	
1688 Aphra Behn, *Oroonoko*	1688–89 The Glorious Revolution; James II exiled and succeeded by his Protestant daughter, Mary, and her husband, William of Orange
1690 John Locke, *An Essay Concerning Human Understanding*	
1700 William Congreve, *The Way of the World*. Mary Astell, *Some Reflections upon Marriage*	
	1702 Death of William III; succession of Anne (Protestant daughter of James II)
1704 Jonathan Swift, *A Tale of a Tub*. Newton, *Opticks*	
	1707 Act of Union with Scotland
	1710 Tories take power
1711 Alexander Pope, *An Essay on Criticism*. Joseph Addison and Sir Richard Steele, *The Spectator* (1711–12, 1714)	
	1714 Death of Queen Anne; George I (great-grandson of James I) becomes the first Hanoverian king; Tory government replaced by Whigs
1716 Lady Mary Wortley Montagu writes her letters from Turkey (1716–18)	
1717 Pope, *The Rape of the Lock*	
1719 Daniel Defoe, *Robinson Crusoe*	
	1720 South Sea Bubble collapses
	1721 Robert Walpole comes to power

TEXTS	CONTEXTS
1726 Swift, *Gulliver's Travels*	
	1727 George I dies; George II succeeds
1728 John Gay, *The Beggar's Opera*	
1733 Pope, *An Essay on Man*	
	1737 Licensing Act censors the stage
1740 Samuel Richardson, *Pamela*	
1742 Henry Fielding, *Joseph Andrews*	1742 Walpole resigns
1743 Pope, *The Dunciad* (final version). William Hogarth, *Marriage A-la-Mode*	
1746 William Collins's *Odes*	1746 Charles Edward Stuart's defeat at Culloden ends the last Jacobite rebellion
1747 Richardson, *Clarissa*	
	1748 Treaty of Aix-la-Chapelle
1749 Fielding, *Tom Jones*	
1751 Thomas Gray, *Elegy Written in a Country Churchyard*	1751 Robert Clive seizes Arcot, the prelude to English control of India
1755 Samuel Johnson, *Dictionary*	
	1756 Beginning of Seven Years War
1759 Johnson, *Rasselas*. Voltaire, *Candide*	1759 James Wolfe's capture of Quebec assures British control of Canada
1760 Laurence Sterne, *Tristram Shandy* (1760–67)	1760 George III succeeds to the throne
1765 Johnson's edition of Shakespeare	
	1768 Captain James Cook voyages to Australia and New Zealand
1770 Oliver Goldsmith, *The Deserted Village*	
	1775 American Revolution (1775–83). James Watt produces steam engines
1776 Adam Smith, *The Wealth of Nations*	
1778 Frances Burney, *Evelina*	
1779 Johnson, *Lives of the Poets* (1779–81)	
	1780 Gordon Riots in London
1783 George Crabbe, *The Village*	1783 William Pitt becomes Prime Minister
1785 William Cowper, *The Task*	

JOHN DRYDEN
1631–1700

Although John Dryden's parents seem to have sided with Parliament against the king, there is no evidence that the poet grew up in a strict Puritan family. His father, a country gentleman of moderate fortune, gave his son a gentleman's education at Westminster School, under the renowned Dr. Richard Busby, who used the rod as a pedagogical aid in imparting a sound knowledge of the learned languages and literatures to his charges (among others John Locke and Matthew Prior). From Westminster, Dryden went to Trinity College, Cambridge, where he took his A.B. in 1654. His first important poem, *Heroic Stanzas* (1659), was written to commemorate the death of Cromwell. The next year, however, in *Astraea Redux*, Dryden joined his countrymen in celebrating the return of Charles II to his throne. During the rest of his life Dryden was to remain entirely loyal to Charles and to his successor, James II.

Dryden is the commanding literary figure of the last four decades of the seventeenth century. Every important aspect of the life of his times—political, religious, philosophical, artistic—finds expression somewhere in his writings. Dryden is the least personal of poets. He is not at all the solitary, subjective poet listening to the murmur of his own voice and preoccupied with his own feelings, but rather a citizen of the world commenting publicly on matters of public concern.

From the beginning to the end of his literary career, Dryden's nondramatic poems are most typically occasional poems, which celebrate particular events of a public character—a coronation, a military victory, a death, or a political crisis. Such poems are social and ceremonial, written not for the self but for the nation. Between 1664 and 1681, however, Dryden was mainly a playwright. The newly chartered theaters needed a modern repertory, and he set out to supply the need. In the style of the time, he produced rhymed heroic plays, in which incredibly noble heroes and heroines face incredibly difficult choices between love and honor; comedies, in which male and female rakes engage in intrigue and bright repartee; and later, libretti for the newly introduced dramatic form, the opera. His one great tragedy, *All for Love* (1677), in blank verse, adapts Shakespeare's *Antony and Cleopatra* to the unities of time, place, and action. As his *An Essay of Dramatic Poesy* (1668) shows, Dryden had studied the works of the great playwrights of Greece and Rome, of the English Renaissance, and of contemporary France, seeking sound theoretical principles on which to construct the new drama that the age demanded. Because he took literature seriously and enjoyed discussing it, he became, almost casually, what Samuel Johnson called him: "the father of English criticism." His abilities as both poet and dramatist brought him to the attention of the king, who in 1668 made him poet laureate. Two years later the post of historiographer royal was added to the laureateship at a combined stipend of £200, enough money to live on.

Between 1678 and 1681, when he was nearing fifty, Dryden discovered his great gift for writing formal verse satire. A quarrel with the playwright Thomas Shadwell prompted the mock-heroic episode *Mac Flecknoe*, probably written in 1678 or 1679 but not published until 1682. Out of the stresses occasioned by the Popish Plot (1678) and its political aftermath came his major political satires, *Absalom and Achitophel* (1681), and *The Medal* (1682), his final attack on the villain of *Absalom and Achitophel*, the earl of Shaftesbury. Twenty years' experience as poet and playwright had prepared him technically for the triumph of *Absalom and Achitophel*. He had mastered the heroic couplet, having fashioned it into an instrument suitable in his hands for every sort of discourse from the thrust and parry of quick logical argument, to lyric feeling, rapid narrative, or forensic declamation. Thanks to this long discipline, he was able in one stride to rival the masters of verse satire: Horace, Juvenal, Persius, in ancient Rome, and Boileau, his French contemporary.

The consideration of religious and political questions that the events of 1678–81 forced on Dryden brought a new seriousness to his mind and works. In 1682 he published *Religio Laici,* a poem in which he examined the grounds of his religious faith and defended the middle way of the Anglican Church against the rationalism of Deism on the one hand and the authoritarianism of Rome on the other. But he had moved closer to Rome than he perhaps realized when he wrote the poem. Charles II died in 1685 and was succeeded by his Catholic brother, James II. Within a year Dryden and his two sons were converted to Catholicism. Though his enemies accused him of opportunism, he proved his sincerity by his steadfast loyalty to the Roman Church after James abdicated and the Protestant William and Mary came in; as a result he was to lose his offices and their much-needed stipends. From his new position as a Roman Catholic, Dryden wrote in 1687 *The Hind and the Panther,* in which a milk-white Hind (the Roman Church) and a spotted Panther (the Anglican Church) eloquently debate theology. The Hind has the better of the argument, but Dryden already knew that James's policies were failing, and with them the Catholic cause in England.

Dryden was now nearing sixty, with a family to support on a much-diminished income. To earn a living, he resumed writing plays and turned to translations. In 1693 appeared his versions of Juvenal and Persius, with the long dedicatory epistle on satire; and in 1697, his greatest achievement in this mode, the works of Virgil. At the very end, two months before his death, came the *Fables Ancient and Modern,* prefaced by one of the finest of his critical essays and made up of translations from Ovid, Boccaccio, and Chaucer.

What was the nature of Dryden's achievement? First and foremost, he brought the pleasures of literature to the ever-increasing reading public of Britain. As a critic and translator, he made many classics available to men and women who lacked a classical education. His canons of taste and theoretical principles would set the standard for the next generation. As a writer of prose, he helped establish a popular new style, shaped to the cadences of good conversation. Johnson praised its apparent artlessness: "every word seems to drop by chance, though it falls into its proper place. Nothing is cold or languid; the whole is airy, animated, and vigorous . . . though all is easy, nothing is feeble; though all seems careless, there is nothing harsh." Although Dryden's plays went out of fashion, his poems did not. His satire inspired the most brilliant verse satirist of the next century, Alexander Pope, and the energy and variety of his metrics launched the long-standing vogue of heroic couplets. Augustan style is at its best in his poems: lively, dignified, precise, and always musical—a flexible instrument of public speech. "By him we were taught *sapere et fari,* to think naturally and express forcibly," Johnson concluded. "What was said of Rome, adorned by Augustus, may be applied by an easy metaphor to English poetry embellished by Dryden, *lateritiam invenit, marmoream reliquit,* he found it brick, and he left it marble."

Song from *Marriage à la Mode*

I

Why should a foolish marriage vow,
    Which long ago was made,
Oblige us to each other now,
    When passion is decayed?
5 We loved, and we loved, as long as we could,
    Till our love was loved out in us both;
But our marriage is dead when the pleasure is fled:
    'Twas pleasure first made it an oath.

2

If I have pleasures for a friend,
10   And farther love in store,
What wrong has he whose joys did end,
   And who could give no more?
'Tis a madness that he should be jealous of me,
   Or that I should bar him of another:
15   For all we can gain is to give ourselves pain,
   When neither can hinder the other.

ca. 1672   1673

Absalom and Achitophel

Absalom and Achitophel   In 1678 a dangerous crisis, both religious and political, threatened to undo the Restoration settlement and to precipitate England once again into civil war. The Popish Plot and its aftermath not only whipped up extreme anti-Catholic passions, but led between 1679 and 1681 to a bitter political struggle between Charles II (whose adherents came to be called Tories) and the earl of Shaftesbury (whose followers were termed Whigs). The issues were nothing less than the prerogatives of the crown and the possible exclusion of the king's Catholic brother, James, duke of York, from his position as heir-presumptive to the throne. Charles's cool courage and brilliant, if unscrupulous, political genius saved the throne for his brother and gave at least temporary peace to his people.

Charles was a Catholic at heart—he received the last rites of that church on his deathbed—and was eager to do what he could do discreetly for the relief of his Catholic subjects, who suffered severe civil and religious disabilities imposed by their numerically superior Protestant compatriots. James openly professed the Catholic religion, an awkward fact politically, for he was next in line of succession because Charles had no legitimate children. The household of the duke, as well as that of Charles's neglected queen, Catherine of Braganza, inevitably became the center of Catholic life and intrigue at court and consequently of Protestant prejudice and suspicion.

No one understood, however, that the situation was explosive until 1678, when Titus Oates (a renegade Catholic convert of infamous character) offered sworn testimony of the existence of a Jesuit plot to assassinate the king, burn London, massacre Protestants, and reestablish the Roman Church.

The country might have kept its head and come to realize (what no historian has doubted) that Oates and his confederates were perjured rascals, as Charles himself quickly perceived. But panic was created by the discovery of the body of a prominent London justice of the peace, Sir Edmund Berry Godfrey, who a few days before had received for safekeeping a copy of Oates's testimony. The murder, immediately ascribed to the Catholics, has never been solved. Fear and indignation reached a hysterical pitch when the seizure of the papers of the duke of York's secretary revealed that he had been in correspondence with the confessor of Louis XIV regarding the reestablishment of the Roman Church in England. Before the terror subsided many innocent men were executed on the increasingly bold and always false evidence of Oates and his accomplices.

The earl of Shaftesbury, the duke of Buckingham, and others quickly took advantage of the situation. With the support of the Commons and the City of London, they moved to exclude the duke of York from the succession. Between 1679 and 1681 Charles and Shaftesbury were engaged in a mighty struggle. The Whigs found a candidate of their own in the king's favorite illegitimate son, the handsome and engaging duke of Monmouth, whom they advanced as a proper successor to his father. They urged Charles to legitimize him, and when he refused, they whispered that there was proof that the king had secretly married Monmouth's mother. The young man allowed himself to be used against his father. He was sent on a triumphant progress through western England, where he was enthusiastically received. Twice an Exclusion Bill nearly passed both houses. But by early 1681 Charles had secured his own position by secretly accepting from Louis XIV a three-year subsidy that made him independent of Parliament, which had tried to force his hand by refusing to vote him funds. He summoned Parliament to meet at Oxford in the spring of 1681, and a few moments after the Commons had passed the Exclusion Bill, in a bold stroke he abruptly dissolved Parliament, which never met again during his reign. Already, as Charles was aware, a reaction had set in against the violence of the Whigs. In midsummer, when he felt it safe to move against his enemies, Shaftesbury was sent to the Tower of London, charged with high treason. In November, the grand jury, packed with Whigs, threw out the indictment, and the earl was free, but his power was broken, and he lived only two more years.

Shortly before the grand jury acted, Dryden published anonymously the first part of *Absalom and Achitophel*, apparently hoping to influence their verdict. The issues in question were grave; the chief actors, the most important men in the realm. Dryden, therefore, could not use burlesque and caricature as had Butler, or the mock heroic as he himself had done in *Mac Flecknoe*. Only a heroic style and manner were appropriate to his weighty material, and the poem is most original in its blending of the heroic and the satiric. Dryden's task called for all his tact and literary skill; he had to mention, but to gloss over, the king's faults: his indolence and love of pleasure; his neglect of his wife, and his devotion to his mistresses—conduct that had left him with many children, but no heir except his Catholic brother. He had to deal gently with Monmouth, whom Charles still loved. And he had to present, or appear to present, the king's case objectively.

The remarkable parallels between the rebellion of Absalom against his father King David (2 Samuel 13–18) had already been remarked in sermons, satires, and pamphlets. Dryden took the hint and gave contemporary events a due distance and additional dignity by approaching them indirectly through their biblical analogues. The poem is famous for its brilliant portraits of the king's enemies and friends, but equally admirable are the temptation scene (which, like other passages, is indebted to *Paradise Lost*) and the remarkably astute analysis of the Popish Plot itself.

A second part of *Absalom and Achitophel* appeared in 1682. Most of it is the work of Nahum Tate, but lines 310–509, which include the devastating portraits of Doeg and Og (two Whig poets, Elkanah Settle and Thomas Shadwell), are certainly by Dryden.

Absalom and Achitophel: A Poem

> In pious times, ere priestcraft did begin,
> Before polygamy was made a sin;
> When man on many multiplied his kind,
> Ere one to one was cursedly confined;
> 5   When nature prompted and no law denied
> Promiscuous use of concubine and bride;
> Then Israel's monarch after Heaven's own heart,[1]
> His vigorous warmth did variously impart

---

1. David ("a man after [God's] own heart," according to 1 Samuel 13.14) represents Charles II.

To wives and slaves; and, wide as his command,
10   Scattered his Maker's image through the land.
Michal,[2] of royal blood, the crown did wear,
A soil ungrateful to the tiller's care:
Not so the rest; for several mothers bore
To godlike David several sons before.
15   But since like slaves his bed they did ascend,
No true succession could their seed attend.
Of all this numerous progeny was none
So beautiful, so brave, as Absalom:[3]
Whether, inspired by some diviner lust,
20   His father got him with a greater gust,°   *relish, pleasure*
Or that his conscious destiny made way,
By manly beauty, to imperial sway.
Early in foreign fields he won renown,
With kings and states allied to Israel's crown:[4]
25   In peace the thoughts of war he could remove,
And seemed as he were only born for love.
Whate'er he did, was done with so much ease,
In him alone 'twas natural to please;
His motions all accompanied with grace;
30   And paradise was opened in his face.
With secret joy indulgent David viewed
His youthful image in his son renewed:
To all his wishes nothing he denied;
And made the charming Annabel[5] his bride.
35   What faults he had (for who from faults is free?)
His father could not, or he would not see.
Some warm excesses which the law forbore,
Were cònstrued youth that purged by boiling o'er:
And Amnon's murther,[6] by a specious name,
40   Was called a just revenge for injured fame.
Thus praised and loved the noble youth remained,
While David, undisturbed, in Sion° reigned.   *London*
But life can never be sincerely° blest;   *wholly*
Heaven punishes the bad, and proves° the best.   *tests*
45   The Jews,° a headstrong, moody, murmuring race,   *English*
As ever tried the extent and stretch of grace;
God's pampered people, whom, debauched with ease,
No king could govern, nor no God could please
(Gods they had tried of every shape and size
50   That god-smiths could produce, or priests devise);[7]
These Adam-wits, too fortunately free,
Began to dream they wanted liberty;[8]

2. One of David's wives, who represents the childless queen, Catherine of Braganza.
3. James Scott, duke of Monmouth (1649–1685).
4. Monmouth had won repute as a soldier fighting
for France against Holland and for Holland against
France.
5. Anne Scott, duchess of Buccleuch (pronounced *Bue-cloo*), a beauty and a great heiress.
6. Absalom killed his half-brother Amnon, who
had raped Absalom's sister Tamar (2 Samuel

13.28–29). The parallel with Monmouth is vague.
He is known to have committed acts of violence in
his youth, but certainly not fratricide.
7. Dryden recalls the political and religious controversies that, since the Reformation, had divided
England and finally caused civil wars.
8. Adam rebelled because he felt that he lacked
("wanted") liberty, because he was forbidden to eat
the fruit of one tree.

And when no rule, no precedent was found,
Of men by laws less circumscribed and bound,
55 They led their wild desires to woods and caves,
And thought that all but savages were slaves.
They who, when Saul was dead, without a blow,
Made foolish Ishbosheth[9] the crown forgo;
Who banished David did from Hebron[1] bring,
60 And with a general shout proclaimed him king:
Those very Jews, who, at their very best,
Their humor° more than loyalty expressed,   *caprice*
Now wondered why so long they had obeyed
An idol monarch, which their hands had made;
65 Thought they might ruin him they could create,
Or melt him to that golden calf,[2] a state.°   *republic*
But these were random bolts;° no formed design   *shots*
Nor interest made the factious crowd to join:
The sober part of Israel, free from stain,
70 Well knew the value of a peaceful reign;
And, looking backward with a wise affright,
Saw seams of wounds, dishonest° to the sight: *disgraceful*
In contemplation of whose ugly scars
They cursed the memory of civil wars.
75 The moderate sort of men, thus qualified,°   *assuaged*
Inclined the balance to the better side;
And David's mildness managed it so well,
The bad found no occasion to rebel.
But when to sin our biased[3] nature leans,
80 The careful Devil is still at hand with means;
And providently pimps for ill desires:
The Good Old Cause[4] revived, a plot requires.
Plots, true or false, are necessary things,
To raise up commonwealths and ruin kings.
85   The inhabitants of old Jerusalem
Were Jebusites;[5] the town so called from them;
And theirs the native right.
But when the chosen people° grew more strong,   *Protestants*
The rightful cause at length became the wrong;
90 And every loss the men of Jebus bore,
They still were thought God's enemies the more.
Thus worn and weakened, well or ill content,
Submit they must to David's government:
Impoverished and deprived of all command,
95 Their taxes doubled as they lost their land;
And, what was harder yet to flesh and blood,
Their gods disgraced, and burnt like common wood.[6]

9. Saul's son; he stands for Richard Cromwell, who succeeded his father as lord protector. "Saul": Oliver Cromwell.
1. Where David reigned over Judah after the death of Saul and before he became king of Israel (2 Samuel 1–5). Charles had been crowned in Scotland in 1651.
2. The image worshiped by the children of Israel during the period that Moses spent on Mount Sinai, receiving the law from God.
3. Inclined (cf. *Mac Flecknoe*, line 189 and n. 5, p. 908).
4. The Commonwealth. Dryden stigmatizes the Whigs by associating them with subversion.
5. Roman Catholics. The original name of Jerusalem (here, London) was Jebus.
6. Such oppressive laws against Roman Catholics date from the time of Elizabeth I.

This set the heathen priesthood[7] in a flame;
For priests of all religions are the same:
100 Of whatsoe'er descent their godhead be,
Stock, stone, or other homely pedigree,
In his defense his servants are as bold,
As if he had been born of beaten gold.
The Jewish rabbins,[8] though their enemies,
105 In this conclude them honest men and wise:
For 'twas their duty, all the learned think,
To espouse his cause, by whom they eat and drink.
From hence began that Plot, the nation's curse,
Bad in itself, but represented worse;
110 Raised in extremes, and in extremes decried;
With oaths affirmed, with dying vows denied;
Not weighed or winnowed by the multitude;
But swallowed in the mass, unchewed and crude.
Some truth there was, but dashed° and brewed with lies, *adulterated*
115 To please the fools, and puzzle all the wise.
Succeeding times did equal folly call,
Believing nothing, or believing all.
The Egyptian rites the Jebusites embraced,
Where gods were recommended by their taste.[9]
120 Such savory deities must needs be good,
As served at once for worship and for food.
By force they could not introduce these gods,
For ten to one in former days was odds;
So fraud was used (the sacrificer's trade):
125 Fools are more hard to conquer than persuade.
Their busy teachers mingled with the Jews,
And raked for converts even the court and stews:° *brothels*
Which Hebrew priests the more unkindly took,
Because the fleece accompanies the flock.[1]
130 Some thought they God's anointed° meant to slay *the king*
By guns, invented since full many a day:
Our author swears it not; but who can know
How far the Devil and Jebusites may go?
This Plot, which failed for want of common sense,
135 Had yet a deep and dangerous consequence:
For, as when raging fevers boil the blood,
The standing lake soon floats into a flood,
And every hostile humor, which before
Slept quiet in its channels, bubbles o'er;
140 So several factions from this first ferment
Work up to foam, and threat the government.
Some by their friends, more by themselves thought wise,
Opposed the power to which they could not rise.
Some had in courts been great, and thrown from thence,

---

7. Roman Catholic clergy.
8. Anglican clergy.
9. Here Dryden sneers at the doctrine of transubstantiation. "Egyptian": French, therefore Catholic.

1. Dryden charges that the Anglican clergy ("Hebrew priests") resented proselytizing by Catholics chiefly because they stood to lose their tithes ("fleece").

145   Like fiends were hardened in impenitence;
       Some, by their monarch's fatal mercy, grown
       From pardoned rebels kinsmen to the throne,
       Were raised in power and public office high;
       Strong bands, if bands ungrateful men could tie.

150   Of these the false Achitophel² was first;
       A name to all succeeding ages cursed:
       For close designs, and crooked counsels fit;
       Sagacious, bold, and turbulent of wit;°   *unruly imagination*
       Restless, unfixed in principles and place;

155   In power unpleased, impatient of disgrace:
       A fiery soul, which, working out its way,
       Fretted the pygmy body to decay,
       And o'er-informed the tenement of clay.³
       A daring pilot in extremity;

160   Pleased with the danger, when the waves went high,
       He sought the storms; but, for a calm unfit,
       Would steer too nigh the sands, to boast his wit.
       Great wits are sure to madness near allied,⁴
       And thin partitions do their bounds divide;

165   Else why should he, with wealth and honor blest,
       Refuse his age the needful hours of rest?
       Punish a body which he could not please;
       Bankrupt of life, yet prodigal of ease?
       And all to leave what with his toil he won,

170   To that unfeathered two-legged thing,⁵ a son;
       Got, while his soul did huddled° notions try;   *confused, hurried*
       And born a shapeless lump, like anarchy.
       In friendship false, implacable in hate,
       Resolved to ruin or to rule the state.

175   To compass this the triple bond⁶ he broke,
       The pillars of the public safety shook,
       And fitted Israel for a foreign yoke;
       Then seized with fear, yet still affecting fame,
       Usurped a patriot's all-atoning name.

180   So easy still it proves in factious times,
       With public zeal to cancel private crimes.
       How safe is treason, and how sacred ill,
       Where none can sin against the people's will!
       Where crowds can wink, and no offense be known,

185   Since in another's guilt they find their own!
       Yet fame deserved, no enemy can grudge;

---

2. Anthony Ashley Cooper, first earl of Shaftesbury (1621–1683). He had served in the parliamentary army and been a member of Cromwell's council of state. He later helped bring back Charles and, in 1670, was made a member of the notorious Cabal Ministry, which formed an alliance with Louis XIV in which England betrayed her ally, Holland, and joined France in war against that country. In 1672 he became lord chancellor, but with the dissolution of the cabal in 1673, he was removed from office. Lines 146–49 apply perfectly to him.

3. The soul is thought of as the animating principle, the force that puts the body in motion. Shaftesbury's body seemed too small to house his fiery, energetic soul.
4. "Great wits": men of genius. That genius and madness are akin is a very old idea.
5. Cf. Plato's definition of a human: "a featherless biped."
6. The triple alliance of England, Sweden, and Holland against France, 1668. Shaftesbury helped to bring about the war against Holland in 1672.

The statesman we abhor, but praise the judge.
In Israel's courts ne'er sat an Abbethdin[7]
With more discerning eyes, or hands more clean;
190 Unbribed, unsought, the wretched to redress;
Swift of dispatch, and easy of access.
Oh, had he been content to serve the crown,
With virtues only proper to the gown;
Or had the rankness of the soil been freed
195 From cockle, that oppressed the noble seed;
David for him his tuneful harp had strung,
And Heaven had wanted one immortal song.[8]
But wild Ambition loves to slide, not stand,
And Fortune's ice prefers to Virtue's land.
200 Achitophel, grown weary to possess
A lawful fame, and lazy happiness,
Disdained the golden fruit to gather free,
And lent the crowd his arm to shake the tree.
Now, manifest of° crimes contrived long since,   detected in
205 He stood at bold defiance with his prince;
Held up the buckler of the people's cause
Against the crown, and skulked behind the laws.
The wished occasion of the Plot he takes;
Some circumstances finds, but more he makes.
210 By buzzing emissaries fills the ears
Of listening crowds with jealousies° and fears   suspicions
Of arbitrary counsels brought to light,
And proves the king himself a Jebusite.
Weak arguments! which yet he knew full well
215 Were strong with people easy to rebel.
For, governed by the moon, the giddy Jews
Tread the same track when she the prime renews;
And once in twenty years, their scribes record,[9]
By natural instinct they change their lord.
220 Achitophel still wants a chief, and none
Was found so fit as warlike Absalom:
Not that he wished his greatness to create
(For politicians neither love nor hate),
But, for he knew his title not allowed,
225 Would keep him still depending on the crowd,
That kingly power, thus ebbing out, might be
Drawn to the dregs of a democracy.[1]
Him he attempts with studied arts to please,
And sheds his venom in such words as these:
230 "Auspicious prince, at whose nativity

7. The chief of the seventy elders who composed the Jewish supreme court. The allusion is to Shaftesbury's serving as lord chancellor from 1672 to 1673. Dryden's praise of Shaftesbury's integrity in this office, by suggesting a balanced judgment, makes his condemnation of the statesman more effective than it might otherwise have been.
8. I.e., David would have had occasion to write one fewer song of praise to heaven. The reference may be to 2 Samuel 22 or to Psalm 4.

9. The moon "renews her prime" when its several phases recur on the same day of the solar calendar—i.e., complete a cycle—as happens approximately every twenty years. The crisis between Charles I and Parliament began to grow acute about 1640; Charles II returned in 1660; it is now 1680 and a full cycle has been completed.
1. To Dryden, "democracy" meant popular government. The "dregs of a democracy" would be mob rule.

Some royal planet[2] ruled the southern sky;
Thy longing country's darling and desire;
Their cloudy pillar and their guardian fire:
Their second Moses, whose extended wand
235 Divides the seas, and shows the promised land;[3]
Whose dawning day in every distant age
Has exercised the sacred prophet's rage:
The people's prayer, the glad diviners' theme,
The young men's vision, and the old men's dream![4]
240 Thee, savior, thee, the nation's vows[5] confess,
And, never satisfied with seeing, bless:
Swift unbespoken pomps thy steps proclaim,
And stammering babes are taught to lisp thy name.
How long wilt thou the general joy detain,
245 Starve and defraud the people of thy reign?
Content ingloriously to pass thy days
Like one of Virtue's fools that feeds on praise;
Till thy fresh glories, which now shine so bright,
Grow stale and tarnish with our daily sight.
250 Believe me, royal youth, thy fruit must be
Or gathered ripe, or rot upon the tree.
Heaven has to all allotted, soon or late,
Some lucky revolution of their fate;
Whose motions if we watch and guide with skill
255 (For human good depends on human will),
Our Fortune rolls as from a smooth descent,
And from the first impression takes the bent;
But, if unseized, she glides away like wind,
And leaves repenting Folly far behind.
260 Now, now she meets you with a glorious prize,
And spreads her locks before her as she flies.[6]
Had thus old David, from whose loins you spring,
Not dared, when Fortune called him, to be king,
At Gath[7] an exile he might still remain,
265 And heaven's anointing[8] oil had been in vain.
Let his successful youth your hopes engage;
But shun the example of declining age;
Behold him setting in his western skies,
The shadows lengthening as the vapors rise.
270 He is not now, as when on Jordan's sand[9] ⎫
The joyful people thronged to see him land, ⎬
Covering the beach, and blackening all the strand; ⎭

---

2. A planet whose influence destines him to kingship.
3. After their exodus from Egypt under the leadership of Moses, whose "extended wand" separated the waters of the Red Sea so that they crossed over on dry land, the Israelites were led in their forty-year wandering in the wilderness by a pillar of cloud by day and a pillar of fire by night (Exodus 13–14).
4. Cf. Joel 2.28.
5. Solemn promises of fidelity.
6. Achitophel gives to Fortune the traditional attributes of the allegorical personification of Opportunity: bald except for a forelock, she can be seized only as she approaches.
7. Brussels, where Charles spent his last years in exile. David took refuge from Saul in Gath (1 Samuel 27.4).
8. After God rejected Saul, he sent Samuel to anoint the boy David, as a token that he should finally come to the throne (1 Samuel 16.1–13).
9. The seashore at Dover, where Charles landed (May 25, 1660).

But, like the Prince of Angels, from his height
Comes tumbling downward with diminished light;[1]
275 Betrayed by one one poor plot to public scorn
(Our only blessing since his cursed return),
Those heaps of people which one sheaf did bind,
Blown off and scattered by a puff of wind.
What strength can he to your designs oppose,
280 Naked of friends, and round beset with foes?
If Pharaoh's[2] doubtful succor he should use,
A foreign aid would more incense the Jews:
Proud Egypt would dissembled friendship bring;
Foment the war, but not support the king:
285 Nor would the royal party e'er unite
With Pharaoh's arms to assist the Jebusite;
Or if they should, their interest soon would break,
And with such odious aid make David weak.
All sorts of men by my successful arts,
290 Abhorring kings, estrange their altered hearts
From David's rule: and 'tis the general cry,
'Religion, commonwealth, and liberty.'[3]
If you, as champion of the public good,
Add to their arms a chief of royal blood,
295 What may not Israel hope, and what applause
Might such a general gain by such a cause?
Not barren praise alone, that gaudy flower
Fair only to the sight, but solid power;
And nobler is a limited command,
300 Given by the love of all your native land,
Than a successive title,[4] long and dark,
Drawn from the moldy rolls of Noah's ark."
    What cannot praise effect in mighty minds,
When flattery soothes, and when ambition blinds!
305 Desire of power, on earth a vicious weed,
Yet, sprung from high, is of celestial seed:
In God 'tis glory; and when men aspire,
'Tis but a spark too much of heavenly fire.
The ambitious youth, too covetous of fame,
310 Too full of angels' metal[5] in his frame,
Unwarily was led from virtue's ways,
Made drunk with honor, and debauched with praise.
Half loath, and half consenting to the ill
(For loyal blood within him struggled still),
315 He thus replied: "And what pretense have I
To take up arms for public liberty?
My father governs with unquestioned right;
The faith's defender, and mankind's delight,
Good, gracious, just, observant of the laws:

1. Cf. the fall of Satan in *Paradise Lost* 1.50–124, which dims the brightness of the archangel. The choice of the undignified word *tumbling* is deliberate.
2. Louis XIV of France.
3. Cf. line 82 and n. 4.

4. A title to the crown based on succession.
5. An alternative spelling of *mettle* (i.e., spirit). But a pun on "metal" is intended, as is obvious from the pun "angel" (a purely intellectual being and a coin). Ambition caused the revolt of the angels in heaven.

320 And heaven by wonders has espoused his cause.
Whom has he wronged in all his peaceful reign?
Who sues for justice to his throne in vain?
What millions has he pardoned of his foes,
Whom just revenge did to his wrath expose?
325 Mild, easy, humble, studious of our good,
Inclined to mercy, and averse from blood;
If mildness ill with stubborn Israel suit,
His crime is God's beloved attribute.
What could he gain, his people to betray,
330 Or change his right for arbitrary sway?
Let haughty Pharaoh curse with such a reign
His fruitful Nile, and yoke a servile train.
If David's rule Jerusalem displease,
The Dog Star[6] heats their brains to this disease.
335 Why then should I, encouraging the bad,
Turn rebel and run popularly mad?
Were he a tyrant, who, by lawless might
Oppressed the Jews, and raised the Jebusite,
Well might I mourn; but nature's holy bands
340 Would curb my spirits and restrain my hands:
The people might assert° their liberty,   claim
But what was right in them were crime in me.
His favor leaves me nothing to require,
Prevents my wishes, and outruns desire.
345 What more can I expect while David lives?
All but his kingly diadem he gives:
And that"—But there he paused; then sighing, said—
"Is justly destined for a worthier head.
For when my father from his toils shall rest
350 And late augment the number of the blest,
His lawful issue shall the throne ascend,
Or the collateral line,[7] where that shall end.
His brother, though oppressed with vulgar spite,
Yet dauntless, and secure of native right,
355 Of every royal virtue stands possessed;
Still dear to all the bravest and the best.
His courage foes, his friends his truth proclaim;
His loyalty the king, the world his fame.
His mercy even the offending crowd will find,
360 For sure he comes of a forgiving kind.[8]
Why should I then repine at heaven's decree,
Which gives me no pretense to royalty?
Yet O that fate, propitiously inclined,
Had raised my birth, or had debased my mind;
365 To my large soul not all her treasure lent,
And then betrayed it to a mean descent!
I find, I find my mounting spirits bold,

6. Sirius, which in midsummer rises and sets with the sun and is thus associated with the maddening heat of the "dog days."
7. In the event of Charles's dying without legiti-mate issue, the throne would constitutionally pass to his brother, James, or his descendants, the "col-lateral line."
8. Race, in the sense of family.

And David's part disdains my mother's mold.
Why am I scanted by a niggard birth?[9]
370   My soul disclaims the kindred of her earth;
And, made for empire, whispers me within,
'Desire of greatness is a godlike sin.'"
        Him staggering so when hell's dire agent found,[1]
While fainting Virtue scarce maintained her ground,
375   He pours fresh forces in, and thus replies:
"The eternal god, supremely good and wise,
Imparts not these prodigious gifts in vain:
What wonders are reserved to bless your reign!
Against your will, your arguments have shown,
380   Such virtue's only given to guide a throne.
Not that your father's mildness I contemn,
But manly force becomes the diadem.
'Tis true he grants the people all they crave;
And more, perhaps, than subjects ought to have:
385   For lavish grants suppose a monarch tame,
And more his goodness than his wit° proclaim.   intelligence
But when should people strive their bonds to break,
If not when kings are negligent or weak?
Let him give on till he can give no more,
390   The thrifty Sanhedrin[2] shall keep him poor;
And every shekel which he can receive,
Shall cost a limb of his prerogative.[3]
To ply him with new plots shall be my care;
Or plunge him deep in some expensive war;
395   Which when his treasure can no more supply,
He must, with the remains of kingship, buy.
His faithful friends our jealousies and fears
Call Jebusites, and Pharaoh's pensioners;
Whom when our fury from his aid has torn,
400   He shall be naked left to public scorn.
The next successor, whom I fear and hate,
My arts have made obnoxious to the state;
Turned all his virtues to his overthrow,
And gained our elders[4] to pronounce a foe.
405   His right, for sums of necessary gold,
Shall first be pawned, and afterward be sold;
Till time shall ever-wanting David draw,
To pass your doubtful title into law:
If not, the people have a right supreme
410   To make their kings; for kings are made for them.
All empire is no more than power in trust,
Which, when resumed, can be no longer just.
Succession, for the general good designed,

9. I.e., why am I limited by a sordid birth?
1. Observe the Miltonic inversion, which helps maintain the epic tone.
2. The highest judicial counsel of the Jews, here, Parliament.
3. The Whigs hoped to limit the special privileges of the Crown (the royal "prerogative") by refusing to vote money to Charles. He circumvented them by living on French subsidies and refusing to summon Parliament.
4. The chief magistrates and rulers of the Jews. Shaftesbury had won over ("gained") country gentlemen and nobles to his hostile view of James.

In its own wrong a nation cannot bind;
415 If altering that the people can relieve,
Better one suffer than a nation grieve.
The Jews well know their power: ere Saul they chose,[5]
God was their king, and God they durst depose.
Urge now your piety,[6] your filial name,
420 A father's right and fear of future fame;
The public good, that universal call,
To which even heaven submitted, answers all.
Nor let his love enchant your generous mind;
'Tis Nature's trick to propagate her kind.
425 Our fond begetters, who would never die,
Love but themselves in their posterity.
Or let his kindness by the effects be tried,
Or let him lay his vain pretense aside.
God said he loved your father; could he bring
430 A better proof than to anoint him king?
It surely showed he loved the shepherd well,
Who gave so fair a flock as Israel.
Would David have you thought his darling son?
What means he then, to alienate[7] the crown?
435 The name of godly he may blush to bear:
'Tis after God's own heart[8] to cheat his heir.
He to his brother gives supreme command;
To you a legacy of barren land,[9]
Perhaps the old harp, on which he thrums his lays,
440 Or some dull Hebrew ballad in your praise.
Then the next heir, a prince severe and wise,
Already looks on you with jealous eyes;
Sees through the thin disguises of your arts,
And marks your progress in the people's hearts.
445 Though now his mighty soul its grief contains,
He meditates revenge who least complains;
And, like a lion, slumbering in the way,
Or sleep dissembling, while he waits his prey,
His fearless foes within his distance draws,
450 Constrains his roaring, and contracts his paws;
Till at the last, his time for fury found,
He shoots with sudden vengeance from the ground;
The prostrate vulgar° passes o'er and spares,   *common people*
But with a lordly rage his hunters tears.
455 Your case no tame expedients will afford:
Resolve on death, or conquest by the sword,
Which for no less a stake than life you draw;
And self-defense is nature's eldest law.
Leave the warm people no considering time;

---

5. Before Saul, the first king of Israel, came to the throne, the Jews were governed by judges. Similarly Oliver Cromwell ("Saul") as lord protector took over the reins of government, after he had dissolved the Rump Parliament in 1653.
6. Dutifulness to a parent.

7. In law, to convey the title to property to another person.
8. An irony (cf. line 7 and n. 1).
9. James was given the title of generalissimo in 1678. In 1679 Monmouth was banished and withdrew to Holland.

460 For then rebellion may be thought a crime.
    Prevail yourself of what occasion gives,
    But try your title while your father lives;
    And that your arms may have a fair pretense,°   *pretext*
    Proclaim you take them in the king's defense;
465 Whose sacred life each minute would expose
    To plots, from seeming friends, and secret foes.
    And who can sound the depth of David's soul?
    Perhaps his fear his kindness may control.
    He fears his brother, though he loves his son,
470 For plighted vows too late to be undone.
    If so, by force he wishes to be gained,
    Like women's lechery, to seem constrained.°   *forced*
    Doubt not; but when he most affects the frown,
    Commit a pleasing rape upon the crown.
475 Secure his person to secure your cause:
    They who possess the prince, possess the laws."
        He said, and this advice above the rest
    With Absalom's mild nature suited best:
    Unblamed of life (ambition set aside),
480 Not stained with cruelty, nor puffed with pride,
    How happy had he been, if destiny
    Had higher placed his birth, or not so high!
    His kingly virtues might have claimed a throne,
    And blest all other countries but his own.
485 But charming greatness since so few refuse,
    'Tis juster to lament him than accuse.
    Strong were his hopes a rival to remove,
    With blandishments to gain the public love;
    To head the faction while their zeal was hot,
490 And popularly prosecute the Plot.
    To further this, Achitophel unites
    The malcontents of all the Israelites;
    Whose differing parties he could wisely join,
    For several ends, to serve the same design:
495 The best (and of the princes some were such),
    Who thought the power of monarchy too much;
    Mistaken men, and patriots in their hearts;
    Not wicked, but seduced by impious arts.
    By these the springs of property were bent,
500 And wound so high, they cracked the government.
    The next for interest sought to embroil the state,
    To sell their duty at a dearer rate;
    And make their Jewish markets of the throne,
    Pretending public good, to serve their own.
505 Others thought kings an useless heavy load,
    Who cost too much, and did too little good.
    These were for laying honest David by,
    On principles of pure good husbandry.°   *economy*
    With them joined all the haranguers of the throng,
510 That thought to get preferment by the tongue.

Who follow next, a double danger bring,
Not only hating David, but the king:
The Solymaean rout,[1] well-versed of old
In godly faction, and in treason bold;
515   Cowering and quaking at a conqueror's sword,
But lofty to a lawful prince restored;
Saw with disdain an ethnic[2] plot begun,
And scorned by Jebusites to be outdone.
Hot Levites[3] headed these; who, pulled before
520   From the ark, which in the Judges' days they bore,
Resumed their cant, and with a zealous cry
Pursued their old beloved theocracy:
Where Sanhedrin and priest enslaved the nation,
And justified their spoils by inspiration:[4]
525   For who so fit for reign as Aaron's race,[5]
If once dominion they could found in grace?
These led the pack; though not of surest scent,
Yet deepest-mouthed[6] against the government.
A numerous host of dreaming saints succeed,
530   Of the true old enthusiastic breed:[7]
'Gainst form and order they their power employ,
Nothing to build, and all things to destroy.
But far more numerous was the herd of such,
Who think too little, and who talk too much.
535   These out of mere instinct, they knew not why,
Adored their fathers' God and property;
And, by the same blind benefit of fate,
The Devil and the Jebusite did hate:
Born to be saved, even in their own despite,
540   Because they could not help believing right.
Such were the tools; but a whole Hydra more
Remains, of sprouting heads too long to score.
Some of their chiefs were princes of the land:
In the first rank of these did Zimri[8] stand;
545   A man so various, that he seemed to be

---

1. I.e., London rabble. Solyma was a name for Jerusalem.

2. Gentile; here, Roman Catholic.

3. I.e., Presbyterian clergymen. The tribe of Levi, assigned to duties in the tabernacle, carried the ark of the covenant during the forty-year sojourn in the wilderness (Numbers 4). Under the Commonwealth ("in the Judges' days") Presbyterianism became the state religion, and its clergy, therefore, "bore the ark." The Act of Uniformity (1662) forced the Presbyterian clergy out of their livings: in short, before the Popish Plot, they had been "pulled from the ark." They are represented here as joining the Whigs in the hope of restoring the commonwealth, "their old beloved theocracy."

4. Observe in these lines the cluster of disparaging words: "cant," "zealous," "inspiration." Dryden shared Samuel Butler's contempt for the irrationality of Dissenters.

5. Priests had to be descendants of Aaron (Exodus 28.1, Numbers 18.7).

6. Loudest. The phrase is applied to hunting dogs.

"Pack" and "scent" sustain the image.

7. "Dreaming saints": a term used by certain Dissenters for those elected to salvation. The extreme fanaticism of the "saints" and their claims to inspiration are characterized as a form of religious madness ("enthusiastic").

8. George Villiers, second duke of Buckingham (1628–1687), wealthy, brilliant, dissolute, and unstable. He had been an influential member of the cabal, but after 1673 had joined Shaftesbury in opposition to the court party. This is the least political of the satirical portraits in the poem. Buckingham had been the chief author of *The Rehearsal* (1671), the play that satirized the heroic play and ridiculed Dryden in the character of Mr. Bayes. Politics gave Dryden an opportunity to retaliate. He comments on this portrait in his *A Discourse Concerning the Original and Progress of Satire*. Dryden had two biblical Zimris in mind: the Zimri destroyed for his lustfulness and blasphemy (Numbers 25) and the conspirator and regicide of 1 Kings 16.8–20 and 2 Kings 9.31.

Not one, but all mankind's epitome:
Stiff in opinions, always in the wrong;
Was everything by starts, and nothing long;
But, in the course of one revolving moon,
550 Was chymist,° fiddler, statesman, and buffoon: chemist
Then all for women, painting, rhyming, drinking,
Besides ten thousand freaks that died in thinking.
Blest madman, who could every hour employ,
With something new to wish, or to enjoy!
555 Railing° and praising were his usual themes;   reviling, abusing
And both (to show his judgment) in extremes:
So over-violent, or over-civil,
That every man, with him, was God or Devil.
In squandering wealth was his peculiar art:
560 Nothing went unrewarded but desert.
Beggared by fools, whom still° he found° too late,   constantly/found out
He had his jest, and they had his estate.
He laughed himself from court; then sought relief
By forming parties, but could ne'er be chief;
565 For, spite of him, the weight of business fell
On Absalom and wise Achitophel:
Thus, wicked but in will, of means bereft,
He left not faction, but of that was left.
    Titles and names 'twere tedious to rehearse
570 Of lords, below the dignity of verse.
Wits, warriors, Commonwealth's men, were the best;
Kind husbands, and mere nobles, all the rest.
And therefore, in the name of dullness, be
The well-hung Balaam and cold Caleb, free;
575 And canting Nadab let oblivion damn,
Who made new porridge for the paschal lamb.[9]
Let friendship's holy band some names assure;
Some their own worth, and some let scorn secure.
Nor shall the rascal rabble here have place,
580 Whom kings no titles gave, and God no grace:
Not bull-faced Jonas,[1] who could statutes draw
To mean rebellion, and make treason law.
But he, though bad, is followed by a worse,
The wretch who heaven's anointed dared to curse:
585 Shimei,[2] whose youth did early promise bring
Of zeal to God and hatred to his king,
Did wisely from expensive sins refrain,

9. The lamb slain during Passover; here, Christ. The identities of Balaam, Caleb, and Nadab have not been certainly established, although various Whig nobles have been suggested. For Balaam see Numbers 22–24; for Caleb, Numbers 13–14; and for Nadab, Leviticus 10.1–2. "Well-hung": fluent of speech or sexually potent or both. "Cold" would contrast with the second meaning of well-hung. "Canting" points to a Nonconformist, as does "new porridge," for Dissenters referred to the Book of Common Prayer contemptuously as "porridge," a hodgepodge, unsubstantial stuff.

1. Sir William Jones, attorney general, had been largely responsible for the passage of the first Exclusion Bill by the House of Commons. He prosecuted the accused in the Popish Plot.
2. Shimei cursed and stoned David when he fled into the wilderness during Absalom's revolt (2 Samuel 16.5–14). His name is used here for one of the two sheriffs of London: Slingsby Bethel, a Whig, former republican, and virulent enemy of Charles. He packed juries with Whigs and so secured the acquittal of enemies of the court, among them Shaftesbury himself.

And never broke the Sabbath, but for gain;
Nor ever was he known an oath to vent,
590   Or curse, unless against the government.
Thus heaping wealth, by the most ready way
Among the Jews, which was to cheat and pray,
The city, to reward his pious hate
Against his master, chose him magistrate.
595   His hand a vare° of justice did uphold;   *staff*
His neck was loaded with a chain of gold.
During his office, treason was no crime;
The sons of Belial[3] had a glorious time;
For Shimei, though not prodigal of pelf,
600   Yet loved his wicked neighbor as himself.
When two or three were gathered to declaim ⎤
Against the monarch of Jerusalem,   ⎬
Shimei was always in the midst of them;   ⎦
And if they cursed the king when he was by,
605   Would rather curse than break good company.
If any durst his factious friends accuse,
He packed a jury of dissenting Jews;
Whose fellow-feeling in the godly cause
Would free the suffering saint from human laws.
610   For laws are only made to punish those
Who serve the king, and to protect his foes.
If any leisure time he had from power
(Because 'tis sin to misemploy an hour),
His business was, by writing, to persuade
615   That kings were useless, and a clog to trade;
And, that his noble style he might refine,
No Rechabite[4] more shunned the fumes of wine.
Chaste were his cellars, and his shrieval board[5]
The grossness of a city feast abhorred:
620   His cooks, with long disuse, their trade forgot;
Cool was his kitchen, though his brains were hot,
Such frugal virtue malice may accuse,
But sure 'twas necessary to the Jews:
For towns once burnt[6] such magistrates require
625   As dare not tempt God's providence by fire.
With spiritual food he fed his servants well,
But free from flesh that made the Jews rebel;
And Moses' laws he held in more account,
For forty days of fasting in the mount.[7]
630   To speak the rest, who better are forgot,
Would tire a well-breathed witness of the Plot.
Yet, Corah,[8] thou shalt from oblivion pass:

3. Sons of wickedness (cf. Milton, *Paradise Lost* 1.490–505). Dryden probably intended a pun on Balliol, the Oxford college in which leading Whigs stayed during the brief and fateful meeting of Parliament at Oxford in 1681.
4. An austere Jewish sect that drank no wine (Jeremiah 35.2–19).
5. Sheriff's dinner table.

6. London burned in 1666.
7. Mount Sinai, where, during a fast of forty days, Moses received the law (Exodus 34.28).
8. Or Korah, a rebellious Levite, swallowed up by the earth because of his crimes (Numbers 16). Corah is Titus Oates, the self-appointed, perjured, and "well-breathed" (long-winded) witness of the plot.

Erect thyself, thou monumental brass,
High as the serpent of thy metal made,[9]
635 While nations stand secure beneath thy shade.
What though his birth were base, yet comets rise
From earthy vapors, ere they shine in skies.
Prodigious actions may as well be done
By weaver's issue,[1] as by prince's son.
640 This arch-attestor for the public good
By that one deed ennobles all his blood.
Who ever asked the witnesses' high race
Whose oath with martyrdom did Stephen[2] grace?
Ours was a Levite, and as times went then,
645 His tribe were God Almighty's gentlemen.
Sunk were his eyes, his voice was harsh and loud,
Sure signs he neither choleric[3] was nor proud:
His long chin proved his wit; his saintlike grace
A church vermilion, and a Moses' face.[4]
650 His memory, miraculously great,
Could plots, exceeding man's belief, repeat;
Which therefore cannot be accounted lies,
For human wit could never such devise.
Some future truths are mingled in his book;
655 But where the witness failed, the prophet spoke:
Some things like visionary flights appear;
The spirit caught him up, the Lord knows where,
And gave him his rabbinical degree,
Unknown to foreign university.[5]
660 His judgment yet his memory did excel;
Which pieced his wondrous evidence so well,
And suited to the temper of the times,
Then groaning under Jebusitic crimes.
Let Israel's foes suspect his heavenly call,
665 And rashly judge his writ apocryphal;[6]
Our laws for such affronts have forfeits made:
He takes his life, who takes away his trade.
Were I myself in witness Corah's place,
The wretch who did me such a dire disgrace
670 Should whet my memory, though once forgot,
To make him an appendix of my plot.
His zeal to heaven made him his prince despise,
And load his person with indignities;
But zeal peculiar privilege affords,
675 Indulging latitude to deeds and words;
And Corah might for Agag's murder[7] call,

---

9. Moses erected a brazen serpent to heal the Jews
bitten by fiery serpents (Numbers 21.4–9). "Brass"
also means impudence or shamelessness.
1. Oates's father, a clergyman, belonged to an
obscure family of ribbon weavers.
2. The first Christian martyr, accused by false witnesses (Acts 6–7).
3. Prone to anger.
4. Moses' face shone when he came down from
Mount Sinai with the tables of the law (Exodus

34.29–30). Oates's face suggests high living, not
spiritual illumination.
5. Oates falsely claimed to be a doctor of divinity
in the University of Salamanca.
6. Not inspired and hence excluded from Holy
Writ.
7. Agag is probably one of the five Catholic peers
executed for the Popish Plot in 1680, most likely
Lord Stafford, against whom Oates fabricated testimony; he is almost certainly not, as is usually sug-

In terms as coarse as Samuel used to Saul.
What others in his evidence did join
(The best that could be had for love or coin),
680   In Corah's own predicament will fall;
For *witness* is a common name to all.
    Surrounded thus with friends of every sort,
Deluded Absalom forsakes the court:
Impatient of high hopes, urged with renown,
685   And fired with near possession of a crown.
The admiring crowd are dazzled with surprise,
And on his goodly person feed their eyes:
His joy concealed, he sets himself to show,
On each side bowing popularly[8] low;
690   His looks, his gestures, and his words he frames,
And with familiar ease repeats their names.
Thus formed by nature, furnished out with arts,
He glides unfelt into their secret hearts.
Then, with a kind compassionating look,
695   And sighs, bespeaking pity ere he spoke,
Few words he said; but easy those and fit,
More slow than Hybla-drops,[9] and far more sweet.
    "I mourn, my countrymen, your lost estate;
Though far unable to prevent your fate:
700   Behold a banished man, for your dear cause
Exposed a prey to arbitrary laws!
Yet oh! that I alone could be undone,
Cut off from empire, and no more a son!
Now all your liberties a spoil are made; ⎫
705   Egypt° and Tyrus° intercept your trade, ⎬   *France/Holland*
And Jebusites your sacred rites invade. ⎭
My father, whom with reverence yet I name,
Charmed into ease, is careless of his fame;
And, bribed with petty sums of foreign gold,
710   Is grown in Bathsheba's[1] embraces old;
Exalts his enemies, his friends destroys;
And all his power against himself employs.
He gives, and let him give, my right away;
But why should he his own, and yours betray?
715   He only, he can make the nation bleed,
And he alone from my revenge is freed.
Take then my tears (with that he wiped his eyes),
'Tis all the aid my present power supplies:
No court-informer can these arms accuse;
720   These arms may sons against their fathers use:
And 'tis my wish, the next successor's reign
May make no other Israelite complain."
        Youth, beauty, graceful action seldom fail;

---

gested, Sir Edmund Berry Godfrey (see headnote, p. 879). "Agag's murder" and Samuel's coarse terms to Saul are in 1 Samuel 15.
8. "So as to please the crowd" (Johnson's *Dictionary*).

9. The famous honey of Hybla in Sicily.
1. With whom David committed adultery (2 Samuel 11); here, Charles II's French mistress, Louise de Kéroualle, duchess of Portsmouth.

But common interest always will prevail;
725 And pity never ceases to be shown
To him who makes the people's wrongs his own.
The crowd (that still believe their kings oppress)
With lifted hands their young Messiah bless:
Who now begins his progress to ordain
730 With chariots, horsemen, and a numerous train;
From east to west his glories he displays,[2]
And, like the sun, the promised land surveys.
Fame runs before him as the morning star,
And shouts of joy salute him from afar:
735 Each house receives him as a guardian god,
And consecrates the place of his abode:
But hospitable treats did most commend
Wise Issachar,[3] his wealthy western friend.
This moving court, that caught the people's eyes,
740 And seemed but pomp, did other ends disguise:
Achitophel had formed it, with intent
To sound the depths, and fathom, where it went,
The people's hearts; distinguish friends from foes,
And try their strength, before they came to blows.
745 Yet all was colored with a smooth pretense
Of specious love, and duty to their prince.
Religion, and redress of grievances,
Two names that always cheat and always please,
Are often urged; and good King David's life
750 Endangered by a brother and a wife.[4]
Thus, in a pageant show, a plot is made,
And peace itself is war in masquerade.
O foolish Israel! never warned by ill,
Still the same bait, and circumvented still!
755 Did ever men forsake their present ease,
In midst of health imagine a disease;
Take pains contingent mischiefs to foresee,
Make heirs for monarchs, and for God decree?
What shall we think![5] Can people give away
760 Both for themselves and sons, their native sway?
Then they are left defenseless to the sword
Of each unbounded, arbitrary lord:
And laws are vain, by which we right enjoy,
If kings unquestioned can those laws destroy.
765 Yet if the crowd be judge of fit and just,
And kings are only officers in trust,
Then this resuming covenant was declared
When kings were made, or is forever barred.
If those who gave the scepter could not tie

2. In 1680 Monmouth made a progress through the west of England, seeking popular support for his cause.
3. Thomas Thynne of Longleat. He entertained Monmouth on his journey in the west. "Wise" is, of course, ironic.
4. Titus Oates had sworn that both James, duke of York, and the queen were involved in a similar plot to poison Charles II.
5. In the passage that follows, Dryden states his political philosophy. He bases the royal authority on a covenant entered into by the governor and the governed.

770 By their own deed their own posterity,
How then could Adam bind his future race?
How could his forfeit on mankind take place?
Or how could heavenly justice damn us all,
Who ne'er consented to our father's fall?

775 Then kings are slaves to those whom they command,
And tenants to their people's pleasure stand.
Add, that the power for property allowed
Is mischievously seated in the crowd;
For who can be secure of private right,

780 If sovereign sway may be dissolved by might?
Nor is the people's judgment always true:
The most may err as grossly as the few;
And faultless kings run down, by common cry,
For vice, oppression, and for tyranny.

785 What standard is there in a fickle rout,
Which, flowing to the mark,° runs faster out?   highwater mark
Nor only crowds, but Sanhedrins may be
Infected with this public lunacy,[6]
And share the madness of rebellious times,

790 To murder monarchs for imagined crimes.[7]
If they may give and take whene'er they please,
Not kings alone (the Godhead's images),
But government itself at length must fall
To nature's state, where all have right to all.

795 Yet, grant our lords the people kings can make,
What prudent men a settled throne would shake?
For whatsoe'er their sufferings were before,
That change they covet makes them suffer more.
All other errors but disturb a state,

800 But innovation is the blow of fate.
If ancient fabrics nod, and threat to fall,
To patch the flaws, and buttress up the wall,
Thus far 'tis duty; but here fix the mark;
For all beyond it is to touch our ark.[8]

805 To change foundations, cast the frame anew,
Is work for rebels, who base ends pursue,
At once divine and human laws control,
And mend the parts by ruin of the whole.
The tampering world is subject to this curse,

810 To physic their disease into a worse.
    Now what relief can righteous David bring?
How fatal 'tis to be too good a king!
Friends he has few, so high the madness grows:
Who dare be such, must be the people's foes:

815 Yet some there were, even in the worst of days;
Some let me name, and naming is to praise.
    In this short file Barzillai[9] first appears;

---

6. The fickle crowd flows and ebbs like the tide, which is pulled back and forth by the moon (hence "lunacy," after the Latin *luna*, or "moon").
7. An allusion to the execution of Charles I.
8. Uzzah was struck dead because he sacrilegiously touched the Ark of the Covenant (2 Samuel

6.6–7).
9. James Butler, duke of Ormond (1610–1688). He was famous for his loyalty to the Stuart cause. He fought for Charles I in Ireland, and when that cause was hopeless, he joined Charles II in his exile abroad. He spent a large fortune on behalf of the

Barzillai, crowned with honor and with years:
Long since, the rising rebels he withstood
820 In regions waste, beyond the Jordan's flood:
Unfortunately brave to buoy the State;
But sinking underneath his master's fate:
In exile with his godlike prince he mourned;
For him he suffered, and with him returned.
825 The court he practiced, not the courtier's art:
Large was his wealth, but larger was his heart:
Which well the noblest objects knew to choose,
The fighting warrior, and recording Muse.
His bed could once a fruitful issue boast;
830 Now more than half a father's name is lost.
His eldest hope,[1] with every grace adorned,
By me (so Heaven will have it) always mourned,
And always honored, snatched in manhood's prime
By unequal fates, and Providence's crime:
835 Yet not before the goal of honor won,
All parts fulfilled of subject and of son; }
Swift was the race, but short the time to run.
O narrow circle, but of power divine,
Scanted in space, but perfect in thy line!
840 By sea, by land, thy matchless worth was known,
Arms thy delight, and war was all thy own:
Thy force, infused, the fainting Tyrians° propped;   *the Dutch*
And haughty Pharaoh found his fortune stopped.
Oh ancient honor! Oh unconquered hand,
845 Whom foes unpunished never could withstand!
But Israel was unworthy of thy name:
Short is the date of all immoderate fame.
It looks as Heaven our ruin had designed,
And durst not trust thy fortune and thy mind.
850 Now, free from earth, thy disencumbered soul
Mounts up, and leaves behind the clouds and starry pole:
From thence thy kindred legions mayst thou bring,
To aid the guardian angel of thy king.
Here stop my Muse, here cease thy painful flight;
855 No pinions can pursue immortal height:
Tell good Barzillai thou canst sing no more,
And tell thy soul she should have fled before:
Or fled she with his life, and left this verse
To hang on her departed patron's hearse?
860 Now take thy steepy flight from heaven, and see
If thou canst find on earth another *he:*
Another *he* would be too hard to find;
See then whom thou canst see not far behind.
Zadoc the priest, whom, shunning power and place,
865 His lowly mind advanced to David's grace:
With him the Sagan of Jerusalem,
Of hospitable soul, and noble stem;

---

king and continued to serve him loyally after the
Restoration.
1. Ormond's son, Thomas, earl of Ossory (1634–

1680), a famous soldier and like his father devoted
to Charles II.

Him of the western dome, whose weighty sense
Flows in fit words and heavenly eloquence.
870 The prophets' sons,[2] by such example led,
To learning and to loyalty were bred:
For colleges on bounteous kinds depend,
And never rebel was to arts a friend.
To these succeed the pillars of the laws,
875 Who best could plead, and best can judge a cause.
Next them a train of loyal peers ascend;
Sharp-judging Adriel, the Muses' friend,
Himself a Muse—in Sanhedrin's debate
True to his prince, but not a slave of state:
880 Whom David's love with honors did adorn,
That from his disobedient son were torn.
Jotham of piercing wit, and pregnant thought,
Indued by nature, and by learning taught
To move assemblies, who but only tried
885 The worse a while, then chose the better side;
Nor chose alone, but turned the balance too;
So much the weight of one brave man can do.
Hushai,[3] the friend of David in distress,
In public storms, of manly steadfastness:
890 By foreign treaties he informed his youth,
And joined experience to his native truth.
His frugal care supplied the wanting throne,
Frugal for that, but bounteous of his own:
'Tis easy conduct when exchequers flow,
895 But hard the task to manage well the low;
For sovereign power is too depressed or high,
When kings are forced to sell, or crowds to buy.
Indulge one labor more, my weary Muse,
For Amiel:[4] who can Amiel's praise refuse?
900 Of ancient race by birth, but nobler yet
In his own worth, and without title great:
The Sanhedrin long time as chief he ruled,
Their reason guided, and their passion cooled:
So dexterous was he in the crown's defense,
905 So formed to speak a loyal nation's sense,
That, as their band was Israel's tribes in small,
So fit was he to represent them all.
Now rasher charioteers the seat ascend,
Whose loose careers his steady skill commend:
910 They like the unequal ruler of the day,
Misguide the seasons, and mistake the way;
While he withdrawn at their mad labor smiles,
And safe enjoys the sabbath of his toils.

---

2. The boys of Westminster School, which Dryden had attended. "Zadoc": William Sancroft, archbishop of Canterbury. "Sagan": Henry Compton, bishop of London. "Him of the western dome": John Dolben, dean of Westminster.

3. Laurence Hyde, earl of Rochester. "Adriel": John Sheffield, earl of Mulgrave. "Jotham": George Savile, marquis of Halifax.

4. Edward Seymour, speaker of the House of Commons.

These were the chief, a small but faithful band ⎫
915   Of worthies, in the breach who dared to stand, ⎬
And tempt the united fury of the land. ⎭
With grief they viewed such powerful engines bent,
To batter down the lawful government:
A numerous faction, with pretended frights,
920   In Sanhedrins to plume the regal rights;
The true successor from the court removed:[5]
The Plot, by hireling witnesses, improved.
These ills they saw, and, as their duty bound,
They showed the king the danger of the wound:
925   That no concessions from the throne would please,
But lenitives[6] fomented the disease;
That Absalom, ambitious of the crown,
Was made the lure to draw the people down;
That false Achitophel's pernicious hate
930   Had turned the Plot to ruin Church and State:
The council violent, the rabble worse;
That Shimei taught Jerusalem to curse.
   With all these loads of injuries oppressed,
And long revolving, in his careful breast,
935   The event of things, at last, his patience tired,
Thus from his royal throne, by Heaven inspired,
The godlike David spoke: with awful fear
His train their Maker in their master hear.
   "Thus long have I, by native mercy swayed,
940   My wrongs dissembled, my revenge delayed:
So willing to forgive the offending age,
So much the father did the king assuage.
But now so far my clemency they slight,
The offenders question my forgiving right.
945   That one was made for many, they contend;
But 'tis to rule; for that's a monarch's end.
They call my tenderness of blood, my fear;
Though manly tempers can the longest bear.
Yet, since they will divert my native course,
950   'Tis time to show I am not good by force.
Those heaped affronts that haughty subjects bring,
Are burdens for a camel, not a king:
Kings are the public pillars of the State,
Born to sustain and prop the nation's weight:
955   If my young Samson will pretend a call
To shake the column, let him share the fall:[7]
But, oh, that yet he would repent and live!
How easy 'tis for parents to forgive!
With how few tears a pardon might be won
960   From nature, pleading for a darling son!
Poor pitied youth, by my paternal care
Raised up to all the height his frame could bear:

---

5. The duke of York had been banished from England.

6. Any medicine that relieves pain.
7. Judges 16.

Had God ordained his fate for empire born,
He would have given his soul another turn:
965   Gulled° with a patriot's name, whose modern sense   *deceived*
Is one that would by law supplant his prince:
The people's brave, the politician's tool;
Never was patriot yet, but was a fool.
Whence comes it that religion and the laws
970   Should more be Absalom's than David's cause?
His old instructor, ere he lost his place,
Was never thought indued with so much grace.[8]
Good heavens, how faction can a patriot paint!
My rebel ever proves my people's saint:
975   Would *they* impose an heir upon the throne?
Let Sanhedrins be taught to give their own.
A king's at least a part of government,
And mine as requisite as their consent;
Without my leave a future king to choose,
980   Infers a right the present to depose:
True, they petition me to approve their choice;
But Esau's hands suit ill with Jacob's voice.[9]
My pious subjects for my safety pray,
Which to secure, they take my power away.
985   From plots and treasons Heaven preserve my years,
But save me most from my petitioners.
Unsatiate as the barren womb or grave;
God cannot grant so much as they can crave.
What then is left but with a jealous eye
990   To guard the small remains of royalty?
The law shall still direct my peaceful sway,
And the same law teach rebels to obey:
Votes shall no more established power control—
Such votes as make a part exceed the whole:
995   No groundless clamors shall my friends remove,
Nor crowds have power to punish ere they prove:
For gods and godlike kings, their care express,
Still to defend their servants in distress.
O that my power to saving were confined:
1000 Why am I forced, like Heaven, against my mind, }
To make examples of another kind?
Must I at length the sword of justice draw?
O curst effects of necessary law!
How ill my fear they by my mercy scan!
1005 Beware the fury of a patient man.
Law they require, let Law then show her face;
They could not be content to look on Grace,
Her hinder parts, but with a daring eye
To tempt the terror of her front and die.[1]
1010 By their own arts, 'tis righteously decreed,
Those dire artificers of death shall bleed.

---

8. The earl of Shaftesbury.
9. Genesis 27.22.

1. Moses was not allowed to see the countenance of Jehovah (Exodus 33.20–23).

Against themselves their witnesses will swear,
Till viper-like their mother Plot they tear:
And suck for nutriment that bloody gore,
1015 Which was their principle of life before.
Their Belial with their Belzebub[2] will fight;
Thus on my foes, my foes shall do me right:
Nor doubt the event; for factious crowds engage,
In their first onset, all their brutal rage.
1020 Then let 'em take an unresisted course,
Retire and traverse, and delude their force:
But when they stand all breathless, urge the fight,
And rise upon 'em with redoubled might:
For lawful power is still superior found,
1025 When long driven back, at length it stands the ground."
    He said. The Almighty, nodding, gave consent;
And peals of thunder shook the firmament.
Henceforth a series of new time began,
The mighty years in long procession ran:
1030 Once more the godlike David was restored,
And willing nations knew their lawful lord.

1681

Mac Flecknoe

Mac Flecknoe   The target of this superb satire, which is cast in the form of a
mock-heroic episode, is Thomas Shadwell (1640–1692), the playwright, with whom
Dryden had been on good terms for a number of years, certainly as late as March
1678. Shadwell considered himself the successor of Ben Jonson and the champion
of the type of comedy that Jonson had written, the "comedy of humors," in which
each character is presented under the domination of a single psychological trait or
eccentricity, his humor. His plays are not without merit, but they are often clumsy
and prolix and certainly much inferior to Jonson's. For many years he had conducted
a public argument with Dryden on the merits of Jonson's comedies, which he thought
Dryden undervalued. Exactly what moved Dryden to attack him is a matter of conjecture: he may simply have grown progressively bored and irritated by Shadwell and
his tedious argument. The poem seems to have been written in late 1678 or 1679
and to have circulated only in manuscript until it was printed in 1682 in a pirated
edition by an obscure publisher. By that time, the two playwrights were alienated by
politics as well as by literary quarrels. Shadwell was a violent Whig and the reputed
author of a sharp attack on Dryden as the Tory author of *Absalom and Achitophel*
and *The Medal*. It was probably for this reason that the printer added the subtitle
referring to Shadwell's Whiggism in the phrase "true-blue-Protestant poet." Political
passions were running high, and sales would be helped if the poem seemed to refer
to the events of the day.

    Whereas Butler had debased and degraded his victims by using burlesque, carica-
ture, and the grotesque, Dryden exposed Shadwell to ridicule by using the devices of
mock epic, which treats the low, mean, or absurd in the grand language, lofty style,
and solemn tone of epic poetry. The obvious disparity between subject and style makes
the satiric point. In 1678, a prolific, untalented writer, Richard Flecknoe, died. Dryden conceived the idea of presenting Shadwell (the self-proclaimed heir of Ben Jonson, the laureate) as the son and successor of Flecknoe—hence *Mac* (i.e., son of)

2. A god of the Philistines. "Belial": the incarnation of all evil.

Flecknoe—from whom he inherits the throne of dullness. Flecknoe in the triple role of king, priest, and poet hails his successor, pronounces a panegyric on his perfect fitness for the throne, anoints and crowns him, foretells his glorious reign, and as he sinks (leaden dullness cannot soar), leaves his mantle to fall symbolically on Shadwell's shoulders. The poem abounds in literary allusions—to Roman legend and history and to the *Aeneid*, to Cowley's fragmentary epic *The Davideis*, to *Paradise Lost*, and to Shadwell's own plays. Biblical allusions add an unexpected dimension of incongruous dignity to the low scene. The coronation takes place in the City, to the plaudits of the citizens, who are fit to admire only what is dull. In 217 lines, Dryden created an image of Shadwell that has fixed his reputation to this day.

Mac Flecknoe

Or a Satire upon the True-Blue-Protestant Poet, T. S.

All human things are subject to decay,
And when fate summons, monarchs must obey.
This Flecknoe found, who, like Augustus,[1] young
Was called to empire, and had governed long;
5   In prose and verse, was owned, without dispute,
Through all the realms of Nonsense, absolute.
This aged prince, now flourishing in peace,
And blest with issue of a large increase,
Worn out with business, did at length debate
10   To settle the succession of the state;
And, pondering which of all his sons was fit
To reign, and wage immortal war with wit,
Cried: " 'Tis resolved; for nature pleads that he
Should only rule, who most resembles me.
15   Sh——[2] alone my perfect image bears,
Mature in dullness from his tender years:
Sh—— alone, of all my sons, is he
Who stands confirmed in full stupidity.
The rest to some faint meaning make pretense,
20   But Sh—— never deviates into sense.
Some beams of wit on other souls may fall,
Strike through, and make a lucid interval;
But Sh——'s genuine night admits no ray,
His rising fogs prevail upon the day.
25   Besides, his goodly fabric[3] fills the eye,
And seems designed for thoughtless majesty:
Thoughtless as monarch oaks that shade the plain,
And, spread in solemn state, supinely reign.
Heywood and Shirley were but types of thee,[4]
30   Thou last great prophet of tautology.[5]

1. In 31 B.C.E. Octavian became the first Roman emperor at the age of thirty-two. He assumed the title Augustus in 27 B.C.E.
2. Thomas Shadwell. The initial and second letter of the name followed by a dash give the appearance, but only the appearance, of protecting Dryden's victim by concealing his name. A common device in the satire of the period.
3. His body. Shadwell was a corpulent man.

4. Thomas Heywood (ca. 1570–1641) and James Shirley (1596–1666), playwrights popular before the closing of the theaters in 1642 but now out of fashion. They are introduced here as "types" (i.e., prefigurings) of Shadwell, in the sense that Solomon was regarded as an Old Testament prefiguring of Christ, the "last [final] great prophet."
5. Unnecessary repetition of meaning in different words.

Even I, a dunce of more renown than they,
Was sent before but to prepare thy way;
And, coarsely clad in Norwich drugget,[6] came
To teach the nations in thy greater name.[7]
35 My warbling lute, the lute I whilom° strung,   *formerly*
When to King John of Portugal[8] I sung,
Was but the prelude to that glorious day,
When thou on silver Thames didst cut thy way,
With well-timed oars before the royal barge,
40 Swelled with the pride of thy celestial charge;
And big with hymn, commander of a host,
The like was ne'er in Epsom blankets tossed.[9]
Methinks I see the new Arion[1] sail,
The lute still trembling underneath thy nail.
45 At thy well-sharpened thumb from shore to shore
The treble squeaks for fear, the basses roar;
Echoes from Pissing Alley Sh—— call,
And Sh—— they resound from Aston Hall.
About thy boat the little fishes throng,
50 As at the morning toast° that floats along.   *sewage*
Sometimes, as prince of thy harmonious band,
Thou wield'st thy papers in thy threshing hand,
St. André's[2] feet ne'er kept more equal time,
Not ev'n the feet of thy own *Psyche's* rhyme;
55 Though they in number as in sense excel:
So just, so like tautology, they fell,
That, pale with envy, Singleton[3] forswore
The lute and sword, which he in triumph bore,
And vowed he ne'er would act Villerius[4] more."
60 Here stopped the good old sire, and wept for joy
In silent raptures of the hopeful boy.
All arguments, but most his plays, persuade,
That for anointed dullness[5] he was made.
    Close to the walls which fair Augusta° bind   *London*
65 (The fair Augusta much to fears inclined),[6]
An ancient fabric,° raised to inform the sight,   *building*
There stood of yore, and Barbican it hight:
A watchtower once; but now, so fate ordains,
Of all the pile an empty name remains.
70 From its old ruins brothel houses rise,

---

6. A coarse woolen cloth. Flecknoe was a Catholic priest.
7. The parallel between Flecknoe, as forerunner of Shadwell, and John the Baptist, as forerunner of Jesus, is made plain in lines 32–34 by the use of details and even words taken from Matthew 3.3–4 and John 1.23.
8. Flecknoe boasted of the patronage of the Portuguese king.
9. A reference to Shadwell's comedy *Epsom Wells* and to the farcical scene in his *Virtuoso*, in which Sir Samuel Hearty is tossed in a blanket.
1. A legendary Greek poet. Returning home by sea, he was robbed and thrown overboard by the sailors, but was saved by a dolphin that had been

charmed by his music.
2. A French dancer who designed the choreography of Shadwell's opera *Psyche* (1675). Dryden's sneer at the mechanical metrics of the songs in *Psyche* is justified.
3. John Singleton (d. 1686), a musician at the Theatre Royal.
4. A character in Sir William Davenant's *Siege of Rhodes* (1656), the first English opera.
5. The anticipated phrase is "anointed *majesty*." English kings are anointed with oil at their coronations.
6. This line alludes to the fears excited by the Popish Plot (cf. *Absalom and Achitophel*, p. 880).

Scenes of lewd loves, and of polluted joys,
Where their vast courts the mother-strumpets keep,
And, undisturbed by watch, in silence sleep.
Near these a Nursery[7] erects its head,
75 Where queens are formed, and future heroes bred;
Where unfledged actors learn to laugh and cry,
Where infant punks° their tender voices try,   *prostitutes*
And little Maximins[8] the gods defy.
Great Fletcher never treads in buskins here,
80 Nor greater Jonson dares in socks[9] appear;
But gentle Simkin[1] just reception finds
Amidst this monument of vanished minds:
Pure clinches° the suburbian Muse affords,   *puns*
And Panton[2] waging harmless war with words.
85 Here Flecknoe, as a place to fame well known,
Ambitiously design'd his Sh——'s throne;
For ancient Dekker[3] prophesied long since,
That in this pile would reign a mighty prince,
Born for a scourge of wit, and flail of sense;
90 To whom true dullness should some *Psyches* owe,
But worlds of *Misers* from his pen should flow;
Humorists and *Hypocrites*[4] it should produce,
Whole Raymond families, and tribes of Bruce.
    Now Empress Fame had published the renown
95 Of Sh——'s coronation through the town.
Roused by report of Fame, the nations meet,
From near Bunhill, and distant Watling Street.[5]
No Persian carpets spread the imperial way,
But scattered limbs of mangled poets lay;
100 From dusty shops neglected authors come,
Martyrs of pies, and relics of the bum.[6]
Much Heywood, Shirley, Ogilby[7] there lay,
But loads of Sh—— almost choked the way.
Bilked stationers for yeomen stood prepared,
105 And Herringman was captain of the guard.[8]
The hoary prince in majesty appeared,
High on a throne of his own labors reared.
At his right hand our young Ascanius sate,
Rome's other hope, and pillar of the state.
110 His brows thick fogs, instead of glories, grace,

7. The name of a training school for young actors.
8. Maximin is the cruel emperor in Dryden's *Tyrannic Love* (1669), notorious for his bombast.
9. "Buskins" and "socks" were the symbols of tragedy and comedy. John Fletcher (1579–1625), the playwright and collaborator with Francis Beaumont (ca. 1584–1616).
1. A popular character in low farces.
2. Said to have been a celebrated punster.
3. Thomas Dekker (ca. 1572–1632), the playwright, whom Jonson had satirized in *The Poetaster*.
4. Three of Shadwell's plays; *The Hypocrite*, a failure, was not published. "Raymond" and "Bruce" (line 93) are characters in *The Humorists* and *The Virtuoso*, respectively.

5. Because Bunhill is about a quarter of a mile and Watling Street little more than half a mile from the site of the Nursery, where the coronation is held, Shadwell's fame is narrowly circumscribed. Moreover, his subjects live in the heart of the City, regarded by men of wit and fashion as the abode of bad taste and middle-class vulgarity.
6. Unsold books eventually went to bakers' shops and privies.
7. John Ogilby, a translator of Homer and Virgil, ridiculed by both Dryden and Pope as a bad poet.
8. "Bilked stationers": cheated publishers, acting as "yeomen" of the guard, led by Henry Herringman, who until 1679 was the publisher of both Shadwell and Dryden.

And lambent dullness played around his face.[9]
As Hannibal did to the altars come,
Sworn by his sire a mortal foe to Rome,[1]
So Sh—— swore, nor should his vow be vain,
115   That he till death true dullness would maintain;
And, in his father's right, and realm's defense,
Ne'er to have peace with wit, nor truce with sense.
The king himself the sacred unction[2] made,
As king by office, and as priest by trade.
120   In his siníster° hand, instead of ball,   *left*
He placed a mighty mug of potent ale;
Love's Kingdom to his right he did convey,
At once his scepter, and his rule of sway;
Whose righteous lore the prince had practiced young,
125   And from whose loins recorded *Psyche* sprung.
His temples, last, with poppies were o'erspread,
That nodding seemed to consecrate his head.[3]
Just at that point of time, if fame not lie,
On his left hand twelve reverend owls did fly.[4]
130   So Romulus, 'tis sung, by Tiber's brook,
Presage of sway from twice six vultures took.
The admiring throng loud acclamations make,
And omens of his future empire take.
The sire then shook the honors[5] of his head,
135   And from his brows damps of oblivion shed
Full on the filial dullness: long he stood, ⎫
Repelling from his breast the raging god; ⎬
At length burst out in this prophetic mood: ⎭
"Heavens bless my son, from Ireland let him reign
140   To far Barbadoes on the western main;[6]
Of his dominion may no end be known,
And greater than his father's be his throne;
Beyond *Love's Kingdom* let him stretch his pen!"
He paused, and all the people cried, "Amen."
145   Then thus continued he: "My son, advance
Still in new impudence, new ignorance.
Success let others teach, learn thou from me
Pangs without birth, and fruitless industry.
Let *Virtuosos* in five years be writ;
150   Yet not one thought accuse thy toil of wit.
Let gentle George[7] in triumph tread the stage,

9. "Ascanius": or Ïulus, son of Aeneas. Virgil referred to him as *"spes altera Romae"* ("Rome's other hope," *Aeneid* 12.168). As Troy fell, he was marked as favored by the gods when a flickering ("lambent") flame played round his head (*Aeneid* 2.680–84).
1. Hannibal, who almost conquered Rome in 216 B.C.E., during the second Punic War, took this oath at the age of nine (Livy 21.1).
2. The sacramental oil, used in the coronation.
3. During the coronation a British monarch holds two symbols of the throne: a globe ("ball") representing the world in the left hand and a scepter in the right. Shadwell's symbols of monarchy are a mug of ale; Flecknoe's dreary play *Love's Kingdom*; and a crown of poppies, which suggest heaviness, dullness, and drowsiness. The poppies also refer obliquely to Shadwell's addiction to opium.
4. Birds of night, appropriate substitutes for the twelve vultures whose flight confirmed to Romulus the destined site of Rome, of which he was founder and king.
5. Ornaments, hence locks.
6. Shadwell's empire is vast but empty.
7. Sir George Etherege (ca. 1635–1691), a writer of brilliant comedies. In the next couplet Dryden names characters from his plays.

Make Dorimant betray, and Loveit rage;
Let Cully, Cockwood, Fopling, charm the pit,
And in their folly show the writer's wit.
155 Yet still thy fools shall stand in thy defense,
And justify their author's want of sense.
Let 'em be all by thy own model made
Of dullness, and desire no foreign aid;
That they to future ages may be known,
160 Not copies drawn, but issue of thy own.
Nay, let thy men of wit too be the same,
All full of thee, and differing but in name.
But let no alien S—dl—y[8] interpose,
To lard with wit[9] thy hungry *Epsom* prose.
165 And when false flowers of rhetoric thou wouldst cull,
Trust nature, do not labor to be dull;
But write thy best, and top; and, in each line,
Sir Formal's[1] oratory will be thine:
Sir Formal, though unsought, attends thy quill,
170 And does thy northern dedications[2] fill.
Nor let false friends seduce thy mind to fame,
By arrogating Jonson's hostile name.
Let father Flecknoe fire thy mind with praise,
And uncle Ogilby thy envy raise.
175 Thou art my blood, where Jonson has no part:
What share have we in nature, or in art?
Where did his wit on learning fix a brand,
And rail at arts he did not understand?
Where made he love in Prince Nicander's vein,[3]
180 Or swept the dust in *Psyche's* humble strain?
Where sold he bargains, 'whip-stitch,[4] kiss my arse,'
Promised a play and dwindled to a farce?[5]
When did his Muse from Fletcher scenes purloin,
As thou whole Eth'rege dost transfuse to thine?
185 But so transfused, as oil on water's flow,
His always floats above, thine sinks below.
This is thy province, this thy wondrous way,
New humors to invent for each new play:
This is that boasted bias[6] of thy mind,
190 By which one way, to dullness, 'tis inclined;
Which makes thy writings lean on one side still,
And, in all changes, that way bends thy will.
Nor let thy mountain-belly make pretense
Of likeness; thine's a tympany[7] of sense.

8. Sir Charles Sedley (1638–1701), wit, rake, poet, and playwright. Dryden hints that he contributed more than the prologue to Shadwell's *Epsom Wells*.
9. This phrase recalls a sentence in Burton's *Anatomy of Melancholy*: "They lard their lean books with the fat of others' works."
1. Sir Formal Trifle, the ridiculous and vapid orator in *The Virtuoso*.
2. Shadwell frequently dedicated his works to the duke of Newcastle and members of his family.
3. In *Psyche*.

4. A nonsense word frequently used by Sir Samuel Hearty in *The Virtuoso*. To "sell bargains" is to answer an innocent question with a coarse or indecent phrase, as in this line.
5. Low comedy that depends largely on situation rather than wit, consistently condemned by Dryden and other serious playwrights.
6. In bowling, the spin given to the bowl that causes it to swerve. Dryden closely parodies a passage in Shadwell's epilogue to *The Humorists*.
7. A swelling in some part of the body caused by wind.

195   A tun° of man in thy large bulk is writ,   *large cask*
     But sure thou'rt but a kilderkin° of wit.   *small cask*
     Like mine, thy gentle numbers feebly creep;
     Thy tragic Muse gives smiles, thy comic sleep.
     With whate'er gall thou sett'st thyself to write,
200   Thy inoffensive satires never bite.
     In thy felonious heart though venom lies,
     It does but touch thy Irish pen,[8] and dies.
     Thy genius calls thee not to purchase fame
     In keen iambics,° but mild anagram.   *sharp satire*
205   Leave writing plays, and choose for thy command
     Some peaceful province in acrostic land.
     There thou may'st wings display and altars raise,
     And torture one poor word ten thousand ways.[9]
     Or, if thou wouldst thy different talent suit,
210   Set thy own songs, and sing them to thy lute."
       He said: but his last words were scarcely heard⎫
     For Bruce and Longville had a trap prepared,   ⎬
     And down they sent the yet declaiming bard.[1] ⎭
     Sinking he left his drugget robe behind,
215   Borne upwards by a subterranean wind.
     The mantle fell to the young prophet's part,[2]
     With double portion of his father's art.

ca. 1679   1682

To the Memory of Mr. Oldham[1]

     Farewell, too little, and too lately known,
     Whom I began to think and call my own:
     For sure our souls were near allied, and thine
     Cast in the same poetic mold with mine.
5   One common note on either lyre did strike,
     And knaves and fools[2] we both abhorred alike.
     To the same goal did both our studies drive;
     The last set out the soonest did arrive.
     Thus Nisus fell upon the slippery place,
10   While his young friend[3] performed and won the race.
     O early ripe! to thy abundant store
     What could advancing age have added more?
     It might (what nature never gives the young)
     Have taught the numbers° of thy native tongue.   *metrics, verse*

8. Dryden accuses Flecknoe and his "son" of being Irish. Ireland suggested only poverty, superstition, and barbarity to 17th-century Londoners.
9. "Wings" and "altars" refer to poems in the shape of these objects as in George Herbert's *Easter Wings* (p. 662) and *The Altar* (p. 661). "Anagram": the transposition of letters in a word so as to make a new one. "Acrostic": a poem in which the first letter of each line, read downward, makes up the name of the person or thing that is the subject of the poem. Dryden is citing instances of triviality and overingenuity in literature.
1. In *The Virtuoso*, Bruce and Longville play this trick on Sir Formal Trifle while he makes a speech.

2. When the prophet Elijah was carried to heaven in a chariot of fire borne on a whirlwind, his mantle fell on his successor, the younger prophet Elisha (2 Kings 2.8–14). Flecknoe, prophet of dullness, naturally cannot ascend, but must sink.
1. John Oldham (1653–1683), the young poet whose *Satires upon the Jesuits* (1681) won Dryden's admiration. This elegy was published in Oldham's *Remains in Verse and Prose* (1684).
2. The objects of satire.
3. Nisus, on the point of winning a footrace, slipped in a pool of blood. His "young friend" was Euryalus (Virgil's *Aeneid* 5.315–39).

15 But satire needs not those, and wit will shine
Through the harsh cadence of a rugged line.[4]
A noble error, and but seldom made,
When poets are by too much force betrayed.
Thy generous fruits, though gathered ere their prime,
20 Still showed a quickness;[5] and maturing time
But mellows what we write to the dull sweets of rhyme.
Once more, hail and farewell;[6] farewell, thou young,
But ah too short, Marcellus[7] of our tongue;
Thy brows with ivy, and with laurels bound;[8]
25 But fate and gloomy night encompass thee around.

1684

A Song for St. Cecilia's Day[1]

I

From harmony, from heavenly harmony
    This universal frame began:
    When Nature underneath a heap
        Of jarring atoms lay,
5   And could not heave her head,
The tuneful voice was heard from high:
        "Arise, ye more than dead."
Then cold, and hot, and moist, and dry,[2]
    In order to their stations leap,
10   And Music's power obey.
From harmony, from heavenly harmony
    This universal frame began:
    From harmony to harmony
Through all the compass of the notes it ran,
15   The diapason[3] closing full in man.

---

4. Dryden repeats the Renaissance idea that the satirist should avoid smoothness and affect rough meters ("harsh cadence").
5. Sharpness of flavor.
6. Dryden echoes the famous words that conclude Catullus's elegy to his brother: "*Atque in perpetuum, frater, ave atque vale*" ("And forever, brother, hail and farewell!").
7. The nephew of Augustus, adopted by him as his successor. After winning military fame as a youth, he died at the age of twenty. Virgil celebrated him in the *Aeneid* 6.854–86. The last line of Dryden's poem is a reminiscence of *Aeneid* 6.866.
8. The poet's wreath (cf. Milton's *Lycidas*, lines 1–2, p. 703).
1. St. Cecilia, a Roman lady, was an early Christian martyr. She has long been regarded as the patroness of music and the supposed inventor of the organ. Celebrations of her festival day (November 22) in England were usually devoted to music and the praise of music, and from about 1683 to 1703 the Musical Society in London annually commemorated it with a religious service and a public concert. This concert always included an ode written and set to music for the occasion, of

which the two by Dryden (*A Song for St. Cecilia's Day*, 1687, and *Alexander's Feast*, 1697) are the most distinguished. G. B. Draghi, an Italian brought to England by Charles II, set this ode to music; but Handel's fine score, composed in 1739, has completely obscured the original setting. This is an irregular ode in the manner of Cowley. In stanzas 3–6, Dryden boldly attempted to suggest in the sounds of his words the characteristic tones of the instruments mentioned.
2. "Nature": created nature, ordered by the Divine Wisdom out of chaos, which Dryden, adopting the physics of the Greek philosopher Epicurus, describes as composed of the warring and discordant ("jarring") atoms of the four elements: earth, fire, water, and air ("cold," "hot," "moist," and "dry").
3. The entire compass of tones in the scale. Dryden is thinking of the Chain of Being, the ordered creation from inanimate nature up to humans, God's latest and final work. The just gradations of notes in a scale are analogous to the equally just gradations in the ascending scale of created beings. Both are the result of harmony.

2

What passion cannot Music raise and quell![4]
  When Jubal struck the corded shell,[5]
  His listening brethren stood around,
  And, wondering, on their faces fell
20   To worship that celestial sound.
Less than a god they thought there could not dwell
   Within the hollow of that shell
   That spoke so sweetly and so well.
What passion cannot Music raise and quell!

3

25   The trumpet's loud clangor
   Excites us to arms,
  With shrill notes of anger,
   And mortal alarms.
  The double double double beat
30   Of the thundering drum
Cries: "Hark! the foes come;
Charge, charge, 'tis too late to retreat."

4

  The soft complaining flute
  In dying notes discovers
35   The woes of hopeless lovers,
Whose dirge is whispered by the warbling lute.

5

  Sharp violins[6] proclaim
Their jealous pangs, and desperation,
Fury, frantic indignation,
40 Depth of pains, and height of passion,
  For the fair, disdainful dame.

6

  But O! what art can teach,
  What human voice can reach,
The sacred organ's praise?
45   Notes inspiring holy love,
Notes that wing their heavenly ways
  To mend the choirs above.

7

Orpheus[7] could lead the savage race;
And trees unrooted left their place,

---

4. The power of music to describe, evoke, or subdue emotion ("passion") is a frequent theme in 17th-century literature. In stanzas 2–6, the poet considers music as awakening religious awe, warlike courage, sorrow for unrequited love, jealousy and fury, and the impulse to worship God.
5. According to Genesis 4.21, Jubal was the inventor of the lyre and the pipe. Dryden imagines Jubal's lyre to have been made of a tortoise shell ("corded shell").
6. A reference to the bright tone of the modern violin, introduced into England at the Restoration. The tone of the old-fashioned viol is much duller.
7. Legendary poet, son of one of the Muses, who played so wonderfully on the lyre that wild beasts ("the savage race") grew tame and followed him, as did even rocks and trees.

50   Sequacious of° the lyre;   *following*
     But bright Cecilia raised the wonder higher:
     When to her organ vocal breath was given,
     An angel heard, and straight appeared,[8]
     Mistaking earth for heaven.

GRAND CHORUS

55   *As from the power of sacred lays*
             The spheres began to move,
         And sung the great Creator's praise[9]
             To all the blest above;
         So, when the last and dreadful hour
60   *This crumbling pageant[1] shall devour,*
         The trumpet shall be heard on high, ⎤
         The dead shall live, the living die, ⎬
         And Music shall untune the sky.[2]   ⎦

1687

Epigram on Milton[1]

Three poets,[2] in three distant ages born,
Greece, Italy, and England did adorn.
The first in loftiness of thought surpassed,
The next in majesty, in both the last:
5   The force of Nature could no farther go;
To make a third, she joined the former two.

1688

CRITICISM

Because Dryden liked to talk about literature, he became a critic, indeed the first comprehensive critic in England. The Elizabethans, largely impelled by the example of Italian humanists, had produced an interesting but unsystematic body of critical writings. Dryden could look back to such pioneer works as George Puttenham's *Art of English Poesy* (1589), Sir Philip Sidney's *Defense of Poesy* (1595), Samuel Daniel's *Defense of Rhyme* (ca. 1603), and Ben Jonson's *Timber, or Discoveries* (1641). These and later writings Dryden knew, as he knew the ancients and the important contemporary French critics, notably Pierre Corneille, Fr. René Rapin, and Nicolas Boileau. Taken as a whole, his critical prefaces and dedications, which appeared between 1664 and 1700, are the work of a man of independent mind who has made his own synthesis of critical canons from wide reading, a great deal of thinking, and the constant prac-

---

8. According to the legend, it was Cecilia's piety, not her music, that brought an angel to visit her.
9. As it was harmony that ordered the universe, so it was angelic song ("sacred lays") that put the celestial bodies ("spheres") in motion. The harmonious chord that results from the traditional "music of the spheres" is a hymn of "praise" sung by created nature to its "Creator."
1. The universe: the stage on which the drama of human salvation has been acted out.

2. The "last trump" of 1 Corinthians 15.52, which will announce the Resurrection and the Last Judgment. Dryden develops his theme of harmony as order in such a way as to give full emphasis of the splendid paradox ("Music shall *untune*") in the final line of the ode.
1. Engraved beneath the portrait of Milton in Jacob Tonson's edition of *Paradise Lost* (1688).
2. I.e., Homer, Virgil, and Milton.

tice of the art of writing. As a critic he is no one's disciple, and he has the saving grace of being always willing to change his mind.

All but a very few of Dryden's critical works (most notably *An Essay of Dramatic Poesy*) grew out of the works to which they served as prefaces: comedies, heroic plays, tragedies, translations, and poems of various sorts. Each work posed problems that Dryden was eager to discuss with his readers, and the topics that he treated proved to be important in the development of the new literature of which he was the principal apologist. He dealt with the processes of literary creation, the poet's relation to tradition, the forms of modern drama, the craft of poetry, and above all the genius of earlier poets: Shakespeare, Jonson, Chaucer, Juvenal, Horace, Homer, and Virgil. For nearly forty years this voice was heard in the land; and when it was finally silenced, a set of critical standards had come into existence and a new age had been given its direction.

From An Essay of Dramatic Poesy[1]

[SHAKESPEARE AND BEN JONSON COMPARED]

"To begin, then, with Shakespeare. He was the man who of all modern, and perhaps ancient poets, had the largest and most comprehensive soul. All the images of Nature were still present to him, and he drew them, not laboriously, but luckily; when he describes anything, you more than see it, you feel it too. Those who accuse him to have wanted learning, give him the greater commendation: he was naturally learned; he needed not the spectacles of books to read Nature; he looked inwards, and found her there. I cannot say he is everywhere alike; were he so, I should do him injury to compare him with the greatest of mankind. He is many times flat, insipid; his comic wit degenerating into clenches, his serious swelling into bombast. But he is always great when some great occasion is presented to him; no man can say he ever had a fit subject for his wit and did not then raise himself as high above the rest of poets,

Quantum lenta solent inter viburna cupressi[2]

The consideration of this made Mr. Hales[3] of Eton say that there was no subject of which any poet ever writ, but he would produce it much better treated of in Shakespeare; and however others are now generally preferred

1. With the reopening of the theaters in 1660, older plays were revived, but despite their power and charm, they seemed old-fashioned. Although new playwrights, ambitious to create a modern English drama, soon appeared, they were uncertain of their direction. What, if anything, useful could they learn from the dramatic practice of the ancients? Should they ignore the English dramatists of the late 16th and early 17th centuries? Should they make their example the vigorous contemporary drama of France? Dryden addresses himself to these and other problems in this essay, his first extended piece of criticism. Its purpose, he tells us, was "chiefly to vindicate the honor of our English writers from the censure of those who unjustly prefer the French before them." Its method is skeptical: Dryden presents several points of view, but imposes none. The form is a dialogue among friends, like the *Tusculan Disputations* or the *Brutus* of Cicero. Crites praises the drama of

the ancients; Eugenius protests against their authority and argues for the idea of progress in the arts; Lisideius urges the excellence of French plays; and Neander, speaking in the climactic position, defends the native tradition and the greatness of Shakespeare, Fletcher, and Jonson. The dialogue takes place on June 3, 1665, in a boat on the Thames. The four friends are rowed downstream to listen to the cannonading of the English and Dutch fleets, engaged in battle off the Suffolk coast. As the gunfire recedes they are assured of victory and order their boatman to return to London, and naturally enough they fall to discussing the number of bad poems that the victory will evoke.
2. As do cypresses among the bending shrubs (Latin; Virgil's *Eclogues* 1.25).
3. The learned John Hales (1584–1656), provost of Eton. He is reputed to have said this to Jonson himself.

before him, yet the age wherein he lived, which had contemporaries with him Fletcher and Jonson, never equaled them to him in their esteem: and in the last king's[4] court, when Ben's reputation was at highest, Sir John Suckling,[5] and with him the greater part of the courtiers, set our Shakespeare far above him. . . .

"As for Jonson, to whose character I am now arrived, if we look upon him while he was himself (for his last plays were but his dotages), I think him the most learned and judicious writer which any theater ever had. He was a most severe judge of himself, as well as others. One cannot say he wanted wit, but rather that he was frugal of it. In his works you find little to retrench[6] or alter. Wit, and language, and humor also in some measure, we had before him; but something of art[7] was wanting to the drama till he came. He managed his strength to more advantage than any who preceded him. You seldom find him making love in any of his scenes or endeavoring to move the passions; his genius was too sullen and saturnine[8] to do it gracefully, especially when he knew he came after those who had performed both to such an height. Humor was his proper sphere:[9] and in that he delighted most to represent mechanic people.[1] He was deeply conversant in the ancients, both Greek and Latin, and he borrowed boldly from them: there is scarce a poet or historian among the Roman authors of those times whom he has not translated in *Sejanus* and *Catiline*.[2] But he has done his robberies so openly, that one may see he fears not to be taxed by any law. He invades authors like a monarch; and what would be theft in other poets is only victory in him. With the spoils of these writers he so represents old Rome to us, in its rites, ceremonies, and customs, that if one of their poets had written either of his tragedies, we had seen less of it than in him. If there was any fault in his language, 'twas that he weaved it too closely and laboriously, in his serious plays:[3] perhaps, too, he did a little too much Romanize our tongue, leaving the words which he translated almost as much Latin as he found them: wherein, though he learnedly followed the idiom of their language, he did not enough comply with the idiom of ours. If I would compare him with Shakespeare, I must acknowledge him the more correct poet, but Shakespeare the greater wit.[4] Shakespeare was the Homer, or father of our dramatic poets; Jonson was the Virgil, the pattern of elaborate writing; I admire him, but I love Shakespeare. To conclude of him; as he has given us the most correct plays, so in the precepts which he has laid down in his *Discoveries,* we have as many and profitable rules for perfecting the stage, as any wherewith the French can furnish us."

1668

4. Charles I.
5. Courtier, poet, playwright, much admired in Dryden's time for his wit and the easy naturalness of his style.
6. Delete.
7. Craftsmanship.
8. Heavy.
9. In Jonson's comedies the characters are seen under the domination of some psychological trait,

ruling passion, or affectation—i.e., some "humor"—that makes them unique and ridiculous.
1. I.e., artisans.
2. Jonson's two Roman plays, dated 1605 and 1611, respectively.
3. This is the reading of the first edition. Curiously enough, in the second edition Dryden altered the phrase to "in his comedies especially."
4. Genius.

From A Discourse Concerning the Original and Progress of Satire[1]

[THE ART OF SATIRE]

* * * How easy is it to call rogue and villain, and that wittily! But how hard to make a man appear a fool, a blockhead, or a knave without using any of those opprobrious terms! To spare the grossness of the names, and to do the thing yet more severely, is to draw a full face, and to make the nose and cheeks stand out, and yet not to employ any depth of shadowing.[2] This is the mystery of that noble trade, which yet no master can teach to his apprentice; he may give the rules, but the scholar is never the nearer in his practice. Neither is it true that this fineness of raillery[3] is offensive. A witty man is tickled while he is hurt in this manner, and a fool feels it not. The occasion of an offense may possibly be given, but he cannot take it. If it be granted that in effect this way does more mischief; that a man is secretly wounded, and though he be not sensible himself, yet the malicious world will find it out for him; yet there is still a vast difference betwixt the slovenly butchering of a man, and the fineness of a stroke that separates the head from the body, and leaves it standing in its place. A man may be capable, as Jack Ketch's[4] wife said of his servant, of a plain piece of work, a bare hanging; but to make a malefactor die sweetly was only belonging to her husband. I wish I could apply it to myself, if the reader would be kind enough to think it belongs to me. The character of Zimri in my *Absalom*[5] is, in my opinion, worth the whole poem: it is not bloody, but it is ridiculous enough; and he, for whom it was intended, was too witty to resent it as an injury. If I had railed,[6] I might have suffered for it justly; but I managed my own work more happily, perhaps more dexterously. I avoided the mention of great crimes, and applied myself to the representing of blindsides, and little extravagancies; to which, the wittier a man is, he is generally the more obnoxious.[7] It succeeded as I wished; the jest went round, and he was laughed at in his turn who began the frolic. * * *

1693

---

1. This passage is an excerpt from the long and rambling preface that served as the dedication of a translation of the satires of the Roman satirists Juvenal and Persius to Charles Sackville, sixth earl of Dorset. The translations were made by Dryden and other writers, among them William Congreve. Dryden traces the origin and development of verse satire in Rome and in a very fine passage contrasts Horace and Juvenal as satiric poets. It is plain that he prefers the "tragic" satire of Juvenal to the urbane and laughing satire of Horace. But in the passage printed here, he praises his own satiric character of Zimri (the duke of Buckingham) in *Absalom and Achitophel* for the very reason that it is modeled on Horatian "raillery," not Juvenalian invective.

2. Early English miniaturists prided themselves on the art of giving roundness to the full face without painting in shadows.

3. Satirical mirth, good-natured satire.

4. A notorious public executioner of Dryden's time (d. 1686). His name later became a generic term for all members of his profession.

5. *Absalom and Achitophel*, lines 544–68 (p. 892).

6. Reviled, abused. Observe that the verb differed in meaning from its noun, defined above.

7. Liable.

APHRA BEHN
1640?–1689

"A woman wit has often graced the stage," Dryden wrote in 1681. Soon after actresses first appeared in English public theaters, there was an even more striking debut by a woman writer who boldly signed her plays and talked back to her critics. In a dozen years, Aphra Behn turned out at least that many plays, discovering fresh dramatic possibilities in casts that included women with warm bodies and clever heads. She also drew attention as a warm and witty poet of love. When writing for the stage became less profitable, she turned to the emerging field of prose fiction, composing a pioneering epistolary novel, *Love Letters Between a Nobleman and His Sister,* and diverse short tales—not to mention a raft of translations from the French, pindarics to her beloved Stuart rulers, compilations, prologues, complimentary verses, all the piecework and puffery that were the stock in trade of the Restoration town wit. She worked in haste and with flair for nearly two decades and more than held her own as a professional writer. In the end, no author of her time—except Dryden himself—proved more versatile, more alive to new currents of thought, or more inventive in recasting fashionable forms.

Much of Behn's life remains a mystery. Although her books have been accompanied—and often all but buried—by volumes of rumor, hard facts are elusive. She was almost certainly from East Kent; she may well have been named Johnson. But she herself seems to have left no record of her date and place of birth, her family name and upbringing, or the identity of the shadowy Mr. Behn whom she reportedly married. Her many references to nuns and convents, as well as praise for prominent Catholic lords (*Oroonoko* is dedicated to one), have prompted speculation that she may have been raised as a Catholic and educated in a convent abroad. Without doubt, she drew on a range of worldly experience that would be closed to women in the more genteel ages to come. The circumstantial detail of *Oroonoko* supports her claim that she was in the new sugar colony of Surinam early in 1664. Perhaps she exaggerated her social position to enhance her tale, but many particulars—from dialect words and the location of plantations to methods of selling and torturing slaves—can be authenticated. During the trade war that broke out in 1665—which left her "vast and charming world" a Dutch prize—Behn traveled to the Low Countries on a spying mission for King Charles II. The king could be lax about payment, however, and Behn had to petition desperately to escape debtor's prison. In 1670 she brought out her first plays, "forced to write for bread," she confessed, "and not ashamed to own it."

In London, Behn flourished in the cosmopolitan world of the playhouse and the court. Dryden and other wits encouraged her; she mixed with actresses and managers and playwrights and exchanged verses with a lively literary set that she called her "cabal." Surviving letters record a passionate, troubled attachment to a lawyer named John Hoyle, a bisexual with libertine views. She kept up with the most advanced thinking and joined public debates with pointed satire against the Whigs. But the festivity of the Restoration world was fading out in bitter party acrimony. In 1682 Behn was placed under arrest for "abusive reflections" on the king's illegitimate son, the Whig duke of Monmouth (Dryden's Absalom). Her Royalist opinions and the immodesty of her public role made her a target; gleeful lampoons declared that she was aging and ill and once again poor. She responded by bringing out her works at a still faster rate, composing *Oroonoko*, her dedication claims, "in a few hours . . . for I never rested my pen a moment for thought." In some last works she recorded her hope that her writings would live: "I value fame as much as if I had been born a hero." When she died she was buried in Westminster Abbey.

"All women together ought to let flowers fall upon the grave of Aphra Behn," Virginia Woolf wrote, "for it was she who earned them the right to speak their minds."

Behn herself spoke her mind. She scorned hypocrisy and calculation in her society and commented freely on religion, science, and philosophy. Moreover, she spoke as a woman. Denied the classical education of most male authors, she dismissed "musty rules" and lessons and relished the immediate human appeal of popular forms. Her first play, *The Forced Marriage,* exposes the bondage of matches arranged for money and status, and many later works invoke the powerful natural force of love, whose energy breaks through conventions. In a range of genres, from simple pastoral songs to complex plots of intrigue, she candidly explores the sexual feelings of women, their schooling in disguise, their need to "love upon the honest square" (for this her work was later denounced as coarse and impure). *Oroonoko* represents another departure for Behn and prose fiction. It achieves something new both in its narrative form and in extending some of her favorite themes to an original subject: the destiny of a black male hero on a world historical stage.

Oroonoko cannot be classified as fact or fiction, realism or romance. In the still unshaped field of prose narrative—where a "history" could mean any story, true or false—Behn combined the attractions of three older forms. First, she presents the work as a memoir, a personal account of what she has heard and seen. According to a friend, Behn had told this tale over and over; perhaps that explains the conversational ease with which she turns back and forth, interpreting faraway scenes for her readers at home. Second, *Oroonoko* is a travel narrative in three parts. It turns west to a new world often extolled as a paradise, then east to Africa and the amorous intrigues of a corrupt old-world court (popular reading fare), then finally west again with its hero across the infamous "Middle Passage"—over which millions of slaves would be transported during the next century—to the conflicts of a raw colonial world. Exotic scenes fascinate Behn, but she wants even more to talk to people and learn about their ways of life. As in imaginary voyages, from Sir Thomas More's *Utopia* to *Gulliver's Travels* and *Rasselas,* encounters with foreign cultures sharply challenge Europeans to reexamine themselves. Behn's primitive Indians and noble Africans live by a code of virtue, by principles of fidelity and honor, that "civilized" Christians often ignore or betray. Oroonoko embodies this code. Above all, the book is his biography. Courageous, high-minded, and great hearted, he rivals the heroes of classical epics and Plutarch's *Lives* and is equally worthy of fame. Nor does he lack gentler virtues. Like the heroes of seventeenth-century heroic dramas and romances, he shines in the company of women and proves his nobility by his passionate and constant love for Imoinda, his ideal counterpart. Yet finally a contradiction dooms Oroonoko: he is at once prince and chattel, a "royal slave."

Behn handles her forms dynamically, drawing out their inner discords and tensions. In the biography, Oroonoko's deepest values are turned against him. His trust in friendship and scrupulous truth to his word expose him to the treachery of Europeans who calculate human worth on a yardstick of profit. A hero cannot survive in such a world. His self-respect demands action, even when he can find no clear path through the tangle of assurances and lies. Moreover, the colony too seems tangled in contradictions. Behn's travel narrative reveals a broken paradise where, in the absence of secure authority, the settlers descend into a series of unstable alliances, improvised power relations, and escalating suspicions. Here every term—friend and foe, tenderness and brutality, savagery and civilization—can suddenly turn into its opposite. And the author also seems caught between worlds. The cultivated Englishwoman who narrates and acts in this memoir thinks highly of her hero's code of honor and shares his contempt for the riffraff who plague him. Yet her own role is ambiguous: she lacks the power to save Oroonoko and might even be viewed as implicated in his downfall. Only as a writer can she take control, preserving the hero in her work.

The story of Oroonoko did not end with Behn. Compassion for the royal slave and outrage at his fate were enlisted in the long battle against the slave trade. Reprinted, translated, serialized, dramatized, and much imitated, *Oroonoko* helped teach a mass audience to feel for all victims of the brutal commerce in human beings. A hundred years later, the popular writer Hannah More testified to the widening influence of the story: "No individual griefs my bosom melt, / For millions feel what Oroonoko felt." Women especially identified with the experience of personal injustice and everyday indignity—the pain of being treated as something less than fully human. Perhaps it is appropriate that the writer who made the suffering of the royal slave famous had known the pride and lowliness of being "a female pen."

Oroonoko, or The Royal Slave[1]

I do not pretend, in giving you the history of this royal slave, to entertain my reader with the adventures of a feigned hero, whose life and fortunes fancy may manage at the poet's pleasure; nor in relating the truth, design to adorn it with any accidents but such as arrived in earnest to him. And it shall come simply into the world, recommended by its own proper merits and natural intrigues, there being enough of reality to support it, and to render it diverting, without the addition of invention.

I was myself an eyewitness to a great part of what you will find here set down, and what I could not be witness of, I received from the mouth of the chief actor in this history, the hero himself, who gave us the whole transactions of his youth; and though I shall omit for brevity's sake a thousand little accidents of his life, which, however pleasant to us, where history was scarce and adventures very rare, yet might prove tedious and heavy to my reader, in a world where he finds diversions for every minute, new and strange. But we who were perfectly charmed with the character of this great man were curious to gather every circumstance of his life.

The scene of the last part of his adventures lies in a colony in America called Surinam,[2] in the West Indies.

But before I give you the story of this gallant slave, 'tis fit I tell you the manner of bringing them to these new colonies, for those they make use of there are not natives of the place; for those we live with in perfect amity, without daring to command 'em, but on the contrary caress 'em with all the brotherly and friendly affection in the world, trading with 'em for their fish, venison, buffaloes,[3] skins, and little rarities; as marmosets, a sort of monkey as big as a rat or weasel but of a marvelous and delicate shape, and has face and hands like a human creature, and *cousheries*,[4] a little beast in the form and fashion of a lion, as big as a kitten, but so exactly made in all parts like that noble beast, that it is it in miniature. Then for little parakeetoes, great parrots, macaws, and a thousand other birds and beasts of wonderful and surprising forms, shapes, and colors. For skins of prodigious snakes, of which there are some threescore yards in length, as is the skin of one that may be seen at his Majesty's antiquaries'; where are also some rare flies[5] of amazing forms and colors, presented to 'em by myself, some as big as my fist, some less, and all of various excellencies, such as art cannot imitate. Then we

---

1. The text, prepared by Joanna Lipking, is based on the 1688 edition, the sole edition published during Behn's lifetime. The critical edition of G. C. Duchovnay (diss., Indiana, 1971), which collates the four 17th-century editions, has been consulted.

2. A British sugar colony on the South American coast east of Venezuela; later Dutch Guiana.

3. Wild oxen of various species.

4. A name appearing in local descriptions, but the animal is not clearly identified; probably the lion-headed marmoset or perhaps the *cujara* (Portuguese), a rodent known as the rice rat.

5. Butterflies.

trade for feathers, which they order into all shapes, make themselves little short habits of 'em, and glorious wreaths for their heads, necks, arms and legs, whose tinctures are unconceivable. I had a set of these presented to me, and I gave 'em to the King's theater, and it was the dress of the Indian Queen,[6] infinitely admired by persons of quality, and were unimitable. Besides these, a thousand little knacks and rarities in nature, and some of art, as their baskets, weapons, aprons, et cetera. We dealt with 'em with beads of all colors, knives, axes, pins and needles, which they used only as tools to drill holes with in their ears, noses, and lips, where they hang a great many little things, as long beads, bits of tin, brass, or silver beat thin, and any shining trinket. The beads they weave into aprons about a quarter of an ell long, and of the same breadth,[7] working them very prettily in flowers of several colors of beads; which apron they wear just before 'em, as Adam and Eve did the fig leaves, the men wearing a long stripe of linen which they deal with us for. They thread these beads also on long cotton threads and make girdles to tie their aprons to, which come twenty times or more about the waist, and then cross, like a shoulder belt, both ways, and round their necks, arms, and legs. This adornment, with their long black hair, and the face painted in little specks or flowers here and there, makes 'em a wonderful figure to behold.

Some of the beauties which indeed are finely shaped, as almost all are, and who have pretty features, are very charming and novel; for they have all that is called beauty, except the color, which is a reddish yellow; or after a new oiling, which they often use to themselves, they are of the color of a new brick, but smooth, soft, and sleek. They are extreme[8] modest and bashful, very shy and nice of being touched. And though they are all thus naked, if one lives forever among 'em there is not to be seen an indecent action or glance; and being continually used to see one another so unadorned, so like our first parents before the Fall, it seems as if they had no wishes; there being nothing to heighten curiosity, but all you can see you see at once, and every moment see, and where there is no novelty there can be no curiosity. Not but I have seen a handsome young Indian dying for love of a very beautiful young Indian maid; but all his courtship was to fold his arms, pursue her with his eyes, and sighs were all his language; while she, as if no such lover were present, or rather, as if she desired none such, carefully guarded her eyes from beholding him, and never approached him but she looked down with all the blushing modesty I have seen in the most severe and cautious of our world. And these people represented to me an absolute idea of the first state of innocence, before man knew how to sin. And 'tis most evident and plain that simple Nature is the most harmless, inoffensive, and virtuous mistress. 'Tis she alone, if she were permitted, that better instructs the world than all the inventions of man. Religion would here but destroy that tranquillity they possess by ignorance, and laws would but teach 'em to know offense, of which now they have no notion. They once made mourning and fasting for the death of the English governor, who had given his hand to come on such a day to 'em and neither came nor sent, believing when once

---

6. The title character in the 1664 heroic play by Sir Robert Howard and John Dryden, which was noted for its lavish production. There are contemporary records of "speckled plumes" and feather headdresses.
7. About a foot square.
8. Extremely.

a man's word was passed, nothing but death could or should prevent his keeping it. And when they saw he was not dead, they asked him what name they had for a man who promised a thing he did not do. The governor told them, such a man was a liar, which was a word of infamy to a gentleman. Then one of 'em replied, "Governor, you are a liar, and guilty of that infamy." They have a native justice which knows no fraud, and they understand no vice or cunning, but when they are taught by the white men. They have plurality of wives, which, when they grow old, they serve those that succeed 'em, who are young, but with a servitude easy and respected; and unless they take slaves in war, they have no other attendants.

Those on that continent where I was had no king, but the oldest war captain was obeyed with great resignation. A war captain is a man who has led them on to battle with conduct[9] and success, of whom I shall have occasion to speak more hereafter, and of some other of their customs and manners, as they fall in my way.

With these people, as I said, we live in perfect tranquillity and good understanding, as it behooves us to do, they knowing all the places where to seek the best food of the country and the means of getting it, and for very small and unvaluable trifles, supply us with what 'tis impossible for us to get; for they do not only in the wood and over the savannas, in hunting, supply the parts of hounds, by swiftly scouring through those almost impassable places, and by the mere activity of their feet run down the nimblest deer and other eatable beasts; but in the water one would think they were gods of the rivers, or fellow citizens of the deep, so rare an art they have in swimming, diving, and almost living in water, by which they command the less swift inhabitants of the floods. And then for shooting, what they cannot take, or reach with their hands, they do with arrows, and have so admirable an aim that they will split almost a hair; and at any distance that an arrow can reach, they will shoot down oranges and other fruit, and only touch the stalk with the dart's point, that they may not hurt the fruit. So that they being, on all occasions, very useful to us, we find it absolutely necessary to caress 'em as friends, and not to treat 'em as slaves; nor dare we do other, their numbers so far surpassing ours in that continent.

Those then whom we make use of to work in our plantations of sugar are Negroes, black slaves altogether, which are transported thither in this manner. Those who want slaves make a bargain with a master or captain of a ship and contract to pay him so much apiece, a matter of twenty pound a head for as many as he agrees for, and to pay for 'em when they shall be delivered on such a plantation. So that when there arrives a ship laden with slaves, they who have so contracted go aboard and receive their number by lot; and perhaps in one lot that may be for ten, there may happen to be three or four men, the rest women and children. Or be there more or less of either sex, you are obliged to be contented with your lot.

Coramantien,[1] a country of blacks so called, was one of those places in which they found the most advantageous trading for these slaves, and thither

---

9. Capacity to lead.

1. Not a country but a British-held fort and slave market on the Gold Coast of Africa, in modern-day Ghana. As the slave trade expanded, the slaves and workers shipped out from the region (who came to be called Cormantines) impressed many European observers by their beauty and bearing, their fierceness in war, and their extreme dignity under captivity or torture.

most of our great traders in that merchandise trafficked; for that nation is very warlike and brave, and having a continual campaign, being always in hostility with one neighboring prince or other, they had the fortune to take a great many captives; for all they took in battle were sold as slaves, at least those common men who could not ransom themselves. Of these slaves so taken, the general only has all the profit; and of these generals, our captains and masters of ships buy all their freights.

The King of Coramantien was himself a man of a hundred and odd years old, and had no son, though he had many beautiful black wives; for most certainly there are beauties that can charm of that color. In his younger years he had had many gallant men to his sons, thirteen of which died in battle, conquering when they fell; and he had only left him for his successor one grandchild, son to one of these dead victors, who, as soon as he could bear a bow in his hand and a quiver at his back, was sent into the field, to be trained up by one of the oldest generals to war; where, from his natural inclination to arms and the occasions given him, with the good conduct of the old general, he became, at the age of seventeen, one of the most expert captains and bravest soldiers that ever saw the field of Mars. So that he was adored as the wonder of all that world, and the darling of the soldiers. Besides, he was adorned with a native beauty so transcending all those of his gloomy race that he struck an awe and reverence even in those that knew not his quality; as he did in me, who beheld him with surprise and wonder, when afterwards he arrived in our world.

He had scarce arrived at his seventeenth year, when fighting by his side, the general was killed with an arrow in his eye, which the Prince Oroonoko (for so was this gallant Moor[2] called) very narrowly avoided; nor had he, if the general, who saw the arrow shot, and perceiving it aimed at the Prince, had not bowed his head between, on purpose to receive it in his own body rather than it should touch that of the Prince, and so saved him.

'Twas then, afflicted as Oroonoko was, that he was proclaimed general in the old man's place; and then it was, at the finishing of that war, which had continued for two years, that the Prince came to court, where he had hardly been a month together from the time of his fifth year to that of seventeen; and 'twas amazing to imagine where it was he learned so much humanity; or to give his accomplishments a juster name, where 'twas he got that real greatness of soul, those refined notions of true honor, that absolute generosity, and that softness that was capable of the highest passions of love and gallantry, whose objects were almost continually fighting men, or those mangled or dead; who heard no sounds but those of war and groans. Some part of it we may attribute to the care of a Frenchman of wit and learning, who, finding it turn to very good account to be a sort of royal tutor to this young black, and perceiving him very ready, apt, and quick of apprehension, took a great pleasure to teach him morals, language, and science, and was for it extremely beloved and valued by him. Another reason was, he loved, when he came from war, to see all the English gentlemen that traded thither, and did not only learn their language but that of the Spaniards also, with whom he traded afterwards for slaves.

I have often seen and conversed with this great man, and been a witness

2. Loosely used for any black-skinned person.

to many of his mighty actions, and do assure my reader the most illustrious courts could not have produced a braver man, both for greatness of courage and mind, a judgment more solid, a wit more quick, and a conversation more sweet and diverting. He knew almost as much as if he had read much. He had heard of and admired the Romans; he had heard of the late civil wars in England, and the deplorable death of our great monarch,[3] and would discourse of it with all the sense and abhorrence of the injustice imaginable. He had an extreme good and graceful mien, and all the civility of a well-bred great man. He had nothing of barbarity in his nature, but in all points addressed himself as if his education had been in some European court.

This great and just character of Oroonoko gave me an extreme curiosity to see him, especially when I knew he spoke French and English, and that I could talk with him. But though I had heard so much of him, I was as greatly surprised when I saw him as if I had heard nothing of him, so beyond all report I found him. He came into the room and addressed himself to me, and some other women, with the best grace in the world. He was pretty tall, but of a shape the most exact that can be fancied. The most famous statuary[4] could not form the figure of a man more admirably turned from head to foot. His face was not of that brown, rusty black which most of that nation are, but a perfect ebony or polished jet. His eyes were the most awful that could be seen, and very piercing, the white of 'em being like snow, as were his teeth. His nose was rising and Roman, instead of African and flat; his mouth the finest shaped that could be seen, far from those great turned lips which are so natural to the rest of the Negroes. The whole proportion and air of his face was so noble and exactly formed that, bating[5] his color, there could be nothing in nature more beautiful, agreeable, and handsome. There was no one grace wanting that bears the standard of true beauty. His hair came down to his shoulders by the aids of art; which was by pulling it out with a quill and keeping it combed, of which he took particular care. Nor did the perfections of his mind come short of those of his person, for his discourse was admirable upon almost any subject; and whoever had heard him speak would have been convinced of their errors, that all fine wit is confined to the white men, especially to those of Christendom, and would have confessed that Oroonoko was as capable even of reigning well, and of governing as wisely, had as great a soul, as politic[6] maxims, and was as sensible of power, as any prince civilized in the most refined schools of humanity and learning, or the most illustrious courts.

This prince, such as I have described him, whose soul and body were so admirably adorned, was (while yet he was in the court of his grandfather), as I said, as capable of love as 'twas possible for a brave and gallant man to be; and in saying that, I have named the highest degree of love, for sure, great souls are most capable of that passion.

I have already said, the old general was killed by the shot of an arrow, by

3. Charles I, beheaded in 1649 during the civil wars between Royalists and Parliamentarians. In 1688, this remark and others would have signaled Behn's ardent support of James II, the last of the Stuart kings, who would be forced into exile within the year.
4. Sculptor.
5. Except for. The singling out of Africans with European looks or moral values is by no means unique to Behn; for example, Edward Long's 1774 *History of Jamaica* reports of the Cormantines that "their features are very different from the rest of the African Negroes, being smaller, and more of the European turn."
6. Shrewd, sagacious.

the side of this prince, in battle, and that Oroonoko was made general. This old dead hero had one only daughter left of his race, a beauty that, to describe her truly, one need say only she was female to the noble male, the beautiful black Venus to our young Mars, as charming in her person as he, and of delicate virtues. I have seen an hundred white men sighing after her, and making a thousand vows at her feet, all vain and unsuccessful. And she was, indeed, too great for any but a prince of her own nation to adore.

Oroonoko coming from the wars (which were now ended), after he had made his court to his grandfather, he thought in honor he ought to make a visit to Imoinda, the daughter of his foster-father, the dead general; and to make some excuses to her, because his preservation was the occasion of her father's death; and to present her with those slaves that had been taken in this last battle, as the trophies of her father's victories. When he came, attended by all the young soldiers of any merit, he was infinitely surprised at the beauty of this fair queen of night, whose face and person was so exceeding all he had ever beheld; that lovely modesty with which she received him; that softness in her look, and sighs, upon the melancholy occasion of this honor that was done by so great a man as Oroonoko, and a prince of whom she had heard such admirable things: the awfulness[7] wherewith she received him, and the sweetness of her words and behavior while he stayed, gained a perfect conquest over his fierce heart, and made him feel the victor could be subdued. So that having made his first compliments, and presented her a hundred and fifty slaves in fetters, he told her with his eyes that he was not insensible of her charms; while Imoinda, who wished for nothing more than so glorious a conquest, was pleased to believe she understood that silent language of newborn love, and from that moment put on all her additions to beauty.

The Prince returned to court with quite another humor than before; and though he did not speak much of the fair Imoinda, he had the pleasure to hear all his followers speak of nothing but the charms of that maid, insomuch that, even in the presence of the old king, they were extolling her and heightening, if possible, the beauties they had found in her. So that nothing else was talked of, no other sound was heard in every corner where there were whisperers, but "Imoinda! Imoinda!"

'Twill be imagined Oroonoko stayed not long before he made his second visit, nor, considering his quality, not much longer before he told her he adored her. I have often heard him say that he admired[8] by what strange inspiration he came to talk things so soft and so passionate, who never knew love, nor was used to the conversation[9] of women; but (to use his own words) he said, most happily some new and till then unknown power instructed his heart and tongue in the language of love, and at the same time, in favor of him, inspired Imoinda with a sense of his passion. She was touched with what he said, and returned it all in such answers as went to his very heart, with a pleasure unknown before. Nor did he use those obligations[1] ill that love had done him, but turned all his happy moments to the best advantage; and as he knew no vice, his flame aimed at nothing but honor, if such a distinction may be made in love; and especially in that country, where men

7. Reverence.
8. Marveled.
9. Company.
1. Benefits.

take to themselves as many as they can maintain, and where the only crime and sin with woman is to turn her off, to abandon her to want, shame, and misery. Such ill morals are only practiced in Christian countries, where they prefer the bare name of religion, and, without virtue or morality, think that's sufficient. But Oroonoko was none of those professors, but as he had right notions of honor, so he made her such propositions as were not only and barely such; but contrary to the custom of his country, he made her vows she should be the only woman he would possess while he lived; that no age or wrinkles should incline him to change, for her soul would be always fine and always young, and he should have an eternal idea in his mind of the charms she now bore, and should look into his heart for that idea when he could find it no longer in her face.

After a thousand assurances of his lasting flame, and her eternal empire over him, she condescended to receive him for her husband, or rather, received him as the greatest honor the gods could do her.

There is a certain ceremony in these cases to be observed, which I forgot to ask him how performed; but 'twas concluded on both sides that, in obedience to him, the grandfather was to be first made acquainted with the design, for they pay a most absolute resignation to the monarch, especially when he is a parent also.

On the other side, the old king, who had many wives and many concubines, wanted not court flatterers to insinuate in his heart a thousand tender thoughts for this young beauty, and who represented her to his fancy as the most charming he had ever possessed in all the long race of his numerous years. At this character his old heart, like an extinguished brand, most apt to take fire, felt new sparks of love and began to kindle; and now grown to his second childhood, longed with impatience to behold this gay thing, with whom, alas! he could but innocently play. But how he should be confirmed she was this wonder, before he used his power to call her to court (where maidens never came, unless for the King's private use), he was next to consider; and while he was so doing, he had intelligence brought him that Imoinda was most certainly mistress to the Prince Oroonoko. This gave him some chagrin; however, it gave him also an opportunity, one day when the Prince was a-hunting, to wait on a man of quality, as his slave and attendant, who should go and make a present to Imoinda as from the Prince; he should then, unknown, see this fair maid, and have an opportunity to hear what message she would return the Prince for his present, and from thence gather the state of her heart and degree of her inclination. This was put in execution, and the old monarch saw, and burned. He found her all he had heard, and would not delay his happiness, but found he should have some obstacle to overcome her heart; for she expressed her sense of the present the Prince had sent her in terms so sweet, so soft and pretty, with an air of love and joy that could not be dissembled, insomuch that 'twas past doubt whether she loved Oroonoko entirely. This gave the old king some affliction, but he salved it with this, that the obedience the people pay their king was not at all inferior to what they paid their gods; and what love would not oblige Imoinda to do, duty would compel her to.

He was therefore no sooner got to his apartment but he sent the royal veil to Imoinda, that is, the ceremony of invitation: he sends the lady he has a mind to honor with his bed a veil, with which she is covered, and secured for the King's use; and 'tis death to disobey, besides held a most impious disobedience.

'Tis not to be imagined the surprise and grief that seized this lovely maid at this news and sight. However, as delays in these cases are dangerous and pleading worse than treason, trembling, and almost fainting, she was obliged to suffer herself to be covered and led away.

They brought her thus to court; and the King, who had caused a very rich bath to be prepared, was led into it, where he sat under a canopy, in state, to receive this longed-for virgin; whom he having commanded should be brought to him, they (after disrobing her) led her to the bath, and making fast the doors, left her to descend. The King, without more courtship, bade her throw off her mantle and come to his arms. But Imoinda, all in tears, threw herself on the marble, on the brink of the bath, and besought him to hear her. She told him, as she was a maid, how proud of the divine glory she should have been, of having it in her power to oblige her king; but as by the laws he could not, and from his royal goodness would not, take from any man his wedded wife, so she believed she should be the occasion of making him commit a great sin, if she did not reveal her state and condition, and tell him she was another's, and could not be so happy to be his.

The King, enraged at this delay, hastily demanded the name of the bold man that had married a woman of her degree without his consent. Imoinda, seeing his eyes fierce and his hands tremble (whether with age or anger, I know not, but she fancied the last), almost repented she had said so much, for now she feared the storm would fall on the Prince. She therefore said a thousand things to appease the raging of his flame, and to prepare him to hear who it was with calmness; but before she spoke, he imagined who she meant, but would not seem to do so, but commanded her to lay aside her mantle and suffer herself to receive his caresses; or by his gods, he swore that happy man whom she was going to name should die, though it were even Oroonoko himself. "Therefore," said he, "deny this marriage, and swear thyself a maid." "That," replied Imoinda, "by all our powers I do, for I am not yet known to my husband." " 'Tis enough," said the King; " 'tis enough to satisfy both my conscience and my heart." And rising from his seat, he went and led her into the bath, it being in vain for her to resist.

In this time the Prince, who was returned from hunting, went to visit his Imoinda, but found her gone; and not only so, but heard she had received the royal veil. This raised him to a storm, and in his madness they had much ado to save him from laying violent hands on himself. Force first prevailed, and then reason. They urged all to him that might oppose his rage, but nothing weighed so greatly with him as the King's old age, uncapable of injuring him with Imoinda. He would give way to that hope, because it pleased him most, and flattered best his heart. Yet this served not altogether to make him cease his different passions, which sometimes raged within him, and sometimes softened into showers. 'Twas not enough to appease him, to tell him his grandfather was old and could not that way injure him, while he retained that awful duty which the young men are used there to pay to their grave relations. He could not be convinced he had no cause to sigh and mourn for the loss of a mistress he could not with all his strength and courage retrieve. And he would often cry, "O my friends! Were she in walled cities or confined from me in fortifications of the greatest strength, did enchantments or monsters detain her from me, I would venture through any hazard to free her. But here, in the arms of a feeble old man, my youth, my violent love, my trade in arms, and all my vast desire of glory avail me nothing. Imoinda is as irrecoverably lost to me as if she were snatched by the cold arms of Death. Oh! she is never to be retrieved. If I would wait tedious years, till fate should bow the old king to his grave, even that would not leave me Imoinda free; but still that custom that makes it so vile a crime for a son to marry his father's wives or mistresses would hinder my happiness, unless I would either ignobly set an ill precedent to my successors, or abandon my country and fly with her to some unknown world, who never heard our story."

But it was objected to him that his case was not the same; for Imoinda being his lawful wife, by solemn contract, 'twas he was the injured man and might if he so pleased take Imoinda back, the breach of the law being on his grandfather's side; and that if he could circumvent him and redeem her from the Otan, which is the palace of the King's women, a sort of seraglio, it was both just and lawful for him so to do.

This reasoning had some force upon him, and he should have been entirely comforted, but for the thought that she was possessed by his grandfather. However, he loved so well that he was resolved to believe what most favored his hope, and to endeavor to learn from Imoinda's own mouth what only she could satisfy him in, whether she was robbed of that blessing which was only due to his faith and love. But as it was very hard to get a sight of the women (for no men ever entered into the Otan but when the King went to entertain himself with some one of his wives or mistresses, and 'twas death at any other time for any other to go in), so he knew not how to contrive to get a sight of her.

While Oroonoko felt all the agonies of love, and suffered under a torment the most painful in the world, the old king was not exempted from his share of affliction. He was troubled for having been forced by an irresistible passion to rob his son[2] of a treasure he knew could not but be extremely dear to him, since she was the most beautiful that ever had been seen, and had besides all the sweetness and innocence of youth and modesty, with a charm of wit surpassing all. He found that, however she was forced to expose her lovely person to his withered arms, she could only sigh and weep there, and think of Oroonoko; and oftentimes could not forbear speaking of him, though her life were, by custom, forfeited by owning her passion. But she spoke not of a lover only, but of a prince dear to him to whom she spoke, and of the praises of a man who, till now, filled the old man's soul with joy at every recital of his bravery, or even his name. And 'twas this dotage on our young hero that gave Imoinda a thousand privileges to speak of him without offending, and this condescension in the old king that made her take the satisfaction of speaking of him so very often.

Besides, he many times inquired how the Prince bore himself; and those of whom he asked, being entirely slaves to the merits and virtues of the Prince, still answered what they thought conduced best to his service; which was to make the old king fancy that the Prince had no more interest in Imoinda, and had resigned her willingly to the pleasure of the King; that he diverted himself with his mathematicians, his fortifications, his officers, and his hunting.

2. I.e., grandson.

This pleased the old lover, who failed not to report these things again to Imoinda, that she might, by the example of her young lover, withdraw her heart, and rest better contented in his arms. But however she was forced to receive this unwelcome news, in all appearance with unconcern and content, her heart was bursting within, and she was only happy when she could get alone, to vent her griefs and moans with sighs and tears.

What reports of the Prince's conduct were made to the King, he thought good to justify as far as possibly he could by his actions, and when he appeared in the presence of the King, he showed a face not at all betraying his heart. So that in a little time, the old man being entirely convinced that he was no longer a lover of Imoinda, he carried him with him in his train to the Otan, often to banquet with his mistress. But as soon as he entered, one day, into the apartment of Imoinda with the King, at the first glance from her eyes, notwithstanding all his determined resolution, he was ready to sink in the place where he stood, and had certainly done so but for the support of Aboan, a young man who was next to him; which, with his change of countenance, had betrayed him, had the King chanced to look that way. And I have observed, 'tis a very great error, in those who laugh when one says a Negro can change color, for I have seen 'em as frequently blush, and look pale, and that as visibly as ever I saw in the most beautiful white. And 'tis certain that both these changes were evident, this day, in both these lovers. And Imoinda, who saw with some joy the change in the Prince's face, and found it in her own, strove to divert the King from beholding either by a forced caress, with which she met him, which was a new wound in the heart of the poor dying Prince. But as soon as the King was busied in looking on some fine thing of Imoinda's making, she had time to tell the Prince with her angry but love-darting eyes that she resented his coldness, and bemoaned her own miserable captivity. Nor were his eyes silent, but answered hers again, as much as eyes could do, instructed by the most tender and most passionate heart that ever loved. And they spoke so well and so effectually, as Imoinda no longer doubted but she was the only delight and the darling of that soul she found pleading in 'em its right of love, which none was more willing to resign than she. And 'twas this powerful language alone that in an instant conveyed all the thoughts of their souls to each other, that[3] they both found there wanted but opportunity to make them both entirely happy. But when he saw another door opened by Onahal, a former old wife of the King's who now had charge of Imoinda, and saw the prospect of a bed of state made ready with sweets and flowers for the dalliance of the King, who immediately led the trembling victim from his sight into that prepared repose, what rage, what wild frenzies seized his heart! which forcing to keep within bounds, and to suffer without noise, it became the more insupportable, and rent his soul with ten thousand pains. He was forced to retire to vent his groans, where he fell down on a carpet and lay struggling a long time, and only breathing now and then, "—O Imoinda!"

When Onahal had finished her necessary affair within, shutting the door, she came forth to wait till the King called; and hearing someone sighing in the other room, she passed on, and found the Prince in that deplorable condition, which she thought needed her aid. She gave him cordials, but all in vain, till finding the nature of his disease by his sighs and naming Imoinda.

3. So that.

She told him, he had not so much cause as he imagined to afflict himself, for if he knew the King so well as she did, he would not lose a moment in jealousy, and that she was confident that Imoinda bore, at this minute, part in his affliction. Aboan was of the same opinion, and both together persuaded him to reassume his courage; and all sitting down on the carpet, the Prince said so many obliging things to Onahal that he half persuaded her to be of his party. And she promised him she would thus far comply with his just desires, that she would let Imoinda know how faithful he was, what he suffered, and what he said.

This discourse lasted till the King called, which gave Oroonoko a certain satisfaction, and with the hope Onahal had made him conceive, he assumed a look as gay as 'twas possible a man in his circumstances could do; and presently after, he was called in with the rest who waited without. The King commanded music to be brought, and several of his young wives and mistresses came all together by his command to dance before him; where Imoinda performed her part with an air and grace so passing all the rest as her beauty was above 'em, and received the present ordained as a prize. The Prince was every moment more charmed with the new beauties and graces he beheld in this fair one. And while he gazed, and she danced, Onahal was retired to a window with Aboan.

This Onahal, as I said, was one of the cast[4] mistresses of the old king; and 'twas these (now past their beauty) that were made guardians or governants[5] to the new and the young ones, and whose business it was to teach them all those wanton arts of love with which they prevailed and charmed heretofore in their turn; and who now treated the triumphing happy ones with all the severity, as to liberty and freedom, that was possible, in revenge of those honors they rob them of; envying them those satisfactions, those gallantries and presents, that were once made to themselves, while youth and beauty lasted, and which they now saw pass regardless by, and paid only to the bloomings. And certainly nothing is more afflicting to a decayed beauty than to behold in itself declining charms that were once adored, and to find those caresses paid to new beauties to which once she laid a claim; to hear 'em whisper as she passes by, "That once was a delicate woman." These abandoned ladies therefore endeavor to revenge all the despites[6] and decays of time on these flourishing happy ones. And 'twas this severity that gave Oroonoko a thousand fears he should never prevail with Onahal to see Imoinda. But, as I said, she was now retired to a window with Aboan.

This young man was not only one of the best quality,[7] but a man extremely well made and beautiful; and coming often to attend the King to the Otan, he had subdued the heart of the antiquated Onahal, which had not forgot how pleasant it was to be in love. And though she had some decays in her face, she had none in her sense and wit; she was there agreeable still, even to Aboan's youth, so that he took pleasure in entertaining her with discourses of love. He knew also that to make his court to these she-favorites was the way to be great, these being the persons that do all affairs and business at court. He had also observed that she had given him glances more tender and inviting than she had done to others of his quality. And now, when he saw

---

4. Cast-off.
5. Female teachers or chaperones.
6. Insults.
7. Rank.

that her favor could so absolutely oblige the Prince, he failed not to sigh in her ear and to look with eyes all soft upon her, and give her hope that she had made some impressions on his heart. He found her pleased at this, and making a thousand advances to him; but the ceremony ending and the King departing broke up the company for that day, and his conversation.

Aboan failed not that night to tell the Prince of his success, and how advantageous the service of Onahal might be to his amour with Imoinda. The Prince was overjoyed with this good news and besought him, if it were possible, to caress her so as to engage her entirely, which he could not fail to do, if he complied with her desires. "For then," said the Prince, "her life lying at your mercy, she must grant you the request you make in my behalf." Aboan understood him, and assured him he would make love so effectually that he would defy the most expert mistress of the art to find out whether he dissembled it or had it really. And 'twas with impatience they waited the next opportunity of going to the Otan.

The wars came on, the time of taking the field approached, and 'twas impossible for the Prince to delay his going at the head of his army to encounter the enemy. So that every day seemed a tedious year till he saw his Imoinda, for he believed he could not live if he were forced away without being so happy. 'Twas with impatience, therefore, that he expected the next visit the King would make, and according to his wish, it was not long.

The parley of the eyes of these two lovers had not passed so secretly but an old jealous lover could spy it; or rather, he wanted not flatterers who told him they observed it. So that the Prince was hastened to the camp, and this was the last visit he found he should make to the Otan; he therefore urged Aboan to make the best of this last effort, and to explain himself so to Onahal that she, deferring her enjoyment of her young lover no longer, might make way for the Prince to speak to Imoinda.

The whole affair being agreed on between the Prince and Aboan, they attended the King, as the custom was, to the Otan, where, while the whole company was taken up in beholding the dancing and antic postures the women-royal made to divert the King, Onahal singled out Aboan, whom she found most pliable to her wish. When she had him where she believed she could not be heard, she sighed to him, and softly cried, "Ah, Aboan! When will you be sensible of my passion? I confess it with my mouth, because I would not give my eyes the lie; and you have but too much already perceived they have confessed my flame. Nor would I have you believe that because I am the abandoned mistress of a king, I esteem myself altogether divested of charms. No, Aboan; I have still a rest[8] of beauty enough engaging, and have learned to please too well not to be desirable. I can have lovers still, but will have none but Aboan." "Madam," replied the half-feigning youth, "you have already, by my eyes, found you can still conquer, and I believe 'tis in pity of me you condescend to this kind confession. But, Madam, words are used to be so small a part of our country courtship, that 'tis rare one can get so happy an opportunity as to tell one's heart, and those few minutes we have are forced to be snatched for more certain proofs of love than speaking and sighing; and such I languish for."

He spoke this with such a tone that she hoped it true, and could not

8. Remnant.

forbear believing it; and being wholly transported with joy, for having subdued the finest of all the King's subjects to her desires, she took from her ears two large pearls and commanded him to wear 'em in his. He would have refused 'em, crying, "Madam, these are not the proofs of your love that I expect; 'tis opportunity, 'tis a lone hour only, that can make me happy." But forcing the pearls into his hand, she whispered softly to him, "Oh! Do not fear a woman's invention, when love sets her a-thinking." And pressing his hand, she cried, "This night you shall be happy. Come to the gate of the orange groves behind the Otan, and I will be ready, about midnight, to receive you." 'Twas thus agreed, and she left him, that no notice might be taken of their speaking together.

The ladies were still dancing, and the King, laid on a carpet, with a great deal of pleasure was beholding them, especially Imoinda, who that day appeared more lovely than ever, being enlivened with the good tidings Onahal had brought her of the constant passion the Prince had for her. The Prince was laid on another carpet at the other end of the room, with his eyes fixed on the object of his soul; and as she turned or moved, so did they, and she alone gave his eyes and soul their motions. Nor did Imoinda employ her eyes to any other use than in beholding with infinite pleasure the joy she produced in those of the Prince. But while she was more regarding him than the steps she took, she chanced to fall, and so near him as that, leaping with extreme force from the carpet, he caught her in his arms as she fell; and 'twas visible to the whole presence[9] the joy wherewith he received her. He clasped her close to his bosom, and quite forgot that reverence that was due to the mistress of a king, and that punishment that is the reward of a boldness of this nature; and had not the presence of mind of Imoinda (fonder of his safety than her own) befriended him, in making her spring from his arms and fall into her dance again, he had at that instant met his death; for the old king, jealous to the last degree, rose up in rage, broke all the diversion, and led Imoinda to her apartment, and sent out word to the Prince to go immediately to the camp, and that if he were found another night in court he should suffer the death ordained for disobedient offenders.

You may imagine how welcome this news was to Oroonoko, whose unseasonable transport and caress of Imoinda was blamed by all men that loved him; and now he perceived his fault, yet cried that for such another moment, he would be content to die.

All the Otan was in disorder about this accident; and Onahal was particularly concerned, because on the Prince's stay depended her happiness, for she could no longer expect that of Aboan. So that ere they departed, they contrived it so that the Prince and he should come both that night to the grove of the Otan, which was all of oranges and citrons, and that there they should wait her orders.

They parted thus, with grief enough, till night, leaving the King in possession of the lovely maid. But nothing could appease the jealousy of the old lover. He would not be imposed on, but would have it that Imoinda made a false step on purpose to fall into Oroonoko's bosom, and that all things looked like a design on both sides; and 'twas in vain she protested her innocence. He was old and obstinate, and left her more than half assured that his fear was true.

9. Company.

The King going to his apartment sent to know where the Prince was, and if he intended to obey his command. The messenger returned and told him, he found the Prince pensive and altogether unpreparing for the campaign, that he lay negligently on the ground, and answered very little. This confirmed the jealousy of the King, and he commanded that they should very narrowly and privately watch his motions, and that he should not stir from his apartment but one spy or other should be employed to watch him. So that the hour approaching wherein he was to go to the citron grove, and taking only Aboan along with him, he leaves his apartment, and was watched to the very gate of the Otan, where he was seen to enter, and where they left him, to carry back the tidings to the King.

Oroonoko and Aboan were no sooner entered but Onahal led the Prince to the apartment of Imoinda, who, not knowing anything of her happiness, was laid in bed. But Onahal only left him in her chamber, to make the best of his opportunity, and took her dear Aboan to her own, where he showed the heighth of complaisance for his prince, when, to give him an opportunity, he suffered himself to be caressed in bed by Onahal.

The Prince softly wakened Imoinda, who was not a little surprised with joy to find him there; and yet she trembled with a thousand fears. I believe he omitted saying nothing to this young maid that might persuade her to suffer him to seize his own, and take the rights of love; and I believe she was not long resisting those arms where she so longed to be; and having opportunity, night and silence, youth, love and desire, he soon prevailed, and ravished in a moment what his old grandfather had been endeavoring for so many months.

'Tis not to be imagined the satisfaction of these two young lovers; nor the vows she made him that she remained a spotless maid till that night, and that what she did with his grandfather had robbed him of no part of her virgin honor, the gods in mercy and justice having reserved that for her plighted lord, to whom of right it belonged. And 'tis impossible to express the transports he suffered, while he listened to a discourse so charming from her loved lips, and clasped that body in his arms for whom he had so long languished; and nothing now afflicted him but his sudden departure from her; for he told her the necessity and his commands, but should depart satisfied in this, that since the old king had hitherto not been able to deprive him of those enjoyments which only belonged to him, he believed for the future he would be less able to injure him; so that abating the scandal of the veil, which was no otherwise so than that she was wife to another, he believed her safe, even in the arms of the King, and innocent; yet would he have ventured at the conquest of the world, and have given it all, to have had her avoided that honor of receiving the royal veil. 'Twas thus, between a thousand caresses, that both bemoaned the hard fate of youth and beauty, so liable to that cruel promotion. 'Twas a glory that could well have been spared here, though desired and aimed at by all the young females of that kingdom.

But while they were thus fondly employed, forgetting how time ran on, and that the dawn must conduct him far away from his only happiness, they heard a great noise in the Otan, and unusual voices of men; at which the Prince, starting from the arms of the frighted Imoinda, ran to a little battle-ax he used to wear by his side, and having not so much leisure as to put on his habit, he opposed himself against some who were already opening the door; which they did with so much violence that Oroonoko was not able to defend it, but was forced to cry out with a commanding voice, "Whoever ye are that have the boldness to attempt to approach this apartment thus rudely, know that I, the Prince Oroonoko, will revenge it with the certain death of him that first enters. Therefore stand back, and know, this place is sacred to love and me this night; tomorrow 'tis the King's."

This he spoke with a voice so resolved and assured that they soon retired from the door, but cried, " 'Tis by the King's command we are come; and being satisfied by thy voice, O Prince, as much as if we had entered, we can report to the King the truth of all his fears, and leave thee to provide for thy own safety, as thou art advised by thy friends."

At these words they departed, and left the Prince to take a short and sad leave of his Imoinda, who, trusting in the strength of her charms, believed she should appease the fury of a jealous king by saying she was surprised, and that it was by force of arms he got into her apartment. All her concern now was for his life, and therefore she hastened him to the camp, and with much ado prevailed on him to go. Nor was it she alone that prevailed; Aboan and Onahal both pleaded, and both assured him of a lie that should be well enough contrived to secure Imoinda. So that at last, with a heart sad as death, dying eyes, and sighing soul, Oroonoko departed and took his way to the camp.

It was not long after the King in person came to the Otan, where, beholding Imoinda with rage in his eyes, he upbraided her wickedness and perfidy, and threatening her royal lover, she fell on her face at his feet, bedewing the floor with her tears and imploring his pardon for a fault which she had not with her will committed, as Onahal, who was also prostrate with her, could testify; that unknown to her, he had broke into her apartment, and ravished her. She spoke this much against her conscience, but to save her own life 'twas absolutely necessary she should feign this falsity. She knew it could not injure the Prince, he being fled to an army that would stand by him against any injuries that should assault him. However, this last thought of Imoinda's being ravished changed the measures of his revenge; and whereas before he designed to be himself her executioner, he now resolved she should not die. But as it is the greatest crime in nature amongst 'em to touch a woman after having been possessed by a son, a father, or a brother, so now he looked on Imoinda as a polluted thing, wholly unfit for his embrace; nor would he resign her to his grandson, because she had received the royal veil. He therefore removes her from the Otan, with Onahal; whom he put into safe hands, with order they should be both sold off as slaves to another country, either Christian or heathen; 'twas no matter where.

This cruel sentence, worse than death, they implored might be reversed; but their prayers were vain, and it was put in execution accordingly, and that with so much secrecy that none, either without or within the Otan, knew anything of their absence or their destiny.

The old king, nevertheless, executed this with a great deal of reluctancy; but he believed he had made a very great conquest over himself, when he had once resolved, and had performed what he resolved. He believed now that his love had been unjust, and that he could not expect the gods, or Captain of the Clouds (as they call the unknown power), should suffer a better consequence from so ill a cause. He now begins to hold Oroonoko excused, and to say he had reason for what he did. And now everybody could assure the King how passionately Imoinda was beloved by the Prince; even those confessed it now, who said the contrary before his flame was abated. So that the King being old, and not able to defend himself in war, and having no sons of all his race remaining alive but only this, to maintain him on his throne; and looking on this as a man disobliged, first by the rape of his mistress, or rather wife; and now by depriving of him wholly of her, he feared, might make him desperate and do some cruel thing, either to himself or his old grandfather, the offender: he began to repent him extremely of the contempt he had, in his rage, put on Imoinda. Besides, he considered he ought in honor to have killed her for this offense, if it had been one. He ought to have had so much value and consideration for a maid of her quality as to have nobly put her to death, and not to have sold her like a common slave, the greatest revenge and the most disgraceful of any; and to which they a thousand times prefer death, and implore it, as Imoinda did, but could not obtain that honor. Seeing therefore it was certain that Oroonoko would highly resent this affront, he thought good to make some excuse for his rashness to him; and to that end he sent a messenger to the camp, with orders to treat with him about the matter, to gain his pardon, and to endeavor to mitigate his grief; but that by no means he should tell him she was sold, but secretly put to death, for he knew he should never obtain his pardon for the other.

When the messenger came, he found the Prince upon the point of engaging with the enemy; but as soon as he heard of the arrival of the messenger, he commanded him to his tent, where he embraced him and received him with joy; which was soon abated by the downcast looks of the messenger, who was instantly demanded the cause by Oroonoko, who, impatient of delay, asked a thousand questions in a breath, and all concerning Imoinda. But there needed little return, for he could almost answer himself of all he demanded, from his sighs and eyes. At last, the messenger casting himself at the Prince's feet, and kissing them with all the submission of a man that had something to implore which he dreaded to utter, he besought him to hear with calmness what he had to deliver to him, and to call up all his noble and heroic courage to encounter with his words, and defend himself against the ungrateful[1] things he must relate. Oroonoko replied, with a deep sigh and a languishing voice, "I am armed against their worst efforts—; for I know they will tell me, Imoinda is no more—and after that, you may spare the rest." Then, commanding him to rise, he laid himself on a carpet, under a rich pavilion, and remained a good while silent, and was hardly heard to sigh. When he was come a little to himself, the messenger asked him leave to deliver that part of his embassy which the Prince had not yet divined. And the Prince cried, "I permit thee—." Then he told him the affliction the old king was in, for the rashness he had committed in his cruelty to Imoinda; and how he deigned to ask pardon for his offense, and to implore the Prince would not suffer that loss to touch his heart too sensibly, which now all the gods could not restore him, but might recompense him in glory, which he begged he would pursue; and that Death, that common revenger of all injuries, would soon even the account between him and a feeble old man.

Oroonoko bade him return his duty to his lord and master, and to assure

1. Offensive.

him, there was no account of revenge to be adjusted between them; if there were, 'twas he was the aggressor, and that Death would be just and, maugre[2] his age, would see him righted; and he was contented to leave his share of glory to youths more fortunate and worthy of that favor from the gods. That henceforth he would never lift a weapon or draw a bow, but abandon the small remains of his life to sighs and tears, and the continual thoughts of what his lord and grandfather had thought good to send out of the world, with all that youth, that innocence, and beauty.

After having spoken this, whatever his greatest officers and men of the best rank could do, they could not raise him from the carpet, or persuade him to action and resolutions of life; but commanding all to retire, he shut himself into his pavilion all that day, while the enemy was ready to engage; and wondering at the delay, the whole body of the chief of the army then addressed themselves to him, and to whom they had much ado to get admittance. They fell on their faces at the foot of his carpet, where they lay and besought him with earnest prayers and tears to lead 'em forth to battle, and not let the enemy take advantages of them; and implored him to have regard to his glory, and to the world, that depended on his courage and conduct. But he made no other reply to all their supplications but this, that he had now no more business for glory; and for the world, it was a trifle not worth his care. "Go," continued he, sighing, "and divide it amongst you; and reap with joy what you so vainly prize, and leave me to my more welcome destiny."

They then demanded what they should do, and whom he would constitute in his room, that the confusion of ambitious youth and power might not ruin their order and make them a prey to the enemy. He replied, he would not give himself the trouble—; but wished 'em to choose the bravest man amongst 'em, let his quality or birth be what it would. "For, O my friends!" said he, "it is not titles make men brave or good, or birth that bestows courage and generosity, or makes the owner happy. Believe this, when you behold Oroonoko, the most wretched and abandoned by fortune of all the creation of the gods." So turning himself about, he would make no more reply to all they could urge or implore.

The army, beholding their officers return unsuccessful, with sad faces and ominous looks that presaged no good luck, suffered a thousand fears to take possession of their hearts, and the enemy to come even upon 'em, before they would provide for their safety by any defense; and though they were assured by some, who had a mind to animate 'em, that they should be immediately headed by the Prince, and that in the meantime Aboan had orders to command as general, yet they were so dismayed for want of that great example of bravery that they could make but a very feeble resistance; and at last downright fled before the enemy, who pursued 'em to the very tents, killing 'em. Nor could all Aboan's courage, which that day gained him immortal glory, shame 'em into a manly defense of themselves. The guards that were left behind about the Prince's tent, seeing the soldiers flee before the enemy and scatter themselves all over the plain, in great disorder, made such outcries as roused the Prince from his amorous slumber, in which he had remained buried for two days without permitting any sustenance to approach him. But in spite of all his resolutions, he had not the constancy of grief to

2. In spite of. Oroonoko is saying that he will die first.

that degree, as to make him insensible of the danger of his army; and in that instant he leaped from his couch and cried, "—Come, if we must die, let us meet Death the noblest way; and 'twill be more like Oroonoko to encounter him at an army's head, opposing the torrent of a conquering foe, than lazily on a couch to wait his lingering pleasure, and die every moment by a thousand wrecking[3] thoughts; or be tamely taken by an enemy, and led a whining, lovesick slave to adorn the triumphs of Jamoan, that young victor, who already is entered beyond the limits I had prescribed him."

While he was speaking, he suffered his people to dress him for the field, and sallying out of his pavilion, with more life and vigor in his countenance than ever he showed, he appeared like some divine power descended to save his country from destruction; and his people had purposely put on him all things that might make him shine with most splendor, to strike a reverend awe into the beholders. He flew into the thickest of those that were pursuing his men, and being animated with despair, he fought as if he came on purpose to die, and did such things as will not be believed that human strength could perform, and such as soon inspired all the rest with new courage and new order. And now it was that they began to fight indeed, and so as if they would not be outdone even by their adored hero; who, turning the tide of the victory, changing absolutely the fate of the day, gained an entire conquest; and Oroonoko having the good fortune to single out Jamoan, he took him prisoner with his own hand, having wounded him almost to death.

This Jamoan afterwards became very dear to him, being a man very gallant and of excellent graces and fine parts; so that he never put him amongst the rank of captives, as they used to do, without distinction, for the common sale or market; but kept him in his own court, where he retained nothing of the prisoner but the name, and returned no more into his own country, so great an affection he took for Oroonoko; and by a thousand tales and adventures of love and gallantry flattered[4] his disease of melancholy and languishment, which I have often heard him say had certainly killed him, but for the conversation of this prince and Aboan, and the French governor he had from his childhood, of whom I have spoken before, and who was a man of admirable wit, great ingenuity and learning, all which he had infused into his young pupil. This Frenchman was banished out of his own country for some heretical notions he held, and though he was a man of very little religion, he had admirable morals and a brave soul.

After the total defeat of Jamoan's army, which all fled, or were left dead upon the place, they spent some time in the camp, Oroonoko choosing rather to remain a while there in his tents than enter into a palace or live in a court where he had so lately suffered so great a loss. The officers, therefore, who saw and knew his cause of discontent, invented all sorts of diversions and sports to entertain their prince; so that what with those amusements abroad and others at home, that is, within their tents, with the persuasions, arguments, and care of his friends and servants that he more peculiarly prized, he wore off in time a great part of that chagrin and torture of despair which the first efforts of Imoinda's death had given him. Insomuch as having received a thousand kind embassies from the King, and invitations to return to court, he obeyed, though with no little reluctancy; and when he did so,

3. Racking.   4. Soothed.

there was a visible change in him, and for a long time he was much more melancholy than before. But time lessens all extremes, and reduces 'em to mediums and unconcern; but no motives or beauties, though all endeavored it, could engage him in any sort of amour, though he had all the invitations to it, both from his own youth and others' ambitions and designs.

Oroonoko was no sooner returned from this last conquest, and received at court with all the joy and magnificence that could be expressed to a young victor, who was not only returned triumphant but beloved like a deity, when there arrived in the port an English ship.

This person[5] had often before been in these countries and was very well known to Oroonoko, with whom he had trafficked for slaves, and had used to do the same with his predecessors.

This commander was a man of a finer sort of address and conversation, better bred and more engaging than most of that sort of men are, so that he seemed rather never to have been bred out of a court than almost all his life at sea. This captain therefore was always better received at court than most of the traders to those countries were; and especially by Oroonoko, who was more civilized, according to the European mode, than any other had been, and took more delight in the white nations, and above all men of parts and wit. To this captain he sold abundance of his slaves, and for the favor and esteem he had for him, made him many presents, and obliged him to stay at court as long as possibly he could. Which the captain seemed to take as a very great honor done him, entertaining the Prince every day with globes and maps, and mathematical discourses and instruments; eating, drinking, hunting, and living with him with so much familiarity that it was not to be doubted but he had gained very greatly upon the heart of this gallant young man. And the captain, in return of all these mighty favors, besought the Prince to honor his vessel with his presence, some day or other, to dinner, before he should set sail; which he condescended to accept, and appointed his day. The captain, on his part, failed not to have all things in a readiness, in the most magnificent order he could possibly. And the day being come, the captain in his boat, richly adorned with carpets and velvet cushions, rowed to the shore to receive the Prince, with another longboat where was placed all his music and trumpets, with which Oroonoko was extremely delighted; who met him on the shore attended by his French governor, Jamoan, Aboan, and about a hundred of the noblest of the youths of the court. And after they had first carried the Prince on board, the boats fetched the rest off; where they found a very splendid treat, with all sorts of fine wines, and were as well entertained as 'twas possible in such a place to be.

The Prince, having drunk hard of punch and several sorts of wine, as did all the rest (for great care was taken they should want nothing of that part of the entertainment), was very merry, and in great admiration of the ship, for he had never been in one before; so that he was curious of beholding every place where he decently might descend. The rest, no less curious, who were not quite overcome with drinking, rambled at their pleasure fore and aft, as their fancies guided 'em. So that the captain, who had well laid his design before, gave the word, and seized on all his guests; they clapping great irons suddenly on the Prince, when he was leaped down in the hold to view

5. The ship's captain.

that part of the vessel, and locking him fast down, secured him. The same treachery was used to all the rest; and all in one instant, in several places of the ship, were lashed fast in irons, and betrayed to slavery. That great design over, they set all hands to work to hoise[6] sail; and with as treacherous and fair a wind, they made from the shore with this innocent and glorious prize, who thought of nothing less than such an entertainment.

Some have commended this act as brave in the captain; but I will spare my sense of it, and leave it to my reader to judge as he pleases.

It may be easily guessed in what manner the Prince resented this indignity, who may be best resembled to a lion taken in a toil; so he raged, so he struggled for liberty, but all in vain; and they had so wisely managed his fetters that he could not use a hand in his defense, to quit himself of a life that would by no means endure slavery, nor could he move from the place where he was tied to any solid part of the ship, against which he might have beat his head, and have finished his disgrace that way. So that being deprived of all other means, he resolved to perish for want of food. And pleased at last with that thought, and toiled and tired by rage and indignation, he laid himself down, and sullenly resolved upon dying, and refused all things that were brought him.

This did not a little vex the captain, and the more so because he found almost all of 'em of the same humor; so that the loss of so many brave slaves, so tall and goodly to behold, would have been very considerable. He therefore ordered one to go from him (for he would not be seen himself) to Oroonoko, and to assure him he was afflicted for having rashly done so unhospitable a deed, and which could not be now remedied, since they were far from shore; but since he resented it in so high a nature, he assured him he would revoke his resolution, and set both him and his friends ashore on the next land they should touch at; and of this the messenger gave him his oath, provided he would resolve to live. And Oroonoko, whose honor was such as he never had violated a word in his life himself, much less a solemn asseveration, believed in an instant what this man said, but replied, he expected for a confirmation of this to have his shameful fetters dismissed. This demand was carried to the captain, who returned him answer that the offense had been so great which he had put upon the Prince that he durst not trust him with liberty while he remained in the ship, for fear lest by a valor natural to him, and a revenge that would animate that valor, he might commit some outrage fatal to himself and the King his master, to whom his vessel did belong. To this Oroonoko replied, he would engage his honor to behave himself in all friendly order and manner, and obey the command of the captain, as he was lord of the King's vessel and general of those men under his command.

This was delivered to the still doubting captain, who could not resolve to trust a heathen, he said, upon his parole,[7] a man that had no sense or notion of the God that he worshipped. Oroonoko then replied, he was very sorry to hear that the captain pretended to the knowledge and worship of any gods who had taught him no better principles than not to credit as he would be credited; but they told him the difference of their faith occasioned that distrust. For the captain had protested to him upon the word of a Christian, and sworn in the name of a great god, which if he should violate, he would

---

6. Hoist.　　　　　　　　　　7. Word of honor.

expect eternal torment in the world to come. "Is that all the obligation he has to be just to his oath?" replied Oroonoko. "Let him know I swear by my honor; which to violate, would not only render me contemptible and despised by all brave and honest men, and so give myself perpetual pain, but it would be eternally offending and diseasing all mankind, harming, betraying, circumventing and outraging all men; but punishments hereafter are suffered by one's self, and the world takes no cognizances whether this god have revenged 'em or not, 'tis done so secretly and deferred so long. While the man of no honor suffers every moment the scorn and contempt of the honester world, and dies every day ignominiously in his fame, which is more valuable than life. I speak not this to move belief, but to show you how you mistake, when you imagine that he who will violate his honor will keep his word with his gods." So turning from him with a disdainful smile, he refused to answer him, when he urged him to know what answer he should carry back to his captain; so that he departed without saying any more.

The captain pondering and consulting what to do, it was concluded that nothing but Oroonoko's liberty would encourage any of the rest to eat, except the Frenchman, whom the captain could not pretend to keep prisoner, but only told him he was secured because he might act something in favor of the Prince, but that he should be freed as soon as they came to land. So that they concluded it wholly necessary to free the Prince from his irons, that he might show himself to the rest; that they might have an eye upon him, and that they could not fear a single man.

This being resolved, to make the obligation the greater, the captain himself went to Oroonoko; where after many compliments, and assurances of what he had already promised, he receiving from the Prince his parole and his hand for his good behavior, dismissed his irons and brought him to his own cabin; where after having treated and reposed him a while, for he had neither eat[8] nor slept in four days before, he besought him to visit those obstinate people in chains, who refused all manner of sustenance, and entreated him to oblige 'em to eat, and assure 'em of their liberty the first opportunity.

Oroonoko, who was too generous not to give credit to his words, showed himself to his people, who were transported with excess of joy at the sight of their darling prince, falling at his feet and kissing and embracing 'em, believing, as some divine oracle, all he assured 'em. But he besought 'em to bear their chains with that bravery that became those whom he had seen act so nobly in arms; and that they could not give him greater proofs of their love and friendship, since 'twas all the security the captain (his friend) could have, against the revenge, he said, they might possibly justly take for the injuries sustained by him. And they all with one accord assured him, they could not suffer enough, when it was for his repose and safety.

After this they no longer refused to eat, but took what was brought 'em, and were pleased with their captivity, since by it they hoped to redeem the Prince, who, all the rest of the voyage, was treated with all the respect due to his birth, though nothing could divert his melancholy; and he would often sigh for Imoinda, and think this a punishment due to his misfortune, in having left that noble maid behind him that fatal night, in the Otan, when he fled to the camp.

---

8. The past form of *eat*.

Possessed with a thousand thoughts of past joys with this fair young person, and a thousand griefs for her eternal loss, he endured a tedious voyage, and at last arrived at the mouth of the river of Surinam, a colony belonging to the King of England, and where they were to deliver some part of their slaves. There the merchants and gentlemen of the country going on board to demand those lots of slaves they had already agreed on, and, amongst those, the overseers of those plantations where I then chanced to be, the captain, who had given the word, ordered his men to bring up those noble slaves in fetters whom I have spoken of; and having put 'em some in one and some in other lots, with women and children (which they call pickaninnies), they sold 'em off as slaves to several merchants and gentlemen; not putting any two in one lot, because they would separate 'em far from each other, not daring to trust 'em together, lest rage and courage should put 'em upon contriving some great action, to the ruin of the colony.

Oroonoko was first seized on, and sold to our overseer, who had the first lot, with seventeen more of all sorts and sizes, but not one of quality with him. When he saw this, he found what they meant, for, as I said, he understood English pretty well; and being wholly unarmed and defenseless, so as it was in vain to make any resistance, he only beheld the captain with a look all fierce and disdainful, upbraiding him with eyes that forced blushes on his guilty cheeks; he only cried, in passing over the side of the ship, "Farewell, sir. 'Tis worth my suffering, to gain so true a knowledge both of you and of your gods by whom you swear." And desiring those that held him to forbear their pains, and telling 'em he would make no resistance, he cried, "Come, my fellow slaves; let us descend, and see if we can meet with more honor and honesty in the next world we shall touch upon." So he nimbly leaped into the boat, and showing no more concern, suffered himself to be rowed up the river with his seventeen companions.

The gentleman that bought him was a young Cornish gentleman whose name was Trefry, a man of great wit and fine learning, and was carried into those parts by the Lord——, Governor,[9] to manage all his affairs. He reflecting on the last words of Oroonoko to the captain, and beholding the richness of his vest,[1] no sooner came into the boat but he fixed his eyes on him; and finding something so extraordinary in his face, his shape and mien, a greatness of look and haughtiness in his air, and finding he spoke English, had a great mind to be inquiring into his quality and fortune; which, though Oroonoko endeavored to hide, by only confessing he was above the rank of common slaves, Trefry soon found he was yet something greater than he confessed, and from that moment began to conceive so vast an esteem for him that he ever after loved him as his dearest brother, and showed him all the civilities due to so great a man.

Trefry was a very good mathematician and a linguist, could speak French and Spanish; and in the three days they remained in the boat (for so long were they going from the ship to the plantation) he entertained Oroonoko so agreeably with his art and discourse, that he was no less pleased with Trefry than he was with the Prince; and he thought himself at least fortunate in this, that since he was a slave, as long as he would suffer himself to remain

---

9. Lord Willoughby of Parham, coproprietor of Surinam by royal grant. John Treffry was his plan-   tation overseer.
1. An outer garment or robe.

so, he had a man of so excellent wit and parts for a master. So that before they had finished their voyage up the river, he made no scruple of declaring to Trefry all his fortunes, and most part of what I have here related, and put himself wholly into the hands of his new friend, whom he found resenting all the injuries were done him, and was charmed with all the greatness of his actions; which were recited with that modesty and delicate sense as wholly vanquished him, and subdued him to his interest. And he promised him on his word and honor, he would find the means to reconduct him to his own country again, assuring him, he had a perfect abhorrence of so dishonorable an action, and that he would sooner have died than have been the author of such a perfidy. He found the Prince was very much concerned to know what became of his friends, and how they took their slavery; and Trefry promised to take care about the inquiring after their condition, and that he should have an account of 'em.

Though, as Oroonoko afterwards said, he had little reason to credit the words of a *backearary*,[2] yet he knew not why, but he saw a kind of sincerity and awful truth in the face of Trefry; he saw an honesty in his eyes, and he found him wise and witty enough to understand honor; for it was one of his maxims, a man of wit could not be a knave or villain.

In their passage up the river they put in at several houses for refreshment, and ever when they landed, numbers of people would flock to behold this man; not but their eyes were daily entertained with the sight of slaves, but the fame of Oroonoko was gone before him, and all people were in admiration of his beauty. Besides, he had a rich habit on, in which he was taken, so different from the rest, and which the captain could not strip him of, because he was forced to surprise his person in the minute he sold him. When he found his habit made him liable, as he thought, to be gazed at the more, he begged Trefry to give him something more befitting a slave, which he did, and took off his robes. Nevertheless, he shone through all; and his osenbrigs (a sort of brown holland[3] suit he had on) could not conceal the graces of his looks and mien, and he had no less admirers than when he had his dazzling habit on. The royal youth appeared in spite of the slave, and people could not help treating him after a different manner, without designing it. As soon as they approached him, they venerated and esteemed him; his eyes insensibly commanded respect, and his behavior insinuated it into every soul. So that there was nothing talked of but this young and gallant slave, even by those who yet knew not that he was a prince.

I ought to tell you that the Christians never buy any slaves but they give 'em some name of their own, their native ones being likely very barbarous and hard to pronounce; so that Mr. Trefry gave Oroonoko that of Caesar, which name will live in that country as long as that (scarce more) glorious one of the great Roman; for 'tis most evident, he wanted[4] no part of the personal courage of that Caesar, and acted things as memorable, had they been done in some part of the world replenished with people and historians that might have given him his due. But his misfortune was to fall in an obscure world, that afforded only a female pen to celebrate his fame; though

---

2. White person or master; a variant of *backra*, from an Ibo word transported with the slaves to Surinam and the Caribbean.

3. Coarse cotton or linen, sometimes called osnaburg, after a German cloth-manufacturing town.
4. Lacked.

I doubt not but it had lived from others' endeavors, if the Dutch, who immediately after his time took that country,[5] had not killed, banished, and dispersed all those that were capable of giving the world this great man's life, much better than I have done. And Mr. Trefry, who designed it, died before he began it, and bemoaned himself for not having undertook it in time.

For the future, therefore, I must call Oroonoko Caesar, since by that name only he was known in our western world, and by that name he was received on shore at Parham House, where he was destined a slave. But if the King himself (God bless him) had come ashore, there could not have been greater expectations by all the whole plantation, and those neighboring ones, than was on ours at that time; and he was received more like a governor than a slave. Notwithstanding, as the custom was, they assigned him his portion of land, his house, and his business, up in the plantation. But as it was more for form than any design to put him to his task, he endured no more of the slave but the name, and remained some days in the house, receiving all visits that were made him, without stirring towards that part of the plantation where the Negroes were.

At last he would needs go view his land, his house, and the business assigned him. But he no sooner came to the houses of the slaves, which are like a little town by itself, the Negroes all having left work, but they all came forth to behold him, and found he was that prince who had, at several times, sold most of 'em to these parts; and from a veneration they pay to great men, especially if they know 'em, and from the surprise and awe they had at the sight of him, they all cast themselves at his feet, crying out in their language, "Live, O King! Long live, O King!" and kissing his feet, paid him even divine homage.

Several English gentleman were with him; and what Mr. Trefry had told 'em was here confirmed, of which he himself before had no other witness than Caesar himself. But he was infinitely glad to find his grandeur confirmed by the adoration of all the slaves.

Caesar, troubled with their over-joy and over-ceremony, besought 'em to rise and to receive him as their fellow slave, assuring them he was no better. At which they set up with one accord a most terrible and hideous mourning and condoling, which he and the English had much ado to appease; but at last they prevailed with 'em, and they prepared all their barbarous music, and everyone killed and dressed something of his own stock (for every family has their land apart, on which, at their leisure times, they breed all eatable things), and clubbing it together,[6] made a most magnificent supper, inviting their *Grandee Captain*, their prince, to honor it with his presence; which he did, and several English with him; where they all waited on him, some playing, others dancing before him all the time, according to the manners of their several nations, and with unwearied industry endeavoring to please and delight him.

While they sat at meat Mr. Trefry told Caesar that most of these young slaves were undone in love with a fine she-slave, whom they had had about six months on their land. The Prince, who never heard the name of love

---

5. In 1667 the Dutch attacked and conquered Surinam, and England ceded it by treaty in exchange for New York.
6. Contributing jointly.

without a sigh, nor any mention of it without the curiosity of examining further into that tale, which of all discourses was most agreeable to him, asked how they came to be so unhappy as to be all undone for one fair slave. Trefry, who was naturally amorous and loved to talk of love as well as anybody, proceeded to tell him, they had the most charming black that ever was beheld on their plantation, about fifteen or sixteen years old, as he guessed; that for his part, he had done nothing but sigh for her ever since she came, and that all the white beauties he had seen never charmed him so absolutely as this fine creature had done; and that no man, of any nation, ever beheld her that did not fall in love with her; and that she had all the slaves perpetually at her feet, and the whole country resounded with the fame of Clemene, "for so," said he, "we have christened her. But she denies us all with such a noble disdain, that 'tis a miracle to see that she, who can give such eternal desires, should herself be all ice and all unconcern. She is adorned with the most graceful modesty that ever beautified youth; the softest sigher—that, if she were capable of love, one would swear she languished for some absent happy man; and so retired, as if she feared a rape even from the god of day,[7] or that the breezes would steal kisses from her delicate mouth. Her task of work some sighing lover every day makes it his petition to perform for her, which she accepts blushing and with reluctancy, for fear he will ask her a look for a recompense, which he dares not presume to hope, so great an awe she strikes into the hearts of her admirers." "I do not wonder," replied the Prince, "that Clemene should refuse slaves, being as you say so beautiful, but wonder how she escapes those who can entertain her as you can do; or why, being your slave, you do not oblige her to yield." "I confess," said Trefry, "when I have, against her will, entertained her with love so long as to be transported with my passion, even above decency, I have been ready to make use of those advantages of strength and force nature has given me. But oh! she disarms me with that modesty and weeping, so tender and so moving that I retire, and thank my stars she overcame me." The company laughed at his civility to a slave, and Caesar only applauded the nobleness of his passion and nature, since that slave might be noble or, what was better, have true notions of honor and virtue in her. Thus passed they this night, after having received from the slaves all imaginable respect and obedience.

The next day Trefry asked Caesar to walk, when the heat was allayed, and designedly carried him by the cottage of the fair slave, and told him she whom he spoke of last night lived there retired. "But," says he, "I would not wish you to approach, for I am sure you will be in love as soon as you behold her." Caesar assured him he was proof against all the charms of that sex, and that if he imagined his heart could be so perfidious to love again, after Imoinda, he believed he should tear it from his bosom. They had no sooner spoke, but a little shock dog[8] that Clemene had presented her, which she took great delight in, ran out; and she, not knowing anybody was there, ran to get it in again, and bolted out on those who were just speaking of her. When seeing them, she would have run in again, but Trefry caught her by the hand and cried, "Clemene, however you fly a lover, you ought to pay some respect to this stranger" (pointing to Caesar). But she, as if she had

7. The sun.
8. A long-haired dog or poodle, especially associated with women of fashion.

resolved never to raise her eyes to the face of a man again, bent 'em the more to the earth when he spoke, and gave the Prince the leisure to look the more at her. There needed no long gazing or consideration to examine who this fair creature was; he soon saw Imoinda all over her; in a minute he saw her face, her shape, her air, her modesty, and all that called forth his soul with joy at his eyes, and left his body destitute of almost life; it stood without motion, and for a minute knew not that it had a being; and I believe he had never come to himself, so oppressed he was with over-joy, if he had not met with this allay, that he perceived Imoinda fall dead in the hands of Trefry. This awakened him, and he ran to her aid and caught her in his arms, where by degrees she came to herself; and 'tis needless to tell with what transports, what ecstasies of joy, they both a while beheld each other, without speaking; then snatched each other to their arms; then gaze again, as if they still doubted whether they possessed the blessing they grasped; but when they recovered their speech, 'tis not to be imagined what tender things they expressed to each other, wondering what strange fate had brought 'em again together. They soon informed each other of their fortunes, and equally bewailed their fate; but at the same time they mutually protested that even fetters and slavery were soft and easy, and would be supported with joy and pleasure, while they could be so happy to possess each other and to be able to make good their vows. Caesar swore he disdained the empire of the world while he could behold his Imoinda; and she despised grandeur and pomp, those vanities of her sex, when she could gaze on Oroonoko. He adored the very cottage where she resided, and said that little inch of the world would give him more happiness than all the universe could do; and she vowed it was a palace, while adorned with the presence of Oroonoko.

Trefry was infinitely pleased with this novel,[9] and found this Clemene was the fair mistress of whom Caesar had before spoke; and was not a little satisfied that heaven was so kind to the Prince as to sweeten his misfortunes by so lucky an accident; and leaving the lovers to themselves, was impatient to come down to Parham House (which was on the same plantation) to give me an account of what had happened. I was as impatient to make these lovers a visit, having already made a friendship with Caesar, and from his own mouth learned what I have related; which was confirmed by his Frenchman, who was set on shore to seek his fortunes, and of whom they could not make a slave, because a Christian, and he came daily to Parham Hill to see and pay his respects to his pupil prince. So that concerning and interesting myself in all that related to Caesar, whom I had assured of liberty as soon as the Governor arrived, I hasted presently to the place where the lovers were, and was infinitely glad to find this beautiful young slave (who had already gained all our esteems, for her modesty and her extraordinary prettiness) to be the same I had heard Caesar speak so much of. One may imagine then we paid her a treble respect; and though, from her being carved in fine flowers and birds all over her body, we took her to be of quality before, yet when we knew Clemene was Imoinda, we could not enough admire her.

I had forgot to tell you that those who are nobly born of that country are so delicately cut and rased[1] all over the forepart of the trunk of their bodies,

9. Novel event or piece of news.
1. Incised. The carving is likened to figured lac-
querwork in the Japanese style and to elaborate "high point" lace.

that it looks as if it were japanned, the works being raised like high point round the edges of the flowers. Some are only carved with a little flower or bird at the sides of the temples, as was Caesar; and those who are so carved over the body resemble our ancient Picts,[2] that are figured in the chronicles, but these carvings are more delicate.

From that happy day Caesar took Clemene for his wife, to the general joy of all people; and there was as much magnificence as the country would afford at the celebration of this wedding: and in a very short time after she conceived with child, which made Caesar even adore her, knowing he was the last of his great race. This new accident made him more impatient of liberty, and he was every day treating with Trefry for his and Clemene's liberty, and offered either gold or a vast quantity of slaves, which should be paid before they let him go, provided he could have any security that he should go when his ransom was paid. They fed him from day to day with promises, and delayed him till the Lord Governor should come; so that he began to suspect them of falsehood, and that they would delay him till the time of his wife's delivery and make a slave of that too, for all the breed is theirs to whom the parents belong. This thought made him very uneasy, and his sullenness gave them some jealousies[3] of him; so that I was obliged, by some persons who feared a mutiny (which is very fatal sometimes in those colonies, that abound so with slaves that they exceed the whites in vast numbers), to discourse with Caesar, and to give him all the satisfaction I possibly could; they knew he and Clemene were scarce an hour in a day from my lodgings, that they eat with me, and that I obliged 'em in all things I was capable of. I entertained him with the lives of the Romans, and great men, which charmed him to my company, and her with teaching her all the pretty works[4] that I was mistress of, and telling her stories of nuns, and endeavoring to bring her to the knowledge of the true God. But of all discourses Caesar liked that the worst, and would never be reconciled to our notions of the Trinity, of which he ever made a jest; it was a riddle, he said, would turn his brain to conceive, and one could not make him understand what faith was. However, these conversations failed not altogether so well to divert him that he liked the company of us women much above the men, for he could not drink, and he is but an ill companion in that country that cannot. So that obliging him to love us very well, we had all the liberty of speech with him, especially myself, whom he called his Great Mistress; and indeed my word would go a great way with him. For these reasons, I had opportunity to take notice to him that he was not well pleased of late as he used to be, was more retired and thoughtful; and told him I took it ill he should suspect we would break our words with him, and not permit both him and Clemene to return to his own kingdom, which was not so long a way but when he was once on his voyage he would quickly arrive there. He made me some answers that showed a doubt in him, which made me ask him what advantage it would be to doubt. It would but give us a fear of him, and possibly compel us to treat him so as I should be very loath to behold; that is, it might occasion his confinement. Perhaps this was not so luckily spoke of me, for I perceived he resented that word, which I strove to soften again in vain. However, he

2. A North British people appearing in histories of England and Scotland.

3. Suspicions.
4. Decorative needlework or other handiwork.

assured me that whatsoever resolutions he should take, he would act nothing upon the white people; and as for myself and those upon that plantation where he was, he would sooner forfeit his eternal liberty, and life itself, than lift his hand against his greatest enemy on that place. He besought me to suffer no fears upon his account, for he could do nothing that honor should not dictate; but he accused himself for having suffered slavery so long; yet he charged that weakness on Love alone, who was capable of making him neglect even glory itself, and for which now he reproaches himself every moment of the day. Much more to this effect he spoke, with an air impatient enough to make me know he would not be long in bondage; and though he suffered only the name of a slave, and had nothing of the toil and labor of one, yet that was sufficient to render him uneasy; and he had been too long idle, who used to be always in action and in arms. He had a spirit all rough and fierce, and that could not be tamed to lazy rest; and though all endeavors were used to exercise himself in such actions and sports as this world afforded, as running, wrestling, pitching the bar,[5] hunting and fishing, chasing and killing tigers[6] of a monstrous size, which this continent affords in abundance, and wonderful snakes, such as Alexander is reported to have encountered at the river of Amazons,[7] and which Caesar took great delight to overcome, yet these were not actions great enough for his large soul, which was still panting after more renowned action.

Before I parted that day with him, I got, with much ado, a promise from him to rest yet a little longer with patience, and wait the coming of the Lord Governor, who was every day expected on our shore; he assured me he would, and this promise he desired me to know was given perfectly in complaisance to me, in whom he had an entire confidence.

After this, I neither thought it convenient to trust him much out of our view, nor did the country, who feared him; but with one accord it was advised to treat him fairly, and oblige him to remain within such a compass, and that he should be permitted as seldom as could be to go up to the plantations of the Negroes or, if he did, to be accompanied by some that should be rather in appearance attendants than spies. This care was for some time taken, and Caesar looked upon it as a mark of extraordinary respect, and was glad his discontent had obliged 'em to be more observant to him. He received new assurance from the overseer, which was confirmed to him by the opinion of all the gentlemen of the country, who made their court to him. During this time that we had his company more frequently than hitherto we had had, it may not be unpleasant to relate to you the diversions we entertained him with, or rather he us.

My stay was to be short in that country, because my father died at sea, and never arrived to possess the honor was designed him (which was lieutenant general of six and thirty islands, besides the continent[8] of Surinam) nor the advantages he hoped to reap by them; so that though we were obliged to continue on our voyage, we did not intend to stay upon the place. Though, in a word, I must say thus much of it, that certainly had his late Majesty, of

5. A game in which players compete in throwing a heavy bar or rod.
6. Wild cats, including the South American jaguar and cougar.
7. Alexander the Great is supposed to have encountered both snakes and Amazons in a campaign against India.
8. "Land not disjoined by the sea from other lands" (Johnson's *Dictionary*).

sacred memory, but seen and known what a vast and charming world he had been master of in that continent, he would never have parted so easily with it to the Dutch. 'Tis a continent whose vast extent was never yet known, and may contain more noble earth than all the universe besides, for, they say, it reaches from east to west, one way as far as China and another to Peru. It affords all things both for beauty and use; 'tis there eternal spring, always the very months of April, May, and June; the shades are perpetual, the trees bearing at once all degrees of leaves and fruit, from blooming buds to ripe autumn: groves of oranges, lemons, citrons, figs, nutmegs, and noble aromatics, continually bearing their fragrancies. The trees appearing all like nosegays adorned with flowers of different kinds; some are all white, some purple, some scarlet, some blue, some yellow; bearing, at the same time, ripe fruit and blooming young, or producing every day new. The very wood of all these trees has an intrinsic value above common timber, for they are, when cut, of different colors, glorious to behold, and bear a price considerable, to inlay withal. Besides this they yield rich balm and gums, so that we make our candles of such an aromatic substance as does not only give a sufficient light, but, as they burn, they cast their perfumes all about. Cedar is the common firing, and all the houses are built with it. The very meat we eat, when set on the table, if it be native, I mean of the country, perfumes the whole room; especially a little beast called an armadilly, a thing which I can liken to nothing so well as a rhinoceros; 'tis all in white armor, so jointed that it moves as well in it as if it had nothing on; this beast is about the bigness of a pig of six weeks old. But it were endless to give an account of all the diverse wonderful and strange things that country affords, and which we took a very great delight to go in search of, though those adventures are oftentimes fatal and at least dangerous. But while we had Caesar in our company on these designs we feared no harm, nor suffered any.

As soon as I came into the country, the best house in it was presented me, called St. John's Hill. It stood on a vast rock of white marble, at the foot of which the river ran a vast depth down, and not to be descended on that side; the little waves still dashing and washing the foot of this rock made the softest murmurs and purlings in the world; and the opposite bank was adorned with such vast quantities of different flowers eternally blowing,[9] and every day and hour new, fenced behind 'em with lofty trees of a thousand rare forms and colors, that the prospect was the most ravishing that fancy can create.[1] On the edge of this white rock, towards the river, was a walk or grove of orange and lemon trees, about half the length of the Mall[2] here, whose flowery and fruit-bearing branches met at the top and hindered the sun, whose rays are very fierce there, from entering a beam into the grove; and the cool air that came from the river made it not only fit to entertain people in, at all the hottest hours of the day, but refreshed the sweet blossoms and made it always sweet and charming; and sure the whole globe of the world cannot show so delightful a place as this grove was. Not all the gardens of boasted Italy can produce a shade to outvie this, which nature had joined with art to render so exceeding fine; and 'tis a marvel to see how such vast

9. Blooming.
1. The original editions read "the most raving that sands can create," altered to "ravishing" in the third edition, which also corrects the next sentence, "fruity bear branches."
2. Fashionable walk in St. James's Park in London.

trees, as big as English oaks, could take footing on so solid a rock and in so little earth as covered that rock; but all things by nature there are rare, delightful, and wonderful. But to our sports.

Sometimes we would go surprising,[3] and in search of young tigers in their dens, watching when the old ones went forth to forage for prey; and oftentimes we have been in great danger and have fled apace for our lives when surprised by the dams. But once, above all other times, we went on this design, and Caesar was with us, who had no sooner stolen a young tiger from her nest but, going off, we encountered the dam, bearing a buttock of a cow which he[4] had torn off with his mighty paw, and going with it towards his den. We had only four women, Caesar, and an English gentleman, brother to Harry Martin, the great Oliverian;[5] we found there was no escaping this enraged and ravenous beast. However, we women fled as fast as we could from it; but our heels had not saved our lives if Caesar had not laid down his cub, when he found the tiger quit her prey to make the more speed towards him, and taking Mr. Martin's sword, desired him to stand aside, or follow the ladies. He obeyed him, and Caesar met this monstrous beast of might, size, and vast limbs, who came with open jaws upon him; and fixing his awful stern eyes full upon those of the beast, and putting himself into a very steady and good aiming posture of defense, ran his sword quite through his breast down to his very heart, home to the hilt of the sword. The dying beast stretched forth her paw, and going to grasp his thigh, surprised with death in that very moment, did him no other harm than fixing her long nails in his flesh very deep, feebly wounded him, but could not grasp the flesh to tear off any. When he had done this, he halloed to us to return, which, after some assurance of his victory, we did, and found him lugging out the sword from the bosom of the tiger, who was laid in her blood on the ground; he took up the cub, and with an unconcern that had nothing of the joy or gladness of a victory, he came and laid the whelp at my feet. We all extremely wondered at his daring, and at the bigness of the beast, which was about the heighth of a heifer but of mighty, great, and strong limbs.

Another time, being in the woods, he killed a tiger which had long infested that part, and borne away abundance of sheep and oxen, and other things that were for the support of those to whom they belonged; abundance of people assailed this beast, some affirming they had shot her with several bullets quite through the body at several times, and some swearing they shot her through the very heart, and they believed she was a devil rather than a mortal thing. Caesar had often said he had a mind to encounter this monster, and spoke with several gentlemen who had attempted her, one crying, "I shot her with so many poisoned arrows," another with his gun in this part of her, and another in that; so that he, remarking all these places where she was shot, fancied still he should overcome her by giving her another sort of a wound than any had yet done; and one day said (at the table), "What trophies and garlands, ladies, will you make me, if I bring you home the heart of this ravenous beast that eats up all your lambs and pigs?" We all promised he should be rewarded at all our hands. So taking a bow, which he choosed out

3. A military term for making sudden raids.
4. The jarring mixture of pronouns in the two accounts of the tigers (wild cats) may suggest a reluctance to use a feminine pronoun in moments of extreme violence. The first account was left uncorrected in all four 17th-century editions.
5. Supporter of Oliver Cromwell.

of a great many, he went up in the wood, with two gentlemen, where he imagined this devourer to be; they had not passed very far in it but they heard her voice, growling and grumbling, as if she were pleased with something she was doing. When they came in view, they found her muzzling in the belly of a new ravished sheep, which she had torn open; and seeing herself approached, she took fast hold of her prey with her forepaws and set a very fierce raging look on Caesar, without offering to approach him, for fear at the same time of losing what she had in possession. So that Caesar remained a good while, only taking aim, and getting an opportunity to shoot her where he designed; 'twas some time before he could accomplish it, and to wound her and not kill her would but have enraged her more, and endangered him. He had a quiver of arrows at his side, so that if one failed he could be supplied; at last, retiring a little, he gave her opportunity to eat, for he found she was ravenous, and fell to as soon as she saw him retire, being more eager of her prey than of doing new mischiefs. When he going softly to one side of her, and hiding his person behind certain herbage that grew high and thick, he took so good aim that, as he intended, he shot her just into the eye, and the arrow was sent with so good a will and so sure a hand that it stuck in her brain, and made her caper and become mad for a moment or two; but being seconded by another arrow, he fell dead upon the prey. Caesar cut him open with a knife, to see where those wounds were that had been reported to him, and why he did not die of 'em. But I shall now relate a thing that possibly will find no credit among men, because 'tis a notion commonly received with us, that nothing can receive a wound in the heart and live; but when the heart of this courageous animal was taken out, there were seven bullets of lead in it, and the wounds seamed up with great scars, and she lived with the bullets a great while, for it was long since they were shot. This heart the conqueror brought up to us, and 'twas a very great curiosity, which all the country came to see, and which gave Caesar occasion of many fine discourses, of accidents in war and strange escapes.

At other times he would go a-fishing; and discoursing on that diversion, he found we had in that country a very strange fish, called a numb eel[6] (an eel of which I have eaten), that while it is alive, it has a quality so cold, that those who are angling, though with a line of never so great a length with a rod at the end of it, it shall, in the same minute the bait is touched by this eel, seize him or her that holds the rod with benumbedness, that shall deprive 'em of sense for a while; and some have fallen into the water, and others dropped as dead on the banks of the rivers where they stood, as soon as this fish touches the bait. Caesar used to laugh at this, and believed it impossible a man could lose his force at the touch of a fish, and could not understand that philosophy,[7] that a cold quality should be of that nature. However, he had a great curiosity to try whether it would have the same effect on him it had on others, and often tried, but in vain. At last the sought for fish came to the bait, as he stood angling on the bank; and instead of throwing away the rod or giving it a sudden twitch out of the water, whereby he might have caught both the eel and have dismissed the rod, before it could have too much power over him, for experiment sake he grasped it but the harder, and fainting fell into the river; and being still possessed of the rod, the tide carried

---

6. Electric eel.
7. "Hypothesis or system upon which natural effects are explained" (Johnson's *Dictionary*).

him, senseless as he was, a great way, till an Indian boat took him up, and perceived when they touched him a numbness seize them, and by that knew the rod was in his hand; which with a paddle (that is, a short oar) they struck away, and snatched it into the boat, eel and all. If Caesar were almost dead with the effect of this fish, he was more so with that of the water, where he had remained the space of going a league, and they found they had much ado to bring him back to life. But at last they did, and brought him home, where he was in a few hours well recovered and refreshed, and not a little ashamed to find he should be overcome by an eel, and that all the people who heard his defiance would laugh at him. But we cheered him up; and he being convinced, we had the eel at supper, which was a quarter of an ell about and most delicate meat, and was of the more value, since it cost so dear as almost the life of so gallant a man.

About this time we were in many mortal fears about some disputes the English had with the Indians, so that we could scarce trust ourselves, without great numbers, to go to any Indian towns or place where they abode, for fear they should fall upon us, as they did immediately after my coming away; and that it was in the possession of the Dutch, who used 'em not so civilly as the English, so that they cut in pieces all they could take, getting into houses and hanging up the mother and all her children about her, and cut a footman I left behind me all in joints, and nailed him to trees.

This feud began while I was there, so that I lost half the satisfaction I proposed, in not seeing and visiting the Indian towns. But one day, bemoaning of our misfortunes upon this account, Caesar told us we need not fear, for if we had a mind to go, he would undertake to be our guard. Some would, but most would not venture; about eighteen of us resolved and took barge, and after eight days arrived near an Indian town. But approaching it, the hearts of some of our company failed, and they would not venture on shore; so we polled who would and who would not. For my part, I said if Caesar would, I would go; he resolved; so did my brother and my woman, a maid of good courage. Now none of us speaking the language of the people, and imagining we should have a half diversion in gazing only and not knowing what they said, we took a fisherman that lived at the mouth of the river, who had been a long inhabitant there, and obliged him to go with us. But because he was known to the Indians, as trading among 'em, and being by long living there become a perfect Indian in color, we, who resolved to surprise 'em by making 'em see something they never had seen (that is, white people), resolved only myself, my brother and woman should go; so Caesar, the fisherman, and the rest, hiding behind some thick reeds and flowers that grew on the banks, let us pass on towards the town, which was on the bank of the river all along. A little distant from the houses, or huts, we saw some dancing, others busied in fetching and carrying of water from the river. They had no sooner spied us but they set up a loud cry, that frighted us at first; we thought it had been for those that should kill us, but it seems it was of wonder and amazement. They were all naked, and we were dressed so as is most commode[8] for the hot countries, very glittering and rich, so that we appeared extremely fine; my own hair was cut short, and I had a taffety cap with black feathers on my head; my brother was in a stuff[9] suit, with silver loops and buttons and abundance of green ribbon. This was all infinitely surprising to

8. Suitable.   9. Woven fabric, worsted.

them, and because we saw them stand still till we approached 'em, we took heart and advanced, came up to 'em, and offered 'em our hands; which they took, and looked on us round about, calling still for more company; who came swarming out, all wondering and crying out "*Tepeeme*," taking their hair up in their hands and spreading it wide to those they called out to, as if they would say (as indeed it signified) "Numberless wonders," or not to be recounted, no more than to number the hair of their heads. By degrees they grew more bold, and from gazing upon us round, they touched us, laying their hands upon all the features of our faces, feeling our breasts and arms, taking up one petticoat, then wondering to see another; admiring our shoes and stockings, but more our garters, which we gave 'em, and they tied about their legs, being laced with silver lace at the ends, for they much esteem any shining things. In fine, we suffered 'em to survey us as they pleased, and we thought they would never have done admiring us. When Caesar and the rest saw we were received with such wonder, they came up to us; and finding the Indian trader whom they knew (for 'tis by these fishermen, called Indian traders, we hold a commerce with 'em, for they love not to go far from home, and we never go to them), when they saw him therefore they set up a new joy, and cried, in their language, "Oh! here's our *tiguamy*, and we shall now know whether those things can speak." So advancing to him, some of 'em gave him their hands and cried, "*Amora tiguamy*," which is as much as, "How do you?" or "Welcome, friend," and all with one din began to gabble to him, and asked if we had sense and wit; if we could talk of affairs of life and war, as they could do; if we could hunt, swim, and do a thousand things they use. He answered 'em, we could. Then they invited us into their houses, and dressed venison and buffalo for us; and going out, gathered a leaf of a tree called a *sarumbo* leaf, of six yards long, and spread it on the ground for a tablecloth; and cutting another in pieces instead of plates, setting us on little bow Indian stools, which they cut out of one entire piece of wood and paint in a sort of japan work. They serve everyone their mess on these pieces of leaves, and it was very good, but too high seasoned with pepper. When we had eat, my brother and I took out our flutes and played to 'em, which gave 'em new wonder; and I soon perceived, by an admiration that is natural to these people, and by the extreme ignorance and simplicity of 'em, it were not difficult to establish any unknown or extravagant religion among them, and to impose any notions or fictions upon 'em. For seeing a kinsman of mine set some paper afire with a burning glass, a trick they had never before seen, they were like to have adored him for a god, and begged he would give them the characters or figures of his name, that they might oppose it against winds and storms; which he did, and they held it up in those seasons, and fancied it had a charm to conquer them, and kept it like a holy relic. They are very superstitious, and called him the great *Peeie*, that is, prophet. They showed us their Indian *Peeie*, a youth of about sixteen years old, as handsome as nature could make a man. They consecrate a beautiful youth from his infancy, and all arts are used to complete him in the finest manner, both in beauty and shape. He is bred to all the little arts and cunning they are capable of, to all the legerdemain tricks and sleight of hand, whereby he imposes upon the rabble, and is both a doctor in physic and divinity; and by these tricks makes the sick believe he sometimes eases their pains, by drawing from the afflicted part little serpents, or odd flies, or worms, or any strange thing; and though they have besides undoubted good remedies for almost all their diseases, they cure the patient more by fancy than by medicines, and make themselves feared, loved, and reverenced. This young *Peeie* had a very young wife, who seeing my brother kiss her, came running and kissed me; after this they kissed one another, and made it a very great jest, it being so novel; and new admiration and laughing went round the multitude, that they never will forget that ceremony, never before used or known. Caesar had a mind to see and talk with their war captains, and we were conducted to one of their houses, where we beheld several of the great captains, who had been at council. But so frightful a vision it was to see 'em no fancy can create; no such dreams can represent so dreadful a spectacle. For my part I took 'em for hobgoblins or fiends rather than men; but however their shapes appeared, their souls were very humane and noble; but some wanted their noses, some their lips, some both noses and lips, some their ears, and others cut through each cheek with long slashes, through which their teeth appeared; they had other several formidable wounds and scars, or rather dismemberings. They had *comitias* or little aprons before 'em, and girdles of cotton, with their knives naked, stuck in it; a bow at their backs and a quiver of arrows on their thighs; and most had feathers on their heads of diverse colors. They cried *"Amora tiguamy"* to us at our entrance, and were pleased we said as much to 'em; they seated us, and gave us drink of the best sort, and wondered, as much as the others had done before, to see us. Caesar was marveling as much at their faces, wondering how they should all be so wounded in war; he was impatient to know how they all came by those frightful marks of rage or malice, rather than wounds got in noble battle. They told us, by our interpreter, that when any war was waging, two men chosen out by some old captain whose fighting was past, and who could only teach the theory of war, these two men were to stand in competition for the generalship, or great war captain; and being brought before the old judges, now past labor, they are asked what they dare do to show they are worthy to lead an army. When he who is first asked, making no reply, cuts off his nose, and throws it contemptibly[1] on the ground; and the other does something to himself that he thinks surpasses him, and perhaps deprives himself of lips and an eye; so they slash on till one gives out, and many have died in this debate. And 'tis by a passive valor they show and prove their activity, a sort of courage too brutal to be applauded by our black hero; nevertheless he expressed his esteem of 'em.

In this voyage Caesar begot so good an understanding between the Indians and the English that there were no more fears or heart-burnings during our stay, but we had a perfect, open, and free trade with 'em. Many things remarkable and worthy reciting we met with in this short voyage, because Caesar made it his business to search out and provide for our entertainment, especially to please his dearly adored Imoinda, who was a sharer in all our adventures; we being resolved to make her chains as easy as we could, and to compliment the Prince in that manner that most obliged him.

As we were coming up again, we met with some Indians of strange aspects; that is, of a larger size and other sort of features than those of our country. Our Indian slaves that rowed us asked 'em some questions, but they could

---

1. With contempt.

not understand us; but showed us a long cotton string with several knots on it, and told us, they had been coming from the mountains so many moons as there were knots. They were habited in skins of a strange beast, and brought along with 'em bags of gold dust, which, as well as they could give us to understand, came streaming in little small channels down the high mountains when the rains fell; and offered to be the convoy to any body or persons that would go to the mountains. We carried these men up to Parham, where they were kept till the Lord Governor came. And because all the country was mad to be going on this golden adventure, the Governor by his letters commanded (for they sent some of the gold to him) that a guard should be set at the mouth of the river of Amazons[2] (a river so called, almost as broad as the river of Thames) and prohibited all people from going up that river, it conducting to those mountains of gold. But we going off for England before the project was further prosecuted, and the Governor being drowned in a hurricane, either the design died, or the Dutch have the advantage of it. And 'tis to be bemoaned what his Majesty lost by losing that part of America.

Though this digression is a little from my story, however since it contains some proofs of the curiosity and daring of this great man, I was content to omit nothing of his character.

It was thus for some time we diverted him; but now Imoinda began to show she was with child, and did nothing but sigh and weep for the captivity of her lord, herself, and the infant yet unborn, and believed if it were so hard to gain the liberty of two, 'twould be more difficult to get that for three. Her griefs were so many darts in the great heart of Caesar; and taking his opportunity one Sunday when all the whites were overtaken in drink, as there were abundance of several trades and slaves for four years[3] that inhabited among the Negro houses, and Sunday was their day of debauch (otherwise they were a sort of spies upon Caesar), he went pretending out of goodness to 'em to feast amongst 'em; and sent all his music, and ordered a great treat for the whole gang, about three hundred Negroes; and about a hundred and fifty were able to bear arms, such as they had, which were sufficient to do execution[4] with spirits accordingly. For the English had none but rusty swords that no strength could draw from a scabbard, except the people of particular quality, who took care to oil 'em and keep 'em in good order. The guns also, unless here and there one, or those newly carried from England, would do no good or harm; for 'tis the nature of that country to rust and eat up iron, or any metals but gold and silver. And they are very unexpert at the bow, which the Negroes and Indians are perfect masters of.

Caesar, having singled out these men from the women and children, made an harangue to 'em of the miseries and ignominies of slavery, counting up all their toils and sufferings, under such loads, burdens, and drudgeries as were fitter for beasts than men, senseless brutes than human souls. He told 'em, it was not for days, months, or years, but for eternity; there was no end to be of their misfortunes. They suffered not like men, who might find a glory and fortitude in oppression, but like dogs that loved the whip and bell,[5] and fawned the more they were beaten. That they had lost the divine quality of

---

2. The mouth of the Amazon, in Brazil, is far distant from Surinam.
3. Tradesmen, and whites who for crimes or debt were indentured for a fixed period.

4. Harm, slaughter.
5. Proverbial for something that distracts from comfort or pleasure, from the protective charm on chariots of triumphing generals in ancient Rome.

men and were become insensible asses, fit only to bear; nay, worse: an ass, or dog, or horse, having done his duty, could lie down in retreat and rise to work again, and while he did his duty endured no stripes; but men, villainous, senseless men such as they, toiled on all the tedious week till Black Friday;[6] and then, whether they worked or not, whether they were faulty or meriting, they promiscuously, the innocent with the guilty, suffered the infamous whip, the sordid stripes, from their fellow slaves, till their blood trickled from all parts of their body, blood whose every drop ought to be revenged with a life of some of those tyrants that impose it. "And why," said he, "my dear friends and fellow sufferers, should we be slaves to an unknown people? Have they vanquished us nobly in fight? Have they won us in honorable battle? And are we by the chance of war become their slaves? This would not anger a noble heart, this would not animate a soldier's soul; no, but we are bought and sold like apes or monkeys, to be the sport of women, fools, and cowards, and the support of rogues, runagades,[7] that have abandoned their own countries for rapine, murders, thefts, and villainies. Do you not hear every day how they upbraid each other with infamy of life, below the wildest savages; and shall we render obedience to such a degenerate race, who have no one human virtue left to distinguish 'em from the vilest creatures? Will you, I say, suffer the lash from such hands?" They all replied, with one accord, "No, no, no; Caesar has spoke like a great captain, like a great king."

After this he would have proceeded, but was interrupted by a tall Negro of some more quality than the rest; his name was Tuscan; who bowing at the feet of Caesar, cried, "My lord, we have listened with joy and attention to what you have said, and, were we only men, would follow so great a leader through the world. But oh! consider, we are husbands and parents too, and have things more dear to us than life, our wives and children, unfit for travel in these unpassable woods, mountains, and bogs; we have not only difficult lands to overcome, but rivers to wade, and monsters to encounter, ravenous beasts of prey—." To this, Caesar replied that honor was the first principle in nature that was to be obeyed; but as no man would pretend to that, without all the acts of virtue, compassion, charity, love, justice, and reason, he found it not inconsistent with that to take an equal care of their wives and children as they would of themselves; and that he did not design, when he led them to freedom and glorious liberty, that they should leave that better part of themselves to perish by the hand of the tyrant's whip. But if there were a woman among them so degenerate from love and virtue to choose slavery before the pursuit of her husband, and with the hazard of her life to share with him in his fortunes, that such a one ought to be abandoned, and left as a prey to the common enemy.

To which they all agreed—and bowed. After this, he spoke of the impassable woods and rivers, and convinced 'em, the more danger, the more glory. He told them that he had heard of one Hannibal, a great captain, had cut his way through mountains of solid rocks;[8] and should a few shrubs oppose them, which they could fire before 'em? No, 'twas a trifling excuse to men resolved to die or overcome. As for bogs, they are with a little labor filled and

---

6. Here a day of customary beating; more widely, a Friday bringing some notable disaster, from students' slang for examination day.

7. Renegades or fugitives.

8. The Carthaginian general and his troops literally hacked their way down the Alps into Italy to attack Rome.

hardened; and the rivers could be no obstacle, since they swam by nature, at least by custom, from their first hour of their birth. That when the children were weary they must carry them by turns, and the woods and their own industry would afford them food. To this they all assented with joy.

Tuscan then demanded what he would do. He said, they would travel towards the sea, plant a new colony, and defend it by their valor; and when they could find a ship, either driven by stress of weather or guided by Providence that way, they would seize it and make it a prize, till it had transported them to their own countries; at least, they should be made free in his kingdom, and be esteemed as his fellow sufferers, and men that had the courage and the bravery to attempt, at least, for liberty; and if they died in the attempt it would be more brave than to live in perpetual slavery.

They bowed and kissed his feet at this resolution, and with one accord vowed to follow him to death. And that night was appointed to begin their march; they made it known to their wives, and directed them to tie their hamaca[9] about their shoulder and under their arm like a scarf, and to lead their children that could go, and carry those that could not. The wives, who pay an entire obedience to their husbands, obeyed, and stayed for 'em where they were appointed. The men stayed but to furnish themselves with what defensive arms they could get; and all met at the rendezvous, where Caesar made a new encouraging speech to 'em, and led 'em out.

But as they could not march far that night, on Monday early, when the overseers went to call 'em all together to go to work, they were extremely surprised to find not one upon the place, but all fled with what baggage they had. You may imagine this news was not only suddenly spread all over the plantation, but soon reached the neighboring ones; and we had by noon about six hundred men they call the militia of the county, that came to assist us in the pursuit of the fugitives. But never did one see so comical an army march forth to war. The men of any fashion would not concern themselves, though it were almost the common cause; for such revoltings are very ill examples, and have very fatal consequences oftentimes in many colonies. But they had a respect for Caesar, and all hands were against the Parhamites, as they called those of Parham plantation, because they did not, in the first place, love the Lord Governor, and secondly they would have it that Caesar was ill used, and baffled with;[1] and 'tis not impossible but some of the best in the country was of his counsel in this flight, and depriving us of all the slaves; so that they of the better sort would not meddle in the matter. The deputy governor,[2] of whom I have had no great occasion to speak, and who was the most fawning fair-tongued fellow in the world and one that pretended the most friendship to Caesar, was now the only violent man against him; and though he had nothing, and so need fear nothing, yet talked and looked bigger than any man. He was a fellow whose character is not fit to be mentioned with the worst of the slaves. This fellow would lead his army forth to meet Caesar, or rather to pursue him; most of their arms were of those sort of cruel whips they call cat with nine tails; some had rusty useless guns for show, others old basket hilts[3] whose blades had never seen the light in this age, and others had long staffs and clubs. Mr. Trefry went along, rather

---

9. Hammock.
1. Cheated.
2. William Byam. There are recorded complaints

against him for high-handedness and from him about insubordination by settlers and slaves.
3. Swords with protective hilt guards.

to be a mediator than a conqueror in such a battle; for he foresaw and knew, if by fighting they put the Negroes into despair, they were a sort of sullen fellows that would drown or kill themselves before they would yield; and he advised that fair means was best. But Byam was one that abounded in his own wit and would take his own measures.

It was not hard to find these fugitives; for as they fled they were forced to fire and cut the woods before 'em, so that night or day they pursued 'em by the light they made and by the path they had cleared. But as soon as Caesar found he was pursued, he put himself in a posture of defense, placing all the women and children in the rear, and himself with Tuscan by his side, or next to him, all promising to die or conquer. Encouraged thus, they never stood to parley, but fell on pell-mell upon the English, and killed some and wounded a good many, they having recourse to their whips as the best of their weapons. And as they observed no order, they perplexed the enemy so sorely with lashing 'em in the eyes; and the women and children seeing their husbands so treated, being of fearful cowardly dispositions, and hearing the English cry out, "Yield and live, yield and be pardoned," they all run in amongst their husbands and fathers, and hung about 'em, crying out, "Yield, yield; and leave Caesar to their revenge"; that by degrees the slaves abandoned Caesar, and left him only Tuscan and his heroic Imoinda; who, grown big as she was, did nevertheless press near her lord, having a bow and a quiver full of poisoned arrows, which she managed with such dexterity that she wounded several, and shot the governor into the shoulder; of which wound he had like to have died, but that an Indian woman, his mistress, sucked the wound and cleansed it from the venom. But however, he stirred not from the place till he had parleyed with Caesar, who he found was resolved to die fighting, and would not be taken; no more would Tuscan, or Imoinda. But he, more thirsting after revenge of another sort than that of depriving him of life, now made use of all his art of talking and dissembling, and besought Caesar to yield himself upon terms which he himself should propose, and should be sacredly assented to and kept by him. He told him, it was not that he any longer feared him, or could believe the force of two men, and a young heroine, could overcome all them, with all the slaves now on their side also; but it was the vast esteem he had for his person, the desire he had to serve so gallant a man, and to hinder himself from the reproach hereafter of having been the occasion of the death of a prince whose valor and magnanimity deserved the empire of the world. He protested to him, he looked upon this action as gallant and brave, however tending to the prejudice of his lord and master, who would by it have lost so considerable a number of slaves; that this flight of his should be looked on as a heat of youth, and rashness of a too forward courage, and an unconsidered impatience of liberty, and no more; and that he labored in vain to accomplish that which they would effectually perform as soon as any ship arrived that would touch on his coast. "So that if you will be pleased," continued he, "to surrender yourself, all imaginable respect shall be paid you; and yourself, your wife, and child, if it be here born, shall depart free out of our land."

But Caesar would hear of no composition;[4] though Byam urged, if he pursued and went on in his design, he would inevitably perish, either by

4. Settlement.

great snakes, wild beasts, or hunger; and he ought to have regard to his wife, whose condition required ease, and not the fatigues of tedious travel, where she could not be secured from being devoured. But Caesar told him, there was no faith in the white men or the gods they adored, who instructed 'em in principles so false that honest men could not live amongst 'em; though no people professed so much, none performed so little; that he knew what he had to do when he dealt with men of honor, but with them a man ought to be eternally on his guard, and never to eat and drink with Christians without his weapon of defense in his hand; and for his own security, never to credit one word they spoke. As for the rashness and inconsiderateness of his action, he would confess the governor is in the right; and that he was ashamed of what he had done, in endeavoring to make those free who were by nature slaves, poor wretched rogues, fit to be used as Christians' tools; dogs, treacherous and cowardly, fit for such masters; and they wanted only but to be whipped into the knowledge of the Christian gods to be the vilest of all creeping things, to learn to worship such deities as had not power to make 'em just, brave, or honest. In fine, after a thousand things of this nature, not fit here to be recited, he told Byam he had rather die than live upon the same earth with such dogs. But Trefry and Byam pleaded and protested together so much that Trefry, believing the governor to mean what he said, and speaking very cordially himself, generously put himself into Caesar's hands, and took him aside and persuaded him, even with tears, to live, by surrendering himself, and to name his conditions. Caesar was overcome by his wit and reasons, and in consideration of Imoinda; and demanding what he desired, and that it should be ratified by their hands in writing, because he had perceived that was the common way of contract between man and man, amongst the whites. All this was performed, and Tuscan's pardon was put in, and they surrender to the governor, who walked peaceably down into the plantation with 'em, after giving order to bury their dead. Caesar was very much toiled with the bustle of the day, for he had fought like a fury; and what mischief was done he and Tuscan performed alone, and gave their enemies a fatal proof that they durst do anything and feared no mortal force.

But they were no sooner arrived at the place where all the slaves receive their punishments of whipping, but they laid hands on Caesar and Tuscan, faint with heat and toil; and surprising them, bound them to two several stakes, and whipped them in a most deplorable and inhuman manner, rending the very flesh from their bones; especially Caesar, who was not perceived to make any moan or to alter his face, only to roll his eyes on the faithless governor, and those he believed guilty, with fierceness and indignation; and to complete his rage, he saw every one of those slaves, who but a few days before adored him as something more than mortal, now had a whip to give him some lashes, while he strove not to break his fetters; though if he had, it were impossible. But he pronounced a woe and revenge from his eyes, that darted fire that 'twas at once both awful and terrible to behold.

When they thought they were sufficiently revenged on him, they untied him, almost fainting with loss of blood from a thousand wounds all over his body, from which they had rent his clothes, and led him bleeding and naked as he was, and loaded him all over with irons; and then rubbed his wounds, to complete their cruelty, with Indian pepper, which had like to have made him raving mad; and in this condition made him so fast to the ground that he could not stir, if his pains and wounds would have given him leave. They spared Imoinda, and did not let her see this barbarity committed towards her lord, but carried her down to Parham and shut her up; which was not in kindness to her, but for fear she should die with the sight, or miscarry, and then they should lose a young slave and perhaps the mother.

You must know, that when the news was brought on Monday morning that Caesar had betaken himself to the woods and carried with him all the Negroes, we were possessed with extreme fear, which no persuasions could dissipate, that he would secure himself till night, and then that he would come down and cut all our throats. This apprehension made all the females of us fly down the river, to be secured; and while we were away they acted this cruelty. For I suppose I had authority and interest enough there, had I suspected any such thing, to have prevented it; but we had not gone many leagues but the news overtook us that Caesar was taken and whipped like a common slave. We met on the river with Colonel Martin, a man of great gallantry, wit, and goodness, and whom I have celebrated in a character of my new comedy[5] by his own name, in memory of so brave a man. He was wise and eloquent and, from the fineness of his parts, bore a great sway over the hearts of all the colony. He was a friend to Caesar, and resented this false dealing with him very much. We carried him back to Parham, thinking to have made an accommodation; when we came, the first news we heard was that the governor was dead of a wound Imoinda had given him; but it was not so well. But it seems he would have the pleasure of beholding the revenge he took on Caesar, and before the cruel ceremony was finished, he dropped down; and then they perceived the wound he had on his shoulder was by a venomed arrow, which, as I said, his Indian mistress healed by sucking the wound.

We were no sooner arrived but we went up to the plantation to see Caesar, whom we found in a very miserable and unexpressible condition; and I have a thousand times admired how he lived, in so much tormenting pain. We said all things to him that trouble, pity, and good nature could suggest, protesting our innocency of the fact and our abhorrence of such cruelties; making a thousand professions of services to him and begging as many pardons for the offenders, till we said so much that he believed we had no hand in his ill treatment; but told us he could never pardon Byam; as for Trefry, he confessed he saw his grief and sorrow for his suffering, which he could not hinder, but was like to have been beaten down by the very slaves for speaking in his defense. But for Byam, who was their leader, their head—and should, by his justice and honor, have been an example to 'em—for him, he wished to live, to take a dire revenge of him, and said, "It had been well for him if he had sacrificed me, instead of giving me the contemptible[6] whip." He refused to talk much, but begging us to give him our hands, he took 'em, and protested never to lift up his to do us any harm. He had a great respect for Colonel Martin, and always took his counsel like that of a parent, and assured him he would obey him in anything but his revenge on Byam. "Therefore," said he, "for his own safety, let him speedily dispatch me; for if I could

---

5. *The Younger Brother, or The Amorous Jilt,* not produced until 1696 despite this piece of promo-tion.

6. Showing contempt.

dispatch myself I would not, till that justice were done to my injured person, and the contempt of a soldier. No, I would not kill myself, even after a whipping, but will be content to live with that infamy, and be pointed at by every grinning slave, till I have completed my revenge; and then you shall see that Oroonoko scorns to live with the indignity that was put on Caesar." All we could do could get no more words from him; and we took care to have him put immediately into a healing bath to rid him of his pepper, and ordered a chirurgeon[7] to anoint him with healing balm, which he suffered; and in some time he began to be able to walk and eat. We failed not to visit him every day, and to that end had him brought to an apartment at Parham.

The governor was no sooner recovered, and had heard of the menaces of Caesar, but he called his council; who (not to disgrace them, or burlesque the government there) consisted of such notorious villains as Newgate[8] never transported; and possibly originally were such who understood neither the laws of God or man, and had no sort of principles to make 'em worthy the name of men; but at the very council table would contradict and fight with one another, and swear so bloodily that 'twas terrible to hear and see 'em. (Some of 'em were afterwards hanged when the Dutch took possession of the place, others sent off in chains.) But calling these special rulers of the nation together, and requiring their counsel in this weighty affair, they all concluded that (Damn 'em) it might be their own cases; and that Caesar ought to be made an example to all the Negroes, to fright 'em from daring to threaten their betters, their lords and masters; and at this rate no man was safe from his own slaves; and concluded, *nemine contradicente*,[9] that Caesar should be hanged.

Trefry then thought it time to use his authority, and told Byam his command did not extend to his lord's plantation, and that Parham was as much exempt from the law as Whitehall;[1] and that they ought no more to touch the servants of the Lord——(who there represented the King's person) than they could those about the King himself; and that Parham was a sanctuary; and though his lord were absent in person, his power was still in being there, which he had entrusted with him as far as the dominions of his particular plantations reached, and all that belonged to it; the rest of the country, as Byam was lieutenant to his lord, he might exercise his tyranny upon. Trefry had others as powerful, or more, that interested themselves in Caesar's life, and absolutely said he should be defended. So turning the governor and his wise council out of doors (for they sat at Parham House), they set a guard upon our landing place, and would admit none but those we called friends to us and Caesar.

The governor having remained wounded at Parham till his recovery was completed, Caesar did not know but he was still there; and indeed, for the most part his time was spent there, for he was one that loved to live at other people's expense; and if he were a day absent, he was ten present there, and used to play and walk and hunt and fish with Caesar. So that Caesar did not at all doubt, if he once recovered strength, but he should find an opportunity of being revenged on him. Though after such a revenge, he could not hope to live, for if he escaped the fury of the English mobile,[2] who perhaps would

---

7. Surgeon.
8. The major London prison, from which criminals were transported to the colonies.
9. No one disagreeing (Latin).

1. The king's palace in London. Treffry stands as Lord Willoughby's deputy on his private land, Byam in the colony at large.
2. Common people or mob.

have been glad of the occasion to have killed him, he was resolved not to survive his whipping; yet he had, some tender hours, a repenting softness, which he called his fits of coward, wherein he struggled with Love for the victory of his heart, which took part with his charming Imoinda there; but for the most part his time was passed in melancholy thought and black designs. He considered, if he should do this deed and die, either in the attempt or after it, he left his lovely Imoinda a prey, or at best a slave, to the enraged multitude; his great heart could not endure that thought. "Perhaps," said he, "she may be first ravished by every brute, exposed first to their nasty lusts and then a shameful death." No; he could not live a moment under that apprehension, too insupportable to be borne. These were his thoughts and his silent arguments with his heart, as he told us afterwards; so that now resolving not only to kill Byam but all those he thought had enraged him, pleasing his great heart with the fancied slaughter he should make over the whole face of the plantation, he first resolved on a deed, that (however horrid it at first appeared to us all), when we had heard his reasons, we thought it brave and just. Being able to walk and, as he believed, fit for the execution of his great design, he begged Trefry to trust him into the air, believing a walk would do him good, which was granted him; and taking Imoinda with him, as he used to do in his more happy and calmer days, he led her up into a wood, where, after (with a thousand sighs, and long gazing silently on her face, while tears gushed, in spite of him, from his eyes) he told her his design first of killing her, and then his enemies, and next himself, and the impossibility of escaping, and therefore he told her the necessity of dying, he found the heroic wife faster pleading for death than he was to propose it, when she found his fixed resolution, and on her knees besought him not to leave her a prey to his enemies. He (grieved to death) yet pleased at her noble resolution, took her up, and embracing her with all the passion and languishment of a dying lover, drew his knife to kill this treasure of his soul, this pleasure of his eyes; while tears trickled down his cheeks, hers were smiling with joy she should die by so noble a hand, and be sent in her own country (for that's their notion of the next world) by him she so tenderly loved and so truly adored in this; for wives have a respect for their husbands equal to what any other people pay a deity, and when a man finds any occasion to quit his wife, if he love her, she dies by his hand; if not, he sells her, or suffers some other to kill her. It being thus, you may believe the deed was soon resolved on; and 'tis not to be doubted but the parting, the eternal leave-taking of two such lovers, so greatly born, so sensible,[3] so beautiful, so young, and so fond, must be very moving, as the relation of it was to me afterwards.

All that love could say in such cases being ended, and all the intermitting irresolutions being adjusted, the lovely, young, and adored victim lays herself down before the sacrificer; while he, with a hand resolved and a heart breaking within, gave the fatal stroke; first cutting her throat, and then severing her yet smiling face from that delicate body, pregnant as it was with fruits of tenderest love. As soon as he had done, he laid the body decently on leaves and flowers, of which he made a bed, and concealed it under the same coverlid of nature; only her face he left yet bare to look on. But when he found she was dead and past all retrieve, never more to bless him with her eyes and soft language, his grief swelled up to rage; he tore, he raved, he

3. Sensitive.

roared, like some monster of the wood, calling on the loved name of Imoinda. A thousand times he turned the fatal knife that did the deed toward his own heart, with a resolution to go immediately after her; but dire revenge, which now was a thousand times more fierce in his soul than before, prevents him; and he would cry out, "No; since I have sacrificed Imoinda to my revenge, shall I lose that glory which I have purchased so dear as at the price of the fairest, dearest, softest creature that ever nature made? No, no!" Then, at her name, grief would get the ascendant of rage, and he would lie down by her side and water her face with showers of tears, which never were wont to fall from those eyes. And however bent he was on his intended slaughter, he had not power to stir from the sight of this dear object, now more beloved and more adored than ever.

He remained in this deploring condition for two days, and never rose from the ground where he had made his sad sacrifice. At last, rousing from her side, and accusing himself with living too long now Imoinda was dead, and that the deaths of those barbarous enemies were deferred too long, he resolved now to finish the great work; but offering to rise, he found his strength so decayed that he reeled to and fro, like boughs assailed by contrary winds; so that he was forced to lie down again, and try to summons all his courage to his aid. He found his brains turned round, and his eyes were dizzy, and objects appeared not the same to him they were wont to do; his breath was short, and all his limbs surprised with a faintness he had never felt before. He had not eat in two days, which was one occasion of this feebleness, but excess of grief was the greatest; yet still he hoped he should recover vigor to act his design, and lay expecting it yet six days longer, still mourning over the dead idol of his heart, and striving every day to rise, but could not.

In all this time you may believe we were in no little affliction for Caesar and his wife; some were of opinion he was escaped never to return; others thought some accident had happened to him. But however, we failed not to send out an hundred people several ways to search for him; a party of about forty went that way he took, among whom was Tuscan, who was perfectly reconciled to Byam. They had not gone very far into the wood but they smelt an unusual smell, as of a dead body; for stinks must be very noisome that can be distinguished among such a quantity of natural sweets as every inch of that land produces. So that they concluded they should find him dead, or somebody that was so. They passed on towards it, as loathsome as it was, and made such a rustling among the leaves that lie thick on the ground, by continual falling, that Caesar heard he was approached; and though he had during the space of these eight days endeavored to rise, but found he wanted strength, yet looking up and seeing his pursuers, he rose and reeled to a neighboring tree, against which he fixed his back; and being within a dozen yards of those that advanced and saw him, he called out to them and bid them approach no nearer, if they would be safe. So that they stood still, and hardly believing their eyes, that would persuade them that it was Caesar that spoke to 'em, so much was he altered, they asked him what he had done with his wife, for they smelt a stink that almost struck them dead. He, pointing to the dead body, sighing, cried, "Behold her there." They put off the flowers that covered her with their sticks, and found she was killed, and cried out, "Oh, monster! that hast murdered thy wife." Then asking him why he did so cruel a deed, he replied, he had no leisure to answer impertinent questions. "You may go back," continued he, "and tell the faithless governor he may thank fortune that I am breathing my last, and that my arm is too feeble to obey my heart in what it had designed him." But his tongue faltering, and trembling, he could scarce end what he was saying. The English, taking advantage by his weakness, cried, "Let us take him alive by all means." He heard 'em; and as if he had revived from a fainting, or a dream, he cried out, "No, gentlemen, you are deceived; you will find no more Caesars to be whipped, no more find a faith in me. Feeble as you think me, I have strength yet left to secure me from a second indignity." They swore all anew, and he only shook his head and beheld them with scorn. Then they cried out, "Who will venture on this single man? Will nobody?" They stood all silent while Caesar replied, "Fatal will be the attempt to the first adventurer, let him assure himself," and at that word, held up his knife in a menacing posture. "Look ye, ye faithless crew," said he, " 'tis not life I seek, nor am I afraid of dying," and at that word cut a piece of flesh from his own throat, and threw it at 'em; "yet still I would live if I could, till I had perfected my revenge. But oh! it cannot be; I feel life gliding from my eyes and heart, and if I make not haste, I shall yet fall a victim to the shameful whip." At that, he ripped up his own belly, and took his bowels and pulled 'em out, with what strength he could; while some, on their knees imploring, besought him to hold his hand. But when they saw him tottering, they cried out, "Will none venture on him?" A bold English cried, "Yes, if he were the devil" (taking courage when he saw him almost dead); and swearing a horrid oath for his farewell to the world, he rushed on him; Caesar, with his armed hand, met him so fairly as stuck him to the heart, and he fell dead at his feet. Tuscan, seeing that, cried out, "I love thee, O Caesar, and therefore will not let thee die, if possible." And running to him, took him in his arms; but at the same time warding a blow that Caesar made at his bosom, he received it quite through his arm; and Caesar having not the strength to pluck the knife forth, though he attempted it, Tuscan neither pulled it out himself nor suffered it to be pulled out, but came down with it sticking in his arm; and the reason he gave for it was, because the air should not get into the wound. They put their hands across, and carried Caesar between six of 'em, fainted as he was, and they thought dead, or just dying; and they brought him to Parham, and laid him on a couch, and had the chirurgeon immediately to him, who dressed his wounds and sewed up his belly, and used means to bring him to life, which they effected. We ran all to see him, and if before we thought him so beautiful a sight, he was now so altered that his face was like a death's head blacked over, nothing but teeth and eyeholes. For some days we suffered nobody to speak to him, but caused cordials to be poured down his throat, which sustained his life; and in six or seven days he recovered his senses. For you must know that wounds are almost to a miracle cured in the Indies, unless wounds in the legs, which rarely ever cure.

When he was well enough to speak, we talked to him, and asked him some questions about his wife, and the reasons why he killed her; and he then told us what I have related of that resolution, and of his parting; and he besought us we would let him die, and was extremely afflicted to think it was possible he might live; he assured us if we did not dispatch him, he would prove very fatal to a great many. We said all we could to make him live, and gave him new assurances; but he begged we would not think so poorly of him, or of his love to Imoinda, to imagine we could flatter him to life again; but the chirurgeon assured him he could not live, and therefore he need not fear. We were all (but Caesar) afflicted at this news; and the sight was gashly;[4] his discourse was sad, and the earthly smell about him so strong that I was persuaded to leave the place for some time (being myself but sickly, and very apt to fall into fits of dangerous illness upon any extraordinary melancholy). The servants and Trefry and the chirurgeons promised all to take what possible care they could of the life of Caesar, and I, taking boat, went with other company to Colonel Martin's, about three days' journey down the river; but I was no sooner gone, but the governor taking Trefry about some pretended earnest business a day's journey up the river, having communicated his design to one Banister, a wild Irishman and one of the council, a fellow of absolute barbarity, and fit to execute any villainy, but was rich: he came up to Parham, and forcibly took Caesar, and had him carried to the same post where he was whipped; and causing him to be tied to it, and a great fire made before him, he told him he should die like a dog, as he was. Caesar replied, this was the first piece of bravery that ever Banister did, and he never spoke sense till he pronounced that word; and if he would keep it, he would declare, in the other world, that he was the only man of all the whites that ever he heard speak truth. And turning to the men that bound him, he said, "My friends, am I to die, or to be whipped?" And they cried, "Whipped! No, you shall not escape so well." And then he replied, smiling, "A blessing on thee," and assured them they need not tie him, for he would stand fixed like a rock, and endure death so as should encourage them to die. "But if you whip me," said he, "be sure you tie me fast."

He had learned to take tobacco; and when he was assured he should die, he desired they would give him a pipe in his mouth, ready lighted, which they did; and the executioner came, and first cut off his members,[5] and threw them into the fire; after that, with an ill-favored knife, they cut his ears, and his nose, and burned them; he still smoked on, as if nothing had touched him. Then they hacked off one of his arms, and still he bore up, and held his pipe; but at the cutting off the other arm, his head sunk, and his pipe dropped, and he gave up the ghost, without a groan or a reproach. My mother and sister were by him all the while, but not suffered to save him, so rude and wild were the rabble, and so inhuman were the justices, who stood by to see the execution, who after paid dearly enough for their insolence. They cut Caesar in quarters, and sent them to several of the chief plantations. One quarter was sent to Colonel Martin, who refused it, and swore he had rather see the quarters of Banister and the governor himself than those of Caesar on his plantations, and that he could govern his Negroes without terrifying and grieving them with frightful spectacles of a mangled king.

Thus died this great man, worthy of a better fate, and a more sublime wit than mine to write his praise; yet, I hope, the reputation of my pen is considerable enough to make his glorious name to survive to all ages, with that of the brave, the beautiful, and the constant Imoinda.

1688

---

4. Ghastly.   5. Genitals.

ANNE FINCH,
COUNTESS OF WINCHILSEA
1661–1720

Born into an ancient country family, Anne Kingsmill became a maid of honor at the court of Charles II. There she met Colonel Heneage Finch; in 1684 they married. During the short reign of James II they prospered at court, but at the king's fall in 1688 they were forced to retire, eventually settling on a beautiful family estate at Eastwell, in Kent, near the south coast of England. Here Colonel Finch became, in 1712, earl of Winchilsea, and here Lady Winchilsea wrote most of her poems, influenced, she said, by "the solitude and security of the country," and by "objects naturally inspiring soft and poetical imaginations." Her *Miscellany Poems on Several Occasions, Written by a Lady* were published in 1713. One poem, *The Spleen*, a description of the mysterious melancholic illness from which she and many other fashionable people suffered, achieved some fame; Pope seems to refer to it when he invokes the goddess Spleen in *The Rape of the Lock*. But Winchilsea's larger reputation began only a century later, when Wordsworth praised her for keeping her eye on external nature and for a style "often admirable, chaste, tender, and vigorous."

The Introduction[1]

> Did I my lines intend for public view,
> How many censures would their faults pursue!
> Some would, because such words they do affect,
> Cry they're insipid, empty, uncorrect.
> 5 And many have attained, dull and untaught,
> The name of wit, only by finding fault.[2]
> True judges might condemn their want of wit;
> And all might say, they're by a woman writ.
> Alas! a woman that attempts the pen,
> 10 Such an intruder on the rights of men,
> Such a presumptuous creature is esteemed,
> The fault can by no virtue be redeemed.
> They tell us we mistake our sex and way;
> Good breeding, fashion, dancing, dressing, play
> 15 Are the accomplishments we should desire;
> To write, or read, or think, or to enquire,
> Would cloud our beauty, and exhaust our time,
> And interrupt the conquests of our prime;
> Whilst the dull manage of a servile house
> 20 Is held by some our utmost art and use.
>   Sure 'twas not ever thus, nor are we told
> Fables,[3] of women that excelled of old;
> To whom, by the diffusive hand of heaven,
> Some share of wit and poetry was given.
> 25 On that glad day on which the Ark[4] returned,

---

1. This preface to Winchilsea's work was never published during her lifetime, for reasons explained in the poem itself.
2. Pronounced *fawt*.

3. Idle stories or lies.
4. The Ark of the Covenant, restored to Jerusalem by David (1 Chronicles 15).

The holy pledge for which the land had mourned,
The joyful tribes attend it on the way,
The Levites do the sacred charge convey,
Whilst various instruments before it play;
30 Here holy virgins in the concert join,[5]
The louder notes to soften and refine,
And with alternate verse[6] complete the hymn divine.
    Lo! the young poet,° after God's own heart,   *David*
By Him inspired and taught the Muses' art,
35 Returned from conquest a bright chorus meets,
That sing his slain ten thousand in the streets.[7]
In such loud numbers[8] they his acts declare,
Proclaim the wonders of his early war,
That Saul upon the vast applause does frown,
40 And feels its mighty thunder shake the crown.
What can the threatened judgment now prolong?[9]
Half of the kingdom is already gone;
The fairest half, whose influence guides the rest,
Have David's empire o'er their hearts confessed.
45   A woman here leads fainting Israel on,
She fights, she wins, she triumphs with a song,[1]
Devout, majestic, for the subject fit,
And far above her arms, exalts her wit,
Then to the peaceful, shady palm withdraws,
50 And rules the rescued nation with her laws.
    How are we fallen! fallen by mistaken rules,
And education's, more than nature's fools;
Debarred from all improvements of the mind,
And to be dull, expected and designed;°   *intended*
55 And if some one would soar above the rest,
With warmer fancy and ambition pressed,
So strong the opposing faction still appears,
The hopes to thrive can ne'er outweigh the fears.
Be cautioned, then, my Muse, and still retired;
60 Nor be despised, aiming to be admired;
Conscious of wants, still with contracted wing,
To some few friends and to thy sorrows sing.
For groves of laurel thou wert never meant;
Be dark enough thy shades, and be thou there content.

1689?   1903

A Nocturnal Reverie

In such a night,[1] when every louder wind
Is to its distant cavern safe confined;

5. Pronounced *jine*.
6. A series of couplets. The choir of virgins, not mentioned in Chronicles, is imagined by Winchilsea as chanting every other line, responsively, as in some of the Psalms.
7. 1 Samuel 18.6–7.
8. Measures of music and verse.
9. What can now stave off the threatened judgment? Saul's doom ("judgment") had been prophesied: God would replace him with a better king.
1. The prophet and judge Deborah sang to praise the Lord for the victory she herself had brought about (Judges 4–5).
1. This phrase, repeated twice below, echoes the same repeated phrase in the night piece that opens act 5 of *The Merchant of Venice*.

And only gentle Zephyr fans his wings,
And lonely Philomel,° still waking, sings;   *nightingale*
5   Or from some tree, famed for the owl's delight,
She, hollowing clear, directs the wanderer right:
In such a night, when passing clouds give place,
Or thinly veil the heavens' mysterious face;
When in some river, overhung with green,
10 The waving moon and trembling leaves are seen;
When freshened grass now bears itself upright,
And makes cool banks to pleasing rest invite,
Whence springs the woodbind, and the bramble-rose,
And where the sleepy cowslip sheltered grows;
15 Whilst now a paler hue the foxglove takes,
Yet checkers still with red the dusky brakes:
When scattered glow-worms, but in twilight fine,
Show trivial beauties watch their hour to shine;
Whilst Salisbury² stands the test of every light,
20 In perfect charms, and perfect virtue bright:
When odors, which declined repelling day,
Through temperate air uninterrupted stray;
When darkened groves their softest shadows wear,
And falling waters we distinctly hear;
25 When through the gloom more venerable shows
Some ancient fabric,° awful in repose,   *edifice*
While sunburnt hills their swarthy looks conceal,
And swelling haycocks thicken up the vale:
When the loosed horse now, as his pasture leads,
30 Comes slowly grazing through the adjoining meads,
Whose stealing pace, and lengthened shade we fear,
Till torn-up forage in his teeth we hear:
When nibbling sheep at large pursue their food,
And unmolested kine rechew the cud;
35 When curlews cry beneath the village walls,
And to her straggling brood the partridge calls;
Their shortlived jubilee the creatures keep,
Which but endures, whilst tyrant man does sleep;
When a sedate content the spirit feels,
40 And no fierce light disturbs, whilst it reveals;
But silent musings urge the mind to seek
Something, too high for syllables to speak;
Till the free soul to a composedness charmed,
Finding the elements of rage disarmed,
45 O'er all below a solemn quiet grown,
Joys in the inferior world,³ and thinks it like her own:
In such a night let me abroad remain,
Till morning breaks, and all's confused again;
Our cares, our toils, our clamors are renewed,
50 Or pleasures, seldom reached, again pursued.

1713

---

2. Probably Lady Salisbury, the daughter of a friend. The sense is that this lady differs from others more trivial, who like glowworms look fine only one hour a day.

3. The world of nature (compared to the world of the soul).

JONATHAN SWIFT
1667–1745

Jonathan Swift—a posthumous child—was born of English parents in Dublin. Through the generosity of an uncle he was educated at Kilkenny School and Trinity College, Dublin, but before he could fix on a career, the troubles that followed upon James II's abdication and subsequent invasion of Ireland drove Swift along with other Anglo-Irish to England. Between 1689 and 1699 he was more or less continuously a member of the household of his kinsman Sir William Temple, an urbane, civilized man, a retired diplomat, and a friend of King William. During these years Swift read widely, rather reluctantly decided on the church as a career and so took orders, and discovered his astonishing gifts as a satirist. About 1696–97 he wrote his powerful satires on corruptions in religion and learning, *A Tale of a Tub* and *The Battle of the Books,* which were published in 1704 and reached their final form only in the fifth edition of 1710. These were the years in which he slowly came to maturity. When, at the age of thirty-two, he returned to Ireland as chaplain to the lord justice, the earl of Berkeley, he had a clear sense of his genius.

For the rest of his life, Swift devoted his talents to politics and religion—not clearly separated at the time—and most of his works in prose were written to further a specific cause. As a clergyman, a spirited controversialist, and a devoted supporter of the Anglican Church he was hostile to all who seemed to threaten it—Deists, free-thinkers, Roman Catholics, Nonconformists, or merely Whig politicians. In 1710 he abandoned the Whigs, because he opposed their indifference to the welfare of the Anglican Church in Ireland and their desire to repeal the Test Act, which required all holders of offices of state to take the Sacrament according to the Anglican rites, thus excluding Roman Catholics and Dissenters. Welcomed by the Tories, he became the most brilliant political journalist of the day, serving the government of Oxford and Bolingbroke as editor of the party organ, the *Examiner,* and as author of its most powerful articles, as well as writing longer pamphlets in support of important policies, such as that favoring the Peace of Utrecht (1713). He was greatly valued by the two ministers, who admitted him to social intimacy, although never to their counsels. The reward of his services was not the English bishopric that he had a right to expect, but the deanship of St. Patrick's Cathedral in Dublin, which came to him in 1713, a year before the death of Queen Anne and the fall of the Tories put an end to all his hopes of preferment in England.

In Ireland, where he lived unwillingly, he became not only an efficient ecclesiastical administrator but also, in 1724, the leader of Irish resistance to English oppression. Under the pseudonym "M. B. Drapier," he published the famous series of public letters that aroused the country to refuse to accept £100,000 in new copper coins (minted in England by William Wood, who had obtained his patent through court corruption), which, it was feared, would further debase the coinage of the already poverty-stricken kingdom. Although his authorship of the letters was known to all Dublin, no one could be found to earn the £300 offered by the government for information as to the identity of the drapier. Swift is still venerated in Ireland as a national hero. He earned the right to refer to himself in the epitaph that he wrote for his tomb as a vigorous defender of liberty.

His last years were less happy. Swift had suffered most of his adult life from what we now recognize as Ménière's disease, which affects the inner ear, causing dizziness, nausea, and deafness. After 1739, when he was seventy-two years old, his infirmities cut him off from his duties as dean, and from then on his social life dwindled. In 1742 guardians were appointed to administer his affairs, and his last three years were spent in gloom and lethargy. But this dark ending should not put his earlier life, so full of energy and humor, into a shadow. The writer of the satires was a man in full control of great intellectual powers.

For all his involvement in public affairs, Swift seems to stand apart from his contemporaries—a striking figure among the statesmen of the time, a writer who towered
above others by reason of his imagination, mordant wit, and emotional intensity. He
has been called a misanthrope, a hater of humanity, and *Gulliver's Travels* has been
considered an expression of savage misanthropy. It is true that Swift proclaimed himself a misanthrope in a letter to Pope, declaring that though he loved individuals, he
hated "that animal called man" in general, and offering a new definition of the species
as not *animal rationale* ("a rational animal") but as merely *animal rationis capax* ("an
animal *capable* of reason"). This, he declared, is the "great foundation" on which his
"misanthropy" was erected. Swift was stating not his hatred of his fellow creatures
but his antagonism to the current optimistic view that human nature is essentially
good. To the "philanthropic" flattery that sentimentalism and Deistic rationalism were
paying to human nature, Swift opposed a more ancient and plausible view: that
human nature is deeply and permanently flawed and that we can do nothing with or
for the human race until we recognize its moral and intellectual limitations. In his
epitaph he spoke of the "fierce indignation" that had torn his heart, an indignation
that found superb expression in his greatest satires. It was provoked by the constant
spectacle of creatures capable of reason, and therefore of reasonable conduct, steadfastly refusing to live up to their capabilities.

Swift is a master of prose. He defined a good style as "proper words in proper
places," a more complex and difficult saying than at first appears. Clear, simple,
concrete diction, uncomplicated syntax, economy and conciseness of language mark
all his writings. His is a style that shuns ornaments and singularity of all kinds, a style
that grows more tense and controlled the more fierce the indignation that it is called
on to express. The virtues of his prose are those of his poetry, which shocks us with
its hard look at the facts of life and the body. It is unpoetic poetry, devoid of, indeed
as often as not mocking at, inspiration, romantic love, cosmetic beauty, easily
assumed literary attitudes, and conventional poetic language. Like the prose, it is
predominantly satiric in purpose, but not without its moments of comedy and light-
heartedness, though written most often not so much to divert as to reform the reader.

A Description of a City Shower

    Careful observers may foretell the hour
(By sure prognostics) when to dread a shower:
While rain depends,[1] the pensive cat gives o'er
Her frolics, and pursues her tail no more.
5 Returning home at night, you'll find the sink°   *sewer*
Strike your offended sense with double stink.
If you be wise, then go not far to dine;
You'll spend in coach hire more than save in wine.
A coming shower your shooting corns presage,
10 Old achés throb, your hollow tooth will rage.
Sauntering in coffeehouse is Dulman seen;
He damns the climate and complains of spleen.[2]
    Meanwhile the South, rising with dabbled wings,
A sable cloud athwart the welkin flings,
15 That swilled more liquor than it could contain,
And, like a drunkard, gives it up again.

1. Impends, is imminent. An example of elevated
diction used frequently throughout the poem to
gain a mock dignity, comically inappropriate to the
homely and realistic subject.
2. It was commonly believed at this time that the

Englishman's tendency to melancholy ("the
spleen") was attributable to the rainy climate.
"Dulman": a type name (from "dull man"), like
Congreve's "Petulant" or "Witwoud."

Brisk Susan whips her linen from the rope,
While the first drizzling shower is borne aslope:
Such is that sprinkling which some careless quean°   wench, slut
20 Flirts on you from her mop, but not so clean:
You fly, invoke the gods; then turning, stop
To rail; she singing, still whirls on her mop.
Not yet the dust had shunned the unequal strife,
But, aided by the wind, fought still for life,
25 And wafted with its foe by violent gust,
'Twas doubtful which was rain and which was dust.
Ah! where must needy poet seek for aid,
When dust and rain at once his coat invade?
Sole coat, where dust cemented by the rain
30 Erects the nap, and leaves a mingled stain.
    Now in contiguous drops the flood comes down,
Threatening with deluge this devoted town.
To shops in crowds the daggled° females fly,   mud-spattered
Pretend to cheapen° goods, but nothing buy.   bargain for
35 The Templar spruce, while every spout's abroach,[3]
Stays till 'tis fair, yet seems to call a coach.
The tucked-up sempstress walks with hasty strides,
While streams run down her oiled umbrella's sides.
Here various kinds, by various fortunes led,
40 Commence acquaintance underneath a shed.
Triumphant Tories and desponding Whigs
Forget their feuds,[4] and join to save their wigs.
Boxed in a chair° the beau impatient sits,   sedan chair
While spouts run clattering o'er the roof by fits,
45 And ever and anon with frightful din
The leather sounds;[5] he trembles from within.
So when Troy chairmen bore the wooden steed,
Pregnant with Greeks impatient to be freed
(Those bully Greeks, who, as the moderns do,
50 Instead of paying chairmen, run them through),[6]
Laocoön struck the outside with his spear,
And each imprisoned hero quaked for fear.[7]
    Now from all parts the swelling kennels[8] flow,
And bear their trophies with them as they go:
55 Filth of all hues and odors seem to tell
What street they sailed from, by their sight and smell.
They, as each torrent drives with rapid force,
From Smithfield or St. Pulchre's shape their course,
And in huge confluence joined at Snow Hill ridge,
60 Fall from the conduit prone to Holborn Bridge.[9]

3. Pouring out water. "The Templar": a young
man engaged in studying law. In the literature of
the period the Templar is usually depicted as
neglecting his professional studies for the sake of
dissipation and the pursuit of literature.
4. The Whig ministry had just fallen and the
Tories, led by Harley and St. John, were forming
the government with which Swift was to be closely
associated until the death of the queen in 1714.
5. The roof of the sedan chair was made of leather.

6. Run them through with their swords. The bully,
always prone to violence, was a familiar figure in
London streets and places of amusement.
7. Aeneid 2.40–53.
8. The open gutters in the middle of the street.
9. An accurate description of the drainage system
of this part of London—the eastern edge of Holborn and West Smithfield, which lie outside the
old walls west and east of Newgate. The great cattle and sheep markets were in Smithfield. The

Sweepings from butchers' stalls, dung, guts, and blood,

Drowned puppies, stinking sprats,° all drenched in mud,   } *small herrings*

Dead cats, and turnip tops, come tumbling down the flood.[1]

1710

Gulliver's Travels   *Gulliver's Travels* is Swift's most enduring satire. Although full of allusions to recent and current events, it still rings true today, for its objects are human failings and the defective political, economic, and social institutions that they call into being. Swift adopts an ancient satirical device: the imaginary voyage. Lemuel Gulliver, the narrator, is a ship's surgeon, a moderately well educated man, kindly, resourceful, cheerful, inquiring, patriotic, truthful, and rather unimaginative— in short, a reasonably decent example of humanity, with whom a reader can readily identify. He undertakes four voyages, all of which end disastrously among "several remote nations of the world." In the first, Gulliver is shipwrecked in the empire of Lilliput, where he finds himself a giant among a diminutive people, charmed by their miniature city and amused by their toylike prettiness. But in the end they prove to be treacherous, malicious, ambitious, vengeful, and cruel. As we read we grow disenchanted with the inhabitants of this fanciful kingdom, and then gradually we begin to recognize our likeness to them, especially in the disproportion between our natural pettiness and our boundless and destructive passions. In the second voyage, Gulliver is abandoned by his shipmates in Brobdingnag, a land of giants, creatures ten times as large as Europeans. Though he fears that such monsters must be brutes, the reverse proves to be the case. Brobdingnag is something of a utopia, governed by a humane and enlightened prince who is the embodiment of moral and political wisdom. In the long interview in which Gulliver pridefully enlarges on the glories of England and its political institutions, the king reduces him to resentful silence by asking questions that reveal the difference between what England is and what it ought to be. In Brobdingnag, Gulliver finds himself a Lilliputian, his pride humbled by his helpless state and his human vanity diminished by the realization that his body must have seemed as disgusting to the Lilliputians as do the bodies of the Brobdingnagians to him.

In the third voyage, to Laputa, Swift is chiefly concerned with attacking extremes of theoretical and speculative reasoning, whether in science, politics, or economics. Much of this voyage is an allegory of political life under the administration of the Whig minister, Sir Robert Walpole. The final voyage sets Gulliver between a race of horses, Houyhnhnms (prounced *Hwín-ims*), who live entirely by reason except for a few well-controlled and muted social affections, and their slaves, the Yahoos, whose bodies are obscene caricatures of the human body and who have no glimmer of reason but are mere creatures of appetite and passion.

When *Gulliver's Travels* first appeared, everyone read it—children for the story and politicians for the satire of current affairs—and ever since it has retained a hold on readers of every kind. Almost unique in world literature, it is simple enough for children, complex enough to carry adults beyond their depth. Swift's art works on many levels. First of all, there is the sheer playfulness of the narrative. Through Gulliver's eyes, we gaze on marvel after marvel: a tiny girl who threads an invisible needle with invisible silk or a white mare who threads a needle between pastern and hoof. The

church of St. Sepulchre ("St. Pulchre's") stood opposite Newgate Prison. Holborn Conduit was at the foot of Snow Hill. It drained into Fleet Ditch, an evil-smelling open sewer, at Holborn Bridge.

1. In Falkner's edition of Swift's *Works* (Dublin, 1735) a note almost certainly suggested by Swift

points to the concluding triplet, with its resonant final alexandrine, as a burlesque of a mannerism of Dryden and other Restoration poets and claims that Swift's ridicule banished the triplet from contemporary poetry.

travels, like a fairy story, transport us to imaginary worlds that function with a perfect, fantastic logic different from our own; Swift exercises our sense of vision. But beyond that, he exercises our perceptions of meaning. In *Gulliver's Travels*, things are seldom what they seem; irony, probing or corrosive, underlies almost every word. In the last chapter, Gulliver insists that the example of the Houyhnhnms has made him incapable of telling a lie—but the oath he swears is quoted from Sinon, whose lies to the Trojans persuaded them to accept the Trojan *horse*. Swift trains us to read alertly, to look beneath the surface. Yet on its deepest level, the book does not offer final meanings, but a question: What is a human being? Voyaging through imaginary worlds, we try to find ourselves. Are we prideful insects or lords of creation? brutes or reasonable beings? In the last voyage, Swift pushes such questions, and Gulliver himself, almost beyond endurance; hating his own humanity, Gulliver forgets who he is. For the reader, however, the outcome cannot be so clear. Swift does not set out to satisfy our minds but to vex and unsettle them. And he leaves us at the moment when the mixed face of humanity—the pettiness of the Lilliputians, the savagery of the Yahoos, the innocence of Gulliver himself—begins to look strangely familiar, like our own faces in a mirror.

Swift's full title for this work was *Travels into Several Remote Nations of the World. In Four Parts. By Lemuel Gulliver, First a Surgeon, and then a Captain of several Ships*. In the first edition (1726), either the bookseller or Swift's friends Charles Ford, Pope, and others, who were concerned in getting the book anonymously into print, altered and omitted so much of the original manuscript (because of its dangerous political implications) that Swift was seriously annoyed. When, in 1735, the Dublin bookseller George Faulkner brought out an edition of Swift's works, the dean seems to have taken pains, surreptitiously, to see that a more authentic version of the work was published. This text is the basis of modern editions.

From Gulliver's Travels

A Letter from Captain Gulliver to His Cousin Sympson[1]

I hope you will be ready to own publicly, whenever you shall be called to it, that by your great and frequent urgency you prevailed on me to publish a very loose and uncorrect account of my travels; with direction to hire some young gentlemen of either University to put them in order, and correct the style, as my Cousin Dampier[2] did by my advice, in his book called *A Voyage round the World*. But I do not remember I gave you power to consent that anything should be omitted, and much less that anything should be inserted: therefore, as to the latter, I do here renounce everything of that kind; particularly a paragraph about her Majesty the late Queen Anne, of most pious and glorious memory; although I did reverence and esteem her more than any of human species. But you, or your interpolator, ought to have considered that as it was not my inclination, so was it not decent to praise any animal of our composition before my master Houyhnhnm; and besides, the fact was altogether false; for to my knowledge, being in England during some part of her Majesty's reign, she did govern by a chief Minister; nay, even by two successively; the first whereof was the Lord of Godolphin, and the sec-

---

1. In this letter, first published in 1735, Swift complains, among other matters, of the alterations in his original text made by the publisher, Benjamin Motte, in the interest of what he considered political discretion.
2. William Dampier (1652–1715), the explorer, whose account of his circumnavigation of the globe Swift had read.

ond the Lord of Oxford; so that you have made me *say the thing that was not.* Likewise, in the account of the Academy of Projectors, and several passages of my discourse to my master Houyhnhnm, you have either omitted some material circumstances, or minced or changed them in such a manner, that I do hardly know mine own work. When I formerly hinted to you something of this in a letter, you were pleased to answer that you were afraid of giving offense; that people in power were very watchful over the press; and apt not only to interpret, but to punish everything which looked like an *innuendo* (as I think you called it). But pray, how could that which I spoke so many years ago, and at above five thousand leagues distance, in another reign, be applied to any of the Yahoos, who now are said to govern the herd; especially, at a time when I little thought on or feared the unhappiness of living under them. Have not I the most reason to complain, when I see these very Yahoos carried by Houyhnhnms in a vehicle, as if these were brutes, and those the rational creatures? And, indeed, to avoid so monstrous and detestable a sight was one principal motive of my retirement hither.[3]

Thus much I thought proper to tell you in relation to yourself, and to the trust I reposed in you.

I do in the next place complain of my own great want of judgment, in being prevailed upon by the intreaties and false reasonings of you and some others, very much against mine own opinion, to suffer my travels to be published. Pray bring to your mind how often I desired you to consider, when you insisted on the motive of public good, that the Yahoos were a species of animals utterly incapable of amendment by precepts or examples; and so it hath proved; for instead of seeing a full stop put to all abuses and corruptions, at least in this little island, as I had reason to expect, behold, after above six months warning, I cannot learn that my book hath produced one single effect according to mine intentions; I desired you would let me know by a letter, when party and faction were extinguished; judges learned and upright; pleaders honest and modest, with some tincture of common sense; and Smithfield[4] blazing with pyramids of law books; the young nobility's education entirely changed; the physicians banished; the female Yahoos abounding in virtue, honor, truth, and good sense; courts and levees of great ministers thoroughly weeded and swept; wit, merit, and learning rewarded; all disgracers of the press in prose and verse, condemned to eat nothing but their own cotton,[5] and quench their thirst with their own ink. These, and a thousand other reformations, I firmly counted upon by your encouragement; as indeed they were plainly deducible from the precepts delivered in my book. And, it must be owned that seven months were a sufficient time to correct every vice and folly to which Yahoos are subject; if their natures had been capable of the least disposition to virtue or wisdom; yet so far have you been from answering mine expectation in any of your letters, that on the contrary, you are loading our carrier every week with libels, and keys, and reflections, and memoirs, and second parts; wherein I see myself accused of reflecting upon great statesfolk; of degrading human nature (for so they have still the confidence to style it) and of abusing the female sex. I find likewise, that the writers of those bundles are not agreed among themselves; for some of them will not

3. To Nottinghamshire.
4. A part of London containing many bookshops.

5. Presumably their paper.

allow me to be author of mine own travels; and others make me author of books to which I am wholly a stranger.

I find likewise that your printer hath been so careless as to confound the times, and mistake the dates of my several voyages and returns; neither assigning the true year, or the true month, or day of the month; and I hear the original manuscript is all destroyed, since the publication of my book. Neither have I any copy left; however, I have sent you some corrections, which you may insert, if ever there should be a second edition; and yet I cannot stand to them, but shall leave that matter to my judicious and candid readers, to adjust it as they please.

I hear some of our sea Yahoos find fault with my sea language, as not proper in many parts, nor now in use. I cannot help it. In my first voyages, while I was young, I was instructed by the oldest mariners, and learned to speak as they did. But I have since found that the sea Yahoos are apt, like the land ones, to become new fangled in their words; which the latter change every year; insomuch, as I remember upon each return to mine own country, their old dialect was so altered, that I could hardly understand the new. And I observe, when any Yahoo comes from London out of curiosity to visit me at mine own house, we neither of us are able to deliver our conceptions in a manner intelligible to the other.[6]

If the censure of Yahoos could any way affect me, I should have great reason to complain that some of them are so bold as to think my book of travels a mere fiction out of mine own brain; and have gone so far as to drop hints that the Houyhnhnms, and Yahoos have no more existence than the inhabitants of Utopia.

Indeed I must confess that as to the people of Lilliput, Brobdingrag (for so the word should have been spelled, and not erroneously Brobdingnag) and Laputa, I have never yet heard of any Yahoo so presumptuous as to dispute their being, or the facts I have related concerning them; because the truth immediately strikes every reader with conviction. And, is there less probability in my account of the Houyhnhnms or Yahoos, when it is manifest as to the latter, there are so many thousands even in this city, who only differ from their brother brutes in Houyhnhnmland, because they use a sort of a jabber, and do not go naked. I wrote for their amendment, and not their approbation. The united praise of the whole race would be of less consequence to me, than the neighing of those two degenerate Houyhnhnms I keep in my stable; because, from these, degenerate as they are, I still improve in some virtues, without any mixture of vice.

Do these miserable animals presume to think that I am so far degenerated as to defend my veracity; Yahoo as I am, it is well known through all Houyhnhnmland, that by the instructions and example of my illustrious master, I was able in the compass of two years (although I confess with the utmost difficulty) to remove that infernal habit of lying, shuffling, deceiving, and equivocating, so deeply rooted in the very souls of all my species; especially the Europeans.

I have other complaints to make upon this vexatious occasion; but I forbear troubling myself or you any further. I must freely confess that since my last

6. Swift was the inveterate enemy of slang.

return, some corruptions of my Yahoo nature have revived in me by conversing with a few of your species, and particularly those of mine own family, by an unavoidable necessity; else I should never have attempted so absurd a project as that of reforming the Yahoo race in this kingdom; but I have now done with all such visionary schemes for ever.

1727?   1735

The Publisher to the Reader

The author of these travels, Mr. Lemuel Gulliver, is my ancient and intimate friend; there is likewise some relation between us by the mother's side. About three years ago Mr. Gulliver, growing weary of the concourse of curious people coming to him at his house in Redriff,[7] made a small purchase of land, with a convenient house, near Newark, in Nottinghamshire, his native country; where he now lives retired, yet in good esteem among his neighbors.

Although Mr. Gulliver were born in Nottinghamshire, where his father dwelt, yet I have heard him say his family came from Oxfordshire; to confirm which, I have observed in the churchyard at Banbury, in that county, several tombs and monuments of the Gullivers.

Before he quitted Redriff, he left the custody of the following papers in my hands, with the liberty to dispose of them as I should think fit. I have carefully perused them three times; the style is very plain and simple; and the only fault I find is that the author, after the manner of travelers, is a little too circumstantial. There is an air of truth apparent through the whole; and indeed the author was so distinguished for his veracity, that it became a sort of proverb among his neighbors at Redriff, when anyone affirmed a thing, to say, it was as true as if Mr. Gulliver had spoke it.

By the advice of several worthy persons, to whom, with the author's permission, I communicated these papers, I now venture to send them into the world; hoping they may be, at least for some time, a better entertainment to our young noblemen, than the common scribbles of politics and party.

This volume would have been at least twice as large, if I had not made bold to strike out innumerable passages relating to the winds and tides, as well as to the variations and bearings in the several voyages; together with the minute descriptions of the management of the ship in storms, in the style of sailors; likewise the account of the longitudes and latitudes, wherein I have reason to apprehend that Mr. Gulliver may be a little dissatisfied; but I was resolved to fit the work as much as possible to the general capacity of readers. However, if my own ignorance in sea affairs shall have led me to commit some mistakes, I alone am answerable for them; and if any traveler hath a curiosity to see the whole work at large, as it came from the hand of the author, I will be ready to gratify him.

As for any further particulars relating to the author, the reader will receive satisfaction from the first pages of the book.

RICHARD SYMPSON

---

7. Rotherhithe, a district in southern London, below Tower Bridge, then frequented by sailors.

Part 1. A Voyage to Lilliput

CHAPTER 1. *The author gives some account of himself and family; his first inducements to travel. He is shipwrecked, and swims for his life; gets safe on shore in the country of Lilliput; is made a prisoner, and carried up the country.*

My father had a small estate in Nottinghamshire; I was the third of five sons. He sent me to Emanuel College in Cambridge, at fourteen years old, where I resided three years, and applied myself close to my studies: but the charge of maintaining me (although I had a very scanty allowance) being too great for a narrow fortune, I was bound apprentice to Mr. James Bates, an eminent surgeon in London, with whom I continued four years; and my father now and then sending me small sums of money, I laid them out in learning navigation, and other parts of the mathematics, useful to those who intend to travel, as I always believed it would be some time or other my fortune to do. When I left Mr. Bates, I went down to my father; where, by the assistance of him and my uncle John, and some other relations, I got forty pounds, and a promise of thirty pounds a year to maintain me at Leyden: there I studied physic[8] two years and seven months, knowing it would be useful in long voyages.

Soon after my return from Leyden, I was recommended by my good master Mr. Bates, to be surgeon to the *Swallow*, Captain Abraham Pannell commander; with whom I continued three years and a half, making a voyage or two into the Levant[9] and some other parts. When I came back, I resolved to settle in London, to which Mr. Bates, my master, encouraged me; and by him I was recommended to several patients. I took part of a small house in the Old Jury; and being advised to alter my condition, I married Mrs.[1] Mary Burton, second daughter to Mr. Edmond Burton, hosier, in Newgate Street, with whom I received four hundred pounds for a portion.

But, my good master Bates dying in two years after, and I having few friends, my business began to fail; for my conscience would not suffer me to imitate the bad practice of too many among my brethren. Having therefore consulted with my wife, and some of my acquaintance, I determined to go again to sea. I was surgeon successively in two ships, and made several voyages, for six years, to the East and West Indies; by which I got some addition to my fortune. My hours of leisure I spent in reading the best authors, ancient and modern, being always provided with a good number of books; and when I was ashore, in observing the manners and dispositions of the people, as well as learning their language; wherein I had a great facility by the strength of my memory.

The last of these voyages not proving very fortunate, I grew weary of the sea, and intended to stay at home with my wife and family. I removed from the Old Jury to Fetter Lane, and from thence to Wapping, hoping to get business among the sailors; but it would not turn to account. After three years' expectation that things would mend, I accepted an advantageous offer

---

8. The University of Leyden, in Holland, was a center for the study of "physic" (medicine).
9. The eastern Mediterranean.

1. "Mrs." (pronounced "Mistress") designated any woman, married or unmarried. "Old Jury": a street (once "Old Jewry") in the City of London.

from Captain William Prichard, master of the *Antelope,* who was making a voyage to the South Sea. We set sail from Bristol, May 4th, 1699, and our voyage at first was very prosperous.

It would not be proper, for some reasons, to trouble the reader with the particulars of our adventures in those seas: let it suffice to inform him, that in our passage from thence to the East Indies we were driven by a violent storm to the northwest of Van Diemen's Land.[2] By an observation, we found ourselves in the latitude of 30 degrees 2 minutes south. Twelve of our crew were dead by immoderate labor, and ill food, the rest were in a very weak condition. On the fifth of November, which was the beginning of summer in those parts, the weather being very hazy, the seamen spied a rock, within half a cable's length of the ship; but the wind was so strong, that we were driven directly upon it, and immediately split. Six of the crew, of whom I was one, having let down the boat into the sea, made a shift to get clear of the ship, and the rock. We rowed by my computation about three leagues, till we were able to work no longer, being already spent with labor while we were in the ship. We therefore trusted ourselves to the mercy of the waves; and in about half an hour the boat was overset by a sudden flurry from the north. What became of my companions in the boat, as well as of those who escaped on the rock, or were left in the vessel, I cannot tell; but conclude they were all lost. For my own part, I swam as fortune directed me, and was pushed forward by wind and tide. I often let my legs drop, and could feel no bottom; but when I was almost gone, and able to struggle no longer, I found myself within my depth; and by this time the storm was much abated. The declivity was so small, that I walked near a mile before I got to the shore, which I conjectured was about eight o'clock in the evening. I then advanced forward near half a mile, but could not discover any sign of houses or inhabitants; at least I was in so weak a condition, that I did not observe them. I was extremely tired, and with that, and the heat of the weather, and about half a pint of brandy that I drank as I left the ship, I found myself much inclined to sleep. I lay down on the grass, which was very short and soft, where I slept sounder than ever I remember to have done in my life, and as I reckoned, above nine hours; for when I awaked, it was just daylight. I attempted to rise, but was not able to stir: for as I happened to lie on my back, I found my arms and legs were strongly fastened on each side to the ground; and my hair, which was long and thick, tied down in the same manner. I likewise felt several slender ligatures across my body, from my armpits to my thighs. I could only look upwards; the sun began to grow hot, and the light offended my eyes. I heard a confused noise about me, but in the posture I lay, could see nothing except the sky. In a little time I felt something alive moving on my left leg, which advancing gently forward over my breast, came almost up to my chin; when bending my eyes downwards as much as I could, I perceived it to be a human creature not six inches high,[3] with a bow and arrow in his hands, and a quiver at his back. In the meantime, I felt at least forty more of the same kind (as I conjectured) following the first. I was in the utmost astonishment, and roared so loud, that they all ran back in a

---

2. Tasmania.
3. Lilliput is scaled, fairly consistently, at one-twelfth of Gulliver's world.

fright; and some of them, as I was afterwards told, were hurt with the falls they got by leaping from my sides upon the ground. However, they soon returned; and one of them, who ventured so far as to get a full sight of my face, lifting up his hands and eyes by way of admiration,[4] cried out in a shrill, but distinct voice, *Hekinah Degul*: the others repeated the same words several times, but I then knew not what they meant. I lay all this while, as the reader may believe, in great uneasiness; at length, struggling to get loose, I had the fortune to break the strings, and wrench out the pegs that fastened my left arm to the ground; for, by lifting it up to my face, I discovered the methods they had taken to bind me; and, at the same time, with a violent pull, which gave me excessive pain, I a little loosened the strings that tied down my hair on the left side; so that I was just able to turn my head about two inches. But the creatures ran off a second time, before I could seize them; whereupon there was a great shout in a very shrill accent; and after it ceased, I heard one of them cry aloud, *Tolgo phonac*; when in an instant I felt above an hundred arrows discharged on my left hand, which pricked me like so many needles; and besides they shot another flight into the air, as we do bombs in Europe, whereof many, I suppose, fell on my body (though I felt them not) and some on my face, which I immediately covered with my left hand. When this shower of arrows was over, I fell a groaning with grief and pain; and then striving again to get loose, they discharged another volley larger than the first, and some of them attempted with spears to stick me in the sides; but, by good luck, I had on me a buff jerkin,[5] which they could not pierce. I thought it the most prudent method to lie still; and my design was to continue so till night, when, my left hand being already loose, I could easily free myself: and as for the inhabitants, I had reason to believe I might be a match for the greatest armies they could bring against me, if they were all of the same size with him that I saw. But fortune disposed otherwise of me. When the people observed I was quiet, they discharged no more arrows: but by the noise increasing, I knew their numbers were greater; and about four yards from me, over-against my right ear, I heard a knocking for above an hour, like people at work; when turning my head that way, as well as the pegs and strings would permit me, I saw a stage erected about a foot and a half from the ground, capable of holding four of the inhabitants, with two or three ladders to mount it: from whence one of them, who seemed to be a person of quality, made me a long speech, whereof I understood not one syllable. But I should have mentioned, that before the principal person began his oration, he cried out three times, *Langro Dehul san*: (these words and the former were afterwards repeated and explained to me). Whereupon immediately about fifty of the inhabitants came, and cut the strings that fastened the left side of my head, which gave me the liberty of turning it to the right, and of observing the person and gesture of him who was to speak. He appeared to be of a middle age, and taller than any of the other three who attended him; whereof one was a page who held up his train, and seemed to be somewhat longer than my middle finger; the other two stood one on each side to support him. He acted every part of an orator, and I could observe many periods[6] of threatenings, and others of promises, pity and kind-

---

4. Wonderment.
5. Leather jacket.

6. In rhetoric, complete, well-constructed sentences.

ness. I answered in a few words, but in the most submissive manner, lifting up my left hand and both my eyes to the sun, as calling him for a witness; and being almost famished with hunger, having not eaten a morsel for some hours before I left the ship, I found the demands of nature so strong upon me, that I could not forbear showing my impatience (perhaps against the strict rules of decency) by putting my finger frequently on my mouth, to signify that I wanted food. The Hurgo (for so they call a great lord, as I afterwards learned) understood me very well. He descended from the stage, and commanded that several ladders should be applied to my sides, on which above an hundred of the inhabitants mounted, and walked towards my mouth, laden with baskets full of meat, which had been provided and sent thither by the King's orders upon the first intelligence he received of me. I observed there was the flesh of several animals, but could not distinguish them by the taste. There were shoulders, legs, and loins shaped like those of mutton, and very well dressed, but smaller than the wings of a lark. I eat them by two or three at a mouthful, and took three loaves at a time, about the bigness of musket bullets. They supplied me as fast as they could, showing a thousand marks of wonder and astonishment at my bulk and appetite. I then made another sign that I wanted drink. They found by my eating that a small quantity would not suffice me; and being a most ingenious people, they slung up with great dexterity one of their largest hogsheads; then rolled it towards my hand, and beat out the top; I drank it off at a draught, which I might well do, for it hardly held half a pint, and tasted like a small wine of Burgundy, but much more delicious. They brought me a second hogshead, which I drank in the same manner, and made signs for more, but they had none to give me. When I had performed these wonders, they shouted for joy, and danced upon my breast, repeating several times as they did at first, *Hekinah Degul*. They made me a sign that I should throw down the two hogsheads, but first warned the people below to stand out of the way, crying aloud, *Borach Mivola*, and when they saw the vessels in the air, there was an universal shout of *Hekinah Degul*. I confess I was often tempted, while they were passing backwards and forwards on my body, to seize forty or fifty of the first that came in my reach, and dash them against the ground. But the remembrance of what I had felt, which probably might not be the worst they could do; and the promise of honor I made them, for so I interpreted my submissive behavior, soon drove out those imaginations. Besides, I now considered myself as bound by the laws of hospitality to a people who had treated me with so much expense and magnificence. However, in my thoughts I could not sufficiently wonder at the intrepidity of these diminutive mortals, who durst venture to mount and walk on my body, while one of my hands was at liberty, without trembling at the very sight of so prodigious a creature as I must appear to them. After some time, when they observed that I made no more demands for meat, there appeared before me a person of high rank from his Imperial Majesty. His Excellency, having mounted on the small of my right leg, advanced forwards up to my face, with about a dozen of his retinue. And producing his credentials under the Signet Royal, which he applied[7] close to my eyes, spoke about ten minutes, without any signs of anger, but with a kind of determinate resolution; often pointing forwards,

7. Brought.

which, as I afterwards found, was towards the capital city, about half a mile distant, whither it was agreed by his Majesty in council that I must be conveyed. I answered in a few words, but to no purpose, and made a sign with my hand that was loose, putting it to the other (but over his Excellency's head, for fear of hurting him or his train) and then to my own head and body, to signify that I desired my liberty. It appeared that he understood me well enough; for he shook his head by way of disapprobation, and held his hand in a posture to show that I must be carried as a prisoner. However, he made other signs to let me understand that I should have meat and drink enough, and very good treatment. Whereupon I once more thought of attempting to break my bonds; but again, when I felt the smart of their arrows upon my face and hands, which were all in blisters, and many of the darts still sticking in them; and observing likewise that the number of my enemies increased; I gave tokens to let them know that they might do with me what they pleased. Upon this the *Hurgo* and his train withdrew, with much civility and cheerful countenances. Soon after I heard a general shout, with frequent repetitions of the words, *Peplom Selan,* and I felt great numbers of the people on my left side relaxing the cords to such a degree, that I was able to turn upon my right, and to ease myself with making water; which I very plentifully did, to the great astonishment of the people, who conjecturing by my motions what I was going to do, immediately opened to the right and left on that side, to avoid the torrent which fell with such noise and violence from me. But before this, they had daubed my face and both my hands with a sort of ointment very pleasant to the smell, which in a few minutes removed all the smart of their arrows. These circumstances, added to the refreshment I had received by their victuals and drink, which were very nourishing, disposed me to sleep. I slept about eight hours, as I was afterwards assured; and it was no wonder; for the physicians, by the Emperor's order, had mingled a sleeping potion in the hogsheads of wine.

It seems that upon the first moment I was discovered sleeping on the ground after my landing, the Emperor had early notice of it by an express; and determined in council that I should be tied in the manner I have related (which was done in the night while I slept), that plenty of meat and drink should be sent me, and a machine prepared to carry me to the capital city.

This resolution perhaps may appear very bold and dangerous, and I am confident would not be imitated by any prince in Europe on the like occasion; however, in my opinion it was extremely prudent as well as generous. For supposing these people had endeavored to kill me with their spears and arrows while I was asleep; I should certainly have awaked with the first sense of smart, which might so far have roused my rage and strength, as to enable me to break the strings wherewith I was tied; after which, as they were not able to make resistance, so they could expect no mercy.

These people are most excellent mathematicians, and arrived to a great perfection in mechanics by the countenance and encouragement of the Emperor, who is a renowned patron of learning. This prince hath several machines fixed on wheels, for the carriage of trees and other great weights. He often builds his largest men of war, whereof some are nine foot long, in the woods where the timber grows, and has them carried on these engines[8]

8. Contrivances.

three or four hundred yards to the sea. Five hundred carpenters and engineers were immediately set at work to prepare the greatest engine they had. It was a frame of wood raised three inches from the ground, about seven foot long and four wide, moving upon twenty-two wheels. The shout I heard was upon the arrival of this engine, which it seems set out in four hours after my landing. It was brought parallel to me as I lay. But the principal difficulty was to raise and place me in this vehicle. Eighty poles, each of one foot high, were erected for this purpose, and very strong cords of the bigness of pack-thread were fastened by hooks to many bandages, which the workmen had girt round my neck, my hands, my body, and my legs. Nine hundred of the strongest men were employed to draw up these cords by many pulleys fastened on the poles; and thus, in less than three hours, I was raised and slung into the engine, and there tied fast. All this I was told, for while the whole operation was performing, I lay in a profound sleep, by the force of that soporiferous[9] medicine infused into my liquor. Fifteen hundred of the Emperor's largest horses, each about four inches and a half high, were employed to draw me towards the metropolis, which, as I said, was half a mile distant.

About four hours after we began our journey, I awaked by a very ridiculous accident; for, the carriage being stopped a while to adjust something that was out of order, two or three of the young natives had the curiosity to see how I looked when I was asleep; they climbed up into the engine, and advancing very softly to my face, one of them, an officer in the guards, put the sharp end of his half-pike a good way up into my left nostril, which tickled my nose like a straw, and made me sneeze violently: whereupon they stole off unperceived, and it was three weeks before I knew the cause of my awaking so suddenly. We made a long march the remaining part of the day, and rested at night with five hundred guards on each side of me half with torches, and half with bows and arrows, ready to shoot me if I should offer to stir. The next morning at sunrise we continued our march, and arrived within two hundred yards of the city gates about noon. The Emperor and all his court came out to meet us, but his great officers would by no means suffer his Majesty to endanger his person by mounting on my body.

At the place where the carriage stopped, there stood an ancient temple, esteemed to be the largest in the whole kingdom, which having been polluted some years before by an unnatural murder,[1] was, according to the zeal of those people, looked on as profane, and therefore had been applied to common use, and all the ornaments and furniture carried away. In this edifice it was determined I should lodge. The great gate fronting to the north was about four foot high, and almost two foot wide, through which I could easily creep. On each side of the gate was a small window not above six inches from the ground: into that on the left side, the King's smiths conveyed fourscore and eleven chains, like those that hang to a lady's watch in Europe, and almost as large, which were locked to my left leg with six and thirty padlocks. Over against this temple, on the other side of the great highway, at twenty foot distance, there was a turret at least five foot high. Here the Emperor ascended with many principal lords of his court, to have an oppor-

9. Inducing unnatural sleep.
1. Presumably a reference to the execution of Charles I, who was sentenced in Westminster Hall.

tunity of viewing me, as I was told, for I could not see them. It was reckoned that above an hundred thousand inhabitants came out of the town upon the same errand; and in spite of my guards, I believe there could not be fewer than ten thousand, at several times, who mounted upon my body by the help of ladders. But a proclamation was soon issued to forbid it upon pain of death. When the workmen found it was impossible for me to break loose, they cut all the strings that bound me; whereupon I rose up with as melancholy a disposition as ever I had in my life. But the noise and astonishment of the people at seeing me rise and walk are not to be expressed. The chains that held my left leg were about two yards long, and gave me not only the liberty of walking backwards and forwards in a semicircle; but, being fixed within four inches of the gate, allowed me to creep in, and lie at my full length in the temple.

CHAPTER 2. *The Emperor of Lilliput, attended by several of the nobility, comes to see the author in his confinement. The Emperor's person and habit described. Learned men appointed to teach the author their language. He gains favor by his mild disposition. His pockets are searched, and his sword and pistols taken from him.*

When I found myself on my feet, I looked about me, and must confess I never beheld a more entertaining prospect. The country round appeared like a continued garden, and the inclosed fields, which were generally forty foot psquare, resembled so many beds of flowers. These fields were intermingled with woods of half a stang,[2] and the tallest trees, as I could judge, appeared to be seven foot high. I viewed the town on my left hand, which looked like the painted scene of a city in a theater.

I had been for some hours extremely pressed by the necessities of nature; which was no wonder, it being almost two days since I had last disburthened myself. I was under great difficulties between urgency and shame. The best expedient I could think on, was to creep into my house, which I accordingly did; and shutting the gate after me, I went as far as the length of my chain would suffer; and discharged my body of that uneasy load. But this was the only time I was ever guilty of so uncleanly an action; for which I cannot but hope the candid reader will give some allowance, after he hath maturely and impartially considered my case, and the distress I was in. From this time my constant practice was, as soon as I rose, to perform that business in open air, at the full extent of my chain, and due care was taken every morning before company came, that the offensive matter should be carried off in wheelbarrows by two servants appointed for that purpose. I would not have dwelt so long upon a circumstance, that perhaps at first sight may appear not very momentous, if I had not thought it necessary to justify my character in point of cleanliness to the world; which I am told some of my maligners have been pleased, upon this and other occasions, to call in question.

When this adventure was at an end, I came back out of my house, having occasion for fresh air. The Emperor was already descended from the tower, and advancing on horseback towards me, which had like to have cost him dear; for the beast, although very well trained, yet wholly unused to such a

---

2. A quarter of an acre.

sight, which appeared as if a mountain moved before him, reared up on his hinder feet: but that prince, who is an excellent horseman, kept his seat, until his attendants ran in, and held the bridle, while his Majesty had time to dismount. When he alighted, he surveyed me round with great admiration, but kept beyond the length of my chains. He ordered his cooks and butlers, who were already prepared, to give me victuals and drink, which they pushed forward in a sort of vehicles upon wheels until I could reach them. I took these vehicles, and soon emptied them all; twenty of them were filled with meat, and ten with liquor; each of the former afforded me two or three good mouthfuls, and I emptied the liquor of ten vessels, which was contained in earthen vials, into one vehicle, drinking it off at a draught; and so I did with the rest. The Empress, and young princes of the blood, of both sexes, attended by many ladies, sat at some distance in their chairs; but upon the accident that happened to the Emperor's horse, they alighted, and came near his person; which I am now going to describe. He is taller, by almost the breadth of my nail, than any of his court, which alone is enough to strike an awe into the beholders. His features are strong and masculine, with an Austrian lip, and arched nose, his complexion olive, his countenance[3] erect, his body and limbs well proportioned, all his motions graceful, and his deportment majestic. He was then past his prime, being twenty-eight years and three quarters old, of which he had reigned about seven, in great felicity, and generally victorious. For the better convenience of beholding him, I lay on my side, so that my face was parallel to his, and he stood but three yards off: however, I have had him since many times in my hand, and therefore cannot be deceived in the description. His dress was very plain and simple, the fashion of it between the Asiatic and the European; but he had on his head a light helmet of gold, adorned with jewels, and a plume on the crest. He held his sword drawn in his hand, to defend himself, if I should happen to break loose; it was almost three inches long, the hilt and scabbard were gold enriched with diamonds. His voice was shrill, but very clear and articulate, and I could distinctly hear it when I stood up. The ladies and courtiers were all most magnificently clad, so that the spot they stood upon seemed to resemble a petticoat spread on the ground, embroidered with figures of gold and silver. His Imperial Majesty spoke often to me, and I returned answers, but neither of us could understand a syllable. There were several of his priests and lawyers present (as I conjectured by their habits) who were commanded to address themselves to me, and I spoke to them in as many languages as I had the least smattering of, which were High and Low Dutch, Latin, French, Spanish, Italian, and Lingua Franca;[4] but all to no purpose. After about two hours the court retired, and I was left with a strong guard, to prevent the impertinence, and probably the malice of the rabble, who were very impatient to crowd about me as near as they durst; and some of them had the impudence to shoot their arrows at me as I sat on the ground by the door of my house, whereof one very narrowly missed my left eye. But the colonel ordered six of the ringleaders to be seized, and thought no punishment so proper as to deliver them bound into my hands, which some of his soldiers accordingly did, pushing them forwards with the butt-ends of their

---

3. Bearing, appearance. Swift may be satirically idealizing George I, whom most of the British thought gross.

4. A jargon, based on Italian, used by traders in the Mediterranean. "High and Low Dutch": German and Dutch.

pikes into my reach; I took them all in my right hand, put five of them into my coat-pocket; and as to the sixth, I made a countenance as if I would eat him alive. The poor man squalled terribly, and the colonel and his officer were in much pain, especially when they saw me take out my penknife: but I soon put them out of fear; for, looking mildly, and immediately cutting the strings he was bound with, I set him gently on the ground, and away he ran. I treated the rest in the same manner, taking them one by one out of my pocket, and I observed both the soldiers and people were highly obliged at this mark of my clemency, which was represented very much to my advantage at court.

Towards night I got with some difficulty into my house, where I lay on the ground, and continued to do so about a fortnight; during which time the Emperor gave orders to have a bed prepared for me. Six hundred beds of the common measure were brought in carriages, and worked up in my house; an hundred and fifty of their beds sewn together made up the breadth and length, and these were four double, which however kept me but very indifferently from the hardness of the floor, that was of smooth stone. By the same computation they provided me with sheets, blankets, and coverlets, tolerable enough for one who had been so long enured to hardships as I.

As the news of my arrival spread through the kingdom, it brought prodigious numbers of rich, idle, and curious people to see me; so that the villages were almost emptied, and great neglect of tillage and household affairs must have ensued, if his Imperial Majesty had not provided by several proclamations and orders of state against this inconveniency. He directed that those who had already beheld me should return home, and not presume to come within fifty yards of my house without license from court; whereby the secretaries of state got considerable fees.

In the mean time, the Emperor held frequent councils to debate what course should be taken with me; and I was afterwards assured by a particular friend, a person of great quality, who was as much in the secret as any, that the court was under many difficulties concerning me. They apprehended[5] my breaking loose, that my diet would be very expensive, and might cause a famine. Sometimes they determined to starve me, or at least to shoot me in the face and hands with poisoned arrows, which would soon dispatch me: but again they considered, that the stench of so large a carcass might produce a plague in the metropolis, and probably spread through the whole kingdom. In the midst of these consultations, several officers of the army went to the door of the great council chamber; and two of them being admitted, gave an account of my behavior to the six criminals above-mentioned; which made so favorable an impression in the breast of his Majesty, and the whole board, in my behalf, that an imperial commission was issued out, obliging all the villages nine hundred yards round the city to deliver in every morning six beeves, forty sheep, and other victuals for my sustenance; together with a proportionable quantity of bread and wine, and other liquors: for the due payment of which his Majesty gave assignments[6] upon his treasury. For this prince lives chiefly upon his own demesnes; seldom except upon great occasions raising any subsidies upon his subjects, who are bound to attend him in his wars at their own expense. An establishment was also made of six

---

5. Anticipated with fear.

6. Formal mandates of revenue.

hundred persons to be my domestics, who had board-wages allowed for their maintenance, and tents built for them very conveniently on each side of my door. It was likewise ordered, that three hundred tailors should make me a suit of clothes after the fashion of the country: that six of his Majesty's greatest scholars should be employed to instruct me in their language: and, lastly, that the Emperor's horses, and those of the nobility, and troops of guards, should be exercised in my sight, to accustom themselves to me. All these orders were duly put in execution; and in about three weeks I made a great progress in learning their language; during which time the Emperor frequently honored me with his visits, and was pleased to assist my masters in teaching me. We began already to converse together in some sort; and the first words I learned, were to express my desire that he would please to give me my liberty; which I every day repeated on my knees.[7] His answer, as I could apprehend, was, that this must be a work of time, not to be thought on without the advice of his council; and that first I must *Lumos kelmin pesso desmar lon emposo*; that is, swear a peace with him and his kingdom. How-ever, that I should be used with all kindness; and he advised me to acquire by my patience and discreet behavior, the good opinion of himself and his subjects. He desired I would not take it ill, if he gave orders to certain proper officers to search me; for probably I might carry about me several weapons, which must needs be dangerous things, if they answered the bulk of so pro-digious a person.[8] I said, his Majesty should be satisfied, for I was ready to strip myself, and turn up my pockets before him. This I delivered part in words, and part in signs. He replied, that by the laws of the kingdom, I must be searched by two of his officers; that he knew this could not be done without my consent and assistance; that he had so good an opinion of my generosity and justice, as to trust their persons in my hands; that whatever they took from me should be returned when I left the country, or paid for at the rate which I would set upon them. I took up the two officers in my hands, put them first into my coat-pockets, and then into every other pocket about me, except my two fobs, and another secret pocket which I had no mind should be searched, wherein I had some little necessaries of no consequence to any but myself. In one of my fobs there was a silver watch, and in the other a small quantity of gold in a purse. These gentlemen, having pen, ink, and paper about them, made an exact inventory of everything they saw; and when they had done, desired I would set them down, that they might deliver it to the Emperor. This inventory I afterwards translated into English, and is word for word as follows.

Imprimis, In the right coat-pocket of the Great Man-Mountain (for so I interpret the words *Quinbus Flestrin*) after the strictest search, we found only one great piece of coarse cloth, large enough to be a foot-cloth for your Majesty's chief room of state. In the left pocket, we saw a huge silver chest, with a cover of the same metal, which we the search-ers were not able to lift. We desired it should be opened; and one of us, stepping into it, found himself up to the mid leg in a sort of dust, some

7. Gulliver's plea for liberty and the threat of star-vation or rebellion he represents to his captors sug-gest the situation of Ireland with respect to England.

8. When the Whigs came into power in 1715, the leading Tories, who included Swift's friends Oxford and Bolingbroke (Robert Harley and Henry St. John) as well as Swift himself, were investigated by a committee of secrecy.

part whereof flying up to our faces, set us both a sneezing for several times together. In his right waistcoat-pocket, we found a prodigious bundle of white thin substances, folded one over another, about the bigness of three men, tied with a strong cable, and marked with black figures; which we humbly conceive to be writings; every letter almost half as large as the palm of our hands. In the left there was a sort of engine, from the back of which were extended twenty long poles, resembling the palisados[9] before your Majesty's court; wherewith we conjecture the Man-Mountain combs his head; for we did not always trouble him with questions, because we found it a great difficulty to make him understand us. In the large pocket on the right side of his middle cover (so I translate the word *ranfu-lo*, by which they meant my breeches) we saw a hollow pillar of iron, about the length of a man, fastened to a strong piece of timber, larger than the pillar; and upon one side of the pillar were huge pieces of iron sticking out, cut into strange figures; which we know not what to make of. In the left pocket, another engine of the same kind. In the smaller pocket on the right side, were several round flat pieces of white and red metal, of different bulk; some of the white, which seemed to be silver, were so large and heavy, that my comrade and I could hardly lift them. In the left pocket were two black pillars irregularly shaped: we could not, without difficulty, reach the top of them as we stood at the bottom of his pocket. One of them was covered, and seemed all of a piece; but at the upper end of the other, there appeared a white round substance, about twice the bigness of our heads. Within each of these was inclosed a prodigious plate of steel; which, by our orders, we obliged him to show us, because we apprehended they might be dangerous engines. He took them out of their cases, and told us, that in his own country his practice was to shave his beard with one of these, and to cut his meat with the other. There were two pockets which we could not enter: these he called his fobs; they were two large slits cut into the top of his middle cover, but squeezed close by the pressure of his belly. Out of the right fob hung a great silver chain, with a wonderful kind of engine at the bottom. We directed him to draw out whatever was at the end of the chain, which appeared to be a globe, half silver, and half of some transparent metal: for on the transparent side we saw certain strange figures circularly drawn, and thought we could touch them, until we found our fingers stopped with that lucid substance. He put this engine to our ears, which made an incessant noise like that of a watermill. And we conjecture it is either some unknown animal, or the god that he worships: but we are more inclined to the latter opinion, because he assured us (if we understood him right, for he expressed himself very imperfectly), that he seldom did any thing without consulting it. He called it his oracle, and said it pointed out the time for every action of his life. From the left fob he took out a net almost large enough for a fisherman, but contrived to open and shut like a purse, and served him for the same use: we found therein several massy pieces of yellow metal, which if they be of real gold, must be of immense value.

Having thus, in obedience to your Majesty's commands, diligently searched all his pockets, we observed a girdle[1] about his waist made of

---

9. Fences of stakes.　　　　1. Belt.

the hide of some prodigious animal; from which, on the left side, hung a sword of the length of five men; and on the right, a bag or pouch divided into cells; each cell capable of holding three of your Majesty's subjects. In one of these cells were several globes or balls of a most ponderous metal, about the bigness of our heads, and required a strong hand to lift them: the other cell contained a heap of certain black grains, but of no great bulk or weight, for we could hold above fifty of them in the palms of our hands.

This is an exact inventory of what we found about the body of the Man-Mountain; who used us with great civility, and due respect to your Majesty's commission. Signed and sealed on the fourth day of the eighty-ninth moon of your Majesty's auspicious reign.

CLEFREN FRELOCK, MARSI FRELOCK.

When this inventory was read over to the Emperor, he directed me to deliver up the several particulars. He first called for my scimitar, which I took out, scabbard and all. In the meantime he ordered three thousand of his choicest troops (who then attended him) to surround me at a distance, with their bows and arrows just ready to discharge: but I did not observe it; for my eyes were wholly fixed upon his Majesty. He then desired me to draw my scimitar, which, although it had got some rust by the sea water, was in most parts exceeding bright. I did so, and immediately all the troops gave a shout between terror and surprise; for the sun shone clear, and the reflection dazzled their eyes, as I waved the scimitar to and fro in my hand. His Majesty, who is a most magnanimous[2] prince, was less daunted than I could expect; he ordered me to return it into the scabbard, and cast it on the ground as gently as I could, about six foot from the end of my chain. The next thing he demanded was one of the hollow iron pillars, by which he meant my pocket-pistols. I drew it out, and at his desire, as well as I could, expressed to him the use of it, and charging it only with powder, which by the closeness of my pouch happened to escape wetting in the sea (an inconvenience that all prudent mariners take special care to provide against), I first cautioned the Emperor not to be afraid; and then I let it off in the air. The astonishment here was much greater than at the sight of my scimitar. Hundreds fell down as if they had been struck dead; and even the Emperor, although he stood his ground, could not recover himself in some time. I delivered up both my pistols in the same manner as I had done my scimitar, and then my pouch of powder and bullets; begging him that the former might be kept from fire; for it would kindle with the smallest spark, and blow up his imperial palace into the air. I likewise delivered up my watch, which the Emperor was very curious to see; and commanded two of his tallest yeomen of the guards to bear it on a pole upon their shoulders, as draymen in England do a barrel of ale. He was amazed at the continual noise it made, and the motion of the minute-hand, which he could easily discern; for their sight is much more acute than ours: he asked the opinions of his learned men about him, which were various and remote, as the reader may well imagine without my repeating; although indeed I could not very perfectly understand them. I then gave up my silver and copper money, my purse with nine large pieces of gold, and

2. Courageous, great-spirited. Magnanimity, the relation (direct or inverse) between the size of the body and the soul, is a central concern of the first two parts of the *Travels*.

some smaller ones; my knife and razor, my comb and silver snuffbox, my handkerchief and journal book. My scimitar, pistols, and pouch, were conveyed in carriages to his Majesty's stores; but the rest of my goods were returned me.

I had, as I before observed, one private pocket which escaped their search, wherein there was a pair of spectacles (which I sometimes use for the weakness of my eyes), a pocket perspective,[3] and several other little conveniences; which, being of no consequence to the Emperor, I did not think myself bound in honor to discover, and I apprehended they might be lost or spoiled if I ventured them out of my possession.

CHAPTER 3. *The author diverts the Emperor and his nobility of both sexes in a very uncommon manner. The diversions of the court of Lilliput described. The author hath his liberty granted him upon certain conditions.*

My gentleness and good behavior had gained so far on the Emperor and his court, and indeed upon the army and people in general, that I began to conceive hopes of getting my liberty in a short time. I took all possible methods to cultivate this favorable disposition. The natives came by degrees to be less apprehensive of any danger from me. I would sometimes lie down, and let five or six of them dance on my hand. And at last the boys and girls would venture to come and play at hide-and-seek in my hair. I had now made a good progress in understanding and speaking their language. The Emperor had a mind one day to entertain me with several of the country shows; wherein they exceed all nations I have known, both for dexterity and magnificence. I was diverted with none so much as that of the rope-dancers, performed upon a slender white thread, extended about two foot, and twelve inches from the ground. Upon which I shall desire liberty, with the reader's patience, to enlarge a little.

This diversion is only practiced by those persons who are candidates for great employments, and high favor, at court. They are trained in this art from their youth, and are not always of noble birth, or liberal education. When a great office is vacant either by death or disgrace (which often happens) five or six of those candidates petition the Emperor to entertain his Majesty and the court with a dance on the rope; and whoever jumps the highest without falling, succeeds in the office. Very often the chief ministers themselves are commanded to show their skill, and to convince the Emperor that they have not lost their faculty. Flimnap,[4] the Treasurer, is allowed to cut a caper on the strait rope, at least an inch higher than any other lord in the whole empire. I have seen him do the summerset several times together upon a trencher[5] fixed on the rope, which is no thicker than a common packthread in England. My friend Reldresal, Principal Secretary for Private Affairs, is, in my opinion, if I am not partial, the second after the Treasurer; the rest of the great officers are much upon a par.

These diversions are often attended with fatal accidents, whereof great numbers are on record. I myself have seen two or three candidates break a limb. But the danger is much greater when the ministers themselves are

---

3. Telescope.
4. Sir Robert Walpole, the Whig head of the government, was notorious in Swift's circle for his
political acrobatics.
5. Plate. "Summerset": somersault.

commanded to show their dexterity; for, by contending to excel themselves and their fellows, they strain so far, that there is hardly one of them who hath not received a fall; and some of them two or three. I was assured, that a year or two before my arrival, Flimnap would have infallibly broke his neck, if one of the King's cushions,[6] that accidentally lay on the ground, had not weakened the force of his fall.

There is likewise another diversion, which is only shown before the Emperor and Empress, and first minister, upon particular occasions. The Emperor lays on a table three fine silken threads of six inches long. One is blue, the other red, and the third green.[7] These threads are proposed as prizes for those persons whom the Emperor hath a mind to distinguish by a peculiar mark of his favor. The ceremony is performed in his Majesty's great chamber of state; where the candidates are to undergo a trial of dexterity very different from the former, and such as I have not observed the least resemblance of in any other country of the old or the new world. The Emperor holds a stick in his hands, both ends parallel to the horizon, while the candidates, advancing one by one, sometimes leap over the stick, sometimes creep under it backwards and forwards several times, according as the stick is advanced or depressed. Sometimes the Emperor holds one end of the stick, and his first minister the other; sometimes the minister has it entirely to himself. Whoever performs his part with most agility, and holds out the longest in *leaping* and *creeping*, is rewarded with the blue-colored silk; the red is given to the next, and the green to the third, which they all wear girt twice round about the middle; and you see few great persons about this court who are not adorned with one of these girdles.

The horses of the army, and those of the royal stables, having been daily led before me, were no longer shy, but would come up to my very feet, without starting. The riders would leap them over my hand as I held it on the ground; and one of the Emperor's huntsmen, upon a large courser, took[8] my foot, shoe and all; which was indeed a prodigious leap. I had the good fortune to divert the Emperor one day after a very extraordinary manner. I desired he would order several sticks of two foot high, and the thickness of an ordinary cane, to be brought me; whereupon his Majesty commanded the master of his woods to give directions accordingly; and the next morning six woodmen arrived with as many carriages, drawn by eight horses to each. I took nine of these sticks, and fixing them firmly in the ground in a quadrangular figure, two foot and a half square, I took four other sticks, and tied them parallel at each corner, about two foot from the ground; then I fastened my handkerchief to the nine sticks that stood erect, and extended it on all sides till it was as tight as the top of a drum; and the four parallel sticks, rising about five inches higher than the handkerchief, served as ledges on each side. When I had finished my work, I desired the Emperor to let a troop of his best horse, twenty-four in number, come and exercise upon this plain. His Majesty approved of the proposal, and I took them up one by one in my hands, ready mounted and armed, with the proper officers to exercise them. As soon as they got into order, they divided into two parties, performed mock skirmishes, discharged blunt arrows, drew their swords, fled and pursued,

---

6. A mistress of George I was supposed to have helped restore Walpole to office in 1721.
7. The Orders of the Garter, the Bath, and the Thistle, conferred for services to the king.
8. Jumped over.

attacked and retired; and in short discovered the best military discipline I ever beheld. The parallel sticks secured them and their horses from falling over the stage; and the Emperor was so much delighted, that he ordered this entertainment to be repeated several days; and once was pleased to be lifted up, and give the word of command; and, with great difficulty, persuaded even the Empress herself to let me hold her in her close chair[9] within two yards of the stage, from whence she was able to take a full view of the whole performance. It was my good fortune that no ill accident happened in these entertainments, only once a fiery horse that belonged to one of the captains pawing with his hoof struck a hole in my handkerchief, and his foot slipping, he overthrew his rider and himself; but I immediately relieved them both; for covering the hole with one hand, I set down the troop with the other, in the same manner as I took them up. The horse that fell was strained in the left shoulder, but the rider got no hurt, and I repaired my handkerchief as well as I could; however, I would not trust to the strength of it any more in such dangerous enterprises.

About two or three days before I was set at liberty, as I was entertaining the court with these kinds of feats, there arrived an express to inform his Majesty that some of his subjects, riding near the place where I was first taken up, had seen a great black substance lying on the ground, very oddly shaped, extending its edges round as wide as his Majesty's bedchamber, and rising up in the middle as high as a man; that it was no living creature, as they at first apprehended, for it lay on the grass without motion, and some of them had walked round it several times; that by mounting upon each other's shoulders, they had got to the top, which was flat and even; and stamping upon it they found it was hollow within; that they humbly conceived it might be something belonging to the Man-Mountain, and if his Majesty pleased, they would undertake to bring it with only five horses. I presently[1] knew what they meant; and was glad at heart to receive this intelligence. It seems upon my first reaching the shore after our shipwreck, I was in such confusion, that before I came to the place where I went to sleep, my hat, which I had fastened with a string to my head while I was rowing, and had stuck on all the time I was swimming, fell off after I came to land; the string, as I conjecture, breaking by some accident which I never observed, but thought my hat had been lost at sea. I intreated his Imperial Majesty to give orders it might be brought to me as soon as possible, describing to him the use and the nature of it: and the next day the wagoners arrived with it, but not in a very good condition; they had bored two holes in the brim, within an inch and half of the edge, and fastened two hooks in the holes; these hooks were tied by a long cord to the harness, and thus my hat was dragged along for above half an English mile: but the ground in that country being extremely smooth and level, it received less damage than I expected.

Two days after this adventure, the Emperor, having ordered that part of his army which quarters in and about his metropolis to be in a readiness, took a fancy of diverting himself in a very singular manner. He desired I would stand like a colossus, with my legs as far asunder as I conveniently could. He then commanded his general (who was an old experienced leader,

---

9. An enclosed or sedan chair.　　　　1. Immediately.

and a great patron of mine) to draw up the troops in close order, and march them under me; the foot[2] by twenty-four in a breast, and the horse by sixteen, with drums beating, colors flying, and pikes advanced. This body consisted of three thousand foot, and a thousand horse. His Majesty gave orders, upon pain of death, that every soldier in his march should observe the strictest decency with regard to my person; which, however, could not prevent some of the younger officers from turning up their eyes as they passed under me. And, to confess the truth, my breeches were at that time in so ill a condition, that they afforded some opportunities for laughter and admiration.

I had sent so many memorials and petitions for my liberty, that his Majesty at length mentioned the matter first in the cabinet, and then in a full council; where it was opposed by none, except Skyresh Bolgolam,[3] who was pleased, without any provocation, to be my mortal enemy. But it was carried against him by the whole board, and confirmed by the Emperor. That minister was *Galbet*, or Admiral of the Realm; very much in his master's confidence, and a person well versed in affairs, but of a morose and sour complexion.[4] However, he was at length persuaded to comply; but prevailed that the articles and conditions upon which I should be set free, and to which I must swear, should be drawn up by himself. These articles were brought to me by Skyresh Bolgolam in person, attended by two under-secretaries, and several persons of distinction. After they were read, I was demanded to swear to the performance of them; first in the manner of my own country, and afterwards in the method prescribed by their laws; which was to hold my right foot in my left hand, to place the middle finger of my right hand on the crown of my head, and my thumb on the tip of my right ear. But because the reader may perhaps be curious to have some idea of the style and manner of expression peculiar to that people, as well as to know the articles upon which I recovered my liberty, I have made a translation of the whole instrument,[5] word for word, as near as I was able; which I here offer to the public.

GOLBASTO MOMAREN EVLAME GURDILO SHEFIN MULLY ULLY GUE, most mighty Emperor of Lilliput, delight and terror of the universe, whose dominions extend five thousand blustrugs (about twelve miles in circumference) to the extremities of the globe; Monarch of all Monarchs; taller than the sons of men; whose feet press down to the center, and whose head strikes against the sun; at whose nod the princes of the earth shake their knees; pleasant as the spring, comfortable as the summer, fruitful as autumn, dreadful as winter. His most sublime Majesty proposeth to the Man-Mountain, lately arrived at our celestial dominions, the following articles, which by a solemn oath he shall be obliged to perform.

First, The Man-Mountain shall not depart from our dominions, without our license under our great seal.

Secondly, He shall not presume to come into our metropolis, without our express order; at which time the inhabitants shall have two hours warning, to keep within their doors.

Thirdly, The said Man-Mountain shall confine his walks to our prin-

---

2. Foot soldiers or infantry.
3. The earl of Nottingham, an enemy of Swift.
4. Disposition.
5. A formal legal document.

cipal high roads; and not offer to walk or lie down in a meadow, or field of corn.

Fourthly, As he walks the said roads, he shall take the utmost care not to trample upon the bodies of any of our loving subjects, their horses, or carriages, nor take any of our said subjects into his hands, without their own consent.

Fifthly, If an express require extraordinary dispatch, the Man-Mountain shall be obliged to carry in his pocket the messenger and horse, a six days' journey once in every moon, and return the said messenger back (if so required) safe to our Imperial Presence.

Sixthly, He shall be our ally against our enemies in the island of Blefuscu, and do his utmost to destroy their fleet, which is now preparing to invade us.

Seventhly, That the said Man-Mountain shall, at his times of leisure, be aiding and assisting to our workmen, in helping to raise certain great stones, towards covering the wall of the principal park, and other our royal buildings.

Eighthly, That the said Man-Mountain shall, in two moons' time, deliver in an exact survey of the circumference of our dominions by a computation of his own paces round the coast.

Lastly, That upon his solemn oath to observe all the above articles, the said Man-Mountain shall have a daily allowance of meat and drink sufficient for the support of 1,728 of our subjects; with free access to our Royal Person, and other marks of our favor. Given at our palace at Belfaborac the twelfth day of the ninety-first moon of our reign.

I swore and subscribed to these articles with great cheerfulness and content, although some of them were not so honorable as I could have wished; which proceeded wholly from the malice of Skyresh Bolgolam the High Admiral: whereupon my chains were immediately unlocked, and I was at full liberty: the Emperor himself in person did me the honor to be by at the whole ceremony. I made my acknowledgements by prostrating myself at his Majesty's feet: but he commanded me to rise; and after many gracious expressions, which, to avoid the censure of vanity, I shall not repeat, he added, that he hoped I should prove a useful servant, and well deserve all the favors he had already conferred upon me, or might do for the future.

The reader may please to observe, that in the last article for the recovery of my liberty, the Emperor stipulates to allow me a quantity of meat and drink, sufficient for the support of 1,728 Lilliputians. Some time after, asking a friend at court how they came to fix on that determinate number, he told me, that his Majesty's mathematicians, having taken the height of my body by the help of a quadrant, and finding it to exceed theirs in the proportion of twelve to one, they concluded from the similarity of their bodies, that mine must contain at least 1,728 of theirs, and consequently would require as much food as was necessary to support that number of Lilliputians. By which, the reader may conceive an idea of the ingenuity of that people, as well as the prudent and exact economy of so great a prince.

CHAPTER 4. *Mildendo, the metropolis of Lilliput, described, together with the Emperor's palace. A conversation between the author and a principal secretary,*

concerning the affairs of that empire; the author's offers to serve the Emperor
in his wars.

The first request I made after I had obtained my liberty, was, that I might
have license to see Mildendo, the metropolis; which the Emperor easily
granted me, but with a special charge to do no hurt, either to the inhabitants,
or their houses. The people had notice by proclamation of my design to visit
the town. The wall which encompassed it is two foot and an half high, and
at least eleven inches broad, so that a coach and horses may be driven very
safely round it; and it is flanked with strong towers at ten foot distance. I
stepped over the great western gate, and passed very gently, and sideling[6]
through the two principal streets, only in my short waistcoat, for fear of
damaging the roofs and eaves of the houses with the skirts of my coat. I
walked with the utmost circumspection, to avoid treading on any stragglers,
who might remain in the streets, although the orders were very strict, that
all people should keep in their houses, at their own peril. The garret windows
and tops of houses were so crowded with spectators, that I thought in all my
travels I had not seen a more populous place. The city is an exact square,
each side of the wall being five hundred foot long. The two great streets,
which run cross and divide it into four quarters, are five foot wide. The lanes
and alleys, which I could not enter, but only viewed them as I passed, are
from twelve to eighteen inches. The town is capable of holding five hundred
thousand souls. The houses are from three to five stories. The shops and
markets well provided.

The Emperor's palace is in the center of the city, where the two great
streets meet. It is enclosed by a wall of two foot high, and twenty foot distant
from the buildings. I had his Majesty's permission to step over this wall; and
the space being so wide between that and the palace, I could easily view it
on every side. The outward court is a square of forty foot, and includes two
other courts: in the inmost are the royal apartments, which I was very desirous to see, but found it extremely difficult; for the great gates, from one
square into another, were but eighteen inches high, and seven inches wide.
Now the buildings of the outer court were at least five foot high; and it was
impossible for me to stride over them, without infinite damage to the pile,
although the walls were strongly built of hewn stone, and four inches thick.
At the same time the Emperor had a great desire that I should see the magnificence of his palace; but this I was not able to do till three days after,
which I spent in cutting down with my knife some of the largest trees in the
royal park, about an hundred yards distance from the city. Of these trees I
made two stools, each about three foot high, and strong enough to bear my
weight. The people having received notice a second time, I went again
through the city to the palace, with my two stools in my hands. When I came
to the side of the outer court, I stood upon one stool, and took the other in
my hand: this I lifted over the roof, and gently set it down on the space
between the first and second court, which was eight foot wide. I then stepped
over the buildings very conveniently from one stool to the other, and drew
up the first after me with a hooked stick. By this contrivance I got into the
inmost court; and lying down upon my side, I applied my face to the windows

6. Sideways.

of the middle stories, which were left open on purpose, and discovered the most splendid apartments that can be imagined. There I saw the Empress, and the young princes in their several lodgings, with their chief attendants about them. Her Imperial Majesty was pleased to smile very graciously upon me and gave me out of the window her hand to kiss.

But I shall not anticipate the reader with farther descriptions of this kind, because I reserve them for a greater work, which is now almost ready for the press; containing a general description of this empire, from its first erection, through a long series of princes, with a particular account of their wars and politics, laws, learning, and religion; their plants and animals, their peculiar manners and customs, with other matters very curious and useful; my chief design at present being only to relate such events and transactions as happened to the public, or to myself, during a residence of about nine months in that empire.

One morning, about a fortnight after I had obtained my liberty, Reldresal, Principal Secretary (as they style him) of Private Affairs, came to my house, attended only by one servant. He ordered his coach to wait at a distance, and desired I would give him an hour's audience; which I readily consented to, on account of his quality, and personal merits, as well as of the many good offices he had done me during my solicitations at court. I offered to lie down, that he might the more conveniently reach my ear; but he chose rather to let me hold him in my hand during our conversation. He began with compliments on my liberty, said he might pretend to some merit in it; but, however, added, that if it had not been for the present situation of things at court, perhaps I might not have obtained it so soon. For, said he, as flourishing a condition as we appear to be in to foreigners, we labor under two mighty evils; a violent faction at home, and the danger of an invasion by a most potent enemy from abroad. As to the first, you are to understand, that for above seventy moons past, there have been two struggling parties in the empire, under the names of *Tramecksan,* and *Slamecksan,*[7] from the high and low heels on their shoes, by which they distinguish themselves.

It is alleged indeed, that the high heels are most agreeable to our ancient constitution: but however this be, his Majesty hath determined to make use of only low heels in the administration of the government and all offices in the gift of the crown; as you cannot but observe; and particularly, that his Majesty's imperial heels are lower at least by a *drurr* than any of his court; (*drurr* is a measure about the fourteenth part of an inch). The animosities between these two parties run so high, that they will neither eat nor drink, nor talk with each other. We compute the *Tramecksan,* or High-Heels, to exceed us in number; but the power is wholly on our side. We apprehend his Imperial Highness, the heir to the crown, to have some tendency towards the High-Heels; at least we can plainly discover one of his heels higher than the other, which gives him a hobble in his gait.[8] Now, in the midst of these intestine disquiets, we are threatened with an invasion from the island of Blefuscu,[9] which is the other great empire of the universe, almost as large and powerful as this of his Majesty. For as to what we have heard you affirm, that there are other kingdoms and states in the world, inhabited by human

---

7. Tory (High Church) and Whig (Low Church).
8. The Prince of Wales (later George II) had

friends in both parties.
9. France.

creatures as large as yourself, our philosophers are in much doubt; and would rather conjecture that you dropped from the moon, or one of the stars; because it is certain, that an hundred mortals of your bulk would, in a short time, destroy all the fruits and cattle of his Majesty's dominions. Besides, our histories of six thousand moons make no mention of any other regions, than the two great empires of Lilliput and Blefuscu. Which two mighty powers have, as I was going to tell you, been engaged in a most obstinate war for six and thirty moons past. It began upon the following occasion. It is allowed on all hands, that the primitive way of breaking eggs before we eat them, was upon the larger end: but his present Majesty's grandfather, while he was a boy, going to eat an egg, and breaking it according to the ancient practice, happened to cut one of his fingers. Whereupon the Emperor his father published an edict, commanding all his subjects, upon great penalties, to break the smaller end of their eggs. The people so highly resented this law, that our histories tell us there have been six rebellions raised on that account; wherein one emperor lost his life, and another his crown.[1] These civil commotions were constantly fomented by the monarchs of Blefuscu; and when they were quelled, the exiles always fled for refuge to that empire. It is computed, that eleven thousand persons have, at several times, suffered death, rather than submit to break their eggs at the smaller end. Many hundred large volumes have been published upon this controversy: but the books of the Big-Endians have been long forbidden, and the whole party rendered incapable by law of holding employments.[2] During the course of these troubles, the emperors of Blefuscu did frequently expostulate by their ambassadors, accusing us of making a schism in religion, by offending against a fundamental doctrine of our great prophet Lustrog, in the fifty-fourth chapter of the *Brundecral* (which is their Alcoran[3]). This, however, is thought to be a mere strain upon the text: for the words are these; *That all true believers shall break their eggs at the convenient end*: and which is the convenient end, seems, in my humble opinion, to be left to every man's conscience, or at least in the power of the chief magistrate[4] to determine. Now the Big-Endian exiles have found so much credit in the Emperor of Blefuscu's court, and so much private assistance and encouragement from their party here at home, that a bloody war hath been carried on between the two empires for six and thirty moons with various success;[5] during which time we have lost forty capital ships, and a much greater number of smaller vessels, together with thirty thousand of our best seamen and soldiers; and the damage received by the enemy is reckoned to be somewhat greater than ours. However, they have now equipped a numerous fleet, and are just preparing to make a descent upon us; and his Imperial Majesty, placing great confidence in your valor and strength, hath commanded me to lay this account of his affairs before you.

I desired the Secretary to present my humble duty to the Emperor, and to let him know, that I thought it would not become me, who was a foreigner,

1. Swift's satirical allegory of the strife between Catholics (Big-Endians) and Protestants (Little-Endians) touches on Henry VIII (who "broke" with the Pope), Charles I (who lost his life), and James II (who lost his crown).
2. The Test Act (1673) prevented Catholics and Nonconformists from holding office unless they accepted the Anglican Sacrament.
3. Koran.
4. Ruler, sovereign. Swift himself accepted the right of the king to determine religious observances.
5. Reminiscent of the War of the Spanish Succession (1701–13).

to interfere with parties; but I was ready, with the hazard of my life, to defend his person and state against all invaders.

CHAPTER 5. *The author by an extraordinary stratagem prevents an invasion. A high title of honor is conferred upon him. Ambassadors arrive from the Emperor of Blefuscu, and sue for peace. The Empress's apartment on fire by an accident; the author instrumental in saving the rest of the palace.*

The empire of Blefuscu is an island situated to the north north-east side of Lilliput, from whence it is parted only by a channel of eight hundred yards wide. I had not yet seen it, and upon this notice of an intended invasion, I avoided appearing on that side of the coast, for fear of being discovered by some of the enemy's ships, who had received no intelligence of me; all intercourse between the two empires having been strictly forbidden during the war, upon pain of death; and an embargo laid by our Emperor upon all vessels whatsoever. I communicated to his Majesty a project I had formed of seizing the enemy's whole fleet; which, as our scouts assured us, lay at anchor in the harbor ready to sail with the first fair wind. I consulted the most experienced seamen upon the depth of the channel, which they had often plumbed; who told me, that in the middle at high water it was seventy *glumgluffs* deep, which is about six foot of European measure; and the rest of it fifty *glumgluffs* at most. I walked to the northeast coast over against Blefuscu; where, lying down behind a hillock, I took out my small pocket perspective glass, and viewed the enemy's fleet at anchor, consisting of about fifty men of war, and a great number of transports: I then came back to my house, and gave order (for which I had a warrant) for a great quantity of the strongest cable and bars of iron. The cable was about as thick as packthread and the bars of the length and size of a knitting-needle. I trebled the cable to make it stronger, and for the same reason I twisted three of the iron bars together, bending the extremities into a hook. Having thus fixed fifty hooks to as many cables, I went back to the northeast coast, and putting off my coat, shoes, and stockings, walked into the sea in my leathern jerkin, about half an hour before high water. I waded with what haste I could, and swam in the middle about thirty yards until I felt the ground; I arrived at the fleet in less than half an hour. The enemy was so frighted when they saw me, that they leaped out of their ships, and swam to shore, where there could not be fewer than thirty thousand souls. I then took my tackling, and fastening a hook to the hole at the prow of each, I tied all the cords together at the end. While I was thus employed, the enemy discharged several thousand arrows, many of which stuck in my hands and face; and besides the excessive smart, gave me much disturbance in my work. My greatest apprehension was for my eyes, which I should have infallibly lost, if I had not suddenly thought of an expedient. I kept, among other little necessaries, a pair of spectacles in a private pocket, which, as I observed before, had escaped the Emperor's searchers. These I took out, and fastened as strongly as I could upon my nose; and thus armed went on boldly with my work in spite of the enemy's arrows; many of which struck against the glasses of my spectacles, but without any other effect, further than a little to discompose them. I had now fastened all the hooks, and taking the knot in my hand, began to pull; but not a ship would stir, for they were all too fast by their anchors, so that the boldest part of my enterprise remained. I therefore let go the cord, and leaving the hooks fixed to the ships, I resolutely cut with my knife the cables that fastened the anchors, receiving about two hundred shots in my face and hands; then I took up the knotted end of the cables to which my hooks were tied; and with great ease drew fifty of the enemy's largest men-of-war after me.

The Blefuscudians, who had not the least imagination of what I intended, were at first confounded with astonishment. They had seen me cut the cables, and thought my design was only to let the ships run adrift, or fall foul on each other: but when they perceived the whole fleet moving in order, and saw me pulling at the end, they set up such a scream of grief and despair, that it is almost impossible to describe or conceive. When I had got out of danger, I stopped a while to pick out the arrows that stuck in my hands and face, and rubbed on some of the same ointment that was given me at my first arrival, as I have formerly mentioned. I then took off my spectacles, and waiting about an hour until the tide was a little fallen, I waded through the middle with my cargo, and arrived safe at the royal port of Lilliput.

The Emperor and his whole court stood on the shore, expecting the issue of this great adventure. They saw the ships move forward in a large half-moon, but could not discern me, who was up to my breast in water. When I advanced to the middle of the channel, they were yet more in pain, because I was under water to my neck. The Emperor concluded me to be drowned, and that the enemy's fleet was approaching in a hostile manner: but he was soon eased of his fears, for the channel growing shallower every step I made, I came in a short time within hearing; and holding up the end of the cable by which the fleet was fastened, I cried in a loud voice, Long live the most puissant Emperor of Lilliput! This great prince received me at my landing with all possible encomiums, and created me a *Nardac* upon the spot, which is the highest title of honor among them.

His Majesty desired I would take some other opportunity of bringing all the rest of his enemy's ships into his ports. And so unmeasurable is the ambition of princes, that he seemed to think of nothing less than reducing the whole empire of Blefuscu into a province, and governing it by a viceroy; of destroying the Big-Endian exiles, and compelling that people to break the smaller end of their eggs, by which he would remain sole monarch of the whole world. But I endeavored to divert him from this design, by many arguments drawn from the topics of policy as well as justice: and I plainly protested, that I would never be an instrument of bringing a free and brave people into slavery. And when the matter was debated in council, the wisest part of the ministry were of my opinion.

This open bold declaration of mine was so opposite to the schemes and politics of his Imperial Majesty, that he could never forgive me; he mentioned it in a very artful manner at council, where I was told that some of the wisest appeared, at least by their silence, to be of my opinion; but others, who were my secret enemies, could not forbear some expressions, which by a side-wind[6] reflected on me. And from this time began an intrigue between his Majesty and a junta of ministers maliciously bent against me, which broke out in less than two months, and had like to have ended in my utter destruc-

6. Indirectly.

tion. Of so little weight are the greatest services to princes, when put into the balance with a refusal to gratify their passions.[7]

About three weeks after this exploit, there arrived a solemn embassy from Blefuscu, with humble offers of a peace; which was soon concluded upon conditions very advantageous to our Emperor; wherewith I shall not trouble the reader. There were six ambassadors, with a train of about five hundred persons; and their entry was very magnificent, suitable to the grandeur of their master, and the importance of their business. When their treaty was finished, wherein I did them several good offices by the credit I now had, or at least appeared to have at court, their Excellencies, who were privately told how much I had been their friend, made me a visit in form. They began with many compliments upon my valor and generosity; invited me to that kingdom in the Emperor their master's name; and desired me to show them some proofs of my prodigious strength, of which they had heard so many wonders; wherein I readily obliged them, but shall not interrupt the reader with the particulars.

When I had for some time entertained their Excellencies to their infinite satisfaction and surprise, I desired they would do me the honor to present my most humble respects to the Emperor their master, the renown of whose virtues had so justly filled the whole world with admiration, and whose royal person I resolved to attend before I returned to my own country. Accordingly, the next time I had the honor to see our Emperor, I desired his general license to wait on the Blefuscudian monarch, which he was pleased to grant me, as I could plainly perceive, in a very cold manner; but could not guess the reason, till I had a whisper from a certain person, that Flimnap and Bolgolam had represented my intercourse with those ambassadors as a mark of disaffection, from which I am sure my heart was wholly free. And this was the first time I began to conceive some imperfect idea of courts and ministers.

It is to be observed, that these ambassadors spoke to me by an interpreter; the languages of both empires differing as much from each other as any two in Europe, and each nation priding itself upon the antiquity, beauty, and energy of their own tongues, with an avowed contempt for that of their neighbor; yet our Emperor, standing upon the advantage he had got by the seizure of their fleet, obliged them to deliver their credentials, and make their speech, in the Lilliputian tongue. And it must be confessed, that from the great intercourse of trade and commerce between both realms, from the continual reception of exiles, which is mutual among them, and from the custom in each empire to send their young nobility and richer gentry to the other, in order to polish themselves, by seeing the world, and understanding men and manners, there are few persons of distinction, or merchants, or seamen, who dwell in the maritime parts, but what can hold conversation in both tongues; as I found some weeks after, when I went to pay my respects to the Emperor of Blefuscu, which in the midst of great misfortunes, through the malice of my enemies, proved a very happy adventure to me, as I shall relate in its proper place.

The reader may remember, that when I signed those articles upon which I recovered my liberty, there were some which I disliked upon account of

7. After a series of British naval victories, the Treaty of Utrecht (1713) had ended the war with France, but the Tory ministers who engineered the peace were subsequently accused of having sold out to the enemy.

their being too servile, neither could any thing but an extreme necessity have forced me to submit. But being now a *Nardac,* of the highest rank in that empire, such offices[8] were looked upon as below my dignity, and the Emperor (to do him justice) never once mentioned them to me. However, it was not long before I had an opportunity of doing his Majesty, at least as I then thought, a most signal service. I was alarmed at midnight with the cries of many hundred people at my door; by which being suddenly awaked, I was in some kind of terror. I heard the word *burglum* repeated incessantly; several of the Emperor's court, making their way through the crowd, intreated me to come immediately to the palace, where her Imperial Majesty's apartment was on fire, by the carelessness of a maid of honor, who fell asleep while she was reading a romance. I got up in an instant; and orders being given to clear the way before me, and it being likewise a moonshine night, I made a shift to get to the palace without trampling on any of the people. I found they had already applied ladders to the walls of the apartment, and were well provided with buckets, but the water was at some distance. These buckets were about the size of a large thimble, and the poor people supplied me with them as fast as they could; but the flame was so violent, that they did little good. I might easily have stifled it with my coat, which I unfortunately left behind me for haste, and came away only in my leathern jerkin. The case seemed wholly desperate and deplorable; and this magnificent palace would have infallibly been burnt down to the ground, if, by a presence of mind, unusual to me, I had not suddenly thought of an expedient. I had the evening before drank plentifully of a most delicious wine, called *glimigrim* (the Blefuscudians call it *flunec,* but ours is esteemed the better sort), which is very diuretic. By the luckiest chance in the world, I had not discharged myself of any part of it. The heat I had contracted by coming very near the flames, and by my laboring to quench them, made the wine begin to operate by urine; which I voided in such a quantity, and applied so well to the proper places, that in three minutes the fire was wholly extinguished; and the rest of that noble pile, which had cost so many ages in erecting, preserved from destruction.

It was now daylight, and I returned to my house, without waiting to congratulate with the Emperor; because, although I had done a very eminent piece of service, yet I could not tell how his Majesty might resent the manner by which I had performed it: for, by the fundamental laws of the realm, it is capital[9] in any person, of what quality soever, to make water within the precincts of the palace. But I was a little comforted by a message from his Majesty, that he would give orders to the Grand Justiciary for passing my pardon in form; which, however, I could not obtain. And I was privately assured, that the Empress, conceiving the greatest abhorrence of what I had done,[1] removed to the most distant side of the court, firmly resolved that those buildings should never be repaired for her use; and, in the presence of her chief confidents, could not forbear vowing revenge.

CHAPTER 6. *Of the inhabitants of Lilliput; their learning, laws, and customs, the manner of educating their children. The author's way of living in that country. His vindication of a great lady.*

---

8. Duties.
9. Punishable by death.
1. Queen Anne, whom Swift called "a royal prude," strongly objected to the coarseness of *A Tale of a Tub.*

Although I intend to leave the description of this empire to a particular treatise, yet in the mean time I am content to gratify the curious reader with some general ideas. As the common size of the natives is somewhat under six inches, so there is an exact proportion in all other animals, as well as plants and trees: for instance, the tallest horses and oxen are between four and five inches in height, the sheep an inch and a half, more or less; their geese about the bigness of a sparrow; and so the several gradations downwards, till you come to the smallest, which, to my sight, were almost invisible; but nature hath adapted the eyes of the Lilliputians to all objects proper for their view: they see with great exactness, but at no great distance. And to show the sharpness of their sight towards objects that are near, I have been much pleased with observing a cook pulling[2] a lark, which was not so large as a common fly; and a young girl threading an invisible needle with invisible silk. Their tallest trees are about seven foot high; I mean some of those in the great royal park, the tops whereof I could but just reach with my fist clinched. The other vegetables[3] are in the same proportion; but this I leave to the reader's imagination.

I shall say but little at present of their learning, which for many ages hath flourished in all its branches among them: but their manner of writing is very peculiar; being neither from the left to the right, like the Europeans; nor from the right to the left, like the Arabians; nor from up to down, like the Chinese; nor from down to up, like the Cascagians;[4] but aslant from one corner of the paper to the other, like ladies in England.

They bury their dead with their heads directly downwards; because they hold an opinion that in eleven thousand moons they are all to rise again; in which period, the earth (which they conceive to be flat) will turn upside down, and by this means they shall, at their resurrection, be found ready standing on their feet. The learned among them confess the absurdity of this doctrine; but the practice still continues, in compliance to the vulgar.

There are some laws and customs in this empire very peculiar; and if they were not so directly contrary to those of my own dear country, I should be tempted to say a little in their justification. It is only to be wished, that they were as well executed. The first I shall mention relateth to informers. All crimes against the state are punished here with the utmost severity; but if the person accused make his innocence plainly to appear upon his trial, the accuser is immediately put to an ignominious death; and out of his goods or lands, the innocent person is quadruply recompensed for the loss of his time, for the danger he underwent, for the hardship of his imprisonment, and for all the charges he hath been at in making his defense. Or, if that fund be deficient, it is largely[5] supplied by the crown. The Emperor doth also confer on him some public mark of his favor; and proclamation is made of his innocence through the whole city.

They look upon fraud as a greater crime than theft, and therefore seldom fail to punish it with death; for they allege, that care and vigilance, with a very common understanding, may preserve a man's goods from thieves; but honesty hath no fence against superior cunning: and since it is necessary that there should be a perpetual intercourse of buying and selling, and deal-

2. Plucking.
3. Plants.

4. Swift's invention.
5. Fully.

ing upon credit, where fraud is permitted or connived at, or hath no law to punish it, the honest dealer is always undone, and the knave gets the advantage. I remember when I was once interceding with the King for a criminal who had wronged his master of a great sum of money, which he had received by order, and ran away with; and happening to tell his Majesty, by way of extenuation, that it was only a breach of trust, the Emperor thought it monstrous in me to offer, as a defense, the greatest aggravation of the crime: and truly, I had little to say in return, farther than the common answer, that different nations had different customs; for, I confess, I was heartily ashamed.

Although we usually call reward and punishment the two hinges upon which all government turns, yet I could never observe this maxim to be put in practice by any nation, except that of Lilliput. Whoever can there bring sufficient proof that he hath strictly observed the laws of his country for seventy-three moons, hath a claim to certain privileges, according to his quality[6] and condition of life, with a proportionable sum of money out of a fund appropriated for that use: he likewise acquires the title of *Snilpall*, or *Legal*, which is added to his name, but doth not descend to his posterity. And these people thought it a prodigious defect of policy among us, when I told them that our laws were enforced only by penalties, without any mention of reward. It is upon this account that the image of Justice, in their courts of judicature, is formed with six eyes, two before, as many behind, and on each side one, to signify circumspection; with a bag of gold open in her right hand, and a sword sheathed in her left, to show she is more disposed to reward than to punish.

In choosing persons for all employments, they have more regard to good morals than to great abilities; for, since government is necessary to mankind, they believe that the common size of human understandings is fitted to some station or other; and that Providence never intended to make the management of public affairs a mystery, to be comprehended only by a few persons of sublime genius, of which there seldom are three born in an age: but they suppose truth, justice, temperance, and the like, to be in every man's power; the practice of which virtues, assisted by experience and a good intention, would qualify any man for the service of his country, except where a course of study is required. But they thought the want of moral virtues was so far from being supplied by superior endowments of the mind, that employments could never be put into such dangerous hands as those of persons so qualified; and at least, that the mistakes committed by ignorance in a virtuous disposition would never be of such fatal consequence to the public weal, as the practices of a man whose inclinations led him to be corrupt, and had great abilities to manage, to multiply, and defend his corruptions.

In like manner, the disbelief of a divine Providence renders a man uncapable of holding any public station; for since kings avow themselves to be the deputies of Providence, the Lilliputians think nothing can be more absurd than for a prince to employ such men as disown the authority under which he acteth.

In relating these and the following laws, I would only be understood to mean the original institutions, and not the most scandalous corruptions into

---

6. Social position.

which these people are fallen by the degenerate nature of man. For as to that infamous practice of acquiring great employments by dancing on the ropes, or badges of favor and distinction by leaping over sticks, and creeping under them, the reader is to observe, that they were first introduced by the grandfather of the Emperor now reigning; and grew to the present height by the gradual increase of party and faction.

Ingratitude is among them a capital crime, as we read it to have been in some other countries; for they reason thus, that whoever makes ill returns to his benefactor, must needs be a common enemy to the rest of mankind, from whom he hath received no obligation; and therefore such a man is not fit to live.

Their notions relating to the duties of parents and children differ extremely from ours. For, since the conjunction of male and female is founded upon the great law of nature, in order to propagate and continue the species, the Lilliputians will needs have it, that men and women are joined together like other animals, by the motives of concupiscence; and that their tenderness towards their young proceedeth from the like natural principle: for which reason they will never allow, that a child is under any obligation to his father for begetting him, or to his mother for bringing him into the world; which, considering the miseries of human life, was neither a benefit in itself, nor intended so by his parents, whose thoughts in their love-encounters were otherwise employed. Upon these, and the like reasonings, their opinion is, that parents are the last of all others to be trusted with the education of their own children: and therefore they have in every town public nurseries, where all parents, except cottagers[7] and laborers, are obliged to send their infants of both sexes to be reared and educated when they come to the age of twenty moons; at which time they are supposed to have some rudiments of docility. These schools are of several kinds, suited to different qualities, and to both sexes. They have certain professors[8] well skilled in preparing children for such a condition of life as befits the rank of their parents, and their own capacities as well as inclinations. I shall first say something of the male nurseries, and then of the female.

The nurseries for males of noble or eminent birth are provided with grave and learned professors, and their several deputies. The clothes and food of the children are plain and simple. They are bred up in the principles of honor, justice, courage, modesty, clemency, religion, and love of their country; they are always employed in some business, except in the times of eating and sleeping, which are very short, and two hours for diversions, consisting of bodily exercises. They are dressed by men until four years of age, and then are obliged to dress themselves, although their quality be ever so great; and the women attendants, who are aged proportionably to ours at fifty, perform only the most menial offices. They are never suffered to converse with servants, but go together in small or greater numbers to take their diversions, and always in the presence of a professor, or one of his deputies; whereby they avoid those early bad impressions of folly and vice to which our children are subject. Their parents are suffered to see them only twice a year; the visit is not to last above an hour; they are allowed to kiss the child at meeting and parting; but a professor, who always standeth by on those occasions, will not

---

7. Agricultural workers, peasants.　　　　8. Professional teachers.

suffer them to whisper, or use any fondling expressions, or bring any presents of toys, sweetmeats, and the like.

The pension from each family for the education and entertainment[9] of a child, upon failure of due payment, is levied by the Emperor's officers.

The nurseries for children of ordinary gentlemen, merchants, traders, and handicrafts, are managed proportionably after the same manner; only those designed for trades are put out apprentices at seven years old; whereas those of persons of quality continue in their exercises until fifteen, which answers to one and twenty with us: but the confinement is gradually lessened for the last three years.

In the female nurseries, the young girls of quality are educated much like the males, only they are dressed by orderly servants of their own sex, but always in the presence of a professor or deputy, until they come to dress themselves, which is at five years old. And if it be found that these nurses ever presume to entertain the girls with frightful or foolish stories, or the common follies practiced by chambermaids among us, they are publicly whipped thrice about the city, imprisoned for a year, and banished for life to the most desolate parts of the country. Thus the young ladies there are as much ashamed of being cowards and fools as the men; and despise all personal ornaments beyond decency and cleanliness: neither did I perceive any difference in their education, made by their difference of sex, only that the exercises of the females were not altogether so robust; and that some rules were given them relating to domestic life, and a smaller compass of learning was enjoined them: for their maxim is, that among people of quality, a wife should be always a reasonable and agreeable companion, because she cannot always be young. When the girls are twelve years old, which among them is the marriageable age, their parents or guardians take them home, with great expressions of gratitude to the professors, and seldom without tears of the young lady and her companions.

In the nurseries of females of the meaner sort, the children are instructed in all kinds of works proper for their sex, and their several degrees:[1] those intended for apprentices are dismissed at seven years old, the rest are kept to eleven.

The meaner families who have children at these nurseries are obliged, besides their annual pension, which is as low as possible, to return to the steward of the nursery a small monthly share of their gettings, to be a portion for the child; and therefore all parents are limited in their expenses by the law. For the Lilliputians think nothing can be more unjust, than that people, in subservience to their own appetites, should bring children into the world, and leave the burthen of supporting them on the public. As to persons of quality, they give security to appropriate a certain sum for each child, suitable to their condition; and these funds are always managed with good husbandry, and the most exact justice.

The cottagers and laborers keep their children at home, their business being only to till and cultivate the earth; and therefore their education is of little consequence to the public; but the old and diseased among them are supported by hospitals: for begging is a trade unknown in this empire.

And here it may perhaps divert the curious reader, to give some account

9. Sustenance.   1. Various social ranks.

of my domestic,[2] and my manner of living in this country, during a residence of nine months and thirteen days. Having a head mechanically turned, and being likewise forced by necessity, I had made for myself a table and chair convenient enough, out of the largest trees in the royal park. Two hundred sempstresses were employed to make me shirts, and linen for my bed and table, all of the strongest and coarsest kind they could get; which, however, they were forced to quilt together in several folds; for the thickest was some degrees finer than lawn. Their linen is usually three inches wide, and three foot make a piece. The sempstresses took my measure as I lay on the ground, one standing at my neck, and another at my mid-leg, with a strong cord extended, that each held by the end, while the third measured the length of the cord with a rule of an inch long. Then they measured my right thumb, and desired no more; for by a mathematical computation, that twice round the thumb is one round the wrist, and so on to the neck and the waist; and by the help of my old shirt, which I displayed on the ground before them for a pattern, they fitted me exactly. Three hundred tailors were employed in the same manner to make me clothes; but they had another contrivance for taking my measure. I kneeled down, and they raised a ladder from the ground to my neck; upon this ladder one of them mounted, and let fall a plumb-line from my collar to the floor, which just answered the length of my coat; but my waist and arms I measured myself. When my clothes were finished, which was done in my house (for the largest of theirs would not have been able to hold them), they looked like the patchwork made by the ladies in England, only that mine were all of a color.

I had three hundred cooks to dress my victuals, in little convenient huts built about my house, where they and their families lived, and prepared me two dishes apiece. I took up twenty waiters in my hand, and placed them on the table; an hundred more attended below on the ground, some with dishes of meat, and some with barrels of wine, and other liquors, slung on their shoulders; all which the waiters above drew up as I wanted, in a very ingenious manner, by certain cords, as we draw the bucket up a well in Europe. A dish of their meat was a good mouthful, and a barrel of their liquor a reasonable draught. Their mutton yields to ours, but their beef is excellent. I have had a sirloin so large, that I have been forced to make three bites of it; but this is rare. My servants were astonished to see me eat it bones and all, as in our country we do the leg of a lark. Their geese and turkeys I usually eat at a mouthful, and I must confess they far exceed ours. Of their smaller fowl I could take up twenty or thirty at the end of my knife.

One day his Imperial Majesty, being informed of my way of living, desired that himself and his royal consort, with the young princes of the blood of both sexes, might have the happiness (as he was pleased to call it) of dining with me. They came accordingly, and I placed them upon chairs of state on my table, just over against me, with their guards about them. Flimnap the Lord High Treasurer attended there likewise, with his white staff; and I observed he often looked on me with a sour countenance, which I would not seem to regard, but eat more than usual, in honor to my dear country, as well as to fill the court with admiration. I have some private reasons to believe, that this visit from his Majesty gave Flimnap an opportunity of doing

2. Household.

me ill offices to his master. That minister had always been my secret enemy, although he outwardly caressed me more than was usual to the moroseness of his nature. He represented to the Emperor the low condition of his treasury; that he was forced to take up money at great discount; that exchequer bills[3] would not circulate under nine per cent below par; that I had cost his Majesty above a million and a half of *sprugs* (their greatest gold coin, about the bigness of a spangle); and upon the whole, that it would be advisable in the Emperor to take the first fair occasion of dismissing me.

I am here obliged to vindicate the reputation of an excellent lady, who was an innocent sufferer upon my account. The Treasurer took a fancy to be jealous of his wife, from the malice of some evil tongues, who informed him that her Grace had taken a violent affection for my person; and the court-scandal ran for some time that she once came privately to my lodging. This I solemnly declare to be a most infamous falsehood, without any grounds, farther than that her Grace was pleased to treat me with all innocent marks of freedom and friendship. I own she came often to my house, but always publicly, nor ever without three more in the coach, who were usually her sister and young daughter, and some particular acquaintance; but this was common to many other ladies of the court. And I still appeal to my servants round, whether they at any time saw a coach at my door without knowing what persons were in it. On those occasions, when a servant had given me notice, my custom was to go immediately to the door; and, after paying my respects, to take up the coach and two horses very carefully in my hands (for if there were six horses, the postillion always unharnessed four) and place them on a table, where I had fixed a moveable rim quite round, of five inches high, to prevent accidents. And I have often had four coaches and horses at once on my table full of company, while I sat in my chair leaning my face towards them; and when I was engaged with one set, the coachmen would gently drive the others round my table. I have passed many an afternoon very agreeably in these conversations. But I defy the Treasurer, or his two informers (I will name them, and let them make their best of it) Clustril and Drunlo, to prove that any person ever came to me *incognito*, except the Secretary Reldresal, who was sent by express command of his Imperial Majesty, as I have before related. I should not have dwelt so long upon this particular, if it had not been a point wherein the reputation of a great lady is so nearly concerned, to say nothing of my own; although I had the honor to be a *Nardac*, which the Treasurer himself is not; for all the world knows he is only a *Clumglum*, a title inferior by one degree, as that of a marquis is to a duke in England; yet I allow he preceded me in right of his post. These false informations, which I afterwards came to the knowledge of, by an accident not proper to mention, made the Treasurer show his lady for some time an ill countenance, and me a worse; for although he was at last undeceived and reconciled to her, yet I lost all credit with him; and found my interest decline very fast with the Emperor himself, who was indeed too much governed by that favorite.

3. Government bills of credit. Walpole was noted as a canny financier.

CHAPTER 7. *The author, being informed of a design to accuse him of high treason, makes his escape to Blefuscu. His reception there.*

Before I proceed to give an account of my leaving this kingdom, it may be proper to inform the reader of a private intrigue which had been for two months forming against me.

I had been hitherto all my life a stranger to courts, for which I was unqualified by the meanness of my condition. I had indeed heard and read enough of the dispositions of great princes and ministers; but never expected to have found such terrible effects of them in so remote a country, governed, as I thought, by very different maxims from those in Europe.

When I was just preparing to pay my attendance on the Emperor of Blefuscu, a considerable person at court (to whom I had been very serviceable at a time when he lay under the highest displeasure of his Imperial Majesty) came to my house very privately at night in a close chair, and without sending his name, desired admittance. The chairmen were dismissed; I put the chair, with his Lordship in it, into my coat-pocket; and giving orders to a trusty servant to say I was indisposed and gone to sleep, I fastened the door of my house, placed the chair on the table, according to my usual custom, and sat down by it. After the common salutations were over, observing his Lordship's countenance full of concern, and enquiring into the reason, he desired I would hear him with patience, in a matter that highly concerned my honor and my life. His speech was to the following effect, for I took notes of it as soon as he left me.

You are to know, said he, that several committees of council have been lately called in the most private manner on your account: and it is but two days since his Majesty came to a full resolution.

You are very sensible that Skyresh Bolgolam (*Galbet,* or High Admiral) hath been your mortal enemy almost ever since your arrival. His original reasons I know not; but his hatred is much increased since your great success against Blefuscu, by which his glory, as Admiral, is obscured. This lord, in conjunction with Flimnap the High Treasurer, whose enmity against you is notorious on account of his lady, Limtoc the General, Lalcon the Chamberlain, and Balmuff the Grand Justiciary, have prepared articles of impeachment against you, for treason, and other capital crimes.[4]

This preface made me so impatient, being conscious of my own merits and innocence, that I was going to interrupt; when he entreated me to be silent, and thus proceeded.

Out of gratitude for the favors you have done me, I procured information of the whole proceedings, and a copy of the articles, wherein I venture my head for your service.

Articles of Impeachment against Quinbus Flestrin
(*the* Man-Mountain).

ARTICLE 1

Whereas, by a statute made in the reign of his Imperial Majesty Calin Deffar Plune, it is enacted, that whoever shall make water within the

---

4. After the Whigs had investigated Oxford and Bolingbroke, both were impeached for high treason, on charges of being sympathetic to the Jacobites and the French.

precincts of the royal palace shall be liable to the pains and penalties of high treason: notwithstanding, the said Quinbus Flestrin, in open breach of the said law, under color of extinguishing the fire kindled in the apartment of his Majesty's most dear imperial consort, did maliciously, traitorously, and devilishly, by discharge of his urine, put out the said fire kindled in the said apartment, lying and being within the precincts of the said royal palace; against the statute in that case provided, etc., against the duty, etc.

ARTICLE 2

That the said Quinbus Flestrin, having brought the imperial fleet of Blefuscu into the royal port, and being afterwards commanded by his Imperial Majesty to seize all the other ships of the said empire of Blefuscu, and reduce that empire to a province, to be governed by a viceroy from hence; and to destroy and put to death not only all the Big-Endian exiles, but likewise all the people of that empire who would not immediately forsake the Big-Endian heresy: he, the said Flestrin, like a false traitor against his most auspicious, serene, Imperial Majesty, did petition to be excused from the said service, upon pretense of unwillingness to force the consciences, or destroy the liberties and lives of an innocent people.

ARTICLE 3

That, whereas certain ambassadors arrived from the court of Blefuscu to sue for peace in his Majesty's court: he the said Flestrin did, like a false traitor, aid, abet, comfort, and divert the said ambassadors; although he knew them to be servants to a prince who was lately an open enemy to his Imperial Majesty, and in open war against his said Majesty.

ARTICLE 4

That the said Quinbus Flestrin, contrary to the duty of a faithful subject, is now preparing to make a voyage to the court and empire of Blefuscu, for which he hath received only verbal license from his Imperial Majesty; and under color of the said license, doth falsely and traitorously intend to take the said voyage, and thereby to aid, comfort, and abet the Emperor of Blefuscu, so late an enemy, and in open war with his Imperial Majesty aforesaid.

There are some other articles, but these are the most important, of which I have read you an abstract.

In the several debates upon this impeachment, it must be confessed that his Majesty gave many marks of his great *lenity;* often urging the services you had done him, and endeavoring to extenuate your crimes. The Treasurer and Admiral insisted that you should be put to the most painful and ignominious death, by setting fire on your house at night; and the General was to attend with twenty thousand men armed with poisoned arrows, to shoot you on the face and hands. Some of your servants were to have private orders to strew a poisonous juice on your shirts and sheets, which would soon make you tear your own flesh, and die in the utmost torture. The General came into the same opinion; so that for a long time there was a majority against you. But his Majesty resolving, if possible, to spare your life, at last brought off[5] the Chamberlain.

Upon this incident, Reldresal, Principal Secretary for Private Affairs, who always approved[6] himself your true friend, was commanded by the Emperor to deliver his opinion, which he accordingly did; and therein justified the good thoughts you have of him. He allowed your crimes to be great; but that still there was room for mercy, the most commendable virtue in a prince, and for which his Majesty was so justly celebrated. He said, the friendship between you and him was so well known to the world, that perhaps the most honorable board might think him partial: however, in obedience to the command he had received, he would freely offer his sentiments. That if his Majesty, in consideration of your services, and pursuant to his own merciful disposition, would please to spare your life, and only give order to put out both your eyes, he humbly conceived, that by this expedient justice might in some measure be satisfied, and all the world would applaud the *lenity* of the Emperor, as well as the fair and generous proceedings of those who have the honor to be his counselors. That the loss of your eyes would be no impediment to your bodily strength, by which you might still be useful to his Majesty. That blindness is an addition to courage, by concealing dangers from us; that the fear you had for your eyes was the greatest difficulty in bringing over the enemy's fleet; and it would be sufficient for you to see by the eyes of the ministers, since the greatest princes do no more.

This proposal was received with the utmost disapprobation by the whole board. Bolgolam, the Admiral, could not preserve his temper; but rising up in fury, said, he wondered how the Secretary durst presume to give his opinion for preserving the life of a traitor: that the services you had performed were, by all true reasons of state, the great aggravation of your crimes; that you, who were able to extinguish the fire by discharge of urine in her Majesty's apartment (which he mentioned with horror), might, at another time, raise an inundation by the same means, to drown the whole palace; and the same strength which enabled you to bring over the enemy's fleet might serve, upon the first discontent, to carry it back: that he had good reasons to think you were a Big-Endian in your heart; and as treason begins in the heart before it appears in overt acts, so he accused you as a traitor on that account, and therefore insisted you should be put to death.

The Treasurer was of the same opinion; he showed to what straits his Majesty's revenue was reduced by the charge of maintaining you, which would soon grow insupportable: that the Secretary's expedient of putting out your eyes was so far from being a remedy against this evil, that it would probably increase it; as it is manifest from the common practice of blinding some kind of fowl, after which they fed the faster, and grew sooner fat: that his sacred Majesty, and the council, who are your judges, were in their own consciences fully convinced of your guilt; which was a sufficient argument to condemn you to death, without the formal proofs required by the strict letter of the law.

But his Imperial Majesty, fully determined against capital punishment,

---

5. Won over. 6. Proved.

was graciously pleased to say, that since the council thought the loss of your eyes too easy a censure, some other may be inflicted hereafter. And your friend the Secretary humbly desiring to be heard again, in answer to what the Treasurer had objected concerning the great charge his Majesty was at in maintaining you, said, that his Excellency, who had the sole disposal of the Emperor's revenue, might easily provide against this evil, by gradually lessening your establishment; by which, for want of sufficient food, you would grow weak and faint, and lose your appetite, and consequently decay and consume in a few months; neither would the stench of your carcass be then so dangerous, when it should become more than half diminished; and immediately upon your death, five or six thousand of his Majesty's subjects might, in two or three days, cut your flesh from your bones, take it away by cart-loads, and bury it in distant parts to prevent infection; leaving the skeleton as a monument of admiration to posterity.

Thus by the great friendship of the Secretary, the whole affair was compromised. It was strictly enjoined, that the project of starving you by degrees should be kept a secret; but the sentence of putting out your eyes was entered on the books; none dissenting except Bolgolam the Admiral, who being a creature of the Empress, was perpetually instigated by her Majesty to insist upon your death; she having borne perpetual malice against you, on account of that infamous and illegal method you took to extinguish the fire in her apartment.

In three days your friend the Secretary will be directed to come to your house, and read before you the articles of impeachment; and then to signify the great lenity and favor of his Majesty and council; whereby you are only condemned to the loss of your eyes, which his Majesty doth not question you will gratefully and humbly submit to; and twenty of his Majesty's surgeons will attend, in order to see the operation well performed, by discharging very sharp-pointed arrows into the balls of your eyes, as you lie on the ground.

I leave to your prudence what measures you will take; and to avoid suspicion, I must immediately return in as private a manner as I came.

His Lordship did so, and I remained alone, under many doubts and perplexities of mind.

It was a custom introduced by this prince and his ministry (very different, as I have been assured, from the practices of former times), that after the court had decreed any cruel execution, either to gratify the monarch's resentment, or the malice of a favorite, the Emperor always made a speech to his whole council, expressing his great lenity and tenderness, as qualities known and confessed by all the world. This speech was immediately published through the kingdom; nor did any thing terrify the people so much as those encomiums on his Majesty's mercy; because it was observed, that the more these praises were enlarged and insisted on, the more inhuman was the punishment, and the sufferer more innocent. Yet as to myself, I must confess, having never been designed for a courtier, either by my birth or education, I was so ill a judge of things, that I could not discover the lenity and favor of this sentence, but conceived it (perhaps erroneously) rather to be rigorous than gentle. I sometimes thought of standing my trial; for although I could not deny the facts alleged in the several articles, yet I hoped they would admit of some extenuations. But having in my life perused many state trials, which I ever observed to terminate as the judges thought fit to direct, I durst not rely on so dangerous a decision, in so critical a juncture, and against such powerful enemies. Once I was strongly bent upon resistance: for while I had liberty, the whole strength of that empire could hardly subdue me, and I might easily with stones pelt the metropolis to pieces; but I soon rejected that project with horror, by remembering the oath I had made to the Emperor, the favors I received from him, and the high title of *Nardac* he conferred upon me. Neither had I so soon learned the gratitude of courtiers, to persuade myself that his Majesty's present severities acquitted me of all past obligations.

At last I fixed upon a resolution, for which it is probable I may incur some censure, and not unjustly; for I confess I owe the preserving my eyes, and consequently my liberty, to my own great rashness and want of experience: because if I had then known the nature of princes and ministers, which I have since observed in many other courts, and their methods of treating criminals less obnoxious than myself, I should with great alacrity and readiness have submitted to so *easy* a punishment. But hurried on by the precipitancy of youth, and having his Imperial Majesty's license to pay my attendance upon the Emperor of Blefuscu, I took this opportunity, before the three days were elapsed, to send a letter to my friend the Secretary, signifying my resolution of setting out that morning for Blefuscu,[7] pursuant to the leave I had got; and without waiting for an answer, I went to that side of the island where our fleet lay. I seized a large man of war, tied a cable to the prow, and lifting up the anchors, I stripped myself, put my clothes (together with my coverlet, which I carried under my arm) into the vessel; and drawing it after me, between wading and swimming, arrived at the royal port of Blefuscu, where the people had long expected me. They lent me two guides to direct me to the capital city, which is of the same name; I held them in my hands until I came within two hundred yards of the gate; and desired them to signify my arrival to one of the secretaries, and let him know, I there waited his Majesty's commands. I had an answer in about an hour, that his Majesty, attended by the royal family, and great officers of the court, was coming out to receive me. I advanced a hundred yards; the Emperor, and his train, alighted from their horses, the Empress and ladies from their coaches; and I did not perceive they were in any fright or concern. I lay on the ground to kiss his Majesty's and the Empress's hand. I told his Majesty that I was come according to my promise, and with the license of the Emperor my master, to have the honor of seeing so mighty a monarch, and to offer him any service in my power, consistent with my duty to my own prince; not mentioning a word of my disgrace, because I had hitherto no regular information of it, and might suppose myself wholly ignorant of any such design; neither could I reasonably conceive that the Emperor would discover the secret while I was out of his power: wherein, however, it soon appeared I was deceived.

I shall not trouble the reader with the particular account of my reception at this court, which was suitable to the generosity of so great a prince; nor of the difficulties I was in for want of a house and bed, being forced to lie on the ground, wrapped up in my coverlet.

7. Before his trial for treason could be held, Bolingbroke had escaped to France.

CHAPTER 8. *The author, by a lucky accident, finds means to leave Blefuscu; and, after some difficulties, returns safe to his native country.*

Three days after my arrival, walking out of curiosity to the northeast coast of the island, I observed, about half a league off, in the sea, somewhat that looked like a boat overturned. I pulled off my shoes and stockings, and wading two or three hundred yards, I found the object to approach nearer by force of the tide; and then plainly saw it to be a real boat, which I supposed might, by some tempest, have been driven from a ship. Whereupon I returned immediately towards the city, and desired his Imperial Majesty to lend me twenty of the tallest vessels he had left after the loss of his fleet, and three thousand seamen under the command of his Vice Admiral. This fleet sailed round, while I went back the shortest way to the coast where I first discovered the boat; I found the tide had driven it still nearer; the seamen were all provided with cordage, which I had beforehand twisted to a sufficient strength. When the ships came up, I stripped myself, and waded till I came within an hundred yards of the boat; after which I was forced to swim till I got up to it. The seamen threw me the end of the cord, which I fastened to a hole in the fore-part of the boat, and the other end to a man of war: but I found all my labor to little purpose; for being out of my depth, I was not able to work. In this necessity, I was forced to swim behind, and push the boat forwards as often as I could, with one of my hands; and the tide favoring me, I advanced so far, that I could just hold up my chin and feel the ground. I rested two or three minutes, and then gave the boat another shove, and so on till the sea was no higher than my armpits. And now the most laborious part being over, I took out my other cables which were stowed in one of the ships, and fastening them first to the boat, and then to nine of the vessels which attended me, the wind being favorable, the seamen towed, and I shoved till we arrived within forty yards of the shore; and waiting till the tide was out, I got dry to the boat, and by the assistance of two thousand men, with ropes and engines, I made a shift to turn it on its bottom, and found it was but little damaged.

I shall not trouble the reader with the difficulties I was under by the help of certain paddles, which cost me ten days making, to get my boat to the royal port of Blefuscu; where a mighty concourse of people appeared upon my arrival, full of wonder at the sight of so prodigious a vessel. I told the Emperor that my good fortune had thrown this boat in my way, to carry me to some place from whence I might return into my native country; and begged his Majesty's orders for getting materials to fit it up, together with license to depart; which, after some kind expostulations, he was pleased to grant.

I did very much wonder, in all this time, not to have heard of any express relating to me from our Emperor to the court of Blefuscu. But I was afterwards given privately to understand, that his Imperial Majesty, never imagining I had the least notice of his designs, believed I was only gone to Blefuscu in performance of my promise, according to the license he had given me, which was well known at our court; and would return in a few days when that ceremony was ended. But he was at last in pain at my long absence; and, after consulting with the Treasurer, and the rest of that cabal, a person of quality was dispatched with the copy of the articles against me. This envoy had instructions to represent to the monarch of Blefuscu the great lenity of his master, who was content to punish me no further than with the loss of my eyes; that I had fled from justice, and if I did not return in two hours, I should be deprived of my title of *Nardac*, and declared a traitor. The envoy further added, that in order to maintain the peace and amity between both empires, his master expected, that his brother of Blefuscu would give orders to have me sent back to Lilliput, bound hand and foot, to be punished as a traitor.

The Emperor of Blefuscu, having taken three days to consult, returned an answer consisting of many civilities and excuses. He said, that as for sending me bound, his brother knew it was impossible; that although I had deprived him of his fleet, yet he owed great obligations to me for many good offices I had done him in making the peace. That however, both their Majesties would soon be made easy; for I had found a prodigious vessel on the shore, able to carry me on the sea, which he had given order to fit up with my own assistance and direction; and he hoped in a few weeks both empires would be freed from so insupportable an incumbrance.

With this answer the envoy returned to Lilliput, and the monarch of Blefuscu related to me all that had passed, offering me at the same time (but under the strictest confidence) his gracious protection, if I would continue in his service; wherein although I believed him sincere, yet I resolved never more to put any confidence in princes or ministers, where I could possibly avoid it; and therefore, with all due acknowledgements for his favorable intentions, I humbly begged to be excused. I told him, that since fortune, whether good or evil, had thrown a vessel in my way, I was resolved to venture myself in the ocean, rather than be an occasion of difference between two such mighty monarchs. Neither did I find the Emperor at all displeased; and I discovered by a certain accident, that he was very glad of my resolution, and so were most of his ministers.

These considerations moved me to hasten my departure somewhat sooner than I intended; to which the court, impatient to have me gone, very readily contributed. Five hundred workmen were employed to make two sails to my boat, according to my directions, by quilting thirteen fold of their strongest linen together. I was at the pains of making ropes and cables, by twisting ten, twenty or thirty of the thickest and strongest of theirs. A great stone that I happened to find, after a long search by the seashore, served me for an anchor. I had the tallow of three hundred cows for greasing my boat, and other uses. I was at incredible pains in cutting down some of the largest timber trees for oars and masts, wherein I was, however, much assisted by his Majesty's ship-carpenters, who helped me in smoothing them, after I had done the rough work.

In about a month, when all was prepared, I sent to receive his Majesty's commands, and to take my leave. The Emperor and royal family came out of the palace; I lay down on my face to kiss his hand, which he very graciously gave me: so did the Empress, and young princes of the blood. His Majesty presented me with fifty purses of two hundred *sprugs* apiece, together with his picture at full length, which I put immediately into one of my gloves, to keep it from being hurt. The ceremonies at my departure were too many to trouble the reader with at this time.

I stored the boat with the carcasses of an hundred oxen, and three hundred sheep, with bread and drink proportionable, and as much meat ready dressed as four hundred cooks could provide. I took with me six cows and two bulls alive, with as many ewes and rams, intending to carry them into my own country, and propagate the breed. And to feed them on board, I had a good bundle of hay, and a bag of corn.[8] I would gladly have taken a dozen of the natives; but this was a thing the Emperor would by no means permit; and besides a diligent search into my pockets, his Majesty engaged my honor not to carry away any of his subjects, although with their own consent and desire.

Having thus prepared all things as well as I was able, I set sail on the twenty-fourth day of September, 1701, at six in the morning; and when I had gone about four leagues to the northward, the wind being at southeast, at six in the evening, I descried a small island about half a league to the northwest. I advanced forward, and cast anchor on the lee-side of the island, which seemed to be uninhabited. I then took some refreshment, and went to my rest. I slept well, and as I conjecture at least six hours; for I found the day broke in two hours after I awaked. It was a clear night; I eat my breakfast before the sun was up; and heaving anchor, the wind being favorable, I steered the same course that I had done the day before, wherein I was directed by my pocket compass. My intention was to reach, if possible, one of those islands which I had reason to believe lay to the northeast of Van Diemen's Land. I discovered nothing all that day; but upon the next, about three in the afternoon, when I had by my computation made twenty-four leagues from Blefuscu, I descried a sail steering to the southeast; my course was due east. I hailed her, but could get no answer; yet I found I gained upon her, for the wind slackened. I made all the sail I could, and in half an hour she spied me, then hung out her ancient,[9] and discharged a gun. It is not easy to express the joy I was in upon the unexpected hope of once more seeing my beloved country, and the dear pledges[1] I had left in it. The ship slackened her sails, and I came up with her between five and six in the evening, September 26; but my heart leapt within me to see her English colors. I put my cows and sheep into my coat-pockets and got on board with all my little cargo of provisions. The vessel was an English merchantman, returning from Japan by the North and South Seas;[2] the captain, Mr. John Biddel of Deptford, a very civil man, and an excellent sailor. We were now in the latitude of 30 degrees south; there were about fifty men in the ship; and here I met an old comrade of mine, one Peter Williams, who gave me a good character to the captain. This gentleman treated me with kindness, and desired I would let him know what place I came from last, and whither I was bound; which I did in few words; but he thought I was raving, and that the dangers I underwent had disturbed my head; whereupon I took my black cattle and sheep out of my pocket, which, after great astonishment, clearly convinced him of my veracity. I then showed him the gold given me by the Emperor of Blefuscu, together with his Majesty's picture at full length, and some other rarities of that country. I gave him two purses of two hundred *sprugs* each, and promised, when we arrived in England, to make him a present of a cow and a sheep big with young.

I shall not trouble the reader with a particular account of this voyage; which was very prosperous for the most part. We arrived in the Downs[3] on

---

8. Wheat, not maize.
9. Flag.
1. Hostages (i.e., his family).

2. North and South Pacific.
3. A rendezvous for ships off the southeast coast of England.

the 13th of April, 1702. I had only one misfortune, that the rats on board carried away one of my sheep; I found her bones in a hole, picked clean from the flesh. The rest of my cattle I got safe on shore, and set them a grazing in a bowling-green at Greenwich, where the fineness of the grass made them feed very heartily, though I had always feared the contrary; neither could I possibly have preserved them in so long a voyage, if the captain had not allowed me some of his best biscuit, which rubbed to powder, and mingled with water, was their constant food. The short time I continued in England, I made a considerable profit by showing my cattle to many persons of quality, and others: and before I began my second voyage, I sold them for six hundred pounds. Since my last return, I find the breed is considerably increased, especially the sheep; which I hope will prove much to the advantage of the woolen manufacture, by the fineness of the fleeces.

I stayed but two months with my wife and family; for my insatiable desire of seeing foreign countries would suffer me to continue no longer. I left fifteen hundred pounds with my wife, and fixed her in a good house at Redriff. My remaining stock I carried with me, part in money, and part in goods, in hopes to improve my fortunes. My eldest uncle, John, had left me an estate in land, near Epping, of about thirty pounds a year; and I had a long lease of the Black Bull in Fetter Lane, which yielded me as much more: so that I was not in any danger of leaving my family upon the parish.[4] My son Johnny, named so after his uncle, was at the grammar school, and a towardly[5] child. My daughter Betty (who is now well married, and has children) was then at her needlework. I took leave of my wife, and boy and girl, with tears on both sides; and went on board the *Adventure,* a merchant-ship of three hundred tons, bound for Surat, Captain John Nicholas of Liverpool, Commander. But my account of this voyage must be referred to the second part of my *Travels.*

Part 2. A Voyage to Brobdingnag

CHAPTER 1. *A great storm described. The longboat sent to fetch water; the Author goes with it to discover the country. He is left on shore, is seized by one of the natives, and carried to a farmer's house. His reception there, with several accidents that happened there. A description of the inhabitants.*

Having been condemned by nature and fortune to an active and restless life, in ten months after my return I again left my native country, and took shipping in the Downs on the 20th day of June, 1702, in the *Adventure,* Captain John Nicholas, a Cornish man, Commander, bound for Surat.[6] We had a very prosperous gale till we arrived at the Cape of Good Hope, where we landed for fresh water, but discovering a leak we unshipped our goods and wintered there; for the Captain falling sick of an ague, we could not leave the Cape till the end of March. We then set sail, and had a good voyage

4. On welfare (living on charity given by the parish).
5. Promising.
6. In India. The geography of the voyage (described next) is simple: The *Adventure,* after sailing up the east coast of Africa to about five degrees south of the equator (the "Line"), is blown past India into the Malay Archipelago, north of the islands of Buru and Ceram. The storm then drives the ship northward and eastward, away from the coast of Siberia ("Great Tartary") into the northeast Pacific, at that time unexplored. Brobdingnag lies somewhere in the vicinity of Alaska.

till we passed the Straits of Madagascar; but having got northward of that island, and to about five degrees south latitude, the winds, which in those seas are observed to blow a constant equal gale between the north and west from the beginning of December to the beginning of May, on the 19th of April began to blow with much greater violence and more westerly than usual, continuing so far twenty days together, during which time we were driven a little to the east of the Molucca Islands and about three degrees northward of the Line, as our Captain found by an observation he took the 2nd of May, at which time the wind ceased, and it was a perfect calm, whereat I was not a little rejoiced. But he, being a man well experienced in the navigation of those seas, bid us all prepare against a storm, which accordingly happened the day following: for a southern wind, called the southern monsoon, began to set in.

Finding it was likely to overblow,[7] we took in our spritsail, and stood by to hand the foresail; but making foul weather, we looked the guns were all fast, and handed the mizzen. The ship lay very broad off, so we thought it better spooning before the sea, than trying or hulling. We reefed the foresail and set him, we hauled aft the foresheet; the helm was hard aweather. The ship wore bravely. We belayed the fore-downhaul; but the sail was split, and we hauled down the yard and got the sail into the ship, and unbound all the things clear of it. It was a very fierce storm; the sea broke strange and dangerous. We hauled off upon the lanyard of the whipstaff, and helped the man at helm. We would not get down our topmast, but let all stand, because she scudded before the sea very well, and we knew that the topmast being aloft, the ship was the wholesomer, and made better way through the sea, seeing we had searoom. When the storm was over, we set foresail and mainsail, and brought the ship to. Then we set the mizzen, main topsail and the fore topsail. Our course was east-northeast, the wind was at southwest. We got the starboard tacks aboard, we cast off our weather braces and lifts; we set in the lee braces, and hauled forward by the weather bowlings, and hauled them tight, and belayed them, and hauled over the mizzen tack to windward, and kept her full and by as near as she would lie.

During this storm, which was followed by a strong wind west-southwest, we were carried by my computation about five hundred leagues to the east, so that the oldest sailor on board could not tell in what part of the world we were. Our provisions held out well, our ship was staunch, and our crew all in good health; but we lay in the utmost distress for water. We thought it best to hold on the same course rather than turn more northerly, which might have brought us to the northwest parts of Great Tartary, and into the frozen sea.

On the 16th day of June, 1703, a boy on the topmast discovered land. On the 17th we came in full view of a great island or continent (for we knew not whether) on the south side whereof was a small neck of land jutting out into the sea, and a creek[8] too shallow to hold a ship of above one hundred tons. We cast anchor within a league of this creek, and our Captain sent a dozen of his men well armed in the longboat, with vessels for water if any could be found. I desired his leave to go with them that I might see the

---

7. This paragraph is taken almost literally from Samuel Sturmy's *Mariner's Magazine* (1669). Swift is ridiculing the use of technical terms by writers of popular voyages.

8. A small bay or cove, affording anchorage.

country and make what discoveries I could. When we came to land we saw no river or spring, nor any sign of inhabitants. Our men therefore wandered on the shore to find out some fresh water near the sea, and I walked alone about a mile on the other side, where I observed the country all barren and rocky. I now began to be weary, and seeing nothing to entertain my curiosity, I returned gently down towards the creek; and the sea being full in my view, I saw our men already got into the boat, and rowing for life to the ship. I was going to hollow after them, although it had been to little purpose, when I observed a huge creature walking after them in the sea as fast as he could; he waded not much deeper than his knees and took prodigious strides, but our men had the start of him half a league, and the sea thereabouts being full of sharp-pointed rocks, the monster was not able to overtake the boat. This I was afterwards told, for I durst not stay to see the issue of that adventure, but ran as fast as I could the way I first went, and then climbed up a steep hill, which gave me some prospect of the country. I found it fully cultivated; but that which first surprised me was the length of the grass, which, in those grounds that seemed to be kept for hay, was about twenty foot high.[9]

I fell into a highroad, for so I took it to be, although it served to the inhabitants only as a footpath through a field of barley. Here I walked on for some time, but could see little on either side, it being now near harvest, and the corn[1] rising at least forty foot. I was an hour walking to the end of this field, which was fenced in with a hedge of at least one hundred and twenty foot high, and the trees so lofty that I could make no computation of their altitude. There was a stile to pass from this field into the next: it had four steps, and a stone to cross over when you came to the utmost. It was impossible for me to climb this stile, because every step was six foot high, and the upper stone above twenty. I was endeavoring to find some gap in the hedge when I discovered one of the inhabitants in the next field advancing towards the stile, of the same size with him whom I saw in the sea pursuing our boat. He appeared as tall as an ordinary spire-steeple, and took about ten yards at every stride, as near as I could guess. I was struck with the utmost fear and astonishment, and ran to hide myself in the corn, from whence I saw him at the top of the stile, looking back into the next field on the right hand; and heard him call in a voice many degrees louder than a speaking trumpet; but the noise was so high in the air that at first I certainly thought it was thunder. Whereupon seven monsters like himself came towards him with reaping hooks in their hands, each hook about the largeness of six scythes. These people were not so well clad as the first, whose servants or laborers they seemed to be. For, upon some words he spoke, they went to reap the corn in the field where I lay. I kept from them at as great a distance as I could, but was forced to move with extreme difficulty, for the stalks of the corn were sometimes not above a foot distant, so that I could hardly squeeze my body betwixt them. However, I made a shift to go forward till I came to a part of the field where the corn had been laid by the rain and wind; here it was impossible for me to advance a step, for the stalks were so interwoven that I could not creep through, and the beards of the fallen ears so strong

9. Swift's intention, not always carried out accurately, is that everything in Brobdingnag should be, in relation to our familiar world, on a scale of ten to one.
1. Wheat.

and pointed that they pierced through my clothes into my flesh. At the same time I heard the reapers not above an hundred yards behind me. Being quite dispirited with toil, and wholly overcome by grief and despair, I lay down between two ridges and heartily wished I might there end my days. I bemoaned my desolate widow and fatherless children; I lamented my own folly and willfulness in attempting a second voyage against the advice of all my friends and relations. In this terrible agitation of mind, I could not forbear thinking of Lilliput, whose inhabitants looked upon me as the greatest prodigy that ever appeared in the world; where I was able to draw an imperial fleet in my hand, and perform those other actions which will be recorded forever in the chronicles of that empire, while posterity shall hardly believe them, although attested by millions. I reflected what a mortification it must prove to me to appear as inconsiderable in this nation as one single Lilliputian would be among us. But this I conceived was to be the least of my misfortunes; for as human creatures are observed to be more savage and cruel in proportion to their bulk, what could I expect but to be a morsel in the mouth of the first among these enormous barbarians who should happen to seize me? Undoubtedly philosophers are in the right when they tell us that nothing is great or little otherwise than by comparison. It might have pleased fortune to let the Lilliputians find some nation where the people were as diminutive with respect to them as they were to me. And who knows but that even this prodigious race of mortals might be equally overmatched in some distant part of the world, whereof we have yet no discovery?

Scared and confounded as I was, I could not forbear going on with these reflections; when one of the reapers approaching within ten yards of the ridge where I lay, made me apprehend that with the next step I should be squashed to death under his foot, or cut in two with his reaping hook. And therefore when he was again about to move, I screamed as loud as fear could make me. Whereupon the huge creature trod short, and looking round about under him for some time, at last espied me as I lay on the ground. He considered a while with the caution of one who endeavors to lay hold on a small dangerous animal in such a manner that it shall not be able either to scratch or to bite him, as I myself have sometimes done with a weasel in England. At length he ventured to take me up behind by the middle between his forefinger and thumb, and brought me within three yards of his eyes, that he might behold my shape more perfectly. I guessed his meaning, and my good fortune gave me so much presence of mind that I resolved not to struggle in the least as he held me in the air about sixty foot from the ground, although he grievously pinched my sides, for fear I should slip through his fingers. All I ventured was to raise mine eyes towards the sun, and place my hands together in a supplicating posture, and to speak some words in an humble melancholy tone, suitable to the condition I then was in. For I apprehended every moment that he would dash me against the ground, as we usually do any little hateful animal which we have a mind to destroy. But my good star would have it that he appeared pleased with my voice and gestures, and began to look upon me as a curiosity, much wondering to hear me pronounce articulate words, although he could not understand them. In the meantime I was not able to forbear groaning and shedding tears and turning my head towards my sides, letting him know, as well as I could, how cruelly I was hurt by the pressure of his thumb and finger. He seemed to apprehend my meaning; for, lifting up the lappet[2] of his coat, he put me gently into it, and immediately ran along with me to his master, who was a substantial farmer, and the same person I had first seen in the field.

The farmer having (as I supposed by their talk) received such an account of me as his servant could give him, took a piece of a small straw about the size of a walking staff, and therewith lifted up the lappets of my coat, which it seems he thought to be some kind of covering that nature had given me. He blew my hairs aside to take a better view of my face. He called his hinds[3] about him, and asked them (as I afterwards learned) whether they had ever seen in the fields any little creature that resembled me. He then placed me softly on the ground upon all four; but I got immediately up, and walked slowly backwards and forwards, to let those people see I had no intent to run away. They all sat down in a circle about me, the better to observe my motions. I pulled off my hat, and made a low bow towards the farmer; I fell on my knees, and lifted up my hands and eyes, and spoke several words as loud as I could; I took a purse of gold out of my pocket, and humbly presented it to him. He received it on the palm of his hand, then applied it close to his eye to see what it was, and afterwards turned it several times with the point of a pin (which he took out of his sleeve), but could make nothing of it. Whereupon I made a sign that he should place his hand on the ground; I then took the purse, and opening it, poured all the gold into his palm. There were six Spanish pieces of four pistoles each, beside twenty or thirty smaller coins. I saw him wet the tip of his little finger upon his tongue, and take up one of my largest pieces, and then another; but he seemed to be wholly ignorant what they were. He made me a sign to put them again into my purse, and the purse again into my pocket, which after offering to him several times, I thought it best to do.

The farmer by this time was convinced I must be a rational creature. He spoke often to me, but the sound of his voice pierced my ears like that of a water mill, yet his words were articulate enough. I answered as loud as I could in several languages, and he often laid his ear within two yards of me, but all in vain, for we were wholly unintelligible to each other. He then sent his servants to their work, and taking his handkerchief out of his pocket, he doubled and spread it on his hand, which he placed flat on the ground with the palm upwards, making me a sign to step into it, as I could easily do, for it was not above a foot in thickness. I thought it my part to obey, and for fear of falling, laid myself at full length upon the handkerchief, with the remainder of which he lapped me up to the head for further security, and in this manner carried me home to his house. There he called his wife, and showed me to her; but she screamed and ran back as women in England do at the sight of a toad or a spider. However, when she had a while seen my behavior, and how well I observed the signs her husband made, she was soon reconciled, and by degrees grew extremely tender of me.

It was about twelve at noon, and a servant brought in dinner. It was only one substantial dish of meat (fit for the plain condition of an husbandman) in a dish of about four-and-twenty foot diameter. The company were the farmer and his wife, three children, and an old grandmother. When they were sat down, the farmer placed me at some distance from him on the table,

---

2. Flap or fold. 3. Farm servants.

which was thirty foot high from the floor. I was in a terrible fright, and kept as far as I could from the edge, for fear of falling. The wife minced a bit of meat, then crumbled some bread on a trencher, and placed it before me. I made her a low bow, took out my knife and fork, and fell to eat; which gave them exceeding delight. The mistress sent her maid for a small dram cup, which held about two gallons, and filled it with drink; I took up the vessel with much difficulty in both hands, and in a most respectful manner drank to her ladyship's health, expressing the words as loud as I could in English; which made the company laugh so heartily that I was almost deafened with the noise. This liquor tasted like a small cider,[4] and was not unpleasant. Then the master made me a sign to come to his trencher side; but as I walked on the table, being in great surprise all the time, as the indulgent reader will easily conceive and excuse, I happened to stumble against a crust, and fell flat on my face, but received no hurt. I got up immediately, and observing the good people to be in much concern, I took my hat (which I held under my arm out of good manners) and waving it over my head, made three huzzas to show I had got no mischief by my fall. But advancing forwards toward my master (as I shall henceforth call him), his youngest son who sat next him, an arch boy of about ten years old, took me up by the legs, and held me so high in the air that I trembled every limb; but his father snatched me from him, and at the same time gave him such a box on the left ear as would have felled an European troop of horse to the earth, ordering him to be taken from the table. But being afraid the boy might owe me a spite, and well remembering how mischievous all children among us naturally are to sparrows, rabbits, young kittens, and puppy dogs, I fell on my knees, and pointing to the boy, made my master to understand, as well as I could, that I desired his son might be pardoned. The father complied, and the lad took his seat again; whereupon I went to him and kissed his hand, which my master took, and made him stroke me gently with it.

In the midst of dinner, my mistress's favorite cat leaped into her lap. I heard a noise behind me like that of a dozen stocking weavers at work; and turning my head, I found it proceeded from the purring of this animal, who seemed to be three times larger than an ox, as I computed by the view of her head and one of her paws, while her mistress was feeding and stroking her. The fierceness of this creature's countenance altogether discomposed me, although I stood at the farther end of the table, about fifty foot off, and although my mistress held her fast for fear she might give a spring and seize me in her talons. But it happened there was no danger, for the cat took not the least notice of me when my master placed me within three yards of her. And as I have been always told, and found true by experience in my travels, that flying or discovering[5] fear before a fierce animal is a certain way to make it pursue or attack you, so I resolved in this dangerous juncture to show no manner of concern. I walked with intrepidity five or six times before the very head of the cat, and came within half a yard of her; whereupon she drew herself back, as if she were more afraid of me. I had less apprehension concerning the dogs, whereof three or four came into the room, as it is usual in farmers' houses; one of which was a mastiff, equal in bulk to four elephants, and a greyhound, somewhat taller than the mastiff, but not so large.

---

4. I.e., weak cider.   5. Revealing.

When dinner was almost done, the nurse came in with a child of a year old in her arms, who immediately spied me, and began a squall that you might have heard from London Bridge to Chelsea, after the usual oratory of infants, to get me for a plaything. The mother out of pure indulgence took me up, and put me towards the child, who presently seized me by the middle, and got my head in his mouth, where I roared so loud that the urchin was frighted and let me drop; and I should infallibly have broke my neck if the mother had not held her apron under me. The nurse to quiet her babe made use of a rattle, which was a kind of hollow vessel filled with great stones, and fastened by a cable to the child's waist: but all in vain, so that she was forced to apply the last remedy by giving it suck. I must confess no object ever disgusted me so much as the sight of her monstrous breast, which I cannot tell what to compare with so as to give the curious reader an idea of its bulk, shape, and color. It stood prominent six foot, and could not be less than sixteen in circumference. The nipple was about half the bigness of my head, and the hue both of that and the dug so varified with spots, pimples, and freckles that nothing could appear more nauseous: for I had a near sight of her, she sitting down the more conveniently to give suck, and I standing on the table. This made me reflect upon the fair skins of our English ladies, who appear so beautiful to us, only because they are of our own size, and their defects not to be seen but through a magnifying glass, where we find by experiment that the smoothest and whitest skins look rough and coarse and ill colored.

I remember when I was at Lilliput, the complexion of those diminutive people appeared to me the fairest in the world; and talking upon this subject with a person of learning there, who was an intimate friend of mine, he said that my face appeared much fairer and smoother when he looked on me from the ground than it did upon a nearer view when I took him up in my hand and brought him close, which he confessed was at first a very shocking sight. He said he could discover great holes in my skin; that the stumps of my beard were ten times stronger than the bristles of a boar, and my complexion made up of several colors altogether disagreeable: although I must beg leave to say for myself that I am as fair as most of my sex and country and very little sunburnt by all my travels. On the other side, discoursing of the ladies in that Emperor's court, he used to tell me one had freckles, another too wide a mouth, a third too large a nose; nothing of which I was able to distinguish. I confess this reflection was obvious enough; which however I could not forbear, lest the reader might think those vast creatures were actually deformed: for I must do them justice to say they are a comely race of people; and particularly the features of my master's countenance, although he were but a farmer, when I beheld him from the height of sixty foot, appeared very well proportioned.

When dinner was done, my master went out to his laborers; and as I could discover by his voice and gesture, gave his wife a strict charge to take care of me. I was very much tired and disposed to sleep, which my mistress perceiving, she put me on her own bed, and covered me with a clean white handkerchief, but larger and coarser than the mainsail of a man-of-war.

I slept about two hours, and dreamed I was at home with my wife and children, which aggravated my sorrows when I awaked and found myself alone in a vast room, between two and three hundred foot wide, and above two hundred high, lying in a bed twenty yards wide. My mistress was gone about her household affairs, and had locked me in. The bed was eight yards from the floor. Some natural necessities required me to get down; I durst not presume to call, and if I had, it would have been in vain with such a voice as mine at so great a distance from the room where I lay to the kitchen where the family kept. While I was under these circumstances, two rats crept up the curtains, and ran smelling backwards and forwards on the bed. One of them came up almost to my face; whereupon I rose in a fright, and drew out my hanger[6] to defend myself. These horrible animals had the boldness to attack me on both sides, and one of them held his forefeet at my collar; but I had the good fortune to rip up his belly before he could do me any mischief. He fell down at my feet; and the other seeing the fate of his comrade, made his escape, but not without one good wound on the back, which I gave him as he fled, and made the blood run trickling from him. After this exploit I walked gently to and fro on the bed, to recover my breath and loss of spirits. These creatures were of the size of a large mastiff, but infinitely more nimble and fierce; so that if I had taken off my belt before I went to sleep, I must have infallibly been torn to pieces and devoured. I measured the tail of the dead rat, and found it to be two yards long, wanting an inch; but it went against my stomach to drag the carcass off the bed, where it lay still bleeding; I observed it had yet some life, but with a strong slash cross the neck, I thoroughly dispatched it.

Soon after, my mistress came into the room, who seeing me all bloody, ran and took me up in her hand. I pointed to the dead rat, smiling and making other signs to show I was not hurt, whereat she was extremely rejoiced, calling the maid to take up the dead rat with a pair of tongs, and throw it out of the window. Then she set me on a table, where I showed her my hanger all bloody, and wiping it on the lappet of my coat, returned it to the scabbard. I was pressed to do more than one thing, which another could not do for me, and therefore endeavored to make my mistress understand that I desired to be set down on the floor; which after she had done, my bashfulness would not suffer me to express myself farther than by pointing to the door, and bowing several times. The good woman with much difficulty at last perceived what I would be at, and taking me up again in her hand, walked into the garden, where she set me down. I went on one side about two hundred yards; and beckoning to her not to look or to follow me, I hid myself between two leaves of sorrel, and there discharged the necessities of nature.

I hope the gentle reader will excuse me for dwelling on these and the like particulars, which however insignificant they may appear to groveling vulgar minds, yet will certainly help a philosopher[7] to enlarge his thoughts and imagination, and apply them to the benefit of public as well as private life, which was my sole design in presenting this and other accounts of my travels to the world; wherein I have been chiefly studious of truth, without affecting any ornaments of learning or of style. But the whole scene of this voyage made so strong an impression on my mind, and is so deeply fixed in my memory, that in committing it to paper I did not omit one material circumstance; however, upon a strict review, I blotted out several passages of less

---

6. A short, broad sword.
7. "Vulgar": commonplace, uncultivated, in contrast to the scientist ("philosopher"); an irony.

moment which were in my first copy, for fear of being censured as tedious and trifling, whereof travelers are often, perhaps not without justice, accused.

CHAPTER 2. *A description of the farmer's daughter. The Author carried to a market town, and then to the metropolis. The particulars of his journey.*

My mistress had a daughter of nine years old, a child of towardly parts for her age, very dexterous at her needle, and skillful in dressing her baby.[8] Her mother and she contrived to fit up the baby's cradle for me against night: the cradle was put into a small drawer of a cabinet, and the drawer placed upon a hanging shelf for fear of the rats. This was my bed all the time I stayed with those people, although made more convenient by degrees as I began to learn their language, and make my wants known. This young girl was so handy, that after I had once or twice pulled off my clothes before her, she was able to dress and undress me, although I never gave her that trouble when she would let me do either myself. She made me seven shirts, and some other linen of as fine cloth as could be got, which indeed was coarser than sackcloth, and these she constantly washed for me with her own hands. She was likewise my schoolmistress to teach me the language: when I pointed to anything, she told me the name of it in her own tongue, so that in a few days I was able to call for whatever I had a mind to. She was very good-natured, and not above forty foot high, being little for her age. She gave me the name of *Grildrig*, which the family took up, and afterwards the whole kingdom. The word imports what the Latins call *nanunculus*, the Italian *homunceletino*,[9] and the English *mannikin*. To her I chiefly owe my preservation in that country: we never parted while I was there; I called her my *Glumdalclitch*, or little nurse: and I should be guilty of great ingratitude if I omitted this honorable mention of her care and affection towards me, which I heartily wish it lay in my power to requite as she deserves, instead of being the innocent but unhappy instrument of her disgrace, as I have too much reason to fear.

It now began to be known and talked of in the neighborhood that my master had found a strange animal in the field, about the bigness of a *splacknuck*, but exactly shaped in every part like a human creature, which it likewise imitated in all its actions: seemed to speak in a little language of its own, had already learned several words of theirs, went erect upon two legs, was tame and gentle, would come when it was called, do whatever it was bid, had the finest limbs in the world, and a complexion fairer than a nobleman's daughter of three years old. Another farmer who lived hard by, and was a particular friend of my master, came on a visit on purpose to inquire into the truth of this story. I was immediately produced, and placed upon a table, where I walked as I was commanded, drew my hanger, put it up again, made my reverence to my master's guest, asked him in his own language how he did, and told him he was welcome, just as my little nurse had instructed me. This man, who was old and dimsighted, put on his spectacles to behold me better, at which I could not forbear laughing very heartily, for

---

8. Doll. "Towardly parts": promising abilities.
9. The Latin and Italian words are Swift's own

coinages, as, of course, are the various words from the Brobdingnagian language.

his eyes appeared like the full moon shining into a chamber at two windows. Our people, who discovered the cause of my mirth, bore me company in laughing, at which the old fellow was fool enough to be angry and out of countenance. He had the character of a great miser, and to my misfortune he well deserved it by the cursed advice he gave my master to show me as a sight upon a market day in the next town, which was half an hour's riding, about two and twenty miles from our house. I guessed there was some mischief contriving when I observed my master and his friend whispering long together, sometimes pointing at me; and my fears made me fancy that I overheard and understood some of their words. But the next morning Glumdalclitch, my little nurse, told me the whole matter, which she had cunningly picked out from her mother. The poor girl laid me on her bosom, and fell a weeping with shame and grief. She apprehended some mischief would happen to me from rude vulgar folks, who might squeeze me to death, or break one of my limbs by taking me in their hands. She had also observed how modest I was in my nature, how nicely I regarded my honor, and what an indignity I should conceive it to be exposed for money as a public spectacle to the meanest of the people. She said her papa and mamma had promised that Grildrig should be hers; but now she found they meant to serve her as they did last year, when they pretended to give her a lamb, and yet, as soon as it was fat, sold it to a butcher. For my own part, I may truly affirm that I was less concerned than my nurse. I had a strong hope, which never left me, that I should one day recover my liberty; and as to the ignominy of being carried about for a monster, I considered myself to be a perfect stranger in the country, and that such a misfortune could never be charged upon me as a reproach, if ever I should return to England; since the King of Great Britain himself, in my condition, must have undergone the same distress.

My master, pursuant to the advice of his friend, carried me in a box the next market day to the neighboring town, and took along with him his little daughter, my nurse, upon a pillion[1] behind him. The box was close on every side, with a little door for me to go in and out, and a few gimlet holes to let in air. The girl had been so careful to put the quilt of her baby's bed into it, for me to lie down on. However, I was terribly shaken and discomposed in this journey, although it were but of half an hour. For the horse went about forty foot at every step, and trotted so high that the agitation was equal to the rising and falling of a ship in a great storm, but much more frequent. Our journey was somewhat further than from London to St. Albans. My master alighted at an inn which he used to frequent; and after consulting a while with the innkeeper, and making some necessary preparations, he hired the *Grultrud*, or crier, to give notice through the town of a strange creature to be seen at the Sign of the Green Eagle, not so big as a *splacknuck* (an animal in that country very finely shaped, about six foot long), and in every part of the body resembling an human creature; could speak several words and perform an hundred diverting tricks.

I was placed upon a table in the largest room of the inn, which might be near three hundred foot square. My little nurse stood on a low stool close to the table, to take care of me, and direct what I should do. My master, to avoid a crowd, would suffer only thirty people at a time to see me. I walked

---

1. A pad attached to the hinder part of a saddle, on which a second person, usually a woman, could ride.

about on the table as the girl commanded; she asked me questions as far as she knew my understanding of the language reached, and I answered them as loud as I could. I turned about several times to the company, paid my humble respects, said they were welcome, and used some other speeches I had been taught. I took up a thimble filled with liquor, which Glumdalclitch had given me for a cup, and drank their health. I drew out my hanger, and flourished with it after the manner of fencers in England. My nurse gave me part of a straw, which I exercised as pike, having learned the art in my youth. I was that day shown to twelve sets of company, and as often forced to go over again with the same fopperies, till I was half dead with weariness and vexation. For those who had seen me made such wonderful reports that the people were ready to break down the doors to come in. My master for his own interest would not suffer anyone to touch me except my nurse; and, to prevent danger, benches were set round the table at such a distance as put me out of everybody's reach. However, an unlucky schoolboy aimed a hazelnut directly at my head, which very narrowly missed me; otherwise, it came with so much violence that it would have infallibly knocked out my brains, for it was almost as large as a small pumpion:[2] but I had the satisfaction to see the young rogue well beaten, and turned out of the room.

My master gave public notice that he would show me again the next market day, and in the meantime he prepared a more convenient vehicle for me, which he had reason enough to do; for I was so tired with my first journey, and with entertaining company for eight hours together, that I could hardly stand upon my legs or speak a word. It was at least three days before I recovered my strength; and that I might have no rest at home, all the neighboring gentlemen from an hundred miles round, hearing of my fame, came to see me at my master's own house. There could not be fewer than thirty persons with their wives and children (for the country is very populous); and my master demanded the rate of a full room whenever he showed me at home, although it were only to a single family. So that for some time I had but little ease every day of the week (except Wednesday, which is their Sabbath) although I were not carried to the town.

My master finding how profitable I was like to be, resolved to carry me to the most considerable cities of the kingdom. Having therefore provided himself with all things necessary for a long journey, and settled his affairs at home, he took leave of his wife; and upon the 17th of August, 1703, about two months after my arrival, we set out for the metropolis, situated near the middle of that empire, and about three thousand miles distance from our house. My master made his daughter Glumdalclitch ride behind him. She carried me on her lap in a box tied about her waist. The girl had lined it on all sides with the softest cloth she could get, well quilted underneath, furnished it with her baby's bed, provided me with linen and other necessaries, and made everything as convenient as she could. We had no other company but a boy of the house, who rode after us with the luggage.

My master's design was to show me in all the towns by the way, and to step out of the road for fifty or an hundred miles to any village or person of quality's house where he might expect custom. We made easy journeys of not above seven or eight score miles a day: for Glumdalclitch, on purpose to

2. Pumpkin.

spare me, complained she was tired with the trotting of the horse. She often took me out of my box at my own desire, to give me air and show me the country, but always held me fast by leading strings. We passed over five or six rivers many degrees broader and deeper than the Nile or the Ganges; and there was hardly a rivulet so small as the Thames at London Bridge. We were ten weeks in our journey, and I was shown in eighteen large towns, besides many large villages and private families.

On the 26th day of October, we arrived at the metropolis, called in their language *Lorbrulgrud*, or Pride of the Universe. My master took a lodging in the principal street of the city, not far from the royal palace, and put out bills in the usual form, containing an exact description of my person and parts. He hired a large room between three and four hundred foot wide. He provided a table sixty foot in diameter, upon which I was to act my part, and palisadoed it round three foot from the edge, and as many high, to prevent my falling over. I was shown ten times a day to the wonder and satisfaction of all people. I could now speak the language tolerably well, and perfectly understood every word that was spoken to me. Besides, I had learned their alphabet, and could make a shift to explain a sentence here and there; for Glumdalclitch had been my instructor while we were at home, and at leisure hours during our journey. She carried a little book in her pocket, not much larger than a Sanson's *Atlas;*[3] it was a common treatise for the use of young girls, giving a short account of their religion: out of this she taught me my letters, and interpreted the words.

CHAPTER 3. *The Author sent for to Court. The Queen buys him of his master, the farmer, and presents him to the King. He disputes with his Majesty's great scholars. An apartment at Court provided for the Author. He is in high favor with the Queen. He stands up for the honor of his own country. His quarrels with the Queen's dwarf.*

The frequent labors I underwent every day made in a few weeks a very considerable change in my health: the more my master got by me, the more unsatiable he grew. I had quite lost my stomach, and was almost reduced to a skeleton. The farmer observed it, and concluding I soon must die, resolved to make as good a hand of me as he could. While he was thus reasoning and resolving with himself, a *Slardral*, or Gentleman Usher, came from Court, commanding my master to carry me immediately thither for the diversion of the Queen and her ladies. Some of the latter had already been to see me and reported strange things of my beauty, behavior, and good sense. Her Majesty and those who attended her were beyond measure delighted with my demeanor. I fell on my knees and begged the honor of kissing her Imperial foot; but this gracious princess held out her little finger towards me (after I was set on a table), which I embraced in both my arms, and put the tip of it, with the utmost respect, to my lip. She made me some general questions about my country and my travels, which I answered as distinctly and in as few words as I could. She asked whether I would be content to live at Court. I bowed down to the board of the table, and humbly answered that I was my master's slave, but if I were at my own disposal, I should be proud to devote

3. I.e., over two feet long and about two feet wide.

my life to her Majesty's service. She then asked my master whether he were willing to sell me at a good price. He, who apprehended I could not live a month, was ready enough to part with me, and demanded a thousand pieces of gold, which were ordered him on the spot, each piece being about the bigness of eight hundred moidores;[4] but, allowing for the proportion of all things between that country and Europe, and the high price of gold among them, was hardly so great a sum as a thousand guineas would be in England. I then said to the Queen, since I was now her Majesty's most humble creature and vassal, I must beg the favor that Glumdalclitch, who had always tended me with so much care and kindness, and understood to do it so well, might be admitted into her service, and continue to be my nurse and instructor. Her Majesty agreed to my petition, and easily got the farmer's consent, who was glad enough to have his daughter preferred at Court; and the poor girl herself was not able to hide her joy. My late master withdrew, bidding me farewell, and saying he had left me in a good service; to which I replied not a word, only making him a slight bow.

The Queen observed my coldness, and when the farmer was gone out of the apartment, asked me the reason. I made bold to tell her Majesty that I owed no other obligation to my late master than his not dashing out the brains of a poor harmless creature found by chance in his field; which obligation was amply recompensed by the gain he had made in showing me through half the kingdom, and the price he had now sold me for. That the life I had since led was laborious enough to kill an animal of ten times my strength. That my health was much impaired by the continual drudgery of entertaining the rabble every hour of the day; and that if my master had not thought my life in danger, her Majesty perhaps would not have got so cheap a bargain. But as I was out of all fear of being ill treated under the protection of so great and good an Empress, the Ornament of Nature, the Darling of the World, the Delight of her Subjects, the Phoenix of the Creation; so I hoped my late master's apprehensions would appear to be groundless, for I already found my spirits to revive by the influence of her most august presence.

This was the sum of my speech, delivered with great improprieties and hesitation; the latter part was altogether framed in the style peculiar to that people, whereof I learned some phrases from Glumdalclitch, while she was carrying me to Court.

The Queen, giving great allowance for my defectiveness in speaking, was however surprised at so much wit and good sense in so diminutive an animal. She took me in her own hand, and carried me to the King, who was then retired to his cabinet.[5] His Majesty, a prince of much gravity, and austere countenance, not well observing my shape at first view, asked the Queen after a cold manner how long it was since she grew fond of a *splacknuck;* for such it seems he took me to be, as I lay upon my breast in her Majesty's right hand. But this princess, who hath an infinite deal of wit and humor, set me gently on my feet upon the scrutore,[6] and commanded me to give his Majesty an account of myself, which I did in a very few words; and Glumdalclitch, who attended at the cabinet door, and could not endure I should be out of

4. Portuguese coins.
5. Private apartment.

6. Writing desk.

her sight, being admitted, confirmed all that had passed from my arrival at her father's house.

The King, although he be as learned a person as any in his dominions, had been educated in the study of philosophy and particularly mathematics; yet when he observed my shape exactly, and saw me walk erect, before I began to speak, conceived I might be a piece of clockwork (which is in that country arrived to a very great perfection) contrived by some ingenious artist. But when he heard my voice, and found what I delivered to be regular and rational, he could not conceal his astonishment. He was by no means satisfied with the relation I gave him of the manner I came into his kingdom, but thought it a story concerted between Glumdalclitch and her father, who had taught me a set of words to make me sell at a higher price. Upon this imagination he put several other questions to me, and still received rational answers, no otherwise defective than by a foreign accent, and an imperfect knowledge in the language, with some rustic phrases which I had learned at the farmer's house, and did not suit the polite style of a court.

His Majesty sent for three great scholars who were then in their weekly waiting (according to the custom in that country). These gentlemen, after they had a while examined my shape with much nicety, were of different opinions concerning me. They all agreed that I could not be produced according to the regular laws of nature, because I was not framed with a capacity of preserving my life, either by swiftness, or climbing of trees, or digging holes in the earth. They observed by my teeth, which they viewed with great exactness, that I was a carnivorous animal; yet most quadrupeds being an overmatch for me, and field mice, with some others, too nimble, they could not imagine how I should be able to support myself, unless I fed upon snails and other insects; which they offered, by many learned arguments, to evince that I could not possibly do. One of them seemed to think that I might be an embryo, or abortive birth. But this opinion was rejected by the other two, who observed my limbs to be perfect and finished, and that I had lived several years, as it was manifested from my beard, the stumps whereof they plainly discovered through a magnifying glass. They would not allow me to be a dwarf, because my littleness was beyond all degrees of comparison; for the Queen's favorite dwarf, the smallest ever known in that kingdom, was nearly thirty foot high. After much debate, they concluded unanimously that I was only *relplum scalcath,* which is interpreted literally, *lusus naturae;* a determination exactly agreeable to the modern philosophy of Europe, whose professors, disdaining the old evasion of *occult causes,* whereby the followers of Aristotle endeavor in vain to disguise their ignorance, have invented this wonderful solution of all difficulties, to the unspeakable advancement of human knowledge.[7]

After this decisive conclusion, I entreated to be heard a word or two. I applied myself to the King, and assured his Majesty that I came from a country which abounded with several millions of both sexes, and of my own stature, where the animals, trees, and houses were all in proportion, and where by consequence I might be as able to defend myself, and to find sus-

7. Swift had contempt for both the medieval Schoolmen, who discussed "occult causes," the unknown causes of observable effects, and modern scientists, who, he believed, often concealed their ignorance by using equally meaningless terms. *"Lusus naturae"*: one of nature's sports, or roughly, freaks.

tenance, as any of his Majesty's subjects could do here; which I took for a full answer to those gentlemen's arguments. To this they only replied with a smile of contempt, saying that the farmer had instructed me very well in my lesson. The King, who had a much better understanding, dismissing his learned men, sent for the farmer, who by good fortune was not yet gone out of town; having therefore first examined him privately, and then confronted him with me and the young girl, his Majesty began to think that what we told him might possibly be true. He desired the Queen to order that a particular care should be taken of me, and was of opinion that Glumdalclitch should still continue in her office of tending me, because he observed we had a great affection for each other. A convenient apartment was provided for her at Court; she had a sort of governess appointed to take care of her education, a maid to dress her, and two other servants for menial offices; but the care of me was wholly appropriated to herself. The Queen commanded her own cabinetmaker to contrive a box that might serve me for a bedchamber, after the model that Glumdalclitch and I should agree upon. This man was a most ingenious artist, and according to my directions, in three weeks finished for me a wooden chamber of sixteen foot square and twelve high, with sash windows, a door, and two closets, like a London bedchamber. The board that made the ceiling was to be lifted up and down by two hinges, to put in a bed ready furnished by her Majesty's upholsterer, which Glumdalclitch took out every day to air, made it with her own hands, and letting it down at night, locked up the roof over me. A nice[8] workman, who was famous for little curiosities, undertook to make me two chairs, with backs and frames, of a substance not unlike ivory, and two tables, with a cabinet to put my things in. The room was quilted on all sides, as well as the floor and the ceiling, to prevent any accident from the carelessness of those who carried me, and to break the force of a jolt when I went in a coach. I desired a lock for my door to prevent rats and mice from coming in: the smith, after several attempts, made the smallest that ever was seen among them, for I have known a larger at the gate of a gentleman's house in England. I made a shift[9] to keep the key in a pocket of my own, fearing Glumdalclitch might lose it. The Queen likewise ordered the thinnest silks that could be gotten, to make me clothes, not much thicker than an English blanket, very cumbersome till I was accustomed to them. They were after the fashion of the kingdom, partly resembling the Persian, and partly the Chinese, and are a very grave, decent habit.

The Queen became so fond of my company that she could not dine without me. I had a table placed upon the same at which her Majesty ate, just at her left elbow, and a chair to sit on. Glumdalclitch stood upon a stool on the floor, near my table, to assist and take care of me. I had an entire set of silver dishes and plates, and other necessaries, which, in proportion to those of the Queen, were not much bigger than what I have seen of the same kind in a London toyshop,[1] for the furniture of a baby-house: these my little nurse kept in her pocket in a silver box and gave me at meals as I wanted them, always cleaning them herself. No person dined with the Queen but the two Princesses Royal, the elder sixteen years old, and the younger at that time thirteen and a month. Her Majesty used to put a bit of meat upon one of my

8. Exact.
9. Contrived.

1. A shop for selling knickknacks.

dishes, out of which I carved for myself; and her diversion was to see me eat in miniature. For the Queen (who had indeed but a weak stomach) took up at one mouthful as much as a dozen English farmers could eat at a meal, which to me was for some time a very nauseous sight. She would craunch the wing of a lark, bones and all, between her teeth, although it were nine times as large as that of a full-grown turkey; and put a bit of bread into her mouth as big as two twelve-penny loaves. She drank out of a golden cup, above a hogshead at a draught. Her knives were twice as long as a scythe set straight upon the handle. The spoons, forks, and other instruments were all in the same proportion. I remember when Glumdalclitch carried me out of curiosity to see some of the tables at Court, where ten or a dozen of these enormous knives and forks were lifted up together, I thought I had never till then beheld so terrible a sight.

It is the custom that every Wednesday (which, as I have before observed, was their Sabbath) the King and Queen, with the royal issue of both sexes, dine together in the apartment of his Majesty, to whom I was now become a favorite; and at these times my little chair and table were placed at his left hand, before one of the salt-cellars. This prince took a pleasure in conversing with me, inquiring into the manners, religion, laws, government, and learn-ing of Europe; wherein I gave him the best account I was able. His appre-hension was so clear, and his judgment so exact, that he made very wise reflections and observations upon all I said. But I confess that after I had been a little too copious in talking of my own beloved country, of our trade and wars by sea and land, of our schisms in religion and parties in the state, the prejudices of his education prevailed so far that he could not forbear taking me up in his right hand, and stroking me gently with the other, after an hearty fit of laughing, asked me whether I were a Whig or a Tory. Then turning to his first minister, who waited behind him with a white staff, near as tall as the mainmast of the *Royal Sovereign*,[2] he observed how contempt-ible a thing was human grandeur, which could be mimicked by such dimin-utive insects as I: "and yet," said he, "I dare engage, these creatures have their titles and distinctions of honor; they contrive little nests and burrows, that they call houses and cities; they make a figure in dress and equipage; they love, they fight, they dispute, they cheat, they betray." And thus he continued on, while my color came and went several times with indignation to hear our noble country, the mistress of arts and arms, the scourge of France, the arbitress of Europe, the seat of virtue, piety, honor, and truth, the pride and envy of the world, so contemptuously treated.

But as I was not in a condition to resent injuries, so, upon mature thoughts, I began to doubt whether I were injured or no. For, after having been accustomed several months to the sight and converse of this people, and observed every object upon which I cast my eyes to be of proportionable magnitude, the horror I had first conceived from their bulk and aspect was so far worn off that if I had then beheld a company of English lords and ladies in their finery and birthday clothes,[3] acting their several parts in the most courtly manner of strutting and bowing and prating, to say the truth, I should have been strongly tempted to laugh as much at them as this King and his grandees did at me. Neither indeed could I forbear smiling at myself

2. One of the largest ships in the Royal Navy. At the English court the lord treasurer bore a white staff as the symbol of his office.

3. Courtiers dressed with special splendor on the monarch's birthday.

when the Queen used to place me upon her hand towards a looking glass, by which both our persons appeared before me in full view together; and there could be nothing more ridiculous than the comparison; so that I really began to imagine myself dwindled many degrees below my usual size.

Nothing angered and mortified me so much as the Queen's dwarf, who being of the lowest stature that was ever in that country (for I verily think he was not full thirty foot high) became so insolent at seeing a creature so much beneath him that he would always affect to swagger and look big as he passed by me in the Queen's antechamber, while I was standing on some table talking with the lords or ladies of the court; and he seldom failed of a smart word or two upon my littleness, against which I could only revenge myself by calling him brother, challenging him to wrestle, and such repartees as are usual in the mouths of Court pages. One day at dinner this malicious little cub was so nettled with something I had said to him that, raising himself upon the frame of Her Majesty's chair, he took me up by the middle, as I was sitting down, not thinking any harm, and let me drop into a large silver bowl of cream, and then ran away as fast as he could. I fell over head and ears, and if I had not been a good swimmer, it might have gone very hard with me; for Glumdalclitch in that instant happened to be at the other end of the room, and the Queen was in such a fright that she wanted presence of mind to assist me. But my little nurse ran to my relief, and took me out, after I had swallowed above a quart of cream. I was put to bed; however, I received no other damage than the loss of a suit of clothes, which was utterly spoiled. The dwarf was soundly whipped, and as further punishment, forced to drink up the bowl of cream into which he had thrown me; neither was he ever restored to favor: for soon after the Queen bestowed him to a lady of high quality, so that I saw him no more, to my very great satisfaction; for I could not tell to what extremity such a malicious urchin might have carried his resentment.

He had before served me a scurvy trick, which set the Queen a laughing, although at the same time she were heartily vexed, and would have immediately cashiered him, if I had not been so generous as to intercede. Her Majesty had taken a marrow bone upon her plate, and after knocking out the marrow, placed the bone again in the dish, erect as it stood before; the dwarf watching his opportunity, while Glumdalclitch was gone to the sideboard, mounted upon the stool she stood on to take care of me at meals, took me up in both hands, and squeezing my legs together, wedged them into the marrow bone above my waist, where I stuck for some time, and made a very ridiculous figure. I believe it was near a minute before anyone knew what was become of me, for I thought it below me to cry out. But, as princes seldom get their meat hot, my legs were not scalded, only my stockings and breeches in a sad condition. The dwarf at my entreaty had no other punishment than a sound whipping.

I was frequently rallied by the Queen upon account of my fearfulness, and she used to ask me whether the people of my country were as great cowards as myself. The occasion was this. The kingdom is much pestered with flies in summer, and these odious insects, each of them as big as a Dunstable lark, hardly gave me any rest while I sat at dinner, with their continual humming and buzzing about my ears. They would sometimes alight upon my victuals, and leave their loathsome excrement or spawn behind, which to me was very visible, although not to the natives of that country, whose large optics were not so acute as mine in viewing smaller objects. Sometimes they would fix upon my nose or forehead, where they stung me to the quick, smelling very offensively; and I could easily trace that viscous matter, which our naturalists tell us enables those creatures to walk with their feet upwards upon a ceiling. I had much ado to defend myself against these detestable animals, and could not forbear starting when they came on my face. It was the common practice of the dwarf to catch a number of these insects in his hand, as schoolboys do among us, and let them out suddenly under my nose, on purpose to frighten me, and divert the Queen. My remedy was to cut them in pieces with my knife as they flew in the air, wherein my dexterity was much admired.

I remember one morning when Glumdalclitch had set me in my box upon a window, as she usually did in fair days to give me air (for I durst not venture to let the box be hung on a nail out of the window, as we do with cages in England), after I had lifted up one of my sashes, and sat down at my table to eat a piece of sweet cake for my breakfast, above twenty wasps, allured by the smell, came flying into the room, humming louder than the drones of as many bagpipes. Some of them seized my cake, and carried it piecemeal away; others flew about my head and face, confounding me with the noise, and putting me in the utmost terror of their stings. However, I had the courage to rise and draw my hanger, and attack them in the air. I dispatched four of them, but the rest got away, and I presently shut my window. These insects were as large as partridges; I took out their stings, found them an inch and a half long, and as sharp as needles. I carefully preserved them all, and having since shown them with some other curiosities in several parts of Europe, upon my return to England I gave three of them to Gresham College,[4] and kept the fourth for myself.

CHAPTER 4. *The country described. A proposal for correcting modern maps. The King's palace, and some account of the metropolis. The Author's way of traveling. The chief temple described.*

I now intend to give the reader a short description of this country, as far as I had traveled in it, which was not above two thousand miles round Lorbrulgrud the metropolis. For the Queen, whom I always attended, never went further when she accompanied the King in his progresses, and there stayed till his Majesty returned from viewing his frontiers. The whole extent of this prince's dominions reacheth about six thousand miles in length, and from three to five in breadth. From whence I cannot but conclude that our geographers of Europe are in a great error by supposing nothing but sea between Japan and California: for it was ever my opinion that there must be a balance of earth to counterpoise the great continent of Tartary; and therefore they ought to correct their maps and charts by joining this vast tract of land to the northwest parts of America, wherein I shall be ready to lend them my assistance.

The kingdom is a peninsula, terminated to the northeast by a ridge of mountains thirty miles high, which are altogether impassable by reason of the volcanoes upon the tops. Neither do the most learned know what sort of mortals inhabit beyond those mountains, or whether they be inhabited at all.

4. The Royal Society, in its earliest years, met in Gresham College.

On the three other sides it is bounded by the ocean. There is not one seaport in the whole kingdom; and those parts of the coasts into which the rivers issue are so full of pointed rocks, and the sea generally so rough, that there is no venturing with the smallest of their boats; so that these people are wholly excluded from any commerce with the rest of the world. But the large rivers are full of vessels, and abound with excellent fish, for they seldom get any from the sea, because the sea fish are of the same size with those in Europe, and consequently not worth catching; whereby it is manifest that nature, in the production of plants and animals of so extraordinary a bulk, is wholly confined to this continent, of which I leave the reasons to be determined by philosophers. However, now and then they take a whale that happens to be dashed against the rocks, which the common people feed on heartily. These whales I have known so large that a man could hardly carry one upon his shoulders; and sometimes for curiosity they are brought in hampers to Lorbrulgrud: I saw one of them in a dish at the King's table, which passed for a rarity, but I did not observe he was fond of it; for I think indeed the bigness disgusted him, although I have seen one somewhat larger in Greenland.

The country is well inhabited, for it contains fifty-one cities, near an hundred walled towns, and a great number of villages. To satisfy my curious reader, it may be sufficient to describe Lorbrulgrud. This city stands upon almost two equal parts on each side the river that passes through. It contains above eight thousand houses, and about six hundred thousand inhabitants. It is in length three *glonglungs* (which make about fifty-four English miles) and two and a half in breadth, as I measured it myself in the royal map made by the King's order, which was laid on the ground on purpose for me, and extended an hundred feet; I paced the diameter and circumference several times barefoot, and computing by the scale, measured it pretty exactly.

The King's palace is no regular edifice, but an heap of buildings about seven miles round: the chief rooms are generally two hundred and forty foot high, and broad and long in proportion. A coach was allowed to Glumdal-clitch and me, wherein her governess frequently took her out to see the town, or go among the shops; and I was always of the party, carried in my box, although the girl at my own desire would often take me out, and hold me in her hand, that I might more conveniently view the houses and the people as we passed along the streets. I reckoned our coach to be about a square of Westminster Hall,[5] but not altogether so high; however, I cannot be very exact. One day the governess ordered our coachman to stop at several shops, where the beggars, watching their opportunity, crowded to the sides of the coach, and gave me the most horrible spectacles that ever an English eye beheld. There was a woman with a cancer in her breast, swelled to a monstrous size, full of holes, in two or three of which I could have easily crept, and covered my whole body. There was a fellow with a wen in his neck, larger than five woolpacks, and another with a couple of wooden legs, each about twenty foot high. But the most hateful sight of all was the lice crawling on their clothes. I could see distinctly the limbs of these vermin with my naked eye, much better than those of an European louse through a microscope,

---

5. The ancient hall, now incorporated into the Houses of Parliament, where the law courts then sat. Swift presumably means the square of its breadth (just under sixty-eight feet).

and their snouts with which they rooted like swine. They were the first I had ever beheld; and I should have been curious enough to dissect one of them if I had proper instruments (which I unluckily left behind me in the ship), although indeed the sight was so nauseous that it perfectly turned my stomach.

Besides the large box in which I was usually carried, the Queen ordered a smaller one to be made for me, of about twelve foot square and ten high, for the convenience of traveling, because the other was somewhat too large for Glumdalclitch's lap, and cumbersome in the coach; it was made by the same artist, whom I directed in the whole contrivance. This traveling closet was an exact square with a window in the middle of three of the squares, and each window was latticed with iron wire on the outside, to prevent accidents in long journeys. On the fourth side, which had no windows, two strong staples were fixed, through which the person that carried me, when I had a mind to be on horseback, put in a leathern belt, and buckled it about his waist. This was always the office of some grave trusty servant in whom I could confide, whether I attended the King and Queen in their progresses, or were disposed to see the gardens, or pay a visit to some great lady or minister of state in the court, when Glumdalclitch happened to be out of order: for I soon began to be known and esteemed among the greatest officers, I suppose more upon account of their Majesties' favor than any merit of my own. In journeys, when I was weary of the coach, a servant on horseback would buckle my box, and place it on a cushion before him; and there I had a full prospect of the country on three sides from my three windows. I had in this closet a field bed and a hammock hung from the ceiling, two chairs and a table, neatly screwed to the floor to prevent being tossed about by the agitation of the horse or the coach. And having been long used to sea voyages, those motions, although sometimes very violent, did not much discompose me.

When I had a mind to see the town, it was always in my traveling closet, which Glumdalclitch held in her lap in a kind of open sedan, after the fashion of the country, borne by four men, and attended by two others in the Queen's livery. The people, who had often heard of me, were very curious to crowd about the sedan; and the girl was complaisant enough to make the bearers stop, and to take me in her hand that I might be more conveniently seen.

I was very desirous to see the chief temple, and particularly the tower belonging to it, which is reckoned the highest in the kingdom. Accordingly one day my nurse carried me thither, but I may truly say I came back disappointed; for the height is not above three thousand foot, reckoning from the ground to the highest pinnacle top; which, allowing for the difference between the size of those people and us in Europe, is no great matter for admiration, nor at all equal in proportion (if I rightly remember) to Salisbury steeple.[6] But, not to detract from a nation to which during my life I shall acknowledge myself extremely obliged, it must be allowed that whatever this famous tower wants in height is amply made up in beauty and strength. For the walls are near an hundred foot thick, built of hewn stone, whereof each is about forty foot square, and adorned on all sides with statues of gods and emperors cut in marble larger than the life, placed in their several niches. I

---

6. One of the most beautiful Gothic steeples in England is that of Salisbury Cathedral, 404 feet high.

measured a little finger which had fallen down from one of these statues, and lay unperceived among some rubbish, and found it exactly four foot and an inch in length. Glumdalclitch wrapped it up in a handkerchief, and carried it home in her pocket to keep among other trinkets, of which the girl was very fond, as children at her age usually are.

The King's kitchen is indeed a noble building, vaulted at top, and about six hundred foot high. The great oven is not so wide by ten paces as the cupola at St. Paul's:[7] for I measured the latter on purpose after my return. But if I should describe the kitchen grate, the prodigious pots and kettles, the joints of meat turning on the spits, with many other particulars, perhaps I should be hardly believed; at least a severe critic would be apt to think I enlarged a little, as travelers are often suspected to do. To avoid which censure, I fear I have run too much into the other extreme, and that if this treatise should happen to be translated into the language of Brobdingnag (which is the general name of that kingdom) and transmitted thither, the King and his people would have reason to complain that I had done them an injury by a false and diminutive representation.

His Majesty seldom keeps above six hundred horses in his stables: they are generally from fifty-four to sixty foot high. But when he goes abroad on solemn days, he is attended for state by a militia guard of five hundred horse, which indeed I thought was the most splendid sight that could be ever beheld, till I saw part of his army in battalia,[8] whereof I shall find another occasion to speak.

CHAPTER 5. *Several adventures that happened to the Author. The execution of a criminal. The Author shows his skill in navigation.*

I should have lived happy enough in that country if my littleness had not exposed me to several ridiculous and troublesome accidents, some of which I shall venture to relate. Glumdalclitch often carried me into the gardens of the court in my smaller box, and would sometimes take me out of it and hold me in her hand, or set me down to walk. I remember, before the dwarf left the Queen, he followed us one day into those gardens; and my nurse having set me down, he and I being close together near some dwarf apple trees, I must needs show my wit by a silly allusion between him and the trees, which happens to hold in their language as it doth in ours. Whereupon, the malicious rogue watching his opportunity, when I was walking under one of them, shook it directly over my head, by which a dozen apples, each of them near as large as a Bristol barrel, came tumbling about my ears; one of them hit me on the back as I chanced to stoop, and knocked me down flat on my face, but I received no other hurt; and the dwarf was pardoned at my desire, because I had given the provocation.

Another day Glumdalclitch left me on a smooth grassplot to divert myself while she walked at some distance with her governess. In the meantime there suddenly fell such a violent shower of hail that I was immediately by the force of it struck to the ground: and when I was down, the hailstones gave me such cruel bangs all over the body as if I had been pelted with tennis balls;[9] however I made a shift to creep on all four, and shelter myself by lying

---

7. The cupola of St. Paul's Cathedral in London is 108 feet in diameter.
8. Battle array.

9. Eighteenth-century tennis balls, unlike the modern, were very hard.

on my face on the lee side of a border of lemon thyme, but so bruised from head to foot that I could not go abroad in ten days. Neither is this at all to be wondered at, because nature in that country observing the same proportion through all her operations, a hailstone is near eighteen hundred times as large as one in Europe; which I can assert upon experience, having been so curious to weigh and measure them.

But a more dangerous accident happened to me in the same garden when my little nurse, believing she had put me in a secure place, which I often entreated her to do that I might enjoy my own thoughts, and having left my box at home to avoid the trouble of carrying it, went to another part of the garden with her governess and some ladies of her acquaintance. While she was absent and out of hearing, a small white spaniel belonging to one of the chief gardeners, having got by accident into the garden, happened to range near the place where I lay. The dog following the scent, came directly up, and taking me in his mouth, ran straight to his master, wagging his tail, and set me gently on the ground. By good fortune he had been so well taught that I was carried between his teeth without the least hurt, or even tearing my clothes. But the poor gardener, who knew me well, and had a great kindness for me, was in a terrible fright. He gently took me up in both his hands, and asked me how I did; but I was so amazed and out of breath that I could not speak a word. In a few minutes I came to myself, and he carried me safe to my little nurse, who by this time had returned to the place where she left me, and was in cruel agonies when I did not appear nor answer when she called; she severely reprimanded the gardener on account of his dog. But the thing was hushed up and never known at court; for the girl was afraid of the Queen's anger; and truly, as to myself, I thought it would not be for my reputation that such a story should go about.

This accident absolutely determined Glumdalclitch never to trust me abroad for the future out of her sight. I had been long afraid of this resolution, and therefore concealed from her some little unlucky adventures that happened in those times when I was left by myself. Once a kite hovering over the garden made a stoop[1] at me, and if I had not resolutely drawn my hanger, and run under a thick espalier, he would have certainly carried me away in his talons. Another time walking to the top of a fresh molehill, I fell to my neck in the hole through which that animal had cast up the earth, and coined some lie, not worth remembering, to excuse myself for spoiling my clothes. I likewise broke my right shin against the shell of a snail, which I happened to stumble over, as I was walking alone, and thinking on poor England.

I cannot tell whether I were more pleased or mortified to observe in those solitary walks that the smaller birds did not appear to be at all afraid of me; but would hop about within a yard distance, looking for worms and other food with as much indifference and security as if no creature at all were near them. I remember a thrush had the confidence to snatch out of my hand with his bill a piece of cake that Glumdalclitch had just given me for my breakfast. When I attempted to catch any of these birds, they would boldly turn against me, endeavoring to pick my fingers, which I durst not venture within their reach; and then they would hop back unconcerned to hunt for worms or snails, as they did before. But one day I took a thick cudgel, and

---

1. Swoop. "Kite": a bird of prey.

threw it with all my strength so luckily at a linnet that I knocked him down, and seizing him by the neck with both my hands, ran with him in triumph to my nurse. However, the bird, who had only been stunned, recovering himself, gave me so many boxes with his wings on both sides of my head and body, though I held him at arm's length, and was out of the reach of his claws, that I was twenty times thinking to let him go. But I was soon relieved by one of our servants, who wrung off the bird's neck, and I had him next day for dinner, by the Queen's command. This linnet, as near as I can remember, seemed to be somewhat larger than an English swan.

The Maids of Honor often invited Glumdalclitch to their apartments, and desired she would bring me along with her, on purpose to have the pleasure of seeing and touching me. They would often strip me naked from top to toe and lay me at full length in their bosoms; wherewith I was much disgusted, because, to say the truth, a very offensive smell came from their skins, which I do not mention or intend to the disadvantage of those excellent ladies, for whom I have all manner of respect; but I conceive that my sense was more acute in proportion to my littleness, and that those illustrious persons were no more disagreeable to their lovers, or to each other, than people of the same quality are with us in England. And, after all, I found their natural smell was much more supportable than when they used perfumes, under which I immediately swooned away. I cannot forget that an intimate friend of mine in Lilliput took the freedom in a warm day, when I had used a good deal of exercise, to complain of a strong smell about me, although I am as little faulty that way as most of my sex: but I suppose his faculty of smelling was as nice with regard to me as mine was to that of this people. Upon this point, I cannot forbear doing justice to the Queen, my mistress, and Glumdalclitch, my nurse, whose persons were as sweet as those of any lady in England.

That which gave me most uneasiness among these Maids of Honor, when my nurse carried me to visit them, was to see them use me without any manner of ceremony, like a creature who had no sort of consequence. For they would strip themselves to the skin and put on their smocks in my presence, while I was placed on their toilet[2] directly before their naked bodies; which, I am sure, to me was very far from being a tempting sight, or from giving me any other emotions than those of horror and disgust. Their skins appeared so coarse and uneven, so variously colored, when I saw them near, with a mole here and there as broad as a trencher, and hairs hanging from it thicker than pack-threads, to say nothing further concerning the rest of their persons. Neither did they at all scruple, while I was by, to discharge what they had drunk, to the quantity of at least two hogsheads, in a vessel that held above three tuns. The handsomest among these Maids of Honor, a pleasant frolicsome girl of sixteen, would sometimes set me astride upon one of her nipples, with many other tricks, wherein the reader will excuse me for not being over particular. But I was so much displeased that I entreated Glumdalclitch to contrive some excuse for not seeing that young lady any more.

One day a young gentleman, who was nephew to my nurse's governess, came and pressed them both to see an execution. It was of a man who had

2. Toilet table.

murdered one of that gentleman's intimate acquaintance. Glumdalclitch was prevailed on to be of the company, very much against her inclination, for she was naturally tender-hearted: and as for myself, although I abhorred such kind of spectacles, yet my curiosity tempted me to see something that I thought must be extraordinary. The malefactor was fixed in a chair upon a scaffold erected for the purpose, and his head cut off at a blow with a sword of about forty foot long. The veins and arteries spouted up such a prodigious quantity of blood, and so high in the air, that the great *jet d'eau* at Versailles was not equal for the time it lasted; and the head, when it fell on the scaffold floor, gave such a bounce,[3] as made me start, although I were at least half an English mile distant.

The Queen, who often used to hear me talk of my sea voyages, and took all occasions to divert me when I was melancholy, asked me whether I understood how to handle a sail or an oar, and whether a little exercise of rowing might not be convenient for my health. I answered that I understood both very well. For although my proper employment had been to be surgeon or doctor to the ship, yet often, upon a pinch, I was forced to work like a common mariner. But I could not see how this could be done in their country, where the smallest wherry was equal to a first-rate man-of-war among us, and such a boat as I could manage would never live in any of their rivers. Her Majesty said, if I would contrive a boat, her own joiner should make it, and she would provide a place for me to sail in. The fellow was an ingenious workman and, by my instructions, in ten days finished a pleasure boat with all its tackling, able conveniently to hold eight Europeans. When it was finished, the Queen was so delighted that she ran with it in her lap to the King, who ordered it to be put in a cistern full of water, with me in it, by way of trial; where I could not manage my two sculls, or little oars, for want of room. But the Queen had before contrived another project. She ordered the joiner to make a wooden trough of three hundred foot long, fifty broad, and eight deep; which being well pitched to prevent leaking, was placed on the floor along the wall in an outer room of the palace. It had a cock near the bottom to let out the water when it began to grow stale, and two servants could easily fill it in half an hour. Here I often used to row for my own diversion, as well as that of the Queen and her ladies, who thought themselves well entertained with my skill and agility. Sometimes I would put up my sail, and then my business was only to steer, while the ladies gave me a gale with their fans; and when they were weary, some of the pages would blow my sail forward with their breath, while I showed my art by steering starboard or larboard as I pleased. When I had done, Glumdalclitch always carried my boat into her closet, and hung it on a nail to dry.

In this exercise I once met an accident which had like to have cost me my life. For one of the pages having put my boat into the trough, the governess who attended Glumdalclitch very officiously[4] lifted me up to place me in the boat; but I happened to slip through her fingers, and should have infallibly fallen down forty foot upon the floor, if by the luckiest chance in the world I had not been stopped by a corking-pin that stuck in the good gentlewoman's stomacher;[5] the head of the pin passed between my shirt and the waistband

---

3. A sudden noise. "*Jet d'eau* at Versailles": this fountain rose over forty feet in the air.
4. Kindly, dutifully.

5. An ornamental covering for the front and upper part of the body. "Corking-pin": a pin of the largest size.

of my breeches, and thus I was held by the middle in the air until Glumdal-clitch ran to my relief.

Another time, one of the servants, whose office it was to fill my trough every third day with fresh water, was so careless to let a huge frog (not perceiving it) slip out of his pail. The frog lay concealed till I was put into my boat, but then seeing a resting place, climbed up, and made it lean so much on one side that I was forced to balance it with all my weight on the other, to prevent overturning. When the frog was got in, it hopped at once half the length of the boat, and then over my head, backwards and forwards, daubing my face and clothes with its odious slime. The largeness of its features made it appear the most deformed animal that can be conceived. How-ever, I desired Glumdalclitch to let me deal with it alone. I banged it a good while with one of my sculls, and at last forced it to leap out of the boat.

But the greatest danger I ever underwent in that kingdom was from a monkey, who belonged to one of the clerks of the kitchen. Glumdalclitch had locked me up in her closet, while she went somewhere upon business or a visit. The weather being very warm, the closet window was left open, as well as the windows in the door of my bigger box, in which I usually lived, because of its largeness and conveniency. As I sat quietly meditating at my table, I heard something bounce in at the closet window, and skip about from one side to the other, whereat, although I was much alarmed, yet I ventured to look out, but stirred not from my seat; and then I saw this frol-icsome animal, frisking and leaping up and down, till at last he came to my box, which he seemed to view with great pleasure and curiosity, peeping in at the door and every window. I retreated to the farther corner of my room, or box, but the monkey looking in at every side, put me into such a fright that I wanted presence of mind to conceal myself under the bed, as I might easily have done. After some time spent in peeping, grinning, and chattering, he at last espied me, and reaching one of his paws in at the door, as a cat does when she plays with a mouse, although I often shifted place to avoid him, he at length seized the lappet of my coat (which, being made of that country cloth, was very thick and strong) and dragged me out. He took me up in his right forefoot, and held me as a nurse does a child she is going to suckle, just as I have seen the same sort of creature do with a kitten in Europe: and when I offered to struggle, he squeezed me so hard that I thought it more prudent to submit. I have good reason to believe that he took me for a young one of his own species, by his often stroking my face very gently with his other paw. In these diversions he was interrupted by a noise at the closet door, as if somebody were opening it, whereupon he sud-denly leaped up to the window at which he had come in, and thence upon the leads and gutters, walking upon three legs, and holding me in the fourth, till he clambered up to a roof that was next to ours. I heard Glumdalclitch give a shriek at the moment he was carrying me out. The poor girl was almost distracted: that quarter of the palace was all in an uproar; the servants ran for ladders; the monkey was seen by hundreds in the court, sitting upon the ridge of a building, holding me like a baby in one of his forepaws and feeding me with the other, by cramming into my mouth some victuals he had squeezed out of the bag on one side of his chaps, and patting me when I would not eat; whereat many of the rabble below could not forebear laughing; neither do I think they justly ought to be blamed, for without question the sight was ridiculous enough to everybody but myself. Some of the people threw up stones, hoping to drive the monkey down; but this was strictly forbidden, or else very probably my brains had been dashed out.

The ladders were now applied, and mounted by several men; which the monkey observing, and finding himself almost encompassed, not being able to make speed enough with his three legs, let me drop on a ridge tile, and made his escape. Here I sat for some time three hundred yards from the ground, expecting every moment to be blown down by the wind, or to fall by my own giddiness, and come tumbling over and over from the ridge to the eaves. But an honest lad, one of my nurse's footmen, climbed up, and putting me into his breeches pocket, brought me down safe.

I was almost choked with the filthy stuff the monkey had crammed down my throat; but my dear little nurse picked it out of my mouth with a small needle, and then I fell a vomiting, which gave me great relief. Yet I was so weak and bruised in the sides with the squeezes given me by this odious animal that I was forced to keep my bed a fortnight. The King, Queen, and all the Court sent every day to inquire after my health, and her Majesty made me several visits during my sickness. The monkey was killed, and an order made that no such animal should be kept about the palace.

When I attended the King after my recovery, to return him thanks for his favors, he was pleased to rally me a good deal upon this adventure. He asked me what my thoughts and speculations were while I lay in the monkey's paw, how I liked the victuals he gave me, his manner of feeding, and whether the fresh air on the roof had sharpened my stomach. He desired to know what I would have done upon such an occasion in my own country. I told his Majesty that in Europe we had no monkeys, except such as were brought for curiosities from other places, and so small that I could deal with a dozen of them together, if they presumed to attack me. And as for that monstrous animal with whom I was so lately engaged (it was indeed as large as an elephant), if my fears had suffered me to think so far as to make use of my hanger (looking fiercely and clapping my hand upon the hilt as I spoke) when he poked his paw into my chamber, perhaps I should have given him such a wound as would have made him glad to withdraw it with more haste than he put it in. This I delivered in a firm tone, like a person who was jealous lest his courage should be called in question. However, my speech produced nothing else besides a loud laughter, which all the respect due to his Majesty from those about him could not make them contain. This made me reflect how vain an attempt it is for a man to endeavor doing himself honor among those who are out of all degree of equality or comparison with him. And yet I have seen the moral of my own behavior very frequent in England since my return, where a little contemptible varlet, without the least title to birth, person, wit, or common sense, shall presume to look with importance, and put himself upon a foot with the greatest persons of the kingdom.

I was every day furnishing the court with some ridiculous story; and Glumdalclitch, although she loved me to excess, yet was arch enough to inform the Queen whenever I committed any folly that she thought would be diverting to her Majesty. The girl, who had been out of order, was carried by her governess to take the air about an hour's distance, or thirty miles from town. They alighted out of the coach near a small footpath in a field, and Glumdalclitch setting down my traveling box, I went out of it to walk. There was a cow dung in the patch, and I must needs try my activity by attempting to leap over it. I took a run, but unfortunately jumped short, and found myself just in the middle up to my knees. I waded through with some difficulty, and one of the footmen wiped me as clean as he could with his handkerchief; for I was filthily bemired, and my nurse confined me to my box till we returned home, where the Queen was soon informed of what had passed and the footmen spread it about the Court, so that all the mirth, for some days, was at my expense.

CHAPTER 6. *Several contrivances of the Author to please the King and Queen. He shows his skill in music. The King inquires into the state of Europe, which the Author relates to him. The King's observations thereon.*

I used to attend the King's levee once or twice a week, and had often seen him under the barber's hand, which indeed was at first very terrible to behold. For the razor was almost twice as long as an ordinary scythe. His Majesty, according to the custom of the country, was only shaved twice a week. I once prevailed on the barber to give me some of the suds or lather, out of which I picked forty or fifty of the strongest stumps of hair. I then took a piece of fine wood, and cut it like the back of a comb, making several holes in it at equal distance with as small a needle as I could get from Glumdalclitch. I fixed in the stumps so artificially,[6] scraping and sloping them with my knife towards the points, that I made a very tolerable comb; which was a seasonable supply, my own being so much broken in the teeth that it was almost useless; neither did I know any artist in that country so nice and exact as would undertake to make me another.

And this puts me in mind of an amusement wherein I spent many of my leisure hours. I desired the Queen's woman to save for me the combings of her Majesty's hair, whereof in time I got a good quantity; and consulting with my friend the cabinetmaker, who had received general orders to do little jobs for me, I directed him to make two chair frames, no larger than those I had in my box, and then to bore little holes with a fine awl round those parts where I designed the backs and seats; through these holes I wove the strongest hairs I could pick out, just after the manner of cane chairs in England. When they were finished, I made a present of them to her Majesty, who kept them in her cabinet, and used to show them for curiosities, as indeed they were the wonder of every one that beheld them. The Queen would have made me sit upon one of these chairs, but I absolutely refused to obey her, protesting I would rather die a thousand deaths than place a dishonorable part of my body on those precious hairs that once adorned her Majesty's head. Of these hairs (as I had always a mechanical genius) I likewise made a neat little purse above five foot long, with her Majesty's name deciphered in gold letters, which I gave to Glumdalclitch by the Queen's consent. To say the truth, it was more for show than use, being not of strength to bear the weight of the larger coins; and therefore she kept nothing in it but some little toys[7] that girls are fond of.

The King, who delighted in music, had frequent consorts[8] at court, to

---

6. Skillfully.
7. Trifles.
8. Concerts.

which I was sometimes carried, and set in my box on a table to hear them; but the noise was so great that I could hardly distinguish the tunes. I am confident that all the drums and trumpets of a royal army, beating and sounding together just at your ears, could not equal it. My practice was to have my box removed from the places where the performers sat, as far as I could, then to shut the doors and windows of it, and draw the window curtains, after which I found their music not disagreeable.

I had learned in my youth to play a little upon the spinet. Glumdalclitch kept one in her chamber, and a master attended twice a week to teach her: I call it a spinet, because it somewhat resembled that instrument, and was played upon in the same manner. A fancy came into my head that I would entertain the King and Queen with an English tune upon this instrument. But this appeared extremely difficult: for the spinet was near sixty foot long, each key being almost a foot wide; so that, with my arms extended, I could not reach to above five keys, and to press them down required a good smart stroke with my fist, which would be too great a labor and to no purpose. The method I contrived was this: I prepared two round sticks about the bigness of common cudgels; they were thicker at one end than the other, and I covered the thicker ends with a piece of a mouse's skin, that by rapping on them I might neither damage the tops of the keys, nor interrupt the sound. Before the spinet a bench was placed, about four foot below the keys, and I was put upon the bench. I ran sideling upon it that way and this, as fast as I could, banging the proper keys with my two sticks; and made a shift to play a jig, to the great satisfaction of both their Majesties: but it was the most violent exercise I ever underwent, and yet I could not strike above sixteen keys, nor, consequently, play the bass and treble together, as other artists do; which was a great disadvantage to my performance.

The King, who, as I before observed, was a prince of excellent understanding, would frequently order that I should be brought in my box and set upon the table in his closet. He would then command me to bring one of my chairs out of the box, and sit down within three yards distance upon the top of the cabinet, which brought me almost to a level with his face. In this manner I had several conversations with him. I one day took the freedom to tell his Majesty that the contempt he discovered towards Europe, and the rest of the world, did not seem answerable to those excellent qualities of mind that he was master of. That reason did not extend itself with the bulk of the body: on the contrary, we observed in our country that the tallest persons were usually least provided with it. That among other animals, bees and ants had the reputation of more industry, art, and sagacity than many of the larger kinds; and that, as inconsiderable as he took me to be, I hoped I might live to do his Majesty some signal service. The King heard me with attention, and began to conceive a much better opinion of me than he had before. He desired I would give him as exact an account of the government of England as I possibly could; because, as fond as princes commonly are of their own customs (for so he conjectured of other monarchs, by my former discourses), he should be glad to hear of anything that might deserve imitation.

Imagine with thyself, courteous reader, how often I then wished for the tongue of Demosthenes or Cicero, that might have enabled me to celebrate the praise of my own dear native country in a style equal to its merits and felicity.

I began my discourse by informing his Majesty that our dominions consisted of two islands, which composed three mighty kingdoms under one sovereign, beside our plantations in America. I dwelt long upon the fertility of our soil, and the temperature[9] of our climate. I then spoke at large upon the constitution of an English Parliament, partly made up of an illustrious body called the House of Peers, persons of the noblest blood, and of the most ancient and ample patrimonies. I described that extraordinary care always taken of their education in arts and arms, to qualify them for being counselors born to the king and kingdom; to have a share in the legislature, to be members of the highest Court of Judicature, from whence there could be no appeal; and to be champions always ready for the defense of their prince and country, by their valor, conduct, and fidelity. That these were the ornament and bulwark of the kingdom, worthy followers of their most renowned ancestors, whose honor had been the reward of their virtue, from which their posterity were never once known to degenerate. To these were joined several holy persons, as part of that assembly, under the title of Bishops, whose peculiar business it is to take care of religion, and of those who instruct the people therein. These were searched and sought out through the whole nation, by the prince and his wisest counselors, among such of the priesthood as were most deservedly distinguished by the sanctity of their lives and the depth of their erudition, who were indeed the spiritual fathers of the clergy and the people.

That the other part of the Parliament consisted of an assembly called the House of Commons, who were all principal gentlemen, freely picked and culled out by the people themselves, for their great abilities and love of their country, to represent the wisdom of the whole nation. And these two bodies make up the most august assembly in Europe, to whom, in conjunction with the prince, the whole legislature is committed.

I then descended to the Courts of Justice, over which the Judges, those venerable sages and interpreters of the law, presided, for determining the disputed rights and properties of men, as well as for the punishment of vice, and protection of innocence. I mentioned the prudent management of our treasury, the valor and achievements of our forces by sea and land. I computed the number of our people, by reckoning how many millions there might be of each religious sect, or political party among us. I did not omit even our sports and pastimes, or any other particular which I thought might redound to the honor of my country. And I finished all with a brief historical account of affairs and events in England for about an hundred years past.

This conversation was not ended under five audiences, each of several hours, and the King heard the whole with great attention, frequently taking notes of what I spoke, as well as memorandums of several questions he intended to ask me.

When I had put an end to these long discourses, his Majesty in a sixth audience consulting his notes, proposed many doubts, queries, and objections, upon every article. He asked what methods were used to cultivate the minds and bodies of our young nobility, and in what kind of business they commonly spent the first and teachable part of their lives. What course was

9. Temperateness.

taken to supply that assembly when any noble family became extinct. What qualifications were necessary in those who were to be created new lords. Whether the humor[1] of the prince, a sum of money to a Court lady or a prime minister, or a design of strengthening a party opposite to the public interest, ever happened to be motives in those advancements. What share of knowledge these lords had in the laws of their country, and how they came by it, so as to enable them to decide the properties of their fellow subjects in the last resort. Whether they were always so free from avarice, partialities, or want that a bribe or some other sinister view could have no place among them. Whether those holy lords I spoke of were constantly promoted to that rank upon account of their knowledge in religious matters, and the sanctity of their lives; had never been compliers with the times while they were common priests, or slavish prostitute chaplains to some nobleman, whose opinions they continued servilely to follow after they were admitted into that assembly.

He then desired to know what arts were practiced in electing those whom I called Commoners. Whether a stranger with a strong purse might not influence the vulgar voters to choose him before their own landlord or the most considerable gentleman in the neighborhood. How it came to pass that people were so violently bent upon getting into this assembly, which I allowed to be a great trouble and expense, often to the ruin of their families, without any salary or pension: because this appeared such an exalted strain of virtue and public spirit that his Majesty seemed to doubt it might possibly not be always sincere; and he desired to know whether such zealous gentlemen could have any views of refunding themselves for the charges and trouble they were at, by sacrificing the public good to the designs of a weak and vicious prince in conjunction with a corrupted ministry. He multiplied his questions, and sifted me thoroughly upon every part of this head, proposing numberless inquiries and objections, which I think it not prudent or convenient to repeat.

Upon what I said in relation to our Courts of Justice, his Majesty desired to be satisfied in several points: and this I was the better able to do, having been formerly almost ruined by a long suit in chancery, which was decreed for me with costs. He asked what time was usually spent in determining between right and wrong, and what degree of expense. Whether advocates and orators had liberty to plead in causes manifestly known to be unjust, vexatious, or oppressive. Whether party in religion or politics were observed to be of any weight in the scale of justice. Whether those pleading orators were persons educated in the general knowledge of equity, or only in provincial, national, and other local customs. Whether they or their judges had any part in penning those laws which they assumed the liberty of interpreting and glossing upon at their pleasure. Whether they had ever at different times pleaded for and against the same cause, and cited precedents to prove contrary opinions. Whether they were a rich or a poor corporation. Whether they received any pecuniary reward for pleading or delivering their opinions. And particularly whether they were ever admitted as members in the lower senate.

1. Whim.

He fell next upon the management of our treasury, and said he thought my memory had failed me, because I computed our taxes at about five or six millions a year, and when I came to mention the issues,[2] he found they sometimes amounted to more than double, for the notes he had taken were very particular in this point; because he hoped, as he told me, that the knowledge of our conduct might be useful to him, and he could not be deceived in his calculations. But if what I told him were true, he was still at a loss how a kingdom could run out of its estate like a private person. He asked me, who were our creditors? and where we should find money to pay them? He wondered to hear me talk of such chargeable and extensive wars; that certainly we must be a quarrelsome people, or live among very bad neighbors, and that our generals must needs be richer than our kings.[3] He asked what business we had out of our own islands, unless upon the score of trade or treaty or to defend the coasts with our fleet. Above all, he was amazed to hear me talk of a mercenary standing army[4] in the midst of peace, and among a free people. He said if we were governed by our own consent in the persons of our representatives, he could not imagine of whom we were afraid, or against whom we were to fight; and would hear my opinion whether a private man's house might not better be defended by himself, his children, and family, than by half a dozen rascals picked up at a venture[5] in the streets for small wages, who might get an hundred times more by cutting their throats.

He laughed at my odd kind of arithmetic (as he was pleased to call it) in reckoning the numbers of our people by a computation drawn from the several sects among us in religion and politics. He said he knew no reason why those who entertain opinions prejudicial to the public should be obliged to change, or should not be obliged to conceal them. And as it was tyranny in any government to require the first, so it was weakness not to enforce the second: for a man may be allowed to keep poisons in his closet, but not to vend them about for cordials.[6]

He observed that among the diversions of our nobility and gentry I had mentioned gaming. He desired to know at what age this entertainment was usually taken up, and when it was laid down; how much of their time it employed; whether it ever went so high as to affect their fortunes; whether mean, vicious people, by their dexterity in that art, might not arrive at great riches, and sometimes keep our very nobles in dependence, as well as habituate them to vile companions, wholly take them from the improvement of their minds, and force them, by the losses they received, to learn and practice that infamous dexterity upon others.

He was perfectly astonished with the historical account I gave him of our affairs during the last century, protesting it was only an heap of conspiracies, rebellions, murders, massacres, revolutions, banishments, the very worst effects that avarice, faction, hypocrisy, perfidiousness, cruelty, rage, madness, hatred, envy, lust, malice, or ambition could produce.

His Majesty in another audience was at the pains to recapitulate the sum of all I had spoken; compared the questions he made with the answers I had

2. Expenditures.

3. An allusion to the enormous fortune gained by the duke of Marlborough, formerly captain-general of the army, whom Swift detested.

4. Since the declaration of the Bill of Rights (1689), a standing army without authorization by Parliament had been illegal. Swift and the Tories in general were vigilant in their opposition to such an army.

5. By chance.

6. Medicines to stimulate the heart, or, equally commonly, liqueurs.

given; then taking me into his hands, and stroking me gently, delivered himself in these words, which I shall never forget, nor the manner he spoke them in. "My little friend Grildrig, you have made a most admirable panegyric upon your country. You have clearly proved that ignorance, idleness, and vice are the proper ingredients for qualifying a legislator. That laws are best explained, interpreted, and applied by those whose interests and abilities lie in perverting, confounding, and eluding them. I observe among you some lines of an institution which in its original might have been tolerable; but these half erased, and the rest wholly blurred and blotted by corruptions. It doth not appear from all you have said how any one virtue is required towards the procurement of any one station among you; much less that men are ennobled on account of their virtue, that priests are advanced for their piety or learning, soldiers for their conduct or valor, judges for their integrity, senators for the love of their country, or counselors for their wisdom. As for yourself," continued the King, "who have spent the greatest part of your life in traveling, I am well disposed to hope you may hitherto have escaped many vices of your country. But by what I have gathered from your own relation, and the answers I have with much pains wringed and extorted from you, I cannot but conclude the bulk of your natives to be the most pernicious race of little odious vermin that nature ever suffered to crawl upon the surface of the earth."

CHAPTER 7. *The Author's love of his country. He makes a proposal of much advantage to the King; which is rejected. The King's great ignorance in politics. The learning of that country very imperfect and confined. Their laws, and military affairs, and parties in the State.*

Nothing but an extreme love of truth could have hindered me from concealing this part of my story. It was in vain to discover my resentments, which were always turned into ridicule: and I was forced to rest with patience while my noble and most beloved country was so injuriously treated. I am heartily sorry as any of my readers can possibly be that such an occasion was given, but this prince happened to be so curious and inquisitive upon every particular that it could not consist either with gratitude or good manners to refuse giving him what satisfaction I was able. Yet thus much I may be allowed to say in my own vindication: that I artfully eluded many of his questions, and gave to every point a more favorable turn by many degrees than the strictness of truth would allow. For I have always borne that laudable partiality to my own country, which Dionysius Halicarnassensis[7] with so much justice recommends to an historian. I would hide the frailties and deformities of my political mother, and place her virtues and beauties in the most advantageous light. This was my sincere endeavor in those many discourses I had with that mighty monarch, although it unfortunately failed of success.

But great allowances should be given to a King who lives wholly secluded from the rest of the world, and must therefore be altogether unacquainted with the manners and customs that most prevail in other nations: the want of which knowledge will ever produce many *prejudices*, and a certain *nar-*

---

7. A Greek rhetorician and historian, who flourished ca. 25 B.C.E. His history of Rome was written to reconcile the Greeks to their Roman masters.

rowness of thinking, from which we and the politer countries of Europe are wholly exempted. And it would be hard indeed if so remote a prince's notions of virtue and vice were to be offered as a standard for all mankind.

To confirm what I have now said, and further to show the miserable effects of a *confined education*, I shall here insert a passage which will hardly obtain belief. In hopes to ingratiate myself farther into his Majesty's favor, I told him of an invention discovered between three and four hundred years ago, to make a certain powder, into an heap of which the smallest spark of fire falling would kindle the whole in a moment, although it were as big as a mountain, and make it all fly up in the air together, with a noise and agitation greater than thunder. That a proper quantity of this powder rammed into an hollow tube of brass or iron, according to its bigness, would drive a ball of iron or lead with such violence and speed as nothing was able to sustain its force. That the largest balls thus discharged would not only destroy whole ranks of an army at once, but batter the strongest walls to the ground; sink down ships with a thousand men in each, to the bottom of the sea; and, when linked together by a chain, would cut through masts and rigging; divide hundreds of bodies in the middle, and lay all waste before them. That we often put this powder into large hollow balls of iron, and discharged them by an engine into some city we were besieging; which would rip up the pavements, tear the houses to pieces, burst and throw splinters on every side, dashing out the brains of all who came near. That I knew the ingredients very well, which were cheap and common; I understood the manner of compounding them, and could direct his workmen how to make those tubes of a size proportionable to all other things in his Majesty's kingdom, and the largest need not be above two hundred foot long; twenty or thirty of which tubes, charged with the proper quantity of powder and balls, would batter down the walls of the strongest town in his dominions in a few hours; or destroy the whole metropolis, if ever it should pretend to dispute his absolute commands. This I humbly offered to his Majesty as a small tribute of acknowledgement in return of so many marks that I had received of his royal favor and protection.

The King was struck with horror at the description I had given of those terrible engines and the proposal I had made. He was amazed how so impotent and groveling an insect as I (these were his expressions) could entertain such inhuman ideas, and in so familiar a manner as to appear wholly unmoved at all the scenes of blood and desolation which I had painted as the common effects of those destructive machines; whereof he said some evil genius, enemy to mankind, must have been the first contriver. As for himself, he protested that although few things delighted him so much as new discoveries in art or in nature, yet he would rather lose half his kingdom than be privy to such a secret, which he commanded me, as I valued my life, never to mention any more.

A strange effect of *narrow principles* and *short views!* that a prince possessed of every quality which procures veneration, love, and esteem; of strong parts, great wisdom, and profound learning; endued with admirable talents for government, and almost adored by his subjects; should from a *nice, unnecessary scruple,* whereof in Europe we can have no conception, let slip an opportunity put into his hands that would have made him absolute master of the lives, the liberties, and the fortunes of his people. Neither do I say this with the least intention to detract from the many virtues of that excellent King, whose character I am sensible will on this account be very much lessened in the opinion of an English reader: but I take this defect among them to have risen from their ignorance; they not having hitherto reduced politics into a science, as the more acute wits of Europe have done. For I remember very well, in a discourse one day with the King, when I happened to say there were several thousand books among us written upon the art of government, it gave him (directly contrary to my intention) a very mean opinion of our understandings. He professed both to abominate and despise all *mystery*, *refinement*, and *intrigue*, either in a prince or a minister. He could not tell what I meant by *secrets of state*, where an enemy or some rival nation were not in the case. He confined the knowledge of governing within very *narrow bounds*: to common sense and reason, to justice and lenity, to the speedy determination of civil and criminal causes, with some other obvious topics which are not worth considering. And he gave it for his opinion that whoever could make two ears of corn or two blades of grass to grow upon a spot of ground where only one grew before would deserve better of mankind and do more essential service to his country than the whole race of politicians[8] put together.

The learning of this people is very defective, consisting only in morality, history, poetry, and mathematics; wherein they must be allowed to excel. But the last of these is wholly applied to what may be useful in life, to the improvement of agriculture and all mechanical arts; so that among us it would be little esteemed. And as to ideas, entities, abstractions, and transcendentals,[9] I could never drive the least conception into their heads.

No law of that country must exceed in words the number of letters in their alphabet, which consists only in two and twenty. But indeed few of them extend even to that length. They are expressed in the most plain and simple terms, wherein those people are not mercurial enough to discover above one interpretation. And to write a comment upon any law is a capital crime. As to the decision of civil causes, or proceedings against criminals, their precedents are so few that they have little reason to boast of any extraordinary skill in either.

They have had the art of printing as well as the Chinese, time out of mind. But their libraries are not very large; for that of the King's, which is reckoned the biggest, doth not amount to above a thousand volumes, placed in a gallery of twelve hundred foot long, from whence I had liberty to borrow what books I pleased. The Queen's joiner had contrived in one of the Glumdalclitch's rooms a kind of wooden machine five and twenty foot high, formed like a standing ladder; the steps were each fifty foot long. It was indeed a movable pair of stairs, the lowest end placed at ten foot distance from the wall of the chamber. The book I had a mind to read was put up leaning against the wall. I first mounted to the upper step of the ladder, and turning my face towards the book began at the top of the page, and so walking to the right and left about eight or ten paces according to the length of the lines, till I had gotten a little below the level of mine eyes, and then descending gradually till I came to the bottom: after which I mounted again, and began the other page

---

8. By *politicians*, Swift means something like our modern political scientists or theorists.

9. In Swift's time, *transcendental* was practically synonymous with *metaphysical*.

in the same manner, and so turned over the leaf, which I could easily do with both my hands, for it was as thick and stiff as a pasteboard, and in the largest folios not above eighteen or twenty foot long.

Their style is clear, masculine, and smooth, but not florid; for they avoid nothing more than multiplying unnecessary words or using various expressions. I have perused many of their books, especially those in history and morality. Among the rest, I was much diverted with a little old treatise, which always lay in Glumdalclitch's bedchamber, and belonged to her governess, a grave elderly gentlewoman, who dealt in writings of morality and devotion. The book treats of the weakness of human kind, and is in little esteem, except among the women and the vulgar. However, I was curious to see what an author of that country could say upon such a subject. This writer went through all the usual topics of European moralists: showing how diminutive, contemptible, and helpless an animal was man in his own nature; how unable to defend himself from the inclemencies of the air, or the fury of wild beasts; how much he was excelled by one creature in strength, by another in speed, by a third in foresight, by a fourth in industry. He added that nature was degenerated in these latter declining ages of the world, and could now produce only small abortive births in comparison of those in ancient times. He said it was very reasonable to think, not only that the species of men were originally much larger, but also that there must have been giants in former ages; which, as it is asserted by history and tradition, so it hath been confirmed by huge bones and skulls casually dug up in several parts of the kingdom, far exceeding the common dwindled race of man in our days. He argued that the very laws of nature absolutely required we should have been made in the beginning of a size more large and robust, not so liable to destruction from every little accident of a tile falling from a house, or a stone cast from the hand of a boy, or of being drowned in a little brook. From this way of reasoning, the author drew several moral applications useful in the conduct of life, but needless here to repeat. For my own part, I could not avoid reflecting how universally this talent was spread, of drawing lectures in morality, or indeed rather matter of discontent and repining, from the quarrels we raise with nature. And I believe, upon a strict inquiry, those quarrels might be shown as ill grounded among us as they are among that people.

As to their military affairs, they boast that the King's army consists of an hundred and seventy-six thousand foot and thirty-two thousand horse: if that may be called an army which is made up of tradesmen in the several cities, and farmers in the country, whose commanders are only the nobility and gentry, without pay or reward. They are indeed perfect enough in their exercises, and under very good discipline, wherein I saw no great merit; for how should it be otherwise, where every farmer is under the command of his own landlord, and every citizen under that of the principal men in his own city, chosen after the manner of Venice by ballot?

I have often seen the militia of Lorbrulgrud drawn out to exercise in a great field near the city, of twenty miles square. They were in all not above twenty-five thousand foot, and six thousand horse; but it was impossible for me to compute their number, considering the space of ground they took up. A cavalier mounted on a large steed might be about an hundred foot high. I have seen this whole body of horse, upon a word of command, draw their swords at once, and brandish them in the air. Imagination can figure nothing so grand, so surprising, and so astonishing. It looked as if ten thousand flashes of lightning were darting at the same time from every quarter of the sky.

I was curious to know how this prince, to whose dominions there is no access from any other country, came to think of armies, or to teach his people the practice of military discipline. But I was soon informed, both by conversation and reading their histories. For in the course of many ages they have been troubled with the same disease to which the whole race of mankind is subject: the nobility often contending for power, the people for liberty, and the King for absolute dominion. All which, however happily tempered by the laws of the kingdom, have been sometimes violated by each of the three parties, and have more than once occasioned civil wars, the last whereof was happily put an end to by this prince's grandfather in a general composition;[1] and the militia, then settled with common consent, hath been ever since kept in the strictest duty.

CHAPTER 8. *The King and Queen make a progress to the frontiers. The Author attends them. The manner in which he leaves the country very particularly related. He returns to England.*

I had always a strong impulse that I should some time recover my liberty, though it were impossible to conjecture by what means, or to form any project with the least hope of succeeding. The ship in which I sailed was the first ever known to be driven within sight of that coast; and the King had given strict orders that if at any time another appeared, it should be taken ashore, and with all its crew and passengers brought in a tumbrel[2] to Lorbrulgrud. He was strongly bent to get me a woman of my own size, by whom I might propagate the breed: but I think I should rather have died than undergone the disgrace of leaving a posterity to be kept in cages like tame canary birds, and perhaps in time sold about the kingdom to persons of quality for curiosities. I was indeed treated with much kindness: I was the favorite of a great King and Queen, and the delight of the whole Court, but it was upon such a foot as ill became the dignity of human kind. I could never forget those domestic pledges I had left behind me. I wanted to be among people with whom I could converse upon even terms, and walk about the streets and fields without fear of being trod to death like a frog or a young puppy. But my deliverance came sooner than I expected, and in a manner not very common; the whole story and circumstances of which I shall faithfully relate.

I had now been two years in this country; and about the beginning of the third, Glumdalclitch and I attended the King and Queen in progress to the south coast of the kingdom. I was carried as usual in my traveling box, which, as I have already described, was a very convenient closet of twelve foot wide. I had ordered a hammock to be fixed by silken ropes from the four corners at the top, to break the jolts when a servant carried me before him on horseback, as I sometimes desired; and would often sleep in my hammock while we were upon the road. On the roof of my closet, set not directly over

1. A political settlement based on general agreement of all parties.　　2. A farm wagon.

the middle of the hammock, I ordered the joiner to cut out a hole of a foot square to give me air in hot weather as I slept, which hole I shut at pleasure with a board that drew backwards and forwards through a groove.

When we came to our journey's end, the King thought proper to pass a few days at a palace he hath near Flanflasnic, a city within eighteen English miles of the seaside. Glumdalclitch and I were much fatigued; I had gotten a small cold, but the poor girl was so ill as to be confined to her chamber. I longed to see the ocean, which must be the only scene of my escape, if ever it should happen. I pretended to be worse than I really was, and desired leave to take the fresh air of the sea with a page whom I was very fond of, and who had sometimes been trusted with me. I shall never forget with what unwillingness Glumdalclitch consented, nor the strict charge she gave the page to be careful of me, bursting at the same time into a flood of tears, as if she had some foreboding of what was to happen. The boy took me out in my box about half an hour's walk from the palace, towards the rocks on the seashore. I ordered him to set me down, and lifting up one of my sashes, cast many a wistful melancholy look towards the sea. I found myself not very well, and told the page that I had a mind to take a nap in my hammock, which I hoped would do me good. I got in, and the boy shut the window close down, to keep out the cold. I soon fell asleep: and all I can conjecture is that while I slept, the page, thinking no danger could happen, went among the rocks to look for birds' eggs; having before observed him from my window searching about, and picking up one or two in the clefts. Be that as it will, I found myself suddenly awaked with a violent pull upon the ring which was fastened at the top of my box for the conveniency of carriage. I felt my box raised very high in the air, and then borne forward with prodigious speed. The first jolt had like to have shaken me out of my hammock, but afterwards the motion was easy enough. I called out several times as loud as I could raise my voice, but all to no purpose. I looked towards my windows, and could see nothing but the clouds and sky. I heard a noise just over my head like the clapping of wings, and then began to perceive the woeful condition I was in; that some eagle had got the ring of my box in his beak, with an intent to let it fall on a rock, like a tortoise in a shell, and then pick out my body and devour it. For the sagacity and smell of this bird enable him to discover his quarry at a great distance, although better concealed than I could be within a two-inch board.

In a little time I observed the noise and flutter of wings to increase very fast, and my box was tossed up and down like a signpost in a windy day. I heard several bangs or buffets, as I thought, given to the eagle (for such I am certain it must have been that held the ring of my box in his beak), and then all on a sudden felt myself falling perpendicularly down for above a minute, but with such incredible swiftness that I almost lost my breath. My fall was topped by a terrible squash, that sounded louder to mine ears than the cataract of Niagara; after which I was quite in the dark for another minute, and then my box began to rise so high that I could see light from the tops of my windows. I now perceived that I was fallen into the sea. My box, by the weight of my body, the goods that were in, and the broad plates of iron fixed for strength at the four corners of the top and bottom, floated above five foot deep in water. I did then and do now suppose that the eagle which flew away with my box was pursued by two or three others, and forced to let me drop while he was defending himself against the rest, who hoped to share in the prey. The plates of iron fastened at the bottom of the box (for those were the strongest) preserved the balance while it fell, and hindered it from being broken on the surface of the water. Every joint of it was well grooved, and the door did not move on hinges, but up and down like a sash; which kept my closet so tight that very little water came in. I got with much difficulty out of my hammock, having first ventured to draw back the slip-board on the roof already mentioned, contrived on purpose to let in air, for want of which I found myself almost stifled.

How often did I then wish myself with my dear Glumdalclitch, from whom one single hour had so far divided me! And I may say with truth that in the midst of my own misfortune, I could not forbear lamenting my poor nurse, the grief she would suffer for my loss, the displeasure of the Queen, and the ruin of her fortune. Perhaps many travelers have not been under greater difficulties and distress than I was at this juncture, expecting every moment to see my box dashed in pieces, or at least overset by the first violent blast or a rising wave. A breach in one single pane of glass would have been immediate death, nor could anything have preserved the windows but the strong lattice wires placed on the outside against accidents in traveling. I saw the water ooze in at several crannies, although the leaks were not considerable, and I endeavored to stop them as well as I could. I was not able to lift up the roof of my closet, which otherwise I certainly should have done, and sat on the top of it, where I might at least preserve myself from being shut up, as I may call it, in the hold. Or, if I escaped these dangers for a day or two, what could I expect but a miserable death of cold and hunger! I was four hours under these circumstances, expecting and indeed wishing every moment to be my last.

I have already told the reader that there were two strong staples fixed upon that side of my box which had no window and into which the servant, who used to carry me on horseback, would put a leathern belt, and buckle it about his waist. Being in this disconsolate state, I heard, or at least thought I heard, some kind of grating noise on that side of my box where the staples were fixed; and soon after I began to fancy that the box was pulled or towed along in the sea; for I now and then felt a sort of tugging, which made the waves rise near the tops of my windows, leaving me almost in the dark. This gave me some faint hopes of relief, although I was not able to imagine how it could be brought about. I ventured to unscrew one of my chairs, which were always fastened to the floor; and having made a hard shift to screw it down again directly under the slipping-board that I had lately opened, I mounted on the chair, and putting my mouth as near as I could to the hole, I called for help in a loud voice, and in all the languages I understood. I then fastened my handkerchief to a stick I usually carried, and thrusting it up the hole, waved it several times in the air, that if any boat or ship were near, the seamen might conjecture some unhappy mortal to be shut up in the box.

I found no effect from all I could do, but plainly perceived my closet to be moved along; and in the space of an hour or better, that side of the box where the staples were, and had no window, struck against something that was hard. I apprehended it to be a rock, and found myself tossed more than ever. I plainly heard a noise upon the cover of my closet, like that of a cable, and the grating of it as it passed through the ring. I then found myself hoisted up by degrees at least three foot higher than I was before. Whereupon I again thrust up my stick and handkerchief, calling for help till I was almost hoarse. In return to which, I heard a great shout repeated three times, giving me such transports of joy as are not to be conceived but by those who feel them. I now heard a trampling over my head, and somebody calling through the hole with a loud voice in the English tongue: "If there be anybody below, let them speak." I answered, I was an Englishman, drawn by ill fortune into the greatest calamity that ever any creature underwent, and begged, by all that was moving, to be delivered out of the dungeon I was in. The voice replied, I was safe, for my box was fastened to their ship; and the carpenter should immediately come and saw an hole in the cover, large enough to pull me out. I answered, that was needless and would take up too much time, for there was no more to be done but let one of the crew put his finger into the ring, and take the box out of the sea into the ship, and so into the captain's cabin. Some of them, upon hearing me talk so wildly, thought I was mad; others laughed; for indeed it never came into my head that I was now got among people of my own stature and strength. The carpenter came, and in a few minutes sawed a passage about four foot square; then let down a small ladder, upon which I mounted, and from thence was taken into the ship in a very weak condition.

The sailors were all in amazement, and asked me a thousand questions, which I had no inclination to answer. I was equally confounded at the sight of so many pygmies, for such I took them to be, after having so long accustomed my eyes to the monstrous objects I had left. But the Captain, Mr. Thomas Wilcocks, an honest, worthy Shropshire man, observing I was ready to faint, took me into his cabin, gave me a cordial to comfort me, and made me turn in upon his own bed, advising me to take a little rest, of which I had great need. Before I went to sleep I gave him to understand that I had some valuable furniture in my box, too good to be lost, a fine hammock, an handsome field bed, two chairs, a table, and a cabinet; that my closet was hung on all sides, or rather quilted with silk and cotton; that if he would let one of the crew bring my closet into his cabin, I would open it before him and show him my goods. The Captain, hearing me utter these absurdities, concluded I was raving; however (I suppose to pacify me), he promised to give order as I desired, and going upon deck, sent some of his men down into my closet, from whence (as I afterwards found) they drew up all my goods and stripped off the quilting; but the chairs, cabinet, and bedstead, being screwed to the floor, were much damaged by the ignorance of the seamen, who tore them up by force. Then they knocked off some of the boards for the use of the ship; and when they had got all they had a mind for, let the hulk drop into the sea, which, by reason of many breaches made in the bottom and sides, sunk to rights.[3] And indeed I was glad not to have been a spectator of the havoc they made, because I am confident it would have sensibly touched me, by bringing former passages into my mind, which I had rather forget.

I slept some hours, but perpetually disturbed with dreams of the place I had left, and the dangers I had escaped. However, upon waking, I found myself much recovered. It was now about eight o'clock at night, and the Captain ordered supper immediately, thinking I had already fasted too long.

---

3. At once; altogether.

He entertained me with great kindness, observing me not to look wildly, or talk inconsistently; and when we were left alone, desired I would give him a relation of my travels, and by what accident I came to be set adrift in that monstrous wooden chest. He said that about twelve o'clock at noon, as he was looking through his glass, he spied it at a distance, and thought it was a sail, which he had a mind to make,[4] being not much out of his course, in hopes of buying some biscuit, his own beginning to fall short. That, upon coming nearer, and finding his error, he sent out his longboat to discover what I was; that his men came back in a fright, swearing they had seen a swimming house. That he laughed at their folly, and went himself in the boat, ordering his men to take a strong cable along with them. That the weather being calm, he rowed round me several times, observed my windows, and the wire lattices that defended them. That he discovered two staples upon one side, which was all of boards, without any passage for light. He then commanded his men to row up to that side, and fastening a cable to one of the staples, ordered his men to tow my chest (as he called it) towards the ship. When it was there, he gave directions to fasten another cable to the ring fixed in the cover, and to raise up my chest with pulleys, which all the sailors were not able to do above two or three foot. He said they saw my stick and handkerchief thrust out of the hole, and concluded that some unhappy man must be shut up in the cavity. I asked whether he or the crew had seen any prodigious birds in the air about the time he first discovered me. To which he answered that, discoursing this matter with the sailors while I was asleep, one of them said he had observed three eagles flying towards the north, but remarked nothing of their being larger than the usual size (which I suppose must be imputed to the great height they were at), and he could not guess the reason of my question. I then asked the Captain how far he reckoned we might be from land; he said, by the best computation he could make, we were at least an hundred leagues. I assured him that he must be mistaken by almost half; for I had not left the country from whence I came above two hours before I dropped into the sea. Whereupon he began again to think that my brain was disturbed, of which he gave me a hint, and advised me to go to bed in a cabin he had provided. I assured him I was well refreshed with his good entertainment and company, and as much in my senses as ever I was in my life. He then grew serious and desired to ask me freely whether I were not troubled in mind by the consciousness of some enormous crime, for which I was punished at the command of some prince, by exposing me in that chest, as great criminals in other countries have been forced to sea in a leaky vessel without provisions; for although he should be sorry to have taken so ill[5] a man into his ship, yet he would engage his word to set me safe on shore in the first port where we arrived. He added that his suspicions were much increased by some very absurd speeches I had delivered at first to the sailors, and afterwards to himself, in relation to my closet or chest, as well as by my odd looks and behavior while I was at supper.

I begged his patience to hear me tell my story, which I faithfully did from the last time I left England to the moment he first discovered me. And as truth always forceth its way into rational minds, so this honest, worthy gentleman, who had some tincture of learning, and very good sense, was imme-

---

4. Overtake.   5. Evil.

diately convinced of my candor and veracity. But further to confirm all I had said, I entreated him to give order that my cabinet should be brought, of which I kept the key in my pocket (for he had already informed me how the seamen disposed of my closet). I opened it in his presence and showed him the small collection of rarities I made in the country from whence I had been so strangely delivered. There was the comb I had contrived out of the stumps of the King's beard, and another of the same materials, but fixed into a paring of her Majesty's thumbnail, which served for the back. There was a collection of needles and pins from a foot to half a yard long; four wasp-stings, like joiners' tacks; some combings of the Queen's hair; a gold ring which one day she made me a present of in a most obliging manner, taking it from her little finger, and throwing it over my head like a collar. I desired the Captain would please to accept this ring in return for his civilities, which he absolutely refused. I showed him a corn that I had cut off with my own hand from a Maid of Honor's toe; it was about the bigness of a Kentish pippin, and grown so hard that, when I returned to England, I got it hollowed into a cup and set in silver. Lastly, I desired him to see the breeches I had then on, which were made of a mouse's skin.

I could force nothing on him but a footman's tooth, which I observed him to examine with great curiosity, and found he had a fancy for it. He received it with abundance of thanks, more than such a trifle could deserve. It was drawn by an unskillful surgeon in a mistake from one of Glumdalclitch's men, who was afflicted with the toothache; but it was as sound as any in his head. I got it cleaned, and put it into my cabinet. It was about a foot long, and four inches in diameter.

The Captain was very well satisfied with this plain relation I had given him, and said he hoped when we returned to England I would oblige the world by putting it in paper and making it public. My answer was that I thought we were already overstocked with books of travels; that nothing could now pass which was not extraordinary; wherein I doubted some authors less consulted truth than their own vanity or interest, or the diversion of ignorant readers. That my story could contain little besides common events, without those ornamental descriptions of strange plants, trees, birds, and other animals, or the barbarous customs and idolatry of savage people, with which most writers abound. However, I thanked him for his good opinion, and promised to take the matter into my thoughts.

He said he wondered at one thing very much, which was to hear me speak so loud, asking me whether the King or Queen of that country were thick of hearing. I told him it was what I had been used to for above two years past, and that I admired[6] as much at the voices of him and his men, who seemed to me only to whisper, and yet I could hear them well enough. But, when I spoke in that country, it was like a man talking in the street to another looking out from the top of a steeple, unless when I was placed on a table, or held in any person's hand. I told him I had likewise observed another thing: that when I first got into the ship, and the sailors stood all about me, I thought they were the most little contemptible creatures I had ever beheld. For indeed while I was in that prince's country, I could never endure to look in a glass after my eyes had been accustomed to such prodigious objects, because the comparison gave me so despicable a conceit[7] of myself. The

---

6. Wondered.   7. Notion.

Captain said that while we were at supper he observed me to look at every-thing with a sort of wonder, and that I often seemed hardly able to contain my laughter; which he knew not well how to take, but imputed it to some disorder in my brain. I answered, it was very true; and I wondered how I could forbear, when I saw his dishes of the size of a silver threepence, a leg of pork hardly a mouthful, a cup not so big as a nutshell; and so I went on, describing the rest of his household stuff and provisions after the same man-ner. For, although the Queen had ordered a little equipage of all things necessary for me while I was in her service, yet my ideas were wholly taken up with what I saw on every side of me, and I winked at my own littleness, as people do at their own faults. The Captain understood my raillery very well, and merrily replied with the old English proverb, that he doubted[8] my eyes were bigger than my belly, for he did not observe my stomach so good, although I had fasted all day; and continuing in his mirth, protested he would have gladly given an hundred pounds to have seen my closet in the eagle's bill, and afterwards in its fall from so great an height into the sea; which would certainly have been a most astonishing object, worthy to have the description of it transmitted to future ages: and the comparison of Phaeton[9] was so obvious, that he could not forbear applying it, although I did not much admire the conceit.

The Captain having been at Tonquin,[1] was in his return to England driven northeastward to the latitude of 44 degrees, and of longitude 143. But meet-ing a trade wind two days after I came on board him, we sailed southward a long time, and coasting New Holland[2] kept our course west-southwest, and then south-southwest till we doubled the Cape of Good Hope. Our voyage was very prosperous, but I shall not trouble the reader with a journal of it. The Captain called in at one or two ports, and sent in his longboat for pro-visions and fresh water; but I never went out of the ship till we came into the Downs, which was on the third day of June, 1706, about nine months after my escape. I offered to leave my goods in security for payment of my freight; but the Captain protested he would not receive one farthing. We took kind leave of each other, and I made him promise he would come to see me at my house in Redriff. I hired a horse and guide for five shillings, which I borrowed of the Captain.

As I was on the road, observing the littleness of the houses, the trees, the cattle, and the people, I began to think myself in Lilliput. I was afraid of trampling on every traveler I met, and often called aloud to have them stand out of the way, so that I had like to have gotten one or two broken heads for my impertinence.

When I came to my own house, for which I was forced to inquire, one of the servants opening the door, I bent down to go in (like a goose under a gate) for fear of striking my head. My wife ran out to embrace me, but I stooped lower than her knees, thinking she could otherwise never be able to reach my mouth. My daughter kneeled to ask my blessing, but I could not see her till she arose, having been so long used to stand with my head and eyes erect to above sixty foot; and then I went to take her up with one hand by the waist. I looked down upon the servants and one or two friends who

---

8. Feared.
9. Son of Helios, the sun god, whose unsuccessful attempt to drive his father's chariot led to his death, when he lost control and was hurled by Zeus from the sky, falling into the river Eridanus, where he drowned.
1. Tonkin, now in Vietnam.
2. Australia.

were in the house, as if they had been pygmies and I a giant. I told my wife she had been too thrifty; for I found she had starved herself and her daughter to nothing. In short, I behaved myself so unaccountably that they were all of the Captain's opinion when he first saw me, and concluded I had lost my wits. This I mention as an instance of the great power of habit and prejudice.

In a little time I and my family and friends came to a right understanding; but my wife protested I should never go to sea any more, although my evil destiny so ordered that she had not power to hinder me; as the reader may know hereafter. In the meantime I here conclude the second part of my unfortunate voyages.

From *Part 3. A Voyage to Laputa, Balnibarbi, Glubbdubdrib, Luggnagg, and Japan*

* * *

[THE FLYING ISLAND OF LAPUTA][3]

CHAPTER 2. *The humors and dispositions of the Laputans described. An account of their learning. Of the King and his court. The author's reception there. The inhabitants subject to fears and disquietudes. An account of the women.*

At my alighting I was surrounded by a crowd of people, but those who stood nearest seemed to be of better quality. They beheld me with all the marks and circumstances of wonder; neither indeed was I much in their debt, having never till then seen a race of mortals so singular in their shapes, habits, and countenances. Their heads were all reclined to the right, or the left; one of their eyes turned inward, and the other directly up to the zenith. Their outward garments were adorned with the figures of suns, moons, and stars, interwoven with those of fiddles, flutes, harps, trumpets, guitars, harpsichords, and many more instruments of music, unknown to us in Europe.[4] I observed here and there many in the habits of servants, with a blown bladder fastened like a flail to the end of a short stick, which they carried in their hands. In each bladder was a small quantity of dried pease or little pebbles (as I was afterwards informed). With these bladders they now and then flapped the mouths and ears of those who stood near them, of which practice I could not then conceive the meaning. It seems, the minds of these people are so taken up with intense speculations, that they neither can speak, or attend to the discourses of others, without being roused by some external taction[5] upon the organs of speech and hearing; for which reason those persons who are able to afford it always keep a flapper (the original is *climenole*) in their family, as one of their domestics; nor ever walk abroad or make visits without him. And the business of this officer is, when two or more persons are in company, gently to strike with his bladder the mouth of him who is to speak, and the right ear of him or them to whom the speaker

3. In the first chapter of part 3 Gulliver starts on his third voyage, but is captured by pirates and set adrift. Just as he is about to despair, a vast flying island appears in the sky, and the inhabitants draw him up with pulleys.
4. The Laputans represent contemporary specu-
lation, deplored by Swift, about abstract theories of science, mathematics, and music. Both the Royal Society and Sir Isaac Newton took an interest in the mathematical basis of music.
5. Touch.

addresseth himself. This flapper is likewise employed diligently to attend his master in his walks, and upon occasion to give him a soft flap on his eyes, because he is always so wrapped up in cogitation, that he is in manifest danger of falling down every precipice, and bouncing his head against every post; and in the streets, of jostling others, or being jostled himself into the kennel.[6]

It was necessary to give the reader this information, without which he would be at the same loss with me, to understand the proceedings of these people, as they conducted me up the stairs to the top of the island, and from thence to the royal palace. While we were ascending, they forgot several times what they were about, and left me to myself, till their memories were again roused by their flappers; for they appeared altogether unmoved by the sight of my foreign habit and countenance, and by the shouts of the vulgar, whose thoughts and minds were more disengaged.

At last we entered the palace, and proceeded into the chamber of presence; where I saw the King seated on his throne, attended on each side by persons of prime quality. Before the throne was a large table filled with globes and spheres, and mathematical instruments of all kinds. His Majesty took not the least notice of us, although our entrance was not without sufficient noise, by the concourse of all persons belonging to the court. But he was then deep in a problem, and we attended at least an hour before he could solve it. There stood by him on each side a young page, with flaps in their hands, and when they saw he was at leisure, one of them gently struck his mouth, and the other his right ear; at which he started like one awaked on the sudden, and looking towards me, and the company I was in, recollected the occasion of our coming, whereof he had been informed before. He spoke some words, whereupon immediately a young man with a flap came up to my side, and flapped me gently on the right ear; but I made signs as well as I could, that I had no occasion for such an instrument; which as I afterwards found gave his Majesty and the whole court a very mean opinion of my understanding. The King, as far as I could conjecture, asked me several questions, and I addressed myself to him in all the languages I had. When it was found that I could neither understand nor be understood, I was conducted by his order to an apartment in his palace (this prince being distinguished above all his predecessors for his hospitality to strangers),[7] where two servants were appointed to attend me. My dinner was brought, and four persons of quality, whom I remembered to have seen very near the King's person, did me the honor to dine with me. We had two courses, of three dishes each. In the first course there was a shoulder of mutton, cut into an equilateral triangle; a piece of beef into a rhomboid; and a pudding into a cycloid. The second course was two ducks, trussed up into the form of fiddles; sausages and pudding resembling flutes and hautboys,[8] and a breast of veal in the shape of a harp. The servants cut our bread into cones, cylinders, parallelograms, and several other mathematical figures.

While we were at dinner, I made bold to ask the names of several things in their language, and those noble persons, by the assistance of their flappers, delighted to give me answers, hoping to raise my admiration of their great

6. Gutter.
7. George I, a patron of music and science, had filled his court with Hanoverians when he came to

England in 1714.
8. Oboes.

abilities, if I could be brought to converse with them. I was soon able to call for bread and drink, or whatever else I wanted.

After dinner my company withdrew, and a person was sent to me by the King's order, attended by a flapper. He brought with him pen, ink, and paper, and three or four books; giving me to understand by signs, that he was sent to teach me the language. We sat together four hours, in which time I wrote down a great number of words in columns, with the translations over against them. I likewise made a shift to learn several short sentences. For my tutor would order one of my servants to fetch something, to turn about, to make a bow, to sit, or stand, or walk, and the like. Then I took down the sentence in writing. He showed me also in one of his books the figures of the sun, moon, and stars, the zodiac, the tropics and polar circles, together with the denominations of many figures of planes and solids. He gave me the names and descriptions of all the musical instruments, and the general terms of art in playing on each of them. After he had left me, I placed all my words with their interpretations in alphabetical order. And thus in a few days, by the help of a very faithful memory, I got some insight into their language.

The word, which I interpret the *Flying* or *Floating Island*, is in the original *Laputa*; whereof I could never learn the true etymology. *Lap* in the old obsolete language signifieth *high*, and *untuh* a *governor*; from which they say by corruption was derived *Laputa*, from *Lapuntuh*. But I do not approve of this derivation, which seems to be a little strained. I ventured to offer to the learned among them a conjecture of my own, that *Laputa* was *quasi Lap outed*; *Lap* signifying properly the dancing of the sunbeams in the sea, and *outed* a wing, which however I shall not obtrude, but submit to the judicious reader.[9]

Those to whom the King had entrusted me, observing how ill I was clad, ordered a tailor to come next morning, and take my measure for a suit of clothes. This operator did his office after a different manner from those of his trade in Europe. He first took my altitude by a quadrant, and then, with rule and compasses, described the dimensions and outlines of my whole body; all which he entered upon paper, and in six days brought my clothes very ill made, and quite out of shape, by happening to mistake a figure in the calculation. But my comfort was, that I observed such accidents very frequent, and little regarded.

During my confinement for want of clothes, and by an indisposition that held me some days longer, I much enlarged my dictionary; and when I went next to court, was able to understand many things the King spoke, and to return him some kind of answers. His Majesty had given orders that the island should move northeast and by east, to the vertical point over Lagado, the metropolis of the whole kingdom, below upon the firm earth. It was about ninety leagues distant, and our voyage lasted four days and a half. I was not in the least sensible of the progressive motion made in the air by the island. On the second morning, about eleven o'clock, the King himself in person, attended by his nobility, courtiers, and officers, having prepared all their musical instruments, played on them for three hours without intermission, so that I was quite stunned with the noise; neither could I possibly guess the meaning, till my tutor informed me. He said, that the people of their island

9. Gulliver overlooks a likelier etymology: Spanish *la puta*, "the whore."

had their ears adapted to hear the music of the spheres, which always played at certain periods; and the court was now prepared to bear their part in whatever instrument they most excelled.

In our journey towards Lagado, the capital city, his Majesty ordered that the island should stop over certain towns and villages, from whence he might receive the petitions of his subjects. And to this purpose, several packthreads were let down with small weights at the bottom. On these packthreads the people strung their petitions, which mounted up directly like the scraps of paper fastened by schoolboys at the end of the string that holds their kite.[1] Sometimes we received wine and victuals from below, which were drawn up by pulleys.

The knowledge I had in mathematics gave me great assistance in acquiring their phraseology, which depended much upon that science and music; and in the latter I was not unskilled. Their ideas are perpetually conversant in lines and figures. If they would, for example, praise the beauty of a woman, or any other animal, they describe it by rhombs, circles, parallelograms, ellipses, and other geometrical terms; or else by words of art drawn from music, needless here to repeat. I observed in the King's kitchen all sorts of mathematical and musical instruments, after the figures of which they cut up the joints that were served to his Majesty's table.

Their houses are very ill built, the walls bevil, without one right angle in any apartment; and this defect ariseth from the contempt they bear for practical geometry; which they despise as vulgar and mechanic, those instructions they give being too refined for the intellectuals of their workmen; which occasions perpetual mistakes. And although they are dextrous enough upon a piece of paper, in the management of the rule, the pencil, and the divider, yet in the common actions and behavior of life I have not seen a more clumsy, awkward, and unhandy people, nor so slow and perplexed in their conceptions upon all other subjects, except those of mathematics and music. They are very bad reasoners, and vehemently given to opposition, unless when they happen to be of the right opinion, which is seldom their case. Imagination, fancy, and invention, they are wholly strangers to, nor have any words in their language by which those ideas can be expressed; the whole compass of their thoughts and mind being shut up within the two forementioned sciences.

Most of them, and especially those who deal in the astronomical part, have great faith in judicial astrology, although they are ashamed to own it publicly. But what I chiefly admired,[2] and thought altogether unaccountable, was the strong disposition I observed in them towards news and politics; perpetually enquiring into public affairs, giving their judgments in matters of state; and passionately disputing every inch of a party opinion. I have indeed observed the same disposition among most of the mathematicians I have known in Europe; although I could never discover the least analogy between the two sciences; unless those people suppose, that because the smallest circle hath as many degrees as the largest, therefore the regulation and management of the world require no more abilities than the handling and turning of a globe. But I rather take this quality to spring from a very

1. Petitioners, that is, might as well go fly a kite. Throughout this section Swift satirizes the "distance" of George I (who spent much of his time in Hanover) from his British subjects.
2. Wondered at.

common infirmity of human nature, inclining us to be more curious and conceited in matters where we have least concern, and for which we are least adapted either by study or nature.

These people are under continual disquietudes, never enjoying a minute's peace of mind; and their disturbances proceed from causes which very little affect the rest of mortals. Their apprehensions arise from several changes they dread in the celestial bodies. For instance; that the earth, by the continual approaches of the sun towards it, must in course of time be absorbed or swallowed up. That the face of the sun will by degrees be encrusted with its own effluvia,[3] and give no more light to the world. That the earth very narrowly escaped a brush from the tail of the last comet, which would have infallibly reduced it to ashes; and that the next, which they have calculated for one and thirty years hence, will probably destroy us.[4] For, if in its perihelion it should approach within a certain degree of the sun (as by their calculations they have reason to dread), it will conceive a degree of heat ten thousand times more intense than that of red-hot glowing iron; and in its absence from the sun, carry a blazing tail ten hundred thousand and fourteen miles long; through which if the earth should pass at the distance of one hundred thousand miles from the nucleus, or main body of the comet, it must in its passage be set on fire, and reduced to ashes. That the sun daily spending its rays without any nutriment to supply them, will at last be wholly consumed and annihilated; which must be attended with the destruction of this earth, and of all the planets that receive their light from it.

They are so perpetually alarmed with the apprehensions of these and the like impending dangers, that they can neither sleep quietly in their beds, nor have any relish for the common pleasures or amusements of life. When they meet an acquaintance in the morning, the first question is about the sun's health, how he looked at his setting and rising, and what hopes they have to avoid the stroke of the approaching comet. This conversation they are apt to run into with the same temper that boys discover in delighting to hear terrible stories of sprites and hobgoblins, which they greedily listen to, and dare not go to bed for fear.

The women of the island have abundance of vivacity; they contemn their husbands, and are exceedingly fond of strangers, whereof there is always a considerable number from the continent below, attending at court, either upon affairs of the several towns and corporations, or their own particular occasions; but are much despised, because they want the same endowments. Among these the ladies choose their gallants: but the vexation is, that they act with too much ease and security; for the husband is always so rapt in speculation, that the mistress and lover may proceed to the greatest familiarities before his face, if he be but provided with paper and implements, and without his flapper at his side.

The wives and daughters lament their confinement to the island, although I think it the most delicious spot of ground in the world; and although they live here in the greatest plenty and magnificence, and are allowed to do whatever they please, they long to see the world, and take the diversions of the metropolis, which they are not allowed to do without a particular license from the King; and this is not easy to be obtained, because the people of

---

3. Sunspots.
4. Halley's comet, some astronomers had feared, might strike the earth on its next appearance (1758). All the disasters that disquiet the Laputans had occurred to English scientists as possible implications of Newtonian theory.

quality have found by frequent experience, how hard it is to persuade their women to return from below. I was told that a great court lady, who had several children, is married to the prime minister, the richest subject in the kingdom, a very graceful person, extremely fond of her, and lives in the finest palace of the island, went down to Lagado, on the pretense of health, there hid herself for several months, till the King sent a warrant to search for her, and she was found in an obscure eating-house all in rags, having pawned her clothes to maintain an old deformed footman, who beat her every day, and in whose company she was taken much against her will. And although her husband received her with all possible kindness, and without the least reproach, she soon after contrived to steal down again with all her jewels, to the same gallant, and hath not been heard of since.

This may perhaps pass with the reader rather for an European or English story, than for one of a country so remote. But he may please to consider, that the caprices of womankind are not limited by any climate or nation; and that they are much more uniform than can be easily imagined.

In about a month's time I had made a tolerable proficiency in their language, and was able to answer most of the King's questions, when I had the honor to attend him. His Majesty discovered not the least curiosity to enquire into the laws, government, history, religion, or manners of the countries where I had been; but confined his questions to the state of mathematics, and received the account I gave him with great contempt and indifference, though often roused by his flapper on each side.[5]

* * *

[THE ACADEMY OF LAGADO][6]
FROM CHAPTER 5.

The first professor I saw was in a very large room, with forty pupils about him. After salutation, observing me to look earnestly upon a frame, which took up the greatest part of both the length and breadth of the room, he said, perhaps I might wonder to see him employed in a project for improving speculative knowledge by practical and mechanical operations. But the world would soon be sensible[7] of its usefulness, and he flattered himself that a more noble, exalted thought never sprang in any other man's head. Everyone knew how laborious the usual method is of attaining to arts and sciences; whereas by his contrivance the most ignorant person at a reasonable charge, and with a little bodily labor, may write books in philosophy, poetry, politics, law, mathematics, and theology, without the least assistance from genius or study. He then led me to the frame, about the sides whereof all his pupils stood in ranks. It was twenty foot square, placed in the middle of the room. The superficies[8] was composed of several bits of wood, about the bigness of a die, but some larger than others. They were all linked together by slender wires. These bits of wood were covered on every square with papers pasted

---

5. In the omitted chapters, Gulliver visits countries that show the consequences of modern learning. After an account of the Flying Island, whose power of motion (derived from a giant magnet or lodestone) allows it to dominate the regions below, he descends to Balnibarbi, a once fertile land now ruined by the fanciful projects of impractical scientists. In the Grand Academy of Lagado he meets many professors who are contriving such perverse "improvements" as making clothes from cobwebs or breeding naked sheep. Then he visits the part of the academy devoted to speculative learning.

6. The Grand Academy of Lagado satirizes the Royal Society of London, an organization founded in 1662 to encourage the pursuit of scientific knowledge. Some of the projects described by Swift resemble the experiments or speculations of British scientists at the time.

7. Aware.

8. Surface.

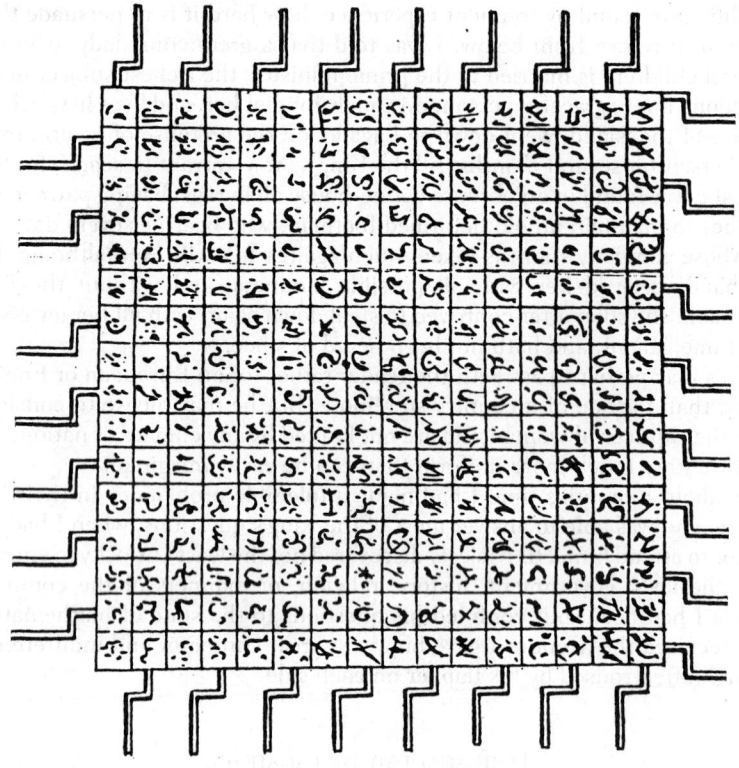

[A PRIMITIVE COMPUTER]

on them; and on these papers were written all the words of their language in their several moods, tenses, and declensions, but without any order. The professor then desired me to observe, for he was going to set his engine at work. The pupils at his command took each of them hold of an iron handle, whereof there were forty fixed round the edges of the frame; and giving them a sudden turn, the whole disposition[9] of the words was entirely changed. He then commanded six and thirty of the lads to read the several lines softly as they appeared upon the frame; and where they found three or four words together that might make part of a sentence, they dictated to the four remaining boys who were scribes. This work was repeated three or four times, and at every turn the engine was so contrived that the words shifted into new places, as the square bits of wood moved upside down.

Six hours a day the young students were employed in this labor; and the professor showed me several volumes in large folio already collected, of broken sentences, which he intended to piece together, and out of those rich materials to give the world a complete body of all arts and sciences; which however might be still improved, and much expedited, if the public would raise a fund for making and employing five hundred such frames in Lagado, and oblige the managers to contribute in common their several[1] collections.

9. Arrangement.   1. Separate.

He assured me, that this invention had employed all his thoughts from his youth, that he had emptied the whole vocabulary into his frame, and made the strictest computation of the general proportion there is in books between the numbers of particles, nouns, and verbs, and other parts of speech.

I made my humblest acknowledgments to this illustrious person for his great communicativeness, and promised if ever I had the good fortune to return to my native country, that I would do him justice, as the sole inventor of this wonderful machine; the form and contrivance of which I desired leave to delineate upon paper as in the figure here annexed. I told him, although it were the custom of our learned in Europe to steal inventions from each other, who had thereby at least this advantage, that it became a controversy which was the right owner, yet I would take such caution, that he should have the honor entire without a rival.

We next went to the school of languages, where three professors sat in consultation upon improving that of their own country.[2]

The first project was to shorten discourse by cutting polysyllables into one, and leaving out verbs and participles, because in reality all things imaginable are but nouns.

The other was a scheme for entirely abolishing all words whatsoever; and this was urged as a great advantage in point of health as well as brevity. For it is plain, that every word we speak is in some degree a diminution of our lungs by corrosion, and consequently contributes to the shortening of our lives. An expedient was therefore offered, that since words are only names for *things*, it would be more convenient for all men to carry about them such *things* as were necessary to express the particular business they are to discourse on. And this invention would certainly have taken place, to the great ease as well as health of the subject, if the women in conjunction with the vulgar and illiterate had not threatened to raise a rebellion, unless they might be allowed the liberty to speak with their tongues, after the manner of their forefathers. Such constant irreconcilable enemies to science[3] are the common people. However, many of the most learned and wise adhere to the new scheme of expressing themselves by *things,* which hath only this inconvenience attending it, that if a man's business be very great, and of various kinds, he must be obliged in proportion to carry a greater bundle of *things* upon his back, unless he can afford one or two strong servants to attend him. I have often beheld two of those sages almost sinking under the weight of their packs, like pedlars among us, who when they met in the streets would lay down their loads, open their sacks, and hold conversation for an hour together, then put up their implements, help each other to resume their burdens, and take their leave.

But for short conversations a man may carry implements in his pockets and under his arms, enough to supply him, and in his house he cannot be at a loss; therefore the room where company meet who practice this art is full of all *things* ready at hand, requisite to furnish matter for this kind of artificial converse.[4]

Another great advantage proposed by this invention was that it would serve

---

2. Many contemporary scientists had proposed a philosophical language that would eliminate the treacherous disparity between words and things and thus allow accurate scientific discourse.

3. Knowledge.

4. The Royal Society had sponsored a collection intended to contain one specimen of every thing in the world.

as an universal language to be understood in all civilized nations, whose goods and utensils are generally of the same kind, or nearly resembling, so that their uses might easily be comprehended. And thus, ambassadors would be qualified to treat with foreign princes or ministers of state to whose tongues they were utter strangers.

I was at the mathematical school, where the master taught his pupils after a method scarce imaginable to us in Europe. The proposition and demonstration were fairly written on a thin wafer, with ink composed of a cephalic tincture.[5] This the student was to swallow upon a fasting stomach, and for three days following eat nothing but bread and water. As the wafer digested, the tincture mounted to his brain, bearing the proposition along with it. But the success hath not hitherto been answerable, partly by some error in the *quantum* or composition, and partly by the perverseness of lads, to whom this bolus[6] is so nauseous that they generally steal aside, and discharge it upwards before it can operate; neither have they been yet persuaded to use so long an abstinence as the prescription requires.[7]

* * *

[THE STRULDBRUGGS]

CHAPTER 10. *The Luggnaggians commended. A particular description of the struldbruggs, with many conversations between the author and some eminent persons upon that subject.*

The Luggnaggians are a polite[8] and generous people, and although they are not without some share of that pride which is peculiar to all eastern countries, yet they show themselves courteous to strangers, especially such who are countenanced by the court. I had many acquaintance among persons of the best fashion, and being always attended by my interpreter, the conversation we had was not disagreeable.

One day in much good company, I was asked by a person of quality, whether I had seen any of their *struldbruggs* or *immortals*. I said I had not; and desired he would explain to me what he meant by such an appellation, applied to a mortal creature. He told me, that sometimes, although very rarely, a child happened to be born in a family with a red circular spot in the forehead, directly over the left eyebrow, which was an infallible mark that it should never die. The spot, as he described it, was about the compass of a silver threepence, but in the course of time grew larger, and changed its color; for at twelve years old it became green, so continued till five and twenty, then turned to a deep blue; at five and forty it grew coal black, and as large as an English shilling; but never admitted any farther alteration. He said these births were so rare, that he did not believe there could be above eleven hundred *struldbruggs* of both sexes in the whole kingdom, of which he computed about fifty in the metropolis, and among the rest a young girl born about three years ago. That these productions were not peculiar to any family, but a mere effect of chance; and the children of the *struldbruggs* themselves were equally mortal with the rest of the people.

5. A solution or dye directed toward the head.
6. A large pill. "*Quantum*": amount.
7. In the omitted chapters Gulliver hears projects for improving politics and offers some of his own. He sails to Glubbdubdrib, the Island of Sorcerers, where he talks with the spirits of the dead; he learns that history is a pack of lies and that humanity has degenerated since ancient times. He is then received by the king of Luggnagg.
8. Refined, cultivated.

I freely own myself to have been struck with inexpressible delight upon hearing this account: and the person who gave it me happening to understand the Balnibarbian language, which I spoke very well, I could not forbear breaking out into expressions perhaps a little too extravagant. I cried out as in a rapture: Happy nation, where every child hath at least a chance for being immortal! Happy people who enjoy so many living examples of ancient virtue, and have masters ready to instruct them in the wisdom of all former ages! But happiest beyond all comparison are those excellent *struldbruggs*, who being born exempt from that universal calamity of human nature, have their minds free and disengaged, without the weight and depression of spirits caused by the continual apprehension of death. I discovered my admiration that I had not observed any of these illustrious persons at court; the black spot on the forehead being so remarkable a distinction, that I could not have easily overlooked it; and it was impossible that his Majesty, a most judicious prince, should not provide himself with a good number of such wise and able counselors. Yet perhaps the virtue of those reverend sages was too strict for the corrupt and libertine manners of a court. And we often find by experience that young men are too opinionative[9] and volatile to be guided by the sober dictates of their seniors. However, since the King was pleased to allow me access to his royal person, I was resolved upon the very first occasion to deliver my opinion to him on this matter freely, and at large by the help of my interpreter; and whether he would please to take my advice or no, yet in one thing I was determined, that his Majesty having frequently offered me an establishment in this country, I would with great thankfulness accept the favor, and pass my life here in the conversation of those superior beings the *struldbruggs*, if they would please to admit me.

The gentleman to whom I addressed my discourse, because (as I have already observed) he spoke the language of Balnibarbi, said to me with a sort of a smile, which usually ariseth from pity to the ignorant, that he was glad of any occasion to keep me among them, and desired my permission to explain to the company what I had spoke. He did so; and they talked together for some time in their own language, whereof I understood not a syllable, neither could I observe by their countenances what impression my discourse had made on them. After a short silence the same person told me, that his friends and mine (so he thought fit to express himself) were very much pleased with the judicious remarks I had made on the great happiness and advantages of immortal life; and they were desirous to know in a particular manner, what scheme of living I should have formed to myself, if it had fallen to my lot to have been born a *struldbrugg*.

I answered, it was easy to be eloquent on so copious and delightful a subject, especially to me who have been often apt to amuse myself with visions of what I should do if I were a king, a general, or a great lord; and upon this very case I had frequently run over the whole system how I should employ myself, and pass the time if I were sure to live forever.

That, if it had been my good fortune to come into the world a *struldbrugg*, as soon as I could discover my own happiness by understanding the difference between life and death, I would first resolve by all arts and methods whatsoever to procure myself riches: in the pursuit of which, by thrift and management, I might reasonably expect in about two hundred years to be

---

9. Speculative, impractical.

the wealthiest man in the kingdom. In the second place, I would from my earliest youth apply myself to the study of arts and sciences, by which I should arrive in time to excel all others in learning. Lastly, I would carefully record every action and event of consequence that happened in the public, impartially draw the characters of the several successions of princes, and great ministers of state; with my own observations on every point. I would exactly set down the several changes in customs, languages, fashions of dress, diet and diversions. By all which acquirements, I should be a living treasury of knowledge and wisdom, and certainly become the oracle of the nation.

I would never marry after threescore, but live in an hospitable manner, yet still on the saving side. I would entertain myself in forming and directing the minds of hopeful young men, by convincing them from my own remembrance, experience and observation, fortified by numerous examples, of the usefulness of virtue in public and private life. But my choice and constant companions should be a set of my own immortal brotherhood, among whom I would elect a dozen from the most ancient down to my own contemporaries. Where any of these wanted fortunes, I would provide them with convenient lodges round my own estate, and have some of them always at my table, only mingling a few of the most valuable among you mortals, whom length of time would harden me to lose with little or no reluctance, and treat your posterity after the same manner; just as a man diverts himself with the annual succession of pinks and tulips in his garden, without regretting the loss of those which withered the preceding year.

These *struldbruggs* and I would mutually communicate our observations and memorials[1] through the course of time; remark the several gradations by which corruption steals into the world, and oppose it in every step, by giving perpetual warning and instruction to mankind; which, added to the strong influence of our own example, would probably prevent that continual degeneracy of human nature, so justly complained of in all ages.

Add to all this, the pleasure of seeing the various revolutions of states and empires; the changes in the lower and upper world;[2] ancient cities in ruins; and obscure villages become the seats of kings. Famous rivers lessening into shallow brooks; the ocean leaving one coast dry, and overwhelming another; the discovery of many countries yet unknown. Barbarity overrunning the politest nations, and the most barbarous becoming civilized. I should then see the discovery of the longitude, the perpetual motion, the universal medicine,[3] and many other great inventions brought to the utmost perfection.

What wonderful discoveries should we make in astronomy, by outliving and confirming our own predictions, by observing the progress and returns of comets, with the changes of motion in the sun, moon and stars.

I enlarged upon many other topics, which the natural desire of endless life and sublunary happiness could easily furnish me with. When I had ended, and the sum of my discourse had been interpreted as before to the rest of the company, there was a good deal of talk among them in the language of the country, not without some laughter at my expense. At last the same gentleman who had been my interpreter said, he was desired by the rest to

1. Memories.
2. Earth and heaven; figuratively, common people and the ruling class. "Revolutions": cycles.
3. The *elixir vitae*, an alchemical formula to pre-

serve life forever, was considered by Swift an impossible dream, like a method for calculating longitude at sea, or a perpetual motion machine.

set me right in a few mistakes, which I had fallen into through the common imbecility[4] of human nature, and upon that allowance was less answerable for them. That this breed of *struldbruggs* was peculiar to their country, for there were no such people either in Balnibarbi or Japan, where he had the honor to be ambassador from his Majesty, and found the natives in both those kingdoms very hard to believe that the fact was possible; and it appeared from my astonishment when he first mentioned the matter to me, that I received it as a thing wholly new, and scarcely to be credited. That in the two kingdoms above mentioned, where during his residence he had conversed very much, he observed long life to be the universal desire and wish of mankind. That whoever had one foot in the grave was sure to hold back the other as strongly as he could. That the oldest had still hopes of living one day longer, and looked on death as the greatest evil, from which nature always prompted him to retreat; only in this island of Luggnagg the appetite for living was not so eager, from the continual example of the *struldbruggs* before their eyes.

That the system of living contrived by me was unreasonable and unjust, because it supposed a perpetuity of youth, health, and vigor, which no man could be so foolish to hope, however extravagant he might be in his wishes. That the question therefore was not whether a man would choose to be always in the prime of youth, attended with prosperity and health; but how he would pass a perpetual life under all the usual disadvantages which old age brings along with it. For although few men will avow their desires of being immortal upon such hard conditions, yet in the two kingdoms before mentioned of Balnibarbi and Japan, he observed that every man desired to put off death for some time longer, let it approach ever so late; and he rarely heard of any man who died willingly, except he were incited by the extremity of grief or torture. And he appealed to me whether in those countries I had traveled, as well as my own, I had not observed the same general disposition.

After this preface he gave me a particular account of the *struldbruggs* among them. He said they commonly acted like mortals, till about thirty years old, after which by degrees they grew melancholy and dejected, increasing in both till they came to fourscore. This he learned from their own confession; for otherwise there not being above two or three of that species born in an age, they were too few to form a general observation by. When they came to fourscore years, which is reckoned the extremity of living in this country, they had not only all the follies and infirmities of other old men, but many more which arose from the dreadful prospect of never dying. They were not only opinionative, peevish, covetous, morose, vain, talkative; but uncapable of friendship, and dead to all natural affection, which never descended below their grandchildren. Envy and impotent desires are their prevailing passions. But those objects against which their envy seems principally directed, are the vices of the younger sort, and the deaths of the old. By reflecting on the former, they find themselves cut off from all possibility of pleasure; and whenever they see a funeral, they lament and repine that others are gone to an harbor of rest, to which they themselves never can hope to arrive. They have no remembrance of anything but what they learned and observed in their youth and middle age, and even that is very imperfect.

---

4. Weakness.

And for the truth or particulars of any fact, it is safer to depend on common traditions than upon their best recollections. The least miserable among them appear to be those who turn to dotage, and entirely lose their memories; these meet with more pity and assistance, because they want[5] many bad qualities which abound in others.

If a *struldbrugg* happen to marry one of his own kind, the marriage is dissolved of course by the courtesy of the kingdom, as soon as the younger of the two comes to be fourscore. For the law thinks it a reasonable indulgence, that those who are condemned without any fault of their own to a perpetual continuance in the world, should not have their misery doubled by the load of a wife.

As soon as they have completed the term of eighty years, they are looked on as dead in law; their heirs immediately succeed to their estates, only a small pittance is reserved for their support; and the poor ones are maintained at the public charge. After that period they are held incapable of any employment of trust or profit; they cannot purchase land, or take leases, neither are they allowed to be witnesses in any cause, either civil or criminal, not even for the decision of meers[6] and bounds.

At ninety they lose their teeth and hair; they have at that age no distinction of taste, but eat and drink whatever they can get, without relish or appetite. The diseases they were subject to still continue without increasing or diminishing. In talking they forget the common appellation of things, and the names of persons, even of those who are their nearest friends and relations. For the same reason they never can amuse themselves with reading, because their memory will not serve to carry them from the beginning of a sentence to the end, and by this defect they are deprived of the only entertainment whereof they might otherwise be capable.

The language of this country being always upon the flux, the *struldbruggs* of one age do not understand those of another; neither are they able after two hundred years to hold any conversation (farther than by a few general words) with their neighbors the mortals; and thus they lie under the disadvantage of living like foreigners in their own country.

This was the account given me of the *struldbruggs,* as near as I can remember. I afterwards saw five or six of different ages, the youngest not above two hundred years old, who were brought to me at several times by some of my friends; but although they were told that I was a great traveler, and had seen all the world, they had not the least curiosity to ask me a question; only desired I would give them *slumskudask,* or a token of remembrance; which is a modest way of begging, to avoid the law that strictly forbids it, because they are provided for by the public, although indeed with a very scanty allowance.

They are despised and hated by all sorts of people; when one of them is born, it is reckoned ominous, and their birth is recorded very particularly; so that you may know their age by consulting the registry, which however hath not been kept above a thousand years past, or at least hath been destroyed by time or public disturbances. But the usual way of computing how old they are, is by asking them what kings or great persons they can remember, and then consulting history; for infallibly the last prince in their mind did not begin his reign after they were fourscore years old.

---

5. Lack.   6. Boundaries.

They were the most mortifying sight I ever beheld; and the women more horrible than the men. Besides the usual deformities in extreme old age, they acquired an additional ghastliness in proportion to their number of years, which is not to be described; and among half a dozen I soon distinguished which was the oldest, although there were not above a century or two between them.

The reader will easily believe, that from what I had heard and seen, my keen appetite for perpetuity of life was much abated. I grew heartily ashamed of the pleasing visions I had formed; and thought no tyrant could invent a death into which I would not run with pleasure from such a life. The King heard of all that had passed between me and my friends upon this occasion, and rallied[7] me very pleasantly; wishing I would send a couple of *struldbruggs* to my own country, to arm our people against the fear of death; but this it seems is forbidden by the fundamental laws of the kingdom; or else I should have been well content with the trouble and expense of transporting them.

I could not but agree, that the laws of this kingdom relating to the *struldbruggs,* were founded upon the strongest reasons, and such as any other country would be under the necessity of enacting in the like circumstances. Otherwise, as avarice is the necessary consequent of old age, those immortals would in time become proprietors of the whole nation, and engross[8] the civil power; which, for want of abilities to manage, must end in the ruin of the public.[9]

* * *

Part 4. A Voyage to the Country of the Houyhnhnms[1]

CHAPTER 1. *The Author sets out as Captain of a ship. His men conspire against him, confine him a long time to his cabin, set him on shore in an unknown land. He travels up into the country. The Yahoos, a strange sort of animal, described. The Author meets two Houyhnhnms.*

I continued at home with my wife and children about five months in a very happy condition, if I could have learned the lesson of knowing when I was well. I left my poor wife big with child, and accepted an advantageous offer made me to be Captain of the *Adventure,* a stout merchantman of 350 tons; for I understood navigation well, and being grown weary of a surgeon's employment at sea, which however I could exercise upon occasion, I took a skillful young man of that calling, one Robert Purefoy, into my ship. We set sail from Portsmouth upon the 7th day of September, 1710; on the 14th we met with Captain Pocock of Bristol, at Tenariff,[2] who was going to the Bay of Campeachy[3] to cut logwood. On the 16th he was parted from us by a storm; I heard since my return that his ship foundered and none escaped, but one cabin boy. He was an honest man and a good sailor, but a little too positive in his own opinions, which was the cause of his destruction, as it hath been of several others. For if he had followed my advice, he might at this time have been safe at home with his family as well as myself.

7. Ridiculed.
8. Absorb, monopolize.
9. In the omitted chapter, Gulliver sails to Japan, where a Dutch ship provides him passage back to Europe.

1. Pronounced *hwin-ims.* The word suggests the neigh characteristic of a horse.
2. Teneriffe, one of the Canary Islands.
3. Campeche, in the Gulf of Mexico.

I had several men died in my ship of calentures,[4] so that I was forced to get recruits out of Barbadoes and the Leeward Islands, where I touched by the direction of the merchants who employed me; which I had soon too much cause to repent, for I found afterwards that most of them had been buccaneers. I had fifty hands on board; and my orders were that I should trade with the Indians in the South Sea, and make what discoveries I could. These rogues whom I had picked up debauched my other men, and they all formed a conspiracy to seize the ship and secure me; which they did one morning, rushing into my cabin, and binding me hand and foot, threatening to throw me overboard, if I offered to stir. I told them I was their prisoner, and would submit. This they made me swear to do, and then unbound me, only fastening one of my legs with a chain near my bed, and placed a sentry at my door with his piece charged, who was commanded to shoot me dead if I attempted my liberty. They sent me down victuals and drink, and took the government of the ship to themselves. Their design was to turn pirates and plunder the Spaniards, which they could not do, till they got more men. But first they resolved to sell the goods in the ship, and then go to Madagascar for recruits, several among them having died since my confinement. They sailed many weeks, and traded with the Indians; but I knew not what course they took, being kept close prisoner in my cabin, and expecting nothing less than to be murdered, as they often threatened me.

Upon the 9th day of May, 1711, one James Welch came down to my cabin; and said he had orders from the Captain to set me ashore. I expostulated with him, but in vain; neither would he so much as tell me who their new Captain was. They forced me into the longboat, letting me put on my best suit of clothes, which were as good as new, and a small bundle of linen, but no arms except my hanger; and they were so civil as not to search my pockets, into which I conveyed what money I had, with some other little necessaries. They rowed about a league, and then set me down on a strand. I desired them to tell me what country it was; they all swore, they knew no more than myself, but said that the Captain (as they called him) was resolved, after they had sold the lading, to get rid of me in the first place where they discovered land. They pushed off immediately, advising me to make haste, for fear of being overtaken by the tide, and bade me farewell.

In this desolate condition I advanced forward, and soon got upon firm ground, where I sat down on a bank to rest myself, and consider what I had best to do. When I was a little refreshed, I went up into the country, resolving to deliver myself to the first savages I should meet, and purchase my life from them by some bracelets, glass rings, and other toys, which sailors usually provide themselves with in those voyages, and whereof I had some about me. The land was divided by long rows of trees, not regularly planted, but naturally growing; there was great plenty of grass, and several fields of oats. I walked very circumspectly for fear of being surprised, or suddenly shot with an arrow from behind, or on either side. I fell into a beaten road, where I saw many tracks of human feet, and some of cows, but most of horses. At last I beheld several animals in a field, and one or two of the same kind sitting in trees. Their shape was very singular, and deformed, which a little

---

4. "A distemper peculiar to sailors, in hot climates; wherein they imagine the sea to be green fields, and will throw themselves into it, if not restrained" (Johnson's *Dictionary*).

discomposed me, so that I lay down behind a thicket to observe them better. Some of them coming forward near the place where I lay, gave me an opportunity of distinctly marking their form. Their heads and breasts were covered with a thick hair, some frizzled and others lank; they had beards like goats, and a long ridge of hair down their backs, and the fore parts of their legs and feet; but the rest of their bodies were bare, so that I might see their skins, which were of a brown buff color. They had no tails, nor any hair at all on their buttocks, except about the anus; which, I presume Nature had placed there to defend them as they sat on the ground; for this posture they used, as well as lying down, and often stood on their hind feet. They climbed high trees, as nimbly as a squirrel, for they had strong extended claws before and behind, terminating in sharp points, and hooked. They would often spring, and bound, and leap with prodigious agility. The females were not so large as the males; they had long lank hair on their heads, and only a sort of down on the rest of their bodies, except about the anus, and pudenda. Their dugs hung between their forefeet, and often reached almost to the ground as they walked. The hair of both sexes was of several colors, brown, red, black, and yellow. Upon the whole, I never beheld in all my travels so disagreeable an animal, or one against which I naturally conceived so strong an antipathy. So that thinking I had seen enough, full of contempt and aversion, I got up and pursued the beaten road, hoping it might direct me to the cabin of some Indian. I had not gone far when I met one of these creatures full in my way, and coming up directly to me. The ugly monster, when he saw me, distorted several ways every feature of his visage, and stared as at an object he had never seen before; then approaching nearer, lifted up his forepaw, whether out of curiosity or mischief, I could not tell; but I drew my hanger, and gave him a good blow with the flat side of it; for I durst not strike him with the edge, fearing the inhabitants might be provoked against me, if they should come to know that I had killed or maimed any of their cattle. When the beast felt the smart, he drew back, and roared so loud, that a herd of at least forty came flocking about me from the near field, howling and making odious faces; but I ran to the body of a tree, and leaning my back against it, kept them off, by waving my hanger. Several of this cursed brood getting hold of the branches behind, leaped up into the tree, from whence they began to discharge their excrements on my head; however, I escaped pretty well, by sticking close to the stem of the tree, but was almost stifled with the filth, which fell about me on every side.

In the midst of this distress, I observed them all to run away on a sudden as fast as they could; at which I ventured to leave the tree, and pursue the road, wondering what it was that could put them into this fright. But looking on my left hand, I saw a horse walking softly in the field; which my persecutors having sooner discovered, was the cause of their flight. The horse started a little when he came near me, but soon recovering himself, looked full in my face with manifest tokens of wonder; he viewed my hands and feet, walking round me several times. I would have pursued my journey, but he placed himself directly in the way, yet looking with a very mild aspect, never offering the least violence. We stood gazing at each other for some time; at last I took the boldness, to reach my hand towards his neck, with a design to stroke it; using the common style and whistle of jockies when they are going to handle a strange horse. But this animal, seeming to receive my civilities with disdain, shook his head, and bent his brows, softly raising up his left forefoot to remove my hand. Then he neighed three or four times, but in so different a cadence, that I almost began to think he was speaking to himself in some language of his own.

While he and I were thus employed, another horse came up; who applying himself to the first in a very formal manner, they gently struck each other's right hoof before, neighing several times by turns, and varying the sound, which seemed to be almost articulate. They went some paces off, as if it were to confer together, walking side by side, backward and forward, like persons deliberating upon some affair of weight; but often turning their eyes towards me, as it were to watch that I might not escape. I was amazed to see such actions and behavior in brute beasts; and concluded with myself that if the inhabitants of this country were endued with a proportionable degree of reason, they must needs be the wisest people upon earth. This thought gave me so much comfort, that I resolved to go forward until I could discover some house or village, or meet with any of the natives, leaving the two horses to discourse together as they pleased. But the first, who was a dapple grey, observing me to steal off, neighed after me in so expressive a tone that I fancied myself to understand what he meant; whereupon I turned back, and came near him, to expect his farther commands; but concealing my fear as much as I could; for I began to be in some pain, how this adventure might terminate; and the reader will easily believe I did not much like my present situation.

The two horses came up close to me, looking with great earnestness upon my face and hands. The grey steed rubbed my hat all round with his right fore hoof, and discomposed it so much that I was forced to adjust it better, by taking it off, and settling it again; whereat both he and his companion (who was a brown bay) appeared to be much surprised; the latter felt the lappet of my coat, and finding it to hang loose about me, they both looked with new signs of wonder. He stroked my right hand, seeming to admire the softness, and color; but he squeezed it so hard between his hoof and his pastern, that I was forced to roar; after which they both touched me with all possible tenderness. They were under great perplexity about my shoes and stockings, which they felt very often, neighing to each other, and using various gestures, not unlike those of a philosopher, when he would attempt to solve some new and difficult phenomenon.

Upon the whole, the behavior of these animals was so orderly and rational, so acute and judicious, that I at last concluded, they must needs be magicians, who had thus metamorphosed themselves upon some design; and seeing a stranger in the way, were resolved to divert themselves with him; or perhaps were really amazed at the sight of a man so very different in habit, feature, and complexion from those who might probably live in so remote a climate. Upon the strength of this reasoning, I ventured to address them in the following manner: "Gentlemen, if you be conjurers, as I have good cause to believe, you can understand any language; therefore I make bold to let your worships know that I am a poor distressed Englishman, driven by his misfortunes upon your coast; and I entreat one of you, to let me ride upon his back, as if he were a real horse, to some house or village, where I can be relieved. In return of which favor, I will make you a present of this knife and bracelet" (taking them out of my pocket). The two creatures stood silent while I spoke, seeming to listen with great attention; and when I had ended, they neighed frequently towards each other, as if they were engaged in serious conversation. I plainly observed, that their language expressed the passions very well, and the words might with little pains be resolved into an alphabet more easily than the Chinese.

I could frequently distinguish the word *Yahoo*,[5] which was repeated by each of them several times; and although it were impossible for me to conjecture what it meant, yet while the two horses were busy in conversation, I endeavored to practice this word upon my tongue; and as soon as they were silent, I boldly pronounced "Yahoo" in a loud voice, imitating, at the same time, as near as I could, the neighing of a horse; at which they were both visibly surprised, and the grey repeated the same word twice, as if he meant to teach me the right accent, wherein I spoke after him as well as I could, and found myself perceivably to improve every time, although very far from any degree of perfection. Then the bay tried me with a second word, much harder to be pronounced; but reducing it to the English orthography, may be spelt thus, *Houyhnhnm.* I did not succeed in this so well as the former, but after two or three farther trials, I had better fortune; and they both appeared amazed at my capacity.

After some farther discourse, which I then conjectured might relate to me, the two friends took their leaves, with the same compliment of striking each other's hoof; and the grey made me signs that I should walk before him; wherein I thought it prudent to comply, till I could find a better director. When I offered to slacken my pace, he would cry, "Hhuun, Hhuun"; I guessed his meaning, and gave him to understand, as well as I could that I was weary, and not able to walk faster; upon which, he would stand a while to let me rest.

CHAPTER 2. *The Author conducted by a Houyhnhnm to his house. The house described. The Author's reception. The food of the Houyhnhnms. The Author in distress for want of meat is at last relieved. His manner of feeding in that country.*

Having traveled about three miles, we came to a long kind of building, made of timber, stuck in the ground, and wattled across; the roof was low, and covered with straw. I now began to be a little comforted, and took out some toys, which travelers usually carry for presents to the savage Indians of America and other parts, in hopes the people of the house would be thereby encouraged to receive me kindly. The horse made me a sign to go in first; it was a large room with a smooth clay floor, and a rack and manger extending the whole length on one side. There were three nags, and two mares, not eating, but some of them sitting down upon their hams, which I very much wondered at; but wondered more to see the rest employed in domestic business. The last seemed but ordinary cattle; however this confirmed my first opinion, that a people who could so far civilize brute animals must needs excel in wisdom all the nations of the world. The grey came in just after, and thereby prevented any ill treatment, which the others might

5. Perhaps compounded from two expressions of disgust, *yah* and *ugh* (or *hoo*), common in the 18th century.

have given me. He neighed to them several times in a style of authority, and received answers.

Beyond this room there were three others, reaching the length of the house, to which you passed through three doors, opposite to each other, in the manner of a vista; we went through the second room towards the third; here the grey walked in first, beckoning me to attend.[6] I waited in the second room, and got ready my presents, for the master and mistress of the house; they were two knives, three bracelets of false pearl, a small looking glass and a bead necklace. The horse neighed three or four times, and I waited to hear some answers in a human voice, but I heard no other returns than in the same dialect, only one or two a little shriller than his. I began to think that this house must belong to some person of great note among them, because there appeared so much ceremony before I could gain admittance. But, that a man of quality should be served all by horses, was beyond my comprehension. I feared my brain was disturbed by my sufferings and misfortunes; I roused myself, and looked about me in the room where I was left alone; this was furnished as the first, only after a more elegant manner. I rubbed my eyes often, but the same objects still occurred. I pinched my arms and sides, to awaken myself, hoping I might be in a dream. I then absolutely concluded that all these appearances could be nothing else but necromancy and magic. But I had no time to pursue these reflections; for the grey horse came to the door, and made me a sign to follow him into the third room; where I saw a very comely mare, together with a colt and foal, sitting on their haunches, upon mats of straw, not unartfully made, and perfectly neat and clean.

The mare soon after my entrance, rose from her mat, and coming up close, after having nicely observed my hands and face, gave me a most contemptuous look; then turning to the horse, I heard the word Yahoo often repeated betwixt them; the meaning of which word I could not then comprehend, although it were the first I had learned to pronounce; but I was soon better informed, to my everlasting mortification: for the horse beckoning to me with his head, and repeating the word, "Hhuun, Hhuun," as he did upon the road, which I understood was to attend him, led me out into a kind of court, where was another building at some distance from the house. Here we entered, and I saw three of those detestable creatures, which I first met after my landing, feeding upon roots, and the flesh of some animals, which I afterwards found to be that of asses and dogs, and now and then a cow dead by accident or disease. They were all tied by the neck with strong withes, fastened to a beam; they held their food between the claws of their forefeet, and tore it with their teeth.

The master horse ordered a sorrel nag, one of his servants, to untie the largest of these animals, and take him into a yard. The beast and I were brought close together; and our countenances diligently compared, both by master and servant, who thereupon repeated several times the word "Yahoo." My horror and astonishment are not to be described, when I observed, in this abominable animal, a perfect human figure; the face of it indeed was flat and broad, the nose depressed, the lips large, and the mouth wide; but these differences are common to all savage nations, where the lineaments of the countenance are distorted by the natives suffering their infants to lie

6. To wait. "Vista": a long, open corridor.

groveling on the earth, or by carrying them on their backs, nuzzling with their face against the mother's shoulders. The forefeet of the Yahoo differed from my hands in nothing else but the length of the nails, the coarseness and brownness of the palms, and the hairiness on the backs. There was the same resemblance between our feet, with the same differences, which I knew very well, although the horses did not, because of my shoes and stockings; the same in every part of our bodies, except as to hairiness and color, which I have already described.

The great difficulty that seemed to stick with the two horses was to see the rest of my body so very different from that of a Yahoo, for which I was obliged to my clothes, whereof they had no conception; the sorrel nag offered me a root, which he held (after their manner, as we shall describe in its proper place) between his hoof and pastern; I took it in my hand, and having smelled it, returned it to him again as civilly as I could. He brought out of the Yahoo's kennel a piece of ass's flesh, but it smelled so offensively that I turned from it with loathing; he then threw it to the Yahoo, by whom it was greedily devoured. He afterwards showed me a wisp of hay, and a fetlock full of oats; but I shook my head, to signify that neither of these were food for me. And indeed, I now apprehended that I must absolutely starve, if I did not get to some of my own species; for as to those filthy Yahoos, although there were few greater lovers of mankind, at that time, than myself, yet I confess I never saw any sensitive being so detestable on all accounts; and the more I came near them, the more hateful they grew, while I stayed in that country. This the master horse observed by my behavior, and therefore sent the Yahoo back to his kennel. He then put his forehoof to his mouth, at which I was much surprised, although he did it with ease, and with a motion that appeared perfectly natural; and made other signs to know what I would eat; but I could not return him such an answer as he was able to apprehend; and if he had understood me, I did not see how it was possible to contrive any way for finding myself nourishment. While we were thus engaged, I observed a cow passing by; whereupon I pointed to her, and expressed a desire to let me go and milk her. This had its effect; for he led me back into the house, and ordered a mare-servant to open a room, where a good store of milk lay in earthen and wooden vessels, after a very orderly and cleanly manner. She gave me a large bowl full, of which I drank very heartily, and found myself well refreshed.

About noon I saw coming towards the house a kind of vehicle, drawn like a sledge by four Yahoos. There was in it an old steed, who seemed to be of quality; he alighted with his hind feet forward, having by accident got a hurt in his left forefoot. He came to dine with our horse, who received him with great civility. They dined in the best room, and had oats boiled in milk for the second course, which the old horse eat warm, but the rest cold. Their mangers were placed circular in the middle of the room, and divided into several partitions, round which they sat on their haunches upon bosses of straw. In the middle was a large rack with angles answering to every partition of the manger. So that each horse and mare eat their own hay, and their own mash of oats and milk, with much decency and regularity. The behavior of the young colt and foal appeared very modest; and that of the master and mistress extremely cheerful and complaisant to their guest. The grey ordered me to stand by him; and much discourse passed between him and his friend concerning me, as I found by the stranger's often looking on me, and the frequent repetition of the word Yahoo.

I happened to wear my gloves; which the master grey observing, seemed perplexed; discovering signs of wonder what I had done to my forefeet; he put his hoof three or four times to them, as if he would signify, that I should reduce them to their former shape, which I presently did, pulling off both my gloves, and putting them into my pocket. This occasioned farther talk, and I saw the company was pleased with my behavior, whereof I soon found the good effects. I was ordered to speak the few words I understood; and while they were at dinner, the master taught me the names for oats, milk, fire, water, and some others which I could readily pronounce after him, having from my youth a great facility in learning languages.

When dinner was done, the master horse took me aside, and by signs and words made me understand the concern he was in that I had nothing to eat. Oats in their tongue are called *hlunnh*. This word I pronounced two or three times; for although I had refused them at first, yet upon second thoughts, I considered that I could contrive to make a kind of bread, which might be sufficient with milk to keep me alive, till I could make my escape to some other country, and to creatures of my own species. The horse immediately ordered a white mare-servant of his family to bring me a good quantity of oats in a sort of wooden tray. These I heated before the fire as well as I could, and rubbed them till the husks came off, which I made a shift to winnow from the grain; I ground and beat them between two stones, then took water, and made them into a paste or cake, which I toasted at the fire, and eat warm with milk. It was at first a very insipid diet, although common enough in many parts of Europe, but grew tolerable by time; and having been often reduced to hard fare in my life, this was not the first experiment I had made how easily nature is satisfied. And I cannot but observe that I never had one hour's sickness, while I staid in this island. It is true, I sometimes made a shift to catch a rabbit, or bird, by springes[7] made of Yahoos' hairs; and I often gathered wholesome herbs, which I boiled, or eat as salads with my bread; and now and then, for a rarity, I made a little butter, and drank the whey. I was at first at a great loss for salt; but custom soon reconciled the want of it; and I am confident that the frequent use of salt among us is an effect of luxury, and was first introduced only as a provocative to drink; except where it is necessary for preserving of flesh in long voyages, or in places remote from great markets. For we observe no animal to be fond of it but man;[8] and as to myself, when I left this country, it was a great while before I could endure the taste of it in anything that I eat.

This is enough to say upon the subject of my diet, wherewith other travelers fill their books, as if the readers were personally concerned whether we fare well or ill. However, it was necessary to mention this matter, lest the world should think it impossible that I could find sustenance for three years in such a country, and among such inhabitants.

When it grew towards evening, the master horse ordered a place for me to lodge in; it was but six yards from the house, and separated from the stable of the Yahoos. Here I got some straw, and covering myself with my own

7. Snares.
8. Gulliver is, of course, in error; many animals require salt.

clothes, slept very sound. But I was in a short time better accommodated, as the reader shall know hereafter, when I come to treat more particularly about my way of living.

CHAPTER 3. *The Author studious to learn the language, the Houyhnhnm his master assists in teaching him. The language described. Several Houyhnhnms of quality come out of curiosity to see the Author. He gives his master a short account of his voyage.*

My principal endeavor was to learn the language, which my master (for so I shall henceforth call him) and his children, and every servant of his house were desirous to teach me. For they looked upon it as a prodigy, that a brute animal should discover such marks of a rational creature. I pointed to every-thing, and enquired the name of it, which I wrote down in my journal book when I was alone, and corrected my bad accent, by desiring those of the family to pronounce it often. In this employment, a sorrel nag, one of the under servants, was very ready to assist me.

In speaking, they pronounce through the nose and throat, and their lan-guage approaches nearest to the High Dutch or German, of any I know in Europe; but is much more graceful and significant. The Emperor Charles V made almost the same observation, when he said, that if he were to speak to his horse, it should be in High Dutch.[9]

The curiosity and impatience of my master were so great, that he spent many hours of his leisure to instruct me. He was convinced (as he afterwards told me) that I must be a Yahoo, but my teachableness, civility, and clean-liness astonished him; which were qualities altogether so opposite to those animals. He was most perplexed about my clothes, reasoning sometimes with himself whether they were a part of my body; for I never pulled them off till the family were asleep, and got them on before they waked in the morning. My master was eager to learn from whence I came; how I acquired those appearances of reason, which I discovered in all my actions; and to know my story from my own mouth, which he hoped he should soon do by the great proficiency I made in learning and pronouncing their words and sentences. To help my memory, I formed all I learned into the English alphabet, and writ the words down with the translations. This last, after some time, I ven-tured to do in my master's presence. It cost me much trouble to explain to him what I was doing; for the inhabitants have not the least idea of books or literature.

In about ten weeks time I was able to understand most of his questions; and in three months could give him some tolerable answers. He was extremely curious to know from what part of the country I came, and how I was taught to imitate a rational creature; because the Yahoos (whom he saw I exactly resembled in my head, hands, and face, that were only visible) with some appearance of cunning, and the strongest disposition to mischief, were observed to be the most unteachable of all brutes. I answered that I came over the sea, from a far place, with many others of my own kind, in a great hollow vessel made of the bodies of trees; that my companions forced me to

---

9. The emperor is supposed to have said that he would speak to his God in Spanish, to his mistress in Italian, and to his horse in German.

land on this coast, and then left me to shift for myself. It was with some difficulty, and by the help of many signs, that I brought him to understand me. He replied that I must needs be mistaken, or that I *said the thing which was not.* (For they have no word in their language to express lying or falsehood.) He knew it was impossible that there could be a country beyond the sea, or that a parcel of brutes could move a wooden vessel whither they pleased upon water. He was sure no Houyhnhnm alive could make such a vessel, or would trust Yahoos to manage it.

The word Houyhnhnm, in their tongue, signifies a Horse; and in its etymology, the Perfection of Nature. I told my master that I was at a loss for expression, but would improve as fast as I could; and hoped in a short time I should be able to tell him wonders. He was pleased to direct his own mare, his colt, and foal, and the servants of the family to take all opportunities of instructing me; and every day for two or three hours, he was at the same pains himself. Several horses and mares of quality in the neighborhood came often to our house, upon the report spread of a wonderful Yahoo, that could speak like a Houyhnhnm, and seemed in his words and actions to discover some glimmerings of reason. These delighted to converse with me; they put many questions, and received such answers as I was able to return. By all which advantages, I made so great a progress, that in five months from my arrival, I understood whatever was spoke, and could express myself tolerably well.

The Houyhnhnms who came to visit my master, out of a design of seeing and talking with me, could hardly believe me to be a right Yahoo, because my body had a different covering from others of my kind. They were astonished to observe me without the usual hair or skin, except on my head, face, and hands; but I discovered that secret to my master, upon an accident, which happened about a fortnight before.

I have already told the reader, that every night when the family were gone to bed, it was my custom to strip and cover myself with my clothes; it happened one morning early, that my master sent for me, by the sorrel nag, who was his valet; when he came, I was fast asleep, my clothes fallen off on one side, and my shirt above my waist. I awaked at the noise he made, and observed him to deliver his message in some disorder; after which he went to my master, and in a great fright gave him a very confused account of what he had seen. This I presently discovered; for going as soon as I was dressed, to pay my attendance upon his honor, he asked me the meaning of what his servant had reported; that I was not the same thing when I slept as I appeared to be at other times; that his valet assured him, some part of me was white, some yellow, at least not so white, and some brown.

I had hitherto concealed the secret of my dress, in order to distinguish myself as much as possible, from that cursed race of Yahoos; but now I found it in vain to do so any longer. Besides, I considered that my clothes and shoes would soon wear out, which already were in a declining condition, and must be supplied by some contrivance from the hides of Yahoos, or other brutes; whereby the whole secret would be known. I therefore told my master, that in the country from whence I came, those of my kind always covered their bodies with the hairs of certain animals prepared by art, as well for decency, as to avoid inclemencies of air both hot and cold; of which, as to my own person I would give him immediate conviction, if he pleased to command me; only desiring his excuse, if I did not expose those parts that Nature taught us to conceal. He said, my discourse was all very strange, but especially the last part; for he could not understand why Nature should teach us to conceal what Nature had given. That neither himself nor family were ashamed of any parts of their bodies; but however I might do as I pleased. Whereupon, I first unbuttoned my coat, and pulled it off. I did the same with my waistcoat; I drew off my shoes, stockings, and breeches. I let my shirt down to my waist, and drew up the bottom, fastening it like a girdle about my middle to hide my nakedness.

My master observed the whole performance with great signs of curiosity and admiration. He took up all my clothes in his pastern, one piece after another, and examined them diligently; he then stroked my body very gently, and looked round me several times; after which he said, it was plain I must be a perfect Yahoo; but that I differed very much from the rest of my species, in the whiteness and smoothness of my skin, my want of hair in several parts of my body, the shape and shortness of my claws behind and before, and my affectation of walking continually on my two hinder feet. He desired to see no more; and gave me leave to put on my clothes again, for I was shuddering with cold.

I expressed my uneasiness at his giving me so often the appellation of Yahoo, an odious animal, for which I had so utter an hatred and contempt. I begged he would forbear applying that word to me, and take the same order in his family, and among his friends whom he suffered to see me. I requested likewise, that the secret of my having a false covering to my body might be known to none but himself, at least as long as my present clothing should last; for as to what the sorrel nag his valet had observed, his honor might command him to conceal it.

All this my master very graciously consented to; and thus the secret was kept till my clothes began to wear out, which I was forced to supply by several contrivances, that shall hereafter be mentioned. In the meantime, he desired I would go on with my utmost diligence to learn their language, because he was more astonished at my capacity for speech and reason, than at the figure of my body, whether it were covered or no; adding that he waited with some impatience to hear the wonders which I promised to tell him.

From thenceforward he doubled the pains he had been at to instruct me; he brought me into all company, and made them treat me with civility, because, as he told them privately, this would put me into good humor, and make me more diverting.

Every day when I waited on him, beside the trouble he was at in teaching, he would ask me several questions concerning myself, which I answered as well as I could; and by those means he had already received some general ideas, although very imperfect. It would be tedious to relate the several steps, by which I advanced to a more regular conversation, but the first account I gave of myself in any order and length was to this purpose:

That, I came from a very far country, as I already had attempted to tell him, with about fifty more of my own species; that we traveled upon the seas, in a great hollow vessel made of wood, and larger than his honor's house. I described the ship to him in the best terms I could; and explained by the help of my handkerchief displayed, how it was driven forward by the wind. That, upon a quarrel among us, I was set on shore on this coast, where I walked forward without knowing whither, till he delivered me from the persecution of those execrable Yahoos. He asked me who made the ship, and how it was possible that the Houyhnhnms of my country would leave it to the management of brutes? My answer was that I durst proceed no farther in my relation, unless he would give me his word and honor that he would not be offended; and then I would tell him the wonders I had so often promised. He agreed; and I went on by assuring him, that the ship was made by creatures like myself, who in all the countries I had traveled, as well as in my own, were the only governing, rational animals; and that upon my arrival hither, I was as much astonished to see the Houyhnhnms act like rational beings, as he or his friends could be in finding some marks of reason in a creature he was pleased to call a Yahoo; to which I owned my resemblance in every part, but could not account for their degenerate and brutal nature. I said farther, that if good fortune ever restored me to my native country, to relate my travels hither, as I resolved to do, everybody would believe that I *said the thing which was not,* that I invented the story out of my own head; and with all possible respect to himself, his family, and friends, and under his promise of not being offended, our countrymen would hardly think it probable, that a Houyhnhnm should be the presiding creature of a nation, and a Yahoo the brute.

CHAPTER 4. *The Houyhnhnms' notion of truth and falsehood. The Author's discourse disapproved by his master. The Author gives a more particular account of himself, and the accidents of his voyage.*

My master heard me with great appearances of uneasiness in his countenance; because *doubting* or *not believing* are so little known in this country, that the inhabitants cannot tell how to behave themselves under such circumstances. And I remember in frequent discourses with my master concerning the nature of manhood, in other parts of the world, having occasion to talk of *lying* and *false representation,* it was with much difficulty that he comprehended what I meant; although he had otherwise a most acute judgment. For he argued thus: that the use of speech was to make us understand one another, and to receive information of facts; now if anyone *said the thing which was not,* these ends were defeated; because I cannot properly be said to understand him; and I am so far from receiving information, that he leaves me worse than in ignorance; for I am led to believe a thing *black* when it is *white,* and *short* when it is *long.* And these were all the notions he had concerning the faculty of *lying,* so perfectly well understood, and so universally practiced among human creatures.

To return from this digression; when I asserted that the Yahoos were the only governing animals in my country, which my master said was altogether past his conception, he desired to know, whether we had Houyhnhnms among us, and what was their employment. I told him we had great numbers; that in summer they grazed in the fields, and in winter were kept in houses, with hay and oats, where Yahoo servants were employed to rub their skins smooth, comb their manes, pick their feet, serve them with food, and make their beds. "I understand you well," said my master; "it is now very plain from all you have spoken, that whatever share of reason the Yahoos pretend to, the Houyhnhnms are your masters; I heartily wish our Yahoos would be so tractable." I begged his honor would please to excuse me from proceeding any farther, because I was very certain that the account he expected from me would be highly displeasing. But he insisted in commanding me to let him know the best and the worst; I told him he should be obeyed. I owned that the Houyhnhnms among us, whom we called Horses, were the most generous[1] and comely animal we had; that they excelled in strength and swiftness; and when they belonged to persons of quality, employed in traveling, racing, and drawing chariots, they were treated with much kindness and care, till they fell into diseases, or became foundered in the feet; but then they were sold, and used to all kind of drudgery till they died; after which their skins were stripped and sold for what they were worth, and their bodies left to be devoured by dogs and birds of prey. But the common race of horses had not so good fortune, being kept by farmers and carriers, and other mean people, who put them to greater labor, and feed them worse. I described as well as I could, our way of riding; the shape and use of a bridle, a saddle, a spur, and a whip; of harness and wheels. I added, that we fastened plates of a certain hard substance called iron at the bottom of their feet, to preserve their hoofs from being broken by the stony ways on which we often traveled.

My master, after some expressions of great indignation, wondered how we dared to venture upon a Houyhnhnm's back; for he was sure, that the weakest servant in his house would be able to shake off the strongest Yahoo; or by lying down, and rolling upon his back, squeeze the brute to death. I answered that our horses were trained up from three or four years old to the several uses we intended them for; that if any of them proved intolerably vicious, they were employed for carriages; that they were severely beaten while they were young for any mischievous tricks; that the males, designed for the common use of riding or draught, were generally castrated about two years after their birth, to take down their spirits, and make them more tame and gentle; that they were indeed sensible of rewards and punishments; but his honor would please to consider that they had not the least tincture of reason any more than the Yahoos in this country.

It put me to the pains of many circumlocutions to give my master a right idea of what I spoke; for their language doth not abound in variety of words, because their wants and passions are fewer than among us. But it is impossible to express his noble resentment at our savage treatment of the Houyhnhnm race; particularly after I had explained the manner and use of castrating horses among us, to hinder them from propagating their kind, and to render them more servile. He said, if it were possible there could be any country where Yahoos alone were endued with reason, they certainly must be the governing animal, because reason will in time always prevail against brutal strength. But, considering the frame of our bodies, and especially of mine, he thought no creature of equal bulk was so ill-contrived for employing that reason in the common offices of life; whereupon he desired to know whether those among whom I lived resembled me or the Yahoos of his country. I assured him that I was as well shaped as most of my age; but the younger and the females were much more soft and tender, and the skins of the latter generally as white as milk. He said I differed indeed from other Yahoos, being

1. Noble.

much more cleanly, and not altogether so deformed; but in point of real advantage, he thought I differed for the worse. That my nails were of no use either to my fore or hinder feet; as to my forefeet, he could not properly call them by that name, for he never observed me to walk upon them; that they were too soft to bear the ground; that I generally went with them uncovered, neither was the covering I sometimes wore on them of the same shape, or so strong as that on my feet behind. That I could not walk with any security; for if either of my hinder feet slipped, I must inevitably fall. He then began to find fault with other parts of my body; the flatness of my face, the prominence of my nose, my eyes placed directly in front, so that I could not look on either side without turning my head; that I was not able to feed myself without lifting one of my forefeet to my mouth; and therefore nature had placed those joints to answer that necessity. He knew not what could be the use of those several clefts and divisions in my feet behind; that these were too soft to bear the hardness and sharpness of stones without a covering made from the skin of some other brute; that my whole body wanted a fence against heat and cold, which I was forced to put on and off every day with tediousness and trouble. And lastly, that he observed every animal in his country naturally to abhor the Yahoos, whom the weaker avoided, and the stronger drove from them. So that supposing us to have the gift of reason, he could not see how it were possible to cure that natural antipathy which every creature discovered against us; nor consequently, how we could tame and render them serviceable. However, he would (as he said) debate the matter no farther, because he was more desirous to know my own story, the country where I was born, and the several actions and events of my life before I came hither.

I assured him how extremely desirous I was that he should be satisfied in every point; but I doubted much whether it would be possible for me to explain myself on several subjects whereof his honor could have no conception, because I saw nothing in his country to which I could resemble them. That however, I would do my best, and strive to express myself by similitudes, humbly desiring his assistance when I wanted proper words; which he was pleased to promise me.

I said, my birth was of honest parents, in an island called England, which was remote from this country, as many days journey as the strongest of his honor's servants could travel in the annual course of the sun. That I was bred a surgeon, whose trade it is to cure wounds and hurts in the body, got by accident or violence. That my country was governed by a female man, whom we called a queen. That I left it to get riches, whereby I might maintain myself and family when I should return. That in my last voyage, I was Commander of the ship and had about fifty Yahoos under me, many of which died at sea, and I was forced to supply them by others picked out from several nations. That our ship was twice in danger of being sunk; the first time by a great storm, and the second, by striking against a rock. Here my master interposed, by asking me, how I could persuade strangers out of different countries to venture with me, after the losses I had sustained, and the hazards I had run. I said, they were fellows of desperate fortunes, forced to fly from the places of their birth, on account of their poverty or their crimes. Some were undone by lawsuits; others spent all they had in drinking, whoring, and gaming; others fled for treason; many for murder, theft, poisoning, robbery, perjury, forgery, coining false money; for committing rapes or sodomy; for flying from their colors, or deserting to the enemy; and most of them had broken prison. None of these durst return to their native countries for fear of being hanged, or of starving in a jail; and therefore were under a necessity of seeking a livelihood in other places.

During this discourse, my master was pleased often to interrupt me. I had made use of many circumlocutions in describing to him the nature of the several crimes, for which most of our crew had been forced to fly their country. This labor took up several days conversation before he was able to comprehend me. He was wholly at a loss to know what could be the use or necessity of practicing those vices. To clear up which I endeavored to give him some ideas of the desire of power and riches; of the terrible effects of lust, intemperance, malice, and envy. All this I was forced to define and describe by putting of cases, and making suppositions. After which, like one whose imagination was struck with something never seen or heard of before, he would lift up his eyes with amazement and indignation. Power, government, war, law, punishment, and a thousand other things had no terms, wherein that language could express them; which made the difficulty almost insuperable to give my master any conception of what I meant; but being of an excellent understanding, much improved by contemplation and converse, he at last arrived at a competent knowledge of what human nature in our parts of the world is capable to perform; and desired I would give him some particular account of that land, which we call Europe, especially, of my own country.

CHAPTER 5. *The Author, at his master's commands, informs him of the state of England. The causes of war among the princes of Europe. The Author begins to explain the English Constitution.*

The reader may please to observe that the following extract of many conversations I had with my master contains a summary of the most material points, which were discoursed at several times for above two years; his honor often desiring fuller satisfaction as I farther improved in the Houyhnhnm tongue. I laid before him, as well as I could, the whole state of Europe; I discoursed of trade and manufactures, of arts and sciences; and the answers I gave to all the questions he made, as they arose upon several subjects, were a fund of conversation not to be exhausted. But I shall here only set down the substance of what passed between us concerning my own country, reducing it into order as well as I can, without any regard to time or other circumstances, while I strictly adhere to truth. My only concern is that I shall hardly be able to do justice to my master's arguments and expressions; which must needs suffer by my want of capacity, as well as by a translation into our barbarous English.

In obedience therefore to his honor's commands, I related to him the Revolution under the Prince of Orange; the long war with France entered into by the said Prince, and renewed by his successor the present queen; wherein the greatest powers of Christendom were engaged, and which still continued. I computed at his request, that about a million of Yahoos might have been killed in the whole progress of it; and perhaps a hundred or more cities taken, and five times as many ships burned or sunk.[2]

---

2. Gulliver relates recent English history: the Glorious Revolution (1688–89) and the War of Spanish Succession (1703–13). He greatly exaggerates the casualties in the war.

He asked me what were the usual causes or motives that made one country to go to war with another. I answered, they were innumerable; but I should only mention a few of the chief. Sometimes the ambition of princes, who never think they have land or people enough to govern; sometimes the corruption of ministers, who engage their master in a war in order to stifle or divert the clamor of the subjects against their evil administration. Difference in opinions hath cost many millions of lives; for instance, whether flesh be bread, or bread be flesh; whether the juice of a certain berry be blood or wine; whether whistling be a vice or a virtue; whether it be better to kiss a post, or throw it into the fire; what is the best color for a coat, whether black, white, red, or grey; and whether it should be long or short, narrow or wide, dirty or clean;[3] with many more. Neither are any wars so furious and bloody, or of so long continuance, as those occasioned by difference in opinion, especially if it be in things indifferent.[4]

Sometimes the quarrel between two princes is to decide which of them shall dispossess a third of his dominions, where neither of them pretend to any right. Sometimes one prince quarreleth with another, for fear the other should quarrel with him. Sometimes a war is entered upon, because the enemy is too strong, and sometimes because he is too weak. Sometimes our neighbors want the things which we have, or have the things which we want; and we both fight, till they take ours or give us theirs. It is a very justifiable cause of war to invade a country after the people have been wasted by famine, destroyed by pestilence, or embroiled by factions amongst themselves. It is justifiable to enter into a war against our nearest ally, when one of his towns lies convenient for us, or a territory of land, that would render our dominions round and compact. If a prince send forces into a nation, where the people are poor and ignorant, he may lawfully put half of them to death, and make slaves of the rest, in order to civilize and reduce them from their barbarous way of living. It is a very kingly, honorable, and frequent practice, when one prince desires the assistance of another to secure him against an invasion, that the assistant, when he hath driven out the invader, should seize on the dominions himself, and kill, imprison, or banish the prince he came to relieve. Alliance by blood or marriage is a sufficient cause of war between princes; and the nearer the kindred is, the greater is their disposition to quarrel. Poor nations are hungry, and rich nations are proud; and pride and hunger will ever be at variance. For these reasons, the trade of a soldier is held the most honorable of all others: because a soldier is a Yahoo hired to kill in cold blood as many of his own species, who have never offended him, as possibly he can.

There is likewise a kind of beggarly princes in Europe, not able to make war by themselves, who hire out their troops to richer nations for so much a day to each man; of which they keep three fourths to themselves, and it is the best part of their maintenance; such are those in many northern parts of Europe.[5]

"What you have told me," said my master, "upon the subject of war, doth indeed discover most admirably the effects of that reason you pretend to. However, it is happy that the shame is greater than the danger; and that

---

3. Gulliver refers to the religious controversies of the Reformation and Counter-Reformation: the doctrine of transubstantiation, the use of music in church services, the veneration of the crucifix, and the wearing of priestly vestments.
4. Of little consequence.
5. A satiric glance at George I, who, as elector of Hanover, had dealt in this trade.

Nature hath left you utterly uncapable of doing much mischief; for your mouths lying flat with your faces, you can hardly bite each other to any purpose, unless by consent. Then, as to the claws upon your feet before and behind, they are so short and tender, that one of our Yahoos would drive a dozen of yours before him. And therefore in recounting the numbers of those who have been killed in battle, I cannot but think that you have *said the thing which is not*."

I could not forbear shaking my head and smiling a little at his ignorance. And, being no stranger to the art of war, I gave him a description of cannons, culverins, muskets, carabines, pistols, bullets, powder, swords, bayonets, battles, sieges, retreats, attacks, undermines, countermines, bombardments, sea fights; ships sunk with a thousand men; twenty thousand killed on each side; dying groans, limbs flying in the air; smoke, noise, confusion, trampling to death under horses' feet; flight, pursuit, victory; fields strewed with carcasses left for food to dogs, and wolves, and birds of prey; plundering, stripping, ravishing, burning, and destroying. And, to set forth the valor of my own dear countrymen, I assured him that I had seen them blow up a hundred enemies at once in a siege, and as many in a ship; and beheld the dead bodies drop down in pieces from the clouds, to the great diversion of all the spectators.

I was going on to more particulars, when my master commanded me silence. He said, whoever understood the nature of Yahoos might easily believe it possible for so vile an animal, to be capable of every action I had named, if their strength and cunning equaled their malice. But, as my discourse had increased his abhorrence of the whole species, so he found it gave him a disturbance in his mind, to which he was wholly a stranger before. He thought his ears being used to such abominable words, might by degrees admit them with less detestation. That, although he hated the Yahoos of this country, yet he no more blamed them for their odious qualities, than he did a *gnnayh* (a bird of prey) for its cruelty, or a sharp stone for cutting his hoof. But, when a creature pretending to reason could be capable of such enormities, he dreaded lest the corruption of that faculty might be worse than brutality itself. He seemed therefore confident, that instead of reason, we were only possessed of some quality fitted to increase our natural vices; as the reflection from a troubled stream returns the image of an ill-shapen body, not only larger, but more distorted.

He added that he had heard too much upon the subject of war, both in this and some former discourses. There was another point which a little perplexed him at present. I had said that some of our crew left their country on account of being ruined by law: that I had already explained the meaning of the word; but he was at a loss how it should come to pass, that the law which was intended for every man's preservation, should be any man's ruin. Therefore he desired to be farther satisfied what I meant by law, and the dispensers thereof, according to the present practice in my own country; because he thought Nature and Reason were sufficient guides for a reasonable animal, as we pretended to be, in showing us what we ought to do, and what to avoid.

I assured his honor that law was a science wherein I had not much conversed, further than by employing advocates, in vain, upon some injustices that had been done me. However, I would give him all the satisfaction I was able.

I said there was a society of men among us, bred up from their youth in the art of proving by words multiplied for the purpose, that white is black, and black is white, according as they are paid. To this society all the rest of the people are slaves.

"For example. If my neighbor hath a mind to my cow, he hires a lawyer to prove that he ought to have my cow from me. I must then hire another to defend my right; it being against all rules of law that any man should be allowed to speak for himself. Now in this case, I who am the true owner lie under two great disadvantages. First, my lawyer being practiced almost from his cradle in defending falsehood is quite out of his element when he would be an advocate for justice, which as an office unnatural, he always attempts with great awkwardness, if not with ill-will. The second disadvantage is that my lawyer must proceed with great caution, or else he will be reprimanded by the judges, and abhorred by his brethren, as one who would lessen the practice of the law. And therefore I have but two methods to preserve my cow. The first is to gain over my adversary's lawyer with a double fee; who will then betray his client, by insinuating that he hath justice on his side. The second way is for my lawyer to make my cause appear as unjust as he can; by allowing the cow to belong to my adversary; and this if it be skillfully done, will certainly bespeak the favor of the bench.

"Now, your honor is to know that these judges are persons appointed to decide all controversies of property, as well as for the trial of criminals; and picked out from the most dextrous lawyers who are grown old or lazy; and having been biased all their lives against truth and equity, lie under such a fatal necessity of favoring fraud, perjury, and oppression, that I have known some of them to have refused a large bribe from the side where justice lay, rather than injure the faculty,[6] by doing anything unbecoming their nature or their office.

"It is a maxim among these lawyers, that whatever hath been done before may legally be done again; and therefore they take special care to record all the decisions formerly made against common justice and the general reason of mankind. These, under the name of *precedents*, they produce as authorities to justify the most iniquitous opinions; and the judges never fail of directing accordingly.

"In pleading, they studiously avoid entering into the merits of the cause; but are loud, violent, and tedious in dwelling upon all circumstances which are not to the purpose. For instance, in the case already mentioned, they never desire to know what claim or title my adversary hath to my cow; but whether the said cow were red or black; her horns long or short; whether the field I graze her in be round or square; whether she were milked at home or abroad; what diseases she is subject to, and the like. After which they consult precedents, adjourn the cause, from time to time, and in ten, twenty, or thirty years come to an issue.

"It is likewise to be observed, that this society hath a peculiar cant and jargon of their own, that no other mortal can understand, and wherein all their laws are written, which they take special care to multiply; whereby they have wholly confounded the very essence of truth and falsehood, of right and wrong; so that it will take thirty years to decide whether the field, left me by my ancestors for six generations, belong to me, or to a stranger three hundred miles off.

6. Profession.

"In the trial of persons accused for crimes against the state, the method is much more short and commendable: the judge first sends to sound the disposition of those in power; after which he can easily hang or save the criminal, strictly preserving all the forms of law."

Here my master interposing said it was a pity that creatures endowed with such prodigious abilities of mind as these lawyers, by the description I gave of them, must certainly be, were not rather encouraged to be instructors of others in wisdom and knowledge. In answer to which, I assured his honor that in all points out of their own trade, they were usually the most ignorant and stupid generation among us, the most despicable in common conversation, avowed enemies to all knowledge and learning; and equally disposed to pervert the general reason of mankind, in every other subject of discourse as in that of their own profession.

CHAPTER 6. *A continuation of the state of England, under Queen Anne. The character of a first minister in the courts of Europe.*

My master was yet wholly at a loss to understand what motives could incite this race of lawyers to perplex, disquiet, and weary themselves by engaging in a confederacy of injustice, merely for the sake of injuring their fellow animals; neither could he comprehend what I meant in saying they did it for hire. Whereupon I was at much pains to describe to him the use of money, the materials it was made of, and the value of the metals; that when a Yahoo had got a great store of this precious substance, he was able to purchase whatever he had a mind to; the finest clothing, the noblest houses, great tracts of land, the most costly meats and drinks; and have his choice of the most beautiful females. Therefore since money alone was able to perform all these feats, our Yahoos thought they could never have enough of it to spend or to save, as they found themselves inclined from their natural bent either to profusion or avarice. That the rich man enjoyed the fruit of the poor man's labor, and the latter were a thousand to one in proportion to the former. That the bulk of our people was forced to live miserably, by laboring every day for small wages to make a few live plentifully. I enlarged myself much on these and many other particulars to the same purpose, but his honor was still to seek,[7] for he went upon a supposition that all animals had a title to their share in the productions of the earth; and especially those who presided over the rest. Therefore he desired I would let him know what these costly meats were, and how any of us happened to want[8] them. Whereupon I enumerated as many sorts as came into my head, with the various methods of dressing them, which could not be done without sending vessels by sea to every part of the world, as well for liquors to drink, as for sauces, and innumerable other conveniencies. I assured him, that this whole globe of earth must be at least three times gone round, before one of our better female Yahoos could get her breakfast, or a cup to put it in. He said, "That must needs be a miserable country which cannot furnish food for its own inhabitants." But what he chiefly wondered at, was how such vast tracts of ground as I described, should be wholly without fresh water, and the people put to the necessity of sending over the sea for drink. I replied that England (the dear place of my nativity) was computed to produce three times the quantity

7. Still did not understand.　　　　　　　　　8. Lack.

of food, more than its inhabitants are able to consume, as well as liquors extracted from grain, or pressed out of the fruit of certain trees, which made excellent drink; and the same proportion in every other convenience of life. But, in order to feed the luxury and intemperance of the males, and the vanity of the females, we sent away the greatest part of our necessary things to other countries, from whence in return we brought the materials of diseases, folly, and vice, to spend among ourselves. Hence it follows of necessity, that vast numbers of our people are compelled to seek their livelihood by begging, robbing, stealing, cheating, pimping, forswearing, flattering, suborning, forging, gaming, lying, fawning, hectoring, voting, scribbling, star gazing, poisoning, whoring, canting, libeling, freethinking, and the like occupations; every one of which terms, I was at much pains to make him understand.

That, wine was not imported among us from foreign countries, to supply the want of water or other drinks, but because it was a sort of liquid which made us merry, by putting us out of our senses; diverted all melancholy thoughts, begat wild extravagant imaginations in the brain, raised our hopes, and banished our fears; suspended every office of reason for a time, and deprived us of the use of our limbs, until we fell into a profound sleep; although it must be confessed, that we always awaked sick and dispirited; and that the use of this liquor filled us with diseases, which made our lives uncomfortable and short.

But beside all this, the bulk of our people supported themselves by furnishing the necessities or conveniencies of life to the rich, and to each other. For instance, when I am at home and dressed as I ought to be, I carry on my body the workmanship of an hundred tradesmen; the building and furniture of my house employ as many more; and five times the number to adorn my wife.

I was going on to tell him of another sort of people, who get their livelihood by attending the sick; having upon some occasions informed his honor that many of my crew had died of diseases. But here it was with the utmost difficulty that I brought him to apprehend what I meant. He could easily conceive that a Houyhnhnm grew weak and heavy a few days before his death; or by some accident might hurt a limb. But that nature, who worketh all things to perfection, should suffer any pains to breed in our bodies, he thought impossible; and desired to know the reason of so unaccountable an evil. I told him, we fed on a thousand things which operated contrary to each other; that we eat when we were not hungry, and drank without the provocation of thirst; that we sat whole nights drinking strong liquors without eating a bit, which disposed us to sloth, inflamed our bodies, and precipitated or prevented digestion. That, prostitute female Yahoos acquired a certain malady, which bred rottenness in the bones of those who fell into their embraces; that this and many other diseases were propagated from father to son; so that great numbers come into the world with complicated maladies upon them; that it would be endless to give him a catalogue of all diseases incident to human bodies; for they could not be fewer than five or six hundred, spread over every limb, and joint; in short, every part, external and intestine, having diseases appropriated to each. To remedy which, there was a sort of people bred up among us, in the profession or pretense of curing the sick. And because I had some skill in the faculty, I would in gratitude to his honor let him know the whole mystery and method by which they proceed.

Their fundamental is that all diseases arise from repletion; from whence they conclude, that a great evacuation of the body is necessary, either through the natural passage, or upwards at the mouth. Their next business is, from herbs, minerals, gums, oils, shells, salts, juices, seaweed, excrements, barks of trees, serpents, toads, frogs, spiders, dead men's flesh and bones, birds, beasts and fishes, to form a composition for smell and taste the most abominable, nauseous, and detestable, that they can possibly contrive, which the stomach immediately rejects with loathing, and this they call a vomit. Or else from the same storehouse, with some other poisonous additions, they command us to take in at the orifice above or below (just as the physician then happens to be disposed) a medicine equally annoying and disgustful to the bowels; which relaxing the belly, drives down all before it; and this they call a purge, or a clyster. For nature (as the physicians allege) having intended the superior anterior orifice only for the intromission of solids and liquids, and the inferior posterior for ejection, these artists ingeniously considering that in all diseases nature is forced out of her seat; therefore to replace her in it, the body must be treated in a manner directly contrary, by interchanging the use of each orifice; forcing solids and liquids in at the anus, and making evacuations at the mouth.

But, besides real diseases, we are subject to many that are only imaginary, for which the physicians have invented imaginary cures; these have their several names, and so have the drugs that are proper for them; and with these our female Yahoos are always infested.

One great excellency in this tribe is their skill at prognostics, wherein they seldom fail; their predictions in real diseases, when they rise to any degree of malignity, generally portending death, which is always in their power, when recovery is not, and therefore, upon any unexpected signs of amendment, after they have pronounced their sentence, rather than be accused as false prophets, they know how to approve[9] their sagacity to the world by a seasonable dose.

They are likewise of special use to husbands and wives, who are grown weary of their mates; to eldest sons, to great ministers of state, and often to princes.

I had formerly upon occasion discoursed with my master upon the nature of government in general, and particularly of our own excellent constitution, deservedly the wonder and envy of the whole world. But having here accidently mentioned a minister of state, he commanded me some time after to inform him what species of Yahoo I particularly meant by that appellation.

I told him that a first or chief minister of state, whom I intended to describe, was a creature wholly exempt from joy and grief, love and hatred, pity and anger; at least makes use of no other passions but a violent desire of wealth, power, and titles; that he applies his words to all uses, except to the indication of his mind; that he never tells a truth, but with an intent that you should take it for a lie; nor a lie, but with a design that you should take it for a truth; that those he speaks worst of behind their backs are in the surest way to preferment; and whenever he begins to praise you to others or

9. Prove.

to yourself, you are from that day forlorn. The worst mark you can receive is a promise, especially when it is confirmed with an oath; after which every wise man retires, and gives over all hopes.

There are three methods by which a man may rise to be chief minister: the first is by knowing how with prudence to dispose of a wife, a daughter, or a sister; the second, by betraying or undermining his predecessor; and the third is by a furious zeal in public assemblies against the corruptions of the court. But a wise prince would rather choose to employ those who practice the last of these methods; because such zealots prove always the most obsequious and subservient to the will and passions of their master. That, these ministers having all employments at their disposal, preserve themselves in power by bribing the majority of a senate or great council; and at last by an expedient called an Act of Indemnity[1] (whereof I described the nature to him) they secure themselves from after reckonings, and retire from the public, laden with the spoils of the nation.

The palace of a chief minister is a seminary to breed up others in his own trade; the pages, lackies, and porter, by imitating their master, become ministers of state in their several districts, and learn to excel in the three principal ingredients, of insolence, lying, and bribery. Accordingly, they have a subaltern court paid to them by persons of the best rank; and sometimes by the force of dexterity and impudence, arrive through several gradations to be successors to their lord.

He is usually governed by a decayed wench, or favorite footman, who are the tunnels through which all graces are conveyed, and may properly be called, in the last resort, the governors of the kingdom.

One day, my master, having heard me mention the nobility of my country, was pleased to make me a compliment which I could not pretend to deserve: that, he was sure, I must have been born of some noble family, because I far exceeded in shape, color, and cleanliness, all the Yahoos of his nation, although I seemed to fail in strength, and agility, which must be imputed to my different way of living from those other brutes; and besides, I was not only endowed with the faculty of speech, but likewise with some rudiments of reason, to a degree, that with all his acquaintance I passed for a prodigy.

He made me observe, that among the Houyhnhnms, the white, the sorrel, and the iron grey were not so exactly shaped as the bay, the dapple grey, and the black; nor born with equal talents of mind, or a capacity to improve them; and therefore continued always in the condition of servants, without ever aspiring to match out of their own race, which in that country would be reckoned monstrous and unnatural.

I made his honor my most humble acknowledgments for the good opinion he was pleased to conceive of me; but assured him at the same time, that my birth was of the lower sort, having been born of plain, honest parents, who were just able to give me a tolerable education; that, nobility among us was altogether a different thing from the idea he had of it; that, our young noblemen are bred from their childhood in idleness and luxury; that, as soon as years will permit, they consume their vigor, and contract odious diseases among lewd females; and when their fortunes are almost ruined, they marry

---

1. An act passed at each session of Parliament to protect ministers of state who in good faith might have acted illegally.

some woman of mean birth, disagreeable person, and unsound constitution, merely for the sake of money, whom they hate and despise. That, the productions of such marriages are generally scrofulous, rickety or deformed children; by which means the family seldom continues above three generations, unless the wife take care to provide a healthy father among her neighbors, or domestics, in order to improve and continue the breed. That a weak diseased body, a meager countenance, and sallow complexion are the true marks of noble blood; and a healthy robust appearance is so disgraceful in a man of quality, that the world concludes his real father to have been a groom or a coachman. The imperfections of his mind run parallel with those of his body; being a composition of spleen, dullness, ignorance, caprice, sensuality, and pride.

Without the consent of this illustrious body, no law can be enacted, repealed, or altered, and these nobles have likewise the decision of all our possessions without appeal.

CHAPTER 7. *The Author's great love of his native country. His master's observations upon the constitution and administration of England, as described by the Author, with parallel cases and comparisons. His master's observations upon human nature.*

The reader may be disposed to wonder how I could prevail on myself to give so free a representation of my own species, among a race of mortals who were already too apt to conceive the vilest opinion of humankind, from that entire congruity betwixt me and their Yahoos. But I must freely confess that the many virtues of those excellent quadrupeds placed in opposite view to human corruptions had so far opened my eyes, and enlarged my understanding, that I began to view the actions and passions of man in a very different light; and to think the honor of my own kind not worth managing;[2] which, besides, it was impossible for me to do before a person of so acute a judgment as my master, who daily convinced me of a thousand faults in myself, whereof I had not the least perception before, and which with us would never be numbered even among human infirmities. I had likewise learned from his example an utter detestation of all falsehood or disguise; and truth appeared so amiable to me, that I determined upon sacrificing everything to it.

Let me deal so candidly with the reader as to confess that there was yet a much stronger motive for the freedom I took in my representation of things. I had not been a year in this country, before I contracted such a love and veneration for the inhabitants, that I entered on a firm resolution never to return to humankind, but to pass the rest of my life among these admirable Houyhnhnms in the contemplation and practice of every virtue; where I could have no example or incitement to vice. But it was decreed by fortune, my perpetual enemy, that so great a felicity should not fall to my share. However, it is now some comfort to reflect that in what I said of my countrymen, I extenuated their faults as much as I durst before so strict an examiner; and upon every article, gave as favorable a turn as the matter would bear. For, indeed, who is there alive that will not be swayed by his bias and partiality to the place of his birth?

2. Taking care of.

I have related the substance of several conversations I had with my master, during the greatest part of the time I had the honor to be in his service; but have indeed for brevity sake omitted much more than is here set down.

When I had answered all his questions, and his curiosity seemed to be fully satisfied; he sent for me one morning early, and commanding me to sit down at some distance (an honor which he had never before conferred upon me), he said he had been very seriously considering my whole story, as far as it related both to myself and my country; that, he looked upon us as a sort of animals to whose share, by what accident he could not conjecture, some small pittance of reason had fallen, whereof we made no other use than by its assistance to aggravate our natural corruptions, and to acquire new ones which nature had not given us. That we disarmed ourselves of the few abilities she had bestowed; had been very successful in multiplying our original wants, and seemed to spend our whole lives in vain endeavors to supply them by our own inventions. That, as to myself, it was manifest I had neither the strength or agility of a common Yahoo; that I walked infirmly on my hinder feet; had found out a contrivance to make my claws of no use or defense, and to remove the hair from my chin, which was intended as a shelter from the sun and the weather. Lastly, that I could neither run with speed, nor climb trees like my brethren (as he called them) the Yahoos in this country.

That our institutions of government and law were plainly owing to our gross defects in reason, and by consequence, in virtue; because reason alone is sufficient to govern a rational creature; which was therefore a character we had no pretense to challenge, even from the account I had given of my own people; although he manifestly perceived, that in order to favor them, I had concealed many particulars, and often *said the thing which was not.*

He was the more confirmed in this opinion, because he observed that I agreed in every feature of my body with other Yahoos, except where it was to my real disadvantage in point of strength, speed, and activity, the shortness of my claws, and some other particulars where Nature had no part; so, from the representation I had given him of our lives, our manners, and our actions, he found as near a resemblance in the disposition of our minds. He said the Yahoos were known to hate one another more than they did any different species of animals; and the reason usually assigned was the odiousness of their own shapes, which all could see in the rest, but not in themselves. He had therefore begun to think it not unwise in us to cover our bodies, and by that invention, conceal many of our deformities from each other, which would else be hardly supportable. But he now found he had been mistaken; and that the dissensions of those brutes in his country were owing to the same cause with ours, as I had described them. For, if (said he) you throw among five Yahoos as much food as would be sufficient for fifty, they will instead of eating peaceably, fall together by the ears, each single one impatient to have all to itself; and therefore a servant was usually employed to stand by while they were feeding abroad, and those kept at home were tied at a distance from each other. That, if a cow died of age or accident, before a Houyhnhnm could secure it for his own Yahoos, those in the neighborhood would come in herds to seize it, and then would ensue such a battle as I had described, with terrible wounds made by their claws on both sides, although they seldom were able to kill one another, for want of such convenient instruments of death as we had invented. At other times the like battles have been fought between the Yahoos of several neighborhoods without any visible cause; those of one district watching all opportunities to surprise the next before they are prepared. But if they find their project hath miscarried, they return home, and for want of enemies, engage in what I call a civil war among themselves.

That, in some fields of his country, there are certain shining stones of several colors, whereof the Yahoos are violently fond; and when part of these stones are fixed in the earth, as it sometimes happeneth, they will dig with their claws for whole days to get them out, and carry them away, and hide them by heaps in their kennels; but still looking round with great caution, for fear their comrades should find out their treasure. My master said he could never discover the reason of this unnatural appetite, or how these stones could be of any use to a Yahoo; but now he believed it might proceed from the same principle of avarice, which I had ascribed to mankind. That he had once, by way of experiment, privately removed a heap of these stones from the place where one of his Yahoos had buried it, whereupon, the sordid animal missing his treasure, by his loud lamenting brought the whole herd to the place, there miserably howled, then fell to biting and tearing the rest; began to pine away, would neither eat nor sleep, nor work, till he ordered a servant privately to convey the stones into the same hole, and hide them as before; which when his Yahoo had found, he presently recovered his spirits and good humor; but took care to remove them to a better hiding place; and hath ever since been a very serviceable brute.

My master farther assured me, which I also observed myself, that in the fields where these shining stones abound, the fiercest and most frequent battles are fought, occasioned by perpetual inroads of the neighboring Yahoos.

He said it was common when two Yahoos discovered such a stone in a field, and were contending which of them should be the proprietor, a third would take the advantage, and carry it away from them both; which my master would needs contend to have some resemblance with our suits at law; wherein I thought it for our credit not to undeceive him; since the decision he mentioned was much more equitable than many decrees among us; because the plaintiff and defendant there lost nothing beside the stone they contended for; whereas our courts of equity would never have dismissed the cause while either of them had anything left.

My master continuing his discourse said there was nothing that rendered the Yahoos more odious, than their undistinguished appetite to devour everything that came in their way, whether herbs, roots, berries, corrupted flesh of animals, or all mingled together; and it was peculiar in their temper, that they were fonder of what they could get by rapine or stealth at a greater distance, than much better food provided for them at home. If their prey held out, they would eat till they were ready to burst, after which nature had pointed out to them a certain root that gave them a general evacuation.

There was also another kind of root very juicy, but something rare and difficult to be found, which the Yahoos sought for with much eagerness, and would suck it with great delight; it produced the same effects that wine hath upon us. It would make them sometimes hug, and sometimes tear one another; they would howl and grin, and chatter, and reel, and tumble, and then fall asleep in the mud.

I did indeed observe that the Yahoos were the only animals in this country subject to any diseases; which however, were much fewer than horses have among us, and contracted not by any ill treatment they meet with, but by the nastiness and greediness of that sordid brute. Neither has their language any more than a general appellation for those maladies; which is borrowed from the name of the beast, and called *Hnea Yahoo*, or the Yahoo's Evil; and the cure prescribed is a mixture of their own dung and urine, forcibly put down the Yahoo's throat. This I have since often known to have been taken with success, and do here freely recommend it to my countrymen, for the public good, as an admirable specific against all diseases produced by repletion.

As to learning, government, arts, manufactures, and the like, my master confessed he could find little or no resemblance between the Yahoos of that country and those in ours. For he only meant to observe what parity there was in our natures. He had heard indeed some curious Houyhnhnms observe that in most herds there was a sort of ruling Yahoo (as among us there is generally some leading or principal stag in a park) who was always more deformed in body, and mischievous in disposition, than any of the rest. That this leader had usually a favorite as like himself as he could get, whose employment was to lick his master's feet and posteriors, and drive the female Yahoos to his kennel; for which he was now and then rewarded with a piece of ass's flesh. This favorite is hated by the whole herd; and therefore to protect himself, keeps always near the person of his leader. He usually continues in office till a worse can be found; but the very moment he is discarded, his successor, at the head of all the Yahoos in that district, young and old, male and female, come in a body, and discharge their excrements upon him from head to foot. But how far this might be applicable to our courts and favorites, and ministers of state, my master said I could best determine.

I durst make no return to this malicious insinuation, which debased human understanding below the sagacity of a common hound, who hath judgment enough to distinguish and follow the cry of the ablest dog in the pack, without being ever mistaken.

My master told me there were some qualities remarkable in the Yahoos, which he had not observed me to mention, or at least very slightly, in the accounts I had given him of humankind. He said, those animals, like other brutes, had their females in common; but in this they differed, that the she-Yahoo would admit the male while she was pregnant; and that the hes would quarrel and fight with the females as fiercely as with each other. Both which practices were such degrees of infamous brutality, that no other sensitive creature ever arrived at.

Another thing he wondered at in the Yahoos was their strange disposition to nastiness and dirt; whereas there appears to be a natural love of cleanliness in all other animals. As to the two former accusations, I was glad to let them pass without any reply, because I had not a word to offer upon them in defense of my species, which otherwise I certainly had done from my own inclinations. But I could have easily vindicated humankind from the imputation of singularity upon the last article, if there had been any swine in that country (as unluckily for me there were not) which although it may be a sweeter quadruped than a Yahoo, cannot I humbly conceive in justice pretend to more cleanliness; and so his honor himself must have owned, if he had seen their filthy way of feeding, and their custom of wallowing and sleeping in the mud.

My master likewise mentioned another quality, which his servants had discovered in several Yahoos, and to him was wholly unaccountable. He said, a fancy would sometimes take a Yahoo, to retire into a corner, to lie down and howl, and groan, and spurn away all that came near him, although he were young and fat, and wanted neither food nor water; nor did the servants imagine what could possibly ail him. And the only remedy they found was to set him to hard work, after which he would infallibly come to himself. To this I was silent out of partiality to my own kind; yet here I could plainly discover the true seeds of spleen,[3] which only seizeth on the lazy, the luxurious, and the rich; who, if they were forced to undergo the same regimen, I would undertake for the cure.

His Honor had farther observed, that a female Yahoo would often stand behind a bank or a bush, to gaze on the young males passing by, and then appear, and hide, using many antic gestures and grimaces; at which time it was observed, that she had a most offensive smell; and when any of the males advanced, would slowly retire, looking back, and with a counterfeit show of fear, run off into some convenient place where she knew the male would follow her.

At other times, if a female stranger came among them, three or four of her own sex would get about her, and stare and chatter, and grin, and smell her all over; and then turn off with gestures that seemed to express contempt and disdain.

Perhaps my master might refine a little in these speculations, which he had drawn from what he observed himself, or had been told by others; however, I could not reflect without some amazement, and much sorrow, that the rudiments of lewdness, coquetry, censure, and scandal, should have place by instinct in womankind.

I expected every moment that my master would accuse the Yahoos of those unnatural appetites in both sexes, so common among us. But Nature it seems hath not been so expert a schoolmistress; and these politer pleasures are entirely the productions of art and reason, on our side of the globe.

CHAPTER 8. *The Author relateth several particulars of the Yahoos. The great virtues of the Houyhnhnms. The education and exercises of their youth. Their general assembly.*

As I ought to have understood human nature much better than I supposed it possible for my master to do, so it was easy to apply the character he gave of the Yahoos to myself and my countrymen; and I believed I could yet make farther discoveries from my own observation. I therefore often begged his honor to let me go among the herds of Yahoos in the neighborhood; to which he always very graciously consented, being perfectly convinced that the hatred I bore those brutes would never suffer me to be corrupted by them; and his honor ordered one of his servants, a strong sorrel nag, very honest and good-natured, to be my guard; without whose protection I durst not

3. Hypochondria.

undertake such adventures. For I have already told the reader how much I was pestered by those odious animals upon my first arrival. I afterwards failed very narrowly three or four times of falling into their clutches, when I happened to stray at any distance without my hanger. And I have reason to believe, they had some imagination that I was of their own species, which I often assisted myself, by stripping up my sleeves, and shewing my naked arms and breast in their sight, when my protector was with me; at which times they would approach as near as they durst, and imitate my actions after the manner of monkeys, but ever with great signs of hatred; as a tame jackdaw with cap and stockings is always persecuted by the wild ones, when he happens to be got among them.

They are prodigiously nimble from their infancy; however, I once caught a young male of three years old, and endeavored by all marks of tenderness to make it quiet; but the little imp fell a squalling, scratching, and biting with such violence, that I was forced to let it go; and it was high time, for a whole troop of old ones came about us at the noise; but finding the cub was safe (for away it ran) and my sorrel nag being by, they durst not venture near us. I observed the young animal's flesh to smell very rank, and the stink was somewhat between a weasel and a fox, but much more disagreeable. I forgot another circumstance (and perhaps I might have the reader's pardon, if it were wholly omitted) that while I held the odious vermin in my hands, it voided its filthy excrements of a yellow liquid substance, all over my clothes; but by good fortune there was a small brook hard by, where I washed myself as clean as I could; although I durst not come into my master's presence until I were sufficiently aired.

By what I could discover, the Yahoos appear to be the most unteachable of all animals, their capacities never reaching higher than to draw or carry burdens. Yet I am of opinion, this defect ariseth chiefly from a perverse, restive disposition. For they are cunning, malicious, treacherous and revengeful. They are strong and hardy, but of a cowardly spirit, and by consequence insolent, abject, and cruel. It is observed that the red-haired of both sexes are more libidinous and mischievous than the rest, whom yet they much exceed in strength and activity.

The Houyhnhnms keep the Yahoos for present use in huts not far from the house; but the rest are sent abroad to certain fields, where they dig up roots, eat several kinds of herbs, and search about for carrion, or sometimes catch weasels and *luhimuhs* (a sort of wild rat) which they greedily devour. Nature hath taught them to dig deep holes with their nails on the side of a rising ground, wherein they lie by themselves; only the kennels of the females are larger, sufficient to hold two or three cubs.

They swim from their infancy like frogs, and are able to continue long under water, where they often take fish, which the females carry home to their young. And upon this occasion, I hope the reader will pardon my relating an odd adventure.

Being one day abroad with my protector the sorrel nag, and the weather exceeding hot, I entreated him to let me bathe in a river that was near. He consented, and I immediately stripped myself stark naked, and went down softly into the stream. It happened that a young female Yahoo standing behind a bank, saw the whole proceeding; and inflamed by desire, as the nag and I conjectured, came running with all speed, and leaped into the water within five yards of the place where I bathed. I was never in my life so terribly frighted; the nag was grazing at some distance, not suspecting any harm. She embraced me after a most fulsome manner; I roared as loud as I could, and the nag came galloping towards me, whereupon she quitted her grasp, with the utmost reluctancy, and leaped upon the opposite bank, where she stood gazing and howling all the time I was putting on my clothes.

This was matter of diversion to my master and his family, as well as of mortification to myself. For now I could no longer deny that I was a real Yahoo, in every limb and feature, since the females had a natural propensity to me as one of their own species; neither was the hair of this brute of a red color (which might have been some excuse for an appetite a little irregular) but black as a sloe, and her countenance did not make an appearance altogether so hideous as the rest of the kind; for I think, she could not be above eleven years old.

Having already lived three years in this country, the reader I suppose will expect that I should, like other travelers, give him some account of the manners and customs of its inhabitants, which it was indeed my principal study to learn.

As these noble Houyhnhnms are endowed by Nature with a general disposition to all virtues, and have no conceptions or ideas of what is evil in a rational creature; so their grand maxim is to cultivate reason, and to be wholly governed by it. Neither is reason among them a point problematical as with us, where men can argue with plausibility on both sides of a question; but strikes you with immediate conviction; as it must needs do where it is not mingled, obscured, or discolored by passion and interest. I remember it was with extreme difficulty that I could bring my master to understand the meaning of the word "opinion," or how a point could be disputable; because reason taught us to affirm or deny only where we are certain; and beyond our knowledge we cannot do either. So that controversies, wranglings, disputes, and positiveness in false or dubious propositions are evils unknown among the Houyhnhnms. In the like manner when I used to explain to him our several systems of natural philosophy,[4] he would laugh that a creature pretending to reason should value itself upon the knowledge of other people's conjectures, and in things, where that knowledge, if it were certain, could be of no use. Wherein he agreed entirely with the sentiments of Socrates, as Plato delivers them, which I mention as the highest honor I can do that prince of philosophers. I have often since reflected what destruction such a doctrine would make in the libraries of Europe; and how many paths to fame would be then shut up in the learned world.

Friendship and benevolence are the two principal virtues among the Houyhnhnms; and these not confined to particular objects, but universal to the whole race. For a stranger from the remotest part is equally treated with the nearest neighbor, and wherever he goes, looks upon himself as at home. They preserve decency and civility in the highest degrees, but are altogether ignorant of ceremony. They have no fondness for their colts or foals; but the care they take in educating them proceedeth entirely from the dictates of reason. And I observed my master to show the same affection to his neighbor's issue that he had for his own. They will have it that Nature teaches

4. Science.

them to love the whole species, and it is reason only that maketh a distinction of persons, where there is a superior degree of virtue.

When the matron Houyhnhnms have produced one of each sex, they no longer accompany with their consorts, except they lose one of their issue by some casualty, which very seldom happens; but in such a case they meet again; or when the like accident befalls a person whose wife is past bearing, some other couple bestows on him one of their own colts, and then go together a second time, until the mother be pregnant. This caution is necessary to prevent the country from being overburdened with numbers. But the race of inferior Houyhnhnms bred up to be servants is not so strictly limited upon this article; these are allowed to produce three of each sex, to be domestics in the noble families.

In their marriages they are exactly careful to choose such colors as will not make any disagreeable mixture in the breed. Strength is chiefly valued in the male, and comeliness in the female; not upon the account of love, but to preserve the race from degenerating; for, where a female happens to excel in strength, a consort is chosen with regard to comeliness. Courtship, love, presents, jointures, settlements, have no place in their thoughts, or terms whereby to express them in their language. The young couple meet and are joined, merely because it is the determination of their parents and friends; it is what they see done every day; and they look upon it as one of the necessary actions in a reasonable being. But the violation of marriage, or any other unchastity, was never heard of; and the married pair pass their lives with the same friendship and mutual benevolence that they bear to all others of the same species who come in their way, without jealousy, fondness, quarreling, or discontent.

In educating the youth of both sexes, their method is admirable, and highly deserveth our imitation. These are not suffered to taste a grain of oats, except upon certain days, till eighteen years old; nor milk, but very rarely; and in summer they graze two hours in the morning, and as many in the evening, which their parents likewise observe; but the servants are not allowed above half that time; and a great part of the grass is brought home, which they eat at the most convenient hours when they can be best spared from work.

Temperance, industry, exercise, and cleanliness are the lessons equally enjoined to the young ones of both sexes; and my master thought it monstrous in us to give the females a different kind of education from the males, except in some articles of domestic management; whereby, as he truly observed, one half of our natives were good for nothing but bringing children into the world; and to trust the care of their children to such useless animals, he said was yet a greater instance of brutality.

But the Houyhnhnms train up their youth to strength, speed, and hardiness, by exercising them in running races up and down steep hills, or over hard stony grounds; and when they are all in a sweat, they are ordered to leap over head and ears into a pond or a river. Four times a year the youth of certain districts meet to show their proficiency in running, and leaping, and other feats of strength or agility; where the victor is rewarded with a song made in his or her praise. On this festival the servants drive a herd of Yahoos into the field, laden with hay, and oats, and milk for a repast to the Houyhnhnms; after which these brutes are immediately driven back again, for fear of being noisome to the assembly.

Every fourth year, at the vernal equinox, there is a representative council of the whole nation, which meets in a plain about twenty miles from our house, and continueth about five or six days. Here they inquire into the state and condition of the several districts; whether they abound or be deficient in hay or oats, or cows or Yahoos? And wherever there is any want (which is but seldom) it is immediately supplied by unanimous consent and contribution. Here likewise the regulation of children is settled: as for instance, if a Houyhnhnm hath two males, he changeth one of them with another who hath two females, and when a child hath been lost by any casualty, where the mother is past breeding, it is determined what family in the district shall breed another to supply the loss.

CHAPTER 9. *A grand debate at the general assembly of the Houyhnhnms, and how it was determined. The learning of the Houyhnhnms. Their buildings. Their manner of burials. The defectiveness of their language.*

One of these grand assemblies was held in my time, about three months before my departure, whither my master went as the representative of our district. In this council was resumed their old debate, and indeed, the only debate that ever happened in their country; whereof my master after his return gave me a very particular account.

The question to be debated was whether the Yahoos should be exterminated from the face of the earth. One of the members for the affirmative offered several arguments of great strength and weight, alleging that, as the Yahoos were the most filthy, noisome, and deformed animal which nature ever produced, so they were the most restive and indocible,[5] mischievous, and malicious; they would privately suck the teats of the Houyhnhnms' cows; kill and devour their cats, trample down their oats and grass, if they were not continually watched; and commit a thousand other extravagancies. He took notice of a general tradition, that Yahoos had not been always in their country, but that many ages ago, two of these brutes appeared together upon a mountain; whether produced by the heat of the sun upon corrupted mud and slime, or from the ooze and froth of the sea, was never known. That these Yahoos engendered, and their brood in a short time grew so numerous as to overrun and infest the whole nation. That the Houyhnhnms to get rid of this evil, made a general hunting, and at last enclosed the whole herd; and destroying the older, every Houyhnhnm kept two young ones in a kennel, and brought them to such a degree of tameness as an animal so savage by nature can be capable of acquiring, using them for draught and carriage. That there seemed to be much truth in this tradition, and that those creatures could not be *ylnhniamshy* (or aborigines of the land) because of the violent hatred the Houyhnhnms as well as all other animals bore them; which although their evil disposition sufficiently deserved, could never have arrived at so high a degree, if they had been aborigines, or else they would have long since been rooted out. That the inhabitants taking a fancy to use the service of the Yahoos, had very imprudently neglected to cultivate the breed of asses, which were a comely animal, easily kept, more tame and orderly, without any offensive smell, strong enough for labor, although they yield to the other

5. Unteachable.

in agility of body; and if their braying be no agreeable sound, it is far preferable to the horrible howlings of the Yahoos.

Several others declared their sentiments to the same purpose, when my master proposed an expedient to the assembly, whereof he had indeed borrowed the hint from me. He approved of the tradition, mentioned by the honorable member, who spoke before; and affirmed, that the two Yahoos said to be first seen among them, had been driven thither over the sea; that coming to land, and being forsaken by their companions, they retired to the mountains, and degenerating by degrees, became in process of time much more savage than those of their own species in the country from whence these two originals came. The reason of his assertion was that he had now in his possession a certain wonderful Yahoo (meaning myself) which most of them had heard of, and many of them had seen. He then related to them how he first found me; that my body was all covered with an artificial composure of the skins and hairs of other animals; that I spoke in a language of my own, and had thoroughly learned theirs; that I had related to him the accidents which brought me thither; that when he saw me without my covering, I was an exact Yahoo in every part, only of a whiter color, less hairy and with shorter claws. He added how I had endeavored to persuade him that in my own and other countries the Yahoos acted as the governing, rational animal, and held the Houyhnhnms in servitude; that he observed in me all the qualities of a Yahoo, only a little more civilized by some tincture of reason, which however was in a degree as far inferior to the Houyhnhnm race as the Yahoos of their country were to me; that among other things, I mentioned a custom we had of castrating Houyhnhnms when they were young, in order to render them tame; that the operation was easy and safe; that it was no shame to learn wisdom from brutes, as industry is taught by the ant, and building by the swallow (for so I translate the world *lyhannh,* although it be a much larger fowl). That this invention might be practiced upon the younger Yahoos here, which, besides rendering them tractable and fitter for use, would in an age put an end to the whole species without destroying life. That in the meantime the Houyhnhnms should be exhorted to cultivate the breed of asses, which, as they are in all respects more valuable brutes, so they have this advantage, to be fit for service at five years old, which the other are not till twelve.

This was all my master thought fit to tell me at that time, of what passed in the grand council. But he was pleased to conceal one particular, which related personally to myself, whereof I soon felt the unhappy effect, as the reader will know in its proper place, and from whence I date all the succeeding misfortunes of my life.

The Houyhnhnms have no letters, and consequently, their knowledge is all traditional. But there happening few events of any moment among a people so well united, naturally disposed to every virtue, wholly governed by reason, and cut off from all commerce with other nations, the historical part is easily preserved without burdening their memories. I have already observed that they are subject to no diseases, and therefore can have no need of physicians. However, they have excellent medicines composed of herbs, to cure accidental bruises and cuts in the pastern or frog of the foot by sharp stones, as well as other maims and hurts in the several parts of the body.

They calculate the year by the revolution of the sun and the moon, but use no subdivisions into weeks. They are well enough acquainted with the motions of those two luminaries, and understand the nature of eclipses; and this is the utmost progress of their astronomy.

In poetry they must be allowed to excel all other mortals; wherein the justness of their similes, and the minuteness, as well as exactness of their descriptions, are indeed inimitable. Their verses abound very much in both of these, and usually contain either some exalted notions of friendship and benevolence, or the praises of those who were victors in races and other bodily exercises. Their buildings, although very rude and simple, are not inconvenient, but well contrived to defend them from all injuries of cold and heat. They have a kind of tree, which at forty years old loosens in the root, and falls with the first storm; it grows very straight, and being pointed like stakes with a sharp stone (for the Houyhnhnms know not the use of iron), they stick them erect in the ground about ten inches asunder, and then weave in oat straw, or sometimes wattles, betwixt them. The roof is made after the same manner, and so are the doors.

The Houyhnhnms use the hollow part between the pastern and the hoof of their forefeet as we do our hands, and this with greater dexterity than I could at first imagine. I have seen a white mare of our family thread a needle (which I lent her on purpose) with that joint. They milk their cows, reap their oats, and do all the work which requires hands in the same manner. They have a kind of hard flints, which by grinding against other stones they form into instruments that serve instead of wedges, axes, and hammers. With tools made of these flints, they likewise cut their hay, and reap their oats, which there groweth naturally in several fields. The Yahoos draw home the sheaves in carriages, and the servants tread them in certain covered huts, to get out the grain, which is kept in stores. They make a rude kind of earthen and wooden vessels, and bake the former in the sun.

If they can avoid casualties, they die only of old age, and are buried in the obscurest places that can be found, their friends and relations expressing neither joy nor grief at their departure; nor does the dying person discover the least regret that he is leaving the world, any more than if he were upon returning home from a visit to one of his neighbors; I remember my master having once made an appointment with a friend and his family to come to his house upon some affair of importance; on the day fixed, the mistress and her two children came very late; she made two excuses, first for her husband, who, as she said, happened that very morning to *lhnuwnh*. The word is strongly expressive in their language, but not easily rendered into English; it signifies, *to retire to his first Mother*. Her excuse for not coming sooner was that her husband dying late in the morning, she was a good while consulting her servants about a convenient place where his body should be laid; and I observed she behaved herself at our house, as cheerfully as the rest. She died about three months after.

They live generally to seventy or seventy-five years, very seldom to fourscore; some weeks before their death they feel a gradual decay, but without pain. During this time they are much visited by their friends, because they cannot go abroad with their usual ease and satisfaction. However, about ten days before their death, which they seldom fail in computing, they return the visits that have been made by those who are nearest in the neighborhood, being carried in a convenient sledge drawn by Yahoos; which vehicle they use, not only upon this occasion, but when they grow old, upon long journeys, or when they are lamed by any accident. And therefore when the dying Houyhnhnms return those visits, they take a solemn leave of their friends, as if they were going to some remote part of the country, where they designed to pass the rest of their lives.

I know not whether it may be worth observing, that the Houyhnhnms have no word in their language to express anything that is evil, except what they borrow from the deformities or ill qualities of the Yahoos. Thus they denote the folly of a servant, an omission of a child, a stone that cuts their feet, a continuance of foul or unseasonable weather, and the like, by adding to each the epithet of Yahoo. For instance, *hhnm Yahoo, whnaholm Yahoo, ynlhmndwihlma Yahoo*, and an ill-contrived house, *ynholmhnmrohlnw Yahoo*.

I could with great pleasure enlarge farther upon the manners and virtues of this excellent people; but intending in a short time to publish a volume by itself expressly upon that subject, I refer the reader thither. And in the meantime, proceed to relate my own sad catastrophe.

CHAPTER 10. *The Author's economy, and happy life among the Houyhnhnms. His great improvement in virtue, by conversing with them. Their conversations. The Author hath notice given him by his master that he must depart from the country. He falls into a swoon for grief, but submits. He contrives and finishes a canoe, by the help of a fellow servant, and puts to sea at a venture.*

I had settled my little economy to my own heart's content. My master had ordered a room to be made for me after their manner, about six yards from the house; the sides and floors of which I plastered with clay, and covered with rush mats of my own contriving; I had beaten hemp, which there grows wild, and made of it a sort of ticking; this I filled with the feathers of several birds I had taken with springes made of Yahoos' hairs, and were excellent food. I had worked two chairs with my knife, the sorrel nag helping me in the grosser and more laborious part. When my clothes were worn to rags, I made myself others with the skins of rabbits, and of a certain beautiful animal about the same size, called *nnuhnoh*, the skin of which is covered with a fine down. Of these I likewise made very tolerable stockings. I soled my shoes with wood which I cut from a tree, and fitted to the upper leather, and when this was worn out, I supplied it with the skins of Yahoos, dried in the sun. I often got honey out of hollow trees, which I mingled with water, or eat it with my bread. No man could more verify the truth of these two maxims, that *Nature is very easily satisfied*; and, that *Necessity is the mother of invention*. I enjoyed perfect health of body, and tranquility of mind; I did not feel the treachery or inconstancy of a friend, nor the inquiries of a secret or open enemy. I had no occasion of bribing, flattering, or pimping to procure the favor of any great man, or of his minion. I wanted no fence against fraud or oppression; here was neither physician to destroy my body, nor lawyer to ruin my fortune; no informer to watch my words and actions, or forge accusations against me for hire; here were no gibers, censurers, backbiters, pickpockets, highwaymen, housebreakers, attorneys, bawds, buffoons, gamesters, politicians, wits, splenetics, tedious talkers, controvertists, ravishers, murderers, robbers, virtuosos;[6] no leaders or followers of party and faction;

---

6. Savants; those who pursue special interests in the arts or sciences.

no encouragers to vice, by seducement or examples; no dungeons, axes, gibbets, whipping posts, or pillories; no cheating shopkeepers or mechanics; no pride, vanity or affectation; no fops, bullies, drunkards, strolling whores, or poxes; no ranting, lewd, expensive wives; no stupid, proud pedants; no importunate, overbearing, quarrelsome, noisy, roaring, empty, conceited, swearing companions; no scoundrels raised from the dust upon the merit of their vices; or nobility thrown into it on account of their virtues; no lords, fiddlers, judges, or dancing masters.

I had the favor of being admitted to several Houyhnhnms, who came to visit or dine with my master; where his honor graciously suffered me to wait in the room, and listen to their discourse. Both he and his company would often descend to ask me questions, and receive my answers. I had also sometimes the honor of attending my master in his visits to others. I never presumed to speak, except in answer to a question; and then I did it with inward regret, because it was a loss of so much time for improving myself; but I was infinitely delighted with the station of an humble auditor in such conversations, where nothing passed but what was useful, expressed in the fewest and most significant words; where (as I have already said) the greatest decency was observed, without the least degree of ceremony; where no person spoke without being pleased himself, and pleasing his companions; where there was no interruption, tediousness, heat, or difference of sentiments. They have a notion, that when people are met together, a short silence doth much improve conversation; this I found to be true; for during those little intermissions of talk, new ideas would arise in their minds, which very much enlivened the discourse. Their subjects are generally on friendship and benevolence; on order and economy; sometimes upon the visible operations of nature, or ancient traditions; upon the bounds and limits of virtue; upon the unerring rules of reason; or upon some determinations, to be taken at the next great assembly; and often upon the various excellencies of poetry. I may add, without vanity, that my presence often gave them sufficient matter for discourse, because it afforded my master an occasion of letting his friends into the history of me and my country, upon which they were all pleased to descant in a manner not very advantageous to human kind; and for that reason I shall not repeat what they said; only I may be allowed to observe that his honor, to my great admiration, appeared to understand the nature of Yahoos much better than myself. He went through all our vices and follies, and discovered many which I had never mentioned to him; by only supposing what qualities a Yahoo of their country, with a small proportion of reason, might be capable of exerting; and concluded, with too much probability, how vile as well as miserable such a creature must be.

I freely confess, that all the little knowledge I have of any value was acquired by the lectures I received from my master, and from hearing the discourses of him and his friends; to which I should be prouder to listen, than to dictate to the greatest and wisest assembly in Europe. I admired the strength, comeliness, and speed of the inhabitants; and such a constellation of virtues in such amiable persons produced in me the highest veneration. At first, indeed, I did not feel that natural awe which the Yahoos and all other animals bear towards them; but it grew upon me by degrees, much sooner than I imagined, and was mingled with a respectful love and gratitude, that they would condescend to distinguish me from the rest of my species.

When I thought of my family, my friends, my countrymen, or human race in general, I considered them as they really were, Yahoos in shape and disposition, perhaps a little more civilized, and qualified with the gift of speech; but making no other use of reason than to improve and multiply those vices, whereof their brethren in this country had only the share that nature allotted them. When I happened to behold the reflection of my own form in a lake or fountain, I turned away my face in horror and detestation of myself, and could better endure the sight of a common Yahoo than of my own person. By conversing with the Houyhnhnms, and looking upon them with delight, I fell to imitate their gait and gesture, which is now grown into a habit; and my friends often tell me in a blunt way, that I trot like a horse; which, however, I take for a great compliment. Neither shall I disown, that in speaking I am apt to fall into the voice and manner of the Houyhnhnms, and hear myself ridiculed on that account without the least mortification.

In the midst of this happiness, when I looked upon myself to be fully settled for life, my master sent for me one morning a little earlier than his usual hour. I observed by his countenance that he was in some perplexity, and at a loss how to begin what he had to speak. After a short silence, he told me, he did not know how I would take what he was going to say; that, in the last general assembly, when the affair of the Yahoos was entered upon, the representatives had taken offense at his keeping a Yahoo (meaning myself) in his family more like a Houyhnhnm than a brute animal. That he was known frequently to converse with me, as if he could receive some advantage of pleasure in my company; that such a practice was not agreeable to reason or nature, or a thing ever heard of before among them. The assembly did therefore exhort him, either to employ me like the rest of my species, or command me to swim back to the place from whence I came. That the first of these expedients was utterly rejected by all the Houyhnhnms who had ever seen me at his house or their own; for, they alleged, that because I had some rudiments of reason, added to the natural pravity[7] of those animals, it was to be feared, I might be able to seduce them into the woody and mountainous parts of the country, and bring them in troops by night to destroy the Houyhnhnms' cattle, as being naturally of the ravenous kind, and averse from labor.

My master added that he was daily pressed by the Houyhnhnms of the neighborhood to have the assembly's exhortation executed, which he could not put off much longer. He doubted[8] it would be impossible for me to swim to another country; and therefore wished I would contrive some sort of vehicle resembling those I had described to him, that might carry me on the sea; in which work I should have the assistance of his own servants, as well as those of his neighbors. He concluded that for his own part he could have been content to keep me in his service as long as I lived; because he found I had cured myself of some bad habits and dispositions, by endeavoring, as far as my inferior nature was capable, to imitate the Houyhnhnms.

I should here observe to the reader, that a decree of the general assembly in this country is expressed by the word *hnhloayn*, which signifies an exhortation, as near as I can render it; for they have no conception how a rational creature can be compelled, but only advised, or exhorted; because no person can disobey reason without giving up his claim to be a rational creature.

7. Corruption.   8. Feared.

I was struck with the utmost grief and despair at my master's discourse; and being unable to support the agonies I was under, I fell into a swoon at his feet; when I came to myself, he told me that he concluded I had been dead (for these people are subject to no such imbecilities of nature). I answered, in a faint voice, that death would have been too great an happiness; that although I could not blame the assembly's exhortation, or the urgency of his friends; yet in my weak and corrupt judgment, I thought it might consist with reason to have been less rigorous. That I could not swim a league, and probably the nearest land to theirs might be distant above an hundred; that many materials, necessary for making a small vessel to carry me off, were wholly wanting in this country, which, however, I would attempt in obedience and gratitude to his honor, although I concluded the thing to be impossible, and therefore looked on myself as already devoted⁹ to destruction. That the certain prospect of an unnatural death was the least of my evils; for, supposing I should escape with life by some strange adventure, how could I think with temper¹ of passing my days among Yahoos, and relapsing into my old corruptions, for want of examples to lead and keep me within the paths of virtue. That I knew too well upon what solid reasons all the determinations of the wise Houyhnhnms were founded, not to be shaken by arguments of mine, a miserable Yahoo; and therefore after presenting him with my humble thanks for the offer of his servants' assistance in making a vessel, and desiring a reasonable time for so difficult a work, I told him I would endeavor to preserve a wretched being; and, if ever I returned to England, was not without hopes of being useful to my own species by celebrating the praises of the renowned Houyhnhnms, and proposing their virtues to the imitation of mankind.

My master in a few words made me a very gracious reply, allowed me the space of two months to finish my boat, and ordered the sorrel nag, my fellow servant (for so at this distance I may presume to call him), to follow my instructions, because I told my master that his help would be sufficient, and I knew he had a tenderness for me.

In his company my first business was to go to that part of the coast where my rebellious crew had ordered me to be set on shore. I got upon a height, and looking on every side into the sea, fancied I saw a small island towards the northeast; I took out my pocket glass, and could then clearly distinguish it about five leagues off, as I computed; but it appeared to the sorrel nag to be only a blue cloud; for, as he had no conception of any country besides his own, so he could not be as expert in distinguishing remote objects at sea, as we who so much converse in that element.

After I had discovered this island, I considered no farther; but resolved, it should, if possible, be the first place of my banishment, leaving the consequence to fortune.

I returned home, and consulting with the sorrel nag, we went into a copse at some distance, where I with my knive, and he with a sharp flint fastened very artificially,² after their manner, to a wooden handle, cut down several oak wattles about the thickness of a walking staff, and some larger pieces. But I shall not trouble the reader with a particular description of my own mechanics; let it suffice to say, that in six weeks time, with the help of the

9. Doomed.
1. Equanimity.
2. Artfully.

sorrel nag, who performed the parts that required most labor, I finished a sort of Indian canoe; but much larger, covering it with the skins of Yahoos, well stitched together, with hempen threads of my own making. My sail was likewise composed of the skins of the same animal; but I made use of the youngest I could get, the older being too tough and thick; and I likewise provided myself with four paddles. I laid in a stock of boiled flesh, of rabbits and fowls; and took with me two vessels, one filled with milk, and the other with water.

I tried my canoe in a large pond near my master's house, and then corrected in it what was amiss, stopping all the chinks with Yahoo's tallow, till I found it staunch, and able to bear me and my freight. And when it was as complete as I could possibly make it, I had it drawn on a carriage very gently by Yahoos, to the seaside, under the conduct of the sorrel nag and another servant.

When all was ready, and the day came for my departure, I took leave of my master and lady, and the whole family, my eyes flowing with tears and my heart quite sunk with grief. But his honor, out of curiosity, and perhaps (if I may speak it without vanity) partly out of kindness, was determined to see me in my canoe; and got several of his neighboring friends to accompany him. I was forced to wait above an hour for the tide, and then observing the wind very fortunately bearing towards the island to which I intended to steer my course, I took a second leave of my master; but as I was going to prostrate myself to kiss his hoof, he did me the honor to raise it gently to my mouth. I am not ignorant how much I have been censured for mentioning this last particular. Detractors are pleased to think it improbable that so illustrious a person should descend to give so great a mark of distinction to a creature so inferior as I. Neither have I forgot how apt some travelers are to boast of extraordinary favors they have received. But, if these censurers were better acquainted with the noble and courteous disposition of the Houyhnhnms, they would soon change their opinion. I paid my respects to the rest of the Houyhnhnms in his honor's company; then getting into my canoe, I pushed off from shore.

CHAPTER 11. *The Author's dangerous voyage. He arrives at New Holland, hoping to settle there. Is wounded with an arrow by one of the natives. Is seized and carried by force into a Portuguese ship. The great civilities of the Captain. The Author arrives at England.*

I began this desperate voyage on February 15, 1714/5,[3] at 9 o'clock in the morning. The wind was very favorable; however, I made use at first only of my paddles; but considering I should soon be weary, and that the wind might probably chop about, I ventured to set up my little sail, and thus, with the help of the tide, I went at the rate of a league and a half an hour, as near as I could guess. My master and his friends continued on the shore, till I was almost out of sight; and I often heard the sorrel nag (who always loved me) crying out, *"Hnuy illa nyha maiah Yahoo"* ("Take care of thyself, gentle Yahoo").

My design was, if possible, to discover some small island uninhabited, yet

3. I.e., 1715, by modern dating. The year began on March 25.

sufficient by my labor to furnish me with necessaries of life, which I would have thought a greater happiness than to be first minister in the politest court of Europe, so horrible was the idea I conceived of returning to live in the society and under the government of Yahoos. For in such a solitude as I desired, I could at least enjoy my own thoughts, and reflect with delight on the virtues of those inimitable Houyhnhnms, without any opportunity of degenerating into the vices and corruptions of my own species.

The reader may remember what I related when my crew conspired against me, and confined me to my cabin, how I continued there several weeks, without knowing what course we took; and when I was put ashore in the longboat, how the sailors told me with oaths, whether true or false, that they knew not in what part of the world we were. However, I did then believe us to be about 10 degrees southward of the Cape of Good Hope, or about 45 degrees southern latitude, as I gathered from some general words I overheard among them, being I supposed to the southeast in their intended voyage to Madagascar. And although this were but little better than conjecture, yet I resolved to steer my course eastward, hoping to reach the southwest coast of New Holland, and perhaps some such island as I desired, lying westward of it. The wind was full west, and by six in the evening I computed I had gone eastward at least eighteen leagues; when I spied a very small island about half a league off, which I soon reached. It was nothing but a rock with one creek, naturally arched by the force of tempests. Here I put in my canoe, and climbing a part of the rock, I could plainly discover land to the east, extending from south to north. I lay all night in my canoe; and repeating my voyage early in the morning, I arrived in seven hours to the southeast point of New Holland. This confirmed me in the opinion I have long entertained, that the maps and charts place this country at least three degrees more to the east than it really is; which thought I communicated many years ago to my worthy friend Mr. Herman Moll,[4] and gave him my reasons for it, although he hath rather chosen to follow other authors.

I saw no inhabitants in the place where I landed; and being unarmed, I was afraid of venturing far into the country. I found some shellfish on the shore, and eat them raw, not daring to kindle a fire, for fear of being discovered by the natives. I continued three days feeding on oysters and limpets, to save my own provisions; and I fortunately found a brook of excellent water, which gave me great relief.

On the fourth day, venturing out early a little too far, I saw twenty or thirty natives upon a height, not above five hundred yards from me. They were stark naked, men, women, and children round a fire, as I could discover by the smoke. One of them spied me, and gave notice to the rest; five of them advanced towards me, leaving the women and children at the fire. I made what haste I could to the shore, and getting into my canoe, shoved off; the savages observing me retreat, ran after me; and before I could get far enough into the sea, discharged an arrow, which wounded me deeply on the inside of my left knee. (I shall carry the mark to my grave.) I apprehended the arrow might be poisoned; and paddling out of the reach of their darts (being a calm day) I made a shift to suck the wound, and dress it as well as I could.

I was at a loss what to do, for I durst not return to the same landing place,

---

4. A famous contemporary map maker.

but stood to the north, and was forced to paddle; for the wind, although very gentle, was against me, blowing northwest. As I was looking about for a secure landing place, I saw a sail to the north northeast, which appearing every minute more visible, I was in some doubt whether I should wait for them or no; but at last my detestation of the Yahoo race prevailed; and turning my canoe, I sailed and paddled together to the south, and got into the same creek from whence I set out in the morning, choosing rather to trust myself among these barbarians than live with European Yahoos. I drew up my canoe as close as I could to the shore, and hid myself behind a stone by the little brook, which, as I have already said, was excellent water.

The ship came within half a league of this creek, and sent out her longboat with vessels to take in fresh water (for the place it seems was very well known), but I did not observe it until the boat was almost on shore; and it was too late to seek another hiding place. The seamen at their landing observed my canoe, and rummaging it all over, easily conjectured that the owner could not be far off. Four of them well armed searched every cranny and lurking hole, till at last they found me flat on my face behind the stone. They gazed a while in admiration at my strange uncouth dress; my coat made of skins, my wooden-soled shoes, and my furred stockings; from whence, however, they concluded I was not a native of the place, who all go naked. One of the seamen in Portuguese bid me rise, and asked who I was. I understood that language very well, and getting upon my feet, said I was a poor Yahoo, banished from the Houyhnhnms, and desired they would please to let me depart. They admired to hear me answer them in their own tongue, and saw by my complexion I must be an European; but were at a loss to know what I meant by Yahoos and Houyhnhnms, and at the same time fell a laughing at my strange tone in speaking, which resembled the neighing of a horse. I trembled all the while betwixt fear and hatred; I again desired leave to depart, and was gently moving to my canoe; but they laid hold on me, desiring to know what country I was of? whence I came? with many other questions. I told them I was born in England, from whence I came about five years ago, and then their country and ours was at peace. I therefore hoped they would not treat me as an enemy, since I meant them no harm, but was a poor Yahoo, seeking some desolate place where to pass the remainder of his unfortunate life.

When they began to talk, I thought I never heard or saw any thing so unnatural; for it appeared to me as monstrous as if a dog or a cow should speak in England, or a Yahoo in Houyhnhnmland. The honest Portuguese were equally amazed at my strange dress, and the odd manner of delivering my words, which however they understood very well. They spoke to me with great humanity, and said they were sure their Captain would carry me *gratis* to Lisbon, from whence I might return to my own country; that two of the seamen would go back to the ship, to inform the Captain of what they had seen, and receive his orders; in the meantime, unless I would give my solemn oath not to fly, they would secure me by force. I thought it best to comply with their proposal. They were very curious to know my story, but I gave them very little satisfaction; and they all conjectured, that my misfortunes had impaired my reason. In two hours the boat, which went laden with vessels of water, returned with the Captain's commands to fetch me on board. I fell on my knees to preserve my liberty; but all was in vain, and the men having tied me with cords, heaved me into the boat, from whence I was taken into the ship, and from thence into the Captain's cabin.

His name was Pedro de Mendez; he was a very courteous and generous person; he entreated me to give some account of myself, and desired to know what I would eat or drink; said I should be used as well as himself, and spoke so many obliging things, that I wondered to find such civilities from a Yahoo. However, I remained silent and sullen; I was ready to faint at the very smell of him and his men. At last I desired something to eat out of my own canoe; but he ordered me a chicken and some excellent wine, and then directed that I should be put to bed in a very clean cabin. I would not undress myself, but lay on the bedclothes; and in half an hour stole out, when I thought the crew was at dinner; and getting to the side of the ship, was going to leap into the sea, and swim for my life, rather than continue among Yahoos. But one of the seamen prevented me, and having informed the Captain, I was chained to my cabin.

After dinner Don Pedro came to me, and desired to know my reason for so desperate an attempt; assured me he only meant to do me all the service he was able; and spoke so very movingly, that at last I descended to treat him like an animal which had some little portion of reason. I gave him a very short relation of my voyage; of the conspiracy against me by my own men; of the country where they set me on shore, and of my five years residence there. All which he looked upon as if it were a dream or a vision; whereat I took great offense; for I had quite forgot the faculty of lying, so peculiar to Yahoos in all countries where they preside, and consequently the disposition of suspecting truth in others of their own species. I asked him whether it were the custom of his country to *say the thing that was not?* I assured him I had almost forgot what he meant by falsehood; and if I had lived a thousand years in Houyhnhnmland, I should never have heard a lie from the meanest servant. That I was altogether indifferent whether he believed me or no; but however, in return for his favors, I would give so much allowance to the corruption of his nature, as to answer any objection he would please to make; and he might easily discover the truth.

The Captain, a wise man, after many endeavors to catch me tripping in some part of my story, at last began to have a better opinion of my veracity. But he added that since I professed so inviolable an attachment to truth, I must give him my word of honor to bear him company in this voyage without attempting anything against my life; or else he would continue me a prisoner till we arrived at Lisbon. I gave him the promise he required; but at the same time protested that I would suffer the greatest hardships rather than return to live among Yahoos.

Our voyage passed without any considerable accident. In gratitude to the Captain I sometimes sat with him at his earnest request, and strove to conceal my antipathy against humankind, although it often broke out; which he suffered to pass without observation. But the greatest part of the day, I confined myself to my cabin, to avoid seeing any of the crew. The Captain had often entreated me to strip myself of my savage dress, and offered to lend me the best suit of clothes he had. This I would not be prevailed on to accept, abhorring to cover myself with anything that had been on the back of a

Yahoo. I only desired he would lend me two clean shirts, which having been washed since he wore them, I believed would not so much defile me. These I changed every second day, and washed them myself.

We arrived at Lisbon, Nov. 5, 1715. At our landing, the Captain forced me to cover myself with his cloak, to prevent the rabble from crowding about me. I was conveyed to his own house; and at my earnest request, he led me up to the highest room backwards.[5] I conjured him to conceal from all persons what I had told him of the Houyhnhnms; because the least hint of such a story would not only draw numbers of people to see me, but probably put me in danger of being imprisoned, or burned by the Inquisition. The Captain persuaded me to accept a suit of clothes newly made; but I would not suffer the tailor to take my measure; however, Don Pedro being almost of my size, they fitted me well enough. He accoutered me with other necessaries, all new, which I aired for twenty-four hours before I would use them.

The Captain had no wife, nor above three servants, none of which were suffered to attend at meals; and his whole deportment was so obliging, added to very good human understanding, that I really began to tolerate his company. He gained so far upon me, that I ventured to look out of the back window. By degrees I was brought into another room, from whence I peeped into the street, but drew my head back in a fright. In a week's time he seduced me down to the door. I found my terror gradually lessened, but my hatred and contempt seemed to increase. I was at last bold enough to walk the street in his company, but kept my nose well stopped with rue, or sometimes with tobacco.

In ten days, Don Pedro, to whom I had given some account of my domestic affairs, put it upon me as a point of honor and conscience that I ought to return to my native country, and live at home with my wife and children. He told me there was an English ship in the port just ready to sail, and he would furnish me with all things necessary. It would be tedious to repeat his arguments, and my contradictions. He said it was altogether impossible to find such a solitary island as I had desired to live in; but I might command in my own house, and pass my time in a manner as recluse as I pleased.

I complied at last, finding I could not do better. I left Lisbon the 24th day of November, in an English merchantman, but who was the Master I never inquired. Don Pedro accompanied me to the ship, and lent me twenty pounds. He took kind leave of me, and embraced me at parting; which I bore as well as I could. During this last voyage I had no commerce with the Master, or any of his men; but pretending I was sick kept close in my cabin. On the fifth of December, 1715, we cast anchor in the Downs about nine in the morning, and at three in the afternoon I got safe to my house at Redriff.

My wife and family received me with great surprise and joy, because they concluded me certainly dead; but I must freely confess, the sight of them filled me only with hatred, disgust, and contempt; and the more, by reflecting on the near alliance I had to them. For although since my unfortunate exile from the Houyhnhnm country, I had compelled myself to tolerate the sight of Yahoos, and to converse with Don Pedro de Mendez; yet my memory and imaginations were perpetually filled with the virtues and ideas of those

5. At the rear.

exalted Houyhnhnms. And when I began to consider that by copulating with one of the Yahoo species, I had become a parent of more, it struck me with the utmost shame, confusion, and horror.

As soon as I entered the house, my wife took me in her arms, and kissed me; at which, having not been used to the touch of that odious animal for so many years, I fell in a swoon for almost an hour. At the time I am writing, it is five years since my last return to England. During the first year I could not endure my wife or children in my presence, the very smell of them was intolerable; much less could I suffer them to eat in the same room. To this hour they dare not presume to touch my bread, or drink out of the same cup; neither was I ever able to let one of them take me by the hand. The first money I laid out was to buy two young stone-horses,[6] which I keep in a good stable, and next to them the groom is my greatest favorite; for I feel my spirits revived by the smell he contracts in the stable. My horses understand me tolerably well; I converse with them at least four hours every day. They are strangers to bridle or saddle; they live in great amity with me, and friendship to each other.

CHAPTER 12. *The Author's veracity. His design in publishing this work. His censure of those travelers who swerve from the truth. The Author clears himself from any sinister ends in writing. His native country commended. The right of the crown to those countries described by the Author is justified. The difficulty of conquering them. The Author takes his last leave of the reader; proposeth his manner of living for the future; gives good advice, and concludeth.*

Thus gentle reader, I have given thee a faithful history of my travels for sixteen years, and above seven months; wherein I have not been so studious of ornament as of truth. I could perhaps like others have astonished thee with strange improbable tales; but I rather chose to relate plain matter of fact in the simplest manner and style; because my principal design was to inform, and not to amuse thee.

It is easy for us who travel into remote countries, which are seldom visited by Englishmen or other Europeans, to form descriptions of wonderful animals both at sea and land. Whereas a traveler's chief aim should be to make men wiser and better, and to improve their minds by the bad as well as good example of what they deliver concerning foreign places.

I could heartily wish a law were enacted, that every traveler, before he were permitted to publish his voyages, should be obliged to make oath before the Lord High Chancellor that all he intended to print was absolutely true to the best of his knowledge; for then the world would no longer be deceived as it usually is, while some writers, to make their works pass the better upon the public, impose the grossest falsities on the unwary reader. I have perused several books of travels with great delight in my younger days; but, having since gone over most parts of the globe, and been able to contradict many fabulous accounts from my own observation, it hath given me a great disgust against this part of reading, and some indignation to see the credulity of mankind so impudently abused. Therefore, since my acquaintance were pleased to think my poor endeavors might not be unacceptable to my coun-

---

6. Stallions.

try, I imposed on myself as a maxim, never to be swerved from, that I would *strictly adhere to truth*; neither indeed can I be ever under the least temptation to vary from it, while I retain in my mind the lectures and example of my noble master, and the other illustrious Houyhnhnms, of whom I had so long the honor to be an humble hearer.

> ——*Nec si miserum Fortuna Sinonem*
> *Finxit, vanum etiam, mendacemque improba finget.*[7]

I know very well how little reputation is to be got by writings which require neither genius nor learning, nor indeed any other talent, except a good memory, or an exact *Journal*. I know likewise, that writers of travels, like dictionary-makers, are sunk into oblivion by the weight and bulk of those who come last, and therefore lie uppermost. And it is highly probable that such travelers who shall hereafter visit the countries described in this work of mine, may be detecting my errors (if there be any) and adding many new discoveries of their own, jostle me out of vogue, and stand in my place, making the world forget that ever I was an author. This indeed would be too great a mortification if I wrote for fame; but, as my sole intention was the Public Good, I cannot be altogether disappointed. For, who can read the virtues I have mentioned in the glorious Houyhnhnms, without being ashamed of his own vices, when he considers himself as the reasoning, governing animal of his country? I shall say nothing of those remote nations where Yahoos preside; amongst which the least corrupted are the Brobdingnagians, whose wise maxims in morality and government it would be our happiness to observe. But I forbear descanting further, and rather leave the judicious reader to his own remarks and applications.

I am not a little pleased that this work of mine can possibly meet with no censurers; for what objections can be made against a writer who relates only plain facts that happened in such distant countries, where we have not the least interest with respect either to trade or negotiations? I have carefully avoided every fault with which common writers of travels are often too justly charged. Besides, I meddle not the least with any party, but write without passion, prejudice, or ill-will against any man or number of men whatsoever. I write for the noblest end, to inform and instruct mankind, over whom I may, without breach of modesty, pretend to some superiority, from the advantages I received by conversing so long among the most accomplished Houyhnhnms. I write without any view towards profit or praise. I never suffer a word to pass that may look like a reflection, or possibly give the least offense even to those who are most ready to take it. So that, I hope, I may with justice pronounce myself an Author perfectly blameless; against whom the tribes of answerers, considerers, observers, reflectors, detecters, remarkers will never be able to find matter for exercising their talents.

I confess it was whispered to me that I was bound in duty as a subject of England, to have given in a memorial[8] to a secretary of state, at my first coming over; because, whatever lands are discovered by a subject, belong to the Crown. But I doubt whether our conquests in the countries I treat of would be as easy as those of Ferdinando Cortez over the naked Americans.

---

7. Nor if Fortune had molded Sinon for misery, will she also in spite mold him as false and lying (Latin; Virgil's *Aeneid* 2.79–80).

8. Statement of facts for government use.

The Lilliputians, I think, are hardly worth the charge of a fleet and army to reduce them; and I question whether it might be prudent or safe to attempt the Brobdingnagians; or, whether an English army would be much at their ease with the Flying Island over their heads. The Houyhnhnms, indeed, appear not to be so well prepared for war, a science to which they are perfect strangers, and especially against missive weapons. However, supposing myself to be a minister of state, I could never give my advice for invading them. Their prudence, unanimity, unacquaintedness with fear, and their love of their country would amply supply all defects in the military art. Imagine twenty thousand of them breaking into the midst of an European army, confounding the ranks, overturning the carriages, battering the warriors' faces into mummy, by terrible yerks[9] from their hinder hoofs: for they would well deserve the character given to Augustus, *Recalcitrat undique tutus*.[1] But instead of proposals for conquering that magnanimous nation, I rather wish they were in a capacity or disposition to send a sufficient number of their inhabitants for civilizing Europe; by teaching us the first principles of Honor, Justice, Truth, Temperance, public Spirit, Fortitude, Chastity, Friendship, Benevolence, and Fidelity. The names of all which virtues are still retained among us in most languages, and are to be met with in modern as well as ancient authors, which I am able to assert from my own small reading.

But I had another reason which made me less forward to enlarge his majesty's dominions by my discoveries: to say the truth, I had conceived a few scruples with relation to the distributive justice of princes upon those occasions. For instance, a crew of pirates are driven by a storm they know not whither; at length a boy discovers land from the topmast; they go on shore to rob and plunder; they see an harmless people, are entertained with kindness, they give the country a new name, they take formal possession of it for the king, they set up a rotten plank or a stone for a memorial, they murder two or three dozen of the natives, bring away a couple more by force for a sample, return home, and get their pardon. Here commences a new dominion acquired with a title by Divine Right. Ships are sent with the first opportunity; the natives driven out or destroyed, their princes tortured to discover their gold; a free license given to all acts of inhumanity and lust; the earth reeking with the blood of its inhabitants: and this execrable crew of butchers employed in so pious an expedition is a *modern colony* sent to convert and civilize an idolatrous and barbarous people.

But this description, I confess, doth by no means affect the British nation, who may be an example to the whole world for their wisdom, care, and justice in planting colonies; their liberal endowments for the advancement of religion and learning; their choice of devout and able pastors to propagate Christianity; their caution in stocking their provinces with people of sober lives and conversations from this the Mother Kingdom; their strict regard to the distribution of justice, in supplying the civil administration through all their colonies with officers of the greatest abilities, utter strangers to corruption: and to crown all, by sending the most vigilant and virtuous governors, who have no other views than the happiness of the people over whom they preside, and the honor of the king their master.

9. Kicks. "Mummy": pulp.
1. He kicks backward, at every point on his guard (Latin; Horace's *Satires* 2.1.20).

But, as those countries which I have described do not appear to have any desire of being conquered, and enslaved, murdered, or driven out by colonies, nor abound either in gold, silver, sugar, or tobacco, I did humbly conceive they were by no means proper objects of our zeal, our valor, or our interest. However, if those whom it may concern, think fit to be of another opinion, I am ready to depose, when I shall be lawfully called, that no European did ever visit these countries before me. I mean, if the inhabitants ought to be believed.

But, as to the formality of taking possession in my sovereign's name, it never came once into my thoughts; and if it had, yet as my affairs then stood, I should perhaps in point of prudence and self-preservation have put it off to a better opportunity.

Having thus answered the only objection that can be raised against me as a traveler, I here take a final leave of my courteous readers, and return to enjoy my own speculations in my little garden at Redriff; to apply those excellent lessons of virtue which I learned among the Houyhnhnms; to instruct the Yahoos of my own family as far as I shall find them docible animals; to behold my figure often in a glass, and thus if possible habituate myself by time to tolerate the sight of a human creature; to lament the brutality of Houyhnhnms in my own country, but always treat their persons with respect, for the sake of my noble master, his family, his friends, and the whole Houyhnhnm race, whom these of ours have the honor to resemble in all their lineaments, however their intellectuals came to degenerate.

I began last week to permit my wife to sit at dinner with me, at the farthest end of a long table; and to answer (but with the utmost brevity) the few questions I ask her. Yet the smell of a Yahoo continuing very offensive, I always keep my nose well stopped with rue, lavender, or tobacco leaves. And although it be hard for a man late in life to remove old habits, I am not altogether out of hopes in some time to suffer a neighbor Yahoo in my company, without the apprehensions I am yet under of his teeth or his claws.

My reconcilement to the Yahoo kind in general might not be so difficult, if they would be content with those vices and follies only which nature hath entitled them to. I am not in the least provoked at the sight of a lawyer, a pickpocket, a colonel, a fool, a lord, a gamester, a politician, a whoremonger, a physician, an evidence,[2] a suborner, an attorney, a traitor, or the like: this is all according to the due course of things. But when I behold a lump of deformity, and diseases both in body and mind, smitten with *pride,* it immediately breaks all the measures of my patience; neither shall I be ever able to comprehend how such an animal and such a vice could tally together. The wise and virtuous Houyhnhnms, who abound in all excellencies that can adorn a rational creature, have no name for this vice in their language, which hath no terms to express anything that is evil, except those whereby they describe the detestable qualities of their Yahoos, among which they were not able to distinguish this of pride, for want of thoroughly understanding human nature, as it showeth itself in other countries, where that animal presides. But I, who had more experience, could plainly observe some rudiments of it among the wild Yahoos.

But the Houyhnhnms, who live under the government of reason, are no

2. Witness.

more proud of the good qualities they possess, than I should be for not wanting a leg or an arm, which no man in his wits would boast of, although he must be miserable without them. I dwell the longer upon this subject from the desire I have to make the society of an English Yahoo by any means not insupportable; and therefore I here entreat those who have any tincture of this absurd vice, that they will not presume to appear in my sight.

1726, 1735

A Modest Proposal[1]

FOR PREVENTING THE CHILDREN OF POOR PEOPLE IN IRELAND FROM BEING A BURDEN TO THEIR PARENTS OR COUNTRY, AND FOR MAKING THEM BENEFICIAL TO THE PUBLIC

It is a melancholy object to those who walk through this great town[2] or travel in the country, when they see the streets, the roads, and cabin doors, crowded with beggars of the female sex, followed by three, four, or six children, all in rags and importuning every passenger for an alms. These mothers, instead of being able to work for their honest livelihood, are forced to employ all their time in strolling to beg sustenance for their helpless infants, who, as they grow up, either turn thieves for want of work, or leave their dear native country to fight for the Pretender in Spain, or sell themselves to the Barbadoes.[3]

I think it is agreed by all parties that this prodigious number of children in the arms, or on the backs, or at the heels of their mothers, and frequently of their fathers, is in the present deplorable state of the kingdom a very great additional grievance; and therefore whoever could find out a fair, cheap, and easy method of making these children sound, useful members of the commonwealth would deserve so well of the public as to have his statue set up for a preserver of the nation.

But my intention is very far from being confined to provide only for the children of professed beggars; it is of a much greater extent, and shall take in the whole number of infants at a certain age who are born of parents in effect as little able to support them as those who demand our charity in the streets.

1. A Modest Proposal is an example of Swift's favorite satiric devices used with superb effect. Irony (from the deceptive adjective modest in the title to the very last sentence) pervades the piece. A rigorous logic deduces ghastly arguments from a premise so quietly assumed that readers assent before they are aware of what that assent implies. Parody, at which Swift is adept, allows him to glance sardonically at the by then familiar figure of the benevolent humanitarian (forerunner of the modern sociologist, social worker, and economic planner) concerned to correct a social evil by means of a theoretically conceived plan. The proposer, as naive as he is apparently logical and kindly, ignores and therefore emphasizes for the reader the enormity of his plan. The whole is an elaboration of a rather trite metaphor: "The English are devouring the Irish." But there is nothing trite about the pamphlet, which expresses in Swift's most controlled style his pity for the oppressed, ignorant, populous, and hungry Catholic peasants of Ireland and his anger at the rapacious English absentee landlords, who were bleeding the country white with the silent approbation of Parliament, ministers, and the crown.
2. Dublin.
3. James Francis Edward Stuart (1688–1766), the son of James II, was claimant ("Pretender") to the throne of England from which the Glorious Revolution had barred his succession. Catholic Ireland was loyal to him, and Irishmen joined him in his exile on the Continent. Because of the poverty in Ireland, many Irishmen emigrated to the West Indies and other British colonies in America; they paid their passage by binding themselves to work for a stated period for one of the planters.

As to my own part, having turned my thoughts for many years upon this important subject, and maturely weighed the several schemes of other projectors,[4] I have always found them grossly mistaken in their computation. It is true, a child just dropped from its dam may be supported by her milk for a solar year, with little other nourishment; at most not above the value of two shillings, which the mother may certainly get, or the value in scraps, by her lawful occupation of begging; and it is exactly at one year old that I propose to provide for them in such a manner as instead of being a charge upon their parents or the parish, or wanting food and raiment for the rest of their lives, they shall on the contrary contribute to the feeding, and partly to the clothing, of many thousands.

There is likewise another great advantage in my scheme, that it will prevent those voluntary abortions, and that horrid practice of women murdering their bastard children, alas, too frequent among us, sacrificing the poor innocent babes, I doubt, more to avoid the expense than the shame, which would move tears and pity in the most savage and inhuman breast.

The number of souls in this kingdom[5] being usually reckoned one million and a half, of these I calculate there may be about two hundred thousand couple whose wives are breeders; from which number I subtract thirty thousand couples who are able to maintain their own children, although I apprehend there cannot be so many under the present distresses of the kingdom; but this being granted, there will remain an hundred and seventy thousand breeders. I again subtract fifty thousand for those women who miscarry, or whose children die by accident or disease within the year. There only remain an hundred and twenty thousand children of poor parents annually born. The question therefore is, how this number shall be reared and provided for, which, as I have already said, under the present situation of affairs, is utterly impossible by all the methods hitherto proposed. For we can neither employ them in handicraft or agriculture; we neither build houses (I mean in the country) nor cultivate land. They can very seldom pick up a livelihood by stealing till they arrive at six years old, except where they are of towardly parts;[6] although I confess they learn the rudiments much earlier, during which time they can however be looked upon only as probationers, as I have been informed by a principal gentleman in the county of Cavan, who protested to me that he never knew above one or two instances under the ages of six, even in a part of the kingdom so renowned for the quickest proficiency in that art.

I am assured by our merchants that a boy or a girl before twelve years old is no salable commodity; and even when they come to this age they will not yield above three pounds, or three pounds and half a crown at most on the Exchange; which cannot turn to account either to the parents or the kingdom, the charge of nutriment and rags having been at least four times that value.

I shall now therefore humbly propose my own thoughts, which I hope will not be liable to the least objection.

I have been assured by a very knowing American of my acquaintance in London, that a young healthy child well nursed is at a year old a most deli-

---

4. Devisers of schemes.
5. Ireland.

6. Promising abilities.

cious, nourishing, and wholesome food, whether stewed, roasted, baked, or boiled; and I make no doubt that it will equally serve in a fricassee or a ragout.[7]

I do therefore humbly offer it to public consideration that of the hundred and twenty thousand children, already computed, twenty thousand may be reserved for breed, whereof only one fourth part to be males, which is more than we allow to sheep, black cattle, or swine; and my reason is that these children are seldom the fruits of marriage, a circumstance not much regarded by our savages, therefore one male will be sufficient to serve four females. That the remaining hundred thousand may at a year old be offered in sale to the persons of quality and fortune through the kingdom, always advising the mother to let them suck plentifully in the last month, so as to render them plump and fat for a good table. A child will make two dishes at an entertainment for friends; and when the family dines alone, the fore or hind quarter will make a reasonable dish, and seasoned with a little pepper or salt will be very good boiled on the fourth day, especially in winter.

I have reckoned upon a medium that a child just born will weigh twelve pounds, and in a solar year if tolerably nursed increaseth to twenty-eight pounds.

I grant this food will be somewhat dear, and therefore very proper for landlords, who, as they have already devoured most of the parents, seem to have the best title to the children.

Infant's flesh will be in season throughout the year, but more plentiful in March, and a little before and after. For we are told by a grave author, an eminent French physician,[8] that fish being a prolific diet, there are more children born in Roman Catholic countries about nine months after Lent than at any other season; therefore, reckoning a year after Lent, the markets will be more glutted than usual, because the number of popish infants is at least three to one in this kingdom; and therefore it will have one other collateral advantage, by lessening the number of Papists among us.

I have already computed the charge of nursing a beggar's child (in which list I reckon all cottagers, laborers, and four fifths of the farmers) to be about two shillings per annum, rags included; and I believe no gentleman would repine to give ten shillings for the carcass of a good fat child, which, as I have said, will make four dishes of excellent nutritive meat, when he hath only some particular friend or his own family to dine with him. Thus the squire will learn to be a good landlord, and grow popular among the tenants; the mother will have eight shillings net profit, and be fit for the work till she produces another child.

Those who are more thrifty (as I must confess the times require) may flay the carcass; the skin of which artificially[9] dressed will make admirable gloves for ladies, and summer boots for fine gentlemen.

As to our city of Dublin, shambles[1] may be appointed for this purpose in the most convenient parts of it, and butchers we may be assured will not be wanting; although I rather recommend buying the children alive, and dressing them hot from the knife as we do roasting pigs.

A very worthy person, a true lover of his country, and whose virtues I highly

---

7. A highly seasoned meat stew.
8. François Rabelais (ca. 1494–1553), a humorist and satirist, by no means grave.
9. Skillfully.
1. Slaughterhouses.

esteem, was lately pleased in discoursing on this matter to offer a refinement upon my scheme. He said that many gentlemen of this kingdom, having of late destroyed their deer, he conceived that the want of venison might be well supplied by the bodies of young lads and maidens, not exceeding fourteen years of age nor under twelve, so great a number of both sexes in every county being now ready to starve for want of work and service; and these to be disposed of by their parents, if alive, or otherwise by their nearest relations. But with due deference to so excellent a friend and so deserving a patriot, I cannot be altogether in his sentiments; for as to the males, my American acquaintance assured me from frequent experience that their flesh was generally tough and lean, like that of our schoolboys, by continual exercise, and their taste disagreeable; and to fatten them would not answer the charge. Then as to the females, it would, I think with humble submission, be a loss to the public, because they soon would become breeders themselves; and besides, it is not improbable that some scrupulous people might be apt to censure such a practice (although indeed very unjustly) as a little bordering upon cruelty; which I confess, hath always been with me the strongest objection against any project, how well soever intended.

But in order to justify my friend, he confessed that this expedient was put into his head by the famous Psalmanazar,[2] a native of the island Formosa, who came from thence to London above twenty years ago, and in conversation told my friend that in his country when any young person happened to be put to death, the executioner sold the carcass to persons of quality as a prime dainty; and that in his time the body of a plump girl of fifteen, who was crucified for an attempt to poison the emperor, was sold to his Imperial Majesty's prime minister of state, and other great mandarins of the court, in joints from the gibbet, at four hundred crowns. Neither indeed can I deny that if the same use were made of several plump young girls in this town, who without one single groat to their fortunes cannot stir abroad without a chair, and appear at the playhouse and assemblies in foreign fineries which they never will pay for, the kingdom would not be the worse.

Some persons of a desponding spirit are in great concern about that vast number of poor people who are aged, diseased, or maimed, and I have been desired to employ my thoughts what course may be taken to ease the nation of so grievous an encumbrance. But I am not in the least pain upon that matter, because it is very well known that they are every day dying and rotting by cold and famine, and filth and vermin, as fast as can be reasonably expected. And as to the younger laborers, they are now in almost as hopeful a condition. They cannot get work, and consequently pine away for want of nourishment to a degree that if at any time they are accidentally hired to common labor, they have not strength to perform it; and thus the country and themselves are happily delivered from the evils to come.

I have too long digressed, and therefore shall return to my subject. I think the advantages by the proposal which I have made are obvious and many, as well as of the highest importance.

For first, as I have already observed, it would greatly lessen the number of Papists, with whom we are yearly overrun, being the principal breeders of the nation as well as our most dangerous enemies; and who stay at home on

2. George Psalmanazar (ca. 1679–1763), a famous impostor. A Frenchman, he imposed himself on English bishops, noblemen, and scientists as a Formosan. He wrote an entirely fictitious account of Formosa, in which he described human sacrifices and cannibalism.

purpose to deliver the kingdom to the Pretender, hoping to take their advantage by the absence of so many good Protestants, who have chosen rather to leave their country than stay at home and pay tithes against their conscience to an Episcopal curate.

Secondly, the poorer tenants will have something valuable of their own, which by law may be made liable to distress,[3] and help to pay their landlord's rent, their corn and cattle being already seized and money a thing unknown.

Thirdly, whereas the maintenance of an hundred thousand children, from two years old and upwards, cannot be computed at less than ten shillings a piece per annum, the nation's stock will be thereby increased fifty thousand pounds per annum, besides the profit of a new dish introduced to the tables of all gentlemen of fortune in the kingdom who have any refinement in taste. And the money will circulate among ourselves, the goods being entirely of our own growth and manufacture.

Fourthly, the constant breeders, besides the gain of eight shillings sterling per annum by the sale of their children, will be rid of the charge of maintaining them after the first year.

Fifthly, this food would likewise bring great custom to taverns, where the vintners will certainly be so prudent as to procure the best receipts for dressing it to perfection, and consequently have their houses frequented by all the fine gentlemen, who justly value themselves upon their knowledge in good eating; and a skillful cook, who understands how to oblige his guests, will contrive to make it as expensive as they please.

Sixthly, this would be a great inducement to marriage, which all wise nations have either encouraged by rewards or enforced by laws and penalties. It would increase the care and tenderness of mothers toward their children, when they were sure of a settlement for life to the poor babes, provided in some sort by the public, to their annual profit instead of expense. We should see an honest emulation among the married women, which of them could bring the fattest child to the market. Men would become as fond of their wives during the time of their pregnancy as they are now of their mares in foal, their cows in calf, or sows when they are ready to farrow; nor offer to beat or kick them (as is too frequent a practice) for fear of a miscarriage.

Many other advantages might be enumerated. For instance, the addition of some thousand carcasses in our exportation of barreled beef, the propagation of swine's flesh, and improvement in the art of making good bacon, so much wanted among us by the great destruction of pigs, too frequent at our tables, which are no way comparable in taste or magnificence to a well-grown, fat, yearling child, which roasted whole will make a considerable figure at a lord mayor's feast or any other public entertainment. But this and many others I omit, being studious of brevity.

Supposing that one thousand families in this city would be constant customers for infants' flesh, besides others who might have it at merry meetings, particularly weddings and christenings, I compute that Dublin would take off annually about twenty thousand carcasses, and the rest of the kingdom (where probably they will be sold somewhat cheaper) the remaining eighty thousand.

I can think of no one objection that will probably be raised against this

3. Distraint, i.e., the seizing, through legal action, of property for the payment of debts and other obligations.

proposal, unless it should be urged that the number of people will be thereby much lessened in the kingdom. This I freely own, and it was indeed one principal design in offering it to the world. I desire the reader will observe, that I calculate my remedy for this one individual kingdom of Ireland and for no other that ever was, is, or I think ever can be upon earth. Therefore let no man talk to me of other expedients: of taxing our absentees at five shillings a pound: of using neither clothes nor household furniture except what is of our own growth and manufacture: of utterly rejecting the materials and instruments that promote foreign luxury: of curing the expensiveness of pride, vanity, idleness, and gaming in our women: of introducing a vein of parsimony, prudence, and temperance: of learning to love our country, in the want of which we differ even from Laplanders and the inhabitants of Topinamboo:[4] of quitting our animosities and factions, nor acting any longer like the Jews, who were murdering one another at the very moment their city was taken:[5] of being a little cautious not to sell our country and conscience for nothing: of teaching landlords to have at least one degree of mercy toward their tenants: lastly, of putting a spirit of honesty, industry, and skill into our shopkeepers; who, if a resolution could now be taken to buy only our native goods, would immediately unite to cheat and exact upon us in the price, the measure, and the goodness, nor could ever yet be brought to make one fair proposal of just dealing, though often and earnestly invited to it.[6]

Therefore I repeat, let no man talk to me of these and the like expedients, till he hath at least some glimpse of hope that there will ever be some hearty and sincere attempt to put them in practice.

But as to myself, having been wearied out for many years with offering vain, idle, visionary thoughts, and at length utterly despairing of success, I fortunately fell upon this proposal, which, as it is wholly new, so it hath something solid and real, of no expense and little trouble, full in our own power, and whereby we can incur no danger in disobliging England. For this kind of commodity will not bear exportation, the flesh being of too tender a consistence to admit a long continuance in salt, although perhaps I could name a country which would be glad to eat up our whole nation without it.[7]

After all, I am not so violently bent upon my own opinion as to reject any offer proposed by wise men, which shall be found equally innocent, cheap, easy, and effectual. But before something of that kind shall be advanced in contradiction to my scheme, and offering a better, I desire the author or authors will be pleased maturely to consider two points. First, as things now stand, how they will be able to find food and raiment for an hundred thousand useless mouths and backs. And secondly, there being a round million of creatures in human figure throughout this kingdom, whose sole subsistence put into a common stock would leave them in debt two millions of pounds sterling, adding those who are beggars by profession to the bulk of farmers, cottagers, and laborers, with their wives and children who are beggars in effect; I desire those politicians who dislike my overture, and may perhaps be so bold to attempt an answer, that they will first ask the parents

---

4. I.e., even Laplanders love their frozen, infertile country and the savage tribes of Brazil love their jungle more than the Anglo-Irish love Ireland.
5. During the siege of Jerusalem by the Roman emperor Titus, who captured and destroyed the city in 70 C.E., bloody fights broke out between

factions of fanatics.
6. Swift himself had made all these proposals in various pamphlets. In editions printed during his lifetime the various proposals were italicized to indicate that Swift is no longer being ironic.
7. I.e., England.

of these mortals whether they would not at this day think it a great happiness to have been sold for food at a year old in the manner I prescribe, and thereby have avoided such a perpetual sense of misfortunes as they have since gone through by the oppression of landlords, the impossibility of paying rent without money or trade, the want of common sustenance, with neither house nor clothes to cover them from the inclemencies of the weather, and the most inevitable prospect of entailing the like or greater miseries upon their breed forever.

I profess, in the sincerity of my heart, that I have not the least personal interest in endeavoring to promote this necessary work, having no other motive than the public good of my country, by advancing our trade, providing for infants, relieving the poor, and giving some pleasure to the rich. I have no children by which I can propose to get a single penny; the youngest being nine years old, and my wife past childbearing.

1729

ALEXANDER POPE
1688–1744

Alexander Pope is the only important writer of his generation who was solely a man of letters. Because he could not, as a Roman Catholic, attend a university, vote, or hold public office, he was excluded from the sort of patronage that was bestowed by statesmen on many writers during the reign of Anne. This disadvantage he turned into a positive good, for the translation of Homer's *Iliad* and *Odyssey,* which he undertook for profit as well as for fame, gave him ample means to live the life of an independent suburban gentleman. After 1718 he lived hospitably in his villa by the Thames at Twickenham (then pronounced *Twit'nam*), entertaining his friends and converting his five acres of land into a diminutive landscape garden. Almost exactly a century earlier, William Shakespeare had earned enough to retire to a country estate at Stratford—but he had been an actor-manager as well as a playwright; Pope was the first English writer to demonstrate that literature alone could be a gainful profession.

Ill health plagued Pope almost from birth. Crippled early by tuberculosis of the bone, he never grew taller than four and a half feet. In later life he suffered from violent headaches and required constant attention from servants. But Pope did not allow his infirmities to hold him back; he was always a master at making the best of what he had. Around 1700 his father, a well-to-do, retired London merchant, moved to a small property at Binfield in Windsor Forest. There, in rural surroundings, young Pope completed his education by reading whatever he pleased, "like a boy gathering flowers in the woods and fields just as they fall in his way"; and there, encouraged by his father, he began to write verse. He was already an accomplished poet in his teens; no English poet has ever been more precocious.

Pope's first striking success as a poet was *An Essay on Criticism* (1711), which brought him Joseph Addison's approval and an intemperate personal attack from the critic John Dennis, who was angered by a casual reference to himself in the poem. *The Rape of the Lock,* both in its original shorter version of 1712 and in its more elaborate version of 1714, proved the author a master not only of metrics and of language but also of witty, urbane satire. In *An Essay on Criticism,* Pope had excelled all his predecessors in writing a didactic poem after the example of Horace; in the *Rape,* he had written the most brilliant mock epic in the language. But there was another vein in Pope's youthful poetry, a tender concern with natural beauty and love. The *Pastorals* (1709), his first publication, and *Windsor Forest* (1713; much of it was written earlier) abound in visual imagery and descriptive passages of ideally ordered nature; they remind us that Pope was an amateur painter. The *Elegy to the Memory of an Unfortunate Lady* and *Eloisa to Abelard,* published in the collected poems of 1717, dwell on the pangs of unhappy lovers (Pope himself never married). And even the long task of translating Homer; the "dull duty" of editing Shakespeare; and in middle age, his preoccupation with ethical and satirical poetry did not make less fine his keen sense of beauty in nature and art.

Pope's early poetry brought him to the attention of the leading wits of the town, with whom he began to associate in the masculine world of coffeehouse and tavern. Most of them were Whigs. But after the fall of the Whigs in 1710 and the formation of the Tory government under Robert Harley (later earl of Oxford) and Henry St. John (later Viscount Bolingbroke) party loyalties bred bitterness among the wits as among the politicians. By 1712, Pope had made the acquaintance of another group of writers, all Tories, who were soon his intimate friends: Jonathan Swift, by then the close associate of Harley and St. John and the principal propagandist for their policies; Dr. John Arbuthnot, physician to the queen, a learned scientist, a wit, and a man of humanity and integrity; John Gay, the poet, who in 1728 was to create *The Beggar's Opera,* the greatest theatrical success of the century; and the poet Thomas Parnell. Through them he became the friend and admirer of Oxford and later the intimate of Bolingbroke. In 1714 this group formed a club for satirizing all sorts of false learning. The friends proposed to write jointly the biography of a learned fool whom they named Martinus Scriblerus (Martin the Scribbler), whose life and opinions would be a running commentary on educated nonsense. Some amusing episodes were later rewritten and published as the *Memoirs of Martinus Scriblerus* (1741). The real importance of the club, however, is that it fostered a satiric temper that would be expressed in such mature works of the friends as *Gulliver's Travels, The Beggar's Opera,* and *The Dunciad.*

"The life of a wit is a warfare on earth," said Pope, generalizing from his own experience. Throughout his career, enemies jealous of his success derided his crippled body as well as his writings. But he was a fighter who struck back, always giving better than he got. Pope's literary warfare began in 1713, when he announced his intention of translating the *Iliad* and sought subscribers to a deluxe edition of the work. Subscribers came in droves, but the Whig writers who surrounded Addison at Button's Coffee House did all they could to discredit the venture. The eventual success of the first published installment of his *Iliad* in 1715 did not obliterate Pope's resentment against Addison and his "little senate"; and he took his revenge in the damaging portrait of Addison (under the name of Atticus), which was later included in the *Epistle to Dr. Arbuthnot* (1735), lines 193–214. The not unjustified attacks on Pope's edition of Shakespeare (1725) by the learned Shakespeare scholar Lewis Theobald (Pope always spelled and pronounced the name "Tibbald" in his satires), led to Theobald's appearance as king of the dunces in *The Dunciad* (1728). In this impressive poem Pope stigmatized his literary enemies as agents of all that he disliked and feared in the tendencies of his time—the vulgarization of taste and the arts consequent on the rapid growth of the reading public and the development of journalism, magazines, and other popular and cheap publications, which spread scandal, sensationalism, and political partisanship—in short the new commercial spirit of the nation that was corrupting not only the arts but, as Pope saw it, the national life itself.

In the 1730s Pope moved on to philosophical, ethical, and political subjects in *An Essay on Man,* the *Epistles to Several Persons,* and the *Imitations of Horace.* The reigns of George I and George II appeared to him, as to Swift and other Tories, a period of rapid moral, political, and cultural deterioration. The agents of decay fed on the rise of moneyed (as opposed to landed) wealth, which accounted for the political corruption encouraged by Sir Robert Walpole and the court party, and the corruption of all aspects of the national life by a vulgar class of *nouveaux riches*. Pope assumed the role of the champion of traditional values: of right reason, humanistic learning, sound art, good taste, and public virtue. It was fortunate that most of his enemies happened to illustrate various degrees of unreason, pedantry, bad art, vulgar taste, and at best, indifferent morals. In such an age, Pope implies, it is impossible for such a man like him—honest, truthful, blunt—not to write satire.

Pope was a master of style. From first to last, his verse is notable for its rhythmic variety, despite the apparently rigid metrical unit—the heroic couplet—in which he wrote; for the precision of meaning and the harmony (or expressive disharmony) of his language; and for the union of maximum conciseness with maximum complexity. Variety and harmony can be observed in even so short a passage as lines 71–76 of the pastoral *Summer* (1709), lines so lyrical that, in *Semele*, Handel set them to music. In the passage quoted below (as also in the following quotation), only those rhetorical stresses that distort the normal iambic flow of the verse have been marked; internal pauses within the line are indicated by single and double bars, alliteration and assonance by italics.

> Óh déign to visit our *for*aken *se*ats,
>
> The mossy *fou*ntains ‖ and the *g*reen *re*treats!
>
> Where'er yóu wálk ‖ cóol gáles shall *f*an the *g*lade,
>
> Trées whére yóu sít ‖ shall crowd into a shade:
>
> Where'er yóu tŕead ‖ the bl*u*shing *f*lowers shall rise,
>
> And all thíngs *f*lóurish where yóu túrn your eyes.

Pope has attained metrical variety by the free substitution of trochees and spondees for the normal iambs; he has achieved rhythmic variety by arranging phrases and clauses (units of syntax and logic) of different lengths within single lines and couplets, so that the passage moves with the sinuous fluency of thought and feeling; and he not only has chosen musical combinations of words but has also subtly modulated the harmony of the passage by unobtrusive patterns of alliteration and assonance.

Contrast with this pastoral passage lines 16–25 of the *Epilogue to the Satires, Dialogue* 2 (1738), in which Pope is not making music but imitating actual conversation so realistically that the metrical pattern and the integrity of the couplet and individual line seem to be destroyed (although in fact they remain in place). In a dialogue with a friend who warns him that his satire is too personal, indeed mere libel, the poet-satirist replies:

> Yé státesmen, | priests of one religion all!
>
> Yé trádesmen vile ‖ in army, court, or hall!
>
> Yé réverend atheists. ‖ F. Scandal! | name them, | Who?
>
>   P. Why that's the thing you bid me not to do.
>
> Whó stárved a sister, ‖ who foreswore a debt,
>
> Í néver named; ‖ the town's inquiring yet.
>
> The poisoning dame—| F. Yóu méan—| P. I don't—| F. Yóu dó.

P. Sée, nów Í kéep the secret, ‖ and nót yóu!

The bribing statesman—‖ F. Hóld, ‖ tóo hígh you go.

P. The bribed elector—‖ F. There you stoop tóo lów.

In such a passage the language and rhythms of poetry merge with the language and rhythms of impassioned living speech.

A fine example of Pope's ability to derive the maximum of meaning from the most economic use of language and image is the description of the manor house in which lives old Cotta, the miser (*Epistle to Lord Bathurst*, lines 187–96):

> Like some lone Chartreuse stands the good old Hall,
> Silence without, and fasts within the wall;
> No raftered roofs with dance and tabor sound,
> No noontide bell invites the country round;
> Tenants with sighs the smokeless towers survey,
> And turn the unwilling steeds another way;
> Benighted wanderers, the forest o'er,
> Curse the saved candle and unopening door;
> While the gaunt mastiff growling at the gate,
> Affrights the beggar whom he longs to eat.

The first couplet of this passage associates the "Hall," symbol of English rural hospitality, with the Grande Chartreuse, the monastery in the French Alps, which, although a place of "silence" and "fasts" for the monks, afforded food and shelter to all travelers. Then the dismal details of Cotta's miserly dwelling provide a stark contrast, and the meaning of the scene is concentrated in the grotesque image of the last couplet: the half-starved watchdog and the frightened beggar confronting each other in mutual hunger.

But another sort of variety derives from Pope's respect for the idea that the different kinds of literature have their different and appropriate styles. Thus *An Essay on Criticism,* an informal discussion of literary theory, is written, like Horace's *Art of Poetry* (a similarly didactic poem), in a plain style, the easy language of well-bred talk. *The Rape of the Lock,* "a heroi-comical poem" (that is, a comic poem that treats trivial material in an epic style), employs the lofty heroic language that John Dryden had perfected in his translation of Virgil and introduces amusing parodies of passages in *Paradise Lost;* parodies later raised to truly Miltonic sublimity and complexity by the conclusion of *The Dunciad. Eloisa to Abelard* renders the brooding, passionate voice of its heroine in a declamatory language, given to sudden outbursts and shifts of tone, that recalls the stage. The grave epistles that make up *An Essay on Man,* a philosophical discussion of such majestic themes as the Creator and His creation, the universe, human nature, society, and happiness, are written in a stately forensic language and tone and constantly employ the traditional rhetorical figures. The *Imitations of Horace,* and above all, the *Epistle to Dr. Arbuthnot,* his finest poem "in the Horatian way," reveal Pope's final mastery of the plain style of Horace's epistles and satires and support his image of himself as the heir of the Roman poet. In short, no other poet of the century can equal Pope in the range of his materials, the diversity of his poetic styles, and the wizardry of his technique.

An Essay on Criticism

There is no pleasanter introduction to the canons of taste in the English Augustan age than Pope's *An Essay on Criticism.* As Addison said in his review in *Spectator* 253, it assembles the "most known and most received observations on the subject of literature and criticism." Pope was attempting to do for his time what Horace, in his *Art of Poetry,* and what Nicolas Boileau (French poet of the age of Louis XIV), in his *L'Art Poétique,* had done for theirs. Horace is Pope's model not only for principles of criticism but also for style, especially in the simple, conversational language and the tone of well-bred ease.

In framing his critical creed, Pope did not try for novelty: he wished merely to give to generally accepted doctrines pleasing and memorable expression and make them useful to modern poets. Here one meets the key words of neoclassical criticism: *wit, Nature, ancients, rules,* and *genius. Wit* in the poem is a word of many meanings—a clever remark or the person who makes it, a conceit, liveliness of mind, inventiveness, fancy, genius, a genius, and poetry itself, among others. *Nature* is an equally ambiguous word, meaning not "things out there" or "the outdoors" but most important that which is representative, universal, permanent in human experience as opposed to the idiosyncratic, the individual, the temporary. In line 21, *Nature* comes close to meaning "intuitive knowledge." In line 52, it means that half-personified power manifested in the cosmic order, which in its modes of working is a model for art. The reverence felt by most Augustans for the great writers of ancient Greece and Rome raised the question how far the authority of these *ancients* extended. Were their works to be received as models to be conscientiously imitated? Were the *rules* received from them or deducible from their works to be accepted as prescriptive laws or merely convenient guides? Was individual *genius* to be bound by what has been conventionally held to be *Nature,* by the authority of the *ancients,* and by the legalistic pedantry of *rules*? Or could it go its own way?

In part 1 of the *Essay,* Pope constructs a harmonious system in which he effects a compromise among all these conflicting forces—a compromise that is typically eighteenth century in spirit. Part 2 analyzes the causes of faulty criticism. Part 3 characterizes the good critic and praises the great critics of the past.

From An Essay on Criticism

Part 1

'Tis hard to say, if greater want of skill
Appear in writing or in judging ill;
But of the two less dangerous is the offense
To tire our patience than mislead our sense.
5 Some few in that, but numbers err in this,
Ten censure° wrong for one who writes amiss;   *judge*
A fool might once himself alone expose,
Now one in verse makes many more in prose.
  'Tis with our judgments as our watches, none
10 Go just alike, yet each believes his own.
In poets as true genius is but rare,
True taste as seldom is the critic's share;
Both must alike from Heaven derive their light,
These born to judge, as well as those to write.
15 Let such teach others who themselves excel,
And censure freely who have written well.
Authors are partial to their wit, 'tis true,
But are not critics to their judgment too?
  Yet if we look more closely, we shall find
20 Most have the seeds of judgment in their mind:
Nature affords at least a glimmering light;
The lines, though touched but faintly, are drawn right.

But as the slightest sketch, if justly traced, ⎱
Is by ill coloring but the more disgraced, ⎰
25   So by false learning is good sense defaced: ⎰
Some are bewildered in the maze of schools,
And some made coxcombs[1] Nature meant but fools.
In search of wit these lose their common sense,
And then turn critics in their own defense:
30   Each burns alike, who can, or cannot write,
Or with a rival's or an eunuch's spite.
All fools have still an itching to deride,
And fain would be upon the laughing side.
If Maevius[2] scribble in Apollo's spite,
35   There are who judge still worse than he can write.
        Some have at first for wits, then poets passed,
Turned critics next, and proved plain fools at last.
Some neither can for wits nor critics pass,
As heavy mules are neither horse nor ass.
40   Those half-learn'd witlings, numerous in our isle,
As half-formed insects on the banks of Nile;[3]
Unfinished things, one knows not what to call,
Their generation's so equivocal:
To tell° them would a hundred tongues require,   reckon, count
45   Or one vain wit's, that might a hundred tire.
        But you who seek to give and merit fame,
And justly bear a critic's noble name,
Be sure yourself and your own reach to know,
How far your genius, taste, and learning go;
50   Launch not beyond your depth, but be discreet,
And mark that point where sense and dullness meet.
        Nature to all things fixed the limits fit,
And wisely curbed proud man's pretending wit.
As on the land while here the ocean gains,
55   In other parts it leaves wide sandy plains;
Thus in the soul while memory prevails,
The solid power of understanding fails;
Where beams of warm imagination play,
The memory's soft figures melt away.
60   One science[4] only will one genius fit,
So vast is art, so narrow human wit.
Not only bounded to peculiar arts,
But oft in those confined to single parts.
Like kings we lose the conquests gained before,
65   By vain ambition still to make them more;
Each might his several province well command,
Would all but stoop to what they understand.
        First follow Nature, and your judgment frame
By her just standard, which is still the same;
70   Unerring Nature, still divinely bright,
One clear, unchanged, and universal light,

1. Superficial pretenders to learning.
2. A silly poet alluded to contemptuously by Virgil in *Eclogue* 3 and by Horace in *Epode* 10.
3. The ancients believed that many forms of life were spontaneously generated in the fertile mud of the Nile.
4. Branch of learning.

Life, force, and beauty must to all impart,
At once the source, and end, and test of art.
Art from that fund each just supply provides,
75 Works without show, and without pomp presides.
In some fair body thus the informing soul
With spirits feeds, with vigor fills the whole,
Each motion guides, and every nerve sustains;
Itself unseen, but in the effects remains.
80 Some, to whom Heaven in wit has been profuse,
Want as much more to turn it to its use;
For wit and judgment often are at strife,
Though meant each other's aid, like man and wife.
'Tis more to guide than spur the Muse's steed,
85 Restrain his fury than provoke his speed;
The wingèd courser,[5] like a generous° horse,   spirited, highly bred
Shows most true mettle when you check his course.
    Those rules of old discovered, not devised,
Are Nature still, but Nature methodized;
90 Nature, like liberty, is but restrained
By the same laws which first herself ordained.
    Hear how learn'd Greece her useful rules indites,
When to repress and when indulge our flights:
High on Parnassus' top her sons she showed,
95 And pointed out those arduous paths they trod;
Held from afar, aloft, the immortal prize,
And urged the rest by equal steps to rise.
Just precepts thus from great examples given,
She drew from them what they derived from Heaven.
100 The generous critic fanned the poet's fire,
And taught the world with reason to admire.
Then criticism the Muse's handmaid proved,
To dress her charms, and make her more beloved:
But following wits from that intention strayed,
105 Who could not win the mistress, wooed the maid;
Against the poets their own arms they turned,
Sure to hate most the men from whom they learned.
So modern 'pothecaries, taught the art
By doctors's bills° to play the doctor's part,   prescriptions
110 Bold in the practice of mistaken rules,
Prescribe, apply, and call their masters fools.
Some on the leaves of ancient authors prey,
Nor time nor moths e'er spoiled so much as they.
Some dryly plain, without invention's aid,
115 Write dull receipts[6] how poems may be made.
These leave the sense their learning to display,
And those explain the meaning quite away.
    You then whose judgment the right course would steer,
Know well each ancient's proper character;
120 His fable,[7] subject, scope° in every page;   aim, purpose

5. Pegasus, associated with the Muses and poetic inspiration.
6. Formulas for preparing a dish; recipes. Pope himself wrote an amusing burlesque, *Receipt to*

Make an Epic Poem, first published in the *Guardian* 78 (1713).
7. Plot or story of a play or poem.

Religion, country, genius of his age:
Without all these at once before your eyes,
Cavil you may, but never criticize.
Be Homer's works your study and delight,
125 Read them by day, and meditate by night;
Thence form your judgment, thence your maxims bring,
And trace the Muses upward to their spring.
Still with itself compared, his text peruse;
And let your comment be the Mantuan Muse.
130   When first young Maro[8] in his boundless mind
A work to outlast immortal Rome designed,
Perhaps he seemed above the critic's law,
And but from Nature's fountains scorned to draw;
But when to examine every part he came,
135 Nature and Homer were, he found, the same.
Convinced, amazed, he checks the bold design, ⎤
And rules as strict his labored work confine ⎬
As if the Stagirite[9] o'erlooked each line.   ⎦
Learn hence for ancient rules a just esteem;
140 To copy Nature is to copy them.
    Some beauties yet no precepts can declare,
For there's a happiness as well as care.[1]
Music resembles poetry, in each   ⎤
Are nameless graces which no methods teach, ⎬
145 And which a master hand alone can reach.   ⎦
If, where the rules not far enough extend
(Since rules were made but to promote their end)
Some lucky license answers to the full
The intent proposed, that license is a rule.
150 Thus Pegasus, a nearer way to take,
May boldly deviate from the common track.
Great wits sometimes may gloriously offend,
And rise to faults true critics dare not mend;
From vulgar bounds with brave disorder part,
155 And snatch a grace beyond the reach of art,
Which, without passing through the judgment, gains
The heart, and all its end at once attains.
In prospects thus, some objects please our eyes, ⎤
Which out of Nature's common order rise,   ⎬
160 The shapeless rock, or hanging precipice.   ⎦
But though the ancients thus their rules invade
(As kings dispense with laws themselves have made)
Moderns, beware! or if you must offend
Against the precept, ne'er transgress its end;
165 Let it be seldom, and compelled by need;
And have at least their precedent to plead.

---

8. Virgil. He was born in a village adjacent to Mantua in Italy, hence "Mantuan Muse." His epic, the *Aeneid,* was modeled on Homer's *Iliad* and *Odyssey* and was considered to be a refinement on the Greek poems. Thus it could be thought of as a commentary ("comment") on Homer's poems.
9. Aristotle, native of Stagira, from whose *Poetics*

later critics formulated strict rules for writing tragedy and the epic.
1. I.e., no rules ("precepts") can explain ("declare") some beautiful effects in a work of art that can be the result only of inspiration or good luck ("happiness"), not of painstaking labor ("care").

The critic else proceeds without remorse,
Seizes your fame, and puts his laws in force.
　　I know there are, to whose presumptuous thoughts
170　Those freer beauties, even in them, seem faults.[2]
Some figures monstrous and misshaped appear,
Considered singly, or beheld too near,
Which, but proportioned to their light or place,
Due distance reconciles to form and grace.
175　A prudent chief not always must display
His powers in equal ranks and fair array,
But with the occasion and the place comply,
Conceal his force, nay seem sometimes to fly.
Those oft are stratagems which errors seem,
180　Nor is it Homer nods, but we that dream.
　　　　Still green with bays each ancient altar stands
Above the reach of sacrilegious hands,
Secure from flames, from envy's fiercer rage,
Destructive war, and all-involving age.
185　See, from each clime the learn'd their incense bring!
Here in all tongues consenting° paeans ring!　　　　　*agreeing, concurring*
In praise so just let every voice be joined,[3]
And fill the general chorus of mankind.
Hail, bards triumphant! born in happier days,
190　Immortal heirs of universal praise!
Whose honors with increase of ages grow,
As streams roll down, enlarging as they flow;
Nations unborn your mighty names shall sound,
And worlds applaud that must not yet be found!
195　Oh, may some spark of your celestial fire,
The last, the meanest of your sons inspire
(That on weak wings, from far, pursues your flights,
Glows while he reads, but trembles as he writes)
To teach vain wits a science little known,
200　To admire superior sense, and doubt their own!

Part 2

　　Of all the causes which conspire to blind
Man's erring judgment, and misguide the mind,
What the weak head with strongest bias rules,
Is pride, the never-failing vice of fools.
205　Whatever Nature has in worth denied,
She gives in large recruits° of needful pride;　　　　　*supplies*
For as in bodies, thus in souls, we find
What wants in blood and spirits, swelled with wind:
Pride, where wit fails, steps in to our defense,
210　And fills up all the mighty void of sense.
If once right reason drives that cloud away,
Truth breaks upon us with resistless day.
Trust not yourself: but your defects to know,

2. Pronounced *fawts*.　　　　　　　　　　3. Pronounced *jined*.

Make use of every friend—and every foe.
215 A little learning is a dangerous thing;
Drink deep, or taste not the Pierian spring.[4]
There shallow draughts intoxicate the brain,
And drinking largely sobers us again.
Fired at first sight with what the Muse imparts,
220 In fearless youth we tempt° the heights of arts,   *attempt*
While from the bounded level of our mind
Short views we take, nor see the lengths behind;
But more advanced, behold with strange surprise
New distant scenes of endless science rise!
225 So pleased at first the towering Alps we try,
Mount o'er the vales, and seem to tread the sky,
The eternal snows appear already past,
And the first clouds and mountains seem the last;
But, those attained, we tremble to survey
230 The growing labors of the lengthened way,
The increasing prospect tires our wandering eyes,
Hills peep o'er hills, and Alps on Alps arise!
  A perfect judge will read each work of wit
With the same spirit that its author writ:
235 Survey the whole, nor seek slight faults to find
Where Nature moves, and rapture warms the mind;
Nor lose, for that malignant dull delight,
The generous pleasure to be charmed with wit.
But in such lays as neither ebb nor flow,
240 Correctly cold, and regularly low,
That, shunning faults, one quiet tenor keep,
We cannot blame indeed—but we may sleep.
In wit, as nature, what affects our hearts
Is not the exactness of peculiar parts;
245 'Tis not a lip, or eye, we beauty call,
But the joint force and full result of all.
Thus when we view some well-proportioned dome[5]
(The world's just wonder, and even thine, O Rome!),
No single parts unequally surprise,
250 All comes united to the admiring eyes:
No monstrous height, or breadth, or length appear;
The whole at once is bold and regular.
  Whoever thinks a faultless piece to see,
Thinks what ne'er was, nor is, nor e'er shall be.
255 In every work regard the writer's end,
Since none can compass more than they intend;
And if the means be just, the conduct true,
Applause, in spite of trivial faults, is due.
As men of breeding, sometimes men of wit,
260 To avoid great errors must the less commit,
Neglect the rules each verbal critic lays,
For not to know some trifles is a praise.

4. The spring in Pieria on Mount Olympus, sacred to the Muses.

5. The dome of St. Peter's, designed by Michelangelo.

Most critics, fond of some subservient art,
Still make the whole depend upon a part:
265 They talk of principles, but notions prize,
And all to one loved folly sacrifice.
    Once on a time La Mancha's knight,[6] they say,
A certain bard encountering on the way,
Discoursed in terms as just, with looks as sage,
270 As e'er could Dennis,[7] of the Grecian stage;
Concluding all were desperate sots and fools
Who durst depart from Aristotle's rules.
Our author, happy in a judge so nice,
Produced his play, and begged the knight's advice;
275 Made him observe the subject and the plot,
The manners, passions, unities; what not?
All which exact to rule were brought about,
Were but a combat in the lists left out.
"What! leave the combat out?" exclaims the knight.
280 "Yes, or we must renounce the Stagirite."
"Not so, by Heaven!" he answers in a rage,
"Knights, squires, and steeds must enter on the stage."
"So vast a throng the stage can ne'er contain."
"Then build a new, or act it in a plain."
285   Thus critics of less judgment than caprice,
Curious,° not knowing, not exact, but nice,°   *laborious/fussy*
Form short ideas, and offend in arts
(As most in manners), by a love to parts.
    Some to conceit[8] alone their taste confine,
290 And glittering thoughts struck out at every line;
Pleased with a work where nothing's just or fit,
One glaring chaos and wild heap of wit.
Poets, like painters, thus unskilled to trace
The naked nature and the living grace,
295 With gold and jewels cover every part,
And hide with ornaments their want of art.
True wit is Nature to advantage dressed,
What oft was thought, but ne'er so well expressed;
Something whose truth convinced at sight we find,
300 That gives us back the image of our mind.
As shades more sweetly recommend the light,
So modest plainness sets off sprightly wit;
For works may have more wit than does them good,
As bodies perish through excess of blood.
305   Others for language all their care express,
And value books, as women men, for dress.
Their praise is still—the style is excellent;
The sense they humbly take upon contènt.°   *mere acquiescence*
Words are like leaves; and where they most abound,

6. Don Quixote. The story comes not from Cervantes's novel, but from a spurious sequel to it by Don Alonzo Fernandez de Avellaneda.
7. John Dennis (1657–1734), although one of the leading critics of the time, was frequently ridiculed by the wits for his irascibility and pomposity. Pope apparently did not know Dennis personally, but his jibe at him in part 3 of this poem made him a bitter enemy.
8. Pointed wit, ingenuity and extravagance, or affectation in the use of figures, especially similes and metaphors.

310   Much fruit of sense beneath is rarely found.
        False eloquence, like the prismatic glass,
        Its gaudy colors spreads on every place;[9]
        The face of Nature we no more survey,
        All glares alike, without distinction gay.

315   But true expression, like the unchanging sun, ⎫
        Clears and improves whate'er it shines upon; ⎬
        It gilds all objects, but it alters none. ⎭
        Expression is the dress of thought, and still
        Appears more decent as more suitable.

320   A vile conceit in pompous words expressed
        Is like a clown° in regal purple dressed: *rustic, boor*
        For different styles with different subjects sort,
        As several garbs with country, town, and court.
        Some by old words to fame have made pretense,

325   Ancients in phrase, mere moderns in their sense.
        Such labored nothings, in so strange a style,
        Amaze the unlearn'd, and make the learned smile;
        Unlucky as Fungoso[1] in the play, ⎫
        These sparks with awkward vanity display ⎬

330   What the fine gentleman wore yesterday; ⎭
        And but so mimic ancient wits at best,
        As apes our grandsires in their doublets dressed.
        In words as fashions the same rule will hold,
        Alike fantastic if too new or old:

335   Be not the first by whom the new are tried,
        Nor yet the last to lay the old aside.
            But most by numbers° judge a poet's song,   *versification*
        And smooth or rough with them is right or wrong.
        In the bright Muse though thousand charms conspire,

340   Her voice is all these tuneful fools admire,
        Who haunt Parnassus but to please their ear,
        Not mend their minds; as some to church repair, ⎫
        Not for the doctrine, but the music there. ⎭
        These equal syllables alone require,

345   Though oft the ear the open vowels tire,[2]
        While expletives[3] their feeble aid do join,
        And ten low words oft creep in one dull line:
        While they ring round the same unvaried chimes,
        With sure returns of still expected rhymes;

350   Where'er you find "the cooling western breeze,"
        In the next line, it "whispers through the trees";
        If crystal streams "with pleasing murmurs creep,"
        The reader's threatened (not in vain) with "sleep";
        Then, at the last and only couplet fraught

355   With some unmeaning thing they call a thought,
        A needless Alexandrine[4] ends the song

9. A very up-to-date scientific reference. Newton's *Optics*, which dealt with the prism and the spectrum, had been published in 1704, although his theories had been known earlier.
1. A character in Ben Jonson's comedy *Every Man out of His Humor* (1599).
2. In lines 345–57 Pope cleverly contrives to make his own metrics or diction illustrate the faults that he is exposing.
3. Words used merely to achieve the necessary number of feet in a line of verse.
4. A line of verse containing six iambic feet; it is illustrated in the next line.

That, like a wounded snake, drags its slow length along.
Leave such to tune their own dull rhymes, and know
What's roundly smooth or languishingly slow;
360   And praise the easy vigor of a line
Where Denham's strength and Waller's sweetness join.[5]
True ease in writing comes from art, not chance,
As those move easiest who have learned to dance.
'Tis not enough no harshness gives offense,
365   The sound must seem an echo to the sense.
Soft is the strain when Zephyr gently blows,
And the smooth stream in smoother numbers flows;
But when loud surges lash the sounding shore,
The hoarse, rough verse should like the torrent roar.
370   When Ajax strives some rock's vast weight to throw,
The line too labors, and the words move slow;
Not so when swift Camilla scours the plain,
Flies o'er the unbending corn, and skims along the main.
Hear how Timotheus'[6] varied lays surprise,
375   And bid alternate passions fall and rise!
While at each change the son of Libyan Jove°   Alexander the Great
Now burns with glory, and then melts with love;
Now his fierce eyes with sparkling fury glow,
Now sighs steal out, and tears begin to flow:
380   Persians and Greeks like turns of nature[7] found
And the world's victor stood subdued by sound!
The power of music all our hearts allow,
And what Timotheus was, is Dryden now.
      Avoid extremes; and shun the fault of such
385   Who still are pleased too little or too much.
At every trifle scorn to take offense:
That always shows great pride, or little sense.
Those heads, as stomachs, are not sure the best,
Which nauseate all, and nothing can digest.
390   Yet let not each gay turn thy rapture move;
For fools admire,° but men of sense approve:[8]   wonder
As things seem large which we through mists descry,
Dullness is ever apt to magnify.
      Some foreign writers, some our own despise;
395   The ancients only, or the moderns prize.
Thus wit, like faith, by each man is applied
To one small sect, and all are damned beside.
Meanly they seek the blessing to confine,
And force that sun but on a part to shine,
400   Which not alone the southern wit sublimes,°   raises up, purifies
But ripens spirits in cold northern climes;
Which from the first has shone on ages past,
Enlights the present, and shall warm the last;
Though each may feel increases and decays,

5. Dryden, whom Pope echoes here, considered Sir John Denham (1615–1669) and Edmund Waller (1606–1687) to have been the principal shapers of the closed pentameter couplet. He had distinguished the "strength" of the one and the "sweetness" of the other.

6. The musician in Dryden's *Alexander's Feast*. Pope retells the story of that poem in the following lines.
7. Alternations of feelings.
8. Judge favorably only after due deliberation.

405 And see now clearer and now darker days.
Regard not then if wit be old or new,
But blame the false and value still the true.
   Some ne'er advance a judgment of their own,
But catch the spreading notion of the town;
410 They reason and conclude by precedent,
And own stale nonsense which they ne'er invent.
Some judge of authors' names, not works, and then
Nor praise nor blame the writings, but the men.
Of all this servile herd the worst is he
415 That in proud dullness joins with quality,[9]
A constant critic at the great man's board,
To fetch and carry nonsense for my lord.
What woeful stuff this madrigal would be
In some starved hackney sonneteer° or me!   *hireling poet*
420 But let a lord once own the happy lines,
How the wit brightens! how the style refines!
Before his sacred name flies every fault,
And each exalted stanza teems with thought!
   The vulgar thus through imitation err;
425 As oft the learn'd by being singular;
So much they scorn the crowd, that if the throng
By chance go right, they purposely go wrong.
So schismatics[1] the plain believers quit,
And are but damned for having too much wit.
430 Some praise at morning what they blame at night,
But always think the last opinion right.
A Muse by these is like a mistress used,
This hour she's idolized, the next abused;
While their weak heads like towns unfortified,
435 'Twixt sense and nonsense daily change their side.
Ask them the cause; they're wiser still, they say;
And still tomorrow's wiser than today.
We think our fathers fools, so wise we grow;
Our wiser sons, no doubt, will think us so.
440 Once school divines[2] this zealous isle o'erspread;
Who knew most sentences[3] was deepest read.
Faith, Gospel, all seemed made to be disputed,
And none had sense enough to be confuted.
Scotists and Thomists now in peace remain
445 Amidst their kindred cobwebs in Duck Lane.[4]
If faith itself has different dresses worn,
What wonder modes in wit should take their turn?
Oft, leaving what is natural and fit,
The current folly proves the ready wit;
450 And authors think their reputation safe,
Which lives as long as fools are pleased to laugh.

---

9. People of high rank.
1. Those who have divided the church on points of theology. Pope stressed the first syllable, the pronunciation approved by Johnson in his *Dictionary*.
2. The medieval theologians, such as the followers of Duns Scotus and St. Thomas Aquinas, mentioned below.
3. Allusion to Peter Lombard's *Book of Sentences*, a book esteemed by Scholastic philosophers.
4. Street where publishers' remainders and secondhand books were sold.

Some valuing those of their own side or mind,
Still make themselves the measure of mankind:
Fondly° we think we honor merit then,   *foolishly*
455   When we but praise ourselves in other men.
Parties in wit attend on those of state,
And public faction doubles private hate.
Pride, Malice, Folly against Dryden rose,
In various shapes of parsons, critics, beaux;
460   But sense survived, when merry jests were past;
For rising merit will buoy up at last.
Might he return and bless once more our eyes,
New Blackmores and new Milbourns must arise.[5]
Nay, should great Homer lift his awful head,
465   Zoilus[6] again would start up from the dead.
Envy will merit, as its shade, pursue,
But like a shadow, proves the substance true;
For envied wit, like Sol eclipsed, makes known
The opposing body's grossness, not its own.
470   When first that sun too powerful beams displays,
It draws up vapors which obscure its rays;
But even those clouds at last adorn its way,
Reflect new glories, and augment the day.
     Be thou the first true merit to befriend;
475   His praise is lost who stays till all commend.
Short is the date, alas! of modern rhymes,
And 'tis but just to let them live betimes.
No longer now that golden age appears,
When patriarch wits survived a thousand years:
480   Now length of fame (our second life) is lost,
And bare threescore is all even that can boast;
Our sons their fathers' failing language see,
And such as Chaucer is, shall Dryden be.[7]
So when the faithful pencil has designed
485   Some bright idea of the master's mind,
Where a new world leaps out at his command,
And ready Nature waits upon his hand;
When the ripe colors soften and unite,
And sweetly melt into just shade and light;
490   When mellowing years their full perfection give,
And each bold figure just begins to live,
The treacherous colors the fair art betray,
And all the bright creation fades away!
     Unhappy wit, like most mistaken things,
495   Atones not for that envy which it brings.
In youth alone its empty praise we boast,
But soon the short-lived vanity is lost;
Like some fair flower the early spring supplies,

---

5. Sir Richard Blackmore, physician and poet, had attacked Dryden for the immorality of his plays; Rev. Luke Milbourn had attacked his translation of Virgil.
6. A Greek critic of the 4th century B.C.E., who wrote a book of carping criticism of Homer.

7. The radical changes that took place in the English language between the death of Chaucer in 1400 and the death of Dryden in 1700 suggested that in another three hundred years Dryden would be unintelligible. Latin seemed the only means of attaining enduring fame.

That gaily blooms, but even in blooming dies.
500   What is this wit, which must our cares employ?
The owner's wife, that other men enjoy;
Then most our trouble still when most admired,
And still the more we give, the more required;
Whose fame with pains we guard, but lose with ease,
505   Sure some to vex, but never all to please;
'Tis what the vicious fear, the virtuous shun,
By fools 'tis hated, and by knaves undone!
     If wit so much from ignorance undergo,
Ah, let not learning too commence its foe!
510   Of old those met rewards who could excel,
And such were praised who but endeavored well;
Though triumphs were to generals only due,
Crowns were reserved to grace the soldiers too.[8]
Now they who reach Parnassus' lofty crown
515   Employ their pains to spurn some others down;
And while self-love each jealous writer rules,
Contending wits become the sport of fools;
But still the worst with most regret commend,
For each ill author is as bad a friend.
520   To what base ends, and by what abject ways,
Are mortals urged through sacred[9] lust of praise!
Ah, ne'er so dire a thirst of glory boast,
Nor in the critic let the man be lost!
Good nature and good sense must ever join;
525   To err is human, to forgive divine . . .

1709   1711

The Rape of the Lock   *The Rape of the Lock* is based on an actual episode
that provoked a quarrel between two prominent Catholic families. Pope's friend John
Caryll, to whom the poem is addressed (line 3), suggested that Pope write it, in the
hope that a little laughter might serve to soothe ruffled tempers. Lord Petre had cut
off a lock of hair from the head of the lovely Arabella Fermor (often spelled "Farmer"
and doubtless so pronounced), much to the indignation of the lady and her relatives.
In its original version of two cantos and 334 lines, published in 1712, *The Rape of
the Lock* was a great success. In 1713 a new version was undertaken against the
advice of Addison, who considered the poem perfect as it was first written. Pope
greatly expanded the earlier version, adding the delightful "machinery" (i.e., the supernatural agents in epic action) of the Sylphs, Belinda's toilet, the card game, and the
visit to the Cave of Spleen in canto 4. In 1717, with the addition of Clarissa's speech
on good humor, the poem assumed its final form.

     With delicate fancy and playful wit, Pope elaborated the trivial episode that occa-
sioned the poem into the semblance of an epic in miniature, the most nearly perfect
heroicomical poem in English. The verse abounds in parodies and echoes of the *Iliad*,
the *Aeneid*, and *Paradise Lost*, thus constantly forcing the reader to compare small
things with great. The familiar devices of epic are observed, but the incidents or

---

8. To celebrate Roman victories, valiant soldiers
were decorated with a variety of crowns.

9. Accursed. The phrase imitates Virgil's *auri sacra
famis*, "accursed hunger for gold" (*Aeneid* 3.57).

characters are beautifully proportioned to the scale of mock epic. The *Rape* tells of war, but it is the drawing-room war between the sexes; it has its heroes and heroines, but they are beaux and belles; it has its supernatural characters ("machinery"), but they are Sylphs (borrowed, as Pope tells us in his engaging dedicatory letter, from Rosicrucian lore)—creatures of the air, the souls of dead coquettes, with tasks appropriate to their nature—or the Gnome Umbriel, once a prude on earth; it has its epic game, played on the "velvet plain" of the card table, its feasting heroes, who sip coffee and gossip, and its battle, fought with the clichés of compliment and conceits, with frowns and angry glances, with snuff and bodkin; it has the traditional epic journey to the underworld—here the Cave of Spleen, emblematic of the ill nature of female hypochondriacs. And Pope creates a world in which these actions take place, a world that is dense with beautiful objects: brocades, ivory and tortoiseshell, cosmetics and diamonds, lacquered furniture, silver teapot, delicate chinaware. It is a world that is constantly in motion and that sparkles and glitters with light, whether the light of the sun or of Belinda's eyes or that light into which the "fluid" bodies of the Sylphs seem to dissolve as they flutter in shrouds and around the mast of Belinda's ship. Though Pope laughs at this world and its creatures—and remembers that a grimmer, darker world surrounds it (3.19–24 and 5.145–48)—he makes us very much aware of its beauty and charm.

The epigraph may be translated, "I was unwilling, Belinda, to ravish your locks; but I rejoice to have conceded this to your prayers" (Martial's *Epigrams* 12.84.1–2). Pope substituted his heroine for Martial's Polytimus. The epigraph is intended to suggest that the poem was published at Miss Fermor's request.

The Rape of the Lock

An Heroi-Comical Poem

Nolueram, Belinda, tuos violare capillos;
sed juvat hoc precibus me tribuisse tuis.
—MARTIAL

TO MRS. ARABELLA FERMOR

MADAM,

It will be in vain to deny that I have some regard for this piece, since I dedicate it to you. Yet you may bear me witness, it was intended only to divert a few young ladies, who have good sense and good humor enough to laugh not only at their sex's little unguarded follies, but at their own. But as it was communicated with the air of a secret, it soon found its way into the world. An imperfect copy having been offered to a bookseller, you had the good nature for my sake to consent to the publication of one more correct; this I was forced to, before I had executed half my design, for the machinery was entirely wanting to complete it.

The machinery, Madam, is a term invented by the critics, to signify that part which the deities, angels, or demons are made to act in a poem; for the ancient poets are in one respect like many modern ladies: let an action be never so trivial in itself, they always make it appear of the utmost importance. These machines I determined to raise on a very new and odd foundation, the Rosicrucian[1] doctrine of spirits.

---

1. A system of arcane philosophy introduced into England from Germany in the 17th century.

I know how disagreeable it is to make use of hard words before a lady; but 'tis so much the concern of a poet to have his works understood, and particularly by your sex, that you must give me leave to explain two or three difficult terms.

The Rosicrucians are a people I must bring you acquainted with. The best account I know of them is in a French book called *Le Comte de Gabalis*,[2] which both in its title and size is so like a novel, that many of the fair sex have read it for one by mistake. According to these gentlemen, the four elements are inhabited by spirits, which they call Sylphs, Gnomes, Nymphs, and Salamanders. The Gnomes or Demons of earth delight in mischief; but the Sylphs, whose habitation is in the air, are the best-conditioned creatures imaginable. For they say, any mortals may enjoy the most intimate familiarities with these gentle spirits, upon a condition very easy to all true adepts, an inviolate preservation of chastity.

As to the following cantos, all the passages of them are as fabulous as the vision at the beginning, or the transformation at the end (except the loss of your hair, which I always mention with reverence). The human persons are as fictitious as the airy ones; and the character of Belinda, as it is now managed, resembles you in nothing but in beauty.

If this poem had as many graces as there are in your person, or in your mind, yet I could never hope it should pass through the world half so uncensured as you have done. But let its fortune be what it will, mine is happy enough, to have given me this occasion of assuring you that I am, with the truest esteem,

MADAM,
Your most obedient, humble servant,
A. POPE

Canto 1

    What dire offense from amorous causes springs,
    What mighty contests rise from trivial things,
    I sing—This verse to Caryll, Muse! is due:
    This, even Belinda may vouchsafe to view:
5   Slight is the subject, but not so the praise,
    If she inspire, and he approve my lays.
    Say what strange motive, Goddess! could compel
    A well-bred lord to assault a gentle belle?
    Oh, say what stranger cause, yet unexplored,
10 Could make a gentle belle reject a lord?
    In tasks so bold can little men engage,
    And in soft bosoms dwells such mighty rage?
    Sol through white curtains shot a timorous ray,
    And oped those eyes that must eclipse the day.
15 Now lapdogs give themselves the rousing shake,
    And sleepless lovers, just at twelve, awake:
    Thrice rung the bell, the slipper knocked the ground,
    And the pressed watch[3] returned a silver sound.

---

2. By the Abbé de Montfaucon de Villars, published in 1670.
3. A watch that chimes the hour and the quarter hour when the stem is pressed down. "Knocked the ground": summons to a maid.

Belinda still her downy pillow pressed,
20 Her guardian Sylph prolonged the balmy rest.
'Twas he had summoned to her silent bed
The morning dream that hovered o'er her head.
A youth more glittering than a birthnight beau[4]
(That even in slumber caused her cheek to glow)
25 Seemed to her ear his winning lips to lay,
And thus in whispers said, or seemed to say:
    "Fairest of mortals, thou distinguished care
Of thousand bright inhabitants of air!
If e'er one vision touched thy infant thought,
30 Of all the nurse and all the priest have taught,
Of airy elves by moonlight shadows seen,
The silver token, and the circled green,[5]
Or virgins visited by angel powers,
With golden crowns and wreaths of heavenly flowers,
35 Hear and believe! thy own importance know,
Nor bound thy narrow views to things below.
Some secret truths, from learned pride concealed,
To maids alone and children are revealed:
What though no credit doubting wits may give?
40 The fair and innocent shall still believe.
Know, then, unnumbered spirits round thee fly,
The light militia of the lower sky:
These, though unseen, are ever on the wing,
Hang o'er the box, and hover round the Ring.[6]
45 Think what an equipage thou hast in air,
And view with scorn two pages and a chair.°   *sedan chair*
As now your own, our beings were of old,
And once enclosed in woman's beauteous mold;
Thence, by a soft transition, we repair
50 From earthly vehicles to these of air.
Think not, when woman's transient breath is fled,
That all her vanities at once are dead:
Succeeding vanities she still regards,
And though she plays no more, o'erlooks the cards.
55 Her joy in gilded chariots, when alive,
And love of ombre,[7] after death survive.
For when the Fair in all their pride expire,
To their first elements[8] their souls retire:
The sprites of fiery termagants in flame
60 Mount up, and take a Salamander's[9] name.
Soft yielding minds to water glide away,
And sip, with Nymphs, their elemental tea.[1]

---

4. Courtiers wore especially fine clothes on the sovereign's birthday.
5. Rings of bright green grass, which are common in England even in winter, were held to be due to the round dances of fairies. According to popular belief fairies skim off the cream from jugs of milk left standing overnight and leave a coin ("silver token") in payment.
6. The "box" in the theater and the fashionable circular drive ("Ring") in Hyde Park.
7. The popular card game (see n. 8, p. 1143).

8. The four elements out of which all things were believed to have been made were fire, water, earth, and air. One or another of these elements was supposed to be predominant in both the physical and the psychological makeup of each human being. In this context they are spoken of as "humors."
9. A lizardlike animal, in antiquity believed to live in fire. Each element was inhabited by a spirit, as the following lines explain.
1. Pronounced *tay*.

The graver prude sinks downward to a Gnome,
In search of mischief still on earth to roam.
65   The light coquettes in Sylphs aloft repair,
And sport and flutter in the fields of air.
    "Know further yet; whoever fair and chaste
Rejects mankind, is by some Sylph embraced:
For spirits, freed from mortal laws, with ease
70   Assume what sexes and what shapes they please.[2]
What guards the purity of melting maids,
In courtly balls, and midnight masquerades,
Safe from the treacherous friend, the daring spark,
The glance by day, the whisper in the dark,
75   When kind occasion prompts their warm desires,
When music softens, and when dancing fires?
'Tis but their Sylph, the wise Celestials know,
Though Honor is the word with men below.
    "Some nymphs there are, too conscious of their face,
80   For life predestined to the Gnomes' embrace.
These swell their prospects and exalt their pride,
When offers are disdained, and love denied:
Then gay ideas° crowd the vacant brain,   showy images
While peers, and dukes, and all their sweeping train,
85   And garters, stars, and coronets[3] appear,
And in soft sounds, 'your Grace'° salutes their ear.   a duchess
'Tis these that early taint the female soul,
Instruct the eyes of young coquettes to roll,
Teach infant cheeks a bidden blush to know,
90   And little hearts to flutter at a beau.
    "Oft, when the world imagine women stray,
The Sylphs through mystic mazes guide their way,
Through all the giddy circle they pursue,
And old impertinence° expel by new.   trifle
95   What tender maid but must a victim fall
To one man's treat, but for another's ball?
When Florio speaks, what virgin could withstand,
If gentle Damon did not squeeze her hand?
With varying vanities, from every part,
100   They shift the moving toyshop[4] of their heart;
Where wigs with wigs, with sword-knots sword-knots strive,
Beaux banish beaux, and coaches coaches drive.
This erring mortals levity may call;
Oh, blind to truth! the Sylphs contrive it all.
105   "Of these am I, who thy protection claim,
A watchful sprite, and Ariel is my name.
Late, as I ranged the crystal wilds of air,
In the clear mirror of thy ruling star
I saw, alas! some dread event impend,
110   Ere to the main this morning sun descend,
But Heaven reveals not what, or how, or where:

---

2. Cf. *Paradise Lost* 1.427–31; this is one of many   3. Emblems of nobility.
allusions to that poem in the *Rape*.   4. A shop stocked with baubles and trifles.

Warned by the Sylph, O pious maid, beware!
This to disclose is all thy guardian can:
Beware of all, but most beware of Man!"
115   He said; when Shock,[5] who thought she slept too long,
Leaped up, and waked his mistress with his tongue.
'Twas then, Belinda, if report say true,
Thy eyes first opened on a billet-doux;
Wounds, charms, and ardors were no sooner read,
120 But all the vision vanished from thy head.
    And now, unveiled, the toilet stands displayed,
Each silver vase in mystic order laid.
First, robed in white, the nymph intent adores,
With head uncovered, the cosmetic powers.
125 A heavenly image in the glass appears;
To that she bends, to that her eyes she rears.
The inferior priestess, at her altar's side,
Trembling begins the sacred rites of Pride.
Unnumbered treasures ope at once, and here
130 The various offerings of the world appear;
From each she nicely culls with curious toil,
And decks the goddess with the glittering spoil.
This casket India's glowing gems unlocks,
And all Arabia breathes from yonder box.
135 The tortoise here and elephant unite,
Transformed to combs, the speckled and the white.
Here files of pins extend their shining rows,
Puffs, powders, patches, Bibles,[6] billet-doux.
Now awful Beauty puts on all its arms;
140 The fair each moment rises in her charms,
Repairs her smiles, awakens every grace,
And calls forth all the wonders of her face;
Sees by degrees a purer blush arise,
And keener lightnings quicken in her eyes.
145 The busy Sylphs surround their darling care,
These set the head, and those divide the hair,
Some fold the sleeve, whilst others plait the gown;
And Betty's[7] praised for labors not her own.

Canto 2

    Not with more glories, in the ethereal plain,
The sun first rises o'er the purpled main,
Than, issuing forth, the rival of his beams
Launched on the bosom of the silver Thames.
5 Fair nymphs and well-dressed youths around her shone,
But every eye was fixed on her alone.
On her white breast a sparkling cross she wore,
Which Jews might kiss, and infidels adore.
Her lively looks a sprightly mind disclose,

5. A long-haired poodle, Belinda's lapdog.
6. It has been suggested that Pope intended here not "Bibles," but "bibelots" (trinkets), but this
interpretation has not gained wide acceptance.
7. Belinda's maid, the "inferior priestess" mentioned in line 127.

10   Quick as her eyes, and as unfixed as those:
      Favors to none, to all she smiles extends;
      Oft she rejects, but never once offends.
      Bright as the sun, her eyes the gazers strike,
      And, like the sun, they shine on all alike.
15   Yet graceful ease, and sweetness void of pride,
      Might hide her faults, if belles had faults to hide:
      If to her share some female errors fall,
      Look on her face, and you'll forget 'em all.
        This nymph, to the destruction of mankind,
20   Nourished two locks which graceful hung behind
      In equal curls, and well conspired to deck
      With shining ringlets her smooth ivory neck.
      Love in these labyrinths his slaves detains,
      And mighty hearts are held in slender chains.
25   With hairy springes[8] we the birds betray,
      Slight lines of hair surprise the finny prey,
      Fair tresses man's imperial race ensnare,
      And beauty draws us with a single hair.
        The adventurous Baron the bright locks admired,
30   He saw, he wished, and to the prize aspired.
      Resolved to win, he meditates the way,
      By force to ravish, or by fraud betray;
      For when success a lover's toil attends,
      Few ask if fraud or force attained his ends.
35   For this, ere Phoebus rose, he had implored
      Propitious Heaven, and every power adored,
      But chiefly Love—to Love an altar built,
      Of twelve vast French romances, neatly gilt.
      There lay three garters, half a pair of gloves,
40   And all the trophies of his former loves.
      With tender billet-doux he lights the pyre,
      And breathes three amorous sighs to raise the fire.
      Then prostrate falls, and begs with ardent eyes
      Soon to obtain, and long possess the prize:
45   The powers gave ear, and granted half his prayer,
      The rest the winds dispersed in empty air.
        But now secure the painted vessel glides,
      The sunbeams trembling on the floating tides,
      While melting music steals upon the sky,
50   And softened sounds along the waters die.
      Smooth flow the waves, the zephyrs gently play,
      Belinda smiled, and all the world was gay.
      All but the Sylph—with careful thoughts oppressed,
      The impending woe sat heavy on his breast.
55   He summons straight his denizens of air;
      The lucid squadrons round the sails repair:
      Soft o'er the shrouds aërial whispers breathe
      That seemed but zephyrs to the train beneath.
      Some to the sun their insect-wings unfold,

---

8. Snares; pronounced *sprĭn-jez*.

60 Waft on the breeze, or sink in clouds of gold.
Transparent forms too fine for mortal sight,
Their fluid bodies half dissolved in light,
Loose to the wind their airy garments flew,
Thin glittering textures of the filmy dew,
65 Dipped in the richest tincture of the skies,
Where light disports in ever-mingling dyes,
While every beam new transient colors flings,
Colors that change whene'er they wave their wings.
Amid the circle, on the gilded mast,
70 Superior by the head was Ariel placed;
His purple[9] pinions opening to the sun,
He raised his azure wand, and thus begun:
"Ye Sylphs and Sylphids, to your chief give ear!
Fays, Fairies, Genïi, Elves, and Daemons, hear!
75 Ye know the spheres and various tasks assigned
By laws eternal to the aërial kind.
Some in the fields of purest ether play,
And bask and whiten in the blaze of day.
Some guide the course of wandering orbs on high,
80 Or roll the planets through the boundless sky.
Some less refined, beneath the moon's pale light
Pursue the stars that shoot athwart the night,
Or suck the mists in grosser air below,
Or dip their pinions in the painted bow,
85 Or brew fierce tempests on the wintry main,
Or o'er the glebe° distill the kindly rain.   cultivated field
Others on earth o'er human race preside,
Watch all their ways, and all their actions guide:
Of these the chief the care of nations own,
90 And guard with arms divine the British Throne.
"Our humbler province is to tend the Fair,
Not a less pleasing, though less glorious care:
To save the powder from too rude a gale,
Nor let the imprisoned essences exhale;
95 To draw fresh colors from the vernal flowers;
To steal from rainbows e'er they drop in showers
A brighter wash;° to curl their waving hairs,   cosmetic lotion
Assist their blushes, and inspire their airs,
Nay oft, in dreams invention we bestow,
100 To change a flounce, or add a furbelow.
"This day black omens threat the brightest fair,
That e'er deserved a watchful spirit's care;
Some dire disaster, or by force or slight,
But what, or where, the Fates have wrapped in night:
105 Whether the nymph shall break Diana's[1] law,
Or some frail china jar receive a flaw,
Or stain her honor, or her new brocade,
Forget her prayers, or miss a masquerade,

9. In 18th-century poetic diction the word might mean bloodred, purple, or simply (as is likely here) brightly colored. The word derives from Virgil's *Eclogue* 9.40, *purpureum.* An example of the Latinate nature of some poetic diction of the period.
1. Diana was the goddess of chastity.

Or lose her heart, or necklace, at a ball;
110 Or whether Heaven has doomed that Shock must fall.
Haste, then, ye spirits! to your charge repair:
The fluttering fan be Zephyretta's care;
The drops[2] to thee, Brillante, we consign;
And, Momentilla, let the watch be thine;
115 Do thou, Crispissa,[3] tend her favorite Lock;
Ariel himself shall be the guard of Shock.
    "To fifty chosen Sylphs, of special note,
We trust the important charge, the petticoat;
Oft have we known that sevenfold fence to fail,
120 Though stiff with hoops, and armed with ribs of whale.
Form a strong line about the silver bound,
And guard the wide circumference around.
    "Whatever spirit, careless of his charge,
His post neglects, or leaves the fair at large,
125 Shall feel sharp vengeance soon o'ertake his sins,
Be stopped in vials, or transfixed with pins,
Or plunged in lakes of bitter washes lie,
Or wedged whole ages in a bodkin's[4] eye;
Gums and pomatums shall his flight restrain,
130 While clogged he beats his silken wings in vain,
Or alum styptics with contracting power
Shrink his thin essence like a riveled[5] flower:
Or, as Ixion[6] fixed, the wretch shall feel
The giddy motion of the whirling mill,
135 In fumes of burning chocolate shall glow,
And tremble at the sea that froths below!"
    He spoke; the spirits from the sails descend;
Some, orb in orb, around the nymph extend;
Some thread the mazy ringlets of her hair;
140 Some hang upon the pendants of her ear:
With beating hearts the dire event they wait,
Anxious, and trembling for the birth of Fate.

Canto 3

    Close by those meads, forever crowned with flowers,
Where Thames with pride surveys his rising towers,
There stands a structure of majestic frame,
Which from the neighboring Hampton[7] takes its name.
5 Here Britain's statesmen oft the fall foredoom
Of foreign tyrants and of nymphs at home;
Here thou, great Anna! whom three realms obey,
Dost sometimes counsel take—and sometimes tea.
    Hither the heroes and the nymphs resort,

---

2. Diamond earrings. Observe the appropriateness of the names of the Sylphs to their assigned functions.
3. From Latin *crispere*, "to curl."
4. A blunt needle with a large eye, used for drawing ribbon through eyelets in the edging of women's garments.

5. To "rivel" is to "contract into wrinkles and corrugations" (Johnson's *Dictionary*).
6. In the Greek myth, he was punished in the underworld by being bound on an everturning wheel.
7. Hampton Court, the royal palace, about fifteen miles up the Thames from London.

10 To taste awhile the pleasures of a court;
In various talk the instructive hours they passed,
Who gave the ball, or paid the visit last;
One speaks the glory of the British Queen,
And one describes a charming Indian screen;
15 A third interprets motions, looks, and eyes;
At every word a reputation dies.
Snuff, or the fan, supply each pause of chat,
With singing, laughing, ogling, and all that.
    Meanwhile, declining from the noon of day,
20 The sun obliquely shoots his burning ray;
The hungry judges soon the sentence sign,
And wretches hang that jurymen may dine;
The merchant from the Exchange returns in peace,
And the long labors of the toilet cease.
25 Belinda now, whom thirst of fame invites,
Burns to encounter two adventurous knights,
At ombre[8] singly to decide their doom,
And swells her breast with conquests yet to come.
Straight the three bands prepare in arms to join,
30 Each band the number of the sacred nine.
Soon as she spreads her hand, the aërial guard
Descend, and sit on each important card:
First Ariel perched upon a Matadore,
Then each according to the rank they bore;
35 For Sylphs, yet mindful of their ancient race,
Are, as when women, wondrous fond of place.
    Behold, four Kings in majesty revered,
With hoary whiskers and a forky beard;
And four fair Queens whose hands sustain a flower,
40 The expressive emblem of their softer power;
Four Knaves in garbs succinct,° a trusty band,   *girded up*
Caps on their heads, and halberts in their hand;
And parti-colored troops, a shining train,
Draw forth to combat on the velvet plain.
45   The skillful nymph reviews her force with care;
"Let Spades be trumps!" she said, and trumps they were.
    Now move to war her sable Matadores,
In show like leaders of the swarthy Moors.
Spadillio first, unconquerable lord!
50 Led off two captive trumps, and swept the board.
As many more Manillio forced to yield,
And marched a victor from the verdant field.
Him Basto followed, but his fate more hard
Gained but one trump and one plebeian card.

8. The game of ombre that Belinda plays against the baron and another young man is too complicated for complete explication here. Pope has carefully arranged the cards so that Belinda wins. The baron's hand is strong enough to be a threat, but the third player's is of little account. The hand is played exactly according to the rules of ombre, and Pope's description of the cards is equally accurate. Each player holds nine cards (line 30). The "Matadores" (line 33), when spades are trump, are "Spadillio" (line 49), the ace of spades; "Manillio" (line 51), the two of spades; and "Basto" (line 53), the ace of clubs. Belinda holds all three of these. (For a more complete description of ombre, see *The Rape of the Lock and Other Poems*, ed. Geoffrey Tillotson, in the Twickenham Edition of Pope's poems, vol. 2, Appendix C.)

55 With his broad saber next, a chief in years,
The hoary Majesty of Spades appears,
Puts forth one manly leg, to sight revealed,
The rest his many-colored robe concealed.
The rebel Knave, who dares his prince engage,
60 Proves the just victim of his royal rage.
Even mighty Pam,[9] that kings and queens o'erthrew
And mowed down armies in the fights of loo,
Sad chance of war! now destitute of aid,
Falls undistinguished by the victor Spade.
65 　Thus far both armies to Belinda yield;
Now to the Baron fate inclines the field.
His warlike amazon her host invades,
The imperial consort of the crown of Spades.
The Club's black tyrant first her victim died,
70 Spite of his haughty mien and barbarous pride.
What boots the regal circle on his head,
His giant limbs, in state unwieldy spread?
That long behind he trails his pompous robe,
And of all monarchs only grasps the globe?
75 　The Baron now his Diamonds pours apace;
The embroidered King who shows but half his face,
And his refulgent Queen, with powers combined,
Of broken troops an easy conquest find.
Clubs, Diamonds, Hearts, in wild disorder seen,
80 With throngs promiscuous strew the level green.
Thus when dispersed a routed army runs,
Of Asia's troops, and Afric's sable sons,
With like confusion different nations fly,
Of various habit, and of various dye,
85 The pierced battalions disunited fall
In heaps on heaps; one fate o'erwhelms them all.
　The Knave of Diamonds tries his wily arts,
And wins (oh, shameful chance!) the Queen of Hearts.
At this, the blood the virgin's cheek forsook,
90 A livid paleness spreads o'er all her look;
She sees, and trembles at the approaching ill,
Just in the jaws of ruin, and Codille.[1]
And now (as oft in some distempered state)
On one nice trick depends the general fate.
95 An Ace of Hearts steps forth: the King unseen
Lurked in her hand, and mourned his captive Queen.
He springs to vengeance with an eager pace,
And falls like thunder on the prostrate Ace.
The nymph exulting fills with shouts the sky,
100 The walls, the woods, and long canals reply.
　O thoughtless mortals! ever blind to fate,
Too soon dejected, and too soon elate:
Sudden these honors shall be snatched away,
And cursed forever this victorious day.

9. The knave of clubs, the highest trump in the　　1. The term applied to losing a hand at cards.
game of loo.

105   For lo! the board with cups and spoons is crowned,
       The berries crackle, and the mill turns round;[2]
       On shining altars of Japan[3] they raise
       The silver lamp; the fiery spirits blaze:
       From silver spouts the grateful liquors glide,
110   While China's earth receives the smoking tide.
       At once they gratify their scent and taste,
       And frequent cups prolong the rich repast.
       Straight hover round the fair her airy band;
       Some, as she sipped, the fuming liquor fanned,
115   Some o'er her lap their careful plumes displayed,
       Trembling, and conscious of the rich brocade.
       Coffee (which makes the politician wise,
       And see through all things with his half-shut eyes)
       Sent up in vapors to the Baron's brain
120   New stratagems, the radiant Lock to gain.
       Ah, cease, rash youth! desist ere 'tis too late,
       Fear the just Gods, and think of Scylla's[4] fate!
       Changed to a bird, and sent to flit in air,
       She dearly pays for Nisus' injured hair!
125   But when to mischief mortals bend their will,
       How soon they find fit instruments of ill!
       Just then, Clarissa drew with tempting grace
       A two-edged weapon from her shining case:
       So ladies in romance assist their knight,
130   Present the spear, and arm him for the fight.
       He takes the gift with reverence, and extends
       The little engine on his fingers' ends;
       This just behind Belinda's neck he spread,
       As o'er the fragrant steams she bends her head.
135   Swift to the Lock a thousand sprites repair,
       A thousand wings, by turns, blow back the hair,
       And thrice they twitched the diamond in her ear,
       Thrice she looked back, and thrice the foe drew near.
       Just in that instant, anxious Ariel sought
140   The close recesses of the virgin's thought;
       As on the nosegay in her breast reclined,
       He watched the ideas rising in her mind,
       Sudden he viewed, in spite of all her art,
       An earthly lover lurking at her heart.
145   Amazed, confused, he found his power expired,
       Resigned to fate, and with a sigh retired.
       The Peer now spreads the glittering forfex° wide,   *scissors*
       To enclose the Lock; now joins it, to divide.
       Even then, before the fatal engine closed,
150   A wretched Sylph too fondly interposed;
       Fate urged the shears, and cut the Sylph in twain

---

2. I.e., coffee is roasted and ground.
3. I.e., small, lacquered tables. "Altars" suggests the ritualistic character of coffee drinking in Belinda's world.
4. Scylla, daughter of Nisus, was turned into a sea bird because, for the sake of her love for Minos of Crete, who was besieging her father's city of Megara, she cut from her father's head the purple lock on which his safety depended. She is not the Scylla of "Scylla and Charybdis."

(But airy substance soon unites again):
The meeting points the sacred hair dissever
From the fair head, forever and forever!
155   Then flashed the living lightning from her eyes,
And screams of horror rend the affrighted skies.
Not louder shrieks to pitying heaven are cast,
When husbands, or when lapdogs breathe their last;
Or when rich china vessels fallen from high,
160 In glittering dust and painted fragments lie!
"Let wreaths of triumph now my temples twine,"
The victor cried, "the glorious prize is mine!
While fish in streams, or birds delight in air,
Or in a coach and six the British fair,
165 As long as *Atalantis*⁵ shall be read,
Or the small pillow grace a lady's bed,
While visits shall be paid on solemn days,
When numerous wax-lights in bright order blaze,
While nymphs take treats, or assignations give,
170 So long my honor, name, and praise shall live!
    "What time would spare, from steel receives its date,
And monuments, like men, submit to fate!
Steel could the labor of the Gods destroy,
And strike to dust the imperial towers of Troy;
175 Steel could the works of mortal pride confound,
And hew triumphal arches to the ground.
What wonder then, fair nymph! thy hairs should feel,
The conquering force of unresisted steel?"

Canto 4

    But anxious cares the pensive nymph oppressed,
And secret passions labored in her breast.
Not youthful kings in battle seized alive,
Not scornful virgins who their charms survive,
5 Not ardent lovers robbed of all their bliss,
Not ancient ladies when refused a kiss,
Not tyrants fierce that unrepenting die,
Not Cynthia when her manteau's° pinned awry,   *wrap*
E'er felt such rage, resentment, and despair,
10 As thou, sad virgin! for thy ravished hair.
    For, that sad moment, when the Sylphs withdrew
And Ariel weeping from Belinda flew,
Umbriel,⁶ a dusky, melancholy sprite
As ever sullied the fair face of light,
15 Down to the central earth, his proper scene,
Repaired to search the gloomy Cave of Spleen.°   *Ill Humor*
    Swift on his sooty pinions flits the Gnome,
And in a vapor reached the dismal dome.
No cheerful breeze this sullen region knows,

---

5. Delariviere Manley's *New Atalantis* (1709) was notorious for its thinly concealed allusions to contemporary scandals.
6. The name suggests shade and darkness.

20   The dreaded east is all the wind that blows.
      Here in a grotto, sheltered close from air,
      And screened in shades from day's detested glare,
      She sighs forever on her pensive bed,
      Pain at her side, and Megrim° at her head.   *headache*
25   Two handmaids wait the throne: alike in place
      But differing far in figure and in face.
      Here stood Ill-Nature like an ancient maid,
      Her wrinkled form in black and white arrayed;
      With store of prayers for mornings, nights, and noons,
30   Her hand is filled; her bosom with lampoons.
        There Affectation, with a sickly mien,
      Shows in her cheek the roses of eighteen,
      Practiced to lisp, and hang the head aside,
      Faints into airs, and languishes with pride,
35   On the rich quilt sinks with becoming woe,
      Wrapped in a gown, for sickness and for show.
      The fair ones feel such maladies as these,
      When each new nightdress gives a new disease.
        A constant vapor[7] o'er the palace flies,
40   Strange phantoms rising as the mists arise;
      Dreadful as hermit's dreams in haunted shades,
      Or bright as visions of expiring maids.
      Now glaring fiends, and snakes on rolling spires,°   *coils*
      Pale specters, gaping tombs, and purple fires;
45   Now lakes of liquid gold, Elysian scenes,
      And crystal domes, and angels in machines.[8]
        Unnumbered throngs on every side are seen
      Of bodies changed to various forms by Spleen.
      Here living teapots stand, one arm held out,
50   One bent; the handle this, and that the spout:
      A pipkin° there, like Homer's tripod,[9] walks;   *earthen pot*
      Here sighs a jar, and there a goose pie talks;
      Men prove with child, as powerful fancy works,
      And maids, turned bottles, call aloud for corks.
55   Safe passed the Gnome through this fantastic band,
      A branch of healing spleenwort[1] in his hand.
      Then thus addressed the Power: "Hail, wayward Queen!
      Who rule the sex to fifty from fifteen:
      Parent of vapors and of female wit,
60   Who give the hysteric or poetic fit,
      On various tempers act by various ways,
      Make some take physic, others scribble plays;
      Who cause the proud their visits to delay,
      And send the godly in a pet to pray.
65   A nymph there is that all your power disdains,
      And thousands more in equal mirth maintains.

---

7. Emblematic of "the vapors," a fashionable hypochondria, melancholy, or peevishness.
8. Mechanical devices used in the theaters for spectacular effects. The catalog of hallucinations draws on the sensational stage effects popular with contemporary audiences.

9. In *Iliad* 18.373–77, Vulcan furnishes the gods with self-propelling "tripods" (three-legged stools).
1. An herb, efficacious against the spleen. Pope alludes to the golden bough that Aeneas and the Cumaean sibyl carry with them for protection into the underworld in *Aeneid* 6.

But oh! if e'er thy Gnome could spoil a grace,
Or raise a pimple on a beauteous face,
Like citron-waters[2] matrons' cheeks inflame,
70 Or change complexions at a losing game;
If e'er with airy horns[3] I planted heads,
Or rumpled petticoats, or tumbled beds,
Or caused suspicion when no soul was rude,
Or discomposed the headdress of a prude,
75 Or e'er to costive lapdog gave disease,
Which not the tears of brightest eyes could ease,
Hear me, and touch Belinda with chagrin:°   ill humor
That single act gives half the world the spleen."
     The Goddess with a discontented air
80 Seems to reject him though she grants his prayer.
A wondrous bag with both her hands she binds,
Like that where once Ulysses held the winds;[4]
There she collects the force of female lungs,
Sighs, sobs, and passions, and the war of tongues.
85 A vial next she fills with fainting fears,
Soft sorrows, melting griefs, and flowing tears.
The Gnome rejoicing bears her gifts away,
Spreads his black wings, and slowly mounts to day.
     Sunk in Thalestris'[5] arms the nymph he found,
90 Her eyes dejected and her hair unbound.
Full o'er their heads the swelling bag he rent,
And all the Furies issued at the vent.
Belinda burns with more than mortal ire,
And fierce Thalestris fans the rising fire.
95 "O wretched maid!" she spread her hands, and cried
(While Hampton's echoes, "Wretched maid!" replied),
"Was it for this you took such constant care
The bodkin, comb, and essence to prepare?
For this your locks in paper durance bound,
100 For this with torturing irons wreathed around?
For this with fillets strained your tender head,
And bravely bore the double loads of lead?[6]
Gods! shall the ravisher display your hair,
While the fops envy, and the ladies stare!
105 Honor forbid! at whose unrivaled shrine
Ease, pleasure, virtue, all, our sex resign.
Methinks already I your tears survey,
Already hear the horrid things they say,
Already see you a degraded toast,
110 And all your honor in a whisper lost!
How shall I, then, your helpless fame defend?

2. Brandy flavored with orange or lemon peel.
3. The symbol of the cuckold, the man whose wife has been unfaithful to him; here "airy," because they exist only in the jealous suspicions of the husband, the victim of the mischievous Umbriel.
4. Aeolus (later conceived of as god of the winds) gave Ulysses a bag containing all the winds adverse to his voyage home. When his ship was in sight of Ithaca, his companions opened the bag and the storms that ensued drove Ulysses far away (*Odyssey* 10.19ff.).
5. The name is borrowed from a queen of the Amazons, hence a fierce and warlike woman.
6. The frame on which the elaborate coiffures of the day were arranged.

'Twill then be infamy to seem your friend!
And shall this prize, the inestimable prize,
Exposed through crystal to the gazing eyes,
115 And heightened by the diamond's circling rays,
On that rapacious hand forever blaze?
Sooner shall grass in Hyde Park Circus grow,
And wits take lodgings in the sound of Bow;[7]
Sooner let earth, air, sea, to chaos fall,
120 Men, monkeys, lapdogs, parrots, perish all!"
        She said; then raging to Sir Plume repairs,
And bids her beau demand the precious hairs
(Sir Plume of amber snuffbox justly vain,
And the nice conduct of a clouded cane).
125 With earnest eyes, and round unthinking face,
He first the snuffbox opened, then the case,
And thus broke out—"My Lord, why, what the devil!
Z——ds! damn the lock! 'fore Gad, you must be civil!
Plague on 't! 'tis past a jest—nay prithee, pox!
130 Give her the hair"—he spoke, and rapped his box.
        "It grieves me much," replied the Peer again,
"Who speaks so well should ever speak in vain.
But by this Lock, this sacred Lock I swear
(Which never more shall join its parted hair;
135 Which never more its honors shall renew,
Clipped from the lovely head where late it grew),
That while my nostrils draw the vital air,
This hand, which won it, shall forever wear."
He spoke, and speaking, in proud triumph spread
140 The long-contended honors[8] of her head.
        But Umbriel, hateful Gnome, forbears not so;
He breaks the vial whence the sorrows flow.
Then see! the nymph in beauteous grief appears,
Her eyes half languishing, half drowned in tears;
145 On her heaved bosom hung her drooping head,
Which with a sigh she raised, and thus she said:
        "Forever cursed be this detested day,
Which snatched my best, my favorite curl away!
Happy! ah, ten times happy had I been,
150 If Hampton Court these eyes had never seen!
Yet am not I the first mistaken maid,
By love of courts to numerous ills betrayed.
Oh, had I rather unadmired remained
In some lone isle, or distant northern land;
155 Where the gilt chariot never marks the way,
Where none learn ombre, none e'er taste bohea![9]
There kept my charms concealed from mortal eye,
Like roses that in deserts bloom and die.
What moved my mind with youthful lords to roam?
160 Oh, had I stayed, and said my prayers at home!

---

7. A person born within sound of the bells of St. Mary-le-Bow in Cheapside is said to be a cockney. No fashionable wit would have so vulgar an address.
8. Ornaments, hence locks; a Latinism.
9. A costly sort of tea.

'Twas this the morning omens seemed to tell;
Thrice from my trembling hand the patch box[1] fell;
The tottering china shook without a wind,
Nay, Poll sat mute, and Shock was most unkind!
165 A Sylph too warned me of the threats of fate,
In mystic visions, now believed too late!
See the poor remnants of these slighted hairs!
My hands shall rend what e'en thy rapine spares.
These in two sable ringlets taught to break,
170 Once gave new beauties to the snowy neck.
The sister lock now sits uncouth, alone,
And in its fellow's fate foresees its own;
Uncurled it hangs, the fatal shears demands,
And tempts once more thy sacrilegious hands.
175 Oh, hadst thou, cruel! been content to seize
Hairs less in sight, or any hairs but these!"

Canto 5

She said: the pitying audience melt in tears.
But Fate and Jove had stopped the Baron's ears.
In vain Thalestris with reproach assails,
For who can move when fair Belinda fails?
5 Not half so fixed the Trojan[2] could remain,
While Anna begged and Dido raged in vain.
Then grave Clarissa graceful waved her fan;
Silence ensued, and thus the nymph began:
"Say, why are beauties praised and honored most,
10 The wise man's passion, and the vain man's toast?
Why decked with all that land and sea afford,
Why angels called, and angel-like adored?
Why round our coaches crowd the white-gloved beaux,
Why bows the side box from its inmost rows?
15 How vain are all these glories, all our pains,
Unless good sense preserve what beauty gains;
That men may say when we the front box grace,
'Behold the first in virtue as in face!'
Oh! if to dance all night, and dress all day,
20 Charmed the smallpox, or chased old age away,
Who would not scorn what housewife's cares produce,
Or who would learn one earthly thing of use?
To patch, nay ogle, might become a saint,
Nor could it sure be such a sin to paint.
25 But since, alas! frail beauty must decay,
Curled or uncurled, since locks will turn to gray;
Since painted, or not painted, all shall fade,
And she who scorns a man must die a maid;
What then remains but well our power to use,

---

1. To hold the ornamental patches of court plaster worn on the face by both sexes.
2. Aeneas, who forsook Dido at the bidding of the gods, despite her reproaches and the supplications of her sister Anna. Virgil compares him to a steadfast oak that withstands a storm (*Aeneid* 4.437–43).

30 And keep good humor still whate'er we lose?
And trust me, dear, good humor can prevail
When airs, and flights, and screams, and scolding fail.
Beauties in vain their pretty eyes may roll;
Charms strike the sight, but merit wins the soul."[3]
35 So spoke the dame, but no applause ensued;
Belinda frowned, Thalestris called her prude.
"To arms, to arms!" the fierce virago cries,
And swift as lightning to the combat flies.
All side in parties, and begin the attack;
40 Fans clap, silks rustle, and tough whalebones crack;
Heroes' and heroines' shouts confusedly rise,
And bass and treble voices strike the skies.
No common weapons in their hands are found,
Like Gods they fight, nor dread a mortal wound.
45 So when bold Homer makes the Gods engage,
And heavenly breasts with human passions rage;
'Gainst Pallas, Mars; Latona, Hermes arms;
And all Olympus rings with loud alarms:
Jove's thunder roars, heaven trembles all around,
50 Blue Neptune storms, the bellowing deeps resound:
Earth shakes her nodding towers, the ground gives way,
And the pale ghosts start at the flash of day!
Triumphant Umbriel on a sconce's[4] height
Clapped his glad wings, and sat to view the fight:
55 Propped on the bodkin spears, the sprites survey
The growing combat, or assist the fray.
While through the press enraged Thalestris flies,
And scatters death around from both her eyes,
A beau and witling perished in the throng,
60 One died in metaphor, and one in song.
"O cruel nymph! a living death I bear,"
Cried Dapperwit, and sunk beside his chair.
A mournful glance Sir Fopling upwards cast,
"Those eyes are made so killing"—was his last.
65 Thus on Maeander's flowery margin lies
The expiring swan, and as he sings he dies.
When bold Sir Plume had drawn Clarissa down,
Chloe stepped in, and killed him with a frown;
She smiled to see the doughty hero slain,
70 But, at her smile, the beau revived again.
Now Jove suspends his golden scales in air,
Weighs the men's wits against the lady's hair;
The doubtful beam long nods from side to side;
At length the wits mount up, the hairs subside.
75 See, fierce Belinda on the Baron flies,
With more than usual lightning in her eyes;
Nor feared the chief the unequal fight to try,
Who sought no more than on his foe to die.

3. The speech is a close parody of Pope's own translation of the speech of Sarpedon to Glaucus, first published in 1709 and slightly revised in his version of the *Iliad* (12.371–96).
4. Candlestick fastened on the wall.

But this bold lord with manly strength endued,
80 She with one finger and a thumb subdued:
Just where the breath of life his nostrils drew,
A charge of snuff the wily virgin threw;
The Gnomes direct, to every atom just,
The pungent grains of titillating dust.
85 Sudden, with starting tears each eye o'erflows,
And the high dome re-echoes to his nose.
   "Now meet thy fate," incensed Belinda cried,
And drew a deadly bodkin[5] from her side.
(The same, his ancient personage to deck,
90 Her great-great-grandsire wore about his neck,
In three seal rings; which after, melted down,
Formed a vast buckle for his widow's gown:
Her infant grandame's whistle next it grew,
The bells she jingled, and the whistle blew;
95 Then in a bodkin graced her mother's hairs,
Which long she wore, and now Belinda wears.)
   "Boast not my fall," he cried, "insulting foe!
Thou by some other shalt be laid as low.
Nor think to die dejects my lofty mind:
100 All that I dread is leaving you behind!
Rather than so, ah, let me still survive,
And burn in Cupid's flames—but burn alive."
   "Restore the Lock!" she cries; and all around
"Restore the Lock!" the vaulted roofs rebound.
105 Not fierce Othello in so loud a strain
Roared for the handkerchief that caused his pain.[6]
But see how oft ambitious aims are crossed,
And chiefs contend till all the prize is lost!
The lock, obtained with guilt, and kept with pain,
110 In every place is sought, but sought in vain:
With such a prize no mortal must be blessed,
So Heaven decrees! with Heaven who can contest?
   Some thought it mounted to the lunar sphere,
Since all things lost on earth are treasured there.
115 There heroes' wits are kept in ponderous vases,
And beaux' in snuffboxes and tweezer cases.
There broken vows and deathbed alms are found,
And lovers' hearts with ends of riband bound,
The courtier's promises, and sick man's prayers,
120 The smiles of harlots, and the tears of heirs,
Cages for gnats, and chains to yoke a flea,
Dried butterflies, and tomes of casuistry.
   But trust the Muse—she saw it upward rise,
Though marked by none but quick, poetic eyes
125 (So Rome's great founder to the heavens withdrew,[7]
To Proculus alone confessed in view);

5. Here, an ornamental hairpin shaped like a dagger.
6. *Othello* 3.4.
7. Romulus, the "founder" and first king of Rome, was snatched to heaven in a storm cloud while reviewing his army in the Campus Martius (Livy 1.16).

A sudden star, it shot through liquid air,
And drew behind a radiant trail of hair.
Not Berenice's locks first rose so bright,[8]
130 The heavens bespangling with disheveled light.
The Sylphs behold it kindling as it flies,
And pleased pursue its progress through the skies.
　　This the beau monde shall from the Mall[9] survey,
And hail with music its propitious ray.
135 This the blest lover shall for Venus take,
And send up vows from Rosamonda's Lake.[1]
This Partridge[2] soon shall view in cloudless skies,
When next he looks through Galileo's eyes;°　　　　　*telescope*
And hence the egregious wizard shall foredoom
140 The fate of Louis, and the fall of Rome.
　　Then cease, bright nymph! to mourn thy ravished hair,
Which adds new glory to the shining sphere!
Not all the tresses that fair head can boast
Shall draw such envy as the Lock you lost.
145 For, after all the murders of your eye,
When, after millions slain, yourself shall die:
When those fair suns shall set, as set they must,
And all those tresses shall be laid in dust,
This Lock the Muse shall consecrate to fame,
150 And 'midst the stars inscribe Belinda's name.

1712　　　　　　　　　　　　　　　　　　　　　　　1714

An Essay on Man

An Essay on Man　Pope's philosophical poem, *An Essay on Man*, is a fragment of an ambitious but never completed scheme for what the poet referred to as his "ethic work," which was to have been a large survey of human nature, society, and morals. The work is dedicated to Henry St. John (pronounced *Sín-jun*), Viscount Bolingbroke (1678–1751), the brilliant, though erratic, secretary of state in the Tory ministry of 1710–14, whom Pope had come to know through Jonathan Swift. After the accession of George I he fled to France, attainted of treason, but was pardoned and allowed to return in 1723. He settled near Pope at Dawley farm and a close friendship developed between the two men. In their conversations Bolingbroke, who fancied himself a philosopher, helped Pope formulate the optimistic system that is expounded in this poem. Yet it is clear that the poem would have been pretty much what it is had the two men never met, for it expresses doctrines widely circulated and generally accepted at the time by enlightened minds throughout Europe. The *Essay* gives memorable expression to ideas about the nature of the universe and our place in it, ideas on which eighteenth-century optimism rested.

Pope's purpose is to "vindicate the ways of God to man," a phrase that consciously echoes *Paradise Lost* 1.26. Like John Milton, Pope faces the problem of the existence of evil in a world presumed to be the creation of a good God. *Paradise Lost* is biblical

8. Berenice, the wife of Ptolemy III, dedicated a lock of her hair to the gods to ensure her husband's safe return from war. It was turned into a constellation.
9. A walk laid out by Charles II in St. James's Park (London), a resort for strollers of all sorts.

1. In St. James's Park; associated with unhappy lovers.
2. John Partridge, an astrologer whose annually published predictions had been amusingly satirized by Swift and other wits in 1708.

in content, Christian in doctrine; *An Essay on Man* avoids all specifically Christian doctrines, not because Pope disbelieved them, but because "man," the subject of the poem, includes millions who never heard of Christianity, and Pope is concerned with the universal. Milton tells a mythological story. Pope writes in abstract terms.

The *Essay* is divided into four epistles. In the first Pope asserts the essential order and goodness of the universe and the rightness of our place in it. The other epistles deal with how we may emulate in our nature and in society the cosmic harmony revealed in the first epistle. The second seeks to show how we may attain a psychological harmony that can become the basis of a virtuous life through the cooperation of self-love and the passions (both necessary to our complete humanity) with reason, the controller and director. The third is concerned with the individual in society, which, it teaches, was created through the cooperation of self-love (the egoistic drives that motivate us) and social love (our dependence on others, our inborn benevolence). The fourth is concerned with happiness, which lies within the reach of all, for it is dependent on virtue, which becomes possible when—though only when—self-love is transmuted into love of others and love of God. Such, in brief summary, are Pope's main ideas, expressed in many phrases so memorable that they have detached themselves from the poem and become part of daily speech.

From An Essay on Man

TO HENRY ST. JOHN, LORD BOLINGBROKE

Epistle 1. Of the Nature and State of Man, With Respect to the Universe

>   Awake, my St. John! leave all meaner things
> To low ambition, and the pride of kings.
> Let us (since life can little more supply
> Than just to look about us and to die)
> 5 Expatiate free° o'er all this scene of man;   *range freely*
> A mighty maze! but not without a plan;
> A wild, where weeds and flowers promiscuous shoot,
> Or garden, tempting with forbidden fruit.
> Together let us beat this ample field,
> 10 Try what the open, what the covert yield;
> The latent tracts, the giddy heights, explore
> Of all who blindly creep, or sightless soar;
> Eye Nature's walks, shoot folly as it flies,
> And catch the manners living as they rise;
> 15 Laugh where we must, be candid° where we can;   *kindly*
> But vindicate the ways of God to man.
>
>   1. Say first, of God above, or man below,
> What can we reason, but from what we know?
> Of man, what see we but his station here,
> 20 From which to reason, or to which refer?
> Through worlds unnumbered though the God be known,
> 'Tis ours to trace him only in our own.
> He, who through vast immensity can pierce,
> See worlds on worlds compose one universe,
> 25 Observe how system into system runs,
> What other planets circle other suns,

What varied being peoples every star,
May tell why Heaven has made us as we are.
But of this frame the bearings, and the ties,
30 The strong connections, nice dependencies,
Gradations just, has thy pervading soul
Looked through? or can a part contain the whole?
   Is the great chain, that draws all to agree,
And drawn supports, upheld by God, or thee?[1]

35   2. Presumptuous man! the reason wouldst thou find,
Why formed so weak, so little, and so blind?
First, if thou canst, the harder reason guess,
Why formed no weaker, blinder, and no less!
Ask of thy mother earth, why oaks are made
40 Taller or stronger than the weeds they shade?
Or ask of yonder argent fields above,
Why Jove's satellites[2] are less than Jove?
   Of systems possible, if 'tis confessed
That Wisdom Infinite must form the best,
45 Where all must full or not coherent be,
And all that rises, rise in due degree;
Then, in the scale of reasoning life, 'tis plain,
There must be, somewhere, such a rank as man:
And all the question (wrangle e'er so long)
50 Is only this, if God has placed him wrong?
   Respecting man, whatever wrong we call,
May, must be right, as relative to all.
In human works, though labored on with pain,
A thousand movements scarce one purpose gain;
55 In God's, one single can its end produce;
Yet serves to second too some other use.
So man, who here seems principal alone,
Perhaps acts second to some sphere unknown,
Touches some wheel, or verges to some goal;
60 'Tis but a part we see, and not a whole.
   When the proud steed shall know why man restrains
His fiery course, or drives him o'er the plains;
When the dull ox, why now he breaks the clod,
Is now a victim, and now Egypt's god:
65 Then shall man's pride and dullness comprehend
His actions', passions', being's use and end;
Why doing, suffering, checked, impelled; and why
This hour a slave, the next a deity.
   Then say not man's imperfect, Heaven in fault;
70 Say rather, man's as perfect as he ought;
His knowledge measured to his state and place,
His time a moment, and a point his space.
If to be perfect in a certain sphere,[3]
What matter, soon or late, or here or there?

---

1. For the chain of being, see Addison's *The Spectator* 519 and lines 207–58.
2. In his *Dictionary,* Johnson notes and condemns

Pope's giving this word four syllables, as in Latin.
3. I.e., in one's "state and place."

75 The blest today is as completely so,
 As who began a thousand years ago.

  3. Heaven from all creatures hides the book of Fate,
 All but the page prescribed, their present state:
 From brutes what men, from men what spirits know:
80 Or who could suffer being here below?
 The lamb thy riot dooms to bleed today,
 Had he thy reason, would he skip and play?
 Pleased to the last, he crops the flowery food,
 And licks the hand just raised to shed his blood.
85 O blindness to the future! kindly given,
 That each may fill the circle marked by Heaven:
 Who sees with equal eye, as God of all,
 A hero perish, or a sparrow fall,
 Atoms or systems° into ruin hurled,   *solar systems*
90 And now a bubble burst, and now a world.
  Hope humbly then; with trembling pinions soar;
 Wait the great teacher Death, and God adore!
 What future bliss, he gives not thee to know,
 But gives that hope to be thy blessing now.
95 Hope springs eternal in the human breast:
 Man never is, but always to be blest:
 The soul, uneasy and confined from home,
 Rests and expatiates in a life to come.
  Lo! the poor Indian, whose untutored mind
100 Sees God in clouds, or hears him in the wind;
 His soul proud Science never taught to stray
 Far as the solar walk, or milky way;
 Yet simple Nature to his hope has given,
 Behind the cloud-topped hill, an humbler heaven;
105 Some safer world in depth of woods embraced,
 Some happier island in the watery waste,
 Where slaves once more their native land behold,
 No fiends torment, no Christians thirst for gold!
 To be, contents his natural desire,
110 He asks no angel's wing, no seraph's fire;
 But thinks, admitted to that equal sky,
 His faithful dog shall bear him company.

  4. Go, wiser thou! and, in thy scale of sense,
 Weigh thy opinion against Providence;
115 Call imperfection what thou fancy'st such,
 Say, here he gives too little, there too much;
 Destroy all creatures for thy sport or gust,[4]
 Yet cry, if man's unhappy, God's unjust;
 If man alone engross not Heaven's high care,
120 Alone made perfect here, immortal there:
 Snatch from his hand the balance and the rod,
 Rejudge his justice, be the God of God!

4. "Sense of tasting" (Johnson's *Dictionary*).

In pride, in reasoning pride, our error lies;
All quit their sphere, and rush into the skies.
125 Pride still is aiming at the blest abodes,
Men would be angels, angels would be gods.
Aspiring to be gods, if angels fell,
Aspiring to be angels, men rebel:
And who but wishes to invert the laws
130 Of order, sins against the Eternal Cause.

5. Ask for what end the heavenly bodies shine,
Earth for whose use? Pride answers, " 'Tis for mine:
For me kind Nature wakes her genial power,
Suckles each herb, and spreads out every flower;
135 Annual for me, the grape, the rose renew
The juice nectareous, and the balmy dew;
For me, the mine a thousand treasures brings;
For me, health gushes from a thousand springs;
Seas roll to waft me, suns to light me rise;
140 My footstool earth, my canopy the skies."
But errs not Nature from this gracious end,
From burning suns when livid deaths descend,
When earthquakes swallow, or when tempests sweep
Towns to one grave, whole nations to the deep?
145 "No," 'tis replied, "the first Almighty Cause
Acts not by partial, but by general laws;
The exceptions few; some change since all began,
And what created perfect?"—Why then man?
If the great end be human happiness,
150 Then Nature deviates; and can man do less?
As much that end a constant course requires
Of showers and sunshine, as of man's desires;
As much eternal springs and cloudless skies,
As men forever temperate, calm, and wise.
155 If plagues or earthquakes break not Heaven's design,
Why then a Borgia, or a Catiline?[5]
Who knows but he whose hand the lightning forms,
Who heaves old ocean, and who wings the storms,
Pours fierce ambition in a Caesar's mind,
160 Or turns young Ammon[6] loose to scourge mankind?
From pride, from pride, our very reasoning springs;
Account for moral, as for natural things:
Why charge we Heaven in those, in these acquit?
In both, to reason right is to submit.
165 Better for us, perhaps, it might appear,
Were there all harmony, all virtue here;
That never air or ocean felt the wind;
That never passion discomposed the mind:

---

5. The Renaissance Italian family of the Borgias was notorious for its crimes: ruthless lust for power, cruelty, rapaciousness, treachery, and murder (especially by poisoning). Cesare Borgia (1476–1507), son of Pope Alexander VI, is here referred to. Lucius Sergius Catiline (ca. 108–62 B.C.E.), an ambitious, greedy, and cruel conspirator against the Roman state, was denounced in Cicero's famous orations before the senate and in the Forum.
6. Alexander the Great.

But ALL subsists by elemental strife;
170　And passions are the elements of life.
The general ORDER, since the whole began,
Is kept in Nature, and is kept in man.

6. What would this man? Now upward will he soar,
And little less than angel, would be more;
175　Now looking downwards, just as grieved appears
To want the strength of bulls, the fur of bears.
Made for his use all creatures if he call,
Say what their use, had he the powers of all?
Nature to these, without profusion, kind,
180　The proper organs, proper powers assigned;
Each seeming want compènsated of course,
Here with degrees of swiftness, there of force;
All in exact proportion to the state;
Nothing to add, and nothing to abate.
185　Each beast, each insect, happy in its own;
Is Heaven unkind to man, and man alone?
Shall he alone, whom rational we call,
Be pleased with nothing, if not blessed with all?
　　The bliss of man (could pride that blessing find)
190　Is not to act or think beyond mankind;
No powers of body or of soul to share,
But what his nature and his state can bear.
Why has not man a microscopic eye?
For this plain reason, man is not a fly.
195　Say what the use, were finer optics given,
To inspect a mite, not comprehend the heaven?
Or touch, if tremblingly alive all o'er,
To smart and agonize at every pore?
Or quick effluvia[7] darting through the brain,
200　Die of a rose in aromatic pain?
If nature thundered in his opening ears,
And stunned him with the music of the spheres,
How would he wish that Heaven had left him still
The whispering zephyr, and the purling rill?
205　Who finds not Providence all good and wise,
Alike in what it gives, and what it denies?

7. Far as creation's ample range extends,
The scale of sensual,° mental powers ascends:　　　　*sensory*
Mark how it mounts, to man's imperial race,
210　From the green myriads in the peopled grass:
What modes of sight betwixt each wide extreme,
The mole's dim curtain, and the lynx's beam:[8]
Of smell, the headlong lioness between,

---

7. According to the philosophy of Epicurus (adopted by Robert Boyle, the chemist, and other 17th-century scientists), the senses are stirred to perception by being bombarded through the pores by steady streams of "effluvia," incredibly thin and tiny—but material—images of the objects that surround us.

8. One of several early theories of vision held that the eye casts a beam of light that makes objects visible.

And hound sagacious[9] on the tainted green:
215 Of hearing, from the life that fills the flood,
To that which warbles through the vernal wood:
The spider's touch, how exquisitely fine!
Feels at each thread, and lives along the line:
In the nice° bee, what sense so subtly true   *exact, accurate*
220 From poisonous herbs extracts the healing dew:
How instinct varies in the groveling swine,
Compared, half-reasoning elephant, with thine!
'Twixt that, and reason, what a nice barrier,[1]
Forever separate, yet forever near!
225 Remembrance and reflection how allied;
What thin partitions sense from thought divide:
And middle natures, how they long to join,
Yet never pass the insuperable line!
Without this just gradation, could they be
230 Subjected, these to those, or all to thee?
The powers of all subdued by thee alone,
Is not thy reason all these powers in one?

    8. See, through this air, this ocean, and this earth,
All matter quick, and bursting into birth.
235 Above, how high progressive life may go!
Around, how wide! how deep extend below!
Vast Chain of Being! which from God began,
Natures ethereal, human, angel, man,
Beast, bird, fish, insect, what no eye can see,
240 No glass can reach! from Infinite to thee,
From thee to nothing.—On superior powers
Were we to press, inferior might on ours:
Or in the full creation leave a void,
Where, one step broken, the great scale's destroyed:
245 From Nature's chain whatever link you strike,
Tenth or ten thousandth, breaks the chain alike.
    And, if each system in gradation roll
Alike essential to the amazing whole,
The least confusion but in one, not all
250 That system only, but the whole must fall.
Let earth unbalanced from her orbit fly,
Planets and suns run lawless through the sky,
Let ruling angels from their spheres be hurled,
Being on being wrecked, and world on world,
255 Heaven's whole foundations to their center nod,
And Nature tremble to the throne of God:
All this dread ORDER break—for whom? for thee?
Vile worm!—oh, madness, pride, impiety!

    9. What if the foot, ordained the dust to tread,
260 Or hand, to toil, aspired to be the head?

---

9. Quick of scent.   1. Pronounced *ba-réer.*

What if the head, the eye, or ear repined
To serve mere engines to the ruling Mind?[2]
Just as absurd, to mourn the tasks or pains,
The great directing MIND of ALL ordains.
265   All are but parts of one stupendous whole,
Whose body Nature is, and God the soul;
That, changed through all, and yet in all the same,
Great in the earth, as in the ethereal frame,
Warms in the sun, refreshes in the breeze,
270   Glows in the stars, and blossoms in the trees,
Lives through all life, extends through all extent,
Spreads undivided, operates unspent,
Breathes in our soul, informs our mortal part,
As full, as perfect, in a hair as heart;
275   As full, as perfect, in vile man that mourns,
As the rapt seraph that adores and burns;
To him no high, no low, no great, no small;
He fills, he bounds, connects, and equals all.

    10. Cease then, nor ORDER imperfection name:
280   Our proper bliss depends on what we blame.
Know thy own point: this kind, this due degree
Of blindness, weakness, Heaven bestows on thee.
Submit—In this, or any other sphere,
Secure to be as blest as thou canst bear:
285   Safe in the hand of one disposing Power,
Or in the natal, or the mortal hour.
All Nature is but art, unknown to thee;
All chance, direction, which thou canst not see;
All discord, harmony not understood;
290   All partial evil, universal good:
And, spite of pride, in erring reason's spite,
One truth is clear: Whatever IS, is RIGHT.

From *Epistle 2. Of the Nature and State of Man With Respect to Himself, as an Individual*

    1. Know then thyself, presume not God to scan;
The proper study of mankind is Man.
Placed on this isthmus of a middle state,
A being darkly wise, and rudely great:
5   With too much knowledge for the skeptic side,
With too much weakness for the Stoic's pride,
He hangs between; in doubt to act, or rest,
In doubt to deem himself a god, or beast;
In doubt his mind or body to prefer,
10   Born but to die, and reasoning but to err;
Alike in ignorance, his reason such,
Whether he thinks too little, or too much:

---

2. Cf. 1 Corinthians 12.14–26.

Chaos of thought and passion, all confused;
Still by himself abused, or disabused;
15   Created half to rise, and half to fall;
Great lord of all things, yet a prey to all;
Sole judge of truth, in endless error hurled:
The glory, jest, and riddle of the world!

          *   *   *   1733

Epistle 2. To a Lady *Epistle 2. To a Lady* is one of four poems that Pope grouped together under the title *Epistles to Several Persons* but that have usually been known by the less appropriate title *Moral Essays*. They were conceived as parts of Pope's ambitious "ethic work," of which only the first part, *An Essay on Man*, was completed. *Epistle* 1 treats the characters of men and *Epistle* 2, the characters of women. The other two epistles are concerned with the use of riches, a subject that engaged Pope's attention during the 1730s, because he distrusted the influence on private morals and public life of the rapidly growing wealth of England under the first Hanoverians.

Epistle 2 combines two literary forms: the satire on women, and the verse letter to a particular person—here Martha Blount (1690–1763), Pope's closest female friend, whose remark in line 2 sets the theme of the poem. The first section (to line 198) sketches a portrait gallery of ladies that illustrates their inconsistency and volatility. As an amateur painter, Pope is fascinated by the problem of catching such contrary types: the affected, the soft-natured, the cunning, the whimsical, the witty, and the silly. The next part of the poem (lines 199–248) develops Pope's favorite theory of the ruling passion—the idea that each person is driven by a single irresistible desire—and argues that women are limited to two passions: love of pleasure and love of power. The final part (line 249 to the end) describes an ideal woman, good-natured, sensible, and well balanced, who is identified with Blount herself.

Like every satire on women, *Epistle* 2 is shaped by stereotypes: women are fickle, frail, and subordinate to men. Yet much of the poem undermines those prejudices by showing the real difficulties of women's lives. "By man's oppression cursed," they waste their talents on trivial pursuits and "die of nothing but a rage to live." The poem shares that restlessness. If women are full of contradictions, so are Pope's couplets, torn between sympathy and satiric bite. The poet finds himself strangely attracted to what he disapproves, and many female readers, then and now, have felt the same way about the poem.

Epistle 2. To a Lady

Of the Characters of Women

Nothing so true as what you once let fall,
"Most women have no characters at all."
Matter too soft a lasting mark to bear,
And best distinguished by black, brown, or fair.
5   How many pictures[1] of one nymph we view,

---

1. Ladies of the 17th and 18th centuries were often painted in the costumes and attitudes of fanciful, mythological, or historical characters.

All how unlike each other, all how true!
Arcadia's countess, here, in ermined pride,
Is, there, Pastora by a fountain side.
Here Fannia, leering on her own good man,
10 And there, a naked Leda with a swan.[2]
Let then the fair one beautifully cry,
In Magdalen's loose hair and lifted eye,
Or dressed in smiles of sweet Cecilia shine,[3]
With simpering angels, palms, and harps divine;
15 Whether the charmer sinner it, or saint it,
If folly grow romantic,° I must paint it.   *extravagant*
     Come then, the colors and the ground[4] prepare!
Dip in the rainbow, trick° her off in air;   *sketch*
Choose a firm cloud, before it fall, and in it
20 Catch, ere she change, the Cynthia[5] of this minute.
     Rufa, whose eye quick-glancing o'er the park,
Attracts each light gay meteor of a spark,°   *beau*
Agrees as ill with Rufa studying Locke,
As Sappho's diamonds with her dirty smock,
25 Or Sappho at her toilet's greasy task,[6]
With Sappho fragrant at an evening masque:
So morning insects that in muck begun,
Shine, buzz, and flyblow[7] in the setting sun.
     How soft is Silia! fearful to offend,
30 The frail one's advocate, the weak one's friend:
To her, Calista proved her conduct nice,
And good Simplicius asks of her advice.
Sudden, she storms! she raves! You tip the wink,
But spare your censure; Silia does not drink.
35 All eyes may see from what the change arose,
All eyes may see—a pimple on her nose.
     Papillia,[8] wedded to her amorous spark,
Sighs for the shades—"How charming is a park!"
A park is purchased, but the fair he sees
40 All bathed in tears—"Oh, odious, odious trees!"
     Ladies, like variegated tulips, show;
'Tis to their changes half their charms we owe;
Their happy spots the nice admirer take,
Fine by defect, and delicately weak.
45 'Twas thus Calypso[9] once each heart alarmed,
Awed without virtue, without beauty charmed;
Her tongue bewitched as oddly as her eyes,
Less wit than mimic, more a wit than wise;
Strange graces still, and stranger flights she had,
50 Was just not ugly, and was just not mad;

---

2. Leda was seduced by Zeus, who approached her in the form of a swan.
3. St. Mary Magdalen and St. Cecilia were often painted in the manner described.
4. The first coatings of paint on the canvas before the figures in the picture are sketched in.
5. One of the names of Diana, goddess of the moon, a notoriously changeable heavenly body.
6. Lady Mary Wortley Montagu, although beau-

tiful as a young woman, became notorious for her slatternly appearance and personal uncleanliness. Both Sappho and Montagu were poets.
7. Deposit their eggs.
8. The name comes from Latin for "butterfly."
9. The name is borrowed from the fascinating goddess who detained Odysseus on her island for seven years after the fall of Troy, thus preventing his return to his kingdom, Ithaca.

Yet ne'er so sure your passion to create,
As when she touched the brink of all we hate.
    Narcissa's[1] nature, tolerably mild,
To make a wash,° would hardly stew a child;   *cosmetic lotion*
55 Has even been proved to grant a lover's prayer,
And paid a tradesman once to make him stare,
Gave alms at Easter, in a Christian trim,
And made a widow happy, for a whim.
Why then declare good nature is her scorn,
60 When 'tis by that alone she can be borne?
Why pique all mortals, yet affect a name?
A fool to pleasure, yet a slave to fame:
Now deep in Taylor and the *Book of Martyrs*,[2]
Now drinking citron with his Grace and Chartres.[3]
65 Now conscience chills her, and now passion burns;
And atheism and religion take their turns;
A very heathen in the carnal part,
Yet still a sad, good Christian at her heart.
    See Sin in state, majestically drunk;
70 Proud as a peeress, prouder as a punk;°   *harlot*
Chaste to her husband, frank° to all beside,   *licentious*
A teeming mistress, but a barren bride.
What then? let blood and body bear the fault,
Her head's untouched, that noble seat of thought:
75 Such this day's doctrine—in another fit
She sins with poets through pure love of wit.
What has not fired her bosom or her brain?
Caesar and Tallboy, Charles[4] and Charlemagne.
As Helluo,[5] late dictator of the feast,
80 The nose of hautgout,[6] and the tip of taste,
Criticked your wine, and analyzed your meat,
Yet on plain pudding deigned at home to eat;
So Philomedé,[7] lecturing all mankind
On the soft passion, and the taste refined,
85 The address, the delicacy—stoops at once,
And makes her hearty meal upon a dunce.
    Flavia's a wit, has too much sense to pray;
To toast our wants and wishes, is her way;
Nor asks of God, but of her stars, to give
90 The mighty blessing, "while we live, to live."

1. Type of extreme self-love. Narcissus, a beautiful youth, fell in love with his own image when he saw it reflected in a fountain.

2. John Foxe's *Acts and Monuments*, usually referred to as Foxe's *Book of Martyrs*, was a household book in most Protestant families in the 17th and 18th centuries. A record of the Protestants who perished for their faith under the persecution of Mary Tudor (1553–58), it was instrumental in keeping anti-Catholic sentiments alive. Jeremy Taylor, 17th-century Anglican divine, whose *Holy Living and Holy Dying* was often reprinted in the 18th century.

3. Francis Chartres was a debauchee often mentioned by Pope. "His Grace" is usually said to be the duke of Wharton, an old enemy of Swift's and a notorious libertine. "Citron": citron water, brandy flavored with lemon or orange peels.

4. "Charles," as F. W. Bateson points out, was a generic name for a footman in the period. "Tallboy": a crude young man in Richard Brome's comedy *The Jovial Crew* (1641) or the opera adapted from the play (1731).

5. Glutton (Latin).

6. "Anything with a strong relish or strong scent, as overkept venison" (Johnson's *Dictionary*).

7. The name is Pope's adaptation of a Greek epithet meaning "laughter-loving," frequently applied to Aphrodite, the goddess of love.

Then all for death, that opiate of the soul!
Lucretia's dagger, Rosamonda's bowl.[8]
Say, what can cause such impotence of mind?
A spark too fickle, or a spouse too kind.
95 Wise wretch! with pleasures too refined to please,
With too much spirit to be e'er at ease,
With too much quickness ever to be taught,
With too much thinking to have common thought:
You purchase pain with all that joy can give,
100 And die of nothing but a rage to live.
    Turn then from wits; and look on Simo's mate,
No ass so meek, no ass so obstinate:
Or her, that owns her faults, but never mends,
Because she's honest, and the best of friends:
105 Or her, whose life the Church and scandal share,
Forever in a passion, or a prayer:
Or her, who laughs at hell, but (like her Grace)
Cries, "Ah! how charming, if there's no such place!"
Or who in sweet vicissitude appears
110 Of mirth and opium, ratafie[9] and tears,
The daily anodyne, and nightly draught,
To kill those foes to fair ones, time and thought.
Woman and fool are two hard things to hit,
For true no-meaning puzzles more than wit.
115   But what are these to great Atossa's[1] mind?
Scarce once herself, by turns all womankind!
Who, with herself, or others, from her birth
Finds all her life one warfare upon earth:
Shines in exposing knaves, and painting fools,
120 Yet is whate'er she hates and ridicules.
No thought advances, but her eddy brain
Whisks it about, and down it goes again.
Full sixty years the world has been her trade,
The wisest fool much time has ever made.
125 From loveless youth to unrespected age,
No passion gratified except her rage.
So much the fury still outran the wit,
The pleasure missed her, and the scandal hit.
Who breaks with her, provokes revenge from hell,
130 But he's a bolder man who dares be well:[2]
Her every turn with violence pursued,
Nor more a storm her hate than gratitude:
To that each passion turns, or soon or late;
Love, if it makes her yield, must make her hate:
135 Superiors? death! and equals? what a curse!
But an inferior not dependent? worse.
Offend her, and she knows not to forgive;

8. According to tradition, the "fair Rosamonda,"
mistress of Henry II, was forced by Queen Eleanor
to drink poison. Lucretia, violated by Tarquin,
committed suicide.
9. "A fine liquor, prepared from the kernels of
apricots and spirits" (Johnson's *Dictionary*).

1. Atossa, daughter of Cyrus, emperor of Persia (d.
529 B.C.E.). If the duchess of Buckinghamshire is
alluded to, the name is appropriate, for she was the
natural daughter of James II.
2. Be in her favor.

Oblige her, and she'll hate you while you live:
But die, and she'll adore you—Then the bust
140 And temple rise—then fall again to dust.
Last night, her lord was all that's good and great;
A knave this morning, and his will a cheat.
Strange! by the means defeated of the ends,
By spirit robbed of power, by warmth of friends,
145 By wealth of followers! without one distress
Sick of herself through very selfishness!
Atossa, cursed with every granted prayer,
Childless with all her children, wants an heir.
To heirs unknown descends the unguarded store,
150 Or wanders, Heaven-directed, to the poor.
　　Pictures like these, dear Madam, to design,
Asks no firm hand, and no unerring line;
Some wandering touches, some reflected light,
Some flying stroke alone can hit 'em right:
155 For how should equal colors do the knack?[3]
Chameleons who can paint in white and black?
　　"Yet Chloe sure was formed without a spot—"
Nature in her then erred not, but forgot.
"With every pleasing, every prudent part,
160 Say, what can Chloe want?"—She wants a heart.
She speaks, behaves, and acts just as she ought;
But never, never, reached one generous thought.
Virtue she finds too painful an endeavor,
Content to dwell in decencies forever.
165 So very reasonable, so unmoved,
As never yet to love, or to be loved.
She, while her lover pants upon her breast,
Can mark[4] the figures on an Indian chest;
And when she sees her friend in deep despair,
170 Observes how much a chintz exceeds mohair.
Forbid it Heaven, a favor or a debt
She e'er should cancel—but she may forget.
Safe is your secret still in Chloe's ear;
But none of Chloe's shall you ever hear.
175 Of all her dears she never slandered one,
But cares not if a thousand are undone.
Would Chloe know if you're alive or dead?
She bids her footman put it in her head.
Chloe is prudent—Would you too be wise?
180 Then never break your heart when Chloe dies.
　　One certain portrait may (I grant) be seen,
Which Heaven has varnished out, and made a *Queen*:[5]
The same forever! and described by all
With truth and goodness, as with crown and ball.
185 Poets heap virtues, painters gems at will,
And show their zeal, and hide their want of skill.

---

3. Do the trick.
4. Pay attention to.

5. Pope refers as usual to Queen Caroline with disapprobation.

'Tis well—but, artists! who can paint or write,
To draw the naked is your true delight.
That robe of quality so struts and swells,
190 None see what parts of Nature it conceals:
The exactest traits of body or of mind,
We owe to models of an humble kind.
If Queensberry[6] to strip there's no compelling,
'Tis from a handmaid we must take a Helen.
195 From peer or bishop 'tis no easy thing
To draw the man who loves his God, or king:
Alas! I copy (or my draft would fail)
From honest Mah'met or plain Parson Hale.[7]
    But grant, in public men sometimes are shown,
200 A woman's seen in private life alone:
Our bolder talents in full light displayed;
Your virtues open fairest in the shade.
Bred to disguise, in public 'tis you hide;
There, none distinguish 'twixt your shame or pride,
205 Weakness or delicacy; all so nice,
That each may seem a virtue, or a vice.
    In men, we various ruling passions find;
In women, two almost divide the kind;
Those, only fixed, they first or last obey,
210 The love of pleasure, and the love of sway.
    That, Nature gives; and where the lesson taught
Is but to please, can pleasure seem a fault?
Experience, this; by man's oppression cursed,
They seek the second not to lose the first.
215 Men, some to business, some to pleasure take;
But every woman is at heart a rake;
Men, some to quiet, some to public strife;
But every lady would be queen for life.
    Yet mark the fate of a whole sex of queens!
220 Power all their end, but beauty all the means:
In youth they conquer, with so wild a rage,
As leaves them scarce a subject in their age:
For foreign glory, foreign joy, they roam;
No thought of peace or happiness at home.
225 But wisdom's triumph is well-timed retreat,
As hard a science to the fair as great!
Beauties, like tyrants, old and friendless grown,
Yet hate repose, and dread to be alone,
Worn out in public, weary every eye,
230 Nor leave one sigh behind them when they die.
    Pleasures the sex, as children birds, pursue,
Still out of reach, yet never out of view,
Sure, if they catch, to spoil the toy at most,
To covet flying, and regret when lost:
235 At last, to follies youth could scarce defend,

6. The duchess of Queensberry, whom Pope valued because of her kindness to his friend John Gay, had been a famous beauty.

7. Dr. Stephen Hales, an Anglican clergyman and friend of Pope. Mahomet was a Turkish servant of George I.

It grows their age's prudence to pretend;
Ashamed to own they gave delight before,
Reduced to feign it, when they give no more:
As hags hold sabbaths, less for joy than spite,
240 So these their merry, miserable night;[8]
Still round and round the ghosts of beauty glide,
And haunt the places where their honor died.
    See how the world its veterans rewards!
A youth of frolics, an old age of cards;
245 Fair to no purpose, artful to no end,
Young without lovers, old without a friend;
A fop their passion, but their prize a sot;
Alive, ridiculous, and dead, forgot!
    Ah friend! to dazzle let the vain design;
250 To raise the thought, and touch the heart be thine!
That charm shall grow, while what fatigues the Ring[9]
Flaunts and goes down, an unregarded thing:
So when the sun's broad beam has tired the sight,
All mild ascends the moon's more sober light,
255 Serene in virgin modesty she shines,
And unobserved the glaring orb declines.
    Oh! blest with temper, whose unclouded ray
Can make tomorrow cheerful as today;
She, who can love a sister's charms, or hear
260 Sighs for a daughter with unwounded ear;
She, who ne'er answers till a husband cools,
Or, if she rules him, never shows she rules;
Charms by accepting, by submitting sways,
Yet has her humor most, when she obeys;
265 Lets fops or fortune fly which way they will;
Disdains all loss of tickets° or Codille;[1]   *lottery tickets*
Spleen, vapors, or smallpox, above them all,
And mistress of herself, though China[2] fall.
    And yet, believe me, good as well as ill,
270 Woman's at best a contradiction still.
Heaven, when it strives to polish all it can
Its last best work, but forms a softer man;
Picks from each sex, to make the favorite blest,
Your love of pleasure, our desire of rest:
275 Blends, in exception to all general rules,
Your taste of follies, with our scorn of fools:
Reserve with frankness, art with truth allied,
Courage with softness, modesty with pride;
Fixed principles, with fancy ever new;
280 Shakes all together, and produces—you.
    Be this a woman's fame: with this unblest,
Toasts live a scorn, and queens may die a jest.
This Phoebus promised (I forget the year)

8. I.e., evenings on which ladies entertained guests. "Sabbaths": obscene rites popularly supposed to be held by witches ("hags").
9. The fashionable drive in Hyde Park.

1. The loss of a hand at the card games of ombre or quadrille.
2. Pope refers punningly to the chinaware that fashionable women collected enthusiastically.

When those blue eyes first opened on the sphere;
285   Ascendant Phoebus watched that hour with care,
Averted half your parents' simple prayer;
And gave you beauty, but denied the pelf
That buys your sex a tyrant o'er itself.
The generous god, who wit and gold refines,
290   And ripens spirits as he ripens mines,[3]
Kept dross for duchesses, the world shall know it,
To you gave sense, good humor, and a poet.

1735, 1744

Epistle to Dr. Arbuthnot

Dr. John Arbuthnot (1667–1735), to whom Pope addressed his best-known verse epistle, was distinguished both as a physician and as a man of wit. He had been one of the liveliest members of the Martinus Scriblerus Club, helping his friends create the character and shape the career of the learned pedant whose memoirs the club had undertaken to write.

Pope had long been meditating such a poem, which was to be both an attack on his detractors and a defense of his own character and career. In his usual way, he had jotted down hints, lines, couplets, and fragments over a period of two decades, but the poem might never have been completed had it not been for two events: Arbuthnot, from his deathbed, wrote to urge Pope to continue his abhorrence of vice and to express it in his writings and, during 1733, Pope was the victim of two bitter attacks by "persons of rank and fortune," as the *Advertisement* has it. The *Verses Addressed to the Imitator of Horace* was the work of Lady Mary Wortley Montagu, helped by her friend Lord Hervey (pronounced *Harvey*), a close friend and confidant of Queen Caroline. *An Epistle to a Doctor of Divinity from a Nobleman at Hampton Court* was the work of Lord Hervey alone. Montagu, it must be admitted, had provocation enough, especially in Pope's recent reference to her in *The First Satire of the Second Book of Horace*, lines 83–84, but Hervey had little to complain of beyond occasional covert references to him as "Lord Fanny." At any rate, the two scurrilous attacks goaded Pope into action, and the poem was completed by the end of the summer of 1734.

The epistle is a masterpiece of poetic rhetoric. The very fact that it is addressed to Arbuthnot, a man generally known to be honest and kind, seems to guarantee the integrity of the *I* of the poem and to diminish the moral stature of his enemies. This acquisition of virtue through association, an effective stroke, is supported by every device of persuasive rhetoric—reasonable argument and emotional appeals, subtly suggestive imagery, and superbly controlled shifts in tone and style—which help sway the reader's judgment to the side of the speaker. The poem opens in the flat language of commonplace prose discourse, tinged with a wry humor and a tone of exasperation: "Shut, shut the door, good John! (fatigued, I said)" and as it progresses it rises or falls in language and style according to the emotions that the speaker expresses—anger, contempt, amusement, sarcasm, mock self-pity, indignation, hatred, affection, gratitude, and tenderness—to return at the end to the homely tone of the opening.

It is not clear that Pope intended the poem to be thought of as a dialogue, as it has usually been printed since Warburton's edition of 1751. The original edition, while suggesting interruptions in the flow of the monologue, kept entirely to the form of a

---

3. Phoebus Apollo, as god of poetry "ripens wit"; as god of the sun, he "ripens mines," for respectable scientific theory held that the sun's rays mature precious metals in the earth.

letter. The introduction of the friend, who speaks from time to time, converts the original letter into a dramatic dialogue.

Epistle to Dr. Arbuthnot

Advertisement

TO THE FIRST PUBLICATION OF THIS *Epistle*

This paper is a sort of bill of complaint, begun many years since, and drawn up by snatches, as the several occasions offered. I had no thoughts of publishing it, till it pleased some persons of rank and fortune (the authors of *Verses to the Imitator of Horace*, and of an *Epistle to a Doctor of Divinity from a Nobleman at Hampton Court*) to attack, in a very extraordinary manner, not only my writings (of which, being public, the public is judge) but my person, morals, and family, whereof, to those who know me not, a truer information may be requisite. Being divided between the necessity to say something of myself, and my own laziness to undertake so awkward a task, I thought it the shortest way to put the last hand to this epistle. If it have anything pleasing, it will be that by which I am most desirous to please, the truth and the sentiment; and if anything offensive, it will be only to those I am least sorry to offend, the vicious or the ungenerous.

Many will know their own pictures in it, there being not a circumstance but what is true; but I have, for the most part, spared their names, and they may escape being laughed at, if they please.

I would have some of them know, it was owing to the request of the learned and candid friend to whom it is inscribed, that I make not as free use of theirs as they have done of mine. However, I shall have this advantage, and honor, on my side, that whereas, by their proceeding, any abuse may be directed at any man, no injury can possibly be done by mine, since a nameless character can never be found out, but by its truth and likeness. P.

P. Shut, shut the door, good John![1] (fatigued, I said),
Tie up the knocker, say I'm sick, I'm dead.
The Dog Star[2] rages! nay 'tis past a doubt
All Bedlam,[3] or Parnassus, is let out:
5   Fire in each eye, and papers in each hand,
They rave, recite, and madden round the land.
   What walls can guard me, or what shades can hide?
They pierce my thickets, through my grot[4] they glide,
By land, by water, they renew the charge,
10 They stop the chariot, and they board the barge.
No place is sacred, not the church is free;
Even Sunday shines no Sabbath day to me:
Then from the Mint[5] walks forth the man of rhyme,

---

1. John Serle, Pope's gardener.
2. Sirius, associated with the period of greatest heat (and hence of madness) because it sets with the sun in late summer. August, in ancient Rome, was the season for reciting poetry.
3. Bethlehem Hospital for the insane, in London.
4. The subterranean passage under the road that

separated his house at Twickenham from his garden became, in Pope's hands, a romantic grotto ornamented with shells and mirrors.
5. A place in Southwark where debtors were free from arrest (they could not be arrested anywhere on Sundays).

Happy! to catch me just at dinner time.
15   Is there a parson, much bemused in beer,
A maudlin poetess, a rhyming peer,
A clerk foredoomed his father's soul to cross,
Who pens a stanza when he should engross?[6]
Is there who, locked from ink and paper,[7] scrawls
20   With desperate charcoal round his darkened walls?
All fly to Twit'nam,[8] and in humble strain
Apply to me to keep them mad or vain.
Arthur,[9] whose giddy son neglects the laws,
Imputes to me and my damned works the cause:
25   Poor Cornus[1] sees his frantic wife elope,
And curses wit, and poetry, and Pope.
    Friend to my life (which did not you prolong,
The world had wanted many an idle song)
What drop or nostrum° can this plague remove?   *medicine*
30   Or which must end me, a fool's wrath or love?
A dire dilemma! either way I'm sped,[2]
If foes, they write, if friends, they read me dead.
Seized and tied down to judge, how wretched I!
Who can't be silent, and who will not lie.
35   To laugh were want of goodness and of grace,
And to be grave exceeds all power of face.
I sit with sad civility, I read
With honest anguish and an aching head,
And drop at last, but in unwilling ears,
40   This saving counsel, "Keep your piece nine years."[3]
    "Nine years!" cries he, who high in Drury Lane,[4]
Lulled by soft zephyrs through the broken pane,
Rhymes ere he wakes, and prints before term[5] ends,
Obliged by hunger and request of friends:
45   "The piece, you think, is incorrect? why, take it,
I'm all submission, what you'd have it, make it."
    Three things another's modest wishes bound,
My friendship, and a prologue, and ten pound.
    Pitholeon[6] sends to me: "You know his Grace,
50   I want a patron; ask him for a place."
Pitholeon libeled me—"but here's a letter
Informs you, sir, 'twas when he knew no better.
Dare you refuse him? Curll[7] invites to dine,

---

6. Write out legal documents.
7. Is there some madman who, locked up without ink or paper . . . ?
8. I.e., Twickenham, Pope's villa on the bank of the Thames, a few miles above Hampton Court.
9. Arthur Moore, whose son, James Moore Smythe, dabbled in literature. Moore Smythe had earned Pope's enmity by using in one of his plays some unpublished lines from Pope's *Epistle 2. To a Lady* in spite of Pope's objections.
1. Latin for "horn," the traditional emblem of the cuckold.
2. "Destroyed; killed" (Johnson's *Dictionary*).
3. The advice of Horace in *Art of Poetry* (line 388).
4. I.e., living in a garret in Drury Lane, site of one

of the theaters and the haunt of the profligate.
5. One of the four annual periods in which the law courts are in session and with which the publishing season coincided.
6. "A foolish poet of Rhodes, who pretended much to Greek" [Pope's note]. He is Leonard Welsted, who translated Longinus and had attacked and slandered Pope (see line 375).
7. Edmund Curll, shrewd and disreputable bookseller, published pirated works, works falsely ascribed to reputable writers, scandalous biographies, and other ephemera. Pope had often attacked him and had assigned to him a low role in *The Dunciad*.

He'll write a *Journal,* or he'll turn divine."[8]
55　Bless me! a packet.—" 'Tis a stranger sues,
A virgin tragedy, an orphan Muse."
If I dislike it, "Furies, death, and rage!"
If I approve, "Commend it to the stage."
There (thank my stars) my whole commission ends,
60　The players and I are, luckily, no friends.
Fired that the house reject him, " 'Sdeath, I'll print it,
And shame the fools—Your interest, sir, with Lintot!"[9]
Lintot, dull rogue, will think your price too much.
"Not, sir, if you revise it, and retouch."
65　All my demurs but double his attacks;
At last he whispers, "Do; and we go snacks."°　　　　　*shares*
Glad of a quarrel, straight I clap the door,
"Sir, let me see your works and you no more."
　'Tis sung, when Midas' ears began to spring
70　(Midas, a sacred person and a king),
His very minister who spied them first,
(Some say his queen) was forced to speak, or burst.[1]
And is not mine, my friend, a sorer case,
When every coxcomb perks them in my face?
75　　A. Good friend, forbear! you deal in dangerous things.
I'd never name queens, ministers, or kings;
Keep close to ears, and those let asses prick;
'Tis nothing——P. Nothing? if they bite and kick?
Out with it, *Dunciad!* let the secret pass,
80　That secret to each fool, that he's an ass:
The truth once told (and wherefore should we lie?)
The queen of Midas slept, and so may I.
　　You think this cruel? take it for a rule,
No creature smarts so little as a fool.
85　Let peals of laughter, Codrus! round thee break,
Thou unconcerned canst hear the mighty crack.
Pit, box, and gallery in convulsions hurled,
Thou stand'st unshook amidst a bursting world.
Who shames a scribbler? break one cobweb through,
90　He spins the slight, self-pleasing thread anew:
Destroy his fib or sophistry, in vain;
The creature's at his dirty work again,
Throned in the center of his thin designs,
Proud of a vast extent of flimsy lines.
95　Whom have I hurt? has poet yet or peer
Lost the arched eyebrow or Parnassian sneer?
And has not Colley[2] still his lord and whore?
His butchers Henley? his freemasons Moore?

---

8. I.e., he will attack Pope in the *London Journal* or write a treatise on theology, as Welsted in fact did.
9. Bernard Lintot, publisher of Pope's Homer and other early works.
1. Midas, king of ancient Lydia, had the bad taste to prefer the flute-playing of Pan to that of Apollo, whereupon the god endowed him with ass's ears. It was his barber (not his wife or his minister) who discovered the secret and whispered it into a hole in the earth. The reference to "queen" and "minister" makes it plain that Pope is alluding to George II, Queen Caroline, and Walpole.
2. Colley Cibber, the laureate. John Henley, known as "Orator" Henley, an independent preacher of marked eccentricity, was popular among the lower orders, especially for his elocution.

Does not one table Bavius still admit?
100   Still to one bishop Philips[3] seem a wit?
Still Sappho[4]——A. Hold! for god's sake—you'll offend.
No names—be calm—learn prudence of a friend.
I too could write, and I am twice as tall;
But foes like these!——P. One flatterer's worse than all.
105   Of all mad creatures, if the learn'd are right,
It is the slaver kills, and not the bite.
A fool quite angry is quite innocent:
Alas! 'tis ten times worse when they repent.

One dedicates in high heroic prose,
110   And ridicules beyond a hundred foes;
One from all Grub Street[5] will my fame defend,
And, more abusive, calls himself my friend.
This prints my letters,[6] that expects a bribe,
And others roar aloud, "Subscribe, subscribe!"[7]
115   There are, who to my person pay their court:
I cough like Horace, and, though lean, am short;
Ammon's great son° one shoulder had too high,   *Alexander the Great*
Such Ovid's nose,[8] and "Sir! you have an eye—"
Go on, obliging creatures, make me see
120   All that disgraced my betters met in me.
Say for my comfort, languishing in bed,
"Just so immortal Maro° held his head":   *Virgil*
And when I die, be sure you let me know
Great Homer died three thousand years ago.

125   Why did I write? what sin to me unknown
Dipped me in ink, my parents', or my own?
As yet a child, nor yet a fool to fame,
I lisped in numbers, for the numbers came.
I left no calling for this idle trade,
130   No duty broke, no father disobeyed.
The Muse but served to ease some friend, not wife,
To help me through this long disease, my life,
To second, Arbuthnot! thy art and care,
And teach the being you preserved, to bear.°   *endure*

135   A. But why then publish? P. Granville the polite,
And knowing Walsh, would tell me I could write;
Well-natured Garth inflamed with early praise,
And Congreve loved, and Swift endured my lays;
The courtly Talbot, Somers, Sheffield, read;
140   Even mitered Rochester would nod the head,

3. The "bishop" is Hugh Boulter, bishop of Armagh; he had employed as his secretary Ambrose Philips (1674–1749), whose insipid simplicity of manner in poetry earned him the nickname of "Namby-Pamby." Bavius, the bad poet alluded to in Virgil's *Eclogue* 3.
4. Lady Mary Wortley Montagu.
5. A term denoting the whole society of literary, political, and journalistic hack writers.
6. In 1726 Curll had surreptitiously acquired and published without permission some of Pope's letters to Henry Cromwell.
7. To ensure the financial success of a work, the public was often asked to "subscribe" to it by taking a certain number of copies before printing was undertaken. Pope's Homer was published in this manner.
8. Ovid's family name, Naso, suggests the Latin word *nasus* ("nose"), hence the pun.

And St. John's self (great Dryden's friends before)
With open arms received one poet more.[9]
Happy my studies, when by these approved!
Happier their author, when by these beloved!
145 From these the world will judge of men and books,
Not from the Burnets, Oldmixons, and Cookes.[1]
    Soft were my numbers; who could take offense
While pure description held the place of sense?
Like gentle Fanny's[2] was my flowery theme,
150 A painted mistress, or a purling stream.
Yet then did Gildon draw his venal quill;[3]
I wished the man a dinner, and sat still.
Yet then did Dennis[4] rave in furious fret;
I never answered, I was not in debt.
155 If want provoked, or madness made them print,
I waged no war with Bedlam or the Mint.
    Did some more sober critic come abroad?
If wrong, I smiled; if right, I kissed the rod.
Pains, reading, study are their just pretense,
160 And all they want is spirit, taste, and sense.
Commas and points they set exactly right,
And 'twere a sin to rob them of their mite.
Yet ne'er one sprig of laurel graced these ribalds,
From slashing Bentley down to piddling Tibbalds.[5]
165 Each wight who reads not, and but scans and spells,
Each word-catcher that lives on syllables,
Even such small critics some regard may claim,
Preserved in Milton's or in Shakespeare's name.
Pretty! in amber to observe the forms
170 Of hairs, or straws, or dirt, or grubs, or worms!
The things, we know, are neither rich nor rare,
But wonder how the devil they got there.
    Were others angry? I excused them too;
Well might they rage; I gave them but their due.
175 A man's true merit 'tis not hard to find;
But each man's secret standard in his mind,
That casting weight[6] pride adds to emptiness,
This, who can gratify? for who can guess?
The bard[7] whom pilfered pastorals renown,

9. The purpose of this list is to establish Pope as the successor of Dryden and thus to place him far above his Grub Street persecutors. George Granville, Lord Lansdowne, poet and statesman; William Walsh, poet and critic; Sir Samuel Garth, physician and mock-epic poet; William Congreve, the playwright; the statesmen Charles Talbot, duke of Shrewsbury; Lord Sommers; John Sheffield, duke of Buckinghamshire; and Francis Atterbury, bishop of Rochester, had all been associated with Dryden in his later years and had all encouraged the young Pope.
1. Thomas Burnet, John Oldmixon, and Thomas Cooke: Pope identifies them in a note as "authors of secret and scandalous history."
2. John, Lord Hervey, whom Pope satirizes in the character of Sporus (lines 305–33).
3. Charles Gildon, minor critic and scribbler, who, Pope believed, early attacked him at the insti-

gation of Addison; hence "venal quill."
4. John Dennis (see An Essay on Criticism, n. 7, p. 1129).
5. Lewis Theobald (1688–1744), whose minute learning in Elizabethan literature had enabled him to expose Pope's defects as an editor of Shakespeare in 1726. Pope made him king of the Dunces in The Dunciad of 1728. Richard Bentley (1662–1742), the eminent classical scholar, seemed to both Pope and Swift the perfect type of the pedant: he is called "slashing" because, in his edition of Paradise Lost (1732), he had set in square brackets all passages that he disliked on the grounds they had been slipped into the poem without the blind poet's knowledge.
6. The weight that turns the scale; here, the "deciding factor."
7. Ambrose Philips, Pope's rival in pastoral poetry in 1709, when their pastorals were published in

180 Who turns a Persian tale for half a crown,
 Just writes to make his barrenness appear,
 And strains from hard-bound brains eight lines a year:
 He, who still wanting, though he lives on theft,
 Steals much, spends little, yet has nothing left;
185 And he who now to sense, now nonsense leaning,
 Means not, but blunders round about a meaning:
 And he whose fustian's so sublimely bad,
 It is not poetry, but prose run mad:
 All these, my modest satire bade translate,
190 And owned that nine such poets made a Tate.[8]
 How did they fume, and stamp, and roar, and chafe!
 And swear, not Addison himself was safe.
  Peace to all such! but were there one whose fires
 True Genius kindles, and fair Fame inspires;
195 Blessed with each talent and each art to please,
 And born to write, converse, and live with ease:
 Should such a man, too fond to rule alone,
 Bear, like the Turk, no brother near the throne;
 View him with scornful, yet with jealous eyes,
200 And hate for arts that caused himself to rise;
 Damn with faint praise, assent with civil leer,
 And without sneering, teach the rest to sneer;
 Willing to wound, and yet afraid to strike,
 Just hint a fault, and hesitate dislike;
205 Alike reserved to blame or to commend,
 A timorous foe, and a suspicious friend;
 Dreading even fools; by flatterers besieged,
 And so obliging that he ne'er obliged;
 Like Cato, give his little senate[9] laws,
210 And sit attentive to his own applause;
 While wits and Templars° every sentence raise,   *law students*
 And wonder with a foolish face of praise—
 Who but must laugh, if such a man there be?
 Who would not weep, if Atticus[1] were he?
215 What though my name stood rubric[2] on the walls
 Or plastered posts, with claps,° in capitals?   *posters*
 Or smoking forth, a hundred hawkers' load,
 On wings of winds came flying all abroad?
 I sought no homage from the race that write;
220 I kept, like Asian monarchs, from their sight:
 Poems I heeded (now berhymed so long)
 No more than thou, great George! a birthday song.

Tonson's 6th *Miscellany*. Philips had also translated some Persian tales (cf. line 100).
8. Nahum Tate, poet laureate from 1692 to 1715.
His popular rewriting of Shakespeare's *King Lear*
provided a happy ending; he wrote most of part 2
of *Absalom and Achitophel*. The line refers to the
old adage that it takes nine tailors to make one
man.
9. Addison's tragedy *Cato* had been a sensational
success in 1713. Pope had written the prologue, in
which occurs the line, "While Cato gives his little

senate laws." The satirical reference here is to
Addison in the role of arbiter of taste among his
friends and admirers, mostly Whigs, at Button's
Coffee House. It was these people who had worked
against the success of Pope's Homer.
1. Pope's satiric pseudonym for Addison; Atticus
(109–32 B.C.E.) was a wealthy man of letters and
a friend of Cicero, known as a wise and disinter-
ested man.
2. In red letters.

I ne'er with wits or witlings passed my days
To spread about the itch of verse and praise;
225 Nor like a puppy daggled through the town
To fetch and carry sing-song up and down;
Nor at rehearsals sweat, and mouthed, and cried,
With handkerchief and orange at my side;
But sick of fops, and poetry, and prate,
230 To Bufo left the whole Castalian[3] state.
　　Proud as Apollo on his forkèd hill,[4]
Sat full-blown Bufo, puffed by every quill;
Fed with soft dedication all day long,
Horace and he went hand in hand in song.
235 His library (where busts of poets dead
And a true Pindar stood without a head)
Received of wits an undistinguished race,
Who first his judgment asked, and then a place:
Much they extolled his pictures, much his seat,[5]
240 And flattered every day, and some days eat:
Till grown more frugal in his riper days,
He paid some bards with port, and some with praise;
To some a dry rehearsal was assigned,
And others (harder still) he paid in kind.
245 Dryden alone (what wonder?) came not nigh;
Dryden alone escaped this judging eye:
But still the great have kindness in reserve;
He helped to bury whom he helped to starve.
　　May some choice patron bless each gray goose quill!
250 May every Bavius have his Bufo still!
So when a statesman wants a day's defense,
Or envy holds a whole week's war with sense,
Or simple pride for flattery makes demands,
May dunce by dunce be whistled off my hands!
255 Blessed be the great! for those they take away,
And those they left me—for they left me Gay;[6]
Left me to see neglected genius bloom,
Neglected die, and tell it on his tomb;
Of all thy blameless life the sole return
260 My verse, and Queensberry weeping o'er thy urn!
Oh, let me live my own, and die so too!
("To live and die is all I have to do")[7]
Maintain a poet's dignity and ease,
And see what friends, and read what books I please;
265 Above a patron, though I condescend
Sometimes to call a minister my friend.
I was not born for courts or great affairs;

3. The Castalian spring on Mount Parnassus was sacred to Apollo and the Muses. "Bufo": a type of tasteless patron of the arts. (*Bufo* means "toad" in Latin.)
4. Mount Parnassus had two peaks, one sacred to Apollo, one to Bacchus.
5. Estate. Pronounced *sate* and rhymed in next line with "eat" (*ate*).
6. John Gay (1685–1732), author of *The Beggar's Opera* and other delightful works, dear friend of Swift and Pope. His failure to obtain patronage from the court intensified Pope's hostility to the Whig administration and the queen. Gay spent the last years of his life under the protection of the duke and duchess of Queensberry.
7. A quotation from John Denham's poem *Of Prudence*.

I pay my debts, believe, and say my prayers,
Can sleep without a poem in my head,
270　Nor know if Dennis be alive or dead.
　　　Why am I asked what next shall see the light?
Heavens! was I born for nothing but to write?
Has life no joys for me? or (to be grave)
Have I no friend to serve, no soul to save?
275　"I found him close with Swift"—"Indeed? no doubt"
Cries prating Balbus, "something will come out."
'Tis all in vain, deny it as I will.
"No, such a genius never can lie still,"
And then for mine obligingly mistakes
280　The first lampoon Sir Will or Bubo[8] makes.
Poor guiltless I! and can I choose but smile,
When every coxcomb knows me by my style?
　　　Cursed be the verse, how well soe'er it flow,
That tends to make one worthy man my foe,
285　Give virtue scandal, innocence a fear,
Or from the soft-eyed virgin steal a tear!
But he who hurts a harmless neighbor's peace,
Insults fallen worth, or beauty in distress,
Who loves a lie, lame slander helps about,
290　Who writes a libel, or who copies out:
That fop whose pride affects a patron's name,
Yet absent, wounds an author's honest fame;
Who can your merit selfishly approve,
And show the sense of it without the love;
295　Who has the vanity to call you friend,
Yet wants the honor, injured, to defend;
Who tells whate'er you think, whate'er you say,
And, if he lie not, must at least betray:
Who to the dean and silver bell can swear,
300　And sees at Cannons what was never there:[9]
Who reads but with a lust to misapply,
Make satire a lampoon, and fiction, lie:
A lash like mine no honest man shall dread,
But all such babbling blockheads in his stead.
305　　Let Sporus[1] tremble—— A. What? that thing of silk,
Sporus, that mere white curd of ass's milk?[2]
Satire or sense, alas! can Sporus feel?
Who breaks a butterfly upon a wheel?
　　　P. Yet let me flap this bug with gilded wings,
310　This painted child of dirt, that stinks and stings;
Whose buzz the witty and the fair annoys,
Yet wit ne'er tastes, and beauty ne'er enjoys;

---

8. Sir William Yonge, Whig politician and poet-aster. George Bubb ("Bubo") Dodington, a Whig patron of letters.
9. Pope's enemies had accused him of satirizing Cannons, the ostentatious estate of the duke of Chandos, in his description of Timon's villa in the *Epistle to Burlington*. This Pope quite justly denied. The bell of Timon's chapel was of silver, and there preached a dean who "never mentions Hell to ears polite."
1. John, Lord Hervey, effeminate courtier and confidant of Queen Caroline (see the headnote to *Epistle to Dr. Arbuthnot*, p. 1168). The original Sporus was a boy, whom the emperor Nero publicly married (see Suetonius's life of Nero in *The Twelve Caesars*).
2. Drunk by invalids.

So well-bred spaniels civilly delight
In mumbling of the game they dare not bite.
315 Eternal smiles his emptiness betray,
As shallow streams run dimpling all the way.
Whether in florid impotence he speaks,
And, as the prompter breathes, the puppet squeaks;
Or at the ear of Eve,[3] familiar toad,
320 Half froth, half venom, spits himself abroad,
In puns, or politics, or tales, or lies,
Or spite, or smut, or rhymes, or blasphemies.
His wit all seesaw between *that* and *this*,
Now high, now low, now master up, now miss,
325 And he himself one vile antithesis.
Amphibious thing! that acting either part,
The trifling head or the corrupted heart,
Fop at the toilet, flatterer at the board,
Now trips a lady, and now struts a lord.
330 Eve's tempter thus the rabbins[4] have expressed,
A cherub's face, a reptile all the rest;
Beauty that shocks you, parts that none will trust,
Wit that can creep, and pride that licks the dust.
    Not fortune's worshiper, nor fashion's fool,
335 Not lucre's madman, nor ambition's tool,
Not proud, nor servile, be one poet's praise,
That if he pleased, he pleased by manly ways:
That flattery, even to kings, he held a shame,
And thought a lie in verse or prose the same:
340 That not in fancy's maze he wandered long,
But stooped[5] to truth, and moralized his song:
That not for fame, but virtue's better end,
He stood the furious foe, the timid friend,
The damning critic, half approving wit,
345 The coxcomb hit, or fearing to be hit;
Laughed at the loss of friends he never had,
The dull, the proud, the wicked, and the mad;
The distant threats of vengeance on his head,
The blow unfelt, the tear he never shed;
350 The tale revived, the lie so oft o'erthrown,
The imputed trash, and dullness not his own;
The morals blackened when the writings 'scape,
The libeled person, and the pictured shape;[6]
Abuse on all he loved, or loved him, spread,
355 A friend in exile, or a father dead;
The whisper, that to greatness still too near,
Perhaps yet vibrates on his Sovereign's ear—
Welcome for thee, fair virtue! all the past:
For thee, fair virtue! welcome even the last!
360   A. But why insult the poor, affront the great?

---

3. The queen; the allusion is to *Paradise Lost* (4.799–809).
4. Scholars of and authorities on Jewish law and doctrine.

5. The falcon is said to "stoop" to its prey when it swoops down and seizes it in flight.
6. Pope's deformity was frequently ridiculed and occasionally caricatured.

P. A knave's a knave to me in every state:
Alike my scorn, if he succeed or fail,
Sporus at court, or Japhet[7] in a jail,
A hireling scribbler, or a hireling peer,
365 Knight of the post[8] corrupt, or of the shire,
If on a pillory, or near a throne,
He gain his prince's ear, or lose his own.
    Yet soft by nature, more a dupe than wit,
Sappho° can tell you how this man was bit:°   *Montagu / deceived*
370 This dreaded satirist Dennis will confess
Foe to his pride, but friend to his distress:[9]
So humble, he has knocked at Tibbald's door,
Has drunk with Cibber, nay, has rhymed for Moore.
Full ten years slandered, did he once reply?
375 Three thousand suns went down on Welsted's lie.
To please a mistress one aspersed his life;
He lashed him not, but let her be his wife.
Let Budgell charge low Grub Street on his quill,
And write whate'er he pleased, except his will;[1]
380 Let the two Curlls of town and court,[2] abuse
His father, mother, body, soul, and muse.
Yet why? that father held it for a rule,
It was a sin to call our neighbor fool;
That harmless mother thought no wife a whore:
385 Hear this, and spare his family, James Moore!
Unspotted names, and memorable long,
If there be force in virtue, or in song.
    Of gentle blood (part shed in honor's cause,
While yet in Britain honor had applause)
390 Each parent sprung——A. What fortune, pray?——P. Their own,
And better got than Bestia's[3] from the throne.
Born to no pride, inheriting no strife,
Nor marrying discord in a noble wife,
Stranger to civil and religious rage,
395 The good man walked innoxious through his age.
No courts he saw, no suits would ever try,
Nor dared an oath,[4] nor hazarded a lie.
Unlearn'd, he knew no schoolman's subtle art,
No language but the language of the heart.
400 By nature honest, by experience wise,
Healthy by temperance, and by exercise;
His life, though long, to sickness passed unknown,
His death was instant, and without a groan.
Oh, grant me thus to live, and thus to die!

---

7. Japhet Crook, a notorious forger.
8. One who lives by selling false evidence.
9. Pope wrote the prologue to Cibber's *Provoked Husband* (1728) when that play was performed for Dennis's benefit, shortly before the old critic died.
1. Eustace Budgell attacked the *Grub Street Journal* for publishing what he took to be a squib by Pope charging him with having forged the will of Dr. Matthew Tindal.
2. I.e., the publisher and Lord Hervey.

3. Probably the duke of Marlborough, whose vast fortune was made through the favor of Queen Anne. The actual Bestia was a corrupt Roman consul.
4. As a Catholic, Pope's father refused to take the Oaths of Allegiance and Supremacy and the oath against the pope. He thus rendered himself vulnerable to the many repressive anti-Catholic laws then in force.

405 Who sprung from kings shall know less joy than I.
    O friend! may each domestic bliss be thine!
Be no unpleasing melancholy mine:
Me, let the tender office long engage,
To rock the cradle of reposing age,
410 With lenient arts extend a mother's breath,
Make languor smile, and smooth the bed of death,
Explore the thought, explain the asking eye,
And keep a while one parent from the sky![5]
On cares like these if length of days attend,
415 May Heaven, to bless those days, preserve my friend,
Preserve him social, cheerful, and serene,
And just as rich as when he served a Queen![6]
    A. Whether that blessing be denied or given,
Thus far was right—the rest belongs to Heaven.

1735

The Dunciad: Book the Fourth

The fourth book of *The Dunciad*, Pope's last major work, was originally intended as a continuation of *An Essay on Man*. To Jonathan Swift, the spiritual ancestor of the poem, Pope confided in 1736 that he was at work on a series of epistles on the uses of human reason and learning, to conclude with "a satire against the misapplication of all these, exemplified by pictures, characters, and examples." But the epistles never appeared; instead, the satire grew until it took their place. As Pope surveyed England in his last years, the complex literary and social order that had sustained him seemed to be crumbling. It was a time for desperate measures, for satire. And the means of retribution was at hand, in the structure of Pope's own *Dunciad*, the long work that had already impaled so many enemies.

The first *Dunciad*, published in three books in 1728, is a mock-epic reply to Pope's critics and other petty authors. Its hero and victim, Lewis Theobald, had attacked Pope's edition of Shakespeare (1725); other victims had offended Pope either by personal abuse or simply by ineptitude. Inspired by Dryden's *Mac Flecknoe, The Dunciad* celebrates the triumph of the hordes of Grub Street. Indeed, so many obscure hacks were mentioned that a *Dunciad Variorum* (1729) was soon required, in which mock-scholarly notes identify the victims, "since it is only in this monument that they must expect to survive." But a modern reader need not catch every reference to enjoy the dazzling wit of the poem, or the sheer sense of fun with which Pope remakes the London literary world into a tiny insane fairground of his own.

The New Dunciad (1742), however, plays a far more serious game: here Pope takes aim at the rot of the whole social fabric. The satire goes deep, and works at many levels, which for convenience may be divided into four. (1) Politics: From 1721 to 1742 England had been ruled by the Whig supremacy of Robert Walpole, first minister. To Pope and his circle, the immensely powerful Walpole (no friend of poets) seemed a crass and greedy vulgarian, like his monarch George II. It is no accident, in the kingdom of *The Dunciad*, that Dulness personified sits on a throne. (2) Society: Just as the action of the *Aeneid* had been the removal of the empire of Troy to Latium, the action of *The Dunciad*, according to Pope, is "the removal of the empire of Dul-

---

5. Pope was a tender and devoted son. His mother had died in 1733, and the earliest version of these lines dates from 1731, when the poet was nursing her through a serious illness.

6. Pope alludes to the fact that Arbuthnot, a man of strict probity, left the queen's service no wealthier than when he entered it.

ness from the City of London to the polite world, Westminster"; that is, the abdication of civility in favor of commerce and financial interests. In modern England, authors write for money, and ministers govern for profit; conspicuous consumption (especially the consumption of paper by scribblers) has replaced the old values of the yeoman and the aristocrat. In 1743, Pope revised the original *Dunciad*, substituting the actor and poet laureate Colley Cibber for Theobald as the hero and incorporating *The New Dunciad* as the fourth book (the version printed here). Dulness, he implies, has achieved her final triumph; Cibber is laureate in England. (3) Education: The word *dunce* is derived from the Scholastic philosopher John Duns Scotus (ca. 1265–1308), whose name had come to stand for silly and useless subtlety, logical hairsplitting. Pope, as an heir of the Renaissance, believes that the central subject of education must always be its relevance for human behavior: "The proper study of mankind is Man," and moral philosophy, the relation of individuals to each other and to the world, should be the teacher's first and last concern. By contrast, Dunces waste their time on grammar (words alone) or the "science" of the collector (things alone); they never comprehend that word and thing, like spirit and matter, are essentially dead unless they join. (4) Religion: At its deepest level, the subject of *The Dunciad* is the undoing of God's creation. Many passages from the fourth book echo *Paradise Lost*, and one of Pope's starting places seems to be Satan's threat to return the world to its original darkness, chaos, and ancient night (*Paradise Lost* 2.968–87). *The Dunciad* ends in a great apocalypse, with a yawn that signals the death of *Logos*; as words have become meaningless, so has the whole creation, which the Lord called forth with words. Here Pope invokes, with terrifying intensity, the old idea that God was the first poet, whose poem was the world, and suggests that the sickness of the word has infected all nature. But there is one consolation: out of non-art itself, out of matter without spirit and substance without essence, the poet creates his own final artistic triumph, and makes a poem.

From The Dunciad

From *Book the Fourth*

Yet, yet a moment, one dim ray of light
Indulge, dread Chaos, and eternal Night!
Of darkness visible[1] so much be lent,
As half to show, half veil the deep intent.
5   Ye Powers![2] whose mysteries restored I sing,
To whom Time bears me on his rapid wing,
Suspend a while your force inertly strong,
Then take at once the poet and the song.
     Now flamed the Dog-star's[3] unpropitious ray,
10   Smote every brain, and withered every bay,[4]
Sick was the sun, the owl forsook his bower,
The moon-struck prophet felt the madding hour:
Then rose the seed[5] of Chaos, and of Night,
To blot out Order, and extinguish Light,
15   Of dull and venal a new world to mold,
And bring Saturnian days of lead and gold.[6]

---

1. Cf. *Paradise Lost* 1.63.
2. Chaos and Night, invoked in place of the Muse, because "the restoration of their empire is the action of the poem" [Pope's note].
3. Sirius, associated with the heat of summer and the madness of poets (see *Epistle to Dr. Arbuthnot*, line 3, p. 1169).

4. The laurel, whose garlands are bestowed on poets.
5. The Goddess Dulness.
6. Saturn ruled during the golden age; the new age of "gold" will be reestablished by the dull and venal.

She mounts the throne: her head a cloud concealed,
In broad effulgence all below revealed,
('Tis thus aspiring Dulness ever shines)
20   Soft on her lap her Laureate son[7] reclines.
    Beneath her foot-stool, Science groans in chains,
And Wit dreads exile, penalties and pains.
There foamed rebellious Logic, gagged and bound,
There, stripped, fair Rhetoric languished on the ground;
25   His blunted arms by Sophistry are born,
And shameless Billingsgate[8] her robes adorn.
Morality, by her false guardians drawn,
Chicane in furs, and Casuistry in lawn,[9]
Gasps, as they straighten at each end the cord,
30   And dies, when Dulness gives her Page[1] the word.

*   *   *

[THE EDUCATOR]

135   Now crowds on crowds around the Goddess press,
Each eager to present the first address.[2]
Dunce scorning dunce beholds the next advance,
But fop shows fop superior complaisance.
When lo! a specter[3] rose, whose index-hand
140   Held forth the virtue of the dreadful wand;
His beavered brow a birchen garland wears,[4]
Dropping with infant's blood, and mother's tears.
O'er every vein a shuddering horror runs;
Eton and Winton shake through all their sons.
145   All flesh is humbled, Westminster's bold race[5]
Shrink, and confess the Genius[6] of the place:
The pale boy-Senator yet tingling stands,
And holds his breeches close with both his hands.
    Then thus. "Since Man from beast by words is known,
150   Words are Man's province, words we teach alone.
When reason doubtful, like the Samian letter,[7]
Points him two ways, the narrower is the better.
Placed at the door of learning, youth to guide,
We never suffer it to stand too wide.
155   To ask, to guess, to know, as they commence,
As fancy opens the quick springs of sense,
We ply the memory, we load the brain,
Bind rebel wit, and double chain on chain,
Confine the thought, to exercise the breath;[8]

7. Colley Cibber, the poet laureate.
8. Fishmarket slang, which now covers the noble science of rhetoric.
9. Chicanery (legal trickery) wears the ermine robe of a judge; casuistry wears the linen sleeves of a bishop.
1. Sir Francis Page, a notorious hanging judge; or court page, used to strangle criminals in Turkey; or page of writing on which a dull author "kills" moral sentiments.
2. The goddess, newly enthroned, is receiving petitions and congratulations.
3. The ghost of Dr. Busby, stern headmaster of Westminster School.

4. He wears a hat (beaver) and a garland of birch twigs, used for flogging. "Wand": cane used for beating.
5. Alumni of Westminster School, with a play on the justices and members of Parliament who meet at Westminster Hall.
6. I.e., admit that Dr. Busby is the presiding deity (Genius).
7. The letter Y, which Pythagoras (a native of Samos) used as an emblem of the different roads of virtue and vice.
8. Students are taught only to recite the classic poets by heart.

160 And keep them in the pale of words till death.
Whate'er the talents, or howe'er designed,
We hang one jingling padlock on the mind:
A poet the first day, he dips his quill;
And what the last? a very poet still.

165 Pity! the charm works only in our wall,
Lost, lost too soon in yonder House or Hall."[9]

*   *   *

[THE TRIUMPH OF DULNESS]

Then blessing all,[1] "Go children of my care!
580 To practice now from theory repair.
All my commands are easy, short, and full:
My sons! be proud, be selfish, and be dull.
Guard my prerogative, assert my throne:
This nod confirms each privilege your own.

585 The cap and switch be sacred to his Grace;[2]
With staff and pumps[3] the Marquis lead the race;
From stage to stage the licensed[4] Earl may run,
Paired with his fellow-charioteer the sun;
The learned baron butterflies design,

590 Or draw to silk Arachne's subtle line;°   *spiderweb*
The Judge to dance his brother Sergeant[5] call;
The Senator at cricket urge the ball;
The Bishop stow (pontific luxury!)
An hundred souls of turkeys in a pie;[6]

595 The sturdy squire to Gallic masters° stoop,   *French chefs*
And drown his lands and manors in a soup.
Others import yet nobler arts from France,
Teach kings to fiddle, and make senates dance.
Perhaps more high some daring son may soar,[7]

600 Proud to my list to add one monarch more;
And nobly conscious, Princes are but things
Born for First Ministers, as slaves for kings,
Tyrant supreme! shall three estates command,
And MAKE ONE MIGHTY DUNCIAD OF THE LAND!"

605 More she had spoke, but yawned—All Nature nods:
What mortal can resist the yawn of Gods?
Churches and chapels instantly it reached;
(St. James's first, for leaden Gilbert[8] preached)
Then catched the schools; the Hall scarce kept awake;

610 The Convocation gaped,[9] but could not speak:
Lost was the Nation's Sense,° nor could be found,   *Parliament*

---

9. The House of Commons and Westminster Hall,
where law cases were heard. The eloquence
learned by rote disappears on occasions for public
speaking.
1. Having conferred her titles, Dulness bids each
of the rulers of England to indulge in the triviality
closest to his heart.
2. His Grace, a duke who loves horse racing, is to
use the cap and switch of a jockey.
3. Footmen, who wore pumps (low-cut shoes for
running), were matched in races.
4. The license required by the owner of a stage-

coach; also privileged or licentious.
5. A lawyer or legislative officer. Formal ceremonies at the Inns of Court are said to have resembled
a country dance, "a call of sergeants."
6. According to Pope, a hundred turkeys had been
"not unfrequently deposited in one Pye in the Bishopric of Durham."
7. A bold, direct attack on Walpole.
8. Dr. John Gilbert, dean of Exeter.
9. The Convocation, an assembly of clergy consulting on ecclesiastical affairs, had been
adjourned since 1717.

While the long solemn unison went round:
Wide, and more wide, it spread o'er all the realm;
Even Palinurus[1] nodded at the helm:

615 The vapor mild o'er each committee crept;
Unfinished treaties in each office slept;
And chiefless armies dozed out the campaign;
And navies yawned for orders on the main.
    O Muse! relate (for you can tell alone,

620 Wits have short memories, and dunces none)
Relate, who first, who last resigned to rest;
Whose heads she partly, whose completely blessed;
What charms could faction, what ambition lull,
The venal quiet, and entrance the dull;

625 'Till drowned was sense, and shame, and right, and wrong—
O sing, and hush the nations with thy song!
. . . .
In vain, in vain,—the all-composing Hour
Resistless falls: The Muse obeys the Power.
She comes! she comes![2] the sable throne behold

630 Of Night primeval, and of Chaos old!
Before her, Fancy's gilded clouds decay,
And all its varying rainbows die away.
Wit shoots in vain its momentary fires,
The meteor drops, and in a flash expires.

635 As one by one, at dread Medea's strain,
The sickening stars fade off the ethereal plain;[3]
As Argus' eyes by Hermes' wand oppressed,
Closed one by one to everlasting rest;[4]
Thus at her felt approach, and secret might,

640 Art after Art goes out, and all is Night.
See skulking Truth to her old cavern fled,[5]
Mountains of casuistry heaped o'er her head!
Philosophy, that leaned on Heaven before,
Shrinks to her second cause,[6] and is no more.

645 Physic[7] of Metaphysic begs defense,
And Metaphysic calls for aid on Sense!
See Mystery[8] to Mathematics fly!
In vain! they gaze, turn giddy, rave, and die.
Religion blushing veils her sacred fires,

650 And unawares Morality expires.
Nor public flame, nor private, dares to shine;
Nor human spark is left, nor glimpse divine!
Lo! thy dread Empire, CHAOS! is restored;
Light dies before thy uncreating word:[9]

1. The pilot of Aeneas's ship; here Walpole.
2. Having triumphed in the contemporary world of affairs, Dulness (like her antitype Christ) has a Second Coming, a prophetic vision in which she extinguishes the light of the arts and sciences.
3. In Seneca's *Medea*, the stars obey the curse of Medea, a magician and avenger.
4. Argus, Hera's hundred-eyed watchman, was charmed to sleep and slain by Hermes.
5. Alluding to the saying of Democritus, that Truth lay at the bottom of a deep well [Pope's note].
6. Science (philosophy) no longer accepts God as the first cause or final explanation of how all things came to be; instead, it accepts only the second or material cause and tries to account for all things by physical principles alone.
7. Natural science in general.
8. A religious truth known only through divine revelation.
9. Cf. God's first creating words in Genesis, "Let there be light."

655   Thy hand, great Anarch! lets the curtain fall;
        And Universal Darkness buries All.

                                                            1743

LADY MARY WORTLEY MONTAGU
1689–1762

In her early teens Lady Mary Pierrepont did something that well-bred young women
were not supposed to do: she secretly taught herself Latin. The act reveals many traits
that would characterize her as a mature woman: curiosity, love of learning, intelligence, ambition, and independence of mind. The eldest daughter of a wealthy Whig
peer, she grew up amid a glittering London circle that included Addison, Steele,
Congreve, and later Pope and Gay. But she was not content to live the life of a dutiful
aristocratic daughter. Unlike most women in her time, she married for love, and when
her husband, Edward Wortley Montagu, was appointed ambassador to Constantinople in 1716, she took the opportunity of traveling through Europe, studying the
language and customs of Turkey, and even visiting harems; her "Turkish Letters,"
published in 1763, would establish her as one of the great letter writers in English.
She also pioneered in introducing smallpox inoculation to England. Returning home
in 1718, she spent unhappy years that included bitter political quarrels with Pope
(who satirized her as "Sappho" in *Epistle 2. To a Lady*) and the gradual failure of her
marriage. Then she fell in love with a young Italian author, Francesco Algarotti. In
1739 she traveled to Italy hoping to see him; but the passion that had kindled in their
letters was quenched when he failed to join her. She spent the rest of her life abroad,
and died soon after returning to London in 1762. Montagu is remembered chiefly
for her letters, but was also admired in her own time as a poet. Her verse, though
often casual, reveals the strong mind of a woman who is not willing to accept the
stereotypes imposed on her by men and who insists on preserving her freedom of
choice. Her sexual candor and punishing wit demand respect; and the poems, like
Montagu herself, are never dull.

The Lover: A Ballad

        At length, by so much importunity pressed,
        Take, (Molly),[1] at once, the inside of my breast;
        This stupid indifference so often you blame
        Is not owing to nature, to fear, or to shame;
5   I am not as cold as a Virgin in lead,[2]
        Nor is Sunday's sermon so strong in my head;
        I know but too well how time flies along,
        That we live but few years and yet fewer are young.

---

1. Molly Skerrett, a friend of Lady Mary, was the
mistress of Sir Robert Walpole. The ideal "lover"
of the title, however, is not to be identified with
any particular person.

2. I.e., an image of the Virgin Mary, either as a
leaden statue or as a stained-glass window framed
in lead.

But I hate to be cheated, and never will buy
10 Long years of repentance for moments of joy.
Oh was there a man (but where shall I find
Good sense and good nature so equally joined?)
Would value his pleasure, contribute to mine,
Not meanly would boast, nor lewdly design,°   plot
15 Not over severe, yet not stupidly vain,
For I would have the power though not give the pain;

No pedant yet learnèd, not rakehelly gay
Or laughing because he has nothing to say,
To all my whole sex obliging and free,
20 Yet never be fond of any but me;
In public preserve the decorums are just,
And show in his eyes he is true to his trust,
Then rarely approach, and respectfully bow,
Yet not fulsomely pert, nor yet foppishly low.

25 But when the long hours of public are past
And we meet with champagne and a chicken at last,
May every fond pleasure that hour endear,
Be banished afar both discretion and fear,
Forgetting or scorning the airs of the crowd
30 He may cease to be formal, and I to be proud,
Till lost in the joy we confess that we live,
And he may be rude, and yet I may forgive.

And that my delight may be solidly fixed,
Let the friend and the lover be handsomely mixed,
35 In whose tender bosom my soul might confide,
Whose kindness can sooth me, whose counsel could guide.
From such a dear lover as here I describe
No danger should fright me, no millions should bribe;
But till this astonishing creature I know,
40 As I long have lived chaste, I will keep myself so.

I never will share with the wanton coquette,
Or be caught by a vain affectation of wit.
The toasters and songsters may try all their art
But never shall enter the pass of my heart.
45 I loathe the lewd rake, the dressed fopling despise;
Before such pursuers the nice° virgin flies;   fastidious
And as Ovid has sweetly in parables told
We harden like trees, and like rivers are cold.[3]

1747

3. In Ovid's *Metamorphoses*, Daphne, to escape Apollo, was turned into a laurel, and Arethusa, escaping Alpheus, became a fountain.

Epistle from Mrs. Yonge to Her Husband[1]

Think not this paper comes with vain pretense
To move your pity, or to mourn th' offense.
Too well I know that hard obdurate heart;
No softening mercy there will take my part,
5   Nor can a woman's arguments prevail,
When even your patron's wise example fails.[2]
But this last privilege I still retain;
Th' oppressed and injured always may complain.
    Too, too severely laws of honor bind
10   The weak submissive sex of womankind.
If sighs have gained or force compelled our hand,
Deceived by art, or urged by stern command,
Whatever motive binds the fatal tie,
The judging world expects our constancy.
15   Just heaven! (for sure in heaven does justice reign,
Though tricks below that sacred name profane)
To you appealing I submit my cause,
Nor fear a judgment from impartial laws.
All bargains but conditional[3] are made;
20   The purchase void, the creditor unpaid;
Defrauded servants are from service free;
A wounded slave regains his liberty.
For wives ill used no remedy remains,
To daily racks condemned, and to eternal chains.
25   From whence is this unjust distinction grown?
Are we not formed with passions like your own?
Nature with equal fire our souls endued,
Our minds as haughty, and as warm our blood;
O'er the wide world your pleasures you pursue,
30   The change is justified by something new;
But we must sigh in silence—and be true.
Our sex's weakness you expose and blame
(Of every prattling fop the common theme),
Yet from this weakness you suppose is due
35   Sublimer virtue than your Cato[4] knew.
Had heaven designed us trials so severe,

1. In 1724 the notorious libertine William Yonge, separated from his wife, Mary, discovered that she (like him) had committed adultery. He sued her lover, Colonel Norton, for damages and collected £1,500. Later that year, according to the law of the time, he petitioned the Houses of Parliament for a divorce. The case was tried in public, Mrs. Yonge's love letters were read aloud, and two men testified that they had found her and Norton "together in naked bed." Yonge was granted the divorce, his wife's dowry, and the greater part of her fortune.

    Although the *Epistle* is obviously based on this sensational affair, it is also a work of imagination. Like Pope's *Eloisa to Abelard*—to which the author himself called Montagu's attention—it takes the form of a heroic epistle, the passionate outcry of an abandoned woman. The poet, entering into the feelings of Mary Yonge, justifies her conduct with reasons both of the heart and of the head. The objects of her attack include the institution of marriage, which binds wives in "eternal chains"; the double standard of morality, which requires chastity from women but not men; the hypocrisy of society, which condemns the very behavior it secretly lusts after; and the craven greed and cruelty of the husband himself. But 18th-century women seldom dared to speak like this in public, and the *Epistle* was not published until the 1970s.
2. Sir Robert Walpole, William Yonge's friend at court, was rumored to tolerate his own wife's infidelities.
3. Only conditionally.
4. The asceticism and self-discipline of the Roman statesman Cato had been emphasized in Addison's famous tragedy *Cato* (1713).

It would have formed our tempers then to bear.
   And I have borne (oh what have I not borne!)
The pang of jealousy, the insults of scorn.
40 Wearied at length, I from your sight remove,
And place my future hopes in secret love.
In the gay bloom of glowing youth retired,
I quit the woman's joy to be admired,
With that small pension your hard heart allows,
45 Renounce your fortune, and release your vows.
To custom (though unjust) so much is due;
I hide my frailty from the public view.
My conscience clear, yet sensible of shame,
My life I hazard, to preserve my fame.
50 And I prefer this low inglorious state ⎫
To vile dependence on the thing I hate— ⎬
But you pursue me to this last retreat.   ⎭
Dragged into light, my tender crime is shown
And every circumstance of fondness known.
55 Beneath the shelter of the law you stand,
And urge my ruin with a cruel hand,
While to my fault thus rigidly severe,
Tamely submissive to the man you fear.[5]
   This wretched outcast, this abandoned wife,
60 Has yet this joy to sweeten shameful life:
By your mean conduct, infamously loose,
You are at once my accuser and excuse.
Let me be damned by the censorious prude
(Stupidly dull, or spiritually lewd),
65 My hapless case will surely pity find
From every just and reasonable mind.
When to the final sentence I submit,
The lips condemn me, but their souls acquit.
   No more my husband, to your pleasures go,
70 The sweets of your recovered freedom know.
Go: court the brittle friendship of the great,
Smile at his board,° or at his levee[6] wait;   *dining table*
And when dismissed, to madam's toilet[7] fly,
More than her chambermaids, or glasses,° lie,   *mirrors*
75 Tell her how young she looks, how heavenly fair,
Admire the lilies and the roses there.
Your high ambition may be gratified,
Some cousin of her own be made your bride,
And you the father of a glorious race
80 Endowed with Ch——l's strength and Low——r's face.[8]

1724   1972

5. I.e., Walpole. Montagu suggests that the whole political establishment of England takes sides against Mary Yonge.
6. Morning reception of visitors.
7. It was fashionable for women like Lady Walpole to receive visitors during the last stages of dressing (their "toilet").
8. General Churchill was rumored to have had an affair with Lady Walpole; Antony Lowther was a notorious gallant. The author implies that William Yonge's next wife may be as untrue as his first. Mary Yonge remarried immediately after her divorce; five years later Yonge himself (whose divorce had made him rich) married the daughter of a baron.

WILLIAM HOGARTH
1697–1764

William Hogarth was a Londoner born and bred; the life of the city, both high and low, fills all his work. His early life was hard. When his father, a writer and teacher, failed in business, the family was confined to the area of the Fleet, the debtor's prison. Hogarth never forgot "the cruel treatment" of his father by booksellers, and he resolved to make his living without relying on dealers; he would always be aggressively independent. Apprenticed as an engraver, he trained himself to sketch scenes quickly or catch them in memory. He also learned to paint, studying with the Serjeant Painter to the King, Sir James Thornhill, whose daughter he married (late in life Hogarth himself would become Serjeant Painter). Gradually he won a reputation for portraits and conversation pieces—group portraits in which members of a family or assembly interact in a social situation. But his popular fame was forged by sets of pictures that told a story: *A Harlot's Progress* (1731–32), *A Rake's Progress* (1734–35), and *Marriage A-la-Mode* (1743–45). First Hogarth painted these Modern Moral Subjects (as he called them), then prints were made and sold in large editions. He also found new ways to market and protect his work; a copyright bill to ban cheap imitations of prints was known as "Hogarth's Act." Despite this success, however, his ambition to redefine British standards of art led to frustration. The high regard and high prices for continental old masters were too well entrenched to be undermined. Hogarth did not get prestigious commissions, and his *Analysis of Beauty* (1753), an effort to fix "the fluctuating ideas of taste" by appealing to practical observations, not academic rules, was poorly received. Political and aesthetic controversies embittered his final years.

Writers have always loved Hogarth's satiric art, and many have claimed him as one of their own. Swift, Fielding, and Sterne associated their work with his; Horace Walpole considered him more "a writer of comedy with a pencil" than a painter; Charles Lamb compared him to Shakespeare; and William Hazlitt included him among the great English comic writers. This emphasis may slight Hogarth's importance in the history of art. His attempts to found a British school that looked at life and nature directly, not through a haze of ideas or reverence for the past, and to give pleasure to common people, not only to critics and connoisseurs, opened the eyes of many artists to come. But Hogarth is also a great storyteller, someone to *read*. Like novels and plays, his pictures have plots and morals; they ask us not only to look but also to think. Yet looking and thinking are always intertwined. The mind delights in riddles, according to Hogarth; and as he revised his work he stuffed in more and more clues, like a mystery writer. A feast of interpretation draws the reader in. So many expressive details crowd the pictures, so many keys to character and meaning, that viewers often become obsessed with figuring them out. Even inanimate objects can speak; playwrights rely on words, as Walpole pointed out, but "it was reserved to Hogarth to write a scene of furniture."

The furniture is particularly eloquent in *Marriage A-la-Mode*; note, for example, the fallen chairs in Plates 2 and 6. Hogarth took special pains with this series. The audience at which he aimed, as well as the subject matter, belonged to high society; and the art too is highly refined. A sinuous line weaves through each picture, leading the reader on, and each piece of bric-a-brac carries a message of lavish excess. Yet the story itself is brutally straightforward. A disastrous forced marriage stands at the center: a rich but miserly merchant buys the worthless son of an aristocrat for his restless daughter, and with nothing in common the couple destroy one another. The crisis of values that Hogarth depicts was bringing about radical changes in English life. In the tension between a fading aristocracy, both morally and financially bankrupt, and an upwardly mobile middle class, greedy for power but culturally insecure, the marriage reflects a society that has lost all sense of right and wrong. The artist plays no favorites. The aristocratic Squanderfields are not only vain, effete, and dissipated but also lacking in taste; the wan mythological paintings on their walls are just the sort of pretentious, overpriced art that Hogarth hates. But the vulgar Dutch art on the merchant's walls (in Plate 6) seems even worse, and his daughter falls for every extravagant, spurious fashion (in Plate 4). Nor do the parasites who live off these easy marks offer any hope. Lawyer and doctor, bawd and servant pave the road to ruin. Hogarth's satire warns against the spreading corruption of modern times, when self-interest eats into marriage and old values die. Look hard, he tells the public. These objects make up the world we live in. We might become these people.

Marriage A-la-Mode

Plate 1. *The Marriage Contract.* Lord Squanderfield points to the family tree, going back to William the Conquerer, that his son will bring to the marriage. Coronets are blazed all over the room, from the top of the canopy at the upper left to the side of the prostrate dog on the lower right. The earl, though hobbled by gout, is proud. But he has run out of money: construction has stopped on the Palladian mansion seen through the window. Sitting across from him, a squinting merchant grasps the marriage settlement. Some of the coins and banknotes he has placed on the table have been taken up by a scrawny usurer, who hands the earl a mortgage in return. At the right the betrothed sit back to back, uncaring as the dogs chained to each other below. The vacuous viscount pinches snuff and gazes at himself in a mirror, which ominously reflects the image of lawyer Silvertongue, who sharpens his pen as he bends unctuously over the bride-to-be. Pouting, she twirls her wedding ring in a handkerchief. Disasters from mythology cover the walls. A bombastic portrait of the earl as Jupiter, astride a cannon, dominates the room; and in a candle sconce on the right Medusa glowers over the scene.

Plate 2. *After the Marriage.* By now the couple are used to ignoring each other. The morning after a spree, the rumpled, exhausted viscount slouches in a chair. His broken sword has dropped on the carpet, and a lapdog sniffs at a woman's cap in his pocket—souvenirs of the night. Lolling and stretching in an unladylike pose, his wife too is half asleep. She has spent the night home but not alone. *Hoyle on Whist* lies before her, cards are scattered on the floor, and the overturned chair, book of music, and violin cases suggest that some player may have departed in haste. A steward carries away a sheaf of bills—only one paid—and the household ledger; a Methodist (*Regeneration* is in his pocket), he petitions heaven to look down on these heathens. Oriental idols decorate the mantel over the fireplace, surmounted by a broken-nosed Roman bust that frowns like the steward and a painting of Cupid playing the bagpipes. On the left, amid the shrubbery of a rococo clock, a cat leers over fish and a Buddha smiles. In the next room, a dozing servant fails to notice that a candle has set fire to a chair. Next to a row of saints, a curtain does not quite cover a bawdy painting from which a naked foot peeps.

Plate 3. *The Scene with the Quack.* The husband has come to this chamber of medical horrors in search of a cure. The pillbox he holds toward the quack has not done its job, and he raises his cane as if with a playful threat. Evidently the little girl who stands between his legs is infected. She dabs a sore on her lip, and her ageless face may hint that she is not as young and pure as she looks. Her cap resembles the cap in Plate 2; she is the husband's mistress. Perhaps the beauty spot on his neck also covers a sore. The bowlegged Monsieur de la Pillule comfortably wipes his glasses; he has seen all this before. Between the two men an angry woman, fortified by a massive hoop skirt, opens a knife. She may be the wife of the quack, defending her man, or else a bawd who resents the charge that her girls are damaged goods. Medical oddities and monstrosities clutter the room, along with portents of death. The viscount's cane points to a cabinet where a wigged head looks at a skeleton that seems to be groping a cadaver; the tripod above evokes a gallows tree. At the far left, in front of a laboratory door, are two of the doctor's inventions: machines for setting bones and uncorking bottles. Their similarity to instruments of torture hints at how useful the doctor's assistance will be.

Plate 4. *The Countess's Levee.* In her bedchamber at rising (*levée;* French), the countess receives some guests and puts on a show. Her husband is now earl (note the coronets), and they have a child (note the rattle on her chair). While a hairdresser curls her locks, she hangs on the words of Silvertongue, who makes himself at home (note his portrait on the upper right wall). Tonight they will be going to a masquerade ball, like the one on the screen he gestures toward; his left hand holds the tickets. At the far right a puffy, bedizened castrato sings, accompanied by a flute. His audience includes a self-absorbed dandy in curl-papers; a man who appreciatively smirks and opens his hand, from which a fan dangles; a snoring husband, holding his riding-crop like a baton; and his enraptured wife, who leans forward as if about to swoon. Unobserved by the others, a black servant, bearing a cup of chocolate, smiles in amazement at these precious airs. At the lower left another black servant, a boy in a turban, grins at gewgaws purchased at an auction. His finger points both to Actaeon's horns, the sign of a cuckold, and to the couple as they arrange their tryst. Wall paintings illustrate unnatural sex: Lot's seduction by his daughters, Jupiter embracing Io, and the rape of Ganymede.

Plate 5. *The Death of the Earl.* The melodramatic tableau at the center, as the earl totters toward death and the countess kneels to beg forgiveness, imitates paintings of Christ descending from the cross while Mary Magdalen mourns. But the surroundings are sordid. At a house of ill repute, the Turk's Head Bagnio, the countess and Silvertongue have been surprised in bed. The earl has broken in (key and socket on the floor) and drawn his sword, and the lawyer has run him through. As the horrified owner and constable enter, under a watchman's lantern, the killer, still in his nightshirt, flees through a window. A fire, outside the picture on the lower right, casts lurid light on the victim; the shadow of the tongs encircles the murder weapon. Costumed as a nun and friar, the lovers have come from a masquerade, and their discarded masks and clothes show they were in haste. Pills (presumably mercury, prescribed for venereal disease) have spilled from an overturned table on the right, beside an advertisement for the bagnio, a corset, and a bundle of firewood. The portrait of a streetwalker, a squirrel perched on her hand, leers over the countess; on the wall behind the earl an uplifted blade is about to sever a child, in the Judgment of Solomon. At the top left St. Luke, the patron of artists, inscribes these transgressions.

Plate 6. *The Death of the Countess.* "Counseller Silvertongues Last Dying Speech," a paper on the floor announces, and a bottle of laudanum has dropped beside it. News of her lover's execution has driven the countess to poison herself. Slumped in a chair, she is already dead; on the far right a doctor steals away. Her father calmly slides the ring from her finger. This is his house; a window with cobwebs and broken panes opens on London Bridge, in the heart of the City. No luxury here. The furnishings are sparse, the floor is bare, and the dining table holds only one egg and a few leftovers, including a pathetic boar's head from which a starving hound is tearing scraps. The art is equally cheap: a pissing boy, a jumbled still life, a pipe set alight by the glowing nose of a drunk. At the center, beneath a coatrack, a stout apothecary (stomach pump and julep in his pocket) points toward the empty bottle in reproof and pokes the servant who brought it—an idiot wearing a coat many sizes too large, the merchant's hand-me-down. The service staff is completed by a withered old woman who holds out the countess's little child for one last hug and kiss. But the mark on the child's cheek and the brace on its leg imply that disease has passed to the next generation. This noble family will have no heir.

SAMUEL JOHNSON
1709–1784

Samuel Johnson was famous as a talker in his own time, and his conversation (preserved by James Boswell and others) has been famous ever since. But his wisdom survives above all in his writings: a few superb poems; the grave *Rambler* essays, which established his reputation as a stylist and a moralist; the lessons about life in *Rasselas* and the *Lives of the Poets*; and literary criticism that ranks among the best in English. The virtues of the talk and the writings are the same. They come hot from a mind well stored with knowledge, searingly honest, humane, and quick to seize the unexpected but appropriate image of truth. Johnson's wit is timeless, for it deals with the great facts of human experience, with hope and happiness and loss and duty and the fear of death. Whatever topic he addresses, whatever the form in which he writes, he holds to one commanding purpose: to see life as it is.

Two examples must suffice here. When Anna Williams wondered why a man should make a beast of himself through drunkenness, Johnson answered that "he who makes a beast of himself gets rid of the pain of being a man." In this reply Williams's tired metaphor is so charged with an awareness of the dark aspects of human life that it comes almost unbearably alive. Such moments characterize Johnson's writings as well. For instance, in reviewing the book of a fatuous would-be philosopher who blandly explained away the pains of poverty by declaring that a kindly providence compensates the poor by making them more hopeful, more healthy, more easily pleased, and less sensitive than the rich, Johnson retorted: "The poor indeed are insensible of many little vexations which sometimes embitter the possessions and pollute the enjoyments of the rich. They are not pained by casual incivility, or mortified by the mutilation of a compliment; but this happiness is like that of a malefactor who ceases to feel the cords that bind him when the pincers are tearing his flesh."

Johnson had himself known the pains of poverty. During his boyhood and youth, his father's financial circumstances steadily worsened, so that he was forced to leave Oxford before he had taken a degree. An early marriage to a well-to-do widow, Elizabeth ("Tetty") Porter, more than twenty years older than he, enabled him to open a school. But the school failed, and he moved to London to make his way as a writer. The years between 1737, when he first arrived there with his pupil David Garrick (later to become the leading actor of his generation), and 1755, when the publication of the *Dictionary* established his reputation, were often difficult. He supported himself at first as best he could by doing hack work for the *Gentleman's Magazine,* but gradually his own original writings began to attract attention.

In 1747 Johnson published the *Plan* of his *Dictionary,* and he spent the the next seven years compiling it—although he had expected to finish it in three. When in 1748 Dr. Adams, a friend from Oxford days, questioned his ability to carry out such a work alone so fast and reminded him that the *Dictionary* of the French Academy had needed forty academicians working for forty years, Johnson replied with humorous jingoism: "Sir, thus it is. This is the proportion. Let me see; forty times forty is sixteen hundred. As three to sixteen hundred, so is the proportion of an Englishman to a Frenchman."

Johnson's achievement in compiling the *Dictionary* seems even greater when we realize that he was writing some of his best essays and poems during the same period. Although the booksellers who published the *Dictionary* paid him what was then the large sum of £1,575, it was not enough to enable him to support his household, buy materials, and pay the wages of the six assistants whom he employed year by year until the task was accomplished. He therefore had to earn more money by writing. In 1749, his early tragedy *Irene* (pronounced *I-re-nĕ*) was produced at long last by his old friend Garrick, by then the manager of Drury Lane. The play was not a success, although Johnson made some profit from it. In the same year appeared his finest poem, *The Vanity of Human Wishes*. With the *Rambler* (1750–52) and the *Idler* (1758–60), two series of periodical essays, Johnson found a devoted audience, but his pleasure was tempered by the death of his wife in 1752. He never remarried.

Boswell said of the *Rambler* essays that "in no writings whatever can be found more bark and steel [i.e., quinine and iron] for the mind." Moral strength and health; the importance of applying reason to experience; the test of virtue by what we do, not what we say or "feel"; faith in God: these are the centers to which Johnson's moral writings always return. What Johnson uniquely offers us is the quality of his understanding of the human condition, based on wide reading but always ultimately referred to his own passionate and often anguished experience. Such understanding had to be fought for again and again.

Johnson is thought of as the great generalizer, but what gives his generalizations strength is that they are rooted in the particulars of his self-knowledge. He had constantly to fight against what he called "filling the mind" with illusions to avoid the call of duty, his own black melancholy, and the realities of life. His theme of themes is expressed in the title *The Vanity of Human Wishes*: the dangerous but all-pervasive power of wishful thinking, the feverish intrusion of desires and hopes that distort reality and lead to false expectations. Almost all of Johnson's major writings—verse satire, moral essay, or the prose fable *Rasselas* (1759)—express this theme. In *Rasselas* it is called "the hunger of imagination, which preys upon life," picturing things as one would like them to be, not as they are. The travelers who are the fable's protagonists pursue some formula for happiness; they reflect our naive hope, against the lessons of experience, that one choice of life will make us happy forever.

During this time of great activity, Johnson developed his characteristic style: the rotund periods, proceeding through balanced or parallel words; phrases or clauses moving to carefully controlled rhythms, in language that is characteristically general, often Latinate, and frequently polysyllabic. It is a style at the opposite extreme from Jonathan Swift's simplicity or Joseph Addison's neatness. In Johnson's writings this style never becomes obscure or turgid, for even a very complex sentence reveals—as it should—the structure of the thought, and the learned words are always precisely used. While reading early scientists to collect words for the *Dictionary*, he developed a new vocabulary: for example, *obtund, exuberate, fugacity,* and *frigorific*. But he used many of these strange words in conversation as well as in his writings, often with a peculiarly Johnsonian felicity, describing the operations of the mind with a scientific precision.

After Johnson received his pension in 1762, he no longer had to write for a living, and because he held that "no man but a blockhead" ever wrote for any other reason, he produced as little as he decently could during the last twenty years of his life. His edition of Shakespeare, long delayed, was published in 1765, with a fine preface and fascinating notes. His last important work is the *Lives of the Poets*, which came out in two parts in 1779 and 1781. These biographical and critical prefaces were commissioned by a group of booksellers who had joined together to publish a large collection of the English poets and who wished to give their venture the prestige that Johnson would lend it. The poets to be included (except for four insisted on by Johnson) were selected by the booksellers according to current fashions. Therefore the collection begins with Abraham Cowley and John Milton and ends with Thomas Gray, and it omits such standard poets as Geoffrey Chaucer, Edmund Spenser, Sir Philip Sidney, John Donne, and Andrew Marvell.

In the *Lives of the Poets* and in the earlier *Life of Richard Savage* (1744), Johnson did much to advance the art of biography in England. Biography had long been associated with panegyrics or scandalous memoirs; and therefore Johnson's insistence on truth, even about the subject's defects, and on concrete, often minute, details was a new departure, disliked by many readers. "The biographical part of literature is what I love most," Johnson said, for he found every biography useful in revealing the human nature that all of us share. His insistence on truth in biography (and knowing that Boswell intended to write his life, he insisted that he should write it truthfully) was owing to his conviction that only a truthful work can be trusted to help us with the business of living.

The ideal poet, according to Johnson, has a genius for making the things we see every day seem new. The same might be said of Johnson himself as a critic. He is our great champion, in criticism, of common sense and the common reader. Without denying the right of the poet to flights of imagination, he also insists that poems must make sense, please readers, and help us not only understand the world but cope with it. Johnson holds poems to the truth, as he sees it: the principles of nature, logic, religion, and morality. Not even Shakespeare can be excused when "he sacrifices virtue to convenience" and "seems to write without any moral purpose." Yet Johnson is no worshiper of authority or mere "correctness." As a critic he is always the empiricist, testing theory by practice. His determination to judge literature by its truth to life, not by abstract rules, is perfectly illustrated by his treatment of the doctrine of the three unities in the *Preface* to Shakespeare. Johnson is never afraid to state the obvious, whether the lack of human interest in *Paradise Lost* or Shakespeare's temptation by puns. But at its best, as in the praise of Milton or Shakespeare, his criticism engages some of the deepest questions about literature: why it endures, and how it helps us endure.

The Vanity of Human Wishes

This poem is an imitation of Juvenal's *Satire 10*. Although it closely follows the order and the ideas of the Latin poem, it remains a very personal work, for Johnson has used the Roman Stoic's satire as a means of expressing his own sense of the tragic and comic in human life. He has tried to reproduce in English verse the qualities he thought especially Juvenalian: stateliness, pointed sentences, and declamatory grandeur. The poem is difficult because of the extreme compactness of the style: every line is forced to convey the greatest possible amount of meaning. Johnson's poetic theory demanded that the poet should deal in the general rather than mere particulars, but he certainly did not intend that the general should fade into the abstract: observe, for example, how he makes abstract nouns concrete, active, and dramatic by using them as subjects of active and dramatic verbs: "Hate *dogs* their flight, and Insult *mocks* their end" (line 78). But the difficulty of the poem is also related to its theme, the difficulty of seeing anything clearly on this earth. In a world of blindness and illusion, human beings must struggle to find a point of view that will not deceive them, and a happiness that can last.

The Vanity of Human Wishes

In Imitation of the Tenth Satire of Juvenal

    Let Observation, with extensive view,
    Survey mankind, from China to Peru;
    Remark each anxious toil, each eager strife,
    And watch the busy scenes of crowded life;
5   Then say how hope and fear, desire and hate
    O'erspread with snares the clouded maze of fate,
    Where wavering man, betrayed by venturous pride
    To tread the dreary paths without a guide,
    As treacherous phantoms in the mist delude,

10 Shuns fancied ills, or chases airy good;
    How rarely Reason guides the stubborn choice,
    Rules the bold hand, or prompts the suppliant voice;
    How nations sink, by darling schemes oppressed,
    When Vengeance listens to the fool's request.
15 Fate wings with every wish the afflictive dart,
    Each gift of nature, and each grace of art;
    With fatal heat impetuous courage glows,
    With fatal sweetness elocution flows,
    Impeachment stops the speaker's powerful breath,
20 And restless fire precipitates on death.
        But scarce observed, the knowing and the bold
    Fall in the general massacre of gold;
    Wide-wasting pest! that rages unconfined,
    And crowds with crimes the records of mankind;
25 For gold his sword the hireling ruffian draws,
    For gold the hireling judge distorts the laws;
    Wealth heaped on wealth, nor truth nor safety buys,
    The dangers gather as the treasures rise.
        Let History tell where rival kings command,
30 And dubious title shakes the madded land,
    When statutes glean the refuse of the sword,
    How much more safe the vassal than the lord;
    Low skulks the hind° beneath the rage of power,   peasant
    And leaves the wealthy traitor[1] in the Tower,
35 Untouched his cottage, and his slumbers sound,
    Though Confiscation's vultures hover round.
        The needy traveler, serene and gay,
    Walks the wild heath, and sings his toil away.
    Does envy seize thee? crush the upbraiding joy,
40 Increase his riches and his peace destroy;
    New fears in dire vicissitude invade,
    The rustling brake° alarms, and quivering shade,   thicket
    Nor light nor darkness bring his pain relief,
    One shows the plunder, and one hides the thief.
45   Yet still one general cry the skies assails,
    And gain and grandeur load the tainted gales;
    Few know the toiling statesman's fear or care,
    The insidious rival and the gaping heir.
        Once more, Democritus,[2] arise on earth,
50 With cheerful wisdom and instructive mirth,
    See motley life in modern trappings dressed,
    And feed with varied fools the eternal jest:
    Thou who couldst laugh where Want enchained Caprice,
    Toil crushed Conceit, and man was of a piece;
55 Where Wealth unloved without a mourner died;
    And scarce a sycophant was fed by Pride;
    Where ne'er was known the form of mock debate,
    Or seen a new-made mayor's unwieldy state;

1. Johnson first wrote "bonny traitor," recalling
the Jacobite uprising of 1745 and the execution of
four of its Scot leaders.

2. A Greek philosopher of the late 5th century
B.C.E., remembered as the "laughing philosopher"
because men's follies only moved him to mirth.

Where change of favorites made no change of laws,
60   And senates heard before they judged a cause;
How wouldst thou shake at Britain's modish tribe,
Dart the quick taunt, and edge the piercing gibe?
Attentive truth and nature to descry,
And pierce each scene with philosophic eye.
65   To thee were solemn toys or empty show
The robes of pleasure and the veils of woe:
All aid the farce, and all thy mirth maintain,
Whose joys are causeless, or whose griefs are vain.
      Such was the scorn that filled the sage's mind,
70   Renewed at every glance on human kind;
How just that scorn ere yet thy voice declare,
Search every state, and canvass every prayer.
      Unnumbered suppliants crowd Preferment's gate,
Athirst for wealth, and burning to be great;
75   Delusive Fortune hears the incessant call,
They mount, they shine, evaporate, and fall.
On every stage the foes of peace attend,
Hate dogs their flight, and Insult mocks their end.
Love ends with hope, the sinking statesman's door
80   Pours in the morning worshiper no more;[3]
For growing names the weekly scribbler lies,
To growing wealth the dedicator flies;
From every room descends the painted face,
That hung the bright palladium[4] of the place;
85   And smoked in kitchens, or in auctions sold,
To better features yields the frame of gold;
For now no more we trace in every line
Heroic worth, benevolence divine:
The form distorted justifies the fall,
90   And Detestation rids the indignant wall.
      But will not Britain hear the last appeal,
Sign her foes' doom, or guard her favorites' zeal?
Through Freedom's sons no more remonstrance rings,
Degrading nobles and controlling kings;
95   Our supple tribes repress their patriot throats,
And ask no questions but the price of votes;
With weekly libels and septennial ale,[5]
Their wish is full to riot and to rail.
      In full-blown dignity, see Wolsey[6] stand,
100 Law in his voice, and fortune in his hand:
To him the church, the realm, their powers consign,
Through him the rays of regal bounty shine;
Turned by his nod the stream of honor flows,

---

3. Statesmen gave interviews and received friends and petitioners at levees, or morning receptions.
4. An image of Pallas Athena, which fell from heaven and was preserved at Troy. Not until it was stolen by Diomedes could the city fall to the Greeks.
5. Ministers and even the king freely bought support by bribing Members of Parliament, who in turn won elections by buying votes. "Weekly libels": politically motivated lampoons published in the weekly newspapers. "Septennial ale": the ale given away by candidates at parliamentary elections, held at least every seven years.
6. Thomas Cardinal Wolsey (ca. 1475–1530), lord chancellor and favorite of Henry VIII. Shakespeare dramatized his fall in *Henry VIII*.

His smile alone security bestows:
105 Still to new heights his restless wishes tower,
Claim leads to claim, and power advances power;
Till conquest unresisted ceased to please,
And rights submitted, left him none to seize.
At length his sovereign frowns—the train of state
110 Mark the keen glance, and watch the sign to hate.
Where'er he turns, he meets a stranger's eye,
His suppliants scorn him, and his followers fly;
At once is lost the pride of awful state,
The golden canopy, the glittering plate,
115 The regal palace, the luxurious board,
The liveried army, and the menial lord.
With age, with cares, with maladies oppressed,
He seeks the refuge of monastic rest.
Grief aids disease, remembered folly stings,
120 And his last sighs reproach the faith of kings.
    Speak thou, whose thoughts at humble peace repine,
Shall Wolsey's wealth, with Wolsey's end be thine?
Or liv'st thou now, with safer pride content,
The wisest justice on the banks of Trent?
125 For why did Wolsey, near the steeps of fate,
On weak foundations raise the enormous weight?
Why but to sink beneath misfortune's blow,
With louder ruin to the gulfs below?
    What gave great Villiers[7] to the assassin's knife,
130 And fixed disease on Harley's closing life?
What murdered Wentworth, and what exiled Hyde,
By kings protected, and to kings allied?
What but their wish indulged in courts to shine,
And power too great to keep or to resign?
135   When first the college rolls receive his name,
The young enthusiast quits his ease for fame;
Through all his veins the fever of renown
Burns from the strong contagion of the gown:
O'er Bodley's dome his future labors spread,
140 And Bacon's[8] mansion trembles o'er his head.
Are these thy views? proceed, illustrious youth,
And Virtue guard thee to the throne of Truth!
Yet should thy soul indulge the generous heat,
Till captive Science yields her last retreat;
145 Should Reason guide thee with her brightest ray,
And pour on misty Doubt resistless day;
Should no false kindness lure to loose delight,
Nor praise relax, nor difficulty fright;

7. George Villiers, first duke of Buckingham, favorite of James I and Charles I, was assassinated in 1628. Mentioned in the following lines: Robert Harley, earl of Oxford, chancellor of the exchequer and later lord treasurer under Queen Anne (1710–14), impeached and imprisoned by the Whigs in 1715. Thomas Wentworth, earl of Strafford, intimate and adviser of Charles I, impeached by the Long Parliament and executed in 1641. Edward Hyde, earl of Clarendon ("to kings allied" because his daughter married James, duke of York), lord chancellor under Charles II (impeached in 1667, he fled to the Continent).
8. Roger Bacon (ca. 1214–1294), scientist and philosopher, taught at Oxford, where his study, according to tradition, would collapse when a man greater than he should appear at Oxford. "Bodley's dome": the Bodleian Library, Oxford.

Should tempting Novelty thy cell refrain,
150 And Sloth effuse her opiate fumes in vain;
Should Beauty blunt on fops her fatal dart,
Nor claim the triumph of a lettered heart;
Should no disease thy torpid veins invade,
Nor Melancholy's phantoms haunt thy shade;
155 Yet hope not life from grief or danger free,
Nor think the doom of man reversed for thee:
Deign on the passing world to turn thine eyes,
And pause a while from letters, to be wise;
There mark what ills the scholar's life assail,
160 Toil, envy, want, the patron,[9] and the jail.
See nations slowly wise, and meanly just,
To buried merit raise the tardy bust.
If dreams yet flatter, once again attend,
Hear Lydiat's life, and Galileo's[1] end.
165   Nor deem, when Learning her last prize bestows,
The glittering eminence exempt from foes;
See when the vulgar 'scapes, despised or awed,
Rebellion's vengeful talons seize on Laud.[2]
From meaner minds, though smaller fines content,
170 The plundered palace or sequestered rent;[3]
Marked out by dangerous parts he meets the shock,
And fatal Learning leads him to the block:
Around his tomb let Art and Genius weep,
But hear his death, ye blockheads, hear and sleep.
175   The festal blazes, the triumphal show,
The ravished standard, and the captive foe,
The senate's thanks, the gazette's pompous tale,
With force resistless o'er the brave prevail.
Such bribes the rapid Greek° o'er Asia whirled,   *Alexander the Great*
180 For such the steady Romans shook the world;
For such in distant lands the Britons shine,
And stain with blood the Danube or the Rhine;
This power has praise that virtue scarce can warm,
Till fame supplies the universal charm.
185 Yet Reason frowns on War's unequal game,
Where wasted nations raise a single name,
And mortgaged states their grandsires' wreaths regret
From age to age in everlasting debt;
Wreaths which at last the dear-bought right convey
190 To rust on medals, or on stones decay.
    On what foundation stands the warrior's pride?
How just his hopes, let Swedish Charles[4] decide;

9. In the first edition, "garret." For the reason of the change see Boswell's *Life of Johnson* (p. 1278).
1. Galileo (1564–1642), famous astronomer, was imprisoned as a heretic by the Inquisition in 1633; he died blind. Thomas Lydiat (1572–1646), Oxford scholar, died impoverished because of his Royalist sympathies.
2. Appointed archbishop of Canterbury by Charles I, William Laud followed rigorously High Church policies and was executed by order of the Long Parliament in 1645.
3. During the Commonwealth, the estates of many Royalists were pillaged and their incomes confiscated ("sequestered") by the state.
4. Charles XII of Sweden (1682–1718). Defeated by the Russians at Pultowa (1709), he escaped to

A frame of adamant, a soul of fire,
No dangers fright him, and no labors tire;
195 O'er love, o'er fear, extends his wide domain,
Unconquered lord of pleasure and of pain;
No joys to him pacific scepters yield,
War sounds the trump, he rushes to the field;
Behold surrounding kings their powers combine,
200 And one capitulate, and one resign;[5]
Peace courts his hand, but spreads her charms in vain;
"Think nothing gained," he cries, "till naught remain,
On Moscow's walls till Gothic standards fly,
And all be mine beneath the polar sky."
205 The march begins in military state,
And nations on his eye suspended wait;
Stern Famine guards the solitary coast,
And Winter barricades the realms of Frost;
He comes, nor want nor cold his course delay—
210 Hide, blushing Glory, hide Pultowa's day:
The vanquished hero leaves his broken bands,
And shows his miseries in distant lands;
Condemned a needy supplicant to wait,
While ladies interpose, and slaves debate.
215 But did not Chance at length her error mend?
Did no subverted empire mark his end?
Did rival monarchs give the fatal wound?
Or hostile millions press him to the ground?
His fall was destined to a barren strand,
220 A petty fortress, and a dubious hand;
He left the name at which the world grew pale,
To point a moral, or adorn a tale.
    All times their scenes of pompous woes afford,
From Persia's tyrant to Bavaria's lord.[6]
225 In gay hostility, and barbarous pride,
With half mankind embattled at his side,
Great Xerxes comes to seize the certain prey,
And starves exhausted regions in his way;
Attendant Flattery counts his myriads o'er,
230 Till counted myriads soothe his pride no more;
Fresh praise is tried till madness fires his mind,
The waves he lashes, and enchains the wind;
New powers are claimed, new powers are still bestowed,
Till rude resistance lops the spreading god;
235 The daring Greeks deride the martial show,
And heap their valleys with the gaudy foe;
The insulted sea with humbler thoughts he gains,

Turkey and tried to form an alliance against Russia with the sultan. Returning to Sweden, he attacked Norway and was killed in the attack on Fredrikshald.
5. Frederick IV of Denmark capitulated to Charles in 1700. Augustus II of Poland resigned his throne to Charles in 1704.

6. The Elector Charles Albert caused the War of the Austrian Succession (1740–48) when he contested the crown of the empire with Maria Theresa ("Fair Austria" in line 245). "Persia's tyrant": Xerxes invaded Greece and was totally defeated in the sea battle off Salamis, 480 B.C.E.

A single skiff to speed his flight remains;
The encumbered oar scarce leaves the dreaded coast
240 Through purple billows and a floating host.
     The bold Bavarian, in a luckless hour,
Tries the dread summits of Caesarean power,
With unexpected legions bursts away,
And sees defenseless realms receive his sway;
245 Short sway! fair Austria spreads her mournful charms,
The queen, the beauty, sets the world in arms;
From hill to hill the beacon's rousing blaze
Spreads wide the hope of plunder and of praise;
The fierce Croatian, and the wild Hussar,[7]
250 With all the sons of ravage crowd the war;
The baffled prince in honor's flattering bloom
Of hasty greatness finds the fatal doom;
His foes' derision, and his subjects' blame,
And steals to death from anguish and from shame.
255   Enlarge my life with multitude of days!
In health, in sickness, thus the suppliant prays;
Hides from himself his state, and shuns to know,
That life protracted is protracted woe.
Time hovers o'er, impatient to destroy,
260 And shuts up all the passages of joy;
In vain their gifts the bounteous seasons pour,
The fruit autumnal, and the vernal flower;
With listless eyes the dotard views the store,
He views, and wonders that they please no more;
265 Now pall the tasteless meats, and joyless wines,
And Luxury with sighs her slave resigns.
Approach, ye minstrels, try the soothing strain,
Diffuse the tuneful lenitives[8] of pain:
No sounds, alas! would touch the impervious ear,
270 Though dancing mountains witnessed Orpheus[9] near;
Nor lute nor lyre his feeble powers attend,
Nor sweeter music of a virtuous friend,
But everlasting dictates crowd his tongue,
Perversely grave, or positively wrong.
275 The still returning tale, and lingering jest,
Perplex the fawning niece and pampered guest,
While growing hopes scarce awe the gathering sneer,
And scarce a legacy can bribe to hear;
The watchful guests still hint the last offense,
280 The daughter's petulance, the son's expense,
Improve his heady rage with treacherous skill,
And mold his passions till they make his will.
     Unnumbered maladies his joints invade,
Lay siege to life and press the dire blockade;
285 But unextinguished avarice still remains,
And dreaded losses aggravate his pains;

7. Hungarian light cavalry.
8. Medicines that relieve pain.

9. A legendary poet who played on the lyre so
beautifully that wild beasts were spellbound.

He turns, with anxious heart and crippled hands,
His bonds of debt, and mortgages of lands;
Or views his coffers with suspicious eyes,
290   Unlocks his gold, and counts it till he dies.
      But grant, the virtues of a temperate prime
Bless with an age exempt from scorn or crime;
An age that melts with unperceived decay,
And glides in modest innocence away;
295   Whose peaceful day Benevolence endears,
Whose night congratulating Conscience cheers;
The general favorite as the general friend:
Such age there is, and who shall wish its end?
      Yet even on this her load Misfortune flings,
300   To press the weary minutes' flagging wings;
New sorrow rises as the day returns,
A sister sickens, or a daughter mourns.
Now kindred Merit fills the sable bier,
Now lacerated Friendship claims a tear;
305   Year chases year, decay pursues decay,
Still drops some joy from withering life away;
New forms arise, and different views engage,
Superfluous lags the veteran[1] on the stage,
Till pitying Nature signs the last release,
310   And bids afflicted Worth retire to peace.
      But few there are whom hours like these await,
Who set unclouded in the gulfs of Fate.
From Lydia's monarch[2] should the search descend,
By Solon cautioned to regard his end,
315   In life's last scene what prodigies surprise,
Fears of the brave, and follies of the wise!
From Marlborough's eyes the streams of dotage flow,
And Swift[3] expires a driveler and a show.
      The teeming mother, anxious for her race,
320   Begs for each birth the fortune of a face:
Yet Vane could tell what ills from beauty spring;
And Sedley[4] cursed the form that pleased a king.
Ye nymphs of rosy lips and radiant eyes,
Whom Pleasure keeps too busy to be wise,
325   Whom Joys with soft varieties invite,
By day the frolic, and the dance by night;
Who frown with vanity, who smile with art,
And ask the latest fashion of the heart;
What care, what rules your heedless charms shall save,
330   Each nymph your rival, and each youth your slave?
Against your fame with Fondness Hate combines,
The rival batters, and the lover mines.

---

1. A veteran of life, not of war.
2. Croesus, the wealthy and fortunate king, was warned by Solon not to count himself happy until he ceased to live. He lost his crown to Cyrus the Great of Persia.
3. Jonathan Swift, who passed the last four years of his life in utter senility. John Churchill, duke of Marlborough, England's brilliant general during most of the War of the Spanish Succession (1702–13).
4. Catherine Sedley, mistress of James II. Anne Vane, mistress of Frederick, prince of Wales (son of George II).

With distant voice neglected Virtue calls,
Less heard and less, the faint remonstrance falls;
335 Tired with contempt, she quits the slippery reign,
And Pride and Prudence take her seat in vain.
In crowd at once, where none the pass defend,
The harmless freedom, and the private friend.
The guardians yield, by force superior plied:
340 To Interest, Prudence; and to Flattery, Pride.
Now Beauty falls betrayed, despised, distressed,
And hissing Infamy proclaims the rest.
    Where then shall Hope and Fear their objects find?
Must dull Suspense corrupt the stagnant mind?
345 Must helpless man, in ignorance sedate,
Roll darkling down the torrent of his fate?
Must no dislike alarm, no wishes rise,
No cries invoke the mercies of the skies?
Inquirer, cease; petitions yet remain,
350 Which Heaven may hear, nor deem religion vain.
Still raise for good the supplicating voice,
But leave to Heaven the measure and the choice.
Safe in his power, whose eyes discern afar
The secret ambush of a specious prayer.
355 Implore his aid, in his decisions rest,
Secure, whate'er he gives, he gives the best.
Yet when the sense of sacred presence fires,
And strong devotion to the skies aspires,
Pour forth thy fervors for a healthful mind,
360 Obedient passions, and a will resigned;
For love, which scarce collective man can fill;[5]
For patience sovereign o'er transmuted ill;
For faith, that panting for a happier seat,
Counts death kind Nature's signal of retreat:
365 These goods for man the laws of Heaven ordain,
These goods he grants, who grants the power to gain;
With these celestial Wisdom calms the mind,
And makes the happiness she does not find.

1749

On the Death of Dr. Robert Levet[1]

Condemned to Hope's delusive mine,
    As on we toil from day to day,
By sudden blasts, or slow decline,
    Our social comforts drop away.

5 Well tried through many a varying year,
    See Levet to the grave descend;

---

5. Which humankind as a whole can hardly over-task.
1. An unlicensed physician, who lived in Johnson's house for many years and who died in 1782.

His practice was among the very poor. Boswell wrote: "He was of a strange grotesque appearance, stiff and formal in his manner, and seldom said a word while any company was present."

Officious,[2] innocent, sincere,
   Of every friendless name the friend.

Yet still he fills Affection's eye,
10   Obscurely wise, and coarsely kind;
Nor, lettered Arrogance, deny
   Thy praise to merit unrefined.

When fainting Nature called for aid,
   And hovering Death prepared the blow,
15   His vigorous remedy displayed
   The power of art without the show.

In Misery's darkest caverns known,
   His useful care was ever nigh,
Where hopeless Anguish poured his groan,
20   And lonely Want retired to die.

No summons mocked by chill delay,
   No petty gain disdained by pride,
The modest wants of every day
   The toil of every day supplied.

25   His virtues walked their narrow round,
   Nor made a pause, nor left a void;
And sure the Eternal Master found
   The single talent well employed.[3]

The busy day, the peaceful night,
30   Unfelt, uncounted, glided by;
His frame was firm, his powers were bright,
   Though now his eightieth year was nigh.

Then with no throbbing fiery pain,
   No cold gradations of decay,
35   Death broke at once the vital chain,
   And freed his soul the nearest way.

1783

Rasselas   Johnson wrote *Rasselas* in January 1759, during the evenings of one week, a remarkable instance of his ability to write rapidly and brilliantly under the pressure of necessity. His mother lay dying in Lichfield. Her son, famous for his *Dictionary,* was nonetheless oppressed by poverty and in great need of ready money with which to make her last days comfortable, pay her funeral expenses, and settle

---

2. "Kind, doing good offices" (Johnson's *Dictionary*).
3. In the parable of the talents (Matthew 25.14–

30), Jesus suggests that salvation will be granted to those who make good use of their abilities, however small.

her small debts. He was paid £100 for the first edition of *Rasselas,* but not in time to attend her deathbed or her funeral.

Rasselas is a philosophical fable cast in the popular form of an Oriental tale, a type of fiction that owed its popularity to the vogue of the *Arabian Nights,* first translated into English in the early eighteenth century. Because the work is a fable, we should not approach it as a novel: psychologically credible characters and a series of intricately involved actions that lead to a necessary resolution and conclusion are not to be found in *Rasselas.* Instead we are meant to reflect on the ideas and to savor the melancholy resonance and intelligence of the stately prose that expresses them. Johnson arranges the incidents of the fable to test a variety of possible solutions to a problem: What choice of life will bring us happiness? (*The Choice of Life* was his working title for the book.) Many ways of life are examined in turn, and each is found wanting. Johnson does not pretend to have solved the problem. Rather, he locates the sources of discontent in a basic principle of human nature: the "hunger of imagination which preys incessantly upon life" (chapter 32) and which lures us to "listen with credulity to the whispers of fancy and pursue with eagerness the phantoms of hope" (chapter 1). The tale is a gentle satire on one of the perennial topics of satirists: the folly of all of us who stubbornly cling to our illusions despite the evidence of experience. *Rasselas* is not all darkness and gloom, for Johnson's theme invites comic as well as tragic treatment, and some of the episodes evoke that laughter of the mind that is the effect of high comedy. In its main theme, however—the folly of cherishing the dream of ever attaining unalloyed happiness in a world that can never wholly satisfy our desires—and in many of the sayings of its characters, especially of the sage Imlac, *Rasselas* expresses some of Johnson's own deepest convictions.

From The History of Rasselas, Prince of Abyssinia

Chapter 1. Description of a Palace in a Valley

Ye who listen with credulity to the whispers of fancy, and pursue with eagerness the phantoms of hope; who expect that age will perform the promises of youth, and that the deficiencies of the present day will be supplied by the morrow—attend to the history of Rasselas, prince of Abyssinia.

Rasselas was the fourth son of the mighty emperor in whose dominions the Father of Waters[1] begins his course; whose bounty pours down the streams of plenty, and scatters over half the world the harvests of Egypt.

According to the custom which has descended from age to age among the monarchs of the torrid zone, Rasselas was confined in a private palace, with the other sons and daughters of Abyssinian royalty, till the order of succession should call him to the throne.

The place which the wisdom or policy of antiquity had destined for the residence of the Abyssinian princes was a spacious valley[2] in the kingdom of Amhara, surrounded on every side by mountains, of which the summits overhang the middle part. The only passage by which it could be entered was a cavern that passed under a rock, of which it has long been disputed whether it was the work of nature or of human industry. The outlet of the cavern was concealed by a thick wood, and the mouth which opened into the valley was

---

1. The Nile.
2. Johnson had read of the Happy Valley in the Portuguese Jesuit Father Lobo's book on Abyssinia, which he translated in 1735. The description in this and the immediately following paragraphs illustrates Johnson's preference for the "general" over the "particular" (see chap. 10). It owes something to the description of the Garden in *Paradise Lost* 4, and Coleridge's *Kubla Khan* owes something to it.

closed with gates of iron, forged by the artificers of ancient days, so massy that no man could, without the help of engines, open or shut them.

From the mountains on every side rivulets descended that filled all the valley with verdure and fertility, and formed a lake in the middle, inhabited by fish of every species, and frequented by every fowl whom nature has taught to dip the wing in water. This lake discharged its superfluities by a stream, which entered a dark cleft of the mountain on the northern side, and fell with dreadful noise from precipice to precipice till it was heard no more.

The sides of the mountains were covered with trees, the banks of the brooks were diversified with flowers; every blast shook spices from the rocks, and every month dropped fruits upon the ground. All animals that bite the grass, or browse the shrub, whether wild or tame, wandered in this extensive circuit, secured from beasts of prey by the mountains which confined them. On one part were flocks and herds feeding in the pastures, on another all the beasts of chase frisking in the lawns; the sprightly kid was bounding on the rocks, the subtle monkey frolicking in the trees, and the solemn elephant reposing in the shade. All the diversities of the world were brought together, the blessings of nature were collected, and its evils extracted and excluded.

The valley, wide and fruitful, supplied its inhabitants with the necessaries of life, and all delights and superfluities were added at the annual visit which the emperor paid his children, when the iron gate was opened to the sound of music, and during eight days everyone that resided in the valley was required to propose whatever might contribute to make seclusion pleasant, to fill up the vacancies of attention, and lessen the tediousness of time. Every desire was immediately granted. All the artificers of pleasure were called to gladden the festivity; the musicians exerted the power of harmony, and the dancers showed their activity before the princes, in hope that they should pass their lives in this blissful captivity, to which those only were admitted whose performance was thought able to add novelty to luxury. Such was the appearance of security and delight which this retirement afforded, that they to whom it was new always desired that it might be perpetual; and as those on whom the iron gate had once closed were never suffered to return, the effect of longer experience could not be known. Thus every year produced new schemes of delight and new competitors for imprisonment.

The palace stood on an eminence, raised about thirty paces above the surface of the lake. It was divided into many squares or courts, built with greater or less magnificence according to the rank of those for whom they were designed. The roofs were turned into arches of massy stone, joined with a cement that grew harder by time, and the building stood from century to century, deriding the solstitial rains and equinoctial hurricanes, without need of reparation.

This house, which was so large as to be fully known to none but some ancient officers, who successively inherited the secrets of the place, was built as if suspicion herself had dictated the plan. To every room there was an open and secret passage; every square had a communication with the rest, either from the upper stories by private galleries, or by subterranean passages from the lower apartments. Many of the columns had unsuspected cavities, in which a long race of monarchs had reposited their treasures. They then closed up the opening with marble, which was never to be removed but in the utmost exigencies of the kingdom, and recorded their accumulations in a book, which was itself concealed in a tower, not entered but by the emperor, attended by the prince who stood next in succession.

Chapter 2. The Discontent of Rasselas in the Happy Valley

Here the sons and daughters of Abyssinia lived only to know the soft vicissitudes of pleasure and repose, attended by all that were skillful to delight, and gratified with whatever the senses can enjoy. They wandered in gardens of fragrance, and slept in the fortresses of security. Every art was practiced to make them pleased with their own condition. The sages who instructed them told them of nothing but the miseries of public life, and described all beyond the mountains as regions of calamity, where discord was always raging, and where man preyed upon man.

To heighten their opinion of their own felicity, they were daily entertained with songs, the subject of which was the *happy valley*. Their appetites were excited by frequent enumerations of different enjoyments, and revelry and merriment was the business of every hour, from the dawn of morning to the close of even.

These methods were generally successful; few of the princes had ever wished to enlarge their bounds, but passed their lives in full conviction that they had all within their reach that art or nature could bestow, and pitied those whom fate had excluded from this seat of tranquility, as the sport of chance and the slaves of misery.

Thus they rose in the morning and lay down at night, pleased with each other and with themselves; all but Rasselas, who, in the twenty-sixth year of his age, began to withdraw himself from their pastimes and assemblies, and to delight in solitary walks and silent meditation. He often sat before tables covered with luxury, and forgot to taste the dainties that were placed before him; he rose abruptly in the midst of the song, and hastily retired beyond the sound of music. His attendants observed the change, and endeavored to renew his love of pleasure. He neglected their officiousness, repulsed their invitations, and spent day after day on the banks of rivulets sheltered with trees, where he sometimes listened to the birds in the branches, sometimes observed the fish playing in the stream, and anon cast his eyes upon the pastures and mountains filled with animals, of which some were biting the herbage, and some sleeping among the bushes.

This singularity of his humor made him much observed. One of the sages, in whose conversation he had formerly delighted, followed him secretly, in hope of discovering the cause of his disquiet. Rasselas, who knew not that anyone was near him, having for some time fixed his eyes upon the goats that were browsing among the rocks, began to compare their condition with his own.

"What," said he, "makes the difference between man and all the rest of the animal creation? Every beast that strays beside me has the same corporal necessities with myself; he is hungry, and crops the grass, he is thirsty, and drinks the stream, his thirst and hunger are appeased, he is satisfied, and sleeps; he rises again, and he is hungry, he is again fed, and is at rest. I am hungry and thirsty like him, but when thirst and hunger cease, I am not at rest; I am, like him, pained with want, but am not, like him, satisfied with fullness. The intermediate hours are tedious and gloomy; I long again to be hungry that I may again quicken my attention. The birds peck the berries or the corn, and fly away to the groves, where they sit in seeming happiness on the branches, and waste their lives in tuning one unvaried series of sounds. I likewise can call the lutanist and the singer, but the sounds that pleased me yesterday weary me today, and will grow yet more wearisome tomorrow. I can discover within me no power of perception which is not glutted with its proper pleasure, yet I do not feel myself delighted. Man has surely some latent sense for which this place affords no gratification, or he has some desires distinct from sense, which must be satisfied before he can be happy."

After this he lifted up his head, and seeing the moon rising, walked towards the palace. As he passed through the fields, and saw the animals around him, "Ye," said he, "are happy, and need not envy me that walk thus among you, burthened with myself; nor do I, ye gentle beings, envy your felicity, for it is not the felicity of man. I have many distresses from which ye are free; I fear pain when I do not feel it; I sometimes shrink at evils recollected, and sometimes start at evils anticipated. Surely the equity of Providence has balanced peculiar sufferings with peculiar enjoyments."

With observations like these the prince amused himself as he returned, uttering them with a plaintive voice, yet with a look that discovered him to feel some complacence in his own perspicacity, and to receive some solace of the miseries of life from consciousness of the delicacy with which he felt, and the eloquence with which he bewailed them. He mingled cheerfully in the diversions of the evening, and all rejoiced to find that his heart was lightened.

Chapter 3. *The Wants of Him That Wants Nothing*

On the next day his old instructor, imagining that he had now made himself acquainted with his disease of mind, was in the hope of curing it by counsel, and officiously sought an opportunity of conference, which the prince, having long considered him as one whose intellects were exhausted, was not very willing to afford. "Why," said he, "does this man thus intrude upon me; shall I be never suffered to forget those lectures which pleased only while they were new, and to become new again must be forgotten?" He then walked into the wood, and composed himself to his usual meditations; when, before his thoughts had taken any settled form, he perceived his pursuer at his side, and was at first prompted by his impatience to go hastily away; but, being unwilling to offend a man whom he had once reverenced and still loved, he invited him to sit down with him on the bank.

The old man, thus encouraged, began to lament the change which had been lately observed in the prince, and to inquire why he so often retired from the pleasures of the palace, to loneliness and silence. "I fly from pleasure," said the prince, "because pleasure has ceased to please; I am lonely because I am miserable, and am unwilling to cloud with my presence the happiness of others." "You, sir," said the sage, "are the first who has complained of misery in the *happy valley*. I hope to convince you that your complaints have no real cause. You are here in full possession of all that the emperor of Abyssinia can bestow; here is neither labor to be endured nor danger to be dreaded, yet here is all that labor or danger can procure or purchase. Look round and tell me which of your wants is without supply; if you want nothing, how are you unhappy?"

"That I want nothing," said the prince, "or that I know not what I want, is the cause of my complaint; if I had any known want, I should have a certain wish; that wish would excite endeavor, and I should not then repine to see the sun move so slowly towards the western mountain, or lament when the day breaks, and sleep will no longer hide me from myself. When I see the kids and the lambs chasing one another, I fancy that I should be happy if I had something to pursue. But, possessing all that I can want, I find one day and one hour exactly like another, except that the latter is still more tedious than the former. Let your experience inform me how the day may now seem as short as in my childhood, while nature was yet fresh and every moment showed me what I never had observed before. I have already enjoyed too much; give me something to desire."

The old man was surprised at this new species of affliction and knew not what to reply, yet was unwilling to be silent. "Sir," said he, "if you had seen the miseries of the world you would know how to value your present state." "Now," said the prince, "you have given me something to desire. I shall long to see the miseries of the world, since the sight of them is necessary to happiness."[3]

* * *

Chapter 6. A Dissertation on the Art of Flying

Among the artists that had been allured into the happy valley, to labor for the accommodation and pleasure of its inhabitants, was a man eminent for his knowledge of the mechanic powers, who had contrived many engines[4] both of use and recreation. By a wheel, which the stream turned, he forced the water into a tower, whence it was distributed to all the apartments of the palace. He erected a pavillion in the garden, around which he kept the air always cool by artificial showers. One of the groves, appropriated to the ladies, was ventilated by fans, to which the rivulet that run through it gave a constant motion; and instruments of soft music were placed at proper distances, of which some played by the impulse of the wind, and some by the power of the stream.

This artist was sometimes visited by Rasselas, who was pleased with every kind of knowledge, imagining that the time would come when all his acquisitions should be of use to him in the open world. He came one day to amuse himself in his usual manner, and found the master busy in building a sailing chariot: he saw that the design was practicable upon a level surface, and with expressions of great esteem solicited its completion. The workman was pleased to find himself so much regarded by the prince, and resolved to gain yet higher honors. "Sir," said he, "you have seen but a small part of what the mechanic sciences can perform. I have been long of opinion, that, instead of the tardy conveyance of ships and chariots, man might use the swifter migration of wings; that the fields of air are open to knowledge, and that only ignorance and idleness need crawl upon the ground."

This hint rekindled the prince's desire of passing the mountains; having seen what the mechanist had already performed, he was willing to fancy that he could do more; yet resolved to inquire further before he suffered hope to afflict him by disappointment. "I am afraid," said he to the artist, "that your

---

3. In chapters 4 and 5, Rasselas dreams about escaping the valley.

4. Machines. "Mechanic powers": the forces that cause things to move.

imagination prevails over your skill, and that you now tell me rather what you wish than what you know. Every animal has his element assigned him; the birds have the air, and man and beasts the earth." "So," replied the mechanist, "fishes have the water, in which yet beasts can swim by nature, and men by art. He that can swim needs not despair to fly: to swim is to fly in a grosser fluid, and to fly is to swim in a subtler. We are only to proportion our power of resistance to the different density of the matter through which we are to pass. You will be necessarily upborn by the air, if you can renew any impulse upon it, faster than the air can recede from the pressure."

"But the exercise of swimming," said the prince, "is very laborious; the strongest limbs are soon wearied; I am afraid the act of flying will be yet more violent, and wings will be of no great use, unless we can fly further than we can swim."

"The labor of rising from the ground," said the artist "will be great, as we see it in the heavier domestic fowls; but, as we mount higher, the earth's attraction, and the body's gravity, will be gradually diminished, till we shall arrive at a region where the man will float in the air without any tendency to fall: no care will then be necessary, but to move forwards, which the gentlest impulse will effect. You, Sir, whose curiosity is so extensive, will easily conceive with what pleasure a philosopher, furnished with wings, and hovering in the sky, would see the earth, and all its inhabitants, rolling beneath him, and presenting to him successively, by its diurnal motion, all the countries within the same parallel. How must it amuse the pendent spectator to see the moving scene of land and ocean, cities and deserts! To survey with equal security the marts of trade, and the fields of battle; mountains infested by barbarians, and fruitful regions gladdened by plenty, and lulled by peace! How easily shall we then trace the Nile through all his passage; pass over to distant regions, and examine the face of nature from one extremity of the earth to the other!"

"All this," said the prince, "is much to be desired, but I am afraid that no man will be able to breathe in these regions of speculation and tranquility. I have been told, that respiration is difficult upon lofty mountains, yet from these precipices, though so high as to produce great tenuity of the air, it is very easy to fall: therefore I suspect, that from any height, where life can be supported, there may be danger of too quick descent."

"Nothing," replied the artist, "will ever be attempted, if all possible objections must be first overcome. If you will favor my project I will try the first flight at my own hazard. I have considered the structure of all volant[5] animals, and find the folding continuity of the bat's wings most easily accommodated to the human form. Upon this model I shall begin my task tomorrow, and in a year expect to tower into the air beyond the malice or pursuit of man. But I will work only on this condition, that the art shall not be divulged, and that you shall not require me to make wings for any but ourselves."

"Why," said Rasselas, "should you envy others so great an advantage? All skill ought to be exerted for universal good; every man has owed much to others, and ought to repay the kindness that he has received."

"If men were all virtuous," returned the artist, "I should with great alacrity

---

5. Able to fly.

teach them all to fly. But what would be the security of the good, if the bad could at pleasure invade them from the sky? Against an army sailing through the clouds neither walls, nor mountains, nor seas, could afford any security. A flight of northern savages might hover in the wind, and light at once with irresistible violence upon the capital of a fruitful region that was rolling under them. Even this valley, the retreat of princes, the abode of happiness, might be violated by the sudden descent of some of the naked nations that swarm on the coast of the southern sea."

The prince promised secrecy, and waited for the performance, not wholly hopeless of success. He visited the work from time to time, observed its progress, and remarked many ingenious contrivances to facilitate motion, and unite levity with strength. The artist was every day more certain that he should leave vultures and eagles behind him, and the contagion of his confidence seized upon the prince.

In a year the wings were finished, and, on a morning appointed, the maker appeared furnished for flight on a little promontory: he waved his pinions a while to gather air, then leaped from his stand, and in an instant dropped into the lake. His wings, which were of no use in the air, sustained him in the water, and the prince drew him to land, half dead with terror and vexation.[6]

* * *

Chapter 10. Imlac's History Continued. A Dissertation upon Poetry

"Wherever I went, I found that poetry was considered as the highest learning, and regarded with a veneration somewhat approaching to that which man would pay to the angelic nature. And yet it fills me with wonder that, in almost all countries, the most ancient poets are considered as the best: whether it be that every other kind of knowledge is an acquisition gradually attained, and poetry is a gift conferred at once; or that the first poetry of every nation surprised them as a novelty, and retained the credit by consent which it received by accident at first; or whether, as the province of poetry is to describe nature and passion, which are always the same, the first writers took possession of the most striking objects for description and the most probable occurrences for fiction, and left nothing to those that followed them, but transcription of the same events, and new combinations of the same images—whatever be the reason, it is commonly observed that the early writers are in possession of nature, and their followers of art; that the first excel in strength and invention, and the latter in elegance and refinement.

"I was desirous to add my name to this illustrious fraternity. I read all the poets of Persia and Arabia, and was able to repeat by memory the volumes that are suspended in the mosque of Mecca. But I soon found that no man was ever great by imitation. My desire of excellence impelled me to transfer my attention to nature and to life. Nature was to be my subject, and men to be my auditors: I could never describe what I had not seen; I could not hope to move those with delight or terror, whose interests and opinions I did not understand.

6. In chapters 7–9, Rasselas comes to know Imlac, a scholar and poet who knows the great world outside the valley and who tells the story of his life.

"Being now resolved to be a poet, I saw everything with a new purpose; my sphere of attention was suddenly magnified; no kind of knowledge was to be overlooked. I ranged mountains and deserts for images and resemblances, and pictured upon my mind every tree of the forest and flower of the valley. I observed with equal care the crags of the rock and the pinnacles of the palace. Sometimes I wandered along the mazes of the rivulet, and sometimes watched the changes of the summer clouds. To a poet nothing can be useless. Whatever is beautiful, and whatever is dreadful, must be familiar to his imagination; he must be conversant with all that is awfully vast or elegantly little. The plants of the garden, the animals of the wood, the minerals of the earth, and meteors of the sky, must all concur to store his mind with inexhaustible variety: for every idea[7] is useful for the enforcement or decoration of moral or religious truth; and he who knows most will have most power of diversifying his scenes, and of gratifying his reader with remote allusions and unexpected instruction.

"All the appearances of nature I was therefore careful to study, and every country which I have surveyed has contributed something to my poetical powers."

"In so wide a survey," said the prince, "you must surely have left much unobserved. I have lived till now within the circuit of these mountains, and yet cannot walk abroad without the sight of something which I have never beheld before, or never heeded."

"The business of a poet," said Imlac, "is to examine, not the individual, but the species; to remark general properties and large appearances; he does not number the streaks of the tulip, or describe the different shades in the verdure of the forest. He is to exhibit in his portraits of nature such prominent and striking features as recall the original to every mind, and must neglect the minuter discriminations, which one may have remarked and another have neglected, for those characteristics which are alike obvious to vigilance and carelessness.

"But the knowledge of nature is only half the task of a poet; he must be acquainted likewise with all the modes of life. His character requires that he estimate the happiness and misery of every condition; observe the power of all the passions in all their combinations, and trace the changes of the human mind, as they are modified by various institutions and accidental influences of climate or custom, from the sprightliness of infancy to the despondence of decrepitude. He must divest himself of the prejudices of his age or country; he must consider right and wrong in their abstracted and invariable state; he must disregard present laws and opinions, and rise to general and transcendental[8] truths, which will always be the same. He must, therefore, content himself with the slow progress of his name, contemn the applause of his own time, and commit his claims to the justice of posterity. He must write as the interpreter of nature and the legislator of mankind, and consider himself as presiding over the thoughts and manners of future generations, as a being superior to time and place.

"His labor is not yet at an end; he must know many languages and many sciences; and, that his style may be worthy of his thoughts, must by incessant

7. Mental image.
8. "General; pervading many particulars" (Johnson's *Dictionary*).

practice familiarize to himself every delicacy of speech and grace of harmony."

Chapter 11. Imlac's Narrative Continued. A Hint on Pilgrimage

Imlac now felt the enthusiastic fit, and was proceeding to aggrandize his own profession, when the prince cried out: "Enough! thou hast convinced me that no human being can ever be a poet. Proceed with thy narration."

"To be a poet," said Imlac, "is indeed very difficult." "So difficult," returned the prince, "that I will at present hear no more of his labors. Tell me whither you went when you had seen Persia."

"From Persia," said the poet, "I traveled through Syria, and for three years resided in Palestine, where I conversed with great numbers of the northern and western nations of Europe, the nations which are now in possession of all power and all knowledge, whose armies are irresistible, and whose fleets command the remotest parts of the globe. When I compared these men with the natives of our own kingdom, and those that surround us, they appeared almost another order of beings. In their countries it is difficult to wish for anything that may not be obtained; a thousand arts, of which we never heard, are continually laboring for their convenience and pleasure; and whatever their own climate has denied them is supplied by their commerce."

"By what means," said the prince, "are the Europeans thus powerful, or why, since they can so easily visit Asia and Africa for trade or conquest, cannot the Asiatics and Africans invade their coasts, plant colonies in their ports, and give laws to their natural princes? The same wind that carries them back would bring us thither."

"They are more powerful, sir, than we," answered Imlac, "because they are wiser; knowledge will always predominate over ignorance, as man governs the other animals. But why their knowledge is more than ours, I know not what reason can be given, but the unsearchable will of the Supreme Being."

"When," said the prince with a sigh, "shall I be able to visit Palestine, and mingle with this mighty confluence of nations? Till that happy moment shall arrive, let me fill up the time with such representations as thou canst give me. I am not ignorant of the motive that assembles such numbers in that place, and cannot but consider it as the center of wisdom and piety, to which the best and wisest men of every land must be continually resorting."

"There are some nations," said Imlac, "that send few visitants to Palestine; for many numerous and learned sects in Europe concur to censure pilgrimage as superstitious, or deride it as ridiculous."

"You know," said the prince, "how little my life has made me acquainted with diversity of opinions. It will be too long to hear the arguments on both sides; you, that have considered them, tell me the result."

"Pilgrimage," said Imlac, "like many other acts of piety, may be reasonable or superstitious, according to the principles upon which it is performed. Long journeys in search of truth are not commanded. Truth, such as is necessary to the regulation of life, is always found where it is honestly sought. Change of place is no natural cause of the increase of piety, for it inevitably produces dissipation of mind. Yet, since men go every day to view the fields where great actions have been performed, and return with stronger impressions of the event, curiosity of the same kind may naturally dispose us to view that country whence our religion had its beginning; and I believe no man surveys those awful scenes without some confirmation of holy resolutions. That the Supreme Being may be more easily propitiated in one place than in another is the dream of idle superstition, but that some places may operate upon our own minds in an uncommon manner is an opinion which hourly experience will justify. He who supposes that his vices may be more successfully combated in Palestine, will, perhaps, find himself mistaken, yet he may go thither without folly; he who thinks they will be more freely pardoned, dishonors at once his reason and religion."

"These," said the prince, "are European distinctions. I will consider them another time. What have you found to be the effect of knowledge? Are those nations happier than we?"

"There is so much infelicity," said the poet, "in the world that scarce any man has leisure from his own distresses to estimate the comparative happiness of others. Knowledge is certainly one of the means of pleasure, as is confessed by the natural desire which every mind feels of increasing its ideas. Ignorance is mere privation, by which nothing can be produced; it is a vacuity in which the soul sits motionless and torpid for want of attraction; and, without knowing why, we always rejoice when we learn, and grieve when we forget. I am therefore inclined to conclude that if nothing counteracts the natural consequence of learning, we grow more happy as our minds take a wider range.

"In enumerating the particular comforts of life, we shall find many advantages on the side of the Europeans. They cure wounds and diseases with which we languish and perish. We suffer inclemencies of weather which they can obviate. They have engines for the despatch of many laborious works, which we must perform by manual industry. There is such communication between distant places that one friend can hardly be said to be absent from another. Their policy removes all public inconveniences; they have roads cut through their mountains, and bridges laid upon their rivers. And, if we descend to the privacies of life, their habitations are more commodious, and their possessions are more secure."

"They are surely happy," said the prince, "who have all these conveniencies, of which I envy none so much as the facility with which separated friends interchange their thoughts."

"The Europeans," answered Imlac, "are less unhappy than we, but they are not happy. Human life is everywhere a state in which much is to be endured, and little to be enjoyed."[9]

* * *

Chapter 15. *The Prince and Princess Leave the Valley, and See Many Wonders*

The prince and princess had jewels sufficient to make them rich whenever they came into a place of commerce, which, by Imlac's direction, they hid in their clothes, and, on the night of the next full moon, all left the valley. The princess was followed only by a single favorite, who did not know whither she was going.

---

9. In chapters 12–14, Rasselas and Imac, assisted by Nekayah, Rasselas's sister, succeed in making a tunnel through the mountain.

They clambered through the cavity, and began to go down on the other side. The princess and her maid turned their eyes towards every part, and, seeing nothing to bound their prospect, considered themselves as in danger of being lost in a dreary vacuity. They stopped and trembled. "I am almost afraid," said the princess, "to begin a journey of which I cannot perceive an end, and to venture into this immense plain where I may be approached on every side by men whom I never saw." The prince felt nearly the same emotions, though he thought it more manly to conceal them.

Imlac smiled at their terrors, and encouraged them to proceed; but the princess continued irresolute till she had been imperceptibly drawn forward too far to return.

In the morning they found some shepherds in the field, who set milk and fruits before them. The princess wondered that she did not see a palace ready for her reception, and a table spread with delicacies; but, being faint and hungry, she drank the milk and ate the fruits, and thought them of a higher flavor than the products of the valley.

They traveled forward by easy journeys, being all unaccustomed to toil or difficulty, and knowing, that though they might be missed, they could not be pursued. In a few days they came into a more populous region, where Imlac was diverted with the admiration which his companions expressed at the diversity of manners, stations and employments.

Their dress was such as might not bring upon them the suspicion of having any thing to conceal, yet the prince, wherever he came, expected to be obeyed, and the princess was frighted, because those that came into her presence did not prostrate themselves before her. Imlac was forced to observe them with great vigilance, lest they should betray their rank by their unusual behavior, and detained them several weeks in the first village to accustom them to the sight of common mortals.

By degrees the royal wanderers were taught to understand that they had for a time laid aside their dignity, and were to expect only such regard as liberality and courtesy could procure. And Imlac, having, by many admonitions, prepared them to endure the tumults of a port, and the ruggedness of the commercial race, brought them down to the seacoast.

The prince and his sister, to whom every thing was new, were gratified equally at all places, and therefore remained for some months at the port without any inclination to pass further. Imlac was content with their stay, because he did not think it safe to expose them, unpracticed in the world, to the hazards of a foreign country.

At last he began to fear lest they should be discovered, and proposed to fix a day for their departure. They had no pretensions to judge for themselves, and referred the whole scheme to his direction. He therefore took passage in a ship to Suez; and, when the time came, with great difficulty prevailed on the princess to enter the vessel. They had a quick and prosperous voyage, and from Suez traveled by land to Cairo.

Chapter 16. They Enter Cairo, and Find Every Man Happy

As they approached the city, which filled the strangers with astonishment, "This," said Imlac to the prince, "is the place where travelers and merchants assemble from all the corners of the earth. You will here find men of every character and every occupation. Commerce is here honorable. I will act as a merchant, and you shall live as strangers, who have no other end of travel than curiosity. It will soon be observed that we are rich; our reputation will procure us access to all whom we shall desire to know; you will see all the conditions of humanity, and enable yourself at leisure to make your *choice of life.*"

They now entered the town, stunned by the noise, and offended by the crowds. Instruction had not yet so prevailed over habit, but that they wondered to see themselves pass undistinguished along the street, and met by the lowest of the people without reverence or notice. The princess could not at first bear the thought of being leveled with the vulgar,[1] and for some days continued in her chamber, where she was served by her favorite, Pekuah, as in the palace of the valley.

Imlac, who understood traffic,[2] sold part of the jewels the next day, and hired a house, which he adorned with such magnificence that he was immediately considered as a merchant of great wealth. His politeness attracted many acquaintance, and his generosity made him courted by many dependents. His table was crowded by men of every nation, who all admired his knowledge, and solicited his favor. His companions, not being able to mix in the conversation, could make no discovery of their ignorance or surprise, and were gradually initiated in the world as they gained knowledge of the language.

The prince had, by frequent lectures, been taught the use and nature of money; but the ladies could not for a long time comprehend what the merchants did with small pieces of gold and silver, or why things of so little use should be received as equivalent to the necessaries of life.

They studied the language two years, while Imlac was preparing to set before them the various ranks and conditions of mankind. He grew acquainted with all who had anything uncommon in their fortune or conduct. He frequented the voluptuous and the frugal, the idle and the busy, the merchants and the men of learning.

The prince being now able to converse with fluency, and having learned the caution necessary to be observed in his intercourse with strangers, began to accompany Imlac to places of resort, and to enter into all assemblies, that he might make his *choice of life.*

For some time he thought choice needless, because all appeared to him equally happy. Wherever he went he met gaiety and kindness, and heard the song of joy or the laugh of carelessness. He began to believe that the world overflowed with universal plenty, and that nothing was withheld either from want or merit; that every hand showered liberality, and every heart melted with benevolence: "And who then," says he, "will be suffered to be wretched?"

Imlac permitted the pleasing delusion, and was unwilling to crush the hope of inexperience, till one day, having sat awhile silent, "I know not," said the prince, "what can be the reason that I am more unhappy than any of our friends. I see them perpetually and unalterably cheerful, but feel my own mind restless and uneasy. I am unsatisfied with those pleasures which I seem most to court; I live in the crowds of jollity, not so much to enjoy company as to shun myself, and am only loud and merry to conceal my sadness."

"Every man," said Imlac, "may, by examining his own mind, guess what

1. Ordinary people.   2. Commerce.

passes in the minds of others; when you feel that your own gaiety is counterfeit, it may justly lead you to suspect that of your companions not to be
sincere. Envy is commonly reciprocal. We are long before we are convinced
that happiness is never to be found, and each believes it possessed by others,
to keep alive the hope of obtaining it for himself. In the assembly where you
passed the last night, there appeared such sprightliness of air, and volatility
of fancy, as might have suited beings of an higher order, formed to inhabit
serener regions, inaccessible to care or sorrow; yet, believe me, prince, there
was not one who did not dread the moment when solitude should deliver
him to the tyranny of reflection."

"This," said the prince, "may be true of others, since it is true of me; yet,
whatever be the general infelicity of man, one condition is more happy than
another, and wisdom surely directs us to take the least evil in the *choice of
life.*"

"The causes of good and evil," answered Imlac, "are so various and uncertain, so often entangled with each other, so diversified by various relations,
and so much subject to accidents which cannot be foreseen, that he who
would fix his condition upon incontestable reasons of preference must live
and die inquiring and deliberating."

"But, surely," said Rasselas, "the wise men, to whom we listen with reverence and wonder, chose that mode of life for themselves which they
thought most likely to make them happy."

"Very few," said the poet, "live by choice. Every man is placed in his present
condition by causes which acted without his foresight, and with which he
did not always willingly cooperate; and therefore you will rarely meet one
who does not think the lot of his neighbor better than his own."

"I am pleased to think," said the prince, "that my birth has given me at
least one advantage over others, by enabling me to determine for myself. I
have here the world before me. I will review it at leisure; surely happiness is
somewhere to be found."

Chapter 17. The Prince Associates with Young Men of Spirit and Gaiety

Rasselas rose next day, and resolved to begin his experiments upon life.
"Youth," cried he, "is the time of gladness: I will join myself to the young
men, whose only business is to gratify their desires, and whose time is all
spent in a succession of enjoyments."

To such societies he was readily admitted, but a few days brought him
back weary and disgusted. Their mirth was without images,[3] their laughter
without motive; their pleasures were gross and sensual, in which the mind
had no part; their conduct was at once wild and mean; they laughed at order
and at law, but the frown of power dejected, and the eye of wisdom abashed
them.

The prince soon concluded, that he should never be happy in a course of
life of which he was ashamed. He thought it unsuitable to a reasonable being
to act without a plan, and to be sad or cheerful only by chance. "Happiness,"
said he, "must be something solid and permanent, without fear and without
uncertainty."

But his young companions had gained so much of his regard by their

3. Ideas.

frankness and courtesy, that he could not leave them without warning and remonstrance. "My friends," said he, "I have seriously considered our manners and our prospects, and find that we have mistaken our own interest. The first years of man must make provision for the last. He that never thinks never can be wise. Perpetual levity must end in ignorance; and intemperance, though it may fire the spirits for an hour, will make life short or miserable. Let us consider that youth is of no long duration, and that in maturer age, when the enchantments of fancy shall cease, and phantoms of delight dance no more about us, we shall have no comforts but the esteem of wise men, and the means of doing good. Let us, therefore, stop, while to stop is in our power: let us live as men who are sometime to grow old, and to whom it will be the most dreadful of all evils not to count their past years but by follies, and to be reminded of their former luxuriance of health only by the maladies which riot has produced."

They stared a while in silence one upon another, and, at last, drove him away by a general chorus of continued laughter.

The consciousness that his sentiments were just, and his intentions kind, was scarcely sufficient to support him against the horror of derision. But he recovered his tranquillity, and pursued his search.

Chapter 18. *The Prince Finds a Wise and Happy Man*

As he was one day walking in the street, he saw a spacious building which all were, by the open doors, invited to enter: he followed the stream of people, and found it a hall or school of declamation, in which professors read lectures to their auditory. He fixed his eye upon a sage raised above the rest, who discoursed with great energy on the government of the passions. His look was venerable, his action graceful, his pronunciation clear, and his diction elegant. He showed with great strength of sentiment and variety of illustration that human nature is degraded and debased, when the lower faculties predominate over the higher; that when fancy, the parent of passion, usurps the dominion of the mind, nothing ensues but the natural effect of unlawful government, perturbation, and confusion; that she betrays the fortresses of the intellect to rebels, and excites her children to sedition against reason, their lawful sovereign. He compared reason to the sun, of which the light is constant, uniform and lasting; and fancy to a meteor, of bright but transitory luster, irregular in its motion, and delusive in its direction.

He then communicated the various precepts given from time to time for the conquest of passion, and displayed the happiness of those who had obtained the important victory, after which man is no longer the slave of fear, nor the fool of hope; is no more emaciated by envy, inflamed by anger, emasculated by tenderness, or depressed by grief; but walks on calmly through the tumults or the privacies of life, as the sun pursues alike his course through the calm or the stormy sky.

He enumerated many examples of heroes immovable by pain or pleasure, who looked with indifference on those modes or accidents to which the vulgar give the names of good and evil. He exhorted his hearers to lay aside their prejudices, and arm themselves against the shafts of malice or misfortune, by invulnerable patience; concluding that this state only was happiness, and that this happiness was in everyone's power.

Rasselas listened to him with the veneration due to the instructions of a superior being, and, waiting for him at the door, humbly implored the liberty of visiting so great a master of true wisdom. The lecturer hesitated a moment, when Rasselas put a purse of gold into his hand, which he received with a mixture of joy and wonder.

"I have found," said the prince at his return to Imlac, "a man who can teach all that is necessary to be known; who, from the unshaken throne of rational fortitude, looks down on the scenes of life changing beneath him. He speaks, and attention watches his lips. He reasons, and conviction closes his periods. This man shall be my future guide; I will learn his doctrines, and imitate his life."

"Be not too hasty," said Imlac, "to trust or to admire the teachers of morality: they discourse like angels, but they live like men."

Rasselas, who could not conceive how any man could reason so forcibly without feeling the cogency of his own arguments, paid his visit in a few days, and was denied admission. He had now learned the power of money, and made his way by a piece of gold to the inner apartment, where he found the philosopher in a room half darkened, with his eyes misty and his face pale. "Sir," said he, "you are come at a time when all human friendship is useless; what I suffer cannot be remedied, what I have lost cannot be supplied. My daughter, my only daughter, from whose tenderness I expected all the comforts of my age, died last night of a fever. My views, my purposes, my hopes are at an end; I am now a lonely being, disunited from society."

"Sir," said the prince, "mortality is an event by which a wise man can never be surprised; we know that death is always near, and it should therefore always be expected." "Young man," answered the philosopher, "you speak like one that has never felt the pangs of separation." "Have you then forgot the precepts," said Rasselas, "which you so powerfully enforced? Has wisdom no strength to arm the heart against calamity? Consider that external things are naturally variable, but truth and reason are always the same." "What comfort," said the mourner, "can truth and reason afford me? Of what effect are they now, but to tell me that my daughter will not be restored?"

The prince, whose humanity would not suffer him to insult misery with reproof, went away, convinced of the emptiness of rhetorical sound, and the inefficacy of polished periods and studied sentences.[4]

Chapter 19. A Glimpse of Pastoral Life

He was still eager upon the same inquiry; and having heard of a hermit that lived near the lowest cataract of the Nile, and filled the whole country with the fame of his sanctity, resolved to visit his retreat, and inquire whether that felicity which public life could not afford was to be found in solitude; and whether a man whose age and virtue made him venerable could teach any peculiar art of shunning evils, or enduring them.

Imlac and the princess agreed to accompany him, and, after the necessary preparations, they began their journey. Their way lay through fields, where shepherds tended their flocks and the lambs were playing upon the pasture. "This," said the poet, "is the life which has been often celebrated for its innocence and quiet; let us pass the heat of the day among the shepherds'

4. Maxims or moral axioms. "Periods": complete sentences.

tents, and know whether all our searches are not to terminate in pastoral simplicity."

The proposal pleased them, and they induced the shepherds, by small presents and familiar questions, to tell their opinion of their own state. They were so rude and ignorant, so little able to compare the good with the evil of the occupation, and so indistinct in their narratives and descriptions, that very little could be learned from them. But it was evident that their hearts were cankered with discontent; that they considered themselves as condemned to labor for the luxury of the rich, and looked up with stupid malevolence toward those that were placed above them.

The princess pronounced with vehemence that she would never suffer these envious savages to be her companions, and that she should not soon be desirous of seeing any more specimens of rustic happiness; but could not believe that all the accounts of primeval pleasures were fabulous, and was yet in doubt whether life had anything that could be justly preferred to the placid gratifications of fields and woods. She hoped that the time would come, when, with a few virtuous and elegant companions, she could gather flowers planted by her own hand, fondle the lambs of her own ewe, and listen, without care, among brooks and breezes, to one of her maidens reading in the shade.

Chapter 20. The Danger of Prosperity

On the next day they continued their journey, till the heat compelled them to look round for shelter. At a small distance they saw a thick wood, which they no sooner entered than they perceived that they were approaching the habitations of men. The shrubs were diligently cut away to open walks where the shades were darkest; the boughs of opposite trees were artificially interwoven; seats of flowery turf were raised in vacant spaces, and a rivulet, that wantoned along the side of a winding path, had its banks sometimes opened into small basins, and its stream sometimes obstructed by little mounds of stone heaped together to increase its murmurs.

They passed slowly through the wood, delighted with such unexpected accommodations, and entertained each other with conjecturing what, or who, he could be, that, in those rude and unfrequented regions, had leisure and art for such harmless luxury.

As they advanced, they heard the sound of music, and saw youths and virgins dancing in the grove; and, going still further, beheld a stately palace built upon a hill surrounded with woods. The laws of eastern hospitality allowed them to enter, and the master welcomed them like a man liberal and wealthy.

He was skilful enough in appearances soon to discern that they were no common guests, and spread his table with magnificence. The eloquence of Imlac caught his attention, and the lofty courtesy of the princess excited his respect. When they offered to depart he entreated their stay, and was the next day still more unwilling to dismiss them than before. They were easily persuaded to stop, and civility grew up in time to freedom and confidence.

The prince now saw all the domestics cheerful, and all the face of nature smiling round the place, and could not forbear to hope that he should find here what he was seeking; but when he was congratulating the master upon his possessions, he answered with a sigh, "My condition has indeed the appearance of happiness, but appearances are delusive. My prosperity puts my life in danger; the Bassa of Egypt is my enemy, incensed only by my wealth and popularity. I have been hitherto protected against him by the princes of the country; but, as the favor of the great is uncertain, I know not how soon my defenders may be persuaded to share the plunder with the Bassa. I have sent my treasures into a distant country, and, upon the first alarm, am prepared to follow them. Then will my enemies riot in my mansion, and enjoy the gardens which I have planted."

They all joined in lamenting his danger, and deprecating his exile; and the princess was so much disturbed with the tumult of grief and indignation, that she retired to her apartment. They continued with their kind inviter a few days longer, and then went forward to find the hermit.

Chapter 21. The Happiness of Solitude. The Hermit's History

They came on the third day, by the direction of the peasants, to the hermit's cell: it was a cavern in the side of a mountain, over-shadowed with palm-trees; at such a distance from the cataract, that nothing more was heard than a gentle uniform murmur, such as composed the mind to pensive meditation, especially when it was assisted by the wind whistling among the branches. The first rude essay of nature had been so much improved by human labor, that the cave contained several apartments, appropriated to different uses, and often afforded lodging to travelers, whom darkness or tempests happened to overtake.

The hermit sat on a bench at the door, to enjoy the coolness of the evening. On one side lay a book with pens and papers, on the other mechanical instruments of various kinds. As they approached him unregarded, the princess observed that he had not the countenance of a man that had found, or could teach, the way to happiness.

They saluted him with great respect, which he repaid like a man not unaccustomed to the forms of courts. "My children," said he, "if you have lost your way, you shall be willingly supplied with such conveniencies for the night as this cavern will afford. I have all that nature requires, and you will not expect delicacies in a hermit's cell."

They thanked him, and, entering, were pleased with the neatness and regularity of the place. The hermit set flesh and wine before them, though he fed only upon fruits and water. His discourse was cheerful without levity, and pious without enthusiasm.[5] He soon gained the esteem of his guests, and the princess repented of her hasty censure.

At last Imlac began thus: "I do not now wonder that your reputation is so far extended; we have heard at Cairo of your wisdom, and came hither to implore your direction for this young man and maiden in the *choice of life*."

"To him that lives well," answered the hermit, "every form of life is good; nor can I give any other rule for choice, than to remove from all apparent evil."

---

5. "A vain belief of private revelation; a vain confidence of divine favor or communication" (Johnson's *Dictionary*).

"He will remove most certainly from evil," said the prince, "who shall devote himself to that solitude which you have recommended by your example."

"I have indeed lived fifteen years in solitude," said the hermit, "but have no desire that my example should gain any imitators. In my youth I professed arms, and was raised by degrees to the highest military rank. I have traversed wide countries at the head of my troops, and seen many battles and sieges. At last, being disgusted by the preferment of a younger officer, and feeling that my vigor was beginning to decay, I resolved to close my life in peace, having found the world full of snares, discord, and misery. I had once escaped from the pursuit of the enemy by the shelter of this cavern, and therefore chose it for my final residence. I employed artificers to form it into chambers, and stored it with all that I was likely to want.

"For some time after my retreat, I rejoiced like a tempest-beaten sailor at his entrance into the harbor, being delighted with the sudden change of the noise and hurry of war, to stillness and repose. When the pleasure of novelty went away, I employed my hours in examining the plants which grow in the valley, and the minerals which I collected from the rocks. But that inquiry is now grown tasteless and irksome. I have been for some time unsettled and distracted: my mind is disturbed with a thousand perplexities of doubt, and vanities of imagination, which hourly prevail upon me, because I have no opportunities of relaxation or diversion. I am sometimes ashamed to think that I could not secure myself from vice, but by retiring from the exercise of virtue, and begin to suspect that I was rather impelled by resentment, than led by devotion, into solitude. My fancy riots in scenes of folly, and I lament that I have lost so much, and have gained so little. In solitude, if I escape the example of bad men, I want likewise the counsel and conversation of the good. I have been long comparing the evils with the advantages of society, and resolve to return into the world tomorrow. The life of a solitary man will be certainly miserable, but not certainly devout."

They heard his resolution with surprise, but, after a short pause, offered to conduct him to Cairo. He dug up a considerable treasure which he had hid among the rocks, and accompanied them to the city, on which, as he approached it, he gazed with rapture.

Chapter 22. The Happiness of a Life Led According to Nature

Rasselas went often to an assembly of learned men, who met at stated times to unbend their minds and compare their opinions. Their manners were somewhat coarse, but their conversation was instructive, and their disputations acute, though sometimes too violent, and often continued till neither controvertist remembered upon what question they began. Some faults were almost general among them; everyone was desirous to dictate to the rest, and everyone was pleased to hear the genius or knowledge of another depreciated.

In this assembly Rasselas was relating his interview with the hermit, and the wonder with which he heard him censure a course of life which he had so deliberately chosen, and so laudably followed. The sentiments of the hearers were various. Some were of opinion that the folly of his choice had been justly punished by condemnation to perpetual perseverance. One of the youngest among them, with great vehemence, pronounced him an hypocrite. Some talked of the right of society to the labor of individuals, and considered retirement as a desertion of duty. Others readily allowed that there was a time when the claims of the public were satisfied, and when a man might properly sequester himself, to review his life and purify his heart.

One, who appeared more affected with the narrative than the rest, thought it likely that the hermit would in a few years go back to his retreat, and perhaps, if shame did not restrain, or death intercept him, return once more from his retreat into the world. "For the hope of happiness," said he, "is so strongly impressed that the longest experience is not able to efface it. Of the present state, whatever it be, we feel and are forced to confess the misery; yet when the same state is again at a distance, imagination paints it as desirable. But the time will surely come when desire will be no longer our torment, and no man shall be wretched but by his own fault."

"This," said a philosopher who had heard him with tokens of great impatience, "is the present condition of a wise man. The time is already come when none are wretched but by their own fault. Nothing is more idle than to inquire after happiness, which nature has kindly placed within our reach. The way to be happy is to live according to nature, in obedience to that universal and unalterable law with which every heart is originally impressed; which is not written on it by precept, but engraven by destiny, not instilled by education, but infused at our nativity. He that lives according to nature will suffer nothing from the delusions of hope, or importunities of desire; he will receive and reject with equability of temper, and act or suffer as the reason of things shall alternately prescribe. Other men may amuse themselves with subtle definitions, or intricate ratiocination. Let them learn to be wise by easier means; let them observe the hind of the forest, and the linnet of the grove; let them consider the life of animals, whose motions are regulated by instinct; they obey their guide, and are happy. Let us therefore, at length, cease to dispute, and learn to live; throw away the encumbrance of precepts, which they who utter them with so much pride and pomp do not understand, and carry with us this simple and intelligible maxim, that deviation from nature is deviation from happiness."

When he had spoken, he looked round him with a placid air, and enjoyed the consciousness of his own beneficence. "Sir," said the prince with great modesty, "as I, like all the rest of mankind, am desirous of felicity, my closest attention has been fixed upon your discourse. I doubt not the truth of a position which a man so learned has so confidently advanced. Let me only know what it is to live according to nature."

"When I find young men so humble and so docile," said the philosopher, "I can deny them no information which my studies have enabled me to afford. To live according to nature, is to act always with due regard to the fitness arising from the relations and qualities of causes and effects; to concur with the great and unchangeable scheme of universal felicity; to cooperate with the general disposition and tendency of the present system of things."

The prince soon found that this was one of the sages whom he should understand less as he heard him longer. He therefore bowed and was silent; and the philosopher, supposing him satisfied, and the rest vanquished, rose up and departed with the air of a man that had co-operated with the present system.[6]

* * *

Chapter 26. The Princess Continues Her Remarks upon Private Life

Nekayah, perceiving her brother's attention fixed, proceeded in her narrative.

"In families where there is or is not poverty, there is commonly discord. If a kingdom be, as Imlac tells us, a great family, a family likewise is a little kingdom, torn with factions and exposed to revolutions. An unpracticed observer expects the love of parents and children to be constant and equal; but this kindness seldom continues beyond the years of infancy: in a short time the children become rivals to their parents. Benefits are allayed[7] by reproaches, and gratitude debased by envy.

"Parents and children seldom act in concert; each child endeavors to appropriate the esteem or fondness of the parents, and the parents, with yet less temptation, betray each other to their children. Thus, some place their confidence in the father, and some in the mother, and by degrees the house is filled with artifices and feuds.

"The opinions of children and parents, of the young and the old, are naturally opposite, by the contrary effects of hope and despondence, of expectation and experience, without crime or folly on either side. The colors of life in youth and age appear different, as the face of nature in spring and winter. And how can children credit the assertions of parents, which their own eyes show them to be false?

"Few parents act in such a manner as much to enforce their maxims by the credit of their lives. The old man trusts wholly to slow contrivance and gradual progression; the youth expects to force his way by genius, vigor, and precipitance. The old man pays regard to riches, and the youth reverences virtue. The old man deifies prudence; the youth commits himself to magnanimity and chance. The young man, who intends no ill, believes that none is intended, and therefore acts with openness and candor; but his father, having suffered the injuries of fraud, is impelled to suspect, and too often allured to practice it. Age looks with anger on the temerity of youth, and youth with contempt on the scrupulosity[8] of age. Thus parents and children, for the greatest part, live on to love less and less; and, if those whom nature has thus closely united are the torments of each other, where shall we look for tenderness and consolation?"

"Surely," said the prince, "you must have been unfortunate in your choice of acquaintance: I am unwilling to believe that the most tender of all relations is thus impeded in its effects by natural necessity."

"Domestic discord," answered she, "is not inevitably and fatally necessary, but yet is not easily avoided. We seldom see that a whole family is virtuous; the good and evil cannot well agree, and the evil can yet less agree with one another. Even the virtuous fall sometimes to variance, when their virtues are

---

6. In chapters 23–25, Rasselas examines court life; and Nekayah, domestic life. She reports her findings to him.
7. To allay is "to join any thing to another, so as

to abate its predominant qualities" (Johnson's *Dictionary*).
8. "Fear of acting in any manner" (Johnson's *Dictionary*).

of different kinds, and tending to extremes. In general, those parents have most reverence who most deserve it; for he that lives well cannot be despised.

"Many other evils infest private life. Some are the slaves of servants whom they have trusted with their affairs. Some are kept in continual anxiety to the caprice of rich relations, whom they cannot please, and dare not offend. Some husbands are imperious, and some wives perverse; and, as it is always more easy to do evil than good, though the wisdom or virtue of one can very rarely make many happy, the folly or vice of one may often make many miserable."

"If such be the general effect of marriage," said the prince, "I shall for the future think it dangerous to connect my interest with that of another, lest I should be unhappy by my partner's fault."

"I have met," said the princess, "with many who live single for that reason; but I never found that their prudence ought to raise envy. They dream away their time without friendship, without fondness, and are driven to rid themselves of the day, for which they have no use, by childish amusements, or vicious delights. They act as beings under the constant sense of some known inferiority that fills their minds with rancor, and their tongues with censure. They are peevish at home, and malevolent abroad; and, as the outlaws of human nature, make it their business and their pleasure to disturb that society which debars them from its privileges. To live without feeling or exciting sympathy, to be fortunate without adding to the felicity of others, or afflicted without tasting the balm of pity, is a state more gloomy than solitude; it is not retreat but exclusion from mankind. Marriage has many pains, but celibacy has no pleasures."

"What then is to be done?" said Rasselas; "the more we inquire, the less we can resolve. Surely he is most likely to please himself that has no other inclination to regard."[9]

* * *

Chapter 29. *The Debate on Marriage Continued*

"The good of the whole," says Rasselas, "is the same with the good of all its parts. If marriage be best for mankind it must be evidently best for individuals, or a permanent and necessary duty must be the cause of evil, and some must be inevitably sacrificed to the convenience of others. In the estimate which you have made of the two states, it appears that the incommodities of a single life are, in a great measure, necessary and certain, but those of the conjugal state accidental and avoidable.

"I cannot forbear to flatter myself that prudence and benevolence will make marriage happy. The general folly of mankind is the cause of general complaint. What can be expected but disappointment and repentance from a choice made in the immaturity of youth, in the ardor of desire, without judgment, without foresight, without inquiry after conformity of opinions, similarity of manners, rectitude of judgment, or purity of sentiment.

"Such is the common process of marriage. A youth and maiden meeting by chance, or brought together by artifice, exchange glances, reciprocate civilities, go home, and dream of one another. Having little to divert atten-

---

9. In chapters 27–29, Rasselas reports on the unhappiness of court life, and he and Nekayah debate whether marriage leads to happiness or misery.

tion, or diversify thought, they find themselves uneasy when they are apart, and therefore conclude that they shall be happy together. They marry, and discover what nothing but voluntary blindness had before concealed; they wear out life in altercations, and charge nature with cruelty.

"From those early marriages proceeds likewise the rivalry of parents and children: the son is eager to enjoy the world before the father is willing to forsake it, and there is hardly room at once for two generations. The daughter begins to bloom before the mother can be content to fade, and neither can forbear to wish for the absence of the other.

"Surely all these evils may be avoided by that deliberation and delay which prudence prescribes to irrevocable choice. In the variety and jollity of youthful pleasures life may be well enough supported without the help of a partner. Longer time will increase experience, and wider views will allow better opportunities of inquiry and selection: one advantage, at least, will be certain; the parents will be visibly older than their children."

"What reason cannot collect," said Nekayah, "and what experiment has not yet taught, can be known only from the report of others. I have been told that late marriages are not eminently happy. This is a question too important to be neglected, and I have often proposed it to those, whose accuracy of remark, and comprehensiveness of knowledge, made their suffrages[1] worthy of regard. They have generally determined that it is dangerous for a man and woman to suspend their fate upon each other, at a time when opinions are fixed, and habits are established; when friendships have been contracted on both sides, when life has been planned into method, and the mind has long enjoyed the contemplation of its own prospects.

"It is scarcely possible that two traveling through the world under the conduct of chance should have been both directed to the same path, and it will not often happen that either will quit the track which custom has made pleasing. When the desultory levity of youth has settled into regularity, it is soon succeeded by pride ashamed to yield, or obstinacy delighting to contend. And even though mutual esteem produces mutual desire to please, time itself, as it modifies unchangeably the external mien, determines likewise the direction of the passions, and gives an inflexible rigidity to the manners. Long customs are not easily broken: he that attempts to change the course of his own life very often labors in vain; and how shall we do that for others which we are seldom able to do for ourselves?"

"But surely," interposed the prince, "you suppose the chief motive of choice forgotten or neglected. Whenever I shall seek a wife, it shall be my first question, whether she be willing to be led by reason?"

"Thus it is," said Nekayah, "that philosophers are deceived. There are a thousand familiar[2] disputes which reason never can decide; questions that elude investigation, and make logic ridiculous; cases where something must be done, and where little can be said. Consider the state of mankind, and inquire how few can be supposed to act upon any occasions, whether small or great, with all the reasons of action present to their minds. Wretched would be the pair above all names of wretchedness, who should be doomed to adjust by reason every morning all the minute detail of a domestic day.

"Those who marry at an advanced age will probably escape the encroach-

1. Opinions.   2. Domestic.

ments of their children; but, in diminution of this advantage, they will be likely to leave them, ignorant and helpless, to a guardian's mercy: or, if that should not happen, they must at least go out of the world before they see those whom they love best either wise or great.

"From their children, if they have less to fear, they have less also to hope, and they lose, without equivalent, the joys of early love, and the convenience of uniting with manners pliant and minds susceptible of new impressions, which might wear away their dissimilitudes by long cohabitation, as soft bodies, by continual attrition, conform their surfaces to each other.

"I believe it will be found that those who marry late are best pleased with their children, and those who marry early with their partners."

"The union of these two affections," said Rasselas, "would produce all that could be wished. Perhaps there is a time when marriage might unite them, a time neither too early for the father, nor too late for the husband."

"Every hour," answered the princess, "confirms my prejudice in favor of the position so often uttered by the mouth of Imlac, 'That nature sets her gifts on the right hand and on the left.' Those conditions, which flatter hope and attract desire, are so constituted that, as we approach one, we recede from another. There are goods so opposed that we cannot seize both, but, by too much prudence, may pass between them at too great a distance to reach either. This is often the fate of long consideration; he does nothing who endeavors to do more than is allowed to humanity. Flatter not yourself with contrarieties of pleasure. Of the blessings set before you make your choice, and be content. No man can taste the fruits of autumn, while he is delighting his scent with the flowers of the spring: no man can, at the same time, fill his cup from the source and from the mouth of the Nile."[3]

* * *

Chapter 31. They Visit the Pyramids

The resolution being thus taken, they set out the next day. They laid tents upon their camels, being resolved to stay among the pyramids till their curiosity was fully satisfied. They traveled gently, turned aside to everything remarkable, stopped from time to time and conversed with the inhabitants, and observed the various appearances of towns ruined and inhabited, of wild and cultivated nature.

When they came to the great pyramid, they were astonished at the extent of the base, and the height of the top. Imlac explained to them the principles upon which the pyramidal form was chosen for a fabric intended to coextend its duration with that of the world; he showed that its gradual diminution gave it such stability as defeated all the common attacks of the elements, and could scarcely be overthrown by earthquakes themselves, the least resistible of natural violence. A concussion that should shatter the pyramid would threaten the dissolution of the continent.

They measured all its dimensions, and pitched their tents at its foot. Next day they prepared to enter its interior apartments, and having hired the common guides, climbed up to the first passage, when the favorite of the princess, looking into the cavity, stepped back and trembled. "Pekuah," said the prin-

---

3. In chapter 30, Imlac proposes a visit to the pyramids.

cess, "of what art thou afraid?" "Of the narrow entrance," answered the lady, "and of the dreadful gloom. I dare not enter a place which must surely be inhabited by unquiet souls. The original possessors of these dreadful vaults will start up before us, and perhaps shut us in forever." She spoke, and threw her arms round the neck of her mistress.

"If all your fear be of apparitions," said the prince, "I will promise you safety. There is no danger from the dead; he that is once buried will be seen no more."

"That the dead are seen no more," said Imlac, "I will not undertake to maintain, against the concurrent and unvaried testimony of all ages, and of all nations. There is no people, rude or learned, among whom apparitions of the dead are not related and believed. This opinion, which perhaps prevails as far as human nature is diffused, could become universal only by its truth; those that never heard of one another would not have agreed in a tale which nothing but experience can make credible. That it is doubted by single cavilers can very little weaken the general evidence; and some who deny it with their tongues confess it by their fears.

"Yet I do not mean to add new terrors to those which have already seized upon Pekuah. There can be no reason why specters should haunt the pyramid more than other places, or why they should have power or will to hurt innocence and purity. Our entrance is no violation of their privileges; we can take nothing from them, how then can we offend them?"

"My dear Pekuah," said the princess, "I will always go before you, and Imlac shall follow you. Remember that you are the companion of the princess of Abyssinia."

"If the princess is pleased that her servant should die," returned the lady, "let her command some death less dreadful than enclosure in this horrid cavern. You know I dare not disobey you; I must go if you command me, but if I once enter, I never shall come back."

The princess saw that her fear was too strong for expostulation or reproof, and, embracing her, told her that she should stay in the tent till their return. Pekuah was yet not satisfied, but entreated the princess not to pursue so dreadful a purpose as that of entering the recesses of the pyramid. "Though I cannot teach courage," said Nekayah, "I must not learn cowardice, nor leave at last undone what I came hither only to do."

Chapter 32. *They Enter the Pyramid*

Pekuah descended to the tents, and the rest entered the pyramid. They passed through the galleries, surveyed the vaults of marble, and examined the chest in which the body of the founder is supposed to have been reposited. They then sat down in one of the most spacious chambers to rest a while before they attempted to return.

"We have now," said Imlac, "gratified our minds with an exact view of the greatest work of man, except the wall of China.

"Of the wall it is very easy to assign the motive. It secured a wealthy and timorous nation from the incursions of barbarians, whose unskillfulness in arts made it easier for them to supply their wants by rapine than by industry, and who from time to time poured in upon the habitations of peaceful commerce, as vultures descend upon domestic fowl. Their celerity and fierceness made the wall necessary, and their ignorance made it efficacious.

"But for the pyramids, no reason has ever been given adequate to the cost and labor of the work. The narrowness of the chambers proves that it could afford no retreat from enemies, and treasures might have been reposited at far less expense with equal security. It seems to have been erected only in compliance with that hunger of imagination which preys incessantly upon life, and must be always appeased by some employment. Those who have already all that they can enjoy must enlarge their desires. He that has built for use till use is supplied, must begin to build for vanity, and extend his plan to the utmost power of human performance, that he may not be soon reduced to form another wish.

"I consider this mighty structure as a monument of the insufficiency of human enjoyments. A king, whose power is unlimited, and whose treasures surmount all real and imaginary wants, is compelled to solace, by the erection of a pyramid, the satiety of dominion and tastelessness of pleasures, and to amuse the tediousness of declining life by seeing thousands laboring without end, and one stone, for no purpose, laid upon another. Whoever thou art, that, not content with a moderate condition, imaginest happiness in royal magnificence, and dreamest that command or riches can feed the appetite of novelty with perpetual gratifications, survey the pyramids, and confess thy folly!"[4]

* * *

Chapter 40. The History of a Man of Learning

They returned to Cairo, and were so well pleased at finding themselves together, that none of them went much abroad. The prince began to love learning, and one day declared to Imlac, that he intended to devote himself to science,[5] and pass the rest of his days in literary solitude.

"Before you make your final choice," answered Imlac, "you ought to examine its hazards, and converse with some of those who are grown old in the company of themselves. I have just left the observatory of one of the most learned astronomers in the world, who has spent forty years in unwearied attention to the motions and appearances of the celestial bodies, and has drawn out his soul in endless calculations. He admits a few friends once a month to hear his deductions and enjoy his discoveries. I was introduced as a man of knowledge worthy of his notice. Men of various ideas and fluent conversation are commonly welcome to those whose thoughts have been long fixed upon a single point, and who find the images of other things stealing away. I delighted him with my remarks, he smiled at the narrative of my travels, and was glad to forget the constellations, and descend for a moment into the lower world.

"On the next day of vacation I renewed my visit, and was so fortunate as to please him again. He relaxed from that time the severity of his rule, and permitted me to enter at my own choice. I found him always busy, and always glad to be relieved. As each knew much which the other was desirous of

---

4. In chapters 33–39, Pekuah—while her friends are in the pyramid—is abducted by a troop of Arabs. The chief is tempted to keep her, but even-tually accepts a ransom and returns her unharmed.
5. Knowledge.

learning, we exchanged our notions with great delight. I perceived that I had every day more of his confidence, and always found new cause of admiration in the profundity of his mind. His comprehension is vast, his memory capacious and retentive, his discourse is methodical, and his expression clear.

"His integrity and benevolence are equal to his learning. His deepest researches and most favorite studies are willingly interrupted for any opportunity of doing good by his counsel or his riches. To his closest retreat, at his most busy moments, all are admitted that want his assistance: 'For though I exclude idleness and pleasure, I will never,' says he, 'bar my doors against charity. To man is permitted the contemplation of the skies, but the practice of virtue is commanded.' "

"Surely," said the princess, "this man is happy."

"I visited him," said Imlac, "with more and more frequency, and was every time more enamored of his conversation: he was sublime without haughtiness, courteous without formality, and communicative without ostentation. I was at first, great princess, of your opinion, thought him the happiest of mankind, and often congratulated him on the blessing that he enjoyed. He seemed to hear nothing with indifference but the praises of his condition, to which he always returned a general answer, and diverted the conversation to some other topic.

"Amidst this willingness to be pleased, and labor to please, I had quickly reason to imagine that some painful sentiment pressed upon his mind. He often looked up earnestly towards the sun, and let his voice fall in the midst of his discourse. He would sometimes, when we were alone, gaze upon me in silence with the air of a man who longed to speak what he was yet resolved to suppress. He would often send for me with vehement injunctions of haste, though, when I came to him, he had nothing extraordinary to say. And sometimes, when I was leaving him, he would call me back, pause a few moments and then dismiss me.

Chapter 41. The Astronomer Discovers[6] the Cause of his Uneasiness

"At last the time came when the secret burst his reserve. We were sitting together last night in the turret of his house, watching the emersion of a satellite of Jupiter. A sudden tempest clouded the sky, and disappointed our observation. We sat a while silent in the dark, and then he addressed himself to me in these words: 'Imlac, I have long considered thy friendship as the greatest blessing of my life. Integrity without knowledge is weak and useless, and knowledge without integrity is dangerous and dreadful. I have found in thee all the qualities requisite for trust, benevolence, experience, and fortitude. I have long discharged an office which I must soon quit at the call of nature, and shall rejoice in the hour of imbecility[7] and pain to devolve it upon thee.'

"I thought myself honored by this testimony, and protested that whatever could conduce to his happiness would add likewise to mine.

" 'Hear, Imlac, what thou wilt not without difficulty credit. I have possessed for five years the regulation of weather, and the distribution of the seasons: the sun has listened to my dictates, and passed from tropic to tropic

6. Reveals. 7. Feebleness.

by my direction; the clouds, at my call, have poured their waters, and the Nile has overflowed at my command; I have restrained the rage of the dogstar, and mitigated the fervors of the crab.[8] The winds alone, of all the elemental powers, have hitherto refused my authority, and multitudes have perished by equinoctial tempests which I found myself unable to prohibit or restrain. I have administered this great office with exact justice, and made to the different nations of the earth an impartial dividend of rain and sunshine. What must have been the misery of half the globe, if I had limited the clouds to particular regions, or confined the sun to either side of the equator?'

Chapter 42. The Opinion of the Astronomer Is Explained and Justified

"I suppose he discovered in me, through the obscurity of the room, some tokens of amazement and doubt, for, after a short pause, he proceeded thus:

" 'Not to be easily credited will neither surprise nor offend me; for I am, probably, the first of human beings to whom this trust has been imparted. Nor do I know whether to deem this distinction a reward or punishment; since I have possessed it I have been far less happy than before, and nothing but the consciousness of good intention could have enabled me to support the weariness of unremitted vigilance.'

" 'How long, Sir', said I, 'has this great office been in your hands?'

" 'About ten years ago,' said he, 'my daily observations of the changes of the sky led me to consider, whether, if I had the power of the seasons, I could confer greater plenty upon the inhabitants of the earth. This contemplation fastened on my mind, and I sat days and nights in imaginary dominion, pouring upon this country and that the showers of fertility, and seconding every fall of rain with a due proportion of sunshine. I had yet only the will to do good, and did not imagine that I should ever have the power.

" 'One day as I was looking on the fields withering with heat, I felt in my mind a sudden wish that I could send rain on the southern mountains, and raise the Nile to an inundation. In the hurry of my imagination I commanded rain to fall, and, by comparing the time of my command, with that of the inundation, I found that the clouds had listened to my lips.'

" 'Might not some other cause,' said I, 'produce this concurrence? the Nile does not always rise on the same day.'

" 'Do not believe,' said he with impatience, 'that such objections could escape me: I reasoned long against my own conviction, and labored against truth with the utmost obstinacy. I sometimes suspected myself of madness, and should not have dared to impart this secret but to a man like you, capable of distinguishing the wonderful from the impossible, and the incredible from the false.'

" 'Why, Sir,' said I, 'do you call that incredible, which you know, or think you know, to be true?'

" 'Because,' said he, 'I cannot prove it by any external evidence; and I know too well the laws of demonstration to think that my conviction ought to influence another, who cannot, like me, be conscious of its force. I therefore

---

8. The fourth sign of the zodiac (Cancer). "The dogstar": Sirius was supposed to cause the heat ("dog days") of summer.

shall not attempt to gain credit by disputation. It is sufficient that I feel this power, that I have long possessed, and every day exerted it. But the life of man is short, the infirmities of age increase upon me, and the time will soon come when the regulator of the year must mingle with the dust. The care of appointing a successor has long disturbed me; the night and the day have been spent in comparisons of all the characters which have come to my knowledge, and I have yet found none so worthy as thyself.

Chapter 43. The Astronomer Leaves Imlac His Directions

" 'Hear therefore, what I shall impart, with attention, such as the welfare of a world requires. If the task of a king be considered as difficult, who has the care only of a few millions, to whom he cannot do much good or harm, what must be the anxiety of him, on whom depends the action of the elements, and the great gifts of light and heat!—Hear me therefore with attention.

" 'I have diligently considered the position of the earth and sun, and formed innumerable schemes in which I changed their situation. I have sometimes turned aside the axis of the earth, and sometimes varied the ecliptic of the sun: but I have found it impossible to make a disposition by which the world may be advantaged; what one region gains, another loses by any imaginable alteration, even without considering the distant parts of the solar system with which we are unacquainted. Do not, therefore, in thy administration of the year, indulge thy pride by innovation; do not please thyself with thinking that thou canst make thyself renowned to all future ages, by disordering the seasons. The memory of mischief is no desirable fame. Much less will it become thee to let kindness or interest prevail. Never rob other countries of rain to pour it on thine own. For us the Nile is sufficient.'

"I promised that when I possessed the power, I would use it with inflexible integrity, and he dismissed me, pressing my hand. 'My heart,' said he, 'will be now at rest, and my benevolence will no more destroy my quiet: I have found a man of wisdom and virtue, to whom I can cheerfully bequeath the inheritance of the sun.' "

The prince heard this narration with very serious regard, but the princess smiled, and Pekuah convulsed herself with laughter. "Ladies," said Imlac, "to mock the heaviest of human afflictions is neither charitable nor wise. Few can attain this man's knowledge, and few practice his virtues; but all may suffer his calamity. Of the uncertainties of our present state, the most dreadful and alarming is the uncertain continuance of reason."

The princess was recollected, and the favorite was abashed. Rasselas, more deeply affected, inquired of Imlac, whether he thought such maladies of the mind frequent, and how they were contracted.

Chapter 44. The Dangerous Prevalence[9] of Imagination

"Disorders of intellect," answered Imlac, "happen much more often than superficial observers will easily believe. Perhaps, if we speak with rigorous exactness, no human mind is in its right state. There is no man whose imag-

---

9. Predominance.

ination does not sometimes predominate over his reason, who can regulate his attention wholly by his will, and whose ideas will come and go at his command. No man will be found in whose mind airy notions do not sometimes tyrannize, and force him to hope or fear beyond the limits of sober probability. All power of fancy over reason is a degree of insanity; but while this power is such as we can control and repress, it is not visible to others, nor considered as any depravation of the mental faculties; it is not pronounced madness but when it comes ungovernable, and apparently influences speech or action.

"To indulge the power of fiction, and send imagination out upon the wing, is often the sport of those who delight too much in silent speculation. When we are alone we are not always busy; the labor of excogitation is too violent to last long; the ardor of inquiry will sometimes give way to idleness or satiety. He who has nothing external that can divert him must find pleasure in his own thoughts, and must conceive himself what he is not; for who is pleased with what he is? He then expatiates in boundless futurity, and culls from all imaginable conditions that which for the present moment he should most desire, amuses his desires with impossible enjoyments, and confers upon his pride unattainable dominion. The mind dances from scene to scene, unites all pleasures in all combinations, and riots in delights which nature and fortune, with all their bounty, cannot bestow.

"In time, some particular train of ideas fixes the attention; all other intellectual gratifications are rejected; the mind, in weariness or leisure, recurs constantly to the favorite conception, and feasts on the luscious falsehood, whenever she is offended with the bitterness of truth. By degrees the reign of fancy is confirmed; she grows first imperious, and in time despotic. Then fictions begin to operate as realities, false opinions fasten upon the mind, and life passes in dreams of rapture or of anguish.

"This, sir, is one of the dangers of solitude, which the hermit has confessed not always to promote goodness, and the astronomer's misery has proved to be not always propitious to wisdom."

"I will no more," said the favorite, "imagine myself the queen of Abyssinia. I have often spent the hours which the princess gave to my own disposal, in adjusting ceremonies and regulating the court; I have repressed the pride of the powerful, and granted the petitions of the poor; I have built new palaces in more happy situations, planted groves upon the tops of mountains, and have exulted in the beneficence of royalty, till, when the princess entered, I had almost forgotten to bow down before her."

"And I," said the princess, "will not allow myself any more to play the shepherdess in my waking dreams. I have often soothed my thoughts with the quiet and innocence of pastoral employments, till I have in my chamber heard the winds whistle, and the sheep bleat; sometimes freed the lamb entangled in the thicket, and sometimes with my crook encountered the wolf. I have a dress like that of the village maids, which I put on to help my imagination, and a pipe on which I play softly, and suppose myself followed by my flocks."

"I will confess," said the prince, "an indulgence of fantastic delight more dangerous than yours. I have frequently endeavored to image the possibility of a perfect government, by which all wrong should be restrained, all vice reformed, and all the subjects preserved in tranquility and innocence. This thought produced innumerable schemes of reformation, and dictated many useful regulations and salutary edicts. This has been the sport, and sometimes the labor, of my solitude; and I start, when I think with how little anguish I once supposed the death of my father and my brothers."

"Such," says Imlac, "are the effects of visionary schemes; when we first form them, we know them to be absurd, but familiarize them by degrees, and in time lose sight of their folly."

Chapter 45. *They Discourse with an Old Man*

The evening was now far past, and they rose to return home. As they walked along the bank of the Nile, delighted with the beams of the moon quivering on the water, they saw at a small distance an old man, whom the prince had often heard in the assembly of the sages. "Yonder," said he, "is one whose years have calmed his passions, but not clouded his reason. Let us close the disquisitions of the night by inquiring what are his sentiments of his own state, that we may know whether youth alone is to struggle with vexation, and whether any better hope remains for the latter part of life."

Here the sage approached and saluted them. They invited him to join their walk, and prattled a while, as acquaintance that had unexpectedly met one another. The old man was cheerful and talkative, and the way seemed short in his company. He was pleased to find himself not disregarded, accompanied them to their house, and, at the prince's request, entered with them. They placed him in the seat of honor, and set wine and conserves before him.

"Sir," said the princess, "an evening walk must give to a man of learning like you pleasures which ignorance and youth can hardly conceive. You know the qualities and the causes of all that you behold, the laws by which the river flows, the periods in which the planets perform their revolutions. Everything must supply you with contemplation, and renew the consciousness of your own dignity."

"Lady," answered he, "let the gay and the vigorous expect pleasure in their excursions; it is enough that age can obtain ease. To me the world has lost its novelty; I look round, and see what I remember to have seen in happier days. I rest against a tree, and consider that in the same shade I once disputed upon the annual overflow of the Nile with a friend who is now silent in the grave. I cast my eyes upward, fix them on the changing moon, and think with pain on the vicissitudes of life. I have ceased to take much delight in physical truth; for what have I to do with those things which I am soon to leave?"

"You may at least recreate[1] yourself," said Imlac, "with the recollection of an honorable and useful life, and enjoy the praise which all agree to give you."

"Praise," said the sage with a sigh, "is to an old man an empty sound. I have neither mother to be delighted with the reputation of her son, nor wife to partake the honors of her husband. I have outlived my friends and my rivals. Nothing is now of much importance; for I cannot extend my interest beyond myself. Youth is delighted with applause, because it is considered as the earnest of some future good, and because the prospect of life is far

---

1. Refresh.

extended; but to me, who am now declining to decrepitude, there is little to be feared from the malevolence of men, and yet less to be hoped from their affection or esteem. Something they may yet take away, but they can give me nothing. Riches would now be useless, and high employment would be pain. My retrospect of life recalls to my view many opportunities of good neglected, much time squandered upon trifles, and more lost in idleness and vacancy. I leave many great designs unattempted, and many great attempts unfinished. My mind is burthened with no heavy crime, and therefore I compose myself to tranquility; endeavor to abstract my thoughts from hopes and cares which, though reason knows them to be vain, still try to keep their old possession of the heart; expect,[2] with serene humility, that hour which nature cannot long delay; and hope to possess, in a better state, that happiness which here I could not find, and that virtue which here I have not attained."

He arose and went away, leaving his audience not much elated with the hope of long life. The prince consoled himself with remarking that it was not reasonable to be disappointed by this account; for age had never been considered as the season of felicity, and if it was possible to be easy in decline and weakness, it was likely that the days of vigor and alacrity might be happy; that the noon of life might be bright, if the evening could be calm.

The princess suspected that age was querulous and malignant, and delighted to repress the expectations of those who had newly entered the world. She had seen the possessors of estates look with envy on their heirs, and known many who enjoy pleasure no longer than they can confine it to themselves.

Pekuah conjectured that the man was older than he appeared, and was willing to impute his complaints to delirious dejection; or else supposed that he had been unfortunate, and was therefore discontented. "For nothing," said she, "is more common than to call our own condition the condition of life."

Imlac, who had no desire to see them depressed, smiled at the comforts which they could so readily procure to themselves, and remembered that, at the same age, he was equally confident of unmingled prosperity, and equally fertile of consolatory expedients. He forbore to force upon them unwelcome knowledge, which time itself would too soon impress. The princess and her lady retired; the madness of the astronomer hung upon their minds, and they desired Imlac to enter upon his office, and delay next morning the rising of the sun.[3]

* * *

Chapter 48. Imlac Discourses on the Nature of the Soul

"What reason," said the prince, "can be given, why the Egyptians should thus expensively preserve those carcasses which some nations consume with fire, others lay to mingle with the earth, and all agree to remove from their sight, as soon as decent rites can be performed?"

"The original of ancient customs," said Imlac, "is commonly unknown; for

2. Await.
3. In chapters 46 and 47, Nekayah, Pekuah, and Rasselas befriend the astronomer and gradually wean him from madness. In search of diversion, all of them visit the catacombs.

the practice often continues when the cause has ceased; and concerning superstitious ceremonies it is vain to conjecture; for what reason did not dictate reason cannot explain. I have long believed that the practice of embalming arose only from tenderness to the remains of relations or friends, and to this opinion I am more inclined, because it seems impossible that this care should have been general: had all the dead been embalmed, their repositories must in time have been more spacious than the dwellings of the living. I suppose only the rich or honorable were secured from corruption, and the rest left to the course of nature.

"But it is commonly supposed that the Egyptians believed the soul to live as long as the body continued undissolved, and therefore tried this method of eluding death."

"Could the wise Egyptians," said Nekayah, "think so grossly of the soul? If the soul could once survive its separation, what could it afterwards receive or suffer from the body?"

"The Egyptians would doubtless think erroneously," said the astronomer, "in the darkness of heathenism, and the first dawn of philosophy. The nature of the soul is still disputed amidst all our opportunities of clearer knowledge: some yet say, that it may be material, who, nevertheless, believe it to be immortal."

"Some," answered Imlac, "have indeed said that the soul is material, but I can scarcely believe that any man has thought it, who knew how to think; for all the conclusions of reason enforce the immateriality of mind, and all the notices of sense and investigations of science concur to prove the unconsciousness of matter.

"It was never supposed that cogitation is inherent in matter, or that every particle is a thinking being. Yet if any part of matter be devoid of thought, what part can we suppose to think? Matter can differ from matter only in form, density, bulk, motion, and direction of motion: to which of these, however varied or combined, can consciousness be annexed? To be round or square, to be solid or fluid, to be great or little, to be moved slowly or swiftly one way or another, are modes of material existence, all equally alien from the nature of cogitation. If matter be once without thought, it can only be made to think by some new modification, but all the modifications which it can admit are equally unconnected with cogitative powers."

"But the materialists," said the astronomer, "urge that matter may have qualities with which we are unacquainted."

"He who will determine," returned Imlac, "against that which he knows, because there may be something which he knows not; he that can set hypothetical possibility against acknowledged certainty, is not to be admitted among reasonable beings. All that we know of matter is, that matter is inert, senseless and lifeless; and if this conviction cannot be opposed but by referring us to something that we know not, we have all the evidence that human intellect can admit. If that which is known may be overruled by that which is unknown, no being, not omniscient, can arrive at certainty."

"Yet let us not," said the astronomer, "too arrogantly limit the Creator's power."

"It is no limitation of omnipotence," replied the poet, "to suppose that one thing is not consistent with another, that the same proposition cannot be at once true and false, that the same number cannot be even and odd, that cogitation cannot be conferred on that which is created incapable of cogitation."

"I know not," said Nekayah, "any great use of this question. Does that immateriality, which, in my opinion, you have sufficiently proved, necessarily include eternal duration?"

"Of immateriality," said Imlac, "our ideas are negative, and therefore obscure. Immateriality seems to imply a natural power of perpetual duration as a consequence of exemption from all causes of decay: whatever perishes, is destroyed by the solution of its contexture,[4] and separation of its parts; nor can we conceive how that which has no parts, and therefore admits no solution, can be naturally corrupted or impaired."

"I know not," said Rasselas, "how to conceive anything without extension: what is extended must have parts, and you allow, that whatever has parts may be destroyed."

"Consider your own conceptions," replied Imlac, "and the difficulty will be less. You will find substance without extension. An ideal form is no less real than material bulk: yet an ideal form has no extension. It is no less certain, when you think on a pyramid, that your mind possesses the idea of a pyramid, than that the pyramid itself is standing. What space does the idea of a pyramid occupy more than the idea of a grain of corn? or how can either idea suffer laceration? As is the effect such is the cause; as thought is, such is the power that thinks; a power impassive and indiscerptible."[5]

"But the Being," said Nekayah, "whom I fear to name, the Being which made the soul, can destroy it."

"He, surely, can destroy it," answered Imlac, "since, however unperishable, it receives from a superior nature its power of duration. That it will not perish by any inherent cause of decay, or principle of corruption, may be shown by philosophy; but philosophy can tell no more. That it will not be annihilated by him that made it, we must humbly learn from higher authority."

The whole assembly stood a while silent and collected. "Let us return," said Rasselas, "from this scene of mortality. How gloomy would be these mansions of the dead to him who did not know that he shall never die; that what now acts shall continue its agency, and what now thinks shall think on for ever. Those that lie here stretched before us, the wise and the powerful of ancient times, warn us to remember the shortness of our present state: they were, perhaps, snatched away while they were busy, like us, in the choice of life."

"To me," said the princess, "the choice of life is become less important; I hope hereafter to think only on the choice of eternity."

They then hastened out of the caverns, and, under the protection of their guard, returned to Cairo.

Chapter 49. The Conclusion, in Which Nothing Is Concluded

It was now the time of the inundation of the Nile: a few days after their visit to the catacombs, the river began to rise.

They were confined to their house. The whole region being under water gave them no invitation to any excursions, and being well supplied with mate-

---

4. Dissolution of its structure. 5. Not to be separated.

rials for talk, they diverted themselves with comparisons of the different forms of life which they had observed, and with various schemes of happiness which each of them had formed.

Pekuah was never so much charmed with any place as the convent of St. Anthony, where the Arab restored her to the princess, and wished only to fill it with pious maidens, and to be made prioress of the order; she was weary of expectation and disgust,[6] and would gladly be fixed in some unvariable state.

The princess thought that, of all sublunary things, knowledge was the best: she desired first to learn all sciences, and then purposed to found a college of learned women, in which she would preside, that, by conversing with the old and educating the young, she might divide her time between the acquisition and communication of wisdom, and raise up for the next age models of prudence, and patterns of piety.

The prince desired a little kingdom, in which he might administer justice in his own person, and see all the parts of government with his own eyes; but he could never fix the limits of his dominion, and was always adding to the number of his subjects.

Imlac and the astronomer were contented to be driven along the stream of life, without directing their course to any particular port.

Of these wishes that they had formed, they well knew that none could be obtained. They deliberated a while what was to be done, and resolved, when the inundation should cease, to return to Abyssinia.[7]

1759

[A Brief to Free a Slave][1]

It must be agreed that in most ages many countries have had part of their inhabitants in a state of slavery; yet it may be doubted whether slavery can ever be supposed the natural condition of man. It is impossible not to conceive that men in their original state were equal; and very difficult to imagine how one would be subjected to another but by violent compulsion. An individual may, indeed, forfeit his liberty by a crime; but he cannot by that crime forfeit the liberty of his children. What is true of a criminal seems true likewise of a captive. A man may accept life from a conquering enemy on condition of perpetual servitude; but it is very doubtful whether he can entail[2] that servitude on his descendants; for no man can stipulate without commission for another. The condition which he himself accepts, his son or

6. Aversion.
7. Probably not, as is often suggested, to the Happy Valley, which the travelers earlier fled as a prison. Presumably the travelers return, with whatever wisdom they have gained but also with their cherished illusions, to share the common destiny of humankind.
1. Samuel Johnson detested slavery and the owners of slaves. Once, "in company with some very grave men at Oxford, his toast was, 'Here's to the next insurrection of the Negroes in the West Indies,'" and in his pamphlet *Taxation No Tyranny*

(1775), he put the American rebels down with a devastating question: "How is it that we hear the loudest yelps for liberty among the drivers of Negroes?" Although slavery had been abolished in England in 1772, serfdom still existed in Scotland, and the British remained heavily involved in the slave trade. In 1777 a black slave, Joseph Knight, sued for freedom from the Scottish master he had escaped. On his behalf Johnson dictated this argument to Boswell.
2. Settle unalterably.

grandson perhaps would have rejected. If we should admit, what perhaps may with more reason be denied, that there are certain relations between man and man which may make slavery necessary and just,[3] yet it can never be proved that he who is now suing for his freedom ever stood in any of those relations. He is certainly subject by no law, but that of violence, to his present master,[4] who pretends no claim to his obedience, but that he bought him from a merchant of slaves, whose right to sell him never was examined. It is said that, according to the constitutions of Jamaica, he was legally enslaved; these constitutions are merely positive;[5] and apparently injurious to the rights of mankind, because whoever is exposed to sale is condemned to slavery without appeal; by whatever fraud or violence he might have been originally brought into the merchant's power. In our own time princes have been sold, by wretches to whose care they were entrusted, that they might have an European education; but when once they were brought to a market in the plantations, little would avail either their dignity or their wrongs. The laws of Jamaica afford a Negro no redress. His color is considered as a sufficient testimony against him. It is to be lamented that moral right should ever give way to political convenience. But if temptations of interest are sometimes too strong for human virtue, let us at least retain a virtue where there is no temptation to quit it. In the present case there is apparent right on one side, and no convenience on the other. Inhabitants of this island can neither gain riches nor power by taking away the liberty of any part of the human species. The sum of the argument is this:—No man is by nature the property of another: The defendant is, therefore, by nature free: The rights of nature must be some way forfeited before they can be justly taken away: That the defendant has by any act forfeited the rights of nature we require to be proved; and if no proof of such forfeiture can be given, we doubt not but the justice of the court will declare him free.[6]

1777   1792

Rambler No. 4

[ON FICTION]

Saturday, *March* 31, 1750

Simul et jucunda et idonea dicere vitae.
—HORACE, *Art of Poetry*, 334
And join both profit and delight in one.
—CREECH

The works of fiction with which the present generation seems more particularly delighted are such as exhibit life in its true state, diversified only by accidents that daily happen in the world, and influenced by passions and qualities which are really to be found in conversing with mankind.

This kind of writing may be termed, not improperly, the comedy of

---

3. Boswell, who strongly disagreed with Johnson's "prejudice" against slavery, argued that "to abolish a *status*, which in all ages GOD has sanctioned, and man has continued, would not only be *robbery* to an innumerable class of our fellow subjects; but it would be extreme cruelty to the African savages."
4. Knight had been kidnapped as a child.
5. Arbitrarily instituted (opposed to *natural* laws).
6. Knight was set free by the Scottish court.

romance, and is to be conducted nearly by the rules of comic poetry. Its province is to bring about natural events by easy means, and to keep up curiosity without the help of wonder: it is therefore precluded from the machines[1] and expedients of the heroic romance, and can neither employ giants to snatch away a lady from the nuptial rites, nor knights to bring her back from captivity; it can neither bewilder its personages in deserts, nor lodge them in imaginary castles.

I remember a remark made by Scaliger upon Pontanus,[2] that all his writings are filled with the same images; and that if you take from him his lilies and his roses, his satyrs and his dryads, he will have nothing left that can be called poetry. In like manner, almost all the fictions of the last age will vanish if you deprive them of a hermit and a wood, a battle and a shipwreck.

Why this wild strain of imagination found reception so long in polite and learned ages, it is not easy to conceive; but we cannot wonder that while readers could be procured, the authors were willing to continue it; for when a man had by practice gained some fluency of language, he had no further care than to retire to his closet, let loose his invention, and heat his mind with incredibilities; a book was thus produced without fear of criticism, without the toil of study, without knowledge of nature, or acquaintance with life.

The task of our present writers is very different; it requires, together with that learning which is to be gained from books, that experience which can never be attained by solitary diligence, but must arise from general converse and accurate observation of the living world. Their performances have, as Horace expresses it, *plus oneris quanto veniae minus,*[3] little indulgence, and therefore more difficulty. They are engaged in portraits of which everyone knows the original, and can detect any deviation from exactness of resemblance. Other writings are safe, except from the malice of learning, but these are in danger from every common reader; as the slipper ill executed was censured by a shoemaker who happened to stop in his way at the Venus of Apelles.[4]

But the fear of not being approved as just copiers of human manners is not the most important concern that an author of this sort ought to have before him. These books are written chiefly to the young, the ignorant, and the idle, to whom they serve as lectures of conduct, and introductions into life. They are the entertainment of minds unfurnished with ideas, and therefore easily susceptible of impressions; not fixed by principles, and therefore easily following the current of fancy; not informed by experience, and consequently open to every false suggestion and partial account.

That the highest degree of reverence should be paid to youth, and that nothing indecent should be suffered to approach their eyes or ears, are precepts extorted by sense and virtue from an ancient writer by no means eminent for chastity of thought.[5] The same kind, though not the same degree, of caution, is required in everything which is laid before them, to secure

---

1. The technical term in neoclassical critical theory for the supernatural agents who intervene in human affairs in epic and tragedy.
2. Julius Caesar Scaliger (1484–1558) criticized the Latin poems of the Italian poet Jovianus Pontanus (1426–1503).
3. *Epistles* 2.1.170.
4. According to Pliny the Younger (*Naturalis His-*

toria 35.85), the Greek painter Apelles of Kos (4th century B.C.E.) corrected the drawing of a sandal after hearing a shoemaker criticize it as faulty, but when the flattered artisan dared to find fault with the drawing of a leg, the artist bade him "stick to his last."
5. Juvenal's *Satires* 14.1–58.

them from unjust prejudices, perverse opinions, and incongruous combinations of images.

In the romances formerly written, every transaction and sentiment was so remote from all that passes among men that the reader was in very little danger of making any applications to himself; the virtues and crimes were equally beyond his sphere of activity; and he amused himself with heroes and with traitors, deliverers and persecutors, as with beings of another species, whose actions were regulated upon motives of their own, and who had neither faults nor excellencies in common with himself.

But when an adventurer is leveled with the rest of the world, and acts in such scenes of the universal drama as may be the lot of any other man, young spectators fix their eyes upon him with closer attention, and hope, by observing his behavior and success, to regulate their own practices when they shall be engaged in the like part.

For this reason these familiar histories may perhaps be made of greater use than the solemnities of professed morality, and convey the knowledge of vice and virtue with more efficacy than axioms and definitions. But if the power of example is so great as to take possession of the memory by a kind of violence, and produce effects almost without the intervention of the will, care ought to be taken that when the choice is unrestrained, the best examples only should be exhibited; and that which is likely to operate so strongly should not be mischievous or uncertain in its effects.

The chief advantage which these fictions have over real life is that their authors are at liberty, though not to invent, yet to select objects, and to cull from the mass of mankind those individuals upon which the attention ought most to be employed; as a diamond, though it cannot be made, may be polished by art, and placed in such situation as to display that luster which before was buried among common stones.

It is justly considered as the greatest excellency of art to imitate nature; but it is necessary to distinguish those parts of nature which are most proper for imitation: greater care is still required in representing life, which is so often discolored by passion or deformed by wickedness. If the world be promiscuously[6] described, I cannot see of what use it can be to read the account; or why it may not be as safe to turn the eye immediately upon mankind as upon a mirror which shows all that presents itself without discrimination.

It is therefore not a sufficient vindication of a character that it is drawn as it appears, for many characters ought never to be drawn; nor of a narrative that the train of events is agreeable to observation and experience, for that observation which is called knowledge of the world will be found much more frequently to make men cunning than good. The purpose of these writings is surely not only to show mankind, but to provide that they may be seen hereafter with less hazard; to teach the means of avoiding the snares which are laid by Treachery for Innocence, without infusing any wish for that superiority with which the betrayer flatters his vanity; to give the power of counteracting fraud without the temptation to practice it; to initiate youth by mock encounters in the art of necessary defense, and to increase prudence without impairing virtue.

Many writers, for the sake of following nature, so mingle good and bad

6. Indiscriminately.

qualities in their principal personages that they are both equally conspicuous; and as we accompany them through their adventures with delight, and are led by degrees to interest ourselves in their favor, we lose the abhorrence of their faults because they do not hinder our pleasure, or perhaps regard them with some kindness for being united with so much merit.

There have been men indeed splendidly wicked, whose endowments threw a brightness on their crimes, and whom scarce any villainy made perfectly detestable because they never could be wholly divested of their excellencies; but such have been in all ages the great corrupters of the world, and their resemblance ought no more to be preserved than the art of murdering without pain.

Some have advanced, without due attention to the consequences of this notion, that certain virtues have their correspondent faults, and therefore that to exhibit either apart is to deviate from probability. Thus men are observed by Swift to be "grateful in the same degree as they are resentful." This principle, with others of the same kind, supposes man to act from a brute impulse, and pursue a certain degree of inclination without any choice of the object; for, otherwise, though it should be allowed that gratitude and resentment arise from the same constitution of the passions, it follows not that they will be equally indulged when reason is consulted; yet, unless that consequence be admitted, this sagacious maxim becomes an empty sound, without any relation to practice or to life.

Nor is it evident that even the first motions to these effects are always in the same proportion. For pride, which produces quickness of resentment, will obstruct gratitude by unwillingness to admit that inferiority which obligation implies; and it is very unlikely that he who cannot think he receives a favor will acknowledge or repay it.

It is of the utmost importance to mankind that positions of this tendency should be laid open and confuted; for while men consider good and evil as springing from the same root, they will spare the one for the sake of the other, and in judging, if not of others at least of themselves, will be apt to estimate their virtues by their vices. To this fatal error all those will contribute who confound the colors of right and wrong, and, instead of helping to settle their boundaries, mix them with so much art that no common mind is able to disunite them.

In narratives where historical veracity has no place, I cannot discover why there should not be exhibited the most perfect idea of virtue; of virtue not angelical, nor above probability (for what we cannot credit, we shall never imitate), but the highest and purest that humanity can reach, which, exercised in such trials as the various revolutions of things shall bring upon it, may, by conquering some calamities and enduring others, teach us what we may hope, and what we can perform. Vice (for vice is necessary to be shown) should always disgust; nor should the graces of gaiety, nor the dignity of courage, be so united with it as to reconcile it to the mind. Wherever it appears, it should raise hatred by the malignity of its practices, and contempt by the meanness of its stratagems: for while it is supported by either parts or spirit, it will be seldom heartily abhorred. The Roman tyrant was content to be hated if he was but feared;[7] and there are thousands of the readers of

---

7. The Emperor Tiberius (see Suetonius's *Lives of the Caesars*).

romances willing to be thought wicked if they may be allowed to be wits. It is therefore to be steadily inculcated that virtue is the highest proof of understanding, and the only solid basis of greatness; and that vice is the natural consequence of narrow thoughts; that it begins in mistake, and ends in ignominy.

Rambler No. 60

[BIOGRAPHY]

Saturday, *October* 13, 1750

—*Quid sit pulchrum, quid turpe, quid utile, quid non,*
Plenius ac melius Chrysippo et Crantore dicit.
—HORACE, *Epistles,* 1.2. 3–4

Whose works the beautiful and base contain,
Of vice and virtue more instructive rules,
Than all the sober sages of the schools.
—FRANCIS

All joy or sorrow for the happiness or calamities of others is produced by an act of the imagination, that realizes the event, however fictitious, or approximates it, however remote, by placing us, for a time, in the condition of him whose fortune we contemplate; so that we feel, while the deception lasts, whatever motions would be excited by the same good or evil happening to ourselves.

Our passions are therefore more strongly moved, in proportion as we can more readily adopt the pains or pleasure proposed to our minds, by recognizing them as once our own, or considering them as naturally incident to our state of life. It is not easy for the most artful writer to give us an interest in happiness or misery, which we think ourselves never likely to feel, and with which we have never yet been made acquainted. Histories of the downfall of kingdoms, and revolutions of empires, are read with great tranquility; the imperial tragedy pleases common auditors only by its pomp of ornament, and grandeur of ideas; and the man whose faculties have been engrossed by business, and whose heart never fluttered but at the rise or fall of stocks, wonders how the attention can be seized, or the affections agitated, by a tale of love.

Those parallel circumstances, and kindred images to which we readily conform our minds, are, above all other writings, to be found in narratives of the lives of particular persons; and therefore no species of writing seems more worthy of cultivation than biography, since none can be more delightful or more useful, none can more certainly enchain the heart by irresistible interest, or more widely diffuse instruction to every diversity of condition.

The general and rapid narratives of history, which involve a thousand fortunes in the business of a day, and complicate innumerable incidents in one great transaction, afford few lessons applicable to private life, which derives its comforts and its wretchedness from the right or wrong management of things, which nothing but their frequency makes considerable, *Parva si non fiunt quotidie*, says Pliny,[1] and which can have no place in those relations

---

1. Pliny the Younger's *Epistles* 3.1. Johnson translates the phrase in the preceding clause.

which never descend below the consultation of senates, the motions of armies, and the schemes of conspirators.

I have often thought that there has rarely passed a life of which a judicious and faithful narrative would not be useful. For, not only every man has in the mighty mass of the world great numbers in the same condition with himself, to whom his mistakes and miscarriages, escapes and expedients, would be of immediate and apparent use; but there is such an uniformity in the state of man, considered apart from adventitious and separable decorations and disguises, that there is scarce any possibility of good or ill, but is common to humankind. A great part of the time of those who are placed at the greatest distance by fortune, or by temper, must unavoidably pass in the same manner; and though, when the claims of nature are satisfied, caprice, and vanity, and accident, begin to produce discriminations and peculiarities, yet the eye is not very heedful or quick, which cannot discover the same causes still[2] terminating their influence in the same effects, though sometimes accelerated, sometimes retarded, or perplexed by multiplied combinations. We are all prompted by the same motives, all deceived by the same fallacies, all animated by hope, obstructed by danger, entangled by desire, and seduced by pleasure.

It is frequently objected to relations of particular lives, that they are not distinguished by any striking or wonderful vicissitudes. The scholar who passed his life among his books, the merchant who conducted only his own affairs, the priest whose sphere of action was not extended beyond that of his duty, are considered as no proper objects of public regard, however they might have excelled in their several stations, whatever might have been their learning, integrity, and piety. But this notion arises from false measures of excellence and dignity, and must be eradicated by considering, that in the esteem of uncorrupted reason, what is of most use is of most value.

It is, indeed, not improper to take honest advantages of prejudice, and to gain attention by a celebrated name; but the business of the biographer is often to pass slightly over those performances and incidents, which produce vulgar greatness, to lead the thoughts into domestic privacies, and display the minute details of daily life, where exterior appendages are cast aside, and men excel each other only by prudence and by virtue. The account of Thuanus[3] is, with great propriety, said by its author to have been written, that it might lay open to posterity the private and familiar character of that man, *cujus ingenium et candorem ex ipsius scriptis sunt olim semper miraturi,* whose candor and genius will to the end of time be by his writings preserved in admiration.

There are many invisible circumstances which, whether we read as inquirers after natural or moral knowledge, whether we intend to enlarge our science, or increase our virtue, are more important than public occurrences. Thus Sallust, the great master of nature, has not forgot, in his account of Catiline,[4] to remark that *his walk was now quick, and again slow,* as an indication of a mind revolving something with violent commotion. Thus the story of Melancthon[5] affords a striking lecture on the value of time, by informing

---

2. Always.
3. Jacques-Auguste de Thou (1553–1617), an important French historian, of whom Nicholas Rigault wrote a brief biography, a sentence of which Johnson quotes and translates below.

4. Sallust, a Roman historian of the 1st century B.C.E., wrote an account of Catiline's conspiracy against the Roman state.
5. Camerarius wrote a life of Melancthon, a German theologian of the 16th century.

us that when he made an appointment, he expected not only the hour, but the minute to be fixed, that the day might not run out in the idleness of suspense; and all the plans and enterprises of De Witt are now of less importance to the world, than that part of his personal character, which represents him as careful of his health, and negligent of his life.[6]

But biography has often been allotted to writers who seem very little acquainted with the nature of their task, or very negligent about the performance. They rarely afford any other account than might be collected from public papers, but imagine themselves writing a life when they exhibit a chronological series of actions or preferments; and so little regard the manners or behavior of their heroes, that more knowledge may be gained of a man's real character, by a short conversation with one of his servants, than from a formal and studied narrative, begun with his pedigree, and ended with his funeral.

If now and then they condescend to inform the world of particular facts, they are not always so happy as to select the most important. I know not well what advantage posterity can receive from the only circumstance by which Tickell has distinguished Addison from the rest of mankind, the irregularity of his pulse:[7] nor can I think myself overpaid for the time spent in reading the life of Malherbe, by being enabled to relate, after the learned biographer,[8] that Malherbe had two predominant opinions; one, that the looseness of a single woman might destroy all her boast of ancient descent; the other, that the French beggars made use very improperly and barbarously of the phrase *noble gentleman*, because either word included the sense of both.

There are, indeed, some natural reasons why these narratives are often written by such as were not likely to give much instruction or delight, and why most accounts of particular persons are barren and useless. If a life be delayed till interest and envy are at an end, we may hope for impartiality, but must expect little intelligence;[9] for the incidents which give excellence to biography are of a volatile and evanescent kind, such as soon escape the memory, and are rarely transmitted by tradition. We know how few can portray a living acquaintance, except by his most prominent and observable particularities, and the grosser features of his mind; and it may be easily imagined how much of this little knowledge may be lost in imparting it, and how soon a succession of copies will lose all resemblance of the original.

If the biographer writes from personal knowledge, and makes haste to gratify the public curiosity, there is danger lest his interest, his fear, his gratitude, or his tenderness, overpower his fidelity, and tempt him to conceal, if not to invent. There are many who think it an act of piety to hide the faults or failings of their friends, even when they can no longer suffer by their detection; we therefore see whole ranks of characters adorned with uniform panegyric, and not to be known from one another, but by extrinsic and casual circumstances. "Let me remember," says Hale, "when I find myself inclined to pity a criminal, that there is likewise a pity due to the country."[1] If we owe regard to the memory of the dead, there is yet more respect to be paid to knowledge, to virtue, and to truth.

---

6. Sir William Temple, characterizing the Dutch statesman John De Witt.
7. From Thomas Tickell's preface to Addison's *Works* (1721).
8. The life of the French poet François de Malherbe (1555–1628) was written by Honorat de Racan.
9. Information.
1. From Gilbert Burnet's *Life and Death of Sir Matthew Hale* (1682).

A Dictionary of the English Language

Before Johnson, no standard dictionary of the English language existed. The lack had troubled speakers of English for some time, both because Italian and French academies had produced major dictionaries of their own tongues and because, in the absence of any authority, English seemed likely to change utterly from one generation to another. Many eighteenth-century authors feared that their own language would soon become obsolete: as Alexander Pope wrote in *An Essay on Criticism*,

> Our sons their fathers' failing language see,
> And such as Chaucer is, shall Dryden be.

A dictionary could help retard such change, and commercially it would be a book that everyone would need to buy. In 1746 a group of London publishers commissioned Johnson, still an unknown author, to undertake the project. He hoped to finish it in three years; it took him nine. But the quantity and quality of work he accomplished, aided only by six part-time assistants, made him famous as "Dictionary Johnson." The *Dictionary* remained a standard reference book for one hundred years.

Johnson's achievement is notable in three respects: its size (forty thousand words), the wealth of illustrative quotations, and the excellence of the definitions. No earlier English dictionary rivaled the scope of Johnson's two large folio volumes. About 114,000 quotations, gathered from the best English writers from Sidney to the eighteenth century, exemplify the usage of words as well as their meanings. Above all, it was the definitions, however, that established the authority of Johnson's *Dictionary*. A small selection is only too likely to concentrate on a few amusing or notorious definitions, but the great majority are full, clear, and totally free from eccentricity. Indeed, many of them are still repeated in modern dictionaries. Language, Johnson knew, cannot be fixed once and for all; many of the words he defines have radically changed meaning since the eighteenth century. Yet Johnson did more than any person of his time to preserve the ideal of a standard English.

From A Dictionary of the English Language

From *Preface*

* * *

A large work is difficult because it is large, even though all its parts might singly be performed with facility; where there are many things to be done, each must be allowed its share of time and labor, in the proportion only which it bears to the whole; nor can it be expected that the stones which form the dome of a temple should be squared and polished like the diamond of a ring.

Of the event of this work, for which, having labored it with so much application, I cannot but have some degree of parental fondness, it is natural to form conjectures. Those who have been persuaded to think well of my design will require that it should fix our language, and put a stop to those alterations which time and chance have hitherto been suffered to make in it without opposition. With this consequence I will confess that I flattered myself for a while;[1] but now begin to fear that I have indulged expectation which neither

---

1. Johnson's *Plan* (1747) had called for "a dictionary by which the pronunciation of our language may be fixed, and its attainment facilitated; by which its purity may be preserved, its use ascertained, and its duration lengthened."

reason nor experience can justify. When we see men grow old and die at a certain time one after another, from century to century, we laugh at the elixir that promises to prolong life to a thousand years; and with equal justice may the lexicographer be derided, who being able to produce no example of a nation that has preserved their words and phrases from mutability, shall imagine that his dictionary can embalm his language and secure it from corruption and decay, that it is in his power to change sublunary nature, or clear the world at once from folly, vanity, and affectation.

With this hope, however, academies have been instituted, to guard the avenues of their languages, to retain fugitives, and repulse intruders; but their vigilance and activity have hitherto been vain; sounds are too volatile and subtle for legal restraints; to enchain syllables, and to lash the wind, are equally the undertakings of pride, unwilling to measure its desires by its strength. The French language has visibly changed under the inspection of the academy;[2] the style of Amelot's translation of father Paul is observed by Le Courayer to be *un peu passé*;[3] and no Italian will maintain that the diction of any modern writer is not perceptibly different from that of Boccace, Machiavel, or Caro.[4]

Total and sudden transformations of a language seldom happen; conquests and migrations are now very rare: but there are other causes of change, which, though slow in their operation, and invisible in their progress, are perhaps as much superior to human resistance as the revolutions of the sky, or intumescence[5] of the tide. Commerce, however necessary, however lucrative, as it depraves the manners, corrupts the language; they that have frequent intercourse with strangers, to whom they endeavor to accommodate themselves, must in time learn a mingled dialect, like the jargon which serves the traffickers[6] on the Mediterranean and Indian coasts. This will not always be confined to the exchange, the warehouse, or the port, but will be communicated by degrees to other ranks of the people, and be at last incorporated with the current speech.

There are likewise internal causes equally forcible. The language most likely to continue long without alteration would be that of a nation raised a little, and but a little, above barbarity, secluded from strangers, and totally employed in procuring the conveniencies of life; either without books, or, like some of the Mahometan countries, with very few: men thus busied and unlearned, having only such words as common use requires, would perhaps long continue to express the same notions by the same signs. But no such constancy can be expected in a people polished by arts, and classed by subordination, where one part of the community is sustained and accommodated by the labor of the other. Those who have much leisure to think, will always be enlarging the stock of ideas, and every increase of knowledge, whether real or fancied, will produce new words, or combinations of words. When the mind is unchained from necessity, it will range after convenience;

2. The French academy, founded to purify the French language, had produced a dictionary in 1694; but revisions were necessary within a few years.
3. A bit old-fashioned (French). Le Courayer's translation (1736) of Father Paolo Sarpi's *History of the Council of Trent* superseded Amelot's (1683).
4. Like Boccaccio (1313–1375) and Machiavelli (1469–1527), Annibale Caro (1507–1566) was a classic Italian stylist whose work had preceded the dictionary published in 1612 by the Italian academy.
5. Swelling.
6. Traders.

when it is left at large in the fields of speculation, it will shift opinions; as any custom is disused, the words that expressed it must perish with it; as any opinion grows popular, it will innovate speech in the same proportion as it alters practice.

As by the cultivation of various sciences, a language is amplified, it will be more furnished with words deflected from their original sense; the geometrician will talk of a courtier's zenith, or the eccentric virtue of a wild hero, and the physician of sanguine expectations and phlegmatic delays.[7] Copiousness of speech will give opportunities to capricious choice, by which some words will be preferred, and others degraded; vicissitudes of fashion will enforce the use of new, or extend the signification of known terms. The tropes[8] of poetry will make hourly encroachments, and the metaphorical will become the current sense: pronunciation will be varied by levity or ignorance, and the pen must at length comply with the tongue; illiterate writers will at one time or other, by public infatuation, rise into renown, who, not knowing the original import of words, will use them with colloquial licentiousness, confound distinction, and forget propriety. As politeness increases, some expressions will be considered as too gross and vulgar for the delicate, others as too formal and ceremonious for the gay and airy; new phrases are therefore adopted, which must, for the same reasons, be in time dismissed. Swift, in his petty treatise on the English language,[9] allows that new words must sometimes be introduced, but proposes that none should be suffered to become obsolete. But what makes a word obsolete, more than general agreement to forbear it? and how shall it be continued, when it conveys an offensive idea, or recalled again into the mouths of mankind, when it has once by disuse become unfamiliar, and by unfamiliarity unpleasing.

There is another cause of alteration more prevalent than any other, which yet in the present state of the world cannot be obviated. A mixture of two languages will produce a third distinct from both, and they will always be mixed, where the chief part of education, and the most conspicuous accomplishment, is skill in ancient or in foreign tongues. He that has long cultivated another language, will find its words and combinations crowd upon his memory; and haste or negligence, refinement or affectation, will obtrude borrowed terms and exotic expressions.

The great pest of speech is frequency of translation. No book was ever turned from one language into another, without imparting something of its native idiom; this is the most mischievous and comprehensive innovation; single words may enter by thousands, and the fabric of the tongue continue the same, but new phraseology changes much at once; it alters not the single stones of the building, but the order[1] of the columns. If an academy should be established for the cultivation of our style, which I, who can never wish to see dependence multiplied, hope the spirit of English liberty will hinder or destroy, let them, instead of compiling grammars and dictionaries, endeavor with all their influence to stop the license of translators, whose

---

7. "Sanguine" and "phlegmatic" once referred only to the physiological predominance of blood or phlegm. "Zenith" (the point of the sky directly overhead) and "eccentric" (deviating from the center) were originally astronomical and geometrical terms.

8. "A change of a word from its original signification" (Johnson's *Dictionary*).
9. *A Proposal for Correcting, Improving, and Ascertaining the English Tongue* (1712). "Petty": little.
1. Architectural mode (Doric, etc.), which determines the style and proportions of columns.

idleness and ignorance, if it be suffered to proceed, will reduce us to babble a dialect of France.

If the changes that we fear be thus irresistible, what remains but to acquiesce with silence, as in the other insurmountable distresses of humanity? It remains that we retard what we cannot repel, that we palliate what we cannot cure. Life may be lengthened by care, though death cannot be ultimately defeated: tongues, like governments, have a natural tendency to degeneration; we have long preserved our constitution, let us make some struggles for our language.

In hope of giving longevity to that which its own nature forbids to be immortal, I have devoted this book, the labor of years, to the honor of my country, that we may no longer yield the palm of philology without a contest to the nations of the continent. The chief glory of every people arises from its authors: whether I shall add anything by my own writings to the reputation of English literature, must be left to time. Much of my life has been lost under the pressures of disease; much has been trifled away; and much has always been spent in provision for the day that was passing over me; but I shall not think my employment useless or ignoble, if by my assistance foreign nations, and distant ages, gain access to the propagators of knowledge, and understand the teachers of truth; if my labors afford light to the repositories of science, and add celebrity to Bacon, to Hooker, to Milton, and to Boyle.[2]

When I am animated by this wish, I look with pleasure on my book, however defective; and deliver it to the world with the spirit of a man that has endeavored well. That it will immediately become popular I have not promised to myself: a few wild blunders and risible absurdities, from which no work of such multiplicity was ever free, may for a time furnish folly with laughter, and harden ignorance in contempt; but useful diligence will at last prevail, and there never can be wanting some who distinguish desert;[3] who will consider that no dictionary of a living tongue ever can be perfect, since while it is hastening to publication, some words are budding, and some falling away; that a whole life cannot be spent upon syntax and etymology, and that even a whole life would not be sufficient; that he, whose design includes whatever language can express, must often speak of what he does not understand; that a writer will sometimes be hurried by eagerness to the end, and sometimes faint with weariness under a task, which Scaliger compares to the labors of the anvil and the mine;[4] that what is obvious is not always known, and what is known is not always present; that sudden fits of inadvertency will surprise vigilance, slight avocations[5] will reduce attention, and casual eclipses of the mind will darken learning; and that the writer shall often in vain trace his memory at the moment of need, for that which yesterday he knew with intuitive readiness, and which will come uncalled into his thoughts tomorrow.

In this work, when it shall be found that much is omitted, let it not be forgotten that much likewise is performed; and though no book was ever spared out of tenderness to the author, and the world is little solicitous to

2. Leading physicist and chemist (1627–1691). "Science": knowledge. Richard Hooker wrote *The Laws of Ecclesiastical Polity* (1594–97), a famous defense of the Church of England.

3. Merit.

4. Joseph Justus Scaliger (1540–1609), a great scholar and lexicographer, wrote Latin verses suggesting that criminals should be condemned to lexicography.

5. Whatever calls one aside.

know whence proceeded the faults of that which it condemns; yet it may gratify curiosity to inform it, that the *English Dictionary* was written with little assistance of the learned, and without any patronage of the great;[6] not in the soft obscurities of retirement, or under the shelter of academic bowers, but amidst inconvenience and distraction, in sickness and in sorrow: and it may repress the triumph of malignant criticism to observe, that if our language is not here fully displayed, I have only failed in an attempt which no human powers have hitherto completed. If the lexicons of ancient tongues, now immutably fixed, and comprised in a few volumes, be yet, after the toil of successive ages, inadequate and delusive; if the aggregated knowledge and cooperating diligence of the Italian academicians did not secure them from the censure of Beni;[7] if the embodied critics of France, when fifty years had been spent upon their work, were obliged to change its economy,[8] and give their second edition another form, I may surely be contented without the praise of perfection, which, if I could obtain, in this gloom of solitude, what would it avail me? I have protracted my work till most of those whom I wished to please have sunk into the grave,[9] and success and miscarriage are empty sounds: I therefore dismiss it with frigid tranquility, having little to fear or hope from censure or from praise.

[SOME DEFINITIONS: A SMALL ANTHOLOGY][1]

ANTHO'LOGY. *n.*

1. A collection of flowers.

To CANT. *v.*

   To talk in the jargon of particular professions, or in any kind of formal affected language, or with a peculiar and studied tone of voice.

> Men *cant* endlessly about *materia forma*; and hunt chimeras by rules of art, or dress up ignorance in words of bulk or sound, which may stop up the mouth of inquiry.—*Glanville's Scepsis Scientifica.*

ENTHU'SIASM. *n.*

1. A vain belief of private revelation; a vain confidence of divine favor or communication.

> *Enthusiasm* is founded neither on reason nor divine revelation, but rises from the conceits of a warmed or overweening brain.—*Locke.*

GE'NIUS. *n.*

1. The protecting or ruling power of men, places, or things.

> And as I awake, sweet music breathe,
> Sent by some spirit to mortals good,
> Or th' unseen *genius* of the wood.—*Milton.*

2. A man endowed with superior faculties.

3. Mental power or faculties.

4. Disposition of nature by which anyone is qualified for some peculiar employment.

5. Nature; disposition.

6. See Johnson's letter to Lord Chesterfield in Boswell's *Life of Johnson* (p. 1277).

7. Paolo Beni's *L'Anticrusca* (1612) violently attacked the first edition of the *Vocabolario* (the Italian dictionary).

8. Organization.

9. Johnson's wife had died three years earlier.

1. Johnson's definitions include etymologies and illustrative quotations, some of which are omitted in this selection.

IMA'GINATION. *n.*

1. Fancy; the power of forming ideal pictures; the power of representing things absent to one's self or others.

2. Conception; image in the mind; idea.

3. Contrivance; scheme.

LEXICO'GRAPHER. *n.*

A writer of dictionaries; a harmless drudge, that busies himself in tracing the original, and detailing the signification of words.

MELANCHO'LY. *n.*

1. A disease, supposed to proceed from a redundance of black bile.

2. A kind of madness, in which the mind is always fixed on one object.

3. A gloomy, pensive, discontented temper.

NA'TURE. *n.*

1. An imaginary being supposed to preside over the material and animal world.

> Thou, *nature*, art my goddess; to thy law
> My services are bound.—*Shakespeare.*

2. The native state or properties of anything, by which it is discriminated from others.

3. The constitution of an animated body.

4. Disposition of mind; temper.

5. The regular course of things.

6. The compass of natural existence.

7. Natural affection, or reverence; native sensations.

8. The state or operation of the material world.

9. Sort; species.

10. Sentiments or images adapted to nature, or comfortable to truth and reality.

11. Physics; the science which teaches the qualities of things.

> *Nature* and *nature's* laws lay hid in night,
> God said, Let Newton be, and all was light.—*Pope.*

NE'TWORK. *n.*

Anything reticulated or decussated, at equal distances, with interstices between the intersections.

OATS. *n.*

A grain, which in England is generally given to horses, but in Scotland supports the people.

PA'STERN. *n.*

1. The knee of an horse.[2]

PA'TRON. *n.*

1. One who countenances, supports, or protects. Commonly a wretch who supports with insolence, and is paid with flattery.

PE'NSION. *n.*

An allowance made to anyone without an equivalent. In England it is generally understood to mean pay given to a state hireling for treason to his country.[3]

---

2. "A lady once asked him how he came to define *Pastern* the *knee* of a horse: instead of making an elaborate defense, as she expected, he at once answered, 'Ignorance, Madam, pure ignorance' " (Boswell).

3. In 1762 Johnson was awarded a pension, but he did not revise the definition in later editions.

SA'TIRE. *n.*

A poem in which wickedness or folly is censured. Proper *satire* is distinguished, by the generality of the reflections, from a *lampoon,* which is aimed against a particular person; but they are too frequently confounded.

TO'RY. *n.*

One who adheres to the ancient constitution of the state, and the apostolical hierarchy of the church of England, opposed to a whig.

The knight is more a *tory* in the country than the town, because it more advances his interest.—*Addison.*

WHIG. *n.*

2. The name of a faction.

Whoever has a true value for church and state, should avoid the extremes of *whig* for the sake of the former, and the extremes of tory on the account of the latter.—*Swift.*

WIT. *n.*

1. The powers of the mind; the mental faculties; the intellects. This is the original signification.

2. Imagination; quickness of fancy.

3. Sentiments produced by quickness of fancy.

4. A man of fancy.

5. A man of genius.

6. Sense; judgment.

7. In the plural. Sound mind; intellect not crazed.

8. Contrivance; stratagem; power of expedients.

1755

The Preface to Shakespeare This is the finest piece of Shakespeare criticism in the eighteenth century; it culminates a critical tradition that began with John Dryden's remarks on Shakespeare and continued as the plays were edited by Nicholas Rowe, Alexander Pope, Lewis Theobald, and William Warburton. Johnson addresses the standard topics: Shakespeare is the poet of nature, not learning; the creator of characters who spring to life; and a writer whose works express the full range of human passions. But the *Preface* also takes a fresh look not only at the plays but at the first principles of criticism. Resisting "bardolatry"—uncritical worship of Shakespeare—Johnson points out his faults as well as his virtues, yet finds that his truth to life, or "just representations of general nature," surpasses that of all other modern writers. The *Preface* is most original when it attacks the long-standing critical reverence for the unities of time and place. What seems real on the stage, Johnson argues, does not depend on artificial rules but on what the mind is willing to imagine.

Johnson's edition of Shakespeare also contained footnotes and brief introductions to each of the plays. Reprinted here are his afterwords on *Twelfth Night* and *King Lear.*

From The Preface to Shakespeare

[SHAKESPEARE'S EXCELLENCE. GENERAL NATURE]

That praises are without reason lavished on the dead, and that the honors due only to excellence are paid to antiquity, is a complaint likely to be always continued by those who, being able to add nothing to truth, hope for eminence from the heresies of paradox; or those who, being forced by disappointment upon consolatory expedients, are willing to hope from posterity what the present age refuses, and flatter themselves that the regard which is yet denied by envy will be at last bestowed by time.

Antiquity, like every other quality that attracts the notice of mankind, has undoubtedly votaries that reverence it not from reason but from prejudice. Some seem to admire indiscriminately whatever has been long preserved, without considering that time has sometimes cooperated with chance; all perhaps are more willing to honor past than present excellence; and the mind contemplates genius through the shades of age, as the eye surveys the sun through artificial opacity. The great contention of criticism is to find the faults of the moderns and the beauties of the ancients. While an author is yet living we estimate his powers by his worst performance; and when he is dead we rate them by his best.

To works, however, of which the excellence is not absolute and definite, but gradual and comparative; to works not raised upon principles demonstrative and scientific, but appealing wholly to observation and experience, no other test can be applied than length of duration and continuance of esteem. What mankind have long possessed they have often examined and compared; and if they persist to value the possession, it is because frequent comparisons have confirmed opinion in its favor. As among the works of nature no man can properly call a river deep or a mountain high, without the knowledge of many mountains and many rivers; so in the productions of genius, nothing can be styled excellent till it has been compared with other works of the same kind. Demonstration[1] immediately displays its power and has nothing to hope or fear from the flux of years; but works tentative and experimental must be estimated by their proportion to the general and collective ability of man, as it is discovered in a long succession of endeavors. Of the first building that was raised, it might be with certainty determined that it was round or square, but whether it was spacious or lofty must have been referred to time. The Pythagorean scale of numbers[2] was at once discovered to be perfect; but the poems of Homer we yet know not to transcend the common limits of human intelligence, but by remarking that nation after nation, and century after century, has been able to do little more than transpose his incidents, new name his characters, and paraphrase his sentiments.

The reverence due to writings that have long subsisted arises, therefore, not from any credulous confidence in the superior wisdom of past ages, or gloomy persuasion of the degeneracy of mankind, but is the consequence of acknowledged and indubitable positions, that what has been longest known has been most considered, and what is most considered is best understood.

The poet of whose works I have undertaken the revision may now begin to assume the dignity of an ancient and claim the privilege of established fame and prescriptive veneration. He has long outlived his century, the term commonly fixed as the test of literary merit.[3] Whatever advantages he might once derive from personal allusions, local customs, or temporary opinions, have for many years been lost; and every topic of merriment or motive of sorrow which the modes of artificial life afforded him now only obscure the

1. "The highest degree of deducible or argumental evidence" (Johnson's *Dictionary*).
2. Pythagoras discovered the ratios that determine the principal intervals of the musical scale.
3. Horace's *Epistles* 2.1.39.

scenes which they once illuminated. The effects of favor and competition are at an end; the tradition of his friendships and his enmities has perished; his works support no opinion with arguments nor supply any faction with invectives; they can neither indulge vanity nor gratify malignity; but are read without any other reason than the desire of pleasure, and are therefore praised only as pleasure is obtained; yet, thus unassisted by interest or passion, they have passed through variations of taste and changes of manners, and, as they devolved from one generation to another, have received new honors at every transmission.

But because human judgment, though it be gradually gaining upon certainty, never becomes infallible, and approbation, though long continued, may yet be only the approbation of prejudice or fashion, it is proper to inquire by what peculiarities of excellence Shakespeare has gained and kept the favor of his countrymen.

Nothing can please many, and please long, but just representations of general nature. Particular manners can be known to few, and therefore few only can judge how nearly they are copied. The irregular combinations of fanciful invention may delight awhile by that novelty of which the common satiety of life sends us all in quest; but the pleasures of sudden wonder are soon exhausted, and the mind can only repose on the stability of truth.

Shakespeare is, above all writers, at least above all modern writers, the poet of nature, the poet that holds up to his readers a faithful mirror of manners and of life. His characters are not modified by the customs of particular places, unpracticed by the rest of the world; by the peculiarities of studies or professions, which can operate but upon small numbers; or by the accidents of transient fashions or temporary opinions: they are the genuine progeny of common humanity, such as the world will always supply and observation will always find. His persons act and speak by the influence of those general passions and principles by which all minds are agitated and the whole system of life is continued in motion. In the writings of other poets a character is too often an individual: in those of Shakespeare it is commonly a species.

It is from this wide extension of design that so much instruction is derived. It is this which fills the plays of Shakespeare with practical axioms and domestic wisdom. It was said of Euripides[4] that every verse was a precept; and it may be said of Shakespeare that from his works may be collected a system of civil and economical prudence. Yet his real power is not shown in the splendor of particular passages, but by the progress of his fable[5] and the tenor of his dialogue; and he that tries to recommend him by select quotations will succeed like the pedant in Hierocles[6] who, when he offered his house to sale, carried a brick in his pocket as a specimen.

It will not easily be imagined how much Shakespeare excels in accommodating his sentiments to real life but by comparing him with other authors. It was observed of the ancient schools of declamation that the more diligently they were frequented, the more was the student disqualified for the world, because he found nothing there which he should ever meet in any other

4. The Greek tragic poet (ca. 480–406 B.C.E.). The observation is Cicero's.
5. Plot. "The series or contexture of events which constitute a poem epic or dramatic" (Johnson's *Dictionary*).
6. Hierocles of Alexandria, a Greek philosopher of the 5th century C.E.

place. The same remark may be applied to every stage but that of Shake-speare. The theater, when it is under any other direction, is peopled by such characters as were never seen, conversing in a language which was never heard, upon topics which will never arise in the commerce of mankind. But the dialogue of this author is often so evidently determined by the incident which produces it, and is pursued with so much ease and simplicity, that it seems scarcely to claim the merit of fiction, but to have been gleaned by diligent selection out of common conversation and common occurrences.

Upon every other stage the universal agent is love, by whose power all good and evil is distributed and every action quickened or retarded. To bring a lover, a lady, and a rival into the fable; to entangle them in contradictory obligations, perplex them with oppositions of interest, and harass them with violence of desires inconsistent with each other; to make them meet in rap-ture, and part in agony; to fill their mouths with hyperbolical joy and out-rageous sorrow; to distress them as nothing human ever was distressed; to deliver them as nothing human ever was delivered, is the business of a mod-ern dramatist. For this, probability is violated, life is misrepresented, and language is depraved. But love is only one of many passions; and as it has no great influence upon the sum of life, it has little operation in the dramas of a poet who caught his ideas from the living world and exhibited only what he saw before him. He knew that any other passion, as it was regular or exorbitant, was a cause of happiness or calamity.

Characters thus ample and general were not easily discriminated and pre-served; yet perhaps no poet ever kept his personages more distinct from each other. I will not say with Pope that every speech may be assigned to the proper speaker,[7] because many speeches there are which have nothing char-acteristical; but perhaps though some may be equally adapted to every per-son, it will be difficult to find that any can be properly transferred from the present possessor to another claimant. The choice is right when there is reason for choice.

Other dramatists can only gain attention by hyperbolical or aggravated characters, by fabulous and unexampled excellence or depravity, as the writ-ers of barbarous romances invigorated the reader by a giant and a dwarf; and he that should form his expectations of human affairs from the play or from the tale would be equally deceived. Shakespeare has no heroes; his scenes are occupied only by men, who act and speak as the reader thinks that he should himself have spoken or acted on the same occasion; even where the agency is supernatural, the dialogue is level with life. Other writers disguise the most natural passions and most frequent incidents so that he who con-templates them in the book will not know them in the world: Shakespeare approximates[8] the remote, and familiarizes the wonderful; the event which he represents will not happen, but, if it were possible, its effects would prob-ably be such as he has assigned; and it may be said that he has not only shown human nature as it acts in real exigencies, but as it would be found in trials to which it cannot be exposed.

This therefore is the praise of Shakespeare, that his drama is the mirror of life; that he who has mazed his imagination in following the phantoms

---

7. In the preface to his edition of Shakespeare's plays (1725).

8. Brings near.

which other writers raise up before him, may here be cured of his delirious ecstasies by reading human sentiments in human language, by scenes from which a hermit may estimate the transactions of the world, and a confessor predict the progress of the passions.

[SHAKESPEARE'S FAULTS. THE THREE DRAMATIC UNITIES]

Shakespeare with his excellencies has likewise faults, and faults sufficient to obscure and overwhelm any other merit. I shall show them in the proportion in which they appear to me, without envious malignity or superstitious veneration. No question can be more innocently discussed than a dead poet's pretensions to renown; and little regard is due to that bigotry which sets candor[9] higher than truth.

His first defect is that to which may be imputed most of the evil in books or in men. He sacrifices virtue to convenience, and is so much more careful to please than to instruct that he seems to write without any moral purpose. From his writings indeed a system of social duty may be selected, for he that thinks reasonably must think morally, but his precepts and axioms drop casually from him; he makes no just distribution of good or evil, nor is always careful to show in the virtuous a disapprobation of the wicked; he carries his persons indifferently through right and wrong, and at the close dismisses them without further care, and leaves their examples to operate by chance. This fault the barbarity of his age cannot extenuate; for it is always a writer's duty to make the world better, and justice is a virtue independent on time or place.

The plots are often so loosely formed that a very slight consideration may improve them, and so carelessly pursued that he seems not always fully to comprehend his own design. He omits opportunities of instructing or delighting which the train of his story seems to force upon him, and apparently rejects those exhibitions which would be more affecting for the sake of those which are more easy.

It may be observed that in many of his plays the latter part is evidently neglected. When he found himself near the end of his work, and in view of his reward, he shortened the labor to snatch the profit. He therefore remits his efforts where he should most vigorously exert them, and his catastrophe is improbably produced or imperfectly represented.

He had no regard to distinction of time or place, but gives to one age or nation, without scruple, the customs, institutions, and opinions of another, at the expense not only of likelihood but of possibility. These faults Pope has endeavored, with more zeal than judgment, to transfer to his imagined interpolators. We need not wonder to find Hector quoting Aristotle, when we see the loves of Theseus and Hippolyta combined with the Gothic mythology of fairies.[1] Shakespeare, indeed, was not the only violator of chronology, for in the same age Sidney, who wanted not the advantages of learning, has, in his *Arcadia*, confounded the pastoral with the feudal times, the days of innocence, quiet, and security with those of turbulence, violence, and adventure.

In his comic scenes he is seldom very successful when he engages his

9. Kindness.
1. In *Troilus and Cressida* 2.2.166 and in *Midsummer Night's Dream*, respectively.

characters in reciprocations of smartness and contests of sarcasm; their jests are commonly gross, and their pleasantry licentious; neither his gentlemen nor his ladies have much delicacy, nor are sufficiently distinguished from his clowns by any appearance of refined manners. Whether he represented the real conversation of his time is not easy to determine: the reign of Elizabeth is commonly supposed to have been a time of stateliness, formality, and reserve; yet perhaps the relaxations of that severity were not very elegant. There must, however, have been always some modes of gaiety preferable to others, and a writer ought to choose the best.

In tragedy his performance seems constantly to be worse as his labor is more. The effusions of passion, which exigence forces out, are for the most part striking and energetic; but whenever he solicits his invention, or strains his faculties, the offspring of his throes is tumor,[2] meanness, tediousness, and obscurity.

In narration he affects a disproportionate pomp of diction and a wearisome train of circumlocution, and tells the incident imperfectly in many words which might have been more plainly delivered in few. Narration in dramatic poetry is naturally tedious, as it is unanimated and inactive, and obstructs the progress of the action; it should therefore always be rapid and enlivened by frequent interruption. Shakespeare found it an encumbrance, and instead of lightening it by brevity, endeavored to recommend it by dignity and splendor.

His declamations or set speeches are commonly cold and weak, for his power was the power of nature; when he endeavored, like other tragic writers, to catch opportunities of amplification and, instead of inquiring what the occasion demanded, to show how much his stores of knowledge could supply, he seldom escapes without the pity or resentment of his reader.

It is incident to him to be now and then entangled with an unwieldy sentiment which he cannot well express, and will not reject; he struggles with it awhile, and, if it continues stubborn, comprises it in words such as occur, and leaves it to be disentangled and evolved[3] by those who have more leisure to bestow upon it.

Not that always where the language is intricate the thought is subtle, or the image always great where the line is bulky; the equality of words to things is very often neglected, and trivial sentiments and vulgar[4] ideas disappoint the attention, to which they are recommended by sonorous epithets and swelling figures.

But the admirers of this great poet have most reason to complain when he approaches nearest to his highest excellence, and seems fully resolved to sink them in dejection and mollify them with tender emotions by the fall of greatness, the danger of innocence, or the crosses of love. What he does best, he soon ceases to do. He is not long soft and pathetic without some idle conceit or contemptible equivocation. He no sooner begins to move than he counteracts himself; and terror and pity, as they are rising in the mind, are checked and blasted by sudden frigidity.

A quibble[5] is to Shakespeare what luminous vapors are to the traveler: he follows it at all adventures; it is sure to lead him out of his way, and sure to

---

2. Inflated grandeur, false magnificence.
3. Unfolded.
4. "Mean; low; being of the common rate" (Johnson's *Dictionary*).
5. Pun.

engulf him in the mire. It has some malignant power over his mind, and its fascinations are irresistible. Whatever be the dignity or profundity of his disquisitions, whether he be enlarging knowledge or exalting affection, whether he be amusing[6] attention with incidents, or enchaining it in suspense, let but a quibble spring up before him, and he leaves his work unfinished. A quibble is the golden apple for which he will always turn aside from his career[7] or stoop from his elevation. A quibble, poor and barren as it is, gave him such delight that he was content to purchase it by the sacrifice of reason, propriety, and truth. A quibble was to him the fatal Cleopatra for which he lost the world, and was content to lose it.

It will be thought strange that in enumerating the defects of this writer, I have not yet mentioned his neglect of the unities; his violation of those laws which have been instituted and established by the joint authority of poets and critics.

For his other deviations from the art of writing, I resign him to critical justice without making any other demand in his favor than that which must be indulged to all human excellence: that his virtues be rated with his failings. But from the censure which this irregularity may bring upon him I shall, with due reverence to that learning which I must oppose, adventure to try how I can defend him.

His histories, being neither tragedies nor comedies, are not subject to any of their laws; nothing more is necessary to all the praise which they expect than that the changes of action be so prepared as to be understood; that the incidents be various and affecting, and the characters consistent, natural, and distinct. No other unity is intended, and therefore none is to be sought.

In his other works he has well enough preserved the unity of action. He has not, indeed, an intrigue regularly perplexed and regularly unraveled: he does not endeavor to hide his design only to discover it, for this is seldom the order of real events, and Shakespeare is the poet of nature: but his plan has commonly what Aristotle requires,[8] a beginning, a middle, and an end; one event is concatenated with another, and the conclusion follows by easy consequence. There are, perhaps, some incidents that might be spared, as in other poets there is much talk that only fills up time upon the stage; but the general system makes gradual advances, and the end of the play is the end of expectation.

To the unities of time and place he has shown no regard; and perhaps a nearer view of the principles on which they stand will diminish their value and withdraw from them the veneration which, from the time of Corneille,[9] they have very generally received, by discovering that they have given more trouble to the poet than pleasure to the auditor.

The necessity of observing the unities of time and place arises from the supposed necessity of making the drama credible. The critics hold it impossible that an action of months or years can be possibly believed to pass in three hours; or that the spectator can suppose himself to sit in the theater

6. "To entertain with tranquility; to fill with thoughts that engage the mind, without distracting it" (Johnson's *Dictionary*).
7. Course of action; the ground on which a race is run. In Greek legend Atalanta refused to marry any man who could not defeat her in a foot race. Hippomenes won her by dropping, as he ran, three of the golden apples of the Hesperides, which she paused to pick up.
8. *Poetics* 7.
9. Pierre Corneille (1606–1684), the French playwright, discussed the unities in his *Discours des trois unités* (1660).

while ambassadors go and return between distant kings, while armies are levied and towns besieged, while an exile wanders and returns, or till he whom they saw courting his mistress shall lament the untimely fall of his son. The mind revolts from evident falsehood, and fiction loses its force when it departs from the resemblance of reality.

From the narrow limitation of time necessarily arises the contraction of place. The spectator who knows that he saw the first act at Alexandria cannot suppose that he sees the next at Rome, at a distance to which not the dragons of Medea[1] could, in so short a time, have transported him; he knows with certainty that he has not changed his place; and he knows that place cannot change itself, that what was a house cannot become a plain, that what was Thebes can never be Persepolis.

Such is the triumphant language with which a critic exults over the misery of an irregular poet, and exults commonly without resistance or reply. It is time, therefore, to tell him by the authority of Shakespeare that he assumes, as an unquestionable principle, a position which, while his breath is forming it into words, his understanding pronounces to be false. It is false that any representation is mistaken for reality; that any dramatic fable in its materiality was ever credible or, for a single moment, was ever credited.

The objection arising from the impossibility of passing the first hour at Alexandria and the next at Rome supposes that when the play opens the spectator really imagines himself at Alexandria, and believes that his walk to the theater has been a voyage to Egypt, and that he lives in the days of Antony and Cleopatra. Surely he that imagines this may imagine more. He that can take the stage at one time for the palace of the Ptolemies may take it in half an hour for the promontory of Actium. Delusion, if delusion be admitted, has no certain limitation; if the spectator can be once persuaded that his old acquaintances are Alexander and Caesar, that a room illuminated with candles is the plain of Pharsalia or the bank of Granicus, he is in a state of elevation above the reach of reason or of truth, and from the heights of empyrean poetry may despise the circumscriptions of terrestrial nature. There is no reason why a mind thus wandering in ecstasy should count the clock, or why an hour should not be a century in that calenture[2] of the brain that can make the stage a field.

The truth is that the spectators are always in their senses, and know, from the first act to the last, that the stage is only a stage, and that the players are only players. They came to hear a certain number of lines recited with just gesture and elegant modulation. The lines relate to some action, and an action must be in some place; but the different actions that complete a story may be in places very remote from each other; and where is the absurdity of allowing that space to represent first Athens, and then Sicily, which was always known to be neither Sicily nor Athens but a modern theater?

By supposition, as place is introduced, time may be extended; the time required by the fable elapses, for the most part, between the acts; for, of so much of the action as is represented, the real and poetical duration is the same. If, in the first act, preparations for war against Mithridates are represented to be made in Rome, the event of the war may, without absurdity,

1. According to legend, Medea fled the scene of her crimes in a chariot drawn by dragons.
2. A delirium produced by tropical heat, which causes sailors to leap into the sea under the delusion that it is a green field.

be represented, in the catastrophe, as happening in Pontus; we know that there is neither war nor preparation for war; we know that we are neither in Rome nor Pontus, that neither Mithridates nor Lucullus are before us. The drama exhibits successive imitations of successive actions; and why may not the second imitation represent an action that happened years after the first, if it be so connected with it that nothing but time can be supposed to intervene? Time is, of all modes of existence, most obsequious[3] to the imagination; a lapse of years is as easily conceived as a passage of hours. In contemplation we easily contract the time of real actions, and therefore willingly permit it to be contracted when we only see their imitation.

It will be asked how the drama moves if it is not credited. It is credited with all the credit due to a drama. It is credited, whenever it moves, as a just picture of a real original; as representing to the auditor what he would himself feel if he were to do or suffer what is there feigned to be suffered or to be done. The reflection that strikes the heart is not that the evils before us are real evils, but that they are evils to which we ourselves may be exposed. If there be any fallacy, it is not that we fancy the players, but that we fancy ourselves, unhappy for a moment; but we rather lament the possibility than suppose the presence of misery, as a mother weeps over her babe when she remembers that death may take it from her. The delight of tragedy proceeds from our consciousness of fiction; if we thought murders and treasons real, they would please no more.

Imitations produce pain or pleasure, not because they are mistaken for realities, but because they bring realities to mind. When the imagination is recreated[4] by a painted landscape, the trees are not supposed capable to give us shade or the fountains coolness; but we consider how we should be pleased with such fountains playing beside us and such woods waving over us. We are agitated in reading the history of *Henry the Fifth;* yet no man takes his book for the field of Agincourt. A dramatic exhibition is a book recited with concomitants that increase or diminish its effect. Familiar comedy is often more powerful on the theater than in the page; imperial tragedy is always less. The humor of Petruchio may be heightened by grimace; but what voice or what gesture can hope to add dignity or force to the soliloquy of Cato?[5]

A play read affects the mind like a play acted. It is therefore evident that the action is not supposed to be real; and it follows that between the acts a longer or shorter time may be allowed to pass, and that no more account of space or duration is to be taken by the auditor of a drama than by the reader of a narrative, before whom may pass in an hour the life of a hero or the revolutions of an empire.

Whether Shakespeare knew the unities and rejected them by design or deviated from them by happy ignorance, it is, I think, impossible to decide and useless to inquire. We may reasonably suppose that, when he rose to notice, he did not want[6] the counsels and admonitions of scholars and critics, and that he at last deliberately persisted in a practice which he might have begun by chance. As nothing is essential to the fable but unity of action, and

---

3. "Obedient; compliant" (Johnson's *Dictionary*).
4. Delighted.
5. In Addison's tragedy *Cato* (5.1), the hero soliloquizes on immortality shortly before committing

suicide. Petruchio is the hero of Shakespeare's comedy *The Taming of the Shrew.*
6. Lack.

as the unities of time and place arise evidently from false assumptions, and, by circumscribing the extent of the drama, lessen its variety, I cannot think it much to be lamented that they were not known by him, or not observed: nor, if such another poet could arise, should I very vehemently reproach him that his first act passed at Venice and his next in Cyprus.[7] Such violations of rules merely positive[8] become the comprehensive genius of Shakespeare, and such censures are suitable to the minute and slender criticism of Voltaire.

> *Non usque adeo permiscuit imis*
> *Longus summa dies, ut non, si voce Metelli*
> *Serventur leges, malint a Caesare tolli.*[9]

Yet when I speak thus slightly of dramatic rules, I cannot but recollect how much wit and learning may be produced against me; before such authorities I am afraid to stand: not that I think the present question one of those that are to be decided by mere authority, but because it is to be suspected that these precepts have not been so easily received but for better reasons than I have yet been able to find. The result of my inquiries, in which it would be ludicrous to boast of impartiality, is that the unities of time and place are not essential to a just drama, that though they may sometimes conduce to pleasure, they are always to be sacrificed to the nobler beauties of variety and instruction; and that a play written with nice observation of critical rules is to be contemplated as an elaborate curiosity, as the product of superfluous and ostentatious art, by which is shown rather what is possible than what is necessary.

He that without diminution of any other excellence shall preserve all the unities unbroken deserves the like applause with the architect who shall display all the orders of architecture in a citadel without any deduction for its strength; but the principal beauty of a citadel is to exclude the enemy, and the greatest graces of a play are to copy nature and instruct life.* * *

[HENRY IV]

None of Shakespeare's plays are more read than the first and second parts of *Henry the Fourth*. Perhaps no author has ever in two plays afforded so much delight. The great events are interesting, for the fate of kingdoms depends upon them; the slighter occurrences are diverting, and, except one or two, sufficiently probable; the incidents are multiplied with wonderful fertility of invention, and the characters diversified with the utmost nicety of discernment, and the profoundest skill in the nature of man.

The prince, who is the hero both of the comic and tragic part, is a young man of great abilities and violent passions, whose sentiments are right, though his actions are wrong; whose virtues are obscured by negligence, and whose understanding is dissipated by levity. In his idle hours he is rather loose than wicked, and when the occasion forces but his latent qualities, he is great without effort, and brave without tumult. The trifler is roused into a hero, and the hero again reposes in the trifler. This character is great, original, and just.[1]

---

7. As is the case in *Othello*.
8. Arbitrary; not natural.
9. Lucan's *Pharsalia* 3.138–40: "The course of time has not wrought such confusion that the laws would not rather be trampled on by Caesar than saved by Metellus."
1. Accurate, well grounded.

Percy is a rugged soldier, choleric and quarrelsome, and has only the soldier's virtues, generosity and courage.

But Falstaff, unimitated, unimitable Falstaff, how shall I describe thee? Thou compound of sense and vice; of sense which may be admired but not esteemed, of vice which may be despised, but hardly detested. Falstaff is a character loaded with faults, and with those faults which naturally produce contempt. He is a thief, and a glutton, a coward, and a boaster, always ready to cheat the weak, and prey upon the poor; to terrify the timorous and insult the defenseless. At once obsequious and malignant, he satirizes in their absence those whom he lives by flattering. He is familiar with the prince only as an agent of vice, but of this familiarity he is so proud as not only to be supercilious and haughty with common men, but to think his interest of importance to the duke of Lancaster. Yet the man thus corrupt, thus despicable, makes himself necessary to the prince that despises him, by the most pleasing of all qualities, perpetual gaiety, by an unfailing power of exciting laughter, which is the more freely indulged, as his wit is not of the splendid or ambitious kind, but consists in easy escapes and sallies of levity, which make sport but raise no envy. It must be observed that he is stained with no enormous or sanguinary crimes, so that his licentiousness is not so offensive but that it may be borne for his mirth.

The moral to be drawn from this representation is that no man is more dangerous than he that with a will to corrupt, hath the power to please; and that neither wit nor honesty ought to think themselves safe with such a companion when they see Henry seduced by Falstaff.

FROM LIVES OF THE POETS

From Milton[1]

[LYCIDAS]

One of the poems on which much praise has been bestowed is *Lycidas*; of which the diction is harsh,[2] the rhymes uncertain, and the numbers unpleasing. What beauty there is, we must therefore seek in the sentiments and images. It is not to be considered as the effusion of real passion; for passion runs not after remote allusions and obscure opinions. Passion plucks no berries from the myrtle and ivy, nor calls upon Arethuse and Mincius, nor tells of "rough satyrs and fauns with cloven heel." Where there is leisure for fiction there is little grief.

In this poem there is no nature, for there is no truth; there is no art, for there is nothing new. Its form is that of a pastoral, easy, vulgar, and therefore disgusting:[3] whatever images it can supply are long ago exhausted; and its inherent improbability always forces dissatisfaction on the mind. When

1. Johnson's treatment of Milton as man and poet gave great offense to many ardent Miltonians in his own day and damaged his reputation as a critic in the following century. He did not admire Milton's character, and he detested his politics and religion. But no one has praised *Paradise Lost* more handsomely. Especially offensive in the 19th century was his attack on *Lycidas*. Johnson disliked modern pastorals, recognizing that the tradition had been worn threadbare. His views on the genre may be read in *Rambler* no. 36 and no. 37.
2. This notorious word does not mean "unmelodious," but "strained, forced, affected, or labored."
3. I.e., displeasing, because its stale conventionality made it "vulgar" by putting it within the reach of the many.

Cowley tells of Hervey that they studied together, it is easy to suppose how much he must miss the companion of his labors and the partner of his discoveries;[4] but what image of tenderness can be excited by these lines!

> We drove afield, and both together heard
> What time the grayfly winds her sultry horn,
> Battening our flocks with the fresh dews of night.

We know that they never drove afield, and that they had no flocks to batten; and though it be allowed that the representation may be allegorical, the true meaning is so uncertain and remote that it is never sought because it cannot be known when it is found.

Among the flocks and copses and flowers appear the heathen deities, Jove and Phoebus, Neptune and Aeolus, with a long train of mythological imagery, such as a college easily supplies. Nothing can less display knowledge or less exercise invention than to tell how a shepherd has lost his companion and must now feed his flocks alone, without any judge of his skill in piping; and how one god asks another god what is become of Lycidas, and how neither god can tell. He who thus grieves will excite no sympathy; he who thus praises will confer no honor.

This poem has yet a grosser fault. With these trifling fictions are mingled the most awful and sacred truths, such as ought never to be polluted with such irreverent combinations. The shepherd likewise is now a feeder of sheep, and afterwards an ecclesiastical pastor, a superintendent of a Christian flock. Such equivocations are always unskillful; but here they are indecent,[5] and at least approach to impiety, of which, however, I believe the writer not to have been conscious.

Such is the power of reputation justly acquired that its blaze drives away the eye from nice examination. Surely no man could have fancied that he read *Lycidas* with pleasure had he not known its author.

[*L'ALLEGRO, IL PENSEROSO*]

Of the two pieces, *L'Allegro* and *Il Penseroso,* I believe opinion is uniform; every man that reads them, reads them with pleasure. The author's design is not, what Theobald[6] has remarked, merely to show how objects derived their colors from the mind, by representing the operation of the same things upon the gay and the melancholy temper, or upon the same man as he is differently disposed; but rather how, among the successive variety of appearances, every disposition of mind takes hold on those by which it may be gratified.

The *cheerful* man hears the lark in the morning; the *pensive* man hears the nightingale in the evening. The *cheerful* man sees the cock strut, and hears the horn and hounds echo in the wood; then walks "not unseen" to observe the glory of the rising sun or listen to the singing milkmaid, and view the labors of the plowman and the mower; then casts his eyes about him over scenes of smiling plenty, and looks up to the distant tower, the residence of some fair inhabitant: thus he pursues rural gaiety through a day of labor

---

4. Cowley's *On the Death of Mr. William Hervey* (1656).
5. Unbecoming, lacking in decorum.

6. Lewis Theobald (1688–1744), the editor of Shakespeare and the enemy of Pope.

or of play, and delights himself at night with the fanciful narratives of superstitious ignorance.

The *pensive* man at one time walks "unseen" to muse at midnight, and at another hears the sullen curfew. If the weather drives him home he sits in a room lighted only by "glowing embers"; or by a lonely lamp outwatches the North Star to discover the habitation of separate souls, and varies the shades of meditation by contemplating the magnificent or pathetic scenes of tragic and epic poetry. When the morning comes, a morning gloomy with rain and wind, he walks into the dark trackless woods, falls asleep by some murmuring water, and with melancholy enthusiasm expects some dream of prognostication or some music played by aerial performers.

Both Mirth and Melancholy are solitary, silent inhabitants of the breast that neither receive nor transmit communication: no mention is therefore made of a philosophical friend or a pleasant companion. The seriousness does not arise from any participation of calamity, nor the gaiety from the pleasures of the bottle.

The man of *cheerfulness* having exhausted the country tries what "towered cities" will afford, and mingles with scenes of splendor, gay assemblies, and nuptial festivities; but he mingles a mere spectator as, when the learned comedies of Jonson or the wild dramas of Shakespeare are exhibited, he attends the theater.

The *pensive* man never loses himself in crowds, but walks the cloister or frequents the cathedral. Milton probably had not yet forsaken the Church.

Both his characters delight in music; but he seems to think that cheerful notes would have obtained from Pluto a complete dismission of Eurydice, of whom solemn sounds only procured a conditional release.

For the old age of Cheerfulness he makes no provision; but Melancholy he conducts with great dignity to the close of life. His Cheerfulness is without levity, and his Pensiveness without asperity.

Through these two poems the images are properly selected and nicely distinguished, but the colors of the diction seem not sufficiently discriminated. I know not whether the characters are kept sufficiently apart. No mirth can, indeed, be found in his melancholy; but I am afraid that I always meet some melancholy in his mirth. They are two noble efforts of imagination.

[*PARADISE LOST*]

Those little pieces may be dispatched without much anxiety; a greater work calls for greater care. I am now to examine *Paradise Lost,* a poem which, considered with respect to design, may claim the first place, and with respect to performance the second, among the productions of the human mind.

By the general consent of critics the first praise of genius is due to the writer of an epic poem, as it requires an assemblage of all the powers which are singly sufficient for other compositions. Poetry is the art of uniting pleasure with truth, by calling imagination to the help of reason. Epic poetry undertakes to teach the most important truths by the most pleasing precepts, and therefore relates some great event in the most affecting manner. History must supply the writer with the rudiments of narration, which he must improve and exalt by a nobler art, must animate by dramatic energy, and diversify by retrospection and anticipation; morality must teach him the exact bounds and different shades of vice and virtue; from policy and the practice of life he has to learn the discriminations of character and the tendency of the passions, either single or combined; and physiology must supply him with illustrations and images. To put these materials to poetical use is required an imagination capable of painting nature and realizing fiction. Nor is he yet a poet till he has attained the whole extension of his language, distinguished all the delicacies of phrase, and all the colors of words, and learned to adjust their different sounds to all the varieties of metrical modulation.

Bossu is of opinion that the poet's first work is to find a *moral,* which his fable is afterwards to illustrate and establish.[7] This seems to have been the process only of Milton: the moral of other poems is incidental and consequent; in Milton's only it is essential and intrinsic. His purpose was the most useful and the most arduous: "to vindicate the ways of God to man";[8] to show the reasonableness of religion, and the necessity of obedience to the Divine Law.

To convey this moral there must be a *fable,* a narration artfully constructed, so as to excite curiosity and surprise expectation. In this part of his work Milton must be confessed to have equaled every other poet. He has involved in his account of the Fall of Man the events which preceded, and those that were to follow it: he has interwoven the whole system of theology with such propriety that every part appears to be necessary, and scarcely any recital is wished shorter for the sake of quickening the progress of the main action.

The subject of an epic poem is naturally an event of great importance. That of Milton is not the destruction of a city, the conduct of a colony, or the foundation of an empire. His subject is the fate of worlds, the revolutions of heaven and of earth; rebellion against the Supreme King raised by the highest order of created beings; the overthrow of their host and the punishment of their crime; the creation of a new race of reasonable creatures; their original happiness and innocence, their forfeiture of immortality, and their restoration to hope and peace.

Great events can be hastened or retarded only by persons of elevated dignity. Before the greatness displayed in Milton's poem all other greatness shrinks away. The weakest of his agents are the highest and noblest of human beings, the original parents of mankind; with whose actions the elements consented; on whose rectitude or deviation of will depended the state of terrestrial nature and the condition of all the future inhabitants of the globe.

Of the other agents in the poem, the chief are such as it is irreverence to name on slight occasions. The rest were lower powers;

> of which the least could wield
> Those elements, and arm him with the force
> Of all their regions;[9]

powers which only the control of Omnipotence restrains from laying creation waste, and filling the vast expanse of space with ruin and confusion. To

---

7. Père le Bossu wrote a treatise on the epic poem, *Traité du Poëme Épique,* 1675, much admired during the late 17th and early 18th centuries.
8. Milton wrote "justify," not "vindicate" (*Paradise*

Lost 1.26). It was Pope, in *An Essay on Man* 1.16, who used "vindicate."
9. *Paradise Lost* 6.221.

display the motives and actions of beings thus superior, so far as human reason can examine them or human imagination represent them, is the task which this mighty poet has undertaken and performed.

In the examination of epic poems much speculation is commonly employed upon the *characters*. The characters in the *Paradise Lost* which admit of examination are those of angels and of man; of angels good and evil, of man in his innocent and sinful state.

Among the angels the virtue of Raphael is mild and placid, of easy condescension and free communication; that of Michael is regal and lofty, and, as may seem, attentive to the dignity of his own nature. Abdiel and Gabriel appear occasionally, and act as every incident requires; the solitary fidelity of Abdiel is very amiably painted.[1]

Of the evil angels the characters are more diversified. To Satan, as Addison observes, such sentiments are given as suit "the most exalted and most depraved being."[2] Milton has been censured by Clarke for the impiety which sometimes breaks from Satan's mouth. For there are thoughts, as he justly remarks, which no observation of character can justify, because no good man would willingly permit them to pass, however transiently, through his own mind.[3] To make Satan speak as a rebel, without any such expressions as might taint the reader's imagination, was indeed one of the great difficulties in Milton's undertaking, and I cannot but think that he has extricated himself with great happiness. There is in Satan's speeches little that can give pain to a pious ear. The language of rebellion cannot be the same with that of obedience. The malignity of Satan foams in haughtiness and obstinacy; but his expressions are commonly general, and no otherwise offensive than as they are wicked.

The other chiefs of the celestial rebellion are very judiciously discriminated in the first and second books; and the ferocious character of Moloch appears, both in the battle and the council, with exact consistency.

To Adam and Eve are given during their innocence such sentiments as innocence can generate and utter. Their love is pure benevolence and mutual veneration; their repasts are without luxury and their diligence without toil. Their addresses to their Maker have little more than the voice of admiration and gratitude. Fruition left them nothing to ask, and Innocence left them nothing to fear.

But with guilt enter distrust and discord, mutual accusation, and stubborn self-defense; they regard each other with alienated minds, and dread their Creator as the avenger of their transgression. At last they seek shelter in his mercy, soften to repentance, and melt in supplication. Both before and after the Fall the superiority of Adam is diligently sustained.

Of the *probable* and the *marvelous*,[4] two parts of a vulgar epic poem which immerge the critic in deep consideration, the *Paradise Lost* requires little to be said. It contains the history of a miracle, of Creation and Redemption; it displays the power and the mercy of the Supreme Being: the probable therefore is marvelous, and the marvelous is probable. The substance of the narrative is truth; and as truth allows no choice, it is, like necessity, superior to rule. To the

---

1. *Paradise Lost* 5.803ff.
2. *Spectator* 303.
3. John Clarke's *Essay upon Study* (1731).

4. Actions in an epic poem that are wonderful because they exceed the probable.

accidental or adventitious parts, as to every thing human, some slight exceptions may be made. But the main fabric is immovably supported.

It is justly remarked by Addison[5] that this poem has, by the nature of its
subject, the advantage above all others, that it is universally and perpetually
interesting. All mankind will, through all ages, bear the same relation to
Adam and to Eve, and must partake of that good and evil which extend to
themselves.

Of the *machinery,* so called from *theòs apò mēkhanēs,*[6] by which is meant
the occasional interposition of supernatural power, another fertile topic of
critical remarks, here is no room to speak, because every thing is done under
the immediate and visible direction of Heaven; but the rule is so far observed
that no part of the action could have been accomplished by any other means.

Of *episodes*[7] I think there are only two, contained in Raphael's relation of
the war in heaven and Michael's prophetic account of the changes to happen
in this world. Both are closely connected with the great action; one was
necessary to Adam as a warning, the other as a consolation.

To the completeness or *integrity* of the design nothing can be objected; it
has distinctly and clearly what Aristotle requires, a beginning, a middle, and
an end. There is perhaps no poem of the same length from which so little
can be taken without apparent mutilation. Here are no funeral games, nor
is there any long description of a shield. The short digressions at the beginning of the third, seventh, and ninth books might doubtless be spared; but
superfluities so beautiful who would take away? or who does not wish that
the author of the *Iliad* had gratified succeeding ages with a little knowledge
of himself? Perhaps no passages are more frequently or more attentively read
than those extrinsic paragraphs; and since the end of poetry is pleasure, that
cannot be unpoetical with which all are pleased.

The questions, whether the action of the poem be strictly *one,*[8] whether
the poem can be properly termed *heroic,* and who is the hero, are raised by
such readers as draw their principles of judgment rather from books than
from reason. Milton, though he entitled *Paradise Lost* only a "poem," yet
calls it himself "heroic song."[9] Dryden, petulantly and indecently, denies the
heroism of Adam because he was overcome; but there is no reason why the
hero should not be unfortunate except established practice, since success
and virtue do not go necessarily together. Cato is the hero of Lucan, but
Lucan's authority will not be suffered by Quintilian to decide. However, if
success be necessary, Adam's deceiver was at last crushed; Adam was
restored to his Maker's favor, and therefore may securely resume his human
rank.

After the scheme and fabric of the poem must be considered its compo-
nent parts, the sentiments, and the diction.

The *sentiments,* as expressive of manners or appropriated to characters,
are for the greater part unexceptionably just. Splendid passages containing
lessons of morality or precepts of prudence occur seldom. Such is the original
formation of this poem that as it admits no human manners till the Fall, it

5. *Spectator* 273.
6. Aristotle's *Poetics* 15.10. *Deus ex machina,* the
intervention of supernatural powers into the affairs
of humans.
7. Incidental but related narratives within an epic

poem. Johnson is citing *Paradise Lost* 5.577ff. and
11.334ff.
8. I.e., a single action dealing with a single character.
9. *Paradise Lost* 9.25.

can give little assistance to human conduct. Its end is to raise the thoughts above sublunary cares or pleasures. Yet the praise of that fortitude, with which Abdiel maintained his singularity of virtue against the scorn of multitudes, may be accommodated to all times; and Raphael's reproof of Adam's curiosity after the planetary motions, with the answer returned by Adam, may be confidently opposed to any rule of life which any poet has delivered.[1]

The thoughts which are occasionally called forth in the progress are such as could only be produced by an imagination in the highest degree fervid and active, to which materials were supplied by incessant study and unlimited curiosity. The heat of Milton's mind might be said to sublimate his learning, to throw off into his work the spirit of science,[2] unmingled with its grosser parts.

He had considered creation in its whole extent, and his descriptions are therefore learned. He had accustomed his imagination to unrestrained indulgence, and his conceptions therefore were extensive. The characteristic quality of his poem is sublimity. He sometimes descends to the elegant, but his element is the great. He can occasionally invest himself with grace; but his natural port is gigantic loftiness. He can please when pleasure is required; but it is his peculiar power to astonish.

He seems to have been well acquainted with his own genius, and to know what it was that Nature had bestowed upon him more bountifully than upon others; the power of displaying the vast, illuminating the splendid, enforcing the awful, darkening the gloomy, and aggravating the dreadful: he therefore chose a subject on which too much could not be said, on which he might tire his fancy without the censure of extravagance.

* * *

The defects and faults of *Paradise Lost*, for faults and defects every work of man must have, it is the business of impartial criticism to discover. As in displaying the excellence of Milton I have not made long quotations, because of selecting beauties there had been no end, I shall in the same general manner mention that which seems to deserve censure; for what Englishman can take delight in transcribing passages, which, if they lessen the reputation of Milton, diminish in some degree the honor of our country?

* * *

The plan of *Paradise Lost* has this inconvenience, that it comprises neither human actions nor human manners. The man and woman who act and suffer are in a state which no other man or woman can ever know. The reader finds no transaction in which he can be engaged, beholds no condition in which he can by any effort of imagination place himself; he has, therefore, little natural curiosity or sympathy.

We all, indeed, feel the effects of Adam's disobedience; we all sin like Adam, and like him must all bewail our offenses; we have restless and insidious enemies in the fallen angels, and in the blessed spirits we have guardians and friends; in the Redemption of mankind we hope to be included: in the description of heaven and hell we are surely interested, as we are all to reside hereafter either in the regions of horror or of bliss.

1. *Paradise Lost* 8.65ff. 2. Knowledge.

But these truths are too important to be new: they have been taught to our infancy; they have mingled with our solitary thoughts and familiar conversation, and are habitually interwoven with the whole texture of life. Being therefore not new they raise no unaccustomed emotion in the mind: what we knew before, we cannot learn; what is not unexpected, cannot surprise.

Of the ideas suggested by these awful scenes, from some we recede with reverence, except when stated hours require their association; and from others we shrink with horror, or admit them only as salutary inflictions, as counterpoises to our interests and passions. Such images rather obstruct the career of fancy than incite it.

Pleasure and terror are indeed the genuine sources of poetry; but poetical pleasure must be such as human imagination can at least conceive, and poetical terror such as human strength and fortitude may combat. The good and evil of Eternity are too ponderous for the wings of wit; the mind sinks under them in passive helplessness, content with calm belief and humble adoration.

Known truths however may take a different appearance, and be conveyed to the mind by a new train of intermediate images. This Milton has undertaken, and performed with pregnancy and vigor of mind peculiar to himself. Whoever considers the few radical positions which the Scriptures afforded him will wonder by what energetic operation he expanded them to such extent and ramified them to so much variety, restrained as he was by religious reverence from licentiousness of fiction.

Here is a full display of the united force of study and genius; of a great accumulation of materials, with judgment to digest and fancy to combine them: Milton was able to select from nature or from story, from ancient fable or from modern science, whatever could illustrate or adorn his thoughts. An accumulation of knowledge impregnated his mind, fermented by study and exalted by imagination.

* * *

But original deficiency cannot be supplied. The want of human interest is always felt. *Paradise Lost* is one of the books which the reader admires and lays down, and forgets to take up again. None ever wished it longer than it is. Its perusal is a duty rather than a pleasure. We read Milton for instruction, retire harassed and overburdened, and look elsewhere for recreation; we desert our master, and seek for companions.

* * *

Dryden remarks that Milton has some flats among his elevations.[3] This is only to say that all the parts are not equal. In every work one part must be for the sake of others; a palace must have passages, a poem must have transitions. It is no more to be required that wit should always be blazing than that the sun should always stand at noon. In a great work there is a vicissitude[4] of luminous and opaque parts, as there is in the world a succession of day and night. Milton, when he has expatiated in the sky, may be allowed sometimes to revisit earth; for what other author ever soared so high or sustained his flight so long?

3. Preface to *Sylvae;* see W. P. Ker (ed.), *Essays*   4. Change.
1.268.

* * *

The highest praise of genius is original invention. Milton cannot be said to have contrived the structure of an epic poem, and therefore owes reverence to that vigor and amplitude of mind to which all generations must be indebted for the art of poetical narration, for the texture of the fable, the variation of incidents, the interposition of dialogue, and all the stratagems that surprise and enchain attention. But of all the borrowers from Homer Milton is perhaps the least indebted. He was naturally a thinker for himself, confident of his own abilities and disdainful of help or hindrance; he did not refuse admission to the thoughts or images of his predecessors, but he did not seek them. From his contemporaries he neither courted nor received support; there is in his writings nothing by which the pride of other authors might be gratified or favor gained, no exchange of praise or solicitation of support. His great works were performed under discountenance and in blindness, but difficulties vanished at his touch; he was born for whatever is arduous; and his work is not the greatest of heroic poems, only because it is not the first.

1779

JAMES BOSWELL
1740–1795

The discovery of a vast number of James Boswell's personal papers (believed until 1925 to have been destroyed by his literary executors) has made it possible to know the author of *The Life of Samuel Johnson* better, perhaps, than we can know any other person, dead or living. His published letters and journals have made modern readers aware of the serious and absurd, the charming and repellent sides of his character. At twenty-three, when he met Johnson, he had already trained himself to listen, to observe, and to remember until he found time to set it all down in writing. Only very rarely, it seems, did he ever take notes of conversations while they were in progress, which might have inhibited the speakers. His unusual memory and disciplined art enabled him to re-create and vividly preserve the many "scenes" that distinguish his journals as they do the *Life*.

Boswell was the elder son of Alexander Boswell of Auchinleck (pronounced *Affléck*) in Ayrshire, a judge who bore the courtesy title of Lord Auchinleck. As a member of an ancient family and heir to its large estate, Boswell was in the technical sense of the term a gentleman, with entrée into the best circles of Edinburgh and London. By temperament he was unstable, emotionally and sexually skittish. By 1769, Boswell was established in what was to prove a successful law practice in Edinburgh and had married his cousin, Margaret Montgomerie. But he kept his ties to London and Johnson. In 1773 he persuaded Johnson to join him in a tour of the Highlands and the Hebrides. Johnson's *Journey to the Western Isles of Scotland* (1775) is a thoughtful account of the way that people live in the Hebrides (though some Scots were offended). Boswell's *Journal of a Tour to the Hebrides* (1785), a preliminary study for the *Life*, is a lively and entertaining diary, approved, at least in part, by Johnson himself.

In 1788, four years after Johnson's death, Boswell abandoned his Scottish practice, moved to London, was admitted to the English bar (but never actually practiced), and often depressed and drunken, began the *Life*. Fortunately he had the help and encouragement of the distinguished literary scholar Edmond Malone, without whose guidance he might never have finished his task. Boswell had an overwhelming amount of material to deal with: his own journals, all of Johnson's letters that he could find, Johnson's voluminous writings, and every scrap of information that his friends would furnish—all of which had to be collected, verified, and somehow reduced to unity.

Although the Johnson of popular legend is largely Boswell's creation, there was much in his life about which Boswell had no firsthand knowledge. At their first meeting, Johnson was fifty-four, a widower, already established as "Dictionary" Johnson and the author of the *Rambler,* and pensioned by the crown. Boswell knew nothing at firsthand of the long, hard years during which Johnson made his way painfully up from obscurity to fame. Hence the *Life* is the portrait of a sage. Its chief glory is conversation: the talk of a man who has experienced broadly, read widely, and observed and reflected on his observations; whose ideas are constantly brought to the test of experience; and whose experience is habitually transmuted into ideas. The book is as large as life and as human as its central character.

From The Life of Samuel Johnson, LL.D.

[PLAN OF THE *LIFE*]

* * * Had Dr. Johnson written his own life, in conformity with the opinion which he has given, that every man's life may be best written by himself;[1] had he employed in the preservation of his own history, that clearness of narration and elegance of language in which he has embalmed so many eminent persons, the world would probably have had the most perfect example of biography that was ever exhibited. But although he at different times, in a desultory manner, committed to writing many particulars of the progress of his mind and fortunes, he never had persevering diligence enough to form them into a regular composition. Of these memorials a few have been preserved; but the greater part was consigned by him to the flames, a few days before his death.

As I had the honor and happiness of enjoying his friendship for upwards of twenty years; as I had the scheme of writing his life constantly in view; as he was well apprised of this circumstance, and from time to time obligingly satisfied my inquiries, by communicating to me the incidents of his early years; as I acquired a facility in recollecting, and was very assiduous in recording, his conversation, of which the extraordinary vigor and vivacity constituted one of the first features of his character; and as I have spared no pains in obtaining materials concerning him, from every quarter where I could discover that they were to be found, and have been favored with the most liberal communications by his friends; I flatter myself that few biographers have entered upon such a work as this with more advantages; independent of literary abilities, in which I am not vain enough to compare myself with some great names who have gone before me in this kind of writing. * * *

Indeed I cannot conceive a more perfect mode of writing any man's life than not only relating all the most important events of it in their order, but interweaving what he privately wrote, and said, and thought; by which mankind are enabled as it were to see him live, and to "live o'er each scene"[2] with

---

1. *Idler* 84.   2. Pope's *Prologue* to Addison's *Cato*, line 4.

him, as he actually advanced through the several stages of his life. Had his other friends been as diligent and ardent as I was, he might have been almost entirely preserved. As it is, I will venture to say that he will be seen in this work more completely than any man who has ever yet lived.

[JOHNSON'S EARLY YEARS. MARRIAGE]

[1729] The "morbid melancholy," which was lurking in his constitution, and to which we may ascribe those particularities and that aversion to regular life, which, at a very early period, marked his character, gathered such strength in his twentieth year as to afflict him in a dreadful manner. While he was at Lichfield, in the college vacation of the year 1729, he felt himself overwhelmed with an horrible hypochondria, with perpetual irritation, fretfulness, and impatience; and with a dejection, gloom, and despair, which made existence misery. From this dismal malady he never afterwards was perfectly relieved; and all his labors, and all his enjoyments, were but temporary interruptions of its baleful influence. He told Mr. Paradise[3] that he was sometimes so languid and inefficient that he could not distinguish the hour upon the town-clock. * * *

[1735] Though Mrs. Porter was double the age of Johnson, and her person and manner, as described to me by the late Mr. Garrick,[4] were by no means pleasing to others, she must have had a superiority of understanding and talents, as she certainly inspired him with a more than ordinary passion; and she having signified her willingness to accept of his hand, he went to Lichfield to ask his mother's consent to the marriage, which he could not but be conscious was a very imprudent scheme, both on account of their disparity of years and her want of fortune. But Mrs. Johnson knew too well the ardor of her son's temper, and was too tender a parent to oppose his inclinations.

I know not for what reason the marriage ceremony was not performed at Birmingham; but a resolution was taken that it should be at Derby, for which place the bride and bridegroom set out on horseback, I suppose in very good humor. But though Mr. Topham Beauclerk[5] used archly to mention Johnson's having told him, with much gravity, "Sir, it was a love marriage on both sides," I have had from my illustrious friend the following curious account of their journey to church upon the nuptial morn:

9th July: "Sir, she had read the old romances, and had got into her head the fantastical notion that a woman of spirit should use her lover like a dog. So, Sir, at first she told me that I rode too fast, and she could not keep up with me; and, when I rode a little slower, she passed me, and complained that I lagged behind. I was not to be made the slave of caprice; and I resolved to begin as I meant to end. I therefore pushed on briskly, till I was fairly out of her sight. The road lay between two hedges, so I was sure she could not miss it; and I contrived that she should soon come up with me. When she did, I observed her to be in tears." * * *

---

3. John Paradise, a member of the Essex Head Club, which Johnson founded in 1783.
4. David Garrick (1717–1779), the most famous actor of his day. In 1736 he was one of Johnson's three pupils in an unsuccessful school at Edial.
5. Pronounced *bo-clare*. A descendant of Charles II and the actress Nell Gwynn, he was brilliant and dissolute.

[THE LETTER TO CHESTERFIELD]

[*1754*] Lord Chesterfield,[6] to whom Johnson had paid the high compliment of addressing to his Lordship the *Plan* of his *Dictionary*, had behaved to him in such a manner as to excite his contempt and indignation. The world has been for many years amused with a story confidently told, and as confidently repeated with additional circumstances, that a sudden disgust was taken by Johnson upon occasion of his having been one day kept long in waiting in his Lordship's antechamber, for which the reason assigned was that he had company with him; and that at last, when the door opened, out walked Colley Cibber;[7] and that Johnson was so violently provoked when he found for whom he had been so long excluded, that he went away in a passion, and never would return. I remember having mentioned this story to George Lord Lyttelton, who told me he was very intimate with Lord Chesterfield; and holding it as a well-known truth, defended Lord Chesterfield, by saying, that Cibber, who had been introduced familiarly by the back stairs, had probably not been there above ten minutes. It may seem strange even to entertain a doubt concerning a story so long and so widely current, and thus implicitly adopted, if not sanctioned, by the authority which I have mentioned; but Johnson himself assured me that there was not the least foundation for it. He told me that there never was any particular incident which produced a quarrel between Lord Chesterfield and him; but that his Lordship's continued neglect was the reason why he resolved to have no connection with him. When the *Dictionary* was upon the eve of publication, Lord Chesterfield, who, it is said, had flattered himself with expectations that Johnson would dedicate the work to him, attempted, in a courtly manner, to soothe, and insinuate himself with the sage, conscious, as it should seem, of the cold indifference with which he had treated its learned author; and further attempted to conciliate him, by writing two papers in *The World*, in recommendation of the work; and it must be confessed that they contain some studied compliments, so finely turned, that if there had been no previous offense, it is probable that Johnson would have been highly delighted. Praise, in general, was pleasing to him; but by praise from a man of rank and elegant accomplishments, he was peculiarly gratified. * * *

This courtly device failed of its effect. Johnson, who thought that "all was false and hollow,"[8] despised the honeyed words, and was even indignant that Lord Chesterfield should, for a moment, imagine that he could be dupe of such an artifice. His expression to me concerning Lord Chesterfield, upon this occasion, was, "Sir, after making great professions, he had, for many years, taken no notice of me; but when my *Dictionary* was coming out, he fell a-scribbling in *The World* about it. Upon which, I wrote him a letter expressed in civil terms, but such as might show him that I did not mind what he said or wrote, and that I had done with him."

This is that celebrated letter of which so much has been said, and about which curiosity has been so long excited, without being gratified. I for many

---

6. Philip Dormer Stanhope, earl of Chesterfield (1694–1773), statesman, wit, man of fashion. His *Letters*, written for the guidance of his natural son, are famous for their worldly good sense and for their expression of the ideal of an 18th-century gentleman.

7. Colley Cibber (1671–1757), playwright, comic actor, and (after 1730) poet laureate. A fine actor but a very bad poet, Cibber was a constant object of ridicule by the wits of the town. Pope made him king of the Dunces in the *Dunciad* of 1743.

8. *Paradise Lost* 2.112.

years solicited Johnson to favor me with a copy of it, that so excellent a composition might not be lost to posterity. He delayed from time to time to give it me; till at last in 1781, when we were on a visit at Mr. Dilly's,[9] at Southill in Bedfordshire, he was pleased to dictate it to me from memory. He afterwards found among his papers a copy of it, which he had dictated to Mr. Baretti,[1] with its title and corrections, in his own handwriting. This he gave to Mr. Langton; adding that if it were to come into print, he wished it to be from that copy. By Mr. Langton's kindness, I am enabled to enrich my work with a perfect transcript of what the world has so eagerly desired to see.

TO THE RIGHT HONORABLE THE EARL OF CHESTERFIELD

February 7, 1755

MY LORD,

I have been lately informed, by the proprietor of *The World,* that two papers, in which my Dictionary is recommended to the public, were written by your Lordship. To be so distinguished, is an honor, which, being very little accustomed to favors from the great, I know not well how to receive, or in what terms to acknowledge.

When, upon some slight encouragement, I first visited your Lordship, I was overpowered, like the rest of mankind, by the enchantment of your address; and could not forbear to wish that I might boast myself *Le vainqueur du vainqueur de la terre*[2]—that I might obtain that regard for which I saw the world contending; but I found my attendance so little encouraged that neither pride nor modesty would suffer me to continue it. When I had once addressed your Lordship in public, I had exhausted all the art of pleasing which a retired and uncourtly scholar can possess. I had done all that I could; and no man is well pleased to have his all neglected, be it ever so little.

Seven years, my Lord, have now passed since I waited in your outward rooms, or was repulsed from your door; during which time I have been pushing on my work through difficulties of which it is useless to complain, and have brought it, at last, to the verge of publication, without one act of assistance, one word of encouragement, or one smile of favor. Such treatment I did not expect, for I never had a patron before.

The shepherd in Virgil grew at last acquainted with Love, and found him a native of the rocks.[3]

Is not a patron, my Lord, one who looks with unconcern on a man struggling for life in the water, and, when he has reached ground, encumbers him with help? The notice which you have been pleased to take of my labors, had it been early, had it been kind; but it has been delayed till I am indifferent, and cannot enjoy it; till I am solitary, and

9. Southill was the country home of Charles and Edward Dilly, publishers. The firm published all of Boswell's serious works and shared in the publication of Johnson's *Lives of the Poets* (1779–81).
1. Giuseppe Baretti, an Italian writer and lexicog-rapher whom Johnson introduced into his circle.
2. The conqueror of the conqueror of the earth (French). From the first line of Scudéry's epic *Alaric* (1654).
3. *Eclogues* 8.44.

cannot impart it; till I am known, and do not want it. I hope it is no very cynical asperity not to confess obligations where no benefit has been received, or to be unwilling that the public should consider me as owing that to a patron which Providence has enabled me to do for myself.

Having carried on my work thus far with so little obligation to any favorer of learning, I shall not be disappointed though I should conclude it, if less be possible, with less; for I have been long wakened from that dream of hope in which I once boasted myself with so much exultation, my Lord, your Lordship's most humble, most obedient servant,

SAM. JOHNSON.

"While this was the talk of the town," says Dr. Adams, in a letter to me, "I happened to visit Dr. Warburton,[4] who finding that I was acquainted with Johnson, desired me earnestly to carry his compliments to him, and to tell him that he honored him for his manly behavior in rejecting these condescensions of Lord Chesterfield, and for resenting the treatment he had received from him, with a proper spirit. Johnson was visibly pleased with this compliment, for he had always a high opinion of Warburton. Indeed, the force of mind which appeared in this letter was congenial with that which Warburton himself amply possessed."

There is a curious minute circumstance which struck me, in comparing the various editions of Johnson's imitations of Juvenal. In the tenth satire, one of the couplets upon the vanity of wishes even for literary distinction stood thus:

> Yet think what ills the scholar's life assail,
> Toil, envy, want, the *garret*, and the jail.

But after experiencing the uneasiness which Lord Chesterfield's fallacious patronage made him feel, he dismissed the word *garret* from the sad group, and in all the subsequent editions the line stands

> Toil, envy, want, the *patron*, and the jail.

[A MEMORABLE YEAR: BOSWELL MEETS JOHNSON]

[1763] This is to me a memorable year; for in it I had the happiness to obtain the acquaintance of that extraordinary man whose memoirs I am now writing; an acquaintance which I shall ever esteem as one of the most fortunate circumstances in my life. * * *

Mr. Thomas Davies the actor, who then kept a bookseller's shop in Russel Street, Covent Garden, told me that Johnson was very much his friend, and came frequently to his house, where he more than once invited me to meet him; but by some unlucky accident or other he was prevented from coming to us. * * *

At last, on Monday the 16th of May, when I was sitting in Mr. Davies's

---

4. William Warburton, bishop of Gloucester, friend and literary executor of Pope, editor of Pope and Shakespeare, theological controversialist.

back parlor, after having drunk tea with him and Mrs. Davies, Johnson unexpectedly came into the shop; and Mr. Davies having perceived him through the glass door in the room in which we were sitting, advancing towards us—he announced his awful approach to me, somewhat in the manner of an actor in the part of Horatio, when he addresses Hamlet on the appearance of his father's ghost, "Look, my Lord, it comes." I found that I had a very perfect idea of Johnson's figure, from the portrait of him painted by Sir Joshua Reynolds soon after he had published his *Dictionary,* in the attitude of sitting in his easy chair in deep meditation, which was the first picture his friend did for him, which Sir Joshua very kindly presented to me, and from which an engraving has been made for this work. Mr. Davies mentioned my name, and respectfully introduced me to him. I was much agitated; and recollecting his prejudice against the Scotch, of which I had heard much, I said to Davies, "Don't tell where I come from."—"From Scotland," cried Davies roguishly. "Mr. Johnson," said I, "I do indeed come from Scotland, but I cannot help it." I am willing to flatter myself that I meant this as light pleasantry to soothe and conciliate him, and not as an humiliating abasement at the expense of my country. But however that might be, this speech was somewhat unlucky; for with that quickness of wit for which he was so remarkable, he seized the expression "come from Scotland," which I used in the sense of being of that country; and, as if I had said that I had come away from it, or left it, retorted, "That, Sir, I find, is what a very great many of your countrymen cannot help." This stroke stunned me a good deal; and when we had sat down, I felt myself not a little embarrassed, and apprehensive of what might come next. He then addressed himself to Davies: "What do you think of Garrick? He has refused me an order for the play for Miss Williams,[5] because he knows the house will be full, and that an order would be worth three shillings." Eager to take any opening to get into conversation with him, I ventured to say, "O Sir, I cannot think Mr. Garrick would grudge such a trifle to you." "Sir," said he, with a stern look, "I have known David Garrick longer than you have done: and I know no right you have to talk to me on the subject." Perhaps I deserved this check; for it was rather presumptuous in me, an entire stranger, to express any doubt of the justice of his animadversion upon his old acquaintance and pupil. I now felt myself much mortified, and began to think that the hope which I had long indulged of obtaining his acquaintance was blasted. And, in truth, had not my ardor been uncommonly strong, and my resolution uncommonly persevering, so rough a reception might have deterred me forever from making any further attempts. Fortunately, however, I remained upon the field not wholly discomfited. * * *

I was highly pleased with the extraordinary vigor of his conversation, and regretted that I was drawn away from it by an engagement at another place. I had, for a part of the evening, been left alone with him, and had ventured to make an observation now and then, which he received very civilly; so that I was satisfied that though there was a roughness in his manner, there was no ill nature in his disposition. Davies followed me to the door, and when I complained to him a little of the hard blows which the great man had given

---

5. Mrs. Anna Williams (1706–1783), a blind poet and friend of Mrs. Johnson. She continued to live in Johnson's house after his wife's death and habit-ually sat up to make tea for him whenever he came home.

me, he kindly took upon him to console me by saying, "Don't be uneasy. I can see he likes you very well."

[FEAR OF DEATH]

[1769] When we were alone, I introduced the subject of death, and endeavored to maintain that the fear of it might be got over. I told him that David Hume said to me, he was no more uneasy to think he should *not be* after this life, than that he *had not been* before he began to exist. JOHNSON. "Sir, if he really thinks so, his perceptions are disturbed; he is mad: if he does not think so, he lies. He may tell you, he holds his finger in the flame of a candle, without feeling pain; would you believe him? When he dies, he at least gives up all he has." BOSWELL. "Foote,[6] Sir, told me, that when he was very ill he was not afraid to die." JOHNSON. "It is not true, Sir. Hold a pistol to Foote's breast, or to Hume's breast, and threaten to kill them, and you'll see how they behave." BOSWELL. "But may we not fortify our minds for the approach of death?" Here I am sensible I was in the wrong, to bring before his view what he ever looked upon with horror; for although when in a celestial frame, in his *Vanity of Human Wishes,* he has supposed death to be "kind Nature's signal for retreat," from this stage of being to "a happier seat," his thoughts upon this awful change were in general full of dismal apprehensions. His mind resembled the vast amphitheater, the Colosseum at Rome. In the center stood his judgment, which, like a mighty gladiator, combated those apprehensions that, like the wild beasts of the arena, were all around in cells, ready to be let out upon him. After a conflict, he drove them back into their dens; but not killing them, they were still assailing him. To my question, whether we might not fortify our minds for the approach of death, he answered, in a passion, "No, Sir, let it alone. It matters not how a man dies, but how he lives. The act of dying is not of importance, it lasts so short a time." He added (with an earnest look), "A man knows it must be so, and submits. It will do him no good to whine."

I attempted to continue the conversation. He was so provoked that he said, "Give us no more of this"; and was thrown into such a state of agitation that he expressed himself in a way that alarmed and distressed me; showed an impatience that I should leave him, and when I was going away, called to me sternly, "Don't let us meet tomorrow." * * *

[JOHNSON FACES DEATH]

Death had always been to him an object of terror; so that, though by no means happy, he still clung to life with an eagerness at which many have wondered. At any time when he was ill, he was very much pleased to be told that he looked better. An ingenious member of the Eumelian Club[7] informs me that upon one occasion when he said to him that he saw health returning to his cheek, Johnson seized him by the hand and exclaimed, "Sir, you are one of the kindest friends I ever had." * * *

About eight or ten days before his death, when Dr. Brocklesby paid him

---

6. Samuel Foote, actor and dramatist, famous for his wit and his skill in mimicry.

7. A club to which Boswell and Reynolds belonged.

his morning visit, he seemed very low and desponding, and said, "I have been as a dying man all night." He then emphatically broke out in the words of Shakespeare:

> "Canst thou not minister to a mind diseased;
> Pluck from the memory a rooted sorrow,
> Raze out the written troubles of the brain,
> And with some sweet oblivious antidote
> Cleanse the stuffed bosom of that perilous stuff
> Which weighs upon the heart?"

To which Dr. Brocklesby readily answered, from the same great poet:

> "Therein the patient
> Must minister to himself."[8]

Johnson expressed himself much satisfied with the application. * * *

Dr. Brocklesby, who will not be suspected of fanaticism, obliged me with the following account:

> "For some time before his death, all his fears were calmed and absorbed by the prevalence of his faith, and his trust in the merits and *propitiation* of Jesus Christ." * * *

Johnson having thus in his mind the true Christian scheme, at once rational and consolatory, uniting justice and mercy in the Divinity, with the improvement of human nature, previous to his receiving the Holy Sacrament in his apartment, composed and fervently uttered this prayer:

> "Almighty and most merciful Father, I am now as to human eyes, it seems, about to commemorate, for the last time, the death of thy Son Jesus Christ, our Saviour and Redeemer. Grant, O Lord, that my whole hope and confidence may be in his merits, and thy mercy; enforce and accept my imperfect repentance; make this commemoration available to the confirmation of my faith, the establishment of my hope, and the enlargement of my charity; and make the death of thy Son Jesus Christ effectual to my redemption. Have mercy upon me, and pardon the multitude of my offenses. Bless my friends; have mercy upon all men. Support me, by thy Holy Spirit, in the days of weakness, and at the hour of death; and receive me, at my death, to everlasting happiness, for the sake of Jesus Christ. Amen."

Having * * * made his will on the 8th and 9th of December, and settled all his worldly affairs, he languished till Monday, the 13th of that month, when he expired, about seven o'clock in the evening, with so little apparent pain that his attendants hardly perceived when his dissolution took place. * * *

1791

---

8. *Macbeth* 5.3.40–46.

THOMAS GRAY
1716–1771

The man who wrote the English poem most loved by what Samuel Johnson called "the common reader" was oddly enough a scholarly recluse who lived the quiet life of a university professor in the stagnant atmosphere of mid-eighteenth-century Cambridge, where toward the end of his life he held the professorship of modern history without feeling called on to give a single lecture. He was educated at Eton, where he made intimate friends—Richard West; Thomas Ashton; and Horace Walpole, the son of the prime minister. After four years at Cambridge he left without a degree to make the grand tour of France and Italy as Walpole's guest. The death of West in 1742 desolated Gray, and memories of West haunt much of his verse. He spent the rest of his life in Cambridge, pursuing his studies and writing delightful letters as well as a handful of poems—including two high-flown Pindaric odes, *The Progress of Poesy* (1754) and *The Bard* (1757).

Most of Gray's poems take part in a contemporary reaction against the finish of Pope's couplets; poets sought a new style, at once intimate and prophetic. Gray held that "the language of the age is never the language of poetry," and often uses archaic diction and distorted syntax. But the *Elegy Written in a Country Churchyard* stands alone in his work. It balances Latinate phrases with living English speech, and the learning of a scholar with a common humanity that everyone can share. Johnson, who did not usually like Gray's poetry, acknowledged that the *Elegy* would live forever:

> The Churchyard abounds with images which find a mirror in every mind, and with sentiments to which every bosom returns an echo. The four stanzas beginning "Yet even these bones" are to me original: I have never seen the notions in any other place; yet he that reads them here, persuades himself that he has always felt them. Had Gray written often thus, it had been vain to blame, and useless to praise him.

Ode on the Death of a Favorite Cat[1]

Drowned in a Tub of Goldfishes

'Twas on a lofty vase's side,
Where China's gayest art had dyed
   The azure flowers that blow;°   *bloom*
Demurest of the tabby kind,
5 The pensive Selima reclined,
   Gazed on the lake below.

Her conscious tail her joy declared;
The fair round face, the snowy beard,
   The velvet of her paws,
10 Her coat, that with the tortoise vies,
Her ears of jet, and emerald eyes,
   She saw; and purred applause.

Still had she gazed; but 'midst the tide
Two angel forms were seen to glide,

---

1. Selima, one of Horace Walpole's cats, had recently drowned in a china cistern. Gray wrote this memorial at Walpole's request.

15   The genii of the stream:
       Their scaly armor's Tyrian° hue   *purple*
       Through richest purple to the view
          Betrayed a golden gleam.

       The hapless nymph with wonder saw:
20   A whisker first and then a claw,
          With many an ardent wish,
       She stretched in vain to reach the prize.
       What female heart can gold despise?
          What cat's averse to fish?

25   Presumptuous maid! with looks intent
       Again she stretched, again she bent,
          Nor knew the gulf between.
       (Malignant Fate sat by and smiled)
       The slippery verge her feet beguiled,
30   She tumbled headlong in.

       Eight times emerging from the flood
       She mewed to every watery god,
          Some speedy aid to send.
       No dolphin came, no nereid° stirred: *sea nymph*
35   Nor cruel Tom, nor Susan[2] heard.
          A favorite has no friend!

       From hence, ye beauties, undeceived,
       Know, one false step is ne'er retrieved,
          And be with caution bold.
40   Not all that tempts your wandering eyes
       And heedless hearts is lawful prize;
          Nor all that glisters gold.

1747   1748

Elegy Written in a Country Churchyard

    The curfew tolls the knell of parting day,
      The lowing herd wind slowly o'er the lea,
    The plowman homeward plods his weary way,
      And leaves the world to darkness and to me.

5   Now fades the glimmering landscape on the sight,
      And all the air a solemn stillness holds,
    Save where the beetle wheels his droning flight,
      And drowsy tinklings lull the distant folds;

    Save that from yonder ivy-mantled tower
10   The moping owl does to the moon complain

2. "Tom" and "Susan" are servants' names.

Of such, as wandering near her secret bower,
    Molest her ancient solitary reign.

Beneath those rugged elms, that yew tree's shade,
    Where heaves the turf in many a moldering heap,
15 Each in his narrow cell forever laid,
    The rude° forefathers of the hamlet sleep.   *untaught*

The breezy call of incense-breathing Morn,
    The swallow twittering from the straw-built shed,
The cock's shrill clarion, or the echoing horn,°   *hunter's horn*
20   No more shall rouse them from their lowly bed.

For them no more the blazing hearth shall burn,
    Or busy housewife ply her evening care;
No children run to lisp their sire's return,
    Or climb his knees the envied kiss to share.

25 Oft did the harvest to their sickle yield,
    Their furrow oft the stubborn glebe° has broke;   *soil, turf*
How jocund did they drive their team afield!
    How bowed the woods beneath their sturdy stroke!

Let not Ambition mock their useful toil,
30   Their homely joys, and destiny obscure;
Nor Grandeur hear with a disdainful smile
    The short and simple annals of the poor.

The boast of heraldry,° the pomp of power,   *noble birth*
    And all that beauty, all that wealth e'er gave,
35 Awaits alike the inevitable hour.
    The paths of glory lead but to the grave.

Nor you, ye proud, impute to these the fault,
    If Memory o'er their tomb no trophies[1] raise,
Where through the long-drawn aisle and fretted[2] vault
40   The pealing anthem swells the note of praise.

Can storied urn[3] or animated° bust   *lifelike*
    Back to its mansion call the fleeting breath?
Can Honor's voice provoke° the silent dust,   *call forth*
    Or Flattery soothe the dull cold ear of Death?

45 Perhaps in this neglected spot is laid
    Some heart once pregnant with celestial fire;
Hands that the rod of empire might have swayed,
    Or waked to ecstasy the living lyre.

1. An ornamental or symbolic group of figures depicting the achievements of the deceased.
2. Decorated with intersecting lines in relief.

3. A funeral urn with an epitaph or pictured story inscribed on it.

But Knowledge to their eyes her ample page
50   Rich with the spoils of time did ne'er unroll;
Chill Penury repressed their noble rage,
    And froze the genial current of the soul.

Full many a gem of purest ray serene,
    The dark unfathomed caves of ocean bear:
55   Full many a flower is born to blush unseen,
    And waste its sweetness on the desert air.

Some village Hampden,[4] that with dauntless breast
    The little tyrant of his fields withstood;
Some mute inglorious Milton here may rest,
60   Some Cromwell guiltless of his country's blood.

The applause of listening senates to command,
    The threats of pain and ruin to despise,
To scatter plenty o'er a smiling land,
    And read their history in a nation's eyes,

65   Their lot forbade: nor circumscribed alone
    Their growing virtues, but their crimes confined;
Forbade to wade through slaughter to a throne,
    And shut the gates of mercy on mankind,

The struggling pangs of conscious truth to hide,
70   To quench the blushes of ingenuous shame,
Or heap the shrine of Luxury and Pride
    With incense kindled at the Muse's flame.

Far from the madding crowd's ignoble strife,
    Their sober wishes never learned to stray;
75   Along the cool sequestered vale of life
    They kept the noiseless tenor of their way.

Yet even these bones from insult to protect
    Some frail memorial still erected nigh,
With uncouth rhymes and shapeless sculpture decked,[5]
80   Implores the passing tribute of a sigh.

Their name, their years, spelt by the unlettered Muse,
    The place of fame and elegy supply:
And many a holy text around she strews,
    That teach the rustic moralist to die.

85   For who to dumb Forgetfulness a prey,
    This pleasing anxious being e'er resigned,
Left the warm precincts of the cheerful day,
    Nor cast one longing lingering look behind?

4. John Hampden (1594–1643), who, both as a private citizen and as a Member of Parliament, zealously defended the rights of the people against the autocratic policies of Charles I.
5. Cf. "the storied urn or animated bust" dedicated inside the church to "the proud" (line 41).

On some fond breast the parting soul relies,
90   Some pious drops the closing eye requires;
Even from the tomb the voice of Nature cries,
      Even in our ashes live their wonted fires.

For thee, who mindful of the unhonored dead
      Dost in these lines their artless tale relate;
95 If chance, by lonely contemplation led,
      Some kindred spirit shall inquire thy fate,

Haply some hoary-headed swain may say,
      "Oft have we seen him at the peep of dawn
Brushing with hasty steps the dews away
100   To meet the sun upon the upland lawn.

"There at the foot of yonder nodding beech
      That wreathes its old fantastic roots so high,
His listless length at noontide would he stretch,
      And pore upon the brook that babbles by.

105 "Hard by yon wood, now smiling as in scorn,
      Muttering his wayward fancies he would rove,
Now drooping, woeful wan, like one forlorn,
      Or crazed with care, or crossed in hopeless love.

"One morn I missed him on the customed hill,
110   Along the heath and near his favorite tree;
Another came; nor yet beside the rill,
      Nor up the lawn, nor at the wood was he;

"The next with dirges due in sad array
      Slow through the churchway path we saw him borne.
115 Approach and read (for thou canst read) the lay,
      Graved on the stone beneath yon aged thorn."

The Epitaph

Here rests his head upon the lap of Earth
    A youth to Fortune and to Fame unknown.
Fair Science° frowned not on his humble birth,   Learning
120   *And Melancholy marked him for her own.*

Large was his bounty, and his soul sincere,
    Heaven did a recompense as largely send:
He gave to Misery all he had, a tear,
    He gained from Heaven ('twas all he wished) a friend.

125   *No farther seek his merits to disclose,*
    Or draw his frailties from their dread abode

(There they alike in trembling hope repose),
    The bosom of his Father and his God.

ca. 1742–50   1751

WILLIAM COLLINS
1721–1759

William Collins was born in Chichester and was educated at Winchester and Oxford.
Coming up to London from the university, he tried to establish himself as an author,
but he was given rather to planning than to writing books. Samuel Johnson later
remembered him affectionately as a man of learning who "loved fairies, genii, giants,
and monsters" and who "delighted to rove through the meanders of enchantment."
In 1746 Collins published *Odes on Several Descriptive and Allegorical Subjects,* his
part in an undertaking, with his friend Joseph Warton, to create a new poetry, more
lyrical and fanciful than that of Alexander Pope's generation. Collins's *Odes* address
personified abstractions (Fear, Pity, the Passions), which are imagined as vivid pres-
ences that overwhelm the poet as he calls them to life. This quest for the sublime
has impressed many later readers of Collins, though contemporaries often found his
poems obscure. Inheriting some money, the poet traveled for a while, but fits of
depression gradually deepened into total debility. He spent his last years in Chichester, forgotten by all but a small circle of loyal friends. By the end of the century,
however, his reputation had grown; the Romantics admired his poems and felt akin
to him. The *Ode to Evening,* which combines a chaste and cool classicism with a
delicate feeling for landscape and mood, is one of the delightful poems of the century.

Ode Written in the Beginning of the Year 1746

How sleep the brave[1] who sink to rest
By all their country's wishes blest!
When Spring, with dewy fingers cold,
Returns to deck their hallowed mold,
5   She there shall dress a sweeter sod
Than Fancy's feet have ever trod.

By fairy hands their knell is rung,
By forms unseen their dirge is sung;
There Honor comes, a pilgrim gray,
10   To bless the turf that wraps their clay,
And Freedom shall awhile repair,
To dwell a weeping hermit there!

1746

---

1. Collins is presumably thinking of those who lost their lives defending England in 1745, when the Scotch
Jacobites, led by Bonnie Prince Charlie, penetrated to within 127 miles of London.

Ode to Evening[1]

If aught of oaten stop, or pastoral song,
May hope, chaste Eve, to soothe thy modest ear,
    Like thy own solemn springs,
    Thy springs and dying gales,
5 O nymph reserved, while now the bright-haired sun
Sits in yon western tent, whose cloudy skirts,
    With brede° ethereal wove,   *embroidery*
    O'erhang his wavy bed:
Now air is hushed, save where the weak-eyed bat,
10 With short shrill shriek flits by on leathern wing,
    Or where the beetle winds
    His small but sullen horn,
As oft he rises 'midst the twilight path,
Against the pilgrim borne in heedless hum:
15   Now teach me, maid composed,
    To breathe some softened strain,
Whose numbers,° stealing through thy darkening vale,   *measures*
May not unseemly with its stillness suit,
    As, musing slow, I hail
20   Thy genial loved return!
For when thy folding-star[2] arising shows
His paly circlet, at his warning lamp
    The fragrant Hours, and elves
    Who slept in flowers the day,
25 And many a nymph who wreaths her brows with sedge,
And sheds the freshening dew, and, lovelier still,
    The pensive Pleasures sweet,
    Prepare thy shadowy car.
Then lead, calm vot'ress, where some sheety lake
30 Cheers the lone heath, or some time-hallowed pile
    Or upland fallows gray
    Reflect its last cool gleam.
But when chill blustering winds, or driving rain,
Forbid my willing feet, be mine the hut
35   That from the mountain's side
    Views wilds, and swelling floods,
And hamlets brown, and dim-discovered spires,
And hears their simple bell, and marks o'er all
    Thy dewy fingers draw
40   The gradual dusky veil.
While Spring shall pour his showers, as oft he wont,
And bathe thy breathing tresses, meekest Eve;
    While Summer loves to sport
    Beneath thy lingering light;
45 While sallow Autumn fills thy lap with leaves;

1. Collins borrowed the metrical structure and the rhymeless lines of this ode from Milton's translation of Horace, *Odes* 1.5 (1673). The text printed here is based on the revised version, published in Dodsley's *Miscellany* (1748).
2. The evening star, which signals the hour for herding the sheep into the sheepfold.

Or Winter, yelling through the troublous air,
    Affrights thy shrinking train,
    And rudely rends thy robes;
So long, sure-found beneath the sylvan shed,
50 Shall Fancy, Friendship, Science, rose-lipped Health,
    Thy gentlest influence own,
    And hymn thy favorite name!

                                     1746, 1748

WILLIAM COWPER
1731–1800

There are no saner poems in the language than William Cowper's, yet they were written by a man who was periodically insane and who, for forty years, lived day to day with the possibility of madness. After attempting suicide in 1763, he believed that he was damned for having committed the unforgivable sin, the "sin against the Holy Ghost." From then on, a refugee from life, he looked for hope in Evangelicalism; and found shelter, first in the pious family of the clergyman, Morley Unwin, and after Unwin's death, with his widow, Mary Unwin, who cared for Cowper until her death in 1796. Their move to rural Olney (pronounced Own-y) in 1768 brought them under the influence of the Evangelical minister John Newton; with him Cowper wrote the famous *Olney Hymns*. But another attack of madness, in 1773, not only frustrated his planned marriage to Mary Unwin but left him convinced for the rest of his life that he had been cast out by God. He never again attended services, and the main purpose of his life thereafter was to divert his mind from numb despair by every possible innocent device. He gardened, he kept pets, he walked, he wrote letters (some of the best of the century), he conversed, he read—and he wrote poetry. When his work was published, it brought him a measure of fame that his modest nature could never have hoped for. In the small world and gentle musings of Cowper's major work, *The Task* (1785), contemporaries recognized their own heartfelt concerns. No poet of the century was more beloved.

The Castaway

Obscurest night involved the sky,
    The Atlantic billows roared,
When such a destined wretch as I,
    Washed headlong from on board,
5 Of friends, of hope, of all bereft,
    His floating home forever left.

No braver chief[1] could Albion boast
    Than he with whom he went,

---

1. George, Lord Anson (1697–1762), in whose *Voyage* (1748), Cowper, years before writing this poem, had read the story of the sailor washed overboard in a storm.

Nor ever ship left Albion's coast,
10   With warmer wishes sent.
He loved them both, but both in vain,
Nor him beheld, nor her again.

Not long beneath the whelming brine,
      Expert to swim, he lay;
15   Nor soon he felt his strength decline,
      Or courage die away;
But waged with death a lasting strife,
Supported by despair of life.

He shouted; nor his friends had failed
20   To check the vessel's course,
But so the furious blast prevailed,
      That, pitiless perforce,
They left their outcast mate behind,
And scudded still before the wind.

25   Some succor yet they could afford;
      And, such as storms allow,
The cask, the coop, the floated cord,
      Delayed not to bestow.
But he (they knew) nor ship, nor shore,
30   Whate'er they gave, should visit more.

Nor, cruel as it seemed, could he
      Their haste himself condemn,
Aware that flight, in such a sea,
      Alone could rescue them;
35   Yet bitter felt it still to die
Deserted, and his friends so nigh.

He long survives, who lives an hour
      In ocean, self-upheld;
And so long he, with unspent power,
40   His destiny repelled;
And ever, as the minutes flew,
Entreated help, or cried, "Adieu!"

At length, his transient respite past,
      His comrades, who before
45   Had heard his voice in every blast,
      Could catch the sound no more.
For then, by toil subdued, he drank
The stifling wave, and then he sank.

No poet wept him; but the page
50   Of narrative sincere,
That tells his name, his worth, his age,
      Is wet with Anson's tear.

And tears by bards or heroes shed
Alike immortalize the dead.

55   I therefore purpose not, or dream,
         Descanting on his fate,
     To give the melancholy theme
         A more enduring date:
     But misery still delights to trace
60   Its semblance in another's case.

     No voice divine the storm allayed,
         No light propitious shone,
     When, snatched from all effectual aid,
         We perished, each alone;
65   But I beneath a rougher sea,
     And whelmed in deeper gulfs than he.

1799   1803

OLAUDAH EQUIANO

ca. 1745–1797

The Interesting Narrative of the Life of Olaudah Equiano, or Gustavus Vassa, the African, Written by Himself, published in 1789, is the classic story of an eighteenth-century African's descent into slavery and rise to freedom. Raised in an Ibo village (in modern Nigeria), Olaudah Equiano was kidnapped by African raiders and sold into slavery. He survived the horrors of the Middle Passage to the New World, where an English naval officer bought him to serve as a cabin boy and renamed him Gustavus Vassa, after a sixteenth-century Swedish hero who freed his people from the Danes (such names concealed the status of a slave, because slavery was frowned on by the British Navy). During years at sea, as well as a period at a London school, Equiano acquired a basic education. He was also baptized, which many slaves expected to make them free. But his hopes were cruelly disappointed when, after six years' service, he was suddenly sold and shipped to the West Indies. There a Quaker merchant, Robert King, purchased him, employed him as a clerk and seaman, and eventually allowed him, in 1766, to buy his freedom. Equiano went back to England, working first as a hairdresser and later voyaging all over the world, even taking part in an effort to find a passage to India by way of the North Pole. In the 1780s he became involved in the abolitionist movement. The story of his life was an important contribution to that movement, not only for its explicit arguments against the slave trade but also for its demonstration that someone born in Africa could be humane, intelligent, a good Christian, and a free and eloquent British subject. The book went through many editions and made Equiano famous. He married an Englishwoman, fathered two daughters, and died in London in 1797.

The *Life of Equiano* combines several literary genres. It is a captivity narrative, a spiritual autobiography, a travel memoir, an adventure story, and an abolitionist tract. The early chapters describe the healthy, cheerful, and virtuous life of Africans, contrasted with European inhumanity, and the later chapters show how much a black man can achieve, when given a chance. Equiano does not disguise the strains of his position as he is pulled between different identities anddifferent worlds. His main-purpose, however, is clearly to force his readers to face the ordeals a slave must endure—to live in his skin. If *Oroonoko* taught Europeans to sympathize with Africans, Equiano taught them that a black man could speak for himself.

From The Interesting Narrative of the Life of Olaudah Equiano, or Gustavus Vassa, the African, Written by Himself

[THE MIDDLE PASSAGE][1]

The first object which saluted my eyes when I arrived on the coast was the sea, and a slave ship, which was then riding at anchor, and waiting for its cargo. These filled me with astonishment, which was soon converted into terror when I was carried on board. I was immediately handled and tossed up to see if I were sound by some of the crew; and I was now persuaded that I had gotten into a world of bad spirits, and that they were going to kill me. Their complexions too differing so much from ours, their long hair, and the language they spoke, (which was very different from any I had ever heard) united to confirm me in this belief. Indeed such were the horrors of my views and fears at the moment, that, if ten thousand worlds had been my own, I would have freely parted with them all to have exchanged my condition with that of the meanest slave in my own country. When I looked round the ship too and saw a large furnace of copper boiling, and a multitude of black people of every description chained together, every one of their countenances expressing dejection and sorrow, I no longer doubted of my fate; and, quite overpowered with horror and anguish, I fell motionless on the deck and fainted. When I recovered a little I found some black people about me, who I believe were some of those who brought me on board, and had been receiv-ing their pay; they talked to me in order to cheer me, but all in vain. I asked them if we were not to be eaten by those white men with horrible looks, red faces, and loose hair. They told me I was not; and one of the crew brought me a small portion of spirituous liquor in a wine glass; but, being afraid of him, I would not take it out of his hand. One of the blacks therefore took it from him and gave it to me, and I took a little down my palate, which, instead of reviving me, as they thought it would, threw me into the greatest con-sternation at the strange feeling it produced, having never tasted any such liquor before. Soon after this the blacks who brought me on board went off, and left me abandoned to despair. I now saw myself deprived of all chance of returning to my native country, or even the least glimpse of hope of gaining the shore, which I now considered as friendly; and I even wished for my former slavery in preference to my present situation, which was filled with horrors of every kind, still heightened by my ignorance of what I was to undergo. I was not long suffered to indulge my grief; I was soon put down under the decks, and there I received such a salutation in my nostrils as I had never experienced in my life; so that, with the loathsomeness of the stench, and crying together, I became so sick and low that I was not able to eat, nor had I the least desire to taste any thing. I now wished for the last

1. After his kidnapping, young Equiano passes from one African master to another. The last of these, a merchant, treats him like a member of the family, until one morning the boy is suddenly wak-ened and hurried away to the seacoast.

friend, death, to relieve me; but soon, to my grief, two of the white men offered me eatables; and, on my refusing to eat, one of them held me fast by the hands, and laid me across I think the windlass, and tied my feet, while the other flogged me severely. I had never experienced any thing of this kind before; and although, not being used to the water, I naturally feared that element the first time I saw it, yet nevertheless, could I have got over the nettings,[2] I would have jumped over the side, but I could not; and, besides, the crew used to watch us very closely who were not chained down to the decks, lest we should leap into the water; and I have seen some of these poor African prisoners most severely cut for attempting to do so, and hourly whipped for not eating. This indeed was often the case with myself. In a little time after, amongst the poor chained men, I found some of my own nation, which in a small degree gave ease to my mind. I inquired of these what was to be done with us; they gave me to understand we were to be carried to these white people's country to work for them. I then was a little revived, and thought, if it were no worse than working, my situation was not so desperate: but still I feared I should be put to death, the white people looked and acted, as I thought, in so savage a manner; for I had never seen among any people such instances of brutal cruelty; and this not only shewn towards us blacks, but also to some of the whites themselves. One white man in particular I saw, when we were permitted to be on deck, flogged so unmercifully with a large rope near the foremast, that he died in consequence of it; and they tossed him over the side as they would have done a brute. This made me fear these people the more; and I expected nothing less than to be treated in the same manner. I could not help expressing my fears and apprehensions to some of my countrymen: I asked them if these people had no country, but lived in this hollow place (the ship): they told me they did not, but came from a distant one. "Then," said I, "how comes it in all our country we never heard of them?" They told me because they lived so very far off. I then asked where were their women? had they any like themselves? I was told they had: "and why," said I, "do we not see them?" they answered, because they were left behind. I asked how the vessel could go? they told me they could not tell; but that there were cloths put upon the masts by the help of the ropes I saw, and then the vessel went on; and the white men had some spell or magic they put in the water when they liked in order to stop the vessel. I was exceedingly amazed at this account, and really thought they were spirits. I therefore wished much to be from amongst them, for I expected they would sacrifice me: but my wishes were vain; for we were so quartered that it was impossible for any of us to make our escape. While we stayed on the coast I was mostly on deck; and one day, to my great astonishment, I saw one of these vessels coming in with the sails up. As soon as the whites saw it, they gave a great shout, at which we were amazed; and the more so as the vessel appeared larger by approaching nearer. At last she came to an anchor in my sight, and when the anchor was let go I and my countrymen who saw it were lost in astonishment to observe the vessel stop; and were now convinced it was done by magic. Soon after this the other ship got her boats out, and they came on board of us, and the people of both ships seemed very glad to see each other. Several of the strangers also shook hands

2. A network of small ropes around the ship kept slaves from jumping overboard.

with us black people, and made motions with their hands, signifying I suppose we were to go to their country; but we did not understand them. At last, when the ship we were in had got in all her cargo, they made ready with many fearful noises, and we were all put under deck, so that we could not see how they managed the vessel. But this disappointment was the least of my sorrow. The stench of the hold while we were on the coast was so intolerably loathsome, that it was dangerous to remain there for any time, and some of us had been permitted to stay on the deck for the fresh air; but now that the whole ship's cargo were confined together, it became absolutely pestilential. The closeness of the place, and the heat of the climate, added to the number in the ship, which was so crowded that each had scarcely room to turn himself, almost suffocated us. This produced copious perspirations, so that the air soon became unfit for respiration, from a variety of loathsome smells, and brought on a sickness among the slaves, of which many died, thus falling victims to the improvident avarice, as I may call it, of their purchasers. This wretched situation was again aggravated by the galling of the chains, now become insupportable; and the filth of the necessary tubs,[3] into which the children often fell, and were almost suffocated. The shrieks of the women, and the groans of the dying, rendered the whole a scene of horror almost inconceivable. Happily perhaps for myself I was soon reduced so low here that it was thought necessary to keep me almost always on deck; and from[4] my extreme youth I was not put in fetters. In this situation I expected every hour to share the fate of my companions, some of whom were almost daily brought upon deck at the point of death, which I began to hope would soon put an end to my miseries. Often did I think many of the inhabitants of the deep much more happy than myself. I envied them the freedom they enjoyed, and as often wished I could change my condition for theirs. Every circumstance I met with served only to render my state more painful, and heighten my apprehensions, and my opinion of the cruelty of the whites. One day they had taken a number of fishes; and when they had killed and satisfied themselves with as many as they thought fit, to our astonishment who were on the deck, rather than give any of them to us to eat as we expected, they tossed the remaining fish into the sea again, although we begged and prayed for some as well as we could, but in vain; and some of my countrymen, being pressed by hunger, took an opportunity, when they thought no one saw them, of trying to get a little privately; but they were discovered, and the attempt procured them some very severe floggings.

One day, when we had a smooth sea and moderate wind, two of my wearied countrymen who were chained together (I was near them at the time), preferring death to such a life of misery, somehow made through the nettings and jumped into the sea; immediately another quite dejected fellow, who, on account of his illness, was suffered to be out of irons, also followed their example; and I believe many more would very soon have done the same if they had not been prevented by the ship's crew, who were instantly alarmed. Those of us that were the most active were in a moment put down under the deck, and there was such a noise and confusion amongst the people of the ship as I never heard before, to stop her, and get the boat out to go after the slaves. However two of the wretches were drowned, but they got the other,

3. Latrines.   4. Because of.

and afterwards flogged him unmercifully for thus attempting to prefer death to slavery. In this manner we continued to undergo more hardships than I can now relate, hardships which are inseparable from this accursed trade. Many a time we were near suffocation from the want of fresh air, which we were often without for whole days together. This, and the stench of the necessary tubs, carried off many. During our passage I first saw flying fishes, which surprised me very much: they used frequently to fly across the ship, and many of them fell on the deck. I also now first saw the use of the quadrant; I had often with astonishment seen the mariners make observations with it, and I could not think what it meant. They at last took notice of my surprise; and one of them, willing to increase it, as well as to gratify my curiosity, made me one day look through it. The clouds appeared to me to be land, which disappeared as they passed along. This heightened my wonder; and I was now more persuaded than ever that I was in another world, and that every thing about me was magic. At last we came in sight of the island of Barbados,[5] at which the whites on board gave a great shout, and made many signs of joy to us. We did not know what to think of this; but as the vessel drew nearer we plainly saw the harbor, and other ships of different kinds and sizes; and we soon anchored amongst them off Bridge Town. Many merchants and planters now came on board, though it was in the evening. They put us in separate parcels,[6] and examined us attentively. They also made us jump, and pointed to the land, signifying we were to go there. We thought by this we should be eaten by these ugly men, as they appeared to us; and, when soon after we were all put down under the deck again, there was much dread and trembling among us, and nothing but bitter cries to be heard all the night from these apprehensions, insomuch that at last the white people got some old slaves from the land to pacify us. They told us we were not to be eaten, but to work, and were soon to go on land, where we should see many of our country people. This report eased us much; and sure enough, soon after we were landed, there came to us Africans of all languages. We were conducted immediately to the merchant's yard, where we were pent up altogether like so many sheep in a fold, without regard to sex or age. As every object was new to me, every thing I saw filled me with surprise. What struck me first was that the houses were built with stories, and in every other respect different from those in Africa; but I was still more astonished on seeing people on horseback. I did not know what this could mean; and indeed I thought these people were full of nothing but magical arts. While I was in this astonishment one of my fellow prisoners spoke to a countryman of his about the horses, who said they were the same kind they had in their country. I understood them, though they were from a distant part of Africa, and I thought it odd I had not seen any horses there; but afterwards, when I came to converse with different Africans, I found they had many horses amongst them, and much larger than those I then saw. We were not many days in the merchant's custody before we were sold after their usual manner, which is this:—On a signal given (as the beat of a drum) the buyers rush at once into the yard where the slaves are confined, and make a choice of that parcel they like best. The noise and clamor with which this is attended, and the eager-

---

5. The easternmost Caribbean island, then an important center for the trade of sugar and slaves.

6. Groups sorted to be sold as one lot.

ness visible in the countenances of the buyers, serve not a little to increase the apprehensions of the terrified Africans, who may well be supposed to consider them as the ministers of that destruction to which they think themselves devoted.[7] In this manner, without scruple, are relations and friends separated, most of them never to see each other again. I remember in the vessel in which I was brought over, in the men's apartment, there were several brothers, who, in the sale, were sold in different lots; and it was very moving on this occasion to see and hear their cries at parting. O, ye nominal Christians! might not an African ask you, learned you this from your God, who says unto you, Do unto all men as you would men should do unto you? Is it not enough that we are torn from our country and friends to toil for your luxury and lust of gain? Must every tender feeling be likewise sacrificed to your avarice? Are the dearest friends and relations, now rendered more dear by their separation from their kindred, still to be parted from each other, and thus prevented from cheering the gloom of slavery with the small comfort of being together and mingling their sufferings and sorrows? Why are parents to lose their children, brothers their sisters, or husbands their wives? Surely this is a new refinement in cruelty, which, while it has no advantage to atone for it, thus aggravates distress, and adds fresh horrors even to the wretchedness of slavery.

* * *

[A FREE MAN][8]

Every day now brought me nearer my freedom, and I was impatient till we proceeded again to sea, that I might have an opportunity of getting a sum large enough to purchase it. I was not long ungratified; for, in the beginning of the year 1766, my master bought another sloop, named the *Nancy*, the largest I had ever seen. She was partly laden, and was to proceed to Philadelphia; our Captain had his choice of three, and I was well pleased he chose this, which was the largest; for, from his having a large vessel, I had more room, and could carry a larger quantity of goods with me. Accordingly, when we had delivered our old vessel, the *Prudence*, and completed the lading of the *Nancy*, having made near three hundred per cent, by four barrels of pork I brought from Charlestown, I laid in as large a cargo as I could, trusting to God's providence to prosper my undertaking. With these views I sailed for Philadelphia. On our passage, when we drew near the land, I was for the first time surprised at the sight of some whales, having never seen any such large sea monsters before; and as we sailed by the land one morning I saw a puppy whale close by the vessel; it was about the length of a wherry boat, and it followed us all the day till we got within the Capes. We arrived safe and in good time at Philadelphia, and I sold my goods there chiefly to the Quakers. They always appeared to be a very honest discreet sort of people, and never attempted to impose on me; I therefore liked them, and ever after chose to deal with them in preference to any others.

---

7. Doomed.
8. Frustrated in his hope to be set free in England, Equiano is shipped to Montserrat, a British colony in the Leeward Islands of the West Indies. Robert King, a prosperous Quaker merchant from Philadelphia, buys him, treats him kindly, and values him as a reliable worker. By being useful to a friendly sea captain, Thomas Farmer, Equiano has opportunities to travel and trade goods for money. Eventually King promises to let him purchase his freedom for his original cost: forty pounds sterling.

One Sunday morning while I was here, as I was going to church, I chanced to pass a meeting house. The doors being open, and the house full of people, it excited my curiosity to go in. When I entered the house, to my great surprise, I saw a very tall woman standing in the midst of them, speaking in an audible voice something which I could not understand. Having never seen anything of this kind before, I stood and stared about me for some time, wondering at this odd scene. As soon as it was over I took an opportunity to make inquiry about the place and people, when I was informed they were called Quakers.[9] I particularly asked what that woman I saw in the midst of them had said, but none of them were pleased to satisfy me; so I quitted them, and soon after, as I was returning, I came to a church crowded with people; the church-yard was full likewise, and a number of people were even mounted on ladders, looking in at the windows. I thought this a strange sight, as I had never seen churches, either in England or the West Indies, crowded in this manner before. I therefore made bold to ask some people the meaning of all this, and they told me the Rev. Mr. George Whitfield[1] was preaching. I had often heard of this gentleman, and had wished to see and hear him; but I had never before had an opportunity. I now therefore resolved to gratify myself with the sight, and I pressed in amidst the multitude. When I got into the church I saw this pious man exhorting the people with the greatest fervor and earnestness, and sweating as much as I ever did while in slavery on Montserrat beach. I was very much struck and impressed with this; I thought it strange I had never seen divines exert themselves in this manner before, and I was no longer at a loss to account for the thin congregations they preached to.

When we had discharged our cargo here, and were loaded again, we left this fruitful land once more, and set sail for Montserrat. My traffic had hitherto succeeded so well with me, that I thought, by selling my goods when we arrived at Montserrat, I should have enough to purchase my freedom. But, as soon as our vessel arrived there, my master came on board, and gave orders for us to go to St. Eustatia,[2] and discharge our cargo there, and from thence proceed for Georgia. I was much disappointed at this; but thinking, as usual, it was of no use to murmur at the decrees of fate, I submitted without repining, and we went to St. Eustatia. After we had discharged our cargo there we took in a live cargo, as we call a cargo of slaves. Here I sold my goods tolerably well; but, not being able to lay out all my money in this small island to as much advantage as in many other places, I laid out only part, and the remainder I brought away with me neat.[3] We sailed from hence for Georgia, and I was glad when we got there, though I had not much reason to like the place from my last adventure in Savannah;[4] but I longed to get back to Montserrat and procure my freedom, which I expected to be able to purchase when I returned. As soon as we arrived here I waited on my careful doctor, Mr. Brady, to whom I made the

9. Quaker meetings are not led by clergy; any male or female worshiper who felt inspired by God could rise to speak.
1. Whitefield (1714–1770), a famous evangelist who helped found Methodism, was in Britain, not Philadelphia, in 1766. It is possible that Equiano had heard him preach the previous year, in Savannah, Georgia. Equiano's later conversion to Meth-

odism will become a dominant theme of his life story.
2. An island in the Netherlands Antilles (West Indies).
3. Intact.
4. The year before, a drunken slave owner and his servant had beaten Equiano so brutally that he nearly died.

most grateful acknowledgments in my power for his former kindness and attention during my illness.

While we were here an odd circumstance happened to the Captain and me, which disappointed us both a good deal. A silversmith, whom we had brought to this place some voyages before, agreed with the Captain to return with us to the West Indies, and promised at the same time to give the Captain a great deal of money, having pretended to take a liking to him, and being, as we thought, very rich. But while we stayed to load our vessel this man was taken ill in a house where he worked, and in a week's time became very bad. The worse he grew the more he used to speak of giving the Captain what he had promised him, so that he expected something considerable from the death of this man, who had no wife or child, and he attended him day and night. I used also to go with the Captain, at his own desire, to attend him; especially when we saw there was no appearance of his recovery; and, in order to recompense me for my trouble, the Captain promised me ten pounds, when he should get the man's property. I thought this would be of great service to me, although I had nearly money enough to purchase my freedom, if I should get safe this voyage to Montserrat. In this expectation I laid out above eight pounds of my money for a suit of superfine clothes to dance with at my freedom, which I hoped was then at hand. We still continued to attend this man, and were with him even on the last day he lived, till very late at night, when we went on board. After we were got to bed, about one or two o'clock in the morning, the Captain was sent for, and informed the man was dead. On this he came to my bed, and, waking me, informed me of it, and desired me to get up and procure a light, and immediately go to him. I told him I was very sleepy, and wished he would take somebody else with him, or else, as the man was dead, and could want no farther attendance, to let all things remain as they were till next morning. "No, no," said he, "we will have the money tonight, I cannot wait till tomorrow; so let us go." Accordingly I got up and struck a light, and away we both went and saw the man as dead as we could wish. The Captain said he would give him a grand burial, in gratitude for the promised treasure; and desired that all the things belonging to the deceased might be brought forth. Among others, there was a nest of trunks of which he had kept the keys whilst the man was ill, and when they were produced we opened them with no small eagerness and expectation; and as there were a great number within one another, with much impatience we took them one out of the other. At last, when we came to the smallest, and had opened it, we saw it was full of papers, which we supposed to be notes; at the sight of which our hearts leapt for joy; and that instant the Captain, clapping his hands, cried out, "Thank God, here it is." But when we took up the trunk, and began to examine the supposed treasure and long-looked-for bounty, (alas! alas! how uncertain and deceitful are all human affairs!) what had we found! While we were embracing a substance we grasped an empty nothing. The whole amount that was in the nest of trunks was only one dollar and a half; and all that the man possessed would not pay for his coffin. Our sudden and exquisite joy was now succeeded by as sudden and exquisite pain; and my Captain and I exhibited, for some time, most ridiculous figures—pictures of chagrin and disappointment! We went away greatly mortified, and left the deceased to do as well as he could for himself, as we had taken so good care of him when alive for nothing. We set sail once more for Montserrat, and arrived there safe; but much out of humor with our friend the silversmith. When we had unladen the vessel, and I had sold my venture, finding myself master of about forty-seven pounds, I consulted my true friend, the Captain, how I should proceed in offering my master the money for my freedom. He told me to come on a certain morning, when he and my master would be at breakfast together. Accordingly, on that morning I went, and met the Captain there, as he had appointed. When I went in I made my obeisance to my master, and with my money in my hand, and many fears in my heart, I prayed him to be as good as his offer to me, when he was pleased to promise me my freedom as soon as I could purchase it. This speech seemed to confound him; he began to recoil; and my heart that instant sank within me. "What," said he, "give you your freedom? Why, where did you get the money? Have you got forty pounds sterling?" "Yes, sir," I answered. "How did you get it?" replied he. I told him, very honestly. The Captain then said he knew I got the money very honestly and with much industry, and that I was particularly careful. On which my master replied, I got money much faster than he did; and said he would not have made me the promise he did if he had thought I should have got money so soon. "Come, come," said my worthy Captain, clapping my master on the back, "Come, Robert" (which was his name), "I think you must let him have his freedom; you have laid your money out very well; you have received good interest for it all this time, and here is now the principal at last. I know Gustavus has earned you more than an hundred a-year, and he will still save you money, as he will not leave you:—Come, Robert, take the money." My master then said, he would not be worse than his promise; and, taking the money, told me to go to the Secretary at the Register Office, and get my manumission[5] drawn up. These words of my master were like a voice from heaven to me: in an instant all my trepidation was turned into unutterable bliss; and I most reverently bowed myself with gratitude, unable to express my feelings, but by the overflowing of my eyes, while my true and worthy friend, the Captain, congratulated us both with a peculiar degree of heartfelt pleasure. As soon as the first transports of my joy were over, and that I had expressed my thanks to these my worthy friends in the best manner I was able, I rose with a heart full of affection and reverence, and left the room, in order to obey my master's joyful mandate of going to the Register Office. As I was leaving the house I called to mind the words of the Psalmist, in the 126th Psalm, and like him, "I glorified God in my heart, in whom I trusted." These words had been impressed on my mind from the very day I was forced from Deptford[6] to the present hour, and I now saw them, as I thought, fulfilled and verified. My imagination was all rapture as I flew to the Register Office, and in this respect, like the apostle Peter[7] (whose deliverance from prison was so sudden and extraordinary, that he thought he was in a vision), I could scarcely believe I was awake. Heavens! who could do justice to my feelings at this moment! Not conquering heroes themselves, in the midst of a triumph—Not the tender mother who had just regained her long-lost infant, and presses it to her heart—Not the weary hungry mariner, at the sight of the desired friendly port—Not the lover, when he once more

5. Release from slavery.
6. The port near London from which Equiano was
sold by his English master.
7. Acts, chap. xii, ver. 9 [Equiano's note].

embraces his beloved mistress, after she had been ravished from his arms!—
All within my breast was tumult, wildness, and delirium! My feet scarcely
touched the ground, for they were winged with joy, and, like Elijah, as he
rose to Heaven,[8] they "were with lightning sped as I went on." Every one I
met I told of my happiness, and blazed about the virtue of my amiable master
and captain.

When I got to the office and acquainted the Register with my errand he
congratulated me on the occasion, and told me he would draw up my manumission for half price, which was a guinea. I thanked him for his kindness;
and having received it and paid him, I hastened to my master to get him to
sign it, that I might be fully released. Accordingly he signed the manumission
that day, so that, before night, I who had been a slave in the morning, trembling at the will of another, was become my own master, and completely free.
I thought this was the happiest day I had ever experienced; and my joy was
still heightened by the blessings and prayers of the sable race, particularly
the aged, to whom my heart had ever been attached with reverence.

As the form of my manumission has something peculiar in it, and expresses
the absolute power and dominion one man claims over his fellow, I shall beg
leave to present it before my readers at full length:

Montserrat.—To all men unto whom these presents shall come: I Robert
King, of the parish of St. Anthony in the said island, merchant, send greeting:
Know ye, that I the aforesaid Robert King, for and in consideration of the
sum of seventy pounds current money of the said island,[9] to me in hand paid,
and to the intent that a negro man-slave, named Gustavus Vassa, shall and
may become free, have manumitted, emancipated, enfranchised, and set
free, and by these presents do manumit, emancipate, enfranchise, and set
free, the aforesaid negro man-slave, named Gustavus Vassa, for ever, hereby
giving, granting, and releasing unto him, the said Gustavus Vassa, all right,
title, dominion, sovereignty, and property, which, as lord and master over
the aforesaid Gustavus Vassa, I had, or now I have, or by any means whatsoever I may or can hereafter possibly have over him the aforesaid negro, for
ever. In witness whereof I the above-said Robert King have unto these presents set my hand and seal, this tenth day of July, in the year of our Lord one
thousand seven hundred and sixty-six.

ROBERT KING

Signed, sealed, and delivered in the presence of Terrylegay, Montserrat.
Registered the within manumission at full length, this eleventh day of July,
1766, in liber D.[1]

TERRYLEGAY, REGISTER.

In short, the fair as well as black people immediately styled me by a new
appellation, to me the most desirable in the world, which was Freeman, and

---

8. 2 Kings 2.11.
9. The equivalent of forty pounds in British money.
1. Book or register D.

at the dances I gave my Georgia superfine blue clothes made no indifferent appearance, as I thought.

* * *

1789

FRANCES BURNEY
1752–1840

People have often made the mistake of underestimating Frances Burney. In person, as in her writing, she seemed a proper, self-effacing lady. Many readers still call her "Fanny," as if familiarity could make her harmless. But she saw through such poses. Sir Joshua Reynolds said that "if he was conscious to himself of any trick, or any affectation, there is nobody he should so much fear as this little Burney!" And Samuel Johnson teased her by claiming that "your shyness, & slyness, & pretending to know nothing, never took *me* in, whatever you may do with others. *I* always knew you for a *toadling!*" (according to legend, little toads may look submissive but actually carry poison). Although her writing crackles with humor, it can be relentless—and some-times cruel—in exposing bad manners or a selfish heart.

She learned quite young how to hide in a crowd. Devoted daughter of Charles Burney, a popular teacher and historian of music, Frances grew up in a large family that gave her many opportunities to study character and mix discreetly in society. Her first novel, *Evelina, or A Young Lady's Entrance into the World* (1778), was written in secret and published anonymously. But delighted readers, including Johnson, Burke, and Hester Thrale, soon found her out and sang her praises; and a second novel, *Cecilia* (1782), confirmed her reputation. Her home life was less happy, however; she and her stepmother disliked each other, and she fell in love with a young clergyman who never got around to proposing. In 1786, to please her father, she accepted a place as a lady-in-waiting at court, where the paralyzing etiquette and lack of inde-pendence tormented her for the next five years, until she finally managed to resign. At forty-one she married a French émigré, General Alexandre Gabriel-Jean-Baptiste d'Arblay. Despite the disapproval of her father—d'Arblay was penniless, Catholic, and politically liberal—the marriage was happy. Madame d'Arblay soon bore a son, and her novel *Camilla* (1796) brought in good money. When she joined her husband in France, in 1802, the Napoleonic wars prevented them from returning to England for ten years; the pain of an outcast dominates her last novel, *The Wanderer, or Female Difficulties* (1814). But she never stopped writing, producing a doctored version of her father's *Memoirs* (1832) and more of the diaries and letters that, edited after her death by a niece, made her famous again.

Burney wrote all her life—not only novels and plays but perpetual letters and jour-nals, recording whatever she saw for friends and family as well as herself. Even the most informal pages display her gifts: a knack for catching character, a wonderful ear for dialogue, wry humor, and a swift pace that carries the reader along from moment to moment. Her special subject is embarrassment—often her own. In scenes like her flight from the king, where she is torn between opposite notions of the right thing to do, shame and comedy mingle. But these trepidations can also be incredibly painful, as in her gripping account of a mastectomy. Despite her propriety, Burney looks at the world and its institutions with the clear eyes of an outsider, aware of the gaps between what people say and what they do. She frees herself to write with utter honesty by pretending, at first, that nobody is going to read her. But her private thoughts are reported so fully and faithfully that, in the end, every reader can share them.

From The Journal and Letters

[FIRST JOURNAL ENTRY]

Poland Street, London, March 27, 1768[1]

To have some account of my thoughts, manners, acquaintance & actions, when the hour arrives in which time is more nimble than memory, is the reason which induces me to keep a journal: a journal in which I must confess my *every* thought, must open my whole heart! But a thing of this kind ought to be addressed to somebody—I must imagine myself to be talking—talking to the most intimate of friends—to one in whom I should take delight in confiding, & remorse in concealment: but who must this friend be?—to make choice of one to whom I can but *half* rely, would be to frustrate entirely the intention of my plan. The only one I could wholly, totally confide in, lives in the same house with me, & not only never *has*, but never *will*, leave me one secret *to* tell her.[2] To whom, then, *must* I dedicate my wonderful, surprising & interesting adventures?—to *whom* dare I reveal my private opinion of my nearest relations? the secret thoughts of my dearest friends? my own hopes, fears, reflections & dislikes?—Nobody!

To Nobody, then, will I write my journal! since to Nobody can I be wholly unreserved—to Nobody can I reveal every thought, every wish of my heart, with the most unlimited confidence, the most unremitting sincerity to the end of my life! For what chance, what accident can end my connections with Nobody? No secret *can* I conceal from No—body, & to No—body can I be *ever* unreserved. Disagreement cannot stop our affection, time itself has no power to end our friendship. The love, the esteem I entertain for Nobody, No-body's self has not power to destroy. From Nobody I have nothing to fear, the secrets sacred to friendship, Nobody will not reveal, when the affair is doubtful, Nobody will not look towards the side least favorable—.

I will suppose you, then, to be my best friend; tho' God forbid you ever should! my dearest companion—& a romantick girl, for mere oddity may perhaps be more sincere—more *tender*—than if you were a friend in propria personæ[3]—in as much as imagination often exceeds reality. In your breast my errors may create pity without exciting contempt; may raise your compassion, without eradicating your love.

From this moment, then, my dear girl—but why, permit me to ask, must a *female* be made Nobody? Ah! my dear, what were this world good for, *were* Nobody a female? And now I have done with *preambulation*.

---

1. This is the first page of Burney's first journal, begun when she was fifteen.
2. Burney's younger sister, Susanna. In 1773, when Burney spent the summer away from home, she began a journal for her sister, and continued it off and on until 1800, when Susanna died.
3. In your own person.

["DOWN WITH HER, BURNEY!"]

Streatham, September 15, 1778[4]

I was then looking over the Life of Cowley, which he had himself given me to read, at the same time that he gave to Mrs. Thrale that of Waller.—They are now *printed,* though they will not be *published* for some time. But he bid me put it away.—"Do," cried he, "put away that now, & *prattle* with us;—I can't make this little Burney prattle,—& I am *sure* she prattles well.—but I shall teach her another lesson than to sit thus silent, before I have done with her."

"To *talk,*" cried I, "is the *only* lesson I shall be backward to learn from you, sir."

Mrs. T. Tomorrow, sir, Mrs. Montagu[5] dines here! & then you will have talk enough.

Dr. Johnson began to seesaw, with a countenance strongly expressive of *inward fun,*—&, after enjoying it some time in silence, he suddenly, & with great animation, turned to me, & cried "*Down* with her, Burney!—*down* with her!—spare her not! attack her, fight her, & *down* with her at once!—*You* are a *rising* wit,—*she* is at the *top,*—& when *I* was beginning the world, & was nothing & nobody, the joy of my life was to fire at all the established wits!—& then, every body loved to hallow[6] me on;—but there is no game *now,* & *now,* every body would be glad to see me *conquered*: but *then,* when I was *new,*—to vanquish the great ones was all the delight of my poor little dear soul!—So at her, Burney!—at her, & *down* with her!"

O how we all hollowed![7] By the way, I must tell you that Mrs. Montagu is in very great estimation here, even with Dr. Johnson himself, when others do not praise her *improperly*: Mrs. Thrale ranks her as the *first of women,* in the literary way.

I should have told you, that Miss Gregory, daughter of the Gregory who wrote the letters, or *Legacy* of advice,[8] lives with Mrs. Montagu, & was invited to accompany her.

"Mark, now," said Dr. Johnson, "if I *contradict* her tomorrow; I am determined, let her say what she will, that I will *not* contradict her."

Mrs. T. Why, to be sure, Sir, you *did* put her a little out of countenance last time she came,—yet you were neither rough, nor cruel, nor ill-natured,—but still, when a lady *changes color,* we imagine her feelings are not quite *composed.*

Dr. J. Why, madam, I won't answer that I sha'n't contradict her again, if she provokes me as she did then; but a *less* provocation I will withstand. I believe I am not high in her good graces already, & I begin (added he, laughing heartily) to tremble for my admission into her new house! I doubt I shall never see the inside of it!

Mrs. Montagu is building a most superb house.

---

4. *Evelina* was published in January 1778 and enthusiastically received. After her authorship became known, Burney was invited to Streatham Park, the country house of Hector and Hester Lynch Thrale. Johnson spent much of his time there and was then writing his *Lives of the Poets.* He and Hester Thrale became fond of Burney.
5. Elizabeth Montagu, known as "Queen of the

Blues" (or bluestockings), a group of intellectual women, was probably the most respected literary woman in England; she had written the famous *Essay on Shakespear* (1769).
6. A cry inciting hunters to the chase.
7. "To shout; to hoot" (Johnson's *Dictionary*).
8. John Gregory, *A Father's Legacy to His Daughters* (1774).

Mrs. T. O, I warrant you! she *fears* you, indeed, but that, you know, is nothing uncommon: & dearly I love to hear your *disquisitions*,—for certainly she is the first woman, for literary knowledge, in England,—& if in *England* I hope I may say in the *world!*

Dr. J. I believe you may, Madam. She diffuses more knowledge in her conversation than any woman I know,—or, indeed, *almost* any man.

Mrs. T. I declare *I* know *no* man equal to her, take away yourself & Burke, for *that* art.—And *you*, who love magnificence, won't quarrel with her, as everybody else does, for her love of finery.

Dr. J. No, I shall not quarrel with her upon that topic. (then, looking earnestly at *me*) "Nay," he added, "it's very handsome."

"What, sir?" cried I, amazed.

"Why your cap:—I have looked at it some time, & I like it much. It has not that vile *bandeau*[9] across it, which I have so often cursed."

Did you ever hear any thing so strange? *Nothing* escapes him. My Daddy Crisp[1] is not more minute in his attentions: nay, I think he is even *less* so.

Mrs. T. Well, sir, that bandeau you quarreled with was worn by every woman at court the last Birth Day,[2]—& I observed that *all* the men found fault with it.

Dr. J. The truth is,—women,—take them in general,—have *no* idea of grace!—Fashion is *all* they think of;—I don't mean Mrs. Thrale & Miss Burney, when I talk of *women!*—*they* are goddesses!—& therefore I except them.

Mrs. T. Lady Ladd never wore the bandeau, & said she never would, because it is unbecoming.

Dr. J. (*laughing*) Did not she? then is Lady Ladd a charming woman, & I have yet hopes of entering into engagements with her!

Mrs. T. Well, as to that, I can't say,—but, to be sure, the only similitude *I* have yet discovered in you, *is* in *size: there* you agree mighty well.

Dr. J. Why if *any* body could have worn the bandeau, it must have been Lady Ladd, for there is *enough* of her to carry it off; but *you* are too *little* for any thing ridiculous; that which seems *nothing* upon a Patagonian,[3] will become very *conspicuous* upon a Lilliputian; & of *you* there is so little in *all*, that one single absurdity would swallow up *half* of you.

Some time after,—when we had all been a few minutes wholly silent, he turned to me, & said "Come, Burney,—shall you & I *study our parts* against[4] Mrs. Montagu comes?"

How would you be entertained, my dear Susy, if I could give you the *manner*, as well as *matter*, of the conversation of this greatest of men.

[ENCOUNTERING THE KING]

Kew Palace, Monday February 2, 1789

What an adventure had I this morning! one that has occasioned me the severest personal terror I ever experienced in my life.

Sir Lucas Pepys still persisting that exercise and air were absolutely necessary to save me from illness, I have continued my walks, varying my gardens

---

9. A narrow headband.
1. Samuel Crisp, an old family friend, had been a mentor to Burney.
2. June 4, the king's birthday.

3. The Indians of Patagonia, whose average height was more than six feet, were commonly thought to be giants.
4. Before.

from Richmond to Kew, according to the accounts I received of the movements of the king. For this I had her majesty's permission, on the representation of Sir Lucas.

This morning, when I received my intelligence of the king from Dr. John Willis,[5] I begged to know where I might walk in safety? "In Kew gardens," he said, "as the king would be in Richmond."

"Should any unfortunate circumstance," I cried, "at any time, occasion my being seen by his majesty, do not mention my name, but let me run off without call or notice."

This he promised. Everybody, indeed, is ordered to keep out of sight.

Taking, therefore, the time I had most at command, I strolled into the gardens. I had proceeded, in my quick way, nearly half the round, when I suddenly perceived, through some trees, two or three figures. Relying on the instructions of Dr. John, I concluded them to be workmen and gardeners; yet tried to look sharp, and in so doing, as they were less shaded, I thought I saw the person of his majesty!

Alarmed past all possible expression, I waited not to know more, but turning back, ran off with all my might. But what was my terror to hear myself pursued!—to hear the voice of the king himself loudly and hoarsely calling after me, "Miss Burney! Miss Burney!"

I protest I was ready to die. I knew not in what state he might be at the time; I only knew the orders to keep out of his way were universal; that the queen would highly disapprove any unauthorized meeting, and that the very action of my running away might deeply, in his present irritable state, offend him. Nevertheless, on I ran, too terrified to stop, and in search of some short passage, for the garden is full of little labyrinths, by which I might escape.

The steps still pursued me, and still the poor hoarse and altered voice rang in my ears:—more and more footsteps resounded frightfully behind me,—the attendants all running, to catch their eager master, and the voices of the two Doctor Willises loudly exhorting him not to heat himself so unmercifully.

Heavens, how I ran! I do not think I should have felt the hot lava from Vesuvius—at least not the hot cinders—had I so run during its eruption. My feet were not sensible that they even touched the ground.

Soon after, I heard other voices, shriller, though less nervous, call out "Stop! stop! stop!"

I could by no means consent; I knew not what was purposed, but I recollected fully my agreement with Dr. John that very morning, that I should decamp if surprised, and not be named.

My own fears and repugnance, also, after a flight and disobedience like this, were doubled in the thought of not escaping; I knew not to what I might be exposed, should the malady be then high, and take the turn of resentment. Still, therefore, on I flew; and such was my speed, so almost incredible to relate or recollect, that I fairly believe no one of the whole party could have overtaken me, if these words, from one of the attendants, had not reached me: "Doctor Willis begs you to stop!"

"I cannot! I cannot!" I answered, still flying on, when he called out "You must, ma'am; it hurts the king to run."

Then, indeed, I stopped—in a state of fear really amounting to agony. I

---

5. In 1788, two years after Burney joined the court, George III began to have fits of delirium or madness (today diagnosed as porphyria, a hereditary disease). He was kept in isolation at Kew, under the control of two physicians, Francis and John Willis.

turned round, I saw the two doctors had got the king between them, and three attendants of Dr. Willis's were hovering about. They all slackened their pace, as they saw me stand still; but such was the excess of my alarm, that I was wholly insensible to the effects of a race which, at any other time, would have required an hour's recruit.[6]

As they approached, some little presence of mind happily came to my command; it occurred to me that, to appease the wrath of my flight, I must now show some confidence. I therefore faced them as undauntedly as I was able, only charging the nearest of the attendants to stand by my side.

When they were within a few yards of me, the king called out, "Why did you run away?"

Shocked at a question impossible to answer, yet a little assured by the mild tone of his voice, I instantly forced myself forward, to meet him, though the internal sensation, which satisfied me this was a step the most proper to appease his suspicions and displeasure, was so violently combated by the tremor of my nerves, that I fairly think I may reckon it the greatest effort of personal courage I have ever made.

The effort answered: I looked up, and met all his wonted benignity of countenance, though something still of wildness in his eyes. Think, however, of my surprise, to feel him put both his hands round my two shoulders, and then kiss my cheek!

I wonder I did not really sink, so exquisite was my affright when I saw him spread out his arms! Involuntarily, I concluded he meant to crush me; but the Willises, who have never seen him till this fatal illness, not knowing how very extraordinary an action this was from him, simply smiled and looked pleased, supposing, perhaps, it was his customary salutation!

I believe, however, it was but the joy of a heart unbridled, now, by the forms and proprieties of established custom and sober reason. To see any of his household thus by accident, seemed such a near approach to liberty and recovery, that who can wonder it should serve rather to elate than lessen what yet remains of his disorder!

He now spoke in such terms of his pleasure in seeing me, that I soon lost the whole of my terror; astonishment to find him so nearly well, and gratification to see him so pleased, removed every uneasy feeling, and the joy that succeeded, in my conviction of his recovery, made me ready to throw myself at his feet to express it . . .

What a scene! how variously was I affected by it! but, upon the whole, how inexpressibly thankful to see him so nearly himself—so little removed from recovery!

[A MASTECTOMY]

Paris, March 22, 1812[7]

Separated as I have now so long—long been from my dearest father—brothers—sisters—nieces, & native friends, I would spare, at least, their kind hearts any grief for me but what they must inevitably feel in reflecting upon the sorrow of such an absence to one so tenderly attached to all her first and

6. Renewal of strength.
7. Burney (now Madame d'Arblay) sent this letter

to Esther Burney, her sister, describing an operation performed the previous September.

forever so dear & regretted ties—nevertheless, if they should hear that I have been dangerously ill from any hand but my own, they might have doubts of my perfect recovery which my own alone can obviate. And how can I hope they will escape hearing what has reached Seville to the south, and Constantinople to the east? from both I have had messages—yet nothing could urge me to this communication till I heard that M. de Boinville had written it to his wife, without any precaution, because in ignorance of my plan of silence.[8] Still I must hope it may never travel to my dearest father—But to you, my beloved Esther, who, living more in the world, will surely hear it ere long, to you I will write the whole history, certain that, from the moment you know any evil has befallen me your kind kind heart will be constantly anxious to learn its extent, & its circumstances, as well as its termination.

About August, in the year 1810, I began to be annoyed by a small pain in my breast, which went on augmenting from week to week, yet, being rather heavy than acute, without causing me any uneasiness with respect to the consequences: Alas, *"what was the ignorance?"* The most sympathizing of partners, however, was more disturbed: not a start, not a wry face, not a movement that indicated pain was unobserved, & he early conceived apprehensions to which I was a stranger. He pressed me to see some surgeon; I revolted from the idea, & hoped, by care & warmth, to make all succor unnecessary. Thus passed some months, during which Madame de Maisonneuve, my particularly intimate friend, joined with M. d'Arblay to press me to consent to an examination. I thought their fears groundless, and could not make so great a conquest over my repugnance. I relate this false confidence, now, as a warning to my dear Esther—my sisters & nieces, should any similar sensations excite similar alarm. M. d'A. now revealed his uneasiness to another of our kind friends, Mme. de Tracy, who wrote to me a long & eloquent letter upon the subject, that began to awaken very unpleasant surmises; & a conference with her ensued, in which her urgency & representations, aided by her long experience of disease, & most miserable existence by art, subdued me, and, most painfully & reluctantly, I ceased to object, & M. d'A. summoned a physician—M. Bourdois? Maria will cry;—No, my dear Maria, I would not give your beau frere[9] that trouble; not him, but Dr. Jouart, the physician of Miss Potts. Thinking but slightly of my statement, he gave me some directions that produced no fruit—on the contrary, I grew worse, & M. d'A. now would take no denial to my consulting M. Dubois, who had already attended & cured me in an abscess of which Maria, my dearest Esther, can give you the history. M. Dubois, the most celebrated surgeon of France, was then appointed accoucheur to the empress, & already lodged in the Tuilleries,[1] & in constant attendance: but nothing could slacken the ardor of M. d'A. to obtain the first advice. Fortunately for his kind wishes, M. Dubois had retained a partial regard for me from the time of his former attendance, &, when applied to through a third person, he took the first moment of liberty, granted by a *promenade* taken by the empress, to come to me. It was now I began to perceive my real danger. M. Dubois

---

8. Because Chastel de Boinville's wife was English, it was likely that news of the illness would spread to the Burney family in England.
9. Brother-in-law. Maria (or Marianne), Esther

Burney's daughter, had married Antoine Bourdois, whose brother was a prominent French physician.
1. The royal palace in Paris. "Accoucheur": obstetrician.

gave me a prescription to be pursued for a month, during which time he could not undertake to see me again, & pronounced nothing—but uttered so many charges to me to be tranquil, & to suffer no uneasiness, that I could not but suspect there was room for terrible inquietude. My alarm was increased by the nonappearance of M. d'A. after his departure. They had remained together some time in the book room, & M. d'A. did not return— till, unable to bear the suspense, I begged him to come back. He, also, sought then to tranquilize me—but in words only; his looks were shocking! his features, his whole face displayed the bitterest woe. I had not, therefore, much difficulty in telling myself what he endeavored not to tell me—that a small operation would be necessary to avert evil consequences!—Ah, my dearest Esther, for this I felt no courage—my dread & repugnance, from a thousand reasons *besides* the pain, almost shook all my faculties, &, for some time, I was rather confounded & stupified than affrighted.—Direful, however, was the effect of this interview; the pains became quicker & more violent, & the hardness of the spot affected increased. I took, but vainly, my prescription, & every symptom grew more serious. * * * A physician was now called in, Dr. Moreau, to hear if he could suggest any new means: but Dr. Larrey had left him no resources untried.[2] A formal consultation now was held, of Larrey, Ribe, & Moreau—&, in fine, I was formally condemned to an operation by all three. I was as much astonished as disappointed—for the poor breast was no where discolored, & not much larger than its healthy neighbor. Yet I felt the evil to be deep, so deep, that I often thought if it could not be dissolved, it could only with life be extirpated. I called up, however, all the reason I possessed, or could assume, & told them—that if they saw no other alternative, I would not resist their opinion & experience:—the good Dr. Larrey, who, during his long attendance had conceived for me the warmest friendship, had now tears in his eyes; from my dread he had expected resistance.[3] * * * Sundry necessary works & orders filled up my time entirely till one o'clock. When all was ready——but Dr. Moreau then arrived, with news that M. Dubois could not attend till three. Dr. Aumont went away—& the coast was clear. This, indeed, was a dreadful interval. I had no longer any thing to do—I had only to think—TWO HOURS thus spent seemed never-ending. I would fain have written to my dearest father—to you, my Esther— to Charlotte, James, Charles—Amelia Lock—but my arm prohibited me. I strolled to the salon—I saw it fitted with preparations, & I recoiled—But I soon returned; to what effect disguise from myself what I must so soon know?—yet the sight of the immense quantity of bandages, compresses, sponges, lint——made me a little sick.—I walked backwards & forwards till I quieted all emotion, & became, by degrees, nearly stupid—torpid, without sentiment or consciousness;—& thus I remained till the clock struck three. A sudden spirit of exertion then returned—I defied my poor arm, no longer worth sparing, & took my long banished pen to write a few words to M. d'A.—& a few more for Alex, in case of a fatal result. These short billets I could only deposit safely, when the cabriolets[4]—one—two—three—four— succeeded rapidly to each other in stopping at the door. Dr. Moreau instantly

2. Dominique-Jean Larrey, "Napoleon's surgeon," is still remembered for his courage on the battlefield and his innovative procedures.
3. One morning, three weeks later, Burney was

suddenly informed that her operation was scheduled for that afternoon. Operations were then performed at home and without anesthetics.
4. Carriages.

entered my room, to see if I were alive. He gave me a wine cordial, & went to the salon. I rang for my maid & nurses—but before I could speak to them, my room, without previous message, was entered by 7 men in black, Dr. Larrey, M. Dubois, Dr. Moreau, Dr. Aumont, Dr. Ribe, & a pupil of Dr. Larrey, & another of M. Dubois. I was now awakened from my stupor—& by a sort of indignation—Why so many? & without leave?—But I could not utter a syllable. M. Dubois acted as commander in chief. Dr. Larrey kept out of sight; M. Dubois ordered a bedstead into the middle of the room. Astonished, I turned to Dr. Larrey, who had promised that an armchair would suffice; but he hung his head, & would not look at me. Two *old mattresses* M. Dubois then demanded, & an old sheet. I now began to tremble violently, more with distaste & horror of the preparations even than of the pain. These arranged to his liking, he desired me to mount the bedstead. I stood suspended, for a moment, whether I should not abruptly escape—I looked at the door, the windows—I felt desperate—but it was only for a moment, my reason then took the command, & my fears & feelings struggled vainly against it. I called to my maid—she was crying, & the two nurses stood, transfixed, at the door. "Let those women all go!" cried M. Dubois. This order recovered me my voice—"No," I cried, "let them stay! qu'elles restent!" This occasioned a little dispute, that re-animated me. The maid, however, & one of the nurses ran off—I charged the other to approach, & she obeyed. M. Dubois now tried to issue his commands *en militaire*,[5] but I resisted all that were resistible—I was compelled, however, to submit to taking off my long robe de chambre,[6] which I had meant to retain—Ah, then, how did I think of my sisters!—not one, at so dreadful an instant, at hand, to protect—adjust—guard me—I regretted that I had refused Mme de Maisonneuve—Mme Chastel—no one upon whom I could rely—my departed angel![7]—how did I think of her!—how did I long—long for my Esther—my Charlotte!—My distress was, I suppose, apparent, though not my wishes, for M. Dubois himself now softened, & spoke soothingly. "Can *you*," I cried, "feel for an operation that, to *you*, must seem so trivial?"—"Trivial?" he repeated—taking up a bit of paper, which he tore, unconsciously, into a million of pieces, "*oui—c'est peu de chose—mais—*"[8] he stammered, & could not go on. No one else attempted to speak, but I was softened myself, when I saw even M. Dubois grow agitated, while Dr. Larrey kept always aloof, yet a glance showed me he was pale as ashes. I knew not, positively, then, the immediate danger, but everything convinced me danger was hovering about me, & that this experiment could alone save me from its jaws. I mounted, therefore, unbidden, the bedstead—& M. Dubois placed me upon the mattress, & spread a cambric handkerchief upon my face. It was transparent, however, & I saw, through it, that the bedstead was instantly surrounded by the 7 men & my nurse. I refused to be held; but when, bright through the cambric, I saw the glitter of polished steel—I closed my eyes. I would not trust to convulsive fear the sight of the terrible incision. A silence the most profound ensued, which lasted for some minutes, during which, I imagine, they took their orders by signs, & made their examination—Oh what a horrible suspension!—I did not breathe—& M. Dubois tried vainly to find any pulse. This

5. In military fashion. Most of the attending physicians had been army surgeons.
6. Dressing gown.

7. Susanna, Burney's favorite sister, had died in 1800.
8. Yes—it is not much—but— (French).

pause, at length, was broken by Dr. Larrey, who, in a voice of solemn melancholy, said "Qui me tiendra ce sein?—"[9]

No one answered; at least not verbally; but this aroused me from my passively submissive state, for I feared they imagined the whole breast infected—feared it too justly—for, again through the cambric, I saw the hand of M. Dubois held up, while his forefinger first described a straight line from top to bottom of the breast, secondly a cross, & thirdly a circle; intimating that the WHOLE was to be taken off. Excited by this idea, I started up, threw off my veil, &, in answer to the demand "Qui me tiendra ce sein?" cried "C'est moi, monsieur!"[1] & I held my hand under it, & explained the nature of my sufferings, which all sprang from one point, though they darted into every part. I was heard attentively, but in utter silence, & M. Dubois then re-placed me as before, &, as before, spread my veil over my face. How vain, alas, my representation! immediately again I saw the fatal finger describe the cross—& the circle. Hopeless, then, desperate, & self-given up, I closed once more my eyes, relinquishing all watching, all resistance, all interference, & sadly resolute to be wholly resigned.

My dearest Esther, & all my dears to whom she communicates this doleful ditty, will rejoice to hear that this resolution once taken, was firmly adhered to, in defiance of a terror that surpasses all description, & the most torturing pain. Yet—when the dreadful steel was plunged into the breast—cutting through veins—arteries—flesh—nerves—I needed no injunctions not to restrain my cries. I began a scream that lasted unintermittingly during the whole time of the incision—& I almost marvel that it rings not in my ears still! so excruciating was the agony. When the wound was made, & the instrument was withdrawn, the pain seemed undiminished, for the air that suddenly rushed into those delicate parts felt like a mass of minute but sharp & forked poniards,[2] that were tearing the edges of the wound—but when again I felt the instrument—describing a curve—cutting against the grain, if I may so say, while the flesh resisted in a manner so forcible as to oppose & tire the hand of the operator, who was forced to change from the right to the left—then, indeed, I thought I must have expired. I attempted no more to open my eyes,—they felt as if hermetically shut, & so firmly closed, that the eyelids seemed indented into the cheeks. The instrument this second time withdrawn, I concluded the operation over. Oh no! presently the terrible cutting was renewed—& worse than ever, to separate the bottom, the foundation of this dreadful gland from the parts to which it adhered. Again all description would be baffled—yet again all was not over.—Dr. Larrey rested but his own hand, &—Oh heaven!—I then felt the knife rackling[3] against the breast bone—scraping it!—This performed, while I yet remained in utterly speechless torture, I heard the voice of Mr. Larrey (all others guarded a dead silence) in a tone nearly tragic, desire every one present to pronounce if any thing more remained to be done. The general voice was Yes—but the finger of Mr. Dubois—which I literally *felt* elevated over the wound, though I saw nothing, & though he touched nothing, so indescribably sensitive was the spot—pointed to some further requisition[4]—& again began the scraping!—and, after this, Dr. Moreau thought he discerned a peccant atom—

9. Who will hold this breast for me? (French).
1. *I will!* (French).
2. Daggers.
3. Raking (?).

4. Necessity. Surgical practice of the time dictated that "the whole diseased structure" be cut out, no matter how long or painful the operation.

and still, & still, M. Dubois demanded atom after atom. My dearest Esther, not for days, not for weeks, but for months I could not speak of this terrible business without nearly again going through it! I could not *think* of it with impunity! I was sick, I was disordered by a single question—even now, 9 months after it is over, I have a headache from going on with the account! & this miserable account, which I began 3 months ago, at least, I dare not revise, nor read, the recollection is still so painful.

To conclude, the evil was so profound, the case so delicate, & the precautions necessary for preventing a return so numerous, that the operation, including the treatment & the dressing, lasted 20 minutes! a time, for sufferings so acute, that was hardly supportable. However, I bore it with all the courage I could exert, & never moved, nor stopped them, nor resisted, nor remonstrated, nor spoke—except once or twice, during the dressings, to say "Ah Messieurs! que je vous plains!—"[5] for indeed I was sensible to the feeling concern with which they all saw what I endured, though my speech was principally—*very* principally meant for Dr. Larrey. Except this, I uttered not a syllable, save, when so often they recommenced, calling out "Avertissez moi,[6] Messieurs! avertissez moi!—" Twice, I believe, I fainted; at least, I have two total chasms in my memory of this transaction, that impede my tying together what passed. When all was done, & they lifted me up that I might be put to bed, my strength was so totally annihilated, that I was obliged to be carried, & could not even sustain my hands & arms, which hung as if I had been lifeless; while my face, as the nurse has told me, was utterly colorless. This removal made me open my eyes—& I then saw my good Dr. Larrey, pale nearly as myself, his face streaked with blood, & its expression depicting grief, apprehension, & almost horror.

When I was in bed, my poor M. d'Arblay—who ought to write you himself his own history of this morning—was called to me—& afterwards our Alex.—

[M. D'ARBLAY'S POSTSCRIPT]

No! No my dearest & ever more dear friends, I shall not make a fruitless attempt. No language could convey what I felt in the deadly course of these seven hours. Nevertheless, every one *of you, my dearest dearest friends,* can guess, must even know it. Alexander had no less feeling, but showed more fortitude. He, perhaps, will be more able to describe to you, nearly at least, the torturing state of my poor heart & soul. Besides, I must own, to you, that these details which were, till just now, quite unknown to me, have almost killed me, & I am only able to thank God that this more than half angel has had the sublime courage to deny herself the comfort I might have offered her, to spare me, not the sharing of her excruciating pains, that was impossible, but the witnessing so terrific a scene, & perhaps the remorse to have rendered it more tragic. For I don't flatter myself I could have got through it—I must confess it.

Thank heaven! She is now surprisingly well, & in good spirits, & we hope to have many many still happy days. May that of peace soon arrive, and enable me to embrace better than with my pen my beloved & ever ever more dear friends of the town & country. Amen. Amen![7]

---

5. How I pity you! (French).
6. Give me warning! (French).
7. The wound healed without infection. Burney

returned to England later in 1812 and lived for twenty-eight years.

Poems in Process

In all ages, some poets have claimed that their poems were not willed but were inspired, whether by a muse, by divine visitation, or by sudden emergence from the author's subconscious mind. But as the poet Richard Aldington has remarked, "genius is not enough; one must also work." The working manuscripts of the greatest writers show that, however involuntary the origin of a poem, vision was usually followed by laborious revision before the work achieved the seeming inevitability of its final form.

Milton is the first major English author for whom we possess drafts of poems indubitably written in his own hand; the excerpt from his manuscript of *Lycidas* shows the extent to which he worked over and expanded his initial attempt. We have increasing numbers of manuscripts written in the eighteenth century, such as those reproduced below from Pope and Johnson. In the early nineteenth century the working drafts of poets began to be widely preserved, and so remain abundantly available.

The examples from major poets that are transcribed here represent various stages in the composition of a poem, and a variety of procedures by individual poets. In all these examples we look on as poets, no matter how rapidly they achieve a result they are willing to let stand, carry on their inevitably tentative efforts to meet the multiple requirements of meaning, syntax, meter, sound pattern, and the constraints imposed by a chosen stanza. And because these are all very good poets, the seeming conflict between the necessities of significance and form results not in the distortion but in the perfecting of the poetic statement.

Our transcriptions from the poets' drafts attempt to reproduce, as accurately as the change from script to print will allow, the appearance of the original manuscript page. A poet's first attempt at a line or phrase is reproduced in larger type, the emendations in smaller type. The line numbers in the headings that identify an excerpt are those of the final form of the complete poem, as reprinted in this anthology, above. The marginal numbers beside the extract from *The Vanity of Human Wishes* are Johnson's own additions.

SELECTED BIBLIOGRAPHY

Autograph Poetry in the English Language, 2 vols., 1973, compiled by P. J. Croft, reproduces and transcribes one or more pages of manuscript in the poet's own hand, from the 14th century to the present time. Volume 1 includes Blake and Burns; volume 2 includes many of the other poets represented in this volume of *The Norton Anthology of English Literature,* from Wordsworth to Dylan Thomas. Books that discuss the process of composition and revision, with examples from the manuscripts and printed versions of poems, are Charles D. Abbott, ed., *Poets at Work,* 1948; Phyllis Bartlett, *Poems in Process,* 1951; A. F. Scott, *The Poet's Craft,* 1957; George Bornstein, *Poetic Remaking: The Art of Browning, Yeats, and Pound,* 1988. In *Word for Word: A Study of Authors' Alterations,* 1965, Wallace Hildick analyzes the composition of prose fiction as well as poems; a shorter version, *Word for Word: The Rewriting of Fiction,* 1965, discusses the revision of novels by George Eliot, Samuel Butler, Hardy, Lawrence, James, and Woolf. *Byron's "Don Juan,"* ed. T. G. Steffan and W. W. Pratt, 4 vols., 1957, transcribes the manuscript drafts; the Cornell Wordsworth, in process, reproduces, transcribes, and discusses various versions of Wordsworth's poems from the first manuscript drafts to the final publication in his lifetime, and the Cornell Yeats, also in process, does the same for Yeats. For facsimiles and transcripts of Keats's poems, see *John Keats: Poetry Manuscripts at Harvard,* ed. Jack Stillinger, 1990. Jon Stallworthy, *Between the Lines: Yeats's Poetry in the Making,* 1963, reproduces and analyzes the sequential drafts of a number of Yeats's major poems. Valerie Eliot has edited

T. S. Eliot's *The Waste Land: A Facsimile and Transcript of the Original Drafts Including the Annotations of Ezra Pound*, 1971, while Dame Helen Gardner has transcribed and analyzed the manuscript drafts of Eliot's *Four Quartets* in *The Composition of Four Quartets*, 1978.

JOHN MILTON
From Lycidas[1]

[Lines 1–14][2]

yet once more O ye laurells and once more

ye myrtl's browne wth Ivie never sere

I come to pluck yor berries harsh and crude

~~before the mellowing yeare~~ and wth forc't fingers rude

~~and crop yor young~~ shatter yor leaves before ye mellowing yeare

bitter constraint, and sad occasion deare

compells me to disturbe yor season due

for ~~young~~ Lycidas is dead, dead ere his prime

young Lycidas and hath not left his peere

       not
who would ∧sing for Lycidas he well knew

himselfe to sing & build the loftie rime

he must not flote upon his watrie beare

unwept, and welter to the parching wind

without the meed of some melodious teare

[Lines 56–63]

ay mee I fondly dreame

~~had yee bin there, for~~ what could that have don?

~~what could the golden hayrd Calliope~~

for her inchaunting son ⸻

~~when shee beheld (the gods farre sighted bee)~~

~~his goarie scalpe rowle downe the Thracian lee~~

✱whome universal nature
might lament
~~and heaven and hel deplore~~
~~when his divine head downe~~
the streame was sent
downe the Swift Hebrus to the
Lesbian shore.

[THE THIRD AND FOLLOWING LINES ARE REWRITTEN ON A SEPARATE PAGE]

✱what could the muse her selfe that Orpheus bore
   the muse her selfe for her inchanting son

~~for her inchanting son~~

           did
whome universal nature ~~might~~ lament

when by the rout that made the hideous roare

      gorie
✱goarie his ~~divine~~ visage down the streame was sent

  downe the swift Hebrus to ye Lesbian shoare.

1. Transcribed from a manuscript of fifty pages in the library of Trinity College, Cambridge. Among the poems written in Milton's own hand are *Lycidas*, *Comus*, seven sonnets, and several other short poems. The manuscript has been photographically reproduced, with printed transcriptions, by W. Aldis Wright, *Facsimile of the Manuscript of Milton's Minor Poems* (Cambridge, England, 1899).
2. This draft is written on a separate page of the manuscript, which also contains drafts of the passages, "What could the muse her selfe" and "Bring the rathe primrose," transcribed below.

[*Lines 132–53*]

Returne Alpheus the dred voice is past
  that shrunk thy streams, returne Sicilian Muse
  and call the vales and bid them hither cast
  thire bells, and flowrets of a thousand hues
  yee vallies low where the mild wispers use

  of shades, and wanton winds, and goshing brooks   ✻ ✻
                          ^u   sparely
  on whose fresh lap the swart starre sparely looks   —faintly   ✻
✻
  bring hither all yor quaint enamel'd eyes   ✻
                                     throw
  that on the greene terfe suck the honied showrs
  and purple all the ground wth vernal flowrs
                               Bring the rathe &c.[3]
  to strew the laureat herse where Lycid' lies
  for so to interpose a little ease
   ✻   fraile
  let our sad thoughts dally wth false surmise   ✻   fraile

[LINES 142–50 ARE DRAFTED ON A SEPARATE PAGE, AS FOLLOWS]

  Bring the rathe primrose that unwedded dies
  collu colouring the pale cheeke of uninjoyd love
  and that sad floure that strove
  to write his owne woes on the vermeil graine
  next adde Narcissus y^t still weeps in vaine
  the woodbine and ye pancie freak't wth jet
  the glowing violet
  the cowslip wan that hangs his pensive head
  and every bud that sorrows liverie weares
                        with
  let Daffadillies fill thire cups teares
  bid Amaranthus all his beautie shed
  to strew the laureat herse &c.

  Bring the rathe primrose that forsaken dies
  the tufted crowtoe and pale Gessamin
                 ^{ye}
  the white pinke, and pansie freakt wth jet
  the glowing violet
               the well-attired woodbine
  the muske rose and the garish columbine
  wth cowslips wan that hang the pensive head
                 ✻   weares ✻   weares
  and every flower that sad escutcheon beares   imbroidrie beares
   &
  2 let daffadillies fill thire cups wth teares
  1 bid Amaranthus all his beauties shed
  to strew &c.

_____

3. I.e., Milton plans to insert here the passage that follows, lines 142–50.

ALEXANDER POPE
From The Rape of the Lock[1]
[*1712 Version: Canto 1, Lines 1–24*]

WHAT dire Offence from Am'rous Causes springs,
    What mighty Quarrels rise from Trivial Things,
      I sing—This Verse to C—l, Muse! is due;
This, ev'n *Belinda* may vouchsafe to view:
Slight is the Subject, but not so the Praise,
If she inspire, and He approve my Lays.
    Say what strange Motive, Goddess! cou'd compel
A well-bred *Lord* t'assault a gentle *Belle?*
Oh say what stranger Cause, yet unexplor'd,
Cou'd make a gentle *Belle* reject a *Lord?*
And dwells such Rage in *softest Bosoms* then?
And lodge such daring Souls in *Little Men?*
    Sol thro' white Curtains did his Beams display,
And op'd those Eyes which brighter shine than they;
Shock just had giv'n himself the rowzing Shake,
And Nymphs prepar'd their *Chocolate* to take;
Thrice the wrought Slipper knock'd against the Ground,
And striking Watches the tenth Hour resound.
Belinda rose, and 'midst attending Dames
Launch'd on the Bosom of the silver *Thames:*
A Train of well-drest Youths around her shone,
And ev'ry Eye was fix'd on her alone;
On her white Breast a sparking *Cross* she wore,
Which *Jews* might kiss, and Infidels adore.

[*Revised Version: Canto 1, Lines 1–22*]

WHAT dire Offence from am'rous Causes springs,
    What mighty Contests rise from trivial Things,
      I sing—This Verse to *Caryll*, Muse! is due;
This, ev'n *Belinda* may vouchsafe to view:
Slight is the Subject, but not so the Praise,
If She inspire, and He approve my Lays.
    Say what strange Motive, Goddess! cou'd compel
A well-bred *Lord* t'assault a gentle *Belle?*
Oh say what stranger Cause, yet unexplor'd,
Cou'd make a gentle *Belle* reject a *Lord?*

1. The first version of *The Rape of the Lock*, published 1712, consisted of two cantos and a total of 334 lines. Two years later, in 1714, Pope published an enlarged version of five cantos and 794 lines, in which he added the supernatural "machinery" of the Sylphs and Gnomes as well as a number of mock-epic episodes. The excerpts reprinted here show how Pope revised and expanded passages that he retained from the first version of the poem. The revised version includes changes that Pope added in later editions of the enlarged text of 1714.

In Tasks so bold, can Little Men engage,
And in soft Bosoms dwells such mighty Rage?
  Sol thro' white Curtains shot a tim'rous Ray,
And op'd those Eyes that must eclipse the Day;
Now Lapdogs give themselves the rowzing Shake,
And sleepless Lovers, just at Twelve, awake:
Thrice rung the Bell, the Slipper knock'd the Ground,
And the press'd Watch return'd a silver Sound.
Belinda still her downy Pillow prest,
Her Guardian *Sylph* prolong'd the balmy Rest.
'Twas he had summon'd to her silent Bed
The Morning-Dream that hover'd o'er her Head.

[*Revised Version: Canto 2, Lines 1–8*]

Not with more Glories, in th' Etherial Plain,
  The Sun first rises o'er the purpled Main,
  Than issuing forth, the Rival of his Beams
Launch'd on the Bosom of the Silver *Thames*.
Fair Nymphs, and well-drest Youths around her shone,
But ev'ry Eye was fix'd on her alone.
On her white Breast a sparkling *Cross* she wore,
Which *Jews* might kiss, and Infidels adore.

From An Essay on Man[1]

[*From the First Manuscript*]

we ourselves
1. Learn ~~then thyself~~, not God presume to scan,
    But
    ~~And~~ know, the Study of Mankind is <u>Man.</u>
Plac'd on this <u>Isthmus</u> of a Middle State,
A Being <u>darkly wise,</u> & <u>rudely great.</u>
With too much <u>knowledge</u> for the <u>Sceptic</u> side,
And too much <u>Weakness</u> for a <u>Stoic's</u> Pride,
He hangs between, uncertain where to rest;
Whether to deem himself a <u>God</u> or <u>Beast;</u>
Whether his <u>Mind</u> or <u>Body</u> to prefer,
Born but to <u>die,</u> & reas'ning but to <u>err;</u>
                    his
Alike in <u>Ignorance,</u> (~~that~~ Reason such)
        ~~Who~~   ~~who thinks~~
Whether he thinks too <u>little</u> or too <u>much</u>:
Chaos of <u>Thought</u> & <u>Passion,</u> all confus'd,
Still by <u>himself</u> abus'd & dis-abus'd:

1. Two of Pope's holograph manuscripts of *An Essay on Man* have survived. The earlier one is at the Pierpont Morgan Library in New York. The second one, at the Houghton Library, Harvard, was evidently intended as a fair copy for printing; but Pope, who was an inveterate reviser, intro- duced some last-minute changes. The passage transcribed here from each of these manuscripts is Pope's famed description of man's "middle state" in the great chain of being; in the published ver- sion, it opens Epistle 2, lines 1–18.

Created half to <u>rise</u>, & half to <u>fall</u>;
Great <u>Lord</u> of all things, yet a <u>prey</u> to all;
Sole <u>Judge</u> of <u>Truth</u>, in endless <u>Error</u> hurl'd;
The <u>Glory</u>, <u>Jest</u>, and <u>Riddle</u> of the World.

[*From the Second Manuscript*][2]

~~Incipit I~~   Know
~~Incipit III~~   ~~Learn~~ we ourselves, not God presume to scan,
The only Science   Convinc'd,
     ~~But know,~~ the Study of Mankind is <u>Man</u>;
(Plac'd on this Isthmus of a Middle State,
A Being darkly wise, and rudely great;
With too much Knowledge for the Sceptic side,
    With
~~And~~ too much Weakness for a Stoic's Pride,
       in doubt to act or
He hangs between, ~~uncertain where to~~ rest,
       Part of
Whether $\overline{T}$o deem himself a God or Beast;
     In doubt
Whether his Mind, or Body to prefer.
  ~~This born~~   ~~that~~
Born but to die, and reas'ning but to err;
Alike in Ignorance, his Reason such,
    Whether he thinks   or too much.
~~Who thinks~~ too little, ~~or who thinks too much:~~
Chaos of Thought and Passion, all confus'd,
Still by himself abus'd and dis-abus'd:
Created half to rise, and half to fall;
Great Lord of all things, yet a prey to all;
Sole Judge of Truth, in endless error hurl'd;
The Glory, Jest, and Riddle of the World!

2. In this version of the manuscript, Pope inserted some marginal glosses. In the right-hand margin (next to the line beginning "Learn we ourselves . . ."), he wrote, "Of Man, as an Individual," while next to the line beginning "Plac'd on this Isthmus . . . ," he wrote, "His Middle Nature." And in the left-hand margin, a little below the line beginning "With too much knowledge . . . ," he wrote, "His Powers, and Imperfections."

SAMUEL JOHNSON

Johnson told Boswell in 1766 that when composing verses "I have generally had them in my mind, perhaps fifty at a time, walking up and down in my room; and then I have written them down, and often, from laziness, have written only half lines. . . . I remember I wrote a hundred lines of *The Vanity of Human Wishes* in a day." When the first manuscript draft of this poem turned up in the 1940s among Boswell's papers at Malahide Castle, it supported Johnson's account, for it had been written and corrected in haste, with only sparse punctuation; also the second half of each line had been filled out, obviously from memory, at some time after the writing of the first half, in a darker ink. In the transcriptions from this manuscript (which is in the collection of Mary Hyde, Somerville, New Jersey), the half-lines and emendations that Johnson added to his initial draft are printed in boldface type.

The draft was written on the right-hand pages of a small homemade pocket book;

some words in the added half-line, impinging on the right margin of the page, had to be completed above or below the line. The two added lines, "See Nations slowly wise . . . the tardy Bust," were written on the blank left-hand page, at the place where they were to be inserted. The numeration of every tenth line was added by Johnson in the manuscript and incorporates these two additional lines.

Johnson published the poem in 1749 and revised it for a second publication in 1755, when it achieved the final form printed in the selections from Johnson, above. It was in 1755 that Johnson introduced his most famous emendation, when, after his disillusionment with Lord Chesterfield as literary patron, he substituted in line 162 the word "patron" for "garret": "Toil, envy, want, the patron, and the jail."

From The Vanity of Human Wishes

[*Lines 135–64*]

When first the College Rolls **receive his nam**^e
The young Enthusiast quits his ease for fame

Quick fires his breast
~~Each act betrays~~ **the fever of renown**
Caught from **the strong Contagion of the Gown**
On Isis banks he waves, from noise **withdrawn**
140 In sober state th' imaginary Lawn
O'er Bodley's Dome **his future Labours spread**
And Bacon's Mansion **trembles o'er his head.**
Are these thy views, **proceed illustrious Youth**
And Virtue guard **thee to the throne of Trut**^h
Yet should th~~y fate~~ Soul indulge the gen'rous
                                              Heat
Till Captive Science **yields her last Retreat**
Should Reason **guide thee with her brightest Ray**
And pour on misty Doubt **resistless day**
Should no false kindness **lure to loose delight**
150 Nor Praise relax, nor **difficulty fright**
Should tempting Novelty **thy cell refrain**
                                              vain
And Sloth's bland opiates **shed their fumes in**
sShould Beuty blunt **on fops her fatal dart**
Nor claim the **triumph of a letter'd heart**
~~S Nor~~ Should no Disease **thy torpid veins invade**
Nor Melancholys Spectres **haunt thy Shade**
                    hope
Yet ~~dream~~ not Life **from Grief or Danger free,**
Nor think the doom of **Man revers'd for thee**
Deign   passing   to
~~Turn~~ on the world ~~awhile~~ turn thine eyes
160 And pause **awhile from Learning to be wise**
There mark what **ill the Scholar's life assail**
                                              the
Toil envy Want ~~a~~ Garret and the Jayl
                    Dreams
If ~~Hope~~ yet flatter **once again attend**
Hear Lydiats life **and Galileo's End.**

e Nations slowly wise, and meanly just,
buried merit raise the tardy Bust.

THOMAS GRAY

There are three manuscript versions of the *Elegy* in Gray's handwriting. The one reproduced here in part is the earliest of these, preserved at Eton College, England; Gray entitled it "Stanzas wrote in a Country Church-Yard."

It is evident that Gray originally intended to conclude his poem at the end of the fifth stanza transcribed below. At some later time he bracketed off the last four stanzas, introduced a transitional stanza that incorporated the last two lines of the original conclusion, and then went on to write a new and much enlarged conclusion to the poem, which includes the closing "Epitaph." A comparison with the final version of the *Elegy,* above, will show that the author deleted some of these added stanzas, and also made a number of verbal changes, in his published texts of the poem.

From Elegy Written in a Country Churchyard

[*Lines 69–128*]

The struggleings Pangs of conscious Truth to hide,
To quench the Blushes of ingenuous Shame,
crown
And at the Shrine of Luxury & Pride
With   by
~~Burn~~ Incense hallowd in the Muse's Flame.
kindled at

The thoughtless World to Majesty may bow
Exalt the brave, & idolize Success
But more to Innocence their Safety owe
Than Power & Genius e'er conspired to bless

And thou, who mindful of the unhonour'd Dead
eir
Dost in these notes thy artless Tale relate
By Night & lonely Contemplation led
To linger in the gloomy Walks of Fate

Hark how the sacred Calm, that broods around
Bids ev'ry fierce tumultuous Passion cease
In still small Accents whisp'ring from the Ground
A grateful Earnest of eternal Peace

No more with Reason & thyself at Strife
Give anxious Cares & endless Wishes room
But thro' the cool sequester'd Vale of Life
Pursue the silent Tenour of thy Doom.

Far from the madding Crowd's ignoble Strife;
Their sober Wishes never knew to stray:
Along the cool sequester'd Vale of Life
noiseless
They kept the silent Tenour of their Way.

Yet even these Bones from Insult to protect
Some frail Memorial still erected nigh

With
~~In~~ uncouth Rhime, & shapeless Sculpture deckt
Implores the passing Tribute of a Sigh.

Their Name, their Years, spelt by th' unletter'd Muse
The Place of Fame, & Epitaph supply,
And many a holy Text around she strews
That teach the rustic Moralist to die.

For who to dumb Forgetfulness a Prey
This pleasing anxious Being e'er resign'd;
Left the warm Precincts of the chearful Day,
Nor cast one longing lingring Look behind?

On some fond Breast the parting Soul relies,
Some pious Drops the closing Eye requires:
Even from the Tomb the Voice of Nature cries,
And buried Ashes glow with social Fires
    For Thee, who mindful &c: as above.[1]

If chance that e'er some pensive Spirit more,
By sympathetic Musings here delay'd,
With vain, tho' kind, Enquiry shall explore
Thy once-loved Haunt, this long-deserted Shade.

Haply some hoary-headed Swain shall say,[2]
Oft have we seen him at the Peep of Dawn
With hasty Footsteps brush the Dews away
On the high Brow of yonder hanging Lawn
Him have we seen the Green-wood Side along,
While o'er the Heath we hied, our Labours done,
Oft as the Woodlark piped her farewell Song
With whistful Eyes pursue the setting Sun.

                      spreading   nodding
Oft at the Foot of yonder hoary Beech
That wreathes its old fantastic Roots so high
His listless Length at Noontide would he stretch,
And pore upon the Brook that babbles by.
    With Gestures quaint now smileing as in Scorn,
               wayward fancies   ~~loved~~ would he
    Mutt'ring his fond Conceits he ~~wont to~~ rove:
      drooping,
    Now woeful wan, ~~he droop'd,~~ as one forlorn
    Or crazed with Care, or cross'd in hopeless Love.
      One Morn we miss'd him on th' accustom'd Hill,
      Along the   near
      By the Heath-~~side,~~ & at his fav'rite Tree.
      Another came, nor yet beside the Rill,
             by
      Nor up the Lawn, nor at the Wood was he.

1. I.e., Gray indicates that the second bracketed stanza, above, is to be inserted here, except that the opening "And thou" is to be altered to "For Thee."

2. At this point in the manuscript Gray ceases to leave a space between the stanzas. The first edition of 1751, at Gray's request, was printed without such spaces. They were, however, inserted in later editions printed during Gray's lifetime.

~~There scatter'd oft, the earliest~~
The next with Dirges meet in sad Array
    by
Slow thro the Church-way Path we saw him born
Approach & read, for thou can'st read the Lay
  Graved carved   yon
Wrote on the Stone beneath that ancient Thorn

                       Year
There scatter'd oft the earliest of y^e ~~Spring~~
            showers of
By Hands unseen are frequent Vi'lets found
  Redbreast
The Robin loves to build & warble there,
And little Footsteps lightly print the Ground.

Here rests his Head upon the Lap of Earth[3]
A Youth to Fortune & to Fame unknown
Fair Science frown'd not on his humble Birth
And Melancholy mark'd him for her own

Large was his Bounty & his Heart sincere;
Heaven did a Recompence as largely send.
He gave to Mis'ry all he had, a Tear.
He gain'd from Heav'n, 'twas all he wish'd, a Friend

No farther seek his Merits to disclose,
  think
Nor seek to draw them from their dread Abode
(His Frailties there in trembling Hope repose)
The Bosom of his Father & his God.

3. These last three stanzas (which Gray in the first edition of 1751 labeled "The Epitaph") are written in the right-hand margin, with the page turned crosswise.

Selected Bibliographies

The Selected Bibliographies consist of a list of Suggested General Readings on English literature, followed by bibliographies for each of the literary periods. For ease of reference, the authors within each period are arranged in alphabetical order.

SUGGESTED GENERAL READINGS

Histories of England and of English Literature

New research and new perspectives have made even the most distinguished of the comprehensive, general histories written in past generations seem outmoded. Innovative research in social, cultural, and political history has made it difficult to write a single, coherent account of England from the Middle Ages to the present, let alone to accommodate in a unified narrative the complex histories of Scotland, Ireland, and Wales. Readers who wish to explore the historical matrix out of which the works of literature collected in this anthology emerged are advised to consult the studies of particular periods listed in the appropriate sections of this bibliography. The multivolume *Oxford History of England* is useful, as are the three-volume *Peoples of the British Isles: A New History*, ed. Stanford Lehmberg, 1992, and the nine-volume *Cambridge Cultural History of Britain*, ed. Boris Ford, 1992. Albert Baugh et al., *A Literary History of England*, rev. 1967, remains a convenient source of factual materials about authors, works, and chronology. Given the cultural centrality of London, readers may find Roy Porter's *London: A Social History*, 1994, valuable. Similar observations may be made about literary history. In the light of such initiatives as women's studies, new historicism, and postcolonialism, the range of authors deemed most significant has expanded in recent years, along with the geographical and conceptual boundaries of literature in English. Attempts to capture in a unified account the great sweep of literature from *Beowulf* to late last night have largely given way to studies of individual genres, carefully delimited time periods, and specific authors. For these more focused accounts, see the listings by period.

Among the large-scale literary surveys, *The Cambridge Guide to Literature in English*, 1993, is useful, as is *The Penguin History of Literature. The Feminist Companion to Literature in English*, ed. Virginia Blain, Isobel Grundy, and Patricia Clements, 1990, is an important resource, and the editorial materials in *The Norton Anthology of*

Literature by Women, 2nd ed., 1996, ed. Sandra M. Gilbert and Susan Gubar, constitute a concise history and set of biographies of women authors since the Middle Ages. *Annals of English Literature, 1475–1950*, rev. 1961, lists important publications year by year, together with the significant literary events for each year. David Daiches, *A Critical History of English Literature*, 2 vols., rev. 1970, provides a running literary appreciation.

Helpful treatments and surveys of English meter, rhyme, and stanza forms are Paul Fussell Jr., *Poetic Meter and Poetic Form*, rev. 1979; Donald Wesling, *The Chances of Rhyme: Device and Modernity*, 1980; Derek Attridge, *The Rhythms of English Poetry*, 1982; Charles O. Hartman, *Free Verse: An Essay in Prosody*, 1983; John Hollander, *Vision and Resonance: Two Senses of Poetic Form*, rev. 1985; and Robert Pinsky, *The Sounds of Poetry: A Brief Guide*, 1998.

On the development of the novel as a form, see Ian Watt, *The Rise of the Novel*, 1957; *The Columbia History of the British Novel*, ed. John Richetti, 1994; and Margaret Doody, *The True Story of the Novel*, 1996. On women novelists and readers, see Nancy Armstrong, *Desire and Domestic Fiction: A Political History of the Novel*, 1987; and Catherine Gallagher, *Nobody's Story: The Vanishing Acts of Women Writers in the Marketplace, 1670–1820*, 1994.

On the history of playhouse design, see Richard Leacroft, *The Development of the English Playhouse: An Illustrated Survey of Theatre Building in England from Medieval to Modern Times*, 1988. For a survey of the plays that have appeared on these and other stages, see Allardyce Nicoll, *British Drama*, rev. 1962, and the eight-volume *Revels History of Drama in English*, gen. eds. Clifford Leech and T. W. Craik, 1975–83.

On some of the key intellectual currents that are at once reflected in and shaped by English literature, Arthur T. Lovejoy's classic studies *The Great Chain of Being*, 1936, and *Essays in the History of Ideas*, 1948, remain valuable, along with such works as Lovejoy and George Boas, *Primitivism and Related Ideas in Antiquity*, 1935; Ernst Kantowicz, *The King's Two Bodies: A Study in Medieval Political Theology*, 1957, new ed. 1997; Richard Popkin, *The History of Skepticism from Erasmus to Descartes*, 1960; M. H. Abrams, *Natural Supernaturalism: Tradition and Revolution in Romantic Literature*, 1971; and Michel Foucault, *Madness and Civilization: A History of Insanity in the Age of Reason*, Eng. trans. 1965, and *The Order of Things: An Archaeology of the Human Sciences*, Eng. trans. 1970.

Reference Works

The single most important tool for the study of literature in English is the *Oxford English Dictionary*, 2nd ed., 1989, also available on CD-ROM. The *OED* is written on historical principles: that is, it attempts not only to describe current word use but also to record the history and development of the language from its origins before the Norman conquest to the present. It thus provides, for familiar as well as archaic and obscure words, the widest possible range of meanings and uses, organized chronologically and illustrated with quotations. Beyond the *OED* there are many other valuable dictionaries, such as *The American Heritage Dictionary*, *The Oxford Dictionary of Etymology*, and an array of reference works from *The Cambridge Encyclopedia of the English Language*, ed. David Crystal, 1995, to guides to specialized vocabularies, slang, regional dialects, and the like.

There is a steady flow of new editions of most major and many minor writers in English, along with a ceaseless outpouring of critical appraisals and scholarship. The *MLA International Bibliography* (also on line) is the best way to keep abreast of the most recent work and to conduct bibliographic searches. *The New Cambridge Bibliography of English Literature* ed. George Watson, 1969–77, updated shorter ed. 1981, is a valuable guide to the huge body of earlier literary criticism and scholarship. *A Guide to English and American Literature*, ed. F. W. Bateson and Harrison Meserole, rev. 1976, is a selected list of editions, as well as scholarly and critical treatments. Further bibliographical aids are described in Arthur G. Kennedy, *A Concise Bibliography for Students of English*, rev. 1972; Richard D. Altick and Andrew Wright, *Selective Bibliography for the Study of English and American Literature* rev. 1979, and James L. Harner, *Literary Research Guide*, rev. 1998.

For compact biographies of English authors, see the multivolume *Dictionary of National Biography*, ed. Leslie Stephen and Sidney Lee, 1885–1900, with supplements that carry the work to 1980; condensed biographies will be found in the *Concise Dictionary of National Biography*, 2 parts (1920, 1988). Handy reference books of authors, works, and various literary terms and allusions are *The Oxford Companion to the Theatre*, Phyllis Hartnoll, rev. 1990; *Princeton Encyclopedia of Poetry and Poetics*, ed. Alex Preminger and others, rev. 1993; and *The Oxford Companion to English Literature*,

ed. Margaret Drabble, rev. 1998. Low-priced handbooks that define and illustrate literary concepts and terms are *The Penguin Dictionary of Literary Terms and Literary Theory*, ed. J. A. Cuddon, 1991; W. F. Thrall and Addison Hibbard, *A Handbook to Literature*, ed. C. Hugh Holman, rev. 1992; *Critical Terms for Literary Study*, ed. Frank Lentricchia and Thomas McLaughlin, rev. 1995; and M. H. Abrams, *A Glossary of Literary Terms*, rev. 1992. On Greek and Roman background, see G. M. Kirkwood, *A Short Guide to Classical Mythology*, 1959; *The Oxford Classical Dictionary*, rev. 1996; and *The Oxford Companion to Classical Literature*, ed. M. C. Howatson and Ian Chilvers, rev. 1993.

Literary Criticism and Theory

Three volumes of the *Cambridge History of Literary Criticism* have been published, 1989–: *Classical Criticism*, ed. George A. Kennedy; *The Eighteenth Century*, ed. H. B. Nisbet and Claude Rawson; and *From Formalism to Poststructuralism*, ed. Raman Selden. See also M. H. Abrams, *The Mirror and the Lamp: Romantic Theory and the Critical Tradition*, 1953; William K. Wimsatt and Cleanth Brooks, *Literary Criticism: A Short History*, 1957; George Watson, *The Literary Critics*, 1962; René Wellek, *A History of Modern Criticism: 1750–1950*, 9 vols., 1955–1993; Frank Lentricchia, *After the New Criticism*, 1980; and *Redrawing the Boundaries: The Transformation of English and American Literary Studies*, ed. Stephen Greenblatt and Giles Gunn, 1992. Raman Selden, Peter Widdowson, and Peter Brooker have written *A Reader's Guide to Contemporary Literary Theory*, 1997.

The following is a selection of books in literary criticism that have been notably influential in shaping modern approaches to English literature and literary forms: Lionel Trilling, *The Liberal Imagination*, 1950; T. S. Eliot, *Selected Essays*, 3rd ed. 1951, and *On Poetry and Poets*, 1957; Erich Auerbach, *Mimesis: The Representation of Reality in Western Literature*, 1953; William Empson, *Seven Types of Ambiguity*, 3rd ed. 1953; William K. Wimsalt, *The Verbal Icon*, 1954; Northrop Frye, *Anatomy of Criticism*, 1957; Wayne C. Booth, *The Rhetoric of Fiction*, 1961, rev. ed. 1983; W. J. Bate, *The Burden of the Past and the English Poet*, 1970; Harold Bloom, *The Anxiety of Influence*, 1973; and Paul de Man, *Allegories of Reading*, 1979.

René Wellek and Austin Warren, *Theory of Literature*, rev. 1970, is a useful introduction to the variety of scholarly and critical approaches to literature up to the time of its publication. Jonathan Culler's *Literary Theory: A Very Short Introduction*, 1997, discusses recurrent issues and debates. Modern feminist literary criticism was fashioned by such works as Particia Meyers Spacks, *The Female Imagination*, 1975; Ellen Moers, *Literary Women*, 1976; Elaine Showalter, *A Literature of Their Own*, 1977; and Sandra Gilbert and Susan Gubar, *The Madwoman in the Attic*, 1979. More recent studies include Jane Gallop, *The Daughter's Seduction: Feminism and Psychoanalysis*, 1982; Gayatri Chakravorty Spivak, *In Other Worlds: Essays in Cultural Politics*, 1987; Sandra Gilbert and Susan Gubar, *No Man's Land: The Place of the Woman Writer in the Twentieth Century*, 2 vols., 1988–89; Barbara Johnson, *A World of Difference*, 1989; Judith Butler, *Gender Trouble*, 1990; and the critical views sampled in Elaine Showalter, *The New Feminist Criticism*, 1985; *Feminist Literary Theory: A Reader*, ed. Mary Eagleton, 2nd ed., 1995; and *Feminisms: An Anthology of Literary Theory and Criticism*, ed. Robyn R. Warhol and Diane Price Herndl, 2nd ed. 1997. Gay and lesbian studies and criticism are represented in *The Lesbian and Gay Studies Reader*, ed. Henry Abelove, Michele Barale, and David Halperin, 1993, and by such books as Eve Sedgwick, *Between Men: English Literature and Male Homosocial Desire*, 1985, and *Epistemology of the Closet*, 1990; Diana Fuss, *Essentially Speaking: Feminism, Nature, and Difference*, 1989; and Gregory Woods, *A History of Gay Literature: The Male Tradition*, 1998. Convenient introductions to structuralist literary criticism include Robert Scholes, *Structuralism in Literature: An Introduction*, 1974, and Jonathan Culler, *Structuralist Poetics*, 1975. The poststructuralist challenges to this approach are discussed in Jonathan Culler, *On Deconstruction*, 1982; Fredric Jameson, *Poststructuralism; or the Cultural Logic of Late Capitalism*, 1991; John McGowan, *Postmodernism and Its Critics*, 1991; and *Beyond Structuralism*, ed. Wendell Harris,

1996. New historicism is represented in Stephen Greenblatt, *Learning to Curse*, 1990, and in the essays collected in *The New Historicism*, ed. Harold Veeser, 1989, and *New Historical Literary Study: Essays on Reproducing Texts, Representing History*, ed. Jeffrey N. Cox and Larry J. Reynolds, 1993. The related social and historical dimension of texts is discussed in Jerome McGann, *Critique of Modern Textual Criticism*, 1983, and D. F. McKenzie, *Bibliography and Sociology of Texts*, 1986. Characteristic of new historicism is an expansion of the field of literary interpretation extended still further in cultural studies; for a broad sampling of the range of interests, see *The Cultural Studies Reader*, ed. Simon During, 1993, and *A Cultural Studies Reader: History, Theory, Practice*, ed. Jessica Munns and Gita Rajan, 1997. This expansion of the field is similarly reflected in postcolonial studies: see *The Post-Colonial Studies Reader*, ed. Bill Ashcroft, Gareth Griffiths, and Helen Tiffin, 1995, and such influential books as Ranajit Guha and Gayatri Chakravorti Spivak, *Selected Subaltern Studies*, 1988; Edward Said, *Culture and Imperialism*, 1993; and Homi Bhabha, *The Location of Culture*, 1994.

Anthologies representing a range of recent approaches include *Modern Criticism and Theory*, ed. David Lodge, 1988, and *Contemporary Literary Criticism*, ed. Robert Con Davis and Ronald Schlieffer, rev. 1998.

THE MIDDLE AGES

Scholarship during this era has been divided into the same three periods as in the General Introduction: Anglo-Saxon England, Anglo-Norman England, and Middle English Literature of the Fourteenth and Fifteenth Centuries. A reference book for the whole era is Joseph Strayer et al., *Dictionary of the Middle Ages*, 1982–.

Anglo-Saxon England

D. Whitelock, *The Beginnings of English Society*, 1952, provides concise historical background for the literature of the period. The most detailed history is F. M. Stenton's authoritative *Anglo-Saxon England*, 3rd ed., 1971. Also highly informative are P. Hunter Blair, *An Introduction to Anglo-Saxon England*, 1956, and *Roman Britain and Early England*, 55 B.C.–A.D. 871, 1963. The classic study of the culture of the primitive Germanic peoples is H. M. Chadwick, *The Heroic Age*, 1912. For those who wish to sample basic historical documents of the period, there is available the translation by G. N. Garmonsway of *The Anglo-Saxon Chronicle*, 1953. *The Age of Bede*, ed. D. H. Farmer, rev. 1983, and *Alfred the Great*, ed. S. Keynes and M. Lapidge, 1983, contain texts documenting two crucial periods of Anglo-Saxon history. Bede's *Ecclesiastical History of the English People* is translated and edited by B. Colgrave and R. A. B.

Mynors, 1969. For studies of Bede, see G. H. Brown, *Bede, the Venerable*, 1987, and J. M. Wallace-Hadrill, *Bede's Ecclesiastical History of the English People: A Historical Commentary*, 1993. A lavishly and finely illustrated introduction to Anglo-Saxon England is *The Anglo-Saxons*, ed. J. Campbell, 1982. C. Fell, *Women in Anglo-Saxon England*, 1984, is pertinent to women's studies. The journal *Anglo-Saxon England* is devoted to all aspects of the history and culture of the period.

All the surviving poetry in Old English is contained in the six volumes edited by G. P. Krapp and E. V. K. Dobbie, *The Anglo-Saxon Poetic Records*, 1931–53, but the absence of glossaries makes this edition difficult for nonspecialists. Excellent texts of the shorter poems translated in this anthology are contained in J. C. Pope, *Seven Old English Poems*, 1966, rev. 1981. The standard text of *Beowulf and the Fight of Finnsburg* is F. Klaeber's 3rd ed., 1950; C. L. Wrenn's edition, *Beowulf, with the Finnsburg Fragment*, rev. W. F. Bolton, 1973, rev. 1988, is very useful; H. D. Chickering Jr. has made a dual-language edition with extensive commentary, and G. B. Jack has prepared *Beowulf: A Student Edition*, 1994. There are individual editions of *The Dream of the Rood* by M. Swanton, 1970; of *The Wanderer* by T. P. Dunning and A. J. Bliss, 1969. *The Wanderer* and *The Wife's Lament* are included in *The*

Old English Elegies: A Critical Edition and Genre Study, ed. A. L. Klinck, 1992. Modern English translations of many of the Old English poems have been published under various titles by R. K. Gordon, C. W. Kennedy, M. Alexander, S. A. J. Bradley, and K. Crossley-Holland. Many translations of *Beowulf* are available. E. T. Donaldson's translation is used in *Beowulf*, A Norton Critical Edition, ed. J. F. Tuso, 1975.

General discussions of Old English literature will be found in Vol. 1 of the *Cambridge History of English Literature*; S. B. Greenfield and D. G. Calder, *New Critical History of Old English Literature*, 1986; C. L. Wrenn, *A Study of Old English Literature*; M. Alexander, *Old English Literature*, 1983; and *The Cambridge Companion to Old English Literature*, ed. M. Godden and M. Lapidge, 1991.

Some useful studies and collections devoted exclusively to Old English poetry are S. B. Greenfield, *The Interpretation of Old English Poems*, 1972; T. A. Shippey, *Old English Verse*, 1972; J. B. Bessinger Jr. and S. J. Kahrl, *Essential Articles for the Study of Old English Poetry*, 1977; D. A. Pearsall, *Old and Middle English Poetry*, 1977; B. C. Raw, *The Art and Background of Old English Poetry*, 1978; *Old English Poetry: Essays on Style*, ed. D. G. Calder, 1979; *The Old English Elegies*, ed. M. Green, 1983; S. B. Greenfield, *Hero and Exile: The Art of Old English Poetry*, 1989; *De Gustibus*, ed. J. M. Foley et al., 1992; *Heroic Poetry in the Anglo-Saxon Period*, ed. H. Damico and J. Leyerle, 1993; *Companion to Old English Poetry*, ed. H. Aertsen and R. H. Bremmer Jr., 1994; and *Old English Shorter Poems: Basic Readings*, ed. K. O'Brien O'Keeffe, 1994.

General collections of essays on Old English literature include *Old English Literature in Context*, ed. J. D. Niles, 1980; *Literature and Learning in Anglo-Saxon England*, ed. M. Lapidge and H. Gneuss, 1985; *Modes of Interpretation in Old English Literature*, ed. P. R. Brown et al., 1986; F. C. Robinson, *The Tomb of Beowulf and Other Essays on Old English*, 1993; and *Studies in English Language and Literature*, ed. M. J. Toswell and E. M. Tyler, 1996.

Some studies of special topics in Old English literature are J. Chance, *Woman as Hero in Old English Literature*, 1986; *New Readings on Women in Old English Literature*, ed. Helen Damico and A. H. Olsen, 1990; A. J. Frantzen, *Desire for Origins: New Language, Old English, and Teaching the Tradition*, 1990; *The Battle of Maldon AD 991*, ed. D. Scragg, 1991; *Class and Gender in Early English Literature*, ed. B. J. Harwood and G. R. Overing, 1994; and *Holy Men, Holy Women: Old English Prose Saints' Lives and Their Contexts*, ed. P. Szarmach, 1996.

Beowulf

Essential backgrounds to the study of the poem are provided by R. W. Chambers, *Beowulf: An Introduction to the Study of the Poem*, 3rd ed., with a supplement by C. L. Wrenn, 1959; and a wide-ranging overview of *Beowulf* scholarship is furnished by *A Beowulf Handbook*, ed. R. E. Bjork and J. D. Niles, 1997. Important critical studies of the poem are found in D. Whitelock, *The Audience of Beowulf*, 1951; A. G. Brodeur, *The Art of Beowulf*, 1959; E. B. Irving Jr., *A Reading of Beowulf*, 1968, *Introduction to Beowulf*, 1969, and *Rereading Beowulf*, 1990; T. A. Shippey, *Beowulf*, 1978; J. D. Niles, *Beowulf: The Poem and Its Tradition*, 1983; G. Clark, *Beowulf*, 1990; J. W. Earl, *Thinking about Beowulf*, 1994; J. M. Hill, *The Cultural World in Beowulf*, 1995; and C. R. Davis, *Beowulf and the Demise of Germanic Legend in England*, 1996.

For anthologies of criticism, see *The Beowulf Poet*, ed. D. K. Fry, 1968; *Beowulf*, A Norton Critical Edition, ed. J. Tuso, 1975; *Interpretations of Beowulf*, ed. R. D. Fulk, 1991; and *Beowulf: Basic Readings*, ed. P. S. Baker, 1995. Special mention should be made of J. R. R. Tolkien's famous lecture, *Beowulf, the Monsters and the Critics*, 1937, reprinted in the anthologies of Fry and Fulk.

Anglo-Norman England

For accounts of the Norman conquest and its historical consequences, see C. Brooke, *From Alfred to Henry III, 871–1272*, 2 vols., 1961; R. A. Brown, *The Normans*, 1984; A. L. Poole, *From Domesday Book to Magna Carta*, 1955; P. Stafford, *A Political and Social History of England in the Tenth and Eleventh Centuries*, 1989; and F. M. Powicke, *The Thirteenth Century, 1216–1307*, 1953. The *Peterborough Chronicle*, a continuation of the *Anglo-Saxon Chronicle* to the year 1154, relates events from the point of view of English monks and can be read in translation in *The Anglo-Saxon Chronicle: a Revised Translation*, ed. by D. Whitelock with D. C. Douglas and S. I. Tucker, 1961, rev. 1965.

Studies of historical writing within the period itself, including the legendary histories of the kings of Britain, are J. S. P. Tatlock, *The Legendary History of Britain*, 1950; R. W. Hanning, *The Vision of History in Early Britain: From Gildas to Geoffrey of Monmouth*, 1966; and M. Otter, *Inventiones: Fiction and Referentiality in Twelfth-Century Historical Writing*.

On **Geoffrey of Monmouth**, in addition to the texts mentioned above, see the translation of his *History of the Kings of Britain* by Lewis Thorpe, 1966; R. W. Leckie Jr., *The Passage of Dominion: Geoffrey of Monmouth and the Periodization of Insular History in the Twelfth Century*, 1981; and M. J. Curley, *Geoffrey of Monmouth*, 1994. The *Brut* by **Layamon** is available in translations by D. G. Bzdyl, 1989; Rosamund Allen, 1992; and in an edition of the Middle English text with facing translation, notes, and commentary by W. R. J. Barron and S. C. Weinberg, 1989. The Arthurian sections of Wace's *Roman de Brut*, translated by Judith Weiss, and of Layamon in Allen's translation are printed together as *The Life of King Arthur*, 1997.

M. D. Legge, *Anglo-Norman Literature and Its*

Background, 1963, is the standard history. The lais of **Marie de France** have been translated by R. H. Hanning and J. Ferrante, 1978, and by G. S. Burgess and K. Busby, 1986. For background and critical interpretations of Marie de France's works, see E. J. Mickel, *Marie de France*, 1974; P. M. Clifford, *Marie de France, Lais*, 1982; and G. S. Burgess, *The Lais of Marie de France*, 1987.

R. M. Wilson's *Early Middle English Literature* focuses primarily on this period. Vol. 1 of the *Oxford History of English Literature*, by J. A. W. Bennett and D. Gray, *Middle English Literature*, 1986, which goes up to 1400 (exclusive of Chaucer), contains excellent discussions of early Middle English texts. Selections of texts from this era with a valuable introduction to the language and annotations are contained in the anthology edited by J. A. W. Bennett and G. V. Smithers, *Early Middle English Verse and Prose*, 2nd ed, 1968.

For discussions of the Arthurian materials in Geoffrey of Monmouth, Wace, Marie de France, and Layamon, see chaps. 4 and 8 to 11 in *Arthurian Literature in the Middle Ages*, ed. R. S. Loomis, 1959.

Middle English Literature of the Fourteenth and Fifteenth Centuries

Histories of the period include G. Holmes, *The Later Middle Ages, 1272–1485*, 1962; M. McKisack, *The Fourteenth Century, 1307–99*, 1959; and E. F. Jacob, *The Fifteenth Century*, 1961. Accounts of life and society during this period are provided by G. G. Coulton in *Chaucer and His England*, 1908, *The Medieval Scene*, 1930, and *Medieval Panorama*, 1938; E. Rickert, *Chaucer's World*, 1948; G. M. Trevelyan, *Chaucer's England and the Early Tudors*, vol. 1 of *The Illustrated English Social History*, 1949; and M. Keen, *English Society in the Later Middle Ages*, 1990. See also the picture books listed under Chaucer. J. Huizinga has written a famous account of the culture and spirit of the late fourteenth to fifteenth centuries, formerly translated as *The Waning of the Middle Ages*, 1924, now available in a fuller text under the more accurate title, *The Autumn of the Middle Ages*, trans. R. J. Payton and U. Mammitzsch, 1996. F. R. H. Du Boulay complements and qualifies Huizinga in *An Age of Ambition*, 1970. Chaps. 6 to 10 in E. Auerbach's *Mimesis: The Representation of Reality in Western Literature*, trans. by W. R. Trask, 1953, although it does not deal with works in this anthology, gives penetrating insights into the reading of medieval texts. C. S. Lewis, *The Discarded Image: An Introduction to Medieval and Renaissance Literature*, 1964, seeks to restore for modern readers the perspective and sensibilities of the earlier age.

For general discussion of late Middle English literature, see the *The Oxford History of English Literature*: J. A. W. Bennett and D. Gray, *Middle English Literature*, 1986, vol. 1, part 2 (up to 1400, exclusive of Chaucer); H. S. Bennett, *Chaucer and the Fifteenth Century*, vol. 2, part 1, 1947, and E. K.

Chambers, *English Literature at the Close of the Middle Ages*, vol. 2, part 2, 1954; also D. A. Pearsall, *Old and Middle English Poetry*, 1977; J. A. Burrow, *Middle English Literature and Its Background*, 1982; and D. S. Brewer, *English Gothic Literature*, 1983.

Critical works devoted to more than one author or genre in the period are G. Kane, *Middle English Literature*, 1951 (chapters on the romances, the religious lyrics, and *Piers Plowman*); J. A. Burrow, *Ricardian Poetry: Chaucer, Gower, Langland, and the Gawain Poet*, 1971; C. Muscatine, *Poetry and Crisis in the Age of Chaucer*, 1972; A. C. Spearing, *Medieval Dream Poetry*, 1976, and *Readings in Medieval Poetry*, 1987; T. Turville-Petre, *The Alliterative Revival*, 1977; *Medieval Literature: Chaucer and the Alliterative Tradition*, vol. 1 of *The New Pelican Guide to English Literature*, ed. Boris Ford, 1982; D. Despres, *Ghostly Sights: Visual Meditation in Late-Medieval Literature*, 1989; S. Justice, *Writing and Rebellion: England in 1381*, 1994; and G. Margherita, *The Romance of Origins: Language and Sexual Difference in Middle English Literature*, 1994. *Middle English Survey: Critical Essays*, ed. E. Vasta, 1965, contains commentary on Langland, *Gawain*, and drama.

For the Middle English language, see Helge Kökeritz, *A Guide to Chaucer's Pronunciation*, 1954; David Burnley, *A Guide to Chaucer's Language*, 1983; and J. A. Burrow and T. Turville-Petre, *A Book of Middle English*, 1996.

The standard bibliography is *A Manual of the Writings in Middle English, 1050–1500*, 6 vols., ed. J. B. Severs, A. E. Hartung, et al., 1967–80, which is based on and supersedes the *Manual* of J. E. Wells, 1916, with nine supplements through 1945.

Geoffrey Chaucer

The standard edition of Chaucer's writing is *The Riverside Chaucer*, 3rd ed., ed. L. D. Benson et al., 1987, based on F. N. Robinson's edition. E. Talbot Donaldson, *Chaucer's Poetry*, 2nd ed., 1975, from which are taken the selections printed here, is helpful to the nonspecialist, as are John H. Fisher, *The Complete Poetry and Prose of Geoffrey Chaucer*, 2nd ed., 1989, and V. A. Kolve and Glending Olson, *The Canterbury Tales: Nine Tales and The "General Prologue,"* Norton Critical Edition, 1989. Vivid presentations of Chaucer in the background of fourteenth-century England are found in D. S. Brewer, *Chaucer and His World*, 1978, which is beautifully illustrated, and *A New Introduction to Chaucer*, 2nd ed., 1998. Pictorial companions to Chaucer's works, especially the *Canterbury Tales*, include R. S. Loomis, *A Mirror of Chaucer's World*, 1965, Maurice Hussey, *Chaucer's World*, 1967, Ian Serraillier, *Chaucer and His World*, 1968, and Roger Hart, *English Life in Chaucer's Day*, 1973.

The raw material for Chaucer's biography is contained in *Chaucer Life-Records*, ed. M. M. Crow and C. C. Olson, 1966. D. R. Howard, *Chaucer: His Life, His Works, His World*, 1987, and D. A. Pearsall, *The Life of Geoffrey Chaucer*, 1992, contain extensive background and interpretation. For succinct accounts of the sources and literary background of Chaucer's works, see R. D. French, *A Chaucer Handbook*, 2nd ed., 1947; reproductions of many of the known sources of the *Canterbury Tales* are contained in *Sources and Analogues of Chaucer's Canterbury Tales*, ed. W. F. Bryan and Germaine Dempster, 1941, 1958. Useful literary materials are collected in R. P. Miller, *Chaucer: Sources and Backgrounds*, 1977. Muriel Bowden, *A Commentary on the General Prologue to the Canterbury Tales*, 1948, provides a wealth of background information on the individual Canterbury pilgrims; see also Jill Mann, *Chaucer and Medieval Estates Satire*, 1973. Various aspects of Chaucer's work are treated by a number of scholars in *Chaucer and Chaucerians*, ed. D. S. Brewer, 1966; *Geoffrey Chaucer (Writers and Their Background)*, ed. D. S. Brewer, 1974; *Companion to Chaucer Studies*, ed. Beryl Rowland, rev. 1979; and *The Cambridge Chaucer Companion*, ed. Piero Boitani and Jill Mann, 1986.

For literary criticism on both *The Canterbury Tales* and other works by Chaucer, the following contain stimulating discussions: G. L. Kittredge, *Chaucer and His Poetry*, 1915; J. L. Lowes, *Geoffrey Chaucer and the Development of His Genius*, 1934; C. Muscatine, *Chaucer and the French Tradition*, 1957; W. C. Curry, *Chaucer and the Medieval Sciences*, rev. 1960; R. O. Payne, *The Key of Remembrance*, 1963; M. Hussey, A. C. Spearing, and J. Winny, *An Introduction to Chaucer*, 1965; E. T. Donaldson, *Speaking of Chaucer*, 1970; T. Ross, *Chaucer's Bawdy*, 1972; D. S. Brewer, *Chaucer*, 3rd ed., 1973; P. Elbow, *Oppositions in Chaucer*, 1975; A. David, *The Strumpet Muse: Art and Morals in Chaucer's Poetry*, 1976; R. Burlin, *Chaucerian Fiction*, 1977; G. Kane, *Chaucer*, 1984; S. Knight, *Geoffrey Chaucer*, 1986; D. Wallace, *Chaucerian Polity: Absolutist Lineages and Associational Forms in England and Italy*, 1997; and R. P. McGerr, *Chaucer's Open Book: Resistance to Closure in Medieval Discourse*, 1998.

Criticism that deals mainly with *The Canterbury Tales* and with earlier commentary on it includes P. Ruggiers, *The Art of The Canterbury Tales*, 1964; D. R. Howard, *The Idea of The Canterbury Tales*, 1976; T. Lawler, *The One and the Many in The Canterbury Tales*, 1980; D. Pearsall, *The Canterbury Tales*, 1985; C. D. Benson, *Chaucer's Drama of Style: Poetic Variety in The Canterbury Tales*, 1986; W. Wetherbee, *Geoffrey Chaucer: The Canterbury Tales*, 1989; H. M. Leicester Jr., *The Disenchanted Self: Representing the Subject in The Canterbury Tales*, 1990; S. Crane, *Gender and Romance in Chaucer's Canterbury Tales*, 1994; and H. Cooper, *The Canterbury Tales*, Oxford Guides to Chaucer, 2nd ed., 1996.

D. W. Robertson's *A Preface to Chaucer*, 1962, is a learned and stimulating introduction to the reading of Chaucer in the light of medieval aesthetic doctrines. V. A. Kolve, *Chaucer and the Imagery of*

Narrative, 1984, relates the first five of the *Canterbury Tales* to medieval art. Several recent books stress the importance of oral delivery, performance, and storytelling in the *Canterbury Tales*: Betsy Bowden, *Chaucer Aloud*, 1987; Carl Lindahl, *Earnest Games: Folkloric Patterns in The Canterbury Tales*, 1987; L. M. Koff, *Chaucer and the Art of Storytelling*, 1988; and J. M. Ganim, *Chaucerian Theatricality*, 1990. The following studies relate Chaucer's works to their social and historical background: Paul Strohm, *Social Chaucer*, 1989; Peggy Knapp, *Chaucer and the Social Contest*, 1990; Peter Brown and Andrew Butcher, *The Age of Saturn: Literature and History in The Canterbury Tales*, 1991; and Lee Patterson, *Chaucer and the Subject of History*, 1991. A pioneer feminist study of Chaucer is Carolyn Dinshaw, *Chaucer's Sexual Poetics*, 1989; see also E. T. Hansen, *Chaucer and the Fictions of Gender*, 1992.

The following are collections of critical essays: *Chaucer: Modern Essays in Criticism*, ed. E. C. Wagenknecht, 1959; *Chaucer Criticism: The Canterbury Tales*, ed. R. J. Schoeck and J. Taylor, 1960; *Discussions of The Canterbury Tales*, ed. C. J. Owen, 1961; *Geoffrey Chaucer: A Critical Anthology*, ed. J. A. Burrow, 1969; and *Geoffrey Chaucer* Contemporary Studies in Literature, ed. G. D. Economou, 1975. See also the prefatory remarks on individual works and tales in *The Riverside Chaucer* and the commentary in E. Talbot Donaldson's anthology, cited above.

Perhaps the most reliable glossary is that edited by Norman Davis et al., 1979. The standard bibliographies are E. P. Hammond, *Chaucer: A Bibliographical Manual*, 1908; D. D. Griffith, *Bibliography of Chaucer*, 1955; W. R. Crawford, *1954–63*, 1967; L. Y. Baird, *1964–73*, 1977; and L. Y. Baird-Lange and H. Schnutgen, *1974–85*, 1988. Two very useful annotated bibliographies are by Mark Allen and J. H. Fisher, *The Essential Chaucer*, 1987, and John Leyerle and Anne Quick, *Chaucer: A Bibliographical Introduction*, 1986. *Studies in the Age of Chaucer*, the journal of The New Chaucer Society, publishes a current bibliography as well as articles on Chaucer and other medieval literature. See also Caroline Spurgeon, *Five Hundred Years of Chaucer Criticism and Allusion, 1357–1900*, 1925.

Julian of Norwich

The standard Middle English text with a wealth of commentary is *A Book of Showings to the Anchoress Julian of Norwich*, 2 vols., ed. Edmund Colledge and James Walsh, 1978. The editors' translation is published as *Julian of Norwich: Showings*, 1978; another translation of the long text by Clifton Walters is published under the title *Revelations of Divine Love*, 1966. Another edition of the long text, ed. G. R. Crampton, 1994, published for TEAMS (Consortium for the Teaching of the Middle Ages) is designed for students.

General studies of mystical writing in England and on the Continent are W. Riehle, *The Middle English Mystics*, trans. B. Standring, 1981; *An Intro-*

duction to the Medieval Mystics of Europe, ed. P. Szarmach, 1984; A. K. Warren, *Anchorites and their Patrons in Medieval England*, 1985; F. Beer, *Women and Mystical Experience in the Middle Ages*, 1992; S. Beckwith, *Christ's Body: Identity, Culture, and Society in Late Medieval Writings*, 1993; and D. Aers and L. Staley, *The Powers of the Holy: Religion, Politics, and Gender in Late Medieval English Culture*, 1996. Studies helpful to understanding the mystical thought of Julian of Norwich are B. Pelphrey, *Christ Our Mother*, 1989, and D. N. Baker, *Julian of Norwich's Showing: From Vision to Book*, 1994.

Sir Thomas Malory

The Winchester manuscript of Malory's *Morte Darthur*, with full commentary and valuable discussion, is given in Eugène Vinaver's *The Works of Sir Thomas Malory*, 3 vols., 2nd ed., 1967; the one-volume edition, Oxford, 1970, contains the text only. The Caxton version is most readily available in *Caxton's Malory*, ed. J. W. Spisak, 1983. Vinaver, *Malory*, 1929, surveys Malory's life and career; see also, P. J. C. Field, *The Life and Times of Sir Thomas Malory*, 1993. Guides to Malory are B. Dillon, *A Malory Handbook*, 1978; Terence McCarthy, *An Introduction to Malory*, rev. ed., 1991; and E. Archibald and A. S. G. Edwards, *A Companion to Malory*, 1996. A number of critical problems in Malory's work, especially its unity, are discussed in three collections of essays by various scholars: *Essays on Malory*, ed. J. A. W. Bennett, 1963, *Malory's Originality*, ed. by R. M. Lumiansky, 1964, and *Studies in Malory*, ed. J. W. Spisak, 1985. Other studies of Malory and the *Morte Darthur* include Mark Lambert, *Malory: Style and Vision in Le Morte Darthur*, 1975; L. D. Benson, *Malory's Morte Darthur*, 1976; and Felicity Riddy, *Sir Thomas Malory*, 1987.

For reference books and discussions of the development and of the political and social significance of the Arthurian tradition in England, see R. S. Loomis, *The Development of Arthurian Romance*, 1963; S. Knight, *Arthurian Literature and Society*, 1983; *The Arthurian Handbook*, ed. N. J. Lacy and G. Ashe, 2nd ed., 1998; *The New Arthurian Encyclopedia*, ed. N. J. Lacy, 1991; *Approaches to Teaching the Arthurian Tradition*, ed. M. Fries and J. Watson, 1992; *Culture and the King: the Social Implications of the Arthurian Legend*, ed. M. Schichtman and J. Carley, 1994; *Arthurian Women: A Casebook*, ed. T. Fenster, 1996; and *King Arthur: A Casebook*, ed. E. D. Kennedy, 1996.

Mystery Plays

E. K. Chambers's classic *The Medieval Stage*, 1905, remains a mine of information, although its views about the evolution of medieval drama are no longer accepted. A new understanding and appreciation of medieval drama begins with O. B. Hardison, *Christian Rite and Christian Drama in the Middle Ages*, 1965; and for the mysteries, with V. A. Kolve, *The Play Called Corpus Christie*, 1966. Rosemary Woolf, *The English Mystery Plays*, 1972, makes detailed comparisons among the extant plays. Individual cycles are studied by Peter Travis in *Dramatic Design in the Chester Cycle*, 1982, and by Martin Stevens in *Four Middle English Mystery Cycles: Textual, Contextual, and Critical Interpretations*, 1987. G. M. Gibson fills in the social and religious background in *The Theater of Devotion: East Anglian Drama and Society in the Late Middle Ages*, 1989. Good selections of Middle English plays are presented by A. C. Cawley, *Everyman and Medieval Miracle Plays*, 1960; by D. M. Bevington, *Medieval Drama*, 1975; and by Peter Happé, *The English Mystery Plays*, 1975. Cawley, *The Wakefield Pageants in the Towneley Cycle*, 1958, has a discussion of the work of the "Wakefield Master" whose hand is seen in the *Second Shepherds' Play*. A collection of critical essays has been made by Jerome Taylor and A. H. Nelson in *Medieval English Drama*, 1972. *Approaches to Teaching Medieval Drama*, ed. Richard Emmerson, 1990, contains essays by many hands and makes up a nontechnical survey of current opinion. For commentary on *Everyman*, see the introduction to A. C. Cawley's 1961 edition and Robert Potter's comprehensive *The English Morality Play: Origins, History, and Influence of a Dramatic Tradition*, 1975.

Sir Gawain and the Green Knight

The standard Middle English edition of the poem is by J. R. R. Tolkien and E. V. Gordon, rev. Norman Davis, 1967. Easier to use are the editions by R. A. Waldron, 1970, rev. for *The Poems of the Pearl Manuscript*, 1978; and by J. A. Burrow, 1972. For a guide to the poems in the manuscript, see A. Putter, *An Introduction to the Gawain-Poet*, 1996, and *A Companion to the Gawain Poet*, ed. D. S. Brewer and J. Gibson, 1997. Discussions of various aspects of the poem appear in Marie Borroff, *Sir Gawain and the Green Knight: A Stylistic and Metrical Study*, 1962; L. D. Benson, *Art and Tradition in Sir Gawain and the Green Knight*, 1965; J. A. Burrow, *A Reading of Sir Gawain and the Green Knight*, 1965; A. C. Spearing, *The Gawain Poet: A Critical Study*, 1971; And W. Clein, *Concepts of Chivalry in Sir Gawain and the Green Knight*, 1984.

Collections of essays have been compiled by R. J. Blanch, *Sir Gawain and Pearl*, 1966, and *Text and Matter: New Critical Perspectives of the Pearl-Poet*, 1991 D. Fox, *Twentieth-Century Interpretations of Sir Gawain and the Green Knight*, 1968; and D. R. Howard and C. K. Zacher, *Critical Studies of Sir Gawain and the Green Knight*, 1968.

THE SIXTEENTH CENTURY

Some important books on society and culture in early modern England are Lawrence Stone, *The Crisis of the Aristocracy, 1558–1641*, 1965, and *The Family, Sex and Marriage in England, 1500–1800*, 1979; Keith Thomas, *Religion and the Decline of Magic*, 1971; J. A. Sharpe, *Early Modern England: A Social History*, 1987; P. G. Emmison, *Elizabethan Life: Disorder*, 1970; David Cressy, *Literacy and the Social Order: Reading and Writing in Tudor and Stuart England*, 1980, and *Birth, Marriage, and Death: Ritual, Religion, and the Life-Cycle in Tudor and Stuart England*, 1997; Keith Wrightson, *English Society, 1580–1680*, 1982; Peter Clark, *The English Alehouse: A Social History, 1200–1830*, 1983; Peter Laslett, *The World We Have Lost, Further Explored*, 1984; Paul Slack, *The Impact of Plague in Tudor and Stuart England*, 1985; Mervyn James, *Society, Politics, and Culture: Studies in Early Modern England*, 1986; Susan Amussen, *An Ordered Society: Gender and Class in Early Modern England*, 1988; Felicity Heal, *Hospitality in Early Modern England*, 1990; Ian Archer, *The Pursuit of Stability: Social Relations in Elizabethan London*, 1991; Illana Ben-Amos, *Adolescence and Youth in Early Modern England*, 1994; Ronald Hutton, *The Rise and Fall of Merry England: The Ritual Year 1400–1700*, 1994; Lena Orlin, *Private Matters and Public Culture in Post-Reformation England*, 1994; and Kim Hall, *Things of Darkness: Economies of Race and Gender in Early Modern England*, 1995.

Useful general studies of the history of the period include J. B. Black, *The Reign of Elizabeth, 1558–1603*, 2nd ed., 1959; G. R. Elton, *England under the Tudors*, 1955, and *Reform and Reformation: England, 1509–1559*, 1977; Conrad Russell, *The Crisis of Parliaments: English History, 1509–1660*, 1971; and John Guy, *Tudor England*, 1988. Political theory in the period is surveyed in Quentin Skinner, *The Foundations of Modern Political Thought*, 2 vols., 1978; and there is an important analysis of the theory of kingship in E. H. Kantorowicz, *The King's Two Bodies*, 1957. Exploration and military history are treated in G. Mattingly, *The Armada*, 1959, and J. A. Williamson, *The Age of Drake*, 4th ed., 1960. For church history and religion, see John Bossy, *The English Catholic Community, 1570–1850*, 1979; Patrick Collinson, *The Religion of Protestants: The Church in English Society, 1559–1625*, 1982, and *The Birthpangs of Protestant England: Religious and Cultural Change in the Sixteenth and Seventeenth Centuries*, 1988; Peter Lake, *Anglicans and Puritans?*, 1988; Debora Shuger, *Habits of Thought in the English Renaissance: Religion, Politics, and the Dominant Culture*, 1990; Eamon Duffy, *The Stripping of the Altars: Traditional Religion in England c. 1400–c. 1580*, 1992; Christopher Haigh, *English Reformations: Religion, Politics, and Society under the Tudors*, 1993; and James Shapiro, *Shakespeare and the Jews*, 1996.

Life at court is described in David Starkey, *The English Court: From the Wars of the Roses to the Civil War*, 1987. Patronage and courtiership, with special reference to literature, are analyzed in David Javitch, *Poetry and Courtliness in Renaissance England*, 1976; *Patronage in the Renaissance*, ed. Guy Fitch Lytle and Stephen Orgel, 1981; and Frank Whigham, *Ambition and Privilege: The Social Tropes of Elizabethan Courtesy Theory*, 1984. On publishing and the book trade, see H. S. Bennett, *English Books and Readers, 1475–1557*, 1952, and *English Books and Readers, 1558–1603*, 1965; Elizabeth L. Eisenstein, *The Printing Press as an Agent of Change*, 2 vols., 1979; and Adrian Johns, *The Nature of the Book: Print and Knowledge in the Making*, 1998.

Several classic studies define the Renaissance in terms of humanism, imitation of the ancients, and individual achievement: Jacob Burckhardt, *The Civilization of the Renaissance*, 1878, rev. 1944; Douglas Bush, *The Renaissance and English Humanism*, 1939; E. M. W. Tillyard, *The Elizabethan World Picture*, 1943; *The Renaissance Philosophy of Man*, ed. Ernst Cassirer et al., 1948; Erwin Panofsky, *Renaissance and Renascences in Western Art*, 2 vols., 1960; and Paul O. Kristeller, *Renaissance Thought*, 2 vols., 1961, 1965. Revisionist analyses by new historicist and cultural materialist critics focus on the interaction of institutions, ideology, and the conditions of cultural production in the social construction of persons and literary texts. Some seminal studies are Stephen Greenblatt, *Renaissance Self-Fashioning*, 1980; *Representing the English Renaissance*, ed. S. Greenblatt, 1988; Richard Helgerson, *Self-Crowned Laureates: Spenser, Jonson, Milton and the Literary System*, 1983, and *Forms of Nationhood: The Elizabethan Writing of England*, 1992; Annabel Patterson, *Censorship and Interpretation: The Conditions of Writing and Reading in Early Modern England*, 1984; Peter Stallybrass and Allon White, *The Politics and Poetics of Transgression*, 1986; and Richard Halpern, *The Poetics of Primitive Accumulation: English Renaissance Culture and the Genealogy of Capital*, 1991. (Others on the theater and on Shakespeare are noted in appropriate sections.)

Science and medicine in this period are discussed in Antonia Mclean, *Humanism and the Rise of Science in Tudor England*, 1972; Roy Porter, *Disease, Medicine and Society in England 1550–1860*, 1987; Thomas Laqueur, *Making Sex: Body and Gender from the Greeks to Freud*, 1990; and Jonathan Sawday, *The Body Emblazoned: Dissection and the Human Body in Renaissance Culture*, 1995. Education is the subject of T. W. Baldwin, *William Shakespere's Small Latine and Lesse Greeke*, 2 vols., 1944, and Kenneth Charlton, *Education in Renaissance England*, 1965. On logic and rhetoric see W. S. Howell, *Logic and Rhetoric in England, 1500–1700*, 1956; Sister Miriam Joseph, *Rhetoric* in Shakespeare's Time, 1962; Frances Yates, The Art of Memory, 1966; and Victoria Kahn, Rhetoric and Skepticism in the Renaissance, 1985.

Some books on Renaissance art and architecture are Marcus Whiffin, An Introduction to Elizabethan and Jacobean Architecture, 1952; J. Buxton, Elizabethan Taste, 1963; Roy Strong, The English Icon: Elizabethan and Jacobean Portraiture, 1969, and The Cult of Elizabeth: Elizabethan Portraiture and Pageantry, 1977; Mark Girouard, Life in the English Country House, 1978; John King, Tudor Royal Iconography: Literature and Art in an Age of Religious Crisis, 1989; Lucy Gent, Picture and Poetry, 1560–1620, 1981; and Norman K. Farmer, Poets and the Visual Arts in Renaissance England, 1984. Renaissance iconology and emblem books often illuminate literary imagery; important studies are Erwin Panofsky, Studies in Iconology, 1939; Rosemary Freeman, English Emblem Books, 1948; Jean Seznec, The Survival of the Pagan Gods, trans. B. F. Sessions, 1963. The attack on religious images is treated by John Phillips, The Reformation of Images: Destruction of Art in England, 1535–1660, 1971; and Ernest B. Gilman, Iconoclasm and Poetry in the English Reformation, 1986.

For Tudor music and musicians in relation to poetry see M. C. Boyd, Elizabethan Music and Music Criticism, 1940; E. H. Fellowes, English Madrigal Verse, rev. 1967; John Stevens, Music and Poetry in the Early Tudor Court, 1961, rpt. 1979; David Price, Patrons and Musicians of the English Renaissance, 1981; and Winifred Meynard, Elizabethan Lyric Poetry and Its Music, 1986. John Hollander studies music as symbol in The Untuning of the Sky: Ideas of Music in English Poetry, 1500–1700, 1961; and Paula Johnson analyzes structural affinities of the two art forms in Form and Transformation in Music and Poetry of the English Renaissance, 1975.

Useful anthologies of Elizabethan literary criticism are G. G. Smith, Elizabethan Critical Essays, 2 vols., 1904, and O. B. Hardison Jr., English Literary Criticism: The Renaissance, 1963. Important studies of Renaissance literary theory and criticism include Rosamond Tuve, Elizabethan and Metaphysical Imagery, 1947; Baxter Hathaway, Marvels and Commonplaces: Renaissance Literary Criticism, 1968; Don C. Allen, Mysteriously Meant: The Rediscovery of Pagan Symbolism and Allegorical Interpretation in the Renaissance, 1970; S. K. Heninger, Touches of Sweet Harmony: Pythagorean Cosmology and Renaissance Poetics, 1974; Margaret W. Ferguson, Trials of Desire: Renaissance Defenses of Poetry, 1983; and Arthur Kinney, Humanist Poetics, 1986.

Some distinguished historical and critical accounts of Renaissance literature include Hallett Smith, Elizabethan Poetry: A Study in Conventions, Meaning, and Expression, 1952, rpt. 1968; C. S. Lewis, English Literature in the Sixteenth Century, Excluding Drama, 1954; Douglas Bush, Mythology and the Renaissance Tradition in English Poetry, rev. 1963; Rosalie Colie, The Resources of Kind: Genre-Theory in the Renaissance, 1973; Thomas M.

Greene, The Light in Troy: Imitation and Discovery in Renaissance Poetry, 1982; Alan Sinfield, Literature in Protestant England, 1560–1660, 1983; and David Norbrook, Poetry and Politics in the English Renaissance, 1984. Important studies of particular Renaissance genres and kinds include J. W. Lever, The Elizabethan Love Sonnet, 1956; Alvin Kernan, The Cankered Muse: Satire of the English Renaissance, 1959; Lily B. Campbell, Divine Poetry and Drama in Sixteenth-Century England, 1959; Angus Fletcher, Allegory: The Theory of a Symbolic Mode, 1964; Douglas L. Peterson, The English Lyric from Wyatt to Donne, 1966; Seventeenth-Century Prose, ed. Stanley Fish, 1971; Patricia Parker, Inescapable Romance, 1979; Anne Ferry, The "Inward" Language: Sonnets of Wyatt, Sidney, Shakespeare, and Donne, 1983; Janel Mueller, The Native Tongue and the Word: Developments in English Prose Style, 1380–1580, 1984; Peter Sacks, The English Elegy: Studies in the Genre from Spenser to Yeats, 1985; Susanne Wofford, The Choice of Achilles: The Ideology of Figure in the Epic, 1992; Arthur Marotti, Manuscript, Print, and the English Renaissance Lyric, 1995; and Paul Alpers, What Is Pastoral?, 1996.

Important studies of stage history, audiences, and the development of dramatic forms include E. K. Chambers, The Elizabethan Stage, 4 vols., 1923; Allardyce Nicoll, British Drama, rev. 1962; Revels History of Drama in English, 8 vols., 1978–83; Muriel D. Bradbrook, A History of Elizabethan Drama, 6 vols., 1935–76; F. T. Bowers, Elizabethan Revenge Tragedy, 1578–1642, 1940; Glynne Wickham, Early English Stages, 1300–1660, 3 vols., 1959–81; Richard Leacroft, The Development of the English Playhouse, 1973; David Bevington, From "Mankind" to Marlowe, 1962; Stephen Orgel, The Illusion of Power: Political Theater in the English Renaissance, 1975, and Impersonations: The Performance of Gender in Shakespeare's England, 1996; Ann Jennalie Cook, The Privileged Playgoers of Shakespeare's London: 1576–1642, 1981; Andrew Gurr, Playgoing in Shakespeare's London, 1987; and Leeds Barroll, Politics, Plague, and Shakespeare's Theater, 1991. Some important studies of drama in relation to contemporary politics and ideology are David Bevington, Tudor Drama and Politics, 1968; Robert Weiman, Shakespeare and the Popular Tradition in the Theater, 1967, rpt. 1987; Jonas Barish, The Antitheatrical Prejudice, 1981; Jonathan Dollimore, Radical Tragedy: Religion, Ideology and Power in the Drama of Shakespeare and his Contemporaries, 1984; Catherine Belsey, The Subject of Tragedy: Identity and Difference in Renaissance Drama, 1985; Jean-Christophe Agnew, Worlds Apart: The Market and the Theatre in Anglo-American Thought, 1550–1750, 1986; Steven Mullaney, The Place of the Stage, 1988; Katharine Maus, Inwardness and Theater in the English Renaissance, 1995; and Louis Montrose, The Purpose of Playing: Shakespeare and the Cultural Politics of the Elizabethan Theatre, 1996.

The many recent studies of the status of women

in early modern England have a distinguished precursor in Alice Clark, *Working Life of Women in the Seventeenth Century*, 1919. On the situation of women in the Renaissance and the achievements of women writers, see Joan Kelly-Gadol, "Did Women Have a Renaissance?" in *Becoming Visible: Women in European History*, ed. R. Bridenthal and C. Koonz, 1977; Ian Maclean, *The Renaissance Notion of Women*, 1980; *Beyond Their Sex: Learned Women of the European Past*, ed. Patricia H. Labalme, 1980; Retha M. Warnicke, *Women of the English Renaissance and Reformation*, 1983; Linda Woodbridge, *Women and the English Renaissance: Literature and the Nature of Womankind, 1540–1640*, 1984; *Rewriting the Renaissance: The Discourses of Sexual Difference in Early Modern Europe*, ed. Margaret Ferguson et al., 1986; Elaine Beilin, *Redeeming Eve: Women Writers of the English Renaissance*, 1987; *The Renaissance Englishwoman in Print: Counterbalancing the Canon*. ed. Anne M. Haselkorn and Betty S. Travitsky, 1990; Constance Jordan, *Renaissance Feminism: Literary Texts and Political Models*, 1990; and Patricia Crawford, *Women and Religion in England, 1500–1720*, 1993. A useful anthology is *The Paradise of Women: Writings by Englishwomen of the Renaissance*, ed. Betty Travitsky, 1981; see also Randall Martin, *Women Writers in Renaissance England*, 1997. On male homosexuality in the period, see Alan Bray, *Homosexuality in Renaissance England*, 1982, and Bruce Smith, *Homosexual Desire in Shakespeare's England*, 1991.

An invaluable tool for the study of early modern literature is the *Oxford English Dictionary*, 2nd ed., 1989, now also on CD-ROM. Also useful are Morris Tilley, *A Dictionary of the Proverbs in England in the Sixteenth and Seventeenth Centuries*, 1950; Richard Jones, *The Triumph of the English Language*, 1953; Richard Lanham, *A Handlist of Rhetorical Terms*, 1968; James Hencke, *Courtesans and Cuckolds: A Glossary of Renaissance Dramatic Bawdy (Exclusive of Shakespeare)*, 1979; Fausto Cercignani, *Shakespeare's Works and Elizabethan Pronunciation*, 1981; Eric Partridge, *Shakespeare's Bawdy*, 3rd ed., 1991; and Charles Barber, *Early Modern English*, rev. ed., 1997.

Michael Drayton
The standard edition is by J. W. Hebel, 5 vols., 1931–41, rpt. 1961; there is a useful selected edition by John Buxton, 1953. The standard biography is B. H. Newdigate, *Michael Drayton and his Circle*, 1941, rpt. 1961. Critical studies include J. A. Berthelot, *Michael Drayton*, 1967; R. F. Hardin, *Michael Drayton and the Passing of Elizabethan England*, 1973; and Jean R. Brink, *Michael Drayton Revisited*, 1990. There are valuable discussions of Drayton in Richard Helgerson, *Forms of Nationhood*, 1992, and Claire McEachern, *The Poetics of English Nationhood, 1590–1612*, 1996.

Queen Elizabeth I
There is no complete edition of Queen Elizabeth's writings. *The Poems of Queen Elizabeth I*, ed.

Leicester Bradner, 1964, prints several of her poems and verse translations. The most inclusive edition of her letters is by G. B. Harrison, 1935; and George P. Rice Jr. prints twenty-one of her speeches in *The Public Speaking of Queen Elizabeth: Selections from her Official Addresses*, 1951, rpt. 1966. Frances Teague surveys Elizabeth's life and writings, and prints a selection of her works, in *Women Writers of the Renaissance and Reformation*, ed. Katharina M. Wilson, 1987; Marc Shell edits and provides an extended commentary on one of her religious translations in *Elizabeth's Glass*, 1993. The standard biography remains J. E. Neale, *Queen Elizabeth I*, 1934, rpt. 1967. Maria Perry has a documentary biography, *The Word of a Prince: The Life of Elizabeth I from Contemporary Documents*, 1990. The queen's significance as political and cultural presence is treated by Frances Yates, *Astraea: The Imperial Theme*, 1975; Marie Axton, *The Queen's Two Bodies: Drama and the Elizabethan Succession*, 1977; Phillippa Berry, *Of Chastity and Power: Elizabethan Literature and the Unmarried Queen*, 1989; and Carole Levin, *"The Heart and Stomach of a King": Elizabeth I and the Politics of Sex and Power*, 1994. Susan Bassnett, *Elizabeth I: A Feminist Perspective*, 1988, approaches the queen's career through her writings; Susan Frye, *Elizabeth I: The Competition for Representation*, 1993, studies Elizabeth's construction of her power within a patriarchal society. *ELR* 23 (1993): 345–54 and 24 (1994): 234–36 survey recent studies of Elizabeth.

The English Bible
Debora Shuger's *The Renaissance Bible: Scholarship, Sacrifice, and Subjectivity*, 1994, is a brilliant analysis of the place of Scripture in a wide range of early modern discourses. Studies of the English Bible include John Coolidge, *The Pauline Renaissance in England: Puritanism and the Bible*, 1970; David Daiches, *The King James Version of the English Bible*, 1968; F. F. Bruce, *History of the Bible in English*, 1978; and A. C. Partridge, *English Biblical Translation*, 1973. William Tyndale's doctrinal treatises were edited by Henry Walter in 1848; there is a modern biography of Tyndale by David Daniell, 1994, and an account of his psychological and literary power in Stephen Greenblatt, *Renaissance Self-Fashioning*, 1980.

The Book of Common Prayer
John Booty edited the 1559 version of the Book of Common Prayer in 1976; Booty also edited *The Godly Kingdom of Tudor England*, 1981, a useful collection of essays on the prayer book, the Book of Homilies, and other Reformation texts.

Mary (Sidney) Herbert, Countess of Pembroke
Margaret P. Hannay et al. edited the *Collected Works*, 2 vols., 1998; there is an important edition of *The Psalms of Sir Philip Sidney and the Countess of Pembroke*, ed J. C. A. Rathmell, 1963. Margaret P. Hannay has written the only literary biography, *Philip's Phoenix*, 1990. Mary Herbert is also one of the three writers treated in Kim Walker, *Women*

Writers of the English Renaissance, 1996. Other important studies are Gary Waller, Mary Sidney, Countess of Pembroke: A Critical Study of Her Writings and Literary Milieu, 1979, and Mary Ellen Lamb, Gender and Authorship in the Sidney Circle, 1990. Recent studies are surveyed in ELR 14 (1984): 426–37 and 24 (1994): 237–38.

Christopher Marlowe

Fredson Bowers has edited the Complete Works, 2 vols., 1973, rev. 1981; R. H. Case has a modern-spelling edition, 6 vols., 1930–33, rpt. 1966; of Roma Gill's projected three-volume edition, the first two volumes appeared in 1987. W. W. Greg edited parallel texts of the two versions of Dr. Faustus in 1950; the two versions have also been edited by David Bevington and Eric Rasmussen, 1993; and Roma Gill edited the A text (our copy text for Faustus) in 1989. Stephen Orgel edited The Complete Poems and Translations of Christopher Marlowe, 1971. For Marlowe's biography see John Bakeless, The Tragicall History of Christopher Marlowe, 2 vols., 1942, and Charles Nicholl, The Reckoning: The Murder of Christopher Marlowe, 1992. Valuable critical studies include Harry Levin, The Overreacher, 1952; Douglas Cole, Suffering and Evil in the Plays of Christopher Marlowe, 1962; Two Renaissance Mythmakers: Christopher Marlowe and Ben Jonson, ed. Alvin B. Kernan, 1977; Marlowe: The Critical Heritage, ed. Millar McLure, 1979; Clifford Leech, Christopher Marlowe: Poet for the Stage, 1986; Simon Shepherd, Marlowe and the Politics of Elizabethan Theatre, 1986; Christopher Marlowe, in the series "Modern Critical Views," ed. Harold Bloom, 1986; C. L. Barber, Creating Elizabethan Tragedy: the Theater of Marlowe and Kyd, 1988. Christopher Marlowe's "Doctor Faustus," in "Modern Critical Interpretations," ed. Harold Bloom, 1988; and Christopher Marlowe and English Renaissance Culture, ed. Darryll Grantley and Peter Roberts, 1996. For Hero and Leander, Louis L. Martz's facsimile of the first edition, 1972, has an important introduction. On the genre, see William Keach, Elizabeth Erotic Narratives, 1977; and Clark Hulse, Metamorphic Verse: The Elizabethan Minor Epic, 1981. Recent studies are surveyed in ELR 7 (1977): 382–99 and 18 (1988): 329–42.

Thomas Nashe

The standard edition, 5 vols., is by R. W. McKerrow, rev. F. P. Wilson, 1958; there are selected editions by Stanley Wells, 1965, and J. B. Steane, 1972. Charles Nicholl has written A Cup of News: The Life of Thomas Nashe, 1984. Useful critical studies include G. R. Hibbard, Thomas Nashe: A Critical Introduction, 1962; Jonathan V. Crewe, Unredeemed Rhetoric: Thomas Nashe and the Scandal of Authorship, 1982; Stephen S. Hilliard, The Singularity of Thomas Nashe, 1986; Lorna Hutson, Thomas Nashe in Context, 1989; and Peter Holbrook, Literature and Degree in Renaissance England: Nashe, Bourgeois Tragedy, Shakespeare, 1994. ELR 25 (1995): 261–64 reviews recent studies.

Sir Walter Ralegh

The collected edition is by William Oldys and Thomas Birch, 8 vols., 1829, rpt. 1965; the standard edition of the poems is by A. M. C. Latham, rev. 1950; a useful edition is Selected Writings, ed. Gerard Hammond, 1984. The Discoverie of the Large, Rich and Bewtiful Empyre of Guiana has been newly edited, with much contextual and interpretive material, by Neil L. Whitehead, 1997. Biographies include Willard M. Wallace, Sir Walter Raleigh, 1959, and Stephen Coote, A Play of Passion, 1993. Noteworthy studies include David B. Quinn, Ralegh and the British Empire, 1947, rpt. 1962; E. A. Strathmann, Sir Walter Ralegh, A Study in Elizabethan Skepticism, 1951; Philip Edwards, Sir Walter Ralegh, 1953, rpt. 1976; F. J. Levy, Tudor Historical Thought, 1967; Stephen Greenblatt, Sir Walter Ralegh, 1973; and Shannon Miller, Invested with Meaning: The Raleigh Circle in the New World, 1998. For guides to scholarship, see Jerry L. Mills, Sir Walter Ralegh: A Reference Guide, 1986, and Christopher Armitage, Sir Walter Ralegh, An Annotated Bibliography, 1987. See also entries under The Wider World.

William Shakespeare

Some important editions of the plays are the Variorum (S. B. Hemingway, ed., 1 Henry IV, 1936, with a supplement by G. B. Evans, 1956); the New Arden (A. R. Humphries, ed., 1 Henry IV, 1960); and David Bevington, ed., 1 Henry IV, 1987. Major studies treating 1 Henry IV are E. M. W. Tillyard, Shakespeare's History Plays, 1944; Irving Ribner, The English History Play in the Age of Shakespeare, rev. 1965; Robert Ornstein, A Kingdom for a Stage: The Achievement of Shakespeare's History Plays, 1972; Phyllis Rackin, Stages of History: Shakespeare's English Chronicles, 1990; and Scott McMillin, Shakespeare in Performance: 1 Henry IV, 1991.

The objects of obsessive critical attention for centuries, Shakespeare's plays have recently been studied from new historicist, feminist, psychoanalytic, and deconstructive perspectives, among others. The range may be sampled in such collections as Representing Shakespeare: New Psychoanalytic Essays, ed. Murray Schwartz and Coppelia Kahn, 1980; Alternative Shakespeares, ed. John Drakakis, 1985; Shakespeare and the Question of Theory, ed. Patricia Parker and Geoffrey Hartman, 1985; Shakespeare Reproduced, ed. Jean Howard and M. O'Connor, 1987; Political Shakespeare, ed. Jonathan Dollimore and Alan Sinfield, 1994; and in such books as Lisa Jardine, Still Harping on Daughters, 1983; Marjorie Garber, Shakespeare's Ghost Writers, 1987; Stephen Greenblatt, Shakespearean Negotiations, 1988; Margreta de Grazia, Shakespeare Verbatim, 1991; Janet Adelman, Suffocating Mothers, 1992; Valerie Traub, Desire and Anxiety, 1992; and Harry Berger Jr., Making Trifles of Terrors, 1997. Notable performance studies include Marvin Rosenberg, The Masks of Lear,

1972; David Bevington, *Action Is Eloquence*, 1984; Michael Goldman, *Acting and Action in Shakespearean Tragedy*, 1985; Peter Donaldson, *Shakespearean Films, Shakespearean Directors*, 1990; and *Shakespeare, the Movie*, ed. Lynda Boose and Richard Burt, 1997.

Hyder Rollins's Variorum edition of the sonnets, 2 vols., 1944, summarizes many commentaries and problems; Stephen Booth's edition, 1977, presents a facsimile of the first edition and a modernized text on facing pages, with elaborate commentary; see, likewise, the Arden Edition (K. Duncan-Jones, ed., 1997) and Helen Vendler, *The Art of Shakespeare's Sonnets*, 1997. Noteworthy criticism of the sonnets and poems includes Stephen Booth, *An Essay on Shakespeare's Sonnets*, 1969; Joel Fineman, *Shakespeare's Perjured Eye: The Invention of Poetic Subjectivity in the Sonnets*, 1986; Heather Dubrow, *Captive Victors: Shakespeare's Narrative Poems and Sonnets*, 1987; Bruce Smith, *Homosexual Desire in Shakespeare's England*, 1991; and Margreta de Grazia, "The Scandal of Shakespeare's Sonnets," in *Shakespeare Survey* 46 (1994): 35–49.

The life and works are treated by E. K. Chambers, *William Shakespeare: A Study of Facts and Problems*, 2 vols., 1930. S. Schoenbaum's important biographical research is recorded in *William Shakespeare: A Documentary Life*, 1975, and *A Compact Documentary Life*, 1977. Some useful aids to scholarship are Geoffrey Bullough, *Narrative and Dramatic Sources of Shakespeare*, 8 vols., 1957–75, and *A New Companion to Shakespeare Studies*, ed. Kenneth Muir and S. Schoenbaum, 1971, rpt. 1976.

Sir Philip Sidney

Oxford editions are standard for everything except the correspondence: the poetry is edited by William A. Ringler Jr., 1962; the *Old Arcadia* by Jean Robertson, 1973; the *New Arcadia* by Victor Skretkowicz, 1987; and the *Miscellaneous Prose* (including the *Defense*) by Katherine Duncan-Jones and Jan Van Dorsten, 1973. Sidney's letters are found in *The Prose Works of Sir Philip Sidney*, 4 vols., ed. Albert Feuillerat, 1912, rpt. 1962, 3: 75–184. There are valuable editions of the *Defense* by Geoffrey Shepherd, 1965, and Van Dorsten, 1966. Maurice Evans edited *The Countess of Pembroke's Arcadia* (the 1593 composite version) in 1977. Useful volumes of selected works are those by David Kalstone, 1970; Duncan-Jones for the Oxford English Authors series, 1989; Catherine Bates (poetry), 1994; and Elizabeth P. Watson, 1997. The earliest biography was by Sidney's friend Fulke Greville, 1652; it is included in Greville's *Prose Works*, ed. John Gouws, 1986. The standard modern biography is Duncan-Jones, *Sir Philip Sidney: Courtier Poet*, 1991. Modern studies of the life and works are John Buxton, *Sir Philip Sidney and the English Renaissance*, 1954, rpt. 1964; James M. Osborn, *Young Philip Sidney*, 1972; and A. C. Hamilton, *Sir Philip Sidney: A Study of His Life and Works*, 1977. Some important critical studies are Walter R. Davis and

Richard Lanham, *Sidney's Arcadia*, 1965; David Kalstone, *Sidney's Poetry: Contexts and Interpretations*, 1965; Neil L. Rudenstine, *Sidney's Poetic Development*, 1967; Andrew Weiner, *Sir Philip Sidney and the Poetics of Protestantism*, 1978; Richard C. McCoy, *Sir Philip Sidney: Rebellion in Arcadia*, 1979; Stephen Greenblatt, "Murdering Peasants: Status, Genre, and the Representation of Rebellion," in *Representations* 1 (1983): 1–29; Joan Rees, *Sir Philip Sidney and "Arcadia,"* 1991; Roland Greene in *Post-Petrarchism*, 1991; and Blair Worden, *The Sound of Virtue: Philip Sidney's "Arcadia" and Elizabethan Politics*, 1996. Dennis Kay edited *Sir Philip Sidney: An Anthology of Modern Criticism*, 1987. *Sidney in Retrospect: Selections from "English Literary Renaissance,"* ed. Arthur F. Kinney, 1988, reprints articles and reviews of recent scholarship from a leading Renaissance journal. Recent studies of *Arcadia* are surveyed in *ELR* 26 (1996): 173–81.

Edmund Spenser

Edwin A. Greenlaw et al. edited a ten-volume Variorum edition, *The Works of Edmund Spenser*, 1932–49. Important editions of *The Faerie Queene* are by A. C. Hamilton, 1977, and Thomas P. Roche Jr., 1978; William A. Oram et al. edited *The Yale Edition of the Shorter Poems of Edmund Spenser*, 1989. The chief biography is *The Life of Edmund Spenser* by Alexander Judson, 1945. Two recent overviews of the life and works are Gary Waller, *Edmund Spenser, A Literary Life*, 1994, and Oram, *Edmund Spenser*, 1997. Important critical studies include C. S. Lewis, *The Allegory of Love*, 1936; Paul J. Alpers, *The Poetry of "The Faerie Queene,"* 1967; Isabel MacCaffrey, *Spenser's Allegory: The Anatomy of Imagination*, 1975; James Nohrnberg, *The Analogy of "The Faerie Queene,"* 1976; Michael O'Connell, *Mirror and Veil: The Historical Dimension of Spenser's "Faerie Queene,"* 1977; Jonathan Goldberg, *Endlesse Worke: Spenser and the Structure of Discourse*, 1981; John Guillory, *Poetic Authority: Spenser, Milton, and Literary History*, 1983; Harry Berger Jr., *Revisionary Play: Studies in the Spenserian Dynamics*, 1988; John N. King, *Spenser's Poetry and the Reformation Tradition*, 1990; Theresa M. Krier, *Gazing on Secret Sights: Spenser, Classical Imitation, and the Decorums of Vision*, 1990; Richard Rambuss, *Spenser's Secret Career*, 1993; Gordon Teskey, *Allegory, Materialism, Violence*, 1994; Lauren Silberman, *Transforming Desire: Erotic Knowledge in Books III and IV of "The Faerie Queene,"* 1995; and Willy Maley, *Salvaging Spenser: Colonialism, Culture, and Identity*, 1997. Hamilton edited *Essential Articles for the Study of Edmund Spenser*, 1972. A wide range of criticism is reprinted in Hugh Maclean and Anne Lake Prescott's Norton Critical Edition, *Edmund Spenser's Poetry*, rev. 1993. Mihoko Suzuki edited a collection of recent *Critical Essays on Edmund Spenser*, 1996; a parallel collection, issued the same year, is *Edmund Spenser*, ed. Andrew Hadfield. A collection that students may find intriguing is

Approaches to Teaching Spenser's "Faerie Queene," ed. David L. Miller and Alexander Dunlop, 1994. The Spenser Encyclopedia, ed. Hamilton et al., 1990, is an invaluable aid. The best guides to recent work are the bibliographies in the encyclopedia and the selected bibliography, with annotations, in Oram's Edmund Spenser.

Henry Howard, Earl of Surrey

The complete edition is by F. M. Padelford, 1928, rpt. 1966; Emrys Jones's excellent selected edition, 1964, is widely used. Tottel's Miscellany is edited by Hyder E. Rollins, 2 vols., rev. 1965. E. R. Casady's biography, 1938, rpt. 1966, and W. R. Sessions's study of the life and works, 1986, bear the same title, Henry Howard, Earl of Surrey. Noteworthy critical studies are Walter R. Davis, "Contexts in Surrey's Poetry," ELR 4 (1974): 40–55; the chapters on Surrey in Alastair Fowler, Conceitful Thought: The Interpretation of English Renaissance Poems, 1975, and Jonathan Crewe, Trials of Authorship: Anterior Forms and Poetic Reconstruction from Wyatt to Shakespeare, 1990, and those on Wyatt and Surrey in Maurice Evans, English Poetry in the Sixteenth Century, rev. 1967; Susanne Woods, Natural Emphasis: English Versification from Chaucer to Dryden, 1984; A. C. Spearing, Medieval to Renaissance in English Poetry, 1985; and Elizabeth Heale, Wyatt, Surrey and Early Tudor Poetry, 1998. Scholarship is surveyed in Clyde W. Jentoft, Sir

Thomas Wyatt and Henry Howard, Earl of Surrey: A Reference Guide, 1980. Reviews of recent studies are in ELR 19 (1989): 389–401 and 28 (1998): 307.

Sir Thomas Wyatt

The most useful edition is by Kenneth Muir and Patricia Thomson, Collected Poems, 1969; others are by Richard C. Harrier, 1975; Joost Daalder, 1975; and R. A. Rebholz, 1978. Tottel's Miscellany is edited by Hyder E. Rollins, 2 vols., rev. 1965. Letters and life records are included in Muir's biography, 1963; Thomson treats both life and works in Sir Thomas Wyatt and His Background, 1964; a more recent, slighter treatment is Stephen M. Foley, Sir Thomas Wyatt, 1990. Critical studies include E. M. W. Tillyard, The Poetry of Sir Thomas Wyatt, 1929, rpt. 1949; Raymond Southall, The Courtly Maker, 1964; Elizabeth W. Pomeroy, The Elizabethan Miscellanies: Their Development and Conventions, 1973; Stephen Greenblatt, Renaissance Self-Fashioning, 1980; Thomas M. Greene, The Light in Troy: Imitation and Discovery in Renaissance Poetry, 1982; and Barbara L. Estrin, Laura: Uncovering Gender and Genre in Wyatt, Donne, and Marvell, 1994. Since the sixteenth century, Wyatt and Surrey have often been discussed in tandem: for some modern instances, see Surrey. Thomson edited Wyatt: The Critical Heritage, 1974. Reviews of recent studies are in ELR 19 (1989): 226–46 and 28 (1998): 307–09.

THE EARLY SEVENTEENTH CENTURY

The journal English Literary Renaissance (ELR) publishes recent studies of individual sixteenth- and seventeenth-century authors and of some literary topics, on an ongoing basis; they are updated periodically. In its winter issue, annually, the journal Studies in English Literature publishes "Recent Studies in the English Renaissance," evaluating the past year's publications. These journals regularly carry important new articles on seventeenth-century topics, as do English Literary History, Representations, The Seventeenth Century, Seventeenth Century News, Renaissance Studies, John Donne Journal, Milton Studies, and Milton Quarterly.

Politics, Society, and Political Thought

Some general histories of the seventeenth century or some part of it are Christopher Hill, The Century of Revolution, 1961; Barry Coward, The Stuart Age: A History of England, 1603–1714, 1980; Derek Hirst, Authority and Conflict: England, 1603–58, 1986; and Austin Woolrych, Commonwealth to Protectorate, 1982. Interpretation of the causes and progress of the English revolution is a contested issue. A series of books by Christopher Hill emphasizes political, social, and ideological conflict: Puritanism and Revolution, 1958; The World Turned Upside Down: Radical Ideas During the English Revolution, 1972; and The Experience of Defeat, 1984.

The "revisionist" view sees this event not as a revolution but as an accidental consequence of politicians' incompetence: it is represented by J. S. Morrill, Seventeenth-Century Britain, 1603–1714, 1980; and Conrad Russell, The Causes of the English Civil War, 1990, and Unrevolutionary England, 1603–1642, 1990. Recent efforts to revise the revisionists include J. P. Sommerville, Politics and Ideology in England, 1603–1640, 1986; Conflict in Early Stuart England: Studies in Religion and Politics, 1603–1642, ed. Richard Cust and Ann Hughes, 1989, and Reviving the English Revolution: Reflections and Elaborations on the Work of Christopher Hill, ed. Geoff Eley and William Hunt, 1988. The complex place of religion, both as doctrine and cultural force, is explored in William Haller, The Rise of Puritanism, 1938; Keith Thomas, Religion and the Decline of Magic: Popular Beliefs in Sixteenth- and Seventeenth-Century England, 1971; Patrick Collinson, The Religion of Protestants: The Church in English Society, 1559–1625, 1982, and The Birthpangs of Protestant England, 1986; and David Underdown, Revel, Riot, and Rebellion: Popular Politics and Culture in England, 1603–1660, 1985. Suggestive essays on the interrelation of events, religion, and culture are collected in Culture and Politics in Early Stuart England, ed. Kevin Sharpe and Peter Lake, 1993.

English society in the seventeenth century was analyzed by the German sociologist Max Weber in a very influential essay, 1904–05, emphasizing the importance of the Protestant doctrine of the calling or vocation for the aspiring capitalist class; that thesis was further developed by R. H. Tawney in *Religion and the Rise of Capitalism*, 1926, but it has been much disputed, notably by H. R. Trevor-Roper. Peter Laslett's book, *The World We Have Lost*, 3rd. ed., 1984, helps in imagining what life was like in a preindustrial society. Studies of early modern society of special interest to students of literature include Lawrence Stone, *The Family, Sex and Marriage in England, 1500–1800*, 1977; Keith Wrightson, *English Society, 1580–1680*, 1982; Susan Amussen, *An Ordered Society: Gender and Class in Early Modern England*, 1988; and Alan Bray, *Homosexuality in Renaissance England*, 1982. Elizabeth Eisenstein, *The Printing Press as an Agent of Change*, 2 vols., 1979, bears directly on the production and transmission of literature. A general study of schools and education in the period is K. Charlton, *Education in Renaissance England*, 1965.

Helpful accounts of political thought in the seventeenth century are found in J. G. A. Pocock's seminal works, *The Ancient Constitution and the Feudal Law*, rev. 1987, and *The Machiavellian Moment: Florentine Political Thought and the Atlantic Republican Tradition*, 1975, as well as in Quentin Skinner, *The Foundations of Modern Political Thought*, 2 vols., 1978, and Richard Tuck, *Philosophy and Government, 1572–1651*, 1993. A useful collection of political treatises in the period has been edited by David Wootton, *Divine Right and Democracy: An Anthology of Political Writing in Stuart England*, 1986. J. H. Burns has edited essays included in *The Cambridge History of Political Thought, 1450–1700*, 1991.

Literature, Culture, and Politics

Several studies focus on the intellectual and cultural milieu of the period as it affects literature. Inherited views of the universe based on hierarchy, order, and analogy, which were still prevalent in poetic imagery, are set forth in E. M. W. Tillyard's concise though oversimplified account, *The Elizabethan World Picture*, 1943. Studies focusing on the challenge of the new science include Rupert Hall, *The Scientific Revolution, 1500–1800*, 1954; William R. Shea, *Galileo's Intellectual Revolution*, 1972; Hans Blumenberg, *The Genesis of the Copernican World*, 1987; and Barbara Shapiro, *Probability and Certainty in Seventeenth-Century England*, 1983. Some sense of the still-powerful influence of the occult—alchemy, magic, hermeticism, and the like—may be gleaned from Wayne Shumaker, *The Occult Sciences in the Renaissance*, 1972. C. A. Patrides and Raymond Waddington have edited a useful collection of essays on various facets of seventeenth-century society and culture, *The Age of Milton: Backgrounds to Seventeenth-Century Literature*, 1980. More focused studies of intellectual currents include Debora Shuger, *Habits*

of Thought in the English Renaissance: Religion, Politics, and the Dominant Culture, 1990; Victoria Kahn, *Machiavellian Rhetoric: From the Counter-Reformation to Milton*, 1994; and John Rogers, *The Matter of Revolution: Science, Poetry, and Politics in the Age of Milton*, 1996. A fine brief account of court culture in the Jacobean and Caroline eras is by Graham Parry, *The Golden Age Restor'd: The Culture of the Stuart Court, 1603–1642*, 1981.

Studies of seventeenth-century literature in relation to political and cultural forces include James Turner, *The Politics of Landscape: Rural Scenery and Society in English Poetry, 1630–1660*, 1979; Annabel Patterson, *Censorship and Interpretation: The Conditions of Writing and Reading in Early Modern England*, 1984; Graham Parry, *Seventeenth Century Poetry: The Social Context*, 1985; Leah Marcus, *The Politics of Mirth: Jonson, Herrick, Milton, Marvell*, 1986; and David Norbrook, *Poetry and Politics in the English Renaissance*, 1984. Several collections of essays treat particular topics and writers in these terms: *The Muses' Common-Weale: Poetry and Politics in the Seventeenth Century*, ed. Claude Summers and Ted-Larry Pebworth, 1988; *The Politics of Discourse: The Literature and History of Seventeenth-Century England*, ed. Kevin Sharpe and Steven Zwicker, 1987; *Patronage, Politics, and Literary Traditions in England, 1558–1658*, ed. Cedric Brown, 1993; and *Religion and Culture in Renaissance England*, ed. C. McEachern and D. Shuger, 1997.

Analyses focusing especially on the Jacobean era are Jonathan Goldberg, *James I and the Politics of Literature: Jonson, Shakespeare, Donne and Their Contemporaries*, 1983; Curtis Perry, *The Making of Jacobean Culture*, 1987; and an important collection of essays edited by Linda Levy Peck, *The Mental World of the Jacobean Court*, 1991. Kevin Sharpe has edited essays pertaining to the Caroline era, *Criticism and Compliment: The Politics of Literature in the England of Charles I*, 1987. Studies treating the literature and culture of the revolutionary era focus on Milton, Marvell, and several royalist poets and prose writers, including Michael Wilding, *Dragon's Teeth: Literature in the English Revolution*, 1987; Nigel Smith, *Literature and Revolution in England, 1640–1660*, 1994, which treats the political uses of various genres; Steven Zwicker, *Lines of Authority: Politics and English Culture, 1649–1689*, 1993; and essays edited by Thomas Healy and Jonathan Sawday, *Literature and the English Civil War*, 1990. Works that attend especially to royalist writers are Raymond Anselment, *Loyalist Resolve: Patient Fortitude in the English Civil War*, 1988; Lois Potter, *Secret Rites and Secret Writing: Royalist Literature, 1641–1660*, 1989; and *Classic and Cavalier: Essays on Jonson and the Sons of Ben*, ed. Claude J. Summers and Ted-Larry Pebworth, 1982. David Norbrook has written an impressive, wide-ranging study of writers who contributed to the emergence of republican thought and culture in England before and during the revolution, *Writing the English Republic: Poetry, Rhetoric and Politics,*

1627–1660, 1999. Joad Raymond has studied the emergence of the newspaper during the revolutionary era in *The Invention of the Newspaper: English Newsbooks 1641–1649*, 1996. Nigel Smith has analyzed the rhetoric and assumptions about language of the revolution's radicals—Quakers, Ranters, Diggers—in *Perfection Proclaimed: Language and Literature in English Radical Religion, 1640–1660*, 1989.

Genre, Style, and Poetics

Valuable perspectives on literary history, the literary institution, and aspects of style in the period are provided in several works. J. E. Spingarn has edited a collection of literary criticism, *Critical Essays of the Seventeenth Century*, reissued, 1957. An illuminating and elegant brief account of the place and uses of genre is supplied by Rosalie Colie in *The Resources of Kind: Genre-Theory in the Renaissance*, 1973. Although the category of Metaphysical poets has generally lost its usefulness, Earl Miner's three volumes provide important surveys of the literature of the era: *The Metaphysical Mode from Donne to Cowley*, 1969; *The Cavalier Mode from Jonson to Cotton*, 1971; and *The Restoration Mode from Milton to Dryden*, 1974. George Parfitt has provided a single-volume survey, *English Poetry of the Seventeenth Century*, 1985. Barbara K. Lewalski, *Protestant Poetics and the Seventeenth-Century Religious Lyric*, 1979, treats the effect of Protestant theology, sermon theory, and devotional practices on poetics and religious poetry, especially Donne, Herbert, Vaughan, and Traherne. Diane McColley has explored the relationship between the poetic language of several major poets and the music of the period in *Poetry and Music in Seventeenth-Century England*, 1997. An important collection of essays that reconsiders canonical poets of period in the light of poststructuralist theory is *Soliciting Interpretation: Literary Theory and Seventeenth-Century Poetry*, ed. Elizabeth D. Harvey and Katharine E. Maus, 1990.

The styles, varieties, and rhetoric of seventeenth-century prose are treated in several important studies: Maurice Croll, in *Style, Rhetoric, and Rhythm: Essays*, ed. J. M. Patrick et al., 1966; Stanley Fish, *Self-Consuming Artifacts: The Experience of Seventeenth-Century Literature*, 1972 (Bacon, Burton, Browne, Milton, Bunyan); Joan Webber, *The Eloquent I: Style and Self in Seventeenth-Century Prose*, 1968; and Roger Pooley, *English Prose of the Seventeenth Century, 1590–1700*, 1992. In *Paradoxia Epidemica*, 1966, Rosalie Colie studied the pervasiveness of paradox in texts of all kinds throughout the century.

Important studies of particular genres in relation to seventeenth-century culture include Rosemary Freeman, *English Emblem Books*, 1948; Paul Delany, *British Autobiography in the Seventeenth Century*, 1969; Ellen Z. Lambert, *Placing Sorrow: A Study of Pastoral Elegy*, 1976; Anthony Low, *Love's Architecture: Devotional Modes in Seventeenth-Century English Poetry*, 1978, and *The Geor-*

gic Revolution, 1985; Paul Salzman, *English Prose Fiction 1558–1700: A Critical History*, 1985; Heather DuBrow, *The Happier Eden: The Politics of Marriage in the Stuart Epithalamium*, 1990; Alastair Fowler, *The Country-House Poem*, 1994; and Amy Boesky, *Founding Fictions: Utopias in Early Modern England*, 1996. Some of the many studies of drama in the Stuart era are Brian Gibbons, *Jacobean City Comedy: A Study of Satiric Plays by Jonson, Marston, and Middleton*, 1968; Margot Heinemann, *Puritanism and Theatre: Thomas Middleton and Opposition Drama Under the Early Stuarts*, 1980; Albert Tricomi, *Anticourt Drama in England, 1603–1642*, 1989; and Richard Strier ed., et al., *The Theatrical City: Culture, Theater, and Politics in London, 1576–1649*, 1995.

Women's Roles and Writing

An important recovery effort is under way in publishing and studying hitherto unknown or little-studied works by early modern women, sometimes highlighting gender issues, sometimes attending to women's self-constructions as patrons and authors, sometimes addressing aesthetic and stylistic matters. Some anthologies of writing by women in (or including) the seventeenth century are *The Paradise of Women*, ed. Betty Travitsky, 1981; *First Feminists: British Women Writers, 1578–1799*, ed. Moira Ferguson, 1985; *Kissing the Rod: An Anthology of Seventeenth-Century Women's Verse*, ed. Germaine Greer et al., 1988; *Women Writers of the Seventeenth Century*, ed. Katharina Wilson and Frank J. Warnke, 1989; and *Her Own Life: Autobiographical Writings by Seventeenth-Century Englishwomen*, ed. Elspeth Graham et al., 1989. An annotated bibliography by Hilda Smith and Susan Cardinale, *Women and the Literature of the Seventeenth Century*, 1900, gives a brief account of all the works by or about women listed in Donald Wing's *Short-Title Catalogue of English books published between 1641 and 1700*. Elaine Hobby in *Virtue of Necessity: English Women's Writing, 1649–88*, 1988, discusses women writers and their several genres, with bibliography. Other important bibliographical resources are Mary Thomas Crane, "Women and the Early Modern Canon: Recent Editions of Works by English Women, 1500–1500," *Renaissance Quarterly* 51 (1998); and recent studies of seventeenth-century women writers by Elizabeth Hageman and Sara Jayne Steen, in *ELR* 14 (1984), 18 (1988), and 24 (1994). Anthologies of texts that illuminate the place of women and women writers in seventeenth-century society are *Half Humankind: Contexts and Texts of the Controversy about Women in England, 1540–1640*, ed. K. Henderson and B. McManus, 1985, and *Daughters, Wives, and Widows: Writings By Men About Women and Marriage in England, 1500–1640*, ed. Joan L. Klein, 1992. Antonia Fraser has written a lively social history of women throughout the century, with many vignettes of particular lives, *The Weaker Vessel*, 1984.

Some important studies and collections of essays

on women, writing, and gender in the period are Linda Woodbridge, *Women and the English Renaissance: Literature and the Nature of Womenkind, 1540–1620,* 1984; *Women in English Society, 1500–1800,* ed. Mary Prior, 1985; *Rewriting the Renaissance: The Discourses of Sexual Difference in Early Modern England,* ed. Margaret Ferguson, Maureen Quilligan, and Nancy Vickers, 1986; and Margaret J. M. Ezell, *The Patriarch's Wife: Literary Evidence and the History of the Family,* 1987. Some of the women writers included in this anthology are treated by Elaine Beilin in *Redeeming Eve: Women Writers of the English Renaissance,* 1987; by Sara Mendelson in *The Mental World of Stuart Women,* 1987; by Tina Krontiris in *Oppositional Voices: Women as Writers and Translators of Literature in the English Renaissance,* 1991; by Barbara K. Lewalski in *Writing Women in Jacobean England,* 1993; and by Louise Schleiner in *Tudor and Stuart Women Writers,* 1994. Phyllis Mack, *Visionary Women: Ecstatic Prophecy in Seventeenth-Century England,* 1992, highlights the emergence of prophecy as a genre for women, especially during the revolution; a complementary study by Bonnelyn Y. Kunze is *Margaret Fell and the Rise of Quakerism,* 1994. Useful collections of essays discussing various women writers are *Ambiguous Realities: Women in the Middle Ages and Renaissance,* ed. Carole Levin and Jeanie Watson, 1987; *The Renaissance Englishwoman in Print: Counterbalancing the Canon,* ed. Anne M. Haselkorn and Travitsky, 1990; Jean Brink, *Privileging Gender in Early Modern England,* 1993; *Women and Literature in Britain, 1500–1700,* ed. Helen Wilcox, 1996; and *Representing Women in Renaissance England,* ed. Claude J. Summers and Ted-Larry Pebworth, 1997.

Margaret Cavendish, Duchess of Newcastle
Kate Lilley has edited *Margaret Cavendish: The Description of a New World Called The Blazing World and Other Writings,* 1992; *The Blazing World* is also included in Paul Salzman's *Anthology of Seventeenth-Century Fiction,* 1991, and he discusses that work in his *English Prose Fiction,* 1985, as does Amy Boesky in *Founding Fictions: Utopias in Early Modern England,* 1996. Two of Cavendish's books have been reprinted in facsimile, *Sociable Letters,* 1969, and *Poems and Fancies,* 1972. There are selections in *Women Writers of the Seventeenth Century,* ed. Katharina Wilson and Frank J. Warnke, and in *Kissing the Rod: An Anthology of Seventeenth-Century Women's Verse* ed. Germaine Greer et al., 1988. Ann Shaver has edited plays by Cavendish in *Convent of Pleasure and Other Plays,* 1999. The best biography is by Kathleen Jones, *A Glorious Fame: The Life of Margaret Cavendish, Duchess of Newcastle, 1623–1673,* 1988. There are substantial scholarly treatments of Cavendish in Hilda Smith, *Reason's Disciples: Seventeenth-Century English Feminists,* 1982; Sara Mendelson, *The Mental World of Stuart Women,* 1987; and Mary Beth Rose, *Women in the Middle Ages and Renaissance,* 1986. Some useful articles are Catherine Gallagher, "Embracing the Absolute: The Politics of the Female Subject in Seventeenth-Century England," in *Genders* 1 (1988): 24–29, and Eve Keller, "Producing Petty Gods: Margaret Cavendish's Critique of Experimental Science," in *English Literary History* 64 (1997): 447–71.

John Donne
The two-volume edition of Donne's *Poems* edited by H. J. C. Grierson, 1912, is still important, although we now have newer Oxford editions of Donne's several genres: *The Divine Poems,* ed. Helen Gardner, 1952, rev. 1978; *The Elegies and the Songs and Sonnets,* ed. Gardner, 1965; *The Satires, Epigrams, and Verse Letters,* ed. Wesley Milgate, 1967; and *The Epithalamions, Anniversaries, and Epicedes,* ed., Milgate, 1978. George Potter and Evelyn Simpson have edited *The Sermons of John Donne,* 10 vols., 1953–62. Donne's meditations were edited by Anthony Raspa, *John Donne: Devotions upon Emergent Occasions,* 1975. There are several single-volume editions of the English poems, one by C. A. Patrides, 1985, rpt. 1994, and another by A. L. Clements, 1966, rev. 1992. A *Donne Variorum* edition is in progress, 1995–, under the general editorship of Gary Stringer; Vol. 6, *Anniversaries and Epicedes,* and Vol. 8, *Epigrams, Epithalamions, Epitaphs, etc.* have been published. The first biography of Donne was by Izaak Walton, 1640. R. C. Bald's *John Donne: A Life,* 1970, is the standard biography. John Carey, *John Donne: Life, Mind, and Art,* 1981, offers a challenging account of the psychological and social factors influencing Donne's life choices and his poetry. Arthur Marotti, *John Donne: Coterie Poet,* 1986, locates Donne in his social milieu and places his poems in relation to the various audiences they addressed.

T. S. Eliot's essay "The Varieties of Metaphysical Poets," in *Selected Essays, 1917–1932,* 1932, rpt. 1969, was influential in setting terms for analyzing Donne over several decades; Cleanth Brook's reading of "The Canonization" in his *Well Wrought Urn,* 1947, is a classic of the New Criticism. Donne is discussed in many accounts of the period—Earl Miner, *The Metaphysical Mode from Donne to Cowley,* 1969; Barbara K. Lewalski, *Protestant Poetics and the Seventeenth-Century Religious Lyric,* 1979; and Jonathan Goldberg, *James I and the Politics of Literature,* 1983—and has invited several valuable individual studies: Donald Guss, *John Donne: Petrarchist,* 1966; Murray Roston, *The Soul of Wit,* 1974; Lewalski, *Donne's Anniversaries and the Poetry of Praise,* 1973; Stevie Davies, *Reassessing John Donne,* 1986; Terry Sherwood, *Fulfilling the Circle,* 1986; Meg Lota Brown, *Donne and the Politics of Conscience,* 1995. Many significant critical essays are collected in *John Donne: Essays in Celebration,* ed. A. J. Smith, 1972; *John Donne: The Critical Heritage,* ed. Smith, 1975–1996; *John Donne and the Seventeenth-Century Metaphysical Poets,* ed. Harold Bloom, 1986; *The Eagle and the*

Dove: Reassessing John Donne, ed. Claude J. Summers and Ted-Larry Pebworth, 1986; and *Critical Essays on John Donne*, ed. Arthur Marotti, 1994.

George Herbert

The standard edition is *The Works of George Herbert*, ed. F. E. Hutchinson, rev. 1945; C. A. Patrides edited a compact edition of *The English Poems*, 1974. Izaak Walton wrote a contemporary *Life of George Herbert*, 1670; there are modern ones by Amy Charles, *A Life of George Herbert*, 1977, and by Stanley Stewart, *George Herbert*, 1986. Besides the general studies mentioned in the general bibliography for the period, several important critical books on Herbert deal with the interrelation of his religion and his art: Rosemund Tuve, *A Reading of George Herbert*, 1952; Joseph Summers, *George Herbert: His Religion and His Art*, 1954; Stanley Fish, *The Living Temple: George Herbert and Catechizing*, 1978; Diana Benet, *Secretary of Praise: The Poetic Vocation of George Herbert*, 1984; Chana Bloch, *Spelling the Word: George Herbert and the Bible*, 1985; Terry Sherwood, *Herbert's Prayerful Art*, 1989; Richard Strier, *Love Known: Theology and Experience in George Herbert's Poetry*, 1983; and Gene E. Veith, *Reformation Spirituality: The Religion of George Herbert*, 1985. Helen Vendler, in *The Poetry of George Herbert*, 1975, focuses on Herbert's exquisite art. Michael Schoenfeldt, in *Prayer and Power: George Herbert and Renaissance Courtship*, 1991, explores the interdependence of social and religious discourse, to advance a cultural poetics of Herbert's lyrics. There are several essay collections all or partly on Herbert: *"Too Rich to Clothe the Sunne": Essays on George Herbert*, ed. Claude Summers and Ted-Larry Pebworth, 1980; *"Bright Shoots of Everlastingness": The Seventeenth-Century Religious Lyric*, ed. Summers and Pebworth, 1987; and *George Herbert: The Critical Heritage*, ed. C. A. Patrides, 1983. Recent studies are surveyed in *ELR* 18 (1988): 460–75.

Robert Herrick

The standard edition is by L. C. Martin, *Robert Herrick: Poems*, 1965. J. Max Patrick also edited the *Complete Poetry of Robert Herrick* in 1963. There are biographical accounts by Roger Rollin, *Robert Herrick*, 1966, and George W. Scott, *Robert Herrick*, 1974. Important critical studies include Robert Deming, *Ceremony and Art: Robert Herrick's Poetry*, 1974; Leigh DeNeef, *"This Poetic Liturgie:" Robert Herrick's Ceremonial Mode*, 1974; Ann Baynes Coiro, *Robert Herrick's Hesperides and the Epigram Book Tradition*, 1988; as well as essays by Leah Marcus in *The Politics of Mirth*, 1986, and by Aschah Guibbory in *The Muses' Common-Weale: Poetry and Politics in the Seventeenth Century*, ed. Claude Summers and Ted-Larry Pebworth, 1988. A collection of essays edited by Roger Rollin and J. Max Patrick, *Trust to Good Verses: Herrick Tercentenary Essays*, appeared in 1978. Recent studies are surveyed in *ELR* 3 (1973): 462–71.

Ben Jonson

A monumental edition of Jonson's *Works* was edited by C. H. Herford and Percy and Evelyn Simpson, 11 vols., 1925–52. The Yale edition and the paperback series known as the New Mermaids provide good modernized and annotated versions of the major plays (one play to a volume). Robert M. Adams has edited *Ben Jonson's Plays and Masques*, 1979, with critical essays. Stephen Orgel has edited *The Complete Masques*, 1969. Handy editions of the verse are by W. B. Hunter, *The Complete Poetry of Ben Jonson*, 1963, and George Parfitt, *Ben Jonson: The Complete Poems*, 1975. There is an edition of *Timber* by Ralph Walker, 1953. David Riggs has written a fine biography, *Ben Jonson: A Life*, 1989.

Important critical studies include Alexander Leggatt, *Ben Jonson: His Vision and His Art*, 1981; Richard Helgerson, *Self-Crowned Laureates: Spenser, Jonson, Milton and the Literary System*, 1983; Katherine E. Maus, *Ben Jonson and the Roman Frame of Mind*, 1984; Robert N. Watson, *Ben Jonson's Parodic Strategy: Literary Imperialism in the Comedies*, 1987; George Rowe, *Distinguishing Jonson*, 1988; Jonathan Haynes, *The Social Relations of Jonson's Theater*, 1992; and Richard Burt, *Licensed by Authority: Ben Jonson and the Discourses of Censorship*, 1993. Works that deal especially with Jonson's poetry are Sara Van den Berg, *The Action of Ben Jonson's Poetry*, 1987, and Robert C. Evans, *Ben Jonson and the Poetics of Patronage*, 1989. Don E. Wayne, *Penshurst: The Semiotics of Place and the Poetics of History*, 1984, locates Jonson's poem in its social and architectural context; Raymond Williams, *The Country and the City*, 1973, places it within a broad social history of movements affecting agriculture and the land.

Stuart court masques, and Jonson's major contribution to them, are analyzed in two essay collections: *The Court Masque*, ed. David Lindley, 1984, and *The Politics of the Stuart Court Masque*, ed. David Bevington and Peter Holbrook, 1998, and by Orgel in *The Illusion of Power: Political Theater in the English Renaissance*, 1975. The fascinating reproduction of drawings and designs for the masques, published by Orgel and Roy Strong in *Inigo Jones: The Theatre of the Stuart Court*, 2 vols., 1973, gives some sense of what masques looked like in presentation. Collections of critical essays on Jonson include *Classic and Cavalier: Essays on Jonson and the Sons of Ben*, ed. Claude J. Summers and Ted-Larry Pebworth, 1982; *Ben Jonson: A Collection of Critical Essays*, ed. Jonas A. Barish, 1963; and *New Perspectives on Ben Jonson*, ed. James Hirsh, 1997.

Aemilia Lanyer

Susanne Woods has edited *The Poems of Aemelia Lanyer: Salve Deus Rex Judaeorum*, 1993, and has also analyzed her life and works in *Lanyer: A Renaissance Woman Poet*, 1999. The important collection of essays edited by Marshall Grossman, *Aemilia*

Lanyer: Gender, Genre, and the Canon, 1998, includes a valuable annotated bibliography. There are chapters on Lanyer in Elaine Beilin, *Redeeming Eve: Women Writers of the English Renaissance*, 1987; Tina Krontiris, *Oppositional Voices: Women as Writers and Translators of Literature in the English Renaissance*, 1991; Barbara K. Lewalski, *Writing Women in Jacobean England*, 1993; and Louise Schleiner, *Tudor and Stuart Women Writers*, 1994. Other notable essays include Mary Ellen Lamb, "Patronage and Class in Aemilia Lanyer's *Salve Deus Rex Judaeorum*," in *Women, Writing, and the Reproduction of Culture*, ed. Jane Donawerth et al., 1999, and Wendy Wall, "The Body of Christ, Aemilia Lanyer's Passion," in her volume, *The Imprint of Gender: Authorship and Publication in the English Renaissance*, 1993.

Richard Lovelace

C. H. Wilkinson edited the *Poems*, 1930, rpt. 1968. Manfred Weidhorn published a biography, *Richard Lovelace*, 1970; and both the life and works are treated in Cyril Hartmann, *The Cavalier Spirit and Its Influence on the Life and Work of Richard Lovelace (1618–1658)*, 1925. Commentary can be found in Earl Miner, *The Cavalier Mode from Jonson to Cotton, 1971*; in Raymond Anselment, " 'Stone Walls' and 'Iron Bars': Richard Lovelace and Seventeenth-Century Prison Literature," in *Renaissance and Reformation* 17 (1993); and in two essay collections edited by Claude J. Summers and Ted-Larry Pebworth: *Classic and Cavalier: Essays on Jonson and the Sons of Ben*, 1982, and *The Wit of Seventeenth-Century Poetry*, 1995. Recent studies are reviewed in *ELR* 7 (1977): 248–52.

Andrew Marvell

The standard edition is *The Poems and Letters of Andrew Marvell*, ed. H. M. Margoliouth, 1927; rev. Pierre Legouis and E. E. Duncan-Jones, 2 vols., 1971. His Restoration prose satires, *The Rehearsal Transpros'd* (2 parts), are edited by D. I. B. Smith, 1971. There are handy editions of Marvell's *Complete Poetry* by George de F. Lord, 1968, rpt. 1984, and Elizabeth Story Donno, 1972. Biographical studies include John Dixon Hunt, *Andrew Marvell: His Life and Writings*, 1978; Patsy Griffin, *The Modest Ambition of Andrew Marvell: A Study of Marvell and His Relation to Lovelace, Fairfax, Cromwell, and Milton*, 1995; and Thomas Wheeler, *Andrew Marvell Revisited*, 1996. Influential studies of his political attitudes and writing in connection with his poetry include John M. Wallace, *Destiny His Choice: The Loyalism of Andrew Marvell*, 1968; Annabel Patterson, *Marvell and the Civic Crown*, 1978; Warren Chernaik, *The Poet's Time: Politics and Religion in the Work of Marvell*, 1983; *The Political Identity of Andrew Marvell*, ed. Conal Condren and A. D. Cousins, 1990; and the important essay by David Norbrook, "Horatian Ode," in *Literature and the English Civil War*, ed. Thomas Healy and Jonathan Sawday, 1990. Important analyses of Marvell's poetic art include Rosalie Colie's elegant and learned study, '*My Ecchoing Song*':

Andrew Marvell's Poetry of Criticism, 1970; Donald Friedman, *Marvell's Pastoral Art*, 1970; Patrick Cullen, *Spenser, Marvell, and Renaissance Pastoral*, 1970; Robert Wilcher, *Andrew Marvell*, 1985; and Christine Rees, *The Judgment of Marvell*, 1989. Donno has edited *Andrew Marvell: The Critical Heritage*, 1978. Important essays dealing with Marvell are included in various tercentenary tributes: *Tercentenary Essays in Honor of Andrew Marvell*, ed. Kenneth Friedenreich, 1977; *Approaches to Marvell*, ed. C. A. Patrides, 1978; and *Andrew Marvell: Essays on the Tercentenary of His Death*, ed. R. L. Brett, 1979. Others are in *Politics of Discourse: The Literature and History of Seventeenth-Century England*, ed. Kevin Sharpe and Steven Zwicker, 1987; in Leah Marcus, *Politics of Mirth: Jonson, Herrick, Milton, Marvell*, 1986; and in Zwicker, *Lines of Authority: Politics and English Culture, 1649–1689*, 1993.

John Milton

The Columbia Milton, *The Works of John Milton*, 18 vols., ed. F. A. Patterson, et al., 1931–40, with its invaluable two-volume index, is the only complete edition of all the poetry and prose, English and Latin. The Yale edition, *Complete Prose Works of John Milton*, 8 vols., ed. Don M. Wolfe et al., 1953–82, supplies excellent historical introductions to all the prose. The single-volume edition, *Complete Poems and Major Prose*, by Merritt Y. Hughes, 1957, is still useful; *The Riverside Milton*, ed. Roy Flannagan, 1998, contains all the poetry and much of the English prose, with updated introductions and bibliography. John Leonard's paperback, *John Milton: The Complete Poems*, 1998, supplies a good text and useful notes; the Longman edition is in two volumes: John Carey, *John Milton: Complete Shorter Poems*, 1972, rev. 1997, and *Paradise Lost*, ed. Alastair Fowler, 1966, rev. 1998. For the prose, C. A. Patrides's paperback edition, *John Milton: Selected Prose*, 1985, offers a judicious selection. Three volumes of the *Variorum Commentary on the Poems of John Milton*, ed. Douglas Bush, et al., 1970–75, have been published, but the volume on *Paradise Lost* is still in process.

The standard biography is William Riley Parker, *Milton: A Biography*, 2 vols., 1968. David Masson's, *The Life of John Milton*, 6 vols. plus index, 1859–91, is still a treasure trove of information about the poet and the period. Christopher Hill's *Milton and the English Revolution*, 1977, has spearheaded an ongoing effort to locate Milton more precisely among his revolutionary contemporaries. Cedric C. Brown's brief biography, *John Milton: A Literary Life*, 1995, offers a useful introduction to the man and his works. Milton is psychoanalyzed by William Kerrigan in *The Sacred Complex: On the Psychogenesis of Paradise Lost*, 1983. The five volumes of J. Milton French's *The Life Records of John Milton*, 1949–58, rpt. 1966, gather much primary material for the life. Gordon Campbell, *A Milton Chronology*, 1997, reexamines records, and adds to these materials. Aids to the study of Milton include the nine-volume *Milton Encyclopedia*, ed. William Hunter et al., 1978–83, with bibliographies and updates in Vol. 9, and *The Cambridge Companion to Milton*, ed. Dennis Danielson, 1989, rev. 1999.

Valuable critical studies that address all or some considerable part of Milton's career and writing include the following: Kerrigan, *The Prophetic Milton*, 1974; Louis L. Martz, *Milton: Poet of Exile*, 1980; Christopher Kendrick, *Milton: A Study in Ideology and Form*, 1986; Marshall Grossman, *"Authors to Themselves": Milton and the Revelation of History*, 1987; Catherine Belsey, *John Milton: Language, Gender, Power*, 1988; Joan Bennett, *Reviving Liberty: Radical Christian Humanism in Milton's Great Poems*, 1989; Loewenstein, *Milton and the Drama of History*, 1990; John T. Shawcross, *John Milton: The Self and the World*, 1993; Sharon Achinstein, *Milton and the Revolutionary Reader*, 1994; Laura Lunger Knoppers, *Historicizing Milton: Spectacle, Power, and Poetry in Restoration England*, 1994; Lana Cable, *Carnal Rhetoric: Milton's Iconoclasm and the Poetics of Desire*, 1995; John Rumrich, *Milton Unbound: Controversy and Reinterpretation*, 1996; and David Norbrook, *Writing the English Republic: Poetry, Rhetoric, and Politics, 1627–1660*, 1999.

Various approaches to Milton over the centuries can be sampled in two volumes edited by Shawcross, *Milton: The Critical Heritage, 1628–1731*, 1970, and *Milton, 1732–1801: The Critical Heritage*, 1972; in *The Romantics on Milton*, ed. Joseph Wittreich, 1970; and in *Milton: A Collection of Critical Essays*, ed. Louis L. Martz, 1966. Useful essay collections include Mary Nyquist and Margaret Ferguson, *Re-Membering Milton: Essays on the Texts and Traditions*, 1988; *Milton in Italy*, ed. Mario Di Cesare, 1991; *John Milton*, ed. Annabel Patterson, 1992; *Literary Milton: Text, Pretext, Context*, ed. Diana Benet and Michael Lieb, 1994; *Of Poetry and Politics: New Essays on Milton and His World*, ed. Paul G. Stanwood, 1995; *Milton and Republicanism*, ed. David Armitage, Armand Himy, and Quentin Skinner, 1995; *Arenas of Conflict: Milton and the Unfettered Mind*, ed. Kristin McColgan and Charles Durham, 1997; and Stephen B. Dobranski and John P. Rumrich, *Milton and Heresy*, 1998. Milton's views of women and various feminist issues are addressed in several of these collections, and centrally in Diane McColley, *Milton's Eve*, 1983; James Grantham Turner, *One Flesh: Paradisal Marriage and Sexual Relations in the Age of Milton*, 1987; Joseph Wittreich, *Feminist Milton*, 1987; and *Milton and the Idea of Woman*, ed. Julia M. Walker, 1988.

Stella Revard has written an excellent account of Milton's shorter poems, including the Latin poems, *Milton and the Tangles of Neaera's Hair: The Making of the 1645 Poems*, 1997. Rosamond Tuve, *Images and Themes in Five Poems by Milton*, 1957, can still illuminate Milton's most important shorter poems. Brown treats Milton's *Comus* and "Lycidas" in their social and political contexts in *John Milton's Aristocratic Entertainments*, 1985. Patrides has

edited a useful collection of essays, *Milton's Lycidas: The Tradition and the Poem*, rev. 1983; and that poem is at the center of Joseph A Wittreich, *Visionary Poetics: Milton's Tradition and His Legacy*, 1980. Milton's prose is discussed in several important books and essays: Arthur Barker, *Milton and the Puritan Dilemma, 1641–1660*, 1942; Thomas A. Kranides, *The Fierce Equation: A Study of Milton's Decorum*, 1964; Joan Webber, *The Eloquent I: Style and Self in Seventeenth-Century Prose*, 1968; Stanley Fish, *Self-Consuming Artifacts*, 1972; Keith W. Staveley, *The Politics of Milton's Prose Style*, 1975; *Achievements of the Left Hand*, ed. Michael Lieb and Shawcross, 1974; Thomas N. Corns, *The Development of Milton's Prose Style*, 1982; and *Politics, Poetics, and Hermeneutics in Milton's Prose*, ed. David Loewenstein and James G. Turner, 1990.

Modern criticism of *Paradise Lost* still engages with issues of interpretation and generic tradition raised in C. S. Lewis, *A Preface to Paradise Lost*, 1942; C. M. Bowra, *From Virgil to Milton*, 1945; and William Empson's provocative attack on the figure of God in the poem, *Milton's God*, rev. 1965. A classic study of Milton's theology in reference to the epic is Maurice Kelley, *This Great Argument: A Study of Milton's De Doctrina Christiana as a Gloss upon Paradise Lost*, 1941; Dennis R. Danielson, *Milton's Good God: A Study in Literary Theodicy*, 1982, revisits that issue. Some important earlier critical books include Joseph Summers, *The Muse's Method: An Introduction to Paradise Lost*, 1962; Christopher Ricks, *Milton's Grand Style*, 1963; Northrop Frye, *The Return to Eden*, 1966; and Fish's very influential reader response criticism, *Surprised by Sin: The Reader in Paradise Lost*, 1967. Collections of critical essays include *Approaches to Paradise Lost*, ed. Patrides, 1968, and *New Essays on Paradise Lost*, ed. Thomas Kranidas, 1969. Concerns in some recent criticism are indicated by the titles: J. M. Evans, *Paradise Lost and the Genesis Tradition*, 1968; Lieb, *The Dialectics of Creation: Patterns of Birth and Regeneration in Paradise Lost*, 1970; John R. Knott, *Milton's Pastoral Vision*, 1971; John Steadman, *Epic and Tragic Structure in Paradise Lost*, 1976; Joan Webber, *Milton and His Epic Tradition*, 1979; Murray Roston, *Milton and the Baroque*, 1980; Maureen Quilligan, *Milton's Spenser: The Politics of Reading*, 1983; Stevie Davies, *Images of Kingship in Paradise Lost*, 1983; Barbara K. Lewalski, *Paradise Lost and the Rhetoric of Literary Forms*, 1985; David Quint, *Epic and Empire: Politics and Generic Form from Virgil to Milton*, 1993; Jason Rosenblatt, *Torah and Law in Paradise Lost*, 1994; and J. Martin Evans, *Milton's Imperial Epic: Paradise Lost and the Discourse of Colonialism*, 1996. Placing Milton's epic in relation to relevant visual traditions is the burden of a beautifully illustrated book by Roland M. Frye, *Milton's Imagery and the Visual Arts: Iconographic Traditions in the Epic Poems*, 1978; and of a broader study by Diane McColley, *A Gust for Paradise: Milton's Eden and the Visual Arts*, 1993.

Milton's brief epic, *Paradise Regained*, is the subject of Lewalski, *Milton's Brief Epic: The Genre, Meaning, and Art of Paradise Regained*, 1966; the poem is treated at some length in Loewenstein, *Milton and the Drama of History*; Knoppers, *Historicizing Milton*; Quint, *Epic and Empire*; Mary Ann Radzinowicz, *Milton's Epics and the Book of Psalms*, 1989; *Calm of Mind*, ed. Joseph Wittreich, 1971; and *The Prison and the Pinnacle*, ed. Balachandra Rajan, 1972, which also contain essays on *Samson Agonistes*. Some important works dealing with Milton's tragedy, *Samson Agonistes*, include William R. Parker, *Milton's Debt to Greek Tragedy in Samson Agonistes*, 1937; Anthony Low, *The Blaze of Noon: A Reading of Samson Agonistes*, 1974; and with reference to competing traditions of interpreting the Samson story, in Wittriech, *Interpreting Samson Agonistes*, 1986. Radzinowicz, *Toward Samson Agonistes: The Growth of Milton's Mind*, 1978, treats themes and concerns in all his writing as leading toward his great tragedy. In 1987 Patrides provided the very useful *Annotated Critical Bibliography of John Milton*.

Katherine Philips

Patrick Thomas has edited *The Collected Works of Katherine Philips: The Matchless Orinda*, 1993. Her translations of Corneille and other French works were edited by Ruth Little, 1991. There are two biographies: Philip W. Souer, *The Matchless Orinda*, 1931, and Patrick Thomas, *Katherine Philips*, 1988. Useful critical studies include Harriette Andreadis, "The Sapphic-Platonics of Katherine Philips, 1632–1664," in *Signs* 15 (1989): 34–60; Elizabeth Hageman, "Katherine Philips: The Matchless Orinda," in *Women Writers of the Renaissance and Reformation*, ed. Katharina M. Wilson, 1987; and Arlene Stiebel, "Subversive Sexuality: Masking the Erotic in Poems by Katherine Philips and Aphra Behn," in *Renaissance Discourses of Desire*, ed. Claude J. Summers and Ted-Larry Pebworth, 1993.

Lady Mary Wroth

Josephine Roberts edited *Poems*, 1983, and also *The First Part of The Countess of Montgomery's Urania*, 1995. Part II of the *Urania* is being published from the manuscript in the Newberry Library. There is a modernized edition of *Poems* edited by R. E. Pritchard, 1996. Wroth's pastoral drama, *Love's Victory*, was edited by Michael Brennan, 1988. There are biographical accounts in Roberts' introductions, and in Kim Walker, *Women Writers of the English Renaissance*, 1996. Critical studies include May Nelson Paulissen, *The Love Sonnets of Lady Mary Wroth: A Critical Introduction*, 1982; Gary Waller, *The Sidney Family Romance: Mary Wroth, William Herbert, and the Early Modern Construction of Gender*, 1993; and Naomi Miller, *Changing the Subject: Mary Wroth and Figurations of Gender in Early Modern England*, 1996. Miller and Waller have also edited a collection of essays, *Reading Mary Wroth: Representing Alternatives in Early Modern England*, 1991. Wroth's works are also treated by Maureen Quilligan in *Unfolded Tales: Essays on Renaissance Romance*, ed. George Logan and Gordon Teskey, 1989; by several hands in *The Renaissance Englishwoman in Print: Counterbalancing the Canon*, ed. Anne M. Haselkorn and Betty Travitsky, 1990; and in Barbara K. Lewalski, *Writing Women in Jacobean England*, 1993. Recent studies are surveyed in *ELR* 18 (1988) and 24 (1994).

THE RESTORATION AND THE EIGHTEENTH CENTURY

In recent decades, historians have placed less emphasis on stories about the ruling classes and their political conflicts and more on the economic and social forces that shape the lives of ordinary people. A good example of this approach is *The Peoples of the British Isles: A New History*, 3 vols., 1992; volume 2, by T. W. Heyck, covers the period from 1688 to 1870. A fuller account is provided by J. R. Jones, *Country and Court; England, 1658–1714*, 1978; W. A. Speck, *Stability and Strife: England, 1714–1760*, 1977; and Ian Christie, *Wars and Revolutions: Britain, 1760–1815*, 1982. Linda Colley, *Britons*, 1992, studies the forging of a new national identity. J. H. Plumb, *England in the Eighteenth Century*, 1950, describes the structure of society, and Roy Porter, *English Society in the Eighteenth Century*, rev. 1990, is a mine of information. John Brewer, *The Pleasures of the Imagination*, 1997, is a wide-ranging history of popular culture. The life and manners of the age are surveyed in *Johnson's England*, 2 vols., ed. A. S. Turberville, 1933; Dorothy Marshall, *English People in the Eighteenth Century*, 1956; and R. B. Schwartz, *Daily Life in Johnson's England*, 1983. *The Birth of a Consumer Society*, 1982, by Neil McKendrick, Brewer, and J. H. Plumb, traces the rise of modern commercialization in the eighteenth century. Useful guides to the historical and cultural contexts of literature include A. R. Humphreys, *The Augustan World*, 1954; Donald Greene, *The Age of Exuberance*, 1970; *The Eighteenth Century*, ed. Pat Rogers, 1978; and James Sambrook, *The Eighteenth Century, 1700–1789*, 2nd ed., 1993.

On the intellectual background of the period, Sir Leslie Stephen, *History of English Thought in the Eighteenth Century*, 2 vols., 1876, remains valuable; so do A. O. Lovejoy, *The Great Chain of Being*, 1942, and *Essays in the History of Ideas*, 1948. Basil Willey, *The Eighteenth Century Background*, 1940, studies ideas about nature, and Keith Thomas, *Man and the Natural World*, 1983, shows the development of a modern sensibility between 1500 and 1800. Gordon Rupp, *Religion in England, 1688–1791*, 1986, is dependable. Volumes 4 to 6 of F. C.

Coplestone, *History of Philosophy*, 1960, deal with the period from Descartes to Kant; Peter Gay, *The Enlightenment: An Interpretation*, 2 vols., 1969, forcefully defends the philosophers of the Age of Reason. Paul Hazard, *The European Mind, 1680–1715*, 1953, and *European Thought in the Eighteenth Century*, 1954, trans. from French by J. L. May, are readable surveys of intellectual movements on the Continent as well as in England. J. W. Johnson, *The Formation of English Neo-Classical Thought*, 1967, and J. M. Levine, *The Battle of the Books: History and Literature in the Augustan Age*, 1991, study the ways that writers came to terms with the past. Burton Feldman and R. D. Richardson, *The Rise of Modern Mythology 1680–1860*, 1972, and Gerald Newman, *The Rise of English Nationalism*, 1987, deal with important new directions of thought. Steven Shapin, *The Scientific Revolution*, 1996, is a brief clear survey. Valuable studies of the influence of scientific ideas include R. F. Jones, *Ancients and Moderns*, 1936; Marjorie Nicolson, *Newton Demands the Muse*, 1946, and *Science and the Imagination*, 1956; and W. P. Jones, *The Rhetoric of Science*, 1966. Myra Reynolds, *The Learned Lady in England, 1650–1760*, 1920, still useful, should be supplemented by Sylvia Myers, *The Bluestocking Circle*, 1990. Sensibility, a set of new ideas and feelings associated especially with women, is the subject of several good books, including Jean Hagstrum, *Sex and Sensibility*, 1970; Janet Todd, *Sensibility: An Introduction*, 1986; John Mullan, *Sentiment and Sociability*, 1988; and G. J. Barker-Benfield, *The Culture of Sensibility*, 1992. Changes in the literary marketplace are illuminated by Pat Rogers, *Grub Street*, 1972; Paula McDowell, *The Women of Grub Street*, 1998; Mark Rose, *Authors and Owners: The Invention of Copyright*, 1993; and Dustin Griffin, *Literary Patronage in England, 1650–1800*, 1996. Martin Price, *To the Palace of Wisdom: Studies in Order and Energy from Dryden to Blake*, 1964; Paul Fussell, *The Rhetorical World of Augustan Humanism*, 1965; W. J. Bate, *The Burden of the Past and the English Poet*, 1970; John Sitter, *Literary Loneliness in Mid-Eighteenth-Century England*, 1982; Howard Weinbrot, *Britannia's Issue: The Rise of British Literature from Dryden to Ossian*, 1993; and Stuart Sherman, *Telling Time: Clocks, Diaries, and English Diurnal Form, 1660–1785*, 1996, are all thoughtful and stimulating studies that relate ideas to literary art.

Good surveys of the literature of the age include George Sherburn, "The Restoration and Eighteenth Century," in *A Literary History of England*, ed. A. C. Baugh, rev. 1967, and *Dryden to Johnson*, ed. Roger Lonsdale, rev. 1987, vol. 4 of the Sphere History of Literature. Far more detailed are three volumes of the *Oxford History of English Literature*: James Sutherland, *English Literature of the Late Seventeenth Century*, 1969; Bonamy Dobrée, *English Literature in the Early Eighteenth Century, 1700–1740*, 1959; and John Butt and Geoffrey Carnall, *English Literature in the Mid-Eighteenth Century*, 1979. On women writers they need to be supple-

mented by Janet Todd, *A Dictionary of British and American Women Writers, 1660–1800*, 1985.

Among books that deal with a single literary mode, James Sutherland, *A Preface to Eighteenth-Century Poetry*, 1948, is a deft introduction, and Eric Rothstein, *Restoration and Eighteenth-Century Poetry, 1660–1780*, 1981, is a fresh, informative survey. Other useful studies include Ian Jack, *Augustan Satire*, 1952; Earl Miner, *The Restoration Mode from Milton to Dryden*, 1974; Rachel Trickett, *The Honest Muse*, 1974; Margaret Doody, *The Daring Muse*, 1985; and Robert Griffin, *Wordsworth's Pope*, 1995. Anne Williams, *Prophetic Strain*, 1984, and Richard Feingold, *Moralized Song*, 1989, both stress the lyricism of eighteenth-century poems. Two anthologies edited by Roger Lonsdale, *The New Oxford Book of Eighteenth Century Verse*, 1984, and *Eighteenth-Century Women Poets*, 1989, have sparked an interest in neglected poems about daily life; Joyce Fullard has edited *Eighteenth-Century Women Poets 1660–1800*, 1990; and David Fairer and Christine Gerrard have edited an annotated anthology, *Eighteenth-Century Poetry*, 1999.

On drama, a good introduction is R. W. Bevis, *English Drama: Restoration and Eighteenth Century, 1660–1789*, 1988. Fuller accounts appear in Allardyce Nicoll, *A History of Restoration Drama 1660–1700*, *A History of Early Eighteenth-Century Drama, 1700–1750*, and *A History of Late Eighteenth-Century Drama, 1750–1800*, rev. 1952; and *The Revels History of Drama in English*, Vol. 5, *1660–1750*, 1976, and Vol. 6, *1750–1880*, 1975. An invaluable store of detailed information is *The London Stage, 1660–1800*, 11 vols., 1960–68, the critical introductions of which have been gathered in five paperback books. Six of the most important plays of the period, together with critical commentary and background material on theaters, staging, and audience, are edited by Scott McMillin in a Norton Critical Edition, *Restoration and Eighteenth-Century Comedy*, 2nd ed., 1997. Two collections, *Restoration Dramatists*, ed. Earl Miner, 1966, and *Restoration Drama*, ed. John Loftis, 1966, provide essays in criticism by various writers; Loftis has also analyzed *Comedy and Society from Congreve to Fielding*, 1959. Walter Graham has surveyed *English Literary Periodicals*, 1930. Letter writing was an important eighteenth-century genre, discussed in *The Familiar Letter in the Eighteenth Century*, ed. Howard Anderson, P. B. Daghlian, and Irvin Ehrenpreis, 1966, and Bruce Redford, *The Converse of the Pen*, 1987. Another important genre, history writing, is examined in Karen O'Brien, *Narratives of Enlightenment*, 1997. D. A. Stauffer, *English Biography before 1700*, 1930, and *The Art of Biography in Eighteenth-Century England*, 2 vols., 1941, are standard surveys; William H. Epstein, *Recognizing Biography*, 1987, is a challenging theoretical study. Bunyan figures prominently in two books on autobiography: John N. Morris, *Versions of the Self*, 1966, and Felicity Nussbaum, *The Autobiographical Subject*, 1989. Patricia Spacks, *Imagining a Self*, 1976, discusses conceptions of personal identity in eighteenth-century autobiographies and novels.

The Cambridge Companion to the Eighteenth-Century Novel, ed. John Richetti, 1996, is a good general survey. E. A. Baker, *The History of the English Novel*, vols. 3–5, 1930–34, assembles many details. A. D. McKillop, *The Early Masters of English Fiction*, 1956, and Clive Probyn, *English Fiction of the Eighteenth Century, 1700–1789*, 1987, offer good introductions to major novelists. Ian Watt, *The Rise of the Novel*, 1957, an influential study of Defoe, Richardson, and Fielding, set off a long discussion that has been joined by Jane Spencer, *The Rise of the Woman Novelist*, 1986; Michael McKeon, *The Origins of the English Novel*, 1987; Nancy Armstong, *Desire and Domestic Fiction*, 1987; J. Paul Hunter, *Before Novels*, 1990; Homer O. Brown, *Institutions of the English Novel from Defoe to Scott*, 1997; and William B. Warner, *Licensing Entertainment*, 1998. Interesting studies of special aspects of fiction include Lennard Davis, *Factual Fictions*, 1983; Terry Castle, *Masquerade and Civilization*, 1986; John Bender, *Imagining the Penitentiary*, 1987; Carol Kay, *Political Constructions*, 1988; and Catherine Gallagher, *Nobody's Story*, 1994, which has chapters on *Oroonoko* and Frances Burney.

The most comprehensive account of eighteenth-century criticism is vol. 4 of *The Cambridge History of Literary Criticism*, ed. H. B. Nisbet and Claude Rawson, 1997, J. E. Spingarn, *Critical Essays of the Seventeenth Century*, vols. 2 and 3, 1908 (the preface is still useful), and Scott Elledge, *Eighteenth-Century Critical Essays*, 2 vols., 1961, are valuable collections. R. S. Crane's "Neo-Classical Criticism," in *A Dictionary of World Literature*, ed. J. T. Shipley, 1943, has not been surpassed. A survey of major critical movements is provided by James Engell, *Forming the Critical Mind: Dryden to Coleridge*, 1989. René Wellek, *A History of Modern Criticism 1750–1950*, vol. 1, 1955, and W. K. Wimsatt and Cleanth Brooks, *Literary Criticism: A Short History*, 1957, review important issues of theory and aesthetics. Raymond Williams, *Keywords: A Vocabulary of Culture and Society*, 1983, examines the changing meanings of critical terms. A feminist perspective is offered by Marilyn Williamson, *Raising Their Voices: British Women Writers, 1650–1750*, 1990. The issues explored by Samuel H. Monk's classic study, *The Sublime*, 1935, have been taken up by many later critics, among them David Morris, *The Religious Sublime*, 1972, and Steven Knapp, *Personification and the Sublime*, 1985. The theory of satire has also been a perennial source of interest, most recently in John Sitter, *Arguments of Augustan Wit*, 1991, and Dustin Griffin, *Satire: A Critical Reintroduction*, 1994. Though primarily concerned with Romantic theory, M. H. Abrams, *The Mirror and the Lamp*, 1953, delves deeply into eighteenth-century critical ideas.

The relation of literature to other arts has been the subject of many instructive studies. Jean Hagstrum, *The Sister Arts*, 1958, compares paintings with poems; John Dixon Hunt, *The Figure in the Landscape*, 1977, deals with poetry, painting, and gardening; and Richard Wendorf, *The Elements of Life*, 1990, compares biography with portrait-painting. Lawrence Lipking discusses the first histories of the arts in *The Ordering of the Arts in Eighteenth-Century England*, 1970; Ronald Paulson, *Breaking and Remaking*, 1989, explores aesthetic practice from 1700 to 1820; and Murray Roston analyzes *Changing Perspectives in Literature and the Visual Arts 1650–1820*, 1990. B. Sprague Allen, *Tides of English Taste 1619–1800*, 2 vols., 1937, on architecture, gardening, and decoration, and Sir Kenneth Clark, *The Gothic Revival*, 2nd ed., 1950, on architecture, chronicle significant changes in style.

Good collections of criticism have been edited by James L. Clifford, *Eighteenth-Century English Literature: Modern Essays in Criticism*, 1959, and Leopold Damrosch, *Modern Essays on Eighteenth-Century Literature*, 1988. Essays that explore new theoretical approaches are collected by Felicity Nussbaum and Laura Brown, *The New Eighteenth Century*, 1987. *Studies in English Literature* devotes its summer issue to the Restoration and the eighteenth century and includes an article reviewing important work published in the preceding year. Finally, for elaborate bibliographies and reviews of eighteenth-century studies, the student may consult the bibliography of English literature, 1660–1800, that has appeared annually since 1926 in *Philological Quarterly* and, since 1976, in yearly volumes, *The Eighteenth Century: A Current Bibliography*.

Aphra Behn

Janet Todd has edited *The Works of Aphra Behn*, 7 vols., 1992–96. The Norton Critical Edition of *Oroonoko*, ed. Joanna Lipking, 1997, includes relevant historical backgrounds and criticism. The paucity of reliable facts about Behn's life prevents any biography from being authoritative, but Maureen Duffy, *The Passionate Shepherdess*, 1977, is worth reading, and Janet Todd, *The Secret Life of Aphra Behn*, 1997, is full of interesting speculations and fresh information. Wylie Sypher, *Guinea's Captive Kings*, 1942, puts *Oroonoko* in the context of antislavery literature. Mary Ann O'Donnell, *Aphra Behn: An Annotated Bibliography*, 1986, is a thorough review of primary and secondary sources through 1985.

James Boswell

Modern revaluations of Boswell began with the publication of *The Private Papers of James Boswell from Malahide Castle*, ed. Geoffrey Scott and Frederick A. Pottle, 18 vols., 1928–34. Pottle described the history of the papers in *Pride and Negligence*, 1981. A trade edition of Boswell's *Journals*, 14 vols., 1950–89, has valuable introductions and notes. The *Letters*, ed. C. B. Tinker, 2 vols., 1924, need to be supplemented by the recovered *Correspondence of James Boswell*, 1966–97, of which seven volumes have been published. The best edition of the *Life of Johnson* is L. F. Powell's revision of G. B. Hill's edition, 6 vols., 1934–64. A good one-volume edition by R. W. Chapman and J. D. Fleeman, 1982, is available in paperback.

F. A. Pottle, *James Boswell, The Earlier Years, 1740–1769*, 1966, and Frank Brady, *James Boswell, The Later Years, 1769–1795*, 1984, are the two halves of the standard biography, judicious and well informed. Pottle, *The Literary Career of James Boswell*, 1929, and Mary Hyde, *The Impossible Friendship: Boswell and Mrs. Thrale*, 1972, are both useful. B. H. Bronson, "Boswell's Boswell," in *Johnson and Boswell*, 1944, is a wise and sympathetic study; and J. L. Smith-Dampier, *Who's Who in Boswell?*, 1935, is a helpful guide through the *Life of Johnson*. Greg Clingham has edited a collection of essays, *New Light on Boswell*, 1991.

Frances Burney
The *Diary and Letters* were first edited in a truncated version by Charlotte Barrett, Burney's niece, 7 vols., 1842–46. The original texts of *The Journals and Letters of Fanny Burney (Madame d'Arblay), 1791–1840*, 12 vols., have been superbly edited by Joyce Hemlow et al., 1972–84. Several volumes of *The Early Journals and Letters of Fanny Burney, 1768–1791*, which will eventually fill ten or twelve volumes, have been edited by Lars Troide et al., 1988–94. There is no standard edition of the novels, but Peter Sabor has edited *The Complete Plays of Frances Burney*, 2 vols., 1995. Joyce Hemlow wrote the standard biography, *The History of Fanny Burney*, 1958, and Margaret Doody's critical biography, *Frances Burney: The Life in the Works*, 1988, is lively and thought provoking.

William Collins
The *Works* of Collins, which amount only to one slim volume, have been well edited by Richard Wendorf and Charles Ryskamp, 1979. Lonsdale's edition (see **Gray**) has copious notes. P. L. Carver, *The Life of a Poet*, 1967, is the fullest biography. Wendorf, *William Collins and Eighteenth-Century English Poetry*, 1981, is a fine critical study.

William Cowper
The *Poems*, 3 vols., have been expertly edited by John D. Baird and Charles Ryskamp, 1980–95. James Sambrook's edition of *The Task and Selected Other Poems*, 1994, has useful notes. James King and Ryskamp have edited Cowper's *Letters and Prose Writings*, 5 vols., 1979–86, and one volume of *Selected Letters*, 1989. King, *William Cowper: A Biography*, 1986, is the best full life; Ryskamp's fine *William Cowper of the Inner Temple, Esq.*, 1959, ends in 1768. Useful critical studies include Morris Golden, *In Search of Stability: The Poetry of William Cowper*, 1960; Vincent Newey, *Cowper's Poetry*, 1982; Martin Priestman, *Cowper's Task*, 1983; and the last chapter of Donald Davie, *The Eighteenth-Century Hymn in England*, 1993.

John Dryden
James A. Winn's *John Dryden and His World*, 1987, is the best biography. G. R. Noyes's edition of the *Poetical Works*, 2nd ed., 1950, includes a good bio-

graphical sketch; and Samuel Johnson's *Life of Dryden* is still worth reading. A fine scholarly edition of the *Works*, launched in 1956, under the general editorship first of E. N. Hooker, then H. T. Swedenberg, and lately Alan Roper, has reached twenty volumes. Keith Walker has edited a useful selected *Works*, 1987. The poems have been edited by James Kinsley, 4 vols., 1958, and the essays by W. P. Ker, 2 vols., 1900, and George Watson, 2 vols., 1962. Paul Hammond's new edition of the poems has useful notes; the first two volumes appeared in 1995.

Mark Van Doren, *John Dryden: A Study of His Poetry*, 1920, remains valuable for its fresh critical responses, as do T. S. Eliot's brief studies, *Homage to John Dryden*, 1924, and *John Dryden the Poet, the Dramatist, and the Critic*, 1932. Important modern criticism includes Arthur Hoffman, *John Dryden's Imagery*, 1962; Alan Roper, *Dryden's Poetic Kingdoms*, 1965; and Earl Miner, *Dryden's Poetry*, 1967. David Hopkins, *John Dryden*, 1986, is a good introduction. Steven Zwicker has studied *Politics and Language in Dryden's Poetry*, 1984. The standard work on Dryden's philosophical and religious ideas is Philip Harth, *Contexts of Dryden's Thought*, 1968, and Harth has also analyzed the politics of *Absalom and Achitophel* in *Pen for a Party*, 1993. Robert Hume analyzes *Dryden's Criticism*, 1970; Edward Pechter, *Dryden's Classical Theory of Literature*, 1975; and John C. Aden brings together *The Critical Opinions of John Dryden, A Dictionary*, 1963, under convenient headings. James Winn has edited *Critical Essays on John Dryden*, 1997.

Olaudah Equiano
A facsimile of the first edition of the *Interesting Narrative* was published by Paul Edwards, 2 vols., 1969. Equiano's later revisions of the *Narrative* and other writings have been edited, with useful notes, by Vincent Carretta, 1995. Carretta includes Equiano as well as other eighteenth-century black authors in a good anthology, *Unchained Voices*, 1996. Angelo Costanzo, *Surprizing Narrative: Olaudah Equiano and the Beginnings of Black Autobiography*, 1987; Keith Sandiford, *Measuring the Moment: Strategies of Protest in Eighteenth-Century Afro-English Writing*, 1988; and Peter Fryer, *Staying Power: The History of Black People in Britain*, 1984, place Equiano amid the debates of his time.

Anne Finch, Countess of Winchilsea
Myra Reynolds added a long biographical introduction to her valuable edition of the *Poems*, 1903, which needs to be supplemented by *The Anne Finch Wellesley Manuscript Poems*, ed. Barbara McGovern and Charles Hinnant, 1998. McGovern has written a good critical biography, *Anne Finch and Her Poetry*, 1992. Hinnant, *The Poetry of Anne Finch*, 1994, is an essay in interpretation.

Thomas Gray
The poems of Gray, Collins, and Goldsmith have been edited, with informative notes, by Roger Lonsdale, 1969. The standard edition of Gray's *Works* remains that of Edmund Gosse, 4 vols., rev. 1902–

6; of the *Correspondence*, that of Paget Toynbee and Leonard Whibley, 3 vols., 1935; of the poems, that of H. W. Starr and J. R. Hendrickson, 1966. R. W. Ketton-Cremer, *Thomas Gray*, 1955, is the best biography. Among critical studies, Henry Weinfield, *The Poet without a Name: Gray's Elegy and the Problem of History*, 1991, is thoughtful and searching, and B. Eugene McCarthy, *Thomas Gray: The Progress of a Poet*, 1997, is a good general introduction. *From Sensibility to Romanticism*, ed. F. W. Hilles and Harold Bloom, 1965, includes studies of the *Elegy* by Ian Jack, B. H. Bronson, and Frank Brady.

William Hogarth

The standard, comprehensive critical biography is Ronald Paulson, *Hogarth*, 3 vols., 1991–93. Jenny Uglow, *Hogarth: A Life and a World*, 1997, is perceptive and lively. Paulson has edited *Hogarth's Graphic Works*, 2 vols., 1970, as well as *The Analysis of Beauty*, 1998. The paintings are catalogued by R. B. Beckett, *Hogarth*, 1949, and the drawings by A. P. Oppé, *The Drawings of William Hogarth*, 1948. Sean Shesgreen has edited *Engravings by Hogarth*, 1973, in a generous and inexpensive format. *Hogarth on High Life*, 1970, illuminates *Marriage A-la-Mode* with the famous eighteenth-century commentaries by Georg Christoph Lichtenberg, translated and edited by Arthur Wensinger with W. B. Coley. David Bindman, *Hogarth*, 1981, is a good brief introduction to the art, and Bindman and Scott Wilcox have edited *Among the Whores and Thieves*, 1997, a collection of essays on Hogarth and *The Beggar's Opera*.

Samuel Johnson

Others among Johnson's friends besides Boswell wrote of him: notably, Hester Lynch Thrale Piozzi, whose *Anecdotes* (1786) have been edited, along with William Shaw's *Anecdotes*, by Arthur Sherbo, 1974; Sir John Hawkins, whose *Life* (1787) has been edited and abridged by Bertram H. Davis, 1961; and Frances Burney (Mme D'Arblay), from whose diary C. B. Tinker extracted the Johnsonian passages in *Dr. Johnson and Fanny Burney*, 1911. Pat Rogers, *The Samuel Johnson Encyclopedia*, 1996, is a handy source of information. James L. Clifford, *Young Sam Johnson*, 1955, and *Dictionary Johnson*, 1979, are well-informed studies of the early and middle years that supplement Boswell's rather sketchy account of Johnson's life before their meeting in 1763. There are fine modern biographies by John Wain, 1975, and W. J. Bate, 1977.

The best collected edition of Johnson's *Works* appeared as long ago as 1825. It is being replaced by an excellent scholarly edition, published by Yale, that has been coming out irregularly since 1958. The poems have been edited by D. N. Smith and E. L. McAdam, 2nd ed. rev. by J. D. Fleeman, 1974. G. B. Hill's editions of *Johnsonian Miscellanies*, 2 vols., 1897, and *The Lives of the Poets*, 3 vols., 1905, are still well worth consulting for their fine notes. Bruce Redford's edition of the *Letters*, 5 vols., 1992–94, is superb. The *Dictionary* is available on CD-ROM, ed. Anne McDermott, 1996.

Robert DeMaria, *The Life of Samuel Johnson*, 1993, and Lawrence Lipking, *Samuel Johnson: The Life of an Author*, 1998, offer critical overviews of Johnson's literary career. Thomas Woodman, *A Preface to Samuel Johnson*, 1993, and *The Cambridge Companion to Samuel Johnson*, ed. Greg Clingham, 1997, are useful guides. Among critical introductions, W. J. Bate, *The Achievement of Samuel Johnson*, 1955, is inspiring, and Paul Fussell, *Samuel Johnson and the Life of Writing*, 1971, is lively. Good specialized studies include W. K. Wimsatt, *The Prose Style of Samuel Johnson*, 1941; Donald J. Greene, *The Politics of Samuel Johnson*, 2nd ed., 1990; Carey McIntosh, *The Choice of Life: Samuel Johnson and the World of Fiction*, 1973; Robert Folkenflik, *Samuel Johnson, Biographer*, 1978; Nicholas Hudson, *Samuel Johnson and Eighteenth-Century Thought*, 1988; and John Cannon, *Samuel Johnson and the Politics of Hanoverian England*, 1994. Joseph E. Brown collected *The Critical Opinions of Samuel Johnson*, 1926. Jean Hagstrum's fine study of *Samuel Johnson's Literary Criticism*, 1952, has been complemented by Leopold Damrosch, *The Uses of Johnson's Criticism*, 1976, and G. F. Parker, *Johnson's Shakespeare*, 1989. DeMaria, *Johnson's Dictionary and the Language of Learning*, 1986, looks at the range of ideas gathered by Johnson, and Allen Reddick has studied *The Making of Johnson's Dictionary, 1746–1773*, rev. 1996. J. L. Clifford and D. J. Greene's survey and bibliography of critical studies, rev. 1970, was updated through 1985 by Greene and J. A. Vance, 1987.

Lady Mary Wortley Montagu

Isobel Grundy's full-scale biography, *Lady Mary Wortley Montagu: Comet of the Enlightenment*, 1999, adds much indeed to Robert Halsband's elegant *Life of Lady Mary Wortley Monagu*, 1956. Halsband also edited *The Complete Letters*, 3 vols., 1965–67; *Selected Letters*, 1970; and with Grundy, *Essays and Poems and Simplicity, a Comedy*, 2nd ed., 1993. Grundy has edited the *Romance Writings*, 1996.

Alexander Pope

There is no reliable complete edition of Pope's works. Although defective in many respects, the Victorian edition by Whitwell Elwin and J. W. Courthope, 10 vols., 1871–89, must still be consulted (with caution). The excellent Twickenham Edition of the poems, 11 vols., 1939–67, a cooperative undertaking by several scholars (under John Butt), includes valuable introductory and critical materials and notes. A convenient selection in a single volume, with selected notes, omits the translations of Homer. *The Prose Works* have been edited in 2 vols., by Norman Ault, 1936, and Rosemary Cowler, 1986.

Maynard Mack, *Alexander Pope: A Life*, 1986, is a full and sympathetic biography. George Sherburn, *Early Career of Alexander Pope*, 1934, and Mack, *The Garden and the City*, 1969, on Pope's later career, are valuable studies. David Foxon, *Pope and* the Early Eighteenth-Century Book Trade, 1991, and Brean Hammond, *Professional Imaginative Writing in England, 1670–1740,* 1997, treat Pope's concern with the business of publication. Howard Erskine-Hill has described *The Social Milieu of Alexander Pope,* 1975, and Valerie Rumbold examined *Women's Place in Pope's World,* 1989. Sherburn's edition of the *Correspondence,* 5 vols., 1956, is standard. R. H. Griffith, *Alexander Pope: A Bibliography,* 2 vols., 1962, is a detailed list of Pope's writings.

A good critical introduction to the poems is Geoffrey Tillotson, *On the Poetry of Pope,* 2nd ed., 1950; and Tillotson, *Pope and Human Nature,* 1958, throws light on a difficult subject. David B. Morris, *Alexander Pope: The Genius of Sense,* 1984, offers fine criticism of individual poems. Reuben A. Brower, *Alexander Pope: The Poetry of Allusion,* 1959, is an enlightening study of Pope's lifelong habit of adapting phrases, images, and ideas from earlier poets, especially those of classical antiquity. Much information is gathered up in Robert W. Rogers, *The Major Satires of Alexander Pope,* 1955. Austin Warren, *Alexander Pope as Critic and Humanist,* 1929, is dated but still useful. Aubrey Williams has analyzed *Pope's Dunciad,* 1955, and John Sitter, *The Poetry of Pope's Dunciad,* 1971. Several essays on Pope are included in Maynard Mack, *Collected in Himself,* 1982. Mack has also edited *Essential Articles for the Study of Alexander Pope,* 1964, and with James Winn, *Pope: Recent Essays,* 1980. *The Enduring Legacy,* ed. G. S. Rousseau and Pat Rogers, 1988, collects new essays on Pope, and Bran Hammond has edited *Pope,* 1996, a critical reader.

Jonathan Swift

Irvin Ehrenpreis's standard, comprehensive biography, *Swift: The Man, His Works, and the Age,* consists of three volumes: *Mr. Swift and His Contemporaries,* 1962, *Dr. Swift,* 1967, and *Dean Swift,* 1983. J. A. Downie, *Jonathan Swift, Political Writer,* 1984, and David Nokes, *Jonathan Swift, A Hypocrite Reversed,* 1985, are good introductions to the life and writings. Louis A. Landa, *Swift and the Church of Ireland,* 1954, is a valuable special study.

The standard edition of the poems is by Sir Harold Williams, 2 vols., 1937, rev., 1958. Pat Rogers's edition of Swift's *Complete Poems,* 1983, is reliable and less expensive. Herbert Davis has edited the prose works in fourteen volumes, 1939–68. Swift's *Correspondence* was edited by Williams, 5 vols., 1963–65. Other distinguished editions include Davis, *The Drapier's Letters,* 1935; Williams, *Journal to Stella,* 2 vols., 1948; A. C. Guthkelch and D. Nichol Smith, *A Tale of a Tub,* 2nd ed., 1958; and Frank H. Ellis, *A Discourse of the Contests and Dissentions between the Nobles and the Commons in Athens and Rome,* 1967. For the Norton Critical Editions series, Robert Greenberg has edited *Gulliver's Travels,* rev. 1971, and with W. B. Piper, *The Writings of Jonathan Swift,* 1973.

Among the abundant critical studies, the student should find especially helpful Ricardo Quintana, *The Mind and Art of Jonathan Swift,* 1936, and *Swift: An Introduction,* 1955. Arthur Case, *Four Essays on Gulliver's Travels,* Herbert Davis, *Jonathan Swift: Essays on his Satire and Other Studies,* 1964; C. J. Rawson, *Gulliver and the Gentle Reader,* 1973; and Robert Phiddian, *Swift's Parodies,* 1995, are all useful. After long neglect, Swift's poems have attracted a wealth of criticism; some of the best has been collected by David Vieth, *Essential Articles for the study of Jonathan Swift's Poetry,* 1984. Three books by Robert C. Elliott, *The Power of Satire,* 1960, *The Shape of Utopia,* 1970, and *The Literary Persona,* 1982, contain interesting chapters on Swift; so do Edward Said, *The World, the Text, and the Critic,* 1983, and Carol Houlihan Flynn, *The Body in Swift and Defoe,* 1990. Two good collections of essays are *Jonathan Swift: A Critical Anthology,* ed. Denis Donoghue, 1971, and *The Character of Swift's Satire,* ed. C. J. Rawson, 1983.

Poetic Forms and
Literary Terminology

Systematic literary theory and criticism in English began in the sixteenth century, at a time when the standard education for upper-class students emphasized the study of the classical languages and literatures. As a consequence, the English words that were introduced to describe meter, figures of speech, and literary genres often derive from Latin and Greek roots.

RHYTHM AND METER

Verse is generally distinguished from prose as a more compressed and more regularly rhythmic form of statement. This approximate truth underlines the importance of **meter** in poetry, as the means by which rhythm is measured and described.

In Latin and Greek, meter was established on a **quantitative** basis, by the regular alternation of long and short syllables (that is, syllables classified according to the time taken to pronounce them). Outside of a few experiments (and the songs of Thomas Campion), this system has never proved congenial to Germanic languages such as English, which distinguish, instead, between **stressed** and **unstressed,** or accented and unaccented syllables. Two varieties of accented stress may be distinguished. On the one hand, there is the natural stress pattern of words themselves; *sýllable* is accented on the first syllable, *deplórable* on the second, and so on. Then there is the sort of stress that indicates rhetorical emphasis. If the sentence "You went to Greece?" is given a pronounced accent on the last word, it implies "Greece (of all places)?" If the accent falls on the first word, it implies "you (of all people)?" The meter of poetry—that is, its rhythm—is ordinarily built up out of a regular recurrence of accents, whether established as **word accents** or **rhetorical accents;** once started, it has (like all rhythm) a tendency to persist in the reader's mind.

The unit that is repeated to give steady rhythm to a poem is called a **foot;** in English it usually consists of accented and unaccented syllables in one of five fairly simple patterns:

The **iambic foot** (or **iamb**) consists of an unstressed followed by a stressed syllable, as in *uníte, repeát,* or *insíst.* Most English verse falls naturally into the iambic pattern.

The **trochaic foot** (**trochee**) inverts this order; it is a stressed followed by an unstressed syllable—for example, *únit, réaper,* or *ínstant.*

The **anapestic foot** (**anapest**) consists of two unstressed syllables followed by a stressed syllable, as in *intercéde, disarránged,* or *Cameróon.*

The **dactylic foot** (**dactyl**) consists of a stressed syllable followed by two unstressed syllables, as in *Wáshington, Écuador,* or *ápplejack.*

The **spondaic foot** (**spondee**) consists of two successive stressed syllables, as in *heartbreak, headline,* or *Kashmir.*

In all the examples above, word accent and the quality of the metrical foot coincide exactly. But the metrical foot may well consist of several words, or, on the other hand, one word may well consist of several metrical feet. *Phótolithógraphy* consists of two dactyls in a single word; *dárk and with spóts on it,* though it consists of six words rather than one, is also two dactyls. When we read a piece of poetry with the intention of discovering its underlying metrical pattern, we are said to **scan** it—that is, we go through it line by line, indicating by conventional signs which are the accented and which the unaccented syllables within the feet. We also count the number of feet in each line; a line is, formally, also called a **verse** (from Latin *versus*, which means one "row" of metrical feet). Verse lengths are conventionally described in terms derived from the Greek:

Monometer: one foot (of rare occurrence)
Dimeter: two feet (also rare)
Trimeter: three feet
Tetrameter: four feet
Pentameter: five feet
Hexameter: six feet (six iambic feet make what is called an **Alexandrine**)
Heptameter: seven feet (also rare)

Samuel Johnson wrote a little parody of simpleminded poets which can be scanned this way:

> Ĭ pút m̆y hát ŭpón m̆y héad
> Ănd wálked ĭntó thĕ Stránd
> Ănd thére Ĭ mét ănóthĕr mán
> Whŏse hát wăs ín hĭs hánd.

The poem is iambic in rhythm, alternating tetrameter and trimeter in the length of the verse-lines. The fact that it scans so nicely is, however, no proof that it is good poetry. Quite the contrary. Many of poetry's most subtle effects are achieved by establishing an underlying rhythm and then varying it by means of a whole series of devices, some dramatic and expressive, others designed simply to lend variety and interest to the verse. A well-known sonnet of Shakespeare's (*116*) begins,

> Let me not to the marriage of true minds
> Admit impediments. Love is not love
> Which alters when it alteration finds,
> Or bends with the remover to remove.

It is possible to read the first line of this poem as mechanical iambic pentameter:

Lĕt mé nŏt tó thĕ márrĭăge óf trŭe mińds

But of course nobody ever reads it that way, except to make a point; read with normal English accent and some sense of what it is saying, the line would form a pattern something like this:

Lĕt mĕ nŏt tŏ thĕ márrĭăge ŏf trúe mińds

which is neither pentameter nor in any way iambic. The second line is a little more iambic, but, read expressively also falls short of pentameter:

Ădmít ĭmpédĭmeńts. Lóve ĭs nŏt lóve

Only in the third and fourth lines of the sonnet do we get verses that read as five iambic feet.

The fact is that perfectly regular metrical verse is easy to write and dull to read. Among the devices in common use for varying too regular a pattern are the insertion of a trochaic foot among iambics, especially at the opening of a line, where the soft first syllable of the iambic foot often needs stiffening (see line 1 of the sonnet above); the more or less free addition of extra unaccented syllables; and the use of **caesura,** or strong grammatical pause within a line (conventionally indicated, in scanning, by the sign ‖). The second line of the sonnet above is a good example of caesura:

Admit impediments. ‖ Love is not love

The strength of the caesura, and its placing in the line, may be varied to produce striking variations of effect. More broadly, the whole relation between the poem's sound- and rhythm-patterns and its pattern as a sequence of assertions (phrases, clauses, sentences) may be manipulated by the poet. Sometimes the statements fit neatly within the lines, so that each line ends with a strong mark of punctuation; they are then known as **end-stopped lines.** Sometimes the sense flows over the ends of the lines, creating **run-on lines;** this process is also known, from the French, as **enjambment** (literally, "straddling").

End-stopped lines (Marlowe, *Hero and Leander*, lines 45–48):

> So lovely fair was Hero, Venus' nun,
> As Nature wept, thinking she was undone,
> Because she took more from her than she left
> And of such wondrous beauty her bereft.

Run-on lines (Keats, *Endymion* 1.89–93):

> Full in the middle of this pleasantness
> There stood a marble altar, with a tress
> Of flowers budded newly; and the dew
> Had taken fairy fantasies to strew
> Daisies upon the sacred sward, . . .

Following the example of such poets as Blake, Rimbaud, and Whitman, many twentieth-century poets have undertaken to write what is called **free** verse—that is, verse which has neither a fixed metrical foot nor (consequently) a fixed number of feet in its lines, but which depends for its rhythm on a pattern of cadences, or the rise and fall of the voice in utterance, or the pattern indicated to the reader's eye by the breaks between the verse lines. As in traditional versification, free verse is printed in short lines instead of with the continuity of prose; it differs from such versification, however, by the fact that its stressed syllables are not organized into a regular metric sequence.

SENSE AND SOUND

The words of which poetic lines—whether free or traditional—are composed cause them to have different sounds and produce different effects. Polysyllables, being pronounced fast, often cause a line to move swiftly; monosyllables, especially when heavy and requiring distinct accents, may cause it to move heavily, as in Milton's famous line (*Paradise Lost* 2.621):

> Rocks, caves, lakes, fens, bogs, dens, and shades of death

Poetic assertions are often dramatized and reinforced by means of **alliteration**—that is, the use of several nearby words or stressed syllables beginning with the same consonant. When Shakespeare writes (*Sonnet 64*),

> Ruin hath taught me thus to ruminate
> That Time will come and take my love away,

the alliterative *r*'s and rich internal echoes of the first line contrast with the sharp anxiety and directness of the alliterative *t*'s in the second. When Dryden starts *Absalom and Achitophel* with the couplet,

> In pious times, ere priestcraft did begin,
> Before polygamy was made a sin,

the satiric undercutting is strongly reinforced by the triple alliteration that links "*p*ious" with "*p*riestcraft" and "*p*olygamy."

Assonance, or repetition of the same or similar vowel sounds within a passage (usually in accented syllables), also serves to enrich it, as in two lines from Keats's *Ode on Melancholy*:

> For shade to shade will come too drowsily,
> And drown the wakeful anguish of the soul.

It is clear that the round, hollow tones of "drowsily," repeated in "drown" and darkening to the full *o*-sound of "soul," have much to do with the effect of the passage. A related device is **consonance,** or the repetition of a pattern of consonants with changes in the intervening vowels—for example: *linger, longer, languor; rider, reader, raider, ruder.*

The use of words that seem to reproduce the sounds they designate (known as **onomatopoeia**) has been much attempted, from Virgil's galloping horse—

Quadrupedante putrem sonitu quatit ungula campum—

through Tennyson's account, in *The Princess*, of

> The moan of doves in immemorial elms,
>   And murmuring of innumerable bees—

to many poems in the present day.

RHYME AND STANZA

Rhyme consists of a repetition of accented sounds in words, usually those falling at the end of verse lines. If the rhyme sound is the very last syllable of the line (*rebound, sound*), the rhyme is called **masculine;** if the accented syllable is followed by an unaccented syllable (*hounding, bounding*), the rhyme is called **feminine.** Rhymes amounting to three or more syllables, like forced rhymes, generally have a comic effect in English, and have been freely used for this purpose, e.g., by Byron (*intellectual, henpecked-you-all*). Rhymes occurring within a single line are called **internal;** for instance, the Mother Goose rhyme "Mary, Mary, quite contrary," or from Coleridge's *Ancient Mariner* ("We were the first that ever burst / Into that silent sea"). **Eye rhymes** are words used as rhymes that look alike but actually sound different (for example, *alone, done; remove, love*); **off rhymes** (sometimes called **partial, imperfect,** or **slant rhymes**) are occasionally the result of pressing exigencies or lack of skill, but are also, at times, used deliberately by modern poets for special effects. For instance, a poem by Wilfred Owen (*Strange Meeting*) contains such paired words (which Owen called "pararhymes") as *years* / *yours* or *tigress* / *progress.*

Blank verse is unrhymed iambic pentameter; until the recent advent of free verse, it was the only unrhymed measure to achieve general popularity in English. Though first used by the earl of Surrey in translating Virgil's *Aeneid*, blank verse was during the sixteenth century employed primarily in plays; *Paradise Lost* was one of the first nondramatic poems in English to use it. But Milton's authority and his success were so great that during the eighteenth and nineteenth centuries blank verse came to be used for a great variety of discursive, descriptive, and philosophical poems—besides remaining the standard metrical form for epics. Thomson's *Seasons*, Cowper's *Task*, Wordsworth's *Prelude*, and Tennyson's *Idylls of the King* were all written in blank verse.

A **stanza** is a recurring unit of a poem, consisting of a number of verses. Certain poems (for example, Dryden's *Alexander's Feast*) have stanzas comprising a variable number of verses, of varying lengths. Others are more regular, and are identified by particular names.

The simplest form of stanza is the **couplet;** it is two lines rhyming together. A single couplet considered in isolation is sometimes called a **distich;** when it expresses a complete thought, ending with a terminal mark of punctuation such as a semicolon or period, it is called a **closed couplet.** The development of very regular end-stopped couplets, their use in so-called heroic tragedies, and their consequent acquisition of the name **heroic couplets** took place for the most part during the mid-seventeenth century. The heroic couplet was the principal form in English neoclassical poems.

Another traditional and challenging form of couplet is the **tetrameter, or four-beat couplet.** All rhymed couplets are hard to manage without monotony; and since, in addition, a four-beat line is hard to divide by caesura without splitting it into two tick-tock dimeters, tetrameter couplets have posed a perpetual challenge to poets, and still provide an admirable finger-exercise for aspiring versifiers. An instance of tetrameter couplets managed with marvelous variety, complexity, and expressiveness is Marvell's *To His Coy Mistress:*

> Thou by the Indian Ganges' side
> Shouldst rubies find; I by the tide
> Of Humber would complain. I would
> Love you ten years before the Flood,
> And you should, if you please, refuse
> Till the conversion of the Jews.

English has not done much with rhymes grouped in threes, but has borrowed from Italian the form known as **terza rima,** in which Dante composed his *Divine Comedy.* This form consists of linked groups of three rhymes according to the following pattern: *aba bcb cdc ded,* etc. Shelley's *Ode to the West Wind* is composed in stanzas of *terza rima,* the poem as a whole ending with a couplet.

Quatrains are stanzas of four lines; the lines usually rhyme alternately, *abab,* or in the second and fourth lines, *abcb.* When they alternate tetrameter and trimeter lines, as in Johnson's little poem about men in hats (above), or as in *Sir Patrick Spens,* they are called **ballad stanza.** Dryden's *Annus Mirabilis* and Gray's *Elegy Written in a Country Churchyard* are in **heroic quatrains;** these rhyme alternately *abab,* and employ five-stress iambic verse throughout. Tennyson used for *In Memoriam* a tetrameter quatrain rhymed *abba,* and FitzGerald translated *The Rubáiyát of Omar Khayyám* into a pentameter quatrain rhymed *aaba;* but these forms have not been widely adopted.

Chaucer's *Troilus and Criseide* is the premier example in English of **rhyme royal,** a seven-line iambic pentameter stanza consisting essentially of a quatrain dovetailed onto two couplets, according to the rhyme scheme *ababbcc* (the fourth line serves both as the final line of the quatrain and as the first line of the first couplet). Closely akin to rhyme royal, but differentiated by an extra *a*-rhyme between the two *b*-rhymes, is **ottava rima,** that is, an eight-line stanza rhyming *abababcc.* As its name suggests, ottava rima is of Italian origin; it was first used in English by Wyatt. Its final couplet, being less prepared for than in rhyme royal, and usually set off as a separate verbal unit, is capable of manifesting a witty snap, for which Byron found good use in *Don Juan.*

The longest and most intricate stanza generally used for narrative purposes in English is that devised by Edmund Spenser for *The Faerie Queene.* The **Spenserian stanza** has nine lines rhyming *ababbcbcc;* the first eight lines are pentameter, the last line an Alexandrine. Slow-moving, intricate of pattern, and very demanding in its rhyme scheme (the *b*-sound recurs four times, the *c*-sound three), the Spenserian stanza has nonetheless appealed widely to poets who seek a rich and complicated metrical form. Keats's *Eve* *of St. Agnes* and Shelley's *Adonais* are brilliantly successful nineteenth-century examples of its use.

The **sonnet,** originally a stanza of Italian origin that has developed into an independent lyric form, is usually defined nowadays as fourteen lines of iambic pentameter. None of the elements in this definition is absolute and in earlier centuries there were sonnets in hexameters (the first of Sidney's *Astrophil and Stella*), and sonnets of as many as twenty lines (Milton's *On the New Forcers of Conscience*). Most, however, approximate the definition. Most Elizabethan sonnets dealt with love; and some poets, like Sidney, Spenser, and Shakespeare, imitated Petrarch in grouping together their sonnets dealing with a particular lady or situation. The term for these gatherings is **sonnet sequences;** the extent to which they tell a sequential story, and the extent to which such stories are autobiographical, vary greatly. Since Elizabethan times, the sonnet has been applied to a wide range of subject matters—religious, political, satiric, moral, and philosophic.

In blank verse or irregularly rhymed verse, where stanzaic divisions do not exist or are indistinct, the poetry sometimes falls into **verse paragraphs,** which are in effect divisions of sense like prose paragraphs. This division can be clearly seen in Milton's *Lycidas* and *Paradise Lost*. An intermediate form, clearly stanzaic but with stanzas of varying patterns of line-length and rhyme, is illustrated by Spenser's *Epithalamion*; in this instance, the division into stanzas is reinforced by a **refrain,** which is simply a line repeated at the end of each stanza. Ballads also customarily have refrains; for example, the refrain of *Lord Randall* is

> mother, make my bed soon,
> For I'm weary wi' hunting, and fain wald lie down.

FIGURATIVE LANGUAGE

The act of bringing words together into rich and vigorous poetic lines is complex and demanding, chiefly because so many variables require control. There is the "thought" of the lines, their verbal texture, their emotional resonance, the developing perspective of the reader—all these to be managed at once. One of the poet's chief resources toward this end is figurative language. Here, as in matters of meter, one may distinguish a great variety of devices, some of which we use in everyday speech without special awareness of their names and natures. When we say someone eats "like a horse" or "like a bird," we are using a **simile,** that is, a comparison marked out by a specific word of likening—"like" or "as." When we omit the word of comparison but imply a likeness—as in the sentence "That hog has guzzled all the champagne"—we are making use of **metaphor.** The **epic simile,** frequent in epic poetry, is an extended simile in which the thing compared is described as an object in its own right, beyond its point of likeness with the main subject. Milton starts to compare Satan to Leviathan, but concludes his simile with the story of a sailor who moored his ship by mistake, one night, to a whale (*Paradise Lost* 1.200–208). Metaphors and similes have been distinguished according to their special effects; they may be, for instance, violent, comic, degrading, decorative, or ennobling.

When we speak of "forty head of cattle" or ask someone to "lend a hand" with a job, we are using **synecdoche,** a figure that substitutes the part for the whole. When we speak of a statement coming "from the White House," or a man much interested in "the turf," (that is, the race-course), we are using **metonymy,** or the substitution of one term for another with which it is closely associated. **Antithesis** is a device for placing opposing ideas in grammatical parallel, as, for example, in the following passage from Alexander Pope's *Rape of the Lock* (5.25–30), where there are more examples of antithesis than there are lines:

> But since, alas! frail beauty must decay,
> Curled or uncurled, since locks will turn to gray;
> Since painted, or not painted, all shall fade,
> And she who scorns a man must die a maid;
> What then remains but well our power to use,
> And keep good humor still whate'er we lose?

   Irony is a verbal device that implies an attitude quite different from (and often opposite to) that which is literally expressed. In Pope's *The Rape of the Lock* (4.131–32), after poor Sir Plume has stammered an incoherent request to return the stolen lock of hair, the Baron answers ironically:

> "It grieves me much," replied the Peer again,
> "Who speaks so well should ever speak in vain."

And when Donne "proves," in *The Canonization,* that he and his mistress are going to found a new religion of love, he seems to be inviting us to take a subtly ironic attitude toward religion as well as love.

   Because it is easy to see through, **hyperbole,** or willful exaggeration, is a favorite device of irony—which is not to say that it may not be "serious" as well. When she hears that a young man is "dying for love" of her, a sensible young woman does not accept this statement literally, but it may convey a serious meaning to her nonetheless. The **pun,** or play on words (known to the learned, sometimes, as **paronomasia**), may also be serious or comic in intent; witness, for example, the famous series of puns on Donne's name in his *Hymn to God the Father.* **Oxymoron** is a conjunction of two terms that in ordinary use are contraries or incompatible—for instance, Milton's famous description of hell as containing "darkness visible" (*Paradise Lost* 1.63). A **paradox** is a statement that seems absurd but turns out to have rational meaning after all, usually in some unexpected sense; Donne speaks of fear being great courage and high valor (*Satire* 3, line 16), and turns out to mean that fear of God is greater courage than any earthly bravery. A **conceit** is a far-fetched and unusually elaborate comparison. Writing in the fourteenth century, the Italian poet Petrarch popularized a great number of conceits handy for use in love poetry, and readily adapted by his English imitators. Wyatt, for example, is using **Petrarchan conceits** when he compares love to a warrior, or the lover's state to that of a storm-tossed ship; and a hundred other sonneteers developed the themes of the lady's stony heart, incendiary glances, and so forth. On the other hand, the **metaphysical conceit** was a more intellectualized, many-leveled comparison, giving a strong sense of the poet's ingenuity in overcoming obstacles—for instance, Donne's comparison of separated lovers to the legs of a compass (A *Valediction: Forbidding Mourning*) or Herbert's comparison of devotion to a pulley, in the poem of that name.

Personification (or in the term derived from Latin **prosopopoeia**) is the attribution of human qualities to an inanimate object (for example, the Sea) or an abstract concept (Freedom); a special variety of it is called (in a term of John Ruskin's invention) the **pathetic fallacy.** When we speak of leaves "dancing" or a lake "smiling," we attribute human traits to nonhuman objects. Ruskin thought this was false and therefore "morbid"; modern criticism tends to view the practice as artistically and morally neutral. A more formal and abstract variety of personification is **allegory,** in which a narrative (such as *Pilgrim's Progress*) is constructed by representing general concepts (Faithfulness, Sin, Despair) as persons who act out the plot. A **fable** (like Chaucer's *The Nun's Priest's Tale*) represents beasts behaving like humans; a **parable** is a brief story, or simply an observation, with strong moral application; and an **exemplum** is a story told to illustrate a point in a sermon.

A special series of devices, nearly obsolete today, used to be available to poets who could count on readers trained in the classics. These were the devices of **classical allusion**—that is, reference to the mythology (stories about the actions of gods and other supernatural beings) of the Greeks and Romans. In their simplest form, the classic **myths** used to provide a repertoire of agreeable stage properties, and a convenient shorthand for expressing emotional attitudes. Picturesque creatures like centaurs, satyrs, and sphinxes, heroes and heroines like Hector and Helen, and the whole pantheon of Olympic deities could be used to make ready reference to a great many aspects of human nature. One does not have to explain the problems of a man who is "cleaning the Augean stables"; if he is afflicted with an "Achilles' heel," or is assailing "Hydra-headed difficulties," his state is clear. These descriptive phrases, making **allusion** to mythological stories, suggest in a phrase situations that would normally require cumbersome explanations. But because it used to be taken for granted that the classical mythology was the common possession of all educated readers, the classic myths entered into English literature as early as Chaucer. In poets like Spenser and Milton, classical allusion becomes a kind of enormously learned game, in which the poet seeks to make his points as indirectly as possible. For instance, Spenser writes in the *Epithalamion*, lines 328–29:

> Lyke as when Jove with fayre Alcmena lay,
> When he begot the great Tirynthian groome.

The mere mention of Alcmena in the first line suggests, to the informed reader, Hercules, the son of Jupiter (Jove) by Alcmena. Spenser's problem in the second line is to find a way of referring to him that is neither redundant nor heavy-handed. "Tirynthian" reminds the reader of Hercules' long connection with the city of Tiryns, stretching our minds (as it were) across his whole career; and "groome" compresses references to a man-child, a servant, and a bridegroom, all of which apply to different aspects of Hercules' history. Thus, far from simply avoiding redundancy, Spenser has enriched, for the reader who possesses the classical information, the whole texture of his verse, thought, and feeling.

SCHOOLS

Literary scholars and critics often group together in **schools** writers who share stylistic traits or thematic concerns. Whether they considered themselves a group doesn't much matter; although in some cases—for example, the Imagists or the Beat poets—the writers themselves have identified themselves as belonging to a group. None of the **Romantic poets** knew they were being romantic, although Hazlitt, Shelley, and other writers of the time recognized shared features that they called "the spirit of the age." The followers of Spenser are known as **Spenserians;** they knew they admired and to some extent wrote like Spenser, but didn't realize that made them a group. **Cavalier** poets are set decisively apart from **Metaphysical** poets, though pretty surely none of the two-dozen-odd men involved knew that was what they were. And so with the **Gothic novelists,** and the so-called **Graveyard School** of the eighteenth century; these schools are generally grouped, defined, and named by scholars and critics after the event.

Intellectual affinities have led some writers to be classified under the names of the philosophical schools of Greece and Rome. These are chiefly the **Epicureans,** who specify that the aim of life and the source of value is pleasure; the **Stoics,** who emphasize stern virtue and the dignified endurance of what cannot be avoided; and the **Skeptics,** who doubt that anything can be known for certain. These categories are useful as capsule descriptions, but they aren't very tidy, as they are omissive, overlap one another, and cut across other categories. Dryden is an author strongly tinged with skepticism, but many of his poems suggest an unabashed epicureanism. *The Vanity of Human Wishes*, by Samuel Johnson, is the classic poem in English of stoic philosophy, but it also expresses a particularly strong coloring of Christian humanism.

TERMS OF LITERARY ART

The following section defines frequently used literary terms, especially frequently used terms that are closely related or tend to be mistaken for each other.

Allegory, Symbol, Emblem, Type. Allegory is a narrative in which the agents, and sometimes also the setting, are personified concepts or character-types, and the plot represents a doctrine or thesis. John Bunyan's *Pilgrim's Progress*, for example, allegorizes the Christian doctrine of salvation by narrating how the character named Christian, warned by Evangelist, flees the City of Destruction and makes his laborious way to the Celestial City; en route he meets such characters as Faithful and the Giant Despair, and passes through places like the Slough of Despond and Vanity Fair. A literary **symbol** is the representation of an object or event which has a further range of reference beyond itself. Examples of sustainedly symbolic poems are William Blake's *The Sick Rose* and William Butler Yeats's *Sailing to Byzantium*. In the sixteenth and seventeenth centuries, an **emblem** was an enigmatic picture of a physical object, to which was attached a motto and a verse explaining its significance. In present-day usage, an emblem is any object which is widely understood to signify an abstract concept; thus a dove is an emblem of peace, and a cross, of Christianity. In what was once a widespread Christian mode of biblical interpretation, a **type** was a person or event in the Old Testament which was regarded as historically real, but also as "prefiguring" a person or event in the New Testament. Thus Adam was often said to be a type of Christ, and the act of Moses in liberating the children of Israel was said to prefigure Christ in freeing men from Satan.

Baroque and **Mannerist** are terms imported into literary study from the history of art, and applied by analogy. Michelangelo is a **baroque** artist; he holds great masses in powerful dynamic tension, his style is heavily ornamented and restless. In these respects he is sometimes compared to Milton. El Greco is a **mannerist,** whose gaunt and distorted figures often seem to be laboring under great spiritual stress, whose light seems to be focused in spots against a dark background. He has been compared to Donne. Analogies of this sort are occasionally suggestive, but can readily deteriorate into parallels that are forced and nominal rather than substantial.

Bathos. See **Pathos,** the **Sublime,** and **Bathos.**

Burlesque and **Mock Heroic** differ in that the former makes its subject ludicrous by directly cutting it down, the latter by inflating it. In Pope's mock-heroic *Dunciad*, the figure of Dulness (Colley Cibber) is given inappropriately heroic dimensions; in Butler's burlesque *Hudibras*, the knightly hero is characterized by low and vulgar attributes, and persistently engages in inappropriately low behavior. Burlesque contributed to the development of the English novel; and during the nineteenth century, when formal drama tended to be stagy and melodramatic, a vigorous burlesque stage flourished in England, making fun of the classics. See **Imitation** and **Parody.**

Catastrophe and **Catharsis.** The **catastrophe** is the conclusion of a play; the word means "down-turning," and is usually applied only to tragedies, in which a frequent kind of catastrophe is the death of the protagonist. (A term for the precipitating final scene that applies both to tragedy and to comedy is **denouement,** which in French means "unknotting.") **Catharsis** in Greek signifies "purgation" or "purification." In Aristotle's *Poetics*, the special effect of tragedy is the "catharsis" of the "emotions of pity and fear" that have been aroused in the audience by the events of the drama.

Chiasmus and **Zeugma.** **Chiasmus** is an inversion of the word order in two parallel phrases, as in John Denham's *Cooper's Hill:* "Strong without rage, without o'erflowing full." **Zeugma** is the use of a single verb or adjective to control two nouns, as in Pope's *The Rape of the Lock:* "Or stain her honor, or her new brocade."

Classic and **Neoclassic.** See **Gothic, Classic, Neoclassic.**

Convention and **Tradition. Conventions** are agreed-upon artistic procedures peculiar to an art form. None of Shakespeare's contemporaries spoke blank verse in everyday life, but characters in his plays do, and the audience accepts it—as the audience at an opera accepts that characters will sing arias to express their feelings. A **tradition** consists of beliefs, attitudes, and ways of representing things that is widely shared by writers over a span of time; it generally includes a number of conventions.

Didactic poetry is designed to teach a branch of knowledge, or to embody in fictional form a moral, religious, or philosophical doctrine. The term is not derogatory. John Milton's *Paradise Lost*, for example, can be called didactic, insofar as it is organized, as Milton claimed in his invocation, to "assert Eternal Providence / And justify the ways of God to men." In the eighteenth century, a number of poets wrote didactic poems called **geor-gics** (modeled on the Roman Virgil's *Georgics* on rural life and farming), which described such applied arts as making cider or running a sugar plantation.

Dramatic irony and **Dramatic monologue** are quite different literary modes. In **dramatic irony** a stage character says something that has one meaning for him, but quite another for the audience who possesses relevant knowledge that the speaker lacks. The **dramatic monologue** is a form that was perfected by Robert Browning in such poems as *My Last Duchess* and *The Bishop Orders His Tomb*. In it, the poetic speaker unintentionally reveals to the reader his character and temperament by what he says, usually to another person whose presence we infer from the utterance of the speaker.

Eclogue. See **Pastorals**.

Emblem. See **Allegory, Symbol, Emblem, Type**.

Epigram, Epigraph, Epitaph. An **epigram** is a short, witty statement in verse or prose. One of Oscar Wilde's characters remarks, "I can resist everything, except temptation." An **epigraph** is an apposite quotation placed at the beginning of a book or a section of it. An **epitaph** is a brief statement about someone who has died; usually, it is intended to be inscribed on a tombstone.

Eulogy and **Elegy.** The **eulogy** is a work of praise, in prose or poetry, for a person either very distinguished or recently dead. In its usual modern sense, an **elegy** is a formal, and usually long, poetic lament for someone who has died. In an extended sense, the term is also used to designate poems on the transience of earthly things (such as the Old English *The Seafarer*) or poetic meditations on mortality (such as Thomas Gray's *Elegy Written in a Country Churchyard*).

Euphemism and **Euphuism. Euphemism,** or "fine speech," is a verbal device for avoiding an unpleasant concept or expression, as when, instead of saying a person "died," we say he "passed away." Euphues was the hero of a prose romance (published 1579–80) by John Lyly; his adventures are recounted in a mannered style full of puns, alliteration, and antithetical "points." Under the name of **Euphuism** this courtly style enjoyed a brief vogue in the Elizabethan era.

Fancy and **Imagination.** The distinction between these two mental powers was central to the literary theory of S. T. Coleridge. **Fancy** (a word directly derived by contraction from "fantasy") was defined by Coleridge as the power of combining several known properties into new combinations; **imagination,** on the other hand, was the faculty of using such properties to create an integral whole that is entirely new.

Folios, Quartos, etc., are terms used to specify the size of book pages. To make a **folio**, a sheet of paper (14" × 20" or larger) is folded just once (producing thereby four pages); **quartos** are folded twice (producing eight pages). Shakespeare's plays were first printed in quartos (often in several different editions), but when they were collected together, in 1623, they appeared as the First Folio edition.

Genre, Decorum. A genre is an established literary form or type, such as stage comedy, the picaresque novel, the epic, the sonnet. Works belonging to a certain genre tend to represent certain characters and events, and to seek a similar effect. **Decorum,** in literary criticism—where it was a central concept from the Renaissance through the eighteenth century—designates the requirement that there should be a propriety, or fitness, in the way that the character, actions, and style are matched to each other in a particular genre. Low characters, actions, and style, for example, were thought appropriate for satire, while epic demanded characters of high estate, engaged in great actions, and speaking in an appropriately high style.

Gothic, Classic, Neoclassic. These terms are used to distinguish prominent tendencies in literature and the other arts. The term **Gothic** originally referred to the Goths, an early Germanic tribe, then came to signify "medieval." In the eighteenth century "Gothic" connoted primitive and irregular work, possessing the qualities of the relatively barbaric North. **Gothic novels** were a very popular type of prose fiction, inaugurated by Horace Walpole's *Castle of Otranto* (1764), usually set in a medieval castle, which aimed to evoke chilling terror from their readers. **Classic** implies lucid, rational, and orderly works, such as are usually attributed to the writers and thinkers in the classic era of the Greeks and Romans. **Neoclassic**— a term often applied to the period in England from 1660 through most of the eighteenth century—implies an ideal of life, art, and thought deliberately modeled on Greek and Roman examples.

Heroic poems, Heroic drama, Heroic couplets. Because they concentrate on the figure of a typical hero (Achilles, Aeneas), epic poems were frequently called "heroic." Trying to transfer epic grandeur to the stage, playwrights of the Restoration period wrote what was called **heroic drama,** but usually achieved only grandiosity. The stately iambic pentameter couplets in which they made their characters speak became known as **heroic couplets.**

Humor. See **Wit** and **Humor.**

Humors and **Temperaments** are psychological terms used by Renaissance writers. It was believed that every person's constitution contained four basic humors: the **choleric** (bile), the **sanguine** (blood), the **phlegmatic** (phlegm), and the **melancholy** (black bile). The **temperament,** or mixture, of these four humors was held to determine both a person's physical condition and a person's type of character. When a particular humor predominated, it pushed the character in that direction: choler = anger; sanguine = geniality; phlegm = cold torpor; and melancholy = gloomy self-absorption.

Imagination. See **Fancy** and **Imagination.**

Imitation and **Parody** are forms in which a literary work refers back to a predecessor. In the eighteenth century, an "imitation" was a poem that deliberately echoed an older work, but adapted it to subject matter in the writer's own era, usually with a satirical aim directed against that subject matter; Alexander Pope, for example, wrote a number of satires on contemporary life that he entitled *Imitations of Horace*. A **parody** imitates the characteristic style and other features of a particular literary work—or else of a particular literary type—but in such a way as to satirize that work, by making it either amusing or ridiculous. *Northanger Abbey* (1818) by Jane Austen was a good-humored parody of the popular horror-narratives known as gothic novels. (See **Burlesque** and **Gothic**.)

Irony, Sarcasm. **Irony** and **sarcasm** are both ways of saying one thing but implying something sharply different, often opposite; they differ, however, in the way they go about doing so. **Sarcasm** is a broad and taunting form of using apparent praise in order in fact to denigrate. The patriarch Job is bitterly sarcastic when he replies to his would-be comforters (12.2), "No doubt but ye are the people, and wisdom shall die with you." On the other hand, Jane Austen, in the first sentence of *Pride and Prejudice*, overstates the case just enough to make it drily **ironic** when she writes, "It is a truth universally acknowledged, that a single man in possession of a good fortune, must be in want of a wife." (See **Irony**, in the section "Figurative Language," above.)

Legend. See **Myth** and **Legend**.

Logic. See **Rhetoric** and **Logic**.

Masque. The **Masque**, which flourished during the reigns of Elizabeth I, James I, and Charles I, was an elaborate court entertainment that combined poetic drama, music, song, dance, and splendid costumes and settings. For a discussion of the English masque, see the introduction to Jonson's *Pleasure Reconciled to Virtue*.

Myth and Legend. **Myths** are hereditary narratives that purport to account, in supernatural terms, for why the world is as it is, and why people act as they do; they also often provide the rules by which people conduct their lives. Myths often spring up to explain rituals, the original meanings of which have been forgotten. A system of related myths is called a **mythology**—a body of supernatural narratives believed to be true by a particular cultural group. The term "myth" is frequently extended to a set of supernatural narratives that are developed by individual poets such as William Blake and W. B. Yeats. Three great mythologies that have been exploited by poets long after they ceased to be believed are the classical (Greek and Roman), the Celtic, and the Germanic. A **legend** is an old and popularly repeated story, of which the protagonist is not supernatural, but a human being. If a hereditary story concerns supernatural beings who are not gods, and the story is not part of a systematic mythology, it is usually classified as a **folktale**.

Naturalism. See **Realism** and **Naturalism**.

Neo-Classic. See **Gothic, Classic, Neoclassic**.

Novel. See **Romance, Novel**.

Ode. A long lyric poem serious in subject and treatment, written in an elevated style and, usually, in an elaborate stanza. See the discussion of English odes in the headnote to Jonson's *Ode on Cary and Morison*.

Pastoral, Eclogue, and **Pastoral Elegy. Pastorals** (from the Latin word for "shepherd") are deliberately conventional poems that project a cultivated poet's nostalgic image of the peace and simplicity of the life of shepherds and other rural folk in an idealized natural setting. The form was established by the Greek poet Theocritus in the third century B.C.E.; it is sometimes also called an **eclogue,** which was the title that the Roman poet Virgil gave to his collection of pastorals. The pastorals by Theocritus and later classical poets often included a poem in which a shepherd mourns the death of a fellow shepherd; from these poems developed the highly conventional **pastoral elegy,** a type that includes such great laments as Milton's *Lycidas* and Shelley's *Adonais*. *Lycidas* is also an example of the extension of the classical pastoral to a Christian range of reference, by way of the use of the term "pastor" (shepherd) for a parish priest or minister and the frequent representation of Christ as "the Good Shepherd."

Pathos, the Sublime, and Bathos. In Greek, **pathos** signified deep feeling, especially suffering; in modern criticism, it is used in a more limited way to signify a scene or passage designed to evoke the feelings of pity or sympathetic sorrow from an audience. An example is the passage in which King Lear is briefly reunited with his daughter Cordelia, beginning

> Pray, do not mock me.
> I am a very foolish fond old man . . .

In the first century the Greek rhetorician Longinus wrote a treatise *On the Sublime,* in which he proposed that sublimity ("loftiness") is the greatest of stylistic qualities in literature; the effect of the sublime on the reader is *elestasis* ("transport"). In 1757 Edmund Burke published a highly influential treatise on *The Sublime and Beautiful,* in which he distinguished the sublime from the beautiful, not as a stylistic quality, but as the representation of objects that are vast, obscure, and powerful, which evoke from the reader a "delightful horror" that combines pleasure and terror. **Bathos** (Greek for "depth") was used by Pope, in a parodic parallel to Longinus' "sublime," to signify an unintentional descent in literature, when an author, straining to be passionate or elevated, overshoots the mark and falls into the trivial or the ridiculous.

Poetic diction, Poetic license, Poetic justice. Poetic diction denotes a distinctive language used by a poet which is not current in the discourse of the age; an example is the deliberately archaic language of Spenser's *The Faerie Queene*. In modern critical discussion, the term is applied especially to the style of eighteenth-century poets who, according to the reigning principle of decorum (see **Decorum**), believed that a poet must adapt the level of his diction to the dignity of the high genres of epic, tragedy, and ode. The results were such phrases as "the finny tribe" for "fish" and "the bleating kind" for "sheep." **Poetic license** designates the freedom of a poet or other literary writer to depart, for special effects, from the norms of common discourse and of literal or historical truth. Examples: the use of archaic words, meter, and rhyme, and the use of other literary conventions. (See **Convention.**) **Poetic justice** was coined by Thomas Rymer, in the later seventeenth century, to denote his claim that a narrative or drama should, at the end, distribute rewards and punishments in proportion to the virtues and vices of each character. No important critic since Rymer has adopted this doctrine, except in a highly qualified way.

Quarto. See **Folios, Quartos.**

Realism and **Naturalism** are both terms applied to prose fictions that aim at a faithful representation of actual existence; they differ, however, in the aspects of that existence that they represent and in the manner in which they represent them. The realistic novel attempts to give the effect of representing ordinary life as it commonly occurs. Realistic novelists such as George Eliot in England and William Dean Howells in America present everyday characters experiencing ordinary events, rendered in great detail. **Naturalism,** which the French novelist Émile Zola developed in the 1870s and later, is based on the philosophy that a human being is merely a higher-order animal, whose character and behavior are determined by heredity and environment. Zola, followed by such later naturalistic novelists as the Americans Frank Norris and Theodore Dreiser, typically represents characters who inherit such compulsive instincts as greed and the sexual drive and are shaped by the social and economic forces of family, class, and the milieu into which they are born. Naturalistic novelists also often display an almost medical candor in describing human activities and bodily functions largely unmentioned in earlier fiction.

Rhetoric and **Logic. Rhetoric** was developed by Greek and Roman theorists as the art of using all available means of persuading an audience, either by speech or in writing; it had a great influence on literary criticism in the Renaissance and through the eighteenth century. Rhetorical theorists developed a detailed analysis of figures of speech, largely as effective means to the overall aim of persuasion. In the present century, however, the analysis of such figures has been excerpted from this rhetorical context and made an independent and central concern of language theorists and literary critics. See **Figurative language. Logic** is the study of the principles of reasoning. Logic may be used to persuade an audience, but it does not, like rhetoric, avail itself of all means of persuasion, emotional as well as rational; instead, logic limits itself to a concern with the formal procedures of reasoning from sound premises to valid conclusions.

Romance and **Novel.** Medieval **romances** were verse narratives of adventure, usually about a knightly hero on a quest to gain a lady's favor, who encounters both natural tribulations and supernatural marvels. The term "romance" has since come to be opposed to realism (see **Realism** and **Naturalism**) and is applied to prose fictions that represent characters and events which are more picturesque, fantastic, adventurous, or heroic than one encounters in ordinary life. The **novel,** as distinguished from the prose romance, undertakes to be a more realistic representation of common life and social relationships and tends to avoid the fantastic, the fabulous, and the realm of high derring-do. (See **Realism.**)

Sarcasm. See **Irony, Sarcasm.**

Satire designates literary forms which diminish or derogate a subject by making it ridiculous and by evoking toward it amusement, or scorn, or indignation. In **formal satire,** such as Alexander Pope's *Moral Essays,* the satire is accomplished in a direct, first-person address, either to the audience or to a listener within the work. **Indirect satire** is not a direct address, but is cast in the form of a fictional narrative, as in Swift's *Gulliver's Travels* or Byron's *Don Juan.* For a discussion of the backgrounds of English satire, see the introduction to Donne's *Satire 3.*

Sublime. See **Pathos, the Sublime,** and **Bathos.**

Symbol. See **Allegory, Symbol, Emblem, Type.**

Tradition. See **Convention** and **Tradition.**

Type. See **Allegory, Symbol, Emblem, Type.**

Wit and **Humor,** in their present use, designate elements in a literary work which are designed to amuse or to excite mirth in the reader or audience. **Wit,** through the seventeenth century, had a broad range of meanings, including general intelligence, mental acuity, and ingenuity in literary invention, especially in a brilliant and paradoxical style. From this last application there derived the most common present use of "wit" to denote a kind of verbal expression that is brief, deft, and contrived to produce a shock of comic surprise; a characteristic form of wit, in this sense, is the epigram. (See **Epigram.**) **Humor** goes back to the ancient theory of the four humors and the application of the term "humorous" to a comically eccentric character who has an imbalance of the humors in his or her temperament. (See **Humors** and **Temperament.**) As we now use the word, **humor** is ascribed both to a comic utterance and to the comic appearance or behavior of a literary character. A humorous utterance, unlike a witty utterance, need not be intended to be comic by the speaker, and is not cast in the neat epigrammatic form of a witty saying. In Shakespeare's *Twelfth Night*, for example, Malvolio's utterances, as well as his appearance and behavior, are all found humorous by the audience, but his utterances are never witty and are humorous despite his own very solemn intentions.

Zeugma. See **Chiasmus** and **Zeugma.**

THE UNIVERSE ACCORDING TO PTOLEMY

Ptolemy was a Roman astronomer of Greek descent, born in Egypt during the second century C.E.; after his death, for nearly fifteen hundred years his account of the design of the universe was accepted as standard. During that long period, the basic pattern underwent many detailed modifications and was fitted out with many astrological and pseudoscientific trappings. But in essence Ptolemy's followers agreed in portraying the earth as the center of the universe, with the sun, planets, and fixed stars set in transparent spheres orbiting around it. In this scheme of things, as modified for Christian usage, Hell was usually placed under the earth's surface at the center of the cosmic globe, while Heaven, the abode of the blessed spirits, was in the outermost, uppermost circle, the empyrean. But in 1543 the Polish astronomer Copernicus proposed an alternative hypothesis—that the earth rotates around the sun, not vice versa; and despite theological opposition, observations with the new telescope and careful mathematical calculations insured ultimate acceptance of the new view.

The map of the Ptolemaic universe represented here is a simplified version of a diagram in Peter Apian's *Cosmography* (1584). In such a diagram, the Firmament is the sphere which contained the fixed stars; the Crystalline Sphere, which contained no heavenly bodies, is a late innovation, included to explain certain anomalies in the observed movement of the heavenly bodies; and the Prime Mover is the sphere which, itself put into motion by God, imparts rotation around the earth to all the other spheres.

Milton, writing in mid-seventeenth century, made use of two universes. The Copernican universe, though he alludes to it, was too large, formless, and unfamiliar to serve as the setting for the war between Heaven and Hell in *Paradise Lost*. He therefore adopted as his setting the Ptolemaic cosmos, but placed Heaven well outside this smaller earth-centered universe, Hell far beneath it, and assigned the vast middle space to Chaos.

Building above stage known as the "Heavens". It contains a windlass for special effects (e.g. descent of enthroned "gods" from the "sky" to the stage).

Flag is flown every playing day.

Two-penny Gallery

A. Curtained recess. (See Dr Faustus I and Volpone I i)
B. Upper stage and windows (see Volpone II i)
C. "Trapdoor to "Hell" area under the stage (traditionally used for appearances of ghosts, etc.)
D. One-penny audience ("groundlings") standing in yard.

Backstage area (called the "Tiring House")

Staircases to galleries

C. Walter Hodges. 1948

PERMISSIONS ACKNOWLEDGMENTS

Aphra Behn: *The Complete Text of OROONOKO*, edited by Joanna Lipking. Copyright © 1993 by Joanna Lipking and W. W. Norton & Company, Inc. Reprinted by permission of W. W. Norton & Company, Inc.

Beowulf: A new translation by Seamus Heaney. Copyright © 2000 by Seamus Heaney. Reprinted with permission of W. W. Norton & Company, Inc.

Frances Burney: *First Journal Entry* (ca. 800 words), from THE EARLY JOURNALS AND LETTERS OF FANNY BURNEY, VOL. 1, edited by Lars E. Troide (1988). Reprinted by permission of Oxford University Press. *"Down with Her, Burney!"* from THE EARLY JOURNALS AND LETTERS OF FANNY BURNEY, VOL. 3, edited by Lars E. Troide & Stewart J. Cooke. *A Mastectomy*, from THE JOURNALS AND LETTERS OF FANNY BURNEY, VOL. 6, edited by Joyce Hemlow. Reprinted with the permission of McGill–Queen's University Press Ltd.

Margaret Lucas Cavendish: Extracts from THE BLAZING WORLD are taken from Margaret Cavendish, Duchess of Newcastle, THE DESCRIPTION OF A NEW WORLD CALLED THE BLAZING WORLD AND OTHER WRITINGS, edited by Kate Lilley (London: Pickering & Chatto). Reprinted by permission of the publisher.

Geoffrey Chaucer: All excerpts are from CHAUCER'S POETRY: AN ANTHOLOGY FOR THE MODERN READER, 2nd ed. by E. T. Donaldson. Copyright © 1958, 1975 by Scott Foresman and Company. Reprinted by permission of Addison-Wesley Longman Educational Publishers, Inc.

Queen Elizabeth: *On Monsieur's Departure* from THE POEMS OF QUEEN ELIZABETH I, edited by Leicester Bradner. Copyright © 1964 by Brown University. Reprinted by permission of the University Press of New England. *Letter to Sir Amyes Paulet* and *Letter to Henry III, King of France* from THE LETTERS OF QUEEN ELIZABETH, edited by G. B. Harrison (Cassell, 1935). Reprinted by permission of David Higham Associates. *The Golden Speech* and *Speech to the Troops at Tilbury* from THE PUBLIC SPEAKING OF QUEEN ELIZABETH: SELECTIONS FROM HER OFFICIAL ADDRESSES, edited by George P. Rice, Jr. (AMS Press, 1966). Reprinted with the permission of AMS Press, Inc.

Sir Gawain: Complete text of SIR GAWAIN AND THE GREEN KNIGHT: A New Verse Translation by Marie Boroff, translator. Copyright © 1967 by W. W. Norton & Company, Inc. Reprinted by permission of W. W. Norton & Company, Inc.

Thomas Gray: From the manuscript of *Elegy Written in a Country Churchyard*. Transcribed by kind permission of the Provost and Fellows of Eton College.

William Hogarth: *Marriage A-la-Mode*, 1745, Plates 1–6, reproduced by permission of the Print Collection, Miriam and Ira D. Wallach Division of Art, Prints and Photographs, The New York Public Library, Astor, Lenox and Tilden Foundations.

Samuel Johnson: Excerpt from the manuscript of *The Vanity of Human Wishes*. Reprinted with permission.

Julian of Norwich: Excerpts reprinted from Julian of Norwich, A BOOK OF SHOWINGS, edited by Edmund Colledge and James Walsh, by permission of the publisher. Copyright © 1978 by the Pontifical Institute of Mediaeval Studies, Toronto.

Layamon: Excerpts from Layamon's BRUT translated by Rosamund Allen. Reprinted by permission of The Orion Publishing Group Ltd. on behalf of the publisher, Everyman.

Marie de France: Translation of LANVAL by Alfred David. Copyright © 2000 by Alfred David. Reprinted with the permission of the translator.

John Milton: Lines from the manuscript of Milton's LYCIDAS. Reprinted with the permission of the Master and Fellows of Trinity College, Cambridge. Excerpts from *Areopagitica* from THE COMPLETE POETRY AND MAJOR PROSE OF MILTON, edited by Merritt Y. Hughes, copyright © 1957. Reprinted by permission of Prentice-Hall, Inc., Upper Saddle River, N.J. From PARADISE LOST: A Norton Critical Edition, Second Edition, edited by Scott Elledge. Copyright © 1993, 1975 by W. W. Norton & Company, Inc. Reprinted by permission of W. W. Norton & Company, Inc.

Lady Mary Wortley Montagu: Poems from LADY MARY WORTLEY MONTAGU, ESSAYS AND POEMS, 1977, Revised 1993, edited by R. Halsband and I. Grundy. Reprinted with permission.

Mystery Plays: *The Chester Play of Noah's Flood* from THE CHESTER MYSTERY CYCLE, edited by R. M. Lumiansky and David Mills. Copyright © 1974. Reprinted by permission of The Council of the Early English Text Society.

Katherine Philips: *A Married State* from NLW Orielton Collection, box 24. Courtesy of The National Library of Wales.

Alexander Pope: From the manuscript of AN ESSAY ON MAN, MS Eng 233.21 transcribed by permission of the Houghton Library, Harvard University, and The Pierpont Morgan Library/Art Resource, NY.

Sir Philip Sidney: Selections from THE POEMS OF SIR PHILIP SIDNEY, edited by William A. Ringler, Jr. (1962). Reprinted by permission of Oxford University Press.

Lady Mary Wroth: Poems reprinted with the permission of Louisiana State University Press from THE POEMS OF LADY MARY WROTH, edited, with an introduction and notes, by Josephine A. Roberts. Copyright © 1983.

Every effort has been made to contact the copyright holders of each of the selections. Rights holders of any selections not credited should contact W. W. Norton & Company, Inc., 500 Fifth Avenue, New York, NY 10110 for a correction to be made in the next reprinting of our work.

Index